Eighteenth Century
Poetry & Prose

Edited by

LOUIS I. BREDVOLD
University of Michigan

ALAN D. McKILLOP
The Rice Institute

LOIS WHITNEY
Russell Sage College

SECOND EDITION

THE RONALD PRESS COMPANY

NEW YORK

Library of Congress Catalog Card Number: 56-7504

TABLE OF CONTENTS

iii

SUPPLEMENT: *FURTHER READINGS*

PREFACE

The purpose ot this volume is to provide representative selections from English prose and poetry of the eighteenth century for undergraduate courses in that period. The texts are presented complete and unabridged; those taken from larger works, such as the *Dunciad*, can be read as independent wholes. It has been the aim of the editors to achieve a balance which would give the student an appreciation of the individual authors at their best and also a comprehensive grasp of the literary developments of a century which, in the history of literature, is conventionally one hundred and forty years long. For obvious reasons, the drama and the novel are not represented.

In this second edition of the anthology the editors have expanded the contents considerably. Additions have been made from Addison, Pope, Swift, Young, Smart, Burke, and Reynolds, with Blake's comments. As in the first edition, spelling and punctuation have been modernized. Texts, notes, introductions, and bibliographies have been reviewed and revised in the light of more recent scholarship.

The extensive notes and introductions should assist the beginning student to understand the texts, but it is hoped that they will also lead him to explore further in the works listed in the bibliographies. A broad survey of the whole period is provided by A. D. McKillop in the general introduction.

L. I. B.
A. D. McK.
L. W.

INTRODUCTION

THE present collection of texts has been planned for a variety of uses, and an introduction need not undertake to tell the reader in advance just what he is going to find or advise him just what he ought to think about "our excellent and indispensable eighteenth century." A brief general survey of such a large area must always be unsatisfactory. Yet the eighteenth century in Western Europe has at least the appearance of being relatively simple and unified, and has thus invited people to make sweeping generalizations about it. As in any other field, no ready-made formula is adequate, yet a plan must be had, if the course of study is to be more than a collection of disconnected impressions and facts. We know in advance that we should give due consideration to the personalities of the writers, the ideas and theories on which they worked, and the times in which they lived; but it takes a good deal of care and tact to know just how much weight to give each of these factors, and how to put them together so that they shall be not a patchwork but an orderly perspective. And the various "-isms" about which the student has heard so much and will hear more—classicism, romanticism, deism, optimism, rationalism, sentimentalism, primitivism—must not be used mechanically as labels or catchwords; we must earn the right to use these terms by understanding, as far as we can, what lies back of them, and what they meant in the actual life of the eighteenth century. Even while we distinguish one from the other, we must try to see them not separately but together, not as clean-cut doctrines or opinions, but as tendencies often followed or attitudes often assumed under the obscure compulsions which determine our social behavior and our artistic tastes. Such a plan of study can never be fully realized, but any steps we may take toward its fulfillment will bring us a rich reward in a better understanding of great literature and of the bases of modern culture.

In the mid-seventeenth century, the nations of western Europe were divided among and within themselves by political and religious differences that broke out into open war—the Civil War in England from 1642, the Thirty Years War between Protestant and Catholic powers on the Continent, and the Wars of the Fronde in France. Statesmen, philosophers, and artists were thus confronted by the same problem: how to reëstablish some kind of working unity after a period of over-sharp cleavages. One way to do this was to set up an absolute authority, and this was what Louis XIV meant when he said, "L'état, c'est moi." The other way was to mediate between conflicting interests and principles. In restoring Charles II to the throne in 1660 the English nation was moved by a deeply felt need for the social and political unity that can be gained only by compromise, but it took another generation to attain that end. Charles's dissolute court represented the temporary triumph of everything that was anti-Puritan; partisan and religious differences came to white heat in the last years of his reign, and James II, whose Catholic convictions kept him from playing the normal rôle of an English monarch as a mediator between and above factions, followed extreme policies which brought about by reaction the Revolution of 1688. In the Revolution settlement both parties, Whig and Tory, had a share, but its practical effect was to bring the Whigs to the fore; the prerogatives of the Crown were limited in the interests of wealth and privilege, and power came to lie chiefly in the hands of a few great families. The cabinet system of government took shape in the successive reigns of William and Anne; amid bitter recrimination and intrigue the grip of the Whigs on Church and State became firmer, save for the Tory regime

of the last four years of Anne (1710-1714), and under Sir Robert Walpole's long
domination (1721-1742) the Opposition was reduced to political impotence. After
the death of Anne, the succession passed to the House of Hanover, and Britain
was ruled for the rest of the century by the mediocre Georges, at worst stupid
and obstinate, at best merely respectable. The personality of the monarch was of
little importance compared with the underlying social situation. The working
principle of eighteenth-century politics was the coöperation of the great landed
Whigs and the newly rich merchants who were riding the crest of a wave of prosperity; this increasingly middle-class regime nurtured the traditional strength
and inertia of John Bull. Even when the Tory policies of George III and his
ministers led to the loss of the American colonies, even when France burst forth
in revolution, the great mass of the English people shifted their position very
slowly, and the era of revolutions produced in Edmund Burke the supreme exponent of British conservatism.

Public opinion and taste became so coherent and powerful that they now determined the fortunes of authors more directly than ever before. From the inner
circles, made up of the coffee-house wits and the men of wealth and position
who might be regarded as possible patrons of letters, the public whom authors
addressed was extended to include additional social groups in town and country.
With the development of party responsibility in the reign of Queen Anne there
came a period when the political affiliations of authors were of great importance,
and when they were often rewarded with political office—Addison, Steele, and
Defoe with the Whigs, Prior and Swift with the Tories. The highly practical
Walpole chose to hire obscure journalists rather than distinguished men of
letters, and the important writers of the second quarter of the century are found
in the Opposition—Pope, Swift, Thomson, Akenside, Johnson, Fielding. In the
mid-century, patronage, whether private or official, was coming to be less important, and the growth of the middle-class reading public was enabling the resolute
journeymen of letters, such as Johnson, Goldsmith, and the major novelists, to
make a living without any important patron but the discriminating public itself.

In general the political and social situation liberated the energy of men and
allowed it to expend itself in private enterprise. While their institutions seemed
to be sunk in lethargy and complacency, eighteenth-century Englishmen were
establishing a great colonial empire overseas, reforming their agriculture, and
initiating modern commerce and industry. The Industrial Revolution, the development of the factory system in place of the older system of domestic industry, came late in the century, and ultimately changed the whole structure of
society and raised problems which are not yet solved, but its full consequences
lie beyond the period of our study. Until the nineteenth century the government
was still in the hands of the hereditary rulers, the large landowners. But many
new fortunes and estates were built up in the eighteenth century and duly taken
into the aristocracy; the governing classes, by making their alliances with trade,
saved themselves from the fate that overtook the aristocracy of France.

Meanwhile the upper classes lived in increasing comfort and luxury, and the
practical arts, such as architecture, landscape gardening, and interior decoration,
were highly cultivated. Our impressions of the age are based largely on these
decorative effects, and on the formal elegance of costume and manners, particularly as we find them in American colonial styles. The eighteenth century appeals to the eye, and the brilliant surface play of its life, as in *The Rape of the
Lock*, has led some to condemn the period as trivial and superficial, while others
admire the styles for their own sake and look no farther than the quaintness and
the charm. But in any case this elegance did not extend beyond the upper
middle class. In the pictures of Hogarth and the realistic writings of Defoe,
Smollett, and Crabbe we are shown the seamy side so vividly that we can never
overlook the slums and the dirt and the vice. But it would not be fair simply to

contrast the fine clothes of the upper classes with the rags of the poor, or the sensible thinking and living of enlightened gentlemen with the brutality and degradation of countless thousands. From the end of the seventeenth century there was a strong movement toward "the reformation of manners," a phrase which came to denote not only a stricter personal morality but also a heightened sense of social responsibility. Charity schools, prison reform, and other philanthropic works are characteristic of the eighteenth century. Addison and Steele sought to mediate between the court and the town, engrafting the courtier's politeness on the citizen's virtue, and their program shows the main line of development. Yet the social thinking of the time was the reverse of revolutionary. What with political stability and economic prosperity, it was generally felt that great issues were settled and that intelligent men could turn their attention to confirming and improving what was already agreed upon.

It is always hard to describe the dominant attitude of an age—such oversimplification distorts the facts—but we may say that the early eighteenth century emphasized the restriction of man's activities to what he was certain to attain and what he was certain would be of use to him. Men professed to be looking for the useful or practical; they thought and wrote toward sharply defined ends, so that their purpose in science was utilitarian and in literature didactic and moralizing.

> Learn then no happiness can be secure,
> Placed in whatever lies beyond our power.
> (Charles Johnson, Medæa)

Man gets on best by considering his limitations earnestly. "Common sense," a feeling that what is possible or desirable for man in general puts sharp limits on the individual, ruled the day; this same doctrine or concept was often called "reason," but it has little in common with the speculative reason of the scientist and the philosopher, so limited is it by the restrictions imposed by the rule of the useful and practical. Rather it leads to distrust of the expert, the specialist, the man who carries on "research." The cardinal doctrine of Swift is that the truth we need must be plain and non-technical, easily attainable by man were it not for his incorrigible pride. A moderate and accessible ideal for man has been set up, but even so, will he keep to it in practice, or will he inevitably yield to overmastering passion? The moralists of the day gave different answers to these questions: over against the optimism and simplicity of such a plain program for human well-being, we have the deep conviction of satirist and cynic that men will never really act on their knowledge of what is good for them, the realist's shrewd observation of actual follies. Swift's Gulliver's Travels, Mandeville's Fable of the Bees, Pope's Essay on Man, and Johnson's Rasselas may all be connected with this central ethical problem—the nature of the limitations on man necessary for the good life, and the chances of his actually living up to them. And characterization in the fiction and drama of the period is more largely determined than ever before by sharply contrasted pairs of ethical opposites—benevolence and selfishness, prudence and imprudence, candor and hypocrisy, sense and sensibility. If this eighteenth century moralizing seems to be thin, bloodless, and trite, it is counterbalanced by a sturdy realism which insists that man and the world are downright ugly facts. Thus a division may be made between the amiable moralists and the rough-handed moralists who urge us to face the truth—Addison and Shaftesbury over against Defoe, Swift, Mandeville, Hogarth, and Smollett. Or ethical optimism and the sense of fact may, however inconsistently, be found in the same men, as in Pope, Fielding, and Richardson.

In an age dominated by such views, what becomes of literature considered as a fine art? The sense of human limitations gave strong support to tradition; the presumption was entirely in favor of what had already been agreed upon, in favor of art forms and rules already established. The more daring achievements of previous ages were accepted and identified with the dictates of "common sense" or "reason." The Renaissance had taken over from classical antiquity the doctrine that the artist was to imitate nature, that is, that his work was to be tested by its conformity with general truths which were at the same time the objects of man's knowledge and the goal of his moral and religious aspirations. In the seventeenth century this doctrine was connected with the cardinal principle of the new science, that the order of reason was the order of nature, that the truth about God, man, and the external world could be expressed in intelligible and immutable laws. After the Baconian vision of a fruitful conquest of nature by experimental science came the program of Descartes, which set up self-evident clarity as the criterion of truth. The work of the Royal Society, established in 1662, and the triumph of Newtonian physics confirmed men's belief in an order of things at once intelligible and actual. The truth thus attained was valued more highly than the disordered data of sensation and imagination or the random movements of the spirit. In the field of religious thought man likewise argued that amid all the diversity of creeds there must be some central unity, since human reason is essentially the same everywhere and at all times; thus man's capacity for arriving at the truth by his own powers will lead him to a knowledge of God. John Locke handed on to the eighteenth century this doctrine of natural and reasonable religion, which was fully expounded by the deists but shared to a large extent by the orthodox. Many churchmen believed that natural religion and revealed religion might exist side by side, complementing or confirming one another, but the emphasis was on the benevolence and intelligence of man rather than on the mysteries of God. The Church became a vested interest, a bulwark of social respectability, and her bishops were often politicians rather than theologians. Locke set the general tone for the new age by his moderate and unenthusiastic attitude, his program of putting reason to work on the practical problems of human life and eschewing flights of fancy and daring speculations. The Enlightenment, as this period of thought has been labeled, was more interested in ethics and politics than in metaphysics and dogmatic theology.

Something akin to the rationalism of the new science and of current thought on religious and social subjects underlay the literary doctrines that are called neo-classical. It has often been pointed out that Pope and his contemporaries were ready to submit to the authority of the ancients not simply because they *were* the ancients, but because they were the exponents of reason; because, in the words of a minor poet, they possessed that true wit which is "in all times and languages the same." This view of the authority of reason in literature was strongly supported by the scientific temper of the age, but literary criticism was still deeply colored by reverence for authority and tradition as such. The early eighteenth century was ready to accept a rationalistic view of life as far as it could be made to support the *status quo*. Reason was called on, not to remake the world but to validate things as they were. Seventeenth century thought had often threatened tradition, and moved toward extreme positions and drastic measures. In literary criticism the rationalistic attitude might be pushed so far as to carry with it the exclusion of imagination from art, and this tendency had appeared in the daring materialistic philosophy of Hobbes. But the Enlightenment recoiled from Hobbes, preferring a moderate and cautious thinker like Locke. For literature and literary criticism this meant that there was to be no break with tradition, not even in the sacred name of reason, only a sensible and tactful modification.

The precepts of neo-classicism go back to the doctrines of Aristotle, Longinus, Horace, and Quintilian as interpreted by the critics of the Italian Renaissance.

Rules supposedly derived from the ancients, such as the unities of time, place, and action in drama, were used as yardsticks to measure the practice of the moderns. The lay-out of an epic was inevitably Homeric or Virgilian; the satirists looked back to Horace and Juvenal; the writer of an ode was virtually restricted to a choice between the Pindaric and the Horatian models. Grammar-school and university curricula, with their exclusive emphasis on Latin and Greek and their endless exercises in Latin prose and verse, made it inevitable that educated men should accept ancient authors as models for imitation. In practice the Latin authors counted for much more than the Greek. But it was only in the hands of relatively unimportant critics that these prescriptions for following the ancients became intolerably severe.

In the middle of the seventeenth century the neo-classical program as laid down by the great French critic Boileau was progressive and enlightened as far as it helped to free the literatures of western Europe from mannered, ornate, and extravagant styles—such a style, for example, as largely persists in the bombast of the Restoration heroic plays. The general change is familiar to students of English poetry as the transition from the metaphysical poets to the clarity and simplicity of Dryden's mature work, and this movement against false wit was continued by Addison and Pope. Along with this change in poetic standards came the evolution of a plain expository prose style which has always been associated with the rise of the new science and its demand for "a close, naked, natural way of speaking; positive expressions, clear senses, a native easiness, bringing all things as near the mathematical plainness as they can." (Sprat, *History of the Royal Society*.) The ideals of the coming age, the converging ideals of poetry and prose, were neatly set forth by an obscure poet of 1646 in the very meter which was to become standard:

> A poet's then exact in every part
> That is born one from Nature, nursed by Art;
> Whose happy mixture both of skill and fate
> Makes the most sudden thought elaborate;
> Whose easy strains a flowing sense does fit,
> Unforced expression and unravished wit;
> Words filled with equal subject such as brings
> To chosen language high and chosen things;
> Harsh reason clear as day, as smooth as steep,
> Glide(s) here like rivers, even still though deep;
> Discord grows music, grief itself delight;
> Horror, when he describes, leaves off to affright;
> Sullen philosophy does learn to go
> In lightest dressings, and becomes them too.[1]

Hackneyed almost beyond quotation are the famous lines on the Thames which Sir John Denham added to his *Cooper's Hill* in 1655 and which express the new ideal of style:

> O could I flow like thee, and make thy stream
> My great example, as it is my theme!
> Though deep, yet clear; though gentle, yet not dull;
> Strong without rage, without o'erflowing full.

Neo-classical theory sought to mediate between nature and art, imagination and reason, delight and instruction. Boileau, Dryden, and Pope all tried to steer some such middle course. We may speak of an Augustan compromise just as easily as we speak of a Victorian compromise. William Minto long ago wrote of the eighteenth century: "If the age was comparatively barren of the higher poetry, the explanation is not to be found in the predominance of narrow and exclusive critical theories."

[1] Verses by J. F. prefixed to Martin Lluelyn's *Men-Miracles* (1646), reprinted by Thomas Hayward in *The British Muse* (1738), iii, 30. and by Ruth C. Wallerstein in *PMLA*, L (1935), 208.

The limitations of neo-classical verse have often been described in terms of meter and diction, and many since William Cowper have been found to reproach the followers of Pope for making poetry a "mere mechanic art." But in the hands of the greater writers the heroic couplet was not necessarily monotonous or mechanical; they did not adopt it blindly, but chose it as a means to an end, and its dominance was never complete. The history of the heroic couplet may be traced in English poetry from the end of the sixteenth century; Drayton, Fairfax in his translation of Tasso's *Jerusalem Delivered,* Sandys in his translation of Ovid, and Ben Jonson in turn used the single closed couplet for the expression of general truths. Denham and Waller give it more uniformity and simplicity, and from their practice develops the critical theory that the standard form of verse should combine Denham's "strength" and Waller's "sweetness." But it was Dryden who truly energized the form and established it as standard. The Restoration experiment in riming heroic plays was a failure, but served to bring home to Dryden the limitations and possibilities of the couplet. His views as to its range are indicated in the conclusion of his Preface to *Religio Laici.*

If any one be so lamentable a critic as to require the smoothness, the numbers, and the turn of heroic poetry in this poem, I must tell him that, if he has not read Horace, I have studied him, and hope the style of his Epistles is not ill imitated here. The expressions of a poem designed purely for instruction ought to be plain and natural, and yet majestic; for here the poet is presumed to be a kind of law-giver, and those three qualities which I have named are proper to the legislative style. The florid, elevated, and figurative way is for the passions; for love and hatred, fear and anger, are begotten in the soul by showing their objects out of their true proportion, either greater than the life, or less; but instruction is to be given by showing them what they naturally are. A man is to be cheated into passion, but to be reasoned into truth.

Accordingly he remarks at the end of the poem:

> And this unpolished, rugged verse I chose,
> As fittest for discourse, and nearest prose.

He draws his distinctions too sharply here, but he indicates the limits—a florid heroic style and a plain expository style—within which both he and Pope worked. Pope, of course, avoids Dryden's tendency toward ruggedness, and seeks to combine smoothness and plain sense; his work in consciously lofty rhetoric is secondary. It need hardly be pointed out to readers of such superb verse as *Absalom and Achitophel,* the lines to Congreve, Pope's Atticus portrait, the conclusion of the *Dunciad,* or the passage on the death of Charles XII in Jonson's *Vanity of Human Wishes* that the modulated rhythms of the perfected couplet express controlled feeling as well as triumphant intellect.

But the passage just quoted from Dryden has some ominous implications about diction. When the poet takes the "florid, elevated, and figurative way" it seems that he is to use fine big words to raise his subject. This program was carried out in the eighteenth century with disastrous results, and laid the poets of the time open to Wordsworth's famous attack, which has perhaps had the effect of making people complain too much of the vicious diction of the school of Dryden and Pope. The second-rate poet, dominated by dry common sense and by sham ideals of gentility and propriety, draws a sharp line between fact and fancy, and thinks of poetic style as the application of extraneous ornament to plain truth. Milton's stately language, Dryden's translation of Virgil, Pope's translation of Homer, and Thomson's *Seasons* furnished a treasury of poetic diction which lesser versifiers used mechanically. They had learned this method at school, where they "imitated" the Latin poets by piecing together tags and epithets from a stock collection. One must not underestimate the pleasure to be found in manipulating a special vocabulary which is supposed to be the property of the elect; but the higher end, as Dr. Johnson explains in his *Life of Dryden,* was to attain generality and dignity, and to avoid the extremes of homeliness and extravagance:

There was . . . before the time of Dryden no poetical diction, no system of words at once refined from the grossness of domestic use, and free from the harshness of terms appropriated to
particular arts. Words too familiar, or too remote, defeat the purpose of a poet. From those sounds
which we hear on small or on coarse occasions, we do not easily receive strong impressions, or
delightful images; and words to which we are nearly strangers, whenever they occur, draw that
attention on themselves which they should transmit to things.

Such a style was adequate for expository verse which dealt with the general traits
of human nature and society, but failed when applied to the homely details of
life and to the description of external nature. The stock horrible examples of
poetic diction are roundabout names for plain things—such as "the whiskered
vermin race" for rats and mice—and passages in which nature is described as
"decked," "enamelled," "painted," and the like. The poet thus puts us off with
a formula instead of getting to the heart of his subject. We are haunted by the
feeling that when he takes to such a style he is neither thinking hard nor feeling
intensely. On the other hand, the versifiers who avoid such paraphrasing and
keep to a direct style—notably, in this collection, Defoe, Swift, Mandeville, and
Green—often seem to sacrifice nobility and dignity for mere shrewdness.

   Neo-classical doctrine emphasized the importance of structure and form rather
than ornament, but here there was a gap between theory and practice. According
to the tradition inherited from the Renaissance, epic and drama were the supreme
forms, but there was no vital epic enterprise in England after the supreme achieve-
ment of *Paradise Lost,* and no great poetic drama. The heroic couplet put a
premium on brilliant or neat phrases; the part often seemed to be greater than
the whole, and only in exceptional cases were elaborate structures built up out
of couplets. Neither Pope nor Dryden worked on a grand scale. At the same time,
an age which subordinated the individual to impersonal norms did not express
itself in short intense poems of personal feeling; the lyric poetry of the period
tends to be trivial and conventional, or at best neat and pensive. A favorite form
was the verse-essay, brilliantly illustrated in the *Religio Laici* and *An Essay on
Man.* More broadly, anything which involved an argument, an explanation, or
the enforcement of a moral could be put into verse—an account of the progress
of this, or the art of that, any popular survey or outline of knowledge. The
modern reader smiles at such "unpoetical" subjects as *The Sugar Cane, The Art
of Preserving Health,* or *The Economy of Monastic Life,* but should remember
that in an age of elaborate restrictions on diction and style the privilege of
experimenting with various matters was sometimes valuable. The preoccupation
with human nature in society was likely to lead poets into satire; indeed, the
satiric spirit of the age, the impulse to pass genial or bitter judgment on the
failings of mankind in the light of an absolute standard of virtue and reason,
was too pervasive to confine itself to direct imitation of Horace and Juvenal.
Consider the indescribably complex variations of the satiric spirit to be found
in Butler, Oldham, Dryden, Swift, Defoe, Addison, Steele, Pope, Young, Mandeville, Green, Fielding, Smollett, Johnson, Churchill, Junius, Burns, Crabbe! The
commentator on men and manners almost instinctively struck a pose of judicious-
ness and turned satirist. An indirect expression of the satirical and critical spirit
is found in burlesque poetry, especially the mock-heroic, which applies a lofty
style to low matter, or at least to incongruous matter. Every accepted form and
style has its burlesque anti-type—the epic in Garth's *Dispensary* and Pope's *Rape
of the Lock,* and the *Dunciad,* the Miltonic style in John Philips's *Splendid
Shilling* and innumerable others, the pastoral in Gay's *Shepherd's Week,* the
opera in his *Beggar's Opera,* the georgic (broadly defined as a poem professing
to tell how to do something) in his *Trivia,* the Spenserian style in Shenstone's
Schoolmistress and many other pieces. Somewhat similarly, we find in Prior and
Gay the cultivation of a witty and playful kind of lyric in which the poet takes

his ease and enjoys the advantages of the form in which he is working without taking full responsibility. It should be remembered too that burlesque drama had a brilliant career from Buckingham's *Rehearsal* (1671) to Sheridan's *The Critic* (1779), and that such great novelists as Fielding and Jane Austen approached prose fiction through burlesque. Burlesque lent itself to the expression of attitudes and moods ranging from the playfulness of a secure age to severe criticism and mordant satire.

Poetry and prose share the same impulse toward satire, moralizing commentary, and half-informal exposition, and this is what led Matthew Arnold to say that the best poets of the time were really "classics of our prose." But this is to underestimate the element of formal art in Augustan poetry, and the pleasure the poet and his readers had in the execution of a project within the limits imposed by a literary form. The poet, accepting a form, works out a "solution" of his problem somewhat as an architect would do. At the same time, the achievements of the great prosemen of the age have the advantage of less conventional ornament and a more direct attack on their problem. New types of writing were developed to meet the requirements of a public that was ready to buy pamphlets, periodicals, non-technical books, and improving stories. Creative impulse and practical purpose united to give the best prose of the time a directness and competence that have never been surpassed. Defoe, Swift, Addison, and Steele, varied as are their accomplishments, all use words and ideas for specific purposes of which they are fully conscious. They transform or even create literary genres to suit their purpose; we talk so much of the uniformity and conventionality of the age that we do not always stop to admire the plasticity and originality of Dryden's critical essays, of Defoe's pamphlets and prose narratives, of the *Spectator's* various performances, of the plain prose of Franklin, Paine, and Cobbett, of Swift's unique satires, of the narrative prose of Fielding, Smollett, and Jane Austen. Even a secondary writer like Mandeville shares their incomparable faculty of getting to the point.

When the pressure toward the point is slightly relaxed, as in the *Spectator* tradition and the major letter-writers (Lady Mary Wortley Montagu, Chesterfield, Walpole, Gray, Cowper) we get the added grace of a prose style which is informal without being ineffectual. Here develops the natural, playful, and witty vein characteristic of much of the best eighteenth century prose—markedly present in Swift, Addison, Gray, Cowper, Walpole, and Goldsmith, seldom carried to excess except in some of Swift's outbursts and in the extravagances of Sterne. The vitality and naturalness of this kind of writing is due to the fact that it approximates the rhythms of cultivated speech. Furthermore, this practical yet urbane prose is adapted to new uses and made a medium for the effective expression of personality, not only in the letter-writers but in the new biography consummately realized by Boswell. To be sure, formal rhetoric was present in eighteenth century prose as in poetry, and sometimes hampered natural and effective expression. In Johnson's *Rambler*, in the stately periods of Gibbon and the eloquence of Burke we are aware of this danger, even as we admire their dignity. With inferior followers of Addison, Pope, and Johnson, the formal style became pompous and perfunctory. There was no sudden shattering of the forms, and the partly spurious stateliness of late eighteenth century worthies stalked on into the nineteenth. American students will find it in the accepted language of politics and patriotism in their own country from the Revolution to the Civil War.

To return to the first half of the eighteenth century, the seriousness and magnitude of the writer's task were freely granted in theory; the power of the imagination was not questioned, though it was sometimes feared; Shakespeare, Homer, and Milton were revered. Nevertheless there was the feeling, characteristic of a prosperous and settled society, that it was better to undertake only modest and definite projects. In short, as has been said, practice rather than theory was limited. It would be easy to make a list of human, or even specifically English interests and attitudes that are underemphasized or omitted in Augustan literature. The life of the common people is not there, save in incidental touches and half-sympathetic burlesque, nor in any large degree the rural background so characteristic of English life, nor the untrammeled expression of personality and temperament, nor the mystical and supernatural side of religion. But in the long run Englishmen were too individual to brook a polite suppression of personality, too much attached to rural and provincial life to accept the absolute social and intellectual domination of London; moreover, they had inherited too much from Puritanism to keep clear of religious ardor and religious gloom.

It was, however, possible for writers to express these interests without raising the cry of rebellion. The Augustan compromise was tolerant enough to give considerable freedom to writers who professed a didactic purpose, and to permit them to work in a fairly wide variety of genres. The most important poetic type evolved during the first half of the century, the descriptive, expository, and meditative blank-verse poem, aroused no critical controversy, though there was a minor debate on the relative merits of the heroic couplet and blank verse. To an age familiar with philosophical and religious verse, with the loco-descriptive poem (as in Denham's *Cooper's Hill*), the pastoral, and the georgic, Thomson's *Seasons* brought pleasures that were at least half-familiar. Thomson extended the subject-matter of poetry without running seriously counter to contemporary views. His independent use of blank verse gave him a workable if not ideal medium for description and exposition. His fine observation of the external world, both in detail and in the large, blended easily with the ideas he took over from contemporary philosophy, theology, and science. Even less consciously radical were the blank-verse sermons of Young and Blair, though the somber rhetoric which they applied to the service of orthodox theology gave expression to moods which had been largely disregarded by Augustan politeness. In the youthful poets of the forties we seem to come closer to a new position, described in the Advertisement to Joseph Warton's *Odes* (1746):

The public has been so much accustomed of late to didactic poetry alone, and essays on moral subjects, that any work where the imagination is much indulged will perhaps not be relished or regarded. The author therefore of these pieces is in some pain lest certain austere critics should think him too fanciful and descriptive. But as he is convinced that the fashion of moralizing in verse has been carried too far, and as he looks upon Invention and Imagination to be the chief faculties of a poet, so he will be happy if the following odes may be looked upon as an attempt to bring back poetry into its right channel.

Largely under the influence of Milton's minor poems a new type of "descriptive and allegorical" ode was developed, and in different ways Akenside, Collins, the Wartons, and Gray all strive in the forties and fifties to achieve concentration of thought and feeling within sharply limited lyric forms. The somewhat abstract intensity of Collins and the finished art of Gray produced the best that the mid-century has to offer. The Wartons, in spite of Joseph's pronouncements, are more remarkable for their assemblage of "natural" themes and for their fertile if inconsistent criticism than for their actual accomplishment.

Warton was premature in calling for a reaction against didactic poetry; the blank-verse didactic and descriptive poem continued to flourish down to the days of Cowper and Wordsworth, but Augustan satire did lose ground in the mid-century. Though there was no coherent movement and no concerted revolt, confused changes in thought and attitude were indicated. In an age of increasing luxury and corruption, there was a strong impulse to reassert the ideal of simplicity. There were grounds for believing that the dominant views represented not a triumph of pure reason but a triumph of convention and artifice. The reaction was toward a doctrine that goodness and truth were to be found not in the standards set by a corrupt society but in the judgments and impulses of the natural man. Such a theory was already in the air. We have seen that the Enlightenment was disposed to teach that reason was the essential element of human nature, but, as Professor Crane has recently pointed out, liberal divines of the late seventeenth century often chose to describe this element as benevolence (without, of course, trying to exclude reason). Such was the groundwork of the doctrine of man's natural sense of beauty and goodness, brilliantly formulated and spread, though by no means originated, by the Earl of Shaftesbury, and later called sentimentalism—a doctrine opposed alike to the extreme Stoic position that man should be controlled by reason to the exclusion of feeling, to the theological dogma of original sin as it had come down from St. Augustine through Calvin, and to the doctrine of man as a creature dominated by selfish passion expounded by Hobbes and Mandeville. Conscious opposition to the latter doctrine determined its early development. At this stage the theory of man's natural goodness was set in opposition to low views of human nature, but it did not necessarily contradict the Augustan acceptance of the best culture and the best society; it might be agreed that this natural endowment needed cultivation and even rigorous training. Thus the theory was expounded in a spirit of correctness rather than of enthusiasm (in spite of Shaftesbury's eloquence); it was not launched as a daring paradox, but as something that was obviously acceptable to an intelligent gentleman. It coincided with current optimism and deistic teaching, and appeared in sermons, plays, essays, and poems without meeting concerted opposition.

But as the age began to suffer from the ennui brought about by excessive formalism, men came to set more and more value on the evidence of natural goodness afforded by the spontaneous movement and expression of the feelings, and to set the feelings in sharp opposition to conventional etiquette and education. At this point, since emotions do not always come to order, genuine feeling is often replaced by a doctrine that man is under a moral obligation to feel, that the one unmistakable proof of virtue is the unbridled expression of sympathy or pity on the slightest provocation. Such is the later development of sentiment into sensibility, a development which destroyed man's sense of proportion and led him away from the symmetry and moderation of neo-classicism. At the same time, the sharp opposition between feeling and convention led the thinker and the poet away from the town and the aristocracy to the country and to humble life, and eventually to the child and to primitive man. Sentimentalism was thus connected with primitivism and with democracy in the widest sense. The locus of natural goodness was the rural retreat or the wilderness. Imagery and ideas drawn from pastoral poetry, from the art of landscape in painting and gardening, and from travel literature came to form a rich complex which delighted those who vaguely sought the "natural," the "simple," the "sublime," and the "pathetic." Much of this is to be found in Thomson and the Wartons, and in the descriptions of delightful retirement in many a minor poet and novelist. Likewise, the emphasis in aesthetic theory was shifted from the formal characteristics of a work of art to the natural and spontaneous action of the minds that created it and enjoyed it; this meant that critics came more and more to talk of enthusiasm rather than good sense, and of original genius (a new phrase in the mid-century) rather than wit. The cult of violent feeling, real or assumed, put new meaning into men's preference for the picturesque, the irregular, the sublime—what came to be called "the Gothic." "Beauty tends more and more to be relegated to the domain of the simple, the harmonious, the unified and the calm, while the pathetic-sublime grows steadily to include unbeautiful ideas and objects and the more turbulent emotions."[2]

[2] S. H. Monk, *The Sublime: A Study of Critical Theories in XVIII-Century England* (New York, 1935), p. 70.

Parallel in some respects to these tendencies, and far more coherent and con-centrated, was the Methodist awakening led by the Wesleys and Whitefield, which was spreading rapidly in the forties. As against the cool common sense and formality of the Established Church, Methodism dwelt on the supernatural and emotional elements in religion, on the intervention of divine grace, and on spir-itual struggle and triumph within the individual soul. The ready response these doctrines found in the hearts of men made Methodism the most important religious and social movement of eighteenth century England, but because it inherited the Puritan distrust of art, and because it reached downward to levels of the population not yet included within the reading public, it colored English literature only gradually and indirectly.

The mid-century, then, saw the subject-matter of literature extended, though this change did not immediately transform the poetry of the time. This genera-tion, indeed, did its freshest work not in poetry but in the development of the novel of manners and sentiment by Fielding and Richardson. In verse, the cult of simplicity and original genius meant a new receptiveness toward poets (Shake-speare, Spenser, Milton) who lay outside the neo-classical sequence from Waller to Pope, and in Akenside and Collins led to a vaguely but enthusiastically con-ceived Hellenic ideal. The extension of literary sympathy, the eagerness to re-discover the genius of the remote past, was strikingly demonstrated when Macpherson foisted the Ossianic poems on the world in the early sixties and when Bishop Percy, following an interest which had always had some currency since Addison's ballad-criticisms in the *Spectator*, published the *Reliques of Ancient English Poetry* in 1765. The scholarly tastes of Gray, Collins, and the Wartons had already moved in the same direction; the new line in poetry and art was bound up with dilettantism and scholarship rather than with ardent speculation or experiment. Criticism was still inconsistent and compromising, but pushed on ahead of creative art; the new impulses were felt and transmitted for the most part by bookish gentlemen living in seclusion. A reckless town-wit like Charles Churchill, who tried to revive the satiric spirit of Dryden, contrasted strangely with his pre-romantic contemporaries. In Shenstone and other agreeable minor writers, poetry was reduced to the dimensions of a harmless diversion in a rural retreat. Thus it came about that Dr. Johnson accused many of his con-temporaries of being silly, affected, and trivial; and in a changed age tried to preserve the old reverence for traditionally enshrined universal truth, combined with a sternly anti-sentimental morality of resignation and disillusion. To such doctrines Johnson's follower and ally, Goldsmith, would in theory subscribe, but the sentimental tinge of *The Deserted Village* shows his susceptibility to current ideas.

Johnson should not be regarded, however, merely as a champion of the lost cause of neo-classicism; his strength lies not so much in his sturdy opposition to the new tendencies as in his power to take in and enjoy the various aspects of human life while he relates them to the first principles of morality and religion. In no other age could a stern moralist and dogmatist have so much enjoyed the spectacle afforded by his own time while making so few concessions to contem-porary fads and follies. Johnson is less the mere man of letters than the other great neo-classical arbiters, Dryden and Pope; his personality is deeper and richer than theirs. In this view of man and society he is very close to Burke; both see how tradition and convention are interwoven in the very fabric of human life. In an age when citizens were being told how fast they were advancing in the march of progress, and how they might go even faster in the crisis of revolution, Johnson and Burke urged on all men of common sense and good will a doctrine of restriction and negation, and denied the possibility of rapid improvement in the individual or in society. The reaction of the English public to the excesses of the French Revolution showed that they spoke for many of their contemporaries. The English liberals who had supported the revolt of the colonists in America were now for the most part forced to take the conservative side, and at the end of the century the British aristocracy and middle classes were still socially and politically old-fashioned. The pro-Revolutionary group in the England of the nineties was a small but articulate minority. The spirit of the age changes, however; there is a sharper formulation of issues; what with Burke on one side and Tom Paine on the other, the line of battle is drawn up.

In this age of sharper division, Cowper, Crabbe, and Burns are close to the average of sentiment and common sense; they represent a kind of consolidation of moderate views of society and nature, a ground swell of deep reflection on man and his destiny which was making itself felt but had not yet found full expression in literature. Cowper is a cultivated gentleman in retirement, writing verse conservative in diction and colored by liberal and humanitarian ideas, but he is more than the amateur sentimentalist; he has been profoundly affected by the evangelical revival, a counter-reformation within the Established Church stimulated by Methodism, and his agonizing religious experiences give a special quality to his poetry. Crabbe is in deliberate reaction from the pastoral dream and from the optimism and complacency of the ruling classes; his sober realism is offered as a corrective to the bookishness and sham-simplicity of pre-romanticism, yet in his refusal to "sacrifice to the Graces" he is clearly not of the old school.

The work of Robert Burns was as solidly based on fact as Crabbe's, as intimately connected with sentimentalism as Cowper's, but ranged far beyond them in its fusion of humorous, emotional, and imaginative power. The Ayrshire plowman was of course hailed as a child of nature by contemporary critics; modern readers must correct this sentimental error by defining his position in the great British tradition of humane letters. The sequence of Scottish poets from Ramsay to Fergusson, the English poets from Milton and Thomson to Shenstone, all contributed to the making of Burns. He did not rebel against a literary code, but energized it and brought out its possibilities; in his work we discover that the hackneyed terms bandied about by the eighteenth-century critics—"nature," "art," "invention," "simplicity"—are more than empty words.

The elder romantics, Wordsworth, Coleridge, Scott, and Southey, were grown men by the year 1800, and their intellectual and artistic development is really part and parcel of the eighteenth century. The compromises of the early and mid-century no longer served the needs of men, and ideas which once seemed tame and harmless now became exciting and dangerous. Where men could formerly give languid and conventional approval to the dream of a primitive golden age or of the natural goodness of man they were now asked to translate such ideas into terms of political equality and democracy. Few men actually made the translation, but even the inert and complacent could not overlook the possibility of revolt. The extreme of revolt was realized by William Blake, who ignores the compromises of the workaday world. Of course his detachment is not absolute; he gives us echoes of the eighteenth-century cult of simplicity and even of such palpable things as Ossianic rhetoric and the revolutions in America and France; there were channels through which occult symbolism and mysticism reached him from other periods and places. But he stands apart as the poet of rebellion and anarchy; he is not interested in saving tradition by modifying it. He should be bracketed with Shelley rather than with any other poet included in this collection; he is not the natural terminus of the century, but comes from without to tell us that there are things in heaven and earth not comprehended in the eighteenth-century view of the world.

To an age like ours, remembering, experiencing, and anticipating one national crisis after another, the eighteenth century may seem at first to be an age of trivialities; but as we continue our study we may come to feel that people who could work so quietly and urbanely had high and exacting standards from which we still have something to learn. We may learn to appreciate in the poetry of the time the same qualities we enjoy in eighteenth century domestic architecture, furniture, painting, and music. We may learn to appreciate the subtlety of individual expression within the conventions of prescribed forms, and may come to realize that literary genius does not necessarily mean an extravagant exploitation of personality. We may even envy in some ways those who lived in such a time. But if at one stage of our initiation we think of the Augustan age as a "place of rest and refreshment" after the excitement of contemporary life, on closer knowledge it will appear that this period is not a mere vacation resort for the soul, but a seed-plot of the ideas that have shaped the modern world, and a serious school in which we can learn much of human nature and of life.

A. D. McK.

SAMUEL BUTLER (1613-1680)

Little is known of Samuel Butler's personality and private life, though his work is stamped with an unmistakable individuality of thought and style. John Aubrey's brief description is this: "He was of a leonine-colored hair, sanguine-choleric, middle sized, strong." Butler was born and educated at Worcester, served as clerk to various Puritan country justices, and was for a time a member of Gray's Inn. All through the Civil wars and the Commonwealth he viewed morosely the extravagances of the Puritan factions, and finally vented his spleen against pedantry and fanaticism in *Hudibras* (published in three parts in 1663, 1664, and 1678). Much of the poem had probably been written before 1660. This powerful satire was enthusiastically received by the court party, but its success did not win for Butler any substantial rewards; he was steward of Ludlow Castle for a short time, and from 1671 to 1674 secretary to George Villiers, Duke of Buckingham, and probably received small sums of government money, but when he died in 1680 his name became a by-word for neglected genius. Three years later, when Dryden was complaining that his government salary and pension were in arrears, he remarked, " 'Tis enough for one age to have neglected Mr. Cowley and starved Mr. Butler."

The seventeenth century abounded in travesty, the treatment of heroic themes in an intentionally ridiculous and vulgar style. But the travesty proper followed a particular poem, such as the *Aeneid*, whereas *Hudibras* takes as its subject-matter the doctrines and controversies of church and state, and then proceeds to substitute for these high matters grotesque and coarse imagery and diction. The Puritan knight Hudibras, accompanied by his squire Ralpho, undertakes to stop a bear-baiting, and later courts a wealthy widow and in furtherance of his suit consults the astrologer Sidrophel. Meanwhile knight and squire disagree on points of faith and practice, and argue elaborately with one another. The intellectual, religious, and political life of man appears as an ignoble series of disputes and violent brawls. Butler's underlying belief in moderation and common sense is to be inferred, but finds no spokesman in *Hudibras*. Like Swift, he never tires of finding ways to deride the unreasonable antics of supposedly rational creatures. The pungent and grotesque style in which he treats of human folly has proved endlessly diverting; he is a master of comic rimes and rhythms; his rugged octosyllables pull up man's pretensions short, and he draws on an immense store of out-of-the-way learning to furnish novel analogies and illustrations. The same intellectual resourcefulness and severe judgment of human absurdities appear in his *Characters*, which remained unpublished until 1759.

Hudibras was learnedly annotated by Zachary Gray (1744); the best modern edition is Waller's (Cambridge, 1905). The miscellaneous remains in prose and verse are important for an understanding of his genius (*Characters and Passages from Note-Books*, ed. Waller [Cambridge, 1908]; *Satires and Miscellaneous Poetry and Prose*, ed. Lamar [Cambridge, 1928]). For an analysis of the method of Hudibrastic burlesque, see Richmond P. Bond, *English Burlesque Poetry 1700-1750* (Cambridge, Mass., 1932), and E. A. Richards, *Hudibras in the Burlesque Tradition* (New York, 1937). See also page 1268.

HUDIBRAS

THE ARGUMENT

Sir Hudibras his passing worth,
The manner how he sallied forth,
His arms and equipage, are shown;
His horse's virtues and his own.
Th' adventure of the bear and fiddle
Is sung, but breaks off in the middle.

When civil fury first grew high,
And men fell out, they knew not why;

When hard words, jealousies, and fears
Set folks together by the ears,
And made them fight, like mad or drunk,
For Dame Religion as for punk;[1]
Whose honesty they all durst swear for,
Though not a man of them knew wherefore;
When gospel-trumpeter, surrounded
With long-eared rout, to battle sounded; 10
And pulpit, drum ecclesiastic,
Was beat with fist instead of a stick;

[1] Prostitute.

Then did Sir Knight abandon dwelling,
And out he rode a-colonelling.
    A wight he was, whose very sight would
Entitle him Mirror of Knighthood,
That never bowed his stubborn knee
To anything but chivalry,
Nor put up blow but that which laid
Right Worshipful on shoulder-blade;   20
Chief of domestic knights and errant,
Either for chartel[2] or for warrant;
Great on the bench, great in the saddle,
That could as well bind o'er as swaddle;[3]
Mighty he was at both of these,
And styled of war as well as peace.
(So some rats of amphibious nature
Are either for the land or water.)
But here our authors make a doubt
Whether he were more wise or stout.   30
Some hold the one, and some the other;
But, howsoe'er they make a pother,
The difference was so small, his brain
Outweighed his rage but half a grain;
Which made some take him for a tool
That knaves do work with, called a fool.
For 't has been held by many, that
As Montaigne, playing with his cat,
Complains she thought him but an ass,
Much more she would Sir Hudibras;   40
(For that's the name our valiant knight
To all his challenges did write).
But they're mistaken very much;
'Tis plain enough he was no such.
We grant, although he had much wit,
H' was very shy of using it,
As being loth to wear it out,
And therefore bore it not about,
Unless on holidays or so,
As men their best apparel do.   50
Beside, 'tis known he could speak Greek
As naturally as pigs squeak;
That Latin was no more difficile,
Than to a blackbird 'tis to whistle.
Being rich in both, he never scanted
His bounty unto such as wanted;
But much of either would afford
To many that had not one word.
For Hebrew roots, although they're found
To flourish most in barren ground,   60
He had such plenty as sufficed
To make some think him circumcised.
And truly so perhaps he was;
'Tis many a pious Christian's case,

[2] Challenge to a duel.
[3] Cudgel.

He was in logic a great critic,
Profoundly skilled in analytic;
He could distinguish and divide
A hair 'twixt south and southwest side;
On either which he would dispute,
Confute, change hands, and still confute.   70
He'd undertake to prove by force
Of argument, a man's no horse;
He'd prove a buzzard is no fowl,
And that a lord may be an owl;
A calf an alderman, a goose a justice,
And rooks committee-men and trustees.
He'd run in debt by disputation,
And pay with ratiocination.
All this by syllogism, true
In mood and figure, he would do.   80
    For rhetoric, he could not ope
His mouth but out there flew a trope;
And when he happened to break off
I' th' middle of his speech, or cough,
H' had hard words ready to show why,
And tell what rules he did it by;
Else, when with greatest art he spoke,
You'd think he talked like other folk;
For all a rhetorician's rules
Teach nothing but to name his tools.   90
But when he pleased to show 't, his speech
In loftiness of sound was rich,
A Babylonish dialect
Which learnèd pedants much affect;
It was a parti-colored dress
Of patched and piebald languages;
'Twas English cut on Greek and Latin,
Like fustian heretofore on satin;
It had an odd promiscuous tone,
As if h' had talked three parts in one;   100
Which made some think, when he did
        gabble,
Th' had heard three labourers of Babel,
Or Cerberus himself pronounce
A leash of languages at once.
This he as volubly would vent,
As if his stock would ne'er be spent;
And truly, to support that charge,
He had supplies as vast and large;
For he could coin or counterfeit
New words with little or no wit;   110
Words so debased and hard, no stone
Was hard enough to touch them on;
And when with hasty noise he spoke 'em,
The ignorant for current took 'em;
That, had the orator who once
Did fill his mouth with pebble stones

When he harangued, but known his phrase,
He would have used no other ways.
   In mathematics he was greater
Than Tycho Brahe or Erra Pater; 120
For he by geometric scale
Could take the size of pots of ale;
Resolve by sines and tangents straight
If bread or butter wanted weight;
And wisely tell what hour o' th' day
The clock does strike, by algebra.
   Besides, he was a shrewd philosopher,
And had read every text and gloss over:
Whate'er the crabbed'st author hath,
He understood b' implicit faith; 130
Whatever skeptic could inquire for,
For every *why* he had a *wherefore*;
Knew more than forty of them do,
As far as words and terms could go;
All which he understood by rote,
And, as occasion served, would quote,
No matter whether right or wrong;
They might be either said or sung.
His notions fitted things so well,
That which was which he could not tell, 140
But oftentimes mistook the one
For th' other, as great clerks have done.
He could reduce all things to acts,
And knew their natures by abstracts;
Where entity and quiddity,
The ghosts of defunct bodies, fly;
Where Truth in person does appear,
Like words congealed in northern air.
He knew what's what, and that's as high
As metaphysic wit can fly. 150
   In school-divinity as able
As he that hight Irrefragable;
A second Thomas, or, at once
To name them all, another Duns;
Profound in all the nominal
And real ways beyond them all;
And with as delicate a hand
Could twist as tough a rope of sand;
And weave fine cobwebs, fit for skull
That's empty when the moon is full; 160
Such as take lodgings in a head
That's to be let unfurnishèd.
He could raise scruples dark and nice,
And after solve 'em in a trice;
As if divinity had catched
The itch on purpose to be scratched;
Or, like a mountebank, did wound
And stab herself with doubts profound,
Only to show with how small pain
The sores of faith are cured again; 170

Although by woeful proof we find
They always leave a scar behind.
He knew the seat of Paradise,
Could tell in what degree it lies,
And, as he was disposed, could prove it
Below the moon, or else above it;
What Adam dreamt of when his bride
Came from her closet in his side;
Whether the devil tempted her
By a High Dutch interpreter; 18
If either of them had a navel;
Who first made music malleable;
Whether the serpent at the Fall
Had cloven feet, or none at all.
All this, without a gloss or comment,
He could unriddle in a moment,
In proper terms, such as men smatter
When they throw out and miss the matter.
   For his religion, it was fit
To match his learning and his wit; 19
'Twas Presbyterian true blue;
For he was of that stubborn crew
Of errant saints whom all men grant
To be the true church militant;
Such as do build their faith upon
The holy text of pike and gun;
Decide all controversies by
Infallible artillery;
And prove their doctrine orthodox,
By apostolic blows and knocks; 20
Call fire and sword and desolation
A godly, thorough reformation,
Which always must be carried on,
And still be doing, never done;
As if religion were intended
For nothing else but to be mended;
A sect whose chief devotion lies
In odd perverse antipathies;
In falling out with that or this,
And finding somewhat still amiss; 21
More peevish, cross, and splenetic,
Than dog distract or monkey sick;
That with more care keep holy-day
The wrong, than others the right way;
Compound for sins they are inclined to,
By damning those they have no mind to;
Still so perverse and opposite,
As if they worshiped God for spite.
The self-same thing they will abhor
One way, and long another for. 220
Free will they one way disavow,
Another, nothing else allow.
All piety consists therein
In them, in other men all sin.

Rather than fail, they will defy
That which they love most tenderly;
Quarrel with minced-pies, and disparage
Their best and dearest friend, plum-por-
    ridge;
Fat pig and goose itself oppose,
And blaspheme custard through the nose. 230
Th' apostles of this fierce religion,
Like Mahomet's, were ass and widgeon,
To whom our knight, by fast instinct
Of wit and temper, was so linked,
As if hypocrisy and nonsense
Had got th' advowson⁴ of his conscience.
    Thus was he gifted, and accoutred,
We mean on th' inside, not the outward:
That next of all we shall discuss;
Then listen, sirs, it follows thus: 240
    His tawny beard was th' equal grace
Both of his wisdom and his face;
In cut and die so like a tile,
A sudden view it would beguile;
The upper part whereof was whey,
The nether orange mixed with gray.
This hairy meteor did denounce
The fall of scepters and of crowns;
With grizzly type did represent
Declining age of government,   250
And tell, with hieroglyphic spade,
Its own grave and the state's were made.
Like Samson's heart-breakers, it grew
In time to make a nation rue;
Though it contributed its own fall,
To wait upon the public downfall;
It was monastic, and did grow
In holy orders by strict vow.
Of rule as sullen and severe
As that of rigid Cordelier,   260
'Twas bound to suffer persecution
And martyrdom with resolution;
T' oppose itself against the hate
And vengeance of th' incensèd state,
In whose defiance it was worn,
Still ready to be pulled and torn,
With red-hot irons to be tortured,
Reviled, and spit upon, and martyred;
Maugre all which 'twas to stand fast
As long as monarchy should last;   270
But when the state should hap to reel,
'Twas to submit to fatal steel,
And fall, as it was consecrate,
A sacrifice to fall of state,
Whose thread of life the Fatal Sisters
Did twist together with its whiskers,

⁴ The patronage of a church living.

And twine so close that Time should never
In life or death their fortunes sever,
But with his rusty sickle mow
Both down together at a blow.   280
    So learnèd Taliacotius, from
The brawny part of porter's bum,
Cut supplemental noses, which
Would last as long as parent breech,
But when the date of Nock was out,
Off dropped the sympathetic snout.
    His back, or rather burthen, showed
As if it stooped with its own load;
For as Aeneas bore his sire
Upon his shoulders through the fire,   290
Our knight did bear no less a pack
Of his own buttocks on his back;
Which now had almost got the upper
Hand of his head, for want of crupper.
To poise this equally, he bore
A paunch of the same bulk before,
Which still he had a special care
To keep well-crammed with thrifty fare,
As white-pot,⁵ buttermilk, and curds,
Such as a country-house affords;   300
With other victual which anon
We further shall dilate upon,
When of his hose we come to treat,
The cupboard where he kept his meat.
    His doublet was of sturdy buff,
And though not sword, yet cudgel-proof,
Whereby 'twas fitter for his use
Who feared no blows but such as bruise.
    His breeches were of rugged woollen,
And had been at the siege of Bullen;   310
To old King Harry so well known,
Some writers held they were his own.
Through they were lined with many a piece
Of ammunition-bread and cheese
And fat black-puddings,⁶ proper food
For warriors that delight in blood.
For, as we said, he always chose
To carry victual in his hose,
That often tempted rats and mice
The ammunition to surprise;   320
And when he put a hand but in
The one or th' other magazine,
They stoutly in defense on 't stood,
And from the wounded foe drew blood;
And till th' were stormed and beaten out,
Ne'er left the fortified redoubt.
And though knights-errant, as some think,
Of old did neither eat nor drink,

⁵ A pudding of milk, eggs, sugar, and bread.
⁶ Sausages of blood and suet.

Because, when thorough deserts vast
And regions desolate they passed,   330
Where belly-timber above ground
Or under was not to be found,
Unless they grazed, there's not one word
Of their provision on record;
Which made some confidently write,
They had no stomachs but to fight.
'Tis false; for Arthur wore in hall
Round table like a farthingal,
On which, with shirt pulled out behind
And eke before, his good knights dined.   340
Though 'twas no table, some suppose,
But a huge pair of round trunk-hose,
In which he carried as much meat
As he and all his knights could eat,
When, laying by their swords and trun-
          cheons,
They took their breakfasts or their nun-
          cheons.
But let that pass at present, lest
We should forget where we digressed,
As learnèd authors use, to whom
We leave 't, and to the purpose come.   350
   His puissant sword unto his side,
Near his undaunted heart, was tied,
With basket-hilt that would hold broth,
And serve for fight and dinner both;
In it he melted lead for bullets,
To shoot at foes, and sometimes pullets,
To whom he bore so fell a grutch,
He ne'er gave quarter t' any such.
The trenchant blade, Toledo trusty,
For want of fighting was grown rusty,   360
And ate into itself for lack
Of somebody to hew and hack:
The peaceful scabbard where it dwelt
The rancor of its edge had felt;
For of the lower end two handful
It had devoured, 'twas so manful,
And so much scorned to lurk in case,
As if it durst not show its face.
In many desperate attempts
Of warrants, exigents, contempts,   370
It had appeared with courage bolder,
Than Sergeant Bum invading shoulder;
Oft had it ta'en possession,
And prisoners too, or made them run.
   This sword a dagger had, his page,
That was but little for his age,
And therefore waited on him so,
As dwarfs upon knights-errant do.
It was a serviceable dudgeon,[7]

   [7] A short dagger.

Either for fighting or for drudging;   380
When it had stabbed, or broke a head,
It would scrape trenchers or chip bread;
Toast cheese or bacon; though it were
To bait a mouse-trap, 'twould not care;
'Twould make clean shoes, and in the earth
Set leeks and onions, and so forth.
It had been 'prentice to a brewer,
Where this and more it did endure,
But left the trade, as many more
Have lately done on the same score.   390
   In th' holsters at his saddle-bow
Two aged pistols he did stow,
Among the surplus of such meat
As in his hose he could not get.
They were upon hard duty still,
And every night stood sentinel,
To guard the magazine in th' hose
From two-legged and from four-legged foes.
   Thus clad and fortified, Sir Knight
From peaceful home set forth to fight.   400
But first with nimble active force
He got on th' outside of his horse.
For having but one stirrup tied
T' his saddle on the further side,
It was so short h' had much ado
To reach it with his desperate toe;
But after many strains and heaves,
He got up to the saddle-eaves,
From whence he vaulted into th' seat
With so much vigor, strength, and heat,   410
That he had almost tumbled over
With his own weight, but did recover
By laying hold on tail and mane,
Which oft he used instead of rein.
   But now we talk of mounting steed,
Before we further do proceed,
It doth behove us to say something
Of that which bore our valiant bumkin.
The beast was sturdy, large, and tall,
With mouth of meal and eyes of wall—   420
I would say eye, for h' had but one,
As most agree, though some say none.
He was well stayed, and in his gait
Preserved a grave, majestic state;
At spur or switch no more he skipped
Or mended pace, than Spaniard whipped,
And yet so fiery, he would bound,
As if he grieved to touch the ground;
That Caesar's horse, who as fame goes,
Had corns upon his feet and toes,   430
Was not by half so tender-hoofed,
Nor trod upon the ground so soft;
And as that beast would kneel and stoop

(Some write) to take his rider up,
So Hudibras his ('tis well known)
Would often do to set him down.
We shall not need to say what lack
Of leather was upon his back,
For that was hidden under pad,
And breech of knight, galled full as bad. 440
His strutting ribs on both sides showed
Like furrows he himself had plowed;
For underneath the skirt of panel,
'Twixt every two there was a channel.
His draggling tail hung in the dirt,
Which on his rider he would flirt,
Still as his tender side he pricked,
With armed heel, or with unarmed, kicked:
For Hudibras wore but one spur,
As wisely knowing could he stir   450
To active trot one side of's horse,
The other would not hang an arse.
    A Squire he had whose name was Ralph,
That in th' adventure went his half,
Though writers, for more statelier tone,
Do call him Ralpho, 'tis all one;
And when we can, with metre safe,
We'll call him so; if not, plain Ralph;
(For rhyme the rudder is of verses,
With which, like ships, they steer their
        courses) :   460
An equal stock of wit and valour
He had laid in, by birth a tailor.
The mighty Tyrian queen, that gained
With subtle shreds a tract of land,
Did leave it with a castle fair
To his great ancestor, her heir;
From him descended cross-legged knights,
Famed for their faith and warlike fights
Against the bloody Cannibal,
Whom they destroyed both great and
        small.   470
This sturdy Squire had, as well
As the bold Trojan knight seen hell,
Not with a counterfeited pass
Of golden bough, but true gold-lace:
His knowledge was not far behind
The Knight's, but of another kind,
And he another way came by't.
Some call it Gift, and some New Light;
A liberal art that costs no pains
Of study, industry, or brains.   480
His wits were sent him for a token,
But in the carriage cracked and broken;
Like commendation nine-pence crooked
With—To and from my love—it looked.
He ne'er considered it, as loth

To look a gift-horse in the mouth,
And very wisely would lay forth
No more upon it than 'twas worth;
But as he got it freely, so
He spent it frank and freely too: 490
For saints themselves will sometimes be,
Of gifts that cost them nothing, free.
By means of this, with hem and cough,
Prolongers to enlightened snuff,
He could deep mysteries unriddle
As easily as thread a needle;
For as of vagabonds we say
That they are ne'er beside their way,
Whate'er men speak by this New Light,
Still they are sure to be i' th' right. 500
'Tis a dark lantern of the Spirit,
Which none see by but those that bear it;
A light that falls down from on high,
For spiritual trades to couzen by;
An *ignis fatuus*, that bewitches,
And leads men into pools and ditches,
To make them dip themselves and sound
For Christendom in dirty pond;
To dive like wild-fowl for salvation,
And fish to catch regeneration.   510
This light inspires and plays upon
The nose of saint, like bagpipe drone,
And speaks through hollow empty soul,
As through a trunk or whispering hole,
Such language as no mortal ear
But spiritual eaves-dropper's can hear:
So Phoebus or some friendly Muse
Into small poets song infuse,
Which they at second-hand rehearse,
Through reed or bagpipe, verse for verse. 520
    Thus Ralph became infallible
As three or four-legged oracle,
The ancient cup, or modern chair,
Spoke truth point-blank, though unaware.
    For mystic learning, wondrous able
In magic, talisman, and cabal,
Whose primitive tradition reaches
As far as Adam's first green breeches;
Deep-sighted in intelligences,
Ideas, atoms, influences;   530
And much of *Terra Incognita*,
Th' intelligible world, could say;
A deep occult philosopher,
As learned as the Wild Irish are,
Or Sir Agrippa, for profound
And solid lying much renowned:
He Anthroposophus and Fludd
And Jacob Behmen understood;
Knew many an amulet and charm,

That would do neither good nor harm; 540
In Rosicrucian lore as learned
As he that *Vere adeptus* earned.
He understood the speech of birds
As well as they themselves do words;
Could tell what subtlest parrots mean,
That speak and think contrary clean;
What member 'tis of whom they talk
When they cry "Rope," and "Walk, knave,
    walk."
He'd extract numbers out of matter,
And keep them in a glass, like water, 550
Of sovereign power to make men wise;
For, dropped in blear thick-sighted eyes,
They'd make them see in darkest night,
Like owls, though purblind in the light.
By help of these (as he professed)
He had First Matter seen undressed:
He took her naked, all alone,
Before one rag of form was on.
The Chaos, too, he had descried,
And seen quite through, or else he lied: 560
Not that of pasteboard, which men show
For groats at fair of Barthol'mew;
But its great grandsire, first o' th' name,
Whence that and Reformation came,
Both cousin-germans, and right able
T' inveigle and draw in the rabble.
But Reformation was, some say,
O' th' younger house to Puppet-play.
He could foretell whats'ever was
By consequence to come to pass; 570
As death of great men, alterations,
Diseases, battles, inundations:
All this without th' eclipse of sun,
Or dreadful comet, he hath done
By inward light, a way as good,
And easy to be understood;
But with more lucky hit than those
That use to make the stars depose,
Like Knights o' th' Post, and falsely charge
Upon themselves what others forge; 580
As if they were consenting to
All mischief in the world men do,
Or, like the devil, did tempt and sway 'em
To rogueries, and then betray 'em.
They'll search a planet's house to know
Who broke and robbed a house below;
Examine Venus and the Moon,
Who stole a thimble and a spoon;
And though they nothing will confess,
Yet by their very looks can guess, 590
And tell what guilty aspect bodes,
Who stole, and who received the goods.

They'll question Mars, and by his look
Detect who 'twas that nimmed a cloak;
Make Mercury confess, and peach
Those thieves which he himself did teach.
They'll find i' th' physiognomies
O' th' planets, all men's destinies,
Like him that took the doctor's bill,
And swallowed it instead o' th' pill; 600
Cast the nativity o' th' question,
And from positions to be guessed on,
As sure as if they knew the moment
Of Native's birth, tell what will come on't.
They'll feel the pulses of the stars,
To find out agues, cough, catarrhs,
And tell what crisis does divine
The rot in sheep, or mange in swine;
In men, what gives or cures the itch,
What makes them cuckolds, poor or
    rich; 610
What gains or loses, hangs or saves;
What makes men great, what fools or
    knaves,
But not what wise, for only of those
The stars (they say) cannot dispose.
No more than can the astrologians;
There they say right, and like true Trojans:
This Ralpho knew, and therefore took
The other course, of which we spoke.
    Thus was th' accomplished Squire endued
With gifts and knowledge perilous shrewd.
Never did trusty squire with knight, 621
Or knight with squire, jump more right.
Their arms and equipage did fit,
As well as virtues, parts, and wit:
Their valors too were of a rate,
And out they sallied at the gate.
    Few miles on horseback had they jogged
But Fortune unto them turned dogged;
For they a sad adventure met,
Of which we now prepare to treat. 630
But ere we venture to unfold
Achievements so resolved and bold,
We should, as learned poets use,
Invoke th' assistance of some Muse,
However critics count it sillier
Than jugglers talking t' a familiar;
We think 'tis no great matter which,
They're all alike, yet we shall pitch
On one that fits our purpose most,
Whom therefore thus do we accost: 640
    Thou that with ale or viler liquors,
Didst inspire Withers, Prynne, and Vicars,
And force them, though it were in spite
Of Nature and their stars, to write;

Who (as we find in sullen writs,
And cross-grained works of modern wits)
With vanity, opinion, want,
The wonder of the ignorant,
The praises of the author, penned
By himself or wit-ensuring friend,   650
The itch of picture in the front,
With bays and wicked rhyme upon't,
(All that is left o' th' Forked Hill
To make men scribble without skill)
Canst make a poet, spite of Fate,
And teach all people to translate,
Though out of languages in which
They understand no part of speech;
Assist me but this once I 'mplore,
And I shall trouble thee no more.   660
    In western clime there is a town,
To those that dwell therein well known;
Therefore there needs no more be said here;
We unto them refer our reader;
For brevity is very good,
When w'are, or are not understood.
To this town people did repair
On days of market or of fair,
And to cracked fiddle and hoarse tabor,
In merriment did drudge and labor: 670
But now a sport more formidable
Had raked together village rabble;
'Twas an old way of recreating,
Which learned butchers call Bear-baiting;
A bold adventurous exercise,
With ancient heroes in high prize;
For authors do affirm it came
From Isthmian or Nemaean game;
Other derive it from the Bear
That's fixed in northern hemisphere,   680
And round about the pole does make
A circle, like a bear at stake,
That at the chain's end wheels about,
And overturns the rabble-rout:
For after solemn proclamation
In the bear's name (as is the fashion
According to the law of arms,
To keep men from inglorious harms)
That none presume to come so near
As forty foot of stake of bear,   690
If any yet be so foolhardy,
T' expose themselves to vain jeopardy,
If they come wounded off and lame,
No honour's got by such a maim,
Although the bear gain much, being bound
In honour to make good his ground
When he's engaged, and take no notice,
If any press upon him, who 'tis,

But lets them know, at their own cost,
That he intends to keep his post.   700
This to prevent and other harms
Which always wait on feats of arms,
(For in the hurry of a fray
'Tis hard to keep out of harm's way)
Thither the Knight his course did steer,
To keep the peace 'twixt dog and bear,
As he believed he was bound to do
In conscience and commission too;
And therefore thus bespoke the Squire:
    "We that are wisely mounted higher   710
Than constables in curule wit,
When on tribunal bench we sit,
Like speculators should foresee,
From Pharos of authority,
Portended mischiefs further than
Low proletarian tithing-men;
And therefore being informed by bruit
That dog and bear are to dispute,
For so of late men fighting name,
Because they often prove the same   720
(For where the first does hap to be,
The last does *coincidere*);
Quantum in nobis, have thought good
To save th' expense of Christian blood,
And try if we by mediation
Of treaty and accommodation
Can end the quarrel, and compose
The bloody duel without blows.
Are not our liberties, our lives,
The laws, religion, and our wives   730
Enough at once to lie at stake
For Covenant and the Cause's sake,
But in that quarrel dogs and bears,
As well as we, must venture theirs?
This feud, by Jesuits invented,
By evil counsel is fomented;
There is a Machiavellian plot
(Though every *nare olfact* it not) [8]
A deep design in't to divide
The well-affected that confide,   740
By setting brother against brother,
To claw and curry one another.
Have we not enemies *plus satis*,[9]
That *cane et angue pejus*[10] hate us?
And shall we turn our fangs and claws
Upon ourselves, without a cause?
That some occult design doth lie
In bloody cynarctomachy
Is plain enough to him that knows

[8] Though every nostril smell it not.
[9] More than enough.
[10] Worse than dog and snake.

How Saints lead Brothers by the nose. 750
I wish myself a pseudo-prophet,
But sure some mischief will come of it,
Unless by providential wit,
Or force, we averruncate it.[11]
For what design, what interest,
Can beast have to encounter beast?
They fight for no espoused Cause,
Frail Privilege, Fundamental Laws,
Nor for a thorough Reformation,
Nor Covenant nor Protestation, 760
Nor Liberty of Consciences,
Nor Lords' and Commons' Ordinances;
Nor for the Church, nor for Church Lands,
To get them in their own no hands;
Nor evil counsellors to bring
To justice, that seduce the King;
Nor for the worship of us men,
Though we have done as much for them.
Th' Egyptians worshipped dogs, and for
Their faith made fierce and zealous war; 770
Others adored a rat, and some
For their church suffered martyrdom;
The Indians fought for the truth
Of th' elephant and monkey's tooth,
And many, to defend that faith,
Fought it out *mordicus*[12] to death;
But no beast ever was so slight,
For man, as for his god, to fight:
They have more wit, alas! and know
Themselves and us better than so. 780
But we, we only do infuse
The rage in them like *boute-feus*;[13]
'Tis our example that instils
In them th' infection of our ills.
For, as some late philosophers
Have well observed, beasts that converse
With man take after him, as hogs
Get pigs all th' year, and bitches dogs;
Just so, by our example, cattle
Learn to give one another battle. 790
We read in Nero's time, the Heathen,
When they destroyed the Christian brethren,
They sewed them in the skins of bears,
And then set dogs about their ears;
From whence, no doubt, th' invention came
Of this lewd antichristian game."
  To this quoth Ralpho, "Verily
The point seems very plain to be;
It is an antichristian game,

Unlawful both in thing and name. 800
First, for the name; the word Bear-baiting
Is carnal, and of man's creating,
For certainly there's no such word
In all the Scripture on record;
Therefore unlawful, and a sin:
And so is (secondly) the thing;
A vile assembly 'tis, that can
No more be proved by Scripture than
Provincial, Classic, National,
Mere human creature-cobwebs all. 810
Thirdly, it is idolatrous;
For when men run a-whoring thus
With their inventions, whatsoe'er
The thing be, whether dog or bear,
It is idolatrous and Pagan,
No less than worshipping of Dagon."
  Quoth Hudibras, "I smell a rat;
Ralpho, thou dost prevaricate:
For though the thesis which thou lay'st
Be true *ad amussim*[14] as thou say'st; 820
(For that bear-baiting should appear
Jure divino[15] lawfuller
Than Synods are, thou dost deny
Totidem verbis,[16] so do I)
Yet there's a fallacy in this;
For if by sly *homoeosis*,
Thou wouldst sophistically imply
Both are unlawful, —I deny."
  "And I" quoth Ralpho, "do not doubt
But bear-baiting may be made out, 830
In gospel times, as lawful as is
Provincial or parochial classis;
And that both are so near of kin,
And like in all, as well as sin,
That put 'em in a bag and shake 'em,
Yourself o' th' sudden would mistake 'em,
And not know which is which, unless
You measure by their wickedness;
For 'tis not hard t' imagine whether 839
O' th' two is worst, though I name neither."
  Quoth Hudibras, "Thou offer'st much,
But art not able to keep touch;
Mira de lente, as 'tis i' th' adage,
Id est, to make a leek a cabbage:
Thou canst at best but overstrain
A paradox and thy own hot brain;
For what can synods have at all,
With bears that's analogical?
Or what relation has debating
Of Church affairs with bear-baiting? 850

[11] Weed it out.
[12] With the teeth.
[13] Firebrand used to set off cannon.

[14] Exactly.
[15] By divine law.
[16] In so many words.

A just comparison still is
Of things *ejusdem generis*;[17]
And then what genus rightly doth
Include and comprehend them both?
If animal, both of us may
As justly pass for bears as they,
For we are animals no less,
Although of different specieses.
But, Ralpho, this in no fit place,
Nor time, to argue out the case;   860
For now the field is not far off
Where we must give the world a proof
Of deeds, not words, and such as suit
Another manner of dispute:
A controversy that affords
Actions for arguments, not words;
Which we must manage at a rate
Of prowess and conduct adequate
To what our place and fame doth promise,
And all the godly expect from us.   870
Nor shall they be deceived, unless
We're slurred and outed by success;
Success, the mark no mortal wit
Or surest hand can always hit:
For whatsoe'er we perpetrate,
We do but row, we are steered by Fate,
Which in success oft disinherits,
For spurious causes, noblest merits.
Great actions are not always true sons
Of great and mighty resolutions;   880
Nor do the bold'st attempts bring forth
Events still equal to their worth;
But sometimes fail, and in their stead
Fortune and cowardice succeed.
Yet we have no great cause to doubt,
Our actions still have borne us out;

17 Of the same kind.

Which though they're known to be so
    ample,
We need no copy from example;
We are not the only person durst
Attempt this province, nor the first.   890
In northern clime a valorous knight
Did whilom kill his bear in fight,
And wound a Fiddler: we have both
Of these the objects of our wroth,
And equal fame and glory from
Th' attempt, or victory to come.
'Tis sung there is a valiant [Mamaluke],
In foreign land ycleped—
To whom we have been oft compared
For person, parts, address, and beard;   900
Both equally reputed stout,
And in the same cause both have fought:
He oft in such attempts as these
Came off with glory and success;
Nor will we fail in th' execution,
For want of equal resolution.
Honor is like a widow, won
With brisk attempt and putting on;
With entering manfully, and urging,
Not slow approaches, like a virgin."   910
    This said, as once the Phrygian knight,
So ours with rusty steel did smite
His Trojan horse, and just as much
He mended pace upon the touch;
But from his empty stomach groaned
Just as that hollow beast did sound,
And angry, answered from behind,
With brandished tail and blast of wind.
So have I seen, with armed heel,
A wight bestride a Commonweal,   920
While still the more he kicked and spurred.
The less the sullen jade has stirred.
                                            [1663]

CHARACTERS

A POLITICIAN

Is a speculative statesman, student in the liberal art of free government, that did all his exercises in the late times of cursed memory at the *Rota*, but is not yet admitted to practice. He is a state-empiric, that has receipts for all the infirmities of governments, but knows nothing of their constitutions, nor how to proportion his dose. He dissects the body-politic into controversies, as anatomists do the body of a man, and mangles every part, only to find out new disputes. He weighs every thing in the balance of property, which at first would turn with the fortieth part of a grain, but since by use is worn so false that it inclines one way more than the other most abominably. He shapes dirty governments on his *Rota* like pipkins, that never prove without some crack or flaw. He is always finding out of expedients, but they are such as light in his way by chance, and nobody else would stoop to take up. The harder he charges his head with politics, the more it recoils and is nearer cracking; for, though in matters of action, the more experience a man has the more he knows, it fares otherways with speculations, in which an error is seldom discovered until it be reduced to practice; and if but one of these creep in among his contemplations, it makes way for others to follow, and the further he pursues his thoughts, the further he is out of his way. He derives the pedigree of government from its first original, and makes it begotten on the body of a woman by the first father, and born with the first child, from whom all that are at present in the world are lineally descended. He is wonderfully enamoured of a Commonwealth because it is like a common whore which every one may have to do with; but cannot abide Monarchy, because it is honest and confined to one. He despises the present government, let it be what it will, and prefers the old Greek and Roman, like those that wear long beards, trunk-hose, and ruffs, but never considers that in that they are more fantastic than those that affect the newest fashions.

A BUMPKIN OR COUNTRY-SQUIRE

Is a clown of rank and degree. He is the growth of his own land, a kind of Autochthonus, like the Athenians, that sprung out of their own ground; or barnacles that grow upon trees in Scotland: his homely education has rendered him a native only of his own soil, and a foreigner to all other places, from which he differs in language, manner of living, and behaviour, which are as rugged as the coat of a colt that has been bred upon a common. The custom of being the best man in his own territories has made him the worst every where else. He assumes the upper end of the table at an ale-house, as his birthright; receives the homage of his company, which are always subordinate, and dispenses ale and communication, like a self-conforming teacher in a conventicle. The chief points he treats on are the memoirs of his dogs and horses, which he repeats as often as a holder-forth, that has but two sermons; to which if he adds the history of his hawks and fishing, he is very painful and laborious. He does his endeavor to appear a drole, but his wit being, like his estate, within the compass of a hedge, is so profound and obscure to a stranger, that it requires a commentary, and is not to be understood without a perfect knowledge of all circumstances of persons and the particular idiom of the place. He has no ambition to appear a person of civil prudence and understanding, more than in putting off a lame infirm jade for sound wind and limb; to which purpose he brings his squirehood and groom to vouch; and, rather than fail, will outswear an affidavit-man. The top of his entertainment is horrible strong beer, which he pours into his guests (as the Dutch did water into our merchants when they tortured them at Amboyna) till they confess they can drink no more; and then he triumphs over them as subdued and vanquished, no less by the strength of his brain, than his drink. When he salutes a man, he lays violent hands upon him, and gripes and shakes him, like a fit of an ague: and, when he accosts a lady, he stamps with his foot, like a French fencer, and makes a longee[1] at her, in which he always misses his aim, too high or too low, and hits her on the nose or chin. He is never without some rough-

[1] lunge.

handed flatterer, that rubs him, like a horse, with a curry-comb, till he kicks and grunts with the pleasure of it. He has old family stories and jests that fell to him with the estate and have been left from heir to heir time out of mind; with these he entertains all comers over and over, and has added some of his own times, which he intends to transmit over to posterity. He has but one way of making all men welcome that come to his house, and that is by making himself and them drunk; while his servants take the same course with theirs, which he approves of as good and faithful service, and the rather because, if he has occasion to tell a strange improbable story, they may be in readiness to vouch with the more impudence and make it a case of conscience to lie as well as drink for his credit. All the heroical glory he aspires to, is but to be reputed a most potent and victorious stealer of deer and beater-up of parks, to which purpose he has compiled commentaries of his own actions that treat of his dreadful adventures in the night, of giving battle in the dark, discomfiting keepers, horsing the deer on his own back, and making off with equal resolution and success. He goes to bawdy-houses to see fashions; that is, to have his pocket picked, and the pox into the bargain.

there being so many that undertake that journey, how few soever arrive at the end of it, they must of necessity jostle, crowd and fall foul upon one another, as we find they do, and therefore he thinks it best, both for himself and the ease of his fellow-travellers, to get out of the common road and leave the more room for those that cannot leap ditches, and if they could, when they are once out, do not know how to get in again so well as he does. He is but a kind of modest Ranter, that believes Christian liberty and natural liberty may very well consist together; for being things of the same kind there can be no possible difference between them, but only in degree, which can never cause the one to destroy the other; and natural liberty being of the elder house, if there be any precedency, ought to have a right to it. He believes obedience is nothing but a civil complacence, that obliges a man no further than saying, "I am your humble servant"; and that uniformity is too like a thing made and complotted to be true. He believes laws are made to punish those only that do not know how to break them discreetly, and to do no man right that has not money or interest to compel them to it; that like foolish magistrates require respect in public, but will endure all manner of affronts in private, especially among friends.

A LATITUDINARIAN

Gives himself the more scope, because he that has the largest conscience is most like, in all probability, to keep within the compass of it: for one that is strait is uneasy, apt to pinch, and will not do half the service that a wider will endure. He does not greatly care to live within the pale of his Church, but had rather have the Church live within his pale. He believes the way to heaven is never the better for being strait, and if it could be made wider it would be much more convenient; for

A FANATIC

Saint Paul was thought by Festus to be mad with too much learning; but the Fanatics of our times are mad with too little. He chooses himself one of the Elect, and packs a Committee of his own Party to judge the twelve Tribes of Israel. The Apostles in the primitive Church worked miracles to confirm and propagate their doctrine; but he thinks to confirm his by working at his trade. He assumes a privilege to impress what text of Scripture he pleases for his own use, and leaves those that make against him for the use of the wicked. His religion, that tends only to faction and sedition, is neither fit for peace nor war, but times of a condition between both; like the sails of a ship that will not endure a storm and are of no use at all in a calm. He believes it has enough of the primitive Christian if it be but persecuted as that was, no matter for the piety or doctrine of it; as if there were nothing required to prove the truth of a religion but the punishment of the professors of it; like the old mathematicians, that were never believed to be profoundly knowing in their profession until they had run through all punishments and just 'scaped the fork. He is all for suffering for religion, but nothing for acting; for he accounts good works no better than encroachments upon the merits of free believing, and a good life the most troublesome and unthrifty way to Heaven. He canonizes himself a Saint in his own life-time, as the more sure and certain way and less troublesome to others. He outgrows ordinances, as a 'prentice that has served out his time does his indentures, and being a freeman supposes himself at liberty to set up what religion he pleases. He calls his own supposed abilities *gifts*, and disposes of himself like a foundation designed to pious uses, although, like others of the same kind, they are always diverted to other purposes. He owes all his *gifts* to his ignorance, as beggars do the alms they receive to their poverty. They are such as the fairies are said to drop in mens' shoes, and when they are discovered to give them over and confer no more; for when his *gifts* are discovered they vanish and come to nothing. He is but a puppet saint that moves he knows not how, and his ignorance is the dull leaden weight that puts all his parts in motion. His outward man is a saint, and his inward man a reprobate; for he carries his vices in his heart, and his religion in his face.

A PLAY-WRITER

Of our times is like a fanatic, that has no wit in ordinary easy things and yet attempts the hardest task of brains in the whole world, only because, whether his play or work please or displease, he is certain to come off better than he deserves, and find some of his own latitude to applaud him, which he could never expect any other way; and is as sure to lose no reputation, because he has none to venture.

> Like gaming rooks, that never stick
> To play for hundreds upon tick,
> 'Cause, if they chance to lose at play,
> Th'ave not one halfpenny to pay;
> And, if they win a hundred pound,
> Gain, if for sixpence they compound.

Nothing encourages him more in his undertaking than his ignorance, for he has not wit enough to understand so much as the difficulty of what he attempts; therefore he runs on boldly like a foolhardy wit, and Fortune, that favors fools and the bold, sometimes takes notice of him for his double capacity, and receives him into her good graces. He has one motive more, and that is the concurrent ignorant judgment of the present age, in which his sottish fopperies pass with applause, like Oliver Cromwell's oratory among fanatics of his own canting inclination. He finds it easier to write in rime than prose; for the world being overcharged with romances, he finds his plots, passions, and repartees ready made to his hand; and if he can but turn them into rime, the thievery is disguised, and they pass for his own wit and invention without question; like a stolen cloak made into a coat, or dyed into another color. Besides this he makes no conscience of stealing any thing that lights in his way, and borrows the advice of so many to correct, enlarge, and amend what he has ill-favoredly patched together, that it becomes like a thing drawn by Council, and none of his own performance, or the son of a whore that has no one certain father. He has very great reason to prefer verse before prose in his compositions; for rime is like lace, that serves excellently well to hide the piecing and coarseness of bad stuff, contributes mightily to the bulk, and makes the less serve by the many impertinencies it commonly requires to make way for it; for very few are endowed with abilities to bring it in on its own account. This he finds to be good husbandry, and a kind of necessary thrift; for they that have but a little ought to make as much of it as they can. His prologue, which is commonly none of his own, is always better than his play, like a piece of cloth that's fine in the beginning and coarse afterwards, though it has but one topic, and that's the same that is used by malefactors, when they are to be tried, to except against as many of the jury as they can.

SAMUEL PEPYS (1633-1703)

The name of Pepys, to many modern readers, has come to signify only a small gossip. His diary, which he secretly kept in shorthand and which was not deciphered until the nineteenth century, is responsible for his popular reputation. It was discovered among the books and papers which he left by will to Magdalene College, Cambridge. It is one of the most amazing and most enjoyable of self-revelations; and it is so frank and honest even in situations where most of us would have tried to deceive ourselves, that Pepys is often regarded as a shallow babbler. But the real Pepys is not to be disposed of so simply as that; such an estimate does not suggest the interesting, and even baffling, problem of his personality. His contemporaries saw in him a man of circumspect respectability, of practical judgment and tact, of unusual devotion and ability in public affairs, one of the most admirable public servants of his day. Modern historians agree that his success and esteem were deserved, especially for his services to the English navy.

After graduating from Cambridge in 1653, he entered the service of his kinsman, Sir Edward Montagu, later first Earl of Sandwich, who figures in the diary as "my Lord." In 1655 he married Elizabeth St. Michel, the fifteen-year-old daughter of a French Huguenot father and an English mother; their happy, though tempestuous, married life is recorded in the *Diary*, and Pepys grieved with a deep repentance for his infidelities when his wife died in 1669. The rapid rise of Pepys in the government service began in 1660 when he and his patron Montagu went with a delegation to Holland to accompany Charles II back to England. His *Diary* records minutely the stages of his success from that time until 1668. He became secretary of the Navy Board in 1660; was appointed to the Tangier Commission in 1662; became surveyor-general of the Victualling Office in 1665; and, as he records faithfully, grew richer every year. In 1668 he was alarmed by the prospect of blindness and bade his *Diary* farewell, but his eyesight was spared him to the end of his life. He served as secretary of the Admiralty from 1672 to 1678 and again from 1684 to 1688. During the excitement of the Popish Plot he came under unjust suspicion and was imprisoned in the Tower from December 1678 to the following March, when he was released for lack of evidence. In 1684 and 1685 he was elected president of the Royal Society, a recognition of the value to the Society of his patronage. Owing to his loyalty to the Stuarts, he retired from public office after the Revolution of 1688. In 1690 he published his notable *Memoirs of the Navy*, which added to the respect which was accorded him by the public in his old age. He died on May 26, 1703.

His library, including the manuscript *Diary*, was left by will to Magdalene College, Cambridge. The *Diary* was first deciphered by the Reverend John Smith and published, with omissions, by Lord Braybrooke in 1825. A more nearly complete edition is by Henry B. Wheatley, 1893-99. Several volumes of letters and miscellaneous papers by Pepys have been published by J. R. Tanner, 1926 and 1928. A famous essay on Pepys by Robert Louis Stevenson is included in his *Familiar Studies of Men and Books*. There are many readable volumes devoted to Pepys, among them H. B. Wheatley, *Samuel Pepys and the World He Lived in* (1880); Gamaliel Bradford, *The Soul of Samuel Pepys* (1924); Arthur Ponsonby, *Samuel Pepys* (English Men of Letters Series, 1928); and John Drinkwater, *Pepys, His Life and Character* (1930). The most elaborate and authoritative biography is by Arthur Bryant (Cambridge, Eng., 1933-38).

DIARY

1660

May 23rd. In the morning came infinity of people on board from the King to go along with him. My Lord, Mr. Crewe, and others, go on shore to meet the King as he comes off from shore, where Sir R. Stayner bringing His Majesty into the boat, I hear His Majesty did with a great deal of affection kiss my Lord upon his first meeting. The King, with the two Dukes and Queen of Bohemia, Princess Royal, and Prince of Orange, came on board, where I in their coming in kissed the King's, Queen's, and Princess's hands having done the other before. Infinite shooting off of the guns, and that in a disorder on purpose, which was better than if it had been otherwise. All day nothing but Lords and persons of honour on board, that we were exceeding full. Dined in a great deal of state, the Royal company by themselves in the coach, which was a blessed sight to see. After dinner the King and Duke altered the name of some of the ships, viz. the *Nazeby* into *Charles*; the *Richard, James*; the *Speaker, Mary*; the *Dunbar* (which was not in company with us), the *Henry*; *Winsly, Happy Return*; *Wakefield, Richmond*; *Lambert*, the *Henrietta*; *Cheriton*, the *Speedwell*; *Bradford*, the *Success*. That done, the Queen, Princess Royal, and Prince of Orange, took leave of the King, and the Duke of York went on board the *London*, and the Duke of Gloucester, the *Swiftsure*. Which done, we weighed anchor, and with a fresh gale and most happy weather we set sail for England. All the afternoon the King walked here and there, up and down (quite contrary to what I thought him to have been), very active and stirring. Upon the quarterdeck he fell into discourse of his escape from Worcester, where it made me ready to weep to hear the stories that he told of his difficulties that he had passed through, as his traveling four days and three nights on foot, every step up to his knees in dirt, with nothing but a green coat and a pair of country breeches on, and a pair of country shoes that made him so sore all over his feet, that he could scarce stir. Yet he was forced to run away from a miller and other company, that took them for rogues. His sitting at table at one place, where the master of the house, that had not seen him in eight years, did know him, but kept it private; when at the same table there was one that had been of his own regiment at Worcester, could not know him, but made him drink the King's health, and said that the King was at least four fingers higher than he. At another place he was by some servants of the house made to drink,

that they might know him not to be a Roundhead, which they swore he was. In another place at his inn, the master of the house, as the King was standing with his hands upon the back of a chair by the fireside, kneeled down and kissed his hand, privately, saying, that he would not ask who he was, but bid God bless him whither he was going. Then the difficulty of getting a boat to get into France, where he was fain to plot with the master thereof to keep his design from the four men and a boy (which was all his ship's company), and so go to Fécamp in France. At Rouen he looked so poorly, that the people went into the rooms before he went away to see whether he had not stolen something or other. . . . The King supped alone in the coach; after that I got a dish, and we four supped in my cabin, as at noon. . . . So to my cabin again, where the company still was, and were talking more of the King's difficulties; as how he was fain to eat a piece of bread and cheese out of a poor boy's pocket; how, at a Catholic house he was fain to lie in the priest's hole a good while in the house for his privacy. Under sail all night, and most glorious weather.

May 24th. Up, and make myself as fine as I could, with the linning stockings on and wide canons that I bought the other day at Hague. Extraordinary press of noble company, and great mirth all the day. . . . Walking upon the decks, where persons of honour all the afternoon, among others, Thomas Killigrew (a merry droll, but a gentleman of great esteem with the King), who told us many merry stories. . . . After this discourse I was called to write a pass for my Lord Mandeville to take up horses to London, which I wrote in the King's name, and carried it to him to sign, which was the first and only one that ever he signed in the ship *Charles*. To bed, coming in sight of land a little before night.

May 25th. By the morning we were come close to the land, and everybody made ready to get on shore. The King and the two Dukes did eat their breakfast before they went; and there being set some ship's diet before them, only to show them the manner of the ship's diet, they eat of nothing else but peas and pork, and boiled beef. I had Mr. Darcy in my cabin; and Dr. Clerke, who eat with me, told me how the King had given £50 to Mr. Shepley for my Lord's servants, and £500 among the officers and common men of the ship. I spoke to the Duke of York about business, who called me Pepys by name, and upon my desire did promise me his future favour. Great expectation of the King's making some knights, but there was none. About noon (though the brigantine that Beale made was there ready to carry him) yet he would go in my Lord's barge with the two Dukes. Our Captain steered, and my Lord went along bare with him. I went, and Mr. Mansell, and one of the King's footmen, and a dog that the King loved, in a boat by ourselves, and so got on shore when the King did, who was received by General Monk with all imaginable love and respect at his entrance upon the land at Dover. Infinite the crowd of people and the gallantry of the horsemen, citizens, and noblemen of all sorts. The Mayor of the town come and give him his white staff, the badge of his place, which the King did give him again. The Mayor also presented him from the town a very rich Bible, which he took, and said it was the thing that he loved above all things in the world. A canopy was provided for him to stand under, which he did, and talked a while with General Monk and others, and so into a stately coach there set for him, and so away through the town towards Canterbury, without making any stay at Dover. The shouting and joy expressed by all is past imagination. Seeing that my Lord did not stir out of his barge, I got into a boat, and so into his barge, and we back to the ship, seeing a man almost drowned that fell into the sea. My Lord almost transported with joy that he had done all this without any the

least blur or obstruction in the world, that could give offense to any, and with the great honour he thought it would be to him. Being overtook by the brigantine, my Lord and we went out of our barge into it, and so went on board with Sir W. Batten and the Vice- and Rear-Admirals. At night, I supped with the Captain, who told me what the King had given us. My Lord returned late, and at his coming did give me order to cause the mark to be gilded, and a crown and C. R. to be made at the head of the coach table, where the King to-day with his own hand did mark his height, which accordingly I caused the painter to do, and is now done, as is to be seen.

1661

April 23rd. About four I rose and got to the Abbey, where I followed Sir J. Denham, the Surveyor, with some company that he was leading in. And with much ado, by the favour of Mr. Cooper, his man, did get up into a great scaffold across the north end of the Abbey, where with a great deal of patience I sat from past four till eleven before the King came in. And a great pleasure it was to see the Abbey raised in the middle, all covered with red, and a throne (that is a chair) and footstool on the top of it; and all the officers of all kinds, so much as the very fiddlers, in red vests. At last comes in the Dean and Prebends of Westminster, with the Bishops (many of them in cloth of gold copes), and after them the Nobility, all in their Parliament robes, which was a most magnificent sight. Then the Duke, and the King with a scepter (carried by my Lord Sandwich) and sword and mond before him, and the crown too. The King in his robes, bare-headed, which was very fine. And after all had placed themselves, there was a sermon and the service; and then in the choir at the high altar, the King passed through all the ceremonies of the Coronation, which to my great grief I and most in the Abbey could not see. The crown being put upon his head, a great shout begun, and he came forth to the throne, and there passed more ceremonies: as taking the oath, and having things read to him by the Bishop; and his lords (who put on their caps as soon as the King put on his crown) and bishops come, and kneeled before him. And three times the King-at-Arms went to the three open places on the scaffold, and proclaimed, that if any one could show any reason why Charles Stuart should not be King of England, that now he should come and speak. And a General Pardon also was read by the Lord Chancellor, and medals flung up and down by my Lord Cornwallis, of silver, but I could not come by any. But so great a noise that I could make but little of the music; and indeed it was lost to everybody. I went out a little while before the King had done all his ceremonies, and went round the Abbey to Westminster Hall, all the way within rails, and 10,000 people with the ground covered with blue cloth; and scaffolds all the way. Into the Hall I got, where it was very fine with hangings and scaffolds one upon another full of brave ladies; and my wife in one little one, on the right hand. Here I staid walking up and down, and at last upon one of the side stalls I stood and saw the King come in with all the persons (but the soldiers) that were yesterday in the cavalcade; and a most pleasant sight it was to see them in their several robes. And the King come in with his crown on, and his scepter in his hand, under a canopy borne up by six silver staves, carried by Barons of the Cinque Ports, and little bells at every end. And after a long time, he got up to the farther end, and all set themselves down at their several tables; and that was also a brave sight: and the King's first course carried up by the Knights of the Bath. And many fine ceremonies there was of the Heralds leading up people before him, and bowing; and my Lord of Albemarle's going to the kitchen and eating a bit of the first dish that was to go to the King's table. But, above all, was these three lords, Northumberland, and Suffolk, and the Duke of Ormond, coming before the courses on horseback, and staying so all dinner-time, and at last bringing up the King's Champion, all in armor on horseback, with his spear and target carried before him. And a Herald proclaims "That if any dare deny Charles Stuart to be lawful King of England, here was a Champion that would fight with him;" and with these words, the Champion flings down his gauntlet, and all this he do three times in his going up towards the King's Table. At last, when he is come, the King drinks to him, and then sends him the cup, which is of gold, and he drinks it off, and then rides back again with the cup in his hand. I went from table to table to see the Bishops and all others at their dinner, and was infinitely pleased with it. And at the Lords' table, I met with William Howe, and he spoke to my Lord for me, and he did give him four rabbits and a pullet, and so Mr. Creed and I got Mr. Minshell to give us some bread, and so we at a stall ate it, as everybody else did what they could get. I took a great deal of pleasure to go up and down, and look upon the ladies, and to hear the music of all sorts, but above all, the 24 violins. About six at night they had dined, and I went up to my wife. And strange it is to think that these two days have held up fair till now that all is done, and the King gone out of the Hall; and then it fell a-raining and thundering and lightening as I have not seen it do for some years: which people did take great notice of; God's blessing of the work of these two days, which is a foolery to take too much notice of such things. I observed little disorder in all this, only the King's footmen had got hold of the canopy, and would keep it from the Barons of the Cinque Ports, which they endeavored to force from them again, but could not do it till my Lord Duke of Albemarle caused it to be put into Sir R. Pye's hand till to-morrow to be decided. At Mr. Bowyer's; a great deal of company, some I knew, others I did not. Here we staid upon the leads and below till it was late, expecting to see the fireworks, but they were not performed to-night: only the City had a light like a glory round about it, with bonfires. At last, I went to King Street, and there sent Crockford to my father's and my house, to tell them I could not come home to-night, because of the dirt, and a coach could not be had. And so I took my wife and Mrs. Frankleyn (who I proffered the civility of lying with my wife at Mrs. Hunt's to-night) to Axe Yard, in which, at the further end, there were three great bonfires, and a great many gallants, men and women; and they laid hold of us, and would have us drink the King's health upon our knees, kneeling upon a faggot, which we all did, they drinking to us one after another, which we thought a strange frolic; but these gallants continued there a great while, and I wondered to see how the ladies did tipple. At last, I sent my wife and her bedfellow to bed, and Mr. Hunt and I went in with Mr. Thornbury (who did give the company all their wine, he being yeoman of the wine-cellar to the King) ; and there, with his wife and two of his sisters, and some gallant sparks that were there, we drank the King's health, and nothing else, till one of the gentlemen fell down stark drunk, and there lay; and I went to my Lord's pretty well. But no sooner a-bed with Mr. Shepley but my head began to turn, and I to vomit, and if ever I was foxed, it was now, which I cannot say yet, because I fell asleep, and slept till morning. Thus did the day end with joy everywhere; and blessed be God, I have not heard of any mischance to anybody through it all, but only to Serjeant Glynne, whose horse fell upon him yesterday, and is like to kill him, which people do please themselves to see how just God is to punish the rogue at such a time as this; he being now one of the King's serjeants, and rode in the cavalcade with Maynard, to whom people wish the same fortune. There was also this night, in King Street, a woman had her eye put out by a boy's flinging a firebrand into the coach. Now, after all this, I can say that, besides the pleasure of the sight of these glorious things, I may now shut my eyes against any other objects, nor for the future trouble myself to see things of state and show, as being sure never to see the like again in this world.

September 7th. Having appointed the young ladies at the Wardrobe to go with them to the play to-day, my wife and I took them to the theater, where we seated ourselves close by the King, and Duke of York, and Madame Palmer, which was great content; and, indeed, I can never enough admire her beauty. And here was *Bartholomew Fair*, with the puppet-show, acted to-day, which had not been these forty years, it being so satirical against Puritanism, they durst not till now, which is strange they should already dare to do it, and the King to countenance it, but I do never a whit like it the better for the puppets, but rather the worse. Thence home with the ladies, it being by reason of our staying a great while for the King's coming, and the length of the play, near nine o'clock before it was done.

1662

August 17th. (Lord's day.) This being the last Sunday that the Presbyterians are to preach, unless they read the new Common Prayer, and renounce the Covenant, I had a mind to hear Dr. Bates's farewell sermon; and walked to St. Dunstan's, where, it not being seven o'clock yet, the doors were not open; and so I walked an hour in the Temple Garden, reading my vows, which it is a great content to me to see how I am a changed man in all respects for the better, since I took them, which the God of Heaven continue to me, and make me thankful for. At eight o'clock I went, and crowded in at a back door among

others, the church being half-full almost before any doors were open publicly, which is the first time that I have
done so these many years; and so got
into the gallery, beside the pulpit, and
heard very well. His text was, "Now
the God of Peace—"; the last Hebrews,
and the 20th verse: he making a
very good sermon, and very little reflections in it to anything of the times.
I was very well pleased with the sight
of a fine lady that I have often seen
walk in Gray's Inn Walks. To Madam
Turner's, and dined with her. She
had heard Parson Herring take his
leave; though he, by reading so much
of the Common Prayer as he did, hath
cast himself out of the good opinion of
both sides. After dinner, to St. Dunstan's again; and the church quite
crowded before I come, which was
just at one o'clock; but I got into the
gallery again, but stood in a crowd.
Dr. Bates pursued his text again very
well; and only at the conclusion told
us, after this manner: "I do believe
that many of you do expect that I
should say something to you in reference to the time, this being the last
time that possibly I may appear here.
You know it is not my manner to
speak anything in the pulpit that is
extraneous to my text and business;
yet this I shall say, that it is not my
opinion, fashion, or humour that keeps
me from complying with what is required of us; but something, after
much prayer, discourse, and study, yet
remains unsatisfied, and commands
me herein. Wherefore, if it is my unhappiness not to receive such an illumination as should direct me to do
otherwise, I know no reason why men
should not pardon me in this world,
as I am confident that God will pardon me for it in the next." And so he
concluded. Parson Herring read a
psalm and chapters before sermon;
and one was the chapter in the Acts,
where the story of Ananias and Sapphira is. And after he had done, says
he, "This is just the case of England at
present. God he bids us to preach, and
men bid us not to preach; and if we

do, we are to be imprisoned and further punished. All that I can say to it
is that I beg your prayers, and the
prayers of all good Christians, for
us." This was all the exposition he
made of the chapter in these very
words, and no more. I was much
pleased with Bates's manner of bringing in the Lord's Prayer after his own;
thus, "In whose comprehensive words
we sum up all our imperfect desires;
saying, 'Our Father,' " &c. I hear most
of the presbyters took their leaves to-
day, and that the City is much dissatisfied with it. I pray God keep peace
among us, and make the bishops
careful of bringing in men in their
rooms, or else all will fly a-pieces; for
bad ones will not go down with the
City.

August 19th. At the office; and Mr.
Coventry did tell us of the duel between Mr. Jermyn, nephew to my
Lord St. Albans, and Colonel Giles
Rawlins, the latter of whom is killed,
and the first mortally wounded, as it
is thought. They fought against Captain Thomas Howard, my Lord Carlisle's brother, and another, unknown;
who, they say, had armor on that they
could not be hurt, so that one of their
swords went up to the hilt against it.
They had horses ready, and are fled.
But what is most strange, Howard
sent one challenge before, but they
could not meet till yesterday at the
old Pall Mall at St. James's, and he
would not till the last tell Jermyn
what the quarrel was; nor do anybody
know. The Court is much concerned
in this fray, and I am glad of it; hoping that it will cause some good laws
against it. After sitting, Sir G. Carteret
did tell me how he had spoke of me
to my Lord Chancellor; and that if
my Lord Sandwich would ask my Lord
Chancellor, he should know what he
had said of me to him to my advantage.

September 29th. . . . To the King's
Theatre, where we saw *Midsummer
Night's Dream*, which I had never
seen before, nor shall ever again, for

it is the most insipid ridiculous play that ever I saw in my life. . . .

December 26th. To the Wardrobe. Hither came Mr. Battersby; and we falling into discourse of a new book of drollery in verse called *Hudibras,* I would needs go find it out, and met with it at the Temple: cost me 2s. 6d. But when I came to read it, it is so silly an abuse of the Presbyter Knight going to the wars, that I am ashamed of it; and by and by meeting at Mr. Townsend's at dinner, I sold it to him for 18d. . . .

December 31st. . . . Thence merry back, Mr. Povy and I, to Whitehall; he carrying me thither on purpose to carry me into the ball this night before the King. All the way he talking very ingeniously, and I find him a fine gentleman, and one that loves to live nobly and neatly, as I perceive by his discourse of his house, pictures, and horses. He brought me first to the Duke's chamber, where I saw him and the Duchess at supper; and thence into the room where the ball was to be, crammed with fine ladies, the greatest of the Court. By and by comes the King and Queen, the Duke and Duchess and all the great ones; and after seating themselves, the King takes out the Duchess of York; and the Duke, the Duchess of Buckingham; the Duke of Monmouth, my Lady Castlemaine; and so other lords other ladies; and they danced the Bransle. After that, the King led a lady a single Coranto; and then the rest of the lords, one after another, other ladies; very noble it was, and great pleasure to see. Then to country dances; the King leading the first, which he called for; which was, says he, "Cuckolds all awry," the old dance of England. Of the ladies that danced, the Duke of Monmouth's mistress, and my Lady Castlemaine, and a daughter of Sir Harry de Vicke's, were the best. The manner was, when the King dances, all the ladies in the room, and the Queen herself, stand up; and indeed he dances rarely, and much better than the Duke of York. . . .

Thus ends this year with great mirth to me and my wife. Our condition being thus:—we are at present spending a night or two at my Lord's lodgings at Whitehall. Our home at the Navy office, which is and hath a pretty while been in good condition, finished and made very convenient. My purse is worth about £650, besides my goods of all sorts, which yet might have been more but for my late layings out upon my house and public assessment, and yet would not have been so much if I had not lived a very orderly life all this year by virtue of the oaths that God put into my heart to take against wine, plays, and other expenses, and to observe for these last twelve months, and which I am now going to renew, I under God owing my present content thereunto. My family is myself and wife, William, my clerk; Jane, my wife's upper maid, but, I think, growing proud and negligent upon it: we must part, which troubles me; Susan, our cook-maid, a pretty willing wench, but no good cook; and Wayneman, my boy, who I am now turning away for his naughty tricks. We have had from the beginning our healths to this day, very well, blessed be God! Public matters stand thus: The King is bringing, as is said, his family, and Navy, and all other his charges, to a less expence. In the mean time, himself following his pleasures more than with good advice he would do; at least, to be seen to all the world to do so. His dalliance with my Lady Castlemaine being public, every day, to his great reproach; and his favouring of none at Court so much as those that are the confidants of his pleasure, as Sir H. Bennet and Sir Charles Barkeley; which, good God! put it into his heart to mend, before he makes himself too much contemned by his people for it! The Duke of Monmouth is in so great splendour at Court, and so dandled by the King, that some doubt, if the King should have no child by the Queen (which there is yet no appearance of), whether he would not be acknowledged for a lawful son; and that there will be a difference follow upon it between the Duke of York and him; which God prevent! My Lord Chancellor is threatened by people to be questioned, the next sitting of the Parliament, by some spirits that do not love to see him so great; but certainly he is a good servant to the King. . . . My Lord Sandwich is still in good esteem, and now keeping his Christmas in the country; and I in good esteem, I think, as any man can be, with him. . . . In fine, for the good condition of myself, wife, family, and estate, in the great degree that it is, and for the public state of the nation, so quiet as it is, the Lord God be praised!

1663

January 6th. (Twelfth day.) . . . To the Duke's house, and there saw *Twelfth Night* acted well, though it be but a silly play, and not relating at all to the name or day. Home, and found all well, only myself somewhat vexed at my wife's neglect in leaving of her scarf, waistcoat, and night-dressings in the coach, to-day, that brought us from Westminster; though, I confess, she did give them to me to look after. It might be as good as 25*s.* loss.

February 6th. To Lincoln's Inn Fields; and it being too soon to go to dinner, I walked up and down, and looked upon the outside of the new theatre building in Covent Garden, which will be very fine. And so to a bookseller's in the Strand, and there bought *Hudibras* again, it being certainly some ill humour to be so against that which all the world cries up to be the example of wit; for which I am resolved once more to read him, and see whether I can find it so or no. . . .

April 4th. After dinner to Hyde Park; Mrs. Wright and I in one coach, and all the rest of the women in Mrs. Turner's; Roger Pepys being gone in haste to the Parliament about the carrying this business of the Papists, in which it seems there is a great contest on both sides. At the Park was the

King, and in another coach my Lady Castlemaine, they greeting one another at every turn. This being my feast, in lieu of what I should have had a few days ago, for the cutting of the stone, very merry at, before and after dinner, and the more for that my dinner was great, and most neatly dressed by our own only maid. We had a fricassee of rabbits and chickens, a leg of mutton boiled, three carps in a dish, a great dish of a side of lamb, a dish of roasted pigeons, a dish of four lobsters, three tarts, a lamprey pie (a most rare pie), a dish of anchovies, good wine of several sorts, and all things mighty noble, and to my great content.

April 20th. To Mr. Grant's. There saw his prints, which he showed me, and indeed are the best collection of anything almost that ever I saw, there being the prints of most of the greatest houses, churches, and antiquities in Italy and France, and brave cuts. I had not time to look them over as I ought. With Sir G. Carteret and Sir John Minnes to my Lord Treasurer's, thinking to have spoken about getting money for paying the Yards; but we found him with some ladies at cards: and so, it being a bad time to speak, we parted. This day the little Duke of Monmouth was married at Whitehall, in the King's chamber; and to-night is a great supper and dancing at his lodgings, near Charing Cross. I observed his coat at the tail of his coach: he gives the arms of England, Scotland, and France quartered upon some other fields; but what it is that speaks his being a bastard I know not.

May 4th. The dancing-master come, whom standing by, seeing him instructing my wife, when he had done with her, he would needs have me try the steps of a coranto; and what with his desire and my wife's importunity, I did begin, and then was obliged to give him entry money 10*s.*, and am become his scholar. The truth is, I think it is a thing very useful for any gentleman. To St. James's, where Mr. Coventry, Sir W. Penn, and I staid for the Duke's coming in, but not coming, we walked to Whitehall; and meeting the King, we followed him into the Park, where Mr. Coventry and he talking of building a new yacht out of his private purse, he having some contrivance of his own. The talk being done, we fell off to Whitehall, leaving the King in the Park; and going back, met the Duke going towards St. James's to meet us. So he turned back again, and to his closet at Whitehall; and there, my Lord Sandwich present, we did our weekly errand, and so broke up; and I to the garden with my Lord Sandwich; after we had sat an hour at the Tangier Committee, and after talking largely of his own businesses, we began to talk how matters are at Court: and though he did not flatly tell me any such thing, yet I do suspect that all is not kind between the King and the Duke, and that the King's fondness to the little Duke do occasion it; and it may be that there is some fear of his being made heir to the crown. But this my Lord did not tell me, but is my guess only; and that my Lord Chancellor is without doubt falling past hopes.

May 11th. On foot to Greenwich, where, going, I was set upon by a great dog, who got hold of my garters, and might have done me hurt; but, Lord! to see in what a maze I was, that, having a sword about me, I never thought of it, or had the heart to make use of it, but might, for want of that courage, have been worried. With Sir W. Penn to St. James's, where we attended the Duke of York: and, among other things, Sir G. Carteret and I had a great dispute about the different value of the pieces of eight rated by Mr. Creed at 4s. and 5d., and by Mr. Pitts at 4s. and 9d., which was the greatest husbandry to the King? he proposing that the greatest sum was; which is as ridiculous a piece of ignorance as could be imagined. However, it is to be argued at the Board, and reported to the Duke next week; which I shall do with advantage, I

hope. I went homeward, after a little discourse with Mr. Pierce, the surgeon, who tells me that my Lady Castlemaine hath now got lodgings near the King's chamber at Court; and that the other day Dr. Clerke and he did dissect two bodies, a man and a woman, before the King, with which the King was highly pleased. I called upon Mr. Crumlum, and did give him the 10s. remaining not laid out, of the £5 I promised him for the school, with which he will buy strings, and golden letters upon the books I did give them.

May 12th. A little angry with my wife for minding nothing now but the dancing-master, having him come twice a day, which is folly.

May 14th. Met Mr. Moore: and with him to an alehouse in Holborn; where in discourse he told me that he fears the King will be tempted to endeavor the setting the crown upon the little Duke, which may cause troubles; which God forbid, unless it be his due! He told me my Lord do begin to settle to business again; and that the King did send for him the other day to my Lady Castlemaine's, to play at cards, where he lost £50; for which I am sorry, though he says my Lord was pleased at it, and said he would be glad at any time to lose £50 for the King to send for him to play, which I do not so well like. This day we received a basket from my sister Pall, made by her, of paper, which hath a great deal of labor in it for country innocent work.

May 18th. I walked to Whitehall, and into the Park, seeing the Queen and Maids of Honor passing through the house, going to the Park. But, above all, Mrs. Stewart is a fine woman, and they say now a common mistress to the King, as my Lady Castlemaine is; which is a great pity. Taking a coach to Mrs. Clerke's— took her, and my wife, and Ashwell, and a Frenchman, a kinsman of hers, to the Park; where we saw many fine faces, and one exceeding handsome, in a white dress over her head, with many others very beautiful. Home, talking much of what we had observed to-day of the poor household stuff of Mrs. Clerke, and her show and flutter that she makes in the world; and pleasing myself in my own house and manner of living more than ever I did, by seeing how much better and more substantially I live than others do.

May 31st. (Lord's day.) After dinner, read part of the new play of *The Five Hours' Adventure*, which though I have seen it twice, yet I never did admire or understand it enough—it being a play of the greatest plot that ever I expect to see. Made up my month's accounts, and find myself clear worth £726. This month the greatest news is the height and heat that the Parliament is in, in inquiring into the revenue, which displeases the Court, and their backwardness to give the King any money. Their inquiring into the selling of places do trouble a great many; among the chief, my Lord Chancellor, against whom particularly it is carried, and Mr. Coventry; for which I am sorry. The King of France was given out to be poisoned and dead; but it proves to be the measles: and he is well, or likely to be soon well again. I find myself growing in the esteem and credit that I have in the office, and I hope falling to my business again will confirm me in it.

1664

February 3rd. . . . In Covent Garden tonight, going to fetch home my wife, I stopped at the great Coffeehouse there, where I never was before: where Dryden, the poet, I knew at Cambridge, and all the wits of the town, and Harris the player, and Mr. Hoole, of our College. And, had I had time then, or could at other times, it will be good coming thither, for there, I perceive, is very witty and pleasant discourse. But I could not tarry, and, as it was late, they were all ready to go away.

February 8th. Mr. Pierce told me how the King still do dote upon his women, even beyond all shame: and that the good Queen will of herself stop before she goes sometimes into her dressing-room, till she knows whether the King be there, for fear he should be, as she hath sometimes taken him, with Mrs. Stewart; and that some of the best parts of the Queen's jointure are, contrary to faith and against the opinion of my Lord Treasurer and his Council, bestowed or rented, I know not how, to my Lord FitzHarding and Mrs. Stewart and others of that crew: that the King do dote infinitely upon the Duke of Monmouth, apparently as one that he intends to have succeed him, God knows what will be the end of it!

December 31st. At the office all the morning, and after dinner there again, dispatched first my letters, and then to my accounts, not of the month but of the whole year also, and was at it till past twelve at night, it being bitter cold; but yet I was well satisfied with my work, and, above all, to find myself, by the great blessing of God, worth £1,349, by which, as I have spent very largely, so I have laid up above £500 this year above what I was worth this day twelvemonth. The Lord make me for ever thankful to his holy name for it! Thence home to eat a little and to bed. Soon as ever the clock struck one, I kissed my wife in the kitchen by the fireside, wishing her a merry new year, observing that I believe I was the first proper wisher of it this year, for I did it as soon as ever the clock struck one.

So ends the old year, I bless God, with great joy to me, not only from my having made so good a year of profit, as having spent £420 and laid up £540, and upwards; but I bless God I never have been in so good plight as to my health in so very cold weather as this is, nor indeed in any hot weather, these ten years, as I am at this day, and have been these four or five months. But I am at a great loss to know whether it be my hare's foot, or taking every morning of a pill of turpentine, or my having left off the wearing of a gown. My family is my wife, in good health, and happy with her; her woman Mercer, a pretty, modest, quiet maid; her chambermaid Bess, her cook-maid Jane, the little girl Susan, and my boy, which I have had about half a year, Tom Edwards, which I took from the King's chapel; and as pretty and loving quiet a family I have as any man in England. My credit in the world and my office grows daily, and I am in good esteem with everybody, I think. My troubles of my uncle's estate pretty well over; but it comes to be of little profit to us, my father being much supported by my purse. But great vexations remain upon my father and me from my brother Tom's death and ill condition, both to our disgrace and discontent, though no great reason for either. Public matters are all in a hurry about a Dutch war. Our preparations great; our provocations against them great; and, after all our presumption, we are now afraid as much of them as we lately contemned them. Everything else in the State quiet, blessed be God! My Lord Sandwich at sea with the fleet, at Portsmouth; sending some about to cruise for taking of ships, which we have done to a great number. This Christmas I judged it fit to look over all my papers and books, and to tear all that I found either boyish or not to be worth keeping, or fit to be seen, if it should please God to take me away suddenly. . . .

1665

January 14th. . . . To the King's house, there to see *Volpone,* a most excellent play; the best I think I ever saw, and well acted. . . .

February 19th. Lay in bed, it being Lord's day, all the morning talking with my wife, sometimes pleased, sometimes displeased, and then up and to dinner. At supper hearing by accident of my maids their letting in a rogueing Scotch woman that haunts

the office, to help them to wash and scour in our house, and that very lately, I fell mightily out, and made my wife, to the disturbance of the house and neighbors, to beat our little girl, and then we shut her down into the cellar, and there she lay all night. So we to bed.

May 28th. (Lord's day.) I hear that Nixon is condemned to be shot to death, for his cowardice, by a Council of War. To Sir Philip Warwick's to dinner, where abundance of company come in unexpectedly; and here I saw one pretty piece of household stuff, as the company increaseth, to put a larger leaf upon an oval table. After dinner, much good discourse with Sir Philip, who, I find, I think a most pious good man, and a professor of a philosophical manner of life, and principles like Epictetus. Thence to my Lady Sandwich's, where, to my shame, I had not been a great while. Here, upon my telling her a story of my Lord Rochester's running away on Friday night last with Mrs. Mallett, the great beauty and fortune of the north, who had supped at Whitehall with Mrs. Stewart, and was going home to her lodgings with her grandfather, my Lord Haly, by coach; and was at Charing Cross seized on by both horse- and foot-men, and forcibly taken from him, and put into a coach with six horses, and two women provided to receive her, and carried away. Upon immediate pursuit, my Lord of Rochester, for whom the King had spoke to the lady often, but with no success, was taken at Uxbridge; but the lady is not yet heard of, and the King mighty angry, and the lord sent to the Tower. Hereupon my Lady did confess to me, as a great secret, her being concerned in this story; for if this match breaks between my Lord Rochester and her, then, by the consent of all her friends, my Lord Hinchingbroke stands fair, and is invited for her. She is worth, and will be at her mother's death, who keeps but a little from her, £2500 per annum. Pray God give a good success to it! But my poor Lady, who is afraid of the sickness, and resolved to be gone into the country, is forced to stay in town a day or two, or three, about it, to see the event of it. Thence to see my Lady Pen, where my wife and I were shown a fine rarity: of fishes kept in a glass of water, that will live so forever; and finely marked they are, being foreign.

1666

June 10th. (Lord's day.) I met with Pierce, the surgeon, who is lately come from the fleet, and tells me that all the commanders, officers, and even the common seamen, do condemn every part of the late conduct of the Duke of Albemarle: both in his fighting at all, running among them in his retreat, and running the ships on ground; so as nothing can be worse spoken of. That Holmes, Spragg, and Smith do all the business, and the old and wiser commanders nothing: so as Sir Thomas Teddiman, whom the King and all the world speak well of, is mightily discontented, as being wholly slighted. He says we lost more after the *Prince* came than before, too. The *Prince* was so maimed as to be forced to be towed home. He says all the fleet confess their being chased home by the Dutch; and yet the body of the Dutch that did it was not above forty sail at most; and yet this put us into the fright, as to bring all our ships on ground. He says, however, that the Duke of Albemarle is as high almost as ever, and pleases himself to think that he hath given the Dutch their bellies full, without sense of what he hath lost us; and talks how he knows now the way to beat them. But he says that even Smith himself, one of his creatures, did himself condemn the late conduct from the beginning to the end. He tells me further how the Duke of York is wholly given up to his new mistress my Lady Denham, going at noonday with all his gentlemen with him to visit her in Scotland Yard; she declaring she will not be his mis-

tress, as Mrs. Price, to go up and down the Privy-stairs, but will be owned publicly; and so she is. Mr. Brouncker, it seems, was the pimp to bring it about; and my Lady Castlemaine, who designs thereby to fortify herself by the Duke; there being a falling-out the other day between the King and her: on this occasion, the Queen, in ordinary talk before the ladies in her drawing-room, did say to my Lady Castlemaine that she feared the King did take cold by staying so late abroad at her house. She answered, before them all, that he did not stay so late abroad with her, for he went betimes thence (though he do not before one, two, or three in the morning), but must stay somewhere else. The King then coming in, and over-hearing, did whisper in the ear aside, and told her she was a bold, impertinent woman, and bid her to be gone out of the Court, and not come again till he sent for her; which she did presently, and went to a lodging in the Pell Mell, and kept there two or three days, and then sent to the King to know whether she might send for her things away out of her house. The King sent to her, she must first come and view them: and so she come, and the King went to her, and all friends again. He tells me she did, in her anger, say she would be even with the King, and print his letters to her; so, putting all together, we are, and are like to be, in a sad condition; we are endeavoring to raise money by borrowing it of the City; but I do not think the City will lend a farthing. Sir G. Carteret and I walked an hour in the churchyard, under Henry the Seventh's Chapel, he being lately come from the fleet; and tells me, as I hear from everybody else, that the management in the late fight was bad, from top to bottom. That several said that this would not have been if my Lord Sandwich had had the ordering of it. Nay, he tells me that certainly, had my Lord Sandwich had the misfortune to have done as they have done, the King could not have saved him. There is, too, nothing but discontent among the officers; and all the old, experienced men are slighted. He tells me, to my question, but as a great secret, that the dividing of the fleet did proceed first from a proposition from the fleet, though agreed to hence; but he confesses it arose from want of due intelligence. He do, however, call the fleet's retreat on Sunday a very honourable one, and that the Duke of Albemarle did do well in it, and it would have been well if he had done it sooner, rather than venture the loss of the fleet and crown, as he must have done, if the *Prince* had not come. He was surprised when I told him I heard that the King did intend to borrow some money of the City, and would know who had spoke of it to me; I told him Sir Ellis Layton this afternoon. He says it is a dangerous discourse, for that the City certainly will not be invited to do it; and then, for the King to ask it and be denied, will be the beginning of our sorrow. He seems to fear we shall all fall to pieces among ourselves. This evening we hear that Sir Christopher Mings is dead of his late wounds; and Sir W. Coventry did commend him to me in a most extraordinary manner. But this day, after three days' trial in vain, and the hazard of the spoiling of the ship in lying till next spring, besides the disgrace of it, news is brought that the *Loyal London* is launched at Deptford.

July 7th. Creed tells me, he finds all things mighty dull at Court; and that they now begin to lie long in bed; it being, as we suppose, not seemly for them to be found playing and gaming as they used to be; nor that their minds are at ease enough to follow those sports, and yet not knowing how to employ themselves, though there be work enough for their thoughts and councils and pains, they keep long in bed. But he thinks with me that there is nothing in the world can help us but the King's personal looking after his business and his officers, and that, with that, we may yet do well; but otherwise must be undone; nobody at this day taking care of anything, nor hath anybody to call him to account for it. To bed; and it proved the hottest night that ever I was in in my life, and thundered and lightened all night long, and rained hard. But, Lord! to see in what fear I lay a good while, hearing of a little noise of somebody walking in the house: so rung the bell, and it was my maids going to bed about one o'clock in the morning. But the fear of being robbed, having so much money in the house, was very great, and is still so, and do much disquiet me.

August 20th. . . . To Deptford by water, reading *Othello, Moor of Venice,* which I ever heretofore esteemed a mighty good play; but having so lately read *The Adventures of Five Hours,* it seems a mean thing. . . .

September 2nd. (Lord's day.) Some of our maids sitting up late last night to get things ready against our feast to-day, Jane called us up about three in the morning, to tell us of a great fire they saw in the City. So I rose and slipped on my night-gown, and went to her window, and thought it to be on the back-side of Mark-lane at the farthest; but, being unused to such fires as followed, I thought it far enough off; and so went to bed again and to sleep. About seven rose again to dress myself, and there looked out at the window, and saw the fire not so much as it was and further off. By and by Jane comes and tells me that she hears that above 300 houses have been burned down to-night by the fire we saw, and that it is now burning down all Fish-street, by London Bridge. So I made myself ready presently, and walked to the Tower, and there got up upon one of the high places, Sir J. Robinson's little son going up with me; and there I did see the houses at that end of the bridge all on fire, and an infinite great fire on this and the other side the end of the bridge; which, among other people, did trouble me for poor little Michell and our Sarah on the bridge. So down, with my heart full of trouble, to the Lieutenant of the Tower, who tells me that it begun this morning in the King's baker's house in Pudding-lane, and that it hath burned St. Magnus's Church and most part of Fish-street already. So I down to the water-side, and there got a boat and through bridge, and there saw a lamentable fire. Poor Michell's house, as far as the Old Swan, already burned that way, and the fire running further, that in a very little time it got as far as the Steele-yard, while I was there. Everybody endeavouring to remove their goods, and flinging into the river or bringing them into lighters that lay off; poor people staying in their houses as long as till the very fire touched them, and then running into boats, or clambering from one pair of stairs by the water-side to another. And among other things, the poor pigeons, I perceive, were loth to leave their houses, but hovered about the windows and balconies till they were, some of them burned, their wings, and fell down. Having stayed, and in an hour's time seen the fire rage every way, and nobody, to my sight, endeavouring to quench it, but to remove their goods, and leave all to the fire, and having seen it get as far as the Steele-yard, and the wind mighty high and driving it into the City; and every thing, after so long a drought, proving combustible, even the very stones of churches, and among other things the poor steeple by which pretty Mrs. —— lives, and whereof my old schoolfellow Elborough is parson, taken fire in the very top, and there burned till it fell down: I to Whitehall (with a gentleman with me who desired to go off from the Tower, to see the fire, in my boat) ; to Whitehall, and there up to the King's closet in the Chapel, where people come about me, and I did give them an account dismayed them all, and word was carried in to the King.

So I was called for, and did tell the King and Duke of York what I saw, and that unless his Majesty did command houses to be pulled down nothing could stop the fire. They seemed much troubled, and the King commanded me to go to my Lord Mayor from him, and command him to spare no houses, but to pull down before the fire every way. . . . At last met my Lord Mayor in Canning-street, like a man spent, with a handkercher about his neck. To the King's message he cried, like a fainting woman, "Lord, what can I do? I am spent: people will not obey me. I have been pulling down houses; but the fire overtakes us faster than we can do it." He must go and refresh himself, having been up all night. So he left me, and I him, and walked home; seeing people all almost distracted, and no manner of means used to quench the fire. The houses, too, so very thick thereabouts, and full of matter for burning, as pitch and tar, in Thames Street; and warehouses of oil, and wines, and brandy, and other things. Here I saw Mr. Isaac Houblon, the handsome man, prettily dressed and dirty at his door at Dowgate, receiving some of his brother's things, whose houses were on fire; and, as he says, have been removed twice already; and he doubts, as it soon proved, that they must be, in a little time, removed from his house also, which was a sad consideration. And to see the churches all filling with goods by people who themselves should have been quietly there at this time. By this time, it was about twelve o'clock; and so home, and there find my guests, who were Mr. Wood and his wife Barbary Sheldon, and also Mr. Moone: she mighty fine, and her husband, for aught I see, a likely man. But Mr. Moone's design and mine, which was to look over my closet, and please him with the sight thereof, which he hath long desired, was wholly disappointed; for we were in great trouble and disturbance at this fire, not knowing what to think of it. However, we had an extraordinary good dinner, and as merry as at this time we could be. While at dinner, Mrs. Batelier came to inquire after Mr. Woolfe and Stanes, who, it seems, are related to them, whose houses in Fish-street are all burned, and they in a sad condition. She would not stay in the fright. Soon as dined, I and Moone away, and walked through the City, the streets full of nothing but people; and horses and carts loaden with goods, ready to run over one another, and removing goods from one burned house to another. They now removing out of Canning Street, which received goods in the morning, into Lombard Street, and further: and, among others, I now saw my little goldsmith Stokes, receiving some friend's goods, whose house itself was burned the day after. We parted at Paul's, he home, and I to Paul's Wharf, where I had appointed a boat to attend me, and took in Mr. Carcasse and his brother, whom I met in the street, and carried them below and above bridge too. And again to see the fire, which was now got further, both below and above, and no likelihood of stopping it. Met with the King and Duke of York in their barge, and with them to Queenhithe, and there called Sir Richard Browne to them. Their order was only to pull down houses apace, and so below bridge at the waterside; but little was or could be done, the fire coming upon them so fast. Good hopes there was of stopping it at the Three Cranes above, and at Buttulph's Wharf below bridge, if care be used; but the wind carries it into the City, so as we know not, by the waterside, what it do there. River full of lighters and boats taking in goods, and good goods swimming in the water; and only I observed that hardly one lighter or boat in three that had the goods of a house in, but there was a pair of virginals in it. Having seen as much as I could now, I away to Whitehall by appointment, and there walked to St. James's Park; and there met my wife, and Creed,

and Wood, and his wife, and walked to my boat; and there upon the water again, and to the fire up and down, it still increasing, and the wind great. So near the fire as we could for smoke; and all over the Thames, with one's face in the wind, you were almost burned with a shower of fire-drops. This is very true: so as houses were burned by these drops and flakes of fire, three or four, nay, five or six houses, one from another. When we could endure no more upon the water, we to a little alehouse on the Bankside, over against the Three Cranes, and there staid till it was dark almost, and saw the fire grow; and, as it grew darker, appeared more and more; and in corners and upon steeples, and between churches and houses, as far as we could see up the hill of the City, in a most horrid, malicious, bloody flame, not like the fine flame of an ordinary fire. Barbary and her husband away before us. We staid till, it being darkish, we saw the fire as only one entire arch of fire from this to the other side the bridge, and in a bow up the hill for an arch of above a mile along: it made me weep to see it. The churches, houses, and all on fire, and flaming at once; and a horrid noise the flames made, and the cracking of houses at their ruin. So home with a sad heart, and there find everybody discoursing and lamenting the fire; and poor Tom Hater come with some few of his goods saved out of his house, which was burned upon Fish Street Hill. I invited him to lie at my house, and did receive his goods; but was deceived in his lying there, the news coming every moment of the growth of the fire; so as we were forced to begin to pack up our own goods, and prepare for their removal; and did by moonshine, it being brave, dry, and moonshine and warm weather, carry much of my goods into the garden; and Mr. Hater and I did remove my money and iron chests into my cellar, as thinking that the safest place. And got my bags of gold into my office, ready to carry away, and my chief papers of accounts also there, and my tallies into a box by themselves. So great was our fear, as Sir W. Batten hath carts come out of the country to fetch away his goods this night. We did put Mr. Hater, poor man! to bed a little; but he got but very little rest, so much noise being in my house, taking down of goods.

1667

February 2nd. I am very well pleased this night with reading a poem I brought home with me last night from Westminster Hall, of Dryden's upon the present war; a very good poem. By and by to dinner, where very good company. Among other discourse, we talked much of Nostradamus his prophecy of these times, and the burning the City of London, some of whose verses are put into Booker's *Almanack* this year; and Sir G. Carteret did tell a story, how at his death he did make the town swear that he should never be dug up, or his tomb opened, after he was buried; but they did after sixty years do it, and upon his breast they found a plate of brass, saying what a wicked and unfaithful people the people of that place were, who after so many vows should disturb and open him such a day and year and hour; which, if true, is very strange.

March 2nd. After dinner, with my wife, to the King's house to see *The Maiden Queen*, a new play of Dryden's, mightily commended for the regularity of it, and the strain and wit; and, the truth is, there is a comical part done by Nell, which is Florimel, that I never can hope ever to see the like done again, by man or woman. The King and Duke of York were at the play. But so great performance of a comical part was never, I believe, in the world before as Nell do this, both as a mad girl, then most and best of all when she comes in like a young gallant; and hath the motions and carriage of a spark the most that ever I saw any man have. It makes me, I confess, admire her.

April 16th. Home to dinner, and in haste to carry my wife to see the new play I saw yesterday, she not knowing it. But there, contrary to expectation, find *The Silent Woman*. . . . I was never more taken with a play than I am with this *Silent Woman*, as old as it is, and as often as I have seen it. There is more wit in it than goes to ten new plays. . . .

1668

September 3rd. To my bookseller's, for Hobbes's *Leviathan*, which is now mightily called for; and what was heretofore sold for 8s. I now give 24s. for, at the second hand, and is sold for 30s., it being a book the Bishops will not let be printed again.

1669

And thus ends all that I doubt I shall ever be able to do with my own eyes in the keeping of my Journal, I being not able to do it any longer, having done now so long as to undo my eyes almost every time that I take a pen in my hand; and, therefore, whatever comes of it, I must forbear: and, therefore, resolve, from this time forward, to have it kept by my people in long-hand, and must therefore be contented to set down no more than is fit for them and all the world to know; or, if there be anything, which cannot be much, now my *amours* to Deb. are past, and my eyes hindering me in almost all other pleasures, I must endeavor to keep a margin in my book open. to add, here and there, a note in short-hand with my own hand.

And so I betake myself to that course, which is almost as much as to see myself go into my grave: for which, and all the discomforts that will accompany my being blind, the good God prepare me!

S. P.

May 31, 1669.

JOHN WILMOT, EARL OF ROCHESTER (1647-1680)

The name of John Wilmot, second Earl of Rochester, has always stood for the worst side of the Restoration; he is remembered as the most brilliant of Charles II's courtiers, the most gifted and reckless of "the mob of gentlemen who wrote with ease." Though it is the practice of contemporary biography to rehabilitate such men, to discover that they are generous and genial at heart and that the very disorganization of their lives shows them to be "modern," it would tax the resources of any biographer to prove that Rochester was not a perfidious bully and libertine. Yet in his verses he shows undeniable wit and power. He is one of the last to speak in the true accent of the seventeenth century cavalier, to which he adds a personal note, as in *The Maimed Debauchee*:

> Should some brave youth (worth being drunk) prove nice,
> And from his fair inviter meanly shrink,
> 'Twould please the ghost of my departed vice,
> If, at my counsel, he repent and drink.

In spite of his indebtedness to the satires of Boileau, he is a pioneer in adapting this neoclassical form to native and individual uses: his *Allusion to Horace: The Tenth Satire of the First Book* shows how the Roman form may be filled with English matter, and his *Satire against Mankind* carries intellectual weight and puts impressively the questions about man's animality and rationality that were to be raised so insistently by Swift and Mandeville.

The one good edition of Rochester is John Hayward's (London, 1926) ; a painstaking biography and bibliography has been compiled by Johannes Prinz (Leipzig, 1927; *Palaestra*, CLIV) . See also page 1268.

A SATIRE AGAINST MANKIND

Were I, who to my cost already am
One of those strange, prodigious creatures, man,
A spirit free to choose for my own share
What sort of flesh and blood I pleased to wear,
I'd be a dog, a monkey, or a bear,
Or anything, but that vain animal,
Who is so proud of being rational.
The senses are too gross, and he'll contrive
A sixth to contradict the other five;
And before certain instinct will prefer   10
Reason, which fifty times for one does err—
Reason, an *ignis fatuus* of the mind,
Which leaves the light of nature, sense, behind.
Pathless and dangerous wandering ways it takes
Through error's fenny bogs and thorny brakes,
Whilst the misguided follower climbs with pain
Mountains of whimsies, heaped in his own brain,
Stumbling from thought to thought, falls headlong down
Into doubt's boundless sea, where, like to drown,
Books bear him up awhile and make him try   20
To swim with bladders of philosophy,
In hopes still to o'ertake the skipping light.
The vapour dances in his dazzled sight
Till, spent, it leaves him to eternal night.
Then old age and experience, hand in hand,
Lead him to death and make him understand
After a search so painful and so long,
That all his life he has been in the wrong.
Huddled in dirt, the reasoning engine lies
Who was so proud, so witty, and so wise.   30
Pride drew him in, as cheats their bubbles catch,
And made him venture to be made a wretch.

His wisdom did his happiness destroy,
Aiming to know the world he should enjoy;
And wit was his vain frivolous pretence
Of pleasing others at his own expense.
For wits are treated just like common
    whores;
First they're enjoyed, and then kicked out
    of doors.
The pleasure past, a threatening doubt re-
    mains,
That frights the enjoyer with succeeding
    pains.   40
Women and men of wit are dangerous
    tools,
And ever fatal to admiring fools.
Pleasure allures, and when the fops escape,
'Tis not that they're beloved, but fortunate,
And therefore what they fear, at heart they
    hate.
But now methinks some formal band and
    beard
Takes me to task: "Come on, sir, I'm pre-
    pared."
"Then, by your favour, anything that's writ
Against this gibing, jingling knack, called
    wit,
Likes me abundantly; but you'll take care
Upon this point, not to be too severe.   51
Perhaps my Muse were fitter for this part,
For I profess, I can be very smart
On wit, which I abhor with all my heart.
I long to lash it in some sharp essay,
But your grand indiscretion bids me stay,
And turns my tide of ink another way.
What rage ferments in your degenerate
    mind
To make you rail at reason and mankind?—
Blest glorious man, to whom alone kind
    Heaven   60
An everlasting soul hath freely given;
Whom his great Maker took such care to
    make
That from himself he did the image take,
And this fair frame in shining reason
    dressed,
To dignify his nature above beast—
Reason, by whose aspiring influence
We take a flight beyond material sense,
Dive into mysteries, then soaring pierce
The flaming limits of the universe,
Search heaven and hell, find out what's
    acted there,   70
And give the world true grounds of hope
    and fear?"

"Hold, mighty man," I cry. "All this we
    know
From the pathetic pen of Ingelo,
From Patrick's *Pilgrim*, Sibb's *Soliloquies*;
And 'tis this very reason I despise,
This supernatural gift, that makes a mite
Think he's the image of the infinite;
Comparing his short life, void of all rest,
To the eternal and the ever blest;
This busy puzzling stirrer up of doubt,   80
That frames deep mysteries, then finds 'em
    out,
Filling with frantic crowds of thinking
    fools,
The reverend bedlams, colleges, and
    schools;
Borne on whose wings, each heavy sot can
    pierce
The limits of the boundless universe.
So charming ointments make an old witch
    fly,
And bear a crippled carcass through the
    sky.
'Tis this exalted power whose business lies
In nonsense and impossibilities;
This made a whimsical philosopher,   90
Before the spacious world his tub prefer;
And we have many modern coxcombs who
Retire to think, 'cause they have naught
    to do.
But thoughts were given for action's govern-
    ment;
Where action ceases, thought's impertinent.
Our sphere of action is life's happiness,
And he that thinks beyond thinks like an
    ass.
Thus whilst against false reasoning I in-
    veigh,
I own right reason, which I would obey—
That reason which distinguishes by sense,
And gives us rules of good and ill from
    thence;   101
That bounds desires with a reforming will
To keep them more in vigour, not to kill.
Your reason hinders, mine helps to enjoy,
Renewing appetites, yours would destroy.
My reason is my friend, yours is a cheat:
Hunger calls out, my reason bids me eat;
Perversely yours, your appetite does mock;
This asks for food; that answers, "What's
    o'clock?"
   "This plain distinction, sir, your doubt
    secures;   110
'Tis not true reason I despise, but yours.

Thus I think reason righted; but for man,
I'll ne'er recant, defend him if you can.
For all his pride and his philosophy,
'Tis evident beasts are, in their degree,
As wise at least, and better far than he.
Those creatures are the wisest who attain
By surest means the ends at which they aim.
If therefore Jowler finds and kills his hare
Better than Meres supplies committee
    chair,   120
Though one's a statesman, th' other but a
    hound,
Jowler in justice will be wiser found.
You see how far man's wisdom here ex-
    tends:
Look next if human nature makes amends,
Whose principles are most generous and
    just,
And to whose morals, you would sooner
    trust.
Be judge yourself, I'll bring it to the test,
Which is the basest creature, man or beast:
Birds feed on birds, beasts on each other
    prey;
But savage man alone does man betray. 130
Pressed by necessity, they kill for food;
Man undoes man to do himself no good.
With teeth and claws by Nature armed
    they hunt
Nature's allowance, to supply their want;
But man with smiles, embraces, friendships,
    praise,
Inhumanly his fellow's life betrays,
With voluntary pains works his distress,
Not through necessity, but wantonness.
For hunger or for love they bite or tear,
Whilst wretched man is still in arms for
    fear: 140
For fear he arms, and is of arms afraid;
From fear to fear successively betrayed.
Base fear, the source whence his best pas-
    sions came,

His boasted honour, and his dear-bought
    fame,
The lust of power, to which he's such a
    slave,
And for the which alone he dares be brave;
To which his various projects are designed,
Which makes him generous, affable, and
    kind;
For which he takes such pains to be thought
    wise,
And screws his actions in a forced dis-
    guise;   150
Leads a most tedious life in misery,
Under laborious, mean hypocrisy.
Look to the bottom of his vast design,
Wherein man's wisdom, power, and glory
    join—
The good he acts, the ill he does endure,
'Tis all from fear, to make himself secure.
Merely for safety, after fame they thirst,
For all men would be cowards if they durst;
And honesty's against all common sense—
Men must be knaves; 'tis in their own
    defence.   160
Mankind 's dishonest; if they think it fair,
Amongst known cheats, to play upon the
    square,
You'll be undone—
Nor can weak truth your reputation save;
The knaves will all agree to call you knave.
Wronged shall he live, insulted o'er, op-
    pressed,
Who dares be less a villain than the rest.
Thus here you see what human nature
    craves,
Most men are cowards, all men should be
    knaves.
The difference lies, as far as I can see,   170
Not in the thing itself, but the degree;
And all the subject-matter of debate,
Is only, who's a knave of the first rate."

[1675]

JOHN DRYDEN (1631-1700)

Dryden is quite properly associated with Pope as one of the two leading representatives of the Classical period in English poetry. But the Classical period was by no means static, and the discerning reader will observe the differences as well as the similarities of the two men. Both as man and artist, Dryden belongs distinctly to the seventeenth century. Many of his characteristic peculiarities of thought and expression are better understood when placed in their proper historical perspective.

Dryden was born in 1631 in Northamptonshire. His family sympathized with the Puritan and Parliamentary side in the Civil War, and an uncle of his held high office under Cromwell. He was educated at Westminster School under the redoubtable Richard Busby, famous for his floggings and for the remarkable way his pupils had of later becoming distinguished men. From Westminster he went to Trinity College, Cambridge, where he received his degree in 1654. He seems to have gone up to London at least as early as 1657, and in 1658 published his *Heroic Stanzas* upon the death of Cromwell. By 1660 he had become intimate with Sir Robert Howard, son of the Earl of Berkshire, whose sister, Lady Elizabeth, he married on December 1, 1663. Dryden was among those who welcomed the Restoration of Charles II with poetical tributes. It had become clear that only the Stuart dynasty could restore a peaceful establishment to the nation, and Dryden, as Dr. Johnson has said, "changed with the nation." It should also be noted that all of Dryden's changes of opinion in religion and politics were uniformly in a conservative direction, and were in that respect consistent.

In 1663 Dryden turned his hand to the theatre and produced during his career a large number of comedies and tragedies. His real ambition was to write an epic, but up to 1680, when political excitement made the theatre unprofitable, he felt obliged to write plays to support his family. In 1670 he was appointed Poet Laureate at a salary of £200, which was augmented in 1677 to £300. Unfortunately, the exchequer of the king was by this time in such a deplorable condition that the Treasury, with the best will in the world, could pay the Poet Laureate only half his annual salary, as they continued to do uniformly until the death of Charles II in 1685. Dryden's appointment was renewed under James II, when all government obligations were paid with regularity.

Up to his fiftieth year Dryden had published almost exclusively drama. His most important poem had been *Annus Mirabilis* (1667), on the London Fire and the Dutch War. It was characteristically occasional, poetry inspired by some external event or situation. But Dryden's full powers were first displayed by his political poems, written during the national crisis following the Popish Plot of 1678; in 1681 he published *Absalom and Achitophel* and in the following year *The Medal*, also on politics, and he entered the sphere of religious as well as political controversy with *Religio Laici*. A fuller account of these political poems, and also of his poems on religion and his conversion to Roman Catholicism, will be found in the introductions to the individual poems.

After the Revolution of 1688 Dryden refused to take the oath of allegiance to the new monarchs, William and Mary, and Thomas Shadwell, the hero of *Mac Flecknoe*, succeeded him as Poet Laureate. Dryden turned for financial support to industrious literary labors, editing miscellanies, translating Virgil and other Classical writers, modernising Chaucer, and writing prologues and occasional pieces. His translations of Juvenal and Persius appeared in 1693, his Virgil in 1697, and the *Fables* from Chaucer and Boccaccio in 1700, just before he died.

Dryden's work is so diversified that his full genius is not appreciated in any single *genre*. His friend Congreve paid tribute to this versatility: "I may venture to say, in general terms, that no man hath written in our language so much, and so various matter, and in so various manners so well . . . what he has done in any one species, or distinct kind, would have been sufficient to have acquired him a great name. If he had written nothing but his Prefaces, or nothing but his Songs, or his Prologues, each of them would have entitled him to the preference and distinction of excelling in his kind." This largeness of his genius is reflected in the energy of his style; he is not the exquisite artist such as Pope, his successor, who worked within a narrower compass. In his *Life of Pope* Dr. Johnson introduced an admirable comparison of the two men which should be read entire, but from which the following excerpt must suffice here: "The style of Dryden is capricious and varied, that of Pope is cautious and uniform: Dryden obeys the motions of his own mind, Pope constrains his mind to his own rules of composition. Dryden is sometimes vehement and rapid; Pope is always smooth, uniform, and gentle. Dryden's page is a natural field rising into inequalities, and diversified by the varied exuberance of abundant vegetation; Pope's is a velvet lawn, shaven by the scythe, and levelled by the roller. Of genius, that power which constitutes a poet; that quality without which judgment is cold and knowledge is inert; that energy which collects, combines, amplifies, and animates; the superiority must, with some hesitation, be allowed to Dryden. . . . If the flights of Dryden therefore are higher, Pope continues longer on the wing. If of Dryden's fire the blaze is brighter, of Pope's the heat is more regular and constant. Dryden often surpasses expectation, and Pope never falls below it. Dryden is read with frequent astonishment, and Pope with perpetual delight." This comparison of the styles of the two men is also suggestive of the difference between the two centuries in which the men lived. And Dryden represents in many ways the vehemence, the complexity, the sweep of the seventeenth century, as well as the effort towards refinement of art and life which we call the Classical movement.

The standard edition of Dryden's works is by Sir Walter Scott (1808), re-edited by George Saintsbury (1882-93). An excellent one-volume edition of the poems is by George R. Noyes (Boston, 1908). W. P. Ker's edition of the critical essays (2 vols., 1900) is indispensable. The best biographies are the extended one by Scott (1808) and the brief one by Saintsbury (1881). Mark Van Doren has published an admirable volume on *The Poetry of John Dryden* (1920, reprinted 1932), and Louis I. Bredvold has studied his intellectual background in *The Intellectual Milieu of John Dryden* (Ann Arbor, 1934). Many of the notes have been condensed from *The Best of Dryden* (1933), edited by Louis I. Bredvold. See also page 1268.

TO MY HONOR'D FRIEND SIR ROBERT HOWARD, ON HIS EXCELLENT POEMS

As there is music uninform'd by art
In those wild notes, which with a merry
        heart
The birds in unfrequented shades express,
Who, better taught at home, yet please us
        less:
So in your verse a native sweetness dwells,
Which shames composure, and its art excels.
Singing no more can your soft numbers
        grace
Than paint adds charms unto a beauteous
        face.
Yet as when mighty rivers gently creep,
Their even calmness does suppose them
        deep,   10
Such is your Muse: no metaphor swell'd
        high
With dangerous boldness lifts her to the
        sky;
Those mounting fancies, when they fall
        again,
Shew sand and dirt at bottom do remain.
So firm a strength, and yet withal so sweet,
Did never but in Samson's riddle meet.
'T is strange each line so great a weight
        should bear,

And yet no sign of toil, no sweat appear.
Either your art hides art, as Stoics feign
Then least to feel, when most they suffer
        pain;   20
And we, dull souls, admire, but cannot see
What hidden springs within the engine be,
Or 't is some happiness that still pursues
Each act and motion of your graceful Muse.
Or is it fortune's work, that in your head
The curious net[1] that is for fancies spread,
Lets thro' its meshes every meaner thought
While rich ideas there are only caught?
Sure that's not all; this is a piece too fair
To be the child of chance, and not of care.
No atoms casually together hurl'd   31
Could e'er produce so beautiful a world.
Nor dare I such a doctrine here admit,
As would destroy the providence of wit.
'T is your strong genius then which does
        not feel
Those weights would make a weaker spirit
        reel.
To carry weight and run so lightly too
Is what alone your Pegasus can do.
Great Hercules himself could ne'er do more,
Than not to feel those heav'ns and gods
        he bore.   40
Your easier odes, which for delight were
        penn'd,
Yet our instruction make their second end;

[1] *Rete mirabile.*

We're both enrich'd and pleas'd, like them
    that woo
At once a beauty and a fortune too.
Of moral knowledge Poesy was queen,
And still she might, had wanton wits not
    been;
Who like ill guardians liv'd themselves at
    large,
And, not content with that, debauch'd their
    charge.
Like some brave captain, your successful
    pen
Restores the Exil'd to her crown again;   50
And gives us hope, that having seen the
    days
When nothing flourish'd but fanatic bays,
All will at length in this opinion rest:
"A sober prince's government is best."
This is not all; your art the way has found
To make improvement of the richest
    ground,
That soil which those immortal laurels bore,
That once the sacred Maro's temples wore.
Elisa's griefs are so express'd by you,   59
They are too eloquent to have been true.
Had she so spoke, Æneas had obey'd
What Dido rather then what Jove had said.
If funeral rites can give a ghost repose,
Your muse so justly has discharged those,
Elisa's shade may now its wand'ring cease,
And claim a title to the fields of peace.
But if Æneas be oblig'd, no less
Your kindness great Achilles doth confess,
Who, dress'd by Statius in too bold a look,
Did ill become those virgin's robes he
    took.   70
To understand how much we owe to you,
We must your numbers with your author's
    view;
Then we shall see his work was lamely
    rough,
Each figure stiff, as if design'd in buff;
His colors laid so thick on every place,
As only shew'd the paint, but hid the face.
But as in perspective we beauties see,
Which in the glass, not in the picture, be;
So here our sight obligingly mistakes
That wealth which his your bounty only
    makes.   80
Thus vulgar dishes are by cooks disguis'd,
More for their dressing than their substance
    priz'd.
Your curious notes[2] so search into that age,

    [2] Annotations on Statius.

When all was fable but the sacred page,
That, since in that dark night we needs
    must stray,
We are at least misled in pleasant way.
But what we most admire, your verse no
    less
The prophet than the poet doth confess.
Ere our weak eyes discern'd the doubtful
    streak
Of light, you saw great Charles his morn-
    ing break.   90
So skilful seamen ken the land from far,
Which shews like mists to the dull pas-
    senger.
To Charles your Muse first pays her duteous
    love,
As still the Ancients did begin from Jove.
With Monk you end, whose name preserv'd
    shall be,
As Rome recorded Rufus' memory,[3]
Who thought it greater honor to obey
His country's interest, than the world to
    sway.
But to write worthy things of worthy men,
Is the peculiar talent of your pen;   100
Yet let me take your mantle up, and I
Will venture in your right to prophesy.

"This work, by merit first of fame secure,
Is likewise happy in its geniture:
For, since 't is born when Charles ascends
    the throne,
It shares at once his fortune and its own."

                                        [1660]

TO MY HONOR'D FRIEND, DR. CHARLETON,

ON HIS LEARNED AND USEFUL
    WORKS; AND MORE PARTICULARLY
    THIS OF STONEHENGE, BY HIM
    RESTOR'D TO THE TRUE FOUNDERS

The longest tyranny that ever sway'd
Was that wherein our ancestors betray'd
Their free-born reason to the Stagirite,
And made his torch their universal light.
So truth, while only one supplied the state,
Grew scarce, and dear, and yet sophisticate;

[3] *Hic situs est Rufus, qui pulso Vindice quon-
dam, Imperium asseruit non sibi sed patriæ.*

Until 't was bought, like emp'ric wares, or
  charms,
Hard words seal'd up with Aristotle's arms.
Columbus was the first that shook his
  throne,
And found a temp'rate in a torrid zone,   10
The fev'rish air fann'd by a cooling breeze,
The fruitful vales set round with shady
  trees;
And guiltless men, who danc'd away their
  time,
Fresh as their groves, and happy as their
  clime.
Had we still paid that homage to a name,
Which only God and Nature justly claim,
The western seas had been our utmost
  bound,
Where poets still might dream the sun was
  drown'd:
And all the stars that shine in southern
  skies
Had been admir'd by none but savage
  eyes.   20
Among th' asserters of free reason's claim,
Th' English are not the least in worth or
  fame.
The world to Bacon does not only owe
Its present knowledge, but its future too.
Gilbert shall live, till loadstones cease to
  draw,
Or British fleets the boundless ocean awe.
And noble Boyle, not less in nature seen,
Than his great brother read in states and
  men.
The circling streams, once thought but
  pools, of blood
(Whether life's fuel or the body's food)   30
From dark oblivion Harvey's name shall
  save;
While Ent keeps all the honour that he
  gave.
Nor are you, learned friend, the least re-
  nown'd;
Whose fame, not circumscrib'd with English
  ground,
Flies like the nimble journeys of the light;
And is, like that, unspent too in its flight.
Whatever truths have been by art or chance
Redeem'd from error, or from ignorance,
Thin in their authors, like rich veins of
  ore,
Your works unite, and still discover more.   40
Such is the healing virtue of your pen,
To perfect cures on books, as well as men.

Nor is this work the least: you well may
  give
To men new vigour, who makes stones to
  live.
Thro' you, the Danes, their short dominion
  lost,
A longer conquest than the Saxons boast.
Stonehenge, once thought a temple, you
  have found
A throne, where kings, our earthly gods,
  were crown'd;
Where by their wond'ring subjects they
  were seen,
Joy'd with their stature and their princely
  mien.   50
Our sovereign here above the rest might
  stand,
And here be chose again to rule the land.
These ruins shelter'd once his sacred
  head,
Then when from Wor'ster's fatal field he
  fled;
Watch'd by the genius of this royal place,
And mighty visions of the Danish race,
His refuge then was for a temple shown:
But, he restor'd, 't is now become a throne.

[1663]

SONGS

FROM TYRANNIC LOVE

Ah how sweet it is to love,
Ah how gay is young desire!
And what pleasing pains we prove
When we first approach love's fire!
  Pains of love be sweeter far
  Than all other pleasures are.

Sighs which are from lovers blown,
Do but gently heave the heart:
Ev'n the tears they shed alone
Cure, like trickling balm, their smart.   10
  Lovers when they lose their breath
  Bleed away in easie death.

Love and time with reverence use,
Treat 'em like a parting friend:
Nor the golden gifts refuse
Which in youth sincere they send:
  For each year their price is more,
  And they less simple than before.

Love like spring-tides full and high
Swells in ev'ry youthful vein: 20
But each tide does less supply,
Till they quite shrink in again:
                              [1670]

FROM MARRIAGE A-LA-MODE

1

Why should a foolish marriage vow
  Which long ago was made,
Oblige us to each other now
  When passion is decay'd?
We lov'd, and we lov'd, as long as we
      cou'd,
  Till our love was lov'd out in us both:
But our marriage is dead, when the pleas-
      ure is fled:
  'Twas pleasure first made it an oath.

2

If I have pleasures for a friend,
  And farther love in store,   10
What wrong has he whose joys did end,
  And who cou'd give no more?
'Tis a madness that he
Shou'd be jealous of me,
Or that I shou'd bar him of another:
For all we can gain is to give our selves
      pain,
When neither can hinder the other.
                              [1672]

FROM THE SPANISH FRYAR

I

Farwell ungratefull traitor,
  Farwell my perjur'd swain,
Let never injur'd creature
  Believe a man again.
The pleasure of possessing
Surpasses all expressing,
But 'tis too short a blessing,
  And love too long a pain.

II

'Tis easie to deceive us
  In pity of your pain,   10
But when we love you leave us
  To rail at you in vain.

Before we have descried it,
There is no bliss beside it,
But she that once has tried it
Will never love again.

III

The passion you pretended
  Was only to obtain
But when the charm is ended
  The charmer you disdain.   20
Your love by ours we measure
Till we have lost our treasure,
But dying is a pleasure,
  When living is a pain.
                              [1681]

PROLOGUE TO THE TEMPEST

As when a tree's cut down, the secret root
Lives under ground, and thence new
      branches shoot,
So from old Shakespeare's honoured dust
      this day
Springs up and buds a new reviving play:
Shakespeare, who (taught by none) did
      first impart
To Fletcher wit, to labouring Jonson art;
He monarch-like, gave those his subjects
      law,
And is that Nature which they paint and
      draw.
Fletcher reach'd that which on his heights
      did grow,
Whilst Jonson crept and gather'd all be-
      low.   10
This did his love, and this his mirth digest:
One imitates him most, the other best.
If they have since out-writ all other men,
'Tis with the drops which fell from Shake-
      speare's pen.
The storm which vanish'd on the neigh-
      b'ring shore
Was taught by Shakespeare's *Tempest* first
      to roar.
That innocence and beauty, which did
      smile
In Fletcher, grew on this *Enchanted Isle.*
But Shakespeare's magic could not copy'd
      be;   19
Within that circle none durst walk but he.

I must confess 'twas bold, nor would you
    now
That liberty to vulgar wits allow,
Which works by magic supernatural things;
But Shakespeare's pow'r is sacred as a
    King's.
Those legends from old priest-hood were
    receiv'd,
And he then writ, as people then believ'd.
But if for Shakespeare we your grace im-
    plore,
We for our theatre shall want it more;
Who by our dearth of youths are forc'd t'
    employ
One of our women to present a boy.   30
And that's a transformation you will say
Exceeding all the magic in the play.
Let none expect in the last act to find
Her sex transform'd from man to woman-
    kind.
Whate'er she was before the play began,
All you shall see of her is perfect man.
Or, if your fancy will be farther led
To find her woman, it must be abed.

                [1670]

EPILOGUE TO THE SECOND PART OF THE CONQUEST OF GRANADA BY THE SPANIARDS

They who have best succeeded on the stage,
Have still conform'd their Genius to their
    Age.
Thus Jonson did mechanic humor show
When men were dull, and conversation
    low.
Then, Comedy was faultless, but 'twas
    coarse;
Cobb's tankard was a jest, and Otter's horse.
And as their Comedy, their Love was mean;
Except, by chance, in some one labour'd
    scene,
Which must atone for an ill-written play,
They rose, but at their height could seldom
    stay.   10
Fame then was cheap, and the first comer
    sped;
And they have kept it since, by being dead,
But, were they now to write, when critics
    weigh

Each line, and ev'ry word, throughout a
    play,
None of 'em, no, not Jonson in his height,
Could pass, without allowing grains for
    weight.
Think it not envy, that these truths are
    told;
Our poet's not malicious, though he's bold.
'Tis not to brand 'em that their faults are
    shown,
But by their errours to excuse his own.   20
If Love and Honour now are higher rais'd,
'Tis not the poet, but the Age is prais'd.
Wit's now arriv'd to a more high degree;
Our native language more refin'd and free;
Our ladies and our men now speak more
    wit
In conversation, than those poets writ.
Then, one of these is, consequently, true;
That what this poet writes comes short of
    you,
And imitates you ill (which most he fears)
Or else his writing is not worse than theirs.
Yet, though you judge (as sure the Critics
    will)   31
That some before him writ with greater
    skill,
In this one praise he has their fame surpast,
To please an age more gallant than the last.

                [1672]

PROLOGUE TO AURENG-ZEBE

Our author by experience finds it true,
'Tis much more hard to please himself than
    you;
And out of no feign'd modesty, this day,
Damns his laborious trifle of a play;
Not that it's worse than what before he
    writ,
But he has now another taste of wit;
And, to confess a truth (though out of
    time,)
Grows weary of his long-loved mistress
    Rhyme.
Passion's too fierce to be in fetters bound,
And Nature flies him like enchanted
    ground: 10
What verse can do he has perform'd in this,
Which he presumes the most correct of his;

But spite of all his pride, a secret shame
Invades his breast at Shakespear's sacred
    name:
Aw'd when he hears his godlike Romans
    rage,
He in a just despair would quit the stage;
And to an age less polish'd, more unskill'd,
Does with disdain the foremost honours
    yield.
As with the greater Dead he dares not
    strive,
He wou'd not match his verse with those
    who live: 20
Let him retire, betwixt two ages cast,
The first of this, and hindmost of the last.
A losing gamester, let him sneak away;
He bears no ready money from the play.
The fate which governs poets, thought it fit,
He shou'd not raise his fortunes by his wit.
The clergy thrive, and the litigious bar;

Dull heroes fatten with the spoils of war:
All southern vices, heav'n be prais'd, are
    here;
But wit's a luxury you think too dear.   30
When you to cultivate the plant are loath,
'Tis a shrewd sign 'twas never of your
    growth:
And wit in Northern climates will not blow,
Except, like orange-trees, 'tis hous'd from
    snow.
There needs no care to put a play-house
    down,
'Tis the most desart place of all the Town:
We and our neighbours, to speak proudly,
    are
Like monarchs, ruin'd with expensive war;
While, like wise English, unconcern'd you
    sit,
And see us play the Tragedy of Wit.   40

[1676]

ABSALOM AND ACHITOPHEL

A POEM

Si propius stes
Te capiat magis.

TO THE READER

'T is not my intention to make an apology for my poem: some will think it needs no excuse, and others will receive none. The design, I am sure, is honest: but he who draws his pen for one party must expect to make enemies of the other. For Wit and Fool are consequents of Whig and Tory; and every man is a knave or an ass to the contrary side. There 's a treasury of merits in the Fanatic Church, as well as in the Papist; and a pennyworth to be had of saintship, honesty, and poetry, for the lewd, the factious, and the blockheads; but the longest chapter in *Deuteronomy* has not curses enough for an anti-Bromingham. My comfort is, their manifest prejudice to my cause will render their judgment of less authority against me. Yet if a poem have a genius, it will force its own reception in the world; for there 's a sweetness in good verse, which tickles even while it hurts, and no man can be heartily angry with him who pleases him against his will. The commendation of adversaries is the greatest triumph of a writer, because it never comes unless extorted. But I can be satisfied on more easy terms: if I happen to please the more moderate sort, I shall be sure of an honest party, and, in all probability, of the best judges; for the least concerned are commonly the least corrupt. And, I confess, I have laid in for those, by rebating the satire (where justice would allow it) from carrying too sharp an edge. They who can criticise so weakly, as to imagine I have done my worst, may be convinced, at their own cost, that I can write severely with more ease than I can gently. I have but laughed at some men's follies, when I could have declaimed against their vices; and other men's virtues I have commended, as freely as I have tax'd their crimes. And now, if you are a malicious reader, I expect you should return upon me that I affect to be thought more impartial than I am. But if men are not to be judged by their professions, God forgive you Commonwealth's-men for professing so plausibly for the government. You cannot be so unconscionable as to charge me for not subscribing of my name; for that would reflect too grossly upon your own party, who never dare, tho' they have the advantage of a jury to secure them. If you like not my poem, the fault may, possibly, be in my writing (tho' 't is hard for an author to judge against himself) ; but, more probably, 't is in your morals, which cannot bear the truth of it. The violent, on both sides, will condemn the character of Absalom, as either too favorably or too hardly drawn. But they are not the violent whom I desire to please. The fault on the right hand is to extenuate, palliate, and indulge; and, to confess freely, I have endeavored to commit it. Besides the respect which I owe his birth, I have a greater for his heroic virtues; and David himself could not be more tender of the young man's life than I would be of his reputation. But since the most excellent natures are always the most easy, and, as being such, are the soonest perverted by ill counsels, especially when baited with fame and glory; 't is no more a wonder that he withstood not the temptations of Achitophel, than it was for Adam not to have resisted the two devils, the serpent and the woman. The conclusion of the story I purposely forbore to prosecute, because I could not obtain from myself to show Absalom unfortunate. The frame of it was cut out but for a picture to the waist, and if the draught be so far true, 't is as much as I designed.

Were I the inventor, who am only the historian, I should certainly conclude the piece with the reconcilement of Absalom to David. And who knows but this may come to pass? Things were not brought to an extremity where I left the story; there seems yet to be room left for a composure; hereafter there may only be for pity. I have not so much as an uncharitable wish against Achitophel, but am content to be accused of a good-natured error, and to hope with Origen, that the Devil himself may at last be saved. For which reason, in this poem, he is neither brought to set his house in order, nor to dispose of his person afterwards as he in wisdom shall think fit. God is infinitely merciful; and his vicegerent is only not so, because he is not infinite.

The true end of satire is the amendment of vices by correction. And he who writes honestly is no more an enemy to the offender, than the physician to the patient, when he prescribes harsh remedies to an inveterate disease; for those are only in order to prevent the chirurgeon's work of an *ense rescindendum*, which I wish not to my very enemies. To conclude all; if the body politic have any analogy to the natural, in my weak judgment, an act of oblivion were as necessary in a hot, distempered state, as an opiate would be in a raging fever.

ABSALOM AND ACHITOPHEL

In pious times, ere priestcraft did begin,
Before polygamy was made a sin;
When man on many multiplied his kind,
Ere one to one was cursedly confin'd;
When nature prompted, and no law denied
Promiscuous use of concubine and bride;
Then Israel's monarch after Heaven's own heart,
His vigorous warmth did, variously, impart
To wives and slaves; and, wide as his command,   9
Scatter'd his Maker's image thro' the land.
Michal, of royal blood, the crown did wear,
A soil ungrateful to the tiller's care:
Not so the rest; for several mothers bore
To godlike David several sons before.
But since like slaves his bed they did ascend,
No true succession could their seed attend.
Of all this numerous progeny was none
So beautiful, so brave, as Absalon:
Whether, inspir'd by some diviner lust,
His father got him with a greater gust,   20
Or that his conscious destiny made way,
By manly beauty, to imperial sway.
Early in foreign fields he won renown,
With kings and states allied to Israel's crown:
In peace the thoughts of war he could remove,
And seem'd as he were only born for love.
Whate'er he did, was done with so much ease,
In him alone 't was natural to please;
His motions all accompanied with grace;
And paradise was open'd in his face.   30
With secret joy indulgent David view'd
His youthful image in his son renew'd:
To all his wishes nothing he denied;
And made the charming Annabel his bride.
What faults he had (for who from faults is free?)
His father could not, or he would not see.
Some warm excesses which the law forbore,
Were construed youth that purg'd by boiling o'er:
And Amnon's murther, by a specious name,
Was call'd a just revenge for injur'd fame.
Thus prais'd and lov'd the noble youth remain'd,   41
While David, undisturb'd, in Sion reign'd.
But life can never be sincerely blest:
Heav'n punishes the bad, and proves the best.
The Jews, a headstrong, moody, murm'ring race,

As ever tried th' extent and stretch of
    grace;
God's pamper'd people, whom, debauch'd
    with ease,
No king could govern, nor no God could
    please;
(Gods they had tried of every shape and
    size,
That god-smiths could produce, or priests
    devise:)   50
These Adam-wits, too fortunately free,
Began to dream they wanted liberty;
And when no rule, no precedent was
    found,
Of men by laws less circumscrib'd and
    bound;
They led their wild desires to woods and
    caves,
And thought that all but savages were
    slaves.
They who, when Saul was dead, without a
    blow,
Made foolish Ishbosheth the crown forego;
Who banish'd David did from Hebron
    bring,
And with a general shout proclaim'd him
    king: 60
Those very Jews, who, at their very best,
Their humor more than loyalty express'd,
Now wonder'd why so long they had obey'd
An idol monarch, which their hands had
    made;
Thought they might ruin him they could
    create,
Or melt him to that golden calf, a State.
But these were random bolts: no form'd
    design,
Nor interest made the factious crowd to
    join:
The sober part of Israel, free from stain,
Well knew the value of a peaceful reign; 70
And, looking backward with a wise affright,
Saw seams of wounds, dishonest to the
    sight:
In contemplation of whose ugly scars
They curs'd the memory of civil wars.
The moderate sort of men, thus qualified,
Inclin'd the balance to the better side;
And David's mildness manag'd it so well,
The bad found no occasion to rebel.
But when to sin our bias'd nature leans,
The careful Devil is still at hand with
    means;   80
And providently pimps for ill desires;

The Good Old Cause reviv'd, a plot re
    quires:
Plots, true or false, are necessary things,
To raise up commonwealths, and ruin kings.
  Th' inhabitants of old Jerusalem
Were Jebusites; the town so call'd from
    them;
And theirs the native right ——
But when the chosen people grew more
    strong,
The rightful cause at length became the
    wrong;
And every loss the men of Jebus bore,   90
They still were thought God's enemies the
    more.
Thus worn and weaken'd, well or ill con-
    tent,
Submit they must to David's government:
Impoverish'd and depriv'd of all command,
Their taxes doubled as they lost their land;
And, what was harder yet to flesh and blood,
Their gods disgrac'd, and burnt like com-
    mon wood.
This set the heathen priesthood in a flame;
For priests of all religions are the same:
Of whatsoe'er descent their godhead be, 100
Stock, stone, or other homely pedigree,
In his defense his servants are as bold,
As if he had been born of beaten gold.
The Jewish rabbins, tho' their enemies,
In this conclude them honest men and
    wise:
For 't was their duty, all the learned think,
T' espouse his cause, by whom they eat and
    drink.
From hence began that Plot, the nation's
    curse,
Bad in itself, but represented worse,
Rais'd in extremes, and in extremes de-
    cried,   110
With oaths affirm'd, with dying vows denied,
Not weigh'd or winnow'd by the multi-
    tude,
But swallow'd in the mass, unchew'd, and
    crude.
Some truth there was, but dash'd and
    brew'd with lies,
To please the fools, and puzzle all the
    wise.
Succeeding times did equal folly call,
Believing nothing, or believing all.
Th' Egyptian rites the Jebusites embrac'd,
Where gods were recommended by their
    taste.

Such sav'ry deities must needs be good, 120
As serv'd at once for worship and for food.
By force they could not introduce these
gods,
For ten to one in former days was odds;
So fraud was us'd (the sacrificer's trade):
Fools are more hard to conquer than per-
suade.
Their busy teachers mingled with the Jews,
And rak'd for converts even the court and
stews:
Which Hebrew priests the more unkindly
took,
Because the fleece accompanies the flock.
Some thought they God's anointed meant
to slay 130
By guns, invented since full many a day:
Our author swears it not; but who can
know
How far the Devil and Jebusites may go?
This Plot, which fail'd for want of com-
mon sense,
Had yet a deep and dangerous conse-
quence:
For, as when raging fevers boil the blood,
The standing lake soon floats into a flood,
And ev'ry hostile humor, which before
Slept quiet in its channels, bubbles o'er;
So several factions from this first ferment
Work up to foam, and threat the govern-
ment. 141
Some by their friends, more by themselves
thought wise,
Oppos'd the pow'r to which they could not
rise.
Some had in courts been great, and thrown
from thence,
Like fiends were harden'd in impenitence.
Some, by their monarch's fatal mercy,
grown
From pardon'd rebels, kinsmen to the
throne,
Were rais'd in pow'r and public office high;
Strong bands, if bands ungrateful men
could tie.
Of these the false Achitophel was first; 150
A name to all succeeding ages curst:
For close designs and crooked counsels fit,
Sagacious, bold, and turbulent of wit,
Restless, unfix'd in principles and place,
In pow'r unpleas'd, impatient of disgrace;
A fiery soul, which, working out its way,
Fretted the pigmy body to decay:
And o'er-inform'd the tenement of clay.

A daring pilot in extremity;
Pleas'd with the danger, when the waves
went high, 160
He sought the storms; but, for a calm unfit,
Would steer too nigh the sands, to boast his
wit.
Great wits are sure to madness near allied,
And thin partitions do their bounds divide;
Else why should he, with wealth and honor
blest,
Refuse his age the needful hours of rest?
Punish a body which he could not please,
Bankrupt of life, yet prodigal of ease?
And all to leave what with his toil he won,
To that unfeather'd two-legg'd thing, a
son: 170
Got, while his soul did huddled notions try;
And born a shapeless lump, like anarchy.
In friendship false, implacable in hate,
Resolv'd to ruin or to rule the State;
To compass this the triple bond he broke;
The pillars of the public safety shook,
And fitted Israel for a foreign yoke:
Then seiz'd with fear, yet still affecting
fame,
Usurp'd a Patriot's all-atoning name.
So easy still it proves in factious times 180
With public zeal to cancel private crimes.
How safe is treason, and how sacred ill,
Where none can sin against the People's
Will!
Where crowds can wink, and no offense be
known,
Since in another's guilt they find their own!
Yet, fame deserv'd, no enemy can grudge;
The statesman we abhor, but praise the
judge.
In Israel's courts ne'er sat an Abbethdin
With more discerning eyes or hands more
clean,
Unbrib'd, unsought, the wretched to re-
dress; 190
Swift of dispatch, and easy of access.
O, had he been content to serve the crown,
With virtues only proper to the gown,
Or had the rankness of the soil been freed
From cockle, that oppress'd the noble seed,
David for him his tuneful harp had strung,
And Heav'n had wanted one immortal
song.
But wild Ambition loves to slide, not stand,
And Fortune's ice prefers to Virtue's land.
Achitophel, grown weary to possess 200
A lawful fame, and lazy happiness,

Disdain'd the golden fruit to gather free
And lent the crowd his arm to shake the
    tree.
Now, manifest of crimes contriv'd long
    since,
He stood at bold defiance with his prince:
Held up the buckler of the people's cause
Against the crown; and skulk'd behind the
    laws.
The wish'd occasion of the Plot he takes;
Some circumstances finds, but more he
    makes.
By buzzing emissaries, fills the ears   210
Of list'ning crowds with jealousies and fears
Of arbitrary counsels brought to light,
And proves the king himself a Jebusite.
Weak arguments! which yet he knew full
    well
Were strong with people easy to rebel.
For, govern'd by the moon, the giddy Jews
Tread the same track when she the prime
    renews:
And once in twenty years, their scribes
    record,
By natural instinct they change their lord.
Achitophel still wants a chief, and none 220
Was found so fit as warlike Absalon:
Not that he wish'd his greatness to create,
(For politicians neither love nor hate,)
But, for he knew his title not allow'd,
Would keep him still depending on the
    crowd,
That kingly pow'r, thus ebbing out, might
    be
Drawn to the dregs of a democracy.
Him he attempts with studied arts to please,
And sheds his venom in such words as
    these:
"Auspicious prince, at whose nativity 230
Some royal planet rul'd the southern sky;
Thy longing country's darling and desire,
Their cloudy pillar and their guardian fire,
Their second Moses, whose extended wand
Divides the seas, and shews the promis'd
    land,
Whose dawning day in every distant age
Has exercis'd the sacred prophets' rage,
The people's pray'r, the glad diviners'
    theme,
The young men's vision, and the old men's
    dream!
Thee, Savior, thee, the nation's vows con-
    fess;   240
And, never satisfied with seeing, bless:

Swift, unbespoken pomps, thy steps pro-
    claim,
And stammering babes are taught to lisp
    thy name.
How long wilt thou the general joy detain,
Starve, and defraud the people of thy reign?
Content ingloriously to pass thy days
Like one of Virtue's fools that feeds on
    praise;
Till thy fresh glories, which now shine so
    bright,
Grow stale and tarnish with our daily sight.
Believe me, royal youth, thy fruit must be
Or gather'd ripe, or rot upon the tree. 251
Heav'n has to all allotted, soon or late,
Some lucky revolution of their fate:
Whose motions if we watch and guide with
    skill,
(For human good depends on human will)
Our Fortune rolls as from a smooth descent,
And from the first impression takes the
    bent:
But, if unseiz'd, she glides away like wind,
And leaves repenting Folly far behind.
Now, now she meets you with a glorious
    prize,   260
And spreads her locks before her as she
    flies.
Had thus old David, from whose loins you
    spring,
Not dar'd, when Fortune call'd him, to be
    king,
At Gath an exile he might still remain,
And Heaven's anointing oil had been in
    vain.
Let his successful youth your hopes engage,
But shun th' example of declining age:
Behold him setting in his western skies,
The shadows lengthening as the vapors rise.
He is not now, as when on Jordan's sand 270
The joyful people throng'd to see him land,
Cov'ring the beach, and black'ning all the
    strand:
But, like the Prince of Angels, from his
    height
Comes tumbling downward with diminish'd
    light:
Betray'd by one poor plot to public scorn,
(Our only blessing since his curst return)
Those heaps of people which one sheaf did
    bind,
Blown off and scatter'd by a puff of wind.
What strength can he to your designs
    oppose,

Naked of friends, and round beset with
    foes? 280
If Pharaoh's doubtful succor he should use,
A foreign aid would more incense the Jews:
Proud Egypt would dissembled friendship
    bring;
Foment the war, but not support the king:
Nor would the royal party e'er unite
With Pharaoh's arms t' assist the Jebusite;
Or if they should, their interest soon would
    break,
And with such odious aid make David weak.
All sorts of men by my successful arts,
Abhorring kings, estrange their alter'd
    hearts 290
From David's rule: and 't is the general cry,
'Religion, commonwealth, and liberty.'
If you, as champion of the public good,
Add to their arms a chief of royal blood,
What may not Israel hope, and what ap-
    plause
Might such a general gain by such a cause?
Not barren praise alone, that gaudy flow'r
Fair only to the sight, but solid pow'r:
And nobler is a limited command,
Giv'n by the love of all your native land, 300
Than a successive title, long and dark,
Drawn from the moldy rolls of Noah's ark."
    What cannot praise effect in mighty
    minds,
When flattery soothes, and when ambition
    blinds!
Desire of pow'r, on earth a vicious weed,
Yet, sprung from high, is of celestial seed;
In God 't is glory: and when men aspire,
'T is but a spark too much of heavenly fire.
Th' ambitious youth, too covetous of fame,
Too full of angels' metal in his frame, 310
Unwarily was led from virtue's ways,
Made drunk with honour, and debauch'd
    with praise.
Half loth, and half consenting to the ill,
(For loyal blood within him struggled still)
He thus replied: "And what pretense have I
To take up arms for public liberty?
My father governs with unquestion'd right;
The faith's defender, and mankind's de-
    light,
Good, gracious, just, observant of the laws;
And Heav'n by wonders has espous'd his
    cause. 320
Whom has he wrong'd in all his peaceful
    reign?
Who sues for justice to his throne in vain?

What millions has he pardon'd of his foes
Whom just revenge did to his wrath expose?
Mild, easy, humble, studious of our good,
Inclin'd to mercy, and averse from blood;
If mildness ill with stubborn Israel suit,
His crime is God's beloved attribute.
What could he gain, his people to betray,
Or change his right for arbitrary sway? 330
Let haughty Pharaoh curse with such a
    reign
His fruitful Nile, and yoke a servile train.
If David's rule Jerusalem displease,
The Dog-star heats their brains to this dis-
    ease.
Why then should I, encouraging the bad,
Turn rebel and run popularly mad?
Were he a tyrant, who, by lawless might
Oppress'd the Jews, and rais'd the Jebusite,
Well might I mourn; but Nature's holy
    bands
Would curb my spirits and restrain my
    hands; 340
The people might assert their liberty;
But what was right in them, were crime in
    me.
His favour leaves me nothing to require,
Prevents my wishes, and outruns desire.
What more can I expect while David lives?
All but his kingly diadem he gives:
And that"—But there he paus'd; then sigh-
    ing, said—
"Is justly destin'd for a worthier head.
For when my father from his toils shall rest
And late augment the number of the
    blest, 350
His lawful issue shall the throne ascend,
Or the *collat'ral* line, where that shall end.
His brother, tho' oppress'd with vulgar
    spite,
Yet dauntless, and secure of native right,
Of every royal virtue stands possess'd;
Still dear to all the bravest and the best.
His courage foes, his friends his truth pro-
    claim;
His loyalty the king, the world his fame.
His mercy ev'n th' offending crowd will
    find,
For sure he comes of a forgiving kind. 360
Why should I then repine at Heaven's de-
    cree
Which gives me no pretense to royalty?
Yet O that fate, propitiously inclin'd,
Had rais'd my birth, or had debas'd my
    mind;

To my large soul not all her treasure lent,
And then betray'd it to a mean descent!
I find, I find my mounting spirits bold,
And David's part disdains my mother's
    mold.
Why am I scanted by a niggard birth?
My soul disclaims the kindred of her
    earth;   370
And, made for empire, whispers me within,
'Desire of greatness is a godlike sin.' "
    Him staggering so when Hell's dire agent
        found,
While fainting Virtue scarce maintain'd her
    ground,
He pours fresh forces in, and thus replies:
"Th' eternal God, supremely good and
    wise,
Imparts not these prodigious gifts in vain;
What wonders are reserv'd to bless your
    reign!
Against your will, your arguments have
    shown,
Such virtue's only giv'n to guide a
    throne.   380
Not that your father's mildness I contemn,
But manly force becomes the diadem.
'T is true he grants the people all they
    crave;
And more, perhaps, than subjects ought to
    have:
For lavish grants suppose a monarch tame
And more his goodness than his wit pro-
    claim.
But when should people strive their bonds
    to break
If not when kings are negligent or weak?
Let him give on till he can give no more,
The thrifty Sanhedrin shall keep him
    poor;   390
And every shekel which he can receive
Shall cost a limb of his prerogative.
To ply him with new plots shall be my care;
Or plunge him deep in some expensive war;
Which, when his treasure can no more
    supply,
He must, with the remains of kingship, buy.
His faithful friends, our jealousies and fears
Call Jebusites, and Pharaoh's pensioners;
Whom when our fury from his aid has torn,
He shall be naked left to public scorn.   400
The next successor, whom I fear and hate,
My arts have made obnoxious to the State;
Turn'd all his virtues to his overthrow,
And gain'd our elders to pronounce a foe.

His right, for sums of necessary gold,
Shall first be pawn'd, and afterwards be
    sold;
Till time shall ever-wanting David draw,
To pass your doubtful title into law.
If not; the people have a right supreme
To make their kings; for kings are made for
    them.   410
All empire is no more than pow'r in trust,
Which, when resum'd, can be no longer
    just.
Succession, for the general good design'd,
In its own wrong a nation cannot bind:
If altering that the people can relieve,
Better one suffer, than a nation grieve.
The Jews well know their pow'r: ere Saul
    they chose,
God was their king, and God they durst
    depose.
Urge now your piety, your filial name,
A father's right, and fear of future fame; 420
The public good, that universal call,
To which even Heav'n submitted, answers
    all.
Nor let his love enchant your generous
    mind;
'T is Nature's trick to propagate her kind.
Our fond begetters, who would never die,
Love but themselves in their posterity.
Or let his kindness by th' effects be tried
Or let him lay his vain pretense aside.
God said he lov'd your father; could he
    bring
A better proof than to anoint him king? 430
It surely shew'd he lov'd the shepherd well,
Who gave so fair a flock as Israel.
Would David have you thought his darling
    son?
What means he then, to alienate the crown?
The name of godly he may blush to bear:
'T is after God's own heart to cheat his heir.
He to his brother gives supreme command;
To you a legacy of barren land:
Perhaps th' old harp, on which he thrums
    his lays:
Or some dull Hebrew ballad in your
    praise.   440
Then the next heir, a prince severe and
    wise,
Already looks on you with jealous eyes,
Sees thro' the thin disguises of your arts,
And marks your progress in the people's
    hearts.
Tho' now his mighty soul its grief contains,

He meditates revenge who least complains;
And, like a lion, slumb'ring in the way,
Or sleep dissembling, while he waits his
    prey,
His fearless foes within his distance draws,
Constrains his roaring, and contracts his
    paws;   450
Till at the last, his time for fury found,
He shoots with sudden vengeance from the
    ground:
The prostrate vulgar passes o'er and spares,
But with a lordly rage his hunters tears.
Your case no tame expedients will afford:
Resolve on death, or conquest by the sword,
Which for no less a stake than life you
    draw,
And self-defense is Nature's eldest law.
Leave the warm people no considering
    time;
For then rebellion may be thought a
    crime.   460
Prevail yourself of what occasion gives,
But try your title while your father lives;
And that your arms may have a fair pre-
    tense,
Proclaim you take them in the king's de-
    fense;
Whose sacred life each minute would ex-
    pose
To plots, from seeming friends, and secret
    foes.
And who can sound the depth of David's
    soul?
Perhaps his fear his kindness may control.
He fears his brother, tho' he loves his son,
For plighted vows too late to be undone.   470
If so, by force he wishes to be gain'd,
Like women's lechery, to seem constrain'd.
Doubt not; but, when he most affects the
    frown,
Commit a pleasing rape upon the crown.
Secure his person to secure your cause;
They who possess the prince, possess the
    laws."
    He said, and this advice above the rest,
With Absalom's mild nature suited best;
Unblam'd of life (ambition set aside)
Not stain'd with cruelty, nor puff'd with
    pride;   480
How happy had he been, if destiny
Had higher plac'd his birth, or not so high!
His kingly virtues might have claim'd a
    throne
And blest all other countries but his own.

But charming greatness since so few refuse,
'T is juster to lament him, than accuse.
Strong were his hopes a rival to remove,
With blandishments to gain the public love,
To head the faction while their zeal was
    hot,
And popularly prosecute the Plot.   490
To farther this, Achitophel unites
The malcontents of all the Israelites:
Whose differing parties he could wisely join,
For several ends, to serve the same design.
The best, and of the princes some were
    such,
Who thought the pow'r of monarchy too
    much;
Mistaken men, and patriots in their hearts;
Not wicked, but seduc'd by impious arts.
By these the springs of property were bent,
And wound so high, they crack'd the gov-
    ernment.   500
The next for interest sought t' embroil the
    State,
To sell their duty at a dearer rate;
And make their Jewish markets of the
    throne,
Pretending public good, to serve their own.
Others thought kings an useless heavy load,
Who cost too much, and did too little good.
These were for laying honest David by,
On principles of pure good husbandry.
With them join'd all th' haranguers of the
    throng
That thought to get preferment by the
    tongue.   510
Who follow next, a double danger bring,
Not only hating David, but the king:
The Solymæan rout; well-vers'd of old
In godly faction, and in treason bold;
Cow'ring and quaking at a conqu'ror's
    sword,
But lofty to a lawful prince restor'd;
Saw with disdain an Ethnic plot begun
And scorn'd by Jebusites to be outdone.
Hot Levites headed these; who, pull'd be-
    fore
From th' ark, which in the Judges' days they
    bore,   520
Resum'd their cant, and with a zealous cry
Pursued their old belov'd Theocracy:
Where Sanhedrin and priest enslav'd the
    nation,
And justified their spoils by inspiration:
For who so fit for reign as Aaron's race,

If once dominion they could found in
    grace?
These led the pack; tho' not of surest scent,
Yet deepest mouth'd against the govern-
    ment.
A numerous host of dreaming saints suc-
    ceed,
Of the true old Enthusiastic breed: 530
'Gainst form and order they their pow'r
    employ,
Nothing to build, and all things to destroy.
But far more numerous was the herd of
    such,
Who think too little, and who talk too
    much.
These, out of mere instinct, they knew not
    why,
Ador'd their fathers' God and property:
And, by the same blind benefit of fate,
The Devil and the Jebusite did hate: 538
Born to be sav'd, even in their own despite,
Because they could not help believing right.
Such were the tools; but a whole Hydra
    more
Remains, of sprouting heads too long to
    score.
Some of their chiefs were princes of the
    land;
In the first rank of these did Zimri stand:
A man so various, that he seem'd to be
Not one, but all mankind's epitome:
Stiff in opinions, always in the wrong;
Was everything by starts, and nothing long;
But, in the course of one revolving moon,
Was chymist, fiddler, statesman, and buf-
    foon: 550
Then all for women, painting, rhyming,
    drinking,
Besides ten thousand freaks that died in
    thinking.
Blest madman, who could every hour em-
    ploy,
With something new to wish, or to enjoy!
Railing and praising were his usual themes;
And both (to show his judgment) in ex-
    tremes:
So over-violent, or over-civil,
That every man, with him, was God or
    Devil.
In squand'ring wealth was his peculiar art:
Nothing went unrewarded, but desert.   560
Beggar'd by fools, whom still he found too
    late:
He had his jest, and they had his estate.

He laugh'd himself from court; then sought
    relief
By forming parties, but could ne'er be chief:
For, spite of him, the weight of business fell
On Absalom and wise Achitophel:
Thus wicked but in will, of means bereft,
He left not faction, but of that was left.
    Titles and names 't were tedious to re-
    hearse
Of lords, below the dignity of verse.   570
Wits, warriors, Commonwealth's-men, were
    the best:
Kind husbands, and mere nobles, all the
    rest.
And therefore, in the name of dulness, be
The well-hung Balaam and cold Caleb,
    free;
And canting Nadab let oblivion damn,
Who made new porridge for the paschal
    lamb.
Let friendship's holy band some names as-
    sure,
Some their own worth, and some let scorn
    secure.
Nor shall the rascal rabble here have place,
Whom kings no titles gave, and God no
    grace: 580
Not bull-fac'd Jonas, who could statutes
    draw
To mean rebellion, and make treason law.
But he, tho' bad, is follow'd by a worse,
The wretch who Heav'n's anointed dar'd to
    curse:
Shimei, whose youth did early promise
    bring
Of zeal to God, and hatred to his king,
Did wisely from expensive sins refrain,
And never broke the Sabbath, but for gain;
Nor ever was he known an oath to vent,
Or curse, unless against the government. 590
Thus, heaping wealth, by the most ready
    way
Among the Jews, which was to cheat and
    pray,
The city, to reward his pious hate
Against his master, chose him magistrate:
His hand a vare of justice did uphold;
His neck was loaded with a chain of gold.
During his office, treason was no crime;
The sons of Belial had a glorious time:
For Shimei, tho' not prodigal of pelf,
Yet lov'd his wicked neighbor as himself. 600
When two or three were gather'd to de-
    claim

Against the monarch of Jerusalem,
Shimei was always in the midst of them;
And if they curs'd the king when he was by,
Would rather curse than break good com-
    pany.
If any durst his factious friends accuse,
He pack'd a jury of dissenting Jews;
Whose fellow-feeling in the godly cause
Would free the suff'ring saint from human
    laws.   610
For laws are only made to punish those
Who serve the king, and to protect his foes.
If any leisure time he had from pow'r,
(Because 't is sin to misemploy an hour)
His bus'ness was, by writing, to persuade
That kings were useless, and a clog to trade:
And, that his noble style he might refine,
No Rechabite more shunn'd the fumes of
    wine.
Chaste were his cellars; and his shrieval
    board
The grossness of a city feast abhorr'd:
His cooks, with long disuse, their trade for-
    got;   620
Cool was his kitchen, tho' his brains were
    hot.
Such frugal virtue malice may accuse.
But sure 't was necessary to the Jews:
For towns once burnt such magistrates re-
    quire
As dare not tempt God's providence by fire.
With spiritual food he fed his servants well,
But free from flesh that made the Jews
    rebel;
And Moses' laws he held in more account,
For forty days of fasting in the mount.   629
    To speak the rest, who better are forgot,
Would tire a well-breath'd witness of the
    Plot:
Yet, Corah, thou shalt from oblivion pass;
Erect thyself, thou monumental brass,
High as the serpent of thy metal made,
While nations stand secure beneath thy
    shade.
What tho' his birth were base, yet comets
    rise
From earthy vapors, ere they shine in skies.
Prodigious actions may as well be done
By weaver's issue, as by prince's son.
This arch-attestor for the public good   640
By that one deed ennobles all his blood.
Who ever ask'd the witness's high race
Whose oath with martyrdom did Stephen
    grace?

Ours was a Levite, and as times went then,
His tribe were God Almighty's gentlemen.
Sunk were his eyes, his voice was harsh and
    loud,
Sure signs he neither choleric was nor
    proud:
His long chin prov'd his wit; his saintlike
    grace
A church vermilion, and a Moses' face.
His memory, miraculously great,   650
Could plots, exceeding man's belief, repeat;
Which therefore cannot be accounted lies,
For human wit could never such devise.
Some future truths are mingled in his book;
But where the witness fail'd, the prophet
    spoke:
Some things like visionary flights appear;
The spirit caught him up, the Lord knows
    where,
And gave him his rabbinical degree,
Unknown to foreign university.
His judgment yet his mem'ry did excel,   660
Which piec'd his wondrous evidence so well,
And suited to the temper of the times,
Then groaning under Jebusitic crimes.
Let Israel's foes suspect his heav'nly call,
And rashly judge his writ apocryphal;
Our laws for such affronts have forfeits
    made:
He takes his life, who takes away his trade.
Were I myself in witness Corah's place,
The wretch who did me such a dire disgrace
Should whet my memory, tho' once forgot,
To make him an appendix of my Plot.   671
His zeal to Heav'n made him his prince
    despise,
And load his person with indignities:
But zeal peculiar privilege affords,
Indulging latitude to deeds and words;
And Corah might for Agag's murther call,
In terms as coarse as Samuel us'd to Saul.
What others in his evidence did join,
(The best that could be had for love or
    coin,)
In Corah's own predicament will fall;   680
For witness is a common name to all.
    Surrounded thus with friends of every
    sort,
Deluded Absalom forsakes the court:
Impatient of high hopes, urg'd with re-
    nown,
And fir'd with near possession of a crown.
Th' admiring crowd are dazzled with sur-
    prise

And on his goodly person feed their eyes:
His joy conceal'd, he sets himself to show,
On each side bowing popularly low;
His looks, his gestures, and his words he
   frames   690
And with familiar ease repeats their names.
Thus form'd by nature, furnish'd out with
   arts,
He glides unfelt into their secret hearts:
Then, with a kind compassionating look,
And sighs, bespeaking pity ere he spoke,
Few words he said; but easy those and fit,
More slow than Hybla-drops, and far more
   sweet.
  "I mourn, my countrymen, your lost
   estate,
Tho' far unable to prevent your fate:
Behold a banish'd man, for your dear cause
Expos'd a prey to arbitrary laws!   701
Yet O! that I alone could be undone,
Cut off from empire, and no more a son!
Now all your liberties a spoil are made;
Egypt and Tyrus intercept your trade,
And Jebusites your sacred rites invade.
My father, whom with reverence yet I
   name,
Charm'd into ease, is careless of his fame:
And, brib'd with petty sums of foreign gold,
Is grown in Bathsheba's embraces old: 710
Exalts his enemies, his friends destroys,
And all his pow'r against himself employs.
He gives, and let him give, my right away;
But why should he his own and yours be-
   tray?
He, only he, can make the nation bleed,
And he alone from my revenge is freed.
Take then my tears (with that he wip'd his
   eyes)
'T is all the aid my present pow'r supplies:
No court-informer can these arms accuse;
These arms may sons against their fathers
   use;   720
And 't is my wish, the next successor's reign
May make no other Israelite complain."
  Youth, beauty, graceful action seldom
   fail:
But common interest always will prevail:
And pity never ceases to be shown
To him who makes the people's wrongs his
   own.
The crowd, that still believe their kings op-
   press,
With lifted hands their young Messiah
   bless:

Who now begins his progress to ordain
With chariots, horsemen, and a num'rous
   train;   730
From east to west his glories he displays,
And, like the sun, the promis'd land surveys.
Fame runs before him as the morning star,
And shouts of joy salute him from afar:
Each house receives him as a guardian god,
And consecrates the place of his abode:
But hospitable treats did most commend
Wise Issachar, his wealthy western friend.
This moving court, that caught the people's
   eyes,
And seem'd but pomp, did other ends dis-
   guise: 740
Achitophel had form'd it, with intent
To sound the depths, and fathom, where it
   went,
The people's hearts; distinguish friends
   from foes,
And try their strength, before they came to
   blows.
Yet all was colour'd with a smooth pretense
Of specious love, and duty to their prince.
Religion, and redress of grievances,
Two names that always cheat and always
   please,
Are often urg'd; and good King David's life
Endanger'd by a brother and a wife.   750
Thus in a pageant show a Plot is made,
And peace itself is war in masquerade.
O foolish Israel! never warn'd by ill!
Still the same bait, and circumvented still!
Did ever men forsake their present ease,
In midst of health imagine a disease;
Take pains contingent mischiefs to foresee,
Make heirs for monarchs, and for God de-
   cree?
What shall we think! Can people give away,
Both for themselves and sons, their native
   sway?   760
Then they are left defenseless to the sword
Of each unbounded, arbitrary lord:
And laws are vain, by which we right enjoy,
If kings unquestion'd can those laws de
   stroy.
Yet if the crowd be judge of fit and just,
And kings are only officers in trust,
Then this resuming cov'nant was declar'd
When kings were made, or is for ever barr'd:
If those who gave the scepter could not tie
By their own deed their own posterity,   770
How then could Adam bind his future race?

How could his forfeit on mankind take
    place?
Or how could heavenly justice damn us all,
Who ne'er consented to our father's fall?
Then kings are slaves to those whom they
    command,
And tenants to their people's pleasure stand.
Add that the pow'r, for property allow'd,
Is mischievously seated in the crowd;
For who can be secure of private right,   779
If sovereign sway may be dissolv'd by might?
Nor is the people's judgment always true:
The most may err as grossly as the few;
And faultless kings run down, by common
    cry,
For vice, oppression, and for tyranny.
What standard is there in a fickle rout,
Which, flowing to the mark, runs faster out?
Nor only crowds, but Sanhedrins may be
Infected with this public lunacy,
And share the madness of rebellious times,
To murther monarchs for imagin'd crimes.
If they may give and take whene'er they
    please,   791
Not kings alone, (the Godhead's images,)
But government itself at length must fall
To nature's state, where all have right to all.
Yet, grant our lords, the People, kings can
    make,
What prudent men a settled throne would
    shake?
For whatsoe'er their sufferings were before,
That change they covet makes them suffer
    more.
All other errors but disturb a state;
But innovation is the blow of fate.   800
If ancient fabrics nod, and threat to fall,
To patch the flaws, and buttress up the wall,
Thus far 't is duty; but here fix the mark:
For all beyond it is to touch our Ark.
To change foundations, cast the frame
    anew,
Is work for rebels who base ends pursue,
At once divine and human laws control,
And mend the parts by ruin of the whole.
The tamp'ring world is subject to this curse,
To physic their disease into a worse.   810
    Now what relief can righteous David
        bring?
How fatal 't is to be too good a king!
Friends he has few, so high the madness
    grows;
Who dare be such, must be the people's
    foes:

Yet some there were, ev'n in the worst of
    days;
Some let me name, and naming is to praise.
    In this short file Barzillai first appears;
Barzillai, crown'd with honour and with
    years:
Long since, the rising rebels he withstood
In regions waste, beyond the Jordan's flood:
Unfortunately brave to buoy the State;   821
But sinking underneath his master's fate:
In exile with his godlike prince he mourn'd,
For him he suffer'd, and with him return'd.
The court he practic'd, not the courtier's
    art:
Large was his wealth, but larger was his
    heart:
Which well the noblest objects knew to
    choose,
The fighting warrior, and recording Muse.
His bed could once a fruitful issue boast;
Now more than half a father's name is
    lost.   830
His eldest hope, with every grace adorn'd,
By me (so Heav'n will have it) always
    mourn'd,
And always honour'd, snatch'd in man-
    hood's prime
B' unequal fates, and Providence's crime:
Yet not before the goal of honour won,
All parts fulfill'd of subject and of son;
Swift was the race, but short the time to run.
O narrow circle, but of pow'r divine,
Scanted in space, but perfect in thy line!
By sea, by land, thy matchless worth was
    known,   840
Arms thy delight, and war was all thy own:
Thy force, infus'd, the fainting Tyrians
    propp'd;
And haughty Pharaoh found his fortune
    stopp'd.
O ancient honor! O unconquer'd hand,
Whom foes unpunish'd never could with-
    stand!
But Israel was unworthy of thy name;
Short is the date of all immoderate fame.
It looks as Heav'n our ruin had design'd,
And durst not trust thy fortune and thy
    mind.
Now, free from earth, thy disencumber'd
    soul   850
Mounts up, and leaves behind the clouds
    and starry pole:
From thence thy kindred legions mayst thou
    bring,

To aid the guardian angel of thy king.
Here stop, my Muse, here cease thy painful
    flight;
No pinions can pursue immortal height:
Tell good Barzillai thou canst sing no more,
And tell thy soul she should have fled
    before,
Or fled she with his life, and left this verse
To hang on her departed patron's hearse?
Now take thy steepy flight from heav'n, and
    see   860
If thou canst find on earth another *he*:
Another *he* would be too hard to find;
See then whom thou canst see not far be-
    hind.
Zadoc the priest, whom, shunning pow'r
    and place,
His lowly mind advanc'd to David's grace:
With him the Sagan of Jerusalem,
Of hospitable soul, and noble stem;
Him of the western dome, whose weighty
    sense
Flows in fit words and heavenly eloquence.
The prophets' sons, by such example led,
To learning and to loyalty were bred: 871
For colleges on bounteous kings depend,
And never rebel was to arts a friend.
To these succeed the pillars of the laws,
Who best could plead, and best can judge a
    cause.
Next them a train of loyal peers ascend:
Sharp-judging Adriel, the Muses' friend;
Himself a Muse:—in Sanhedrin's debate
True to his prince, but not a slave of state:
Whom David's love with honours did adorn,
That from his disobedient son were torn. 881
Jotham of piercing wit, and pregnant
    thought,
Endued by nature, and by learning taught
To move assemblies, who but only tried
The worse a while, then chose the better
    side;
Nor chose alone, but turn'd the balance too;
So much the weight of one brave man can
    do.
Hushai, the friend of David in distress,
In public storms, of manly steadfastness: 889
By foreign treaties he inform'd his youth,
And join'd experience to his native truth.
His frugal care supplied the wanting
    throne;
Frugal for that, but bounteous of his own:
'T is easy conduct when exchequers flow,
But hard the task to manage well the low;

For sovereign power is too depress'd or
    high,
When kings are forc'd to sell, or crowds to
    buy.
Indulge one labor more, my weary Muse,
For Amiel: who can Amiel's praise refuse?
Of ancient race by birth, but nobler yet 900
In his own worth, and without title great:
The Sanhedrin long time as chief he rul'd,
Their reason guided, and their passion
    cool'd:
So dext'rous was he in the crown's defense,
So form'd to speak a loyal nation's sense,
That, as their band was Israel's tribes in
    small,
So fit was he to represent them all.
Now rasher charioteers the seat ascend,
Whose loose careers his steady skill com-
    mend:
They, like th' unequal ruler of the day, 910
Misguide the seasons, and mistake the way;
While he withdrawn at their mad labour
    smiles,
And safe enjoys the sabbath of his toils.
    These were the chief; a small but faithful
    band
Of worthies, in the breach who dar'd to
    stand
And tempt th' united fury of the land.
With grief they view'd such powerful en-
    gines bent
To batter down the lawful government:
A numerous faction, with pretended frights,
In Sanhedrins to plume the regal rights; 920
The true successor from the court remov'd;
The Plot, by hireling witnesses, improv'd.
These ills they saw, and, as their duty
    bound,
They show'd the king the danger of the
    wound;
That no concessions from the throne would
    please,
But lenitives fomented the disease;
That Absalom, ambitious of the crown,
Was made the lure to draw the people
    down;
That false Achitophel's pernicious hate
Had turn'd the Plot to ruin Church and
    State;   930
The council violent, the rabble worse:
That Shimei taught Jerusalem to curse.
    With all these loads of injuries oppress'd,
And long revolving in his careful breast

Th' event of things; at last, his patience
tir'd,
Thus from his royal throne, by Heav'n in-
spir'd,
The godlike David spoke; with awful fear
His train their Maker in their master hear.
"Thus long have I, by native mercy
sway'd,
My wrongs dissembled, my revenge delay'd;
So willing to forgive th' offending age; 941
So much the father did the king assuage.
But now so far my clemency they slight,
Th' offenders question my forgiving right.
That one was made for many, they contend;
But 't is to rule, for that's a monarch's end.
They call my tenderness of blood, my fear,
Tho' manly tempers can the longest bear.
Yet, since they will divert my native course,
'T is time to shew I am not good by force.
Those heap'd affronts that haughty subjects
bring, 951
Are burthens for a camel, not a king.
Kings are the public pillars of the State,
Born to sustain and prop the nation's
weight:
If my young Samson will pretend a call
To shake the column, let him share the fall:
But O that yet he would repent and live!
How easy 't is for parents to forgive!
With how few tears a pardon might be won
From nature, pleading for a darling son! 960
Poor pitied youth, by my paternal care
Rais'd up to all the height his frame could
bear:
Had God ordain'd his fate for empire born,
He would have giv'n his soul another turn:
Gull'd with a Patriot's name, whose modern
sense
Is one that would by law supplant his
prince;
The people's brave, the politician's tool;
Never was Patriot yet, but was a fool.
Whence comes it that religion and the laws
Should more be Absalom's than David's
cause? 970
His old instructor, ere he lost his place,
Was never thought indued with so much
grace.
Good heav'ns, how faction can a Patriot
paint!
My rebel ever proves my people's saint.
Would *they* impose an heir upon the
throne?
Let Sanhedrins be taught to give their own.

A king 's at least a part of government,
And mine as requisite as their consent:
Without my leave a future king to choose,
Infers a right the present to depose. 980
True, they petition me t' approve their
choice:
But Esau's hands suit ill with Jacob's voice.
My pious subjects for my safety pray;
Which to secure, they take my pow'r away.
From plots and treasons Heav'n preserve
my years,
But save me most from my petitioners!
Unsatiate as the barren womb or grave;
God cannot grant so much as they can crave.
What then is left, but with a jealous eye
To guard the small remains of royalty? 990
The law shall still direct my peaceful sway,
And the same law teach rebels to obey:
Votes shall no more establish'd pow'r con-
trol,
Such votes as make a part exceed the whole:
No groundless clamors shall my friends re-
move
Nor crowds have pow'r to punish ere they
prove;
For gods and godlike kings their care ex-
press,
Still to defend their servants in distress.
O that my pow'r to saving were confin'd:
Why am I forc'd, like Heav'n, against my
mind, 1000
To make examples of another kind?
Must I at length the sword of justice draw?
O curst effects of necessary law!
How ill my fear they by my mercy scan!
Beware the fury of a patient man.
Law they require, let Law then shew her
face;
They could not be content to look on Grace,
Her hinder parts, but with a daring eye
To tempt the terror of her front, and die.
By their own arts, 't is righteously de-
creed, 1010
Those dire artificers of death shall bleed.
Against themselves their witnesses will
swear,
Till viper-like their mother Plot they tear,
And suck for nutriment that bloody gore,
Which was their principle of life before.
Their Belial with their Belzebub will fight;
Thus on my foes, my foes shall do me right.
Nor doubt th' event; for factious crowds
engage

In their first onset, all their brutal rage.
Then let 'em take an unresisted course; 1020
Retire, and traverse, and delude their force:
But, when they stand all breathless, urge the
    fight,
And rise upon 'em with redoubled might;
For lawful pow'r is still superior found,
When long driv'n back, at length it stands
    the ground."

He said. Th' Almighty, nodding, gave con-
    sent;
And peals of thunder shook the firmament.
Henceforth a series of new time began,
The mighty years in long procession ran:
Once more the godlike David was restor'd,
And willing nations knew their lawful
    lord.   1031

[1681]

THE MEDAL

A SATIRE AGAINST SEDITION

Per Graium populos, mediæque per Elidis urbem
Ibat ovans, divumque sibi poscebat honorem.

EPISTLE TO THE WHIGS

For to whom can I dedicate this poem, with so much justice as to you? 'T is the representation of your own hero: 't is the picture drawn at length, which you admire and prize so much in little. None of your ornaments are wanting; neither the landscape of the Tower, nor the rising sun; nor the Anno Domini of your new sovereign's coronation. This must needs be a grateful undertaking to your whole party; especially to those who have not been so happy as to purchase the original. I hear the graver has made a good market of it: all his kings are bought up already; or the value of the remainder so enhanced, that many a poor Polander who would be glad to worship the image, is not able to go to the cost of him, but must be content to see him here. I must confess I am no great artist; but signpost painting will serve the turn to remember a friend by, especially when better is not to be had. Yet for your comfort the lineaments are true; and tho' he sate not five times to me, as he did to B., yet I have consulted history, as the Italian painters do, when they would draw a Nero or a Caligula; tho' they have not seen the man, they can help their imagination by a statue of him, and find out the colouring from Suetonius and Tacitus. Truth is, you might have spared one side of your Medal: the head would be seen to more advantage if it were placed on a spike of the Tower, a little nearer to the sun, which would then break out to better purpose.

You tell us in your preface to the *No-Protestant Plot*, that you shall be forced hereafter to leave off your modesty: I suppose you mean that little which is left you; for it was worn to rags when you put out this Medal. Never was there practiced such a piece of notorious impudence in the face of an established government. I believe when he is dead you will wear him in thumb-rings, as the Turks did Scanderbeg, as if there were virtue in his bones to preserve you against monarchy. Yet all this while you pretend not only zeal for the public good, but a due veneration for the person of the king. But all men who can see an inch before them may easily detect those gross fallacies. That it is necessary for men in your circumstances to pretend both, is granted you; for without them there could be no ground to raise a faction. But I would ask you one civil question, what right has any man among you, or any association of men, (to come nearer to you,) who, out of Parliament, cannot be considered in a public capacity, to meet as you daily do in factious clubs, to vilify the government in your discourses, and to libel it in all your writings? Who made you judges in Israel? Or how is it consistent with your zeal of the public welfare to promote sedition? Does your definition of *loyal*, which is to serve the king according to the laws, allow you the license of traducing the executive power with which you own he is invested? You complain that his Majesty has lost the love and confidence of his people; and by your very urging it you endeavor, what in you lies, to make him lose them. All good subjects abhor the thought of arbitrary power, whether it be in one or many: if you were the patriots you would seem, you would not at this rate incense the multitude to assume it; for no sober man can fear it, either from the king's disposition, or his practice, or even, where you would odiously lay it, from his ministers. Give us leave to enjoy the government and the benefit of laws under which we were born, and which we desire to transmit to our posterity. You are not the trustees of the public liberty; and if you have not right to petition in a crowd, much less have you to intermeddle in the management of affairs, or to arraign what you do not like, which in effect is every-thing that is done by the king and council. Can you imagine that any reasonable man will believe you respect the person of his Majesty, when 't is apparent that your seditious pamphlets are stuffed with particular reflections on him? If you have the confidence to deny this, 't is easy to be evinc'd from a thousand passages, which I only forbear to quote, because I desire they should die, and be forgotten. I have perused many of your papers, and to show you that I have, the third part of your *No-Protestant Plot* is much of it stolen from your dead author's pamphlet, call'd *The Growth of Popery*; as manifestly as Milton's *Defense of the English People* is from Buchanan, *De Jure Regni apud Scotos*; or your first Covenant and new Association from the Holy League of the French Guisards. Anyone who reads Davila may trace your practices all along. There were the same pretenses for reformation and loyalty, the same aspersions of the king, and the same grounds of a rebellion. I know not whether you will take the historian's word, who says it was reported that Poltrot, a Huguenot, murther'd Francis, Duke of Guise, by the instigations of Theodore Beza, or that it was a Huguenot minister, otherwise call'd a Presbyterian, (for our Church abhors so devilish a tenet,) who first writ a treatise of the lawfulness of deposing and murthering kings of a different persuasion in religion; but I am able to prove, from the doctrine of Calvin, and principles of Buchanan, that they set the people above the magistrate; which, if I mistake not, is your own fundamental, and which carries your loyalty no farther than your liking. When a vote of the House of Commons goes on your side, you are as ready to observe it as if it were passed into a law; but when you are pinched with any former, and yet unrepealed act of parliament, you declare that in some cases you will not be oblig'd by it. The passage is in the same third part of the *No-Protestant Plot*, and is too plain to be denied. The late copy of your intended Association, you neither wholly justify nor condemn; but as the Papists, when they are unopposed, fly out into all the pageantries of worship; but in times of war, when they are hard pressed by arguments, lie close intrenched behind the Council of Trent: so now, when your affairs are in a low condition, you dare not pretend that to be a legal combination, but whensoever you are afloat, I doubt not but it will be maintained and justified to purpose. For indeed there is nothing to defend it but the sword; 't is the proper time to say anything, when men have all things in their power.

In the mean time, you would fain be nibbling at a parallel betwixt this Association and that in the time of Queen Elizabeth. But there is this small difference betwixt them, that the ends of the one are directly opposite to the other: one with the queen's approbation and conjunction, as head of it; the other without either the consent or knowledge of the king, against whose authority it is manifestly designed. Therefore you do well to have recourse to your last evasion, that it was contrived by your enemies, and shuffled into the papers that were seized; which yet you see the nation is not so easy to believe as your own jury; but the matter is not difficult, to find twelve men in Newgate who would acquit a malefactor.

I have one only favour to desire of you at parting, that when you think of answering this poem, you would employ the same pens against it, who have combated with so much success against *Absalom and Achitophel*; for then you may assure yourselves of a clear victory, without the least reply. Rail at me abundantly; and, not to break a custom, do it without wit: by this method you will gain a considerable point, which is, wholly to waive the answer of my arguments. Never own the bottom of your principles, for fear they should be treason. Fall severely on the miscarriages of government; for if scandal be not allowed, you are no freeborn subjects. If God has not blest you with the talent of rhyming, make use of my poor stock and welcome: let your verses run upon my feet; and, for the utmost refuge of notorious blockheads, reduced to the last extremity of sense, turn my own lines upon me, and, in utter despair of your own satire, make me satirize myself. Some of you have been driven to this bay already; but, above all the rest, commend me to the Non-conformist parson, who writ the *Whip and Key*. I am afraid it is not read so much as the piece deserves, because the bookseller is every week crying help at the end of his gazette, to get it off. You see I am charitable enough to do him a kindness, that it may be published as well as printed; and that so much skill in Hebrew derivations may not lie for waste paper in the shop. Yet I half suspect he went no farther for his learning, than the index of Hebrew names and etymologies, which is printed at the end of some English Bibles. If Achitophel signify the brother of a fool, the author of that poem will pass with his readers for the next of kin. And perhaps 't is the relation that makes the kindness. Whatever the verses are, buy 'em up, I beseech you, out of pity; for I hear the conventicle is shut up, and the brother of Achitophel out of service.

Now footmen, you know, have the generosity to make a purse for a member of their society, who has had his livery pulled over his ears; and even Protestant socks are bought up among you, out of veneration to the name. A dissenter in poetry from sense and English will make as good a Protestant rhymer, as a dissenter from the Church of England a Protestant parson. Besides, if you encourage a young beginner, who knows but he may elevate his style a little above the vulgar epithets of profane, and saucy Jack, and atheistic scribbler, with which he treats me, when the fit of enthusiasm is strong upon him; by which well-mannered and charitable expressions I was certain of his sect before I knew his name. What would you have more of a man? He has damned me in your cause from Genesis to the Revelations; and has half the texts of both the Testaments against me, if you will be so civil to yourselves as to take him for your interpreter, and not to take them for Irish witnesses. After all, perhaps you will tell me that you retained him only for the opening of your cause, and that your main lawyer is yet behind. Now if it so happen he meet with no more reply than his predecessors, you may either conclude that I trust to the goodness of my cause, or fear my adversary, or disdain him, or what you please, for the short on 't is, 't is indifferent to your humble servant, whatever your party says or thinks of him.

THE MEDAL

Of all our antic sights and pageantry
Which English idiots run in crowds to see,
The Polish Medal bears the prize alone:
A monster, more the favorite of the town
Than either fairs or theaters have shown.
Never did art so well with nature strive,
Nor ever idol seem'd so much alive:
So like the man; so golden to the sight,
So base within, so counterfeit and light.
One side is fill'd with title and with face; 10
And, lest the king should want a regal place,
On the reverse, a tow'r the town surveys,
O'er which our mounting sun his beams
   displays.
The word, pronounc'd aloud by shrieval
   voice,
Lætamur, which, in Polish, is *rejoice.*
The day, month, year, to the great act are
   join'd,
And a new canting holiday design'd.
Five days he sate for every cast and look;
Four more than God to finish Adam took.
But who can tell what essence angels are 20
Or how long Heav'n was making Lucifer?
O could the style that copied every grace
And plow'd such furrows for an eunuch
   face,
Could it have form'd his ever-changing will,
The various piece had tir'd the graver's
   skill!
A martial hero first, with early care
Blown, like a pigmy by the winds, to war.
A beardless chief, a rebel, ere a man,
(So young his hatred to his prince began.)
Next this, (how wildly will ambition steer!)
A vermin wriggling in th' usurper's ear. 31
Bart'ring his venal wit for sums of gold,
He cast himself into the saintlike mold;

Groan'd, sigh'd, and pray'd, while godliness
   was gain,
The loudest bagpipe of the squeaking train.
But, as 't is hard to cheat a juggler's eyes,
His open lewdness he could ne'er disguise.
There split the saint: for hypocritic zeal
Allows no sins but those it can conceal. 39
Whoring to scandal gives too large a scope;
Saints must not trade; but they may inter-
   lope.
Th' ungodly principle was all the same;
But a gross cheat betrays his partner's game.
Besides, their pace was formal, grave, and
   slack;
His nimble wit outran the heavy pack.
Yet still he found his fortune at a stay,
Whole droves of blockheads choking up his
   way:
They took, but not rewarded, his advice;
Villain and wit exact a double price.
Pow'r was his aim; but, thrown from that
   pretense, 50
The wretch turn'd loyal in his own defense,
And malice reconcil'd him to his prince.
Him in the anguish of his soul he serv'd,
Rewarded faster still than he deserv'd.
Behold him, now exalted into trust;
His counsel's oft convenient, seldom just;
Ev'n in the most sincere advice he gave
He had a grudging still to be a knave.
The frauds he learnt in his fanatic years
Made him uneasy in his lawful gears: 60
At best as little honest as he could,
And, like white witches, mischievously good.
To his first bias longingly he leans,
And *rather* would be great by wicked means.
Thus, fram'd for ill, he loos'd our Triple
   hold;
(Advice unsafe, precipitous, and bold.)
From hence those tears! that Ilium of our
   woe!

Who helps a pow'rful friend, forearms a
    foe.
What wonder if the waves prevail so far,
When he cut down the banks that made the
    bar?   70
Seas follow but their nature to invade,
But he by art our native strength betray'd.
So Samson to his foe his force confess'd,
And, to be shorn, lay slumb'ring on her
    breast.
But, when this fatal counsel, found too late,
Expos'd its author to the public hate;
When his just sovereign, by no impious way.
Could be seduc'd to arbitrary sway;
Forsaken of that hope, he shifts the sail,
Drives down the current with a pop'lar
    gale;   80
And shews the fiend confess'd without a veil.
He preaches to the crowd that pow'r is lent,
But not convey'd to kingly government;
That claims successive bear no binding
    force;
That coronation oaths are things of course;
Maintains the multitude can never err;
And sets the people in the papal chair.
The reason 's obvious: *int'rest never lies*;
The most have still their int'rest in their
    eyes;
The pow'r is always theirs, and pow'r is ever
    wise.   90
Almighty crowd, thou shorten'st all dispute;
Pow'r is thy essence; wit thy attribute!
Nor faith nor reason make thee at a stay,
Thou leap'st o'er all eternal truths in thy
    Pindaric way!
Athens no doubt did righteously decide,
When Phocion and when Socrates were
    tried;
As righteously they did those dooms repent;
Still they were wise, whatever way they
    went.
Crowds err not, tho' to both extremes they
    run;
To kill the father and recall the son.   100
Some think the fools were most, as times
    went then,
But now the world 's o'erstock'd with pru-
    dent men.
The common cry is ev'n religion's test:
The Turk's is at Constantinople best,
Idols in India, Popery at Rome,
And our own worship only true at home.
And true, but for the time; 't is hard to
    know

How long we please it shall continue so;
This side to-day, and that to-morrow burns;
So all are God-a'mighties in their turns. 110
A tempting doctrine, plausible and new:
What fools our fathers were, if this be true!
Who, to destroy the seeds of civil war,
Inherent right in monarchs did declare:
And, that a lawful pow'r might never cease,
Secur'd succession, to secure our peace.
Thus property and sovereign sway, at last
In equal balances were justly cast:
But this new Jehu spurs the hot-mouth'd
    horse;
Instructs the beast to know his native force,
To take the bit between his teeth, and fly 121
To the next headlong steep of anarchy.
Too happy England, if our good we knew;
Would we possess the freedom we pursue!
The lavish government can give no more;
Yet we repine; and plenty makes us poor.
God tried us once; our rebel fathers fought;
He glutted 'em with all the pow'r they
    sought,
Till, master'd by their own usurping brave,
The freeborn subject sunk into a slave.   130
We loathe our manna, and we long for
    quails;
Ah, what is man, when his own wish pre-
    vails!
How rash, how swift to plunge himself in
    ill;
Proud of his pow'r, and boundless in his
    will!
That kings can do no wrong we must be-
    lieve;
None can they do, and must they all re-
    ceive?
Help, Heav'n! or sadly we shall see an hour,
When neither wrong nor right are in their
    pow'r!
Already they have lost their best defense,
The benefit of laws which they dispense: 140
No justice to their righteous cause allow'd;
But baffled by an arbitrary crowd;
And medals grav'd, their conquest to record,
The stamp and coin of their adopted lord.
    The man who laugh'd but once, to see an
    ass
Mumbling to make the crossgrain'd thistles
    pass,
Might laugh again, to see a jury chaw
The prickles of unpalatable law.
The witnesses that, leech-like, liv'd on
    blood,

Sucking for them were med'cinally good; 150
But when they fasten'd on *their* fester'd
    sore,
Then justice and religion they forswore,
Their maiden oaths debauch'd into a whore.
Thus men are rais'd by factions, and de-
    cried;
And rogue and saint distinguish'd by their
    side.
They rack ev'n scripture to confess their
    cause,
And plead a call to preach in spite of laws.
But that 's no news to the poor injur'd page,
It has been us'd as ill in every age;
And is constrain'd, with patience, all to
    take;   160
For what defense can Greek and Hebrew
    make?
Happy who can this talking trumpet seize;
They make it speak whatever sense they
    please!
'T was fram'd at first our oracle t' enquire;
But since our sects in prophecy grow higher,
The text inspires not them, but they the
    text inspire.
    London, thou great *emporium* of our isle,
O thou too bounteous, thou too fruitful
    Nile!
How shall I praise or curse to thy desert!
Or separate thy sound, from thy corrupted
    part!   170
I call'd thee Nile; the parallel will stand:
Thy tides of wealth o'erflow the fatten'd
    land;
Yet monsters from thy large increase we
    find
Engender'd on the slime thou leav'st be-
    hind.
Sedition has not wholly seiz'd on thee,
Thy nobler parts are from infection free.
Of Israel's tribes thou hast a numerous
    band,
But still the Canaanite is in the land.
Thy military chiefs are brave and true,
Nor are thy disenchanted burghers few. 180
The head is loyal which thy heart com-
    mands,
But what 's a head with two such gouty
    hands?
The wise and wealthy love the surest way,
And are content to thrive and to obey.
But wisdom is to sloth too great a slave;
None are so busy as the fool and knave.

Those let me curse; what vengeance will
    they urge,
Whose ordures neither plague nor fire can
    purge;
Nor sharp experience can to duty bring,
Nor angry Heaven, nor a forgiving king! 190
In gospel-phrase their chapmen they betray;
Their shops are dens, the buyer is their
    prey.
The knack of trades is living on the spoil;
They boast, ev'n when each other they be-
    guile.
Customs to steal is such a trivial thing,
That 't is their charter to defraud their
    king.
All hands unite of every jarring sect;
They cheat the country first, and then in-
    fect.
They for God's cause their monarchs dare
    dethrone,
And they 'll be sure to make his cause their
    own.   200
Whether the plotting Jesuit laid the plan
Of murd'ring kings, or the French Puritan,
Our sacrilegious sects their guides outgo,
And kings and kingly pow'r would murder
    too.
    What means their trait'rous combination
    less,
Too plain t' evade, too shameful to confess!
But treason is not own'd when 't is descried;
Successful crimes alone are justified.
The men, who no conspiracy would find,
Who doubts, but had it taken, they had
    join'd?   210
Join'd in a mutual cov'nant of defense,
At first without, at last against their prince?
If sovereign right by sovereign pow'r they
    scan,
The same bold maxim holds in God and
    man:
God were not safe; his thunder could they
    shun,
He should be forc'd to crown another Son.
Thus, when the heir was from the vineyard
    thrown,
The rich possession was the murd'rers' own.
In vain to sophistry they have recourse:
By proving theirs no plot, they prove 't is
    worse;   220
Unmask'd rebellion, and audacious force;
Which tho' not actual, yet all eyes may see
'T is working in th' immediate pow'r to be;

For from pretended grievances they rise,
First to dislike, and after to despise;
Then, Cyclop-like, in human flesh to deal,
Chop up a minister at every meal;
Perhaps not wholly to melt down the king,
But clip his regal rights within the ring.
From thence t' assume the pow'r of peace
    and war; 230
And ease him by degrees of public care.
Yet, to consult his dignity and fame,
He should have leave to exercise the name,
And hold the cards while commons play'd
    the game.
For what can pow'r give more than food
    and drink,
To live at ease, and not be bound to think?
These are the cooler methods of their crime,
But their hot zealots think 't is loss of time:
On utmost bounds of loyalty they stand,
And grin and whet like a Croatian band, 240
That waits impatient for the last command.
Thus outlaws open villainy maintain,
They steal not, but in squadrons scour the
    plain;
And, if their pow'r the passengers subdue,
The most have right, the wrong is in the
    few.
Such impious axioms foolishly they show,
For in some soils republics will not grow:
Our temp'rate isle will no extremes sustain
Of pop'lar sway or arbitrary reign,
But slides between them both into the
    best; 250
Secure in freedom, in a monarch blest.
And tho' the climate, vex'd with various
    winds,
Works thro' our yielding bodies on our
    minds,
The wholesome tempest purges what it
    breeds,
To recommend the calmness that succeeds.
    But thou, the pander of the people's
    hearts,
(O crooked soul, and serpentine in arts!)
Whose blandishments a loyal land have
    whor'd,
And broke the bonds she plighted to her
    lord;
What curses on thy blasted name will
    fall! 260
Which age to age their legacy shall call;
For all must curse the woes that must de-
    scend on all.
Religion thou hast none; thy *mercury*

Has pass'd thro' every sect, or theirs thro'
    thee.
But what thou giv'st, that venom still re-
    mains;
And the pox'd nation feels thee in their
    brains.
What else inspires the tongues and swells
    the breasts
Of all thy bellowing renegado priests,
That preach up thee for God; dispense thy
    laws;
And with thy stum ferment their fainting
    cause? 270
Fresh fumes of madness raise, and toil and
    sweat
To make the formidable cripple great?
Yet should thy crimes succeed, should law-
    less pow'r
Compass those ends thy greedy hopes de-
    vour,
Thy canting friends thy mortal foes would
    be,
Thy God and theirs will never long agree;
For thine (if thou hast any) must be one
That lets the world and humankind alone;
A jolly god, that passes hours too well
To promise heav'n, or threaten us with
    hell; 280
That unconcern'd can at rebellion sit,
And wink at crimes he did himself commit.
A tyrant theirs; the heav'n their priesthood
    paints
A conventicle of gloomy sullen saints;
A heav'n like Bedlam, slovenly and sad,
Foredoom'd for souls with false religion
    mad.
    Without a vision poets can foreshow
What all but fools by common sense may
    know:
If true succession from our Isle should fail,
And crowds profane with impious arms
    prevail, 290
Not thou, nor those thy factious arts engage,
Shall reap that harvest of rebellious rage,
With which thou flatter'st thy decrepit age
The swelling poison of the sev'ral sects,
Which, wanting vent, the nation's health in-
    fects,
Shall burst its bag; and, fighting out their
    way,
The various venoms on each other prey.
The presbyter, puff'd up with spiritual
    pride,

Shall on the necks of the lewd nobles ride,
His brethren damn, the civil pow'r defy,　300
And parcel out republic prelacy.
But short shall be his reign; his rigid yoke
And tyrant pow'r will puny sects provoke,
And frogs and toads, and all the tadpole
　　train,
Will croak to Heav'n for help from this de-
　　vouring crane.
The cut-throat sword and clamorous gown
　　shall jar,
In sharing their ill-gotten spoils of war;
Chiefs shall be grudg'd the part which they
　　pretend,
Lords envy lords, and friends with every
　　friend
About their impious merit shall contend. 310
The surly commons shall respect deny,
And justle peerage out with property.
Their gen'ral either shall his trust betray,
And force the crowd to arbitrary sway;
Or they, suspecting his ambitious aim,
In hate of kings shall cast anew the frame;
And thrust out Collatine that bore their
　　name.
　　Thus inborn broils the factions would
　　　engage,
Or wars of exil'd heirs, or foreign rage,
Till halting vengeance overtook our age; 320
And our wild labours wearied into rest,
Reclin'd us on a rightful monarch's breast.
　　　Pudet hæc opprobria, vobis
　Et dici potuisse, et non potuisse refelli.
　　　　　　　　　　　　　　　　[1682]

MAC FLECKNOE

OR, A SATIRE UPON THE TRUE-BLUE-
PROTESTANT POET

T. S.

All human things are subject to decay,
And when Fate summons, monarchs must
　　obey.
This Flecknoe found, who, like Augustus,
　　young
Was call'd to empire, and had govern'd
　　long:
In prose and verse, was own'd, without dis-
　　pute,

Thro' all the realms of *Nonsense*, absolute.
This aged prince, now flourishing in peace,
And blest with issue of a large increase,
Worn out with business, did at length de-
　　bate
To settle the succession of the State;　10
And, pond'ring which of all his sons was fit
To reign, and wage immortal war with wit,
Cried: " 'T is resolv'd; for Nature pleads,
　　that he
Should only rule, who most resembles me.
Sh—— alone my perfect image bears,
Mature in dulness from his tender years:
Sh—— alone of all my sons is he
Who stands confirm'd in full stupidity.
The rest to some faint meaning make pre-
　　tense,
But Sh—— never deviates into sense.　20
Some beams of wit on other souls may fall,
Strike thro', and make a lucid interval;
But Sh——'s genuine night admits no ray,
His rising fogs prevail upon the day.
Besides, his goodly fabric fills the eye,
And seems design'd for thoughtless majesty:
Thoughtless as monarch oaks that shade the
　　plain,
And, spread in solemn state, supinely reign.
Heywood and Shirley were but types of
　　thee,
Thou last great prophet of tautology.　30
Even I, a dunce of more renown than they,
Was sent before but to prepare thy way;
And coarsely clad in Norwich drugget came
To teach the nations in thy greater name.
My warbling lute, the lute I whilom strung,
When to King John of Portugal I sung,
Was but the prelude to that glorious day,
When thou on silver Thames didst cut thy
　　way,
With well-tim'd oars before the royal barge,
Swell'd with the pride of thy celestial
　　charge;　40
And big with hymn, commander of a host,
The like was ne'er in Epsom blankets toss'd.
Methinks I see the new Arion sail,
The lute still trembling underneath thy
　　nail.
At thy well-sharpen'd thumb from shore to
　　shore
The treble squeaks for fear, the basses roar;
Echoes from Pissing Alley Sh—— call,
And Sh——they resound from Aston Hall.

About thy boat the little fishes throng,
As at the morning toast that floats along. 50
Sometimes, as prince of thy harmonious
    band,
Thou wield'st thy papers in thy threshing
    hand.
St. André's feet ne'er kept more equal time,
Not ev'n the feet of thy own *Psyche's*
    rhyme:
Tho' they in number as in sense excel,
So just, so like tautology, they fell,
That, pale with envy, Singleton forswore
The lute and sword, which he in triumph
    bore,
And vow'd he ne'er would act Villerius
    more."
Here stopp'd the good old sire, and wept
    for joy   60
In silent raptures of the hopeful boy.
All arguments, but most his plays, persuade,
That for anointed dulness he was made.
    Close to the walls which fair Augusta
    bind,
(The fair Augusta much to fears inclin'd)
An ancient fabric rais'd t' inform the sight,
There stood of yore, and Barbican it hight:
A watchtower once; but now, so fate or-
    dains,
Of all the pile an empty name remains.
From its old ruins brothel-houses rise,   70
Scenes of lewd loves, and of polluted joys,
Where their vast courts the mother-strum-
    pets keep,
And, undisturb'd by watch, in silence sleep.
Near these a Nursery erects its head,
Where queens are form'd, and future heroes
    bred;
Where unfledg'd actors learn to laugh and
    cry,
Where infant punks their tender voices try,
And little Maximins the gods defy.
Great Fletcher never treads in buskins here,
Nor greater Jonson dares in socks appear;   80
But gentle Simkin just reception finds
Amidst this monument of vanish'd minds:
Pure clinches the suburbian Muse affords,
And Panton waging harmless war with
    words.
Here Flecknoe, as a place to fame well
    known,
Ambitiously design'd his Sh——'s throne;
For ancient Dekker prophesied long since,
That in this pile should reign a mighty
    prince,

Born for a scourge of wit, and flail of sense,
To whom true dulness should some *Psyches*
    owe,   90
But worlds of *Misers* from his pen should
    flow;
Humorists and *Hypocrites* it should produce,
Whole Raymond families, and tribes of
    Bruce.
    Now Empress Fame had publish'd the re-
    nown
Of Sh——'s coronation thro' the town.
Rous'd by report of Fame, the nations meet,
From near Bunhill, and distant Watling
    Street.
No Persian carpets spread th' imperial way,
But scatter'd limbs of mangled poets lay;
From dusty shops neglected authors
    come,   100
Martyrs of pies, and relics of the bum.
Much Heywood, Shirley, Ogleby there lay,
But loads of Sh—— almost chok'd the way.
Bilk'd stationers for yeomen stood prepar'd
And Herringman was captain of the guard.
The hoary prince in majesty appear'd,
High on a throne of his own labours rear'd.
At his right hand our young Ascanius sat,
Rome's other hope, and pillar of the State.
His brows thick fogs, instead of glories,
    grace,   110
And lambent dulness play'd around his face.
As Hannibal did to the altars come,
Sworn by his sire a mortal foe to Rome;
So Sh—— swore, nor should his vow be vain,
That he till death true dulness would main-
    tain;
And, in his father's right, and realm's de-
    fense,
Ne'er to have peace with wit, nor truce with
    sense.
The king himself the sacred unction made,
As king by office, and as priest by trade.
In his sinister hand, instead of ball,   120
He plac'd a mighty mug of potent ale;
Love's Kingdom to his right he did convey,
At once his scepter, and his rule of sway;
Whose righteous lore the prince had prac-
    tic'd young
And from whose loins recorded *Psyche*
    sprung.
His temples, last, with poppies were o'er-
    spread,
That nodding seem'd to consecrate his head:

Just at that point of time, if fame not lie,
On his left hand twelve reverend owls did
      fly.
So Romulus, 't is sung, by Tiber's brook, 130
Presage of sway from twice six vultures
      took.
Th' admiring throng loud acclamations
      make,
And omens of his future empire take.
The sire then shook the honours of his head,
And from his brows damps of oblivion shed
Full on the filial dulness: long he stood,
Repelling from his breast the raging god;
At length burst out in this prophetic mood:
   "Heavens bless my son, from Ireland let
      him reign
To far Barbadoes on the western main; 140
Of his dominion may no end be known,
And greater than his father's be his throne;
Beyond *Love's Kingdom* let him stretch his
      pen!"
He paus'd, and all the people cried,
      "Amen."
Then thus continued he: "My son, advance
Still in new impudence, new ignorance.
Success let others teach, learn thou from me
Pangs without birth, and fruitless industry.
Let *Virtuosos* in five years be writ;
Yet not one thought accuse thy toil of
      wit.   150
Let gentle George in triumph tread the
      stage,
Make Dorimant betray, and Loveit rage;
Let Cully, Cockwood, Fopling, charm the
      pit,
And in their folly shew the writer's wit.
Yet still thy fools shall stand in thy defense
And justify their author's want of sense.
Let 'em be all by thy own model made
Of dulness, and desire no foreign aid,
That they to future ages may be known,
Not copies drawn, but issue of thy own. 160
Nay, let thy men of wit too be the same,
All full of thee, and differing but in name.
But let no alien S—dl—y interpose,
To lard with wit thy hungry *Epsom* prose.
And when false flowers of rhetoric thou
      wouldst cull,
Trust nature, do not labor to be dull;
But write thy best, and top; and, in each
      line,
Sir Formal's oratory will be thine:
Sir Formal, tho' unsought, attends thy quill,

And does thy northern dedications fill. 170
Nor let false friends seduce thy mind to
      fame,
By arrogating Jonson's hostile name.
Let father Flecknoe fire thy mind with
      praise,
And uncle Ogleby thy envy raise.
Thou art my blood, where Jonson has no
      part:
What share have we in nature, or in art?
Where did his wit on learning fix a brand,
And rail at arts he did not understand?
Where made he love in Prince Nicander's
      vein,
Or swept the dust in *Psyche's* humble
      strain?   180
Where sold he bargains, 'whip-stitch, kiss
      my arse,'
Promis'd a play and dwindled to a farce?
When did his Muse from Fletcher scenes
      purloin,
As thou whole Eth'rege dost transfuse to
      thine?
But so transfus'd, as oil on water's flow,
His always floats above, thine sinks below.
This is thy province, this thy wondrous way,
New humours to invent for each new play:
This is that boasted bias of thy mind,
By which one way, to dulness, 't is in-
      clin'd,   190
Which makes thy writings lean on one side
      still,
And, in all changes, that way bends thy will.
Nor let thy mountain-belly make pretense
Of likeness; thine 's a tympany of sense.
A tun of man in thy large bulk is writ,
But sure thou 'rt but a kilderkin of wit.
Like mine, thy gentle numbers feebly creep;
Thy tragic Muse gives smiles, thy comic
      sleep.
With whate'er gall thou sett'st thyself to
      write,
Thy inoffensive satires never bite.   200
In thy felonious heart tho' venom lies,
It does but touch thy Irish pen, and dies.
Thy genius calls thee not to purchase fame
In keen iambics, but mild anagram.
Leave writing plays, and choose for thy
      command
Some peaceful province in acrostic land.
There thou may'st wings display, and altars
      raise.

And torture one poor word ten thousand
ways;
Or, if thou wouldst thy diff'rent talents suit,
Set thy own songs, and sing them to thy
lute."   210
He said: but his last words were scarcely
heard,
For Bruce and Longvil had a trap prepar'd,

And down they sent the yet declaiming
bard.
Sinking he left his drugget robe behind,
Borne upwards by a subterranean wind.
The mantle fell to the young prophet's
part,
With double portion of his father's art.
                                              [1682]

RELIGIO LAICI

OR, A LAYMAN'S FAITH

A POEM

Ornari res ipsa negat, contenta doceri.

THE PREFACE

A poem with so bold a title, and a name prefixed from which the handling of so serious a subject would not be expected, may reasonably oblige the author to say somewhat in defense both of himself and of his undertaking. In the first place, if it be objected to me that, being a layman, I ought not to have concerned myself with speculations which belong to the profession of divinity, I could answer that perhaps laymen, with equal advantages of parts and knowledge, are not the most incompetent judges of sacred things; but, in the due sense of my own weakness and want of learning, I plead not this; I pretend not to make myself a judge of faith in others, but only to make a confession of my own; I lay no unhallowed hand upon the ark, but wait on it, with the reverence that becomes me, at a distance. In the next place I will ingenuously confess that the helps I have used in this small treatise were many of them taken from the works of our own reverend divines of the Church of England; so that the weapons with which I combat irreligion are already consecrated; tho' I suppose they may be taken down as lawfully as the sword of Goliah was by David, when they are to be employed for the common cause, against the enemies of piety. I intend not by this to entitle them to any of my errors, which yet, I hope, are only those of charity to mankind; and such as my *own* charity has caused me to commit, that of *others* may more easily excuse. Being naturally inclined to scepticism in philosophy, I have no reason to impose my opinions in a subject which is above it; but whatever they are, I submit them with all reverence to my Mother Church, accounting them no further mine, than as they are authorized, or at least uncondemned by her. And, indeed, to secure myself on this side, I have used the necessary precaution of showing this paper before it was published to a judicious and learned friend, a man indefatigably zealous in the service of the Church and State; and whose writings have highly deserved of both. He was pleased to approve the body of the discourse, and I hope he is more my friend than to do it out of complaisance. 'T is true, he had too good a taste to like it all; and amongst some other faults recommended to my second view what I have written, perhaps too boldly, on St. Athanasius, which he advis'd me wholly to omit. I am sensible enough that I had done more *prudently* to have followed his opinion; but then I could not have satisfied myself that I had done honestly not to have written what was my own. It has always been my *thought* that heathens who never did, nor without miracle could, hear of the name of Christ, were yet in a possibility of salvation. Neither will it enter easily into my belief that, before the coming of our Savior, the whole world, excepting only the Jewish nation, should lie under the inevitable necessity of everlasting punishment, for want of that revelation which was confined to so small a spot of ground as that of Palestine. Among the sons of Noah we read of one only who was accursed; and if a blessing in the ripeness of time was reserved for Japhet, (of whose progeny we are,) it seems unaccountable to me why so many generations of the same offspring, as preceded our Savior in the flesh, should be all involved in one common condemnation, and yet that their posterity should be entitled to the hopes of salvation: as if a Bill of Exclusion had passed only on the fathers, which debarred not the sons from their succession. Or that so many ages had been *deliver'd over* to hell, and so many *reserv'd* for heaven, and that the Devil had the first choice, and God the next. Truly I am apt to think that the revealed religion which was taught by Noah to all his sons might continue for some ages in the whole posterity. That afterwards it was included wholly in the family of Sem is manifest; but when the progenies of Cham and Japhet swarmed into colonies, and those colonies were subdivided into many others, in process of time their descendants lost by little and little the primitive and purer rites of divine worship, retaining only the notion of one deity; to which succeeding generations added others; for men took their degrees in those ages from conquerors to gods. Revelation being thus eclipsed to almost all mankind, the Light of Nature, as the next in dignity, was substituted; and that is it which St. Paul concludes to be the rule of the heathens, and by which they are hereafter to be judged. If my supposition be true, then the consequence which I have assumed in my poem may be also true: namely, that Deism, or the principles of natural worship, are only the faint remnants or dying flames of revealed religion in the posterity of Noah: and that our modern philosophers, nay, and some of our philosophizing divines, have too much exalted the faculties of our souls, when they have maintained that by their force mankind has been able to find out that there is one supreme agent or intellectual being which we call God; that praise and prayer are his due worship; and the rest of those deducements, which I am confident are the remote effects of revelation, and unattainable by our discourse; I mean as simply considered, and without the benefit of divine illumination. So that we have not lifted up ourselves to God by the weak pinions of our reason, but he has been pleased to descend to us; and what Socrates said of him, what Plato writ, and the rest of the heathen philosophers of several nations, is all no more than the twilight of Revelation, after the sun of it was set in the race of Noah. That there is something above us, some principle of *motion*, our reason can apprehend, tho' it cannot discover what it is, by its own virtue. And indeed 't is very improbable that we, who by the strength of our faculties cannot enter into the knowledge of any *being*, not so much as of our *own*, should be able to find out by them that supreme nature, which we cannot otherwise define than by saying it is infinite; as if infinite were definable, or infinity a subject for our narrow understanding. They who would prove religion by reason do but weaken the cause which they endeavour to support: 't is to take away the pillars from our faith, and to prop it only with a twig; 't is to design a tower like that of Babel, which, if it were possible (as it is not) to reach heaven, would come to nothing by the confusion of the workmen. For every man is building a several way; impotently conceited of his own model and his own materials: reason is always striving, and always at a loss; and of necessity it must so come to pass, while 't is exercised about that which is not its proper object. Let us be content at last to know God by his own methods; at least, so much of him as he is pleased to reveal to us in the sacred Scriptures; to apprehend them to be the word of God is all our reason has to do; for all beyond it is the work of faith, which is the seal of heaven impressed upon our human understanding.

And now for what concerns the holy bishop Athanasius, the preface of whose creed seems inconsistent with my opinion; which is, that heathens may possibly be saved: in the first place I desire it may be considered that it is the preface only, not the creed itself, which (till I am better informed) is of too hard a digestion for my charity. 'T is not that I am ignorant how many several texts of Scripture seemingly support that cause; but neither am I ignorant how all those texts may receive a kinder and more mollified interpretation. Every man who is read in Church history knows *that* belief was drawn up after a long contestation with Arius concerning the divinity of our blessed Savior, and his being one substance with the Father; and that, thus compiled, it was sent abroad among the Christian churches, as a kind of test, which whosoever took was looked on as an orthodox believer. 'T is manifest from hence that the heathen part of the empire was not concerned in it; for its business was not to distinguish betwixt pagans and Christians, but betwixt heretics and true believers. This, well considered, takes off the heavy weight of censure, which I would willingly avoid from so venerable a man; for if this proportion, 'whosoever will be saved,' be restrain'd only to those to whom it was intended, and for whom it was composed, I mean the Christians; then the anathema reaches not the heathens, who had never heard of Christ, and were nothing interested in that dispute. After all, I am far from blaming even that prefatory addition to the creed, and as far from caviling at the continuation of it in the liturgy of the Church, where, on the days appointed, 't is publicly read: for I suppose there is the same reason for it now, in opposition to the Socinians, as there was then against the Arians; the one being a heresy which seems to have been refined out of the other; and with how much more plausibility of reason it combats our religion, with so much more caution to be avoided; and therefore the prudence of our Church is to be commended, which has interposed her authority for the recommendation of this creed. Yet, to such as are grounded in the true belief, those explanatory creeds, the Nicene and this of Athanasius, might perhaps be spared; for what is supernatural will always be a mystery in spite of exposition, and, for my own part, the plain Apostles' Creed is most suitable to my weak understanding, as the simplest diet is the most easy of digestion.

I have dwelt longer on this subject than I intended, and longer than, perhaps, I ought; for having laid down, as my foundation, that the Scripture is a rule; that in all things needful to salvation it is clear, sufficient, and ordained by God Almighty for that purpose, I have left myself no right to interpret obscure places, such as concern the possibility of eternal happiness to heathens; because whatsoever is obscure is concluded not necessary to be known.

But, by asserting the Scripture to be the canon of our faith, I have unavoidably created to myself two sorts of enemies: the Papists indeed, more directly, because they have kept the Scripture from us, what they could; and have reserved to themselves a right of interpreting what they have delivered under the pretense of infallibility: and the Fanatics more collaterally, because they have assumed what amounts to an infallibility in the private spirit; and have detorted those texts of Scripture which are not necessary to salvation, to the damnable uses of sedition, disturbance, and destruction of the civil government. To begin with the Papists, and to speak freely, I think them the less dangerous, at least in appearance, to our present State, for not only the penal laws are in force against them, and their number is contemptible; but also their peerage and commons are excluded from parliaments, and consequently those laws in no probability of being repealed. A general and uninterrupted plot of their clergy, ever since the Reformation, I suppose all Protestants believe. For 't is not reasonable to think but that so many of their orders, as were outed from their fat possessions, would endeavor a reëntrance against those whom they account heretics. As for the late design, Mr. Coleman's letters, for aught I know, are the best evidence; and what they discover, without wiredrawing their sense, or malicious glosses, all men of reason conclude credible. If there be anything more than this required of me, I must believe it as well as I am able, in spite of the witnesses, and out of a decent conformity to the votes of parliament; for I suppose the Fanatics will not allow the Private Spirit in this case: here the infallibility is at least in one part of the government; and our understanding as well as our wills are represented. But to return to the Roman Catholics, how can we be secure from the practice of Jesuited Papists in that religion? For not two or three of that order, as some of them would impose upon us, but almost the whole body of them, are of opinion that their infallible master has a right over kings, not only in spirituals but temporals. Not to name Mariana, Bellarmine, Emanuel Sa, Molina, Santarel, Simancha, and at least twenty others of foreign countries; we can produce, of our own nation, Campian, and Doleman or Parsons: besides many are named whom I have not read, who all of them attest this doctrine, that the Pope can depose and give away the right of any sovereign prince, *si vel paulum deflexerit,* if he shall never so little warp; but if he once comes to be excommunicated, then the bond of obedience is taken off from subjects; and they may and ought to drive him, like another Nebuchadnezzar, *ex hominum Christianorum dominatu,* from exercising dominion over Christians; and to this they are bound by virtue of divine precept, and by all the ties of conscience under no less penalty than damnation. If they answer me (as a learned priest has lately written) that this doctrine of the Jesuits is not *de fide;* and that consequently they are not obliged by it, they must pardon me if I think they have said nothing to the purpose; for 't is a maxim in their Church, where points of faith are not decided, and that doctors are of contrary opinions, they may follow which part they please; but more safely the most received and most authorized. And their champion Bellarmine has told the world, in his *Apology,* that the king of England is a vassal to the Pope, *ratione directi dominii,* and that he holds in villanage of his Roman landlord. Which is no new claim put in for England. Our chronicles are his authentic witnesses that King John was deposed by the same plea, and Philip Augustus admitted tenant. And which makes the more for Bellarmine, the French king was again ejected when our king submitted to the Church, and the crown received under the sordid condition of a vassalage.

'T is not sufficient for the more moderate and well-meaning Papists (of which I doubt not there are many) to produce the evidences of their loyalty to the late king, and to declare their innocency in this Plot: I will grant their behavior in the first to have been as loyal and as brave as they desire; and will be willing to hold them excused as to the second, (I mean when it comes to my turn, and after my betters; for 't is a madness to be sober alone, while the nation continues drunk;) but that saying of their Father Cres, is still running in my head, that they may be dispensed with in their obedience to an heretic prince, while the necessity of the times shall oblige them to it: for that (as another of them tells us) is only the effec. of Christian prudence; but when once they shall get power to shake him off, an heretic i. no lawful king, and consequently to rise against him is no rebellion. I should be glad, therefore, that they would follow the advice which was charitably given them by a reverend prelate of our Church; namely, that they would join in a public act of disowning and detesting those Jesuitic principles; and subscribe to all doctrines which deny the Pope's authority of deposing kings, and releasing subjects from their oath of allegiance: to which I should think they might easily be induced, if it be true that this present Pope has condemned the doctrine of king-killing, (a thesis of the Jesuits,) amongst others, *ex cathedra*, (as they call it,) or in open consistory.

Leaving them, therefore, in so fair a way (if they please themselves) of satisfying all reasonable men of their sincerity and good meaning to the government, I shall make bold to consider that other extreme of our religion, I mean the Fanatics, or Schismatics, of the English Church. Since the Bible has been translated into our tongue, they have used it so, as if their business was not to be saved but to be damned by its contents. If we consider only them, better had it been for the English nation that it had still remained in the original Greek and Hebrew, or at least in the honest Latin of St. Jerome, than that several texts in it should have been prevaricated to the destruction of that government which put it into so ungrateful hands.

How many heresies the first translation of Tyndal produced in few years, let my Lord Herbert's *History of Henry the Eighth* inform you; insomuch that for the gross errors in it, and the great mischiefs it occasioned, a sentence passed on the first edition of the Bible, too shameful almost to be repeated. After the short reign of Edward the Sixth, (who had continued to carry on the Reformation on other principles than it was begun,) everyone knows that not only the chief promoters of that work, but many others whose consciences would not dispense with Popery, were forced, for fear of persecution, to change climates: from whence returning at the beginning of Queen Elizabeth's reign, many of them who had been in France, and at Geneva, brought back the rigid opinions and imperious discipline of Calvin, to graff upon our Reformation. Which, tho' they cunningly concealed at first, (as well knowing how nauseously that drug would go down in a lawful monarchy, which was prescribed for a rebellious commonwealth,) yet they always kept it in reserve; and were never wanting to themselves either in court or parliament, when either they had any prospect of a numerous party of Fanatic members in the one, or the encouragement of any favorite in the other, whose covetousness was gaping at the patrimony of the Church. They who will consult the works of our venerable Hooker, or the account of his life, or more particularly the letter written to him on this subject by George Cranmer, may see by what gradations they proceeded: from the dislike of cap and surplice, the very next step was admonitions to the parliament against the whole government ecclesiastical; then came out volumes in English and Latin in defense of their tenets; and immediately practices were set on foot to erect their discipline without authority. Those not succeeding, satire and railing was the next; and Martin Mar-prelate (the Marvell of those times) was the first Presbyterian scribbler who sanctified libels and scurrility to the use of the Good Old Cause. Which was done (says my author) upon this account; that (their serious treatises having been fully answered and refuted) they might compass by railing what they had lost by reasoning; and, when their cause was sunk in court and parliament, they might at least hedge in a stake amongst the rabble: for to their ignorance all things are wit which are abusive. But if Church and State were made the theme, then the doctoral degree of wit was to be taken at Billingsgate: even the most saintlike of the party, tho' they durst not excuse this contempt and vilifying of the government, yet were pleased, and grinned at it with a pious smile, and called it a judgment of God against the hierarchy. Thus Sectaries, we may see, were born with teeth, foul-mouth'd and scurrilous from their infancy; and if spiritual pride, venom, violence, contempt of superiors, and slander, had been the marks of orthodox belief, the Presbytery and the rest of our Schismatics, which are their spawn, were always the most visible Church in the Christian world.

'T is true, the government was too strong at that time for a rebellion; but to show what proficiency they had made in Calvin's school, even *then* their mouths watered at it; for two of their gifted brotherhood, (Hacket and Coppinger,) as the story tells us, got up into a pease-cart and harangued the people, to dispose them to an insurrection, and to establish their discipline by force: so that, however it comes about that now they celebrate Queen Elizabeth's birthnight as that of their saint and patroness, yet then they were for doing the work of the Lord by arms against her; and, in all probability, they wanted but a Fanatic lord mayor and two sheriffs of their party, to have compassed it.

Our venerable Hooker, after many admonitions which he had given them, toward the end of his preface breaks out into this prophetic speech: "There is in every one of these considerations most just cause to fear, lest our hastiness to embrace a thing of so perilous consequence" (meaning the Presbyterian discipline) "should cause posterity to feel those evils, which as yet are more easy for us to prevent, than they would be for them to remedy."

How fatally this Cassandra has foretold, we know too well by sad experience: the seeds were sown in the time of Queen Elizabeth, the bloody harvest ripened in the reign of King Charles the Martyr; and, because all the sheaves could not be carried off without shedding some of the loose grains, another crop is too like to follow; nay, I fear 't is unavoidable if the conventiclers be permitted still to scatter.

A man may be suffered to quote an adversary to our religion, when he speaks truth; and 't is the observation of Maimbourg, in his *History of Calvinism*, that wherever that discipline was planted and embraced, rebellion, civil war, and misery attended it. And how indeed should it happen otherwise? Reformation of Church and State has always been the ground of our divisions in England. While we were Papists, our Holy Father rid us, by pretending authority out of the Scriptures to depose princes; when we shook off his authority, the Sectaries furnished themselves with the same weapons; and out of the same magazine, the Bible: so that the Scriptures, which are in themselves the greatest security of governors, as commanding express obedience to them, are now turned to their destruction; and never since the Reformation has there wanted a text of their interpreting to authorize a rebel. And 't is to be noted by the way that the doctrines of king-killing and deposing, which have been taken up only by the worst party of the Papists, the most frontless flatterers of the Pope's authority, have been espoused, defended, and are still maintained by the whole body of Nonconformists and Republicans. 'T is but dubbing themselves the people of God, which 't is the interest of their preachers to tell them they are, and their own interest to believe; and after that, they cannot dip into the Bible, but one text or another will turn up for their purpose; if they are under persecution, (as they call it,) then that is a mark of their election; if they flourish, then God works miracles for their deliverance, and the saints are to possess the earth.

They may think themselves to be too roughly handled in this paper; but I, who know best how far I could have gone on this subject, must be bold to tell them they are spared: tho' at the same time I am not ignorant that they interpret the mildness of a writer to them, as they do the mercy of the government; in the one they think it fear, and conclude it weakness in the other. The best way for them to confute me is, as I have advised the Papists, to disclaim their principles and renounce their practices. We shall all be glad to think them true Englishmen when they obey the king, and true Protestants when they conform to the Church discipline.

It remains that I acquaint the reader that the verses were written for an ingenious young gentleman, my friend, upon his translation of the *Critical History of the Old Testament*, composed by the learned Father Simon: the verses therefore are addressed to the translator of that work, and the style of them is, what it ought to be, epistolary.

If anyone be so lamentable a critic as to require the smoothness, the numbers, and the turn of heroic poetry in this poem, I must tell him that, if he has not read Horace, I have studied him, and hope the style of his *Epistles* is not ill imitated here. The expressions of a poem designed purely for instruction ought to be plain and natural, and yet majestic; for here the poet is presumed to be a kind of lawgiver, and those three qualities which I have named are proper to the legislative style. The florid, elevated, and figurative way is for the passions; for love and hatred, fear and anger, are begotten in the soul by showing their objects out of their true proportion, either greater than the life, or less; but instruction is to be given by showing them what they naturally are. A man is to be cheated into passion, but to be reasoned into truth.

RELIGIO LAICI

Dim as the borrow'd beams of moon and
    stars
To lonely, weary, wand'ring travelers
Is Reason to the soul: and, as on high
Those rolling fires discover but the sky,

Not light us here; so Reason's glimmering
    ray
Was lent, not to assure our doubtful way,
But guide us upward to a better day.
And as those nightly tapers disappear
When day's bright lord ascends our hem-
    isphere;

So pale grows Reason at Religion's sight; 10
So dies, and so dissolves in supernatural
    light.
Some few, whose lamp shone brighter, have
    been led
From cause to cause, to Nature's secret
    head;
And found that one first principle must be:
But what, or who, that UNIVERSAL HE;
Whether some soul encompassing this ball,
Unmade, unmov'd; yet making, moving all;
Or various atoms' interfering dance
Leapt into form, (the noble work of
    chance;)
Or this great All was from eternity;   20
Not ev'n the Stagirite himself could see,
And Epicurus guess'd as well as he.
As blindly grop'd they for a future state,
As rashly judg'd of providence and fate:
[1] But least of all could their endeavours find
What most concern'd the good of human-
    kind;
For happiness was never to be found,
But vanish'd from 'em, like enchanted
    ground.
One thought content the good to be en-
    joy'd:
This every little accident destroy'd: 30
The wiser madmen did for virtue toil,
A thorny, or at best a barren soil:
In pleasure some their glutton souls would
    steep,
But found their line too short, the well too
    deep,
And leaky vessels which no bliss could keep.
Thus anxious thoughts in endless circles
    roll,
Without a center where to fix the soul;
In this wild maze their vain endeavours
    end:
How can the less the greater comprehend?
Or finite reason reach Infinity?   40
For what could fathom GOD were more than
    He.
[2] The Deist thinks he stands on firmer
    ground,
Cries: "Εὕρεκα, the mighty secret 's found:
God is that spring of good; supreme and
    best;
We, made to serve, and in that service
    blest."

[1] Opinions of the several sects of philosophers
concerning the *Summum Bonum*.
[2] System of Deism.

If so, some rules of worship must be given,
Distributed alike to all by Heaven:
Else God were partial, and to some denied
The means his justice should for all pro-
    vide.
This general worship is to PRAISE and
    PRAY,   50
One part to borrow blessings, one to pay;
And when frail nature slides into offense,
The sacrifice for crimes is penitence.
Yet, since th' effects of Providence, we find,
Are variously dispens'd to humankind;
That vice triumphs, and virtue suffers here,
(A brand that sovereign justice cannot
    bear;)
Our reason prompts us to a future state,
The last appeal from fortune and from fate:
Where God's all-righteous ways will be de-
    clar'd,   60
The bad meet punishment, the good re-
    ward.
[3] Thus man by his own strength to heaven
    would soar,
And would not be oblig'd to God for more.
Vain, wretched creature, how art thou mis-
    led
To think thy wit these godlike notions bred!
These truths are not the product of thy
    mind,
But dropp'd from Heaven, and of a nobler
    kind.
Reveal'd Religion first inform'd thy sight,
And Reason saw not, till Faith sprung the
    light.
Hence all thy natural worship takes the
    source: 70
'T is Revelation what thou think'st Dis-
    course.
Else, how com'st thou to see these truths so
    clear,
Which so obscure to heathens did appear?
Not Plato these, nor Aristotle found;
[4] Nor he whose wisdom oracles renown'd.
Hast thou a wit so deep, or so sublime,
Or canst thou lower dive, or higher climb?
Canst thou, by Reason, more of Godhead
    know
Than Plutarch, Seneca, or Cicero?
Those giant wits, in happier ages born,   80
(When arms and arts did Greece and Rome
    adorn,)

[3] Of reveal'd Religion.
[4] Socrates.

Knew no such system; no such piles could raise
Of natural worship, built on pray'r and praise,
To One Sole GOD:
Nor did remorse, to expiate sin, prescribe,
But slew their fellow creatures for a bribe:
The guiltless victim groan'd for their offense,
And cruelty and blood was penitence.
If sheep and oxen could atone for men,
Ah! at how cheap a rate the rich might sin!   90
And great oppressors might Heaven's wrath beguile
By offering his own creatures for a spoil!
    Dar'st thou, poor worm, offend Infinity?
And must the terms of peace be given by thee?
Then thou art Justice in the last appeal;
Thy easy God instructs thee to rebel:
And, like a king remote, and weak, must take
What satisfaction thou art pleas'd to make.
    But if there be a pow'r too just and strong
To wink at crimes, and bear unpunish'd wrong;   100
Look humbly upward, see his will disclose
The forfeit first, and then the fine impose:
A mulct thy poverty could never pay
Had not eternal wisdom found the way
And with celestial wealth supplied thy store:
His justice makes the fine, his mercy quits the score.
See God descending in thy human frame;
Th' offended suff'ring in th' offender's name;
All thy misdeeds to Him imputed see,
And all His righteousness devolv'd on thee.   110
    For granting we have sinn'd, and that th' offense
Of man is made against Omnipotence,
Some price that bears proportions must be paid,
And infinite with infinite be weigh'd.
See then the Deist lost: remorse for vice,
Not paid, or paid, inadequate in price:
What farther means can Reason now direct,
Or what relief from human wit expect?
That shows us sick; and sadly are we sure
Still to be sick, till Heav'n reveal the cure: 120

If then Heav'n's will must needs be understood,
(Which must, if we want cure, and Heaven be good,)
Let all records of will reveal'd be shown;
With Scripture all in equal balance thrown,
And our one Sacred Book will be that one.
    Proof needs not here, for whether we compare
That impious, idle, superstitious ware
Of rites, lustrations, offerings (which before,
In various ages, various countries bore)
With Christian faith and virtues, we shall find   130
None answ'ring the great ends of humankind,
But this one rule of life; that shows us best
How God may be appeas'd, and mortals blest.
Whether from length of time its worth we draw,
The world is scarce more ancient than the law:
Heav'n's early care prescrib'd for every age;
First, in the soul, and after, in the page.
Or, whether more abstractedly we look,
Or on the writers, or the written book,
Whence, but from heav'n, could men unskill'd in arts,   140
In several ages born, in several parts,
Weave such agreeing truths? or how, or why,
Should all conspire to cheat us with a lie?
Unask'd their pains, ungrateful their advice,
Starving their gain, and martyrdom their price.
    If on the book itself we cast our view,
Concurrent heathens prove the story true;
The doctrine, miracles; which must convince,
For Heav'n in them appeals to human sense:
And tho' they prove not, they confirm the cause,   150
When what is taught agrees with nature's laws.
    Then for the style, majestic and divine,
It speaks no less than God in every line:
Commanding words; whose force is still the same
As the first fiat that produc'd our frame.
All faiths beside or did by arms ascend,

Or sense indulg'd has made mankind their
  friend:
This only doctrine does our lusts oppose,
Unfed by nature's soil, in which it grows;
Cross to our interests, curbing sense and
  sin;   160
Oppress'd without, and undermin'd within,
It thrives thro' pain; its own tormentors
  tires;
And with a stubborn patience still aspires.
To what can Reason such effects assign,
Transcending nature, but to laws divine?
Which in that sacred volume are contain'd;
Sufficient, clear, and for that use ordain'd.
  [5] But stay: the Deist here will urge anew,
No supernatural worship can be true:
Because a general law is that alone   170
Which must to all, and everywhere, be
  known:
A style so large as not this Book can claim,
Nor aught that bears reveal'd Religion's
  name.
'T is said the sound of a Messiah's birth
Is gone thro' all the habitable earth;
But still that text must be confin'd alone
To what was then inhabited, and known:
And what provision could from thence ac-
  crue
To Indian souls, and worlds discover'd new?
In other parts it helps, that, ages past,   180
The Scriptures there were known, and were
  embrac'd,
Till Sin spread once again the shades of
  night:
What 's that to these who never saw the
  light?
  [6] Of all objections this indeed is chief
To startle Reason, stagger frail Belief:
We grant, 't is true, that Heav'n from
  human sense
Has hid the secret paths of Providence;
But boundless wisdom, boundless mercy,
  may
Find ev'n for those bewilder'd souls a way:
If from his nature foes may pity claim,   190
Much more may strangers who ne'er heard
  his name.
And tho' no name be for salvation known,
But that of his eternal Son's alone;
Who knows how far transcending goodness
  can
Extend the merits of that Son to man?

Who knows what reasons may his mercy
  lead,
Or ignorance invincible may plead?
Not only charity bids hope the best,
But more the great apostle has express'd:
That if the Gentiles (whom no law in-
  spir'd)   200
By nature did what was by law requir'd;
They, who the written rule had never
  known,
Were to themselves both rule and law alone:
To Nature's plain indictment they shall
  plead,
And by their conscience be condemn'd or
  freed.
Most righteous doom! because a rule re-
  veal'd
Is none to those from whom it was con-
  ceal'd.
Then those who follow'd Reason's dictates
  right,
Liv'd up, and lifted high their natural light;
With Socrates may see their Maker's face, 210
While thousand rubric-martyrs want a place.
  Nor does it balk my charity, to find
Th' Egyptian bishop of another mind:
For tho' his creed eternal truth contains,
'T is hard for man to doom to endless pains
All who believ'd not all his zeal requir'd,
Unless he first could prove he was inspir'd.
Then let us either think he meant to say
This faith, where publish'd, was the only
  way;
Or else conclude that, Arius to confute, 220
The good old man, too eager in dispute,
Flew high; and, as his Christian fury rose,
Damn'd all for heretics who durst oppose.
  [7] Thus far my charity this path has tried,
(A much unskilful, but well-meaning
  guide:)
Yet what they are, ev'n these crude thoughts
  were bred
By reading that, which better thou hast
  read:
Thy matchless author's work: which thou,
  my friend,
By well translating better dost commend:
Those youthful hours which of thy equals
  most   230
In toys have squander'd, or in vice have lost,
Those hours hast thou to nobler use em-
  ploy'd;

[5] Objection of the Deist.
[6] The objection answer'd.

[7] Digression to the translator of Father Simon's *Critical History of the Old Testament.*

And the severe delights of truth enjoy'd.
Witness this weighty book, in which appears
The crabbed toil of many thoughtful years,
Spent by thy author in the sifting care
Of Rabbins' old sophisticated ware
From gold divine, which he who well can
    sort
May afterwards make algebra a sport:
A treasure which, if country curates buy, 240
They Junius and Tremellius may defy:
Save pains in various readings and transla-
    tions,
And without Hebrew make most learn'd
    quotations:
A work so full with various learning
    fraught,
So nicely ponder'd, yet so strongly wrought,
As nature's height and art's last hand re-
    quir'd:
As much as man could compass, uninspir'd.
Where we may see what errors have been
    made
Both in the copier's and translator's trade;
How Jewish, Popish interests have pre-
    vail'd, 250
And where infallibility has fail'd.
  For some, who have his secret meaning
    guess'd,
Have found our author not too much a
    priest:
For fashion-sake he seems to have recourse
To Pope, and councils, and tradition's
    force;
But he that old traditions could subdue,
Could not but find the weakness of the new:
If Scripture, tho' deriv'd from heav'nly
    birth,
Has been but carelessly preserv'd on earth;
If God's own people, who of God before 260
Knew what we know, and had been prom-
    is'd more,
In fuller terms, of Heaven's assisting care,
And who did neither time nor study spare
To keep this book untainted, unperplex'd,
Let in gross errors to corrupt the text,
Omitted paragraphs, embroil'd the sense,
With vain traditions stopp'd the gaping
    fence,
Which every common hand pull'd up with
    ease:
What safety from such brushwood-helps as
    these?
If written words from time are not se-
    cur'd, 270

How can we think have oral sounds en-
    dur'd?
Which thus transmitted, if one mouth has
    fail'd,
Immortal lies on ages are entail'd;
And that some such have been, is prov'd too
    plain;
If we consider interest, Church, and gain.
  [8] "O, but," says one, "tradition set aside.
Where can we hope for an unerring guide?
For since th' original Scripture has been lost,
All copies disagreeing, maim'd the most,
Or Christian faith can have no certain
    ground, 280
Or truth in Church tradition must be
    found."
  Such an omniscient Church we wish in-
    deed;
'T were worth both Testaments; and cast
    in the Creed:
But if this mother be a guide so sure,
As can all doubts resolve, all truth secure,
Then her infallibility as well
Where copies are corrupt or lame can tell;
Restore lost canon with as little pains,
As truly explicate what still remains:
Which yet no council dare pretend to
    do, 290
Unless like Esdras they could write it new:
Strange confidence, still to interpret true,
Yet not be sure that all they have explain'd,
Is in the blest original contain'd.
More safe, and much more modest 't is, to
    say
God would not leave mankind without a
    way;
And that the Scriptures, tho' not every-
    where
Free from corruption, or entire, or clear,
Are uncorrupt, sufficient, clear, entire,
In all things which our needful faith re-
    quire. 300
If others in the same glass better see,
'T is for themselves they look, but not for
    me:
For MY salvation must its doom receive,
Not from what OTHERS but what I believe.
  [9] Must all tradition then be set aside?
This to affirm were ignorance or pride.
Are there not many points, some needful
    sure

[8] Of the infallibility of tradition in general.
[9] Objection in behalf of tradition, urg'd by
Father Simon.

To saving faith, that Scripture leaves ob-
    scure?
Which every sect will wrest a several way
(For what one sect interprets, all sects
    may) :   310
We hold, and say we prove from Scripture
    plain,
That Christ is GOD; the bold Socinian
From the same Scripture urges he 's but MAN.
Now what appeal can end th' important
    suit;
Both parts talk loudly, but the rule is mute.
  Shall I speak plain, and in a nation free
Assume an honest layman's liberty?
I think (according to my little skill,
To my own Mother Church submitting
    still)
That many have been sav'd, and many
    may,   320
Who never heard this question brought in
    play.
Th' unletter'd Christian, who believes in
    gross,
Plods on to heaven, and ne'er is at a loss;
For the strait gate would be made straiter
    yet,
Were none admitted there but men of wit.
The few by nature form'd, with learning
    fraught,
Born to instruct, as others to be taught,
Must study well the sacred page; and see
Which doctrine, this, or that, does best
    agree
With the whole tenor of the work divine, 330
And plainliest points to Heaven's reveal'd
    design:
Which exposition flows from genuine sense,
And which is forc'd by wit and eloquence.
Not that tradition's parts are useless here,
When general, old, disinteress'd and clear:
That ancient Fathers thus expound the page
Gives truth the reverend majesty of age,
Confirms its force, by biding every test;
For best authorities, next rules, are best.
And still the nearer to the spring we go, 340
More limpid, more unsoil'd the waters flow.
Thus, first traditions were a proof alone,
Could we be certain such they were, so
    known:
But since some flaws in long descent may be,
They make not truth, but probability.
Even Arius and Pelagius durst provoke
To what the centuries preceding spoke.
Such difference is there in an oft-told tale:

But truth by its own sinews will prevail.
Tradition written therefore more com-
    mends   350
Authority, than what from voice descends;
And this, as perfect as its kind can be,
Rolls down to us the sacred history,
Which, from the Universal Church receiv'd,
Is tried, and after for itself believ'd.
  [10] The partial Papists would infer from
    hence
Their Church, in last resort, should judge
    the sense.
[11] But first they could assume, with won-
    drous art,
Themselves to be the whole, who are but
    part
Of that vast frame, the Church; yet grant
    they were   360
The handers down, can they from thence
    infer
A right t' interpret? or would they alone
Who brought the present, claim it for their
    own?
The book 's a common largess to mankind,
Not more for them than every man de-
    sign'd;
The welcome news is in the letter found;
The carrier 's not commission'd to expound.
It speaks itself, and what it does contain,
In all things needful to be known, is plain.
  In times o'er grown with rust and ig-
    norance,   370
A gainful trade their clergy did advance;
When want of learning kept the laymen
    low,
And none but priests were authoriz'd to
    know;
When what small knowledge was, in them
    did dwell,
And he a god who could but read or spell:
Then Mother Church did mightily prevail:
She parcell'd out the Bible by retail;
But still expounded what she sold or gave,
To keep it in her power to damn and save:
Scripture was scarce, and, as the market
    went,   380
Poor laymen took salvation on content;
As needy men take money, good or bad:
God's word they had not, but the priest's
    they had.
Yet, whate'er false conveyances they made,
The lawyer still was certain to be paid.

[10] The second objection.
[11] Answer to the objection.

In those dark times they learn'd their knack
  so well,
That by long use they grew infallible:
At last, a knowing age began t' enquire
If they the Book, or that did them inspire;
And, making narrower search, they found,
  tho' late, 390
That what they thought the priest's was
  their estate,
Taught by the will produc'd, (the written
  word,)
How long they had been cheated on record.
Then every man who saw the title fair
Claim'd a child's part, and put in for a
  share;
Consulted soberly his private good,
And sav'd himself as cheap as e'er he could.
  'T is true, my friend, (and far be flattery
  hence,)
This good had full as bad a consequence:
The book thus put in every vulgar hand, 400
Which each presum'd he best could under-
  stand,
The common rule was made the common
  prey,
And at the mercy of the rabble lay.
The tender page with horny fists was gall'd,
And he was gifted most that loudest bawl'd:
The spirit gave the doctoral degree,
And every member of a company
Was of his trade and of the Bible free.
Plain truths enough for needful use they
  found,
But men would still be itching to ex-
  pound: 410
Each was ambitious of th' obscurest place,
No measure ta'en from knowledge, all from
  GRACE.
Study and pains were now no more their
  care;
Texts were explain'd by fasting and by
  prayer:
This was the fruit the private spirit brought,
Occasion'd by great zeal and little thought.
While crowds unlearn'd, with rude devotion
  warm,
About the sacred viands buzz and swarm,
The fly-blown text creates a crawling brood;
And turns to maggots what was meant for
  food. 420
A thousand daily sects rise up and die;
A thousand more the perish'd race supply:
So all we make of Heaven's discover'd will
Is, not to have it, or to use it ill.

The danger 's much the same; on several
  shelves
If others wreck us, or we wreck ourselves.
  What then remains, but, waiving each
  extreme,
The tides of ignorance and pride to stem?
Neither so rich a treasure to forego;
Nor proudly seek beyond our pow'r to
  know: 430
Faith is not built on disquisitions vain;
The things we must believe are few and
  plain:
But since men will believe more than they
  need,
And every man will make himself a creed,
In doubtful questions 't is the safest way
To learn what unsuspected ancients say;
For 't is not likely we should higher soar
In search of heav'n, than all the Church
  before:
Nor can we be deceiv'd, unless we see
The Scripture and the Fathers disagree. 440
If, after all, they stand suspected still,
(For no man's faith depends upon his will)
'T is some relief that points not clearly
  known
Without much hazard may be let alone:
And after hearing what our Church can say,
If still our Reason runs another way,
That private Reason 't is more just to curb,
Than by disputes the public peace disturb.
For points obscure are of small use to learn:
But common quiet is mankind's concern. 450
  Thus have I made my own opinions clear;
Yet neither praise expect, nor censure fear:
And this unpolish'd, rugged verse, I chose,
As fittest for discourse, and nearest prose;
For while from sacred truth I do not swerve,
Tom Sternhold's, or Tom Sha—ll's rhymes
  will serve.
                                   [1682]

TO THE MEMORY OF
MR. OLDHAM

Farewell, too little, and too lately known,
Whom I began to think and call my own:
For sure our souls were near allied, and
  thine
Cast in the same poetic mold with mine.
One common note on either lyre did strike.

And knaves and fools we both abhorr'd
    alike.
To the same goal did both our studies drive;
The last set out the soonest did arrive.
Thus Nisus fell upon the slippery place,
While his young friend perform'd and won
    the race.   10
O early ripe! to thy abundant store
What could advancing age have added
    more?
It might (what nature never gives the
    young)
Have taught the numbers of thy native
    tongue.
But satire needs not those, and wit will
    shine
Thro' the harsh cadence of a rugged line:
A noble error, and but seldom made,
When poets are by too much force betray'd.
Thy generous fruits, tho' gather'd ere their
    prime,   19
Still show'd a quickness; and maturing time
But mellows what we write to the dull
    sweets of rhyme.
Once more, hail and farewell; farewell,
    thou young,
But ah too short, Marcellus of our tongue;
Thy brows with ivy, and with laurels
    bound;
But fate and gloomy night encompass thee
    around.

                                            [1684]

TO THE PIOUS MEMORY
OF THE ACCOMPLISH'D
YOUNG LADY, MRS.
ANNE KILLIGREW

EXCELLENT IN THE TWO SISTER-ARTS
OF POESY AND PAINTING, AN ODE

                          I

Thou youngest virgin-daughter of the skies,
Made in the last promotion of the blest;
Whose palms, new pluck'd from paradise,
In spreading branches more sublimely rise,
Rich with immortal green above the rest:
Whether, adopted to some neighboring star,
Thou roll'st above us in thy wand'ring race,
    Or, in procession fix'd and regular,

Mov'd with the heavens' majestic pace;
Or, call'd to more superior bliss,   10
Thou tread'st, with seraphims, the vast
    abyss:
Whatever happy region is thy place,
Cease thy celestial song a little space;
(Thou wilt have time enough for hymns
    divine,
    Since heav'n's eternal year is thine.)
Hear then a mortal Muse thy praise re-
    hearse,
    In no ignoble verse;
But such as thy own voice did practice here,
When thy first fruits of poesy were giv'n,
To make thyself a welcome inmate there; 20
    While yet a young probationer,
    And candidate of heav'n.

                          II

If by traduction came thy mind,
Our wonder is the less to find
A soul so charming from a stock so good;
Thy father was transfus'd into thy blood:
So wert thou born into the tuneful strain,
(An early, rich, and inexhausted vein.)
    But if thy preëxisting soul
    Was form'd, at first, with myriads more, 30
It did thro' all the mighty poets roll,
    Who Greek or Latin laurels wore,
And was that Sappho last, which once it was
    before.
    If so, then cease thy flight, O heav'n-born
    mind!
Thou hast no dross to purge from thy
    rich ore;
Nor can thy soul a fairer mansion find,
Than was the beauteous frame she left
    behind:
Return, to fill or mend the choir of thy
    celestial kind.

                          III

May we presume to say, that at thy birth
New joy was sprung in heav'n, as well as
    here on earth?   40
For sure the milder planets did combine
On thy auspicious horoscope to shine,
And ev'n the most malicious were in
    trine.
Thy brother-angels at thy birth
    Strung each his lyre, and tun'd it high,
    That all the people of the sky

Might know a poetess was born on earth.
  And then, if ever, mortal ears
Had heard the music of the spheres!
And if no clust'ring swarm of bees   50
On thy sweet mouth distill'd their golden
    dew,
  'T was that such vulgar miracles
  Heav'n had not leisure to renew:
For all the blest fraternity of love
Solemniz'd there thy birth, and kept thy
    holiday above.

IV

O gracious God! how far have we
Profan'd thy heav'nly gift of poesy!
Made prostitute and profligate the Muse,
Debas'd to each obscene and impious use,
Whose harmony was first ordain'd above   60
For tongues of angels, and for hymns of
    love!
O wretched we! why were we hurried down
  This lubric and adult'rate age,
  (Nay, added fat pollutions of our own,)
    T' increase the steaming ordures of the
    stage?
What can we say t' excuse our *second fall?*
Let this thy *vestal,* Heav'n, atone for all:
Her Arethusian stream remains unsoil'd,
Unmix'd with foreign filth, and undefil'd;
Her wit was more than man, her innocence
    a child!   70

V

Art she had none, yet wanted none;
  For nature did that want supply:
  So rich in treasures of her own,
  She might our boasted stores defy:
Such noble vigour did her verse adorn
That it seem'd borrow'd, where 't was only
    born.
Her morals too were in her bosom bred,
  By great examples daily fed,
What in the best of books, her father's life,
    she read.
And to be read herself she need not fear;   80
Each test, and ev'ry light, her Muse will
    bear,
Tho' Epictetus with his lamp were there.
Ev'n love (for love sometimes her Muse ex-
    press'd)
Was but a lambent flame which play'd
  about her breast,

Light as the vapors of a morning dream:
So cold herself, whilst she such warmth ex-
    press'd,
'T was Cupid bathing in Diana's stream.

VI

Born to the spacious empire of the Nine,
Onc would have thought she should have
    been content
To manage well that mighty government;   90
But what can young ambitious souls con-
    fine?
  To the next realm she stretch'd her sway,
  For painture near adjoining lay,
A plenteous province, and alluring prey.
  A chamber of dependences was fram'd,
  (As conquerors will never want pretense,
    When arm'd, to justify th' offense,)
And the whole fief in right of poetry she
    claim'd.
The country open lay without defense;   99
For poets frequent inroads there had made,
  And perfectly could represent
  The shape, the face, with ev'ry lineament;
And all the large demains which the *Dumb
    Sister* sway'd,
  All bow'd beneath her government;
  Receiv'd in triumph wheresoe'er she
    went.
Her pencil drew whate'er her soul design'd,
And oft the happy draught surpass'd the
    image in her mind.
  The sylvan scenes of herds and flocks,
  And fruitful plains and barren rocks,
  Of shallow brooks that flow'd so clear   110
  The bottom did the top appear;
  Of deeper too and ampler floods,
  Which, as in mirrors, show'd the woods;
  Of lofty trees, with sacred shades,
  And perspectives of pleasant glades,
  Where nymphs of brightest form appear,
  And shaggy satyrs standing near,
  Which them at once admire and fear:
  The ruins too of some majestic piece,
  Boasting the pow'r of ancient Rome, or
    Greece,   120
  Whose statues, friezes, columns broken
    lie,
  And, tho' defac'd, the wonder of the eye:
  What nature, art, bold fiction, e'er durst
    frame,
  Her forming hand gave feature to the
    name.

So strange a concourse ne'er was seen be-
        fore,
But when the peopled ark the whole crea-
        tion bore.

VII

The scene then chang'd: with bold
        erected look
Our martial king the sight with reverence
        strook;
For, not content t' express his outward part,
Her hand call'd out the image of his heart:
His warlike mind, his soul devoid of fear, 131
His high-designing thoughts were figur'd
        there,
As when, by magic, ghosts are made appear.
    Our Phœnix queen was portray'd too so
        bright,
Beauty alone could beauty take so right:
Her dress, her shape, her matchless grace,
Were all observ'd, as well as heav'nly face.
With such a peerless majesty she stands,
As in that day she took the crown from sa-
        cred hands;
Before a train of heroines was seen,   140
In beauty foremost, as in rank the queen.
Thus nothing to her genius was denied,
    But like a ball of fire the further thrown,
    Still with a greater blaze she shone,
And her bright soul broke out on ev'ry side.
What next she had design'd, Heaven only
        knows;
To such immod'rate growth her conquest
        rose
That fate alone its progress could oppose.

VIII

Now all those charms, that blooming
        grace,
The well-proportion'd shape, and beauteous
        face,   150
Shall never more be seen by mortal eyes:
In earth the much-lamented virgin lies!
    Not wit, nor piety could fate prevent;
    Nor was the cruel Destiny content
    To finish all the murder at a blow,
    To sweep at once her life and beauty too;
But, like a harden'd felon, took a pride
    To work more mischievously slow,
And plunder'd first, and then destroy'd.
O double sacrilege on things divine,   160
To rob the relic, and deface the shrine!
    But thus Orinda died:

Heav'n, by the same disease, did both trans-
        late;
As equal were their souls, so equal was their
        fate.

IX

Meantime her warlike brother on the seas
    His waving streamers to the winds dis-
        plays,
And vows for his return, with vain devotion,
        pays.
    Ah, generous youth, that wish forbear,
    The winds too soon will waft thee here!
Slack all thy sails, and fear to come,   170
Alas, thou know'st not, thou art wreck'd at
        home!
No more shalt thou behold thy sister's face,
Thou hast already had her last embrace.
But look aloft, and if thou kenn'st from far
Among the Pleiads a new kindled star;
If any sparkles than the rest more bright,
'T is she that shines in that propitious light.

X

When in mid-air the golden trump shall
        sound,
    To raise the nations under ground;
    When in the Valley of Jehosaphat   180
The judging God shall close the book of
        fate,
    And there the last assizes keep
    For those who wake and those who
        sleep;
    When rattling bones together fly
    From the four corners of the sky;
When sinews o'er the skeletons are spread,
Those cloth'd with flesh, and life inspires
        the dead;
The sacred poets first shall hear the sound,
And foremost from the tomb shall bound,
For they are cover'd with the lightest
        ground;   190
And straight, with inborn vigour, on the
        wing,
Like mounting larks, to the new morning
        sing.
There thou, sweet saint, before the choir
        shalt go,
As harbinger of heav'n, the way to show,
The way which thou so well hast learn'd
        below.
                                               [1685]

THE HIND AND THE PANTHER

A POEM IN THREE PARTS

—Antiquam exquirite matrem.
Et vera, incessu, patuit dea.— } VIRG.

TO THE READER

The nation is in too high a ferment for me to expect either fair war, or even so much as fair quarter, from a reader of the opposite party. All men are engaged either on this side or that; and tho' conscience is the common word which is given by both, yet if a writer fall among enemies, and cannot give the marks of their conscience, he is knocked down before the reasons of his own are heard. A preface, therefore, which is but a bespeaking of favour, is altogether useless. What I desire the reader should know concerning me, he will find in the body of the poem, if he have but the patience to peruse it. Only this advertisement let him take beforehand, which relates to the merits of the cause. No general characters of parties (call 'em either sects or churches) can be so fully and exactly drawn, as to comprehend all the several members of 'em; at least all such as are received under that denomination. For example, there are some of the Church by law established who envy not liberty of conscience to Dissenters; as being well satisfied that, according to their own principles, they ought not to persecute them. Yet these, by reason of their fewness, I could not distinguish from the numbers of the rest, with whom they are embodied in one common name. On the other side, there are many of our sects, and more indeed than I could reasonably have hoped, who have withdrawn themselves from the communion of the Panther, and embraced this gracious indulgence of his Majesty in point of toleration. But neither to the one nor the other of these is this satire any way intended: 't is aimed only at the refractory and disobedient on either side; for those who are come over to the royal party are consequently supposed to be out of gunshot. Our physicians have observed that, in process of time, some diseases have abated of their virulence, and have in a manner worn out their malignity, so as to be no longer mortal; and why may not I suppose the same concerning some of those who have formerly been enemies to kingly government, as well as Catholic religion? I hope they have now another notion of both, as having found, by comfortable experience, that the doctrine of persecution is far from being an article of our faith.

'T is not for any private man to censure the proceedings of a foreign prince; but, without suspicion of flattery, I may praise our own, who has taken contrary measures, and those more suitable to the spirit of Christianity. Some of the Dissenters, in their addresses to his Majesty, have said, *that he has restored God to his empire over conscience.* I confess I dare not stretch the figure to so great a boldness; but I may safely say that conscience is the royalty and prerogative of every private man. He is absolute in his own breast, and accountable to no earthly power for that which passes only betwixt God and him. Those who are driven into the fold are, generally speaking, rather made hypocrites than converts.

This indulgence being granted to all the sects, it ought in reason to be expected that they should both receive it, and receive it thankfully. For at this time of day to refuse the benefit, and adhere to those whom they have esteemed their persecutors, what is it else, but publicly to own, that they suffered not before for conscience sake, but only out of pride and obstinacy, to separate from a Church for those impositions, which they now judge may be lawfully obeyed? After they have so long contended for their classical ordination, (not to speak of rites and ceremonies,) will they at length submit to an episcopal? If they can go so far out of complaisance to their old enemies, methinks a little reason should persuade 'em to take another step, and see whither that would lead 'em.

Of the receiving this toleration thankfully I shall say no more, than that they ought, and I doubt not they will consider from what hands they received it. 'T is not from a Cyrus, a heathen prince, and a foreigner, but from a Christian king, their native sovereign; who expects a return *in specie* from them, that the kindness which he has graciously shown them may be retaliated on those of his own persuasion.

As for the poem in general, I will only thus far satisfy the reader, that it was neither imposed on me, nor so much as the subject given me by any man. It was written during the last winter and the beginning of this spring, tho' with long interruptions of ill health and other hindrances. About a fortnight before I had finished it, his Majesty's Declaration for Liberty of Conscience came abroad: which if I had so soon expected, I might have spared myself the labor of writing many things which are contained in the third part of it. But I was always in some hope that the Church of England might have been persuaded to have taken off the penal laws and the Test, which was one design of the poem when I proposed to myself the writing of it.

'T is evident that some part of it was only occasional, and not first intended. I mean that defense of myself to which every honest man is bound, when he is injuriously attacked in print; and I refer myself to the judgment of those who have read the *Answer to the Defense of the late King's Papers*, and that of the *Duchess*, (in which last I was concerned,) how charitably I have been represented there. I am now informed both of the author and supervisors of his pamphlet, and will reply when I think he can affront me; for I am of Socrates's opinion, that all creatures cannot. In the mean time let him consider, whether he deserved not a more severe reprehension than I gave him formerly, for using so little respect to the memory of those whom he pretended to answer; and, at his leisure, look out for some original *Treatise of Humility*, written by any Protestant in English, (I believe I may say in any other tongue:) for the magnified piece of Duncomb on that subject, which either he must mean, or none, and with which another of his fellows has upbraided me, was translated from the Spanish of Rodriguez; tho' with the omission of the seventeenth, the twenty-fourth, the twenty-fifth, and the last chapter, which will be found in comparing of the books.

He would have insinuated to the world that her late Highness died not a Roman Catholic. He declares himself to be now satisfied to the contrary, in which he has given up the cause: for matter of fact was the principal debate betwixt us. In the mean time, he would dispute the motives of her change; how preposterously, let all men judge, when he seemed to deny the subject of the controversy, the change itself. And because I would not take up this ridiculous challenge, he tells the world I cannot argue; but he may as well infer, that a Catholic cannot fast, because he will not take up the cudgels against Mrs. James, to confute the Protestant religion.

I have but one word more to say concerning the poem as such, and abstracting from the matters, either religious or civil, which are handled in it. The *first part*, consisting most in general characters and narration, I have endeavored to raise, and give it the majestic turn of heroic poesy. The *second*, being matter of dispute, and chiefly concerning Church authority, I was obliged to make as plain and perspicuous as possibly I could; yet not wholly neglecting the numbers, tho' I had not frequent occasions for the magnificence of verse. The *third*, which has more of the nature of domestic conversation, is, or ought to be, more free and familiar than the two former.

There are in it two *episodes*, or *fables*, which are interwoven with the main design; so that they are properly parts of it, tho' they are also distinct stories of themselves. In both of these I have made use of the commonplaces of *satire*, whether true or false, which are urged by the members of the one Church against the other: at which I hope no reader of either party will be scandalized, because they are not of my invention, but as old, to my knowledge, as the times of Boccace and Chaucer on the one side, and as those of the Reformation on the other.

THE HIND AND THE PANTHER

THE FIRST PART

A milk-white Hind, immortal and un-
    chang'd,
Fed on the lawns, and in the forest rang'd;
Without unspotted, innocent within,
She fear'd no danger, for she knew no sin.
Yet had she oft been chas'd with horns and
    hounds
And Scythian shafts; and many winged
    wounds
Aim'd at her heart; was often forc'd to fly,
And doom'd to death, tho' fated not to die.
    Not so her young; for their unequal line
Was hero's make, half human, half divine.
Their earthly mold obnoxious was to fate, 11
Th' immortal part assum'd immortal state.
Of these a slaughter'd army lay in blood,
Extended o'er the Caledonian wood,
Their native walk; whose vocal blood arose,
And cried for pardon on their perjur'd
    foes.

Their fate was fruitful, and the sanguine
    seed,
Endued with souls, increas'd the sacred
    breed.
So captive Israel multiplied in chains,
A numerous exile, and enjoy'd her pains. 20
With grief and gladness mix'd, their mother
    view'd
Her martyr'd offspring, and their race re-
    new'd;
Their corps to perish, but their kind to last,
So much the deathless plant the dying fruit
    surpass'd.
    Panting and pensive now she rang'd
    alone,
And wander'd in the kingdoms, once her
    own.
The common hunt, tho' from their rage
    restrain'd
By sov'reign pow'r, her company disdain'd;
Grinn'd as they pass'd, and with a glaring
    eye
Gave gloomy signs of secret enmity. 30
'T is true, she bounded by, and tripp'd so
    light,
They had not time to take a steady sight,
For Truth has such a face and such a mien,
As to be lov'd needs only to be seen.
    The bloody Bear, an *Independent* beast,
Unlick'd to form, in groans her hate ex-
    press'd.
Among the timorous kind the *Quaking
    Hare*
Profess'd neutrality, but would not swear.
Next her the *buffoon* Ape, as atheists use,
Mimick'd all sects, and had his own to
    choose: 40
Still when the Lion look'd, his knees he
    bent,
And paid at church a courtier's compliment.
    The bristled *Baptist* Boar, impure as he,
(But whiten'd with the foam of sanctity,)
With fat pollutions fill'd the sacred place,
And mountains level'd in his furious race:
So first rebellion founded was in grace.
But since the mighty ravage which he made
In German forests had his guilt betray'd,
With broken tusks, and with a borrow'd
    name, 50
He shunn'd the vengeance, and conceal'd
    the shame;
So lurk'd in sects unseen. With greater guile
False Reynard fed on consecrated spoil:
The graceless beast by Athanasius first

Was chas'd from Nice; then, by Socinus
    nurs'd,
His impious race their blasphemy renew'd,
And nature's King thro' nature's optics
    view'd.
Revers'd, they view'd him lessen'd to their
    eye,
Nor in an infant could a God descry: 59
New swarming sects to this obliquely tend,
Hence they began, and here they all will
    end.
    What weight of ancient witness can pre-
    vail,
If private reason hold the public scale?
But, gracious God, how well dost thou pro-
    vide
For erring judgments an unerring guide!
Thy throne is darkness in th' abyss of light,
A blaze of glory that forbids the sight.
O teach me to believe thee thus conceal'd,
And search no farther than thyself reveal'd;
But her alone for my director take, 70
Whom thou hast promis'd never to forsake!
My thoughtless youth was wing'd with vain
    desires,
My manhood, long misled by wand'ring
    fires,
Follow'd false lights; and when their
    glimpse was gone,
My pride struck out new sparkles of her
    own.
Such was I, such by nature still I am,
Be thine the glory, and be mine the shame.
Good life be now my task: my doubts are
    done:
(What more could fright my faith, than
    Three in One?)
Can I believe eternal God could lie 80
Disguis'd in mortal mold and infancy?
That the great Maker of the world could
    die?
And after that trust my imperfect sense
Which calls in question his omnipotence?
Can I my reason to my faith compel,
And shall my sight, and touch, and taste
    rebel?
Superior faculties are set aside,
Shall their subservient organs be my guide?
Then let the moon usurp the rule of day, 89
And winking tapers show the sun his way;
For what my senses can themselves perceive,
I need no revelation to believe.
Can they who say the host should be de-
    scried

By sense, define a body glorified?
Impassible, and penetrating parts?
Let them declare by what mysterious arts
He shot that body thro' th' opposing might
Of bolts and bars impervious to the light,
And stood before his train confess'd in open
    sight.
   For since thus wondrously he pass'd, 't is
    plain,   100
One single place two bodies did contain.
And sure the same Omnipotence as well
Can make one body in more places dwell.
Let Reason then at her own quarry fly,
But how can finite grasp Infinity?
  'T is urg'd again that faith did first com-
    mence
By miracles, which are appeals to sense,
And thence concluded, that our sense must
    be
The motive still of credibility.
For latter ages must on former wait,   110
And what began belief, must propagate.
  But winnow well this thought, and you
    shall find
'T is light as chaff that flies before the wind.
Were all those wonders wrought by pow'r
    divine,
As means or ends of some more deep design?
Most sure as means, whose end was this
    alone,
To prove the Godhead of th' eternal Son.
God thus asserted: man is to believe
Beyond what sense and reason can conceive,
And for mysterious things of faith rely   120
On the proponent, Heav'n's authority.
If then our faith we for our guide admit,
Vain is the farther search of human wit,
As when the building gains a surer stay,
We take th' unuseful scaffolding away.
Reason by sense no more can understand;
The game is play'd into another hand.
Why choose we then like bilanders to creep
Along the coast, and land in view to keep,
When safely we may launch into the deep?
In the same vessel which our Savior bore, 131
Himself the pilot, let us leave the shore,
And with a better guide a better world ex-
    plore.
Could he his Godhead veil with flesh and
    blood
And not veil these again to be our food?
His grace in both is equal in extent,
The first affords us life, the second nourish-
    ment.

And if he can, why all this frantic pain
To construe what his clearest words contain,
And make a riddle what he made so plain?
To take up half on trust, and half to try, 141
Name it not faith, but bungling bigotry.
Both knave and fool the merchant we may
    call,
To pay great sums, and to compound the
    small:
For who would break with Heav'n, and
    would not break for all?
Rest then, my soul, from endless anguish
    freed:
Nor sciences thy guide, nor sense thy creed.
Faith is the best ensurer of thy bliss;
The bank above must fail before the ven-
    ture miss.
But heav'n and heav'n-born faith are far
    from thee,   150
Thou first apostate to divinity.
Unkennel'd range in thy Polonian plains;
A fiercer foe th' insatiate Wolf remains.
  Too boastful Britain, please thyself no
    more,
That beasts of prey are banish'd from thy
    shore:
The Bear, the Boar, and every savage name,
Wild in effect, tho' in appearance tame,
Lay waste thy woods, destroy thy blissful
    bow'r,
And, muzzled tho' they seem, the mutes de-
    vour.   159
More haughty than the rest, the wolfish race
Appear with belly gaunt, and famish'd face:
Never was so deform'd a beast of grace.
His ragged tail betwixt his legs he wears,
Close clapp'd for shame; but his rough crest
    he rears,
And pricks up his predestinating ears.
His wild disorder'd walk, his haggard eyes,
Did all the bestial citizens surprise.
Tho' fear'd and hated, yet he rul'd a while,
As captain or companion of the spoil.   169
Full many a year his hateful head had been
For tribute paid, nor since in Cambria seen:
The last of all the litter scap'd by chance,
And from Geneva first infested France.
Some authors thus his pedigree will trace,
But others write him of an upstart race:
Because of Wycliffe's brood no mark he
    brings
But his innate antipathy to kings.
These last deduce him from th' Helvetian
    kind.

Who near the Leman lake his consort lin'd:
That fi'ry Zuinglius first th' affection bred,
And meager Calvin bless'd the nuptial bed.
[1] In Israel some believe him whelp'd long
    since,   182
When the proud Sanhedrin oppress'd the
    prince,
Or, since he will be Jew, derive him high'r,
When Corah with his brethren did conspire
From Moses' hand the sov'reign sway to
    wrest,
And Aaron of his ephod to divest:
Till opening earth made way for all to pass,
And could not bear the burden of a class.
The Fox and he came shuffled in the dark,
If ever they were stow'd in Noah's ark: 191
Perhaps not made; for all their barking
    train
The Dog (a common species) will contain.
And some wild curs, who from their masters
    ran,
Abhorring the supremacy of man,
In woods and caves the rebel-race began.
    O happy pair, how well have you in-
    creas'd!
What ills in Church and State have you
    redress'd!
With teeth untried, and rudiments of claws,
Your first essay was on your native laws: 200
Those having torn with ease, and trampled
    down,
Your fangs you fasten'd on the miter'd
    crown,
And freed from God and monarchy your
    town.
What tho' your native kennel still be small,
Bounded betwixt a puddle and a wall;
Yet your victorious colonies are sent
Where the north ocean girds the continent.
Quicken'd with fire below, your monsters
    breed
In fenny Holland, and in fruitful Tweed:
And, like the first, the last effects to be 210
Drawn to the dregs of a democracy.
As, where in fields the fairy rounds are seen,
A rank sour herbage rises on the green;
So, springing where these midnight elves
    advance,
Rebellion prints the footsteps of the dance.
Such are their doctrines, such contempt they
    show
To Heav'n above, and to their prince below,
As none but traitors and blasphemers know.

[1] *Vid.* pref. to Heylin's *Hist. of Presb.*

God, like the tyrant of the skies, is plac'd,
And kings, like slaves, beneath the crowd
    debas'd.   220
So fulsome is their food that flocks refuse
To bite; and only dogs for physic use.
As, where the lightning runs along the
    ground,
No husbandry can heal the blasting wound,
Nor bladed grass, nor bearded corn suc-
    ceeds,
But scales of scurf and putrefaction breeds:
Such wars, such waste, such fiery tracks of
    dearth
Their zeal has left, and such a teemless
    earth.
But as the poisons of the deadliest kind 229
Are to their own unhappy coasts confin'd;
As only Indian shades of sight deprive,
And magic plants will but in Colchos thrive;
So Presbyt'ry and pestilential zeal
Can only flourish in a commonweal.
    From Celtic woods is chas'd the *wolfish*
    crew;
But ah! some pity e'en to brutes is due:
Their native walks, methinks, they might
    enjoy,
Curb'd of their native malice to destroy.
Of all the tyrannies on humankind,   239
The worst is that which persecutes the mind.
Let us but weigh at what offense we strike,
'T is but because we cannot think alike.
In punishing of this, we overthrow
The Laws of Nations and of Nature too.
Beasts are the subjects of tyrannic sway,
Where still the stronger on the weaker prey;
Man only of a softer mold is made,
Not for his fellows' ruin, but their aid:
Created kind, beneficent, and free,
The noble image of the Deity.   250
    One portion of informing fire was giv'n
To brutes, th' inferior family of heav'n:
The smith divine, as with a careless beat,
Struck out the mute creation at a heat;
But, when arriv'd at last to human race,
The Godhead took a deep consid'ring space;
And, to distinguish man from all the rest,
Unlock'd the sacred treasures of his breast;
And mercy mix'd with reason did impart,
One to his head, the other to his heart: 260
Reason to rule, but mercy to forgive:
The first is law, the last prerogative.
And like his mind his outward form ap-
    pear'd,
When, issuing naked to the wond'ring herd,

He charm'd their eyes; and, for they lov'd,
        they fear'd:
Not arm'd with horns of arbitrary might,
Or claws to seize their furry spoils in fight,
Or with increase of feet t' o'ertake 'em in
        their flight;
Of easy shape, and pliant ev'ry way;
Confessing still the softness of his clay,   270
And kind as kings upon their coronation
        day;
With open hands, and with extended space
Of arms, to satisfy a large embrace.
Thus kneaded up with milk, the new-made
        man
His kingdom o'er his kindred world began;
Till knowledge misapplied, misunderstood,
And pride of empire sour'd his balmy blood.
Then, first rebelling, his own stamp he
        coins;
The murth'rer Cain was latent in his loins:
And blood began its first and loudest cry 280
For diff'ring worship of the Deity.
Thus persecution rose, and farther space
Produc'd the mighty hunter of his race.
Not so the blessed Pan his flock increas'd,
Content to fold 'em from the famish'd
        beast:
Mild were his laws; the Sheep and harmless
        Hind
Were never of the persecuting kind.
Such pity now the pious Pastor shows,
Such mercy from the British Lion flows,
That both provide protection for their foes.
    O happy regions, Italy and Spain,   291
Which never did those monsters entertain!
The Wolf, the Bear, the Boar, can there ad-
        vance
No native claim of just inheritance.
And self-preserving laws, severe in show,
May guard their fences from th' invading
        foe.
Where birth has plac'd 'em, let 'em safely
        share
The common benefit of vital air.
Themselves unharmful, let them live un-
        harm'd;
Their jaws disabled, and their claws dis-
        arm'd: 300
Here, only in nocturnal howlings bold,
They dare not seize the Hind, nor leap the
        fold.
Mcre pow'rful, and as vigilant as they,
The Lion awfully forbids the prey.

Their rage repress'd, tho' pinch'd with
        famine sore,
They stand aloof, and tremble at his roar:
Much is their hunger, but their fear is
        more.
    These are the chief; to number o'er the
        rest,
And stand, like Adam, naming ev'ry beast,
Were weary work: nor will the Muse de-
        scribe   310
A slimy-born and sun-begotten tribe;
Who, far from steeples and their sacred
        sound,
In fields their sullen conventicles found.
These gross, half-animated lumps I leave;
Nor can I think what thoughts they can
        conceive.
But if they think at all, 't is sure no high'r
Than matter, put in motion, may aspire:
Souls that can scarce ferment their mass of
        clay;
So drossy, so divisible are they,
As would but serve pure bodies for allay: 320
Such souls as shards produce, such beetle
        things
As only buzz to heav'n with ev'ning wings;
Strike in the dark, offending but by chance,
Such are the blindfold blows of ignorance.
They know not beings, and but hate a
        name;
To them the Hind and Panther are the
        same.
    The Panther, sure the noblest, next the
        Hind,
And fairest creature of the spotted kind;
O, could her inborn stains be wash'd away,
She were too good to be a beast of prey! 330
How can I praise, or blame, and not offend,
Or how divide the frailty from the friend!
Her faults and virtues lie so mix'd that she
Nor wholly stands condemn'd, nor wholly
        free.
Then, like her injur'd Lion, let me speak:
He cannot bend her, and he would not
        break.
Unkind already, and estrang'd in part,
The Wolf begins to share her wand'ring
        heart.
Tho' unpolluted yet with actual ill,
She half commits, who sins but in her will.
If, as our dreaming Platonists report,   341
There could be spirits of a middle sort,
Too black for heav'n, and yet too white for
        hell,

Who just dropp'd halfway down, nor lower
  fell;
So pois'd, so gently she descends from high,
It seems a soft dismission from the sky.
Her house not ancient, whatsoe'er pretense
Her clergy heralds make in her defense;
A second century not halfway run,
Since the new honours of her blood begun.
A Lion, old, obscene, and furious made   351
By lust, compress'd her mother in a shade;
Then, by a left-hand marriage, weds the
  dame,
Cov'ring adult'ry with a specious name:
So Schism begot; and Sacrilege and she,
A well-match'd pair, got graceless Heresy.
God's and kings' rebels have the same good
  cause,
To trample down divine and human laws;
Both would be call'd reformers, and their
  hate
Alike destructive both to Church and State:
The fruit proclaims the plant; a lawless
  prince   361
By luxury reform'd incontinence;
By ruins, charity; by riots, abstinence.
Confessions, fasts, and penance set aside;
O, with what ease we follow such a guide,
Where souls are starv'd, and senses gratified!
Where marriage pleasures midnight pray'r
  supply,
And matin bells (a melancholy cry)
Are tun'd to merrier notes, *increase* and
  multiply!
Religion shows a rosy-color'd face;   370
Not hatter'd out with drudging works of
  grace:
A downhill reformation rolls apace.
What flesh and blood would crowd the nar-
  row gate,
Or, till they waste their pamper'd paunches,
  wait?
All would be happy at the cheapest rate.
  Tho' our lean faith these rigid laws has
  giv'n,
The full-fed Mussulman goes fat to heav'n;
For his Arabian prophet with delights
Of sense allur'd his Eastern proselytes.
The jolly Luther, reading him, began   380
T' interpret Scriptures by his Alcoran;
To grub the thorns beneath our tender feet,
And make the paths of paradise more sweet:
Bethought him of a wife ere halfway gone,
(For 't was uneasy travailing alone;)
And, in this masquerade of mirth and love,

Mistook the bliss of heav'n for Bacchanals
  above.
Sure he presum'd of praise, who came to
  stock
Th' ethereal pastures with so fair a flock;
Burnish'd, and batt'ning on their food, to
  show   390
The diligence of careful herds below.
  Our Panther, tho' like these she chang'd
  her head,
Yet, as the mistress of a monarch's bed,
Her front erect with majesty she bore,
The crosier wielded, and the miter wore.
Her upper part of decent discipline
Show'd affectation of an ancient line;
And Fathers, councils, Church and Church's
  head,
Were on her reverend phylacteries read.
But what disgrac'd and disavow'd the rest,
Was Calvin's brand, that stigmatiz'd the
  beast.   401
Thus, like a creature of a double kind,
In her own labyrinth she lives confin'd.
To foreign lands no sound of her is come,
Humbly content to be despis'd at home.
Such is her faith; where good cannot be had,
At least she leaves the refuse of the bad:
Nice in her choice of ill, tho' not of best,
And least deform'd, because reform'd the
  least.
In doubtful points betwixt her diff'ring
  friends,   410
Where one for substance, one for sign con-
  tends,
Their contradicting terms she strives to
  join;
Sign shall be substance, substance shall be
  sign.
A real presence all her sons allow,
And yet 't is flat idolatry to bow,
Because the Godhead 's there they know not
  how.
Her novices are taught that bread and wine
Are but the visible and outward sign,
Receiv'd by those who in communion join;
But th' inward grace, or the thing signified,
His blood and body, who to save us died, 421
The faithful this thing signified receive.
What is 't those faithful then partake or
  leave?
For what is signified and understood,
Is, by her own confession, flesh and blood.
Then, by the same acknowledgment, we
  know

They take the sign, and take the substance
    too.
The lit'ral sense is hard to flesh and blood,
But nonsense never can be understood.
    Her wild belief on ev'ry wave is toss'd; 430
But sure no Church can better morals boast.
True to her king her principles are found;
O that her practice were but half so sound!
Steadfast in various turns of state she stood,
And seal'd her vow'd affection with her
    blood;
Nor will I meanly tax her constancy,
That int'rest or obligement made the tie
(Bound to the fate of murder'd monarchy.)
Before the sounding ax so falls the vine,
Whose tender branches round the poplar
    twine.   440
She chose her ruin, and resign'd her life,
In death undaunted as an Indian wife:
A rare example! but some souls we see
Grow hard, and stiffen with adversity:
Yet these by fortune's favours are undone,
Resolv'd, into a baser form they run,
And bore the wind, but cannot bear the sun.
Let this be Nature's frailty, or her fate,
Or² Isgrim's counsel, her new-chosen mate;
Still she's the fairest of the fallen crew, 450
No mother more indulgent, but the true.
    Fierce to her foes, yet fears her force to
    try,
Because she wants innate authority;
For how can she constrain them to obey,
Who has herself cast off the lawful sway?
Rebellion equals all, and those who toil
In common theft will share the common
    spoil.
Let her produce the title and the right
Against her old superiors first to fight;
If she reform by text, ev'n that 's as plain
For her own rebels to reform again.   461
As long as words a diff'rent sense will bear,
And each may be his own interpreter,
Our airy faith will no foundation find;
The word 's a weathercock for ev'ry wind:
The Bear, the Fox, the Wolf, by turns pre-
    vail,
The most in pow'r supplies the present gale.
The wretched Panther cries aloud for aid
To Church and councils, whom she first be-
    tray'd;
No help from Fathers or tradition's train,
Those ancient guides she taught us to dis-
    dain.   471
    ² The Wolf.

And by that Scripture which she once
    abus'd
To reformation, stands herself accus'd.
What bills for breach of laws can she prefer,
Expounding which she owns herself may
    err?
And, after all her winding ways are tried,
If doubts arise, she slips herself aside
And leaves the private conscience for the
    guide.
If then that conscience set th' offender free,
It bars her claim to Church authority.   480
How can she censure, or what crime pre-
    tend,
But Scripture may be construed to defend?
Ev'n those whom for rebellion she transmits
To civil pow'r, her doctrine first acquits;
Because no disobedience can ensue,
Where no submission to a judge is due;
Each judging for himself, by her consent,
Whom thus absolv'd she sends to punish-
    ment.
Suppose the magistrate revenge her cause,
'T is only for transgressing human laws.   490
How answ'ring to its end a Church is made,
Whose pow'r is but to counsel and per-
    suade?
O solid rock, on which secure she stands!
Eternal house, not built with mortal hands!
O sure defense against th' infernal gate,
A patent during pleasure of the state!
    Thus is the Panther neither lov'd nor
    fear'd,
A mere mock queen of a divided herd;
Whom soon by lawful pow'r she might con-
    trol,
Herself a part submitted to the whole.   500
Then, as the moon who first receives the
    light
By which she makes our nether regions
    bright,
So might she shine, reflecting from afar
The rays she borrow'd from a better star;
Big with the beams which from her mother
    flow,
And reigning o'er the rising tides below:
Now, mixing with a savage crowd, she goes,
And meanly flatters her invet'rate foes;
Rul'd while she rules, and losing ev'ry hour
Her wretched remnants of precarious pow'r.
    One evening, while the cooler shade she
    sought,   511
Revolving many a melancholy thought,

Alone she walk'd, and look'd around in
    vain,
With rueful visage, for her vanish'd train:
None of her sylvan subjects made their
    court;
Levées and couchées pass'd without resort.
So hardly can usurpers manage well
Those whom they first instructed to rebel:
More liberty begets desire of more;
The hunger still increases with the store. 520
Without respect they brush'd along the
    wood,
Each in his clan, and, fill'd with loathsome
    food,
Ask'd no permission to the neighb'ring
    flood.
The Panther, full of inward discontent,
Since they would go, before 'em wisely went;
Supplying want of pow'r by drinking first,
As if she gave 'em leave to quench their
    thirst.
Among the rest, the Hind, with fearful face,
Beheld from far the common wat'ring place,
Nor durst approach; till with an awful roar
The sovereign Lion bade her fear no more.
Encourag'd thus she brought her younglings
    nigh,   532
Watching the motions of her patron's eye,
And drank a sober draught; the rest amaz'd
Stood mutely still, and on the stranger gaz'd;
Survey'd her part by part, and sought to
    find
The ten-horn'd monster in the harmless
    Hind,
Such as the Wolf and Panther had design'd.
They thought at first they dream'd; for 't
    was offense
With them to question certitude of sense,
Their guide in faith; but nearer when they
    drew,   541
And had the faultless object full in view,
Lord, how they all admir'd her heav'nly
    hue!
Some, who before her fellowship disdain'd,
Scarce, and but scarce, from inborn rage re-
    strain'd,
Now frisk'd about her, and old kindred
    feign'd.
Whether for love or int'rest, ev'ry sect
Of all the savage nation show'd respect:
The viceroy Panther could not awe the herd;
The more the company, the less they fear'd.
The surly Wolf with secret envy burst,   551

Yet could not howl; the Hind had seen him
    first:
But what he durst not speak, the Panther
    durst.
    For when the herd, suffic'd, did late repair
To ferny heaths, and to their forest lair,
She made a mannerly excuse to stay,
Proff'ring the Hind to wait her half the way:
That, since the sky was clear, an hour of
    talk
Might help her to beguile the tedious walk.
With much good will the motion was em-
    brac'd,   560
To chat a while on their adventures pass'd;
Nor had the grateful Hind so soon forgot
Her friend and fellow-suff'rer in the Plot.
Yet wond'ring how of late she grew
    estrang'd,
Her forehead cloudy, and her count'nance
    chang'd,
She thought this hour th' occasion would
    present
To learn her secret cause of discontent,
Which well she hop'd might be with ease
    redress'd,
Consid'ring her a well-bred civil beast,
And more a gentlewoman than the rest.   570
After some common talk what rumors ran,
The lady of the spotted muff began.

[1687]

A SONG FOR ST. CECILIA'S
DAY, 1687

I

From harmony, from heav'nly harmony
    This universal frame began:
    When Nature underneath a heap
      Of jarring atoms lay,
    And could not heave her head,
The tuneful voice was heard from high:
    "Arise, ye more than dead."
Then cold, and hot, and moist, and dry
In order to their stations leap,
    And Music's pow'r obey.   10
From harmony, from heav'nly harmony
    This universal frame began:
    From harmony to harmony
Thro' all the compass of the notes it ran,
The diapason closing full in Man.

II

What passion cannot Music raise and quell!
   When Jubal struck the corded shell,
His list'ning brethren stood around,
And, wond'ring, on their faces fell
To worship that celestial sound: 20
Less than a god they thought there could
      not dwell
   Within the hollow of that shell,
   That spoke so sweetly and so well.
What passion cannot Music raise and quell!

III

   The trumpet's loud clangor
     Excites us to arms
   With shrill notes of anger
    And mortal alarms.
   The double double double beat
    Of the thund'ring drum   30
Cries: "Hark! the foes come;
Charge, charge, 't is too late to retreat."

IV

   The soft complaining flute
   In dying notes discovers
   The woes of hopeless lovers,
Whose dirge is whisper'd by the warbling
     lute.

V

   Sharp violins proclaim
Their jealous pangs, and desperation,
Fury, frantic indignation,
Depth of pains, and height of passion,   46
   For the fair, disdainful dame.

VI

   But O! what art can teach,
   What human voice can reach
The sacred organ's praise?
   Notes inspiring holy love,
Notes that wing their heav'nly ways
   To mend the choirs above.

VII

Orpheus could lead the savage race,
And trees unrooted left their place,
   Sequacious of the lyre;   50

But bright Cecilia rais'd the wonder high'r:
When to her organ vocal breath was giv'n,
An angel heard, and straight appear'd,
   Mistaking earth for heav'n.

GRAND CHORUS

   As from the pow'r of sacred lays
    The spheres began to move,
   And sung the great Creator's praise
    To all the blessed above;
So, when the last and dreadful hour
This crumbling pageant shall devour, 60
The trumpet shall be heard on high,
The dead shall live, the living die,
And Music shall untune the sky.

LINES PRINTED UNDER THE ENGRAVED PORTRAIT OF MILTON,

IN TONSON'S FOLIO EDITION OF THE "PARADISE LOST," 1688

Three poets, in three distant ages born,
Greece, Italy, and England, did adorn.
The first in loftiness of thought surpass'd,
The next in majesty, in both the last:
The force of Nature could no farther go;
To make a third she join'd the former two.

TO MY DEAR FRIEND MR. CONGREVE, ON HIS COMEDY CALL'D THE DOUBLE-DEALER

Well then, the promis'd hour is come at last;
The present age of wit obscures the past:
Strong were our sires, and as they fought
   they writ,
Conqu'ring with force of arms, and dint of
   wit;
Theirs was the giant race, before the Flood;
And thus, when Charles return'd, our em-
   pire stood.
Like Janus he the stubborn soil manur'd,
With rules of husbandry the rankness cur'd:
Tam'd us to manners, when the stage was
   rude,

And boist'rous English wit with art indued.
Our age was cultivated thus at length,   11
But what we gain'd in skill we lost in
    strength.
Our builders were with want of genius
    cursed;
The second temple was not like the first:
Till you, the best Vitruvius, come at length,
Our beauties equal, but excel our strength.
Firm Doric pillars found your solid base,
The fair Corinthian crowns the higher
    space:
Thus all below is strength, and all above is
    grace.
In easy dialogue is Fletcher's praise;   20
He mov'd the mind, but had not power to
    raise.
Great Jonson did by strength of judgment
    please,
Yet, doubling Fletcher's force, he wants his
    ease.
In diff'ring talents both adorn'd their age;
One for the study, t'other for the stage:
But both to Congreve justly shall submit,
One match'd in judgment, both o'ermatch'd
    in wit.
In him all beauties of this age we see,
Etherege his courtship, Southerne's purity,
The satire, wit, and strength of Manly
    Wycherley.   30
All this in blooming youth you have
    achiev'd,
Nor are your foil'd contemporaries griev'd.
So much the sweetness of your manners
    move,
We cannot envy you, because we love.
Fabius might joy in Scipio, when he saw
A beardless consul made against the law,
And join his suffrage to the votes of Rome,
Tho' he with Hannibal was overcome.
Thus old Romano bow'd to Raphael's fame,
And scholar to the youth he taught became.
    O that your brows my laurel had sustain'd;
Well had I been depos'd, if you had reign'd!
The father had descended for the son;   43
For only you are lineal to the throne.
Thus, when the state one Edward did de-
    pose,
A greater Edward in his room arose.
But now, not I, but poetry is curst;
For Tom the Second reigns like Tom the
    First.
But let 'em not mistake my patron's part
Nor call his charity their own desert.   50

Yet this I prophesy: thou shalt be seen,
(Tho' with some short parenthesis be
    tween:)
High on the throne of wit; and, seated
    there,
Nor mine (that's little) but thy laurel wear.
Thy first attempt an early promise made;
That early promise this has more than paid.
So bold, yet so judiciously you dare,
That your least praise, is to be regular.
Time, place, and action may with pains be
    wrought,
But Genius must be born, and never can be
    taught.   60
This is your portion, this your native store:
Heav'n, that but once was prodigal before,
To *Shakespeare* gave as much; she cou'd not
    give him more.
    Maintain your post: that 's all the fame
    you need;
For 'tis impossible you shou'd proceed.
Already I am worn with cares and age,
And just abandoning th' ungrateful stage:
Unprofitably kept at heav'n's expense,
I live a rent-charge on his providence:
But you, whom ev'ry Muse and Grace
    adorn,   70
Whom I foresee to better fortune born,
Be kind to my remains; and oh defend,
Against your judgment, your departed
    friend!
Let not th' insulting foe my fame pursue;
But shade those laurels which descend to
    you:
And take for tribute what these lines ex-
    press;
You merit more; nor cou'd my love do less.
                                        [1694]

ALEXANDER'S FEAST

OR, THE POWER OF MUSIC; AN ODE
IN HONOUR OF ST. CECILIA'S DAY:

1697

I

'T was at the royal feast, for Persia won
        By Philip's warlike son:
        Aloft in awful state
        The godlike hero sate
        On his imperial throne:

His valiant peers were plac'd around;
Their brows with roses and with myrtles
      bound:
(So should desert in arms be crown'd.)
The lovely Thais, by his side,
Sate like a blooming Eastern bride   10
In flow'r of youth and beauty's pride.
   Happy, happy, happy pair!
     None but the brave,
     None but the brave,
     None but the brave deserves the fair.

CHORUS

   Happy, happy, happy pair!
     None but the brave,
     None but the brave,
     None but the brave deserves the fair.

II

Timotheus, plac'd on high   20
   Amid the tuneful choir,
   With flying fingers touch'd the lyre:
The trembling notes ascend the sky,
     And heav'nly joys inspire.
The song began from Jove,
Who left his blissful seats above,
(Such is the pow'r of mighty love.)
A dragon's fiery form belied the god:
Sublime on radiant spires he rode,
When he to fair Olympia press'd;   30
   And while he sought her snowy breast:
Then, round her slender waist he curl'd,
And stamp'd an image of himself, a sov'reign
     of the world.
The list'ning crowd admire the lofty sound,
"A present deity," they shout around:
"A present deity," the vaulted roofs rebound.
     With ravish'd ears
     The monarch hears,
     Assumes the god,
     Affects to nod,   40
And seems to shake the spheres.

CHORUS

     With ravish'd ears
     The monarch hears,
     Assumes the god,
     Affects to nod,
And seems to shake the spheres.

III

The praise of Bacchus then the sweet mu-
     sician sung,
   Of Bacchus ever fair and ever young:
   The jolly god in triumph comes;
   Sound the trumpets; beat the drums; 50
     Flush'd with a purple grace
     He shews his honest face:
Now give the hautboys breath; he comes, he
     comes.
   Bacchus, ever fair and young
   Drinking joys did first ordain;
   Bacchus' blessings are a treasure,
   Drinking is the soldier's pleasure;
     Rich the treasure,
     Sweet the pleasure,
     Sweet is pleasure after pain.   60

CHORUS

   Bacchus' blessings are a treasure,
   Drinking is the soldier's pleasure;
     Rich the treasure,
     Sweet the pleasure,
     Sweet is pleasure after pain.

IV

   Sooth'd with the sound, the king grew
     vain;
     Fought all his battles o'er again;
And thrice he routed all his foes; and thrice
     he slew the slain.
The master saw the madness rise,
His glowing cheeks, his ardent eyes;   70
And, while he heav'n and earth defied,
Chang'd his hand, and check'd his pride.
   He chose a mournful Muse,
     Soft pity to infuse;
He sung Darius great and good,
     By too severe a fate,
Fallen, fallen, fallen, fallen,
     Fallen from his high estate,
     And welt'ring in his blood;
Deserted, at his utmost need   80
By those his former bounty fed;
On the bare earth expos'd he lies,
With not a friend to close his eyes.
With downcast looks the joyless victor sate,
   Revolving in his alter'd soul
     The various turns of chance below;
   And, now and then, a sigh he stole,
     And tears began to flow.

CHORUS

Revolving in his alter'd soul
  The various turns of chance below;   90
And, now and then, a sigh he stole,
  And tears began to flow.

V

The mighty master smil'd to see
That love was in the next degree;
'T was but a kindred sound to move,
For pity melts the mind to love.
  Softly sweet, in Lydian measures,
  Soon he sooth'd his soul to pleasures.
"War," he sung, "is toil and trouble;
Honor, but an empty bubble.   100
  Never ending, still beginning,
  Fighting still, and still destroying:
  If the world be worth thy winning,
  Think, O think it worth enjoying.
  Lovely Thais sits beside thee,
  Take the good the gods provide thee."
The many rend the skies with loud applause;
So Love was crown'd, but Music won the
    cause.
  The prince, unable to conceal his pain,
    Gaz'd on the fair   110
    Who caus'd his care,
  And sigh'd and look'd, sigh'd and look'd,
  Sigh'd and look'd, and sigh'd again:
At length, with love and wine at once op-
    press'd,
The vanquish'd victor sunk upon her breast.

CHORUS

The prince, unable to conceal his pain,
    Gaz'd on the fair
    Who caus'd his care,
  And sigh'd and look'd, sigh'd and look'd,
  Sigh'd and look'd, and sigh'd again: 120
At length, with love and wine at once op-
    press'd,
The vanquish'd victor sunk upon her breast.

VI

Now strike the golden lyre again:
A louder yet, and yet a louder strain.
Break his bands of sleep asunder,
And rouse him, like a rattling peal of thun-
    der.
  Hark, hark, the horrid sound

Has rais'd up his head:
  As awak'd from the dead,
  And amaz'd, he stares around.   130
"Revenge, revenge!" Timotheus cries,
  "See the Furies arise!
  See the snakes that they rear,
  How they hiss in their hair,
  And the sparkles that flash from their eyes!
  Behold a ghastly band,
  Each a torch in his hand!
Those are Grecian ghosts, that in battle were
    slain,
  And unburied remain
  Inglorious on the plain: 140
  Give the vengeance due
  To the valiant crew.
Behold how they toss their torches on high,
  How they point to the Persian abodes,
And glitt'ring temples of their hostile gods!"
The princes applaud, with a furious joy;
And the king seiz'd a flambeau with zeal to
    destroy;
  Thais led the way,
  To light him to his prey,   149
And, like another Helen, fir'd another Troy.

CHORUS

And the king seiz'd a flambeau with zeal to
    destroy;
  Thais led the way,
  To light him to his prey,
And, like another Helen, fir'd another Troy.

VII

  Thus long ago,
  Ere heaving bellows learn'd to blow,
  While organs yet were mute;
  Timotheus, to his breathing flute,
    And sounding lyre,
Could swell the soul to rage, or kindle soft
    desire.   160
  At last, divine Cecilia came,
  Inventress of the vocal frame;
The sweet enthusiast, from her sacred store,
  Enlarg'd the former narrow bounds,
  And added length to solemn sounds,
With nature's mother wit, and arts unknown
    before.
  Let old Timotheus yield the prize,
    Or both divide the crown:
  He rais'd a mortal to the skies;
  She drew an angel down.   170

GRAND CHORUS

At last, divine Cecilia came,
Inventress of the vocal frame;
The sweet enthusiast, from her sacred store,
Enlarg'd the former narrow bounds,
And added length to solemn sounds,

With nature's mother wit, and arts unknown
before.
Let old Timotheus yield the prize,
Or both divide the crown:
He rais'd a mortal to the skies;
She drew an angel down.   180

AN ESSAY OF DRAMATIC POESY

TO THE READER

The drift of the ensuing Discourse was chiefly to vindicate the honour of our English writers, from the censure of those who unjustly prefer the French before them. This I intimate, lest any should think me so exceedingly vain, as to teach others an art which they understand much better than myself. But if this incorrect Essay, written in the country without the help of books or advice of friends, shall find any acceptance in the world, I promise to myself a better success of the Second Part, wherein I shall more fully treat of the virtues and faults of the English poets, who have written either in this, the epic, or the lyric way.

It was that memorable day, in the first summer of the late war, when our navy engaged the Dutch; a day wherein the two most mighty and best appointed fleets which any age had ever seen, disputed the command of the greater half of the globe, the commerce of nations, and the riches of the universe: while these vast floating bodies, on either side, moved against each other in parallel lines, and our countrymen, under the happy conduct of his Royal Highness, went breaking, by little and little, into the line of the enemies; the noise of the cannon from both navies reached our ears about the City, so that all men being alarmed with it, and in a dreadful suspense of the event, which they knew was then deciding, every one went following the sound as his fancy led him; and leaving the town almost empty, some took towards the park, some cross the river, others down it; all seeking the noise in the depth of silence.

Among the rest, it was the fortune of Eugenius, Crites, Lisideius, and Neander, to be in company together; three of them persons whom their wit and quality have made known to all the town; and whom I have chose to hide under these borrowed names, that they may not suffer by so ill a relation as I am going to make of their discourse.

Taking then a barge, which a servant of Lisideius had provided for them, they made haste to shoot the bridge, and left behind them that great fall of waters which hindered them from hearing what they desired: after which, having disengaged themselves from many vessels which rode at anchor in the Thames, and almost blocked up the passage towards Greenwich, they ordered the watermen to let fall their oars more gently; and then, every one favoring his own curiosity with a strict silence, it was not long ere they perceived the air to break about them like the noise of distant thunder, or of swallows in a chimney: those little undulations of sound, though seeming to retain somewhat of their first horror, which they had betwixt the fleets. After they had attentively listened till such time as the sound by little and little went from them, Eugenius, lifting up his head, and taking notice of it, was the first who congratulated to the rest that happy omen of our Nation's victory: adding, that we had but this to desire in confirmation of it, that we might hear no more of that noise, which was now leaving the English coast. When the rest had concurred in the same opinion, Crites, a person of a sharp judgment, and somewhat too delicate a taste in wit, which the world have mistaken in him for ill-nature, said, smiling to us, that if the concernment of this battle had not been so exceeding great, he could scarce have wished the victory at the price he knew he must pay for it, in being subject to the reading and hearing of so many ill verses as he was sure would be made on that subject. Adding that no argument could 'scape some of those eternal rhymers, who watch a battle with more diligence that the ravens and birds of prey; and the worst of them surest to be first in upon the quarry: while the better able, either out of modesty writ not at all, or set that due value upon their poems, as to let them be often desired and long expected. "There are some of those impertinent people of whom you speak," answered Lisideius, "who to my knowledge are already provided, either way, that they can produce not only a Panegyric upon the victory, but, if need be, a Funeral Elegy on the Duke; wherein, after they have crowned his valor with many laurels, they will at last deplore the odds under which he fell, concluding that his courage deserved a better destiny." All the company smiled at the conceit of Lisideius; but Crites, more eager than before, began to make particular exceptions against some writers, and said, the public magistrate ought to send betimes to forbid them; and that it concerned the peace and quiet of all honest people, that ill poets should be as well silenced as seditious preachers. "In my opinion," replied Eugenius, "you pursue your point too far; for as to my own particular, I am so great a lover of poesy, that I could wish them all rewarded who attempt but to do well; at least, I would not have them worse used than one of their brethren was by Sylla the Dictator:—*Quem in concione vidimus* (says Tully), *cum ei libellum malus poeta de populo subjecisset, quod epigramma in eum fecisset tantummodo alternis versibus longiusculis, statim ex iis rebus quas tunc vendebat jubere ei praemium tribui, sub ea conditione ne quid postea scriberet.*" "I could wish with all my heart," replied Crites, "that many whom we know were as bountifully thanked upon the same condition,—that they would never trouble us again. For amongst others, I have a moral apprehension of two poets, whom this victory, with the help of both her wings, will never be able to escape." "'Tis easy to guess whom you intend," said Lisideius; "and without naming them, I ask you, if one of them does not perpetually pay us with clenches upon words, and a certain clownish kind of raillery? if now and then he does not offer at a catachresis or Clevelandism, wresting and torturing a word into another meaning: in fine, if he be not one of those whom the French would call *un mauvais buffon*; one who is so much a well-willer to the satire, that he intends at least to spare no man; and though he cannot strike a blow to hurt any, yet he ought to be punished for the malice of the action, as our witches are justly hanged, because they think themselves to be such; and suffer deservedly for believing they did mischief, because they meant it." "You have described him," said Crites, "so exactly, that I am afraid to come after you with my other extremity of poetry. He is one of those who, having had some advantage of education and converse, knows better than the other what a poet should be, but puts it into practice more unluckily than any man; his style and matter are every where alike: he is the most calm, peaceable writer you ever read: he never disquiets your passions with the least concernment, but still leaves you in as even a temper as he found you; he is a very Leveller in poetry: he creeps along with ten little words in every line, and helps out his numbers with *For to*, and *Unto*, and all the pretty expletives he can find, till he drags them to the end of another line; while the sense is left tired half way behind it: he doubly starves all his verses, first for want of thought, and then of expression; his poetry neither has wit in it, nor seems to have it; like him in Martial:

Pauper videri Cinna *vult, et est pauper.*

"He affects plainness, to cover his

want of imagination: when he writes the serious way, the highest flight of his fancy is some miserable antithesis, or seeming contradiction; and in the comic he is still reaching at some thin conceit, the ghost of a jest, and that too flies before him, never to be caught; these swallows which we see before us on the Thames are the just resemblance of his wit: you may observe how near the water they stoop, how many proffers they make to dip, and yet how seldom they touch it; and when they do, it is but the surface: they skim over it but to catch a gnat, and then mount into the air and leave it."

"Well, gentlemen," said Eugenius, "you may speak your pleasure of these authors; but though I and some few more about the town may give you a peaceable hearing, yet assure yourselves, there are multitudes who would think you malicious and them injured: especially him whom you first described; he is the very Withers of the city: they have bought more editions of his works than would serve to lay under all their pies at the Lord Mayor's Christmas. When his famous poem first came out in the year 1660, I have seen them reading it in the midst of 'Change time; nay so vehement they were at it, that they lost their bargain by the candles' ends; but what will you say if he has been received amongst great persons? I can assure you he is, this day, the envy of one who is lord in the art of quibbling, and who does not take it well that any man should intrude so far into his province." "All I would wish," replied Crites, "is, that they who love his writings, may still admire him, and his fellow poet: *Qui Bavium non odit, etc.*, is curse sufficient." "And farther," added Lisideius, "I believe there is no man who writes well, but would think he had hard measure, if their admirers should praise anything of his: *Nam quos contemnimus, eorum quoque laudes contemnimus*." "There are so few who write well in this age," says Crites, "that methinks any praises

should be welcome; they neither rise to the dignity of the last age, nor to any of the Ancients: and we may cry out of the writers of this time, with more reason than Petronius of his, *Pace vestra liceat dixisse, primi omnium eloquentium perdidistis:* you have debauched the true old poetry so far, that Nature, which is the soul of it, is not in any of your writings."

"If your quarrel," said Eugenius, "to those who now write, be grounded only on your reverence to antiquity, there is no man more ready to adore those great Greeks and Romans than I am: but on the other side, I cannot think so contemptibly of the age in which I live, or so dishonourably of my own country, as not to judge we equal the Ancients in most kinds of poesy, and in some surpass them; neither know I any reason why I may not be as zealous for the reputation of our age as we find the Ancients themselves were in reference to those who lived before them. For you hear your Horace saying,

Indignor quidquam reprehendi, non quia crasse
Compositum, illepideve putetur, sed quia nuper.

And after:

Si meliora dies, ut vina, poemata reddit,
Scire velim, pretim chartis quotus arroget annus?

"But I see I am engaging in a wide dispute, where the arguments are not like to reach close on either side; for Poesy is of so large an extent, and so many both of the Ancients and Moderns have done well in all kinds of it, that in citing one against the other, we shall take up more time this evening than each man's occasions will allow him: therefore I would ask Crites to what part of poesy he would confine his arguments, and whether he would defend the general cause of the Ancients against the Moderns, or oppose any age of the Moderns against this of ours?"

Crites, a little while considering upon this demand, told Eugenius, that if he pleased, he would limit their dispute to Dramatic Poesy; in which he thought it not difficult to prove, either that the Ancients were superior to the Moderns, or the last age to this of ours.

Eugenius was somewhat surprised, when he heard Crites make this choice of that subject. "For ought I see," said he, "I have undertaken a harder province than I imagined; for though I never judged the plays of the Greek or Roman poets comparable to ours, yet, on the other side, those we now see acted come short of many which were written in the last age: but my comfort is, if we are overcome, it will be only by our own countrymen: and if we yield to them in this one part of poesy, we more surpass them in all the other: for in the epic or lyric way, it will be hard for them to show us one such amongst them, as we have many now living, or who lately were: they can produce nothing so courtly writ, or which expresses so much the conversation of a gentleman, as Sir John Suckling; nothing so even, sweet, and flowing as Mr. Waller; nothing so majestic, so correct, as Sir John Denham; nothing so elevated, so copious, and full of spirit as Mr. Cowley; as for the Italian, French, and Spanish plays, I can make it evident, that those who now write surpass them; and that the Drama is wholly ours."

All of them were thus far of Eugenius his opinion, that the sweetness of English verse was never understood or practised by our fathers; even Crites himself did not much oppose it; and every one was willing to acknowledge how much our poesy is improved by the happiness of some writers yet living; who first taught us to mould our thoughts into easy and significant words,—to retrench the superfluities of expression,—and to make our rhyme so properly a part of the verse, that it should never mislead the sense, but itself be led and governed by it.

Eugenius was going to continue this discourse, when Lisideius told him that it was necessary, before they proceeded further, to take a standing measure of their controversy; for how was it possible to be decided who writ the best plays, before we know what a play should be? But, this once agreed on by both parties, each might have recourse to it, either to prove his own advantages, or to discover the failings of his adversary.

He had no sooner said this, but all desired the favour of him to give the definition of a play; and they were the more importunate, because neither Aristotle, nor Horace, nor any other, who had writ of that subject, had ever done it.

Lisideius, after some modest denials, at last confessed he had a rude notion of it; indeed, rather a description than a definition; but which served to guide him in his private thoughts, when he was to make a judgment of what others writ: that he conceived a play ought to be, *A just and lively image of human nature, representing its passions and humours, and the changes of fortune to which it is subject, for the delight and instruction of mankind.*

This definition, though Crites raised a logical objection against it— that it was only *a genere et fine,* and so not altogether perfect, was yet well received by the rest; and after they had given order to the watermen to turn their barge, and row softly, that they might take the cool of the evening in their return, Crites, being desired by the company to begin, spoke on behalf of the Ancients, in this manner:—

"If confidence presage a victory, Eugenius, in his own opinion, has already triumphed over the Ancients: nothing seems more easy to him, than to overcome those whom it is our greatest praise to have imitated well; for we do not only build upon their foundations, but by their models. Dramatic Poesy had time enough, reckoning from Thespis (who first invented it) to Aristophanes, to be born, to grow up, and to flourish in maturity. It has been observed of arts and sciences, that in one and the same century they have arrived to great perfection; and no wonder, since every age has a kind of universal genius, which inclines those that live in it to some particular studies: the work then, being pushed on by many hands, must of necessity go forward.

"Is it not evident, in these last hundred years, when the study of philosophy has been the business of all the Virtuosi in Christendom, that almost a new Nature has been revealed to us? That more errors of the school have been detected, more useful experiments in philosophy have been made, more noble secrets in optics, medicine, anatomy, astronomy, discovered, than in all those credulous and doting ages from Aristotle to us? —so true it is, that nothing spreads more fast than science, when rightly and generally cultivated.

"Add to this, the more than common emulation that was in those times of writing well; which though it be found in all ages and all persons that pretend to the same reputation, yet Poesy, being then in more esteem than now it is, had greater honours decreed to the professors of it, and consequently the rivalship was more high between them; they had judges ordained to decide their merit, and prizes to reward it; and historians have been diligent to record of Eschylus, Euripides, Sophocles, Lycophron, and the rest of them, both who they were that vanquished in these wars of the theatre, and how often they were crowned: while the Asian kings and Grecian commonwealths scarce afforded them a nobler subject than the unmanly luxuries of a debauched court, or giddy intrigues of a factious city:—*Alit aemulatio ingenia* (says Paterculus) *et nunc invidia, nunc admiratio incitationem accendit:* Emulation is the spur of wit; and sometimes envy, sometimes admiration, quickens our endeavours.

"But now, since the rewards of honour are taken away, that virtuous emulation is turned into direct malice; yet so slothful, that it contents itself to condemn and cry down others, without attempting to do better: it is a reputation too unprofitable, to take the necessary pains for it; yet, wishing they had it, that desire is incitement enough to hinder others from it. And this, in short, Eugenius, is the reason why you have now so few good poets, and so many severe judges. Certainly, to imitate the Ancients well, much labour and long study is required; which pains, I have already shown, our poets would want encouragement to take, if yet they had ability to go through the work. Those Ancients have been faithful imitators and wise observers of that Nature which is so torn and ill represented in our plays; they have handed down to us a perfect resemblance of her; which we, like ill copiers, neglecting to look on, have rendered monstrous, and disfigured. But, that you may know how much you are indebted to those your masters, and be ashamed to have so ill requited them, I must remember you, that all the rules by which we practise the Drama at this day (either such as relate to the justness and symmetry of the plot, or the episodical ornaments, such as descriptions, narrations, and other beauties, which are not essential to the play), were delivered to us from the observations which Aristotle made, of those poets, who either lived before him, or were his contemporaries: we have added nothing of our own, except we have the confidence to say our wit is better; of which, none boast in this our age, but such as understand not theirs. Of that book which Aristotle has left us, περὶ τῆς Ποιητικῆς, Horace his *Art of Poetry* is an excellent comment, and, I believe, restores to us that Second Book of his concerning *Comedy*, which is wanting in him.

"Out of these two have been extracted the famous Rules, which the French call *Des Trois Unités*, or, The Three Unities, which ought to be observed in every regular play; namely, of Time, Place, and Action.

"The Unity of Time they comprehend in twenty-four hours, the compass of a natural day, or as near it as it can be contrived; and the reason of it is obvious to every one,—that the time of the feigned action, or fable of the play, should be proportioned as near as can be to the duration of that time in which it is represented: since, therefore, all plays are acted on the theatre in the space of time much within the compass of twenty-four hours, that play is to be thought the nearest imitation of nature, whose plot or action is confined within that time; and, by the same rule which concludes this general proportion of time, it follows, that all the parts of it are (as near as may be) to be equally subdivided; namely, that one act take not up the supposed time of half a day, which is out of proportion to the rest; since the other four are then to be straitened within the compass of the remaining half: for it is unnatural that one act, which being spoke or written is not longer than the rest, should be supposed longer by the audience; it is therefore the poet's duty, to take care that no act should be imagined to exceed the time in which it is represented on the stage; and that the intervals and inequalities of time be supposed to fall out between the acts.

"This rule of time, how well it has been observed by the Ancients, most of their plays will witness; you see them in their tragedies (wherein to follow this rule is certainly most difficult), from the very beginning of their plays, falling close into that part of the story which they intend for the action or principal object of it, leaving the former part to be delivered by narration: so that they set the audience, as it were, at the post where the race is to be concluded; and, saving them the tedious expectation of seeing the poet set out and ride the beginning of the course, they suffer you not to behold him, till he is in sight of the goal, and just upon you.

"For the second Unity, which is that of Place, the Ancients meant by it, that the scene ought to be continued through the play, in the same place where it was laid in the beginning: for, the stage on which it is represented being but one and the same place, it is unnatural to conceive it many,—and those far distant from one another. I will not deny but, by the variation of painted scenes, the fancy, which in these cases will contribute to its own deceit, may sometimes imagine it several places, with some appearance of probability; yet it still carries the greater likelihood of truth if those places be supposed so near each other as in the same town or city; which may all be comprehended under the larger denomination of one place; for a greater distance will bear no proportion to the shortness of time which is allotted, in the acting, to pass from one of them to another; for the observation of this, next to the Ancients, the French are to be most commended. They tie themselves so strictly to the Unity of Place that you never see in any of their plays a scene changed in the middle of an act: if the act begins in a garden, a street, or chamber, 'tis ended in the same place; and that you may know it to be the same, the stage is so supplied with persons, that it is never empty all the time: he who enters second, has business with him who was on before; and before the second quits the stage, a third appears who has business with him. This Corneille calls *la liaison des scènes*, the continuity or joining of the scenes: and 'tis a good mark of a well-contrived play, when all the persons are known to each other, and every one of them has some affairs with all the rest.

"As for the third Unity, which is that of Action, the Ancients meant no other by it than what the logicians do by their *finis*, the end or scope of any action; that which is the first in intention, and last in execution: now the poet is to aim at one great and complete action, to the carrying on of which all things in his play, even the very obstacles, are to be subservient; and the reason of this is as evident as any of the former. For two actions equally laboured and driven on by the writer, would destroy the unity of the poem; it would be no longer one play, but two: not but that there may be many actions in a play, as Ben Jonson has observed in his *Discoveries*; but they must be all subservient to the great one, which our language happily expresses in the name of *under-plots*: such as in Terence's *Eunuch* is the difference and reconcilement of Thais and Phædria, which is not the chief business of the play but promotes the marriage of Chærea and Chremes's sister, principally intended by the poet. There ought to be but one action, says Corneille, that is, one complete action, which leaves the mind of the audience in a full repose; but this cannot be brought to pass but by many other imperfect actions, which conduce to it, and hold the audience in a delightful suspense of what will be.

"If by these rules (to omit many other drawn from the precepts and practice of the Ancients) we should judge our modern plays, 'tis probable that few of them would endure the trial: that which should be the business of a day, takes up in some of them an age; instead of one action, they are the epitomes of a man's life; and for one spot of ground, which the stage should represent, we are sometimes in more countries than the map can show us.

"But if we allow the Ancients to have contrived well, we must acknowledge them to have written better. Questionless we are deprived of a great stock of wit in the loss of Menander among the Greek poets, and of Cæcilius, Afranius, and Varius, among the Romans; we may guess at Menander's excellency by the plays of Terence, who translated some of his; and yet wanted so much of

him, that he was called by C. Cæsar the half-Menander; and may judge of Varius, by the testimonies of Horace, Martial, and Velleius Paterculus. 'Tis probable that these, could they be recovered, would decide the controversy; but so long as Aristophanes and Plautus are extant, while the tragedies of Euripides, Sophocles, and Seneca, are in our hands, I can never see one of those plays which are now written but it increases my admiration of the Ancients. And yet I must acknowledge further, that to admire them as we ought, we should understand them better than we do. Doubtless many things appear flat to us, the wit of which depended on some custom or story, which never came to our knowledge; or perhaps on some criticism in their language, which being so long dead, and only remaining in their books, 'tis not possible they should make us understand perfectly. To read Macrobius, explaining the propriety and elegancy of many words in Virgil, which I had before passed over without consideration as common things, is enough to assure me that I ought to think the same of Terence; and that in the purity of his style (which Tully so much valued that he ever carried his works about him) there is yet left in him great room for admiration, if I knew but where to place it. In the meantime I must desire you to take notice that the greatest man of the last age, Ben Jonson, was willing to give place to them in all things: he was not only a professed imitator of Horace, but a learned plagiary of all the others; you track him everywhere in their snow: if Horace, Lucan, Petronius Arbiter, Seneca, and Juvenal, had their own from him, there are few serious thoughts which are new in him: you will pardon me, therefore, if I presume he loved their fashion, when he wore their clothes. But since I have otherwise a great veneration for him, and you, Eugenius, prefer him above all other poets, I will use no farther argument to you than his example:

I will produce before you Father Ben, dressed in all the ornaments and colours of the Ancients; you will need no other guide to our party, if you follow him; and whether you consider the bad plays of our age, or regard the good plays of the last, both the best and the worst of the modern poets will equally instruct you to admire the Ancients."

Crites had no sooner left speaking, but Eugenius, who had waited with some impatience for it, thus began:

"I have observed in your speech, that the former part of it is convincing as to what the Moderns have profited by the rules of the Ancients; but in the latter you are careful to conceal how much they have excelled them; we own all the helps we have from them, and want neither veneration nor gratitude, while we acknowledge that, to overcome them, we must make use of the advantages we have received from them: but to these assistances we have joined our own industry; for, had we sat down with a full imitation of them, we might then have lost somewhat of the old perfection, but never acquired any that was new. We draw not therefore after their lines, but those of Nature; and having the life before us, besides the experience of all they knew, it is no wonder if we hit some airs and features which they have missed. I deny not what you urge of arts and sciences, that they have flourished in some ages more than others; but your instance in philosophy makes for me: for if natural causes be more known now than in the time of Aristotle, because more studied, it follows that poesy and other arts may, with the same pains, arrive still nearer to perfection; and, that granted, it will rest for you to prove that they wrought more perfect images of human life than we; which seeing in your discourse you have avoided to make good, it shall now be my task to show you some part of their defects, and some few excellencies of the Moderns. And I think there is none among us

can imagine I do it enviously, or with purpose to detract from them; for what interest of fame or profit can the living lose by the reputation of the dead? On the other side, it is a great truth which Velleius Paterculus affirms: *Audita visis libentius laudamus; et præsentia invidia, præterita admiratione prosequimur; et his nos obrui, illis instrui credimus:* that praise or censure is certainly the most sincere, which unbribed posterity shall give us.

"Be pleased then in the first place to take notice that the Greek poesy, which Crites has affirmed to have arrived to perfection in the reign of the Old Comedy, was so far from it that the distinction of it into acts was not known to them; or if it were, it is yet so darkly delivered to us that we cannot make it out.

"All we know of it is from the singing of their Chorus; and that too is so uncertain, that in some of their plays we have reason to conjecture they sung more than five times. Aristotle indeed divides the integral parts of a play into four. First, the *Protasis*, or entrance, which gives light only to the characters of the persons, and proceeds very little into any part of the action. Secondly, the *Epitasis*, or working up of the plot; where the play grows warmer, the design or action of it is drawing on, and you see something promising that it will come to pass. Thirdly, the *Catastasis*, called by the Romans, *Status*, the height and full growth of the play: we may call it properly the counter-turn, which destroys that expectation, imbroils the action in new difficulties, and leaves you far distant from that hope in which it found you; as you may have observed in a violent stream resisted by a narrow passage,—it runs round to an eddy, and carries back the waters with more swiftness than it brought them on. Lastly, the *Catastrophe*, which the Grecians called λύσις the French *le dénouement*, and we the discovery, or unravelling of the plot: there you see all things set-

tling again upon their first foundations; and, the obstacles which hindered the design or action of the play
once removed, it ends with that resemblance of truth and nature, that
the audience are satisfied with the
conduct of it. Thus this great man
delivered to us the image of a play;
and I must confess it is so lively, that
from thence much light has been de- 10
rived to the forming it more perfectly
into acts and scenes: but what poet
first limited to five the number of the
acts, I know not; only we see it so
firmly established in the time of Horace, that he gives it for a rule in comedy,—*Neu brevior quinto, neu sit
productior actu.* So that you see the
Grecians cannot be said to have con-
summated this art; writing rather by 20
entrances than by acts, and having
rather a general indigested notion of
a play, than knowing how and where
to bestow the particular graces of it.

"But since the Spaniards at this day
allow but three acts, which they call
Jornadas, to a play, and the Italians
in many of theirs follow them, when
I condemn the Ancients, I declare it
is not altogether because they have 30
not five acts to every play, but because they have not confined themselves to one certain number: it is
building an house without a model;
and when they succeeded in such undertakings, they ought to have sacrificed to Fortune, not to the Muses.

"Next, for the plot, which Aristotle
called Τὸ μύθος and often τῶν
πραγμάτων σύνθεσις and from him the 40
Romans Fabula; it has already been
judiciously observed by a late writer,
that in their tragedies it was only
some tale derived from Thebes or
Troy, or at least something that happened in those two ages; which was
worn so threadbare by the pens of all
the epic poets, and even by tradition
itself of the talkative Greeklings (as
Ben Jonson calls them), that before 50
it came upon the stage it was already
known to all the audience: and the
people, so soon as ever they heard the
name of Œdipus, knew as well as the

poet, that he had killed his father by
a mistake, and committed incest with
his mother, before the play; that they
were now to hear of a great plague,
an oracle, and the ghost of Laius: so
that they sat with a yawning kind
of expectation, till he was to come
with his eyes pulled out, and speak
a hundred or more verses in a tragic
tone, in complaint of his misfortunes.
But one Œdipus, Hercules, or Medea,
had been tolerable: poor people,
they escaped not so good cheap; they
had still the *chapon bouillé* set before them, till their appetites were
cloyed with the same dish, and, the
novelty being gone, the pleasure vanished; so that one main end of Dra- 20
matic Poesy in its definition, which
was to cause delight, was of consequence destroyed.

"In their comedies, the Romans
generally borrowed their plots from
the Greek poets; and theirs was commonly a little girl stolen or wandered
from her parents, brought back unknown to the city, there got with
child by some lewd young fellow,
who, by the help of his servant, cheats 30
his father; and when her time comes,
to cry,—*Juno Lucina, fer opem,*—one
or other sees a little box or cabinet
which was carried away with her, and
so discovers her to her friends, if some
god do not prevent it, by coming
down in a machine, and taking the
thanks of it to himself.

"By the plot you may guess much
of the characters of the persons. An 40
old father, who would willingly, before he dies, see his son well married;
his debauched son, kind in his nature
to his mistress, but miserably in want
of money; a servant or slave, who has
so much wit to strike in with him,
and help to dupe his father; a brag-
gadochio captain, parasite, and a lady
of pleasure.

"As for the poor honest maid, on 50
whom the story is built, and who
ought to be one of the principal actors in the play, she is commonly a
mute in it: she has the breeding of
the old Elizabeth way, which was for

maids to be seen and not to be heard; and it is enough you know she is willing to be married, when the fifth act requires it.

"These are plots built after the Italian mode of houses, you see through them all at once: the characters are indeed the imitation of Nature, but so narrow, as if they had imitated only an eye or an hand, and did not dare to venture on the lines of a face, or the proportion of a body.

"But in how strait a compass soever they have bounded their plots and characters, we will pass it by, if they have regularly pursued them, and perfectly observed those three Unities of Time, Place, and Action; the knowledge of which you say is derived to us from them. But in the first place give me leave to tell you, that the Unity of Place, however it might be practised by them, was never any of their rules: we neither find it in Aristotle, Horace, or any who have written of it, till in our age the French poets first made it a precept of the stage. The Unity of Time, even Terence himself, who was the best and most regular of them, has neglected: his *Heautontimorumenos*, or *Self-Punisher*, takes up visibly two days, says Scaliger, the two first acts concluding the first day, the three last the day ensuing; and Euripides, in tying himself to one day, has committed an absurdity never to be forgiven him; for in one of his tragedies he has made Theseus go from Athens to Thebes, which was about forty English miles, under the walls of it to give battle, and appear victorious in the next act; and yet, from the time of his departure to the return of the Nuntius, who gives the relation of his victory, Aethra and the Chorus have but thirty-six verses; which is not for every mile a verse.

"The like error is as evident in Terence his *Eunuch*, when Laches, the old man, enters by mistake into the house of Thais; where, betwixt his exit and the entrance of Pythias, who comes to give ample relation of the disorders he has raised within. Parmeno, who was left upon the stage, has not above five lines to speak. *C'est bien employer un temps si court*, says the French poet, who furnished me with one of the observations: and almost all their tragedies will afford us examples of the like nature.

"It is true, they have kept the continuity, or, as you called it *liaison des scènes*, somewhat better: two do not perpetually come in together, talk, and go out together; and other two succeed them, and do the same throughout the act, which the English call by the name of single scenes; but the reason is, because they have seldom above two or three scenes, properly so called, in every act; for it is to be accounted a new scene, not only every time the stage is empty; but every person who enters, though to others makes it so; because he introduces a new business. Now the plots of their plays being narrow, and the persons few, one of their acts was written in a less compass than one of our well-wrought scenes; and yet they are often deficient even in this. To go no further than Terence; you find in the *Eunuch*, Antipho entering single in the midst of the third act, after Chremes and Pythias were gone off; in the same play you have likewise Dorias beginning the fourth act alone; and after she had made a relation of what was done at the Soldiers' entertainment (which by the way was very inartificial, because she was presumed to speak directly to the audience, and to acquaint them with what was necessary to be known, but yet should have been so contrived by the poet as to have been told by persons of the drama to one another, and so by them to have come to the knowledge of the people), she quits the stage, and Phædria enters next, alone likewise: he also gives you an account of himself, and of his returning from the country, in monologue: to which unnatural way of narration Terence is subject in all his plays. In his *Adel-*

phi, or *Brothers*, Syrus and Demea enter after the scene was broken by the departure of Sostrata, Geta, and Canthara; and indeed you can scarce look unto any of his comedies, where you will not presently discover the same interruption.

"But as they have failed both in laying of their plots, and in the management, swerving from the rules of their own art by misrepresenting Nature to us, in which they have ill satisfied one intention of a play, which was delight; so in the instructive part they have erred worse: instead of punishing vice and rewarding virtue, they have often shewn a prosperous wickedness, and unhappy piety: they have set before us a bloody image of revenge in Medea, and given her dragons to convey her safe from punishment; a Priam and Astyanax murdered, and Cassandra ravished, and the lust and murder ending in the victory of him who acted them: in short, there is no indecorum in any of our modern plays, which if I would excuse, I could not shadow with some authority from the Ancients.

"And one farther note of them let me leave you: tragedies and comedies were not writ then as they are now, promiscuously, by the same person; but he who found his genius bending to the one, never attempted the other way. This is so plain, that I need not instance to you, that Aristophanes, Plautus, Terence, never any of them writ a tragedy; Æschylus, Euripides, Sophocles, and Seneca, never meddled with comedy: the sock and buskin were not worn by the same poet. Having then so much care to excel in one kind, very little is to be pardoned them, if they miscarried in it; and this would lead me to the consideration of their wit, had not Crites given me sufficient warning not to be too bold in my judgment of it; because, the languages being dead, and many of the customs and little accidents on which it depended lost to us, we are not competent judges of it. But though I grant that here and there

we may miss the application of a proverb or a custom, yet a thing well said will be wit in all languages; and though it may lose something in translation, yet to him who reads it in the original, 'tis still the same: he has an idea of its excellency, though it cannot pass from his mind into any other expression or words than those in which he finds it. When Phædria, in the *Eunuch*, had a command from his mistress to be absent two days, and, encouraging himself to go through with it, said, *Tandem ego non illa caream, si sit opus, vel totum triduum?*—Parmeno, to mock the softness of his master, lifting up his hands and eyes, cries out, as it were in admiration, *Hui! universum triduum!* the elegancy of which *universum*, though it cannot be rendered in our language, yet leaves an impression on our souls: but this happens seldom in him; in Plautus oftener, who is infinitely too bold in his metaphors and coining words, out of which many times his wit is nothing; which questionless was one reason why Horace falls upon him so severely in those verses:

Sed proavi nostri Plautinos et numeros et
Laudavere sales, nimium patienter utrumque.
Ne dicam stolide.

For Horace himself was cautious to obtrude a new word on his readers, and makes custom and common use the best measure of receiving it into our writings:

Multa renascentur quae nunc cecidere, ca-
  dentque
Quae nunc sunt in honore vocabula, si volet
  usus,
Quem penes arbitrium est, et jus, et norma
  loquendi.

"The not observing this rule is that which the world has blamed in our satirist, Cleveland: to express a thing hard and unnaturally, is his new way of elocution. 'Tis true, no poet but may sometimes use a catachresis: Virgil does it—

Mistaque ridenti colocasia fundet acantho—

in his eclogue of Pollio; and in his seventh *Æneid*:

. . . . . . mirantur et undae,
Miratur nemus insuetum fulgentia longe
Scuta virum fluvio pictasque innare carinas.

And Ovid once so modestly, that he
asks leave to do it:

. . . . . . quem, si verbo audacia detur,
Haud metuam summi dixisse Palatia caeli.

calling the court of Jupiter by the
name of Augustus his palace; though   10
in another place he is more bold,
where he says,—*et longas visent Capi-*
tolia pompas. But to do this always,
and never be able to write a line without it, though it may be admired by
some few pedants, will not pass upon
those who know that wit is best conveyed to us in the most easy language;
and is most to be admired when a
great thought comes dressed in words   20
so commonly received, that it is understood by the meanest apprehensions, as the best meat is the most
easily digested: but we cannot read
a verse of Cleveland's without making a face at it, as if every word were
a pill to swallow: he gives us many
times a hard nut to break our teeth,
without a kernel for our pains. So
that there is this difference betwixt   30
his Satires and doctor Donne's; that
the one gives us deep thoughts in
common language, though rough cadence; the other gives us common
thoughts in abstruse words: 'tis true,
in some places his wit is independent
of his words, as in that of the *Rebel*
Scot:

Had Cain been Scot, God would have chang'd
*   his doom;*   40
Not forc'd him wander, but confin'd him
*   home.*

"*Si sic omnia dixisset!* This is wit
in all languages: it is like Mercury,
never to be lost or killed:—and so \that
other—

For Beauty, like white powder, makes no
*   noise,*
And yet the silent hypocrite destroys.

You see the last line is highly meta-   50
phorical, but it is so soft and gentle,
that it does not shock us as we read
it.

"But, to return from whence I have
digressed, to the consideration of the
Ancients' writing, and their wit; (of
which by this time you will grant us
in some measure to be fit judges).
Though I see many excellent thoughts
in Seneca, yet he of them who had a
genius most proper for the stage, was
Ovid; he had a way of writing so fit
to stir up a pleasing admiration and
concernment, which are the objects
of a tragedy, and to show the various
movements of a soul combating betwixt two different passions, that had
he lived in our age, or in his own
could have writ with our advantages,
no man but must have yielded to
him; and therefore I am confident the
Medea is none of his: for, though I
esteem it for the gravity and senten-
tiousness of it, which he himself concludes to be suitable to a tragedy,—
Omne genus scripti gravitate tragœdia
vincit,—yet it moves not my soul
enough to judge that he, who in the
epic way wrote things so near the
drama as the story of Myrrha, of
Caunus and Biblis, and the rest,
should stir up no more concernment
where he most endeavoured it. The
master-piece of Seneca I hold to be
that scene in the *Troades*, where
Ulysses is seeking for Astyanax to kill
him: there you see the tenderness of
a mother so represented in Andro-
mache, that it raises compassion to a
high degree in the reader, and bears
the nearest resemblance of anything
in the tragedies of the Ancients to the
excellent scenes of passion in Shakespeare, or in Fletcher: for love-scenes,
you will find few among them; their
tragic poets dealt not with that soft
passion, but with lust, cruelty, revenge, ambition, and those bloody actions they produced; which were more
capable of raising horror than compassion in an audience: leaving love
untouched, whose gentleness would
have tempered them; which is the
most frequent of all the passions, and
which, being the private concernment
of every person, is soothed by view-

ing its own image in a public entertainment.

"Among their comedies, we find a scene or two of tenderness, and that where you would least expect it, in Plautus; but to speak generally, their lovers say little, when they see each other, but *anima mea, vita mea*: ζωὴ καὶ Ψυχῆ as the women in Juvenal's time used to cry out in the fury of their kindness. Any sudden gust of passion (as an ecstasy of love in an unexpected meeting) cannot better be expressed than in a word and a sigh, breaking one another. Nature is dumb on such occasions; and to make her speak would be to represent her unlike herself. But there are a thousand other concernments of lovers, as jealousies, complaints, contrivances, and the like, where not to open their minds at large to each other, were to be wanting to their own love, and to the expectation of the audience; who watch the movements of their minds, as much as the changes of their fortunes. For the imaging of the first is properly the work of a poet; the latter he borrows from the historian."

Eugenius was proceeding in that part of his discourse, when Crites interrupted him. "I see," said he, "Eugenius and I are never like to have this question decided betwixt us; for he maintains, the Moderns have acquired a new perfection in writing; I can only grant they have altered the mode of it. Homer described his heroes men of great appetites, lovers of beef broiled upon the coals, and good fellows; contrary to the practice of the French Romances, whose heroes neither eat, nor drink, nor sleep, for love. Virgil makes Æneas a bold avower of his own virtues:

Sum pius Æneas, fama super aethera notus;

which, in the civility of our poets is the character of a fanfaron or Hector: for with us the knight takes occasion to walk out, or sleep, to avoid the vanity of telling his own story, which the trusty 'squire is ever to perform for him. So in their love-scenes, of which Eugenius spoke last, the Ancients were more hearty, were more talkative: they writ love as it was then the mode to make it; and I will grant thus much to Eugenius, that perhaps one of their poets had he lived in our *age, si foret hoc nostrum fato delapsus in œvum* (as Horace says of Lucilius), he had altered many things; not that they were not natural before, but that he might accommodate himself to the age in which he lived. Yet in the meantime, we are not to conclude anything rashly against those great men, but preserve to them the dignity of masters, and give that honour to their memories, *quos Libitina sacravit,* part of which we expect may be paid to us in future times."

This moderation of Crites, as it was pleasing to all the company, so it put an end to that dispute; which Eugenius, who seemed to have the better of the argument, would urge no farther: but Lisideius, after he had acknowledged himself of Eugenius his opinion concerning the Ancients, yet told him, he had forborne, till his discourse were ended, to ask him why he preferred the English plays above those of other nations? and whether we ought not to submit our stage to the exactness of our next neighbors?

"Though," said Eugenius, "I am at all times ready to defend the honour of my country against the French, and to maintain, we are as well able to vanquish them with our pens, as our ancestors have been with their swords; yet, if you please," added he, looking upon Neander, "I will commit this cause to my friend's management; his opinion of our plays is the same with mine, and besides, there is no reason, that Crites and I, who have now left the stage, should re-enter so suddenly upon it; which is against the laws of comedy."

"If the question had been stated," replied Lisideius, "who had writ best, the French or English, forty years ago, I should have been of your opinion, and adjudged the honour to our own nation; but since that time" (said he, turning towards Neander), "we have been so long together bad English-men that we had not leisure to be good poets. Beaumont, Fletcher, Jon-son (who were only capable of bring-ing us to that degree of perfection which we have), were just then leav-ing the world; as if in an age of so much horror, wit, and those milder studies of humanity, had no farther business among us. But the Muses, who ever follow peace, went to plant in another country: it was then that the great Cardinal Richelieu began to take them into his protection; and that, by his encouragement, Corneille, and some other Frenchmen, reformed their theatre (which before was as much below ours, as it now surpasses it and the rest of Europe). But be-cause Crites in his discourse for the Ancients has prevented me, by observ-ing many rules of the stage which the Moderns have borrowed from them, I shall only, in short, demand of you, whether you are not convinced that of all nations the French have best observed them? In the Unity of Time you find them so scrupulous that it yet remains a dispute among their poets, whether the artificial day of twelve hours, more or less, be not meant by Aristotle, rather than the natural one of twenty-four; and con-sequently, whether all plays ought not to be reduced into that compass. This I can testify, that in all their dramas writ within these last twenty years and upwards, I have not ob-served any that have extended the time to thirty hours: in the Unity of Place they are full as scrupulous; for many of their critics limit it to that very spot of ground where the play is supposed to begin; none of them ex-ceed the compass of the same town or city. The Unity of Action in all plays is yet more conspicuous; for they do not burden them with under-plots, as the English do: which is the reason why many scenes of our tragi-come-dies carry on a design that is nothing of kin to the main plot; and that we see two distinct webs in a play, like

those in ill-wrought stuffs; and two actions, that is, two plays, carried on together, to the confounding of the audience; who, before they are warm in their concernments for one part, are diverted to another; and by that means espouse the interest of neither. From hence likewise it arises that the one half of our actors are not known to the other. They keep their dis-tances, as if they were Montagues and Capulets, and seldom begin an ac-quaintance till the last scene of the fifth act, when they are all to meet upon the stage. There is no theatre in the world has anything so absurd as the English tragi-comedy; 'tis a drama of our own invention, and the fashion of it is enough to proclaim it so; here a course of mirth, there an-other of sadness and passion, and a third of honour, and a duel: thus, in two hours and a half, we run through all the fits of Bedlam. The French af-fords you as much variety on the same day, but they do it not so unseason-ably, or *mal à propos*, as we: our poets present you the play and the farce together; and our stages still re-tain somewhat of the original civility of the Red Bull:

Atque ursum et pugiles media inter carmina poscunt.

The end of tragedies or serious plays, says Aristotle, is to beget admiration, compassion, or concernment; but are not mirth and compassion things in-compatible? and is it not evident that the poet must of necessity destroy the former by intermingling of the latter? that is, he must ruin the sole end and object of his tragedy, to introduce somewhat that is forced into it, and is not of the body of it. Would you not think that physician mad, who, having prescribed a purge, should immediately order you to take re-stringents?

"But to leave our plays, and return to theirs. I have noted one great ad-vantage they have had in the plotting of their tragedies; that is, they are always grounded upon some known history: according to that of Horace, *Ex noto fictum carmen sequar*; and in that they have so imitated the Ancients that they have surpassed them. For the Ancients, as was observed before, took for the foundation of their plays some poetical fiction, such as under that consideration could move but little concernment in the audience, because they already knew the event of it. But the French goes farther:

Atque ita mentitur, sic veris falsa remiscet Primo ne medium, medio ne discrepet imum.

He so interweaves truth with probable fiction, that he puts a pleasing fallacy upon us; mends the intrigues of fate, and dispenses with the severity of history, to reward that virtue which has been rendered to us there unfortunate. Sometimes the story has left the success so doubtful that the writer is free, by the privilege of a poet, to take that which of two or more relations will best suit with his design: as for example, in the death of Cyrus, whom Justin and some others report to have perished in the Scythian war, but Xenophon affirms to have died in his bed of extreme old age. Nay more, when the event is past dispute, even then we are willing to be deceived, and the poet, if he contrives it with appearance of truth, has all the audience of his party; at least during the time his play is acting; so naturally we are kind to virtue, when our own interest is not in question, that we take it up as the general concernment of mankind. On the other side, if you consider the historical plays of Shakespeare, they are rather so many chronicles of kings, or the business many times of thirty or forty years, cramped into a representation of two hours and a half; which is not to imitate or paint Nature, but rather to draw her in miniature, to take her in little; to look upon her through the wrong end of a perspective, and receive her images not only much less, but infinitely more imperfect than the life: this, instead of making a play delightful, renders it ridiculous:—

Quodcunque ostendis mihi sic, incredulus odi.

For the spirit of man cannot be satisfied but with truth, or at least verisimility; and a poem is to contain, if not τὰ ἔτυμα yet ἐτύμοισιν ὁμοῖα as one of the Greek poets has expressed it.

"Another thing in which the French differ from us and from the Spaniards, is that they do not embarrass, or cumber themselves with too much plot; they only represent so much of a story as will constitute one whole and great action sufficient for a play; we, who undertake more, do but multiply adventures which, not being produced from one another, as effects from causes, but barely following, constitute many actions in the drama, and consequently make it many plays.

"But by pursuing closely one argument, which is not cloyed with many turns, the French have gained more liberty for verse, in which they write; they have leisure to dwell on a subject which deserves it; and to represent the passions (which we have acknowledged to be the poet's work), without being hurried from one thing to another, as we are in the plays of Calderon, which we have seen lately upon our theatres under the name of Spanish plots. I have taken notice but of one tragedy of ours whose plot has that uniformity and unity of design in it, which I have commended in the French; and that is *Rollo*, or rather, under the name of Rollo, the Story of Bassianus and Geta in Herodian: there indeed the plot is neither large nor intricate, but just enough to fill the minds of the audience, not to cloy them. Besides, you see it founded upon the truth of history, only the time of the action is not reduceable to the strictness of the rules; and you see in some places a little farce mingled, which is below the dignity of the other parts, and in this all our poets are extremely peccant: even Ben Jonson himself, in *Sejanus* and *Catiline*, has given us this oleo of a play, this unnatural mixture of comedy and tragedy; which to me sounds just as ridiculously as the history of David with the merry humours of Golia's. In *Sejanus* you may take notice of the scene betwixt Livia and the physician, which is a pleasant satire upon the artificial helps of beauty: in *Catiline* you may see the parliament of women; the little envies of them to one another; and all that passes betwixt Curio and Fulvia: scenes admirable in their kind, but of an ill mingle with the rest.

"But I return again to the French writers, who, as I have said, do not burden themselves too much with plot, which has been reproached to them by an ingenious person of our nation as a fault; for, he says, they commonly make but one person considerable in a play; they dwell on him, and his concernments, while the rest of the persons are only subservient to set him off. If he intends this by it, that there is one person in the play who is of greater dignity than the rest, he must tax, not only theirs, but those of the Ancients, and which he would be loth to do, the best of ours; for it is impossible but that one person must be more conspicuous in it than any other, and consequently the greatest share in the action must devolve on him. We see it so in the management of all affairs; even in the most equal aristocracy, the balance cannot be so justly poised but some one will be superior to the rest, either in parts, fortune, interest, or the consideration of some glorious exploit; which will reduce the greatest part of business into his hands.

"But, if he would have us to imagine, that in exalting one character the rest of them are neglected, and that all of them have not some share or other in the action of the play, I desire him to produce any of Corneille's tragedies, wherein every person, like so many servants in a well-governed family, has not some employment, and who is not necessary to the carrying on of the plot, or at least to your understanding it.

"There are indeed some protatick persons in the Ancients, whom they make use of in their plays, either to hear or give the relation: but the French avoid this with great address, making their narrations only to, or by such, who are some way interested in the main design. And now I am speaking of relations, I cannot take a fitter opportunity to add this in favour of the French, that they often use them with better judgment and more *à propos* than the English do. Not that I commend narrations in general, but there are two sorts of them. One, of those things which are antecedent to the play, and are related to make the conduct of it more clear to us. But 'tis a fault to choose such subjects for the stage as will force us on that rock because we see they are seldom listened to by the audience and that is many times the ruin of the play; for, being once let pass without attention, the audience can never recover themselves to understand the plot: and indeed it is somewhat unreasonable that they should be put to so much trouble, as that, to comprehend what passes in their sight, they must have recourse to what was done, perhaps, ten or twenty years ago.

"But there is another sort of relations, that is, of things happening in the action of the play, and supposed to be done behind scenes; and this is many times both convenient and beautiful; for by it the French avoid the tumult to which we are subject in England, by representing duels, battles, and the like; which renders our stage too like the theatres where they fight prizes. For what is more ridiculous than to represent an army with a drum and five men behind it; all which the hero of the other side is to drive in before him; or to see a duel fought, and one slain with two or three thrusts of the foils, which we know are so blunted that we might give a man an hour to kill another in good earnest with them.

"I have observed that in all our tragedies, the audience cannot forbear laughing when the actors are to die;

it is the most comic part of the whole play. All *passions* may be lively represented on the stage, if to the well-writing of them the actor supplies a good commanded voice, and limbs that move easily, and without stiffness; but there are many *actions* which can never be imitated to a just height: dying especially is a thing which none but a Roman gladiator could naturally perform on the stage, when he did not imitate or represent, but do it; and therefore it is better to limit the representation of it.

"The words of a good writer, which describe it lively, will make a deeper impression of belief in us than all the actor can insinuate into us, when he seems to fall dead before us; as a poet in the description of a beautiful garden, or a meadow, will please our imagination more than the place itself can please our sight. When we see death represented, we are convinced it is but fiction; but when we hear it related, our eyes, the strongest witnesses, are wanting, which might have undeceived us; and we are all willing to favour the sleight, when the poet does not too grossly impose on us. They therefore who imagine these relations would make no concernment in the audience, are deceived, by confounding them with the other, which are of things antecedent to the play: those are made often in cold blood, as I may say, to the audience; but these are warmed with our concernments, which were before awakened in the play. What the philosophers say of motion, that, when it is once begun, it continues of itself, and will do so to eternity, without some stop put to it, is clearly true on this occasion: the soul being already moved with the characters and fortunes of those imaginary persons, continues going of its own accord; and we are no more weary to hear what becomes of them when they are not on the stage, than we are to listen to the news of an absent mistress. But it is objected, that if one part of the play may be related, then why not all? I

answer, some parts of the action are more fit to be represented, some related. Corneille says judiciously that the poet is not obliged to expose to view all particular actions which conduce to the principal: he ought to select such of them to be seen, which will appear with the greatest beauty, either by the magnificence of the show, or the vehemence of passions which they produce, or some other charm which they have in them; and let the rest arrive to the audience by narration. 'Tis a great mistake in us to believe the French present no part of the action on the stage; every alteration or crossing of a design, every new-sprung passion, and turn of it, is a part of the action, and much the noblest, except we conceive nothing to be action till the players come to blows: as if the painting of the hero's mind were not more properly the poet's work than the strength of his body. Nor does this anything contradict the opinion of Horace, where he tells us,

Segnius irritant animos demissa per aurem,
Quam quae sunt oculis subjecta fidelibus.

For he says immediately after,

. . . . Non tamen intus
Digna geri promes in scenam; multaque tolles
Ex oculis quae mox narret facundia praesens.

Among which many he recounts some:

Nec pueros coram populo Medea trucidet,
Aut in avem Progne mutetur, Cadmus in
*   anguem, etc.*

That is, those actions which by reason of their cruelty will cause aversion in us, or by reason of their impossibility, unbelief, ought either wholly to be avoided by a poet, or only delivered by narration. To which we may have leave to add, such as, to avoid tumult (as was before hinted), or to reduce the plot into a more reasonable compass of time, or for defect of beauty in them, are rather to be related than presented to the eye. Examples of all these kinds are frequent, not only among all the ancients, but in the best received of our English poets. We find Ben Jonson using them in his *Magnetic Lady*, where one comes out from dinner, and relates the quarrels and disorders of it, to save the undecent appearance of them on the stage, and to abbreviate the story; and this in express imitation of Terence, who had done the same before him in his *Eunuch*, where Pythias makes the like relation of what had happened within at the Soldiers' entertainment. The relations likewise of Sejanus's death, and the prodigies before it, are remarkable; the one of which was hid from sight, to avoid the horror and tumult of the representation; the other, to shun the introducing of things impossible to be believed. In that excellent play, *The King and no King*, Fletcher goes yet farther; for the whole unravelling of the plot is done by narration in the fifth act, after the manner of the Ancients; and it moves great concernment in the audience, though it be only a relation of what was done many years before the play. I could multiply other instances, but these are sufficient to prove that there is no error in choosing a subject which requires this sort of narrations; in the ill management of them, there may.

"But I find I have been too long in this discourse, since the French have many other excellencies not common to us; as that you never see any of their plays end with a conversion, or simple change of will, which is the ordinary way which our poets use to end theirs. It shows little art in the conclusion of a dramatic poem, when they who have hindered the felicity during the four acts, desist from it in the fifth, without some powerful cause to take them off their design; and though I deny not but such reasons may be found, yet it is a path that is cautiously to be trod, and the poet is to be sure he convinces the audience that the motive is strong enough. As for example, the conversion of the Usurer in *The Scornful Lady* seems to me a little forced; for, being an Usurer,

which implies a lover of money to the highest degree of covetousness,—and such the poet has represented him,— the account he gives for the sudden change is, that he has been duped by the wild young fellow; which in reason might render him more wary another time, and make him punish himself with harder fare and coarser clothes, to get up again what he had lost: but that he should look on it as a judgment, and so repent, we may expect to hear in a sermon, but I should never endure it in a play.

"I pass by this; neither will I insist on the care they take that no person after his first entrance shall ever appear, but the business which brings him upon the stage shall be evident; which rule, if observed, must needs render all the events in the play more natural; for there you see the probability of every accident, in the cause that produced it; and that which appears chance in the play, will seem so reasonable to you, that you will there find it almost necessary: so that in the exit of the actor you have a clear account of his purpose and design in the next entrance (though, if the scene be well wrought, the event will commonly deceive you) ; for there is nothing so absurd, says Corneille, as for an actor to leave the stage only because he has no more to say.

"I should now speak of the beauty of their rhyme, and the just reason I have to prefer that way of writing in tragedies before ours in blank verse; but because it is partly received by us, and therefore not altogether peculiar to them, I will say no more of it in relation to their plays. For our own, I doubt not but it will exceedingly beautify them; and I can see but one reason why it should not generally obtain, that is, because our poets write so ill in it. This indeed may prove a more prevailing argument than all others which are used to destroy it, and therefore I am only troubled when great and judicious poets, and those who are acknowledged such, have writ or spoke against it: as for others, they are to be answered by that one sentence of an ancient author:—*Sed ut primo ad consequendos eos quos priores ducimus, accendimur, ita ubi aut proeteriri, aut aequari eos posse desperavimus, studium cum spe senescit: quod, scilicet, assequi non potest, sequi desinit: . . . praeteritoque eo in quo eminere non possumus, aliquid in quo nitamur, con-   10 quirimus."

Lisideius concluded in this manner; and Neander, after a little pause, thus answered him:

"I shall grant Lisideius, without much dispute, a great part of what he has urged against us; for I acknowledge that the French contrive their plots more regularly, and observe the laws of comedy, and decorum of the   20 stage (to speak generally), with more exactness than the English. Farther, I deny not but he has taxed us justly in some irregularities of ours, which he has mentioned; yet, after all, I am of opinion that neither our faults nor their virtues are considerable enough to place them above us.

"For the lively imitation of Nature being in the definition of a play, those   30 which best fulfil that law ought to be esteemed superior to the others. 'Tis true, those beauties of the French poesy are such as will raise perfection higher where it is, but are not sufficient to give it where it is not: they are indeed the beauties of a statue, but not of a man, because not animated with the soul of Poesy, which is imitation of humour and passions: and   40 this Lisideius himself, or any other, however biassed to their party, cannot but acknowledge, if he will either compare the humours of our comedies, or the characters of our serious plays, with theirs. He who will look upon theirs which have been written till these last ten years, or thereabouts, will find it a hard matter to pick out two or three passable humours   50 amongst them. Corneille himself, their arch-poet, what has he produced except *The Liar*, and you know how it was cried up in France; but when it

came upon the English stage, though well translated, and that part of Dorant acted to so much advantage as I am confident it never received in its own country, the most favourable to it would not put it in competition with many of Fletcher's or Ben Jonson's. In the rest of Corneille's comedies you have little humour; he tells you himself, his way is, first to show two lovers in good intelligence with each other; in the working up of the play to embroil them by some mistake, and in the latter end to clear it, and reconcile them.

"But of late years Moliere, the younger Corneille, Quinault, and some others, have been imitating afar off the quick turns and graces of the English stage. They have mixed their serious plays with mirth, like our tragi-comedies, since the death of Cardinal Richelieu; which Lisideius and many others not observing, have commended that in them for a virtue which they themselves no longer practise. Most of their new plays are, like some of ours, derived from the Spanish novels. There is scarce one of them without a veil, and a trusty Diego, who drolls much after the rate of *The Adventures*. But their humours, if I may grace them with that name, are so thin-sown, that never above one of them comes up in any play. I dare take upon me to find more variety of them in some one play of Ben Jonson's than in all theirs together; as he who has seen *The Alchemist, The Silent Woman,* or *Bartholomew-Fair,* cannot but acknowledge with me.

"I grant the French have performed what was possible on the ground-work of the Spanish plays; what was pleasant before, they have made regular: but there is not above one good play to be writ on all those plots; they are too much alike to please often; which we need not the experience of our own stage to justify. As for their new way of mingling mirth with serious plot, I do not, with Lisideius, condemn the thing, though I cannot approve their manner of doing it. He tells us, we cannot so speedily recollect ourselves after a scene of great passion and concernment, as to pass to another of mirth and humour, and to enjoy it with any relish: but why should he imagine the soul of man more heavy than his senses? Does not the eye pass from an unpleasant object to a pleasant in a much shorter time than is required to this? and does not the unpleasantness of the first commend the beauty of the latter? The old rule of logic might have convinced him, that contraries, when placed near, set off each other. A continued gravity keeps the spirit too much bent; we must refresh it sometimes, as we bait in a journey that we may go on with greater ease. A scene of mirth, mixed with tragedy, has the same effect upon us which our music has betwixt the acts; which we find a relief to us from the best plots and language of the stage, if the discourses have been long. I must therefore have stronger arguments, ere I am convinced that compassion and mirth in the same subject destroy each other; and in the mean time cannot but conclude, to the honour of our nation, that we have invented, increased, and perfected a more pleasant way of writing for the stage, than was ever known to the Ancients or Moderns of any nation, which is tragi-comedy.

"And this leads me to wonder why Lisideius and many others should cry up the barrenness of the French plots above the variety and copiousness of the English. Their plots are single; they carry on one design, which is pushed forward by all the actors, every scene in the play contributing and moving towards it. Our plays, besides the main design, have under-plots, or by-concernments, of less considerable persons and intrigues, which are carried on with the notion of the main plot: as they say the orb of the fixed stars, and those of the planets, though they have motions of their own, are whirled about by the motion of the *primum mobile*, in which they are contained. That similitude expresses much of the English stage; for if contrary motions may be found in nature to agree; if a planet can go east and west at the same time;—one way by virtue of his own motion, the other by the force of the First Mover;—it will not be difficult to imagine how the under-plot, which is only different, not contrary to the great design, may naturally be conducted along with it.

"Eugenius has already shown us, from the confession of the French poets, that the Unity of Action is sufficiently preserved, if all the imperfect actions of the play are conducing to the main design; but when those petty intrigues of a play are so ill ordered, that they have no coherence with the other, I must grant that Lisideius has reason to tax that want of due connection; for co-ordination in a play is as dangerous and unnatural as in a state. In the meantime he must acknowledge, our variety, if well ordered, will afford a greater pleasure to the audience.

"As for his other argument, that by pursuing one single theme they gain an advantage to express and work up the passions, I wish any example he could bring from them would make it good; for I confess their verses are to me the coldest I have ever read. Neither, indeed, is it possible for them, in the way they take, so to express passion, as that the effects of it should appear in the concernment of an audience, their speeches being so many declamations, which tire us with the length; so that instead of persuading us to grieve for their imaginary heroes, we are concerned for our own trouble, as we are in tedious visits of bad company; we are in pain till they are gone. When the French stage came to be reformed by Cardinal Richelieu, those long harangues were introduced to comply with the gravity of a churchman. Look upon the *Cinna* and the *Pompey*; they are not so properly to be called plays, as long discourses of reason of state; and *Polieucte* in matters of religion is as solemn as the long stops upon our organs. Since that time it is grown into a custom, and their actors speak by the hour-glass, like our parsons; nay, they account it the grace of their parts, and think themselves disparaged by the poet, if they may not twice or thrice in a play entertain the audience with a speech of an hundred lines. I deny not but this may suit well enough with the French; for as we, who are a more sullen people, come to be diverted at our plays, so they, who are of an airy and gay temper, come thither to make themselves more serious: and this I conceive to be one reason why comedies are more pleasing to us, and tragedies to them. But to speak generally: it cannot be denied that short speeches and replies are more apt to move the passions and beget concernment in us, than the other; for it is unnatural for any one in a gust of passion to speak long together, or for another in the same condition to suffer him, without interruption. Grief and passion are like floods raised in little brooks by a sudden rain; they are quickly up; and if the concernment be poured unexpectedly in upon us, it overflows us; but a long sober shower gives them leisure to run out as they came in, without troubling the ordinary current. As for Comedy, repartee is one of its chiefest graces; the greatest pleasure of the audience is a chase of wit, kept up on both sides, and swiftly managed. And this our forefathers, if not we, have had in Fletcher's plays, to a much higher degree of perfection than the French poets can, reasonably, hope to reach.

"There is another part of Lisideius his discourse, in which he rather excused our neighbors than commended them; that is, for aiming only to make one person considerable in their plays. 'Tis very true what he has urged, that one character in all plays, even without the poet's care, will have advantage of all the others; and that the design of the whole drama will chiefly depend on it. But this hinders not that there may be more shining characters in the play: many persons of a second magnitude, nay, some so very near, so almost equal to the first, that greatness may be opposed to greatness, and all the persons be made considerable, not only by their quality, but their action. 'Tis evident that the more the persons are, the greater will be the variety of the plot. If then the parts are managed so regularly, that the beauty of the whole be kept entire, and that the variety become not a perplexed and confused mass of accidents, you will find it infinitely pleasing to be led in a labyrinth of design, where you see some of your way before you, yet discern not the end till you arrive at it. And that all this is practicable, I can produce for examples many of our English plays: as *The Maid's Tragedy*, *The Alchemist*, *The Silent Woman*: I was going to have named *The Fox*, but that the unity of design seems not exactly observed in it; for there appear two actions in the play; the first naturally ending with the fourth act; the second forced from it in the fifth: which yet is the less to be condemned in him, because the disguise of Volpone, though it suited not with his character as a crafty or covetous person, agreed well enough with that of a voluptuary; and by it the poet gained the end at which he aimed, the punishment of vice, and the reward of virtue, both which that disguise produced. So that to judge equally of it, it was an excellent fifth act, but not so naturally proceeding from the former.

"But to leave this, and pass to the latter part of Lisideius his discourse, which concerns relations: I must acknowledge with him, that the French have reason to hide that part of the action which would occasion too much tumult on the stage, and to choose rather to have it made known by narration to the audience. Farther, I think it very convenient, for the reasons he has given, that all incredible actions were removed; but whether custom has so insinuated itself into our countrymen, or nature has so formed them to fierceness, I know not, but they will scarcely suffer combats and other objects of horror to be taken from them. And indeed, the indecency of tumults is all which can be objected against fighting: for why may not our imagination as well suffer itself to be deluded with the probability of it, as with any other thing in the play? For my part, I can with as great ease persuade myself that the blows are given in good earnest, as I can that they who strike them are kings or princes, or those persons which they represent. For objects of incredibility, I would be satisfied from Lisideius, whether we have any so removed from all appearance of truth, as are those of Corneille's *Andromede*; a play which has been frequented the most of any he has writ. If the Perseus, or the son of a heathen god, the Pegasus, and the Monster, were not capable to choke a strong belief, let him blame any representation of ours hereafter. Those indeed were objects of delight; yet the reason is the same as to the probability: for he makes it not a Ballette or masque, but a play, which is to resemble truth. But for death, that it ought not to be represented, I have, besides the arguments alleged by Lisideius, the authority of Ben Jonson, who has forborne it in his tragedies; for both the death of Sejanus and Catiline are related: though in the latter I cannot but observe one irregularity of that great poet; he has removed the scene in the same act from Rome to Catiline's army, and from thence again to Rome; and besides, has allowed a very inconsiderable time, after Catiline's speech, for the striking of the battle, and the return of Petreius, who is to relate the event of it to the senate: which I should not animadvert on him, who was otherwise a painful observer of τὸ πρέπον or the *decorum* of the stage, if he had not used extreme severity in his judgment on the incomparable Shakespeare for the same fault.—To conclude on this subject of relations; if we are to be blamed for showing too much of the action, the French are as faulty for discovering too little of it: a mean betwixt both should be observed by every judicious writer, so as the audience may neither be left unsatisfied by not seeing what is beautiful, or shocked by beholding what is either incredible or undecent.

"I hope I have already proved in this discourse, that though we are not altogether so punctual as the French in observing the laws of comedy, yet our errors are so few, and little, and those things wherein we excel them so considerable, that we ought of right to be preferred before them. But what will Lisideius say, if they themselves acknowledge they are too strictly bounded by those laws, for breaking which he has blamed the English? I will allege Corneille's words, as I find them in the end of his Discourse of the Three Unities: *Il est facile aux spéculatifs d' estre sévères, etc.* ' 'Tis easy for speculative persons to judge severely; but if they would produce to public view ten or twelve pieces of this nature, they would perhaps give more latitude to the rules than I have done, when by experience they had known how much we are limited and constrained by them, and how many beauties of the stage they banished from it.' To illustrate a little what he has said: By their servile observations of the Unities of Time and Place, and integrity of scenes, they have brought on themselves that dearth of plot, and narrowness of imagination, which may be observed in all their plays. How many beautiful accidents might naturally happen in two or three days, which cannot arrive with any probability in the compass of twenty-four hours? There is time to be allowed also for maturity of design, which, amongst great and prudent persons, such as are often represented in Tragedy, cannot, with any likelihood of truth, be brought to pass at so short a warning. Farther: by tying themselves strictly to the Unity of Place, and unbroken scenes, they are forced many times to omit some beauties which cannot be shown where the act began; but might if the scene were interrupted, and the stage cleared for the persons to enter in another place; and therefore the French poets are often forced upon absurdities; for if the act begins in a chamber, all the persons in the play must have some business or other to come thither, or else they are not to be shown that act; and sometimes their characters are very unfitting to appear there: as, suppose it were the king's bed-chamber; yet the meanest man in the tragedy must come and dispatch his business there, rather than in the lobby, or courtyard (which is fitter for him), for fear the stage should be cleared, and the scenes broken. Many times they fall by it in a greater inconvenience; for they keep their scenes unbroken, and yet change the place; as in one of their newest plays, where the act begins in the street. There a gentleman is to meet his friend; he sees him with his man, coming out from his father's house they talk together, and the first goes out: the second, who is a lover, has made an appointment with his mistress; she appears at the window, and then we are to imagine the scene lies under it. This gentleman is called away, and leaves his servant with his mistress; presently her father is heard from within; the young lady is afraid the serving-man should be discovered, and thrusts him into a place of safety, which is supposed to be her closet. After this, the father enters to the daughter, and now the scene is in a house, for he is seeking from one room to another for this poor Philipin, or French Diego, who is heard from within, drolling and breaking many a miserable conceit on the subject of his sad condition. In this ridiculous manner the play goes forward, the stage being never empty all the while: so that the street, the window, the houses, and the closet, are made to walk about, and the persons to stand still. Now what, I beseech you, is more easy than to write a regular French play, or more difficult than to write an irregular English one, like those of Fletcher, or of Shakespeare?

"If they content themselves, as Corneille did, with some flat design, which, like an ill riddle, is found out ere it be half proposed, such plots we can make every way regular, as easily as they; but whenever they endeavour to rise to any quick turns and counterturns of plot, as some of them have attempted, since Corneille's plays have been less in vogue, you see they write as irregularly as we, though they cover it more speciously. Hence the reason is perspicuous why no French plays, when translated, have, or ever can succeed on the English stage. For, if you consider the plots, our own are fuller of variety; if the writing, ours are more quick and fuller of spirit; and therefore 'tis a strange mistake in those who decry the way of writing plays in verse, as if the English therein imitated the French. We have borrowed nothing from them; our plots are weaved in English looms: we endeavour therein to follow the variety and greatness of characters which are derived to us from Shakspeare and Fletcher; the copiousness and well-knitting of the intrigues we have from Jonson; and for the verse itself we have English precedents of elder date than any of Corneille's plays. Not to name our old comedies before Shakspeare, which were all writ in verse of six feet, or Alexandrines, such as the French now use,— I can show in Shakspeare many scenes of rhyme together, and the like in Ben Jonson's tragedies: in *Catiline* and *Sejanus* sometimes thirty or forty lines,—I mean besides the Chorus, or the monologues; which, by the way, showed Ben no enemy to this way of writing, especially if you read his *Sad Shepherd*, which goes sometimes on rhyme, sometimes on blank verse, like an horse who eases himself on trot and amble. You find him likewise commending Fletcher's pastoral of *The Faithful Shepherdess*, which is for the most part rhyme, though not refined to that purity to which it hath since been brought. And these examples are enough to clear us from a servile imitation of the French.

"But to return whence I have digressed: I dare boldly affirm these two things of the English drama; First, that we have many plays of ours as regular as any of theirs, and which, besides, have more variety of plot and characters; and secondly, that in most of the irregular plays of Shakspeare or Fletcher (for Ben Jonson's are for the most part regular), there is a more masculine fancy and greater spirit in the writing than there is in any of the French. I could produce, even in Shakspeare's and Fletcher's works, some plays which are almost exactly formed; as *The Merry Wives of Windsor,* and *The Scornful Lady*: but because (generally speaking) Shakspeare, who writ first, did not perfectly observe the laws of Comedy, and Fletcher, who came nearer to perfection, yet through carelessness made many faults; I will take the pattern of a perfect play from Ben Jonson, who was a careful and learned observer of the dramatic laws, and from all his comedies I shall select *The Silent Woman*; of which I will make a short examen, according to those rules which the French observe."

As Neander was beginning to examine *The Silent Woman*, Eugenius, earnestly regarding him; "I beseech you, Neander," said he, "gratify the company, and me in particular, so far, as before you speak of the play, to give us a character of the author; and tell us frankly your opinion, whether you do not think all writers, both French and English, ought to give place to him."

"I fear," replied Neander, "that in obeying your commands I shall draw some envy on myself. Besides, in performing them, it will be first necessary to speak somewhat of Shakspeare and Fletcher, his rivals in poesy; and one of them, in my opinion, at least his equal, perhaps his superior.

"To begin, then, with Shakspeare. He was the man who of all modern, and perhaps ancient poets, had the largest and most comprehensive soul. All the images of Nature were still present to him, and he drew them, not laboriously, but luckily; when he describes anything, you more than see it, you feel it too. Those who accuse him to have wanted learning, give him the greater commendation: he was naturally learned; he needed not the spectacles of books to read Nature; he looked inwards, and found her there. I cannot say he is everywhere alike; were he so, I should do him injury to compare him with the greatest of mankind. He is many times flat, insipid; his comic wit degenerating into clenches, his serious swelling into bombast. But he is always great, when some great occasion is presented to him; no man can say he ever had a fit subject for his wit, and did not then raise himself as high above the rest of poets,

Quantum lenta solent inter viburna cupressi.

The consideration of this made Mr. Hales of Eaton say, that there was no subject of which any poet ever writ, but he would produce it much better done in Shakspeare; and however others are now generally preferred before him, yet the age wherein he lived, which had contemporaries with him Fletcher and Jonson, never equalled them to him in their esteem: and in the last king's court, when Ben's reputation was at highest, Sir John Suckling, and with him the greater part of the courtiers, set our Shakspeare far above him.

"Beaumont and Fletcher, of whom I am next to speak, had, with the advantage of Shakspeare's wit, which was their precedent, great natural gifts, improved by study: Beaumont especially being so accurate a judge of plays, that Ben Jonson, while he lived, submitted all his writings to his censure, and, 'tis thought, used his judgment in correcting, if not contriving, all his plots. What value he had for him, appears by the verses he writ to him; and therefore I need speak no farther of it. The first play that brought Fletcher and him in esteem was their *Philaster*: for before that, they had written two or three very unsuccessfully, as the like is reported of Ben Jonson, before he writ *Every Man in his Humour*. Their plots were generally more regular than Shakspeare's, especially those which were made before Beaumont's death; and they understood and imitated the conversation of gentlemen much better; whose wild debaucheries, and quickness of wit in repartees, no poet before them could paint as they have done. Humour, which Ben Jonson derived from particular persons, they made it not their business to describe; they represented all the passions very lively, but above all, love. I am apt to believe the English language in them arrived to its highest perfection: what words have since been taken in, are rather superfluous than ornamental. Their plays are now the most pleasant and frequent entertainments of the stage; two of theirs being acted through the year for one of Shakspeare's or Jonson's: the reason is, because there is a certain gaiety in their comedies, and pathos in their more serious plays, which suit generally with all men's humours. Shakspeare's language is likewise a little obsolete, and Ben Jonson's wit comes short of theirs.

"As for Jonson, to whose character I am now arrived, if we look upon him while he was himself (for his last plays were but his dotages), I think him the most learned and judicious writer which any theatre ever had. He was a most severe judge of himself, as well as others. One cannot say he wanted wit, but rather that he was frugal of it. In his works you find little to retrench or alter. Wit, and language, and humour also in some measure, we had before him; but something of art was wanting to the Drama till he came. He managed his strength to more advantage than any who preceded him. You seldom find

him making love in any of his scenes, or endeavouring to move the passions; his genius was too sullen and saturnine to do it gracefully, especially when he knew he came after those who had performed both to such an height. Humour was his proper sphere; and in that he delighted most to represent mechanic people. He was deeply conversant in the Ancients, both Greek and Latin, and he borrowed boldly from them: there is scarce a poet or historian among the Roman authors of those times whom he has not translated in *Sejanus* and *Catiline*. But he has done his robberies so openly, that one may see he fears not to be taxed by any law. He invades authors like a monarch; and what would be theft in other poets, is only victory in him. With the spoils of these writers he so represents old Rome to us, in its rites, ceremonies, and customs, that if one of their poets had written either of his tragedies, we had seen less of it than in him. If there was any fault in his language, 'twas that he weaved it too closely and laboriously, in his comedies especially: perhaps, too, he did a little too much Romanize our tongue, leaving the words which he translated almost as much Latin as he found them: wherein, though he learnedly followed their language, he did not enough comply with the idiom of ours. If I would compare him with Shakspeare, I must acknowledge him the more correct poet, but Shakspeare the greater wit. Shakspeare was the Homer, or father of our dramatic poets; Jonson was the Virgil, the pattern of elaborate writing; I admire him, but I love Shakspeare. To conclude of him; as he has given us the most correct plays, so in the precepts which he has laid down in his *Discoveries*, we have as many and profitable rules for perfecting the stage, as any wherewith the French can furnish us.

"Having thus spoken of the author, I proceed to the examination of his comedy, *The Silent Woman*.

Examen of the Silent Woman

"To begin first with the length of the action; it is so far from exceeding the compass of a natural day, that it takes not up an artificial one. 'Tis all included in the limits of three hours and a half, which is no more than is required for the presentment on the stage: a beauty perhaps not much observed; if it had, we should not have looked on the Spanish translation of *Five Hours* with so much wonder. The scene of it is laid in London; the latitude of place is almost as little as you can imagine; for it lies all within the compass of two houses, and after the first act, in one. The continuity of scenes is observed more than in any of our plays, except his own *Fox* and *Alchemist.* They are not broken above twice or thrice at most in the whole comedy; and in the two best of Corneille's plays, the *Cid* and *Cinna,* they are interrupted once. The action of the play is entirely one; the end or aim of which is the settling Morose's estate on Dauphine. The intrigue of it is the greatest and most noble of any pure unmixed comedy in any language; you see in it many persons of various characters and humours, and all delightful. As first, Morose, or an old man, to whom all noise but his own talking is offensive. Some who would be thought critics, say this humour of his is forced: but to remove that objection, we may consider him first to be naturally of a delicate hearing, as many are, to whom all sharp sounds are unpleasant; and secondly, we may attribute much of it to the peevishness of his age, or the wayward authority of an old man in his own house, where he may make himself obeyed; and to this the poet seems to allude in his name Morose. Besides this, I am assured from divers persons, that Ben Jonson was actually acquainted with such a man, one altogether as ridiculous as he is here represented. Others say, it is not enough to find one man of such an humour; it must be common to more, and the more common the more natural. To prove this, they instance in the best of comical characters, Falstaff. There are many men resembling him; old, fat, merry, cowardly, drunken, amorous, vain, and lying. But to convince these people, I need but tell them that humour is the ridiculous extravagance of conversation, wherein one man differs from all others. If then it be common, or communicated to many, how differs it from other men's? or what indeed causes it to be ridiculous so much as the singularity of it? As for Falstaff, he is not properly one humour, but a miscellany of humours or images, drawn from so many several men: that wherein he is singular is his wit, or those things he says *praeter expectatum*, unexpected by the audience; his quick evasions, when you imagine him surprised, which, as they are extremely diverting of themselves, so receive a great addition from his person; for the very sight of such an unwieldy old debauched fellow is a comedy alone. And here, having a place so proper for it, I cannot but enlarge somewhat upon this subject of humour into which I am fallen. The ancients had little of it in their comedies; for the τὸ γελοῖον of the Old Comedy, of which Aristophanes was chief, was not so much to imitate a man, as to make the people laugh at some odd conceit, which had commonly somewhat of unnatural or obscene in it. Thus, when you see Socrates brought upon the stage, you are not to imagine him made ridiculous by the imitation of his actions, but rather by making him perform something very unlike himself; something so childish and absurd, as by comparing it with the gravity of the true Socrates, makes a ridiculous object for the spectators. In their New Comedy which succeeded, the poets sought indeed to express the ἦθος as in their Tragedies the πάθος of mankind. But this ἦθος contained only the general characters of men and manners; as old men, lovers, serving-

men, courtezans, parasites, and such
other persons as we see in their comedies; all which they made alike: that
is, one old man or father, one lover,
one courtezan, so like another, as if
the first of them had begot the rest of
every sort: *Ex homine hunc natum
dicas.* The same custom they observed
likewise in their tragedies. As for the
French, though they have the word
humeur among them, yet they have
small use of it in their comedies or
farces; they being but ill imitations of
the *ridiculum*, or that which stirred
up laughter in the Old Comedy. But
among the English 'tis otherwise:
where by humour is meant some extravagant habit, passion, or affection,
particular (as I said before) to some
one person, by the oddness of which,
he is immediately distinguished from
the rest of men; which being lively
and naturally represented, most frequently begets that malicious pleasure
in the audience which is testified by
laughter; as all things which are deviations from customs are ever the
aptest to produce it: though by the
way this laughter is only accidental,
as the person represented is fantastic
or bizarre; but pleasure is essential to
it, as the imitation of what is natural.
The description of these humours,
drawn from the knowledge and observation of particular persons, was
the peculiar genius and talent of Ben
Jonson; to whose play I now return.

"Besides Morose, there are at least
nine or ten different characters, and
humours in *The Silent Woman*; all
which persons have several concernments of their own, yet are all used
by the poet to the conducting of the
main design to perfection. I shall not
waste time in commending the writing of this play; but I will give you
my opinion, that there is more wit and
acuteness of fancy in it than in any of
Ben Jonson's. Besides that he has
here described the conversation of
gentlemen in the persons of True-
Wit, and his friends, with more gaiety,
air, and freedom, than in the rest of
his comedies. For the contrivance of

the plot, 'tis extreme, elaborate, and
yet withal easy; for the λύσις or unty-
ing of it, 'tis so admirable, that when
it is done, no one of the audience
would think the poet could have
missed it; and yet it was concealed so
much before the last scene, that any
other way would sooner have entered
into your thoughts. But I dare not
take upon me to commend the fabric
of it, because it is altogether so full of
art, that I must unravel every scene
in it to commend it as I ought. And
this excellent contrivance is still the
more to be admired, because 'tis comedy, where the persons are only of
common rank, and their business private, not elevated by passions or high
concernments, as in serious plays.
Here every one is a proper judge of all
he sees, nothing is represented but
that with which he daily converses:
so that by consequence all faults lie
open to discovery, and few are pardonable. 'Tis this which Horace has
judiciously observed:

Creditur, ex medio quia res arcessit, habere
Sudoris minimum; sed habet Comedia tanto
Plus oneris, quanto veniae minus.

But our poet who was not ignorant of
these difficulties has made use of all
advantages; as he who designs a large
leap takes his rise from the highest
ground. One of these advantages is
that which Corneille has laid down as
the greatest which can arrive to any
poem, and which he himself could
never compass above thrice in all his
plays; viz., the making choice of some
signal and long-expected day, whereon
the action of the play is to depend.
This day was that designed by
Dauphine for the settling of his
uncle's estate upon him; which to
compass, he contrives to marry him.
That the marriage had been plotted
by him long beforehand, is made evident by what he tells True-wit in the
second act, that in one moment he had
destroyed what he had been raising
many months.

"There is another artifice of the
poet, which I cannot here omit, be-

cause by the frequent practice of it in his comedies he has left it to us almost as a rule; that is, when he has any character or humour wherein he would show a *coup de Maistre,* or his highest skill, he recommends it to your observation by a pleasant description of it before the person first appears. Thus, in *Bartholomew-Fair* he gives you the pictures of Numps and Cokes, and in this those of Daw, Lafoole, Morose, and the Collegiate Ladies; all of which you hear described before you see them. So that before they come upon the stage, you have a longing expectation of them, which prepares you to receive them favourably; and when they are there, even from their first appearance you are so far acquainted with them, that nothing of their humour is lost to you.

"I will observe yet one thing further of this admirable plot; the business of it rises in every act. The second is greater than the first; the third than the second; and so forward to the fifth. There too you see, till the very last scene, new difficulties arising to obstruct the action of the play; and when the audience is brought into despair that the business can naturally be effected, then, and not before, the discovery is made. But that the poet might entertain you with more variety all this while, he reserves some new characters to show you, which he opens not till the second and third act; in the second Morose, Daw, the Barber, and Otter; in the third the Collegiate Ladies: all which he moves afterwards in by-walks, or under-plots, as diversions to the main design, lest it should grow tedious, though they are still naturally joined with it, and somewhere or other subservient to it. Thus, like a skilful chess-player, by little and little he draws out his men, and makes his pawns of use to his greater persons.

"If this comedy and some others of his were translated into French prose (which would now be no wonder to them, since Molière has lately given

them plays out of verse, which have not displeased them), I believe the controversy would soon be decided betwixt the two nations, even making them the judges. But we need not call our heroes to our aid. Be it spoken to the honour of the English, our nation can never want in any age such who are able to dispute the empire of wit with any people in the universe. And though the fury of a civil war, and power for twenty years together abandoned to a barbarous race of men, enemies of all good learning, had buried the muses under the ruins of monarchy; yet with the restoration of our happiness, we see revived Poesy lifting up its head, and already shaking off the rubbish which lay so heavy on it. We have seen since his Majesty's return, many dramatic poems which yield not to those of any foreign nation, and which deserve all laurels but the English. I will set aside flattery and envy: it cannot be denied but we have had some little blemish either in the plot or writing of all those plays which have been made within these seven years; (and perhaps there is no nation in the world so quick to discern them, or so difficult to pardon them, as ours) : yet if we can persuade ourselves to use the candour of that poet, who, though the most severe of critics, has left us this caution by which to moderate our censures—

. . . . . *ubi plura nitent in carmine, non ego paucis*
Offendar maculis;—

if, in consideration of their many and great beauties, we can wink at some slight and little imperfections, if we, I say, can be thus equal to ourselves, I ask no favour from the French. And if I do not venture upon any particular judgment of our late plays, 'tis out of the consideration which an ancient writer gives me: *vivorum, ut magna admiratio, ita censura difficilis:* betwixt the extremes of admiration and malice, 'tis hard to judge uprightly of the living. Only I think it may be per-

mitted me to say, that as it is no lessening to us to yield to some plays, and
those not many, of our own nation in
the last age, so can it be no addition to
pronounce of our present poets, that
they have far surpassed all the ancients, and the modern writers of other
countries."

This was the substance of what was
then spoken on that occasion; and Lisideius, I think, was going to reply, when
he was prevented thus by Crites: "I
am confident," said he, "that the most
material things that can be said have
been already urged on either side; if
they have not, I must beg of Lisideius
that he will defer his answer till another time: for I confess I have a joint
quarrel to you both, because you have
concluded, without any reason given
for it, that rhyme is proper for the
stage. I will not dispute how ancient
it hath been among us to write this
way; perhaps our ancestors knew no
better till Shakespeare's time. I will
grant it was not altogether left by him,
and that Fletcher and Ben Jonson used
it frequently in their Pastorals, and
sometimes in other plays. Farther, I
will not argue whether we received it
originally from our own countrymen,
or from the French; for that is an inquiry of as little benefit, as theirs, who,
in the midst of the late plague, were
not so solicitous to provide against it,
as to know whether we had it from the
malignity of our own air, or by transportation from Holland. I have therefore only to affirm, that it is not allowable in serious plays; for comedies, I
find you already concluding with me.
To prove this, I might satisfy myself
to tell you, how much in vain it is for
you to strive against the stream of the
people's inclination; the greatest part
of which are prepossessed so much
with those excellent plays of Shakespeare, Fletcher, and Ben Jonson, which
have been written out of rhyme, that
except you could bring them such as
were written better in it, and those too
by persons of equal reputation with
them, it will be impossible for you to
gain your cause with them, who will

still be judges. This it is to which, in
fine, all your reasons must submit. The
unanimous consent of an audience is
so powerful, that even Julius Caesar
(as Macrobius reports of him), when
he was perpetual dictator, was not able
to balance it on the other side; but
when Laberius, a Roman Knight, at
his request contended in the *Mime*
with another poet, he was forced to
cry out, *Etiam favente me victus es,
Laberi*. But I will not on this occasion
take the advantage of the greater number, but only urge such reasons against
rhyme, as I find in the writings of
those who have argued for the other
way. First, then, I am of opinion that
rhyme is unnatural in a play, because
dialogue there is presented as the effect
of sudden thought: for a play is the
imitation of Nature; and since no
man, without premeditation, speaks in
rhyme, neither ought he to do it on
the stage. This hinders not but the
fancy may be there elevated to an
higher pitch of thought than it is in
ordinary discourse; for there is a probability that men of excellent and quick
parts may speak noble things *ex tempore:* but those thoughts are never fet-
tered with the numbers or sound of
verse without study, and therefore it
cannot be but unnatural to present
the most free way of speaking in that
which is the most constrained. For this
reason, says Aristotle, 'tis best to write
tragedy in that kind of verse which is
the least such, or which is nearest
prose: and this amongst the Ancients
was the Iambic, and with us is blank
verse, or the measure of verse kept
exactly without rhyme. These numbers
therefore are fittest for a play; the
others for a paper of verses, or a poem;
blank verse being as much below them
as rhyme is improper for the Drama.
And if it be objected that neither are
blank verses made *ex tempore*, yet, as
nearest nature, they are still to be preferred.—But there are two particular
exceptions, which many besides myself
have had to verse; by which it will appear yet more plainly how improper it
is in plays. And the first of them is

grounded on that very reason for which some have commended rhyme; they say, the quickness of repartees in argumentative scenes receives an ornament from verse. Now what is more unreasonable than to imagine that a man should not only imagine the Wit, but the rhyme too, upon the sudden? This nicking of him who spoke before both in sound and measure, is so great an happiness, that you must at least suppose the persons of your play to be born poets: *Arcades omnes, et cantare pares, et respondere parati:* they must have arrived to the degree of *quicquid conabar dicere;*—to make verses almost whether they will or no. If they are anything below this, it will look rather like the design of two, than the answer of one: it will appear that your actors hold intelligence together; that they perform their tricks like fortune-tellers, by confederacy. The hand of art will be too visible in it, against that maxim of all professions—*Ars est celare artem,* that it is the greatest perfection of art to keep itself undiscovered. Nor will it serve you to object, that however you manage it, 'tis still known to be a play; and, consequently, the dialogue of two persons understood to be the labour of one poet. For a play is still an imitation of Nature; we know we are to be deceived, and we desire to be so; but no man ever was deceived but with a probability of truth; for who will suffer a gross lie to be fastened on him? Thus we sufficiently understand that the scenes which represent cities and countries to us are not really such, but only painted on boards and canvas; but shall that excuse the ill painture or designment of them? Nay, rather ought they not be laboured with so much the more diligence and exactness, to help the imagination? since the mind of man does naturally tend to truth; and therefore the nearer anything comes to the imitation of it, the more it pleases.

"Thus, you see, your rhyme is incapable of expressing the greatest thoughts naturally, and the lowest it

cannot with any grace: for what is more unbefitting the majesty of verse, than to call a servant, or bid a door be shut in rhyme? and yet you are often forced on this miserable necessity. But verse, you say, circumscribes a quick and luxuriant fancy, which would extend itself too far on every subject, did not the labour which is required to well-turned and polished rhyme, set bounds to it. Yet this argument, if granted, would only prove that we may write better in verse, but not more naturally. Neither is it able to evince that; for he who wants judgment to confine his fancy in blank verse, may want it as much in rhyme: and he who has it will avoid errors in both kinds. Latin verse was as great a confinement to the imagination of those poets as rhyme to ours; and yet you find Ovid saying too much on every subject. *Nescivit* (says Seneca) *quod bene cessit relinquere:* of which he gives you one famous instance in his description of the deluge:

Omnia pontus erat, deerant quoque litora ponto.
Now all was sea, nor had that sea a shore.

Thus Ovid's fancy was not limited by verse, and Virgil needed not verse to have bounded his.

"In our own language we see Ben Jonson confining himself to what ought to be said, even in the liberty of blank verse; and yet Corneille, the most judicious of the French poets, is still varying the same sense an hundred ways, and dwelling eternally on the same subject, though confined by rhyme. Some other exceptions I have to verse; but since these I have named are for the most part already public, I conceive it reasonable they should first be answered."

"It concerns me less than any," said Neander (seeing he had ended), "to reply to this discourse; because when I should have proved that verse may be natural in plays, yet I should always be ready to confess, that those which I have written in this kind come short of that perfection which is required. Yet since you are pleased I should undertake this province, I will do it, though with all imaginable respect and deference, both to that person from whom you have borrowed your strongest arguments, and to whose judgment, when I have said all, I finally submit. But before I proceed to answer your objections, I must first remember you, that I exclude all Comedy from my defence; and next that I deny not but blank verse may be also used; and content myself only to assert, that in serious plays where the subject and characters are great, and the plot unmixed with mirth, which might allay or divert these concernments which are produced, rhyme is there as natural and more effectual than blank verse.

"And now having laid down this as a foundation,—to begin with Crites, I must crave leave to tell him, that some of his arguments against rhyme reach no farther than, from the faults or defects of ill rhyme, to conclude against the use of it in general. May not I conclude against blank verse by the same reason? If the words of some poets who write in it are either ill chosen, or ill placed, which makes not only rhyme, but all kind of verse in any language unnatural, shall I, for their vicious affectation, condemn those excellent lines of Fletcher, which are written in that kind? Is there anything in rhyme more constrained than this line in blank verse?—*I heaven invoke, and strong resistance make;* where you see both the clauses are placed unnaturally, that is, contrary to the common way of speaking, and that without the excuse of a rhyme to cause it: yet you would think me very ridiculous, if I should accuse the stubbornness of blank verse for this, and not rather the stiffness of the poet. Therefore, Crites, you must either prove that words, though well chosen, and duly placed, yet render not rhyme natural in itself; or that, however natural and easy the rhyme may be, yet it is not proper for a play. If you insist on the former part, I would ask you, what other conditions are required to make rhyme natural in itself, besides an election of apt words, and a right disposition of them? For the due choice of your words expresses your sense naturally, and the due placing them adapts the rhyme to it. If you object that one verse may be made for the sake of another; though both the words and rhyme be apt, I answer, it cannot possibly so fall out; for either there is a dependence of sense betwixt the first line and the second, or there is none: if there be that connection, then in the natural position of the words the latter line must of necessity flow from the former; if there be no dependence, yet still the due ordering of words makes the last line as natural in itself as the other: so that the necessity of a rhyme never forces any but bad or lazy writers to say what they would not otherwise. 'Tis true, there is both care and art required to write in verse. A good poet never establishes the first line till he has sought out such a rhyme as may fit the sense, already prepared to heighten the second: many times the close of the sense falls into the middle of the next verse, or farther off, and he may often prevail himself of the same advantages in English which Virgil had in Latin, he may break off in the hemistich, and begin another line. Indeed, the not observing these two last things makes plays which are writ in verse so tedious: for though, most commonly, the sense is to be confined to the couplet, yet nothing that does *perpetuo tenore fluere,* run in the same channel, can please always. 'Tis like the murmuring of a stream, which not varying in the fall, causes at first attention, at last drowsiness. Variety of cadences is the best rule; the greatest help to the actors, and refreshment to the audience.

"If then verse may be made natural in itself, how becomes it unnatural in a play? You say the stage is the representation of Nature, and no man in ordinary conversation speaks in rhyme. But you foresaw when you said this, that it might be answered—neither does any man speak in blank verse, or in measure without rhyme. Therefore you concluded, that which is nearest Nature is still to be preferred. But you took no notice that rhyme might be made as natural as blank verse, by the well placing of the words, etc. All the difference between them, when they are both correct, is, the sound in one, which the other wants; and if so, the sweetness of it, and all the advantage resulting from it, which are handled in the Preface to *The Rival Ladies,* will yet stand good. As for that place of Aristotle, where he says, plays should be writ in that kind of verse which is nearest prose, it makes little for you; blank verse being properly but measured prose. Now measure alone, in any modern language, does not constitute verse; those of the Ancients in Greek and Latin consisted in quantity of words, and a determinate number of feet. But when, by the inundation of the Goths and Vandals into Italy, new languages were introduced, and barbarously mingled with the Latin, of which the Italian, Spanish, French, and ours (made out of them and the Teutonic) are dialects, a new way of poesy was practised; new, I say, in those countries, for in all probability it was that of the conquerors in their own nations: at least we are able to prove, that the eastern people have used it from all antiquity. This new way consisted in measure or number of feet, and rhyme; the sweetness of rhyme, and observation of accent, supplying the place of quantity in words, which could neither exactly be observed by those barbarians, who knew not the rules of it, neither was it suitable to their tongues, as it had been to the Greek and Latin. No man is tied in modern poesy to observe any farther rule in the feet of his verse, but that they be dissyllables; whether Spondee, Trochee, or Iambic, it matters not; only he is obliged to rhyme: neither do the Spanish, French, Italian, or Germans, acknowledge at all, or very rarely, any such kind of poesy as blank verse amongst them. There-

fore, at most 'tis but a poetic prose, a *sermo pedestris;* and as such, most fit for comedies, where I acknowledge rhyme to be improper.—Farther; as to that quotation of Aristotle, our couplet verses may be rendered as near prose as blank verse itself, by using those advantages I lately named,—as breaks in an hemistich, or running the sense into another line,—thereby making art and order appear as loose and free as nature: or not tying ourselves to couplets strictly, we may use the benefit of the Pindaric way practised in *The Siege of Rhodes;* where the numbers vary, and the rhyme is disposed carelessly, and far from often chiming. Neither is that other advantage of the Ancients to be despised, of changing the kind of verse when they please, with the change of the scene, or some new entrance; for they confine not themselves always to iambics, but extend their liberty to all lyric numbers, and sometimes even to hexameter. But I need not go so far to prove that rhyme, as it succeeds to all other offices of Greek and Latin verse, so especially to this of plays, since the custom of nations at this day confirms it; the French, Italian, and Spanish tragedies are generally writ in it; and sure the universal consent of the most civilised parts of the world, ought in this, as it doth in other customs, to include the rest.

"But perhaps you may tell me, I have proposed such a way to make rhyme natural, and consequently proper to plays, as is unpracticable; and that I shall scarce find six or eight lines together in any play, where the words are so placed and chosen as is required to make it natural. I answer, no poet need constrain himself at all times to it. It is enough he makes it his general rule; for I deny not but sometimes there may be a greatness in placing the words otherwise; and sometimes they may sound better; sometimes also the variety itself is excuse enough. But if, for the most part, the words be placed as they are in the negligence of prose, it is sufficient to denominate the way practicable; for we esteem that to be such, which in the trial oftener succeeds than misses. And thus far you may find the practice made good in many plays: where you do not, remember still, that if you cannot find six natural rhymes together, it will be as hard for you to produce as many lines in blank verse, even among the greatest of our poets, against which I cannot make some reasonable exception.

"And this, Sir, calls to my remembrance the beginning of your discourse, where you told us we should never find the audience favourable to this kind of writing, till we could produce as good plays in rhyme as Ben Jonson, Fletcher, and Shakspeare had writ out of it. But it is to raise envy to the living, to compare them with the dead. They are honoured, and almost adored by us, as they deserve; neither do I know any so presumptuous of themselves as to contend with them. Yet give me leave to say thus much, without injury to their ashes; that not only we shall never equal them, but they could never equal themselves, were they to rise and write again. We acknowledge them our fathers in wit; but they have ruined their estates themselves, before they came to their children's hands. There is scarce an humour, a character, or any kind of plot, which they have not used. All comes sullied or wasted to us: and were they to entertain this age, they could not now make so plenteous treatments out of such decayed fortunes. This therefore will be a good argument to us, either not to write at all, or to attempt some other way. There is no bays to be expected in their walks: *tentanda via est, qua me quoque possum tollere humo.*

"This way of writing in verse they have only left free to us; our age is arrived to a perfection in it, which they never knew; and which (if we may guess by what of theirs we have seen in verse, as *The Faithful Shepherdess,* and *Sad Shepherd*) 'tis probable they never could have reached. For the genius of every age is different;

and though ours excel in this, I deny not but to imitate Nature in that perfection which they did in prose, is a greater commendation than to write in verse exactly. As for what you have added—that the people are not generally inclined to like this way, if it were true, it would be no wonder, that betwixt the shaking off an old habit, and the introducing of a new, there should be difficulty. Do we not see them stick to Hopkins' and Sternhold's psalms, and forsake those of David, I mean Sandys his translation of them? If by the people you understand the multitude, the οἱ πολλοί, 'tis no matter what they think; they are sometimes in the right, sometimes in the wrong; their judgment is a mere lottery. *Est ubi plebs recte putat, est ubi peccat.* Horace says it of the vulgar, judging poesy. But if you mean the mixed audience of the populace and the noblesse, I dare confidently affirm that a great part of the latter sort are already favourable to verse; and that no serious plays written since the King's return have been more kindly received by them than *The Siege of Rhodes,* the *Mustapha, The Indian Queen,* and *Indian Emperor.*

"But I come now to the inference of your first argument. You said that the dialogue of plays is presented as the effect of sudden thought, but no man speaks suddenly, or *ex tempore,* in rhyme; and you inferred from thence, that rhyme, which you acknowledge to be proper to epic poesy, cannot equally be proper to dramatic, unless we could suppose all men born so much more than poets, that verses should be made in them, not by them.

"It has been formerly urged by you, and confessed by me, that since no man spoke any kind of verse *ex tempore,* that which was nearest Nature was to be preferred. I answer you, therefore, by distinguishing betwixt what is nearest to the nature of Comedy, which is the imitation of common persons and ordinary speaking, and what is nearest to the nature of a serious play: this last is indeed the representation of Nature.

but 'tis Nature wrought up to a higher pitch. The plot, the characters, the wit, the passions, the descriptions, are all exalted above the level of common converse, as high as the imagination of the poet can carry them, with proportion to verisimility. Tragedy, we know, is wont to image to us the minds and fortunes of noble persons, and to portray these exactly; heroic rhyme is nearest Nature, as being the noblest kind of modern verse.

Indignatur enim privatis et prope socco
Dignis carminibus narrari coena Thyestae,

says Horace: and in another place,

Effutire leves indigna tragaedia versus.

Blank verse is acknowledged to be too low for a poem, nay more, for a paper of verses; but if too low for an ordinary sonnet, how much more for Tragedy, which is by Aristotle, in the dispute betwixt the epic poesy and the dramatic, for many reasons he there alleges, ranked above it?

"But setting this defence aside, your argument is almost as strong against the use of rhyme in poems as in plays; for the epic way is everywhere interlaced with dialogue, or discoursive scenes; and therefore you must either grant rhyme to be improper there, which is contrary to your assertion, or admit it into plays by the same title which you have given it to poems. For though tragedy be justly preferred above the other, yet there is a great affinity between them, as may easily be discovered in that definition of a play which Lisideius gave us. The *genus* of them is the same—a just and lively image of human nature, in its actions, passions, and traverses of fortune: so is the end—namely, for the delight and benefit of mankind. The characters and persons are still the same, viz., the greatest of both sorts; only the manner of acquainting us with those actions, passions, and fortunes, is different. Tragedy performs it *viva voce*, or by action, in dialogue; wherein it excels the Epic Poem, which does it chiefly by narration. and therefore is not so lively an image of human nature. However, the agreement betwixt them is such, that if rhyme be proper for one, it must be for the other. Verse, 'tis true, is not the effect of sudden thought; but this hinders not that sudden thought may be represented in verse, since those thoughts are such as must be higher than Nature can raise them without premeditation, especially to a continuance of them, even out of verse; and consequently you cannot imagine them to have been sudden either in the poet or in the actors. A play, as I have said, to be like Nature, is to be set above it; as statues which are placed on high are made greater than the life, that they may descend to the sight in their just proportion.

"Perhaps I have insisted too long on this objection; but the clearing of it will make my stay shorter on the rest. You tell us, Crites, that rhyme appears most unnatural in repartees, or short replies: when he who answers (it being presumed he knew not what the other would say, yet) makes up that part of the verse which was left incomplete, and supplies both the sound and measure of it. This, you say, looks rather like the confederacy of two, than the answer of one.

"This, I confess, is an objection which is in every man's mouth, who loves not rhyme: but suppose, I beseech you, the repartee were made only in blank verse, might not part of the same argument be turned against you? for the measure is as often supplied there as it is in rhyme; the latter half of the hemistich as commonly made up, or a second line subjoined as a reply to the former; which any one leaf in Jonson's plays will sufficiently clear to you. You will often find in the Greek tragedians, and in Seneca, that when a scene grows up into the warmth of repartees, which is the close fighting of it, the latter part of the trimeter is supplied by him who answers; and yet it was never observed as a fault in them by any of the ancient or modern critics. The case is the same in our verse, as it was in theirs; rhyme to us being in lieu of quantity to them. But if no latitude is to be allowed a poet, you take from him not only his licence of *quidlibet audendi*, but you tie him up in a straiter compass than you would a philosopher. This is in deed *Musas colere severiores*. You would have him follow Nature, but he must follow her on foot: you have dismounted him from his Pegasus. But you tell us, this supplying the last half of a verse, or adjoining a whole second to the former, looks more like the design of two, than the answer of one. Supposing we acknowledge it: how comes this confederacy to be more displeasing to you, than in a dance which is well contrived? You see there the united design of many persons to make up one figure: after they have separated themselves in many petty divisions, they rejoin one by one into a gross: the confederacy is plain amongst them, for chance could never produce anything so beautiful; and yet there is nothing in it that shocks your sight. I acknowledge the hand of art appears in repartee, as of necessity it must in all kind of verse. But there is also the quick and poignant brevity of it (which is an high imitation of Nature in those sudden gusts of passion) to mingle with it; and this, joined with the cadency and sweetness of the rhyme, leaves nothing in the soul of the hearer to desire. 'Tis an art which appears; but it appears only like the shadowings of painture, which being to cause the rounding of it, cannot be absent; but while that is considered, they are lost: so while we attend to the other beauties of the matter, the care and labour of the rhyme is carried from us or at least drowned in its own sweetness, as bees are sometimes buried in their honey. When a poet has found the repartee, the last perfection he can add to it, is to put it into verse. However good the thought may be, however apt the words in which 'tis couched, yet he finds himself at a little unrest, while rhyme is wanting: he cannot leave it till that comes naturally, and then is at ease, and sits down contented.

"From replies, which are the most elevated thoughts of verse, you pass to those which are most mean, and which are common with the lowest of household conversation. In these, you say, the majesty of verse suffers. You instance in the calling of a servant, or commanding a door to be shut, in rhyme. This, Crites, is a good observation of yours, but no argument; for it proves no more but that such thoughts should be waiv'd as often as may be, by the address of the poet. But suppose they are necessary in the places where he uses them, yet there is no need to put them into rhyme. He may place them in the beginning of a verse, and break it off, as unfit, when so debased, for any other use: or granting the worst, that they require more room than the hemistich will allow, yet still there is a choice to be made of the best words, and least vulgar (provided they be apt), to express such thoughts. Many have blamed rhyme in general, for this fault, when the poet with a little care might have redressed it. But they do it with no more justice than if English Poesy should be made ridiculous for the sake of the Water Poet's rhymes. Our language is noble, full, and significant; and I know not why he who is master of it may not clothe ordinary things in it as decently as the Latin, if he use the same diligence in his choice of words: *delectus verborum origo est eloquentiae*. It was the saying of Julius Caesar, one so curious in his, that none of them can be changed but for a worse. One would think, *unlock the door*, was a thing as vulgar as could be spoken; and yet Seneca could make it sound high and lofty in his Latin:

> *Reserate clusos regii postes laris.*
> Set wide the palace gates.

"But I turn from this conception, both because it happens not above twice or thrice in any play that those vulgar thoughts are used; and then too, were there no other apology to be made, yet the necessity of them, which is alike in all kind of writing, may excuse them. For if they are little and mean in rhyme, they are of consequence such in blank verse. Besides that the great eagerness and precipitation with which they are spoken, makes us rather mind the substance than the dress; that for which they are spoken, rather than what is spoken. For they are always the effect of some hasty concernment, and something of consequence depends on them.

"Thus, Crites, I have endeavoured to answer your objections; it remains only that I should vindicate an argument for verse, which you have gone about to overthrow. It had formerly been said that the easiness of blank verse renders the poet too luxuriant, but that the labour of rhyme bounds and circumscribes an over-fruitful fancy; the sense there being commonly confined to the couplet, and the words so ordered that the rhyme naturally follows them, not they the rhyme. To this you answered, that it was no argument to the question in hand; for the dispute was not which way a man may write best, but which is most proper for the subject on which he writes.

"First, give me leave, Sir, to remember you that the argument against which you raised this objection was only secondary: it was built on this hypothesis, that to write in verse was proper for serious plays. Which supposition being granted (as it was briefly made out in that discourse, by showing how verse might be made natural), it asserted, that this way of writing was an help to the poet's judgment, by putting bounds to a wild overflowing fancy. I think, therefore, it will not be hard for me to make good what it was to prove on that supposition. But you add, that were this let pass, yet he who wants judgment in the liberty of his fancy, may as well show the defect of it when he is confined to verse; for he who has judgment will avoid errors, and he who has it not, will commit them in all kinds of writing.

"This argument, as you have taken it from a most acute person, so I confess it carries much weight in it: but by using the word judgment here indefinitely, you seem to have put a fallacy upon us. I grant, he who has judgment, that is, so profound, so strong, or rather so infallible a judgment, that he needs no helps to keep it always poised and upright, will commit no faults either in rhyme or out of it. And on the other extreme, he who has a judgment so weak and crazed that no helps can correct or amend it, shall write scurvily out of rhyme, and worse in it. But the first of these judgments is nowhere to be found, and the latter is not fit to write at all. To speak therefore of judgment as it is in the best poets; they who have the greatest proportion of it, want other helps than from it, within. As for example, you would be loth to say that he who is endued with a sound judgment has no need of History, Geography, or Moral Philosophy, to write correctly. Judgment is indeed the master-workman in a play; but he requires many subordinate hands, many tools to his assistance. And verse I affirm to be one of these; 'tis a rule and line by which he keeps his building compact and even, which otherwise lawless imagination would raise either irregularly or loosely; at least, if the poet commits errors with this help, he would make greater and more without it: 'tis, in short, a slow and painful, but the surest kind of working. Ovid, whom you accuse for luxuriancy in verse, had perhaps been farther guilty of it, had he writ in prose. And for your instance of Ben Jonson, who, you say, writ exactly without the help of rhyme; you are to remember, 'tis only an aid to a luxuriant fancy, which his was not: as he did not want imagination, so none ever said he had much to spare. Neither was verse then refined so much, to be an help to that age, as it is to ours. Thus then the second thoughts being usually the best, as receiving the maturest digestion from judgment, and the last and most mature product of those thoughts being artful and laboured verse, it may be well inferred, that verse is a great help to a luxuriant fancy; and this is what that argument which you opposed was to evince."

Neander was pursuing this discourse so eagerly that Eugenius had called to him twice or thrice, ere he took notice that the barge stood still, and that they were at the foot of Somerset Stairs, where they had appointed it to land. The company were all sorry to separate so soon, though a great part of the evening was already spent; and stood awhile looking back on the water, upon which the moonbeams played, and made it appear like floating quicksilver: at last they went up through a crowd of French people, who were merrily dancing in the open air, and nothing concerned for the noise of guns which had alarmed the town that afternoon. Walking thence together to the Piazze, they parted here; Eugenius and Lisideius to some pleasant appointment they had made, and Crites and Neander to their several lodgings.

SIR WILLIAM TEMPLE (1628-1699)

Temple played an important rôle in history as a diplomat, especially in strengthening the Protestant interest in Europe to counterbalance the increasing power of Louis XIV. In 1668 he concluded the Triple Alliance between England, Holland, and Sweden. He was chiefly responsible for the marriage in 1677 of Princess Mary to William of Orange, which later had such a profound influence on English history through the political establishment of the Revolution of 1688. In domestic politics he was less successful; in 1679 he endeavored to prevent the crisis in government which seemed threatening with the division of the nation into Whigs and Tories, but his proposals were rejected. Deeply disappointed, he gave up public affairs and retired to his estate at Moor Park, devoting himself henceforth to writing his memoirs and essays and leading a cultivated life of leisure among his books. It was here that Jonathan Swift joined his household as secretary.

As a man of the world, Temple carried his learning with ease and grace, but he preferred, as he said, old wine, old friends, and old books. In his essay *On Ancient and Modern Learning* (1690) he took the side of the Ancients in the controversy which had already been raging in Paris as to whether the Moderns had excelled the Ancients in the sciences and arts. The essay was not valuable in itself, as Temple's scholarship was more genteel than penetrating or critical; but the controversy it raised in England stimulated Richard Bentley, one of the greatest Greek scholars of any age, to publish a masterly *Dissertation on the Epistles of Phalaris*; more important still, it inspired Swift to write that masterpiece of parody and banter, *The Battle of the Books*. In the essay *Of Poetry* Temple's partisanship with the Ancients is clearly expressed, but the eighteenth-century reader was more interested in the revelation of a hitherto-neglected Norse literature and in Temple's defence of some of those characteristically English literary qualities which were scorned by gentlemen of the purest Parisian taste. Here, as also in the attention he called in another essay to the beauties of Oriental gardening, his influence upon the following century was distinctly liberal. His reputation as an artist in prose was high, and Dr. Johnson declared that he "was the first writer who gave cadence to English prose,"—by which we must understand that kind of cadence which the eighteenth century enjoyed best.

The *Essays on Ancient and Modern Learning and on Poetry* were edited by J. E. Spingarn (Oxford, 1909). There were numerous editions of Temple's *Works* in the eighteenth century. Among essays on him should be noted Charles Lamb's "The Genteel Style in Writing," in *Last Essays of Elia* (1833), and T. B. Macaulay's "Life and Writings of Temple" (1838). Two small readable volumes are by M. L. R. Beavan (Oxford, 1908) and E. S. Lyttel (Oxford, 1908). Temple's relation to the thought of his time has been studied by Clara Marburg in *Sir William Temple; a Seventeenth Century "Libertin"* (New Haven, 1932).

OF POETRY (1690)

The two common shrines to which most men offer up the application of their thoughts and their lives are profit and pleasure; and by their devotions to either of these, they are vulgarly distinguished into two sects, and called either busy or idle men. Whether these terms differ in meaning or only in sound, I know very well may be disputed, and with appearance enough, since the covetous man takes perhaps as much pleasure in his gains as the voluptuous does in his luxury, and would not pursue his business unless he were pleased with it, upon the last account of what he most wishes and desires, nor would care for the increase of his fortunes unless he proposed thereby that of his pleasures, too, in one kind or other, so that pleasure may be said to be his end, whether he will allow to find it in his pursuit or no. Much ado there has been, many words spent, or (to speak with more respect to the ancient philosophers) many disputes have been raised upon this argument, I think to little purpose, and that all has been rather an exercise of wit than an inquiry after truth, and all controversies that can never end had better perhaps never begin. The best is to take words as they are most commonly spoken and meant, like coin as it most currently passes, without raising scruples upon the weight or the allay, unless the cheat or the defect be gross and evident. Few things in the world, or none, will bear too much refining; a thread too fine spun will easily break, and the point of a needle too finely filed. The usual acceptation takes profit and pleasure for two different things, and not only calls the followers or votaries of them by several names of busy and idle men, but distinguishes the faculties of the mind that are conversant about them, calling the operations of the first wisdom, and of the other wit, which is a Saxon word that is used to express what the Spaniards and Italians call *ingenio*, and the French, *esprit*, both from the Latin; but I think wit more peculiarly signifies that of poetry, as may occur upon remarks of the runic language. To the first of these are attributed the inventions or productions of things generally esteemed the most necessary, useful, or profitable to human life, either in private possessions or public institutions; to the other, those writings or discourses which are the most pleasing or entertaining to all that read or hear them. Yet, according to the opinion of those that link them together, as the inventions of sages and lawgivers themselves do please as well as profit those who follow them, so those of poets instruct and profit as well as please such as are conversant in them; and the happy mixture of both these makes the excellency in both those compositions, and has given occasion for esteeming, or at least for calling, heroic virtue and poetry divine.

The names given to poets, both in Greek and Latin, express the same opinion of them in those nations: the Greek signifying makers or creators, such as raise admirable frames and fabrics out of nothing, which strike with wonder and with pleasure the eyes and imaginations of those who behold them; the Latin makes the same word common to poets and to prophets. Now, as creation is the first attribute and highest operation of divine power, so is prophecy the greatest emanation of divine spirit in the world. As the names in those two learned languages, so the causes of poetry, are by the writers of them made to be divine, and to proceed from a celestial fire or divine inspiration; and by the vulgar opinions, recited or related to in many passages of those authors, the effects of poetry were likewise thought divine and supernatural, and power of charms and enchantments were ascribed to it.

Carmina vel caelo possunt deducere lunam,
Carminibus Circe socios mutavit Ulyssis,
Frigidus in pratis cantando rumpitur anguis.

But I can easily admire poetry, and yet without adoring it: I can allow it to arise from the greatest excellency of natural temper or the greatest race of native genius, without exceeding the reach of what is human, or giving it any approaches of divinity, which is, I doubt, debased or dishonored by ascribing to it anything that is in the compass of our action or even comprehension, unless it be raised by an immediate influence from itself. I cannot allow poetry to be more divine in its effects than in its causes, nor any operation produced by it to be more than purely natural, or to deserve any other sort of wonder than those of music or of natural magic, however any of them have appeared to minds little versed in the speculations of nature, of occult qualities, and the force of numbers or of sounds. Whoever talks of drawing down the moon from heaven by force of verses or of charms either believes not himself or too easily believes what others told him, or perhaps follows an opinion begun by the practice of some poet upon the facility of some people—who, knowing the time when an eclipse would happen, told them he would by his charms call down the moon at such an hour, and was by them thought to have performed it.

When I read that charming description in Virgil's Eighth Eclogue of all sorts of charms and fascinations by verses, by images, by knots, by numbers, by fire, by herbs, employed upon occasion of a violent passion from a jealous or disappointed love, I have recourse to the strong impressions of fables and of poetry, to the easy mistakes of popular opinions, to the force of imagination, to the secret virtues of several herbs, and to the powers of sounds. And I am sorry the natural history or account of fascination has not employed the pen of some person of such excellent wit and deep thought and learning as Casaubon, who writ that curious and useful treatise of *Enthusiasm*, and by it discovered the hidden or mistaken sources of that delusion so frequent in all regions and religions of the world, and which had so fatally spread over our country in that age in which this treatise was so seasonably published. 'Tis much to be lamented that he lived not to complete that work in the Second Part he promised, or that his friends neglected the publishing it, if it were left in papers, though loose and unfinished. I think a clear account of enthusiasm and fascination from their natural causes would very much deserve from mankind in general as well as from the commonwealth of learning, might perhaps prevent many public disorders, and save the lives of many innocent deluded or deluding people, who suffer so frequently upon account of witches and wizards. I have seen many miserable examples of this kind in my youth at home; and though the humor or fashion be a good deal worn out of the world within thirty or forty years past, yet it still remains in several remote parts of Germany, Sweden, and some other countries.

But to return to the charms of poetry, if the forsaken lover in that eclogue of Virgil had expected only from the force of her verses or her charms, what is the burden of the song, to bring Daphnis home from the town where he was gone and engaged in a new amour; if she had pretended only to revive an old fainting flame, or to damp a new one that was kindling in his breast, she might, for aught I know, have compassed such ends by the power of such charms, and without other than very natural enchantments. For there is no question but true poetry may have the force to raise passions and to allay them, to change and to extinguish them, to temper joy and grief, to raise love and fear, nay, to turn fear into boldness, and love into indifference and into hatred itself; and I easily believe that the disheartened Spartans were new animated, and recovered their lost courage, by the songs of Tyrtaeus, that the cruelty and revenge of Phalaris were changed by the odes of Stesichorus into the greatest kindness and esteem, and that many men were as passionately enamored by the charms of Sappho's wit and poetry as by those of beauty in Flora or Thais; for 'tis not only beauty gives love, but love gives beauty to the object that raises it; and if the possession be strong enough, let it come from what it will, there is always beauty enough in the person that gives it. Nor is it any great wonder that such force should be found in poetry, since in it are assembled all the powers of eloquence, of music, and of picture, which are all allowed to make so strong impressions upon human minds. How far men have been affected with all or any of these needs little proof or testimony. The examples have been known enough in Greece and Italy, where some have fallen downright in love with the ravishing beauties of a lovely object drawn by the skill of admirable painter; nay, painters themselves have fallen in love with some of their own productions, and doted on them as on a mistress or a fond child, which distinguishes among the Italians the several pieces that are done by the same hand into several degrees of those made *con studio, con diligenza,* or *con amore,* whereof the last are ever the most excelling. But there needs no more instances of this kind than the stories related and believed by the best authors as known and undisputed; of the two young Grecians, one whereof ventured his life to be locked up all night in the temple, and satisfy his passion with the embraces and enjoyment of a statue of Venus, that was there set up and designed for another sort of adoration; the other pined away and died for being hindered his perpetually gazing, admiring, and embracing a statue at Athens.

The powers of music are either felt and known by all men, and are allowed to work strangely upon the mind and the body, the passions and the blood, to raise joy and grief, to give pleasure and pain, to cure diseases and the mortal sting of the tarantula, to give motions to the feet as well as the heart, to compose disturbed thoughts, to assist and heighten devotion itself. We need no recourse to the fables of Orpheus or Amphion, or the force of their music upon fishes and beasts: 'tis enough that we find the charming of serpents and the cure or allay of an evil spirit or possession attributed to it in Sacred Writ.

For the force of eloquence that so often raised and appeased the violence of popular commotions and caused such convulsions in the Athenian state, no man need more to make him acknowledge it than to consider Caesar, one of the greatest and wisest of mortal men, come upon the tribunal full of hatred and revenge, and with a determined resolution to condemn Labienus, yet upon the force of Cicero's eloquence, in an oration for his defense, begin to change countenance, turn pale, shake to that degree that the papers he held fell out of his hand, as if he had been frighted with words that never was so with blows, and at last change all his anger into clemency, and acquit the brave criminal instead of condemning him.

Now, if the strength of these three mighty powers be united in poetry, we need not wonder that such virtues and such honors have been attributed to it that it has been thought to be inspired, or has been called divine; and yet I think it will not be disputed that the force of wit and of reasoning, the height of conceptions and expressions, may be found in poetry as well as in oratory, the life and spirit of representation or picture as much as in painting, and the force of sounds as well as in music; and how far these three natural powers together may extend, and to what effect, even such as may be mistaken for supernatural or magical, I leave it to such men to consider whose thoughts turn to such speculations as these, or who by their native temper and genius are in some degree disposed to receive the impressions of them. For my part, I do not wonder that the famous Doctor Harvey, when he was reading Virgil, should sometimes throw him down upon the table, and say he had a devil, nor that the learned Meric Casaubon should find such charming pleasures and emotions as he describes upon the reading some parts of Lucretius; that so many should cry, and with downright tears, at some tragedies of Shakespeare, and so many more should feel such turns or curdling of their blood upon the reading or hearing some excellent pieces of poetry, nor that Octavia fell into a swound at the recital made by Virgil of those verses in the Sixth of his *Æneids.*

This is enough to assert the powers of poetry, and discover the ground of those opinions of old which derived it from divine inspiration, and gave it so great a share in the supposed effects of sorcery or magic. But as the old romances seem to lessen the honor of true prowess and valor in their knights by giving such a part in all their chief adventures to enchantment, so the true excellency and just esteem of poetry seems rather debased than exalted by the stories or belief of the charms performed by it, which among the northern nations grew so strong and so general that about five or six hundred years ago all the runic poetry came to be decried, and those ancient characters in which they were written to be abolished by the zeal of bishops and even by orders and decrees of state, which has given a great maim, or rather an irrecoverable loss, to the story of those northern kingdoms, the seat of our ancestors in all the western parts of Europe.

The more true and natural source of poetry may be discovered by observing to what god this inspiration was ascribed by the ancients, which was Apollo, or the Sun, esteemed among them the god of learning in general, but more particularly of music and of poetry. The mystery of this fable means, I suppose, that a certain noble and vital heat of temper, but especially of the brain, is the true spring of these two arts or sciences. This was that celestial fire which gave such a pleasing motion and agitation to the minds of those men that have been so much admired in the world, that raises such infinite images of things so agreeable and delightful to mankind. By the influence of this sun are produced those golden and inexhausted mines of invention, which has furnished the world with treasures so highly esteemed and so universally known and used in all the regions that have yet been discovered. From this arises that elevation of genius which can never be produced by any art or study, by pains or by industry, which cannot be taught by precepts or examples, and therefore is agreed by all to be the pure and free gift of Heaven or of Nature, and to be a fire kindled out of some hidden spark of the very first conception.

But though invention be the mother of poetry, yet this child is like all others born naked, and must be nourished with care, clothed with exactness and elegance, educated with industry, instructed with art, improved by application, corrected with severity, and accomplished with labour and with time, before it arrives at any great perfection or growth. 'Tis certain that no composition requires so many gifts of nature and so many improvements of learning and of art. For there must be an universal genius, of great compass as well as great elevation. There must be a sprightly imagination or fancy, fertile in a thousand productions, ranging over infinite ground, piercing into every corner, and by the light of that true poetical fire discovering a thousand little bodies or images in the world, and similitudes among them, unseen to common eyes, and which could not be discovered without the rays of that sun.

Besides the heat of invention and liveliness of wit, there must be the coldness of good sense and soundness of judgment, to distinguish between things and conceptions which at first sight or upon short glances seem alike, to choose among infinite productions of wit and fancy which are worth preserving and cultivating, and which are better stifled in the birth or thrown away when they are born, as not worth bringing up. Without the forces of wit all poetry is flat and languishing; without the succors of judgment 'tis wild and extravagant. The true wonder of poesy is that such contraries must meet to compose it: a genius both penetrating and solid; in expression both delicacy and force; and the frame or fabric of a true poem must have something both sublime and just, amazing and agreeable. There must be a great agitation of mind to invent, a great calm to judge and correct; there must be upon the same tree, and at the same time, both flower and fruit. To work up this metal into exquisite figure, there must be employed the fire, the hammer, the chisel, and the file. There must be a general knowledge both of nature and of arts; and to go the lowest that can be, there are required genius, judgment, and application; for without this last all the rest will not serve turn, and none ever was a great poet that applied himself much to anything else.

When I speak of poetry, I mean not an ode or an elegy, a song or a satire, nor by a poet the composer of any of these, but of a just poem; and after all I have said, 'tis no wonder there should be so few that appeared in any parts or any ages of the world, or that such as have should be so much admired, and have almost divinity ascribed to them and to their works.

Whatever has been among those who are mentioned with so much praise or admiration by the ancients, but are lost to us, and unknown any further than their names, I think no man has been so bold among those that remain to question the title of Homer and Virgil, not only to the first rank, but to the supreme dominion in this state, and from whom, as the great lawgivers as well as princes, all the laws and orders of it are or may be derived. Homer was without dispute the most universal genius that has been known in the world, and Virgil the most accomplished. To the first must be allowed the most fertile invention, the richest vein, the most general knowledge, and the most lively expression: to the last, the noblest ideas, the justest institution, the wisest conduct, and the choicest elocution. To speak in the painters' terms, we find in the works of Homer the most spirit, force, and life; in those of Virgil, the best design, the truest proportions, and the greatest grace: the coloring in both seems equal, and, indeed, in both is admirable. Homer had more fire and rapture, Virgil more light and swiftness; or at least the poetical fire was more raging in one, but clearer in the other, which makes the first more amazing and the latter more agreeable. The ore was richer in one, but in t'other more refined, and better allayed to make up excellent work. Upon the whole, I think it must be confessed that Homer was of the two, and perhaps of all others, the vastest, the sublimest, and the most wonderful genius; and that he has been generally

so esteemed, there cannot be a greater testimony given than what has been by some observed, that not only the greatest masters have found in his works the best and truest principles of all their sciences or arts, but that the noblest nations have derived from them the original of their several races, though it be hardly yet agreed whether his story be true or fiction. In short, these two immortal poets must be allowed to have so much excelled in their kinds as to have exceeded all comparison, to have even extinguished emulation, and in a manner confined true poetry not only to their two languages, but to their very persons. And I am apt to believe so much of the true genius of poetry in general, and of its elevation in these two particulars, that I know not whether of all the numbers of mankind that live within the compass of a thousand years, for one man that is born capable of making such a poet as Homer or Virgil, there may not be a thousand born capable of making as great generals of armies or ministers of state as any the most renowned in story.

I do not here intend to make a further critique upon poetry, which were too great a labor, nor to give rules for it, which were as great a presumption. Besides, there has been so much paper blotted upon these subjects in this curious and censuring age that 'tis all grown tedious or repetition. The modern French wits (or pretenders) have been very severe in their censures and exact in their rules, I think to very little purpose; for I know not why they might not have contented themselves with those given by Aristotle and Horace, and have translated them rather than commented upon them, for all they have done has been no more, so as they seem, by their writings of this kind, rather to have valued themselves than improved anybody else. The truth is, there is something in the genius of poetry too libertine to be confined to so many rules; and whoever goes about to subject it to such constraints loses both its spirit and grace, which are ever native, and never learnt, even of the best masters. 'Tis as if, to make excellent honey, you should cut off the wings of your bees, confine them to their hive or their stands, and lay flowers before them, such as you think the sweetest and like to yield the finest extraction; you had as good pull out their stings, and make arrant drones of them. They must range through fields as well as gardens, choose such flowers as they please, and by proprieties and scents they only know and distinguish. They must work up their cells with admirable art, extract their honey with infinite labor, and sever it from the wax with such distinction and choice as belongs to none but themselves to perform or to judge.

It would be too much mortification to these great arbitrary rulers among the French writers or our own to observe the worthy productions that have been formed by their rules, the honor they have received in the world, or the pleasure they have given mankind. But to comfort them, I do not know there was any great poet in Greece after the rules of that art laid down by Aristotle, nor in Rome after those by Horace, which yet none of our moderns pretend to have outdone. Perhaps Theocritus and Lucan may be alleged against this assertion; but the first offered no further than at idyls or eclogues; and the last, though he must be avowed for a true and a happy genius, and to have made some very high flights, yet he is so unequal to himself, and his muse is so young, that his faults are too noted to allow his pretenses. *Feliciter audet* is the true character of Lucan, as of Ovid, *Lusit amabiliter*. After all, the utmost that can be achieved or, I think, pretended by any rules in this art is but to hinder some men from being very ill poets, but not to make any man a very good one. To judge who is so, we need go no further for instruction than three lines of Horace:

Ille meum qui pectus inaniter angit,
Irritat, mulcet, falsis terroribus implet,
Ut Magus, et modo me Thebis, modo ponit
    Athenis.

He is a poet,

Who vainly anguishes my breast,
Provokes, allays, and with false terror fills,
Like a magician, and now sets me down
In Thebes, and now in Athens.

Whoever does not affect and move the same present passions in you that he represents in others, and at other times raise images about you, as a conjuror is said to do spirits, transport you to the places and to the persons he describes, cannot be judged to be a poet, though his measures are never so just, his feet never so smooth, or his sounds never so sweet.

But instead of critique or rules concerning poetry, I shall rather turn my thoughts to the history of it, and observe the antiquity, the uses, the changes, the decays, that have attended this great empire of wit.

It is, I think, generally agreed to have been the first sort of writing that has been used in the world, and in several nations to have preceded the very invention or usage of letters. This last is certain in America, where the first Spaniards met with many strains of poetry, and left several of them translated into their language, which seem to have flowed from a true poetic vein before any letters were known in those regions. The same is probable of the Scythians, the Grecians, and the Germans. Aristotle says the Agathyrsi had their laws all in verse; and Tacitus, that they had no annals nor records but what were so; and for the Grecian oracles delivered in them, we have no certain account when they began, but rather reason to believe it was before the introduction of letters from Phœnicia among them. Pliny tells it, as a thing known, that Pherecides was the first who writ prose in the Greek tongue, and that he lived about the time of Cyrus, whereas Homer and Hesiod lived some hundreds of years before that age, and Orpheus, Linus, Musæus, some hundreds before them: and of the Sybils, several were before any of those, and in times as well as places whereof we have no clear records now remaining. What Solon and Pythagoras writ is said to have been in verse, who were something older than Cyrus; and before them were Archilocus, Simonides, Tyrtæus, Sappho, Stesichorus, and several other poets famous in their times. The same thing is reported of Chaldæa, Syria, and China; among the ancient Western Goths, our ancestors, the runic poetry seems to have been as old as their letters; and their laws, their precepts of wisdom as well as their records, their religious rites as well as their charms and incantations, to have been all in verse.

Among the Hebrews, and even in Sacred Writ, the most ancient is by some learned men esteemed to be the Book of Job, and that it was written before the time of Moses, and that it was a translation into Hebrew, out of the old Chaldæan or Arabian language. It may probably be conjectured that he was not a Jew, from the place of his abode, which appears to have been seated between the Chaldæans on one side and the Sabæans (who were of Arabia) on the other; and by many passages of that admirable and truly inspired poem, the author seems to have lived in some parts near the mouth of Euphrates, or the Persian Gulf, where he contemplated the wonders of the deep as well as the other works of nature common to those regions. Nor is it easy to find any traces of the Mosaical rites or institutions, either in the divine worship or the morals related to in those writings: for not only sacrifices and praises were much more ancient in religious service than the age of Moses; but the opinion of one deity, and adored without any idol or representation, was professed and received among the ancient Persians and Etruscans and Chaldæans. So that if Job was an Hebrew, 'tis probable he may have been of the race of Heber, who lived in Chaldæa, or of Abraham, who is supposed to have left

that country for the profession or worship of one God, rather than from the branch of Isaac and Israel, who lived in the land of Canaan. Now, I think it is out of controversy that the Book of Job was written originally in verse, and was a poem upon the subject of the justice and power of God, and in vindication of His providence against the common arguments of atheistical men, who took occasion to dispute it from the usual events of human things, by which so many ill and impious men seem happy and prosperous in the course of their lives, and so many pious and just men seem miserable or afflicted. The Spanish translation of the Jews in Ferrara, which pretends to render the Hebrew, as near as could be, word for word, and for which all translators of the Bible since have had great regard, gives us the two first chapters and the last from the seventh verse in prose, as an historical introduction and conclusion of the work, and all the rest in verse, except the transitions from one part or person of this sacred dialogue to another.

But if we take the Books of Moses to be the most ancient in the Hebrew tongue, yet the song of Moses may probably have been written before the rest; as that of Deborah, before the Book of Judges, being praises sung to God upon the victories or successes of the Israelites, related in both. And I never read the last without observing in it as true and noble strains of poetry and picture as in any other language whatsoever, in spite of all disadvantages from translations into so different tongues and common prose. If an opinion of some learned men, both modern and ancient, could be allowed, that Esdras was the writer or compiler of the first historical parts of the Old Testament, though from the same divine inspiration as that of Moses and the other prophets, then the Psalms of David would be the first writings we find in Hebrew; and next to them, the Song of Solomon, which was written when he was young, and Ecclesiastes when he was old. So that from all sides, both sacred and profane, it appears that poetry was the first sort of writing known and used in the several nations of the world.

It may seem strange, I confess, upon the first thought, that a sort of style so regular and so difficult should have grown in use before the other so easy and so loose: but if we consider what the first end of writing was, it will appear probable from reason as well as experience; for the true and general end was but the help of memory in preserving that of words and of actions, which would otherwise have been lost and soon vanish away with the transitory passage of human breath and life. Before the discourses and disputes of philosophers began to busy or amuse the Grecian wits, there was nothing written in prose but either laws, some short sayings of wise men, or some riddles, parables, or fables, wherein were couched by the ancients many strains of natural or moral wisdom and knowledge, and besides these some short memorials of persons, actions, and of times. Now, 'tis obvious enough to conceive how much easier all such writings should be learnt and remembered in verse than in prose, not only by the pleasure of measures and of sounds, which gives a great impression to memory, but by the order of feet, which makes a great facility of tracing one word after another, by knowing what sort of foot or quantity must necessarily have preceded or followed the words we retain and desire to make up.

This made poetry so necessary before letters were invented, and so convenient afterwards; and shows that the great honour and general request wherein it has always been has not proceeded only from the pleasure and delight, but likewise from the usefulness and profit of poetical writings.

This leads me naturally to the subjects of poetry, which have been generally praise, instruction, story, love, grief, and reproach. Praise was the subject of all the songs and psalms mentioned in Holy Writ, of the hymns of Orpheus, of Homer, and many others; of the *carmina secularia* in Rome, composed all and designed for the honour of their gods; of Pindar, Stesichorus, and Tyrtæus, in the praises of virtue or virtuous men. The subject of Job is instruction concerning the attributes of God and the works of nature. Those of Simonides, Phocillides, Theognis, and several other of the smaller Greek poets, with what passes for Pythagoras, are instructions in morality; the first book of Hesiod and Virgil's *Georgics*, in agriculture, and Lucretius in the deepest natural philosophy. Story is the proper subject of heroic poems, as Homer and Virgil in their inimitable *Iliads* and *Æneids*; and fable, which is a sort of story, in the *Metamorphosis* of Ovid. The lyric poetry has been chiefly conversant about love, though turned often upon praise too; and the vein of pastorals and eclogues has run the same course, as may be observed in Theocritus, Virgil, and Horace, who was, I think, the first and last of true lyric poets among the Latins. Grief has been always the subject of elegy, and reproach that of satire. The dramatic poesy has been composed of all these, but the chief end seems to have been instruction, and under the disguise of fables or the pleasure of story to show the beauties and the rewards of virtue, the deformities and misfortunes of punishment of vice; by examples of both, to encourage one, and deter men from the other; to reform ill customs, correct ill manners, and moderate all violent passions. These are the general subjects of both parts, though comedy give us but the images of common life, and tragedy those of the greater and more extraordinary passions and actions among men. To go further upon this subject would be to tread so beaten paths that to travel in them only raises dust, and is neither of pleasure nor of use.

For the changes that have happened in poetry, I shall observe one ancient, and the others that are modern will be too remarkable, in the declines or decays of this great Empire of Wit.

The first change of poetry was made by translating it into prose, or clothing it in those loose robes or common veils that disguised or covered the true beauty of its features and exactness of its shape. This was done first by Æsop in Greek, but the vein was much more ancient in the eastern regions, and much in vogue, as we may observe in the many parables used in the Old Testament as well as in the New. And there is a book of fables, of the sort of Æsop's, translated out of Persian, and pretended to have been so into that language out of the ancient Indian; but though it seems genuine of the eastern countries, yet I do not take it to be so old nor to have so much spirit as the Greek. The next succession of poetry in prose seems to have been in the Miletian tales, which were a sort of little pastoral romances; and though much in request in old Greece and Rome, yet we have no examples that I know of them, unless it be the *Longi Pastoralia*, which gives a taste of the great delicacy and pleasure that was found so generally in those sort of tales. The last kind of poetry in prose is that which in latter ages has overrun the world under the name of romances, which though it seems modern and a production of the Gothic genius, yet the writing is ancient. The remainders of Petronius Arbiter seem to be of this kind, and that which Lucian calls his *True History*. But the most ancient that passes by the name is Heliodorus, famous for the author's choosing to lose his bishopric rather than disown that child of his wit. The true spirit or vein of ancient poetry in this kind seems to shine most in Sir Philip Sidney, whom I esteem both the greatest poet and the noblest genius of any that have left writings behind them and published in ours or any other modern language—a person born capable not only of forming the greatest ideas, but of leaving the noblest examples, if the length of his life had been equal to the excellence of his wit and his virtues.

With him I leave the discourse of ancient poetry, and to discover the decays of this empire must turn to that of the modern, which was introduced after the decays or rather extinction of the old, as if, true poetry being dead, an apparition of it walked about. This mighty change arrived by no smaller occasions nor more ignoble revolutions than those which destroyed the ancient empire and government of Rome, and erected so many new ones upon their ruins, by the invasions and conquests or the general inundations of the Goths, Vandals, and other barbarous or northern nations, upon those parts of Europe that had been subject to the Romans. After the conquests made by Caesar upon Gaul and the nearer parts of Germany, which were continued and enlarged in the times of Augustus and Tiberius by their lieutenants or generals, great numbers of Germans and Gauls resorted to the Roman armies, and to the city itself, and habituated themselves there, as many Spaniards, Syrians, Grecians had done before, upon the conquest of those countries. This mixture soon corrupted the purity of the Latin tongue, so that in Lucan, but more in Seneca, we find a great and harsh allay entered into the style of the Augustan Age. After Trajan and Adrian had subdued many German and Scythian nations on both sides of the Danube, the commerce of those barbarous people grew very frequent with the Romans; and I am apt to think that the little verses ascribed to Adrian were in imitation of the runic poetry. The *Scythicas Pati Pruinas* of Florus shows their race or climate, and the first rhyme that ever I read in Latin, with little allusions of letters or syllables, is in that of Adrian at his death:

> *O Animula vagula, blandula,*
> *Quæ nunc abibis in loca?*
> *Pallidula, lurida, timidula,*
> *Nec, ut soles, dabis joca.*

'Tis probable, the old spirit of poetry being lost or frighted away by those long and bloody wars with such barbarous enemies, this new ghost began to appear in its room even about that age, or else that Adrian, who affected that piece of learning as well as others, and was not able to reach the old vein, turned to a new one, which his expeditions into those countries made more allowable in an emperor, and his example recommended to others. In the time of Boethius, who lived under Theodoric in Rome, we find the Latin poetry smell rank of this Gothic imitation, and the old vein quite seared up.

After that age learning grew every day more and more obscured by that cloud of ignorance which, coming from the north and increasing with the numbers and successes of those barbarous people, at length overshadowed all Europe for so long together. The Roman tongue began itself to fail or be disused, and by its corruption made way for the generation of three new languages, in Spain, Italy, and France. The course of the princes and nobles, who were of the conquering nations, for several ages used their Gothic, or Franc, or Saxon tongues, which were mingled with those of Germany, where some of the Goths had sojourned long, before they proceeded to their conquests of the more southern or western parts. Wherever the Roman colonies had long remained and their language had been generally spoken, the common people used that still, but vitiated with the base allay of their provincial speech. This in Charlemagne's time was called in France *Rustica Romana*, and in Spain, during the Gothic reigns there, *Romance;* but in England, from whence all the Roman soldiers, and great numbers of the Britains most accustomed to their commerce and language, had been drained for the defense of Gaul against the barbarous nations that invaded it about the time of Valentinian, that tongue (being wholly extinguished, as well as their own) made way for the entire use of the Saxon language. With these changes the ancient poetry was wholly lost in all these countries, and a new sort grew up by degrees, which was called by a name of rhymes, with an easy change of the Gothic word *runes*, and not from the Greek *rythmes*, as is vulgarly supposed.

Runes was properly the name of the ancient Gothic letters or characters, which were invented first or introduced by Odin, in the colony or kingdom of the Getes or Goths, which he planted in the north-west parts and round the Baltic Sea, as has been before related. But because all the writings they had among them for many ages were in verse, it came to be the common name of all sorts of poetry among the Goths, and the writers or composers of them were called *runers*, or *rymers*. They had likewise another name for them, or for some sorts of them, which was *vüses*, or *wises*; and because the sages of that nation expressed the best of their thoughts, and what learning and prudence they had, in these kind of writings, they that succeeded best and with most applause were termed *wise-men*, the good sense or learning or useful knowledge contained in them was called *wisdom*, and the pleasant or facetious vein among them was called *wit*, which was applied to all spirit or race of poetry, where it was found in any men, and was generally pleasing to those that heard or read them.

Of these runes there were in use among the Goths above a hundred several sorts, some composed in longer, some in shorter lines, some equal and others unequal, with many different cadences, quantities, or feet, which in the pronouncing make many different sorts of original or natural tunes. Some were framed with allusions of words or consonance of syllables or of letters, either in the same line, or in the distich, or by alternate succession and resemblance, which made a sort of jingle that pleased the ruder ears of that people. And because their language was composed most of monosyllables and of so great numbers, many must end in the same sound; another sort of runes were made with the care and study of ending two lines, or each other of four lines, with words of the same sound, which being the easiest, requiring less art and needing less spirit, because a certain chime in the sounds supplied that want and pleased common ears, this in time grew the most general among all the Gothic colonies in Europe, and made rhymes or runes pass for the modern poetry in these parts of the world.

This was not used only in their modern languages, but, during those ignorant ages, even in that barbarous Latin which remained, and was preserved among the monks and priests, to distinguish them by some show of learning from the laity, who might well admire it, in what degree soever, and reverence the professors, when they themselves could neither write nor read, even in their own language; I mean, not only the vulgar laymen, but even the generality of nobles, barons, and princes among them; and this lasted till the ancient learning and languages began to be restored in Europe about two hundred years ago.

The common vein of the Gothic runes was what is termed dithyrambic, and was of a raving or rambling sort of wit or invention, loose and flowing, with little art or confinement to any certain measures or rules; yet some of it wanted not the true spirit of poetry in some degree, or that natural inspiration which has been said to arise from some spark of poetical fire wherewith particular men are born. And such as it was, it served the turn, not only to please, but even to charm the ignorant and barbarous vulgar, where it was in use. This made the runers among the Goths as much in request and admired as any of the ancient and most celebrated poets were among the learned nations; for among the blind, he that has one eye is a prince. They were as well as the others thought inspired, and the charms of their runic conceptions were generally esteemed divine, or magical at least.

The subjects of them were various, but commonly the same with those already observed in the true ancient poetry. Yet this vein was chiefly employed upon the records of bold and martial actions, and the praises of valiant men that had fought successfully or died bravely; and these songs or ballads were usually sung at feasts, or in circles of young or idle persons, and served to inflame the humour of war, of slaughter, and of spoils among them. More refined honour or love had little in the lives or actions of those fierce people and bloody times. Honour among them consisted in victory, and love in rapes and in lust.

But as the true flame of poetry was rare among them, and the rest was but wild fire that sparkled or rather crackled a while, and soon went out with little pleasure or gazing of the beholders, those runers who could not raise admiration by the spirit of their poetry endeavored to do it by another, which was that of enchantments: this came in to supply the defect of that sublime and marvelous which has been found both in poetry and prose among the learned ancients. The Gothic runers, to gain and establish the credit and admiration of their rhymes, turned the use of them very much to incantations and charms, pretending by them to raise storms, to calm the seas, to cause terror in their enemies, to transport themselves in the air, to conjure spirits, to cure diseases, and stanch bleeding wounds, to make women kind or easy, and men hard or invulnerable, as one of their most ancient runers affirms of himself and his own achievements, by force of these magical arms. The men or women who were thought to perform such wonders or enchantments were, from *vüses*, or *wises*, the name of those verses wherein their charms were conceived, called *wizards* or *witches*.

Out of this quarry seem to have been raised all those trophies of enchantment that appear in the whole fabric of the old Spanish romances, which were the productions of the Gothic wit among them during their reign; and after the conquests of Spain by the Saracens, they were applied to the long wars between them and the

Christians. From the same perhaps may be derived all the visionary tribe of fairies, elves, and goblins, of sprites and of bullbeggars, that serve not only to fright children into whatever their nurses please, but sometimes, by lasting impressions, to disquiet the sleeps and the very lives of men and women, till they grow to years of discretion; and that, God knows, is a period of time which some people arrive to but very late, and perhaps others never. At least, this belief prevailed so far among the Goths and their races that all sorts of charms were not only attributed to their runes or verses, but to their very characters; so that, about the eleventh century, they were forbidden and abolished in Sweden, as they had been before in Spain, by civil and ecclesiastical commands or constitutions; and what has been since recovered of that learning or language has been fetched as far as Iceland itself.

How much of this kind and of this credulity remained even to our own age may be observed by any man that reflects, so far as thirty or forty years, how often avouched, and how generally credited, were the stories of fairies, sprites, witchcrafts, and enchantments. In some parts of France, and not longer ago, the common people believed certainly there were *lougaroos*, or men turned into wolves; and I remember several Irish of the same mind. The remainders are woven into our very language: *Mara,* in old runic was a goblin that seized upon men asleep in their beds, and took from them all speech and motion; *Old Nicka* was a sprite that came to strangle people who fell into the water; *Bo* was a fierce Gothic captain, son of Odin, whose name was used by his soldiers when they would fright or surprise their enemies; and the proverb of rhyming rats to death came, I suppose, from the same root.

There were, not longer since than the time I have mentioned, some remainders of the runic poetry among the Irish. The great men of their septs, among the many offices of their family,

which continued always in the same races, had not only a physician, a huntsman, a smith, and such like, but a poet and a tale-teller. The first recorded and sung the actions of their ancestors, and entertained the company at feasts: the latter amused them with tales when they were melancholy and could not sleep. And a very gallant gentleman of the north of Ireland has told me of his own experience, that, in his wolf-huntings there, when he used to be abroad in the mountains three or four days together, and lay very ill a-nights, so as he could not well sleep, they would bring him one of these tale-tellers, that, when he lay down, would begin a story of a king, or a giant, a dwarf and a damosel, and such rambling stuff, and continue it all night long in such an even tone that you heard it going on whenever you awaked; and he believed nothing any physicians give could have so good and so innocent effect, to make men sleep in any pains or distempers of body or mind. I remember, in my youth, some persons of our country to have said grace in rhymes, and others their constant prayers; and 'tis vulgar enough that some deeds or conveyances of land have been so since the Conquest.

In such poor wretched weeds as these was poetry clothed, during those shades of ignorance that overspread all Europe for so many ages after the sunset of the Roman learning and empire together, which were succeeded by so many new dominions or plantations of the Gothic swarms, and by a new face of customs, habit, language, and almost of nature. But upon the dawn of a new day, and the resurrection of other sciences, with the two learned languages, among us, this of poetry began to appear very early, though very unlike itself, and in shapes as well as clothes, in humour and in spirit, very different from the ancient. It was now all in rhyme, after the Gothic fashion; for indeed none of the several dialects of that language or allay would bear the composure of such feet and measures as were in use among the Greeks and Latins; and some that attempted it soon left it off, despairing of success. Yet, in this new dress, poetry was not without some charms, especially those of grace and sweetness, and the ore begun to shine in the hands and works of the first refiners. Petrarch, Ronsard, Spenser met with much applause upon the subjects of love, praise, grief, reproach. Ariosto and Tasso entered boldly upon the scene of heroic poems, but, having not wings for so high flights, began to learn of the old ones, fell upon their imitations, and chiefly of Virgil, as far as the force of their genius or disadvantage of new languages and customs would allow. The religion of the Gentiles had been woven into the contexture of all the ancient poetry with a very agreeable mixture, which made the moderns affect to give that of Christianity a place also in their poems. But the true religion was not found to become fiction so well as a false had done, and all their attempts of this kind seemed rather to debase religion than to heighten poetry. Spenser endeavored to supply this with morality, and to make instruction instead of story the subject of an epic poem. His execution was excellent, and his flights of fancy very noble and high, but his design was poor, and his moral lay so bare that it lost the effect: 'tis true, the pill was gilded, but so thin that the color and the taste were too easily discovered.

After these three, I know none of the moderns that have made any achievements in heroic poetry worth recording. The wits of the age soon left off such bold adventures, and turned to other veins, as if, not worthy to sit down at the feast, they contented themselves with the scraps, with songs and sonnets, with odes and elegies, with satires and panegyrics, and what we call copies of verses upon any subjects or occasions, wanting either genius or application for nobler or more laborious productions, as painters that cannot succeed in great pieces turn to miniature.

But the modern poets, to value this small coin, and make it pass, though of so much a baser metal than the old, gave it a new mixture from two veins which were little known or little esteemed among the ancients. There were indeed certain fairies in the old regions of poetry, called Epigrams, which seldom reached above the stature of two or four or six lines, and which, being so short, were all turned upon conceit, or some sharp hits of fancy or wit. The only ancient of this kind among the Latins were the *Priapeia*, which were little voluntaries or extemporaries written upon the ridiculous wooden statues of Priapus among the gardens of Rome. In the decays of the Roman learning and wit as well as language, Martial, Ausonius, and others fell into this vein, and applied it indifferently to all subjects, which was before restrained to one, and dressed it something more cleanly than it was born. This vein of conceit seemed proper for such scraps or splinters into which poetry was broken, and was so eagerly followed as almost to overrun all that was composed in our several modern languages. The Italian, the French, the Spanish, as well as English, were for a great while full of nothing else but conceit. It was an ingredient that gave taste to compositions which had little of themselves; 'twas a sauce that gave point to meat that was flat, and some life to colors that were fading; and, in short, those who could not furnish spirit supplied it with this salt, which may preserve things or bodies that are dead, but is, for aught I know, of little use to the living, or necessary to meats that have much or pleasing tastes of their own. However it were, this vein first overflowed our modern poetry, and with so little distinction or judgment that we would have conceit as well as rhyme in every two lines, and run through all our long scribbles as well as the short, and the whole body of the poem, whatever it is. This was just as if a building should be nothing but ornament, or clothes nothing but trimming; as if a face should be covered over with black patches, or a gown with spangles; which is all I shall say of it.

Another vein which has entered and helped to corrupt our modern poesy is that of ridicule, as if nothing pleased but what made one laugh, which yet come from two very different affections of the mind; for as men have no disposition to laugh at things they are most pleased with, so they are very little pleased with many things they laugh at.

But this mistake is very general, and such modern poets as found no better way of pleasing thought they could not fail of it by ridiculing. This was encouraged by finding conversation run so much into the same vein, and the wits in vogue to take up with that part of it which was formerly left to those that were called fools, and were used in great families only to make the company laugh. What opinion the Romans had of this character appears in those lines of Horace:

——*Absentem qui rodit amicum,*
Qui non defendit alio culpante, solutos,
Qui captat risus hominum famamque dicacis,
Fingere qui non visa potest, commissa tacere
Qui nequit, hic niger est, hunc tu, Romane,
  caveto.

And 'tis pity the character of a wit in one age should be so like that of a black in another.

Rabelais seems to have been father of the ridicule, a man of excellent and universal learning as well as wit; and though he had too much game given him for satire in that age, by the customs of courts and of convents, of processes and of wars, of schools and of camps, of romances and legends, yet he must be confessed to have kept up his vein of ridicule by saying many things so malicious, so smutty, and so profane, that either a prudent, a modest, or a pious man could not have afforded, though he had never so much of that coin about him; and it were to be wished that the wits who have fol-

lowed his vein had not put too much value upon a dress that better understandings would not wear, at least in public, and upon a compass they gave themselves which other men would not take. The matchless writer of *Don Quixote* is much more to be admired for having made up so excellent a composition of satire or ridicule without those ingredients, and seems to be the best and highest strain that ever was or will be reached by that vein.

It began first in verse with an Italian poem, called *La Secchia Rapita*, was pursued by Scarron in French with his *Virgil Travestie*, and in English by Sir John Minnes, *Hudibras*, and Cotton, and with greater height of burlesque in the English than, I think, in any other language. But let the execution be what it will, the design, the custom, and example are very pernicious to poetry, and indeed to all virtue and good qualities among men, which must be disheartened by finding how unjustly and undistinguished they fall under the lash of raillery, and this vein of ridiculing the good as well as the ill, the guilty and the innocent together. 'Tis a very poor though common pretense to merit, to make it appear by the faults of other men. A mean wit or beauty may pass in a room where the rest of the company are allowed to have none; 'tis something to sparkle among diamonds, but to shine among pebbles is neither credit nor value worth the pretending.

Besides these two veins brought in to supply the defects of the modern poetry, much application has been made to the smoothness of language or style, which has at the best but the beauty of coloring in a picture, and can never make a good one without spirit and strength. The Academy set up by Cardinal Richelieu to amuse the wits of that age and country, and divert them from raking into his politics and ministry, brought this in vogue: and the French wits have for the last age been in a manner wholly turned to the refinement of their language, and indeed with such success that it can hardly be excelled, and runs equally through their verse and their prose. The same vein has been likewise much cultivated in our modern English poetry; and by such poor recruits have the broken forces of this empire been of late made up; with what success, I leave to be judged by such as consider it in the former heights and the present declines both of power and of honour; but this will not discourage, however it may affect, the true lovers of this mistress, who must ever think her a beauty in rags as well as in robes.

Among these many decays, there is yet one sort of poetry that seems to have succeeded much better with our moderns than any of the rest, which is dramatic, or that of the stage. In this the Italian, the Spanish, and the French have all had their different merit, and received their just applauses. Yet I am deceived if our English has not in some kind excelled both the modern and ancient, which has been by force of a vein natural perhaps to our country, and which with us is called *humour*, a word peculiar to our language too, and hard to be expressed in any other; nor is it, that I know of, found in any foreign writers, unless it be Molière, and yet his itself has too much of the farce to pass for the same with ours. Shakespeare was the first that opened this vein upon our stage, which has run so freely and so pleasantly ever since that I have often wondered to find it appear so little upon any others, being a subject so proper for them, since humour is but a picture of particular life, as comedy is of general; and though it represents dispositions and customs less common, yet they are not less natural than those that are more frequent among men; for if humour itself be forced, it loses all the grace; which has been indeed the fault of some of our poets most celebrated in this kind.

It may seem a defect in the ancient stage that the characters introduced were so few, and those so common, as a covetous old man, an amourous

young, a witty wench, a crafty slave, a bragging soldier. The spectators met nothing upon the stage but what they met in the streets and at every turn. All the variety is drawn only from different and uncommon events, whereas if the characters are so too, the diversity and the pleasure must needs be the more. But as of most general customs in a country there is usually some ground from the nature of the people or the climate, so there may be amongst us for this vein of our stage, and a greater variety of humour in the picture, because there is a greater variety in the life. This may proceed from the native plenty of our soil, the unequalness of our climate, as well as the ease of our government, and the liberty of professing opinions and factions, which perhaps our neighbors may have about them, but are forced to disguise, and thereby they may come in time to be extinguished. Plenty begets wantonness and pride: wantonness is apt to invent, and pride scorns to imitate. Liberty begets stomach or heart, and stomach will not be constrained. Thus we come to have more originals, and more that appear what they are; we have more humour, because every man follows his own, and takes a pleasure, perhaps a pride, to show it.

On the contrary, where the people are generally poor, and forced to hard labour, their actions and lives are all of a piece; where they serve hard masters, they must follow his examples as well as commands, and are forced upon imitation in small matters as well as obedience in great: so that some nations look as if they were cast all by one mold, or cut out all by one pattern—at least the common people in one, and the gentlemen in another: they seem all of a sort in their habits, their customs, and even their talk and conversation, as well as in the application and pursuit of their actions and their lives.

Besides all this, there is another sort of variety amongst us, which arises from our climate and the dispositions it naturally produces. We are not only more unlike one another than any nation I know, but we are more unlike ourselves too at several times, and owe to our very air some ill qualities as well as many good. We may allow some distempers incident to our climate since so much health, vigour, and length of life have been generally ascribed to it; for among the Greek and Roman authors themselves, we shall find the Britons observed to live the longest, and the Egyptians the shortest, of any nations that were known in those ages. Besides, I think none will dispute the native courage of our men and beauty of our women, which may be elsewhere as great in particulars, but nowhere so in general; they may be (what is said of diseases) as acute in other places, but with us they are epidemical. For my own part, who have conversed much with men of other nations, and such as have been both in great employments and esteem, I can say very impartially that I have not observed among any so much true genius as among the English: nowhere more sharpness of wit, more pleasantness of humour, more range of fancy, more penetration of thought or depth of reflection among the better sort: nowhere more goodness of nature and of meaning, nor more plainness of sense and of life than among the common sort of country people, nor more blunt courage and honesty than among our seamen.

But, with all this, our country must be confessed to be what a great foreign physician called it, the Region of Spleen, which may arise a good deal from the great uncertainty and many sudden changes of our weather in all seasons of the year. And how much these affect the heads and hearts, especially of the finest tempers, is hard to be believed by men whose thoughts are not turned to such speculations. This makes us unequal in our humours, inconstant in our passions, uncertain in our ends, and even in our desires. Besides, our different opinions in religion and the factions they have raised or animated for fifty years past have had an ill effect upon our manners and customs, inducing more avarice, ambition, disguise, with the usual consequences of them, than were before in our constitution. From all this it may happen that there is nowhere more true zeal in the many different forms of devotion, and yet nowhere more knavery under the shows and pretenses. There are nowhere so many disputers upon religion, so many reasoners upon government, so many refiners in politics, so many curious inquisitives, so many pretenders to business and state-employments, greater porers upon books, nor plodders after wealth. And yet nowhere more abandoned libertines, more refined luxurists, extravagant debauchees, conceited gallants, more dabblers in poetry as well as in politics, in philosophy, and in chemistry. I have had several servants far gone in divinity, others in poetry; have known, in the families of some friends, a keeper deep in the Rosycrucian principles, and a laundress firm in those of Epicurus. What effect soever such a composition or medley of humours among us may have upon our lives or our government, it must needs have a good one upon our stage, and has given admirable play to our comical wits: so that in my opinion there is no vein of that sort, either ancient or modern, which excels or equals the humour of our plays. And for the rest, I cannot but observe, [to] the honour of our country, that the good qualities amongst us seem to be natural, and the ill ones more accidental, and such as would be easily changed by the examples of princes and by the precepts of laws; such, I mean, as should be designed to form manners, to restrain excesses, to encourage industry, to prevent men's expenses beyond their fortunes, to countenance virtue, and raise that true esteem due to plain sense and common honesty.

But to spin off this thread which is already grown too long: what honour and request the ancient poetry has lived in may not only be observed from the universal reception and use in all nations from China to Peru, from Scythia to Arabia, but from the esteem of the best and the greatest men as well as the vulgar. Among the Hebrews, David and Solomon, the wisest kings, Job and Jeremiah, the holiest men, were the best poets of their nation and language. Among the Greeks, the two most renowned sages and lawgivers were Lycurgus and Solon, whereof the last is known to have excelled in poetry, and the first was so great a lover of it that to his care and industry we are said by some authors to owe the collection and preservation of the loose and scattered pieces of Homer in the order wherein they have since appeared. Alexander is reported neither to have traveled nor slept without those admirable poems always in his company. Phalaris, that was inexorable to all other enemies, relented at the charms of Stesichorus his Muse. Among the Romans, the last and great Scipio passed the soft hours of his life in the conversation of Terence, and was thought to have a part in the composition of his comedies. Caesar was an excellent poet as well as orator, and composed a poem in his voyage from Rome to Spain, relieving the tedious difficulties of his march with the entertainments of his Muse. Augustus was not only a patron, but a friend and companion, of Virgil and Horace, and was himself both an admirer of poetry and a pretender too, as far as his genius would reach or his busy scene allow. 'Tis true, since his age we have few such examples of great princes favouring or affecting poetry, and as few perhaps of great poets deserving it. Whether it be that the fierceness of the Gothic humours, or noise of their perpetual wars, frighted it away, or that the unequal mixture of the modern languages would not bear it, certain it is that the great heights and excellency both of poetry and music fell with the Roman learning and empire, and have never since recovered the admiration and

applauses that before attended them. Yet such as they are amongst us, they must be confessed to be the softest and sweetest, the most general and most innocent amusements of common time and life. They still find room in the courts of princes and the cottages of shepherds. They serve to revive and animate the dead calm of poor or idle lives, and to allay or divert the violent passions and perturbations of the greatest and the busiest men. And both these effects are of equal use to human life; for the mind of man is like the sea, which is neither agreeable to the beholder nor the voyager in a calm or in a storm, but is so to both when a little agitated by gentle gales; and so the mind, when moved by soft and easy passions or affections. I know very well that many, who pretend to be wise by the forms of being grave, are apt to despise both poetry and music as toys and trifles too light for the use or entertainment of serious men. But whoever find themselves wholly insensible to these charms would, I think, do well to keep their own counsel, for fear of reproaching their own temper, and bringing the goodness of their natures, if not of their understandings, into question. It may be thought at least an ill sign, if not an ill constitution, since some of the Fathers went so far as to esteem the love of music a sign of predestination, as a thing divine, and reserved for the felicities of Heaven itself. While this world lasts, I doubt not but the pleasure and request of these two entertainments will do so too; and happy those that content themselves with these or any other so easy and so innocent, and do not trouble the world or other men, because they cannot be quiet themselves, though nobody hurts them!

When all is done, human life is, at the greatest and the best, but like a froward child, that must be played with and humoured a little to keep it quiet till it falls asleep, and then the care is over.

JOHN POMFRET (1667-1702)

Samuel Johnson said of Pomfret's *The Choice*, "Perhaps no composition in our language has been oftener perused." The prodigious popularity in the eighteenth century of a poem now to be found only in a few anthologies can doubtless be explained by its thoroughly representative character. Pomfret was typical of the cultured, genteel, ease-loving clergymen of the Church of England of his time, and his poem, in the graceful couplets of his day, celebrates at once the pleasures of the intellectual dilettante in retirement and the virtues of the Aristotelian mean so dear to the neo-classicist. Even his house is to be "Built uniform, not little, nor too great." He was a Bedfordshire clergyman, educated at Queens College, Cambridge, where he took his M.A. in 1688. He published *Poems on Several Occasions* in 1699. In 1700 *The Choice* was issued anonymously and roused immediate interest and speculation, the most interesting rumor being that it was partially suggested by the way of life of Sir William Temple. It went through four more editions in 1701 and helped to carry the sale of *Miscellany Poems on Several Occasions* published in 1702, the year of Pomfret's death. Perhaps Leigh Hunt catches the slender charm of *The Choice* as well as anyone who has written of it:

> I have been reading Pomfret's *Choice* this spring,
> A pretty kind of—sort of—kind of thing,
> Not much a verse, and poem not at all,
> Yet, as they say, extremely natural.
> And yet I know not. There's a skill in pies,
> In raising crusts as well as galleries;
> And he's the poet, more or less, who knows
> The charm that hallows the least thing from prose,
> And dresses it in its mild singing clothes.
>
> (From *The Choice*)

THE CHOICE

If heaven the grateful liberty would give
That I might choose my method how to live,
And all those hours propitious fate should lend,
In blissful ease and satisfaction spend:
  Near some fair town I'd have a private seat,
Built uniform, not little, nor too great:
Better if on a rising ground it stood;
Fields on this side, on that a neighbouring wood;
It should within no other things contain
But what were useful, necessary, plain: 10
Methinks 'tis nauseous, and I'd ne'er endure
The needless pomp of gaudy furniture.
A little garden, grateful to the eye,
And a cool rivulet run murmuring by,
On whose delicious banks a stately row
Of shady limes or sycamores should grow;
At the end of which a silent study placed
Should be with all the noblest authors graced:

Horace and Virgil, in whose mighty lines
Immortal wit and solid learning shines; 20
Sharp Juvenal, and amorous Ovid too,
Who all the turns of love's soft passion knew;
He that with judgment reads his charming lines,
In which strong art with stronger nature joins,
Must grant his fancy does the best excel,
His thoughts so tender and expressed so well;
With all those moderns, men of steady sense,
Esteemed for learning and for eloquence.
In some of these, as fancy should advise,
I'd always take my morning exercise: 30
For sure no minutes bring us more content
Than those in pleasing, useful studies spent.
  I'd have a clear and competent estate,
That I might live genteelly, but not great;
As much as I could moderately spend,
A little more, sometimes to oblige a friend.
Nor should the sons of poverty repine
Too much at fortune, they should taste of mine;
And all that objects of true pity were

145

Should be relieved with what my wants could
    spare.   40
For that our Maker has too largely given
Should be returned, in gratitude to heaven.
A frugal plenty should my table spread,
With healthy, not luxurious dishes fed:
Enough to satisfy, and something more
To feed the stranger and the neighbouring
    poor.
Strong meat indulges vice, and pampering
    food
Creates diseases and inflames the blood.
But what's sufficient to make nature strong
And the bright lamp of life continue long 50
I'd freely take, and as I did possess,
The bounteous Author of my plenty bless.
  I'd have a little vault, but always stored
With the best wines each vintage could af-
    ford.
Wine whets the wit, improves its native
    force,
And gives a pleasant flavour to discourse:
By making all our spirits debonair
Throws off the lees, the sediment of care.
But as the greatest blessing heaven lends
May be debauched and serve ignoble ends, 60
So, but too oft, the grape's refreshing juice
Does many mischievous effects produce.
My house should no such rude disorders
    know
As from high drinking consequently flow.
Nor would I use what was so kindly given
To the dishonour of indulgent heaven.
If any neighbor came, he should be free,
Used with respect, and not uneasy be
In my retreat, or to himself or me.
What freedom, prudence, and right reason
    give   70
All men may with impunity receive:
But the least swerving from their rule's too
    much,
For, what's forbidden us, 'tis death to touch.
  That life may be more comfortable yet,
And all my joys refined, sincere and great,
I'd choose two friends, whose company
    would be
A great advance to my felicity:
Well born, of humours suited to my own;
Discreet, and men, as well as books, have
    known.
Brave, generous, witty, and exactly free   80
From loose behaviour or formality.
Airy and prudent, merry, but not light;
Quick in discerning, and in judging right.

Secret they should be, faithful to their trust;
In reasoning cool, strong, temperate and
    just;
Obliging, open, without huffing, brave,
Brisk in gay talking, and in sober, grave;
Close in dispute, but not tenacious, tried
By solid reason, and let that decide;
Not prone to lust, revenge, or envious hate,
Nor busy meddlers with intrigues of state; 91
Strangers to slander, and sworn foes to spite:
Not quarrelsome, but stout enough to fight;
Loyal and pious, friends to Caesar, true
As dying martyrs to their Maker too.
In their society, I could not miss
A permanent, sincere, substantial bliss.
  Would bounteous heaven once more in-
    dulge, I'd choose
(For who would so much satisfaction lose
As witty nymphs in conversation give)   100
Near some obliging, modest fair to live;
For there's that sweetness in a female mind
Which in a man's we cannot hope to find,
That by a secret but a powerful art
Winds up the springs of life, and does im-
    part
Fresh vital heat to the transported heart.
  I'd have her reason all her passions sway;
Easy in company, in private gay:
Coy to a fop, to the deserving free,
Still constant to herself, and just to me.   110
A soul she should have for great actions fit;
Prudence and wisdom to direct her wit:
Courage to look bold danger in the face,
No fear, but only to be proud or base:
Quick to advise, by an emergence pressed,
To give good counsel, or to take the best.
I'd have the expression of her thoughts be
    such
She might not seem reserved nor talk too
    much;
That shows a want of judgment and of sense:
More than enough is but impertinence.   120
Her conduct regular, her mirth refined,
Civil to strangers, to her neighbours kind;
Averse to vanity, revenge, and pride,
In all the methods of deceit untried;
So faithful to her friend, and good to all,
No censure might upon her actions fall;
Then would even envy be compelled to say
She goes the least of womankind astray.
  To this fair creature I'd sometimes retire,
Her conversation would new joys inspire; 130
Give life an edge so keen, no surly care
Would venture to assault my soul, or dare

Near my retreat to hide one secret snare.
But so divine, so noble a repast
I'd seldom and with moderation taste;
For highest cordials all their virtue lose
By a too frequent and too bold an use:
And what would cheer the spirits in distress
Ruins our health, when taken to excess.
    I'd be concerned in no litigious jar, 140
Beloved by all, not vainly popular;
Whate'er assistance I had power to bring
To oblige my country, or to serve my king,
Whene'er they called, I'd readily afford
My tongue, my pen, my counsel, or my
    sword.
Lawsuits I'd shun, with as much studious
    care
As I would dens where hungry lions are,
And rather put up injuries than be
A plague to him who'd be a plague to me.
I value quiet at a price too great 150

To give for my revenge so dear a rate;
For what do we by all our bustle gain
But counterfeit delight, for real pain?
    If heaven a date of many years would give,
Thus I'd in pleasure, ease, and plenty live;
And as I near approached the verge of life,
Some kind relation, for I'd have no wife,
Should take upon him all my worldly care
While I did for a better state prepare.
Then I'd not be with any trouble vexed, 160
Nor have the evening of my days perplexed;
But by a silent and a peaceful death,
Without a sigh, resign my aged breath:
And when committed to the dust, I'd have
Few tears, but friendly, dropped into my
    grave.
Then would my exit so propitious be,
All men would wish to live and die like me
                     [1700]

MATTHEW PRIOR (1664-1721)

Matthew Prior came of a good Dorsetshire family which had gone down in the world. One day, so the story goes, the Earl of Dorset found him as a boy reading Horace in a tavern kept by his uncle in Whitehall, and thus Prior found a patron and a career. He was educated at Westminster School and at St. John's College, Cambridge; with his schoolfellow Charles Montagu, later Earl of Halifax, he wrote a burlesque of Dryden's *Hind and the Panther—The Hind and the Panther transversed to the story of the Country Mouse and the City Mouse* (1687). With an appointment as Secretary to the English Ambassador at The Hague, he began a long diplomatic career; he took an important part in negotiating the Peace of Ryswick between France and England in 1697, and seems to have had the confidence of King William. Under Queen Anne he is found in the Tory camp, a follower of Bolingbroke and Harley and an associate of Swift. While the Tory administration was bringing to an end the War of the Spanish Succession by negotiating the Peace of Utrecht, Prior was active as England's chief diplomatic representative at Paris. But he went down to political ruin with the rest of the Tories at the death of Queen Anne, and was arrested and severely examined by the Whig House of Commons. To help him in his distress, Pope, Arbuthnot, Gay, Swift, and other friends promoted the publication by subscription of his *Poems on Several Occasions* (dated 1718, published 1719). Prior describes the contents of this famous volume as "public panegyrics, amorous odes, serious reflections, or idle tales, the product of his leisure hours, who had business enough upon his hands, and was only a poet by accident." The pose of the gentlemanly amateur is characteristic; nevertheless Prior's work is versatile, "correct" in the eighteenth century sense, and in its way important. The "public panegyrics" are political pieces of no value; the "serious reflections" include his longest poems, the didactic *Solomon on the Vanity of the World,* and the curious *Alma,* which treats of human nature in sprightly Hudibrastic couplets. Prior was genuinely interested in the philosophical ideas of his time, and seems to have been inclined to skeptical views derived from the Montaigne tradition. He was also a connoisseur and collector of paintings. But it is on his light verse that his reputation rests. He writes artificial lyrics in the tradition associated with the Greek poet Anacreon, who bequeathed to later writers the apparatus of Cupid and his arrows, Venus and her doves, flames and myrtle wreaths. We may also call him Horatian, if we add that he had the urbanity and good sense but not the mellowness and personal depth of Horace. He is master of an informal style which never breaks down in spite of its apparent negligence, and for which he finds the ideal meter in his swinging anapests and easy octosyllabic couplets. If we compare the two answers to *Cloe Jealous* we see that Prior was conscious that the artificiality of his lyric forms should be tempered by common-sense informality. The "idle tales" of which he speaks are witty and sometimes licentious pieces, with the savor of shrewd realism about them. *An Epitaph, An English Padlock,* and the charming *Jinny the Just* may serve to show his estimate of human nature, cynical without bitterness, avoiding alike excessive hope and excessive despair.

Writings, ed. A. R. Waller (2 vols., Cambridge, Eng., 1905, 1907); F. Bickley, *Life of Matthew Prior* (1914); L. G. Wickham Legg, *Matthew Prior* (Cambridge, Eng., 1921); H. Bunker Wright, "Matthew Prior: A Supplement to His Biography," *Northwestern Univ. Summaries of Doctoral Dissertations,* V (1937), 34–38; C. K. Eves, *Matthew Prior: Poet and Diplomatist* (1939).

TO A LADY: SHE REFUSING TO CONTINUE A DISPUTE WITH ME, AND LEAVING ME IN THE ARGUMENT

Spare, generous victor, spare the slave,
  Who did unequal war pursue;
That more than triumph he might have,
  In being overcome by you.

In the dispute whate'er I said,
  My heart was by my tongue belied;
And in my looks you might have read
  How much I argued on your side.

You, far from danger as from fear,
  Might have sustained an open fight,   10
For seldom your opinions err;
  Your eyes are always in the right.

Why, fair one, would you not rely
  On Reason's force with Beauty's joined?
Could I their prevalence deny,
  I must at once be deaf and blind.

Alas! not hoping to subdue,
  I only to the fight aspired;
To keep the beauteous foe in view
  Was all the glory I desired.   20

But she, howe'er of victory sure,
  Contemns the wreath too long delayed,
And, armed with more immediate power,
  Calls cruel silence to her aid.

Deeper to wound, she shuns the fight;
  She drops her arms, to gain the field;
Secures her conquest by her flight,
  And triumphs, when she seems to yield.

So when the Parthian turned his steed,
  And from the hostile camp withdrew,   30
With cruel skill the backward reed
  He sent; and as he fled, he slew.

[1704]

TO A CHILD OF QUALITY FIVE YEARS OLD

Lords, knights, and squires, the numerous
    band
  That wear the fair Miss Mary's fetters,
Were summoned by her high command,
  To show their passions by their letters.

My pen amongst the rest I took,
  Lest those bright eyes that cannot read
Should dart their kindling fires, and look
  The power they have to be obeyed.

Nor quality nor reputation
  Forbid me yet my flame to tell;   10
Dear five years old befriends my passion,
  And I may write till she can spell.

For while she makes her silk-worms beds
  With all the tender things I swear,
Whilst all the house my passion reads,
  In papers round her baby's hair,

She may receive and own my flame,
  For though the strictest prudes should
    know it,
She'll pass for a most virtuous dame,
  And I for an unhappy poet.   20

Then too, alas! when she shall tear
  The lines some younger rival sends,
She'll give me leave to write, I fear,
  And we shall still continue friends;

For, as our different ages move,
  'Tis so ordained, would fate but mend it!
That I shall be past making love
  When she begins to comprehend it.

[1704]

AN ENGLISH PADLOCK

Miss Danaë, when fair and young
(As Horace has divinely sung)
Could not be kept from Jove's embrace
By doors of steel and walls of brass.
The reason of the thing is clear,
Would Jove the naked truth aver:
Cupid was with him of the party,
And showed himself sincere and hearty;
For, give that whipster but his errand,
He takes my Lord Chief Justice' warrant;   10
Dauntless as Death away he walks;
Breaks the doors open; snaps the locks;
Searches the parlour, chamber, study;
Nor stops, till he has Culprit's body.
  Since this has been authentic truth,
By Age delivered down to Youth,
Tell us, mistaken husband, tell us,
Why so mysterious, why so jealous?

Does the restraint, the bolt, the bar
Make us less curious, her less fair?   20
The spy which does this treasure keep,
Does she ne'er say her prayers, nor sleep?
Does she to no excess incline?
Does she fly music, mirth, and wine?
Or have not gold and flattery power
To purchase one unguarded hour?
    Your care does further yet extend:
That spy is guarded by your friend.—
But has this friend nor eye, nor heart?
May he not feel the cruel dart   30
Which, soon or late, all mortals feel?
May he not, with too tender zeal,
Give the fair prisoner cause to see
How much he wishes she were free?
May he not craftily infer
The rules of friendship too severe,
Which chain him to a hated trust?
Which make him wretched, to be just?
And may not she, this darling she,
Youthful and healthy, flesh and blood,   40
Easy with him, ill-used by thee,
Allow this logic to be good?
    "Sir, will your questions never end?
I trust to neither spy nor friend.
In short, I keep her from the sight
Of every human face."—"She'll write."—
"From pen and paper she's debarred.—"
"Has she a bodkin and a card?
She'll prick her mind."—"She will, you say:
But how shall she that mind convey?   50
I keep her in one room: I lock it:
The key (look here) is in this pocket."
"The key-hole, is that left?"—"Most certain."
"She'll thrust her letter through—*Sir Martin*."
"Dear angry friend, what must be done?
Is there no way?"—There is but one.
Send her abroad; and let her see,
That all this mingled mass, which she
Being forbidden longs to know,
Is a dull farce, an empty show,   60
Powder, and pocket-glass, and beau;
A staple of romance and lies,
False tears, and real perjuries:
Where sighs and looks are bought and sold;
And love is made but to be told:
Where the fat bawd and lavish heir
The spoils of ruined beauty share;
And youth seduced from friends and fame,
Must give up age to want and shame.
Let her behold the frantic scene,   70

The women wretched, false the men:
And when, these certain ills to shun,
She would to thy embraces run,
Receive her with extended arms;
Seem more delighted with her charms;
Wait on her to the park and play;
Put on good humour; make her gay;
Be to her virtues very kind;
Be to her faults a little blind;
Let all her ways be unconfined,   80
And clap your padlock—on her mind.

                                    [1705]

A SIMILE

Dear Thomas, didst thou never pop
Thy head into a tin-man's shop?
There, Thomas, didst thou never see
('Tis but by way of simile)
A squirrel spend his little rage
In jumping round a rolling cage?
The cage, as either side turned up,
Striking a ring of bells a-top?—
    Moved in the orb, pleased with the
        chimes,
The foolish creature thinks he climbs: 10
But here or there, turn wood or wire,
He never gets two inches higher.
    So fares it with those merry blades,
That frisk it under Pindus' shades:
In noble songs and lofty odes,
They tread on stars and talk with gods;
Still dancing in an airy round,
Still pleased with their own verses' sound,
Brought back, how fast so'er they go,
Always aspiring, always low.   20

                                    [1706]

TO CLOE WEEPING

See, whilst thou weep'st, fair Cloe, see
The world in sympathy with thee.
The cheerful birds no longer sing;
Each drops his head and hangs his wing.
The clouds have bent their bosom lower,
And shed their sorrows in a shower.
The brooks beyond their limits flow,
And louder murmurs speak their woe.
The nymphs and swains adopt thy cares;

They heave thy sighs and weep thy tears. 10
Fantastic nymph! that grief should move
Thy heart, obdurate against love.
Strange tears! whose power can soften all
But that dear breast on which they fall.

[1709]

AN ODE

The merchant, to secure his treasure,
  Conveys it in a borrowed name;
Euphelia serves to grace my measure,
  But Cloe is my real flame.

My softest verse, my darling lyre,
  Upon Euphelia's toilet lay;
When Cloe noted her desire
  That I should sing, that I should play.

My lyre I tune, my voice I raise,
  But with my numbers mix my sighs; 10
And whilst I sing Euphelia's praise,
  I fix my soul on Cloe's eyes.

Fair Cloe blushed; Euphelia frowned;
  I sung and gazed; I played and trembled;
And Venus to the Loves around
  Remarked, how ill we all dissembled.

[1718]

CLOE JEALOUS

Forbear to ask me why I weep,
  Vexed Cloe to her shepherd said:
'Tis for my two poor straggling sheep,
  Perhaps, or for my squirrel dead.

For mind I what you late have writ?
  Your subtle questions and replies,
Emblems to teach a female wit
  The ways where changing Cupid flies.

Your riddle, purposed to rehearse
  The general power that beauty has: 10
But why did no peculiar verse
  Describe one charm of Cloe's face?

The glass which was at Venus' shrine
  With such mysterious sorrow laid;
The garland (and you call it mine)
  Which showed how youth and beauty
    fade—

Ten thousand trifles light as these
  Nor can my rage nor anger move;
She should be humble who would please,
  And she must suffer who can love. 20

When in my glass I chanced to look,
  Of Venus what did I implore?
That every grace which thence I took,
  Should know to charm my Damon more.

Reading thy verse; who heeds, said I,
  If here or there his glances flew?
Oh, free forever be his eye,
  Whose heart to me is always true!

My bloom indeed, my little flower
  Of beauty quickly lost its pride; 30
For severed from its native bower
  It on thy glowing bosom died.

Yet cared I not, what might presage
  Or withering wreath or fleeting youth:
Love I esteemed more strong than age,
  And time less permanent than truth.

Why then I weep, forbear to know:
  Fall uncontrolled my tears, and free:
O Damon, 'tis the only woe,
  I ever yet concealed from thee. 40

The secret wound with which I bleed
  Shall lie wrapped up, even in my hearse:
But on my tombstone thou shalt read
  My answer to thy dubious verse.

[1718]

A BETTER ANSWER (TO CLOE JEALOUS)

Dear Cloe, how blubbered is that pretty face!
  Thy cheek all on fire, and thy hair all uncurled!
Prithee quit this caprice; and (as old Falstaff says)
  Let us e'en talk a little like folks of this world.

How canst thou presume, thou hast leave to destroy
   The beauties, which Venus but lent to thy keeping?
Those looks were designed to inspire love and joy;
   More ordinary eyes may serve people for weeping.

To be vexed at a trifle or two that I writ,
   Your judgment at once and my passion you wrong: 10
You take that for fact which will scarce be found wit:
   Od's life! must one swear to the truth of a song?

What I speak, my fair Cloe, and what I write, shows
   The difference there is betwixt nature and art;
I court others in verse, but I love thee in prose;
   And they have my whimsies, but thou hast my heart.

The god of us verse-men (you know, child) the Sun,
   How after his journeys he sets up his rest;
If at morning o'er earth 'tis his fancy to run,
   At night he reclines on his Thetis's breast.   20

So when I am wearied with wandering all day,
   To thee my delight in the evening I come;
No matter what beauties I saw in my way—
   They were but my visits, but thou art my home.

Then finish, dear Cloe, this pastoral war;
   And let us like Horace and Lydia agree:
For thou art a girl as much brighter than her,
   As he was a poet sublimer than me.

                                                    [1718]

AN EPITAPH

Interred beneath this marble stone,
Lie sauntering Jack and idle Joan.
While rolling threescore years and one
Did round this globe their courses run,
If human things went ill or well,
If changing empires rose or fell,
The morning passed, the evening came,
And found this couple still the same.
They walked and eat, good folks—what then?
Why then they walked and eat again.   10
They soundly slept the night away;
They did just nothing all the day;
And having buried children four,
Would not take pains to try for more.
Nor sister either had, nor brother;
They seemed just tallied for each other.
   Their moral and economy
Most perfectly they made agree;
Each virtue kept its proper bound,
Nor trespassed on the other's ground.   20
Nor fame nor censure they regarded;
They neither punished nor rewarded.
He cared not what the footmen did;
Her maids she neither praised, nor chid;
So every servant took his course,
And bad at first, they all grew worse.
Slothful disorder filled his stable,
And sluttish plenty decked her table.
Their beer was strong; their wine was port;
Their meal was large; their grace was short.
They gave the poor the remnant-meat,   31
Just when it grew not fit to eat.
   They paid the church and parish rate,
And took, but read not the receipt;
For which they claimed their Sunday's due,
Of slumbering in an upper pew.
   No man's defects sought they to know;
So never made themselves a foe.
No man's good deeds did they commend;
So never raised themselves a friend.   40
Nor cherished they relations poor,

That might decrease their present store;
Nor barn nor house did they repair,
That might oblige their future heir.
  They neither added nor confounded;
They neither wanted nor abounded.
Each Christmas they accompts did clear,
And wound their bottom¹ round the year.
Nor tear nor smile did they employ
At news of public grief or joy.   50
When bells were rung, and bonfires made,
If asked they ne'er denied their aid:

  ¹ A ball of thread.

Their jug was to the ringers carried,
Whoever either died or married.
Their billet at the fire was found,
Whoever was deposed, or crowned.
  Nor good, nor bad, nor fools, nor wise;
They would not learn, nor could advise:
Without love, hatred, joy, or fear,
They led—a kind of—as it were: 60
Nor wished, nor cared, nor laughed, nor
    cried;
And so they lived; and so they died.

[1718]

ANNE FINCH, COUNTESS OF WINCHILSEA (1661-1720)

Anne Kingsmill was born in Hampshire in 1661. She was one of the maids of honor to Mary of Modena (the second wife of the Duke of York, afterwards James II) and married Colonel Heneage Finch, who was in the retinue of the same household. When James was driven from his throne in 1688 they remained loyal to the Stuart cause and were thereafter completely cut off from court life and politics. Soon they found refuge at Eastwell Park, Kent, the beautiful country estate of the young Earl of Winchilsea. Colonel Finch was his uncle, and succeeded to the title in 1712. At Eastwell Park, Anne Finch became the center of a literary coterie of gentlefolk, and wrote agreeable verses under the name of "Ardelia." Her work was circulated in manuscript, and she did not appear in print until Charles Gildon printed her pindaric ode, *The Spleen*, in 1701. She was known to the great wits of the day, Pope, Swift, and Gay, but she was never drawn into the literary life of the town; it is to her advantage that she never acquired the literary smartness of the Augustans. Much of her work, such as her fables, pindarics, and plays, consists of uninspired literary exercises, but in the small group of poems represented in the following selections she shows a subtle power in rendering natural impressions, a quiet delicacy, which give her an assured place among the minor poets. Wordsworth rediscovered her for later English readers, and his praise of her *Nocturnal Reverie* in the *Essay Supplementary to the Preface* (1815) remains the cornerstone of her reputation.

Poems, ed. Myra Reynolds (Chicago, 1903) [the definitive edition]; *Minor Poets of the Eighteenth Century,* ed. H. I'A. Fausset (Everyman's Library); Reuben A. Brower, "Lady Winchilsea and the Poetic Tradition of the Seventeenth Century," *SP*, XLII (1945), 61-80.

TO THE ECHO

IN A CLEAR NIGHT UPON ASTROP WALKS

Say, lovely nymph, where dost thou dwell?
Where is that secret sylvan seat,
That melancholy, sweet retreat
From whence thou dost these notes repel,
And moving syllables repeat?
O lovely nymph, our joys to swell,
Thy hollow leafy mansion tell;
Or if thou only charm'st the ear
And never wilt to sight appear,
But dost alone in voice excel,   10
Still with it fix us here,
Where Cynthia lends her gentle light,
Whilst the appeased, expanded air
A passage for thee does prepare,
And Strephon's tuneful voice invite
Thine a soft part with him to bear.
O Pleasure! when thou'dst take a flight
Beyond thy common, mortal height,
When to thy sphere above thou'dst press,
And men like angels thou wouldst bless, 20
Thy season be like this fair night,
And harmony thy dress.

[1903]

THE BIRD

Kind bird, thy praises I design;
Thy praises like thy plumes should shine;
Thy praises should thy life outlive,
Could I the fame I wish thee give.
Thou my domestic music art,
And dearest trifle of my heart.
Soft in thy notes and in thy dress,
Softer than numbers can express,
Softer than love, softer than light
When just escaping from the night,   10
When first she rises, unarrayed,
And steals a passage through the shade;
Softer than air, or flying clouds
Which Phoebus' glory thinly shrouds,
Gay as the spring, gay as the flowers
When lightly strewed with pearly showers.
Ne'er to the woods shalt thou return,
Nor thy wild freedom shalt thou mourn.
Thou to my bosom shalt repair,
And find a safer shelter there;   20
There shalt thou watch, and should I sleep,
My heart, thy charge, securely keep.
Love, who a stranger is to me,
Must by thy wings be kin to thee:
So painted o'er, so seeming fair,
So soft his first addresses are,

Thy guard he ne'er can pass unseen.
Thou, surely thou hast often been,
Whilst yet a wanderer in the grove,
A false accomplice with this Love,   30
In the same shade hast thou not sate,
And seen him work some wretch's fate?
Hast thou not soothed him in the wrong,
And graced the mischief with a song,
Tuning thy loud conspiring voice
O'er falling lovers to rejoice?
If so, thy wicked faults redeem
In league with me, no truce with him
Do thou admit, but warn my heart,
And all his sly designs impart,   40
Lest to that breast by craft he get
Which has defied and braved him yet.

[1903]

THE TREE

Fair tree! for thy delightful shade
'Tis just that some return be made;
Sure, some return is due from me
To thy cool shadows and to thee.
When thou to birds dost shelter give,
Thou music dost from them receive;
If travelers beneath thee stay,
Till storms have worn themselves away,
That time in praising thee they spend,
And thy protecting power commend;   10
The shepherd here, from scorching freed,
Tunes to thy dancing leaves his reed;
Whilst his loved nymph in thanks bestows
Her flowery chaplets on thy boughs.
Shall I then only silent be,
And no return be made by me?
No: let this wish upon thee wait,
And still to flourish be thy fate;
To future ages mayst thou stand,
Untouched by the rash workman's hand, 20
Till that large stock of sap is spent
Which gives thy summer's ornament;
Till the fierce winds that vainly strive
To shock thy greatness whilst alive,
Shall on thy lifeless hour attend,
Prevent the axe, and grace thy end:
Their scattered strength together call,

And to the clouds proclaim thy fall,
Who then their evening dews may spare,
When thou no longer art their care,   30
But shalt, like ancient heroes, burn,
And some bright hearth be made thy urn.

[1903]

TO THE NIGHTINGALE

Exert thy voice, sweet harbinger of spring!
    This moment is thy time to sing,
    This moment I attend to praise,
And set my numbers to thy lays.
    Free as thine shall be my song,
    As thy music, short or long.
Poets, wild as thee, were born,
    Pleasing best when unconfined,
    When to please is least designed,
Soothing but their cares to rest;   10
    Cares do still their thoughts molest,
    And still the unhappy poet's breast,
Like thine, when best he sings, is placed
    against a thorn.

She begins. Let all be still!
    Muse, thy promise now fulfil!
Sweet, oh sweet! still sweeter yet!
Can thy words such accents fit,
Canst thou syllables refine,
Melt a sense that shall retain
Still some spirit of the brain,   20
Till with sounds like these it join?
    'Twill not be! then change thy note,
    Let division shake thy throat.
Hark! division now she tries,
Yet as far the Muse outflies.
    Cease then, prithee, cease thy tune!
    Trifler, wilt thou sing till June?
Till thy business all lies waste,
And the time of building's past?
    Thus we poets that have speech,   30
Unlike what thy forests teach,
    If a fluent vein be shown
    That's transcendent to our own,
Criticize, reform, or preach,
Or censure what we cannot reach.

[1713]

A NOCTURNAL REVERIE

In such a night, when every louder wind
Is to its distant cavern safe confined;
And only gentle Zephyr fans his wings,

And lonely Philomel, still waking, sings;
Or from some tree, famed for the owl's delight,
She, hollowing clear, directs the wanderer right;
In such a night, when passing clouds give place,
Or thinly veil the heavens' mysterious face;
When in some river overhung with green,
The waving moon and trembling leaves are seen;   10
When freshened grass now bears itself upright,
And makes cool banks to pleasing rest invite,
Whence springs the woodbine and the bramble-rose,
And where the sleepy cowslip sheltered grows;
Whilst now a paler hue the foxglove takes,
Yet checkers still with red the dusky brakes,
When scattered glow-worms, but in twilight fine,
Show trivial beauties watch their hour to shine;
Whilst Salisbury stands the test of every light,
In perfect charms and perfect virtue bright;   20
When odours which declined repelling day
Through temperate air uninterrupted stray;
When darkened groves their softest shadows wear,
And falling waters we distinctly hear;
When through the gloom more venerable shows
Some ancient fabric, awful in repose,
While sunburnt hills their swarthy looks conceal,
And swelling haycocks thicken up the vale;
When the loosed horse now, as his pasture leads,
Comes slowly grazing through the adjoining meads,   30
Whose stealing pace and lengthened shade we fear,
Till torn up forage in his teeth we hear;
When nibbling sheep at large pursue their food,
And unmolested kine rechew the cud;
When curlews cry beneath the village walls,
And to her straggling brood the partridge calls;
Their short-lived jubilee the creatures keep,
Which but endures whilst tyrant man does sleep;
When a sedate content the spirit feels,
And no fierce light disturbs, whilst it reveals,   40
But silent musings urge the mind to seek
Something too high for syllables to speak;
Till the free soul to a composedness charmed,
Finding the elements of rage disarmed,
O'er all below, a solemn quiet grown,
Joys in the inferior world and thinks it like her own:
In such a night let me abroad remain,
Till morning breaks, and all's confused again:
Our cares, our toils, our clamours are renewed,
Or pleasures, seldom reached, again pursued.

[1713]

DANIEL DEFOE (1660?-1731)

Millions of readers know Defoe only as the name on the title-page of one of the world's most successful books. But Defoe's own history, obscure though it still is in some of its phases, is in itself a sort of sordid underworld mystery story. He seems to have been gifted with the shrewd practical sense of a successful tradesman, but he failed in business. He had the intense moral and political convictions of a Whig and a Dissenter, and yet for nearly twenty years he sold his talents to successive ministries, Whig and Tory, as an undercover political agent and journalist. Although his moral convictions were so earnest that he seriously advocated tearing down the theatres of London as the best way of reforming them, in his own fictional biographies he could pander to the weakness of popular taste. He is a strange mixture of success and failure, of devotion to principle and unscrupulous grasping at profits. Recent research has uncovered much new information about him, but the mystery of his real self may never be revealed.

He was distinctly a middle-class type, raised in a Presbyterian family, educated at a Dissenters' academy, and naturally attracted at an early age to trade. His first business expanded to a magnificent scale, and when he went bankrupt in 1692 his deficit totalled £17,000. After a period of hiding to avoid imprisonment for debt, he compounded with his creditors and started fresh with the manufacture of brick and tile, a venture which also ended in bankruptcy about 1702. Sharp-witted as he was, he seems to have been beset by financial difficulties until his death.

His first important publication, *An Essay On Projects* (1698), was of help in advancing his reputation, but his real taste of fame came a few years later. He was an ardent admirer of William III., and when a poem appeared attacking the king of England as a foreigner, Defoe replied with his *True-Born Englishman* (1701). In unpolished, but forceful, verse Defoe pointed out that Englishmen, especially the nobility and gentry who were so ready to sneer at the foreign birth of William III., were themselves descended from various foreign invaders of England. The poem attracted wide attention, and the defender of the king seemed about to rise on the tide of fortune. But in 1702 William died, and Defoe moreover published an anonymous pamphlet which had disastrous results. *The Shortest Way with the Dissenters* was an ironical defence of the extreme Anglicans who wanted to force the Dissenters by law to conform to the Established Church. But the irony was unperceived in the heat of the ensuing controversy, and when the real authorship was discovered both Anglicans and Dissenters regarded themselves as imposed upon. The outcry was general, the government ordered his arrest for sedition, and Defoe went into hiding. In 1703 he was convicted and sentenced to jail and pillory. It is now known that he was released in November, 1703, through the good offices of Robert Harley, and that it was as Harley's secret political agent that he began his *Review* in 1704.

From this point on the career of Defoe is too complicated for anything but a general summary. The *Review* changed its politics with the changes in the ministries, until Defoe dropped it in 1713. After that he was involved in a succession of journalistic enterprises, and, always posing as the aggrieved enemy of the government, he even managed at times to edit or control the organs of the opposition to keep them harmless. His own statement of this amazing journalistic feat was discovered in 1864 among the documents in the State Paper Office. His duplicity was, indeed, more and more suspected by his public, and by 1719 his services in this way were accordingly becoming of very little value to the ministry.

He was now approaching sixty, and looking for a new source of income. He turned, among other things, to the composition of faked confessions and autobiographies, in which category must be placed *Robinson Crusoe* (1719), *Moll Flanders* and *A Journal of the Plague Year* (1722), and his other so-called "novels." These works were not novels in the usual sense; as first published they purported to be truth, not fiction. The illusion which Defoe aimed at in them is consequently not what we call "realism" in fiction, but rather actuality, as in a biography or newspaper story. The name of Defoe did not, and could not, appear on his title-pages, inasmuch as it was his intention to make the books pass for authentic memoirs of his characters. The purpose of this deception was of course merely greater sales. But Defoe's genius appears in the fact that the world has come to recognize a whole series of these journalistic "fakes" as literature.

Defoe's deficiencies in education and culture are apparent when we compare him with Addison and Steele, who were as deeply interested in the middle class as he, but whose work has a charm and urbanity, a richness of allusion, and a delicacy of thought and phrasing which we look for in vain in Defoe. He has the limitations of his class, with a leaning towards the plebeian. His mind was retentive of minute details and he had acquired through the years an enormous mass of such practical knowledge as is the delight of modern realistic novelists and their readers. All this he could put down in plain and home-spun English, vigorous and idiomatic, such English as was not inappropriate to his unlearned characters. For the illusion of his style is as convincing as the illusion of his matter.

Defoe published more than two hundred books and pamphlets which have never been reprinted; but his novels are available in several collected editions. The best introduction is still W. P. Trent's *Defoe: How to Know Him* (Indianapolis, 1916), the fruit of years of research. Paul Dottin has written a comprehensive study, *Daniel Defoe et ses Romans* (3 vols., Paris, 1924), and Thomas Wright's *Life of Daniel Defoe* (revised edition, 1931) is useful for biographical information, but has been superseded in some respects by a new biography by James R. Sutherland (London, 1937). A standard work on Defoe's methods of composing his fiction is A. W. Secord's *Studies in the Narrative Method of Defoe* (Urbana, Illinois, 1924). See also page 1268.

AN ESSAY ON PROJECTS
(1698)

Of Academies

We have in England fewer of these than in any part of the world, at least where learning is in so much esteem. But to make amends, the two great seminaries we have are, without comparison, the greatest—I won't say the best—in the world; and though much might be said here concerning universities in general, and foreign academies in particular, I content myself with noting that part in which we seem defective. The French, who justly value themselves upon erecting the most celebrated academy of Europe, owe the lustre of it very much to the great encouragement the kings of France have given to it. And one of the members, making a speech at his entrance, tells you, "That 'tis not the least of the glories of their invincible monarch to have engrossed all the learning of the world in that sublime body."

The peculiar study of the Academy of Paris has been to refine and correct their own language, which they have done to that happy degree that we see it now spoken in all the courts of Christendom as the language allowed to be most universal.

I had the honour once to be a member of a small society, who seemed to offer at this noble design in England; but the greatness of the work and the modesty of the gentlemen concerned prevailed with them to desist an enterprise which appeared too great for private hands to undertake. We want indeed a Richelieu to commence such a work; for I am persuaded were there such a genius in our kingdom to lead the way, there would not want capacities who could carry on the work to a glory equal to all that has gone before them. The English tongue is a subject not at all less worthy the labour of such a society than the French, and capable of a much greater perfection. The learned among the French will own that the comprehensiveness of expression is a glory in which the English tongue not only equals, but excels its neighbours. Rapin, St. Evremont, and the most eminent French authors have acknowledged it; and my Lord Roscommon, who is allowed to be a good judge of English, because he wrote it as exactly as any ever did, expresses what I mean in these lines:—

"For who did ever in French authors see
  The comprehensive English energy?
The weighty bullion of one sterling line,
  Drawn to French wire, would through
    whole pages shine."

"And if our neighbours will yield us, as their greatest critic has done, the preference for sublimity and nobleness of style, we will willingly quit all pretensions to their insignificant gaiety."

'Tis a great pity that a subject so noble should not have some as noble to attempt it; and for a method, what greater can be set before us than the Academy of Paris, which, to give the French their due, stands foremost among all the great attempts in the learned part of the world.

The present King of England, of whom we have seen the whole world writing panegyrics and encomiums, and whom his enemies, when their interest does not silence them, are apt to say more of than ourselves; as in the war he has given surprising instances of a greatness of spirit more than common, so in peace, I dare say with submission, he shall never have an opportunity to illustrate his memory more than by such a foundation; by which he shall have opportunity to darken the glory of the French King in peace, as he has by his daring attempts in the war.

Nothing but pride loves to be flattered, and that only as it is a vice which blinds us to our own imperfections. I think princes as particularly unhappy in having their good actions magnified, as their evil actions covered. But King William, who has already won praise by the steps of dangerous virtue, seems reserved for some actions which are above the touch of flattery, whose praise is in themselves.

And such would this be; and because I am speaking of a work which seems to be proper only for the hand of the King himself, I shall not presume to carry on this chapter to the model as I have done in other subjects. Only thus far:—

That a society be erected by the King himself, if His Majesty thought fit, and composed of none but persons of the first figure in learning; and 'twere to be wished our gentry were so much lovers of learning that birth might always be joined with capacity.

The work of this society should be to encourage polite learning, to polish and refine the English tongue, and advance the so much neglected faculty of correct language, to establish purity and propriety of style, and to purge it from all the irregular additions that ignorance and affectation have introduced; and all those innovations in speech, if I may call them such, which some dogmatic writers have the confidence to foster upon their native language, as if their authority were sufficient to make their own fancy legitimate.

By such a society I dare say the true glory of our English style would appear, and among all the learned part of the world be esteemed, as it really is, the noblest and most comprehensive of all the vulgar languages in the world.

Into this society should be admitted none but persons eminent for learning, and yet none, or but very few, whose business or trade was learning. For I may be allowed, I suppose, to say we have seen many great scholars, mere learned men, and graduates in the last degree of study, whose English has been far from polite, full of stiffness and affectation, hard words, and long unusual coupling of syllables and sentences, which sound harsh and untunable to the ear, and shock the reader both in expression and understanding.

In short, there should be room in this society for neither clergyman, physician, or lawyer. Not that I would put an affront upon the learning of any of those honourable employments, much less upon their persons. But if I do think that their several professions do naturally and severally prescribe habits of speech to them peculiar to their practice, and prejudicial to the study I speak of, I believe I do them no wrong. Nor do I deny but there may be, and now are, among some of all those professions men of style and language, great masters of

English, whom few men will undertake to correct; and where such do at any time appear, their extraordinary merit should find them a place in this society; but it should be rare, and upon very extraordinary occasions, that such be admitted.

I would therefore have this society wholly composed of gentlemen, whereof twelve to be of the nobility, if possible, and twelve private gentlemen, and a class of twelve to be left open for mere merit, let it be found in who or what sort it would, which should lie as the crown of their study, who have done something eminent to deserve it. The voice of this society should be sufficient authority for the usage of words, and sufficient also to expose the innovations of other men's fancies; they should preside with a sort of judicature over the learning of the age, and have liberty to correct and censure the exorbitance of writers, especially of translators. The reputation of this society would be enough to make them the allowed judges of style and language; and no author would have the impudence to coin without their authority. Custom, which is now our best authority for words, would always have its original here, and not be allowed without it. There should be no more occasion to search for derivations and constructions, and it would be as criminal then to coin words as money.

The exercises of this society would be lectures on the English tongue, essays on the nature, original, usage, authorities, and differences of words, on the propriety, purity, and cadence of style, and of the politeness and manner in writing, reflections upon irregular usages, and corrections of erroneous customs in words; and, in short, everything that would appear necessary to the bringing our English tongue to a due perfection, and our gentlemen to a capacity of writing like themselves; to banish pride and pedantry, and silence the impudence and impertinence of young authors. whose ambition is to be known, though it be by their folly. . . .

Under this head of Academies I might bring in a project for—

AN ACADEMY FOR WOMEN.

I have often thought of it as one of the most barbarous customs in the world, considering us as a civilized and a Christian country, that we deny the advantages of learning to women. We reproach the sex every day with folly and impertinence, while I am confident, had they the advantages of education equal to us, they would be guilty of less than ourselves.

One would wonder, indeed, how it should happen that women are conversible at all, since they are only beholden to natural parts for all their knowledge. Their youth is spent to teach them to stitch and sew or make baubles. They are taught to read indeed, and perhaps to write their names or so, and that is the height of a woman's education. And I would but ask any who slight the sex for their understanding, what is a man (a gentleman, I mean) good for that is taught no more?

I need not give instances, or examine the character of a gentleman with a good estate and of a good family and with tolerable parts, and examine what figure he makes for want of education.

The soul is placed in the body like a rough diamond, and must be polished, or the lustre of it will never appear: and it is manifest that as the rational soul distinguishes us from brutes, so education carries on the distinction and makes some less brutish than others. This is too evident to need any demonstration. But why then should women be denied the benefit of instruction? If knowledge and understanding had been useless additions to the sex, God Almighty would never have given them capacities, for He made nothing needless. Besides, I would ask such what they can see in ignorance that they should think it a necessary ornament to a woman? or how much worse is a wise woman than a fool? or what has the woman done to forfeit the privilege of being taught? Does she plague us with her pride and impertinence? Why did we not let her learn, that she might have had more wit? Shall we upbraid women with folly, when it is only the error of this inhuman custom that hindered them being made wiser?

The capacities of women are supposed to be greater and their senses quicker than those of the men; and what they might be capable of being bred to is plain from some instances of female wit, which this age is not without; which upbraids us with injustice, and looks as if we denied women the advantages of education for fear they should vie with the men in their improvements.

To remove this objection, and that women might have at least a needful opportunity of education in all sorts of useful learning, I propose the draught of an Academy for that purpose.

I know it is dangerous to make public appearances of the sex. They are not either to be confined or exposed; the first will disagree with their inclinations and the last with their reputations, and therefore it is somewhat difficult; and I doubt a method proposed by an ingenious lady in a little book called "Advice to the Ladies" would be found impracticable, for, saving my respect to the sex, the levity, which perhaps is a little peculiar to them, at least in their youth, will not bear the restraint; and I am satisfied nothing but the height of bigotry can keep up a nunnery. Women are extravagantly desirous of going to heaven, and will punish their pretty bodies to get thither; but nothing else will do it, and even in that case sometimes it falls out that nature will prevail.

When I talk, therefore, of an academy for women, I mean both the model, the teaching, and the government different from what is proposed by that ingenious lady, for whose proposal I have a very great esteem, and also a great opinion of her wit; different, too, from all sorts of religious confinement, and, above all, from vows of celibacy.

Wherefore the academy I propose should differ but little from public schools, wherein such ladies as were willing to study should have all the advantages of learning suitable to their genius.

But since some severities of discipline more than ordinary would be absolutely necessary to preserve the reputation of the house, that persons of quality and fortune might not be afraid to venture their children thither, I shall venture to make a small scheme by way of essay.

The house I would have built in a form by itself, as well as in a place by itself.

The building should be of three plain fronts, without any jettings or bearing-work, that the eye might at a glance see from one coin to the other; the gardens walled in the same triangular figure, with a large moat, and but one entrance.

When thus every part of the situation was contrived as well as might be for discovery, and to render intriguing dangerous, I would have no guards, no eyes, no spies set over the ladies, but shall expect them to be tried by the principles of honour and strict virtue.

And if I am asked why, I must ask pardon of my own sex for giving this reason for it:—

I am so much in charity with women, and so well acquainted with men, that 'tis my opinion there needs no other care to prevent intriguing than to keep the men effectually away; for though inclination, which we prettily call love, does sometimes move a little too visibly in the sex, and frailty often follows, yet I think, verily, custom, which we miscall modesty, has so far the ascendant over the sex, that solicitation always goes before it.

Custom with women 'stead of virtue rules;
It leads the wisest and commands the fools;
For this alone, when inclinations reign,
Though virtue's fled, will acts of vice restrain.
Only by custom 'tis that virtue lives,
And love requires to be asked before it gives.
For that which we call modesty is pride;
They scorn to ask, and hate to be denied.
'Tis custom thus prevails upon their want;
They'll never beg what asked they easily
    grant;
And when the needless ceremony's over,   10
Themselves the weakness of the sex discover.
If then desires are strong and nature free,
Keep from her men and opportunity;
Else 'twill be vain to curb her by restraint,
But keep the question off, you keep the saint.

In short, let a woman have never such a coming principle, she will let you ask before she complies, at least if she be a woman of any honour.

Upon this ground I am persuaded such measures might be taken that the ladies might have all the freedom in the world within their own walls, and yet no intriguing, no indecencies, nor scandalous affairs happen; and in order to this the following customs and laws should be observed in the colleges, of which I would propose one at least in every county in England, and about ten for the City of London.

After the regulation of the form of the building as before:—

(1.) All the ladies who enter into the house should set their hands to the orders of the house, to signify their consent to submit to them.

(2.) As no woman should be received but who declared herself willing, and that it was the act of her choice to enter herself, so no person should be confined to continue there a moment longer than the same voluntary choice inclined her.

(3.) The charges of the house being to be paid by the ladies, every one that entered should have only this encumbrance, that she should pay for the whole year, though her mind should change as to her continuance.

(4.) An Act of Parliament should make it felony without clergy for any man to enter by force or fraud into the house, or to solicit any woman, *though it were to marry*, while she was

in the house. And this law would by no means be severe, because any woman who was willing to receive the addresses of a man might discharge herself of the house when she pleased; and, on the contrary, any woman who had occasion, might discharge herself of the impertinent addresses of any person she had an aversion to by entering into the house.

In this house,

The persons who enter should be taught all sorts of breeding suitable to both their genius and their quality, and in particular music and dancing, which it would be cruelty to bar the sex of, because they are their darlings; but besides this, they should be taught languages, as particularly French and Italian; and I would venture the injury of giving a woman more tongues than one.

They should, as a particular study, be taught all the graces of speech and all the necessary air of conversation, which our common education is so defective in that I need not expose it. They should be brought to read books, and especially history, and so to read as to make them understand the world, and be able to know and judge of things when they hear of them.

To such whose genius would lead them to it I would deny no sort of learning; but the chief thing in general is to cultivate the understandings of the sex, that they may be capable of all sorts of conversation; that their parts and judgments being improved, they may be as profitable in their conversation as they are pleasant.

Women, in my observation, have little or no difference in them, but as they are or are not distinguished by education. Tempers indeed may in some degree influence them, but the main distinguishing part is their breeding.

The whole sex are generally quick and sharp. I believe I may be allowed to say generally so, for you rarely see them lumpish and heavy when they are children, as boys will often be. If a woman be well-bred, and taught the proper management of her natural wit, she proves generally very sensible and retentive; and without partiality, a woman of sense and manners is the finest and most delicate part of God's creation; the glory of her Maker, and the great instance of His singular regard to man, His darling creature, to whom He gave the best gift either God could bestow or man receive. And it is the sordidest piece of folly and ingratitude in the world to withhold from the sex the due lustre which the advantages of education gives to the natural beauty of their minds.

A woman well bred and well taught, furnished with the additional accomplishments of knowledge and behaviour, is a creature without comparison; her society is the emblem of sublimer enjoyments; her person is angelic and her conversation heavenly; she is all softness and sweetness, peace, love, wit, and delight. She is every way suitable to the sublimest wish, and the man that has such a one to his portion has nothing to do but to rejoice in her and be thankful.

On the other hand, suppose her to be the very same woman, and rob her of the benefit of education, and it follows thus:—

If her temper be good, want of education makes her soft and easy.

Her wit, for want of teaching, makes her impertinent and talkative.

Her knowledge, for want of judgment and experience, makes her fanciful and whimsical.

If her temper be bad, want of breeding makes her worse, and she grows haughty, insolent, and loud.

If she be passionate, want of manners makes her termagant and a scold, which is much at one with lunatic.

If she be proud, want of discretion (which still is breeding) makes her conceited, fantastic, and ridiculous.

And from these she degenerates to be turbulent, clamorous, noisy, nasty, and the devil.

Methinks mankind for their own sakes, since, say what we will of the women, we all think fit one time or other to be concerned with them, should take some care to breed them up to be suitable and serviceable, if they expected no such thing as delight from them. Bless us! what care do we take to breed up a good horse and to break him well, and what a value do we put upon him when it is done, and all because he should be fit for our use; and why not a woman? Since all her ornaments and beauty without suitable behaviour is a cheat in nature, like the false tradesman who puts the best of his goods uppermost that the buyer may think the rest are of the same goodness.

Beauty of the body, which is the women's glory, seems to be now unequally bestowed, and Nature, or rather Providence, to lie under some scandal about it, as if it was given a woman for a snare to men, and so make a kind of a she-devil of her; because, they say, exquisite beauty is rarely given with wit, more rarely with goodness of temper, and never at all with modesty. And some, pretending to justify the equity of such a distribution, will tell us 'tis the effect of the justice of Providence in dividing particular excellences among all His creatures, share and share alike, as it were, that all might for something or other be acceptable to one another, else some would be despised.

I think both these notions false, and yet the last, which has the show of respect to Providence, is the worst, for it supposes Providence to be indigent and empty, as if it had not wherewith to furnish all the creatures it had made, but was fain to be parsimonious in its gifts, and distribute them by piecemeal for fear of being exhausted.

If I might venture my opinion against an almost universal notion, I would say most men mistake the proceedings of Providence in this case, and all the world at this day are mistaken in their practice about it. And because the assertion is very bold, I desire to explain myself.

That Almighty First Cause which

made us all is certainly the fountain of excellence, as it is of being, and by an invisible influence could have diffused equal qualities and perfections to all the creatures it has made, as the sun does its light, without the least ebb or diminution to Himself, and has given indeed to every individual sufficient to the figure His providence had designed him in the world.

I believe it might be defended if I should say that I do suppose God has given to all mankind equal gifts and capacities in that He has given them all souls equally capable, and that the whole difference in mankind proceeds either from accidental difference in the make of their bodies or from the foolish difference of education.

1. From accidental difference in bodies. I would avoid discoursing here of the philosophical position of the soul in the body. But if it be true, as philosophers do affirm, that the understanding and memory is dilated or contracted according to the accidental dimensions of the organ through which it is conveyed, then, though God has given a soul as capable to me as another, yet if I have any natural defect in those parts of the body by which the soul should act, I may have the same soul infused as another man, and yet he be a wise man and I a very fool. For example, if a child naturally have a defect in the organ of hearing, so that he could never distinguish any sound, that child shall never be able to speak or read, though it have a soul capable of all the accomplishments in the world. The brain is the centre of the soul's actings, where all the distinguishing faculties of it reside; and it is observable a man who has a narrow contracted head, in which there is not room for the due and necessary operations of nature by the brain, is never a man of very great judgment; and that proverb, "A great head and little wit," is not meant by nature, but is a reproof upon sloth, as if one should, by way of wonder, say, "Fie, fie! you that have a great head have but little wit;

that's strange! that must certainly be your own fault." From this notion I do believe there is a great matter in the breed of men and women—not that wise men shall always get wise children, but I believe strong and healthy bodies have the wisest children, and sickly, weakly bodies affect the wits as well as the bodies of their children. We are easily persuaded to believe this in the breeds of horses, cocks, dogs, and other creatures, and I believe it is as visible in men.

But to come closer to the business, the great distinguishing difference which is seen in the world between men and women is in their education, and this is manifested by comparing it with the difference between one man or woman and another.

And herein it is that I take upon me to make such a bold assertion that all the world are mistaken in their practice about women; for I cannot think that God Almighty ever made them so delicate, so glorious creatures, and furnished them with such charms, so agreeable and so delightful to mankind, with souls capable of the same accomplishments with men, and all to be only stewards of our houses, *cooks and slaves*.

Not that I am for exalting the female government in the least; but, in short, I would have men take women for companions, and educate them to be fit for it. A woman of sense and breeding will scorn as much to encroach upon the prerogative of the man as a man of sense will scorn to oppress *the weakness of the woman*. But if the women's souls were refined and improved by teaching, that word would be lost; to say, the weakness of the sex as to judgment, would be nonsense, for ignorance and folly would be no more to be found among women than men. I remember a passage which I heard from a very fine woman; she had wit and capacity enough, an extraordinary shape and face, and a great fortune, but had been cloistered up all her time, and for fear of being stolen, had not had the liberty of being taught the common necessary knowledge of women's affairs; and when she came to converse in the world, her natural wit made her so sensible of the want of education, that she gave this short reflection on herself:—"I am ashamed to talk with my very maids," says she, "for I don't know when they do right or wrong. I had more need go to school than be married."

I need not enlarge on the loss the defect of education is to the sex, nor argue the benefit of the contrary practice; it is a thing will be more easily granted than remedied. This chapter is but an essay at the thing, and I refer the practice to those happy days, if ever they shall be, when men shall be wise enough to mend it.

A TRUE RELATION OF THE APPARITION OF MRS. VEAL,

THE NEXT DAY AFTER HER DEATH, TO ONE MRS. BARGRAVE, AT CANTERBURY, THE 8TH OF SEPTEMBER, 1705.

(1706)

THE PREFACE

This relation is matter of fact, and attended with such circumstances as may induce any reasonable man to believe it. It was sent by a gentleman, a justice of peace at Maidstone, in Kent, and a very intelligent person, to his friend in London, as it is here worded; which discourse is attested by a very sober and understanding gentleman, who had it from his kinswoman, who lives in Canterbury, within a few doors of the house in which the within-named Mrs. Bargrave lived; and who he believes to be of so discerning a spirit, as not to be put upon by any fallacy, and who positively assured him that the whole matter as it is related and laid down is really true, and what she herself had in the same words, as near as may be, from Mrs. Bargrave's own mouth,

who, she knows, had no reason to invent and publish such a story, or any design to forge and tell a lie, being a woman of much honesty and virtue, and her whole life a course, as it were, of piety. The use which we ought to make of it is to consider that there is a life to come after this, and a just God who will retribute to every one according to the deeds done in the body, and therefore to reflect upon our past course of life we have led in the world; that our time is short and uncertain; and that if we would escape the punishment of the ungodly and receive the reward of the righteous, which is the laying hold of eternal life, we ought, for the time to come to return to God by a speedy repentance, ceasing to do evil, and learning to do well; to seek after God early, if haply He may be found of us, and lead such lives for the future as may be well pleasing in His sight.

A RELATION, &c.

This thing is so rare in all its circumstances, and on so good authority, that my reading and conversation have not given me anything like it. It is fit to gratify the most ingenious and serious inquirer. Mrs. Bargrave is the person to whom Mrs. Veal appeared after her death; she is my intimate friend, and I can avouch for her reputation for these last fifteen or sixteen years, on my own knowledge; and I can confirm the good character she had from her youth to the time of my acquaintance; though since this relation she is calumniated by some people that are friends to the brother of Mrs. Veal who appeared, who think the relation of this appearance to be a reflection, and endeavour what they can to blast Mrs. Bargrave's reputation, and to laugh the story out of countenance. But by the circumstances thereof, and the cheerful disposition of Mrs. Bargrave, notwithstanding the ill-usage of a very wicked husband, there is not the least sign of dejection in her face; nor did I ever hear her let fall a desponding or murmuring expression; nay, not when actually under her husband's barbarity, which I have been witness to, and several other persons of undoubted reputation.

Now you must know Mrs. Veal was a maiden gentlewoman of about thirty years of age, and for some years last past had been troubled with fits, which were perceived coming on her by her going off from her discourses very abruptly to some impertinence. She was maintained by an only brother, and kept his house in Dover. She was a very pious woman, and her brother a very sober man, to all appearance; but now he does all he can to null or quash the story. Mrs. Veal was intimately acquainted with Mrs. Bargrave from her childhood. Mrs. Veal's circumstances were then mean; her father did not take care of his children as he ought, so that they were exposed to hardships; and Mrs. Bargrave in those days had as unkind a father, though she wanted neither for food nor clothing, whilst Mrs. Veal wanted for both, insomuch that she would often say, "Mrs. Bargrave, you are not only the best, but the only friend I have in the world; and no circumstance in life shall ever dissolve my friendship." They would often condole each other's adverse fortunes, and read together "Drelincourt upon Death," and other good books; and so, like two Christian friends, they comforted each other under their sorrow.

Some time after Mr. Veal's friends got him a place in the custom-house at Dover, which occasioned Mrs. Veal, by little and little, to fall off from her intimacy with Mrs. Bargrave, though there never was any such thing as a quarrel; but an indifferency came on by degrees, till at last Mrs. Bargrave had not seen her in two years and a half; though about a twelve-month of the time Mrs. Bargrave had been absent from Dover, and this last half-year had been in Canterbury about two months of the time, dwelling in a house of her own.

In this house, on the 8th of September 1705, she was sitting alone, in the forenoon, thinking over her unfortunate life, and arguing herself into a due resignation to Providence, though her condition seemed hard. "And," said she, "I have been provided for hitherto, and doubt not but I shall be still; and am well satisfied that my afflictions shall end when it is most fit for me"; and then took up her sewing-work, which she had no sooner done but she hears a knocking at the door. She went to see who was there, and this proved to be Mrs. Veal, her old friend, who was in a riding-habit; at that moment of time the clock struck twelve at noon.

"Madam," says Mrs. Bargrave, "I am surprised to see you, you have been so long a stranger"; but told her she was glad to see her, and offered to salute her, which Mrs. Veal complied with, till their lips almost touched; and then Mrs. Veal drew her hand across her own eyes and said, "I am not very well," and so waived it. She told Mrs. Bargrave she was going a journey, and had a great mind to see her first. "But," says Mrs. Bargrave, "how came you to take a journey alone? I am amazed at it, because I know you have a good brother." "Oh," says Mrs. Veal, "I gave my brother the slip, and came away, because I had so great a desire to see you before I took my journey." So Mrs. Bargrave went in with her into another room within the first, and Mrs. Veal set her down in an elbow-chair, in which Mrs. Bargrave was sitting when she heard Mrs. Veal knock. Then says Mrs. Veal, "My dear friend, I am come to renew our old friendship again, and beg your pardon for my breach of it; and if you can forgive me, you are the best of women." "Oh," says Mrs. Bargrave, "do not mention such a thing. I have not had an uneasy thought about it; I can easily forgive it." "What did you think of me?" said Mrs. Veal. Says Mrs. Bargrave, "I thought you were like the rest of the world, and that prosperity had made you forget yourself and me." Then Mrs. Veal reminded Mrs. Bargrave of the many friendly offices she did in her former days, and much of the conversation they had with each other in the times of their adversity; what books they read, and what comfort in particular they received from "Drelincourt's Book of Death," which was the best, she said, on that subject ever written. She also mentioned Dr. Sherlock, the two Dutch books which were translated, written upon Death, and several others; but Drelincourt, she said, had the clearest notions of death and of the future state of any who had handled that subject. Then she asked Mrs. Bargrave whether she had Drelincourt. She said, "Yes." Says Mrs. Veal, "Fetch it." And so Mrs. Bargrave goes upstairs and brings it down. Says Mrs. Veal, "Dear Mrs. Bargrave, if the eyes of our faith were as open as the eyes of our body, we should see numbers of angels about us for our guard. The notions we have of heaven now are nothing like to what it is, as Drelincourt says. Therefore be comforted under your afflictions, and believe that the Almighty has a particular regard to you, and that your afflictions are marks of God's favour; and when they have done the business they are sent for, they shall be removed from you. And believe me, my dear friend, believe what I say to you, one minute of future happiness will infinitely reward you for all your sufferings; for I can never believe" (and claps her hands upon her knees with great earnestness, which indeed ran through most of her discourse) "that ever God will suffer you to spend all your days in this afflicted state; but be assured that your afflictions shall leave you, or you them, in a short time." She spake in that pathetical and heavenly manner that Mrs. Bargrave wept several times, she was so deeply affected with it.

Then Mrs. Veal mentioned Dr. Horneck's "Ascetic," at the end of which he gives an account of the lives of the primitive Christians. Their pattern she recommended to our imitation, and said, "Their conversation was not like this of our age; for now," says she, "there is nothing but frothy, vain discourse, which is far different from theirs. Theirs was to edification, and to build one another up in faith; so that they were not as we are, nor are we as they were; but," said she, "we ought to do as they did. There was a hearty friendship among them; but where is it now to be found?" Says Mrs. Bargrave, "It is hard indeed to find a true friend in these days." Says Mrs. Veal, "Mr. Norris has a fine copy of verses, called 'Friendship in Perfection,' which I wonderfully admire. Have you seen the book?" says Mrs. Veal. "No," says Mrs. Bargrave, "but I have the verses of my own writing out." "Have you?" says Mrs. Veal; "then fetch them." Which she did from above-stairs, and offered them to Mrs. Veal to read, who refused, and waived the thing, saying holding down her head would make it ache; and then desired Mrs. Bargrave to read them to her, which she did. As they were admiring "Friendship," Mrs. Veal said, "Dear Mrs. Bargrave I shall love you for ever." In these verses there is twice used the word Elysian. "Ah!" says Mrs. Veal, "these poets have such names for heaven!" She would often draw her hand across her own eyes and say, "Mrs. Bargrave, do not you think I am mightily impaired by my fits?" "No," says Mrs. Bargrave, "I think you look as well as ever I knew you."

After all this discourse, which the apparition put in much finer words than Mrs. Bargrave said she could pretend to, and as much more than she can remember, for it cannot be thought that an hour and three-quarters' conversation could be retained, though the main of it she thinks she does, she said to Mrs. Bargrave she would have her write a letter to her brother, and tell him she would have him give rings to such and such, and that there was a purse of gold in her cabinet, and that she would have two broad pieces given to her cousin Watson.

Talking at this rate, Mrs. Bargrave thought that a fit was coming upon her, and so placed herself in a chair just before her knees, to keep her from falling to the ground, if her fits should occasion it (for the elbow-chair, she thought, would keep her from falling on either side) ; and to divert Mrs. Veal, as she thought, took hold of her gown-sleeve several times and commended it. Mrs. Veal told her it was a scoured silk, and newly made up. But for all this, Mrs. Veal persisted in her request, and told Mrs. Bargrave that she must not deny her, and she would have her tell her brother all their conversation when she had an opportunity. "Dear Mrs. Veal," said Mrs. Bargrave, "this seems so impertinent that I cannot tell how to comply with it; and what a mortifying story will our conversation be to a young gentleman? Why," says Mrs. Bargrave, "it is much better, methinks, to do it yourself." "No," says Mrs. Veal, "though it seems impertinent to you now, you will see more reason for it hereafter." Mrs. Bargrave then, to satisfy her importunity, was going to fetch a pen and ink, but Mrs. Veal said, "Let it alone now, but do it when I am gone; but you must be sure to do it"; which was one of the last things she enjoined her at parting. So she promised her.

Then Mrs. Veal asked for Mrs. Bargrave's daughter. She said she was not at home, "But if you have a mind to see her," says Mrs. Bargrave, "I'll send for her." "Do," says Mrs. Veal. On which she left her, and went to a neighbour's to see for her; and by the time Mrs. Bargrave was returning, Mrs. Veal was got without the door into the street, in the face of the beast-market, on a Saturday (which is market-day), and stood ready to part, as soon as Mrs. Bargrave came to her. She asked her why she was in such haste. She said she must be going,

though perhaps she might not go her journey until Monday; and told Mrs. Bargrave she hoped she should see her again at her cousin Watson's before she went whither she was going. Then she said she would take her leave of her, and walked from Mrs. Bargrave in her view, till a turning interrupted the sight of her, which was three-quarters after one in the afternoon.

Mrs. Veal died the 7th of September, at twelve o'clock at noon, of her fits, and had not above four hours' sense before death, in which time she received the sacrament. The next day after Mrs. Veal's appearing, being Sunday, Mrs. Bargrave was so mightily indisposed with a cold and a sore throat, that she could not go out that day; but on Monday morning she sent a person to Captain Watson's to know if Mrs. Veal was there. They wondered at Mrs. Bargrave's inquiry, and sent her word that she was not there, nor was expected. At this answer, Mrs. Bargrave told the maid she had certainly mistook the name or made some blunder. And though she was ill, she put on her hood, and went herself to Captain Watson's, though she knew none of the family, to see if Mrs. Veal was there or not. They said they wondered at her asking, for that she had not been in town; they were sure, if she had, she would have been there. Says Mrs. Bargrave, "I am sure she was with me on Saturday almost two hours." They said it was impossible; for they must have seen her, if she had. In comes Captain Watson while they are in dispute, and said that Mrs. Veal was certainly dead, and her escutcheons were making. This strangely surprised Mrs. Bargrave, who went to the person immediately who had the care of them, and found it true. Then she related the whole story to Captain Watson's family, and what gown she had on, and how striped, and that Mrs. Veal told her it was scoured. Then Mrs. Watson cried out, "You have seen her indeed, for none knew but Mrs. Veal and myself that the gown was scoured." And Mrs. Watson owned that she described the gown exactly; "for," said she, "I helped her to make it up." This Mrs. Watson blazed all about the town, and avouched the demonstration of the truth of Mrs. Bargrave's seeing Mrs. Veal's apparition; and Captain Watson carried two gentlemen immediately to Mrs. Bargrave's house to hear the relation from her own mouth. And when it spread so fast that gentlemen and persons of quality, the judicious and sceptical part of the world, flocked in upon her, it at last became such a task that she was forced to go out of the way; for they were in general extremely well satisfied of the truth of the thing, and plainly saw that Mrs. Bargrave was no hypochondriac, for she always appears with such a cheerful air and pleasing mien, that she has gained the favour and esteem of all the gentry, and it is thought a great favour if they can but get the relation from her own mouth. I should have told you before that Mrs. Veal told Mrs. Bargrave that her sister and brother-in-law were just come down from London to see her. Says Mrs. Bargrave, "How came you to order matters so strangely?" "It could not be helped," said Mrs. Veal. And her brother and sister did come to see her, and entered the town of Dover just as Mrs. Veal was expiring. Mrs. Bargrave asked her whether she would drink some tea. Says Mrs. Veal, "I do not care if I do; but I'll warrant you this mad fellow" (meaning Mrs. Bargrave's husband) "has broken all your trinkets." "But," says Mrs. Bargrave, "I'll get something to drink in for all that." But Mrs. Veal waived it, and said, "It is no matter; let it alone"; and so it passed.

All the time I sat with Mrs. Bargrave, which was some hours, she recollected fresh sayings of Mrs. Veal. And one material thing more she told Mrs. Bargrave—that old Mr. Breton allowed Mrs. Veal ten pounds a year, which was a secret, and unknown to Mrs. Bargrave till Mrs. Veal told it her. Mrs. Bargrave never varies in her story, which puzzles those who doubt of the truth or are unwilling to believe it. A servant in the neighbour's yard adjoining to Mrs. Bargrave's house heard her talking to somebody an hour of the time Mrs. Veal was with her. Mrs. Bargrave went out to her next neighbour's the very moment she parted with Mrs. Veal, and told her what ravishing conversation she had with an old friend, and told the whole of it. Drelincourt's "Book of Death" is, since this happened, bought up strangely. And it is to be observed that, notwithstanding all the trouble and fatigue Mrs. Bargrave has undergone upon this account, she never took the value of a farthing, nor suffered her daughter to take anything of anybody, and therefore can have no interest in telling the story.

But Mr. Veal does what he can to stifle the matter, and said he would see Mrs. Bargrave; but yet it is certain matter of fact that he has been at Captain Watson's since the death of his sister, and yet never went near Mrs. Bargrave; and some of his friends report her to be a liar, and that she knew of Mr. Breton's ten pounds a year. But the person who pretends to say so has the reputation of a notorious liar among persons whom I know to be of undoubted credit. Now, Mr. Veal is more of a gentleman than to say she lies, but says a bad husband has crazed her. But she needs only present herself and it will effectually confute that pretence. Mr. Veal says he asked his sister on her deathbed whether she had a mind to dispose of anything, and she said no. Now, the things which Mrs. Veal's apparition would have disposed of were so trifling, and nothing of justice aimed at in their disposal, that the design of it appears to me to be only in order to make Mrs. Bargrave so to demonstrate the truth of her appearance, as to satisfy the world of the reality thereof as to what she had seen and heard, and to secure her reputation among the reasonable and understanding part of mankind. And then again Mr. Veal owns that there was a purse of gold; but it was not found in her cabinet, but in a comb-box. This looks improbable; for that Mrs. Watson owned that Mrs. Veal was so very careful of the key of the cabinet that she would trust nobody with it; and if so, no doubt she would not trust her gold out of it. And Mrs. Veal's often drawing her hand over her eyes, and asking Mrs. Bargrave whether her fits had not impaired her, looks to me as if she did it on purpose to remind Mrs. Bargrave of her fits, to prepare her not to think it strange that she should put her upon writing to her brother to dispose of rings and gold, which looks so much like a dying person's request; and it took accordingly with Mrs. Bargrave, as the effects of her fits coming upon her; and was one of the many instances of her wonderful love to her and care of her that she should not be affrighted, which indeed appears in her whole management, particularly in her coming to her in the daytime, waiving the salutation, and when she was alone, and then the manner of her parting to prevent a second attempt to salute her.

Now, why Mr. Veal should think this relation a reflection, as it is plain he does by his endeavouring to stifle it, I cannot imagine, because the generality believe her to be a good spirit, her discourse was so heavenly. Her two great errands were to comfort Mrs. Bargrave in her affliction, and to ask her forgiveness for the breach of friendship, and with a pious discourse to encourage her. So that after all to suppose that Mrs. Bargrave could hatch such an invention as this from Friday noon to Saturday noon, supposing that she knew of Mrs. Veal's death the very first moment, without

jumbling circumstances, and without any interest too, she must be more witty, fortunate, and wicked too than any indifferent person, I dare say, will allow. I asked Mrs. Bargrave several times if she was sure she felt the gown. She answered modestly, "If my senses are to be relied on, I am sure of it." I asked her if she heard a sound when she clapped her hands upon her knees. She said she did not remember she did, but said she appeared to be as much a substance as I did, who talked with her. "And I may," said she, "be as soon persuaded that your apparition is talking to me now as that I did not really see her; for I was under no manner of fear, and received her as a friend, and parted with her as such. I would not," says she, "give one farthing to make any one believe it; I have no interest in it. Nothing but trouble is entailed upon me for a long time, for aught I know; and had it not come to light by accident, it would never have been made public." But now she says she will make her own private use of it, and keep herself out of the way as much as she can; and so she has done since. She says she had a gentleman who came thirty miles to her to hear the relation, and that she had told it to a room full of people at a time. Several particular gentlemen have had the story from Mrs Bargrave's own mouth.

This thing has very much affected me, and I am as well satisfied as I am of the best grounded matter of fact. And why we should dispute matter of fact because we cannot solve things of which we have no certain or demonstrative notions, seems strange to me. Mrs. Bargrave's authority and sincerity alone would have been undoubted in any other case.

JONATHAN SWIFT (1667-1745)

For the modern reader Jonathan Swift still exercises a personal and intellectual power beyond all his contemporaries. His life was extremely unhappy but also highly successful, if the profound and disturbing impression which he has always made on the minds of his fellow men can be called success. The son of an Englishman who had settled in Ireland, he was educated at Kilkenny Grammar School and at Trinity College, Dublin. He was necessarily in a position of dependence, first on the uncle who gave him money for his schooling, and then on Sir William Temple (see above, p. 127), with whom he lived at Moor Park, Surrey, during the last decade of the seventeenth century. The cultured Temple was not a congenial master, but helped to initiate the surly young scholar into the world of wit and polite learning. On Temple's behalf he entered into the controversy on the ancients and the moderns with *The Battle of the Books*; on his own behalf he expressed his view of man and life fully in the incomparable *Tale of a Tub*, where his genius appears in its full force. These works, not published until 1704, were written in the years 1696-98. In this same memorable decade Swift formed his life-long attachment to Hester Johnson, his "Stella," also a member of Temple's household. Swift's relations with Stella are enigmatic, and biographers still debate the question whether he married her; it can only be said here that of all human beings she came closest to touching his heart.

On Temple's death Swift had nothing to show for his services but some small church livings in Ireland. He could not be content with the retired life that was thus open to him; he sought action in public life, and in the early years of Queen Anne he made friends with the great wits and entered into political controversy. He found time to play in his fashion; characteristic of his grim wit are the pamphlets he wrote under the name of "Isaac Bickerstaff" against the almanac-maker Partridge, whose death he predicted and duly announced in spite of the protests of his victim. His central position in politics was a defence of the prerogatives of the Church; on this ground he savagely assailed deists and dissenters, and changed his politics from Whig to Tory in 1710. For three years he was chief pamphleteer of the Tory administration of Harley and St. John, and prided himself on being on an intimate footing with the great. The *Journal to Stella* gives us a day by day record of this period. Politics estranged him from Addison and Steele, and only the friendships of the Scriblerus Club, with Prior, Arbuthnot, Pope, Gay, and Parnell, held firm. In 1714 the death of Queen Anne dashed the hopes of the Tories, and Swift withdrew in disgust to Dublin, where he spent the rest of his life as Dean of St. Patrick's Cathedral. Misanthrope though he was, he won popularity among the Irish by defending their economic and political interests against the English government. When a man named Wood was granted the right to issue an inferior copper coinage for Ireland, Swift blocked the scheme with his famous *Drapier's Letters* (1724) and scored a great political triumph. But he suffered from chronic ill health; he chafed at the provincial society of Ireland, and his chief interest was the expression of his conviction of human triviality and folly. From 1721 to 1725 he worked on *Gulliver's Travels*, which he brought out after a visit to England in 1726. Here, however it is to be interpreted, is his final word on man as an individual and man in society. *Gulliver* and the *Miscellanies* which Pope and Swift published in 1727 are the outcome of the old projects of the Scriblerus Club.

Thenceforward he put all his literary work under the heading of "bagatelles"—trifles with which to beguile the time and to play on the surface of life, since beneath are only unreason and despair. "Life is a ridiculous tragedy, which is the worst kind of composition," he wrote to Pope in 1731. He jotted down *A Complete Collection of Genteel and Ingenious Conversation*, a remarkable record of trite colloquialisms, and the ironical *Directions to Servants*. His invincible command of the plain phrase appears in verse as well as prose. Dryden is said to have told him that he would never be a poet, but no one can deny that the author of *Verses on the Death of Dr. Swift*, *The Beast's Confession*, and *The Day of Judgment* uses verse to terrible effect. His literary career was virtually closed with the great poems of the early 30's. His latter state is described in some words to Pope: "I desire you will look upon me as a man worn with years, and sunk by public as well as personal vexation. I have entirely lost my memory, uncapable of conversation by a cruel deafness, which has lasted almost a year, and I despair of any cure." In 1742 he was declared of unsound mind, and in 1745 he died.

Swift is of his age in his devotion to the ideals of simple reason and good sense, his distrust of fantasy and speculation, his social and religious conservatism, and his inclination toward the use of burlesque forms for the purposes of satire. But he upholds his ideas and applies his literary devices with a passionate and scornful intensity which is unparalleled in any age. His philosophy, so far as he had one, can be expressed in words which sound like Augustan commonplace: right reason is uniform and simple, and man as far as he is rational has the good life within his grasp. And at least man is capable of reason. How, then, can he fall short of attaining a rational ideal? Some of Swift's contemporaries, notably Shaftesbury, give a hopeful and optimistic answer to this question. But Swift devotes himself to explaining in what various ways, by what various illusions, perversities, and follies, man sins against the clear light of nature and his better judgment. He pours his scorn on enthusiasm (fanaticism or zeal), selfish passion, the workings of imagination, the subleties of speculative thought, the endless toil of scholarship and scientific research, the crooked ways of politics, and especially on the vileness of the human body and the preposterous pride of the human animal. These are the themes of *A Tale of a Tub* and *Gulliver*. The world that man makes for himself is a world of error. The history of human institutions shows us that man is morally depraved and intellectually the prey of illusion. There is something of the Yahoo in every man, and in the realm of thought and imagination he dwells on appearances, not realities. In the famous "Digression on Madness" Swift ironically sets forth the "clothes philosophy," according to which surfaces and shows are all that exist; there is no inside to the universe. But this is really a myth or a parable rather than a metaphysical view; it is Swift's vision of a world without reason. In a somewhat parallel way, the Yahoo is Swift's vision of a humanity without reason. At the same time, it should not be assumed that Swift is a complete skeptic or pessimist. A positive standard is assumed, though Swift will not flatter us by the assurance that we have almost reached it or that our chances of reaching it are very good; as a satirist, he is moved to blame rather than praise. In *A Tale of a Tub* and *An Argument against Abolishing Christianity* the ideal of a true church must be present to make the argument intelligible. In *A Modest Proposal* it is humane indignation at the plight of the poor people of Ireland that gives meaning to Swift's savagery. Recent criticism has emphasized the fact that in his most important works Swift assumes a rôle or dons a mask, and speaks ironically or dramatically; his own views are not identical with the final disillusion and misanthropy of Gulliver, and cannot be fully expressed in terms of sheer disgust at Yahoos and complete acceptance of the "horse sense" of the Houyhnhnms. No one would deny that there is an underlying passion and violence in Swift which runs counter to the neo-classical compromise; no editor can explain away the contradiction between right reason and original sin in Swift's conception of man. He is not a speculative thinker but a pungent and profound commentator on life from the point of view of disillusioned good sense, and, by virtue of his clarity of vision and power of plain speech, a supreme master of prose.

Prose Works, ed. Temple Scott (12 vols., 1897-1908) ; *Prose Works,* ed. Herbert Davis (Oxford, 1939-   ) ; *Satires and Personal Writings, Gulliver's Travels, etc.,* ed. W. A. Eddy (2 vols., 1932-33) ; *Poems,* ed. Harold Williams (3 vols., Oxford, 1937) ; *Correspondence,* ed. F. E. Ball (6 vols., 1910-14) ; *Letters to Charles Ford,* ed. D. Nichol Smith (Oxford, 1935) ; *Journal to Stella,* ed. Harold Williams (2 vols., Oxford, 1948) ; *A Tale of a Tub* and *The Battle of the Books,* ed. A. C. Guthkelch and D. Nichol Smith (Oxford, 1920) ; *Gulliver's Travels,* ed. Harold Williams (1926); ed. A. E. Case (1938) ; *Drapier's Letters,* ed. Herbert Davis (Oxford, 1935) ; *Memoirs of Martinus Scriblerus,* ed. Charles Kerby-Miller (New Haven, 1950) ; Sir Henry Craik, *Life* (2 vols., 1894) ; Carl Van Doren, *Swift* (1930) ; Herbert Davis, *Stella* (1942) ; J. Middleton Murry, *Jonathan Swift: A Critical Biography* (1954) [often inaccurate, but stimulating]; Émile Pons, *Swift: les années de jeunesse et le 'Conte du tonneau'* (Strasbourg, 1925) [important]; Ricardo Quintana, *The Mind and Art of Jonathan Swift* (1936, rev. ed. 1953) [a standard work]; "Situational Satire: A Commentary on the Method of Swift," *Univ. of Toronto Quarterly,* XVII (1948), 30-36; John F. Ross, *Swift and Defoe* (Berkeley and Los Angeles, 1941) ; Herbert Davis, *The Satire of Jonathan Swift* (1947); Miriam Starkman, *Swift's Satire on Learning in A Tale of A Tub* (Princeton, 1950) ; J. M. Bullitt, *Jonathan Swift and the Anatomy of Satire* (Cambridge, Mass., 1953) .

For additional readings in Swift see pages 1082-1123.

BAUCIS AND PHILEMON

In ancient times, as story tells,
The saints would often leave their cells,
And stroll about, but hide their quality,
To try good people's hospitality.

It happened on a winter night,
As authors of the legend write,
Two brother hermits, saints by trade,
Taking their tour in masquerade,
Disguised in tattered habits, went
To a small village down in Kent;   10
Where, in the strollers' canting strain,
They begged from door to door in vain;
Tried every tone might pity win,
But not a soul would let them in.

Our wandering saints in woeful state,
Treated at this ungodly rate,
Having through all the village passed,
To a small cottage came at last;
Where dwelt a good honest old yeoman,
Called in the neighbourhood Philemon,   20
Who kindly did these saints invite
In his poor hut to pass the night:
And then the hospitable sire
Bid Goody Baucis mend the fire;
While he from out the chimney took
A flitch of bacon off the hook;
And freely from the fattest side
Cut out large slices to be fried:
Then stepped aside to fetch 'em drink,
Filled a large jug up to the brink;   30
And saw it fairly twice go round:
Yet (what is wonderful) they found
'Twas still replenished to the top,
As if they ne'er had touched a drop.
The good old couple was amazed,
And often on each other gazed:
For both were frighted to the heart,
And just began to cry,—"What art!"
Then softly turned aside to view,
Whether the lights were burning blue.   40
The gentle Pilgrims, soon aware on't,
Told 'em their calling, and their errant:
"Good folks, you need not be afraid,
We are but saints," the hermits said:
"No hurt shall come to you or yours:
But, for that pack of churlish boors,
Not fit to live on Christian ground,
They and their houses shall be drowned:
Whilst you shall see your cottage rise,
And grow a church before your eyes."   50
They scarce had spoke, when fair and soft,
The roof began to mount aloft;

Aloft rose every beam and rafter,
The heavy wall climbed slowly after.
The chimney widened, and grew higher,
Became a steeple with a spire.

The kettle to the top was hoist,
And there stood fastened to a joist;
But with the upside down, to show
Its inclinations for below: 60
In vain; for a superior force
Applied at bottom, stops its course,
Doomed ever in suspense to dwell,
'Tis now no kettle, but a bell.

A wooden jack, which had almost
Lost, by disuse, the art to roast,
A sudden alteration feels,
Increased by new intestine wheels:
And, what exalts the wonder more,
The number made the motion slower.   70
The flyer, though't had leaden feet,
Turned round so quick, you scarce could
      see't;
But slackened by some secret power,
Now hardly moves an inch an hour.
The jack and chimney, near allied,
Had never left each other's side;
The chimney to a steeple grown,
The jack would not be left alone,
But up against the steeple reared,
Became a clock, and still adhered: 80
And still its love to household cares
By a shrill voice at noon declares,
Warning the cook-maid not to burn
That roast meat which it cannot turn.

The groaning chair began to crawl
Like an huge snail along the wall;
There stuck aloft, in public view,
And with small change a pulpit grew.

The porringers, that in a row
Hung high and made a glittering show,   90
To a less noble substance changed,
Were now but leathern buckets ranged.

The ballads pasted on the wall,
Of Joan of France and English Moll,
Fair Rosamond and Robin Hood,
The Little Children in the Wood,
Now seemed to look abundance better,
Improved in picture, size, and letter,
And high in order placed, describe
The heraldry of every tribe.   100

A bedstead of the antique mode,
Compact of timber many a load,
Such as our ancestors did use,
Was metamorphosed into pews;

Which still their ancient nature keep,
By lodging folks disposed to sleep.
   The cottage, by such feats as these,
Grown to a church by just degrees,
The hermits then desired their host
To ask for what he fancied most.   110
Philemon, having paused a while,
Returned 'em thanks in homely style;
Then said, "My house is grown so fine,
Methinks I still would call it mine:
I'm old, and fain would live at ease;
Make me the parson, if you please."
   He spoke, and presently he feels
His grazier's coat fall down his heels;
He sees, yet hardly can believe,
About each arm a pudding-sleeve;   120
His waistcoat to a cassock grew,
And both assumed a sable hue;
But being old, continued just
As threadbare, and as full of dust.
His talk was now of tithes and dues;
He smoked his pipe, and read the news;
Knew how to preach old sermons next,
Vamped in the preface and the text;
At christenings well could act his part,
And had the service all by heart;   130
Wished women might have children fast,
And thought whose sow had farrowed last:
Against dissenters would repine,
And stood up firm for right divine:
Found his head filled with many a system,
But classic authors,—he ne'er missed 'em.
   Thus having furbished up a parson,
Dame Baucis next they played their farce on;
Instead of homespun coifs were seen
Good pinners edged with colberteen: 140
Her petticoat transformed apace,
Became black satin flounced with lace.

Plain Goody would no longer down,
'Twas Madam, in her grogram gown.
Philemon was in great surprise,
And hardly could believe his eyes,
Amazed to see her look so prim;
And she admired as much at him.
   Thus, happy in their change of life,
Were several years this man and wife;   150
When on a day, which proved their last,
Discoursing o'er old stories past,
They went by chance, amidst their talk,
To the churchyard to take a walk;
When Baucis hastily cried out,
"My dear, I see your forehead sprout!"
"Sprout," quoth the man, "what's this you
      tell us?
I hope you don't believe me jealous:
But yet, methinks, I feel it true;
And really, yours is budding too—   160
Nay,—now I cannot stir my foot:
It feels as if 'twere taking root."
   Description would but tire my Muse:
In short, they both were turned to yews.
   Old Goodman Dobson of the green
Remembers he the trees has seen;
He'll talk of them from noon to night,
And goes with folks to show the sight;
On Sundays, after evening prayer,
He gathers all the parish there;   170
Points out the place of either yew;
Here Baucis, there Philemon grew:
Till once, a parson of our town,
To mend his barn, cut Baucis down;
At which, 'tis hard to be believed
How much the other tree was grieved,
Grew scrubby, died a-top, was stunted;
So the next parson stubbed and burnt it.
                              [1706, 1709]

A DESCRIPTION OF THE MORNING

Now hardly here and there an hackney-coach
Appearing, showed the ruddy morn's approach.
Now Betty from her master's bed had flown,
And softly stole to discompose her own;
The slip-shod 'prentice from his master's door
Had pared the dirt, and sprinkled round the floor.
Now Moll had whirled her mop with dexterous airs,
Prepared to scrub the entry and the stairs.
The youth with broomy stumps began to trace
The kennel-edge, where wheels had worn the place.   10
The small-coal man was heard with cadence deep,

Till drowned in shriller notes of chimney-sweep:
Duns at his lordship's gate began to meet;
And brickdust Moll had screamed through half the street.
The turnkey now his flock returning sees,
Duly let out a-nights to steal for fees:
The watchful bailiffs take their silent stands,
And schoolboys lag with satchels in their hands.

[*1709*, 1709]

A DESCRIPTION OF A CITY SHOWER

Careful observers may foretell the hour
(By sure prognostics) when to dread a shower.
While rain depends, the pensive cat gives o'er
Her frolics, and pursues her tail no more.
Returning home at night, you'll find the sink
Strike your offended sense with double stink.
If you be wise, then go not far to dine;
You'll spend in coach-hire more than save in wine.
A coming shower your shooting corns presage,
Old aches throb, your hollow tooth will rage: 10
Sauntering in coffee-house is Dulman seen;
He damns the climate and complains of spleen.
   Meanwhile the South, rising with dabbled wings,
A sable cloud athwart the welkin flings,
That swilled more liquor than it could contain,
And, like a drunkard, gives it up again.
Brisk Susan whips her linen from the rope,
While the first drizzling shower is borne aslope:
Such is that sprinkling which some careless quean
Flirts on you from her mop, but not so clean: 20
You fly, invoke the gods; then turning, stop
To rail; she singing, still whirls on her mop,
Not yet the dust had shunned the unequal strife,
But, aided by the wind, fought still for life,
And wafted with its foe by violent gust,
'Twas doubtful which was rain and which was dust.
Ah! where must needy poet seek for aid,
When dust and rain at once his coat invade?
His only coat, where dust confused with rain
Roughen the nap, and leave a mingled stain.   30
   Now in contiguous drops the flood comes down,
Threatening with deluge this devoted town.
To shops in crowds the daggled females fly,
Pretend to cheapen goods, but nothing buy.
The Templar spruce, while every spout's abroach,
Stays till 'tis fair, yet seems to call a coach.
The tucked-up sempstress walks with hasty strides,
While streams run down her oiled umbrella's sides.
Here various kinds, by various fortunes led,
Commence acquaintance underneath a shed.   40
Triumphant Tories and desponding Whigs

Forget their feuds, and join to save their wigs.
Boxed in a chair the beau impatient sits,
While spouts run clattering o'er the roof by fits,
And ever and anon with frightful din
The leather sounds; he trembles from within.
So when Troy chairmen bore the wooden steed,
Pregnant with Greeks impatient to be freed
(Those bully Greeks, who, as the moderns do,
Instead of paying chairmen, run them through),   50
Laocoön struck the outside with his spear,
And each imprisoned hero quaked for fear.
    Now from all parts the swelling kennels flow,
And bear their trophies with them as they go:
Filth of all hues and odours seem to tell
What street they sailed from, by their sight and smell.
They, as each torrent drives with rapid force,
From Smithfield or St. Pulchre's shape their course,
And in huge confluent join at Snow Hill ridge,
Fall from the conduit prone to Holborn Bridge.   60
Sweeping from butchers' stalls, dung, guts, and blood,
Drowned puppies, stinking sprats, all drenched in mud,
Dead cats and turnip-tops come tumbling down the flood.
                                        [1710]

ON STELLA'S BIRTHDAY

Stella this day is thirty-four
(We shan't dispute a year or more) —
However, Stella, be not troubled,
Although thy size and years are doubled,
Since first I saw thee at sixteen,
The brightest virgin on the green,
So little is thy form declined;
Made up so largely in thy mind.
    Oh, would it please the gods, to split
Thy beauty, size, and years, and wit;   10
No age could furnish out a pair
Of nymphs so graceful, wise, and fair:
With half the lustre of your eyes,
With half your wit, your years, and size.
And then, before it grew too late,
How should I beg of gentle Fate
(That either nymph might have her swain)
To split my worship too in twain.
                            [1719, 1727]

STELLA'S BIRTHDAY

MARCH 13, 1726-27

This day, whate'er the Fates decree,
Shall still be kept with joy by me:

This day then let us not be told
That you are sick, and I grown old;
Nor think on our approaching ills,
And talk of spectacles and pills;
To-morrow will be time enough
To hear such mortifying stuff.
Yet, since from reason may be brought
A better and more pleasing thought,   10
Which can, in spite of all decays,
Support a few remaining days;
From not the gravest of divines
Accept for once some serious lines.
    Although we now can form no more
Long schemes of life, as heretofore,
Yet you, while time is running fast,
Can look with joy on what is past.
    Were future happiness and pain
A mere contrivance of the brain;   20
As atheists argue, to entice
And fit their proselytes for vice
(The only comfort they propose,
To have companions in their woes),
Grant this the case; yet sure 'tis hard
That virtue, styled its own reward,
And by all sages understood
To be the chief of human good,
Should acting, die, nor leave behind
Some lasting pleasure in the mind,   30
Which by remembrance will assuage

Grief, sickness, poverty, and age;
And strongly shoot a radiant dart
To shine through life's declining part.
    Say, Stella, feel you no content,
Reflecting on a life well spent?
Your skilful hand employed to save
Despairing wretches from the grave;
And then supporting with your store
Those whom you dragged from death before;
So Providence on mortals waits,   41
Preserving what it first creates;
Your generous boldness to defend
An innocent and absent friend;
That courage which can make you just
To merit humbled in the dust;
The detestation you express
For vice in all its glittering dress;
That patience under torturing pain,
Where stubborn Stoics would complain: 50
    Must these like empty shadows pass,
Or forms reflected from a glass,
Or mere chimaeras in the mind,
That fly, and leave no marks behind?
Does not the body thrive and grow
By food of twenty years ago?
And, had it not been still supplied,
It must a thousand times have died.
Then who with reason can maintain
That no effects of food remain?   60
And is not virtue in mankind
The nutriment that feeds the mind;
Upheld by each good action past,
And still continued by the last?
Then who with reason can pretend
That all effects of virtue end?
    Believe me, Stella, when you show
That true contempt for things below,
Nor prize your life for other ends
Than merely to oblige your friends;   70
Your former actions claim their part,
And join to fortify your heart.
For Virtue in her daily race,
Like Janus, bears a double face;
Looks back with joy where she has gone,
And therefore goes with courage on.
She at your sickly couch will wait,
And guide you to a better state.
    Oh then, whatever Heaven intends,
Take pity on your pitying friends!   80
Nor let your ills affect your mind,
To fancy they can be unkind.
Me, surely me, you ought to spare,
Who gladly would your sufferings share;
Or give my scrap of life to you,

And think it far beneath your due;
You, to whose care so oft I owe
That I'm alive to tell you so.

[1727]

THE BEASTS' CONFESSION TO THE PRIEST, ON OBSERVING HOW MOST MEN MISTAKE THEIR OWN TALENTS

When beasts could speak (the learned say
They still can do so every day),
It seems, they had religion then,
As much as now we find in men.
It happened, when a plague broke out
(Which therefore made them more devout),
The king of brutes (to make it plain,
Of quadrupeds I only mean)
By proclamation gave command,
That every subject in the land   10
Should to the priest confess their sins;
And thus the pious wolf begins:
"Good father, I must own with shame,
That often I have been to blame:
I must confess, on Friday last,
Wretch that I was! I broke my fast:
But I defy the basest tongue
To prove I did my neighbour wrong;
Or ever went to seek my food
By rapine, theft, or thirst of blood." 20
    The ass, approaching next, confessed,
That in his heart he loved a jest:
A wag he was, he needs must own,
And could not let a dunce alone:
Sometimes his friend he would not spare,
And might perhaps be too severe:
But yet, the worst that could be said,
He was a *wit* both born and bred;
And, if it be a sin or shame,
Nature alone must bear the blame: 30
One fault he hath, is sorry for't,
His ears are half a foot too short;
Which could he to the standard bring,
He'd show his face before the king;
Then for his voice, there's none disputes
That he's the nightingale of brutes.
    The swine with contrite heart allowed,
His shape and beauty made him proud;
In diet was perhaps too nice,
But gluttony was ne'er his vice;   40

In every turn of life content,
And meekly took what fortune sent:
Inquire through all the parish round,
A better neighbour ne'er was found;
His vigilance might some displease;
'Tis true he hated sloth like pease.

  The mimic ape began his chatter,
How evil tongues his life bespatter:
Much of the censuring world complained,
Who said his gravity was feigned: 50
Indeed, the strictness of his morals
Engaged him in an hundred quarrels:
He saw, and he was grieved to see't,
His zeal was sometimes indiscreet;
He found his virtues too severe
For our corrupted times to bear;
Yet such a lewd licentious age
Might well excuse a Stoic's rage.

  The goat advanced with decent pace,
And first excused his youthful face;   60
Forgiveness begged that he appeared
('Twas Nature's fault) without a beard.
'Tis true, he was not much inclined
To fondness for the female kind;
Not, as his enemies object,
From chance, or natural defect;
Not by his frigid constitution,
But through a pious resolution;
For he had made a holy vow
Of chastity, as monks do now;   70
Which he resolved to keep forever hence,
As strictly too, as doth his reverence.

  Apply the tale, and you shall find,
How just it suits with human kind.
Some faults we own: but, can you guess?
—Why, virtues carried to excess,
Wherewith our vanity endows us,
Though neither foe nor friend allows us.

  The lawyer swears, you may rely on't,
He never squeezed a needy client;   80
And this he makes his constant rule,
For which his brethren call him fool:
His conscience always was so nice,
He freely gave the poor advice;
By which he lost, he may affirm,
A hundred fees last Easter term.
While others of the learned robe
Would break the patience of a Job;
No pleader at the bar could match
His diligence and quick dispatch;   90
Ne'er kept a cause, he well may boast,
Above a term or two at most.

  The cringing knave who seeks a place
Without success, thus tells his case:

Why should he longer mince the matter?
He failed because he could not flatter;
He had not learned to turn his coat,
Nor for a party give his vote:
His crime he quickly understood;
Too zealous for the nation's good: 100
He found the ministers resent it,
Yet could not for his heart repent it.

  The chaplain vows he cannot fawn,
Though it would raise him to the lawn:
He passed his hours among his books;
You find it in his meagre looks:
He might, if he were worldly wise,
Preferment get and spare his eyes:
But owned he had a stubborn spirit,
That made him trust alone to merit;   110
Would rise by merit to promotion;
Alas! a mere chimeric notion.

  The doctor, if you will believe him,
Confessed a sin; and God forgive him!
Called up at midnight, ran to save
A blind old beggar from the grave:
But see how Satan spreads his snares;
He quite forgot to say his prayers.
He cannot help it for his heart
Sometimes to act the parson's part: 120
Quotes from the Bible many a sentence,
That moves his patients to repentance;
And, when his medicines do no good,
Supports their minds with heavenly food,
At which, however well intended,
He hears the clergy are offended;
And grown so bold behind his back,
To call him hypocrite and quack.
In his own church he keeps a seat;
Says grace before and after meat;   130
And calls, without affecting airs,
His household twice a day to prayers.
He shuns apothecaries' shops,
And hates to cram the sick with slops;
He scorns to make his art a trade,
Nor bribes my lady's favourite maid.
Old nurse-keepers would never hire
To recommend him to the squire;
Which others, whom he will not name,
Have often practised to their shame.   140

  The statesman tells you with a sneer,
His fault is to be too sincere;
And, having no sinister ends,
Is apt to disoblige his friends.
The nation's good, his master's glory,
Without regard to Whig or Tory,
Were all the schemes he had in view;
Yet he was seconded by few:

Though some had spread a thousand lies,
'Twas *he* defeated the Excise.   150
'Twas known, though he had borne asper-
   sion,
That standing troops were his aversion:
His practice was, in every station,
To serve the king and please the nation.
Though hard to find in every case
The fittest man to fill a place,
His promises he ne'er forgot,
But took memorials on the spot:
His enemies, for want of charity,
Said he affected popularity: 160
'Tis true, the people understood
That all he did was for their good;
Their kind affections he has tried;
No love is lost on either side.
He came to court with fortune clear,
Which now he runs out every year:
Must, at the rate that he goes on,
Inevitably be undone:
Oh! if his Majesty would please
To give him but a writ of ease,   170
Would grant him license to retire,
As it hath long been his desire,
By fair accounts it would be found,
He's poorer by ten thousand pound.
He owns, and hopes it is no sin,
He ne'er was partial to his kin;
He thought it base for men in stations
To crowd the court with their relations;
His country was his dearest mother,
And every virtuous man his brother;   180
Through modesty or awkward shame
 (For which he owns himself to blame) ,
He found the wisest men he could,
Without respect to friends or blood;

Nor ever acts on private views,
When he hath liberty to choose.
   The sharper swore he hated play,
Except to pass an hour away:
And well he might; for, to his cost,
By want of skill he always lost;   190
He heard there was a club of cheats,
Who had contrived a thousand feats;
Could change the stock, or cog a die,
And thus deceive the sharpest eye:
Nor wonder how his fortune sunk,
His brothers fleece him when he's drunk.
   I own the moral not exact;
Besides, the tale is false in fact;
And so absurd that could I raise up
From fields Elysian fabling Aesop,   200
I would accuse him to his face
For libelling the four-foot race.
Creatures of every kind but ours
Well comprehend their natural powers;
While we, whom reason ought to sway,
Mistake our talents every day.
The ass was never known so stupid
To act the part of Tray or Cupid;
Nor leaps upon his master's lap,
There to be stroked, and fed with pap,   210
As Aesop would the world persuade;
He better understands his trade:
Nor comes, whene'er his lady whistles,
But carries loads, and feeds on thistles.
Our author's meaning, I presume, is
A creature *bipes et implumis*;
Wherein the moralist designed
A compliment on humankind:
For here he owns that now and then
Beasts may *degenerate* into men.   220

[*1732-33*, 1738]

VERSES ON THE DEATH OF DR. SWIFT, OCCASIONED BY READING A MAXIM IN ROCHEFOUCAULD

Dans l'adversité de nos meilleurs amis nous trouvons toujours quelque chose, qui ne nous deplaît pas.[1]

As Rochefoucauld his maxims drew
From nature, I believe them true:
They argue no corrupted mind
In him; the fault is in mankind.
   This maxim more than all the rest
Is thought too base for human breast:
"In all distresses of our friends

We first consult our private ends;
While Nature, kindly bent to ease us,
Points out some circumstance to please us."
   If this perhaps your patience move,   11
Let reason and experience prove.

[1] In the adversity of our best friends we always find something that does not displease us.

We all behold with envious eyes
Our equal raised above our size.
Who would not at a crowded show
Stand high himself, keep others low?
I love my friend as well as you,
But why should he obstruct my view?
Then let me have the higher post;
Suppose it but an inch at most.   20
    If in a battle you should find
One, whom you love of all mankind,
Had some heroic action done,
A champion killed, or trophy won;
Rather than thus be overtopped,
Would you not wish his laurels cropped?
    Dear honest Ned is in the gout,
Lies racked with pain, and you without:
How patiently you hear him groan!
How glad, the case is not your own!   30
    What poet would not grieve to see
His brethren write as well as he?
But rather than they should excel,
He'd wish his rivals all in hell.
    Her end when Emulation misses,
She turns to envy, stings, and hisses:
The strongest friendship yields to pride,
Unless the odds be on our side.
    Vain humankind! fantastic race!
Thy various follies who can trace?   40
Self-love, ambition, envy, pride,
Their empire in our hearts divide.
Give others riches, power, and station;
'Tis all on me an usurpation;
I have no title to aspire,
Yet, when you sink, I seem the higher.
In Pope I cannot read a line,
But with a sigh I wish it mine:
When he can in one couplet fix
More sense than I can do in six,   50
It gives me such a jealous fit,
I cry, "Pox take him and his wit!"
    I grieve to be outdone by Gay
In my own humourous biting way.
Arbuthnot is no more my friend,
Who dares to irony pretend,
Which I was born to introduce,
Refined it first, and showed its use.
St. John, as well as Pulteney, knows
That I had some repute for prose;   60
And, till they drove me out of date,
Could maul a minister of state.
If they have mortified my pride,
And made me throw my pen aside;
If with such talents Heaven hath blessed 'em,
Have I not reason to detest 'em?

To all my foes, dear Fortune, send
Thy gifts, but never to my friend:
I tamely can endure the first,
But this with envy makes me burst.   70
    Thus much may serve by way of proem;
Proceed we therefore to our poem.
    The time is not remote, when I
Must by the course of nature die;
When, I foresee, my special friends
Will try to find their private ends:
Though it is hardly understood
Which way my death can do them good,
Yet thus, methinks, I hear 'em speak:
"See how the Dean begins to break!   80
Poor gentleman! he droops apace!
You plainly find it in his face.
That old vertigo in his head
Will never leave him till he's dead.
Besides, his memory decays;
He recollects not what he says;
He cannot call his friends to mind;
Forgets the place where last he dined;
Plies you with stories o'er and o'er;
He told them fifty times before.   90
How does he fancy we can sit
To hear his out-of-fashion wit?
But he takes up with younger folks,
Who for his wine will bear his jokes.
Faith, he must make his stories shorter,
Or change his comrades once a quarter;
In half the time he talks them round,
There must another set be found.
    "For poetry, he's past his prime;
He takes an hour to find a rhyme;   100
His fire is out, his wit decayed,
His fancy sunk, his Muse a jade.
I'd have him throw away his pen;—
But there's no talking to some men."
    And then their tenderness appears
By adding largely to my years:
"He's older than he would be reckoned,
And well remembers Charles the Second.
He hardly drinks a pint of wine;
And that, I doubt, is no good sign.   110
His stomach, too, begins to fail;
Last year we thought him strong and hale;
But now he's quite another thing;
I wish he may hold out till spring."
They hug themselves, and reason thus:
"It is not yet so bad with us."
    In such a case they talk in tropes,
And by their fears express their hopes.
Some great misfortune to portend
No enemy can match a friend.   120

With all the kindness they profess,
The merit of a lucky guess
(When daily how-d'ye's come of course,
And servants answer, "Worse and worse!")
Would please 'em better, than to tell
That God be praised! the Dean is well.
Then he who prophesied the best,
Approves his foresight to the rest:
"You know I always feared the worst,
And often told you so at first." 130
He'd rather choose that I should die,
Than his prediction prove a lie.
Not one foretells I shall recover,
But all agree to give me over.

Yet, should some neighbour feel a pain
Just in the parts where I complain,
How many a message would he send!
What hearty prayers that I should mend!
Inquire what regimen I kept;
What gave me ease, and how I slept, 140
And more lament, when I was dead,
Then all the snivellers round my bed.

My good companions, never fear;
For though you may mistake a year,
Though your prognostics run too fast,
They must be verified at last.

Behold the fatal day arrive!
"How is the Dean?"—"He's just alive."
Now the departing prayer is read.
"He hardly breathes"—"The Dean is dead."

Before the passing-bell begun, 151
The news through half the town has run.
"Oh! may we all for death prepare!
What has he left? and who's his heir?"
"I know no more than what the news is;
'Tis all bequeathed to public uses."
"To public use! a perfect whim!
What had the public done for him?
Mere envy, avarice, and pride:
He gave it all—but first he died. 160
And had the Dean in all the nation
No worthy friend, no poor relation?
So ready to do strangers good,
Forgetting his own flesh and blood?"

Now Grub Street wits are all employed;
With elegies the town is cloyed;
Some paragraph in every paper
To curse the Dean, or bless the Drapier.

The doctors, tender of their fame,
Wisely on me lay all the blame. 170
"We must confess his case was nice;
But he would never take advice.
Had he been ruled, for aught appears,
He might have lived these twenty years:

For, when we opened him, we found,
That all his vital parts were sound."

From Dublin soon to London spread,
'Tis told at court, "The Dean is dead."
Kind Lady Suffolk, in the spleen,
Runs laughing up to tell the Queen. 180
The Queen, so gracious, mild, and good,
Cries, "Is he gone? 'tis time he should.
He's dead, you say; why, let him rot:
I'm glad the medals were forgot.
I promised him, I own; but when?
I only was a princess then;
But now, as consort of a king,
You know, 'tis quite a different thing."

Now Chartres, at Sir Robert's levee,
Tells with a sneer the tidings heavy: 190
"Why, is he dead without his shoes?"
Cries Bob, "I'm sorry for the news:
Oh, were the wretch but living still,
And in his place my good friend Will!
Or had a mitre on his head,
Provided Bolingbroke were dead!"

Now Curll his shop from rubbish drains:
Three genuine tomes of Swift's remains!
And then, to make them pass the glibber,
Revised by Tibbalds, Moore, and Cibber. 200
He'll treat me as he does my betters,
Publish my will, my life, my letters;
Revive the libels born to die,
Which Pope must bear, as well as I.

Here shift the scene, to represent
How those I love my death lament.
Poor Pope will grieve a month, and Gay
A week, and Arbuthnot a day.
St. John himself will scarce forbear
To bite his pen, and drop a tear. 210
The rest will give a shrug, and cry,
"I'm sorry—but we all must die!"
Indifference clad in wisdom's guise
All fortitude of mind supplies:
For how can stony bowels melt
In those who never pity felt?
When we are lashed, they kiss the rod,
Resigning to the will of God.

The fools, my juniors by a year,
Are tortured with suspense and fear; 220
Who wisely thought my age a screen,
When death approached, to stand between:
The screen removed, their hearts are trem-
bling;
They mourn for me without dissembling.

My female friends, whose tender hearts
Have better learned to act their parts,
Receive the news in doleful dumps:

"The Dean is dead (and what is trumps?)
Then, Lord have mercy on his soul!
(Ladies, I'll venture for the vole.)   230
Six deans, they say, must bear the pall.
(I wish I knew what king to call.)
Madam, your husband will attend
The funeral of so good a friend?"
"No, madam, 'tis a shocking sight;
And he's engaged to-morrow night:
My Lady Club would take it ill,
If he should fail her at quadrille.
He loved the Dean— (I lead a heart)
But dearest friends, they say, must part.   240
His time was come; he ran his race;
We hope he's in a better place."
   Why do we grieve that friends should die?
No loss more easy to supply.
One year is past; a different scene!
No further mention of the Dean,
Who now, alas! no more is missed,
Than if he never did exist.
Where's now this favourite of Apollo?
Departed:—and his works must follow,   250
Must undergo the common fate;
His kind of wit is out of date.
   Some country squire to Lintot goes,
Inquires for Swift in verse and prose.
Says Lintot, "I have heard the name;
He died a year ago."—"The same."
He searches all the shop in vain.
"Sir, you may find them in Duck Lane:
I sent them, with a load of books,
Last Monday to the pastry-cook's.   260
To fancy they could live a year!
I find you're but a stranger here.
The Dean was famous in his time,
And had a kind of knack at rhyme.
His way of writing now is past:
The town has got a better taste.
I keep no antiquated stuff;
But spick and span I have enough.
Pray do but give me leave to show 'em:
Here's Colley Cibber's birthday poem.   270
This ode you never yet have seen
By Stephen Duck upon the Queen.
Then here's a letter finely penned
Against the *Craftsman* and his friend;
It clearly shows that all reflection
On ministers is disaffection.
Next, here's Sir Robert's vindication,
And Mr. Henley's last oration.
The hawkers have not got them yet:
Your honour please to buy a set?   280

"Here's Woolston's tracts, the twelfth edi-
      tion;
'Tis read by every politician:
The country members, when in town,
To all their boroughs send them down;
You never met a thing so smart;
The courtiers have them all by heart;
Those maids of honour (who can read)
Are taught to use them for their creed.
The reverend author's good intention
Has been rewarded with a pension.   290
He does an honour to his gown,
By bravely running priestcraft down;
He shows, as sure as God's in Gloucester,
That Jesus was a grand impostor;
That all his miracles were cheats,
Performed as jugglers do their feats:
The Church had never such a writer;
A shame he has not got a mitre!"
   Suppose me dead; and then suppose
A club assembled at the Rose;   300
Where, from discourse of this and that,
I grow the subject of their chat.
And while they toss my name about,
With favour some, and some without,
One, quite indifferent in the cause,
My character impartial draws:
   "The Dean, if we believe report,
Was never ill received at court.
As for his works in verse and prose,
I own myself no judge of those;   310
Nor can I tell what critics thought 'em:
But this I know, all people bought 'em,
As with a moral view designed
To cure the vices of mankind;
And, if he often missed his aim,
The world must own it, to their shame;
The praise is his, and theirs the blame."
   "Sir, I have heard another story:
He was a most confounded Tory,
And grew, or he is much belied,   320
Extremely dull, before he died."
   "Can we the Drapier then forget?
Is not our nation in his debt?
'Twas he that writ the Drapier's letters!"—
   "He should have left them for his betters,
We had a hundred abler men,
Nor need depend upon his pen.
Say what you will about his reading,
You never can defend his breeding;
Who in his satires running riot,   330
Could never leave the world in quiet;
Attacking, when he took the whim,
Court, city, camp—all one to him.

"But why should he, except he slobbered,
Offend our patriot, great Sir Robert,
Whose counsels aid the sovereign power
To save the nation every hour?
What scenes of evil he unravels
In satires, libels, lying travels!
Not sparing his own clergy-cloth,   340
But eats into it, like a moth!"
  "His vein, ironically grave,
Exposed the fool and lashed the knave,
To steal a hint was never known,
But what he writ was all his own.
  "He never thought an honour done him,
Because a duke was proud to own him,
Would rather slip aside and choose
To talk with wits in dirty shoes;
Despised the fools with stars and garters,   350
So often seen caressing Chartres.
He never courted men in station,
Nor persons held in admiration;
Of no man's greatness was afraid,
Because he sought for no man's aid.
Though trusted long in great affairs,
He gave himself no haughty airs;
Without regarding private ends,
Spent all his credit for his friends;
And only chose the wise and good;   360
No flatterers, no allies in blood;
But succoured virtue in distress,
And seldom failed of good success;
As numbers in their hearts must own,
Who, but for him, had been unknown.
  "With princes kept a due decorum,
But never stood in awe before 'em.
He followed David's lesson just;
In princes never put thy trust:
And would you make him truly sour,   370
Provoke him with a slave in power.
The Irish senate if you named,
With what impatience he declaimed!
Fair Liberty was all his cry,
For her he stood prepared to die;
For her he boldly stood alone;
For her he oft exposed his own.
Two kingdoms, just as faction led,
Had set a price upon his head,
But not a traitor could be found,   380
To sell him for six hundred pound.
  "Had he but spared his tongue and pen,
He might have rose like other men;
But power was never in his thought,
And wealth he valued not a groat:
Ingratitude he often found,
And pitied those who meant the wound;

But kept the tenour of his mind,
To merit well of human kind:
Nor made a sacrifice of those   390
Who still were true, to please his foes.
He laboured many a fruitless hour,
To reconcile his friends in power;
Saw mischief by a faction brewing,
While they pursued each other's ruin.
But finding vain was all his care,
He left the court in mere despair.
  "And, oh! how short are human schemes!
Here ended all our golden dreams.
What St. John's skill in state affairs,   400
What Ormond's valour, Oxford's cares,
To save their sinking country lent,
Was all destroyed by one event.
Too soon that precious life was ended,
On which alone our weal depended.
When up a dangerous faction starts,
With wrath and vengeance in their hearts;
By solemn League and Covenant bound,
To ruin, slaughter, and confound;
To turn religion to a fable,   410
And make the government a Babel;
Pervert the laws, disgrace the gown,
Corrupt the senate, rob the crown;
To sacrifice old England's glory,
And make her infamous in story:
When such a tempest shook the land,
How could unguarded Virtue stand?
With horror, grief, despair, the Dean
Beheld the dire destructive scene:
His friends in exile, or the Tower,   420
Himself within the frown of power,
Pursued by base envenomed pens,
Far to the land of slaves and fens;
A servile race in folly nursed,
Who truckle most, when treated worst.
  "By innocence and resolution,
He bore continual persecution;
While numbers to preferment rose,
Whose merits were, to be his foes;
When even his own familiar friends,   430
Intent upon their private ends,
Like renegadoes now he feels,
Against him lifting up their heels.
  "The Dean did, by his pen, defeat
An infamous destructive cheat;
Taught fools their interest how to know,
And gave them arms to ward the blow.
Envy has owned it was his doing,
To save that hapless land from ruin;
While they who at the steerage stood,   440
And reaped the profit, sought his blood.

"To save them from their evil fate,
In him was held a crime of state.
A wicked monster on the bench,
Whose fury blood could never quench;
As vile and profligate a villain,
As modern Scroggs, or old Tresilian;
Who long all justice had discarded,
Nor feared he God, nor man regarded;
Vowed on the Dean his rage to vent,   450
And make him of his zeal repent:
But Heaven his innocence defends,
The grateful people stand his friends;
Not strains of law, nor judge's frown,
Nor topics brought to please the crown,
Nor witness hired, nor jury picked,
Prevail to bring him in convict.
   "In exile, with a steady heart,
He spent his life's declining part;
Where folly, pride, and faction sway   460
Remote from St. John, Pope, and Gay."
   "Alas, poor Dean! his only scope
Was to be held a misanthrope,
This into general odium drew him,
Which if he liked, much good may't do him.
His zeal was not to lash our crimes,
But discontent against the times:
For had we made him timely offers
To raise his post, or fill his coffers,
Perhaps he might have truckled down,   470
Like other brethren of his gown.
For party he would scarce have bled:
I say no more—because he's dead.
What writings has he left behind?
I hear they're of a different kind;
A few in verse; but most in prose—
Some high-flown pamphlets, I suppose;
All scribbled in the worst of times,
To palliate his friend Oxford's crimes,
To praise Queen Anne, nay more defend
    her,   480
As never favouring the Pretender;
Or libels yet concealed from sight,
Against the court to show his spite;
Perhaps his travels, part the third;
A lie at every second word—
Offensive to a loyal ear:
But not one sermon, you may swear."
   "His friendships there, to few confined,
Were always of the middling kind;
No fools of rank, a mongrel breed,   490
Who fain would pass for lords indeed:
Where titles give no right or power,
And peerage is a withered flower;

He would have held it a disgrace,
If such a wretch had known his face.
On rural squires, that kingdom's bane,
He vented oft his wrath in vain;
[Biennial] squires to market brought;
Who sell their souls, and [votes] for naught;
The [nation stripped], go joyful back,   500
To [rob] the church, their tenants rack,
Go snacks with [rogues and rapparees],
And keep the peace to pick up fees;
In every job to have a share,
A jail or barrack to repair;
And turn the tax for public roads,
Commodious to their own abodes.
   "Perhaps I may allow the Dean
Had too much satire in his vein;
And seemed determined not to starve it,   510
Because no age could more deserve it.
Yet malice never was his aim;
He lashed the vice, but spared the name;
No individual could resent,
Where thousands equally were meant;
His satire points at no defect,
But what all mortals may correct;
For he abhorred that senseless tribe
Who call it humour when they gibe:
He spared a hump, or crooked nose,   520
Whose owners set not up for beaux.
True genuine dullness moved his pity,
Unless it offered to be witty.
Those who their ignorance confessed,
He ne'er offended with a jest;
But laughed to hear an idiot quote
A verse from Horace learned by rote.
   "Vice, if it e'er can be abashed,
Must be or ridiculed or lashed.
If you resent it, who's to blame?   530
He neither knew you nor your name.
Should vice expect to 'scape rebuke,
Because its owner is a duke?
   "He knew an hundred pleasant stories,
With all the turns of Whigs and Tories;
Was cheerful to his dying day;
And friends would let him have his way.
   "He gave the little wealth he had
To build a house for fools and mad;
And showed by one satiric touch,   540
No nation wanted it so much.
That kingdom he hath left his debtor,
I wish it soon may have a better.
And since you dread no farther lashes,
Methinks you may forgive his ashes."

                                     [*1731*, *1739*]

THE DAY OF JUDGMENT

Once, with a whirl of thought oppressed,
I sunk from reverie to rest.
An horrid vision seized my head;
I saw the graves give up their dead!
Jove, armed with terrors, burst the skies,
The thunder roars, the lightning flies!
Confused, amazed, its fate unknown,
The world stands trembling at his throne!
While each pale sinner hangs his head,
Jove, nodding shook the heavens and said: 10

"Offending race of human kind,
By nature, custom, learning, blind;
You who through frailty slipped aside,
And you who never fell—through pride;
And you by differing churches shammed,
Who come to see each other damned
(So some folks told you, but they knew
No more of Jove's designs than you) —
The world's mad business now is o'er,
And I resent those pranks no more.   20
I to such blockheads set my wit!
I damn such fools!—Go, go, you're *bit*."
                                      [*1731?* 1773]

A TALE OF A TUB

SECTION IX

A DIGRESSION CONCERNING THE ORIGINAL, THE
USE, AND IMPROVEMENT OF MADNESS, IN A
COMMONWEALTH

Nor shall it any ways detract from
the just reputation of this famous
sect, that its rise and institution are 10
owing to such an author as I have
described Jack to be—a person whose
intellectuals were overturned, and his
brain shaken out of its natural position; which we commonly suppose to
be a distemper, and call by the name
of *madness* or *frenzy*. For, if we take
a survey of the greatest actions that
have been performed in the world,
under the influence of single men, 20
which are, the establishment of new
empires by conquest, the advance and
progress of new schemes in philosophy, and the contriving, as well as the
propagating, of new religions, we
shall find the authors of them all to
have been persons whose natural reason hath admitted great revolutions,
from their diet, their education, the
prevalency of some certain temper, together with the particular influence 30
of air and climate. Besides, there is
something individual in human
minds that easily kindles at the accidental approach and collision of certain circumstances, which, though of
paltry and mean appearance, do often
flame out into the greatest emergencies of life. For great turns are not
always given by strong hands, but by
lucky adaption and at proper seasons;
and it is of no import where the fire
was kindled, if the vapour has once
got up into the brain. For the *upper
region* of man is furnished like the
middle region of the air; the materials
are formed from causes of the widest
difference, yet produce at last the
same substance and effect. Mists arise
from the earth, steams from dunghills,
exhalations from the sea, and smoke
from fire; yet all clouds are the same
in composition as well as consequences, and the fumes issuing from
a jakes will furnish as comely and useful a vapour as incense from an altar.
Thus far, I suppose, will easily be
granted me; and then it will follow
that, as the face of nature never produces rain but when it is overcast and
disturbed, so human understanding,
seated in the brain, must be troubled
and overspread by vapours, ascending
from the lower faculties to water the
invention and render it fruitful. Now,
although these vapours (as it hath
been already said) are of as various
original as those of the skies, yet the
crops they produce differ both in kind
and degree, merely according to the
soil. I will produce two instances to
prove and explain what I am now advancing.
A certain great prince raised a
mighty army, filled his coffers with infinite treasures, provided an invincible fleet, and all this. without giving
the least part of his design to his

greatest ministers, or his nearest favourites. Immediately the whole world
was alarmed; the neighbouring
crowns in trembling expectation, towards what point the storm would
burst; the small politicians everywhere forming profound conjectures.
Some believed he had laid a scheme
for universal monarchy; others, after
much insight, determined the matter
to be a project for pulling down the
pope, and setting up the reformed religion, which had once been his own.
Some, again, of a deeper sagacity, sent
him into Asia to subdue the Turk,
and recover Palestine. In the midst
of all these projects and preparations,
a certain state-surgeon, gathering the
nature of the disease by these symptoms, attempted the cure, at one blow
performed the operation, broke the
bag, and out flew the vapour; nor did
anything want to render it a complete
remedy, only that the prince unfortunately happened to die in the performance. Now, is the reader exceeding curious to learn from whence this
vapour took its rise, which had so long
set the nations at a gaze? What secret
wheel, what hidden spring, could put
into motion so wonderful an engine?
It was afterwards discovered, that the
movement of this whole machine had
been directed by an absent female,
whose eyes had raised a protuberancy,
and, before emission, she was removed
into an enemy's country. What should
an unhappy prince do in such ticklish
circumstances as these? He tried in
vain the poet's never-failing receipt
of *corpora quaeque*; for

Idque petit corpus mens unde est saucia
   amore:
Unde feritur, eo tendit, gestitque coire.
                              —Lucr.

Having to no purpose used all
peaceable endeavours, the collected
part of the semen, raised and inflamed, became adust, converted to
choler, turned head upon the spinal
duct, and ascended to the brain. The
very same principle that influences a
bully to break the windows of a whore
who has jilted him, naturally stirs up
a great prince to raise mighty armies,
and dream of nothing but sieges, battles, and victories.

             ——Teterrima belli
             Causa——

   The other instance is what I have
read somewhere in a very ancient author, of a mighty king, who, for the
space of above thirty years, amused
himself to take and lose towns; beat
armies, and be beaten; drive princes
out of their dominions; fright children from their bread and butter;
burn, lay waste, plunder, dragoon,
massacre subject and stranger, friend
and foe, male and female. 'Tis recorded, that the philosophers of each
country were in grave dispute upon
causes natural, moral, and political,
to find out where they should assign
an original solution of this phenomenon. At last, the vapour or spirit,
which animated the hero's brain, being in perpetual circulation, seized
upon that region of the human body,
so renowned for furnishing the *zibeta
occidentalis*, and, gathering there
into a tumour, left the rest of the
world for that time in peace. Of such
mighty consequence it is where those
exhalations fix, and of so little from
whence they proceed. The same spirits, which in their superior progress
would conquer a kingdom, descending upon the anus, conclude in a
fistula.

   Let us next examine the great in-
troducers of new schemes in philosophy, and search till we can find from
what faculty of the soul the disposition arises in mortal man, of taking
it into his head to advance new systems, with such an eager zeal, in
things agreed on all hands impossible
to be known; from what seeds this
disposition springs, and to what quality of human nature these grand innovators have been indebted for their
number of disciples. Because it is
plain, that several of the chief among
them, both ancient and modern, were
usually mistaken by their adversaries,
and indeed by all, except their own
followers, to have been persons crazed,
or out of their wits; having generally

proceeded, in the common course of their words and actions, by a method very different from the vulgar dictates of unrefined reason; agreeing for the most part in their several models, with their present undoubted successors in the *Academy of Modern Bedlam*, (whose merits and principles I shall farther examine in due place). Of this kind were *Epicurus, Diogenes, Apollonius, Lucretius, Paracelsus, Descartes,* and others, who, if they were now in the world, tied fast, and separate from their followers, would, in this our undistinguishing age, incur manifest danger of phlebotomy, and whips, and chains, and the dark chambers, and straw. For what man, in the natural state or course of thinking, did ever conceive it in his power to reduce the notions of all mankind exactly to the same length, and breadth, and height of his own? Yet this is the first humble and civil design of all innovators in the empire of reason. Epicurus modestly hoped that, one time or other, a certain fortuitous concourse of all men's opinions, after perpetual justlings, the sharp with the smooth, the light and the heavy, the round and the square, would, by certain *clinamina*, unite in the notions of atoms and void, as these did in the originals of all things. Cartesius reckoned to see, before he died, the sentiments of all philosophers, like so many lesser stars in his romantic system, rapt and drawn within his own vortex. Now, I would gladly be informed, how it is possible to account for such imaginations as these in particular men, without recourse to my phenomenon of vapours, ascending from the lower faculties to overshadow the brain, and there distilling into conceptions, for which the narrowness of our mother-tongue has not yet assigned any other name besides that of madness or frenzy. Let us therefore now conjecture how it comes to pass that none of these great prescribers do ever fail providing themselves and their notions with a number of implicit disciples. And, I think, the reason is easy to be as-

signed: for there is a peculiar *string* in the harmony of human understanding, which in several individuals is exactly of the same tuning. This, if you can dexterously screw up to its right key, and then strike gently upon it, whenever you have the good fortune to light among those of the same pitch, they will, by a secret necessary sympathy, strike exactly at the same time. And in this one circumstance lies all the skill or luck of the matter; for, if you chance to jar the string among those who are either above or below your own height, instead of subscribing to your doctrine, they will tie you fast, call you mad, and feed you with bread and water. It is therefore a point of the nicest conduct, to distinguish and adapt this noble talent, with respect to the differences of persons and of times. Cicero understood this very well, when writing to a friend in England, with a caution, among other matters, to beware of being cheated by our hackney-coachman (who, it seems, in those days were as arrant rascals as they are now) has these remarkable words: *Est quod gaudeas te in ista loca venisse, ubi aliquid sapere viderere.* For, to speak a bold truth, it is a fatal miscarriage so ill to order affairs, as to pass for a fool in one company when in another you might be treated as a philosopher. Which I desire some certain gentlemen of my acquaintance to lay up in their hearts, as a very seasonable *innuendo*.

This, indeed, was the fatal mistake of that worthy gentleman, my most ingenious friend, Mr. Wotton: a person in appearance ordained for great designs as well as performances, whether you will consider his notions or his looks. Surely no man ever advanced into the public with fitter qualifications of body and mind, for the propagation of a new religion. Oh, had those happy talents, misapplied to vain philosophy, been turned into their proper channels of dreams and visions, where distortion of mind and countenance are of such sovereign use, the base detracting world would not then have dared to report that something is amiss, that his brain has undergone an unlucky shake; which even his brother modernists themselves, like ungrates, do whisper so loud that it reaches up to the very garret I am now writing in.

Lastly, whosoever pleases to look into the fountains of enthusiasm, from whence, in all ages, have eternally proceeded such fattening streams, will find the spring-head to have been as troubled and muddy as the current; of such great emolument is a tincture of this vapour, which the world calls madness, that without its help the world would not only be deprived of those two great blessings, conquests and systems, but even all mankind would unhappily be reduced to the same belief in things invisible. Now, the former *postulatum* being held, that it is of no import from what originals this vapour proceeds, but either in what angles it strikes and spreads over the understanding, or upon what species of brain it ascends; it will be a very delicate point to cut the feather, and divide the several reasons to a nice and curious reader, how this numerical difference in the brain can produce effects of so vast a difference from the same vapour, as to be the sole point of individuation between Alexander the Great, Jack of Leyden, and Monsieur Descartes. The present argument is the most abstracted that ever I engaged in; it strains my faculties to their highest stretch; and I desire the reader to attend with the utmost perpensity, for I now proceed to unravel this knotty point.

There is in mankind a certain*
      * * * *
  * * * * * * * *
Hic multa * * * * * *
desiderantur. * * * * * *
   * * * And this I take to be a clear solution of the matter.

* Here is another defect in the manuscript, but I think the author did wisely, and that the matter which thus strained his faculties, was not worth a solution; and it were well if all metaphysical cobweb problems were not otherwise answered. [Swift, 1710.]

Having therefore so narrowly passed through this intricate difficulty, the reader will, I am sure, agree with me in the conclusion, that if the moderns mean by madness only a disturbance or transposition of the brain by force of certain vapours issuing up from the lower faculties, then has this madness been the parent of all those mighty revolutions that have happened in empire, in philosophy, and in religion. For the brain, in its natural position and state of serenity, disposeth its owner to pass his life in the common forms, without any thought of subduing multitudes to his own power, his reasons, or his visions; and the more he shapes his understanding by the pattern of human learning, the less he is inclined to form parties after his particular notions, because that instructs him in his private infirmities as well as in the stubborn ignorance of the people. But when a man's fancy gets *astride* on his reason; when imagination is at cuffs with the senses, and common understanding as well as common sense is kicked out of doors; the first proselyte he makes is himself; and when that is once compassed, the difficulty is not so great in bringing over others; a strong delusion always operating from without as vigorously as from within. For cant and vision are to the ear and the eye, the same that tickling is to the touch. Those entertainments and pleasures we most value in life, are such as dupe and play the wag with the senses. For, if we take an examination of what is generally understood by happiness, as it has respect either to the understanding or the senses, we shall find all its properties and adjuncts will herd under this short definition, that it is a perpetual possession of being well deceived. And, first, with relation to the mind or understanding, 'tis manifest what mighty advantages fiction has over truth; and the reason is just at our elbow, because imagination can build nobler scenes, and produce more wonderful revolutions than fortune or nature will be at expense to furnish. Nor is mankind so much to blame in his choice thus determining him, if we consider that the debate merely lies between things past and things conceived; and so the question is only this: whether things that have place in the imagination, may not as properly be said to exist, as those that are seated in the memory, which may be justly held in the affirmative, and very much to the advantage of the former, since this is acknowledged to be the womb of things, and the other allowed to be no more than the grave. Again, if we take this definition of happiness, and examine it with reference to the senses, it will be acknowledged wonderfully adapt. How fading and insipid do all objects accost us that are not conveyed in the vehicle of delusion! How shrunk is everything, as it appears in the glass of nature! So that if it were not for the assistance of artificial mediums, false lights, refracted angles, varnish and tinsel, there would be a mighty level in the felicity and enjoyments of mortal men. If this were seriously considered by the world, as I have a certain reason to suspect it hardly will, men would no longer reckon among their high points of wisdom, the art of exposing weak sides, and publishing infirmities; an employment, in my opinion, neither better nor worse than that of unmasking, which, I think, has never been allowed fair usage, either in the world or the playhouse.

In the proportion that credulity is a more peaceful possession of the mind than curiosity; so far preferable is that wisdom, which converses about the surface, to that pretended philosophy, which enters into the depth of things and then comes gravely back with informations and discoveries, that in the inside they are good for nothing. The two senses to which all objects first address themselves, are the sight and the touch; these never examine farther than the colour, the shape, the size, and whatever other qualities dwell, or are drawn by art upon the outward of bodies; and then comes reason officiously with tools for cutting, and opening, and mangling, and piercing, offering to demonstrate, that they are not of the same consistence quite through. Now I take all this to be the last degree of perverting nature; one of whose eternal laws it is, to put her best furniture forward. And therefore, in order to save the charges of all such expensive anatomy for the time to come, I do here think fit to inform the reader that in such conclusions as these, reason is certainly in the right, and that in most corporeal beings, which have fallen under my cognizance, the outside has been infinitely preferable to the in; whereof I have been farther convinced from some late experiments. Last week I saw a woman flayed, and you will hardly believe how much it altered her person for the worse. Yesterday I ordered the carcass of a beau to be stripped in my presence, when we were all amazed to find so many unsuspected faults under one suit of clothes. Then I laid open his brain, his heart, and his spleen; but I plainly perceived at every operation, that the farther we proceeded, we found the defects increase upon us in number and bulk; from all which, I justly formed this conclusion to myself; that whatever philosopher or projector can find out an art to solder and patch up the flaws and imperfections of nature, will deserve much better of mankind, and teach us a more useful science, than that so much in present esteem, of widening and exposing them, (like him who held anatomy to be the ultimate end of physic). And he, whose fortunes and dispositions have placed him in a convenient station to enjoy the fruits of this noble art; he that can, with Epicurus, content his ideas with the films and images that fly off upon his senses from the superficies of things; such a man, truly wise, creams off nature, leaving the sour and the dregs for philosophy and reason to lap up. This is the sublime and refined point of felicity, called the possession of being well deceived; the serene peaceful state of being a fool among knaves.

But to return to madness. It is certain, that, according to the system I have above deduced, every species thereof proceeds from a redundancy of vapours; therefore, as some kinds of frenzy give double strength to the sinews, so there are of other species, which add vigour, and life, and spirit to the brain. Now, it usually happens, that these active spirits, getting possession of the brain, resemble those that haunt other waste and empty dwellings, which, for want of business, either vanish, and carry away a piece of the house, or else stay at home, and fling it all out of the windows. By which, are mystically displayed the two principal branches of madness, and which some philosophers, not considering so well as I, have mistook to be different in their causes, over hastily assigning the first to deficiency and the other to redundance.

I think it therefore manifest, from what I have here advanced, that the main point of skill and address is to furnish employment for this redundancy of vapour and prudently to adjust the season of it; by which means, it may certainly become of cardinal and catholic emolument in a commonwealth. Thus one man, choosing a proper juncture, leaps into a gulf, from whence proceeds a hero, and is called the saver of his country; another achieves the same enterprise, but, unluckily timing it, has left the brand of madness fixed as a reproach upon his memory; upon so nice a distinction, are we taught to repeat the name of Curtius with reverence and love, that of Empedocles with hatred and contempt. Thus also it is usually conceived, that the elder Brutus only personated the fool and madman for the good of the public; but this was nothing else than a redundancy of the same vapour long misapplied, called by the Latins, *ingenium par negotiis*, or, (to translate it as nearly as I can) a sort of frenzy, never in its right ele-

ment, till you take it up in the business of the state.

Upon all which, and many other reasons of equal weight, though not equally curious, I do here gladly embrace an opportunity I have long sought for, of recommending it as a very noble undertaking to Sir Edward Seymour, Sir Christopher Musgrave, Sir John Bowls, John How, Esq., and other patriots concerned, that they would move for leave to bring in a bill for appointing commissioners to inspect into Bedlam, and the parts adjacent; who shall be empowered to send for persons, papers, and records, to examine into the merits and qualifications of every student and professor, to observe with utmost exactness their several dispositions and behaviour, by which means, duly distinguishing and adapting their talents, they might produce admirable instruments for the several offices in a state, * * * * * civil, and military, proceeding in such methods as I shall here humbly propose. And I hope the gentle reader will give some allowance to my great solicitudes in this important affair, upon account of the high esteem I have borne that honourable society, whereof I had some time the happiness to be an unworthy member.

Is any student tearing his straw in piece-meal, swearing and blaspheming, biting his grate, foaming at the mouth, and emptying his pisspot in the spectators' faces? Let the right worshipful the commissioners of inspection give him a regiment of dragoons, and send him into Flanders among the rest. Is another eternally talking, sputtering, gaping, bawling in a sound without period or article? What wonderful talents are here mislaid! Let him be furnished immediately with a green bag and papers, and threepence in his pocket, and away with him to Westminster Hall. You will find a third gravely taking the dimensions of his kennel, a person of foresight and insight, though kept quite in the dark; for why, like Moses, *ecce cornuta erat ejus facies*. He walks duly in one pace, entreats your penny with due gravity and ceremony, talks much of hard times, and taxes, and the whore of Babylon, bars up the wooden window of his cell constantly at eight o'clock, dreams of fire, and shoplifters, and court-customers, and privileged places. Now, what a figure would all these acquirements amount to, if the owner were sent into the city among his brethren! Behold a fourth, in much and deep conversation with himself, biting his thumbs at proper junctures, his countenance checkered with business and design, sometimes walking very fast, with his eyes nailed to a paper that he holds in his hands; a great saver of time, somewhat thick of hearing, very short of sight, but more of memory; a man ever in haste, a great hatcher and breeder of business, and excellent at the famous art of whispering nothing; a huge idolator of monosyllables and procrastination, so ready to give his word to everybody, that he never *keeps* it; one that has forgot the common meaning of words, but an admirable retainer of the sound; extremely subject to the looseness, for his occasions are perpetually calling him away. If you approach his grate in his familiar intervals; "Sir," says he, "give me a penny, and I'll sing you a song; but give me the penny first," (hence comes the common saying, and commoner practice, of parting with money for a song). What a complete system of court skill is here described in every branch of it, and all utterly lost with wrong application! Accost the hole of another kennel, first stopping your nose, you will behold a surly, gloomy, nasty, slovenly mortal. . . . The student of this apartment is very sparing of his words, but somewhat over-liberal of his breath. He holds his hand out ready to receive your penny, and immediately upon receipt withdraws to his former occupations. Now, is it not amazing to think, the society of Warwick Lane should have no more concern for the recovery of so useful a member; who, if one may judge from these appearances, would become the greatest ornament to that illustrious body? Another student struts up fiercely to your teeth, puffing with his lips, half squeezing out his eyes, and very graciously holds you out his hand to kiss. The keeper desires you not to be afraid of this professor, for he will do you no hurt; to him alone is allowed the liberty of the ante-chamber, and the orator of the place gives you to understand that this solemn person is a tailor run mad with pride. This considerable student is adorned with many other qualities, upon which at present I shall not farther enlarge. . . . Hark in your ear . . . I am strangely mistaken, if all his address, his emotions, and his airs, would not then be very natural, and in their proper element.

THE BATTLE OF THE BOOKS

[EPISODE OF THE SPIDER AND THE BEE]

Things were at this crisis, when a material accident fell out. For, upon the highest corner of a large window, there dwelt a certain spider, swollen up to the first magnitude by the destruction of infinite numbers of flies, whose spoils lay scattered before the gates of his palace, like human bones before the cave of some giant. The avenues to his castle were guarded with turnpikes and palisadoes, all after the modern way of fortification. After you had passed several courts, you came to the centre, wherein you might behold the constable himself in his own lodgings, which had windows fronting to each avenue, and ports to sally out, upon all occasions of prey or defence. In this mansion he had for some time dwelt in peace and plenty, without danger to his person by swallows from above, or to his palace, by brooms from below; when it was the pleasure of fortune to conduct thither a wandering bee, to whose curiosity a broken pane in the glass had discovered itself, and in he went; where, expatiating a while, he at last happened to alight upon one of the outward walls of the spider's citadel; which, yielding to the unequal weight, sunk down to the very foundation. Thrice he endeavoured to force his passage, and thrice the centre shook. The spider within, feeling the terrible convulsion, supposed at first that nature was approaching to her final dissolution; or else, that Beelzebub, with all his legions, was come to revenge the death of many thousands of his subjects, whom his enemy had slain and devoured. However, he at length valiantly resolved to issue forth, and meet his fate. Meanwhile the bee had acquitted himself of his toils, and, posted securely at some distance, was employed in cleansing his wings, and disengaging them from the ragged remnants of the cobweb. By this time the spider was adventured out, when, beholding the chasms, and ruins, and dilapidations of his fortress, he was very near at his wit's end; he stormed and swore like a madman, and swelled till he was ready to burst. At length, casting his eye upon the bee, and wisely gathering causes from events, (for they knew each other by sight): "A plague split you," said he, "for a giddy son of a whore! Is it you, with a vengeance, that have made this litter here? Could not you look before you, and be d——d? Do you think I have nothing else to do (in the devil's name) but to mend and repair after your arse?"—"Good words, friend," said the bee (having now pruned himself, and being disposed to droll), "I'll give you my hand and word to come near your kennel no more; I was never in such a confounded pickle since I was born."—"Sirrah," replied the spider, "if it were not for breaking an old custom in our family, never to stir abroad against an enemy, I should come and teach you better manners."—"I pray have patience," said the bee, "or you'll spend your substance, and, for aught I see, you

may stand in need of it all, toward the repair of your house."—"Rogue, rogue," replied the spider, "yet, methinks you should have more respect to a person, whom all the world allows to be so much your betters."— "By my troth," said the bee, "the comparison will amount to a very good jest, and you will do me a favour to let me know the reasons that all the world is pleased to use in so hopeful a dispute." At this the spider, having swelled himself into the size and posture of a disputant, began his argument in the true spirit of controversy, with resolution to be heartily scurrilous and angry, to urge on his own reasons, without the least regard to the answers or objections of his opposite, and fully predetermined in his mind against all conviction.

"Not to disparage myself," said he, "by the comparison with such a rascal, what art thou but a vagabond without house or home, without stock or inheritance? Born to no possession of your own, but a pair of wings and a drone-pipe. Your livelihood is a universal plunder upon nature; a freebooter over fields and gardens; and, for the sake of stealing, will rob a nettle as readily as a violet. Whereas I am a domestic animal, furnished with a native stock within myself. This large castle (to show my improvements in the mathematics) is all built with my own hands, and the materials extracted altogether out of my own person."

"I am glad," answered the bee, "to hear you grant at least that I am come honestly by my wings and my voice; for then, it seems, I am obliged to Heaven alone for my flights and my music; and Providence would never have bestowed on me two such gifts, without designing them for the noblest ends. I visit indeed all the flowers and blossoms of the field and garden; but whatever I collect from thence, enriches myself, without the least injury to their beauty, their smell, or their taste. Now, for you and your skill in architecture, and other mathematics, I have little to say: In that building of yours there might, for aught I know, have been labour and method enough; but, by woful experience for us both, 'tis too plain, the materials are naught, and I hope you will henceforth take warning, and consider duration and matter, as well as method and art. You boast, indeed, of being obliged to no other creature, but of drawing and spinning out all from yourself; that is to say, if we may judge of the liquor in the vessel by what issues out, you possess a good plentiful store of dirt and poison in your breast; and, though I would by no means lessen or disparage your genuine stock of either, yet, I doubt you are somewhat obliged, for an increase of both, to a little foreign assistance. Your inherent portion of dirt does not fail of acquisitions, by sweepings exhaled from below; and one insect furnishes you with a share of poison to destroy another. So that, in short, the question comes all to this—Whether is the nobler being of the two, that which, by a lazy contemplation of four inches round, by an overweening pride, which feeding and engendering on itself, turns all into excrement and venom, producing nothing at all, but flybane and a cobweb; or that which, by an universal range, with long search, much study, true judgment, and distinction of things, brings home honey and wax."

This dispute was managed with such eagerness, clamour, and warmth, that the two parties of books, in arms below, stood silent a while, waiting in suspense what would be the issue, which was not long undetermined: For the bee, grown impatient at so much loss of time, fled straight away to a bed of roses, without looking for a reply, and left the spider, like an orator, collected in himself, and just prepared to burst out.

It happened upon this emergency, that Æsop broke silence first. He had been of late most barbarously treated by a strange effect of the regent's humanity, who had tore off his title-page, sorely defaced one half of his leaves, and chained him fast among a shelf of Moderns. Where, soon discovering how high the quarrel was like to proceed, he tried all his arts, and turned himself to a thousand forms. At length, in the borrowed shape of an ass, the regent mistook him for a Modern; by which means he had time and opportunity to escape to the Ancients, just when the spider and the bee were entering into their contest, to which he gave his attention with a world of pleasure; and when it was ended, swore in the loudest key, that in all his life he had never known two cases so parallel and adapt to each other, as that in the window, and this upon the shelves. "The disputants," said he. "have admirably managed the dispute between them, have taken in the full strength of all that is to be said on both sides, and exhausted the substance of every argument *pro* and *con*. It is but to adjust the reasonings of both to the present quarrel, then to compare and apply the labours and fruits of each, as the bee has learnedly deduced them, and we shall find the conclusion fall plain and close upon the Moderns and us. For, pray, gentlemen, was ever anything so modern as the spider in his air, his turns, and his paradoxes? He argues in the behalf of you his brethren and himself, with many boastings of his native stock and great genius; that he spins and spits wholly from himself, and scorns to own any obligation or assistance from without. Then he displays to you his great skill in architecture, and improvement in the mathematics. To all this the bee, as an advocate, retained by us the Ancients, thinks fit to answer—that, if one may judge of the great genius or inventions of the Moderns by what they have produced, you will hardly have countenance to bear you out, in boasting of either. Erect your schemes with as much method and skill as you please; yet if the materials be nothing but dirt, spun out of your own entrails (the guts of modern brains) the edifice will conclude at last in a cobweb, the duration of which, like that of other spiders' webs, may be imputed to their being forgotten, or neglected, or hid in a corner. For anything else of genuine that the Moderns may pretend to, I cannot recollect; unless it be a large vein of wrangling and satire, much of a nature and substance with the spider's poison; which, however they pretend to spit wholly out of themselves, is improved by the same arts, by feeding upon the insects and vermin of the age. As for us the Ancients, we are content, with the bee, to pretend to nothing of our own, beyond our wings and our voice, that is to say, our flights and our language. For the rest, whatever we have got, has been by infinite labour and search, and ranging through every corner of nature; the difference is, that, instead of dirt and poison, we have rather chosen to fill our hives with honey and wax, thus furnishing mankind with the two noblest of things, which are sweetness and light."

AN ARGUMENT

to prove that the

ABOLISHING OF CHRISTIANITY IN ENGLAND

may, as things now stand, be attended with some inconveniences, and perhaps not produce those many good effects proposed thereby.

WRITTEN IN THE YEAR 1708.

I am very sensible what a weakness and presumption it is, to reason against the general humour and disposition of the world. I remember it was with great justice, and a due regard to the freedom both of the public and the press, forbidden upon several penalties to write, or discourse, or lay wagers against the Union, even before it was confirmed by parliament, because that was looked upon as a design, to oppose the current of the people, which, besides the folly of it, is a manifest breach of the fundamental law that makes this majority of opinion the voice of God. In like manner, and for the very same reasons, it may perhaps be neither safe nor prudent to argue against the abolishing of Christianity, at a juncture when all parties appear so unanimously determined upon the point, as we cannot but allow from their actions, their discourses, and their writings. However, I know not how, whether from the affection of singularity, or the perverseness of human nature, but so it unhappily falls out, that I cannot be entirely of this opinion. Nay, though I were sure an order were issued for my immediate prosecution by the attorney-general, I should still confess that in the present posture of our affairs at home or abroad, I do not yet see the absolute necessity of extirpating the Christian religion from among us.

This perhaps may appear too great a paradox even for our wise and paradoxical age to endure; therefore I shall handle it with all tenderness, and with the utmost deference to that great and profound majority which is of another sentiment.

And yet the curious may please to observe how much the genius of a nation is liable to alter in half an age: I have heard it affirmed for certain by some very old people that the contrary opinion was even in their memories as much in vogue as the other is now; and that a project for the abolishing of Christianity would then have appeared as singular, and been thought as absurd, as it would be at this time to write or discourse in its defence.

Therefore I freely own that all appearances are against me. The system of the Gospel, after the fate of other systems, is generally antiquated and exploded; and the mass or body of the common people, among whom it seems to have had its latest credit, are now grown as much ashamed of it as their betters; opinions, like fashions, always descending from those of quality to the middle sort, and thence to the vulgar, where at length they are dropped and vanish.

But here I would not be mistaken, and must therefore be so bold as to borrow a distinction from the writers on the other side, when they make a difference between nominal and real Trinitarians. I hope no reader imagines me so weak to stand up in the defence of real Christianity, such as used in primitive times (if we may believe the authors of those ages) to have an influence upon men's belief and actions: to offer at the restoring of that would indeed be a wild project; it would be to dig up foundations; to destroy at one blow all the wit, and half the learning of the kingdom; to break the entire frame and constitution of things; to ruin trade, extinguish arts and sciences with the professors of them; in short, to turn our courts, exchanges, and shops into deserts; and would be full as absurd as the proposal of Horace, where he advises the Romans all in a body to leave their city and seek a new seat in some remote part of the world, by way of cure for the corruption of their manners.

Therefore I think this caution was in itself altogether unnecessary, (which I have inserted only to prevent all possibility of cavilling) since every candid reader will easily understand my discourse to be intended only in defence of nominal Christianity, the other having been for some time wholly laid aside by general consent as utterly inconsistent with our present schemes of wealth and power.

But why we should therefore cast off the name and title of Christians, although the general opinion and resolution be so violent for it, I confess I cannot (with submission) apprehend the consequence necessary. However, since the undertakers propose such wonderful advantages to the nation by this project, and advance many plausible objections against the system of Christianity, I shall briefly consider the strength of both, fairly allow them their greatest weight, and offer such answers as I think most reasonable. After which I will beg leave to show what inconveniences may possibly happen by such an innovation, in the present posture of our affairs.

First, One great advantage proposed by the abolishing of Christianity is, that it would very much enlarge and establish liberty of conscience, that great bulwark of our nation, and of the protestant religion, which is still too much limited by priestcraft, notwithstanding all the good intentions of the legislature, as we have lately found by a severe instance. For it is confidently reported, that two young gentlemen of real hopes, bright wit, and profound judgment, who upon a thorough examination of causes and effects, and by the mere force of natural abilities, without the least tincture of learning, having made a discovery, that there was no God, and generously communicating their thoughts for the good of the public, were some time ago, by an unparalleled severity, and upon I know not what obsolete law, broke for blasphemy. And as it hath been wisely observed, if persecution once begins, no man alive knows how far it may reach, or where it will end.

In answer to all which, with deference to wiser judgments, I think this rather shows the necessity of a nominal religion among us. Great wits love to be free with the highest objects; and if they cannot be allowed a God to revile or renounce, they will speak evil of dignities, abuse the government, and reflect upon the ministry; which I am sure few will deny to be of much more pernicious consequence, according to the saying of Tiberius, *Deorum offensa diis curæ.* As to the particular fact related, I think it is not fair to argue from one instance, perhaps another cannot be produced; yet (to the comfort of all those who may be apprehensive of persecution) blasphemy we know is freely spoken a million of times in every coffeehouse and tavern, or wherever else good company meet. It must be allowed indeed, that to break an English freeborn officer only for blasphemy, was, to speak the gentlest of such an action, a very high strain of absolute power. Little can be said in excuse for the general, perhaps he was afraid it might give offence to the allies among whom, for aught we know, it may be the custom of the country to believe a God. But if he argued, as some have done, upon a mistaken principle, that an officer who is guilty of speaking blasphemy, may some time or other proceed so far as to raise a mutiny, the consequence is by no means to be admitted; for, surely the commander of an English army is likely to be but ill obeyed, whose soldiers fear and reverence him as little as they do a Deity.

It is further objected against the gospel system, that it obliges men to the belief of things too difficult for free-thinkers, and such who have shaken off the prejudices that usually cling to a confined education. To which I answer, that men should be cautious, how they raise objections which reflect upon the wisdom of the nation. Is not everybody freely allowed to believe whatever he pleases, and to publish his belief to the world whenever he thinks fit, especially if it serves to strengthen the party which is in the right? Would any indifferent foreigner, who should read the trumpery lately written by Asgil, Tindal, Toland, Coward, and forty more, imagine the Gospel to be our rule of faith, and confirmed by parliaments? Does any man either believe, or say he believes, or desire to have it thought that he says he believes one syllable of the matter? And is any man worse received upon that score, or does he find his want of nominal faith a disadvantage to him in the pursuit of any civil or military employment? What if there be an old dormant statute or two against him, are they not now obsolete, to a degree, that Empson and Dudley themselves if they were now alive, would find it impossible to put them in execution?

It is likewise urged that there are by computation in this kingdom above ten thousand parsons, whose revenues, added to those of my lords the bishops, would suffice to maintain at least two hundred young gentlemen of wit and pleasure, and free-thinking, enemies to priestcraft, narrow principles, pedantry, and prejudices; who might be an ornament to the Court and Town: And then, again, so great a number of able [-bodied] divines might be a recruit to our fleet and armies. This indeed appears to be a consideration of some weight: but then, on the other side, several things deserve to be considered likewise: as, first, whether it may not be thought necessary that in certain tracts of country, like what we call parishes, there shall be one man at least of abilities to read and write. Then it seems a wrong computation, that the revenues of the Church throughout this island would be large enough to maintain two hundred young gentlemen, or even half that number, after the present refined way of living; that is, to allow each of them such a rent, as in the modern form of speech, would make them easy. But still there is in this project a greater mischief behind; and we ought to beware of the woman's folly, who killed the hen that every morning laid her a golden egg. For, pray what would become of the race of men in the next age, if we had nothing to trust to beside the scrofulous, consumptive productions, furnished by our men of wit and pleasure, when, having squandered away their vigour, health and estates, they are forced by some disagreeable marriage to piece up their broken fortunes, and entail rottenness and politeness on their posterity? Now here are ten thousand persons reduced by the wise regulations of Henry the Eighth, to the necessity of a low diet and moderate exercise, who are the only great restorers of our breed, without which the nation would in an age or two become one great hospital.

Another advantage proposed by the abolishing of Christianity is the clear gain of one day in seven, which is now entirely lost, and consequently the kingdom one seventh less considerable in trade, business, and pleasure; besides the loss to the public of so many stately structures now in the hands of the clergy, which might be converted into playhouses, exchanges, market-houses, common dormitories, and other public edifices.

I hope I shall be forgiven a hard word, if I call this a perfect *cavil*. I readily own there hath been an old custom time out of mind, for people to assemble in the churches every Sunday, and that shops are still frequently shut, in order, as it is conceived, to preserve the memory of that ancient practice, but how this can prove a hindrance to business or pleasure, is hard to imagine. What if the men of pleasure are forced, one day in the week, to game at home instead of the chocolate-house? Are not the taverns and coffee-houses open? Can there be a more convenient season for taking a dose of physic? Are fewer claps got upon Sundays than other days? Is not that the chief day for traders to sum up the accounts of the week, and for lawyers to prepare their briefs? But I would fain know how it can be pretended that the churches are misapplied? Where are more appointments and rendezvouzes of gallantry? Where more care to appear in the foremost box with greater advantage of dress? Where more meetings for business? Where more bargains driven of all sorts? And where so many conveniences or incitements to sleep?

There is one advantage greater than any of the foregoing, proposed by the abolishing of Christianity: that it will utterly extinguish parties among us, by removing those factious distinctions of High and Low Church, of Whig and Tory, Presbyterian and Church of England, which are now so many mutual clogs upon public proceedings, and are apt to prefer the gratifying themselves, or depressing their adversaries, before the most important interest of the state.

I confess, if it were certain that so great an advantage would redound to the nation by this expedient, I would submit and be silent: but will any man say, that if the words *whoring, drinking, cheating, lying, stealing,* were by act of parliament ejected out of the English tongue and dictionaries, we should all awake next morning chaste and temperate, honest and just, and lovers of truth? Is this a fair consequence? Or, if the physicians would forbid us to pronounce the words *pox, gout, rheumatism* and *stone,* would that expedient serve like so many talismans to destroy the diseases themselves? Are party and faction rooted in men's hearts no deeper than phrases borrowed from religion, or founded upon no firmer principles? And is our language so poor that we cannot find other terms to express them? Are *envy, pride, avarice* and *ambition* such ill nomenclators, that they cannot furnish appellations for their owners? Will not *heydukes* and *mamalukes, mandarins* and *patshaws,* or any other words formed at pleasure, serve to distinguish those who are in the ministry from others who would be in it if they could? What, for instance, is easier than to vary the form of speech, and instead of the word *church,* make it a question in politics, whether the Monument be in danger? Because religion was nearest at hand to furnish a few convenient phrases, is our invention so barren we can find no other? Suppose, for argument sake, that the Tories favoured Margarita, the Whigs Mrs. Tofts, and the Trimmers Valentini, would not *Margaritians, Toftians* and *Valentinians* be very tolerable marks of distinction? The *Prasini* and *Veniti,* two most virulent factions in Italy, began (if I remember right) by a distinction of colours in ribbons, which we might do with as good a grace about the dignity of the blue and the green, and would serve as properly to divide the Court, the Parliament, and the Kingdom between them, as any terms of art whatsoever borrowed from religion. And therefore I think there is little force in this objection against Christianity, or prospect of so great an advantage as is proposed in the abolishing of it.

'Tis again objected, as a very absurd ridiculous custom, that a set of men should be suffered, much less employed and hired, to bawl one day in seven against the lawfulness of those methods most in use toward the pursuit of greatness, riches and pleasure, which are the constant practice of all men alive on the other six. But this objection is, I think, a little unworthy so refined an age as ours. Let us argue this matter calmly: I appeal to the breast of any polite freethinker, whether in the pursuit of gratifying a predominant passion he hath not always felt a wonderful incitement, by reflecting it was a thing forbidden: and therefore we see, in order to cultivate this taste, the wisdom of the nation hath taken special care that the ladies should be furnished with prohibited silks, and the men with prohibited wine. And indeed, it were to be wished that some other prohibitions were promoted, in order to improve the pleasures of the town; which, for want of such expedients begin already, as I am told, to flag and grow languid, giving way daily to cruel inroads from the spleen.

'Tis likewise proposed as a great advantage to the public that if we once discard the system of the Gospel, all religion will of course be banished for ever; and consequently, along with it, those grievous prejudices of education, which under the names of *virtue, conscience, honour, justice,* and the like, are so apt to disturb the peace of human minds, and the notions whereof are so hard to be eradicated by right reason or freethinking, sometimes during the whole course of our lives.

Here first I observe how difficult it is to get rid of a phrase which the world is once grown fond of, though the occasion that first produced it be entirely taken away. For several years past, if a man had but an ill-favoured

nose, the deep-thinkers of the age would some way or other contrive to impute the cause to the prejudice of his education. From this fountain were said to be derived all our foolish notions of justice, piety, love of our country, all our opinions of God, or a future state, Heaven, Hell, and the like: and there might formerly perhaps have been some pretence for this charge. But so effectual care hath been since taken to remove those prejudices, by an entire change in the methods of education, that (with honour I mention it to our polite innovators) the young gentlemen who are now on the scene, seem to have not the least tincture of those infusions, or string of those weeds; and, by consequence, the reason for abolishing nominal Christianity upon that pretext, is wholly ceased.

For the rest, it may perhaps admit a controversy, whether the banishing of all notions of religion whatsoever, would be convenient for the vulgar. Not that I am in the least of opinion with those who hold religion to have been the invention of politicians, to keep the lower part of the world in awe by the fear of invisible powers; unless mankind were then very different from what it is now: For I look upon the mass or body of our people here in England to be as freethinkers, that is to say, as staunch unbelievers, as any of the highest rank. But I conceive some scattered notions about a superior power to be of singular use for the common people, as furnishing excellent materials to keep children quiet when they grow peevish, and providing topics of amusement in a tedious winter-night.

Lastly, 'tis proposed as a singular advantage, that the abolishing of Christianity will very much contribute to the uniting of Protestants, by enlarging the terms of communion so as to take in all sorts of dissenters, who are now shut out of the pale upon account of a few ceremonies which all sides confess to be things indifferent: that this alone will effectually answer the great ends of a scheme for comprehension, by opening a large noble gate, at which all bodies may enter; whereas the chaffering with dissenters, and dodging about this or t'other ceremony, is but like opening a few wickets, and leaving them at jar, by which no more than one can get in at a time, and that, not without stooping, and sideling, and squeezing his body.

To all this I answer that there is one darling inclination of mankind, which usually affects to be a retainer to religion, though she be neither its parent, its godmother, or its friend; I mean the spirit of opposition, that lived long before Christianity, and can easily subsist without it. Let us, for instance, examine wherein the opposition of sectaries among us consists, we shall find Christianity to have no share in it at all. Does the Gospel any where prescribe a starched, squeezed countenance, a stiff, formal gait, a singularity of manners and habit, or any affected modes of speech different from the reasonable part of mankind? Yet, if Christianity did not lend its name to stand in the gap, and to employ or divert these humours, they must of necessity be spent in contraventions to the laws of the land, and disturbance of the public peace. There is a portion of enthusiasm assigned to every nation, which, if it hath not proper objects to work on, will burst out, and set all into a flame. If the quiet of a state can be bought by only flinging men a few ceremonies to devour, it is a purchase no wise man would refuse. Let the mastiffs amuse themselves about a sheep's skin stuffed with hay, provided it will keep them from worrying the flock. The institution of convents abroad seems in one point a strain of great wisdom, there being few irregularities in human passions, which may not have recourse to vent themselves in some of those orders, which are so many retreats for the speculative, the melancholy, the proud, the silent, the politic and the morose, to spend them-

selves, and evaporate the noxious particles; for each of whom we in this island are forced to provide a several sect of religion, to keep them quiet: and whenever Christianity shall be abolished, the legislature must find some other expedient to employ and entertain them. For what imports it how large a gate you open, if there will be always left a number who place a pride and a merit in not coming in?

Having thus considered the most important objections against Christianity and the chief advantages proposed by the abolishing thereof, I shall now with equal deference and submission to wiser judgments as before, proceed to mention a few inconveniences that may happen, if the Gospel should be repealed; which perhaps the projectors may not have sufficiently considered.

And first, I am very sensible how much the gentlemen of wit and pleasure are apt to murmur, and be choked at the sight of so many draggled-tail parsons, that happen to fall in their way, and offend their eyes; but at the same time, these wise reformers do not consider what an advantage and felicity it is, for great wits to be always provided with objects of scorn and contempt, in order to exercise and improve their talents, and divert their spleen from falling on each other or on themselves; especially when all this may be done without the least imaginable danger to their persons.

And to urge another argument of a parallel nature: if Christianity were once abolished, how could the freethinkers, the strong reasoners, and the men of profound learning, be able to find another subject so calculated in all points whereon to display their abilities? What wonderful productions of wit should we be deprived of, from those whose genius by continual practice hath been wholly turned upon raillery and invectives against religion, and would therefore never be able to shine or distinguish themselves upon any other subject! We are daily complaining of the great decline of wit among us, and would we take away the greatest, perhaps the only, topic we have left? Who would ever have suspected Asgil for a wit, or Toland for a philosopher, if the inexhaustible stock of Christianity had not been at hand to provide them with materials? What other subject, through all art or nature, could have produced Tindal for a profound author, or furnished him with readers? It is the wise choice of the subject that alone adorns and distinguishes the writer. For, had a hundred such pens as these been employed on the side of religion, they would have immediately sunk into silence and oblivion.

Nor do I think it wholly groundless, or my fears altogether imaginary, that the abolishing of Christianity may perhaps bring the Church into danger, or at least put the senate to the trouble of another securing vote. I desire I may not be mistaken; I am far from presuming to affirm or think that the Church is in danger at present, or as things now stand; but we know not how soon it may be so when the Christian religion is repealed. As plausible as this project seems, there may a dangerous design lurk under it: Nothing can be more notorious, than that the Atheists, Deists, Socinians, Antitrinitarians, and other subdivisions of freethinkers, are persons of little zeal for the present ecclesiastical establishment: Their declared opinion is for repealing the Sacramental Test; they are very indifferent with regard to ceremonies; nor do they hold the *jus divinum* of Episcopacy. Therefore this may be intended as one politic step toward altering the constitution of the Church established, and setting up Presbytery in the stead, which I leave to be further considered by those at the helm.

In the last place, I think nothing can be more plain, than that by this expedient, we shall run into the evil we chiefly pretend to avoid; and that

the abolishment of the Christian religion will be the readiest course we can take to introduce popery. And I am the more inclined to this opinion, because we know it has been the constant practice of the Jesuits to send over emissaries with instructions to personate themselves members of the several prevailing sects among us. So it is recorded, that they have at sundry times appeared in the guise of Presbyterians, Anabaptists, Independents and Quakers, according as any of these were most in credit; so, since the fashion hath been taken up of exploding religion, the popish missionaries have not been wanting to mix with the freethinkers; among whom, Toland the great oracle of the Antichristians is an Irish priest, the son of an Irish priest; and the most learned and ingenious author of a book called "The Rights of the Christian Church," was in a proper juncture reconciled to the Romish faith, whose true son, as appears by a hundred passages in his treatise, he still continues. Perhaps I could add some others to the number; but the fact is beyond dispute, and the reasoning they proceed by is right: for, supposing Christianity to be extinguished, the people will never be at ease till they find out some other method of worship; which will as infallibly produce superstition, as this will end in popery.

And therefore, if notwithstanding all I have said, it still be thought necessary to have a bill brought in for repealing Christianity, I would humbly offer an amendment; that instead of the word, Christianity, may be put religion in general; which I conceive will much better answer all the good ends proposed by the projectors of it. For, as long as we leave in being a God and his providence, with all the necessary consequences which curious and inquisitive men will be apt to draw from such premises, we do not strike at the root of the evil, though we should ever so effectually annihilate the present scheme of the Gospel: for of what use is freedom of thought, if it will not produce freedom of action, which is the sole end, how remote soever in appearance, of all objections against Christianity? And, therefore, the freethinkers consider it as a sort of edifice, wherein all the parts have such a mutual dependence on each other, that if you happen to pull out one single nail, the whole fabric must fall to the ground. This was happily expressed by him who had heard of a text brought for proof of the Trinity, which in an ancient manuscript was differently read; he thereupon immediately took the hint, and by a sudden deduction of a long *sorites*, most logically concluded; "Why, if it be as you say, I may safely whore and drink on, and defy the parson." From which, and many the like instances easy to be produced, I think nothing can be more manifest than that the quarrel is not against any particular points of hard digestion in the Christian system, but against religion in general; which, by laying restraints on human nature, is supposed the great enemy to the freedom of thought and action.

Upon the whole, if it shall still be thought for the benefit of Church and State, that Christianity be abolished, I conceive, however, it may be more convenient to defer the execution to a time of peace, and not venture in this conjuncture to disoblige our allies, who, as it falls out, are all Christians, and many of them, by the prejudices of their education, so bigoted, as to place a sort of pride in the appellation. If upon being rejected by them, we are to trust an alliance with the Turk, we shall find ourselves much deceived: for, as he is too remote, and generally engaged in war with the Persian emperor, so his people would be more scandalized at our infidelity, than our Christian neighbours. For they are not only strict observers of religious worship, but what is worse, believe a God; which is more than required of us even while we preserve the name of Christians.

To conclude: Whatever some may think of the great advantages to trade by this favourite scheme, I do very much apprehend, that in six months time after the act is passed for the extirpation of the Gospel, the Bank, and East-India Stock, may fall at least one *per cent*. And since that is fifty times more than ever the wisdom of our age thought fit to venture for the preservation of Christianity, there is no reason we should be at so great a loss, merely for the sake of destroying it.

GULLIVER'S TRAVELS

For Part II of *Gulliver's Travels* see pages 1085–1123.

A VOYAGE TO THE COUNTRY OF THE HOUYHNHNMS

CHAP. I

The author sets out as Captain of a ship. His men conspire against him, confine him a long time to his cabin, set him on shore in an unknown land. He travels up into the country. The Yahoos, *a strange sort of animal, described. The author meets two Houyhnhnms.*

I continued at home with my wife and children about five months in a very happy condition, if I could have learned the lesson of knowing when I was well. I left my poor wife big with child, and accepted an advantageous offer made me to be Captain of the *Adventure*, a stout merchantman of 350 tons: for I understood navigation well, and being grown weary of a surgeon's employment at sea, which however I could exercise upon occasion, I took a skilful young man of that calling, one Robert Purefoy, into my ship. We set sail from Portsmouth upon the seventh day of September, 1710; on the fourteenth we met with Captain Pocock of Bristol, at Teneriffe, who was going to the bay of Campechy, to cut logwood. On the sixteenth, he was parted from us by a storm; I heard since my return, that his ship foundered and none escaped but one cabin boy. He was an honest man, and a good sailor, but a little too positive in his own opinions, which was the cause of his destruction, as it hath been of several others. For if he had followed my advice, he might have been safe at home with his family at this time, as well as myself.

I had several men died in my ship of calentures, so that I was forced to get recruits out of Barbadoes, and the Leeward Islands, where I touched by the direction of the merchants who employed me, which I had soon too much cause to repent: for I found afterwards that most of them had been buccaneers. I had fifty hands on board, and my orders were, that I should trade with the Indians in the South Sea, and make what discoveries I could. These rogues whom I had picked up debauched my other men, and they all formed a conspiracy to seize the ship and secure me; which they did one morning, rushing into my cabin, and binding me hand and foot, threatening to throw me overboard, if I offered to stir. I told them I was their prisoner, and would submit. This they made me swear to do, and then they unbound me, only fastening one of my legs with a chain near my bed, and placed a sentry at my door with his piece charged, who was commanded to shoot me dead, if I attempted my liberty. They sent me down victuals and drink, and took the government of the ship to themselves. Their design was to turn pirates, and plunder the Spaniards, which they could not do, till they got more men. But first they resolved to sell the goods in the ship, and then go to Madagascar for recruits, several among them having died since my confinement. They sailed many weeks, and traded with the Indians, but I knew not what course they took, being kept a close prisoner in my cabin, and expecting nothing less than to be murdered, as they often threatened me.

Upon the ninth day of May, 1711, one James Welch came down to my cabin; and said he had orders from the Captain to set me ashore. I ex-

postulated with him, but in vain; neither would he so much as tell me who their new Captain was. They forced me into the long-boat, letting me put on my best suit of clothes, which were as good as new, and a small bundle of linen, but no arms except my hanger; and they were so civil as not to search my pockets, into which I conveyed what money I had, with some other little necessaries. They rowed about a league, and then set me down on a strand. I desired them to tell me what country it was. They all swore, they knew no more than myself, but said, that the Captain (as they called him) was resolved, after they had sold the lading, to get rid of me in the first place where they could discover land. They pushed off immediately, advising me to make haste, for fear of being overtaken by the tide, and so bade me farewell.

In this desolate condition I advanced forward, and soon got upon firm ground, where I sat down on a bank to rest myself, and consider what I had best to do. When I was a little refreshed, I went up into the country, resolving to deliver myself to the first savages I should meet, and purchase my life from them by some bracelets, glass rings, and other toys which sailors usually provide themselves with in those voyages, and whereof I had some about me. The land was divided by long rows of trees, not regularly planted, but naturally growing; there was great plenty of grass, and several fields of oats. I walked very circumspectly for fear of being surprised, or suddenly shot with an arrow from behind or on either side. I fell into a beaten road, where I saw many tracks of human feet, and some of cows, but most of horses. At last I beheld several animals in a field, and one or two of the same kind sitting in trees. Their shape was very singular, and deformed, which a little discomposed me, so that I lay down behind a thicket to observe them better. Some of them coming forward near the place where I lay, gave me an opportunity of distinctly marking their form. Their heads and breasts were covered with a thick hair, some frizzled and others lank; they had beards like goats, and a long ridge of hair down their backs, and the fore parts of their legs and feet, but the rest of their bodies were bare, so that I might see their skins, which were of a brown buff colour. They had no tails, nor any hair at all on their buttocks, except about the anus; which, I presume, nature had placed there to defend them as they sat on the ground; for this posture they used, as well as lying down, and often stood on their hind feet. They climbed high trees, as nimbly as a squirrel, for they had strong extended claws before and behind, terminating in sharp points, and hooked. They would often spring, and bound, and leap with prodigious agility. The females were not so large as the males; they had long lank hair on their heads, but none on their faces, nor anything more than a sort of down on the rest of their bodies, except about the anus, and pudenda. Their dugs hung between their fore-feet, and often reached almost to the ground as they walked. The hair of both sexes was of several colours, brown, red, black, and yellow. Upon the whole, I never beheld in all my travels so disagreeable an animal, nor one against which I naturally conceived so strong an antipathy. So that thinking I had seen enough, full of contempt and aversion, I got up and pursued the beaten road, hoping it might direct me to the cabin of some Indian. I had not got far when I met one of these creatures full in my way, and coming up directly to me. The ugly monster, when he saw me, distorted several ways every feature of his visage, and stared as at an object he had never seen before; then approaching nearer, lifted up his fore-paw, whether out of curiosity or mischief, I could not tell. But I drew my hanger, and gave him a good blow with the flat side of it,

for I durst not strike with the edge, fearing the inhabitants might be provoked against me, if they should come to know, that I had killed or maimed any of their cattle. When the beast felt the smart, he drew back, and roared so loud, that a herd of at least forty came flocking about me from the next field, howling and making odious faces; but I ran to the body of a tree, and leaning my back against it, kept them off by waving my hanger. Several of this cursed brood getting hold of the branches behind, leapt up into the tree, from whence they began to discharge their excrements on my head; however, I escaped pretty well, by sticking close to the stem of the tree, but was almost stifled with the filth, which fell about me on every side.

In the midst of this distress, I observed them all to run away on a sudden as fast as they could, at which I ventured to leave the tree, and pursue the road, wondering what it was that could put them into this fright. But looking on my left hand, I saw a horse walking softly in the field; which my persecutors having sooner discovered, was the cause of their flight. The horse started a little when he came near me, but soon recovering himself, looked full in my face with manifest tokens of wonder: he viewed my hands and feet, walking round me several times. I would have pursued my journey, but he placed himself directly in the way, yet looking with a very mild aspect, never offering the least violence. We stood gazing at each other for some time; at last I took the boldness to reach my hand towards his neck, with a design to stroke it, using the common style and whistle of jockeys when they are going to handle a strange horse. But this animal seeming to receive my civilities with disdain, shook his head, and bent his brows, softly raising up his right forefoot to remove my hand. Then he neighed three or four times, but in so different a cadence, that I almost be-

gan to think he was speaking to himself in some language of his own.

While he and I were thus employed,
another horse came up; who applying himself to the first in a very formal manner, they gently struck each
other's right hoof before, neighing
several times by turns, and varying
the sound, which seemed to be almost
articulate. They went some paces off, 10
as if it were to confer together, walking side by side, backward and forward, like persons deliberating upon
some affair of weight, but often turning their eyes towards me, as it were
to watch that I might not escape. I
was amazed to see such actions and
behaviour in brute beasts, and concluded with myself, that if the inhabitants of this country were endued 20
with a proportionable degree of reason, they must needs be the wisest
people upon earth. This thought gave
me so much comfort, that I resolved
to go forward until I could discover
some house or village, or meet with
any of the natives, leaving the two
horses to discourse together as they
pleased. But the first, who was a dap-
ple gray, observing me to steal off, 30
neighed after me in so expressive a
tone, that I fancied myself to understand what he meant; whereupon I
turned back, and came near him, to
expect his farther commands: but
concealing my fear as much as I could,
for I began to be in some pain, how
this adventure might terminate; and
the reader will easily believe I did
not much like my present situation. 40

The two horses came up close to
me, looking with great earnestness
upon my face and hands. The gray
steed rubbed my hat all round
with his right fore-hoof, and discomposed it so much that I was forced
to adjust it better, by taking it off,
and settling it again; whereat both
he and his companion (who was a
brown bay) appeared to be much sur- 50
prised: the latter felt the lappet of
my coat, and finding it to hang loose
about me, they both looked with new
signs of wonder. He stroked my right

hand, seeming to admire the softness
and colour; but he squeezed it so hard
between his hoof and his pastern, that
I was forced to roar; after which they
both touched me with all possible
tenderness. They were under great
perplexity about my shoes and stockings, which they felt very often, neighing to each other, and using various
gestures, not unlike those of a phi- 10
losopher, when he would attempt to
solve some new and difficult phenomenon.

Upon the whole, the behaviour of
these animals was so orderly and rational, so acute and judicious, that I
at last concluded, they must needs be
magicians, who had thus metamorphosed themselves upon some design,
and seeing a stranger in the way, 20
were resolved to divert themselves
with him; or perhaps were really
amazed at the sight of a man so very
different in habit, feature, and complexion from those who might probably live in so remote a climate. Upon
the strength of this reasoning, I ventured to address them in the following manner: Gentlemen, if you be
conjurers, as I have good cause to 30
believe, you can understand any language; therefore I make bold to let
your worships know, that I am a poor
distressed Englishman, driven by his
misfortunes upon your coast, and I
entreat one of you, to let me ride
upon his back, as if he were a real
horse, to some house or village, where
I can be relieved. In return of which
favour, I will make you a present of 40
this knife and bracelet, (taking them
out of my pocket). The two creatures
stood silent while I spoke, seeming to
listen with great attention; and when
I had ended, they neighed frequently
towards each other, as if they were
engaged in serious conversation. I
plainly observed, that their language
expressed the passions very well, and
the words might with little pains be 50
resolved into an alphabet more easily
than the Chinese.

I could frequently distinguish the
word *Yahoo*, which was repeated by

each of them several times; and although it was impossible for me to conjecture what it meant, yet while the two horses were busy in conversation, I endeavoured to practise this word upon my tongue; and as soon as they were silent, I boldly pronounced *Yahoo* in a loud voice, imitating, at the same time, as near as I could, the neighing of a horse; at which they were both visibly surprised, and the gray repeated the same word twice, as if he meant to teach me the right accent, wherein I spoke after him as well as I could, and found myself perceivably to improve every time, though very far from any degree of perfection. Then the bay tried me with a second word, much harder to be pronounced; but reducing it to the English orthography, may be spelt thus, *houyhnhnm*. I did not succeed in this so well as the former, but after two or three farther trials, I had better fortune; and they both appeared amazed at my capacity.

After some further discourse, which I then conjectured might relate to me, the two friends took their leaves, with the same compliment of striking each other's hoof; and the gray made me signs that I should walk before him, wherein I thought it prudent to comply, till I could find a better director. When I offered to slacken my pace, he would cry *Hhuun, Hhuun*; I guessed his meaning, and gave him to understand, as well as I could, that I was weary, and not able to walk faster; upon which, he would stand a while to let me rest.

CHAP. II

The author conducted by a Houyhnhnm *to his house. The house described. The author's reception. The food of the* Houyhnhnms. *The author in distress for want of meat, is at last relieved. His manner of feeding in this country.*

Having travelled about three miles, we came to a long kind of building, made of timber, stuck in the ground, and wattled across; the roof was low, and covered with straw. I now began

to be a little comforted, and took out some toys, which travellers usually carry for presents to the savage Indians of America and other parts, in hopes the people of the house would be thereby encouraged to receive me kindly. The horse made me a sign to go in first; it was a large room with a smooth clay floor, and a rack and manger extending the whole length on one side. There were three nags, and two mares, not eating, but some of them sitting down upon their hams, which I very much wondered at; but wondered more to see the rest employed in domestic business. The last seemed but ordinary cattle; however, this confirmed my first opinion, that a people who could so far civilize brute animals, must needs excel in wisdom all the nations of the world. The gray came in just after, and thereby prevented any ill treatment, which the others might have given me. He neighed to them several times in a style of authority, and received answers.

Beyond this room there were three others, reaching the length of the house, to which you passed through three doors, opposite to each other, in the manner of a vista; we went through the second room towards the third; here the gray walked in first, beckoning me to attend: I waited in the second room, and got ready my presents for the master and mistress of the house: they were two knives, three bracelets of false pearl, a small looking-glass, and a bead necklace. The horse neighed three or four times, and I waited to hear some answers in a human voice, but I heard no other returns, than in the same dialect, only one or two a little shriller than his. I began to think that this house must belong to some person of great note among them, because there appeared so much ceremony before I could gain admittance. But, that a man of quality should be served all by horses, was beyond my comprehension. I feared my brain was disturbed by my sufferings and misfortunes: I roused myself, and looked about me in the room where I was left alone; this was furnished like the first, only after a more elegant manner. I rubbed my eyes often, but the same objects still occurred. I pinched my arms and sides, to awake myself, hoping I might be in a dream. I then absolutely concluded, that all these appearances could be nothing else but necromancy and magic. But I had no time to pursue these reflections; for the gray horse came to the door, and made me a sign to follow him into the third room, where I saw a very comely mare, together with a colt and foal, sitting on their haunches, upon mats of straw, not unartfully made, and perfectly neat and clean.

The mare soon after my entrance, rose from her mat, and coming up close, after having nicely observed my hands and face, gave me a most contemptuous look; then turning to the horse, I heard the word *Yahoo* often repeated betwixt them; the meaning of which word I could not then comprehend, although it were the first I had learned to pronounce; but I was soon better informed, to my everlasting mortification: for the horse beckoning to me with his head, and repeating the word *Hhuun, Hhuun,* as he did upon the road, which I understood was to attend him, led me out into a kind of court, where was another building at some distance from the house. Here we entered, and I saw three of those detestable creatures, which I first met after my landing, feeding upon roots, and the flesh of some animals, which I afterwards found to be that of asses and dogs, and now and then a cow dead by accident or disease. They were all tied by the neck with strong withes, fastened to a beam; they held their food between the claws of their fore-feet, and tore it with their teeth.

The master horse ordered a sorrel nag, one of his servants, to untie the largest of these animals, and take him into the yard. The beast and I were brought close together, and our countenances diligently compared, both by master and servant, who thereupon repeated several times the word *Yahoo*. My horror and astonishment are not to be described, when I observed, in this abominable animal, a perfect human figure: the face of it indeed was flat and broad, the nose depressed, the lips large, and the mouth wide. But these differences are common to all savage nations, where the lineaments of the countenance are distorted by the natives suffering their infants to be grovelling on the earth, or by carrying them on their backs, nuzzling with their face against the mother's shoulders. The fore-feet of the *Yahoo* differed from my hands in nothing else but the length of the nails, the coarseness and brownness of the palms, and the hairiness on the backs. There was the same resemblance between our feet, with the same differences, which I knew very well, though the horses did not, because of my shoes and stockings; the same in every part of our bodies, except as to hairiness and colour, which I have already described.

The great difficulty that seemed to stick with the two horses, was, to see the rest of my body so very different from that of a *Yahoo*, for which I was obliged to my clothes, whereof they had no conception. The sorrel nag offered me a root, which he held (after their manner, as we shall describe in its proper place) between his hoof and pastern; I took it in my hand, and having smelt it, returned it to him again as civilly as I could. He brought out of the *Yahoo's* kennel a piece of ass's flesh, but it smelt so offensively that I turned from it with loathing: he then threw it to the *Yahoo*, by whom it was greedily devoured. He afterwards showed me a wisp of hay, and a fetlock full of oats; but I shook my head, to signify, that neither of these were food for me. And indeed, I now apprehended that I must absolutely starve, if I did not get to some of my own species; for as to those filthy *Yahoos*, although there were few greater lovers of mankind, at that time, than myself, yet I confess I never saw any sensitive being so detestable on all accounts; and the more I came near them, the more hateful they grew, while I stayed in that country. This the master horse observed by my behaviour, and therefore sent the *Yahoo* back to his kennel. He then put his fore-hoof to his mouth, at which I was much surprised, although he did it with ease, and with a motion that appeared perfectly natural, and made other signs to know what I would eat; but I could not return him such an answer as he was able to apprehend; and if he had understood me, I did not see how it was possible to contrive any way for finding myself nourishment. While we were thus engaged, I observed a cow passing by, whereupon I pointed to her, and expressed a desire to let me go and milk her. This had its effect; for he led me back into the house, and ordered a mare-servant to open a room, where a good store of milk lay in earthen and wooden vessels, after a very orderly and cleanly manner. She gave me a large bowl full, of which I drank very heartily, and found myself well refreshed.

About noon I saw coming towards the house a kind of vehicle, drawn like a sledge by four *Yahoos*. There was in it an old steed, who seemed to be of quality; he alighted with his hind-feet forward, having by accident got a hurt in his left fore-foot. He came to dine with our horse, who received him with great civility. They dined in the best room, and had oats boiled in milk for the second course, which the old horse eat warm, but the rest cold. Their mangers were placed circular in the middle of the room, and divided into several partitions, round which they sat on their haunches upon bosses of straw. In the middle was a large rack with angles answering to every partition of the manger; so that each horse and mare eat their own hay, and their own mash of oats and milk, with much decency

and regularity. The behaviour of the young colt and foal appeared very modest, and that of the master and mistress extremely cheerful and complaisant to their guest. The gray ordered me to stand by him, and much discourse passed between him and his friend concerning me, as I found by the stranger's often looking on me, and the frequent repetition of the word *Yahoo*.

I happened to wear my gloves, which the master gray observing, seemed perplexed, discovering signs of wonder what I had done to my forefeet; he put his hoof three or four times to them, as if he would signify, that I should reduce them to their former shape, which I presently did, pulling off both my gloves, and putting them into my pocket. This occasioned farther talk, and I saw the company was pleased with my behaviour, whereof I soon found the good effects. I was ordered to speak the few words I understood, and while they were at dinner, the master taught me the names for oats, milk, fire, water, and some others; which I could readily pronounce after him, having from my youth a great facility in learning languages.

When dinner was done, the master horse took me aside, and by signs and words made me understand the concern that he was in, that I had nothing to eat. Oats in their tongue are called *hlunnh*. This word I pronounced two or three times; for although I had refused them at first, yet upon second thoughts, I considered that I could contrive to make of them a kind of bread, which might be sufficient with milk to keep me alive, till I could make my escape to some other country, and to creatures of my own species. The horse immediately ordered a white mare-servant of his family to bring me a good quantity of oats in a sort of wooden tray. These I heated before the fire as well as I could, and rubbed them till the husks came off, which I made a shift to winnow from the grain; I ground and beat them between two stones, then took water, and made them into a paste or cake, which I toasted at the fire, and ate warm with milk. It was at first a very insipid diet, though common enough in many parts of Europe, but grew tolerable by time; and having been often reduced to hard fare in my life, this was not the first experiment I had made how easily nature is satisfied. And I cannot but observe, that I never had one hour's sickness, while I stayed in this island. 'Tis true, I sometimes made a shift to catch a rabbit, or bird, by springes made of *Yahoo's* hairs, and I often gathered wholesome herbs, which I boiled, and eat as salads with my bread, and now and then, for a rarity, I made a little butter, and drank the whey. I was at first at a great loss for salt; but custom soon reconciled the want of it; and I am confident that the frequent use of salt among us is an effect of luxury, and was first introduced only as a provocative to drink; except where it is necessary for preserving of flesh in long voyages, or in places remote from great markets. For we observe no animal to be fond of it but man: and as to myself, when I left this country, it was a great while before I could endure the taste of it in anything that I eat.

This is enough to say upon the subject of my diet, wherewith other travellers fill their books, as if the readers were personally concerned whether we fared well or ill. However, it was necessary to mention this matter, lest the world should think it impossible that I could find sustenance for three years in such a country, and among such inhabitants.

When it grew towards evening, the master horse ordered a place for me to lodge in; it was but six yards from the house, and separated from the stable of the *Yahoos*. Here I got some straw, and covering myself with my own clothes, slept very sound. But I was in a short time better accommodated, as the reader shall know here-after, when I come to treat more particularly about my way of living.

The author studious to learn the language, the Houyhnhnm *his master assists in teaching him. The language described. Several* Houyhnhnms *of quality come out of curiosity to see the author. He gives his master a short account of his voyage.*

My principal endeavour was to learn the language, which my master (for so I shall henceforth call him), and his children, and every servant of his house, were desirous to teach me. For they looked upon it as a prodigy that a brute animal should discover such marks of a rational creature. I pointed to every thing, and enquired the name of it, which I wrote down in my journal-book when I was alone, and corrected my bad accent by desiring those of the family to pronounce it often. In this employment, a sorrel nag, one of the under servants, was very ready to assist me.

In speaking, they pronounce through the nose and throat, and their language approaches nearest to the High-Dutch, or German, of any I know in Europe; but is much more graceful and significant. The Emperor Charles V. made almost the same observation, when he said, that if he were to speak to his horse, it should be in High-Dutch.

The curiosity and impatience of my master were so great, that he spent many hours of his leisure to instruct me. He was convinced (as he afterwards told me) that I must be a *Yahoo,* but my teachableness, civility, and cleanliness, astonished him; which were qualities altogether so opposite to those animals. He was most perplexed about my clothes, reasoning sometimes with himself, whether they were a part of my body: for I never pulled them off till the family were asleep, and got them on before they waked in the morning. My master was eager to learn from whence I came, how I acquired those appearances of reason, which I discovered in all my actions, and to know my story from my own mouth, which he hoped he should soon do by the great proficiency I made in learning and pronouncing their words and sentences. To help my memory, I formed all I learned into the English alphabet, and writ the words down with the translations. This last, after some time, I ventured to do in my master's presence. It cost me much trouble to explain to him what I was doing; for the inhabitants have not the least idea of books or literature.

In about ten weeks time I was able to understand most of his questions, and in three months could give him some tolerable answers. He was extremely curious to know from what part of the country I came, and how I was taught to imitate a rational creature, because the *Yahoos* (whom he saw I exactly resembled in my head, hands, and face, that were only visible), with some appearance of cunning, and the strongest disposition to mischief, were observed to be the most unteachable of all brutes. I answered, that I came over the sea from a far place, with many others of my own kind, in a great hollow vessel made of the bodies of trees: that my companions forced me to land on this coast, and then left me to shift for myself. It was with some difficulty, and by the help of many signs, that I brought him to understand me. He replied, that I must needs be mistaken, or that I *said the thing which was not.* (For they have no word in their language to express lying or falsehood.) He knew it was impossible that there could be a country beyond the sea, or that a parcel of brutes could move a wooden vessel whither they pleased upon water. He was sure no *Houyhnhnm* alive could make such a vessel, nor would trust *Yahoos* to manage it.

The word *Houyhnhnm,* in their tongue, signifies a *horse,* and in its etymology, *the perfection of nature.* I told my master, that I was at a loss for expression, but would improve as

fast as I could; and hoped in a short time I should be able to tell him wonders: he was pleased to direct his own mare, his colt and foal, and the servants of the family, to take all opportunities of instructing me, and every day for two or three hours, he was at the same pains himself. Several horses and mares of quality in the neighbourhood came often to our house upon the report spread of a wonderful *Yahoo,* that could speak like a *Houyhnhnm,* and seemed in his words and actions to discover some glimmerings of reason. These delighted to converse with me; they put many questions, and received such answers, as I was able to return. By all these advantages, I made so great a progress, that in five months from my arrival, I understood whatever was spoke, and could express myself tolerably well.

The *Houyhnhnms* who came to visit my master, out of a design of seeing and talking with me, could hardly believe me to be a right *Yahoo,* because my body had a different covering from others of my kind. They were astonished to observe me without the usual hair or skin, except on my head, face, and hands; but I discovered that secret to my master, upon an accident, which happened about a fortnight before.

I have already told the reader, that every night when the family were gone to bed, it was my custom to strip and cover myself with my clothes: it happened one morning early, that my master sent for me, by the sorrel nag, who was his valet; when he came, I was fast asleep, my clothes fallen off on one side, and my shirt above my waist. I awaked at the noise he made, and observed him to deliver his message in some disorder; after which he went to my master, and in a great fright gave him a very confused account of what he had seen. This I presently discovered; for going as soon as I was dressed, to pay my attendance upon his Honour, he asked me the meaning of what his servant had reported, that I was not the same thing when I slept as I appeared to be at other times; that his valet assured him, some part of me was white, some yellow, at least not so white, and some brown.

I had hitherto concealed the secret of my dress, in order to distinguish myself, as much as possible, from that cursed race of *Yahoos*; but now I found it in vain to do so any longer. Besides, I considered that my clothes and shoes would soon wear out, which already were in a declining condition, and must be supplied by some contrivance from the hides of *Yahoos* or other brutes; whereby the whole secret would be known. I therefore told my master, that in the country from whence I came, those of my kind always covered their bodies with the hairs of certain animals prepared by art, as well for decency, as to avoid the inclemencies of air, both hot and cold; of which, as to my own person, I would give him immediate conviction, if he pleased to command me: only desiring his excuse, if I did not expose those parts, that nature taught us to conceal. He said my discourse was all very strange, but especially the last part; for he could not understand, why nature should teach us to conceal what nature had given. That neither himself nor family were ashamed of any parts of their bodies; but however I might do as I pleased. Whereupon, I first unbuttoned my coat, and pulled it off. I did the same with my waistcoat; I drew off my shoes, stockings, and breeches. I let my shirt down to my waist, and drew up the bottom, fastening it like a girdle about my middle to hide my nakedness.

My master observed the whole performance with great signs of curiosity and admiration. He took up all my clothes in his pastern, one piece after another, and examined them diligently; he then stroked my body very gently, and looked round me several times, after which he said, it was plain I must be a perfect *Yahoo*; but that I differed very much from the rest of my species, in the softness and whiteness and smoothness of my skin, my want of hair in several parts of my body, the shape and shortness of my claws behind and before, and my affectation of walking continually on my two hinder feet. He desired to see no more, and gave me leave to put on my clothes again, for I was shuddering with cold.

I expressed my uneasiness at his giving me so often the appellation of *Yahoo*, an odious animal, for which I had so utter a hatred and contempt. I begged he would forbear applying that word to me, and take the same order in his family, and among his friends whom he suffered to see me. I requested likewise, that the secret of my having a false covering to my body might be known to none but himself, at least as long as my present clothing should last; for as to what the sorrel nag his valet had observed, his Honour might command him to conceal it.

All this my master very graciously consented to, and thus the secret was kept till my clothes began to wear out, which I was forced to supply by several contrivances, that shall hereafter be mentioned. In the meantime, he desired I would go on with my utmost diligence to learn their language, because he was more astonished at my capacity for speech and reason, than at the figure of my body, whether it were covered or no; adding, that he waited with some impatience to hear the wonders which I promised to tell him.

From thenceforward he doubled the pains he had been at to instruct me; he brought me into all company, and made them treat me with civility, because, as he told them, privately, this would put me into good humour, and make me more diverting.

Every day when I waited on him, beside the trouble he was at in teaching, he would ask me several questions concerning myself, which I answered as well as I could; and by these means he had already received some general ideas, though very imperfect. It would be tedious to relate the several steps by which I advanced to a more regular conversation: but the first account I gave of myself in any order and length, was to this purpose:

That I came from a very far country, as I already had attempted to tell him, with about fifty more of my own species; that we travelled upon the seas, in a great hollow vessel made of wood, and larger than his Honour's house. I described the ship to him in the best terms I could, and explained by the help of my handkerchief displayed, how it was driven forward by the wind. That upon a quarrel among us, I was set on shore on this coast, where I walked forward without knowing whither, till he delivered me from the persecution of those execrable *Yahoos*. He asked me, who made the ship, and how it was possible that the *Houyhnhnms* of my country would leave it to the management of brutes? My answer was, that I durst proceed no further in my relation, unless he would give me his word and honour that he would not be offended, and then I would tell him the wonders I had so often promised. He agreed; and I went on by assuring him, that the ship was made by creatures like myself, who in all the countries I had travelled, as well as in my own were the only governing, rational animals; and that upon my arrival hither, I was as much astonished to see the *Houyhnhnms* act like rational beings, as he or his friends could be in finding some marks of reason in a creature he was pleased to call a *Yahoo*, to which I owned my resemblance in every part, but could not account for their degenerate and brutal nature. I said farther, that if good fortune ever restored me to my native country, to relate my travels hither, as I resolved to do, everybody would believe that I *said the thing which was not*; that I invented the story out of my own head; and with all possible respect to himself, his family and friends, and under his promise of not being offended, our

countrymen would hardly think it probable, that a *Houyhnhnm* should be the presiding creature of a nation, and a *Yahoo* the brute.

CHAP. IV

The Houyhnhnm's *notion of truth and falsehood. The author's discourse disapproved by his master. The author gives a more particular account of himself, and the accidents of his voyage.*

My master heard me with great appearances of uneasiness in his countenance, because *doubting*, or *not believing*, are so little known in this country, that the inhabitants cannot tell how to behave themselves under such circumstances. And I remember in frequent discourses with my master concerning the nature of manhood, in other parts of the world, having occasion to talk of *lying* and *false representation*, it was with much difficulty that he comprehended what I meant, although he had otherwise a most acute judgment. For he argued thus: that the use of speech was to make us understand one another, and to receive information of facts; now if any one *said the thing which was not*, these ends were defeated; because I cannot properly be said to understand him; and I am so far from receiving information, that he leaves me worse than in ignorance, for I am led to believe a thing black when it is white, and short when it is long. And these were all the notions he had concerning that faculty of *lying*, so perfectly well understood, and so universally practised, among human creatures.

To return from this digression; when I asserted that the *Yahoos* were the only governing animals in my country, which my master said was altogether past his conception, he desired to know, whether we had *Houyhnhnms* among us, and what was their employment: I told him, we had great numbers, that in summer they grazed in the fields, and in winter were kept in houses, with hay and oats, where *Yahoo* servants were employed to rub their skins smooth, comb their manes, pick their feet, serve them with food, and make their beds. I understand you well, said my master, it is now very plain, from all you have spoken, that whatever share of reason the *Yahoos* pretend to, the *Houyhnhnms* are your masters; I heartily wish our *Yahoos* would be so tractable. I begged his Honour would please to excuse me from proceeding any farther, because I was very certain that the account he expected from me would be highly displeasing. But he insisted in commanding me to let him know the best and the worst: I told him, he should be obeyed. I owned, that the *Houyhnhnms* among us, whom we called horses, were the most generous and comely animals we had, that they excelled in strength and swiftness; and when they belonged to persons of quality, employed in travelling, racing, or drawing chariots, they were treated with much kindness and care, till they fell into diseases, or became foundered in the feet; and then they were sold, and used to all kind of drudgery till they died; after which their skins were stripped and sold for what they were worth, and their bodies left to be devoured by dogs and birds of prey. But the common race of horses had not so good fortune, being kept by farmers and carriers, and other mean people, who put them to greater labour, and fed them worse. I described, as well as I could, our way of riding, the shape and use of a bridle, a saddle, a spur, and a whip, of harness and wheels. I added, that we fastened plates of a certain hard substance called iron at the bottom of their feet, to preserve their hoofs from being broken by the stony ways on which we often travelled.

My master, after some expressions of great indignation, wondered how we dared to venture upon a *Houyhnhnm's* back, for he was sure, that the weakest servant in his house would be able to shake off the strongest *Yahoo*, or by lying down, and rolling on his back, squeeze the brute to death. I answered, that our horses were trained up from three or four years old to the several uses we intended them for; that if any of them proved intolerably vicious, they were employed for carriages; that they were severely beaten while t h e y were young, for any mischievous tricks; that the males, designed for common use of riding or draught, were generally castrated about two years after their birth, to take down their spirits, and make them more tame and gentle; that they were indeed sensible of rewards and punishments; but his Honour would please to consider, that they had not in the least tincture of reason any more than the *Yahoos* in this country.

It put me to the pains of many circumlocutions to give my master a right idea of what I spoke; for their language doth not abound in variety of words, because their wants and passions are fewer than among us. But it is impossible to express his noble resentment at our savage treatment of the *Houyhnhnm* race, particularly after I had explained the manner and use of castrating horses among us, to hinder them from propagating their kind, and to render them more servile. He said, if it were possible there could be any country where *Yahoos* alone were endued with reason, they certainly must be the governing animal, because reason will in time always prevail against brutal strength. But, considering the frame of our bodies, and especially of mine, he thought no creature of equal bulk was so ill-contrived, for employing that reason in the common offices of life; whereupon he desired to know whether those among whom I lived resembled me or the *Yahoos* of his country. I assured him, that I was as well shaped as most of my age; but the younger and the females were much more soft and tender, and the skins of the latter generally as white as milk. He said, I differed indeed from other *Yahoos*, being much more cleanly, and not altogether so deformed, but, in point of real advantage, he thought I differed for the worse. That my nails were of no use either to my fore or hinder-feet; as to my fore-feet, he could not properly call them by that name, for he never observed me to walk upon them; that they were too soft to bear the ground; that I generally went with them uncovered, neither was the covering I sometimes wore on them, of the same shape, or so strong as that on my feet behind. That I could not walk with any security, for if either of my hinder-feet slipped, I must inevitably fall. He then began to find fault with other parts of my body, the flatness of my face, the prominence of my nose, my eyes placed directly in front, so that I could not look on either side without turning my head: that I was not able to feed myself, without lifting one of my fore-feet to my mouth: and therefore nature had placed those joints to answer that necessity. He knew not what could be the use of those several clefts and divisions in my feet behind; that these were too soft to bear the hardness and sharpness of stones without a covering made from the skin of some other brute; that my whole body wanted a fence against heat and cold, which I was forced to put on and off every day with tediousness and trouble. And lastly, that he observed every animal in this country naturally to abhor the *Yahoos*, whom the weaker avoided, and the stronger drove from them. So that supposing us to have the gift of reason, he could not see how it were possible to cure that natural antipathy which every creature discovered against us; nor consequently, how we could tame and render them serviceable. However, he would, (as he said,) debate the matter no farther, because he was more desirous to know my own story, the country where I was born, and the several actions and events of my life before I came hither.

I assured him, how extremely desirous I was that he should be satisfied on every point; but I doubted much, whether it would be possible for me to explain myself on several subjects whereof his Honour could have no conception, because I saw nothing in his country to which I could resemble them. That however, I would do my best, and strive to express myself by similitudes, humbly desiring his assistance when I wanted proper words; which he was pleased to promise me.

I said, my birth was of honest parents in an island called England, which was remote from this country, as many days' journey as the strongest of his Honour's servants could travel in the annual course of the sun. That I was bred a surgeon, whose trade it is to cure wounds and hurts in the body, got by accident or violence; that my country was governed by a female man, whom we called a Queen. That I left it to get riches, whereby I might maintain myself and family when I should return. That, in my last voyage, I was Commander of the ship, and had about fifty *Yahoos* under me, many of which died at sea, and I was forced to supply them by others picked out from several nations. That our ship was twice in danger of being sunk; the first time by a great storm, and the second, by striking against a rock. Here my master interposed, by asking me, how I could persuade strangers out of different countries to venture with me, after the losses I had sustained, and the hazards I had run. I said, they were fellows of desperate fortunes, forced to fly from the places of their birth, on account of their poverty or their crimes. Some were undone by lawsuits; others spent all they had in drinking, whoring and gaming; others fled for treason; many for murder, theft, poisoning, robbery, perjury, forgery, coining false money, for committing rapes or sodomy, for flying from their colours, or deserting to the enemy, and most of them had broken prison; none of these durst return to their native countries for fear of being hanged, or of starving in a jail; and therefore were under the necessity of seeking a livelihood in other places.

During this discourse, my master was pleased to interrupt me several times; I had made use of many circumlocutions in describing to him the nature of the several crimes, for which most of our crew had been forced to fly their country. This labour took up several days' conversation, before he was able to comprehend me. He was wholly at a loss to know what could be the use or necessity of practising those vices. To clear up which I endeavoured to give some ideas of the desire of power and riches, of the terrible effects of lust, intemperance, malice and envy. All this I was forced to define and describe by putting of cases, and making of suppositions. After which, like one whose imagination was struck with something never seen or heard of before, he would lift up his eyes with amazement and indignation. Power, government, war, law, punishment, and a thousand other things had no terms, wherein that language could express them, which made the difficulty almost insuperable to give my master any conception of what I meant. But being of an excellent understanding, much improved by contemplation and converse, he at last arrived at a competent knowledge of what human nature in our parts of the world is capable to perform, and desired I would give him some particular account of that land which we call Europe, but especially of my own country.

CHAP. V

The author, at his master's commands, informs him of the state of England. The causes of war among the princes of Europe. The author begins to explain the English constitution.

The reader may please to observe, that the following extract of many conversations I had with my master, contains a summary of the most material points, which were discoursed at several times for above two years; his Honour often desiring fuller satisfaction as I farther improved in the *Houyhnhnm* tongue. I laid before him, as well as I could, the whole state of Europe; I discoursed of trade and manufactures, of arts and sciences; and the answers I gave to all the questions he made, as they arose upon several subjects, were a fund of conversation not to be exhausted. But I shall here only set down the substance of what passed between us concerning my own country, reducing it into order as well as I can, without any regard to time or other circumstances, while I strictly adhere to truth. My only concern is, that I shall hardly be able to do justice to my master's arguments and expressions, which must needs suffer by my want of capacity, as well as by a translation into our barbarous English.

In obedience, therefore, to his Honour's commands, I related to him the Revolution under the Prince of Orange; the long war with France entered into by the said prince, and renewed by his successor, the present Queen, wherein the greatest powers of Christendom were engaged, and which still continued: I computed at his request, that about a million of *Yahoos* might have been killed in the whole progress of it; and perhaps a hundred or more cities taken, and five times as many ships burnt or sunk.

He asked me what were the usual causes or motives that made one country go to war with another. I answered they were innumerable; but I should only mention a few of the chief. Sometimes the ambition of princes, who never think they have land or people enough to govern; sometimes the corruption of ministers, who engage their master in a war in order to stifle or divert the clamour of the subjects against their evil administration. Difference in opinions hath cost many millions of lives: for instance, whether flesh be bread, or bread be flesh; whether the juice of a certain berry be blood or wine; whether whistling be a vice or a virtue; whether it be better to kiss a post, or throw it into the fire; what is the best colour for a coat, whether black, white, red, or gray; and whether it should be long or short, narrow or wide, dirty or clean; with many more. Neither are any wars so furious and bloody, or of so long continuance, as those occasioned by difference in opinion, especially if it be in things indifferent.

Sometimes the quarrel between two princes is to decide which of them shall dispossess a third of his dominions, where neither of them pretend to any right. Sometimes one prince quarrelleth with another, for fear the other should quarrel with him. Sometimes a war is entered upon, because the enemy is too strong, and sometimes because he is too weak. Sometimes our neighbours want the things which we have, or have the things which we want; and we both fight, till they take ours or give us theirs. It is a very justifiable cause of a war to invade a country after the people have been wasted by famine, destroyed by pestilence, or embroiled by factions among themselves. It is justifiable to enter into war against our nearest ally, when one of his towns lies convenient for us, or a territory of land, that would render our dominions round and compact. If a prince sends forces into a nation, where the people are poor and ignorant, he may lawfully put half of them to death, and make slaves of the rest, in order to civilize and reduce them from their barbarous way of living. It is a very kingly, honourable, and frequent practice, when one prince desires the assistance of another to secure him against an invasion, that the assistant, when he hath driven out the invader, should seize on the dominions himself, and kill, imprison or banish the prince he came to relieve. Alliance by blood or marriage, is a frequent cause of war between princes; and the nearer the kindred is, the greater is their disposition to quarrel: poor nations are hungry, and rich nations are proud; and pride and hunger will ever be at variance. For these reasons, the trade of a soldier is held the most honourable of

all others; because a soldier is a *Yahoo* hired to kill in cold blood as many of his own species, who have never offended him, as possibly he can.

There is likewise a kind of beggarly princes in Europe, not able to make war by themselves, who hire out their troops to richer nations, for so much a day to each man; of which they keep three fourths to themselves, and it is the best part of their maintenance; such are those in many northern parts of Europe.

What you have told me, (said my master) upon the subject of war, does indeed discover most admirably the effects of that reason you pretend to: however, it is happy that the shame is greater than the danger; and that nature hath left you utterly uncapable of doing much mischief.

For your mouths lying flat with your faces, you can hardly bite each other to any purpose, unless by consent. Then as to the claws upon your feet before and behind, they are so short and tender, that one of our *Yahoos* would rive a dozen of yours before him. And therefore in recounting the numbers of those who have been killed in battle, I cannot but think that you have *said the thing which is not*.

I could not forbear shaking my head, and smiling a little at his ignorance. And being no stranger to the art of war, I gave him a description of cannons, culverins, muskets, carabines, pistols, bullets, powder, swords, bayonets, battles, sieges, retreats, attacks, undermines, countermines, bombardments, sea fights; ships sunk with a thousand men, twenty thousand killed on each side; dying groans, limbs flying in the air, smoke, noise, confusion, trampling to death under horses' feet; flight, pursuit, victory; fields strewed with carcases left for food to dogs, and wolves, and birds of prey; plundering, stripping, ravishing, burning and destroying. And to set forth the valour of my own dear countrymen, I assured him, that I had seen them blow up a hundred enemies **at** once in a siege, and as many in a ship, and beheld the dead bodies drop down in pieces from the clouds, to the great diversion of the spectators.

I was going on to more particulars, when my master commanded me silence. He said, whoever understood the nature of *Yahoos* might easily believe it possible for so vile an animal, to be capable of every action I had named, if their strength and cunning equalled their malice. But as my discourse had increased his abhorrence of the whole species, so he found it gave him a disturbance in his mind, to which he was wholly a stranger before. He thought his ears being used to such abominable words, might by degrees admit them with less detestation. That although he hated the *Yahoos* of this country, yet he no more blamed them for their odious qualities, than he did a *gnnayh* (a bird of prey) for its cruelty, or a sharp stone for cutting his hoof. But when a creature pretending to reason, could be capable of such enormities, he dreaded lest the corruption of that faculty might be worse than brutality itself. He seemed therefore confident, that instead of reason, we were only possessed of some quality fitted to increase our natural vices; as the reflection from a troubled stream returns the image of an ill-shapen body, not only larger, but more distorted.

He added, that he had heard too much upon the subject of war, both in this, and some former discourses. There was another point which a little perplexed him at present. I had informed him, that some of our crew left their country on account of being ruined by *Law*; that I had already explained the meaning of the word; but he was at a loss how it should come to pass, that the law which was intended for every man's preservation, should be any man's ruin. Therefore he desired to be farther satisfied what I meant by law, and the dispensers thereof, according to the present practice in my own country; because he thought nature and reason were suffi-

cient guides for a reasonable animal, as we pretended to be, in showing us what we ought to do, and what to avoid.

I assured his Honour, that law was a science wherein I had not much conversed, further than by employing advocates, in vain, upon some injustices that had been done me: however, I would give him all the satisfaction I was able.

I said, there was a society of men among us, bred up from their youth in the art of proving by words multiplied for the purpose, that white is black, and black is white, according as they are paid. To this society all the rest of the people are slaves. For example, if my neighbour hath a mind to my cow, he hires a lawyer to prove that he ought to have my cow from me. I must then hire another to defend my right, it being against all rules of law that any man should be allowed to speak for himself. Now in this case, I, who am the right owner, lie under two great disadvantages. First, my lawyer, being practised almost from his cradle in defending falsehood, is quite out of his element when he would be an advocate for justice, which as an office unnatural, he always attempts with great awkwardness, if not with ill-will. The second disadvantage is, that my lawyer must proceed with great caution, or else he will be reprimanded by the judges, and abhorred by his brethren, as one that would lessen the practice of the law. And therefore I have but two methods to preserve my cow. The first is, to gain over my adversary's lawyer with a double fee; who will then betray his client, by insinuating that he hath justice on his side. The second way is for my lawyer to make my cause appear as unjust as he can, by allowing the cow to belong to my adversary: and this, if it be skilfully done, will certainly bespeak the favour of the bench.

Now, your Honour is to know, that these judges are persons appointed to decide all controversies of property, as well as for the trial of criminals, and picked out from the most dexterous lawyers, who are grown old or lazy, and having been biassed all their lives against truth and equity, lie under such a fatal necessity of favouring fraud, perjury, and oppression, that I have known several of them refuse a large bribe from the side where justice lay, rather than injure the faculty, by doing any thing unbecoming their nature or their office.

It is a maxim among these lawyers, that whatever hath been done before, may legally be done again: and therefore they take special care to record all the decisions formerly made against common justice, and the general reason of mankind. These, under the name of *precedents*, they produce as authorities, to justify the most iniquitous opinions; and the judges never fail of directing accordingly.

In pleading, they studiously avoid entering into the merits of the cause; but are loud, violent, and tedious in dwelling upon all circumstances which are not to the purpose. For instance, in the case already mentioned: they never desire to know what claim or title my adversary hath to my cow; but whether the said cow were red or black; her horns long or short; whether the field I graze her in be round or square; whether she was milked at home or abroad; what diseases she is subject to, and the like; after which they consult precedents, adjourn the cause from time to time, and in ten, twenty, or thirty years, come to an issue.

It is likewise to be observed, that this society hath a peculiar cant and jargon of their own, that no other mortal can understand, and wherein all their laws are written, which they take special care to multiply; whereby they have wholly confounded the very essence of truth and falsehood, of right and wrong; so that it will take thirty years to decide whether the field left me by my ancestors for six generations belongs to me, or to a stranger three hundred miles off.

In the trial of persons accused for crimes against the state, the method is much more short and commendable: the judge first sends to sound the disposition of those in power, after which he can easily hang or save the criminal, strictly preserving all due forms of law.

Here my master interposing, said it was a pity, that creatures endowed with such prodigious abilities of mind as these lawyers, by the description I gave of them, must certainly be, were not rather encouraged to be instructors of others in wisdom and knowledge. In answer to which, I assured his Honour, that in all points out of their own trade, they were usually the most ignorant and stupid generation among us, the most despicable in common conversation, avowed enemies to all knowledge and learning, and equally disposed to pervert the general reason of mankind in every other subject of discourse, as in that of their own profession.

CHAP. VI

A continuation of the state of England, *under Queen* Anne. *The character of a first minister in the courts of* Europe.

My master was yet wholly at a loss to understand what motives could incite this race of lawyers to perplex, disquiet, and weary themselves, and engage in a confederacy of injustice, merely for the sake of injuring their fellow-animals; neither could he comprehend what I meant in saying they did it for hire. Whereupon I was at much pains to describe to him the use of money, the materials it was made of, and the value of the metals; that when a *Yahoo* had got a great store of this precious substance, he was able to purchase whatever he had a mind to; the finest clothing, the noblest houses, great tracts of land, the most costly meats and drinks, and have his choice of the most beautiful females. Therefore since money alone was able to perform all these feats, our *Yahoos* thought they could never have enough of it to spend or to save, as they found themselves inclined from their natural bent either to profusion or avarice. That the rich man enjoyed the fruit of the poor man's labour, and the latter were a thousand to one in proportion to the former. That the bulk of our people were forced to live miserably, by labouring every day for small wages to make a few live plentifully. I enlarged myself much on these and many other particulars to the same purpose; but his Honour was still to seek; for he went upon a supposition that all animals had a title to their share in the productions of the earth, and especially those who presided over the rest. Therefore he desired I would let him know, what these costly meats were, and how any of us happened to want them. Whereupon I enumerated as many sorts as came into my head, with the various methods of dressing them, which could not be done without sending vessels by sea to every part of the world, as well for liquors to drink, as for sauces, and innumerable other conveniences. I assured him, that this whole globe of earth must be at least three times gone round, before one of our better female *Yahoos* could get her breakfast, or a cup to put it in. He said, that must needs be a miserable country which cannot furnish food for its own inhabitants. But what he chiefly wondered at, was how such vast tracts of ground as I described should be wholly without fresh water, and the people put to the necessity of sending over the sea for drink. I replied, that England (the dear place of my nativity) was computed to produce three times the quantity of food, more than its inhabitants are able to consume, as well as liquors extracted from grain, or pressed out of the fruit of certain trees, which made excellent drink, and the same proportion in every other convenience of life. But, in order to feed the luxury and intemperance of the males, and the vanity of the females, we sent away the greatest part of our necessary things to other countries, from whence in re-

turn we brought the materials of diseases, folly, and vice, to spend among ourselves. Hence it follows of necessity, that vast numbers of our people are compelled to seek their livelihood by begging, robbing, stealing, cheating, pimping, forswearing, flattering, suborning, forging, gaming, lying, fawning, hectoring, voting, scribbling, star-gazing, poisoning, whoring, canting, libelling, freethinking, and the like occupations: every one of which terms, I was at much pains to make him understand.

That wine was not imported among us from foreign countries, to supply the want of water or other drinks, but because it was a sort of liquid which made us merry, by putting us out of our senses; diverted all melancholy thoughts, begat wild extravagant imaginations in the brain, raised our hopes, and banished our fears, suspended every office of reason for a time, and deprived us of the use of our limbs, till we fell into a profound sleep; although it must be confessed, that we always awaked sick and dispirited and that the use of this liquor filled us with diseases, which made our lives uncomfortable and short.

But beside all this, the bulk of our people supported themselves by furnishing the necessities or conveniences of life to the rich, and to each other. For instance, when I am at home and dressed as I ought to be, I carry on my body the workmanship of an hundred tradesmen; the building and furniture of my house employ as many more, and five times the number to adorn my wife.

I was going on to tell him of another sort of people, who get their livelihood by attending the sick, having upon some occasions informed his Honour that many of my crew had died of diseases. But here it was with the utmost difficulty, that I brought him to apprehend what I meant. He could easily conceive, that a *Houyhnhnm* grew weak and heavy a few days before his death, or by some accident might hurt a limb. But that nature, who works all things to perfection, should suffer any pains to breed in our bodies, he thought impossible, and desired to know the reason of so unaccountable an evil. I told him, we fed on a thousand things which operated contrary to each other; that we eat when we were not hungry, and drank without the provocation of thirst; that we sat whole nights drinking strong liquors without eating a bit, which disposed us to sloth, inflamed our bodies, and precipitated or prevented digestion. That prostitute female *Yahoos* acquired a certain malady, which bred rottenness in the bones of those who fell into their embraces; that this and many other diseases, were propagated from father to son, so that great numbers come into the world with complicated maladies upon them; that it would be endless to give him a catalogue of all diseases incident to human bodies; for they would not be fewer than five or six hundred, spread over every limb and joint; in short, every part, external and intestine, having diseases appropriated to each. To remedy which, there was a sort of people bred up among us, in the profession or pretence of curing the sick. And because I had some skill in the faculty, I would in gratitude to his Honour, let him know the whole mystery and method by which they proceed.

Their fundamental is, that all diseases arise from repletion, from whence they conclude, that a great evacuation of the body is necessary, either through the natural passage, or upwards at the mouth. Their next business is, from herbs, minerals, gums, oils, shells, salts, juices, seaweed, excrements, barks of trees, serpents, toads, frogs, spiders, dead men's flesh and bones, birds, beasts and fishes, to form a composition for smell and taste the most abominable, nauseous and detestable, they can possibly contrive, which the stomach immediately rejects with loathing; and this they call a vomit; or else from the same store-house, with some other poisonous additions, they command us to take in at the orifice above or below (just as the physician then happens to be disposed) a medicine equally annoying and disgustful to the bowels; which relaxing the belly, drives down all before it, and this they call a purge, or a clyster. For nature (as the physicians allege) having intended the superior anterior orifice only for the intromission of solids and liquids, and the inferior posterior for ejection, these artists ingeniously considering that in all diseases nature is forced out of her seat, therefore to replace her in it, the body must be treated in a manner directly contrary, by interchanging the use of each orifice; forcing solids and liquids in at the anus, and making evacuations at the mouth.

But, besides real diseases, we are subject to many that are only imaginary, for which the physicians have invented imaginary cures; these have their several names, and so have the drugs that are proper for them, and with these our female *Yahoos* are always infested.

One great excellency in this tribe is their skill at prognostics, wherein they seldom fail; their predictions in real diseases, when they rise to any degree of malignity, generally portending death, which is always in their power, when recovery is not: and therefore, upon any unexpected signs of amendment, after they have pronounced their sentence, rather than be accused as false prophets, they know how to approve their sagacity to the world by a seasonable dose.

They are likewise of special use to husbands and wives, who are grown weary of their mates; to eldest sons, to great ministers of state, and often to princes.

I had formerly upon occasion discoursed with my master upon the nature of government in general, and particularly of our own excellent constitution, deservedly the wonder and envy of the whole world. But having here accidentally mentioned a minister of state, he commanded me some time after to inform him, what species of *Yahoo* I particularly meant by that appellation.

I told him, that a First or Chief Minister of State, who was the person I intended to describe, was a creature wholly exempt from joy and grief, love and hatred, pity and anger; at least makes use of no other passions but a violent desire of wealth, power, and titles; that he applies his words to all uses, except to the indication of his mind; that he never tells a truth, but with an intent that you should take it for a lie; nor a lie, but with a design that you should take it for a truth; that those he speaks worst of behind their backs, are in the surest way of preferment; and whenever he begins to praise you to others or to yourself, you are from that day forlorn. The worst mark you can receive is a promise, especially when it is confirmed with an oath; after which every wise man retires, and gives over all hopes.

There are three methods by which a man may rise to be chief minister: the first is, by knowing how with prudence to dispose of a wife, a daughter, or a sister: the second, by betraying or undermining his predecessor: and the third is, by a furious zeal in public assemblies against the corruptions of the court. But a wise prince would rather choose to employ those who practise the last of these methods; because such zealots prove always the most obsequious and subservient to the will and passions of their master. That these ministers having all employments at their disposal, preserve themselves in power, by bribing the majority of a senate or great council; and at last, by an expedient called an Act of Indemnity (whereof I described the nature to him) they secure themselves from after-reckonings, and retire from the public, laden with the spoils of the nation.

The palace of a chief minister, is a seminary to breed up others in his own trade: the pages, lackeys, and porters, by imitating their master, become ministers of state in their several districts, and learn to excel in the three principal ingredients, of insolence, lying, and bribery. Accordingly, they have a subaltern court paid to them by persons of the best rank, and sometimes by the force of dexterity and impudence, arrive through several gradations to be successors to their lord.

He is usually governed by a decayed wench, or favourite footman, who are the tunnels through which all graces are conveyed, and may properly be called, in the last resort, the governors of the kingdom.

One day in discourse my master, having heard me mention the nobility of my country, was pleased to make me a compliment which I could not pretend to deserve: that he was sure I must have been born of some noble family, because I far exceeded in shape, colour, and cleanliness, all the *Yahoos* of his nation, although I seemed to fail in strength and agility, which must be imputed to my different way of living from those other brutes; and besides, I was not only endowed with the faculty of speech, but likewise with some rudiments of reason, to a degree, that with all his acquaintance I passed for a prodigy.

He made me observe, that among the *Houyhnhnms*, the white, the sorrel, and the iron-gray, were not so exactly shaped as the bay, the dapple-gray, and the black; nor born with equal talents of mind, or a capacity to improve them; and therefore continued always in the condition of servants, without ever aspiring to match out of their own race, which in that country would be reckoned monstrous and unnatural.

I made his Honour my most humble acknowledgments for the good opinion he was pleased to conceive of me; but assured him at the same time, that my birth was of the lower sort, having been born of plain honest parents, who were just able to give me a tolerable education; that nobility among us was altogether a different thing from the idea he had of it; that our young noblemen are bred from their childhood in idleness and luxury; that as soon as years will permit, they consume their vigour, and contract odious diseases among lewd females; and when their fortunes are almost ruined, they marry some woman of mean birth, disagreeable person, and unsound constitution, merely for the sake of money, whom they hate and despise. That the productions of such marriages are generally scrofulous, ricketty, or deformed children; by which means the family seldom continues above three generations, unless the wife takes care to provide a healthy father among her neighbours or domestics, in order to improve and continue the breed. That a weak diseased body, a meagre countenance, and sallow complexion, are the true marks of noble blood; and a healthy robust appearance is so disgraceful in a man of quality, that the world concludes his real father to have been a groom or a coachman. The imperfections of his mind run parallel with those of his body, being a composition of spleen, dullness, ignorance, caprice, sensuality and pride.

Without the consent of this illustrious body, no law can be enacted, repealed, or altered; and these nobles have likewise the decision of all our possessions without appeal.

CHAP. VII

The author's great love of his native country. His master's observations upon the constitution and administration of England, as described by the author, with parallel cases and comparisons. His master's observations upon human nature.

The reader may be disposed to wonder how I could prevail on myself to give so free a representation of my own species, among a race of mortals who are already too apt to conceive the vilest opinion of human kind, from that entire congruity betwixt me and their *Yahoos*. But I must freely confess, that the many virtues of those excellent quadrupeds placed in opposite view to human corruptions, had so far opened mine eyes and enlarged my understanding, that I began to view the actions and passions of man in a very different light, and to think the honour of my own kind not worth managing, which, besides, it was impossible for me to do before a person of so acute a judgment as my master, who daily convinced me of a thousand faults in myself, whereof I had not the least perception before, and which with us would never be numbered even among human infirmities. I had likewise learned from his example an utter detestation of all falsehood or disguise, and truth appeared so amiable to me, that I determined upon sacrificing every thing to it.

Let me deal so candidly with the reader, as to confess, that there was yet a much stronger motive for the freedom I took in my representation of things. I had not been a year in this country, before I contracted such a love and veneration for the inhabitants, that I entered on a firm resolution never to return to human kind, but to pass the rest of my life among these admirable *Houyhnhnms* in the contemplation and practice of every virtue; where I could have no example or incitement to vice. But it was decreed by fortune, my perpetual enemy, that so great a felicity should not fall to my share. However, it is now some comfort to reflect, that in what I said of my countrymen, I extenuated their faults as much as I durst before so strict an examiner, and upon every article gave as favourable a turn as the matter would bear. For, indeed, who is there alive that will not be swayed by his bias and partiality to the place of his birth?

I have related the substance of several conversations I had with my master, during the greatest part of the time I had the honour to be in his service, but have indeed for brevity's sake omitted much more than is here set down.

When I had answered all his questions, and his curiosity seemed to be fully satisfied; he sent for me one morning early, and commanding me to sit down at some distance (an honour which he had never before conferred upon me), he said, he had been very seriously considering my whole story, as far as it related both to myself and my country; that he looked upon us as a sort of animals to whose share, by what accident he could not conjecture, some small pittance of reason had fallen, whereof we made no other use than by its assistance to aggravate our natural corruptions, and to acquire new ones, which nature had not given us. That we disarmed ourselves of the few abilities she had bestowed, had been very successful in multiplying our original wants, and seemed to spend our whole lives in vain endeavours to supply them by our own inventions. That as to myself, it was manifest I had neither the strength or agility of a common *Yahoo*; that I walked infirmly on my hinder feet; had found out a contrivance to make my claws of no use or defence, and to remove the hair from my chin, which was intended as a shelter from the sun and the weather. Lastly, that I could neither run with speed, nor climb trees like my brethren (as he called them) the *Yahoos* in this country.

That our institutions of government and law were plainly owing to our gross defects in reason, and by consequence, in virtue; because reason alone is sufficient to govern a rational creature; which was therefore a character we had no pretence to challenge, even from the account I had given of my own people; although he manifestly perceived, that in order to favour them, I had concealed many particulars, and often *said the thing which was not*.

He was the more confirmed in this opinion, because he observed, that as I agreed in every feature of my body with other *Yahoos*, except where it was to my real disadvantage in point of strength, speed and activity, the shortness of my claws, and some other particulars where nature had no part; so from the representation I had given him of our lives, our manners, and our actions, he found as near a resemblance in the disposition of our minds. He said the *Yahoos* were known to hate one another more than they did any different species of animals; and the reason usually assigned was, the odiousness of their own shapes, which all could see in the rest, but not in themselves. He had therefore begun to think it not unwise in us to cover our bodies, and by that invention conceal many of our own deformities from each other, which would else be hardly supportable. But he now found he had been mistaken, and that the dissensions of those brutes in his country were owing to the same cause with ours, as I had described them. For if (said he), you throw among five *Yahoos* as much food as would be sufficient for fifty, they will, instead of eating peaceably, fall together by the ears, each single one impatient to have all to itself; and therefore a servant was usually employed to stand by while they were feeding abroad, and those kept at home were tied at a distance from each other: that if a cow died of age or accident, before a *Houyhnhnm* could secure it for his own *Yahoos*, those in the neighbourhood would come in herds to seize it, and then would ensue such a battle as I had described, with terrible wounds made by their claws on both sides, although they seldom were able to kill one another, for want of such convenient instruments of death as we had invented. At other times the like battles have been fought between the *Yahoos* of several neighbourhoods without any visible cause; those of one district watching all opportunities to surprise the next before they are prepared. But if they find their project hath miscarried, they return home, and, for want of enemies, engage in what I call a civil war among themselves.

That in some fields of his country,

there are certain shining stones of several colours, whereof the *Yahoos* are violently fond, and when part of these stones is fixed in the earth, as it sometimes happeneth, they will dig with their claws for whole days to get them out, then carry them away, and hide them by heaps in their kennels; but still looking round with great caution, for fear their comrades should find out their treasure. My master said, he could never discover the reason of this unnatural appetite, or how these stones could be of any use to a *Yahoo*; but now he believed it might proceed from the same principle of avarice which I had ascribed to mankind: that he had once, by way of experiment, privately removed a heap of these stones from the place where one of his *Yahoos* had buried it: whereupon, the sordid animal missing his treasure, by his loud lamenting brought the whole herd to the place, there miserably howled, then fell to biting and tearing the rest, began to pine away, would neither eat, nor sleep, nor work, till he ordered a servant privately to convey the stones into the same hole, and hide them as before; which when his *Yahoo* had found, he presently recovered his spirits and good humour, but took care to remove them to a better hiding place, and hath ever since been a very serviceable brute.

My master farther assured me, which I also observed myself, that in the fields where the shining stones abound, the fiercest and most frequent battles are fought, occasioned by perpetual inroads of the neighbouring *Yahoos*.

He said, it was common when two *Yahoos* discovered such a stone in a field, and were contending which of them should be the proprietor, a third would take the advantage, and carry it away from them both; which my master would needs contend to have some kind of resemblance with our suits at law; wherein I thought it for our credit not to undeceive him; since the decision he mentioned was much more equitable than many decrees among us; because the plaintiff and defendant there lost nothing beside the stone they contended for, whereas our courts of equity would never have dismissed the cause while either of them had any thing left.

My master continuing his discourse, said, there was nothing that rendered the *Yahoos* more odious, than their undistinguishing appetite to devour every thing that came in their way, whether herbs, roots, berries, the corrupted flesh of animals, or all mingled together: and it was peculiar in their temper, that they were fonder of what they could get by rapine or stealth at a greater distance, than much better food provided for them at home. If their prey held out, they would eat till they were ready to burst, after which nature had pointed out to them a certain root that gave them a general evacuation.

There was also another kind of root very juicy, but somewhat rare and difficult to be found, which the *Yahoos* sought for with much eagerness, and would suck it with great delight; it produced in them the same effects that wine hath upon us. It would make them sometimes hug, and sometimes tear one another; they would howl and grin, and chatter, and reel, and tumble, and then fall asleep in the mud.

I did indeed observe, that the *Yahoos* were the only animals in this country subject to any diseases; which, however, were much fewer than horses have among us, and contracted not by any ill-treatment they meet with, but by the nastiness and greediness of that sordid brute. Neither has their language any more than a general appellation for those maladies, which is borrowed from the name of the beast, and called *Hnea-Yahoo*, or *Yahoo's evil*, and the cure prescribed is a mixture of their own dung and urine forcibly put down the *Yahoo's* throat. This I have since often known to have been taken with success, and do here freely recommend it to my countrymen, for the public good, as an admirable specific against all diseases produced by repletion.

As to learning, government, arts, manufactures, and the like, my master confessed he could find little or no resemblance between the *Yahoos* of that country and those in ours. For he only meant to observe what parity there was in our natures. He had heard indeed some curious *Houyhnhnms* observe, that in most herds there was a sort of ruling *Yahoo* (as among us there is generally some leading or principal stag in a park), who was always more deformed in body, and mischievous in disposition, than any of the rest. That this leader had usually a favourite as like himself as he could get, whose employment was to lick his master's feet and posteriors, and drive the female *Yahoos* to his kennel; for which he was now and then rewarded with a piece of ass's flesh. This favourite is hated by the whole herd, and therefore to protect himself, keeps always near the person of his leader. He usually continues in office till a worse can be found; but the very moment he is discarded, his successor, at the head of all the *Yahoos* in that district, young and old, male and female, come in a body, and discharge their excrements upon him from head to foot. But how far this might be applicable to our courts and favourites, and ministers of state, my master said I could best determine.

I durst make no return to this malicious insinuation which debased human understanding below the sagacity of a common hound, who has judgment enough to distinguish and follow the cry of the ablest dog in the pack, without being ever mistaken.

My master told me, there were some qualities remarkable in the *Yahoos*, which he had not observed me to mention, or at least very slightly, in the accounts I had given him of human kind. He said, those animals, like other brutes, had their females in common; but in this they differed, that the she-*Yahoo* would admit the male while she was pregnant; and that the hees would quarrel and fight with the females as fiercely as with each other. Both which practices were such degrees of infamous brutality, that no other sensitive creature ever arrived at.

Another thing he wondered at in the *Yahoos*, was their strange disposition to nastiness and dirt, whereas there appears to be a natural love of cleanliness in all other animals. As to the two former accusations, I was glad to let them pass without any reply, because I had not a word to offer upon them in defence of my species, which otherwise I certainly had done from my own inclinations. But I could have easily vindicated human kind from the imputation of singularity upon the last article, if there had been any swine in that country (as unluckily for me there were not), which although it may be a sweeter quadruped than a *Yahoo*, cannot I humbly conceive in justice pretend to more cleanliness; and so his Honour himself must have owned, if he had seen their filthy way of feeding, and their custom of wallowing and sleeping in the mud.

My master likewise mentioned another quality which his servants had discovered in several *Yahoos*, and to him was wholly unaccountable. He said, a fancy would sometimes take a *Yahoo* to retire into a corner, to lie down and howl, and groan, and spurn away all that came near him, although he were young and fat, wanted neither food nor water; nor did the servants imagine what could possibly ail him. And the only remedy they found was to set him to hard work, after which he would infallibly come to himself. To this I was silent out of partiality to my own kind; yet here I could plainly discover the true seeds of spleen, which only seizeth on the lazy, the luxurious, and the rich; who, if they were forced to undergo the same regimen, I would undertake for the cure.

His Honour had further observed, that a female *Yahoo* would often stand behind a bank or a bush, to gaze on the young males passing by, and then appear, and hide, using many antic gestures and grimaces, at which time it was observed, that she had a most offensive smell; and when any of the males advanced, would slowly retire, looking often back, and with a counterfeit show of fear, run off into some convenient place where she knew the male would follow her.

At other times if a female stranger came among them, three or four of her own sex would get about her, and stare and chatter, and grin, and smell her all over; and then turn off with gestures that seemed to express contempt and disdain.

Perhaps my master might refine a little in these speculations, which he had drawn from what he observed himself, or had been told him by others; however, I could not reflect without some amazement, and much sorrow, that the rudiments of lewdness, coquetry, censure, and scandal, should have place by instinct in womankind.

I expected every moment, that my master would accuse the *Yahoos* of those unnatural appetites in both sexes, so common among us. But nature, it seems, hath not been so expert a school-mistress; and these politer pleasures are entirely the productions of art and reason, on our side of the globe.

CHAP. VIII.

The author relates several particulars of the Yahoos. *The great virtues of the* Houyhnhnms. *The education and exercise of their youth. Their general assembly.*

As I ought to have understood human nature much better than I supposed it possible for my master to do, so it was easy to apply the character he gave of the *Yahoos* to myself and my countrymen; and I believed I could yet make farther discoveries from my own observation. I therefore often begged his Honour to let

me go among the herds of *Yahoos* in the neighbourhood, to which he always very graciously consented, being perfectly convinced that the hatred I bore those brutes would never suffer me to be corrupted by them; and his Honour ordered one of his servants, a strong sorrel nag, very honest and good-natured to be my guard, without whose protection I durst not undertake such adventures. For I have already told the reader how much I was pestered by those odious animals upon my first arrival. And I afterwards failed very narrowly three or four times of falling into their clutches, when I happened to stray at any distance without my hanger. And I have reason to believe they had some imagination that I was of their own species, which I often assisted myself, by stripping up my sleeves, and showing my naked arms and breast in their sight, when my protector was with me. At which times they would approach as near as they durst, and imitate my actions after the manner of monkeys, but ever with great signs of hatred; as a tame jack-daw with cap and stockings, is always persecuted by the wild ones, when he happens to be got among them.

They are prodigiously nimble from their infancy; however, I once caught a young male of three years old, and endeavoured by all marks of tenderness to make it quiet; but the little imp fell a squalling and scratching, and biting with such violence, that I was forced to let it go; and it was high time, for a whole troop of old ones came about us at the noise, but finding the cub was safe (for away it ran), and my sorrel nag being by, they durst not venture near us. I observed the young animal's flesh to smell very rank, and the stink was somewhat between a weasel and a fox, but much more disagreeable. I forgot another circumstance (and perhaps I might have the reader's pardon if it were wholly omitted), that while I held the odious vermin in my hands, it voided its filthy excrements of a yellow liquid substance, all over my clothes; but by good fortune there was a small brook hard by, where I washed myself as clean as I could; although I durst not come into my master's presence, until I were sufficiently aired.

By what I could discover, the *Yahoos* appear to be the most unteachable of all animals, their capacities never reaching higher than to draw or carry burdens. Yet I am of opinion, this defect ariseth chiefly from a perverse, restive disposition. For they are cunning, malicious, treacherous, and revengeful. They are strong and hardy, but of a cowardly spirit, and by consequence, insolent, abject, and cruel. It is observed, that the red-haired of both sexes are more libidinous and mischievous than the rest, whom yet they much exceed in strength and activity.

The *Houyhnhnms* keep the *Yahoos* for present use in huts not far from the house; but the rest are sent abroad to certain fields, where they dig up roots, eat several kinds of herbs, and search about for carrion, or sometimes catch weasels and *luhimuhs* (a sort of wild rat), which they greedily devour. Nature hath taught them to dig deep holes with their nails on the side of a rising ground, wherein they lie by themselves; only the kennels of the females are larger, sufficient to hold two or three cubs.

They swim from their infancy like frogs, and are able to continue long under water, where they often take fish, which the females carry home to their young. And upon this occasion, I hope the reader will pardon my relating an odd adventure.

Being one day abroad with my protector the sorrel nag, and the weather exceeding hot, I entreated him to let me bathe in a river that was near. He consented, and I immediately stripped myself stark naked, and went down softly into the stream. It happened that a young female *Yahoo*, standing behind a bank, saw the whole proceeding, and inflamed by desire, as the nag and I conjectured, came running with all speed, and leaped into the water, within five yards of the place where I bathed. I was never in my life so terribly frighted; the nag was grazing at some distance, not suspecting any harm. She embraced me after a most fulsome manner; I roared as loud as I could, and the nag came galloping towards me, whereupon she quitted her grasp, with the utmost reluctancy, and leaped upon the opposite bank, where she stood gazing and howling all the time I was putting on my clothes.

This was matter of diversion to my master and his family, as well as of mortification to myself. For now I could no longer deny that I was a real *Yahoo* in every limb and feature, since the females had a natural propensity to me, as one of their own species. Neither was the hair of this brute of a red colour (which might have been some excuse for an appetite a little irregular), but black as a sloe, and her countenance did not make an appearance altogether so hideous as the rest of the kind; for, I think, she could not be above eleven years old.

Having already lived three years in this country, the reader I suppose will expect, that I should, like other travellers, give him some account of the manners and customs of its inhabitants, which it was indeed my principal study to learn.

As these noble *Houyhnhnms* are endowed by nature with a general disposition to all virtues, and have no conceptions or ideas of what is evil in a rational creature, so their grand maxim is, to cultivate reason, and to be wholly governed by it. Neither is reason among them a point problematical as with us, where men can argue with plausibility on both sides of the question; but strikes you with immediate conviction; as it must needs do where it is not mingled, obscured, or discoloured by passion and interest. I remember it was with extreme difficulty that I could bring my master to understand the meaning of the word *opinion*, or how a point could be disputable; because reason taught us to affirm or deny only where we are certain; and beyond our knowledge we cannot do either. So that controversies, wranglings, disputes, and positiveness in false or dubious propositions, are evils unknown among the *Houyhnhnms*. In the like manner when I used to explain to him our several systems of natural philosophy, he would laugh that a creature pretending to reason, should value itself upon the knowledge of other people's conjectures, and in things, where that knowledge, if it were certain, could be of no use. Wherein he agreed entirely with the sentiments of Socrates, as Plato delivers them; which I mention as the highest honour I can do that prince of philosophers. I have often since reflected what destruction such a doctrine would make in the libraries of Europe; and how many paths to fame would be then shut up in the learned world.

Friendship and benevolence are the two principal virtues among the *Houyhnhnms*: and these not confined to particular objects, but universal to the whole race. For a stranger from the remotest part is equally treated with the nearest neighbour, and wherever he goes, looks upon himself as at home. They preserve decency and civility in the highest degrees, but are altogether ignorant of ceremony. They have no fondness for their colts or foals, but the care they take in educating them proceeds entirely from the dictates of reason. And I observed my master to show the same affection to his neighbour's issue that he had for his own. They will have it that nature teaches them to love the whole species, and it is reason only that maketh a distinction of persons, where there is a superior degree of virtue.

When the matron *Houyhnhnms* have produced one of each sex, they no longer accompany with their consorts, except they lose one of their issue by some casualty, which very seldom happens: but in such a case they meet again, or when the like accident befalls a person whose wife is past bearing, some other couple bestow him one of their own colts, and then go together again till the mother is pregnant. This caution is necessary to prevent the country from being overburthened with numbers. But the race of inferior *Houyhnhnms* bred up to be servants is not so strictly limited upon this article; these are allowed to produce three of each sex, to be domestics in the noble families.

In their marriages they are exactly careful to choose such colours as will not make any disagreeable mixture in the breed. Strength is chiefly valued in the male, and comeliness in the female; not upon the account of love, but to preserve the race from degenerating; for where a female happens to excel in strength, a consort is chosen with regard to comeliness. Courtship, love, presents, jointures, settlements, have no place in their thoughts; or terms whereby to express them in their language. The young couple meet and are joined, merely because it is the determination of their parents and friends: it is what they see done every day, and they look upon it as one of the necessary actions in a reasonable being. But the violation of marriage, or any other unchastity, was never heard of: and the married pair pass their lives with the same friendship, and mutual benevolence that they bear to all others of the same species, who come in their way; without jealousy, fondness, quarrelling, or discontent.

In educating the youth of both sexes, their method is admirable, and highly deserves our imitation. These are not suffered to taste a grain of oats, except upon certain days, till eighteen years old; nor milk, but very rarely; and in summer they graze two hours in the morning, and as many in the evening, which their parents likewise observe; but the servants are not allowed above half that time, and a great part of their grass is brought home, which they eat at the most convenient hours, when they can be best spared from work.

Temperance, industry, exercise and cleanliness, are the lessons equally enjoined to the young ones of both sexes: and my master thought it monstrous in us to give the females a different kind of education from the males, except in some articles of domestic management; whereby as he truly observed, one half of our natives were good for nothing but bringing children into the world: and to trust the care of our children to such useless animals, he said, was yet a greater instance of brutality.

But the *Houyhnhnms* train up their youth to strength, speed, and hardiness, by exercising them in running races up and down steep hills, and over hard stony grounds; and when they are all in a sweat, they are ordered to leap over head and ears into a pond or a river. Four times a year the youth of a certain district meet to show their proficiency in running and leaping, and other feats of strength and agility; where the victor is rewarded with a song made in his or her praise. On this festival the servants drive a herd of *Yahoos* into the field, laden with hay, and oats, and milk, for a repast to the *Houyhnhnms*; after which, these brutes are immediately driven back again, for fear of being noisome to the assembly.

Every fourth year, at the vernal equinox, there is a representative council of the whole nation, which meets in a plain about twenty miles from our house, and continueth about five or six days. Here they enquire into the state and condition of the several districts; whether they abound or be deficient in hay or oats, or cows or *Yahoos*? And wherever there is any want (which is but seldom) it is immediately supplied by unanimous consent and contribution. Here likewise the regulation of children is settled: as for instance, if a *Houyhnhnm* hath two males, he changeth one of them with another that hath two females; and when a child hath been lost by any casualty, where the mother is past breeding, it is determined what family in the district shall breed another to supply the loss.

CHAP. IX

A grand debate at the general assembly of the Houyhnhnms, *and how it was determined. The learning of the* Houyhnhnms. *Their buildings. Their manner of burials. The defectiveness of their language.*

One of these grand assemblies was held in my time, about three months before my departure, whither my master went as the representative of our district. In this council was resumed their old debate, and indeed, the only debate which ever happened in that country; whereof my master after his return gave me a very particular account.

The question to be debated, was, whether the *Yahoos* should be exterminated from the face of the earth. One of the members for the affirmative offered several arguments of great strength and weight, alleging, that as the *Yahoos* were the most filthy, noisome, and deformed animal which nature ever produced, so they were the most restive and indocible, mischievous and malicious: they would privately suck the teats of the *Houyhnhnm's* cows, kill and devour their cats, trample down their oats and grass, if they were not continually watched, and commit a thousand other extravagances. He took notice of a general tradition, that *Yahoos* had not been always in their country; but, that many ages ago, two of these brutes appeared together upon a mountain; whether produced by the heat of the sun upon corrupted mud and slime, or from the ooze and froth of the sea, was never known. That these *Yahoos* engendered, and their brood in a short time grew so numerous as to overrun and infest the whole nation. That the *Houyhnhnms* to get rid of this evil, made a general hunting, and at last enclosed the whole herd; and destroying the elder, every *Houyhnhnm* kept two young ones in a kennel, and brought them to such a degree of tameness, as an animal so savage by nature can be capable of acquiring; using them for draught and carriage. That there seemed to be much truth in this tradition, and that those creatures could not be *Ylnhniamshy* (or *aborigines* of the land), because of the violent hatred the *Houyhnhnms*, as well as all other animals, bore them; which although their evil disposition sufficiently deserved, could never have arrived at so high a degree, if they had been aborigines, or else they would have long since been rooted out. That the inhabitants taking a fancy to use the service of the *Yahoos*, had very imprudently neglected to cultivate the breed of asses, which were a comely animal, easily kept, more tame and orderly, without any offensive smell, strong enough for labour, although they yield to the other in agility of body; and if their braying be no agreeable sound, it is far preferable to the horrible howlings of the *Yahoos*.

Several others declared their sentiments to the same purpose, when my master proposed an expedient to the assembly, whereof he had indeed borrowed the hint from me. He approved of the tradition mentioned by the honourable member, who spoke before, and affirmed, that the two *Yahoos* said to be first seen among them, had been driven thither over the sea; that coming to land, and being forsaken by their companions, they retired to the mountains, and degenerating by degrees, became in process of time, much more savage than those of their own species in the country from whence these two originals came. The reason of this assertion was, that he had now in his possession a certain wonderful *Yahoo*, (meaning myself) which most of them had heard of, and many of them had seen. He then related to them, how he first found me; that my body was all covered with an artificial composure of the skins and hairs of other animals; that I spoke in a language of my own, and had thoroughly

learned theirs: that I had related to him the accidents which brought me thither: that when he saw me without my covering, I was an exact *Yahoo* in every part, only of a whiter colour, less hairy, and with shorter claws. He added, how I had endeavoured to persuade him, that in my own and other countries the *Yahoos* acted as the governing, rational animal, and held the *Houyhnhnms* in servitude: that he observed in me all the qualities of a *Yahoo*, only a little more civilized by some tincture of reason, which however was in a degree as far inferior to the *Houyhnhnm* race, as the *Yahoos* of their country were to me: that, among other things, I mentioned a custom we had of castrating *Houyhnhnms* when they were young, in order to render them tame; that the operation was easy and safe; that it was no shame to learn wisdom from brutes, as industry is taught by the ant, and building by the swallow. (For so I translate the word *lyhannh*, although it be a much larger fowl.) That this invention might be practised upon the younger *Yahoos* here, which, besides rendering them tractable and fitter for use, would in an age put an end to the whole species without destroying life. That in the mean time the *Houyhnhnms* should be exhorted to cultivate the breed of asses, which, as they are in all respects more valuable brutes, so they have this advantage, to be fit for service at five years old, which the others are not till twelve.

This was all my master thought fit to tell me at that time, of what passed in the grand council. But he was pleased to conceal one particular, which related personally to myself, whereof I soon felt the unhappy effect, as the reader will know in its proper place, and from whence I date all the succeeding misfortunes of my life.

The *Houyhnhnms* have no letters, and consequently their knowledge is all traditional. But there happening few events of any moment among a people so well united, naturally disposed to every virtue, wholly governed by reason, and cut off from all commerce with other nations, the historical part is easily preserved without burthening their memories. I have already observed, that they are subject to no diseases and therefore can have no need of physicians. However, they have excellent medicines composed of herbs, to cure accidental bruises and cuts in the pastern or frog of the foot by sharp stones, as well as other maims and hurts in the several parts of the body.

They calculate the year by the revolution of the sun and moon, but use no subdivisions into weeks. They are well enough acquainted with the motions of those two luminaries, and understand the nature of eclipses; and this is the utmost progress of their astronomy.

In poetry they must be allowed to excell all other mortals; wherein the justness of their similes, and the minuteness, as well as exactness of their descriptions, are indeed inimitable. Their verses abound very much in both of these, and usually contain either some exalted notions of friendship and benevolence, or the praises of those who were victors in races, and other bodily exercises. Their buildings, although very rude and simple, are not inconvenient, but well contrived to defend them from all injuries of cold and heat. They have a kind of tree, which at forty years old loosens in the root, and falls with the first storm: it grows very straight, and being pointed like stakes with a sharp stone (for the *Houyhnhnms* know not the use of iron), they stick them erect in the ground about ten inches asunder, and then weave in oat-straw, or sometimes wattles betwixt them. The roof is made after the same manner, and so are the doors.

The *Houyhnhnms* use the hollow part between the pastern and the hoof of their fore-feet, as we do our hands, and this with greater dexterity than I could at first imagine. I have seen a white mare of our family thread a needle (which I lent her on purpose) with that joint. They milk their cows, reap their oats, and do all the work which requires hands, in the same manner. They have a kind of hard flints, which by grinding against other stones, they form into instruments, that serve instead of wedges, axes, and hammers. With tools made of these flints, they likewise cut their hay, and reap their oats, which there groweth naturally in several fields: the *Yahoos* draw home the sheaves in carriages, and the servants tread them in certain covered huts, to get out the grain, which is kept in stores. They make a rude kind of earthen and wooden vessels, and bake the former in the sun.

If they can avoid casualties, they die only of old age, and are buried in the obscurest places that can be found, their friends and relations expressing neither joy nor grief at their departure; nor does the dying person discover the least regret that he is leaving the world, any more than if he were upon returning home from a visit to one of his neighbours. I remember my master having once made an appointment with a friend and his family to come to his house upon some affair of importance, on the day fixed, the mistress and her two children came very late; she made two excuses, first for her husband, who, as she said, happened that very morning to *lhnuwnh*. The word is strongly expressive in their language, but not easily rendered into English; it signifies, *to retire to his first mother*. Her excuse for not coming sooner, was, that her husband dying late in the morning, she was a good while consulting her servants about a convenient place where his body should be laid; and I observed she behaved herself at our house as cheerfully as the rest. She died about three months after.

They live generally to seventy or seventy-five years, very seldom to fourscore: some weeks before their death they feel a gradual decay, but without pain. During this time they are much visited by their friends, because they cannot go abroad with their usual ease and satisfaction. However, about ten days before their death, which they seldom fail in computing, they return the visits that have been made them by those who are nearest in the neighbourhood, being carried in a convenient sledge drawn by *Yahoos*; which vehicle they use, not only upon this occasion, but when they grow old, upon long journeys, or when they are lamed by any accident. And therefore when the dying *Houyhnhnms* return those visits, they take a solemn leave of their friends, as if they were going to some remote part of the country, where they designed to pass the rest of their lives.

I know not whether it may be worth observing, that the *Houyhnhnms* have no word in their language to express any thing that is evil, except what they borrow from the deformities or ill qualities of the *Yahoos*. Thus they denote the folly of a servant, an omission of a child, a stone that cuts their feet, a continuance of foul or unseasonable weather, and the like, by adding to each the epithet of *Yahoo*. For instance, *Hhnm Yahoo, Whnaholm Yahoo, Ynlhmndwihlma Yahoo*, and an ill-contrived house *Ynholmhnmrohlnw Yahoo*.

I could with great pleasure enlarge further upon the manners and virtues of this excellent people; but intending in a short time to publish a volume by itself expressly upon that subject, I refer the reader thither. And in the mean time, proceed to relate my own sad catastrophe.

CHAP. X

The author's economy, and happy life among the Houyhnhnms. *His great improvement in virtue by conversing with them. Their conversations. The author hath notice given him by his master that he must depart from the country. He falls into a swoon for grief, but submits. He contrives and finishes a canoe, by the help of a fellow-servant, and puts to sea at a venture.*

I had settled my little economy to my own heart's content. My master had ordered a room to be made for me after their manner, about six yards from the house; the sides and floor of which I plastered with clay, and covered with rush-mats of my own contriving; I had beaten hemp, which there grows wild, and made of it a sort of ticking: this I filled with the feathers of several birds I had taken with springes made of *Yahoos'* hairs, and were excellent food. I had worked two chairs with my knife, the sorrel nag helping me in the grosser and more laborious part. When my clothes were worn to rags, I made myself others with the skins of rabbits, and of a certain beautiful animal about the same size, called *nnuhnoh*, the skin of which is covered with a fine down. Of these I likewise made very tolerable stockings. I soled my shoes with wood which I cut from a tree, and fitted to the upper leather, and when this was worn out, I supplied it with the skins of *Yahoos* dried in the sun. I often got honey out of hollow trees, which I mingled with water, or eat with my bread. No man could more verify the truth of these two maxims, *That nature is very easily satisfied; and That necessity is the mother of invention.* I enjoyed perfect health of body, and tranquillity of mind; I did not feel the treachery or inconstancy of a friend, nor the injuries of a secret or open enemy. I had no occasion of bribing, flattering or pimping, to procure the favour of any great man or of his minion. I wanted no fence against fraud or oppression; here was neither physician to destroy my body, nor lawyer to ruin my fortune; no informer to watch my words and actions, or forge accusations against me for hire: here were no gibers, censurers, backbiters, pickpockets, highwaymen, housebreakers, attorneys, bawds, buffoons, gamesters, politicians, wits, splenetics, tedious talkers, controvertists, ravishers, murderers, robbers, virtuosos; no leaders or followers of party and faction; no encouragers to vice, by seducement or examples; no dungeon, axes, gibbets, whipping-posts, or pillories; no cheating shop-keepers or mechanics; no pride, vanity, or affectation; no fops, bullies, drunkards, strolling whores, or poxes; no ranting lewd, expensive wives; no stupid, proud pedants; no importunate, overbearing, quarrelsome, noisy, roaring, empty, conceited, swearing companions; no scoundrels, raised from the dust for the sake of their vices, or nobility thrown into it on account of their virtues; no lords, fiddlers, judges, or dancing-masters.

I had the favour of being admitted to several *Houyhnhnms*, who came to visit or dine with my master; where his Honour graciously suffered me to wait in the room, and listen to their discourse. Both he and his company would often descend to ask me questions, and receive my answers. I had also sometimes the honour of attending my master in his visits to others. I never presumed to speak, except in answer to a question; and then I did it with inward regret, because it was a loss of so much time for improving myself: but I was infinitely delighted with the station of an humble auditor in such conversations, where nothing passed but what was useful, expressed in the fewest and most significant words; where (as I have already said) the greatest decency was observed, without the least degree of ceremony; where no person spoke without being pleased himself, and pleasing his companions; where there was no interruption, tediousness, heat, or difference of sentiments. They had a notion, that when people are met together, a short silence doth much improve conversation: this I found to be true; for during those little intermissions of talk, new ideas would arise in their minds, which very much enlivened the discourse. Their subjects are generally on friendship and benevolence, or order and economy; sometimes upon the visible operations of nature, or ancient traditions; upon the bounds and limits of virtue; upon the unerring rules of reason, or upon some determinations to be taken at the next great assembly; and often upon the various excellencies of poetry. I may add, without vanity, that my presence often gave them sufficient matter for discourse, because it afforded my master an occasion of letting his friends into the history of me and my country, upon which they were all pleased to descant in a manner not very advantageous to human kind; and for that reason I shall not repeat what they said: only I may be allowed to observe, that his Honour, to my great admiration, appeared to understand the nature of *Yahoos* much better than myself. He went through all our vices and follies, and discovered many which I had never mentioned to him, by only supposing what qualities a *Yahoo* of their country, with a small proportion of reason, might be capable of exerting; and concluded, with too much probability, how vile as well as miserable such a creature must be.

I freely confess, that all the little knowledge I have of any value, was acquired by the lectures I received from my master, and from hearing the discourses of him and his friends; to which I should be prouder to listen, than to dictate to the greatest and wisest assembly in Europe. I admired the strength, comeliness, and speed of the inhabitants; and such a constellation of virtues in such amiable persons produced in me the highest veneration. At first, indeed, I did not feel that natural awe which the *Yahoos* and all other animals bear towards them; but it grew upon me by degrees, much sooner than I imagined, and was mingled with a respectful love and gratitude, that they would condescend to distinguish me from the rest of my species.

When I thought of my family, my friends, my countrymen, or human race in general, I considered them as they really were, *Yahoos* in shape and disposition, perhaps a little more civilized, and qualified with the gift of speech, but making no other use of reason, than to improve and multiply those vices, whereof their brethren in this country had only the share that nature allotted them. When I happened to behold the reflection of my own form in a lake or fountain, I turned away my face in horror and detestation of myself, and could better endure the sight of a common *Yahoo*, than of my own person. By conversing with the *Houyhnhnms*, and looking upon them with delight, I fell to imitate their gait and gesture, which is now grown into a habit, and my friends often tell me in a blunt way, that *I trot like a horse*; which, however, I take for a great compliment. Neither shall I disown, that in speaking I am apt to fall into the voice and manner of the *Houyhnhnms*, and hear myself ridiculed on that account without the least mortification.

In the midst of all this happiness, and when I looked upon myself to be fully settled for life, my master sent for me one morning a little earlier than his usual hour. I observed by his countenance that he was in some perplexity, and at a loss how to begin what he had to speak. After a short silence, he told me, he did not know how I would take what he was going to say; that in the last general assembly, when the affair of the *Yahoos* was entered upon, the representatives had taken offence at his keeping a *Yahoo* (meaning myself) in his family more like a *Houyhnhnm* than a brute animal. That he was known frequently to converse with me, as if he could receive some advantage or pleasure in my company; that such a practice was not agreeable to reason or nature, or a thing ever heard of before among them. The assembly did therefore exhort him, either to employ me like the rest of my species, or command me to swim back to the place from whence I came. That the first of these expedients was utterly rejected by all the *Houyhnhnms* who had ever seen me at his house or their own: for they alleged, that because I had some rudiments of reason, added to the natural pravity of those animals, it was to be

feared, I might be able to seduce them into the woody and mountainous parts of the country, and bring them in troops by night to destroy the *Houyhnhnms'* cattle, as being naturally of the ravenous kind, and averse from labour.

My master added, that he was daily pressed by the *Houyhnhnms* of the neighbourhood to have the assembly's exhortation executed, which he could not put off much longer. He doubted it would be impossible for me to swim to another country, and therefore wished I would contrive some sort of vehicle resembling those I had described to him, that might carry me on the sea; in which work I should have the assistance of his own servants, as well as those of his neighbours. He concluded, that for his own part, he could have been content to keep me in his service as long as I lived; because he found I had cured myself of some bad habits and dispositions, by endeavouring, as far as my inferior nature was capable, to imitate the *Houyhnhnms*.

I should here observe to the reader, that a decree of the general assembly in this country is expressed by the word *hnhloayn*, which signifies an exhortation, as near as I can render it; for they have no conception how a rational creature can be compelled, but only advised, or exhorted; because no person can disobey reason, without giving up his claim to be a rational creature.

I was struck with the utmost grief and despair at my master's discourse; and being unable to support the agonies I was under, I fell into a swoon at his feet; when I came to myself, he told me, that he concluded I had been dead (for these people are subject to no such imbecilities of nature). I answered, in a faint voice, that death would have been too great an happiness; that although I could not blame the assembly's exhortation, or the urgency of his friends; yet, in my weak and corrupt judgment, I thought it might consist with reason to have been less rigorous. That I could not swim a league, and probably the nearest land to theirs might be distant above an hundred: that many materials, necessary for making a small vessel to carry me off, were wholly wanting in this country, which, however, I would attempt in obedience and gratitude to his Honour, although I concluded the thing to be impossible, and therefore looked on myself as already devoted to destruction. That the certain prospect of an unnatural death was the least of my evils: for, supposing I should escape with life by some strange adventure, how could I think with temper, of passing my days among *Yahoos*, and relapsing into my old corruptions, for want of examples to lead and keep me within the paths of virtue. That I knew too well upon what solid reasons all the determinations of the wise *Houyhnhnms* were founded, not to be shaken by arguments of mine, a miserable *Yahoo*; and therefore, after presenting him with my humble thanks for the offer of his servants' assistance in making a vessel, and desiring a reasonable time for so difficult a work, I told him I would endeavour to preserve a wretched being; and, if ever I returned to England, was not without hopes of being useful to my own species, by celebrating the praises of the renowned *Houyhnhnms*, and proposing their virtues to the imitation of mankind.

My master in a few words made me a very gracious reply, allowed me the space of two months to finish my boat; and ordered the sorrel nag, my fellow-servant (for so at this distance I may presume to call him) to follow my instructions, because I told my master, that his help would be sufficient, and I knew he had a tenderness for me.

In his company my first business was to go to that part of the coast where my rebellious crew had ordered me to be set on shore. I got upon a height, and looking on every side into the sea, fancied I saw a small island, towards the north-east: I took out my pocket-glass, and could then clearly distinguish it about five leagues off, as I computed; but it appeared to the sorrel nag to be only a blue cloud: for, as he had no conception of any country beside his own, so he could not be as expert in distinguishing remote objects at sea, as we who so much converse in that element.

After I had discovered this island, I considered no farther; but resolved it should, if possible, be the first place of my banishment, leaving the consequence to fortune.

I returned home, and consulting with the sorrel nag, we went into a copse at some distance, where I with my knife, and he with a sharp flint fastened very artificially, after their manner, to a wooden handle, cut down several oak wattles about the thickness of a walking-staff, and some larger pieces. But I shall not trouble the reader with a particular description of my own mechanics; let it suffice to say, that in six weeks time, with the help of the sorrel nag, who performed the parts that required most labour, I finished a sort of Indian canoe, but much larger, covering it with the skins of *Yahoos* well stitched together, with hempen threads of my own making. My sail was likewise composed of the skins of the same animal; but I made use of the youngest I could get, the older being too tough and thick; and I likewise provided myself with four paddles. I laid in a stock of boiled flesh, of rabbits and fowls, and took with me two vessels, one filled with milk, and the other with water.

I tried my canoe in a large pond near my master's house, and then corrected in it what was amiss; stopping all the chinks with *Yahoos'* tallow, till I found it staunch, and able to bear me, and my freight. And when it was as complete as I could possibly make it, I had it drawn on a carriage very gently by *Yahoos* to the sea-side, under the conduct of the sorrel nag, and another servant.

When all was ready, and the day came for my departure, I took leave of my master and lady, and the whole family, my eyes flowing with tears, and my heart quite sunk with grief. But his Honour, out of curiosity, and, perhaps (if I may speak it without vanity), partly out of kindness, was determined to see me in my canoe, and got several of his neighbouring friends to accompany him. I was forced to wait above an hour for the tide, and then observing the wind very fortunately bearing towards the island, to which I intended to steer my course, I took a second leave of my master: but as I was going to prostrate myself to kiss his hoof, he did me the honour to raise it gently to my mouth. I am not ignorant how much I have been censured for mentioning this last particular. Detractors are pleased to think it improbable, that so illustrious a person should descend to give so great a mark of distinction to a creature so inferior as I. Neither have I forgot, how apt some travellers are to boast of extraordinary favours they have received. But if these censurers were better acquainted with the noble and courteous disposition of the *Houyhn-hnms*, they would soon change their opinion.

I paid my respects to the rest of the *Houyhnhnms* in his Honour's company; then getting into my canoe, I pushed off from shore.

CHAP. XI

The author's dangerous voyage. He arrives at New Holland, *hoping to settle there. Is wounded with an arrow by one of the natives. Is seized and carried by force into a* Portuguese *ship. The great civilities of the Captain. The author arrives at England.*

I began this desperate voyage on February 15, 1714-15, at 9 o'clock in the morning. The wind was very favourable; however, I made use at first only of my paddles; but considering I should soon be weary, and that the wind might chop about, I ventured to set up my little sail; and thus, with the help of the tide, I went at the rate of a league and a half an hour, as

near as I could guess. My master and his friends continued on the shore, till I was almost out of sight; and I often heard the sorrel nag (who always loved me) crying out, *Hnuy illa nyha majah Yahoo.* Take care of thyself, gentle *Yahoo.*

My design was, if possible, to discover some small island uninhabited, yet sufficient by my labour to furnish me with the necessaries of life, which I would have thought a greater happiness than to be first minister in the politest court of Europe; so horrible was the idea I conceived of returning to live in the society and under the government of *Yahoos.* For in such a solitude as I desired, I could at least enjoy my own thoughts, and reflect with delight on the virtues of those inimitable *Houyhnhnms*, without any opportunity of degenerating into the vices and corruptions of my own species.

The reader may remember what I related when my crew conspired against me, and confined me to my cabin. How I continued there several weeks, without knowing what course we took; and when I was put ashore in the long-boat, how the sailors told me with oaths, whether true or false, that they knew not in what part of the world we were. However, I did then believe us to be about ten degrees southward of the Cape of Good Hope, or about 45 degrees southern latitude, as I gathered from some general words I overheard among them, being I supposed to the southeast in their intended voyage to Madagascar. And although this were but little better than conjecture, yet I resolved to steer my course eastward, hoping to reach the southwest coast of New Holland, and perhaps some such island as I desired, lying westward of it. The wind was full west, and by six in the evening I computed I had gone eastward at least eighteen leagues, when I spied a very small island about half a league off, which I soon reached. It was nothing but a rock with one creek, naturally arched by the force of tempests. Here I put in my canoe, and climbing up a part of the rock, I could plainly discover land to the east, extending from south to north. I lay all night in my canoe; and repeating my voyage early in the morning, I arrived in seven hours to the southeast point of New Holland. This confirmed me in the opinion I have long entertained, that the maps and charts place this country at least three degrees more to the east than it really is; which thought I communicated many years ago to my worthy friend Mr. Herman Moll, and gave him my reasons for it, although he hath rather chosen to follow other authors.

I saw no inhabitants in the place where I landed, and being unarmed, I was afraid of venturing far into the country. I found some shellfish on the shore, and eat them raw, not daring to kindle a fire, for fear of being discovered by the natives. I continued three days feeding on oysters and limpets, to save my own provisions; and I fortunately found a brook of excellent water, which gave me great relief.

On the fourth day, venturing out early a little too far, I saw twenty or thirty natives upon a height, not above five hundred yards from me. They were stark naked men, women, and children round a fire, as I could discover by the smoke. One of them spied me, and gave notice to the rest; five of them advanced towards me, leaving the women and children at the fire. I made what haste I could to the shore, and getting into my canoe, shoved off: the savages observing me retreat, ran after me; and before I could get far enough into the sea, discharged an arrow, which wounded me deeply on the inside of my left knee (I shall carry the mark to my grave). I apprehended the arrow might be poisoned, and paddling out of the reach of their darts (being a calm day), I made a shift to suck the wound, and dress it as well as I could. I was at a loss what to do, for I durst not return to the same landing-place, but stood to the north, and was forced to paddle; for the wind, though very gentle, was against me, blowing northwest. As I was looking about for a secure landing-place, I saw a sail to the north-northeast, which appearing every minute more visible, I was in some doubt whether I should wait for them or no; but at last my detestation of the *Yahoo* race prevailed, and turning my canoe, I sailed and paddled together to the south, and got into the same creek from whence I set out in the morning, choosing rather to trust myself among these barbarians, than live with European *Yahoos*. I drew up my canoe as close as I could to the shore, and hid myself behind a stone by the little brook, which, as I have already said, was excellent water.

The ship came within half a league of this creek, and sent her long-boat with vessels to take in fresh water (for the place it seems was very well known), but I did not observe it till the boat was almost on shore, and it was too late to seek another hiding-place. The seamen at their landing observed my canoe, and rummaging it all over, easily conjectured that the owner could not be far off. Four of them, well armed, searched every cranny and lurking-hole, till at last they found me flat on my face behind the stone. They gazed awhile in admiration at my strange uncouth dress; my coat made of skins, my wooden-soled shoes, and my furred stockings; from whence, however, they concluded I was not a native of the place, who all go naked. One of the seamen in Portuguese bid me rise, and asked who I was. I understood that language very well, and getting upon my feet, said, I was a poor *Yahoo*, banished from the *Houyhnhnms*, and desired they would please to let me depart. They admired to hear me answer them in their own tongue, and saw by my complexion I must be an European; but were at a loss to know what I meant by *Yahoos* and *Houy-*

hnhnms, and at the same time fell a-laughing at my strange tone in speaking, which resembled the neighing of a horse. I trembled all the while betwixt fear and hatred: I again desired leave to depart, and was gently moving to my canoe; but they laid hold of me, desiring to know what country I was of? whence I came? with many other questions. I told them, I was born in England, from whence I came about five years ago, and then their country and ours were at peace. I therefore hoped they would not treat me as an enemy, since I meant them no harm, but was a poor *Yahoo,* seeking some desolate place where to pass the remainder of his unfortunate life.

When they began to talk, I thought I never heard or saw any thing so unnatural; for it appeared to me as monstrous as if a dog or a cow should speak in England, or a *Yahoo* in *Houyhnhnmland.* The honest Portuguese were equally amazed at my strange dress, and the odd manner of delivering my words, which however they understood very well. They spoke to me with great humanity, and said they were sure their Captain would carry me *gratis* to Lisbon, from whence I might return to my own country; that two of the seamen would go back to the ship, inform the Captain of what they had seen, and receive his orders; in the meantime, unless I would give my solemn oath not to fly, they would secure me by force. I thought it best to comply with their proposal. They were very curious to know my story, but I gave them very little satisfaction; and they all conjectured, that my misfortunes had impaired my reason. In two hours the boat, which went loaden with vessels of water, returned with the Captain's command to fetch me on board. I fell on my knees to preserve my liberty; but all was in vain, and the men having tied me with cords, heaved me into the boat, from whence I was taken into the ship, and from thence into the Captain's cabin.

His name was Pedro de Mendez;

he was a very courteous and generous person; he entreated me to give some account of myself, and desired to know what I would eat or drink; said, I should be used as well as himself, and spoke so many obliging things, that I wondered to find such civilities from a *Yahoo.* However, I remained silent and sullen; I was ready to faint at the very smell of him and his men. At last I desired something to eat out of my own canoe; but he ordered me a chicken and some excellent wine, and then directed that I should be put to bed in a very clean cabin. I would not undress myself, but lay on the bed-clothes, and in half an hour stole out, when I thought the crew was at dinner, and getting to the side of the ship was going to leap into the sea, and swim for my life, rather than continue among *Yahoos.* But one of the seamen prevented me, and having informed the Captain, I was chained to my cabin.

After dinner Don Pedro came to me, and desired to know my reason for so desperate an attempt; assured me he only meant to do me all the service he was able; and spoke so very movingly, that at last I descended to treat him like an animal which had some little portion of reason. I gave him a very short relation of my voyage; of the conspiracy against me by my own men; of the country where they set me on shore, and of my five years residence there. All which he looked upon as if it were a dream or a vision; whereat I took great offence; for I had quite forgot the faculty of lying, so peculiar to *Yahoos* in all countries where they preside, and, consequently the disposition of suspecting truth in others of their own species. I asked him, whether it were the custom in his country to *say the thing that was not?* I assured him I had almost forgot what he meant by falsehood, and if I had lived a thousand years in *Houyhnhnmland,* I should never have heard a lie from the meanest servant; that I was altogether indifferent whether he believed me or no; but, however, in return for his favours, I would give so much allowance to the corruption of his nature, as to answer any objection he would please to make, and then he might easily discover the truth.

The Captain, a wise man, after many endeavours to catch me tripping in some part of my story, at last began to have a better opinion of my veracity. But he added, that since I professed so inviolable an attachment to truth, I must give him my word of honour to bear him company in this voyage, without attempting any thing against my life, or else he would continue me a prisoner till we arrived at Lisbon. I gave him the promise he required; but at the same time protested that I would suffer the greatest hardships rather than return to live among *Yahoos*.

Our voyage passed without any considerable accident. In gratitude to the Captain I sometimes sat with him at his earnest request, and strove to conceal my antipathy to human kind, although it often broke out, which he suffered to pass without observation. But the greatest part of the day, I confined myself to my cabin, to avoid seeing any of the crew. The Captain had often entreated me to strip myself of my savage dress, and offered to lend me the best suit of clothes he had. This I would not be prevailed on to accept, abhorring to cover myself with any thing that had been on the back of a *Yahoo*. I only desired he would lend me two clean shirts, which having been washed since he wore them, I believed would not so much defile me. These I changed every second day, and washed them myself.

We arrived at Lisbon, Nov. 5, 1715. At our landing the Captain forced me to cover myself with his cloak, to prevent the rabble from crowding about me. I was conveyed to his own house, and at my earnest request, he led me up to the highest room backwards. I conjured him to conceal from all persons what I had told him of the *Houyhnhnms*, because the least hint of such a story would not only draw numbers of people to see me, but probably put me in danger of being imprisoned, or burnt by the Inquisition. The Captain persuaded me to accept a suit of clothes newly made; but I would not suffer the tailor to take my measure; however, Don Pedro being almost of my size, they fitted me well enough. He accoutred me with other necessaries all new, which I aired for twenty-four hours before I would use them.

The Captain had no wife, nor above three servants, none of which were suffered to attend at meals, and his whole deportment was so obliging, added to very good *human* understanding, that I really began to tolerate his company. He gained so far upon me, that I ventured to look out of the back window. By degrees I was brought into another room, from whence I peeped into the street, but drew my head back in a fright. In a week's time he seduced me down to the door. I found my terror gradually lessened, but my hatred and contempt seemed to increase. I was at last bold enough to walk the street in his company, but kept my nose well stopped with rue, or sometimes with tobacco.

In ten days, Don Pedro, to whom I had given some account of my domestic affairs, put it upon me as a matter of honour and conscience, that I ought to return to my native country, and live at home with my wife and children. He told me there was an English ship in the port just ready to sail, and he would furnish me with all things necessary. It would be tedious to repeat his arguments, and my contradictions. He said it was altogether impossible to find such a solitary island as I desired to live in; but I might command in my own house, and pass my time in a manner as recluse as I pleased.

I complied at last, finding I could not do better. I left Lisbon the 24th day of November, in an English merchant-man, but who was the master I never inquired. Don Pedro accompanied me to the ship, and lent me twenty pounds. He took kind leave of me and embraced me at parting, which I bore as well as I could. During this last voyage I had no commerce with the master or any of his men; but pretending I was sick, kept close in my cabin. On the fifth of December, 1715, we cast anchor in the Downs about nine in the morning, and at three in the afternoon I got safe to my house at Redriff.

My wife and family received me with great surprise and joy, because they concluded me certainly dead, but I must freely confess the sight of them filled me only with hatred, disgust, and contempt, and the more by reflecting on the near alliance I had to them. For, although since my unfortunate exile from the *Houyhnhnm* country, I had compelled myself to tolerate the sight of *Yahoos*, and to converse with Don Pedro de Mendex; yet my memory and imagination were perpetually filled with the virtues and ideas of those exalted *Houyhnhnms*. And when I began to consider, that by copulating with one of the *Yahoo* species I had become a parent of more, it struck me with the utmost shame, confusion, and horror.

As soon as I entered the house, my wife took me in her arms, and kissed me; at which, having not been used to the touch of that odious animal for so many years, I fell in a swoon for almost an hour. At the time I am writing it is five years since my last return to England: during the first year, I could not endure my wife or children in my presence, the very smell of them was intolerable; much less could I suffer them to eat in the same room. To this hour they dare not presume to touch my bread, or drink out of the same cup, neither was I ever able to let one of them take me by the hand. The first money I laid out was to buy two young stonehorses, which I keep in a good stable, and next to them the groom is my greatest favourite; for I feel my spirits revived by the smell he contracts in the stable. My horses understand me tolerably well; I converse with them at least four hours every day. They are strangers to bridle or saddle; they live in great amity with me, and friendship to each other.

CHAP. XII

The author's veracity. His design in publishing this work. His censure of those travellers who swerve from the truth. The author clears himself from any sinister ends in writing. An objection answered. The method of planting colonies. His native country commended. The right of the Crown to those countries described by the author, is justified. The difficulty of conquering them. The author takes his last leave of the reader; proposeth his manner of living for the future, gives good advice, and concludeth.

Thus, gentle reader, I have given thee a faithful history of my travels for sixteen years and above seven months; wherein I have not been so studious of ornament as of truth. I could perhaps like others have astonished thee with strange improbable tales; but I rather chose to relate plain matter of fact in the simplest manner and style; because my principal design was to inform, and not to amuse thee.

It is easy for us who travel into remote countries, which are seldom visited by Englishmen or other Europeans, to form descriptions of wonderful animals both at sea and land. Whereas a traveller's chief aim should be to make men wiser and better, and to improve their minds by the bad as well as good example of what they deliver concerning foreign places.

I could heartily wish a law was enacted, that every traveller, before he were permitted to publish his voyages, should be obliged to make oath before the Lord High Chancellor that all he intended to print was absolutely true to the best of his knowledge; for then the world would no longer be deceived as it usually is, while some writers, to make their works pass the better upon the public, impose the grossest falsities on the unwary reader. I have perused several books of travels with great delight in my younger days; but having since gone over most parts of the globe, and been able to contradict many fabulous accounts from my own observation, it hath given me a great disgust against this part of reading, and some indignation to see the credulity of mankind so impudently abused. Therefore since my acquaintance were pleased to think my poor endeavours might not be unacceptable to my country, I imposed on myself as a maxim, never to be swerved from, that I would *strictly adhere to truth*; neither indeed can I be ever under the least temptation to vary from it, while I retain in my mind the lectures and example of my noble master, and the other illustrious *Houyhnhnms*, of whom I had so long the honour to be an humble hearer.

—Nec si miserum Fortuna Sinonem
Finxit, vanum etiam mendacemque improba
 finget.

I know very well how little reputation is to be got by writings which require neither genius nor learning, nor indeed any other talent, except a good memory, or an exact journal. I know likewise, that writers of travels, like dictionary-makers, are sunk into oblivion by the weight and bulk of those who come last, and therefore lie uppermost. And it is highly probable, that such travellers who shall hereafter visit the countries described in this work of mine, may, by detecting my errors (if there be any), and adding many new discoveries of their own, justle me out of vogue, and stand in my place, making the world forget that ever I was an author. This indeed would be too great a mortification if I wrote for fame: but, as my sole intention was the PUBLIC GOOD, I cannot be altogether disappointed. For who can read of the virtues I have mentioned in the glorious *Houyhnhnms*, without being ashamed of his own vices, when he considers himself as the reasoning, governing animal of his country? I shall say nothing of those remote nations where *Yahoos* preside; amongst which the least corrupted are the *Brobdingnagians*, whose wise maxims in morality and government it would be our happiness to observe. But I forbear descanting farther, and rather leave the judicious reader to his own remarks and applications.

I am not a little pleased that this work of mine can possibly meet with no censurers: for what objections can be made against a writer who relates only plain facts that happened in such distant countries, where we have not the least interest with respect either to trade or negotiations? I have carefully avoided every fault with which common writers of travels are often too justly charged. Besides, I meddle not the least with any party, but write without passion, prejudice, or ill-will against any man or number of men whatsoever. I write for the noblest end, to inform and instruct mankind, over whom I may, without breach of modesty, pretend to some superiority, from the advantages I received by conversing so long among the most accomplished *Houyhnhnms*. I write without any view towards profit or praise. I never suffer a word to pass that may look like reflection, or possibly give the least offence even to those who are most ready to take it. So that I hope I may with justice pronounce myself an author perfectly blameless, against whom the tribes of answerers, considerers, observers, reflecters, detecters, remarkers, will never be able to find matter for exercising their talents.

I confess, it was whispered to me, that I was bound in duty as a subject of England, to have given in a memorial to a Secretary of State, at my first coming over; because, whatever lands are discovered by a subject, belong to the Crown. But I doubt whether our conquests in the countries I treat of, would be as easy as those of Ferdinando Cortez over the naked Americans. The *Lilliputians*, I think, are hardly worth the charge of a fleet and army to reduce them; and I question whether it might be prudent or safe to attempt the *Brobdingnagians*; or whether an English army would be much at their ease with the Flying Island over their heads. The *Houyhnhnms*, indeed, appear not to be so well prepared for war, a science to which they are perfect strangers, and especially against missive weapons. However, supposing myself to be a minister of state, I could never give my advice for invading them. Their prudence, unanimity, unacquaintedness with fear, and their love of their country, would amply supply all defects in the military art. Imagine twenty thousand of them breaking into the midst of an European army, confounding the ranks, overturning the carriages, battering the warriors' faces into mummy by terrible yerks from their hinder hoofs; for they would well deserve the character given to Augustus; *Recalcitrat undique tutus*. But instead of proposals for conquering that magnanimous nation, I rather wish they were in a capacity or disposition to send a sufficient number of their inhabitants for civilizing Europe, by teaching us the first principles of honour, justice, truth, temperance, public spirit, fortitude, chastity, friendship, benevolence, and fidelity. The names of all which virtues are still retained among us in most languages, and are to be met with in modern as well as ancient authors; which I am able to assert from my own small reading.

But I had another reason which made me less forward to enlarge his Majesty's dominions by my discoveries. To say the truth, I had conceived a few scruples with relation to the distributive justice of princes upon those occasions. For instance, a crew of pirates are driven by a storm they know not whither; at length a boy discovers lands from the topmast; they go on shore to rob and plunder; they see an harmless people, are entertained with kindness, they give the country a new name, they take formal possession of it for their king, they set up a rotten plank or a stone for a memorial, they murder two or three dozen of the natives, bring away a couple more by force for a sample, return home, and get their pardon. Here commences a new dominion acquired with a title by *divine right*. Ships are sent with the first opportunity; the natives driven out or destroyed, their princes tortured to discover their gold; a free license given to all acts of inhumanity and lust, the earth reeking with the blood of its inhabitants: and this execrable crew of butchers employed in so pious an expedition, is a *modern colony* sent to convert and civilize an idolatrous and barbarous people.

But this description, I confess, doth by no means affect the British nation, who may be an example to the whole world for their wisdom, care, and justice in planting colonies; their liberal endowments for the advancement of religion and learning; their choice of devout and able pastors to propagate Christianity; their caution in stocking their provinces with people of sober lives and conversations from this the mother kingdom; their strict regard to the distribution of justice, in supplying the civil administration through all their colonies with officers of the greatest abilities, utter strangers to corruption; and to crown all, by sending the most vigilant and virtuous governors, who have no other views, than the happiness of the people over whom they preside, and the honour of the King their master.

But, as those countries which I have described do not appear to have any desire of being conquered, and enslaved, murdered or driven out by colonies; nor abound either in gold, silver, sugar, or tobacco; I did humbly conceive, they were by no means proper objects of our zeal, our valour, or our interest. However, if those whom it may concern think fit to be of another opinion, I am ready to depose, when I shall be lawfully called, that no European did ever visit these countries before me. I mean, if the inhabitants ought to be believed.

But, as to the formality of taking possession in my Sovereign's name, it never came once into my thoughts; and if it had, yet as my affairs then stood, I should perhaps in point of prudence and self-preservation, have put it off to a better opportunity.

Having thus answered the only objection that can ever be raised against me as a traveller, I here take a final leave of all my courteous readers, and return to enjoy my own speculations in my little garden at Redriff, to apply those excellent lessons of virtue which I learned among the *Houyhnhnms*; to instruct the *Yahoos* of my own family as far as I shall find them docible animals; to behold my figure often in a glass, and thus if possible habituate myself by time to tolerate the sight of a human creature: to lament the brutality of *Houyhnhnms* in my own country, but always treat their persons with respect, for the sake of my noble master, his family, his friends, and the whole *Houyhnhnm* race, whom these of ours have the honour to resemble in all their lineaments, however their intellectuals came to degenerate.

I began last week to permit my wife to sit at dinner with me, at the farthest end of a long table; and to answer (but with the utmost brevity) the few questions I asked her. Yet the smell of a *Yahoo* continuing very offensive, I always keep my nose well stopped with rue, lavender, or tobacco leaves. And although it be hard for a man late in life to remove old habits, I am not altogether out of hopes in some time to suffer a neighbour *Yahoo* in my company, without the apprehensions I am yet under of his teeth or his claws.

My reconcilement to the *Yahoo*-kind in general might not be so difficult, if they would be content with those vices and follies only which nature hath entitled them to. I am not in the least provoked at the sight of a lawyer, a pick-pocket, a colonel, a fool, a lord, a gamester, a politician, a whore-monger, a physician, an evidence, a suborner, an attorney, a traitor, or the like; this is all according to the due course of things: but when I behold a lump of deformity, and diseases both in body and mind, smitten with *pride*, it immediately breaks all the measures of my patience; neither shall I ever be able to comprehend how such an animal and such a vice could tally together. The wise and virtuous *Houyhnhnms*, who abound in all excellencies that can adorn a rational creature, have no name for this vice in their language, which hath no terms to express any thing that is evil, except those whereby they describe the detestable qualities of their *Yahoos*, among which they were not able to distinguish this of pride, for want of thoroughly understanding human nature, as it showeth itself in other countries, where that animal presides. But I, who had more experience, could plainly observe some rudiments of it among the wild *Yahoos*.

But the *Houyhnhnms*, who live under the government of reason, are no more proud of the good qualities they possess, than I should be for not wanting a leg or an arm, which no man in his wits would boast of, although he must be miserable without them. I dwell the longer upon this subject from the desire I have to make the society of an English *Yahoo* by any means not insupportable; and therefore I here entreat those who have any tincture of this absurd vice, that they will not presume to come in my sight.

A MODEST PROPOSAL

FOR PREVENTING THE CHILDREN OF POOR PEOPLE IN IRELAND FROM BEING A BURDEN TO THEIR PARENTS OR COUNTRY, AND FOR MAKING THEM BENEFICIAL TO THE PUBLIC.

It is a melancholy object to those who walk through this great town, or travel in the country, when they see the streets, the roads, and cabin-doors crowded with beggars of the female sex, followed by three, four, or six children, *all in rags,* and importuning every passenger for an alms. These mothers instead of being able to work for their honest livelihood, are forced to employ all their time in strolling, to beg sustenance for their helpless infants, who, as they grow up, either turn thieves for want of work, or leave their dear Native Country to fight for the Pretender in Spain, or sell themselves to the Barbadoes.

I think it is agreed by all parties, that this prodigious number of children, in the arms, or on the backs, or at the heels of their mothers, and frequently of their fathers, is in the present deplorable state of the kingdom a very great additional grievance; and therefore whoever could find out a fair, cheap and easy method of making these children sound useful members of the commonwealth would deserve so well of the public, as to have his statue set up for a preserver of the nation.

But my intention is very far from being confined to provide only for the children of professed beggars, it is of a much greater extent, and shall take in the whole number of infants at a certain age, who are born of parents in effect as little able to support them, as those who demand our charity in the streets.

As to my own part, having turned my thoughts, for many years, upon this important subject, and maturely weighed the several schemes of other projectors, I have always found them grossly mistaken in their computation. It is true a child, just dropped from its dam, may be supported by her milk for a solar year with little other nourishment, at most not above the value of two shillings, which the mother may certainly get, or the value in scraps, by her lawful occupation of begging, and it is exactly at one year old that I propose to provide for them, in such a manner, as, instead

of being a charge upon their parents, or the parish, or wanting food and raiment for the rest of their lives, they shall, on the contrary, contribute to the feeding and partly to the clothing of many thousands.

There is likewise another great advantage in my scheme, that it will prevent those voluntary abortions, and that horrid practice of women murdering their bastard children, alas, too frequent among us, sacrificing the poor innocent babes, I doubt, more to avoid the expense, than the shame, which would move tears and pity in the most savage and inhuman breast.

The number of souls in this kingdom being usually reckoned one million and a half, of these I calculate there may be about two hundred thousand couple whose wives are breeders, from which number I subtract thirty thousand couple, who are able to maintain their own children, although I apprehend there cannot be so many under the present distresses of the kingdom, but this being granted, there will remain an hundred and seventy thousand breeders. I again subtract fifty thousand for those women who miscarry, or whose children die by accident, or disease within the year. There only remain an hundred and twenty thousand children of poor parents annually born: the question therefore is, how this number shall be reared, and provided for, which, as I have already said, under the present situation of affairs, is utterly impossible by all the methods hitherto proposed, for we can neither employ them in handicraft, or agriculture; we neither build houses, (I mean in the country) nor cultivate land: they can very seldom pick up a livelihood by stealing till they arrive at six years old, except where they are of towardly parts, although, I confess they learn the rudiments much earlier, during which time, they can however be properly looked upon only as *probationers,* as I have been informed by a principal gentleman in the County of Cavan, who protested to me, that he never knew above one or two instances under the age of six, even in a part of the kingdom so renowned for the quickest proficiency in that art.

I am assured by our merchants, that a boy or a girl, before twelve years old, is no saleable commodity, and even when they come to this age, they will not yield above three pounds, or three pounds and half-a-crown at most on the Exchange, which cannot turn to account either to the parents or kingdom, the charge of nutriment and rags having been at least four times that value.

I shall now therefore humbly propose my own thoughts, which I hope will not be liable to the least objection.

I have been assured by a very knowing American of my acquaintance in London, that a young healthy child well nursed is at a year old a most delicious, nourishing, and wholesome food, whether stewed, roasted, baked, or boiled, and I make no doubt that it will equally serve in a fricassee, or ragout.

I do therefore humbly offer it to public consideration, that of the hundred and twenty thousand children, already computed, twenty thousand may be reserved for breed, whereof only one fourth part to be males, which is more than we allow to sheep, black-cattle, or swine, and my reason is that these children are seldom the fruits of marriage, a circumstance not much regarded by our savages, therefore one male will be sufficient to serve four females. That the remaining hundred thousand may at a year old be offered in sale to the persons of quality, and fortune, through the kingdom, always advising the mother to let them suck plentifully in the last month, so as to render them plump, and fat for a good table. A child will make two dishes at an entertainment for friends, and when the family dines alone, the fore or hind quarter will make a reasonable dish, and seasoned with a little pepper or salt will be very good boiled on the fourth day, especially in winter.

I have reckoned upon a medium, that a child just born will weigh 12 pounds, and in a solar year if tolerably nursed increaseth to 28 pounds.

I grant this food will be somewhat dear, and therefore very proper for landlords, who, as they have already devoured most of the parents, seem to have the best title to the children.

Infants' flesh will be in season throughout the year, but more plentiful in March, and a little before and after, for we are told by a grave author, an eminent French Physician, that fish being a prolific diet, there are more children born in Roman Catholic countries about nine months after Lent, than at any other season; therefore reckoning a year after Lent, the markets will be more glutted than usual, because the number of Popish infants is at least three to one in this kingdom, and therefore it will have one other collateral advantage by lessening the number of Papists among us.

I have already computed the charge of nursing a beggar's child (in which list I reckon all cottagers, labourers, and four-fifths of the farmers) to be about two shillings *per annum*, rags included, and I believe no gentleman would repine to give ten shillings for the carcass of a good fat child, which, as I have said, will make four dishes of excellent nutritive meat, when he hath only some particular friend, or his own family to dine with him. Thus the Squire will learn to be a good landlord, and grow popular among his tenants, the mother will have eight shillings net profit, and be fit for work till she produces another child.

Those who are more thrifty (as I must confess the times require) may flay the carcass; the skin of which, artificially dressed, will make admirable gloves for ladies, and summer boots for fine gentlemen.

As to our City of Dublin, shambles may be appointed for this purpose, in the most convenient parts of it, and butchers we may be assured will not be wanting, although I rather recommend buying the children alive, and dressing them hot from the knife, as we do roasting pigs.

A very worthy person, a true lover of his country, and whose virtues I highly esteem, was lately pleased, in discoursing on this matter, to offer a refinement upon my scheme. He said, that many gentlemen of this kingdom, having of late destroyed their deer, he conceived that the want of venison might be well supplied by the bodies of young lads and maidens, not exceeding fourteen years of age, nor under twelve, so great a number of both sexes in every country being now ready to starve, for want of work and service: and these to be disposed of by their parents if alive, or otherwise by their nearest relations. But with due deference to so excellent a friend, and so deserving a patriot, I cannot be altogether in his sentiments; for as to the males, my American acquaintance assured me from frequent experience, that their flesh was generally tough and lean, like that of our schoolboys, by continual exercise, and their taste disagreeable, and to fatten them would not answer the charge. Then as to the females, it would, I think with humble submission, be a loss to the public, because they soon would become breeders themselves: and besides, it is not improbable that some scrupulous people might be apt to censure such a practice, (although indeed very unjustly) as a little bordering upon cruelty, which, I confess, hath always been with me the strongest objection against any project, however so well intended.

But in order to justify my friend, he confessed that this expedient was put into his head by the famous Psalmanazar, a native of the island Formosa, who came from thence to London, above twenty years ago, and in conversation told my friend, that in his country when any young person happened to be put to death, the executioner sold the carcass to persons of quality, as a prime dainty, and that, in his time, the body of a plump girl of fifteen, who was crucified for an attempt to poison the emperor, was sold to his Imperial Majesty's Prime Minister of State, and other great Mandarins of the Court, in joints from the gibbet, at four hundred crowns. Neither indeed can I deny, that if the same use were made of several plump young girls in this town, who, without one single groat to their fortunes, cannot stir abroad without a chair, and appear at the playhouse, and assemblies in foreign fineries, which they never will pay for, the kingdom would not be the worse.

Some persons of a desponding spirit are in great concern about that vast number of poor people, who are aged, diseased, or maimed, and I have been desired to employ my thoughts what course may be taken, to ease the nation of so grievous an encumbrance. But I am not in the least pain upon that matter, because it is very well known, that they are every day dying, and rotting, by cold, and famine, and filth, and vermin, as fast as can be reasonably expected. And as to the younger labourers they are now in almost as hopeful a condition. They cannot get work, and consequently pine away for want of nourishment, to a degree, that if at any time they are accidentally hired to common labour, they have not strength to perform it; and thus the country and themselves are in a fair way of being soon delivered from the evils to come.

I have too long digressed, and therefore shall return to my subject. I think the advantages by the proposal which I have made are obvious and many, as well as of the highest importance.

For first, as I have already observed, it would greatly lessen the number of Papists, with whom we are yearly over-run, being the principal breeders of the nation, as well as our most dangerous enemies, and who stay at home on purpose with a design to deliver the kingdom to the Pretender, hoping to take their advantage by the absence of so many good Protestants, who have chosen rather to leave their country, than stay at home, and pay tithes against their conscience, to an Episcopal curate.

Secondly, The poorer tenants will have something valuable of their own, which by law may be made liable to distress, and help to pay their land-lords rent, their corn and cattle being already seized, and *money a thing unknown.*

Thirdly, Whereas the maintenance of an hundred thousand children, from two years old, and upwards, cannot be computed at less than ten shillings a piece *per annum*, the na-tion's stock will be thereby increased fifty thousand pounds *per annum*, be-sides the profit of a new dish, intro-duced to the tables of all gentlemen of fortune in the kingdom, who have any refinement in taste, and the money will circulate among ourselves, the goods being entirely of our own growth and manufacture.

Fourthly, The constant breeders, besides the gain of eight shillings sterling *per annum*, by the sale of their children, will be rid of the charge of maintaining them after the first year.

Fifthly, This food would likewise bring great custom to taverns, where the vintners will certainly be so pru-dent as to procure the best receipts for dressing it to perfection, and conse-quently have their houses frequented by all the fine gentlemen, who justly value themselves upon their knowl-edge in good eating; and a skilful cook, who understands how to oblige his guests will contrive to make it as expensive as they please.

Sixthly, This would be a great in-ducement to marriage, which all wise nations have either encouraged by re-wards, or enforced by laws and penal-ties. It would increase the care and tenderness of mothers toward their children, when they were sure of a settlement for life, to the poor babes, provided in some sort by the public

to their annual profit instead of ex-pense. We should see an honest emu-lation among the married women, which of them could bring the fattest child to the market; men would be-come as fond of their wives, during the time of their pregnancy, as they are now of their mares in foal, their cows in calf, or sows when they are ready to farrow, nor offer to beat or kick them (as it is too frequent a practice) for fear of a miscarriage.

Many other advantages might be enumerated: For instance, the addi-tion of some thousand carcasses in our exportation of barrelled beef; the propagation of swine's flesh, and im-provement in the art of making good bacon, so much wanted among us by the great destruction of pigs, too fre-quent at our tables, which are no way comparable in taste, or magnificence to a well-grown, fat yearling child, which roasted whole will make a con-siderable figure at a Lord Mayor's feast, or any other public entertain-ment. But this, and many others I omit, being studious of brevity.

Supposing that one thousand fami-lies in this city, would be constant customers for infants' flesh, besides others who might have it at merry-meetings, particularly weddings and christenings, I compute that Dublin would take off annually about twenty thousand carcasses, and the rest of the kingdom (where probably they will be sold somewhat cheaper) the re-maining eighty thousand.

I can think of no one objection, that will possibly be raised against this proposal, unless it should be urged that the number of peo-ple will be thereby much lessened in the kingdom. This I freely own, and was indeed one principal design in offering it to the world. I desire the reader will observe, that I cal-culate my remedy *for this one indi-vidual Kingdom of Ireland, and for no other that ever was, is, or, I think, ever can be upon earth.* Therefore let no man talk to me of other expedi-ents: *Of taxing our absentees at five shillings a pound: Of using neither clothes, nor household furniture, except what is of our own growth and manufacture: Of utterly rejecting the materials and instruments that promote foreign luxury: Of curing the expensiveness of pride, vanity, idleness, and gaming in our women: Of introducing a vein of parsimony, prudence and temperance: Of learning to love our Country, wherein we differ even from* LAPLANDERS, *and the inhabitants of* TOPINAMBOO: *Of quitting our animosities and factions, nor act any longer like the Jews, who were murdering one another at the very moment their city was taken: Of being a little cautious not to sell our country and consciences for nothing: Of teaching landlords to have at least one degree of mercy toward their tenants. Lastly, of putting a spirit of honesty, industry, and skill into our shopkeepers, who, if a resolution could now be taken to buy our native goods, would immediately unite to cheat and exact upon us in the price, the measure, and the goodness, nor could ever yet be brought to make one fair proposal of just dealing, though often and earnestly invited to it.*

Therefore I repeat, let no man talk to me of these and the like expedients, till he hath at least some glimpse of hope that there will ever be some hearty and sincere attempt to put them in practice.

But as to myself, having been wearied out for many years with offering vain, idle, visionary thoughts, and at length utterly despairing of success, I fortunately fell upon this proposal, which as it is wholly new, so it hath something solid and real, of no expense and little trouble, full in our own power, and whereby we can incur no danger in *disobliging* ENGLAND. For this kind of commodity will not bear exportation, the flesh being of too tender a consistence, to admit a long continuance in salt, *although perhaps I could name a country, which would be glad to eat up our whole nation without it.*

After all I am not so violently bent upon my own opinion, as to reject any offer, proposed by wise men, which shall be found equally innocent, cheap, easy and effectual. But before something of that kind shall be advanced in contradiction to my scheme, and offering a better, I desire the author, or authors will be pleased maturely to consider two points. First, as things now stand, how they will be able to find food and raiment for an hundred thousand useless mouths and backs. And secondly, there being a round million of creatures in human figure, throughout this kingdom, whose whole subsistence put into a common stock would leave them in debt two millions of pounds sterling; adding those who are beggars by profession to the bulk of farmers, cottagers, and labourers with their wives and children, who are beggars in effect; I desire those politicians who dislike my overture, and may perhaps be so bold to attempt an answer, that they will first ask the parents of these mortals, whether they would not at this day think it a great happiness to have been sold for food at a year old, in the manner I prescribe, and thereby have avoided such a perpetual scene of misfortunes, as they have since gone through, by the oppression of landlords, the impossibility of paying rent without money or trade, the want of common sustenance, with neither house nor clothes to cover them from the inclemencies of the weather, and the most inevitable prospect of entailing the like, or greater miseries upon their breed for ever.

I profess in the sincerity of my heart that I have not the least personal interest in endeavouring to promote this necessary work, having no other motive than the *public good of my country, by advancing our trade, providing for infants, relieving the poor, and giving some pleasure to the rich.* I have no children, by which I can propose to get a single penny; the youngest being nine years old, and my wife past child-bearing.

[*For additional readings in Swift see pages 1083–1123.*]

RICHARD STEELE (1672-1729) and JOSEPH ADDISON (1672-1719)

The literary partnership of Steele and Addison is one of the happiest in the annals of English letters. In temperament they differed greatly, but in their aims and tastes they were in the main united, and by their collaboration on *The Tatler* and *The Spectator* they achieved a success and influence such as would probably have been beyond the reach of either one alone. The dashing, impulsive, sometimes erratic, Irishman could contribute a warm human touch to everything he wrote; the more restrained and sedate Englishman was surer and steadier in tone. But both were intent on reforming English taste and manners by means of light banter and gentle persuasion; both were deeply sympathetic with the moral attitude of the rapidly-growing middle class; and both aimed also to reconcile this popular audience to the best elements of the inherited English culture of the more courtly or aristocratic tradition.

In their lives, as in their literary labors, they were often associated. They were schoolmates at the Charterhouse in London. Both went up to Oxford. But Steele characteristically ran away from his college, enlisted under an assumed name in the Life Guards in London, and—his identity and ability being soon discovered—rose to the rank of captain. He became a familiar figure in the circles of the coffee-house wits, a member of the distinguished Kit-Cat Club, and eventually found himself succumbing to the temptations of fashionable London life. To strengthen his own resistance he wrote a small volume, *The Christian Hero* (1701), on the theme that only Christian doctrine can give a man the moral heroism necessary in the face of such temptations. In the same year he produced his first play, *The Funeral*, which, like his later comedies, provided the audience with a combination of entertainment and moral improvement. In 1706 Steele was appointed gentleman in waiting to Prince George of Denmark, the husband of Queen Anne, and in 1707 to the editorship of the *London Gazette*, the official organ of the government. In 1707 he was married to Mary Scurlock, the "dear Prue" of his famous letters, who was his second wife. But in spite of this apparent prosperity, Steele was always embarrassed by his weakness for living beyond his means. In 1709 he started an essay periodical, *The Tatler*, partly for the purpose of replenishing his purse.

Addison, meanwhile, had been arriving by a different route. He distinguished himself at Oxford, where it was generally believed he was destined for the church. He became Fellow of Magdalen College, was permitted by the elderly John Dryden to contribute to his translation of Virgil, and attained a high reputation for his Latin verse. But in 1699 the ministry sought him out as a man of promise for public employment and offered him a pension to prepare himself for such a career by travel abroad. Addison accepted this change in his prospects and spent several years on the Continent. But in 1703 his pension was stopped and all plans cancelled, owing to the political changes incident to the death of William III. His next opportunity came in 1704, when he was asked to write a poem celebrating the victory of Blenheim, and the success of *The Campaign* launched him on a political career. In 1706 he became under-secretary of state, and he sat in the Commons from 1708 until his death. During these years both Addison and Steele formed an intimacy with Swift, who was in London from time to time on business on behalf of the church in Ireland; from Swift's papers against the astrologer Partridge Steele borrowed the pseudonym "Isaac Bickerstaff" for *The Tatler*.

In 1709 Addison went to Ireland for a short period as secretary to Lord Wharton, the Lord Lieutenant, whom Swift detested. While there he read the early *Tatlers*, which were coming out three times a week from April 12, 1709. Detecting Steele's authorship, he began to send contributions, which were gratefully accepted. *The Tatler*, however, shows in its contents as well as in its title the predominant impress of the personality of Steele. On January 2, 1711, it was discontinued, and on March 1 of the same year appeared the first number of a new paper, *The Spectator*, which was published six times a week until December 6, 1712. As the title and the first number indicate, Addison was the dominant influence in this publication, and his contributions to it outnumber those of Steele.

248

Regarding the later careers of the two men, little need be said here. After 1710 both were prevented by their Whig politics from continuing their intimacy with Swift, or with forming any close friendships with Pope, Gay, Arbuthnot, and other wits of the Tory circle. The suspicions arising between Addison and Pope, the blame for which must fall in part on Addison, inspired Pope's great satirical portrait of Addison in the *Epistle to Arbuthnot*. Addison held some political offices of importance after the accession of George I, and in 1716 married the countess dowager of Warwick. He died in 1719 and was buried in West-minister Abbey. Steele continued his busy career in journalism and politics, was knighted in 1715, wrote a notable sentimental comedy in *The Conscious Lovers* (1722), and constantly strove to disengage himself from chronic financial difficulties which finally forced him to retire from London to some property in Wales in 1724. He died in 1729.

After their publication in periodical form, the *Tatler* and *Spectator* were reprinted with some revision in details in collected volumes, and went through many editions. They came to represent for the next hundred years the very type and excellence of the periodical essay, and innumerable imitations ran their brief courses, not only in England, but in France, Germany, and almost all other European countries. Their prestige and popularity were due in part to the perfect style and tone of the papers; they were easy and natural without being unduly familiar or colloquial; they were graceful without being artificial; they set a high and pleasing standard of journalistic manners for an age that was deeply interested in manners in journalism as well as elsewhere. Even a slight acquaintance with English journals before and after Steele and Addison, and with their protestations in their papers, reveals with what determination they set themselves against the inevitable temptations of the popular press.

The most thoroughly annotated edition of the *Tatler* is by G. A. Aitken (4 vols., 1898), who also edited the *Spectator* (8 vols., 1898). An excellent edition of the *Spectator* by G. Gregory Smith (8 vols., 1897-98) is also available in Everyman's Library. G. A. Aitken is the author of a voluminous and authoritative biography of Steele (2 vols., 1889), but there is no similar life of Addison. W. J. Courthope's volume on Addison (1884) in the English Men of Letters Series is brief, but competent, and the first chapter, on the reformation accomplished by Addison and Steele in the national manners and sentiments, is especially valuable. There is no complete edition of Steele's works; a collected edition of Addison by Bishop Hurd in six volumes is best consulted in the reprints of 1856 and later. For the history of periodicals see W. J. Graham, *English Literary Periodicals* (1930) and G. S. Marr, *Periodical Essayists of the Eighteenth Century* (1925). For additional readings see pages 1125-1129.

THE TATLER

No. 1   Tuesday, April 12, 1709.
[Steele]

Quicquid agunt homines . . . nostri farrago libelli.
                                    Juvenal, *Satires*, I, 85, 86.

Though the other papers which are published for the use of the good people of England have certainly very wholesome effects, and are laudable in their particular kinds, they do not seem to come up to the main design of such narrations, which, I humbly presume, should be principally intended for the use of politic persons, who are so public spirited as to neglect their own affairs to look into transactions of State. Now these gentlemen, for the most part, being men of strong zeal and weak intellects, it

is both a charitable and necessary work to offer something, whereby such worthy and well-affected members of the commonwealth may be instructed, after their reading, *what to think;* which shall be the end and purpose of this my paper: wherein I shall from time to time report and consider all matters of what kind soever that shall occur to me, and publish such my advices and reflections every Tuesday, Thursday, and Saturday in the week for the convenience of the post. I have also resolved to have something which may be of entertainment to the fair sex, in honour of whom I have taken the title of this paper. I therefore earnestly desire all persons, without distinction, to take it in for the present gratis, and hereafter at the price of one penny, forbidding all hawkers to take more for it at their peril. And I desire all persons to consider, that I am at a very great charge for proper materials for this work, as well as that before I resolved upon it, I had settled a correspondence in all parts of the known and knowing world. And forasmuch as this globe is not trodden upon by mere drudges of business only, but that men of spirit and genius are justly to be esteemed as considerable agents in it, we shall not, upon a dearth of news, present you with musty foreign edicts, or dull proclamations, but shall divide our relation of the passages which occur in action or discourse throughout this town, as well as elsewhere, under such dates of places as may prepare you for the matter you are to expect, in the following manner:

All accounts of gallantry, pleasure, and entertainment, shall be under the article of White's Chocolate-house; poetry, under that of Will's Coffee-house; learning, under the title of Grecian; foreign and domestic news, you will have from St. James's Coffee-house; and what else I shall on any other subject offer, shall be dated from my own apartment.

I once more desire my readers to consider that as I cannot keep an ingenious man to go daily to Will's under twopence each day merely for his charges, to White's under sixpence, nor to the Grecian without allowing him some plain Spanish, to be as able as others at the learned table; and that a good observer cannot speak with even Kidney at St. James's without clean linen; I say, these considerations will, I hope, make all persons willing to comply with my humble request (when my gratis stock is exhausted) of a penny a piece; especially since they are sure of some proper amusement, and that it is impossible for me to want means to entertain them, having, besides the helps of my own parts, the power of divination, and that I can, by casting a figure, tell you all that will happen before it comes to pass.

But this last faculty I shall use very sparingly, and speak of but few things until they are passed, for fear of divulging matters which may offend our superiors.

White's Chocolate-house, April 7.

The deplorable condition of a very pretty gentleman, who walks here at the hours when men of quality first appear, is what is very much lamented. His history is, that on the 9th of September, 1705, being in his one and twentieth year, he was washing his teeth at a tavern window in Pall Mall, when a fine equipage passed by, and in it a young lady, who looked up at him; away goes the coach, and the young gentleman pulled off his night-cap, and instead of rubbing his gums, as he ought to do out of the window till about four o'clock, he sits him down, and spoke not a word till twelve at night; after which he began to inquire, if anybody knew the lady. The company asked, "What lady?" But he said no more until they broke up at six in the morning. All the ensuing winter he went from church to church every Sunday, and from playhouse to playhouse every night in the week, but could never find the original of the picture which dwelt in his bosom. In a word, his attention to anything but his passion, was utterly gone. He has lost all the money he ever played for, and been confuted in every argument he has entered upon since the moment he first saw her. He is of a noble family, has naturally a very good air, and is of a frank, honest temper: but this passion has so extremely mauled him, that his features are set and uninformed, and his whole visage is deadened by a long absence of thought. He never appears in any alacrity, but when raised by wine; at which time he is sure to come hither, and throw away a great deal of wit on fellows, who have no sense further than just to observe, that our poor lover has most understanding when he is drunk, and is least in his senses when he is sober.

Will's Coffee-house, April 8.

On Thursday last was presented, for the benefit of Mr. Betterton, the celebrated comedy, called "Love for Love." Those excellent players, Mrs. Barry, Mrs. Bracegirdle, and Mr. Doggett, though not at present concerned in the house, acted on that occasion. There has not been known so great a concourse of persons of distinction as at that time; the stage itself was covered with gentlemen and ladies, and when the curtain was drawn, it discovered even there a very splendid audience. This unusual encouragement, which was given to a play for the advantage of so great an actor, gives an undeniable instance, that the true relish for manly entertainments and rational pleasures is not wholly lost. All the parts were acted to perfection; the actors were careful of their carriage, and no one was guilty of the affectation to insert witticisms of his own, but a due respect was had to the audience, for encouraging this accomplished player. It is not now doubted but plays will revive, and take their usual place in the opinion of persons of wit and merit, notwithstanding their late apostacy in favour of dress and sound.

This place is very much altered since Mr. Dryden frequented it; where you used to see songs, epigrams, and satires in the hands of every man you met, you have now only a pack of cards; and instead of the cavils about the turn of the expression, the elegance of the style, and the like, the learned now dispute only about the truth of the game. But, however the company is altered, all have shown a great respect for Mr. Betterton: and the very gaming part of this house have been so much touched with a sense of the uncertainty of human affairs (which alter with themselves every moment) that in this gentle-

man, they pitied Mark Antony of Rome, Hamlet of Denmark, Mithridates of Pontus, Theodosius of Greece, and Henry the Eighth of England. It is well known he has been in the condition of each of those illustrious personages for several hours together, and behaved himself in those high stations, in all the changes of the scene, with suitable dignity. For these reasons, we intend to repeat this favour to him on a proper occasion, lest he who can instruct us so well in personating feigned sorrows, should be lost to us by suffering under real ones. The town is at present in very great expectation of seeing a comedy, now in rehearsal, which is the twenty-fifth production of my honoured friend Mr. Thomas D'Urfey; who, besides his great abilities in the dramatic, has a peculiar talent in the lyric way of writing, and that with a manner wholly new and unknown to the ancient Greeks and Romans, wherein he is but faintly imitated in the translations of the modern Italian operas.

St. James's Coffee-house, April 11.

Letters from the Hague of the 16th say, that Major-General Cadogan was gone to Brussels, with orders to disperse proper instructions for assembling the whole force of the Allies in Flanders in the beginning of the next month. The late offers concerning peace were made in the style of persons who think themselves upon equal terms. But the Allies have so just a sense of their present advantages, that they will not admit of a treaty, except France offers what is more suitable to her present condition. At the same time we make preparations, as if we were alarmed by a greater force than that which we are carrying into the field. Thus this point seems now to be argued sword in hand. This was what a great general alluded to, when being asked the names of those who were to be plenipotentiaries for the ensuing peace, answered, with a serious air, "There are about a hundred thousand of us." Mr. Kidney, who has the ear of the greatest politicians that come hither, tells me, there is a mail come in to-day with letters, dated Hague, April 19, N. S., which say, a design of bringing part of our troops into the field at the latter end of this month, is now altered to a resolution of marching towards the camp about the 20th of the next. There happened the other day, in the road of Scheveling, an engagement between a privateer of Zealand and one of Dunkirk. The Dunkirker, carrying 33 pieces of cannon, was taken and brought into the Texel. It is said, the courier of Monsieur Rouillé is returned to him from the Court of France. Monsieur Vendôme being reinstated in the favour of the Duchess of Burgundy, is to command in Flanders.

Mr. Kidney added that there were letters of the 17th from Ghent, which give an account that the enemy had formed a design to surprise two battalions of the Allies which lay at Alost; but those battalions received advice of their march, and retired to Dendermond. Lieutenant-General Wood appeared on this occasion at the head of 5000 foot, and 1000 horse, upon which the enemy withdrew, without making any further attempt.

From my own Apartment.

I am sorry I am obliged to trouble the public with so much discourse upon a matter which I at the very first mentioned as a trifle—viz., the death of Mr. Partridge, under whose name there is an almanac come out for the year 1709, in one page of which it is asserted by the said John Partridge, that he is still living, and that not only so, but that he was also living some time before, and even at the instant when I writ of his death. I have in another place, and in a paper by itself, sufficiently convinced this man that he is dead, and if he has any

shame, I don't doubt but that by this time he owns it to all his acquaintance: for though the legs and arms, and whole body of that man may still appear and perform their animal functions; yet since, as I have elsewhere observed, his art is gone, the man is gone. I am, as I said, concerned, that this little matter should make so much noise; but since I am engaged, I take myself obliged in honour to go on in my lucubrations, and by the help of these arts of which I am master, as well as my skill in astrological speculations, I shall, as I see occasion, proceed to confute other dead men, who pretend to be in being, that they are actualy deceased. I therefore give all men fair warning to mend their manners, for I shall from time to time print bills of mortality; and I beg the pardon of all such who shall be named therein, if they who are good for nothing, shall find themselves in the number of the deceased.

No. 21   Saturday, May 28, 1709.
[Steele]

White's Chocolate-house, May 26.

A gentleman has writ to me out of the country a very civil letter, and said things which I suppress with great violence to my vanity. There are many terms in my narratives which he complains want explaining, and has therefore desired, that, for the benefit of my country readers, I would let him know what I mean by a Gentleman, a Pretty Fellow, a Toast, a Coquette, a Critic, a Wit, and all other appellations of those now in the gayer world, who are in possession of these several characters; together with an account of those who unfortunately pretend to them. I shall begin with him we usually call a Gentleman, or man of conversation.

It is generally thought that warmth of imagination, quick relish of pleasure, and a manner of becoming it, are the most essential qualities for forming this sort of man. But any one that is much in company will observe, that the height of good breeding is shown rather in never giving offence, than in doing obliging things. Thus, he that never shocks you, though he is seldom entertaining, is more likely to keep your favour than he who often entertains, and sometimes displeases you. The most necessary talent therefore in a man of conversation, which is what we ordinarily intend by a fine gentleman, is a good judgment. He that has this in perfection, is master of his companion, without letting him see it; and has the same advantage over men of any other qualifications whatsoever, as one that can see would have over a blind man of ten times his strength.

This is what makes Sophronius the darling of all who converse with him, and the most powerful with his acquaintance of any man in town. By the light of this faculty, he acts with great ease and freedom among the men of pleasure, and acquits himself with skill and despatch among the men of business. All which he performs with so much success, that, with as much discretion in life as any man ever had, he neither is, nor appears, cunning. But as he does a good office, if he ever does it, with readiness and alacrity; so he denies what he does not care to engage in, in a manner that convinces you that you ought not to have asked it. His judgment is so good and unerring, and accompanied with so cheerful a spirit, that his conversation is a continual feast, at which he helps some, and is helped by others, in such a manner that the equality of society is perfectly kept up, and every man obliges as much as he is obliged: for it is the greatest and justest skill in a man of superior understanding, to know how to be on a level with his companions. This sweet disposition runs through all the actions of Sophronius, and makes his company desired by women, without being envied by men. Sophronius would be as just as

he is, if there were no law; and would be as discreet as he is, if there were no such thing as calumny.

In imitation of this agreeable being, is made that animal we call a Pretty Fellow; who being just able to find out that what makes Sophronius acceptable, is a natural behaviour; in order to the same reputation, makes his own an artificial one. Jack Dimple is his perfect mimic, whereby he is of course the most unlike him of all men living. Sophronius just now passed into the inner room directly forward: Jack comes as fast after as he can for the right and left looking-glass, in which he had but just approved himself by a nod at each, and marched on. He will meditate within for half an hour, till he thinks he is not careless enough in his air, and come back to the mirror to recollect his forgetfulness.

Will's Coffee-house, May 27.

This night was acted the comedy, called, "The Fox;" but I wonder the modern writers do not use their interest in the house to suppress such representations. A man that has been at this, will hardly like any other play during the season: therefore I humbly move, that the writings, as well as dresses, of the last age, should give way to the present fashion. We are come into a good method enough (if we were not interrupted in our mirth by such an apparition as a play of Jonson's) to be entertained at more ease, both to the spectator and the writer, than in the days of old. It is no difficulty to get hats, and swords, and wigs, and shoes, and everything else, from the shops in town, and make a man show himself by his habit, without more ado, to be a counsellor, a fop, a courtier, or a citizen, and no be obliged to make those characters talk in different dialects to be distinguished from each other. This is cer-

tainly the surest and best way of writing: but such a play as this makes a
man for a month after overrun with
criticism, and inquire, what every man
on the stage said? What had such a
one to do to meddle with such a
thing? How came the other, who was
bred after this or that manner, to
speak so like a man conversant among
a different people? These questions   10
rob us of all our pleasure; for at this
rate, no one sentence in a play should
be spoken by any one character, which
could possibly enter into the head of
any other man represented in it; but
every sentiment should be peculiar to
him only who utters it. Laborious
Ben's works will bear this sort of inquisition; but if the present writers
were thus examined, and the offences   20
against this rule cut out, few plays
would be long enough for the whole
evening's entertainment.

But I don't know how they did in
those old times: this same Ben Jonson has made every one's passion in
this play be towards money, and yet
not one of them expresses that desire,
or endeavours to obtain it any way
but what is peculiar to him only: one   30
sacrifices his wife, another his profession, another his posterity from the
same motive; but their characters are
kept so skilfully apart, that it seems
prodigious their discourses should
rise from the invention of the same
author.

But the poets are a nest of hornets,
and I'll drive these thoughts no farther, but must mention some hard   40
treatment I am like to meet with from
my brother-writers. I am credibly informed, that the author of a play,
called "Love in a Hollow Tree," has
made some remarks upon my late discourse on "The Naked Truth." I cannot blame a gentleman for writing
against any error; it is for the good
of the learned world. But I would
have the thing fairly left between us   50
two, and not under the protection of
patrons. But my intelligence is that he

has dedicated his treatise to the Honourable Mr. Ed——d H——rd.

From my own Apartment, May 27.

"To Isaac Bickerstaff, Esq.
York, May 16, 1709.

"Sir,
"Being convinced as the whole
world is, how infallible your predictions are, and having the honour to
be your near relation, of the Staffian
family, I was under great concern at
one of your predictions relating to
yourself, wherein you foretold your
own death would happen on the 17th
instant, unless it were prevented by
the assistance of well-disposed people:
I have therefore prevailed on my own
modesty to send you a piece of news,
which may serve instead of Goddard's
Drops, to keep you alive for two days,
till nature be able to recover itself, or
till you meet with some better help
from other hands. Therefore, without
further ceremony, I will go on to relate
a singular adventure just happened in
the place where I am writing, wherein
it may be highly useful for the public
to be informed.

"Three young ladies of our town
were on Saturday last indicted for
witchcraft. The witnesses against the
first deposed upon oath before Justice
Bindover, that she kept spirits locked
up in vessels, which sometimes appeared in flames of blue fire; that she
used magical herbs, with some of
which she drew in hundreds of men
daily to her, who went out from her
presence all inflamed, their mouths
parched, and a hot steam issuing
from them, attended with a grievous
stench; that many of the said men
were by the force of that herb metamorphosed into swine, and lay wallowing in the kennels for twenty-four
hours, before they could reassume
their shapes or their senses.

"It was proved against the second
that she cut off by night the limbs
from dead bodies that were hanged,
and was seen to dig holes in the
ground, to mutter some conjuring

words, and bury pieces of the flesh, after the usual manner of witches.

"The third was accused for a notorious piece of sorcery, long practised by hags, of moulding up pieces of dough into the shapes of men, women, and children; then heating them at a gentle fire, which had a sympathetic power to torment the bowels of those in the neighbourhood.

"This was the sum of what was objected against the three ladies, who indeed had nothing to say in their own defence, but downright denying the facts, which is like to avail very little when they come upon their trials.

"But the parson of our parish, a strange refractory man, will believe nothing of all this; so that the whole town cries out, 'Shame! that one of his coat should be such an atheist!' and design to complain of him to the bishop. He goes about very oddly to solve the matter. He supposes that the first of these ladies keeping a brandy and tobacco shop, the fellows went out smoking, and got drunk towards evening, and made themselves beasts. He says, the second is a butcher's daughter, and sometimes brings a quarter of mutton from the slaughterhouse overnight against a market-day, and once buried a bit of beef in the ground, as a known receipt to cure warts on her hands. The parson affirms, that the third sells gingerbread, which, to please the children, she is forced to stamp with images before it is baked; and if it burns their guts, it is because they eat too much, or do not drink after it.

"These are the answers he gives to solve these wonderful phenomena; upon which I shall not animadvert, but leave it among the philosophers: and so wishing you all success in your undertakings for the amendment of the world, I remain,

"Dear Cousin,
"Your most affectionate Kinsman,
"and humble Servant,
"Ephraim Bedstaff."

"P.S.—Those who were condemned to death among the Athenians, were obliged to take a dose of poison, which made them die upwards, seizing first upon their feet, making them cold and insensible, and so ascending gradually, till it reached the vital parts. I believe your death, which you foretold would happen on the 17th instant, will fall out the same way, and that your distemper hath already seized on you, and makes progress daily. The lower part of you, that is, the advertisements, is dead; and these have risen for these ten days last past, so that they now take up almost a whole paragraph. Pray, sir, do your endeavour to drive this distemper as much as possible to the extreme parts, and keep it there, as wise folks do the gout; for if it once gets into your stomach, it will soon fly up into your head, and you are a dead man."

St. James's Coffee-house, May 27.

We hear from Leghorn that Sir Edward Whitaker, with five men-of-war, four transports, and two fire-ships, was arrived at that port, and Admiral Byng was suddenly expected. Their squadrons being joined, they design to sail directly for Final, to transport the reinforcements lodged in those parts, to Barcelona.

They write from Milan, that Count Thaun arrived there on the 16th instant, N.S., and proceeded on his journey to Turin on the 21st, in order to concert such measures with his royal highness, as shall appear necessary for the operations of the ensuing campaign.

Advices from Dauphiné say, that the troops of the Duke of Savoy began already to appear in those valleys, whereof he made himself master the last year; and that the Duke of Berwick applied himself with all imaginable diligence to secure the passes of the mountains by ordering entrenchments to be made towards Briançon, Tourneau, and the Valley of Queiras. That general has also been at Marseilles and Toulon, to hasten the transportation of the corn and provisions designed for his army.

Letters from Vienna, bearing date May 23, N.S., import that the Cardinal of Saxe-Zeits and the Prince of Lichtenstein were preparing to set out for Presburgh, to assist at the Diet of the States of Hungary, which 10 is to be assembled at that place on the 25th of this month. General Heister would shortly appear at the head of his army at Trentschin, which place is appointed for the general rendezvous of the Imperial forces in Hungary; from whence he will advance to lay siege to Neuhausel: in the meantime, reinforcements, with a great train of artillery, are marching the 20 same way. The King of Denmark arrived on the 10th instant at Innspruck, and on the 26th at Dresden, under a triple discharge of the artillery of that place; but his Majesty refused the ceremonies of a public entry.

Our letters from the Upper Rhine say that the Imperial army began to form itself at Etlingen; where the re- 30 spective deputies of the Elector Palatine, the Prince of Baden Durlach, the Bishopric of Spires, &c. were assembled, and had taken the necessary measures for the provision of forage, the security of the country against the incursions of the enemy, and laying a bridge over the Rhine. Several vessels laden with corn are daily passing before Frankfort for the Lower 40 Rhine.

Letters from Poland inform us, that a detachment of Muscovite cavalry, under the command of General Infland, had joined the confederate army; and the infantry commanded by General Goltz, was expected to come up within few days. These succours will amount to 20,000 men.

Our last advices from the Hague, 50 dated June the 4th, N.S., say, that they expected a courier from the French Court with the ratification of the preliminaries that night or the

day following. His Grace the Duke of Marlborough will set out for Brussels on Wednesday or Thursday next, if the despatches which are expected from Paris don't alter his resolutions. Letters from Majorca confirm the honourable capitulation of the castle of Alicant, and also the death of the governor, Major-General Richards, 10 Colonel Sibourg, and Major Vignolles, who were all buried in the ruins of that place, by the springing of their great mine, which did, it seems, more execution than was reported. Monsieur Torcy passed through Mons in his return, and had there a long conference with the Elector of Bavaria; after which, that prince spoke publicly of the treat- 20 ment he had from France with the utmost indignation.

Any person that shall come publicly abroad in a fantastical habit, contrary to the present mode and fashion, except Don Diego Dismallo, or any other out of poverty, shall have his name and dress inserted in our next.

N.B.—Mr. How'd'call is desired to 30 leave off those buttons.

THE SPECTATOR

No. 1.

[Addison.] Thursday, March 1, 17$_{11}^{10}$

Non fumum ex fulgore, sed ex fumo dare lucem
Cogitat, ut speciosa dehinc miracula promat.—Horace, *Ars Poetica*, 143.

I have observed, that a reader seldom peruses a book with pleasure, till he knows whether the writer of it be a black or fair man, of a mild or cholerick disposition, married or a bachelor, with other particulars of the 50 like nature, that conduce very much to the right understanding of an author. To gratify this curiosity, which is so natural to a reader, I design this paper, and my next, as prefatory discourses to my following writings, and shall give some account in them of the several persons that are engaged in this work. As the chief trouble of compiling, digesting, and correcting will fall to my share, I must do myself the justice to open the work with my own history.

I was born to a small hereditary estate, which, according to the tradition of the village where it lies, was bounded by the same hedges and ditches in William the Conqueror's time that it is at present, and has been delivered down from father to son whole and entire, without the loss or acquisition of a single field or meadow, during the space of six hundred years. There runs a story in the family, that when my mother was gone with child of me about three months, she dreamt that she was brought to bed of a judge: Whether this might proceed from a law-suit which was then depending in the family, or my father's being a Justice of the Peace, I cannot determine; for I am not so vain as to think it presaged any dignity that I should arrive at in my future life, though that was the interpretation which the neighbourhood put upon it. The gravity of my behaviour at my very first appearance in the world, and all the time that I sucked, seemed to favour my mother's dream: For, as she had often told me, I threw away my rattle before I was two months old, and would not make use of my coral till they had taken away the bells from it.

As for the rest of my infancy, there being nothing in it remarkable, I shall pass it over in silence. I find that, during my nonage, I had the reputation of a very sullen youth, but was always a favourite of my school-master, who used to say, that my parts were solid and would wear well. I had not been long at the university, before I distinguished myself by a most profound silence; for during the space of eight years, excepting in the public exercises of the college, I scarce uttered the quantity of an hundred words;

and indeed do not remember that I ever spoke three sentences together in my whole life. Whilst I was in this learned body I applied myself with so much diligence to my studies, that there are very few celebrated books, either in the learned or the modern tongues, which I am not acquainted with.

Upon the death of my father I was resolved to travel into foreign countries, and therefore left the university, with the character of an odd unaccountable fellow that had a great deal of learning, if I would but show it. An insatiable thirst after knowledge carried me into all the countries of Europe, in which there was any thing new or strange to be seen; nay, to such a degree was my curiosity raised, that having read the controversies of some great men concerning the antiquities of Egypt, I made a voyage to Grand Cairo on purpose to take the measure of a pyramid; and as soon as I had set myself right in that particular, returned to my native country with great satisfaction.

I have passed my latter years in this city, where I am frequently seen in most public places, tho' there are not above half a dozen of my select friends that know me; of whom my next paper shall give a more particular account. There is no place of general resort, wherein I do not often make my appearance; sometimes I am seen thrusting my head into a round of politicians at Will's, and listening with great attention to the narratives that are made in those little circular audiences. Sometimes I smoke a pipe at Child's; and whilst I seem attentive to nothing but the *Postman,* overhear the conversation of every table in the room. I appear on Sunday nights at St. James's Coffee-house and sometimes join the little committee of politics in the inner room, as one who comes there to hear and improve. My face is likewise very well known at the Grecian, the Cocoa-Tree, and in the theatres both of Drury Lane and the Haymarket. I have been taken for a merchant upon the Exchange for above these ten years, and sometimes pass for a Jew in the assembly of stock-jobbers at Jonathan's. In short, wherever I see a cluster of people I always mix with them, though I never open my lips but in my own club.

Thus I live in the world, rather as a Spectator of Mankind, than as one of the species; by which means I have made my self a speculative statesman, soldier, merchant, and artizan, without ever meddling with any practical part in life. I am very well versed in the theory of an husband, or a father, and can discern the errors in the economy, business and diversion of others, better than those who are engaged in them; as standers-by discover blots, which are apt to escape those who are in the game. I never espoused any party with violence, and am resolved to observe an exact neutrality between the Whigs and Tories, unless I shall be forced to declare myself by the hostilities of either side. In short, I have acted in all the parts of my life as a looker-on, which is the character I intend to preserve in this paper.

I have given the reader just so much of my history and character as to let him see I am not altogether unqualified for the business I have undertaken. As for other particulars in my life and adventures, I shall insert them in following papers, as I shall see occasion. In the meantime, when I consider how much I have seen, read and heard, I begin to blame my own taciturnity; and since I have neither time nor inclination to communicate the fulness of my heart in speech, I am resolved to do it in writing, and to print myself out, if possible, before I die. I have been often told by my friends that it is pity so many useful discoveries which I have made, should be in the possession of a silent man. For this reason, therefore, I shall publish a sheet-full of thoughts every morning, for the benefit of my contemporaries; and if I can any way con-

tribute to the diversion or improvement of the country in which I live, I shall leave it, when I am summoned out of it, with the secret satisfaction of thinking that I have not lived in vain.

There are three very material points which I have not spoken to in this paper, and which, for several important reasons, I must keep to my self, at least for some time: I mean, an account of my name, my age, and my lodgings. I must confess I would gratify my reader in anything that is reasonable; but as for these three particulars, though I am sensible they might tend very much to the embellishment of my paper, I cannot yet come to a resolution of communicating them to the public. They would indeed draw me out of that obscurity which I have enjoyed for many years, and expose me in public places to several salutes and civilities, which have been always very disagreeable to me; for the greatest pain I can suffer, is the being talked to, and being stared at. It is for this reason likewise, that I keep my complexion and dress, as very great secrets; though it is not impossible, but I may make discoveries of both, in the progress of the work I have undertaken.

After having been thus particular upon myself, I shall in to-morrow's paper give an account of those gentlemen who are concerned with me in this work. For, as I have before intimated, a plan of it is laid and concerted (as all other matters of importance are) in a club. However, as my friends have engaged me to stand in the front, those who have a mind to correspond with me, may direct their Letters *To the* SPECTATOR, *at Mr. Buckley's in Little Britain.* For I must further acquaint the reader, that though our club meets only on Tuesdays and Thursdays, we have appointed a committee to sit every night, for the inspection of all such papers as may contribute to the advancement of the public zeal. **C**

No. 2.
[Steele.]   Friday, March 2.

———*Ast alii sex*
Vel plures uno conclamant ore.—Juvenal
    Satires, VII, 167.

The first of our society is a gentleman of Worcestershire, of ancient descent, a baronet, his name Sir ROGER
DE COVERLEY. His great grandfather   10
was inventor of that famous country-
dance which is called after him. All
who know that shire are very well acquainted with the parts and merits of
Sir ROGER. He is a gentleman that is
very singular in his behaviour, but his
singularities proceed from his good
sense, and are contradictions to the
manners of the world, only as he
thinks the world is in the wrong.   20
However, this humour creates him no
enemies, for he does nothing with
sourness or obstinacy, and his being
unconfined to modes and forms,
makes him but the readier and more
capable to please and oblige all who
know him. When he is in town he
lives in Soho Square: It is said, he
keeps himself a bachelor by reason he
was crossed in love, by a perverse   30
beautiful widow of the next county to
him. Before this disappointment, Sir
ROGER was what you call a fine gentleman, had often supped with my
Lord Rochester and Sir George Etherege, fought a duel upon his first
coming to town, and kicked Bully
Dawson in a public coffee-house for
calling him youngster. But being ill
used by the above-mentioned widow,   40
he was very serious for a year and a
half; and though, his temper being
naturally jovial, he at last got over it,
he grew careless of himself, and never
dressed afterwards; he continues to
wear a coat and doublet of the same
cut that were in fashion at the time
of his repulse, which, in his merry
humours, he tells us has been in and
out twelve times since he first wore it. 50
'Tis said Sir ROGER grew humble in
his desires after he had forgot this
cruel beauty, insomuch that it is re-

ported he has frequently offended
in point of chastity with beggars and
gypsies: but this is looked upon by his
friends rather as matter of raillery
than truth. He is now in his fifty-sixth
year, cheerful, gay, and hearty, keeps
a good house both in town and country; a great lover of mankind; but
there is such a mirthful cast in his behaviour, that he is rather beloved than
esteemed: His tenants grow rich, his
servants look satisfied, all the young
women profess love to him, and the
young men are glad of his company.
When he comes into a house he calls
the servants by their names, and talks
all the way up stairs to a visit. I
must not omit that Sir ROGER is a
Justice of the Quorum: that he fills   20
the chair at a Quarter Session with
great abilities, and three months ago
gained universal applause by explaining a passage in the Game Act.
The gentleman next in esteem and
authority among us, is another bachelor, who is a member of the Inner
Temple; a man of great probity, wit,
and understanding; but he has chosen
his place of residence rather to obey   30
the direction of an old humoursome
father, than in pursuit of his own inclinations. He was placed there to
study the laws of the land, and is the
most learned of any of the house in
those of the stage. Aristotle and
Longinus are much better understood
by him than Littleton or Coke. The
father sends up every post questions
relating to marriage-articles, leases,   40
and tenures, in the neighbourhood,
all which questions he agrees with an
attorney to answer and take care of in
the lump. He is studying the passions
themselves, when he should be inquiring into the debates among men
which arise from them. He knows the
argument of each of the orations of
Demosthenes and Tully, but not one
Case in the Reports of our own   50
Courts. No one ever took him for a
fool, but none, except his intimate
friends, know he has a great deal of
wit. This turn makes him at once both

disinterested and agreeable. As few of his thoughts are drawn from business, they are most of them fit for conversation. His taste of books is a little too just for the age he lives in; he has read all, but approves of very few. His familiarity with the customs, manners, actions, and writings of the ancients, makes him a very delicate observer of what occurs to him in the present world. He is an excellent critic, and the time of the play is his hour of business; exactly at five he passes through New Inn, crosses through Russell Court, and takes a turn at Will's till the play begins; he has his shoes rubbed and his periwig powdered at the barber's as you go into the Rose. It is for the good of the audience when he is at a play, for the actors have an ambition to please him.

The person of next consideration is Sir ANDREW FREEPORT, a merchant of great eminence in the city of London. A person of indefatigable industry, strong reason, and great experience. His notions of trade are noble and generous, and (as every rich man has usually some sly way of jesting, which would make no great figure were he not a rich man) he calls the Sea the British Common. He is acquainted with commerce in all its parts, and will tell you that it is a stupid and barbarous way to extend dominion by arms; for true power is to be got by arts and industry. He will often argue, that if this part of our trade were well cultivated, we should gain from one nation; and if another, from another. I have heard him prove, that diligence makes more lasting acquisitions than valour, and that sloth has ruined more nations than the sword. He abounds in several frugal maxims, among which the greatest favourite is, "A penny saved is a penny got." A general trader of good sense, is pleasanter company than a general scholar; and Sir ANDREW having a natural unaffected eloquence, the perspicuity of his discourse gives the same pleasure that

wit would in another man. He has made his fortunes himself; and says that England may be richer than other kingdoms, by as plain methods as he himself is richer than other men; though at the same time I can say this of him, that there is not a point in the compass but blows home a ship in which he is an owner.

Next to Sir ANDREW in the club-room sits Captain SENTRY, a gentleman of great courage, good understanding, but invincible modesty. He is one of those that deserve very well, but are very awkward at putting their talents within the observation of such as should take notice of them. He was some years a captain, and behaved himself with great gallantry in several engagements, and at several sieges; but having a small estate of his own, and being next heir to Sir ROGER, he has quitted a way of life in which no man can rise suitably to his merit, who is not something of a courtier as well as a soldier. I have heard him often lament, that in a profession where merit is placed in so conspicuous a view, impudence should get the better of modesty. When he has talked to this purpose I never heard him make a sour expression, but frankly confess that he left the world, because he was not fit for it. A strict honesty and an even regular behaviour, are in themselves obstacles to him that must press through crowds, who endeavour at the same end with himself, the favour of a commander. He will however in his way of talk excuse generals for not disposing according to men's desert, or inquiring into it: for, says he, that great man who has a mind to help me, has as many to break through to come at me, as I have to come at him. Therefore he will conclude that the man who would make a figure, especially in a military way, must get over all false modesty, and assist his patron against the importunity of other pretenders by a proper assurance in his own vindication. He says it is a civil cowardice to be backward in asserting what you ought to expect, as it is a military fear to be slow in attacking when it is your duty. With this candour does the gentleman speak of himself and others. The same frankness runs through all his conversation. The military part of his life has furnished him with many adventures, in the relation of which he is very agreeable to the company; for he is never overbearing, though accustomed to command men in the utmost degree below him; nor ever too obsequious, from an habit of obeying men highly above him.

But that our society may not appear a set of humourists unacquainted with the gallantries and pleasures of the age, we have among us the gallant WILL HONEYCOMB, a gentleman who according to his years should be in the decline of his life, but having ever been very careful of his person, and always had a very easy fortune, time has made but very little impression, either by wrinkles on his forehead or traces in his brain. His person is well turned, of a good height. He is very ready at that sort of discourse with which men usually entertain women. He has all his life dressed very well, and remembers habits as others do men. He can smile when one speaks to him, and laughs easily. He knows the history of every mode, and can inform you from which of the French king's wenches our wives and daughters had this manner of curling their hair, that way of placing their hoods; whose frailty was covered by such a sort of petticoat, and whose vanity to show her foot made that part of the dress so short in such a year. In a word all his conversation and knowledge has been in the female world. As other men of his age will take notice to you what such a minister said upon such and such an occasion, he will tell you when the Duke of Monmouth danced at court such a woman was then smitten, another was taken with him at the head of his troop in the Park. In all these important relations, he has

ever about the same time received a kind glance or a blow of a fan from some celebrated beauty, mother of the present Lord Such-a-one. If you speak of a young commoner that said a lively thing in the House, he starts up, "He has good blood in his veins, Tom Mirabell begot him, the rogue cheated me in that affair; that young fellow's mother used me more like a dog than any woman I ever made advances to." This way of talking of his very much enlivens the conversation among us of a more sedate turn, and I find there is not one of the company, but my self, who rarely speak at all, but speaks of him as of that sort of man who is usually called a well-bred fine gentleman. To conclude his character, where women are not concerned, he is an honest worthy man.

I cannot tell whether I am to account him whom I am next to speak of as one of our company; for he visits us but seldom, but when he does it adds to every man else a new enjoyment of himself. He is a clergyman, a very philosophic man, of general learning, great sanctity of life, and the most exact good breeding. He has the misfortune to be of a very weak constitution, and consequently cannot accept of such cares and business as preferments in his function would oblige him to. He is therefore among divines what a chamber-counsellor is among lawyers. The probity of his mind, and the integrity of his life, create him followers, as being eloquent or loud advances others. He seldom introduces the subject he speaks upon; but we are so far gone in years that he observes, when he is among us, an earnestness to have him fall on some divine topic, which he always treats with much authority, as one who has no interests in this world, as one who is hastening to the object of all his wishes, and conceives hope from his decays and infirmities. These are my ordinary companions. **R**

No. 5.
[Addison.]   Tuesday, March 6.

Spectatum admissi risum teneatis?
—Horace, *Ars Poetica*, 5.

An opera may be allowed to be extravagantly lavish in its decorations, as its only design is to gratify the senses, and keep up an indolent attention in the audience. Common sense, however, requires that there should be nothing in the scenes and machines which may appear childish and absurd. How would the wits of King Charles's time have laughed, to have seen Nicolini exposed to a tempest in robes of ermine, and sailing in an open boat upon a sea of pasteboard? What a field of raillery would they have been let into, had they been entertained with painted dragons spitting wildfire, enchanted chariots drawn by Flanders mares, and real cascades in artificial landscapes? A little skill in criticism would inform us that shadows and realities ought not to be mixed together in the same piece; and that scenes which are designed as the representations of nature should be filled with resemblances, and not with the things themselves. If one would represent a wide champaign country filled with herds and flocks, it would be ridiculous to draw the country only upon the scenes, and to crowd several parts of the stage with sheep and oxen. This is joining together inconsistencies, and making the decoration partly real and partly imaginary. I would recommend what I have here said, to the directors, as well as to the admirers, of our modern opera.

As I was walking in the streets about a fortnight ago, I saw an ordinary fellow carrying a cage full of little birds upon his shoulder; and, as I was wondering with myself what use he would put them to, he was met very luckily by an acquaintance, who had the same curiosity. Upon his asking him what he had upon his shoulder, he told him that he had been buying sparrows for the opera. Sparrows for the opera, says his friend, licking his lips, what, are they to be roasted? No, no, says the other, they are to enter towards the end of the first act, and to fly about the stage.

This strange dialogue awakened my curiosity so far that I immediately bought the opera, by which means I perceived that the sparrows were to act the part of singing birds in a delightful grove: though upon a nearer inquiry I found the sparrows put the same trick upon the audience, that Sir Martin Mar-all practised upon his mistress; for, though they flew in sight, the music proceeded from a concert of flageolets and bird-calls which was planted behind the scenes. At the same time I made this discovery, I found by the discourse of the actors, that there were great designs on foot for the improvement of the opera; that it had been proposed to break down a part of the wall, and to surprise the audience with a party of an hundred horse, and that there was actually a project of bringing the New River into the house, to be employed in jetteaus and water-works. This project, as I have since heard, is postponed till the summer season; when it is thought the coolness that proceeds from fountains and cascades will be more acceptable and refreshing to people of quality. In the mean time, to find out a more agreeable entertainment for the winter season, the opera of *Rinaldo* is filled with thunder and lightning, illuminations and fireworks; which the audience may look upon without catching cold, and indeed without much danger of being burnt; for there are several engines filled with water, and ready to play at a minute's warning, in case any such accident should happen. However, as I have a very great friendship for the owner of this theatre, I hope that he has been wise enough to *insure* his house before he would let this opera be acted in it.

It is no wonder that those scenes

should be very surprising, which were contrived by two poets of different nations, and raised by two magicians of different sexes. Armida (as we are told in the argument) was an Amazonian enchantress, and poor Signior Cassani (as we learn from the persons represented) a Christian conjurer (*Mago Christiano*). I must confess I am very much puzzled to find how an Amazon should be versed in the black art, of how a good Christian, for such is the part of the magician, should deal with the devil.

To consider the poets after the conjurers, I shall give you a taste of the Italian, from the first lines of his preface. *Eccoti, benigno lettore, un parto di poche sere, che se ben nato di notte, non è però aborto di tenebre, mà si farà conoscere figlio d' Apollo con qualche raggio di Parnasso. Behold, gentle reader, the birth of a few evenings, which, though it be the offspring of the night, is not the abortive of darkness, but will make itself known to be the son of Apollo, with a certain ray of Parnassus.* He afterwards proceeds to call Minheer Hendel the Orpheus of our age, and to acquaint us, in the same sublimity of style, that he composed this opera in a fortnight. Such are the wits, to whose tastes we so ambitiously conform ourselves. The truth of it is, the finest writers among the modern Italians express themselves in such a florid form of words, and such tedious circumlocutions, as are used by none but pedants in our own country; and at the same time fill their writings with such poor imaginations and conceits, as our youths are ashamed of before they have been two years at the university. Some may be apt to think that it is the difference of genius which produces this difference in the works of the two nations; but to show there is nothing in this, if we look into the writings of the old Italians, such as Cicero and Virgil, we shall find that the English writers, in their way of thinking and expressing themselves, resemble those authors much more than the modern

Italians pretend to do. And as for the poet himself, from whom the dreams of this opera are taken, I must entirely agree with Monsieur Boileau, that one verse in Virgil is worth all the *clinquant*, or tinsel, of Tasso.

But to return to the sparrows; there have been so many flights of them let loose in this opera, that it is feared the house will never get rid of them, and that in other plays they may make their entrance in very wrong and improper scenes, so as to be seen flying in a lady's bed-chamber, or perching upon a king's throne; besides the inconveniences which the heads of the audience may sometimes suffer from them. I am credibly informed, that there was once a design of casting into an opera the Story of Whittington and his cat, and that in order to it there had been got together a great quantity of mice; but Mr. Rich, the proprietor of the playhouse, very prudently considered that it would be impossible for the cat to kill them all, and that consequently the princes of his stage might be as much infested with mice, as the prince of the island was before the cat's arrival upon it; for which reason he would not permit it to be acted in his house. And indeed I cannot blame him; for, as he said very well upon that occasion, I do not hear that any of the performers in our opera pretend to equal the famous Pied Piper, who made all the mice of a great town in Germany follow his music, and by that means cleared the place of those little noxious animals.

Before I dismiss this paper, I must inform my reader, that I hear there is a treaty on foot with London and Wise (who will be appointed gardeners of the playhouse) to furnish the opera of *Rinaldo and Armida* with an orange-grove; and that the next time it is acted, the singing birds will be personated by tom-tits, the undertakers being resolved to spare neither pains nor money, for the gratification of the audience.   C

No. 58.
[Addison.]   Monday, May 7.

Ut pictura poesis erit.–Horace, *Ars Poetica,*
  361.

Nothing is so much admired, and so little understood, as wit. No author that I know of has written professedly upon it; and as for those who make any mention of it, they only treat on the subject as it has accidentally fallen in their way, and that too in little short reflections, or in general declamatory flourishes, without entering into the bottom of the matter. I hope therefore I shall perform an acceptable work to my countrymen, if I treat at large upon this subject; which I shall endeavour to do in a manner suitable to it, that I may not incur the censure which a famous critic bestows upon one who had written a treatise upon the sublime in a low groveling style. I intend to lay aside a whole week for this undertaking, that the scheme of my thoughts may not be broken and interrupted: and I dare promise myself, if my readers will give me a week's attention, that this great city will be very much changed for the better by next Saturday night. I shall endeavour to make what I say intelligible to ordinary capacities; but if my readers meet with any paper that in some parts of it may be a little out of their reach, I would not have them discouraged, for they may assure themselves the next shall be much clearer.

As the great and only end of these my speculations is to banish vice and ignorance out of the territories of Great Britain, I shall endeavour as much as possible to establish among us a taste of polite writing. It is with this view that I have endeavoured to set my readers right in several points relating to operas and tragedies; and shall from time to time impart my notions of comedy, as I think they may tend to its refinement and perfection. I find by my bookseller that these papers of criticism, with that upon humour, have met with a more kind reception than indeed I could have hoped for from such subjects; for which reason I shall enter upon my present undertaking with greater cheerfulness.

In this, and one or two following papers, I shall trace out the history of false wit, and distinguish the several kinds of it as they have prevailed in different ages of the world. This I think the more necessary at present, because I observed there were attempts on foot last winter to revive some of those antiquated modes of wit that have been long exploded out of the commonwealth of letters. There were several satires and panegyrics handed about in acrostic, by which means some of the most arrant undisputed blockheads about the town began to entertain ambitious thoughts, and to set up for polite authors. I shall therefore describe at length those many arts of false wit, in which a writer does not show himself a man of a beautiful genius, but of great industry.

The first species of false wit which I have met with is very venerable for its antiquity, and has produced several pieces which have lived very near as long as the *Iliad* itself: I mean those short poems printed among the minor Greek poets, which resemble the figure of an egg, a pair of wings, an axe, a shepherd's pipe, and an altar.

As for the first, it is a little oval poem, and may not improperly be called a scholar's egg. I would endeavour to hatch it, or, in more intelligible language, to translate it into English, did not I find the interpretation of it very difficult; for the author seems to have been more intent upon the figure of his poem, than upon the sense of it.

The pair of wings consist of twelve verses, or rather feathers, every verse decreasing gradually in its measure according to its situation in the wing. The subject of it (as in the rest of the poems which follow) bears some remote affinity with the figure, for it describes a god of love, who is always painted with wings.

The axe methinks would have been a good figure for a lampoon, had the edge of it consisted of the most satirical parts of the work; but as it is in the original, I take it to have been nothing else but the poesy of an axe which was consecrated to Minerva, and was thought to have been the same that Epeus made use of in the building of the Trojan horse; which is a hint I shall leave to the consideration of the critics. I am apt to think that the poesy was written originally upon the axe, like those which our modern cutlers inscribe upon their knives; and that therefore the poesy still remains in its ancient shape, though the axe itself is lost.

The shepherd's pipe may be said to be full of music, for it is composed of nine different kinds of verses, which by their several lengths resemble the nine stops of the old musical instrument, that is likewise the subject of the poem.

The altar is inscribed with the Epitaph of Troilus, the son of Hecuba; which, by the way, makes me believe, that these false pieces of wit are much more ancient than the authors to whom they are generally ascribed; at least I will never be persuaded, that so fine a writer as Theocritus could have been the author of any such simple works.

It was impossible for a man to succeed in these performances who was not a kind of painter, or at least a designer: he was first of all to draw the outline of the subject which he intended to write upon, and afterwards conform the description to the figure of his subject. The poetry was to contract or dilate itself according to the mould in which it was cast. In a word, the verses were to be cramped or extended to the dimensions of the frame that was prepared for them; and to undergo the fate of those persons whom the tyrant Procrustes used to lodge in his iron bed; if they were too short he stretched them on a rack.

and if they were too long chopped off a part of their legs, till they fitted the couch which he had prepared for them.

Mr. Dryden hints at this obsolete kind of wit in one of the following verses in his *MacFleckno*, which an English reader cannot understand, who does not know that there are those little poems abovementioned in the shape of wings and altars.

——*Choose for thy Command*
Some peaceful province in acrostic land;
There may'st thou wings display, and altars raise,
And torture one poor word a thousand ways.

This fashion of false wit was revived by several poets of the last age, and in particular may be met with among Mr. Herbert's poems; and, if I am not mistaken, in the translation of Du Bartas. I do not remember any other kind of work among the moderns which more resembles the performances I have mentioned, than that famous picture of King Charles I. which has the whole book of Psalms written in the lines of the face and the hair of the head. When I was last at Oxford I perused one of the whiskers; and was reading the other, but could not go so far in it as I would have done, by reason of the impatience of my friends and fellow-travellers, who all of them pressed to see such a piece of curiosity. I have since heard, that there is now an eminent writing-master in town, who has transcribed all the Old Testament in a full-bottomed periwig; and if the fashion should introduce the thick kind of wigs which were in vogue some few years ago, he promises to add two or three supernumerary locks that shall contain all the Apocrypha. He designed this wig originally for King William, having disposed of the two books of Kings in the two forks of the foretop; but that glorious monarch dying before the wig was finished, there is a space left in it for the face of any one that has a mind to purchase it.

But to return to our ancient poems

in picture, I would humbly propose, for the benefit of our modern smatterers in poetry, that they would imitate their brethren among the ancients in those ingenious devices. I have communicated this thought to a young poetical lover of my acquaintance, who intends to present his mistress with a copy of verses made in the shape of her fan; and, if he tells me true, has already finished the three first sticks of it. He has likewise promised me to get the measure of his mistress's marriage-finger, with a design to make a poesy in the fashion of a ring which shall exactly fit it. It is so very easy to enlarge upon a good hint, that I do not question but my ingenious readers will apply what I have said to many other particulars; and that we shall see the town filled in a very little time with poetical tippets, handkerchiefs, snuff-boxes, and the like female-ornaments. I shall therefore conclude with a word of advice to those admirable English authors who call themselves pindaric writers, that they would apply themselves to this kind of wit without loss of time, as being provided better than any other poets with verses of all sizes and dimensions.　　　　　　　　　　C

No. 70.
[Addison.]　　　　Monday, May 21.

Interdum vulgus rectum videt,
—Horace, *Epistles,* I, ii, 63.

When I travelled, I took a particular delight in hearing the songs and fables that are come from father to son, and are most in vogue among the common people of the countries through which I passed; for it is impossible that any thing should be universally tasted and approved by a multitude, though they are only the rabble of a nation, which hath not in it some peculiar aptness to please and gratify the mind of man. Human nature is the same in all reasonable creatures; and whatever falls in with it,

will meet with admirers amongst readers of all qualities and conditions. Molière, as we are told by Monsieur Boileau, used to read all his comedies to an old woman who was his housekeeper, as she sat with him at her work by the chimney corner; and could foretell the success of his play in the theatre, from the reception it met at his fireside; for he tells us the audience always followed the old woman, and never failed to laugh in the same place.

I know nothing which more shows the essential and inherent perfection of simplicity of thought, above that which I call the Gothic manner in writing, than this, that the first pleases all kinds of palates, and the latter only such as have formed to themselves a wrong artificial taste upon little fanciful authors and writers of epigram. Homer, Virgil, or Milton, so far as the language of their poems is understood, will please a reader of plain common sense, who would neither relish nor comprehend an epigram of Martial, or a poem of Cowley: so, on the contrary, an ordinary song or ballad that is the delight of the common people, cannot fail to please all such readers as are not unqualified for the entertainment by their affectation or ignorance; and the reason is plain, because the same paintings of nature which recommend it to the most ordinary reader, will appear beautiful to the most refined.

The old song of *Chevy Chase* is the favourite ballad of the common people of England; and Ben Jonson used to say he had rather have been the author of it than of all his works. Sir Philip Sidney in his discourse of poetry speaks of it in the following words: *I never heard the old Song of Piercy and Douglas, that I found not my heart more moved than with a trumpet; and yet it is sung by some blind crowder with no rougher voice than rude style; which being so evil apparelled in the dust and cobweb of that uncivil age, what would it work trimmed in the gorgeous eloquence of*

Pindar? For my own part, I am so professed an admirer of this antiquated song, that I shall give my reader a critique upon it, without any further apology for so doing.

The greatest modern critics have laid it down as a rule, that an heroic poem should be founded upon some important precept of morality, adapted to the constitution of the country in which the poet writes. Homer and Virgil have formed their plans in this view. As Greece was a collection of many governments, who suffered very much among themselves, and gave the Persian emperor, who was their common enemy, many advantages over them by their mutual jealousies and animosities, Homer, in order to establish among them an union, which was so necessary for their safety, grounds his poem upon the discords of the several Grecian princes who were engaged in a confederacy against an Asiatic prince, and the several advantages which the enemy gained by such their discords. At the time the poem we are now treating of was written, the dissensions of the barons, who were then so many petty princes, ran very high, whether they quarrelled among themselves, or with their neighbours, and produced unspeakable calamities to the country. The poet, to deter men from such unnatural contentions, describes a bloody battle and dreadful scene of death, occasioned by the mutual feuds which reigned in the families of an English and Scotch nobleman. That he designed this for the instruction of his poem, we may learn from his four last lines, in which, after the example of the modern tragedians, he draws from it a precept for the benefit of his readers.

God save the king, and bless the land
In plenty, joy, and peace;
And grant henceforth that foul debate
'Twixt noblemen may cease.

The next point observed by the greatest heroic poets, hath been to celebrate persons and actions which do honour to their country: Thus Virgil's hero was the founder of Rome, Homer's a Prince of Greece; and for this reason Valerius Flaccus and Statius, who were both Romans, might be justly derided for having chosen the expedition of the Golden Fleece, and the wars of Thebes, for the subjects of their epic writings.

The poet before us has not only found out an hero in his own country, but raises the reputation of it by several beautiful incidents. The English are the first who take the field, and the last who quit it. The English bring only fifteen hundred to the battle, the Scotch two thousand. The English keep the field with fifty-three: the Scotch retire with fifty-five: all the rest on each side being slain in battle. But the most remarkable circumstance of this kind, is the different manner in which the Scotch and English kings receive the news of this fight, and of the great men's deaths who commanded in it.

This news was brought to Edinburgh,
  Where Scotland's king did reign,
That brave Earl Douglas suddenly
  Was with an arrow slain.

O heavy news, King James did say,
  Scotland can witness be,
I have not any captain more
  Of such account as he.

Like tidings to King Henry came
  Within as short a space,
That Piercy of Northumberland
  Was slain in Chevy Chase.

Now God be with him, said our king,
  Sith 'twill no better be,
I trust I have within my realm
  Five hundred as good as he.

Yet shall not Scot nor Scotland say
  But I will vengeance take,
And be revenged on them all
  For brave Lord Piercy's sake.

This vow full well the king performed
  After on Humble-down,
In one day fifty knights were slain
  With lords of great renown.

And of the rest of small account
  Did many thousands die, &c.

At the same time that our poet shows a laudable partiality to his country-

men, he represents the Scots after a
manner not unbecoming so bold and
brave a people.

> Earl Douglas on a milk-white stead,
>   Most like a baron bold,
>   Rode foremost of the company
>   Whose armour shone like gold.

His sentiments and actions are every
way suitable to an hero. One of us
two, says he, must die: I am an earl
as well as yourself, so that you can
have no pretence for refusing the combat. However, says he, 'tis pity, and
indeed would be a sin, that so many
innocent men should perish for our
sakes; rather let you and I end our
quarrel in single fight.

> E'er thus I will out-braved be,
>   One of us two shall die;
>   I know thee well, an earl thou art,
>   Lord Piercy, so am I.

> But trust me, Piercy, pity it were,
>   And great offence, to kill
>   Any of these our harmless men,
>   For they have done no ill.

> Let thou and I the battle try,
>   And set our men aside;
>   Accurst be he, Lord Piercy said,
>   By whom this is denied.

When these brave men had distinguished themselves in the battle and
in single combat with each other, in
the midst of a generous parley, full of
heroic sentiments, the Scotch earl
falls; and with his dying words encourages his men to revenge his death,
representing to them, as the most bitter circumstance of it, that his rival
saw him fall.

> With that there came an arrow keen
>   Out of an English bow,
>   Which struck Earl Douglas to the heart
>   A deep and deadly blow.

> Who never spoke more words than these,
>   Fight on, my merry men all,
>   For why, my life is at an end,
>   Lord Piercy sees my fall.

Merry men, in the language of those
times, is no more than a cheerful word
for companions and fellow-soldiers. A
passage in the eleventh book of Virgil's *Æneid* is very much to be admired, where Camilla in her last

agonies, instead of weeping over the
wound she had received, as one might
have expected from a warrior of her
sex, considers only (like the hero of
whom we are now speaking) how the
battle should be continued after her
death.

> Tum sic expirans, &c.
> A gathering mist o'erclouds her cheerful eyes,
> And from her cheeks the rosy colour flies,
> Then, turns to her, whom, of her female
>   train,
> She trusted most, and thus she speaks with
>   pain:

> *Acca, 'tis past! He swims before my sight,*
> *Inexorable Death: and claims his right.*
> *Bear my last words to Turnus, fly with speed,*
> *And bid him timely to my charge succeed:*
> *Repel the Trojans, and the town relieve;*
> *Farewell ——*

Turnus did not die in so heroic a
manner; though our poet seems to
have had his eye upon Turnus's
speech in the last verse.

> Lord Piercy sees my fall.

> ——Vicisti, et victum tendere palmas
> Ausonii videre—

Earl Piercy's lamentation over his
enemy is generous, beautiful, and passionate; I must only caution the
reader not to let the simplicity of the
style, which one may well pardon in
so old a poet, prejudice him against
the greatness of the thought.

> Then leaving life Earl Piercy took
>   The dead man by the hand,
>   And said, Earl Douglas for thy life
>   Would I had lost my land.

> O Christ! My very heart doth bleed
>   With sorrow for thy sake;
>   For sure a more renowned knight
>   Mischance did never take.

That beautiful line *Taking the dead
man by the hand,* will put the reader
in mind of Æneas's behaviour towards
Lausus, whom he himself had slain as
he came to the rescue of his aged
father.

> At ver ut vultum vidit morientis, et ora,
> Ora modis Anchisiades pallentia miris,
> Ingemuit, miserans graviter, dextramque te-
>   tendit. &c.

The pious prince beheld young Lausus dead;
He grieved, he wept; then grasped his hand,
  and said,
Poor hapless youth! What praises can be
  paid
To worth so great ——

I shall take another opportunity to consider the other parts of this old song.

No. 81.
[Addison.]   Saturday, June 2, 1711.

Qualis ubi audito venantum murmure tigris
Horruit in maculas ——
            —Statius, *Thebaid*, II, 128.

About the middle of last winter I went to see an opera at the Theatre in the Haymarket, where I could not but take notice of two parties of very fine women that had placed themselves in the opposite side boxes, and seemed drawn up in a kind of battle array one against another. After a short survey of them, I found they were *patched* differently; the faces, on one hand, being spotted on the right side of the forehead, and those upon the other on the left. I quickly perceived that they cast hostile glances upon one another; and that their patches were placed in those different situations, as party signals to distinguish friends from foes. In the middle boxes, between these two opposite bodies, were several ladies who patched indifferently on both sides of their faces, and seemed to sit there with no other intention but to see the opera. Upon inquiry I found, that the body of Amazons on my right hand, were Whigs; and those on my left, Tories; and that those who had placed themselves in the middle boxes were a neutral party, whose faces had not yet declared themselves. These last, however, as I afterwards found, diminished daily, and took their party with one side or the other; insomuch that I observed in several of them, the patches which were before dispersed equally, are now all gone over to the

Whig or Tory side of the face. The censorious say that the men whose hearts are aimed at are very often the occasions that one part of the face is thus dishonoured, and lies under a kind of disgrace, while the other is so much set off and adorned by the owner; and that the patches turn to the right or to the left, according to the principles of the man who is most in favour. But whatever may be the motives of a few fantastical coquets, who do not patch for the public good, so much as for their own private advantage; it is certain that there are several women of honour who patch out of principle, and with an eye to the interest of their country. Nay, I am informed, that some of them adhere so steadfastly to their party, and are so far from sacrificing their zeal for the public to their passion for any particular person, that in a late draught of marriage articles a lady has stipulated with her husband that, whatever his opinions are, she shall be at liberty to patch on which side she pleases.

I must here take notice, that Rosalinda, a famous Whig partizan, has most unfortunately a very beautiful mole on the Tory part of her forehead; which, being very conspicuous, has occasioned many mistakes, and given an handle to her enemies to misrepresent her face, as though it had revolted from the Whig interest. But whatever this natural patch may seem to intimate, it is well known that her notions of government are still the same. This unlucky mole, however, has misled several coxcombs; and, like the hanging out of false colours, made some of them converse with Rosalinda in what they thought the spirit of her party, when on a sudden she has given them an unexpected fire, that has sunk them all at once. If Rosalinda is unfortunate in her mole, Nigranilla is as unhappy in a pimple, which forces her, against her inclinations, to patch on the Whig side.

I am told that many virtuous matrons, who formerly have been taught to believe that this artificial spotting of the face was unlawful, are now reconciled by a zeal for their cause, to what they could not be prompted by a concern for their beauty. This way of declaring war upon one another, puts me in mind of what is reported of the tigress, that several spots rise in her skin when she is angry; or as Mr. Cowley has imitated the verses that stand as the motto of this Paper,

—— She swells with angry pride,
And calls forth all her spots on ev'ry side.

When I was in the theatre the time above-mentioned, I had the curiosity to count the patches on both sides, and found the Tory patches to be about twenty stronger than the Whig; but to make amends for this small inequality, I the next morning found the whole puppet-show filled with faces spotted after the Whiggish manner. Whether or no the ladies had retreated hither in order to rally their forces I cannot tell; but the next night they came in so great a body to the opera, that they outnumbered the enemy.

This account of party patches will, I am afraid, appear improbable to those who live at a distance from the fashionable world; but as it is a distinction of a very singular nature, and what perhaps may never meet with a parallel, I think I should not have discharged the office of a faithful Spectator had I not recorded it.

I have, in former papers, endeavoured to expose this party rage in women, as it only serves to aggravate the hatreds and animosities that reign among men, and in a great measure deprives the fair sex of those peculiar charms with which nature has endowed them.

When the Romans and Sabines were at war, and just upon the point of giving battle, the women, who were allied to both of them, interposed with so many tears and entreaties that they prevented the mutual slaughter which threatened both parties, and united them together in a firm and lasting peace.

I would recommend this noble example to our British ladies, at a time when their country is torn with so many unnatural divisions that if they continue, it will be a misfortune to be born in it. The Greeks thought it so improper for women to interest themselves in competitions and contentions, that for this reason, among others, they forbade them, under pain of death, to be present at the Olympic games, notwithstanding these were the public diversions of all Greece.

As our English women excel those of all nations in beauty, they should endeavour to outshine them in all other accomplishments proper to the sex, and to distinguish themselves as tender mothers and faithful wives, rather than as furious partizans. Female virtues are of a domestic turn. The family is the proper province for private women to shine in. If they must be showing their zeal for the public, let it not be against those who are perhaps of the same family, or at least of the same religion or nation, but against those who are the open, professed, undoubted enemies of their faith, liberty, and country. When the Romans were pressed with a foreign enemy, the ladies voluntarily contributed all their rings and jewels to assist the government under a public exigence; which appeared so laudable an action in the eyes of their countrymen, that from thenceforth it was permitted by a law to pronounce public orations at the funeral of a woman in praise of the deceased person, which till that time was peculiar to men. Would our English ladies, instead of sticking on a patch against those of their own country, show themselves so truly public-spirited as to sacrifice every one her necklace against the common enemy, what decrees ought not to be made in favour of them?

Since I am recollecting upon this subject such passages as occur to my memory out of ancient authors, I cannot omit a sentence in the celebrated funeral oration of Pericles, which he made in honour of those brave Athenians that were slain in a fight with the Lacedemonians. After having addressed himself to the several ranks and orders of his country men, and shown them how they should behave themselves in the public cause, he turns to the female part of his audience; "And as for you (says he) I shall advise you in very few words. Aspire only to those virtues that are peculiar to your sex; follow your natural modesty, and think it your greatest commendation not to be talked of one way or other." **C**

No. 105.
[Addison.] Saturday, June 30.

—— Id arbitror
Adprime in vita esse utile, ut nequid nimis.
—Terence, *Andria,* I, 60-61.

My friend WILL HONEYCOMB values himself very much upon what he calls the knowledge of mankind, which has cost him many disasters in his youth; for WILL reckons every misfortune that he has met with among the women, and every encounter among the men, as parts of his education, and fancies he should never have been the man he is, had not he broke windows, knocked down constables, disturbed honest people with his midnight serenades, and beat up a lewd woman's quarters, when he was a young fellow. The engaging in adventures of this nature, WILL calls the studying of mankind; and terms this knowledge of the town, the knowledge of the world. WILL ingenuously confesses, that for half his life his head ached every morning with reading of men overnight; and at present comforts himself under certain pains which he endures from time to time, that without them he could not have been acquainted with the gallantries of the age. This WILL looks upon as the learning of a gentleman, and regards all other kinds of science as the ac-

complishments of one whom he calls a scholar, a bookish man, or a philosopher.

For these reasons WILL shines in mixed company, where he has the discretion not to go out of his depth, and has often a certain way of making his real ignorance appear a seeming one. Our club, however, has frequently caught him tripping, at which times they never spare him. For as WILL often insults us with the knowledge of the town, we sometimes take our revenge upon him by our knowledge of books.

He was last week producing two or three letters which he writ in his youth to a coquet lady. The raillery of them was natural, and well enough for a mere man of the town; but, very unluckily, several of the words were wrong spelt. WILL laughed this off at first as well as he could, but finding himself pushed on all sides, and especially by the Templar, he told us, with a little passion, that he never liked pedantry in spelling, and that he spelt like a gentleman, and not like a scholar: upon this WILL had recourse to his old topic of showing the narrow spiritedness, the pride, and ignorance of pedants; which he carried so far, that upon my retiring to my lodgings, I could not forbear throwing together such reflections as occurred to me upon that subject.

A man who has been brought up among books, and is able to talk of nothing else, is a very indifferent companion, and what we call a pedant. But, methinks, we should enlarge the title, and give it everyone that does not know how to think out of his profession, and particular way of life. What is a greater pedant than a mere man of the town? Bar him the playhouses, a catalogue of the reigning beauties, and an account of a few fashionable distempers that have befallen him, and you strike him dumb. How many a pretty gentleman's knowledge lies all within the verge of the court? He will tell you the names of the principal favourites, repeat the shrewd sayings of a man of quality, whisper an intrigue that is not yet blown upon by common fame; or, if the sphere of his observations is a little larger than ordinary, will perhaps enter into all the incidents, turns, and revolutions in a game of ombre. When he has gone thus far he has shown you the whole circle of his accomplishments, his parts are drained, and he is disabled from any farther conversation. What are these but rank pedants? and yet these are the men who value themselves most on their exemption from the pedantry of colleges.

I might here mention the military pedant, who always talks in a camp, and is storming towns, making lodgments, and fighting battles from one end of the year to the other. Every thing he speaks smells of gunpowder; if you take away his artillery from him, he has not a word to say for himself. I might likewise mention the law pedant, that is perpetually putting cases, repeating the transactions of Westminster Hall, wrangling with you upon the most indifferent circumstances of life, and not to be convinced of the distance of a place, or of the most trival point in conversation, but by dint of argument. The state pedant is wrapt up in news, and lost in politics. If you mention either of the kings of Spain or Poland, he talks very notably; but if you go out of the *Gazette*, you drop him. In short, a mere Courtier, a mere Soldier, a mere Scholar, a mere anything, is an insipid pedantic character, and equally ridiculous.

Of all the species of pedants, which I have mentioned, the book pedant is much the most supportable; he has at least an exercised understanding, and a head which is full though confused, so that a man who converses with him may often receive from him hints of things that are worth knowing, and what he may possibly turn to his own advantage, though they are of little use to the owner. The worst kind of pedants among learned men are such

as are naturally endued with a very small share of common sense, and have read a great number of books without taste or distinction.

The truth of it is, learning, like travelling, and all other methods of improvement, as it finishes good sense, so it makes a silly man ten thousand times more insufferable, by supplying variety of matter to his impertinence, and giving him an opportunity of abounding in absurdities.

Shallow pedants cry up one another much more than men of solid and useful learning. To read the titles they give an editor, or collator of a manuscript, you would take him for the glory of the commonwealth of letters, and the wonder of his age; when perhaps upon examination you find that he has only rectified a Greek particle, or laid out a whole sentence in proper commas.

They are obliged indeed to be thus lavish of their praises, that they may keep one another in countenance; and it is no wonder if a great deal of knowledge, which is not capable of making a man wise, has a natural tendency to make him vain and arrogant.   L

No. 106.
[Addison.]   Monday, July 2.

——Hinc tibi copia
Manabit ad plenum benigno
*   Ruris honorum opulenta cornu.*
          —Horace, *Odes*, I, xvii, 14.

Having often received an invitation from my friend Sir ROGER DE COVERLEY to pass away a month with him in the country, I last week accompanied him thither, and am settled with him for some time at his country house, where I intend to form several of my ensuing speculations. Sir ROGER, who is very well acquainted with my humour, lets me rise and go to bed when I please, dine at his own table or in my chamber as I think fit, sit still and say nothing without bidding me be merry. When the gentlemen of the country come to see him, he only shows me at a distance: as I have been walking in his fields I have observed them stealing a sight of me over an hedge, and have heard the knight desiring them not to let me see them, for that I hated to be stared at.

I am the more at ease in Sir ROGER'S family, because it consists of sober and staid persons; for as the knight is the best master in the world, he seldom changes his servants; and as he is beloved by all about him, his servants never care for leaving him: by this means his domestics are all in years, and grown old with their master. You would take his *valet-de-chambre* for his brother, his butler is grey-headed, his groom is one of the gravest men that I have ever seen, and his coachman has the looks of a privy-counsellor. You see the goodness of the master even in the old house-dog, and in a gray pad that is kept in the stable with great care and tenderness out of regard to his past services, though he has been useless for several years.

I could not but observe with a great deal of pleasure the joy that appeared in the countenances of these ancient domestics upon my friend's arrival at his country seat. Some of them could not refrain from tears at the sight of their old master; every one of them pressed forward to do something for him, and seemed discouraged if they were not employed. At the same time the good old knight, with a mixture of the father and the master of the family, tempered the inquiries after his own affairs with several kind questions relating to themselves. This humanity and good nature engages every body to him, so that when he is pleasant upon any of them, all his family are in good humour, and none so much as the person whom he diverts himself with: on the contrary, if he coughs, or betrays any infirmity of old age, it is easy for a stander-by to ob-

serve a secret concern in the looks of all his servants.

My worthy friend has put me under the particular care of his butler, who is a very prudent man, and, as well as the rest of his fellow-servants, wonderfully desirous of pleasing me, because they have often heard their master talk of me as of his particular friend.

My chief companion, when Sir ROGER is diverting himself in the woods or the fields, is a very venerable man who is ever with Sir ROGER, and has lived at his house in the nature of a chaplain above thirty years. This gentleman is a person of good sense and some learning, of a very regular life and obliging conversation: he heartily loves Sir ROGER, and knows that he is very much in the old knight's esteem; so that he lives in the family rather as a relation than a dependant.

I have observed in several of my papers, that my friend SIR ROGER, amidst all his good qualities, is something of an humourist; and that his virtues, as well as imperfections, are as it were tinged by a certain extravagance, which makes them particularly *his*, and distinguishes them from those of other men. This cast of mind, as it is generally very innocent in itself, so it renders his conversation highly agreeable, and more delightful than the same degree of sense and virtue would appear in their common and ordinary colours. As I was walking with him last night, he asked me how I liked the good man whom I have just now mentioned? and without staying for my answer, told me that he was afraid of being insulted with Latin and Greek at his own table; for which reason, he desired a particular friend of his at the university to find him out a clergyman rather of plain sense than much learning, of a good aspect, a clear voice, a sociable temper, and, if possible, a man that understood a little of backgammon. "My friend," says Sir ROGER, "found me out this gentleman, who, besides the endowments required of him, is, they tell me, a good scholar, though he does not show it. I have given him the parsonage of the parish; and because I know his value, have settled upon him a good annuity for life. If he outlives me, he shall find that he was higher in my esteem than perhaps he thinks he is. He has now been with me thirty years; and though he does not know I have taken notice of it, has never in all that time asked any thing of me for himself, though he is every day soliciting me for something in behalf of one or other of my tenants his parishioners. There has not been a law-suit in the parish since he has lived among them. If any dispute arises, they apply themselves to him for the decision; if they do not acquiesce in his judgment, which I think never happened above once, or twice at most, they appeal to me. At his first settling with me, I made him a present of all the good sermons which have been printed in English, and only begged of him that every Sunday he would pronounce one of them in the pulpit. Accordingly, he has digested them into such a series, that they follow one another naturally, and make a continued system of practical divinity."

As Sir ROGER was going on in his story, the gentleman we were talking of came up to us; and upon the knight's asking him who preached tomorrow (for it was Saturday night) told us, the Bishop of St. Asaph in the morning, and Doctor South in the afternoon. He then showed us his list of preachers for the whole year, where I saw with a great deal of pleasure Archbishop Tillotson, Bishop Saunderson, Doctor Barrow, Doctor Calamy, with several living authors who have published discourses of practical divinity. I no sooner saw this venerable man in the pulpit, but I very much approved of my friend's insisting upon the qualifications of a good aspect and a clear voice; for I was so charmed with the gracefulness of his figure and delivery, as well as with

the discourses he pronounced, that I think I never passed any time more to my satisfaction. A sermon repeated after this manner, is like the composition of a poet in the mouth of a graceful actor.

I could heartily wish that more of our country clergy would follow this example; and instead of wasting their spirits in laborious compositions of their own, would endeavour after a handsome elocution, and all those other talents that are proper to enforce what has been penned by greater masters. This would not only be more easy to themselves, but more edifying to the people. L

No. 108.
[Addison.]   Wednesday, July 4.

Gratis anhelans, multa agendo nihil agens.
          —Phædrus, *Fables,* V, 3.

As I was yesterday morning walking with Sir ROGER before his house, a country fellow brought him a huge fish, which, he told him, Mr. William Wimble had caught that very morning; and that he presented it, with his service, to him, and intended to come and dine with him. At the same time he delivered a letter, which my friend read to me as soon as the messenger left him.

"Sir ROGER,
I desire you to accept of a jack, which is the best I have caught this season. I intend to come and stay with you a week, and see how the perch bite in the Black River. I observed, with some concern, the last time I saw you upon the bowling-green, that your whip wanted a lash to it: I will bring half a dozen with me that I twisted last week, which I hope will serve you all the time you are in the country. I have not been out of the saddle for six days last past, having been at Eton with Sir John's eldest son. He takes to his learning hugely.
     I am,
          Sir,
               Your humble servant,
                    Will Wimble."

This extraordinary letter, and message that accompanied it, made me very curious to know the character and quality of the gentleman who sent them; which I found to be as follows: Will Wimble is younger brother to a baronet, and descended of the ancient family of the Wimbles. He is now between forty and fifty; but being bred to no business and born to no estate, he generally lives with his elder brother as superintendent of his game. He hunts a pack of dogs better than any man in the country, and is very famous for finding out a hare. He is extremely well versed in all the little handicrafts of an idle man: he makes a May-fly to a miracle; and furnishes the whole country with angle-rods. As he is a good-natured officious fellow, and very much esteemed upon account of his family, he is a welcome guest at every house, and keeps up a good correspondence among all the gentlemen about him. He carries a tulip-root in his pocket from one to another, or exchanges a puppy between a couple of friends that live perhaps in the opposite sides of the county. Will is a particular favorite of all the young heirs, whom he frequently obliges with a net that he has weaved, or a setting-dog that he has *made* himself: he now and then presents a pair of garters of his own knitting to their mothers or sisters; and raises a great deal of mirth among them, by enquiring as often as he meets them *how they wear?* These gentlemanlike manufactures and obliging little humours, make Will the darling of the country.

Sir ROGER was proceeding in the character of him, when we saw him make up to us, with two or three hazel-twigs in his hand that he had cut in Sir ROGER's woods, as he came through them, in his way to the house. I was very much pleased to observe on one side the hearty and sincere welcome with which Sir ROGER received him, and on the other the secret joy which his guest discovered at sight of the good old knight. After

the first salutes were over, Will desired Sir ROGER to lend him one of his servants to carry a set of shuttle-cocks he had with him in a little box to a lady that lived about a mile off, to whom it seems he had promised such a present for above this half year. Sir ROGER's back was no sooner turned, but honest Will began to tell me of a large cock pheasant that he had sprung in one of the neighbouring woods, with two or three other adventures of the same nature. Odd and uncommon characters are the game that I look for, and most delight in; for which reason I was as much pleased with the novelty of the person that talked to me, as he could be for his life with the springing of a pheasant, and therefore listened to him with more than ordinary attention.

In the midst of his discourse the bell rung to dinner, where the gentleman I have been speaking of had the pleasure of seeing the huge jack, he had caught, served up for the first dish in a most sumptuous manner. Upon our sitting down to it he gave us a long account how he had hooked it, played with it, foiled it, and at length drew it out upon the bank, with several other particulars that lasted all the first course. A dish of wild-fowl that came afterwards furnished conversation for the rest of the dinner, which concluded with a late invention of Will's for improving the quail-pipe.

Upon withdrawing into my room after dinner, I was secretly touched with compassion towards the honest gentleman that had dined with us; and could not but consider with a great deal of concern, how so good an heart and such busy hands were wholly employed in trifles; that so much humanity should be so little beneficial to others, and so much industry so little advantageous to himself. The same temper of mind and application to affairs might have recommended him to the public esteem, and have raised his fortune in another station of life. What good to his country or himself might not a trader or merchant have done with such useful though ordinary qualifications?

Will Wimble's is the case of many a younger brother of a great family, who had rather see their children starve like gentlemen, than thrive in a trade or profession that is beneath their quality. This humour fills several parts of Europe with pride and beggary. It is the happiness of a trading nation, like ours, that the younger sons, though uncapable of any liberal art or profession, may be placed in such a way of life, as may perhaps enable them to vie with the best of their family: accordingly we find several citizens that were launched into the world with narrow fortunes, rising by an honest industry to greater estates than those of their elder brothers. It is not improbable but Will was formerly tried at divinity, law, or physic; and that finding his genius did not lie that way, his parents gave him up at length to his own inventions: but certainly, however improper he might have been for studies of a higher nature, he was perfectly well turned for the occupations of trade and commerce. As I think this is a point which cannot be too much inculcated, I shall desire my reader to compare what I have here written with what I have said in my twenty-first speculation.   L

No. 120.
[Addison.]   Wednesday, July 18.

. . . *Equidem credo, quia sit divinitus illis Ingenium* . . .—Virgil *Georgics*, I, 415.

My friend Sir ROGER is very often merry with me, upon my passing so much of my time among his poultry: he has caught me twice or thrice looking after a bird's nest, and several times sitting an hour or two together near an hen and chickens. He tells me he believes I am personally acquainted with every fowl about his house; calls such a particular cock my favourite; and frequently complains that his ducks and geese have more of my company than himself.

I must confess I am infinitely delighted with those speculations of nature which are to be made in a country life; and as my reading has very much lain among books of natural history, I cannot forbear recollecting upon this occasion the several remarks which I have met with in authors, and comparing them with what falls under my own observation: the arguments for Providence drawn from the natural history of animals, being in my opinion demonstrative.

The make of every kind of animal is different from that of every other kind; and yet there is not the least turn in the muscles or twist in the fibres of any one, which does not render them more proper for that particular animal's way of life than any other cast or texture of them would have been.

The most violent appetites in all creatures are *lust* and *hunger*: The first is a perpetual call upon them to propagate their kind; the latter, to preserve themselves.

It is astonishing to consider the different degrees of care that descend from the parent to the young, so far as is absolutely necessary for the leaving a posterity. Some creatures cast their eggs as chance directs them, and think of them no farther, as insects and several kinds of fish; others of a nicer frame, find out proper beds to deposit them in, and there leave them; as the serpent, the crocodile, and ostrich: others hatch their eggs and tend the birth, till it is able to shift for itself.

What can we call the principle which directs every different kind of bird to observe a particular plan in the structure of its nest, and directs all of the same species to work after the same model? It cannot be *imitation*; for though you hatch a crow under a hen, and never let it see any of the works of its own kind, the nest it makes shall be the same, to the laying of a stick, with all the other nests of the same species. It cannot be *reason*; for were animals indued with it to as great a degree as man, their buildings would be as different as ours, according to the different conveniences that they would propose to themselves.

Is it not remarkable, that the same temper of weather which raises this genial warmth in animals, should cover the trees with leaves and the fields with grass for their security and concealment, and produce such infinite swarms of insects for the support and sustenance of their respective broods?

Is it not wonderful, that the love of the parent should be so violent while it lasts; and that it should last no longer than is necessary for the preservation of the young?

The violence of this natural love is exemplified by a very barbarous experiment; which I shall quote at length as I find it in an excellent author, and hope my readers will pardon the mentioning such an instance of cruelty, because there is nothing can so effectually show the strength of that principle in animals of which I am here speaking. "A person who was well skilled in dissections opened a bitch, and as she lay in the most exquisite tortures offered her one of her young puppies, which she immediately fell a licking; and for the time seemed insensible of her own pain: on the removal, she kept her eye fixt on it, and began a wailing sort of cry, which seemed rather to proceed from the loss of her young one, than the sense of her own torments."

But notwithstanding this natural love in brutes is much more violent and intense than in rational creatures, Providence has taken care that it should be no longer troublesome to the parent than it is useful to the young; for so soon as the wants of the latter cease, the mother withdraws her fondness and leaves them to provide for themselves: and what is a very remarkable circumstance in this part of instinct, we find that the love of the parent may be lengthened out beyond its usual time if the preservation of the species requires it; as we may see in birds that drive away their young as soon as they are able to get their livelihood, but continue to feed them if they are tied to the nest or confined within a cage, or by any other means appear to be out of a condition of supplying their own necessities.

This natural love is not observed in animals to ascend from the young to the parent, which is not at all necessary for the continuance of the species: nor indeed in reasonable creatures does it rise in any proportion, as it spreads itself downwards; for in all family affection, we find protection granted and favours bestowed, are greater motives to love and tenderness; than safety, benefits, or life received.

One would wonder to hear sceptical men disputing for the reason of animals, and telling us it is only our pride and prejudices that will not allow them the use of that faculty.

Reason shows itself in all occurrences of life; whereas the brute makes no discovery of such a talent, but in what immediately regards his own preservation, or the continuance of his species. Animals in their generation are wiser than the sons of men; but their wisdom is confined to a few particulars, and lies in a very narrow compass. Take a brute out of his instinct, and you find him wholly deprived of understanding. To use an instance that comes often under observation:—

With what caution does the hen provide herself a nest in places unfrequented, and free from noise and disturbance? When she has laid her eggs in such a manner that she can cover them, what care does she take in turning them frequently, that all parts may partake of the vital warmth? When she leaves them to provide for her necessary sustenance. how punctually does she return before they have time to cool, and become incapable of producing an animal? In the summer you see her giving herself greater freedoms, and quitting her care for above two hours together; but in winter, when the rigour of the season would chill the principles of life, and destroy the young one, she grows more assiduous in her attendance, and stays away but half the time. When the birth approaches, with how much nicety and attention does she help the chick to break its prison? Not to take notice of her covering it from the injuries of the weather, providing it proper nourishment, and teaching it to help itself; nor to mention her forsaking the nest, if after the usual time of reckoning the young one does not make its appearance. A chemical operation could not be followed with greater art or diligence, than is seen in the hatching of a chick; though there are many other birds that show an infinitely greater sagacity in all the forementioned particulars.

But at the same time the hen, that has all this seeming ingenuity (which is indeed absolutely necessary for the propagation of the species), considered in other respects, is without the least glimmerings of thought or common sense. She mistakes a piece of chalk for an egg, and sits upon it in the same manner: she is insensible of any increase or diminution in the number of those she lays: she does not distinguish between her own and those of another species; and when the birth appears of never so different a bird, will cherish it for her own. In all these circumstances, which do not carry an immediate regard to the subsistence of herself or her species, she is a very idiot.

There is not in my opinion any thing more mysterious in nature than this instinct in animals, which thus rises above reason, and falls infinitely short of it. It cannot be accounted for by any properties in matter, and at the same time works after so odd a manner, that one cannot think it the

faculty of an intellectual being. For my own part, I look upon it as upon the principle of gravitation in bodies, which is not to be explained by any known qualities inherent in the bodies themselves, nor from any laws of mechanism, but, according to the best notions of the greatest philosophers, is an immediate impression from the First Mover, and the Divine Energy acting in the creatures.   L

No. 122.
[Addison.]   Friday, July 20.

Comes jucundus in via pro vehiculo est.
—Publius Syrus, *Fragments.*

A man's first care should be to avoid the reproaches of his own heart; his next, to escape the censures of the world. If the last interferes with the former, it ought to be entirely neglected; but otherwise, there cannot be a greater satisfaction to an honest mind, than to see those approbations which it gives itself seconded by the applauses of the public. A man is more sure of his conduct, when the verdict which he passes upon his own behaviour is thus warranted, and confirmed by the opinion of all that know him.

My worthy friend Sir ROGER is one of those who is not only at peace within himself, but beloved and esteemed by all about him. He receives a suitable tribute for his universal benevolence to mankind, in the returns of affection and goodwill, which are paid him by every one that lives within his neighbourhood. I lately met with two or three odd instances of that general respect which is shown to the good old knight. He would needs carry Will Wimble and myself with him to the County Assizes. As we were upon the road Will Wimble joined a couple of plain men who rid before us, and conversed with them for some time; during which my friend Sir ROGER acquainted me with their characters.

The first of them, says he, that has a spaniel by his side, is a yeoman of about an hundred pounds a year, an honest man. He is just within the Game Act, and qualified to kill an hare or a pheasant. He knocks down a dinner with his gun twice or thrice a week; and by that means lives much cheaper than those who have not so good an estate as himself. He would be a good neighbour if he did not destroy so many partridges: in short, he is a very sensible man; shoots flying; and has been several times foreman of the Petty Jury.

The other that rides along with him is Tom Touchy, a fellow famous for *taking the law* of every body. There is not one in the town where he lives that he has not sued at a Quarter Sessions. The rogue had once the impudence to go to law with the widow. His head is full of costs, damages, and ejectments: he plagued a couple of honest gentlemen so long for a trespass in breaking one of his hedges, till he was forced to sell the ground it enclosed to defray the charges of the prosecution: his father left him fourscore pounds a year; but he has cast and been cast so often, that he is not now worth thirty. I suppose he is going upon the old business of the willow tree.

As Sir ROGER was giving me this account of Tom Touchy, Will Wimble and his two companions stopped short till we came up to them. After having paid their respects to Sir Roger, Will told him that Mr. Touchy and he must appeal to him upon a dispute that arose between them. Will, it seems, had been giving his fellow traveler an account of his angling one day in such a hole; when Tom Touchy, instead of hearing out his story, told him, that Mr. Such-an-one, if he pleased, might *take the law of him* for fishing in that part of the river. My friend Sir ROGER heard them both, upon a round trot; and after having paused some time told them, with the air of a man who would not give his judgment rashly, that *much*

might be said on both sides. They were neither of them dissatisfied with the knight's determination because neither of them found himself in the wrong by it: upon which we made the best of our way to the assizes.

The court was sat before Sir ROGER came, but notwithstanding all the justices had taken their places upon the bench, they made room for the old knight at the head of them; who for his reputation in the country took occasion to whisper in the judge's ear, that *he was glad his lordship had met with so much good weather in his circuit.* I was listening to the proceedings of the court with much attention, and infinitely pleased with that great appearance and solemnity which so properly accompanies such a public administration of our laws; when, after about an hour's sitting, I observed to my great surprise, in the midst of a trial, that my friend Sir ROGER was getting up to speak. I was in some pain for him, till I found he had acquitted himself of two or three sentences, with a look of much business and great intrepidity.

Upon his first rising the court was hushed, and a general whisper ran among the country people that Sir ROGER *was up.* The speech he made was so little to the purpose, that I shall not trouble my readers with an account of it; and I believe was not so much designed by the knight himself to inform the court, as to give him a figure in my eye, and keep up his credit in the country.

I was highly delighted, when the court rose, to see the gentlemen of the country gathering about my old friend, and striving who should compliment him most; at the same time that the ordinary people gazed upon him at a distance, not a little admiring his courage, that was not afraid to speak to the judge.

In our return home we met with a very odd accident, which I cannot forbear relating, because it shows how desirous all who know Sir ROGER are of giving him marks of their esteem.

When we were arrived upon the verge of his estate, we stopped at a little inn to rest ourselves and our horses. The man of the house had it seems been formerly a servant in the knight's family; and to do honour to his old master, had some time since, unknown to Sir ROGER, put him up in a sign-post before the door; so that *The Knight's Head* had hung out upon the road about a week before he himself knew anything of the matter. As soon as Sir ROGER was acquainted with it, finding that his servant's indiscretion proceeded wholly from affection and goodwill, he only told him that he had made him too high a compliment; and when the fellow seemed to think that could hardly be, added with a more decisive look, that it was too great an honour for any man under a duke; but told him at the same time that it might be altered with a very few touches, and that he himself would be at the charge of it. Accordingly they got a painter by the knight's directions to add a pair of whiskers to the face, and by a little aggravation of the features to change it into *The Saracen's Head*. I should not have known this story, had not the innkeeper upon Sir ROGER's alighting told him in my hearing, that his honour's head was brought back last night with the alterations that he had ordered to be made in it. Upon this my friend with his usual cheerfulness related the particulars abovementioned, and ordered the head to be brought into the room. I could not forbear discovering greater expressions of mirth than ordinary upon the appearance of this monstrous face, under which, notwithstanding it was made to frown and stare in a most extraordinary manner, I could still discover a distant resemblance of my old friend. Sir ROGER, upon seeing me laugh, desired me to tell him truly if I thought it possible for people to know him in that disguise. I at first kept my usual silence; but upon the knight's conjuring me to tell him whether it was not still more like him-

self than a Saracen, I composed my countenance in the best manner I could, and replied, *that much might be said on both sides.*

These several adventures, with the knight's behaviour in them, gave me as pleasant a day as ever I met with in any of my travels.　　　　L

No. 157.
[Steele.]　　　　Thursday, August 30.

. . . *Genius natale comes qui temperat astrum,*
Naturae deus humanae, mortalis in unum
Quodque caput. . . .
　　　　—Horace, *Epistles*, II, ii, 187.

I am very much at a loss to express by any word that occurs to me in our language that which is understood by *indoles* in Latin. The natural disposition to any particular art, science, profession, or trade, is very much to be consulted in the care of youth, and studied by men for their own conduct when they form to themselves any scheme of life. It is wonderfully hard indeed for a man to judge of his own capacity impartially; that may look great to me which may appear little to another, and I may be carried by fondness towards myself so far, as to attempt things too high for my talents and accomplishments: but it is not methinks so very difficult a matter to make a judgment of the abilities of others, especially of those who are in their infancy. My commonplace book directs me on this occasion to mention the dawning of greatness in Alexander, who being asked in his youth to contend for a prize in the Olympic games, answered he would if he had kings to run against him. Cassius, who was one of the conspirators against Cæsar, gave as great a proof of his temper, when in his childhood he struck a playfellow, the son of Sylla, for saying his father was master of the Roman people. Scipio is reported to have answered (when some flatterers at supper were asking him what the Romans should do for a general after his death), Take Marius. Marius was then a very boy, and had given no instances of his valour; but it was visible to Scipio from the manners of the youth, that he had a soul formed for the attempt and execution of great undertakings. I must confess I have very often with much sorrow bewailed the misfortune of the children of Great Britain, when I consider the ignorance and undiscerning of the generality of school-masters. The boasted liberty we talk of is but a mean reward for the long servitude, the many heartaches and terrors, to which our childhood is exposed in going through a grammar-school: many of these stupid tyrants exercise their cruelty without any manner of distinction of the capacities of children, or the intention of parents in their behalf. There are many excellent tempers which are worthy to be nourished and cultivated with all possible diligence and care, that were never designed to be acquainted with Aristotle, Tully, or Virgil; and there are as many who have capacities for understanding every word those great persons have writ, and yet were not born to have any relish of their writings. For want of this common and obvious discerning in those who have the care of youth, we have so many hundred unaccountable creatures every age whipped up into great scholars, that are for ever near a right understanding, and will never arrive at it. These are the scandal of letters, and these are generally the men who are to teach others. The sense of shame and honour is enough to keep the world itself in order without corporal punishment, much more to train the minds of uncorrupted and innocent children. It happens, I doubt not, more than once in a year, that a lad is chastised for a blockhead, when it is good apprehension that makes him incapable of knowing what his teacher means: a brisk imagination very often may suggest an error, which a lad could not have fallen into if he had

been as heavy in conjecturing as his master in explaining: but there is no mercy even towards a wrong interpretation of his meaning; the sufferings of the scholar's body are to rectify the mistakes of his mind.

I am confident that no boy who will not be allured to letters without blows, will ever be brought to any thing with them. A great or good mind must necessarily be the worse for such indignities; and it is a sad change to lose of its virtue for the improvement of its knowledge. No one who has gone through what they call a great school, but must remember to have seen children of excellent and ingenuous natures (as has afterwards appeared in their manhood); I say no man has passed through this way of education, but must have seen an ingenuous creature expiring with shame, with pale looks, beseeching sorrow, and silent tears, throw up its honest eyes, and kneel on its tender knees to an inexorable blockhead, to be forgiven the false quantity of a word in making a Latin verse: the child is punished, and the next day he commits a like crime, and so a third with the same consequence. I would fain ask any reasonable man whether this lad, in the simplicity of his native innocence, full of shame, and capable of any impression from that grace of soul, was not fitter for any purpose in this life, than after that spark of virtue is extinguished in him, though he is able to write twenty verses in an evening?

Seneca says, after his exalted way of talking, *As the immortal gods never learnt any virtue, tho' they are indued with all that is good; so there are some men who have so natural a propensity to what they should follow, that they learn it almost as soon as they hear it.* Plants and vegetables are cultivated into the production of finer fruit than they would yield without that care; and yet we cannot entertain hopes of producing a tender conscious spirit into acts of virtue, without the same methods as is used to cut timber, or give new shape to a piece of stone.

It is wholly to this dreadful practice that we may attribute a certain hardness and ferocity which some men, though liberally educated, carry about them in all their behaviour. To be bred like a gentleman, and punished like a malefactor, must, as we see it does, produce that illiberal sauciness which we see sometimes in men of letters.

The Spartan boy who suffered the fox (which he had stolen and hid under his coat) to eat into his bowels, I dare say had not half the wit or petulance which we learn at great schools among us: but the glorious sense of honour, or rather fear of shame, which he demonstrated in that action, was worth all the learning in the world without it.

It is methinks a very melancholy consideration, that a little negligence can spoil us, but great industry is necessary to improve us; the most excellent natures are soon depreciated, but evil tempers are long before they are exalted into good habits. To help this by punishments, is the same thing as killing a man to cure him of a distemper; when he comes to suffer punishment in that one circumstance, he is brought below the existence of a rational creature, and is in the state of a brute that moves only by the admonition of stripes. But since this custom of educating by the lash is suffered by the gentry of Great Britain, I would prevail only that honest heavy lads may be dismissed from slavery sooner than they are at present, and not whipped on to their fourteenth or fifteenth year, whether they expect any progress from them or not. Let the child's capacity be forthwith examined, and he sent to some mechanic way of life, without respect to his birth, if nature designed him for nothing higher; let him go before he has innocently suffered, and is debased into a dereliction of mind for being what it is no guilt to be, a

plain man. I would not here be supposed to have said, that our learned men of either robe who have been whipped at school, are not still men of noble and liberal minds; but I am sure they had been much more so than they are, had they never suffered that infamy.

But though there is so little care, as I have observed, taken, or observation made of the natural strain of men, it is no small comfort to me, as a SPECTATOR, that there is any right value set upon the *bona indoles* of other animals; as appears by the following advertisement handed about the county of Lincoln, and subscribed by Enos Thomas, a person whom I have not the honour to know, but suppose to be profoundly learned in horseflesh:

A chestnut horse called Cæsar, *bred by* James Darcey, *Esq. at* Sedbury *near* Richmond *in the County of* York; *his grandam was his old royal mare, and got by* Blunderbuss, *which was got by* Hemsly Turk, *and he got by Mr.* Courant's *Arabian, which got Mr.* Minshul's Jewstrump. *Mr.* Cæsar *sold him to a nobleman (coming five years old, when he had but one sweat) for three hundred guineas. A guinea a leap and trial, and a shilling the man.*
T   Enos Thomas.

No. 159.
[Addison.] Saturday, September 1.

. . . *Omnem, quae nunc obducta tuenti Mortales hebetat visus tibi, & humida circum Caligat, nubem eripiam.* . . .
                    —Virgil, *Æneid*, II, 604-6.

When I was at Grand Cairo I picked up several Oriental manuscripts, which I have still by me. Among others I met with one, entitled *The Visions of Mirzah*, which I have read over with great pleasure. I intend to give it to the public when I have no other entertainment for them; and shall begin with the first vision, which I have translated word for word as follows:

On the fifth day of the moon, which according to the custom of my forefathers I always keep holy, after having washed myself and offered up my morning devotions, I ascended the high hills of Bagdat, in order to pass the rest of the day in meditation and prayer. As I was here airing myself on the tops of the mountains, I fell into a profound contemplation on the vanity of human life; and passing from one thought to another, Surely, said I, man is but a shadow and life a dream. Whilst I was thus musing, I cast my eyes towards the summit of a rock that was not far from me, where I discovered one in the habit of a shepherd, with a little musical instrument in his hand. As I looked upon him he applied it to his lips, and began to play upon it. The sound of it was exceeding sweet, and wrought into a variety of tunes that were inexpressibly melodious, and altogether different from any thing I had ever heard. They put me in mind of those heavenly airs that are played to the departed souls of good men upon their first arrival in paradise, to wear out the impressions of the last agonies, and qualify them for the pleasures of that happy place. My heart melted away in secret raptures.

I had been often told that the rock before me was the haunt of a genius; and that several had been entertained with music who had passed by it, but never heard that the musician had before made himself visible. When he had raised my thoughts, by those transporting airs which he played, to taste the pleasures of his conversation, as I looked upon him like one astonished, he beckoned to me, and by the waving of his hand directed me to approach the place where he sat. I drew near with that reverence which is due to a superior nature; and as my heart was entirely subdued by the captivating strains I had heard, I fell

down at his feet and wept. The genius smiled upon me with a look of compassion and affability that familiarized him to my imagination, and at once dispelled all the fears and apprehensions with which I approached him. He lifted me from the ground, and taking me by the hand, Mirzah, said he, I have heard thee in thy soliloquies, follow me.

He then led me to the highest pinnacle of the rock, and placing me on the top of it, Cast thy eyes eastward, said he, and tell me what thou seest. I see, said I, a huge valley and a prodigious tide of water rolling through it. The valley that thou seest, said he, is the vale of misery, and the tide of water that thou seest is part of the great tide of eternity. What is the reason, said I, that the tide I see rises out of a thick mist at one end, and again loses itself in a thick mist at the other? What thou seest, said he, is that portion of eternity which is called time, measured out by the sun, and reaching from the beginning of the world to its consummation. Examine now, said he, this sea that is bounded with darkness at both ends, and tell me what thou discoverest in it. I see a bridge, said I, standing in the midst of the tide. The bridge thou seest, said he, is human life; consider it attentively. Upon a more leisurely survey of it, I found that it consisted of threescore and ten entire arches, with several broken arches, which added to those that were entire, made up the number about an hundred. As I was counting the arches, the genius told me that this bridge consisted at first of a thousand arches; but that a great flood swept away the rest, and left the bridge in the ruinous condition I now beheld it. But tell me further, said he, what thou discoverest on it. I see multitudes of people passing over it, said I, and a black cloud hanging on each end of it. As I looked more attentively, I saw several of the passengers dropping through the bridge, into the great tide that flowed underneath it; and upon further examination, perceived there were innumerable trap-doors that lay concealed in the bridge, which the passengers no sooner trod upon, but they fell through them into the tide and immediately disappeared. These hidden pitfalls were set very thick at the entrance of the bridge, so that throngs of people no sooner broke through the cloud, but many of them fell into them. They grew thinner towards the middle, but multiplied and lay closer together towards the end of the arches that were entire.

There were indeed some persons, but their number was very small, that continued a kind of hobbling march on the broken arches, but fell through one after another, being quite tired and spent with so long a walk.

I passed some time in the contemplation of this wonderful structure, and the great variety of objects which it presented. My heart was filled with a deep melancholy to see several dropping unexpectedly in the midst of mirth and jollity, and catching at everything that stood by them to save themselves. Some were looking up towards the heavens in a thoughtful posture, and in the midst of a speculation stumbled and fell out of sight. Multitudes were very busy in the pursuit of bubbles that glittered in their eyes and danced before them, but often when they thought themselves within the reach of them their footing failed and down they sunk. In this confusion of objects, I observed some with scimitars in their hands, and others with urinals, who ran to and fro upon the bridge, thrusting several persons on trap-doors which did not seem to lie in their way, and which they might have escaped had they not been thus forced upon them.

The genius seeing me indulge myself in this melancholy prospect, told me I had dwelt long enough upon it: Take thine eyes off the bridge, said he, and tell me if thou yet seest any thing thou dost not comprehend.

Upon looking up, What mean, said I, those great flights of birds that are perpetually hovering about the bridge, and settling upon it from time to time? I see vultures, harpies, ravens, cormorants; and among many other feathered creatures several little winged boys, that perch in great numbers upon the middle arches. These, said the genius, are envy, avarice, superstition, despair, love, with the like cares and passions that infest human life.

I here fetched a deep sigh, Alas, said I, man was made in vain! How is he given away to misery and mortality! tortured in life, and swallowed up in death! The genius being moved with compassion towards me, bid me quit so uncomfortable a prospect. Look no more, said he, on man in the first stage of his existence, in his setting out for eternity; but cast thine eye on that thick mist into which the tide bears the several generations of mortals that fall into it. I directed my sight as I was ordered, and (whether or no the good genius strengthened it with any supernatural force, or dissipated part of the mist that was before too thick for the eye to penetrate) I saw the valley opening at the further end, and spreading forth into an immense ocean, that had a huge rock of adamant running through the midst of it, and dividing it into two equal parts. The clouds still rested on one half of it, insomuch that I could discover nothing in it: but the other appeared to me a vast ocean planted with innumerable islands, that were covered with fruits and flowers, and interwoven with a thousand little shining seas that ran among them. I could see persons dressed in glorious habits, with garlands upon their heads, passing among the trees, lying down by the sides of fountains, or resting on beds of flowers; and could hear a confused harmony of singing birds, falling waters, human voices, and musical instruments. Gladness grew in me upon the discovery of so delightful a scene. I wished for the wings of an eagle, that I might fly away to those happy seats; but the genius told me there was no passage to them, except through the gates of death that I saw opening every moment upon the bridge. The islands, said he, that lie so fresh and green before thee, and with which the whole face of the ocean appears spotted as far as thou canst see, are more in number than the sands on the seashore; there are myriads of islands behind those which thou here discoverest, reaching further than thine eye or even thine imagination can extend it self. These are the mansions of good men after death, who according to the degree and kinds of virtue in which they excelled, are distributed among these several islands, which abound with pleasures of different kinds and degrees, suitable to the relishes and perfections of those who are settled in them; every island is a paradise accommodated to its respective inhabitants. Are not these, O Mirzah, habitations worth contending for? Does life appear miserable, that gives thee opportunities of earning such a reward? Is death to be feared, that will convey thee to so happy an existence? Think not man was made in vain, who has such an eternity reserved for him. I gazed with inexpressible pleasure on these happy islands. At length, said I, show me now, I beseech thee, the secrets that lie hid under those dark clouds which cover the ocean on the other side of the rock of adamant. The genius making me no answer, I turned about to address myself to him a second time, but I found that he had left me; I then turned again to the vision which I had been so long contemplating, but instead of the rolling tide, the arched bridge, and the happy islands, I saw nothing but the long hollow valley of Bagdat, with oxen, sheep, and camels grazing upon the sides of it.

The End of the first Vision of Mirzah.
C

No. 160.
[Addison.] Monday, September 3.

. . . Cui mens divinior, atque os Magna sonaturum, des nominis hujus honorem.—Horace, *Satires*, I, iv, 43-44.

There is no character more frequently given to a writer, than that of being a genius. I have heard many a little sonneteer called a *fine genius*. There is not an heroic scribbler in the nation, that has not his admirers who think him a *great genius*; and as for your smatterers in tragedy, there is scarce a man among them who is not cried up by one or other for a *prodigious genius*.

My design in this paper is to consider what is properly a great genius, and to throw some thoughts together on so uncommon a subject.

Among great geniuses, those few draw the admiration of all the world upon them, and stand up as the prodigies of mankind, who by the mere strength of natural parts, and without any assistance of art or learning, have produced works that were the delight of their own times and the wonder of posterity. There appears something nobly wild and extravagant in these great natural geniuses, that is infinitely more beautiful than all the turn and polishing of what the French call a *bel esprit*, by which they would express a genius refined by conversation, reflection, and the reading of the most polite authors. The greatest genius which runs through the arts and sciences, takes a kind of tincture from them, and falls unavoidably into imitation.

Many of these great natural geniuses that were never disciplined and broken by rules of art, are to be found among the ancients, and in particular among those of the more eastern parts of the world. Homer has innumerable flights that Virgil was not able to reach, and in the Old Testament we find several passages more elevated and sublime than any in

Homer. At the same time that we allow a greater and more daring genius to the ancients, we must own that the greatest of them very much failed in, or, if you will, that they were much above the nicety and correctness of the moderns. In their similitudes and allusions, provided there was a likeness, they did not much trouble themselves about the decency of the comparison: Thus Solomon resembles the nose of his beloved to the tower of Lebanon which looketh toward Damascus; as the coming of a thief in the night, is a similitude of the same kind in the New Testament. It would be endless to make collections of this nature: Homer illustrates one of his heroes encompassed with the enemy, by an ass in a field of corn that has his sides belaboured by all the boys of the village without stirring a foot for it; and another of them tossing to and fro in his bed and burning with resentment, to a piece of flesh broiled on the coals. This particular failure in the ancients, opens a large field of raillery to the little wits, who can laugh at an indecency but not relish the sublime in these sorts of writings. The present Emperor of Persia, conformable to this Eastern way of thinking, amidst a great many pompous titles, denominates himself the Sun of Glory, and the *Nutmeg of Delight*. In short, to cut off all cavilling against the ancients, and particularly those of the warmer climates, who had most heat and life in their imaginations, we are to consider that the rule of observing what the French call the *bienséance* in an allusion, has been found out of latter years and in the colder regions of the world; where we would make some amends for our want of force and spirit, by a scrupulous nicety and exactness in our compositions. Our countryman Shakespeare was a remarkable instance of this first kind of great geniuses.

I cannot quit this head without observing that Pindar was a great genius of the first class, who was hurried on by a natural fire and impetuosity to vast conceptions of things, and noble sallies of imagination. At the same time, can anything be more ridiculous than for men of a sober and moderate fancy to imitate this poet's way of writing in those monstrous compositions which go among us under the name of Pindarics? When I see people copying works, which, as Horace has represented them, are singular in their kind and inimitable; when I see men following irregularities by rule, and by the little tricks of art straining after the most unbounded flights of nature, I cannot but apply to them that passage in Terence.

. . . incerta hæc si tu postules
Ratione certa facere, nihilo plus agas,
Quam si des operam, ut cum ratione insanias.

In short a modern pindaric writer compared with Pindar, is like a sister among the Camisars compared with Virgil's Sybil: there is the distortion, grimace, and outward figure, but nothing of that divine impulse which raises the mind above itself, and makes the sounds more than human.

There is another kind of great geniuses which I shall place in a second class, not as I think them inferior to the first, but only for distinction's sake as they are of a different kind. This second class of great geniuses are those that have formed themselves by rules, and submitted the greatness of their natural talents to the corrections and restraints of art. Such among the Greeks were Plato and Aristotle, among the Romans Virgil and Tully, among the English Milton and Sir Francis Bacon.

The genius in both these classes of authors may be equally great, but shows itself after a different manner. In the first it is like a rich soil in a happy climate, that produces a whole wilderness of noble plants rising in a thousand beautiful landscapes without any certain order or regularity. In the other it is the same rich soil under the same happy climate, that has been laid out in walks and parterres, and cut into shape and beauty by the skill of the gardener.

The great danger in these latter kind of geniuses, is, lest they cramp their own abilities too much by imitation, and form themselves altogether upon models, without giving the full play to their own natural parts. An imitation of the best authors is not to compare with a good original; and I believe we may observe that very few writers make an extraordinary figure in the world, who have not something in their way of thinking or expressing themselves that is peculiar to them and entirely their own.

It is odd to consider what great geniuses are sometimes thrown away upon trifles.

"I once saw a shepherd," says a famous Italian author, "who used to divert himself in his solitudes with tossing up eggs and catching them again without breaking them; in which he had arrived to so great a degree of perfection, that he would keep up four at a time for several minutes together playing in the air, and falling into his hand by turns. I think," says the author, "I never saw a greater severity than in this man's face; for by his wonderful perseverance and application, he had contracted the seriousness and gravity of a privy-councillour; and I could not but reflect with myself, that the same assiduity and attention, had they been rightly applied, might have made him a greater mathematician than Archimedes."   C

No. 174.
[Steele.] Wednesday, September 19.

Haec memini et victum frustra contendere Thyrsin.—Virgil, Eclogues, VII, 69.

There is scarce any thing more common than animosities between parties that cannot subsist but by their agreement: this was well represented in the sedition of the members of the human body in the old Roman fable. It is often the case of lesser confederate states against a superior power, which are hardly held together though their unanimity is necessary for their common safety: and this is always the case of the landed and trading interest of Great Britain; the trader is fed by the product of the land, and the landed man cannot be clothed but by the skill of the trader; and yet those interests are ever jarring.

We had last winter an instance of this at our club, in Sir ROGER DE COV-ERLEY and Sir ANDREW FREEPORT, between whom there is generally a constant, though friendly, opposition of opinions. It happened that one of the company, in an historical discourse, was observing, that Carthaginian faith was a proverbial phrase to intimate breach of leagues. Sir ROGER said it could hardly be otherwise: that the Carthaginians were the greatest traders in the world; and as gain is the chief end of such a people, they never pursue any other: the means to it are never regarded; they will, if it comes easily, get money honestly; but if not, they will not scruple to attain it by fraud or cosenage: and indeed what is the whole business of the trader's account, but to overreach him who trusts to his memory? But were that not so, what can there great and noble be expected from him whose attention is for ever fixed upon balancing his books, and watching over his expenses? And at best, let frugality and parsimony be the virtues of the merchant, how much is his punctual dealing below a gentleman's charity to the poor, or hospitality among his neighbours?

CAPTAIN SENTRY observed Sir ANDREW very diligent in hearing Sir ROGER, and had a mind to turn the discourse, by taking notice in general from the highest to the lowest parts of human society, there was a secret, though unjust way among men, of indulging the seeds of ill-nature and envy, by comparing their own state of life to that of another, and grudging the approach of their neighbour to their own happiness; and on the other side, he who is the less at his ease repines at the other who, he thinks, has unjustly the advantage over him. Thus the civil and military list look upon each other with much ill-nature; the soldier repines at the courtier's power, and the courtier rallies the soldier's honour; or, to come to lower instances, the private men in the horse and foot of an army, the carmen and coachmen in the city-streets, mutually look upon each other with ill-will, when they are in competition for quarters or the way in their respective motions.

It is very well, good Captain, interrupted Sir ANDREW: You may attempt to turn the discourse, if you think fit, but I must however have a word or two with Sir ROGER; who, I see, thinks he has paid me off, and been very severe upon the merchant. I shall not, continued he, at this time remind Sir ROGER of the great and noble monuments of charity and public spirit which have been erected by merchants since the Reformation, but at present content my self with what he allows us, parsimony and frugality. If it were consistent with the quality of so ancient a baronet as Sir ROGER, to keep an account or measure things by the most infallible way, that of numbers, he would prefer our parsimony to his hospitality. If to drink so many hogsheads is to be hospitable, we do not contend for the fame of that virtue; but it would be worth while to consider, whether so many artificers at work ten days together by my appointment, or so many peasants made merry on Sir ROGER's charge, are the men more obliged: I believe the families of the artificers will thank me, more than the households of the peasants shall Sir ROGER. Sir ROGER gives to his men, but I place mine above the necessity or obligation of my bounty. I am in very little pain for the Roman proverb upon the Carthaginian traders;

the Romans were their professed enemies: I am only sorry no Carthaginian histories have come to our hands; we might have been taught perhaps by them some proverbs against the Roman generosity, in fighting for and bestowing other people's goods. But since Sir ROGER has taken occasion from an old proverb to be out of humour with merchants, it should be no offence to offer one not quite so old in their defence. When a man happens to break in Holland, they say of him that *he has not kept true accounts*. This phrase, perhaps, among us would appear a soft or humorous way of speaking, but with that exact nation it bears the highest reproach; for a man to be mistaken in the calculation of his expense, in his ability to answer future demands, or to be impertinently sanguine in putting his credit to too great adventure, are all instances of as much infamy, as with gayer nations to be failing in courage or common honesty.

Numbers are so much the measure of everything that is valuable, that it is not possible to demonstrate the success of any action, or the prudence of any undertaking, without them. I say this in answer to what Sir ROGER is pleased to say, that little that is truly noble can be expected from one who is ever poring on his cash-book or balancing his accounts. When I have my returns from abroad, I can tell to a shilling by the help of numbers the profit or loss by my adventure; but I ought also to be able to show that I had reason for making it, either from my own experience or that of other people, or from a reasonable presumption that my returns will be sufficient to answer my expense and hazard; and this is never to be done without the skill of numbers. For instance, if I am to trade to Turkey, I ought beforehand to know the demand of our manufactures there as well as of their silks in England, and the customary prices that are given for both in each country. I ought to have a clear knowledge of these matters beforehand, that I may presume upon sufficient returns to answer the charge of the cargo I have fitted out, the freight and assurance out and home, the customs to the Queen, and the interest of my own money, and besides all these expenses a reasonable profit to myself. Now what is there of scandal in this skill? What has the merchant done that he should be so little in the good graces of Sir ROGER? he throws down no man's enclosures, and tramples upon no man's corn; he takes nothing from the industrious labourer; he pays the poor man for his work; he communicates his profit with mankind; by the preparation of his cargo and the manufacture of his returns, he furnishes employment and subsistence to greater numbers than the richest nobleman; and even the nobleman is obliged to him for finding out foreign markets for the produce of his estate, and for making a great addition to his rents; and yet 'tis certain that none of all these things could be done by him without the exercise of his skill in numbers.

This is the economy of the merchant, and the conduct of the gentleman must be the same, unless by scorning to be the steward, he resolves the steward shall be the gentleman. The gentleman no more than the merchant is able without the help of numbers to account for the success of any action, or the prudence of any adventure. If, for instance, the chase is his whole adventure, his only returns must be the stag's horns in the great hall, and the fox's nose upon the stable door. Without doubt Sir ROGER knows the full value of these returns; and if beforehand he had computed the charges of the chase, a gentleman of his discretion would certainly have hanged up all his dogs, he would never have brought back so many fine horses to the kennel, he would never have gone so often like a blast over fields of corn. If such too had been the conduct of all his ancestors, he might truly have boasted at this day that the antiquity of his family had

never been sullied by a trade; a merchant had never been permitted with his whole estate to purchase a room for his picture in the gallery of the COVERLEYS, or to claim his descent from the maid of honour. But 'tis very happy for Sir ROGER that the merchant paid so dear for his ambition. 'Tis the misfortune of many other gentlemen to turn out of the seats of their ancestors, to make way for such new masters as have been more exact in their accounts than themselves; and certainly he deserves the estate a great deal better who has got it by his industry, than he who has lost it by his negligence.

No. 249.
[Addison.] Saturday, December 15.

Γέλως ἄκαιρος ἐν βροτοῖς δεινὸν κακόν.
—Frag. Vet. Poet.

When I make choice of a subject that has not been treated of by others, I throw together my reflections on it without any order or method, so that they may appear rather in the looseness and freedom of an essay, than in the regularity of a set discourse. It is after this manner that I shall consider laughter and ridicule in my present paper.

Man is the merriest species of the creation, all above and below him are serious. He sees things in a different light from other beings, and finds his mirth rising from objects which perhaps cause something like pity or displeasure in higher natures. Laughter is indeed a very good counterpoise to the spleen; and it seems but reasonable that we should be capable of receiving joy from what is no real good to us, since we can receive grief from what is no real evil.

I have in my forty-seventh paper raised a speculation on the notion of a modern philosopher, who describes the first motive of laughter to be a secret comparison which we make between ourselves and the persons we laugh at; or, in other words, that satisfaction which we receive from the opinion of some pre-eminence in ourselves, when we see the absurdities of another, or when we reflect on any past absurdities of our own. This seems to hold in most cases, and we may observe that the vainest part of mankind are the most addicted to this passion.

I have read a sermon of a conventual in the Church of Rome, on those words of the wise man, *I said of laughter it is mad, and of mirth what does it?* Upon which he laid it down as a point of doctrine, that laughter was the effect of original sin, and that Adam could not laugh before the Fall.

Laughter, while it lasts, slackens and unbraces the mind, weakens the faculties, and causes a kind of remissness, and dissolution in all the powers of the soul. And thus far it may be looked upon as a weakness in the composition of human nature. But if we consider the frequent reliefs we receive from it, and how often it breaks the gloom which is apt to depress the mind and damp our spirits, with transient unexpected gleams of joy, one would take care not to grow too wise for so great a pleasure of life.

The talent of turning men into ridicule, and exposing to laughter those one converses with, is the qualification of little ungenerous tempers. A young man with this cast of mind cuts himself off from all manner of improvement. Everyone has his flaws and weaknesses; nay, the greatest blemishes are often found in the most shining characters; but what an absurd thing is it to pass over all the valuable parts of a man, and fix our attention on his infirmities; to observe his imperfections more than his virtues; and to make use of him for the sport of others, rather than for our own improvement.

We therefore very often find that persons the most accomplished in ridicule are those who are very shrewd at hitting a blot, without exerting any thing masterly in themselves. As there

are many eminent critics who never writ a good line, there are many admirable buffoons that animadvert upon every single defect in another, without ever discovering the least beauty of their own. By this means these unlucky little wits often gain reputation in the esteem of vulgar minds, and raise themselves above persons of much more laudable characters.

If the talent of ridicule were employed to laugh men out of vice and folly, it might be of some use to the world; but instead of this, we find that it is generally made use of to laugh men out of virtue and good sense, by attacking every thing that is solemn and serious, decent and praiseworthy in human life.

We may observe, that in the first ages of the world, when the great souls and masterpieces of human nature were produced, men shined by a noble simplicity of behaviour, and were strangers to those little embellishments which are so fashionable in our present conversation. And it is very remarkable, that notwithstanding we fall short at present of the ancients in poetry, painting, oratory, history, architecture, and all the noble arts and sciences which depend more upon genius than experience, we exceed them as much in doggerel, humour, burlesque, and all the trivial arts of ridicule. We meet with more raillery among the moderns, but more good sense among the ancients.

The two great branches of ridicule in writing are comedy and burlesque. The first ridicules persons by drawing them in their proper characters, the other by drawing them quite unlike themselves. Burlesque is therefore of two kinds, the first represents mean persons in the accoutrements of heroes, the other describes great persons acting and speaking, like the basest among the people. *Don Quixote* is an instance of the first, and Lucian's gods of the second. It is a dispute among the critics, whether burlesque poetry runs best in heroic verse, like that of the *Dispensary,* or in doggerel, like that of *Hudibras.* I think where the low character is to be raised the heroic is the proper measure, but when an hero is to be pulled down and degraded, it is done best in doggerel.

If *Hudibras* had been set out with as much wit and humour in heroic verse as he is in doggerel, he would have made a much more agreeable figure than he does; though the generality of his readers are so wonderfully pleased with the double rhymes, that I do not expect many will be of my opinion in this particular.

I shall conclude this essay upon laughter with observing that the metaphor of laughing, applied to fields and meadows when they are in flower, or to trees when they are in blossom, runs through all languages; which I have not observed of any other metaphor, excepting that of fire, and burning, when they are applied to love. This shows that we naturally regard laughter, as what is both in itself amiable and beautiful. For this reason likewise Venus has gained the title of Φιλομμειδής, the laughter-loving dame, as Waller has translated it, and is represented by Horace as the goddess who delights in laughter. Milton, in a joyous assembly of imaginary persons, has given us a very poetical figure of laughter. His whole band of mirth is so finely described that I shall set down the passage at length.

But come thou goddess fair and free,
In heaven ycleped Euphrosyne,
And by men, heart-easing mirth,
Whom lovely Venus at a birth
With two sister graces more
To ivy-crowned Bacchus bore:
Haste thee nymph, and bring with thee
Jest and youthful jollity,
Quips and cranks, and wanton wiles,
Nods, and becks, and wreathed smiles,
Such as hang on Hebe's cheek,
And love to live in dimple sleek;
Sport that wrinkled care derides,
And laughter holding both his sides.
Come, and trip it as you go
On the light fantastic toe,
And in thy right hand lead with thee,
The mountain nymph, sweet Liberty;
And if I give thee honour due,

Mirth, admit me of thy crew
To live with her, and live with thee,
In unreproved pleasures free.

C

No. 263.
[Steele.] Tuesday, January 1, 1712.

Gratulor . . . quod eum quem necesse erat diligere, qualiscunque esset, talem habemus, ut libenter quoque diligamus.—
Trebonius apud Tull.

Mr. SPECTATOR,

I am the happy father of a very towardly son, in whom I do not only see my life, but also my manner of life, renewed. It would be extremely beneficial to society, if you would frequently resume subjects which serve to bind these sort of relations faster, and endear the ties of blood with those of good-will, protection, observance, indulgence and veneration. I would, methinks, have this done after an uncommon method, and do not think any one, who is not capable of writing a good play, fit to undertake a work wherein there will necessarily occur so many secret instincts, and biases of human nature, which would pass unobserved by common eyes. I thank Heaven I have no outrageous offense against my own excellent parents to answer for, but when I am now and then alone, and look back upon my past life, from my earliest infancy to this time, there are many faults which I committed that did not appear to me, even till I myself became a father. I had not till then a notion of the earnings of heart, which a man has when he sees his child do a laudable thing, or the sudden damp which seizes him when he fears he will act something unworthy. It is not to be imagined, what a remorse touched me for a long train of childish negligences of my mother, when I saw my wife the other day look out of the window, and turn as pale as ashes upon seeing my younger boy sliding upon the ice. These slight intimations will give you to understand, that there are numberless little crimes, which children take no notice of while they are doing, which, upon reflection, when they shall themselves become fathers, they will look upon with the utmost sorrow and contrition that they did not regard, before those whom they offended were to be no more seen. How many thousand things do I remember, which would have highly pleased my father, and I omitted for no other reason, but that I thought what he proposed the effect of humour and old age, which I am now convinced had reason and good sense in it. I cannot now go into the parlour to him, and make his heart glad with an account of a matter which was of no consequence, but that I told it, and acted in it. The good man and woman are long since in their graves, who used to sit and plot the welfare of us their children, while, perhaps, we were sometimes laughing at the old folks at another end of the house. The truth of it is, were we merely to follow nature in these great duties of life, though we have a strong instinct towards the performing of them, we should be on both sides very deficient. Age is so unwelcome to the generality of mankind, and growth towards manhood so desirable to all, that resignation to decay is too difficult a task in the father; and deference, amidst the impulse of gay desires, appears unreasonable to the son. There are so few who can grow old with a good grace, and yet fewer who can come slow enough into the world, that a father, were he to be actuated by his desires, and a son, were he to consult himself only, could neither of them behave himself as he ought to the other. But when reason interposes against instinct, where it would carry either out of the interests of the other, there arises that happiest intercourse of good offices between those dearest relations of human life. The father, according to the opportunities which are offered to him, is throwing down blessings on the son, and the son endeavouring to appear the worthy offspring of such a father. It is after this manner that Camillus and his first-born dwell together.

Camillus enjoys a pleasing and indolent old age, in which passion is subdued, and reason exalted. He waits the day of his dissolution with a resignation mixed with delight, and the son fears the accession of his father's fortune with diffidence, lest he should not enjoy or become it as well as his predecessor. Add to this, that the father knows he leaves a friend to the children of his friends, an easy landlord to his tenants, and an agreeable companion to his acquaintance. He believes his son's behaviour will make him frequently remembered, but never wanted. This commerce is so well cemented, that without the pomp of saying, *Son, be a friend to such a one when I am gone,* Camillus knows, being in his favour, is direction enough to the grateful youth who is to succeed him, without the admonition of his mentioning it. These gentlemen are honoured in all their neighbourhood, and the same effect which a court has on the manners of a kingdom, their characters have on all who live within the influence of them.

My son and I are not of fortune to communicate our good actions or intentions to so many as these gentlemen do; but I will be bold to say, my son has, by the applause and approbation which his behaviour towards me has gained him, occasioned that many an old man, besides myself, has rejoiced. Other men's children follow the example of mine, and I have the inexpressible happiness of overhearing our neighbours, as we ride by, point to their children, and say with a voice of joy, There they go.

You cannot, Mr. SPECTATOR, pass your time better, than in insinuating the delights which these relations well regarded bestow upon each other. Ordinary passages are no longer such, but mutual love gives an importance to the most indifferent things, and a merit to actions the most insignificant. When we look round the world, and observe the many misunderstandings which are created by the malice and insinuation of the meanest servants between people thus related, how necessary will it appear that it were inculcated that men would be upon their guard to support a constancy of affection, and that grounded upon the principles of reason, not the impulses of instinct.

It is from the common prejudices which men receive from their parents, that hatreds are kept alive from one generation to another; and when men act by instinct, hatreds will descend when good offices are forgotten. For the degeneracy of human life is such, that our anger is more easily transferred to our children than our love. Love always gives something to the object it delights in, and anger spoils the person against whom it is moved of something laudable in him: from this degeneracy, therefore, and a sort of self-love, we are more prone to take up the ill-will of our parents, than to follow them in their friendships.

One would think there should need no more to make men keep up this sort of relation with the utmost sanctity, than to examine their own hearts. If every father remembered his own thoughts and inclinations when he was a son, and every son remembered what he expected from his father, when he himself was in a state of dependence, this one reflection would preserve men from being dissolute or rigid in these several capacities. The power and subjection between them when broken, make them more emphatically tyrants and rebels against each other, with greater cruelty of heart than the disruption of states and empires can possibly produce. I shall end this application to you with two letters which passed between a mother and son very lately, and are as follows:

"Dear FRANK,

If the pleasures, which I have the grief to hear you pursue in town, do not take up all your time, do not deny your mother so much of it, as to read seriously this letter. You said before Mr. Letacre, that an old woman might live very well in the country upon half my jointure, and that your father was a fond fool to give me a rent-charge of eight hundred a year to the prejudice of his son. What Letacre said to you upon that occasion, you ought to have borne with more decency, as he was your father's well-beloved servant, than to have called him *country putt*. In the first place, Frank, I must tell you I will have my rent duly paid, for I will make up to your sisters for the partiality I was guilty of, in making your father do so much as he has done for you. I may, it seems, live upon half my jointure! I lived upon much less, Frank, when I carried you from place to place in these arms, and could neither eat, dress, or mind any thing for feeding and tending you a weakly child, and shedding tears when the convulsions you were then troubled with returned upon you. By my care you outgrew them, to throw away the vigour of your youth in the arms of harlots, and deny your mother what is not yours to detain. Both your sisters are crying to see the passion which I smother; but if you please to go on thus like a gentleman of the town, and forget all regards to yourself and family, I shall immediately enter upon your estate for the arrear due to me, and without one tear more contemn you for forgetting the fondness of your mother, as much as you have the example of your father. O Frank, do I live to omit writing myself,

Your Affectionate Mother,
A. T."

"Madam,

I will come down to morrow and pay the money on my knees. Pray write so no more. I will take care you never shall, for I will be forever hereafter

Your most dutiful son,
F. T.

I will bring down new heads for my sisters. Pray let all be forgotten."
                                                                    T

No. 267.
[Addison.]   Saturday, January 5.

Cedite Romani scriptores, cedite Graii.
—Propertius, *Elegies*, III, xxvi (34), 65.

There is nothing in nature so irksome as general discourses, especially when they turn chiefly upon words. For this reason I shall waive the discussion of that point which was started some years since, Whether Milton's *Paradise Lost* may be called an heroic poem? Those who will not give it that title, may call it (if they please) a *divine poem*. It will be sufficient to its perfection, if it has in it all the beauties of the highest kind of poetry; and as for those who allege it is not an heroic poem, they advance no more to the diminution of it, than if they should say Adam is not Æneas, nor Eve Helen.

I shall therefore examine it by the rules of epic poetry, and see whether it falls short of the *Iliad* or *Æneid*, in the beauties which are essential to that kind of writing. The first thing to be considered in an epic poem, is the fable, which is perfect or imperfect, according as the action which it relates is more or less so. This action should have three qualifications in it. First, it should be but one action. Secondly, it should be an entire action; and thirdly, it should be a great action. To consider the action of the *Iliad*, *Æneid*, and *Paradise Lost*, in these three several lights. Homer to preserve the unity of his action hastens into the midst of things, as Horace has observed: had he gone up to Leda's egg, or begun much later, even at the rape of Helen, or the investing of Troy, it is manifest that the story of the poem would have been a series of several actions. He therefore opens his poem with the discord of his princes, and with great art interweaves in the several succeeding parts of it, an account of every thing mate-

rial which relates to them, and had passed before that fatal dissension. After the same manner Æneas makes his first appearance in the Tyrrhene seas, and within sight of Italy, because the action proposed to be celebrated was that of his settling himself in Latium. But because it was necessary for the reader to know what had happened to him in the taking of Troy, and in the preceding parts of his voyage, Virgil makes his hero relate it by way of episode in the second and third books of the *Æneid*. The contents of both which books come before those of the first book in the thread of the story, though for preserving of this unity of action, they follow them in the disposition of the poem. Milton, in imitation of these two great poets, opens his *Paradise Lost*, with an infernal council plotting the fall of man, which is the action he proposed to celebrate; and as for those great actions which preceded, in point of time, the battle of the angels, and the creation of the world (which would have entirely destroyed the unity of his principal action, had he related them in the same order that they happened), he cast them into the fifth, sixth, and seventh books, by way of episode to this noble poem.

Aristotle himself allows, that Homer has nothing to boast of as to the unity of his fable, though at the same time that great critic and philosopher endeavours to palliate this imperfection in the Greek poet, by imputing it in some measure to the very nature of an epic poem. Some have been of opinion, that the *Æneid* labours also in this particular, and has episodes which may be looked upon as excrescences rather than as parts of the action. On the contrary, the poem which we have now under our consideration, hath no other episodes than such as naturally arise from the subject, and yet is filled with such a multitude of astonishing incidents, that it gives us at the same time a pleasure of the greatest variety, and of the greatest simplicity.

I must observe also, that as Virgil in the poem which was designed to celebrate the original of the Roman empire, has described the birth of its great rival, the Carthaginian commonwealth: Milton with the like art in his poem on the Fall of Man, has related the fall of those angels who are his professed enemies. Besides the many other beauties in such an episode. its running parallel with the great action of the poem, hinders it from breaking the unity so much as another episode would have done, that had not so great an affinity with the principal subject. In short, this is the same kind of beauty which the critics admire in the *Spanish Fryar,* or the *Double Discovery,* where the two different plots look like counterparts and copies of one another.

The second qualification required in the action of an epic poem is, that it should be an *entire* action. An action is entire when it is complete in all its parts; or as Aristotle describes it, when it consists of a beginning, a middle, and an end. Nothing should go before it, be intermixed with it, or follow after it, that is not related to it. As on the contrary, no single step should be omitted in that just and regular process which it must be supposed to take from its original to its consummation. Thus we see the anger of Achilles in its birth, its continuance and effects; and Æneas's settlement in Italy, carried on through all the oppositions in his way to it both by sea and land. The action in Milton excels (I think) both the former in this particular: we see it contrived in hell, executed upon earth, and punished by heaven. The parts of it are told in the most distinct manner, and grow out of one another in the most natural method.

The third qualification of an epic poem is its *greatness.* The anger of Achilles was of such consequence, that it embroiled the kings of Greece, destroyed the heroes of Troy, and engaged all the gods in factions. Æneas's settlement in Italy produced the Cæsars, and gave birth to the Roman Empire. Milton's subject was still greater than either of the former; it does not determine the fate of single persons or nations, but of a whole species. The united powers of hell are joined together for the destruction of mankind, which they effected in part, and would have completed, had not omnipotence itself interposed. The principal actors are man in his greatest perfection, and woman in her highest beauty. Their enemies are the fallen angels: the Messiah their friend, and the Almighty their protector. In short, everything that is great in the whole circle of being, whether within the verge of nature, or out of it, has a proper part assigned it in this noble poem.

In poetry, as in architecture, not only the whole, but the principal members, and every part of them, should be great. I will not presume to say, that the book of games in the *Æneid,* or that in the *Iliad,* are not of this nature, nor to reprehend Virgil's simile of the top, and many other of the same nature in the *Iliad,* as liable to any censure in this particular; but I think we may say, without derogating from those wonderful performances, that there is an unquestionable magnificence in every part of *Paradise Lost,* and indeed a much greater than could have been formed upon any pagan system.

But Aristotle, by the greatness of the action, does not only mean that it should be great in its nature, but also in its duration, or in other words, that it should have a due length in it, as well as what we properly call greatness. The just measure of the kind of magnitude, he explains by the following similitude. An animal, no bigger than a mite, cannot appear perfect to the eye, because the sight takes it in at once, and has only a confused idea of the whole, and not a distinct idea of all its parts: if on the contrary you should suppose an animal of ten thousand furlongs in length, the eye would be so filled with a single part of it, that it could not give the mind an idea of the whole. What these animals are to the eye, a very short or a very long action would be to the memory. The first would be, as it were, lost and swallowed up by it, and the other difficult to be contained in it. Homer and Virgil have shown their principal art in this particular; the action of the *Iliad*, and that of the *Æneid*, were in themselves exceeding short, but are so beautifully extended and diversified by the invention of episodes, and the machinery of gods, with the like poetical ornaments, that they make up an agreeable story sufficient to employ the memory without overcharging it. Milton's action is enriched with such a variety of circumstances, that I have taken as much pleasure in reading the contents of his books, as in the best invented story I ever met with. It is possible, that the traditions on which the *Iliad* and *Æneid* were built, had more circumstances in them than the history of the Fall of Man, as it is related in Scripture. Besides it was easier for Homer and Virgil to dash the truth with fiction, as they were in no danger of offending the religion of their country by it. But as for Milton, he had not only a very few circumstances upon which to raise his poem, but was also obliged to proceed with the greatest caution in every thing that he added out of his own invention. And, indeed, notwithstanding all the restraints he was under, he has filled his story with so many surprising incidents, which bear so close an analogy with what is delivered in Holy Writ, that it is capable of pleasing the most delicate reader, without giving offence to the most scrupulous.

The modern critics have collected from several hints in the *Iliad* and *Æneid* the space of time, which is taken up by the action of each of those poems; but as a great part of Milton's story was transacted in regions that lie out of the reach of the sun and the sphere of day, it is impos-

sible to gratify the reader with such a calculation, which indeed would be more curious than instructive; none of the critics, either ancient or modern, having laid down rules to circumscribe the action of an epic poem with any determined number of years, days or hours.

This Piece of Criticism on Milton's Paradise Lost shall be carried on in the following Saturdays' Papers. L

No. 361.
[Addison.] Thursday, April 24.

Tartaream intendit vocem, qua protinus omnis
Contremuit domus.
—Altered from Virgil, *Æneid*, VII, 514-15.

I have lately received the following letter from a country gentleman.

"Mr. SPECTATOR,

The night before I left London I went to see a play, called *The Humorous Lieutenant*. Upon the rising of the curtain I was very much surprised with the great concert of cat-calls which was exhibited that evening, and began to think with myself that I had made a mistake, and gone to a music meeting instead of the playhouse. It appeared indeed a little odd to me to see so many persons of quality of both sexes assembled together at a kind of catterwauling; for I can not look upon that performance to have been any thing better, whatever the musicians themselves might think of it. As I had no acquaintance in the house to ask questions of, and was forced to go out of town early the next morning, I could not learn the secret of this matter. What I would therefore desire of you is, to give some account of this strange instrument, which I found the company called a cat-call; and particularly to let me know whether it be a piece of music lately come from Italy. For my own part, to be free with you, I would rather hear an English fiddle; though I durst not show my dislike whilst I was in the playhouse, it being my chance to sit the very next man to one of the performers.

I am, Sir,
Your most affectionate Friend and
    Servant,
        John Shallow, Esq."

In compliance with Squire Shallow's requests, I design this paper as a dissertation upon the cat-call. In order to make myself a master of the subject, I purchased one the beginning of last week, though not without great difficulty, being informed at two or three toy-shops that the players had lately bought them all up. I have since consulted many learned antiquaries in relation to its original, and find them very much divided among themselves upon that particular. A Fellow of the Royal Society, who is my good friend, and a great proficient in the mathematical part of music, concludes from the simplicity of its make, and the uniformity of its sound, that the cat-call is older than any of the inventions of Jubal. He observes very well, that musical instruments took their first rise from the notes of birds, and other melodious animals; and what, says he, was more natural than for the first ages of mankind to imitate the voice of a cat that lived under the same roof with them? He added that the cat had contributed more to harmony than any other animal; as we are not only beholden to her for this wind instrument, but for our string music in general.

Another virtuoso of my acquaintance will not allow the cat-call to be older than Thespis, and is apt to think it appeared in the world soon after the ancient comedy; for which reason it has still a place in our dramatic entertainments: nor must I here omit what a very curious gentleman, who is lately returned from his travels, has more than once assured me, namely, that there was lately dug up at Rome the Statue of a Momus, who holds an instrument in his right hand

very much resembling our modern cat-call.

There are others who ascribe this invention to Orpheus, and look upon the cat-call to be one of those instruments which that famous musician made use of to draw the beasts about him. It is certain, that the roasting of a cat does not call together a greater audience of that species, than this instrument, if dexterously played upon in proper time and place.

But notwithstanding these various and learned conjectures, I cannot forbear thinking that the cat-call is originally a piece of English music. Its resemblance to the voice of some of our British songsters, as well as the use of it, which is peculiar to our nation, confirms me in this opinion. It has at least received great improvements among us, whether we consider the instrument itself, or those several quavers and graces which are thrown into the playing of it. Every one might be sensible of this, who heard that remarkable overgrown cat-call which was placed in the center of the pit, and presided over all the rest at the celebrated performance lately exhibited in Drury Lane.

Having said thus much concerning the original of the cat-call, we are in the next place to consider the use of it. The cat-call exerts itself to most advantage in the British theatre: it very much improves the sound of nonsense, and often goes along with the voice of the actor who pronounces it, as the violin or harpsichord accompanies the Italian recitativo.

It has often supplied the place of the ancient Chorus, in the words of Mr. * * *. In short, a bad poet has as great an antipathy to a cat-call as many people have to a real cat.

Mr. Collier, in his ingenious essay upon music, has the following passage:

I believe 'tis possible to invent an instrument that shall have a quite contrary effect to those martial ones now in use. An instrument that shall sink the spirits, and shake the nerves, and curdle the blood, and inspire despair, and cowardice and consternation, at a surprising rate. 'Tis probable the roaring of lions, the warbling of cats and scritch-owls, together with a mixture of the howling of dogs, judiciously imitated and compounded, might go a great way in this invention. Whether such anti-music as this might not be of service in a camp, I shall leave to the military men to consider.

What this learned gentleman supposes in speculation, I have known actually verified in practice. The cat-call has struck a damp into generals, and frightened heroes off the stage. At the first sound of it I have seen a crowned head tremble, and a princess fall into fits. The Humourous Lieutenant himself could not stand it; nay, I am told that even Almanzor looked like a mouse, and trembled at the voice of this terrifying instrument.

As it is of a dramatic nature, and peculiarly appropriated to the stage, I can by no means approve the thought of that angry lover, who, after an unsuccessful pursuit of some years, took leave of his mistress in a serenade of cat-calls.

I must conclude this paper with the account I have lately received of an ingenious artist, who has long studied this instrument, and is very well versed in all the rules of the drama. He teaches to play on it by book, and to express by it the whole art of criticism. He has his bass and his treble cat-call; the former for tragedy, the latter for comedy; only in tragi-comedies they may both play together in concert. He has a particular squeak to denote the violation of each of the unities, and has different sounds to show whether he aims at the poet or the player. In short, he teaches the smut-note, the fustian-note, the stupid-note, and has composed a kind of air that may serve as an act-tune to an incorrigible play, and which takes in the whole compass of the cat-call.

L

No. 409.
[Addison.]   Thursday, June 19.

. . Musaeo contingere cuncta lepore.
—Lucretius, I, 933.

Gracian very often recommends *the fine Taste,* as the utmost perfection of an accomplished man. As this word arises very often in conversation, I shall endeavour to give some account of it, and to lay down rules how we may know whether we are possessed of it, and how we may acquire that fine taste of writing, which is so much talked of among the polite world.

Most languages make use of this metaphor, to express that faculty of the mind, which distinguishes all the most concealed faults and nicest perfections in writing. We may be sure this metaphor would not have been so general in all tongues, had there not been a very great conformity between that mental taste, which is the subject of this paper, and that sensitive taste which gives us a relish of every different flavour that affects the palate. Accordingly we find, there are as many degrees of refinement in the intellectual faculty, as in the sense, which is marked out by this common denomination.

I knew a person who possessed the one in so great a perfection, that after having tasted ten different kinds of tea, he would distinguish, without seeing the colour of it, the particular sort which was offered him; and not only so, but any two sorts of them that were mixt together in an equal proportion; nay, he has carried the experiment so far, as upon tasting the composition of three different sorts, to name the parcels from whence the three several ingredients were taken. A man of a fine taste in writing will discern after the same manner, not only the general beauties and imperfections of an author, but discover the several ways of thinking and expressing himself, which diversify him from all other authors, with the several foreign infusions of thought and language, and the particular authors from whom they were borrowed.

After having thus far explained what is generally meant by a fine taste in writing, and shown the propriety of the metaphor which is used on this occasion, I think I may define it to be *that faculty of the soul, which discerns the beauties of an author with pleasure, and the imperfections with dislike.* If a man would know whether he is possessed of this faculty, I would have him read over the celebrated works of antiquity, which have stood the test of so many different ages and countries; or those works among the moderns, which have the sanction of the politer part of our contemporaries. If upon the perusal of such writings he does not find himself delighted in an extraordinary manner, or if, upon reading the admired passages in such authors, he finds a coldness and indifference in his thoughts, he ought to conclude, not (as is too usual among tasteless readers) that the author wants those perfections which have been admired in him, but that he himself wants the faculty of discovering them.

He should, in the second place, be very careful to observe, whether he tastes the distinguishing perfections, or, if I may be allowed to call them so, the specific qualities of the author whom he peruses; whether he is particularly pleased with Livy for his manner of telling a story, with Sallust for his entering into those internal principles of action which arise from the characters and manners of the persons he describes, or with Tacitus for his displaying those outward motives of safety and interest, which give birth to the whole series of transactions which he relates.

He may likewise consider, how differently he is affected by the same thought, which presents itself in a great writer, from what he is when he finds it delivered by a person of an ordinary genius. For there is as much difference in apprehending a thought clothed in Cicero's language, and that of a common author, as in seeing an object by the light of a taper, or by the light of the sun.

It is very difficult to lay down rules for the acquirement of such a taste as that I am here speaking of. The faculty must in some degree be born with us, and it very often happens, that those who have other qualities in perfection are wholly void of this. One of the most eminent mathematicians of the age has assured me, that the greatest pleasure he took in reading Virgil, was in examining Æneas his voyage by the map; as I question not but many a modern compiler of history would be delighted with little more in that divine author, than the bare matters of fact.

But notwithstanding this faculty must in some measure be born with us, there are several methods for cultivating and improving it, and without which it will be very uncertain, and of little use to the person that possesses it. The most natural method for this purpose is to be conversant among the writings of the most polite authors. A man who has any relish for fine writing, either discovers new beauties, or receives stronger impressions from the masterly strokes of a great author every time he peruses him: besides that, he naturally wears himself into the same manner of speaking and thinking.

Conversation with men of a polite genius is another method for improving our natural taste. It is impossible for a man of the greatest parts to consider any thing in its whole extent, and in all its variety of lights. Every man, besides those general observations which are to be made upon an author, forms several reflections that are peculiar to his own manner of thinking; so that conversation will naturally furnish us with hints which we did not attend to, and make us enjoy other men's parts and reflections as well as our own. This is the best reason I can give for the observation which several have made, that men of great genius in the same way of writing, seldom rise up singly, but at certain periods of time appear together, and in a body; as they did at Rome in the reign of Augustus, and in Greece about the age of Socrates. I cannot think that Corneille, Racine, Molière, Boileau, La Fontaine, Bruyere, Bossu, or the Daciers, would have written so well as they have done, had they not been friends and contemporaries.

It is likewise necessary for a man who would form to himself a finished taste of good writing, to be well versed in the works of the best critics both ancient and modern. I must confess that I could wish there were authors of this kind, who beside the mechanical rules which a man of very little taste may discourse upon, would enter into the very spirit and soul of fine writing, and show us the several sources of that pleasure which rises in the mind upon the perusal of a noble work. Thus although in poetry it be absolutely necessary that the unities of time, place and action, with other points of the same nature, should be thoroughly explained and understood; there is still something more essential to the art, something that elevates and astonishes the fancy, and gives a greatness of mind to the reader, which few of the critics besides Longinus have considered.

Our general taste in England is for epigram, turns of wit, and forced conceits, which have no manner of influ-

ence, either for the bettering or enlarging the mind of him who reads them, and have been carefully avoided by the greatest writers, both among the ancients and moderns. I have endeavoured in several of my speculations to banish this Gothic taste, which has taken possession among us. I entertained the town for a week together with an essay upon wit, in which I endeavoured to detect several of those false kinds which have been admired in the different ages of the world; and at the same time to show wherein the nature of true wit consists. I afterwards gave an instance of the great force which lies in a natural simplicity of thought to affect the mind of the reader, from such vulgar pieces as have little else besides this single qualification to recommend them. I have likewise examined the works of the greatest poet which our nation or perhaps any other has produced, and particularized most of those rational and manly beauties which give a value to that divine work. I shall next Saturday enter upon an essay *on the Pleasures of the Imagination,* which, though it shall consider that subject at large, will perhaps suggest to the reader what it is that gives a beauty to many passages of the finest writers both in prose and verse. As an undertaking of this nature is entirely new, I question not but it will be received with candour. O

[*For additional readings see pages 1125–1129.*]

THOMAS TICKELL (1685-1740)

Thomas Tickell, fellow of Queen's College, Oxford, was a friend of Edward Young and John Philips, and from 1712 one of the most prominent members of Addison's "little senate." Thus he was led to praise Ambrose Philips's *Pastorals* and to undertake a translation of the *Iliad* in rivalry with Pope. This project received Addison's support, and had an important part in the estrangement of Pope and Addison. Tickell continued to be Addison's political and literary henchman, and was entrusted with the duty of editing his works after his death in 1719. To this edition, published in 1721, Tickell prefixed his best and most famous poem, *To the Earl of Warwick on the Death of Mr. Addison*. For the last sixteen years of his life he was secretary to the Lord Lieutenant of Ireland.

A detailed account of his life and friendships, with many new documents, is to be found in R. E. Tickell's *Thomas Tickell and the Eighteenth Century Poets (1685-1740)* (London, 1931).

TO THE EARL OF WARWICK ON THE DEATH OF MR. ADDISON

If dumb too long the drooping Muse hath
    stayed,
And left her debt to Addison unpaid,
Blame not her silence, Warwick, but be-
    moan,
And judge, O judge my bosom by your own.
What mourner ever felt poetic fires?
Slow comes the verse that real woe inspires;
Grief unaffected suits but ill with art,
Or flowing numbers with a bleeding heart.
    Can I forget the dismal night that gave
My soul's best part forever to the grave?   10
How silent did his old companions tread,
By midnight lamps, the mansions of the
    dead,
Through breathing statues, then unheeded
    things,
Through rows of warriors and through walks
    of kings!
What awe did the slow solemn knell inspire,
The pealing organ and the pausing choir,
The duties by the lawn-robed prelate paid,
And the last words, that dust to dust con-
    veyed!
While speechless o'er thy closing grave we
    bend,
Accept these tears, thou dear departed
    friend: 20

O gone forever, take this long adieu,
And sleep in peace next thy loved Mon-
    tague!
    To strew fresh laurels let the task be mine,
A frequent pilgrim at thy sacred shrine;
Mine with true sighs thy absence to bemoan,
And grave with faithful epitaphs thy stone.
If e'er from me thy loved memorial part,
May shame afflict this alienated heart;
Of thee forgetful if I form a song,   29
My lyre be broken, and untuned my tongue,
My griefs be doubled, from thy image free,
And mirth a torment, unchastised by thee.
    Oft let me range the gloomy aisles alone
(Sad luxury! to vulgar minds unknown)
Along the walls where speaking marbles
    show
What worthies form the hallowed mould be-
    low;
Proud names who once the reins of empire
    held,
In arms who triumphed or in arts excelled;
Chiefs graced with scars and prodigal of
    blood;   39
Stern patriots who for sacred freedom stood;
Just men by whom impartial laws were
    given;
And saints who taught and led the way to
    Heaven.
Ne'er to these chambers where the mighty
    rest,
Since their foundation, came a nobler guest,

301

Nor e'er was to the bowers of bliss conveyed
A fairer spirit or more welcome shade.
   In what new region, to the just assigned,
What new employments please the unbodied
      mind?
A wingèd Virtue, through the ethereal sky,
From world to world unwearied does he fly?
Or curious trace the long laborious maze   51
Of Heaven's decrees, where wondering an-
      gels gaze?
Does he delight to hear bold Seraphs tell
How Michael battled and the Dragon fell?
Or, mixed with milder Cherubim, to glow
In hymns of love, not ill essayed below?
Or dost thou warn poor mortals left behind,
A task well suited to thy gentle mind?
Oh, if sometimes thy spotless form descend,
To me thy aid, thou guardian genius, lend!
When rage misguides me or when fear
      alarms,   61
When pain distresses or when pleasure
      charms,
In silent whisperings purer thoughts impart,
And turn from ill a frail and feeble heart;
Lead through the paths thy virtue trod be-
      fore,
Till bliss shall join, nor death can part us
      more.
   That awful form (which, so ye heavens
      decree,
Must still be loved and still deplored by me)
In nightly visions seldom fails to rise,
Or, roused by fancy, meets my waking eyes.
If business calls, or crowded courts invite, 71
The unblemished statesman seems to strike
      my sight;
If in the stage I seek to soothe my care,
I meet his soul, which breathes in Cato there;
If pensive to the rural shades I rove,
His shape o'ertakes me in the lonely grove;
'Twas there of just and good he reasoned
      strong,
Cleared some great truth or raised some
      serious song;
There patient showed us the wise course to
      steer,
A candid censor and a friend severe;   80
There taught us how to live, and (O, too
      high
The price for knowledge!) taught us how to
      die.
   Thou hill, whose brow the antique struc-
      tures grace,

Reared by bold chiefs of Warwick's noble
      race,
Why, once so loved, whene'er thy bower ap-
      pears,
O'er my dim eyeballs glance the sudden
      tears?
How sweet were once thy prospects fresh and
      fair,
Thy sloping walks and unpolluted air!
How sweet the glooms beneath thy aged
      trees,
Thy noontide shadow and thy evening
      breeze!   90
His image thy forsaken bowers restore;
Thy walks and airy prospects charm no
      more;
No more the summer in thy glooms allayed,
Thy evening breezes and thy noonday shade.
   From other ills, however fortune frowned,
Some refuge in the Muse's art I found;
Reluctant now I touch the trembling string,
Bereft of him who taught me how to sing;
And these sad accents, murmured o'er his
      urn,   99
Betray that absence they attempt to mourn.
Oh, must I then (now fresh my bosom bleeds,
And Craggs in death to Addison succeeds)
The verse, begun to one lost friend, prolong,
And weep a second in the unfinished song!
   These works divine, which, on his death
      bed laid,
To thee, O Craggs! the expiring sage con-
      veyed,
Great but ill-omened monument of fame,
Nor he survived to give, nor thou to claim.
Swift after him thy social spirit flies,
And close to his, how soon! thy coffin lies. 110
Blessed pair! whose union future bards shall
      tell
In future tongues—each other's boast! fare-
      well!
Farewell! whom joined in fame, in friend-
      ship tried,
No chance could sever, nor the grave divide.
                                            [1721]

COLIN AND LUCY

Of Leinster, famed for maidens fair,
   Bright Lucy was the grace;
Nor e'er did Liffy's limpid stream
   Reflect a fairer face;

Till luckless love and pining care
  Impaired her rosy hue,
Her dainty lip, her damask cheek,
  And eyes of glossy blue.

Ah! have you seen a lily pale
  When beating rains descend?   10
So drooped this slow-consuming maid,
  Her life now near its end.

By Lucy warned, of flattering swains
  Take heed, ye easy fair!
Of vengeance due to broken vows,
  Ye flattering swains, beware!

Three times all in the dead of night
  A bell was heard to ring;
And at her window shrieking thrice,
  The raven flapped his wing.   20

Full well the love-lorn maiden knew
  The solemn-boding sound,
And thus in dying words bespoke
  The virgins weeping round.

"I hear a voice you cannot hear
  That cries I must not stay;
I see a hand you cannot see,
  That beckons me away.

"Of a false swain and broken heart,
  In early youth I die: 30
Am I to blame because the bride
  Is twice as rich as I?

"Ah, Colin, give not her thy vows—
  Vows due to me alone!
Nor thou, rash girl, receive his kiss,
  Nor think him all thy own!

"To-morrow in the church to wed,
  Impatient both prepare:

But know, false man, and know, fond maid,
  Poor Lucy will be there.   40

"Then bear my corse, ye comrades dear,
  The bridegroom blithe to meet;
He in his wedding-trim so gay,
  I in my winding-sheet!"

She spoke, she died, her corse was borne
  The bridegroom blithe to meet;
He in his wedding-trim so gay,
  She in her winding-sheet.

What then were Colin's dreadful thoughts?
  How were these nuptials kept?   50
The brides-men flocked round Lucy dead,
  And all the village wept!

Compassion, shame, remorse, despair,
  At once his bosom swell:
The damps of death bedewed his brow,
  He groaned, he shook, he fell.

From the vain bride—a bride no more—
  The varying crimson fled;
When, stretched beside her rival's corse,
  She saw her lover dead.   60

He to his Lucy's new-made grave,
  Conveyed by trembling swains,
In the same mould, beneath one sod,
  Forever now remains.

Oft at this place the constant hind
  And plighted maid are seen;
With garlands gay and true-love knots
  They deck the sacred green.

But, swain forsworn, whoe'er thou art,
  This hallowed ground forbear!   70
Remember Colin's dreadful fate,
  And fear to meet him there.

                    [*1724? 1725*]

JOHN PHILIPS (1676-1709)

John Philips, the fourth of six sons of the clergyman, Dr. Stephen Philips, was educated at Winchester, and Christ Church, Oxford. At both institutions he seems to have been a great favorite for the simplicity and modesty of his nature and for his poetic and scholarly gifts. As a student he fell under the spell of Milton's poetry, and when he came to write poetry himself his special contribution to eighteenth-century literature was in calling the attention of his age—the age of the heroic couplet—to the qualities of Milton's blank verse. He was in fact a forerunner of the later so-called "Miltonic School." He imitated Milton seriously in his *Blenheim*, a poem suggested to him by the Tory ministers, Harley and St. John, as an offset to Addison's celebration of the same victory from the Whig point of view in his *Campaign*. There is much of the manner of Milton also in Philips' *Cyder*, a poem written on the pattern of Virgil's *Georgics*. It celebrates the process of cider-making from the raising of apples to the finished product and in so doing set the style for such later informational poems as Dyer's *The Fleece* and Somerville's *The Chase*. But by far the most successful and influential of Philips' imitations of Milton is his burlesque of the Miltonic manner in *The Splendid Shilling*. The heightened language of *Paradise Lost*, the elaborate similes, the rich embroidery of proper names are all delightfully called to mind. Addison called *The Splendid Shilling* "the finest burlesque poem in the British language" (*Tatler*, No. 249), and Johnson thus explains its success: "To degrade the sounding words and stately construction of Milton, by an application to the lowest and most trivial things, gratifies the mind with a momentary triumph over that grandeur which hitherto held its captives in admiration." (*Life of John Philips*.)

The *Splendid Shilling* was first published without authorization in 1701, and correctly published by the author in 1705. There is a new edition of the complete poems edited by M. G. Lloyd Thomas: *The Poems of John Philips*, Oxford, 1927.

THE SPLENDID SHILLING

AN IMITATION OF MILTON

Happy the man who, void of cares and strife,
In silken or in leathern purse retains
A Splendid Shilling: he nor hears with pain
New oysters cried, nor sighs for cheerful ale;
But with his friends, when nightly mists arise,
To Juniper's, Magpye, or Town-Hall repairs:
Where, mindful of the nymph whose wanton eye
Transfixed his soul and kindled amorous flames,
Chloe, or Phyllis, he each circling glass   9
Wisheth her health, and joy, and equal love.
Meanwhile he smokes, and laughs at merry tale,
Or pun ambiguous, or conundrum quaint.
But I, whom griping penury surrounds,
And hunger, sure attendant upon want,
With scanty offals, and small acid tiff[1]
(Wretched repast!) my meagre corpse sustain:
Then solitary walk, or doze at home
In garret vile, and with a warming puff
Regale chilled fingers; or from tube as black
As winter chimney or well polished jet   20
Exhale Mundungus, ill-perfuming scent:
Not blacker tube nor of a shorter size
Smokes Cambro-Britain (versed in pedigree,
Sprung from Cadwalader and Arthur, kings
Full famous in romantic tale) when he
O'er many a craggy hill and barren cliff,
Upon a cargo of famed Cestrian cheese
High over-shadowing rides, with a design
To vend his wares, or at the Arvonian mart,
Or Maridunum, or the ancient town   30
Yclept Brechinia, or where Vaga's stream
Encircles Ariconium, fruitful soil,
Whence flow nectareous wines, that well may vie

[1] Weak liquor.

304

With Massic, Setin, or renowned Falern.
  Thus while my joyless minutes tedious
    flow
With looks demure and silent pace, a dun,
Horrible monster! hated by gods and men,
To my aërial citadel ascends;
With vocal heel thrice thundering at my
    gates,   39
With hideous accent thrice he calls; I know
The voice ill-boding and the solemn sound.
What should I do? or whither turn? Amazed,
Confounded, to the dark recess I fly
Of woodhole; straight my bristling hairs
    erect
Through sudden fear; a chilly sweat bedews
My shuddering limbs, and, wonderful to tell,
My tongue forgets her faculty of speech,
So horrible he seems; his faded brow
Entrenched with many a frown and conic
    beard
And spreading band, admired by modern
    saints,   50
Disastrous acts forebode; in his right hand
Long scrolls of paper solemnly he waves,
With characters and figures dire inscribed
Grievous to mortal eyes; (ye gods avert
Such plagues from righteous men!) behind
    him stalks
Another monster, not unlike himself,
Sullen of aspect, by the vulgar called
A catchpole,[2] whose polluted hands the gods
With force incredible and magic charms
Erst have indued; if he his ample palm   60
Should haply on ill-fated shoulder lay
Of debtor, straight his body to the touch
Obsequious, as whilom knights were wont,
To some enchanted castle is conveyed,
Where gates impregnable and coercive
    chains
In durance strict detain him, till in form
Of money Pallas sets the captive free.
  Beware, ye debtors, when ye walk beware,
Be circumspect; oft with insidious ken
This caitiff eyes your steps aloof, and oft   70
Lies perdue in a nook or gloomy cave,
Prompt to enchant some inadvertent wretch
With his unhallowed touch. So, poets sing,
Grimalkin, to domestic vermin sworn
An everlasting foe, with watchful eye
Lies nightly brooding o'er a chinky gap,
Protending her fell claws, to thoughtless
    mice

[2] Sheriff's officer.

Sure ruin. So her disemboweled web
Arachne in a hall or kitchen spreads,
Obvious to vagrant flies: she secret stands   80
Within her woven cell; the humming prey,
Regardless of their fate, rush on the toils
Inextricable, nor will aught avail
Their arts, nor arms, nor shapes of lovely
    hue:
The wasp insidious, and the buzzing drone,
And butterfly proud of expanded wings
Distinct with gold, entangled in her snares,
Useless resistance make. With eager strides
She towering flies to her expected spoils;
Then with envenomed jaws the vital blood 90
Drinks of reluctant foes, and to her cave
Their bulky carcasses triumphant drags.
  So pass my days. But when nocturnal
    shades
This world envelop, and the inclement air
Persuades men to repel benumbing frosts
With pleasant wines and crackling blaze of
    wood,
Me lonely sitting, nor the glimmering light
Of make-weight candle, nor the joyous talk
Of loving friend delights; distressed, forlorn,
Amidst the horrors of the tedious night   100
Darkling I sigh, and feed with dismal
    thoughts
My anxious mind; or sometimes mournful
    verse
Indite, and sing of groves and myrtle shades,
Or desperate lady near a purling stream,
Or lover pendent on a willow tree.
Meanwhile I labour with eternal drought,
And restless wish and rave; my parched
    throat
Finds no relief, nor heavy eyes repose:
But if a slumber haply does invade
My weary limbs, my fancy's still awake,   110
Thoughtful of drink, and eager in a dream
Tipples imaginary pots of ale;
In vain; awake, I find the settled thirst
Still gnawing, and the pleasant phantom
    curse.
  Thus do I live from pleasure quite de-
    barred,
Nor taste the fruits that the sun's genial rays
Mature, John-apple, nor the downy peach,
Nor walnut in rough-furrowed coat secure,
Nor medlar, fruit delicious in decay.
Afflictions great! yet greater still remain: 120
My galligaskins[3] that have long withstood

[3] Breeches.

The winter's fury and encroaching frosts,
By time subdued, (what will not time sub-
　　due!)
An horrid chasm disclose, with orifice
Wide, discontinuous; at which the winds
Eurus and Auster, and the dreadful force
Of Boreas, that congeals the Cronian waves,
Tumultuous enter with dire chilling blasts
Portending agues. Thus a well-fraught ship
Long sailed secure, or through the Aegean
　　deep,　　130
Or the Ionian, till cruising near
The Lilybean shore, with hideous crush
On Scylla or Charybdis, dangerous rocks,

She strikes rebounding, whence the shattered
　　oak,
So fierce a shock unable to withstand,
Admits the sea; in at the gaping side
The crowding waves gush with impetuous
　　rage,
Resistless, overwhelming; horrors seize
The mariners, death in their eyes appears,
They stare, they lave, they pump, they swear,
　　they pray:　　140
Vain efforts! still the battering waves rush in
Implacable, till deluged by the foam,
The ship sinks foundering in the vast abyss.

[1701]

AMBROSE PHILIPS (1674-1749)

Ambrose Philips, a member of Addison's "little senate," is remembered in literary history for the *Pastorals* which stirred Pope's jealousy and inspired Gay's *Shepherd's Week*, and for his poems in praise of childhood, which earned for him the nickname "Namby Pamby," bestowed by Henry Carey. Philips was probably the editor of a pioneer collection of old ballads (1723-25), and he adapted Racine's *Andromaque* under the title of *The Distressed Mother*.

Poems, ed. Mary G. Segar (Oxford, 1937).

TO MISS CHARLOTTE PULTENEY, IN HER MOTHER'S ARMS

Timely blossom, infant fair,
Fondling of a happy pair,
Every morn and every night
Their solicitous delight;
Sleeping, waking, still at ease,
Pleasing, without skill to please,
Little gossip, blithe and hale,
Tattling many a broken tale,
Singing many a tuneless song,
Lavish of a heedless tongue,　　　　　　　10
Simple maiden, void of art,
Babbling out the very heart,
Yet abandoned to thy will,
Yet imagining no ill,
Yet too innocent to blush;
Like the linlet in the bush,
To the mother-linnet's note
Moduling[1] her slender throat,
Chirping forth thy pretty joys;
Wanton in the change of toys,　　　　　　　20
Like the linnet green, in May,
Flitting to each bloomy spray;
Wearied then, and glad of rest,
Like the linlet in the nest.
This thy present happy lot,
This, in time, will be forgot;
Other pleasures, other cares,
Ever-busy Time prepares;
And thou shalt in thy daughter see
This picture once resembled thee.　　　　　　　30

[*1724, 1725*]

[1] Modulating.

GEORGE BERKELEY (1685-1753)

George Berkeley was one of the most brilliant writers and subtle thinkers among English philosophers. His one famous poem was inspired by his project of founding a college in the Bermudas for the benefit of the English colonists and the natives. He spent three years at Newport, Rhode Island, vainly awaiting the government grant of money, returned to England in 1732, and spent the rest of his life as bishop of Cloyne, in Ireland.

Benjamin Rand, *Berkeley's American Sojourn* (Cambridge, Mass., 1932); Bonamy Dobrée, "Berkeley as a Man of Letters," *Hermathena*, LXXXII (1953), 49-75.

VERSES ON THE PROSPECT OF PLANTING ARTS AND LEARNING IN AMERICA

The Muse, disgusted at an age and clime
  Barren of every glorious theme,
In distant lands now waits a better time,
  Producing subjects worthy fame:

In happy climes where from the genial sun
  And virgin earth such scenes ensue,
The force of art by nature seems outdone,
  And fancied beauties by the true:

In happy climes, the seat of innocence,
  Where nature guides and virtue rules, 10
Where men shall not impose for truth and
    sense
  The pedantry of courts and schools:

There shall be sung another golden age,
  The rise of empire and of arts,
The good and great inspiring epic rage,
  The wisest heads and noblest hearts.

Not such as Europe breeds in her decay;
  Such as she bred when fresh and young,
When heavenly flame did animate her clay,
  By future poets shall be sung. 20

Westward the course of empire takes its way;
  The four first acts already past,
A fifth shall close the drama with the day;
  Time's noblest offspring is the last.

[1752]

ANTHONY ASHLEY COOPER, Third Earl of Shaftesbury (1671-1713)

Shaftesbury must be read by modern students of the eighteenth century for his historical, rather than intrinsic, importance. His style is too dilute and too "genteel" for modern taste, and his ideas have been assimilated by greater and more profound thinkers. But he is representative of a development of great importance in the history of modern taste and sentiment, and his influence was pervasive not only in England, but in France, Germany, Italy, and other European countries. Montesquieu, indeed, declared that the four great poets of the world are Plato, Malebranche, Shaftesbury, and Montaigne.

Shaftesbury belonged to the Whig aristocracy, his grandfather, the first earl, having been the first leader of the Whig party and the Achitophel of Dryden's famous poem. From childhood his health was delicate, and his character and tastes may be accounted for in part by his sheltered existence. He was educated privately, under the general supervision of John Locke, whose friendship with the family began with the first earl. The boy was taught to converse in Greek and Latin, and when he entered Winchester at eleven he could read anything in the classics with ease. At the age of fifteen he was sent on the usual Grand Tour of the Continent, after which he preferred to continue his studies at home rather than enter any university.

Although he had a distaste for the rough life of politics, he was in the House of Commons from 1695 to 1698, and in 1699, on the death of his father, took his seat on the Whig side in the House of Lords. Ill health sent him to Italy in 1711, where he died in 1713.

As a fruit of his retired studies he wrote a number of essays which were collected in three volumes in 1711, under the comprehensive title *Characteristics of Men, Manners, Opinions, Times*. This collection gives a first appearance of a rambling and chaotic miscellany, but it is in fact a leisurely exposition of a small group of interrelated ideas; it is an attempt to defend philosophical idealism by an analysis of the constitution of human nature. Shaftesbury was repelled by the cynicism so common in the seventeenth century, represented by Hobbes and La Rochefoucauld among others, who held that man is essentially selfish, is incapable of anything but selfishness, and that all our so-called virtues are really only disguised selfish desires. He also rejected the current Libertine contention that no values are determinable and that vice and virtue are merely conventional ideas. Plato, Marcus Aurelius, Epictetus, and the Cambridge Platonists had bred him up in nobler and more generous sentiments, and had fostered in his nature ideas more becoming to a gentleman. This idea of the gentleman, with noble and refined tastes in philosophy and conduct as well as in the arts, appeared to Shaftesbury to be truly regulative. To philosophize, he said, "is but to carry good-breeding a step higher. For the accomplishment of breeding is, to learn whatever is decent in company or beautiful in arts; and the sum of philosophy is, to learn what is just in society and beautiful in Nature and the order of the world." Such a gentleman, he assumed, believes in the reality of the true, the good, and the beautiful.

But the problem always arises as to how we can establish standards for determining the true, the good, and the beautiful. Shaftesbury's answer was that the gentleman of true cultivation perceives these values immediately, by a sort of taste which makes it unnecessary, and even undesirable, to argue about them. We must be guided in conduct by an intuitive "moral sense." Shaftesbury therefore reduced the problem of standards to a subjectivism which in his later disciples often became mere emotionalism. In nature poetry, especially, his conception of virtue as an emotional state is traceable in the widely accepted belief in Nature as a moral teacher.

The *Characteristics* are available in many editions of the eighteenth century and in a modern reprint edited by J. M. Robertson (London, 1900). An excellent volume, but long out of print, is T. Fowler's *Shaftesbury and Hutcheson* (London, 1882). For the influence of Shaftesbury on English poetry consult two important articles by C. A. Moore, "Shaftesbury and the Ethical Poets in England," in *Publications of the Modern Language Association*, June 1916; and "The Return to Nature in the English Poetry of the Eighteenth Century," in *Studies in Philology*, July 1917. See also page 1269.

CHARACTERISTICS

AN INQUIRY CONCERNING VIRTUE OR MERIT

BOOK I

PART III

SECTION I

The nature of virtue consisting (as has been explained) in a certain just disposition or proportionable affection of a rational creature towards the moral objects of right and wrong, nothing can possibly in such a creature exclude a principle of virtue, or render it ineffectual, except what

1. Either takes away the natural and just sense of right and wrong;
2. Or creates a wrong sense of it;
3. Or causes the right sense to be opposed by contrary affections.

On the other side, nothing can assist or advance the principle of virtue except what either in some manner nourishes and promotes a sense of right and wrong, or preserves it genuine and uncorrupt, or causes it when such to be obeyed, by subduing and subjecting the other affections to it.

We are to consider, therefore, how any of the above-mentioned opinions on the subject of a Deity may influence in these cases, or produce either of these three effects.

1. As to the first case, the taking away the natural sense of right and wrong.

It will not surely be understood that by this is meant the taking away the notion of what is good or ill in the species or society. For of the reality of such a good and ill, no rational creature can possibly be insensible. Every one discerns and owns a public interest, and is conscious of what affects his fellowship or community. When we say, therefore, of a creature "that he has wholly lost the sense of right and wrong," we suppose that being able to discern the good and ill of his species, he has at the same time no concern for either, nor any sense of excellency or baseness in any moral action relat-

ing to one or the other. So that except merely with respect to a private and narrowly confined self-good, 'tis supposed there is in such a creature no liking or dislike of manners; no admiration or love of anything as morally good, nor hatred of anything as morally ill, be it ever so unnatural or deformed.

There is in reality no rational creature whatsoever who knows not that when he voluntarily offends or does harm to any one, he cannot fail to create an apprehension and fear of like harm, and consequently a resentment and animosity in every creature who observes him. So that the offender must needs be conscious of being liable to such treatment from every one as if he had in some degree offended all.

Thus offence and injury are always known as punishable by every one; and equal behaviour (which is therefore called merit) as rewardable and well-deserving from every one. Of this even the wickedest creature living must have a sense. So that if there be any further meaning in this sense of right and wrong; if in reality there be any sense of this kind which an absolute wicked creature has not; it must consist in a real antipathy or aversion to injustice or wrong, and in a real affection or love towards equity and right for its own sake, and on the account of its own natural beauty and worth.

'Tis impossible to suppose a mere sensible creature originally so ill-constituted and unnatural as that, from the moment he comes to be tried by sensible objects, he should have no one good passion towards his kind, no foundation either of pity, love, kindness, or social affection. 'Tis full as impossible to conceive that a rational creature coming first to be tried by rational objects, and receiving into his mind the images or representations of justice, generosity, gratitude, or other virtue, should have no liking of these or dislike of their contraries, but be found absolutely indifferent towards whatsoever is presented to him of this sort. A soul, indeed, may as well be without sense as without admiration in the things of which it has any knowledge. Coming therefore to a capacity of seeing and admiring in this new way, it must needs find a beauty and a deformity as well in actions, minds, and tempers, as in figures, sounds, or colours. If there be no real amiableness or deformity in moral acts, there is at least an imaginary one ot full force. Though perhaps the thing itself should not be allowed in Nature, the imagination or fancy of it must be allowed to be from Nature alone. Nor can anything besides art and strong endeavour, with long practice and meditation, overcome such a natural prevention or prepossession of the mind in favour of this moral distinction.

Sense of right and wrong therefore being as natural to us as natural affection itself, and being a first principle in our constitution and make, there is no speculative opinion, persuasion, or belief, which is capable immediately or directly to exclude or destroy it. That which is of original and pure nature, nothing beside contrary habit and custom (a second nature) is able to displace. And this affection being an original one of earliest rise in the soul or affectionate part, nothing beside contrary affection, by frequent check and control, can operate upon it, so as either to diminish it in part or destroy it in the whole.

'Tis evident in what relates to the frame and order of our bodies, that no particular odd mien or gesture, which is either natural to us and consequent to our make, or accidental and by habit acquired, can possibly be overcome by our immediate disapprobation, or the contrary bent of our will ever so strongly set against it. Such a change cannot be effected without extraordinary means, and the intervention of art and method, a strict attention, and repeated check. And even thus, Nature we find is hardly mastered, but lies sullen, and ready to revolt on the first occasion. Much more is this the mind's case in respect of that natural affection and anticipating fancy which makes the sense of right and wrong. 'Tis impossible that this can instantly, or without much force and violence, be effaced, or struck out of the natural temper, even by means of the most extravagant belief or opinion in the world.

Neither Theism therefore, nor Atheism, nor Daemonism, nor any religious or irreligious belief of any kind being able to operate immediately or directly in this case, but indirectly, by the intervention of opposite or of favourable affections casually excited by any such belief, we may consider of this effect in our last case, where we come to examine the agreement or disagreement of other affections with this natural and moral one which relates to right and wrong.

SECTION II

2. As to the second case, viz. the wrong sense or false imagination of right and wrong.

This can proceed only from the force of custom and education in opposition to Nature, as may be noted in those countries where, according to custom or politic institution, certain actions naturally foul and odious are repeatedly viewed with applause, and honour ascribed to them. For thus 'tis possible that a man, forcing himself, may eat the flesh of his enemies, not only against his stomach, but against his nature, and think it nevertheless both right and honourable, as supposing it to be of considerable service to his community, and capable of advancing the name and spreading the terror of his nation.

But to speak of the opinions relating to a Deity, and what effect they may have in this place. As to atheism, it does not seem that it can directly have any effect at all towards the setting up a false species of right or wrong. For notwithstanding a man may through custom, or by licentiousness of practice, favoured by atheism, come in time to lose much of his natural moral sense, yet it does not seem that atheism should of itself be the cause of any estimation or valuing of anything as fair, noble, and deserving, which was the contrary. It can never, for instance, make it be thought that the being able to eat man's flesh, or commit bestiality, is good and excellent in itself. But this is certain, that by means of corrupt religion or superstition, many things the most horridly unnatural and inhuman come to be received as excellent, good, and laudable in themselves.

Nor is this a wonder. For wherever anything, in its nature odious and abominable, is by religion advanced, as the supposed will or pleasure of a supreme Deity, if in the eye of the believer it appears not indeed in any respect the less ill or odious on this account, then must the Deity of necessity bear the blame, and be considered as a being naturally ill and odious, however courted and solicited through mistrust and fear. But this is what religion, in the main, forbids us to imagine. It everywhere prescribes esteem and honour in company with worship and adoration. Whensoever therefore it teaches the love and admiration of a Deity who has any apparent character of ill, it teaches at the same time a love and admiration of that ill, and causes that to be taken for good and amiable which is in itself horrid and detestable.

For instance, if Jupiter be he who is adored and reverenced, and if his history represents him amorously inclined, and permitting his desires of this kind to wander in the loosest manner, 'tis certain that his worshippers, believing this history to be literally and strictly true, must of course be taught a greater love of amorous and wanton acts. If there be a religion which teaches the adoration and love of a God whose character it is to be captious and of high resentment, subject to wrath and anger, furious, re-

vengeful, and revenging himself, when offended, on others than those who gave the offence; and if there be added to the character of this God a fraudulent disposition, encouraging deceit and treachery amongst men, favourable to a few, though for slight causes, and cruel to the rest, 'tis evident that such a religion as this being strongly enforced must of necessity raise even an approbation and respect towards the vices of this kind, and breed a suitable disposition, a capricious, partial, revengeful, and deceitful temper. For even irregularities and enormities of a heinous kind must in many cases appear illustrious to one who considers them in a being admired and contemplated with the highest honour and veneration.

This indeed must be allowed, that if in the cult or worship of such a Deity there be nothing beyond common form, nothing beside what proceeds from mere example, custom, constraint, or fear; if there be, at the bottom, no real heartiness, no esteem or love implied, the worshipper perhaps may not be much misled as to his notion of right and wrong. If in following the precepts of his supposed God, or doing what he esteems necessary towards the satisfying of such his Deity, he is compelled only by fear, and, contrary to his inclination, performs an act which he secretly detests as barbarous and unnatural, then has he an apprehension or sense still of right and wrong, and, according to what has been already observed, is sensible of ill in the character of his God, however cautious he may be of pronouncing anything on this subject, or so thinking of it as to frame any formal or direct opinion in the case. But if by insensible degrees, as he proceeds in his religious faith and devout exercise, he comes to be more and more reconciled to the malignity, arbitrariness, partiality, or revengefulness of his believed Deity, his reconciliation with these qualities themselves will soon grow in proportion, and the most cruel, unjust, and barbarous acts will, by the power of this example, be often considered by him not only as just and lawful, but as divine and worthy of imitation.

For whoever thinks there is a God, and pretends formally to believe that he is just and good, must suppose that there is independently such a thing as justice and injustice, truth and falsehood, right and wrong, according to which he pronounces that God is just, righteous, and true. If the mere will, decree, or law of God be said absolutely to constitute right and wrong, then are these latter words of no significancy at all. For thus, if each part of a contradiction were affirmed for truth by the Supreme Power, they would consequently become true. Thus if one person were decreed to suffer for another's fault, the sentence would be just and equitable. And thus, in the same manner, if arbitrarily and without reason some beings were destined to endure perpetual ill, and others as constantly to enjoy good, this also would pass under the same denomination. But to say of anything that it is just or unjust on such a foundation as this, is to say nothing, or to speak without a meaning.

And thus it appears that where a real devotion and hearty worship is paid to a Supreme Being, who in his history or character is represented otherwise than as really and truly just and good, there must ensue a loss of rectitude, a disturbance of thought, and a corruption of temper and manners in the believer. His honesty will of necessity be supplanted by his zeal, whilst he is thus unnaturally influenced, and rendered thus immorally devout.

To this we need only add, that as the ill character of a God does injury to the affections of men, and disturbs and impairs the natural sense of right and wrong, so, on the other hand, nothing can more highly contribute to the fixing of right apprehensions, and a sound judgment or sense of right and wrong, than to be-lieve a God who is ever and on all accounts represented such as to be actually a true model and example of the most exact justice and highest goodness and worth. Such a view of divine providence and bounty extended to all, and expressed in a constant good affection towards the whole, must of necessity engage us, within our compass and sphere, to act by a like principle and affection. And having once the good of our species or public in view, as our end or aim, 'tis impossible we should be misguided by any means to a false apprehension or sense of right or wrong.

As to this second case therefore, religion (according as the kind may prove) is capable of doing great good or harm, and atheism nothing positive in either way. For however it may be indirectly an occasion of men's losing a good and sufficient sense of right and wrong, it will not, as atheism merely, be the occasion of setting up a false species of it, which only false religion or fantastical opinion, derived commonly from superstition and credulity, is able to effect.

SECTION III

Now as to the last case, the opposition made by other affections to the natural sense of right and wrong.

'Tis evident that a creature having this sort of sense or good affection in any degree must necessarily act according to it, if it happens not to be opposed, either by some settled sedate affection towards a conceived private good, or by some sudden, strong, and forcible passion, as of lust or anger, which may not only subdue the sense of right and wrong, but the very sense of private good itself, and over-rule even the most familiar and received opinion of what is conducing to self-interest.

But it is not our business in this place to examine the several means or methods by which this corruption is introduced or increased. We are to consider only how the opinions concerning a Deity can influence one way or another.

That it is possible for a creature capable of using reflection to have a liking or dislike of moral actions, and consequently a sense of right and wrong, before such time as he may have any settled notion of a God, is what will hardly be questioned; it being a thing not expected, or any way possible, that a creature such as man, arising from his childhood slowly and gradually to several degrees of reason and reflection, should at the very first be taken up with those speculations or more refined sort of reflections, about the subject of God's existence.

Let us suppose a creature who, wanting reason and being unable to reflect, has notwithstanding many good qualities and affections, as love to his kind, courage, gratitude, or pity. 'Tis certain that if you give to this creature a reflecting faculty, it will at the same instant approve of gratitude, kindness, and pity; be taken with any show or representation of the social passion, and think nothing more amiable than this, or more odious than the contrary. And this is to be capable of virtue, and to have a sense of right and wrong.

Before the time, therefore, that a creature can have any plain or positive notion one way or other concerning the subject of a God, he may be supposed to have an apprehension or sense of right and wrong, and be possessed of virtue and vice in different degrees, as we know by experience of those who, having lived in such places and in such a manner as never to have entered into any serious thoughts of religion, are nevertheless very different among themselves, as to their characters of honesty and worth: some being naturally modest, kind, friendly, and consequently lovers of kind and friendly actions; others proud, harsh, cruel, and consequently inclined to admire rather the acts of violence and mere power.

Now as to the belief of a Deity, and how men are influenced by it, we may consider, in the first place, on what account men yield obedience, and act in conformity to such a supreme Being. It must be either in the way of his power, as presupposing some disadvantage or benefit to accrue from him; or in the way of his excellency and worth, as thinking it the perfection of nature to imitate and resemble him.

If (as in the first case) there be a belief or conception of a Deity who is considered only as powerful over his creature, and enforcing obedience to his absolute will by particular rewards and punishments; and if on this account, through hope merely of reward, or fear of punishment, the creature be incited to do the good he hates, or restrained from doing the ill to which he is not otherwise in the least degree averse, there is in this case (as has been already shown) no virtue or goodness whatsoever. The creature, notwithstanding his good conduct, is intrinsically of as little worth as if he acted in his natural way, when under no dread or terror of any sort. There is no more of rectitude, piety, or sanctity in a creature thus reformed, than there is meekness or gentleness in a tiger strongly chained, or innocence and sobriety in a monkey under the discipline of the whip. For however orderly and well those animals, or man himself upon like terms, may be induced to act, whilst the will is neither gained nor the inclination wrought upon, but awe alone prevails and forces obedience, the obedience is servile, and all which is done through it merely servile. The greater degree of such a submission or obedience is only the greater servility, whatever may be the object. For whether such a creature has a good master or an ill one, he is neither more nor less servile in his own nature. Be the master or superior ever so perfect or excellent, yet the greater submission caused in this case, through this sole principle or motive, is only the lower and more abject servitude, and implies the greater wretchedness and meanness in the creature, who has those passions of self-love so predominant, and is in his temper so vicious and defective as has been explained.

As to the second case. If there be a belief or conception of a Deity who is considered as worthy and good, and admired and reverenced as such, being understood to have, besides mere power and knowledge, the highest excellence of nature, such as renders him justly amiable to all; and if in the manner this Sovereign and mighty Being is represented, or as he is historically described, there appears in him a high and eminent regard to what is good and excellent, a concern for the good of all, and an affection of benevolence and love towards the whole, such an example must undoubtedly serve (as above explained) to raise and increase the affection towards virtue, and help to submit and subdue all other affections to that alone.

Nor is this good effected by example merely. For where the theistical belief is entire and perfect, there must be a steady opinion of the superintendency of a supreme Being, a witness and spectator of human life, and conscious of whatsoever is felt or acted in the universe; so that in the perfectest recess or deepest solitude there must be One still presumed remaining with us, whose presence singly must be of more moment than that of the most august assembly on earth. In such a presence, 'tis evident that as the shame of guilty actions must be the greatest of any, so must the honour be of well-doing, even under the unjust censure of a world. And in this case 'tis very apparent how conducing a perfect theism must be to virtue, and how great deficiency there is in atheism.

What the fear of future punishment and hope of future reward, added to this belief, may further contribute towards virtue, we come now to consider more particularly. So much in the meanwhile may be gathered from what has been said above, that neither this fear nor hope can possibly be of the kind called good affections, such as are acknowledged the springs and sources of all actions truly good. Nor can this fear or hope, as above intimated, consist in reality with virtue or goodness, if it either stands as essential to any moral performance, or as a considerable motive to any act, of which some better affection ought alone to have been a sufficient cause.

It may be considered withal, that in this religious sort of discipline, the principle of self-love, which is naturally so prevailing in us, being no way moderated or restrained, but rather improved and made stronger every day by the exercise of the passions in a subject of more extended self-interest, there may be reason to apprehend lest the temper of this kind should extend itself in general through all the parts of life. For if the habit be such as to occasion, in every particular, a stricter attention to self good and private interest, it must insensibly diminish the affections towards public good or the interest of society, and introduce a certain narrowness of spirit, which (as some pretend) is peculiarly observable in the devout persons and zealots of almost every religious persuasion.

This, too, must be confessed: that if it be true piety to love God for his own sake, the over-solicitous regard to private good expected from him must of necessity prove a diminution of piety. For whilst God is beloved only as the cause of private good, he is no otherwise beloved than as any other instrument or means of pleasure by any vicious creature. Now the more there is of this violent affection towards private good, the less room is there for the other sort towards goodness itself, or any good and deserving object, worthy of love and admiration for its own sake, such as God is universally acknowledged, or at least by the generality of civilised or refined worshippers.

'Tis in this respect that the strong desire and love of life may also prove an obstacle to piety, as well as to virtue and public love. For the stronger this affection is in any one, the less will he be able to have true resignation, or submission to the rule and order of the Deity. And if that which he calls resignation depends only on the expectation of infinite retribution or reward, he discovers no more worth or virtue here than in any other bargain of interest. The meaning of his resignation being only this, "That he resigns his present life and pleasures conditionally, for that which he himself confesses to be beyond an equivalent: eternal living in a state of highest pleasure and enjoyment."

But notwithstanding the injury which the principle of virtue may possibly suffer by the increase of the selfish passion in the way we have been mentioning, 'tis certain, on the other side, that the principle of fear of future punishment, and hope of future reward, how mercenary or servile soever it may be accounted, is yet in many circumstances a great advantage, security, and support to virtue.

It has been already considered, that notwithstanding there may be implanted in the heart a real sense of right and wrong, a real good affection towards the species or society, yet by the violence of rage, lust, or any other counter-working passion, this good affection may frequently be controlled and overcome. Where therefore there is nothing in the mind capable to render such ill passions the objects of its aversion, and cause them earnestly to be opposed, 'tis apparent how much a good temper in time must suffer, and a character by degrees change for the worse. But if religion, interposing, creates a belief that the ill passions of this kind, no less than their consequent actions, are the objects of a Deity's animadversion, 'tis certain that such a belief must prove a seasonable remedy against vice, and

be in a particular manner advantageous to virtue. For a belief of this kind must be supposed to tend considerably towards the calming of the mind, and disposing or fitting the person to a better recollection of himself, and to a stricter observance of that good and virtuous principle which needs only his attention to engage him wholly in its party and interest.

And as this belief of a future reward and punishment is capable of supporting those who through ill practice are like to apostatize from virtue, so when by ill opinion and wrong thought the mind itself is bent against the honest course, and debauched even to an esteem and deliberate preference of a vicious one, the belief of the kind mentioned may prove on this occasion the only relief and safety.

A person, for instance, who has much of goodness and natural rectitude in his temper, but withal so much softness or effeminacy as unfits him to bear poverty, crosses, or adversity, if by ill fortune he meets with many trials of this kind, it must certainly give a sourness and distaste to his temper, and make him exceedingly averse to that which he may falsely presume the occasion of such calamity or ill. Now if his own thoughts, or the corrupt insinuations of other men, present it often to his mind "that his honesty is the occasion of this calamity, and that if he were delivered from this restraint of virtue and honesty, he might be much happier," 'tis very obvious that his esteem of these good qualities must in proportion diminish every day as the temper grows uneasy and quarrels with itself. But if he opposes to this thought the consideration "that honesty carries with it, if not a present, at least a future advantage, such as to compensate that loss of private good which he regrets," then may this injury to his good temper and honest principle be prevented, and his love or affection towards honesty and virtue remain as it was before.

In the same manner, where instead of regard or love there is rather an aversion to what is good and virtuous (as, for instance, where lenity and forgiveness are despised, and revenge highly thought of and beloved), if there be this consideration added, "That lenity is, by its rewards, made the cause of a greater self-good and enjoyment than what is found in revenge," that very affection of lenity and mildness may come to be industriously nourished, and the contrary passion depressed. And thus temperance, modesty, candour, benignity, and other good affections, however despised at first, may come at last to be valued for their own sakes, the contrary species rejected, and the good and proper object beloved and prosecuted, when the reward or punishment is not so much as thought of.

Thus in a civil state or public we see that a virtuous administration, and an equal and just distribution of rewards and punishments, is of the highest service, not only by restraining the vicious, and forcing them to act usefully to society, but by making virtue to be apparently the interest of every one, so as to remove all prejudices against it, create a fair reception for it, and lead men into that path which afterwards they cannot easily quit. For thus a people raised from barbarity or despotic rule, civilised by laws, and made virtuous by the long course of a lawful and just administration, if they chance to fall suddenly under any misgovernment of unjust and arbitrary power, they will on this account be the rather animated to exert a stronger virtue in opposition to such violence and corruption. And even where, by long and continued arts of a prevailing tyranny, such a people are at last totally oppressed, the scattered seeds of virtue will for a long time remain alive, even to a second generation, ere the utmost force of misapplied rewards and punishments can bring

them to the abject and compliant state of long-accustomed slaves.

But though a right distribution of justice in a government be so essential a cause of virtue, we must observe in this case that it is example which chiefly influences mankind, and forms the character and disposition of a people. For a virtuous administration is in a manner necessarily accompanied with virtue in the magistrate. Otherwise it could be of little effect, and of no long duration. But where it is sincere and well established, there virtue and the laws must necessarily be respected and beloved. So that, as to punishments and rewards, their efficacy is not so much from the fear or expectation which they raise, as from a natural esteem of virtue and detestation of villainy, which is awakened and excited by these public expressions of the approbation and hatred of mankind in each case. For in the public executions of the greatest villains we see generally that the infamy and odiousness of their crime, and the shame of it before mankind, contribute more to their misery than all besides; and that it is not the immediate pain of death itself which raises so much horror either in the sufferers or spectators, as that ignominious kind of death which is inflicted for public crimes and violations of justice and humanity.

And as the case of reward and punishment stands thus in the public, so, in the same manner, as to private families. For slaves and mercenary servants, restrained and made orderly by punishment and the severity of their master, are not on this account made good or honest. Yet the same master of the family using proper rewards and gentle punishments towards his children, teaches them goodness, and by this help instructs them in a virtue which afterwards they practise upon other grounds, and without thinking of a penalty or bribe. And this is what we call a liberal education and a liberal service; the contrary service and obedience, whether towards God or man, being illiberal and unworthy of any honour or commendation.

In the case of religion, however, it must be considered that if by the hope of reward be understood the love and desire of virtuous enjoyment, or of the very practice and exercise of virtue in another life, the expectation or hope of this kind is so far from being derogatory to virtue, that it is an evidence of our loving it the more sincerely and for its own sake. Nor can this principle be justly called selfish; for if the love of virtue be not mere self-interest, the love and desire of life for virtue's sake cannot be esteemed so. But if the desire of life be only through the violence of that natural aversion to death, if it be through the love of something else than virtuous affection, or through the unwillingness of parting with something else than what is purely of this kind, then is it no longer any sign or token of real virtue.

Thus a person loving life for life's sake and virtue not at all, may by the promise or hope of life, and fear of death or other evil, be induced to practise virtue, and even endeavour to be truly virtuous by a love of what he practises. Yet neither is this very endeavour to be esteemed a virtue. For though he may intend to be virtuous, he is not become so for having only intended or aimed at it through love of the reward. But as soon as he is come to have any affection towards what is morally good, and can like or affect such good for its own sake, as good and amiable in itself, then is he in some degree good and virtuous, and not till then.

Such are the advantages or disadvantages which accrue to virtue from reflection upon private good or interest. For though the habit of selfishness and the multiplicity of interested views are of little improvement to real merit or virtue, yet there is a necessity for the preservation of virtue, that it should be thought to have

no quarrel with true interest and self-enjoyment.

Whoever, therefore, by any strong persuasion or settled judgment, thinks in the main that virtue causes happiness and vice misery, carries with him that security and assistance to virtue which is required. Or though he has no such thought, nor can believe virtue his real interest, either with respect to his own nature and constitution, or the circumstances of human life, yet if he believes any supreme powers concerned in the present affairs of mankind, immediately interposing in behalf of the honest and virtuous against the impious and unjust, this will serve to preserve in him, however, that just esteem of virtue which might otherwise considerably diminish. Or should he still believe little of the immediate interposition of Providence in the affairs of this present life, yet if he believes a God dispensing rewards and punishments to vice and virtue in a future, he carries with him still the same advantage and security, whilst his belief is steady and nowise wavering or doubtful. For it must be observed, that an expectation and dependency so miraculous and great as this, must naturally take off from other inferior dependencies and encouragements. Where infinite rewards are thus enforced, and the imagination strongly turned towards them, the other common and natural motives to goodness are apt to be neglected and lose much by disuse. Other interests are hardly so much as computed, whilst the mind is thus transported in the pursuit of a high advantage, and self-interest so narrowly confined within ourselves. On this account, all other affections towards friends, relations, or mankind are often slightly regarded as being worldly and of little moment in respect of the interest of our soul. And so little thought is there of any immediate satisfaction arising from such good offices of life, that it is customary with many devout people zealously to decry all temporal advantages of goodness, all natural benefits of virtue, and magnifying the contrary happiness of a vicious state, to declare "that except only for the sake of future reward and fear of future punishment, they would divest themselves of all goodness at once, and freely allow themselves to be most immoral and profligate." From whence it appears that in some respects there can be nothing more fatal to virtue than the weak and uncertain belief of a future reward and punishment. For the stress being laid wholly here, if this foundation come to fail, there is no further prop or security to men's morals. And thus virtue is supplanted and betrayed.

Now as to atheism; though it be plainly deficient and without remedy, in the case of ill judgment on the happiness of virtue, yet it is not, indeed, of necessity the cause of any such ill judgment. For without an absolute assent to any hypothesis of theism, the advantages of virtue may possibly be seen and owned, and a high opinion of it established in the mind. However, it must be confessed that the natural tendency of atheism is very different.

'Tis in a manner impossible to have any great opinion of the happiness of virtue without conceiving high thoughts of the satisfaction resulting from the generous admiration and love of it; and nothing beside the experience of such a love is likely to make this satisfaction credited. The chief ground and support therefore of this opinion of happiness in virtue must arise from the powerful feeling of this generous moral affection, and the knowledge of its power and strength. But this is certain, that it can be no great strengthening to the moral affection, no great support to the pure love of goodness and virtue, to suppose there is neither goodness nor beauty in the Whole itself; nor any example or precedent of good affection in any superior Being. Such a belief must tend rather to the weaning the affections from anything amiable or self-worthy, and to the suppress-

ing the very habit and familiar custom of admiring natural beauties, or whatever in the order of things is according to just design, harmony, and proportion. For how little disposed must a person be to love or admire anything as orderly in the universe who thinks the universe itself a pattern of disorder? How unapt to reverence or respect any particular subordinate beauty of a part, when even the Whole itself is thought to want perfection, and to be only a vast and infinite deformity?

Nothing indeed can be more melancholy than the thought of living in a distracted universe, from whence many ills may be suspected, and where there is nothing good or lovely which presents itself, nothing which can satisfy in contemplation, or raise any passion besides that of contempt, hatred, or dislike. Such an opinion as this may by degrees embitter the temper, and not only make the love of virtue to be less felt, but help to impair and ruin the very principle of virtue, *viz.* natural and kind affection.

Upon the whole, whoever has a firm belief of a God whom he does not merely call good, but of whom in reality he believes nothing beside real good, nothing beside what is truly suitable to the exactest character of benignity and goodness; such a person believing rewards or retributions in another life, must believe them annexed to real goodness and merit, real villainy and baseness, and not to any accidental qualities or circumstances, in which respect they cannot properly be styled rewards or punishments, but capricious distributions of happiness or unhappiness to creatures. These are the only terms on which the belief of a world to come can happily influence the believer. And on these terms, and by virtue of this belief, man perhaps may retain his virtue and integrity, even under the hardest thoughts of human nature, when either by any ill circumstance or untoward doctrine he is brought to that unfortunate opinion of Virtue's being naturally an enemy to happiness in life.

This, however, is an opinion which cannot be supposed consistent with sound theism. For whatever be decided as to a future life, or the rewards and punishments of hereafter, he who, as a sound theist, believes a reigning mind sovereign in Nature, and ruling all things with the highest perfection of goodness, as well as of wisdom and power, must necessarily believe virtue to be naturally good and advantageous. For what could more strongly imply an unjust ordinance, a blot and imperfection in the general constitution of things, than to suppose virtue the natural ill, and vice the natural good of any creature?

And now, last of all, there remains for us to consider a yet further advantage to virtue, in the theistical belief above the atheistical. The proposition may at first sight appear over-refined, and of a sort which is esteemed too nicely philosophical. But after what has been already examined, the subject perhaps may be more easily explained.

There is no creature, according to what has been already proved, who must not of necessity be ill in some degree, by having any affection or aversion in a stronger degree than is suitable to his own private good, or that of the system to which he is joined. For in either case the affection is ill and vicious. Now if a rational creature has that degree of aversion which is requisite to arm him against any particular misfortune, and alarm him against the approach of any calamity, this is regular and well. But if after the misfortune is happened, his aversion continues still, and his passion rather grows upon him, whilst he rages at the accident and exclaims against his private fortune or lot, this will be acknowleded both vicious in present and for the future, as it affects the temper, and disturbs that easy course of the affections on which virtue and goodness so much depend. On the other side, the patient enduring of the calamity, and the bearing up of the mind under it, must be acknowledged immediately virtuous and preservative of virtue. Now, according to the hypothesis of those who exclude a general mind, it must be confessed there can nothing happen in the course of things to deserve either our admiration and love or our anger and abhorrence. However, as there can be no satisfaction at the best in thinking upon what atoms and chance produce, so upon disastrous occasions, and under the circumstances of a calamitous and hard fortune, 'tis scarce possible to prevent a natural kind of abhorrence and spleen, which will be entertained and kept alive by the imagination of so perverse an order of things. But in another hypothesis (that of perfect theism) it is understood "that whatever the order of the world produces, is in the main both just and good." Therefore in the course of things in this world, whatever hardship of events may seem to force from any rational creature a hard censure of his private condition or lot, he may by reflection nevertheless come to have patience, and to acquiesce in it. Nor is this all. He may go further still in this reconciliation, and from the same principle may make the lot itself an object of his good affection, whilst he strives to maintain this generous fealty, and stands so well disposed towards the laws and government of his higher country.

Such an affection must needs create the highest constancy in any state of sufferance, and make us in the best manner support whatever hardships are to be endured for virtue's sake. And as this affection must of necessity cause a greater acquiescence and complacency with respect to ill accidents, ill men, and injuries, so of course it cannot fail of producing still a greater equality, gentleness, and benignity in the temper. Consequently the affection must be a truly good one, and a creature the more truly good and virtuous by possessing it. For whatsoever is the occasion or means of more affectionately uniting a rational creature to his part in society, and causes him to prosecute the public good or interest of his species with more zeal and affection than ordinary, is undoubtedly the cause of more than ordinary virtue in such a person.

This too is certain, that the admiration and love of order, harmony, and proportion, in whatever kind, is naturally improving to the temper, advantageous to social affection, and highly assistant to virtue, which is itself no other than the love of order and beauty in society. In the meanest subjects of the world, the appearance of order gains upon the mind and draws the affection towards it. But if the order of the world itself appears just and beautiful, the admiration and esteem of order must run higher, and the elegant passion or love of beauty, which is so advantageous to virtue, must be the more improved by its exercise in so ample and magnificent a subject. For 'tis impossible that such a divine order should be contemplated without ecstasy and rapture, since in the common subjects of science and the liberal arts, whatever is according to just harmony and proportion is so transporting to those who have any knowledge or practice in the kind.

Now if the subject and ground of this divine passion be not really just or adequate (the hypothesis of theism being supposed false) the passion still in itself is so far natural and good, as it proves an advantage to virtue and goodness, according to what has been above demonstrated. But if, on the other side, the subject of this passion be really adequate and just (the hypothesis of theism being real, and not imaginary), then is the passion also just, and becomes absolutely due and requisite in every rational creature.

Hence we may determine justly the relation which Virtue has to Piety, the first being not complete but in the latter, since where the latter is wanting, there can neither be the same benignity, firmness, or constancy, the same good composure of the affections or uniformity of mind.

And thus the perfection and height of virtue must be owing to the belief of a God.

MISCELLANY III

CHAPTER II

Explanation of a taste continued—Ridiculers of it—Their wit and sincerity—Application of the taste to affairs of government and politics—Imaginary characters in the State —Young nobility and gentry—Pursuit of beauty—Preparation for philosophy.

By this time, surely, I must have proved myself sufficiently engaged in the project and design of our self-discoursing author, whose defence I have undertaken. His pretension, as plainly appears in this third treatise is to recommend morals on the same foot with what in a lower sense is called manners, and to advance philosophy (as harsh a subject as it may appear) on the very foundation of what is called agreeable and polite. And 'tis in this method and management that, as his interpreter or paraphrast, I have proposed to imitate and accompany him, as far as my miscellaneous character will permit.

Our joint endeavour, therefore, must appear this: to show "that nothing which is found charming or delightful in the polite world, nothing which is adopted as pleasure or entertainment, of whatever kind, can any way be accounted for, supported, or established, without the pre-establishment or supposition of a certain taste." Now a taste or judgment, 'tis supposed, can hardly come ready formed with us into the world. Whatever principles or materials of this kind we may possibly bring with us, whatever good faculties, senses, or anticipating sensations and imaginations may be of Nature's growth, and arise properly of themselves, without our art, promotion, or assistance, the general idea which is formed of all this management and the clear notion we attain of what is preferable and principal in all these subjects of choice and estimation will not, as I imagine, by any person be taken for innate. Use, practice, and culture must precede the understanding and wit of such an advanced size and growth as this. A legitimate and just taste can neither be begotten, made, conceived, or produced without the antecedent labour and pains of criticism.

For this reason we presume not only to defend the cause of critics, but to declare open war against those indolent supine authors, performers, readers, auditors, actors or spectators who, making their humour alone the rule of what is beautiful and agreeable, and having no account to give of such their humour or odd fancy, reject the criticising or examining art, by which alone they are able to discover the true beauty and worth of every object.

According to that affected ridicule which these insipid remarkers pretend to throw upon just critics, the enjoyment of all real arts or natural beauty would be entirely lost; even in behaviour and manners we should at this rate become in time as barbarous as in our pleasures and diversions. I would presume it, however, of these critic-haters, that they are not yet so uncivilised or void of all social sense as to maintain "that the most barbarous life or brutish pleasure is as desirable as the most polished or refined."

For my own part, when I have heard sometimes men of reputed ability join in with that effeminate plaintive tone of invective against critics, I have really thought they had it in their fancy to keep down the growing geniuses of the youth, their rivals, by turning them aside from that examination and search, on which all good performance as well as good judgment depends. I have seen many a time a well-bred man, who had himself a real good taste, give way with a malicious complaisance to the hu-

mour of a company, where, in favour chiefly of the tender sex, this soft languishing contempt of critics and their labours has been the subject set afoot. "Wretched creatures! (says one) impertinent things, these critics, as ye call them! As if one could not know what was agreeable or pretty without their help. 'Tis fine, indeed, that one should not be allowed to fancy for oneself. Now should a thousand critics tell me that Mr. A.——'s new play was not the wittiest in the world, I would not mind them one bit."

This our real man of wit hears patiently, and adds, perhaps of his own, "that he thinks it truly somewhat hard, in what relates to people's diversion and entertainment, that they should be obliged to choose what pleased others and not themselves." Soon after this he goes himself to the play, finds one of his effeminate companions commending or admiring at a wrong place. He turns to the next person who sits by him, and asks privately, "what he thinks of his companion's relish."

Such is the malice of the world! They who by pains and industry have acquired a real taste in arts, rejoice in their advantage over others, who have either none at all or such as renders them ridiculous. At an auction of books or pictures, you shall hear these gentlemen persuading every one "to bid for what he fancies." But at the same time they would be soundly mortified themselves if, by such as they esteemed good judges, they should be found to have purchased by a wrong fancy or ill taste. The same gentleman who commends his neighbour for ordering his garden or apartment as his humour leads him, takes care his own should be so ordered as the best judgments would advise. Being once a judge himself, or but tolerably knowing in these affairs, his aim is not "to change the being of things, and bring truth and Nature to his humour; but, leaving Nature and truth just as he found them, to accommodate his humour and fancy to their standard." Would he do this in a yet higher case, he might in reality become as wise and great a man as he is already a refined and polished gentleman. By one of these tastes he understands how to lay out his garden, model his house, fancy his equipage, appoint his table; by the other he learns of what value these amusements are in life, and of what importance to a man's freedom, happiness, and self-enjoyment. For if he would try effectually to acquire the real science or taste of life, he would certainly discover "that a right mind and generous affection had more beauty and charm than all other symmetries in the world besides." And "that a grain of honesty and native worth was of more value than all the adventitious ornaments, estates, or preferments; for the sake of which some of the better sort so oft turn knaves, forsaking their principles and quitting their honour and freedom for a mean, timorous, shifting state of gaudy servitude."

A little better taste (were it a very little) in the affair of life itself would, if I mistake not, mend the manners and secure the happiness of some of our noble countrymen, who come with high advantage and a worthy character into the public. But ere they have long engaged in it, their worth unhappily becomes venal. Equipages, titles, precedencies, staffs, ribbons, and other such glittering ware are taken in exchange for inward merit, honour, and a character.

This they may account perhaps a shrewd bargain. But there will be found very untoward abatements in it when the matter comes to be experienced. They may have descended in reality from ever so glorious ancestors, patriots, and sufferers for their nation's liberty and welfare; they may have made their entrance into the world upon this bottom of anticipated fame and honour; they may have been advanced on this account to dignities which they were thought to have deserved. But when induced to change

their honest measures, and sacrifice their cause and friends to an imaginary private interest, they will soon find, by experience, that they have lost the relish and taste of life; and for insipid wretched honours of a deceitful kind have unhappily exchanged an amiable and sweet honour, of a sincere and lasting relish and good savour. They may, after this, act farces as they think fit, and hear qualities and virtues assigned to them under the titles of graces, excellencies, honours, and the rest of this mock praise and mimical appellation. They may even with serious looks be told of honour and worth, their principle, and their country; but they know better within themselves, and have occasion to find that after all the world too knows better, and that their few friends and admirers have either a very shallow wit or a very profound hypocrisy.

'Tis not in one party alone that these purchases and sales of honour are carried on. I can represent to myself a noted patriot and reputed pillar of the religious part of our constitution, who having by many and long services and a steady conduct gained the reputation of thorough zeal with his own party, and of sincerity and honour with his very enemies, on a sudden (the time being come that the fulness of his reward was set before him) submits complacently to the proposed bargain, and sells himself for what he is worth, in a vile, detestable old age, to which he has reserved the infamy of betraying both his friends and country.

I can imagine, on the other side, one of a contrary party, a noted friend to liberty in Church and State; an abhorrer of the slavish dependency on courts, and of the narrow principles of bigots. Such a one, after many public services of note, I can see wrought upon, by degrees, to seek court preferment, and this too under a patriot character. But having perhaps tried this way with less success, he is obliged to change his character, and become a royal flatterer, a courtier against his nature; submitting himself and suing, in so much the meaner degree, as his inherent principles are well known at court and to his new adopted party, to whom he feigns himself a proselyte.

The greater the genius or character is of such a person, the greater is his slavery and heavier his load. Better had it been that he had never discovered such a zeal for public good, or signalised himself in that party which can with least grace make sacrifices of national interests to a crown, or to the private will, appetite, or pleasure of a prince. For supposing such a genius as this had been to act his part of courtship in some foreign and absolute court, how much less infamous would his part have proved? how much less slavish, amidst a people who were all slaves? Had he peradventure been one of that forlorn begging troop of gentry extant in Denmark or Sweden, since the time that those nations lost their liberties; had he lived out of a free nation and happily balanced constitution; had he been either conscious of no talent in the affairs of government or of no opportunity to exert any such to the advantage of mankind: where had been the mighty shame, if perhaps he had employed some of his abilities in flattering like others, and paying the necessary homage required for safety's sake and self-preservation, in absolute and despotic governments? The taste, perhaps, in strictness, might still be wrong, even in this hard circumstance; but how inexcusable in a quite contrary one! For let us suppose our courtier not only an Englishman, but of the rank and stem of those old English patriots who were wont to curb the licentiousness of our court, arraign its flatterers, and purge away those poisons from the ear of princes; let us suppose him of a competent fortune and moderate appetites, without any apparent luxury or lavishment in his manners: what shall we, after this, bring in excuse, or as an apology, for such a choice as his? How shall we explain this pre-

posterous relish, this odd preference of subtlety and indirectness to true wisdom, open honesty, and uprightness?

'Tis easier, I confess, to give account of this corruption of taste in some noble youth of a more sumptuous, gay fancy; supposing him born truly great and of honourable descent, with a generous free mind, as well as ample fortune. Even these circumstances themselves may be the very causes perhaps of his being thus ensnared. The elegance of his fancy in outward things may have made him overlook the worth of inward character and proportion: and the love of grandeur and magnificence, wrong turned, may have possessed his imagination over-strongly with such things as frontispieces, parterres, equipages, trim varlets in parti-coloured clothes, and others in gentlemen's apparel,— magnanimous exhibitions of honour and generosity! "In town, a palace and suitable furniture! In the country the same, with the addition of such edifices and gardens as were unknown to our ancestors, and are unnatural to such a climate as Great Britain!"

Meanwhile the year runs on, but the year's income answers not its expense. For "which of these articles can be retrenched? Which way take up, after having thus set out?" A princely fancy has begot all this, and a princely slavery and court dependence must maintain it.

The young gentleman is now led into a chase, in which he will have slender capture, though toil sufficient. He is himself taken. Nor will he so easily get out of that labyrinth, to which he chose to commit his steps, rather than to the more direct and plainer paths in which he trod before. "Farewell that generous, proud spirit, which was wont to speak only what it approved, commend only whom it thought worthy, and act only what it thought right! Favourites must be now observed; little engines of power attended on and loathsomely caressed; an honest man dreaded, and every free tongue or pen abhorred as dangerous and reproachful." For till our gentleman is become wholly prostitute and shameless; till he is brought to laugh at public virtue, and the very notion of common good; till he has openly renounced all principles of honour and honesty, he must in good policy avoid those to whom he lies so much exposed, and shun that commerce and familiarity which was once his chief delight.

Such is the sacrifice made to a wrong pride and ignorant self-esteem, by one whose inward character must necessarily, after this manner, become as mean and abject as his outward behaviour insolent and intolerable.

There are another sort of suitors to powers, and traffickers of inward worth and liberty for outward gain, whom one would be naturally drawn to compassionate. They are themselves of a humane, compassionate, and friendly nature, well-wishers to their country and mankind. They could, perhaps, even embrace poverty contentedly rather than submit to anything diminutive either of their inward freedom or national liberty. But what they can bear in their own persons they cannot bring themselves to bear in the persons of such as are to come after them. Here the best and noblest of affections are borne down by the excess of the next best, those of tenderness for relations and near friends.

Such captives as these would disdain, however, to devote themselves to any prince or ministry whose ends were wholly tyrannical and irreconcilable with the true interest of their nation. In other cases of a less degeneracy, they may bow down perhaps in the temple of Rimmon, support the weight of their supine lords, and prop the steps and ruining credit of their corrupt patrons.

This is drudgery sufficient for such honest natures, such as by hard fate alone could have been made dishonest. But as for pride or insolence on the account of their outward advancement and seeming elevation, they are so far from anything resembling it

that one may often observe what is very contrary in these fairer characters of men. For though perhaps they were known somewhat rigid and severe before, you see them now grown in reality submissive and obliging. Though in conversation formerly dogmatical and overbearing on the points of State and government, they are now the patientest to hear, the least forward to dictate, and the readiest to embrace any entertaining subject of discourse, rather than that of the public and their own personal advancement.

Nothing is so near virtue as this behaviour; and nothing so remote from it, nothing so sure a token of the most profligate manners, as the contrary. In a free government, 'tis so much the interest of every one in place, who profits by the public, to demean himself with modesty and submission, that to appear immediately the more insolent and haughty on such an advancement is the mark only of a contemptible genius, and of a want of true understanding, even in the narrow sense of interest and private good.

Thus we see, after all, that 'tis not merely what we call principle, but a taste which governs men. They may think for certain, "this is right, or that wrong": they may believe "this a crime, or that a sin; this punishable by man, or that by God": yet if the savour of things lies cross to honesty; if the fancy be florid and the appetite high towards the subaltern beauties and lower order of worldly symmetries and proportions, the conduct will infallibly turn this latter way.

Even conscience, I fear, such as is owing to religious discipline, will make but a slight figure where this taste is set amiss. Among the vulgar, perhaps, it may do wonders. A devil and a hell may prevail where a jail and gallows are thought insufficient. But such is the nature of the liberal, polished, and refined part of mankind. So far are they from the mere simplicity of babes and sucklings that, instead of applying the notion of a future reward or punishment to their immediate behaviour in society, they are apt much rather, through the whole course of their lives, to show evidently that they look on the pious narrations to be indeed no better than children's tales or the amusement of the mere vulgar:—

Esse aliquos Manes, et subterranea regna,
Nec pueri credunt, nisi qui nondum aere
      lavantur.

Something therefore should, methinks, be further thought of in behalf of our generous youths towards the correcting of their taste or relish in the concerns of life. For this at last is what will influence. And in this respect the youth alone are to be regarded. Some hopes there may be still conceived of these. The rest are confirmed and hardened in their way. A middle-aged knave (however devout or orthodox) is but a common wonder; an old one is no wonder at all; but a young one is still (thank heaven!) somewhat extraordinary. And I can never enough admire what was said once by a worthy man at the first appearance of one of these young able prostitutes, "that he even trembled at the sight, to find nature capable of being turned so soon; and that he boded greater calamity to his country from this single example of young villainy than from the practices and arts of all the old knaves in being."

Let us therefore proceed in this view, addressing ourselves to the grown youth of our polite world. Let the appeal be to these whose relish is retrievable, and whose taste may yet be formed in morals, as it seems to be already in exterior manners and behaviour.

That there is really a standard of this latter kind will immediately, and on the first view, be acknowledged. The contest is only, "which is right; which the unaffected carriage and just demeanour; and which the affected and false." Scarce is there any one who pretends not to know and to decide what is well-bred and handsome.

There are few so affectedly clownish as absolutely to disown good breeding, and renounce the notion of a beauty in outward manners and deportment. With such as these, wherever they should be found, I must confess I could scarce be tempted to bestow the least pains or labour towards convincing them of a beauty in inward sentiments and principles.

Whoever has any impression of what we call gentility or politeness is already so acquainted with the decorum and grace of things that he will readily confess a pleasure and enjoyment in the very survey and contemplation of this kind. Now if in the way of polite pleasure the study and love of beauty be essential, the study and love of symmetry and order, on which beauty depends, must also be essential in the same respect.

'Tis impossible we can advance the least in any relish or taste of outward symmetry and order, without acknowledging that the proportionate and regular state is the truly prosperous and natural in every subject. The same features which make deformity create incommodiousness and disease. And the same shapes and proportions which make beauty afford advantage by adapting to activity and use. Even in the imitative or designing arts (to which our author so often refers) the truth or beauty of every figure or statue is measured from the perfection of Nature in her just adapting of every limb and proportion to the activity, strength, dexterity, life and vigour of the particular species or animal designed.

Thus beauty and truth are plainly joined with the notion of utility and convenience, even in the apprehension of every ingenious artist, the architect, the statuary, or the painter. 'Tis the same in the physician's way. Natural health is the just proportion, truth, and regular course of things in a constitution. 'Tis the inward beauty of the body. And when the harmony and just measures of the rising pulses, the circulating humours, and the moving airs or spirits, are disturbed or lost, deformity enters, and with it, calamity and ruin.

Should not this (one would imagine) be still the same case and hold equally as to the mind? Is there nothing there which tends to disturbance and dissolution? Is there no natural tenour, tone, or order of the passions or affections? No beauty or deformity in this moral kind? Or allowing that there really is, must it not, of consequence, in the same manner imply health or sickliness, prosperity or disaster? Will it not be found in this respect, above all, "that what is beautiful is harmonious and proportionable;* what is harmonious and pro-

portionable is true; and what is at once both beautiful and true is, of consequence, agreeable and good?"

Where then is this beauty or harmony to be found? How is this symmetry to be discovered and applied? Is it any other art than that of philosophy or the study of inward numbers and proportions which can exhibit this in life? If no other, who then can possibly have a taste of this kind, without being beholden to philosophy? Who can admire the outward beauties and not recur instantly to the inward, which are the most real and essential, the most naturally affecting, and of the highest pleasure, as well as profit and advantage?

---

* This is the honestum, the pulchrum, τὸ καλόν, on which our author lays the stress of virtue, and the merits of this cause; as well in his other Treatises as in this of *Soliloquy* here commented. This beauty the Roman orator, in his rhetorical way, and in the majesty of style, could express no otherwise than as a mystery. "Honestum igitur id intelligimus, quod tale est, ut, detracta omni utilitate, sine ullis praemiis fructibusve, per seipsum possit jure laudari. Quod quale sit, non tam definitione qua sum usus intelligi potest (quanquam ali quantum potest) quam communi omnium judicio, et optimi cujusque studiis, atque factis; qui permulta ob eam unam causam faciunt, quia decet, quia rectum, quia honestum est; etsi nullum consecuturum emolumentum vident." ["by *right* therefore I understand what is such that, apart from expediency, without any reward or profit, it can properly be praised on its own account. What sort of thing that is, may be understood, not so much from the definition I have given (though to some extent it may be so understood) as from the general agreement of all, and from the enthusiasm and acts of the best men; they do many a thing for this one reason, that it is becoming, is proper, is right, even though they see no gain likely to follow."—Cicero, *De Finibus*, ii, 45.] Our author, on the other side, having little of the orator, and less of the constraint of formality belonging to some graver characters, can be more familiar on this occasion; and accordingly descending without the least scruple into whatever style or humour, he refuses to make the least difficulty or mystery of this matter. He pretends, on this head, to claim the assent not only of orators, poets, and the higher virtuosi, but even of the beaux themselves, and such as go no farther than the dancing-master to seek for grace and beauty. He pretends, we see, to

fetch this natural idea from as familiar amusements as dress, equipage, the tiring-room, or toy-shop. And thus in his proper manner of soliloquy or self-discourse, we may imagine him running on, beginning perhaps with some particular scheme or fancied scale of beauty, which, according to his philosophy, he strives to erect by distinguishing, sorting, and dividing into things animate, inanimate, and mixed, as thus:—

In the inanimate: beginning from those regular figures and symmetries with which children are delighted, and proceeding gradually to the proportions of architecture and the other arts. The same in respect of sounds and music. From beautiful stones, rocks, minerals, to vegetables, woods, aggregate parts of the world, seas, rivers, mountains, vales. The globe. Celestial bodies and their order. The higher architecture of Nature. Nature herself considered as inanimate and passive.

In the animate: from animals and their several kinds, tempers, sagacities, to men. And from single persons of men, their private characters, understandings, geniuses, dispositions, manners, to public societies, communities or commonwealths. From flocks, herds, and other natural assemblages or groups of living creatures, to human intelligencies and correspondencies, or whatever is higher in the kind. The correspondence, union and harmony of Nature herself, considered as animate and intelligent.

In the mixed: as in a single person (a body and a mind) the union and harmony of this kind, which constitutes the real person; and the friendship, love, or whatever other affection is formed on such an object. A household, a city or nation, with certain lands, buildings, and other appendices or local ornaments which jointly form that agreeable idea of home, family, country.

"And what of this?" says an airy spark, no

In so short a compass does that learning and knowledge lie on which manners and life depend. 'Tis we ourselves create and form our taste. If we resolve to have it just, 'tis in our power. We may esteem and resolve, approve and disapprove, as we would wish. For who would not rejoice to be always equal and consonant to himself, and have constantly that opinion of things which is natural and proportionable? But who dares search opinion to the bottom, or call in question his early and prepossessing taste? Who is so just to himself as to recall his fancy from the power of fashion

friend to meditation or deep thought. "What means this catalogue or scale, as you are pleased to call it?" "Only, sir, to satisfy myself that I am not alone or single in a certain fancy I have of a thing called beauty; that I have almost the whole world for my companions; and that each of us admirers and earnest pursuers of beauty (such as in a manner we all are) if peradventure we take not a certain sagacity along with us, we must err widely, range extravagantly, and run ever upon a false scent. We may (in the sportsman's phrase) have many hares afoot, but shall stick to no real game, nor be fortunate in any capture which may content us.

"See with what ardour and vehemence the young man, neglecting his proper race and fellow-creatures, and forgetting what is decent, handsome, or becoming in human affairs, pursues these species in those common objects of his affection, a horse, a hound, a hawk! What doting on these beauties! What admiration of the kind itself! And of the particular animal, what care, and in a manner idolatry and consecration, when the beast beloved is (as often happens) even set apart from use, and only kept to gaze on and feed the enamoured fancy with highest delight! See in another youth, not so forgetful of human kind, but remembering it still in a wrong way! a φιλόκαλος of another sort, a Chaerea. Quam elegans formarum spectator! See as to other beauties, where there is no possession, no enjoyment or reward, but barely seeing and admiring; as in the virtuoso-passion, the love of painting and the designing arts of every kind so often observed. How fares it with our princely genius, our grandee who assembles all these beauties, and within the bounds of his sumptuous palace incloses all these graces of a thousand kinds? What pains! study! science! Behold the disposition and order of these finer sorts of apartments, gardens, villas! The kind of harmony to the eye from the various shapes and colours agreeably mixed and ranged in lines, intercrossing without confusion, and fortunately coincident. A parterre, cypresses, groves, wilderness. Statues here and there of virtue, fortitude, temperance. Heroes' busts, philosophers' heads, with suitable mottoes and inscriptions. Solemn representations of things deeply natural—caves, grottoes, rocks, urns and obelisks in retired places and disposed at proper distances and points of sight, with all those symmetries which silently express a reigning order, peace, harmony, and beauty! . . . But what is there answerable to this in the minds of the possessors? What possession or propriety is theirs? What constancy or security of enjoyment? What peace, what harmony within?"

Thus our monologist, or self-discoursing author, in his usual strain, when incited to the search of Beauty and the Decorum by vulgar admiration and the universal acknowledgment of the species in outward things, and in the meaner and subordinate subjects. By this inferior species, it seems, our strict inspector disdains to be allured; and refusing to be captivated by anything less than the superior, original, and genuine kind, he walks at leisure, without emotion, in deep philosophical reserve, through all these pompous scenes; passes unconcernedly by those court pageants, the illustrious and much envied potentates of the place; overlooks the rich, the great, and even the fair, feeling no other astonishment than what is accidentally raised in him by the view of these impostures and of this specious snare. For here he observes those gentlemen chiefly to be caught and fastest held who are the highest ridiculers of such reflections as his own, and who in the very height of this ridicule prove themselves the impotent contemners of a species which, whether they will or no, they ardently pursue, some in a face and certain regular lines or features, others in a palace and apartments, others in an equipage and dress. "O effeminacy, effeminacy! Who would imagine this could be the vice of such as appear no inconsiderable men? But person is a subject of flattery which reaches beyond the bloom of youth. The experienced senator and aged general can in our days dispense with a toilet and take his outward form into a very extraordinary adjustment and regulation. All embellishments are affected, besides the true. And thus, led by example, whilst we run in search of elegancy and neatness, pursuing beauty, and adding, as we imagine, more lustre and value to our own person, we grow, in our real character and true self, deformed and monstrous, servile and abject, stooping to the lowest terms of courtship, and sacrificing all internal proportion, all intrinsic and real beauty and worth for the sake of things which carry scarce a shadow of the kind." [Shaftesbury.]

and education to that of reason? Could we, however, be thus courageous, we should soon settle in ourselves such an opinion of good as would secure to us an invariable, agreeable, and just taste in life and manners.

Thus have I endeavoured to tread in my author's steps, and prepare the reader for the serious and downright philosophy which even in this last commented treatise, our author keeps still as a mystery and dares not formally profess. His pretence has been to advise authors and polish styles, but his aim has been to correct manners and regular lives. He has affected soliloquy, as pretending only to censure himself, but he has taken occasion to bring others into his company and make bold with personages and characters of no inferior rank. He has given scope enough to raillery and humour, and has intrenched very largely on the province of us miscellanarian writers. But the reader is now about to see him in a new aspect, "a formal and professed philosopher, a system-writer, a dogmatist and expounder." *Habes confitentem reum.*

So to his philosophy I commit him. Though, according as my genius at present disposition will permit, I intend still to accompany him at a distance, keep him in sight, and convoy him, the best I am able, through the dangerous seas he is about to pass.

THE APOSTROPHE TO NATURE, FROM THE MORALISTS

Ye fields and woods, my refuge from the toilsome world of business, receive me in your quiet sanctuaries, and favour my retreat and thoughtful solitude! Ye verdant plains, how gladly I salute ye! Hail all ye blissful mansions! known seats! delightful prospects! Majestic beauties of this earth, and all ye rural powers and graces! Blessed be ye chaste abodes of happiest mortals, who here in peaceful innocence enjoy a life unenvied, though divine; whilst with its blessed tranquillity it affords a happy leisure and retreat for man, who, made for contemplation, and to search his own and other natures, may here best meditate the cause of things, and, placed amidst the various scenes of Nature, may nearer view her works.

O glorious nature! supremely fair and sovereignly good! all-loving and all lovely, all divine! whose looks are so becoming and of such infinite grace; whose study brings such wisdom, and whose contemplation such delight; whose every single work affords an ampler scene, and is a nobler spectacle than all which ever art presented! O mighty Nature! wise substitute of Providence! impowered creatress! Or thou impowering Deity, supreme creator! Thee I invoke and thee alone adore. To thee this solitude, this place, these rural meditations are sacred: whilst thus inspired with harmony of thought, though unconfined by words, and in loose numbers, I sing of Nature's order in created beings, and celebrate the beauties which resolve in thee, the source and principle of all beauty and perfection.

Thy being is boundless, unsearchable, impenetrable. In thy immensity all thought is lost, fancy gives over its flight, and wearied imagination spends itself in vain, finding no coast nor limit of this ocean, nor, in the widest tract through which it soars, one point yet nearer the circumference than the first centre whence it parted. Thus having oft essayed, thus sallied forth into the wide expanse, when I return again within myself, struck with the sense of this so narrow being and of the fulness of that immense one, I dare no more behold the amazing depths nor sound the abyss of Deity.

Yet since by thee, O sovereign mind, I have been formed such as I am, intelligent and rational, since the peculiar dignity of my nature is to know and contemplate thee, permit that with due freedom I exert those faculties with which thou hast adorned me. Bear with my venturous and bold approach. And since nor vain curiosity, nor fond conceit, nor love of aught save thee alone inspires me with such thought as these, be thou my assistant and guide me in this pursuit, whilst I venture thus to tread the labyrinth of wide Nature and endeavour to trace thee in thy works.

BERNARD MANDEVILLE (1670-1733)

Bernard Mandeville came to England from Holland. Eventually one of the most famous of a long line of illustrious Mandevilles, he was baptized at Rotterdam, November 20, 1670. He decided early to follow medicine, the profession of his father, his grandfather and great-grandfather. He took the degree of Doctor of Medicine at the University of Leyden in 1691, although his university career had not been without excursions into the field of philosophy. It was not long after this that he went to London, ostensibly to learn the language, but he found the country and its people so congenial that he settled there, married an Englishwoman, practiced his profession and wrote for the rest of his life until his death in 1733. We have very little biographical information for this part of his life. He seems to have been well thought of in his profession but his professional reputation was eclipsed by his fame and popularity—perhaps notoriety—as a writer.

By far Mandeville's most important work is his *Fable of the Bees*. The starting point of this work was a poem which Mandeville published anonymously in 1705, called *The Grumbling Hive: or Knaves Turned Honest*. The witty and provocative paradoxes of this poem not only made it immediately popular but aroused much discussion. In 1714 Mandeville republished *The Grumbling Hive* with a commentary and an essay entitled "An Enquiry into the Origin of Moral Virtue," and called the whole *The Fable of the Bees: or Private Vices, Public Benefits*. The great storm of objection to Mandeville's opinions did not come, however, until 1723 when he added his attack on charity schools and another essay directed chiefly against Shaftesbury called "A Search into the Nature of Society." Churchmen and philosophers published letters, sermons, and even whole books of attack on the *Fable*, and the more they attacked it the more it was read. In 1728 Mandeville added Part II, consisting of a preface and six dialogues in which he further amplified and defended his ideas. The two parts were finally published together in 1733.

The epitome of Mandeville's thought, and the paradox that caused so much consternation, lies in his sub-title, "Private Vices, Public Benefits." In an age of commercial and industrial expansion, Mandeville, the realist, forced Englishmen to see that their practice was no longer in harmony with the system of morals which they were preaching in their churches. They wished England to be prosperous and commercially influential, but they wished Englishmen to be frugal and strictly virtuous. This, said Mandeville, is an impossibility. "Great wealth and foreign treasure," he wrote, "will ever scorn to come among men unless you'll admit their inseparable companions, avarice and luxury: where trade is considerable, fraud will intrude. To be at once well-bred and sincere is no less than a contradiction; and therefore while man advances in knowledge, and his manners are polished, we must expect to see at the same time his desires enlarged, his appetites refined, and his vices increased." In other words Mandeville said in effect to his contemporaries, "You can take your choice between national prosperity and an ethics that demands the conquest of the selfish impulses and the subordination of the passions to reason; but you cannot have both." Incidentally Mandeville's vigorous thinking laid the foundation for many social and economic theories that came into favor later in the century, such as utilitarianism, and the economic doctrines of the division of labor, free trade, and *laissez faire* doctrines, later so ably developed by Adam Smith.

The best editing and discussion of the *Fable of the Bees* is to be found in the edition by F. B. Kaye, Oxford, 1924.

THE GRUMBLING HIVE: OR, KNAVES TURNED HONEST

A spacious hive well stocked with bees,
That lived in luxury and ease,
And yet as famed for laws and arms

As yielding large and early swarms
Was counted the great nursery
Of sciences and industry.
No bees had better government,
More fickleness, or less content:
They were not slaves to tyranny
Nor ruled by wild democracy,   10

But kings that could not wrong because
Their power was circumscribed by laws.
    These insects lived like men, and all
Our actions they performed in small:
They did whatever's done in town,
And what belongs to sword or gown,
Though the artful works by nimble slight
Of minute limbs 'scaped human sight,
Yet we've no engines, labourers,
Ships, castles, arms, artificers,   20
Craft, science, shop, or instrument,
But they had an equivalent,
Which, since their language is unknown,
Must be called, as we do our own.
As grant that, among other things,
They wanted dice, yet they had kings,
And those had guards, from whence we may
Justly conclude, they had some play,
Unless a regiment be shown
Of soldiers, that make use of none.   30
    Vast numbers thronged the fruitful hive,
Yet those vast numbers made them thrive;
Millions endeavouring to supply
Each other's lust and vanity;
While other millions were employed
To see their handiworks destroyed.
They furnished half the universe,
Yet had more work than labourers.
Some with vast stocks and little pains
Jumped into business of great gains;   40
And some were damned to scythes and
                        spades,
And all those hard laborious trades
Where willing wretches daily sweat
And wear out strength and limbs to eat;
While others followed mysteries
To which few folks bind 'prentices,
That want no stock but that of brass
And may set up without a cross,
As sharpers, parasites, pimps, players,
Pickpockets, coiners, quacks, soothsayers,   50
And all those that in enmity
With downright working, cunningly
Convert to their own use the labour
Of their good-natured heedless neighbour.
These were called knaves, but bar the name,
The grave industrious were the same:
All trades and places knew some cheat;
No calling was without deceit.
    The lawyers, of whose art the basis
Was raising feuds and splitting cases,   60
Opposed all registers that cheats
Might make more work with dipped estates;
⌐er't unlawful that one's own

Without a law-suit should be known.
They kept off hearings wilfully
To finger the refreshing fee;
And to defend a wicked cause
Examined and surveyed the laws,
As burglars shops and houses do
To find out where they'd best break through.
    Physicians valued fame and wealth   71
Above the drooping patient's health
Or their own skill: the greatest part
Studied, instead of rules of art,
Grave pensive looks and dull behaviour
To gain the apothecary's favour,
The praise of midwives, priests, and all
That served at birth or funeral;
To bear with the ever-talking tribe
And hear my lady's aunt prescribe;   80
With formal smile, and kind "How d'ye,"
To fawn on all the family;
And, which of all the greatest curse is,
To endure the impertinence of nurses.
    Among the many priests of Jove,
Hired to draw blessings from above,
Some few were learned and eloquent,
But thousands hot and ignorant:
Yet all passed muster that could hide
Their sloth, lust, avarice, and pride,   90
For which they were as famed as tailors
For cabbage, or for brandy sailors;
Some, meagre-looked and meanly clad,
Would mystically pray for bread,
Meaning by that an ample store,
Yet literally received no more;
And while these holy drudges starved,
The lazy ones, for which they served,
Indulged their ease with all the graces
Of health and plenty in their faces.   100
    The soldiers that were forced to fight,
If they survived, got honour by it,
Though some that shunned the bloody fray
Had limbs shot off, that ran away:
Some valiant generals fought the foe;
Others took bribes to let them go:
Some ventured always where 'twas warm,
Lost now a leg and then an arm,
Till quite disabled and put by
They lived on half their salary,   110
While others never came in play
And stayed at home for double pay.
    Their kings were served, but knavishly,
Cheated by their own ministry;
Many that for their welfare slaved
Robbing the very crown they saved:
Pensions were small and they lived high,

Yet boasted of their honesty,
Calling, whene'er they strained their right,
The slippery trick a perquisite;   120
And when folks understood their cant
They changed that for emolument,
Unwilling to be short or plain
In anything concerning gain;
For there was not a bee but would
Get more, I won't say than he should,
But than he dared to let them know
That paid for't; as your gamesters do
That, though at fair play, ne'er will own
Before the losers what they've won.   130

But who can all their frauds repeat?
The very stuff which in the street
They sold for dirt to enrich the ground
Was often by the buyers found
Sophisticated with a quarter
Of good-for-nothing stones and mortar,
Though Flail had little cause to mutter
Who sold the other salt for butter.

Justice herself, famed for fair dealing,
By blindness had not lost her feeling;   140
Her left hand, which the scales should hold,
Had often dropped 'em, bribed with gold;
And though she seemed impartial
Where punishment was corporal,
Pretended to a regular course
In murder and all crimes of force;
Though some, first pilloried for cheating,
Were hanged in hemp of their own beating,
Yet it was thought the sword she bore
Checked but the desperate and the poor, 150
That, urged by mere necessity,
Were tied up to the wretched tree
For crimes which not deserved that fate,
But to secure the rich and great.

Thus every part was full of vice,
Yet the whole mass a paradise;
Flattered in peace and feared in wars,
They were the esteem of foreigners,
And lavish of their wealth and lives,
The balance of all other hives.   160
Such were the blessings of that state;
Their crimes conspired to make them great:
And virtue, who from politics
Had learned a thousand cunning tricks,
Was, by their happy influence,
Made friends with vice; and ever since,
The worst of all the multitude
Did something for the common good.

This was the state's craft that maintained
The whole of which each part complained:
This, as in music harmony.   171

Made jarrings in the main agree;
Parties directly opposite
Assist each other, as 'twere for spite;
And temperance with sobriety
Serve drunkenness and gluttony.

The root of evil, avarice,
That damned ill-natured baneful vice,
Was slave to prodigality,
That noble sin; whilst luxury   180
Employed a million of the poor,
And odious pride a million more:
Envy itself, and vanity,
Were ministers of industry;
Their darling folly, fickleness,
In diet, furniture and dress,
That strange ridiculous vice, was made
The very wheel that turned the trade.
Their laws and clothes were equally
Objects of mutability;   190
For what was well done for a time
In half a year became a crime;
Yet while they altered thus their laws,
Still finding and correcting flaws,
They mended by inconstancy
Faults which no prudence could foresee.

Thus vice nursed ingenuity
Which, joined with time and industry,
Had carried life's conveniencies,
Its real pleasures, comforts, ease,   200
To such a height, the very poor
Lived better than the rich before,
And nothing could be added more.

How vain is mortal happiness!
Had they but known the bounds of bliss,
And that perfection here below
Is more than gods can well bestow,
The grumbling brutes had been content
With ministers and government.
But they, at every ill success,   210
Like creatures lost without redress,
Cursed politicians, armies, fleets,
While every one cried, "Damn the cheats,"
And would, though conscious of his own,
In others barb'rously bear none.

One that had got a princely store
By cheating master, king, and poor,
Dared cry aloud, "The land must sink
For all its fraud." And whom d'ye think
The sermonizing rascal chid?   220
A glover that sold lamb for kid.

The least thing was not done amiss,
Or crossed the public business,
But all the rogues cried brazenly,
"Good gods, had we but honesty!"

Mercury smiled at the impudence,
And others called it want of sense,
Always to rail at what they loved:
But Jove, with indignation moved,
At last in anger swore he'd rid   230
The bawling hive of fraud; and did.
The very moment it departs,
And honesty fills all their hearts;
There shows them, like the instructive tree,
Those crimes which they're ashamed to see,
Which now in silence they confess
By blushing at their ugliness,
Like children that would hide their faults
And by their color own their thoughts,
Imagining, when they're looked upon,   240
That others see what they have done.
    But, Oh ye gods! What consternation,
How vast and sudden was the alteration!
In half an hour, the nation round,
Meat fell a penny in the pound.
The mask hypocrisy's flung down
From the great statesman to the clown:
And some in borrowed looks well known
Appeared like strangers in their own.
The bar was silent from that day,   250
For now the willing debtors pay
Even what's by creditors forgot,
Who quitted them that had it not.
Those that were in the wrong stood mute
And dropped the patched vexatious suit,
On which, since nothing less can thrive
Than lawyers in an honest hive,
All, except those that got enough,
With inkhorns by their sides trooped off.
    Justice hanged some, set others free,   260
And after jail delivery,
Her presence being no more required,
With all her train and pomp retired.
First marched some smiths with locks and
        grates,
Fetters and doors with iron plates;
Next jailers, turnkeys, and assistants;
Before the goddess, at some distance,
Her chief and faithful minister,
Squire Catch, the law's great finisher,
Bore not the imaginary sword   270
But his own tools, an axe and cord;
Then on a cloud the hoodwinked fair,
Justice herself, was pushed by air:
About her chariot, and behind,
Were sergeants, bums of every kind,
Tip-staffs, and all those officers
That squeeze a living out of tears.
    Though physic lived while folks were ill,

None would prescribe but bees of skill,
Which, through the hive dispersed so wide
That none of them had need to ride,   281
Waved vain disputes, and strove to free
The patients of their misery;
Left drugs in cheating countries grown,
And used the product of their own,
Knowing the gods sent no disease
To nations without remedies.
    Their clergy roused from laziness
Laid not their charge on journey-bees,
But served themselves, exempt from vice, 290
The gods with prayer and sacrifice;
All those that were unfit, or knew
Their service might be spared, withdrew:
Nor was there business for so many,
If the honest stand in need of any;
Few only with the high-priest stayed,
To whom the rest obedience paid;
Himself employed in holy cares,
Resigned to others state affairs.
He chased no starveling from his door,   300
Nor pinched the wages of the poor;
But at his house the hungry's fed,
The hireling finds unmeasured bread,
The needy traveler board and bed.
    Among the king's great ministers
And all the inferior officers
The change was great; for frugally
They now lived on their salary.
That a poor bee should ten times come
To ask his due, a trifling sum,   310
And by some well-hired clerk be made
To give a crown, or ne'er be paid,
Would now be called a downright cheat,
Though formerly a perquisite.
All places managed first by three
Who watched each other's knavery
And often for a fellow feeling
Promoted one another's stealing,
Are happily supplied by one,
By which some thousands more are gone.   320
    No honour now could be content
To live and owe for what was spent;
Liveries in brokers' shops are hung;
They part with coaches for a song,
Sell stately horses by whole sets,
And country houses to pay debts.
    Vain cost is shunned as much as fraud;
They have no forces kept abroad,
Laugh at the esteem of foreigners
And empty glory got by wars;   330
They fight, but for their country's sake.

When right or liberty's at stake.
  Now mind the glorious hive, and see
How honesty and trade agree.
The show is gone, it thins apace,
And looks with quite another face,
For 'twas not only that they went
By whom vast sums were yearly spent,
But multitudes that lived on them
Were daily forced to do the same.   340
In vain to other trades they'd fly;
All were o'erstocked accordingly.
  The price of land and houses falls;
Miraculous palaces whose walls,
Like those of Thebes, were raised by play
Are to be let; while the once gay,
Well-seated household gods would be
More pleased to expire in flames, than see
The mean inscription on the door
Smile at the lofty ones they bore.   350
The building trade is quite destroyed;
Artificers are not employed;
No limner for his art is famed;
Stone-cutters, carvers are not named.
  Those that remained, grown temperate,
    strive,
Not how to spend, but how to live,
And, when they paid their tavern score,
Resolved to enter it no more:
No vintner's jilt in all the hive
Could wear now cloth of gold, and thrive; 360
Nor Torcol such vast sums advance
For Burgundy and Ortelans;
The courtier's gone that with his miss
Supped at his house on Chrismas peas,
Spending as much in two hours stay,
As keeps a troop of horse a day.
  The haughty Chloe, to live great
Had made her husband rob the state;
But now she sells her furniture,
Which the Indies had been ransacked for; 370
Contracts the expensive bill of fare,
And wears her strong suit a whole year:
The slight and fickle age is past,
And clothes, as well as fashions, last.
Weavers, that joined rich silk with plate,
And all the trades subordinate
Are gone. Still peace and plenty reign,
And everything is cheap, though plain:
Kind nature, free from gardeners force,
Allows all fruits in her own course;   380
But rarities cannot be had
Where pains to get them are not paid.
  As pride and luxury decrease,

So by degrees they leave the seas.
Not merchants now, but companies
Remove whole manufactories.
All arts and crafts neglected lie;
Content, the bane of industry,
Makes them admire their homely store
And neither seek nor covet more.   390
  So few in the vast hive remain,
The hundredth part they can't maintain
Against the insults of numerous foes,
Whom yet they valiantly oppose,
Till some well-fenced retreat is found,
And here they die or stand their ground.
No hireling in their army's known;
But bravely fighting for their own,
Their courage and integrity
At last were crowned with victory.   400
  They triumphed not without their cost,
For many thousand bees were lost.
Hardened with toils and exercise,
They counted ease itself a vice,
Which so improved their temperance
That, to avoid extravagance,
They flew into a hollow tree,
Blest with content and honesty.

The Moral

  Then leave complaints: fools only strive
To make a great an honest hive.   410
To enjoy the world's conveniencies,
Be famed in war, yet live in ease,
Without great vices is a vain
Utopia seated in the Brain.
Fraud, luxury, and pride must live,
While we the benefits receive:
Hunger's a dreadful plague, no doubt,
Yet who digests or thrives without?
Do we not owe the growth of wine
To the dry, shabby, crooked vine?   420
Which, while its shoots neglected stood,
Choked other plants, and ran to wood;
But blessed us with its noble fruit
As soon as it was tied and cut:
So vice is beneficial found,
When it's by justice lopped and bound;
Nay, where the people would be great,
As necessary to the state
As hunger is to make 'em eat.
Bare virtue can't make nations live   430
In splendor; they, that would revive
A Golden Age, must be as free
For acorns as for honesty.

[1705]

THE FABLE OF THE BEES

AN ENQUIRY INTO THE ORIGIN OF MORAL VIRTUE

All untaught animals are only solicitous of pleasing themselves, and naturally follow the bent of their own inclinations, without considering the good or harm that from their being pleased will accrue to others. This is the reason, that in the wild state of Nature those creatures are fittest to live peaceably together in great numbers, that discover the least of understanding, and have the fewest appetites to gratify; and consequently no species of animals is, without the curb of government, less capable of agreeing long together in multitudes than that of man; yet such are his qualities, whether good or bad, I shall not determine, that no creature besides himself can ever be made sociable. But being an extraordinary selfish and headstrong, as well as cunning animal, however he may be subdued by superior strength, it is impossible by force alone to make him tractable, and receive the improvements he is capable of.

The chief thing, therefore, which lawgivers and other wise men, that have laboured for the establishment of society, have endeavoured, has been to make the people they were to govern, believe, that it was more beneficial for every body to conquer than indulge his appetites, and much better to mind the public than what seemed his private interest. As this has always been a very difficult task, so no wit or eloquence has been left untried to compass it; and the moralists and philosophers of all ages employed their utmost skill to prove the truth of so useful an assertion. But whether mankind would have ever believed it or not, it is not likely that any body could have persuaded them to disapprove of their natural inclinations, or prefer the good of others to their own, if at the same time he had not showed them an equivalent to be enjoyed as a reward for the violence, which by so doing they of necessity must commit upon themselves. Those that have undertaken to civilize mankind, were not ignorant of this; but being unable to give so many real rewards as would satisfy all persons for every individual action, they were forced to contrive an imaginary one, that as a general equivalent for the trouble of self-denial should serve on all occasions, and without costing any thing either to themselves or others, be yet a most acceptable recompense to the receivers.

They thoroughly examined all the strength and frailties of our nature, and observing that none were either so savage as not to be charmed with praise, or so despicable as patiently to bear contempt, justly concluded, that flattery must be the most powerful argument that could be used to human creatures. Making use of this bewitching engine, they extolled the excellency of our nature above other animals, and setting forth with unbounded praises the wonders of our sagacity and vastness of understanding, bestowed a thousand encomiums on the rationality of our souls, by the help of which we were capable of performing the most noble achievements. Having by this artful way of flattery insinuated themselves into the hearts of men, they began to instruct them in the notions of honour and shame, representing the one as the worst of all evils, and the other as the highest good to which mortals could aspire: which being done, they laid before them how unbecoming it was the dignity of such sublime creatures to be solicitous about gratifying those appetites, which they had in common with brutes, and at the same time unmindful of those higher qualities that gave them the pre-eminence over all visible beings. They indeed confessed, that those impulses of nature were very pressing; that it was troublesome to resist, and very difficult wholly to subdue them. But this they only used as an argument to demonstrate, how glorious the conquest of them was on the one hand, and how scandalous on the other not to attempt it.

To introduce, moreover, an emulation amongst men, they divided the whole species into two classes, vastly differing from one another: the one consisted of abject, low-minded people, that always hunting after immediate enjoyment, were wholly incapable of self-denial, and without regard to the good of others, had no higher aim than their private advantage; such as being enslaved by voluptuousness, yielded without resistance to every gross desire, and made no use of their rational faculties but to heighten their sensual pleasure. These vile groveling wretches, they said, were the dross of their kind, and having only the shape of men, differed from brutes in nothing but their outward figure. But the other class was made up of lofty high-spirited creatures, that free from sordid selfishness, esteemed the improvements of the mind to be their fairest possessions; and setting a true value upon themselves, took no delight but in embellishing that part in which their excellency consisted; such as despising whatever they had in common with irrational creatures, opposed by the help of reason their most violent inclinations; and making a continual war with themselves to promote the peace of others, aimed at no less than the public welfare and the conquest of their own passion.

Fortior est qui se quàm qui fortissima vincit mœnia — — — —

These they called the true representatives of their sublime species, exceeding in worth the first class by more degrees, than that itself was superior to the beasts of the field.

As in all animals that are not too imperfect to discover pride, we find, that the finest and such as are the most beautiful and valuable of their kind, have generally the greatest share of it; so in man, the most perfect of animals, it is so inseparable from his very essence (how cunningly soever some may learn to hide or disguise it)

that without it the compound he is made of would want one of the chiefest ingredients: which, if we consider, it is hardly to be doubted but lessons and remonstrances, so skilfully adapted to the good opinion man has of himself, as those I have mentioned, must, if scattered amongst a multitude not only gain the assent of most of them, as to the speculative part, but likewise induce several, especially the fiercest, most resolute, and best among them, to endure a thousand inconveniences, and undergo as many hardships, that they may have the pleasure of counting themselves men of the second class, and consequently appropriating to themselves all the excellences they have heard of it.

From what has been said, we ought to expect in the first place that the heroes who took such extraordinary pains to master some of their natural appetites, and preferred the good of others to any visible interest of their own, would not recede an inch from the fine notions they had received concerning the dignity of rational creatures; and having ever the authority of the government on their side, with all imaginable vigour assert the esteem that was due to those of the second class, as well as their superiority over the rest of their kind. In the second, that those who wanted a sufficient stock of either pride or resolution to buoy them up in mortifying of what was dearest to them, followed the sensual dictates of nature, would yet be ashamed of confessing themselves to be those despicable wretches that belonged to the inferior class, and were generally reckoned to be so little removed from brutes; and that therefore in their own defence they would say as others did, and hiding their own imperfections as well as they could, cry up self-denial and public-spiritedness as much as any: for it is highly probable that some of them, convinced by the real proofs of fortitude and self-conquest they had seen, would admire in others what they found wanting in themselves: others be afraid of the resolution and prowess of those of the second class, and that all of them were kept in awe by the power of their rulers; wherefore it is reasonable to think, that none of them (whatever they thought in themselves) would dare openly contradict, what by every body else was thought criminal to doubt of.

This was (or at least might have been) the manner after which savage man was broke; from whence it is evident, that the first rudiments of morality, broached by skilful politicians, to render men useful to each other as well as tractable, were chiefly contrived that the ambitious might reap the more benefit from, and govern vast numbers of them with the greater ease and security. This foundation of politics being once laid, it is impossible that man should long remain uncivilized: For even those who only strove to gratify their appetites, being continually crossed by others of the same stamp, could not but observe, that whenever they checked their inclinations or but followed them with more circumspection, they avoided a world of troubles, and often escaped many of the calamities that generally attended the too eager pursuit after pleasure.

First, they received, as well as others, the benefit of those actions that were done for the good of the whole society, and consequently could not forbear wishing well to those of the superior class that performed them. Secondly, the more intent they were in seeking their own advantage, without regard to others, the more they were hourly convinced, that none stood so much in their way as those that were most like themselves.

It being the interest then of the very worst of them, more than any, to preach up public-spiritedness, that they might reap the fruits of the labour and self-denial of others, and at the same time indulge their own appetites with less disturbance, they agreed with the rest, to call every thing, which, without regard to the public, man should commit to gratify any of his appetites, VICE; if in that action there could be observed the least prospect, that it might either be injurious to any of the society, or ever render himself less serviceable to others: and to give the name of VIRTUE to every performance, by which man, contrary to the impulse of nature, should endeavour the benefit of others, or the conquest of his own passions out of a rational ambition of being good.

It shall be objected, that no society was ever any ways civilized before the major part had agreed upon some worship or other of an over-ruling power, and consequently that the notions of good and evil, and the distinction between *Virtue* and *Vice*, were never the contrivance of politicians, but the pure effect of religion. Before I answer this objection, I must repeat what I have said already, that in this *Enquiry into the Origin of Moral Virtue*, I speak neither of Jews or Christians, but man in his state of nature and ignorance of the true Deity; and then I affirm, that the idolatrous superstitions of all other nations, and the pitiful notions they had of the Supreme Being, were incapable of exciting man to virtue, and good for nothing but to awe and amuse a rude and unthinking multitude. It is evident from history, that in all considerable societies, how stupid or ridiculous soever people's received notions have been, as to the Deities they worshipped, human nature has ever exerted itself in all its branches, and that there is no earthly wisdom or moral virtue, but at one time or other men have excelled in it in all monarchies and commonwealths, that for riches and power have been any ways remarkable.

The Ægyptians, not satisfied with having deified all the ugly monsters they could think on, were so silly as to adore the onions of their own sowing; yet at the same time their country was the most famous nursery of arts and sciences in the world, and themselves more eminently skilled in the deepest mysteries of nature than any nation has been since.

No states or kingdoms under heaven have yielded more or greater patterns in all sorts of moral virtues than the Greek and Roman Empires, more especially the latter; and yet how loose, absurd and ridiculous were their sentiments as to sacred matters? For without reflecting on the extravagant number of their deities, if we only consider the infamous stories they fathered upon them, it is not to be denied but that their religion, far from teaching men the conquest of their passions, and the way to virtue, seemed rather contrived to justify their appetites, and encourage their vices. But if we would know what made 'em excel in fortitude, courage and magnanimity, we must cast our eyes on the pomp of their triumphs, the magnificence of their monuments and arches; their trophies, statues, and inscriptions; the variety of their military crowns, their honours decreed to the dead, public encomiums on the living, and other imaginary rewards they bestowed on men of merit; and we shall find, that what carried so many of them to the utmost pitch of self-denial, was nothing but their policy in making use of the most effectual means that human pride could be flattered with.

It is visible then that it was not any heathen religion or other idolatrous superstition, that first put man upon crossing his appetites and subduing his dearest inclinations, but the skilful management of wary politicians; and the nearer we search into human nature, the more we shall be convinced, that the moral virtues are the political offspring which flattery begot upon pride.

There is no man of what capacity or penetration soever, that is wholly proof against the witchcraft of flattery, if artfully performed, and suited to his abilities. Children and fools will swallow personal praise, but those that are more cunning, must be managed with greater circumspection;

and the more general the flattery is, the less it is suspected by those it is levelled at. What you say in commendation of a whole town is received with pleasure by all the inhabitants: speak in commendation of Letters in general, and every man of learning will think himself in particular obliged to you. You may safely praise the employment a man is of, or the country he was born in; because you give him an opportunity of screening the joy he feels upon his own account, under the esteem which he pretends to have for others.

It is common among cunning men, that understand the power which flattery has upon pride, when they are afraid they shall be imposed upon, to enlarge, tho' much against their conscience, upon the honour, fair dealing and integrity of the family, country, or sometimes the profession of him they suspect; because they know that men often will change their resolution, and act against their inclination, that they may have the pleasure of continuing to appear in the opinion of some, what they are conscious not to be in reality. Thus sagacious moralists draw men like angels, in hopes that the pride at least of some will put 'em upon copying after the beautiful originals which they are represented to be.

When the incomparable Sir Richard Steele, in the usual elegance of his easy style, dwells on the praises of his sublime species, and with all the embellishments of rhetoric sets forth the excellency of human nature, it is impossible not to be charmed with his happy turns of thought, and the politeness of his expressions. But tho' I have been often moved by the force of his eloquence, and ready to swallow the ingenious sophistry with pleasure, yet I could never be so serious, but reflecting on his artful encomiums I thought on the tricks made use of by the women that would teach children to be mannerly. When an awkward girl, before she can either speak or go, begins after many entreaties to make the first rude essays of curt'sying, the nurse falls in an ecstasy of praise; *There's a delicate curt'sy! O fine Miss! There's a pretty lady! Mama! Miss can make a better curt'sy than her sister Molly!* The same is echoed over by the maids, whilst Mama almost hugs the child to pieces; only Miss Molly, who being four years older knows how to make a very handsome curt'sy, wonders at the perverseness of their judgment, and swelling with indignation, is ready to cry at the injustice that is done her, till, being whispered in the ear that it is only to please the baby, and that she is a woman, she grows proud at being let into the secret, and rejoicing at the superiority of her understanding, repeats what has been said with large additions, and insults over the weakness of her sister, whom all this while she fancies to be the only bubble among them. These extravagant praises would by any one, above the capacity of an infant, be called fulsome flatteries, and, if you will, abominable lies, yet experience teaches us, that by the help of such gross encomiums, young misses will be brought to make pretty curt'sies, and behave themselves womanly much sooner, and with less trouble, than they would without them. 'Tis the same with boys, whom they'll strive to persuade, that all fine gentlemen do as they are bid, and that none but beggar boys are rude, or dirty their clothes; nay, as soon as the wild brat with his untaught fist begins to fumble for his hat, the mother, to make him pull it off, tells him before he is two years old, that he is a man; and if he repeats that action when she desires him, he's presently a captain, a Lord Mayor, a King, or something higher if she can think of it, till egged on by the force of praise, the little urchin endeavours to imitate man as well as he can, and strains all his faculties to appear what his shallow noddle imagines he is believed to be.

The meanest wretch puts an ines-timable value upon himself, and the highest wish of the ambitious man is to have all the world, as to that particular, of his opinion: so that the most insatiable thirst after fame that ever hero was inspired with, was never more than an ungovernable greediness to engross the esteem and admiration of others in future ages as well as his own; and (what mortification soever this truth might be to the second thoughts of an Alexander or a Cæsar) the great recompence in view, for which the most exalted minds have with so much alacrity sacrificed their quiet, health, sensual pleasures, and every inch of themselves, has never been any thing else but the breath of man, the aerial coin of praise. Who can forbear laughing when he thinks on all the great men that have been so serious on the subject of that Macedonian madman, his capacious soul, that mighty heart, in one corner of which, according to Lorenzo Gratian, the world was so commodiously lodged, that in the whole there was room for six more? Who can forbear laughing, I say, when he compares the fine things that have been said of Alexander, with the end he proposed to himself from his vast exploits, to be proved from his own mouth; when the vast pains he took to pass the Hydaspes forced him to cry out, *Oh ye Athenians, could you believe what dangers I expose my self to, to be praised by you!* To define then the reward of glory in the amplest manner, the most that can be said of it, is, that it consists in a superlative felicity which a man, who is conscious of having performed a noble action, enjoys in self-love, whilst he is thinking on the applause he expects of others.

But here I shall be told, that besides the noisy toils of war and public bustle of the ambitious, there are noble and generous actions that are performed in silence; that virtue being its own reward, those who are really good have a satisfaction in their consciousness of being so, which is all the recompence they expect from the most worthy performances; that among the heathens there have been men, who, when they did good to others, were so far from coveting thanks and applause, that they took all imaginable care to be for ever concealed from those on whom they bestowed their benefits, and consequently that pride has no hand in spurring man on to the highest pitch of self-denial.

In answer to this I say, that it is impossible to judge of a man's performance, unless we are thoroughly acquainted with the principle and motive from which he acts. Pity, tho' it is the most gentle and the least mischievous of all our passions, is yet as much a frailty of our nature, as anger, pride, or fear. The weakest minds have generally the greatest share of it, for which reason none are more compassionate than women and children. It must be owned, that of all our weaknesses it is the most amiable, and bears the greatest resemblance to virtue; nay, without a considerable mixture of it the society could hardly subsist: but as it is an impulse of nature, that consults neither the public interest nor our own reason, it may produce evil as well as good. It has helped to destroy the honour of virgins, and corrupted the integrity of judges; and whoever acts from it as a principle, what good soever he may bring to the society, has nothing to boast of but that he has indulged a passion that has happened to be beneficial to the public. There is no merit in saving an innocent babe ready to drop into the fire: the action is neither good nor bad, and what benefit soever the infant received, we only obliged ourselves; for to have seen it fall, and not strove to hinder it, would have caused a pain, which

self-preservation compelled us to prevent: nor has a rich prodigal, that happens to be of a commiserating temper, and loves to gratify his passions, greater virtue to boast of when he relieves an object of compassion with what to himself is a trifle.

But such men, as without complying with any weakness of their own, can part from what they value themselves, and, from no other motive but their love to goodness, perform a worthy action in silence: such men, I confess, have acquired more refined notions of virtue than those I have hitherto spoke of; yet even in these (with which the world has yet never swarmed) we may discover no small symptoms of pride, and the humblest man alive must confess, that the reward of a virtuous action, which is the satisfaction that ensues upon it, consists in a certain pleasure he procures to himself by contemplating on his own worth: which pleasure, together with the occasion of it, are as certain signs of pride, as looking pale and trembling at any imminent danger, are the symptoms of fear.

If the too scrupulous reader should at first view condemn these notions concerning the origin of moral virtue, and think them perhaps offensive to Christianity, I hope he'll forbear his censures, when he shall consider, that nothing can render the unsearchable depth of the Divine Wisdom more conspicuous, than that *Man*, whom Providence had designed for Society, should not only by his own frailties and imperfections be led into the road to temporal happiness, but likewise receive, from a seeming necessity of natural causes, a tincture of that knowledge, in which he was afterwards to be made perfect by the True Religion, to his eternal welfare.

ALEXANDER POPE (1688-1744)

A poet of our own day of very considerable reputation for fine technique has recently written of Pope that he is, "in his two finest poems, perhaps the most flawless artist out race has yet produced." (Edith Sitwell, *Alexander Pope*, London, 1930.) And indeed his poetry is well calculated not only to win the respect but repay the study of our contemporary poets with their renewed concern for perfection of texture, for nicety in timing, for the fine tempering of assonance with dissonance. Pope had inherited from the seventeenth century an artistic conscience which became more and more exigent as his powers developed, and in the end outstripped that of his great predecessor and model, Dryden. It is gratifying to find some of the appreciation for his beauty of texture, which was so generously awarded him in his own day, coming back to him in ours.

Many of the episodes of Pope's literary career are so entangled in controversy that there is very little of it that can be told briefly, although the main outlines of his life are very simple. Born in 1688 of middle-aged Catholic parents, he went through life with two handicaps, a weak constitution and the very considerable civil restrictions to which Catholics were then subjected. It is probable that the world has been a gainer by at least the second handicap, for of necessity Pope was more purely the literary artist and less the political tool and controversialist than many of his contemporaries. In fact he remained through life free from patronage of any sort, being one of the first writers to earn a very respectable income from his published works. After a somewhat desultory education at various Catholic schools Pope moved with his family to Binfield near Windsor Forest in 1700. There followed some of the happiest years of his life, when, as he told Spence, "I took to reading by myself, for which I had a very great eagerness and enthusiasm, especially for poetry: and in a few years I had dipped into a great number of the English, French, Italian, Latin, and Greek poets. This I did without any design, but that of pleasing myself: and got the languages, by hunting after the stories in the several poets I read; rather than read the books to get the languages." The Binfield years saw the composition also of such important early works as the *Essay on Criticism* and *The Rape of the Lock*. The family remained at Binfield until 1716 when there was a threatened increase in the already heavy taxes levied on Catholics, and Pope's father felt obliged to give up his house. In order to better the family's financial state, Pope had already begun his translation of Homer. This undertaking gave him a large enough income so that after several years at Chiswick he was able to buy a small estate at Twickenham on the Thames. There he remained to his death in 1744, a gracious host to many distinguished guests.

Very early in the Binfield period, Pope says when he was sixteen, he composed his *Pastorals* and thereby won the attention and friendship of such men as Walsh, Wycherley, Congreve, and Betterton. The poet Walsh seems to have been particularly helpful to Pope in forming his literary standards. These first friends were much older than Pope and most of them passed out of his life fairly early, but he never lacked for close friends. Although he is perhaps more popularly known by his literary quarrels than by his friendships, he seems to have had an especial gift for friendship and numbered many of the most notable people of the period among his devoted admirers. Perhaps the shortest-lived friendship was that with Addison and his group at Button's Coffee-house, which had definitely cooled as early as 1715 for reasons too complex to go into here. But for the Tory group with which Pope became intimate about this same time—Swift, Arbuthnot, Gay, Parnell, Bolingbroke, and others who formed the Scriblerus Club—there was no cooling in affection to the end of his life. Not only were these men united by common political leanings but by a common attitude toward their world, an attitude characterized by Dr. Arbuthnot, the moving spirit of the Scriblerus Club, as a "disdain and abhorrence of vice," but a disdain which expressed itself in gay and witty satire rather than in Jeremiads. One has only to consider the three works which were being produced under Pope's roof at Twickenham in the summer of 1726 to appreciate the harmony of purpose in the group: Pope was writing his *Dunciad*, Gay his *Beggar's Opera*, and Swift was seeing *Gulliver's Travels* through the press. The spirit of much of their less serious writing was well expressed by Pope in his letter to Swift on the publication of one of Pope's and Swift's joint miscellanies: "I am prodigiously pleased with this joint volume, in which, methinks, we look like friends side by side, serious and merry by turns, conversing interchangeably, and walking down hand in hand to posterity, not in the stiff forms of learned authors, flattering each other, and setting the rest of mankind at naught, but in a free, unimportant, natural, easy manner, diverting others just as we diverted ourselves." (March 8, 1727) But behind this gaiety lurked a serious purpose. "I know nothing that moves strongly but satire," wrote Pope in another letter, "and those who are ashamed of nothing else, are so of being ridiculous. I fancy, if we three [Swift, Bolingbroke, and Pope] were together but for three years, some good might be done even upon this age." ([April, 1732])

Pope's literary career falls into three periods. The first period includes the early descriptive poetry, the *Pastorals*, 1709, and *Windsor Forest*, 1713; the *Essay on Criticism*, 1711; *The Rape of the Lock*, 1714; and the prose essays which Pope contributed to *The Guardian* in 1713 and 1714. This period may be said to end with the first collected edition of his poems in 1717, in which appeared for the first time the *Elegy to the Memory of an Unfortunate Lady* and *Eloisa to Abelard*. Four years before, however, the second period of translation and editing had really begun with the first work on the translation of Homer in 1713. For a number of years Pope did very little else but work on his translation of Homer and his edition of Shakespeare. The latter was finished in 1725 and the former in 1726, and Pope was at last free to turn his hand to other things.

The last period began with Pope's most savage satire, *The Dunciad*, 1728-1743, in which Pope paid off his enemies for attacks that had been going on for years on his poetry, his person, his family, and finally his *Odyssey* and *Shakespeare*. And satire, as seen further in his *Imitations of Horace* and various epistles, is perhaps the dominant note throughout this final period, but in the thirties a graver note is struck, probably through the influence of Bolingbroke. Pope wrote to Swift, "You call your satires, libels: I would call my satires, epistles. They will consist more of morality than of wit, and grow graver, which you will call duller. I shall leave it to my antagonists to be witty, if they can, and content myself to be useful, and in the right." (April 2, 1733) And again, "I have only one piece of mercy to beg of you; do not laugh at my gravity, but permit me to wear the beard of a philosopher, till I pull it off, and make a jest of it myself." (Sept. 15, 1734) These were the years of the *Essay on Man*, 1733-1734, which was designed as the first part of a much larger work on morality and government, the only other parts of which to be realized were the *Moral Essays*, 1731-1735. A more particular account of the circumstances of the writing of these various poems will be found in the notes.

The first complete edition of Pope's works to incorporate his latest revisions was that published by Warburton in 1751. The Elwin and Courthope edition, London, 1871-1889, in ten volumes, is the nearest to an authentic and complete modern edition but it is far from satisfactory. An excellent small edition called *The Best of Pope*, edited by George Sherburn, 1931, is valuable for its introduction and notes. Early biographical material is to be found in Giles Jacob, *Historical Account of the Lives and Writings of Our Most Considerable English Poets*, 1720; Theophilus Cibber, *The Lives of the Poets of Great Britain and Ireland to the Time of Swift*, 1753; Dr. Johnson, *Lives of the Poets*, 1781; and Joseph Spence, *Anecdotes, Observations, and Characters of Books and Men, Collected from the Conversation of Mr. Pope, and Other Eminent Persons of his Time*, edited by S. W. Singer, 1820. There are however so many disputed points in Pope's life that the student had best consult the only really judicious and authentic biography which has yet come out, George Sherburn's *The Early Career of Alexander Pope*, Oxford, 1934, and R. H. Griffith, *Alexander Pope. A Bibliography*, Austin, Texas, 1922, 1927. Edith Sitwell's *Alexander Pope*, London, 1930, Chapter XVIII, is a stimulating appreciation of the poetry. Articles helpful in the interpretation of the poems have been suggested in the notes in connection with the individual poems.

For additional readings in Pope see pages 1131-1141.

SUMMER:

THE SECOND PASTORAL, OR ALEXIS

To Dr. Garth

A Shepherd's Boy (he seeks no better name)
Led forth his flocks along the silver Thame,
Where dancing sunbeams on the waters
    played,
And verdant alders formed a quivering
    shade.
Soft as he mourned, the streams forgot to
    flow,
The flocks around a dumb compassion show,
The Naiads wept in every watery bower,
And Jove consented in a silent shower.

  Accept, O Garth, the muse's early lays,
That adds this wreath of ivy to thy bays;   10
Hear what from love unpractised hearts en-
    dure,
From love, the sole disease thou canst not
    cure.

  "Ye shady beeches, and ye cooling streams,
Defence from Phœbus', not from Cupid's
    beams,
To you I mourn, nor to the deaf I sing,
The woods shall answer, and their echo ring.
The hills and rocks attend my doleful lay,
Why art thou prouder and more hard than
    they?
The bleating sheep with my complaints
    agree,
They parched with heat, and I inflamed by
    thee.   20
The sultry Sirius burns the thirsty plains,
While in thy heart eternal winter reigns.

  "Where stray ye, muses, in what lawn or
    grove,
While your Alexis pines in hopeless love?
In those fair fields where sacred Isis glides,
Or else where Cam his winding vales divides?
As in the crystal spring I view my face,
Fresh rising blushes paint the watery glass;
But since those graces please thy eyes no
    more,   29
I shun the fountains which I sought before.
Once I was skilled in every herb that grew,
And every plant that drinks the morning
    dew;
Ah, wretched shepherd, what avails thy art,
To cure thy lambs, but not to heal thy heart!

  "Let other swains attend the rural care,
Feed fairer flocks, or richer fleeces shear:

But nigh yon mountain let me tune my lays,
Embrace my love, and bind my brows with
    bays.
That flute is mine which Colin's tuneful
    breath
Inspired when living, and bequeathed in
    death;   40
He said, 'Alexis, take this pipe, the same
That taught the groves my Rosalinda's
    name.'
But now the reeds shall hang on yonder tree,
Forever silent, since despised by thee.
Oh! were I made by some transforming
    power
The captive bird that sings within thy bower!
Then might my voice thy listening ears em-
    ploy,
And I those kisses he receives, enjoy.

  "And yet my numbers please the rural
    throng,
Rough satyrs dance, and Pan applauds the
    song: 50
The nymphs, forsaking every cave and
    spring,
Their early fruit, and milk-white turtles
    bring;
Each amorous nymph prefers her gifts in
    vain,
On you their gifts are all bestowed again.
For you the swains the fairest flowers design,
And in one garland all their beauties join;
Accept the wreath which you deserve alone,
In whom all beauties are comprised in one.

  "See what delights in sylvan scenes ap-
    pear!   59
Descending gods have found Elysium here.
In woods bright Venus with Adonis strayed,
And chaste Diana haunts the forest shade.
Come, lovely nymph, and bless the silent
    hours,
When swains from shearing seek their
    nightly bowers,
When weary reapers quit the sultry field,
And crowned with corn their thanks to Ceres
    yield.
This harmless grove no lurking viper hides,
But in my breast the serpent love abides.
Here bees from blossoms sip the rosy dew,
But your Alexis knows no sweets but you.   70
Oh, deign to visit our forsaken seats,
The mossy fountains, and the green retreats!
Where'er you walk, cool gales shall fan the
    glade;

Trees, where you sit, shall crowd into a
    shade;
Where'er you tread, the blushing flowers
    shall rise,
And all things flourish where you turn your
    eyes.
Oh, how I long with you to pass my days,
Invoke the muses, and resound your praise!
Your praise the birds shall chant in every
    grove,
And winds shall waft it to the powers above,
But would you sing, and rival Orpheus'
    strain,   81
The wondering forests soon should dance
    again;
The moving mountains hear the powerful
    call,
And headlong streams hang glistening in
    their fall!
"But see, the shepherds shun the noonday
    heat;
The lowing herds to murmuring brooks re-
    treat;
To closer shades the panting flocks remove;
Ye Gods! and is there no relief for love?
But soon the sun with milder rays descends
To the cool ocean, where his journey ends: 90
On me love's fiercer flames for ever prey,
By night he scorches, as he burns by day."

                [1704? 1709]

AN ESSAY ON CRITICISM

PART I

'Tis hard to say if greater want of skill
Appear in writing or in judging ill;
But, of the two, less dangerous is the offence
To tire our patience, than mislead our sense.
Some few in that, but numbers err in this;
Ten censure wrong for one who writes amiss;
A fool might once himself alone expose;
Now one in verse makes many more in prose.
'Tis with our judgments as our watches:
    none
Go just alike, yet each believes his own.   10
In poets as true genius is but rare,
True taste as seldom is the critic's share;
Both must alike from heaven derive their
    light,
These born to judge, as well as those to write.
Let such teach others who themselves excel,

And censure freely who have written well.
Authors are partial to their wit, 'tis true,
But are not critics to their judgment too?
  Yet if we look more closely, we shall find
Most have the seeds of judgment in their
    mind: 20
Nature affords at least a glimmering light;
The lines, though touched but faintly, are
    drawn right.
But as the slightest sketch, if justly traced,
Is by ill-colouring but the more disgraced,
So by false learning is good sense defaced:
Some are bewildered in the maze of schools,
And some made coxcombs nature meant but
    fools.
In search of wit these lose their common
    sense,
And then turn critics in their own defence:
Each burns alike, who can, or cannot write,
Or with a rival's, or an eunuch's spite.   31
All fools have still an itching to deride,
And fain would be upon the laughing side.
If Mævius scribble in Apollo's spite,
There are who judge still worse than he can
    write.
  Some have at first for wits, then poets
    passed,
Turned critics next, and proved plain fools
    at last.
Some neither can for wits nor critics pass,
As heavy mules are neither horse nor ass.
Those half-learned witlings, numerous in
    our isle,   40
As half-formed insects on the banks of Nile;
Unfinished things, one knows not what to
    call,
Their generation's so equivocal;
To tell 'em would a hundred tongues re-
    quire,
Or one vain wit's, that might a hundred tire.
  But you who seek to give and merit fame,
And justly bear a critic's noble name,
Be sure yourself and your own reach to know,
How far your genius, taste, and learning go;
Launch not beyond your depth, but be dis-
    creet,   50
And mark that point where sense and dul-
    ness meet.
  Nature to all things fixed the limits fit,
And wisely curbed proud man's pretending
    wit.
As on the land while here the ocean gains,
In other parts it leaves wide sandy plains;
Thus in the soul while memory prevails,

The solid power of understanding fails;
Where beams of warm imagination play,
The memory's soft figures melt away.
One science only will one genius fit;   60
So vast is art, so narrow human wit—
Not only bounded to peculiar arts,
But oft in those confined to single parts.
Like kings we lose the conquests gained before,
By vain ambition still to make them more;
Each might his several province well command,
Would all but stoop to what they understand.
    First follow nature, and your judgment frame
By her just standard, which is still the same:
Unerring nature, still divinely bright,   70
One clear, unchanged, and universal light,
Life, force, and beauty, must to all impart,
At once the source, and end, and test of art.
Art from that fund each just supply provides,
Works without show, and without pomp presides;
In some fair body thus the informing soul
With spirits feeds, with vigour fills the whole,
Each motion guides, and every nerve sustains;
Itself unseen, but in the effects remains.
Some, to whom Heaven in wit has been profuse,   80
Want as much more, to turn it to its use;
For wit and judgment often are at strife,
Though meant each other's aid, like man and wife
'Tis more to guide, than spur the muse's steed,
Restrain his fury, than provoke his speed;
The wingèd courser, like a generous horse,
Shows most true mettle when you check his course.
    Those rules of old discovered, not devised,
Are nature still, but nature methodised;
Nature, like liberty, is but restrained   90
By the same laws which first herself ordained.
    Hear how learned Greece her useful rules indites,
When to repress, and when indulge our flights:
High on Parnassus' top her sons she showed,
And pointed out those arduous paths they trod;
Held from afar, aloft, the immortal prize,
And urged the rest by equal steps to rise.

Just precepts thus from great examples given,
She drew from them what they derived from heaven.   99
The generous critic fanned the poet's fire,
And taught the world with reason to admire.
Then criticism the muses' handmaid proved,
To dress her charms, and make her more beloved:
But following wits from that intention strayed;
Who could not win the mistress, wooed the maid;
Against the poets their own arms they turned,
Sure to hate most the men from whom they learned.
So modern 'pothecaries, taught the art
By doctor's bills to play the doctor's part,
Bold in the practice of mistaken rules,   110
Prescribe, apply, and call their masters fools.
Some on the leaves of ancient authors prey,
Nor time nor moths e'er spoiled so much as they.
Some dryly plain, without invention's aid,
Write dull receipts how poems may be made.
These leave the sense, their learning to display,
And those explain the meaning quite away.
    You then whose judgment the right course would steer,
Know well each ancient's proper character;
His fable, subject, scope in every page;   120
Religion, country, genius of his age:
Without all these at once before your eyes,
Cavil you may, but never criticise.
Be Homer's works your study and delight,
Read them by day, and meditate by night;
Thence form your judgment, thence your maxims bring,
And trace the muses upward to their spring.
Still with itself compared, his text peruse,
And let your comment be the Mantuan muse.
    When first young Maro in his boundless mind   130
A work to outlast immortal Rome designed,
Perhaps he seemed above the critic's law,
And but from nature's fountains scorned to draw;
But when to examine every part he came,
Nature and Homer were, he found, the same.
Convinced, amazed, he checks the bold design;
And rules as strict his laboured work confine,

As if the Stagirite o'erlooked each line.
Learn hence for ancient rules a just esteem;
To copy nature is to copy them. 140
  Some beauties yet no precepts can declare,
For there's a happiness as well as care.
Music resembles poetry, in each
Are nameless graces which no methods teach,
And which a master-hand alone can reach.
If, where the rules not far enough extend,
(Since rules were made but to promote their
    end)
Some lucky licence answer to the full
The intent proposed, that licence is a rule.
Thus Pegasus, a nearer way to take, 150
May boldly deviate from the common track;
From vulgar bounds with brave disorder
    part,
And snatch a grace beyond the reach of art,
Which without passing through the judg-
    ment, gains
The heart, and all its end at once attains.
In prospects thus, some objects please our
    eyes,
Which out of nature's common order rise,
The shapeless rock, or hanging precipice.
Great wits sometimes may gloriously offend,
And rise to faults true critics dare not
    mend. 160
But though the ancients thus their rules in-
    vade,
(As kings dispense with laws themselves have
    made)
Moderns, beware! or if you must offend
Against the precept, ne'er transgress its end;
Let it be seldom, and compelled by need;
And have, at least, their precedent to plead.
The critic else proceeds without remorse,
Seizes your fame, and puts his laws in force.
  I know there are, to whose presumptuous
    thoughts
Those freer beauties, even in them, seem
    faults. 179
Some figures monstrous and mis-shaped ap-
    pear,
Considered singly, or beheld too near,
Which, but proportioned to their light, or
    place,
Due distance reconciles to form and grace.
A prudent chief not always must display
His powers in equal ranks, and fair array,
But with the occasion and the place comply,
Conceal his force, nay seem sometimes to fly.
Those oft are stratagems which error seem,
Nor is it Homer nods, but we that dream. 180

Still green with bays each ancient altar
    stands,
Above the reach of sacrilegious hands,
Secure from flames, from envy's fiercer rage,
Destructive war, and all-involving age.
See, from each clime the learned their in-
    cense bring!
Hear, in all tongues consenting pæans ring!
In praise so just let every voice be joined,
And fill the general chorus of mankind.
Hail, bards triumphant! born in happier
    days,
Immortal heirs of universal praise! 190
Whose honours with increase of ages grow,
As streams roll down, enlarging as they flow;
Nations unborn your mighty names shall
    sound,
And worlds applaud that must not yet be
    found!
Oh, may some spark of your celestial fire,
The last, the meanest of your sons inspire,
(That on weak wings, from far, pursues your
    flights;
Glows while he reads, but trembles as he
    writes)
To teach vain wits a science little known,
To admire superior sense, and doubt their
    own! 200

PART II

Of all the causes which conspire to blind
Man's erring judgment, and misguide the
    mind,
What the weak head with strongest bias rules
Is pride, the never-failing vice of fools.
Whatever nature has in worth denied,
She gives in large recruits of needful pride;
For as in bodies, thus in souls, we find
What wants in blood and spirits, swelled
    with wind:
Pride, where wit fails, steps in to our defence,
And fills up all the mighty void of sense. 210
If once right reason drives that cloud away,
Truth breaks upon us with resistless day.
Trust not yourself; but your defects to know
Make use of every friend—and every foe.
  A little learning is a dangerous thing;
Drink deep, or taste not the Pierian spring:
There shallow draughts intoxicate the brain,
And drinking largely sobers us again.
Fired at first sight with what the muse im-
    parts,

In fearless youth we tempt the heights of
  arts,   220
While from the bounded level of our mind
Short views we take, nor see the lengths be-
  hind;
But more advanced, behold with strange sur-
  prise
New distant scenes of endless science rise!
So pleased at first the towering Alps we try,
Mount o'er the vales, and seem to tread the
  sky;
The eternal snows appear already past,
And the first clouds and mountains seem the
  last;
But, those attained, we tremble to survey
The growing labours of the lengthened way;
The increasing prospect tires our wandering
  eyes,   231
Hills peep o'er hills, and Alps on Alps arise!
  A perfect judge will read each work of wit
With the same spirit that its author writ:
Survey the whole, nor seek slight faults to
  find
Where nature moves, and rapture warms the
  mind;
Nor lose, for that malignant dull delight,
The generous pleasure to be charmed with
  wit.
But in such lays as neither ebb, nor flow,
Correctly cold, and regularly low,   240
That shunning faults, one quiet tenour keep,
We cannot blame indeed——but we may
  sleep.
In wit, as nature, what affects our hearts
Is not the exactness of peculiar parts;
'Tis not a lip, or eye, we beauty call,
But the joint force and full result of all.
Thus when we view some well-proportioned
  dome,
(The world's just wonder, and even thine,
  O Rome!)
No single parts unequally surprise,
All comes united to the admiring eyes;   250
No monstrous height, or breadth, or length
  appear;
The whole at once is bold, and regular.
  Whoever thinks a faultless piece to see,
Thinks what ne'er was, nor is, nor e'er shall
  be.
In every work regard the writer's end,
Since none can compass more than they in-
  tend;
And if the means be just, the conduct true,
Applause, in spite of trivial faults, is due;

As men of breeding, sometimes men of wit,
To avoid great errors, must the less commit:
Neglect the rules each verbal critic lays,   261
For not to know some trifles, is a praise.
Most critics, fond of some subservient art,
Still make the whole depend upon a part;
They talk of principles, but notions prize,
And all to one loved folly sacrifice.
  Once on a time, La Mancha's knight, they
  say,
A certain bard encountering on the way,
Discoursed in terms as just, with looks as
  sage,
As e'er could Dennis of the Grecian stage;   270
Concluding all were desperate sots and fools,
Who durst depart from Aristotle's rules.
Our author, happy in a judge so nice,
Produced his play, and begged the knight's
  advice;
Made him observe the subject, and the plot,
The manners, passions, unities—what not?
All which, exact to rule, were brought about,
Were but a combat in the lists left out.
"What! leave the combat out?" exclaims the
  knight;
"Yes, or we must renounce the Stagirite."   280
"Not so by Heaven," he answers in a rage,
"Knights, squires, and steeds, must enter on
  the stage."
"So vast a throng the stage can ne'er con-
  tain."
"Then build a new, or act it in a plain."
  Thus critics, of less judgment than caprice,
Curious not knowing, not exact but nice,
Form short ideas, and offend in arts
(As most in manners) by a love to parts.
  Some to conceit alone their taste confine,
And glittering thoughts struck out at every
  line;   290
Pleased with a work where nothing's just or
  fit,
One glaring chaos and wild heap of wit.
Poets like painters, thus, unskilled to trace
The naked nature and the living grace,
With gold and jewels cover every part,
And hide with ornaments their want of art.
True wit is nature to advantage dressed,
What oft was thought, but ne'er so well ex-
  pressed;
Something, whose truth convinced at sight
  we find,
That gives us back the image of our mind.   300
As shades more sweetly recommend the light,
So modest plainness sets off sprightly wit;

For works may have more wit than does 'em
    good,
As bodies perish through excess of blood.
    Others for language all their care express,
And value books, as women men, for dress:
Their praise is still,—the style is excellent:
The sense, they humbly take upon content.
Words are like leaves; and where they most
    abound,
Much fruit of sense beneath is rarely found:
False eloquence, like the prismatic glass, 311
Its gaudy colours spreads on every place;
The face of nature we no more survey,
All glares alike, without distinction gay:
But true expression, like the unchanging
    sun,
Clears and improves whate'er it shines upon;
It gilds all objects, but it alters none.
Expression is the dress of thought, and still
Appears more decent as more suitable;
A vile conceit in pompous words expressed,
Is like a clown in regal purple dressed: 321
For different styles with different subjects
    sort,
As several garbs with country, town, and
    court.
Some by old words to fame have made pre-
    tence,
Ancients in phrase, mere moderns in their
    sense;
Such laboured nothings, in so strange a style,
Amaze the unlearned, and make the learned
    smile.
Unlucky, as Fungoso in the play,
These sparks with awkward vanity display
What the fine gentleman wore yesterday; 330
And but so mimic ancient wits at best,
As apes our grandsires, in their doublets
    dressed.
In words as fashions the same rule will hold;
Alike fantastic if too new or old:
Be not the first by whom the new are tried,
Nor yet the last to lay the old aside.
    But most by numbers judge a poet's song;
And smooth or rough with them is right or
    wrong:
In the bright muse though thousand charms
    conspire,
Her voice is all these tuneful fools admire,
Who haunt Parnassus but to please their
    ear,   341
Not mend their minds; as some to church
    repair,
Not for the doctrine, but the music there.

These equal syllables alone require,
Though oft the ear the open vowels tire;
While expletives their feeble aid do join,
And ten low words oft creep in one dull line:
While they ring round the same unvaried
    chimes,
With sure returns of still expected rhymes;
Where'er you find "the cooling western
    breeze,"   350
In the next line, it "whispers through the
    trees";
If crystal streams "with pleasing murmurs
    creep,"
The reader's threatened (not in vain) with
    "sleep";
Then, at the last and only couplet fraught
With some unmeaning thing they call a
    thought,
A needless Alexandrine ends the song
That, like a wounded snake, drags its slow
    length along.
Leave such to tune their own dull rhymes,
    and know
What's roundly smooth or languishingly
    slow;
And praise the easy vigour of a line,   360
Where Denham's strength and Waller's
    sweetness join.
True ease in writing comes from art, not
    chance,
As those move easiest who have learned to
    dance.
'Tis not enough no harshness gives offence;
The sound must seem an echo to the sense:
Soft is the strain when Zephyr gently blows,
And the smooth stream in smoother numbers
    flows;
But when loud surges lash the sounding
    shore,
The hoarse, rough verse should like the tor-
    rent roar:
When Ajax strives some rock's vast weight to
    throw,   370
The line too labours, and the words move
    slow;
Not so, when swift Camilla scours the plain,
Flies o'er the unbending corn, and skims
    along the main.
Hear how Timotheus' varied lays surprise,
And bid alternate passions fall and rise!
While, at each change, the son of Libyan
    Jove
Now burns with glory, and then melts with
    love,

Now his fierce eyes with sparkling fury glow,
Now sighs steal out, and tears begin to flow:
Persians and Greeks like turns of nature found, 380
And the world's victor stood subdued by sound!
The power of music all our hearts allow,
And what Timotheus was, is Dryden now.
   Avoid extremes, and shun the fault of such,
Who still are pleased too little or too much.
At every trifle scorn to take offence;
That always shows great pride or little sense;
Those heads, as stomachs, are not sure the best,
Which nauseate all, and nothing can digest.
Yet let not each gay turn thy rapture move;
For fools admire, but men of sense approve:
As things seem large which we through mists descry, 392
Dulness is ever apt to magnify.
   Some foreign writers, some our own despise;
The ancients only, or the moderns prize.
Thus wit, like faith, by each man is applied
To one small sect, and all are damned beside.
Meanly they seek the blessing to confine,
And force that sun but on a part to shine,
Which not alone the southern wit sublimes,
But ripens spirits in cold northern climes; 401
Which from the first has shone on ages past,
Enlights the present, and shall warm the last;
Though each may feel increases and decays,
And see now clearer and now darker days.
Regard not then if wit be old or new,
But blame the false, and value still the true.
   Some ne'er advance a judgment of their own,
But catch the spreading notion of the town;
They reason and conclude by precedent, 410
And own stale nonsense which they ne'er invent.
Some judge of authors' names, not works, and then
Nor praise nor blame the writings, but the men.
Of all this servile herd the worst is he
That in proud dulness joins with quality;
A constant critic at the great man's board,
To fetch and carry nonsense for my lord.
What woeful stuff this madrigal would be,
In some starved hackney sonneteer, or me?
But let a lord once own the happy lines, 420
How the wit brightens! how the style refines!

Before his sacred name flies every fault,
And each exalted stanza teems with thought!
   The vulgar thus through imitation err;
As oft the learned by being singular;
So much they scorn the crowd, that if the throng
By chance go right, they purposely go wrong;
So schismatics the plain believers quit,
And are but damned for having too much wit.
Some praise at morning what they blame at night, 430
But always think the last opinion right.
A muse by these is like a mistress used,
This hour she's idolised, the next abused;
While their weak heads, like towns unfortified,
'Twixt sense and nonsense daily change their side.
Ask them the cause; they're wiser still, they say;
And still to-morrow's wiser than to-day.
We think our fathers fools, so wise we grow;
Our wiser sons, no doubt, will think us so.
Once school-divines this zealous isle o'erspread; 440
Who knew most sentences, was deepest read;
Faith, gospel, all, seemed made to be disputed,
And none had sense enough to be confuted:
Scotists and Thomists now in peace remain,
Amidst their kindred cobwebs in Duck Lane.
If faith itself has different dresses worn,
What wonder modes in wit should take their turn?
Oft, leaving what is natural and fit,
The current folly proves the ready wit;
And authors think their reputation safe, 450
Which lives as long as fools are pleased to laugh.
   Some, valuing those of their own side or mind,
Still make themselves the measure of mankind:
Fondly we think we honour merit then,
When we but praise ourselves in other men.
Parties in wit attend on those of state,
And public faction doubles private hate.
Pride, Malice, Folly, against Dryden rose,
In various shapes of parsons, critics, beaux;
But sense survived, when merry jests were past; 460
For rising merit will buoy up at last.

Might he return, and bless once more our
eyes,
New Blackmores and new Milbournes must
arise:
Nay, should great Homer lift his awful head,
Zoilus again would start up from the dead.
Envy will merit, as its shade, pursue;
But like a shadow, proves the substance true;
For envied wit, like Sol eclipsed, makes
known
The opposing body's grossness, not its own.
When first that sun too powerful beams dis-
plays,   470
It draws up vapours which obscure its rays;
But even those clouds at last adorn its way,
Reflect new glories, and augment the day.

Be thou the first true merit to befriend;
His praise is lost who stays till all commend.
Short is the date, alas, of modern rhymes,
And 'tis but just to let them live betimes.
No longer now that golden age appears,
When patriarch wits survived a thousand
years:
Now length of fame (our second life) is lost,
And bare threescore is all even that can
boast;   481
Our sons their fathers' failing language see,
And such as Chaucer is, shall Dryden be.
So when the faithful pencil has designed
Some bright idea of the master's mind,
Where a new world leaps out at his com-
mand,
And ready nature waits upon his hand;
When the ripe colours soften and unite,
And sweetly melt into just shade and light;
When mellowing years their full perfection
give,   490
And each bold figure just begins to live,
The treacherous colours the fair art betray,
And all the bright creation fades away!

Unhappy wit, like most mistaken things,
Atones not for that envy which it brings.
In youth alone its empty praise we boast,
But soon the short-lived vanity is lost:
Like some fair flower the early spring sup-
plies,
That gaily blooms, but even in blooming
dies.
What is this wit, which must our cares em-
ploy?   500
The owner's wife, that other men enjoy;
Then most our trouble still when most ad-
mired,

And still the more we give, the more re-
quired;
Whose fame with pains we guard, but lose
with ease,
Sure some to vex, but never all to please;
'Tis what the vicious fear, the virtuous shun;
By fools 'tis hated, and by knaves undone!

If wit so much from ignorance undergo,
Ah let not learning too commence its foe!
Of old, those met rewards who could excel,
And such were praised who but endeavoured
well;   511
Though triumphs were to generals only due,
Crowns were reserved to grace the soldiers
too.
Now they who reach Parnassus' lofty crown
Employ their pains to spurn some others
down;
And while self-love each jealous writer rules,
Contending wits become the sport of fools;
But still the worst with most regret commend,
For each ill author is as bad a friend.
To what base ends, and by what abject ways,
Are mortals urged through sacred lust of
praise!   521
Ah, ne'er so dire a thirst of glory boast,
Nor in the critic let the man be lost.
Good nature and good sense must ever join;
To err is human; to forgive, divine.

But if in noble minds some dregs remain
Not yet purged off, of spleen and sour dis-
dain,
Discharge that rage on more provoking
crimes,
Nor fear a dearth in these flagitious times.
No pardon vile obscenity should find,   530
Though wit and art conspire to move your
mind;
But dullness with obscenity must prove
As shameful sure as impotence in love.
In the fat age of pleasure, wealth, and ease,
Sprung the rank weed, and thrived with
large increase:
When love was all an easy monarch's care;
Seldom at council, never in a war:
Jilts ruled the state, and statesmen farces
writ;
Nay wits had pensions, and young lords had
wit:
The fair sate panting at a courtier's play, 540
And not a mask went unimproved away:
The modest fan was lifted up no more,
And virgins smiled at what they blushed be-
fore.

The following licence of a foreign reign
Did all the dregs of bold Socinus drain;
Then unbelieving priests reformed the nation,
And taught more pleasant methods of salvation;
Where Heaven's free subjects might their rights dispute,
Lest God himself should seem too absolute:
Pulpits their sacred satire learned to spare,
And vice admired to find a flatterer there!
Encouraged thus, wit's Titans braved the skies,   552
And the press groaned with licensed blasphemies.
These monsters, critics! with your darts engage,
Here point your thunder, and exhaust your rage!
Yet shun their fault, who, scandalously nice,
Will needs mistake an author into vice;
All seems infected that the infected spy,
As all looks yellow to the jaundiced eye.

PART III

  Learn then what morals critics ought to show,   560
For 'tis but half a judge's task, to know.
'Tis not enough, taste, judgment, learning, join;
In all you speak, let truth and candor shine:
That not alone what to your sense is due
All may allow, but seek your friendship too.
  Be silent always when you doubt your sense,
And speak, though sure, with seeming diffidence:
Some positive, persisting fops we know,
Who, if once wrong, will needs be always so;
But you, with pleasure own your errors past,
And make each day a critic on the last.   571
  'Tis not enough, your counsel still be true;
Blunt truths more mischief than nice falsehoods do;
Men must be taught as if you taught them not,
And things unknown proposed as things forgot.
Without good breeding, truth is disapproved;
That only makes superior sense beloved.
  Be niggards of advice on no pretence,
For the worst avarice is that of sense.

With mean complacence ne'er betray your trust,   580
Nor be so civil as to prove unjust.
Fear not the anger of the wise to raise;
Those best can bear reproof, who merit praise.
  'Twere well might critics still this freedom take,
But Appius reddens at each word you speak,
And stares tremendous, with a threatening eye,
Like some fierce tyrant in old tapestry.
Fear most to tax an honourable fool,
Whose right it is, uncensured, to be dull;
Such, without wit, are poets when they please,   590
As without learning they can take degrees.
Leave dangerous truths to unsuccessful satires,
And flattery to fulsome dedicators,
Whom, when they praise, the world believes no more,
Than when they promise to give scribbling o'er.
'Tis best sometimes your censure to restrain,
And charitably let the dull be vain:
Your silence there is better than your spite,
For who can rail so long as they can write?
Still humming on, their drowsy course they keep,   600
And lashed so long, like tops, are lashed asleep.
False steps but help them to renew the race,
As, after stumbling, jades will mend their pace.
What crowds of these, impenitently bold,
In sounds and jingling syllables grown old.
Still run on poets, in a raging vein,
Even to the dregs and squeezings of the brain,
Strain out the last dull droppings of their sense,
And rhyme with all the rage of impotence.
  Such shameless bards we have; and yet 'tis true,   610
There are as mad abandoned critics too.
The bookful blockhead, ignorantly read,
With loads of learned lumber in his head,
With his own tongue still edifies his ears,
And always listening to himself appears.
All books he reads, and all he reads assails,
From Dryden's *Fables* down to Durfey's *Tales.*

With him, most authors steal their works, or
    buy;
Garth did not write his own *Dispensary*.
Name a new play, and he's the poet's friend,
Nay, showed his faults—but when would
    poets mend?   621
No place so sacred from such fops is barred,
Nor is Paul's church more safe than Paul's
    churchyard:
Nay, fly to altars; there they'll talk you dead,
For fools rush in where angels fear to tread.
Distrustful sense with modest caution speaks;
It still looks home, and short excursions
    makes;
But rattling nonsense in full volleys breaks,
And never shocked, and never turned aside,
Bursts out, resistless, with a thundering tide.
    But where's the man who counsel can be-
    stow,   631
Still pleased to teach, and yet not proud to
    know?
Unbiased or by favor or by spite;
Not dully prepossessed nor blindly right;
Though learned, well-bred; and though well-
    bred, sincere;
Modestly bold, and humanly severe:
Who to a friend his faults can freely show,
And gladly praise the merit of a foe?
Blest with a taste exact, yet unconfined;
A knowledge both of books and human kind:
Generous converse; a soul exempt from
    pride;   641
And love to praise, with reason on his side?
    Such once were critics; such the happy few,
Athens and Rome in better ages knew.
The mighty Stagirite first left the shore,
Spread all his sails, and durst the deeps ex-
    plore;
He steered securely, and discovered far,
Led by the light of the Mæonian Star.
Poets, a race long unconfined and free,
Still fond and proud of savage liberty,   650
Received his laws, and stood convinced 'twas
    fit,
Who conquered nature, should preside o'er
    wit.
    Horace still charms with graceful negli-
    gence,
And without method talks us into sense;
Will, like a friend, familiarly convey
The truest notions in the easiest way.
He, who supreme in judgment as in wit,
Might boldly censure as he boldly writ,

Yet judged with coolness, though he sung
    with fire;
His precepts teach but what his works in-
    spire.   660
Our critics take a contrary extreme;
They judge with fury, but they write with
    phlegm:
Nor suffers Horace more in wrong transla-
    tions
By wits, than critics in as wrong quotations
    See Dionysius Homer's thoughts refine,
And call new beauties forth from every line!
Fancy and art in gay Petronius please,
The scholar's learning, with the courtier's
    ease.
    In grave Quintilian's copious work we find
The justest rules and clearest method joined:
Thus useful arms in magazines we place,   671
All ranged in order, and disposed with grace,
But less to please the eye, than arm the hand,
Still fit for use, and ready at command.
    Thee, bold Longinus! all the Nine inspire,
And bless their critic with a poet's fire.
An ardent judge, who zealous in his trust,
With warmth gives sentence, yet is always
    just;   678
Whose own example strengthens all his laws,
And is himself that great sublime he draws.
    Thus long succeeding critics justly reigned,
Licence repressed, and useful laws ordained.
Learning and Rome alike in empire grew,
And arts still followed where her eagles flew;
From the same foes, at last, both felt their
    doom,
And the same age saw learning fall, and
    Rome.
With tyranny, then superstition joined,
As that the body, this enslaved the mind;
Much was believed, but little understood,
And to be dull was construed to be good;   690
A second deluge learning thus o'errun,
And the monks finished what the Goths be-
    gun.
    At length Erasmus, that great injured
    name,
(The glory of the priesthood, and the
    shame!)
Stemmed the wild torrent of a barbarous age,
And drove those holy Vandals off the stage.
    But see! each muse, in Leo's golden days,
Starts from her trance, and trims her with-
    ered bays;
Rome's ancient genius, o'er its ruins spread,

Shakes off the dust, and rears his reverend
    head. 700
Then sculpture and her sister arts revive;
Stones leaped to form, and rocks began to
    live;
With sweeter notes each rising temple rung;
A Raphael painted, and a Vida sung.
Immortal Vida, on whose honoured brow
The poet's bays and critic's ivy grow:
Cremona now shall ever boast thy name,
As next in place to Mantua, next in fame!
    But soon by impious arms from Latium
        chased,
Their ancient bounds the banished muses
    passed; 710
Thence arts o'er all the northern world ad-
    vance,
But critic-learning flourished most in France:
The rules a nation, born to serve, obeys;
And Boileau still in right of Horace sways.
But we, brave Britons, foreign laws despised,
And kept unconquered, and uncivilised;
Fierce for the liberties of wit, and bold,
We still defied the Romans, as of old.
Yet some there were, among the sounder few
Of those who less presumed, and better
    knew, 720
Who durst assert the juster ancient cause,
And here restored wit's fundamental laws.
Such was the muse, whose rules and practice
    tell,
"Nature's chief master-piece is writing well."
Such was Roscommon, not more learned
    than good,
With manners generous as his noble blood;
To him the wit of Greece and Rome was
    known,
And every author's merit, but his own.
Such late was Walsh—the muse's judge and
    friend,
Who justly knew to blame or to commend;
To failings mild, but zealous for desert, 731
The clearest head, and the sincerest heart.
This humble praise, lamented shade! re-
    ceive,
This praise at least a grateful muse may give:
The muse, whose early voice you taught to
    sing,
Prescribed her heights, and pruned her ten-
    der wing,
(Her guide now lost) no more attempts to
    rise,
But in low numbers short excursions tries:

Content, if hence the unlearned their wants
    may view,
The learned reflect on what before they
    knew: 740
Careless of censure, nor too fond of fame;
Still pleased to praise, yet not afraid to
    blame;
Averse alike to flatter, or offend;
Not free from faults, nor yet too vain to
    mend.

                [1711]

THE RAPE OF THE LOCK

CANTO I

What dire offence from amorous causes
    springs,
What mighty contests rise from trivial things,
I sing—This verse to Caryll, Muse! is due:
This, even Belinda may vouchsafe to view:
Slight is the subject, but not so the praise,
If she inspire, and he approve my lays.
    Say what strange motive, Goddess! could
        compel
A well-bred lord to assault a gentle belle?
O say what stranger cause, yet unexplored,
Could make a gentle belle reject a lord? 10
In tasks so bold, can little men engage,
And in soft bosoms dwells such mighty rage?
    Sol through white curtains shot a timorous
        ray,
And oped those eyes that must eclipse the
    day:
Now lap-dogs give themselves the rousing
    shake,
And sleepless lovers, just at twelve, awake:
Thrice rung the bell, the slipper knocked the
    ground,
And the pressed watch returned a silver
    sound.
Belinda still her downy pillow pressed,
Her guardian sylph prolonged the balmy
    rest: 20
'Twas he had summoned to her silent bed
The morning-dream that hovered o'er her
    head;
A Youth more glittering than a birth-night
    beau,
(That even in slumber caused her cheek to
    glow)
Seemed to her ear his winning lips to lay.

And thus in whispers said, or seemed to say:
"Fairest of mortals, thou distinguished
care
Of thousand bright inhabitants of air!
If e'er one vision touched thy infant thought,
Of all the nurse and all the priest have
taught;   30
Of airy elves by moonlight shadows seen,
The silver token, and the circled green,
Or virgins visited by angel-powers,
With golden crowns and wreaths of heav-
enly flowers;
Hear and believe! thy own importance know,
Nor bound thy narrow views to things below.
Some secret truths, from learnèd pride con-
cealed,
To maids alone and children are revealed:
What though no credit doubting wits may
give?
The fair and innocent shall still believe.   40
Know, then, unnumbered Spirits round thee
fly,
The light militia of the lower sky:
These, though unseen, are ever on the wing,
Hang o'er the box, and hover round the
Ring.
Think what an equipage thou hast in air,
And view with scorn two pages and a chair.
As now your own, our beings were of old,
And once inclosed in woman's beauteous
mould;
Thence, by a soft transition, we repair
From earthly vehicles to these of air.   50
Think not, when woman's transient breath
is fled,
That all her vanities at once are dead;
Succeeding vanities she still regards,
And though she plays no more, o'erlooks the
cards.
Her joy in gilded chariots, when alive,
And love of ombre, after death survive.
For when the fair in all their pride expire,
To their first elements their souls retire:
The sprites of fiery termagants in flame
Mount up, and take a salamander's name. 60
Soft yielding minds to water glide away,
And sip, with nymphs, their elemental tea.
The graver prude sinks downward to a
gnome,
In search of mischief still on earth to roam.
The light coquettes in sylphs aloft repair,
And sport and flutter in the fields of air.
"Know further yet: whoever fair and
chaste

Rejects mankind, is by some sylph embraced;
For spirits, freed from mortal laws, with ease
Assume what sexes and what shapes they
please.   70
What guards the purity of melting maids,
In courtly balls, and midnight masquerades,
Safe from the treacherous friend, the daring
spark,
The glance by day, the whisper in the dark,
When kind occasion prompts their warm de-
sires,
When music softens, and when dancing fires?
'Tis but their sylph, the wise celestials know,
Though honour is the word with men below.
"Some nymphs there are, too conscious of
their face,
For life predestined to the gnomes' embrace.
These swell their prospects and exalt their
pride,   81
When offers are disdained, and love denied:
Then gay ideas crowd the vacant brain,
While peers, and dukes, and all their sweep-
ing train,
And garters, stars, and coronets appear,
And in soft sounds, 'Your Grace' salutes their
ear.
'Tis these that early taint the female soul,
Instruct the eyes of young coquettes to roll,
Teach infant cheeks a bidden blush to know,
And little hearts to flutter at a beau.   90
"Oft, when the world imagine women
stray,
The sylphs through mystic mazes guide their
way;
Through all the giddy circle they pursue,
And old impertinence expel by new.
What tender maid but must a victim fall
To one man's treat, but for another's ball?
When Florio speaks what virgin could with-
stand,
If gentle Damon did not squeeze her hand?
With varying vanities, from every part,
They shift the moving toyshop of their heart;
Where wigs with wigs, with sword-knots
sword-knots strive,   101
Beaux banish beaux, and coaches coaches
drive.
This erring mortals levity may call;
Oh blind to truth! the sylphs contrive it all.
"Of these am I, who thy protection claim,
A watchful sprite, and Ariel is my name.
Late, as I ranged the crystal wilds of air,
In the clear mirror of thy ruling star
I saw, alas! some dread event impend.

Ere to the main this morning sun descend,
But Heaven reveals not what, or how, or
      where: 111
Warned by the sylph, O pious maid, beware!
This to disclose is all thy guardian can:
Beware of all, but most beware of man!"
      He said; when Shock, who thought she
         slept too long,
Leaped up, and waked his mistress with his
      tongue.
'Twas then, Belinda, if report say true,
Thy eyes first opened on a billet-doux;
Wounds, charms, and ardors were no sooner
      read,
But all the vision vanished from thy head.
      And now, unveiled, the toilet stands dis-
         played,   121
Each silver vase in mystic order laid.
First, robed in white, the nymph intent
      adores,
With head uncovered, the cosmetic powers.
A heavenly image in the glass appears,
To that she bends, to that her eyes she rears;
Th' inferior priestess, at her altar's side,
Trembling begins the sacred rites of pride.
Unnumbered treasures ope at once, and
      here   129
The various offerings of the world appear;
From each she nicely culls with curious toil,
And decks the Goddess with the glittering
      spoil.
This casket India's glowing gems unlocks,
And all Arabia breathes from yonder box.
The tortoise here and elephant unite,
Transformed to combs, the speckled, and the
      white.
Here files of pins extend their shining rows,
Puffs, powders, patches, Bibles, billet-doux.
Now awful beauty puts on all its arms;
The fair each moment rises in her charms,
Repairs her smiles, awakens every grace,   141
And calls forth all the wonders of her face;
Sees by degrees a purer blush arise,
And keener lightnings quicken in her eyes.
The busy sylphs surround their darling care,
These set the head, and those divide the hair,
Some fold the sleeve, whilst others plait the
      gown;
And Betty's praised for labours not her own.

CANTO II

Not with more glories, in the ethereal plain,
The sun first rises o'er the purpled main,

Than, issuing forth, the rival of his beams
Launched on the bosom of the silver
      Thames.
Fair nymphs and well-dressed youths around
      her shone,
But every eye was fixed on her alone.
On her white breast a sparkling cross she
      wore,
Which Jews might kiss, and infidels adore.
Her lively looks a sprightly mind disclose,
Quick as her eyes, and as unfixed as those; 10
Favours to none, to all she smiles extends;
Oft she rejects, but never once offends.
Bright as the sun, her eyes the gazers strike,
And, like the sun, they shine on all alike.
Yet graceful ease, and sweetness void of
      pride,
Might hide her faults, if belles had faults to
      hide;
If to her share some female errors fall,
Look on her face, and you'll forget 'em all.
      This nymph, to the destruction of man-
         kind,
Nourished two locks, which graceful hung
      behind   20
In equal curls, and well conspired to deck
With shining ringlets the smooth ivory neck.
Love in these labyrinths his slaves detains,
And mighty hearts are held in slender chains.
With hairy springes we the birds betray,
Slight lines of hair surprise the finny prey,
Fair tresses man's imperial race ensnare,
And beauty draws us with a single hair.
      The adventurous Baron the bright locks
         admired;
He saw, he wished, and to the prize aspired.
Resolved to win, he meditates the way,   31
By force to ravish, or by fraud betray;
For when success a lover's toil attends,
Few ask, if fraud or force attained his ends.
      For this, ere Phœbus rose, he had implored
Propitious heaven, and every power adored,
But chiefly Love—to Love an altar built,
Of twelve vast French romances, neatly gilt.
There lay three garters, half a pair of gloves;
And all the trophies of his former loves;   40
With tender billet-doux he lights the pyre,
And breathes three amorous sighs to raise the
      fire.
Then prostrate falls, and begs with ardent
      eyes
Soon to obtain, and long possess the prize;
The powers gave ear, and granted half his
      prayer,

The rest, the winds dispersed in empty air.
But now secure the painted vessel glides,
The sunbeams trembling on the floating
    tides:
While melting music steals upon the sky,
And softened sounds along the waters die; 50
Smooth flow the waves, the zephyrs gently
    play,
Belinda smiled, and all the world was gay.
All but the sylph—with careful thoughts op-
    pressed,
The impending woe sat heavy on his breast.
He summons straight his denizens of air;
The lucid squadrons round the sails repair;
Soft o'er the shrouds aërial whispers breathe,
That seemed but zephyrs to the train be-
    neath.
Some to the sun their insect-wings unfold, 59
Waft on the breeze, or sink in clouds of gold;
Transparent forms, too fine for mortal sight,
Their fluid bodies half dissolved in light,
Loose to the wind their airy garments flew,
Thin glittering textures of the filmy dew,
Dipped in the richest tincture of the skies,
Where light disports in ever-mingling dyes,
While every beam new transient colours
    flings,
Colours that change whene'er they wave
    their wings.
Amid the circle, on the gilded mast,
Superior by the head, was Ariel placed;   70
His purple pinions opening to the sun,
He raised his azure wand, and thus begun:
"Ye sylphs and sylphids, to your chief give
    ear!
Fays, fairies, genii, elves, and demons, hear!
Ye know the spheres and various tasks as-
    signed
By laws eternal to the aërial kind.
Some in the fields of purest ether play,
And bask and whiten in the blaze of day.
Some guide the course of wandering orbs on
    high,
Or roll the planets through the boundless
    sky.   80
Some less refined, beneath the moon's pale
    light
Pursue the stars that shoot athwart the night,
Or suck the mists in grosser air below,
Or dip their pinions in the painted bow,
Or brew fierce tempests on the wintry main,
Or o'er the glebe distil the kindly rain.
Others on earth o'er human race preside.

Watch all their ways, and all their actions
    guide:
Of these the chief the care of nations own,
And guard with arms divine the British
    throne.   90
"Our humbler province is to tend the fair,
Not a less pleasing, though less glorious care;
To save the powder from too rude a gale,
Nor let the imprisoned essences exhale;
To draw fresh colours from the vernal
    flowers;
To steal from rainbows e'er they drop in
    showers
A brighter wash; to curl their waving hairs,
Assist their blushes, and inspire their airs;
Nay oft, in dreams, invention we bestow,
To change a flounce, or add a furbelow.   100
"This day, black omens threat the bright-
    est fair
That e'er deserved a watchful spirit's care;
Some dire disaster, or by force, or slight;
But what, or where, the fates have wrapped
    in night.
Whether the nymph shall break Diana's law,
Or some frail china jar receive a flaw;
Or stain her honour, or her new brocade;
Forget her prayers, or miss a masquerade;
Or lose her heart, or necklace, at a ball;
Or whether Heaven has doomed that Shock
    must fall.   110
Haste, then, ye spirits! to your charge repair.
The fluttering fan be Zephyretta's care;
The drops to thee, Brillante, we consign;
And, Momentilla, let the watch be thine;
Do thou, Crispissa, tend her favorite lock;
Ariel himself shall be the guard of Shock.
"To fifty chosen sylphs, of special note,
We trust the important charge, the petticoat:
Oft have we known that seven-fold fence to
    fail,
Though stiff with hoops, and armed with
    ribs of whale;   120
Form a strong line about the silver bound,
And guard the wide circumference around.
"Whatever spirit, careless of his charge,
His post neglects, or leaves the fair at large,
Shall feel sharp vengeance soon o'ertake his
    sins,
Be stopped in vials, or transfixed with pins;
Or plunged in lakes of bitter washes lie,
Or wedged whole ages in a bodkin's eye:
Gums and pomatums shall his flight restrain,
While clogged he beats his silken wings in
    vain;   130

Or alum styptics with contracting power
Shrink his thin essence like a rivelled flower:
Or, as Ixion fixed, the wretch shall feel
The giddy motion of the whirling mill,
In fumes of burning chocolate shall glow,
And tremble at the sea that froths below!"
   He spoke; the spirits from the sails descend;
Some, orb in orb, around the nymph extend;
Some thrid the mazy ringlets of her hair;
Some hang upon the pendants of her ear; 140
With beating hearts the dire event they wait,
Anxious, and trembling for the birth of Fate.

CANTO III

Close by those meads, forever crowned with
   flowers,
Where Thames with pride surveys his rising
   towers,
There stands a structure of majestic frame,
Which from the neighboring Hampton takes
   its name.
Here Britain's statesmen oft the fall fore-
   doom
Of foreign tyrants and of nymphs at home;
Here thou, great Anna! whom three realms
   obey,
Dost sometimes counsel take—and sometimes
   tea.
   Hither the heroes and the nymphs resort,
To taste awhile the pleasures of a court;   10
In various talk the instructive hours they
   passed,
Who gave the ball, or paid the visit last;
One speaks the glory of the British Queen,
And one describes a charming Indian screen;
A third interprets motions, looks, and eyes;
At every word a reputation dies.
Snuff, or the fan, supply each pause of chat,
With singing, laughing, ogling, *and all that.*
   Meanwhile, declining from the noon of
   day,
The sun obliquely shoots his burning ray; 20
The hungry judges soon the sentence sign,
And wretches hang that jurymen may dine;
The merchant from the Exchange returns in
   peace,
And the long labours of the toilet cease.
Belinda now, whom thirst of fame invites,
Burns to encounter two adventurous knights,
At ombre singly to decide their doom;
And swells her breast with conquests yet to
   come.

Straight the three bands prepare in arms to
   join,
Each band the number of the sacred Nine. 30
Soon as she spreads her hand, the aërial
   guard
Descend, and sit on each important card:
First Ariel perched upon a Matadore,
Then each, according to the rank they bore;
For sylphs, yet mindful of their ancient race,
Are, as when women, wondrous fond of
   place.
   Behold, four kings in majesty revered,
With hoary whiskers and a forky beard;
And four fair queens whose hands sustain a
   flower,   39
The expressive emblem of their softer power;
Four knaves in garbs succinct, a trusty band,
Caps on their heads, and halberts in their
   hand;
And particolored troops, a shining train,
Draw forth to combat on the velvet plain.
   The skilful nymph reviews her force with
   care:
"Let spades be trumps!" she said, and trumps
   they were.
   Now move to war her sable Matadores,
In show like leaders of the swarthy Moors.
Spadillio first, unconquerable lord!
Led off two captive trumps, and swept the
   board.   50
As many more Manillio forced to yield,
And marched a victor from the verdant field.
Him Basto followed, but his fate more hard
Gained but one trump and one plebeian
   card.
With his broad sabre next, a chief in years,
The hoary majesty of spades appears,
Puts forth one manly leg, to sight revealed;
The rest, his many-colored robe concealed.
The rebel knave, who dares his prince en-
   gage,
Proves the just victim of his royal rage. 60
Even mighty Pam, that kings and queens
   o'erthrew
And mowed down armies in the fights of loo,
Sad chance of war! now destitute of aid,
Falls undistinguished by the victor spade!
   Thus far both armies to Belinda yield;
Now to the Baron fate inclines the field.
His warlike Amazon her host invades,
The imperial consort of the crown of spades.
The club's black tyrant first her victim died,
Spite of his haughty mien, and barbarous
   pride: 70

What boots the regal circle on his head,
His giant limbs, in state unwieldy spread;
That long behind he trails his pompous robe,
And, of all monarchs, only grasps the globe?
  The Baron now his diamonds pours apace;
The embroidered king who shows but half
    his face,
And his refulgent queen, with powers com-
    bined
Of broken troops an easy conquest find.
Clubs, diamonds, hearts, in wild disorder
    seen,
With throngs promiscuous strow the level
    green.   80
Thus when dispersed a routed army runs,
Of Asia's troops, and Afric's sable sons,
With like confusion different nations fly,
Of various habit, and of various dye,
The pierced battalions disunited fall,
In heaps on heaps; one fate o'erwhelms them
    all.
  The knave of diamonds tries his wily arts,
And wins (oh shameful chance!) the queen
    of hearts.
At this, the blood the virgin's cheek forsook,
A livid paleness spreads o'er all her look; 90
She sees, and trembles at the approaching ill,
Just in the jaws of ruin, and codille.
And now (as oft in some distempered state)
On one nice trick depends the general fate.
An ace of hearts steps forth: The king un-
    seen
Lurked in her hand, and mourned his cap-
    tive queen:
He springs to vengeance with an eager pace,
And falls like thunder on the prostrate ace.
The nymph exulting fills with shouts the
    sky;   99
The walls, the woods, and long canals reply.
  Oh thoughtless mortals! ever blind to fate,
Too soon dejected, and too soon elate.
Sudden, these honours shall be snatched
    away,
And cursed forever this victorious day.
  For lo! the board with cups and spoons is
    crowned,
The berries crackle, and the mill turns
    round;
On shining altars of japan they raise
The silver lamp; the fiery spirits blaze:
From silver spouts the grateful liquors glide,
While China's earth receives the smoking
    tide: 110
At once they gratify their scent and taste,

And frequent cups prolong the rich repast.
Straight hover round the fair her airy band;
Some, as she sipped, the fuming liquor
    fanned,
Some o'er her lap their careful plumes dis-
    played,
Trembling, and conscious of the rich bro-
    cade.
Coffee, (which makes the politician wise,
And see through all things with his half-shut
    eyes)
Sent up in vapours to the Baron's brain
New stratagems, the radiant lock to gain. 120
Ah cease, rash youth! desist ere 'tis too late,
Fear the just gods, and think of Scylla's fate!
Changed to a bird, and sent to flit in air,
She dearly pays for Nisus' injured hair!
  But when to mischief mortals bend their
    will,
How soon they find fit instruments of ill!
Just then, Clarissa drew with tempting grace
A two-edged weapon from her shining case:
So ladies in romance assist their knight, 128
Present the spear, and arm him for the fight.
He takes the gift with reverence, and extends
The little engine on his fingers' ends;
This just behind Belinda's neck he spread,
As o'er the fragrant steams she bends her
    head.
Swift to the lock a thousand sprites repair,
A thousand wings, by turns, blow back the
    hair;
And thrice they twitched the diamond in her
    ear;
Thrice she looked back, and thrice the foe
    drew near.
Just in that instant, anxious Ariel sought
The close recesses of the virgin's thought; 140
As on the nosegay in her breast reclined,
He watched the ideas rising in her mind,
Sudden he viewed, in spite of all her art,
An earthly lover lurking at her heart,
Amazed, confused, he found his power ex-
    pired,
Resigned to fate, and with a sigh retired.
  The Peer now spreads the glittering forfex
    wide,
To inclose the lock; now joins it, to divide.
Even then, before the fatal engine closed,
A wretched sylph too fondly interposed; 150
Fate urged the shears, and cut the sylph in
    twain,
(But airy substance soon unites again)

The meeting points the sacred hair dissever
From the fair head, forever, and forever!
    Then flashed the living lightning from her
        eyes,
And screams of horror rend the affrighted
    skies.
Not louder shrieks to pitying Heaven are
    cast,
When husbands, or when lap-dogs breathe
    their last;
Or when rich China vessels fallen from high,
In glittering dust and painted fragments lie!
    "Let wreaths of triumph now my temples
        twine,"   161
The victor cried; "the glorious prize is mine!
While fish in streams, or birds delight in air,
Or in a coach and six the British fair,
As long as *Atalantis* shall be read,
Or the small pillow grace a lady's bed,
While visits shall be paid on solemn days,
When numerous wax-lights in bright order
    blaze,
While nymphs take treats, or assignations
    give,
So long my honour, name, and praise shall
    live!   170
What time would spare, from steel receives
    its date,
And monuments, like men, submit to fate!
Steel could the labour of the gods destroy,
And strike to dust the imperial towers of
    Troy;
Steel could the works of mortal pride con-
    found,
And hew triumphal arches to the ground.
What wonder then, fair nymph! thy hairs
    should feel
The conquering force of unresisted steel?"

CANTO IV

But anxious cares the pensive nymph op-
    pressed,
And secret passions laboured in her breast.
Not youthful kings in battle seized alive,
Not scornful virgins who their charms sur-
    vive,
Not ardent lovers robbed of all their bliss,
Not ancient ladies when refused a kiss,
Not tyrants fierce that unrepenting die,
Not Cynthia when her manteau's pinned
    awry,
E'er felt such rage, resentment, and despair,

As thou, sad virgin! for thy ravished hair.   1c
    For, that sad moment, when the sylphs
        withdrew
And Ariel weeping from Belinda flew,
Umbriel, a dusky, melancholy sprite,
As ever sullied the fair face of light,
Down to the central earth, his proper scene,
Repaired to search the gloomy Cave of
    Spleen.
    Swift on his sooty pinions flits the gnome,
And in a vapour reached the dismal dome.
No cheerful breeze this sullen region knows,
The dreaded east is all the wind that blows.
Here in a grotto, sheltered close from air,   21
And screened in shades from day's detested
    glare,
She sighs forever on her pensive bed,
Pain at her side, and Megrim at her head.
    Two handmaids wait the throne: alike in
        place,
But differing far in figure and in face.
Here stood Ill-nature like an ancient maid,
Her wrinkled form in black and white ar-
    rayed;
With store of prayers, for mornings, nights,
    and noons,
Her hand is filled; her bosom with lampoons.
    There Affectation, with a sickly mien,   31
Shows in her cheek the roses of eighteen,
Practised to lisp, and hang the head aside,
Faints into airs, and languishes with pride,
On the rich quilt sinks with becoming woe,
Wrapped in a gown, for sickness, and for
    show.
The fair ones feel such maladies as these,
When each new night-dress gives a new dis-
    ease.
    A constant vapour o'er the palace flies,
Strange phantoms rising as the mists arise; 40
Dreadful, as hermit's dreams in haunted
    shades,
Or bright as visions of expiring maids.
Now glaring fiends, and snakes on rolling
    spires,
Pale spectres, gaping tombs, and purple fires.
Now lakes of liquid gold, Elysian scenes,
And crystal domes, and angels in machines.
    Unnumbered throngs on every side are
        seen,
Of bodies changed to various forms by
    Spleen.
Here living teapots stand, one arm held out,
One bent; the handle this, and that the
    spout: 50

A pipkin there, like Homer's tripod walks;
Here sighs a jar, and there a goose-pie talks;
Men prove with child, as powerful fancy
    works,
And maids turned bottles, call aloud for
    corks.
  Safe passed the gnome through this fantas-
    tic band,
A branch of healing spleenwort in his hand.
Then thus addressed the power: "Hail, way-
    ward Queen!
Who rule the sex to fifty from fifteen:
Parent of vapours and of female wit,
Who give the hysteric or poetic fit,   60
On various tempers act by various ways,
Make some take physic, others scribble plays;
Who cause the proud their visits to delay,
And send the godly in a pet to pray.
A nymph there is, that all thy power disdains,
And thousands more in equal mirth main-
    tains.
But oh! if e'er thy gnome could spoil a grace,
Or raise a pimple on a beauteous face,
Like citron-waters matrons' cheeks inflame,
Or change complexions at a losing game;   70
If e'er with airy horns I planted heads,
Or rumpled petticoats, or tumbled beds,
Or caused suspicion when no soul was rude,
Or discomposed the head-dress of a prude,
Or e'er to costive lap-dog gave disease,
Which not the tears of brightest eyes could
    ease:
Hear me, and touch Belinda with chagrin,
That single act gives half the world the
    spleen."
  The goddess with a discontented air
Seems to reject him, though she grants his
    prayer.   80
A wondrous bag with both her hands she
    binds,
Like that where once Ulysses held the winds;
There she collects the force of female lungs,
Sighs, sobs, and passions, and the war of
    tongues.
A vial next she fills with fainting fears,
Soft sorrows, melting griefs, and flowing
    tears.
The gnome rejoicing bears her gifts away,
Spreads his black wings, and slowly mounts
    to day.
  Sunk in Thalestris' arms the nymph he
    found,
Her eyes dejected and her hair unbound.   90
Full o'er their heads the swelling bag he rent,

And all the Furies issued at the vent.
Belinda burns with more than mortal ire,
And fierce Thalestris fans the rising fire.
"Oh wretched maid!" she spread her hands,
    and cried,
(While Hampton's echoes, "Wretched
    maid!" replied)
"Was it for this you took such constant care
The bodkin, comb, and essence to prepare?
For this your locks in paper durance bound,
For this with torturing irons wreathed
    around?   100
For this with fillets strained your tender
    head,
And bravely bore the double loads of lead?
Gods! shall the ravisher display your hair,
While the fops envy, and the ladies stare!
Honour forbid! at whose unrivalled shrine
Ease, pleasure, virtue, all our sex resign.
Methinks already I your tears survey,
Already hear the horrid things they say,
Already see you a degraded toast,
And all your honour in a whisper lost!   110
How shall I, then, your helpless fame defend?
'Twill then be infamy to seem your friend!
And shall this prize, the inestimable prize,
Exposed through crystal to the gazing eyes,
And heightened by the diamond's circling
    rays,
On that rapacious hand forever blaze?
Sooner shall grass in Hyde Park Circus grow,
And wits take lodgings in the sound of Bow;
Sooner let earth, air, sea, to chaos fall,   119
Men, monkeys, lap-dogs, parrots, perish all!"
  She said; then raging to Sir Plume repairs,
And bids her beau demand the precious hairs
(Sir Plume of amber snuff-box justly vain,
And the nice conduct of a clouded cane) ;
With earnest eyes, and round unthinking
    face,
He first the snuff-box opened, then the case,
And thus broke out—"My Lord, why, what
    the devil?
Z—ds! damn the lock! 'fore Gad, you must
    be civil!
Plague on't! 'tis past a jest—nay prithee, pox!
Give her the hair"—he spoke, and rapped his
    box.   130
  "It grieves me much," replied the Peer
    again,
"Who speaks so well should ever speak in
    vain.
But by this lock, this sacred lock, I swear,
(Which never more shall join its parted hair·

Which never more its honours shall renew,
Clipped from the lovely head where late it
grew)
That while my nostrils draw the vital air,
This hand, which won it, shall forever wear."
He spoke, and speaking, in proud triumph
spread
The long-contended honours of her head. 140
But Umbriel, hateful gnome! forbears not
so;
He breaks the vial whence the sorrows flow.
Then see! the nymph in beauteous grief ap-
pears,
Her eyes half-languishing, half-drowned in
tears;
On her heaved bosom hung her drooping
head,
Which, with a sigh, she raised; and thus she
said:
"Forever cursed be this detested day,
Which snatched my best, my favorite curl
away!
Happy! ah ten times happy had I been,
If Hampton Court these eyes had never seen!
Yet am not I the first mistaken maid, 151
By love of courts to numerous ills betrayed.
Oh had I rather unadmired remained
In some lone isle, or distant northern land;
Where the gilt chariot never marks the way,
Where none learn ombre, none e'er taste
bohea!
There kept my charms concealed from mor-
tal eye,
Like roses that in deserts bloom and die.
What moved my mind with youthful lords to
roam?
Oh had I stayed, and said my prayers at
home! 160
'Twas this, the morning omens seemed to
tell,
Thrice from my trembling hand the patch-
box fell;
The tottering china shook without a wind,
Nay, Poll sat mute, and Shock was most un-
kind!
A sylph too warned me of the threats of fate,
In mystic visions, now believed too late!
See the poor remnants of these slighted hairs!
My hands shall rend what even thy rapine
spares:
These in two sable ringlets taught to break,
Once gave new beauties to the snowy neck;
The sister-lock now sits uncouth, alone, 171
And in its fellow's fate foresees its own;

Uncurled it hangs, the fatal shears demands,
And tempts once more, thy sacrilegious
hands.
Oh hadst thou, cruel! been content to seize
Hairs less in sight, or any hairs but these!"

CANTO V

She said: the pitying audience melt in tears;
But Fate and Jove had stopped the Baron's
ears.
In vain Thalestris with reproach assails,
For who can move when fair Belinda fails?
Not half so fixed the Trojan could remain,
While Anna begged and Dido raged in vain.
Then grave Clarissa graceful waved her fan;
Silence ensued, and thus the nymph began:
"Say why are beauties praised and hon-
oured most,
The wise man's passion, and the vain man's
toast?   10
Why decked with all that land and sea afford,
Why angels called, and angel-like adored?
Why round our coaches crowd the white-
gloved beaux,
Why bows the side-box from its inmost rows?
How vain are all these glories, all our pains,
Unless good sense preserve what beauty
gains:
That men may say, when we the front-box
grace:
'Behold the first in virtue as in face!'
Oh! if to dance all night, and dress all day,
Charmed the smallpox, or chased old age
away;   20
Who would not scorn what housewife's cares
produce,
Or who would learn one earthly thing of use?
To patch, nay ogle, might become a saint,
Nor could it sure be such a sin to paint.
But since, alas! frail beauty must decay,
Curled or uncurled, since locks will turn to
grey;
Since painted, or not painted, all shall fade,
And she who scorns a man, must die a maid;
What then remains but well our power to
use,
And keep good humour still whate'er we
lose?   30
And trust me, dear! good humour can pre-
vail,
When airs, and flights, and screams, and
scolding fail.
Beauties in vain their pretty eyes may roll;

Charms strike the sight, but merit wins the
    soul."
  So spoke the dame, but no applause en-
    sued;
Belinda frowned, Thalestris called her
    prude.
"To arms, to arms!" the fierce virago cries,
And swift as lightning to the combat flies.
All side in parties, and begin the attack;
Fans clap, silks rustle, and tough whalebones
    crack;   40
Heroes' and heroines' shouts confusedly rise,
And bass and treble voices strike the skies.
No common weapons in their hands are
    found,
Like gods they fight, nor dread a mortal
    wound.
  So when bold Homer makes the gods en-
    gage,
And heavenly breasts with human passions
    rage;
'Gainst Pallas, Mars; Latona, Hermes arms;
And all Olympus rings with loud alarms:
Jove's thunder roars, heaven trembles all
    around,
Blue Neptune storms, the bellowing deeps
    resound: 50
Earth shakes her nodding towers, the ground
    gives way,
And the pale ghosts start at the flash of day!
  Triumphant Umbriel on a sconce's height
Clapped his glad wings, and sate to view the
    fight:
Propped on their bodkin spears, the sprites
    survey
The growing combat, or assist the fray.
  While through the press enraged Thales-
    tris flies,
And scatters death around from both her
    eyes,
A beau and witling perished in the throng,
One died in metaphor, and one in song. 60
"O cruel nymph! a living death I bear,"
Cried Dapperwit, and sunk beside his chair.
A mournful glance Sir Fopling upwards cast,
"Those eyes are made so killing"—was his
    last.
Thus on Mæander's flowery margin lies
The expiring swan, and as he sings he dies.
  When bold Sir Plume had drawn Clarissa
    down,
Chloe stepped in, and killed him with a
    frown;
She smiled to see the doughty hero slain,

But, at her smile, the beau revived again. 70
  Now Jove suspends his golden scales in air,
Weighs the men's wits against the lady's hair;
The doubtful beam long nods from side to
    side;
At length the wits mount up, the hairs sub-
    side.
  See, fierce Belinda on the Baron flies,
With more than usual lightning in her eyes:
Nor feared the chief the unequal fight to try,
Who sought no more than on his foe to die.
But this bold lord with manly strength en-
    dued,   79
She with one finger and a thumb subdued:
Just where the breath of life his nostrils drew,
A charge of snuff the wily virgin threw;
The gnomes direct, to every atom just,
The pungent grains of titillating dust.
Sudden, with starting tears each eye o'er-
    flows,
And the high dome re-echoes to his nose.
  "Now meet thy fate," incensed Belinda
    cried,
And drew a deadly bodkin from her side.
(The same, his ancient personage to deck,
Her great great grandsire wore about his
    neck,   90
In three seal-rings; which after, melted down,
Formed a vast buckle for his widow's gown:
Her infant grandame's whistle next it grew,
The bells she jingled, and the whistle blew;
Then in a bodkin graced her mother's hairs,
Which long she wore, and now Belinda
    wears.)
  "Boast not my fall," he cried, "insulting
    foe!
Thou by some other shalt be laid as low,
Nor think, to die dejects my lofty mind:
All that I dread is leaving you behind! 100
Rather than so, ah let me still survive,
And burn in Cupid's flames—but burn alive."
  "Restore the lock!" she cries; and all
    around
"Restore the lock!" the vaulted roofs re-
    bound.
Not fierce Othello in so loud a strain
Roared for the handkerchief that caused his
    pain.
But see how oft ambitious aims are crossed,
And chiefs contend 'till all the prize is lost!
The lock, obtained with guilt, and kept with
    pain,   109
In every place is sought, but sought in vain:
With such a prize no mortal must be blessed.

So Heaven decrees! with Heaven who can
　　contest?
　Some thought it mounted to the lunar
　　sphere,
Since all things lost on earth are treasured
　　there.
There heroes' wits are kept in ponderous
　　vases,
And beaux' in snuff-boxes and tweezer-cases.
There broken vows and death-bed alms are
　　found,
And lovers' hearts with ends of riband
　　bound,
The courtier's promises, and sick man's
　　prayers,
The smiles of harlots, and the tears of heirs,
Cages for gnats, and chains to yoke a flea, 121
Dried butterflies, and tomes of casuistry.
　But trust the Muse—she saw it upward rise,
Though marked by none but quick, poetic
　　eyes:
(So Rome's great founder to the heavens
　　withdrew,
To Proculus alone confessed in view)
A sudden star, it shot through liquid air,
And drew behind a radiant trail of hair.
Not Berenice's locks first rose so bright,
The heavens bespangling with dishevelled
　　light. 130
The sylphs behold it kindling as it flies,
And pleased pursue its progress through the
　　skies.
　This the beau monde shall from the Mall
　　survey,
And hail with music its propitious ray.
This the blest lover shall for Venus take,
And send up vows from Rosamonda's lake.
This Partridge soon shall view in cloudless
　　skies,
When next he looks through Galileo's eyes;
And hence the egregious wizard shall fore-
　　doom
The fate of Louis, and the fall of Rome. 140
　Then cease, bright nymph! to mourn thy
　　ravished hair,
Which adds new glory to the shining sphere!
Not all the tresses that fair head can boast,
Shall draw such envy as the lock you lost.
For, after all the murders of your eye,
When, after millions slain, yourself shall die:
When those fair suns shall set, as set they
　　must,
And all those tresses shall be laid in dust, 148

This lock, the Muse shall consecrate to fame,
And 'midst the stars inscribe Belinda's name.

[*1711, 1713, 1714*]

ELEGY

TO THE MEMORY OF AN UNFORTU-
NATE LADY

What beckoning ghost, along the moonlight
　　shade
Invites my steps, and points to yonder glade?
'Tis she!—but why that bleeding bosom
　　gored?
Why dimly gleams the visionary sword?
O ever beauteous, ever friendly! tell,
Is it in heaven a crime to love too well?
To bear too tender or too firm a heart,
To act a lover's or a Roman's part?
Is there no bright reversion in the sky,
For those who greatly think, or bravely die? 10
　Why bade ye else, ye powers! her soul
　　aspire
Above the vulgar flight of low desire?
Ambition first sprung from your blest abodes,
The glorious fault of angels and of gods;
Thence to their images on earth it flows,
And in the breasts of kings and heroes glows.
Most souls, 'tis true, but peep out once an
　　age,
Dull sullen prisoners in the body's cage:
Dim lights of life, that burn a length of
　　years
Useless, unseen, as lamps in sepulchres; 20
Like Eastern Kings a lazy state they keep,
And close confined to their own palace,
　　sleep.
　From these perhaps (ere nature bade her
　　die)
Fate snatched her early to the pitying sky.
As into air the purer spirits flow,
And separate from their kindred dregs be-
　　low;
So flew the soul to its congenial place,
Nor left one virtue to redeem her race.
　But thou, false guardian of a charge too
　　good, 29
Thou, mean deserter of thy brother's blood!
See on these ruby lips the trembling breath,
These cheeks now fading at the blast of
　　death:

Cold is that breast which warmed the world
    before,
And those love-darting eyes must roll no
    more.
Thus, if eternal justice rules the ball,
Thus shall your wives, and thus your chil-
    dren fall;
On all the line a sudden vengeance waits,
And frequent hearses shall besiege your
    gates.
There passengers shall stand, and pointing
    say,
(While the long funerals blacken all the
    way)   40
"Lo these were they whose souls the furies
    steeled,
And cursed with hearts unknowing how to
    yield.
Thus unlamented pass the proud away,
The gaze of fools, and pageant of a day!
So perish all, whose breast ne'er learned to
    glow
For others' good, or melt at others' woe."
  What can atone (O ever-injured shade!)
Thy fate unpitied, and thy rites unpaid?
No friend's complaint, no kind domestic tear
Pleased thy pale ghost, or graced thy mourn-
    ful bier.   50
By foreign hands thy dying eyes were closed,
By foreign hands thy decent limbs composed,
By foreign hands thy humble grave adorned,
By strangers honoured, and by strangers
    mourned!
What though no friends in sable weeds ap-
    pear,
Grieve for an hour, perhaps, then mourn a
    year,
And bear about the mockery of woe
To midnight dances, and the public show?
What though no weeping loves thy ashes
    grace,
Nor polished marble emulate thy face?   60
What though no sacred earth allow thee
    room,
Nor hallowed dirge be muttered o'er thy
    tomb?
Yet shall thy grave with rising flowers be
    dressed,
And the green turf lie lightly on thy breast:
There shall the morn her earliest tears be-
    stow,
There the first roses of the year shall blow;
While angels with their silver wings o'er-
    shade

The ground, now sacred by thy reliques
    made.
So peaceful rests, without a stone, a name,
What once had beauty, titles, wealth, and
    fame.   70
How loved, how honoured once, avails thee
    not,
To whom related, or by whom begot;
A heap of dust alone remains of thee,
'Tis all thou art, and all the proud shall be!
  Poets themselves must fall, like those they
    sung,
Deaf the praised ear, and mute the tuneful
    tongue.
Even he, whose soul now melts in mournful
    lays,
Shall shortly want the generous tear he pays;
Then from his closing eyes thy form shall
    part,
And the last pang shall tear thee from his
    heart,   80
Life's idle business at one gasp be o'er,
The muse forgot, and thou be loved no
    more!

                 [1717]

ELOÏSA TO ABELARD

In these deep solitudes and awful cells,
Where heavenly-pensive Contemplation
    dwells,
And ever musing Melancholy reigns;
What means this tumult in a vestal's veins?
Why rove my thoughts beyond this last re-
    treat?
Why feels my heart its long-forgotten heat?
Yet, yet I love!—From Abelard it came,
And Eloïsa yet must kiss the name.
  Dear fatal name! rest ever unrevealed,
Nor pass these lips in holy silence sealed: 10
Hide it, my heart, within that close disguise,
Where mixed with God's, his loved idea lies:
O write it not, my hand—the name appears
Already written—wash it out, my tears!
In vain lost Eloïsa weeps and prays,
Her heart still dictates, and her hand obeys.
  Relentless walls! whose darksome round
    contains
Repentant sighs and voluntary pains:
Ye rugged rocks! which holy knees have
    worn;

Ye grots and caverns shagged with horrid
    thorn!   20
Shrines! where their vigils pale-eyed virgins
    keep,
And pitying saints, whose statues learn to
    weep!
Though cold like you, unmoved and silent
    grown,
I have not yet forgot myself to stone.
All is not Heaven's while Abelard has part,
Still rebel nature holds out half my heart;
Nor prayers nor fasts its stubborn pulse re-
    strain,
Nor tears for ages taught to flow in vain.
Soon as thy letters trembling I unclose,
That well-known name awakens all my woes.
Oh name forever sad! forever dear!   31
Still breathed in sighs, still ushered with a
    tear.
I tremble too, where'er my own I find,
Some dire misfortune follows close behind.
Line after line my gushing eyes o'erflow,
Led through a sad variety of woe:
Now warm in love, now withering in my
    bloom,
Lost in a convent's solitary gloom!
There stern religion quenched the unwilling
    flame,
There died the best of passions, love and
    fame.   40
    Yet write, oh write me all, that I may join
Griefs to thy griefs, and echo sighs to thine.
Nor foes nor fortune take this power away;
And is my Abelard less kind than they?
Tears still are mine, and those I need not
    spare,
Love but demands what else were shed in
    prayer;
No happier task these faded eyes pursue;
To read and weep is all they now can do.
    Then share thy pain, allow that sad relief;
Ah, more than share it, give me all thy grief.
Heaven first taught letters for some wretch's
    aid,   51
Some banished lover or some captive maid;
They live, they speak, they breathe what love
    inspires,
Warm from the soul, and faithful to its fires,
The virgin's wish without her fears impart,
Excuse the blush, and pour out all the heart,
Speed the soft intercourse from soul to soul,
And waft a sigh from Indus to the pole.
    Thou know'st how guiltless first I met thy
    flame,

When love approached me under friend-
    ship's name;   60
My fancy formed thee of angelic kind,
Some emanation of the all-beauteous Mind.
Those smiling eyes, attempering every ray,
Shone sweetly lambent with celestial day.
Guiltless I gazed; Heaven listened while you
    sung;
And truths divine came mended from that
    tongue.
From lips like those what precept failed to
    move?
Too soon they taught me 'twas no sin to love:
Back through the paths of pleasing sense I
    ran,
Nor wished an angel whom I loved a man. 70
Dim and remote the joys of saints I see,
Nor envy them that heaven I lose for thee.
    How oft, when pressed to marriage, have I
    said,
Curse on all laws but those which love has
    made?
Love, free as air, at sight of human ties,
Spreads his light wings, and in a moment
    flies.
Let wealth, let honour, wait the wedded
    dame,
August her deed, and sacred be her fame;
Before true passion all those views remove,
Fame, wealth, and honour! what are you to
    love?   80
The jealous god, when we profane his fires,
Those restless passions in revenge inspires,
And bids them make mistaken mortals groan,
Who seek in love for aught but love alone.
Should at my feet the world's great master
    fall,
Himself, his throne, his world, I'd scorn 'em
    all:
Not Cæsar's empress would I deign to prove;
No, make me mistress to the man I love;
If there be yet another name more free,
More fond than mistress, make me that to
    thee!   90
Oh! happy state! when souls each other draw,
When love is liberty, and nature law:
All then is full, possessing, and possessed,
No craving void left aching in the breast:
Even thought meets thought, ere from the
    lips it part,
And each warm wish springs mutual from
    the heart.
This sure is bliss (if bliss on earth there be)

And once the lot of Abelard and me.
  Alas, how changed! what sudden horrors
    rise!
A naked lover bound and bleeding lie!   100
Where, where was Eloïse? her voice, her
    hand,
Her poniard, had opposed the dire com-
    mand.
Barbarian, stay! that bloody stroke restrain;
The crime was common, common be the
    pain.
I can no more; by shame, by rage suppressed,
Let tears and burning blushes speak the rest.
  Canst thou forget that sad, that solemn
    day,
When victims at yon altar's foot we lay?
Canst thou forget what tears that moment
    fell,
When, warm in youth, I bade the world fare-
    well?   110
As with cold lips I kissed the sacred veil,
The shrines all trembled, and the lamps grew
    pale:
Heaven scarce believed the conquest it sur-
    veyed,
And saints with wonder heard the vows I
    made.
Yet then, to those dread altars as I drew,
Not on the Cross my eyes were fixed, but you:
Not grace, or zeal, love only was my call,
And if I lose thy love, I lose my all.
Come! with thy looks, thy words, relieve my
    woe;
Those still at least are left thee to bestow. 120
Still on that breast enamoured let me lie,
Still drink delicious poison from thy eye,
Pant on thy lip, and to thy heart be pressed;
Give all thou canst—and let me dream the
    rest.
Ah no! instruct me other joys to prize,
With other beauties charm my partial eyes,
Full in my view set all the bright abode,
And make my soul quit Abelard for God.
  Ah, think at least thy flock deserves thy
    care,
Plants of thy hand, and children of thy
    prayer.   130
From the false world in early youth they fled,
By thee to mountains, wilds, and deserts led.
You raised these hallowed walls; the desert
    smiled,
And Paradise was opened in the wild.
No weeping orphan saw his father's stores
Our shrines irradiate, or emblaze the floors;

No silver saints, by dying misers given,
Here bribed the rage of ill-requited Heaven:
But such plain roofs as piety could raise,
And only vocal with the Maker's praise.   140
In these lone walls (their days eternal
    bound)
These moss-grown domes with spiry turrets
    crowned,
Where awful arches make a noonday night,
And the dim windows shed a solemn light;
Thy eyes diffused a reconciling ray,
And gleams of glory brightened all the day.
But now no face divine contentment wears,
'Tis all blank sadness, or continual tears.
See how the force of others' prayers I try,
(O pious fraud of amorous charity!)   150
But why should I on others' prayers depend?
Come thou, my father, brother, husband,
    friend!
Ah let thy handmaid, sister, daughter move,
And all those tender names in one, thy love!
The darksome pines that o'er yon rocks re-
    clined
Wave high, and murmur to the hollow wind,
The wandering streams that shine between
    the hills,
The grots that echo to the tinkling rills,
The dying gales that pant upon the trees,
The lakes that quiver to the curling breeze;
No more these scenes my meditation aid,   161
Or lull to rest the visionary maid.
But o'er the twilight groves and dusky caves,
Long-sounding aisles, and intermingled
    graves,
Black Melancholy sits, and round her throws
A death-like silence, and a dead repose:
Her gloomy presence saddens all the scene,
Shades every flower, and darkens every green,
Deepens the murmur of the falling floods,
And breathes a browner horror on the woods
  Yet here forever, ever must I stay;   171
Sad proof how well a lover can obey!
Death, only death, can break the lasting
    chain;
And here, even then, shall my cold dust
    remain,
Here all its frailties, all its flames resign,
And wait till 'tis no sin to mix with thine.
  Ah wretch! believed the spouse of God in
    vain,
Confessed within the slave of love and man
Assist me, Heaven! but whence arose that
    prayer?
Sprung it from piety, or from despair?   180

Even here, where frozen chastity retires,
Love finds an altar for forbidden fires.
I ought to grieve, but cannot what I ought;
I mourn the lover, not lament the fault;
I view my crime, but kindle at the view,
Repent old pleasures, and solicit new;
Now turned to Heaven, I weep my past of-
    fence,
Now think of thee, and curse my innocence.
Of all affliction taught a lover yet,
'Tis sure the hardest science to forget! 190
How shall I lose the sin, yet keep the sense,
And love the offender, yet detest the offence?
How the dear object from the crime remove,
Or how distinguish penitence from love?
Unequal task! a passion to resign,
For hearts so touched, so pierced, so lost as
    mine.
Ere such a soul regains its peaceful state,
How often must it love, how often hate!
How often hope, despair, resent, regret, 199
Conceal, disdain,—do all things but forget.
But let Heaven seize it, all at once 'tis fired:
Not touched, but rapt; not wakened, but in-
    spired!
Oh come! oh teach me nature to subdue,
Renounce my love, my life, myself—and you.
Fill my fond heart with God alone, for he
Alone can rival, can succeed to thee.
    How happy is the blameless vestal's lot!
The world forgetting, by the world forgot:
Eternal sunshine of the spotless mind!
Each prayer accepted, and each wish re-
    signed; 210
Labour and rest, that equal periods keep;
"Obedient slumbers that can wake and
    weep";
Desires composed, affections ever even;
Tears that delight, and sighs that waft to
    Heaven.
Grace shines around her with serenest beams,
And whispering angels prompt her golden
    dreams.
For her the unfading rose of Eden blooms,
And wings of seraphs shed divine perfumes,
For her the Spouse prepares the bridal ring,
For her white virgins hymeneals sing, 220
To sounds of heavenly harps she dies away,
And melts in visions of eternal day.
    Far other dreams my erring soul employ,
Far other raptures, of unholy joy:
When at the close of each sad, sorrowing day,
Fancy restores what vengeance snatched
    away,

Then conscience sleeps, and leaving nature
    free,
All my loose soul unbounded springs to thee.
Oh curst, dear horrors of all-conscious night!
How glowing guilt exalts the keen delight!
Provoking demons all restraint remove, 231
And stir within me every source of love.
I hear thee, view thee, gaze o'er all thy
    charms,
And round thy phantom glue my clasping
    arms.
I wake:—no more I hear, no more I view,
The phantom flies me, as unkind as you.
I call aloud; it hears not what I say:
I stretch my empty arms; it glides away.
To dream once more I close my willing eyes;
Ye soft illusions, dear deceits, arise! 240
Alas, no more! methinks we wandering go
Through dreary wastes, and weep each
    other's woe,
Where round some mouldering tower pale
    ivy creeps,
And low-browed rocks hang nodding o'er the
    deeps.
Sudden you mount, you beckon from the
    skies;
Clouds interpose, waves roar, and winds
    arise.
I shriek, start up, the same sad prospect find,
And wake to all the griefs I left behind.
    For thee the fates, severely kind, ordain
A cool suspense from pleasure and from
    pain; 250
Thy life a long dead calm of fixed repose;
No pulse that riots, and no blood that glows.
Still as the sea, ere winds were taught to blow,
Or moving spirit bade the waters flow;
Soft as the slumbers of a saint forgiven,
And mild as opening gleams of promised
    Heaven.
    Come, Abelard! for what hast thou to
    dread?
The torch of Venus burns not for the dead.
Nature stands checked; religion disapproves;
Even thou art cold—yet Eloïsa loves. 260
Ah hopeless, lasting flames! like those that
    burn
To light the dead, and warm the unfruitful
    urn.
    What scenes appear where'er I turn my
    view?
The dear ideas, where I fly, pursue,
Rise in the grove, before the altar rise,
Stain all my soul, and wanton in my eyes.

I waste the matin lamp in sighs for thee,
Thy image steals between my God and me,
Thy voice I seem in every hymn to hear,
With every bead I drop too soft a tear.   270
When from the censer clouds of fragrance
    roll,
And swelling organs lift the rising soul,
One thought of thee puts all the pomp to
    flight,
Priests, tapers, temples, swim before my
    sight;
In seas of flame my plunging soul is drowned,
While altars blaze, and angels tremble round.
    While prostrate here in humble grief I lie,
Kind, virtuous drops just gathering in my
    eye,
While praying, trembling, in the dust I roll,
And dawning grace is opening on my soul:
Come, if thou darest, all charming as thou
    art!   281
Oppose thyself to Heaven; dispute my heart;
Come, with one glance of those deluding eyes
Blot out each bright idea of the skies;
Take back that grace, those sorrows, and
    those tears;
Take back my fruitless penitence and
    prayers;
Snatch me, just mounting, from the blest
    abode;
Assist the fiends, and tear me from my God!
    No, fly me, fly me, far as pole from pole;
Rise Alps between us! and whole oceans roll!
Ah, come not, write not, think not once of
    me,   291
Nor share one pang of all I felt for thee.
Thy oaths I quit, thy memory resign;
Forget, renounce me, hate whate'er was
    mine.
Fair eyes, and tempting looks (which yet I
    view!)
Long loved, adored ideas, all adieu!
Oh Grace serene! oh virtue heavenly fair!
Divine oblivion of low-thoughted care!
Fresh blooming Hope, gay daughter of the
    sky!
And Faith, our early immortality!   300
Enter, each mild, each amicable guest;
Receive, and wrap me in eternal rest!
    See in her cell sad Eloïsa spread,
Propped on some tomb, a neighbour of the
    dead.
In each low wind methinks a spirit calls,
And more than echoes talk along the walls.
Here, as I watched the dying lamps around,

From yonder shrine I heard a hollow sound.
"Come, sister, come!" it said, or seemed to
    say,
"Thy place is here, sad sister, come away!   310
Once like thyself, I trembled, wept, and
    prayed,
Love's victim then, though now a sainted
    maid:
But all is calm in this eternal sleep;
Here grief forgets to groan, and love to weep;
Even superstition loses every fear,
For God, not man, absolves our frailties
    here."
    I come, I come! prepare your roseate bow-
    ers,
Celestial palms, and ever-blooming flowers.
Thither, where sinners may have rest, I go,
Where flames refined in breasts seraphic
    glow: 320
Thou, Abelard! the last sad office pay,
And smooth my passage to the realms of day;
See my lips tremble, and my eyeballs roll,
Suck my last breath, and catch my flying
    soul!
Ah no—in sacred vestments mayst thou stand,
The hallowed taper trembling in thy hand,
Present the Cross before my lifted eye,
Teach me at once, and learn of me to die.
Ah then, thy once loved Eloïsa see!
It will be then no crime to gaze on me.   330
See from my cheek the transient roses fly!
See the last sparkle languish in my eye!
Till every motion, pulse, and breath be o'er;
And even my Abelard be loved no more.
O Death all-eloquent! you only prove
What dust we dote on, when 'tis man we love.
    Then too, when fate shall thy fair frame
    destroy,
(That cause of all my guilt, and all my joy)
In trance ecstatic may thy pangs be drowned,
Bright clouds descend, and angels watch thee
    round,   340
From opening skies may streaming glories
    shine,
And saints embrace thee with a love like
    mine.
    May one kind grave unite each hapless
    name,
And graft my love immortal on thy fame!
Then, ages hence, when all my woes are o'er,
When this rebellious heart shall beat no
    more;
If ever chance two wandering lovers brings
To Paraclete's white walls and silver springs,

O'er the pale marble shall they join their
    heads,
And drink the falling tears each other sheds;
Then sadly say, with mutual pity moved,   351
"Oh may we never love as these have loved!"
From the full choir when loud hosannas rise,
And swell the pomp of dreadful sacrifice,
Amid that scene if some relenting eye
Glance on the stone where our cold relics lie,
Devotion's self shall steal a thought from
    Heaven,
One human tear shall drop and be forgiven.
And sure, if fate some future bard shall join
In sad similitude of griefs to mine,   360
Condemned whole years in absence to de-
    plore,
And image charms he must behold no more;
Such if there be, who loves so long, so well,
Let him our sad, our tender story tell;
The well-sung woes will soothe my pensive
    ghost;
He best can paint 'em who shall feel 'em
    most.

[1717]

AN ESSAY ON MAN

EPISTLE I

Awake, my St. John! leave all meaner things
To low ambition, and the pride of kings.
Let us (since Life can little more supply
Than just to look about us and to die)
Expatiate[1] free o'er all this scene of Man;
A mighty maze! but not without a plan;
A wild, where weeds and flowers promiscuous
    shoot;
Or garden, tempting with forbidden fruit.
Together let us beat this ample field,
Try what the open, what the covert yield;   10
The latent tracts, the giddy heights, explore
Of all who blindly creep, or sightless soar;
Eye nature's walks, shoot folly as it flies,
And catch the manners living as they rise;
Laugh where we must, be candid where we
    can,
But vindicate the ways of God to man.
  I. Say first, of God above, or man below,
What can we reason but from what we know?
Of man, what see we but his station here,
From which to reason, or to which refer?   20
  [1] Wander, roam.

Through worlds unnumbered though the God
    be known,
'Tis ours to trace him only in our own.
He who through vast immensity can pierce,
See worlds on worlds compose one universe,
Observe how system into system runs,
What other planets circle other suns,
What varied being peoples every star,
May tell why Heaven has made us as we are.
But of this frame the bearings and the ties,
The strong connections, nice dependencies,   30
Gradations just, has thy pervading soul
Looked through? or can a part contain the
    whole?
  Is the great chain that draws all to agree,
And drawn supports, upheld by God, or thee?
  II. Presumptuous man! the reason wouldst
    thou find,
Why formed so weak, so little, and so blind?
First, if thou canst, the harder reason guess,
Why formed no weaker, blinder, and no less!
Ask of thy mother earth, why oaks are made
Taller or stronger than the weeds they shade!
Or ask of yonder argent fields above,   41
Why Jove's satellites are less than Jove!
  Of systems possible, if 'tis confessed
That wisdom infinite must form the best,
Where all must full or not coherent be,
And all that rises, rise in due degree;
Then, in the scale of reasoning life, 'tis plain,
There must be, somewhere, such a rank as
    man:
And all the question (wrangle e'er so long)
Is only this, if God has placed him wrong.   50
  Respecting man, whatever wrong we call,
May, must be right, as relative to all.
In human works, though laboured on with pain,
A thousand movements scarce one purpose
    gain;
In God's, one single can its end produce;
Yet serves to second too some other use.
So man, who here seems principal alone,
Perhaps acts second to some sphere unknown,
Touches some wheel, or verges to some goal;
'Tis but a part we see, and not a whole.   60
  When the proud steed shall know why man
    restrains
His fiery course, or drives him o'er the plains:
When the dull ox, why now he breaks the clod,
Is now a victim, and now Egypt's god:
Then shall man's pride and dullness compre-
    hend
His actions', passions', being's, use and end;
Why doing, suffering, checked, impelled; and
    why

This hour a slave, the next a deity.
  Then say not man's imperfect, Heaven in
    fault;
Say rather, man's as perfect as he ought: 70
His knowledge measured to his state and
    place;
His time a moment, and a point his space.
If to be perfect in a certain sphere,
What matter, soon or late, or here or there?
The blessed to-day is as completely so,
As who began a thousand years ago.
  III. Heaven from all creatures hides the
    book of fate,
All but the page prescribed, their present
    state;
From brutes what men, from men what spirits
    know,
Or who could suffer being here below?   80
The lamb thy riot dooms to bleed to-day,
Had he thy reason, would he skip and play?
Pleased to the last, he crops the flowery food,
And licks the hand just raised to shed his
    blood.
Oh blindness to the future! kindly given,
That each may fill the circle marked by
    Heaven:
Who sees with equal eye, as God of all,
A hero perish, or a sparrow fall,
Atoms or systems into ruin hurled,
And now a bubble burst, and now a world.   90
  Hope humbly then; with trembling pinions
    soar;
Wait the great teacher Death; and God adore.
What future bliss, he gives not thee to know,
But gives that hope to be thy blessing now.
Hope springs eternal in the human breast;
Man never is, but always to be blessed;
The soul, uneasy and confined from home,
Rests and expatiates in a life to come.
  Lo, the poor Indian! whose untutored mind
Sees God in clouds, or hears him in the wind;
His soul, proud science never taught to stray
Far as the solar walk or milky way;   102
Yet simple nature to his hope has given,
Behind the cloud-topped hill, an humbler
    heaven;
Some safer world in depth of woods embraced,
Some happier island in the watery waste,
Where slaves once more their native land be-
    hold,
No fiends torment, no Christians thirst for gold.
To be, contents his natural desire;
He asks no angel's wing, no seraph's fire;   110
But thinks, admitted to that equal sky,

His faithful dog shall bear him company.
  IV. Go, wiser thou! and, in thy scale of sense,
Weigh thy opinion against Providence;
Call imperfection what thou fanciest such;
Say, here he gives too little, there too much:
Destroy all creatures for thy sport or gust,
Yet cry, If man's unhappy, God's unjust;
If man alone engross not Heaven's high care,
Alone made perfect here, immortal there: 120
Snatch from his hand the balance and the rod,
Re-judge his justice, be the God of God.
In pride, in reasoning pride, our error lies;
All quit their sphere, and rush into the skies,
Pride still is aiming at the blessed abodes,
Men would be angels, angels would be gods.
Aspiring to be gods, if angels fell,
Aspiring to be angels, men rebel:
And who but wishes to invert the laws
Of order, sins against the Eternal Cause.   130
  V. Ask for what end the heavenly bodies
    shine,
Earth for whose use? Pride answers, "'Tis for
    mine:
For me kind nature wakes her genial[2] power,
Suckles each herb, and spreads out every
    flower;
Annual for me, the grape, the rose renew
The juice nectareous and the balmy dew;
For me, the mine a thousand treasures brings;
For me, health gushes from a thousand springs;
Seas roll to waft me, suns to light me rise;
My footstool earth, my canopy the skies."   140
  But errs not nature from this gracious end,
From burning suns when livid deaths descend,
When earthquakes swallow, or when tempests
    sweep
Towns to one grave, whole nations to the
    deep?
"No," 'tis replied, "the first Almighty Cause
Acts not by partial but by general laws;
The exceptions few; some change since all be-
    gan:
And what created perfect?"—Why then man?
If the great end be human happiness,   149
Then nature deviates; and can man do less?
As much that end a constant course requires
Of showers and sunshine, as of man's desires;
As much eternal springs and cloudless skies,
As men forever temperate, calm, and wise.
If plagues or earthquakes break not Heaven's
    design,
Why then a Borgia, or a Catiline?
Who knows but he, whose hand the lightning
    forms,
  [2] Life-giving.

Who heaves old ocean, and who wings the
    storms;
Pours fierce ambition in a Cæsar's mind,
Or turns young Ammon loose to scourge man-
    kind?   160
From pride, from pride, our very reasoning
    springs;
Account for moral, as for natural things:
Why charge we Heaven in those, in these ac-
    quit?
In both, to reason right is to submit.
    Better for us, perhaps, it might appear,
Were there all harmony, all virtue here;
That never air or ocean felt the wind;
That never passion discomposed the mind.
But all subsists by elemental strife,
And passions are the elements of life. 170
The general order, since the whole began,
Is kept in nature, and is kept in man.
    VI. What would this man? Now upward
    will he soar,
And little less than angel, would be more;
Now looking downwards, just as grieved ap-
    pears
To want the strength of bulls, the fur of bears.
Made for his use all creatures if he call,
Say what their use, had he the powers of all?
Nature to these, without profusion, kind, 179
The proper organs, proper powers assigned;
Each seeming want compensated of course,
Here with degrees of swiftness, there of force;
All in exact proportion to the state;
Nothing to add, and nothing to abate.
Each beast, each insect, happy in its own:
Is Heaven unkind to man, and man alone?
Shall he alone, whom rational we call,
Be pleased with nothing, if not blessed with
    all?
    The bliss of man (could pride that blessing
    find)
Is not to act or think beyond mankind; 190
No powers of body or of soul to share,
But what his nature and his state can bear.
Why has not man a microscopic eye?
For this plain reason, man is not a fly.
Say what the use, were finer optics given,
To inspect a mite, not comprehend the heaven?
Or touch, if tremblingly alive all o'er,
To smart and agonize at every pore?
Or quick effluvia darting through the brain,
Die of a rose in aromatic pain? 200
If nature thundered in his opening ears,
And stunned him with the music of the
    spheres,

How would he wish that Heaven had left him
    still
The whispering zephyr, and the purling rill?
Who finds not Providence all good and wise,
Alike in what it gives, and what denies?
    VII. Far as creation's ample range extends,
The scale of sensual, mental powers ascends:
Mark how it mounts, to man's imperial race,
From the green myriads in the peopled grass:
What modes of sight betwixt each wide ex-
    treme,   211
The mole's dim curtain and the lynx's beam:
Of smell, the headlong lioness between,
And hound sagacious on the tainted green:
Of hearing, from the life that fills the flood,
To that which warbles through the vernal
    wood:
The spider's touch, how exquisitely fine!
Feels at each thread, and lives along the line:
In the nice bee, what sense so subtly true
From poisonous herbs extracts the healing
    dew?   220
How instinct varies in the grovelling swine,
Compared, half-reasoning elephant, with
    thine!
'Twixt that, and reason, what a nice barrier,
Forever separate, yet forever near!
Remembrance and reflection how allied;
What thin partitions sense from thought di-
    vide:
And middle natures, how they long to join,
Yet never pass the insuperable line!
Without this just gradation, could they be
Subjected, these to those, or all to thee? 230
The powers of all subdued by thee alone,
Is not thy reason all these powers in one?
    VIII. See through this air, this ocean, and
    this earth,
All matter quick, and bursting into birth.
Above, how high, progressive life may go!
Around, how wide! how deep extend below!
Vast chain of being! which from God began,
Natures ethereal, human, angel, man,
Beast, bird, fish, insect, what no eye can see,
No glass can reach; from infinite to thee, 240
From thee to nothing.—On superior powers
Were we to press, inferior might on ours:
Or in the full creation leave a void,
Where, one step broken, the great scale's de-
    stroyed:
From nature's chain whatever link you strike,
Tenth or ten thousandth, breaks the chain
    alike.
    And, if each system in gradation roll
Alike essential to the amazing whole,

The least confusion but in one, not all
That system only, but the whole must fall. 250
Let earth unbalanced from her orbit fly,
Planets and suns run lawless through the sky;
Let ruling angels from their spheres be hurled,
Being on being wrecked, and world on world;
Heaven's whole foundations to their centre
    nod,
And nature tremble to the throne of God.
All this dread order break—for whom? for
    thee?
Vile worm!—Oh madness! pride! impiety!
    IX. What if the foot, ordained the dust to
        tread,
Or hand, to toil, aspired to be the head? 260
What if the head, the eye, or ear repined
To serve mere engines to the ruling mind?
Just as absurd for any part to claim
To be another, in this general frame:
Just as absurd, to mourn the tasks or pains
The great directing mind of all ordains.
    All are but parts of one stupendous whole,
Whose body nature is, and God the soul;
That, changed through all, and yet in all the
    same,
Great in the earth, as in the ethereal frame,
Warms in the sun, refreshes in the breeze, 271
Glows in the stars, and blossoms in the trees,
Lives through all life, extends through all ex-
    tent,
Spreads undivided, operates unspent;
Breathes in our soul, informs our mortal part,
As full, as perfect, in a hair as heart:
As full, as perfect, in vile man that mourns,
As the rapt seraph that adores and burns:
To him no high, no low, no great, no small;
He fills, he bounds, connects, and equals all.
    X. Cease then, nor order imperfection
        name; 281
Our proper bliss depends on what we blame.
Know thy own point: this kind, this due de-
    gree
Of blindness, weakness, Heaven bestows on
    thee.
Submit.—In this, or any other sphere,
Secure to be as blessed as thou canst bear:
Safe in the hand of one disposing Power,
Or in the natal or the mortal hour.
All nature is but art, unknown to thee;
All chance, direction, which thou canst not
    see; 290
All discord, harmony not understood;
All partial evil, universal good:
And, spite of pride, in erring reason's spite,
One truth is clear, WHATEVER IS, IS RIGHT.

EPISTLE II

I. Know then thyself, presume not God to
    scan;
The proper study of mankind is man.
Placed on this isthmus of a middle state,
A being darkly wise, and rudely great:
With too much knowledge for the sceptic side,
With too much weakness for the stoic's pride,
He hangs between, in doubt to act or rest;
In doubt to deem himself a god, or beast;
In doubt his mind or body to prefer;
Born but to die, and reasoning but to err; 10
Alike in ignorance, his reason such,
Whether he thinks too little or too much:
Chaos of thought and passion, all confused;
Still by himself abused or disabused;
Created half to rise and half to fall;
Great lord of all things, yet a prey to all;
Sole judge of truth, in endless error hurled:
The glory, jest, and riddle of the world!
    Go, wondrous creature! mount where sci-
        ence guides,
Go, measure earth, weigh air, and state the
        tides; 20
Instruct the planets in what orbs to run,
Correct old time, and regulate the sun;
Go, soar with Plato to the empyreal sphere,
To the first good, first perfect, and first fair;
Or tread the mazy round his followers trod,
And quitting sense call imitating God;
As Eastern priests in giddy circles run,
And turn their heads to imitate the sun.
Go, teach Eternal Wisdom how to rule—
Then drop into thyself, and be a fool! 30
    Superior beings, when of late they saw
A mortal man unfold all nature's law,
Admired such wisdom in an earthly shape,
And showed a Newton as we show an ape.
    Could he whose rules the rapid comet bind,
Describe or fix one movement of his mind?
Who saw its fires here rise, and there descend,
Explain his own beginning, or his end?
Alas what wonder! man's superior part
Unchecked may rise, and climb from art to
        art; 40
But when his own great work is but begun,
What reason weaves, by passion is undone.
    Trace science then, with modesty thy guide;
First strip off all her equipage of pride;
Deduct what is but vanity, or dress,
Or learning's luxury, or idleness;
Or tricks to show the stretch of human brain,
Mere curious pleasure, or ingenious pain;

Expunge the whole, or lop the excrescent
    parts
Of all our vices have created arts;   50
Then see how little the remaining sum,
Which served the past, and must the times to
    come!
  II. Two principles in human nature reign:
Self-love, to urge, and reason, to restrain;
Nor this a good, nor that a bad we call,
Each works its end, to move or govern all:
And to their proper operation still,
Ascribe all good; to their improper, ill.
  Self-love, the spring of motion, acts the soul;
Reason's comparing balance rules the whole.
Man, but for that, no action could attend, 61
And but for this, were active to no end:
Fixed like a plant on his peculiar spot,
To draw nutrition, propagate, and rot;
Or, meteor-like, flame lawless through the
    void,
Destroying others, by himself destroyed.
  Most strength the moving principle re-
    quires;
Active its task, it prompts, impels, inspires.
Sedate and quiet the comparing lies,
Formed but to check, deliberate, and advise.
Self-love still stronger, as its objects nigh; 71
Reason's at distance, and in prospect lie:
That sees immediate good by present sense;
Reason, the future and the consequence.
Thicker than arguments, temptations throng,
At best more watchful this, but that more
    strong.
The action of the stronger to suspend,
Reason still use, to reason still attend.
Attention, habit and experience gains;
Each strengthens reason, and self-love re-
    strains.   80
  Let subtle schoolmen teach these friends to
    fight,
More studious to divide than to unite;
And grace and virtue, sense and reason split,
With all the rash dexterity of wit.
Wits, just like fools, at war about a name,
Have full as oft no meaning, or the same.
Self-love and reason to one end aspire,
Pain their aversion, pleasure their desire;
But greedy that, its object would devour;
This taste the honey, and not wound the
    flower: 90
Pleasure, or wrong or rightly understood,
Our greatest evil, or our greatest good.
  III. Modes of self-love the passions we may
    call;
'Tis real good, or seeming, moves them all;

But since not every good we can divide,
And reason bids us for our own provide,
Passions, though selfish, if their means be fair,
List under reason, and deserve her care;
Those, that imparted, court a nobler aim,
Exalt their kind, and take some virtue's name.
  In lazy apathy let stoics boast   101
Their virtue fixed; 'tis fixed as in a frost;
Contracted all, retiring to the breast;
But strength of mind is exercise, not rest:
The rising tempest puts in act the soul;
Parts it may ravage, but preserves the whole.
On life's vast ocean diversely we sail,
Reason the card, but passion is the gale;
Nor God alone in the still calm we find;
He mounts the storm, and walks upon the
    wind.   110
  Passions, like elements, though born to fight,
Yet, mixed and softened, in his work unite:
These 'tis enough to temper and employ;
But what composes man, can man destroy?
Suffice that reason keep to nature's road,
Subject, compound them, follow her and God.
Love, hope, and joy, fair pleasure's smiling
    train,
Hate, fear, and grief, the family of pain,
These mixed with art, and to due bounds con-
    fined,
Make and maintain the balance of the mind:
The lights and shades whose well accorded
    strife   121
Gives all the strength and colour of our life.
  Pleasures are ever in our hands or eyes;
And when in act they cease, in prospect rise;
Present to grasp, and future still to find,
The whole employ of body and of mind.
All spread their charms, but charm not all
    alike;
On different senses different objects strike;
Hence different passions more or less inflame,
As strong or weak, the organs of the frame; 130
And hence one master passion in the breast,
Like Aaron's serpent, swallows up the rest.
  As man, perhaps, the moment of his breath,
Receives the lurking principle of death;
The young disease that must subdue at length
Grows with his growth, and strengthens with
    his strength:
So, cast and mingled with his very frame,
The mind's disease, its ruling passion, came;
Each vital humour which should feed the
    whole
Soon flows to this, in body and in soul: 140
Whatever warms the heart or fills the head,
As the mind opens and its functions spread,

Imagination plies her dangerous art,
And pours it all upon the peccant part.
   Nature its mother, habit is its nurse;
Wit, spirit, faculties, but make it worse;
Reason itself but gives it edge and power,
As heaven's blessed beam turns vinegar more
         sour.
   We, wretched subjects though to lawful
         sway,
In this weak queen some favorite still obey:
Ah! if she lend not arms, as well as rules, 151
What can she more than tell us we are fools?
Teach us to mourn our nature, not to mend,
A sharp accuser but a helpless friend!
Or from a judge turn pleader, to persuade
The choice we make, or justify it made;
Proud of an easy conquest all along,
She but removes weak passions for the strong:
So, when small humours gather to a gout,
The doctor fancies he has driven them out. 160
   Yes, nature's road must ever be preferred;
Reason is here no guide, but still a guard;
'Tis hers to rectify, not overthrow,
And treat this passion more as friend than foe:
A mightier power the strong direction sends,
And several men impels to several ends:
Like varying winds, by other passions tossed,
This drives them constant to a certain coast.
Let power or knowledge, gold or glory, please,
Or (oft more strong than all) the love of ease;
Through life 'tis followed, even at life's ex-
         pense;   171
The merchant's toil, the sage's indolence,
The monk's humility, the hero's pride,
All, all alike, find reason on their side.
   The Eternal Art educing good from ill,
Grafts on this passion our best principle:
'Tis thus the mercury of man is fixed,
Strong grows the virtue with his nature mixed;
The dross cements what else were too refined,
And in one interest body acts with mind. 180
   As fruits ungrateful to the planter's care
On savage stocks inserted, learn to bear;
The surest virtues thus from passions shoot,
Wild nature's vigor working at the root.
What crops of wit and honesty appear
From spleen, from obstinacy, hate, or fear!
See anger, zeal and fortitude supply;
Even avarice, prudence; sloth, philosophy;
Lust, through some certain strainers well re-
         fined,
Is gentle love, and charms all womankind; 190
Envy, to which the ignoble mind's a slave,
Is emulation in the learned or brave;
Nor virtue, male or female, can we name,

But what will grow on pride, or grow on
         shame.
   Thus Nature gives us (let it check our pride)
The virtue nearest to our vice allied:
Reason the bias turns to good from ill,
And Nero reigns a Titus, if he will.
The fiery soul abhorred in Catiline,
In Decius charms, in Curtius is divine: 200
The same ambition can destroy or save,
And makes a patriot as it makes a knave.
   IV. This light and darkness in our chaos
         joined,
What shall divide? The God within the mind.
   Extremes in nature equal ends produce;
In man they join to some mysterious use;
Though each by turns the other's bound in-
         vade,
As, in some well-wrought picture, light and
         shade,
And oft so mix, the difference is too nice
Where ends the virtue, or begins the vice. 210
   Fools! who from hence into the notion fall,
That vice or virtue there is none at all.
If white and black blend, soften, and unite
A thousand ways, is there no black or white?
Ask your own heart, and nothing is so plain;
'Tis to mistake them, costs the time and pain.
   V. Vice is a monster of so frightful mien,
As, to be hated, needs but to be seen;
Yet seen too oft, familiar with her face,
We first endure, then pity, then embrace.   220
But where the extreme of vice, was ne'er
         agreed:
Ask where's the north? at York, 'tis on the
         Tweed;
In Scotland, at the Orcades; and there,
At Greenland, Zembla, or the Lord knows
         where.
No creature owns it in the first degree,
But thinks his neighbour further gone than he;
Even those who dwell beneath its very zone,
Or never feel the rage, or never own;
What happier natures shrink at with affright,
The hard inhabitant contends is right.   230
   VI. Virtuous and vicious every man must be,
Few in the extreme, but all in the degree;
The rogue and fool, by fits, is fair and wise;
And even the best, by fits, what they despise.
'Tis but by parts we follow good or ill,
For, vice or virtue, self directs it still;
Each individual seeks a several goal,
But Heaven's great view is one, and that the
         whole.
That counter-works each folly and caprice;
That disappoints the effect of every vice; 240

That, happy frailties to all ranks applied,
Shame to the virgin, to the matron pride,
Fear to the statesman, rashness to the chief,
To kings presumption, and to crowds belief:
That, virtue's ends from vanity can raise,
Which seeks no interest, no reward but praise;
And build on wants and on defects of mind,
The joy, the peace, the glory of mankind.
  Heaven forming each on other to depend,
A master, or a servant, or a friend,   250
Bids each on other for assistance call,
Till one man's weakness grows the strength of
    all.
Wants, frailties, passions, closer still ally
The common interest, or endear the tie.
To these we owe true friendship, love sincere,
Each home-felt joy that life inherits here;
Yet from the same we learn, in its decline,
Those joys, those loves, those interests to re-
    sign;
Taught half by reason, half by mere decay,
To welcome death and calmly pass away.   260
  Whate'er the passion, knowledge, fame, or
    pelf,
Not one will change his neighbour with himself.
The learned is happy nature to explore,
The fool is happy that he knows no more,
The rich is happy in the plenty given,
The poor contents him with the care of Heaven.
See the blind beggar dance, the cripple sing,
The sot a hero, lunatic a king;
The starving chemist in his golden views
Supremely blessed, the poet in his Muse.   270
  See some strange comfort every state attend,
And pride bestowed on all, a common friend;
See some fit passion every age supply,
Hope travels through, nor quits us when we
    die.
Behold the child, by nature's kindly law,
Pleased with a rattle, tickled with a straw;
Some livelier plaything gives his youth de-
    light,
A little louder, but as empty quite;
Scarfs, garters, gold, amuse his riper stage,   279
And beads and prayerbooks are the toys of age;
Pleased with this bauble still, as that before;
'Til tired he sleeps, and life's poor play is o'er.
  Meanwhile opinion gilds with varying rays
Those painted clouds that beautify our days;
Each want of happiness by hope supplied,
And each vacuity of sense by pride:
These build as fast as knowledge can destroy;
In folly's cup still laughs the bubble, joy;
One prospect lost, another still we gain,
And not a vanity is given in vain;   290

Even mean self-love becomes, by force divine,
The scale to measure others' wants by thine.
See! and confess, one comfort still must rise,
'Tis this, though man's a fool, yet God is wise.

EPISTLE III

Here then we rest: "The Universal Cause
Acts to one end, but acts by various laws."
In all the madness of superfluous health,
The trim of pride, the impudence of wealth,
Let this great truth be present night and day;
But most be present, if we preach or pray.
  I. Look round our world; behold the chain
    of love
Combining all below and all above.
See plastic nature working to this end,
The single atoms each to other tend,   10
Attract, attracted to, the next in place
Formed and impelled its neighbour to em-
    brace.
See matter next, with various life endued,
Press to one centre still, the general good.
See dying vegetables life sustain,
See life dissolving vegetate again:
All forms that perish other forms supply,
(By turns we catch the vital breath, and die)
Like bubbles on the sea of matter born,
They rise, they break, and to that sea return.
Nothing is foreign: parts relate to whole;   21
One all-extending, all-preserving soul
Connects each being, greatest with the least;
Made beast in aid of man, and man of beast;
All served, all serving: nothing stands alone;
The chain holds on, and where it ends, un-
    known.
  Has God, thou fool! worked solely for thy
    good,
Thy joy, thy pastime, thy attire, thy food?
Who for thy table feeds the wanton fawn,
For him as kindly spread the flowery lawn. 30
Is it for thee the lark ascends and sings?
Joy tunes his voice, joy elevates his wings.
Is it for thee the linnet pours his throat?
Loves of his own and raptures swell the note.
The bounding steed you pompously bestride,
Shares with his lord the pleasure and the pride.
Is thine alone the seed that strews the plain?
The birds of heaven shall vindicate their grain.
Thine the full harvest of the golden year?
Part pays, and justly, the deserving steer: 40
The hog, that ploughs not nor obeys thy call,
Lives on the labours of this lord of all.
  Know, nature's children all divide her care:

The fur that warms a monarch, warmed a
    bear.
While man exclaims, "See all things for my
    use!"
"See man for mine!" replies a pampered
    goose;
And just as short of reason he must fall
Who thinks all made for one, not one for all.
  Grant that the powerful still the weak con-
    trol;
Be man the wit and tyrant of the whole: 50
Nature that tyrant checks; he only knows,
And helps, another creature's wants and woes.
Say, will the falcon, stooping from above,
Smit with her varying plumage, spare the
    dove?
Admires the jay the insect's gilded wings?
Or hears the hawk when Philomela sings?
Man cares for all: to birds he gives his woods,
To beasts his pastures, and to fish his floods;
For some his interest prompts him to provide,
For more his pleasure, yet for more his pride:
All feed on one vain patron, and enjoy   61
The extensive blessing of his luxury.
That very life his learnèd hunger craves,
He saves from famine, from the savage saves;
Nay, feasts the animal he dooms his feast,
And, till he ends the being, makes it blessed;
Which sees no more the stroke, or feels the
    pain,
Than favoured man by touch ethereal slain.
The creature had his feast of life before,   69
Thou too must perish, when thy feast is o'er!
  To each unthinking being, Heaven, a friend,
Gives not the useless knowledge of its end:
To man imparts it; but with such a view
As, while he dreads it, makes him hope it too:
The hour concealed, and so remote the fear,
Death still draws nearer, never seeming near.
Great standing miracle! that Heaven assigned
Its only thinking thing this turn of mind.
  II. Whether with reason or with instinct
    blessed,
Know, all enjoy that power which suits them
    best;   80
To bliss alike by that direction tend,
And find the means proportioned to their end.
Say, where full instinct is the unerring guide,
What pope or council can they need beside?
Reason, however able, cool at best,
Cares not for service, or but serves when
    pressed,
Stays till we call, and then not often near;
But honest instinct comes a volunteer,
Sure never to o'ershoot. but just to hit;

While still too wide or short is human wit;   90
Sure by quick nature happiness to gain,
Which heavier reason labours at in vain,
This too serves always, reason never long;
One must go right, the other may go wrong.
See then the acting and comparing powers
One in their nature, which are two in ours;
And reason raise o'er instinct as you can,
In this 'tis God directs, in that 'tis man.
  Who taught the nations of the field and
    wood   99
To shun their poison, and to choose their food?
Prescient, the tides or tempests to withstand,
Build on the wave, or arch beneath the sand?
Who made the spider parallels design,
Sure as Demoivre, without rule or line?
Who bid the stork, Columbus-like, explore
Heavens not his own, and worlds unknown be-
    fore?
Who calls the council, states the certain day,
Who forms the phalanx, and who points the
    way?
  III. God in the nature of each being founds
Its proper bliss, and sets its proper bounds; 110
But as he framed a whole, the whole to bless,
On mutual wants built mutual happiness:
So from the first, eternal order ran,
And creature linked to creature, man to man.
Whate'er of life all-quickening ether keeps,
Or breathes through air, or shoots beneath the
    deeps
Or pours profuse on earth, one nature feeds
The vital flame, and swells the genial seeds.
Not man alone, but all that roam the wood,
Or wing the sky, or roll along the flood,   120
Each loves itself, but not itself alone,
Each sex desires alike, till two are one.
Nor ends the pleasure with the fierce embrace;
They love themselves a third time in their
    race.
Thus beast and bird their common charge at-
    tend,
The mothers nurse it, and the sires defend;
The young dismissed to wander earth or air,
There stops the instinct, and there ends the
    care;
The link dissolves, each seeks a fresh embrace,
Another love succeeds, another race.   130
A longer care man's helpless kind demands;
That longer care contracts more lasting bands;
Reflection, reason, still the ties improve,
At once extend the interest, and the love;
With choice we fix, with sympathy we burn;
Each virtue in each passion takes its turn;

And still new needs, new helps, new habits
    rise,
That graft benevolence on charities.
Still as one brood, and as another rose,
These natural love maintained, habitual those:
The last, scarce ripened into perfect man, 141
Saw helpless him from whom their life began:
Memory and forecast just returns engage,
That pointed back to youth, this on to age;
While pleasure, gratitude, and hope, com-
    bined,
Still spread the interest, and preserved the
    kind.
    IV. Nor think, in nature's state they blindly
    trod;
The state of nature was the reign of God:
Self-love and social at her birth began,
Union the bond of all things, and of man. 150
Pride then was not; nor arts, that pride to aid;
Man walked with beast, joint tenant of the
    shade;
The same his table, and the same his bed;
No murder clothed him, and no murder fed.
In the same temple, the resounding wood,
All vocal beings hymned their equal God:
The shrine with gore unstained, with gold un-
    dressed,
Unbribed, unbloody, stood the blameless
    priest:
Heaven's attribute was universal care,
And man's prerogative to rule, but spare. 160
Ah! how unlike the man of times to come!
Of half that live the butcher and the tomb;
Who, foe to nature, hears the general groan,
Murders their species, and betrays his own.
But just disease to luxury succeeds,
And every death its own avenger breeds;
The fury-passions from that blood began,
And turned on man a fiercer savage, man.
    See him from nature rising slow to art!
To copy instinct then was reason's part; 170
Thus then to man the voice of Nature spake—
"Go, from the creatures thy instructions take:
Learn from the birds what food the thickets
    yield;
Learn from the beasts the physic of the field;
Thy arts of building from the bee receive;
Learn of the mole to plough, the worm to
    weave;
Learn of the little nautilus to sail,
Spread the thin oar, and catch the driving
    gale.
Here too all forms of social union find,
And hence let reason, late, instruct mankind:
Here subterranean works and cities see; 181

There towns aërial on the waving tree.
Learn each small people's genius, policies,
The ant's republic, and the realm of bees;
How those in common all their wealth be-
    stow,
And anarchy without confusion know;
And these forever, though a monarch reign,
Their separate cells and properties maintain.
Mark what unvaried laws preserve each state,
Laws wise as nature and as fixed as fate. 190
In vain thy reason finer webs shall draw,
Entangle justice in her net of law,
And right, too rigid, harden into wrong;
Still for the strong too weak, the weak too
    strong.
Yet go! and thus o'er all the creatures sway,
Thus let the wiser make the rest obey;
And, for those arts mere instinct could afford,
Be crowned as monarchs, or as gods adored."
    V. Great Nature spoke; observant men
    obeyed;
Cities were built, societies were made: 200
Here rose one little state; another near
Grew by like means, and joined, through love
    or fear.
Did here the trees with ruddier burdens bend,
And there the streams in purer rills descend?
What war could ravish, commerce could be-
    stow,
And he returned a friend, who came a foe.
Converse and love mankind might strongly
    draw,
When love was liberty, and nature law.
Thus states were formed; the name of king
    unknown,
Till common interest placed the sway in one.
'Twas virtue only (or in arts or arms, 211
Diffusing blessings, or averting harms)
The same which in a sire the sons obeyed,
A prince the father of a people made.
    VI. Till then, by nature crowned, each
    patriarch sate,
King, priest, and parent of his growing state;
On him, their second Providence, they hung,
Their law his eye, their oracle his tongue.
He from the wondering furrow called the food
Taught to command the fire, control the
    flood, 220
Draw forth the monsters of the abyss pro-
    found,
Or fetch the aërial eagle to the ground.
Till drooping, sickening, dying they began
Whom they revered as God to mourn as man:
Then, looking up from sire to sire, explored
One great first father, and that first adored.

Or plain tradition that this all begun,
Conveyed unbroken faith from sire to son;
The worker from the work distinct was known,
And simple reason never sought but one: 230
Ere wit oblique had broke that steady light,
Man, like his Maker, saw that all was right;
To virtue, in the paths of pleasure, trod,
And owned a father when he owned a God.
Love all the faith, and all the allegiance then,
For nature knew no right divine in men,
No ill could fear in God; and understood
A sovereign being but a sovereign good.
True faith, true policy, united ran,
This was but love of God, and this of man. 240
  Who first taught souls enslaved, and realms
    undone,
The enormous faith of many made for one;
That proud exception to all nature's laws,
To invert the world, and counter-work its
    cause?
Force first made conquest, and that conquest,
    law;
Till superstition taught the tyrant awe,
Then shared the tyranny, then lent it aid,
And gods of conquerors, slaves of subjects
    made:
She 'midst the lightning's blaze, and thun-
    der's sound,
When rocked the mountains, and when
    groaned the ground, 250
She taught the weak to bend, the proud to
    pray,
To power unseen, and mightier far than they:
She from the rending earth and bursting skies
Saw gods descend and fiends infernal rise;
Here fixed the dreadful, there the blessed
    abodes;
Fear made her devils, and weak hope her gods;
Gods partial, changeful, passionate, unjust,
Whose attributes were rage, revenge, or lust;
Such as the souls of cowards might conceive,
And, formed like tyrants, tyrants would be-
    lieve. 260
Zeal then, not charity, became the guide;
And hell was built on spite, and heaven on
    pride,
Then sacred seemed the ethereal vault no
    more;
Altars grew marble then, and reeked with
    gore:
Then first the flamen tasted living food;
Next his grim idol smeared with human blood;
With heaven's own thunders shook the world
    below,

And played the god an engine on his foe.
  So drives self-love, through just and through
    unjust,
To one man's power, ambition, lucre, lust: 270
The same self-love, in all, becomes the cause
Of what restrains him, government and laws.
For, what one likes if others like as well,
What serves one will, when many wills rebel?
How shall he keep, what, sleeping or awake,
A weaker may surprise, a stronger take?
His safety must his liberty restrain;
All join to guard what each desires to gain.
Forced into virtue thus by self-defence,
Even kings learned justice and benevolence;
Self-love forsook the path it first pursued, 281
And found the private in the public good.
  'Twas then the studious head or generous
    mind,
Follower of God or friend of humankind,
Poet or patriot, rose but to restore
The faith and moral nature gave before;
Re-lumed her ancient light, not kindled new;
If not God's image, yet his shadow drew:
Taught power's due use to people and to kings
Taught nor to slack, nor strain its tender
    strings; 290
The less, or greater, set so justly true,
That touching one must strike the other too;
Till jarring interests of themselves create
The according music of a well-mixed state.
Such is the world's great harmony, that springs
From order, union, full consent of things;
Where small and great, where weak and
    mighty, made
To serve, not suffer, strengthen, not invade—
More powerful each as needful to the rest,
And, in proportion as it blesses, blessed— 300
Draw to one point, and to one centre bring
Beast, man, or angel, servant, lord, or king.
  For forms of government let fools contest;
Whate'er is best administered is best:
For modes of faith let graceless zealots fight;
His can't be wrong whose life is in the right:
In faith and hope the world will disagree,
But all mankind's concern is charity:
All must be false that thwart this one great
    end 309
And all of God, that bless mankind or mend.
  Man, like the generous vine, supported lives;
The strength he gains is from the embrace he
    gives.
On their own axis as the planets run,
Yet make at once their circle round the sun,
So two consistent motions act the soul,

And one regards itself, and one the whole.
Thus God and nature linked the general
   frame,
And bade self-love and social be the same.

EPISTLE IV

O happiness! our being's end and aim!
Good, pleasure, ease, content! whate'er thy
   name:
That something still which prompts the eter-
   nal sigh,
For which we bear to live, or dare to die,
Which still so near us, yet beyond us lies,
O'erlooked, seen double, by the fool, and
   wise—
Plant of celestial seed! if dropped below,
Say, in what mortal soil thou deign'st to grow?
Fair opening to some court's propitious shine,
Or deep with diamonds in the flaming mine?
Twined with the wreaths Parnassian laurels
   yield,   11
Or reaped in iron harvests of the field?
Where grows?—where grows it not? If vain
   our toil,
We ought to blame the culture, not the soil;
Fixed to no spot is happiness sincere,
'Tis nowhere to be found, or everywhere;
'Tis never to be bought, but always free,
And fled from monarchs, St. John! dwells
   with thee.
   I. Ask of the learned the way? The learned
   are blind;
This bids to serve, and that to shun mankind;
Some place the bliss in action, some in ease, 21
Those call it pleasure, and contentment these;
Some sunk to beasts, find pleasure end in pain;
Some swelled to gods, confess even virtue vain;
Or indolent, to each extreme they fall,
To trust in everything, or doubt of all.
   Who thus define it, say they more or less
Than this, that happiness is happiness?
   II. Take nature's path, and mad opinion's
   leave;   29
All states can reach it and all heads conceive;
Obvious her goods, in no extreme they dwell;
There needs but thinking right and meaning
   well;
And mourn our various portions as we please,
Equal is common sense, and common ease.
   Remember, man, "the Universal Cause
Acts not by partial, but by general laws;"
And makes what happiness we justly call
Subsist not in the good of one, but all.
There's not a blessing individuals find,

But some way leans and hearkens to the kind:
No bandit fierce, no tyrant mad with pride, 41
No caverned hermit, rests self-satisfied:
Who most to shun or hate mankind pretend,
Seek an admirer or would fix a friend:
Abstract what others feel, what others think
All pleasures sicken and all glories sink:
Each has his share; and who would more ob-
   tain,
Shall find, the pleasure pays not half the pain.
   Order is Heaven's first law; and this con-
   fessed,   49
Some are, and must be, greater than the rest,
More rich, more wise; but who infers from
   hence
That such are happier, shocks all common
   sense.
Heaven to mankind impartial we confess,
If all are equal in their happiness;
But mutual wants this happiness increase;
All nature's difference keeps all nature's peace.
Condition, circumstance is not the thing;
Bliss is the same in subject or in king,
In who obtain defence, or who defend,
In him who is, or him who finds a friend: 60
Heaven breathes through every member of
   the whole
One common blessing, as one common soul.
But fortune's gifts if each alike possessed,
And each were equal, must not all contest?
If then to all men happiness was meant,
God in externals could not place content.
   Fortune her gifts may variously dispose,
And these be happy called, unhappy those;
But Heaven's just balance equal will appear,
While those are placed in hope, and these in
   fear: 70
Nor present good or ill, the joy or curse,
But future views of better or of worse.
   O sons of earth! attempt ye still to rise,
By mountains piled on mountains, to the skies?
Heaven still with laughter the vain toil surveys,
And buries madmen in the heaps they raise.
   III. Know, all the good that individuals
   find,
Or God and nature meant to mere mankind,
Reason's whole pleasure, all the joys of sense,
Lie in three words—health, peace, and com-
   petence.   80
But health consists with temperance alone;
And peace, O virtue! peace is all thy own.
The good or bad the gifts of fortune gain,
But these less taste them as they worse obtain.
Say, in pursuit of profit or delight,

Who risk the most, that take wrong means, or
    right?
Of vice or virtue, whether blessed or cursed,
Which meets contempt, or which compassion
    first?
Count all the advantage prosperous vice at-
    tains,
'Tis but what virtue flies from and disdains; 90
And grant the bad what happiness they would,
One they must want, which is, to pass for good.
    Oh blind to truth, and God's whole scheme
    below,
Who fancy bliss to vice, to virtue woe!
Who sees and follows that great scheme the
    best,
Best knows the blessing, and will most be
    blessed.
But fools the good alone unhappy call,
For ills or accidents that chance to all.
See Falkland dies, the virtuous and the just!
See godlike Turenne prostrate on the dust! 100
See Sidney bleeds amid the martial strife!
Was this their virtue, or contempt of life?
Say, was it virtue, more though heaven ne'er
    gave,
Lamented Digby! sunk thee to the grave?
Tell me, if virtue made the son expire,
Why, full of days and honour, lives the sire?
Why drew Marseille's good bishop purer
    breath,
When nature sickened, and each gale was
    death?
Or why so long (in life if long can be)
Lent Heaven a parent to the poor and me? 110
    What makes all physical or moral ill?
There deviates nature, and here wanders will.
God sends not ill; if rightly understood,
Or partial ill is universal good,
Or change admits, or nature lets it fall;
Short, and but rare, till man improved it all.
We just as wisely might of heaven complain
That righteous Abel was destroyed by Cain,
As that the virtuous son is ill at ease
When his lewd father gave the dire disease. 120
Think we, like some weak prince, the Eternal
    Cause
Prone for his favourites to reverse his laws?
    IV. Shall burning Ætna, if a sage requires,
Forget to thunder, and recall her fires?
On air or sea new motions be impressed,
O blameless Bethel! to relieve thy breast?
When the loose mountain trembles from on
    high,
Shall gravitation cease, if you go by?
Or some old temple, nodding to its fall, 129

For Chartres' head reserve the hanging wall?
    V. But still this world (so fitted for the
        knave)
Contents us not. A better shall we have?
A kingdom of the just then let it be,
But first consider how those just agree.
The good must merit God's peculiar care;
But who but God can tell us who they are?
One thinks on Calvin Heaven's own spirit fell;
Another deems him instrument of hell;
If Calvin feel Heaven's blessing, or its rod,
This cries there is, and that, there is no God.
What shocks one part will edify the rest, 141
Nor with one system can they all be blessed.
The very best will variously incline,
And what rewards your virtue, punish mine.
Whatever is, is right.—This world, 'tis true,
Was made for Cæsar—but for Titus too;
And which more blessed? who chained his
        country, say,
Or he whose virtue sighed to lose a day?
    "But sometimes virtue starves, while vice is
        fed."
What then? Is the reward of virtue bread? 150
That, vice may merit, 'tis the price of toil;
The knave deserves it, when he tills the soil,
The knave deserves it, when he tempts the
        main,
Where folly fights for kings, or dives for gain.
The good man may be weak, be indolent;
Nor is his claim to plenty, but content.
But grant him riches, your demand is o'er?
    "No—shall the good want health, the good
        want power?"
Add health and power and every earthly
        thing,
    "Why bounded power? why private? why no
        king?" 160
Nay, why external for internal given?
Why is not man a god, and earth a heaven?
Who ask and reason thus, will scarce conceive
God gives enough, while he has more to give:
Immense the power, immense were the de-
        mand;
Say, at what part of nature will they stand?
    VI. What nothing earthly gives, or can de-
        stroy,
The soul's calm sunshine and the heart-felt joy,
Is virtue's prize: A better would you fix?
Then give humility a coach and six, 170
Justice a conqueror's sword, or truth a gown,
Or public spirit its great cure, a crown.
Weak, foolish man! will Heaven reward us
    there

With the same trash mad mortals wish for
        here?
The boy and man an individual makes,
Yet sigh'st thou now for apples and for cakes?
Go, like the Indian, in another life
Expect thy dog, thy bottle, and thy wife;
As well as dream such trifles are assigned,
As toys and empires, for a godlike mind.   180
Rewards that either would to virtue bring
No joy, or be destructive of the thing:
How oft by these at sixty are undone
The virtues of a saint at twenty-one!
To whom can riches give repute, or trust
Content or pleasure, but the good and just?
Judges and senates have been bought for gold,
Esteem and love were never to be sold.
O fool! to think God hates the worthy mind,
The lover and the love of humankind,   190
Whose life is healthful, and whose conscience
        clear,
Because he wants a thousand pounds a year.
  Honour and shame from no condition rise;
Act well your part, there all the honour lies.
Fortune in men has some small difference
        made,
One flaunts in rags, one flutters in brocade;
The cobbler aproned, and the parson gowned,
The friar hooded, and the monarch crowned.
"What differ more," you cry, "than crown
        and cowl?"
I'll tell you, friend! a wise man and a fool.   200
You'll find, if once the monarch acts the monk,
Or, cobbler-like, the parson will be drunk,
Worth makes the man, and want of it the
        fellow;
The rest is all but leather or prunella.[1]
  Stuck o'er with titles and hung round with
        strings,
That thou mayst be by kings, or whores of
        kings.
Boast the pure blood of an illustrious race,
In quiet flow from Lucrece to Lucrece:
But by your fathers' worth if yours you rate,
Count me those only who were good and great.
Go! if your ancient but ignoble blood   211
Has crept through scoundrels ever since the
        flood,
Go! and pretend your family is young;
Nor own your fathers have been fools so long.
What can ennoble sots, or slaves, or cowards?
Alas! not all the blood of all the Howards.
  Look next on greatness; say where great-
        ness lies?

[1] Clergymen's gowns were often made of this
material.

"Where, but among the heroes and the wise?"
Heroes are much the same, the point's agreed,
From Macedonia's madman to the Swede;   220
The whole strange purpose of their lives, to
        find,
Or make, an enemy of all mankind!
Not one looks backward, onward still he goes,
Yet ne'er looks forward farther than his nose.
No less alike the politic and wise;
All sly slow things, with circumspective eyes:
Men in their loose unguarded hours they take,
Not that themselves are wise, but others weak.
But grant that those can conquer, these can
        cheat;
'Tis phrase absurd to call a villain great: 230
Who wickedly is wise, or madly brave,
Is but the more a fool, the more a knave.
Who noble ends by noble means obtains,
Or failing, smiles in exile or in chains,
Like good Aurelius let him reign, or bleed
Like Socrates, that man is great indeed.
  What's fame? a fancied life in others' breath,
A thing beyond us, even before our death.
Just what you hear, you have, and what's un-
        known
The same (my Lord) if Tully's, or your own.
All that we feel of it begins and ends   241
In the small circle of our foes or friends;
To all beside as much an empty shade
An Eugene living, as a Cæsar dead;
Alike or when, or where, they shone, or shine,
Or on the Rubicon, or on the Rhine.
A wit's a feather, and a chief a rod;
An honest man's the noblest work of God.
Fame but from death a villain's name can
        save,
As justice tears his body from the grave;   250
When what to oblivion better was resigned,
Is hung on high, to poison half mankind.
All fame is foreign, but of true desert;
Plays round the head, but comes not to the
        heart:
One self-approving hour whole years out-
        weighs
Of stupid starers, and of loud huzzas;
And more true joy Marcellus exiled feels,
Than Cæsar with a senate at his heels.
  In parts superior what advantage lies?
Tell, for you can, what is it to be wise?   260
'Tis but to know how little can be known;
To see all others' faults, and feel our own:
Condemned in business or in arts to drudge,
Without a second, or without a judge:

Truths would you teach, or save a sinking land,
All fear, none aid you, and few understand.
Painful preëminence! yourself to view
Above life's weakness, and its comforts too.
　Bring then these blessings to a strict account;
Make fair deductions; see to what they mount:
How much of other each is sure to cost; 271
How each for other oft is wholly lost;
How inconsistent greater goods with these;
How sometimes life is risked, and always ease:
Think, and if still the things thy envy call,
Say, wouldst thou be the man to whom they
　　fall?
To sigh for ribbands if thou art so silly,
Mark how they grace Lord Umbra, or Sir
　　Billy:
Is yellow dirt the passion of thy life?
Look but on Gripus, or on Gripus' wife: 280
If parts allure thee, think how Bacon shined,
The wisest, brightest, meanest of mankind:
Or ravished with the whistling of a name,
See Cromwell, damned to everlasting fame!
If all, united, thy ambition call,
From ancient story learn to scorn them all.
There, in the rich, the honoured, famed, and
　　great,
See the false scale of happiness complete!
In hearts of kings, or arms of queens who lay,
How happy! those to ruin, these betray. 290
Mark by what wretched steps their glory
　　grows,
From dirt and sea-weed as proud Venice rose;
In each how guilt and greatness equal ran,
And all that raised the hero, sunk the man:
Now Europe's laurels on their brows behold,
But stained with blood, or ill exchanged for
　　gold:
Then see them broke with toils, or sunk in ease,
Or infamous for plundered provinces.
Oh wealth ill-fated! which no act of fame 299
E'er taught to shine, or sanctified from shame!
What greater bliss attends their close of life?
Some greedy minion, or imperious wife.
The trophied arches, storied halls invade
And haunt their slumbers in the pompous
　　shade.
Alas! not dazzled with their noon-tide ray,
Compute the morn and evening to the day;
The whole amount of that enormous fame,
A tale, that blends their glory with their
　　shame!
　VII. Know then this truth (enough for man
　　to know)

"Virtue alone is happiness below." 310
The only point where human bliss stands still,
And tastes the good without the fall to ill;
Where only merit constant pay receives,
Is blessed in what it takes, and what it gives;
The joy unequalled, if its end it gain,
And if it lose, attended with no pain:
Without satiety, though e'er so blessed,
And but more relished as the more distressed:
The broadest mirth unfeeling folly wears,
Less pleasing far than virtue's very tears: 320
Good, from each object, from each place ac-
　　quired,
Forever exercised, yet never tired;
Never elated, while one man's oppressed;
Never dejected, while another's blessed;
And where no wants, no wishes can remain,
Since but to wish more virtue, is to gain.
　See the sole bliss Heaven could on all be-
　　stow!
Which who but feels can taste, but thinks can
　　know:
Yet poor with fortune, and with learning blind,
The bad must miss; the good, untaught, will
　　find; 330
Slave to no sect, who takes no private road,
But looks through Nature up to Nature's God;
Pursues that chain which links the immense
　　design,
Joins heaven and earth, and mortal and di-
　　vine;
Sees, that no being any bliss can know,
But touches some above, and some below;
Learns, from this union of the rising whole,
The first, last purpose of the human soul;
And knows, where faith, law, morals, all be-
　　gan
All end, in love of God, and love of man. 340
　For him alone, hope leads from goal to goal,
And opens still, and opens on his soul;
Till lengthened on to faith, and unconfined,
It pours the bliss that fills up all the mind.
He sees why nature plants in man alone
Hope of known bliss, and faith in bliss un-
　　known:
(Nature, whose dictates to no other kind
Are given in vain, but what they seek they
　　find)
Wise is her present; she connects in this
His greatest virtue with his greatest bliss; 350
At once his own bright prospect to be blest,
And strongest motive to assist the rest.
　Self-love thus pushed to social, to divine

Gives thee to make thy neighbour's blessing
thine.
Is this too little for the boundless heart?
Extend it, let thy enemies have part:
Grasp the whole worlds of reason, life, and
sense,
In one close system of benevolence:
Happier as kinder, in whate'er degree,
And height of bliss but height of charity. 360
   God loves from whole to parts: but human
soul
Must rise from individual to the whole.
Self-love but serves the virtuous mind to wake,
As the small pebble stirs the peaceful lake;
The centre moved, a circle straight succeeds,
Another still, and still another spreads;
Friend, parent, neighbour, first it will embrace;
His country next; and next all human race;
Wide and more wide, the o'erflowings of the
mind
Take every creature in, of every kind; 370
Earth smiles around, with boundless bounty
blest,
And Heaven beholds its image in his breast.
   Come, then, my friend! my genius! come
along;
O master of the poet, and the song!
And while the muse now stoops, or now as-
cends,
To man's low passions, or their glorious ends,
Teach me, like thee, in various nature wise,
To fall with dignity, with temper rise;
Formed by thy converse, happily to steer
From grave to gay, from lively to severe; 380
Correct with spirit, eloquent with ease,
Intent to reason, or polite to please.
Oh! while along the stream of time thy name
Expanded flies, and gathers all its fame,
Say, shall my little bark attendant sail,
Pursue the triumph, and partake the gale?
When statesmen, heroes, kings in dust repose,
Whose sons shall blush their fathers were thy
foes,
Shall then this verse to future age pretend 389
Thou wert my guide, philosopher, and friend?
That urged by thee, I turned the tuneful art
From sounds to things, from fancy to the heart;
For wit's false mirror held up nature's light;
Showed erring pride, WHATEVER IS, IS RIGHT;
That REASON, PASSION, answer one great aim;
That true SELF-LOVE and SOCIAL are the same;
That VIRTUE only makes our bliss below;
And all our knowledge is, OURSELVES TO KNOW.

[1733-34]

THE UNIVERSAL PRAYER

DEO OPT. MAX.

Father of all! in every age,
  In every clime adored,
By saint, by savage, and by sage,
  Jehovah, Jove, or Lord!

Thou Great First Cause, least understood:
  Who all my sense confined
To know but this, that Thou art good,
  And that myself am blind;

Yet gave me, in this dark estate,
  To see the good from ill; 10
And binding nature fast in fate,
  Left free the human will.

What conscience dictates to be done,
  Or warns me not to do,
This, teach me more than hell to shun,
  That, more than heaven pursue.

What blessings thy free bounty gives,
  Let me not cast away;
For God is payed when man receives,
  To enjoy is to obey. 20

Yet not to earth's contracted span
  Thy goodness led me bound,
Or think Thee Lord alone of man,
  When thousand worlds are round:

Let not this weak, unknowing hand
  Presume thy bolts to throw,
And deal damnation round the land,
  On each I judge thy foe.

If I am right, thy grace impart,
  Still in the right to stay; 30
If I am wrong, oh teach my heart
  To find that better way.

Save me alike from foolish pride,
  Or impious discontent,
At aught thy wisdom has denied,
  Or aught thy goodness lent.

Teach me to feel another's woe,
  To hide the fault I see;
That mercy I to others show,
  That mercy show to me. 40

Mean though I am, not wholly so,
Since quickened by thy breath;
Oh lead me wheresoe'er I go,
Through this day's life or death.

This day, be bread and peace my lot:
All else beneath the sun,
Thou knowest if best bestowed or not;
And let Thy will be done.

To thee, whose temple is all space,
Whose altar earth, sea, skies,   50
One chorus let all being raise,
All nature's incense rise!

[1738]

MORAL ESSAYS

EPISTLE IV

OF THE USE OF RICHES

TO RICHARD BOYLE, EARL OF BURLINGTON

'Tis strange, the miser should his cares em-
ploy
To gain those riches he can ne'er enjoy:
Is it less strange, the prodigal should waste
His wealth, to purchase what he ne'er can
taste?
Not for himself he sees, or hears, or eats;
Artists must choose his pictures, music,
meats;
He buys for Topham, drawings and designs,
For Pembroke, statues, dirty gods, and coins;
Rare monkish manuscripts for Hearne alone,
And books for Mead, and butterflies for
Sloane.   10
Think we all these are for himself? no more
Than his fine wife, alas! or finer whore.
For what has Virro painted, built, and
planted?
Only to show, how many tastes he wanted.
What brought Sir Visto's ill got wealth to
waste?
Some demon whispered, "Visto! have a
taste."
Heaven visits with a taste the wealthy fool,
And needs no rod but Ripley with a rule.
See! sportive fate, to punish awkward pride,
Bids Bubo build, and sends him such a
guide—   20

A standing sermon, at each year's expense,
That never coxcomb reached magnificence!
You show us, Rome was glorious, not pro-
fuse,
And pompous buildings once were things of
use.
Yet shall, my lord, your just, your noble rules
Fill half the land with imitating fools,
Who random drawings from your sheets shall
take,
And of one beauty many blunders make;
Load some vain church with old theatric
state,
Turn arcs of triumph to a garden-gate,   30
Reverse your ornaments, and hang them all
On some patched doghole eked with ends
of wall;
Then clap four slices of pilaster on't,
That, laced with bits of rustic, makes a front;
Shall call the winds through long arcades to
roar,
Proud to catch cold at a Venetian door;
Conscious they act a true Palladian part,
And, if they starve, they starve by rules of
art.
Oft have you hinted to your brother peer
A certain truth, which many buy too dear: 40
Something there is more needful than ex-
pense,
And something previous even to taste—'tis
sense:
Good sense, which only is the gift of Heaven,
And though no science, fairly worth the
seven:
A light, which in yourself you must perceive;
Jones and Le Nôtre have it not to give.
To build, to plant, whatever you intend,
To rear the column, or the arch to bend,
To swell the terrace, or to sink the grot;
In all, let nature never be forgot.   50
But treat the goddess like a modest fair,
Nor over-dress, nor leave her wholly bare;
Let not each beauty everywhere be spied,
Where half the skill is decently to hide.
He gains all points who pleasingly con-
founds,
Surprises, varies, and conceals the bounds.
Consult the genius of the place in all,
That tells the waters or to rise or fall,
Or helps the ambitious hill the heavens to
scale,
Or scoops in circling theatres the vale;   60
Calls in the country, catches opening glades,

Joins willing woods, and varies shades from
　　　shades;
Now breaks, or now directs, the intending
　　　lines;
Paints as you plant, and as you work designs.
　Still follow sense, of every art the soul,
Parts answering parts shall slide into a
　　　whole,
Spontaneous beauties all around advance,
Start even from difficulty, strike from chance;
Nature shall join you; time shall make it
　　　grow
A work to wonder at—perhaps a Stowe.　　70
　　Without it, proud Versailles! thy glory
　　　falls,
And Nero's terraces desert their walls;
The vast parterres a thousand hands shall
　　　make,
Lo! Cobham comes, and floats them with a
　　　lake:
Or cut wide views through mountains to the
　　　plain,
You'll wish your hill or sheltered seat again.
Even in an ornament its place remark,
Nor in an hermitage set Dr. Clarke.
　Behold Villario's ten years' toil complete;
His quincunx[1] darkens, his espaliers meet;
The wood supports the plain, the parts
　　　unite,　　　　　　　　　　　　　81
And strength of shade contends with strength
　　　of light;
A waving glow the bloomy beds display,
Blushing in bright diversities of day,
With silver-quivering rills mæandered o'er—
Enjoy them, you! Villario can no more;
Tired of the scene parterres and fountains
　　　yield,
He finds at last he better likes a field.
　　Through his young woods how pleased
　　　Sabinus strayed,
Or sat delighted in the thickening shade,　　90
With annual joy the reddening shoots to
　　　greet,
Or see the stretching branches long to meet!
His son's fine taste an opener vista loves,
Foe to the dryads of his father's groves;
One boundless green or flourished carpet
　　　views,
With all the mournful family of yews;
The thriving plants ignoble broomsticks
　　　made,
Now sweep those alleys they were born to
　　　shade.

[1] An arrangement of trees in fives.

　At Timon's Villa let us pass a day,
Where all cry out, "What sums are thrown
　　　away!"　　　　　　　　　　　　100
So proud, so grand; of that stupendous air,
Soft and agreeable come never there.
Greatness, with Timon, dwells in such a
　　　draught
As brings all Brobdignag before your
　　　thought.
To compass this, his building is a town,
His pond an ocean, his parterre a down:
Who but must laugh, the master when he
　　　sees,
A puny insect, shivering at a breeze!
Lo, what huge heaps of littleness around!
The whole, a laboured quarry above
　　　ground;
Two cupids squirt before; a lake behind　111
Improves the keenness of the northern wind.
His gardens next your admiration call,
On every side you look, behold the wall!
No pleasing intricacies intervene,
No artful wildness to perplex the scene;
Grove nods at grove, each alley has a brother,
And half the platform just reflects the other.
The suffering eye inverted nature sees,
Trees cut to statues, statues thick as trees;　120
With here a fountain, never to be played;
And there a summer-house that knows no
　　　shade;
Here Amphitrite sails through myrtle bow-
　　　ers;
There gladiators fight, or die in flowers;
Unwatered see the drooping sea-horse
　　　mourn,
And swallows roost in Nilus' dusty urn.
　My lord advances with majestic mien,
Smit with the mighty pleasure, to be seen:
But soft,—by regular approach,—not yet,—
First through the length of yon hot terrace
　　　sweat;　　　　　　　　　　　　130
And when up ten steep slopes you've dragged
　　　your thighs,
Just at his study door he'll bless your eyes.
　His study! with what authors is it stored?
In books, not authors, curious is my lord;
To all their dated backs he turns you round:
These Aldus printed, those Du Sueil has
　　　bound.
Lo, some are vellum, and the rest as good
For all his lordship knows, but they are wood
For Locke or Milton 'tis in vain to look,　137
These shelves admit not any modern book.
And now the chapel's silver bell you hear,

That summons you to all the pride of prayer;
Light quirks of music, broken and uneven,
Make the soul dance upon a jig to Heaven.
On painted ceilings you devoutly stare,
Where sprawl the saints of Verrio or La-
    guerre,
On gilded clouds in fair expansion lie,
And bring all paradise before your eye.
To rest, the cushion and soft dean invite,
Who never mentions hell to ears polite.   150
  But hark! the chiming clocks to dinner
    call;
A hundred footsteps scrape the marble hall;
The rich buffet well coloured serpents grace,
And gaping Tritons spew to wash your face.
Is this a dinner? this a genial room?
No, 'tis a temple, and a hecatomb.
A solemn sacrifice, performed in state,
You drink by measure, and to minutes eat.
So quick retires each flying course, you'd
    swear
Sancho's dread doctor and his wand were
    there.   160
Between each act the trembling salvers ring,
From soup to sweet-wine, and God bless the
    King.
In plenty starving, tantalized in state,
And complaisantly helped to all I hate,
Treated, caressed, and tired, I take my leave,
Sick of his civil pride from morn to eve;
I curse such lavish cost, and little skill,
And swear no day was ever passed so ill.
  Yet hence the poor are clothed, the hun-
    gry fed;
Health to himself, and to his infants bread
The labourer bears: What his hard heart de-
    nies,   171
His charitable vanity supplies.
  Another age shall see the golden ear
Embrown the slope, and nod on the parterre,
Deep harvests bury all his pride has planned,
And laughing Ceres re-assume the land.
  Who then shall grace, or who improve the
    soil?
Who plants like Bathurst, or who builds like
    Boyle.
'Tis use alone that sanctifies expense,
And splendour borrows all her rays from
    sense.   180
  His father's acres who enjoys in peace,
Or makes his neighbours glad, if he increase;
Whose cheerful tenants bless their yearly
    toil,
Yet to their lord owe more than to the soil;

Whose ample lawns are not ashamed to feed
The milky heifer and deserving steed;
Whose rising forests, not for pride or show,
But future buildings, future navies, grow—
Let his plantations stretch from down to
    down,
First shade a country, and then raise a town.
  You too proceed! make falling arts your
    care,   191
Erect new wonders, and the old repair;
Jones and Palladio to themselves restore,
And be whate'er Vitruvius was before:
'Til kings call forth the ideas of your mind,
(Proud to accomplish what such hands de-
    signed,)
Bid harbours open, public ways extend,
Bid temples, worthier of the God, ascend;
Bid the broad arch the dangerous flood con-
    tain,
The mole projected break the roaring main;
Back to his bounds their subject sea com-
    mand,   201
And roll obedient rivers through the land:
These honours peace to happy Britain
    brings;
These are imperial works, and worthy kings.

                                      [1731]

EPISTLE TO
DR. ARBUTHNOT

P. Shut, shut the door, good John! fatigued,
    I said;
Tie up the knocker, say I'm sick, i'm dead.
The Dog Star rages! nay 'tis past a doubt,
All Bedlam, or Parnassus, is let out:
Fire in each eye, and papers in each hand,
They rave, recite, and madden round the
    land.
  What walls can guard me, or what shades
    can hide?
They pierce my thickets, through my grot
    they glide;
By land, by water, they renew the charge;
They stop the chariot, and they board the
    barge.   10
No place is sacred, not the church is free;
Even Sunday shines no sabbath-day to me;
Then from the Mint walks forth the man of
    rhyme,
Happy to catch me just at dinner time.
  Is there a parson much bemused in beer,

A maudlin poetess, a rhyming peer,
A clerk, foredoomed his father's soul to cross,
Who pens a stanza, when he should engross?
Is there who, locked from ink and paper,
    scrawls
With desperate charcoal round his darkened
    walls? 20
All fly to Twit'nam, and in humble strain
Apply to me, to keep them mad or vain.
Arthur, whose giddy son neglects the laws,
Imputes to me and my damned works the
    cause;
Poor Cornus sees his frantic wife elope,
And curses wit, and poetry, and Pope.
    Friend to my life! (which did not you pro-
        long,
The world had wanted many an idle song)
What drop or nostrum can this plague re-
    move?
Or which must end me, a fool's wrath or
    love? 30
A dire dilemma! either way I'm sped;
If foes, they write, if friends, they read me
    dead.
Seized and tied down to judge, how wretched
    I!
Who can't be silent, and who will not lie.
To laugh, were want of goodness and of
    grace,
And to be grave, exceeds all power of face.
I sit with sad civility, I read
With honest anguish and an aching head;
And drop at last, but in unwilling ears,
This saving counsel, "Keep your piece nine
    years." 40
    "Nine years!" cries he, who high in Drury
        Lane,
Lulled by soft zephyrs through the broken
    pane,
Rhymes ere he wakes, and prints before term
    ends,
Obliged by hunger, and request of friends:
"The piece, you think, is incorrect? why,
    take it;
I'm all submission, what you'd have it, make
    it."
    Three things another's modest wishes
        bound,
My friendship, and a prologue, and ten
    pound.
    Pitholeon sends to me: "You know his
        Grace,
I want a patron; ask him for a place." 50
"Pitholeon libelled me,"—"But here's a letter

Informs you, sir, 'twas when he knew no
    better.
Dare you refuse him? Curll invites to dine;
He'll write a journal, or he'll turn divine."
    Bless me! a packet.—" 'Tis a stranger sues,
A virgin tragedy, an orphan muse."
If I dislike it, "Furies, death and rage!"
If I approve, "Commend it to the stage."
There (thank my stars) my whole commis-
    sion ends;
The players and I are, luckily, no friends. 60
Fired that the house reject him, " 'Sdeath I'll
    print it,
And shame the fools——Your interest, sir,
    with Lintot!"
"Lintot, dull rogue! will think your price too
    much."
"Not, sir, if you revise it, and retouch."
All my demurs but double his attacks;
At last he whispers, "Do, and we go snacks."
Glad of a quarrel, straight I clap the door;
"Sir, let me see your works and you no more."
'Tis sung, when Midas' ears began to
    spring,
(Midas, a sacred person and a king) 70
His very minister who spied them first,
(Some say his queen) was forced to speak, or
    burst.
And is not mine, my friend, a sorer case,
When every coxcomb perks them in my face?
A. Good friend, forbear! you deal in dan-
    gerous things.
I'd never name queens, ministers, or kings;
Keep close to ears, and those let asses prick;
'Tis nothing— P. Nothing? if they bite and
    kick?
Out with it, Dunciad! let the secret pass,
That secret to each fool, that he's an ass: 80
The truth once told (and wherefore should
    we lie?)
The queen of Midas slept, and so may I.
    You think this cruel? take it for a rule,
No creature smarts so little as a fool.
Let peals of laughter, Codrus! round thee
    break,
Thou unconcerned canst hear the mighty
    crack:
Pit, box, and gallery in convulsions hurled,
Thou standest unshook amidst a bursting
    world.
Who shames a scribbler? break one cobweb
    through,
He spins the slight, self-pleasing thread
    anew: 90

Destroy his fib or sophistry, in vain,
The creature's at his dirty work again,
Throned in the centre of his thin designs,
Proud of a vast extent of flimsy lines!
Whom have I hurt? has poet yet, or peer,
Lost the arched eye-brow, or Parnassian
   sneer?
And has not Colley still his lord, and whore?
His butchers, Henley? his free-masons,
   Moore?
Does not one table Bavius still admit?
Still to one bishop Philips seem a wit? 100
Still Sappho— A. Hold! for God's sake—
   you'll offend;
No names—be calm—learn prudence of a
   friend!
I too could write, and I am twice as tall;
But foes like these— P. One flatterer's worse
   than all.
Of all mad creatures, if the learned are right,
It is the slaver kills, and not the bite.
A fool quite angry is quite innocent;
Alas! 'tis ten times worse when they repent.
   One dedicates in high heroic prose,
And ridicules beyond a hundred foes: 110
One from all Grub Street will my fame de-
   fend,
And, more abusive, calls himself my friend.
This prints my *Letters*, that expects a bribe,
And others roar aloud, "Subscribe, sub-
   scribe."
   There are who to my person pay their
   court:
I cough like Horace, and, though lean, am
   short;
Ammon's great son one shoulder had too
   high,
Such Ovid's nose, and "Sir! you have an
   eye"—
Go on, obliging creatures, make me see
All that disgraced my betters, met in me. 120
Say for my comfort, languishing in bed,
"Just so immortal Maro held his head":
And when I die, be sure you let me know
Great Homer died three thousand years ago.
   Why did I write? what sin to me unknown
Dipped me in ink, my parents', or my own?
As yet a child, nor yet a fool to fame,
I lisped in numbers, for the numbers came.
I left no calling for this idle trade,
No duty broke, no father disobeyed. 130
The muse but served to ease some friend, not
   wife,

To help me through this long disease, my
   life,
To second, Arbuthnot! thy art and care,
And teach the being you preserved, to bear.
   But why then publish? Granville the po-
   lite,
And knowing Walsh, would tell me I could
   write;
Well-natured Garth inflamed with early
   praise;
And Congreve loved, and Swift endured my
   lays;
The courtly Talbot, Somers, Sheffield read;
Even mitred Rochester would nod the head,
And St. John's self (great Dryden's friends
   before) 141
With open arms received one poet more.
Happy my studies, when by these approved!
Happier their author, when by these be-
   loved!
From these the world will judge of men and
   books,
Not from the Burnets, Oldmixons, and
   Cookes.
   Soft were my numbers; who could take
   offence,
While pure description held the place of
   sense?
Like gentle Fanny's was my flowery theme,
A painted mistress, or a purling stream. 150
Yet then did Gildon draw his venal quill;—
I wished the man a dinner, and sat still.
Yet then did Dennis rave in furious fret;
I never answered,—I was not in debt.
If want provoked, or madness made them
   print,
I waged no war with Bedlam or the Mint.
   Did some more sober critic come abroad;
If wrong, I smiled; if right, I kissed the rod.
Pains, reading, study, are their just pretence,
And all they want is spirit, taste, and sense.
Commas and points they set exactly right, 161
And 'twere a sin to rob them of their mite.
Yet ne'er one sprig of laurel graced these
   ribalds,
From slashing Bentley down to pidling Tib-
   balds:
Each wight, who reads not, and but scans
   and spells,
Each word-catcher, that lives on syllables,
Even such small critics some regard may
   claim,
Preserved in Milton's or in Shakespeare's
   name.

Pretty! in amber to observe the forms
Of hairs, or straws, or dirt, or grubs, or
    worms!   170
The things, we know, are neither rich nor
    rare,
But wonder how the devil they got there.
  Were others angry, I excused them too;
Well might they rage, I gave them but their
    due.
A man's true merit 'tis not hard to find;
But each man's secret standard in his mind,
That casting-weight pride adds to emptiness,
This, who can gratify? for who can guess?
The bard whom pilfered pastorals renown,
Who turns a Persian tale for half a crown, 180
Just writes to make his barrenness appear,
And strains, from hard-bound brains, eight
    lines a year;
He who still wanting, though he lives on
    theft,
Steals much, spends little, yet has nothing
    left;
And he who now to sense, now nonsense
    leaning,
Means not, but blunders round about a
    meaning;
And he whose fustian 's so sublimely bad,
It is not poetry, but prose run mad:
All these, my modest satire bade translate,
And owned that nine such poets made a
    Tate.   190
How did they fume, and stamp, and roar,
    and chafe!
And swear, not Addison himself was safe.
  Peace to all such! but were there one whose
    fires
True genius kindles, and fair fame inspires;
Blessed with each talent and each art to
    please,
And born to write, converse, and live with
    ease:
Should such a man, too fond to rule alone,
Bear, like the Turk, no brother near the
    throne;   198
View him with scornful, yet with jealous eyes,
And hate for arts that caused himself to rise;
Damn with faint praise, assent with civil leer,
And without sneering, teach the rest to sneer;
Willing to wound, and yet afraid to strike,
Just hint a fault, and hesitate dislike;
Alike reserved to blame, or to commend,
A timorous foe, and a suspicious friend;
Dreading even fools, by flatterers besieged,
And so obliging, that he ne'er obliged;

Like Cato, give his little senate laws,
And sit attentive to his own applause;   21
While wits and templars every sentence raise,
And wonder with a foolish face of praise—
Who but must laugh, if such a man there be?
Who would not weep, if Atticus were he?
  What though my name stood rubric on the
    walls,
Or plastered posts, with claps, in capitals?
Or smoking forth, a hundred hawkers' load,
On wings of winds came flying all abroad?
I sought no homage from the race that write;
I kept, like Asian monarchs, from their sight;
Poems I heeded (now be-rhymed so long) 22
No more than thou, great George! a birthday
    song.
I ne'er with wits or witlings passed my days,
To spread about the itch of verse and praise;
Nor like a puppy, daggled through the town,
To fetch and carry sing-song up and down;
Nor at rehearsals sweat, and mouthed, and
    cried,
With handkerchief and orange at my side;
But sick of fops, and poetry, and prate,
To Bufo left the whole Castalian state.   230
  Proud as Apollo on his forked hill,
Sat full-blown Bufo, puffed by every quill;
Fed with soft dedication all day long,
Horace and he went hand in hand in song.
His library (where busts of poets dead
And a true Pindar stood without a head,)
Received of wits an undistinguished race,
Who first his judgment asked, and then a
    place:
Much they extolled his pictures, much his
    seat,
And flattered every day, and some days
    eat: 240
Till grown more frugal in his riper days,
He paid some bards with port, and some
    with praise;
To some a dry rehearsal was assigned,
And others (harder still) he paid in kind.
Dryden alone (what wonder?) came not
    nigh;
Dryden alone escaped this judging eye:
But still the great have kindness in reserve;
He helped to bury whom he helped to starve.
  May some choice patron bless each grey
    goose quill!
May every Bavius have his Bufo still!   250
So, when a statesman wants a day's defence,
Or envy holds a whole week's war with sense,
Or simple pride for flattery makes demands,

May dunce by dunce be whistled off my
    hands!
Blessed be the great! for those they take
    away,
And those they left me—for they left me Gay;
Left me to see neglected genius bloom,
Neglected die, and tell it on his tomb:
Of all thy blameless life the sole return
My verse, and Queensberry weeping o'er thy
    urn!   260
    Oh let me live my own, and die so too!
(To live and die is all I have to do:)
Maintain a poet's dignity and ease,
And see what friends, and read what books I
    please;
Above a patron, though I condescend
Sometimes to call a minister my friend.
I was not born for courts or great affairs;
I pay my debts, believe, and say my prayers;
Can sleep without a poem in my head,
Nor know if Dennis be alive or dead.   270
    Why am I asked what next shall see the
    light?
Heavens! was I born for nothing but to
    write?
Has life no joys for me? or, (to be grave)
Have I no friend to serve, no soul to save?
"I found him close with Swift"—"Indeed? no
    doubt,"
Cries prating Balbus, "something will come
    out."
'Tis all in vain, deny it as I will.
"No, such a genius never can lie still;"
And then for mine obligingly mistakes   279
The first lampoon Sir Will or Bubo makes.
Poor guiltless I! and can I choose but smile,
When every coxcomb knows me by my style?
    Cursed be the verse, how well soe'er it
    flow,
That tends to make one worthy man my foe,
Give virtue scandal, innocence a fear,
Or from the soft-eyed virgin steal a tear!
But he who hurts a harmless neighbour's
    peace,
Insults fallen worth, or beauty in distress,
Who loves a lie, lame slander helps about,
Who writes a libel, or who copies out: 290
That fop, whose pride affects a patron's
    name,
Yet absent, wounds an author's honest fame:
Who can your merit selfishly approve,
And show the sense of it without the love;
Who has the vanity to call you friend,

Yet wants the honour, injured, to defend;
Who tells whate'er you think, whate'er you
    say,
And, if he lie not, must at least betray;
Who to the dean, and silver bell can swear,
And sees at Canons what was never there; 300
Who reads, but with a lust to misapply,
Make satire a lampoon, and fiction, lie.
A lash like mine no honest man shall dread,
But all such babbling blockheads in his stead.
    Let Sporus tremble— A. What? that
    thing of silk,
Sporus, that mere white curd of ass's milk?
Satire or sense, alas! can Sporus feel?
Who breaks a butterfly upon a wheel?
P. Yet let me flap this bug with gilded wings,
This painted child of dirt, that stinks and
    stings;   310
Whose buzz the witty and the fair annoys,
Yet wit ne'er tastes, and beauty ne'er enjoys:
So well-bred spaniels civilly delight
In mumbling of the game they dare not bite.
Eternal smiles his emptiness betray,
As shallow streams run dimpling all the way,
Whether in florid impotence he speaks,
And, as the prompter breathes, the puppet
    squeaks;
Or at the ear of Eve, familiar toad,
Half froth, half venom, spits himself abroad,
In puns, or politics, or tales, or lies,   321
Or spite, or smut, or rhymes, or blasphemies,
His wit all see-saw, between that and this,
Now high, now low, now master up, now
    miss,
And he himself one vile antithesis.
Amphibious thing! that acting either part,
The trifling head or the corrupted heart,
Fop at the toilet, flatterer at the board,
Now trips a lady, and now struts a lord.
Eve's tempter thus the rabbins have ex-
    pressed,   330
A cherub's face, a reptile all the rest;
Beauty that shocks you, parts that none will
    trust,
Wit that can creep, and pride that licks the
    dust.
    Not fortune's worshipper, nor fashion's
    fool,
Not lucre's madman, nor ambition's tool,
Not proud, nor servile;—be one poet's praise,
That, if he pleased, he pleased by manly
    ways:
That flattery, even to kings, he held a shame,

And thought a lie in verse or prose the same;
That not in fancy's maze he wandered long,
But stooped to truth, and moralized his
     song;   341
That not for fame, but virtue's better end,
He stood the furious foe, the timid friend,
The damning critic, half approving wit,
The coxcomb hit, or fearing to be hit;
Laughed at the loss of friends he never had,
The dull, the proud, the wicked, and the
     mad;
The distant threats of vengeance on his head
The blow unfelt, the tear he never shed;   349
The tale revived, the lie so oft o'erthrown,
The imputed trash and dulness not his own;
The morals blackened when the writings
     'scape,
The libelled person, and the pictured shape;
Abuse, on all he loved, or loved him, spread,
A friend in exile, or a father dead;
The whisper that, to greatness still too near,
Perhaps yet vibrates on his Sovereign's ear:—
Welcome for thee, fair virtue! all the past;
For thee, fair virtue! welcome even the last!
    A. But why insult the poor, affront the
     great?   360
P. A knave 's a knave, to me, in every state:
Alike my scorn, if he succeed or fail,
Sporus at court, or Japhet in a jail,
A hireling scribbler, or a hireling peer,
Knight of the post corrupt, or of the shire;
If on a pillory, or near a throne,
He gain his prince's ear, or lose his own.
    Yet soft by nature, more a dupe than wit,
Sappho can tell you how this man was bit;
This dreaded satirist Dennis will confess   370
Foe to his pride, but friend to his distress:
So humble, he has knocked at Tibbald's
     door,
Has drunk with Cibber, nay, has rhymed for
     Moore.
Full ten years slandered, did he once reply?
Three thousand suns went down on Wel-
     sted's lie.
To please a mistress one aspersed his life;
He lashed him not, but let her be his wife.
Let Budgell charge low Grub Street on his
     quill,
And write whate'er he pleased, except his
     will;
Let the two Curlls of town and court, abuse
His father, mother, body, soul, and muse.   381
Yet why? that father held it for a rule

It was a sin to call our neighbour fool:
That harmless mother thought no wife a
     whore:
Hear this, and spare his family, James
     Moore!
Unspotted names, and memorable long!
If there be force in virtue, or in song.
    Of gentle blood (part shed in honour's
     cause,
While yet in Britain honour had applause)
Each parent sprung— A. What fortune,
     pray?— P. Their own,   390
And better got, than Bestia's from the
     throne.
Born to no pride, inheriting no strife,
Nor marrying discord in a noble wife,
Stranger to civil and religious rage,
The good man walked innoxious through his
     age.
No courts he saw, no suits would ever try,
Nor dared an oath, nor hazarded a lie.
Unlearned, he knew no schoolman's subtle
     art,
No language but the language of the heart.
By nature honest, by experience wise,   400
Healthy by temperance and by exercise;
His life, though long, to sickness passed un-
     known,
His death was instant, and without a groan.
Oh grant me thus to live, and thus to die!
Who sprung from kings shall know less joy
     than I.
    O friend! may each domestic bliss be
     thine!
Be no unpleasing melancholy mine:
Me, let the tender office long engage,
To rock the cradle of reposing age,
With lenient arts extend a mother's breath,
Make languor smile, and smooth the bed of
     death,   411
Explore the thought, explain the asking eye,
And keep a while one parent from the sky!
On cares like these if length of days attend,
May Heaven, to bless those days, preserve
     my friend,
Preserve him social, cheerful, and serene,
And just as rich as when he served a Queen.
A. Whether that blessing be denied or
     given,
Thus far was right, the rest belongs to
     Heaven.

                                           [1735]

THE FIRST EPISTLE OF THE SECOND BOOK
OF HORACE: TO AUGUSTUS

ADVERTISEMENT

The reflections of Horace, and the judgments passed in his Epistle to Augustus seemed so seasonable to the present times that I could not help applying them to the use of my own country. The author thought them considerable enough to address them to his Prince; whom he paints with all the great and good qualities of a monarch upon whom the Romans depended for the increase of an absolute empire. But to make the poem entirely English I was willing to add one or two of those which contribute to the happiness of a free people, and are consistent with the welfare of our neighbours.

This Epistle will show the learned world to have fallen into two mistakes: one, that Augustus was a patron of poets in general; whereas he not only prohibited all but the best writers to name him, but recommended that care even to the civil magistrate: *Admonebat prætores ne paterentur nomen suum obsolefieri,* etc. The other, that this piece was only a general discourse of poetry; whereas it was an apology for the poets, in order to render Augustus more their patron. Horace here pleads the cause of his contemporaries, first against the taste of the town, whose humour it was to magnify the authors of the preceding age; secondly agai.ist the court and nobility, who encouraged only the writers for the theatre: and lastly against the Emperor himself, who had conceived them of little use to the government. He shows (by a view of the progress of learning, and the change of taste among the Romans) that the introduction of the polite arts of Greece had given the writers of his time great advantages over their predecessors; that their morals were much improved, and the licence of those ancient poets restrained; that satire and comedy were become more just and useful; that whatever extravagances were left on the stage were owing to the ill taste of the nobility; that poets, under due regulations, were in many respects useful to the state, and concludes, that it was upon them the Emperor himself must depend for his fame with posterity.

We may further learn from this Epistle that Horace made his court to this great Prince by vriting with a decent freedom toward him, with a just contempt of his low flatterers and with a manly regard to his own character.   POPE.

While you, great Patron of Mankind! sustain
The balanced world, and open all the main;
Your country, chief, in arms abroad defend,
At home, with morals, arts, and laws amend;
How shall the muse from such a monarch steal
An hour, and not defraud the public weal?

Edward and Henry, now the boast of fame,
And virtuous Alfred, a more sacred name,
After a life of generous toils endured,
The Gaul subdued, or property secured,   10
Ambition humbled, mighty cities stormed,
Or laws established, and the world reformed;
Closed their long glories with a sigh, to find
The unwilling gratitude of base mankind!
All human virtue, to its latest breath,
Finds envy never conquered but by death.
The great Alcides, every labour passed
Had still this monster to subdue at last.
Sure fate of all, beneath whose rising ray
Each star of meaner merit fades away!   20
Oppressed we feel the beam directly beat;
Those suns of glory please not till they set.
      To thee the world its present homage pays,

The harvest early, but mature the praise:
Great friend of liberty! in kings a name
Above all Greek, above all Roman fame:
Whose word is truth, as sacred and revered,
As Heaven's own oracles from altars heard.
Wonder of kings! like whom, to mortal eyes
None e'er has risen, and none e'er shall rise. 30
      Just in one instance, be it yet confessed
Your people, Sir, are partial in the rest;
Foes to all living worth except your own,
And advocates for folly dead and gone.
Authors, like coins, grow dear as they grow
      old;
It is the rust we value, not the gold.
Chaucer's worst ribaldry is learned by rote,
And beastly Skelton heads of houses quote:
One likes no language but the *Faery Queen*;
A Scot will fight for *Christ's Kirk o' the Green*: 40
And each true Briton is to Ben so civil,
He swears the Muses met him at the Devil.
      Though justly Greece her eldest sons ad-
      mires,
Why should not we be wiser than our sires?

In every public virtue we excel:
We build, we paint, we sing, we dance as well,
And learned Athens to our art must stoop,
Could she behold us tumbling through a hoop.
    If time improve our wit as well as wine,
Say at what age a poet grows divine?   50
Shall we, or shall we not, account him so,
Who died, perhaps, an hundred years ago?
End all dispute; and fix the year precise
When British bards begin to immortalize?
    "Who lasts a century can have no flaw,
I hold that wit a classic, good in law."
    Suppose he wants a year, will you com-
        pound?
And shall we deem him ancient, right and
        sound,
Or damn to all eternity at once,
At ninety-nine, a modern and a dunce?   60
    "We shall not quarrel for a year or two;
By courtesy of England, he may do."
    Then by the rule that made the horsetail bare,
I pluck out year by year, as hair by hair,
And melt down ancients like a heap of snow:
While you, to measure merits, look in Stow,
And estimating authors by the year,
Bestow a garland only on a bier.
    Shakespeare (whom you and every play-
        house bill
Style the divine, the matchless, what you will)
For gain, not glory, winged his roving flight, 71
And grew immortal in his own despite.
Ben, old and poor, as little seemed to heed
The life to come, in every poet's creed.
Who now reads Cowley? if he pleases yet,
His moral pleases, not his pointed wit;
Forgot his epic, nay Pindaric art,
But still I love the language of his heart.
    "Yet surely, surely, these were famous men!
What boy but hears the sayings of old Ben? 80
In all debates where critics bear a part,
Not one but nods, and talks of Jonson's art,
Of Shakespeare's nature, and of Cowley's wit;
How Beaumont's judgment checked what
        Fletcher writ;
How Shadwell hasty, Wycherley was slow;
But, for the passions, Southern sure and Rowe.
These, only these, support the crowded stage,
From eldest Heywood down to Cibber's age."
    All this may be; the people's voice is odd;
It is, and it is not, the voice of God.   90
To *Gammer Gurton* if it give the bays,
And yet deny the *Careless Husband* praise,
Or say our fathers never broke a rule;
Why then, I say, the public is a fool.
But let them own, that greater faults than we

They had, and greater virtues, I'll agree.
Spenser himself affects the obsolete,
And Sidney's verse halts ill on Roman feet;
Milton's strong pinion now not Heaven can
        bound,
Now serpent-like, in prose he sweeps the
        ground;   100
In quibbles, angel and archangel join,
And God the Father turns a school-divine.
Not that I'd lop the beauties from his book,
Like slashing Bentley with his desperate hook,
Or damn all Shakespeare like the affected fool
At court, who hates whate'er he read at school.
    But for the wits of either Charles's days,
The mob of gentlemen who wrote with ease;
Sprat, Carew, Sedley, and a hundred more,
(Like twinkling stars the miscellanies o'er) 110
One simile that solitary shines
In the dry desert of a thousand lines,
Or lengthened thought that gleams through
        many a page,
Has sanctified whole poems for an age.
I lose my patience, and I own it too,
When works are censured, not as bad but new;
While if our elders break all reason's laws,
These fools demand not pardon, but applause.
    On Avon's bank, where flowers eternal
        blow,
If I but ask if any weed can grow?   120
One tragic sentence if I dare deride,
Which Betterton's grave action dignified,
Or well-mouthed Booth with emphasis pro-
        claims
(Though but, perhaps, a muster-roll of names),
How will our fathers rise up in a rage,
And swear all shame is lost in George's age!
You'd think no fools disgraced the former
        reign,
Did not some grave examples yet remain,
Who scorn a lad should teach his father skill,
And, having once been wrong, will be so still.
He who to seem more deep than you or I, 131
Extols old bards, or Merlin's Prophecy,
Mistake him not; he envies, not admires,
And to debase the sons, exalts the sires.
Had ancient times conspired to disallow
What then was new, what had been ancient
        now?
Or what remained, so worthy to be read
By learned critics, of the mighty dead?
    In days of ease, when now the weary sword
Was sheathed, and luxury with Charles re-
        stored,   140
In every taste of foreign courts improved,
"All, by the King's example, lived and loved."

Then peers grew proud in horsemanship to
    excel,
Newmarket's glory rose, as Britain's fell;
The soldier breathed the gallantries of France,
And every flowery courtier writ romance.
Then marble, softened into life, grew warm,
And yielding metal flowed to human form:
Lely on animated canvas stole
The sleepy eye that spoke the melting soul. 150
No wonder then, when all was love and sport,
The willing Muses were debauched at court:
On each enervate string they taught the note
To pant or tremble through an eunuch's
    throat.
    But Britain, changeful as a child at play,
Now calls in princes, and now turns away:
Now Whig, now Tory, what we loved we hate;
Now all for pleasure, now for church and
    state;
Now for prerogative, and now for laws;
Effects unhappy! from a noble cause.   160
    Time was, a sober Englishman would knock
His servants up, and rise by five o'clock,
Instruct his family in every rule,
And send his wife to church, his son to school.
To worship like his fathers was his care,
To teach their frugal virtues to his heir,
To prove that luxury could never hold,
And place, on good security, his gold.
Now times are changed, and one poetic itch
Has seized the court and city, poor and rich:
Sons, sires, and grandsires, all will wear the
    bays,   171
Our wives read Milton, and our daughters
    plays,
To theatres, and to rehearsals throng,
And all our grace at table is a song.
I, who so oft renounce the Muses, lie,
Not ——'s self e'er tells more fibs than I;
When sick of Muse, our follies we deplore,
And promise our best friends to rhyme no
    more;
We wake next morning in a raging fit,
And call for pen and ink to show our wit. 180
    He served a 'prenticeship who sets up shop;
Ward tried on puppies and the poor, his drop;
Even Radcliffe's doctors travel first to France,
Nor dare to practise till they've learned to
    dance.
Who builds a bridge that never drove a pile?
(Should Ripley venture, all the world would
    smile)
But those who cannot write, and those who
    can

All rhyme, and scrawl, and scribble, to a man.
    Yet, Sir, reflect, the mischief is not great;
These madmen never hurt the church or state:
Sometimes the folly benefits mankind;   191
And rarely avarice taints the tuneful mind.
Allow him but his plaything of a pen,
He ne'er rebels, or plots, like other men:
Flight of cashiers, or mobs, he'll never mind,
And knows no losses while the Muse is kind.
To cheat a friend, or ward, he leaves to Peter;
The good man heaps up nothing but mere
    metre,
Enjoys his garden and his book in quiet;
And then—a perfect hermit in his diet.   200
    Of little use the man you may suppose,
Who says in verse what others say in prose:
Yet let me show a poet's of some weight,
And (though no soldier) useful to the state.
What will a child learn sooner than a song?
What better teach a foreigner the tongue?
What's long or short, each accent where to
    place,
And speak in public with some sort of grace.
I scarce can think him such a worthless thing,
Unless he praise some monster of a king; 210
Or virtue or religion turn to sport,
To please a lewd or unbelieving court.
Unhappy Dryden!—In all Charles's days,
Roscommon only boasts unspotted bays;
And in our own (excuse some courtly stains)
No whiter page than Addison remains.
He, from the taste obscene reclaims our youth,
And sets the passions on the side of truth,
Forms the soft bosom with the gentlest art,
And pours each human virtue in the heart. 220
Let Ireland tell how wit upheld her cause,
Her trade supported, and supplied her laws;
And leave on Swift this grateful verse en-
    graved,
"The rights a court attacked, a poet saved."
Behold the hand that wrought a nation's cure,
Stretched to relieve the idiot and the poor,
Proud vice to brand, or injured worth adorn,
And stretch the ray to ages yet unborn.
Not but there are, who merit other palms;
Hopkins and Sternhold glad the heart with
    Psalms: 230
The boys and girls whom charity maintains,
Implore your help in these pathetic strains:
How could devotion touch the country pews,
Unless the gods bestowed a proper Muse?
Verse cheers their leisure, verse assists their
    work,
Verse prays for peace, or sings down pope and
    Turk.

The silenced preacher yields to potent strain,
And feels that grace his prayer besought in
    vain;
The blessing thrills through all the labouring
    throng,
And Heaven is won by violence of song. 240
  Our rural ancestors, with little blessed,
Patient of labour when the end was rest,
Indulged the day that housed their annual
    grain,
With feasts, and offerings, and a thankful
    strain:
The joy their wives, their sons, and servants
    share,
Ease of their toil, and partners of their care:
The laugh, the jest, attendants on the bowl,
Smoothed every brow, and opened every soul:
With growing years the pleasing licence grew,
And taunts alternate innocently flew. 250
But times corrupt, and nature, ill-inclined,
Produced the point that left a sting behind;
Till friend with friend, and families at strife,
Triumphant malice raged through private
    life.
Who felt the wrong, or feared it, took the
    alarm,
Appealed to law, and Justice lent her arm.
At length, by wholesome dread of statutes
    bound,
The poets learned to please, and not to wound:
Most warped to flattery's side; but some, more
    nice, 259
Preserved the freedom, and forbore the vice.
Hence satire rose, that just the medium hit,
And heals with morals what it hurts with wit.
  We conquered France, but felt our captive's
    charms;
Her arts victorious triumphed o'er our arms;
Britain to soft refinements less a foe,
Wit grew polite, and numbers learned to flow.
Waller was smooth; but Dryden taught to join
The varying verse, the full-resounding line,
The long majestic march, and energy divine.
Though still some traces of our rustic vein 270
And splay-foot verse remained, and will re-
    main.
Late, very late, correctness grew our care,
When the tired nation breathed from civil war.
Exact Racine, and Corneille's noble fire,
Showed us that France had something to ad-
    mire.
Not but the tragic spirit was our own,
And full in Shakespeare, fair in Otway shone:
But Otway failed to polish or refine,
And fluent Shakespeare scarce effaced a line.

Even copious Dryden wanted, or forgot, 280
The last and greatest art, the art to blot.
Some doubt, if equal pains or equal fire
The humbler Muse of comedy require.
But in known images of life, I guess
The labour greater, as the indulgence less.
Observe how seldom even the best succeed:
Tell me if Congreve's fools are fools indeed?
What pert, low dialogue has Farquhar writ!
How Van wants grace, who never wanted wit!
The stage how loosely does Astræa tread, 290
Who fairly puts all characters to bed!
And idle Cibber, how he breaks the laws,
To make poor Pinky eat with vast applause!
But fill their purse, our poet's work is done,
Alike to them, by pathos or by pun.
  O you! whom vanity's light bark conveys
On fame's mad voyage by the wind of praise,
With what a shifting gale your course you ply,
Forever sunk too low, or borne too high!
Who pants for glory finds but short repose; 300
A breath revives him, or a breath o'erthrows.
Farewell the stage! if just as thrives the play,
The silly bard grows fat, or falls away.
  There still remains, to mortify a wit,
The many-headed monster of the pit:
A senseless, worthless, and unhonoured crowd,
Who, to disturb their betters mighty proud,
Clattering their sticks before ten lines are
    spoke,
Call for the farce, the bear, or the black joke.
What dear delight to Britons farce affords! 310
Ever the taste of mobs, but now of lords;
(Taste, that eternal wanderer, which flies
From heads to ears, and now from ears to
    eyes.)
The play stands still; damn action and dis-
    course,
Back fly the scenes, and enter foot and horse;
Pageants on pageants, in long order drawn,
Peers, heralds, bishops, ermine, gold and
    lawn;
The champion too! and, to complete the jest,
Old Edward's armour beams on Cibber's
    breast.
With laughter sure Democritus had died, 320
Had he beheld an audience gape so wide.
Let bear or elephant be e'er so white,
The people, sure, the people are the sight!
Ah luckless poet! stretch thy lungs and roar,
That bear or elephant shall heed thee more;
While all its throats the gallery extends,
And all the thunder of the pit ascends!
Loud as the wolves, on Orcas' stormy steep,
Howl to the roarings of the Northern deep.

Such is the shout, the long-applauding note,
At Quin's high plume, or Oldfield's petticoat;
Or when from Court a birthday suit bestowed,
Sinks the lost actor in the tawdry load.   333
Booth enters—hark! the universal peal!
"But has he spoken?" Not a syllable.
What shook the stage, and made the people
      stare?
Cato's long wig, flowered gown, and lacquered
      chair.

Yet lest you think I rally more than teach,
Or praise malignly arts I cannot reach,
Let me for once presume to instruct the times,
To know the poet from the man of rhymes: 341
'Tis he, who gives my breast a thousand pains,
Can make me feel each passion that he feigns;
Enrage, compose, with more than magic art,
With pity and with terror tear my heart;
And snatch me o'er the earth or through the
      air,
To Thebes, to Athens, when he will, and
      where.

But not this part of the poetic state.
Alone deserves the favour of the great:
Think of those authors, Sir, who would rely 350
More on a reader's sense than gazer's eye.
Or who shall wander where the Muses sing?
Who climb their mountain, or who taste their
      spring?
How shall we fill a library with wit,
When Merlin's Cave is half unfurnished yet?
My liege! why writers little claim your
      thought,
I guess; and with their leave, will tell the
      fault:
We poets are (upon a poet's word)
Of all mankind, the creatures most absurd:
The season, when to come, and when to go, 360
To sing, or cease to sing, we never know;
And if we will recite nine hours in ten,
You lose your patience, just like other men.
Then too we hurt ourselves when to defend
A single verse, we quarrel with a friend;
Repeat unasked; lament, the wit's too fine
For vulgar eyes, and point out every line.
But most, when straining with too weak a
      wing,
We needs will write epistles to the King; 369
And from the moment we oblige the town,
Expect a place, or pension from the crown;
Or dubbed historians by express command,
To enroll your triumphs o'er the seas and land,
Be called to court to plan some work divine.

As once for Louis, Boileau and Racine.
Yet think, great Sir! (so many virtues shown)
Ah think, what poet best may make them
      known?
Or choose at least some minister of grace,
Fit to bestow the Laureate's weighty place.
Charles, to late times to be transmitted fair,
Assigned his figure to Bernini's care;   381
And great Nassau to Kneller's hand decreed
To fix him graceful on the bounding steed;
So well in paint and stone they judged of
      merit:
But kings in wit may want discerning spirit.
The hero William, and the martyr Charles,
One knighted Blackmore, and one pensioned
      Quarles;
Which made old Ben, and surly Dennis swear,
"No Lord's anointed, but a Russian bear."
Not with such majesty, such bold relief, 390
The forms august, of king, or conquering chief,
E'er swelled on marble; as in verse have shined
(In polished verse) the manners and the mind.
Oh! could I mount on the Mæonian wing,
Your arms, your actions, your repose to sing!
What seas you traversed, and what fields you
      fought!
Your country's peace, how oft, how dearly
      bought!
How barbarous rage subsided at your word,
And nations wondered while they dropped
      the sword!
How, when you nodded, o'er the land and
      deep,   400
Peace stole her wing, and wrapped the world
      in sleep;
Till earth's extremes your mediation own,
And Asia's tyrants tremble at your throne—
But verse, alas! your Majesty disdains;
And I'm not used to panegyric strains:
The zeal of fools offends at any time,
But most of all, the zeal of fools in rhyme.
Besides, a fate attends on all I write,
That when I aim at praise, they say I bite.
A vile encomium doubly ridicules;   410
There's nothing blackens like the ink of fools.
If true, a woeful likeness; and if lies,
"Praise undeserved is scandal in disguise:"
Well may he blush, who gives it, or receives;
And when I flatter, let my dirty leaves
(Like journals, odes, and such forgotten things
As Eusden, Philips, Settle, writ of kings)
Clothe spice, line trunks, or fluttering in a row,
Befringe the rails of Bedlam and Soho.

[1737]

THE DUNCIAD

To Dr. Jonathan Swift

BOOK THE FIRST

The mighty mother, and her son, who brings
The Smithfield Muses to the ear of kings,
I sing. Say you, her instruments the great!
Called to this work by Dullness, Jove, and
    Fate:
You by whose care, in vain decried and cursed,
Still Dunce the second reigns like Dunce the
    first;
Say, how the goddess bade Britannia sleep,
And poured her spirit o'er the land and deep.
    In eldest time, ere mortals writ or read, 9
Ere Pallas issued from the Thund'rer's head,
Dullness o'er all possessed her ancient right,
Daughter of Chaos and eternal Night:
Fate in their dotage this fair idiot gave,
Gross as her sire, and as her mother grave,
Laborious, heavy, busy, bold, and blind,
She ruled, in native anarchy, the mind.
    Still her old empire to restore she tries,
For, born a goddess, Dullness never dies.
    O thou! whatever title please thine ear,
Dean, Drapier, Bickerstaff, or Gulliver! 20
Whether thou choose Cervantes' serious air,
Or laugh and shake in Rabelais' easy chair,
Or praise the court, or magnify mankind,
Or thy grieved country's copper chains un-
    bind;
From thy Bœotia though her power retires,
Mourn not, my Swift, at aught our realm
    acquires.
Here pleased behold her mighty wings out-
    spread
To hatch a new Saturnian age of lead.
    Close to those walls where Folly holds her
    throne,
And laughs to think Monroe would take her
    down, 30
Where o'er the gates, by his famed father's
    hand,
Great Cibber's brazen, brainless brothers
    stand;
One cell there is, concealed from vulgar eye,
The Cave of Poverty and Poetry.
Keen, hollow winds howl through the bleak
    recess,
Emblem of music caused by emptiness.
Hence bards like Proteus long in vain tied
    down,

Escape in monsters, and amaze the town.
Hence miscellanies spring, the weekly boast
Of Curll's chaste press, and Lintot's rubric
    post: 40
Hence hymning Tyburn's elegiac lines,
Hence journals, medleys, mercuries, maga-
    zines;
Sepulchral lies, our holy walls to grace,
And New Year odes, and all the Grub Street
    race.
    In clouded majesty here Dullness shone;
Four guardian Virtues, round, support her
    throne:
Fierce champion Fortitude, that knows no
    fears
Of hisses, blows, or want, or loss of ears:
Calm Temperance, whose blessings those par-
    take 49
Who hunger and who thirst for scribbling sake:
Prudence, whose glass presents the approach-
    ing jail:
Poetic Justice, with her lifted scale,
Where, in nice balance, truth with gold she
    weighs,
And solid pudding against empty praise.
    Here she beholds the chaos dark and deep,
Where nameless somethings in their causes
    sleep,
Till genial Jacob, or a warm third day,
Call forth each mass, a poem, or a play:
How hints, like spawn, scarce quick in embryo
    lie, 59
How new-born nonsense first is taught to cry,
Maggots half-formed in rhyme exactly meet,
And learn to crawl upon poetic feet.
Here one poor word an hundred clenches
    makes,
And ductile Dullness new meanders takes;
There motley images her fancy strike,
Figures ill paired, and similes unlike.
She sees a mob of metaphors advance,
Pleased with the madness of the mazy dance;
How Tragedy and Comedy embrace;
How Farce and Epic get a jumbled race; 70
How Time himself stands still at her com-
    mand,
Realms shift their place, and ocean turns to
    land.
Here gay description Egypt glads with show-
    ers,
Or gives to Zembla fruits, to Barca flowers;
Glittering with ice here hoary hills are seen,
There painted valleys of eternal green;
In cold December fragrant chaplets blow,

And heavy harvests nod beneath the snow.
  All these and more the cloud-compelling
    queen
Beholds through fogs, that magnify the scene.
She, tinselled o'er in robes of varying hues, 81
With self-applause her wild creation views;
Sees momentary monsters rise and fall,
And with her own fools-colours gilds them all.
'Twas on the day when * * rich and grave,
Like Cimon, triumphed both on land and
    wave:
(Pomps without guilt, of bloodless swords and
    maces,
Glad chains, warm furs, broad banners, and
    broad faces)
Now night descending, the proud scene was
    o'er, 90
But lived in Settle's numbers one day more.
Now mayors and shrieves all hushed and sati-
    ate lay,
Yet ate, in dreams, the custard of the day;
While pensive poets painful vigils keep,
Sleepless themselves, to give their readers
    sleep.
Much to the mindful queen the feast recalls
What city swans once sung within the walls;
Much she revolves their arts, their ancient
    praise,
And sure succession down from Heywood's
    days.
She saw, with joy, the line immortal run, 99
Each sire impressed and glaring in his son:
So watchful Bruin forms, with plastic care,
Each growing lump, and brings it to a bear.
She saw old Prynne in restless Daniel shine,
And Eusden eke out Blackmore's endless line;
She saw slow Philips creep like Tate's poor
    page,
And all the mighty mad in Dennis rage.
  In each she marks her image full expressed,
But chief in Bays's monster-breeding breast:
Bays, formed by nature stage and town to
    bless,
And act, and be, a coxcomb with success. 110
Dullness with transport eyes the lively Dunce,
Remembering she herself was pertness once.
Now (shame to fortune!) an ill run at play
Blanked his bold visage, and a thin third day:
Swearing and supperless the hero sate,
Blasphemed his gods, the dice, and damned
    his fate;
Then gnawed his pen, then dashed it on the
    ground,
Sinking from thought to thought, a vast pro-
    found!

Plunged for his sense, but found no bottom
    there; 119
Yet wrote and floundered on in mere despair.
Round him much embryo, much abortion lay,
Much future ode, and abdicated play;
Nonsense precipitate, like running lead,
That slipped through cracks and zigzags of the
    head;
All that on Folly Frenzy could beget,
Fruits of dull heat, and sooterkins of wit.
Next, o'er his books his eyes began to roll,
In pleasing memory of all he stole,
How here he sipped, how there he plundered
    snug, 129
And sucked all o'er like an industrious bug.
Here lay poor Fletcher's half-eat scenes, and
    here
The frippery of crucified Molière;
There hapless Shakespeare, yet of Tibbald
    sore,
Wished he had blotted for himself before.
The rest on outside merit but presume,
Or serve (like other fools) to fill a room;
Such with their shelves as due proportion hold,
Or their fond parents dressed in red and gold;
Or where the pictures for the page atone,
And Quarles is saved by beauties not his own.
Here swells the shelf with Ogilby the great;
There, stamped with arms, Newcastle shines
    complete: 142
Here all his suffering brotherhood retire,
And 'scape the martyrdom of jakes and fire:
A Gothic library! of Greece and Rome
Well purged, and worthy Settle, Banks, and
    Broome.
  But, high above, more solid learning shone,
The classics of an age that heard of none;
There Caxton slept, with Wynkyn at his side,
One clasped in wood, and one in strong cow-
    hide, 150
There saved by spice, like mummies, many a
    year,
Dry bodies of divinity appear;
De Lyra there a dreadful front extends,
And here the groaning shelves Philemon bends.
  Of these twelve volumes, twelve of amplest
    size,
Redeemed from tapers and defrauded pies,
Inspired he seizes; these an altar raise;
An hecatomb of pure unsullied lays
That altar crowns; a folio commonplace
Founds the whole pile, of all his works the
    base; 160
Quartos, octavos, shape the lessening pyre;

A twisted birthday ode completes the spire.
   Then he: "Great tamer of all human art!
First in my care, and ever at my heart;
Dullness! whose good old cause I yet defend,
With whom my muse began, with whom shall
      end,
E'er since Sir Fopling's periwig was praise,
To the last honours of the butt and bays:
O thou! of business the directing soul!
To this our head like bias to the bowl,   170
Which, as more ponderous, made its aim more
      true,
Obliquely waddling to the mark in view:
O! ever gracious to perplexed mankind,
Still spread a healing mist before the mind;
And, lest we err by wit's wild dancing light,
Secure us kindly in our native night.
Or, if to wit a coxcomb make pretence,
Guard the sure barrier between that and sense;
Or quite unravel all the reasoning thread,
And hang some curious cobweb in its stead!
As, forced from wind-guns, lead itself can fly,
And ponderous slugs cut swiftly through the
      sky;   182
As clocks to weight their nimble motion owe,
The wheels above urged by the load below:
Me emptiness, and dullness could inspire,
And were my elasticity and fire.
Some demon stole my pen (forgive the of-
      fence)
And once betrayed me into common sense:
Else all my prose and verse were much the
      same;   189
This prose on stilts, that poetry fallen lame.
Did on the stage my fops appear confined?
My life gave ampler lessons to mankind.
Did the dead letter unsuccessful prove?
The brisk example never failed to move.
Yet sure, had Heaven decreed to save the
      state,
Heaven had decreed these works a longer date.
Could Troy be saved by any single hand,
This grey-goose weapon must have made her
      stand.
What can I now? my Fletcher cast aside,
Take up the Bible, once my better guide?   200
Or tread the path by venturous heroes trod,
This box my thunder, this right hand my God?
Or chaired at White's amidst the doctors sit,
Teach oaths to gamesters, and to nobles wit?
Or bidst thou rather party to embrace?
(A friend to party thou, and all her race;
'Tis the same rope at different ends they twist;
To Dullness Ridpath is as dear as Mist.)
Shall I, like Curtius, desperate in my zeal,

O'er head and ears plunge for the Common-
      weal?   210
Or rob Rome's ancient geese of all their glo-
      ries,
And cackling save the monarchy of Tories?
Hold—to the minister I more incline;
To serve his cause, O Queen! is serving thine.
And see! thy very gazetteers give o'er,
Even Ralph repents, and Henley writes no
      more.
What then remains? Ourself. Still, still remain
Cibberian forehead, and Cibberian brain.
This brazen brightness, to the 'squire so dear;
This polished hardness, that reflects the peer:
This arch absurd, that wit and fool delights;
This mess, tossed up of Hockley Hole and
      White's;   222
Where dukes and butchers join to wreathe my
      crown,
At once the bear and fiddle of the town.
   "O born in sin, and forth in folly brought!
Works damned, or to be damned! (your fa-
      ther's fault)
Go, purified by flames ascend the sky,
My better and more Christian progeny!
Unstained, untouched, and yet in maiden
      sheets;
While all your smutty sisters walk the streets.
Ye shall not beg, like gratis-given Bland,   231
Sent with a pass, and vagrant through the
      land;
Not sail with Ward, to ape-and-monkey climes,
Where vile Mundungus trucks for viler rhymes:
Not sulphur-tipped, emblaze an alehouse fire;
Not wrap up oranges, to pelt your sire!
O! pass more innocent, in infant state,
To the mild limbo of our father Tate:
Or peaceably forgot, at once be blessed
In Shadwell's bosom with eternal rest!   240
Soon to that mass of nonsense to return,
Where things destroyed are swept to things
      unborn."
   With that, a tear (portentous sign of grace!)
Stole from the master of the sevenfold face;
And thrice he lifted high the birthday brand,
And thrice he dropped it from his quivering
      hand;
Then lights the structure, with averted eyes:
The rolling smoke involves the sacrifice.
The opening clouds disclose each work by
      turns:
Now flames the Cid, and now Perolla burns;   250
Great Cæsar roars, and hisses in the fires;
King John in silence modestly expires;
No merit now the dear Nonjuror claims,

Molière's old stubble in a moment flames.
Tears gushed again, as from pale Priam's eyes
When the last blaze sent Ilion to the skies.
    Roused by the light, old Dullness heaved
        the head,
Then snatched a sheet of *Thule* from her bed,
Sudden she flies, and whelms it o'er the pyre;
Down sink the flames, and with a hiss expire.
    Her ample presence fills up all the place; 261
A veil of fogs dilates her awful face:
Great in her charms! as when on shrieves and
        mayors
She looks, and breathes herself into their airs.
She bids him wait her to her sacred dome:
Well pleased he entered, and confessed his
        home.
So spirits ending their terrestrial race
Ascend, and recognize their native place.
This the great mother dearer held than all 269
The clubs of quidnuncs, or her own Guildhall:
Here stood her opium, here she nursed her
        owls,
And here she planned the imperial seat of
        fools.
    Here to her chosen all her works she shows;
Prose swelled to verse, verse loitering into
        prose:
How random thoughts now meaning chance
        to find,
Now leave all memory of sense behind;
How prologues into prefaces decay,
And these to notes are frittered quite away:
How index-learning turns no student pale,
Yet holds the eel of science by the tail: 280
How, with less reading than makes felons
        'scape,
Less human genius than God gives an ape,
Small thanks to France, and none to Rome or
        Greece,
A vast, vamped, future, old, revived, new
        piece,
'Twixt Plautus, Fletcher, Shakespeare, and
        Corneille,
Can make a Cibber, Tibbald, or Ozell.
    The Goddess then, o'er his anointed head,
With mystic words, the sacred opium shed.
And lo! her bird (a monster of a fowl,
Something betwixt a Heideggre and owl) 290
Perched on his crown. "All hail! and hail
        again,
My son: the promised land expects thy reign.

Know, Eusden thirsts no more for sack or
        praise;
He sleeps among the dull of ancient days;
Safe, where no critics damn, no duns molest,
Where wretched Withers, Ward, and Gildon
        rest,
And high-born Howard, more majestic sire,
With Fool of Quality completes the quire.
Thou, Cibber! thou, his laurel shalt support;
Folly, my son, has still a friend at court. 300
Lift up your gates, ye princes, see him come!
Sound, sound, ye viols; be the cat-call dumb!
Bring, bring the madding bay, the drunken
        vine;
The creeping, dirty, courtly ivy join.
And thou! his aide-de-camp, lead on my sons,
Light-armed with points, antitheses, and puns.
Let bawdry, Billingsgate, my daughters dear,
Support his front, and oaths bring up the rear:
And under his, and under Archer's wing,
Gaming and Grub Street skulk behind the
        King. 310
    "Oh! when shall rise a monarch all our own,
And I, a nursing mother, rock the throne;
'Twixt prince and people close the curtain
        draw,
Shade him from light, and cover him from
        law;
Fatten the courtier, starve the learnèd band,
And suckle armies, and dry-nurse the land:
Till senates nod to lullabies divine,
And all be sleep, as at an ode of thine."
    She ceased. Then swells the Chapel Royal
        throat:
"God save King Cibber!" mounts in every
        note. 320
Familiar White's, "God save King Colley!"
        cries;
"God save King Colley!" Drury Lane replies:
To Needham's quick the voice triumphal rode,
But pious Needham dropped the name of God;
Back to the Devil the last echoes roll,
And "Coll!" each butcher roars at Hockley
        Hole.
So when Jove's block descended from on
        high
(As sings thy great forefather Ogilby)
Loud thunder to its bottom shook the bog,
And the hoarse nation croaked, "God save
        King Log!" 330
                              [1728, 1743]

THE GUARDIAN

No. 173.   September 29, 1713.

Nec sera comantem
Narcissum, aut flexi tacuissem vimen Acanthi,
Pallentesque hederas, et amantes littora myr-
tos.   —Virgil, *Georgics*, IV, 122.

I lately took a particular friend of mine to my house in the country, not without some apprehension that it could afford little entertainment to a man of his polite taste, particularly in architecture and gardening, who had so long been conversant with all that is beautiful and great in either. But it was a pleasant surprise to me to hear him often declare he had found in my little retirement that beauty which he always thought wanting in the most celebrated seats (or, if you will, villas) of the nation. This he described to me in those verses with which Martial begins one of his epigrams:—

Baiana nostri villa, Besse, Faustini.
Non otiosis ordinata myrtetis,
Viduaque platano, tonsilique buxeto,
Ingrata lati spatia detinet campi;
Sed rure vero, barbaroque laetatur.

There is certainly something in the amiable simplicity of unadorned Nature that spreads over the mind a more noble sort of tranquillity, and a loftier sensation of pleasure, than can be raised from the nicer scenes of art.

This was the taste of the ancients in their gardens, as we may discover from the descriptions extant of them. The two most celebrated wits of the world have each of them left us a particular picture of a garden, wherein those great masters being wholly unconfined, and painting at pleasure, may be thought to have given a full idea of what they esteemed most excellent in this way. These (one may observe) consist entirely of the useful part of horticulture, fruit trees, herbs, water, &c. The pieces I am speaking of are Virgil's account of the garden of the old Corycian, and Homer's of that of Alcinous in the seventh Odyssey, to which I refer the reader.

Sir William Temple has remarked that this garden of Homer contains all the justest rules and provisions which can go toward composing the best gardens. Its extent was four acres, which, in those times of simplicity, was looked upon as a large one, even for a prince. It was inclosed all round for defence; and for conveniency joined close to the gates of the palace.

He mentions next the trees, which were standards, and suffered to grow to their full height. The fine description of the fruits that never failed, and the eternal zephyrs, is only a more noble and poetical way of expressing the continual succession of one fruit after another throughout the year.

The vineyard seems to have been a plantation distinct from the garden; as also the beds of greens mentioned afterwards at the extremity of the inclosure, in the usual place of our kitchen gardens.

The two fountains are disposed very remarkably. They rose within the inclosure, and were brought in by conduits or ducts; one of them to water all parts of the gardens, and the other underneath the palace into the town, for the service of the public.

How contrary to this simplicity is the modern practice of gardening! We seem to make it our study to recede from Nature, not only in the various tonsure of greens into the most regular and formal shapes, but even in monstrous attempts beyond the reach of the art itself: we run into sculpture, and are yet better pleased to have our trees in the most awkward figures of men and animals, than in the most regular of their own.

Hinc et nexilibus videas e frondibus hortos,
Implexos late muros, et moenia circum
Porrigere, et latas e ramis surgere turres;
Deflexam et myrtum in puppes, atque aerea rostra:
In buxisque undare fretum, atque e rore rudentes.
Parte alia frondere suis tentoria castris;
Scutaque, spiculaque, et jaculantia citra vallos.

I believe it is no wrong observation.

that persons of genius, and those who are most capable of art, are always most fond of Nature; as such are chiefly sensible that all art consists in the imitation and study of Nature. On the contrary, people of the common level of understanding are principally delighted with the little niceties and fantastical operations of art, and constantly think that finest which is least natural. A citizen is no sooner proprietor of a couple of yews, but he entertains thoughts of erecting them into giants, like those of Guildhall. I know an eminent cook, who beautified his country seat with a coronation dinner in greens, where you see the Champion flourishing on horseback at one end of the table, and the Queen in perpetual youth at the other.

For the benefit of all my loving countrymen of this curious taste, I shall here publish a catalogue of greens to be disposed of by an eminent town gardener, who has lately applied to me upon this head. He represents, that for the advancement of a politer sort of ornament in the villas and gardens adjacent to this great city, and in order to distinguish those places from the mere barbarous countries of gross nature, the world stands much in need of a virtuoso gardener, who has a turn to sculpture, and is thereby capable of improving upon the ancients, in the imagery of evergreens. I proceed to his catalogue:—

Adam and Eve in Yew; Adam a little shattered by the fall of the Tree of Knowledge in the great storm; Eve and the Serpent very flourishing.
Noah's ark in Holly, the ribs a little damaged for want of water.
The Tower of Babel, not yet finished.
St. George in Box; his arm scarce long enough, but will be in a condition to stick the Dragon by next April.
A green Dragon of the same, with a tail of Ground Ivy for the present.
N.B. These two not to be sold separately.
Edward the Black Prince in Cypress.
A Laurustine Bear in blossom, with a Juniper Hunter in berries.
A pair of Giants, stunted, to be sold cheap.
A Queen Elizabeth in Phyllirea, a little inclining to the green sickness, but of full growth.

Another Queen Elizabeth in Myrtle, which was very forward, but miscarried by being too near a Savine.
An old Maid of Honour in Wormwood.
A topping Ben Jonson in Laurel.
Divers eminent modern Poets in Bays, somewhat blighted, to be disposed of a pennyworth.
A quick-set Hog shot up into a Porcupine, by being forgot a week in rainy weather.
A Lavender Pig, with Sage growing in his belly.
A pair of Maidenheads in Firr, in great forwardness.

He also cutteth family pieces of men, women, and children, so that any gentleman may have his lady's effigies in myrtle, or his own in hornbeam.

Thy wife shall be as the fruitful vine, and thy children as olive branches round thy table.

PREFACE TO THE WORKS OF SHAKESPEARE

It is not my design to enter into a criticism upon this author; though to do it effectually and not superficially, would be the best occasion that any just writer could take, to form the judgment and taste of our nation. For of all English poets Shakespeare must be confessed to be the fairest and fullest subject for criticism, and to afford the most numerous, as well as most conspicuous instances, both of beauties and faults of all sorts. But this far exceeds the bounds of a Preface, the business of which is only to give an account of the fate of his works, and the disadvantages under which they have been transmitted to us. We shall hereby extenuate many faults which are his, and clear him from the imputation of many which are not: a design, which though it can be no guide to future critics to do him justice in one way, will at least be sufficient to prevent their doing him an injustice in the other.

I cannot however but mention some of his principal and characteristic excellences, for which (notwithstanding his defects) he is justly and universally elevated above all other dramatic writers. Not that this is the proper place of praising him, but because I would not omit any occasion of doing it.

If ever any author deserved the name of an *original*, it was Shakespeare. Homer himself drew not his art so immediately from the fountains of Nature; it proceeded through Egyptian strainers and channels, and came to him not without some tincture of the learning, or some cast of the models, of those before him. The poetry of Shakespeare was inspiration indeed; he is not so much an imitator, as an instrument, of Nature; and 'tis not so just to say that he speaks from her, as that she speaks through him.

His *characters* are so much Nature herself, that 'tis a sort of injury to call them by so distant a name as copies of her. Those of other poets have a constant resemblance, which shows that they received them from one another, and were but multipliers of the same image; each picture like a mock-rainbow is but the reflection of a reflection. But every single character in Shakespeare is as much an individual, as those in life itself; it is as impossible to find any two alike; and such as from their relation or affinity in any respect appear most to be twins, will upon comparison be found remarkably distinct. To this life and variety of character, we must add the wonderful preservation of it; which is such throughout his plays, that, had all the speeches been printed without the very names of the persons, I believe one might have applied them with certainty to every speaker.

The *power over our passions* was never possessed in a more eminent degree, or displayed in so different instances. Yet all along, there is seen no labour, no pains to raise them; no preparation to guide our guess to the effect, or be perceived to lead toward it. But the heart swells, and the tears burst out, just at the proper places. We are surprised the moment we weep; and yet upon reflection find the passion so just, that we should be surprised if we had not wept, and wept at that very moment.

How astonishing is it again, that the passions directly opposite to these, laughter and spleen, are no less at his command! that he is not more a master of the great than of the ridiculous in human nature; of our noblest tendernesses, than of our vainest foibles; of our strongest emotions, than of our idlest sensations!

Nor does he only excel in the passions: in the coolness of reflection and reasoning he is full as admirable. His *sentiments* are not only in general the most pertinent and judicious upon every subject; but by a talent very peculiar, something between penetration and felicity, he hits upon that particular point on which the bent of each argument turns, or the force of each motive depends. This is perfectly amazing, from a man of no education or experience in those great and public scenes of life which are usually the subject of his thoughts, so that he seems to have known the world by intuition, to have looked through human nature at one glance, and to be the only author that gives ground for a very new opinion, that the philosopher and even the man of the world, may be *born*, as well as the poet.

It must be owned that with all these great excellences, he has almost as great defects; and that as he has certainly written better, so he has perhaps written worse, than any other. But I think I can in some measure account for these defects, from several causes and accidents; without which it is hard to imagine that so large and so enlightened a mind could ever have been susceptible of them. That all these contingencies should unite to his disadvantage seems to me almost as singularly unlucky, as that so many various (nay contrary) talents should meet in one man, was happy and extraordinary.

It must be allowed that stage-poetry of all other, is more particularly levelled to please the populace, and its success more immediately depending upon the common suffrage. One cannot therefore wonder, if Shakespeare, having at his first appearance no other aim in his writings than to procure a subsistence, directed his endeavours solely to hit the taste and humour that then prevailed. The audience was generally composed of the meaner sort of people; and therefore the images of life were to be drawn from those of their own rank. Accordingly we find, that not our author's only, but almost all the old comedies have their scene among tradesmen and mechanics; and even their historical plays strictly follow the common old stories or vulgar traditions of that kind of people. In tragedy, nothing was so sure to surprise and cause admiration, as the most strange, unexpected, and consequently most unnatural, events and incidents; the most exaggerated thoughts; the most verbose and bombast expression; the most pompous rhymes, and thundering versification. In comedy, nothing was so sure to please as mean buffoonery, vile ribaldry, and unmannerly jests of fools and clowns. Yet even in these our author's wit buoys up, and is borne above his subject; his genius in those low parts is like some prince of a romance in the disguise of a shepherd or peasant; a certain greatness and spirit now and then break out, which manifest his higher extraction and qualities.

It may be added, that not only the common audience had no notion of the rules of writing, but few even of the better sort piqued themselves upon any great degree of knowledge or nicety that way; till Ben Jonson, getting possession of the stage, brought critical learning into vogue. And that this was not done without difficulty, may appear from those frequent lessons (and indeed almost declamations) which he was forced to prefix to his first plays, and put into the mouth of his actors, the *Grex*, *Chorus*, etc., to remove the prejudices,

and inform the judgment of his hearers. Till then, our authors had no thoughts of writing on the model of the ancients: their tragedies were only histories in dialogue, and their comedies followed the thread of any novel as they found it, no less implicitly than if it had been true history.

To judge therefore of Shakespeare by Aristotle's rules, is like trying a man by the laws of one country, who acted under those of another. He writ to the *people*; and writ at first without patronage from the better sort, and therefore without aims of pleasing them: without assistance or advice from the learned, as without the advantage of education or acquaintance among them; without that knowledge of the best models, the ancients to inspire him with an emulation of them; in a word, without any views of reputation, and of what poets are pleased to call immortality, some or all of which have encouraged the vanity, or animated the ambition, of other writers.

Yet it must be observed, that when his performances had merited the protection of his prince, and when the encouragement of the court had succeeded to that of the town, the works of his riper years are manifestly raised above those of his former. The dates of his plays sufficiently evidence that his productions improved, in proportion to the respect he had for his auditors. And I make no doubt this observation would be found true in every instance, were but editions extant from which we might learn the exact time when every piece was composed, and whether writ for the town, or the court.

Another cause (and no less strong than the former) may be deduced from our author's being a *player*, and forming himself first upon the judgments of that body of men whereof he was a member. They have ever had a standard to themselves, upon other principles than those of Aristotle. As they live by the majority, they know no rule but that of pleasing the present humour, and complying with the wit in fashion; a consideration which brings all their judgment to a short point. Players are just such judges of what is *right*, as tailors are of what is *graceful*. And in this view it will be but fair to allow, that most of our author's faults are less to be ascribed to his wrong judgment as a poet, than to his right judgment as a player.

By these men it was thought a praise to Shakespeare, that he scarce ever *blotted a line*. This they industriously propagated, as appears from what we are told by Ben Jonson in his *Discoveries*, and from the preface of Heminges and Condell to the first folio edition. But in reality (however it has prevailed) there never was a more groundless report, or to the contrary of which there are more undeniable evidences. As the comedy of the *Merry Wives of Windsor*, which he entirely new writ; the *History of Henry VI.* which was first published under the title of *The Contention of York and Lancaster*; and that of *Henry V.* extremely improved; that of *Hamlet* enlarged to almost as much again as at first, and many others. I believe the common opinion of his want of learning proceeded from no better ground. This too might be thought a praise by some, and to this his errors have as injudiciously been ascribed by others. For 'tis certain, were it true, it could concern but a small part of them; the most are such as are not properly defects, but superfœtations, and arise not from want of learning or reading, but from want of thinking or judging; or rather (to be more just to our author) from a compliance to those wants in others. As to a wrong choice of the subject, a wrong conduct of the incidents, false thoughts, forced expressions, etc., if these are not to be ascribed to the foresaid accidental reasons, they must be charged upon the poet himself, and there is no help for it. But I think the two disadvantages which I have mentioned (to be obliged to please the lowest of people, and to keep the worst

of company) if the consideration be extended as far as it reasonably may, will appear sufficient to mislead and depress the greatest genius upon earth. Nay the more modesty with which such a one is endued, the more he is in danger of submitting and conforming to others, against his own better judgment.

But as to his want of learning, it may be necessary to say something more. There is certainly a vast difference between learning and languages. How far he was ignorant of the latter, I cannot determine; but 'tis plain he had much reading at least, if they will not call it learning. Nor is it any great matter, if a man has knowledge, whether he has it from one language or from another. Nothing is more evident than that he had a taste of natural philosophy, mechanics, ancient and modern history, poetical learning and mythology. We find him very knowing in the customs, rites, and manners of antiquity. In *Coriolanus* and *Julius Caesar*, not only the spirit, but manners, of the Romans are exactly drawn; and still a nicer distinction is shown between the manners of the Romans in the time of the former, and of the latter. His reading in the ancient historians is no less conspicuous, in many references to particular passages; and the speeches copied from Plutarch in *Coriolanus* may, I think, as well be made an instance of his learning, as those copied from Cicero in *Catiline*, of Ben Jonson's. The manners of other nations in general, the Egyptians, Venetians, French, etc., are drawn with equal propriety. Whatever object of nature, or branch of science, he either speaks of or describes, it is always with competent, if not extensive knowledge; his descriptions are still exact; all his metaphors appropriated, and remarkably drawn from the true nature and inherent qualities of each subject. When he treats of ethic or politic, we may constantly observe a wonderful justness of distinction, as well as extent of comprehension. No one is more a master of the poetical story, or has more frequent allusions to the various parts of it; Mr. Waller (who has been celebrated for this last particular) has not shown more learning this way than Shakespeare. We have translations from Ovid published in his name, among those poems which pass for his, and for some of which we have undoubted authority (being published by himself, and dedicated to his noble patron, the Earl of Southampton). He appears also to have been conversant in Plautus, from whom he has taken the plot of one of his plays; he follows the Greek authors, and particularly Dares Phrygius, in another (although I will not pretend to say in which language he read them). The modern Italian writers of novels he was manifestly acquainted with; and we may conclude him to be no less conversant with the ancients of his own country, from the use he has made of Chaucer in *Troilus and Cressida,* and in the *Two Noble Kinsmen,* if that play be his, as there goes a tradition it was (and indeed it has little resemblance of Fletcher, and more of our author than some of those which have been received as genuine).

I am inclined to think this opinion proceeded originally from the zeal of the partizans of our author and Ben Jonson, as they endeavoured to exalt the one at the expense of the other. It is ever the nature of parties to be in extremes; and nothing is so probable, as that because Ben Jonson had much the most learning, it was said on the one hand that Shakespeare had none at all; and because Shakespeare had much the most wit and fancy, it was retorted on the other that Jonson wanted both. Because Shakespeare borrowed nothing, it was said that Ben Jonson borrowed everything. Because Jonson did not write extempore, he was reproached with being a year about every piece; and because Shakespeare wrote with ease and rapidity, they cried he never once made a blot. Nay the spirit of opposition ran so high, that whatever those of the one

side objected to the other was taken at the rebound and turned into praises; as injudiciously, as their antagonists before had made them objections.

Poets are always afraid of envy; but sure they have as much reason to be afraid of admiration. They are the Scylla and Charybdis of authors; those who escape one, often fall by the other. *Pessimum genus inimicorum laudantes,* says Tacitus; and Virgil desires to wear a charm against those who praise a poet without rule or reason.

Si ultra placitum laudarit, baccare frontem Cingite, ne vati noceat.

But however this contention might be carried on by the partizans on either side, I cannot help thinking these two great poets were good friends, and lived on amicable terms, and in offices of society with each other. It is an acknowledged fact, that Ben Jonson was introduced upon the stage, and his first works encouraged, by Shakespeare. And after his death, that author writes *To the memory of his beloved Mr. William Shakespeare,* which shows as if the friendship had continued through life. I cannot for my own part find any thing invidious or sparing in those verses, but wonder Mr. Dryden was of that opinion. He exalts him not only above all his contemporaries, but above Chaucer and Spenser, whom he will not allow to be great enough to be ranked with him; and challenges the names of Sophocles, Euripides, and Aeschylus, nay all Greece and Rome at once, to equal him; and (which is very particular) expressly vindicates him from the imputation of wanting art, not enduring that all his excellences should be attributed to Nature. It was remarkable, too, that the praise he gives him in his *Discoveries* seems to proceed from a personal kindness; he tells us that he loved the man, as well as honoured his memory; celebrates the honesty, openness, and frankness of his temper; and only distinguishes, as he reasonably ought, between the real merit of the author, and the silly and derogatory applauses of the players. Ben Jonson might indeed be sparing in his commendations (though certainly he is not so in this instance), partly from his own nature, and partly from judgment. For men of judgment think they do any man more service in praising him justly, than lavishly. I say, I would fain believe they were friends, though the violence and ill-breeding of their followers and flatterers were enough to give rise to the contrary report. I would hope that it may be with parties, both in wit and state, as with those monsters described by the poets; and that their heads at least may have something human, though their bodies and tails are wild beasts and serpents.

As I believe that what I have mentioned gave rise to the opinion of Shakespeare's want of learning; so what has continued it down to us may have been the many blunders and illiteracies of the first publishers of his works. In these editions their ignorance shines in almost every page; nothing is more common than *Actus tertia. Exit omnes. Enter three witches solus.* Their French is as bad as their Latin, both in construction and spelling; their very Welsh is false. Nothing is more likely than that those palpable blunders of Hector's quoting Aristotle, with others of that gross kind, sprung from the same root, it not being at all credible that these could be the errors of any man who had the least tincture of a school, or the least conversation with such as had. Ben Jonson (whom they will not think partial to him) allows him at least to have had *some* Latin; which is utterly inconsistent with mistakes like these. Nay the constant blunders in proper names of persons and places, are such as must have proceeded from a man who had not so much as read any history, in any language, so could not be Shakespeare's.

I shall now lay before the reader some of those almost innumerable er-

rors, which have risen from one source, the ignorance of the players, both as his actors, and as his editors. When the nature and kinds of these are enumerated and considered, I dare to say that not Shakespeare only, but Aristotle or Cicero, had their works undergone the same fate, might have appeared to want sense as well as learning.

It is not certain that any one of his plays was published by himself. During the time of his employment in the theatre, several of his pieces were printed separately in quarto. What makes me think that most of these were not published by him, is the excessive carelessness of the press; every page is so scandalously false spelled, and almost all the learned or unusual words so intolerably mangled, that it's plain there either was no corrector to the press at all, or one totally illiterate. If any were supervised by himself, I should fancy the two parts of *Henry the 4th* and *Midsummer-Night's Dream* might have been so, because I find no other printed with any exactness; and (contrary to the rest) there is very little variation in all the subsequent editions of them. There are extant two prefaces, to the first quarto edition of *Troilus and Cressida* in 1609, and to that of *Othello*; by which it appears, that the first was published without his knowledge or consent, and even before it was acted, so late as seven or eight years before he died, and that the latter was not printed till after his death. The whole number of genuine plays which we have been able to find printed in his lifetime, amounts but to eleven. And of some of these, we meet with two or more editions by different printers, each of which has whole heaps of trash different from the other; which I should fancy was occasioned by their being taken from different copies, belonging to different playhouses.

ers, Heminges and Condell, in 1623, seven years after his decease. They declare that all the other editions were stolen and surreptitious, and affirm theirs to be purged from the errors of the former. This is true as to the literal errors, and no other; for in all respects else it is far worse than the quartos.

First, because the additions of trifling and bombast passages are in this edition far more numerous. For whatever had been added, since those quartos, by the actors, or had stolen from their mouths into the written parts, were from thence conveyed into the printed text, and all stand charged upon the author. He himself complained of this usage in *Hamlet*, where he wishes that *those who play the Clowns would speak no more than is set down for them.* (Act iii. Sc. iv.) But as a proof that he could not escape it, in the old editions of *Romeo and Juliet* there is no hint of a great number of the mean conceits and ribaldries now to be found there. In others, the low scenes of mobs, plebeians and clowns, are vastly shorter than at present. And I have seen one in particular (which seems to have belonged to the playhouse, by having the parts divided with lines, and the actors' names in the margin) where several of those very passages were added in a written hand, which are since to be found in the folio.

In the next place, a number of beautiful passages which are extant in the first single editions, are omitted in this; as it seems without any other reason, than their willingness to shorten some scenes, these men (as it was said of Procrustes) either lopping, or stretching an author, to make him just fit for their stage.

This edition is said to be printed from the *original copies.* I believe they meant those which had lain ever since the author's days in the playhouse, and had from time to time been cut, or added to, arbitrarily. It appears that this edition, as well as the quartos, was printed (at least partly) from no better copies than the *prompter's book,* or *piece-meal parts* written out for the use of the actors, for in some places their very names are through carelessness set down instead of the *personae dramatis.* And in others the notes of direction to the property-men for their movables, and to the players for their entries, are inserted into the text, through the ignorance of the transcribers.

The plays not having been before so much as distinguished by acts and scenes, they are in this edition divided according as they played them; often where there is no pause in the action, or where they thought fit to make a breach in it, for the sake of music, masques, or monsters.

Sometimes the scenes are transposed and shuffled backward and forward; a thing which could no otherwise happen, but by their being taken from separate and piece-meal written parts.

Many verses are omitted entirely, and others transposed; from whence invincible obscurities have arisen, past the guess of any commentator to clear up, but just where the accidental glimpse of an old edition enlightens us.

Some characters were confounded and mixed, or two put into one, for want of a competent number of actors. Thus in the quarto edition of *Midsummer Night's Dream,* Act v. Shakespeare introduces a kind of Master of the revels called Philostratus, all whose part is given to another character (that of Aegeus) in the subsequent editions. So also in *Hamlet* and *King Lear.* This too makes it probable that the prompter's books were what they called the original copies.

From liberties of this kind, many speeches also were put into the mouths of wrong persons, where the author now seems chargeable with making them speak out of character; or sometimes perhaps for no better reason, than that a governing player, to have the mouthing of some favourite speech himself, would snatch it from the unworthy lips of an underling.

Prose from verse they did not know, and they accordingly printed one for the other throughout the volume.

Having been forced to say so much of the players, I think I ought in justice to remark that the judgment, as well as condition, of that class of people was then far inferior to what it is in our days. As then the best playhouses were inns and taverns (the Globe, the Hope, the Red Bull, the Fortune, etc.) , so the top of the profession were then mere players, not gentlemen of the stage. They were led into the buttery by the steward, not placed at the lord's table, or lady's toilette; and consequently were entirely deprived of those advantages they now enjoy, in the familiar conversation of our nobility, and an intimacy (not to say dearness) with people of the first condition.

From what has been said, there can be no question but had Shakespeare published his works himself (especially in his latter time, and after his retreat from the stage) , we should not only be certain which are genuine, but should find in those that are, the errors lessened by some thousands. If I may judge from all the distinguishing marks of his style, and his manner of thinking and writing, I make no doubt to declare that those wretched plays, *Pericles, Locrine, Sir John Old-castle, Yorkshire Tragedy, Lord Cromwell, The Puritan,* and *London Prodigal,* cannot be admitted as his. And I should conjecture of some of the others (particularly *Love's Labour's Lost, The Winter's Tale,* and *Titus Andronicus*) that only some characters, single scenes, or perhaps a few particular passages, were of his hand. It is very probable what occasioned some plays to be supposed Shakespeare's was only this: that they were pieces produced by unknown authors, or fitted up for the theatre while it was under his administration; and no owner claiming them, they were adjudged to him, as they give

strays to the lord of the manor: a mistake which (one may also observe) it was not for the interest of the house to remove. Yet the players themselves, Heminges and Condell, afterwards did Shakespeare the justice, to reject those eight plays in their edition; though they were then printed in his name, in everybody's hands, and acted with some applause (as we learn from what Ben Jonson says of *Pericles* in his Ode on the *New Inn*) . That *Titus Andronicus* is one of this class I am the rather induced to believe, by finding the same author openly express his contempt of it in the *Induction to Bartholomew-Fair,* in the year 1614, when Shakespeare was yet living. And there is no better authority for these latter sort, than for the former, which were equally published in his lifetime.

If we give into this opinion, how many low and vicious parts and passages might no longer reflect upon this great genius, but appear unworthily charged upon him? And even in those which are really his, how many faults may have been unjustly laid to his account from arbitrary additions, expunctions, transpositions of scenes and lines, confusion of characters and persons, wrong application of speeches, corruptions of innumerable passages by the ignorance, and wrong corrections of them again by the impertinence of his first editors? From one or other of these considerations, I am verily persuaded, that the greatest and the grossest part of what are thought his errors would vanish, and leave his character in a light very different from that disadvantageous one, in which it now appears to us.

This is the state in which Shakespeare's writings lie at present; for, since the above-mentioned folio edition, all the rest have implicitly followed it, without having recourse to any of the former, or ever making the comparison between them. It is impossible to repair the injuries already done him; too much time has elapsed, and the materials are too few.

In what I have done I have rather given a proof of my willingness and desire, than of my ability, to do him justice. I have discharged the dull duty of an editor, to my best judgment, with more labour than I expect thanks, with a religious abhorrence of all innovation, and without any indulgence to my private sense or conjecture. The method taken in this edition will show itself. The various readings are fairly put in the margin, so that every one may compare them; and those I have preferred into the text are constantly *ex fide codicum,* upon authority. The alterations or additions which Shakespeare himself made, are taken notice of as they occur. Some suspected passages which are excessively bad (and which seem interpolations by being so inserted that one can entirely omit them without any chasm, or deficiency in the context) are degraded to the bottom of the page; with an asterisk referring to the places of their insertion. The scenes are marked so distinctly that every removal of place is specified; which is more necessary in this author than any other, since he shifts them more frequently; and sometimes without attending to this particular, the reader would have met with obscurities. The more obsolete or unusual words are explained. Some of the most shining passages are distinguished by commas in the margin; and where the beauty lay not in particulars but in the whole, a star is prefixed to the scene. This seems to me a shorter and less ostentatious method of performing the better half of criticism (namely the pointing out an author's excellences) than to fill a whole paper with citations of fine passages, with general applauses, or empty exclamations at the tail of them. There is also subjoined a catalogue of those first editions by which the greater part of the various readings and of the corrected passages are authorised (most of which are such as carry their own evidence along with them). These editions now hold the place of originals, and are the only materials left to repair the deficiencies or restore the corrupted sense of the author. I can only wish that a greater number of them (if a greater were ever published) may yet be found, by a search more successful than mine, for the better accomplishment of this end.

I will conclude by saying of Shakespeare, that with all his faults, and with all the irregularity of his drama, one may look upon his works, in comparison of those that are more finished and regular, as upon an ancient majestic piece of Gothic architecture, compared with a neat modern building. The latter is more elegant and glaring, but the former is more strong and more solemn. It must be allowed that in one of these there are materials enough to make many of the other. It has much the greater variety, and much the nobler apartments; though we are often conducted to them by dark, odd, and uncouth passages. Nor does the whole fail to strike us with greater reverence, though many of the parts are childish, ill-placed, and unequal to its grandeur.

JOHN GAY (1685-1732)

John Gay, born at Barnstaple, Devon, 1685, was apprenticed in his youth to a London mercer. His early poems, *Wine* (1708), *Rural Sports* (1713), and *The Fan* (1713), failed to lift him from obscurity, but at the same time he was making important friends among men of letters and the aristocracy. Pope and Swift esteemed him highly, and kept insisting that his noble friends and the Government should do something for him. The indolent, self-indulgent poet came to feel that he was being shabbily treated, and when he failed to get a suitable sinecure at the accession of George II, was bitterly offended at the Court and the Walpole administration. Like Edward Young, he wasted years in suing for favor.

Yet, except for political preferment, Gay enjoyed all the kinds of success possible for a man of letters in his day. He was a docile friend of the great wits, and got help from them in developing a vein of realistic humor in his verse. *The Shepherd's Week* (1714) was perhaps connected with Pope's campaign against the *Pastorals* of Ambrose Philips; the burlesque intention freed Gay from the conventionalities of *Rural Sports*. *Trivia, or the Art of Walking the Streets of London* (1716) certainly owes something to the vigorous realism of Swift (see "A Description of the Morning," "A Description of a City Shower") and the milder realism of Addison and Steele. Gay's circle of friends was so wide that he made about £1000 when he published his poems by subscription in 1720; this money he immediately lost in South Sea Stock. His *Fables* appeared in 1727, and earned him a position in elementary schoolbooks for a century or more. *The Beggar's Opera* (1728) derives from Swift's earlier suggestion of a "Newgate pastoral" to follow *The Shepherd's Week;* the timeliness and cleverness of the piece, with its amusing burlesque of current operatic form, its neat and cynical lyrics, and its identification of Walpole with the gallant highwayman Macheath, took the town by storm. Thus Gay came to enjoy popular success of the widest kind. Even when the sequel *Polly* was forbidden production for political reasons, he made £1200 from the sale of the work. In his latter years he was almost entirely under the care of his generous friends, the Duke and the Duchess of Queensberry.

Gay fell far short of the solidity and intellectual power of the great Augustans, and the friendship of Pope and Swift probably led them to exaggerate his merits. Except in his charming and witty songs, his work lacks style and finish. His was a lax, passive temperament, with a talent for using current materials as "copy" for readable if not distinguished verse. He was interested in the portrayal of every-day life, and to this extent he worked toward later developments in the poetry and fiction of the century. But in spite of his amused observation of the actualities of life, he did not understand his subjects thoroughly or feel them deeply. Nevertheless there is a place in literature for the writer who makes easy transcriptions, and later readers have enjoyed the surface-play of life in the first quarter of the eighteenth century as rendered by John Gay.

G. C. Faber's edition of Gay's *Poetical Works* (Oxford University Press, 1926) is definitive. Much has been written about *The Beggar's Opera* (see W. E. Schultz, *Gay's Beggar's Opera* [New Haven, 1923]), but there is no full-length life except Lewis Melville's scrappy and superficial *Life and Letters of John Gay* (London, 1921). Readers of *Trivia* will find much material in W. H. Irving, *John Gay's London* (Cambridge, U. S. A., 1928). See also page 1269.

ON A MISCELLANY OF POEMS

TO BERNARD LINTOT

*Ipsa varietate tentamus efficere ut alia aliis; quaedam
fortasse omnibus placeant.*[1]

PLIN. EPIST. [IV, xiv.]

As when some skilful cook, to please each guest,
Would in one mixture comprehend a feast,
With due proportion and judicious care
He fills each dish with different sorts of fare,
Fishes and fowl deliciously unite,
To feast at once the taste, the smell, and sight;
  So, Bernard, must a miscellany be
Compounded of all kinds of poetry;
The Muses' olio,[2] which all tastes may fit,
And treat each reader with his darling wit.   10
  Wouldst thou for miscellanies raise thy fame,
And bravely rival Jacob's mighty name,
Let all the Muses in the piece conspire;
The lyric bard must strike the harmonious lyre;
Heroic strains must here and there be found,
And nervous sense be sung in lofty sound;
Let elegy in moving numbers flow,
And fill some pages with melodious woe;
Let not your amorous songs too numerous prove,
Nor glut thy reader with abundant love;   20
Satire must interfere, whose pointed rage
May lash the madness of a vicious age;
Satire, the Muse that never fails to hit,
For if there's scandal, to be sure there's wit.
Tire not our patience with Pindaric lays;
Those swell the piece, but very rarely please:
Let short-breathed epigram its force confine,
And strike at follies in a single line.
Translations should throughout the work be sown,
And Homer's godlike Muse be made our own;   30
Horace in useful numbers should be sung,
And Virgil's thoughts adorn the British tongue;
Let Ovid tell Corinna's hard disdain,
And at her door in melting notes complain;
His tender accents pitying virgins move,
And charm the listening ear with tales of love.
Let every classic in the volume shine,
And each contribute to thy great design:
Through various subjects let the reader range,
And raise his fancy with a grateful change;   40
Variety's the source of joy below,
From whence still fresh revolving pleasures flow.

[1] I try by this variety to hit different tastes with different pieces, and provide a few, perhaps, which may please everybody.
[2] A mixed dish.

In books and love, the mind one end pursues,
And only change the expiring flame renews.
  Where Buckingham will condescend to give,
That honoured piece to distant times must live;
When noble Sheffield strikes the trembling strings,
The little loves rejoice, and clap their wings;
"Anacreon lives," they cry; "the harmonious swain
Retunes the lyre, and tries his wonted strain;   50
'Tis he,—our lost Anacreon lives again!"
But when the illustrious poet soars above
The sportive revels of the god of love,
Like Maro's Muse he takes a loftier flight,
And towers beyond the wondering Cupid's sight.
  If thou wouldst have thy volume stand the test,
And of all others be reputed best,
Let Congreve teach the listening groves to mourn,
As when he wept o'er fair Pastora's urn.
  Let Prior's Muse with softening accents move,   60
Soft as the strains of constant Emma's love;
Or let his fancy choose some jovial theme,
As when he told Hans Carvel's jealous dream;
Prior the admiring reader entertains,
With Chaucer's humour and with Spenser's strains.
  Waller in Granville lives; when Mira sings,
With Waller's hand he strikes the sounding strings;
With sprightly turns his noble genius shines,
And manly sense adorns his easy lines.
  On Addison's sweet lays attention waits,   70
And silence guards the place while he repeats;
His Muse alike on every subject charms,
Whether she paints the god of love, or arms;
In him, pathetic Ovid sings again,
And Homer's *Iliad* shines in his *Campaign*.
  Whenever Garth shall raise his sprightly song,
Sense flows in easy numbers from his tongue;
Great Phoebus in his learned son we see,
Alike in physic, as in poetry.
  When Pope's harmonious Muse with pleasure roves,   80
Amidst the plains, the murmuring streams, and groves,
Attentive Echo, pleased to hear his songs,
Through the glad shade each warbling note prolongs;
His various numbers charm our ravished ears,
His steady judgment far outshoots his years,
And early in the youth the god appears.
  From these successful bards collect thy strains,
And praise with profit shall reward thy pains:
Then, while calves-leather binding bears the sway,
And sheepskin to its sleeker gloss gives way;   90
While neat old Elzevir is reckoned better
Than Pirate Hills' brown sheets and scurvy letter;
While print-admirers careful Aldus choose
Before John Morphew, or the weekly news:
So long shall live thy praise in books of fame,
And Tonson yield to Lintot's lofty name.

[1712]

THE SHEPHERD'S WEEK

THURSDAY; OR, THE SPELL

Hobnelia

Hobnelia, seated in a dreary vale,
In pensive mood rehearsed her piteous tale;
Her piteous tale the winds in sighs bemoan,
And pining Echo answers groan for groan.
  I rue the day, a rueful day, I trow,
The woeful day, a day indeed of woe!
When Lubberkin to town his cattle drove,
A maiden fine bedight he happed to love;
The maiden fine bedight his love retains,
And for the village he forsakes the plains.   10
Return, my Lubberkin, these ditties hear;
Spells will I try, and spells shall ease my care.
  With my sharp heel I three times mark the ground,
  And turn me thrice around, around, around.
  When first the year, I heard the cuckoo sing,
And call with welcome note the budding spring,
I straightway set a-running with such haste,
Deborah, that won the smock, scarce ran so fast.
Till spent for lack of breath, quite weary grown,
Upon a rising bank I sat adown,   20
Then doffed my shoe, and by my troth, I swear,
Therein I spied this yellow frizzled hair,
As like to Lubberkin's in curl and hue,
As if upon his comely pate it grew.
  With my sharp heel I three times mark the ground,
  And turn me thrice around, around, around.
  At eve last Midsummer no sleep I sought,
But to the field a bag of hemp-seed brought;
I scattered round the seed on every side,
And three times in a trembling accent cried,   30
This hemp-seed with my virgin hand I sow,
Who shall my true-love be, the crop shall mow.
I straight looked back, and if my eyes speak truth,
With his keen scythe behind me came the youth.
  With my sharp heel I three times mark the ground,
  And turn me thrice around, around, around.
  Last Valentine, the day when birds of kind
Their paramours with mutual chirpings find;
I rearly[1] rose, just at the break of day,
Before the sun had chased the stars away;   40
Afield I went, amid the morning dew,
To milk my kine (for so should huswives do) ;
Thee first I spied, and the first swain we see,
In spite of fortune shall our true-love be;
See, Lubberkin, each bird his partner take,
And canst thou then thy sweetheart dear forsake?

[1] Early.

With my sharp heel I three times mark the ground,
And turn me thrice around, around, around.
Last May Day fair I searched to find a snail
That might my secret lover's name reveal;   50
Upon a gooseberry bush a snail I found,
For always snails near sweetest fruit abound.
I seized the vermin, home I quickly sped,
And on the hearth the milk-white embers spread.
Slow crawled the snail, and if I right can spell
In the soft ashes marked a curious L:
Oh, may this wondrous omen lucky prove!
For L is found in *Lubberkin* and *Love.*
    With my sharp heel I three times mark the ground,
    And turn me thrice around, around, around.   60
    Two hazel-nuts I threw into the flame,
And to each nut I gave a sweetheart's name.
This with the loudest bounce me sore amazed,
That in a flame of brightest colour blazed.
As blazed the nut so may thy passion grow,
For 'twas thy nut that did so brightly glow.
    With my sharp heel I three times mark the ground,
    And turn me thrice around, around, around.
    As peascods once I plucked, I chanced to see
One that was closely filled with three times three,   70
Which when I cropped I safely home conveyed,
And o'er my door the spell in secret laid.
My wheel I turned, and sung a ballad new,
While from the spindle I the fleeces drew;
The latch moved up, when who should first come in,
But in his proper person,—Lubberkin!
I broke my yarn surprised the sight to see,
Sure sign that he would break his word with me.
Eftsoons I joined it with my wonted sleight,
So may again his love with mine unite!   80
    With my sharp heel I three times mark the ground,
    And turn me thrice around, around, around.
    This lady-fly I take from off the grass,
Whose spotted back might scarlet red surpass.
Fly, Lady-Bird, *north, south, or east or west,*
Fly where the man is found that I love best.
He leaves my hand, see, to the west he's flown,
To call my true-love from the faithless town.
    With my sharp heel I three times mark the ground,
    And turn me thrice around, around, around.   90
    I pare this pippin round and round again,
My shepherd's name to flourish on the plain.
I fling the unbroken paring o'er my head,
Upon the grass a perfect L is read:
Yet on my heart a fairer L is seen
Than what the paring marks upon the green.
    With my sharp heel I three times mark the ground,
    And turn me thrice around, around, around.
    This pippin shall another trial make.
See, from the core two kernels brown I take;   100

This on my cheek for Lubberkin is worn,
And Boobyclod on t' other side is borne.
But Boobyclod soon drops upon the ground,
A certain token that his love's unsound,
While Lubberkin sticks firmly to the last;
Oh, were his lips to mine but joined so fast!
  With my sharp heel I three times mark the ground,
  And turn me thrice around, around, around.
  As Lubberkin once slept beneath a tree,
I twitched his dangling garter from his knee;   110
He wist not when the hempen string I drew,
Now mine I quickly doff of inkle[2] blue;
Together fast I tie the garters twain,
And while I knit the knot repeat this strain:
Three times a true-love's knot I tie secure,
Firm be the knot, firm may his love endure.
  With my sharp heel I three times mark the ground,
  And turn me thrice around, around, around.
  As I was wont, I trudged last market-day
To town, with new-laid eggs preserved in hay.   120
I made my market long before 'twas night;
My purse grew heavy and my basket light.
Straight to the 'pothecary's shop I went,
And in love-powder all my money spent;
Behap what will, next Sunday after prayers,
When to the alehouse Lubberkin repairs,
These golden flies into his mug I'll throw,
And soon the swain with fervent love shall glow.
  With my sharp heel I three times mark the ground,
  And turn me thrice around, around, around.   130
But hold—our Lightfoot barks, and cocks his ears;
O'er yonder stile see Lubberkin appears.
He comes, he comes, Hobnelia's not bewrayed,
Nor shall she crowned with willow die a maid.
He vows, he swears, he'll give me a green gown;
Oh dear! I fall adown, adown, adown!

FRIDAY; OR, THE DIRGE

Bumkinet, Grubbinol

Bumkinet. Why, Grubbinol, dost thou so wistful seem?
There's sorrow in thy look, if right I deem.
'Tis true, yon oaks with yellow tops appear,
And chilly blasts begin to nip the year;
From the tall elm a shower of leaves is borne,
And their lost beauty riven beeches mourn.
Yet even this season pleasance blithe affords,
Now the squeezed press foams with our apple hoards.
Come, let us hie, and quaff a cheery bowl;
Let cider new wash sorrow from thy soul.   10
  Grubbinol. Ah Bumkinet! since thou from hence wert gone,
From these sad plains all merriment is flown;

---

[2] Linen tape.

Should I reveal my grief, 'twould spoil thy cheer,
And make thine eye o'erflow with many a tear.
   Bumkinet. Hang sorrow! Let's to yonder hut repair,
And with trim sonnets cast away our care.
Gillian of Croydon well thy pipe can play,
Thou sing'st most sweet, *O'er hills and far away.*
Of *Patient Grissel* I devise to sing,
And catches quaint shall make the valleys ring.   20
Come, Grubbinol, beneath this shelter come,
From hence we view our flocks securely roam.
   Grubbinol. Yes, blithesome lad, a tale I mean to sing,
But with my woe shall distant valleys ring,
The tale shall make our kidlings droop their head,
For woe is me!—our Blouzelind is dead.
   Bumkinet. Is Blouzelinda dead? farewell my glee!
No happiness is now reserved for me.
As the wood-pigeon coos without his mate,
So shall my doleful dirge bewail her fate.   30
Of Blouzelinda fair I mean to tell,
The peerless maid that did all maids excel.
   Henceforth the morn shall dewy sorrow shed,
And evening tears upon the grass be spread;
The rolling streams with watery grief shall flow,
And winds shall moan aloud—when loud they blow.
Henceforth, as oft as autumn shall return,
The dropping trees, whene'er it rains, shall mourn;
This season quite shall strip the country's pride,
For 'twas in autumn Blouzelinda died.   40
   Where'er I gad, I Blouzelind shall view;
Woods, dairy, barn, and mows our passion knew.
When I direct my eyes to yonder wood,
Fresh rising sorrow curdles in my blood.
Thither I've often been the damsel's guide,
When rotten sticks our fuel have supplied;
There I remember how her fagots large,
Were frequently these happy shoulders' charge.
Sometimes this crook drew hazel boughs adown,
And stuffed her apron wide with nuts so brown;   50
Or when her feeding hogs had missed their way,
Or wallowing 'mid a feast of acorns lay,
The untoward creatures to the sty I drove,
And whistled all the way—or told my love.
   If by the dairy's hatch I chance to hie,
I shall her goodly countenance espy,
For there her goodly countenance I've seen,
Set off with kerchief starched and pinners[1] clean.
Sometimes like wax she rolls the butter round,
Or with the wooden lily prints the pound.   60
Whilom I've seen her skim the clouted cream,
And press from spongy curds the milky stream.
But now, alas! these ears shall hear no more
The whining swine surround the dairy door;
No more her care shall fill the hollow tray,

---

[1] A close-fitting cap with two long flaps.

To fat the guzzling hogs with floods of whey.
Lament, ye swine, in grunting spend your grief,
For you, like me, have lost your sole relief.
　　When in the barn the sounding flail I ply,
Where from her sieve the chaff was wont to fly,　　　　7(
The poultry there will seem around to stand,
Waiting upon her charitable hand.
No succour meet the poultry now can find,
For they, like me, have lost their Blouzelind.
　　Whenever by yon barley mow I pass,
Before my eyes will trip the tidy lass.
I pitched the sheaves (oh, could I do so now!)
Which she in rows piled on the growing mow.
There every deal[2] my heart by love was gained,
There the sweet kiss my courtship has explained.　　　80
Ah, Blouzelind! that mow I ne'er shall see,
But thy memorial will revive in me.
　　Lament, ye fields, and rueful symptoms show!
Henceforth let not the smelling primrose grow;
Let weeds instead of butter-flowers[3] appear,
And meads, instead of daisies, hemlock bear;
For cowslips sweet let dandelions spread,
For Blouzelinda, blithesome maid, is dead!
Lament, ye swains, and o'er her grave bemoan,
And spell ye right this verse upon her stone:　　　　90
Here Blouzelinda *lies—Alas, alas!*
Weep shepherds—and remember flesh is grass.
　　Grubbinol. Albeit thy songs are sweeter to mine ear,
Than to the thirsty cattle rivers clear;
Or winter porridge to the labouring youth,
Or buns and sugar to the damsel's tooth;
Yet Blouzelinda's name shall tune my lay;
Of her I'll sing for ever and for aye.
　　When Blouzelind expired, the wether's bell
Before the drooping flock tolled forth her knell;　　　100
The solemn deathwatch clicked the hour she died,
And shrilling crickets in the chimney cried;
The boding raven on her cottage sate,
And with hoarse croaking warned us of her fate;
The lambkin, which her wonted tendance bred,
Dropped on the plains that fatal instant dead;
Swarmed on a rotten stick the bees I spied,
Which erst I saw when Goody Dobson died.
　　How shall I void of tears her death relate!
While on her darling' bed her mother sate,　　　　11(
These words the dying Blouzelinda spoke,
And of the dead let none the will revoke:
"Mother," quoth she, "let not the poultry need,
And give the goose wherewith to raise her breed;
Be these my sister's care—and every morn
Amid the ducklings let her scatter corn;
The sickly calf that's housed, be sure to tend,

[2] Entirely.
[3] Buttercups.

Feed him with milk, and from bleak colds defend.
Yet e'er I die—see, Mother, yonder shelf,
There secretly I've hid my worldly pelf.   120
Twenty good shillings in a rag I laid,
Be ten the parson's, for my sermon paid.
The rest is yours—my spinning-wheel and rake,
Let Susan keep for her dear sister's sake;
My new straw hat that's trimly lined with green,
Let Peggy wear, for she's a damsel clean.
My leathern bottle, long in harvests tried,
Be Grubbinol's—this silver ring beside:
Three silver pennies and a ninepence bent,
A token kind, to Bumkinet is sent."   130
Thus spoke the maiden, while her mother cried,
And peaceful, like the harmless lamb, she died.

   To show their love, the neighbours far and near
Followed with wistful look the damsel's bier.
Sprigged rosemary the lads and lasses bore,
While dismally the parson walked before.
Upon her grave the rosemary they threw,
The daisy, butter-flower, and endive blue.

   After the good man warned us from his text,
That none could tell whose turn would be the next,   140
He said that Heaven would take her soul, no doubt,
And spoke the hourglass in her praise—quite out.

   To her sweet memory flowery garlands strung,
O'er her now empty seat aloft were hung.
With wicker rods we fenced her tomb around,
To ward from man and beast the hallowed ground,
Lest her new grave the parson's cattle raze,
For both his horse and cow the churchyard graze.

   Now we trudged homeward to her mother's farm,
To drink new cider mulled, with ginger warm.   150
For Gaffer Treadwell told us by the bye,
Excessive sorrow is exceeding dry.

   While bulls bear horns upon their curlèd brow,
Or lasses with soft strokings milk the cow;
While paddling ducks the standing lake desire,
Or battening hogs roll in the sinking mire;
While moles the crumbled earth in hillocks raise,
So long shall swains tell Blouzelinda's praise.

   Thus wailed the louts in melancholy strain,
Till bonny Susan sped across the plain;   160
They seized the lass in apron clean arrayed,
And to the alehouse forced the willing maid;
In ale and kisses they forget their cares,
And Susan Blouzelinda's loss repairs.

SATURDAY; OR, THE FLIGHTS

Bowzybeus.

Sublimer strains, O rustic Muse, prepare;
Forget awhile the barn and dairy's care;

Thy homely voice to loftier numbers raise;
The drunkard's flights require sonorous lays;
With Bowzybeus' songs exalt thy verse,
While rocks and woods the various notes rehearse.
 'Twas in the season when the reapers' toil
Of the ripe harvest 'gan to rid the soil;
Wide through the field was seen a goodly rout;
Clean damsels bound the gathered sheaves about;   **10**
The lads with sharpened hook and sweating brow
Cut down the labours of the winter plow.
To the near hedge young Susan steps aside;
She feigned her coat or garter was untied;
Whate'er she did, she stooped adown unseen,
And merry reapers, what they list, will ween.
Soon she rose up, and cried with voice so shrill
That echo answered from the distant hill;
The youths and damsels ran to Susan's aid,
Who thought some adder had the lass dismayed.   **20**
 There fast asleep they Bowzybeus spied,
His hat and oaken staff lay close beside—
That Bowzybeus who could sweetly sing,
Or with the rosined bow torment the string;
That Bowzybeus who with finger's speed
Could call soft warblings from the breathing reed;
That Bowzybeus who with jocund tongue
Ballads and roundelays and catches sung.
They loudly laugh to see the damsel's fright,
And in disport surround the drunken wight.   **30**
 Ah, Bowzybee, why didst thou stay so long?
The mugs were large, the drink was wondrous strong!
Thou shouldst have left the fair before 'twas night,
But thou satst toping till the morning light.
 Cicely, brisk maid, steps forth before the rout,
And kissed with smacking lip the snoring lout.
For custom says whoe'er this venture proves,
For such a kiss demands a pair of gloves.
By her example Dorcas bolder grows,
And plays a tickling straw within his nose.   **40**
He rubs his nostril, and in wonted joke
The sneering swains with stammering speech bespoke:
"To you, my lads, I'll sing my carols o'er.
As for the maids,—I've something else in store."
 No sooner 'gan he raise his tuneful song,
But lads and lasses round about him throng.
Not ballad-singer placed above the crowd
Sings with a note so shrilling sweet and loud,
Nor parish clerk who calls the psalm so clear,
Like Bowzybeus soothes the attentive ear.   **50**
 Of Nature's laws his carols first begun,
Why the grave owl can never face the sun,
For owls, as swains observe, detest the light,
And only sing and seek their prey by night;
How turnips hide their swelling heads below,
And how the closing coleworts upwards grow;

How Will-a-Wisp misleads night-faring clowns,
O'er hills, and sinking bogs, and pathless downs.
Of stars he told that shoot with shining trail,
And of the glow-worm's light that gilds his tail.   60
He sung where woodcocks in the summer feed,
And in what climates they renew their breed;
Some think to northern coasts their flight they tend,
Or to the moon in midnight hours ascend;
Where swallows in the winter's season keep,
And how the drowsy bat and dormouse sleep;
How Nature does the puppy's eyelid close,
Till the bright sun has nine times set and rose,
For huntsmen by their long experience find,
That puppies still nine rolling suns are blind.   70
　　Now he goes on, and sings of fairs and shows,
For still new fairs before his eyes arose;
How pedlars' stalls with glittering toys are laid,
The various fairings of the country maid.
Long silken laces hang upon the twine,
And rows of pins and amber bracelets shine;
How the tight lass, knives, combs, and scissors spies,
And looks on thimbles with desiring eyes.
Of lotteries next with tuneful note he told,
Where silver spoons are won and rings of gold.   80
The lads and lasses trudge the street along,
And all the fair is crowded in his song.
The mountebank now treads the stage, and sells
His pills, his balsams, and his ague-spells;
Now o'er and o'er the nimble tumbler springs,
And on the rope the venturous maiden swings;
Jack Pudding[1] in his parti-coloured jacket
Tosses the glove, and jokes at every packet.
Of raree-shows[2] he sung, and Punch's feats,
Of pockets picked in crowds, and various cheats.   90
　　Then sad he sung the Children in the Wood.
Ah, barbarous uncle, stained with infant blood!
How blackberries they plucked in deserts wild,
And fearless at the glittering falchion smiled;
Their little corps the robin redbreasts found,
And strewed with pious bill the leaves around.
Ah, gentle birds! if this verse lasts so long,
Your names shall live forever in my song.
　　For buxom Joan he sung the doubtful strife,
How the sly sailor made the maid a wife.   100
　　To louder strains he raised his voice, to tell
What woeful wars in Chevy Chase befell,
When Percy drove the deer with hound and horn,
Wars to be wept by children yet unborn!
Ah, Witherington, more years thy life had crowned,
If thou hadst never heard the horn or hound!
Yet shall the Squire who fought on bloody stumps,
By future bards be wailed in doleful dumps.

[1] The clown.
[2] Peep-shows.

All in the land of Essex next he chants,
How to sleek mares starch Quakers turn gallants;   116
How the grave brother stood on bank so green.
Happy for him if mares had never been!
   Then he was seized with a religious qualm,
And on a sudden, sung the hundredth psalm.
   He sung of Taffey Welsh, and Sawney Scot,
Lillibullero and the Irish Trot.
Why should I tell of Bateman or of Shore,
Or Wantley's Dragon slain by valiant Moore,
The bower of Rosamond, or Robin Hood,
And how the grass now grows where Troy town stood?   120
   His carols ceased: the listening maids and swains
Seem still to hear some soft imperfect strains.
Sudden he rose, and as he reels along
Swears kisses sweet should well reward his song.
The damsels laughing fly; the giddy clown
Again upon a wheat-sheaf drops adown;
The power that guards the drunk, his sleep attends,
Till, ruddy, like his face, the sun descends.

[1714]

TRIVIA

OR, THE ART OF WALKING THE STREETS OF LONDON

Quo te Moeri pedes? An, quo via ducit, in Urbem?[1]—Virgil, *Ecl.* ix, 1

Book II

OF WALKING THE STREETS BY DAY

Thus far the Muse has traced in useful lays,
The proper implements for wintry ways;
Has taught the walker, with judicious eyes,
To read the various warnings of the skies
Now venture, Muse, from home, to range the town,
And for the public safety risk thy own.
   For ease and for dispatch the morning's best;
No tides of passengers the street molest.
You'll see a draggled damsel, here and there,
From Billingsgate her fishy traffic bear;   10
On doors the sallow milkmaid chalks her gains;
Ah, how unlike the milkmaid of the plains!
Before proud gates attending asses bray,
Or arrogate with solemn pace the way;
These grave physicians with their milky cheer
The love-sick maid and dwindling beau repair;
Here rows of drummers stand in martial file,
And with their vellum thunder shake the pile,
To greet the new-made bride. Are sounds like these
The proper prelude to a state of peace?   20

[1] Where are you going, Moerus? To the city, whither this road leads?

Now Industry awakes her busy sons;
Full charged with news the breathless hawker runs.
Shops open, coaches roll, carts shake the ground,
And all the streets with passing cries resound.
   If clothed in black you tread the busy town,
Or if distinguished by the reverend gown,
Three trades avoid: oft in the mingling press
The barber's apron soils the sable dress;
Shun the perfumer's touch with cautious eye,
Nor let the baker's step advance too nigh.   30
Ye walkers too that youthful colours wear,
Three sullying trades avoid with equal care:
The little chimney-sweeper skulks along,
And marks with sooty stains the heedless throng;
When small-coal murmurs in the hoarser throat,
From smutty dangers guard thy threatened coat;
The dustman's cart offends thy clothes and eyes,
When through the street a cloud of ashes flies;
But whether black or lighter dyes are worn,
The chandler's basket, on his shoulder borne,   40
With tallow spots thy coat; resign the way,
To shun the surly butcher's greasy tray,
Butchers, whose hands are dyed with blood's foul stain,
And always foremost in the hangman's train.
   Let due civilities be strictly paid.
The wall surrender to the hooded maid;
Nor let thy sturdy elbow's hasty rage
Jostle the feeble steps of trembling age;
And when the porter bends beneath his load,
And pants for breath, clear thou the crowded road.   50
But, above all, the groping blind direct,
And from the pressing throng the lame protect.
You'll sometimes meet a fop, of nicest tread,
Whose mantling peruke veils his empty head;
At every step he dreads the wall to lose,
And risks, to save a coach, his red-heeled shoes;
Him, like the miller, pass with caution by,
Lest from his shoulder clouds of powder fly.
But when the bully, with assuming pace,
Cocks his broad hat, edged round with tarnished lace, 60
Yield not the way; defy his strutting pride,
And thrust him to the muddy kennel's[2] side;
He never turns again, nor dares oppose,
But mutters coward curses as he goes.
   If drawn by business to a street unknown,
Let the sworn porter point thee through the town;
Be sure observe the signs, for signs remain,
Like faithful landmarks to the walking train.
Seek not from 'prentices to learn the way;
Those fabling boys will turn thy steps astray;   70
Ask the grave tradesman to direct thee right;
He ne'er deceives, but when he profits by't.
   Where famed St. Giles's ancient limits spread,

[2] Gutter's

An inrailed column rears its lofty head;
Here to seven streets seven dials count the day,
And from each other catch the circling ray.
Here oft the peasant, with enquiring face,
Bewildered, trudges on from place to place;
He dwells on every sign with stupid gaze,
Enters the narrow alley's doubtful maze,   80
Tries every winding court and street in vain,
And doubles o'er his weary steps again.
Thus hardy Theseus, with intrepid feet,
Traversed the dangerous labyrinth of Crete;
But still the wandering passes forced his stay,
Till Ariadne's clue unwinds the way.
But do not thou, like that bold chief, confide
Thy venturous footsteps to a female guide;
She'll lead thee with delusive smiles along,   90
Dive in thy fob, and drop thee in the throng.
   When waggish boys the stunted besom ply
To rid the slabby[3] pavement, pass not by
E'er thou hast held their hands; some heedless flirt
Will overspread thy calves with spattering dirt.
Where porters' hogsheads roll from carts aslope,
Or brewers down steep cellars stretch the rope,
Where counted billets are by carmen tossed,
Stay thy rash step, and walk without the post.
   Where elevated o'er the gaping crowd,
Clasped in the board[4] the perjured head is bowed,   100
Betimes retreat; here thick as hailstones pour
Turnips, and half-hatched eggs (a mingled shower)
Among the rabble rain; some random throw
May with the trickling yolk thy cheek o'erflow.
   Though expedition bids, yet never stray
Where no ranged posts defend the rugged way.
Here laden carts with thundering wagons meet,
Wheels clash with wheels, and bar the narrow street;
The lashing whip resounds, the horses strain,
And blood in anguish bursts the swelling vein.   110
O barbarous men, your cruel breasts assuage!
Why vent ye on the generous steed your rage?
Does not his service earn your daily bread?
Your wives, your children by his labours fed!
If, as the Samian taught, the soul revives,
And, shifting seats, in other bodies lives;
Severe shall be the brutal coachman's change,
Doomed in a hackney horse the town to range:
Carmen, transformed, the groaning load shall draw,
Whom other tyrants with the lash shall awe.   120
   Who would of Watling Street the dangers share,
When the broad pavement of Cheapside is near?
Or who that rugged street would traverse o'er,
That stretches, O Fleet Ditch, from thy black shore
To the Tower's moated walls? Here steams ascend

³ Muddy.
⁴ Pillory.

That in mixed fumes the wrinkled nose offend.
Where chandlers cauldrons boil, where fishy prey
Hide the wet stall, long absent from the sea,
And where the cleaver chops the heifer's spoil,
And where huge hogsheads sweat with trainy oil,⁵   130
Thy breathing nostril hold; but how shall I
Pass, where in piles Cornavian cheeses lie—
Cheese, that the table's closing rites denies,
And bids me with the unwilling chaplain rise.
    O bear me to the paths of fair Pell Mell!
Safe are thy pavements, grateful is thy smell!
At distance rolls along the gilded coach,
Nor sturdy carmen on thy walks encroach;
No lets would bar thy ways were chairs denied,
The soft supports of laziness and pride;   140
Shops breathe perfumes, through sashes ribbons glow,
The mutual arms of ladies and the beau.
Yet still even here, when rains the passage hide,
Oft the loose stone spurts up a muddy tide
Beneath thy careless foot; and from on high,
Where masons mount the ladder, fragments fly;
Mortar and crumbled lime in showers descend,
And o'er thy head destructive tiles impend.
    But sometimes let me leave the noisy roads,
And silent wander in the close abodes
Where wheels ne'er shake the ground; there pensive stray,   150
In studious thought, the long uncrowded way.
Here I remark each walker's different face,
And in their look their various business trace.
The broker here his spacious beaver wears;
Upon his brow sit jealousies and cares;
Bent on some mortgage (to avoid reproach)
He seeks by-streets, and saves the expensive coach.
Soft, at low doors, old letchers tap their cane,
For fair recluse, that travels Drury Lane;   160
Here roams uncombed the lavish rake, to shun
His Fleet Street draper's everlasting dun.
    Careful observers, studious of the town,
Shun the misfortunes that disgrace the clown;
Untempted, they contemn the juggler's feats,
Pass by the Mews, nor try the thimble's cheats.
When drays bound high, they never cross behind,
Where bubbling yeast is blown by gusts of wind:
And when up Ludgate Hill huge carts move slow,
Far from the straining steeds securely go,   170
Whose dashing hoofs behind them fling the mire,
And mark with muddy blots the gazing squire.
The Parthian thus his javelin backward throws,
And as he flies infests pursuing foes.
    The thoughtless wits shall frequent forfeits pay,
Who 'gainst the sentry's box discharge their tea.
Do thou some court or secret corner seek,
Nor flush with shame the passing virgin's cheek.

⁵ Whale oil.

Yet let me not descend to trivial song,
Nor vulgar circumstance my verse prolong.   180
Why should I teach the maid when torrents pour,
Her head to shelter from the sudden shower?
Nature will best her ready hand inform,
With her spread petticoat to fence the storm.
Does not each walker know the warning sign,
When wisps of straw depend upon the twine
Cross the close street—that then the paver's art
Renews the ways, denied to coach and cart?
Who knows not that the coachman lashing by,
Oft with his flourish cuts the heedless eye;   190
And when he takes his stand, to wait a fare,
His horses' foreheads shun the winter's air?
Nor will I roam when summer's sultry rays
Parch the dry ground and spread with dust the ways;
With whirling gusts the rapid atoms rise,
Smoke o'er the pavement, and involve the skies.
　　Winter my theme confines; whose nitry wind
Shall crust the slabby mire, and kennels bind;[6]
She bids the snow descend in flaky sheets,
And in her hoary mantle clothe the streets.   200
Let not the virgin tread these slippery roads;
The gathering fleece the hollow patten[7] loads;
But if thy footsteps slide with clotted frost,
Strike off the breaking balls against the post.
On silent wheel the passing coaches roll;
Oft look behind, and ward the threatening pole.
In hardened orbs the schoolboy moulds the snow,
To mark the coachman with a dexterous throw.
Why do ye, boys, the kennel's surface spread,
To tempt with faithless pass the matron's tread?   210
How can ye laugh to see the damsel spurn,[8]
Sink in your frauds, and her green stocking mourn?
At White's the harnessed chairman idly stands,
And swings around his waist his tingling hands:
The sempstress speeds to 'Change with red-tipped nose;
The Belgian stove beneath her footstool glows;
In half-whipped muslin needles useless lie,
And shuttle-cocks across the counter fly.
These sports warm harmless; why then will ye prove,
Deluded maids, the dangerous flame of love?   220
　　Where Covent Garden's famous temple stands,
That boasts the work of Jones' immortal hands;
Columns with plain magnificence appear,
And graceful porches lead along the square;
Here oft my course I bend, when lo! from far
I spy the furies of the football war:
The 'prentice quits his shop to join the crew;
Increasing crowds the flying game pursue.
Thus, as you roll the ball o'er snowy ground,

[6] Freeze the gutters.
[7] Overshoe or sandal, with a wooden sole mounted on an oval iron ring.
[8] Kick out, i.e., slip suddenly.

The gathering globe augments with every round.   230
But whither shall I run? the throng draws nigh;
The ball now skims the street, now soars on high;
The dexterous glazier strong returns the bound,
And jingling sashes on the penthouse sound.
    O roving Muse, recall that wondrous year,
When winter reigned in bleak Britannia's air;
When hoary Thames, with frosted osiers crowned,
Was three long moons in icy fetters bound.
The waterman, forlorn along the shore,
Pensive reclines upon his useless oar,   240
Sees harnessed steeds desert the stony town,
And wander roads unstable, not their own:
Wheels o'er the hardened waters smoothly glide,
And raze with whitened tracks the slippery tide.
Here the fat cook piles high the blazing fire,
And scarce the spit can turn the steer entire.
Booths sudden hide the Thames, long streets appear,
And numerous games proclaim the crowded fair.
So when a general bids the martial train
Spread their encampment o'er the spacious plain,   250
Thick-rising tents a canvas city build,
And the loud dice resound through all the field.
    'Twas here the matron found a doleful fate:
Let elegiac lay the woe relate,
Soft as the breath of distant flutes, at hours
When silent evening closes up the flowers;
Lulling as falling water's hollow noise;
Indulging grief, like Philomela's voice.
    Doll every day had walked these treacherous roads;
Her neck grew warped beneath autumnal loads   260
Of various fruit; she now a basket bore—
That head, alas! shall basket bear no more.
Each booth she frequent passed in quest of gain,
And boys with pleasure heard her shrilling strain.
Ah, Doll! all mortals must resign their breath,
And industry itself submit to death!
The cracking crystal yields, she sinks, she dies;
Her head, chopped off, from her lost shoulders flies;
"Pippins" she cried, but death her voice confounds,
And "pip-pip-pip" along the ice resounds.   270
So when the Thracian furies Orpheus tore,
And left his bleeding trunk deformed with gore,
His severed head floats down the silver tide,
His yet warm tongue for his lost consort cried;
"Eurydice," with quivering voice he mourned,
And Heber's banks "Eurydice" returned.
    But now the western gale the flood unbinds,
And blackening clouds move on with warmer winds.
The wooden town its frail foundation leaves,
And Thames' full urn rolls down his plenteous waves;   280
From every penthouse streams the fleeting snow,
And with dissolving frost the pavements flow.
    Experienced men, inured to city ways,

Need not the calendar to count their days.
When through the town with slow and solemn air,
Led by the nostril, walks the muzzled bear,
Behind him moves majestically dull,
The pride of Hockley Hole, the surly bull;
Learn hence the periods of the week to name;
Mondays and Thursdays are the days of game.   290
    When fishy stalls with double store are laid—
The golden-bellied carp, the broad-finned maid,
Red-speckled trouts, the salmon's silver jowl,
The jointed lobster, and unscaly sole,
And luscious scallops, to allure the tastes
Of rigid zealots to delicious fasts—
Wednesdays and Fridays you'll observe from hence,
Days, when our sires were doomed to abstinence.
    When dirty waters from balconies drop,
And dexterous damsels twirl the sprinkling mop,   300
And cleanse the spattered sash, and scrub the stairs,
Know, Saturday's conclusive morn appears.
    Successive cries the seasons' change declare,
And mark the monthly progress of the year.
Hark, how the streets with treble voices ring,
To sell the bounteous product of the spring!
Sweet-smelling flowers, and elder's early bud,
With nettle's tender shoots, to cleanse the blood:
And when June's thunder cools the sultry skies,
Even Sundays are profaned by mackerel cries.   310
    Walnuts the fruiterer's hand in autumn stain;
Blue plums and juicy pears augment his gain;
Next oranges the longing boys entice,
To trust their copper fortunes to the dice.
    When rosemary, and bays, the poet's crown,
Are bawled in frequent cries through all the town,
Then judge the festival of Christmas near,
Christmas, the joyous period of the year.
Now with bright holly all your temples strow,
With laurel green and sacred mistletoe.   320
Now, heaven-born Charity, thy blessings shed;
Bid meagre Want uprear her sickly head;
Bid shivering limbs be warm; let plenty's bowl
In humble roofs make glad the needy soul.
See, see, the heaven-born maid her blessings shed;
Lo! meagre Want uprears her sickly head;
Clothed are the naked, and the needy glad,
While selfish Avarice alone is sad.
    Proud coaches pass, regardless of the moan
Of infant orphans, and the widow's groan;   330
While Charity still moves the walker's mind,
His liberal purse relieves the lame and blind.
Judiciously thy halfpence are bestowed,
Where the laborious beggar sweeps the road.
Whate'er you give, give ever at demand,
Nor let old age long stretch his palsied hand.
Those who give late, are importuned each day,

And still are teased because they still delay.
If e'er the miser durst his farthings spare,
He thinly spreads them through the public square,   340
Where, all beside the rail, ranged beggars lie,
And from each other catch the doleful cry;
With heaven, for twopence, cheaply wipes his score,
Lifts up his eyes, and hastes to beggar more.
    Where the brass knocker, wrapped in flannel band,
Forbids the thunder of the footman's hand,
The upholder,9 rueful harbinger of death,
Waits with impatience for the dying breath;
As vultures o'er a camp, with hovering flight,
Snuff up the future carnage of the fight.   350
Here canst thou pass, unmindful of a prayer,
That heaven in mercy may thy brother spare?
    Come, F——, sincere, experienced friend,
Thy briefs, thy deeds, and even thy fees suspend;
Come, let us leave the Temple's silent walls;
Me business to my distant lodging calls;
Through the long Strand together let us stray;
With thee conversing, I forget the way.
Behold that narrow street which steep descends,
Whose building to the slimy shore extends;   360
Here Arundel's famed structure reared its frame;
The street alone retains an empty name:
Where Titian's glowing paint the canvas warmed,
And Raphael's fair design with judgment charmed,
Now hangs the bellman's song, and pasted here
The coloured prints of Overton appear.
Where statues breathed, the work of Phidias' hands,
A wooden pump or lonely watch-house stands.
There Essex' stately pile adorned the shore,
There Cecil's, Bedford's, Villiers', now no more.   370
Yet Burlington's fair palace still remains;
Beauty within, without proportion reigns.
Beneath his eye declining art revives,
The wall with animated picture lives;
There Handel strikes the strings, the melting strain
Transports the soul, and thrills through every vein;
There oft I enter (but with cleaner shoes)
For Burlington's beloved by every Muse.
    O ye associate walkers, O my friends,
Upon your state what happiness attends!   380
What though no coach to frequent visit rolls,
Nor for your shilling chairmen sling their poles;
Yet still your nerves rheumatic pains defy,
Nor lazy jaundice dulls your saffron eye;
No wasting cough discharges sounds of death,
Nor wheezing asthma heaves in vain for breath;
Nor from your restless couch is heard the groan
Of burning gout, or sedentary stone.
Let others in the jolting coach confide,
Or in the leaky boat the Thames divide;   390

Undertaker.

Or, boxed within the chair, contemn the street,
And trust their safety to another's feet;
Still let me walk; for oft the sudden gale
Ruffles the tide, and shifts the dangerous sail.
Then shall the passenger too late deplore
The whelming billow, and the faithless oar;
The drunken chairman in the kennel spurns,
The glasses shatters, and his charge o'erturns.
Who can recount the coach's various harms,
The legs disjointed, and the broken arms?   400
   I've seen a beau, in some ill-fated hour,
When o'er the stones choked kennels swell the shower,
In gilded chariot loll; he with disdain
Views spattered passengers all drenched in rain;
With mud filled high, the rumbling cart draws near;
Now rule thy prancing steeds, laced charioteer!
The dustman lashes on with spiteful rage;
His ponderous spokes thy painted wheel engage;
Crushed is thy pride, down falls the shrieking beau,
The slabby pavement crystal fragments strow;   410
Black floods of mire the embroidered coat disgrace,
And mud enwraps the honours of his face.
So when dread Jove the son of Phoebus hurled,
Scarred with dark thunder, to the nether world,
The headstrong coursers tore the silver reins,
And the sun's beamy ruin gilds the plains.
   If the pale walker pant with weakening ills,
His sickly hand is stored with friendly bills:
From hence he learns the seventh-born doctor's fame,
From hence he learns the cheapest tailor's name.   420
   Shall the large mutton smoke upon your boards?
Such Newgate's copious market best affords.
Wouldst thou with mighty beef augment thy meal?
Seek Leadenhall; St. James's sends thee veal.
Thames Street gives cheeses; Covent Garden fruits;
Moorfields old books; and Monmouth Street old suits.
Hence mayst thou well supply the wants of life,
Support thy family, and clothe thy wife.
   Volumes on sheltered stalls expanded lie,
And various science lures the learned eye;   430
The bending shelves with ponderous scholiasts groan,
And deep divines to modern shops unknown;
Here, like the bee, that on industrious wing
Collects the various odours of the spring,
Walkers at leisure learning's flowers may spoil,
Nor watch the wasting of the midnight oil,
May morals snatch from Plutarch's tattered page,
A mildewed Bacon, or Stagyra's sage.
Here sauntering 'prentices o'er Otway weep,
O'er Congreve smile, or over D—— sleep;   440
Pleased sempstresses the Lock's famed Rape unfold,
And Squirts read Garth, till apozems[10] grow cold.
   O Lintot, let my labours obvious lie,

[10] Medicine in the form of a liquid extract.

Ranged on thy stall, for every curious eye;
So shall the poor these precepts *gratis* know,
And to my verse their future safeties owe.
    What walker shall his mean ambition fix
On the false lustre of a coach and six?
Let the vain virgin, lured by glaring show,
Sigh for the liveries of the embroidered beau.   450
    See yon bright chariot on its harness swing,
With Flanders mares, and on an arched spring;
That wretch, to gain an equipage and place,
Betrayed his sister to a lewd embrace.
This coach that with the blazoned 'scutcheon glows,
Vain of his unknown race, the coxcomb shows.
Here the bribed lawyer, sunk in velvet, sleeps;
The starving orphan, as he passes, weeps;
There flames a fool, begirt with tinselled slaves,
Who wastes the wealth of a whole race of knaves.   460
That other, with a clustering train behind,
Owes his new honours to a sordid mind.
This next in court-fidelity excels,
The public rifles, and his country sells.
May the proud chariot never be my fate,
If purchased at so mean, so dear a rate;
O rather give me sweet content on foot,
Wrapped in my virtue, and a good surtout![11]

¹¹ Overcoat.

[1716]

SWEET WILLIAM'S FAREWELL TO BLACK-EYED SUSAN

A BALLAD

All in the I owns the fleet was moored,
    The streamers waving in the wind,
When black-eyed Susan came aboard.
    "Oh! where shall I my true love find?
Tell me, ye jovial sailors, tell me true,
If my sweet William sails among the crew."

William, who high upon the yard
    Rocked with the billow to and fro,
Soon as her well-known voice he heard,
    He sighed and cast his eyes below;   10
The cord slides swiftly through his glowing
        hands,
And quick as lightning on the deck he stands.

So the sweet lark, high-poised in air,
    Shuts close his pinions to his breast,
(If, chance, his mate's shrill call he hear)
    And drops at once into her nest.
The noblest Captain in the British fleet
Might envy William's lip those kisses sweet.

"O Susan, Susan, lovely dear,
    My vows shall ever true remain;   20
Let me kiss off that falling tear;
    We only part to meet again.
Change, as ye list, ye winds! my heart shall be
The faithful compass that still points to thee.

"Believe not what the landmen say,
    Who tempt with doubts thy constant
        mind;
They'll tell thee, sailors, when away,
    In every port a mistress find.
Yes, yes, believe them when they tell thee so,
For thou art present wheresoe'er I go.   30

"If to far India's coast we sail,
    Thy eyes are seen in diamonds bright,
Thy breath is Afric's spicy gale,
    Thy skin is ivory, so white.
Thus every beauteous object that I view,
Wakes in my soul some charm of lovely Sue.

"Though battle call me from thy arms,
    Let not my pretty Susan mourn;
Though cannons roar, yet safe from harms,
    William shall to his dear return.   40

Love turns aside the balls that round me fly,
Lest precious tears should drop from Susan's
         eye."

         The boatswain gave the dreadful word,
            The sails their swelling bosom spread,
         No longer must she stay aboard;
            They kissed, she sighed, he hung his
               head;
Her lessening boat unwilling rows to land;
"Adieu!" she cries, and waved her lily hand.

                                    [1720]

TO A LADY ON HER PASSION
FOR OLD CHINA

      What ecstasies her bosom fire!
How her eyes languish with desire!
How blessed, how happy should I be,
Were that fond glance bestowed on me!
New doubts and fears within me war:
What rival's near? A China jar.
      China's the passion of her soul;
A cup, a plate, a dish, a bowl
Can kindle wishes in her breast,
Inflame with joy, or break her rest.   10
      Some gems collect; some medals prize,
And view the rust with lovers' eyes;
Some court the stars at midnight hours;
Some dote on Nature's charms in flowers!
But every beauty I can trace
In Laura's mind, in Laura's face;
My stars are in this brighter sphere,
My lily and my rose is here.
      Philosophers more grave than wise
Hunt science down in butterflies;   20
Or fondly poring on a spider,
Stretch human contemplation wider;
Fossils give joy to Galen's soul;
He digs for knowledge like a mole;
In shells so learned, that all agree
No fish that swims knows more than he!
In such pursuits if wisdom lies,
Who, Laura, shall thy taste despise?
      When I some antique jar behold,
Or white, or blue, or specked with gold,   30
Vessels so pure and so refined
Appear the types of womankind:
Are they not valued for their beauty,
Too fair, too fine for household duty,
With flowers and gold and azure dyed,
Of every house the grace and pride?

How white, how polished is their skin,
And valued most when only seen!
She who before was highest prized,
Is for a crack or flaw despised;   40
I grant they're frail, yet they're so rare,
The treasure cannot cost too dear!
But man is made of coarser stuff,
And serves convenience well enough;
He's a strong earthen vessel, made
For drudging, labour, toil, and trade;
And when wives lose their other self,
With ease they bear the loss of Delf.
      Husbands more covetous than sage
Condemn this China-buying rage;   50
They count that woman's prudence little,
Who sets her heart on things so brittle.
But are those wise men's inclinations
Fixed on more strong, more sure founda-
      tions?
If all that's frail we must despise,
No human view or scheme is wise.
Are not Ambition's hopes as weak?
They swell like bubbles, shine, and break.
A courtier's promise is so slight,
'Tis made at noon, and broke at night.   60
What pleasure's sure? The miss you keep
Breaks both your fortune and your sleep.
The man who loves a country life
Breaks all the comforts of his wife;
And if he quit his farm and plough,
His wife in town may break her vow.
Love, Laura, love, while youth is warm,
For each new winter breaks a charm;
And woman's not like China sold,
But cheaper grows in growing old;   70
Then quickly choose the prudent part,
Or else you break a faithful heart.

                                    [1725]

SONG

         O ruddier than the cherry,
         O sweeter than the berry,
            O nymph more bright
            Than moonshine night,
         Like kidlings blithe and merry.
         Ripe as the melting cluster,
         No lily has such lustre,
               Yet hard to tame,
               As raging flame,
         And fierce as storms that bluster.   10

                                    [1732]

THOMAS PARNELL (1679-1718)

Thomas Parnell, a graduate of Trinity College, Dublin, took holy orders and held livings in Ireland. He provided the "Essay on the Life, Writings, and Learning of Homer" prefixed to Pope's *Iliad*, and otherwise aided Pope in the translation and commentary. Along with Pope, Arbuthnot, Swift, and Gay, he had a share in the projects of the Scriblerus Club. After his death, his poems were published by Pope, with a fine dedicatory tribute to his memory. Parnell's grace and finish of style appear to better advantage in his light lyrics and skilful octosyllabics than in his use of the heroic couplet. *The Hermit*, a piece beloved of eighteenth-century moralists, shows how neo-classical mannerisms encumber a plain narrative. Goldsmith's *Life of Parnell*, with its preference of the *Night-Piece on Death* to Gray's *Elegy*, has helped to sustain the poet's modest reputation. Goldsmith further says of Parnell: "His poetical language is not less correct than his subjects are pleasing. He found it at that period in which it was brought to its highest pitch of refinement; and ever since his time it has been gradually declining." This comment has at least historical interest, and, carefully interpreted, may help us to a better understanding of Augustan and post-Augustan views of poetry.

Parnell's verse is accessible in *Minor Poets of the Eighteenth Century*, ed. H. I'A. Fausset (Everyman's Library). Of earlier editions the most important is that by G. A. Aitken (London, 1894, Aldine edition).

A HYMN TO CONTENTMENT

"Lovely, lasting peace of mind!
Sweet delight of humankind!
Heavenly-born, and bred on high,
To crown the favourites of the sky
With more of happiness below
Than victors in a triumph know!
Whither, oh whither art thou fled,
To lay thy meek, contented head?
What happy region dost thou please
To make the seat of calms and ease?   10
"Ambition searches all its sphere
Of pomp and state, to meet thee there.
Increasing avarice would find
Thy presence in its gold enshrined.
The bold adventurer ploughs his way
Through rocks amidst the foaming sea,
To gain thy love; and then perceives
Thou wert not in the rocks and waves.
The silent heart which grief assails
Treads soft and lonesome o'er the vales,   20
Sees daisies open, rivers run,
And seeks, as I have vainly done,
Amusing thought; but learns to know
That solitude's the nurse of woe.
No real happiness is found

In trailing purple o'er the ground;
Or in a soul exalted high,
To range the circuit of the sky,
Converse with stars above, and know
All nature in its forms below;   30
The rest it seeks, in seeking dies,
And doubts at last, for knowledge, rise.
"Lovely, lasting Peace, appear!
This world itself, if thou art here,
Is once again with Eden blessed,
And man contains it in his breast."
'Twas thus, as under shade I stood,
I sung my wishes to the wood,
And lost in thought, no more perceived
The branches whisper as they waved;   40
It seemed as all the quiet place
Confessed the presence of the Grace;
When thus she spoke—"Go rule thy will,
Bid thy wild passions all be still,
Know God—and bring thy heart to know
The joys which from religion flow:
Then every Grace shall prove its guest,
And I'll be there to crown the rest."
Oh! by yonder mossy seat,
In my hours of sweet retreat,   50
Might I thus my soul employ,
With sense of gratitude and joy!
Raised as ancient prophets were,
In heavenly vision, praise, and prayer;

Pleasing all men, hurting none,
Pleased and blessed with God alone!
Then, while the gardens take my sight
With all the colours of delight,
While silver waters glide along,
To please my ear and court my song,   60
I'll lift my voice, and tune my string,
And Thee, great Source of Nature, sing.
    The sun that walks his airy way,
To light the world and give the day;
The moon that shines with borrowed light;
The stars that gild the gloomy night;
The seas that roll unnumbered waves;
The wood that spreads its shady leaves;
The field whose ears conceal the grain,
The yellow treasure of the plain;   70
All of these, and all I see,
Should be sung, and sung by me:
They speak their Maker as they can.
But want and ask the tongue of man.
    Go search among your idle dreams,
Your busy or your vain extremes;
And find a life of equal bliss,
Or own the next begun in this.

[1714]

SONG

When thy beauty appears,
    In its graces and airs,
All bright as an angel new dropped from the
        sky;
    At distance I gaze, and am awed by my
        fears
    So strangely you dazzle my eye!

But when without art,
    Your kind thoughts you impart,
When your love runs in blushes through every
        vein;
    When it darts from your eyes, when it
        pants in your heart,
    Then I know you're a woman again.   10

There's a passion and pride
    In our sex, she replied,
And thus (might I gratify both) I would do;
    Still an angel appear to each lover beside,
    But still be a woman to you.

[1721]

A NIGHT-PIECE ON DEATH

By the blue taper's trembling light,
No more I waste the wakeful night,
Intent with endless view to pore
The schoolmen and the sages o'er:
Their books from wisdom widely stray,
Or point at best the longest way.
I'll seek a readier path, and go
Where wisdom's surely taught below.
    How deep yon azure dyes the sky,
Where orbs of gold unnumbered lie,   10
While through their ranks in silver pride
The nether crescent seems to glide!
The slumbering breeze forgets to breathe;
The lake is smooth and clear beneath,
Where once again the spangled show
Descends to meet our eyes below.
The grounds which on the right aspire,
In dimness from the view retire:
The left presents a place of graves,
Whose wall the silent water laves.   20
That steeple guides thy doubtful sight
Among the livid gleams of night.
There pass, with melancholy state,
By all the solemn heaps of fate,
And think, as softly-sad you tread
Above the venerable dead,
"Time was, like thee they life possessed,
And time shall be, that thou shalt rest."
    Those graves, with bending osier bound,
That nameless heave the crumbled ground,
Quick to the glancing thought disclose   31
Where Toil and Poverty repose.
    The flat smooth stones that bear a name,
The chisel's slender help to fame,
(Which ere our set of friends decay
Their frequent steps may wear away),
A middle race of mortals own,
Men half ambitious, all unknown.
    The marble tombs that rise on high,
Whose dead in vaulted arches lie,   40
Whose pillars swell with sculptured stones,
Arms, angels, epitaphs, and bones,
These, all the poor remains of state,
Adorn the rich, or praise the great,
Who while on earth in fame they live,
Are senseless of the fame they give.
    Hah! while I gaze, pale Cynthia fades;
The bursting earth unveils the shades!
All slow, and wan, and wrapped with
        shrouds,
They rise in visionary crowds,   50
And all with sober accent cry,
"Think, mortal, what it is to die!"

Now from yon black and funeral yew,
That bathes the charnel-house with dew,
Methinks I hear a voice begin;
(Ye ravens, cease your croaking din!
Ye tolling clocks, no time resound
O'er the long lake and midnight ground!)
It sends a peal of hollow groans,
Thus speaking from among the bones: 60
"When men my scythe and darts supply,
How great a king of fears am I!
They view me like the last of things;
They make, and then they dread, my stings.
Fools! if you less provoked your fears,
No more my spectre-form appears.
Death's but a path that must be trod,
If man would ever pass to God;
A port of calms, a state of ease
From the rough rage of swelling seas.   70
    "Why then thy flowing sable stoles,
Deep pendent cypress, mourning poles,
Loose scarfs to fall athwart thy weeds,
Long palls, drawn hearses, covered steeds,
And plumes of black, that, as they tread,
Nod o'er the 'scutcheons of the dead?
    "Nor can the parted body know,
Nor wants the soul, these forms of woe.
As men who long in prison dwell,
With lamps that glimmer round the cell,   80
Whene'er their suffering years are run,
Spring forth to greet the glittering sun:
Such joy, though far transcending sense,
Have pious souls at parting hence.
On earth, and in the body placed,
A few, and evil, years they waste;
But when their chains are cast aside,
See the glad scene unfolding wide,
Clap the glad wing, and tower away,
And mingle with the blaze of day."   90

[1721]

SONG

My days have been so wondrous free,
    The little birds that fly
With careless ease from tree to tree,
    Were but as blessed as I.

Ask gliding waters, if a tear
    Of mine increased their stream?
Or ask the flying gales, if e'er
    I lent one sigh to them?

But now my former days retire,
    And I'm by beauty caught;   10
The tender chains of sweet desire
    Are fixed upon my thought.

Ye nightingales, ye twisting pines!
    Ye swains that haunt the grove!
Ye gentle echoes, breezy winds!
    Ye close retreats of love!

With all of nature, all of art,
    Assist the dear design;
Oh teach a young, unpractised heart
    To make my Nancy mine!   20

The very thought of change I hate,
    As much as of despair;
Nor ever covet to be great,
    Unless it be for her.

'Tis true, the passion in my mind
    Is mixed with soft distress;
Yet while the fair I love is kind,
    I cannot wish it less.

[1721]

ALLAN RAMSAY (1685?-1758)

Although Allan Ramsay was born and spent his early years at Leadhills, Crawford, Lanarkshire, most of his life was passed in Edinburgh. He was at first apprenticed to a wig-maker, but before 1725 he became a bookseller. His interest in Scottish literature and the facility at writing occasional verse which he showed among his boon companions led natu-rally to this change of occupation. He opened one of the first circulating libraries in Great Britain, was concerned in dramatic productions in Edinburgh, and in general stood for a liberal and secular view of life as opposed to the austerities of the Scottish Kirk. With inno-cent vanity, he thought of himself as the compeer of the great wits of London.

Like Scott, Ramsay was an editor of the earlier literature of his country; like Burns, he collected and rewrote traditional Scottish songs. His *Ever Green* (1724) was mostly drawn from the collection of Middle Scots poems known as the Bannatyne Manuscript, with the addition of some other pieces, such as *Hardyknute*. He treated his texts very freely and slipped in some of his own work; his interests were not scholarly, but patriotic. In his *Tea-Table Miscellany* (1724-37) he rewrote, often for the worse, many traditional songs. He lacked the narrative power of Scott and the lyrical power of Burns.

But much can be forgiven him for his shrewd and hearty humor and his abundant knowl-edge of the ways of his people. His work at times reminds us of John Gay's; both writers have a keen eye for the details of low life in town or country, and both use the pastoral form for realistic ends. In 1720 Ramsay published a humorous eclogue, *Patie and Roger;* in 1723 a sequel, *Jenny and Meggy*. These became the first and second scenes of the five-act pastoral drama called *The Gentle Shepherd* (1725), Ramsay's most famous work. His pri-mary interest was in the racy dialogue and vivid detail of his rustic scenes; the romantic plot of the completed drama is by comparison perfunctory. Perfunctory, too, was his re-writing of *The Gentle Shepherd* as a ballad-opera in 1728. Nevertheless the vitality of the piece is attested by the fact that it was acted by the people of Lothian, where its scenes are laid, well into the nineteenth century.

An amiable partiality for Ramsay appears among his countrymen. In his own day Hamil ton of Gilbertfield hailed him thus:

> O famed and celebrated Allan!
> Renowned Ramsay! canty callan![1]
> There's neither Hielandman nor Lawlan,
>   In poetrie,
> But may as soon ding doun Tantallan[2]
>   As match wi' thee.

The same rhymes and sentiments appear in some lines on pastoral poetry found among Burns's papers, though not certainly written by him:

> In this braw age o' wit and lear,[3]
> Will nane the Shepherd's whistle mair
> Blaw sweetly in its native air,
>   And rural grace;
> And, wi' the far-famed Grecian, share
>   A rival place?
> Yes! there is ane; a Scottish callan!
> There's ane; come forrit,[4] honest Allan!
> Thou need na jouk behint the hallan,[5]
>   A chiel sae clever;
> The teeth o' time may gnaw Tantallan,
>   But thou's forever.

[1] Merry youth.
[2] Knock down Tantallan, a strong castle in East Lothian.
[3] Learning.
[4] Forward.
[5] Hide behind the partition.

There is no recent edition of Ramsay; J. Logie Robertson has edited a convenient volume of selections (London, 1887). The biography has been carefully worked out by Andrew Gibson, *New Light on Allan Ramsay* (Edinburgh, 1927), and Burns Martin, *Allan Ramsay: A Study of His Life and Works* (Cambridge, U. S. A., 1931). See also page 1269.

THE YOUNG LAIRD AND EDINBURGH KATY

Now wat ye wha I met yestreen,
    Coming down the street, my jo?
My mistress, in her tartan screen,[1]
    Fou bonny, braw, and sweet, my jo.
"My dear," quoth I, "thanks to the night,
    That never wished a lover ill,
Since ye're out of your mither's sight,
    Lets tak a walk up to the Hill.

"O Katy! wiltu gang wi' me,
    And leave the dinsome town a while?   10
The blossom's sprouting frae the tree,
    And a' the simmer's gawn to smile.
The mavis, nightingale, and lark,—
    The bleating lambs and whistling hind,—
In ilka dale, green, shaw[2] and park,
    Will nourish health, and glad ye'r mind.

"Soon as the clear goodman of day
    Bends[3] his morning draught of dew,
We'll gae to some burnside and play,
    And gather flowers to busk[4] ye'r brow.   20
We'll pou the daisies on the green,
    The lucken gowans[5] frae the bog;
Between hands now and then we'll lean,
    And sport upo' the velvet fog.[6]

"There's up into a pleasant glen,
    A wee piece frae my father's tower,
A canny,[7] saft, and flowery den
    Which circling birks has formed a bower:
Whene'er the sun grows high and warm,
    We'll to the cawler[8] shade remove;   30
There will I lock thee in mine arms,
    And love and kiss, and kiss and love."
                                        [1719]

[1] Scarf.
[2] Grove.
[3] Drinks.
[4] Adorn.
[5] Globe flowers.
[6] Moss.
[7] Cozy, comfortable.
[8] Fresh.

KATY'S ANSWER

My mither's ay glowran[1] o'er me,
Though she did the same before me;
    I canna get leave
    To look at my love,
Or else she'll be like to devour me.

Right fain wad I take ye'r offer,
Sweet sir, but I'll tine my tocher;[2]
    Then, Sandy, ye'll fret,
    And wyte[3] ye'r poor Kate,
Whene'er ye keek[4] in your toom[5] coffer.   10

For though my father has plenty
Of siller and plenishing dainty,
    Yet he's unco sweer[6]
    To twin[7] wi' his gear;
And sae we hae need to be tenty.[8]
Tutor my parents wi' caution,
Be wylie in ilka motion;
    Brag well o' ye'r land,
    And there's my leal hand;
Win them, I'll be at your devotion.   20
                                        [1719]

[1] Gazing, looking.
[2] Lose my dowry.
[3] Scold, blame.
[4] Peep.
[5] Empty.
[6] Very loth.
[7] Part.
[8] Careful.

THE POET'S WISH: AN ODE

Frae great Apollo, poet, say,
What is thy wish, what wadst thou hae
When thou bows at his shrine?
Not Carse o' Gowrie's fertile field,
Nor a' the flocks the Grampians yield,
    That are baith sleek and fine:
Not costly things brought frae afar,
    As ivory, pearl, and gems;
Nor those fair straths[1] that watered are

[1] Wide valleys.

With Tay and Tweed's smooth streams. 10
  Which gently and daintily
  Eat down the flowery braes;
  As greatly and quietly
  They wimple² to the seas.

Whaefever by his canny fate
Is master of a good estate,
That can ilk thing afford,
Let him enjoy't withouten care,
And with the wale³ of curious fare
  Cover his ample board.   20
Much dawted⁴ by the gods is he
  Wha to the Indian plain
Successfu' ploughs the wally⁵ sea
  And safe returns again,
    With riches that hitches
    Him high aboon the rest
    Of sma' fowk, and a' fowk
    That are wi' poortith⁶ prest.

For me I can be well content
To eat my bannock⁷ on the bent,⁸   30
And kitchen't wi' fresh air;⁹
Of lang-kail¹⁰ I can make a feast,
And cantily had up my crest,
  And laugh at dishes rare.
Nought frae Apollo I demand,
  But through a lengthened life
My outer fabric firm may stand,
  And saul clear without strife.
    May he then but gie then
    Those blessings for my skair,¹¹   40
    I'll fairly and squairly
    Quite a' and seek nae mair.
          [1721]

² Meander.
³ The choicest.
⁴ Favored.
⁵ Tempestuous.
⁶ Poverty.
⁷ Thick round cake.
⁸ Open field.
⁹ With fresh air for sauce.
¹⁰ Uncut cabbage.
¹¹ Share.

AN THOU WERE MY AIN THING

An thou were my ain thing,
I would love thee, I would love thee:
An thou were my ain thing,
  How dearly would I love thee.

Like bees that suck the morning dew
Frae flowers of sweetest scent and hue,
Sae wad I dwell upo' thy mou,
  And gar¹ the gods envy me.
    An thou were, &c.

Sae lang's I had the use of light,   10
I'd on thy beauties feast my sight,
Syne in saft whispers through the night
  I'd tell how much I lo'ed thee.
    An thou were, &c.

How fair and ruddy is my Jean!
She moves a goddess o'er the green.
Were I a king, thou should be queen,
  Nane but mysel aboon thee.
    An thou were, &c.

I'd grasp thee to this breast of mine,   20
Whilst thou like ivy or the vine
Around my stronger limbs should twine,
  Formed hardy to defend thee.
    An thou were, &c.

Time's on the wing and will not stay,
In shining youth let's make our hay,
Since love admits of no delay,
  O! let na scorn undo thee.
    An thou were, &c.

While love does at his altar stand,   30
Hae there's my heart, gie me thy hand,
And with ilk smile thou shalt command
  The will of him wha loves thee.
    An thou were, &c.
          [1724]

¹ Make.

SANG

My Peggy is a young thing,
  Just entered in her teens,
Fair as the day and sweet as May,
Fair as the day and always gay.
  My Peggy is a young thing,
    And I'm not very auld,
  Yet well I like to meet her at
    The wawking¹ of the fauld.

My Peggy speaks sa sweetly,
  Whene'er we meet alane,   10
¹ Watching.

I wish nae mair to lay my care,
I wish nae mair of a' that's rare.
My Peggy speaks sae sweetly,
To a' the lave[2] I'm cauld;
But she gars a' my spirits glow
At wawking of the fauld.

My Peggy smiles sae kindly,
Whene'er I whisper love,
That I look down on a' the town,
That I look down upon a crown.   20
My Peggy smiles sae kindly,
It makes me blythe and bauld,
Rest.

And naething gi'es me sic delight,
As wawking of the fauld.

My Peggy sings sae saftly,
When on my pipe I play;
By a' the rest it is confest,
By a' the rest that she sings best.
My Peggy sings sae saftly,
And in her sangs are tald,   30
With innocence, the wale[3] of sense,
At wawking of the fauld.

[1729?]

[3] The best of sense.

HENRY CAREY (1687?-1743)

Henry Carey was a musician and song-writer of London, an industrious composer of farces and operettas. The little we know of him suggests that he was one of the merriest of the laborers in Grub Street, even though his end was poverty and suicide. His poems have been edited by F. T. Wood (London, 1930).

THE BALLAD OF SALLY IN OUR ALLEY

Of all the girls that are so smart,
  There's none like pretty Sally;
She is the darling of my heart,
  And she lives in our alley:
There is no lady in the land
  Is half so sweet as Sally;
She is the darling of my heart,
  And she lives in our alley.

Her father he makes cabbage-nets,
  And through the streets does cry'em;   10
Her mother she sells laces long,
  To such as please to buy'em;
But sure such folks could ne'er beget
  So sweet a girl as Sally;
She is the darling of my heart,
  And she lives in our alley.

When she is by, I leave my work
  (I love her so sincerely);
My master comes, like any Turk,
  And bangs me most severely;   20
But let him bang his bellyful,
  I'll bear it all for Sally;
She is the darling of my heart,
  And she lives in our alley.

Of all the days that's in the week,
  I dearly love but one day,
And that's the day that comes betwixt
  A Saturday and Monday;

For then I'm dressed, all in my best,
  To walk abroad with Sally;   38
She is the darling of my heart,
  And she lives in our alley.

My master carries me to church,
  And often am I blamed,
Because I leave him in the lurch,
  As soon as text is named:
I leave the church in sermon time,
  And slink away to Sally;
She is the darling of my heart,
  And she lives in our alley.   40

When Christmas comes about again,
  O then I shall have money;
I'll hoard it up, and box and all
  I'll give it to my honey:
And would it were ten thousand pounds,
  I'd give it all to Sally;
She is the darling of my heart,
  And she lives in our alley.

My master and the neighbours all
  Make game of me and Sally;   50
And (but for her) I'd better be
  A slave, and row a galley:
But when my seven long years are out,
  O then I'll marry Sally!
O then we'll wed, and then we'll bed;
  But not in our alley!

                    [before 1719]

WILLIAM HAMILTON OF BANGOUR (1704-1754)

William Hamilton of Bangour, Linlithgowshire, Scotland, is remembered only for this lyric, which he contributed to Ramsay's *Tea-Table Miscellany*. He took part in the Jacobite rising of 1745 and spent the last years of his life in France.

THE BRAES OF YARROW

IN IMITATION OF THE ANCIENT SCOTTISH MANNER

A. Busk[1] ye, busk ye, my bonny bonny bride,
    Busk ye, busk ye, my winsome marrow![2]
    Busk ye, busk ye, my bonny bonny bride,
    And think nae mair on the braes of Yarrow.

B. Where gat ye that bonny bonny bride?
    Where gat ye that winsome marrow?
A. I gat her where I dare na weel be seen—
    Puing the birks[3] on the braes of Yarrow.

    Weep not, weep not, my bonny bonny bride,
    Weep not, weep not, my winsome marrow,   10
    Nor let thy heart lament to leive
    Puing the birks on the braes of Yarrow.

B. Why does she weep, thy bonny bonny bride?
    Why does she weep, thy winsome marrow?
    And why dare ye nae mair weel be seen
    Puing the birks on the braes of Yarrow?

A. Lang maun she weep, lang maun she, maun she weep,
    Lang maun she weep with dule[4] and sorrow,
    And lang maun I nae mair weel be seen
    Puing the birks on the braes of Yarrow·   20

    For she has tint[5] her luver, luver dear—
    Her luver dear, the cause of sorrow;
    And I hae slain the comeliest swain
    That e'er pued birks on the braes of Yarrow.

    Why runs thy stream, O Yarrow, Yarrow, red?
    Why on thy braes heard the voice of sorrow?

[1] Dress or make ready.
[2] Mate.
[3] Pulling the birches.
[4] Grief.
[5] Lost.

And why yon melancholious weids
    Hung on the bonny birks of Yarrow?

What's yonder floats on the rueful, rueful flude?
    What's yonder floats? O dule and sorrow!   30
'Tis he, the comely swain I slew
    Upon the duleful braes of Yarrow.

Wash, O wash his wounds, his wounds in tears,
    His wounds in tears, with dule and sorrow,
And wrap his limbs in mourning weeds,
    And lay him on the braes of Yarrow.

Then build, then build, ye sisters, sisters sad,
    Ye sisters sad, his tomb with sorrow,
And weep around in waeful wise,
    His helpless fate on the braes of Yarrow.   40

Curse ye, curse ye his useless, useless shield,
    My arm that wrought the deed of sorrow,
The fatal spear that pierced his breast,
    His comely breast, on the braes of Yarrow.

Did I not warn thee, not to, not to luve?
    And warn from fight? but to my sorrow,
Too rashly bauld, a stronger arm
    Thou mett'st, and fell'st on the braes of Yarrow.

C. Sweet smells the birk, green grows, green grows the grass.
    Yellow on Yarrow's bank the gowan,[6]   50
Fair hangs the apple frae the rock,
    Sweet the wave of Yarrow flowan.

A. Flows Yarrow sweet? as sweet, as sweet flows Tweed,
    As green its grass, its gowan yellow,
As sweet smells on its braes the birk,
    The apple frae its rock as mellow.

Fair was thy luve, fair, fair indeed thy luve,
    In flowery bands thou him didst fetter;
Though he was fair and weel beluved again,
    Than me he never luved thee better.   60

Busk ye, then busk, my bonny bonny bride,
    Busk ye, busk ye, my winsome marrow,
Busk ye, and luve me on the banks of Tweed,
    And think nae mair on the braes of Yarrow.

C. How can I busk a bonny bonny bride?
    How can I busk a winsome marrow?
How luve him upon the banks of Tweed,
    That slew my luve on the braes of Yarrow?

O Yarrow fields, may never, never rain
    Nor dew thy tender blossoms cover.   70

[6] Daisy.

For there was basely slain my luve,
   My luve, as he had not been a lover.

The boy put on his robes, his robes of green,
   His purple vest, 'twas my awn sewing:
Ah! wretched me! I little, little kenned
   He was in these to meet his ruin.

The boy took out his milk-white, milk-white steed,
   Unheedful of my dule and sorrow:
But ere the to-fall of the night
   He lay a corpse on the braes of Yarrow.   80

Much I rejoiced that waeful, waeful day;
   I sang, my voice the woods returning:
But lang ere night the spear was flown
   That slew me luve, and left me mourning.

What can my barbarous, barbarous father do,
   But with his cruel rage pursue me?
My luver's blood is on thy spear,
   How canst thou, barbarous man, then woo me?

My happy sisters may be, may be proud,
   With cruel, and ungentle scoffin',   90
May bid me seek on Yarrow's braes
   My luver nailed in his coffin.

My brother Douglas may upbraid, upbraid,
   And strive with threatening words to muve me:
My luver's blood is on thy spear,
   How canst thou ever bid me luve thee?

Yes, yes, prepare the bed, the bed of luve;
   With bridal sheets my body cover;
Unbar, ye bridal maids, the door;
   Let in the expected husband lover.   100

But who the expected husband, husband is?
   His hands, methinks, are bathed in slaughter:
Ah me! what ghastly spectre's yon
   Comes, in his pale shroud, bleeding after?

Pale as he is here lay him, lay him down,
   O lay his cold head on my pillow;
Take aff, take aff, these bridal weids,
   And crown my careful head with willow.

Pale though thou art, yet best, yet best beluved,
   O could my warmth to life restore thee!   110
Yet lie all night between my breists;
   No youth lay ever there before thee.

Pale, pale indeed, O luvely, luvely youth!
   Forgive, forgive so foul a slaughter,

And lie all night between my breists;
No youth shall ever lie there after.

A. Return, return, O mournful, mournful bride,
Return, and dry thy useless sorrow;
Thy luver heeds naught of thy sighs,
He lies a corpse on the braes of Yarrow. 120

[1724]

JOHN DYER (1699-1757)

John Dyer, poet and painter, was in his youth a member of the London literary circle which included James Thomson, Richard Savage, and Aaron Hill. After abandoning the profession of law for the study of art, he traveled about Wales and later went to Italy. *Grongar Hill* (1726) reflects his delight in the landscape of his native Carmarthenshire, South Wales, but he never fulfilled the promise he showed in this charming piece and its companion poem, *The Country Walk.* Later he entered the Church, and published two comparatively dull blank-verse poems, *The Ruins of Rome* (1740) and *The Fleece* (1757). The former is comparable in thought and inspiration to Thomson's *Liberty*; the latter gives an elaborate account of the British woolen industry in a style which suggests the more pedestrian parts of *The Seasons.* Nevertheless Wordsworth praises both *The Fleece* and *Grongar Hill* in his graceful sonnet *To the Poet John Dyer.* Dyer's work is included in *Minor Poets of the Eighteenth Century,* ed. H. I'A. Fausset (Everyman's Library).

GRONGAR HILL

Silent nymph, with curious eye!
Who, the purple evening, lie
On the mountain's lonely van,[1]
Beyond the noise of busy man,
Painting fair the form of things,
While the yellow linnet sings;
Or the tuneful nightingale
Charms the forest with her tale;
Come with all thy various hues,
Come, and aid thy sister Muse;   10
Now while Phoebus riding high
Gives lustre to the land and sky!
Grongar Hill invites my song,
Draw the landscape bright and strong;
Grongar, in whose mossy cells
Sweetly musing Quiet dwells;
Grongar, in whose silent shade,
For the modest Muses made,
So oft I have, the evening still,
At the fountain of a rill,   20
Sate upon a flowery bed,
With my hand beneath my head;
While strayed my eyes o'er Towy's flood,
Over mead and over wood,
From house to house, from hill to hill,
Till Contemplation had her fill.
    About his checkered sides I wind,
And leave his brooks and meads behind,
And groves, and grottoes where I lay,
And vistas shooting beams of day;   30
Wide and wider spreads the vale,
As circles on a smooth canal;

[1] Height, summit (a Welsh word).

The mountains round—unhappy fate,
Sooner or later, of all height—
Withdraw their summits from the skies,
And lessen as the others rise;
Still the prospect wider spreads,
Adds a thousand woods and meads,
Still it widens, widens still,
And sinks the newly-risen hill.   40
    Now I gain the mountain's brow,
What a landscape lies below!
No clouds, no vapours intervene,
But the gay, the open scene
Does the face of Nature show
In all the hues of heaven's bow,
And, swelling to embrace the light,
Spreads around beneath the sight.
    Old castles on the cliffs arise,
Proudly towering in the skies!   50
Rushing from the woods, the spires
Seem from hence ascending fires!
Half his beams Apollo sheds
On the yellow mountain-heads,
Gilds the fleeces of the flocks,
And glitters on the broken rocks!
    Below me trees unnumbered rise,
Beautiful in various dyes:
The gloomy pine, the poplar blue,
The yellow beech, the sable yew,   60
The slender fir that taper grows,
The sturdy oak with broad-spread boughs.
And beyond the purple grove,
Haunt of Phyllis, queen of love!
Gaudy as the opening dawn,
Lies a long and level lawn,
On which a dark hill, steep and high,
Holds and charms the wandering eye!

146

Deep are his feet in Towy's flood,
His sides are clothed with waving wood, 70
And ancient towers crown his brow,
That cast an awful look below;
Whose ragged walls the ivy creeps,
And with her arms from falling keeps;
So both a safety from the wind
On mutual dependence find.
   'Tis now the raven's bleak abode;
'Tis now the apartment of the toad;
And there the fox securely feeds;
And there the poisonous adder breeds, 80
Concealed in ruins, moss, and weeds,
While, ever and anon, there falls
Huge heaps of hoary mouldered walls.
Yet Time has seen, that lifts the low,
And level lays the lofty brow,
Has seen this broken pile complete,
Big with the vanity of state;
But transient is the smile of Fate!
A little rule, a little sway,
A sunbeam in a winter's day, 90
Is all the proud and mighty have
Between the cradle and the grave.
   And see the rivers, how they run
Through woods and meads, in shade and sun;
Sometimes swift, sometimes slow,
Wave succeeding wave, they go
A various journey to the deep,
Like human life to endless sleep!
Thus is Nature's vesture wrought,
To instruct our wandering thought; 100
Thus she dresses green and gay,
To disperse our cares away.
   Ever charming, ever new,
When will the landscape tire the view!
The fountain's fall, the river's flow,
The woody valleys warm and low;
The windy summit, wild and high,
Roughly rushing on the sky;
The pleasant seat, the ruined tower,
The naked rock, the shady bower, 110
The town and village, dome and farm,
Each give each a double charm,
As pearls upon an Ethiop's arm.
   See on the mountain's southern side,

Where the prospect opens wide,
Where the evening gilds the tide,
How close and small the hedges lie!
What streaks of meadows cross the eye!
A step methinks may pass the stream,
So little distant dangers seem; 120
So we mistake the future's face,
Eyed through Hope's deluding glass;
As yon summits soft and fair,
Clad in colours of the air,
Which to those who journey near,
Barren, brown, and rough appear;
Still we tread the same coarse way,
The present's still a cloudy day.
   Oh, may I with myself agree,
And never covet what I see, 130
Content me with an humble shade,
My passions tamed, my wishes laid;
For while our wishes wildly roll,
We banish quiet from the soul;
'Tis thus the busy beat the air,
And misers gather wealth and care.
   Now, even now, my joys run high,
As on the mountain turf I lie;
While the wanton Zephyr sings,
And in the vale perfumes his wings; 140
While the waters murmur deep,
While the shepherd charms his sheep,
While the birds unbounded fly,
And with music fill the sky;
Now, even now, my joys run high.
   Be full, ye courts, be great who will;
Search for Peace with all your skill;
Open wide the lofty door;
Seek her on the marble floor;
In vain you search, she is not there; 150
In vain ye search the domes of Care!
Grass and flowers Quiet treads,
On the meads and mountain-heads,
Along with Pleasure, close allied,
Ever by each other's side:
And often, by the murmuring rill,
Hears the thrush, while all is still,
Within the groves of Grongar Hill.

                           [1726]

JAMES THOMSON (1700-1748)

James Thomson's literary success was immediate and lasting. He brought to readers of his own day a fresh experience of poetry, and much of his work can still be read with pleasure. Without dramatic or lyrical power, without wit or satire, he made his way by combining sensitiveness and good sense. He appealed to an age that liked to find familiar ideas expressed in verse, and was also ready to enjoy a dignified poetic version of the phenomena of external nature.

Thomson was born at Ednam, Roxburghshire, spent his boyhood at Southdean ("Sooden") in the same border county, and was educated at Edinburgh with a view to entering the ministry. In 1725 he came up to London: he published *Winter* in 1726 and on its success the rest of *The Seasons* soon followed—*Summer* (1727), *Spring* (1728), and *Autumn* in the first collected edition (1730). From the beginning he made friends and found patrons, and thereafter led a fairly comfortable and sheltered life. He made the Grand Tour as traveling companion to Charles Talbot, son of the Solicitor General, and in *Liberty* (1735-36) attempted a broad view of political and cultural history inspired by his travels. This unsuccessful poem indicates his connection with the Whig opposition to Walpole, shown also in his poem *Britannia* (1729), and in his dramas, especially the masque of *Alfred* (1740). He was an adherent of Frederick, Prince of Wales, and a close friend of Lord Lyttelton, who had great influence both in literary and political circles. From 1736 he lived in a suburban retreat between Kew and Richmond.

Thomson's two most important poems are *The Seasons*, which appeared in a thoroughly revised form in 1744, and *The Castle of Indolence*, which "after fourteen or fifteen years" was published in the year of his death. *The Seasons* set for a century the model of a descriptive-didactic poem in blank verse. Locodescriptive poems such as Denham's *Cooper's Hill* and Pope's *Windsor Forest*, the important influence of Virgil's *Georgics*, and the Miltonic tradition of the religious-sublime set precedents for combining extensive description with far-ranging commentary and generalization. The descriptions of external nature are now the most esteemed parts of *The Seasons*. We enjoy the passages in which he paints with a sweeping but accurate brush the changes in weather and landscape. We appreciate his sensitiveness to movement, light, and shade, his intimate knowledge of country life and the ways of animals and birds. His contemporaries delighted in this part of his work also, although they were not disposed, as some modern critics are, to put him at the head of a school of rural and natural poetry as opposed to the urban and artificial school of Pope. Such an opposition is superficial, even though it is supported by some passages in Thomson's own Preface to the second edition of *Winter* (printed below). His readers found in Thomson as great a purveyor of artificial language as Pope himself; they were satisfied with his swelling Miltonic phrases and Latinized diction, and found it easier to borrow from his artificial vocabulary than to match his accurate observation. More justifiably, they favored his expositions of scientific subjects, his frequent transitions from the particular to the general, from natural objects to Nature. Second-rate as these expository passages may now appear, they were an essential part of his plan:

> To me be Nature's volume broad displayed;
> And to peruse its all-instructing page,
> Or, haply catching inspiration thence,
> Some easy passage, raptured, to translate,
> My sole delight; as through the falling gloom
> Pensive I stray, or with the rising dawn,
> On Fancy's eagle-wing excursive soar.

Thus Thomson draws no sharp line between description on the one hand and scientific and philosophical exposition on the other. He is a popularizer of doctrines drawn from contemporary philosophers, theologians, and scientists, particularly from Shaftesbury, Newton, and the physico-theological manuals which used the new science in the service of religion. His *Poem Sacred to the Memory of Sir Isaac Newton* (1727) expresses his delight in the vision of a universe perfectly ordered by natural law which is at the same time divine, and the phenomena described in *The Seasons* are considered as parts of this system. The influence of science encourages him in exact description and explanation of the world about him; the influence of Shaftesbury irradiates this description with sympathy and benevolence.

The Seasons is superficially Miltonic, *The Castle of Indolence* profoundly Spenserian. Thomson's genial love of the senses, his enjoyment of the play of his own temperament find expression in this delightful allegory; the charms of Indolence lure him beyond the real world of *The Seasons* to imaginative reverie. As the Advertisement prefixed to the poem indicates, Spenserian imitations were expected to verge on the ludicrous, but the humor of the first canto does not break the poetic spell. The second canto, however, reverts to the commonplace theme of Britain's progress in commerce and industry. Such inconsistencies are characteristic of Thomson. In somewhat the same way, his appreciation of simple natural life under primitive conditions conflicts with his enthusiasm for the economic progress of Britain; his conception of a God of and in nature cannot be easily reconciled with the God of orthodox Christianity. It was just this receptive temper, however, these varied interests and enthusiasms, that won for him such wide acceptance in the eighteenth century.

Complete Poetical Works, ed. J. Logie Robertson (Oxford, 1908); *The Seasons*, ed. O. Zippel (Palaestra LXVI; Berlin, 1908) [variorum edition]; excellent biographies by Léon Morel (Paris, 1895), G. C. Macaulay (English Men of Letters), Douglas Grant (1951); C. A. Moore "Shaftesbury and the Ethical Poets in England," *PMLA*, XXXI (1916), 264-325, reprinted in *Backgrounds of English Literature 1700-1760* (Minneapolis, 1953); Herbert Drennon [studies of Thomson and Newtonianism], *Univ. of Chicago Abstracts of Theses*, Humanistic Series, VII (1930), 523-28; *PMLA*, XLIX (1934), 71-80; *ibid.*, LIII (1938), 1094-1101; *SP*, XXXI (1934), 453-71; *ES*, LXVIII (1934), 397-449; *PQ*, XIV (1935), 70-82; A. D. McKillop, *The Background of Thomson's "Seasons"* (Minneapolis, 1942); *The Background of Thomson's "Liberty"* (Rice Institute Pamphlet, XXXVIII, 1951); Marjorie Nicolson, *Newton Demands the Muse* (Princeton, 1946); H. N. Fairchild, *Religious Trends in English Poetry*, I (1939), II, xi; E. R. Wasserman, *Elizabethan Poetry in the Eighteenth Century* (Urbana, Ill. 1947) [for *The Castle of Indolence*].

A POEM SACRED TO THE MEMORY OF SIR ISAAC NEWTON

Shall the great soul of Newton quit this earth
To mingle with his stars, and every Muse,
Astonished into silence, shun the weight
Of honours due to his illustrious name?
But what can man? Even now the sons of light,
In strains high-warbled to seraphic lyre,
Hail his arrival on the coast of bliss.
Yet am not I deterred, though high the theme,
And sung to harps of angels, for with you,
Ethereal flames! ambitious, I aspire
In Nature's general symphony to join.

And what new wonders can ye show your guest,
Who, while on this dim spot where mortals toil
Clouded in dust, from motion's simple laws
Could trace the secret hand of Providence,
Wide-working through this universal frame?
  Have ye not listened while he bound the suns
And planets to their spheres, the unequal task
Of humankind till then? Oft had they rolled
O'er erring man the year, and oft disgraced   20
The pride of schools, before their course was known
Full in its causes and effects to him.
All-piercing sage! who sat not down and dreamed
Romantic schemes, defended by the din
Of specious words, and tyranny of names;
But, bidding his amazing mind attend,
And with heroic patience years on years
Deep-searching, saw at last the system dawn,
And shine, of all his race, on him alone.
  What were his raptures then! how pure! how strong!   30
And what the triumphs of old Greece and Rome,
By his diminished, but the pride of boys
In some small fray victorious! when instead
Of shattered parcels of this earth usurped
By violence unmanly, and sore deeds
Of cruelty and blood, Nature herself
Stood all subdued by him, and open laid
Her every latent glory to his view.
    All intellectual eye, our solar round
First gazing through, he, by the blended power   40
Of gravitation and projection, saw
The whole in silent harmony revolve.
From unassisted vision hid, the moons
To cheer remoter planets numerous poured,
By him in all their mingled tracts were seen.
He also fixed the wandering Queen of Night,
Whether she wanes into a scanty orb,
Or, waxing broad, with her pale shadowy light
  In a soft deluge overflows the sky.
Her every motion clear-discerning, he   50
Adjusted to the mutual main and taught
Why now the mighty mass of water swells
Resistless, heaving on the broken rocks,
And the full river turning—till again
The tide revertive, unattracted, leaves
A yellow waste of idle sands behind.
    Then, breaking hence, he took his ardent flight
Through the blue infinite; and every star
Which the clear concave of a winter's night
Pours on the eye, or astronomic tube,   60
Far stretching, snatches from the dark abyss,
Or such as farther in successive skies
To fancy shine alone, at his approach
Blazed into suns, the living centre each
Of an harmonious system—all combined,
And ruled unerring by that single power

Which draws the stone projected to the ground.
O unprofuse magnificence divine!
O wisdom truly perfect! thus to call
From a few causes such a scheme of things,   70
Effects so various, beautiful, and great,
An universe complete! And O beloved
Of Heaven! whose well purged penetrative eye
The mystic veil transpiercing, inly scanned
The rising, moving, wide-established frame.
     He, first of men, with awful wing pursued
The comet through the long elliptic curve,
As round innumerous worlds he wound his way,
Till, to the forehead of our evening sky
Returned, the blazing wonder glares anew,   80
And o'er the trembling nations shakes dismay.
     The heavens are all his own, from the wide rule
Of whirling vortices and circling spheres
To their first great simplicity restored.
The schools astonished stood; but found it vain
To keep at odds with demonstration strong,
And, unawakened, dream beneath the blaze
Of truth. At once their pleasing visions fled,
With the gay shadows of the morning mixed,
When Newton rose, our philosophic sun!   90
     The aërial flow of sound was known to him,
From whence it first in wavy circles breaks,
Till the touched organ takes the meaning in.
Nor could the darting beam of speed immense
Escape his swift pursuit and measuring eye.
Even light itself, which every thing displays,
Shone undiscovered, till his brighter mind
Untwisted all the shining robe of day;
And from the whitening undistinguished blaze,
Collecting every ray into his kind,   100
To the charmed eye educed the gorgeous train
Of parent-colours. First the flaming red
Sprung vivid forth; the tawny orange next;
And next delicious yellow; by whose side
Fell the kind beams of all-refreshing green;
Then the pure blue, that swells autumnal skies,
Ethereal played; and then, of sadder hue,
Emerged the deepened indigo, as when
The heavy-skirted evening droops with frost;
While the last gleamings of refracted light   110
Died in the fainting violet away.
These, when the clouds distil the rosy shower,
Shine out distinct adown the watery bow;
While o'er our heads the dewy vision bends
Delightful, melting on the fields beneath.
Myriads of mingling dyes from these result,
And myriads still remain—infinite source
Of beauty, ever flushing, ever new.
     Did ever poet image aught so fair,
Dreaming in whispering groves by the hoarse brook,   120
Or prophet, to whose rapture Heaven descends?

Even now the setting sun and shifting clouds,
Seen, Greenwich, from thy lovely heights, declare
How just, how beauteous the refractive law.
　　The noiseless tide of time, all bearing down
To vast eternity's unbounded sea,
Where the green islands of the happy shine,
He stemmed alone: and to the source (involved
Deep in primeval gloom) ascending, raised
His lights at equal distances, to guide   130
Historian wildered on his darksome way.
　　But who can number up his labours? who
His high discoveries sing? When but a few
Of the deep-studying race can stretch their minds
To what he knew—in fancy's lighter thought
How shall the Muse then grasp the mighty theme?
　　What wonder thence that his devotion swelled
Responsive to his knowledge? For could he
Whose piercing mental eye diffusive saw
The finished university of things   140
In all its order, magnitude, and parts,
Forbear incessant to adore that Power
Who fills, sustains, and actuates the whole?
　　Say, ye who best can tell, ye happy few,
Who saw him in the softest lights of life,
All unwithheld, indulging to his friends
The vast unborrowed treasures of his mind,
Oh, speak the wondrous man! how mild, how calm,
How greatly humble, how divinely good,
How firm established on eternal truth;   150
Fervent in doing well, with every nerve
Still pressing on, forgetful of the past,
And panting for perfection; far above
Those little cares and visionary joys
That so perplex the fond impassioned heart
Of ever cheated, ever trusting man.
This, Conduitt, from thy rural hours we hope,
As through the pleasing shade where Nature pours
Her every sweet in studious ease you walk,
The social passions smiling at thy heart,   160
That glows with all the recollected sage.
　　And you, ye hopeless gloomy-minded tribe,
You who, unconscious of those nobler flights
That reach impatient at immortal life,
Against the prime endearing privilege
Of being dare contend,—say, can a soul
Of such extensive, deep, tremendous powers,
Enlarging still, be but a finer breath
Of spirits dancing through their tubes awhile,
And then forever lost in vacant air?   170
　　But hark! methinks I hear a warning voice,
Solemn as when some awful change is come,
Sound through the world—"'Tis done!—the measure's full;
And I resign my charge."—Ye mouldering stones
That build the towering pyramid, the proud
Triumphal arch, the monument effaced

By ruthless ruin, and what'er supports
The worshipped name of hoar antiquity—
Down to the dust! What grandeur can ye boast,
While Newton lifts his column to the skies,   180
Beyond the waste of time? Let no weak drop
Be shed for him. The virgin in her bloom
Cut off, the joyous youth, and darling child—
These are the tombs that claim the tender tear
And elegiac song. But Newton calls
For other notes of gratulation high,
That now he wanders through those endless worlds
He here so well descried, and wondering talks,
And hymns their Author with his glad compeers.
    O Britain's boast! whether with angels thou   190
Sittest in dread discourse, or fellow-blessed,
Who joy to see the honour of their kind;
Or whether, mounted on cherubic wing,
Thy swift career is with the whirling orbs,
Comparing things with things, in rapture lost,
And grateful adoration for that light
So plenteous rayed into thy mind below
From Light Himself; oh, look with pity down
On humankind, a frail erroneous race!
Exalt the spirit of a downward world!   200
O'er thy dejected country chief preside,
And be her Genius called! her studies raise,
Correct her manners, and inspire her youth;
For, though depraved and sunk, she brought thee forth,
And glories in thy name! she points thee out
To all her sons, and bids them eye thy star;
While in expectance of the second life,
When time shall be no more, thy sacred dust
Sleeps with her kings and dignifies the scene.

[1727]

HYMN ON SOLITUDE

Hail, mildly pleasing Solitude,
Companion of the wise and good,
But from whose holy piercing eye
The herd of fools and villains fly.
Oh! how I love with thee to walk,
And listen to thy whispered talk,
Which innocence and truth imparts,
And melts the most obdurate hearts.
    A thousand shapes you wear with ease,
And still in every shape you please.   10
Now wrapt in some mysterious dream,
A lone philosopher you seem;
Now quick from hill to vale you fly,
And now you sweep the vaulted sky;
A shepherd next, you haunt the plain,
And warble forth your oaten strain:

A lover now, with all the grace
Of that sweet passion in your face;
Then, calmed to friendship, you assume
The gentle looking Hertford's bloom,   20
As, with her Musidora, she
(Her Musidora fond of thee)
Amid the long-withdrawing vale
Awakes the rivalled nightingale.
    Thine is the balmy breath of morn,
Just as the dew-bent rose is born;
And, while meridian fervours beat,
Thine is the woodland dumb retreat;
But chief, when evening scenes decay
And the faint landscape swims away,   30
Thine is the doubtful soft decline,
And that best hour of musing thine.
    Descending angels bless thy train,
The virtues of the sage and swain—

Plain Innocence, in white arrayed,
Before thee lifts her fearless head;
Religion's beams around thee shine
And cheer thy glooms with light divine;
About thee sports sweet Liberty,
And rapt Urania sings to thee.   40
  Oh, let me pierce thy secret cell,
And in thy deep recesses dwell!

Perhaps from Norwood's oak-clad hill,
When Meditation has her fill,
I just may cast my careless eyes
Where London's spiry turrets rise,
Think of its crimes, its cares, its pain.
Then shield me in the woods again.

                                        [*1725*, 1729]

THE SEASONS

FROM THE PREFACE TO *WINTER*

I am neither ignorant nor concerned how much one may suffer in the opinion of several persons of great gravity and character by the study and pursuit of poetry.

Although there may seem to be some appearance of reason for the present contempt of it as managed by the most part of our modern writers, yet that any man should seriously declare against that divine art is really amazing. It is declaring against the most charming power of imagination, the most exalting force of thought, the most affecting touch of sentiment—in a word, against the very soul of all learning and politeness. It is affronting the universal taste of mankind, and declaring against what has charmed the listening world from Moses down to Milton. In fine, it is even declaring against the sublimest passages of the inspired writings themselves, and what seems to be the peculiar language of Heaven.

The truth of the case is this: these weak-sighted gentlemen cannot bear the strong light of poetry and the finer and more amusing scene of things it displays. But must those therefore whom Heaven has blessed with the discerning eye shut it to keep them company?

It is pleasant enough, however, to observe frequently in these enemies of poetry an awkward imitation of it. They sometimes have their little brightnesses when the opening glooms will permit. Nay, I have seen their heaviness on some occasions deign to turn friskish and witty, in which they make just such another figure as Æsop's ass when he began to fawn. To complete the absurdity, they would even in their efforts against poetry fain be poetical; like those gentlemen that reason with a great deal of zeal and severity against reason.

That there are frequent and notorious abuses of poetry is as true as that the best things are most liable to that misfortune; but is there no end of that clamorous argument against the use of things from the abuse of them? and yet I hope that no man who has the least sense of shame in him will fall into it after the present sulphureous attacker of the stage.

To insist no further on this head, let Poetry once more be restored to her ancient truth and purity; let her be inspired from Heaven, and in return her incense ascend thither; let her exchange her low, venal, trifling, subjects for such as are fair, useful, and magnificent; and let her execute these so as at once to please, instruct, surprise, and astonish: and then of necessity the most inveterate ignorance and prejudice shall be struck dumb, and poets yet become the delight and wonder of mankind.

But this happy period is not to be expected, till some long-wished, illustrious man of equal power and beneficence rise on the wintry world of letters: one of a genuine and unbounded greatness and generosity of mind; who, far above all the pomp and pride of fortune, scorns the little, addressful flatterer; pierces through the disguised, designing villain; discountenances all the reigning fopperies of a tasteless age; and who, stretching his views into late futurity, has the true interest of virtue, learning, and mankind entirely at heart—a character so nobly desirable that to an honest heart it is almost incredible so few should have the ambition to deserve it.

Nothing can have a better influence towards the revival of poetry than the choosing of great and serious subjects, such as at once amuse the fancy, enlighten the head, and warm the heart. These give a weight and dignity to the poem, nor is the pleasure—I should say rapture—both the writer and the reader feels unwarranted by reason or followed by repentant disgust. To be able to write on a dry, barren theme is looked upon by some as the sign of a happy, fruitful genius:—fruitful indeed! like one of the pendant gardens in Cheapside, watered every morning by the hand of the Alderman himself. And what are we commonly entertained with on these occasions save forced, unaffecting fancies, little, glittering prettinesses, mixed turns of wit and expression, which are as widely different from native poetry as buffoonery is from the perfection of human thinking? A genius fired with the charms of truth and nature is tuned to a sublimer pitch, and scorns to associate with such subjects.

I cannot more emphatically recommend this poetical ambition than by the four following lines from Mr. Hill's poem, called *The Judgment Day*, which is so singular an instance of it:—

> For me, suffice it to have taught my Muse,
> The tuneful triflings of her tribe to shun;
> And raised her warmth such heavenly themes to choose
> As in past ages the best garlands won.

I know no subject more elevating, more amusing, more ready to awake the poetical enthusiasm, the philosophical reflection, and the moral sentiment, than the works of Nature. Where can we meet with such variety, such beauty, such magnificence? All that enlarges and transports the soul? What more inspiring than a calm, wide survey of them? In every dress Nature is greatly charming—whether she puts on the crimson robes of the morning, the strong effulgence of noon, the sober suit of the evening, or the deep sables of blackness and tempest! How gay looks the spring! how glorious the summer! how pleasing the autumn! and how venerable the winter!— But there is no thinking of these things without breaking out into poetry; which is, by the bye, a plain and undeniable argument of their superior excellence.

For this reason the best, both ancient and modern, poets have been passionately fond of retirement and solitude. The wild romantic country was their delight. And they seem never to have been more happy than when, lost in unfrequented fields, far from the little busy world, they were at leisure to meditate, and sing the works of Nature.

The book of Job, that noble and ancient poem, which even strikes so forcibly through a mangling translation, is crowned with a description of the grand works of Nature; and that, too, from the mouth of their Almighty Author.

It was this devotion to the works of Nature that, in his Georgics, inspired the rural Virgil to write so inimitably; and who can forbear joining with him in this declaration of his, which has been the rapture of ages? . . .

> Me may the Muses, my supreme delight!
> Whose priest I am, smit with immense desire,
> Snatch to their care; the starry tracts disclose,
> The sun's distress, the labours of the moon;
> Whence the earth quakes; and by what force the deeps
> Heave at the rocks, then on themselves reflow;
> Why winter suns to plunge in ocean speed;
> And what retards the lazy summer night.
> But, lest I should these mystic truths attain,
> If the cold current freezes round my heart,
> The country me, the brooky vales may please
> Mid woods and streams unknown.

[1726]

WINTER

THE ARGUMENT

The subject proposed. Address to the Earl of Wilmington. First approach of Winter. According to the natural course of the season, various storms described. Rain. Wind. Snow. The driving of the snows: a man perishing among them; whence reflections on the wants and miseries of human life. The wolves descending from the Alps and Apennines. A winter evening described: as spent by philosophers; by the country people; in the city. Frost. A view of Winter within the polar circle. A thaw. The whole concluding with moral reflections on a future state.

> See, Winter comes to rule the varied year
> Sullen and sad, with all his rising train—

Vapours, and clouds, and storms. Be these my theme—
These, that exalt the soul to solemn thought
And heavenly musing. Welcome, kindred glooms!
Cogenial horrors, hail! With frequent foot,
Pleased have I, in my cheerful morn of life,
When nursed by careless solitude I lived
And sung of Nature with unceasing joy,
Pleased have I wandered through your rough domain;   10
Trod the pure virgin-snows, myself as pure;
Heard the winds roar, and the big torrent burst;
Or seen the deep-fermenting tempest brewed
In the grim evening sky. Thus passed the time,
Till through the lucid chambers of the south
Looked out the joyous Spring—looked out and smiled.
    To thee, the patron of this first essay,
The Muse, O Wilmington! renews her song.
Since has she rounded the revolving year:
Skimmed the gay Spring; on eagle-pinions borne,   20
Attempted through the Summer-blaze to rise;
Then swept o'er Autumn with the shadowy gale,
And now among the wintry clouds again,
Rolled in the doubling storm, she tries to soar,
To swell her note with all the rushing winds,
To suit her sounding cadence to the floods;
As is her theme, her numbers wildly great.
Thrice happy, could she fill thy judging ear
With bold description and with manly thought!
Nor art thou skilled in awful schemes alone,   30
And how to make a mighty people thrive;
But equal goodness, sound integrity,
A firm, unshaken, uncorrupted soul
Amid a sliding age, and burning strong,
Not vainly blazing, for thy country's weal,
A steady spirit, regularly free—
These, each exalting each, the statesman light
Into the patriot; these, the public hope
And eye to thee converting, bid the Muse
Record what envy dares not flattery call.   40
    Now, when the cheerless empire of the sky
To Capricorn the Centaur-Archer yields,
And fierce Aquarius stains the inverted year—
Hung o'er the farthest verge of heaven, the sun
Scarce spreads o'er ether the dejected day.
Faint are his gleams, and ineffectual shoot
His struggling rays in horizontal lines
Through the thick air; as clothed in cloudy storm,
Weak, wan, and broad, he skirts the southern sky;
And, soon descending, to the long dark night,   50
Wide-shading all, the prostrate world resigns.
Nor is the night unwished, while vital heat,
Light, life, and joy the dubious day forsake.
Meantime, in sable cincture, shadows vast,
Deep-tinged and damp, and congregated clouds,
And all the vapoury turbulence of heaven
Involve the face of things. Thus Winter falls.

A heavy gloom oppressive o'er the world,
Through Nature shedding influence malign,
And rouses up the seeds of dark disease.   60
The soul of man dies in him, loathing life,
And black with more than melancholy views.
The cattle droop, and o'er the furrowed land,
Fresh from the plough, the dun discoloured flocks,
Untended spreading, crop the wholesome root.
Along the woods, along the moorish fens,
Sighs the sad genius of the coming storm;
And up among the loose disjointed cliffs
And fractured mountains wild, the brawling brook
And cave, presageful, send a hollow moan,   70
Resounding long in listening Fancy's ear.
    Then comes the father of the tempest forth,
Wrapped in black glooms. First, joyless rains obscure
Drive through the mingling skies with vapour foul,
Dash on the mountain's brow, and shake the woods
That grumbling wave below. The unsightly plain
Lies a brown deluge; as the low-bent clouds
Pour flood on flood, yet unexhausted still
Combine, and, deepening into night, shut up
The day's fair face. The wanderers of heaven,   80
Each to his home, retire, save those that love
To take their pastime in the troubled air,
Or skimming flutter round the dimply pool.
The cattle from the untasted fields return
And ask, with meaning low, their wonted stalls,
Or ruminate in the contiguous shade.
Thither the household feathery people crowd,
The crested cock, with all his female train,
Pensive and dripping; while the cottage-hind
Hangs o'er the enlivening blaze, and taleful there   90
Recounts his simple frolic; much he talks,
And much he laughs, nor recks the storm that blows
Without, and rattles on his humble roof.
    Wide o'er the brim, with many a torrent swelled,
And the mixed ruin of its banks o'erspread,
At last the roused-up river pours along:
Resistless, roaring, dreadful, down it comes,
From the rude mountain and the mossy wild,
Tumbling through rocks abrupt, and sounding far;
Then o'er the sanded valley floating spreads,   100
Calm, sluggish, silent; till again, constrained
Between two meeting hills, it bursts a way
Where rocks and woods o'erhang the turbid stream;
There, gathering triple force, rapid and deep,
It boils and wheels and foams and thunders through.
    Nature! great parent! whose unceasing hand
Rolls round the seasons of the changeful year,
How mighty, how majestic are thy works!
With what a pleasing dread they swell the soul,
That sees astonished, and astonished sings!   110
Ye too, ye winds! that now begin to blow
With boisterous sweep, I raise my voice to you.

Where are your stores, ye powerful beings! say,
Where your aërial magazines reserved
To swell the brooding terrors of the storm?
In what far-distant region of the sky,
Hushed in deep silence, sleep you when 'tis calm?
    When from the pallid sky the sun descends,
With many a spot, that o'er his glaring orb
Uncertain wanders, stained; red fiery streaks   120
Begin to flush around. The reeling clouds
Stagger with dizzy poise, as doubting yet
Which master to obey; while, rising slow,
Blank in the leaden-coloured east, the moon
Wears a wan circle round her blunted horns.
Seen through the turbid fluctuating air,
The stars obtuse emit a shivering ray,
Or frequent seem to shoot athwart the gloom,
And long behind them trail the whitening blaze.
Snatched in short eddies, plays the withered leaf,   130
And on the flood the dancing feather floats.
With broadened nostrils to the sky upturned,
The conscious heifer snuffs the stormy gale.
Even as the matron, at her nightly task,
With pensive labour draws the flaxen thread,
The wasted taper and the crackling flame
Foretell the blast. But chief the plumy race,
The tenants of the sky, its changes speak.
Retiring from the downs, where all day long
They picked their scanty fare, a blackening train   140
Of clamorous rooks thick-urge their weary flight,
And seek the closing shelter of the grove.
Assiduous in his bower, the wailing owl
Plies his sad song. The cormorant on high
Wheels from the deep and screams along the land.
Loud shrieks the soaring hern, and with wild wing
The circling sea-fowl cleave the flaky clouds.
Ocean, unequal pressed, with broken tide
And blind commotion heaves; while from the shore,
Eat into caverns by the restless wave,   150
And forest-rustling mountain, comes a voice
That, solemn-sounding, bids the world prepare.
Then issues forth the storm with sudden burst,
And hurls the whole precipitated air
Down in a torrent. On the passive main
Descends the ethereal force, and with strong gust
Turns from its bottom the discoloured deep.
Through the black night that sits immense around,
Lashed into foam, the fierce-conflicting brine
Seems o'er a thousand raging waves to burn.   160
Meantime the mountain-billows, to the clouds
In dreadful tumult swelled, surge above surge,
Burst into chaos with tremendous roar,
And anchored navies from their stations drive,
Wild as the winds, across the howling waste
Of mighty waters; now the inflated wave
Straining they scale, and now impetuous shoot

Into the secret chambers of the deep,
The wintry Baltic thundering o'er their heads.
Emerging thence again, before the breath   170
Of full-exerted heaven they wing their course,
And dart on distant coasts—if some sharp rock
Or shoal insidious break not their career,
And in loose fragments fling them floating round.
   Nor less at land the loosened tempest reigns.
The mountain thunders, and its sturdy sons
Stoop to the bottom of the rocks they shade.
Lone on the midnight steep, and all aghast,
The dark wayfaring stranger breathless toils,
And, often falling, climbs against the blast.   180
Low waves the rooted forest, vexed, and sheds
What of its tarnished honours yet remain—
Dashed down and scattered by the tearing wind's
Assiduous fury, its gigantic limbs.
Thus struggling through the dissipated grove,
The whirling tempest raves along the plain;
And, on the cottage thatched or lordly roof
Keen-fastening, shakes them to the solid base.
Sleep frighted flies; and round the rocking dome,
For entrance eager, howls the savage blast.   190
Then too, they say, through all the burdened air
Long groans are heard, shrill sounds, and distant sighs,
That, uttered by the demon of the night,
Warn the devoted wretch of woe and death.
   Huge Uproar lords it wide. The clouds, commixed
With stars, swift-gliding sweep along the sky.
All Nature reels: till Nature's King, who oft
Amid tempestuous darkness dwells alone,
And on the wings of the careering wind
Walks dreadfully serene, commands a calm;   200
Then straight air, sea, and earth are hushed at once.
   As yet 'tis midnight deep. The weary clouds,
Slow-meeting, mingle into solid gloom.
Now, while the drowsy world lies lost in sleep,
Let me associate with the serious Night,
And Contemplation, her sedate compeer;
Let me shake off the intrusive cares of day,
And lay the meddling senses all aside.
   Where now, ye lying vanities of life!
Ye ever-tempting, ever-cheating train!   210
Where are you now? and what is your amount?
Vexation, disappointment, and remorse.
Sad, sickening thought! and yet deluded man,
A scene of crude disjointed visions past,
And broken slumbers, rises still resolved,
With new-flushed hopes, to run the giddy round.
   Father of light and life! thou Good Supreme!
O teach me what is good! teach me Thyself!
Save me from folly, vanity, and vice,
From every low pursuit; and feed my soul   220
With knowledge, conscious peace, and virtue pure—
Sacred, substantial, never-fading bliss!

The keener tempests come, and, fuming dun
From all the livid east or piercing north,
Thick clouds ascend, in whose capacious womb
A vapoury deluge lies, to snow congealed.
Heavy they roll their fleecy world along,
And the sky saddens with the gathered storm.
Through the hushed air the whitening shower descends,
At first thin-wavering, till at last the flakes   230
Fall broad and wide and fast, dimming the day
With a continual flow. The cherished fields
Put on their winter-robe of purest white.
'Tis brightness all, save where the new snow melts
Along the mazy current. Low the woods
Bow their hoar head; and, ere the languid sun
Faint from the west emits his evening ray,
Earth's universal face, deep-hid and chill,
Is one wild dazzling waste, that buries wide
The works of man. Drooping, the labourer-ox   240
Stands covered o'er with snow, and then demands
The fruit of all his toil. The fowls of heaven,
Tamed by the cruel season, crowd around
The winnowing store, and claim the little boon
Which Providence assigns them. One alone,
The redbreast, sacred to the household gods,
Wisely regardful of the embroiling sky,
In joyless fields and thorny thickets leaves
His shivering mates, and pays to trusted man
His annual visit. Half afraid, he first   250
Against the window beats; then brisk alights
On the warm hearth; then, hopping o'er the floor,
Eyes all the smiling family askance,
And pecks, and starts, and wonders where he is—
Till, more familiar grown, the table-crumbs
Attract his slender feet. The foodless wilds
Pour forth their brown inhabitants. The hare,
Though timorous of heart, and hard beset
By death in various forms, dark snares, and dogs,
And more unpitying men, the garden seeks,   260
Urged on by fearless want. The bleating kind
Eye the bleak heaven, and next the glistening earth,
With looks of dumb despair; then, sad-dispersed,
Dig for the withered herb through heaps of snow.
Now, shepherds, to your helpless charge be kind;
Baffle the raging year, and fill their pens
With food at will; lodge them below the storm,
And watch them strict, for, from the bellowing east,
In this dire season, oft the whirlwind's wing
Sweeps up the burden of whole wintry plains   270
In one wide waft, and o'er the hapless flocks,
Hid in the hollow of two neighbouring hills,
The billowy tempest whelms, till, upward urged,
The valley to a shining mountain swells,
Tipped with a wreath high-curling in the sky.
As thus the snows arise, and, foul and fierce,
All Winter drives along the darkened air,

In his own loose-revolving fields the swain
Disastered stands; sees other hills ascend,
Of unknown joyless brow, and other scenes,   280
Of horrid prospect, shag the trackless plain;
Nor finds the river nor the forest, hid
Beneath the formless wild, but wanders on
From hill to dale, still more and more astray,
Impatient flouncing through the drifted heaps,
Stung with the thoughts of home—the thoughts of home
Rush on his nerves and call their vigour forth
In many a vain attempt. How sinks his soul!
What black despair, what horror fills his heart,
When, for the dusky spot which fancy feigned   290
His tufted cottage rising through the snow,
He meets the roughness of the middle waste,
Far from the track and blest abode of man,
While round him night resistless closes fast,
And every tempest, howling o'er his head,
Renders the savage wilderness more wild.
Then throng the busy shapes into his mind
Of covered pits, unfathomably deep,
A dire descent! beyond the power of frost;
Of faithless bogs; of precipices huge,   300
Smoothed up with snow; and (what is land unknown,
What water) of the still unfrozen spring,
In the loose marsh or solitary lake,
Where the fresh fountain from the bottom boils.
These check his fearful steps; and down he sinks
Beneath the shelter of the shapeless drift,
Thinking o'er all the bitterness of death,
Mixed with the tender anguish nature shoots
Through the wrung bosom of the dying man—
His wife, his children, and his friends unseen.   310
In vain for him the officious wife prepares
The fire fair-blazing and the vestment warm;
In vain his little children, peeping out
Into the mingling storm, demand their sire
With tears of artless innocence. Alas!
Nor wife nor children more shall he behold,
Nor friends, nor sacred home. On every nerve
The deadly winter seizes, shuts up sense,
And, o'er his inmost vitals creeping cold,
Lays him along the snows a stiffened corse,   320
Stretched out and bleaching in the northern blast.
   Ah! little think the gay licentious proud,
Whom pleasure, power, and affluence surround—
They who their thoughtless hours in giddy mirth,
And wanton, often cruel, riot waste—
Ah! little think they, while they dance along,
How many feel, this very moment, death
And all the sad variety of pain;
How many sink in the devouring flood,
Or more devouring flame; how many bleed,   330
By shameful variance betwixt man and man;
How many pine in want, and dungeon glooms,

Shut from the common air and common use
Of their own limbs; how many drink the cup
Of baleful grief, or eat the bitter bread
Of misery; sore pierced by wintry winds,
How many shrink into the sordid hut
Of cheerless poverty; how many shake
With all the fiercer tortures of the mind,
Unbounded passion, madness, guilt, remorse—   340
Whence, tumbled headlong from the height of life,
They furnish matter for the Tragic Muse;
Even in the vale, where wisdom loves to dwell,
With friendship, peace, and contemplation joined,
How many, racked with honest passions, droop
In deep retired distress; how many stand
Around the death-bed of their dearest friends,
And point the parting anguish! Thought fond man
Of these, and all the thousand nameless ills
That one incessant struggle render life,   350
One scene of toil, of suffering, and of fate,
Vice in his high career would stand appalled,
And heedless rambling Impulse learn to think;
The conscious heart of Charity would warm,
And her wide wish Benevolence dilate;
The social tear would rise, the social sigh;
And into clear perfection, gradual bliss,
Refining still, the social passions work.
    And here can I forget the generous band
Who, touched with human woe, redressive searched   360
Into the horrors of the gloomy jail?
Unpitied and unheard where misery moans,
Where sickness pines, where thirst and hunger burn,
And poor misfortune feels the lash of vice;
While in the land of liberty—the land
Whose every street and public meeting glow
With open freedom—little tyrants raged,
Snatched the lean morsel from the starving mouth,
Tore from cold wintry limbs the tattered weed,
Even robbed them of the last of comforts, sleep,   370
The free-born Briton to the dungeon chained,
Or, as the lust of cruelty prevailed,
At pleasure marked him with inglorious stripes,
And crushed out lives, by secret barbarous ways,
That for their country would have toiled or bled.
O great design! if executed well,
With patient care and wisdom-tempered zeal.
Ye sons of mercy! yet resume the search;
Drag forth the legal monsters into light,
Wrench from their hands Oppression's iron rod,   380
And bid the cruel feel the pains they give.
Much still untouched remains; in this rank age,
Much is the patriot's weeding hand required.
The toils of law—what dark insidious men
Have cumbrous added to perplex the truth
And lengthen simple justice into trade—
How glorious were the day that saw these broke,

And every man within the reach of right!
By wintry famine roused, from all the tract
Of horrid mountains which the shining Alps   390
And wavy Apennines and Pyrenees
Branch out stupendous into distant lands,
Cruel as death, and hungry as the grave!
Burning for blood, bony, and gaunt, and grim!
Assembling wolves in raging troops descend;
And, pouring o'er the country, bear along,
Keen as the north wind sweeps the glossy snow.
All is their prize. They fasten on the steed,
Press him to earth, and pierce his mighty heart.
Nor can the bull his awful front defend,   400
Or shake the murdering savages away.
Rapacious, at the mother's throat they fly,
And tear the screaming infant from her breast.
The godlike face of man avails him naught.
Even Beauty, force divine! at whose bright glance
The generous lion stands in softened gaze,
Here bleeds, a hapless undistinguished prey.
But if, apprised of the severe attack,
The country be shut up, lured by the scent,
On churchyards drear (inhuman to relate!)   410
The disappointed prowlers fall, and dig
The shrouded body from the grave, o'er which,
Mixed with foul shades and frighted ghosts, they howl.
    Among those hilly regions where, embraced
In peaceful vales, the happy Grisons dwell,
Oft, rushing sudden from the loaded cliffs,
Mountains of snow their gathering terrors roll.
From steep to steep loud thundering down they come,
A wintry waste in dire commotion all;
And herds and flocks and travellers and swains,   420
And sometimes whole brigades of marching troops,
Or hamlets sleeping in the dead of night,
Are deep beneath the smothering ruin whelmed.
    Now, all amid the rigours of the year,
In the wild depth of winter, while without
The ceaseless winds blow ice, be my retreat,
Between the groaning forest and the shore,
Beat by the boundless multitude of waves,
A rural, sheltered, solitary scene,
Where ruddy fire and beaming tapers join   430
To cheer the gloom. There studious let me sit,
And hold high converse with the mighty dead—
Sages of ancient time, as gods revered,
As gods beneficent, who blessed mankind
With arts and arms, and humanized a world.
Roused at the inspiring thought, I throw aside
The long-lived volume, and deep-musing hail
The sacred shades that slowly rising pass
Before my wondering eyes. First Socrates,
Who, firmly good in a corrupted state,   440
Against the rage of tyrants single stood,
Invincible! calm reason's holy law,

That voice of God within the attentive mind,
Obeying, fearless or in life or death—
Great moral teacher! wisest of mankind!
Solon the next, who built his commonweal
On equity's wide base; by tender laws
A lively people curbing, yet undamped
Preserving still that quick peculiar fire,
Whence in the laurelled field of finer arts,   450
And of bold freedom, they unequalled shone,
The pride of smiling Greece and humankind.
Lycurgus then, who bowed beneath the force
Of strictest discipline, severely wise,
All human passions. Following him I see,
As at Thermopylae he glorious fell,
The firm devoted chief who proved by deeds
The hardest lesson which the other taught.
Then Aristides lifts his honest front;
Spotless of heart, to whom the unflattering voice   460
Of freedom gave the noblest name of Just;
In pure majestic poverty revered;
Who, even his glory to his country's weal
Submitting, swelled a haughty rival's fame.
Reared by his care, of softer ray appears
Cimon, sweet-souled; whose genius, rising strong,
Shook off the load of young debauch; abroad
The scourge of Persian pride, at home the friend
Of every worth and every splendid art;
Modest and simple in the pomp of wealth.   470
Then the last worthies of declining Greece,
Late-called to glory, in unequal times,
Pensive appear. The fair Corinthian boast,
Timoleon, tempered happy, mild, and firm,
Who wept the brother while the tyrant bled;
And, equal to the best, the Theban pair,
Whose virtues, in heroic concord joined,
Their country raised to freedom, empire, fame.
He too, with whom Athenian honour sunk,
And left a mass of sordid lees behind,—   480
Phocion the Good; in public life severe,
To virtue still inexorably firm;
But when, beneath his low illustrious roof,
Sweet peace and happy wisdom smoothed his brow,
Not friendship softer was, nor love more kind.
And he, the last of old Lycurgus' sons,
The generous victim to that vain attempt
To save a rotten state—Agis, who saw
Even Sparta's self to servile avarice sunk.
The two Achaian heroes close the train—   490
Aratus, who a while relumed the soul
Of fondly lingering liberty in Greece;
And he, her darling, as her latest hope,
The gallant Philopoemen, who to arms
Turned the luxurious pomp he could not cure,
Or toiling in his farm, a simple swain,
Or bold and skilful thundering in the field.

Of rougher front, a mighty people come,
A race of heroes! in those virtuous times
Which knew no stain, save that with partial flame 500
Their dearest country they too fondly loved.
Her better founder first, the Light of Rome,
Numa, who softened her rapacious sons;
Servius, the king who laid the solid base
On which o'er earth the vast republic spread.
Then the great consuls venerable rise:
The public father who the private quelled,
As on the dread tribunal, sternly sad;
He whom his thankless country could not lose,
Camillus, only vengeful to her foes; 510
Fabricius, scorner of all-conquering gold,
And Cincinnatus, awful from the plough;
Thy willing victim, Carthage! bursting loose
From all that pleading Nature could oppose,
From a whole city's tears, by rigid faith
Imperious called, and honour's dire command;
Scipio, the gentle chief, humanely brave,
Who soon the race of spotless glory ran,
And, warm in youth, to the poetic shade
With friendship and philosophy retired; 520
Tully, whose powerful eloquence a while
Restrained the rapid fate of rushing Rome;
Unconquered Cato, virtuous in extreme;
And thou, unhappy Brutus, kind of heart,
Whose steady arm, by awful virtue urged,
Lifted the Roman steel against thy friend.
Thousands besides the tribute of a verse
Demand, but who can count the stars of heaven?
Who sing their influence on this lower world?
Behold, who yonder comes! in sober state, 530
Fair, mild, and strong as is a vernal sun:
'Tis Phoebus' self, or else the Mantuan swain!
Great Homer too appears, of daring wing,
Parent of song! and equal by his side,
The British Muse; joined hand in hand they walk,
Darkling, full up the middle steep to fame.
Nor absent are those shades, whose skilful touch
Pathetic drew the impassioned heart, and charmed
Transported Athens with the moral scene;
Nor those who tuneful waked the enchanting lyre. 540
First of your kind! society divine!
Still visit thus my nights, for you reserved,
And mount my soaring soul to thoughts like yours.
Silence, thou lonely power! the door be thine;
See on the hallowed hour that none intrude,
Save a few chosen friends who sometimes deign
To bless my humble roof with sense refined,
Learning digested well, exalted faith,
Unstudied wit, and humour ever gay.
Or from the Muses' hill will Pope descend, 550
To raise the sacred hour, to bid it smile,
And with the social spirit warm the heart;

For, though not sweeter his own Homer sings,
Yet is his life the more endearing song.
　Where art thou, Hammond? thou the darling pride,
The friend and lover of the tuneful throng!
Ah! why, dear youth, in all the blooming prime
Of vernal genius, where, disclosing fast,
Each active worth, each manly virtue lay,
Why wert thou ravished from our hope so soon?   560
What now avails that noble thirst of fame
Which stung thy fervent breast? that treasured store
Of knowledge, early gained? that eager zeal
To serve thy country, glowing in the band
Of youthful patriots who sustain her name?
What now, alas! that life-diffusing charm
Of sprightly wit? that rapture for the Muse,
That heart of friendship and that soul of joy,
Which bade with softest light thy virtues smile?
Ah! only showed to check our fond pursuits,   570
And teach our humbled hopes that life is vain!
　Thus in some deep retirement would I pass
The winter-glooms with friends of pliant soul,
Or blithe or solemn, as the theme inspired:
With them would search if nature's boundless frame
Was called, late-rising, from the void of night,
Or sprung eternal from the Eternal Mind;
Its life, its laws, its progress, and its end.
Hence larger prospects of the beauteous whole
Would gradual open on our opening minds,   580
And each diffusive harmony unite
In full perfection to the astonished eye.
Then would we try to scan the moral world,
Which, though to us it seems embroiled, moves on
In higher order, fitted and impelled
By Wisdom's finest hand, and issuing all
In general good. The sage Historic Muse
Should next conduct us through the deeps of time,
Show us how empire grew, declined, and fell
In scattered states; what makes the nations smile,   590
Improves their soil, and gives them double suns;
And why they pine beneath the brightest skies,
In Nature's richest lap. As thus we talked,
Our hearts would burn within us, would inhale
That portion of divinity, that ray
Of purest Heaven which lights the public soul
Of patriots and of heroes. But, if doomed
In powerless humble fortune to repress
These ardent risings of the kindling soul,
Then, even superior to ambition, we   600
Would learn the private virtues—how to glide
Through shades and plains along the smoothest stream
Of rural life; or, snatched away by hope
Through the dim spaces of futurity,
With earnest eye anticipate those scenes
Of happiness and wonder, where the mind,
In endless growth and infinite ascent,

Rises from state to state, and world to world.
But, when with these the serious thought is foiled,
We, shifting for relief, would play the shapes   610
Of frolic Fancy; and incessant form
Those rapid pictures, that assembled train
Of fleet ideas, never joined before,
Whence lively Wit excites to gay surprise,
Or folly-painting Humour, grave himself,
Calls laughter forth, deep-shaking every nerve.
　　Meantime the village rouses up the fire;
While, well attested and as well believed,
Heard solemn, goes the goblin-story round,
Till superstitious horror creeps o'er all.   620
Or frequent in the sounding hall they wake
The rural gambol. Rustic mirth goes round—
The simple joke that takes the shepherd's heart,
Easily pleased; the long loud laugh sincere;
The kiss, snatched hasty from the sidelong maid
On purpose guardless, or pretending sleep;
The leap, the slap, the haul; and, shook to notes
Of native music, the respondent dance.
Thus jocund fleets with them the winter night.
　　The city swarms intense. The public haunt,   630
Full of each theme and warm with mixed discourse,
Hums indistinct. The sons of riot flow
Down the loose stream of false enchanted joy
To swift destruction. On the rankled soul
The gaming fury falls; and in one gulf
Of total ruin, honour, virtue, peace,
Friends, families, and fortune headlong sink.
Up-springs the dance along the lighted dome,
Mixed and evolved a thousand sprightly ways.
The glittering court effuses every pomp;   640
The circle deepens; beamed from gaudy robes,
Tapers, and sparkling gems, and radiant eyes,
A soft effulgence o'er the palace waves—
While, a gay insect in his summer shine,
The fop, light-fluttering, spreads his mealy wings.
　　Dread o'er the scene the ghost of Hamlet stalks;
Othello rages; poor Monimia mourns;
And Belvidera pours her soul in love.
Terror alarms the breast; the comely tear
Steals o'er the cheek; or else the Comic Muse   650
Holds to the world a picture of itself,
And raises sly the fair impartial laugh.
Sometimes she lifts her strain, and paints the scenes
Of beauteous life—whate'er can deck mankind,
Or charm the heart, in generous Bevil showed.
　　O thou whose wisdom, solid yet refined,
Whose patriot virtues, and consummate skill
To touch the finer springs that move the world,
Joined to whate'er the Graces can bestow,
And all Apollo's animating fire,   660
Give thee with pleasing dignity to shine
At once the guardian, ornament, and joy

Of polished life—permit the rural Muse,
O Chesterfield, to grace with thee her song.
Ere to the shades again she humbly flies,
Indulge her fond ambition, in thy train
(For every Muse has in thy train a place)
To mark thy various full-accomplished mind—
To mark that spirit which with British scorn
Rejects the allurements of corrupted power;   670
That elegant politeness which excels,
Even in the judgment of presumptuous France,
The boasted manners of her shining court;
That wit, the vivid energy of sense,
The truth of nature, which with Attic point,
And kind well-tempered satire, smoothly keen,
Steals through the soul and without pain corrects.
Or, rising thence with yet a brighter flame,
Oh, let me hail thee on some glorious day,
When to the listening senate ardent crowd   680
Britannia's sons to hear her pleaded cause!
Then, dressed by thee, more amiably fair,
Truth the soft robe of mild persuasion wears;
Thou to assenting reason giv'st again
Her own enlightened thoughts: called from the heart,
The obedient passions on thy voice attend;
And even reluctant party feels a while
Thy gracious power, as through the varied maze
Of eloquence, now smooth, now quick, now strong,
Profound and clear, you roll the copious flood.   690
    To thy loved haunt return, my happy Muse:
For now, behold! the joyous winter days,
Frosty, succeed; and through the blue serene,
For sight too fine, the ethereal nitre flies,
Killing infectious damps, and the spent air
Storing afresh with elemental life.
Close crowds the shining atmosphere, and binds
Our strengthened bodies in its cold embrace,
Constringent; feeds and animates our blood;
Refines our spirits, through the new-strung nerves   700
In swifter sallies darting to the brain—
Where sits the soul, intense, collected, cool,
Bright as the skies, and as the season keen.
All nature feels the renovating force
Of Winter—only to the thoughtless eye
In ruin seen. The frost-concocted glebe
Draws in abundant vegetable soul,
And gathers vigour for the coming year;
A stronger glow sits on the lively cheek,
Of ruddy fire; and luculent along   710
The purer rivers flow; their sullen deeps,
Transparent, open to the shepherd's gaze,
And murmur hoarser at the fixing frost.
    What art thou, Frost? and whence are thy keen stores
Derived, thou secret all-invading power,
Whom even the illusive fluid cannot fly?
Is not thy potent energy, unseen,

Myriads of little salts, or hooked, or shaped
Like double wedges, and diffused immense
Through water, earth, and ether? Hence at eve,   **720**
Steamed eager from the red horizon round,
With the fierce rage of Winter deep suffused,
An icy gale, oft shifting, o'er the pool
Breathes a blue film, and in its mid-career
Arrests the bickering stream. The loosened ice,
Let down the flood and half dissolved by day,
Rustles no more; but to the sedgy bank
Fast grows, or gathers round the pointed stone,
A crystal pavement, by the breath of heaven
Cemented firm; till, seized from shore to shore,   **730**
The whole imprisoned river growls below.
Loud rings the frozen earth, and hard reflects
A double noise; while, at his evening watch,
The village dog deters the nightly thief;
The heifer lows; the distant waterfall
Swells in the breeze; and with the hasty tread
Of traveller the hollow-sounding plain
Shakes from afar. The full ethereal round,
Infinite worlds disclosing to the view,
Shines out intensely keen, and, all one cope   **740**
Of starry glitter, glows from pole to pole.
From pole to pole the rigid influence falls
Through the still night, incessant, heavy, strong,
And seizes nature fast. It freezes on,
Till morn, late-rising o'er the drooping world,
Lifts her pale eye unjoyous. Then appears
The various labour of the silent night:
Prone from the dripping eave and dumb cascade,
Whose idle torrents only seem to roar,
The pendent icicle; the frost-work fair,   **750**
Where transient hues and fancied figures rise;
Wide-spouted o'er the hill the frozen brook,
A livid tract, cold-gleaming on the morn;
The forest bent beneath the plumy wave;
And by the frost refined the whiter snow
Incrusted hard, and sounding to the tread
Of early shepherd, as he pensive seeks
His pining flock, or from the mountain top,
Pleased with the slippery surface, swift descends.
   On blithesome frolics bent, the youthful swains,   **760**
While every work of man is laid at rest,
Fond o'er the river crowd, in various sport
And revelry dissolved; where, mixing glad,
Happiest of all the train! the raptured boy
Lashes the whirling top. Or, where the Rhine
Branched out in many a long canal extends,
From every province swarming, void of care,
Batavia rushes forth; and, as they sweep
On sounding skates a thousand different ways
In circling poise swift as the winds along,   **770**
The then gay land is maddened all to joy.
Nor less the northern courts, wide o'er the snow.

Pour a new pomp. Eager, on rapid sleds,
Their vigorous youth in bold contention wheel
The long-resounding course. Meantime, to raise
The manly strife, with highly blooming charms
Flushed by the season, Scandinavia's dames
Or Russia's buxom daughters glow around.
　　Pure, quick, and sportful is the wholesome day,
But soon elapsed. The horizontal sun   780
Broad o'er the south hangs at his utmost noon,
And ineffectual strikes the gelid cliff.
His azure gloss the mountain still maintains,
Nor feels the feeble touch. Perhaps the vale
Relents awhile to the reflected ray;
Or from the forest falls the clustered snow,
Myriads of gems, that in the waving gleam
Gay-twinkle as they scatter. Thick around
Thunders the sport of those who with the gun,
And dog impatient bounding at the shot,   790
Worse than the season desolate the fields,
And, adding to the ruins of the year,
Distress the footed or the feathered game.
　　But what is this? Our infant Winter sinks
Divested of his grandeur should our eye
Astonished shoot into the frigid zone,
Where for relentless months continual Night
Holds o'er the glittering waste her starry reign.
There, through the prison of unbounded wilds,
Barred by the hand of Nature from escape,   800
Wide roams the Russian exile. Naught around
Strikes his sad eye but deserts lost in snow,
And heavy-loaded groves, and solid floods
That stretch athwart the solitary vast
Their icy horrors to the frozen main,
And cheerless towns far distant—never blessed,
Save when its annual course the caravan
Bends to the golden coast of rich Cathay,
With news of humankind. Yet there life glows;
Yet, cherished there, beneath the shining waste   810
The furry nations harbour—tipped with jet,
Fair ermines spotless as the snows they press;
Sables of glossy black; and, dark-embrowned,
Or beauteous freaked with many a mingled hue,
Thousands besides, the costly pride of courts.
There, warm together pressed, the trooping deer
Sleep on the new-fallen snows; and, scarce his head
Raised o'er the heapy wreath, the branching elk
Lies slumbering sullen in the white abyss.
The ruthless hunter wants nor dogs nor toils,   820
Nor with the dread of sounding bows he drives
The fearful flying race—with ponderous clubs,
As weak against the mountain-heaps they push
Their beating breast in vain, and piteous bray,
He lays them quivering on the ensanguined snows,
And with loud shouts rejoicing bears them home.
There, through the piny forest half-absorpt.

Rough tenant of these shades, the shapeless bear,
With dangling ice all horrid, stalks forlorn;
Slow-paced, and sourer as the storms increase,   830
He makes his bed beneath the inclement drift,
And, with stern patience, scorning weak complaint,
Hardens his heart against assailing want.
   Wide o'er the spacious regions of the north,
That see Boötes urge his tardy wain,
A boisterous race, by frosty Caurus pierced,
Who little pleasure know and fear no pain,
Prolific swarm. They once relumed the flame
Of lost mankind in polished slavery sunk;
Drove martial horde on horde, with dreadful sweep   840
Resistless rushing o'er the enfeebled south,
And gave the vanquished world another form.
Not such the sons of Lapland: wisely they
Despise the insensate barbarous trade of war;
They ask no more than simple Nature gives;
They love their mountains and enjoy their storms.
No false desires, no pride-created wants,
Disturb the peaceful current of their time,
And through the restless ever-tortured maze
Of pleasure or ambition bid it rage.   850
Their reindeer form their riches. These their tents,
Their robes, their beds, and all their homely wealth
Supply, their wholesome fare, and cheerful cups.
Obsequious at their call, the docile tribe
Yield to the sled their necks, and whirl them swift
O'er hill and dale, heaped into one expanse
Of marbled snow, or, far as eye can sweep,
With a blue crust of ice unbounded glazed.
By dancing meteors then, that ceaseless shake
A waving blaze refracted o'er the heavens,   860
And vivid moons, and stars that keener play
With doubled lustre from the radiant waste,
Even in the depth of polar night they find
A wondrous day —enough to light the chase
Or guide their daring steps to Finland fairs.
Wished Spring returns; and from the hazy south,
While dim Aurora slowly moves before,
The welcome sun, just verging up at first,
By small degrees extends the swelling curve;
Till, seen at last for gay rejoicing months,   870
Still round and round his spiral course he winds,
And, as he nearly dips his flaming orb,
Wheels up again and re-ascends the sky.
In that glad season, from the lakes and floods,
Where pure Niëmi's fairy mountains rise,
And fringed with roses Tenglio rolls his stream,
They draw the copious fry. With these at eve
They cheerful-loaded to their tents repair,
Where, all day long in useful cares employed,
Their kind unblemished wives the fire prepare.   880
Thrice happy race! by poverty secured
From legal plunder and rapacious power,

In whom fell interest never yet has sown
The seeds of vice, whose spotless swains ne'er knew
Injurious deed, nor, blasted by the breath
Of faithless love, their blooming daughters woe.
    Still pressing on, beyond Tornea's lake,
And Hecla flaming through a waste of snow,
And farthest Greenland, to the pole itself,
Where, failing gradual, life at length goes out,   890
The Muse expands her solitary flight;
And, hovering o'er the wild stupendous scene,
Beholds new seas beneath another sky.
Throned in his palace of cerulean ice,
Here Winter holds his unrejoicing court,
And through his airy hall the loud misrule
Of driving tempest is forever heard;
Here the grim tyrant meditates his wrath;
Here arms his winds with all-subduing frost;
Moulds his fierce hail, and treasures up his snows,   900
With which he now oppresses half the globe.
    Thence winding eastward to the Tartar's coast,
She sweeps the howling margin of the main,
Where, undissolving from the first of time,
Snows swell on snows amazing to the sky;
And icy mountains high on mountains piled
Seem to the shivering sailor from afar,
Shapeless and white, an atmosphere of clouds.
Projected huge and horrid o'er the surge,
Alps frown on Alps; or, rushing hideous down,   910
As if old Chaos was again returned,
Wide-rend the deep and shake the solid pole.
Ocean itself no longer can resist
The binding fury; but, in all its rage
Of tempest taken by the boundless frost,
Is many a fathom to the bottom chained,
And bid to roar no more—a bleak expanse
Shagged o'er with wavy rocks, cheerless, and void
Of every life, that from the dreary months
Flies conscious southward. Miserable they!   920
Who, here entangled in the gathering ice,
Take their last look of the descending sun;
While, full of death and fierce with tenfold frost,
The long long night, incumbent o'er their heads,
Falls horrible! Such was the Briton's fate,
As with first prow (what have not Britons dared?)
He for the passage sought, attempted since
So much in vain, and seeming to be shut
By jealous Nature with eternal bars.
In these fell regions, in Arzina caught,   930
And to the stony deep his idle ship
Immediate sealed, he with his hapless crew,
Each full exerted at his several task,
Froze into statues—to the cordage glued
The sailor, and the pilot to the helm.
    Hard by these shores, where scarce his freezing stream
Rolls the wild Oby, live the last of men;

And, half enlivened by the distant sun,
That rears and ripens man as well as plants,
Here human nature wears its rudest form.   940
Deep from the piercing season sunk in caves,
Here by dull fires and with unjoyous cheer
They waste the tedious gloom: immersed in furs
Doze the gross race—nor sprightly jest nor song
Nor tenderness they know, nor aught of life
Beyond the kindred bears that stalk without—
Till Morn at length, her roses drooping all,
Sheds a long twilight brightening o'er their fields,
And calls the quivered savage to the chase.

What cannot active government perform,   950
New-moulding man? Wide-stretching from these shores,
A people savage from remotest time,
A huge neglected empire, one vast mind
By Heaven inspired from Gothic darkness called.
Immortal Peter! first of monarchs! He
His stubborn country tamed,—her rocks, her fens,
Her floods, her seas, her ill-submitting sons;
And, while the fierce barbarian he subdued,
To more exalted soul he raised the man.
Ye shades of ancient heroes, ye who toiled   960
Through long successive ages to build up
A labouring plan of state, behold at once
The wonder done! behold the matchless prince!
Who left his native throne, where reigned till then
A mighty shadow of unreal power;
Who greatly spurned the slothful pomp of courts;
And, roaming every land, in every port
His sceptre laid aside, with glorious hand
Unwearied plying the mechanic tool,
Gathered the seeds of trade, of useful arts,   970
Of civil wisdom, and of martial skill.
Charged with the stores of Europe home he goes!
Then cities rise amid the illumined waste;
O'er joyless deserts smiles the rural reign;
Far-distant flood to flood is social joined;
The astonished Euxine hears the Baltic roar;
Proud navies ride on seas that never foamed
With daring keel before; and armies stretch
Each way their dazzling files, repressing here
The frantic Alexander of the north,   980
And awing there stern Othman's shrinking sons.
Sloth flies the land, and ignorance and vice,
Of old dishonour proud; it glows around,
Taught by the royal hand that roused the whole,
One scene of arts, of arms, of rising trade—
For, what his wisdom planned and power enforced,
More potent still his great example showed.

Muttering, the winds at eve with blunted point
Blow hollow-blustering from the south. Subdued,
The frost resolves into a trickling thaw.   990
Spotted the mountains shine; loose sleet descends,
And floods the country round. The rivers swell,

Of bonds impatient. Sudden from the hills,
O'er rocks and woods, in broad brown cataracts,
A thousand snow-fed torrents shoot at once;
And, where they rush, the wide-resounding plain
Is left one slimy waste. Those sullen seas,
That wash the ungenial pole, will rest no more
Beneath the shackles of the mighty north,
But, rousing all their waves, resistless heave.   1000
And hark! the lengthening roar continuous runs
Athwart the rifted deep; at once it bursts,
And piles a thousand mountains to the clouds.
Ill fares the bark, with trembling wretches charged,
That, tossed amid the floating fragments, moors
Beneath the shelter of an icy isle,
While night o'erwhelms the sea, and horror looks
More horrible. Can human force endure
The assembled mischiefs that besiege them round?—
Heart-gnawing hunger, fainting weariness,   1010
The roar of winds and waves, the crush of ice,
Now ceasing, now renewed with louder rage,
And in dire echoes bellowing round the main.
More to embroil the deep, Leviathan
And his unwieldy train in dreadful sport
Tempest the loosened brine; while through the gloom
Far from the bleak inhospitable shore,
Loading the winds, is heard the hungry howl
Of famished monsters, there awaiting wrecks.
Yet Providence, that ever-waking Eye,   1020
Looks down with pity on the feeble toil
Of mortals lost to hope, and lights them safe
Through all this dreary labyrinth of fate.
      'Tis done! Dread Winter spreads his latest glooms,
And reigns tremendous o'er the conquered year.
How dead the vegetable kingdom lies!
How dumb the tuneful! Horror wide extends
His desolate domain. Behold, fond man!
See here thy pictured life; pass some few years,
Thy flowering Spring, thy Summer's ardent strength,   1030
Thy sober Autumn fading into age,
And pale concluding Winter comes at last
And shuts the scene. Ah! whither now are fled
Those dreams of greatness? those unsolid hopes
Of happiness? those longings after fame?
Those restless cares? those busy bustling days?
Those gay-spent festive nights? those veering thoughts,
Lost between good and ill, that shared thy life?
All now are vanished! Virtue sole survives—
Immortal, never-failing friend of man,   1040
His guide to happiness on high. And see!
'Tis come, the glorious morn! the second birth
Of heaven and earth! awakening Nature hears
The new-creating word, and starts to life
In every heightened form, from pain and death
Forever free. The great eternal scheme,
Involving all, and in a perfect whole

Uniting, as the prospect wider spreads,
To reason's eye refined clears up apace,
Ye vainly wise! ye blind presumptuous! now,   1050
Confounded in the dust, adore that Power
And Wisdom—oft arraigned: see now the cause
Why unassuming worth in secret lived
And died neglected; why the good man's share
In life was gall and bitterness of soul;
Why the lone widow and her orphans pined
In starving solitude, while Luxury
In palaces lay straining her low thought
To form unreal wants; why heaven-born Truth
And Moderation fair wore the red marks   1060
Of Superstition's scourge; why licensed Pain,
That cruel spoiler, that embosomed foe,
Embittered all our bliss. Ye good distressed!
Ye noble few! who here unbending stand
Beneath life's pressure, yet bear up a while,
And what your bounded view, which only saw
A little part, deemed evil, is no more.
The storms of wintry time will quickly pass,
And one unbounded Spring encircle all.

[1726–46]

A HYMN

These, as they change, Almighty Father! these
Are but the varied God. The rolling year
Is full of Thee. Forth in the pleasing Spring
Thy beauty walks, Thy tenderness and love.
Wide flush the fields; the softening air is balm;
Echo the mountains round; the forest smiles;
And every sense, and every heart, is joy.
Then comes Thy glory in the Summer-months,
With light and heat refulgent. Then Thy sun
Shoots full perfection through the swelling year: 10
And oft Thy voice in dreadful thunder speaks,
And oft, at dawn, deep noon, or falling eve,
By brooks and groves, in hollow-whispering gales.
Thy bounty shines in Autumn unconfined,
And spreads a common feast for all that lives.
In Winter awful Thou! with clouds and storms
Around Thee thrown, tempest o'er tempest rolled,
Majestic darkness! On the whirlwind's wing
Riding sublime, Thou bidst the world adore,
And humblest nature with Thy northern blast.   20
    Mysterious round! what skill, what force divine,
Deep-felt in these appear! a simple train,
Yet so delightful mixed, with such kind art,
Such beauty and beneficence combined,
Shade unperceived so softening into shade,
And all so forming an harmonious whole
That, as they still succeed, they ravish still.

But, wandering oft with brute unconscious gaze,
Man marks not Thee, marks not the mighty hand
That ever busy wheels the silent spheres,   30
Works in the secret deep, shoots steaming thence
The fair profusion that o'erspreads the Spring,
Flings from the sun direct the flaming day,
Feeds every creature, hurls the tempest forth,
And, as on earth this grateful change revolves,
With transport touches all the springs of life.
    Nature, attend! join every living soul
Beneath the spacious temple of the sky,
In adoration join; and ardent raise
One general song! To Him, ye vocal gales,   40
Breathe soft, whose Spirit in your freshness breathes:
Oh! talk of Him in solitary glooms,
Where, o'er the rock, the scarcely-waving pine
Fills the brown shade with a religious awe.
And ye, whose bolder note is heard afar,
Who shake the astonished world, lift high to Heaven
The impetuous song, and say from whom you rage.
His praise, ye brooks, attune, ye trembling rills;
And let me catch it as I muse along.
Ye headlong torrents, rapid and profound;   50
Ye softer floods, that lead the humid maze
Along the vale; and thou, majestic main,
A secret world of wonders in thyself,
Sound His stupendous praise, whose greater voice
Or bids you roar or bids your roarings fall.
Soft-roll your incense, herbs, and fruits, and flowers,
In mingled clouds to Him, whose sun exalts,
Whose breath perfumes you, and whose pencil paints.
Ye forests, bend; ye harvests, wave to Him—
Breathe your still song into the reaper's heart   60
As home he goes beneath the joyous moon.
Ye that keep watch in heaven, as earth asleep
Unconscious lies, effuse your mildest beams,
Ye constellations! while your angels strike
Amid the spangled sky the silver lyre.
Great source of day! best image here below
Of thy Creator, ever pouring wide
From world to world the vital ocean round!
On nature write with every beam His praise.
The thunder rolls: be hushed the prostrate world,   70
While cloud to cloud returns the solemn hymn.
Bleat out afresh, ye hills; ye mossy rocks,
Retain the sound; the broad responsive low,
Ye valleys, raise; for the Great Shepherd reigns,
And His unsuffering kingdom yet will come.
Ye woodlands all, awake: a boundless song
Burst from the groves; and, when the restless day,
Expiring, lays the warbling world asleep,
Sweetest of birds, sweet Philomela! charm
The listening shades, and teach the night His praise!   80
Ye, chief, for whom the whole creation smiles,
At once the head, the heart, the tongue of all,

Crown the great hymn! In swarming cities vast,
Assembled men, to the deep organ join
The long-resounding voice, oft breaking clear
At solemn pauses through the swelling bass;
And, as each mingling flame increases each,
In one united ardour rise to Heaven.
Or, if you rather choose the rural shade,
And find a fane in every sacred grove,   90
There let the shepherd's flute, the virgin's lay,
The prompting seraph, and the poet's lyre
Still sing the God of Seasons as they roll.
For me, when I forget the darling theme,
Whether the blossom blows, the summer-ray
Russets the plain, inspiring Autumn gleams,
Or Winter rises in the blackening east,
Be my tongue mute, may fancy paint no more,
And, dead to joy, forget my heart to beat!

Should fate command me to the farthest verge   100
Of the green earth, to distant barbarous climes,
Rivers unknown to song, where first the sun
Gilds Indian mountains, or his setting beam
Flames on the Atlantic isles, 'tis naught to me;
Since God is ever present, ever felt,
In the void waste as in the city full,
And where He vital spreads there must be joy.
When even at last the solemn hour shall come,
And wing my mystic flight to future worlds,
I cheerful will obey; there, with new powers,   110
Will rising wonders sing: I cannot go
Where Universal Love not smiles around,
Sustaining all yon orbs and all their sons;
From seeming evil still educing good,
And better thence again, and better still,
In infinite progression. But I lose
Myself in Him, in light ineffable!
Come then, expressive Silence, muse His praise.

[1730–46]

RULE, BRITANNIA!

When Britain first, at Heaven's command,
  Arose from out the azure main,
This was the charter of the land,
  And guardian angels sung this strain—
    "Rule, Britannia, rule the waves;
    Britons never will be slaves."

The nations, not so blessed as thee,
  Must in their turns to tyrants fall;
While thou shalt flourish great and free,
  The dread and envy of them all.   10
    "Rule," &c.

Still more majestic shalt thou rise,
  More dreadful from each foreign stroke;
As the loud blast that tears the skies
  Serves but to root thy native oak.
    "Rule," &c.

Thee haughty tyrants ne'er shall tame;
  All their attempts to bend thee down
Will but arouse thy generous flame,
  But work their woe and thy renown.   20
    "Rule," &c.

To thee belongs the rural reign;
  Thy cities shall with commerce shine;

All thine shall be the subject main,
 And every shore it circles thine.
    "Rule," &c.

The Muses, still with freedom found,
 Shall to thy happy coast repair:

Blessed isle! with matchless beauty crowned,
 And manly hearts to guard the fair.   30
    "Rule, Britannia, rule the waves;
    Britons never will be slaves."

[1740]

THE CASTLE OF INDOLENCE

ADVERTISEMENT

This poem being writ in the manner of Spenser, the obsolete words, and a simplicity of diction in some of the lines which borders on the ludicrous, were necessary to make the imitation more perfect. And the style of that admirable poet, as well as the measure in which he wrote, are as it were appropriated by custom to all allegorical poems writ in our language—just as in French the style of Marot, who lived under Francis I, has been used in tales and familiar epistles by the politest writers of the age of Louis XIV.

CANTO I

The Castle hight of Indolence,
  And its false luxury;
Where for a little time, alas!
  We lived right jollily.

I

O mortal man, who livest here by toil,
 Do not complain of this thy hard estate;
 That like an emmet thou must ever moil
 Is a sad sentence of an ancient date:
 And, certes, there is for it reason great;
 For though sometimes it makes thee weep and wail,
 And curse thy stars, and early drudge and late,
 Withouten that would come an heavier bale,
Loose life, unruly passions, and diseases pale.

II

In lowly dale, fast by a river's side,   10
 With woody hill o'er hill encompassed round,
 A most enchanting wizard did abide,
 Than whom a fiend more fell is nowhere found.
 It was, I ween, a lovely spot of ground;
 And there a season atween June and May,
 Half pranked with spring, with summer half imbrowned,
 A listless climate made, where, sooth to say,
No living wight could work, ne carèd even for play.

III

Was naught around but images of rest:
 Sleep-soothing groves, and quiet lawns between;   20
 And flowery beds that slumbrous influence kest,[1]

_____
[1] Cast.

From poppies breathed; and beds of pleasant green,
Where never yet was creeping creature seen.
Meantime unnumbered glittering streamlets played,
And hurlèd everywhere their waters sheen;
That, as they bickered through the sunny glade,
Though restless still themselves, a lulling murmur made.

IV

Joined to the prattle of the purling rills,
Were heard the lowing herds along the vale,
And flocks loud-bleating from the distant hills,   30
And vacant[2] shepherds piping in the dale:
And now and then sweet Philomel would wail,
Or stock-doves plain amid the forest deep,
That drowsy rustled to the sighing gale;
And still a coil[3] the grasshopper did keep:
Yet all these sounds yblent[4] inclined all to sleep.

V

Full in the passage of the vale, above,
A sable, silent, solemn forest stood;
Where naught but shadowy forms were seen to move,
As Idless fancied in her dreaming mood.   40
And up the hills, on either side, a wood
Of blackening pines, aye waving to and fro,
Sent forth a sleepy horror through the blood;
And where this valley winded out below,
The murmuring main was heard, and scarcely heard, to flow.

VI

A pleasing land of drowsyhed it was:
Of dreams that wave before the half-shut eye;
And of gay castles in the clouds that pass,
Forever flushing round a summer sky:
There eke the soft delights, that witchingly   50
Instil a wanton sweetness through the breast,
And the calm pleasures always hovered nigh;
But whate'er smacked of noyance or unrest
Was far far off expelled from this delicious nest.

VII

The landskip such, inspiring perfect ease;
Where Indolence (for so the wizard hight)
Close-hid his castle mid embowering trees,
That half shut out the beam of Phoebus bright,
And made a kind of checkered day and night.
Meanwhile, unceasing at the massy gate,   60
Beneath a spacious palm, the wicked wight

[2] Carefree.
[3] Disturbance, noise.
[4] Blended.

Was placed; and, to his lute, of cruel fate
And labour harsh complained, lamenting man's estate.

VIII

Thither continual pilgrims crowded still
From all the roads of earth that pass thereby:
For, as they chaunced to breathe[5] on neighbouring hill,
The freshness of this valley smote their eye,
And drew them ever and anon more nigh,
Till clustering round the enchanter false they hung,
Ymolten with his siren melody;   70
While o'er the enfeebling lute his hand he flung,
And to the trembling chord these tempting verses sung:

IX

"Behold! ye pilgrims of this earth, behold!
See all but man with unearned pleasure gay.
See her bright robes the butterfly unfold,
Broke from her wintry tomb in prime of May.
What youthful bride can equal her array?
Who can with her for easy pleasure vie?
From mead to mead with gentle wing to stray,
From flower to flower on balmy gales to fly,   80
Is all she has to do beneath the radiant sky.

X

"Behold the merry minstrels of the morn,
The swarming songsters of the careless grove,
Ten thousand throats that, from the flowering thorn,
Hymn their good God, and carol sweet of love,
Such grateful kindly raptures them emove!
They neither plough nor sow; ne, fit for flail,
E'er to the barn the nodding sheaves they drove;
Yet theirs each harvest dancing in the gale,
Whatever crowns the hill, or smiles along the vale.   90

XI

"Outcast of Nature, man! the wretched thrall
Of bitter-dropping sweat, of sweltry pain,
Of cares that eat away thy heart with gall,
And of the vices, an inhuman train,
That all proceed from savage thirst of gain:
For when hard-hearted Interest first began
To poison earth, Astraea left the plain;
Guile, Violence, and Murder seized on man,
And, for soft milky streams, with blood the rivers ran.

XII

"Come, ye, who still the cumbrous load of life   100
Push hard up hill; but, as the farthest steep

[5] Pause to take breath.

You trust to gain, and put an end to strife,
Down thunders back the stone with mighty sweep,
And hurls your labours to the valley deep,
Forever vain: come, and withouten fee
I in oblivion will your sorrows steep,
Your cares, your toils; will steep you in a sea
Of full delight—O come, ye weary wights, to me!

XIII

"With me, you need not rise at early dawn,
To pass the joyless day in various stounds;[6]   110
Or, louting[7] low, on upstart fortune fawn,
And sell fair honour for some paltry pounds;
Or through the city take your dirty rounds,
To cheat, and dun, and lie, and visit pay,
Now flattering base, now giving secret wounds;
Or prowl in courts of law for human prey,
In venal senate thieve, or rob on broad highway.

XIV

"No cocks, with me, to rustic labour call,
From village on to village sounding clear;
To tardy swain no shrill-voiced matrons squall;   120
No dogs, no babes, no wives to stun your ear;
No hammers thump; no horrid blacksmith sear,
Ne noisy tradesman your sweet slumbers start
With sounds that are a misery to hear:
But all is calm as would delight the heart
Of Sybarite of old, all nature, and all art.

XV

"Here naught but candour reigns, indulgent ease,
Good-natured lounging, sauntering up and down;
They who are pleased themselves must always please;
On others' ways they never squint a frown,   130
Nor heed what haps in hamlet or in town.
Thus, from the source of tender Indolence,
With milky blood the heart is overflown,
Is soothed and sweetened by the social sense;
For interest, envy, pride, and strife are banished hence.

XVI

"What, what is virtue but repose of mind?
A pure ethereal calm that knows no storm,
Above the reach of wild ambition's wind,
Above those passions that this world deform,
And torture man, a proud malignant worm!   140
But here, instead, soft gales of passion play,
And gently stir the heart, thereby to form

---

[6] Painful efforts.
[7] Bowing.

A quicker sense of joy; as breezes stray
Across the enlivened skies, and make them still more gay.

XVII

"The best of men have ever loved repose:
They hate to mingle in the filthy fray;
Where the soul sours, and gradual rancour grows,
Imbittered more from peevish day to day.
Even those whom Fame has lent her fairest ray,
The most renowned of worthy wights of yore,   150
From a base world at last have stolen away:
So Scipio, to the soft Cumaean shore
Retiring, tasted joy he never knew before.

XVIII

"But if a little exercise you choose,
Some zest for ease, 'tis not forbidden here.
Amid the groves you may indulge the Muse,
Or tend the blooms and deck the vernal year;
Or softly stealing with your watery gear
Along the brooks, the crimson-spotted fry
You may delude: the whilst, amused,[8] you hear   160
Now the hoarse stream, and now the zephyr's sigh,
Attunèd to the birds, and woodland melody.

XIX

"O grievous folly! to heap up estate,
Losing the days you see beneath the sun;
When, sudden, comes blind unrelenting fate,
And gives the untasted portion you have won
With ruthless toil, and many a wretch undone,
To those who mock you, gone to Pluto's reign,
There with sad ghosts to pine and shadows dun:
But sure it is of vanities most vain,   170
To toil for what you here untoiling may obtain."

XX

He ceased. But still their trembling ears retained
The deep vibrations of his witching song;
That, by a kind of magic power, constrained
To enter in, pell-mell, the listening throng.
Heaps poured on heaps, and yet they slipped along
In silent ease: as when, beneath the beam
Of summer moons, the distant woods among,
Or by some flood all silvered with the gleam,
The soft-embodied fays through airy portal stream.   180

XXI

By the smooth demon so it ordered was,
And here his baneful bounty first began;

[8] In a pleasant reverie.

Though some there were who would not further pass,
And his alluring baits suspected han.
The wise distrust the too fair-spoken man.
Yet through the gate they cast a wishful eye:
Not to move on, perdie, is all they can;
For, do their very best, they cannot fly,
But often each way look, and often sorely sigh.

XXII

When this the watchful wicked wizard saw,   190
With sudden spring he leaped upon them strait;
And, soon as touched by his unhallowed paw,
They found themselves within the cursèd gate,
Full hard to be repassed, like that of Fate.
Not stronger were of old the giant-crew,
Who sought to pull high Jove from regal state,
Though feeble wretch he seemed, of sallow hue:
Certes, who bides his grasp, will that encounter rue.

XXIII

For whomsoe'er the villain takes in hand,
Their joints unknit, their sinews melt apace;   200
As lithe they grow as any willow-wand,
And of their vanished force remains no trace:
So when a maiden fair, of modest grace,
In all her buxom blooming May of charms,
Is seizèd in some losel's⁹ hot embrace,
She waxeth very weakly as she warms,
Then sighing yields her up to love's delicious harms.

XXIV

Waked by the crowd, slow from his bench arose
A comely full-spread porter, swoln with sleep:
His calm, broad, thoughtless aspect breathed repose;   210
And in sweet torpor he was plungèd deep,
Ne could himself from ceaseless yawning keep;
While o'er his eyes the drowsy liquor ran,
Through which his half-waked soul would faintly peep.
Then, taking his black staff, he called his man,
And roused himself as much as rouse himself he can.

XXV

The lad leaped lightly at his master's call.
He was, to weet, a little roguish page,
Save sleep and play who minded naught at all,
Like most the untaught striplings of his age.   220
This boy he kept each band to disengage,
Garters and buckles, task for him unfit,
But ill-becoming his grave personage,

⁹ Libertine's.

And which his portly paunch would not permit.
So this same limber page to all performèd it.

XXVI

Meantime the master-porter wide displayed
Great store of caps, of slippers, and of gowns,
Wherewith he those who entered in arrayed,
Loose as the breeze that plays along the downs,
And waves the summer woods when evening frowns.   230
O fair undress, best dress! it checks no vein,
But every flowing limb in pleasure drowns,
And heightens ease with grace. This done, right fain
Sir Porter sat him down, and turned to sleep again.

XXVII

Thus easy robed, they to the fountain sped,
That in the middle of the court up-threw
A stream, high-spouting from its liquid bed,
And falling back again in drizzly dew:
There each deep draughts, as deep he thirsted, drew;
It was a fountain of Nepenthe rare: 240
Whence, as Dan Homer sings, huge pleasaunce grew,
And sweet oblivion of vile earthly care,
Fair gladsome waking thoughts, and joyous dreams more fair.

XXVIII

This rite performed, all inly pleased and still,
Withouten trump was proclamation made:—
"Ye sons of Indolence, do what you will;
And wander where you list, through hall or glade;
Be no man's pleasure for another's staid:
Let each as likes him best his hours employ,
And cursed be he who minds his neighbour's trade!   250
Here dwells kind ease, and unreproving joy:
He little merits bliss who others can annoy."

XXIX

Strait of these endless numbers, swarming round
As thick as idle motes in sunny ray,
Not one eftsoons[10] in view was to be found,
But every man strolled off his own glad way.
Wide o'er this ample court's blank area,
With all the lodges that thereto pertained,
No living creature could be seen to stray;
While solitude and perfect silence reigned: 260
So that to think you dreamt you almost was constrained.

XXX

As when a shepherd of the Hebrid Isles,
Placed far amid the melancholy main,

(Whether it be lone fancy him beguiles,
Or that aërial beings sometimes deign
To stand embodied to our senses plain)
Sees on the naked hill, or valley low,
The whilst in ocean Phoebus dips his wain,
A vast assembly moving to and fro;
Then all at once in air dissolves the wondrous show.   270

XXXI

Ye gods of quiet, and of sleep profound,
Whose soft dominion o'er this castle sways,
And all the widely-silent places round,
Forgive me, if my trembling pen displays
What never yet was sung in mortal lays.
But how shall I attempt such arduous string?
I who have spent my nights and nightly days
In this soul-deadening place, loose-loitering—
Ah! how shall I for this uprear my moulted wing?

XXXII

Come on, my Muse, nor stoop to low despair,   280
Thou imp[11] of Jove, touched by celestial fire!
Thou yet shalt sing of war, and actions fair,
Which the bold sons of Britain will inspire;
Of ancient bards thou yet shalt sweep the lyre;
Thou yet shalt tread in tragic pall the stage,
Paint love's enchanting woes, the hero's ire,
The sage's calm, the patriot's noble rage,
Dashing corruption down through every worthless age.

XXXIII

The doors, that knew no shrill alarming bell,
Ne cursèd knocker plied by villain's hand,   290
Self-opened into halls where, who can tell
What elegance and grandeur wide expand
The pride of Turkey and of Persia land?
Soft quilts on quilts, on carpets carpets spread,
And couches stretch around in seemly band,
And endless pillows rise to prop the head;
So that each spacious room was one full-swelling bed.

XXXIV

And everywhere huge covered tables stood,
With wines high-flavoured and rich viands crowned;
Whatever sprightly juice or tasteful food   300
On the green bosom of this earth are found,
And all old Ocean genders in his round—
Some hand unseen these silently displayed,
Even undemanded by a sign or sound;

[11] Child, offspring.

You need but wish, and, instantly obeyed,
Fair-ranged the dishes rose, and thick the glasses played.

XXXV

Here freedom reigned without the least alloy;
Nor gossip's tale, nor ancient maiden's gall,
Nor saintly spleen durst murmur at our joy,
And with envenomed tongue our pleasures pall.   310
For why? There was but one great rule for all;
To wit, that each should work his own desire,
And eat, drink, study, sleep, as it may fall,
Or melt the time in love, or wake the lyre,
And carol what, unbid, the Muses might inspire.

XXXVI

The rooms with costly tapestry were hung,
Where was inwoven many a gentle tale,
Such as of old the rural poets sung
Or of Arcadian or Sicilian vale:
Reclining lovers in the lonely dale   320
Poured forth at large the sweetly tortured heart;
Or, looking tender passion, swelled the gale,
And taught charmed echo to resound their smart;
While flocks, woods, streams around, repose and peace impart.

XXXVII

Those pleased the most, where, by a cunning hand,
Depeinten was the patriarchal age;
What time Dan Abraham left the Chaldee land,
And pastured on from verdant stage to stage,
Where fields and fountains fresh could best engage.
Toil was not then. Of nothing took they heed,   330
But with wild beasts the silvan war to wage,
And o'er vast plains their herds and flocks to feed:
Blest sons of nature they: true golden age indeed!

XXXVIII

Sometimes the pencil, in cool airy halls,
Bade the gay bloom of vernal landskips rise,
Or autumn's varied shades imbrown the walls:
Now the black tempest strikes the astonished eyes;
Now down the steep the flashing torrent flies;
The trembling sun now plays o'er ocean blue,
And now rude mountains frown amid the skies;   340
Whate'er Lorrain light-touched with softening hue,
Or savage Rosa dashed, or learnèd Poussin drew.

XXXIX

Each sound too here to languishment inclined,
Lulled the weak bosom, and inducèd ease,

Aërial music in the warbling wind,
At distance rising oft, by small degrees,
Nearer and nearer came, till o'er the trees
It hung, and breathed such soul-dissolving airs
As did, alas! with soft perdition please:
Entangled deep in its enchanting snares,   35 4
The listening heart forgot all duties and all cares.

XL

A certain music, never known before,
Here lulled the pensive melancholy mind;
Full easily obtained. Behoves no more,
But sidelong to the gently-waving wind
To lay the well-tuned instrument reclined;
From which, with airy flying fingers light,
Beyond each mortal touch the most refined,
The god of winds drew sounds of deep delight:
Whence, with just cause, The Harp of Aeolus it hight.   360

XLI

Ah me! what hand can touch the strings so fine?
Who up the lofty diapason roll
Such sweet, such sad, such solemn airs divine,
Then let them down again into the soul?
Now rising love they fanned; now pleasing dole
They breathed, in tender musings, through the heart;
And now a graver sacred strain they stole,
As when seraphic hands an hymn impart:
Wild warbling nature all, above the reach of art!

XLII

Such the gay splendor, the luxurious state,   570
Of Caliphs old, who on the Tygris' shore,
In mighty Bagdat, populous and great,
Held their bright court, where was of ladies store;
And verse, love, music still the garland wore:
When sleep was coy, the bard in waiting there
Cheered the lone midnight with the Muse's lore;
Composing music bade his dreams be fair,
And music lent new gladness to the morning air.

XLIII

Near the pavilions where we slept, still ran
Soft-tinkling streams, and dashing waters fell,   380
And sobbing breezes sighed, and oft began
(So worked the wizard) wintry storms to swell,
As heaven and earth they would together mell:[12]
At doors and windows, threatening, seemed to call
The demons of the tempest, growling fell;

[12] Mingle.

Yet the least entrance found they none at all;
Whence sweeter grew our sleep, secure in massy hall.

XLIV

And hither Morpheus sent his kindest dreams,
Raising a world of gayer tinct and grace;
O'er which were shadowy cast Elysian gleams,   390
That played in waving lights from place to place,
And shed a roseate smile on nature's face.
Not Titian's pencil e'er could so array,
So fleece with clouds the pure ethereal space;
Ne could it e'er such melting forms display,
As loose on flowery beds all languishingly lay.

XLV

No, fair illusions! artful phantoms, no!
My Muse will not attempt your fairyland:
She has no colours that like you can glow;
To catch your vivid scenes too gross her hand.   400
But sure it is, was ne'er a subtler band
Than these same guileful angel-seeming sprites,
Who thus in dreams voluptuous, soft, and bland,
Poured all the Arabian heaven upon our nights,
And blessed them oft besides with more refined delights.

XLVI

They were in sooth a most enchanting train,
Even feigning virtue; skilful to unite
With evil good, and strew with pleasure pain.
But, for those fiends whom blood and broils delight,
Who hurl the wretch as if to hell outright   410
Down, down black gulfs where sullen waters sleep,
Or hold him clambering all the fearful night
On beetling cliffs, or pent in ruins deep—
They, till due time should serve, were bid far hence to keep.

XLVII

Ye guardian spirits, to whom man is dear,
From these foul demons shield the midnight gloom!
Angels of fancy and of love, be near,
And o'er the wilds of sleep diffuse a bloom;
Evoke the sacred shades of Greece and Rome,
And let them virtue with a look impart: 420
But chief, awhile, oh, lend us from the tomb
Those long-lost friends for whom in love we smart,
And fill with pious awe and joy-mixed woe the heart!

XLVIII

Or are you sportive?—Bid the morn of youth
Rise to new light, and beam afresh the days

Of innocence, simplicity, and truth,
To cares estranged, and manhood's thorny ways.
What transport, to retrace our boyish plays,
Our easy bliss, when each thing joy supplied—
The woods, the mountains, and the warbling maze   430
Of the wild brooks! But, fondly wandering wide,
My Muse, resume the task that yet doth thee abide

XLIX

One great amusement of our household was,
In a huge crystal magic globe to spy,
Still as you turned it, all things that do pass
Upon this ant-hill earth; where constantly
Of idly-busy men the restless fry
Run bustling to and fro with foolish haste
In search of pleasures vain, that from them fly,
Or which, obtained, the caitiffs dare not taste: 440
When nothing is enjoyed, can there be greater waste?

L

Of Vanity the Mirror this was called.
Here you a muckworm of the town might see
At his dull desk, amid his ledgers stalled,
Eat up with carking care and penurie,
Most like to carcase parched on gallow-tree.
"A penny savèd is a penny got"—
Firm to this scoundrel maxim keepeth he,
Ne of its rigour will he bate a jot,
Till it has quenched his fire, and banishèd his pot.   450

LI

Strait from the filth of this low grub, behold!
Comes fluttering forth a gaudy spendthrift heir,
All glossy gay, enamelled all with gold,
The silly tenant of the summer-air.
In folly lost, of nothing takes he care;
Pimps, lawyers, stewards, harlots, flatterers vile,
And thieving tradesmen him among them share:
His father's ghost from Limbo-lake the while
Sees this, which more damnation does upon him pile.

LII

This globe portrayed the race of learnèd men,   460
Still at their books, and turning o'er the page
Backwards and forwards: oft they snatch the pen
As if inspired, and in a Thespian rage;
Then write and blot, as would your ruth engage.
Why, authors, all this scrawl and scribbling sore?
To lose the present, gain the future age,
Praisèd to be when you can hear no more,
And much enriched with fame when useless worldly store.

LIII

Then would a splendid city rise to view,
With carts, and cars, and coaches roaring all: 470
Wide-poured abroad, behold the prowling crew;
See how they dash along from wall to wall!
At every door, hark how they thundering call!
Good Lord! what can this eager rout excite?
Why? Each on each to prey, by guile or gall;
With flattery these, with slander those, to blight,
And make new tiresome parties for the coming night.

LIV

The puzzling sons of party next appeared,
In dark cabals and nightly juntos met;
And now they whispered close, now shrugging reared   480
The important shoulder; then, as if to get
New light, their twinkling eyes were inward set.
No sooner Lucifer recalls affairs,
Than forth they various rush in mighty fret;
When lo! pushed up to power, and crowned their cares,
In comes another set, and kicketh them down stairs.

LV

But what most showed the vanity of life
Was to behold the nations all on fire,
In cruel broils engaged and deadly strife:
Most Christian kings, inflamed by black desire,   490
With honourable ruffians in their hire,
Cause war to rage, and blood around to pour.
Of this sad work when each begins to tire,
They sit them down just where they were before,
Till for new scenes of woe peace shall their force restore.

LVI

To number up the thousands dwelling here,
An useless were, and eke an endless task—
From kings, and those who at the helm appear,
To gipsies brown, in summer-glades who bask.
Yea, many a man, perdie, I could unmask,   500
Whose desk and table make a solemn show
With tape-tied trash, and suits of fools that ask
For place or pension, laid in decent row;
But these I passen by, with nameless numbers moe.

LVII

Of all the gentle tenants of the place,
There was a man of special grave remark:
A certain tender gloom o'erspread his face,
Pensive, not sad; in thought involved, not dark:
As soote this man could sing as morning-lark,

And teach the noblest morals of the heart;   510
But these his talents were yburied stark;
Of the fine stores he nothing would impart,
Which or boon Nature gave or Nature-painting Art.

LVIII

To noontide shades incontinent he ran,
Where purls the brook with sleep-inviting sound;
Or, when Dan Sol to slope his wheels began,
Amid the broom he basked him on the ground,
Where the wild thyme and camomile are found:
There would he linger till the latest ray
Of light sat trembling on the welkin's bound;   520
Then homeward through the twilight shadows stray,
Sauntering and slow. So had he passèd many a day.

LIX

Yet not in thoughtless slumber were they passed:
For oft the heavenly fire, that lay concealed
Emongst the sleeping embers, mounted fast,
And all its native light anew revealed.
Oft as he traversed the cerulean field,
And marked the clouds that drove before the wind,
Ten thousand glorious systems would he build,
Ten thousand great ideas filled his mind;   530
But with the clouds they fled, and left no trace behind.

LX

With him was sometimes joined in silent walk
(Profoundly silent for they never spoke),
One shyer still, who quite detested talk:
Oft, stung by spleen, at once away he broke
To groves of pine and broad o'ershadowing oak;
There, inly thrilled, he wandered all alone,
And on himself his pensive fury wroke,
Ne ever uttered word, save when first shone
The glittering star of eve—"Thank Heaven! the day is done."   540

LXI

Here lurked a wretch who had not crept abroad
For forty years, ne face of mortal seen—
In chamber brooding like a loathly toad;
And sure his linen was not very clean.
Through secret loophole, that had practised been
Near to his bed, his dinner vile he took;
Unkempt, and rough, of squalid face and mien,
Our castle's shame! whence, from his filthy nook,
We drove the villain out for fitter lair to look.

LXII

One day there chaunced into these halls to rove   550
A joyous youth, who took you at first sight;

Him the wild wave of pleasure hither drove,
Before the sprightly tempest tossing light:
Certes, he was a most engaging wight,
Of social glee, and wit humane though keen,
Turning the night to day and day to night:
For him the merry bells had rung, I ween,
If, in this nook of quiet, bells had ever been.

LXIII

But not even pleasure to excess is good:
What most elates then sinks the soul as low: 560
When spring-tide joy pours in with copious flood,
The higher still the exulting billows flow,
The farther back again they flagging go
And leave us grovelling on the dreary shore.
Taught by this son of joy, we found it so;
Who, whilst he staid, kept in a gay uproar
Our maddened castle all, the abode of sleep no more;

LXIV

As when in prime of June a burnished fly,
Sprung from the meads, o'er which he sweeps along,
Cheered by the breathing bloom and vital sky,   570
Tunes up amid these airy halls his song,
Soothing at first the gay reposing throng:
And oft he sips their bowl; or, nearly drowned,
He, thence recovering, drives their beds among,
And scares their tender sleep with trump profound;
Then out again he flies, to wing his mazy round.

LXV

Another guest there was, of sense refined,
Who felt each worth,—for every worth he had;
Serene yet warm, humane yet firm his mind,
As little touched as any man's with bad: 580
Him through their inmost walks the Muses lad,
To him the sacred love of Nature lent;
And sometimes would he make our valley glad.
Whenas we found he would not here be pent,
To him the better sort this friendly message sent:—

LXVI

"Come, dwell with us! true son of virtue, come!
But if, alas! we cannot thee persuade
To lie content beneath our peaceful dome,
Ne ever more to quit our quiet glade;
Yet, when at last thy toils, but ill apaid,   590
Shall dead thy fire and damp its heavenly spark,
Thou wilt be glad to seek the rural shade,
There to indulge the Muse, and nature mark:
We then a lodge for thee will rear in Hagley Park."

LXVII

Here whilom ligged[13] the Esopus of the age;
But called by fame, in soul yprickèd deep,
A noble pride restored him to the stage,
And roused him like a giant from his sleep.
Even from his slumbers we advantage reap:
With double force the enlivened scene he wakes,   600
Yet quits not nature's bounds. He knows to keep
Each due decorum: now the heart he shakes,
And now with well-urged sense the enlightened judgment takes.

LXVIII

A bard here dwelt, more fat than bard beseems,
Who, void of envy, guile, and lust of gain,
On virtue still, and nature's pleasing themes,
Poured forth his unpremeditated strain,
The world forsaking with a calm disdain:
Here laughed he careless in his easy seat;
Here quaffed, encircled with the joyous train;   610
Oft moralizing sage; his ditty sweet
He loathèd much to write, ne carèd to repeat.

LXIX

Full oft by holy feet our ground was trod;
Of clerks good plenty here you mote espy.
A little, round, fat, oily man of God
Was one I chiefly marked among the fry:
He had a roguish twinkle in his eye,
And shone all glistening with ungodly dew,
If a tight damsel chaunced to trippen by;
Which when observed, he shrunk into his mew,   620
And straight would recollect his piety anew.

LXX

Nor be forgot a tribe who minded naught
(Old inmates of the place) but state affairs:
They looked, perdie, as if they deeply thought,
And on their brow sat every nation's cares.
The world by them is parcelled out in shares,
When in the Hall of Smoke they congress hold,
And the sage berry sun-burnt Mocha bears
Has cleared their inward eye: then, smoke-enrolled,
Their oracles break forth, mysterious as of old.   630

LXXI

Here languid Beauty kept her pale-faced court:
Bevies of dainty dames of high degree
From every quarter hither made resort;
Where, from gross mortal care and business free,

[13] Formerly lay.

They lay poured out in ease and luxury.
Or, should they a vain show of work assume,
Alas! and well-a-day! what can it be?
To knot, to twist, to range the vernal bloom;
But far is cast the distaff, spinning-wheel, and loom.

LXXII

Their only labour was to kill the time;   640
And labour dire it is, and weary woe.
They sit, they loll, turn o'er some idle rhyme;
Then, rising sudden, to the glass they go,
Or saunter forth with tottering step and slow:
This soon too rude an exercise they find;
Strait on the couch their limbs again they throw,
Where, hours on hours, they sighing lie reclined,
And court the vapoury god soft-breathing in the wind.

LXXIII

Now must I mark the villainy we found,
But ah! too late, as shall eftsoons be shewn.   650
A place here was, deep, dreary, under ground;
Where still our inmates, when unpleasing grown,
Diseased and loathsome, privily were thrown.
Far from the light of heaven they languished there,
Unpitied, uttering many a bitter groan;
For of these wretches taken was no care:
Fierce fiends and hags of hell their only nurses were.

LXXIV

Alas the change! from scenes of joy and rest
To this dark den, where sickness tossed alway.
Here Lethargy, with deadly sleep opprest,   660
Stretched on his back, a mighty lubbard lay,
Heaving his sides, and snorèd night and day:
To stir him from his traunce it was not eath,[14]
And his half-opened eyne he shut straitway;
He led, I wot, the softest way to death,
And taught withouten pain and strife to yield the breath.

LXXV

Of limbs enormous, but withal unsound,
Soft-swoln and pale, here lay the Hydropsy:
Unwieldy man! with belly monstrous round,
Forever fed with watery supply;   670
For still he drank, and yet he still was dry.
And moping here did Hypochondria sit,
Mother of Spleen, in robes of various dye,
Who vexèd was full oft with ugly fit;
And some her frantic deemed, and some her deemed a wit.

[14] Easy.

LXXVI

A lady proud she was, of ancient blood,
Yet oft her fear her pride made crouchen low:
She felt, or fancied in her fluttering mood,
All the diseases which the spittles[15] know,
And sought all physic which the shops bestow,   680
And still new leeches and new drugs would try,
Her humour ever wavering to and fro;
For sometimes she would laugh, and sometimes cry,
Then sudden waxèd wroth; and all she knew not why.

LXXVII

Fast by her side a listless maiden pined,
With aching head and squeamish heart-burnings;
Pale, bloated, cold, she seemed to hate mankind,
Yet loved in secret all forbidden things.
And here the Tertian[16] shakes his chilling wings;
The sleepless Gout here counts the crowing cocks—   690
A wolf now gnaws him, now a serpent stings:
Whilst Apoplexy crammed Intemperance knocks
Down to the ground at once, as butcher felleth ox.

[*1733?–48*, 1748]

[15] Hospitals
[16] Fever and ague recurring every other day.

MATTHEW GREEN (1696-1737)

Matthew Green was an obscure clerk in the London Custom House, and during his lifetime his modest efforts in verse were known only to a few of his friends. He reacted from his Quaker upbringing and distrusted what his age called "enthusiasm," yet he always admired the plain and quiet doctrine of the Friends, and kept enough of their unworldliness to look askance at the ways in which men rose in Church and State. On the other hand, he was worldly enough to enjoy the spectacle of life, and he was of his time in professing to seek a middle way which should avoid the extremes of boredom and extravagance. His one important piece, *The Spleen,* is a minor literary triumph because of the personal sincerity and unobtrusive vigor which lie back of his shrewd dry sense and wit. The poem was published in the year of his death, and quietly made its way. Pope, Walpole, Gray and other men of taste esteemed it. The modern reader is likely to agree with Dr. Johnson that *The Spleen* is versified wit rather than poetry, but other eighteenth-century critics thought that it was both. Thus Walpole wrote: "This is as original a poem as ever was written. It has the wit of Butler with the ease of Prior without imitating either, and though so poetic all the images are taken from the streets of London."

The slender collection of Green's verse may be found in *Minor Poets of the Eighteenth Century,* ed. H. I'A. Fausset (Everyman's Library). *The Spleen* has been edited with notes by W. H. Williams (London, 1936).

THE SPLEEN

AN EPISTLE TO MR. CUTHBERT JACKSON

This motley piece to you I send,
Who always were a faithful friend;
Who, if disputes should happen hence,
Can best explain the author's sense;
And, anxious for the public weal,
Do what I sing so often feel.
   The want of method pray excuse,
Allowing for a vapoured Muse;
Nor to a narrow path confined,
Hedge in by rules a roving mind.   10
   The child is genuine; you can trace
Throughout, the sire's transmitted face.
Nothing is stolen; my Muse, though mean,
Draws from the spring she finds within,
Nor vainly buys what Gildon sells,
Poetic buckets for dry wells.
   School-helps I want, to climb on high,
Where all the ancient treasures lie,
And there unseen commit a theft
On wealth in Greek exchequers left.   20
Then where? from whom? what can I steal,
Who only with the moderns deal?
This were attempting to put on
Raiment from naked bodies won;

They safely sing before a thief,
They cannot give who want relief;
Some few excepted, names well known,
And justly laureled with renown,
Whose stamp of genius marks their ware,
And theft detects: of theft beware;   30
From Moore so lashed, example fit,
Shun petty larceny in wit.
   First know, my friend, I do not mean
To write a treatise on the spleen,
Nor to prescribe when nerves convulse,
Nor mend the alarum watch, your pulse.
If I am right, your question lay,
What course I take to drive away
The day-mare Spleen, by whose false pleas
Men prove mere suicides in ease,   40
And how I do myself demean
In stormy world to live serene.
   When by its magic lantern spleen
With frightful figures spread life's scene,
And threatening prospects urged my fears,
A stranger to the luck of heirs;
Reason, some quiet to restore,
Showed part was substance, shadow more;
With spleen's dead weight though heavy grown,
In life's rough tide I sunk not down,   50
But swam, till Fortune threw a rope,
Buoyant on bladders filled with hope.
   I always choose the plainest food
To mend viscidity of blood.

Hail! water-gruel, healing power,
Of easy access to the poor;
Thy help love's confessors implore,
And doctors secretly adore;
To thee I fly, by thee dilute—
Through veins my blood doth quicker shoot,
And by swift current throws off clean   61
Prolific particles of spleen.

I never sick by drinking grow,
Nor keep myself a cup too low,
And seldom Chloe's lodgings haunt,
Thirsty of spirits which I want.

Hunting I reckon very good
To brace the nerves and stir the blood,
But after no field-honours itch,
Achieved by leaping hedge and ditch.   70
While spleen lies soft relaxed in bed,
Or o'er coal-fires inclines the head,
Hygeia's sons with hound and horn
And jovial cry awake the Morn.
These see her from the dusky plight,
Smeared by the embraces of the Night,
With roral wash redeem her face,
And prove herself of Titan's race,
And, mounting in loose robes the skies,
Shed light and fragrance as she flies.   80
Then horse and hound fierce joy display,
Exulting at the hark-away,[1]
And in pursuit o'er tainted ground
From lungs robust field-notes resound.
Then, as St. George the dragon slew,
Spleen pierced, trod down, and dying view;
While all the spirits are on wing,
And woods and hills and valleys ring.

To cure the mind's wrong bias, spleen,
Some recommend the bowling green;   90
Some, hilly walks; all, exercise;
Fling but a stone, the giant dies.
Laugh and be well. Monkeys have been
Extreme good doctors for the spleen;
And kitten, if the humour hit,
Has harlequined away the fit.

Since mirth is good in this behalf,
At some particulars let us laugh:
Witlings, brisk fools, cursed with half sense
That stimulates their impotence,   100
Who buzz in rhyme, and like blind flies
Err with their wings for want of eyes;
Poor authors worshipping a calf,
Deep tragedies that make us laugh,
A strict dissenter saying grace,
A lecturer preaching for a place,
Folks, things prophetic to dispense,

[1] A shout encouraging the hounds in the chase.

Making the past the future tense,
The popish dubbing of a priest,
Fine epitaphs on knaves deceased,   110
Green-aproned Pythonissa's rage,
Great Aesculapius on his stage,
A miser starving to be rich,
The prior of Newgate's dying speech,
A jointured widow's ritual state,
Two Jews disputing tête-à-tête,
New almanacs composed by seers,
Experiments on felons' ears,
Disdainful prudes, who ceaseless ply
The superb muscle of the eye,   120
A coquette's April-weather face,
A Queenborough mayor behind his mace,
And fops in military show,
Are sovereign for the case in view.

If spleen-fogs rise at close of day,
I clear my evening with a play,
Or to some concert take my way.
The company, the shine of lights,
The scenes of humour, music's flights,
Adjust and set the soul to rights.   130
Life's moving pictures, well-wrought plays,
To others' grief attention raise;
Here, while the tragic fictions glow,
We borrow joy by pitying woe;
There gaily comic scenes delight,
And hold true mirrors to our sight.
Virtue, in charming dress arrayed,
Calling the passions to her aid,
When moral scenes just actions join,
Takes shape, and shows her face divine.   140

Music has charms, we all may find,
Ingratiate deeply with the mind.
When art does sound's high power advance,
To music's pipe the passions dance;
Motions unwilled its powers have shown,
Tarantulated by a tune.
Many have held the soul to be
Nearly allied to harmony.
Her have I known indulging grief,
And shunning company's relief,   150
Unveil her face, and looking round,
Own, by neglecting sorrow's wound,
The consanguinity of sound.

In rainy days keep double guard,
Or spleen will surely be too hard;
Which, like those fish by sailors met,
Fly highest while their wings are wet.
In such dull weather, so unfit
To enterprise a work of wit,
When clouds one yard of azure sky   160
That's fit for simile, deny,
I dress my face with studious looks,

And shorten tedious hours with books.
But if dull fogs invade the head,
That memory minds not what is read,
I sit in window dry as ark,
And on the drowning world remark;
Or to some coffee-house I stray
For news, the manna of a day,
And from the hipped discourses gather   170
That politics go by the weather;
Then seek good-humoured tavern chums,
And play at cards, but for small sums;
Or with the merry fellows quaff,
And laugh aloud with them that laugh;
Or drink a joco-serious cup
With souls who've took their freedom up,
And let my mind, beguiled by talk,
In Epicurus' garden walk,
Who thought it heaven to be serene;   180
Pain, hell; and purgatory, spleen.
    Sometimes I dress, with women sit,
And chat away the gloomy fit;
Quit the stiff garb of serious sense,
And wear a gay impertinence,
Nor think nor speak with any pains,
But lay on fancy's neck the reins,
Talk of unusual swell of waist
In maid of honour loosely laced,
And beauty borrowing Spanish red,   190
And loving pair with separate bed,
And jewels pawned for loss of game,
And then redeemed by loss of fame;
Of Kitty (aunt left in the lurch
By grave pretence to go to church)
Perceived in hack with lover fine,
Like Will and Mary on the coin;
And thus in modish manner we,
In aid of sugar, sweeten tea.
    Permit, ye fair, your idol form,   200
Which e'en the coldest heart can warm,
May with its beauties grace my line,
While I bow down before its shrine,
And your thronged altars with my lays
Perfume, and get by giving praise.
With speech so sweet, so sweet a mien
You excommunicate the spleen,
Which fiend-like flies the magic ring
You form with sound, when pleased to sing;
Whate'er you say, howe'er you move,   210
We look, we listen, and approve.
Your touch, which gives to feeling bliss,
Our nerves officious throng to kiss;
By Celia's pat, on their report,
The grave-aired soul, inclined to sport,
Renounces wisdom's sullen pomp,
And loves the floral game, to romp.

But who can view the pointed rays,
That from black eyes scintillant blaze?
Love on his throne of glory seems   220
Encompassed with satellite beams.
But when blue eyes, more softly bright,
Diffuse benignly humid light,
We gaze, and see the smiling loves,
And Cytherea's gentle doves,
And raptured fix in such a face
Love's mercy-seat and throne of grace.
Shine but on age, you melt its snow;
Again fires long extinguished glow,
And, charmed by witchery of eyes,   230
Blood long congealèd liquefies!
True miracle, and fairly done
By heads which are adored while on.
    But oh, what pity 'tis to find
Such beauties both of form and mind,
By modern breeding much debased,
In half the female world at least!
Hence I with care such lotteries shun,
Where, a prize missed, I'm quite undone,
And han't, by venturing on a wife,   240
Yet run the greatest risk in life.
    Mothers and guardian aunts, forbear
Your impious pains to form the fair,
Nor lay out so much cost and art,
But to deflower the virgin heart,
Of every folly fostering-bed
By quickening heat of custom bred.
Rather than by your culture spoiled,
Desist, and give us nature wild,
Delighted with a hoyden soul   250
Which truth and innocence control.
Coquettes, leave off affected arts,
Gay fowlers at a flock of hearts;
Woodcocks to shun your snares have skill,
You show so plain you strive to kill.
In love the artless catch the game,
And they scarce miss who never aim.
    The world's great Author did create
The sex to fit the nuptial state,
And meant a blessing in a wife   260
To solace the fatigues of life,
And old inspired times display
How wives could love and yet obey.
Then truth and patience of control
And housewife arts adorned the soul;
And charms, the gift of nature, shone;
And jealousy, a thing unknown;
Veils were the only masks they wore;
Novels (receipts to make a whore)
Nor ombre nor quadrille they knew,   270
Nor Pam's puissance felt at loo.
Wise men did not, to be thought gay,

Then compliment their power away;
But lest, by frail desires misled,
The girls forbidden paths should tread,
Of ignorance raised the safe high wall;
But we haw-haws,[2] that show them all.
Thus we at once solicit sense,
And charge them not to break the fence.

   Now, if untired, consider, friend,   280
What I avoid to gain my end.
I never am at meeting[3] seen,
Meeting, that region of the spleen;
The broken heart, the busy fiend,
The inward call, on spleen depend.

   Law, licensed breaking of the peace,
To which vacation is disease;
A gipsy diction[4] scarce known well
By the magi, who law-fortunes tell,
I shun; nor let it breed within   290
Anxiety, and that the spleen;
Law, grown a forest, where perplex
The mazes, and the brambles vex;
Where its twelve verderers[5] every day
Are changing still the public way,
Yet if we miss our path and err,
We grievous penalties incur,
And wanderers tire, and tear their skin,
And then get out where they went in.

   I never game, and rarely bet,   300
Am loth to lend, or run in debt.
No compter-writs[6] me agitate,
Who moralizing pass the gate,
And there mine eyes on spendthrifts turn,
Who vainly o'er their bondage mourn.
Wisdom, before beneath their care,
Pays her upbraiding visits there,
And forces folly through the grate
Her panegyric to repeat.
This view, profusely when inclined,   310
Enters a caveat in the mind;
Experience joined with common sense
To mortals is a providence.

   Passion, as frequently is seen,
Subsiding settles into spleen.
Hence, as the plague of happy life,
I run away from party strife.
A prince's cause, a church's claim,
I've known to raise a mighty flame,
And priest, as stoker, very free   320

[2] A sunk fence bounding park or garden.
[3] Religious assemblies of dissenters.
[4] Outlandish jargon.
[5] Officers who supervised the King's forests.
[6] A warrant to commit a prisoner to one of
the compters or counters, debtors' prisons in
London.

To throw in peace and charity.
   That tribe whose practicals decree
Small beer the deadliest heresy;
Who, fond of pedigree, derive
From the most noted whore alive;
Who own wine's old prophetic aid,
And love the mitre Bacchus made,
Forbid the faithful to depend
On half-pint drinkers for a friend,
And in whose gay red-lettered face   330
We read good living more than grace:
Nor they so pure and so precise,
Immaculate as their white of eyes,
Who for the spirit hug the spleen,
Phylactered throughout all their mien;
Who their ill-tasted home-brewed prayer
To the state's mellow forms prefer;
Who doctrines, as infectious, fear,
Which are not steeped in vinegar,
And samples of heart-chested grace   340
Expose in show-glass of the face,
Did never me as yet provoke
Either to honour band and cloak,
Or deck my hat with leaves of oak.

   I rail not with mock-patriot grace
At folks, because they are in place,
Nor, hired to praise with stallion pen,
Serve the ear-lechery of men;
And to avoid religious jars
The laws are my expositors,   350
Which in my doubting mind create
Conformity to Church and State.
I go, pursuant to my plan,
To Mecca with the caravan,
And think it right in common sense
Both for diversion and defence.

   Reforming schemes are none of mine;
To mend the world's a vast design;
Like theirs who tug in little boat
To pull to them the ship afloat,   360
While to defeat their laboured end,
At once both wind and stream contend;
Success herein is seldom seen,
And zeal, when baffled, turns to spleen.

   Happy the man who, innocent,
Grieves not at ills he can't prevent;
His skiff does with the current glide,
Not puffing pulled against the tide.
He, paddling by the scuffing crowd,
Sees unconcerned life's wager rowed,   370
And when he can't prevent foul play,
Enjoys the folly of the fray.

   By these reflections I repeal
Each hasty promise made in zeal.
When gospel propagators say

We're bound our great light to display,
And Indian darkness drive away,
Yet none but drunken watchmen send
And scoundrel link-boys for that end;
When they cry up this holy war,   380
Which every Christian should be for,
Yet such as owe the law their ears,
We find employed as engineers;
This view my forward zeal so shocks,
In vain they hold the money-box.
At such a conduct, which intends
By vicious means such virtuous ends,
I laugh off spleen, and keep my pence
From spoiling Indian innocence.
Yet philosophic love of ease   390
I suffer not to prove disease,
But rise up in the virtuous cause
Of a free press and equal laws.
The press restrained! nefandous thought!
In vain our sires have nobly fought;
While free from force the press remains,
Virtue and Freedom cheer our plains,
And Learning largesses bestows,
And keeps uncensured open house.
We to the nation's public mart   400
Our works of wit and schemes of art,
And philosophic goods this way,
Like water carriage, cheap convey.
This tree, which knowledge so affords,
Inquisitors with flaming swords
From lay-approach with zeal defend,
Lest their own paradise should end.
The press from her fecundous womb
Brought forth the arts of Greece and Rome;
Her offspring, skilled in logic war,   410
Truth's banner waved in open air;
The monster Superstition fled,
And hid in shades its Gorgon head,
And lawless power the long-kept field.
By reason quelled, was forced to yield.
This nurse of arts, and freedom's fence
To chain, is treason against sense;
And, Liberty, thy thousand tongues
None silence, who design no wrongs;
For those that use the gag's restraint,   420
First rob, before they stop complaint.
Since disappointment galls within,
And subjugates the soul to spleen,
Most schemes, as money-snares, I hate,
And bite not at projector's bait.
Sufficient wrecks appear each day,
And yet fresh fools are cast away.
Ere well the bubbled can turn round,
Their painted vessel runs aground;
Or in deep seas it oversets   430

By a fierce hurricane of debts;
Or helm-directors in one trip,
Freight first embezzled, sink the ship.
Such was of late a corporation,
The brazen serpent of the nation,
Which, when hard accidents distressed,
The poor must look at to be blessed,
And thence expect, with paper sealed
By fraud and usury, to be healed.
I in no soul-consumption wait   440
Whole years at levees of the great,
And hungry hopes regale the while
On the spare diet of a smile.
There you may see the idol stand
With mirror in his wanton hand;
Above, below, now here, now there
He throws about the sunny glare.
Crowds pant, and press to seize the prize,
The gay delusion of their eyes.
When Fancy tries her limning skill   450
To draw and colour at her will,
And raise and round the figures well,
And show her talent to excel,
I guard my heart, lest it should woo
Unreal beauties Fancy drew,
And disappointed, feel despair
At loss of things that never were.
When I lean politicians mark
Grazing on ether in the Park;
Who, e'er on wing with open throats,   460
Fly at debates, expresses, votes,
Just in the manner swallows use,
Catching their airy food of news;
Whose latrant stomachs oft molest
The deep-laid plans their dreams suggest;
Or see some poet pensive sit,
Fondly mistaking spleen for wit,
Who, though short-winded, still will aim
To sound the epic trump of Fame;
Who still on Phoebus' smiles will dote   470
Nor learn conviction from his coat;
I bless my stars, I never knew
Whimsies which, close pursued, undo,
And have from old experience been
Both parent and the child of spleen.
These subjects of Apollo's state,
Who from false fire derive their fate,
With airy purchases undone
Of lands, which none lend money on,
Born dull, had followed thriving ways,   480
Nor lost one hour to gather bays.
Their fancies first delirious grew,
And scenes ideal took for true.
Fine to the sight Parnassus lies,
And with false prospects cheats their eyes;

The fabled goods the poets sing,
A season of perpetual spring,
Brooks, flowery fields, and groves of trees,
Affording sweets and similes,
Gay dreams inspired in myrtle bowers,   490
And wreaths of undecaying flowers,
Apollo's harp with airs divine,
The sacred music of the Nine,
Views of the temple raised to Fame,
And for a vacant niche proud aim,
Ravish their souls, and plainly show
What Fancy's sketching power can do.
They will attempt the mountain steep,
Where on the top, like dreams in sleep,
The Muses revelations show,   500
That find men cracked, or make them so.
  You, friend, like me, the trade of rhyme
Avoid, elaborate waste of time,
Nor are content to be undone,
And pass for Phoebus' crazy son.
Poems, the hop-grounds of the brain,
Afford the most uncertain gain;
And lotteries never tempt the wise
With blanks so many to a prize.
I only transient visits pay,   510
Meeting the Muses in my way,
Scarce known to the fastidious dames,
Nor skilled to call them by their names.
Nor can their passports in these days
Your profit warrant, or your praise.
On poems by their dictates writ,
Critics as sworn appraisers, sit,
And, mere upholsterers, in a trice
On gems and painting set a price.
These tailoring artists for our lays   520
Invent cramped rules, and with strait stays
Striving free Nature's shape to hit,
Emaciate sense, before they fit.
  A commonplace and many friends
Can serve the plagiary's ends,
Whose easy vamping talent lies,
First wit to pilfer, then disguise.
Thus some, devoid of art and skill
To search the mine on Pindus' hill,
Proud to aspire and workmen grow,   530
By genius doomed to stay below,
For their own digging show the town
Wit's treasure brought by others down.
Some wanting, if they find a mine,
An artist's judgment to refine,
On fame precipitately fixed,
The ore with baser metals mixed
Melt down, impatient of delay,
And call the vicious mass a play.
All these engage to serve their ends   540

A band select of trusty friends,
Who, lessoned right, extol the thing,
As Psapho taught his birds to sing;
Then to the ladies they submit,
Returning officers on wit;
A crowded house their presence draws,
And on the beaux imposes laws,
A judgment in its favour ends.
When all the panel are its friends;
Their natures merciful and mild   550
Have from mere pity saved the child;
In bulrush ark the bantling found
Helpless, and ready to be drowned,
They have preserved by kind support,
And brought the baby-muse to court.
  But there's a youth that you can name,
Who needs no leading strings to fame,
Whose quick maturity of brain
The birth of Pallas may explain,
Dreaming of whose depending fate,   560
I heard Melpomene debate:
"This, this is he, that was foretold
Should emulate our Greeks of old.
Inspired by me with sacred art,
He sings, and rules the varied heart;
If Jove's dread anger he rehearse,
We hear the thunder in his verse;
If he describe love turned to rage,
The Furies riot on his page;
If he fair liberty and law   570
By ruffian power expiring draw,
The keener passions then engage
Aright, and sanctify their rage;
If he attempt disastrous love,
We hear those plaints that wound the grove;
Within the kinder passions glow,
And tears distilled from pity flow."
  From the bright vision I descend,
And my deserted theme attend.
  Me never did ambition seize,   580
Strange fever most inflamed by ease!
The active lunacy of pride,
That courts jilt Fortune for a bride,
This paradise tree, so fair and high,
I view with no aspiring eye;
Like aspen shake the restless leaves,
And Sodom-fruit our pains deceives,
Whence frequent falls give no surprise,
But fits of spleen, called growing wise.
Greatness in glittering forms displayed   590
Affects weak eyes much used to shade,
And by its falsely envied scene
Gives self-debasing fits of spleen.
We should be pleased that things are so,
Who do for nothing see the show,

And, middle-sized, can pass between
Life's hubbub safe, because unseen,
And midst the glare of greatness trace
A watery sunshine in the face,
And pleasures fled to, to redress   600
The sad fatigue of idleness.
     Contentment, parent of delight,
So much a stranger to our sight,
Say, goddess, in what happy place
Mortals behold thy blooming face;
Thy gracious auspices impart,
And for thy temple choose my heart.
They whom thou deignest to inspire
Thy science learn, to bound desire;
By happy alchemy of mind   610
They turn to pleasure all they find;
They both disdain in outward mien
The grave and solemn garb of spleen,
And meretricious arts of dress,
To feign a joy, and hide distress;
Unmoved when the rude tempest blows,
Without an opiate they repose,
And covered by your shield, defy
The whizzing shafts that round them fly;
Nor, meddling with the gods' affairs,   620
Concern themselves with distant cares;
But place their bliss in mental rest,
And feast upon the good possessed.
     Forced by soft violence of prayer,
The blithesome goddess soothes my care;
I feel the deity inspire,
And thus she models my desire:
Two hundred pounds half-yearly paid,
Annuity securely made,
A farm some twenty miles from town,   630
Small, tight, salubrious, and my own;
Two maids that never saw the town,
A serving-man not quite a clown,
A boy to help to tread the mow,
And drive, while t'other holds the plough;
A chief, of temper formed to please,
Fit to converse, and keep the keys,
And better to preserve the peace,
Commissioned by the name of niece;
With understandings of a size   640
To think their master very wise.
May heaven (it's all I wish for) send
One genial room to treat a friend,
Where decent cupboard, little plate,
Display benevolence, not state.
And may my humble dwelling stand
Upon some chosen spot of land;
A pond before full to the brim,
Where cows may cool and geese may swim;
Behind, a green like velvet neat,   650

Soft to the eye, and to the feet,
Where odorous plants in evening fair
Breathe all around ambrosial air,
From Eurus, foe to kitchen ground,
Fenced by a slope with bushes crowned,
Fit dwelling for the feathered throng,
Who pay their quit-rents with a song;
With opening views of hill and dale,
Which sense and fancy too regale,
Where the half-cirque which vision bounds,
Like amphitheatre surrounds;   661
And woods impervious to the breeze,
Thick phalanx of embodied trees,
From hills through plains in dusk array
Extended far, repel the day.
Here stillness, height, and solemn shade
Invite, and contemplation aid;
Here nymphs from hollow oaks relate
The dark decrees and will of fate,
And dreams beneath the spreading beech 670
Inspire, and docile fancy teach;
While, soft as breezy breath of wind,
Impulses rustle through the mind:
Here Dryads, scorning Phoebus' ray,
While Pan melodious pipes away,
In measured motions frisk about,
Till old Silenus puts them out.
There see the clover, pea, and bean
Vie in variety of green;
Fresh pastures speckled o'er with sheep,   680
Brown fields their fallow sabbaths keep,
Plump Ceres golden tresses wear,
And poppy top-knots deck her hair,
And silver streams through meadows stray,
And Naiads on the margin play,
And lesser nymphs on side of hills
From plaything urns pour down the rills.
     Thus sheltered, free from care and strife,
May I enjoy a calm through life;
See faction, safe in low degree,   690
As men at land see storms at sea,
And laugh at miserable elves,
Not kind so much as to themselves,
Cursed with such souls of base alloy
As can possess but not enjoy;
Debarred the pleasure to impart
By avarice, sphincter of the heart;
Who wealth, hard earned by guilty cares,
Bequeath untouched to thankless heirs.
May I, with look ungloomed by guile,   700
And wearing virtue's livery-smile,
Prone the distressèd to relieve,
And little trespasses forgive,
With income not in Fortune's power,
And skill to make a busy hour,

With trips to town life to amuse,
To purchase books, and hear the news,
To see old friends, brush off the clown,
And quicken taste at coming down,
Unhurt by sickness' blasting rage,   710
And slowly mellowing in age,
When fate extends its gathering gripe,
Fall off like fruit grown fully ripe,
Quit a worn being without pain,
Perhaps to blossom soon again.
   But now more serious see me grow,
And what I think, my Memmius, know.
   The enthusiast's hope and raptures wild
Have never yet my reason foiled.
His springy soul dilates like air,   720
When free from weight of ambient care,
And, hushed in meditation deep,
Slides into dreams, as when asleep;
Then, fond of new discoveries grown,
Proves a Columbus of her own,
Disdains the narrow bounds of place,
And through the wilds of endless space,
Borne up on metaphysic wings,
Chases light forms and shadowy things,
And, in the vague excursion caught,   730
Brings home some rare exotic thought.
The melancholy man such dreams,
As brightest evidence, esteems;
Fain would he see some distant scene
Suggested by his restless spleen,
And fancy's telescope applies
With tinctured glass to cheat his eyes.
Such thoughts as love the gloom of night
I close examine by the light;
For who, though bribed by gain to lie,   740
Dare sunbeam-written truths deny,
And execute plain common sense
On faith's mere hearsay evidence?
   That superstition mayn't create,
And club its ills with those of fate,
I many a notion take to task,
Made dreadful by its visor-mask.
Thus scruple, spasm of the mind,
Is cured, and certainty I find;
Since optic reason shows me plain,   750
I dreaded spectres of the brain,
And legendary fears are gone,
Though in tenacious childhood sown.
Thus in opinions I commence
Freeholder in the proper sense,
And neither suit nor service do,
Nor homage to pretenders show,
Who boast themselves by spurious roll
Lords of the manor of the soul;
Preferring sense, from chin that's bare,   760

To nonsense throned in whiskered hair.
   To thee, Creator uncreate,
O Entium Ens[7] divinely great!—
Hold, Muse, nor melting pinions try,
Nor near the blazing glory fly,
Nor straining break thy feeble bow,
Unfeathered arrows far to throw;
Through fields unknown nor madly stray,
Where no ideas mark the way.
With tender eyes, and colours faint,   770
And trembling hands forbear to paint.
Who, features veiled by light can hit?
Where can, what has no outline, sit?
My soul, the vain attempt forego!
Thyself, the fitter subject, know!
He wisely shuns the bold extreme,
Who soon lays by the unequal theme,
Nor runs, with wisdom's Sirens caught,
On quicksand swallowing shipwrecked
     thought,
But, conscious of his distance, gives   780
Mute praise, and humble negatives.
In one, no object of our sight,
Immutable and infinite,
Who can't be cruel or unjust,
Calm and resigned, I fix my trust;
To him my past and present state
I owe, and must my future fate.
A stranger into life I'm come,
Dying may be our going home,
Transported here by angry Fate,   790
The convicts of a prior state;
Hence I no anxious thoughts bestow
On matters I can never know.
Through life's foul ways like vagrant passed.
He'll grant a settlement at last,
And with sweet ease the wearied crown,
By leave to lay his being down.
If doomed to dance the eternal round
Of life no sooner lost than found,
And dissolution soon to come,   800
Like sponge, wipes out life's present sum,
But can't our state of power bereave
An endless series to receive;
Then, if hard dealt with here by fate,
We balance in another state,
And consciousness must go along,
And sign the acquittance for the wrong.
He for his creatures must decree
More happiness than misery,
Or be supposèd to create,   810
Curious to try, what 'tis to hate,
And do an act, which rage infers,
   [7] Being of Beings.

'Cause lameness halts, or blindness errs.
　Thus, thus I steer my bark, and sail
On even keel with gentle gale;
At helm I make my reason sit,
My crew of passions all submit.
If dark and blustering prove some nights,
Philosophy puts forth her lights;
Experience holds the cautious glass,　　820
To shun the breakers, as I pass,
And frequent throws the wary lead,
To see what dangers may be hid;
And once in seven years I'm seen

At Bath or Tunbridge to careen.
Though pleased to see the dolphins play,
I mind my compass and my way.
With store sufficient for relief,
And wisely still prepared to reef,
Nor wanting the dispersive bowl　　830
Of cloudy weather in the soul,
I make (may heaven propitious send
Such wind and weather to the end)
Neither becalmed nor over-blown,
Life's voyage to the world unknown.

[1737]

ISAAC WATTS (1674-1748)

Isaac Watts was born at Southampton and educated at a dissenting academy in London. He became one of the most eminent dissenting divines of his day, but poor health limited his active work as a clergyman, and the last half of his life was spent in comfortable retirement in the family of his benefactors Sir Thomas and Lady Abney. He published many sermons, textbooks, and manuals, and poetry was always one of his chief interests. As Dr. Johnson said, he "was one of the first authors that taught the Dissenters to court attention by the graces of language." His views on the religious mission of poetry are interestingly expressed in the Preface to *Horae Lyricae* (1706) (see Chalmer's *English Poets*, xiii, 13-20). But while his more pretentious literary efforts are forgotten, his hymns have been universally used in the evangelical worship of English-speaking countries. He may indeed be said to have made the transition from the older metrical versions of the Psalms to the hymn as since sung by Protestant congregations. He dwells on the awful might and inscrutable will of God; characteristic titles in his *Horae Lyricae* are "Worshiping with Fear" and "God's Dominion and Decrees." But his austere Calvinistic doctrine is colored by an underlying gentleness and sympathy. His homely *Divine and Moral Songs,* a collection of hymns and other verse for children, has passed through hundreds of editions in Great Britain and America.

Recent discussions of the literary aspects of his work: Thomas Wright, *Isaac Watts and Contemporary Hymn-writers* (London, 1914); F. Palmer, "Isaac Watts," *Harvard Theological Review,* XII (1919), 371-403; V. de Sola Pinto, "Isaac Watts and the Adventurous Muse," *Essays and Studies by Members of the English Association,* XX (1935), 86-107. See also page 1269.

THE DAY OF JUDGMENT

AN ODE ATTEMPTED IN ENGLISH SAPPHIC

When the fierce north wind with his airy forces
Rears up the Baltic to a foaming fury,
And the red lightning with a storm of hail comes
    Rushing amain down,

How the poor sailors stand amazed and tremble,
While the hoarse thunder, like a bloody trumpet,
Roars a loud onset to the gaping waters,
    Quick to devour them!

Such shall the noise be and the wild disorder,
(If things eternal may be like these earthly)
Such the dire terror, when the great Archangel
    Shakes the creation,

Tears the strong pillars of the vault of heaven,
Breaks up old marble, the repose of princes;
See the graves open, and the bones arising,
    Flames all around 'em!

Hark, the shrill outcries of the guilty wretches!
Lively bright horror and amazing anguish
Stare through their eyelids, while the living worm lies
    Gnawing within them.

    10

    20

Thoughts like old vultures prey upon their heart-strings,
And the smart twinges, when the eye beholds the
Lofty Judge frowning, and a flood of vengeance
                  Rolling afore him.

Hopeless immortals! how they scream and shiver,
While devils push them to the pit wide-yawning
Hideous and gloomy, to receive them headlong
                  Down to the center.

Stop here, my fancy: (all away ye horrid
Doleful ideas); come, arise to Jesus;   30
How He sits God-like! and the saints around him
                  Throned, yet adoring!

Oh may I sit there when he comes triumphant
Dooming the nations! then ascend to glory
While our hosannas all along the passage
                  Shout the Redeemer.
                        [1706]

THE HAZARD OF LOVING
THE CREATURES

Where'er my flattering passions rove,
  I find a lurking snare;
'Tis dangerous to let loose our love
  Beneath the Eternal Fair.

Souls whom the tie of friendship binds
  And partners of our blood,
Seize a large portion of our minds,
  And leave the less for God.

Nature has soft but powerful bands,
  And Reason she controls;   10
While children with their little hands
  Hang closest to our souls.

Thoughtless they act the old serpent's part;
  What tempting things they be!
Lord, how they twine about our heart,
  And draw it off from thee!

Our hasty wills rush blindly on
  Where rising passion rolls,
And thus we make our fetters strong
  To bind our slavish souls.   20

Dear Sovereign, break these fetters off,
  And set our spirits free;
God in himself is bliss enough,
  For we have all in thee.
            [1706]

CRUCIFIXION TO THE
WORLD BY THE CROSS
OF CHRIST

When I survey the wondrous cross
On which the Prince of Glory died,
My richest gain I count but loss,
And pour contempt on all my pride.

Forbid it, Lord, that I should boast
Save in the death of Christ my God;
All the vain things that charm me most,
I sacrifice them to his blood.

See from his head, his hands, his feet,
Sorrow and Love flow mingled down;   10
Did e'er such Love and Sorrow meet?
Or thorns compose so rich a crown?

His dying crimson like a robe
Spreads o'er his body on the tree;
Then am I dead to all the globe,
And all the globe is dead to me.

Were the whole realm of Nature mine,
That were a present far too small;
Love so amazing, so divine,
Demands my soul, my life, my all.   20
            [1707]

A PROSPECT OF HEAVEN
MAKES DEATH EASY

There is a land of pure delight
　Where saints immortal reign;
Infinite day excludes the night,
　And pleasures banish pain.

There everlasting spring abides,
　And never-withering flowers;
Death like a narrow sea divides
　This heavenly land from ours.

Sweet fields beyond the swelling flood
　Stand dressed in living green:　　10
So to the Jews old Canaan stood,
　While Jordan rolled between.

But timorous mortals start and shrink
　To cross this narrow sea,
And linger shivering on the brink,
　And fear to launch away.

Oh could we make our doubts remove,
　These gloomy doubts that rise,
And see the Canaan that we love,
　With unbeclouded eyes;　　20

Could we but climb where Moses stood
　And view the landscape o'er,
Not Jordan's stream, nor Death's cold flood,
　Should fright us from the shore.

[1707]

MAN FRAIL AND GOD
ETERNAL

Our God, our help in ages past,
　Our hope for years to come,
Our shelter from the stormy blast,
　And our eternal home:

Under the shadow of thy throne
　Thy saints have dwelt secure;
Sufficient is thine arm alone,
　And our defence is sure.

Before the hills in order stood,
　Or earth received her frame,　　10
From everlasting thou art God,
　To endless years the same.

Thy word commands our flesh to dust,
　"Return, ye sons of men:"
All nations rose from earth at first,
　And turn to earth again.

A thousand ages in thy sight
　Are like an evening gone;
Short as the watch that ends the night
　Before the rising sun.　　20

The busy tribes of flesh and blood
　With all their lives and cares
Are carried downwards by thy flood,
　And lost in following years.

Time like an ever-rolling stream
　Bears all its sons away;
They fly forgotten as a dream
　Dies at the opening day.

Like flowery fields the nations stand
　Pleased with the morning light;　　30
The flowers beneath the mower's hand
　Lie withering e'er 'tis night.

Our God, our help in ages past,
　Our hope for years to come,
Our shelter from the stormy blast,
　And our eternal home.

[1719]

A CRADLE HYMN

Hush, my dear, lie still and slumber;
Holy angels guard thy bed!
Heavenly blessings without number
Gently falling on thy head.

Sleep, my babe; thy food and raiment,
House and home thy friends provide;
All without thy care or payment,
All thy wants are well supplied.

How much better thou'rt attended
Than the Son of God could be,　　10
When from Heaven he descended,
And became a child like thee!

Soft and easy is thy cradle;
Coarse and hard thy Saviour lay,
When his birth-place was a stable,
And his softest bed was hay.

Blessed Babe! what glorious features,
Spotless fair, divinely bright!
Must he dwell with brutal creatures?
How could angels bear the sight?   20

Was there nothing but a manger
Cursed sinners could afford,
To receive the heavenly Stranger?
Did they thus affront their Lord?

Soft, my child; I did not chide thee,
Though my song might sound too hard;
'Tis thy $\left\{\begin{array}{l}\text{Mother}^1\\\text{Nurse that}\end{array}\right\}$ sits beside thee
And her arm shall be thy guard.

Yet to read the shameful story,
How the Jews abused their King,   30
How they served the Lord of Glory,
Makes me angry while I sing.

See the kinder shepherds round him,
Telling wonders from the sky;
There they sought him, there they found him,
With his Virgin-Mother by.

¹ Here you may use the words, Brother, Sister,
Neighbour, Friend. &c.

See the lovely Babe a-dressing;
Lovely Infant, how he smiled!
When he wept, the Mother's blessing
Soothed and hushed the holy Child.   40

Lo, he slumbers in his manger,
Where the horned oxen fed;
Peace, my darling, here's no danger,
Here's no ox anear thy bed.

'Twas to save thee, child, from dying,
Save my dear from burning flame,
Bitter groans, and endless crying,
That my blest Redeemer came.

Mayst thou live to know and fear him,
Trust and love him all thy days!   50
Then go dwell forever near him,
See his face, and sing his praise!

I could give thee thousand kisses,
Hoping what I most desire;
Not a mother's fondest wishes
Can to greater joys aspire.

[1720]

CHARLES WESLEY (1707-1788)

Charles Wesley, with his elder brother John, had a leading part in the great religious awakening of the eighteenth century which was nicknamed Methodism. From his student days at Oxford and his missionary journey to Georgia with his brother, his life was full of zealous and practical labor as religious reformer and itinerant preacher. The evangelical movement had profound effects on the national life and so on literature, but its early apostles did not approach literature in the leisurely manner of the typical eighteenth-century clergyman. Though the Wesleys had the training of men of letters, and though John Wesley's *Journal* is sufficient testimony to his command of style, they worked mostly through the medium of the hymn and the sermon. Charles Wesley had the larger share in the voluminous collections of hymns which he and his brother published in and after the year 1739. They are said to have written about 6500 hymns, some 500 of which are in present use. The modern English hymn dates from Addison and Watts. For congregational use the requirements were simple diction and construction, resonant lines, the reiteration of plain gospel truth, and the expression of sentiments that could be understood and shared by the many. In these qualities Charles Wesley is preëminent among English hymn-writers.

The great mass of religious verse written by the two brothers is collected in the *Poetical Works,* 13 vols. (London, 1868-72). See also F. L. Wiseman's study, *Charles Wesley, Evangelist and Poet* (New York, 1932). See also page 1269.

WRESTLING JACOB

Come, O Thou Traveller unknown,
  Whom still I hold, but cannot see;
My company before is gone,
  And I am left alone with Thee;
With Thee all night I mean to stay,
And wrestle till the break of day.

I need not tell Thee who I am,
  My misery or sin declare;
Thyself hast called me by my name;
  Look on Thy hands, and read it there!
But who, I ask Thee, who art Thou?   11
Tell me Thy name, and tell me now!

In vain Thou strugglest to get free,
  I never will unloose my hold;
Art Thou the Man that died for me?
  The secret of Thy love unfold.
Wrestling, I will not let Thee go,
Till I Thy name, Thy nature know.

Wilt Thou not yet to me reveal
  Thy new, unutterable name?   20
Tell me, I still beseech Thee, tell;
  To know it now, resolved I am:
Wrestling, I will not let Thee go,
Till I Thy name, Thy nature know.

'Tis all in vain to hold Thy tongue,
  Or touch the hollow of my thigh;
Though every sinew be unstrung,
  Out of my arms Thou shalt not fly;
Wrestling, I will not let Thee go,
Till I Thy name, Thy nature know.   30

What though my shrinking flesh complain,
  And murmur to contend so long?
I rise superior to my pain;
  When I am weak, then I am strong:
And when my all of strength shall fail,
I shall with the God-Man prevail.

My strength is gone; my nature dies;
  I sink beneath Thy weighty hand,
Faint to revive, and fall to rise;
  I fall, and yet by faith I stand: 40
I stand, and will not let Thee go,
Till I Thy name, Thy nature know.

Yield to me now, for I am weak,
  But confident in self-despair;
Speak to my heart, in blessings speak;
  Be conquered by my instant prayer!
Speak, or Thou never hence shalt move,
And tell me if Thy name is Love!

'Tis Love! 'tis Love! Thou diedst for me!
  I hear Thy whisper in my heart!   50

The morning breaks, the shadows flee;
 Pure universal Love Thou art!
To me, to all, Thy bowels move;
Thy nature and Thy name is Love!

My prayer hath power with God; the grace
 Unspeakable I now receive;
Through faith I see Thee face to face,
 I see Thee face to face, and live:
In vain I have not wept and strove;
Thy nature and Thy name is Love. 60

I know Thee, Saviour, who thou art;
 Jesus, the feeble sinner's friend!
Nor wilt Thou with the night depart,
 But stay, and love me to the end.
Thy mercies never shall remove;
Thy nature and Thy name is Love.

The Sun of Righteousness on me
 Hath rose, with healing in His wings;
Withered my nature's strength, from Thee
 My soul its life and succour brings; 70
My help is all laid up above;
Thy nature and Thy name is Love.

Contented now upon my thigh
 I halt, till life's short journey end;
All helplessness, all weakness, I
 On Thee alone for strength depend;
Nor have I power from Thee to move;
Thy nature and Thy name is Love.

Lame as I am, I take the prey;
 Hell, earth, and sin, with ease o'ercome;
I leap for joy, pursue my way, 81
 And as a bounding hart fly home;
Through all eternity to prove,
Thy nature and Thy name is Love.

      [1742]

IN TEMPTATION

Jesu, Lover of my soul,
 Let me to Thy bosom fly,

While the nearer waters roll,
 While the tempest still is high!
Hide me, O my Saviour, hide,
 Till the storm of life is past;
Safe into the haven guide;
 O receive my soul at last!

Other refuge have I none;
 Hangs my helpless soul on Thee; 10
Leave, ah! leave me not alone,
 Still support and comfort me!
All my trust on Thee is stayed,
 All my help from Thee I bring:
Cover my defenceless head
 With the shadow of Thy wing!

Wilt Thou not regard my call?
 Wilt Thou not accept my prayer?
Lo! I sink, I faint, I fall!
 Lo! on Thee I cast my care! 20
Reach me out Thy gracious hand!
 While I of Thy strength receive,
Hoping against hope I stand,
 Dying, and behold I live!

Thou, O Christ, art all I want;
 More than all in Thee I find:
Raise the fallen, cheer the faint,
 Heal the sick, and lead the blind!
Just and holy is Thy Name;
 I am all unrighteousness; 30
False and full of sin I am,
 Thou art full of truth and grace.

Plenteous grace with Thee is found,
 Grace to cover all my sin;
Let the healing streams abound;
 Make and keep me pure within!
Thou of Life the Fountain art,
 Freely let me take of Thee;
Spring Thou up within my heart!
 Rise to all eternity! 40

      [1749]

EDWARD YOUNG (1683-1765)

In his early days Young appears as a minor Augustan wit who cultivated his acquaintance with Addison and other Oxford men and Whig leaders in order to obtain preferment in law or politics. Following the literary fashions of the time, he wrote in turn religious verse (*The Last Day*, 1713; *Paraphrase of Job*, 1719), bombastic tragedy (*Busiris*, 1719; *Revenge*, 1721), and, more successfully, a brilliant though conventional series of satires (*The Universal Passion*, 1725-28). In 1724 he took holy orders and continued his quest for preferment. He was ordained rector of Welwyn, Hertfordshire, in 1730, where he spent the rest of his long life.

Personal bereavement, disappointed ambition, theological study, and fully matured poetic power all had their share in the making of his most famous poem, *The Complaint; or Night Thoughts on Life, Death, and Immortality* (1742-46). Moved by the successive deaths of Lucia, Philander, and Narcissa (shadowy individuals who do not correspond exactly to the members of Young's own family circle), the poet undertakes a long blank-verse discussion of mortality and immortality. He dramatizes his own sorrow, and thus gives his work a personal center; he puts his meditations in an appropriate nocturnal setting, though he barely suggests the terrors of the tomb. The eighteenth century made the most of these suggestions, and found in Young an exponent of sentimental melancholy and even of Gothic terror. The *Night Thoughts* had for many readers the appeal of a personal elegy (compare Pope's *Elegy to the Memory of an Unfortunate Lady*), or even of the more didactic parts of a novel (compare the death of Richardson's Clarissa). But Young himself was largely interested in the arguments and meditations which develop from the situation. It has been shown that his defense of the cardinal doctrine of immortality follows the lines of current theological discussion (Isabel St. John Bliss, "Young's *Night Thoughts* in Relation to Contemporary Christian Apologetics," *PMLA*, XLIX [1934], 37-70). His poem follows the programs of meditation recommended by manuals of devotion: systematic meditation in retirement on the great truths of Christianity was constantly urged as a religious duty. Meditation might also be "sudden and occasional," and Young's plan combines the "set and deliberate" method with the "occasional." He follows established categories, "the Soliloquy and Complaint," "the Soliloquy and Aspiration," "the Resolution," "the Consolation." His ethical views, centering in the definition of virtue as enlightened self-interest, were likewise current commonplaces. He sets forth the mixed nature and doubtful destiny of man in an epigrammatic and paradoxical style which makes him at times as quotable as Pope. He alternately magnifies and belittles the tragedy of death, alternately mourns the loss of what is past and exults in the infinite possibilities of the future. The latter theme is highly characteristic of Young, and the progressivism of the *Night Thoughts* leads directly to the ardent faith in human powers which he expresses in his brilliant plea for original genius in poetry, *Conjectures on Original Composition* (1759). Readers of later times have suspected Young of being hollow and insincere; his wit is often forced and his rhetoric often bombastic. But we cannot deny his resourcefulness and energy, or overlook the historical interest of a poem which has pleased so many generations of readers.

Complete Works (2 vols., 1854); *Poetical Works*, ed. J. Mitford (Aldine edition); W. Thomas, *Le poète Edward Young* (Paris, 1901); H. C. Shelley, *Life and Letters of Edward Young* (1914); George Eliot, *Worldliness and Other-Worldliness: The Poet Young* (1857) [marks the decline of Young's reputation]; H. Pettit, "Preface to a Bibliography of Young's *Night Thoughts*," *Univ. of Colorado Studies in the Humanities*, II (1945), 215-22.

For additional readings see pages 1143–1157.

THE COMPLAINT, OR NIGHT THOUGHTS ON LIFE, DEATH, AND IMMORTALITY

NIGHT I

Tired Nature's sweet restorer, balmy Sleep!
He, like the world, his ready visit pays
Where Fortune smiles; the wretched he forsakes;
Swift on his downy pinion flies from woe,

And lights on lids unsullied with a tear.
From short (as usual) and disturbed repose,
I wake: how happy they who wake no more!
Yet that were vain, if dreams infest the grave.
I wake, emerging from a sea of dreams
Tumultuous; where my wrecked desponding thought   10
From wave to wave of fancied misery
At random drove, her helm of reason lost.
Though now restored, 'tis only change of pain,
(A bitter change!) severer for severe.
The day too short for my distress; and Night,
Even in the zenith of her dark domain,
Is sunshine to the colour of my fate.
    Night, sable goddess! from her ebon throne,
In rayless majesty now stretches forth
Her leaden scepter o'er a slumbering world.   20
Silence, how dead! and darkness, how profound!
Nor eye nor listening ear an object finds;
Creation sleeps. 'Tis as the general pulse
Of life stood still, and Nature made a pause;
An awful pause! prophetic of her end.
And let her prophecy be soon fulfilled;
Fate! drop the curtain; I can lose no more.
    Silence and Darkness! solemn sisters! twins
From ancient Night, who nurse the tender thought
To reason, and on reason build resolve,   30
(That column of true majesty in man),
Assist me: I will thank you in the grave;
The grave, your kingdom: there this frame shall fall
A victim sacred to your dreary shrine.
But what are ye?—Thou who didst put to flight
Primeval silence, when the morning stars,
Exulted, shouted o'er the rising ball;
O Thou, whose word from solid darkness struck
That spark, the sun; strike wisdom from my soul;
My soul, which flies to Thee, her trust, her treasure,   40
As misers to their gold, while others rest.
    Through this opaque of nature and of soul,
This double night, transmit one pitying ray,
To lighten and to cheer. Oh, lead my mind,
(A mind that fain would wander from its woe),
Lead it through various scenes of life and death;
And from each scene, the noblest truths inspire.
Nor less inspire my conduct than my song;
Teach my best reason, reason; my best will
Teach rectitude; and fix my firm resolve   50
Wisdom to wed, and pay her long arrear:
Nor let the phial of thy vengeance, poured
On this devoted head, be poured in vain.
    The bell strikes one. We take no note of time
But from its loss. To give it then a tongue
Is wise in man. As if an angel spoke,
I feel the solemn sound. If heard aright,
It is the knell of my departed hours:
Where are they? With the years beyond the flood.

It is the signal that demands dispatch: 60
How much is to be done? My hopes and fears
Start up alarmed, and o'er life's narrow verge
Look down—on what? a fathomless abyss;
A dread eternity! how surely mine!
And can eternity belong to me,
Poor pensioner on the bounties of an hour?
  How poor, how rich, how abject, how august,
How complicate, how wonderful is man!
How passing wonder He who made him such!
Who centered in our make such strange extremes! 70
From different natures marvellously mixed,
Connection exquisite of distant worlds!
Distinguished link in being's endless chain!
Midway from nothing to the Deity!
A beam ethereal, sullied and absorpt!
Though sullied and dishonoured, still divine!
Dim miniature of greatness absolute!
An heir of glory! a frail child of dust!
Helpless immortal! insect infinite!
A worm! a god!—I tremble at myself, 80
And in myself am lost! At home a stranger,
Thought wanders up and down, surprised, aghast,
And wondering at her own: how reason reels!
Oh, what a miracle to man is man,
Triumphantly distressed! what joy, what dread!
Alternately transported and alarmed!
What can preserve my life? or what destroy?
An angel's arm can't snatch me from the grave;
Legions of angels can't confine me there.
  'Tis past conjecture; all things rise in proof: 90
While o'er my limbs sleep's soft dominion spread,
What though my soul fantastic measures trod
O'er fairy fields; or mourned along the gloom
Of pathless woods; or down the craggy steep
Hurled headlong, swam with pain the mantled pool;
Or scaled the cliff, or danced on hollow winds,
With antic shapes, wild natives of the brain?
Her ceaseless flight, though devious, speaks her nature
Of subtler essence than the trodden clod;
Active, aërial, towering, unconfined, 100
Unfettered with her gross companion's fall.
Even silent night proclaims my soul immortal;
Even silent night proclaims eternal day.
For human weal, Heaven husbands all events;
Dull sleep instructs, nor sport vain dreams in vain.
  Why then their loss deplore, that are not lost?
Why wanders wretched thought their tombs around,
In infidel distress? Are angels there?
Slumbers, raked up in dust, ethereal fire?
  They live! they greatly live a life on earth 110
Unkindled, unconceived; and from an eye
Of tenderness let heavenly pity fall
On me, more justly numbered with the dead.
This is the desert, this the solitude:

How populous, how vital, is the grave!
This is creation's melancholy vault,
The vale funereal, the sad cypress gloom;
The land of apparitions, empty shades!
All, all on earth is shadow, all beyond
Is substance; the reverse is Folly's creed: 120
How solid all, where change shall be no more!
    This is the bud of being, the dim dawn,
The twilight of our day, the vestibule.
Life's theatre as yet is shut, and Death,
Strong Death, alone can heave the massy bar,
This gross impediment of clay remove,
And makes us embryos of existence free.
From real life, but little more remote
Is he, not yet a candidate for light,
The future embryo, slumbering in his sire.   130
Embryos we must be, till we burst the shell,
Yon ambient azure shell, and spring to life,
The life of gods, oh transport! and of man.
    Yet man, fool man! here buries all his thoughts;
Inters celestial hopes without one sigh.
Prisoner of earth, and pent beneath the moon,
Here pinions all his wishes; winged by Heaven
To fly at infinite; and reach it there,
Where seraphs gather immortality,
On life's fair tree, fast by the throne of God.   140
What golden joys ambrosial clustering glow
In His full beam, and ripen for the just,
Where momentary ages are no more!
Where time, and pain, and chance, and death expire!
And is it in the flight of threescore years,
To push eternity from human thought,
And smother souls immortal in the dust?
A soul immortal, spending all her fires,
Wasting her strength in strenuous idleness,
Thrown into tumult, raptured or alarmed   150
At aught this scene can threaten or indulge,
Resembles ocean into tempest wrought,
To waft a feather or to drown a fly.
    Where falls this censure? It o'erwhelms myself;
How was my heart incrusted by the world!
Oh, how self-fettered was my groveling soul!
How, like a worm, was I wrapped round and round
In silken thought, which reptile Fancy spun,
Till darkened Reason lay quite clouded o'er
With soft conceit of endless comfort here,   160
Nor yet put forth her wings to reach the skies!
    Night-visions may befriend (as sung above):
Our waking dreams are fatal. How I dreamt
Of things impossible! (Could sleep do more?)
Of joys perpetual in perpetual change!
Of stable pleasures on the tossing wave!
Eternal sunshine in the storms of life!
How richly were my noontide trances hung
With gorgeous tapestries of pictured joys!

Joy behind joy, in endless perspective!   176
Till at Death's toll, whose restless iron tongue
Calls daily for his millions at a meal,
Starting I woke, and found myself undone.
Where now my frenzy's pompous furniture?
The cobwebbed cottage, with its ragged wall
Of mouldering mud, is royalty to me!
The spider's most attenuated thread
Is cord, is cable, to man's tender tie
On earthly bliss; it breaks at every breeze.
 Oh, ye blest scenes of permanent delight!   180
Full above measure! lasting beyond bound!
A perpetuity of bliss is bliss.
Could you, so rich in rapture, fear an end,
That ghastly thought would drink up all your joy,
And quite unparadise the realms of light.
Safe are you lodged above these rolling spheres,
The baleful influence of whose giddy dance
Sheds sad vicissitude on all beneath.
Here teems with revolutions every hour;
And rarely for the better; or the best,   190
More mortal than the common births of Fate.
Each Moment has its sickle, emulous
Of Time's enormous scythe, whose ample sweep
Strikes empires from the root; each Moment plays
His little weapon in the narrower sphere
Of sweet domestic comfort, and cuts down
The fairest bloom of sublunary bliss.
 Bliss! sublunary bliss!—proud words, and vain!
Implicit treason to divine decree!
A bold invasion of the rights of Heaven!   200
I clasped the phantoms, and I found them air.
Oh, had I weighed it ere my fond embrace!
What darts of agony had missed my heart!
 Death! great proprietor of all! 'tis thine
To tread out empire and to quench the stars.
The sun himself by thy permission shines,
And one day thou shalt pluck him from his sphere.
Amid such mighty plunder, why exhaust
Thy partial quiver on a mark so mean?
Why thy peculiar rancour wreaked on me?   210
Insatiate archer! could not one suffice?
Thy shaft flew thrice; and thrice my peace was slain;
And thrice, ere thrice yon moon had filled her horn.
O Cynthia! why so pale? dost thou lament
Thy wretched neighbour? Grieve to see thy wheel
Of ceaseless change outwhirled in human life?
How wanes my borrowed bliss! from Fortune's smile
Precarious courtesy! not virtue's sure,
Self-given, solar ray of sound delight.
 In every varied posture, place, and hour,   220
How widowed every thought of every joy!
Thought, busy thought! too busy for my peace!
Through the dark postern of time long elapsed
Led softly, by the stillness of the night—

Led like a murderer (and such it proves!)
Strays (wretched rover!) o'er the pleasing past;
In quest of wretchedness perversely strays;
And finds all desert now; and meets the ghosts
Of my departed joys; a numerous train!
I rue the riches of my former fate;   230
Sweet comfort's blasted clusters I lament;
I tremble at the blessings once so dear;
And every pleasure pains me to the heart.
   Yet why complain? or why complain for one?
Hangs out the sun his lustre but for me,
The single man? Are angels all beside?
I mourn for millions: 'tis the common lot;
In this shape or in that has fate entailed
The mother's throes on all of woman born,
Not more the children, than sure heirs, of pain.   240
   War, famine, pest, volcano, storm, and fire,
Intestine broils, Oppression with her heart
Wrapped up in triple brass, besiege mankind.
God's image disinherited of day,
Here, plunged in mines, forgets a sun was made.
There, beings deathless as their haughty lord,
Are hammered to the galling oar for life;
And plough the winter's wave, and reap despair.
Some, for hard masters, broken under arms,
In battle lopped away, with half their limbs,   250
Beg bitter bread through realms their valour saved,
If so the tyrant, or his minion, doom.
Want and incurable Disease (fell pair!)
On hopeless multitudes remorseless seize
At once; and make a refuge of the grave.
How groaning hospitals eject their dead!
What numbers groan for sad admission there!
What numbers, once in Fortune's lap high-fed,
Solicit the cold hand of Charity!
To shock us more, solicit it in vain!   260
Ye silken sons of Pleasure! since in pains
You rue more modish visits, visit here,
And breathe from your debauch: give, and reduce
Surfeit's dominion o'er you; but, so great
Your impudence, you blush at what is right.
   Happy! did sorrow seize on such alone.
Not prudence can defend or virtue save;
Disease invades the chastest temperance;
And punishment the guiltless; and alarm
Through thickest shades pursues the fond of peace.   270
Man's caution often into danger turns,
And, his guard falling, crushes him to death.
Not Happiness itself makes good her name!
Our very wishes give us not our wish.
How distant oft the thing we doat on most,
From that for which we doat, felicity!
The smoothest course of nature has its pains;
And truest friends, through error, wound our rest.
Without misfortune, what calamities!

And what hostilities, without a foe!   280
Nor are foes wanting to the best on earth.
But endless is the list of human ills,
And sighs might sooner fail, than cause to sigh.
    A part how small of the terraqueous globe
Is tenanted by man! the rest a waste,
Rocks, deserts, frozen seas, and burning sands:
Wild haunts of monsters, poisons, stings, and death.
Such is earth's melancholy map! But, far
More sad! this earth is a true map of man.
So bounded are its haughty lord's delights   290
To woe's wide empire; where deep troubles toss,
Loud sorrows howl, envenomed passions bite,
Ravenous calamities our vitals seize,
And threatening Fate wide opens to devour.
    What then am I, who sorrow for myself?
In age, in infancy, from others' aid
Is all our hope; to teach us to be kind.
That, Nature's first, last lesson to mankind;
The selfish heart deserves the pain it feels;
More generous sorrow, while it sinks, exalts;   300
And conscious virtue mitigates the pang.
Nor virtue, more than prudence, bids me give
Swoln thought a second channel; who divide,
They weaken too, the torrent of their grief.
Take then, O world! thy much-indebted tear;
How sad a sight is human happiness,
To those whose thought can pierce beyond an hour!
O thou! whate'er thou art, whose heart exults!
Wouldst thou I should congratulate thy fate?
I know thou wouldst; thy pride demands it from me.   310
Let thy pride pardon what thy nature needs,
The salutary censure of a friend.
Thou happy wretch! by blindness art thou blessed;
By dotage dandled to perpetual smiles.
Know, smiler! at thy peril art thou pleased;
Thy pleasure is the promise of thy pain.
Misfortune, like a creditor severe,
But rises in demand for her delay;
She makes a scourge of past prosperity,
To sting thee more and double thy distress.   320
    Lorenzo, Fortune makes her court to thee;
Thy fond heart dances, while the siren sings.
Dear is thy welfare; think me not unkind;
I would not damp, but to secure thy joys.
Think not that fear is sacred to the storm;
Stand on thy guard against the smiles of Fate.
Is Heaven tremendous in its frowns? Most sure;
And in its favours formidable too:
Its favours here are trials, not rewards;
A call to duty, not discharge from care;   330
And should alarm us, full as much as woes;
Awake us to their cause and consequence;
And make us tremble, weighed with our desert;
Awe Nature's tumult and chastise her joys,

Lest while we clasp, we kill them; nay, invert
To worse than simple misery, their charms.
Revolted joys, like foes in civil war,
Like bosom friendships to resentments soured,
With rage envenomed rise against our peace.
Beware what earth calls happiness; beware   340
All joys, but joys that never can expire.
Who builds on less than an immortal base,
Fond as he seems, condemns his joys to death.
   Mine died with thee, Philander! thy last sigh
Dissolved the charm; the disenchanted earth
Lost all her lustre. Where her glittering towers?
Her golden mountains, where? all darkened down
To naked waste; a dreary vale of tears:
The great magician's dead! Thou poor, pale piece
Of outcast earth, in darkness! what a change   350
From yesterday! Thy darling hope so near
(Long-laboured prize!), oh, how ambition flushed
Thy glowing cheek! ambition truly great,
Of virtuous praise. Death's subtle seed within,
(Sly, treacherous miner!) working in the dark,
Smiled at thy well-concerted scheme, and beckoned
The worm to riot on that rose so red,
Unfaded ere it fell—one moment's prey!
   Man's foresight is conditionally wise;
Lorenzo, wisdom into folly turns   360
Oft, the first instant its idea fair
To labouring thought is born. How dim our eye!
The present moment terminates our sight;
Clouds, thick as those on doomsday, drown the next;
We penetrate, we prophesy in vain.
Time is dealt out by particles; and each,
Ere mingled with the streaming sands of life,
By fate's inviolable oath is sworn
Deep silence, "Where eternity begins."
   By Nature's law, what may be, may be now;   370
There's no prerogative in human hours.
In human hearts what bolder thought can rise
Than man's presumption on to-morrow's dawn?
Where is to-morrow? In another world.
For numbers this is certain; the reverse
Is sure to none; and yet on this perhaps,
This peradventure, infamous for lies,
As on a rock of adamant, we build
Our mountain hopes; spin out eternal schemes,
As we the fatal sisters could outspin,   380
And, big with life's futurities, expire.
   Not even Philander had bespoke his shroud.
Nor had he cause; a warning was denied:
How many fall as sudden, not as safe!
As sudden, though for years admonished home.
Of human ills the last extreme beware—
Beware, Lorenzo! a slow-sudden death.
How dreadful that deliberate surprise!
Be wise to-day; 'tis madness to defer;

Next day the fatal precedent will plead;   390
Thus on, till wisdom is pushed out of life.
Procrastination is the thief of time;
Year after year it steals, till all are fled,
And to the mercies of a moment leaves
The vast concerns of an eternal scene.
If not so frequent, would not this be strange?
That 'tis so frequent, this is stranger still.
   Of man's miraculous mistakes, this bears
The palm, "That all men are about to live,"
Forever on the brink of being born.   400
All pay themselves the compliment to think
They one day shall not drivel: and their pride
On this reversion takes up ready praise;
At least, their own; their future selves applauds;
How excellent that life they ne'er will lead!
Time lodged in their own hands is Folly's vails;[1]
That lodged in Fate's, to Wisdom they consign;
The thing they can't but purpose, they postpone;
'Tis not in folly, not to scorn a fool;
And scarce in human wisdom to do more.   410
All promise is poor dilatory man,
And that through every stage: when young, indeed,
In full content we sometimes nobly rest,
Unanxious for ourselves; and only wish,
As duteous sons, our fathers were more wise.
At thirty man suspects himself a fool;
Knows it at forty, and reforms his plan;
At fifty chides his infamous delay,
Pushes his prudent purpose to resolve;
In all the magnanimity of thought   420
Resolves; and re-resolves; then dies the same.
   And why? Because he thinks himself immortal.
All men think all men mortal, but themselves;
Themselves, when some alarming shock of Fate
Strikes through their wounded hearts the sudden dread;
But their hearts wounded, like the wounded air,
Soon close; where passed the shaft, no trace is found.
As from the wing no scar the sky retains,
The parted wave no furrow from the keel;
So dies in human hearts the thought of death.   430
Even with the tender tear which Nature sheds
O'er those we love, we drop it in their grave.
Can I forget Philander? That were strange!
Oh, my full heart—But should I give it vent,
The longest night, though longer far, would fail,
And the lark listen to my midnight song.
   The sprightly lark's shrill matin wakes the morn;
Grief's sharpest thorn hard-pressing on my breast,
I strive, with wakeful melody, to cheer
The sullen gloom, sweet Philomel! like thee,   440
And call the stars to listen: every star
Is deaf to mine, enamoured of thy lay.
Yet be not vain; there are, who thine excel,

[1] Tips, gratuities.

And charm through distant ages: wrapped in shade,
Prisoner of darkness! to the silent hours,
How often I repeat their rage divine,
To lull my griefs, and steal my heart from woe!
I roll their raptures, but not catch their fire.
Dark, though not blind, like thee, Maeonides!
Or, Milton! thee; ah, could I reach your strain!   450
Or his, who made Maeonides our own,
Man too he sung: immortal man I sing;
Oft bursts my song beyond the bounds of life;
What now but immortality can please?
Oh, had he pressed his theme, pursued the track,
Which opens out of darkness into day!
Oh, had he, mounted on his wing of fire,
Soared where I sink, and sung immortal man!
How had it blessed mankind, and rescued me!

[1742]

[For additional readings in Young see pages 1143–1157.]

ROBERT BLAIR (1699-1746)

Robert Blair was educated at Edinburgh University, was ordained minister of Athelstaneford, East Lothian, in 1731, and spent the rest of his life in that obscure parish. In 1741 and 1742 he submitted the manuscript of his one important poem, *The Grave,* written for the most part before 1731, to the distinguished clergymen Isaac Watts and Philip Doddridge, and through their good offices it was published in 1743. It appealed to the same public that was reading the first book of Young's *Night Thoughts* and was soon to welcome James Hervey's *Meditations and Contemplations among the Tombs.* Before 1800 it was reprinted at least forty times in Great Britain and America. William Blake's fine drawings to illustrate the poem were published in 1808.

Blair treats with some literary distinction the commonplaces about death which are characteristic of Puritan preaching and pious elegy. He writes a popular sermon in verse, and strives for emphasis and vigor rather than for subtlety and good taste. He avoids the Miltonic meter and diction of Thomson, and models his blank verse on the moralizing passages in such dramatists as Dryden, Lee, and Rowe. The poem is full of verbal echoes of his reading, but he adapts his borrowings with considerable skill. He dwells on the macabre imagery of churchyard and tomb, and he ends with the theme of Christian hope and consolation; his characteristic vein, however, is a grimly satirical treatment of the heedlessness and vanity of mortal man.

A thorough study of the poem has been made by Carl Müller, *Robert Blair's 'Grave' und die Grabes- und Nachtdichtung* (Weimar, 1909). For the general background consult John W. Draper, *The Funeral Elegy and the Rise of English Romanticism* (New York, 1929), Amy L. Reed, *The Background of Gray's Elegy* (New York, 1924), and Paul van Tieghem, "La poésie de la nuit et des tombeaux," in *Le Préromantisme,* ii (Paris, 1930).

THE GRAVE

The house appointed for all living.—Job, xxx, 23

Whilst some affect the sun and some the shade,
Some flee the city, some the hermitage,
Their aims as various as the roads they take
In journeying through life—the task be mine
To paint the gloomy horrors of the tomb,
The appointed place of rendezvous, where all
These travellers meet. Thy succours I implore,
Eternal King! whose potent arm sustains
The keys of hell and death. The Grave, dread thing!
Men shiver when thou'rt named; Nature, appalled,   10
Shakes off her wonted firmness. Ah! how dark
Thy long-extended realms and rueful wastes,
Where naught but silence reigns, and night, dark night,
Dark as was chaos ere the infant sun
Was rolled together, or had tried his beams
Athwart the gloom profound! The sickly taper
By glimmering through thy low-browed misty vaults
(Furred round with mouldy damps and ropy slime)
Lets fall a supernumerary horror,
And only serves to make thy night more irksome.   20
Well do I know thee by thy trusty yew,

Cheerless, unsocial plant! that loves to dwell
Midst skulls and coffins, epitaphs and worms;
Where light-heeled ghosts and visionary shades,
Beneath the wan cold moon (as fame reports)
Embodied thick, perform their mystic rounds.
No other merriment, dull tree! is thine.
   See yonder hallowed fane—the pious work
Of names once famed, now dubious or forgot,
And buried midst the wreck of things which were;   30
There lie interred the more illustrious dead.
The wind is up—hark! how it howls! Methinks
Till now I never heard a sound so dreary.
Doors creak, and windows clap, and night's foul bird,
Rooked[1] in the spire, screams loud; the gloomy aisles,
Black-plastered, and hung round with shreds of 'scutcheons
And tattered coats of arms, send back the sound
Laden with heavier airs, from the low vaults,
The mansions of the dead. Roused from their slumbers,
In grim array the grisly spectres rise,   40
Grin horrible, and obstinately sullen
Pass and repass, hushed as the foot of night.
Again the screech-owl shrieks—ungracious sound!
I'll hear no more; it makes one's blood run chill.
   Quite round the pile, a row of reverend elms
(Coeval near with that) all ragged show,
Long lashed by the rude winds; some rift half down
Their branchless trunks, others so thin at top
That scarce two crows could lodge in the same tree.
Strange things, the neighbours say, have happened here: 50
Wild shrieks have issued from the hollow tombs;
Dead men have come again, and walked about;
And the great bell has tolled, unrung, untouched.
(Such tales their cheer, at wake or gossiping,
When it draws near to witching time of night.)
   Oft in the lone churchyard at night I've seen,
By glimpse of moonshine checkering through the trees,
The school-boy, with his satchel in his hand,
Whistling aloud to bear his courage up,
And lightly tripping o'er the long flat stones   60
(With nettles skirted and with moss o'ergrown)
That tell in homely phrase who lie below.
Sudden he starts, and hears, or thinks he hears,
The sound of something purring at his heels;
Full fast he flies, and dares not look behind him,
Till out of breath he overtakes his fellows;
Who gather round, and wonder at the tale
Of horrid apparition, tall and ghastly,
That walks at dead of night, or takes his stand
O'er some new-opened grave, and (strange to tell!)   70
Evanishes at crowing of the cock.
   The new-made widow too I've sometimes spied,
Sad sight! slow moving o'er the prostrate dead;
Listless she crawls along in doleful black,
Whilst bursts of sorrow gush from either eye,

[1] Cowering.

Fast falling down her now untasted cheek.
Prone on the lowly grave of the dear man
She drops; whilst busy-meddling memory
In barbarous succession musters up
The past endearments of their softer hours,   8ʳ
Tenacious of its theme. Still, still she thinks
She sees him, and indulging the fond thought,
Clings yet more closely to the senseless turf,
Nor heeds the passenger who looks that way.
    Invidious Grave—how dost thou rend in sunder
Whom love has knit, and sympathy made one!
A tie more stubborn far than nature's band.
Friendship! mysterious cement of the soul!
Sweetener of life, and solder of society!
I owe thee much. Thou hast deserved from me   90
Far, far beyond what I can ever pay.
Oft have I proved the labours of thy love,
And the warm efforts of the gentle heart,
Anxious to please. Oh, when my friend and I
In some thick wood have wandered heedless on,
Hid from the vulgar eye, and sat us down
Upon the sloping cowslip-covered bank,
Where the pure limpid stream has slid along
In grateful errors through the underwood,
Sweet-murmuring—methought the shrill-tongued thrush   100
Mended his song of love; the sooty blackbird
Mellowed his pipe and softened every note;
The eglantine smelled sweeter, and the rose
Assumed a dye more deep; whilst every flower
Vied with its fellow plant in luxury
Of dress. Oh, then the longest summer's day
Seemed too, too much in haste; still the full heart
Had not imparted half; 'twas happiness
Too exquisite to last! Of joys departed,
Not to return, how painful the remembrance!   110
    Dull Grave! thou spoil'st the dance of youthful blood,
Strik'st out the dimple from the cheek of mirth,
And every smirking feature from the face;
Branding our laughter with the name of madness.
Where are the jesters now? the men of health
Complexionally pleasant? Where the droll,
Whose every look and gesture was a joke
To clapping theatres and shouting crowds,
And made even thick-lipped musing Melancholy
To gather up her face into a smile   120
Before she was aware? Ah! sullen now,
And dumb as the green turf that covers them!
    Where are the mighty thunderbolts of war,
The Roman Cæsars and the Grecian chiefs,
The boast of story? Where the hot-brained youth,
Who the tiara at his pleasure tore
From kings of all the then discovered globe,
And cried, forsooth, because his arm was hampered,
And had not room enough to do its work?
Alas, how slim—dishonourably slim—   136

And crammed into a space we blush to name!
Proud Royalty! How altered in thy looks!
How blank thy features, and how wan thy hue!
Son of the morning! whither art thou gone?
Where hast thou hid thy many-spangled head,
And the majestic menace of thine eyes,
Felt from afar? Pliant and powerless now;
Like new-born infant wound up in his swathes,
Or victim tumbled flat upon its back,
That throbs beneath the sacrificer's knife;   140
Mute must thou bear the strife of little tongues,
And coward insults of the base-born crowd,
That grudge a privilege thou never hadst,
But only hoped for in the peaceful grave—
Of being unmolested and alone!
Arabia's gums and odoriferous drugs,
And honours by the heralds duly paid
In mode and form, even to a very scruple;
(Oh cruel irony!) these come too late,
And only mock whom they were meant to honour!   150
Surely there's not a dungeon-slave that's buried
In the highway, unshrouded and uncoffined,
But lies as soft and sleeps as sound as he.
Sorry preëminence of high descent
Above the vulgar-born, to rot in state!

But see! the well-plumed hearse comes nodding on,
Stately and slow; and properly attended
By the whole sable tribe, that painful watch
The sick man's door, and live upon the dead,
By letting out their persons by the hour   160
To mimic sorrow, when the heart's not sad.
How rich the trappings, now they're all unfurled
And glittering in the sun! Triumphant entries
Of conquerors, and coronation pomps
In glory scarce exceed. Great gluts of people
Retard the unwieldy show, whilst from the casements
And houses' tops, ranks behind ranks close-wedged
Hang bellying o'er. But tell us, why this waste?
Why this ado in earthing up a carcass
That's fallen into disgrace, and in the nostril   170
Smells horrible? Ye undertakers! tell us,
Midst all the gorgeous figures you exhibit,
Why is the principal concealed, for which
You make this mighty stir? 'Tis wisely done;
What would offend the eye in a good picture,
The painter casts discreetly into shades.

Proud lineage! now how little thou appearest!
Below the envy of the private man!
Honour, that meddlesome officious ill,
Pursues thee even to death, nor there stops short!   180
Strange persecution, when the grave itself
Is no protection from rude sufferance!

Absurd! to think to overreach the grave,
And from the wreck of names to rescue ours!
The best-concerted schemes men lay for fame

Die fast away; only themselves die faster.
The far-famed sculptor and the laurelled bard,
Those bold insurancers of deathless fame,
Supply their little feeble aids in vain—
The tapering pyramid, the Egyptian's pride,   190
And wonder of the world, whose spiky top
Has wounded the thick cloud, and long outlived
The angry shaking of the winter's storm;
Yet, spent at last by the injuries of heaven,
Shattered with age and furrowed o'er with years,
The mystic cone, with hieroglyphics crusted,
Gives way. Oh, lamentable sight! At once
The labour of whole ages lumbers down,
A hideous and misshapen length of ruins!
Sepulchral columns wrestle but in vain   200
With all-subduing Time; her cankering hand
With calm deliberate malice wasteth them.
Worn on the edge of days, the brass consumes,
The busto moulders, and the deep-cut marble,
Unsteady to the steel, gives up its charge!
Ambition, half convicted of her folly,
Hangs down the head, and reddens at the tale.
    Here all the mighty troublers of the earth,
Who swam to sovereign rule through seas of blood,
The oppressive, sturdy, man-destroying villains   210
Who ravaged kingdoms and laid empires waste
And in a cruel wantonness of power
Thinned states of half their people, and gave up
To want the rest; now, like a storm that's spent,
Lie hushed, and meanly sneak behind thy covert.
Vain thought! to hide them from the general scorn
That haunts and dogs them like an injured ghost
Implacable! Here too the petty tyrant
Of scant domains geographer ne'er noticed,
And, well for neighbouring grounds, of arm as short;   220
Who fixed his iron talons on the poor,
And gripped them like some lordly beast of prey,
Deaf to the forceful cries of gnawing hunger,
And piteous plaintive voice of misery
(As if a slave was not a shred of nature,
Of the same common nature with his lord)
Now tame and humble, like a child that's whipped,
Shakes hands with dust, and calls the worm his kinsman;
Nor pleads his rank and birthright. Under ground
Precedency's a jest; vassal and lord,   230
Grossly familiar, side by side consume.
    When self-esteem, or others' adulation,
Would cunningly persuade us we were something
Above the common level of our kind,
The Grave gainsays the smooth-complexioned flattery,
And with blunt truth acquaints us what we are.
    Beauty! thou pretty plaything! dear deceit!
That steals so softly o'er the stripling's heart,
And gives it a new pulse unknown before!
The Grave discredits thee. Thy charms expunged,   240

Thy roses faded, and thy lilies soiled,
What hast thou more to boast of? Will thy lovers
Flock round thee now, to gaze and do thee homage?
Methinks I see thee with thy head low laid;
Whilst, surfeited upon thy damask cheek,
The high-fed worm, in lazy volumes rolled,
Riots unscared. For this was all thy caution?
For this thy painful labours at thy glass,
To improve those charms and keep them in repair,
For which the spoiler thanks thee not? Foul feeder!   250
Coarse fare and carrion please thee full as well,
And leave as keen a relish on the sense.
Look, how the fair one weeps! The conscious tears
Stand thick as dew-drops on the bells of flowers—
Honest effusion! The swoln heart in vain
Works hard to put a gloss on its distress.
    Strength too! thou surly and less gentle boast
Of those that laugh loud at the village ring!
A fit of common sickness pulls thee down
With greater ease than e'er thou didst the stripling   260
That rashly dared thee to the unequal fight.
What groan was that I heard? Deep groan indeed,
With anguish heavy-laden! let me trace it:
From yonder bed it comes, where the strong man,
By stronger arm belaboured, gasps for breath
Like a hard-hunted beast. How his great heart
Beats thick! his roomy chest by far too scant
To give the lungs full play! What now avail
The strong-built sinewy limbs and well-spread shoulders?
See how he tugs for life and lays about him,   270
Mad with his pain! Eager he catches hold
Of what comes next to hand and grasps it hard,
Just like a creature drowning! Hideous sight!
Oh! how his eyes stand out and stare full ghastly!
Whilst the distemper's rank and deadly venom
Shoots like a burning arrow 'cross his bowels
And drinks his marrow up. Heard you that groan?
It was his last. See how the great Goliah,
Just like a child that brawled itself to rest,
Lies still! What mean'st thou then, O mighty boaster,   280
To vaunt of nerves of thine? What means the bull,
Unconscious of his strength, to play the coward,
And flee before a feeble thing like man,
That, knowing well the slackness of his arm,
Trusts only in the well-invented knife?
    With study pale and midnight vigils spent,
The star-surveying sage close to his eye
Applies the sight-invigorating tube,
And, travelling through the boundless length of space,
Marks well the courses of the far-seen orbs,   290
That roll with regular confusion there,
In ecstasy of thought. But ah, proud man!
Great heights are hazardous to the weak head;
Soon, very soon, thy firmest footing fails,
And down thou dropp'st into that darksome place

Where nor device nor knowledge ever came.
Here the tongue-warrior lies, disabled now,
Disarmed, dishonoured, like a wretch that's gagged,
And cannot tell his ail to passers-by!
Great man of language! whence this mighty change, 300
This dumb despair, and drooping of the head?
Though strong Persuasion hung upon thy lip,
And sly Insinuation's softer arts
In ambush lay about thy flowing tongue,
Alas, how chop-fallen now! thick mists and silence
Rest like a weary cloud upon thy breast,
Unceasing. Ah, where is the lifted arm,
The strength of action and the force of words,
The well-turned period and the well-tuned voice,
With all the lesser ornaments of phrase? 310
Ah, fled forever, as they ne'er had been!
Razed from the book of fame; or, more provoking,
Perchance some hackney hunger-bitten scribbler
Insults thy memory, and blots thy tomb
With long flat narrative or duller rhymes,
With heavy halting pace that drawl along—
Enough to rouse a dead man into rage,
And warm with red resentment the wan cheek!
Here the great masters of the healing art,
These mighty mock-defrauders of the tomb, 320
Spite of their juleps and catholicons,[2]
Resign to fate! Proud Aesculapius' son,
Where are thy boasted implements of art,
And all thy well-crammed magazines of health?
Nor hill nor vale, as far as ship could go,
Nor margin of the gravel-bottomed brook
Escaped thy rifling hand; from stubborn shrubs
Thou wrungst their shy retiring virtues out,
And vexed them in the fire. Nor fly, nor insect,
Nor writhy snake, escaped thy deep research. 330
But why this apparatus? why this cost?
Tell us, thou doughty keeper from the grave,
Where are thy recipes and cordials now,
With the long list of vouchers for thy cures?
Alas, thou speakest not. The bold impostor
Looks not more silly when the cheat's found out.
Here the lank-sided miser, worst of felons,
Who meanly stole (discreditable shift)
From back and belly too their proper cheer,
Eased of a tax it irked the wretch to pay 340
To his own carcass, now lies cheaply lodged,
By clamorous appetites no longer teased,
Nor tedious bills of charges and repairs.
But ah, where are his rents, his comings-in?
Ay, now you've made the rich man poor indeed!
Robbed of his gods, what has he left behind?
O cursed lust of gold, when for thy sake
The fool throws up his interest in both worlds,

[2] Universal remedies.

First starved in this, then damned in that to come!
   How shocking must thy summons be, O Death,   350
To him that is at ease in his possessions;
Who, counting on long years of pleasure here,
Is quite unfurnished for that world to come!
In that dread moment how the frantic soul
Raves round the walls of her clay tenement,
Runs to each avenue, and shrieks for help,
But shrieks in vain! How wishfully she looks
On all she's leaving, now no longer here!
A little longer, yet a little longer,
Oh, might she stay to wash away her stains,   360
And fit her for her passage! mournful sight!
Her very eyes weep blood, and every groan
She heaves is big with horror, but the foe,
Like a stanch murderer steady to his purpose,
Pursues her close through every lane of life;
Nor misses once the track, but presses on,
Till, forced at last to the tremendous verge,
At once she sinks to everlasting ruin!
   Sure 'tis a serious thing to die! My soul,
What a strange moment must it be when, near   370
Thy journey's end, thou hast the gulf in view!
That awful gulf no mortal e'er repassed
To tell what's doing on the other side!
Nature runs back and shudders at the sight,
And every life-string bleeds at thoughts of parting!
For part they must—body and soul must part:
Fond couple! linked more close than wedded pair.
This wings its way to its Almighty Source,
The witness of its actions, now its judge;
That drops into the dark and noisome grave,   380
Like a disabled pitcher of no use.
   If death was nothing, and naught after death,
If when men died, at once they ceased to be,
Returning to the barren womb of nothing
Whence first they sprung, then might the debauchee
Untrembling mouth the heavens; then might the drunkard
Reel over his full bowl, and when 'tis drained
Fill up another to the brim, and laugh
At the poor bugbear Death; then might the wretch
That's weary of the world and tired of life,   390
At once give each inquietude the slip
By stealing out of being when he pleased,
And by what way, whether by hemp or steel.
Death's thousand doors stand open. Who could force
The ill-pleased guest to sit out his full time,
Or blame him if he goes? Sure he does well
That helps himself as timely as he can,
When able. But if there is an hereafter—
And that there is, conscience, uninfluenced
And suffered to speak out, tells every man—   400
Then must it be an awful thing to die;
More horrid yet, to die by one's own hand!
Self-murder! Name it not; our island's shame,
That makes her the reproach of neighbouring states.

Shall Nature, swerving from her earliest dictate,
Self-preservation, fall by her own act?
Forbid it, Heaven! Let not, upon disgust,
The shameless hand be foully crimsoned o'er
With blood of its own lord! Dreadful attempt,
Just reeking from self-slaughter, in a rage   410
To rush into the presence of our Judge;
As if we challenged him to do his worst,
And mattered not his wrath! Unheard-of tortures
Must be reserved for such: these herd together;
The common damned shun their society,
And look upon themselves as fiends less foul.
Our time is fixed, and all our days are numbered;
How long, how short, we know not—this we know:
Duty requires we calmly wait the summons,
Nor dare to stir till Heaven shall give permission;   420
Like sentries that must keep their destined stand,
And wait the appointed hour till they're relieved.
Those only are the brave that keep their ground,
And keep it to the last. To run away
Is but a coward's trick; to run away
From this world's ills, that at the very worst
Will soon blow o'er, thinking to mend ourselves
By boldly venturing on a world unknown,
And plunging headlong in the dark—'tis mad!
No frenzy half so desperate as this.   430
    Tell us, ye dead! will none of you, in pity
To those you left behind, disclose the secret?
Oh! that some courteous ghost would blab it out
What 'tis you are, and we must shortly be.
I've heard that souls departed have sometimes
Forewarned men of their death. 'Twas kindly done
To knock and give the alarum. But what means
This stinted charity? 'Tis but lame kindness
That does its work by halves. Why might you not
Tell us what 'tis to die? Do the strict laws   440
Of your society forbid your speaking
Upon a point so nice? I'll ask no more.
Sullen, like lamps in sepulchres, your shine
Enlightens but yourselves. Well—'tis no matter;
A very little time will clear up all,
And make us learned as you are, and as close.
    Death's shafts fly thick! Here falls the village swain,
And there his pampered lord! The cup goes round,
And who so artful as to put it by?
'Tis long since Death had the majority,   450
Yet, strange, the living lay it not to heart.
See yonder maker of the dead man's bed,
The sexton, hoary-headed chronicle,
Of hard unmeaning face, down which ne'er stole
A gentle tear, with mattock in his hand
Digs through whole rows of kindred and acquaintance,
By far his juniors. Scarce a skull's cast up,
But well he knew its owner and can tell
Some passage of his life. Thus hand in hand

The sot has walked with Death twice twenty years;   460
And yet ne'er younker on the green laughs louder,
Or clubs a smuttier tale; when drunkards meet,
None sings a merrier catch or lends a hand
More willing to his cup. Poor wretch! he minds not
That soon some trusty brother of the trade
Shall do for him what he has done for thousands.
   On this side and on that, men see their friends
Drop off like leaves in autumn; yet launch out
Into fantastic schemes, which the long livers
In the world's hale and undegenerate days   470
Could scarce have leisure for.—Fools that we are!
Never to think of death and of ourselves
At the same time!—as if to learn to die
Were no concern of ours. Oh! more than sottish,
For creatures of a day in gamesome mood
To frolic on eternity's dread brink,
Unapprehensive; when, for aught we know,
The very first swoln surge shall sweep us in!
Think we, or think we not, time hurries on
With a resistless unremitting stream,   480
Yet treads more soft than e'er did midnight thief,
That slides his hand under the miser's pillow
And carries off his prize. What is this world?
What but a spacious burial-field unwalled,
Strewed with death's spoils, the spoils of animals
Savage and tame, and full of dead men's bones!
The very turf on which we tread, once lived,
And we that live must lend our carcasses
To cover our own offspring; in their turns
They too must cover theirs. 'Tis here all meet!   490
The shivering Icelander and sun-burnt Moor,
Men of all climes, that never met before,
And of all creeds, the Jew, the Turk, and Christian.
Here the proud prince, and favourite yet prouder,
His sovereign's keeper and the people's scourge,
Are huddled out of sight. Here lie abashed
The great negotiators of the earth,
And celebrated masters of the balance,
Deep read in stratagems and wiles of courts;
Now vain their treaty-skill—Death scorns to treat.   500
Here the o'erloaded slave flings down his burden
From his galled shoulders; and when the cruel tyrant,
Will all his guards and tools of power about him,
Is meditating new unheard-of hardships,
Mocks his short arm, and quick as thought escapes,
Where tyrants vex not and the weary rest.
Here the warm lover, leaving the cool shade,
The tell-tale echo, and the babbling stream,
(Time out of mind the favourite seats of love),
Fast by his gentle mistress lays him down,   510
Unblasted by foul tongue. Here friends and foes
Lie close, unmindful of their former feuds;
The lawn-robed prelate and plain presbyter,
Erewhile that stood aloof, as shy to meet,

Familiar mingle here, like sister-streams
That some rude interposing rock had split.
Here is the large-limbed peasant; here the child
Of a span long, that never saw the sun,
Nor pressed the nipple, strangled in life's porch.
Here is the mother with her sons and daughters,   520
The barren wife, and long-demurring maid,
Whose lonely unappropriated sweets
Smiled like yon knot of cowslips on the cliff,
Not to be come at by the willing hand.
Here are the prude severe, and gay coquette,
The sober widow, and the young green virgin,
Cropped like a rose before 'tis fully blown,
Or half its worth disclosed. Strange medley here!
Here garrulous old age winds up his tale;
And jovial youth, of lightsome vacant heart,   530
Whose every day was made of melody,
Hears not the voice of mirth; the shrill-tongued shrew,
Meek as the turtle-dove, forgets her chiding.
Here are the wise, the generous, and the brave;
The just, the good, the worthless, the profane;
The downright clown, and perfectly well-bred;
The fool, the churl, the scoundrel, and the mean;
The supple statesman, and the patriot stern;
The wrecks of nations, and the spoils of time,
With all the lumber of six thousand years!   540
    Poor man! how happy once in thy first state,
When yet but warm from thy great Maker's hand
He stamped thee with his image, and well pleased
Smiled on his last fair work! Then all was well.
Sound was the body, and the soul serene;
Like two sweet instruments, ne'er out of tune,
That play their several parts. Nor head nor heart
Offered to ache, nor was there cause they should,
For all was pure within. No fell remorse,
Nor anxious castings up of what might be,   550
Alarmed his peaceful bosom. Summer seas
Show not more smooth when kissed by southern winds,
Just ready to expire. Scarce importuned,
The generous soil with a luxuriant hand
Offered the various produce of the year,
And everything most perfect in its kind.
Blessed, thrice blessed days! But ah, how short!
Blessed as the pleasing dreams of holy men;
But fugitive, like those, and quickly gone.
Oh, slippery state of things! What sudden turns,   560
What strange vicissitudes, in the first leaf
Of man's sad history! To-day most happy,
And ere to-morrow's sun has set, most abject!
How scant the space between these vast extremes!
Thus fared it with our sire; not long he enjoyed
His Paradise! Scarce had the happy tenant
Of the fair spot due time to prove its sweets,
Or sum them up, when straight he must be gone,
Ne'er to return again! And must he go?

Can naught compound for the first dire offence   570
Of erring man? Like one that is condemned,
Fain would he trifle time with idle talk,
And parley with his fate. But 'tis in vain;
Not all the lavish odours of the place,
Offered in incense, can procure his pardon,
Or mitigate his doom. A mighty angel
With flaming sword forbids his longer stay,
And drives the loiterer forth; nor must he take
One last and farewell round. At once he lost
His glory and his God! If mortal now,   580
And sorely maimed, no wonder—man has sinned!
Sick of his bliss, and bent on new adventures,
Evil he would needs try, nor tried in vain.
Dreadful experiment! destructive measure!
Where the worst thing could happen, is success!
Alas! too well he sped; the good he scorned
Retired reluctant, like an ill-used ghost,
Not to return; or if it did, its visits,
Like those of angels, short, and far between;
Whilst the black demon, with his hell-'scaped train,   590
Admitted once into its better room,
Grew loud and mutinous, nor would be gone;
Lording it o'er the man, who now too late
Saw the rash error which he could not mend;
An error fatal not to him alone,
But to his future sons, his fortune's heirs.
Inglorious bondage! human nature groans
Beneath a vassalage so vile and cruel,
And its vast body bleeds through every vein.
    What havoc hast thou made, foul monster, Sin!   600
Greatest and first of ills! the fruitful parent
Of woes of all dimensions! But for thee,
Sorrow had never been. All-noxious thing,
Of vilest nature! Other sorts of evils
Are kindly circumscribed, and have their bounds.
The fierce volcano, from its burning entrails
That belches molten stone and globes of fire,
Involved in pitchy clouds of smoke and stench,
Mars the adjacent fields for some leagues round,
And there it stops. The big-swoln inundation,   610
Of mischief more diffusive, raving loud,
Buries whole tracts of country, threatening more;
But that too has its shore it cannot pass.
More dreadful far than these, sin has laid waste,
Not here and there a country, but a world;
Dispatching at a wide-extended blow
Entire mankind, and for their sakes defacing
A whole creation's beauty with rude hands;
Blasting the foodful grain, the loaded branches,
And marking all along its way with ruin.   620
Accursed thing! Oh, where shall Fancy find
A proper name to call thee by, expressive
Of all thy horrors! Pregnant womb of ills!
Of temper so transcendently malign

That toads and serpents of most deadly kind
Compared to thee are harmless! Sicknesses
Of every size and symptom, racking pains,
And bluest plagues, are thine! See how the fiend
Profusely scatters the contagion round:
Whilst deep-mouthed Slaughter, bellowing at her heels,   630
Wades deep in blood new-spilt; yet for to-morrow
Shapes out new work of great uncommon daring,
And inly pines till the dread blow is struck.
    But hold! I've gone too far; too much discovered
My father's nakedness and Nature's shame.
Here let me pause, and drop an honest tear,
One burst of filial duty and condolence,
O'er all those ample deserts Death hath spread,
This chaos of mankind! O great man-eater!
Whose every day is carnival, not sated yet!   640
Unheard of epicure, without a fellow!
The veriest gluttons do not always cram;
Some intervals of abstinence are sought
To edge the appetite—thou seekest none!
Methinks the countless swarms thou hast devoured,
And thousands that each hour thou gobblest up,
This, less than this, might gorge thee to the full.
But ah! rapacious still, thou gap'st for more;
Like one, whole days defrauded of his meals,
On whom lank Hunger lays her skinny hand,   650
And whets to keenest eagerness his cravings;
As if diseases, massacres, and poison,
Famine, and war, were not thy caterers!
    But know that thou must render up thy dead,
And with high interest too!—They are not thine,
But only in thy keeping for a season,
Till the great promised day of restitution;
When loud diffusive sound from brazen trump
Of strong-lunged cherub shall alarm thy captives,
And rouse the long, long sleepers into life,   660
Daylight, and liberty.—
Then must thy gates fly open, and reveal
The mines that lay long forming under ground,
In their dark cells immured; but now full ripe,
And pure as silver from the crucible,
That twice has stood the torture of the fire,
And inquisition of the forge. We know
The illustrious Deliverer of mankind,
The Son of God, thee foiled. Him in thy power
Thou couldst not hold; self-vigorous he rose,   670
And, shaking off thy fetters, soon retook
Those spoils his voluntary yielding lent.
Sure pledge of our releasement from thy thrall—
Twice twenty days he sojourned here on earth,
And showed himself alive to chosen witnesses,
By proofs so strong that the most slow-assenting
Had not a scruple left. This having done,
He mounted up to Heaven. Methinks I see him
Climb the aërial heights, and glide along

Athwart the severing clouds; but the faint eye,   680
Flung backwards in the chase, soon drops its hold,
Disabled quite, and jaded with pursuing.
Heaven's portals wide expand to let him in,
Nor are his friends shut out; as some great prince
Not for himself alone procures admission,
But for his train; it was his royal will
That where he is there should his followers be.
Death only lies between, a gloomy path,
Made yet more gloomy by our coward fears!
But not untrod, nor tedious; the fatigue   690
Will soon go off. Besides, there's no by-road
To bliss. Then why, like ill-conditioned children,
Start we at transient hardships in the way
That leads to purer air and softer skies,
And a ne'er-setting sun? Fools that we are!
We wish to be where sweets unwithering bloom,
But straight our wish revoke, and will not go.
So have I seen, upon a summer's even,
Fast by the rivulet's brink, a youngster play:
How wishfully he looks to stem the tide!   700
This moment resolute, next unresolved;
At last he dips his foot, but as he dips
His fears redouble, and he runs away
From the inoffensive stream, unmindful now
Of all the flowers that paint the further bank,
And smiled so sweet of late.—Thrice welcome Death!
That after many a painful bleeding step
Conducts us to our home, and lands us safe
On the long-wished-for shore. Prodigious change!
Our bane turned to a blessing! Death disarmed   710
Loses her fellness quite; all thanks to him
Who scourged the venom out! Sure the last end
Of the good man is peace. How calm his exit!
Night-dews fall not more gently to the ground,
Nor weary worn-out winds expire so soft.
Behold him in the evening-tide of life,
A life well spent, whose early care it was
His riper years should not upbraid his green;
By unperceived degrees he wears away,
Yet like the sun seems larger at his setting!   720
High in his faith and hopes, look how he reaches
After the prize in view, and, like a bird
That's hampered, struggles hard to get away!
Whilst the glad gates of sight are wide expanded
To let new glories in, the first fair fruits
Of the fast-coming harvest. Then—oh then
Each earth-born joy grows vile or disappears,
Shrunk to a thing of naught. Oh, how he longs
To have his passport signed and be dismissed!
'Tis done, and now he's happy! The glad soul   730
Has not a wish uncrowned. E'en the lag[3] flesh
Rests too in hope of meeting once again
Its better half, never to sunder more.

³ Lagging, tardy.

Nor shall it hope in vain; the time draws on
When not a single spot of burial-earth
Whether on land or in the spacious sea,
But must give back its long-committed dust
Inviolate, and faithfully shall these
Make up the full account; not the least atom
Embezzled or mislaid of the whole tale.   746
Each soul shall have a body ready-furnished,
And each shall have his own. Hence, ye profane!
Ask not how this can be. Sure the same power
That reared the piece at first, and took it down,
Can re-assemble the loose scattered parts,
And put them as they were. Almighty God
Has done much more, nor is his arm impaired
Through length of days; and what he can he will:
His faithfulness stands bound to see it done.
When the dread trumpet sounds, the slumbering dust,   750
Not unattentive to the call, shall wake;
And every joint possess its proper place,
With a new elegance of form, unknown
To its first state. Nor shall the conscious soul
Mistake its partner; but, amidst the crowd
Singling its other half, into its arms
Shall rush with all the impatience of a man
That's new come home, who having long been absent,
With haste runs over every different room,
In pain to see the whole. Thrice happy meeting!   760
Nor time nor death shall ever part them more.
    'Tis but a night, a long and moonless night,
We make the grave our bed, and then are gone.
    Thus at the shut of even, the weary bird
Leaves the wide air, and in some lonely brake
Cowers down and dozes till the dawn of day;
Then claps his well-fledged wings and bears away.

                        [c. 1730, 1743]

MARK AKENSIDE (1721-1770)

Mark Akenside, born of humble parents in Newcastle-upon-Tyne, attracted attention as a youthful poet and was sent by benevolent friends to the University of Edinburgh, where he studied first theology and then medicine. The combination is significant; it was Akenside's wide interest in religion, philosophy, science, and art that prompted him to publish *The Pleasures of Imagination*, with great success, in 1744. He also joined the opposition to Walpole at this time, and wrote ardently of patriotism and liberty. In his *Odes* (1745) these political ideas blend with his enthusiasm for Greek and Roman antiquity. He slightly anticipates the more vital classicism of Collins, and may have had some influence on the greater poet. His later career is of less importance for literature; he practised medicine with indifferent success, wrote some neat odes and inscriptions, and elaborately revised *The Pleasures of Imagination*.

This poem is of more importance to the historian of ideas than to the student of literature. It has been in bad repute among critics because of its pompous, frigid, and clumsy style; and it commits the error, common among eighteenth century writers of blank verse, of assuming that a poet who announces that he is going to write about the sublime and beautiful makes his work *ipso facto* sublime and beautiful. Nevertheless Akenside responds sensitively and intelligently to current ideas, combines them elaborately, and expounds them with some power. His title and some of his central ideas come from Addison's series of papers in the *Spectator* (Nos. 411-421); he follows the example of James Thomson and other poets in writing expository blank verse inspired in part by the new science; he draws largely on Shaftesbury and Plato and gives an elaborate exposition of the idea of the chain or scale of being, which realizes the ideal of a perfect universe by exemplifying all degrees of perfection. From Shaftesbury in particular he takes the conception of the harmony, at once natural and divine, of the true, the good, and the beautiful. Some speculative originality appears in his view that the chain of being is not immutable, that the divine hand is still at work, evolving new species.

> Nor content,
> By one exertion of creative power
> His goodness to reveal; through every age,
> Through every moment up the track of time
> His parent-hand with ever-new increase
> Of happiness and virtue has adorned
> The vast harmonious frame: his parent-hand,
> From the mute shell-fish gasping on the shore,
> To men, to angels, to celestial minds
> Forever leads the generations on
> To higher scenes of being; while supplied
> From day to day with his enlivening breath,
> Inferior orders in succession rise
> To fill the void below.
>
> (*Pleasures of Imagination*, ii, 337-50.)

Less interesting to us, but just as characteristic of his thought, is his preference of Athenian elegance to Gothic barbarism, and his announced intention to "tune to Attic themes the British lyre."

There is no recent edition of Akenside; the Aldine edition (1835 and repr.) may still be used. Interesting for Akenside's anticipation of modern science is G. R. Potter's article, "Mark Akenside, Prophet of Evolution," *Modern Philology*, xxiv (1926), 55-64. For bibliography, see Iolo A. Williams, *Seven XVIIIth Century Bibliographies* (London, 1924).

THE PLEASURES OF IMAGINATION

ARGUMENT OF THE FIRST BOOK

The subject proposed. Difficulty of treating it poetically. The ideas of the divine mind, the origin of every quality pleasing to the imagination. The natural variety of constitution in the minds of men; with its final cause. The idea of a fine imagination, and the state of the mind in the enjoyment of those pleasures which it affords. All the primary pleasures of the imagination result from the perception of greatness, or wonderfulness, or beauty in objects. The pleasure from greatness, with its final cause. Pleasure from novelty or wonderfulness, with its final cause. Pleasure from beauty, with its final cause. The connection of beauty with truth and good, applied to the conduct of life. Invitation to the study of moral philosophy. The different degrees of beauty in different species of objects: colour; shape; natural concretes; vegetables; animals; the mind. The sublime, the fair, the wonderful of the mind. The connection of the imagination and the moral faculty. Conclusion.

BOOK THE FIRST

With what attractive charms this goodly frame
Of nature touches the consenting hearts
Of mortal men; and what the pleasing stores
Which beauteous imitation thence derives
To deck the poet's or the painter's toil,
My verse unfolds. Attend, ye gentle powers
Of musical delight! and while I sing
Your gifts, your honours, dance around my strain.
Thou, smiling queen of every tuneful breast,
Indulgent Fancy! from the fruitful banks   10
Of Avon, whence thy rosy fingers cull
Fresh flowers and dews to sprinkle on the turf
Where Shakespeare lies, be present; and with thee
Let Fiction come, upon her vagrant wings
Wafting ten thousand colours through the air,
Which by the glances of her magic eye
She blends and shifts at will through countless forms,
Her wild creation. Goddess of the lyre,
Which rules the accents of the moving sphere,
Wilt thou, eternal Harmony! descend   20
And join this festive train? for with thee comes
The guide, the guardian of their lovely sports,
Majestic Truth; and where Truth deigns to come,
Her sister Liberty will not be far.
Be present, all ye Genii who conduct
The wandering footsteps of the youthful bard,
New to your springs and shades; who touch his ear
With finer sounds; who heighten to his eye
The bloom of nature, and before him turn
The gayest, happiest attitude of things.   30

Oft have the laws of each poetic strain
The critic-verse employed; yet still unsung
Lay this prime subject, though importing most
A poet's name: for fruitless is the attempt,
By dull obedience and by creeping toil
Obscure to conquer the severe ascent
Of high Parnassus. Nature's kindling breath

Must fire the chosen genius; Nature's hand
Must string his nerves, and imp his eagle-wings,
Impatient of the painful steep, to soar   40
High as the summit; there to breathe at large
Ethereal air, with bards and sages old,
Immortal sons of praise. These flattering scenes,
To this neglected labour court my song;
Yet not unconscious what a doubtful task
To paint the finest features of the mind,
And to most subtile and mysterious things
Give colour, strength, and motion. But the love
Of Nature and the Muses bids explore,
Through secret paths erewhile untrod by man,   50
The fair poetic region, to detect
Untasted springs, to drink inspiring draughts,
And shade my temples with unfading flowers
Culled from the laureate vale's profound recess,
Where never poet gained a wreath before.

From Heaven my strains begin; from Heaven descends
The flame of genius to the human breast,
And love and beauty, and poetic joy
And inspiration. Ere the radiant sun
Sprang from the east, or 'mid the vault of night   60
The moon suspended her serener lamp;
Ere mountains, woods, or streams adorned the globe,
Or Wisdom taught the sons of men her lore;
Then lived the Almighty One: then, deep-retired
In his unfathomed essence, viewed the forms,
The forms eternal of created things;
The radiant sun, the moon's nocturnal lamp,
The mountains, woods and streams, the rolling globe,
And Wisdom's mien celestial. From the first
Of days, on them his love divine he fixed,   70
His admiration: till in time complete,
What he admired and loved, his vital smile
Unfolded into being. Hence the breath
Of life informing each organic frame,
Hence the green earth and wild resounding waves;
Hence light and shade alternate, warmth and cold,
And clear autumnal skies and vernal showers,
And all the fair variety of things.

But not alike to every mortal eye
Is this great scene unveiled. For since the claims   80
Of social life to different labours urge
The active powers of man, with wise intent
The hand of Nature on peculiar minds
Imprints a different bias, and to each
Decrees its province in the common toil.
To some she taught the fabric of the sphere,
The changeful moon, the circuit of the stars,
The golden zones of heaven; to some she gave
To weigh the moment of eternal things,
Of time and space and fate's unbroken chain,   90

And will's quick impulse; others by the hand
She led o'er vales and mountains, to explore
What healing virtue swells the tender veins
Of herbs and flowers; or what the beams of morn
Draw forth, distilling from the clifted rind
In balmy tears. But some to higher hopes
Were destined; some within a finer mold
She wrought, and tempered with a purer flame.
To these the Sire Omnipotent unfolds
The world's harmonious volume, there to read   100
The transcript of himself. On every part
They trace the bright impressions of his hand:
In earth or air, the meadow's purple stores,
The moon's mild radiance, or the virgin's form
Blooming with rosy smiles, they see portrayed
That uncreated beauty which delights
The Mind Supreme. They also feel her charms,
Enamoured; they partake the eternal joy.

    For as old Memnon's image, long renowned
By fabling Nilus, to the quivering touch   110
Of Titan's ray, with each repulsive string
Consenting, sounded through the warbling air
Unbidden strains, even so did Nature's hand
To certain species of external things,
Attune the finer organs of the mind:
So the glad impulse of congenial powers,
Or of sweet sound, or fair proportioned form,
The grace of motion, or the bloom of light,
Thrills through imagination's tender frame,
From nerve to nerve; all naked and alive   120
They catch the spreading rays; till now the soul
At length discloses every tuneful spring,
To that harmonious movement from without
Responsive. Then the inexpressive strain
Diffuses its enchantment: Fancy dreams
Of sacred fountains and Elysian groves,
And vales of bliss; the intellectual power
Bends from his awful throne a wondering ear,
And smiles; the passions, gently soothed away,
Sink to divine repose, and love and joy   130
Alone are waking; love and joy, serene
As airs that fan the summer. Oh, attend,
Whoe'er thou art, whom these delights can touch,
Whose candid bosom the refining love
Of Nature warms, oh, listen to my song;
And I will guide thee to her favourite walks,
And teach thy solitude her voice to hear,
And point her loveliest features to thy view.

    Know then, whate'er of Nature's pregnant stores,
Whate'er of mimic Art's reflected forms   140
With love and admiration thus inflame
The powers of Fancy, her delighted sons
To three illustrious orders have referred;

Three sister-graces, whom the painter's hand,
The poet's tongue confesses: the sublime,
The wonderful, the fair. I see them dawn!
I see the radiant visions, where they rise,
More lovely than when Lucifer displays
His beaming forehead through the gates of morn,
To lead the train of Phoebus and the spring.   150

    Say, why was man so eminently raised
Amid the vast creation; why ordained
Through life and death to dart his piercing eye,
With thoughts beyond the limit of his frame;
But that the Omnipotent might send him forth
In sight of mortal and immortal powers,
As on a boundless theatre, to run
The great career of justice; to exalt
His generous aim to all diviner deeds;
To chase each partial purpose from his breast;   160
And through the mists of passion and of sense,
And through the tossing tide of chance and pain,
To hold his course unfaltering, while the voice
Of truth and virtue, up the steep ascent
Of nature, calls him to his high reward,
The applauding smile of Heaven? Else wherefore burns
In mortal bosoms this unquenchèd hope,
That breathes from day to day sublimer things,
And mocks possession? Wherefore darts the mind,
With such resistless ardour to embrace   170
Majestic forms; impatient to be free,
Spurning the gross control of wilful might;
Proud of the strong contention of her toils;
Proud to be daring? Who but rather turns
To heaven's broad fire his unconstrainèd view,
Than to the glimmering of a waxen flame?
Who that, from Alpine heights, his labouring eye
Shoots round the wide horizon, to survey
Nilus or Ganges rolling his bright wave
Through mountains, plains, through empires black with shade 180
And continents of sand; will turn his gaze
To mark the windings of a scanty rill
That murmurs at his feet? The high-born soul
Disdains to rest her heaven-aspiring wing
Beneath its native quarry. Tired of earth
And this diurnal scene, she springs aloft
Through fields of air; pursues the flying storm;
Rides on the volleyed lightning through the heavens;
Or, yoked with whirlwinds and the northern blast,
Sweeps the long tract of day. Then high she soars   190
The blue profound, and hovering round the sun
Beholds him pouring the redundant stream
Of light; beholds his unrelenting sway
Bend the reluctant planets to absolve
The fated rounds of time. Thence far effused
She darts her swiftness up the long career
Of devious comets; through its burning signs

Exulting measures the perennial wheel
Of nature, and looks back on all the stars,
Whose blended light, as with a milky zone,   200
Invests the orient. Now amazed she views
The empyreal waste, where happy spirits hold,
Beyond this concave heaven, their calm abode;
And fields of radiance, whose unfading light
Has travelled the profound six thousand years,
Nor yet arrives in sight of mortal things.
Even on the barriers of the world untired
She meditates the eternal depth below;
Till half recoiling, down the headlong steep
She plunges; soon o'erwhelmed and swallowed up   210
In that immense of being. There her hopes
Rest at the fated goal. For from the birth
Of mortal man, the Sovereign Maker said
That not in humble nor in brief delight,
Not in the fading echoes of renown,
Power's purple robes, nor Pleasure's flowery lap,
The soul should find enjoyment: but from these
Turning disdainful to an equal good,
Through all the ascent of things enlarge her view,
Till every bound at length should disappear,   220
And infinite perfection close the scene.

Call now to mind what high capacious powers
Lie folded up in man; how far beyond
The praise of mortals, may the eternal growth
Of nature to perfection half divine
Expand the blooming soul? What pity then
Should sloth's unkindly fogs depress to earth
Her tender blossom; choke the streams of life,
And blast her spring! Far otherwise designed
Almighty wisdom; nature's happy cares   230
The obedient heart far otherwise incline.
Witness the sprightly joy when aught unknown
Strikes the quick sense, and wakes each active power
To brisker measures: witness the neglect
Of all familiar prospects, though beheld
With transport once; the fond attentive gaze
Of young astonishment; the sober zeal
Of age, commenting on prodigious things.
For such the bounteous providence of Heaven,
In every breast implanting this desire   240
Of objects new and strange, to urge us on
With unremitted labour to pursue
Those sacred stores that wait the ripening soul
In Truth's exhaustless bosom. What need words
To paint its power? For this the daring youth
Breaks from his weeping mother's anxious arms,
In foreign climes to rove: the pensive sage,
Heedless of sleep or midnight's harmful damp,
Hangs o'er the sickly taper; and untired
The virgin follows, with enchanted step,   250
The mazes of some wild and wondrous tale,

From morn to eve; unmindful of her form,
Unmindful of the happy dress that stole
The wishes of the youth, when every maid
With envy pined. Hence, finally, by night
The village matron, round the blazing hearth,
Suspends the infant audience with her tales,
Breathing astonishment! of witching rhymes
And evil spirits; of the death-bed call
Of him who robbed the widow and devoured   260
The orphan's portion; of unquiet souls
Risen from the grave to ease the heavy guilt
Of deeds in life concealed; of shapes that walk
At dead of night, and clank their chains, and wave
The torch of hell around the murderer's bed.
At every solemn pause the crowd recoil
Gazing each other speechless, and congealed
With shivering sighs: till eager for the event,
Around the beldame all arrect they hang,
Each trembling heart with grateful terrors quelled.   270

But lo! disclosed in all her smiling pomp,
Where Beauty onward moving claims the verse
Her charms inspire: the freely-flowing verse
In thy immortal praise, O form divine,
Smooths her mellifluent stream. Thee, Beauty, thee
The regal dome, and thy enlivening ray
The mossy roofs adore: thou, better sun!
Forever beamest on the enchanted heart
Love and harmonious wonder and delight
Poetic. Brightest progeny of Heaven!   280
How shall I trace thy features? where select
The roseate hues to emulate thy bloom?
Haste then, my song, through Nature's wide expanse,
Haste then, and gather all her comeliest wealth,
Whate'er bright spoils the florid earth contains,
Whate'er the waters or the liquid air,
To deck thy lovely labour. Wilt thou fly
With laughing Autumn to the Atlantic isles,
And range with him the Hesperian field, and see
Where'er his fingers touch the fruitful grove,   290
The branches shoot with gold; where'er his step
Marks the glad soil, the tender clusters grow
With purple ripeness, and invest each hill
As with the blushes of an evening sky?
Or wilt thou rather stoop thy vagrant plume,
Where gliding through his daughter's honoured shades,
The smooth Penéus from his glassy flood
Reflects purpureal Tempe's pleasant scene?
Fair Tempe! haunt beloved of sylvan powers,
Of Nymphs and Fauns; where in the golden age   300
They played in secret on the shady brink
With ancient Pan: while round their choral steps
Young Hours and genial Gales with constant hand
Showered blossoms, odours, showered ambrosial dews,
And spring's Elysian bloom. Her flowery store

To thee nor Tempe shall refuse; nor watch
Of winged Hydra guard Hesperian fruits
From thy free spoil. Oh bear then, unreproved,
Thy smiling treasures to the green recess
Where young Dione stays. With sweetest airs   310
Entice her forth to lend her angel form
For Beauty's honoured image. Hither turn
Thy graceful footsteps; hither, gentle maid,
Incline thy polished forehead; let thy eyes
Effuse the mildness of their azure dawn;
And may the fanning breezes waft aside
Thy radiant locks: disclosing, as it bends
With airy softness from the marble neck,
The cheek fair-blooming, and the rosy lip,
Where winning smiles and pleasures sweet as love,   320
With sanctity and wisdom, tempering blend
Their soft allurement. Then the pleasing force
Of Nature, and her kind parental care
Worthier I'd sing: then all the enamoured youth,
With each admiring virgin, to my lyre
Should throng attentive, while I point on high
Where Beauty's living image, like the morn
That wakes in Zephyr's arms the blushing May,
Moves onward; or as Venus, when she stood
Effulgent on the pearly car, and smiled,   330
Fresh from the deep, and conscious of her form,
To see the Tritons tune their vocal shells,
And each cerulean sister of the flood
With loud acclaim attend her o'er the waves,
To seek the Idalian bower. Ye smiling band
Of youths and virgins, who through all the maze
Of young desire with rival steps pursue
This charm of beauty; if the pleasing toil
Can yield a moment's respite, hither turn
Your favourable ear, and trust my words.   340
I do not mean to wake the gloomy form
Of Superstition dressed in Wisdom's garb,
To damp your tender hopes; I do not mean
To bid the jealous thunderer fire the heavens,
Or shapes infernal rend the groaning earth
To fright you from your joys: my cheerful song
With better omens calls you to the field,
Pleased with your generous ardour in the chase,
And warm like you. Then tell me, for ye know,
Does Beauty ever deign to dwell where health   350
And active use are strangers? Is her charm
Confessed in aught whose most peculiar ends
Are lame and fruitless? Or did Nature mean
This pleasing call the herald of a lie;
To hide the shame of discord and disease,
And catch with fair hypocrisy the heart
Of idle Faith? Oh no! with better cares
The indulgent mother, conscious how infirm
Her offspring tread the paths of good and ill,
By this illustrious image, in each kind   360

Still most illustrious where the object holds
Its native powers most perfect, she by this
Illumes the headstrong impulse of Desire,
And sanctifies his choice. The generous glebe
Whose bosom smiles with verdure, the clear tract
Of streams delicious to the thirsty soul,
The bloom of nectared fruitage ripe to sense,
And every charm of animated things,
Are only pledges of a state sincere,
The integrity and order of their frame,   370
When all is well within, and every end
Accomplished. Thus was Beauty sent from Heaven,
The lovely ministress of truth and good
In this dark world: for Truth and Good are one,
And Beauty dwells in them, and they in her,
With like participation. Wherefore then,
O sons of earth! would ye dissolve the tie?
O wherefore, with a rash impetuous aim,
Seek ye those flowery joys with which the hand
Of lavish Fancy paints each flattering scene   380
Where Beauty seems to dwell, nor once inquire
Where is the sanction of eternal truth,
Or where the seal of undeceitful good,
To save your search from folly! Wanting these,
Lo! Beauty withers in your void embrace,
And with the glittering of an idiot's toy
Did Fancy mock your vows. Nor let the gleam
Of youthful hope that shines upon your hearts
Be chilled or clouded at this awful task,
To learn the lore of undeceitful good   390
And truth eternal. Though the poisonous charms
Of baleful Superstition guide the feet
Of servile numbers through a dreary way
To their abode, through deserts, thorns, and mire;
And leave the wretched pilgrim all forlorn,
To muse at last amid the ghostly gloom
Of graves, and hoary vaults, and cloistered cells;
To walk with spectres through the midnight shade,
And to the screaming owl's accursed song
Attune the dreadful workings of his heart;   400
Yet be not ye dismayed. A gentler star
Your lovely search illumines. From the grove
Where Wisdom talked with her Athenian sons,
Could my ambitious hand entwine a wreath
Of Plato's olive with the Mantuan bay,
Then should my powerful verse at once dispel
Those monkish horrors; then in light divine
Disclose the Elysian prospect, where the steps
Of those whom nature charms through blooming walks,
Through fragrant mountains and poetic streams,   410
Amid the train of sages, heroes, bards,
Led by their winged Genius and the choir
Of laureled science and harmonious art,
Proceed exulting to the eternal shrine,
Where Truth conspicuous with the sister twins,

The undivided partners of her sway,
With Good and Beauty reigns. Oh let not us,
Lulled by luxurious Pleasure's languid strain,
Or crouching to the frowns of bigot Rage,
Oh let us not a moment pause to join   420
That godlike band. And if the gracious power
Who first awakened my untutored song,
Will to my invocation breathe anew
The tuneful spirit; then through all our paths,
Ne'er shall the sound of this devoted lyre
Be wanting; whether on the rosy mead,
When summer smiles, to warn the melting heart
Of Luxury's allurement; whether firm
Against the torrent and the stubborn hill
To urge bold virtue's unremitted nerve,   430
And wake the strong divinity of soul
That conquers chance and fate; or whether struck
For sounds of triumph, to proclaim her toils
Upon the lofty summit, round her brow
To twine the wreath of incorruptive praise;
To trace her hallowed light through future worlds,
And bless Heaven's image in the heart of man.

Thus with a faithful aim have we presumed,
Adventurous, to delineate Nature's form;
Whether in vast, majestic pomp arrayed,   440
Or dressed for pleasing wonder, or serene
In Beauty's rosy smile. It now remains,
Through various being's fair-proportioned scale,
To trace the rising lustre of her charms,
From their first twilight, shining forth at length
To full meridian splendour. Of degree
The least and lowliest, in the effusive warmth
Of colours mingling with a random blaze,
Doth beauty dwell. Then higher in the line
And variation of determined shape,   450
Where truth's eternal measures mark the bound
Of circle, cube, or sphere. The third ascent
Unites this varied symmetry of parts
With colour's bland allurement; as the pearl
Shines in the concave of its azure bed,
And painted shells indent their speckled wreath.
Then more attractive rise the blooming forms
Through which the breath of Nature has infused
Her genial power to draw with pregnant veins
Nutritious moisture from the bounteous earth,   460
In fruit and seed prolific: thus the flowers
Their purple honours with the spring resume;
And such the stately tree which autumn bends
With blushing treasures. But more lovely still
Is Nature's charm, where to the full consent
Of complicated members, to the bloom
Of colour, and the vital change of growth,
Life's holy flame and piercing sense are given,
And active motion speaks the tempered soul:

So moves the bird of Juno; so the steed   470
With rival ardour beats the dusty plain,
And faithful dogs with eager airs of joy
Salute their fellows. Thus doth beauty dwell
There most conspicuous, even in outward shape,
Where dawns the high expression of a mind:
By steps conducting our enraptured search
To the eternal origin, whose power,
Through all the unbounded symmetry of things,
Like rays effulging from the parent sun,
This endless mixture of her charms diffused.   480
Mind, mind alone, (bear witness, earth and heaven!)
The living fountains in itself contains
Of beauteous and sublime: here hand in hand,
Sit paramount the Graces; here enthroned,
Celestial Venus, with divinest airs,
Invites the soul to never-fading joy.
Look then abroad through nature, to the range
Of planets, suns, and adamantine spheres
Wheeling unshaken through the void immense;
And speak, O man! does this capacious scene   490
With half that kindling majesty dilate
Thy strong conception, as when Brutus rose
Refulgent from the stroke of Caesar's fate,
Amid the crowd of patriots; and his arm
Aloft extending, like eternal Jove
When guilt brings down the thunder, called aloud
On Tully's name, and shook his crimson steel,
And bade the father of his country, hail?
For lo! the tyrant prostrate on the dust,
And Rome again is free! Is aught so fair   500
In all the dewy landscapes of the spring,
In the bright eye of Hesper or the morn,
In nature's fairest forms, is aught so fair
As virtuous friendship? as the candid blush
Of him who strives with fortune to be just?
The graceful tear that streams for others' woes?
Or the mild majesty of private life,
Where Peace with ever-blooming olive crowns
The gate; where Honour's liberal hands effuse
Unenvied treasures, and the snowy wings   510
Of Innocence and Love protect the scene?
Once more search, undismayed, the dark profound
Where nature works in secret; view the beds
Of mineral treasure, and the eternal vault
That bounds the hoary ocean; trace the forms
Of atoms moving with incessant change
Their elemental round; behold the seeds
Of being, and the energy of life
Kindling the mass with ever-active flame:
Then to the secrets of the working mind   520
Attentive turn; from dim oblivion call
Her fleet, ideal band; and bid them, go!
Break through time's barrier, and o'ertake the hour
That saw the heavens created: then declare

If aught were found in those external scenes
To move thy wonder now. For what are all
The forms which brute, unconscious matter wears,
Greatness of bulk, or symmetry of parts?
Not reaching to the heart, soon feeble grows
The superficial impulse; dull their charms,   530
And satiate soon, and pall the languid eye.
Not so the moral species, nor the powers
Of genius and design; the ambitious mind
There sees herself; by these congenial forms
Touched and awakened, with intenser act
She bends each nerve, and meditates well-pleased
Her features in the mirror. For of all
The inhabitants of earth, to man alone
Creative Wisdom gave to lift his eye
To truth's eternal measures; then to frame   540
The sacred laws of action and of will,
Discerning justice from unequal deeds,
And temperance from folly. But beyond
This energy of truth, whose dictates bind
Assenting reason, the benignant sire,
To deck the honoured paths of just and good,
Has added bright imagination's rays:
Where Virtue, rising from the awful depth
Of Truth's mysterious bosom, doth forsake
The unadorned condition of her birth;   550
And dressed by Fancy in ten thousand hues,
Assumes a various feature, to attract,
With charms responsive to each gazer's eye,
The hearts of men. Amid his rural walk,
The ingenuous youth, whom solitude inspires
With purest wishes, from the pensive shade
Beholds her moving, like a virgin muse
That wakes her lyre to some indulgent theme
Of harmony and wonder: while among
The herd of servile minds, her strenuous form   560
Indignant flashes on the patriot's eye,
And through the rolls of memory appeals
To ancient honour, or in act serene,
Yet watchful, raises the majestic sword
Of public power, from dark ambition's reach
To guard the sacred volume of the laws.

    Genius of ancient Greece! whose faithful steps
Well pleased I follow through the sacred paths
Of nature and of science; nurse divine
Of all heroic deeds and fair desires!
Oh! let the breath of thy extended praise
Inspire my kindling bosom to the height
Of this untempted theme. Nor be my thoughts
Presumptuous counted, if amid the calm
That soothes this vernal evening into smiles,
I steal impatient from the sordid haunts
Of strife and low ambition, to attend
Thy sacred presence in the sylvan shade.

By their malignant footsteps ne'er profaned.
Descend, propitious! to my favoured eye;   580
Such in thy mien, thy warm, exalted air,
As when the Persian tyrant, foiled and stung
With shame and desperation, gnashed his teeth
To see thee rend the pageants of his throne;
And at the lightning of thy lifted spear
Crouched like a slave. Bring all thy martial spoils,
Thy palms, thy laurels, thy triumphal songs,
Thy smiling band of arts, thy godlike sires
Of civil wisdom, thy heroic youth
Warm from the schools of glory. Guide my way   590
Through fair Lyceum's walk, the green retreats
Of Academus, and the thymy vale,
Where oft enchanted with Socratic sounds,
Ilissus pure devolved his tuneful stream
In gentler murmurs. From the blooming store
Of these auspicious fields, may I unblamed
Transplant some living blossoms to adorn
My native clime: while far above the flight
Of fancy's plume aspiring, I unlock
The springs of ancient wisdom! while I join   600
Thy name, thrice honoured! with the immortal praise
Of nature, while to my compatriot youth
I point the high example of thy sons,
And tune to Attic themes the British lyre.

[1744]

WILLIAM SHENSTONE (1714-1763)

Among the secondary writers of the time William Shenstone is preeminently the "man of taste." He studied at Pembroke College, Oxford, and saw something of the world, but after 1745 he lived on his family estate, the Leasowes, near Birmingham. Here he tried to realize the eighteenth century dream of a rural retreat in which a sensitive and fastidious soul might securely enjoy the pleasures of art, nature, and friendship. (Compare Pomfret's *Choice*.) He practised landscape gardening in the new or natural style which was superseding French formality; the Leasowes rivaled the fame of Lord Lyttelton's estate at Hagley, near by, and many visitors came to admire Shenstone's winding walks, artfully arranged trees, and studied vistas. He also studied music, collected prints, exchanged pleasant letters with his coterie of friends, and wrote verse which at its worst is perfunctory and trifling, at its best graceful, melodious, and charming. His discriminating taste appears in the help he gave his friend Robert Dodsley in the editing of the *Collection of Poems* known by Dodsley's name, the most important miscellany of the mid-century; some years later he gave Bishop Percy indispensable aid in the preparation of the *Reliques of Ancient Poetry*. His wit and shrewdness are displayed in his letters and his *Essays on Men and Manners*.

Shenstone's verse is in the rococo style, an elegant and artificial mode that does not strike deep or work on a large scale. He depends largely on the conventions of the type he has chosen—elegy, love-song, inscription, pastoral, or Spenserian imitation—and he gets his effects by metrical skill and a good taste which keeps him from pushing things too far. The distress of Corydon in the *Pastoral Ballad* cannot discompose the suavity of his phrase:

> Ye shepherds, give ear to my lay,
> And take no more heed of my sheep:
> They have nothing to do but to stray;
> I have nothing to do but to weep.
> Yet do not my folly reprove;
> She was fair—and my passion begun;
> She smiled—and I could not but love;
> She is faithless—and I am undone.

But Shenstone's artificially sheltered life leads to ennui and disillusion, and he sometimes exchanges "pleasing melancholy" for a deeper note, which is heard in the famous lines *Written at an Inn at Henley*.

The mood of Shenstone's most successful poem, *The Schoolmistress*, is complicated by the fact that it is a Spenserian imitation. The poet could safely indulge his fondness for Spenser by burlesquing him, and in the same way he could gently deprecate and yet satisfy his interest in this delightful scene from humble life. It is characteristic of Shenstone's restrained art that he here counterbalances and enhances sentimental sympathy with humor. He neatly describes the tone of his poem by saying that it is intended to be "somewhat more grave than Pope's *Alley* [a coarse imitation of Spenser] and a good deal less than Mr. Thomson's *Castle of Indolence*."

Poetical Works, ed. C. C. Clarke (1880) ; *Letters*, ed. D. Mallam (Minneapolis, 1939) ; ed. Marjorie Williams (Oxford, 1939) ; A. I. Hazeltine, *A Study of William Shenstone and of His Critics* (Menasha, 1918) ; E. M. Purkis, *William Shenstone: Poet and Landscape Gardener* (Wolverhampton, 1931) ; Marjorie Williams, *William Shenstone* (Birmingham, 1935) ; A. R Humphreys, *William Shenstone* (Cambridge, 1937) ; *Shenstone's Miscellany 1759-1763*, ed. Ian Gordon (Oxford, 1952) ; Iolo A. Williams, *Seven xviii^{th} Century Bibliographies* (1924) ; E. R. Wasserman, *Elizabethan Poetry in the Eighteenth Century* (Urbana, Ill., 1947) [for *The Schoolmistress*].

THE SCHOOLMISTRESS

IN IMITATION OF SPENSER

Auditae voces, vagitus et ingens,
Infantumque animae flentes in limine primo.[1]
—Virgil [*Aeneid*, vi, 426-47]

ADVERTISEMENT

What particulars in Spenser were imagined most proper for the author's imitation on this occasion are, his language, his simplicity, his manner of description, and a peculiar tenderness of sentiment remarkable throughout his works.

Ah me! full sorely is my heart forlorn,
To think how modest worth neglected lies,
While partial Fame doth with her blasts adorn
Such deeds alone, as pride and pomp disguise;
Deeds of ill sort, and mischievous emprize!
Lend me thy clarion, goddess! let me try
To sound the praise of merit. ere it dies;
Such as I oft have chauncèd to espy,
Lost in the dreary shades of dull obscurity.

In every village marked with little spire,   10
Embowered in trees, and hardly known to fame,
There dwells, in lowly shed and mean attire,
A matron old, whom we schoolmistress name;
Who boasts unruly brats with birch to tame;
They grieven sore, in piteous durance pent,
Awed by the power of this relentless dame;
And ofttimes, on vagaries idly bent,
For unkempt hair, or task unconned, are sorely shent.[2]

And all in sight doth rise a birchen tree,
Which Learning near her little dome did stowe;[3]   20
Whilom a twig of small regard to see,
Though now so wide its waving branches flow,
And work the simple vassals mickle woe;
For not a wind might curl the leaves that blew,
But their limbs shuddered, and their pulse beat low;
And, as they looked, they found their horror grew,
And shaped it into rods, and tingled at the view.

So have I seen (who has not, may conceive)
A lifeless phantom near a garden placed;
So doth it wanton birds of peace bereave,   30
Of sport, of song, of pleasure, of repast;
They start, they stare, they wheel, they look aghast:
Sad servitude! such comfortless annoy
May no bold Briton's riper age e'er taste!
Ne superstition clog his dance of joy,
Ne vision empty, vain, his native bliss destroy.

[1] Voices are heard, and loud wailing—the spirits of infants weeping at the very threshold.
[2] Scolded.
[3] Place.

Near to this dome is found a patch so green,
On which the tribe their gambols do display;
And at the door imprisoning board is seen,
Lest weakly wights of smaller size should stray;   40
Eager, perdie, to bask in sunny day!
The noises intermixed, which thence resound,
Do learning's little tenement betray:
Where sits the dame, disguised in look profound,
And eyes her fairy throng, and turns her wheel around.

Her cap, far whiter than the driven snow,
Emblem right meet of decency does yield:
Her apron dyed in grain, as blue, I trowe,
As is the harebell that adorns the field:
And in her hand, for scepter, she does wield   50
Tway birchen sprays: with anxious fear entwined,
With dark distrust, and sad repentance filled;
And steadfast hate, and sharp affliction joined,
And fury uncontrolled, and chastisement unkind.

Few but have kenned, in semblance meet portrayed,
The childish faces of old Eol's train,
Libs, Notus, Auster: these in frowns arrayed,
How then would fare or earth, or sky, or main,
Were the stern god to give his slaves the rein?
And were not she rebellious breasts to quell,   60
And were not she her statutes to maintain,
The cot no more, I ween, were deemed the cell
Where comely peace of mind, and decent order dwell.

A russet stole was o'er her shoulders thrown;
A russet kirtle fenced the nipping air;
'Twas simple russet, but it was her own;
'Twas her own country bred the flock so fair;
'Twas her own labor did the fleece prepare;
And, sooth to say, her pupils ranged around,
Through pious awe, did term it passing rare;   70
For they in gaping wonderment abound,
And think, no doubt, she been the greatest wight on ground.

Albeit ne flattery did corrupt her truth,
Ne pompous title did debauch her ear;
Goody, good-woman, gossip, n'aunt, forsooth,
Or dame, the sole additions[4] she did hear;
Yet these she challenged, these she held right dear;
Ne would esteem him act as mought behove,
Who should not honored eld with these revere:
For never title yet so mean could prove,   80
But there was eke a mind which did that title love.

One ancient hen she took delight to feed,
The plodding pattern of the busy dame;
Which, ever and anon, impelled by need,
Into her school, begirt with chickens, came;

[4] Titles.

Such favor did her past deportment claim;
And, if neglect had lavished on the ground
Fragment of bread, she would collect the same;
For well she knew, and quaintly could expound,
What sin it were to waste the smallest crumb she found.   90

Herbs too she knew, and well of each could speak
That in her garden sipped the silvery dew;
Where no vain flower disclosed a gaudy streak,
But herbs for use and physic, not a few,
Of gray renown, within those borders grew:
The tufted basil, pun-provoking thyme,
Fresh baum, and marigold of cheerful hue;
The lowly gill,[5] that never dares to climb
And more I fain would sing, disdaining here to rhyme.

Yet euphrasy[6] may not be left unsung,   100
That gives dim eyes to wander leagues around;
And pungent radish, biting infant's tongue;
And plantain ribbed, that heals the reaper's wound;
And marjoram sweet, in shepherd's posie found;
And lavender whose spikes of azure bloom
Shall be erewhile in arid bundles bound,
To lurk amidst the labors of her loom,
And crown her kerchiefs clean with mickle rare perfume.

And here trim rosmarine, that whilom crowned
The daintiest garden of the proudest peer;   110
Ere, driven from its envied site, it found
A sacred shelter for its branches here;
Where edged with gold its glittering skirts appear.
Oh, wassel days! Oh, customs meet and well!
Ere this was banished from its lofty sphere:
Simplicity then sought this humble cell,
Nor ever would she more with thane and lordling dwell.

Here oft the dame, on Sabbath's decent eve,
Hymnèd such psalms as Sternhold forth did mete;
If winter 'twere, she to her hearth did cleave,   120
But in her garden found a summer seat:
Sweet melody! to hear her then repeat
How Israel's sons, beneath a foreign king,
While taunting foemen did a song entreat,
All, for the nonce untuning every string,
Uphung their useless lyres—small heart had they to sing.

For she was just, and friend to virtuous lore,
And passed much time in truly virtuous deed;
And, in those elfins' ears, would oft deplore
The times when truth by popish rage did bleed,   130
And tortious[7] death was true devotion's meed;
And simple faith in iron chains did mourn,

[5] Ground ivy.
[6] Eyebright.
[7] Wrongful, unjust.

That nould on wooden image place her creed;
And lawny[8] saints in smoldering flames did burn:
Ah! dearest Lord, forefend thilk days should e'er return.

In elbow-chair, like that of Scottish stem
By the sharp tooth of cankering eld defaced,
In which, when he receives his diadem,
Our sovereign prince and liefest liege is placed,
The matron sate; and some with rank she graced,   140
(The source of children's and of courtiers' pride!)
Redressed affronts, for vile affronts there passed,
And warned them not the fretful to deride,
But love each other dear, whatever them betide.

Right well she knew each temper to descry,
To thwart the proud, and the submiss to raise;
Some with vile copper prize exalt on high,
And some entice with pittance small of praise;
And other some with baleful sprig she 'frays:
Even absent, she the reins of power doth hold,   150
While with quaint arts the giddy crowd she sways;
Forewarned, if little bird their pranks behold,
'Twill whisper in her ear, and all the scene unfold.

Lo now with state she utters the command!
Eftsoons the urchins to their tasks repair;
Their books of stature small they take in hand,
Which with pellucid horn securèd are,
To save from finger wet the letters fair;
The work so gay, that on their back is seen,
St. George's high achievements does declare;   160
On which thilk wight that has y-gazing been
Kens the forthcoming rod, unpleasing sight, I ween!

Ah, luckless he, and born beneath the beam
Of evil star! it irks me whilst I write!
As erst the bard by Mulla's silver stream,
Oft, as he told of deadly dolorous plight,
Sighed as he sung, and did in tears indite.
For brandishing the rod, she doth begin
To loose the brogues, the stripling's late delight!
And down they drop; appears his dainty skin,   170
Fair as the furry coat of whitest ermilin.[9]

Oh, ruthful scene! when from a nook obscure,
His little sister doth his peril see:
All playful as she sate, she grows demure;
She finds full soon her wonted spirits flee;
She meditates a prayer to set him free;
Nor gentle pardon could this dame deny,
(If gentle pardon could with dames agree)
To her sad grief that swells in either eye,
And wrings her so that all for pity she could die.   180

Clad in lawn. a fine material used especially for bishops' sleeves
[9] Ermine.

Not longer can she now her shrieks command,
And hardly she forbears, through awful fear,
To rushen forth, and, with presumptuous hand,
To stay harsh justice in its mid-career.
On thee she calls, on thee her parent dear!
(Ah! too remote to ward the shameful blow!)
She sees no kind domestic visage near,
And soon a flood of tears begins to flow,
And gives a loose at last to unavailing woe.

But ah! what pen his piteous plight may trace?   190
Or what device his loud laments explain?
The form uncouth of his disguisèd face?
The pallid hue that dyes his looks amain?
The plenteous shower that does his cheek distain?
When he, in abject wise, implores the dame,
Ne hopeth aught of sweet reprieve to gain;
Or when from high she levels well her aim,
And through the thatch his cries each falling stroke proclaim.

The other tribe, aghast, with sore dismay,
Attend, and conn their tasks with mickle care: 200
By turns, astonied, every twig survey,
And from their fellow's hateful wounds beware,
Knowing, I wist, how each the same may share;
Till fear has taught them a performance meet,
And to the well-known chest the dame repair;
Whence oft with sugared cates[10] she doth 'em greet,
And gingerbread y-rare; now, certes, doubly sweet!

See to their seats they hye with merry glee,
And in beseemly order sitten there;
All but the wight of bum y-gallèd, he   210
Abhorreth bench, and stool, and fourm,[11] and chair;
(This hand in mouth y-fixed, that rends his hair;)
And eke with snubs[12] profound, and heaving breast,
Convulsions intermitting! does declare
His grievous wrong, his dame's unjust behest,
And scorns her offered love, and shuns to be caressed.

His face besprent[13] with liquid crystal shines,
His blooming face, that seems a purple flower
Which low to earth its drooping head declines,
All smeared and sullied by a vernal shower.   220
Oh, the hard bosoms of despotic power!
All, all, but she, the author of his shame,
All, all, but she, regret this mournful hour:
Yet hence the youth, and hence the flower shall claim,
If so I deem aright, transcending worth and fame.

Behind some door, in melancholy thought,
Mindless of food, he, dreary caitiff! pines;

[10] Cakes.
[11] Bench.
[12] Sobs.
[13] Sprinkled.

Ne for his fellows' joyaunce careth aught,
But to the wind all merriment resigns;
And deems it shame, if he to peace inclines;   230
And many a sullen look ascance is sent,
Which for his dame's annoyance he designs;
And still the more to pleasure him she's bent,
The more doth he, perverse, her 'haviour past resent.

Ah me! how much I fear lest pride it be!
But if that pride it be, which thus inspires,
Beware, ye dames, with nice discernment see,
Ye quench not too the sparks of nobler fires:
Ah! better far than all the Muses' lyres,
All coward arts, is valor's generous heat;   240
The firm fixed breast which fit and right requires,
Like Vernon's patriot soul; more justly great
Than craft that pimps for ill, or flowery false deceit.

Yet nursed with skill, what dazzling fruits appear!
Even now sagacious foresight points to show
A little bench of heedless bishops here,
And there a chancellor in embryo,
Or bard sublime, if bard may e'er be so,
As Milton, Shakespeare, names that ne'er shall die!
Though now he crawl along the ground so low,   250
Nor weeting how the Muse should soar on high,
Wisheth, poor starveling elf! his paper kite may fly.

And this perhaps, who, censuring the design,
Low lays the house which that of cards doth build,
Shall Dennis be! if rigid fates incline,
And many an epic to his rage shall yield;
And many a poet quit the Aonian field;
And, soured by age, profound he shall appear,
As he who now with 'sdainful fury thrilled
Surveys mine work; and levels many a sneer,   260
And furls his wrinkly front, and cries, "What stuff is here!"

But now Dan Phoebus gains the middle sky,
And Liberty unbars her prison door;
And like a rushing torrent out they fly,
And now the grassy cirque han covered o'er
With boisterous revel rout and wild uproar;
A thousand ways in wanton rings they run;
Heaven shield their short-lived pastimes, I implore!
For well may freedom, erst so dearly won,
Appear to British elf more gladsome than the sun.   270

Enjoy, poor imps! enjoy your sportive trade;
And chase gay flies, and cull the fairest flowers,
For when my bones in grass-green sods are laid;
For never may ye taste more careless hours
In knightly castles or in ladies' bowers.
Oh, vain to seek delight in earthly thing!
But most in courts where proud ambition towers;

Deluded wight! who weens fair peace can spring
Beneath the pompous dome of kesar[14] or of king.

See in each sprite some various bent appear!   280
These rudely carol most incondite lay;
Those sauntering on the green, with jocund leer
Salute the stranger passing on his way;
Some builden fragile tenements of clay;
Some to the standing lake their courses bend,
With pebbles smooth at duck and drake to play;
Thilk to the huxter's savory cottage tend,
In pastry kings and queens the allotted mite to spend.

Here, as each season yields a different store,
Each season's stores in order rangèd been;   290
Apples with cabbage-net y-covered o'er,
Galling full sore the unmoneyed wight, are seen;
And gooseb'rie clad in livery red or green;
And here of lovely dye, the Catherine pear,
Fine pear! as lovely for thy juice, I ween:
Oh, may no wight e'er pennyless come there,
Lest smit with ardent love he pine with hopeless care!

See! cherries here, ere cherries yet abound,
With thread so white in tempting posies tied,
Scattering like blooming maid their glances round,   300
With pampered look draw little eyes aside;
And must be bought, though penury betide.
The plum all azure and the nut all brown,
And here each season do those cakes abide,
Whose honored names the inventive city own,
Rendering through Britain's isle Salopia's praises known.

Admired Salopia! that with venial pride
Eyes her bright form in Severn's ambient wave,
Famed for her loyal cares in perils tried,
Her daughters lovely, and her striplings brave: 310
Ah! midst the rest, may flowers adorn his grave,
Whose art did first these dulcet cates display!
A motive fair to Learning's imps he gave,
Who cheerless o'er her darkling region stray;
Till reason's morn arise, and light them on their way.

[1737-48]

[14] Emperor.

WRITTEN AT AN INN AT HENLEY

To thee, fair Freedom! I retire
From flattery, cards, and dice, and din;
Nor art thou found in mansions higher
Than the low cot or humble inn.

'Tis here with boundless power I reign;
And every health which I begin,
Converts dull port to bright champagne;
Such freedom crowns it, at an inn.

I fly from pomp, I fly from plate,
I fly from Falsehood's specious grin;   16

Freedom I love and form I hate,
  And choose my lodgings at an inn.

Here, waiter! take my sordid ore,
  Which lackeys else might hope to win;
It buys what courts have not in store;
  It buys me freedom at an inn.

Whoe'er has travelled life's dull round,
  Where'er his stages may have been,
May sigh to think he still has found
  The warmest welcome at an inn.   20

                              [*1751*, *1758*]

SLENDER'S GHOST

Beneath a churchyard yew,
  Decayed and worn with age,
At dusk of eve methought I spied
Poor Slender's ghost, that whimpering cried,
  "O sweet! O sweet Anne Page!"

Ye gentle bards, give ear!
  Who talk of amorous rage,
Who spoil the lily, rob the rose,
Come learn of me to weep your woes:
  "O sweet! O sweet Anne Page!"   10

Why should such labored strains
  Your formal Muse engage?
I never dreamed of flame or dart,
That fired my breast or pierced my heart,
  But sighed, "O sweet Anne Page!"

And you, whose lovesick minds
  No medicine can assuage!
Accuse the leech's art no more,
But learn of Slender to deplore:
  "O sweet! O sweet Anne Page!"   20

And ye, whose souls are held
  Like linnets in a cage!
Who talk of fetters, links, and chains,
Attend and imitate my strains:
  "O sweet! O sweet Anne Page!"

And you, who boast or grieve,
  What horrid wars ye wage!
Of wounds received from many an eye,
Yet mean as I do, when I sigh,
  "O sweet! O sweet Anne Page!"   30

Hence every fond conceit
  Of shepherd or of sage;

'Tis Slender's voice, 'tis Slender's way,
Expresses all you have to say:
  "O sweet! O sweet Anne Page!"
                                        [*1758*]

INSCRIPTION: ON A TABLET AGAINST A ROOT-HOUSE

Here, in cool grot and mossy cell,
We rural fays and fairies dwell;
Though rarely seen by mortal eye,
When the pale moon, ascending high,
Darts through yon limes her quivering beams,
We frisk it near these crystal streams.

Her beams, reflected from the wave,
Afford the light our revels crave;
The turf, with daisies broidered o'er,
Exceeds, we wot, the Parian floor;   10
Nor yet for artful strains we call,
But listen to the water's fall.

Would you then taste our tranquil scene,
Be sure your bosoms be serene;
Devoid of hate, devoid of strife,
Devoid of all that poisons life:
And much it 'vails you in their place,
To graft the love of human race.

And tread with awe these favored bowers,
Nor wound the shrubs, nor bruise the flowers;
So may your path with sweets abound;   21
So may your couch with rest be crowned!
But harm betide the wayward swain,
Who dares our hallowed haunts profane!
                                        [*1755*]

INSCRIPTION: ON THE BACK OF A GOTHIC SEAT

Shepherd, wouldst thou here obtain
Pleasure unalloyed with pain?
Joy that suits the rural sphere?
Gentle shepherd, lend an ear.

Learn to relish calm delight,
Verdant vales and fountains bright;
Trees that nod on sloping hills,
Caves that echo tinkling rills.

If thou canst no charm disclose
In the simplest bud that blows,   10
Go, forsake thy plain and fold;
Join the crowd and toil for gold.

Tranquil pleasures never cloy;
Banish each tumultuous joy;
All but love—for love inspires
Fonder wishes, warmer fires.

Love and all its joys be thine—
Yet, ere thou the reins resign,
Hear what reason seems to say,
Hear attentive, and obey: 20

"Crimson leaves the rose adorn,
But beneath 'em lurks a thorn;
Fair and flowery is the brake,
Yet it hides the vengeful snake.

"Think not she whose empty pride
Dares the fleecy garb deride,
Think not she who, light and vain,
Scorns the sheep, can love the swain.

"Artless deed and simple dress
Mark the chosen shepherdess;   30
Thoughts by decency controlled,
Well conceived and freely told.

"Sense that shuns each conscious air,
Wit that falls ere well aware;
Generous pity, prone to sigh
If her kid or lambkin die.

"Let not lucre, let not pride,
Draw thee from such charms aside;
Have not those their proper sphere?
Gentler passions triumph here.   40

"See, to sweeten thy repose,
The blossom buds, the fountain flows;
Lo! to crown thy healthful board,
All that milk and fruits afford.

"Seek no more—the rest is vain;
Pleasure ending soon in pain;
Anguish lightly gilded o'er;
Close thy wish, and seek no more."

[*1745*, *1758*]

JOSEPH WARTON (1722-1800)—
THOMAS WARTON THE YOUNGER
(1728-1790)

The work of the poetical family of the Wartons covers almost the whole span of the eighteenth century, and furnishes a valuable index to the current fashions and changing tastes of several generations. Thomas Warton the Elder (1688-1745) was a fellow of Magdalen College, Oxford, Professor of Poetry in that university, and afterwards vicar of Basingstoke, Hampshire. His slender output of verse, not collected until 1748 but written for the most part much earlier, shows little poetic power, but includes Miltonic, Spenserian, and Chaucerian imitations, and even two Scandinavian odes; and thus may be fairly accounted an early example of the pre-romantic tendency to seek new models and themes for poetry. He had a direct and important influence on the work of his sons, so that we may speak of a "school of the Wartons." Joseph was educated at Winchester School and at Oriel College, Oxford, and eventually became headmaster of Winchester. Thomas was tutored by his father and passed a life of learned leisure as an Oxford don, holding the Professorship of Poetry which was almost a family perquisite. William Collins was their schoolfellow and friend. Collins and Joseph Warton wrote and published their odes almost simultaneously, and longed for a revival of imagination and passion on what they conceived to be the ancient Greek model. Joseph's *Enthusiast* (1744) and Thomas's *Pleasures of Melancholy* (1747) are surveys in Miltonic blank verse of the poetic themes which were gaining popularity in the 1740's—the moods of *Il Penseroso*, the cult of wild nature and of ruins, the preference for primitive over civilized life. We must remember, however, that in the Wartons these preferences represent bookish and amateur enthusiasm rather than profound conviction.

Both men achieved greater distinction as students of literature than as poets. Joseph's most important work is his *Essay on the Genius and Writings of Pope* (i—1756; ii—1782), which is to be interpreted not as an uncompromising attack on Pope but as an attempt to give a just estimate of his work on the basis of a broad view of English poetry. He places Pope not with Spenser, Shakespeare, and Milton, but next below Milton and just above Dryden. Thomas Warton shows more scholarship than critical power in his *Observations on the Fairy Queen* (1754), his love for Spenser conflicting with his genuine respect for neo-classical rules. His monumental *History of English Poetry* (1774-81) shows his wide though unsystematic learning and his genial antiquarianism. The best of his later poems, such as *The Crusade*, *The Grave of King Arthur*, and the sonnet *Written in a Blank Leaf of Dugdale's Monasticon*, are brilliant footnotes to his medieval studies. In the *Verses on Sir Joshua Reynolds's Painted Window* he characteristically halts between the romantic and the classical, reminding himself that his delight in the Middle Ages may lure him away from universal and rational standards.

> Thy powerful hand has broke the Gothic chain,
> And brought my bosom back to truth again;
> To truth, by no peculiar taste confined,
> Whose universal pattern strikes mankind;
> To truth, whose bold and unresisted aim
> Checks frail caprice, and fashion's fickle claim;
> To truth, whose charms deception's magic quell,
> And bind coy Fancy in a stronger spell.
>
> . . . .
>
> Reynolds, 'tis thine, from the broad window's height,
> To add new lustre to religious light
> Not of its pomp to strip this ancient shrine,
> But bid that pomp, with purer radiance shine;

559

With arts unknown before, to reconcile
The willing Graces to the Gothic pile.

Convenient selections and a bibliography are to be found in Eric Partridge, *The Three Wartons* (London, 1927). The *Poems on Several Occasions* of Thomas Warton the Elder have been reproduced by the Facsimile Text Society, New York, 1930. Clarissa Rinaker's *Thomas Warton* (Urbana, Ill., 1916) is a fully documented biographical and critical study. See also page 1269.

THE ENTHUSIAST: OR, THE LOVER OF NATURE

Ye green-robed Dryads, oft at dusky eve
By wondering shepherds seen, to forests brown,
To unfrequented meads, and pathless wilds,
Lead me from gardens decked with art's vain pomps.
Can gilt alcoves, can marble-mimic gods,
Parterres embroidered, obelisks, and urns
Of high relief; can the long, spreading lake,
Or vista lessening to the sight; can Stowe
With all her Attic fanes, such raptures raise,
As the thrush-haunted copse, where lightly leaps   10
The fearful fawn the rustling leaves along,
And the brisk squirrel sports from bough to bough,
While from an hollow oak the busy bees
Hum drowsy lullabies? The bards of old,
Fair Nature's friends, sought such retreats, to charm
Sweet Echo with their songs; oft too they met,
In summer evenings, near sequestered bowers,
Or Mountain-Nymph, or Muse, and eager learned
The moral strains she taught to mend mankind.
As to a secret grot Egeria stole   20
With patriot Numa, and in silent night
Whispered him sacred laws, he listening sat
Rapt with her virtuous voice; old Tiber leaned
Attentive on his urn, and hushed his waves.
    Rich in her weeping country's spoils, Versailles
May boast a thousand fountains, that can cast
The tortured waters to the distant heavens;
Yet let me choose some pine-topped precipice
Abrupt and shaggy, whence a foamy stream,
Like Anio, tumbling roars; or some bleak heath,   30
Where straggling stand the mournful juniper,
Or yew-tree scathed; while in clear prospect round,
From the grove's bosom spires emerge, and smoke
In bluish wreaths ascends, ripe harvests wave,
Herds low, and straw-roofed cots appear, and streams
Beneath the sunbeams twinkle. The shrill lark,
That wakes the woodman to his early task,
Or love-sick Philomel, whose luscious lays
Soothe lone night-wanderers, the moaning dove
Pitied by listening milkmaid, far excel   40
The deep-mouthed viol, the soul-lulling lute,
And battle-breathing trumpet. Artful sounds!
That please not like the choristers of air,
When first they hail th'approach of laughing May.

Creative Titian, can thy vivid strokes,
Or thine, O graceful Raphael, dare to vie
With the rich tints that paint the breathing mead?
The thousand-coloured tulip, violet's bell
Snow-clad and meek, the vermil-tinctured rose,
And golden crocus? Yet with these the maid,   50
Phillis or Phoebe, at a feast or wake,
Her jetty locks enamels; fairer she,
In innocence and home-spun vestments dressed,
Than if cerulean sapphires at her ears
Shone pendant, or a precious diamond-cross
Heaved gently on her panting bosom white.
     Yon Shepherd idly stretched on the rude rock,
Listening to dashing waves, and sea-mew's clang
High-hovering o'er his head, who views beneath
The dolphin dancing o'er the level brine,   60
Feels more true bliss than the proud admiral,
Amid his vessels bright with burnished gold
And silken streamers, though his lordly nod
Ten thousand war-worn mariners revere.
And great Aeneas gazed with more delight
On the rough mountain shagged with horrid shades,
(Where cloud-compelling Jove, as fancy dreamed,
Descending shook his direful Aegis black)
Than if he entered the high Capitol
On golden columns reared, a conquered world   70
Contributing to deck its stately head:
More pleased he slept in poor Evander's cot
On shaggy skins, lulled by sweet nightingales,
Than if a Nero, in an age refined,
Beneath a gorgeous canopy had placed
His royal guest, and bade his minstrels sound
Soft slumbrous Lydian airs to soothe his rest.
     Happy the first of men, ere yet confined
To smoky cities; who in sheltering groves,
Warm caves, and deep-sunk valleys lived and loved,   80
By cares unwounded; what the sun and showers,
And genial earth untillaged could produce,
They gathered grateful, or the acorn brown,
Or blushing berry; by the liquid lapse
Of murmuring waters called to slake their thirst,
Or with fair Nymphs their sun-brown limbs to bathe;
With Nymphs who fondly clasped their favourite youths,
Unawed by shame, beneath the beechen shade,
Nor wiles nor artificial coyness knew.
Then doors and walls were not; the melting maid   90
Nor frowns of parents feared nor husband's threats;
Nor had cursed gold their tender hearts allured;
Then beauty was not venal. Injured Love,
O whither, god of raptures, art thou fled?
While Avarice waves his golden wand around,
Abhorred magician, and his costly cup
Prepares with baneful drugs, to enchant the souls
Of each low-thoughted fair to wed for gain.
     What though unknown to those primeval sires,

The well-arched dome, peopled with breathing forms　　　100
By fair Italia's skilful hand, unknown
The shapely column, and the crumbling busts
Of awful ancestors in long descent?
Yet why should man mistaken deem it nobler
To dwell in palaces and high-roofed halls
Than in God's forests, architect supreme!
Say, is the Persian carpet, than the field's
Or meadow's mantle gay, more richly woven;
Or softer to the votaries of ease,
Than bladed grass, perfumed with dew-dropped flowers?　　110
O taste corrupt! that luxury and pomp
In specious names of polished manners veiled,
Should proudly banish Nature's simple charms.
Though the fierce North oft smote with iron whip
Their shivering limbs, though oft the bristly boar
Or hungry lion woke them with their howls,
And scared them from their moss-grown caves to rove,
Houseless and cold in dark, tempestuous nights;
Yet were not myriads in embattled fields
Swept off at once, nor had the raving seas　　　　　　120
O'erwhelmed the foundering bark and helpless crew;
In vain the glassy ocean smiled to tempt
The jolly sailor, unsuspecting harm,
For commerce was unknown. Then want and pine
Sunk to the grave their fainting limbs; but us
Excess and endless riot doom to die.
They cropped the poisonous herb unweetingly,
But wiser we spontaneously provide
Rare powerful roots, to quench life's cheerful lamp.
What are the lays of artful Addison,　　　　　　　　130
Coldly correct, to Shakespeare's warblings wild?
Whom on the winding Avon's willowed banks
Fair Fancy found, and bore the smiling babe
To a close cavern: (still the shepherds show
The sacred place, whence with religious awe
They hear, returning from the field at eve,
Strange whisperings of sweet music through the air)
Here. as with honey gathered from the rock,
She fed the little prattler, and with songs
Oft soothed his wondering ears, with deep delight　　140
On her soft lap he sat, and caught the sounds.
Oft near some crowded city would I walk,
Listening the far-off noises, rattling cars,
Loud shouts of joy, sad shrieks of sorrow, knells
Full slowly tolling, instruments of trade,
Striking mine ears with one deep-swelling hum.
Or wandering near the sea, attend the sounds
Of hollow winds, and ever-beating waves.
Even when wild tempests swallow up the plains,
And Boreas' blasts, big hail, and rains combine　　　150
To shake the groves and mountains, would I sit,
Pensively musing on the outrageous crimes
That wake Heaven's vengeance: at such solemn hours,
Demons and goblins through the dark air shriek,
While Hecate with her black-browed sisters nine

Rides o'er the earth, and scatters woes and deaths.
Then, too, they say, in drear Egyptian wilds
The lion and the tiger prowl for prey
With roarings loud! The listening traveler
Starts fear-struck, while the hollow-echoing vaults   160
Of pyramids increase the deathful sounds.
   But let me never fail in cloudless nights,
When silent Cynthia in her silver car
Through the blue concave slides, when shine the hills,
Twinkle the streams, and woods look tipped with gold,
To seek some level mead, and there invoke
Old Midnight's sister, Contemplation sage,
(Queen of the rugged brow and stern-fixed eye)
To lift my soul above this little earth,
This folly-fettered world; to purge my ears,   170
That I may hear the rolling planets' song,
And tuneful-turning spheres: If this debarred,
The little fays that dance in neighbouring dales,
Sipping the night-dew, while they laugh and love,
Shall charm me with aërial notes. As thus
I wander musing, lo, what awful forms
Yonder appear! sharp-eyed Philosophy
Clad in dun robes, an eagle on his wrist,
First meets my eye; next virgin Solitude
Serene, who blushes at each gazer's sight;   180
Then Wisdom's hoary head, with crutch in hand,
Trembling, and bent with age; last Virtue's self
Smiling, in white arrayed, who with her leads
Fair Innocence, that prattles by her side,
A naked boy! Harassed with fear I stop,
I gaze, when Virtue thus—"Whoe'er thou art,
Mortal, by whom I deign to be beheld,
In these my midnight-walks; depart, and say
That henceforth I and my immortal train
Forsake Britannia's isle; who fondly stoops   190
To Vice, her favourite paramour."—She spoke,
And as she turned, her round and rosy neck,
Her flowing train, and long, ambrosial hair,
Breathing rich odours, I enamoured view.
   Oh, who will bear me then to western climes,
(Since Virtue leaves our wretched land) to shades
Yet unpolluted with Iberian swords;
With simple Indian swains, that I may hunt
The boar and tiger through savannahs wild?
There fed on dates and herbs, would I despise   200
The far-fetched cates of luxury, and hoards
Of narrow-hearted Avarice; nor heed
The distant din of the tumultuous world.
So when rude whirlwinds rouse the roaring main,
Beneath fair Thetis sits, in coral caves,
Serenely gay, nor sinking sailors' cries
Disturb her sportive Nymphs, who round her form
The light fantastic dance, or for her hair
Weave rosy crowns, or with according lutes
Grace the soft warbles of her honeyed voice.   210

[1744]

ODE I. TO FANCY

O Parent of each lovely Muse,
Thy spirit o'er my soul diffuse,
O'er all my artless songs preside,
My footsteps to thy temple guide,
To offer at thy turf-built shrine,
In golden cups no costly wine,
No murdered fatling of the flock,
But flowers and honey from the rock.
O Nymph with loosely-flowing hair,
With buskined leg, and bosom bare,   10
Thy waist with myrtle-girdle bound,
Thy brows with Indian feathers crowned,
Waving in thy snowy hand
An all-commanding magic wand,
Of power to bid fresh gardens blow
'Midst cheerless Lapland's barren snow,
Whose rapid wings thy flight convey
Through air, and over earth and sea,
While the vast, various landscape lies
Conspicuous to thy piercing eyes—   20
O lover of the desert, hail!
Say, in what deep and pathless vale,
Or on what hoary mountain's side,
'Midst falls of water you reside,
'Midst broken rocks, a rugged scene,
With green and grassy dales between,
'Midst forests dark of aged oak,
Ne'er echoing with the woodman's stroke,
Where never human art appeared,
Nor even one straw-roofed cot was reared,   30
Where Nature seems to sit alone,
Majestic on a craggy throne;
Tell me the path, sweet wanderer, tell,
To thy unknown sequestered cell,
Where woodbines cluster round the door,
Where shells and moss o'erlay the floor,
And on whose top an hawthorn blows,
Amid whose thickly-woven boughs,
Some nightingale still builds her nest,
Each evening warbling thee to rest;   40
Then lay me by the haunted stream
Wrapt in some wild, poetic dream,
In converse while methinks I rove
With Spenser through a fairy grove;
Till suddenly awoke, I hear
Strange whispered music in my ear,
And my glad soul in bliss is drowned,
By the sweetly-soothing sound!
Me, Goddess, by the right hand lead,
Sometimes through the yellow mead,   50
Where Joy and white-robed Peace resort,
And Venus keeps her festive court,

Where Mirth and Youth each evening meet
And lightly trip with nimble feet,
Nodding their lily-crownèd heads,
Where Laughter rose-lipped Hebe leads;
Where Echo walks steep hills among,
Listening to the shepherd's song:
Or sometimes in thy fiery car
Transport me to the rage of war;   60
There whirl me o'er the hills of slain,
Where Tumult and Destruction reign;
Where mad with pain, the wounded steed
Tramples the dying and the dead;
Where giant Terror stalks around,
With sullen joy surveys the ground,
And pointing to the ensanguined field,
Shakes his dreadful Gorgon-shield!
Then guide me from this horrid scene
To high-arched walks and alleys green,   70
Where lovely Laura walks, to shun
The fervours of the mid-day sun;
The pangs of absence, O remove,
For thou canst place me near my love,
Canst fold in visionary bliss,
And let me think I steal a kiss,
While her ruby lips dispense
Luscious nectar's quintessence!
When young-eyed Spring profusely throws
From her green lap the pink and rose,   80
When the soft turtle of the dale,
To Summer tells her tender tale,
When Autumn cooling caverns seeks,
And stains with wine his jolly cheeks,
When Winter, like poor pilgrim old,
Shakes his silver beard with cold,
At every season let my ear
Thy solemn whispers, Fancy, hear.
O warm, enthusiastic maid,
Without thy powerful, vital aid,   90
That breathes an energy divine,
That gives a soul to every line,
Ne'er may I strive with lips profane
To utter an unhallowed strain,
Nor dare to touch the sacred string,
Save when with smiles thou bidd'st me sing.
O hear our prayer, O hither come
From thy lamented Shakespeare's tomb,
On which thou lov'st to sit at eve,
Musing o'er your darling's grave;   100
O queen of numbers, once again
Animate some chosen swain,
Who, filled with unexhausted fire,
May boldly smite the sounding lyre,
Who with some new, unequalled song,
May rise above the rhyming throng,
O'er all our listening passions reign,

O'erwhelm our souls with joy and pain,
With terror shake, with pity move,
Rouse with revenge, or melt with love.   110
O deign to attend his evening walk,
With him in groves and grottoes talk;
Teach him to scorn with frigid art
Feebly to touch th' unraptured heart;

Like lightning, let his mighty verse
The bosom's inmost foldings pierce;
With native beauties win applause,
Beyond cold critics' studied laws:
O let each Muse's fame increase,
O bid Britannia rival Greece!   120

[1746]

THE PLEASURES OF MELANCHOLY

Mother of musings, Contemplation sage,
Whose mansion is upon the topmost cliff
Of cloud-capped Teneriff, in secret bower;
Where ever wrapped in meditation high,
Thou hear'st unmoved, in dark tempestuous night,
The loud winds howl around, the beating rain
And the big hail in mingling storm descend
Upon his horrid brow; but when the skies
Unclouded shine, and through the blue serene
Pale Cynthia rolls her silver-axled car,   10
Then ever looking on the spangled vault
Raptured thou sitt'st, while murmurs indistinct
Of distant billows soothe thy pensive ear
With hoarse and hollow sounds; secure, self-blessed,
Oft too thou listen'st to the wild uproar
Of fleets encountering, that in whispers low
Ascends the rocky summit, where thou dwell'st
Remote from man, conversing with the spheres—
Oh lead me, black-browed Eve, to solemn glooms
Congenial with my soul, to cheerless shades,   20
To ruined seats, to twilight cells and bowers,
Where thoughtful Melancholy loves to muse,
Her favourite midnight haunts. The laughing scenes
Of purple Spring, where all the wanton train
Of Smiles and Graces seem to lead the dance
In sportive round, while from their hands they shower
Ambrosial blooms and flowers, no longer charm;
Tempe, no more I court thy balmy breeze;
Adieu green vales! embroidered meads adieu!
Beneath yon ruined abbey's moss-grown piles   30
Oft let me sit, at twilight hour of eve,
Where through some western window the pale moon
Pours her long-levelled rule of streaming light;
While sullen sacred silence reigns around,
Save the lone screech-owl's note, whose bower is built
Amid the mouldering caverns dark and damp,
And the calm breeze, that rustles in the leaves
Of flaunting ivy, that with mantle green
Invests some sacred tower. Or let me tread
Its neighbouring walk of pines, where strayed of old   40
The cloistered brothers: through the gloomy void
That far extends beneath their ample arch
As on I tread, religious horror wraps

My soul in dread repose. But when the world
Is clad in Midnight's raven-coloured robe,
In hollow charnel let me watch the flame
Of taper dim, while airy voices talk
Along the glimmering walls, or ghostly shape
At distance seen, invites with beckoning hand
My lonesome steps, through the far-winding vaults.   50
Nor undelightful is the solemn noon
Of night, when haply wakeful from my couch
I start: lo, all is motionless around!
Roars not the rushing wind; the sons of men
And every beast in mute oblivion lie;
All Nature's hushed in silence and in sleep.
Oh then how fearful is it to reflect
That through the solitude of the still globe
No being wakes but me! till stealing Sleep
My drooping temples bathes in opiate dews.   60
Nor then let dreams, of wanton Folly born,
My senses lead through flowery paths of joy;
But let the sacred Genius of the night
Such mystic visions send as Spenser saw,
When through bewildering Fancy's magic maze
To the bright regions of the fairy world
Soared his creative mind: or Milton knew,
When in abstracted thought he first conceived
All Heaven in tumult, and the Seraphim
Come towering, armed in adamant and gold.   70
    Let others love the summer evening's smiles,
As listening to some distant waterfall
They mark the blushes of the streaky west:
I choose the pale December's foggy glooms;
Then, when the sullen shades of evening close,
Where through the room a blindly glimmering gleam
The dying embers scatter, far remote
From Mirth's mad shouts, that through the lighted roof
Resound with festive echo, let me sit,
Blessed with the lowly cricket's drowsy dirge.   80
Then let my contemplative thought explore
This fleeting state of things, the vain delights,
The fruitless toils, that still elude our search,
As through the wilderness of life we rove.
This sober hour of silence will unmask
False Folly's smiles, that like the dazzling spells
Of wily Comus, cheat the unweeting eye
With blear illusion, and persuade to drink
The charmed cup, that Reason's mintage fair
Unmoulds, and stamps the monster on the man.   90
Eager we taste, but in the luscious draught
Forget the poisonous dregs that lurk beneath.
    Few know that elegance of soul refined,
Whose soft sensation feels a quicker joy
From Melancholy's scenes, than the dull pride
Of tasteless splendour and magnificence
Can e'er afford. Thus Eloise, whose mind
Had languished to the pangs of melting love,

More secret transport found, as on some tomb
Reclined she watched the tapers of the dead,   100
Or through the pillared aisles, amid the shrines
Of imaged saints, and intermingled graves,
Which scarce the storied windows dim disclosed,
Musing she wandered; than Cosmelia finds,
As through the Mall in silken pomp arrayed,
She floats amid the gilded sons of dress,
And shines the fairest of the assembled Belles.
   When azure noon-tide cheers the daedal globe,
And the glad regent of the golden day
Rejoices in his bright meridian bower,   110
How oft my wishes ask the night's return,
That best befriends the melancholy mind!
Hail, sacred Night! to thee my song I raise!
Sister of ebon-sceptered Hecate, hail!
Whether in congregated clouds thou wrapp'st
Thy viewless chariot, or with silver crown
Thy beaming head encirclest, ever hail!
What though beneath thy gloom the Lapland witch
Oft celebrates her moon-eclipsing rites;
Though Murder wan, beneath thy shrouding shade   120
Oft calls her silent votaries to devise
Of blood and slaughter, while by one blue lamp
In secret conference sits the listening band,
And start at each low wind, or wakeful sound:
What though thy stay the pilgrim curses oft,
As all benighted in Arabian wastes
He hears the howling wilderness resound
With roaming monsters, while on his hoar head
The black-descending tempest ceaseless beats;
Yet more delightful to my pensive mind   130
Is thy return, than bloomy Morn's approach,
When from the portals of the saffron East
She sheds fresh roses and ambrosial dews.
Yet not ungrateful is the Morn's approach,
When dropping wet she comes, and clad in clouds,
While through the damp air scowls the peevish South,
And the dusk landscape rises dim to view.
The afflicted songsters of the saddened groves
Hail not the sullen gloom, but silent droop;
The waving elms that ranged in thick array   140
Enclose with stately row some rural hall
Are mute, nor echo with the clamours hoarse
Of rooks rejoicing on their hoary boughs:
While to the shed the dripping poultry crowd,
A mournful train: secure the village-hind
Hangs o'er the crackling blaze, nor tempts the storm;
Rings not the high wood with enlivening shouts
Of early hunter: all is silence drear;
And deepest sadness wraps the face of things.
   Through Pope's soft song though all the Graces breathe,   150
And happiest art adorn his Attic page;
Yet does my mind with sweeter transport glow,
As at the foot of some hoar oak reclined,

In magic Spenser's wildly-warbled song
I see deserted Una wander wide
Through wasteful solitudes and lurid heaths,
Weary, forlorn—than when the fated fair,
Upon the bosom bright of silver Thames,
Launches in all the lustre of brocade,
Amid the splendours of the laughing sun.   160
The gay description palls upon the sense,
And coldly strikes the mind with feeble bliss.
   Oh, wrap me then in shades of darksome pine,
Bear me to caves by desolation brown,
To dusky vales and hermit-haunted rocks!
And hark, methinks, resounding from the gloom,
The voice of Melancholy strikes mine ear:
"Come, leave the busy trifles of vain life,
And let these twilight mansions teach thy mind
The joys of musing and of solemn thought."   170
   Ye youths of Albion's beauty-blooming isle,
Whose brows have worn the wreath of luckless love,
Is there a pleasure like the pensive mood,
Whose magic wont to soothe your softened souls?
Oh, tell how rapturous is the deep-felt bliss
To melt to Melody's assuasive voice,
Careless to stray the midnight mead along,
And pour your sorrows to the pitying moon,
Oft interrupted by the bird of woe!
To muse by margin of romantic stream,   180
To fly to solitudes, and there forget
The solemn dullness of the tedious world,
Till in abstracted dreams of fancy lost,
Eager you snatch the visionary fair,
And on the phantom feast your cheated gaze!
Sudden you start—the imagined joys recede,
The same sad prospect opens on your sense;
And naught is seen but deep-extended trees
In hollow rows, and your awakened ear
Again attends the neighbouring fountain's sound.   190
These are delights that absence drear has made
Familiar to my soul, ere since the form
Of young Sapphira, beauteous as the Spring,
When from her violet-woven couch awaked
By frolic Zephyr's hand, her tender cheek
Graceful she lifts, and blushing from her bower,
Issues to clothe in gladsome-glistering green
The genial globe, first met my dazzled sight.
These are delights unknown to minds profane,
And which alone the pensive soul can taste.   200
   The tapered choir, at midnight hour of prayer,
Oft let me tread, while to the according voice
The many-sounding organ peals on high,
In full-voiced chorus through the embowed roof;
Till all my soul is bathed in ecstasies,
And lapped in Paradise. Or let me sit
Far in some distant aisle of the deep dome,
There lonesome listen to the solemn sounds,

Which, as they lengthen through the Gothic vaults,
In hollow murmurs reach my ravished ear, 210
   Nor let me fail to cultivate my mind
With the soft thrillings of the tragic Muse,
Divine Melpomene, sweet Pity's nurse,
Queen of the stately step and flowing pall.
Now let Monimia mourn with streaming eyes
Her joys incestuous, and polluted love:
Now let Calista dye the desperate steel
Within her bosom, for lost innocence,
Unable to behold a father weep.
Or Jaffeir kneel for one forgiving look; 220
Nor seldom let the Moor on Desdemone
Pour the misguided threats of jealous rage.
By soft degrees the manly torrent steals
From my swoln eyes, and at a brother's woe
My big heart melts in sympathizing tears.
   What are the splendours of the gaudy court,
Its tinsel trappings, and its pageant pomps?
To me far happier seems the banished lord
Amid Siberia's unrejoicing wilds
Who pines all lonesome, in the chambers hoar 230
Of some high castle shut, whose windows dim
In distant ken discover trackless plains,
Where Winter ever drives his icy car;
While still repeated objects of his view,
The gloomy battlements, and ivied towers
That crown the solitary dome, arise;
While from the topmost turret the slow clock,
Far heard along the inhospitable wastes
With sad-returning chime, awakes new grief;
Than is the satrap whom he left behind 240
In Moscow's regal palaces, to drown
In ease and luxury the laughing hours.
   Illustrious objects strike the gazer's mind
With feeble bliss, and but allure the sight,
Nor rouse with impulse quick the feeling heart.
Thus, seen by shepherd from Hymettus' brow,
What painted landscapes spread their charms beneath!
Here palmy groves, amid whose umbrage green
The unfading olive lifts her silver head,
Resounding once with Plato's voice, arise: 250
Here vine-clad hills unfold their purple stores,
Here fertile vales their level lap expand,
Amid whose beauties glistering Athens towers.
Though through the graceful seats Ilissus roll
His sage-inspiring flood, whose fabled banks
The spreading laurel shades, though roseate Morn
Pour all her splendours on the empurpled scene,
Yet feels the musing hermit truer joys,
As from the cliff that o'er his cavern hangs,
He views the piles of fallen Persepolis 260
In deep arrangement hide the darksome plain.
Unbounded waste! the mouldering Obelisk
Here, like a blasted oak, ascends the clouds;

Here Parian domes their vaulted halls disclose
Horrid with thorn, where lurks the secret thief,
Whence flits the twilight-loving bat at eve,
And the deaf adder wreathes her spotted train,
The dwellings once of Elegance and Art.
Here temples rise, amid whose hallowed bounds
Spires the black pine, while through the naked street,   270
Haunt of the tradeful merchant, springs the grass:
Here columns heaped on prostrate columns, torn
From their firm base, increase the mouldering mass.
Far as the sight can pierce, appear the spoils
Of sunk magnificence: a blended scene
Of moles, fanes, arches, domes, and palaces,
Where, with his brother Horror, Ruin sits.
     Oh come then, Melancholy, queen of thought,
Oh come with saintly look and stedfast step,
From forth thy cave embowered with mournful yew,   280
Where ever to the curfew's solemn sound
Listening thou sitt'st, and with thy cypress bind
Thy votary's hair, and seal him for thy son.
But never let Euphrosyne beguile
With toys of wanton mirth my fixèd mind,
Nor with her primrose garlands strew my paths.
What though with her the dimpled Hebe dwells,
With young-eyed Pleasure, and the loose-robed Joy;
Though Venus, mother of the Smiles and Loves,
And Bacchus, ivy-crowned, in myrtle bower   290
With her in dance fantastic beat the ground:
What though 'tis hers to calm the blue serene,
And at her presence mild the lowering clouds
Disperse in air, and o'er the face of heaven
New day diffusive glows at her approach;
Yet are these joys that Melancholy gives,
By Contemplation taught, her sister sage,
Than all her witless revels happier far.
     Then ever, beauteous Contemplation, hail!
From thee began, auspicious maid, my song,   300
With thee shall end: for thou art fairer far
Than are the nymphs of Cirrha's mossy grot;
To loftier rapture thou canst wake the thought,
Than all the fabling Poet's boasted powers.
Hail, queen divine! whom, as tradition tells,
Once in his evening walk a Druid found
Far in a hollow glade of Mona's woods,
And piteous bore with hospitable hand
To the close shelter of his oaken bower.
There soon the sage admiring marked the dawn   310
Of solemn musing in thy pensive thought;
For when a smiling babe, you loved to lie
Oft deeply listening to the rapid roar
Of wood-hung Meinai, stream of Druids old,
That laved his hallowed haunt with dashing wave.
                         [1745, 1747]

THE CRUSADE

ADVERTISEMENT

King Richard the First, celebrated for his achievements in the Crusades, was no less distinguished for his patronage of the Provençal minstrels and his own compositions in their species of poetry. Returning from one of his expeditions in the Holy Land in disguise, he was imprisoned in a castle of Leopold, Duke of Austria. His favourite minstrel, Blondel de Nesle, having traversed all Germany in search of his master, at length came to a castle in which he found there was only one prisoner, whose name was unknown. Suspecting that he had made the desired discovery, he seated himself under a window of the prisoner's apartment; and began a song or ode which the King and himself had formerly composed together. When the prisoner, who was King Richard, heard the song, he knew that Blondel must be the singer; and when Blondel paused about the middle, the King began the remainder and completed it. The following ode is supposed to be the joint composition of the minstrel and King Richard.

Bound for holy Palestine,
Nimbly we brushed the level brine,
All in azure steel arrayed;
O'er the wave our weapons played,
And made the dancing billows glow;
High upon the trophied prow,
Many a warrior-minstrel swung
His sounding harp, and boldly sung:
  "Syrian virgins, wail and weep,
English Richard ploughs the deep!   10
Tremble, watchmen, as ye spy,
From distant towers, with anxious eye,
The radiant range of shield and lance
Down Damascus' hills advance:
From Sion's turrets as afar
Ye ken the march of Europe's war!
Saladin, thou paynim king,
From Albion's isle revenge we bring!
On Acon's spiry citadel,
Though to the gale thy banners swell,   20
Pictured with the silver moon;
England shall end thy glory soon!
In vain, to break our firm array,
Thy brazen drums hoarse discord bray:
Those sounds our rising fury fan:
English Richard in the van,
On to victory we go,
A vaunting infidel the foe."
  Blondel led the tuneful band,
And swept the wire with glowing hand.   30
Cyprus, from her rocky mound,
And Crete, with piny verdure crowned,
Far along the smiling main
Echoed the prophetic strain.
  Soon we kissed the sacred earth
That gave a murdered Saviour birth;
Then, with ardour fresh endued,
Thus the solemn song renewed:

  "Lo, the toilsome voyage past,
Heaven's favoured hills appear at last!   40
Object of our holy vow,
We tread the Tyrian valleys now.
From Carmel's almond-shaded steep
We feel the cheering fragrance creep:
O'er Engaddi's shrubs of balm
Waves the date-empurpled palm;
See Lebanon's aspiring head
Wide his immortal umbrage spread!
Hail, Calvary, thou mountain hoar,
Wet with our Redeemer's gore!   50
Ye trampled tombs, ye fanes forlorn,
Ye stones, by tears of pilgrims worn;
Your ravished honours to restore,
Fearless we climb this hostile shore!
And thou, the sepulchre of God!
By mocking pagans rudely trod,
Bereft of every awful rite,
And quenched thy lamps that beamed so
    bright;
For thee, from Britain's distant coast,
Lo, Richard leads his faithful host!   60
Aloft in his heroic hand,
Blazing, like the beacon's brand,
O'er the far-affrighted fields,
Resistless Kaliburn he wields.
Proud Saracen, pollute no more
The shrines by martyrs built of yore!
From each wild mountain's trackless crown
In vain thy gloomy castles frown:
Thy battering engines, huge and high,
In vain our steel-clad steeds defy;   70
And, rolling in terrific state,
On giant-wheels harsh thunders grate.
When eve has hushed the buzzing camp,
Amid the moonlight vapours damp,
Thy necromantic forms in vain

Haunt us on the tented plain:
We bid those spectre-shapes avaunt,
Ashtaroth, and Termagaunt!
With many a demon, pale of hue,
Doomed to drink the bitter dew   80
That drops from Macon's sooty tree,
'Mid the dread grove of ebony.
Nor magic charms, nor fiends of hell,

The Christian's holy courage quell.
"Salem, in ancient majesty
Arise, and lift thee to the sky!
Soon on thy battlements divine
Shall wave the badge of Constantine.
Ye Barons, to the sun unfold
Our Cross with crimson wove and gold!"   90
[1777]

SONNET III

WRITTEN IN A BLANK LEAF OF DUGDALE'S MONASTICON

Deem not devoid of elegance the sage,
By Fancy's genuine feelings unbeguiled,
Of painful Pedantry the poring child;
Who turns, of these proud domes, the historic page,
Now sunk by Time, and Henry's fiercer rage.
Thinkst thou the warbling Muses never smiled
On his lone hours? Ingenuous views engage
His thought, on themes, unclassic falsely styled,
Intent. While cloistered Piety displays
Her mouldering roll, the piercing eye explores
New manners, and the pomp of elder days,
Whence culls the pensive bard his pictured stores.
Nor rough nor barren are the winding ways
Of hoar Antiquity, but strown with flowers.
[1777]

SONNET IV

WRITTEN AT STONEHENGE

Thou noblest monument of Albion's isle!
Whether by Merlin's aid, from Scythia's shore,
To Amber's fatal plain Pendragon bore,
Huge frame of giant-hands, the mighty pile,
To entomb his Britons slain by Hengist's guile:
Or Druid priests, sprinkled with human gore,
Taught mid thy massy maze their mystic lore:
Or Danish chiefs, enriched with savage spoil,
To Victory's idol vast, an unhewn shrine,
Reared the rude heap: or in thy hallowed round   10
Repose the kings of Brutus' genuine line;
Or here those kings in solemn state were crowned:
Studious to trace thy wondrous origin,
We muse on many an ancient tale renowned.
[1777]

SONNET VIII

ON KING ARTHUR'S ROUND TABLE AT WINCHESTER

Where Venta's Norman castle still uprears
  Its raftered hall, that o'er the grassy foss,
  And scattered flinty fragments clad in moss,
  On yonder steep in naked state appears;
High hung remains, the pride of war-like years,
  Old Arthur's Board: on the capacious round
  Some British pen has sketched the names renowned,
  In marks obscure, of his immortal peers.
Though joined by magic skill, with many a rhyme,
  The Druid frame, unhonoured, falls a prey   10
  To the slow vengeance of the wizard Time,
  And fade the British characters away;
Yet Spenser's page, that chants in verse sublime
  Those Chiefs, shall live unconscious of decay.

[1777]

WILLIAM COLLINS (1721-1759)

To the lyric poet in the second quarter of the eighteenth century tradition offered the Pindaric ode for exalted subjects, the Horatian ode for a variety of urbane, personal, and meditative themes, the elegy, and, for elegance and brevity, the "song." Chiefly under the influence of *L'Allegro* and *Il Penseroso* a new type appeared, the "descriptive and allegorical ode," which, as the name implied, centered about a personified abstraction treated in a descriptive or pictorial way. In the 1740's Joseph and Thomas Warton and their more illustrious friend William Collins had a main hand in developing this newer mode.

William Collins was born in 1721 at Chichester, Sussex, and was educated at Winchester School and at Queen's and Magdalen Colleges, Oxford. While he was still at Oxford he published his conventional *Persian Eclogues* (1742) and his *Epistle to Sir Thomas Hanmer on his Edition of Shakespeare's Works* (1743). Coming up to London in 1744 he plunged into various literary and scholarly projects; among other things he planned a *Review of the Advancement of Learning* and a commentary on Aristotle's *Poetics*. Meanwhile he and Joseph Warton were writing odes which at one time they planned to publish in a joint volume; instead, Warton's *Odes on Various Subjects* and Collins's *Odes on Several Descriptive and Allegorical Subjects* appeared separately but almost simultaneously at the end of the year 1746. Collins was deeply mortified at the failure of his *Odes*. He won no popular success during his lifetime, although he formed important literary friendships with Thomson and Johnson, and with lesser men like John Gilbert Cooper, John Home, and Christopher Smart. His last publication was his *Ode Occasioned by the Death of Mr. Thomson* (1749); in the same year he addressed to John Home his superb *Ode on the Popular Superstitions of the Highlands of Scotland*, which remained in manuscript until 1788. In 1750 he was still laying literary plans and writing poems which have been lost—notably an *Ode on the Music of the Grecian Theatre* and an *Epistle to the Editor of Fairfax his Translation of Tasso*. But soon afterwards his career was cut short by a mental disorder which passed from extreme depression to violent insanity; his latter years were a lingering tragedy, and he died at Chichester in 1759, obscure and wretched.

Although Collins's odes never attain warmth and personal intimacy, they achieve certain effects which are unsurpassed in eighteenth-century poetry—the delicate and pensive melody of the *Ode Written in the Beginning of the Year 1746*, the emotionally suffused landscape of the *Ode to Evening*, the vigorous allegory of *The Passions* and the *Ode on the Poetical Character*, and the rich romanticism of the *Ode on the Popular Superstitions of the Highlands of Scotland*. He believes that poetry should be freely imagined and passionately felt, that it should be blessed with "some divine excess," but he is hampered by abstraction and formalism in his quest for his own ideal. Like Gray, he is a scholarly poet who works with set forms; he turns to Greek rather than Latin themes and models, and strives toward a genuine classicism. But, as Dr. Johnson tells us, his tastes incline him also to the medieval and romantic. Like Spenser and Milton, though on a much smaller scale, he draws his inspiration both from classical and medieval sources, and his love for those poets has a profound basis in his tastes and personality. In 1749 and 1750 he was on the threshold of a new period in which, as the *Ode on the Superstitions* indicates, he would have made even richer and fuller use of his enthusiastic scholarship. He was on the point of doing work which would have occupied in his career the place which *The Progress of Poesy* and *The Bard* occupy in Gray's.

Poems, ed. W. C. Bronson (Boston, 1898); ed. E. Blunden (1929); P. L. Carver, "Notes on the Life of William Collins," *N & Q*, CLXXVII (1939); H. W. Garrod, *Collins* (Oxford, 1928); A. S. P. Woodhouse, "Collins in the Eighteenth Century," *TLS*, Oct. 16, 1930, p. 838; "Collins and the Creative Imagination," *Studies in English by Members of University College* (Toronto, 1931); E. G. Ainsworth, *Poor Collins* (Ithaca, 1937); Norman Maclean, "From Action to Image, Theories of the Lyric in the Eighteenth Century," in *Critics and Criticism*, ed. R. S. Crane (Chicago, 1952) [for Gray and Collins]; R. M. Myers, "Neo-classical Criticism of the Ode for Music," *PMLA*, XLII (1947), 399-421 [for *The Passions*]; Iolo A. Williams, *Seven xviiith Century Bibliographies* (1924).

A SONG FROM SHAKE-SPEARE'S CYMBELINE

SUNG BY GUIDERUS AND ARVIRAGUS
OVER FIDELE, SUPPOSED TO BE DEAD

To fair Fidele's grassy tomb
  Soft maids and village hinds shall bring
Each opening sweet of earliest bloom,
  And rifle all the breathing spring.

No wailing ghost shall dare appear
  To vex with shrieks this quiet grove;
But shepherd lads assemble here,
  And melting virgins own their love.

No withered witch shall here be seen,
  No goblins lead their nightly crew; 10
The female fays shall haunt the green,
  And dress thy grave with pearly dew.

The redbreast oft at evening hours
  Shall kindly lend his little aid,
With hoary moss, and gathered flowers,
  To deck the ground where thou art laid.

When howling winds and beating rain
  In tempests shake the sylvan cell,
Or midst the chase on every plain,
  The tender thought on thee shall dwell. 20

Each lonely scene shall thee restore,
  For thee the tear be duly shed;
Beloved till life could charm no more,
  And mourned till Pity's self be dead.
            [1744]

ODE TO PITY

O thou, the friend of man, assigned
With balmy hands his wounds to bind,
  And charm his frantic woe;
When first Distress, with dagger keen,
Broke forth to waste his destined scene,
  His wild unsated foe!

By Pella's bard, a magic name,
By all the griefs his thought could frame,
  Receive my humble rite:
Long, Pity, let the nations view   10
Thy sky-worn robes of tenderest blue,
  And eyes of dewy light!

But wherefore need I wander wide
To old Ilissus' distant side,
  Deserted stream, and mute?
Wild Arun too has heard thy strains,
And Echo, midst my native plains,
  Been soothed by Pity's lute.

There first the wren thy myrtles shed
On gentlest Otway's infant head,   20
  To him thy cell was shown;
And while he sung the female heart,
With youth's soft notes unspoiled by art,
  Thy turtles mixed their own.

Come, Pity, come! By Fancy's aid,
E'en now my thoughts, relenting maid,
  Thy temple's pride design;
Its southern site, its truth complete,
Shall raise a wild enthusiast heat
  In all who view the shrine.   30

There Picture's toils shall well relate
How chance, or hard involving fate,
  O'er mortal bliss prevail;
The buskined Muse shall near her stand,
And sighing prompt her tender hand,
  With each disastrous tale.

There let me oft, retired by day,
In dreams of passion melt away,
  Allowed with thee to dwell;
There waste the mournful lamp of night, 40
Till, Virgin, thou again delight
  To hear a British shell!
            [1746]

ODE TO FEAR

STROPHE

Thou to whom the world unknown,
With all its shadowy shapes, is shown;

Who seest appalled the unreal scene,
While Fancy lifts the veil between—
    Ah Fear! ah frantic Fear!
    I see, I see thee near!
I know thy hurried step, thy haggard eye!
Like thee I start, like thee disordered fly,
For, lo, what monsters in thy train appear!
Danger, whose limbs of giant mold   10
What mortal eye can fixed behold?
Who stalks his round, an hideous form,
Howling amidst the midnight storm;
Or throws him on the ridgy steep
Of some loose-hanging rock to sleep;
And with him thousand phantoms joined,
Who prompt to deeds accursed the mind;
And those, the fiends, who near allied,
O'er Nature's wounds and wrecks preside;
Whilst Vengeance in the lurid air   20
Lifts her red arm, exposed and bare;
On whom that ravening brood of Fate,
Who lap the blood of Sorrow, wait;
Who, Fear, this ghastly train can see,
And look not madly wild, like thee?

EPODE

In earliest Greece, to thee, with partial choice,
    The grief-full Muse addressed her infant tongue;
    The maids and matrons, on her awful voice,
    Silent and pale, in wild amazement hung.

Yet he, the bard who first invoked thy name,   30
    Disdained in Marathon its power to feel;
For not alone he nursed the poet's flame,
    But reached from Virtue's hand the patriot's steel.

But who is he whom later garlands grace,
    Who left awhile o'er Hybla's dews to rove,
With trembling eyes thy dreary steps to trace,
    Where thou and Furies shared the baleful grove?

Wrapped in thy cloudy veil, the incestuous queen
    Sighed the sad call her son and husband heard,
When once alone it broke the silent scene,   40
    And he, the wretch of Thebes, no more appeared.

O Fear, I know thee by my throbbing heart;
    Thy withering power inspired each mournful line;
Though gentle Pity claim her mingled part,
    Yet all the thunders of the scene are thine!

ANTISTROPHE

Thou who such weary lengths hast past,
Where wilt thou rest, mad Nymph, at last?

Say, wilt thou shroud in haunted cell,
Where gloomy Rape and Murder dwell?
    Or in some hollowed seat,   50
    'Gainst which the big waves beat,
Hear drowning seamen's cries, in tempests brought?
Dark power, with shuddering, meek, submitted thought,
    Be mine to read the visions old
    Which thy awakening bards have told;
    And, lest thou meet my blasted view,
    Hold each strange tale devoutly true;
    Ne'er be I found, by thee o'erawed,
    In that thrice-hallowed eve abroad,
    When ghosts, as cottage maids believe,   60
    Their pebbled beds permitted leave;
    And goblins haunt, from fire, or fen,
    Or mine, or flood, the walks of men!

    O thou, whose spirit most possessed
    The sacred seat of Shakespeare's breast!
    By all that from thy prophet broke,
    In thy divine emotions spoke;
    Hither again thy fury deal,
    Teach me but once like him to feel,
    His cypress wreath my meed decree,   70
    And I, O Fear, will dwell with thee!

                    [1746]

ODE TO SIMPLICITY

    O thou by Nature taught
    To breathe her genuine thought,
In numbers warmly pure and sweetly strong;
    Who first, on mountains wild,
    In Fancy, loveliest child,
Thy babe or Pleasure's, nursed the powers of song!

    Thou, who with hermit heart
    Disdain'st the wealth of art,
And gauds, and pageant weeds, and trailing pall;
    But com'st a decent maid,
    In Attic robe arrayed,
O chaste unboastful nymph, to thee I call!

    By all the honeyed store
    On Hybla's thymy shore;
By all her blooms and mingled murmurs dear;
    By her whose lovelorn woe,
    In evening musings slow,
Soothed sweetly sad Electra's poet's ear:

    By old Cephisus deep,
    Who spread his wavy sweep
In warbled wanderings round thy green retreat:

On whose enamelled side,
When holy Freedom died,
No equal haunt allured thy future feet:

O sister meek of Truth,
To my admiring youth,
Thy sober aid and native charms infuse!
The flowers that sweetest breathe,
Though Beauty culled the wreath,
Still ask thy hand to range their ordered hues.   30

While Rome could none esteem
But virtue's patriot theme,
You loved her hills, and led her laureate band;
But stayed to sing alone
To one distinguished throne,
And turned thy face, and fled her altered land.

No more, in hall or bower,
The Passions own thy power;
Love, only Love her forceless numbers mean:
For thou hast left her shrine;   40
Nor olive more, nor vine,
Shall gain thy feet to bless the servile scene.

Though taste, though genius bless
To some divine excess,
Faints the cold work till thou inspire the whole;
What each, what all supply,
May court, may charm, our eye;
Thou, only thou, canst raise the meeting soul!

Of these let others ask,
To aid some mighty task;   50
I only seek to find thy temperate vale,
Where oft my reed might sound
To maids and shepherds round,
And all thy sons, O Nature, learn my tale.

[1746]

ODE ON THE POETICAL CHARACTER

STROPHE

As once—if not with light regard
I read aright that gifted bard,
(Him whose school above the rest
His loveliest Elfin Queen has blessed)—
One, only one, unrivalled fair,
Might hope the magic girdle wear,
At solemn turney hung on high,
The wish of each love-darting eye;

Lo! to each other nymph in turn applied,
As if, in air unseen, some hovering hand, 10
Some chaste and angel friend to virgin fame
With whispered spell had burst the starting
band,
It left unblessed her loathed dishonored side;
Happier, hopeless fair, if never
Her baffled hand with vain endeavor
Had touched that fatal zone to her denied!
Young Fancy thus, to me divinest name,
To whom, prepared and bathed in Heaven,
The cest[1] of amplest power is given:
To few the godlike gift assigns,   20
[1] Girdle.

To gird their blessed prophetic loins,
And gaze her visions wild, and feel unmixed
   her flame!

EPODE

The band, as fairy legends say,
Was wove on that creating day,
When He who called with thought to birth
Yon tented sky, this laughing earth,
And dressed with springs, and forests tall,
And poured the main engirting all,
Long by the loved enthusiast wooed,
Himself in some diviner mood,   30
Retiring, sate with her alone,
And placed her on his sapphire throne,
The whiles, the vaulted shrine around,
Seraphic wires were heard to sound,
Now sublimest triumph swelling,
Now on love and mercy dwelling;
And she, from out the veiling cloud,
Breathed her magic notes aloud:
And thou, thou rich-haired Youth of Morn,
And all thy subject life was born!   40
The dangerous Passions kept aloof,
Far from the sainted growing woof,
But near it sate ecstatic Wonder,
Listening the deep applauding thunder,
And Truth, in sunny vest arrayed,
By whose the tarsel's[2] eyes were made;
All the shadowy tribes of Mind
In braided dance their murmurs joined,
And all the bright uncounted Powers
Who feed on Heaven's ambrosial flowers.   50
Where is the bard whose soul can now
Its high presuming hopes avow?
Where he who thinks, with rapture blind,
This hallowed work for him designed?

ANTISTROPHE

High on some cliff, to Heaven up-piled,
Of rude access, of prospect wild,
Where, tangled round the jealous steep,
Strange shades o'erbrow the valleys deep,

  [2] Falcon's.

And holy genii guard the rock,
Its glooms embrown, its springs unlock,   60
While on its rich ambitious head
An Eden, like his own, lies spread,
I view that oak, the fancied glades among,
By which as Milton lay, his evening ear,
From many a cloud that dropped ethereal
   dew,
Nigh sphered in Heaven its native strains
   could hear;
On which that ancient trump he reached was
   hung:
   Thither oft, his glory greeting,
   From Waller's myrtle shades retreating,
With many a vow from Hope's aspiring
   tongue,   70
My trembling feet his guiding steps pursue;
   In vain—such bliss to one alone,
   Of all the sons of soul was known,
   And Heaven and Fancy, kindred powers,
Have now o'erturned the inspiring bowers,
Or curtained close such scene from every
   future view.

               [1746]

ODE

WRITTEN IN THE BEGINNING OF THE YEAR 1746

How sleep the brave, who sink to rest,
By all their country's wishes blessed!
When Spring, with dewy fingers cold,
Returns to deck their hallowed mold,
She there shall dress a sweeter sod
Than Fancy's feet have ever trod.

By fairy hands their knell is rung;
By forms unseen their dirge is sung;
There Honor comes, a pilgrim gray,
To bless the turf that wraps their clay,   10
And Freedom shall awhile repair,
To dwell a weeping hermit there!

               [1746]

ODE TO EVENING

If aught of oaten stop or pastoral song
May hope, chaste Eve, to soothe thy modest **ear,**
   Like thy own solemn springs,
   Thy springs and dying gales,

O nymph reserved, while now the bright-haired sun
Sits in yon western tent, whose cloudy skirts,
   With brede[1] ethereal wove,
   O'erhang his wavy bed—

Now air is hushed, save where the weak-eyed bat,
With short shrill shriek, flits by on leathern wing;   **10**
   Or where the beetle winds
   His small but sullen horn,

As oft he rises 'midst the twilight path,
Against the pilgrim borne in heedless hum—
   Now teach me, maid composed,
   To breathe some softened strain,

Whose numbers, stealing through thy darkening vale,
May not unseemly with its stillness suit,
   As musing slow I hail
   Thy genial loved return!   **20**

For when thy folding-star arising shows
His paly circlet, at his warning lamp
   The fragrant Hours, and elves
   Who slept in flowers the day,

And many a nymph who wreathes her brows with sedge,
And sheds the freshening dew, and, lovelier still,
   The pensive Pleasures sweet
   Prepare thy shadowy car.

Then lead, calm votaress, where some sheety lake
Cheers the lone heath, or some time-hallowed pile   **30**
   Or upland fallows gray
   Reflect its last cool gleam.

But when chill blustering winds or driving rain
Forbid my willing feet, be mine the hut
   That from the mountain's side
   Views wilds, and swelling floods,

And hamlets brown, and dim-discovered spires,
And hears their simple bell, and marks o'er all
   Thy dewy fingers draw
   The gradual dusky veil.   **40**

While Spring shall pour his showers, as oft he wont,
And bathe thy breathing tresses, meekest Eve;
   While Summer loves to sport
   Beneath thy lingering light;

While sallow Autumn fills thy lap with leaves;
Or Winter, yelling through the troublous air,
   Affrights thy shrinking train,
   And rudely rends thy robes;

[1] Braid, embroidery.

So long, sure-found beneath the sylvan shed,
Shall Fancy, Friendship, Science, rose-lipped Health, 50
  Thy gentlest influence own,
  And hymn thy favorite name!

[1746]

THE PASSIONS: AN ODE FOR MUSIC

When Music, heavenly maid, was young,
While yet in early Greece she sung,
The Passions oft, to hear her shell,
Thronged around her magic cell,
Exulting, trembling, raging, fainting,
Possessed beyond the Muse's painting;
By turns they felt the glowing mind
Disturbed, delighted, raised, refined;

Till once, 'tis said, when all were fired,
Filled with fury, rapt, inspired, 10
From the supporting myrtles round
They snatched her instruments of sound,
And as they oft had heard apart
Sweet lessons of her forceful art,
Each, for madness ruled the hour,
Would prove his own expressive power.

First Fear his hand, its skill to try,
  Amid the chords bewildered laid,
And back recoiled, he knew not why,
  Even at the sound himself had made. 20

Next Anger rushed: his eyes, on fire,
  In lightnings owned his secret stings;
In one rude clash he struck the lyre,
  And swept with hurried hand the strings.

With woeful measures wan Despair—
  Low sullen sounds—his grief beguiled,
A solemn, strange, and mingled air;
  'Twas sad by fits, by starts 'twas wild.

But thou, O Hope, with eyes so fair,
  What was thy delightful measure? 30
Still it whispered promised pleasure,
  And bade the lovely scenes at distance hail!
Still would her touch the strain prolong,
  And from the rocks, the woods, the vale,
She called on Echo still through all the song;
  And, where her sweetest theme she chose,
  A soft responsive voice was heard at every close,
And Hope, enchanted, smiled, and waved her golden hair.

And longer had she sung,—but with a frown
  Revenge impatient rose; 40

He threw his blood-stained sword in thunder down,
    And with a withering look
    The war-denouncing[1] trumpet took,
And blew a blast so loud and dread,
Were ne'er prophetic sounds so full of woe.
    And ever and anon he beat
    The doubling drum with furious heat;

And though sometimes each dreary pause between,
    Dejected Pity at his side
    Her soul-subduing voice applied,   50
    Yet still he kept his wild unaltered mien,
While each strained ball of sight seemed bursting from his head.

Thy numbers, Jealousy, to naught were fixed,
    Sad proof of thy distressful state;
Of differing themes the veering song was mixed,
    And now it courted Love, now raving called on Hate.

With eyes upraised, as one inspired,
Pale Melancholy sate retired,
And from her wild sequestered seat,
In notes by distance made more sweet,   60
Poured through the mellow horn her pensive soul:
    And dashing soft from rocks around,
    Bubbling runnels joined the sound;
Through glades and glooms the mingled measure stole,
Or o'er some haunted stream, with fond delay,
    Round an holy calm diffusing,
    Love of peace and lonely musing,
In hollow murmurs died away.

But oh how altered was its sprightlier tone,
When Cheerfulness, a nymph of healthiest hue,   70
    Her bow across her shoulder flung,
    Her buskins gemmed with morning dew,
Blew an inspiring air, that dale and thicket rung,
    The hunter's call to Faun and Dryad known!
    The oak-crowned Sisters, and their chaste-eyed Queen,
    Satyrs and sylvan boys were seen,
    Peeping from forth their alleys green;
Brown Exercise rejoiced to hear,
    And Sport leaped up, and seized his beechen spear.

Last came Joy's ecstatic trial,   80
He, with viny crown advancing,
    First to the lively pipe his hand addressed,
But soon he saw the brisk awakening viol,
    Whose sweet entrancing voice he loved the best.
    They would have thought who heard the strain,
    They saw in Tempe's vale her native maids,
    Amidst the festal sounding shades,
To some unwearied minstrel dancing,
    While, as his flying fingers kissed the strings.

[1] War-announcing.

Love framed with Mirth a gay fantastic round, 90
Loose were her tresses seen, her zone unbound,
And he amidst his frolic play,
As if he would the charming air repay,
Shook thousand odors from his dewy wings.

O Music, sphere-descended maid,
Friend of Pleasure, Wisdom's aid,
Why, goddess, why, to us denied,
Lay'st thou thy ancient lyre aside?
As in that loved Athenian bower
You learned an all-commanding power, 100
Thy mimic soul, O nymph endeared,
Can well recall what then it heard.
Where is thy native simple heart,
Devote to Virtue, Fancy, Art?
Arise as in that elder time,
Warm, energic, chaste, sublime!
Thy wonders, in that godlike age,
Fill thy recording Sister's page—
'Tis said, and I believe the tale,
Thy humblest reed could more prevail, 110
Had more of strength, diviner rage,
Than all which charms this laggard age,
E/en all at once together found,
Caecilia's mingled world of sound—
Oh bid our vain endeavors cease;
Revive the just designs of Greece;
Return in all thy simple state;
Confirm the tales her sons relate!

[1746]

ODE ON THE DEATH OF MR. THOMSON

The scene of the following stanzas is supposed to lie on the Thames near Richmond

In yonder grave a Druid lies,
  Where slowly winds the stealing wave;
The year's best sweets shall duteous rise
  To deck its poet's sylvan grave.

In yon deep bed of whispering reeds
  His airy harp shall now be laid,
That he, whose heart in sorrow bleeds,
  May love through life the soothing shade.

Then maids and youths shall linger here,
  And while its sounds at distance swell, 10
Shall sadly seem in Pity's ear
  To hear the woodland pilgrim's knell.

Remembrance oft shall haunt the shore
  When Thames in summer wreathes is dressed,
And oft suspend the dashing oar,
  To bid his gentle spirit rest!

And oft, as Ease and Health retire
  To breezy lawn, or forest deep,
The friend shall view yon whitening spire,
  And 'mid the varied landscape weep. 20

But thou who own'st that earthy bed,
  Ah! what will every dirge avail;
Or tears which Love and Pity shed,
  That mourn beneath the gliding sail?

Yet lives there one whose heedless eye
  Shall scorn thy pale shrine glimmering near?
With him, sweet bard, may Fancy die,
  And Joy desert the blooming year.

But thou, lorn stream, whose sullen tide
  No sedge-crowned sisters now attend,   30
Now waft me from the green hill's side,
  Whose cold turf hides the buried friend!

And see, the fairy valleys fade;
  Dun night has veiled the solemn view!
Yet once again, dear parted shade,
  Meek Nature's child, again adieu!

The genial meads, assigned to bless
  Thy life, shall mourn thy early doom;
Their hinds and shepherd-girls shall dress
  With simple hands thy rural tomb.   40

Long, long, thy stone and pointed clay
  Shall melt the musing Briton's eyes;
"O! vales and wild woods," shall he say,
  "In yonder grave your Druid lies!"

[1749]

ODE ON THE POPULAR SUPERSTITIONS OF THE HIGHLANDS OF SCOTLAND

CONSIDERED AS THE SUBJECT OF POETRY

I

H——, thou return'st from Thames, whose naiads long
  Have seen thee lingering with a fond delay,
  'Mid those soft friends, whose hearts, some future day,
Shall melt, perhaps, to hear thy tragic song.
Go, not unmindful of that cordial youth
  Whom, long endeared, thou leav'st by Lavant's side;
Together let us wish him lasting truth,
  And joy untainted with his destined bride.
Go! nor regardless, while these numbers boast
  My short-lived bliss, forget my social name;   10
But think, far off, how, on the southern coast,
  I met thy friendship with an equal flame!
Fresh to that soil thou turn'st, whose every vale
  Shall prompt the poet, and his song demand:
To thee thy copious subjects ne'er shall fail;
  Thou need'st but take the pencil to thy hand,
And paint what all believe who own thy genial land.

II

There must thou wake perforce thy Doric quill;
  'Tis Fancy's land to which thou sett'st thy feet;
  Where still, 'tis said, the fairy people meet,   20
Beneath each birken shade, on mead or hill.
There each trim lass that skims the milky store
  To the swart tribes their creamy bowls allots;
By night they sip it round the cottage door,
  While airy minstrels warble jocund notes.
There every herd by sad experience knows
  How, winged with fate, their elf-shot arrows fly,
When the sick ewe her summer food foregoes,
  Or, stretched on earth, the heart-smit heifers lie.
Such airy beings awe the untutored swain: 30
  Nor thou, though learned, his homelier thoughts neglect;
Let thy sweet Muse the rural faith sustain;

These are the themes of simple, sure effect,
That add new conquests to her boundless reign,
And fill with double force her heart-commanding strain.

III

Even yet preserved, how often mayst thou hear,
    Where to the pole the boreal mountains run,
    Taught by the father to his listening son,
Strange lays whose power had charmed a Spenser's ear.
At every pause, before thy mind possessed,   40
    Old Runic bards shall seem to rise around,
With uncouth lyres, in many-colored vest,
    Their matted hair with boughs fantastic crowned:
Whether thou bidd'st the well-taught hind repeat
    The choral dirge that mourns some chieftain brave,
When every shrieking maid her bosom beat,
    And strewed with choicest herbs his scented grave;
Or whether, sitting in the shepherd's shiel,[1]
    Thou hear'st some sounding tale of war's alarms;
When at the bugle's call, with fire and steel,   50
    The sturdy clans poured forth their bony swarms,
And hostile brothers met, to prove each other's arms.

IV

'Tis thine to sing how, framing hideous spells,
    In Sky's lone isle, the gifted wizard seer,
    Lodged in the wintry cave with [   ]
Or in the depth of Uist's dark forests dwells:
How they whose sight such dreary dreams engross,
    With their own visions oft astonished droop,
    When, o'er the watery strath[2] of quaggy moss
They see the gliding ghosts unbodied troop;   60
    Or, if in sports, or on the festive green,
Their [   ] glance some fated youth descry,
    Who now perhaps in lusty vigor seen,
And rosy health, shall soon lamented die.
    For them the viewless forms of air obey,
    Their bidding heed, and at their beck repair:
They know what spirit brews the stormful day,
And, heartless, oft like moody madness stare
To see the phantom train their secret work prepare.

V

[This stanza, comprising lines 70–86, was missing in the manuscript.]

VI

[The first eight lines of this stanza, lines 87–94 of the poem, were missing in the manuscript.]

What though far off, from some dark dell espied,
    His glimmering mazes cheer the excursive sight,

[1] A temporary shepherd's hut.
[2] A wide valley.

Yet turn, ye wanderers, turn your steps aside,
  Nor trust the guidance of that faithless light;
For, watchful, lurking 'mid the unrustling reed,
  At those mirk hours the wily monster lies,   100
And listens oft to hear the passing steed,
  And frequent round him rolls his sullen eyes,
If chance his savage wrath may some weak wretch surprise.

VII

Ah, luckless swain, o'er all unblessed indeed!
  Whom late bewildered in the dank, dark fen,
  Far from his flocks and smoking hamlet then,
To that sad spot [   ]
  On him, enraged, the fiend, in angry mood,
Shall never look with pity's kind concern,
  But instant, furious, raise the whelming flood   110
O'er its drowned bank, forbidding all return!
  Or, if he meditate his wished escape
To some dim hill, that seems uprising near,
  To his faint eye the grim and grisly shape,
In all its terrors clad, shall wild appear.
  Meantime the watery surge shall round him rise,
Poured sudden forth from every swelling source!
  What now remains but tears and hopeless sigh?
His fear-shook limbs have lost their youthly force,
And down the waves he floats, a pale and breathless corse!   120

VIII

For him in vain his anxious wife shall wait,
  Or wander forth to meet him on his way;
For him in vain at to-fall of the day,
  His babes shall linger at the unclosing gate!
Ah, ne'er shall he return! Alone, if night
  Her travelled limbs in broken slumbers steep,
With drooping willows dressed, his mournful sprite
  Shall visit sad, perchance, her silent sleep;
Then he, perhaps, with moist and watery hand,
  Shall fondly seem to press her shuddering cheek,   130
And with his blue-swoln face before her stand,
  And, shivering cold, these piteous accents speak:
"Pursue, dear wife, thy daily toils pursue,
  At dawn or dusk, industrious as before;
Nor e'er of me one helpless thought renew,
While I lie weltering on the osiered shore,
Drowned by the kelpie's wrath, nor e'er shall aid thee more!"

IX

Unbounded is thy range; with varied style
  Thy Muse may, like those feathery tribes which spring
  From their rude rocks, extend her skirting wing   140
Round the moist marge of each cold Hebrid isle,
  To that hoar pile which still its ruins shows;

In whose small vaults a pigmy-folk is found,
    Whose bones the delver with his spade upthrows,
And culls them, wondering, from the hallowed ground!
Or thither where, beneath the showery West,
    The mighty kings of three fair realms are laid;
Once foes, perhaps, together now they rest;
    No slaves revere them, and no wars invade:
Yet frequent now, at midnight's solemn hour,   150
    The rifted mounds their yawning cells unfold,
And forth the monarchs stalk with sovereign power,
    In pageant robes, and wreathed with sheeny gold,
And on their twilight tombs aërial council hold.

X

But, oh, o'er all, forget not Kilda's race,
    On whose bleak rocks, which brave the wasting tides,
    Fair Nature's daughter, Virtue, yet abides.
Go! just, as they, their blameless manners trace!
    Then to my ear transmit some gentle song.
Of those whose lives are yet sincere and plain,   160
    Their bounded walks the rugged cliffs along,
And all their prospect but the wintry main.
    With sparing temperance, at the needful time,
They drain the sainted spring; or, hunger-pressed,
    Along the Atlantic rock undreading climb,
And of its eggs despoil the solan's nest.
    Thus, blessed in primal innocence, they live
Sufficed and happy with that frugal fare
    Which tasteful toil and hourly danger give.
Hard is their shallow soil, and bleak and bare;   170
    Nor ever vernal bee was heard to murmur there!

XI

Nor need'st thou blush that such false themes engage
    Thy gentle mind, of fairer stores possessed;
    For not alone they touch the village breast,
But filled in elder time, the historic page.
    There Shakespeare's self, with every garland crowned,
[   ]
    In musing hour his wayward Sisters found,
And with their terrors dressed the magic scene.
    From them he sung, when, 'mid his bold design,   180
Before the Scot, afflicted and aghast,
    The shadowy kings of Banquo's fated line
Through the dark cave in gleamy pageant passed.
    Proceed, nor quit the tales which, simply told,
Could once so well my answering bosom pierce;
    Proceed—in forceful sounds and colors bold
The native legends of thy land rehearse;
To such adapt thy lyre, and suit thy powerful verse.

XII

In scenes like these, which, daring to depart
   From sober truth, are still to nature true,   190
And call forth fresh delight to Fancy's view,
The heroic muse employed her Tasso's art!
   How have I trembled, when, at Tancred's stroke,
Its gushing blood the gaping cypress poured!
   When each live plant with mortal accents spoke,
And the wild blast upheaved the vanished sword!
   How have I sat, when piped the pensive wind,
To hear his harp by British Fairfax strung!
   Prevailing poet! whose undoubting mind
Believed the magic wonders which he sung!   200
   Hence at each sound imagination glows!
[   ]
   Hence his warm lay with softest sweetness flows!
Melting it flows, pure, numerous, strong, and clear,
And fills the impassioned heart, and wins the harmonious ear!

XIII

All hail, ye scenes that o'er my soul prevail!
Ye [   ] friths and lakes, which, far away,
   Are by smooth Annan filled or pastoral Tay,
Or Don's romantic springs; at distance, hail!
The time shall come, when I, perhaps, may tread   210
   Your lowly glens, o'erhung with spreading broom;
Or, o'er your stretching heaths, by Fancy led;
   [   ]
Then will I dress once more the faded bower,
   Where Jonson sat in Drummond's [   ] shade;
Or crop, from Tiviot's dale, each [   ]
   And mourn, on Yarrow's banks, [   ]
Meantime, ye Powers that on the plains which bore
   The cordial youth, on Lothian's plains, attend!—
Where'er he dwell, on hill or lowly muir,   220
   To him I lose, your kind protection lend,
And, touched with love like mine, preserve my absent friend!
                            [*1749, 1788*]

THOMAS GRAY (1716-1771)

Thomas Gray was a scholar and what the eighteenth century called a virtuoso—a man with a wide range of interests in literature, art, and science who kept clear of the faults of the professionally learned. The virtuoso was in danger of becoming superficial and affected, as we see in the case of Gray's friend Horace Walpole, an especially brilliant example of the type; but Gray himself combined what was best in eighteenth-century culture—good taste, simple and symmetrical form, moral seriousness—with a sensitiveness and delicacy all his own. Although he will always be remembered for his poetry, poetry was only one of his interests. Matthew Arnold's famous essay represents him as a sensitive soul ill-adapted to the time in which he lived, a romantic genius who might have done greater things if he had lived in another period. Against this it may be urged that the times helped Gray more than they hindered him, that he was by temperament better fitted to be an eighteenth-century virtuoso than a nineteenth-century apostle or prophet. During a lifetime of leisure, to be sure, he wrote very little verse; but that was because he was fastidious, not because the age prevented him from writing more. He found time and opportunity to do and to enjoy many things. Thus, he was one of the greatest of English letter-writers, and made the personal letter a consummate medium for self-expression.

Gray was the son of a London merchant, but his mother's family had a professional and university background. During his schooldays at Eton his closest friends were Horace Walpole, Richard West, and Thomas Ashton. After he and Walpole had finished their studies at Cambridge they traveled together in France and Italy, and Gray's manifold interests appeared in his discriminating enjoyment of French literature, Alpine scenery, and Italian art. The two friends quarreled in Italy, and Gray returned to England alone. For a time he lived in melancholy retirement with his mother and sister at Stoke Poges, Buckinghamshire, and there, during the summer of 1742, he wrote his first important poems—the odes *On the Spring* and *On a Distant Prospect of Eton College*, the *Hymn to Adversity*, and the sonnet on the death of Richard West. The *Elegy Written in a Country Churchyard* was possibly, though by no means certainly, begun at this time also. Deeply personal impulses underlie these poems, but for the most part they are concealed by formal diction and impersonal moralizing. Gray thought of poetry not as a direct transcript of the inner life, but as a distillation of thought and feeling in choice and stately phrase.

After 1742 Gray lived at Cambridge, first at his own college Peterhouse, and later at Pembroke. Here he carried on his varied studies in history, literature, music, and natural science. We can follow his uneventful life in his delightful correspondence with a small circle of friends, notably Walpole, with whom he was now reconciled, and later with Mason, Stonehewer, Wharton, and Norton Nicholls. Meanwhile he wrote very little verse, and shrank from publishing what he did write. The *Elegy* appeared almost against his will in 1751, and perhaps no single poem in English literature ever established its author's reputation more promptly and securely. The "divine truisms" of the *Elegy* are classic in their form and in their spirit of resignation to destiny, but the rigidity of this austere teaching is softened, without being broken, by the poet's sensitiveness and his sympathy with humble humanity. The poetical labors of a decade are included in the *Six Poems* of 1753, brought out through the good offices of Walpole.

In the following years Gray worked on his two great Pindaric odes, and published them, again at the insistence of his friends, in 1757. His earlier works had been chiefly concerned with moral generalities, but he now turned to his historical studies for new material and inspiration. In *The Progress of Poesy* he uses a hackneyed formula, but invests it with new dignity; in *The Bard* his Celtic studies give him a picturesque framework for a grandiose survey of English history. Unlike his earlier verse, these poems were regarded as obscure and difficult by contemporary readers. Both are based on the idea that mankind from earliest times has been visited by the highest poetic inspiration, but this early inspiration is not exalted at the expense of later poetry. In style, diction, and structure, the two odes are stately, artificial, and thus "classical." Gray's interest in early poetry was further stimulated by James Macpherson's *Fragments of Ancient Poetry Collected in the Highlands* (1760), the first of the so-called translations from Ossian. Thereafter he made his fragmentary translations of Welsh and Norse poems, and these chips from his workshop are interesting evidence of the changing taste of the times. His journal of his tour to the Lake Country in 1769 is the most important record we have of several such tours in England and Scotland, significant of his delight in wild and picturesque scenery. He died at Cambridge in 1771, and was buried at Stoke Poges.

  Gray's work is animated with the true critical spirit; he unites wide appreciation with keen judgment, and his casual comments on literary subjects give us some of the best criticism of the century. It is this fine critical sense that makes him a better balanced poet than Collins, with whom he has often been compared. Both are learned poets who look back to Greek models, their primary care always for diction and form. Thus they sacrifice freedom and spontaneity. Gray's ideal is expressed in one of his letters to Mason (January 13, 1758): "Extreme conciseness of expression, yet pure, perspicuous, and musical, is one of the grand beauties of lyric poetry." He adds, "This I have always aimed at, and never could attain." Nevertheless, in meditative lyric and Pindaric ode he was the greatest master of his century.

  Works, ed. E. Gosse (4 vols., revised ed. 1902-6); *Selections,* ed. W. L. Phelps (Boston, 1894); *English Poems,* ed. D. C. Tovey (Cambridge, 1898); *Elegy,* ed. F. G. Stokes (Oxford, 1929); *Correspondence,* ed. P. Toynbee and L. Whibley (3 vols., Oxford, 1935); E. Gosse, *Gray* (1882, English Men of Letters) [untrustworthy]; Matthew Arnold, "Thomas Gray," *Essays in Criticism* (Second Series, 1888); R. Martin, *Essai sur Thomas Gray* (1934) [full and authoritative]; *Chronologie de la vie et de l'oeuvre de Thomas Gray* (1931); R. W. Ketton-Cremer, *Thomas Gray* (1955); W. P. Jones, *Thomas Gray, Scholar* (Cambridge, Mass., 1937); H. W. Starr, *Gray as a Literary Critic* (Philadelphia, 1941); Lord David Cecil, essays in *Two Quiet Lives* (1948), *Poets and Story-Tellers* (1949); Amy L. Reed, *The Background of Gray's Elegy* (1924); W. P. Jones, "The Contemporary Reception of Gray's Odes," *MP,* XXVIII (1930), 61-82; C. S. Northup, *Bibliography of Thomas Gray* (New Haven, 1917); H. W. Starr, *Bibliography of Thomas Gray 1917-1951* (Philadelphia, 1953).

SONNET

ON THE DEATH OF MR. RICHARD WEST

In vain to me the smiling mornings shine,
  And reddening Phœbus lifts his golden fire;
The birds in vain their amorous descant join,
  Or cheerful fields resume their green attire;
These ears, alas! for other notes repine,
  A different object do these eyes require;
My lonely anguish melts no heart but mine,
  And in my breast the imperfect joys expire.
Yet morning smiles the busy race to cheer,
  And new-born pleasure brings to happier men;   10
The fields to all their wonted tribute bear;
  To warm their little loves the birds complain:
I fruitless mourn to him that cannot hear,
  And weep the more, because I weep in vain.

                                      [*1742*, 1775]

ODE ON A DISTANT PROSPECT OF ETON COLLEGE

Ἄνθρωπος᾽ ἱκανὴ πρόφασις εἰς τὸ δυστυχεῖν.[1]
Menander

Ye distant spires, ye antique towers,
That crown the watery glade,
Where grateful Science still adores
Her Henry's holy Shade;
And ye, that from the stately brow
Of Windsor's heights the expanse below
Of grove, of lawn, of mead survey,
Whose turf, whose shade, whose flowers among
Wanders the hoary Thames along
His silver-winding way: 10

Ah, happy hills! ah, pleasing shade!
Ah, fields beloved in vain!
Where once my careless childhood strayed,
A stranger yet to pain!
I feel the gales that from ye blow
A momentary bliss bestow,
As, waving fresh their gladsome wing,
My weary soul they seem to soothe,
And, redolent of joy and youth,
To breathe a second spring.   20

Say, Father Thames, for thou hast seen
Full many a sprightly race
Disporting on thy margent green
The paths of pleasure trace;
Who foremost now delight to cleave
With pliant arm thy glassy wave?
The captive linnet which enthrall?
What idle progeny succeed
To chase the rolling circle's speed,
Or urge the flying ball?   30

While some on earnest business bent
Their murmuring labors ply
'Gainst graver hours, that bring constraint
To sweeten liberty;
Some bold adventurers disdain
The limits of their little reign,
And unknown regions dare descry;
Still as they run they look behind;
They hear a voice in every wind,
And snatch a fearful joy.   40

Gay hope is theirs, by fancy fed,
Less pleasing when possessed;

[1] I am a man, a sufficient excuse for being unhappy.

The tear forgot as soon as shed,
The sunshine of the breast;
Theirs buxom health of rosy hue,
Wild wit, invention ever new,
And lively cheer of vigor born;
The thoughtless day, the easy night,
The spirits pure, the slumbers light,
That fly the approach of morn.   50

Alas, regardless of their doom,
The little victims play!
No sense have they of ills to come,
Nor care beyond to-day!
Yet see how all around 'em wait
The ministers of human fate,
And black Misfortune's baleful train!
Ah, show them where in ambush stand
To seize their prey the murderous band!
Ah, tell them they are men!   60

These shall the fury Passions tear,
The vultures of the mind,
Disdainful Anger, pallid Fear,
And Shame that skulks behind;
Or pining Love shall waste their youth,
Or Jealousy with rankling tooth,
That inly gnaws the secret heart,
And Envy wan, and faded Care,
Grim-visaged comfortless Despair,
And Sorrow's piercing dart.   70

Ambition this shall tempt to rise,
Then whirl the wretch from high,
To bitter Scorn a sacrifice,
And grinning Infamy.
The stings of Falsehood those shall try,
And hard Unkindness' altered eye,
That mocks the tear it forced to flow;
And keen Remorse with blood defiled,
And moody Madness laughing wild
Amid severest woe.   80

Lo, in the vale of years beneath
A grisly troop are seen,
The painful family of Death,
More hideous than their queen:
This racks the joints, this fires the veins,
That every laboring sinew strains,
Those in the deeper vitals rage;
Lo, Poverty, to fill the band,
That numbs the soul with icy hand,
And slow-consuming Age.   90

To each his sufferings; all are men,
Condemned alike to groan—

The tender for another's pain,
The unfeeling for his own.
Yet, ah! why should they know their fate,
Since sorrow never comes too late,
And happiness too swiftly flies?
Thought would destroy their paradise.
No more; where ignorance is bliss,
'Tis folly to be wise.   100

[*1742*, 1747]

HYMN TO ADVERSITY

—Ζῆνα
Τὸν φρονεῖν βροτοὺς ὁδώ-
σαντα, τῷ πάθει μαθὰν
Θέντα κυρίως ἔχειν.[1]
Aeschylus, *Agamem.* 167-71

Daughter of Jove, relentless power,
Thou tamer of the human breast,
Whose iron scourge and torturing hour
The bad affright, afflict the best!
Bound in thy adamantine chain
The proud are taught to taste of pain,
And purple tyrants vainly groan
With pangs unfelt before, unpitied and alone.

When first thy sire to send on earth
Virtue, his darling child, designed,   10
To thee he gave the heavenly birth,
And bade to form her infant mind.
Stern rugged nurse! thy rigid lore
With patience many a year she bore;
What sorrow was, thou badst her know,
And from her own she learned to melt at
          others' woe.

[1] Zeus, who leads mortals to understanding,
who has established as a fixed ordinance that
wisdom comes by suffering.

Scared at thy frown terrific, fly
Self-pleasing Folly's idle brood,
Wild Laughter, Noise, and thoughtless Joy,
And leave us leisure to be good.   20
Light they disperse, and with them go
The summer friend, the flattering foe;
By vain Prosperity received,
To her they vow their truth, and are again
          believed.

Wisdom in sable garb arrayed,
Immersed in rapturous thought profound,
And Melancholy, silent maid,
With leaden eye, that loves the ground,
Still on thy solemn steps attend;
Warm Charity, the general friend,   30
With Justice, to herself severe,
And Pity, dropping soft the sadly-pleasing
          tear.

Oh, gently on thy suppliant's head,
Dread Goddess, lay thy chastening hand!
Not in thy Gorgon terrors clad,
Nor circled with the vengeful band
(As by the impious thou art seen)
With thundering voice, and threatening mien,
With screaming Horror's funeral cry,   39
Despair, and fell Disease, and ghastly Poverty.

Thy form benign, O Goddess, wear,
Thy milder influence impart;
Thy philosophic train be there
To soften, not to wound, my heart;
The generous spark extinct revive,
Teach me to love and to forgive,
Exact my own defects to scan,
What others are to feel, and know myself a
          man.

[*1742*, 1753]

ELEGY

WRITTEN IN A COUNTRY CHURCHYARD

The curfew tolls the knell of parting day,
     The lowing herd wind slowly o'er the lea,
     The ploughman homeward plods his weary way,
          And leaves the world to darkness and to me.

Now fades the glimmering landscape on the sight,
     And all the air a solemn stillness holds,

Save where the beetle wheels his droning flight,
   And drowsy tinklings lull the distant folds;

Save that from yonder ivy-mantled tower
   The moping owl does to the moon complain   10
Of such as, wandering near her secret bower,
   Molest her ancient solitary reign.

Beneath those rugged elms, that yew-tree's shade,
   Where heaves the turf in many a moldering heap,
Each in his narrow cell forever laid,
   The rude forefathers of the hamlet sleep.

The breezy call of incense-breathing morn,
   The swallow twittering from the straw-built shed,
The cock's shrill clarion, or the echoing horn,
   No more shall rouse them from their lowly bed.   20

For them no more the blazing hearth shall burn,
   Or busy housewife ply her evening care:
No children run to lisp their sire's return,
   Or climb his knees the envied kiss to share.

Oft did the harvest to their sickle yield;
   Their furrow oft the stubborn glebe has broke;
How jocund did they drive their team afield!
   How bowed the woods beneath their sturdy stroke!

Let not Ambition mock their useful toil,
   Their homely joys, and destiny obscure;   30
Nor Grandeur hear with a disdainful smile
   The short and simple annals of the poor.

The boast of heraldry, the pomp of power,
   And all that beauty, all that wealth e'er gave,
Awaits alike the inevitable hour:
   The paths of glory lead but to the grave.

Nor you, ye proud, impute to these the fault,
   If Memory o'er their tomb no trophies raise,
Where through the long-drawn aisle and fretted vault
   The pealing anthem swells the note of praise.   40

Can storied urn or animated bust
   Back to its mansion call the fleeting breath?
Can Honor's voice provoke the silent dust,
   Or Flattery soothe the dull, cold ear of Death?

Perhaps in this neglected spot is laid
   Some heart once pregnant with celestial fire;
Hands that the rod of empire might have swayed,
   Or waked to ecstasy the living lyre.

But Knowledge to their eyes her ample page,
   Rich with the spoils of time, did ne'er unroll;   50

Chill Penury repressed their noble rage,
　　And froze the genial current of the soul.

Full many a gem of purest ray serene,
　　The dark unfathomed caves of ocean bear:
Full many a flower is born to blush unseen,
　　And waste its sweetness on the desert air.

Some village Hampden, that with dauntless breast
　　The little tyrant of his fields withstood;
Some mute, inglorious Milton here may rest,
　　Some Cromwell, guiltless of his country's blood.　　　　　　60

The applause of listening senates to command,
　　The threats of pain and ruin to despise,
To scatter plenty o'er a smiling land,
　　And read their history in a nation's eyes,

Their lot forbade: nor circumscribed alone
　　Their growing virtues, but their crimes confined;
Forbade to wade through slaughter to a throne,
　　And shut the gates of mercy on mankind;

The struggling pangs of conscious truth to hide,
　　To quench the blushes of ingenuous shame,　　　　　　70
Or heap the shrine of Luxury and Pride
　　With incense kindled at the Muse's flame.

Far from the madding crowd's ignoble strife,
　　Their sober wishes never learned to stray;
Along the cool, sequestered vale of life
　　They kept the noiseless tenor of their way.

Yet even these bones from insult to protect,
　　Some frail memorial still erected nigh,
With uncouth rhymes and shapeless sculpture decked,
　　Implores the passing tribute of a sigh.　　　　　　80

Their name, their years, spelt by the unlettered Muse,
　　The place of fame and elegy supply;
And many a holy text around she strews,
　　That teach the rustic moralist to die.

For who, to dumb forgetfulness a prey,
　　This pleasing anxious being e'er resigned,
Left the warm precincts of the cheerful day,
　　Nor cast one longing lingering look behind?

On some fond breast the parting soul relies,
　　Some pious drops the closing eye requires;　　　　　　90
E'en from the tomb the voice of Nature cries,
　　E'en in our ashes live their wonted fires.

For thee who, mindful of the unhonored dead,
　　Dost in these lines their artless tale relate;

If chance, by lonely contemplation led,
  Some kindred spirit shall inquire thy fate,—

Haply some hoary-headed swain may say,
  "Oft have we seen him at the peep of dawn
Brushing with hasty steps the dews away,
  To meet the sun upon the upland lawn.   100

"There at the foot of yonder nodding beech
  That wreathes its old fantastic roots so high,
His listless length at noontide would he stretch,
  And pore upon the brook that babbles by.

"Hard by yon wood, now smiling as in scorn,
  Muttering his wayward fancies he would rove;
Now drooping, woeful-wan, like one forlorn,
  Or crazed with care, or crossed in hopeless love.

"One morn I missed him on the customed hill,
  Along the heath, and near his favorite tree;   110
Another came; nor yet beside the rill,
  Nor up the lawn, nor at the wood was he;

"The next, with dirges due, in sad array,
  Slow through the church-way path we saw him borne.
Approach and read (for thou canst read) the lay,
  Graved on the stone beneath yon aged thorn."

THE EPITAPH

Here rests his head upon the lap of earth,
  A youth to Fortune and to Fame unknown;
Fair Science frowned not on his humble birth,
  And Melancholy marked him for her own.   120

Large was his bounty, and his soul sincere;
  Heaven did a recompense as largely send:
He gave to Misery (all he had), a tear;
  He gained from Heaven ('twas all he wished) a friend.

No farther seek his merits to disclose,
  Or draw his frailties from their dread abode,
(There they alike in trembling hope repose,)
  The bosom of his Father and his God.

[*1742?–1750, 1751*]

STANZAS TO MR. BENTLEY

In silent gaze the tuneful choir among,
  Half pleased, half blushing, let the Muse
    admire,
While Bentley leads her sister-art along,
  And bids the pencil answer to the lyre.
See, in their course, each transitory thought

Fixed by his touch a lasting essence take;
  Each dream, in fancy's airy coloring wrought,
To local symmetry and life awake!

The tardy rhymes that used to linger on,
  To censure cold, and negligent of fame,   10
In swifter measures animated run,
  And catch a lustre from his genuine flame.

Ah! could they catch his strength, his easy
  grace,
His quick creation, his unerring line;
The energy of Pope they might efface,
  And Dryden's harmony submit to mine.

But not to one in this benighted age
  Is that diviner inspiration given,
That burns in Shakespeare's or in Milton's
  page,
The pomp and prodigality of Heaven. 20

As when, conspiring in the diamond's blaze,
  The meaner gems that singly charm the
    sight
Together dart their intermingled rays,
  And dazzle with a luxury of light.

Enough for me, if to some feeling breast,
  My lines a secret sympathy ——;
And as their pleasing influence —— ,
  A sigh of soft reflection ——.

                                    [c. 1752, 1775]

THE PROGRESS OF POESY

A PINDARIC ODE

Φωνᾶντα συνετοῖσιν ἐς
Δὲ τὸ πᾶν ἑρμηνέων χατίζει[1].
                                    Pindar, Olymp. II

I—1

Awake, Aeolian lyre, awake,
And give to rapture all thy trembling strings.
From Helicon's harmonious springs
A thousand rills their mazy progress take;
The laughing flowers that round them blow
Drink life and fragrance as they flow.
Now the rich stream of music winds along,
Deep, majestic, smooth, and strong,
Through verdant vales and Ceres' golden reign;
Now rolling down the steep amain,   10
Headlong, impetuous, see it pour;
The rocks and nodding groves rebellow to the roar.

I—2

Oh! Sovereign of the willing soul,
Parent of sweet and solemn-breathing airs,
Enchanting shell! the sullen Cares
And frantic Passions hear thy soft control.
On Thracia's hills the Lord of War
Has curbed the fury of his car,
And dropped his thirsty lance at thy command.
Perching on the sceptered hand   20
Of Jove, thy magic lulls the feathered king,
With ruffled plumes and flagging wing;
Quenched in dark clouds of slumber lie
The terror of his beak, and lightnings of his eye.

I—3

Thee the voice, the dance, obey,
Tempered to thy warbled lay.

[1] Vocal to the intelligent, but for the world at large requiring interpreters.

O'er Idalia's velvet-green
The rosy-crownèd Loves are seen
On Cytherea's day;
With antic Sports, and blue-eyed Pleasures,   30
Frisking light in frolic measures;
Now pursuing, now retreating,
Now in circling troops they meet,
To brisk notes in cadence beating
Glance their many-twinkling feet.
Slow melting strains their queen's approach declare;
Where'er she turns the Graces homage pay.
With arms sublime that float upon the air,
In gliding state she wins her easy way;
O'er her warm cheek and rising bosom move   40
The bloom of young desire and purple light of love.

II—1

Man's feeble race what ills await,
Labor, and penury, the racks of pain,
Disease, and sorrow's weeping train,
And death, sad refuge from the storms of fate!
The fond complaint, my song, disprove,
And justify the laws of Jove.
Say, has he given in vain the heavenly Muse?
Night, and all her sickly dews,
Her spectres wan, and birds of boding cry   50
He gives to range the dreary sky;
Till down the eastern cliffs afar
Hyperion's march they spy, and glittering shafts of war.

II—2

In climes beyond the solar road,
Where shaggy forms o'er ice-built mountains roam,
The Muse has broke the twilight-gloom
To cheer the shivering native's dull abode.
And oft, beneath the odorous shade
Of Chili's boundless forests laid,
She deigns to hear the savage youth repeat   60
In loose numbers wildly sweet
Their feather-cinctured chiefs and dusky loves.
Her track, where'er the goddess roves,
Glory pursue, and generous shame,
The unconquerable mind, and Freedom's holy flame.

II—3

Woods that wave o'er Delphi's steep,
Isles that crown the Aegean deep,
Fields that cool Ilissus laves,
Or where Maeander's amber waves
In lingering labyrinths creep,   70
How do your tuneful echoes languish,
Mute, but to the voice of anguish!

Where each old poetic mountain
Inspiration breathed around,
Every shade and hallowed fountain
Murmured deep a solemn sound;
Till the sad Nine in Greece's evil hour
Left their Parnassus for the Latian plains.
Alike they scorn the pomp of tyrant Power,
And coward Vice, that revels in her chains.   80
When Latium had her lofty spirit lost,
They sought, O Albion! next, thy sea-encircled coast.

III—1

Far from the sun and summer-gale,
In thy green lap was Nature's darling laid,
What time, where lucid Avon strayed,
To him the mighty mother did unveil
Her awful face; the dauntless child
Stretched forth his little arms, and smiled.
"This pencil take," she said, "whose colors clear
Richly paint the vernal year;   90
Thine too these golden keys, immortal boy!
This can unlock the gates of joy;
Of horror that, and thrilling fears,
Or ope the sacred source of sympathetic tears."

III—2

Nor second he that rode sublime
Upon the seraph-wings of ecstasy,
The secrets of the abyss to spy.
He passed the flaming bounds of place and time;
The living throne, the sapphire-blaze,
Where angels tremble while they gaze,   100
He saw; but blasted with excess of light,
Closed his eyes in endless night.
Behold where Dryden's less presumptuous car,
Wide o'er the fields of glory bear
Two coursers of ethereal race,
With necks in thunder clothed, and long-resounding pace.

III—3

Hark, his hands the lyre explore!
Bright-eyed Fancy, hovering o'er,
Scatters from her pictured urn
Thoughts that breathe and words that burn.   110
But ah! 'tis heard no more—
O lyre divine, what daring spirit
Wakes thee now? Though he inherit
Nor the pride nor ample pinion
That the Theban Eagle bear,
Sailing with supreme dominion
Through the azure deep of air;
Yet oft before his infant eyes would run

Such forms as glitter in the Muse's ray
With orient hues, unborrowed of the sun;   120
Yet shall he mount, and keep his distant way
Beyond the limits of a vulgar fate—
Beneath the good how far—but far above the great.

[*1754,* *1757*]

THE BARD

A PINDARIC ODE

I—I

"Ruin seize thee, ruthless King!
Confusion on thy banners wait,
Though fanned by conquest's crimson wing
They mock the air with idle state.
Helm, nor hauberk's twisted mail,
Nor even thy virtues, tyrant, shall avail
To save thy secret soul from nightly fears,
From Cambria's curse, from Cambria's tears!"
Such were the sounds that o'er the crested pride
Of the first Edward scattered wild dismay,   10
As down the steep of Snowdon's shaggy side
He wound with toilsome march his long array.
Stout Glo'ster stood aghast in speechless trance;
"To arms!" cried Mortimer, and couched his quivering lance.

I—2

On a rock whose haughty brow
Frowns o'er old Conway's foaming flood,
Robed in the sable garb of woe,
With haggard eyes the poet stood
(Loose his beard and hoary hair
Streamed, like a meteor, to the troubled air),   20
And with a master's hand and prophet's fire
Struck the deep sorrows of his lyre.
"Hark, how each giant oak and desert cave
Sighs to the torrent's awful voice beneath!
O'er thee, O King! their hundred arms they wave,
Revenge on thee in hoarser murmurs breathe;
Vocal no more, since Cambria's fatal day,
To high-born Hoel's harp, or soft Llewellyn's lay.

I—3

"Cold is Cadwallo's tongue,
That hushed the stormy main;   30
Brave Urien sleeps upon his craggy bed;
Mountains, ye mourn in vain
Modred, whose magic song
Made huge Plinlimmon bow his cloud-topped head.

On dreary Arvon's shore they lie,
Smeared with gore, and ghastly pale;
Far, far aloof the affrighted ravens sail;
The famished eagle screams, and passes by.
Dear lost companions of my tuneful art,
Dear as the light that visits these sad eyes,   40
Dear as the ruddy drops that warm my heart,
Ye died amidst your dying country's cries—
No more I weep. They do not sleep.
On yonder cliffs, a grisly band,
I see them sit; they linger yet,
Avengers of their native land;
With me in dreadful harmony they join,
And weave with bloody hands the tissue of thy line.

II—I

"'Weave the warp, and weave the woof,
The winding-sheet of Edward's race.   50
Give ample room, and verge enough
The characters of hell to trace.
Mark the year, and mark the night,
When Severn shall re-echo with affright
The shrieks of death through Berkeley's roofs that ring,
Shrieks of an agonizing king!
She-wolf of France, with unrelenting fangs,
That tear'st the bowels of thy mangled mate,
From thee be born, who o'er thy country hangs,
The scourge of Heaven. What terrors round him wait!   60
Amazement in his van, with Flight combined,
And Sorrow's faded form, and Solitude behind.

II—2

"'Mighty victor, mighty lord,
Low on his funeral couch he lies!
No pitying heart, no eye, afford
A tear to grace his obsequies.
Is the Sable Warrior fled?
Thy son is gone. He rests among the dead.
The swarm that in thy noon-tide beam were born?
Gone to salute the rising morn.   70
Fair laughs the morn, and soft the zephyr blows,
While proudly riding o'er the azure realm
In gallant trim the gilded vessel goes;
Youth on the prow, and Pleasure at the helm;
Regardless of the sweeping whirlwind's sway,
That, hushed in grim repose, expects his evening prey.

II—3

"'Fill high the sparkling bowl,
The rich repast prepare;
Reft of a crown, he yet may share the feast;
Close by the regal chair   80

Fell Thirst and Famine scowl
A baleful smile upon their baffled guest.
Heard ye the din of battle bray,
Lance to lance, and horse to horse?
Long years of havoc urge their destined course,
And through the kindred squadrons mow their way.
Ye towers of Julius, London's lasting shame,
With many a foul and midnight murder fed,
Revere his consort's faith, his father's fame,
And spare the meek usurper's holy head.   90
Above, below, the rose of snow,
Twined with her blushing foe, we spread;
The bristled boar in infant-gore
Wallows beneath the thorny shade.
Now, brothers, bending o'er the accursed loom,
Stamp we our venegance deep, and ratify his doom.

III—1

"'Edward, lo! to sudden fate
(Weave we the woof: the thread is spun)
Half of thy heart we consecrate.
(The web is wove. The work is done.)'—   100
Stay, oh stay! nor thus forlorn
Leave me unblessed, unpitied, here to mourn!
In yon bright track that fires the western skies,
They melt, they vanish from my eyes.
But oh! what solemn scenes on Snowdon's height,
Descending slow, their glittering skirts unroll?
Visions of glory, spare my aching sight!
Ye unborn ages, crowd not on my soul!
No more our long-lost Arthur we bewail.
All hail, ye genuine kings, Britannia's issue, hail!   110

III—2

"Girt with many a baron bold
Sublime their starry fronts they rear;
And gorgeous dames, and statesmen old
In bearded majesty, appear.
In the midst a form divine!
Her eye proclaims her of the Briton line;
Her lion-port, her awe-commanding face,
Attempered sweet to virgin-grace.
What strings symphonious tremble in the air,
What strains of vocal transport round her play!   120
Hear from the grave, great Taliessin, hear;
They breathe a soul to animate thy clay.
Bright Rapture calls, and soaring, as she sings,
Waves in the eye of Heaven her many-colored wings.

III—3

"The verse adorn again
Fierce War, and faithful Love,

And Truth severe, by fairy Fiction dressed.
In buskined measures move
Pale Grief, and pleasing Pain,
With Horror, tyrant of the throbbing breast.   130
A voice, as of the cherub-choir,
Gales from blooming Eden bear;
And distant warblings lessen on my ear,
That lost in long futurity expire.
Fond impious man, think'st thou yon sanguine cloud,
Raised by thy breath, has quenched the orb of day?
To-morrow he repairs the golden flood,
And warms the nations with redoubled ray.
Enough for me: with joy I see
The different doom our fates assign.   140
Be thine despair, and sceptered care;
To triumph, and to die, are mine."
He spoke, and headlong from the mountain's height
Deep in the roaring tide he plunged to endless night.

[*1754–57*, 1757]

THE FATAL SISTERS

Now the storm begins to lower,
(Haste, the loom of hell prepare!)
Iron-sleet of arrowy shower
Hurtles in the darkened air.

Glittering lances are the loom,
Where the dusky warp we strain,
Weaving many a soldier's doom,
Orkney's woe and Randver's bane.

See the grisly texture grow,
('Tis of human entrails made!)   10
And the weights that play below,
Each a gasping warrior's head.

Shafts for shuttles, dipped in gore,
Shoot the trembling cords along.
Sword, that once a monarch bore,
Keep the tissue close and strong.

Mista black, terrific maid,
Sangrida, and Hilda, see,
Join the wayward work to aid;
'Tis the woof of victory.   20

Ere the ruddy sun be set,
Pikes must shiver, javeline sing,
Blade with clattering buckler meet,
Hauberk crash, and helmet ring.

(Weave the crimson web of war!)
Let us go, and let us fly

Where our friends the conflict share,
Where they triumph, where they die.

As the paths of fate we tread,
Wading through the ensanguined field;
Gondula and Geira, spread   31
O'er the youthful king your shield.

We the reins to slaughter give;
Ours to kill, and ours to spare;
Spite of danger he shall live.
(Weave the crimson web of war!)

They whom once the desert beach
Pent within its bleak domain,
Soon their ample sway shall stretch
O'er the plenty of the plain.   40

Low the dauntless earl is laid,
Gored with many a gaping wound;
Fate demands a nobler head;
Soon a king shall bite the ground.

Long his loss shall Eirin weep,
Ne'er again his likeness see;
Long her strains in sorrow steep,
Strains of immortality!

Horror covers all the heath;
Clouds of carnage blot the sun.   50
Sisters, weave the web of death;
Sisters, cease, the work is done.

Hail the task, and hail the hands!
Songs of joy and triumph sing!
Joy to the victorious bands,
Triumph to the younger king.

Mortal, thou that hear'st the tale,
Learn the tenor of our song.
Scotland, through each winding vale
Far and wide the notes prolong.   60

Sisters, hence with spurs of speed;
Each her thundering falchion wield;
Each bestride her sable steed.
Hurry, hurry to the field!
                    [*1761*, 1768]

THE DESCENT OF ODIN

AN ODE FROM THE NORSE TONGUE

Up rose the King of Men with speed,
And saddled straight his coal-black steed;
Down the yawning steep he rode,
That leads to Hela's drear abode.
Him the Dog of Darkness spied,
His shaggy throat he opened wide,
While from his jaws, with carnage filled,
Foam and human gore distilled;
Hoarse he bays with hideous din,
Eyes that glow and fangs that grin;   10
And long pursues, with fruitless yell,
The Father of the powerful spell.
Onward still his way he takes,
(The groaning earth beneath him shakes,)
Till full before his fearless eyes
The portals nine of hell arise.

Right against the eastern gate,
By the moss-grown pile he sate;
Where long of yore to sleep was laid
The dust of the prophetic maid.   20
Facing to the northern clime,
Thrice he traced the runic rhyme;
Thrice pronounced, in accents dread,
The thrilling verse that wakes the dead;
Till from out the hollow ground
Slowly breathed a sullen sound.

Prophetess. What call unknown, what charms
        presume
To break the quiet of the tomb?
Who thus afflicts my troubled sprite,
And drags me from the realms of night?   30

Long on these moldering bones have beat
The winter's snow, the summer's heat,
The drenching dews, and driving rain!
Let me, let me sleep again.
Who is he, with voice unblessed,
That calls me from the bed of rest?

Odin. A traveller, to thee unknown,
Is he that calls, a warrior's son.
Thou the deeds of light shalt know;
Tell me what is done below,   40
For whom yon glittering board is spread,
Dressed for whom yon golden bed.

Prophetess. Mantling in the goblet see
The pure beverage of the bee;[1]
O'er it hangs the shield of gold;
'Tis the drink of Balder bold:
Balder's head to death is given.
Pain can reach the sons of Heaven!
Unwilling I my lips unclose;
Leave me, leave me to repose.   50

Odin. Once again my call obey.
Prophetess, arise, and say,
What dangers Odin's child await;
Who the author of his fate.

Prophetess. In Hoder's hand the hero's doom;
His brother sends him to the tomb.
Now my weary lips I close;
Leave me, leave me to repose.

Odin. Prophetess, my spell obey,
Once again arise, and say,   60
Who the avenger of his guilt;
By whom shall Hoder's blood be spilt.

Prophetess. In the caverns of the west,
By Odin's fierce embrace compressed,
A wondrous boy shall Rinda bear
Who ne'er shall comb his raven hair,
Nor wash his visage in the stream,
Nor see the sun's departing beam;
Till he on Hoder's corse shall smile
Flaming on the funeral pile.   70
Now my weary lips I close;
Leave me, leave me to repose.

Odin. Yet awhile my call obey.
Prophetess, awake, and say,
What virgins these, in speechless woe,
That bend to earth their solemn brow,
That their flaxen tresses tear,

    [1] Mead.

And snowy veils, that float in air.
Tell me whence their sorrows rose;
Then I leave thee to repose.   80

Prophetess. Ha! no traveller art thou!
King of Men, I know thee now,
Mightiest of a mighty line—

Odin. No boding maid of skill divine
Art thou, nor prophetess of good;
But mother of the giant-brood!

Prophetess. Hie thee hence, and boast at home
That never shall enquirer come
To break my iron-sleep again,
Till Lok has burst his tenfold chain.   90
Never, till substantial Night
Has reassumed her ancient right;
Till wrapped in flames, in ruin hurled,
Sinks the fabric of the world.

                                    [*1761,* 1768]

LETTERS

I. TO RICHARD WEST

You must know that I do not take degrees, and, after this term, shall have nothing more of college impertinences to undergo, which I trust will be some pleasure to you, as it is a great one to me. I have endured lectures daily and hourly since I came last, supported by the hopes of being shortly at full liberty to give myself up to my friends and classical companions, who, poor souls! though I see them fallen into great contempt with most people here, yet I cannot help sticking to them, and out of a spirit of obstinacy (I think) love them the better for it; and indeed, what can I do else? Must I plunge into metaphysics? Alas, I cannot see in the dark; nature has not furnished me with the optics of a cat. Must I pore upon mathematics? Alas, I cannot see in too much light; I am no eagle. It is very possible that two and two make four, but I would not give four farthings to demonstrate this ever so clearly; and if these be the profits of life, give me the amusements of it. The people I behold all around me, it seems, know all this and more, and yet I do not know one of them who inspires me with any ambition of being like him. Surely it was of this place, now Cambridge, but formerly known by the name of Babylon, that the prophet spoke when he said, "the wild beasts of the desert shall dwell there, and their houses shall be full of doleful creatures, and owls shall build there, and satyrs shall dance there; their forts and towers shall be a den for ever, a joy of wild asses; there shall the great owl make her nest, and lay and hatch and gather under her shadow; it shall be a court of dragons; the screech owl also shall rest there, and find for herself a place of rest." You see here is a pretty collection of desolate animals, which is verified in this town to a tittle, and perhaps it may also allude to your habitation, for you know all types may be taken by abundance of handles; however, I defy your owls to match mine.

If the default of your spirits and nerves be nothing but the effect of the hyp, I have no more to say. We all must submit to that wayward Queen; I too in no small degree own her sway,

I feel her influence while I speak her power.

But if it be a real distemper, pray take more care of your health, if not for your own at least for our sakes, and do not be so soon weary of this little world. I do not know what refined friendships you may have contracted in the other, but pray do not be in a hurry to see your acquaintance above; among your terrestrial familiars, however, though I say it that should not say it, there positively is not one that has a greater esteem for you than—
                    Yours most sincerely, etc.
PETERHOUSE, December, 1736.

II. TO HORACE WALPOLE

I was hindered in my last, and so could not give you all the trouble I would have done. The description of a road, which your coach wheels have so often honoured, it would be needless to give you; suffice it that I arrived safe at my uncle's, a great hunter in imagination; his dogs take up every chair in the house, so I am forced to stand at this present writing; and though the gout forbids him galloping after them in the field, yet he continues still to regale his ears and nose with their comfortable noise and stink. He holds me mighty cheap, I perceive, for walking when I should ride, and reading when I should hunt. My comfort amidst all this is, that I have at the distance of half a mile, through a green lane, a forest (the vulgar call it a common) all my own, at least as good as so, for I spy no human thing in it but myself. It is a little chaos of mountains and precipices; mountains, it is true, that do not ascend much above the clouds, nor are the declivities quite so amazing as Dover Cliff; but just such hills as people who love their necks as well as I do may venture to climb, and crags that give the eye as much pleasure as if they were more dangerous. Both vale and hill are covered over with most venerable beeches, and other very reverend vegetables, that, like most other ancient people, are always dreaming out their old stories to the winds,

And as they bow their hoary tops relate,
In murm'ring sounds, the dark decrees of
    fate;
While visions, as poetic eyes avow,
Cling to each leaf and swarm on every bough.

At the foot of one of these squats ME I (*il penseroso*) and there grow to the trunk for a whole morning. The timorous hare and sportive squirrel gambol around me like Adam in paradise before he had an Eve; but I think he did not use to read Virgil, as I commonly do there. In this situation I often converse with my Horace, aloud too, that is talk to you, but I do not remember that I ever heard you answer me. I beg pardon for taking all the conversation to myself, but it is entirely your own fault. We have old Mr. Southern at a gentleman's house a little way off, who often comes to see us; he is now seventy-seven years old, and has almost wholly lost his memory; but is as agreeable as an old man can be, at least I persuade myself so when I look at him, and think of Isabella and Oroonoko. I shall be in town in about three weeks. Adieu.

[August, 1736.]

III. TO HIS MOTHER

AMIENS, April 1, N.S. 1739.

As we made but a very short journey to-day, and came to our inn early, I sit down to give you some account of our expedition. On the 29th (according to the style here) we left Dover at twelve at noon, and with a pretty brisk gale, which pleased everybody mighty well, except myself, who was extremely sick the whole time, we reached Calais by five. The weather changed, and it began to snow hard the minute we got into the harbour, where we took the boat and soon landed. Calais is an exceeding old, but very pretty town, and we hardly saw anything there that was not so new and so different from England, that it surprised us agreeably. We went the next morning to the great church, and were at high Mass (it being Easter Monday). We saw also the convents of the Capuchins, and the nuns of St. Dominic; with these last we held much conversation, especially with an English nun, a Mrs. Davis, of whose work I sent you, by the return of the pacquet, a letter-case to remember her by. In the afternoon we took a post-chaise (it still snowing very hard) for Boulogne, which was only eighteen miles further. This chaise is a strange sort of conveyance, of much greater use than beauty, resembling an ill-shaped chariot, only with the door opening before instead of the side; three horses draw it, one between the shafts, and the other two on each side, on one of which the postillion rides, and drives too. This vehicle will, upon occasion, go fourscore miles a-day, but Mr. Walpole, being in no hurry, chooses to make easy journeys of it, and they are easy ones indeed; for the motion is much like that of a sedan, we go about six miles an hour, and commonly change horses at the end of it. It is true they are no very graceful steeds, but they go well, and through roads which they say are bad for France, but to me they seem gravel walks and bowling greens; in short it would be the finest travelling in the world, were it not for the inns, which are mostly terrible places indeed. But to describe our progress somewhat more regularly, we came into Boulogne when it was almost dark, and went out pretty early on Tuesday morning; so that all I can say about it is, that it is a large, old, fortified town, with more English in it than French. On Tuesday we were to go to Abbéville, seventeen leagues, or fifty-one short English miles; but by the way we dined at Montreuil, much to our hearts' content, on stinking mutton cutlets, addled eggs, and ditch water. Madame the hostess made her appearance in long lappets of bone lace and a sack of linsey-woolsey. We supped and lodged pretty well at Abbéville, and had time to see a little of it before we came out this morning. There are seventeen convents in it, out of which we saw the chapels of Minims and the Carmelite nuns. We are now come further thirty miles to Amiens, the chief city of the province of Picardy. We have seen the cathedral which is just what that of Canterbury must have been before the reformation. It is about the same size, a huge Gothic building, beset on the outside with thousands of small statues, and within adorned with beautiful painted windows, and a vast number of chapels dressed out in all their finery of altarpieces, embroidery, gilding, and marble. Over the high altar are preserved, in a very large wrought shrine of massy gold, the relics of St. Firmin, their patron saint. We went also to the chapels of the Jesuits and Ursuline nuns, the latter of which is very richly adorned. To-morrow we shall lie at Clermont, and next day reach Paris. The country we have passed through hitherto has been flat, open, but agreeably diversified with villages, fields well-cultivated, and little rivers. On every hillock is a wind-mill, a crucifix, or a Virgin Mary dressed in flowers, and a sarcenet robe; one sees not many people or carriages on the road; now and then indeed you meet a strolling friar, a countryman with his great muff, or a woman riding astride on a little ass, with short petticoats, and a great head-dress of blue wool. . . .

IV. TO HIS MOTHER

LYONS, Oct. 13, N.S. 1739.

It is now almost five weeks since I left Dijon, one of the gayest and most agreeable little cities of France, for Lyons, its reverse in all these particulars. It is the second in the kingdom in bigness and rank, the streets excessively narrow and nasty; the houses immensely high and large (that, for instance, where we are lodged has twenty-five rooms on a floor, and that for five stories) ; it swarms with inhabitants like Paris itself, but chiefly a mercantile people, too much given up to commerce, to think of their own, much less of a stranger's diversions. We have no acquaintance in the town, but such English as happen to be passing through here. on their way to Italy and the south, which at present happen to be near thirty in number. It is a fortnight since we set out from hence upon a little excursion to Geneva. We took the longest road, which lies through Savoy, on purpose to see a famous monastery, called the grand Chartreuse, and had no reason to think our time lost. After having travelled seven days very slow (for we did not change horses, it being impossible for a chaise to go post in these roads) we arrived at a little village, among the mountains of Savoy, called Echelles; from thence we proceeded on horses, who are used to the way, to the mountain of the Chartreuse. It is six miles to the top; the road runs winding up it, commonly not six feet broad; on one hand is the rock, with woods of pine-trees hanging over head; on the other, a monstrous precipice, almost perpendicular, at the bottom of which rolls a torrent, that sometimes tumbling among the fragments of stone that have fallen from on high, and sometimes precipitating itself down vast descents with a noise like thunder, which is still made greater by the echo from the mountains on each side, concurs to form one of the most solemn, the most romantic, and the most astonishing scenes I ever beheld. Add to this the strange views made by the crags and cliffs on the other hand; the cascades that in many places throw themselves from the very summit down into the vale, and the river below; and many other particulars impossible to describe; you will conclude we had no occasion to repent our pains. This place St. Bruno chose to retire to, and upon its very top founded the aforesaid convent, which is the superior of the whole order. When we came there, the two fathers, who are commissioned to entertain strangers (for the rest must neither speak one to another, nor to any one else), received us very kindly; and set before us a repast of dried fish, eggs, butter, and fruits, all excellent in their kind, and extremely neat. They pressed us to spend the night there, and to stay some days with them; but this we could not do, so they led us about their house, which is, you must think, like a little city; for there are 100 fathers, besides 300 servants, that make their clothes, grind their corn, press their wine, and do everything among themselves. The whole is quiet, orderly, and simple; nothing of finery, but the wonderful decency, and the strange situation, more than supply the place of it. In the evening we descended by the same

way, passing through many clouds that were then forming themselves on the mountain's side. Next day we continued our journey by Chamberry, which, though the chief city of the duchy, and residence of the King of Sardinia, when he comes into this part of his dominions, makes but a very mean and insignificant appearance; we lay at Aix, once famous for its hot baths, and the next night at Annecy; the day after, by noon, we got to Geneva. I have not time to say anything about it, nor of our solitary journey back again. . . .

V. TO WEST

TURIN, Nov. 16, N.S., 1739.

After eight days' journey through Greenland, we arrived at Turin. You approach it by a handsome avenue of nine miles long, and quite strait. The entrance is guarded by certain vigilant dragons, called Douâniers, who mumbled us for some time. The city is not large, as being a place of strength, and consequently confined within its fortifications; it has many beauties and some faults; among the first are streets all laid out by the line, regular uniform buildings, fine walks that surround the whole, and in general a good lively clean appearance. But the houses are of brick plastered, which is apt to want repairing; the windows of oiled paper, which is apt to be torn; and everything very slight, which is apt to tumble down. There is an excellent opera, but it is only in the carnival; balls every night, but only in the carnival; masquerades too, but only in the carnival. This carnival lasts only from Christmas to Lent; one half of the remaining part of the year is passed in remembering the last, the other in expecting the future carnival. We cannot well subsist upon such slender diet, no more than upon an execrable Italian comedy, and a puppet-show, called *Rappresentazione d'un' anima dannata,* which, I think, are all the present diversions of the place; except the Marquise de Cavaillac's Conversazione, where one goes to see people play at ombre and taroc, a game with seventy-two cards all painted with suns, and moons, and devils and monks. Mr. Walpole has been at court; the family are at present at a country palace, called La Venerie. The palace here in town is the very quintessence of gilding and looking-glass; inlaid floors, carved panels, and painting, wherever they could stick a brush. I own I have not, as yet, anywhere met with those grand and simple works of art that are to amaze one, and whose sight one is to be the better for; but those of Nature have astonished me beyond expression. In our little journey up to the Grande Chartreuse, I do not remember to have gone ten paces without an exclamation, that there was no restraining: not a precipice, not a torrent, not a cliff, but is pregnant with religion and poetry. There are certain scenes that would awe an atheist into belief, without the help of other argument. One need not have a very fantastic imagination to see spirits there at noon-day. You have Death perpetually before your eyes, only so far removed as to compose the mind without frighting it. I am well persuaded St. Bruno was a man of no common genius to choose such a situation for his retirement, and perhaps should have been a disciple of his, had I been born in his time. You may believe Abelard and Heloïse were not forgot upon this occasion. If I do not mistake, I saw you too every now and then at a distance along the trees; *il me semble, que j'ai vu ce chien de visage là quelque part.* You seemed to call to me from the other side of the precipice, but the noise of the river below was so great, that I really could not distinguish what you said; it seemed to have a cadence like verse. In your next you will be so good to let me know what it was. The week we have since passed among the Alps has not equalled the single day upon that mountain, because the winter was rather too far advanced, and the

weather a little foggy. However, it did not want its beauties; the savage rudeness of the view is inconceivable without seeing it. I reckoned in one day thirteen cascades, the least of which was, I dare say, one hundred feet in height. . . . We set out for Genoa in two days' time.

VI. TO WEST

TIVOLI, May 20, 1740.
This day being in the palace of his Highness the Duke of Modena, he laid his most serene commands upon me to write to Mr. West, and said he thought it for his glory, that I should draw up an inventory of all his most serene possessions for the said West's perusal.—*Imprimis,* a house, being in circumference a quarter of a mile, two feet and an inch; the said house containing the following particulars, to wit, a great room. Item, another great room; item, a bigger room; item, another room; item, a vast room; item, a sixth of the same; a seventh ditto; an eighth as before; a ninth as abovesaid; a tenth (see No. 1); item, ten more such, besides twenty besides, which, not to be too particular, we shall pass over. The said rooms contain nine chairs, two tables, five stools, and a cricket. From whence we shall proceed to the garden, containing two millions of superfine laurel hedges, a clump of cypress trees, and half the river Teverone, that pisses into two thousand several chamberpots. Finis. —Dame Nature desired me to put in a list of her little goods and chattels, and, as they were small, to be very minute about them. She has built here three or four little mountains, and laid them out in an irregular semicircle; from certain others behind, at a greater distance, she has drawn a canal, into which she has put a little river of hers, called Anio; she has cut a huge cleft between the two innermost of her four hills, and there she has left it to its own disposal; which she has no sooner done, but, like a heedless chit, it tumbles headlong

down a declivity fifty feet perpendicular, breaks itself all to shatters, and is converted into a shower of rain, where the sun forms many a bow, red, green, blue, and yellow. To get out of our metaphors without any further trouble, it is the most noble sight in the world. The weight of that quantity of waters, and the force they fall with, have worn the rocks they throw themselves among into a thousand irregular crags, and to a vast depth. In this channel it goes boiling along with a mighty noise till it comes to another steep, where you see it a second time come roaring down (but first you must walk two miles farther) a greater height than before, but not with that quantity of waters; for by this time it has divided itself, being crossed and opposed by the rocks, into four several streams, each of which in emulation of the great one, will tumble down too; and it does tumble down, but not from an equally elevated place; so that you have at one view all these cascades intermixed with groves of olive and little woods, the mountains rising behind them, and on the top of one (that which forms the extremity of one of the half-circle's horns) is seated the town itself. At the very extremity of that extremity, on the brink of the precipice, stands the Sybils' temple, the remains of a little rotunda, surrounded with its portico, above half of whose beautiful Corinthian pillars are still standing and entire; all this on one hand. On the other, the open Campagna of Rome, here and there a little castle on a hillock, and the city itself on the very brink of the horizon, indistinctly seen (being eighteen miles off) except the dome of St. Peter's; which, if you look out of your window, wherever you are, I suppose, you can see. I did not tell you that a little below the first fall, on the side of the rock, and hanging over that torrent, are little ruins which they show you for Horace's house, a curious situation to observe the

"Præceps Anio, & Tiburni lucus, & uda
Mobilibus pomaria rivis."

Mæcenas did not care for such a noise, it seems, and built him a house (which they also carry one to see) so situated that it sees nothing at all of the matter, and for anything he knew there might be no such river in the world. Horace had another house on the other side of the Teverone, opposite the Mæcenas's; and they told us there was a bridge of communication, by which *"andava il detto Signor per trastullarsi coll istesso Orazio."* In coming hither we crossed the Aquæ Albulæ, a vile little brook that stinks like a fury, and they say it has stunk so these thousand years. I forgot the Piscina of Quintilius Varus, where he used to keep certain little fishes. This is very entire, and there is a piece of the aqueduct that supplied it too; in the garden below is old Rome, built in little, just as it was, they say. There are seven temples in it, and no houses at all: they say there were none.

May 21.

We have had the pleasure of going twelve miles out of our way to Palestrina. It has rained all day as if heaven and us were coming together. See my honesty, I do not mention a syllable of the temple of Fortune, because I really did not see it; which, I think, is pretty well for an old traveller. So we returned along the Via Prænestina, saw the Lacus Gabinus and Regillus, where, you know, Castor and Pollux appeared upon a certain occasion. And many a good old tomb we left on each hand, and many an aqueduct,

Dumb are whose fountains, and their channels dry.

There are, indeed, two whole modern ones, works of popes, that run about thirty miles a-piece in length; one of them conveys still the famous Aqua Virgo to Rome, and adds vast beauty to the prospect. So we came to Rome again, where waited for us a *splendidissimo regalo* of letters; in one of which came You, with your huge characters and wide intervals, staring. I would have you to know, I expect you should take a handsome crow-quill when you write to me, and not leave room for a pin's point in four sides of a sheet royal. Do you but find matter, I will find spectacles.

I have more time than I thought, and I will employ it in telling you about a ball that we were at the other evening. Figure to yourself a Roman villa; all its little apartments thrown open, and lighted up to the best advantage. At the upper end of the gallery, a fine concert, in which La Diamantina, a famous virtuosa, played on the violin divinely and sung angelically; Giovannino and Pasqualini (great names in musical story) also performed miraculously. On each side were ranged all the secular *grand monde* of Rome, the ambassadors, princesses, and all that. Among the rest *Il Serenissimo Pretendente* (as the Mantova gazette calls him) displayed his rueful length of person, with his two young ones, and all his ministry around him. *"Poi nacque un grazioso ballo,"* where the world danced, and I sat in a corner regaling myself with iced fruits, and other pleasant rinfrescatives.

VII. TO HIS MOTHER

NAPLES, June 17, 1740.

Our journey hither was through the most beautiful part of the finest country in the world; and every spot of it, on some account or other, famous for these three thousand years past. The season has hitherto been just as warm as one would wish it; no unwholesome airs, or violent heats, yet heard of. The people call it a backward year, and are in pain about their corn, wine, and oil; but we, who are neither corn, wine, nor oil, find it very agreeable. Our road was through Velletri, Cisterna, Terracina, Capua, and Aversa, and so to Naples. The minute one leaves his holiness's dominions, the face of things begins to change

from wide uncultivated plains to olive groves and well-tilled fields of corn, intermixed with ranks of elms, every one of which has its vine twining about it, and hanging in festoons between the rows from one tree to another. The great old fig-trees, the oranges in full bloom, and myrtles in every hedge, make one of the delightfullest scenes you can conceive; besides that, the roads are wide, well-kept, and full of passengers, a sight I have not beheld this long time. My wonder still increased upon entering the city, which I think, for number of people, outdoes both Paris and London. The streets are one continued market, and thronged with populace so much that a coach can hardly pass. The common sort are a jolly lively kind of animals, more industrious than Italians usually are; they work till evening; then take their lute or guitar (for they all play) and walk about the city, or upon the sea-shore with it, to enjoy the fresco. One sees their little brown children jumping about stark-naked, and the bigger ones dancing with castanets, while others play on the cymbal to them. Your maps will show you the situation of Naples; it is on the most lovely bay in the world, and one of the calmest seas. It has many other beauties besides those of nature. We have spent two days in visiting the remarkable places in the country round it, such as the bay of Baiæ, and its remains of antiquity; the lake Avernus, and the Solfatara, Charon's grotto, etc. We have been in the Sybil's cave and many other strange holes underground (I only name them, because you may consult Sandys' travels); but the strangest hole I ever was in, has been to-day at a place called Portici, where his Sicilian majesty has a country-seat. About a year ago, as they were digging, they discovered some parts of ancient buildings above thirty feet deep in the ground. Curiosity led them on, and they have been digging ever since; the passage they have made, with all its turnings and windings, is now more than a mile long. As you walk, you see parts of an amphitheatre, many houses adorned with marble columns, and incrusted with the same; the front of a temple, several arched vaults of rooms painted in fresco. Some pieces of painting have been taken out from hence, finer than anything of the kind before discovered, and with these the king has [10] adorned his palace; also a number of statues, medals, and gems; and more are dug out every day. This is known to be a Roman town, that in the emperor Titus's time was overwhelmed by a furious eruption of Mount Vesuvius, which is hard by. The wood and beams remain so perfect that you may see the grain; but burnt to a coal, and dropping into [20] dust upon the least touch. We were to-day at the foot of that mountain, which at present smokes only a little, where we saw the materials that fed the stream of fire, which about four years since ran down its side. We have but a few days longer to stay here; too little in conscience for such a place. . . .

VIII. TO WEST

London, April, Thursday [1742].

You are the first who ever made a Muse of a cough; to me it seems a much more easy task to versify in one's sleep (that indeed you were of old famous for) than for want of it. Not the wakeful nightingale (when she had a cough) ever sung so sweetly. I [40] give you thanks for your warble, and wish you could sing yourself to rest. These wicked remains of your illness will sure give way to warm weather and gentle exercise; which I hope you will not omit as the season advances. Whatever low spirits and indolence, the effect of them, may advise to the contrary, I pray you add five steps to your walk daily for my sake; by the [50] help of which, in a month's time, I propose to set you on horseback.

I talked of the *Dunciad* as concluding you had seen it; if you have

not, do you choose I should get and send it you? I have myself, upon your recommendation, been reading *Joseph Andrews*. The incidents are ill laid and without invention; but the characters have a great deal of nature, which always pleases even in her lowest shapes. Parson Adams is perfectly well; so is Mrs. Slipslop, and the story [10] of Wilson; and throughout he shows himself well read in stage-coaches, country squires, inns, and inns of court. His reflections upon high people and low people, and misses and masters, are very good. However the exaltedness of some minds (or rather, as I shrewdly suspect, their insipidity and want of feeling or observation) may make them insensible to these [20] light things (I mean such as characterize and paint nature), yet surely they are as weighty and much more useful than your grave discourses upon the mind, the passions, and what not. Now as the paradisaical pleasures of the Mahometans consist in playing upon the flute and lying with houris, be mine to read eternal new romances of Marivaux and Crébillon.

You are very good in giving yourself the trouble to read and find fault with my long harangues. Your freedom (as you call it) has so little need of apologies, that I would scarce excuse your treating me any otherwise; which, whatever compliment it might be to my vanity, would be making a very ill one to my understanding. As to matter of style, I have this to say: The language of the age is never the language of poetry, except among the French, whose verse, where the thought or image does not support it, differs in nothing from prose. Our poetry, on the contrary, has a language peculiar to itself; to which almost every one that has written has added something by enriching it with foreign idioms and derivatives; nay sometimes words of their own composition [50] or invention. Shakespeare and Milton have been great creators this way; and no one more licentious than Pope or Dryden, who perpetually borrow expressions from the former. Let me give you some instances from Dryden, whom everybody reckons a great master of our poetical tongue.—Full of *museful mopeings*—unlike the *trim* of love—a pleasant *beverage*—a *roundelay* of love—stood silent in his *mood*—with knots and *knares* deformed—his *ireful mood*—in proud *array*—his *boon* was granted—and *disarray* and shameful rout—*wayward* but wise—*furbished* for the field—the *foiled dodderd* oaks— —*disherited*—*smouldering* flames—*retchless* of laws—*crones* old and ugly—the *beldam* at his side—the *grandamhag*—*villanize* his father's fame.——But they are infinite; and our language not being a settled thing (like the French) has an undoubted right to words of an hundred years old, provided antiquity have not rendered them unintelligible. In truth, Shakespeare's language is one of his principal beauties; and he has no less advantage over your Addisons and Rowes in this, than in those other great excellences you mention. Every word in him is a picture. Pray put me the following lines into the tongue of our modern dramatics:

But I, that am not shaped for sportive tricks,
Nor made to court an amorous looking-glass:
I, that am rudely stampt, and want love's
         majesty
To strut before a wanton ambling nymph:
I, that am curtail'd of this fair proportion,
Cheated of feature by dissembling nature,
Deform'd, unfinish'd, sent before my time
Into this breathing world, scarce half made
         up.

And what follows. To me they appear untranslatable; and if this be the case, our language is greatly degenerated. However, the affectation of imitating Shakespeare may doubtless be carried too far; and is no sort of excuse for sentiments ill-suited or speeches ill-timed, which I believe is a little the case with me. I guess the most faulty expressions may be these—*silken* son of *dalliance*—*drowsier* pretensions—wrinkled *beldams*—*arched* the hearer's brow and *riveted* his eyes in *fearful extasie*. These are easily altered or omitted: and indeed if the thoughts

be wrong or superfluous, there is nothing easier than to leave out the whole. The first ten or twelve lines are, I believe, the best; and as for the rest, I was betrayed into a good deal of it by Tacitus; only what he has said in five words, I imagine I have said in fifty lines. Such is the misfortune of imitating the inimitable. Now, if you are of my opinion, *una litura* may do the business better than a dozen; and you need not fear unravelling my web. I am a sort of spider; and have little else to do but spin it over again, or creep to some other place and spin there. Alas! for one who has nothing to do but amuse himself, I believe my amusements are as little amusing as most folks'. But no matter; it makes the hours pass; and is better than ἐν ἀμαθίᾳ καὶ ἀμουσίᾳ καταβιῶναι. Adieu.

IX. TO HORACE WALPOLE

CAMBRIDGE, February 10, 1751.

As you have brought me into a little sort of distress, you must assist me, I believe. to get out of it as well as I can. Yesterday I had the misfortune of receiving a letter from certain gentlemen (as their bookseller expresses it), who have taken the *Magazine of Magazines* into their hands. They tell me that an *ingenious* poem, called "Reflections in a Country Churchyard," has been communicated to them, which they are printing forthwith; that they are informed that the *excellent* author of it is I by name, and that they beg not only his *indulgence*, but the *honour* of his correspondence, etc. As I am not at all disposed to be either so indulgent, or so correspondent, as they desire, I have but one bad way left to escape the honour they would inflict upon me; and therefore am obliged to desire you would make Dodsley print it immediately (which may be done in less than a week's time) from your copy, but without my name, in what form is most convenient for him, but on his best paper and character; he must correct the press himself, and print it without any interval between the stanzas, because the sense is in some places continued beyond them; and the title must be,—"*Elegy, wrote in a Country Churchyard.*" If he would add a line or two to say it came into his hands by accident, I should like it better. If you behold the *Mag. of Mags* in the light that I do, you will not refuse to give yourself this trouble on my account, which you have taken of your own accord before now. If Dodsley do not do this immediately, he may as well let it alone.

X. TO RICHARD HURD

STOKE, August 25, 1757.

I do not know why you should thank me for what you had a right and title to; but attribute it to the excess of your politeness, and the more so, because almost no one else has made me the same compliment. As your acquaintance in the University (you say) do me the honour to admire, it would be ungenerous in me not to give them notice, that they are doing a very unfashionable thing; for all people of condition are agreed not to admire, nor even to understand. One very great man, writing to an acquaintance of his and mine, says that he had read them seven or eight times; and that now, when he next sees him, he shall not have above thirty questions to ask. Another (a peer) believes that the last stanza of the second ode relates to King Charles the First and Oliver Cromwell. Even my friends tell me they do not succeed, and write me moving topics of consolation on that head. In short, I have heard of nobody but an actor and a doctor of divinity that profess their esteem for them. Oh yes, a lady of quality (a friend of Mason's), who is a great reader. She knew there was a compliment to Dryden, but never suspected there was anything said about Shakespeare or Milton, till it was explained to her; and wishes that there had been titles prefixed to tell what they were about.

From this mention of Mason's name you may think, perhaps, we are great correspondents. No such thing; I have not heard from him these two months. I will be sure to scold in my own name, as well as in yours. I rejoice to hear you are so ripe for the press, and so voluminous; not for my own sake only, whom you flatter with the hopes of seeing your labours both public and private, but for yours too; for to be employed is to be happy. This principle of mine (and I am convinced of its truth) has, as usual, no influence on my practice. I am alone, and *ennuyé* to the last degree, yet do nothing. Indeed I have one excuse; my health (which you have so kindly enquired after) is not extraordinary, ever since I came hither. It is no great malady, but several little ones, that seem brewing no good to me.

It will be a particular pleasure to me to hear whether Content dwells in Leicestershire, and how she entertains herself there. Only do not be too happy, nor forget entirely the quiet ugliness of Cambridge. I am, dear sir,
Your friend and obliged humble servant,

T. GRAY.

XI. TO MR. STONEHEWER

[Stoke], August 18, 1758.

I am as sorry as you seem to be, that our acquaintance harped so much on the subject of materialism when I saw him with you in town, because it was plain to which side of the long-debated question he inclined. That we are indeed mechanical and dependent beings, I need no other proof than my own feelings; and from the same feelings I learn, with equal conviction, that we are not *merely* such: that there is a power within that struggles against the force and bias of that mechanism, commands its motion, and, by frequent practice, reduces it to that ready obedience which we call *habit*; and all this in conformity to a preconceived opinion (no matter whether right or wrong) to that least material of all agents, a thought. I have known many in his case who, while they thought they were conquering an old prejudice, did not perceive they were under the influence of one far more dangerous; one that furnishes us with a ready apology for all our worst actions, and opens to us a full license for doing whatever we please; and yet these very people were not at all the more indulgent to other men (as they naturally should have been); their indignation to such as offended them, their desire of revenge on anybody that hurt them was nothing mitigated: in short, the truth is, they wished to be persuaded of that opinion for the sake of its convenience, but were not so in their heart; and they would have been glad (as they ought in common prudence) that nobody else should think the same, for fear of the mischief that might ensue to themselves. His French author I never saw, but have read fifty in the same strain, and shall read no more. I can be wretched enough without them. They put me in mind of the Greek sophist that got immortal honour by discoursing so feelingly on the miseries of our condition, that fifty of his audience went home and hanged themselves; yet he lived himself (I suppose) many years after in very good plight.

You say you cannot conceive how Lord Shaftesbury came to be a philosopher in vogue; I will tell you. First, he was a lord; 2dly, he was as vain as any of his readers; 3dly, men are very prone to believe what they do not understand; 4thly, they will believe anything at all, provided they are under no obligation to believe it; 5thly, they love to take a new road, even when that road leads nowhere; 6thly, he was reckoned a fine writer, and seemed always to mean more than he said. Would you have any more reasons? An interval of above forty years has pretty well destroyed the charm. A dead lord ranks but with commoners: vanity is no longer interested in the

matter, for the new road has become an old one. The mode of free-thinking is like that of ruffs and farthingales, and has given place to the mode of not thinking at all; once it was reckoned graceful half to discover and half conceal the mind, but now we have been long accustomed to see it quite naked; primness and affectation of style, like the good breeding of Queen Anne's court, has turned to hoydening and rude familiarity.

XII. TO DR. WHARTON

DEAR DOCTOR,

I cannot say anything to you about Mason, whose motions I am entirely a stranger to, and have not once heard from him since he left London, till (the 3d of this month) a letter came, in which he tells me that Gaskrath is at Aston with him, and that the latter end of the month, or the beginning of the next, he shall be in town, as he goes into waiting the last fortnight in October. Lord Holderness, has sent him no less than four expresses (literally so) with public news, good and bad, which has made him of infinite importance in the eyes of that neighbourhood. I cannot pretend, therefore, to guess whether he will be able to come to you. I am sorry to tell you that I try in vain to execute your commission about tapestry. What is so bad as wry-mouthed histories? and yet for this they ask me at least double the price you talk of. I have seen nothing neither that would please me at any price. Yet I allow tapestry (if at all tolerable) to be a very proper furniture for your sort of house; but doubt if any bargain of that kind is to be met with, except at some old mansion-sale in the country, where people will disdain tapestry, because they hear that paper is all the fashion. Stonehewer has been in Northamptonshire till now; as you told me the subject of your letter, I did not send it thither to him, besides that, he was every day expected in town. At last he is come, and has it, but I have not yet seen him; he is gone to-day (I believe) to Portsmouth to receive a Morocco ambassador, but returns very shortly. There is one advantage in getting into your abbey at Christmas time, that it will be at its worst, and if you can bear it then, you need not fear for the rest of the year. Mr. Walpole has lately made a new bed-chamber, which as it is in the best taste of anything he has yet done, and in your own Gothic way, I must describe a little. You enter by a peaked door at one corner of the room (out of a narrow winding passage, you may be sure) into an alcove, in which the bed is to stand, formed by a screen of pierced work opening by one large arch in the middle to the rest of the chamber, which is lighted at the other end by a bow-window of three bays, whose tops are of rich painted glass in mosaic. The ceiling is covered and fretted in star and quatre-foil compartments, with roses at the intersections, all is *papier-mâché*. The chimney on your left is the high altar in the cathedral of Rouen (from whence the screen also is taken), consisting of a low surbased arch between two octagon towers, whose pinnacles almost reach the ceiling, all of niche-work; the chairs and dressing-table are real carved ebony, picked up at auctions. The hangings uniform, purple paper, hung all over with the court of Henry the VIII, copied after the Holbeins in the queen's closet at Kensington, in black and gold frames. The bed is to be either from Burleigh (for Lord Exeter is new-furnishing it, and means to sell some of his original household stuff) of the rich old tarnished embroidery; or if that is not to be had, and it must be new, it is to be a cut velvet with a dark purple pattern on a stone-colour satin ground, and deep mixed fringes and tassels. There's for you, but I want you to see it. In the meantime I live in the Musæum, and write volumes of antiquity. I have got (out of the original ledger-book of the signet) King Richard the Third's oath to Elizabeth, late *calling herself Queen*

of England, to prevail upon her to come out of sanctuary with her five daughters. His grant to Lady Hastings and her son, dated six weeks after he had cut off her husband's head. A letter to his mother, another to his chancellor, to persuade his solicitor-general not to marry Jane Shore then in Ludgate by his command. Sir Thomas Wyat's defence at his trial, when accused by Bishop Bonner of high treason; Lady Purbeck and her son's remarkable case, and several more odd things unknown to our historians. When I come home I have a great heap of the Conway Papers (which is a secret) to read and make out. In short, I am up to the ears.

. . . .

I believe I shall go on Monday to Stoke for a time, where Lady Cobham has been dying. My best respects to Mrs. Wharton. Believe me ever

Faithfully yours,

T. G.

Southampton Row, Sept. 18, 1759.

XIII. TO DR. WHARTON

[June, 1760.]

Dear Doctor,

I heard yesterday from your old friend Mr. Field, that Mrs. Wharton had brought you a son, and as I sincerely hope this may be some addition to your happiness, I heartily congratulate you both on the occasion. Another thing I rejoice in, is to know that you not only grow reconciled to your scene, but discover beauties round you that once were deformities. I am persuaded the whole matter is, to have always something going forward. Happy they that can create a rose-tree, or erect a honeysuckle; that can watch the brood of a hen, or see a fleet of their own ducklings launch into the water! It is with a sentiment of envy that I speak it, who never shall have even a thatched roof of my own, nor gather a strawberry, but in Covent Garden. I will not believe in the *vocality* of Old Park till next sum-

mer, when perhaps I may trust my
own ears.

. . .

We are in great alarms about Quebec; the force in the town was not
3000 men, sufficient to defend the
place (naturally strong) against any
attack of the French forces, unfurnished as they must be for a formal   10
siege; but by no means to meet them
in the field. This however is what
Murray has chosen to do, whether
from rashness, or deceived by false intelligence, I cannot tell. The returns
of our loss are undoubtedly false, for
we have above 100 officers killed or
taken. All depends upon the arrival
of our garrison from Louisbourg,
which was daily expected. But even   20
that (unless they bring provisions
with them) may increase the distress;
for at the time when we were told of
the plenty and cheapness of all things
at Quebec, I am assured a piece of
fresh meat could not be had for twenty
guineas.

If you have seen Stonhewer, he has
probably told you of my old Scotch
(or rather Irish) poetry. I am gone   30
mad about them. They are said to be
translations (literal and in prose)
from the *Erse* tongue, done by one
Macpherson, a young clergyman in
the Highlands. He means to publish
a collection he has of these specimens
of antiquity, if it be antiquity; but
what plagues me is, I cannot come at
any certainty on that head. I was so
struck, so *extasié*, with their infinite   40
beauty, that I writ into Scotland to
make a thousand enquiries. The letters I have in return are ill wrote, ill
reasoned, unsatisfactory, calculated
(one would imagine) to deceive one,
and yet not cunning enough to do it
cleverly. In short, the whole external
evidence would make one believe
these fragments (for so he calls them,
though nothing can be more entire)   50
counterfeit; but the internal is so
strong on the other side, that I am resolved to believe them genuine, spite
of the devil and the kirk. It is impos-

sible to convince me that they were
invented by the same man that writes
me these letters. On the other hand, it
is almost as hard to suppose, if they
are original, that he should be able to
translate them so admirably. What
can one do? Since Stonehewer went, I
have received another of a very different and inferior kind (being merely
descriptive), much more modern than
the former (he says), yet very old too.
This too in its way is extremely fine.
In short, this man is the very dæmon
of poetry, or he has lighted on a treasure hid for ages. The Welsh poets are
also coming to light. I have seen a discourse in MS. about them (by one Mr.
Evans, a clergyman) with specimens
of their writings. This is in Latin, and
though it don't approach the other,
there are fine scraps among it.

You will think I am grown mighty
poetical of a sudden; you would think
so still more, if you knew there was a
satire printed against me and Mason
jointly; it is called "Two Odes": the
one is inscribed to Obscurity (that is
me), the other to Oblivion. It tells me
what I never heard before; for (speaking of himself) the author says though
he has

Nor the pride, nor self-opinion,
That possess the happy pair,
Each of taste the fav'rite minion,
Prancing thro' the desert air:
Yet shall he mount, with classic housings
        grac'd,
By help mechanic of equestrian block;
And all unheedful of the Critic's mock,
Spur his light courser o'er the bounds of
        Taste.

The writer is a Mr. Colman, who
published the *Connoisseur*, nephew
to the late Lady Bath, and a friend of
Garrick's. I believe his odes sell no
more than mine did, for I saw a heap
of them lie in a bookseller's window,
who recommended them to me as a
very pretty thing.

If I did not mention *Tristram* to
you, it was because I thought I had
done so before. There is much good
fun in it, and humour sometimes hit,
and sometimes missed. I agree with
your opinion of it, and shall see the

two future volumes with pleasure. Have you read his sermons (with his own comic figure at the head of them)? They are in the style, I think, most proper for the pulpit, and show a very strong imagination and a sensible heart. But you see him often tottering on the verge of laughter, and ready to throw his periwig in the face of his audience. Now for my season. 10

April 10. I observed the elm putting out.
12. That and the pear looked green. Therm. at 62.
13. Very fine; white poplar and willow put out.
15. Standard pear (sheltered) in full bloom.
18. Lime and hornbeam green.
19. Swallow flying.
20. Therm. at 60. Wind S.W. Skylark, chaffinch, thrush, mew, and robin singing. Horse-chestnut, wild-briar, bramble, and sallow had spread their leaves; hawthorn and lilac had formed their blossoms; blackthorn, double-flowered peach and pears in full bloom; double jonquils, hyacinths, anemones, single wall-flowers, and auriculas, in flower. In the fields—dog violets, daisies, dandelions, butter-cups, red-archangel, and shepherd's purse. 30

21. Almond out of bloom, and spreading its leaves.
26. Lilacs flowering.
May 1. Gentianella in flower.
2. Pear goes off; apple blows. Therm. at 63. Wind N.E.; still fair and dry.
3. Evening and all night hard rain.
4. Therm. at 40. Wind N.E.; rain.
11. Very fine. Wind N.E. Horse-chestnut in full bloom; walnut and vine spread; lilacs, Persian jasmine, tulips, wall-flowers, pheasant-eye, lily-in-the-valley, in flower. In the fields—furze, cowslips, hare-bells, and cow-parsnip.
13. Jasmine and acacia spread. Fine weather.
18. Showery. Wind high.
19. Same. Therm. at 56.
20. Thunder, rain, 54.
21. Rain, wind N.E., 52.
31. Green peas 15d. a quart.
June 1. Therm. at 78.
2. Scarlet strawberries, duke-cherries. Hay-making here.
3. Wind S.S.E. Therm. at 84 (the highest I ever saw it), it was at noon, since which, till last week, we had hot dry weather; now it rains like mad. Cherries and strawberries in bushels.

I believe there is no fear of war with Spain.

JAMES BOSWELL (1740-1795)

Boswell has had the misfortune of being easily misunderstood and undervalued, not because of any subtlety in his character, but, on the contrary, because the contradictions of his nature lie on the surface. It is so easy to condescend to "Jamie" or "Bozzy" and to justify our condescension by reference to his egregious faults. It is more profitable to endeavor to understand his remarkable power of winning the sincere friendship of the men whom he esteemed most in England and on the Continent.

He was the son of a distinguished Scotch judge, and was privileged from his youth to move in the best society that Edinburgh or Glasgow had to offer. But he desired to meet the great beyond his fatherland. He spent some months in London, contrived to meet Dr. Johnson, for whom he had the profoundest regard, and in spite of all obstacles had the friendship sealed before he went on his travels. On his tour of the Continent he added Rousseau, Voltaire, John Wilkes, and General Paoli to his list of distinguished friends. In 1773 he was elected to Johnson's Literary Club, although he could come to London for only a short season each year, and henceforth Edmund Malone and Sir Joshua Reynolds became his faithful friends.

As a man of letters, also, Boswell was cultivating an avocation, and the quantity of his publication is surprising. His most notable works are the *Account of Corsica* (1768), the *Journal of a Tour to the Hebrides with Dr. Johnson* (1785), and, of course, the *Life of Dr Johnson*. The *Life* was conceived by Boswell early in his connection with Johnson, and on his visits to London he systematically gathered material for it in his note-books. It was his intention to produce a new type of biography which would present the man himself, not merely facts about him. "I am absolutely certain," he wrote to his friend Temple, "that *my* mode of biography, which gives not only a *history* of Johnson's *visible* progress through the world, and of his publications, but a *view* of his mind, in his letters and conversations, is the most perfect that can be conceived, and will be *more* of a *Life* than any work that has ever yet appeared." But the execution of such a task, as well as the first conception of it, requires a special genius, and Boswell knew how to select the revealing and characteristic passages that make Johnson more intimately known to us than almost any man of the past.

Immediately after Johnson's death, memoirs and anecdotes began to appear in periodicals and in volumes; the most notable of these is Mrs. Piozzi's *Anecdotes of Dr. Johnson* (1786); Boswell did not permit himself to be hurried by such competitors, and his *Life* appeared in 1791; a second edition, enlarged, was published in 1793, and a third, with additions prepared by Boswell, was seen through the press by Edmund Malone in 1799, after Boswell's death. Through the efforts of Professor Tinker there was discovered at Malahide Castle, near Dublin, Boswell's "black box" containing a mass of letters and journals, which were purchased by an American, Col. Ralph Isham. Besides these documents, published as *Private Papers*, additional Boswell manuscripts were found at Malahide in 1930, 1937, and 1940, and at Fettercairn House, near Aberdeen, in 1930 and 1931. This entire body of material has now passed into the possession of Yale University and is in process of publication.

Journal of a Tour to Corsica, ed. S. C. Roberts (Cambridge, Eng., 1923); *Journal of a Tour to the Hebrides*, ed. F. A. Pottle and Charles H. Bennett (1938); *Life of Johnson*, ed. G. B. Hill (6 vols., Oxford, 1887; rev. L. F. Powell, 6 vols., Oxford, 1934-40); *Private Papers from Malahide Castle*, ed. G. Scott and F. A. Pottle (18 vols., Mount Vernon, N.Y., 1928-34); *Index to the Private Papers*, ed. F. A. Pottle and others (1937); *London Journal, 1762-63*, ed. F. A. Pottle (1950); *Boswell in Holland, 1763-64*, ed. F. A. Pottle (1952); *Boswell on the Grand Tour: Germany and Switzerland, 1764* (1953); *Letters*, ed. Chauncey B. Tinker (2 vols., Oxford, 1924); F. A. Pottle, *The Literary Career of James Boswell* (Oxford, 1929); Bertrand H. Bronson, *Johnson and Boswell: Three Essays* (Berkeley, 1944; repr. Cambridge, Eng. 1946); C. B. Tinker, *Young Boswell* (1922). See also page 1269.

THE LIFE OF SAMUEL JOHNSON, LL.D.

To write the Life of him who excelled all mankind in writing the lives of others, and who, whether we consider his extraordinary endowments, or his various works, has been equalled by few in any age, is an arduous, and may be reckoned in me a presumptuous task.

Had Dr. Johnson written his own life, in conformity with the opinion which he has given, that every man's life may be best written by himself; had he employed in the preservation of his own history, that clearness of narration and elegance of language in which he has embalmed so many eminent persons, the world would probably have had the most perfect example of biography that was ever exhibited. But although he at different times, in a desultory manner, committed to writing many particulars of the progress of his mind and fortunes, he never had persevering diligence enough to form them into a regular composition. Of these memorials a few have been preserved; but the greater part was consigned by him to the flames, a few days before his death.

As I had the honour and happiness of enjoying his friendship for upwards of twenty years; as I had the scheme of writing his life constantly in view; as he was well apprised of this circumstance, and from time to time obligingly satisfied my inquiries, by communicating to me the incidents of his early years; as I acquired a facility in recollecting, and was very assiduous in recording, his conversation, of which the extraordinary vigour and vivacity constituted one of the first features of his character; and as I have spared no pains in obtaining materials concerning him, from every quarter where I could discover that they were to be found, and have been favoured with the most liberal communications by his friends; I flatter myself that few biographers have entered upon such a work as this, with more advantages; independent of literary abilities, in which I am not vain enough to compare myself with some great names who have gone before me in this kind of writing.

. . .

Instead of melting down my materials into one mass, and constantly speaking in my own person, by which I might have appeared to have more merit in the execution of the work, I have resolved to adopt and enlarge upon the excellent plan of Mr. Mason, in his Memoirs of Gray. Wherever narrative is necessary to explain, connect, and supply, I furnish it to the best of my abilities; but in the chronological series of Johnson's life, which I trace as distinctly as I can, year by year, I produce, wherever it is in my power, his own minutes, letters or conversation, being convinced that this mode is more lively, and will make my readers better acquainted with him, than even most of those were who actually knew him, but could know him only partially; whereas there is here an accumulation of intelligence from various points, by which his character is more fully understood and illustrated.

Indeed I cannot conceive a more perfect mode of writing any man's life, than not only relating all the most important events of it in their order, but interweaving what he privately wrote, and said, and thought; by which mankind are enabled as it were to see him live, and to "live o'er each scene" with him, as he actually advanced through the several stages of his life. Had his other friends been as diligent and ardent as I was, he might have been almost entirely preserved. As it is, I will venture to say that he will be seen in this work more completely than any man who has ever yet lived.

And he will be seen as he really was; for I profess to write, not his panegyric, which must be all praise, but his Life; which, great and good as he was, must not be supposed to be entirely perfect. To be as he was, is indeed subject of panegyric enough to any man in this state of being; but in every picture there should be shade as well as light, and when I delineate him without reserve, I do what he himself recommended, both by his precept and his example.

"If the biographer writes from personal knowledge, and makes haste to gratify the public curiosity, there is danger lest his interest, his fear, his gratitude, or his tenderness overpower his fidelity, and tempt him to conceal, if not to invent. There are many who think it an act of piety to hide the faults or failings of their friends, even when they can no longer suffer by their detection; we therefore see whole ranks of characters adorned with uniform panegyric, and not to be known from one another but by extrinsic and casual circumstances. 'Let me remember, (says Hale,) when I find myself inclined to pity a criminal, that there is likewise a pity due to the country.' If we owe regard to the memory of the dead, there is yet more respect to be paid to knowledge, to virtue and to truth."

What I consider as the peculiar value of the following work, is, the quantity it contains of Johnson's conversation; which is universally acknowledged to have been eminently instructive and entertaining; and of which the specimens that I have given upon a former occasion, have been received with so much approbation, that I have good grounds for supposing that the world will not be indifferent to more ample communications of a similar nature.

That the conversation of a celebrated man, if his talents have been exerted in conversation, will best display his character, is, I trust, too well established in the judgment of mankind, to be at all shaken by a sneering observation of Mr. Mason, in his *Memoirs of Mr. William Whitehead,* in which there is literally no *Life,* but a mere dry narrative of facts. I do not think it was quite necessary to attempt a depreciation of what is universally esteemed, because it was not to be found in the immediate object of the ingenious writer's pen; for in truth, from a man so still and so tame, as to be contented to pass many years as the domestic companion of a superannuated lord and lady, conversation could no more be expected, than from a Chinese mandarin on a chimneypiece, or the fantastic figures on a gilt leather screen.

If authority be required, let us appeal to Plutarch, the prince of ancient biographers. Οὔτε ταῖς ἐπιφανεστάταις πράξεσι πάντως ἔνεστι δήλωσις ἀρετῆς ἢ κακίας, ἀλλὰ πρᾶγμα βραχὺ πολλάκις, καὶ ῥῆμα, καὶ παιδιά τις ἔμφασιν ἤθους ἐποίησεν μᾶλλον ἢ μάχαι μυριόνεκροι, καὶ παρατάξεις αἱ μέγισται, καὶ πολιορκίαι πόλεων. "Nor is it always in the most distinguished achievements that men's virtues or vices may be best discerned; but very often an action of small note, a short saying, or a jest, shall distinguish a person's real character more than the greatest sieges, or the most important battles."

To this may be added the sentiments of the very man whose life I am about to exhibit.

"The business of the biographer is often to pass slightly over those performances and incidents which produce vulgar greatness, to lead the thoughts into domestic privacies, and display the minute details of daily life, where exterior appendages are cast aside, and men excel each other only by prudence and by virtue. The account of Thuanus is with great propriety said by its author to have been written, that it might lay open to posterity the private and familiar character of that man, *cujus ingenium et candorem ex ipsius scriptis sunt olim semper miraturi,* whose candour and genius will to the end of time be by his writings preserved in admiration.

"There are many invisible circumstances, which whether we read as inquirers after natural or moral knowledge, whether we intend to enlarge our science, or increase our virtue, are more important than public occurrences. Thus Sallust, the great master of nature, has not forgot in his account of Catiline to remark, that his walk was now quick, and again slow, as an indication of a mind revolving with violent commotion. Thus the story of Melanchthon affords a striking lecture on the value of time, by informing us, that when he had made an appointment, he expected not only the hour, but the minute to be fixed, that the day might not run out in the idleness of suspense; and all the plans and enterprises of De Witt are now of less importance to the world than that part of his personal character, which represents him as careful of his health, and negligent of his life.

"But biography has often been allotted to writers, who seem very little acquainted with the nature of their task, or very negligent about the performance. They rarely afford any other account than might be collected from public papers, but imagine themselves writing a life, when they exhibit a chronological series of actions or preferments; and have so little regard to the manners or behaviour of their heroes, that more knowledge may be gained of a man's real character, by a short conversation with one of his servants, than from a formal and studied narrative, begun with his pedigree, and ended with his funeral.

"There are indeed, some natural reasons why these narratives are often written by such as were not likely to give much instruction or delight, and why most accounts of particular persons are barren and useless. If a life be delayed till interest and envy are at an end, we may hope for impartiality, but must expect little intelligence; for the incidents which give excellence to biography are of a volatile and evanescent kind, such as soon escape the memory, and are transmitted by tradition. We know how few can portray a living acquaintance,

except by his most prominent and observable particularities, and the grosser features of his mind; and it may be easily imagined how much of this little knowledge may be lost in imparting it, and how soon a succession of copies will lose all resemblance of the original."

I am fully aware of the objections which may be made to the minuteness on some occasions of my detail of Johnson's conversation, and how happily it is adapted for the petty exercise of ridicule, by men of superficial understanding and ludicrous fancy; but I remain firm and confident in my opinion, that minute particulars are frequently characteristic, and always amusing, when they relate to a distinguished man. I am therefore exceedingly unwilling that any thing, however slight, which my illustrious friend thought it worth his while to express, with any degree of point, should perish. For this almost superstitious reverence, I have found very old and venerable authority, quoted by our great modern prelate, Secker, in whose tenth sermon there is the following passage:

"*Rabbi David Kimchi,* a noted Jewish Commentator, who lived about five hundred years ago, explains that passage in the first Psalm, *His leaf also shall not wither,* from Rabbins yet older than himself, thus: That *even the idle talk,* so he expresses it, *of a good man ought to be regarded;* the most superfluous things he saith are always of some value. And other ancient authors have the same phrase, nearly in the same sense."

Of one thing I am certain, that considering how highly the small portion which we have of the table-talk and other anecdotes of our celebrated writers is valued, and how earnestly it is regretted that we have not more, I am justified in preserving rather too many of Johnson's sayings, than too few; especially as from the diversity of dispositions it cannot be known with certainty beforehand, whether what may seem trifling to some, and perhaps to the collector himself, may not be most agreeable to many; and the greater number that an author can please in any degree, the more pleasure does there arise to a benevolent mind.

To those who are weak enough to think this a degrading task, and the time and labour which have been devoted to it misemployed, I shall content myself with opposing the authority of the greatest man of any age, JULIUS CÆSAR, of whom Bacon observes, that "in his book of Apothegms which he collected, we see that he esteemed it more honour to make himself but a pair of tables, to take the wise and pithy words of others, than to have every word of his own to be made an apothegm or an oracle."

Having said thus much by way of introduction, I commit the following pages to the candour of the Public.

From the year 1744: Ætat. 35.

It does not appear that he wrote any thing in 1744 for the *Gentleman's Magazine* but the Preface. His *Life of Baretier* was now re-published in a pamphlet by itself. But he produced one work this year, fully sufficient to maintain the high reputation which he had acquired. This was *The Life of Richard Savage*; a man, of whom it is difficult to speak impartially, without wondering that he was for some time the intimate companion of Johnson; for his character was marked by profligacy, insolence, and ingratitude: yet, as he undoubtedly had a warm and vigorous, though unregulated mind, had seen life in all its varieties, and been much in the company of the statesmen and wits of his time, he could communicate to Johnson an abundant supply of such materials as his philosophical curiosity most eagerly desired; and as Savage's misfortunes and misconduct had reduced him to the lowest state of wretchedness as a writer for bread, his visits to St. John's Gate naturally brought Johnson and him together.

It is melancholy to reflect, that Johnson and Savage were sometimes in such extreme indigence, that they could not pay for a lodging; so that they have wandered together whole nights in the streets. Yet in these almost incredible scenes of distress, we may suppose that Savage mentioned many of the anecdotes with which Johnson afterwards enriched the life of his unhappy companion, and those of other poets.

He told Sir Joshua Reynolds, that one night in particular, when Savage and he walked around St. James's-square for want of a lodging, they were not at all depressed by their situation; but in high spirits and brimful of patriotism, traversed the square for several hours, inveighed against the minister, and "resolved they would *stand by their country.*"

I am afraid, however, that by associating with Savage, who was habituated to the dissipation and licentiousness of the town, Johnson, though his good principles remained steady, did not entirely preserve that conduct, for which, in days of greater simplicity, he was remarked by his friend Mr. Hector; but was imperceptibly led into some indulgencies which occasioned much distress to his virtuous mind.

That Johnson was anxious that an authentic and favourable account of his extraordinary friend should first get possession of the public attention, is evident from a letter which he wrote in the *Gentleman's Magazine* for August of the year preceding its publication.

"MR. URBAN,—As your collections show how often you have owed the ornaments of your poetical pages to the correspondence of the unfortunate and ingenious Mr. Savage, I doubt not but you have so much regard to his memory as to encourage any design that may have a tendency to the preservation of it from insults or calumnies; and therefore, with some degree of assurance, intreat you to inform the public, that his life will speedily be published by a person who was favoured with his confidence, and received from himself an account of most of the transactions which he proposes to mention, to the time of his retirement to Swansea in Wales.

"From that period, to his death in the prison of Bristol, the account will be continued from materials still less liable to objection; his own letters, and those of his friends, some of which will be inserted in the work, and abstracts of others subjoined in the margin.

"It may be reasonably imagined, that others may have the same design; but as it is not credible that they can obtain the same materials, it must be expected they will supply from invention the want of intelligence; and that under the title of 'The Life of Savage,' they will publish only a novel, filled with romantic adventures, and imaginary amours. You may therefore, perhaps, gratify the lovers of truth and wit, by giving me leave to inform them in your Magazine, that my account will be published in 8vo. by Mr. Roberts, in Warwick-lane."

[*No signature.*]

In February, 1744, it accordingly came forth from the shop of Roberts, between whom and Johnson I have not traced any connection, except the casual one of this publication. In Johnson's *Life of Savage,* although it must be allowed that its moral is the reverse of—"*Respicere exemplar vitæ morumque jubebo,*" a very useful lesson is inculcated, to guard men of warm passions from a too free indulgence of them; and the various incidents are related in so clear and animated a manner, and illuminated throughout with so much philosophy, that it is one of the most interesting narratives in the English language. Sir Joshua Reynolds told me, that upon his return from Italy he met with it in Devonshire, knowing nothing of its author, and began to read it while he was standing with his arm leaning against a chimney-piece. It seized his attention so strongly, that, not being able to lay down the book

till he had finished it, when he attempted to move, he found his arm totally benumbed. The rapidity with which this work was composed, is a wonderful circumstance. Johnson has been heard to say, "I wrote forty-eight of the printed octavo pages of the *Life of Savage* at a sitting; but then I sat up all night."

He exhibits the genius of Savage to the best advantage in the specimens of his poetry which he has selected, some of which are of uncommon merit. We, indeed, occasionally find such vigour and such point, as might make us suppose that the generous aid of Johnson had been imparted to his friend. Mr. Thomas Warton made this remark to me; and, in support of it, quoted from the poem entitled *The Bastard,* a line, in which the fancied superiority of one "stamped in Nature's mint with extasy," is contrasted with a regular lawful descendant of some great and ancient family:

"No tenth transmitter of a foolish face."

But the fact is, that this poem was published some years before Johnson and Savage were acquainted.

It is remarkable, that in this biographical disquisition there appears a very strong symptom of Johnson's prejudice against players; a prejudice which may be attributed to the following causes: first, the imperfection of his organs, which were so defective that he was not susceptible of the fine impressions which theatrical excellence produces upon the generality of mankind; secondly, the cold rejection of his tragedy; and, lastly, the brilliant success of Garrick, who had been his pupil, who had come to London at the same time with him, not in a much more prosperous state than himself, and whose talents he undoubtedly rated low, compared with his own. His being outstripped by his pupil in the race of immediate fame, as well as of fortune, probably made him feel some indignation, as thinking that whatever might be Garrick's merits in his art, the reward was too great when compared with what the most successful efforts of literary labour could attain. At all periods of his life Johnson used to talk contemptuously of players; but in this work he speaks of them with peculiar acrimony; for which, perhaps, there was formerly too much reason from the licentious and dissolute manners of those engaged in that profession. It is but justice to add, that in our own time such a change has taken place, that there is no longer room for such an unfavourable distinction.

His schoolfellow and friend, Dr. Taylor, told me a pleasant anecdote of Johnson's triumphing over his pupil David Garrick. When that great actor had played some little time at Goodman's Fields, Johnson and Taylor went to see him perform, and afterwards passed the evening at a tavern with him and old Giffard. Johnson, who was ever depreciating stage-players, after censuring some mistakes in emphasis which Garrick had committed in the course of that night's acting, said, "The players, Sir, have got a kind of rant, with which they run on, without any regard either to accent or emphasis." Both Garrick and Giffard were offended at this sarcasm, and endeavoured to refute it; upon which Johnson rejoined, "Well now, I'll give you something to speak, with which you are little acquainted, and then we shall see how just my observation is. That shall be the criterion. Let me hear you repeat the ninth Commandment, 'Thou shalt not bear false witness against thy neighbour.' " Both tried at it, said Dr. Taylor, and both mistook the emphasis, which should be upon *not* and *false witness*. Johnson put them right, and enjoyed his victory with great glee.

Johnson's partiality for Savage made him entertain no doubt of his story, however extraordinary and improbable. It never occurred to him to

question his being the son of the Countess of Macclesfield, of whose unrelenting barbarity he so loudly complained, and the particulars of which are related in so strong and affecting a manner in Johnson's life of him. Johnson was certainly well warranted in publishing his narrative, however offensive it might be to the lady and her relations, because her alleged unnatural and cruel conduct to her son, and shameful avowal of guilt, were stated in a *Life of Savage* now lying before me, which came out so early as 1727, and no attempt had been made to confute it, or to punish the author or printer as a libeller: but for the honour of human nature, we should be glad to find the shocking tale not true; and, from a respectable gentleman connected with the lady's family; I have received such information and remarks, as joined to my own inquiries, will, I think, render it at least somewhat doubtful, especially when we consider that it must have originated from the person himself who went by the name of Richard Savage.

If the maxim *falsum in uno, falsum in omnibus*, were to be received without qualification, the credit of Savage's narrative, as conveyed to us, would be annihilated; for it contains some assertions which, beyond a question, are not true.

1. In order to induce a belief that Earl Rivers, on account of a criminal connection with whom, Lady Macclesfield is said to have been divorced from her husband, by Act of Parliament, had a peculiar anxiety about the child which she bore to him, it is alleged, that his Lordship gave him his own name, and had it duly recorded in the register of St. Andrew's, Holborn. I have carefully inspected that register, but no such entry is to be found.

2. It is stated, that "Lady Macclesfield having lived for some time upon very uneasy terms with her husband, thought a public confession of adultery the most obvious and expeditious

method of obtaining her liberty;" and Johnson, assuming this to be true, stigmatizes her with indignation, as "the wretch who had, without scruple, proclaimed herself an adulteress." But I have perused the Journals of both houses of Parliament at the period of her divorce, and there find it authentically ascertained, that so far from voluntarily submitting to the ignominius charge of adultery, she made a strenuous defence by her Counsel; the bill having been first moved 15th January, 1697, in the House of Lords, and proceeded on, (with various applications for time to bring up witnesses at a distance, &c.) at intervals, till the 3d of March, when it passed. It was brought to the Commons, by a message from the Lords, the 5th of March, proceeded on the 7th, 10th, 11th, 14th, and 15th, on which day, after a full examination of witnesses on both sides, and hearing of Counsel, it was reported without amendments, passed, and carried to the Lords.

That Lady Macclesfield was convicted of the crime of which she was accused, cannot be denied; but the question now is, whether the person calling himself Richard Savage was her son.

It has been said, that when Earl Rivers was dying, and anxious to provide for all his natural children, he was informed by Lady Macclesfield that her son by him was dead. Whether, then, shall we believe that this was a malignant lie, invented by a mother to prevent her own child from receiving the bounty of his father, which was accordingly the consequence, if the person whose life Johnson wrote, was her son; or shall we not rather believe that the person who then assumed the name of Richard Savage was an impostor, being in reality the son of the shoemaker, under whose wife's care Lady Macclesfield's child was placed; that after the death of the real Richard Savage, he attempted to personate him; and that the fraud being known to Lady Mac-

clesfield, he was therefore repulsed by her with just resentment?

There is a strong circumstance in support of the last supposition, though it has been mentioned as an aggravation of Lady Macclesfield's unnatural conduct, and that is, her having prevented him from obtaining the benefit of a legacy left to him by Mrs. Lloyd his god-mother. For if there was such a legacy left, his not being able to obtain payment of it, must be imputed to his consciousness that he was not the real person. The just inference should be, that by the death of Lady Macclesfield's child before its god-mother, the legacy became lapsed, and therefore that Johnson's Richard Savage was an impostor. If he had a title to the legacy, he could not have found any difficulty in recovering it; for had the executors resisted his claim, the whole costs, as well as the legacy, must have been paid by them, if he had been the child to whom it was given.

The talents of Savage, and the mingled fire, rudeness, pride, meanness, and ferocity of his character, concur in making it credible that he was fit to plan and carry on an ambitious and daring scheme of imposture, similar instances of which have not been wanting in higher spheres, in the history of different countries, and have had a considerable degree of success.

Yet, on the other hand, to the companion of Johnson, (who through whatever medium he was conveyed into this world,—be it ever so doubtful "To whom related, or by whom begot," was, unquestionably, a man of no common endowments), we must allow the weight of general repute as to his *Status* or parentage, though illicit; and supposing him to be an impostor, it seems strange that Lord Tyrconnel, the nephew of Lady Macclesfield, should patronize him, and even admit him as a guest in his family. Lastly, it must ever appear very suspicious, that three different accounts of the Life of Richard Savage, one published in *The Plain Dealer,* in 1724, another in 1727, and another by the powerful pen of Johnson, in 1744, and all of them while Lady Macclesfield was alive, should, notwithstanding the severe attacks upon her, have been suffered to pass without any public and effectual contradiction.

I have thus endeavoured to sum up the evidence upon the case, as fairly as I can; and the result seems to be, that the world must vibrate in a state of uncertainty as to what was the truth.

This digression, I trust, will not be censured, as it relates to a matter exceedingly curious, and very intimately connected with Johnson, both as a man and an author.

From the year 1754: Ætat. 45.

The *Dictionary*, we may believe, afforded Johnson full occupation this year. As it approached to its conclusion, he probably worked with redoubled vigor, as seamen increase their exertion and alacrity when they have a near prospect of their haven.

Lord Chesterfield, to whom Johnson had paid the high compliment of addressing to his Lordship the *Plan* of his *Dictionary*, had behaved to him in such a manner as to excite his contempt and indignation. The world has been for many years amused with a story confidently told, and as confidently repeated with additional circumstances, that a sudden disgust was taken by Johnson upon occasion of his having been one day kept long in waiting in his Lordship's antechamber, for which the reason assigned was, that he had company with him; and that at last, when the door opened, out walked Colley Cibber; and that Johnson was so violently provoked when he found for whom he had been so long excluded, that he went away in a passion, and never would return. I remember having mentioned this story to George Lord Lyttelton, who told me, he was very intimate with Lord Chesterfield; and holding it as a well-known truth, de-

fended Lord Chesterfield, by saying, that "Cibber, who had been introduced familiarly by the back-stairs, had probably not been there above ten minutes." It may seem strange even to entertain a doubt concerning a story so long and so widely current, and thus implicitly adopted, if not sanctioned, by the authority which I have mentioned; but Johnson himself assured me, that there was not the least foundation for it. He told me, that there never was any particular incident which produced a quarrel between Lord Chesterfield and him; but that his Lordship's continued neglect was the reason why he resolved to have no connection with him. When the *Dictionary* was upon the eve of publication, Lord Chesterfield, who, it is said, had flattered himself with expectations that Johnson would dedicate the work to him, attempted, in a courtly manner, to sooth, and insinuate himself with the Sage, conscious, as it should seem, of the cold indifference with which he had treated its learned author; and further attempted to conciliate him, by writing two papers in *The World*, in recommendation of the work; and it must be confessed, that they contain some studied compliments, so finely turned, that if there had been no previous offence, it is probable that Johnson would have been highly delighted. Praise, in general, was pleasing to him; but by praise from a man of rank and elegant accomplishments, he was peculiarly gratified.

This courtly device failed of its effect. Johnson, who thought that "all was false and hollow," despised the honeyed words, and was even indignant that Lord Chesterfield should, for a moment, imagine that he could be the dupe of such an artifice. His expression to me concerning Lord Chesterfield, upon this occasion, was, "Sir, after making great professions, he had, for many years, taken no notice of me; but when my *Dictionary* was coming out, he fell a scribbling in *The World* about it. Upon which, I wrote him a letter expressed in civil terms, but such as might shew him that I did not mind what he said or wrote, and that I had done with him."

This is that celebrated letter of which so much has been said, and about which curiosity has been so long excited, without being gratified. I for many years solicited Johnson to favor me with a copy of it, that so excellent a composition might not be lost to posterity. He delayed from time to time to give it me; till at last in 1781, when we were on a visit at Mr. Dilly's, at Southill in Bedfordshire, he was pleased to dictate it to me from memory. He afterwards found among his papers a copy of it, which he had dictated to Mr. Baretti, with its title and corrections, in his own handwriting. This he gave to Mr. Langton; adding that if it were to come into print, he wished it to be from that copy. By Mr. Langton's kindness, I am enabled to enrich my work with a perfect transcript of what the world has so eagerly desired to see.

"TO THE RIGHT HONOURABLE THE EARL OF CHESTERFIELD.

February 7, 1755.

"MY LORD, I have been lately informed, by the proprietor of *The World*, that two papers, in which my Dictionary is recommended to the public, were written by your Lordship. To be so distinguished, is an honour, which, being very little accustomed to favours from the great, I know not well how to receive, or in what terms to acknowledge.

"When, upon some slight encouragement, I first visited your Lordship, I was overpowered, like the rest of mankind, by the enchantment of your address; and could not forbear to wish that I might boast myself *Le vainqueur du vainqueur de la terre;*— that I might obtain that regard for which I saw the world contending; but I found my attendance so little encouraged, that neither pride nor modesty would suffer me to continue it. When I had once addressed your Lordship in public, I had exhausted all the art of pleasing which a retired and uncourtly scholar can possess. I had done all that I could; and no man is well pleased to have his all neglected, be it ever so little.

"Seven years, my Lord, have now passed since I waited in your outward rooms, or was repulsed from your door; during which time I have been pushing on my work through difficulties of which it is useless to complain, and have brought it, at last, to the verge of publication, without one act of assistance, one word of encouragement, or one smile of favour. Such treatment I did not expect, for I never had a patron before.

"The shepherd in Virgil grew at last acquainted with Love, and found him a native of the rocks.

"Is not a patron, my Lord, one who looks with unconcern on a man struggling for life in the water, and, when he has reached ground, encumbers him with help? The notice which you have been pleased to take of my labours, had it been early, had been kind; but it has been delayed till I am indifferent, and cannot enjoy it; till I am solitary, and cannot impart it; till I am known, and do not want it. I hope it is no very cynical asperity not to confess obligations where no benefit has been received, or to be unwilling that the public should consider me as owing that to a patron, which Providence has enabled me to do for myself.

"Having carried on my work thus far with so little obligation to any favourer of learning, I shall not be disappointed though I should conclude it, if less be possible, with less; for I have been long wakened from that dream of hope, in which I once boasted myself with so much exultation,

My Lord,
"Your Lordship's most humble
"Most obedient servant,
"SAM. JOHNSON."

"While this was the talk of the town." says Dr. Adams, in a letter to me, "I happened to visit Dr. Warburton, who, finding that I was acquainted with Johnson, desired me earnestly to carry his compliments to him, and to tell him that he honoured him for his manly behaviour in rejecting these condescensions of Lord Chesterfield, and for resenting the treatment he had received from him, with a proper spirit. Johnson was visibly pleased with this compliment, for he had always a high opinion of Warburton. Indeed, the force of mind which appeared in this letter was congenial with that which Warburton himself amply possessed.

There is a curious minute circumstance which struck me, in comparing the various editions of Johnson's *Imitations of Juvenal*. In the tenth *Satire* one of the couplets upon the vanity of wishes even for literary distinction stood thus:

Yet think what ills the scholar's life assail,
Toil, envy, want, the *garret*, and the jail.

But after experiencing the uneasiness which Lord Chesterfield's fallacious patronage made him feel, he dismissed the word *garret* from the sad group, and in all the subsequent editions the line stands,

Toil, envy, want, the *patron*, and the jail.

That Lord Chesterfield must have been mortified by the lofty contempt, and polite, yet keen, satire with which Johnson exhibited him to himself in this letter, it is impossible to doubt. He, however, with that glossy duplicity which was his constant study, affected to be quite unconcerned. Dr. Adams mentioned to Mr. Robert Dodsley that he was sorry Johnson had written his letter to Lord Chesterfield. Dodsley, with the true feelings of trade, said he was very sorry too; for that he had a property in the *Dictionary*, to which his Lordship's patronage might have been of consequence. He then told Mr. Adams that Lord Chesterfield had shown him the letter. "I should have imagined," replied Dr. Adams, "that Lord Chesterfield would have concealed it." "Poh!" said Dodsley, "do you think a letter from Johnson could hurt Lord Chesterfield? Not at all, sir. It lay upon his table, where anybody might see it. He read it to me; said, 'This man has great powers,' pointed out the severest passages, and observed how well they were expressed." This air of indifference, which imposed upon the worthy Dodsley, was certainly nothing but a specimen of that dissimulation which Lord Chesterfield inculcated as one of the most essential lessons for the conduct of life. His Lordship endeavoured to justify himself to Dodsley from the charges brought against him by Johnson; but we may judge of the flimsiness of his defence, from his having excused his neglect of Johnson by saying that he had heard he had changed his lodgings, and did not know where he lived; as if there could have been the smallest difficulty to inform himself of that circumstance, by enquiring in the literary circle with which his Lordship was well acquainted, and was, indeed, himself, one of its ornaments.

Dr. Adams expostulated with Johnson, and suggested that his not being admitted when he called on him was probably not to be imputed to Lord Chesterfield; for his Lordship had declared to Dodsley that he would have turned off the best servant he ever had, if he had known that he denied him to a man who would have been always more than welcome; and in confirmation of this, he insisted on Lord Chesterfield's general affability and easiness of access, especially to literary men. "Sir," said Johnson, "that is not Lord Chesterfield; he is the proudest man this day existing." "No," said Dr. Adams, "there is one person, at least, as proud; I think, by your own account, you are the prouder man of the two." "But mine," replied Johnson instantly, "was *defensive* pride." This, as Dr. Adams well observed, was one of those happy turns for which he was so remarkably ready.

Johnson having now explicitly avowed his opinion of Lord Chesterfield, did not refrain from expressing himself concerning that nobleman with pointed freedom: "This man," said he, "I thought had been a lord among wits; but I find he is only a wit among lords!" And when his *Letters* to his natural son were published, he observed that "they teach the morals of a whore, and the manners of a dancing-master."

The character of "a respectable Hottentot," in Lord Chesterfield's letters, has been generally understood to be meant for Johnson, and I have no doubt that it was. But I remember when the literary property of those letters was contested in the Court of Session in Scotland, and Mr. Henry Dundas, one of the counsel for the proprietors, read this character as an exhibition of Johnson, Sir David Dalrymple, Lord Hailes, one of the judges, maintained, with some warmth, that it was not intended as a portrait of Johnson, but of a late noble lord, distinguished for abstruse science. I have heard Johnson himself talk of the character, and say that it was meant for George, Lord Lyttelton, in which I could by no means agree; for his Lordship had nothing of that violence which is a conspicuous feature in the composition. Finding that my illustrious friend could bear to have it supposed that it might be meant for him, I said, laughingly, that there was one trait which unquestionably did not belong to him: "He throws his meat anywhere but down his throat." "Sir," said he, "Lord Chesterfield never saw me eat in his life."

From the year 1759: Ætat. 50.

In 1759, in the month of January, his mother died at the great age of ninety, an event which deeply affected him; not that "his mind had acquired no firmness by the contemplation of mortality"; but that his reverential affection for her was not abated by years, as indeed he retained all his tender feelings even to the latest period of his life. I have been told that he regretted much his not having gone to visit his mother for several years, previous to her death. But he was constantly engaged in literary labours which confined him to London; and though he had not the comfort of seeing his aged parent, he contributed liberally to her support.

Soon after this event, he wrote his *Rasselas, Prince of Abyssinia;* concerning the publication of which Sir John Hawkins guesses vaguely and idly, instead of having taken the trouble to inform himself with authentic precision. Not to trouble my readers with a repetition of the Knight's reveries, I have to mention, that the late Mr. Strahan the printer told me, that Johnson wrote it, that with the profits he might defray the expense of his mother's funeral, and pay some little debts which she had left. He told Sir Joshua Reynolds that he composed it in the evenings of one week, sent it to the press in portions as it was written, and had never since read it over. Mr. Strahan, Mr. Johnston, and Mr. Dodsley purchased it for a hundred pounds, but afterwards paid him twenty-five pounds more, when it came to a second edition.

Considering the large sums which have been received for compilations, and works requiring not much more genius than compilations, we cannot but wonder at the very low price which he was content to receive for this admirable performance; which, though he had written nothing else, would have rendered his name immortal in the world of literature. None of his writings has been so extensively diffused over Europe; for it has been translated into most, if not all, of the modern languages. This Tale, with all the charms of oriental imagery, and all the force and beauty of which the English language is capable, leads us through the most important scenes of human life, and shows us that this stage of our being is full of "vanity and vexation of spirit." To those who look no further than the present life, or who maintain that human nature has not fallen from the state in which it was created, the instruction of this sublime story will be of no avail. But they who think justly, and feel with strong sensibility, will listen with eagerness and admiration to its truth and wisdom. Voltaire's *Candide*, written to refute the system of Optimism, which it has accomplished with brilliant success, is wonderfully similar in its plan and conduct to Johnson's *Rasselas*; insomuch, that I have heard Johnson say, that if they had not been published so closely one after the other that there was not time for imitation, it would have been in vain to deny that the scheme of that which came latest was taken from the other. Though the proposition illustrated by both these works was the same, namely, that in our present state there is more evil than good, the intention of the writers was very different. Voltaire, I am afraid, meant only by wanton profaneness to obtain a sportive victory over religion, and to discredit the belief of a superintending Providence: Johnson meant, by showing the unsatisfactory nature of things temporal, to direct the hopes of man to things eternal. *Rasselas,* as was observed to me by a very accomplished lady, may be considered as a more enlarged and more deeply philosophical discourse in prose, upon the interesting truth, which in his *Vanity of Human Wishes* he had so successfully enforced in verse.

The fund of thinking which this work contains is such, that almost every sentence of it may furnish a subject of long meditation. I am not satisfied if a year passes without my having read it through; and at every perusal, my admiration of the mind which produced it is so highly raised, that I can scarcely believe that I had the honour of enjoying the intimacy of such a man.

. . . .

From the Year 1763: Ætat. 54.

This is to me a memorable year; for in it I had the happiness to obtain the acquaintance of that extraordinary man whose memoirs I am now writing; an acquaintance which I shall ever esteem as one of the most fortunate circumstances in my life. Though then but two-and-twenty, I had for several years read his works with delight and instruction, and had the highest reverence for their author, which had grown up in my fancy into a kind of mysterious veneration, by figuring to myself a state of solemn elevated abstraction, in which I supposed him to live in the immense metropolis of London. Mr. Gentleman, a native of Ireland, who passed some years in Scotland as a player, and as an instructor in the English language, a man whose talents and worth were depressed by misfortunes, had given me a representation of the figure and manner of DICTIONARY JOHNSON! as he was then generally called; and during my first visit to London, which was for three months in 1760, Mr. Derrick the poet, who was Gentleman's friend and countryman, flattered me with hopes that he would introduce me to Johnson, an honour of which I was very ambitious. But he never found an opportunity; which made me doubt that he had promised to do what was not in his power; till Johnson some years afterwards told me, "Derrick, Sir, might very well have introduced you. I had a kindness for Derrick, and am sorry he is dead."

. . . .

Mr. Thomas Davies the actor, who then kept a bookseller's shop in Russel-street, Covent-garden, told me that Johnson was very much his friend, and came frequently to his house, where he more than once invited me to meet him; but by some unlucky accident or other he was prevented from coming to us.

Mr. Thomas Davies was a man of

good understanding and talents, with the advantage of a liberal education. Though somewhat pompous, he was an entertaining companion; and his literary performances have no inconsiderable share of merit. He was a friendly and very hospitable man. Both he and his wife, (who has been celebrated for her beauty,) though upon the stage for many years, maintained an uniform decency of character; and Johnson esteemed them, and lived in as easy an intimacy with them, as with any family which he used to visit. Mr. Davies recollected several of Johnson's remarkable sayings, and was one of the best of the many imitators of his voice and manner, while relating them. He increased my impatience more and more to see the extraordinary man whose works I highly valued, and whose conversation was reported to be so peculiarly excellent.

At last, on Monday the 16th of May, when I was sitting in Mr. Davies's back-parlour, after having drunk tea with him and Mrs. Davies, Johnson unexpectedly came into the shop; and Mr. Davies having perceived him through the glass-door in the room in which we were sitting, advancing towards us,—he announced his awful approach to me, somewhat in the manner of an actor in the part of Horatio, when he addresses Hamlet on the appearance of his father's ghost, "Look, my Lord, it comes." I found that I had a very perfect idea of Johnson's figure, from the portrait of him painted by Sir Joshua Reynolds soon after he had published his *Dictionary*, in the attitude of sitting in his easy chair in deep meditation, which was the first picture his friend did for him, which Sir Joshua very kindly presented to me, and from which an engraving has been made for this work. Mr. Davies mentioned my name, and respectfully introduced me to him. I was much agitated; and recollecting his prejudice against the Scotch, of which I had heard much, I said to Davies, "Don't tell where I come from."—"From Scot-

land," cried Davies roguishly. "Mr. Johnson, (said I) I do indeed come from Scotland, but I cannot help it." I am willing to flatter myself that I meant this as light pleasantry to soothe and conciliate him, and not as an humiliating abasement at the expense of my country. But however that might be, this speech was somewhat unlucky; for with that quickness of wit for which he was so remarkable, he seized the expression "come from Scotland," which I used in the sense of being of that country; and, as if I had said that I had come away from it, or left it, retorted, "That, Sir, I find, is what a very great many of your countrymen cannot help." This stroke stunned me a good deal; and when we had sat down, I felt myself not a little embarrassed, and apprehensive of what might come next. He then addressed himself to Davies: "What do you think of Garrick? He has refused me an order for the play for Miss Williams, because he knows the house will be full, and that an order would be worth three shillings." Eager to take any opening to get into conversation with him, I ventured to say, "O, Sir, I cannot think Mr. Garrick would grudge such a trifle to you." "Sir, (said he, with a stern look,) I have known David Garrick longer than you have done: and I know no right you have to talk to me on the subject." Perhaps I deserved this check; for it was rather presumptuous in me, an entire stranger, to express any doubt of the justice of his animadversion upon his old acquaintance and pupil. I now felt myself much mortified, and began to think that the hope which I had long indulged of obtaining his acquaintance was blasted. And, in truth, had not my ardour been uncommonly strong, and my resolution uncommonly persevering, so rough a reception might have deterred me for ever from making any further attempts. Fortunately, however, I remained upon the field not wholly discomfited; and was soon rewarded by hearing some of his conversation, of which I preserved the following short minute, without marking the questions and observations by which it was produced.

"People (he remarked) may be taken in once, who imagine that an author is greater in private life than other men. Uncommon parts require uncommon opportunities for their exertion."

"In barbarous society, superiority of parts is of real consequence. Great strength or great wisdom is of much value to an individual. But in more polished times there are people to do every thing for money; and then there are a number of other superiorities, such as those of birth and fortune, and rank, that dissipate men's attention, and leave no extraordinary share of respect for personal and intellectual superiority. This is wisely ordered by Providence, to preserve some equality among mankind."

"Sir, this book (*The Elements of Criticism*, which he had taken up,) is a pretty essay, and deserves to be held in some estimation, though much of it is chimerical."

Speaking of one who with more than ordinary boldness attacked public measures and the royal family, he said,

"I think he is safe from the law, but he is an abusive scoundrel; and instead of applying to my Lord Chief Justice to punish him, I would send half a dozen footmen and have him well ducked."

"The notion of liberty amuses the people of England, and helps to keep off the *tædium vitæ*. When a butcher tells you that *his heart bleeds for his country*, he has, in fact, no uneasy feeling."

"Sheridan will not succeed at Bath with his oratory. Ridicule has gone down before him, and, I doubt, Derrick is his enemy."

"Derrick may do very well, as long as he can outrun his character; but the moment his character gets up with him, it is all over."

It is, however, but just to record,

that some years afterwards, when I reminded him of this sarcasm, he said, "Well, but Derrick has now got a character that he need not run away from."

I was highly pleased with the extraordinary vigour of his conversation, and regretted that I was drawn away from it by an engagement at another place. I had, for a part of the evening, been left alone with him, and had ventured to make an observation now and then, which he received very civilly; so that I was satisfied that though there was a roughness in his manner, there was no ill-nature in his disposition. Davies followed me to the door, and when I complained to him a little of the hard blows which the great man had given me, he kindly took upon him to console me by saying, "Don't be uneasy. I can see he likes you very well."

A few days afterwards I called on Davies, and asked him if he thought I might take the liberty of waiting on Mr. Johnson at his Chambers in the Temple. He said I certainly might, and that Mr. Johnson would take it as a compliment. So upon Tuesday the 24th of May, after having been enlivened by the witty sallies of Messieurs Thornton, Wilkes, Churchill and Lloyd, with whom I had passed the morning, I boldly repaired to Johnson. His Chambers were on the first floor of No. 1, Inner-Temple-lane, and I entered them with an impression given me by the Reverend Dr. Blair, of Edinburgh, who had been introduced to him not long before, and described his having "found the Giant in his den"; an expression, which, when I came to be pretty well acquainted with Johnson, I repeated to him, and he was diverted at this picturesque account of himself. Dr. Blair had been presented to him by Dr. James Fordyce. At this time the controversy concerning the pieces published by Mr. James Macpherson, as translations of *Ossian*, was at its height. Johnson had all along denied their authenticity; and, what was still more provoking to their admirers, maintained that they had no merit. The subject having been introduced by Dr. Fordyce, Dr. Blair, relying on the internal evidence of their antiquity, asked Dr. Johnson whether he thought any man of a modern age could have written such poems? Johnson replied, "Yes, Sir, many men, many women, and many children." Johnson, at this time, did not know that Dr. Blair had just published a *Dissertation*, not only defending their authenticity, but seriously ranking them with the poems of Homer and Virgil; and when he was afterwards informed of this circumstance, he expressed some displeasure at Dr. Fordyce's having suggested the topic, and said, "I am not sorry that they got thus much for their pains. Sir, it was like leading one to talk of a book when the author is concealed behind the door."

He received me very courteously; but, it must be confessed, that his apartment, and furniture, and morning dress, were sufficiently uncouth. His brown suit of clothes looked very rusty; he had on a little old shrivelled unpowdered wig, which was too small for his head; his shirt-neck and knees of his breeches were loose; his black worsted stockings ill drawn up; and he had a pair of unbuckled shoes by way of slippers. But all these slovenly particularities were forgotten the moment that he began to talk. Some gentlemen, whom I do not recollect, were sitting with him; and when they went away, I also rose; but he said to me, "Nay, don't go." "Sir, (said I,) I am afraid that I intrude upon you. It is benevolent to allow me to sit and hear you." He seemed pleased with this compliment, which I sincerely paid him, and answered, "Sir, I am obliged to any man who visits me." I have preserved the following short minute of what passed this day:—

"Madness frequently discovers itself merely by unnecessary deviation from the usual modes of the world. My poor friend Smart showed the disturbance of his mind, by falling upon his knees, and saying his prayers in the street, or in any other unusual place. Now although, rationally speaking, it is greater madness not to pray at all, than to pray as Smart did, I am afraid there are so many who do not pray, that their understanding is not called in question."

Concerning this unfortunate poet, Christopher Smart, who was confined in a mad-house, he had, at another time, the following conversation with Dr. Burney:—BURNEY. "How does poor Smart do, Sir; is he likely to recover?" JOHNSON. "It seems as if his mind had ceased to struggle with the disease; for he grows fat upon it." BURNEY. "Perhaps, Sir, that may be from want of exercise." JOHNSON. "No, Sir; he has partly as much exercise as he used to have, for he digs in the garden. Indeed, before his confinement, he used for exercise to walk to the ale-house; but he was *carried* back again. I did not think he ought to be shut up. His infirmities were not noxious to society. He insisted on people praying with him; and I'd as lief pray with Kit Smart as any one else. Another charge was, that he did not love clean linen; and I have no passion for it."—Johnson continued: "Mankind have a great aversion to intellectual labour; but even supposing knowledge to be easily attainable, more people would be content to be ignorant than would take even a little trouble to acquire it."

"The morality of an action depends on the motive from which we act. If I fling half a crown to a beggar with intention to break his head, and he picks it up and buys victuals with it, the physical effect is good; but, with respect to me, the action is very wrong. So, religious exercises, if not performed with an intention to please GOD, avail us nothing. As our Saviour says of those who perform them from other motives, 'Verily they have their reward.'"

"The Christian religion has very strong evidences. It, indeed, appears in some degree strange to reason; but in History we have undoubted facts, against which, reasoning *à priori*, we have more arguments than we have for them; but then, testimony has great weight, and casts the balance. I would recommend to every man whose faith is yet unsettled, Grotius, —Dr. Pearson,—and Dr. Clarke."

Talking of Garrick, he said, "He is the first man in the world for sprightly conversation."

When I rose a second time he again pressed me to stay, which I did.

He told me, that he generally went abroad at four in the afternoon, and seldom came home till two in the morning. I took the liberty to ask if he did not think it wrong to live thus, and not make more use of his great talents. He owned it was a bad habit. On reviewing, at the distance of many years, my journal of this period, I wonder how, at my first visit, I ventured to talk to him so freely, and that he bore it with so much indulgence.

Before we parted, he was so good as to promise to favour me with his company one evening at my lodgings; and, as I took my leave, shook me cordially by the hand. It is almost needless to add, that I felt no little elation at having now so happily established an acquaintance of which I had been so long ambitious.

My readers will, I trust, excuse me for being thus minutely circumstantial, when it is considered that the acquaintance of Dr. Johnson was to me a most valuable acquisition, and laid the foundation of whatever instruction and entertainment they may receive from my collections concerning the great subject of the work which they are now perusing.

.　.　.　.　.

My next meeting with Johnson was on Friday the 1st of July, when he and I and Dr. Goldsmith supped together at the Mitre. I was before this time pretty well acquainted with Goldsmith, who was one of the brightest ornaments of the Johnsonian school.

Goldsmith's respectful attachment to Johnson was then at its height; for his own literary reputation had not yet distinguished him so much as to excite a vain desire of competition with his great Master. He had increased my admiration of the goodness of Johnson's heart, by incidental remarks in the course of conversation, such as, when I mentioned Mr. Levet, whom he entertained under his roof, "He is poor and honest, which is recommendation enough to Johnson"; and when I wondered that he was very kind to a man of whom I had heard a very bad character, "He is now become miserable, and that insures the protection of Johnson."

Goldsmith attempted this evening to maintain, I suppose from an affectation of paradox, "that knowledge was not desirable on its own account, for it often was a source of unhappiness." JOHNSON. "Why, Sir, that knowledge may in some cases produce unhappiness, I allow. But, upon the whole, knowledge, *per se,* is certainly an object which every man would wish to attain, although, perhaps, he may not take the trouble necessary for attaining it."

Dr. John Campbell, the celebrated political and biographical writer, being mentioned, Johnson said, "Campbell is a man of much knowledge, and has a good share of imagination. His *Hermippus Redivivus* is very entertaining, as an account of the Hermetic philosophy, and as furnishing a curious history of the extravagancies of the human mind. If it were merely imaginary it would be nothing at all. Campbell is not always rigidly careful of truth in his conversation; but I do not believe there is any thing of this carelessness in his books. Campbell is a good man, a pious man. I am afraid he has not been in the inside of a church for many years; but he never passes a church without pulling off his hat. This shows that he has good principles. I used to go pretty often to Campbell's on a Sunday evening till I began to consider that the shoals of Scotchmen who flocked about him might probably say, when any thing of mine was well done, "Ay, ay, he has learnt this of CAWMELL!"

He talked very contemptuously of Churchill's poetry, observing, that "it had a temporary currency, only from its audacity of abuse, and being filled with living names, and that it would sink into oblivion." I ventured to hint that he was not quite a fair judge, as Churchill had attacked him violently. JOHNSON. "Nay, Sir, I am a very fair judge. He did not attack me violently till he found I did not like his poetry; and his attack on me shall not prevent me from continuing to say what I think of him, from an apprehension that it may be ascribed to resentment. No, Sir, I called the fellow a blockhead at first, and I will call him a blockhead still. However, I will acknowledge that I have a better opinion of him now, than I once had; for he has shown more fertility than I expected. To be sure, he is a tree that cannot produce good fruit: he only bears crabs. But, Sir, a tree that produces a great many crabs is better than a tree which produces only a few."

In this depreciation of Churchill's poetry I could not agree with him. It is very true that the greatest part of it is upon the topics of the day, on which account, as it brought him great fame and profit at the time, it must proportionally slide out of the public attention as other occasional objects succeed. But Churchill had extraordinary vigour both of thought and expression. His portraits of the players will ever be valuable to the true lovers of the drama; and his strong caricatures of several eminent men of his age, will not be forgotten by the curious. Let me add, that there are in his works many passages which are of a general nature; and his *Prophecy of Famine* is a poem of no ordinary merit. It is, indeed, falsely injurious to Scotland, but therefore may be allowed a greater share of invention.

. . . . .

Let me here apologize for the imperfect manner in which I am obliged to exhibit Johnson's conversation at this period. In the early part of my acquaintance with him, I was so wrapt in admiration of his extraordinary colloquial talents, and so little accustomed to his peculiar mode of expression, that I found it extremely difficult to recollect and record his conversation with its genuine vigour and vivacity. In progress of time, when my mind was, as it were, *strongly impregnated with the Johnsonian æther,* I could, with much more facility and exactness, carry in my memory and commit to paper the exuberant variety of his wisdom and wit.

At this time *Miss* Williams, as she was then called, though she did not reside with him in the Temple under his roof, but had lodgings in Bolt-court, Fleet-street, had so much of his attention, that he every night drank tea with her before he went home, however late it might be, and she always sat up for him. This, it may be fairly conjectured, was not alone a proof of his regard for *her,* but of his own unwillingness to go into solitude, before that unseasonable hour at which he had habituated himself to expect the oblivion of repose. Dr. Goldsmith, being a privileged man, went with him this night, strutting away, and calling to me with an air of superiority, like that of an esoteric over an exoteric disciple of a sage of antiquity, "I go to Miss Williams." I confess, I then envied him this mighty privilege, of which he seemed so proud; but it was not long before I obtained the same mark of distinction.

On Tuesday the 5th of July, I again visited Johnson. He told me he had looked into the poems of a pretty voluminous writer, Mr. (now Dr.) John Ogilvie, one of the Presbyterian ministers of Scotland, which had lately come out, but could find no thinking in them. BOSWELL. "Is there not imagination in them, Sir?" JOHNSON. "Why, Sir, there is in them what *was* imagination, but it is no more imagination in *him,* than sound is sound in the echo. And his diction too is not his own. We have long ago seen *white-robed innocence,* and *flower-bespangled meads."*

Talking of London, he observed, "Sir, if you wish to have a just notion of the magnitude of this city, you must not be satisfied with seeing its great streets and squares, but must survey the innumerable little lanes and courts. It is not in the showy evolutions of buildings, but in the multiplicity of human habitations which are crowded together, that the wonderful immensity of London consists."
—I have often amused myself with thinking how different a place London is to different people. They, whose narrow minds are contracted to the consideration of some one particular pursuit, view it only through that medium. A politician thinks of it merely as the seat of government in its different departments; a grazier, as a vast market for cattle; a mercantile man, as a place where a prodigious deal of business is done upon 'Change; a dramatic enthusiast, as the grand scene of theatrical entertainments; a man of pleasure, as an assemblage of taverns, and the great emporium for ladies of easy virtue. But the intellectual man is struck with it, as comprehending the whole of human life in all its variety, the contemplation of which is inexhaustible.

On Wednesday, July 6, he was engaged to sup with me at my lodgings in Downing-street, Westminster. But on the preceding night my landlord having behaved very rudely to me and some company who were with me, I had resolved not to remain another night in his house. I was exceedingly uneasy at the awkward appearance I supposed I should make to Johnson and the other gentlemen whom I had invited, not being able to receive them at home, and being obliged to order supper at the Mitre. I went to Johnson in the morning,

and talked of it as a serious distress. He laughed, and said, "Consider, Sir, how insignificant this will appear a twelvemonth hence."—Were this consideration to be applied to most of the little vexatious incidents of life, by which our quiet is too often disturbed, it would prevent many painful sensations. I have tried it frequently, with good effect. "There is nothing (continued he) in this mighty misfortune; nay, we shall be better at the Mitre." I told him that I had been at Sir John Fielding's office, complaining of my landlord, and had been informed, that though I had taken my lodgings for a year, I might, upon proof of his bad behaviour, quit them when I pleased, without being under an obligation to pay rent for any longer time than while I possessed them. The fertility of Johnson's mind could show itself even upon so small a matter as this. "Why, Sir, (said he,) I suppose this must be the law, since you have been told so in Bow-street. But, if your landlord could hold you to your bargain, and the lodgings should be yours for a year, you may certainly use them as you think fit. So, Sir, you may quarter two life-guardsmen upon him; or you may send the greatest scoundrel you can find into your apartments; or you may say that you want to make some experiments in natural philosophy, and may burn a large quantity of asafœtida in his house."

I had as my guests this evening at the Mitre tavern, Dr. Johnson, Dr. Goldsmith, Mr. Thomas Davies, Mr. Eccles, an Irish gentleman, for whose agreeable company I was obliged to Mr. Davies, and the Reverend Mr. John Ogilvie, who was desirous of being in company with my illustrious friend, while I, in my turn, was proud to have the honour of showing one of my countrymen upon what easy terms Johnson permitted me to live with him.

Goldsmith, as usual, endeavoured, with too much eagerness, to *shine,* and disputed very warmly with Johnson against the well-known maxim of the British constitution, "the King can do no wrong"; affirming, that "what was morally false could not be politically true; and as the King might, in the exercise of his regal power, command and cause the doing of what was wrong, it certainly might be said, in sense and in reason, that he could do wrong." JOHNSON. "Sir, you are to consider, that in our constitution, according to its true principles, the King is the head; he is supreme; he is above everything, and there is no power by which he can be tried. Therefore, it is, Sir, that we hold the King can do no wrong; that whatever may happen to be wrong in government may not be above our reach, by being ascribed to Majesty. Redress is always to be had against oppression, by punishing the immediate agents. The King, though he should command, cannot force a Judge to condemn a man unjustly; therefore it is the Judge whom we prosecute and punish. Political institutions are formed upon the consideration of what will most frequently tend to the good of the whole, although now and then exceptions may occur. Thus it is better in general that a nation should have a supreme legislative power, although it may at times be abused. And then, Sir, there is this consideration, that *if the abuse be enormous, Nature will rise up, and claiming her original rights, overturn a corrupt political system.*" I mark this animated sentence with peculiar pleasure, as a noble instance of that truly dignified spirit of freedom which ever glowed in his heart, though he was charged with slavish tenets by superficial observers; because he was at all times indignant against that false patriotism, that pretended love of freedom, that unruly restlessness, which is inconsistent with the stable authority of any good government.

This generous sentiment, which he uttered with great fervour, struck me exceedingly, and stirred my blood to that pitch of fancied resistance, the possibility of which I am glad to keep in mind, but to which I trust I never shall be forced.

"Great abilities (said he) are not requisite for an historian; for in historical composition, all the greatest powers of the human mind are quiescent. He has facts ready to his hand; so there is no exercise of invention. Imagination is not required in any high degree; only about as much as is used in the lower kinds of poetry. Some penetration, accuracy, and colouring will fit a man for the task, if he can give the application which is necessary."

"Bayle's *Dictionary* is a very useful work for those to consult who love the biographical part of literature, which is what I love most."

Talking of the eminent writers in Queen Anne's reign, he observed, "I think Dr. Arbuthnot the first man among them. He was the most universal genius, being an excellent physician, a man of deep learning, and a man of much humour. Mr. Addison was, to be sure, a great man; his learning was not profound; but his morality, his humour, and his elegance of writing, set him very high."

Mr. Ogilvie was unlucky enough to choose for the topic of his conversation the praises of his native country. He began with saying, that there was very rich land round Edinburgh. Goldsmith, who had studied physic there, contradicted this, very untruly, with a sneering laugh. Disconcerted a little by this, Mr. Ogilvie then took new ground, where, I suppose, he thought himself perfectly safe; for he observed, that Scotland had a great many noble wild prospects. JOHNSON. "I believe, Sir, you have a great many. Norway, too, has noble wild prospects; and Lapland is remarkable for prodigious noble wild prospects. But, Sir, let me tell you, the noblest prospect which a Scotchman ever sees, is the high road that leads him to England!" This unexpected and pointed sally produced a roar of applause. After all, however, those, who admire the rude grandeur of Nature, cannot deny it to Caledonia.

On Saturday, July 9, I found Johnson surrounded with a numerous levee, but have not preserved any part of his conversation. On the 14th we had another evening by ourselves at the Mitre. It happening to be a very rainy night, I made some commonplace observations on the relaxation of nerves and depression of spirits which such weather occasioned; adding, however, that it was good for the vegetable creation. Johnson, who, as we have already seen, denied that the temperature of the air had any influence on the human frame, answered, with a smile of ridicule, "Why yes, Sir, it is good for vegetables, and for the animals who eat those vegetables, and for the animals who eat those animals." This observation of his aptly enough introduced a good supper; and I soon forgot, in Johnson's company, the influence of a moist atmosphere.

Feeling myself now quite at ease as his companion, though I had all possible reverence for him, I expressed a regret that I could not be so easy with my father, though he was not much older than Johnson, and certainly however respectable had not more learning and greater abilities to depress me. I asked him the reason of this. JOHNSON. "Why, Sir, I am a man of the world. I live in the world, and I take, in some degree, the colour of the world as it moves along. Your father is a Judge in a remote part of the island, and all his notions are taken from the old world. Besides, Sir, there must always be a struggle between a father and son, while one aims at power and the other at independence." I said, I was afraid my father would force me to be a lawyer. JOHNSON. "Sir, you need not be afraid of his forcing you to be a laborious practising lawyer; that is not in his power. For as the proverb says, 'One man may lead a horse to the water, but twenty cannot make him drink.' He may be displeased that you are not

what he wishes you to be; but that displeasure will not go far. If he insists only on your having as much law as is necessary for a man of property, and then endeavours to get you into Parliament, he is quite in the right."

He enlarged very convincingly upon the excellence of rhyme over blank verse in English poetry. I mentioned to him that Dr. Adam Smith, in his lectures upon composition, when I studied under him in the College of Glasgow, had maintained the same opinion strenuously, and I repeated some of his arguments. JOHNSON. "Sir, I was once in company with Smith, and we did not take to each other; but had I known that he loved rhyme as much as you tell me he does, I should have HUGGED him."

Talking of those who denied the truth of Christianity, he said, "It is always easy to be on the negative side. If a man were now to deny that there is salt upon the table, you could not reduce him to an absurdity. Come, let us try this a little further. I deny that Canada is taken, and I can support my denial by pretty good arguments. The French are a much more numerous people than we; and it is not likely that they would allow us to take it. 'But the ministry have assured us, in all the formality of The Gazette, that it is taken.'—Very true. But the ministry have put us to an enormous expense by the war in America, and it is their interest to persuade us that we have got something for our money.—'But the fact is confirmed by thousands of men who were at the taking of it.'—Ay, but these men have still more interest in deceiving us. They don't want that you should think the French have beat them, but that they have beat the French. Now suppose you should go over and find that it is really taken, that would only satisfy yourself; for when you come home we will not believe you. We will say, you have been bribed.—Yet, Sir, notwithstanding all these plausible objections, we have no doubt that Canada is really ours. Such is the weight of common testimony. How much stronger are the evidences of the Christian religion!"

"Idleness is a disease which must be combated; but I would not advise a rigid adherence to a particular plan of study. I myself have never persisted in any plan for two days together. A man ought to read just as inclination leads him; for what he reads as a task will do him little good. A young man should read five hours in a day, and so may acquire a great deal of knowledge."

To a man of vigorous intellect and arduous curiosity like his own, reading without a regular plan may be beneficial; though even such a man must submit to it, if he would attain a full understanding of any of the sciences.

To such a degree of unrestrained frankness had he now accustomed me, that in the course of this evening I talked of the numerous reflections which had been thrown out against him on account of his having accepted a pension from his present Majesty. "Why, Sir, (said he, with a hearty laugh,) it is a mighty foolish noise that they make. I have accepted of a pension as a reward which has been thought due to my literary merit; and now that I have this pension, I am the same man in every respect that I have ever been; I retain the same principles. It is true, that I cannot now curse (smiling) the House of Hanover; nor would it be decent for me to drink King James's health in the wine that King George gives me money to pay for. But, Sir, I think that the pleasure of cursing the House of Hanover, and drinking King James's health, are amply overbalanced by three hundred pounds a year."

There was here, most certainly, an affectation of more Jacobitism than he really had; and indeed an intention of admitting, for the moment, in a much greater extent than it really existed, the charge of disaffection imputed to him by the world, merely for the purpose of showing how dexterously he could repel an attack, even though he were placed in the most disadvantageous position; for I have heard him declare, that if holding up his right hand would have secured victory at Culloden to Prince Charles's army, he was not sure he would have held it up; so little confidence had he in the right claimed by the House of Stuart, and so fearful was he of the consequences of another revolution on the throne of Great-Britain; and Mr. Topham Beauclerk assured me, he had heard him say this before he had his pension. At another time he said to Mr. Langton, "Nothing has ever offered, that has made it worth my while to consider the question fully." He, however, also said to the same gentleman, talking of King James the Second, "It was become impossible for him to reign any longer in this country." He no doubt had an early attachment to the House of Stuart; but his zeal had cooled as his reason strengthened. Indeed I heard him once say, that "after the death of a violent Whig, with whom he used to contend with great eagerness, he felt his Toryism much abated." I suppose he meant Mr. Walmsley.

Yet there is no doubt that at earlier periods he was wont often to exercise both his pleasantry and ingenuity in talking Jacobitism. My much respected friend, Dr. Douglas, now Bishop of Salisbury, has favoured me with the following admirable instance from his Lordship's own recollection. One day when dining at old Mr. Langton's where Miss Roberts, his niece, was one of the company, Johnson, with his usual complacent attention to the fair sex, took her by the hand and said, "My dear, I hope you are a Jacobite." Old Mr. Langton, who, though a high and steady Tory, was attached to the present Royal Family, seemed offended, and asked Johnson, with great warmth, what he could mean by putting such a question to his niece? "Why, Sir, (said Johnson) I meant no offense to your niece, I meant her a great compliment. A Jacobite, Sir, believes in the divine right of Kings. He that believes in the divine right of Kings believes in a Divinity. A Jacobite believes in the divine right of Bishops. He that believes in the divine right of Bishops believes in the divine authority of the Christian religion. Therefore, Sir, a Jacobite is neither an Atheist nor a Deist. That cannot be said of a Whig; for *Whiggism is a negation of all principle.*"

He advised me, when abroad, to be as much as I could with the Professors in the universities, and with the Clergy; for from their conversation I might expect the best accounts of every thing in whatever country I should be, with the additional advantage of keeping my learning alive.

It will be observed, that when giving me advice as to my travels, Dr. Johnson did not dwell upon cities, and palaces, and pictures, and shows, and Arcadian scenes. He was of Lord Essex's opinion, who advises his kinsman Roger Earl of Rutland, "rather to go an hundred miles to speak with one wise man, than five miles to see a fair town."

I described to him an impudent fellow from Scotland, who affected to be a savage, and railed at all established systems. JOHNSON. "There is nothing surprising in this, Sir. He wants to make himself conspicuous. He would tumble in a hogstye, as long as you looked at him and called to him to come out. But let him alone, never mind him, and he'll soon give it over."

I added, that the same person maintained that there was no distinction between virtue and vice. JOHNSON. "Why, Sir, if the fellow does not think as he speaks, he is lying; and I see not what honour he can propose to himself from having the character of a liar. But if he does really think that there is no distinction between virtue and vice, why, Sir, when he leaves our houses let us count our spoons."

He recommended to me to keep a journal of my life, full and unre-

served. He said it would be a very good exercise, and would yield me great satisfaction when the particulars were faded from my remembrance. I was uncommonly fortunate in having had a previous coincidence of opinion with him upon this subject, for I had kept such a journal for some time; and it was no small pleasure to me to have this to tell him, and to receive his approbation. He counselled me to keep it private, and said I might surely have a friend who would burn it in case of my death. From this habit I have been enabled to give the world so many anecdotes, which would otherwise have been lost to posterity. I mentioned that I was afraid I put into my journal too many little incidents. JOHNSON. "There is nothing, Sir, too little for so little a creature as man. It is by studying little things that we attain the great art of having as little misery and as much happiness as possible."

Next morning Mr. Dempster happened to call on me, and was so much struck even with the imperfect account which I gave him of Dr. Johnson's conversation, that to his honour be it recorded, when I complained that drinking port and sitting up late with him affected my nerves for some time after, he said, "One had better be palsied at eighteen than not keep company with such a man."

On Tuesday, July 18, I found tall Sir Thomas Robinson sitting with Johnson. Sir Thomas said, that the king of Prussia valued himself upon three things;—upon being a hero, a musician, and an author. JOHNSON. "Pretty well, Sir, for one man. As to his being an author, I have not looked at his poetry; but his prose is poor stuff. He writes just as you might suppose Voltaire's footboy to do, who has been his amanuensis. He has such parts as the valet might have, and about as much of the colouring of the style as might be got by transcribing his works." When I was at Ferney, I repeated this to Voltaire, in order to reconcile him somewhat to Johnson, whom he, in affecting the English mode of expression, had previously characterized as "a superstitious dog"; but after hearing such a criticism on Frederick the Great, with whom he was then on bad terms, he exclaimed, "An honest fellow!"

But I think the criticism much too severe; for the *Memoirs of the House of Brandenburgh* are written as well as many works of that kind. His poetry, for the style of which he himself makes a frank apology, "*Jargonnant un François barbare*," though fraught with pernicious ravings of infidelity, has, in many places, great animation, and in some a pathetic tenderness.

Upon this contemptuous animadversion on the King of Prussia, I observed to Johnson, "It would seem then, Sir, that much less parts are necessary to make a King, than to make an Author; for the King of Prussia is confessedly the greatest King now in Europe, yet you think he makes a very poor figure as an Author."

Mr. Levet this day showed me Dr. Johnson's library, which was contained in two garrets over his Chambers, where Lintot, son of the celebrated bookseller of that name, had formerly his warehouse. I found a number of good books, but very dusty and in great confusion. The floor was strewed with manuscript leaves, in Johnson's own handwriting, which I beheld with a degree of veneration, supposing they perhaps might contain portions of *The Rambler* or of *Rasselas*. I observed an apparatus for chemical experiments, of which Johnson was all his life very fond. The place seemed to be very favourable for retirement and meditation. Johnson told me, that he went up thither without mentioning it to his servant, when he wanted to study secure from interruption; for he would not allow his servant to say he was not at home when he really was. "A servant's strict regard for truth, (said he) must be weakened by such a practice. A philosopher may know that it is merely a

form of denial; but few servants are such nice distinguishers. If I accustom a servant to tell a lie for *me*, have I not reason to apprehend that he will tell many lies for *himself*." I am, however, satisfied that every servant, of any degree of intelligence, understands saying his master is not at home, not at all as the affirmation of a fact, but as customary words, intimating that his master wishes not to be seen; so that there can be no bad effect from it.

Mr. Temple, now vicar of St. Gluvias, Cornwall, who had been my intimate friend for many years, had at this time chambers in Farrar's-buildings, at the bottom of Inner Temple-lane, which he kindly lent me upon my quitting my lodgings, he being to return to Trinity Hall, Cambridge. I found them particularly convenient for me, as they were so near Dr. Johnson's.

On Wednesday, July 20, Dr. Johnson, Mr. Dempster, and my uncle Dr. Boswell, who happened to be now in London, supped with me at these chambers. JOHNSON. "Pity is not natural to man. Children are always cruel. Savages are always cruel. Pity is acquired and improved by the cultivation of reason. We may have uneasy sensations from seeing a creature in distress, without pity; for we have not pity unless we wish to relieve them. When I am on my way to dine with a friend, and finding it late, have bid the coachman make haste, if I happen to attend when he whips his horses, I may feel unpleasantly that the animals are put to pain, but I do not wish him to desist. No, Sir, I wish him to drive on."

Mr. Alexander Donaldson, bookseller of Edinburgh, had for some time opened a shop in London, and sold his cheap editions of the most popular English books, in defiance of the supposed common-law right of Literary Property. Johnson, though he concurred in the opinion which was afterwards sanctioned by a judgment of the House of Lords, that there was no such right, was at this time very angry that the booksellers of London, for whom he uniformly professed much regard, should suffer from an invasion of what they had ever considered to be secure: and he was loud and violent against Mr. Donaldson. "He is a fellow who takes advantage of the law to injure his brethren; for, notwithstanding that the statute secures only fourteen years of exclusive right, it has always been understood by *the trade,* that he, who buys the copyright of a book from the author, obtains a perpetual property; and upon that belief, numberless bargains are made to transfer that property after the expiration of the statutory term. Now Donaldson, I say, takes advantage here, of people who have really an equitable title from usage; and if we consider how few of the books, of which they buy the property, succeed so well as to bring profit, we should be of opinion that the term of fourteen years is too short; it should be sixty years." DEMPSTER. "Donaldson, Sir, is anxious for the encouragement of literature. He reduces the price of books, so that poor students may buy them." JOHNSON, (laughing). "Well, Sir, allowing that to be his motive, he is no better than Robin Hood, who robbed the rich in order to give to the poor."

It is remarkable, that when the great question concerning Literary Property came to be ultimately tried before the supreme tribunal of this country, in consequence of the very spirited exertions of Mr. Donaldson, Dr. Johnson was zealous against a perpetuity; but he thought that the term of the exclusive right of authors should be considerably enlarged. He was then for granting a hundred years.

The conversation now turned upon Mr. David Hume's style. JOHNSON. "Why, Sir, his style is not English; the structure of his sentences is French. Now the French structure and the English structure may, in the nature of things, be equally good. But if you allow that the English language is established, he is wrong. My name might originally have been Nicholson, as well as Johnson; but were you to call me Nicholson now, you would call me very absurdly."

Rousseau's treatise on the inequality of mankind was at this time a fashionable topic. It gave rise to an observation by Mr. Dempster, that the advantages of fortune and rank were nothing to a wise man, who ought to value only merit. JOHNSON. "If man were a savage, living in the woods by himself, this might be true; but in civilized society we all depend upon each other, and our happiness is very much owing to the good opinion of mankind. Now, Sir, in civilized society, external advantages make us more respected. A man with a good coat upon his back meets with a better reception than he who has a bad one. Sir, you may analyse this, and say what is there in it? But that will avail you nothing, for it is a part of a general system. Pound St. Paul's Church into atoms, and consider any single atom; it is, to be sure, good for nothing: but, put all these atoms together, and you have St. Paul's Church. So it is with human felicity, which is made up of many ingredients, each of which may be shown to be very insignificant. In civilized society, personal merit will not serve you so much as money will. Sir, you may make the experiment. Go into the street, and give one man a lecture on morality, and another a shilling, and see which will respect you most. If you wish only to support nature, Sir William Petty fixes your allowance at three pounds a year; but as times are much altered, let us call it six pounds. This sum will fill your belly, shelter you from the weather, and even get you a strong and lasting coat, supposing it to be made of good bull's hide. Now, Sir, all beyond this is artificial, and is desired in order to obtain a greater degree of respect from our fellow-creatures. And, Sir, if six hundred pounds a year procure a man more consequence, and, of course, more happiness than six pounds a year, the same proportion will hold as to six thousand, and so on as far as opulence can be carried. Perhaps he who has a large fortune may not be so happy as he who has a small one; but that must proceed from other causes than from his having the large fortune: for, *cœteris paribus,* he who is rich in a civilized society, must be happier than he who is poor; as riches, if properly used, (and it is a man's own fault if they are not,) must be productive of the highest advantages. Money, to be sure, of itself is of no use; for its only use is to part with it. Rousseau, and all those who deal in paradoxes, are led away by a childish desire of novelty. When I was a boy, I used always to choose the wrong side of a debate, because most ingenious things, that is to say, most new things, could be said upon it. Sir, there is nothing for which you may not muster up more plausible arguments, than those which are urged against wealth and other external advantages. Why, now, there is stealing; why should it be thought a crime? When we consider by what unjust methods property has been often acquired, and that what was unjustly got it must be unjust to keep, where is the harm in one man's taking the property of another from him? Besides, Sir, when we consider the bad use that many people make of their property, and how much better use the thief may make of it, it may be defended as a very allowable practice. Yet, Sir, the experience of mankind has discovered stealing to be so very bad a thing, that they make no scruple to hang a man for it. When I was running about this town a very poor fellow, I was a great arguer for the advantages of poverty; but I was, at the same time, very sorry to be poor. Sir, all the arguments which are brought to represent poverty as no evil, show it to be evidently a great evil. You never find people labouring to convince you that you may live very happily upon a plentiful fortune. —So you hear people talking how miserable a King must be; and yet they all wish to be in his place."

It was suggested that Kings must be unhappy, because they are deprived of the greatest of all satisfactions, easy and unreserved society. JOHNSON. "That is an ill-founded notion. Being a King does not exclude a man from such society. Great Kings have always been social. The King of Prussia, the only great King at present, is very social. Charles the Second, the last King of England who was a man of parts, was social; and our Henrys and Edwards were all social."

Mr. Dempster having endeavoured to maintain that intrinsic merit *ought* to make the only distinction amongst mankind. JOHNSON. "Why, Sir, mankind have found that this cannot be. How shall we determine the proportion of intrinsic merit? Were that to be the only distinction amongst mankind, we should soon quarrel about the degrees of it. Were all distinctions abolished, the strongest would not long acquiesce, but would endeavour to obtain a superiority by their bodily strength. But, Sir, as subordination is very necessary for society, and contentions for superiority very dangerous, mankind, that is to say, all civilized nations, have settled it upon a plain invariable principle. A man is born to hereditary rank; or his being appointed to certain offices, gives him a certain rank. Subordination tends greatly to human happiness. Were we all upon an equality, we should have no other enjoyment than mere animal pleasure."

I said, I considered distinction of rank to be of so much importance in civilized society, that if I were asked on the same day to dine with the first duke in England, and with the first man in Britain for genius, I should hesitate which to prefer. JOHNSON. "To be sure, Sir, if you were to dine only once, and it were never to be known where you dined, you would choose rather to dine with the first man for genius; but to gain most respect, you should dine with the first duke in England. For nine people in ten that you meet with, would have a higher opinion of you for having dined with a duke; and the great genius himself would receive you better, because you had been with the great duke."

He took care to guard himself against any possible suspicion that his settled principles of reverence for rank and respect for wealth were at all owing to mean or interested motives; for he asserted his own independence as a literary man. "No man (said he) who ever lived by literature, has lived more independently than I have done." He said he had taken longer time than he needed to have done in composing his *Dictionary*. He received our compliments upon that great work with complacency, and told us that the *Academia della Crusca* could scarcely believe that it was done by one man.

Next morning I found him alone, and have preserved the following fragments of his conversation. Of a gentleman who was mentioned, he said, "I have not met with any man for a long time who has given me such general displeasure. He is totally unfixed in his principles, and wants to puzzle other people." I said his principles had been poisoned by a noted infidel writer, but that he was, nevertheless, a benevolent good man. JOHNSON. "We can have no dependence upon that instinctive, that constitutional goodness which is not founded upon principle. I grant you that such a man may be a very amiable member of society. I can conceive him placed in such a situation that he is not much tempted to deviate from what is right; and as every man prefers virtue, when there is not some strong incitement to transgress its precepts, I can conceive him doing nothing wrong. But if such a man stood in need of money, I should not like to trust him; and I should certainly not trust him with young ladies, for *there* there is always temptation. Hume, and other sceptical innovators, are vain men, and

will gratify themselves at any expense. Truth will not afford sufficient food to their vanity; so they have betaken themselves to error. Truth, Sir, is a cow which will yield such people no more milk, and so they are gone to milk the bull. If I could have allowed myself to gratify my vanity at the expense of truth, what fame might I have acquired. Every thing which Hume has advanced against Christianity had passed through my mind long before he wrote. Always remember this, that after a system is well settled upon positive evidence, a few partial objections ought not to shake it. The human mind is so limited, that it cannot take in all the parts of a subject, so that there may be objections raised against any thing. There are objections against a *plenum,* and objections against a *vacuum*; yet one of them must certainly be true."

I mentioned Hume's argument against the belief of miracles, that it is more probable that the witnesses to the truth of them are mistaken, or speak falsely, than that the miracles should be true. JOHNSON. "Why, Sir, the great difficulty of proving miracles should make us very cautious in believing them. But let us consider; although GOD has made Nature to operate by certain fixed laws, yet it is not unreasonable to think that he may suspend those laws, in order to establish a system highly advantageous to mankind. Now the Christian religion is a most beneficial system, as it gives us light and certainty where we were before in darkness and doubt. The miracles which prove it are attested by men who had no interest in deceiving us; but who, on the contrary, were told that they should suffer persecution, and did actually lay down their lives in confirmation of the truth of the facts which they asserted. Indeed, for some centuries the heathens did not pretend to deny the miracles; but said they were performed by the aid of evil spirits. This is a circumstance of great weight. Then, Sir, when we take the proofs derived from prophecies which have been so exactly fulfilled, we have most satisfactory evidence. Supposing a miracle possible, as to which, in my opinion, there can be no doubt, we have as strong evidence for the miracles in support of Christianity, as the nature of the thing admits."

At night Mr. Johnson and I supped in a private room at the Turk's Head coffee-house, in the Strand. "I encourage this house (said he;) for the mistress of it is a good civil woman, and has not much business."

"Sir, I love the acquaintance of young people; because, in the first place, I don't like to think myself growing old. In the next place, young acquaintances must last longest, if they do last; and then, Sir, young men have more virtue than old men; they have more generous sentiments in every respect. I love the young dogs of this age: they have more wit and humour and knowledge of life than we had; but then the dogs are not so good scholars. Sir, in my early years I read very hard. It is a sad reflection, but a true one, that I knew almost as much at eighteen as I do now. My judgment, to be sure, was not so good; but I had all the facts. I remember very well, when I was at Oxford, an old gentleman said to me, 'Young man, ply your book diligently now, and acquire a stock of knowledge; for when years come upon you, you will find that poring upon books will be but an irksome task.'"

This account of his reading, given by himself in plain words, sufficiently confirms what I have already advanced upon the disputed question as to his application. It reconciles any seeming inconsistency in his way of talking upon it at different times; and shows that idleness and reading hard were with him relative terms, the import of which, as used by him, must be gathered from a comparison with what scholars of different degrees of ardour and assiduity have been known to do. And let it be remembered, that he was now talking spontaneously,

and expressing his genuine sentiments; whereas at other times he might be induced from his spirit of contradiction, or more properly from his love of argumentative contest, to speak lightly of his own application to study. It is pleasing to consider that the old gentleman's gloomy prophecy as to the irksomeness of books to men of an advanced age, which is too often fulfilled, was so far from being verified in Johnson, that his ardour for literature never failed, and his last writings had more ease and vivacity than any of his earlier productions.

He mentioned to me now, for the first time, that he had been distressed by melancholy, and for that reason had been obliged to fly from study and meditation to the dissipating variety of life. Against melancholy he recommended constant occupation of mind, a great deal of exercise, moderation in eating and drinking, and especially to shun drinking at night. He said melancholy people were apt to fly to intemperance for relief, but that it sunk them much deeper in misery. He observed, that labouring men who work hard, and live sparingly, are seldom or never troubled with low spirits.

He again insisted on the duty of maintaining subordination of rank. "Sir, I would no more deprive a nobleman of his respect, than of his money. I consider myself as acting a part in the great system of society, and I do to others as I would have them to do to me. I would behave to a nobleman as I should expect he would behave to me, were I a nobleman and he Sam. Johnson. Sir, there is one Mrs. Macaulay in this town, a great republican. One day when I was at her house, I put on a very grave countenance, and said to her, 'Madam, I am now become a convert to your way of thinking. I am convinced that all mankind are upon an equal footing; and to give you an unquestionable proof, Madam, that I am in earnest, here is a very sensible, civil, well-behaved fellow-citizen, your footman; I desire that he may be allowed to sit down and dine with us.' I thus, Sir, showed her the absurdity of the levelling doctrine. She has never liked me since. Sir, your levellers wish to level *down* as far as themselves; but they cannot bear levelling *up* to themselves. They would all have some people under them; why not then have some people above them?" I mentioned a certain author who disgusted me by his forwardness, and by showing no deference to noblemen into whose company he was admitted. JOHNSON. "Suppose a shoemaker should claim an equality with him, as he does with a lord; how he would stare. 'Why, Sir, do you stare? (says the shoemaker,) I do great service to society. 'Tis true I am paid for doing it; but so are you, Sir: and I am sorry to say it, paid better than I am, for doing something not so necessary, for mankind could do better without your books, than without my shoes.' Thus, Sir, there would be a perpetual struggle for precedence, were there no fixed invariable rules for the distinction of rank, which creates no jealousy, as it is allowed to be accidental."

He said, Dr. Joseph Warton was a very agreeable man, and his *Essay on the Genius and Writings of Pope,* a very pleasing book. I wondered that he delayed so long to give us the continuation of it. JOHNSON. "Why, Sir, I suppose he finds himself a little disappointed, in not having been able to persuade the world to be of his opinion as to Pope."

We have now been favoured with the concluding volume, in which, to use a parliamentary expression, he has *explained,* so as not to appear quite so adverse to the opinion of the world, concerning Pope, as was at first thought; and we must all agree that his work is a most valuable accession to English literature.

A writer of deserved eminence being mentioned, Johnson said, "Why, Sir, he is a man of good parts, but being originally poor, he has got a love of mean company and low jocularity; a very bad thing, Sir. To laugh

is good, as to talk is good. But you ought no more to think it enough if you laugh, than you are to think it enough if you talk. You may laugh in as many ways as you talk; and surely *every* way of talking that is practised cannot be esteemed."

I spoke of Sir James Macdonald as a young man of most distinguished merit, who united the highest reputation at Eton and Oxford, with the patriarchal spirit of a great Highland Chieftain. I mentioned that Sir James had said to me, that he had never seen Mr. Johnson, but he had a great respect for him, though at the same time it was mixed with some degree of terror. JOHNSON. "Sir, if he were to be acquainted with me, it might lessen both."

The mention of this gentleman led us to talk of the Western Islands of Scotland, to visit which he expressed a wish that then appeared to me a very romantic fancy, which I little thought would be afterwards realized. He told me, that his father had put Martin's account of those islands into his hands when he was very young, and that he was highly pleased with it; that he was particularly struck with the St. Kilda man's notion that the high church of Glasgow had been hollowed out of a rock; a circumstance to which old Mr. Johnson had directed his attention. He said he would go to the Hebrides with me, when I returned from my travels, unless some very good companion should offer when I was absent, which he did not think probable; adding, "There are few people to whom I take so much to as you." And when I talked of my leaving England, he said with a very affectionate air, "My dear Boswell, I should be very unhappy at parting, did I think we were not to meet again." I cannot too often remind my readers, that although such instances of his kindness are doubtless very flattering to me, yet I hope my recording them will be ascribed to a better motive than to vanity; for they afford unquestionable evidence of his tenderness and complacency, which some, while they were forced to acknowledge his great powers, have been so strenuous to deny.

He maintained that a boy at school was the happiest of human beings. I supported a different opinion, from which I have never yet varied, that a man is happier; and I enlarged upon the anxiety and sufferings which are endured at school. JOHNSON. "Ah! Sir, a boy's being flogged is not so severe as a man's having the hiss of the world against him. Men have a solicitude about fame; and the greater share they have of it, the more afraid they are of losing it." I silently asked myself, "Is it possible that the great SAMUEL JOHNSON really entertains any such apprehension, and is not confident that his exalted fame is established upon a foundation never to be shaken?"

He this evening drank a bumper to Sir David Dalrymple, "as a man of worth, a scholar, and a wit." "I have (said he) never heard of him except from you; but let him know my opinion of him: for as he does not show himself much in the world, he should have the praise of the few who hear of him."

On Tuesday, July 26, I found Mr. Johnson alone. It was a very wet day, and I again complained of the disagreeable effects of such weather. JOHNSON. "Sir, this is all imagination, which physicians encourage; for man lives in air, as a fish lives in water; so that if the atmosphere press heavy from above, there is an equal resistance from below. To be sure, bad weather is hard upon people who are obliged to be abroad; and men cannot labour so well in the open air in bad weather, as in good; but, Sir, a smith or a tailor, whose work is within doors, will surely do as much in rainy weather, as in fair. Some very delicate frames, indeed, may be affected by wet weather; but not common constitutions."

We talked of the education of children; and I asked him what he thought was best to teach them first. JOHNSON. "Sir, it is no matter what you teach them first, any more than what leg you shall put into your breeches first. Sir, you may stand disputing which is best to put in first, but in the mean time your breech is bare. Sir, while you are considering which of two things you should teach your child first, another boy has learnt them both."

On Thursday, July 28, we again supped in private at the Turk's Head coffee-house. JOHNSON. "Swift has a higher reputation than he deserves. His excellence is strong sense; for his humour, though very well, is not remarkably good. I doubt whether *The Tale of a Tub* be his; for he never owned it, and it is much above his usual manner.

"Thomson, I think, had as much of the poet about him as most writers. Every thing appeared to him through the medium of his favourite pursuit. He could not have viewed those two candles burning but with a poetical eye."

"Has not —— a great deal of wit, Sir?" JOHNSON. "I do not think so, Sir. He is, indeed, continually attempting wit, but he fails. And I have no more pleasure in hearing a man attempting wit and failing, than in seeing a man trying to leap over a ditch and tumbling into it."

He laughed heartily, when I mentioned to him a saying of his concerning Mr. Thomas Sheridan, which Foote took a wicked pleasure to circulate. "Why, Sir, Sherry is dull, naturally dull; but it must have taken him a great deal of pains to become what we now see him. Such an excess of stupidity, Sir, is not in Nature." "So (said he,) I allowed him all his own merit."

He now added, "Sheridan cannot bear me. I bring his declamation to a point. I ask him a plain question, 'What do you mean to teach?' Besides, Sir, what influence can Mr. Sheridan have upon the languages of this great country, by his narrow exertions? Sir, it is burning a farthing candle at Dover, to show light at Calais."

Talking of a young man who was uneasy from thinking that he was very deficient in learning and knowledge, he said, "A man has no reason to complain who holds a middle place, and has many below him; and perhaps he has not six of his years above him;— perhaps not one. Though he may not know any thing perfectly, the general mass of knowledge that he has acquired is considerable. Time will do for him all that is wanting."

The conversation then took a philosophical turn. JOHNSON. "Human experience, which is constantly contradicting theory, is the great test of truth. A system, built upon the discoveries of a great many minds, is always of more strength, than what is produced by the mere workings of any one mind, which, of itself, can do little. There is not so poor a book in the world that would not be a prodigious effort were it wrought out entirely by a single mind, without the aid of prior investigators. The French writers are superficial; because they are not scholars, and so proceed upon the mere power of their own minds; and we see how very little power they have."

"As to the Christian religion, Sir, besides the strong evidence which we have for it, there is a balance in its favour from the number of great men who have been convinced of its truth, after a serious consideration of the question. Grotius was an acute man, a lawyer, a man accustomed to examine evidence, and he was convinced. Grotius was not a recluse, but a man of the world, who certainly had no bias to the side of religion. Sir Isaac Newton set out an infidel, and came to be a very firm believer."

He this evening again recommended to me to perambulate Spain. I said it would amuse him to get a letter from me dated at Salamancha. JOHNSON. "I love the University of Salamancha; for when the Spaniards were in doubt as to the lawfulness of

their conquering America, the University of Salamancha gave it as their opinion that it was not lawful." He spoke this with great emotion, and with that generous warmth which dictated the lines in his *London*, against Spanish encroachment.

. . . .

I again begged his advice as to my method of study at Utrecht. "Come, (said he) let us make a day of it. Let us go down to Greenwich and dine, and talk of it there." The following Saturday was fixed for this excursion.

As we walked along the Strand tonight arm in arm, a woman of the town accosted us, in the usual enticing manner. "No, no, my girl, (said Johnson) it won't do." He, however, did not treat her with harshness, and we talked of the wretched life of such women; and agreed, that much more misery than happiness, upon the whole, is produced by illicit commerce between the sexes.

On Saturday, July 30, Dr. Johnson and I took a sculler at the Temple-stairs, and set out for Greenwich. I asked him if he really thought a knowledge of the Greek and Latin languages an essential requisite to a good education. JOHNSON. "Most certainly, Sir; for those who know them have a very great advantage over those who do not. Nay, Sir, it is wonderful what a difference learning makes upon people even in the common intercourse of life, which does not appear to be much connected with it." "And yet, (said I) people go through the world very well, and carry on the business of life to good advantage, without learning." JOHNSON. "Why, Sir, that may be true in cases where learning cannot possibly be of any use; for instance, this boy rows us as well without learning, as if he could sing the song of Orpheus to the Argonauts, who were the first sailors." He then called to the boy, "What would you give, my lad, to know about the Argonauts?" "Sir, (said the boy,) I would give what I have." Johnson was much pleased with his answer, and we gave him a double fare. Dr. Johnson then turning to me, "Sir (said he) a desire of knowledge is the natural feeling of mankind; and every human being, whose mind is not debauched, will be willing to give all that he has to get knowledge."

We landed at the Old Swan, and walked to Billingsgate, where we took oars, and moved smoothly along the silver Thames. It was a very fine day. We were entertained with the immense number and variety of ships that were lying at anchor, and with the beautiful country on each side of the river.

I talked of preaching, and of the great success which those called Methodists have. JOHNSON. "Sir, it is owing to their expressing themselves in a plain and familiar manner, which is the only way to do good to the common people, and which clergymen of genius and learning ought to do from a principle of duty, when it is suited to their congregations; a practice for which they will be praised by men of sense. To insist against drunkenness as a crime, because it debases reason, the noblest faculty of man, would be of no service to the common people: but to tell them that they may die in a fit of drunkenness, and show them how dreadful that would be, cannot fail to make a deep impression. Sir, when your Scotch clergy give up their homely manner, religion will soon decay in that country." Let this observation, as Johnson meant it, be ever remembered.

I was much pleased to find myself with Johnson at Greenwich, which he celebrates in his *London* as a favourite scene. I had the poem in my pocket, and read the lines aloud with enthusiasm:

"On Thames's banks in silent thought we
    stood:
Where Greenwich smiles upon the silver
    flood:
Pleas'd with the seat which gave ELIZA birth,
We kneel, and kiss the consecrated earth."

He remarked that the structure of Greenwich hospital was too magnificent for a place of charity, and that its parts were too much detached to make one great whole.

Buchanan, he said, was a very fine poet; and observed, that he was the first who complimented a lady, by ascribing to her the different perfections of the heathen goddesses; but that Johnston improved upon this, by making his lady, at the same time, free from their defects.

He dwelt upon Buchanan's elegant verses to Mary Queen of Scots, *Nympha Caledoniæ*, &c., and spoke with enthusiasm of the beauty of Latin verse. "All the modern languages (said he) cannot furnish so melodious a line as

"Formosam resonare doces Amarillida silvas."

Afterwards he entered upon the business of the day, which was to give me his advice as to a course of study. And here I am to mention with much regret, that my record of what he said is miserably scanty. I recollect with admiration an animating blaze of eloquence, which roused every intellectual power in me to the highest pitch, but must have dazzled me so much, that my memory could not preserve the substance of his discourse; for the note which I find of it is no more than this:—"He ran over the grand scale of human knowledge; advised me to select some particular branch to excel in, but to acquire a little of every kind." The defect of my minutes will be fully supplied by a long letter upon the subject which he favoured me with, after I had been some time at Utrecht, and which my readers will have the pleasure to peruse in its proper place.

We walked in the evening in Greenwich Park. He asked me, I suppose, by way of trying my disposition, "Is not this very fine?" Having no exquisite relish of the beauties of Nature, and being more delighted with "the busy hum of men," I answered,

"Yes, Sir; but not equal to Fleet-street." JOHNSON. "You are right, Sir."

I am aware that many of my readers may censure my want of taste. Let me, however, shelter myself under the authority of a very fashionable baronet in the brilliant world, who, on his attention being called to the fragrance of a May evening in the country, observed, "This may be very well; but, for my part, I prefer the smell of a flambeau at the playhouse."

We staid so long at Greenwich, that our sail up the river, in our return to London, was by no means so pleasant as in the morning; for the night air was so cold that it made me shiver. I was the more sensible of it from having sat up all the night before, recollecting and writing in my journal what I thought worthy of preservation; an exertion, which, during the first part of my acquaintance with Johnson, I frequently made. I remember having sat up four nights in one week, without being much incommoded in the day time.

Johnson, whose robust frame was not in the least affected by the cold, scolded me, as if my shivering had been a paltry effeminacy, saying, "Why do you shiver?" Sir William Scott, of the Commons, told me, that when he complained of a head-ache in the post-chaise, as they were travelling together to Scotland, Johnson treated him in the same manner: "At your age, Sir, I had no head-ache." It is not easy to make allowance for sensations in others, which we ourselves have not at the time. We must all have experienced how very differently we are affected by the complaints of our neighbours, when we are well and when we are ill. In full health, we can scarcely believe that they suffer much; so faint is the image of pain upon our imagination: when softened by sickness, we readily sympathize with the sufferings of others.

We concluded the day at the Turk's Head coffee-house very socially. He was pleased to listen to a particular account which I gave him of my fam-ily, and of its hereditary estate, as to the extent and population of which he asked questions, and made calculations; recommending, at the same time, a liberal kindness to the tenantry, as people over whom the proprietor was placed by Providence. He took delight in hearing my description of the romantic seat of my ancestors. "I must be there, Sir, (said he) and we will live in the old castle; and if there is not a room in it remaining, we will build one." I was highly flattered, but could scarcely indulge a hope that Auchinleck would indeed be honoured by his presence, and celebrated by a description, as it afterwards was, in his *Journey to the Western Islands*.

After we had again talked of my setting out for Holland, he said, "I must see thee out of England; I will accompany you to Harwich." I could not find words to express what I felt upon this unexpected and very great mark of his affectionate regard.

Next day, Sunday, July 31, I told him I had been that morning at a meeting of the people called Quakers, where I had heard a woman preach. JOHNSON. "Sir, a woman's preaching is like a dog's walking on his hinder legs. It is not done well; but you are surprised to find it done at all."

On Tuesday, August 2 (the day of my departure from London having been fixed for the 5th,) Dr. Johnson did me the honour to pass a part of the morning with me at my chambers. He said, that "he always felt an inclination to do nothing." I observed, that it was strange to think that the most indolent man in Britain had written the most laborious work, *The English Dictionary*.

I mentioned an imprudent publication, by a certain friend of his, at an early period of life, and asked him if he thought it would hurt him. JOHNSON. "No, Sir; not much. It may, perhaps, be mentioned at an election."

I had now made good my title to be a privileged man, and was carried by him in the evening to drink tea with Miss Williams, whom, though under the misfortune of having lost her sight, I found to be agreeable in conversation; for she had a variety of literature, and expressed herself well; but her peculiar value was the intimacy in which she had long lived with Johnson, by which she was well acquainted with his habits, and knew how to lead him on to talk.

After tea he carried me to what he called his walk, which was a long narrow paved court in the neighbourhood, overshadowed by some trees. There we sauntered a considerable time; and I complained to him that my love of London and of his company was such, that I shrunk almost from the thought of going away, even to travel, which is generally so much desired by young men. He roused me by manly and spirited conversation. He advised me, when settled in any place abroad, to study with an eagerness after knowledge, and to apply to Greek an hour every day; and when I was moving about, to read diligently the great book of mankind.

On Wednesday, August 3, we had our last social evening at the Turk's Head coffee-house, before my setting out for foreign parts. I had the misfortune, before we parted, to irritate him unintentionally. I mentioned to him how common it was in the world to tell absurd stories of him, and to ascribe to him very strange sayings. JOHNSON. "What do they make me say, Sir?" BOSWELL. "Why, Sir, as an instance very strange indeed, (laughing heartily as I spoke,) David Hume told me, you said that you would stand before a battery of cannon, to restore the Convocation to its full powers." Little did I apprehend that he had actually said this: but I was soon convinced of my error; for, with a determined look, he thundered out "And would I not, Sir? Shall the Presbyterian *Kirk* of Scotland have its General Assembly, and the Church of England be denied its Convocation?" He was walking up and down the room while I told him the anecdote; but when he uttered this explosion of

high-church zeal, he had come close to my chair, and his eyes flashed with indignation. I bowed to the storm, and diverted the force of it, by leading him to expatiate on the influence which religion derived from maintaining the church with great external respectability.

I must not omit to mention that he this year wrote *The Life of Ascham*, and the Dedication to the Earl of Shaftesbury, prefixed to the edition of that writer's English works, published by Mr. Bennet.

On Friday, August 5, we set out early in the morning in the Harwich stage coach. A fat elderly gentlewoman, and a young Dutchman, seemed the most inclined among us to conversation. At the inn where we dined, the gentlewoman said that she had done her best to educate her children; and particularly, that she had never suffered them to be a moment idle. JOHNSON. "I wish, madam, you would educate me too; for I have been an idle fellow all my life." "I am sure, Sir, (said she) you have not been idle." JOHNSON. "Nay, madam, it is very true; and that gentleman there (pointing to me,) has been idle. He was idle at Edinburgh. His father sent him to Glasgow, where he continued to be idle. He then came to London, where he has been very idle; and now he is going to Utrecht, where he will be as idle as ever." I asked him privately how he could expose me so. JOHNSON. "Poh, poh! (said he) they knew nothing about you, and will think of it no more." In the afternoon the gentlewoman talked violently against the Roman Catholics, and of the horrors of the Inquisition. To the utter astonishment of all the passengers but myself, who knew that he could talk upon any side of a question, he defended the Inquisition, and maintained, that "false doctrine should be checked on its first appearance; that the civil power should unite with the church in punishing those who dared to attack the established religion, and that such only were punished by the Inquisition." He had in his pocket *Pomponius Mela de situ Orbis,* in which he read occasionally, and seemed very intent upon ancient geography. Though by no means niggardly, his attention to what was generally right was so minute, that having observed at one of the stages that I ostentatiously gave a shilling to the coachman, when the custom was for each passenger to give only six-pence, he took me aside and scolded me, saying that what I had done would make the coachman dissatisfied with all the rest of the passengers, who gave him no more than his due. This was a just reprimand; for in whatever way a man may indulge his generosity or his vanity in spending his money, for the sake of others he ought not to raise the price of any article for which there is a constant demand.

He talked of Mr. Blacklock's poetry, so far as it was descriptive of visible objects; and observed, that "as its author had the misfortune to be blind, we may be absolutely sure that such passages are combinations of what he has remembered of the works of other writers who could see. That foolish fellow, Spence, has laboured to explain philosophically how Blacklock may have done, by means of his own faculties, what it is impossible he should do. The solution, as I have given it, is plain. Suppose, I know a man to be so lame that he is absolutely incapable to move himself, and I find him in a different room from that in which I left him; shall I puzzle myself with idle conjectures, that, perhaps, his nerves have by some unknown change all at once become effective? No, Sir; it is clear how he got into a different room: he was *carried.*"

Having stopped a night at Colchester, Johnson talked of that town with veneration, for having stood a siege for Charles the First. The Dutchman alone now remained with us. He spoke English tolerably well; and thinking to recommend himself to us by expatiating on the superiority of the criminal jurisprudence of this country over that of Holland, he inveighed against the barbarity of putting an accused person to the torture, in order to force a confession. But Johnson was as ready for this, as for the Inquisition. "Why, Sir, you do not, I find, understand the law of your own country. The torture in Holland is considered as a favour to an accused person; for no man is put to the torture there, unless there is as much evidence against him as would amount to conviction in England. An accused person among you, therefore, has one chance more to escape punishment, than those who are tried among us."

At supper this night he talked of good eating with uncommon satisfaction. "Some people (said he,) have a foolish way of not minding, or pretending not to mind, what they eat. For my part, I mind my belly very studiously, and very carefully; for I look upon it, that he who does not mind his belly will hardly mind anything else." He now appeared to me *Jean Bull philosophe,* and he was, for the moment, not only serious but vehement. Yet I have heard him, upon other occasions, talk with great contempt of people who were anxious to gratify their palates; and the 206th number of his *Rambler* is a masterly essay against gulosity. His practice, indeed, I must acknowledge, may be considered as casting the balance of his different opinions upon this subject; for I never knew any man who relished good eating more than he did. When at table, he was totally absorbed in the business of the moment; his looks seemed riveted to his plate; nor would he, unless when in very high company, say one word, or even pay the least attention to what was said by others, till he had satisfied his appetite, which was so fierce, and indulged with such intenseness, that while in the act of eating, the veins of his forehead swelled, and generally a strong perspiration was visible. To those whose sensations were delicate, this could not but be disgusting; and it was doubtless not very suitable to the character of a philosopher, who should be distinguished by self-command. But it must be owned, that Johnson, though he could be rigidly abstemious, was not a *temperate* man either in eating or drinking. He could refrain, but he could not use moderately. He told me, that he had fasted two days without inconvenience, and that he had never been hungry but once. They who beheld with wonder how much he eat upon all occasions when his dinner was to his taste, could not easily conceive what he must have meant by hunger; and not only was he remarkable for the extraordinary quantity which he eat, but he was, or affected to be, a man of very nice discernment in the science of cookery. He used to descant critically on the dishes which had been at table where he had dined or supped, and to recollect very minutely what he had liked. I remember, when he was in Scotland, his praising *"Gordon's palates,"* (a dish of palates at the Honourable Alexander Gordon's) with a warmth of expression which might have done honour to more important subjects. "As for Maclaurin's imitation of a *made dish*, it was a wretched attempt." He about the same time was so much displeased with the performances of a nobleman's French cook, that he exclaimed with vehemence, "I'd throw such a rascal into the river"; and he then proceeded to alarm a lady at whose house he was to sup, by the following manifesto of his skill: "I, Madam, who live at a variety of good tables, am a much better judge of cookery, than any person who has a very tolerable cook, but lives much at home; for his palate is gradually adapted to the taste of his cook; whereas, Madam, in trying by a wider range, I can more exquisitely judge." When invited to dine, even with an intimate friend, he was not pleased if something better than a plain dinner was not prepared for him. I have heard him say on such an occasion,

"This was a good dinner enough, to be sure; but it was not a dinner to *ask* a man to." On the other hand, he was wont to express, with great glee, his satisfaction when he had been entertained quite to his mind. One day when we had dined with his neighbour and landlord in Bolt-court, Mr. Allen, the printer, whose old housekeeper had studied his taste in every thing, he pronounced this eulogy: "Sir, we could not have had a better dinner had there been a *Synod of Cooks.*"

While we were left by ourselves, after the Dutchman had gone to bed, Dr. Johnson talked of that studied behaviour which many have recommended and practised. He disapproved of it; and said, "I never considered whether I should be a grave man, or a merry man, but just let inclination, for the time, have its course."

He flattered me with some hopes that he would, in the course of the following summer, come over to Holland, and accompany me in a tour through the Netherlands.

I teased him with fanciful apprehensions of unhappiness. A moth having fluttered round the candle, and burnt itself, he laid hold of this little incident to admonish me; saying, with a sly look, and in a solemn but quiet tone, "That creature was its own tormentor, and I believe its name was BOSWELL."

Next day we got to Harwich to dinner; and my passage in the packet-boat to Helvoetsluys being secured, and my baggage put on board, we dined at our inn by ourselves. I happened to say it would be terrible if he should not find a speedy opportunity of returning to London, and be confined to so dull a place. JOHNSON. "Don't, Sir, accustom yourself to use big words for little matters. It would *not* be *terrible*, though I *were* to be detained some time here." The practice of using words of disproportionate magnitude, is, no doubt, too frequent every where; but, I think, most re-markable among the French, of which, all who have travelled in France must have been struck with innumerable instances.

We went and looked at the church, and having gone into it and walked up to the altar, Johnson, whose piety was constant and fervent, sent me to my knees, saying "Now that you are going to leave your native country, recommend yourself to the protection of your CREATOR and REDEEMER."

After we came out of the church, we stood talking for some time to-gether of Bishop Berkeley's ingenious sophistry to prove the non-existence of matter, and that every thing in the universe is merely ideal. I observed, that though we are satisfied his doc-trine is not true, it is impossible to refute it. I shall never forget the alacrity with which Johnson answered, striking his foot with mighty force against a large stone, till he re-bounded from it, "I refute it *thus*." This was a stout exemplification of the *first truths* of Père Bouffier, or the *original principles* of Reid and of Beattie; without admitting which, we can no more argue in metaphysics, than we can argue in mathematics without axioms. To me it is not con-ceivable how Berkeley can be an-swered by pure reasoning; but I know that the nice and difficult task was to have been undertaken by one of the most luminous minds of the present age, had not politics "turned him from calm philosophy aside." What an ad-mirable display of subtilty, united with brilliance, might his contending with Berkeley have afforded us! How must we, when we reflect on the loss of such an intellectual feast, regret that he should be characterized as the man,

"Who born for the universe narrow'd his mind,
And to party gave up what was meant for mankind?"

My revered friend walked down with me to the beach, where we em-braced and parted with tenderness.

and engaged to correspond by letters. I said, "I hope, Sir, you will not forget me in my absence." JOHNSON. "Nay, Sir, it is more likely you should forget me, than that I should forget you." As the vessel put out to sea, I kept my eyes upon him for a considerable time, while he remained rolling his majestic frame in his usual manner: and at last I perceived him walk back into the town, and he disappeared.

. . . . .

From the Year 1766: Ætat. 57.

I returned to London in February, and found Dr. Johnson in a good house in Johnson's Court, Fleet-street, in which he had accommodated Miss Williams with an apartment on the ground floor, while Mr. Levet occu-pied his post in the garret: his faith-ful Francis was still attending upon him. He received me with much kind-ness. The fragments of our first con-versation, which I have preserved, are these: I told him that Voltaire, in a conversation with me, had distin-guished Pope and Dryden thus:— "Pope drives a handsome chariot, with a couple of neat trim nags; Dryden a coach, and six stately horses." JOHN-SON. "Why, Sir, the truth is, they both drive coaches and six; but Dryden's horses are either galloping or stum-bling: Pope's go at a steady even trot." He said of Goldsmith's *Traveller*, which had been published in my ab-sence, "There has not been so fine a poem since Pope's time."

And here it is proper to settle, with authentic precision, what has long floated in public report, as to John-son's being himself the author of a considerable part of that poem. Much no doubt, both of the sentiments and expression, were derived from conver-sation with him; and it was certainly submitted to his friendly revision: but in the year 1783, he, at my re-quest, marked with a pencil the lines which he had furnished, which are only line 420th,

"To stop too fearful, and too faint to go";

and the concluding ten lines, except the last couplet but one, which I distinguish by the Italic character:

"How small of all that human hearts endure,
That part which kings or laws can cause or cure.
Still to ourselves in every place consign'd,
Our own felicity we make or find;
With secret course, which no loud storms annoy,
Glides the smooth current of domestic joy:
The lifted axe, the agonizing wheel,
Luke's iron crown, and Damien's bed of steel,
To men remote from power, but rarely known,
Leave reason, faith, and conscience, all our own."

He added, "These are all of which I can be sure." They bear a small proportion to the whole, which consists of four hundred and thirty-eight verses. Goldsmith, in the couplet which he inserted, mentions *Luke* as a person well known, and superficial readers have passed it over quite smoothly; while those of more attention have been as much perplexed by *Luke*, as by *Lydiat*, in *The Vanity of Human Wishes.* The truth is, that Goldsmith himself was in a mistake. In the *Respublica Hungarica*, there is an account of a desperate rebellion in the year 1514, headed by two brothers, of the name of *Zeck*, George and Luke. When it was quelled, *George*, not *Luke*, was punished by his head being encircled with a red-hot iron crown: "*coroná candescente ferreá coronatur.*" The same severity of torture was exercised on the Earl of Athol, one of the murderers of King James I, of Scotland.

Dr. Johnson at the same time favoured me by marking the lines which he furnished to Goldsmith's *Deserted Village*, which are only the last four:

"That trade's proud empire hastes to swift decay,
As ocean sweeps the labour'd mole away:
While self-dependent power can time defy,
As rocks resist the billows and the sky."

Talking of education, "People have now a-days, (said he,) got a strange opinion that every thing should be taught by lectures. Now, I cannot see that lectures can do so much good as reading the books from which the lectures are taken. I know nothing that can be best taught by lectures, except where experiments are to be shown. You may teach chemistry by lectures. —You might teach making of shoes by lectures!"

At night I supped with him at the Mitre tavern, that we might renew our social intimacy at the original place of meeting. But there was now a considerable difference in his way of living. Having had an illness, in which he was advised to leave off wine, he had, from that period, continued to abstain from it, and drank only water, or lemonade.

I told him that a foreign friend of his, whom I had met with abroad, was so wretchedly perverted to infidelity, that he treated the hopes of immortality with brutal levity; and said, "As man dies like a dog, let him lie like a dog." JOHNSON. "*If* he dies like a dog, *let* him lie like a dog." I added, that this man said to me, "I hate mankind, for I think myself one of the best of them, and I know how bad I am." JOHNSON. "Sir, he must be very singular in his opinion, if he thinks himself one of the best of men; for none of his friends think him so."—He said, "no honest man could be a Deist; for no man could be so after a fair examination of the proofs of Christianity." I named Hume. JOHNSON. "No, Sir; Hume owned to a clergyman in the bishopric of Durham, that he had never read the New Testament with attention." I mentioned Hume's notion, that all who are happy are equally happy; a little miss with a new gown at a dancing school ball, a general at the head of a victorious army, and an orator, after having made an eloquent speech in a great assembly. JOHNSON. "Sir, that all who are happy, are equally happy, is not true. A peasant and a philosopher may be equally *satisfied*, but not equally *happy.* Happiness consists in the multiplicity of agreeable consciousness. A peasant has not capacity for having equal happiness with a philosopher." I remember this very question very happily illustrated in opposition to Hume, by the Reverend Mr. Robert Brown, at Utrecht. "A small drinking-glass and a large one, (said he,) may be equally full; but the large one holds more than the small."

Dr. Johnson was very kind this evening, and said to me, "You have now lived five-and-twenty years, and you have employed them well." "Alas, Sir, (said I,) I fear not. Do I know history? Do I know mathematics? Do I know law?" JOHNSON. "Why, Sir, though you may know no science so well as to be able to teach it, and no profession so well as to be able to follow it, your general mass of knowledge of books and men renders you very capable to make yourself master of any science, or fit yourself for any profession." I mentioned that a gay friend had advised me against being a lawyer, because I should be excelled by plodding block-heads. JOHNSON. "Why, Sir, in the formulary and statutory part of law, a plodding block-head may excel; but in the ingenious and rational part of it a plodding block-head can never excel."

I talked of the mode adopted by some to rise in the world, by courting great men, and asked him whether he had ever submitted to it. JOHNSON. "Why, Sir, I never was near enough to great men, to court them. You may be prudently attached to great men and yet independent. You are not to do what you think wrong; and, Sir, you are to calculate, and not pay too dear for what you get. You must not give a shilling's worth of court for sixpence worth of good. But if you can get a shilling's worth of good for sixpence worth of court, you are a fool if you do not pay court."

He said, "If convents should be allowed at all, they should only be retreats for persons unable to serve the public, or who have served it. It is our first duty to serve society, and, after we have done that, we may attend wholly to the salvation of our own souls. A youthful passion for abstracted devotion should not be encouraged."

I introduced the subject of second sight, and other mysterious manifestations; the fulfilment of which, I suggested, might happen by chance. JOHNSON. "Yes, Sir; but they have happened so often, that mankind have agreed to think them not fortuitous."

I talked to him a great deal of what I had seen in Corsica, and of my intention to publish an account of it. He encouraged me by saying, "You cannot go to the bottom of the subject; but all that you tell us will be new to us. Give us as many anecdotes as you can."

Our next meeting at the Mitre was on Saturday the 15th of February, when I presented to him my old and most intimate friend, the Reverend Mr. Temple, then of Cambridge. I having mentioned that I had passed some time with Rousseau in his wild retreat, and having quoted some remark made by Mr. Wilkes, with whom I had spent many pleasant hours in Italy, Johnson said (sarcastically,) "It seems, Sir, you have kept very good company abroad, Rousseau and Wilkes!" Thinking it enough to defend one at a time, I said nothing as to my gay friend, but answered with a smile, "My dear Sir, you don't call Rousseau bad company. Do you really think him a bad man?" JOHNSON. "Sir, if you are talking jestingly of this, I don't talk with you. If you mean to be serious, I think him one of the worst of men; a rascal who ought to be hunted out of society, as he has been. Three or four nations have expelled him; and it is a shame that he is protected in this country." BOSWELL. "I don't deny, Sir, but that his novel may, perhaps, do harm; but I cannot think his intention was bad." JOHNSON. "Sir, that will not do. We cannot prove any man's intention to be bad. You may shoot a man through the head, and say you intended to miss him; but the Judge will order you to be hanged. An alleged want of intention, when evil is committed, will not be allowed in a court of justice. Rousseau, Sir, is a very bad man. I would sooner sign a sentence for his transportation, than that of any felon who has gone from the Old Bailey these many years. Yes, I should like to have him work in the plantations." BOSWELL. "Sir, do you think him as bad a man as Voltaire?" JOHNSON. "Why, Sir, it is difficult to settle the proportion of iniquity between them."

This violence seemed very strange to me, who had read many of Rousseau's animated writings with great pleasure, and even edification; had been much pleased with his society, and was just come from the Continent, where he was very generally admired. Nor can I yet allow that he deserves the very severe censure which Johnson pronounced upon him. His absurd preference of savage to civilized life, and other singularities, are proofs rather of a defect in his understanding, than of any depravity in his heart. And notwithstanding the unfortunate opinion which many worthy men have expressed of his *"Profession de Foi du Vicaire Savoyard,"* I cannot help admiring it as the performance of a man full of sincere reverential submission to Divine Mystery, though beset with perplexing doubts; a state of mind to be viewed with pity rather than with anger.

On his favourite subject of subordination, Johnson said, "So far is it from being true that men are naturally equal, that no two people can be half an hour together, but one shall acquire an evident superiority over the other."

I mentioned the advice given us by philosophers, to console ourselves, when distressed or embarrassed, by thinking of those who are in a worse situation than ourselves. This, I observed, could not apply to all, for there must be some who have nobody worse than they are. JOHNSON. "Why, to be sure, Sir, there are; but they don't know it. There is no being so poor and so contemptible, who does

not think there is somebody still poorer, and still more contemptible."

As my stay in London at this time was very short, I had not many opportunities of being with Dr. Johnson; but I felt my veneration for him in no degree lessened, by my having seen *multorum hominum mores et urbes.* On the contrary, by having it in my power to compare him with many of the most celebrated persons of other countries, my admiration of his extraordinary mind was increased and confirmed.

The roughness, indeed, which sometimes appeared in his manners, was more striking to me now, from my having been accustomed to the studied smooth complying habits of the Continent; and I clearly recognized in him, not without respect for his honest conscientious zeal, the same indignant and sarcastical mode of treating every attempt to unhinge or weaken good principles.

One evening when a young gentleman teased him with an account of the infidelity of his servant, who, he said, would not believe the scriptures, because he could not read them in the original tongues, and be sure that they were not invented, "Why, foolish fellow, (said Johnson,) has he any better authority for almost every thing that he believes?" BOSWELL. "Then the vulgar, Sir, never can know they are right, but must submit themselves to the learned." JOHNSON. "To be sure, Sir. The vulgar are the children of the State, and must be taught like children." BOSWELL. "Then, Sir, a poor Turk must be a Mahometan, just as a poor Englishman must be a Christian?" JOHNSON. "Why, yes, Sir; and what then? This now is such stuff as I used to talk to my mother, when I first began to think myself a clever fellow; and she ought to have whipped me for it."

Another evening Dr. Goldsmith and I called on him, with the hope of prevailing on him to sup with us at the Mitre. We found him indisposed, and resolved not to go abroad. "Come then (said Goldsmith,) we will not go to the Mitre to-night, since we cannot have the big man with us." Johnson then called for a bottle of port, of which Goldsmith and I partook, while our friend, now a water-drinker, sat by us. GOLDSMITH. "I think, Mr. Johnson, you don't go near the theatres now. You give yourself no more concern about a new play, than if you had never had any thing to do with the stage." JOHNSON. "Why, Sir, our tastes greatly alter. The lad does not care for the child's rattle, and the old man does not care for the young man's whore." GOLDSMITH. "Nay, Sir, but your Muse was not a whore." JOHNSON. "Sir, I do not think she was. But as we advance in the journey of life, we drop some of the things which have pleased us; whether it be that we are fatigued and don't choose to carry so many things any farther, or that we find other things which we like better." BOSWELL. "But, Sir, why don't you give us something in some other way?" GOLDSMITH. "Ay, Sir, we have a claim upon you." JOHNSON. "No, Sir, I am not obliged to do any more. No man is obliged to do as much as he can do. A man is to have part of his life to himself. If a soldier has fought a good many campaigns, he is not to be blamed if he retires to ease and tranquillity. A physician, who has practised long in a great city, may be excused if he retires to a small town, and takes less practice. Now, Sir, the good I can do by my conversation bears the same proportion to the good I can do by my writings, that the practice of a physician, retired to a small town, does to his practice in a great city." BOSWELL. "But I wonder, Sir, you have not more pleasure in writing than in not writing." JOHNSON. "Sir, you *may* wonder."

He talked of making verses, and observed, "The great difficulty is to know when you have made good ones. When composing, I have generally had them in my mind, perhaps fifty at a time, walking up and down in my room; and then I have written them down,

and often, from laziness, have written only half lines. I have written a hundred lines in a day. I remember I wrote a hundred lines of *The Vanity of Human Wishes* in a day. Doctor, (turning to Goldsmith,) I am not quite idle; I made one line t'other day; but I made no more." GOLDSMITH. "Let us hear it; we'll put a bad one to it." JOHNSON. "No, Sir, I have forgot it."

Such specimens of the easy and playful conversation of the great Dr. Samuel Johnson are, I think, to be prized; as exhibiting the little varieties of a mind so enlarged and so powerful when objects of consequence required its exertions, and as giving us a minute knowledge of his character and modes of thinking.

. . . .

From the year 1767: Ætat. 58.

In February, 1767, there happened one of the most remarkable incidents of Johnson's life, which gratified his monarchical enthusiasm, and which he loved to relate with all its circumstances, when requested by his friends. This was his being honoured by a private conversation with his Majesty, in the library at the Queen's house. He had frequently visited those splendid rooms and noble collection of books, which he used to say was more numerous and curious than he supposed any person could have made in the time which the King had employed. Mr. Barnard, the librarian, took care that he should have every accommodation that could contribute to his ease and convenience, while indulging his literary taste in that place; so that he had here a very agreeable resource at leisure hours.

His Majesty having been informed of his occasional visits, was pleased to signify a desire that he should be told when Dr. Johnson came next to the library. Accordingly, the next time that Johnson did come, as soon as he was fairly engaged with a book, on which, while he sat by the fire, he seemed quite intent, Mr. Barnard stole round to the apartment where the King was, and, in obedience to his Majesty's commands, mentioned that Dr. Johnson was then in the library. His Majesty said he was at leisure, and would go to him; upon which Mr. Barnard took one of the candles that stood on the King's table, and lighted his Majesty through a suite of rooms, till they came to a private door into the library, of which his Majesty had the key. Being entered, Mr. Barnard stepped forward hastily to Dr. Johnson, who waᶜ still in a profound study, and whispered him, "Sir, here is the King." Johnson started up, and stood still. His Majesty approached him, and at oncᴇ was courteously easy.

His Majesty began by observing, that he understood he came sometimes to the library; and then mentioning his having heard that the Doctor had been lately at Oxford, asked him if he was not fond of going thither. To which Johnson answered, that he was indeed fond of going to Oxford sometimes, but was likewise glad to come back again. The King then asked him what they were doing at Oxford. Johnson answered, he could not much commend their diligence, but that in some respects they were mended, for they had put their press under better regulations, and were at that time printing Polybius. He was then asked whether there were better libraries at Oxford or Cambridge. He answered, he believed the Bodleian was larger than any they had at Cambridge; at the same time adding, "I hope, whether we have more books or not than they have at Cambridge, we shall make as good use of them as they do." Being asked whether All-Souls or Christ-Church library was the largest, he answered, "All-Souls library is the largest we have, except the Bodleian." "Aye, (said the King,) that is the public library."

His Majesty enquired if he was then writing any thing. He answered, he was not, for he had pretty well told the world what he knew, and must now read to acquire more knowledge. The King, as it should seem with a view to urge him to rely on his own stores as an original writer, and to continue his labours, then said, "I do not think you borrow much from any body." Johnson said, he thought he had already done his part as a writer. "I should have thought so too, (said the King,) if you had not written so well."—Johnson observed to me, upon this, that "No man could have paid a handsomer compliment; and it was fit for a King to pay. It was decisive." When asked by another friend, at Sir Joshua Reynolds's, whether he made any reply to this high compliment, he answered, "No, Sir. When the King had said it, it was to be so. It was not for me to bandy civilities with my Sovereign." Perhaps no man who had spent his whole life in courts could have shown a more nice and dignified sense of true politeness, than Johnson did in this instance.

His Majesty having observed to him that he supposed he must have read a great deal; Johnson answered, that he thought more than he read; that he had read a great deal in the early part of his life, but having fallen into ill health, he had not been able to read much, compared with others: for instance, he said he had not read much, compared with Dr. Warburton. Upon which the King said, that he heard Dr. Warburton was a man of such general knowledge, that you could scarce talk with him on any subject on which he was not qualified to speak; and that his learning resembled Garrick's acting, in its universality. His Majesty then talked of the controversy between Warburton and Lowth, which he seemed to have read, and asked Johnson what he thought of it. Johnson answered, "Warburton has most general, most scholastic learning; Lowth is the more correct scholar. I do not know which of them calls names best." The King was pleased to say he was of the same opinion; adding, "You do not think, then, Dr. Johnson, that there was much argument in the case." Johnson said, he did not think there was. "Why truly, (said the King,) when once it comes to calling names, argument is pretty well at an end."

His Majesty then asked him what he thought of Lord Lyttelton's *History*, which was then just published. Johnson said, he thought his style pretty good, but that he had blamed Henry the Second rather too much. "Why, (said the King,) they seldom do these things by halves." "No, Sir, (answered Johnson,) not to Kings." But fearing to be misunderstood, he proceeded to explain himself; and immediately subjoined, "That for those who spoke worse of Kings than they deserved, he could find no excuse; but that he could more easily conceive how some might speak better of them than they deserved, without any ill intention; for, as Kings had much in their power to give, those who were favoured by them would frequently, from gratitude, exaggerate their praises; and as this proceeded from a good motive, it was certainly excusable, as far as error could be excusable."

The King then asked him what he thought of Dr. Hill. Johnson answered, that he was an ingenious man, but had no veracity; and immediately mentioned, as an instance of it, an assertion of that writer, that he had seen objects magnified to a much greater degree by using three or four microscopes at a time, than by using one. "Now, (added Johnson,) every one acquainted with microscopes knows, that the more of them he looks through, the less the object will appear." "Why (replied the King,) this is not only telling an untruth, but telling it clumsily; for, if that be the case, every one who can look through a microscope will be able to detect him."

"I now, (said Johnson to his friends, when relating what had passed) began to consider that I was depreciating this man in the estimation of his Sovereign, and thought it was time for me to say something that

might be more favourable." He added therefore, that Dr. Hill was, notwithstanding, a very curious observer; and if he would have been contented to tell the world no more than he knew, he might have been a very considerable man, and needed not to have recourse to such mean expedients to raise his reputation.

The King then talked of literary journals, mentioned particularly the *Journal des Savans*, and asked Johnson if it was well done. Johnson said, it was formerly very well done, and gave some account of the persons who began it, and carried it on for some years; enlarging, at the same time, on the nature and use of such works. The King asked him if it was well done now. Johnson answered, he had no reason to think that it was. The King then asked him if there were any other literary journals published in this kingdom, except the *Monthly* and *Critical Reviews*; and on being answered there were no other, his Majesty asked which of them was the best: Johnson answered, that the *Monthly Review* was done with most care, the *Critical* upon the best principles; adding that the authors of the *Monthly Review* were enemies to the Church. This the King said he was sorry to hear.

The conversation next turned on the Philosophical Transactions, when Johnson observed, that they had now a better method of arranging their materials than formerly. "Aye, (said the King,) they are obliged to Dr. Johnson for that"; for his Majesty had heard and remembered the circumstance, which Johnson himself had forgot.

His Majesty expressed a desire to have the literary biography of this country ably executed, and proposed to Dr. Johnson to undertake it. Johnson signified his readiness to comply with his Majesty's wishes.

During the whole of this interview, Johnson talked to his Majesty with profound respect, but still in his firm manly manner, with a sonorous voice, and never in that subdued tone which is commonly used at the levee and in the drawing-room. After the King withdrew, Johnson showed himself highly pleased with his Majesty's conversation, and gracious behaviour. He said to Mr. Barnard, "Sir, they may talk of the King as they will; but he is the finest gentleman I have ever seen." And he afterwards observed to Mr. Langton, "Sir, his manners are those of as fine a gentleman as we may suppose Lewis the Fourteenth or Charles the Second."

At Sir Joshua Reynolds's, where a circle of Johnson's friends was collected round him to hear his account of this memorable conversation, Dr. Joseph Warton, in his frank and lively manner, was very active in pressing him to mention the particulars. "Come now, Sir, this is an interesting matter; do favour us with it." Johnson, with great good humour, complied.

He told them, "I found his Majesty wished I should talk, and I made it my business to talk. I find it does a man good to be talked to by his Sovereign. In the first place, a man cannot be in a passion—." Here some question interrupted him, which is to be regretted, as he certainly would have pointed out and illustrated many circumstances of advantage, from being in a situation, where the powers of the mind are at once excited to vigorous exertion, and tempered by reverential awe.

During all the time in which Dr. Johnson was employed in relating to the circle at Sir Joshua Reynolds's the particulars of what passed between the King and him, Dr. Goldsmith remained unmoved upon a sofa at some distance, affecting not to join in the least in the eager curiosity of the company. He assigned as a reason for his gloom and seeming inattention, that he apprehended Johnson had relinquished his purpose of furnishing him with a Prologue to his play, with the hopes of which he had been flattered; but it was strongly suspected that he was fretting with chagrin and envy at the singular honour Dr. Johnson had lately enjoyed. At length, the frankness and simplicity of his natural character prevailed. He sprung from the sofa, advanced to Johnson, and in a kind of flutter, from imagining himself in the situation which he had just been hearing described, exclaimed, "Well, you acquitted yourself in this conversation better than I should have done; for I should have bowed and stammered through the whole of it."

.   .   .   .

From the year 1773: Ætat. 64.

On Friday, May 7, I breakfasted with him at Mr. Thrale's in the Borough. While we were alone, I endeavoured as well as I could to apologize for a lady who had been divorced from her husband by act of Parliament. I said, that he had used her very ill, had behaved brutally to her, and that she could not continue to live with him without having her delicacy contaminated; that all affection for him was thus destroyed; that the essence of conjugal union being gone, there remained only a cold form, a mere civil obligation; that she was in the prime of life, with qualities to produce happiness; that these ought not to be lost; and, that the gentleman on whose account she was divorced had gained her heart while thus unhappily situated. Seduced, perhaps, by the charms of the lady in question, I thus attempted to palliate what I was sensible could not be justified; for when I had finished my harangue, my venerable friend gave me a proper check: "My dear Sir, never accustom your mind to mingle virtue and vice. The woman's a whore, and there's an end on't."

He described the father of one of his friends thus: "Sir, he was so exuberant a talker at public meeting, that the gentlemen of his county were afraid of him. No business could be done for his declamation."

He did not give me full credit when I mentioned that I had carried on a short conversation by signs with some

Esquimaux who were then in London, particularly with one of them who was a priest. He thought I could not make them understand me. No man was more incredulous as to particular facts, which were at all extraordinary; and therefore no man was more scrupulously inquisitive, in order to discover the truth.

I dined with him this day at the house of my friends, Messieurs Edward and Charles Dilly, booksellers in the Poultry: there were present, their elder brother Mr. Dilly of Bedfordshire, Dr. Goldsmith, Mr. Langton, Mr. Claxton, Reverend Dr. Mayo, a dissenting minister, the Reverend Mr. Toplady, and my friend the Reverend Mr. Temple.

Hawkesworth's compilation of the voyages to the South Sea being mentioned; JOHNSON. "Sir, if you talk of it as a subject of commerce, it will be gainful; if as a book that is to increase human knowledge, I believe there will not be much of that. Hawkesworth can tell only what the voyagers have told him; and they have found very little, only one new animal, I think." BOSWELL. "But many insects, Sir." JOHNSON. "Why, Sir, as to insects, Ray reckons of British insects twenty thousand species. They might have staid at home and discovered enough in that way."

Talking of birds, I mentioned Mr. Daines Barrington's ingenious Essay against the received notion of their migration. JOHNSON. "I think we have as good evidence for the migration of woodcocks as can be desired. We find they disappear at a certain time of the year, and appear again at a certain time of the year; and some of them, when weary in their flight, have been known to alight on the rigging of ships far out at sea." One of the company observed, that there had been instances of some of them found in summer in Essex. JOHNSON. "Sir, that strengthens our argument. *Exceptio probat regulam.* Some being found shows, that, if all remained, many would be found. A few sick or lame

ones may be found." GOLDSMITH. "There is a partial migration of the swallows; the stronger ones migrate, the others do not."

BOSWELL. "I am well assured that the people of Otaheite who have the bread tree, the fruit of which serves them for bread, laughed heartily when they were informed of the tedious process necessary with us to have bread;—plowing, sowing, harrowing, reaping, threshing, grinding, baking." JOHNSON. "Why, Sir, all ignorant savages will laugh when they are told of the advantages of civilized life. Were you to tell men who live without houses, how we pile brick upon brick, and rafter upon rafter, and that after a house is raised to a certain height, a man tumbles off a scaffold, and breaks his neck; he would laugh heartily at our folly in building; but it does not follow that men are better without houses. No, Sir, (holding up a slice of a good loaf,) this is better than the bread tree."

He repeated an argument, which is to be found in his *Rambler*, against the notion that the brute creation is endowed with the faculty of reason: "birds build by instinct; they never improve; they build their first nest as well as any one they ever build." GOLDSMITH. "Yet we see if you take away a bird's nest with the eggs in it, she will make a slighter nest and lay again." JOHNSON. "Sir, that is because at first she has full time and makes her nest deliberately. In the case you mention she is pressed *to* lay, and must therefore make her nest quickly, and consequently it will be slight." GOLDSMITH. "The nidification of birds is what is least known in natural history, though one of the most curious things in it."

I introduced the subject of toleration. JOHNSON. "Every society has a right to preserve public peace and order, and therefore has a good right to prohibit the propagation of opinions which have a dangerous tendency. To say the *magistrate* has this right, is using an inadequate word:

it is the *society* for which the magistrate is agent. He may be morally or theologically wrong in restraining the propagation of opinions which he thinks dangerous, but he is politically right." MAYO. "I am of opinion, Sir, that every man is entitled to liberty of conscience in religion; and that the magistrate cannot restrain that right." JOHNSON. "Sir, I agree with you. Every man has a right to liberty of conscience, and with that the magistrate cannot interfere. People confound liberty of thinking with liberty of talking; nay, with liberty of preaching. Every man has a physical right to think as he pleases; for it cannot be discovered how he thinks. He has not a moral right, for he ought to inform himself, and think justly. But, Sir, no member of a society has a right to *teach* any doctrine contrary to what the society holds to be true. The magistrate, I say, may be wrong in what he thinks: but while he thinks himself right, he may and ought to enforce what he thinks." MAYO. "Then, Sir, we are to remain always in error, and truth never can prevail; and the magistrate was right in persecuting the first Christians." JOHNSON. "Sir, the only method by which religious truth can be established is by martyrdom. The magistrate has a right to enforce what he thinks; and he who is conscious of the truth has a right to suffer. I am afraid there is no other way of ascertaining the truth but by persecution on the one hand and enduring it on the other." GOLDSMITH. "But how is a man to act, Sir? Though firmly convinced of the truth of his doctrine, may he not think it wrong to expose himself to persecution? Has he a right to do so? Is it not, as it were, committing voluntary suicide?" JOHNSON. "Sir, as to voluntary suicide, as you call it, there are twenty thousand men in an army who will go without scruple to be shot at, and mount a breach for five-pence a day." GOLDSMITH. "But have they a moral right to do this?" JOHNSON. "Nay, Sir, if you will not take the universal opinion of mankind, I have nothing to say. If mankind cannot defend their own way of thinking, I cannot defend it. Sir, if a man is in doubt whether it would be better for him to expose himself to martyrdom or not, he should not do it. He must be convinced that he has a delegation from heaven." GOLDSMITH. "I would consider whether there is the greater chance of good or evil upon the whole. If I see a man who had fallen into a well, I would wish to help him out; but if there is a greater probability that he shall pull me in, than that I shall pull him out, I would not attempt it. So were I to go to Turkey, I might wish to convert the Grand Signor to the Christian faith; but when I considered that I should probably be put to death without effectuating my purpose in any degree, I should keep myself quiet." JOHNSON. "Sir, you must consider that we have perfect and imperfect obligations. Perfect obligations, which are generally not to do something, are clear and positive: as, 'thou shalt not kill.' But charity, for instance, is not definable by limits. It is a duty to give to the poor; but no man can say how much another should give to the poor, or when a man has given too little to save his soul. In the same manner it is a duty to instruct the ignorant, and of consequence to convert infidels to Christianity; but no man in the common course of things is obliged to carry this to such a degree as to incur the danger of martyrdom, as no man is obliged to strip himself to the shirt in order to give to charity. I have said that a man must be persuaded that he has a particular delegation from heaven." GOLDSMITH. "How is this to be known? Our first reformers, who were burnt for not believing bread and wine to be CHRIST"—JOHNSON. (interrupting him) "Sir, they were not burnt for not believing bread and wine to be CHRIST, but for insulting those who did believe it. And, Sir, when the first reformers began, they did not intend to be martyred: as many of them ran away as could."

BOSWELL. "But, Sir, there was your countryman, Elwal, who you told me challenged King George with his blackguards, and his red-guards." JOHNSON. "My countryman, Elwal, Sir, should have been put in the stocks; a proper pulpit for him; and he'd have had a numerous audience. A man who preaches in the stocks will always have hearers enough." BOSWELL. "But Elwal thought himself in the right." JOHNSON. "We are not providing for mad people; there are places for them in the neighbourhood." (meaning Moorfields.) MAYO. "But, Sir, is it not very hard that I should not be allowed to teach my children what I really believe to be the truth?" JOHNSON. "Why, Sir, you might contrive to teach your children *extrà scandalum*; but, Sir, the magistrate, if he knows it, has a right to restrain you. Suppose you teach your children to be thieves?" MAYO. "This is making a joke of the subject." JOHNSON. "Nay, Sir, take it thus:—that you teach them the community of goods: for which there are as many plausible arguments as for most erroneous doctrines. You teach them that all things at first were in common, and that no man had a right to anything but as he laid his hands upon it; and that this still is, or ought to be, the rule amongst mankind. Here; Sir, you sap a great principle in society,—property. And don't you think the magistrate would have a right to prevent you? Or, suppose you should teach your children the notion of the Adamites, and they should run naked into the streets, would not the magistrate have a right to flog 'em into their doublets?" MAYO. "I think the magistrate has no right to interfere till there is some overt act." BOSWELL. "So, Sir, though he sees an enemy to the state charging a blunderbuss, he is not to interfere till it is fired off?" MAYO. "He must be sure of its direction against the state." JOHNSON. "The magistrate is to judge of that.—He has no right to restrain your thinking, because the evil centers in yourself. If a man were sitting at this table, and

chopping off his fingers, the magistrate, as guardian of the community, has no authority to restrain him, however he might do it from kindness as a parent.—Though, indeed, upon more consideration, I think he may; as it is probable, that he who is chopping off his own fingers, may soon proceed to chop off those of other people. If I think it right to steal Mr. Dilly's plate, I am a bad man; but he can say nothing to me. If I make an open declaration that I think so, he will keep me out of his house. If I put forth my hand, I shall be sent to Newgate. This is the gradation of thinking, preaching, and acting: if a man thinks erroneously, he may keep his thoughts to himself, and nobody will trouble him; if he preaches erroneous doctrine, society may expel him; if he acts in consequence of it, the law takes place, and he is hanged." MAYO. "But, Sir, ought not Christians to have liberty of conscience?" JOHNSON. "I have already told you so, Sir. You are coming back to where you were." BOSWELL. "Dr. Mayo is always taking a return post-chaise, and going the stage over again. He has it at half price." JOHNSON. "Dr. Mayo, like other champions for unlimited toleration, has got a set of words. Sir, it is no matter, politically, whether the magistrate be right or wrong. Suppose a club were to be formed, to drink confusion to King George the Third, and a happy restoration to Charles the Third, this would be very bad with respect to the State; but every member of that club must either conform to its rules, or be turned out of it. Old Baxter, I remember, maintains, that the magistrate should 'tolerate all things that are tolerable.' This is no good definition of toleration upon any principle; but it shows that he thought some things were not tolerable." TOPLADY. "Sir, you have untwisted this difficult subject with great dexterity."

During this argument, Goldsmith sat in restless agitation, from a wish to get in and *shine*. Finding himself excluded, he had taken his hat to go away, but remained for some time with it in his hand, like a gamester, who at the close of a long night, lingers for a little while, to see if he can have a favourable opening to finish with success. Once when he was beginning to speak, he found himself overpowered by the loud voice of Johnson, who was at the opposite end of the table, and did not perceive Goldsmith's attempt. Thus disappointed of his wish to obtain the attention of the company, Goldsmith in a passion threw down his hat, looking angrily at Johnson, and exclaiming in a bitter tone, "*Take it.*" When Toplady was going to speak, Johnson uttered some sound, which led Goldsmith to think that he was beginning again, and taking the words from Toplady. Upon which, he seized this opportunity of venting his own envy and spleen, under the pretext of supporting another person. "Sir, (said he to Johnson,) the gentleman has heard you patiently for an hour; pray allow us now to hear him." JOHNSON. (sternly,) "Sir, I was not interrupting the gentleman. I was only giving him a signal of my attention. Sir, you are impertinent." Goldsmith made no reply, but continued in the company for some time.

A gentleman present ventured to ask Dr. Johnson if there was not a material difference as to toleration of opinions which lead to action, and opinions merely speculative; for instance, would it be wrong in the magistrate to tolerate those who preach against the doctrine of the TRINITY? Johnson was highly offended, and said, "I wonder, Sir, how a gentleman of your piety can introduce this subject in a mixed company." He told me afterwards, that the impropriety was, that perhaps some of the company might have talked on the subject in such terms as might have shocked him; or he might have been forced to appear in their eyes a narrow-minded man. The gentleman, with submissive deference, said he had only hinted at the question from a desire to hear Dr. Johnson's opinion upon it. JOHNSON.

"Why then, Sir, I think that permitting men to preach any opinion contrary to the doctrine of the established church tends, in a certain degree, to lessen the authority of the church, and consequently, to lessen the influence of religion." "It may be considered, (said the gentleman,) whether it would not be politic to tolerate in such a case." JOHNSON. "Sir, we have been talking of *right*: this is another question. I think it is *not* politic to tolerate in such a case."

.   .   .

From the year 1776: Ætat. 67.

I am now to record a very curious incident in Dr. Johnson's Life, which fell under my own observation; of which *pars magna fui*, and which I am persuaded will, with the liberal-minded, be much to his credit.

My desire of being acquainted with celebrated men of every description, had made me, much about the same time, obtain an introduction to Dr. Samuel Johnson and to John Wilkes, Esq. Two men more different could perhaps not be selected out of all mankind. They had even attacked one another with some asperity in their writings; yet I lived in habits of friendship with both. I could fully relish the excellence of each; for I have ever delighted in that intellectual chemistry, which can separate good qualities from evil in the same person.

Sir John Pringle, "mine own friend and my Father's friend," between whom and Dr. Johnson I in vain wished to establish an acquaintance, as I respected and lived in intimacy with both of them, observed to me once, very ingeniously, "It is not in friendship as in mathematics, where two things, each equal to a third, are equal between themselves. You agree with Johnson as a middle quality, and you agree with me as a middle quality; but Johnson and I should not agree." Sir John was not sufficiently flexible; so I desisted; knowing, indeed, that the repulsion was equally strong on the part of Johnson; who, I know not from what cause, unless his being a Scotchman, had formed a very erroneous opinion of Sir John. But I conceived an irresistible wish, if possible, to bring Dr. Johnson and Mr. Wilkes together. How to manage it, was a nice and difficult matter.

My worthy booksellers and friends, Messieurs Dilly in the Poultry, at whose hospitable and well-covered table I have seen a greater number of literary men, than at any other, except that of Sir Joshua Reynolds, had invited me to meet Mr. Wilkes and some more gentlemen on Wednesday, May 15. "Pray (said I,) let us have Dr. Johnson."—"What with Mr. Wilkes? not for the world, (said Mr. Edward Dilly:) Dr. Johnson would never forgive me."—"Come, (said I,) if you'll let me negotiate for you, I will be answerable that all shall go well." DILLY. "Nay, if you will take it upon you, I am sure I shall be very happy to see them both here."

Notwithstanding the high veneration which I entertained for Dr. Johnson, I was sensible that he was sometimes a little actuated by the spirit of contradiction, and by means of that I hoped I should gain my point. I was persuaded that if I had come upon him with a direct proposal, "Sir, will you dine in company with Jack Wilkes?" he would have flown into a passion, and would probably have answered, "Dine with Jack Wilkes, Sir! I'd as soon dine with Jack Ketch." I therefore, while we were sitting quietly by ourselves at his house in an evening, took occasion to open my plan thus:—"Mr. Dilly, Sir, sends his respectful compliments to you, and would be happy if you would do him the honour to dine with him on Wednesday next along with me, as I must soon go to Scotland." JOHNSON. "Sir, I am obliged to Mr. Dilly. I will wait upon him—" BOSWELL. "Provided, Sir, I suppose, that the company which he is to have, is agreeable to you." JOHNSON. "What do you mean, Sir? What do you take me for? Do you think I am so ignorant of the

world, as to imagine that I am to prescribe to a gentleman what company he is to have at his table?" BOSWELL. "I beg your pardon, Sir, for wishing to prevent you from meeting people whom you might not like. Perhaps he may have some of what he calls his patriotic friends with him." JOHNSON. "Well, Sir, and what then? What care I for his *patriotic friends*? Poh!" BOSWELL. "I should not be surprised to find Jack Wilkes there." JOHNSON "And if Jack Wilkes *should* be there, what is that to *me*, Sir? My dear friend, let us have no more of this. I am sorry to be angry with you; but really it is treating me strangely to talk to me as if I could not meet any company whatever, occasionally." BOSWELL. "Pray forgive me, Sir: I meant well. But you shall meet whoever comes, for me." Thus, I secured him, and told Dilly that he would find him very well pleased to be one of his guests on the day appointed.

Upon the much-expected Wednesday, I called on him about half an hour before dinner, as I often did when we were to dine out together, to see that he was ready in time, and to accompany him. I found him buffeting his books, as upon a former occasion, covered with dust, and making no preparation for going abroad. "How is this, Sir? (said I.) Don't you recollect that you are to dine at Mr. Dilly's?" JOHNSON. "Sir, I did not think of going to Dilly's: it went out of my head. I have ordered dinner at home with Mrs. Williams." BOSWELL. "But, my dear Sir, you know you were engaged to Mr. Dilly, and I told him so. He will expect you, and will be much disappointed if you don't come." JOHNSON. "You must talk to Mrs. Williams about this."

Here was a sad dilemma. I feared that what I was so confident I had secured would yet be frustrated. He had accustomed himself to show Mrs. Williams such a degree of humane attention, as frequently imposed some restraint upon him; and I knew that if she should be obstinate, he would not stir. I hastened down stairs to the blind lady's room, and told her I was in great uneasiness, for Dr. Johnson had engaged to me to dine this day at Mr. Dilly's, but that he had told me he had forgotten his engagement, and had ordered dinner at home. "Yes, Sir, (said she, pretty peevishly,) Dr. Johnson is to dine at home."— "Madam, (said I,) his respect for you is such, that I know he will not leave you unless you absolutely desire it. But as you have so much of his company, I hope you will be good enough to forego it for a day; as Mr. Dilly is a very worthy man, has frequently had agreeable parties at his house for Dr. Johnson, and will be vexed if the Doctor neglects him to-day. And then, Madam, be pleased to consider my situation; I carried the message, and I assured Mr. Dilly that Dr. Johnson was to come, and no doubt he has made a dinner, and invited a company, and boasted of the honour he expected to have. I shall be quite disgraced if the Doctor is not there." She gradually softened to my solicitations, which were certainly as earnest as most entreaties to ladies upon any occasion, and was graciously pleased to empower me to tell Dr. Johnson, "That all things considered, she thought he should certainly go." I flew back to him, still in dust, and careless of what should be the event, "indifferent in his choice to go or stay;" but as soon as I had announced to him Mrs. Williams' consent, he roared, "Frank, a clean shirt," and was very soon dressed. When I had him fairly seated in a hackney-coach with me, I exulted as much as a fortune-hunter who has got an heiress into a post-chaise with him to set out for Gretna-Green.

When we entered Mr. Dilly's drawing room, he found himself in the midst of a company he did not know. I kept myself snug and silent, watching how he would conduct himself. I observed him, whispering to Mr. Dilly, "Who is that gentleman, Sir?"— "Mr. Arthur Lee."—JOHNSON. "Too, too, too," (under his breath,) which was one of his habitual mutterings. Mr. Arthur Lee could not but be very obnoxious to Johnson, for he was not only a *patriot* but an *American*. He was afterwards minister from the United States at the court of Madrid. "And who is the gentleman in lace?"— "Mr. Wilkes, Sir." This information confounded him still more; he had some difficulty to restrain himself, and taking up a book, sat down upon a window-seat and read, or at least kept his eye upon it intently for some time, till he composed himself. His feelings, I dare say, were awkward enough. But he no doubt recollected his having rated me for supposing that he could be at all disconcerted by any company, and he, therefore, resolutely set himself to behave quite as an easy man of the world, who could adapt himself at once to the disposition and manners of those whom he might chance to meet.

The cheering sound of "Dinner is upon the table," dissolved his reverie, and we *all* sat down without any symptom of ill humour. There were present, besides Mr. Wilkes, and Mr. Arthur Lee, who was an old companion of mine when he studied physic at Edinburgh, Mr. (now, Sir John) Miller, Dr. Lettsom, and Mr. Slater the druggist. Mr. Wilkes placed himself next to Dr. Johnson, and behaved to him with so much attention and politeness, that he gained upon him insensibly. No man eat more heartily than Johnson, or loved better what was nice and delicate. Mr. Wilkes was very assiduous in helping him to some fine veal. "Pray give me leave, Sir:—It is better here—A little of the brown— Some fat, Sir—A little of the stuffing —Some gravy—Let me have the pleasure of giving you some butter—Allow me to recommend a squeeze of this orange;—or the lemon, perhaps, may have more zest."—"Sir, Sir, I am obliged to you, Sir," cried Johnson, bowing, and turning his head to him with a look for some time of "surly virtue," but, in a short while, of complacency.

Foote being mentioned, Johnson said, "He is not a good mimic." One of the company added, "A merry Andrew, a buffoon." JOHNSON. "But he has wit too, and is not deficient in ideas, or in fertility and variety of imagery, and not empty of reading; he has knowledge enough to fill up his part. One species of wit he has in an eminent degree, that of escape. You drive him into a corner with both hands; but he's gone, Sir, when you think you have got him—like an animal that jumps over your head. Then he has a great range for wit; he never lets truth stand between him and a jest, and he is sometimes mighty coarse. Garrick is under many restraints from which Foote is free." WILKES. "Garrick's wit is more like Lord Chesterfield's." JOHNSON. "The first time I was in company with Foote was at Fitzherbert's. Having no good opinion of the fellow, I was resolved not to be pleased; and it is very difficult to please a man against his will. I went on eating my dinner pretty sullenly, affecting not to mind him. But the dog was so very comical, that I was obliged to lay down my knife and fork, throw myself back upon my chair, and fairly laugh it out. No, Sir, he was irresistible. He upon one occasion experienced, in an extraordinary degree, the efficacy of his powers of entertaining. Amongst the many and various modes which he tried of getting money, he became a partner with a small-beer brewer, and he was to have a share of the profits for procuring customers amongst his numerous acquaintance. Fitzherbert was one who took his small-beer; but it was so bad that the servants resolved not to drink it. They were at some loss how to notify their resolution, being afraid of offending their master, who they knew liked Foote much as a companion. At last they fixed upon a little black boy, who was rather a favourite, to be their deputy, and deliver their remonstrance; and having invested him with the whole authority of the kitchen, he was to inform Mr. Fitzherbert, in all

their names, upon a certain day, that they would drink Foote's small-beer no longer. On that day Foote happened to dine at Fitzherbert's, and this boy served at table; he was so delighted with Foote's stories, and merriment, and grimace, that when he went down stairs, he told them, 'This is the finest man I have ever seen. I will not deliver your message. I will drink his small-beer.'"

Somebody observed that Garrick could not have done this. WILKES. "Garrick would have made the small-beer still smaller. He is now leaving the stage; but he will play *Scrub* all his life." I knew that Johnson would let nobody attack Garrick but himself, as Garrick once said to me, and I had heard him praise his liberality; so to bring out his commendation of his celebrated pupil, I said, loudly, "I have heard Garrick is liberal." JOHNSON. "Yes, Sir, I know that Garrick has given away more money than any man in England that I am acquainted with, and that not from ostentatious views. Garrick was very poor when he began life; so when he came to have money, he probably was very unskilful in giving away, and saved when he should not. But Garrick began to be liberal as soon as he could; and I am of opinion, the reputation of avarice which he has had, has been very lucky for him, and prevented his having many enemies. You despise a man for avarice, but do not hate him. Garrick might have been much better attacked for living with more splendour than is suitable to a player: if they had had the wit to have assaulted him in that quarter, they might have galled him more. But they have kept clamouring about his avarice, which has rescued him from much obloquy and envy."

Talking of the great difficulty of obtaining authentic information for biography, Johnson told us, "When I was a young fellow I wanted to write the *Life of Dryden*, and in order to get materials, I applied to the only two persons then alive who had seen him: these were old Swinney, and old

Cibber. Swinney's information was no more than this, 'That at Will's coffee-house Dryden had a particular chair for himself, which was set by the fire in winter, and was then called his winter-chair; and that it was carried out for him to the balcony in summer, and was then called his summer-chair.' Cibber could tell no more but 'That he remembered him a decent old man, arbiter of critical disputes at Will's.' You are to consider that Cibber was then at a great distance from Dryden, had perhaps one leg only in the room, and durst not draw in the other." BOSWELL. "Yet Cibber was a man of observation?" JOHNSON. "I think not." BOSWELL. "You will allow his *Apology* to be well done." JOHNSON. "Very well done, to be sure, Sir. That book is a striking proof of the justice of Pope's remark:

'Each might his several province well command,
Would all but stoop to what they understand.'"

BOSWELL. "And his plays are good." JOHNSON. "Yes; but that was his trade; *l'esprit du corps:* he had been all his life among players and play-writers. I wondered that he had so little to say in conversation, for he had kept the best company, and learned all that can be got by the ear. He abused Pindar to me, and then showed me an Ode of his own, with an absurd couplet, making a linnet soar on an eagle's wing. I told him that when the ancients made a simile, they always made it like something real."

Mr. Wilkes remarked, that "among all the bold flights of Shakspeare's imagination, the boldest was making Birnam-wood march to Dunsinane; creating a wood where there never was a shrub; a wood in Scotland! ha! ha! ha!" And he also observed, that "the clannish slavery of the Highlands of Scotland was the single exception to Milton's remark of 'The Mountain Nymph, sweet Liberty,' being worshipped in all hilly countries."— "When I was at Inverary (said he,)

on a visit to my old friend, Archibald Duke of Argyle, his dependents con-gratulated me on being such a fa-vourite of his Grace. I said, 'It is then, gentlemen, truly lucky for me; for if I had displeased the Duke, and he had wished it, there is not a Camp-bell among you but would have been ready to bring John Wilkes's head to him in a charger. It would have been only

'Off with his head! So much for Aylesbury.

I was then member for Aylesbury."

Dr. Johnson and Mr. Wilkes talked of the contested passage in Horace's *Art of Poetry, "Difficile est propriè communia dicere."* Mr. Wilkes, ac-cording to my note, gave the inter-pretation thus: "It is difficult to speak with propriety of common things; as, if a poet had to speak of Queen Caroline drinking tea, he must endeavour to avoid the vulgarity of cups and saucers." But upon reading my note, he tells me that he meant to say, that "the word *communia*, being a Roman law term, signifies here things *communis juris*, that is to say, what have never yet been treated by any body; and this appears clearly from what followed,

'—Tuque
Rectiùs Iliacum carmen deducis in actus,
Quàm si proferres ignota indictaque primus.'

You will easier make a tragedy out of the *Iliad* than on any subject not han-dled before." JOHNSON. "He means that it is difficult to appropriate to particular persons qualities which are common to all mankind, as Homer has done."

WILKES. "We have no City-Poet now: that is an office which has gone into disuse. The last was Elkanah Settle. There is something in *names* which one cannot help feeling. Now *Elkanah Settle* sounds so *queer*, who can expect much from that name? We should have no hesitation to give it for John Dryden, in preference to Elkanah Settle, from the names only, without knowing their different merits." JOHNSON. "I suppose, Sir, Settle did as well for Aldermen in his time, as John Home could do now. Where did Beckford and Trecothick learn English?"

Mr. Arthur Lee mentioned some Scotch who had taken possession of a barren part of America, and wondered why they should choose it. JOHNSON. "Why, Sir, all barrenness is compara-tive. The *Scotch* would not know it to be barren." BOSWELL. "Come, come, he is flattering the English. You have now been in Scotland, Sir, and say if you did not see meat and drink enough there." JOHNSON. "Why yes, Sir; meat and drink enough to give the inhabitants sufficient strength to run away from home." All these quick and lively sallies were said sportively, quite in jest, and with a smile, which showed that he meant only wit. Upon this topic he and Mr. Wilkes could per-fectly assimilate; here was a bond of union between them, and I was con-scious that as both of them had visited Caledonia, both were fully satisfied of the strange narrow ignorance of those who imagine that it is a land of fam-ine. But they amused themselves with persevering in the old jokes. When I claimed a superiority for Scotland over England in one respect, that no man can be arrested there for a debt merely because another swears it against him; but there must first be the judgment of a court of law ascer-taining its justice; and that a seizure of the person, before judgment is ob-tained, can take place only, if his creditor should swear that he is about to fly from the country, or, as it is technically expressed, is *in medita-tione fugæ*: WILKES. "That, I should think, may be safely sworn of all the Scotch nation." JOHNSON. (to Mr. Wilkes) "You must know, Sir, I lately took my friend Boswell and showed him genuine civilized life in an Eng-lish provincial town. I turned him loose at Lichfield, my native city, that he might see for once real civility: for you know he lives among savages in Scotland, and among rakes in Lon-don." WILKES. "Except when he is with grave, sober, decent people like you and me." JOHNSON. (smiling,) "And we ashamed of him."

They were quite frank and easy. Johnson told the story of his asking Mrs. Macaulay to allow her footman to sit down with them, to prove the ridiculousness of the argument for the equality of mankind; and he said to me afterwards, with a nod of satis-faction, "You saw Mr. Wilkes ac-quiesced." Wilkes talked with all im-aginable freedom of the ludicrous title given to the Attorney-General, *Diabo-lus Regis*; adding, "I have reason to know something about that officer; for I was prosecuted for a libel." Johnson, who many people would have sup-posed must have been furiously angry at hearing this talked of so lightly, said not a word. He was now, *indeed*, "a good-humoured fellow."

After dinner we had an accession of Mrs. Knowles, the Quaker lady, well known for her various talents, and of Mr. Alderman Lee. Amidst some pa-triotic groans, somebody (I think the Alderman) said, "Poor old England is lost." JOHNSON. "Sir, it is not so much to be lamented that Old England is lost, as that the Scotch have found it." WILKES. "Had Lord Bute governed Scotland only, I should not have taken the trouble to write his eulogy, and dedicate *Mortimer* to him."

Mr. Wilkes held a candle to show a fine print of a beautiful female figure which hung in the room, and pointed out the elegant contour of the bosom with the finger of an arch connoisseur. He afterwards, in a conversation with me, waggishly insisted, that all the time Johnson showed visible signs of a fervent admiration of the corre-sponding charms of the fair Quaker.

This record, though by no means so perfect as I could wish, will serve to give a notion of a very curious inter-view, which was not only pleasing at the time, but had the agreeable and benignant effect of reconciling any animosity, and sweetening any acidity, which in the various bustle of political contest, had been produced in the minds of two men, who though widely different, had so many things in common—classical learning, modern literature, wit, and humour, and ready repartee—that it would have been much to be regretted if they had been for ever at a distance from each other.

Mr. Burke gave me much credit for this successful *negotiation*; and pleasantly said, that "there was nothing to equal it in the whole history of the *Corps Diplomatique*."

I attended Dr. Johnson home, and had the satisfaction to hear him tell Mrs. Williams how much he had been pleased with Mr. Wilkes's company, and what an agreeable day he had passed.

. . . .

From the year 1778: Ætat. 69.

On Wednesday, April 15, I dined with Dr. Johnson at Mr. Dilly's, and was in high spirits, for I had been a good part of the morning with Mr. Orme, the able and eloquent historian of Hindostan, who expressed a great admiration of Johnson. "I do not care (said he,) on what subject Johnson talks; but I love better to hear him talk than any body. He either gives you new thoughts, or a new colouring. It is a shame to the nation that he has not been more liberally rewarded. Had I been George the Third, and thought as he did about America, I would have given Johnson three hundred a year for his *Taxation no Tyranny*" alone. I repeated this, and Johnson was much pleased with such praise from such a man as Orme.

At Mr. Dilly's to-day were Mrs. Knowles, the ingenious Quaker lady, Miss Seward, the poetess of Lichfield, the Reverend Dr. Mayo, and the Rev. Mr. Beresford, Tutor to the Duke of Bedford. Before dinner Dr. Johnson seized upon Mr. Charles Sheridan's *Account of the late Revolution in Sweden,* and seemed to read it ravenously, as if he devoured it, which was to all appearance his method of studying. "He knows how to read bet-ter than any one (said Mrs. Knowles;) he gets at the substance of a book directly; he tears out the heart of it.' He kept it wrapt up in the tablecloth in his lap during the time of dinner, from an avidity to have one entertainment in readiness when he should have finished another; resembling (if I may use so coarse a simile) a dog who holds a bone in his paws in reserve, while he eats something else which has been thrown to him.

The subject of cookery having been very naturally introduced at a table where Johnson, who boasted of the niceness of his palate, owned that "he always found a good dinner," he said, "I could write a better book of cookery than has ever yet been written; it should be a book upon philosophical principles. Pharmacy is now made much more simple. Cookery may be made so too. A prescription which is now compounded of five ingredients, had formerly fifty in it. So in cookery, if the nature of the ingredients be well known, much fewer will do. Then as you cannot make a bad meat good, I would tell what is the best butcher's meat, the best beef, the best pieces; how to choose young fowls; the proper seasons of different vegetables; and then how to roast and boil, and compound." DILLY. "Mrs. Glasse's *Cookery*, which is the best, was written by Dr. Hill. Half the trade know this." JOHNSON. "Well, Sir. This shows how much better the subject of cookery may be treated by a philosopher. I doubt if the book be written by Dr. Hill; for, in Mrs. Glasse's *Cookery*, which I have looked into, salt-petre and sal-prunella are spoken of as different substances, whereas sal-prunella is only salt-petre burnt on charcoal; and Hill could not be ignorant of this. However, as the greatest part of such a book is made by transcription, this mistake may have been carelessly adopted. But you shall see what a Book of Cookery I shall make! I shall agree with Mr. Dilly for the copyright." MISS SEWARD. "That would be Hercules with the distaff indeed."

JOHNSON. "No, Madam. Women can spin very well; but they cannot make a good book of Cookery."

JOHNSON. "O! Mr. Dilly—you must know that an English Benedictine Monk at Paris has translated *The Duke of Berwick's Memoirs,* from the original French, and has sent them to me to sell. I offered them to Strahan, who sent them back with his answer:—'That the first book he had published was the *Duke of Berwick's Life,* by which he had lost: and he hated the name.'—Now I honestly tell you, that Strahan has refused them; but I also honestly tell you, that he did it upon no principle, for he never looked into them." DILLY. "Are they well translated, Sir?" JOHNSON. "Why, Sir, very well—in a style very current and very clear. I have written to the Benedictine to give me an answer upon two points—What evidence is there that the letters are authentic? (for if they are not authentic they are nothing;) —And how long will it be before the original French is published? For if the French edition is not to appear for a considerable time, the translation will be almost as valuable as an original book. They will make two volumes in octavo; and I have undertaken to correct every sheet as it comes from the press." Mr. Dilly desired to see them, and said he would send for them. He asked Dr. Johnson if he would write a Preface to them. JOHNSON. "No, Sir. The Benedictines were very kind to me, and I'll do what I undertook to do; but I will not mingle my name with them. I am to gain nothing by them. I'll turn them loose upon the world, and let them take their chance." DR. MAYO. "Pray, Sir, are Ganganelli's letters authentic?" JOHNSON. "No, Sir. Voltaire put the same question to the editor of them, that I did to Macpherson— Where are the originals?"

Mrs. Knowles affected to complain that men had much more liberty allowed them than women. JOHNSON. "Why, Madame, women have all the liberty they should wish to have. We have all the labour and the danger, and the women all the advantage. We go to sea, we build houses, we do everything, in short, to pay our court to the women." MRS. KNOWLES. "The Doctor reasons very wittily, but not convincingly. Now, take the instance of building; the mason's wife, if she is ever seen in liquor, is ruined; the mason may get himself drunk as often as he pleases, with little loss of character; nay, may let his wife and children starve." JOHNSON. "Madame, you must consider, if the mason does get himself drunk, and let his wife and children starve, the parish will oblige him to find security for their maintenance. We have different modes of restraining evil. Stocks for the men, a ducking-stool for women, and a pound for beasts. If we require more perfection from women than from ourselves, it is doing them honour. And women have not the same temptations that we have: they may always live in virtuous company; men must mix in the world indiscriminately. If a woman has no inclination to do what is wrong being secured from it is no restraint to her. I am at liberty to walk into the Thames; but if I were to try it, my friends would restrain me in Bedlam, and I should be obliged to them." MRS. KNOWLES. "Still, Doctor, I cannot help thinking it a hardship that more indulgence is allowed to men than to women. It gives a superiority to men, to which I do not see how they are entitled." JOHNSON. "It is plain, Madam, one or other must have the superiority. As Shakespeare says, 'If two men ride on a horse, one must ride behind.'" DILLY. "I suppose, Sir, Mrs. Knowles would have them to ride in panniers, one on each side." JOHNSON. "Then, Sir, the horse would throw them both." MRS. KNOWLES. "Well, I hope that in another world the sexes will be equal." BOSWELL. "That is being too ambitious, Madam. *We* might as well desire to be equal with the angels. We shall all, I hope, be happy in a future state, but we must not expect to be all happy in the same degree. It is enough if we be happy according to our several capacities. A worthy carman will get to heaven as well as Sir Isaac Newton. Yet, though equally good, they will not have the same degrees of happiness." JOHNSON. "Probably not."

Upon this subject I had once before sounded him, by mentioning the late Reverend Mr. Brown, of Utrecht's, image; that a great and small glass, though equally full, did not hold an equal quantity; which he threw out to refute David Hume's saying, that a little miss, going to a dance at a ball, in a fine new dress, was as happy as a great orator, after having made an eloquent and applauded speech. After some thought, Johnson said, "I come over to the parson." As an instance of coincidence of thinking, Mr. Dilly told me, that Dr. King, a late dissenting minister in London, said to him, upon the happiness in a future state of good men of different capacities, "A pail does not hold so much as a tub; but, if it be equally full, it has no reason to complain. Every Saint in heaven will have as much happiness as he can hold." Mr. Dilly thought this a clear, though a familiar illustration of the phrase, "One star differeth from another in brightness."

Dr. Mayo having asked Johnson's opinion of Soame Jenyns's *View of the Internal Evidence of the Christian Religion*;—JOHNSON. "I think it a pretty book; not very theological indeed; and there seems to be an affectation of ease and carelessness, as if it were not suitable to his character to be very serious about the matter." BOSWELL. "He may have intended this to introduce his book the better among genteel people, who might be unwilling to read too grave a treatise. There is a general levity in the age. We have physicians now with bag-wigs; may we not have airy divines, at least somewhat less solemn in their appearance than they used to be?" JOHNSON. "Jenyns might mean as you say." BOSWELL. "*You* should like his book, Mrs. Knowles, as it maintains,

as you *friends* do, that courage is not a Christian virtue." MRS. KNOWLES. "Yes, indeed, I like him there; but I cannot agree with him, that friendship is not a Christian virtue." JOHNSON. "Why, Madam, strictly speaking, he is right. All friendship is preferring the interest of a friend, to the neglect, or, perhaps, against the interest of others; so that an old Greek said, 'He that has *friends* has *no friend.*' Now Christianity recommends universal benevolence, to consider all men as our brethren, which is contrary to the virtue of friendship, as described by the ancient philosophers. Surely, Madam, your sect must approve of this; for, you call all men *friends.*" MRS. KNOWLES. "We are commanded to do good to all men, 'but especially to them who are of the household of Faith.'" JOHNSON. "Well, Madam. The household of Faith is wide enough." MRS. KNOWLES. "But, Doctor, our Saviour had twelve Apostles, yet there was *one* whom he *loved*. John was called 'the disciple whom JESUS *loved.*'" JOHNSON. (with eyes sparkling benignantly,) "Very well, indeed, Madam. You have said very well." BOSWELL. "A fine application. Pray, Sir, had you ever thought of it?" JOHNSON. "I had not, Sir."

From this pleasing subject, he, I know not how or why, made a sudden transition to one upon which he was a violent aggressor; for he said, "I am willing to love all mankind, *except an American:*" and his inflammable corruption bursting into horrid fire, he "breathed out threatenings and slaughter," calling them, "Rascals—Robbers—Pirates;" and exclaiming, he'd "burn and destroy them." Miss Seward, looking to him with mild but steady astonishment, said, "Sir, this is an instance that we are always most violent against those whom we have injured."—He was irritated still more by this delicate and keen reproach; and roared out another tremendous volley, which one might fancy could be heard across the Atlantic. During this tempest I sat in great uneasiness, lamenting his heat of temper; till, by degrees, I diverted his attention to other topics.

DR. MAYO. (to Dr. Johnson,) "Pray, Sir, have you read *Edwards, of New England, on Grace?*" JOHNSON. "No, Sir." BOSWELL. "It puzzled me so much as to the freedom of the human will, by stating, with wonderful acute ingenuity, our being actuated by a series of motives which we cannot resist, that the only relief I had was to forget it." MAYO. "But he makes the proper distinction between moral and physical necessity." BOSWELL. "Alas, Sir, they come both to the same thing. You may be bound as hard by chains when covered by leather, as when the iron appears. The argument for the moral necessity of human actions is always, I observe, fortified by supposing universal prescience to be one of the attributes of the Deity." JOHNSON. "You are surer that you are free, than you are of prescience; you are surer that you can lift up your finger or not as you please, than you are of any conclusion from a deduction of reasoning. But let us consider a little the objection from prescience. It is certain I am either to go home to-night or not; that does not prevent my freedom." BOSWELL. "That it is certain you are *either* to go home or not, does not prevent your freedom; because the liberty of choice between the two is compatible with that certainty. But if *one* of these events be certain *now,* you have no *future* power of volition. If it be certain you are to go home to-night, you *must* go home." JOHNSON. "If I am well acquainted with a man, I can judge with great probability how he will act in any case, without his being restrained by my judging. GOD may have this probability increased to certainty." BOSWELL. "When it is increased to *certainty,* freedom ceases, because that cannot be certainly foreknown, which is not certain at the time; but if it be certain at the time, it is a contradiction in terms to maintain that there can be afterwards any *contingency* dependent upon the ex-

ercise of will or any thing else." JOHNSON. "All theory is against the freedom of the will; all experience for it."— I did not push the subject any farther. I was glad to find him so mild in discussing a question of the most abstract nature, involved with theological tenets, which he generally would not suffer to be in any degree opposed.

He as usual defended luxury; "You cannot spend money in luxury without doing good to the poor. Nay, you do more good to them by spending it in luxury, than by giving it: for by spending it in luxury, you make them exert industry, whereas by giving it, you keep them idle. I own, indeed, there may be more virtue in giving it immediately in charity, than in spending it in luxury; though there may be a pride in that too." Miss Seward asked, if this was not Mandeville's doctrine of "private vices public benefits." JOHNSON. "The fallacy of that book is, that Mandeville defines neither vices nor benefits. He reckons among vices everything that gives pleasure. He takes the narrowest system of morality, monastic morality, which holds pleasure itself to be a vice, such as eating salt with our fish, because it makes it eat better; and he reckons wealth as a public benefit, which is by no means always true. Pleasure of itself is not a vice. Having a garden, which we all know to be perfectly innocent, is a great pleasure. At the same time, in this state of being there are many pleasures vices, which however are so immediately agreeable that we can hardly abstain from them. The happiness of Heaven will be, that pleasure and virtue will be perfectly consistent. Mandeville puts the case of a man who gets drunk in an alehouse; and says it is a public benefit, because so much money is got by it to the public. But it must be considered, that all the good gained by this, through the gradation of alehousekeeper, brewer, maltster, and farmer, is overbalanced by the evil caused to the man and his family by his getting drunk. This is the way to try what is vicious, by ascertaining whether more evil than good is produced by it upon the whole, which is the case in all vice. It may happen that good is produced by vice; but not as vice; for instance, a robber may take money from its owner, and give it to one who will make a better use of it. Here is good produced; but not by the robbery as robbery, but as translation of property. I read Mandeville forty, or, I believe, fifty years ago. He did not puzzle me; he opened my views into real life very much. No, it is clear that the happiness of society depends on virtue. In Sparta, theft was allowed by general consent: theft, therefore, was *there* not a crime, but then there was no security; and what a life must they have had, when there was no security. Without truth there must be a dissolution of society. As it is, there is so little truth, that we are almost afraid to trust our ears; but how should we be, if falsehood were multiplied ten times? Society is held together by communication and information; and I remember this remark of Sir Thomas Brown's, 'Do the devils lie? No; for then Hell could not subsist.'"

Talking of Miss ———, a literary lady, he said, "I was obliged to speak to Miss Reynolds, to let her know that I desired she would not flatter me so much." Somebody now observed, "She flatters Garrick." JOHNSON. "She is in the right to flatter Garrick. She is in the right for two reasons; first, because she has the world with her, who have been praising Garrick these thirty years; and secondly, because she is rewarded for it by Garrick. Why should she flatter *me*? I can do nothing for her. Let her carry her praise to a better market. (Then turning to Mrs. Knowles.) You, Madam, have been flattering me all the evening; I wish you would give Boswell a little now. If you knew his merit as well as I do, you would say a great deal; he is the best travelling companion in the world."

Somebody mentioned the Reverend Mr. Mason's prosecution of Mr. Murray, the bookseller, for having inserted in a collection of *Gray's Poems,* only fifty lines, of which Mr. Mason had still the exclusive property, under the statute of Queen Anne; and that Mr. Mason had persevered, notwithstanding his being requested to name his own terms of compensation. Johnson signified his displeasure at Mr. Mason's conduct very strongly; but added, by way of showing that he was not surprised at it, "Mason's a Whig." MRS. KNOWLES. (not hearing distinctly,) "What! a Prig, Sir?" JOHNSON. "Worse, Madam; a Whig! But he is both."

I expressed a horror at the thought of death. MRS. KNOWLES. "Nay, thou should'st not have a horror for what is the gate of life." JOHNSON. (standing upon the hearth rolling about, with a serious, solemn, and somewhat gloomy air,) "No rational man can die without uneasy apprehension." MRS. KNOWLES. "The Scriptures tell us, 'The righteous shall have *hope* in his death.'" JOHNSON. "Yes, Madam; that is, he shall not have despair. But, consider, his hope of salvation must be founded on the terms on which it is promised that the mediation of our SAVIOUR shall be applied to us,— namely, obedience; and where obedience has failed, then, as suppletory to it, repentance. But what man can say that his obedience has been such, as he would approve of in another, or even in himself upon close examination, or that his repentance has not been such as to require being repented of? No man can be sure that his obedience and repentance will obtain salvation." MRS. KNOWLES. "But divine intimation of acceptance may be made to the soul." JOHNSON "Madam it may; but I should not think the better of a man who should tell me on his death-bed he was sure of salvation. A man cannot be sure himself that he has divine intimation of acceptance; much less can he make others sure that he has it." BOSWELL.

"Then, Sir, we must be contented to acknowledge that death is a terrible thing." JOHNSON. "Yes, Sir. I have made no approaches to a state which can look on it as not terrible." MRS. KNOWLES. (seeming to enjoy a pleasing serenity in the persuasion of benignant divine light,) "Does not St. Paul say, 'I have fought the good fight of faith, I have finished my course; henceforth is laid up for me a crown of life?" JOHNSON. "Yes, Madam; but here was a man inspired, a man who had been converted by supernatural interposition." BOSWELL. "In prospect death is dreadful; but in fact we find that people die easy." JOHNSON. "Why, Sir, most people have not *thought* much of the matter, so cannot *say* much, and it is supposed they die easy. Few believe it certain they are then to die; and those who do, set themselves to behave with resolution, as a man does who is going to be hanged. He is not the less unwilling to be hanged." MISS SEWARD. "There is one mode of the fear of death, which is certainly absurd; and that is the dread of annihilation, which is only a pleasing sleep without a dream." JOHNSON. "It is neither pleasing, nor sleep; it is nothing. Now mere existence is so much better than nothing, that one would rather exist even in pain, than not exist." BOSWELL. "If annihilation be nothing, then existing in pain is not a comparative state, but is a positive evil, which I cannot think we should choose. I must be allowed to differ here; and it would lessen the hope of a future state founded on the argument, that the Supreme Being, who is good as he is great, will hereafter compensate for our present sufferings in this life. For if existence, such as we have it here, be comparatively a good, we have no reason to complain, though no more of it should be given to us. But if our only state of existence were in this world, then we might with some reason complain that we are so dissatisfied with our enjoyments compared with our desires." JOHNSON. "The lady confounds annihilation, which is nothing, with the apprehension of it, which is dreadful. It is in the apprehension of it that the horror of annihilation consists."

Of John Wesley, he said, "He can talk well on any subject." BOSWELL. "Pray, Sir, what has he made of his story of a ghost?" JOHNSON. "Why, Sir, he believes it; but not on sufficient authority. He did not take time enough to examine the girl. It was at Newcastle, where the ghost was said to have appeared to a young woman several times, mentioning something about the right to an old house, advising application to be made to an attorney, which was done; and, at the same time, saying the attorney would do nothing, which proved to be the fact. 'This (says John,) is a proof that a ghost knows our thoughts.' Now (laughing,) it is not necessary to know our thoughts, to tell that an attorney will sometimes do nothing. Charles Wesley, who is a more stationary man, does not believe the story. I am sorry that John did not take more pains to inquire into the evidence for it." MISS SEWARD. (with an incredulous smile,) "What, Sir! about a ghost?" JOHNSON. (with solemn vehemence,) "Yes, Madam: this is a question which, after five thousand years, is yet undecided; a question, whether in theology or philosophy, one of the most important that can come before the human understanding."

Mrs. Knowles mentioned, as a proselyte to Quakerism, Miss ————, a young lady well known to Dr. Johnson, for whom he had shown much affection; while she ever had, and still retained, a great respect for him. Mrs. Knowles at the same time took an opportunity of letting him know "that the amiable young creature was sorry at finding that he was offended at her leaving the Church of England and embracing a simpler faith"; and, in the gentlest and most persuasive manner, solicited his kind indulgence for what was sincerely a matter of conscience. JOHNSON. (frowning very angrily,) "Madam, she is an odious wench. She could not have any proper conviction that it was her duty to change her religion, which is the most important of all subjects, and should be studied with all care, and with all the helps we can get. She knew no more of the Church which she left, and that which she embraced, than she did of the difference between the Copernican and Ptolemaic systems." MRS. KNOWLES. "She had the New Testament before her." JOHNSON. "Madam, she could not understand the New Testament, the most difficult book in the world, for which the study of a life is required." MRS. KNOWLES. "It is clear as to essentials." JOHNSON. "But not as to controversial points. The heathens were easily converted, because they had nothing to give up; but we ought not, without very strong conviction indeed, to desert the religion in which we have been educated. That is the religion given you, the religion in which it may be said Providence has placed you. If you live conscientiously in that religion you may be safe. But error is dangerous indeed, if you err when you choose a religion for yourself." MRS KNOWLES. "Must we then go by implicit faith?" JOHNSON. "Why, Madam, the greatest part of our knowledge is implicit faith; and as to religion, have we heard all that a disciple of Confucius, all that a Mahometan, can say for himself?" He then rose again into passion, and attacked the young proselyte in the severest terms of reproach, so that both the ladies seemed to be much shocked.

[1791]

SAMUEL JOHNSON (1709-1784)

In his famous essay on Johnson published in 1831, Macaulay remarked that "the reputation of those writings, which he probably expected to be immortal, is every day fading, while those peculiarities of manner and that careless table-talk the memory of which, he probably thought, would die with him, are likely to be remembered as long as the English language is spoken in any quarter of the globe." Like most of this essay, this remark is half truth and half prejudice. It is true that a first acquaintance with Johnson is perhaps best begun through Boswell; but a good reader of Boswell is sure to look into the writings of Johnson, and, looking in, to find that this is the same Johnson as in Boswell. There is more formality of manner, but the matter is the same, as even Macaulay admitted. Those who are interested in Johnson's shrewd wisdom, may peruse *The Rambler* with pleasure; and *Rasselas* is one of the most bracing tonics in all literature.

Johnson was made comfortable by a pension in 1762, when he was fifty-three years old, and it was the year following that Boswell met him in the back-parlor of Davies' book-shop. Johnson did not care to recall his experiences during the years of his struggle, and Boswell is comparatively meagre on that period. Our main impression is of a man schooled to stern realities by constant physical infirmities and by poverty even to its direst form. He was the son of a humble bookseller in the small cathedral town of Lichfield. He went up to Oxford with unusual preparation and should have distinguished himself there, but was too poor to remain and take his degree. He tried teaching school, but disliked it, and in 1737 went up to London to try a literary career. With him came his friend and former pupil, David Garrick, who soon rose to fame and affluence as the foremost actor of the age, whereas Johnson continued to drudge for years as a hack-writer. His poem *London* (1738) won praise from Pope, but no attention from the public. He planned an edition of Shakespeare, but this project was realized only late in his life. His fame began to grow with his poem, *The Vanity of Human Wishes* (1749); and *The Rambler* (1750-52), an essay periodical, added to the public esteem but did not reach a large audience until after its publication in book form. The general public was probably most deeply impressed by his *Dictionary*, the plan of which had been published in 1747, but which was not completed until 1755. From April, 1758, he wrote for two years a paper, *The Idler*, for a weekly newpaper, and *Rasselas* appeared in 1759. In 1762 he received a government pension of £300, as was carefully explained to him, not for what he was to do, but for what he had done. He was henceforth at leisure to have his talk out, and Boswell appeared to record it.

In 1764 he was introduced to the Thrales, who provided for him a sort of second home at their suburban residence at Streatham. Boswell induced him to tour Scotland in 1773 and Johnson recorded his impressions in the *Journey to the Western Islands of Scotland* (1775). In 1777 he undertook for the booksellers a series of *Lives of the English Poets*, published in 1779-81. These productions of his old age have some of the ease and informality of his conversation and are for this reason preferred over the more stately periods of *The Rambler*. He died in 1784 and was buried in Westminster Abbey.

Those who have only a superficial acquaintance with Johnson often picture him as an ill-mannered and egotistical tyrant, properly nicknamed "The Great Bear." But, as Goldsmith said, he had nothing of the bear but the skin. His charities are well known to all readers of Boswell. Fanny Burney's *Diary* shows us his gentleness and graciousness of manner in the company of ladies. He bore his manifold ills with a manliness which is touching and inspiriting; he never whined, as his contemporary Rousseau so often did under less provocation. His sincere piety, untainted by unction, commands the respect of men of all creeds. In whatever direction we explore the nature of Johnson, we find him genuine. He does not flatter our weaknesses, he exposes our self-delusions, he insists on the harsh realities; but he never derogates from the dignity of humanity. His orthodox Christianity disciplined his nature and sustained him in a world where, as he said in *Rasselas*, there is little to be enjoyed and much to be endured. He was full of eccentricities which amuse us, but the true Johnsonian regards the great man with mingled affection and reverence.

In one respect it is misleading to label the period the "age of Johnson," inasmuch as Johnson was a severe critic of many of the popular tendencies of his time. He deplored the polemic against civilization that was being carried on by Rousseau and others. He disagreed with the sentimental view of human nature which argued that humanity is good in proportion as it is natural. In literature he could be severe on the old-fashioned rule of the "three unities" in drama as well as on the new-fashioned rage for blank verse and magniloquent Pindaric odes. He was almost alone in his ridicule of the tawdry Ossianic forgeries of Macpherson. In politics he was a Tory, maintaining that Whiggism is at bottom a philosophy of political disintegration, and that the Devil was the first Whig. He was especially stern with those who talked theoretically in favor of doctrines which they had not carefully thought out. Considering the extent to which his conversation has been recorded, it is remarkable that his utterances should be so generally consistent with one another. The true student of Johnson will not be content with enjoyment of the delightful anecdotes, but will seek also to understand that body of principles which informs Johnson's personality and intellectual character.

Works, ed. Sir John Hawkins (15 vols., 1787-89); (11 vols., Oxford, 1825); Selected Prose and Poetry, ed. B. H. Bronson (1952); Rasselas, ed. O. F. Emerson (1895); ed. R. W. Chapman (Oxford, 1927); Journey to the Western Islands of Scotland, ed. R. W. Chapman (1924) (with Boswell's Journal of a Tour to the Hebrides); Lives of the Poets, ed. G. B. Hill (3 vols., Oxford, 1905); Poems, ed. D. Nichol Smith and E. L. McAdam (Oxford, 1941); Prefaces and Dedications, ed. A. T. Hazen (New Haven, 1937); Letters, ed. G. B. Hill (2 vols., Oxford, 1897); ed. R. W. Chapman (3 vols., Oxford, 1952); Critical Opinions, ed. J. E. Brown (Princeton, 1926); Life, see Boswell, p. 619; Johnsonian Miscellanies, ed. G. B. Hill (2 vols., Oxford, 1897); A. L. Reade, Johnsonian Gleanings (10 parts, 1909-46); W. Raleigh, Six Essays on Johnson (Oxford, 1910).

PROLOGUE

SPOKEN BY MR. GARRICK AT THE OPENING OF THE THEATRE
IN DRURY LANE, 1747

When Learning's triumph o'er her barbarous foes
First reared the stage, immortal Shakespeare rose;
Each change of many-colored life he drew,
Exhausted worlds, and then imagined new:
Existence saw him spurn her bounded reign,
And panting Time toiled after him in vain.
His powerful strokes presiding Truth impressed,
And unresisted Passion stormed the breast.
 Then Jonson came, instructed from the school
To please in method and invent by rule;   10
His studious patience and laborious art
By regular approach essayed the heart;
Cold Approbation gave the lingering bays,
For those who durst not censure, scarce could praise.
A mortal born, he met the general doom,
But left, like Egypt's kings, a lasting tomb.
 The wits of Charles found easier ways to fame,
Nor wished for Jonson's art, or Shakespeare's flame;
Themselves they studied; as they felt, they writ;
Intrigue was plot, obscenity was wit.   20
Vice always found a sympathetic friend;
They pleased their age, and did not aim to mend.
Yet bards like these aspired to lasting praise,
And proudly hoped to pimp in future days.
Their cause was general, their supports were strong,

    Their slaves were willing, and their reign was long:
Till Shame regained the post that Sense betrayed,
And Virtue called Oblivion to her aid.
    Then, crushed by rules, and weakened as refined,
For years the power of Tragedy declined;   30
From bard to bard the frigid caution crept,
Till Declamation roared while Passion slept;
Yet still did Virtue deign the stage to tread;
Philosophy remained though Nature fled;
But forced at length her ancient reign to quit,
She saw great Faustus lay the ghost of Wit;
Exulting Folly hailed the joyous day,
And Pantomime and song confirmed her sway.
    But who the coming changes can presage,
And mark the future periods of the stage?   40
Perhaps if skill could distant times explore,
New Behns, new Durfeys, yet remain in store;
Perhaps where Lear has raved, and Hamlet died,
On flying cars new sorcerers may ride;
Perhaps (for who can guess the effects of chance?)
Here Hunt may box, or Mahomet may dance.
    Hard is his lot, that, here by fortune placed,
Must watch the wild vicissitudes of taste;
With every meteor of caprice must play,
And chase the new-blown bubbles of the day.   50
Ah! let not censure term our fate our choice,
The stage but echoes back the public voice;
The drama's laws, the drama's patrons give,
For we that live to please, must please to live.
    Then prompt no more the follies you decry,
As tyrants doom their tools of guilt to die;
'Tis yours this night to bid the reign commence
Of rescued Nature and reviving Sense;
To chase the charms of Sound, the pomp of Show,
For useful Mirth and salutary Woe;   60
Bid scenic Virtue form the rising age,
And Truth diffuse her radiance from the stage.

[1747]

THE VANITY OF HUMAN WISHES

IN IMITATION OF THE TENTH SATIRE OF JUVENAL

    Let Observation, with extensive view,
Survey mankind from China to Peru;
Remark each anxious toil, each eager strife,
And watch the busy scenes of crowded life;
Then say how hope and fear, desire and hate,
O'erspread with snares the clouded maze of fate,
Where wavering man, betrayed by venturous pride
To tread the dreary paths without a guide,
As treacherous phantoms in the mist delude,
Shuns fancied ills, or chases airy good.   10

How rarely Reason guides the stubborn choice,
Rules the bold hand, or prompts the suppliant voice;
How nations sink, by darling schemes oppressed,
When Vengeance listens to the fool's request.
Fate wings with every wish the afflictive dart,
Each gift of nature, and each grace of art;
With fatal heat impetuous courage glows,
With fatal sweetness elocution flows;
Impeachment stops the speaker's powerful breath,
And restless fire precipitates on death.   20

But scarce observed, the knowing and the bold
Fall in the general massacre of gold;
Wide-wasting pest! that rages unconfined,
And crowds with crimes the records of mankind:
For gold his sword the hireling ruffian draws;
For gold the hireling judge distorts the laws;
Wealth heaped on wealth, nor truth nor safety buys,
The dangers gather as the treasures rise.

Let history tell, where rival kings command,
And dubious title shakes the madded land,   30
When statutes glean the refuse of the sword,
How much more safe the vassal than the lord;
Low skulks the hind beneath the rage of power,
And leaves the wealthy traitor in the Tower;
Untouched his cottage, and his slumbers sound,
Though confiscation's vultures hover round.

The needy traveller, serene and gay,
Walks the wild heath, and sings his toil away.
Does envy seize thee? crush the upbraiding joy,
Increase his riches, and his peace destroy;   40
New fears in dire vicissitude invade,
The rustling brake alarms, and quivering shade;
Nor light nor darkness bring his pain relief,
One shows the plunder, and one hides the thief.

Yet still one general cry the skies assails,
And gain and grandeur load the tainted gales;
Few know the toiling statesman's fear or care,
The insidious rival and the gaping heir.

Once more, Democritus, arise on earth,
With cheerful wisdom and instructive mirth,   50
See motley life in modern trappings dressed,
And feed with varied fools the eternal jest:
Thou who couldst laugh where want enchained caprice,
Toil crushed conceit, and man was of a piece;
Where wealth unloved without a mourner died,
And scarce a sycophant was fed by pride;
Where ne'er was known the form of mock debate,
Or seen a new-made mayor's unwieldy state;
Where change of favorites made no change of laws,
And senates heard before they judged a cause;   60
How wouldst thou shake at Britain's modish tribe,
Dart the quick taunt, and edge the piercing gibe,
Attentive truth and nature to descry,
And pierce each scene with philosophic eye!
To thee were solemn toys or empty show

The robes of pleasure and the veils of woe;
All aid the farce, and all thy mirth maintain,
Whose joys are causeless, or whose griefs are vain.
    Such was the scorn that filled the sage's mind,
Renewed at every glance on human kind;   70
How just that scorn ere yet thy voice declare,
Search every state, and canvass every prayer.
    Unnumbered suppliants crowd Preferment's gate,
Athirst for wealth, and burning to be great;
Delusive Fortune hears the incessant call,
They mount, they shine, evaporate, and fall.
On every stage the foes of peace attend;
Hate dogs their flight, and insult mocks their end.
Love ends with hope; the sinking statesman's door
Pours in the morning worshipper no more;   80
For growing names the weekly scribbler lies,
To growing wealth the dedicator flies;
From every room descends the painted face,
That hung the bright Palladium of the place,
And, smoked in kitchens or in auctions sold,
To better features yields the frame of gold;
For now no more we trace in every line
Heroic worth, benevolence divine:
The form distorted justifies the fall,
And detestation rids the indignant wall.   90
    But will not Britain hear the last appeal,
Sign her foes' doom, or guard her favorites' zeal?
Through Freedom's sons no more remonstrance rings,
Degrading nobles and controlling kings;
Our supple tribes repress their patriot throats,
And ask no questions but the price of votes;
With weekly libels and septennial ale,
Their wish is full to riot and to rail.
    In full-blown dignity see Wolsey stand,
Law in his voice, and fortune in his hand·   100
To him the church, the realm, their powers consign,
Through him the rays of regal bounty shine,
Still to new heights his restless wishes tower,
Claim leads to claim, and power advances power;
Till conquest unresisted ceased to please,
And rights submitted, left him none to seize.
At length his sovereign frowns—the train of state
Mark the keen glance, and watch the sign to hate.
Where'er he turns he meets a stranger's eye,
His suppliants scorn him, and his followers fly;   110
At once is lost the pride of awful state,
The golden canopy, the glittering plate,
The regal palace, the luxurious board,
The liveried army, and the menial lord.
With age, with cares, with maladies oppressed,
He seeks the refuge of monastic rest.
Grief aids disease, remembered folly stings,
And his last sighs reproach the faith of kings.
    Speak thou, whose thoughts at humble peace repine,
Shall Wolsey's wealth, with Wolsey's end, be thine?   120

Or liv'st thou now, with safer pride content,
The wisest justice on the banks of Trent?
For why did Wolsey near the steeps of fate
On weak foundations raise the enormous weight?
Why but to sink beneath misfortune's blow,
With louder ruin to the gulfs below?
    What gave great Villiers to the assassin's knife,
And fixed disease on Harley's closing life?
What murdered Wentworth, and what exiled Hyde,
By kings protected and to kings allied?   130
What but their wish indulged in courts to shine,
And power too great to keep or to resign?
    When first the college rolls receive his name,
The young enthusiast quits his ease for fame;
Through all his veins the fever of renown
Burns from the strong contagion of the gown;
O'er Bodley's dome his future labors spread,
And Bacon's mansion trembles o'er his head.
Are these thy views? Proceed, illustrious youth,
And Virtue guard thee to the throne of Truth!   140
Yet should thy soul indulge the generous heat,
Till captive Science yields her last retreat;
Should Reason guide thee with her brightest ray,
And pour on misty Doubt resistless day;
Should no false Kindness lure to loose delight,
Nor Praise relax, nor Difficulty fright;
Should tempting Novelty thy cell refrain,
And Sloth effuse her opiate fumes in vain;
Should Beauty blunt on fops her fatal dart,
Nor claim the triumph of a lettered heart;   150
Should no disease thy torpid veins invade,
Nor Melancholy's phantoms haunt thy shade;
Yet hope not life from grief or danger free,
Nor think the doom of man reversed for thee:
Deign on the passing world to turn thine eyes,
And pause awhile from letters, to be wise;
There mark what ills the scholar's life assail,
Toil, envy, want, the patron, and the jail.
See nations slowly wise, and meanly just,
To buried merit raise the tardy bust.   160
If dreams yet flatter, once again attend,
Hear Lydiat's life, and Galileo's end.
    Nor deem, when Learning her last prize bestows,
The glittering eminence exempt from woes;
See, when the vulgar 'scape, despised or awed,
Rebellion's vengeful talons seize on Laud.
From meaner minds, though smaller fines content,
The plundered palace or sequestered rent;
Marked out by dangerous parts he meets the shock,
And fatal Learning leads him to the block: 170
Around his tomb let Art and Genius weep,
But hear his death, ye blockheads, hear and sleep.
    The festal blazes, the triumphal show,
The ravished standard, and the captive foe,
The senate's thanks, the gazette's pompous tale,

With force resistless o'er the brave prevail.
Such bribes the rapid Greek o'er Asia whirled;
For such the steady Romans shook the world;
For such in distant lands the Britons shine,
And stain with blood the Danube or the Rhine;   180
This power has praise that virtue scarce can warm,
Till fame supplies the universal charm.
Yet Reason frowns on War's unequal game,
Where wasted nations raise a single name,
And mortgaged states their grandsires' wreaths regret,
From age to age in everlasting debt;
Wreaths which at last the dear-bought right convey
To rust on medals, or on stones decay.
    On what foundation stands the warrior's pride,
How just his hopes, let Swedish Charles decide;   190
A frame of adamant, a soul of fire,
No dangers fright him and no labors tire;
O'er love, o'er fear, extends his wide domain,
Unconquered lord of pleasure and of pain;
No joys to him pacific sceptres yield;
War sounds the trump, he rushes to the field;
Behold surrounding kings their power combine,
And one capitulate, and one resign;
Peace courts his hand, but spreads her charms in vain;
"Think nothing gained," he cries, "till naught remain,   200
On Moscow's walls till Gothic standards fly,
And all be mine beneath the polar sky."
The march begins in military state,
And nations on his eye suspended wait;
Stern Famine guards the solitary coast,
And Winter barricades the realms of Frost;
He comes, nor want nor cold his course delay;—
Hide, blushing Glory, hide Pultowa's day!
The vanquished hero leaves his broken bands,
And shows his miseries in distant lands;   210
Condemned a needy supplicant to wait,
While ladies interpose and slaves debate.
But did not Chance at length her error mend?
Did no subverted empire mark his end?
Did rival monarchs give the fatal wound?
Or hostile millions press him to the ground?
His fall was destined to a barren strand,
A petty fortress, and a dubious hand;
He left the name at which the world grew pale,
To point a moral or adorn a tale.   220
    All times their scenes of pompous woes afford,
From Persia's tyrant to Bavaria's lord.
In gay hostility and barbarous pride,
With half mankind embattled at his side,
Great Xerxes comes to seize the certain prey,
And starves exhausted regions in his way;
Attendant Flattery counts his myriads o'er,
Till counted myriads soothe his pride no more;
Fresh praise is tried till madness fires his mind;
The waves he lashes, and enchains the wind;   230

New powers are claimed, new powers are still bestowed,
Till rude resistance lops the spreading god;
The daring Greeks deride the martial show,
And heap their valleys with the gaudy foe;
The insulted sea with humbler thoughts he gains;
A single skiff to speed his flight remains;
The encumbered oar scarce leaves the dreaded coast
Through purple billows and a floating host.
   The bold Bavarian, in a luckless hour,
Tries the dread summits of Caesarean power,   240
With unexpected legions bursts away,
And sees defenceless realms receive his sway;
Short sway! fair Austria spreads her mournful charms;
The queen, the beauty, sets the world in arms;
From hill to hill the beacons' rousing blaze
Spreads wide the hope of plunder and of praise;
The fierce Croatian, and the wild Hussar,
And all the sons of ravage crowd the war;
The baffled prince in honor's flattering bloom
Of hasty greatness finds the fatal doom,   250
His foes' derision, and his subjects' blame,
And steals to death from anguish and from shame.
   "Enlarge my life with multitude of days!"
In health, in sickness, thus the suppliant prays;
Hides from himself his state, and shuns to know
That life protracted is protracted woe.
Time hovers o'er, impatient to destroy,
And shuts up all the passages of joy:
In vain their gifts the bounteous seasons pour,
The fruit autumnal and the vernal flower;   260
With listless eyes the dotard views the store,
He views, and wonders that they please no more;
Now pall the tasteless meats and joyless wines,
And Luxury with sighs her slave resigns.
Approach, ye minstrels, try the soothing strain,
Diffuse the tuneful lenitives of pain:
No sounds, alas, would touch the impervious ear,
Though dancing mountains witnessed Orpheus near;
Nor lute nor lyre his feeble powers attend,
Nor sweeter music of a virtuous friend,   270
But everlasting dictates crowd his tongue,
Perversely grave or positively wrong.
The still returning tale and lingering jest
Perplex the fawning niece and pampered guest,
While growing hopes scarce awe the gathering sneer,
And scarce a legacy can bribe to hear;
The watchful guests still hint the last offence,
The daughter's petulance, the son's expense,
Improve his heady rage with treacherous skill,
And mold his passions till they make his will.   280
   Unnumbered maladies his joints invade,
Lay siege to life, and press the dire blockade;
But unextinguished avarice still remains,
And dreaded losses aggravate his pains;
He turns, with anxious heart and crippled hands.

His bonds of debt and mortgages of lands;
Or views his coffers with suspicious eyes,
Unlocks his gold, and counts it till he dies.
　　But grant, the virtues of a temperate prime
Bless with an age exempt from scorn or crime;   290
An age that melts with unperceived decay,
And glides in modest innocence away;
Whose peaceful day Benevolence endears,
Whose night congratulating Conscience cheers;
The general favorite as the general friend:
Such age there is, and who shall wish its end?
　　Yet even on this her load Misfortune flings,
To press the weary minutes' flagging wings:
New sorrow rises as the day returns;
A sister sickens, or a daughter mourns.   300
Now kindred Merit fills the sable bier,
Now lacerated Friendship claims a tear.
Year chases year, decay pursues decay,
Still drops some joy from withering life away;
New forms arise, and different views engage,
Superfluous lags the veteran on the stage,
Till pitying Nature signs the last release,
And bids afflicted Worth retire to peace.
　　But few there are whom hours like these await,
Who set unclouded in the gulfs of fate.   310
From Lydia's monarch should the search descend,
By Solon cautioned to regard his end,
In life's last scene what prodigies surprise,
Fears of the brave, and follies of the wise!
From Marlborough's eyes the streams of dotage flow,
And Swift expires a driveller and a show.
　　The teeming mother, anxious for her race,
Begs for each birth the fortune of a face;
Yet Vane could tell what ills from beauty spring,
And Sedley cursed the form that pleased a king.   320
Ye nymphs of rosy lips and radiant eyes,
Whom Pleasure keeps too busy to be wise,
Whom joys with soft varieties invite,
By day the frolic, and the dance by night,
Who frown with vanity, who smile with art,
And ask the latest fashion of the heart,
What care, what rules your heedless charms shall save,
Each nymph your rival, and each youth your slave?
Against your fame with fondness hate combines,
The rival batters, and the lover mines.   330
With distant voice neglected Virtue calls,
Less heard and less, the faint remonstrance falls;
Tired with contempt, she quits the slippery reign,
And Pride and Prudence take her seat in vain.
In crowd at once, where none the pass defend,
The harmless freedom, and the private friend.
The guardians yield, by force superior plied;
By Interest, Prudence; and by Flattery, Pride.
Now Beauty falls betrayed, despised, distressed,
And hissing Infamy proclaims the rest.   340

Where then shall Hope and Fear their objects find?
Must dull Suspense corrupt the stagnant mind?
Must helpless man, in ignorance sedate,
Roll darkling down the torrent of his fate?
Must no dislike alarm, no wishes rise,
No cries attempt the mercies of the skies?
Inquirer, cease; petitions yet remain
Which Heaven may hear, nor deem religion vain.
Still raise for good the supplicating voice,
But leave to Heaven the measure and the choice.   350
Safe in his power, whose eyes discern afar
The secret ambush of a specious prayer;
Implore his aid, in his decisions rest,
Secure whate'er he gives, he gives the best.
Yet, when the sense of sacred presence fires,
And strong devotion to the skies aspires,
Pour forth thy fervors for a healthful mind,
Obedient passions, and a will resigned;
For love, which scarce collective man can fill;
For patience, sovereign o'er transmuted ill;   360
For faith, that, panting for a happier seat,
Counts death kind Nature's signal of retreat:
These goods for man the laws of Heaven ordain,
These goods he grants, who grants the power to gain;
With these celestial Wisdom calms the mind,
And makes the happiness she does not find.

[1749]

LINES

WRITTEN IN RIDICULE OF CERTAIN POEMS PUBLISHED IN 1777

Wheresoe'er I turn my view,
All is strange, yet nothing new;
Endless labor all along,
Endless labor to be wrong;

Phrase that time has flung away,
Uncouth words in disarray,
Tricked in antique ruff and bonnet,
Ode, and elegy, and sonnet.

[1777, 1786]

ON THE DEATH OF MR. ROBERT LEVET

Condemned to Hope's delusive mine,
As on we toil from day to day,

By sudden blasts, or slow decline,
Our social comforts drop away.

Well tried through many a varying year,
See Levet to the grave descend,
Officious,[1] innocent, sincere,
Of every friendless name the friend.

Yet still he fills Affection's eye,
Obscurely wise and coarsely kind;   10
Nor, lettered Arrogance, deny
Thy praise to merit unrefined.

When fainting Nature called for aid.
And hovering Death prepared the blow,
His vigorous remedy displayed
The power of art without the show.

In Misery's darkest caverns known,
His useful care was ever nigh,
Where hopeless Anguish poured his groan,
And lonely Want retired to die.   20

[1] Full of good offices.

No summons mocked by chill delay,
  No petty gain disdained by pride;
The modest wants of every day
  The toil of every day supplied.

His virtues walked their narrow round,
  Nor made a pause, nor left a void;
And sure the Eternal Master found
  The single talent well employed.

The busy day, the peaceful night,
  Unfelt, uncounted, glided by;   30
His frame was firm, his powers were bright,
  Though now his eightieth year was high.

Then with no throbbing, fiery pain,
  No cold gradations of decay,
Death broke at once the vital chain,
  And freed his soul the nearest way.

                                        [1782, 1783]

THE RAMBLER

[THE COMEDY OF ROMANCE]

No. 4.   SATURDAY, March 31, 1750

Simul et jucunda et idonea dicere vitæ.
          —HOR. *Art of Poetry*, 334.

And join both profit and delight in one.
                              —CREECH.

The works of fiction, with which 10
the present generation seems more
particularly delighted, are such as exhibit life in its true state, diversified
only by accidents that daily happen
in the world, and influenced by passions and qualities which are really
to be found in conversing with mankind.

This kind of writing may be
termed, not improperly, the comedy 20
of romance, and is to be conducted
nearly by the rules of comic poetry.
Its province is to bring about natural
events by easy means, and to keep up
curiosity without the help of wonder:
it is therefore precluded from the machines and expedients of the heroic
romance, and can neither employ
giants to snatch away a lady from the
nuptial rites, nor knights to bring her 30
back from captivity; it can neither
bewilder its personages in deserts, nor
lodge them in imaginary castles.

I remember a remark made by Scaliger upon Pontanus, that all his writings are filled with the same images;
and that if you take from him his
lilies and his roses, his satyrs and his
dryads, he will have nothing left that
can be called poetry. In like manner, 40
almost all the fictions of the last age

will vanish, if you deprive them of a
hermit and a wood, a battle and a
shipwreck.

Why this wild strain of imagination
found reception so long in polite and
learned ages, it is not easy to conceive; but we cannot wonder that
while readers could be procured, the
authors were willing to continue it;
for when a man had by practice
gained some fluency of language, he
had no further care than to retire to
his closet, let loose his invention, and
heat his mind with incredibilities; a
book was thus produced without fear
of criticism, without the toil of study,
without knowledge of nature, or acquaintance with life.

The task of our present writers is
very different; it requires, together
with that learning which is to be
gained from books, that experience
which can never be attained by solitary diligence, but must arise from
general converse and accurate observation of the living world. Their
performances have, as Horace expresses it, *"plus oneris quantum veniæ
minus,"* little indulgence, and therefore more difficulty. They are engaged
in portraits of which every one knows
the original, and can detect any deviation from exactness of resemblance.
Other writings are safe, except from
the malice of learning, but these are
in danger from every common reader;
as the slipper ill executed was censured by a shoemaker who happened
to stop in his way at the Venus of
Apelles.

But the fear of not being approved

as just copiers of human manners, is not the most important concern that an author of this sort ought to have before him. These books are written chiefly to the young, the ignorant, and the idle, to whom they serve as lectures of conduct, and introductions into life. They are the entertainment of minds unfurnished with ideas, and therefore easily susceptible of impressions; not fixed by principles, and therefore easily following the current of fancy; not informed by experience, and consequently open to every false suggestion and partial account.

That the highest degree of reverence should be paid to youth, and that nothing indecent should be suffered to approach their eyes or ears, are precepts extorted by sense and virtue from an ancient writer, by no means eminent for chastity of thought. The same kind, though not the same degree, of caution, is required in everything which is laid before them, to secure them from unjust prejudices, perverse opinions, and incongruous combinations of images.

In the romances formerly written, every transaction and sentiment was so remote from all that passes among men, that the reader was in very little danger of making any applications to himself; the virtues and crimes were equally beyond his sphere of activity; and he amused himself with heroes and with traitors, deliverers and persecutors, as with beings of another species, whose actions were regulated upon motives of their own, and who had neither faults nor excellencies in common with himself.

But when an adventurer is levelled with the rest of the world, and acts in such scenes of the universal drama, as may be the lot of any other man, young spectators fix their eyes upon him with closer attention, and hope, by observing his behaviour and success, to regulate their own practices, when they shall be engaged in the like part.

For this reason these familiar histories may perhaps be made of greater use than the solemnities of professed morality, and convey the knowledge of vice and virtue with more efficacy than axioms and definitions. But if the power of example is so great as to take possession of the memory by a kind of violence, and produce effects almost without the intervention of the will, care ought to be taken, that, when the choice is unrestrained, the best examples only should be exhibited; and that which is likely to operate so strongly, should not be mischievous or uncertain in its effects.

The chief advantage which these fictions have over real life is, that their authors are at liberty, though not to invent, yet to select objects, and to cull from the mass of mankind, those individuals upon which the attention ought most to be employed; as a diamond, though it cannot be made, may be polished by art, and placed in such situation, as to display that lustre which before was buried among common stones.

It is justly considered as the greatest excellency of art, to imitate nature; but it is necessary to distinguish those parts of nature which are most proper for imitation: greater care is still required in representing life, which is so often discoloured by passion, or deformed by wickedness. If the world be promiscuously described, I cannot see of what use it can be to read the account; or why it may not be as safe to turn the eye immediately upon mankind as upon a mirror which shows all that presents itself without discrimination.

It is therefore not a sufficient vindication of a character, that it is drawn as it appears; for many characters ought never to be drawn: nor of a narrative, that the train of events is agreeable to observation and experience; for that observation which is called knowledge of the world will be found much more frequently to make men cunning than good. The purpose of these writings is surely not only to show mankind, but to provide that they may be seen hereafter with less hazard; to teach the means of avoiding the snares which are laid by TREACHERY for INNOCENCE, without infusing any wish for that superiority with which the betrayer flatters his vanity; to give the power of counteracting fraud, without the temptation to practice it; to initiate youth by mock encounters in the art of necessary defense, and to increase prudence without impairing virtue.

Many writers, for the sake of following nature, so mingle good and bad qualities in their principal personages, that they are both equally conspicuous; and as we accompany them through their adventures with delight, and are led by degrees to interest ourselves in their favour, we lose the abhorrence of their faults, because they do not hinder our pleasure, or perhaps regard them with some kindness, for being united with so much merit.

There have been men indeed splendidly wicked, whose endowments threw a brightness on their crimes, and whom scarce any villainy made perfectly detestable, because they never could be wholly divested of their excellencies; but such have been in all ages the great corrupters of the world, and their resemblance ought no more to be preserved, than the art of murdering without pain.

Some have advanced, without due attention to the consequence of this notion, that certain virtues have their correspondent faults, and therefore that to exhibit either apart is to deviate from probability. Thus men are observed by Swift to be "grateful in the same degree as they are resentful." This principle, with others of the same kind, supposes man to act from a brute impulse, and pursue a certain degree of inclination, without any choice of the object; for, otherwise, though it should be allowed that gratitude and resentment arise from the same constitution of the passions, it follows not that they will be equally indulged when reason is consulted; yet, unless that consequence be admitted, this sagacious maxim becomes an empty sound, without any relation to practice or to life.

Nor is it evident that even the first motions to these effects are always in the same proportion. For pride, which produces quickness of resentment, will obstruct gratitude, by unwillingness to admit that inferiority which obligation implies; and it is very unlikely that he who cannot think he receives a favour, will acknowledge or repay it.

It is of the utmost importance to mankind that positions of this tendency should be laid open and confuted; for while men consider good and evil as springing from the same root, they will spare the one for the sake of the other, and in judging, if not of others at least of themselves, will be apt to estimate their virtues by their vices. To this fatal error all those will contribute who confound the colours of right and wrong, and, instead of helping to settle their boundaries, mix them with so much art, that no common mind is able to disunite them.

In narratives where historical veracity has no place, I cannot discover why there should not be exhibited the most perfect idea of virtue; of virtue not angelical, nor above probability—for what we cannot credit, we shall never imitate—but the highest and purest that humanity can reach, which, exercised in such trials as the various revolutions of things shall bring upon it, may, by conquering some calamities, and enduring others, teach us what we may hope, and what we can perform. Vice, for vice is necessary to be shown, should always disgust; nor should the graces of gaiety, nor the dignity of courage, be so united with it, as to reconcile it to the mind. Wherever it appears, it should raise hatred by the malignity of its practices, and contempt by the meanness of its stratagems: for while it is supported by either parts or spirit, it will be seldom heartily abhorred. The Roman tyrant was content to be hated, if he was but feared; and there are thousands of the readers of romances willing to be thought wicked, if they may be allowed to be wits. It is therefore to be steadily inculcated, that virtue is the highest proof of understanding, and the only solid basis of greatness; and that vice is the natural consequence of narrow thoughts; that it begins in mistake, and ends in ignominy.

THE IDLER

[A VERY SMALL CRITIC]

No. 60.   SATURDAY, *June* 9, 1759

Criticism is a study by which men grow important and formidable at very small expense. The power of invention has been conferred by nature upon few, and the labour of learning those sciences which may, by mere labour, be obtained, is too great to be willingly endured; but every man can exert such judgment as he has upon the works of others; and he whom nature has made weak, and idleness keeps ignorant, may yet support his vanity by the name of a critic.

I hope it will give comfort to great numbers who are passing through the world in obscurity, when I inform them how easily distinction may be obtained. All the other powers of literature are coy and haughty; they must be long courted, and at last are not always gained; but Criticism is a goddess easy of access, and forward of advance, who will meet the slow, and encourage the timorous; the want of meaning she supplies with words, and the want of spirit she recompenses with malignity.

This profession has one recommendation peculiar to itself, that it gives vent to malignity without real mischief. No genius was ever blasted by the breath of critics. The poison which, if confined, would have burst the heart, fumes away in empty hisses, and malice is set at ease with very lit-

tle danger to merit. The critic is the only man whose triumph is without another's pain, and whose greatness does not rise upon another's ruin.

To a study at once so easy and so reputable, so malicious and so harmless, it cannot be necessary to invite my readers by a long or laboured exhortation; it is sufficient, since all would be critics if they could, to show by one eminent example, that all can be critics if they will.

Dick Minim, after the common course of puerile studies, in which he was no great proficient, was put an apprentice to a brewer, with whom he had lived two years, when his uncle died in the city, and left him a large fortune in the stocks. Dick had for six months before used the company of the lower players, of whom he had learned to scorn a trade, and being now at liberty to follow his genius, he resolved to be a man of wit and humour. That he might be properly initiated in his new character, he frequented the coffee-houses near the theatres, where he listened very diligently, day after day, to those who talked of language and sentiments, and unities and catastrophes, till by slow degrees he began to think that he understood something of the stage, and hoped in time to talk himself.

But he did not trust so much to natural sagacity as wholly to neglect the help of books. When the theatres were shut, he retired to Richmond with a few select writers, whose opinions he impressed upon his memory by unwearied diligence; and, when he returned with other wits to the town, was able to tell, in very proper phrases, that the chief business of art is to copy nature; that a perfect writer is not to be expected, because genius decays as judgment increases; that the great art is the art of blotting; and that, according to the rule of Horace, every piece should be kept nine years.

Of the great authors he now began to display the characters, laying down, as an universal position, that all had beauties and defects. His opinion was that Shakspeare, committing himself wholly to the impulse of nature, wanted that correctness which learning would have given him; and that Jonson, trusting to learning, did not sufficiently cast his eye on nature. He blamed the stanza of Spenser, and could not bear the hexameters of Sidney. Denham and Waller he held the first reformers of English numbers; and thought that if Waller could have obtained the strength of Denham, or Denham the sweetness of Waller, there had been nothing wanting to complete a poet. He often expressed his commiseration of Dryden's poverty, and his indignation at the age which suffered him to write for bread; he repeated with rapture the first lines of *All for Love*, but wondered at the corruption of taste which could bear any thing so unnatural as rhyming tragedies. In Otway he found uncommon powers of moving the passions, but was disgusted by his general negligence, and blamed him for making a conspirator his hero; and never concluded his disquisition without remarking how happily the sound of the clock is made to alarm the audience. Southern would have been his favourite, but that he mixes comic with tragic scenes, intercepts the natural course of the passions, and fills the mind with a wild confusion of mirth and melancholy. The versification of Rowe he thought too melodious for the stage, and too little varied in different passions. He made it the great fault of Congreve, that all his persons were wits, and that he always wrote with more art than nature. He considered *Cato* rather as a poem than a play, and allowed Addison to be the complete master of allegory and grave humour, but paid no great deference to him as a critic. He thought the chief merit of Prior was in his easy tales and lighter poems, though he allowed that his *Solomon* had many noble sentiments elegantly expressed. In Swift he discovered an inimitable vein of irony, and an easiness which all would hope and few would attain.

Pope he was inclined to degrade from a poet to a versifier, and thought his numbers rather luscious than sweet. He often lamented the neglect of *Phædra and Hippolytus*, and wished to see the stage under better regulations.

These assertions passed commonly uncontradicted; and if now and then an opponent started up, he was quickly repressed by the suffrages of the company, and Minim went away from every dispute with elation of heart and increase of confidence.

He now grew conscious of his abilities, and began to talk of the present state of dramatic poetry; wondered what was become of the comic genius which supplied our ancestors with wit and pleasantry, and why no writer could be found that durst now venture beyond a farce. He saw no reason for thinking that the vein of humour was exhausted, since we live in a country where liberty suffers every character to spread itself to its utmost bulk, and which therefore produces more originals than all the rest of the world together. Of tragedy he concluded business to be the soul, and yet often hinted that love predominates too much upon the modern stage.

He was now an acknowledged critic, and had his own seat in a coffee-house, and headed a party in the pit. Minim has more vanity than ill-nature, and seldom desires to do much mischief; he will, perhaps, murmur a little in the ear of him that sits next him, but endeavours to influence the audience to favour, by clapping when an actor exclaims, "Ye gods!" or laments the misery of his country.

By degrees he was admitted to rehearsals; and many of his friends are of opinion that our present poets are indebted to him for their happiest thoughts; by his contrivance the bell was rung twice in *Barbarossa*, and by his persuasion the author of *Cleone* concluded his play without a couplet; for what can be more absurd, said Minim, than that part of a play should be rhymed, and part written in blank verse? And by what acquisition of faculties is the speaker, who never could find rhymes before, enabled to rhyme at the conclusion of an act?

He is the great investigator of hidden beauties, and is particularly delighted when he finds "the sound an echo to the sense." He has read all our poets with particular attention to this delicacy of versification, and wonders at the supineness with which their works have been hitherto perused, so that no man has found the sound of a drum in this distich:

And pulpit, drum ecclesiastic,
Was beat with fist instead of a stick;

and that the wonderful lines upon honour and a bubble have hitherto passed without notice:

Honour is like the glassy bubble
Which costs philosophers such trouble;
Where, one part cracked, the whole does fly,
And wits are cracked to find out why.

In these verses, says Minim, we have two striking accommodations of the sound to the sense. It is impossible to utter the two lines emphatically without an act like that which they describe; *bubble* and *trouble* causing a momentary inflation of the cheeks by the retention of the breath, which is afterwards forcibly emitted, as in the practice of *blowing bubbles*. But the greatest excellence is in the third line, which is *cracked* in the middle, to express a crack, and then shivers into monosyllables. Yet has this diamond lain neglected with common stones, and among the innumerable admirers of *Hudibras* the observation of this superlative passage has been reserved for the sagacity of Minim.

[DICK MINIM, *continued*]

No. 61.   SATURDAY, *June* 16, 1759

Mr. Minim had now advanced himself to the zenith of critical reputation; when he was in the pit, every eye in the boxes was fixed upon him; when he entered his coffee-house, he was surrounded by circles of candidates, who passed their novitiate of literature under his tuition: his opinion was asked by all who had no opinion of their own, and yet loved to debate and decide; and no composition was supposed to pass in safety to posterity, till it had been secured by Minim's approbation.

Minim professes great admiration of the wisdom and munificence by which the academies of the continent were raised; and often wishes for some standard of taste, for some tribunal, to which merit may appeal from caprice, prejudice, and malignity. He has formed a plan for an academy of criticism, where every work of imagination may be read before it is printed, and which shall authoritatively direct the theatres what pieces to receive or reject, to exclude or to revive.

Such an institution would, in Dick's opinion, spread the fame of English literature over Europe, and make London the metropolis of elegance and politeness, the place to which the learned and ingenious of all countries would repair for instruction and improvement, and where nothing would any longer be applauded or endured that was not conformed to the nicest rules, and finished with the highest elegance.

Till some happy conjunction of the planets shall dispose our princes or ministers to make themselves immortal by such an academy, Minim contents himself to preside four nights in a week in a critical society selected by himself, where he is heard without contradiction, and whence his judgment is disseminated through "the great vulgar and the small."

When he is placed in the chair of criticism, he declares loudly for the noble simplicity of our ancestors, in opposition to the petty refinements and ornamental luxuriance. Sometimes he is sunk in despair, and perceives false delicacy daily gaining ground, and sometimes brightens his countenance with a gleam of hope, and predicts the revival of the true sublime. He then fulminates his loudest censures against the monkish barbarity of rhyme; wonders how beings that pretend to reason can be pleased with one line always ending like another; tells how unjustly and unnaturally sense is sacrificed to sound; how often the best thoughts are mangled by the necessity of confining or extending them to the dimensions of a couplet; and rejoices that genius has, in our days, shaken off the shackles which had encumbered it so long. Yet he allows that rhyme may sometimes be borne, if the lines be often broken, and the pauses judiciously diversified.

From blank verse he makes an easy transition to Milton, whom he produces as an example of the slow advance of lasting reputation. Milton is the only writer in whose books Minim can read forever without weariness. What cause it is that exempts this pressure from satiety he has long and diligently inquired, and believes it to consist in the perpetual variation of the numbers, by which the ear is gratified and the attention awakened. The lines that are commonly thought rugged and unmusical, he conceives to have been written to temper the melodious luxury of the rest, or to express things by a proper cadence, for he scarcely finds a verse that has not this favourite beauty; he declares that he could shiver in a hot-house when he reads that

<blockquote>
                    the ground
Burns frore, and cold performs th' effect of
    fire;
</blockquote>

and that, when Milton bewails his blindness, the verse,

<blockquote>
So thick a drop serene has quenched these
    orbs
</blockquote>

has, he knows not how, something that strikes him with an obscure sensation, like that which he fancies would be felt from the sound of darkness.

Minim is not so confident of his rules of judgment as not very eagerly to catch new light from the name of the author. He is commonly so prudent as to spare those whom he cannot resist, unless, as will sometimes happen, he finds the public combined against them. But a fresh pretender to fame he is strongly inclined to censure, till his own honour requires that he commend him. Till he knows the success of a composition, he intrenches himself in general terms: there are some new thoughts and beautiful passages, but there is likewise much which he would have advised the author to expunge. He has several favourite epithets, of which he has never settled the meaning, but which are very commodiously applied to books which he has not read, or cannot understand. One is *manly*, another is *dry*, another *stiff*, and another *flimsy*; sometimes he discovers delicacy of style and sometimes meets with *strange expressions*.

He is never so great, or so happy, as when a youth of promising parts is brought to receive his directions for the prosecution of his studies. He then puts on a very serious air; he advises the pupil to read none but the best authors, and when he finds one congenial to his own mind, to study his beauties, but avoid his faults; and, when he sits down to write, to consider how his favourite author would think at the present time on the present occasion. He exhorts him to catch those moments when he finds his thoughts expanded and his genius exalted, but to take care lest imagination hurry him beyond the bounds of nature. He holds diligence the mother of success; yet enjoins him, with great earnestness, not to read more than he can digest, and not to confuse his mind by pursuing studies of contrary tendencies. He tells him that every man has his genius, and that Cicero could never be a poet. The boy retires illuminated, resolved to follow his genius, and to think how Milton would have thought; and Minim feasts upon his own beneficence, till another day brings another pupil.

THE HISTORY OF RASSELAS, PRINCE OF ABYSSINIA

CHAPTER I

DESCRIPTION OF A PALACE IN A VALLEY

Ye who listen with credulity to the whispers of fancy, and pursue with eagerness the phantoms of hope; who expect that age will perform the promises of youth, and that the deficiencies of the present day will be supplied by the morrow,—attend to the history of Rasselas, prince of Abyssinia.

Rasselas was the fourth son of the mighty emperor in whose dominions the Father of Waters begins his course; whose bounty pours down the streams of plenty, and scatters over half the world the harvests of Egypt.

According to the custom which has descended from age to age among the monarchs of the torrid zone, Rasselas was confined in a private palace, with the other sons and daughters of Abyssinian royalty, till the order of succession should call him to the throne.

The place which the wisdom or policy of antiquity had destined for the residence of the Abyssinian princes, was a spacious valley in the kingdom of Amhara, surrounded on every side by mountains, of which the summits overhang the middle part. The only passage by which it could be entered was a cavern that passed under a rock, of which it has long been disputed whether it was the work of nature or of human industry. The outlet of the cavern was concealed by a thick wood, and the mouth which opened into the valley was closed with gates of iron, forged by the artificers of ancient days, so massy that no man could, without the help of engines, open or shut them.

From the mountains on every side rivulets descended that filled all the valley with verdure and fertility, and formed a lake in the middle, inhab-ited by fish of every species, and frequented by every fowl whom nature has taught to dip the wing in water. This lake discharged its superfluities by a stream, which entered a dark cleft of the mountain on the northern side, and fell with dreadful noise from precipice to precipice till it was heard no more.

The sides of the mountains were covered with trees, the banks of the brooks were diversified with flowers; every blast shook spices from the rocks, and every month dropped fruits upon the ground. All animals that bite the grass, or browse the shrub, whether wild or tame, wandered in this extensive circuit, secured from beasts of prey by the mountains which confined them. On one part were flocks and herds feeding in the pastures, on another all the beasts of chase frisking in the lawns; the sprightly kid was bounding on the rocks, the subtle monkey frolicking in the trees, and the solemn elephant reposing in the shade. All the diversities of the world were brought together, the blessings of nature were collected, and its evils extracted and excluded.

The valley, wide and fruitful, supplied its inhabitants with the necessaries of life, and all delights and superfluities were added at the annual visit which the emperor paid his children, when the iron gate was opened to the sound of music, and during eight days everyone that resided in the valley was required to propose whatever might contribute to make seclusion pleasant, to fill up the vacancies of attention, and lessen the tediousness of time. Every desire was immediately granted. All the artificers of pleasure were called to gladden the festivity; the musicians exerted the power of harmony, and the dancers showed their activity before the princes, in hope that they should pass their lives in this blissful captivity, to which those only were admitted whose performance was thought able to add novelty to luxury. Such was the appearance of security and delight which this retirement afforded, that they to whom it was new always desired that it might be perpetual; and as those on whom the iron gate had once closed were never suffered to return, the effect of longer experience could not be known. Thus every year produced new schemes of delight and new competitors for imprisonment.

The palace stood on an eminence, raised about thirty paces above the surface of the lake. It was divided into many squares or courts, built with greater or less magnificence according to the rank of those for whom they were designed. The roofs were turned into arches of massy stone, joined with a cement that grew harder by time, and the building stood from century to century, deriding the solstitial rains and equinoctial hurricanes, without need of reparation.

This house, which was so large as to be fully known to none but some ancient officers, who successively inherited the secrets of the place, was built as if suspicion herself had dictated the plan. To every room there was an open and secret passage; every square had a communication with the rest, either from the upper stories by private galleries, or by subterranean passages from the lower apartments. Many of the columns had unsuspected cavities, in which a long race of monarchs had reposited their treasures. They then closed up the opening with marble, which was never to be removed but in the utmost exigencies of the kingdom, and recorded their accumulations in a book, which was itself concealed in a tower, not entered but by the emperor, attended by the prince who stood next in succession.

CHAPTER II

THE DISCONTENT OF RASSELAS IN THE HAPPY VALLEY

Here the sons and daughters of Abyssinia lived only to know the soft vicissitudes of pleasure and repose, attended by all that were skilful to delight, and gratified with whatever the senses can enjoy. They wandered in gardens of fragrance, and slept in the fortresses of security. Every art was practised to make them pleased with their own condition. The sages who instructed them told them of nothing but the miseries of public life, and described all beyond the mountains as regions of calamity, where discord was always raging, and where man preyed upon man.

To heighten their opinion of their own felicity, they were daily entertained with songs, the subject of which was the *happy valley*. Their appetites were excited by frequent enumerations of different enjoyments, and revelry and merriment was the business of every hour, from the dawn of morning to the close of even.

These methods were generally successful; few of the princes had ever wished to enlarge their bounds, but passed their lives in full conviction that they had all within their reach that art or nature could bestow, and pitied those whom fate had excluded from this seat of tranquillity, as the sport of chance and the slaves of misery.

Thus they rose in the morning and lay down at night, pleased with each other and with themselves, all but Rasselas, who, in the twenty-sixth year of his age, began to withdraw himself from their pastimes and assemblies, and to delight in solitary walks and silent meditation. He often sat before tables covered with luxury, and forgot to taste the dainties that were placed before him; he rose abruptly in the midst of the song, and hastily retired beyond the sound of music. His attendants observed the change, and endeavoured to renew his love of pleasure. He neglected their officiousness, repulsed their invitations, and spent day after day on the banks of rivulets sheltered with trees, where he sometimes listened to the birds in the branches, sometimes observed the fish playing in the stream, and anon cast his eyes upon the pastures and mountains filled with animals, of which some were biting the herbage, and some sleeping among the bushes.

This singularity of his humour made him much observed. One of the sages, in whose conversation he had formerly delighted, followed him secretly, in hope of discovering the cause of his disquiet. Rasselas, who knew not that anyone was near him, having for some time fixed his eyes upon the goats that were browsing among the rocks, began to compare their condition with his own.

"What," said he, "makes the difference between man and all the rest of the animal creation? Every beast that strays beside me has the same corporal necessities with myself; he is hungry, and crops the grass, he is thirsty, and drinks the stream, his thirst and hunger are appeased, he is satisfied, and sleeps; he rises again, and he is hungry, he is again fed, and is at rest. I am hungry and thirsty like him, but when thirst and hunger cease, I am not at rest; I am, like him, pained with want, but am not, like him, satisfied with fulness. The intermediate hours are tedious and gloomy; I long again to be hungry that I may again quicken my attention. The birds peck the berries or the corn, and fly away to the groves, where they sit in seeming happiness on the branches, and waste their lives in tuning one unvaried series of sounds. I likewise can call the lutanist and the singer, but the sounds that pleased me yesterday weary me to-day, and will grow yet more wearisome to-morrow. I can discover within me no power of perception which is not glutted with its proper pleasure, yet I do not feel myself delighted. Man has surely some latent sense for which this place affords no gratification, or he has some desires distinct from sense, which must be satisfied before he can be happy."

After this he lifted up his head, and seeing the moon rising, walked towards the palace. As he passed through the fields, and saw the animals around him, "Ye," said he, "are happy, and need not envy me that walk thus among you, burthened with myself; nor do I, ye gentle beings, envy your felicity, for it is not the felicity of man. I have many distresses from which ye are free; I fear pain when I do not feel it; I sometimes shrink at evils recollected, and sometimes start at evils anticipated. Surely the equity of Providence has balanced peculiar sufferings with peculiar enjoyments."

With observations like these the prince amused himself as he returned, uttering them with a plaintive voice, yet with a look that discovered him to feel some complacence in his own perspicacity, and to receive some solace of the miseries of life from consciousness of the delicacy with which he felt, and the eloquence with which he bewailed them. He mingled cheerfully in the diversions of the evening, and all rejoiced to find that his heart was lightened.

CHAPTER III

THE WANTS OF HIM THAT WANTS NOTHING

On the next day his old instructor, imagining that he had now made himself acquainted with his disease of mind, was in the hope of curing it by counsel, and officiously sought an opportunity of conference, which the prince, having long considered him as one whose intellects were exhausted, was not very willing to afford. "Why," said he, "does this man thus intrude upon me; shall I be never suffered to forget those lectures which pleased only while they were new, and to become new again must be forgotten?" He then walked into the wood, and composed himself to his usual meditations; when, before his thoughts had taken any settled form, he perceived his pursuer at his side, and was at first prompted by his impatience to go hastily away; but, being unwilling to offend a man whom he had once reverenced and still loved, he invited him to sit down with him on the bank.

The old man, thus encouraged, began to lament the change which had been lately observed in the prince, and to inquire why he so often retired from the pleasures of the palace, to loneliness and silence. "I fly from pleasure," said the prince, "because pleasure has ceased to please; I am lonely because I am miserable, and am unwilling to cloud with my presence the happiness of others." "You, sir," said the sage, "are the first who has complained of misery in the *happy valley*. I hope to convince you that your complaints have no real cause. You are here in full possession of all that the emperor of Abyssinia can bestow; here is neither labour to be endured nor danger to be dreaded, yet here is all that labour or danger can procure or purchase. Look round and tell me which of your wants is without supply; if you want nothing, how are you unhappy?"

"That I want nothing," said the prince, "or that I know not what I want, is the cause of my complaint; if I had any known want, I should have a certain wish; that wish would excite endeavour, and I should not then repine to see the sun move so slowly towards the western mountain, or lament when the day breaks, and sleep will no longer hide me from myself. When I see the kids and the lambs chasing one another, I fancy that I should be happy if I had something to pursue. But, possessing all that I can want, I find one day and one hour exactly like another, except that the latter is still more tedious than the former. Let your experience inform me how the day may now seem as short as in my childhood, while nature was yet fresh and every moment showed me what I never had observed before. I have already enjoyed too much; give me something to desire."

The old man was surprised at this new species of affliction and knew not what to reply, yet was unwilling to be silent. "Sir," said he, "if you had seen the miseries of the world you would know how to value your present state." "Now," said the prince, "you have given me something to desire. I shall long to see the miseries of the world, since the sight of them is necessary to happiness."

CHAPTER IV

THE PRINCE CONTINUES TO GRIEVE AND MUSE

At this time the sound of music proclaimed the hour of repast and the conversation was concluded. The old man went away sufficiently discontented to find that his reasonings had produced the only conclusion which they were intended to prevent. But in the decline of life shame and grief are of short duration: whether it be that we bear easily what we have borne long; or that, finding ourselves in age less regarded, we less regard others; or that we look with slight regard upon afflictions to which we know that the hand of death is about to put an end.

The prince, whose views were extended to a wider space, could not speedily quiet his emotions. He had been before terrified at the length of life which nature promised him, because he considered that in a long time much must be endured; he now rejoiced in his youth, because in many years much might be done.

This first beam of hope that had been ever darted into his mind, rekindled youth in his cheeks and doubled the lustre of his eyes. He was fired with the desire of doing something, though he knew not yet with distinctness either end or means.

He was now no longer gloomy and unsocial; but, considering himself as master of a secret stock of happiness which he could enjoy only by concealing it, he affected to be busy in all schemes of diversion, and endeavoured to make others pleased with the state of which he himself was weary. But pleasures can never be so multiplied or continued as not to leave much of life unemployed; there were many hours, both of the night and day, which he could spend without suspicion in solitary thought. The load of life was much lightened; he went eagerly into the assemblies, because he supposed the frequency of his presence necessary to the success of his purposes; he retired gladly to privacy, because he had now a subject of thought.

His chief amusement was to picture to himself that world which he had never seen; to place himself in various conditions; to be entangled in imaginary difficulties, and to be engaged in wild adventures; but his benevolence always terminated his projects in the relief of distress, the detection of fraud, the defeat of oppression, and the diffusion of happiness.

Thus passed twenty months of the life of Rasselas. He busied himself so intensely in visionary bustle that he forgot his real solitude; and, amidst hourly preparations for the various incidents of human affairs, neglected to consider by what means he should mingle with mankind.

One day, as he was sitting on a bank, he feigned to himself an orphan virgin robbed of her little portion by a treacherous lover, and crying after him for restitution and redress. So strongly was the image impressed upon his mind, that he started up in the maid's defense, and ran forward to seize the plunderer with all the eagerness of real pursuit. Fear naturally quickens the flight of guilt. Rasselas could not catch the fugitive with his utmost efforts; but resolving to weary by perseverance him whom he could not surpass in speed, he pressed on till the foot of the mountain stopped his course.

Here he recollected himself, and smiled at his own useless impetuosity. Then raising his eyes to the mountain, "This," said he, "is the fatal obstacle that hinders at once the enjoyment of pleasure and the exercise of virtue. How long is it that my hopes and wishes have flown beyond this boundary of my life, which yet I never have attempted to surmount?"

Struck with this reflection, he sat down to muse, and remembered that since he first resolved to escape from his confinement, the sun had passed twice over him in his annual course. He now felt a degree of regret with which he had never been before acquainted. He considered how much might have been done in the time which had passed, and left nothing real behind it. He compared twenty months with the life of man. "In life," said he, "is not to be counted the ignorance of infancy, or imbecility of age. We are long before we are able to think, and we soon cease from the power of acting. The true period of human existence may be reasonably estimated at forty years, of which I have mused away the four and twentieth part. What I have lost was certain, for I have certainly possessed it; but of twenty months to come, who can assure me?"

The consciousness of his own folly pierced him deeply, and he was long before he could be reconciled to himself. "The rest of my time," said he, "has been lost by the crime or folly of my ancestors, and the absurd institutions of my country. I remember it with disgust, yet without remorse; but the months that have passed since new light darted into my soul, since I formed a scheme of reasonable felicity, have been squandered by my own fault. I have lost that which can never be restored; I have seen the sun rise and set for twenty months, an idle gazer on the light of heaven. In this time the birds have left the nest of their mother, and committed themselves to the woods and to the skies; the kid has forsaken the teat, and learned by degrees to climb the rocks in quest of independent sustenance. I only have made no advances, but am still helpless and ignorant. The moon, by more than twenty changes, admonished me of the flux of life; the stream that rolled before my feet upbraided my inactivity. I sat feasting on intellectual luxury, regardless alike of the examples of the earth, and the instructions of the planets. Twenty months are passed; who shall restore them!"

These sorrowful meditations fastened upon his mind; he passed four months in resolving to lose no more time in idle resolves, and was awakened to more vigorous exertion by hearing a maid, who had broken a porcelain cup, remark that what cannot be repaired is not to be regretted.

This was obvious; and Rasselas reproached himself that he had not discovered it, having not known, or not considered, how many useful hints are obtained by chance, and how often the mind, hurried by her own ardour to distant views, neglects the truths that lie open before her. He for a few hours regretted his regret, and from that time bent his whole mind upon the means of escaping from the valley of happiness.

CHAPTER V

THE PRINCE MEDITATES HIS ESCAPE

He now found that it would be very difficult to effect that which it was very easy to suppose effected. When he looked round about him, he saw himself confined by the bars of nature, which had never yet been broken, and by the gate, through which none that once had passed it were ever able to return. He was now impatient as an eagle in a grate. He passed week after week in clambering the mountains, to see if there was any aperture which the bushes might conceal, but found all the summits inaccessible by their prominence. The iron gate he despaired to open; for it was not only secured with all the power of art, but was always watched by successive sentinels, and was, by its position, exposed to the perpetual observation of all the inhabitants.

He then examined the cavern through which the waters of the lake were discharged; and, looking down at a time when the sun shone strongly upon its mouth, he discovered it to be full of broken rocks, which, though they permitted the stream to flow through many narrow passages, would stop any body of solid bulk. He returned discouraged and dejected; but, having now known the blessing of hope, resolved never to despair.

In these fruitless searches he spent ten months. The time, however, passed cheerfully away: in the morning he rose with new hope, in the evening applauded his own diligence, and in the night slept sound after his fatigue. He met a thousand amusements which beguiled his labour, and diversified his thoughts. He discerned the various instincts of animals and properties of plants, and found the place replete with wonders, of which he purposed to solace himself with the contemplation, if he should never be able to accomplish his flight, rejoicing that his endeavours, though yet unsuccessful, had supplied him with a source of inexhaustible inquiry.

But his original curiosity was not yet abated; he resolved to obtain some knowledge of the ways of men. His wish still continued, but his hope grew less. He ceased to survey any longer the walls of his prison, and spared to search by new toils for interstices which he knew could not be found, yet determined to keep his design always in view, and lay hold on any expedient that time should offer.

CHAPTER VI

A DISSERTATION ON THE ART OF FLYING

Among the artists that had been allured into the happy valley, to labour for the accommodation and pleasure of its inhabitants, was a man eminent for his knowledge of the mechanic powers, who had contrived many engines both of use and recreation. By a wheel which the stream turned, he forced the water into a tower, whence it was distributed to all the apartments of the palace. He erected a pavilion in the garden, around which he kept the air always cool by artificial showers. One of the groves, appropriated to the ladies, was ventilated by fans, to which the rivulet that ran through it gave a constant motion; and instruments of soft music were placed at proper distances, of which some played by the impulse of the wind, and some by the power of the stream.

This artist was sometimes visited by Rasselas, who was pleased with every kind of knowledge, imagining that the time would come when all his acquisitions should be of use to him in the open world. He came one day to amuse himself in his usual manner, and found the master busy in building a sailing chariot. He saw that the design was practicable upon a level surface, and with expressions of great esteem solicited its completion. The workman was pleased to find himself so much regarded by the prince, and resolved to gain yet higher honours. "Sir," said he, "you have seen but a small part of what the mechanic sciences can perform. I have been long of opinion that, instead of the tardy conveyance of ships and chariots, man might use the swifter migration of wings; that the fields of air are open to knowledge, and that only ignorance and idleness need crawl upon the ground."

This hint rekindled the prince's desire of passing the mountains; having seen what the mechanist had already performed, he was willing to fancy that he could do more, yet resolved to inquire further before he suffered hope to afflict him by disappointment. "I am afraid," said he to the artist, "that your imagination prevails over your skill, and that you now tell me rather what you wish than what you know. Every animal has his element assigned him; the birds have the air, and man and beasts the earth." "So," replied the mechanist, "fishes have the water in which yet beasts can swim by nature, and men by art. He that can

swim needs not despair to fly; to swim is to fly in a grosser fluid, and to fly is to swim in a subtler. We are only to proportion our power of resistance to the different density of the matter through which we are to pass. You will be necessarily upborne by the air, if you can renew any impulse upon it faster than the air can recede from the pressure."

"But the exercise of swimming," said the prince, "is very laborious; the strongest limbs are soon wearied; I am afraid the act of flying will be yet more violent, and wings will be of no great use, unless we can fly further than we can swim."

"The labour of rising from the ground," said the artist, "will be great, as we see it in the heavier domestic fowls; but as we mount higher, the earth's attraction and the body's gravity will be gradually diminished, till we shall arrive at a region where the man will float in the air without any tendency to fall; no care will then be necessary but to move forwards, which the gentlest impulse will effect. You, sir, whose curiosity is so extensive, will easily conceive with what pleasure a philosopher, furnished with wings and hovering in the sky, would see the earth and all its inhabitants rolling beneath him, and presenting to him successively, by its diurnal motion, all the countries within the same parallel. How must it amuse the pendent spectator to see the moving scene of land and ocean, cities and deserts! to survey with equal security the marts of trade and the fields of battle, mountains infested by barbarians, and fruitful regions gladdened by plenty, and lulled by peace! How easily shall we then trace the Nile through all his passage; pass over to distant regions, and examine the face of nature from one extremity of the earth to the other!"

"All this," said the prince, "is much to be desired; but I am afraid that no man will be able to breathe in these regions of speculation and tranquillity. I have been told that respiration is difficult upon lofty mountains, yet from these precipices, though so high as to produce great tenuity of the air, it is very easy to fall; therefore I suspect that from any height where life can be supported, there may be danger of too quick descent."

"Nothing," replied the artist, "will ever be attempted, if all possible objections must be first overcome. If you will favour my project, I will try the first flight at my own hazard. I have considered the structure of all volant animals, and find the folding continuity of the bat's wings most easily accommodated to the human form. Upon this model I shall begin my task to-morrow, and in a year expect to tower into the air beyond the malice or pursuit of man. But I will work only on this condition, that the art shall not be divulged, and that you shall not require me to make wings for any but ourselves."

"Why," said Rasselas, "should you envy others so great an advantage? All skill ought to be exerted for universal good; every man has owed much to others, and ought to repay the kindness that he has received."

"If men were all virtuous," returned the artist, "I should with great alacrity teach them all to fly. But what would be the security of the good, if the bad could at pleasure invade them from the sky? Against an army sailing through the clouds, neither walls, nor mountains, nor seas could afford any security. A flight of northern savages might hover in the wind, and light at once with irresistible violence upon the capital of a fruitful region that was rolling under them. Even this valley, the retreat of princes, the abode of happiness, might be violated by the sudden descent of some of the naked nations that swarm on the coasts of the southern sea."

The prince promised secrecy, and waited for the performance, not wholly hopeless of success. He visited the work from time to time, observed its progress, and remarked many ingenious contrivances to facilitate mo-

tion and unite levity with strength. The artist was every day more certain that he should leave vultures and eagles behind him, and the contagion of his confidence seized upon the prince.

In a year the wings were finished; and, on a morning appointed, the maker appeared, furnished for flight, on a little promontory: he waved his pinions a while to gather air, then leaped from his stand, and in an instant dropped into the lake. His wings, which were of no use in the air, sustained him in the water, and the prince drew him to land half dead with terror and vexation.

CHAPTER VII

THE PRINCE FINDS A MAN OF LEARNING

The prince was not much afflicted by this disaster, having suffered himself to hope for a happier event, only because he had no other means of escape in view. He still persisted in his design to leave the happy valley by the first opportunity.

His imagination was now at a stand; he had no prospect of entering into the world, and, notwithstanding all his endeavours to support himself, discontent by degrees preyed upon him, and he began again to lose his thoughts in sadness, when the rainy season, which in these countries is periodical, made it inconvenient to wander in the woods.

The rain continued longer and with more violence than had been ever known; the clouds broke on the surrounding mountains, and the torrents streamed into the plain on every side, till the cavern was too narrow to discharge the water. The lake overflowed its banks, and all the level of the valley was covered with the inundation. The eminence on which the palace was built, and some other spots of rising ground, were all that the eye could now discover. The herds and flocks left the pastures, and both the wild beasts and the tame retreated to the mountains.

This inundation confined all the princes to domestic amusements, and the attention of Rasselas was particularly seized by a poem, which Imlac rehearsed upon the various conditions of humanity. He commanded the poet to attend him in his apartment, and recite his verses a second time; then entering into familiar talk, he thought himself happy in having found a man who knew the world so well, and could so skilfully paint the scenes of life. He asked a thousand questions about things to which, though common to all other mortals, his confinement from childhood had kept him a stranger. The poet pitied his ignorance, and loved his curiosity, and entertained him from day to day with novelty and instruction, so that the prince regretted the necessity of sleep, and longed till the morning should renew his pleasure.

As they were sitting together, the prince commanded Imlac to relate his history, and to tell by what accident he was forced, or by what motive induced, to close his life in the happy valley. As he was going to begin his narrative, Rasselas was called to a concert, and obliged to restrain his curiosity till the evening.

CHAPTER VIII

THE HISTORY OF IMLAC

The close of the day is, in the regions of the torrid zone, the only season of diversion and entertainment, and it was therefore midnight before the music ceased and the princesses retired. Rasselas then called for his companion, and required him to begin the story of his life.

"Sir," said Imlac, "my history will not be long; the life that is devoted to knowledge passes silently away, and is very little diversified by events. To talk in public, to think in solitude, to read and to hear, to inquire and answer inquiries, is the business of a scholar. He wanders about the world without pomp or terror, and is neither known nor valued but by men like himself.

"I was born in the kingdom of Goiama, at no great distance from the fountain of the Nile. My father was a wealthy merchant, who traded between the inland countries of Afric and the ports of the Red Sea. He was honest, frugal, and diligent, but of mean sentiments and narrow comprehension; he desired only to be rich, and to conceal his riches, lest he should be spoiled by the governors of the province."

"Surely," said the prince, "my father must be negligent of his charge, if any man in his dominions dares take that which belongs to another. Does he not know that kings are accountable for injustice permitted as well as done? If I were emperor, not the meanest of my subjects should be oppressed with impunity. My blood boils when I am told that a merchant durst not enjoy his honest gains, for fear of losing them by the rapacity of power. Name the governor who robbed the people, that I may declare his crimes to the emperor!"

"Sir," said Imlac, "your ardour is the natural effect of virtue animated by youth; the time will come when you will acquit your father, and perhaps hear with less impatience of the governor. Oppression is, in the Abyssinian dominions, neither frequent nor tolerated; but no form of government has been yet discovered by which cruelty can be wholly prevented. Subordination supposes power on one part, and subjection on the other; and if power be in the hands of men, it will sometimes be abused. The vigilance of the supreme magistrate may do much, but much will still remain undone. He can never know all the crimes that are committed, and can seldom punish all that he knows."

"This," said the prince, "I do not understand; but I had rather hear thee than dispute. Continue thy narration."

"My father," proceeded Imlac, "originally intended that I should have no other education than such as might qualify me for commerce; and discovering in me great strength of memory, and quickness of apprehension, often declared his hope that I should be some time the richest man in Abyssinia."

"Why," said the prince, "did thy father desire the increase of his wealth, when it was already greater than he durst discover or enjoy? I am unwilling to doubt thy veracity, yet inconsistencies cannot both be true."

"Inconsistencies," answered Imlac, "cannot both be right; but, imputed to man, they may both be true. Yet diversity is not inconsistency. My father might expect a time of greater security. However, some desire is necessary to keep life in motion, and he whose real wants are supplied must admit those of fancy."

"This," said the prince, "I can in some measure conceive. I repent that I interrupted thee."

"With this hope," proceeded Imlac, "he sent me to school; but when I had once found the delight of knowledge, and felt the pleasure of intelligence and the pride of invention, I began silently to despise riches, and determined to disappoint the purpose of my father, whose grossness of conception raised my pity. I was twenty years old before his tenderness would expose me to the fatigue of travel, in which time I had been instructed, by successive masters, in all the literature of my native country. As every hour taught me something new, I lived in a continual course of gratifications; but, as I advanced towards manhood, I lost much of the reverence with which I had been used to look on my instructors; because, when the lesson was ended, I did not find them wiser or better than common men.

"At length my father resolved to initiate me in commerce, and, opening one of his subterranean treasuries, counted out ten thousand pieces of gold. 'This, young man,' said he, 'is the stock with which you must negotiate. I began with less than the fifth part, and you see how diligence and parsimony have increased it. This is your own, to waste or to improve. If you squander it by negligence or caprice, you must wait for my death before you will be rich; if in four years you double your stock, we will thenceforward let subordination cease, and live together as friends and partners; for he shall always be equal with me, who is equally skilled in the art of growing rich.'

"We laid our money upon camels, concealed in bales of cheap goods, and travelled to the shore of the Red Sea. When I cast my eye on the expanse of waters, my heart bounded like that of a prisoner escaped. I felt an unextinguishable curiosity kindle in my mind, and resolved to snatch this opportunity of seeing the manners of other nations, and of learning sciences unknown in Abyssinia.

"I remembered that my father had obliged me to the improvement of my stock not by a promise which I ought not to violate, but by a penalty which I was at liberty to incur; and therefore determined to gratify my predominant desire, and, by drinking at the fountains of knowledge, to quench the thirst of curiosity.

"As I was supposed to trade without connection with my father, it was easy for me to become acquainted with the master of a ship, and procure a passage to some other country. I had no motives of choice to regulate my voyage; it was sufficient for me that, wherever I wandered, I should see a country which I had not seen before. I therefore entered a ship bound for Surat, having left a letter for my father declaring my intention."

CHAPTER IX

THE HISTORY OF IMLAC CONTINUED

"When I first entered upon the world of waters, and lost sight of land, I looked round about me with pleasing terror, and thinking my soul enlarged by the boundless prospect, imagined that I could gaze round for ever without satiety; but in a short time I grew weary of looking on barren uniformity, where I could only see again what I had already seen. I then descended into the ship, and doubted for a while whether all my future pleasures would not end, like this in disgust and disappointment. 'Yet surely,' said I, 'the ocean and the land are very different; the only variety of water is rest and motion, but the earth has mountains and valleys, deserts and cities; it is inhabited by men of different customs and contrary opinions; and I may hope to find variety in life, though I should miss it in nature.'

"With this thought I quieted my mind, and amused myself during the voyage, sometimes by learning from the sailors the art of navigation, which I have never practised, and sometimes by forming schemes for my conduct in different situations, in not one of which I have been ever placed.

"I was almost weary of my naval amusements when we landed safely at Surat. I secured my money and, purchasing some commodities for show, joined myself to a caravan that was passing into the inland country. My companions, for some reason or other, conjecturing that I was rich, and, by my inquiries and admiration, finding that I was ignorant, considered me as a novice whom they had a right to cheat, and who was to learn, at the usual expense, the art of fraud. They exposed me to the theft of servants and the exaction of officers, and saw me plundered upon false pretences, without any advantage to themselves but that of rejoicing in the superiority of their own knowledge."

"Stop a moment," said the prince; "is there such depravity in man as that he should injure another without benefit to himself? I can easily conceive that all are pleased with superiority; but your ignorance was merely accidental, which, being neither your crime nor your folly, could afford them no reason to applaud themselves; and the knowledge which they had, and which you wanted, they might as effectually have shown by warning, as betraying you."

"Pride," said Imlac, "is seldom delicate; it will please itself with very mean advantages, and envy feels not its own happiness but when it may be compared with the misery of others. They were my enemies, because they grieved to think me rich; and my oppressors, because they delighted to find me weak."

"Proceed," said the prince; "I doubt not of the facts which you relate, but imagine that you impute them to mistaken motives."

"In this company," said Imlac, "I arrived at Agra, the capital of Indostan, the city in which the Great Mogul commonly resides. I applied myself to the language of the country, and in a few months was able to converse with the learned men, some of whom I found morose and reserved, and others easy and communicative; some were unwilling to teach another what they had with difficulty learned themselves; and some showed that the end of their studies was to gain the dignity of instructing.

"To the tutor of the young princes I recommended myself so much, that I was presented to the emperor as a man of uncommon knowledge. The emperor asked me many questions concerning my country and my travels; and though I cannot now recollect anything that he uttered above the power of a common man, he dismissed me astonished at his wisdom and enamoured of his goodness.

"My credit was now so high, that the merchants with whom I had travelled applied to me for recommendations to the ladies of the court. I was surprised at their confidence of solicitation, and gently reproached them with their practices on the road. They heard me with cold indifference, and showed no tokens of shame or sorrow.

"They then urged their request with the offer of a bribe; but what I would not do for kindness I would not do for money, and refused them, not because they had injured me, but because I would not enable them to injure others; for I knew they would have made use of my credit to cheat those who should buy their wares.

"Having resided at Agra till there was no more to be learned, I travelled into Persia, where I saw many remains of ancient magnificence, and observed many new accommodations of life. The Persians are a nation eminently social, and their assemblies afforded me daily opportunities of remarking characters and manners, and of tracing human nature through all its variations.

"From Persia I passed into Arabia, where I saw a nation at once pastoral and warlike; who live without any settled habitation; whose only wealth is their flocks and herds; and who have yet carried on through all ages an hereditary war with all mankind, though they neither covet nor envy their possessions."

CHAPTER X

IMLAC'S HISTORY CONTINUED. A DISSERTATION UPON POETRY

"Wherever I went, I found that poetry was considered as the highest learning, and regarded with a veneration somewhat approaching to that which man would pay to the angelic nature. And yet it fills me with wonder that, in almost all countries, the most ancient poets are considered as the best: whether it be that every other kind of knowledge is an acquisition gradually attained, and poetry is a gift conferred at once; or that the first poetry of every nation surprised them as a novelty, and retained the credit by consent which it received by accident at first; or whether, as the province of poetry is to describe nature and passion, which are always the same, the first writers took possession of the most striking objects for description and the most probable occurrences for fiction, and left nothing to those that followed them, but transcription of the same events, and new combinations of the same images. Whatever be the reason, it is commonly observed that the early writers are in possession of nature, and their followers of art; that the first excel in strength and invention, and the latter in elegance and refinement.

"I was desirous to add my name to this illustrious fraternity. I read all the poets of Persia and Arabia, and was able to repeat by memory the volumes that are suspended in the mosque of Mecca. But I soon found that no man was ever great by imitation. My desire of excellence impelled me to transfer my attention to nature and to life. Nature was to be my subject, and men to be my auditors: I could never describe what I had not seen; I could not hope to move those with delight or terror, whose interests and opinions I did not understand.

"Being now resolved to be a poet, I saw everything with a new purpose; my sphere of attention was suddenly magnified; no kind of knowledge was to be overlooked. I ranged mountains and deserts for images and resemblances, and pictured upon my mind every tree of the forest and flower of the valley. I observed with equal care the crags of the rock and the pinnacles of the palace. Sometimes I wandered along the mazes of the rivulet, and sometimes watched the changes of the summer clouds. To a poet nothing can be useless. Whatever is beautiful, and whatever is dreadful, must be familiar to his imagination; he must be conversant with all that is awfully vast or elegantly little. The plants of the garden, the animals of the wood, the minerals of the earth, and meteors of the sky, must all concur to store his mind with inexhaustible variety: for every idea is useful for the enforcement or decoration of moral or religious truth; and he who knows most will have most power of diversifying his scenes, and of gratifying his reader with remote allusions and unexpected instruction.

"All the appearances of nature I was therefore careful to study, and every country which I have surveyed has contributed something to my poetical powers."

"In so wide a survey," said the prince, "you must surely have left much unobserved. I have lived till now within the circuit of these mountains, and yet cannot walk abroad without the sight of something which I have never beheld before, or never heeded."

"The business of a poet," said Imlac, "is to examine, not the individual, but the species; to remark general properties and large appearances; he does not number the streaks of the tulip, or describe the different shades in the verdure of the forest. He is to exhibit in his portraits of nature such prominent and striking features as recall the original to every mind, and must neglect the minuter discriminations, which one may have remarked and another have neglected, for those characteristics which are alike obvious to vigilance and carelessness.

"But the knowledge of nature is only half the task of a poet; he must be acquainted likewise with all the modes of life. His character requires that he estimate the happiness and misery of every condition; observe the power of all the passions in all their combinations, and trace the changes of the human mind, as they are modified by various institutions and accidental influences of climate or custom, from the sprightliness of infancy to the despondence of decrepitude. He must divest himself of the prejudices of his age or country; he must consider right and wrong in their abstracted and invariable state; he must disregard present laws and opinions, and rise to general and transcendental truths, which will always be the same. He must, therefore, content himself with the slow progress of his name, contemn the applause of his own time, and commit his claims to the justice of posterity. He must write as the interpreter of nature and the legislator of mankind, and consider himself as presiding over the thoughts and manners of future generations, as a being superior to time and place.

"His labour is not yet at an end; he must know many languages and many sciences; and, that his style may be worthy of his thoughts, must by incessant practice familiarize to himself every delicacy of speech and grace of harmony."

CHAPTER XI

IMLAC'S NARRATIVE CONTINUED. A HINT ON PILGRIMAGE

Imlac now felt the enthusiastic fit, and was proceeding to aggrandize his own profession, when the prince cried out: "Enough! thou hast convinced me that no human being can ever be a poet. Proceed with thy narration."

"To be a poet," said Imlac, "is indeed very difficult." "So difficult," returned the prince, "that I will at present hear no more of his labours. Tell me whither you went when you had seen Persia."

"From Persia," said the poet, "I travelled through Syria, and for three years resided in Palestine, where I conversed with great numbers of the northern and western nations of Europe, the nations which are now in possession of all power and all knowledge, whose armies are irresistible, and whose fleets command the remotest parts of the globe. When I compared these men with the natives of our own kingdom, and those that surround us, they appeared almost another order of beings. In their countries it is difficult to wish for anything that may not be obtained; a thousand arts, of which we never heard, are continually labouring for their convenience and pleasure; and whatever their own climate has denied them is supplied by their commerce."

"By what means," said the prince, "are the Europeans thus powerful, or why, since they can so easily visit Asia and Africa for trade or conquest, cannot the Asiatics and Africans invade their coasts, plant colonies in their ports, and give laws to their natural princes? The same wind that carries them back would bring us thither."

"They are more powerful, sir, than we," answered Imlac, "because they are wiser; knowledge will always predominate over ignorance, as man governs the other animals. But why their knowledge is more than ours, I know not what reason can be given, but the unsearchable will of the Supreme Being."

"When," said the prince with a sigh, "shall I be able to visit Palestine, and mingle with this mighty confluence of nations? Till that happy moment shall arrive, let me fill up the time with such representations as thou canst give me. I am not ignorant of the motive that assembles such numbers in that place, and cannot but consider it as the centre of wisdom and piety, to which the best and wisest men of every land must be continually resorting."

"There are some nations," said Imlac, "that send few visitants to Palestine; for many numerous and learned sects in Europe concur to censure pilgrimage as superstitious, or deride it as ridiculous."

"You know," said the prince, "how little my life has made me acquainted with diversity of opinions. It will be too long to hear the arguments on both sides; you, that have considered them, tell me the result."

"Pilgrimage," said Imlac, "like many other acts of piety, may be reasonable or superstitious, according to the principles upon which it is performed. Long journeys in search of truth are not commanded. Truth, such as is necessary to the regulation of life, is always found where it is honestly sought. Change of place is no natural cause of the increase of piety, for it inevitably produces dissipation of mind. Yet, since men go every day to view the fields where great actions have been performed, and return with stronger impressions of the event, curiosity of the same kind may naturally

dispose us to view that country whence our religion had its beginning; and I believe no man surveys those awful scenes without some confirmation of holy resolutions. That the Supreme Being may be more easily propitiated in one place than in another, is the dream of idle superstition, but that some places may operate upon our own minds in an uncommon manner, is an opinion which hourly experience will justify. He who supposes that his vices may be more successfully combated in Palestine, will, perhaps, find himself mistaken, yet he may go thither without folly; he who thinks they will be more freely pardoned, dishonours at once his reason and religion."

"These," said the prince, "are European distinctions. I will consider them another time. What have you found to be the effect of knowledge? Are those nations happier than we?"

"There is so much infelicity," said the poet, "in the world, that scarce any man has leisure from his own distresses to estimate the comparative happiness of others. Knowledge is certainly one of the means of pleasure, as is confessed by the natural desire which every mind feels of increasing its ideas. Ignorance is mere privation, by which nothing can be produced; it is a vacuity in which the soul sits motionless and torpid for want of attraction; and, without knowing why, we always rejoice when we learn, and grieve when we forget. I am therefore inclined to conclude, that if nothing counteracts the natural consequence of learning, we grow more happy as our minds take a wider range.

"In enumerating the particular comforts of life, we shall find many advantages on the side of the Europeans. They cure wounds and diseases with which we languish and perish. We suffer inclemencies of weather which they can obviate. They have engines for the despatch of many laborious works, which we must perform by manual industry. There is such communication between distant places, that one friend can hardly be said to be absent from another. Their policy removes all public inconveniencies; they have roads cut through their mountains, and bridges laid upon their rivers. And, if we descend to the privacies of life, their habitations are more commodious, and their possessions are more secure."

"They are surely happy," said the prince, "who have all these conveniencies, of which I envy none so much as the facility with which separated friends interchange their thoughts."

"The Europeans," answered Imlac, "are less unhappy than we, but they are not happy. Human life is everywhere a state in which much is to be endured, and little to be enjoyed."

CHAPTER XII

THE STORY OF IMLAC CONTINUED

"I am not yet willing," said the prince, "to suppose that happiness is so parsimoniously distributed to mortals; nor can believe but that, if I had the choice of life, I should be able to fill every day with pleasure. I would injure no man, and should provoke no resentment; I would relieve every distress, and should enjoy the benedictions of gratitude. I would choose my friends among the wise, and my wife among the virtuous; and therefore should be in no danger from treachery or unkindness. My children should by my care be learned and pious, and would repay to my age what their childhood had received. What would dare to molest him who might call on every side to thousands enriched by his bounty, or assisted by his power? And why should not life glide quietly away in the soft reciprocation of protection and reverence? All this may be done without the help of European refinements, which appear by their effects to be rather specious than useful. Let us leave them, and pursue our journey."

"From Palestine," said Imlac, "I passed through many regions of Asia;

in the more civilized kingdoms as a trader, and among the barbarians of the mountains as a pilgrim. At last I began to long for my native country, that I might repose after my travels and fatigues in the places where I had spent my earliest years, and gladden my old companions with the recital of my adventures. Often did I figure to myself those with whom I had sported away the gay hours of dawning life, sitting round me in its evening, wondering at my tales and listening to my counsels.

"When this thought had taken possession of my mind, I considered every moment as wasted which did not bring me nearer to Abyssinia. I hastened into Egypt, and, notwithstanding my impatience, was detained ten months in the contemplation of its ancient magnificence, and in inquiries after the remains of its ancient learning. I found in Cairo a mixture of all nations; some brought thither by the love of knowledge, some by the hope of gain, and many by the desire of living after their own manner without observation, and of lying hid in the obscurity of multitudes; for, in a city, populous as Cairo, it is possible to obtain at the same time the gratifications of society, and the secrecy of solitude.

"From Cairo I travelled to Suez, and embarked on the Red Sea, passing along the coast till I arrived at the port from which I had departed twenty years before. Here I joined myself to a caravan, and re-entered my native country.

"I now expected the caresses of my kinsmen, and the congratulations of my friends, and was not without hope that my father, whatever value he had set upon riches, would own with gladness and pride a son who was able to add to the felicity and honour of the nation. But I was soon convinced that my thoughts were vain. My father had been dead fourteen years, having divided his wealth among my brothers, who were removed to some other provinces. Of my companions, the greater part was in the grave; of the rest, some could with difficulty remember me, and some considered me as one corrupted by foreign manners.

"A man used to vicissitudes is not easily dejected. I forgot, after a time, my disappointment, and endeavoured to recommend myself to the nobles of the kingdom; they admitted me to their tables, heard my story, and dismissed me. I opened a school, and was prohibited to teach. I then resolved to sit down in the quiet of domestic life, and addressed a lady that was fond of my conversation, but rejected my suit because my father was a merchant.

"Wearied at last with solicitation and repulses, I resolved to hide myself forever from the world, and depend no longer on the opinion or caprice of others. I waited for the time when the gate of the *happy valley* should open, that I might bid farewell to hope and fear. The day came; my performance was distinguished with favour, and I resigned myself with joy to perpetual confinement."

"Hast thou here found happiness at last?" said Rasselas. "Tell me, without reserve; art thou content with thy condition, or dost thou wish to be again wandering and inquiring? All the inhabitants of this valley celebrate their lot, and at the annual visit of the emperor invite others to partake of their felicity."

"Great prince," said Imlac, "I shall speak the truth; I know not one of all your attendants who does not lament the hour when he entered this retreat. I am less unhappy than the rest, because I have a mind replete with images which I can vary and combine at pleasure. I can amuse my solitude by the renovation of the knowledge which begins to fade from my memory, and by recollection of the accidents of my past life. Yet all this ends in the sorrowful consideration that my acquirements are now useless, and that none of my pleasures can be again enjoyed. The rest, whose minds have no impression but of the present moment,

are either corroded by malignant passions, or sit stupid in the gloom of perpetual vacancy."

"What passions can infest those," said the prince, "who have no rivals? We are in a place where impotence precludes malice, and where all envy is repressed by community of enjoyments."

"There may be community," said Imlac, "of material possessions, but there can never be community of love or of esteem. It must happen that one will please more than another; he that knows himself despised will always be envious; and still more envious and malevolent, if he is condemned to live in the presence of those who despise him. The invitations by which they allure others to a state which they feel to be wretched, proceed from the natural malignity of hopeless misery. They are weary of themselves, and of each other, and expect to find relief in new companions. They envy the liberty which their folly has forfeited, and would gladly see all mankind imprisoned like themselves.

"From this crime, however, I am wholly free. No man can say that he is wretched by my persuasion. I look with pity on the crowds who are annually soliciting admission to captivity, and wish that it were lawful for me to warn them of their danger."

"My dear Imlac," said the prince, "I will open to thee my whole heart. I have long meditated an escape from the happy valley. I have examined the mountains on every side, but find myself insuperably barred; teach me the way to break my prison; thou shalt be the companion of my flight, the guide of my rambles, the partner of my fortune, and my sole director in the *choice of life*."

"Sir," answered the poet, "your escape will be difficult, and perhaps you may soon repent your curiosity. The world, which you figure to yourself smooth and quiet as the lake in the valley, you will find a sea foaming with tempests, and boiling with whirlpools: you will be sometimes overwhelmed by the waves of violence, and sometimes dashed against the rocks of treachery. Amidst wrongs and frauds, competitions and anxieties, you will wish a thousand times for these seats of quiet, and willingly quit hope to be free from fear."

"Do not seek to deter me from my purpose," said the prince. "I am impatient to see what thou hast seen; and since thou art thyself weary of the valley, it is evident that thy former state was better than this. Whatever be the consequence of my experiment, I am resolved to judge with my own eyes of the various conditions of men, and then to make deliberately my *choice of life.*"

"I am afraid," said Imlac, "you are hindered by stronger restraints than my persuasions; yet, if your determination is fixed, I do not counsel you to despair. Few things are impossible to diligence and skill."

CHAPTER XIII

RASSELAS DISCOVERS THE MEANS OF ESCAPE

The prince now dismissed his favourite to rest, but the narrative of wonders and novelties filled his mind with perturbation. He revolved all that he had heard, and prepared innumerable questions for the morning.

Much of his uneasiness was now removed. He had a friend to whom he could impart his thoughts, and whose experience could assist him in his designs. His heart was no longer condemned to swell with silent vexation. He thought that even the *happy valley* might be endured with such a companion, and that, if they could range the world together, he should have nothing further to desire.

In a few days the water was discharged, and the ground dried. The prince and Imlac then walked out together, to converse without the notice of the rest. The prince, whose thoughts were always on the wing, as he passed by the gate said, with a countenance of sorrow, "Why art thou so strong, and why is man so weak?"

"Man is not weak," answered his companion; "knowledge is more than equivalent to force. The master of mechanics laughs at strength. I can burst the gate, but cannot do it secretly. Some other expedient must be tried."

As they were walking on the side of the mountain, they observed that the conies, which the rain had driven from their burrows, had taken shelter among the bushes, and formed holes behind them, tending upwards in an oblique line. "It has been the opinion of antiquity," said Imlac, "that human reason borrowed many arts from the instinct of animals; let us, therefore, not think ourselves degraded by learning from the cony. We may escape by piercing the mountain in the same direction. We will begin where the summit hangs over the middle part, and labour upward till we shall issue out beyond the prominence."

The eyes of the prince, when he heard this proposal, sparkled with joy. The execution was easy, and the success certain.

No time was now lost. They hastened early in the morning to choose a place proper for their mine. They clambered with great fatigue among crags and brambles, and returned without having discovered any part that favoured their design. The second and the third day were spent in the same manner, and with the same frustration. But, on the fourth, they found a small cavern concealed by a thicket, where they resolved to make their experiment.

Imlac procured instruments proper to hew stone and remove earth, and they fell to their work on the next day with more eagerness than vigour. They were presently exhausted by their efforts, and sat down to pant upon the grass. The prince, for a moment, appeared to be discouraged. "Sir," said his companion, "practice will enable us to continue our labour for a longer time. Mark, however, how far we have advanced, and you will find that our toil will some time have an end. Great works are performed, not by strength, but perseverance; yonder palace was raised by single stones, yet you see its height and spaciousness. He that shall walk with vigour three hours a day, will pass in seven years a space equal to the circumference of the globe."

They returned to their work day after day, and in a short time found a fissure in the rock, which enabled them to pass far with very little obstruction. This Rasselas considered as a good omen. "Do not disturb your mind," said Imlac, "with other hopes or fears than reason may suggest; if you are pleased with prognostics of good, you will be terrified likewise with tokens of evil, and your whole life will be a prey to superstition. Whatever facilitates our work is more than an omen, it is a cause of success. This is one of those pleasing surprises which often happen to active resolution. Many things difficult to design prove easy to performance."

CHAPTER XIV

RASSELAS AND IMLAC RECEIVE AN UNEXPECTED VISIT

They had now wrought their way to the middle, and solaced their toil with the approach of liberty, when the prince, coming down to refresh himself with air, found his sister Nekayah standing before the mouth of the cavity. He started and stood confused, afraid to tell his design, and yet hopeless to conceal it. A few moments determined him to repose on her fidelity, and secure her secrecy by a declaration without reserve.

"Do not imagine," said the princess, "that I came hither as a spy. I had observed from my window, that you and Imlac directed your walk every day towards the same point, but I did not suppose you had any better reason for the preference than a cooler shade, or more fragrant bank, nor followed you with any other design than

to partake of your conversation. Since, then, not suspicion, but fondness has detected you, let me not lose the advantage of my discovery. I am equally weary of confinement with yourself, and not less desirous of knowing what is done or suffered in the world. Permit me to fly with you from this tasteless tranquillity, which will yet grow more loathsome when you have left me. You may deny me to accompany you, but cannot hinder me from following."

The prince, who loved Nekayah above his other sisters, had no inclination to refuse her request, and grieved that he had lost an opportunity of showing his confidence by a voluntary communication. It was therefore agreed that she should leave the valley with them, and that, in the mean time, she should watch, lest any other straggler should, by chance or curiosity, follow them to the mountain.

At length their labour was at an end; they saw light beyond the prominence, and, issuing to the top of the mountain, beheld the Nile, yet a narrow current, wandering beneath them.

The prince looked round with rapture, anticipated all the pleasures of travel, and in thought was already transported beyond his father's dominions. Imlac, though very joyful at his escape, had less expectation of pleasure in the world, which he had before tried, and of which he had been weary.

Rasselas was so much delighted with a wider horizon, that he could not soon be persuaded to return into the valley. He informed his sister that the way was open, and that nothing now remained but to prepare for their departure.

CHAPTER XV

THE PRINCE AND PRINCESS LEAVE THE VALLEY, AND SEE MANY WONDERS

The prince and princess had jewels sufficient to make them rich whenever they came into a place of commerce, which, by Imlac's direction, they hid in their clothes, and on the night of the next full moon all left the valley. The princess was followed only by a single favourite, who did not know whither she was going.

They clambered through the cavity, and began to go down on the other side. The princess and her maid turned their eyes towards every part, and seeing nothing to bound their prospect, considered themselves as in danger of being lost in a dreary vacuity. They stopped and trembled. "I am almost afraid," said the princess, "to begin a journey of which I cannot perceive an end, and to venture into this immense plain, where I may be approached on every side by men whom I never saw." The prince felt nearly the same emotions, though he thought it more manly to conceal them.

Imlac smiled at their terrors, and encouraged them to proceed; but the princess continued irresolute, till she had been imperceptibly drawn forward too far to return.

In the morning they found some shepherds in the field, who set milk and fruits before them. The princess wondered that she did not see a palace ready for her reception, and a table spread with delicacies; but, being faint and hungry, she drank the milk and eat the fruits, and thought them of a higher flavour than the products of the valley.

They travelled forward by easy journeys, being all unaccustomed to toil or difficulty, and knowing that, though they might be missed, they could not be pursued. In a few days they came into a more populous region, where Imlac was diverted with the admiration which his companions expressed at the diversity of manners, stations, and employments.

Their dress was such as might not bring upon them the suspicion of having anything to conceal; yet the prince, wherever he came, expected to be obeyed, and the princess was frighted because those that came into her presence did not prostrate themselves before her. Imlac was forced to observe them with great vigilance, lest they should betray their rank by their unusual behaviour, and detained them several weeks in the first village to accustom them to the sight of common mortals.

By degrees the royal wanderers were taught to understand that they had for a time laid aside their dignity, and were to expect only such regard as liberality and courtesy could procure. And Imlac, having by many admonitions prepared them to endure the tumults of a port, and the ruggedness of the commercial race, brought them down to the sea-coast.

The prince and his sister, to whom everything was new, were gratified equally at all places, and therefore remained for some months at the port without any inclination to pass further. Imlac was content with their stay, because he did not think it safe to expose them, unpractised in the world, to the hazards of a foreign country.

At last he began to fear lest they should be discovered, and proposed to fix a day for their departure. They had no pretensions to judge for themselves, and referred the whole scheme to his direction. He therefore took passage in a ship to Suez; and, when the time came, with great difficulty prevailed on the princess to enter the vessel. They had a quick and prosperous voyage, and from Suez travelled by land to Cairo.

CHAPTER XVI

THEY ENTER CAIRO, AND FIND EVERY MAN HAPPY

As they approached the city, which filled the strangers with astonishment, "This," said Imlac to the prince, "is the place where travellers and merchants assemble from all the corners of the earth. You will here find men of every character and every occupation. Commerce is here honourable. I will act as a merchant, and you shall live as strangers, who have no other end of travel than curiosity. It will soon be observed that we are rich; our reputation will procure us access to all whom we shall desire to know; you will see all the conditions of humanity, and enable yourself at leisure to make your *choice of life.*"

They now entered the town, stunned by the noise, and offended by the crowds. Instruction had not yet so prevailed over habit, but that they wondered to see themselves pass undistinguished along the street, and met by the lowest of the people without reverence or notice. The princess could not at first bear the thought of being levelled with the vulgar, and for some days continued in her chamber, where she was served by her favourite, Pekuah, as in the palace of the valley.

Imlac, who understood traffic, sold part of the jewels the next day, and hired a house, which he adorned with such magnificence, that he was immediately considered as a merchant of great wealth. His politeness attracted many acquaintance, and his generosity made him courted by many dependents. His table was crowded by men of every nation, who all admired his knowledge, and solicited his favour. His companions, not being able to mix in the conversation, could make no discovery of their ignorance or surprise, and were gradually initiated in the world as they gained knowledge of the language.

The prince had, by frequent lectures, been taught the use and nature of money; but the ladies could not for a long time comprehend what the merchants did with small pieces of gold and silver, or why things of so little use should be received as equivalent to the necessaries of life.

They studied the language two years, while Imlac was preparing to set before them the various ranks and conditions of mankind. He grew acquainted with all who had anything uncommon in their fortune or conduct. He frequented the voluptuous

and the frugal, the idle and the busy, the merchants and the men of learning.

The prince being now able to converse with fluency, and having learned the caution necessary to be observed in his intercourse with strangers, began to accompany Imlac to places of resort, and to enter into all assemblies, that he might make his *choice of life.*

For some time he thought choice needless, because all appeared to him equally happy. Wherever he went he met gaiety and kindness, and heard the song of joy or the laugh of carelessness. He began to believe that the world overflowed with universal plenty, and that nothing was withheld either from want or merit; that every hand showered liberality, and every heart melted with benevolence: "And who then," says he, "will be suffered to be wretched?"

Imlac permitted the pleasing delusion, and was unwilling to crush the hope of inexperience, till one day, having sat awhile silent, "I know not," said the prince, "what can be the reason that I am more unhappy than any of our friends. I see them perpetually and unalterably cheerful, but feel my own mind restless and uneasy. I am unsatisfied with those pleasures which I seem most to court; I live in the crowds of jollity, not so much to enjoy company as to shun myself, and am only loud and merry to conceal my sadness."

"Every man," said Imlac, "may, by examining his own mind, guess what passes in the minds of others; when you feel that your own gaiety is counterfeit, it may justly lead you to suspect that of your companions not to be sincere. Envy is commonly reciprocal. We are long before we are convinced that happiness is never to be found, and each believes it possessed by others, to keep alive the hope of obtaining it for himself. In the assembly where you passed the last night, there appeared such sprightliness of air, and volatility of fancy, as might have suited beings of an higher order, formed to inhabit serener regions, inaccessible to care or sorrow; yet, believe me, prince, there was not one who did not dread the moment when solitude should deliver him to the tyranny of reflection."

"This," said the prince, "may be true of others, since it is true of me; yet, whatever be the general infelicity of man, one condition is more happy than another, and wisdom surely directs us to take the least evil in the *choice of life*."

"The causes of good and evil," answered Imlac, "are so various and uncertain, so often entangled with each other, so diversified by various relations, and so much subject to accidents which cannot be foreseen, that he who would fix his condition upon incontestable reasons of preference, must live and die inquiring and deliberating."

"But, surely," said Rasselas, "the wise men, to whom we listen with reverence and wonder, chose that mode of life for themselves which they thought most likely to make them happy."

"Very few," said the poet, "live by choice. Every man is placed in his present condition by causes which acted without his foresight, and with which he did not always willingly cooperate; and therefore you will rarely meet one who does not think the lot of his neighbour better than his own."

"I am pleased to think," said the prince, "that my birth has given me at least one advantage over others, by enabling me to determine for myself. I have here the world before me. I will review it at leisure; surely happiness is somewhere to be found."

CHAPTER XVII

THE PRINCE ASSOCIATES WITH YOUNG MEN OF SPIRIT AND GAIETY

Rasselas rose next day, and resolved to begin his experiments upon life. "Youth," cried he, "is the time of gladness; I will join myself to the young men, whose only business is to gratify their desires, and whose time is all spent in a succession of enjoyments."

To such societies he was readily admitted, but a few days brought him back weary and disgusted. Their mirth was without images, their laughter without motive; their pleasures were gross and sensual, in which the mind had no part; their conduct was at once wild and mean; they laughed at order and at law, but the frown of power dejected, and the eye of wisdom abashed them.

The prince soon concluded that he should never be happy in a course of life of which he was ashamed. He thought it unsuitable to a reasonable being to act without a plan, and to be sad or cheerful only by chance. "Happiness," said he, "must be something solid and permanent, without fear and without uncertainty."

But his young companions had gained so much of his regard by their frankness and courtesy, that he could not leave them without warning and remonstrance. "My friends," said he, "I have seriously considered our manners and our prospects, and find that we have mistaken our own interest. The first years of man must make provision for the last. He that never thinks, never can be wise. Perpetual levity must end in ignorance; and intemperance, though it may fire the spirits for an hour, will make life short or miserable. Let us consider that youth is of no long duration, and that in maturer age, when the enchantments of fancy shall cease, and phantoms of delight dance no more about us, we shall have no comforts but the esteem of wise men, and the means of doing good. Let us therefore stop while to stop is in our power. Let us live as men who are some time to grow old, and to whom it will be the most dreadful of all evils not to count their past years but by follies, and to be reminded of their former luxuriance of health only by the maladies which riot has produced."

They stared a while in silence one upon another, and at last drove him away by a general chorus of continued laughter.

The consciousness that his sentiments were just, and his intentions kind, was scarcely sufficient to support him against the horror of derision. But he recovered his tranquillity, and pursued his search.

CHAPTER XVIII

THE PRINCE FINDS A WISE AND HAPPY MAN

As he was one day walking in the street, he saw a spacious building which all were, by the open doors, invited to enter: he followed the stream of people, and found it a hall or school of declamation, in which professors read lectures to their auditory. He fixed his eye upon a sage raised above the rest, who discoursed with great energy on the government of the passions. His look was venerable, his action graceful, his pronunciation clear, and his diction elegant. He showed with great strength of sentiment and variety of illustration, that human nature is degraded and debased, when the lower faculties predominate over the higher; that when fancy, the parent of passion, usurps the dominion of the mind, nothing ensues but the natural effect of unlawful government, perturbation and confusion; that she betrays the fortresses of the intellect to rebels, and excites her children to sedition against reason, their lawful sovereign. He compared reason to the sun, of which the light is constant, uniform, and lasting; and fancy to a meteor, of bright but transitory lustre, irregular in its motion, and delusive in its direction. He then communicated the various precepts given from time to time for the conquest of passion, and displayed the happiness of those who had obtained the important victory, after which man is no longer the slave of fear, nor the fool of hope; is no more emaciated by envy, inflamed by anger,

emasculated by tenderness, or depressed by grief; but walks on calmly through the tumults or the privacies of life, as the sun pursues alike his course through the calm or the stormy sky.

He enumerated many examples of heroes immovable by pain or pleasure, who looked with indifference on those modes or accidents to which the vulgar give the names of good and evil. He exhorted his hearers to lay aside their prejudices, and arm themselves against the shafts of malice or misfortune, by invulnerable patience; concluding that this state only was happiness, and that his happiness was in everyone's power.

Rasselas listened to him with the veneration due to the instructions of a superior being, and, waiting for him at the door, humbly implored the liberty of visiting so great a master of true wisdom. The lecturer hesitated a moment, when Rasselas put a purse of gold into his hand, which he received with a mixture of joy and wonder.

"I have found," said the prince at his return to Imlac, "a man who can teach all that is necessary to be known; who, from the unshaken throne of rational fortitude, looks down on the scenes of life changing beneath him. He speaks, and attention watches his lips. He reasons, and conviction closes his periods. This man shall be my future guide; I will learn his doctrines, and imitate his life."

"Be not too hasty," said Imlac, "to trust or to admire the teachers of morality: they discourse like angels, but they live like men."

Rasselas, who could not conceive how any man could reason so forcibly without feeling the cogency of his own arguments, paid his visit in a few days, and was denied admission. He had now learned the power of money, and made his way by a piece of gold to the inner apartment, where he found the philosopher in a room half darkened, with his eyes misty and his face pale. "Sir," said he, "you are come at a time when all human friendship is useless; what I suffer cannot be remedied, what I have lost cannot be supplied. My daughter, my only daughter, from whose tenderness I expected all the comforts of my age, died last night of a fever. My views, my purposes, my hopes are at an end; I am now a lonely being, disunited from society."

"Sir," said the prince, "mortality is an event by which a wise man can never be surprised; we know that death is always near, and it should therefore always be expected." "Young man," answered the philosopher, "you speak like one that has never felt the pangs of separation." "Have you then forgot the precepts," said Rasselas, "which you so powerfully enforced? Has wisdom no strength to arm the heart against calamity? Consider, that external things are naturally variable, but truth and reason are always the same." "What comfort," said the mourner, "can truth and reason afford me? Of what effect are they now, but to tell me that my daughter will not be restored?"

The prince, whose humanity would not suffer him to insult misery with reproof, went away, convinced of the emptiness of rhetorical sound, and the inefficacy of polished periods and studied sentences.

CHAPTER XIX

A GLIMPSE OF PASTORAL LIFE

He was still eager upon the same inquiry; and having heard of a hermit that lived near the lowest cataract of the Nile, and filled the whole country with the fame of his sanctity, resolved to visit his retreat, and inquire whether that felicity which public life could not afford was to be found in solitude; and whether a man whose age and virtue made him venerable, could teach any peculiar art of shunning evils, or enduring them.

Imlac and the princess agreed to accompany him, and, after the necessary preparations, they began their journey. Their way lay through fields, where shepherds tended their flocks and the lambs were playing upon the pasture. "This," said the poet, "is the life which has been often celebrated for its innocence and quiet; let us pass the heat of the day among the shepherds' tents, and know whether all our searches are not to terminate in pastoral simplicity."

The proposal pleased them, and they induced the shepherds, by small presents and familiar questions, to tell their opinion of their own state. They were so rude and ignorant, so little able to compare the good with the evil of the occupation, and so indistinct in their narratives and descriptions, that very little could be learned from them. But it was evident that their hearts were cankered with discontent; that they considered themselves as condemned to labour for the luxury of the rich, and looked up with stupid malevolence toward those that were placed above them.

The princess pronounced with vehemence, that she would never suffer these envious savages to be her companions, and that she should not soon be desirous of seeing any more specimens of rustic happiness; but could not believe that all the accounts of primeval pleasures were fabulous, and was yet in doubt whether life had anything that could be justly preferred to the placid gratifications of fields and woods. She hoped that the time would come, when, with a few virtuous and elegant companions, she could gather flowers planted by her own hand, fondle the lambs of her own ewe, and listen without care, among brooks and breezes, to one of her maidens reading in the shade.

CHAPTER XX

THE DANGER OF PROSPERITY

On the next day they continued their journey, till the heat compelled them to look round for shelter. At a small distance they saw a thick wood, which they no sooner entered than they perceived that they were approaching the habitations of men. The shrubs were diligently cut away to open walks where the shades were darkest; the boughs of opposite trees were artificially interwoven; seats of flowery turf were raised in vacant spaces, and a rivulet that wantoned along the side of a winding path, had its banks sometimes opened into small basins, and its stream sometimes obstructed by little mounds of stone heaped together to increase its murmurs.

They passed slowly through the wood, delighted with such unexpected accommodations, and entertained each other with conjecturing what, or who, he could be that, in those rude and unfrequented regions, had leisure and art for such harmless luxury.

As they advanced they heard the sound of music, and saw youths and virgins dancing in the grove; and, going still further, beheld a stately palace built upon a hill surrounded with woods. The laws of eastern hospitality allowed them to enter, and the master welcomed them like a man liberal and wealthy.

He was skilful enough in appearances soon to discern that they were no common guests, and spread his table with magnificence. The eloquence of Imlac caught his attention, and the lofty courtesy of the princess excited his respect. When they offered to depart, he entreated their stay, and was the next day still more unwilling to dismiss them than before. They were easily persuaded to stop, and civility grew up in time to freedom and confidence.

The prince now saw all the domestics cheerful, and all the face of nature smiling round the place, and could not forbear to hope that he should find here what he was seeking; but when he was congratulating the master upon his possessions, he answered with a sigh, "My condition has

indeed the appearance of happiness, but appearances are delusive. My prosperity puts my life in danger; the Bassa of Egypt is my enemy, incensed only by my wealth and popularity. I have been hitherto protected against him by the princes of the country; but, as the favour of the great is uncertain, I know not how soon my defenders may be persuaded to share the plunder with the Bassa. I have sent my treasures into a distant country, and, upon the first alarm, am prepared to follow them. Then will my enemies riot in my mansion, and enjoy the gardens which I have planted."

They all joined in lamenting his danger, and deprecating his exile; and the princess was so much disturbed with the tumult of grief and indignation, that she retired to her apartment. They continued with their kind inviter a few days longer, and then went forward to find the hermit.

CHAPTER XXI

THE HAPPINESS OF SOLITUDE. THE HERMIT'S HISTORY

They came on the third day, by the direction of the peasants, to the hermit's cell. It was a cavern in the side of a mountain, overshadowed with palm trees; at such a distance from the cataract, that nothing more was heard than a gentle uniform murmur, such as composed the mind to pensive meditation, especially when it was assisted by the wind whistling among the branches. The first rude essay of nature had been so much improved by human labour that the cave contained several apartments appropriated to different uses, and often afforded lodging to travellers, whom darkness or tempests happened to overtake.

The hermit sat on a bench at the door, to enjoy the coolness of the evening. On one side lay a book with pens and papers, on the other mechanical instruments of various kinds.

As they approached him unregarded, the princess observed that he had not the countenance of a man that had found, or could teach, the way to happiness.

They saluted him with great respect, which he repaid like a man not unaccustomed to the forms of courts. "My children," said he, "if you have lost your way, you shall be willingly supplied with such conveniences for the night as this cavern will afford. I have all that nature requires, and you will not expect delicacies in a hermit's cell."

They thanked him, and entering, were pleased with the neatness and regularity of the place. The hermit set flesh and wine before them, though he fed only upon fruits and water. His discourse was cheerful without levity, and pious without enthusiasm. He soon gained the esteem of his guests, and the princess repented of her hasty censure.

At last Imlac began thus: "I do not now wonder that your reputation is so far extended; we have heard at Cairo of your wisdom, and came hither to implore your direction for this young man and maiden in the *choice of life*."

"To him that lives well," answered the hermit, "every form of life is good; nor can I give any other rule for choice than to remove from all apparent evil."

"He will remove most certainly from evil," said the prince, "who shall devote himself to that solitude which you have recommended by your example."

"I have indeed lived fifteen years in solitude," said the hermit, "but have no desire that my example should gain any imitators. In my youth I professed arms, and was raised by degrees to the highest military rank. I have traversed wide countries at the head of my troops, and seen many battles and sieges. At last, being disgusted by the preferment of a younger officer, and feeling that my vigour was beginning to decay, I resolved to close my life in peace, having found the world full of snares, discord, and misery. I had once escaped from the pursuit of the enemy by the shelter of this cavern, and therefore chose it for my final residence. I employed artificers to form it into chambers, and stored it with all that I was likely to want.

"For some time after my retreat, I rejoiced like a tempest-beaten sailor at his entrance into the harbour, being delighted with the sudden change of the noise and hurry of war to stillness and repose. When the pleasure of novelty went away, I employed my hours in examining the plants which grow in the valley, and the minerals which I collected from the rocks. But that inquiry is now grown tasteless and irksome. I have been for some time unsettled and distracted: my mind is disturbed with a thousand perplexities of doubt, and vanities of imagination, which hourly prevail upon me, because I have no opportunities of relaxation or diversion. I am sometimes ashamed to think that I could not secure myself from vice but by retiring from the exercise of virtue, and begin to suspect that I was rather impelled by resentment, than led by devotion, into solitude. My fancy riots in scenes of folly, and I lament that I have lost so much, and have gained so little. In solitude, if I escape the example of bad men, I want likewise the counsel and conversation of the good. I have been long comparing the evils with the advantages of society, and resolved to return into the world to-morrow. The life of a solitary man will be certainly miserable, but not certainly devout."

They heard his resolution with surprise, but after a short pause, offered to conduct him to Cairo. He dug up a considerable treasure which he had hid among the rocks, and accompanied them to the city, on which, as he approached it, he gazed with rapture.

CHAPTER XXII

THE HAPPINESS OF A LIFE LED ACCORDING TO NATURE

Rasselas went often to an assembly of learned men, who met at stated times to unbend their minds and compare their opinions. Their manners were somewhat coarse, but their conversation was instructive, and their disputations acute, though sometimes too violent, and often continued till neither controvertist remembered upon what question they began. Some faults were almost general among them; everyone was desirous to dictate to the rest, and everyone was pleased to hear the genius or knowledge of another depreciated.

In this assembly Rasselas was relating his interview with the hermit, and the wonder with which he heard him censure a course of life which he had so deliberately chosen, and so laudably followed. The sentiments of the hearers were various. Some were of opinion that the folly of his choice had been justly punished by condemnation to perpetual perseverance. One of the youngest among them, with great vehemence, pronounced him an hypocrite. Some talked of the right of society to the labour of individuals, and considered retirement as a desertion of duty. Others readily allowed that there was a time when the claims of the public were satisfied, and when a man might properly sequester himself, to review his life and purify his heart.

One, who appeared more affected with the narrative than the rest, thought it likely that the hermit would in a few years go back to his retreat, and perhaps, if shame did not restrain, or death intercept him, return once more from his retreat into the world. "For the hope of happiness," said he, "is so strongly impressed, that the longest experience is not able to efface it. Of the present state, whatever it be, we feel and are forced to confess the misery; yet when the same state is again at a distance, imagination paints it as desirable. But the time will surely come, when desire will be no longer our torment, and no man shall be wretched but by his own fault."

"This," said a philosopher who had heard him with tokens of great impatience, "is the present condition of a wise man. The time is already come, when none are wretched but by their own fault. Nothing is more idle than to inquire after happiness, which nature has kindly placed within our reach. The way to be happy is to live according to nature, in obedience to that universal and unalterable law with which every heart is originally impressed; which is not written on it by precept, but engraven by destiny, not instilled by education, but infused at our nativity. He that lives according to nature will suffer nothing from the delusions of hope, or importunities of desire; he will receive and reject with equability of temper, and act or suffer as the reason of things shall alternately prescribe. Other men may amuse themselves with subtle definitions, or intricate ratiocination. Let them learn to be wise by easier means; let them observe the hind of the forest, and the linnet of the grove; let them consider the life of animals, whose motions are regulated by instinct; they obey their guide, and are happy. Let us therefore, at length, cease to dispute, and learn to live; throw away the encumbrance of precepts, which they who utter them with so much pride and pomp do not understand, and carry with us this simple and intelligible maxim, that deviation from nature is deviation from happiness."

When he had spoken, he looked round him with a placid air, and enjoyed the consciousness of his own beneficence. "Sir," said the prince with great modesty, "as I, like all the rest of mankind, am desirous of felicity, my closest attention has been fixed upon your discourse. I doubt not the truth of a position which a man so learned has so confidently advanced. Let me only know what it is to live according to nature."

"When I find young men so humble and so docile," said the philosopher, "I can deny them no information which my studies have enabled me to afford. To live according to nature, is to act always with due regard to the fitness arising from the relations and qualities of causes and effects; to concur with the great and unchangeable scheme of universal felicity; to co-operate with the general disposition and tendency of the present system of things."

The prince soon found that this was one of the sages whom he should understand less as he heard him longer. He therefore bowed and was silent; and the philosopher, supposing him satisfied, and the rest vanquished, rose up and departed with the air of a man that had co-operated with the present system.

CHAPTER XXIII

THE PRINCE AND HIS SISTER DIVIDE BETWEEN THEM THE WORK OF OBSERVATION

Rasselas returned home full of reflections, doubtful how to direct his future steps. Of the way to happiness he found the learned and simple equally ignorant; but, as he was yet young, he flattered himself that he had time remaining for more experiments and further inquiries. He communicated to Imlac his observations and his doubts, but was answered by him with new doubts, and remarks that gave him no comfort. He therefore discoursed more frequently and freely with his sister, who had yet the same hope with himself, and always assisted him to give some reason why, though he had been hitherto frustrated, he might succeed at last.

"We have hitherto," said she, "known but little of the world; we have never yet been either great or mean. In our own country, though we had royalty, we had no power, and in

this we have not yet seen the private recesses of domestic peace. Imlac favours not our search, lest we should in time find him mistaken. We will divide the task between us; you shall try what is to be found in the splendour of courts, and I will arrange the shades of humbler life. Perhaps command and authority may be the supreme blessings, as they afford most opportunities of doing good; or perhaps what this world can give may be found in the modest habitations of middle fortune, too low for great designs, and too high for penury and distress."

CHAPTER XXIV

THE PRINCE EXAMINES THE HAPPINESS OF HIGH STATIONS

Rasselas applauded the design, and appeared next day with a splendid retinue at the court of the Bassa. He was soon distinguished for his magnificence, and admitted, as a prince whose curiosity had brought him from distant countries, to an intimacy with the great officers, and frequent conversation with the Bassa himself.

He was at first inclined to believe, that the man must be pleased with his own condition whom all approached with reverence, and heard with obedience, and who had the power to extend his edicts to a whole kingdom. "There can be no pleasure," said he, "equal to that of feeling at once the joy of thousands all made happy by wise administration. Yet, since by the law of subordination this sublime delight can be in one nation but the lot of one, it is surely reasonable to think, that there is some satisfaction more popular and accessible, and that millions can hardly be subjected to the will of a single man, only to fill his particular breast with incommunicable content."

These thoughts were often in his mind, and he found no solution of the difficulty. But as presents and civilities gained him more familiarity, he found that almost every man who stood high in employment hated all the rest, and was hated by them, and that their lives were a continual succession of plots and detections, stratagems and escapes, faction and treachery. Many of those who surrounded the Bassa were sent only to watch and report his conduct; every tongue was muttering censure, and every eye was searching for a fault.

At last the letters of revocation arrived, the Bassa was carried in chains to Constantinople, and his name was mentioned no more.

"What are we now to think of the prerogatives of power?" said Rasselas to his sister; "is it without any efficacy to good, or is the subordinate degree only dangerous, and the supreme safe and glorious? Is the Sultan the only happy man in his dominions, or is the Sultan himself subject to the torments of suspicion and the dread of enemies?"

In a short time the second Bassa was deposed. The Sultan that had advanced him was murdered by the Janissaries, and his successor had other views and different favourites.

CHAPTER XXV

THE PRINCESS PURSUES HER INQUIRY WITH MORE DILIGENCE THAN SUCCESS

The princess, in the meantime, insinuated herself into many families; for there are few doors through which liberality, joined with good humour, cannot find its way. The daughters of many houses were airy and cheerful, but Nekayah had been too long accustomed to the conversation of Imlac and her brother to be much pleased with childish levity and prattle which had no meaning. She found their thoughts narrow, their wishes low, and their merriment often artificial. Their pleasures, poor as they were, could not be preserved pure, but were embittered by petty competitions and worthless emulation. They were always jealous of the beauty of each other; of a quality to which solicitude can add nothing, and from which detraction can take nothing away. Many were in love with triflers like themselves, and many fancied that they were in love when in truth they were only idle. Their affection was seldom fixed on sense or virtue, and therefore seldom ended but in vexation. Their grief, however, like their joy, was transient; everything floated in their mind unconnected with the past or future, so that one desire easily gave way to another, as a second stone, cast into the water, effaces and confounds the circles of the first.

With these girls she played as with inoffensive animals, and found them proud of her countenance, and weary of her company.

But her purpose was to examine more deeply, and her affability easily persuaded the hearts that were swelling with sorrow to discharge their secrets in her ear; and those whom hope flattered, or prosperity delighted, often courted her to partake their pleasures.

The princess and her brother commonly met in the evening in a private summer-house on the bank of the Nile, and related to each other the occurrences of the day. As they were sitting together, the princess cast her eyes upon the river that flowed before her. "Answer," said she, "great Father of Waters, thou that rollest thy floods through eighty nations, to the invocations of the daughter of thy native king. Tell me if thou waterest, through all thy course, a single habitation from which thou dost not hear the murmurs of complaint?"

"You are then," said Rasselas, "not more successful in private houses than I have been in courts." "I have, since the last partition of our provinces," said the princess, "enabled myself to enter familiarly into many families, where there was the fairest show of prosperity and peace, and know not one house that is not haunted by some fury that destroys its quiet.

"I did not seek ease among the poor, because I concluded that there it could not be found. But I saw many poor, whom I had supposed to live in affluence. Poverty has, in large cities, very different appearances; it is often concealed in splendour and often in extravagance. It is the care of a very great part of mankind to conceal their indigence from the rest; they support themselves by temporary expedients, and every day is lost in contriving for the morrow.

"This, however, was an evil which, though frequent, I saw with less pain, because I could relieve it. Yet some have refused my bounties, more offended with my quickness to detect their wants, than pleased with my readiness to succour them; and others, whose exigencies compelled them to admit my kindness, have never been able to forgive their benefactress. Many, however, have been sincerely grateful without the ostentation of gratitude, or the hope of other favours."

CHAPTER XXVI

THE PRINCESS CONTINUES HER REMARKS UPON
PRIVATE LIFE

Nekayah, perceiving her brother's attention fixed, proceeded in her narrative.

"In families where there is or is not poverty, there is commonly discord. If a kingdom be, as Imlac tells us, a great family, a family likewise is a little kingdom, torn with factions and exposed to revolutions. An unpractised observer expects the love of parents and children to be constant and equal; but this kindness seldom continues beyond the years of infancy: in a short time the children become rivals to their parents. Benefits are allayed by reproaches, and gratitude debased by envy.

"Parents and children seldom act in concert; each child endeavours to appropriate the esteem or fondness of the parents, and the parents, with yet less temptation, betray each other to their children. Thus, some place their confidence in the father, and some in the mother, and by degrees the house is filled with artifices and feuds.

"The opinions of children and parents, of the young and the old, are naturally opposite, by the contrary effects of hope and despondence, of expectation and experience, without crime or folly on either side. The colours of life in youth and age appear different, as the face of nature in spring and winter. And how can children credit the assertions of parents, which their own eyes show them to be false?

"Few parents act in such a manner as much to enforce their maxims by the credit of their lives. The old man trusts wholly to slow contrivance and gradual progression; the youth expects to force his way by genius, vigour, and precipitance. The old man pays regard to riches, and the youth reverences virtue. The old man deifies prudence; the youth commits himself to magnanimity and chance. The young man, who intends no ill, believes that none is intended, and therefore acts with openness and candour; but his father, having suffered the injuries of fraud, is impelled to suspect, and too often allured to practise it. Age looks with anger on the temerity of youth, and youth with contempt on the scrupulosity of age. Thus parents and children, for the greatest part, live on to love less and less; and, if those whom nature has thus closely united are the torments of each other, where shall we look for tenderness and consolation?"

"Surely," said the prince, "you must have been unfortunate in your choice of acquaintance: I am unwilling to believe that the most tender of all relations is thus impeded in its effects by natural necessity."

"Domestic discord," answered she, "is not inevitably and fatally necessary, but yet is not easily avoided. We seldom see that a whole family is virtuous: the good and evil cannot well agree, and the evil can yet less agree with one another. Even the virtuous fall sometimes to variance, when their virtues are of different kinds, and tending to extremes. In general, those parents have most reverence who most deserve it; for he that lives well can-not be despised.

"Many other evils infest private 10 life. Some are the slaves of servants whom they have trusted with their affairs. Some are kept in continual anxiety to the caprice of rich rela-tions, whom they cannot please, and dare not offend. Some husbands are imperious, and some wives perverse; and, as it is always more easy to do evil than good, though the wisdom or virtue of one can very rarely make many happy, the folly or vice of one 20 man often make many miserable."

"If such be the general effect of marriage," said the prince, "I shall for the future think it dangerous to connect my interest with that of an-other, lest I should be unhappy by my partner's fault."

"I have met," said the princess, "with many who live single for that reason; but I never found that their 30 prudence ought to raise envy. They dream away their time without friendship, without fondness, and are driven to rid themselves of the day, for which they have no use, by child-ish amusements, or vicious delights. They act as beings under the constant sense of some known inferiority, that fills their minds with rancour, and their tongues with censure. They are 40 peevish at home, and malevolent abroad; and, as the outlaws of hu-man nature, make it their business and their pleasure to disturb that soci-ety which debars them from its privi-leges. To live without feeling or exciting sympathy, to be fortunate without adding to the felicity of others, or afflicted without tasting the balm of pity, is a state more gloomy 50 than solitude; it is not retreat but exclusion from mankind. Marriage has many pains, but celibacy has no pleasures."

"What then is to be done?" said Rasselas; "the more we inquire, the less we can resolve. Surely he is most likely to please himself that has no other inclination to regard."

CHAPTER XXVII

DISQUISITION UPON GREATNESS

The conversation had a short pause. The prince, having considered his sis-ter's observations, told her that she had surveyed life with prejudice, and supposed misery where she did not find it. "Your narrative," says he, "throws yet a darker gloom upon the prospects of futurity: the predictions of Imlac were but faint sketches of 20 the evils painted by Nekayah. I have been lately convinced that quiet is not the daughter of grandeur, or of power; that her presence is not to be bought by wealth, nor enforced by conquest. It is evident, that as any man acts in a wider compass, he must be more exposed to opposition from enmity, or miscarriage from chance. Whoever has many to please or to 30 govern, must use the ministry of many agents, some of whom will be wicked, and some ignorant; by some he will be misled, and by others betrayed. If he gratifies one he will offend another; those that are not favoured will think themselves injured; and, since favours can be conferred but upon few, the greater number will be always dis-contented."

"The discontent," said the princess, 40 "which is thus unreasonable, I hope that I shall always have spirit to de-spise, and you power to repress."

"Discontent," answered Rasselas, "will not always be without reason under the most just or vigilant ad-ministration of public affairs. None, however attentive, can always dis-cover that merit which indigence or faction may happen to obscure; and 50 none, however powerful, can always reward it. Yet he that sees inferior desert advanced above him, will nat-urally impute that preference to partiality or caprice; and, indeed, it can scarcely be hoped that any man, however magnanimous by nature, or exalted by condition, will be able to persist forever in fixed and inexorable justice of distribution. He will sometimes indulge his own affections, and sometimes those of his favourites; he will permit some to please him who can never serve him; he will discover in those whom he loves qualities which in reality they do not possess; and to those from whom he receives pleasure, he will in his turn endeavour to give it. Thus will recommendations sometimes prevail which were purchased by money, or by the more destructive bribery of flattery and servility.

"He that has much to do will do something wrong, and of that wrong must suffer the consequences; and, if it were possible that he should always act rightly, yet when such numbers are to judge of his conduct, the bad will censure and obstruct him by malevolence, and the good sometimes by mistake.

"The highest stations cannot therefore hope to be the abodes of happiness, which I would willingly believe to have fled from thrones and palaces to seats of humble privacy and placid obscurity. For what can hinder the satisfaction, or intercept the expectations, of him whose abilities are adequate to his employment, who sees with his own eyes the whole circuit of his influence, who chooses by his own knowledge all whom he trusts, and whom none are tempted to deceive by hope or fear? Surely he has nothing to do but to love and to be loved, to be virtuous and to be happy."

"Whether perfect happiness would be procured by perfect goodness," said Nekayah, "this world will never afford an opportunity of deciding. But this, at least, may be maintained, that we do not always find visible happiness in proportion to visible virtue. All natural, and almost all political evils are incident alike to the bad and

good; they are confounded in the misery of a famine, and not much distinguished in the fury of a faction; they sink together in a tempest, and are driven together from their country by invaders. All that virtue can afford is quietness of conscience, a steady prospect of a happier state; this may enable us to endure calamity with patience, but remember that patience must suppose pain."

CHAPTER XXVIII

RASSELAS AND NEKAYAH CONTINUE THEIR CONVERSATION

"Dear princess," said Rasselas, "you fall into the common errors of exaggeratory declamation, by producing in a familiar disquisition examples of national calamities, and scenes of extensive misery, which are found in books rather than in the world, and which, as they are horrid, are ordained to be rare. Let us not imagine evils which we do not feel, nor injure life by misrepresentations. I cannot bear that querulous eloquence which threatens every city with a siege like that of Jerusalem, that makes famine attend on every flight of locusts, and suspends pestilence on the wings of every blast that issues from the south.

"On necessary and inevitable evils which overwhelm kingdoms at once, all disputation is vain; when they happen they must be endured. But it is evident that these bursts of universal distress are more dreaded than felt; thousands and ten thousands flourish in youth, and wither in age, without the knowledge of any other than domestic evils, and share the same pleasures and vexations, whether their kings are mild or cruel, whether the armies of their country pursue their enemies, or retreat before them. While courts are disturbed with intestine competitions, and ambassadors are negotiating in foreign countries, the smith still plies his anvil and the husbandman drives his plow forward; the necessaries of life are required and obtained; and the successive business of the seasons continues to make its wonted revolutions.

"Let us cease to consider what, perhaps, may never happen, and what, when it shall happen, will laugh at human speculation. We will not endeavour to modify the motions of the elements or to fix the destiny of kingdoms. It is our business to consider what beings like us may perform, each labouring for his own happiness by promoting within his circle, however narrow, the happiness of others.

"Marriage is evidently the dictate of nature; men and women were made to be companions of each other, and therefore I cannot be persuaded but that marriage is one of the means of happiness."

"I know not," said the princess, "whether marriage be more than one of the innumerable modes of human misery. When I see and reckon the various forms of connubial infelicity, the unexpected causes of lasting discord, the diversities of temper, the oppositions of opinion, the rude collisions of contrary desire where both are urged by violent impulses, the obstinate contests of disagreeing virtues where both are supported by consciousness of good intention, I am sometimes disposed to think, with the severer casuists of most nations, that marriage is rather permitted than approved, and that none, but by the instigation of a passion too much indulged, entangle themselves with indissoluble compacts."

"You seem to forget," replied Rasselas, "that you have, even now, represented celibacy as less happy than marriage. Both conditions may be bad, but they cannot both be worst. Thus it happens, when wrong opinions are entertained, that they mutually destroy each other, and leave the mind open to truth."

"I did not expect," answered the princess, "to hear that imputed to falsehood which is the consequence only of frailty. To the mind, as to the eye, it is difficult to compare with exactness objects vast in their extent, and various in their parts. Where we see or conceive the whole at once, we readily note the discriminations and decide the preference; but of two systems, of which neither can be surveyed by any human being in its full compass of magnitude and multiplicity of complication, where is the wonder that, judging of the whole by parts, I am alternately affected by one and the other as either presses on my memory or fancy? We differ from ourselves, just as we differ from each other, when we see only part of the question, as in the multifarious relations of politics and morality; but when we perceive the whole at once, as in numerical computations, all agree in one judgment, and none ever varies his opinion."

"Let us not add," said the prince, "to the other evils of life the bitterness of controversy, nor endeavour to vie with each other in subtleties of argument. We are employed in a search, of which both are equally to enjoy the success, or suffer by the miscarriage; it is therefore fit that we assist each other. You surely conclude too hastily from the infelicity of marriage against its institution. Will not the misery of life prove equally that life cannot be the gift of heaven? The world must be peopled by marriage, or peopled without it."

"How the world is to be peopled," returned Nekayah, "is not my care, and needs not be yours. I see no danger that the present generation should omit to leave successors behind them; we are not now inquiring for the world, but for ourselves."

CHAPTER XXIX

THE DEBATE ON MARRIAGE CONTINUED

"The good of the whole," says Rasselas, "is the same with the good of all its parts. If marriage be best for mankind, it must be evidently best for individuals, or a permanent and necessary duty must be the cause of evil, and some must be inevitably sacrificed to the convenience of others. In the estimate which you have made of the two states, it appears that the incommodities of a single life are, in a great measure, necessary and certain, but those of the conjugal state accidental and avoidable.

"I cannot forbear to flatter myself, that prudence and benevolence will make marriage happy. The general folly of mankind is the cause of general complaint. What can be expected but disappointment and repentance from a choice made in the immaturity of youth, in the ardour of desire, without judgment, without foresight, without inquiry after conformity of opinions, similarity of manners, rectitude of judgment, or purity of sentiment?

"Such is the common process of marriage. A youth and maiden meeting by chance, or brought together by artifice, exchange glances, reciprocate civilities, go home and dream of one another. Having little to divert attention, or diversify thought, they find themselves uneasy when they are apart, and therefore conclude that they shall be happy together. They marry, and discover what nothing but voluntary blindness had before concealed; they wear out life in altercations, and charge nature with cruelty.

"From those early marriages proceeds likewise the rivalry of parents and children: the son is eager to enjoy the world before the father is willing to forsake it, and there is hardly room at once for two generations. The daughter begins to bloom before the mother can be content to fade, and neither can forbear to wish for the absence of the other.

"Surely all these evils may be avoided by that deliberation and delay which prudence prescribes to irrevocable choice. In the variety and jollity of youthful pleasures, life may be well enough supported without the help of a partner. Longer time will increase experience, and wider views will allow better opportunities of inquiry and selection; one advantage at least will be certain: the parents will be visibly older than their children."

"What reason cannot collect," said Nekayah, "and what experiment has not yet taught, can be known only from the report of others. I have been told that late marriages are not eminently happy. This is a question too important to be neglected, and I have often proposed it to those whose accuracy of remark, and comprehensiveness of knowledge, made their suffrages worthy of regard. They have generally determined, that it is dangerous for a man and woman to suspend their fate upon each other, at a time when opinions are fixed, and habits are established; when friendships have been contracted on both sides, when life has been planned into method, and the mind has long enjoyed the contemplation of its own prospects.

"It is scarcely possible that two, travelling through the world under the conduct of chance, should have been both directed to the same path, and it will not often happen that either will quit the track which custom has made pleasing. When the desultory levity of youth has settled into regularity, it is soon succeeded by pride ashamed to yield, or obstinacy delighting to contend. And even though mutual esteem produces mutual desire to please, time itself, as it modifies unchangeably the external mien, determines likewise the direction of the passions, and gives an inflexible rigidity to the manners. Long customs are not easily broken; he that attempts to change the course of his own life very often labours in vain; and how shall we do that for others, which we are seldom able to do for ourselves?"

"But surely," interposed the prince, "you suppose the chief motive of choice forgotten or neglected. Whenever I shall seek a wife, it shall be my first question, whether she be willing to be led by reason."

"Thus it is," said Nekayah, "that philosophers are deceived. There are a thousand familiar disputes which reason never can decide; questions that elude investigation, and make logic ridiculous; cases where something must be done, and where little can be said. Consider the state of mankind, and inquire how few can be supposed to act upon any occasions, whether small or great, with all the reasons of action present to their minds. Wretched would be the pair, above all names of wretchedness, who should be doomed to adjust by reason every morning all the minute detail of a domestic day.

"Those who marry at an advanced age will probably escape the encroachments of their children; but, in diminution of this advantage, they will be likely to leave them ignorant and helpless to a guardian's mercy; or, if that should not happen, they must at least go out of the world before they see those whom they love best either wise or great.

"From their children, if they have less to fear, they have less also to hope, and they lose, without equivalent, the joys of early love, and the convenience of uniting with manners pliant, and minds susceptible of new impressions, which might wear away their dissimilitudes by long cohabitation, as soft bodies, by continual attrition, conform their surfaces to each other.

"I believe it will be found that those who marry late are best pleased with their children, and those who marry early with their partners."

"The union of these two affections," said Rasselas, "would produce all that could be wished. Perhaps there is a time when marriage might unite them, a time neither too early for the father, nor too late for the husband."

"Every hour," answered the princess, "confirms my prejudice in favour of the position so often uttered by the mouth of Imlac, that nature sets her gifts on the right hand and on the left. Those conditions which flatter hope and attract desire are so constituted, that, as we approach one, we recede from another. There are goods so opposed that we cannot seize both, but, by too much prudence, may pass between them at too great a distance to reach either. This is often the fate of long consideration; he does nothing who endeavours to do more than is allowed to humanity. Flatter not yourself with contrarieties of pleasure. Of the blessings set before you, make your choice and be content. No man can taste the fruits of autumn while he is delighting his scent with the flowers of the spring; no man can at the same time fill his cup from the source and from the mouth of the Nile."

CHAPTER XXX

IMLAC ENTERS, AND CHANGES THE CONVERSATION

Here Imlac entered, and interrupted them. "Imlac," said Rasselas, "I have been taking from the princess the dismal history of private life, and am almost discouraged from further search."

"It seems to me," said Imlac, "that while you are making the choice of life, you neglect to live. You wander about a single city, which, however large and diversified, can now afford few novelties, and forget that you are in a country famous among the earliest monarchies for the power and wisdom of its inhabitants; a country where the sciences first dawned that illuminate the world, and beyond which the arts cannot be traced of civil society or domestic life.

"The old Egyptians have left behind them monuments of industry and power, before which all European magnificence is confessed to fade away. The ruins of their architecture are the schools of modern builders, and from the wonders which time has spared we may conjecture, though uncertainly, what it has destroyed."

"My curiosity," said Rasselas, "does not very strongly lead me to survey piles of stone, or mounds of earth; my business is with man. I came hither not to measure fragments of temples, or trace choked aqueducts, but to look upon the various scenes of the present world."

"The things that are now before us," said the princess, "require attention, and deserve it. What have I to do with the heroes or the monuments of ancient times? with times which never can return, and heroes whose form of life was different from all that the present condition of mankind requires or allows?"

"To know anything," returned the poet, "we must know its effects; to see men, we must see their works, that we may learn what reason has dictated, or passion has incited, and find what are the most powerful motives of action. To judge rightly of the present, we must oppose it to the past; for all judgment is comparative, and of the future nothing can be known. The truth is that no mind is much employed upon the present; recollection and anticipation fill up almost all our moments. Our passions are joy and grief, love and hatred, hope and fear. Of joy and grief the past is the object, and the future of hope and fear; even love and hatred respect the past, for the cause must have been before the effect.

"The present state of things is the consequence of the former, and it is natural to inquire what were the sources of the good that we enjoy, or the evil that we suffer. If we act only for ourselves, to neglect the study of history is not prudent; if we are entrusted with the care of others, it is not just. Ignorance, when it is voluntary, is criminal; and he may properly be charged with evil, who refused to learn how he might prevent it.

"There is no part of history so generally useful as that which relates the progress of the human mind, the gradual improvement of reason, the successive advances of science, the vicissitudes of learning and ignorance, which are the light and darkness of thinking beings, the extinction and resuscitation of arts, and all the revolutions of the intellectual world. If accounts of battles and invasions are peculiarly the business of princes, the useful or elegant arts are not to be neglected; those who have kingdoms to govern, have understandings to cultivate.

"Example is always more efficacious than precept. A soldier is formed in war, and a painter must copy pictures. In this, contemplative life has the advantage; great actions are seldom seen, but the labours of art are always at hand for those who desire to know what art has been able to perform.

"When the eye or the imagination is struck with any uncommon work, the next transition of an active mind is to the means by which it was performed. Here begins the true use of such contemplation; we enlarge our comprehension by new ideas, and perhaps recover some art lost to mankind, or learn what is less perfectly known in our own country. At least we compare our own with former times, and either rejoice at our improvements, or, what is the first motion towards good, discover our defects."

"I am willing," said the prince, "to see all that can deserve my search." "And I," said the princess, "shall rejoice to learn something of the manners of antiquity."

"The most pompous monument of Egyptian greatness, and one of the most bulky works of manual industry," said Imlac, "are the pyramids—fabrics raised before the time of history, and of which the earliest narratives afford us only uncertain traditions. Of these the greatest is still standing, very little injured by time."

"Let us visit them to-morrow," said Nekayah. "I have often heard of the pyramids, and shall not rest till I have seen them, within and without, with my own eyes."

CHAPTER XXXI

THEY VISIT THE PYRAMIDS

The resolution being thus taken, they set out the next day. They laid tents upon their camels, being resolved to stay among the pyramids till their curiosity was fully satisfied. They travelled gently, turned aside to everything remarkable, stopped from time to time and conversed with the inhabitants, and observed the various appearances of towns ruined and inhabited, of wild and cultivated nature.

When they came to the great pyramid, they were astonished at the extent of the base, and the height of the top. Imlac explained to them the principles upon which the pyramidal form was chosen for a fabric intended to co-extend its duration with that of the world; he showed that its gradual diminution gave it such stability as defeated all the common attacks of the elements, and could scarcely be overthrown by earthquakes themselves, the least resistible of natural violence. A concussion that should shatter the pyramid would threaten the dissolution of the continent.

They measured all its dimensions, and pitched their tents at its foot. Next day they prepared to enter its interior apartments, and having hired the common guides, climbed up to the first passage, when the favourite of the princess, looking into the cavity, stepped back and trembled. "Pekuah," said the princess, "of what art thou afraid?" "Of the narrow entrance," answered the lady, "and of the dreadful gloom. I dare not enter a place which must surely be inhabited by unquiet souls. The original possessors of these dreadful vaults will start up before us, and perhaps shut us in for ever." She spoke, and threw her arms round the neck of her mistress.

"If all your fear be of apparitions," said the prince, "I will promise you safety. There is no danger from the dead; he that is once buried will be seen no more."

"That the dead are seen no more," said Imlac, "I will not undertake to maintain, against the concurrent and unvaried testimony of all ages, and of all nations. There is no people, rude or learned, among whom apparitions of the dead are not related and believed. This opinion, which perhaps prevails as far as human nature is diffused, could become universal only by its truth; those that never heard of one another would not have agreed in a tale which nothing but experience can make credible. That it is doubted by single cavillers can very little weaken the general evidence; and some who deny it with their tongues, confess it by their fears.

"Yet I do not mean to add new terrors to those which have already seized upon Pekuah. There can be no reason why spectres should haunt the pyramid more than other places, or why they should have power or will to hurt innocence and purity. Our entrance is no violation of their privileges; we can take nothing from them, how then can we offend them?"

"My dear Pekuah," said the princess, "I will always go before you, and Imlac shall follow you. Remember that you are the companion of the princess of Abyssinia."

"If the princess is pleased that her servant should die," returned the lady, "let her command some death less dreadful than enclosure in this horrid cavern. You know I dare not disobey you; I must go if you command me, but if I once enter, I never shall come back."

The princess saw that her fear was too strong for expostulation or reproof, and, embracing her, told her that she should stay in the tent till their return. Pekuah was yet not satisfied, but entreated the princess not to pursue so dreadful a purpose as that of entering the recesses of the pyramid. "Though I cannot teach courage," said Nekayah, "I must not learn cowardice, nor leave at last undone what I came hither only to do."

CHAPTER XXXII

THEY ENTER THE PYRAMID

Pekuah descended to the tents, and the rest entered the pyramid. They passed through the galleries, surveyed the vaults of marble, and examined the chest in which the body of the founder is supposed to have been reposited. They then sat down in one of the most spacious chambers to rest a while before they attempted to return.

"We have now," said Imlac, "gratified our minds with an exact view of the greatest work of man, except the wall of China.

"Of the wall it is very easy to assign the motive. It secured a wealthy and timorous nation from the incursions of barbarians, whose unskilfulness in arts made it easier for them to supply their wants by rapine than by industry, and who from time to time poured in upon the habitations of peaceful commerce, as vultures descend upon domestic fowl. Their celerity and fierceness made the wall necessary, and their ignorance made it efficacious.

"But for the pyramids, no reason has ever been given adequate to the cost and labour of the work. The narrowness of the chambers proves that it could afford no retreat from enemies, and treasures might have been reposited at far less expense with equal security. It seems to have been erected only in compliance with that hunger of imagination which preys incessantly upon life, and must be always appeased by some employment. Those who have already all that they can enjoy must enlarge their desires. He that has built for use till use is supplied, must begin to build for vanity, and extend his plan to the utmost power of human performance, that he may not be soon reduced to form another wish.

"I consider this mighty structure as a monument of the insufficiency of human enjoyments. A king, whose power is unlimited, and whose treasures surmount all real and imaginary wants, is compelled to solace, by the erection of a pyramid, the satiety of dominion and tastelessness of pleasures, and to amuse the tediousness of declining life by seeing thousands labouring without end, and one stone, for no purpose, laid upon another. Whoever thou art, that, not content with a moderate condition, imaginest happiness in royal magnificence, and dreamest that command or riches can feed the appetite of novelty with perpetual gratifications, survey the pyramids, and confess thy folly!"

CHAPTER XXXIII

THE PRINCESS MEETS WITH AN UNEXPECTED MISFORTUNE

They rose up, and returned through the cavity at which they had entered; and the princess prepared for her favourite a long narrative of dark labyrinths, and costly rooms, and of the different impressions which the varieties of the way had made upon her. But when they came to their train, they found every one silent and dejected; the men discovered shame and fear in their countenances, and the women were weeping in the tents.

What had happened they did not try to conjecture but immediately inquired. "You had scarcely entered into the pyramid," said one of the attendants, "when a troop of Arabs rushed upon us; we were too few to resist them, and too slow to escape. They were about to search the tents, set us on our camels, and drive us along before them, when the approach of some Turkish horsemen put them to flight; but they seized the lady Pekuah with her two maids, and carried them away. The Turks are now pursuing them by our instigation, but I fear they will not be able to overtake them."

The princess was overpowered with surprise and grief. Rasselas, in the first heat of his resentment, ordered his servants to follow him, and prepared to pursue the robbers with his sabre in his hand. "Sir," said Imlac, "what can you hope from violence or valour? The Arabs are mounted on horses trained to battle and retreat; we have only beasts of burthen. By leaving our present station we may lose the princess, but cannot hope to regain Pekuah."

In a short time the Turks returned, having not been able to reach the enemy. The princess burst out into new lamentations, and Rasselas could scarcely forbear to reproach them with cowardice; but Imlac was of opinion that the escape of the Arabs was no addition to their misfortune, for perhaps they would have killed their captives rather than have resigned them.

CHAPTER XXXIV

THEY RETURN TO CAIRO WITHOUT PEKUAH

There was nothing to be hoped from longer stay. They returned to Cairo repenting of their curiosity, censuring the negligence of the government, lamenting their own rashness, which had neglected to procure a guard, imagining many expedients by which the loss of Pekuah might have been prevented, and resolving to do something for her recovery, though none could find anything proper to be done.

Nekayah retired to her chamber, where her women attempted to comfort her, by telling her that all had their troubles, and that lady Pekuah had enjoyed much happiness in the world for a long time, and might reasonably expect a change of fortune. They hoped that some good would befall her wheresoever she was, and that their mistress would find another friend who might supply her place.

The princess made them no answer, and they continued the form of condolence, not much grieved in their hearts that the favourite was lost.

Next day the prince presented to the Bassa a memorial of the wrong which he had suffered, and a petition for redress. The Bassa threatened to punish the robbers, but did not attempt to catch them, nor indeed could any account or description be given by which he might direct the pursuit.

It soon appeared that nothing would be done by authority. Governors, being accustomed to hear of more crimes than they can punish, and more wrongs than they can redress, set themselves at ease by indiscriminate negligence, and presently forget the request when they lose sight of the petitioner.

Imlac then endeavoured to gain some intelligence by private agents. He found many who pretended to an exact knowledge of all the haunts of the Arabs, and to regular correspondence with their chiefs, and who readily undertook the recovery of Pekuah. Of these, some were furnished with money for their journey, and came back no more; some were liberally paid for accounts which a few days discovered to be false. But the princess would not suffer any means, however improbable, to be left untried. While she was doing something, she kept her hope alive. As one expedient failed, another was suggested; when one messenger returned unsuccessful, another was despatched to a different quarter.

Two months had now passed, and of Pekuah nothing had been heard; the hopes which they had endeavoured to raise in each other grew more languid, and the princess, when she saw nothing more to be tried, sunk down inconsolable in hopeless dejection. A thousand times she reproached herself with the easy compliance by which she permitted her favourite to stay behind her. "Had not my fondness," said she "lessened my authority, Pekuah had not dared to talk of her terrors. She ought to have feared me more than spectres. A severe look would have overpowered her; a peremptory command would have compelled obedience. Why did foolish indulgence prevail upon me? Why did I not speak, and refuse to hear?"

"Great princess," said Imlac, "do not reproach yourself for your virtue, or consider that as blamable by which evil has accidentally been caused. Your tenderness for the timidity of Pekuah was generous and kind. When we act according to our duty, we commit the event to Him by whose laws our actions are governed, and who will suffer none to be finally punished for obedience. When, in prospect of some good, whether natural or moral, we break the rules prescribed us, we withdraw from the direction of superior wisdom, and take all consequences upon ourselves. Man cannot so far know the connection of causes and events, as that he may venture to do wrong in order to do right. When we pursue our end by lawful means, we may always console our miscarriage by the hope of future recompense. When we consult only our own policy, and attempt to find a nearer way to good, by overleaping the settled boundaries of right and wrong, we cannot be happy even by success, because we cannot escape the consciousness of our fault; but, if we miscarry, the disappointment is irremediably embittered. How comfortless is the sorrow of him who feels at once the pangs of guilt, and the vexation of calamity which guilt has brought upon him!

"Consider, princess, what would have been your condition if the lady Pekuah had entreated to accompany you, and, being compelled to stay in the tents, had been carried away; or how would you have borne the thought, if you had forced her into the pyramid, and she had died before you in agonies of terror?"

"Had either happened," said Nekayah, "I could not have endured life till now: I should have been tortured to madness by the remembrance of such cruelty, or must have pined away in abhorrence of myself."

"This, at least," said Imlac, "is the present reward of virtuous conduct, that no unlucky consequence can oblige us to repent it."

CHAPTER XXXV

THE PRINCESS LANGUISHES FOR WANT OF PEKUAH

Nekayah, being thus reconciled to herself, found that no evil is insupportable but that which is accompanied with consciousness of wrong. She was, from that time, delivered from the violence of tempestuous sorrow, and sunk into silent pensiveness and gloomy tranquillity. She sat from morning to evening recollecting all that had been done or said by her Pekuah, treasured up with care every trifle on which Pekuah had set an accidental value, and which might recall to mind any little incident or careless conversation. The sentiments of her whom she now expected to see no more, were treasured in her memory as rules of life, and she deliberated to no other end than to conjecture on any occasion, what would have been the opinion and counsel of Pekuah.

The women by whom she was attended knew nothing of her real condition, and therefore she could not talk to them but with caution and reserve. She began to remit her curiosity, having no great care to collect notions which she had no convenience of uttering. Rasselas endeavoured first to comfort, and afterward to divert her; he hired musicians, to whom she seemed to listen, but did not hear them, and procured masters to instruct her in various arts, whose lectures, when they visited her again, were again to be repeated. She had lost her taste of pleasure, and her ambition of excellence; and her mind, though forced into short excursions, always recurred to the image of her friend.

Imlac was every morning earnestly enjoined to renew his inquiries, and was asked every night whether he had yet heard of Pekuah, till, not being able to return the princess the answer that she desired, he was less and less willing to come into her presence. She observed his backwardness, and commanded him to attend her. "You are not," said she, "to confound impatience with resentment, or to suppose that I charge you with negligence, because I repine at your unsuccessfulness. I do not much wonder at your absence; I know that the unhappy are never pleasing, and that all naturally avoid the contagion of misery. To hear complaints is wearisome alike to the wretched and the happy; for who would cloud by adventitious grief the short gleams of gaiety which life allows us? or who, that is struggling under his own evils, will add to them the miseries of another?

"The time is at hand when none shall be disturbed any longer by the sighs of Nekayah; my search after happiness is now at an end. I am resolved to retire from the world, with all its flatteries and deceits, and will hide myself in solitude, without any other care than to compose my thoughts, and regulate my hours by a constant succession of innocent occupations, till, with a mind purified from all earthly desires, I shall enter into that state to which all are hastening, and in which I hope again to enjoy the friendship of Pekuah."

"Do not entangle your mind," said Imlac, "by irrevocable determinations, nor increase the burthen of life by a voluntary accumulation of misery; the weariness of retirement will continue or increase when the loss of Pekuah is forgotten. That you have been deprived of one pleasure, is no very good reason for rejection of the rest."

"Since Pekuah was taken from me," said the princess, "I have no pleasure to reject or to retain. She that has no one to love or trust has little to hope. She wants the radical principle of happiness. We may, perhaps, allow that what satisfaction this world can afford, must arise from the conjunction of wealth, knowledge, and goodness. Wealth is nothing but as it is bestowed, and knowledge nothing but as it is communicated; they must therefore be imparted to others, and to whom could I now delight to impart them? Goodness affords the only comfort which can be enjoyed without a partner, and goodness may be practised in retirement."

"How far solitude may admit goodness, or advance it, I shall not," replied Imlac, "dispute at present. Remember the confession of the pious hermit. You will wish to return into the world, when the image of your companion has left your thoughts." "That time," said Nekayah, "will never come. The generous frankness, the modest obsequiousness, and the faithful secrecy of my dear Pekuah will always be more missed, as I shall live longer to see vice and folly."

"The state of a mind oppressed with a sudden calamity," said Imlac, "is like that of the fabulous inhabitants of the new-created earth, who, when the first night came upon them, supposed that day never would return. When the clouds of sorrow gather over us, we see nothing beyond them, nor can imagine how they will be dispelled; yet a new day succeeded to the night, and sorrow is never long without a dawn of ease. But they who restrain themselves from receiving comfort, do as the savages would have done, had they put out their eyes when it was dark. Our minds, like our bodies, are in continual flux; something is hourly lost, and something acquired. To lose much at once is inconvenient to either, but while the vital powers remain uninjured, nature will find the means of reparation. Distance has the same effect on the mind as on the eye; and while we glide along the stream of time, whatever we leave behind us is always lessening, and that which we approach increasing in magnitude. Do not suffer life to stagnate; it will grow muddy for want of motion. Commit yourself again to the current of the world. Pekuah will vanish by degrees; you will meet in your way some other favourite, or learn to diffuse yourself in general conversation."

"At least," said the prince, "do not despair before all remedies have been tried. The inquiry after the unfortunate lady is still continued, and shall be carried on with yet greater diligence, on condition that you will promise to wait a year for the event, without any unalterable resolution."

Nekayah thought this a reasonable demand, and made the promise to her brother, who had been advised by Imlac to require it. Imlac had, indeed, no great hope of regaining Pekuah; but he supposed that if he could secure the interval of a year, the princess would be then in no danger of a cloister.

CHAPTER XXXVI

PEKUAH IS STILL REMEMBERED. THE PROGRESS OF SORROW

Nekayah, seeing that nothing was omitted for the recovery of her favourite, and having by her promise set her intention of retirement at a distance, began imperceptibly to return to common cares and common pleasures. She rejoiced without her own consent at the suspension of her sorrows, and sometimes caught herself, with indignation, in the act of turning away her mind from the remembrance of her whom yet she resolved never to forget.

She then appointed a certain hour of the day for meditation on the merits and fondness of Pekuah, and for some weeks retired constantly at the time fixed, and returned with her eyes swollen and her countenance clouded. By degrees she grew less scrupulous, and suffered any important and pressing avocation to delay the tribute of daily tears. She then yielded to less occasions; sometimes forgot what she

was, indeed, afraid to remember, and at last wholly released herself from the duty of periodical affliction.

Her real love of Pekuah was yet not diminished. A thousand occurrences brought her back to memory, and a thousand wants, which nothing but the confidence of friendship can supply, made her frequently regretted. She, therefore, solicited Imlac never to desist from inquiry, and to leave no art of intelligence untried, that at least she might have the comfort of knowing that she did not suffer by negligence or sluggishness. "Yet what," said she, "is to be expected from our pursuit of happiness, when we find the state of life to be such, that happiness itself is the cause of misery? Why should we endeavour to attain that of which the possession cannot be secured? I shall henceforward fear to yield my heart to excellence, however bright, or to fondness, however tender, lest I should lose again what I have lost in Pekuah."

CHAPTER XXXVII

THE PRINCESS HEARS NEWS OF PEKUAH

In seven months, one of the messengers, who had been sent away upon the day when the promise was drawn from the princess, returned, after many unsuccessful rambles, from the borders of Nubia, with an account that Pekuah was in the hands of an Arab chief, who possessed a castle or fortress on the extremity of Egypt. The Arab, whose revenue was plunder, was willing to restore her, with her two attendants, for two hundred ounces of gold.

The price was no subject of debate. The princess was in ecstasies when she heard that her favourite was alive and might so cheaply be ransomed. She could not think of delaying for a moment Pekuah's happiness or her own, but entreated her brother to send back the messenger with the sum required. Imlac, being consulted, was not very confident of the veracity of the relator, and was still more doubtful of the Arab's faith, who might, if he were too liberally trusted, detain at once the money and the captives. He thought it dangerous to put themselves in the power of the Arab by going into his district, and could not expect that the rover would so much expose himself as to come into the lower country, where he might be seized by the forces of the Bassa.

It is difficult to negotiate where neither will trust. But Imlac, after some deliberation, directed the messenger to propose that Pekuah should be conducted by ten horsemen to the monastery of St. Anthony, which is situated in the deserts of Upper Egypt, where she should be met by the same number, and her ransom should be paid.

That no time might be lost, as they expected that the proposal would not be refused, they immediately began their journey to the monastery; and, when they arrived, Imlac went forward with the former messenger to the Arab's fortress. Rasselas was desirous to go with them; but neither his sister nor Imlac would consent. The Arab, according to the custom of his nation, observed the laws of hospitality with great exactness to those who put themselves into his power, and in a few days brought Pekuah with her maids, by easy journeys, to their place appointed, where receiving the stipulated price, he restored her with great respect to liberty and her friends, and undertook to conduct them back towards Cairo beyond all danger of robbery or violence.

The princess and her favourite embraced each other with transport too violent to be expressed, and went out together to pour the tears of tenderness in secret, and exchange professions of kindness and gratitude. After a few hours they returned into the refectory of the convent, where, in the presence of the prior and his brethren, the prince required of Pekuah the history of her adventures.

CHAPTER XXXVIII

THE ADVENTURES OF THE LADY PEKUAH

"At what time, and in what manner, I was forced away," said Pekuah, "your servants have told you. The suddenness of the event struck me with surprise, and I was at first rather stupefied than agitated with any passion of either fear or sorrow. My confusion was increased by the speed and tumult of our flight, while we were followed by the Turks, who, as it seemed, soon despaired to overtake us, or were afraid of those whom they made a show of menacing.

"When the Arabs saw themselves out of danger, they slackened their course, and as I was less harassed by external violence, I began to feel more uneasiness in my mind. After some time we stopped near a spring shaded with trees in a pleasant meadow, where we were set upon the ground, and offered such refreshments as our masters were partaking. I was suffered to sit with my maids apart from the rest, and none attempted to comfort or insult us. Here I first began to feel the full weight of my misery. The girls sat weeping in silence, and from time to time looked on me for succour. I knew not to what condition we were doomed, nor could conjecture where would be the place of our captivity, or whence to draw any hope of deliverance. I was in the hands of robbers and savages, and had no reason to suppose that their pity was more than their justice, or that they would forbear the gratification of any ardour of desire, or caprice of cruelty. I, however, kissed my maids, and endeavoured to pacify them by remarking that we were yet treated with decency, and that, since we were now carried beyond pursuit, there was no danger of violence to our lives.

"When we were to be set again on horseback, my maids clung round me, and refused to be parted; but I commanded them not to irritate those who had us in their power. We travelled the remaining part of the day through an unfrequented and pathless country, and came by moonlight to the side of a hill, where the rest of the troop was stationed. Their tents were pitched and their fires kindled, and our chief was welcomed as a man much beloved by his dependents.

"We were received into a large tent, where we found women who had attended their husbands in the expedition. They set before us the supper which they had provided, and I eat it rather to encourage my maids, than to comply with any appetite of my own. When the meat was taken away, they spread the carpets for repose. I was weary, and hoped to find in sleep that remission of distress which nature seldom denies. Ordering myself, therefore, to be undressed, I observed that the women looked very earnestly upon me, not expecting, I suppose, to see me so submissively attended. When my upper vest was taken off, they were apparently struck with the splendour of my clothes, and one of them timorously laid her hand upon the embroidery. She then went out, and in a short time came back with another woman, who seemed to be of higher rank, and greater authority. She did, at her entrance, the usual act of reverence, and, taking me by the hand, placed me in a smaller tent, spread with finer carpets, where I spent the night quietly with my maids.

"In the morning, as I was sitting on the grass, the chief of the troop came towards me. I rose up to receive him, and he bowed with great respect. 'Illustrious lady,' said he, 'my fortune is better than I had presumed to hope; I am told by my women that I have a princess in my camp.' 'Sir,' answered I, 'your women have deceived themselves and you; I am not a princess, but an unhappy stranger who intended soon to have left this country, in which I am now to be imprisoned forever.' 'Whoever or whencesoever you are,' returned the Arab, 'your dress, and that of your servants, show your rank to be high, and your wealth to be great. Why should you, who can so easily procure your ransom, think yourself in danger of perpetual captivity? The purpose of my incursions is to increase my riches, or, more properly, to gather tribute. The sons of Ishmael are the natural and hereditary lords of this part of the continent, which is usurped by late invaders and low-born tyrants, from whom we are compelled to take by the sword what is denied to justice. The violence of war admits no distinction; the lance, that is lifted at guilt and power, will sometimes fall on innocence and gentleness.'

" 'How little,' said I, 'did I expect that yesterday it should have fallen upon me!'

" 'Misfortunes,' answered the Arab, 'should always be expected. If the eye of hostility could learn reverence or pity, excellence like yours had been exempt from injury. But the angels of affliction spread their toils alike for the virtuous and the wicked, for the mighty and the mean. Do not be disconsolate: I am not one of the lawless and cruel rovers of the desert; I know the rules of civil life; I will fix your ransom, give a passport to your messenger, and perform my stipulation with nice punctuality.'

"You will easily believe that I was pleased with his courtesy; and finding that his predominant passion was desire of money, I began now to think my danger less, for I knew that no sum would be thought too great for the release of Pekuah. I told him that he should have no reason to charge me with ingratitude, if I was used with kindness, and that any ransom which could be expected for a maid of common rank would be paid, but that he must not persist to rate me as a princess. He said he would consider what he should demand, and then, smiling, bowed and retired.

"Soon after the women came about me, each contending to be more officious than the other, and my maids themselves were served with reverence. We travelled onward by short journeys. On the fourth day the chief told me that my ransom must be two hundred ounces of gold; which I not only promised him, but told him that I would add fifty more, if I and my maids were honourably treated.

"I never knew the power of gold before. From that time I was the leader of the troop. The march of every day was longer or shorter as I commanded, and the tents were pitched where I chose to rest. We now had camels and other conveniences for travel; my own women were always at my side, and I amused myself with observing the manners of the vagrant nations, and with viewing remains of ancient edifices, with which these deserted countries appear to have been, in some distant age, lavishly embellished.

"The chief of the band was a man far from illiterate; he was able to travel by the stars or the compass, and had marked, in his erratic expeditions, such places as are most worthy the notice of a passenger. He observed to me that buildings are always best preserved in places little frequented, and difficult of access; for, when once a country declines from its primitive splendour, the more inhabitants are left, the quicker ruin will be made. Walls supply stones more easily than quarries, and palaces and temples will be demolished, to make stables of granite, and cottages of porphyry."

CHAPTER XXXIX

THE ADVENTURES OF PEKUAH CONTINUED

"We wandered about in this manner for some weeks, whether, as our chief pretended, for my gratification, or, as I rather suspected, for some convenience of his own. I endeavoured to appear contented where sullenness and resentment would have been of no use, and that endeavor conduced much to the calmness of my mind; but my heart was always with Nekayah, and the troubles of the night much overbalanced the amusements of the day. My women, who threw all their cares upon their mistress, set their minds at ease from the time when they saw me treated with respect, and gave themselves up to the incidental alleviations of our fatigue without solicitude or sorrow. I was pleased with their pleasure, and animated with their confidence. My condition had lost much of its terror, since I found that the Arab ranged the country merely to get riches. Avarice is an uniform and tractable vice: other intellectual distempers are different in different constitutions of mind; that which soothes the pride of one will offend the pride of another; but to the favour of the covetous there is a ready way; bring money, and nothing is denied.

"At last we came to the dwelling of our chief, a strong and spacious house built with stone in an island of the Nile, which lies, as I was told, under the tropic. 'Lady,' said the Arab, 'you shall rest after your journey a few weeks in this place, where you are to consider yourself as sovereign. My occupation is war; I have therefore chosen this obscure residence, from which I can issue unexpected, and to which I can retire unpursued. You may now repose in security; here are few pleasures, but here is no danger.' He then led me into the inner apartments, and seating me on the richest couch, bowed to the ground. His women, who considered me as a rival, looked on me with malignity; but being soon informed that I was a great lady detained only for my ransom, they began to vie with each other in obsequiousness and reverence.

"Being again comforted with new assurances of speedy liberty, I was for some days diverted from impatience by the novelty of the place. The turrets overlooked the country to a great distance, and afforded a view of many windings of the stream. In the day I wandered from one place to another, as the course of the sun varied the splendour of the prospect, and saw many things which I had never seen before. The crocodiles and river-horses are common in this unpeopled region, and I often looked upon them with terror, though I knew that they could not hurt me. For some time I expected to see mermaids and tritons, which, as Imlac has told me, the European travellers have stationed in the Nile, but no such beings ever appeared, and the Arab, when I inquired after them, laughed at my credulity.

"At night the Arab always attended me to a tower set apart for celestial observations, where he endeavoured to teach me the names and courses of the stars. I had no great inclination to this study; but an appearance of attention was necessary to please my instructor, who valued himself for his skill; and, in a little while, I found some employment requisite to beguile the tediousness of time, which was to be passed always amidst the same objects. I was weary of looking in the morning on things from which I had turned away weary in the evening; I therefore was at last willing to observe the stars rather than do nothing, but could not always compose my thoughts, and was very often thinking on Nekayah, when others imagined me contemplating the sky. Soon after, the Arab went upon another expedition, and then my only pleasure was to talk with my maids about the accident by which we were carried away, and the happiness that we should all enjoy at the end of our captivity."

"There were women in your Arab's fortress," said the princess, "why did you not make them your companions, enjoy their conversation, and partake their diversions? In a place where they found business or amusement, why should you alone sit corroded with idle melancholy? or why could not you bear, for a few months, that condition to which they were condemned for life?"

"The diversions of the women," answered Pekuah, "were only childish play, by which the mind, accustomed to stronger operations, could not be kept busy. I could do all which they delighted in doing by powers merely sensitive, while my intellectual faculties were flown to Cairo. They ran from room to room, as a bird hops from wire to wire in his cage. They danced for the sake of motion, as lambs frisk in a meadow. One sometimes pretended to be hurt, that the rest might be alarmed, or hid herself, that another might seek her. Part of their time passed in watching the progress of light bodies that floated on the river, and part in marking the various forms into which clouds broke in the sky.

"Their business was only needle-work, in which I and my maids sometimes helped them; but you know that the mind will easily straggle from the fingers, nor will you suspect that captivity and absence from Nekayah could receive solace from silken flowers.

"Nor was much satisfaction to be hoped from their conversation; for of what could they be expected to talk? They had seen nothing, for they had lived from early youth in that narrow spot; of what they had not seen they could have no knowledge, for they could not read. They had no ideas but of the few things that were within their view, and had hardly names for anything but their clothes and their food. As I bore a superior character, I was often called to terminate their quarrels, which I decided as equitably as I could. If it could have amused me to hear the complaints of each against the rest, I might have been often detained by long stories; but the motives of their animosity were so small that I could not listen without intercepting the tale."

"How," said Rasselas, "can the Arab, whom you represented as a man of more than common accomplishments, take any pleasure in his seraglio, when it is filled only with women like these? Are they exquisitely beautiful?"

"They do not," said Pekuah, "want that unaffecting and ignoble beauty which may subsist without sprightliness or sublimity, without energy of thought or dignity of virtue. But to a man like the Arab such beauty was only a flower casually plucked and carelessly thrown away. Whatever pleasures he might find among them, they were not those of friendship or society. When they were playing about him, he looked on them with inattentive superiority; when they vied for his regard, he sometimes turned away disgusted. As they had no knowledge, their talk could take nothing from the tediousness of life; as they had no choice, their fondness, or appearance of fondness, excited in him neither pride nor gratitude; he was not exalted in his own esteem by the smiles of a woman who saw no other man, nor was much obliged by that regard, of which he could never know the sincerity, and which he might often perceive to be exerted, not so much to delight him as to pain a rival. That which he gave, and they received, as love, was only a careless distribution of superfluous time, such love as man can bestow upon that which he despises, such as has neither hope nor fear, neither joy nor sorrow."

"You have reason, lady, to think yourself happy," said Imlac, "that you have been thus easily dismissed. How could a mind, hungry for knowledge, be willing, in an intellectual famine, to lose such a banquet as Pekuah's conversation?"

"I am inclined to believe," answered Pekuah, "that he was for some time in suspense; for, notwithstanding his promise, whenever I proposed to despatch a messenger to Cairo, he found some excuse for delay. While I was detained in his house, he made many incursions into the neighbouring countries, and perhaps he would have refused to discharge me, had his plunder been equal to his wishes. He returned always courteous, related his adventures, delighted to hear my observations, and endeavoured to advance my acquaintance with the stars.

When I importuned him to send away my letters, he soothed me with professions of honour and sincerity; and, when I could be no longer decently denied, put his troop again in motion, and left me to govern in his absence. I was much afflicted by this studied procrastination, and was sometimes afraid that I should be forgotten; that you would leave Cairo, and I must end my days in an island of the Nile.

"I grew at last hopeless and dejected, and cared so little to entertain him, that he for a while more frequently talked with my maids. That he should fall in love with them, or with me, might have been equally fatal, and I was not much pleased with the growing friendship. My anxiety was not long; for, as I recovered some degree of cheerfulness, he returned to me, and I could not forbear to despise my former uneasiness.

"He still delayed to send for my ransom, and would perhaps never have determined, had not your agent found his way to him. The gold, which he would not fetch, he could not reject when it was offered. He hastened to prepare for our journey hither, like a man delivered from the pain of an intestine conflict. I took leave of my companions in the house, who dismissed me with cold indifference."

Nekayah having heard her favourite's relation, rose and embraced her, and Rasselas gave her an hundred ounces of gold, which she presented to the Arab for the fifty that were promised.

CHAPTER XL

THE HISTORY OF A MAN OF LEARNING

They returned to Cairo, and were so well pleased at finding themselves together, that none of them went much abroad. The prince began to love learning, and one day declared to Imlac that he intended to devote himself to science, and pass the rest of his days in literary solitude.

"Before you make your final choice," answered Imlac, "you ought to examine its hazards, and converse with some of those who are grown old in the company of themselves. I have just left the observatory of one of the most learned astronomers in the world, who has spent forty years in unwearied attention to the motions and appearances of the celestial bodies, and has drawn out his soul in endless calculations. He admits a few friends once a month to hear his deductions and enjoy his discoveries. I was introduced as a man of knowledge worthy of his notice. Men of various ideas, and fluent conversation, are commonly welcome to those whose thoughts have been long fixed upon a single point, and who find the images of other things stealing away. I delighted him with my remarks; he smiled at the narrative of my travels, and was glad to forget the constellations, and descend for a moment into the lower world.

"On the next day of vacation I renewed my visit, and was so fortunate as to please him again. He relaxed from that time the severity of his rule, and permitted me to enter at my own choice. I found him always busy, and always glad to be relieved. As each knew much which the other was desirous of learning, we exchanged our notions with great delight. I perceived that I had every day more of his confidence, and always found new cause of admiration in the profundity of his mind. His comprehension is vast, his memory capacious and retentive, his discourse is methodical, and his expression clear.

"His integrity and benevolence are equal to his learning. His deepest researches and most favourite studies are willingly interrupted for any opportunity of doing good by his counsel or his riches. To his closest retreat, at his most busy moments, all are admitted that want his assistance; 'For though I exclude idleness and pleas-

ure, I will never,' says he, 'bar my doors against charity. To man is permitted the contemplation of the skies, but the practice of virtue is commanded.'"

"Surely," said the princess, "this man is happy."

"I visited him," said Imlac, "with more and more frequency, and was every time more enamoured of his conversation; he was sublime without haughtiness, courteous without formality, and communicative without ostentation. I was at first, great princess, of your opinion, thought him the happiest of mankind, and often congratulated him on the blessing that he enjoyed. He seemed to hear nothing with indifference but the praises of his condition, to which he always returned a general answer, and diverted the conversation to some other topic.

"Amidst this willingness to be pleased, and labour to please, I had quickly reason to imagine that some painful sentiment pressed upon his mind. He often looked up earnestly towards the sun, and let his voice fall in the midst of his discourse. He would sometimes, when we were alone, gaze upon me in silence with the air of a man who longed to speak what he was yet resolved to suppress. He would often send for me with vehement injunctions of haste, though, when I came to him, he had nothing extraordinary to say. And sometimes, when I was leaving him, would call me back, pause a few moments, and then dismiss me."

CHAPTER XLI

THE ASTRONOMER DISCOVERS THE CAUSE OF HIS UNEASINESS

"At last the time came when the secret burst his reserve. We were sitting together last night in the turret of his house, watching the emersion of a satellite of Jupiter. A sudden tempest clouded the sky, and disappointed our observation. We sat awhile silent in the dark, and then he addressed himself to me in these words: 'Imlac, I have long considered thy friendship as the greatest blessing of my life. Integrity without knowledge is weak and useless, and knowledge without integrity is dangerous and dreadful. I have found in thee all the qualities requisite for trust,—benevolence, experience, and fortitude. I have long discharged an office which I must soon quit at the call of nature, and shall rejoice in the hour of imbecility and pain to devolve it upon thee.'

"I thought myself honoured by this testimony, and protested that whatever could conduce to his happiness would add likewise to mine.

"'Hear, Imlac, what thou wilt not without difficulty credit. I have possessed for five years the regulation of weather, and the distribution of the seasons. The sun has listened to my dictates, and passed from tropic to tropic by my direction; the clouds at my call have poured their waters, and the Nile has overflowed at my command; I have restrained the rage of the Dog-star, and mitigated the fervours of the Crab. The winds alone, of all the elemental powers, have hitherto refused my authority, and multitudes have perished by equinoctial tempests which I found myself unable to prohibit or restrain. I have administered this great office with exact justice, and made to the different nations of the earth an impartial dividend of rain and sunshine. What must have been the misery of half the globe, if I had limited the clouds to particular regions, or confined the sun to either side of the equator?'"

CHAPTER XLII

THE OPINION OF THE ASTRONOMER IS
EXPLAINED AND JUSTIFIED

"I suppose he discovered in me, through the obscurity of the room, some tokens of amazement and doubt, for, after a short pause, he proceeded thus:

"'Not to be easily credited will neither surprise nor offend me; for I am probably the first of human beings to whom this trust has been imparted. Nor do I know whether to deem this distinction a reward or punishment; since I have possessed it I have been far less happy than before, and nothing but the consciousness of good intention could have enabled me to support the weariness of unremitted vigilance.'

"'How long, sir,' said I, 'has this great office been in your hands?'

"'About ten years ago,' said he, 'my daily observations of the changes of the sky led me to consider whether, if I had the power of the seasons, I could confer greater plenty upon the inhabitants of the earth. This contemplation fastened on my mind, and I sat days and nights in imaginary dominion, pouring upon this country and that the showers of fertility, and seconding every fall of rain with a due proportion of sunshine. I had yet only the will to do good, and did not imagine that I should ever have the power.

"'One day, as I was looking on the fields withering with heat, I felt in my mind a sudden wish that I could send rain on the southern mountains, and raise the Nile to an inundation. In the hurry of my imagination I commanded rain to fall, and, by comparing the time of my command with that of the inundation, I found that the clouds had listened to my lips.'

"'Might not some other cause,' said I, 'produce this concurrence? The Nile does not always rise on the same day.'

"'Do not believe,' said he, with impatience, 'that such objections could escape me; I reasoned long against my own conviction, and laboured against truth with the utmost obstinacy. I sometimes suspected myself of madness, and should not have dared to impart this secret but to a man like you, capable of distinguishing the wonderful from the impossible, and the incredible from the false.'

"'Why, sir,' said I, 'do you call that

incredible, which you know, or think you know, to be true?'

" 'Because,' said he, 'I cannot prove it by any external evidence; and I know too well the laws of demonstration to think that my conviction ought to influence another, who cannot, like me, be conscious of its force. I, therefore, shall not attempt to gain credit by disputation. It is sufficient that I feel this power, that I have long possessed, and every day exerted it. But the life of man is short, the infirmities of age increase upon me, and the time will soon come, when the regulator of the year must mingle with the dust. The care of appointing a successor has long disturbed me; the night and the day have been spent in comparisons of all the characters which have come to my knowledge, and I have yet found none so worthy as thyself.' "

CHAPTER XLIII

THE ASTRONOMER LEAVES IMLAC HIS DIRECTIONS

" 'Hear therefore, what I shall impart with attention, such as the welfare of a world requires. If the task of a king be considered as difficult, who has the care only of a few millions, to whom he cannot do much good or harm, what must be the anxiety of him on whom depend the action of the elements and the great gifts of light and heat! Hear me therefore with attention.

" 'I have diligently considered the position of the earth and sun, and formed innumerable schemes in which I changed their situation. I have sometimes turned aside the axis of the earth, and sometimes varied the ecliptic of the sun; but I have found it impossible to make a disposition by which the world may be advantaged; what one region gains, another loses by any imaginable alteration, even without considering the distant parts of the solar system with which we are unacquainted. Do not, therefore, in thy administration of the year, indulge thy pride by innovation; do not please thyself with thinking, that thou canst make thyself renowned to all future ages by disordering the seasons. The memory of mischief is no desirable fame. Much less will it become thee to let kindness or interest prevail. Never rob other countries of rain to pour it on thine own. For us the Nile is sufficient.'

"I promised that, when I possessed the power, I would use it with inflexible integrity; and he dismissed me, pressing my hand. 'My heart,' said he, 'will be now at rest, and my benevolence will no more destroy my quiet; I have found a man of wisdom and virtue, to whom I can cheerfully bequeath the inheritance of the sun.' "

The prince heard this narration with very serious regard; but the princess smiled, and Pekuah convulsed herself with laughter. "Ladies," said Imlac, "to mock the heaviest of human afflictions is neither charitable nor wise. Few can attain this man's knowledge, and few practise his virtues, but all may suffer his calamity. Of the uncertainties of our present state, the most dreadful and alarming is the uncertain continuance of reason."

The princess was recollected, and the favourite was abashed. Rasselas, more deeply affected, inquired of Imlac, whether he thought such maladies of the mind frequent, and how they were contracted.

CHAPTER XLIV

THE DANGEROUS PREVALENCE OF IMAGINATION

"Disorders of intellect," answered Imlac, "happen much more often than superficial observers will easily believe. Perhaps, if we speak with rigorous exactness, no human mind is in its right state. There is no man whose imagination does not sometimes predominate over his reason, who can regulate his attention wholly by his will, and whose ideas will come and go at his command. No man will be found in whose mind airy notions do not sometimes tyrannize, and force him to hope or fear beyond the limits of sober probability. All power of fancy over reason is a degree of insanity; but while this power is such as we can control and repress, it is not visible to others, nor considered as any depravation of the mental faculties; it is not pronounced madness but when it comes ungovernable, and apparently influences speech or action.

"To indulge the power of fiction, and send imagination out upon the wing, is often the sport of those who delight too much in silent speculation. When we are alone we are not always busy; the labour of excogitation is too violent to last long; the ardour of inquiry will sometimes give way to idleness or satiety. He who has nothing external that can divert him must find pleasure in his own thoughts, and must conceive himself what he is not; for who is pleased with what he is? He then expatiates in boundless futurity, and culls from all imaginable conditions that which for the present moment he should most desire, amuses his desires with impossible enjoyments, and confers upon his pride unattainable dominion. The mind dances from scene to scene, unites all pleasures in all combinations, and riots in delights which nature and fortune, with all their bounty, cannot bestow.

"In time, some particular train of ideas fixes the attention; all other intellectual gratifications are rejected; the mind, in weariness or leisure, recurs constantly to the favourite conception, and feasts on the luscious falsehood, whenever she is offended with the bitterness of truth. By degrees the reign of fancy is confirmed; she grows first imperious, and in time despotic. Then fictions begin to operate as realities, false opinions fasten upon the mind, and life passes in dreams of rapture or of anguish.

"This, sir, is one of the dangers of solitude, which the hermit has confessed not always to promote goodness, and the astronomer's misery has proved to be not always propitious to wisdom."

"I will no more," said the favourite, "imagine myself the queen of Abyssinia. I have often spent the hours which the princess gave to my own disposal, in adjusting ceremonies and regulating the court; I have repressed the pride of the powerful, and granted the petitions of the poor; I have built new palaces in more happy situations, planted groves upon the tops of mountains, and have exulted in the beneficence of royalty, till, when the princess entered, I had almost forgotten to bow down before her."

"And I," said the princess, "will not allow myself any more to play the shepherdess in my waking dreams. I have often soothed my thoughts with the quiet and innocence of pastoral employments, till I have in my chamber heard the winds whistle, and the sheep bleat; sometimes freed the lamb entangled in the thicket, and sometimes with my crook encountered the wolf. I have a dress like that of the village maids, which I put on to help my imagination, and a pipe on which I play softly, and suppose myself followed by my flocks."

"I will confess," said the prince, "an indulgence of fantastic delight more dangerous than yours. I have frequently endeavoured to image the possibility of a perfect government, by which all wrong should be restrained, all vice reformed, and all the subjects preserved in tranquillity and innocence. This thought produced innumerable schemes of reformation, and dictated many useful regulations and salutary edicts. This has been the sport, and sometimes the labour, of my solitude; and I start, when I think with how little anguish I once supposed the death of my father and my brothers."

"Such," says Imlac, "are the effects of visionary schemes; when we first form them, we know them to be absurd, but familiarize them by degrees, and in time lose sight of their folly."

The evening was now far past, and they rose to return home. As they walked along the bank of the Nile, delighted with the beams of the moon quivering on the water, they saw at a small distance an old man, whom the prince had often heard in the assembly of the sages. "Yonder," said he, "is one whose years have calmed his passions, but not clouded his reason. Let us close the disquisitions of the night by inquiring what are his sentiments of his own state, that we may know whether youth alone is to struggle with vexation, and whether any better hope remains for the latter part of life."

Here the sage approached and saluted them. They invited him to join their walk, and prattled a while, as acquaintance that had unexpectedly met one another. The old man was cheerful and talkative, and the way seemed short in his company. He was pleased to find himself not disregarded, accompanied them to their house, and, at the prince's request, entered with them. They placed him in the seat of honour, and set wine and conserves before him.

"Sir," said the princess, "an evening walk must give to a man of learning like you pleasures which ignorance and youth can hardly conceive. You know the qualities and the causes of all that you behold, the laws by which the river flows, the periods in which the planets perform their revolutions. Everything must supply you with contemplation, and renew the consciousness of your own dignity."

"Lady," answered he, "let the gay and the vigorous expect pleasure in their excursions; it is enough that age can obtain ease. To me the world has lost its novelty; I look round, and see what I remember to have seen in hap-

pier days. I rest against a tree, and consider that in the same shade I once disputed upon the annual overflow of the Nile with a friend who is now silent in the grave. I cast my eyes upward, fix them on the changing moon, and think with pain on the vicissitudes of life. I have ceased to take much delight in physical truth; for what have I to do with those things which I am soon to leave?"

"You may at least recreate yourself," said Imlac, "with the recollection of an honourable and useful life, and enjoy the praise which all agree to give you."

"Praise," said the sage with a sigh, "is to an old man an empty sound. I have neither mother to be delighted with the reputation of her son, nor wife to partake the honours of her husband. I have outlived my friends and my rivals. Nothing is now of much importance; for I cannot extend my interest beyond myself. Youth is delighted with applause, because it is considered as the earnest of some future good, and because the prospect of life is far extended; but to me, who am now declining to decrepitude, there is little to be feared from the malevolence of men, and yet less to be hoped from their affection or esteem. Something they may yet take away, but they can give me nothing. Riches would now be useless, and high employment would be pain. My retrospect of life recalls to my view many opportunities of good neglected, much time squandered upon trifles, and more lost in idleness and vacancy. I leave many great designs unattempted, and many great attempts unfinished. My mind is burthened with no heavy crime, and therefore I compose myself to tranquillity; endeavour to abstract my thoughts from hopes and cares which, though reason knows them to be vain, still try to keep their old possession of the heart; expect, with serene humility, that hour which nature cannot long delay; and hope to possess, in a better state, that happiness which here I could not find, and that virtue which here I have not attained."

He arose and went away, leaving his audience not much elated with the hope of long life. The prince consoled himself with remarking that it was not reasonable to be disappointed by this account; for age had never been considered as the season of felicity, and if it was possible to be easy in decline and weakness, it was likely that the days of vigour and alacrity might be happy; that the noon of life might be bright, if the evening could be calm.

The princess suspected that age was querulous and malignant, and delighted to repress the expectations of those who had newly entered the world. She had seen the possessors of estates look with envy on their heirs, and known many who enjoy pleasure no longer than they can confine it to themselves.

Pekuah conjectured that the man was older than he appeared, and was willing to impute his complaints to delirious dejection; or else supposed that he had been unfortunate, and was therefore discontented. "For nothing," said she, "is more common than to call our own condition the condition of life."

Imlac, who had no desire to see them depressed, smiled at the comforts which they could so readily procure to themselves, and remembered that, at the same age, he was equally confident of unmingled prosperity, and equally fertile of consolatory expedients. He forbore to force upon them unwelcome knowledge, which time itself would too soon impress. The princess and her lady retired; the madness of the astronomer hung upon their minds, and they desired Imlac to enter upon his office, and delay next morning the rising of the sun.

CHAPTER XLVI

THE PRINCESS AND PEKUAH VISIT THE ASTRONOMER

The princess and Pekuah having talked in private of Imlac's astron-omer, thought his character at once so amiable and so strange, that they could not be satisfied without a nearer knowledge; and Imlac was requested to find the means of bringing them together.

This was somewhat difficult; the philosopher had never received any visits from women, though he lived in a city that had in it many Europeans, who followed the manners of their own countries, and many from other parts of the world, that lived there with European liberty. The ladies would not be refused, and several schemes were proposed for the accomplishment of their design. It was proposed to introduce them as strangers in distress, to whom the sage was always accessible; but, after some deliberation, it appeared that by this artifice no acquaintance could be formed, for their conversation would be short, and they could not decently importune him often. "This," said Rasselas, "is true; but I have yet a stronger objection against the misrepresentation of your state. I have always considered it as treason against the great republic of human nature, to make any man's virtues the means of deceiving him, whether on great or little occasions. All imposture weakens confidence, and chills benevolence. When the sage finds that you are not what you seemed, he will feel the resentment natural to a man who, conscious of great abilities, discovers that he has been tricked by understandings meaner than his own, and perhaps the distrust, which he can never afterwards wholly lay aside, may stop the voice of counsel, and close the hand of charity; and where will you find the power of restoring his benefactions to mankind, or his peace to himself?"

To this no reply was attempted, and Imlac began to hope that their curiosity would subside; but next day Pekuah told him she had now found an honest pretence for a visit to the astronomer, for she would solicit permission to continue under him the studies in which she had been initiated by the Arab, and the princess might go with her, either as a fellow-student, or because a woman could not decently come alone. "I am afraid," said Imlac, "that he will be soon weary of your company; men advanced far in knowledge do not love to repeat the elements of their art, and I am not certain that even of the elements, as he will deliver them, connected with inferences, and mingled with reflections, you are a very capable auditress." "That," said Pekuah, "must be my care; I ask of you only to take me thither. My knowledge is, perhaps, more than you imagine it, and, by concurring always with his opinions, I shall make him think it greater than it is."

The astronomer, in pursuance of this resolution, was told that a foreign lady, travelling in search of knowledge, had heard of his reputation, and was desirous to become his scholar. The uncommonness of the proposal raised at once his surprise and curiosity, and when, after a short deliberation, he consented to admit her, he could not stay without impatience till the next day.

The ladies dressed themselves magnificently, and were attended by Imlac to the astronomer, who was pleased to see himself approached with respect by persons of so splendid an appearance. In the exchange of the first civilities he was timorous and bashful; but when the talk became regular, he recollected his powers, and justified the character which Imlac had given. Inquiring of Pekuah, what could have turned her inclination toward astronomy, he received from her a history of her adventure at the pyramid, and of the time passed in the Arab's island. She told her tale with ease and elegance, and her conversation took possession of his heart. The discourse was then turned to astronomy: Pekuah displayed what she knew; he looked upon her as a prodigy of genius, and entreated her not to desist from a study which she had so happily begun.

They came again and again, and were every time more welcome than before. The sage endeavoured to amuse them, that they might prolong their visits, for he found his thoughts grow brighter in their company; the clouds of solicitude vanished by degrees, as he forced himself to entertain them, and he grieved when he was left, at their departure, to his old employment of regulating the seasons.

The princess and her favourite had now watched his lips for several months, and could not catch a single word from which they could judge whether he continued, or not, in the opinion of his preternatural commission. They often contrived to bring him to an open declaration; but he easily eluded all their attacks, and on which side soever they pressed him, escaped from them to some other topic.

As their familiarity increased, they invited him often to the house of Imlac, where they distinguished him by extraordinary respect. He began gradually to delight in sublunary pleasures. He came early, and departed late; laboured to recommend himself by assiduity and compliance; excited their curiosity after new arts, that they might still want his assistance; and when they made any excursion of pleasure or inquiry, entreated to attend them.

By long experience of his integrity and wisdom, the prince and his sister were convinced that he might be trusted without danger; and lest he should draw any false hopes from the civilities which he received, discovered to him their condition, with the motives of their journey, and required his opinion on the choice of life.

"Of the various conditions which the world spreads before you, which you shall prefer," said the sage, "I am not able to instruct you. I can only tell that I have chosen wrong. I have passed my time in study without experience; in the attainment of sciences which can, for the most part, be but remotely useful to mankind. I have purchased knowledge at the expense of all the common comforts of life; I have missed the endearing elegance of female friendship, and the happy commerce of domestic tenderness. If I have obtained any prerogative above other students, they have been accompanied with fear, disquiet, and scrupulosity; but even of these prerogatives, whatever they were, I have, since my thoughts have been diversified by more intercourse with the world, begun to question the reality. When I have been for a few days lost in pleasing dissipation, I am always tempted to think that my inquiries have ended in error, and that I have suffered much, and suffered it in vain."

Imlac was delighted to find that the sage's understanding was breaking through its mists, and resolved to detain him from the planets till he should forget his task of ruling them, and reason should recover its original influence.

From this time the astronomer was received into familiar friendship, and partook of all their projects and pleasures; his respect kept him attentive, and the activity of Rasselas did not leave much time unengaged. Something was always to be done; the day was spent in making observations, which furnished talk for the evening, and the evening was closed with a scheme for the morrow.

The sage confessed to Imlac, that since he had mingled in the gay tumults of life, and divided his hours by a succession of amusements, he found the conviction of his authority over the skies fade gradually from his mind, and began to trust less to an opinion which he never could prove to others, and which he now found subject to variation, from causes in which reason had no part. "If I am accidentally left alone for a few hours," said he, "my inveterate persuasion rushes upon my soul, and my thoughts are chained down by some irresistible violence; but they are soon disentangled by the prince's conversation, and instantaneously released at the entrance of Pekuah. I am like a man habitually afraid of spectres, who is set at ease by a lamp, and wonders at the dread which harassed him in the dark; yet, if his lamp be extinguished, feels again the terrors which he knows that when it is light he shall feel no more. But I am sometimes afraid lest I indulge my quiet by criminal negligence, and voluntarily forget the great charge with which I am entrusted. If I favour myself in a known error, or am determined by my own ease in a doubtful question of this importance, how dreadful is my crime!"

"No disease of the imagination," answered Imlac, "is so difficult of cure as that which is complicated with the dread of guilt; fancy and conscience then act interchangeably upon us, and so often shift their places, that the illusions of one are not distinguished from the dictates of the other. If fancy presents images not moral or religious, the mind drives them away when they give it pain; but when melancholic notions take the form of duty, they lay hold on the faculties without opposition, because we are afraid to exclude or banish them. For this reason the superstitious are often melancholy, and the melancholy almost always superstitious.

"But do not let the suggestions of timidity overpower your better reason; the danger of neglect can be but as the probability of the obligation, which, when you consider it with freedom, you find very little, and that little growing every day less. Open your heart to the influence of the light, which from time to time breaks in upon you. When scruples importune you, which you in your lucid moments know to be vain, do not stand to parley, but fly to business or to Pekuah; and keep this thought always prevalent, that you are only one atom of the mass of humanity, and have neither such virtue nor vice, as that

you should be singled out for supernatural favours or afflictions."

CHAPTER XLVII

THE PRINCE ENTERS, AND BRINGS A NEW TOPIC

"All this," said the astronomer, "I
have often thought, but my reason has
been so long subjugated by an un-
controllable and overwhelming idea,
that it durst not confide in its own
decisions. I now see how fatally I betrayed my quiet, by suffering chimeras to prey upon me in secret; but
melancholy shrinks from communication, and I never found a man before
to whom I could impart my troubles,
though I had been certain of relief. I
rejoice to find my own sentiments
confirmed by yours, who are not easily
deceived, and can have no motive or
purpose to deceive. I hope that time
and variety will dissipate the gloom
that has so long surrounded me, and
the latter part of my days will be spent
in peace."

"Your learning and virtue," said
Imlac, "may justly give you hopes."

Rasselas then entered with the
princess and Pekuah, and inquired
whether they had contrived any new
diversion for the next day. "Such,"
said Nekayah, "is the state of life, that
none are happy but by the anticipation of change: the change itself is
nothing; when we have made it, the
next wish is to change again. The
world is not yet exhausted; let me see
something to-morrow which I never
saw before."

"Variety," said Rasselas, "is so necessary to content, that even the happy
valley disgusted me by the recurrence
of its luxuries; yet I could not forbear
to reproach myself with impatience,
when I saw the monks of St. Anthony
support, without complaint, a life, not
of uniform delight, but uniform hardship."

"Those men," answered Imlac, "are
less wretched in their silent convent
than the Abyssinian princes in their
prison of pleasure. Whatever is done
by the monks is incited by an adequate and reasonable motive. Their
labour supplies them with necessaries;
it therefore cannot be omitted, and is
certainly rewarded. Their devotion
prepares them for another state, and
reminds them of its approach, while
it fits them for it. Their time is regularly distributed; one duty succeeds
another, so that they are not left open
to the distraction of unguided choice,
nor lost in the shades of listless inactivity. There is a certain task to be
performed at an appropriated hour;
and their toils are cheerful, because
they consider them as acts of piety, by
which they are always advancing towards endless felicity."

"Do you think," said Nekayah,
"that the monastic rule is a more holy
and less imperfect state than any
other? May not he equally hope for
future happiness who converses
openly with mankind, who succours
the distressed by his charity, instructs
the ignorant by his learning, and contributes by his industry to the general
system of life; even though he should
omit some of the mortifications which
are practised in the cloister, and allow
himself such harmless delights as his
condition may place within his reach?"

"This," said Imlac, "is a question
which has long divided the wise, and
perplexed the good. I am afraid to
decide on either part. He that lives
well in the world is better than he
that lives well in a monastery. But,
perhaps, everyone is not able to stem
the temptations of public life; and if
he cannot conquer, he may properly
retreat. Some have little power to do
good, and have likewise little strength
to resist evil. Many are weary of their
conflicts with adversity, and are willing to eject those passions which have
long busied them in vain. And many
are dismissed by age and diseases from
the more laborious duties of society.
In monasteries the weak and timorous may be happily sheltered, the
weary may repose, and the penitent
may meditate. Those retreats of prayer
and contemplation have something so
congenial to the mind of man, that,

perhaps, there is scarcely one that does not purpose to close his life in pious abstraction, with a few associates serious as himself."

"Such," said Pekuah, "has often been my wish, and I have heard the princess declare that she should not willingly die in a crowd."

"The liberty of using harmless pleasures," proceeded Imlac, "will not be disputed; but it is still to be examined what pleasures are harmless. The evil of any pleasure that Nekayah can image is not in the act itself, but in its consequences. Pleasure, in itself harmless, may become mischievous by endearing to us a state which we know to be transient and probatory, and withdrawing our thoughts from that, of which every hour brings us nearer to the beginning, and of which no length of time will bring us to the end. Mortification is not virtuous in itself, nor has any other use, but that it disengages us from the allurements of sense. In the state of future perfection to which we all aspire, there will be pleasure without danger, and security without restraint."

The princess was silent, and Rasselas, turning to the astronomer, asked him whether he could not delay her retreat, by showing her something which she had not seen before.

"Your curiosity," said the sage, "has been so general, and your pursuit of knowledge so vigorous, that novelties are not now very easily to be found; but what you can no longer procure from the living may be given by the dead. Among the wonders of this country are the catacombs, or the ancient repositories in which the bodies of the earliest generations were lodged, and where, by the virtue of the gums which embalmed them, they yet remain without corruption."

"I know not," said Rasselas, "what pleasure the sight of the catacombs can afford; but, since nothing else is offered, I am resolved to view them, and shall place this with many other things which I have done because I would do something."

They hired a guard of horsemen, and the next day visited the catacombs. When they were about to descend into the sepulchral caves, "Pekuah," said the princess, "we are now again invading the habitations of the dead; I know that you will stay behind; let me find you safe when I return." "No, I will not be left," answered Pekuah, "I will go down between you and the prince."

They then all descended, and roved with wonder through the labyrinth of subterraneous passages, where the bodies were laid in rows on either side.

CHAPTER XLVIII

IMLAC DISCOURSES ON THE NATURE OF THE SOUL

"What reason," said the prince, "can be given why the Egyptians should thus expensively preserve those carcasses which some nations consume with fire, others lay to mingle with the earth, and all agree to remove from their sight, as soon as decent rites can be performed?"

"The original of ancient customs," said Imlac, "is commonly unknown, for the practice often continues when the cause has ceased; and concerning superstitious ceremonies it is vain to conjecture, for what reason did not dictate, reason cannot explain. I have long believed that the practice of embalming arose only from tenderness to the remains of relations or friends, and to this opinion I am more inclined, because it seems impossible that this care should have been general; had all the dead been embalmed, their repositories must in time have been more spacious than the dwellings of the living. I suppose only the rich or honourable were secured from corruption, and the rest left to the course of nature.

"But it is commonly supposed that the Egyptians believed the soul to live as long as the body continued undissolved, and therefore tried this method of eluding death."

"Could the wise Egyptians," said Nekayah, "think so grossly of the soul? If the soul could once survive its separation, what could it afterwards receive or suffer from the body?"

"The Egyptians would doubtless think erroneously," said the astronomer, "in the darkness of heathenism, and the first dawn of philosophy. The nature of the soul is still disputed amidst all our opportunities of clearer knowledge; some yet say that it may be material, who, nevertheless, believe it to be immortal."

"Some," answered Imlac, "have indeed said that the soul is material, but I can scarcely believe that any man has thought it, who knew how to think; for all the conclusions of reason enforce the immateriality of mind, and all the notices of sense and investigations of science concur to prove the unconsciousness of matter.

"It was never supposed that cogitation is inherent in matter, or that every particle is a thinking being. Yet, if any part of matter be devoid of thought, what part can we suppose to think? Matter can differ from matter only in form, density, bulk, motion, and direction of motion. To which of these, however varied or combined, can consciousness be annexed? To be round or square, to be solid or fluid, to be great or little, to be moved slowly or swiftly one way or another, are modes of material existence, all equally alien from the nature of cogitation. If matter be once without thought, it can only be made to think by some new modification; but all the modifications which it can admit are equally unconnected with cogitative powers."

"But the materialists," said the astronomer, "urge that matter may have qualities with which we are unacquainted."

"He who will determine," returned Imlac, "against that which he knows, because there may be something which he knows not; he that can set hypothetical possibility against acknowledged certainty, is not to be admitted among reasonable beings. All that we know of matter is, that matter is inert, senseless, and lifeless; and if this conviction cannot be opposed but by referring us to something that we know not, we have all the evidence that human intellect can admit. If that which is known may be overruled by that which is unknown, no being, not omniscient, can arrive at certainty."

"You let us not," said the astronomer, "too arrogantly limit the Creator's power."

"It is no limitation of omnipotence," replied the poet, "to suppose that one thing is not consistent with another, that the same proposition cannot be at once true and false, that the same number cannot be even and odd, that cogitation cannot be conferred on that which is created incapable of cogitation."

"I know not," said Nekayah, "any great use of this question. Does that immateriality, which in my opinion you have sufficiently proved, necessarily include eternal duration?"

"Of immateriality," said Imlac, "our ideas are negative, and therefore obscure. Immateriality seems to imply a natural power of perpetual duration as a consequence of exemption from all causes of decay: whatever perishes is destroyed by the solution of its contexture, and separation of its parts; nor can we conceive how that which has no parts, and therefore admits no solution, can be naturally corrupted or impaired."

"I know not," said Rasselas, "how to conceive anything without extension; what is extended must have parts, and you allow that whatever has parts may be destroyed."

"Consider your own conceptions," replied Imlac, "and the difficulty will be less. You will find substance without extension. An ideal form is no less real than material bulk; yet an ideal form has no extension. It is no less certain, when you think on a pyramid, that your mind possesses the idea of a pyramid, than that the pyramid it-self is standing. What space does the idea of a pyramid occupy more than the idea of a grain of corn? or how can either idea suffer laceration? As is the effect, such is the cause; as thought is, such is the power that thinks, a power impassive and indiscerptible."*

"But the Being," said Nekayah, "whom I fear to name, the Being which made the soul, can destroy it."

"He, surely, can destroy it," answered Imlac, "since, however unperishable, it receives from a superior nature its power of duration. That it will not perish by any inherent cause of decay, or principle of corruption, may be shown by philosophy; but philosophy can tell no more. That it will not be annihilated by him that made it, we must humbly learn from higher authority."

The whole assembly stood awhile silent and collected. "Let us return," said Rasselas, "from this scene of mortality. How gloomy would be these mansions of the dead to him who did not know that he shall never die; that what now acts shall continue its agency, and what now thinks shall think on forever. Those that lie here stretched before us, the wise and the powerful of ancient times, warn us to remember the shortness of our present state; they were, perhaps, snatched away while they were busy, like us, in the choice of life."

"To me," said the princess, "the choice of life is become less important; I have hereafter to think only on the choice of eternity."

They then hastened out of the caverns, and, under the protection of their guard, returned to Cairo.

CHAPTER XLIX

THE CONCLUSION, IN WHICH NOTHING IS
CONCLUDED

It was now the time of the inundation of the Nile: a few days after their

* incapable of division.

visit to the catacombs, the river began to rise.

They were confined to their house. The whole region being under water gave them no invitation to any excursions, and being well supplied with materials for talk, they diverted themselves with comparisons of the different forms of life which they had observed, and with various schemes of happiness which each of them had formed.

Pekuah was never so much charmed with any place as the convent of St. Anthony, where the Arab restored her to the princess, and wished only to fill it with pious maidens, and to be made prioress of the order; she was weary of expectation and disgust, and would gladly be fixed in some unvariable state.

The princess thought that, of all sublunary things, knowledge was the best: she desired first to learn all sciences, and then purposed to found a college of learned women, in which she would preside, that, by conversing with the old and educating the young, she might divide her time between the acquisition and communication of wisdom, and raise up for the next age models of prudence, and patterns of piety.

The prince desired a little kingdom, in which he might administer justice in his own person, and see all the parts of government with his own eyes; but he could never fix the limits of his dominion, and was always adding to the number of his subjects.

Imlac and the astronomer were contented to be driven along the stream of life, without directing their course to any particular port.

Of these wishes that they had formed, they well knew that none could be obtained. They deliberated a while what was to be done, and resolved, when the inundation should cease, to return to Abyssinia.

[1759]

CHRISTOPHER SMART (1722-1771)

Christopher Smart, a "little, smart, black-eyed man," according to the *Cambridge Chronicler*, in his fifty years of life first created for himself a brilliant reputation at Cambridge, where he was Fellow of Pembroke College from 1745 to 1749, and then through the effects of drink, idleness, and a growing religious mania, sank to a seven-year period of insanity (1756-63), and finally to confinement for debt in King's Bench Prison, where he died in 1771.

Until fairly recently, Smart's literary reputation has rested solely on his masterpiece, "A Song to David," which he wrote during his period of insanity and published on his release in 1763. New editions of "A Song to David" and of his other poems, and especially the publication of another manuscript, *Jubilate Agno* (see page 1159) from the same period, have greatly increased contemporary interest in Smart. The latter poem is long, often baffling, sometimes unintentionally humorous, sometimes consciously so; often it is far from being poetry at all, but in many passages it rises to great heights. It was originally preserved by William Hayley, a friend of Cowper and Blake, perhaps as a useful illustration of religious mania. Or so Mr. William Force Stead, who found and published the manuscript in 1939, under the title of *Rejoice in the Lamb*, conjectures.

Both "A Song to David" and *Jubilate Agno* are rhapsodies in praise of God. "For I am the Lord's News-Writer—the scribe-evangelist," Smart writes in the latter poem, "For by the grace of God I am the Reviver of ADORATION amongst ENGLISH-MEN." In *Jubilate Agno* Smart summons out of his incredibly well-stocked mind a goodly share of all creation to worship God—beasts, insects, fish, plants, minerals, saints and sinners; "A Song to David" is the refinement and perfection of all that is best in the former. The reader who is aroused and interested by these selections would do well to look for further examples in Smart's poems of his love of childhood, his sympathetic knowledge of animals, his religious concepts so close to Blake's, his simple, direct, often naïve religious expression, and finally his experiments in tone coloring and what looks like an anticipation of sprung rhythms: "Let Ross, house of Ross rejoice with the Great Flabber Dabber Flat Clapping Fish with hands."

Collected Poems, ed. N. Callan (2 vols., 1949) ; *Poems*, ed. R. Brittain (Princeton, 1950) ; *A Song to David and Other Poems*, ed. P. Serle (Melbourne, 1923) ; *Rejoice in the Lamb; A Song from Bedlam*, ed. W. F. Stead (1939) ; *Hymns for the Amusement of Children* (Oxford, 1947) [reproduction of the Bodleian Library copy of 3d ed., London, 1775]; *Jubilate Agno*, ed. W. H. Bond (Cambridge, Mass., 1954) ; K. A. McKenzie, *Christopher Smart, sa Vie et ses Oeuvres* (Paris, 1925) ; R. B. Botting, "Christopher Smart in London," *Research Studies of the State College of Washington*, VII (1939), 3-54; E. G. Ainsworth and C. E. Noyes, *Christopher Smart: A Biographical and Critical Study* (Columbia, Mo., 1943) ; G. J. Gray, *Bibliography of the Writings of Christopher Smart, with Biographical References, Transactions of the Bibliographical Society*, VI (1903).

A SONG TO DAVID

O thou, that sitt'st upon a throne,
With harp of high majestic tone,
  To praise the King of kings;
And voice of heaven-ascending swell,
Which, while its deeper notes excel,
  Clear as a clarion rings:

To bless each valley, grove, and coast,
And charm the cherubs to the post
  Of gratitude in throngs;
To keep the days on Zion's mount,   10
And send the year to his account,
  With dances and with songs:

O Servant of God's holiest charge,
The minister of praise at large,
  Which thou mayst now receive;
From thy blessed mansion hail and hear,
From topmost eminence appear
  To this the wreath I weave.

Great, valiant, pious, good, and clean,
Sublime, contemplative, serene,   20
  Strong, constant, pleasant, wise!
Bright effluence of exceeding grace;
Best man!—the swiftness and the race,
  The peril and the prize!

Great—from the lustre of his crown,
From Samuel's horn and God's renown,
  Which is the people's voice;

For all the host, from rear to van,
Applauded and embraced the man—
   The man of God's own choice.   30

Valiant—the word, and up he rose—
The fight—he triumphed o'er the foes
   Whom God's just laws abhor;
And armed in gallant faith he took
Against the boaster, from the brook,
   The weapons of the war.

Pious—magnificent and grand;
'Twas he the famous temple planned:
   (The seraph in his soul)
Foremost to give his Lord his dues,   40
Foremost to bless the welcome news,
   And foremost to condole.

Good—from Jehudah's genuine vein,
From God's best nature good in grain,
   His aspect and his heart;
To pity, to forgive, to save,
Witness En-gedi's conscious cave,
   And Shimei's blunted dart.

Clean—if perpetual prayer be pure,
And love, which could itself inure   50
   To fasting and to fear—
Clean in his gestures, hands, and feet,
To smite the lyre, the dance complete,
   To play the sword and spear.

Sublime—invention ever young,
Of vast conception, towering tongue,
   To God the eternal theme;
Notes from yon exaltations caught,
Unrivaled royalty of thought,
   O'er meaner strains supreme.   60

Contemplative—on God to fix
His musings, and above the six
   The sabbath-day he blessed;
'Twas then his thoughts self-conquest pruned,
And heavenly melancholy tuned,
   To bless and bear the rest.

Serene—to sow the seeds of peace,
Remembering, when he watched the fleece,
   How sweetly Kidron purled—
To further knowledge, silence vice,   70
And plant perpetual paradise
   When God had calmed the world.

Strong—in the Lord, who could defy
Satan, and all his powers that lie
   In sempiternal night;
And hell and horror and despair
Were as the lion and the bear
   To his undaunted might.

Constant—in love to God the Truth,
Age, manhood, infancy, and youth—   80
   To Jonathan his friend
Constant, beyond the verge of death;
And Ziba and Mephibosheth
   His endless fame attend.

Pleasant—and various as the year;
Man, soul, and angel, without peer,
   Priest, champion, sage and boy;
In armour, or in ephod clad,
His pomp, his piety was glad;
   Majestic was his joy.   90

Wise—in recovery from his fall,
Whence rose his eminence o'er all,
   Of all the most reviled;
The light of Israel in his ways,
Wise are his precepts, prayer, and praise
   And counsel to his child.

His Muse, bright angel of his verse,
Gives balm for all the thorns that pierce,
   For all the pangs that rage;
Blessed light, still gaining on the gloom,   100
The more than Michael of his bloom,
   The Abishag of his age.

He sang of God—the mighty source
Of all things—the stupendous force
   On which all strength depends;
From whose right arm, beneath whose eyes,
All period, power, and enterprize
   Commences, reigns, and ends.

Angels—their ministry and meed,
Which to and fro with blessings speed,   110
   Or with their citterns wait;
Where Michael with his millions bows,
Where dwells the seraph and his spouse,
   The cherub and her mate.

Of man—the semblance and effect
Of God and love—the saint elect
   For infinite applause—
To rule the land, and briny broad,
To be laborious in his laud,
   And heroes in his cause.   120

The world—the clustering spheres he made,
The glorious light, the soothing shade,
  Dale, champaign, grove, and hill;
The multitudinous abyss,
Where Secrecy remains in bliss,
  And Wisdom hides her skill.

Trees, plants, and flowers—of virtuous root;
  Gem yielding blossom, yielding fruit,
  Choice gums and precious balm;
Bless ye the nosegay in the vale,   130
And with the sweetness of the gale
  Enrich the thankful psalm.

Of fowl—e'en every beak and wing
Which cheer the winter, hail the spring,
  That live in peace or prey;
They that make music, or that mock,
The quail, the brave domestic cock,
  The raven, swan, and jay.

Of fishes—every size and shape,
Which nature frames of light escape,   140
  Devouring man to shun:
The shells are in the wealthy deep,
The shoals upon the surface leap,
  And love the glancing sun.

Of beasts—the beaver plods his task;
While the sleek tigers roll and bask,
  Nor yet the shades arouse:
Her cave the mining coney scoops;
Where o'er the mead the mountain stoops,
  The kids exult and browse.   150

Of gems—their virtue and their price,
Which hid in earth from man's device,
  Their darts of lustre sheathe;
The jasper of the master's stamp,
The topaz blazing like a lamp
  Among the mines beneath.

Blessed was the tenderness he felt
When to his graceful harp he knelt,
  And did for audience call;
When Satan with his hand he quelled,   160
And in serene suspense he held
  The frantic throes of Saul.

His furious foes no more maligned
As he such melody divined,
  And sense and soul detained;
Now striking strong, now soothing soft,
He sent the godly sounds aloft,
  Or in delight refrained.

When up to heaven his thoughts he piled,
From fervent lips fair Michael smiled,   170
  As blush to blush she stood;
And chose herself the queen, and gave
Her utmost from her heart, "so brave,
  And plays his hymns so good."

The pillars of the Lord are seven,
Which stand from earth to topmost heaven;
  His wisdom drew the plan;
His Word accomplished the design,
From brightest gem to deepest mine,
  From Christ enthroned to man.   180

Alpha, the cause of causes, first
In station, fountain, whence the burst
  Of light and blaze of day;
Whence bold attempt and brave advance,
Have motion, life, and ordinance,
  And heaven itself its stay.

Gamma supports the glorious arch
On which angelic legions march,
  And is with sapphires paved;
Thence the fleet clouds are sent adrift,   190
And thence the painted folds, that lift
  The crimson veil, are waved.

Eta with living sculpture breathes,
With verdant carvings, flowery wreathes
  Of never-wasting bloom;
In strong relief his goodly base
All instruments of labour grace,
  The trowel, spade, and loom.

Next Theta stands to the Supreme—
Who formed, in number, sign, and scheme,
  The illustrious lights that are;   201
And one addressed his saffron robe,
And one, clad in a silver globe,
  Held rule with every star.

Iota's tuned to choral hymns
Of those that fly, while he that swims
  In thankful safety lurks;
And foot, and chapitre, and niche,
The various histories enrich
  Of God's recorded works.   210

Sigma presents the social droves,
With him that solitary roves,
  And man of all the chief;
Fair on whose face, and stately frame,
Did God impress his hallowed name,
  For ocular belief.

Omega! Greatest and the best,
Stands sacred to the day of rest,
  For gratitude and thought;
Which blessed the world upon his pole, 220
And gave the universe his goal,
  And closed the infernal draught.

O David, scholar of the Lord!
Such is thy science, whence reward
  And infinite degree;
O strength, O sweetness, lasting ripe!
God's harp thy symbol, and thy type
  The lion and the bee!

There is but One who ne'er rebelled,
But One by passion unimpelled, 230
  By pleasures unenticed;
He from himself his semblance sent,
Grand object of his own content,
  And saw the God in Christ.

"Tell them I am," Jehova said
To Moses; while earth heard in dread,
  And smitten to the heart,
At once above, beneath, around,
All nature, without voice or sound,
  Replied, "O Lord, Thou art." 240

Thou art—to give and to confirm,
For each his talent and his term;
  All flesh thy bounties share:
Thou shalt not call thy brother fool;
The porches of the Christian school
  Are meekness, peace, and prayer.

Open, and naked of offence,
Man's made of mercy, soul, and sense;
  God armed the snail and wilk;
Be good to him that pulls thy plough; 250
Due food and care, due rest, allow
  For her that yields thee milk.

Rise up before the hoary head,
And God's benign commandment dread,
  Which says thou shalt not die:
"Not as I will, but as thou wilt,"
Prayed he whose conscience knew no guilt;
  With whose blessed pattern vie.

Use all thy passions!—love is thine,
And joy, and jealousy divine; 260
  Thine hope's eternal fort,
And care thy leisure to disturb,
With fear concupiscence to curb,
  And rapture to transport.

Act simply, as occasion asks:
Put mellow wine in seasoned casks;
  Till not with ass and bull:
Remember thy baptismal bond;
Keep from commixtures foul and fond,
  Nor work thy flax with wool. 270

Distribute: pay the Lord his tithe,
And make the widow's heartstrings blithe;
  Resort with those that weep:
As you from all and each expect,
For all and each thy love direct,
  And render as you reap.

The slander and its bearer spurn,
And propagating praise sojourn
  To make thy welcome last;
Turn from old Adam to the New; 280
By hope futurity pursue;
  Look upwards to the past.

Control thine eye, salute success,
Honour the wiser, happier bless,
  And for thy neighbour feel;
Grutch not of Mammon and his leaven,
Work emulation up to heaven
  By knowledge and by zeal.

O David, highest in the list
Of worthies, on God's ways insist, 290
  The genuine word repeat:
Vain are the documents of men,
And vain the flourish of the pen
  That keeps the fool's conceit.

Praise above all—for praise prevails;
Heap up the measure, load the scales,
  And good to goodness add:
The generous soul her Saviour aids,
But peevish obloquy degrades;
  The Lord is great and glad. 300

For Adoration all the ranks
Of angels yield eternal thanks,
  And David in the midst;
With God's good poor, which, last and least
In man's esteem, thou to thy feast,
  O blessed bride-groom, bidst.

For adoration seasons change,
And order, truth, and beauty range,
  Adjust, attract, and fill:
The grass the polyanthus checks; 310
And polished porphyry reflects,
  By the descending rill.

Rich almonds colour to the prime
For adoration; tendrils climb,
   And fruit trees pledge their gems;
And Ivis with her gorgeous vest
Builds for her eggs her cunning nest,
   And bell-flowers bow their stems.

With vinous syrups cedars spout;
From rocks pure honey gushing out,   320
   For adoration springs:
All scenes of painting crowd the map
Of nature; to the mermaid's pap
   The scaled infant clings.

The spotted ounce and playsome cubs
Run rustling 'mongst the flowering shrubs,
   And lizards feed the moss;
For adoration beasts embark,
While waves upholding halcyon's ark
   No longer roar and toss.   330

While Israel sits beneath his fig,
With coral root and amber sprig
   The weaned adventurer sports;
Where to the palm the jasmine cleaves,
For adoration 'mongst the leaves
   The gale his peace reports.

Increasing days their reign exalt,
Nor in the pink and mottled vault
   The opposing spirits tilt;
And, by the coasting reader spied,   340
The silverlings and crusions glide
   For adoration gilt.

For adoration ripening canes
And cocoa's purest milk detains
   The western pilgrim's staff;
Where rain in clasping boughs enclosed,
And vines with oranges disposed,
   Embower the social laugh.

Now labour his reward receives,
For adoration counts his sheaves   350
   To peace, her bounteous prince;
The nectarine his strong tint imbibes,
And apples of ten thousand tribes,
   And quick peculiar quince.

The wealthy crops of whitening rice,
'Mongst thyine woods and groves of spice,
   For adoration grow;
And, marshalled in the fencèd land,
The peaches and pomegranates stand,
   Where wild carnations blow.   360

The laurels with the winter strive;
The crocus burnishes alive
   Upon the snow-clad earth:
For adoration myrtles stay
To keep the garden from dismay,
   And bless the sight from dearth.

The pheasant shows his pompous neck;
And ermine, jealous of a speck,
   With fear eludes offence:
The sable, with his glossy pride,   370
For adoration is descried,
   Where frosts the wave condense.

The cheerful holly, pensive yew,
And holy thorn, their trim renew;
   The squirrel hoards his nuts:
All creatures batten o'er their stores,
And careful nature all her doors
   For adoration shuts.

For adoration, David's psalms
Lift up the heart to deeds of alms;   380
   And he who kneels and chants,
Prevails his passions to control,
Finds meat and medicine to the soul,
   Which for translation pants.

For adoration, beyond match,
The scholar bulfinch aims to catch
   The soft flute's ivory touch;
And, careless on the hazel spray,
The daring redbreast keeps at bay
   The damsel's greedy clutch.   390

For adoration, in the skies,
The Lord's philosopher espies
   The Dog, the Ram, and Rose;
The planet's ring, Orion's sword;
Nor is his greatness less adored
   In the vile worm that glows.

For adoration on the strings
The western breezes work their wings,
   The captive ear to soothe.—
Hark! 'tis a voice—how still and small—   400
That makes the cataracts to fall,
   Or bids the sea be smooth.

For adoration, incense comes
From bezoar, and Arabian gums;
   And on the civet's fur.
But as for prayer, or ere it faints,
Far better is the breath of saints
   Than galbanum and myrrh.

For adoration, from the down
Of damsons to the anana's crown,   410
   God sends to tempt the taste;
And while the luscious zest invites
The sense, that in the scene delights,
   Commands desire be chaste.

For adoration, all the paths
Of grace are open, all the baths
   Of purity refresh;
And all the rays of glory beam
To deck the man of God's esteem,
   Who triumphs o'er the flesh.   420

For adoration, in the dome
Of Christ the sparrows find an home;
   And on his olives perch:
The swallow also dwells with thee,
O man of God's humility,
   Within his Saviour's Church.

Sweet is the dew that falls betimes,
And drops upon the leafy limes;
   Sweet Hermon's fragrant air:
Sweet is the lily's silver bell,   430
And sweet the wakeful tapers smell
   That watch for early prayer.

Sweet the young nurse with love intense,
Which smiles o'er sleeping innocence;
   Sweet when the lost arrive:
Sweet the musician's ardour beats,
While his vague mind's in quest of sweets,
   The choicest flowers to hive.

Sweeter in all the strains of love,
The language of thy turtle dove,   440
   Paired to thy swelling chord;
Sweeter with every grace endued,
The glory of thy gratitude,
   Respired unto the Lord.

Strong is the horse upon his speed;
Strong in pursuit the rapid glede,
   Which makes at once his game:
Strong the tall ostrich on the ground;
Strong through the turbulent profound
   Shoots xiphias to his aim.   450

Strong is the lion—like a coal
His eye-ball—like a bastion's mole
   His chest against the foes:
Strong, the gier-eagle on his sail,
Strong against tide, the enormous whale
   Emerges as he goes.

But stronger still, in earth and air,
And in the sea, the man of prayer;
   And far beneath the tide;
And in the seat to faith assigned,   460
Where ask is have, where seek is find,
   Where knock is open wide.

Beauteous the fleet before the gale;
Beauteous the multitudes in mail,
   Ranked arms and crested heads:
Beauteous the garden's umbrage mild,
Walk, water, meditated wild,
   And all the bloomy beds.

Beauteous the moon full on the lawn;
And beauteous, when the veil's withdrawn,
   The virgin to her spouse: 471
Beauteous the temple decked and filled,
When to the heaven of heavens they build
   Their heart-directed vows.

Beauteous, yea beauteous more than these,
The shepherd king upon his knees,
   For his momentous trust;
With wish of infinite conceit,
For man, beast, mute, the small and great,
   And prostrate dust to dust.   480

Precious the bounteous widow's mite;
And precious, for extreme delight,
   The largess from the churl:
Precious the ruby's blushing blaze,
And alba's blessed imperial rays,
   And pure cerulean pearl.

Precious the penitential tear;
And precious is the sigh sincere,
   Acceptable to God:
And precious are the winning flowers,   490
In gladsome Israel's feast of bowers,
   Bound on the hallowed sod.

More precious that diviner part
Of David, even the Lord's own heart,
   Great, beautiful, and new:
In all things where it was intent,
In all extremes, in each event,
   Proof—answering true to true.

Glorious the sun in mid career;
Glorious the assembled fires appear;   500
   Glorious the comet's train:
Glorious the trumpet and alarm;
Glorious the almighty stretched-out arm;
   Glorious the enraptured main:

Glorious the northern lights astream;
Glorious the song, when God's the theme;
 Glorious the thunder's roar:
Glorious hosanna from the den;
Glorious the catholic amen;
 Glorious the martyr's gore: 510

Glorious—more glorious is the crown
Of Him that brought salvation down
 By meekness, called thy Son;
Thou that stupendous truth believed,
And now the matchless deed's achieved,
 Determined, dared, and done.

          [1763]

JAMES MACPHERSON (1736-1796)

James Macpherson was in his youth an obscure schoolmaster in southern Inverness-shire; he wrote mediocre verse and showed some interest in the Gaelic poetry of his district, though his knowledge of the language was imperfect. In 1759 he met John Home, who had long cherished the idea that great primitive poetry was to be found in the Highlands and had fired the poet William Collins with his enthusiasm (see Collins's *Ode on the Superstitions of the Highlands of Scotland*). At the instance of Home and his friend Hugh Blair, Professor of Rhetoric at Edinburgh, Macpherson published *Fragments of Ancient Poetry Collected in the Highlands of Scotland and Translated from the Gaelic or Erse Language* (1760). According to the theories of his sponsors, such fragments pointed to the existence of a great primitive epic. He set out on Highland tours in quest of such material and duly published *Fingal, An Ancient Epic* (1761, dated 1762), and *Temora, An Epic Poem* (1763). The collective edition is called *The Poems of Ossian*. Over the question of the authenticity of these works there raged a great controversy which lasted well into the nineteenth century: at one extreme was Dr. Johnson, who declared that Macpherson was a mere forger who had made up his "ancient poems" out of whole cloth; at the other extreme were ardent Scots like Blair, who maintained that the texts were actual translations of ancient originals. The whole debate belongs to Celtic scholarship rather than to literary criticism; it has long been agreed that Macpherson did not translate, paraphrase, or follow continuously any Gaelic texts; but that his work does have some links, however slender, with traditional material actually current in the Highlands.

But it is the tremendous popularity, not the ultimate origin, of Ossian that is important for the student of literature. The appeal to eighteenth-century primitivism and sentimentalism was irresistible. The imagination of Macpherson's generation was captivated by the thought of a great Celtic bard who rivaled Homer. The misty and generalized landscape, which has some relations to the actual Highland scene, was Macpherson's own contribution. He avoided the barbaric and uncouth, and submerged narrative and description in a flood of vague sententious melancholy which was wholly to the taste of readers familiar with the grave-yard school of poetry. His rhythmic prose derives in part from the Old Testament and from Milton. Much of it sounds like windy rhetoric now, but in the late eighteenth century it was argued that either Macpherson or Ossian must be a great genius and that one or the other was entitled to the highest literary honors. Men of taste like Gray found something in Ossian to which we no longer respond. The Highland poems had even more influence on the Continent than in Great Britain. Goethe found in the song of Selma a fitting expression of Werther's stormier moods; and, just as Alexander the Great carried Homer with him on his campaigns, so Napoleon carried the works of Ossian in the widely read Italian version of Cesarotti.

Poems of Ossian, ed. W. Sharp (Edinburgh, 1926); *Ossian*, ed. O. L. Jiriczek (3 vols., Heidelberg, 1940) [facsimile edition, with full critical apparatus]; T. B. Saunders, *Life and Letters* (1894); W. A. Craigie, "The Ossianic Ballads," *Scottish Review*, XXXIV (1899), 260-90; A. Nutt, *Ossian and the Ossianic Literature* (1899); J. S. Smart, *James Macpherson: An Episode in Literature* (1905); P. Van Tieghem, *Ossian en France* (2 vols., Paris, 1917); "Ossian et l'ossianisme au XVIIIe siècle," in his *Le Préromantisme*, I (Paris, 1924); D. S. Thomson, *The Gaelic Sources of Macpherson's Ossian* (Edinburgh, 1952); G. F. Black, "Macpherson's Ossian and the Ossianic Controversy: A Contribution towards a Bibliography," *Bulletin of the New York Public Library*, XXX (1926), 424-39; 508-24.

CARTHON, A POEM

ARGUMENT

This poem is complete, and the subject of it, as of most of Ossian's compositions, tragical. In the time of Comhal, the son of Trathal, and father of the celebrated Fingal, Clessámmor the son of Thaddu and brother of Morna, Fingal's mother, was driven by a storm into the river Clyde [Clutha], on the banks of which stood Balclutha, a town belonging to the Britons between the walls. He was hospitably received by Reuthámir, the principal man in the place, who gave him Moina, his only daughter, in marriage. Reuda, the son of Cormo, a Briton who was in love with Moina, came to Reuthámir's house, and behaved haughtily towards Clessámmor. A quarrel ensued, in which Reuda was killed; the Britons who attended him pressed so hard on Clessámmor that he was obliged to throw himself into the Clyde, and swim to his ship. He hoisted sail, and the wind, being favourable, bore him out to sea. He often endeavoured to return, and carry off his beloved Moina by night; but the wind continuing contrary, he was forced to desist.

Moina, who had been left with child by her husband, brought forth a son, and died soon after.—Reuthámir named the child Carthon—*i.e. the murmur of waves*, from the storm which carried off Clessámmor, his father, who was supposed to have been cast away. When Carthon was three years old, Comhal, the father of Fingal, in one of his expeditions against the Britons, took and burned Balclutha. Reuthámir was killed in the attack: and Carthon was carried safe away by his nurse, who fled farther into the country of the Britons. Carthon, coming to man's estate, was resolved to revenge the fall of Balclutha on Comhal's posterity. He set sail from the Clyde, and, falling on the coast of Morven, defeated two of Fingal's heroes who came to oppose his progress. He was at last unwittingly killed by his father, Clessámmor, in a single combat. This story is the foundation of the present poem, which opens on the night preceding the death of Carthon, so that what passed before is introduced by way of episode. The poem is addressed to Malvina, the daughter of Toscar.

A tale of the times of old! The deeds of days of other years!

The murmur of thy streams, O Lora! brings back the memory of the past. The sound of thy woods, Garmallar, is lovely in mine ear. Dost thou not behold, Malvina, a rock with its head of heath? Three aged pines bend from its face; green is the narrow plain at its feet; there the flower of the mountain grows, and shakes its white head in the breeze. The thistle 10 is there alone, shedding its aged beard. Two stones, half sunk in the ground, show their heads of moss. The deer of the mountain avoids the place, for he beholds a dim ghost standing there. The mighty lie, O Malvina! in the narrow plain of the rock.

A tale of the times of old! the deeds of days of other years!

Who comes from the land of strangers, with his thousands around him? the sunbeam pours 20 its bright stream before him; his hair meets the wind of his hills. His face is settled from war. He is calm as the evening beam that looks from the cloud of the west, on Cona's silent vale. Who is it but Comhal's son, the king of mighty deeds! He beholds his hills with joy, he bids a thousand voices rise. "Ye have fled over your fields, ye sons of the distant land! The king of the world sits in his hall, and hears of his people's flight. He lifts his red eye of 30 pride; he takes his father's sword. Ye have fled over your fields, sons of the distant land!"

Such were the words of the bards, when they came to Selma's halls. A thousand lights from the stranger's land rose in the midst of the people. The feast is spread around; the night passed away in joy. "Where is the noble Clessámmor?" said the fair-haired Fingal.

"Where is the brother of Morna, in the hour of my joy? Sullen and dark he passes his days in the vale of echoing Lora: but, behold, he comes from the hill, like a steed in his strength, who finds his companions in the breeze, and tosses his bright mane in the wind. Blessed be the soul of Clessámmor, why so long from Selma?"

"Returns the chief," said Clessámmor, "in the midst of his fame? Such was the renown of Comhal in the battles of his youth. Often did we pass over Carun to the land of the strangers; our swords returned, not unstained with blood; nor did the kings of the world rejoice. Why do I remember the times of our war? My hair is mixed with gray. My hand forgets to bend the bow; I lift a lighter spear. Oh, that my joy would return, as when I first beheld the maid; the white-bosomed daughter of the strangers, Moina, with the dark blue eyes!"

"Tell," said the mighty Fingal, "the tale of thy youthful days. Sorrow, like a cloud on the sun, shades the soul of Clessámmor. Mournful are thy thoughts, alone on the banks of the roaring Lora. Let us hear the sorrow of thy youth, and the darkness of thy days!"

"It was in the days of peace," replied the great Clessámmor, "I came in my bounding ship, to Balclutha's walls of towers. The winds had roared behind my sails, and Clutha's streams received my dark-bosomed ship. Three days I remained in Reuthámir's halls, and saw his daughter, that beam of light. The joy of the shell went round, and the aged hero gave the fair. Her breasts were like foam on the wave, and her eyes like stars of light; her hair was dark as the raven's wing; her soul was generous and mild. My love for Moina was great; my heart poured forth in joy.

"The son of a stranger came, a chief who loved the white-bosomed Moina. His words were mighty in the hall; he often half-unsheathed his sword. 'Where,' said he, 'is the mighty Comhal, the restless wanderer of the heath? Comes he with his host to Balclutha, since Clessámmor is so bold?' 'My soul,' I replied, 'O warrior! burns in a light of its own. I stand without fear in the midst of thousands, though the valiant are distant far. Stranger! thy words are mighty, for Clessámmor is alone. But my sword trembles by my side, and longs to glitter in my hand. Speak no more of Comhal, son of the winding Clutha!'

"The strength of his pride arose. We fought; he fell beneath my sword. The banks of Clutha heard his fall; a thousand spears glittered around. I fought; the strangers prevailed; I plunged into the stream of Clutha. My white sails rose over the waves, and I bounded on the dark-blue sea. Moina came to the shore, and rolled the red eye of her tears: her loose hair flew on the wind; and I heard her mournful, distant cries. Often did I turn my ship; but the winds of the East prevailed. Nor Clutha ever since have I seen, nor Moina of the dark-brown hair. She fell in Balclutha, for I have seen her ghost. I knew her as she came through the dusky night, along the murmur of Lora; she was like the new moon seen through the gathered mist, when the sky pours down its flaky snow, and the world is silent and dark."

"Raise. ye bards," said the mighty Fingal, "the praise of unhappy Moina. Call her ghost, with your songs, to our hills, that she may rest with the fair of Morven, the sunbeams of other days, the delight of heroes of old. I have seen the walls of Balclutha, but they were desolate. The fire had resounded in the halls; and the voice of the people is heard no more. The stream of Clutha was removed from its place, by the fall of the walls. The thistle shook there its lonely head; the moss whistled to the wind. The fox looked out from the windows; the rank grass of the wall waved round its head. Desolate is the dwelling of Moina; silence is in the house of her fathers. Raise the song of mourning, O bards! over the land of strangers. They have but fallen before us, for one day we must fall. Why dost thou build the hall, son of the winged days? Thou lookest from thy towers to-day; yet a few years, and the blast of the desert comes; it howls in thy empty court, and

whistles round thy half-worn shield. And let the blast of the desert come! we shall be renowned in our day! The mark of my arm shall be in battle; my name in the song of bards. Raise the song; send round the shell: let joy be heard in my hall. When thou, sun of heaven shalt fail! if thou shalt fail, thou mighty light! if thy brightness is for a season, like Fingal, our fame shall survive thy beams!"

Such was the song of Fingal, in the day of his joy. His thousand bards leaned forward from their seats, to hear the voice of the king. It was like the music of harps on the gale of the spring. Lovely were thy thoughts, O Fingal! Why had not Ossian the strength of thy soul? But thou standest alone, my father! Who can equal the king of Selma?

The night passed away in song; morning returned in joy. Thy mountains showed their gray heads; the blue face of ocean smiled. The white wave is seen tumbling round the distant rock; a mist rose slowly from the lake. It came in the figure of an aged man along the silent plain. Its large limbs did not move in steps, for a ghost supported it in mid-air. It came towards Selma's hall, and dissolved in a shower of blood.

The king alone beheld the sight; he foresaw the death of the people. He came in silence to his hall, and took his father's spear. The mail rattled on his breast. The heroes rose around. They looked in silence on each other, marking the eyes of Fingal. They saw battle in his face: the death of armies on his spear. A thousand shields at once are placed on their arms; they drew a thousand swords. The hall of Selma brightened around. The clang of arms ascends. The gray dogs howl in their place. No word is among the mighty chiefs. Each marked the eyes of the king, and half-assumed his spear.

"Sons of Morven," began the king, "this is no time to fill the shell. The battle darkens near us; death hovers over the land. Some ghost, the friend of Fingal, has forewarned us of the foe. The sons of the stranger come from the darkly rolling sea. For, from the water, came the sight of Morven's gloomy danger. Let each assume his heavy spear, each gird on his father's sword. Let the dark helmet rise on every head; the mail pour its lightning from every side. The battle gathers like a storm; soon shall ye hear the roar of death."

The hero moved on before his host, like a cloud before a ridge of green fire, when it pours on the sky of night, and mariners foresee a storm. On Cona's rising heath they stood: the white-bosomed maids beheld them above like a grove; they foresaw the death of the youth, and looked towards the sea with fear. The white wave deceived them for distant sails; the tear is on their cheek! The sun rose on the sea, and we beheld a distant fleet. Like the mist of the ocean they came, and poured their youth upon the coast. The chief was among them, like the stag in the midst of the 10 herd. His shield is studded with gold; stately strode the king of spears. He moved toward Selma; his thousands moved behind.

"Go, with a song of peace," said Fingal; "go, Ullin, to the king of swords. Tell him that we are mighty in war; that the ghosts of our foes are many. But renowned are they who have feasted in my halls; they show the arms of my fathers in a foreign land: the sons of the strangers wonder, and bless the friends of Morven's 20 race; for our names have been heard afar: the kings of the world shook in the midst of their host."

Ullin went with his song. Fingal rested on his spear: he saw the mighty foe in his armour: he blessed the stranger's son. "How stately art thou, son of the sea!" said the king of woody Morven. "Thy sword is a beam of fire by thy side; thy spear is a pine that defies the storm. The varied face of the moon is not broader 30 than thy shield. Ruddy is thy face of youth! soft the ringlets of thy hair! But this tree may fall, and his memory be forgot! The daughter of the stranger will be sad, looking to the rolling sea: the children will say, 'We see a ship; perhaps it is the king of Balclutha.' The tear starts from their mother's eye. Her thoughts are of him who sleeps in Morven."

Such were the words of the king, when Ullin came to the mighty Carthon; he threw 40 down the spear before him; he raised the song of peace. "Come to the feast of Fingal, Carthon, from the rolling sea! partake of the feast of the king, or lift the spear of war! The ghosts of our foes are many: but renowned are the friends of Morven! Behold that field, O Carthon! Many a green hill rises there, with mossy stones and rustling grass: these are the tombs of Fingal's foes, the sons of the rolling sea!"

"Dost thou speak to the weak in arms!" said Carthon, "bard of the woody Morven? Is my face pale for fear, son of the peaceful song? Why, then, dost thou think to darken my soul with the tales of those who fell? My arm has

fought in battle; my renown is known afar. Go to the feeble in arms, bid them yield to Fingal. Have not I seen the fallen Balclutha? And shall I feast with Comhal's son—? Comhal, who threw his fire in the midst of my father's hall? I was young, and knew not the cause, why the virgins wept. The columns of smoke pleased mine eye, when they rose above my walls! I often looked back with gladness when my friends fled along the hill. But when the years of my youth came on, I beheld the moss of my fallen walls. My sight arose with the morning, and my tears descended with night. 'Shall I not fight,' I said to my soul, 'against the children of my foes?' And I will fight, O bard! I feel the strength of my soul."

His people gathered around the hero, and drew at once their shining swords. He stands in the midst, like a pillar of fire, the tear half-starting from his eye; for he thought of the fallen Balclutha. The crowded pride of his soul arose. Sidelong he looked up to the hill, where our heroes shone in arms; the spear trembled in his hand. Bending forward, he seemed to threaten the king.

"Shall I," said Fingal to his soul, "meet, at once, the youth? Shall I stop him in the midst of his course, before his fame shall arise? But the bard hereafter may say, when he sees the tomb of Carthon, 'Fingal took his thousands to battle, before the noble Carthon fell.' No, bard of the times to come! thou shalt not lessen Fingal's fame. My heroes will fight the youth, and Fingal behold the war. If he overcomes, I rush, in my strength, like the roaring stream of Coma. Who of my chiefs will meet the son of the rolling sea? Many are his warriors on the coast, and strong is his ashen spear!"

Cathul rose in his strength, the son of the mighty Lormar: three hundred youths attend the chief, the race of his native streams. Feeble was his arm against Carthon: he fell, and his heroes fled. Connal resumed the battle, but he broke his heavy spear; he lay bound on the field; Carthon pursued his people.

"Clessámmor!" said the king of Morven, "where is the spear of thy strength? Will thou behold Connal bound; thy friend, at the stream of Lora? Rise, in the light of thy steel, companion of valiant Comhal! Let the youth of Balclutha feel the strength of Morven's race." He rose in the strength of his steel, shaking his grisly locks. He fitted the steel to his side; he rushed, in the pride of valour.

Carthon stood on a rock; he saw the hero

rushing on. He loved the dreadful joy of his face—his strength, in the locks of age! "Shall I lift that spear," he said, "that never strikes but once a foe? Or shall I, with the words of peace, preserve the warrior's life? Stately are his steps of age! lovely the remnant of his years! Perhaps it is the husband of Moina; the father of car-borne Carthon. Often have I heard that he dwelt at the echoing stream of Lora." But 10

Such were his words, when Clessámmor came, and lifted high his spear. The youth received it on his shield, and spoke the words of peace. "Warrior of the aged locks! Is there no youth to lift the spear? Hast thou no son to raise the shield before his father to meet the arm of youth? Is the spouse of thy love no more? or weeps she over the tombs of thy sons? Art thou of the kings of men? What will be the fame of my sword shouldst thou fall?" 20 "It will be great, thou son of pride!" began the tall Clessámmor. "I have been renowned in battle; but I never told my name to a foe. Yield to me, son of the wave, then shalt thou know, that the mark of my sword is in many a field." "I never yielded, king of spears!" replied the noble pride of Carthon: "I have also fought in war; I behold my future fame. Despise me not, thou chief of men! my arm, my spear is strong. Retire among thy friends; let 30 younger heroes fight." "Why dost thou wound my soul?" replied Clessámmor, with a tear. "Age does not tremble on my hand; I still can lift the sword. Shall I fly in Fingal's sight—in the sight of him I love? Son of the sea! I never fled: exalt thy pointed spear."

They fought like two contending winds, that strive to roll the wave. Carthon bade his spear to err; he still thought that the foe was the spouse of Moina. He broke Clessámmor's 40 beamy spear in twain: he seized his shining sword. But as Carthon was binding the chief, the chief drew the dagger of his fathers. He saw the foe's uncovered side, and opened there a wound.

Fingal saw Clessámmor low: he moved in the sound of his steel. The host stood silent in his presence; they turned their eyes to the king. He came like the sullen noise of a storm before the winds arise: the hunter hears it in 50 the vale, and retires to the cave of the rock. Carthon stood in his place; the blood is rushing down his side; he saw the coming down of the king; his hopes of fame arose. But pale was his cheek; his hair flew loose; his helmet shook on high; the force of Carthon failed, but his soul was strong.

Fingal beheld the hero's blood; he stopped the uplifted spear. "Yield, king of swords!" said Comhal's son; "I behold thy blood. Thou hast been mighty in battle, and thy fame shall never fade." "Art thou the king so far renowned?" replied the car-borne Carthon. "Art thou the light of death, that frightens the kings of the world? But why should Carthon ask? for he is like the stream of his hills, strong as a river in his course, swift as the eagle of heaven. Oh that I had fought with the king, that my fame might be great in song! that the hunter, beholding my tomb, might say, 'He fought with the mighty Fingal.' But Carthon dies unknown; he has poured out his force on the weak."

"But thou shalt not die unknown," replied the king of woody Morven: "my bards are many, O Carthon! Their songs descend to future times. The children of years to come shall hear the fame of Carthon, when they sit round the burning oak, and the night is spent in songs of old. The hunter, sitting in the heath, shall hear the rustling blast, and, raising his eyes, behold the rock where Carthon fell. He shall turn to his son, and show the place where the mighty fought: 'There the king of Balclutha fought, like the strength of a thousand streams.' "

Joy rose in Carthon's face: he lifted his heavy eyes. He gave his sword to Fingal, to lie within his hall, that the memory of Balclutha's king might remain in Morven. The battle ceased along the field, the bard had sung the song of peace. The chiefs gathered round the falling Carthon; they heard his words with sighs. Silent they leaned on their spears, while Balclutha's hero spoke. His hair sighed in the wind, and his voice was sad and low.

"King of Morven," Carthon said, "I fall in the midst of my course. A foreign tomb receives, in youth, the last of Reuthámir's race. Darkness dwells in Balclutha: the shadows of grief in Crathmo. But raise my remembrance on the banks of Lora, where my fathers dwelt. Perhaps the husband of Moina will mourn over his fallen Carthon." His words reached the heart of Clessámmor; he fell in silence on his son. The host stood darkened around; no voice is on the plain. Night came; the moon, from the east, looked on the mournful field; but still they stood, like a silent grove that lifts its head on Gormal, when the loud winds are laid, and dark autumn is on the plain.

Three days they mourned above Carthon; on the fourth his father died. In the narrow plain of the rock they lie; a dim ghost defends their tomb. There lovely Moina is often seen, when the sunbeam darts on the rock, and all around is dark. There she is seen, Malvina! but not like the daughters of the hill. Her robes are from the stranger's land; and she is still 10 alone!

Fingal was sad for Carthon; he commanded his bards to mark the day when shadowy autumn returned. And often did they mark the day, and sing the hero's praise. "Who comes so dark from the ocean's roar, like autumn's shadowy cloud? Death is trembling in his hand! his eyes are flames of fire! Who roars along dark Lora's heath? Who but Carthon, king of swords! The people fall! see how he 20 strides, like the sullen ghost of Morven! But there he lies, a goodly oak which sudden blasts overturned! When shalt thou rise, Balclutha's joy? When, Carthon, shalt thou arise? Who comes so dark from ocean's roar, like autumn's shadowy cloud?" Such were the words of the bards, in the day of their mourning. Ossian often joined their voice, and added to their song. My soul has been mournful for Carthon; he fell in the days of his youth: and 30 thou, O Clessámmor! where is thy dwelling in the wind? Has the youth forgot his wound? Flies he on clouds with thee? I feel the sun, O Malvina! leave me to my rest. Perhaps they may come to my dreams; I think I hear a feeble voice! The beam of heaven delights to shine on the grave of Carthon: I feel it warm around!

O thou that rollest above, round as the shield of my fathers! Whence are thy beams, O sun! thy everlasting light? Thou comest forth in thy awful beauty; the stars hide themselves in the sky; the moon, cold and pale, sinks in the western wave. But thou thyself movest alone; who can be a companion of thy course? The oaks of the mountains fall; the mountains themselves decay with years; the ocean shrinks and grows again; the moon herself is lost in heaven: but thou art forever the same, rejoicing in the brightness of thy course. When the world is dark with tempests, when thunder rolls and lightning flies, thou lookest in thy beauty from the clouds, and laughest at the storm. But to Ossian thou lookest in vain; for he beholds thy beams no more; whether thy yellow hair flows on the eastern clouds, or thou tremblest at the gates of the west. But thou art, perhaps, like me, for a season; thy years will have an end. Thou shalt sleep in thy clouds, careless of the voice of the morning. Exult then, O sun, in the strength of thy youth! Age is dark and unlovely; it is like the glimmering light of the moon, when it shines through broken clouds, and the mist is on the hills; the blast of the north is on the plain; the traveller shrinks in the midst of his journey.

[1760]

CHARLES CHURCHILL (1731-1764)

During the sixties and seventies of the eighteenth century in England, political controversy ran high. Ephemeral periodicals sprang into existence, the tools of parties and individuals, all of them full of scurrilous abuse of the other party. It was the hey-day of satirical verse. Of all the poets or near-poets who made a living by interesting the public by the wit or the audacity of their attack, Charles Churchill is one of the few who are still remembered. From 1761 until his early death from dissipation in 1764, Charles Churchill was the public favorite in this type of writing, partly because of the vigor and brilliance of his verse and partly because of the popularity of the issues which he supported.

In 1761, Pitt, beloved of the people, had been forced to resign his office as secretary of state by the disregard by the Privy Council of his advice on the conduct of the war. This resignation put the Scottish Earl of Bute, Pitt's chief antagonist, in power. Immediately there was a popular outcry against Bute. Attacks from all sides were unremitting until his resignation early in 1763. It was not simply that he was personally unpopular and that his policies were disliked; he was a Scotsman, and Londoners were watching with growing consternation the taking over of important administrative offices in England by the Scots. Buckingham palace was called satirically Holyrood because of the numbers of Scottish office-seekers who were invading it. All the old antagonisms between England and Scotland were revived. Such was the occasion of Churchill's popular *Prophecy of Famine, a Scots Pastoral*, published in January, 1763. It will be seen that the satire is much more than a voicing of English distrust of Scotland. It begins with an attack on the artificialities of English pastoral poetry, and it parodies, in the dialogue between the pessimist, Sawney, and the optimist, Jockey, the first scene of Allan Ramsay's *Gentle Shepherd*.

Among Churchill's other satires are *The Rosciad*, 1761, an attack on London actors and acting; *The Ghost*, 1762-63, which made capital of the Cock-Lane Ghost episode in London; *The Duellist*, 1764, which attacked political enemies of Churchill's co-editor of the *North Briton*, John Wilkes; *Gotham*, 1764, which attempted to set forth the "idea of a patriot king"; and *The Candidate*, 1764, attacking Lord Sandwich and Cambridge University.

An excellent biographical sketch of Churchill is Joseph M. Beatty's "An Essay in Critical Biography—Charles Churchill," *Publications of the Modern Language Association*, XXXV (1920), 226-46. His poems have recently been edited by James Laver, in *Poems of Charles Churchill*, two volumes, 1933. J. M. Beatty's "The Political Satires of Charles Churchill," *Studies in Philology*, XVI (1919), 303-33, will also be found useful.

THE PROPHECY OF FAMINE

A SCOTS PASTORAL

When Cupid first instructs his darts to fly
From the sly corner of some cook-maid's eye,
The stripling raw, just entered in his teens,
Receives the wound, and wonders what it means;
His heart like dripping melts, and new desire
Within him stirs, each time she stirs the fire;
Trembling and blushing, he the fair one views,
And fain would speak, but can't—without a Muse.
　　So to the sacred mount he takes his way,
Prunes his young wings, and tunes his infant lay;
His oaten reed to rural ditties frames,
To flocks and rocks, to hills and rills, proclaims,

In simplest notes, and all unpolished strains,
The loves of nymphs, and eke the loves of swains.
    Clad, as your nymphs were always clad of yore,
In rustic weeds—a cook-maid now no more—
Beneath an aged oak Lardella lies,
Green moss her couch; her canopy the skies.
From aromatic shrubs the roguish gale
Steals young perfumes, and wafts them through the vale.   20
The youth, turned swain, and skilled in rustic lays,
Fast by her side his amorous descant plays.
Herds low, flocks bleat, pies chatter, ravens scream,
And the full chorus dies a-down the stream.
The streams, with music freighted, as they pass
Present the fair Lardella with a glass,
And Zephyr, to complete the love-sick plan,
Waves his light wings and serves her for a fan.
    But when maturer Judgment takes the lead,
These childish toys on Reason's altar bleed;   30
Formed after some great man, whose name breeds awe,
Whose every sentence Fashion makes a law,
Who on mere credit his vain trophies rears,
And founds his merit on our servile fears;
Then we discard the workings of the heart,
And nature's banished by mechanic art;
Then, deeply read, our reading must be shown;
Vain is that knowledge which remains unknown:
Then Ostentation marches to our aid,
And lettered Pride stalks forth in full parade;   40
Beneath their care behold the work refine,
Pointed each sentence, polished every line.
Trifles are dignified, and taught to wear
The robes of ancients with a modern air;
Nonsense with classic ornaments is graced,
And passes current with the stamp of taste.
    Then the rude Theocrite is ransacked o'er,
And courtly Maro called from Mincio's shore;
Sicilian Muses on our mountains roam,
Easy and free as if they were at home;   50
Nymphs, Naiads, Nereids, Dryads, Satyrs, Fauns,
Sport in our floods and trip it o'er our lawns;
Flowers which once flourished fair in Greece and Rome,
More fair revive in England's meads to bloom;
Skies without cloud exotic suns adorn,
And roses blush, but blush without a thorn;
Landscapes unknown to dowdy Nature rise,
And new creations strike our wondering eyes.
    For bards like these, who neither sing nor say,
Grave without thought, and without feeling gay,   60
Whose numbers in one even tenor flow,
Attuned to pleasure, and attuned to woe;
Who, if plain Common-sense her visit pays,
And mars one couplet in their happy lays,
As at some ghost affrighted, start and stare,
And ask the meaning of her coming there;
For bards like these a wreath shall Mason bring,

Lined with the softest down of Folly's wing;
In Love's pagoda shall they ever doze,
And Gisbal kindly rock them to repose;
My Lord—to letters as to faith most true—
At once their patron and example too—
Shall quaintly fashion his love-laboured dreams,
Sigh with sad winds, and weep with weeping streams,
Curious in grief (for real grief, we know,
Is curious to dress up the tale of woe),
From the green umbrage of some Druid's seat
Shall his own works in his own way repeat.
   Me, whom no Muse of heavenly birth inspires,
No judgment tempers when rash genius fires;
Who boast no merit but mere knack of rhyme,
Short gleams of sense, and satire out of time;
Who cannot follow where trim fancy leads
By prattling streams, o'er flower-empurpled meads;
Who often, but without success, have prayed
For apt Alliteration's artful aid;
Who would, but cannot, with a master's skill,
Coin fine new epithets, which mean no ill;
Me, thus uncouth, thus every way unfit
For pacing poesy, and ambling wit,
Taste with contempt beholds, nor deigns to place
Amongst the lowest of her favoured race.
   Thou, Nature, art my goddess—to thy law
Myself I dedicate—hence, slavish awe,
Which bends to fashion, and obeys the rules
Imposed at first, and since observed by fools.
Hence those vile tricks which mar fair Nature's hue,
And bring the sober matron forth to view,
With all that artificial, tawdry glare
Which virtue scorns, and none but strumpets wear.
Sick of those pomps, those vanities, that waste
Of toil, which critics now mistake for taste,
Of false refinements sick, and laboured ease,
Which Art, too thinly veiled, forbids to please,
By Nature's charms (inglorious truth!) subdued,
However plain her dress, and 'haviour rude,
To northern climes my happier course I steer,
Climes where the goddess reigns throughout the year;
Where, undisturbed by Art's rebellious plan,
She rules the loyal laird and faithful clan.
To that rare soil, where virtues clustering grow,
What mighty blessings doth not England owe?
What wagon-loads of courage, wealth, and sense,
Doth each revolving day import from thence!
To us she gives, disinterested friend,
Faith without fraud, and Stuarts without end.
When we prosperity's rich trappings wear,
Come not her generous sons and take a share?
And if, by some disastrous turn of fate,
Change should ensue, and ruin seize the state,
Shall we not find, safe in that hallowed ground,

70

80

90

100

110

120

Such refuge as the holy martyr found?
　Nor less our debt in science, though denied
By the weak slaves of prejudice and pride.
Thence came the Ramsays, names of worthy note,
Of whom one paints as well as t'other wrote;
Whence, Home, disbanded from the sons of prayer
For loving plays, though no dull dean was there;
Thence issued forth, at great Macpherson's call,
That old, new, epic pastoral, Fingal;   130
Thence Malloch, friend alike of church and state,
Of Christ and Liberty, by grateful Fate
Raised to rewards, which, in a pious reign,
All daring infidels should seek in vain;
Thence simple bards, by simple prudence taught,
To this wise town by simple patrons brought,
In simple manner utter simple lays,
And take, with simple pensions, simple praise.
　Waft me, some Muse, to Tweed's inspiring stream,
Where all the little Loves and Graces dream; 140
Where, slowly winding, the dull waters creep,
And seem themselves to own the power of sleep;
Where on the surface lead, like feathers, swims;
There let me bathe my yet unhallowed limbs,
As once a Syrian bathed in Jordan's flood,
Wash off my native stains, correct that blood
Which mutinies at call of English pride,
And, deaf to prudence, rolls a patriot tide.
　From solemn thought which overhangs the brow
Of patriot care, when things are—God knows how; 150
From nice trim points, where Honour, slave to rule,
In compliment to folly plays the fool;
From those gay scenes, where mirth exalts his power,
And easy humour wings the laughing hour;
From those soft better moments, when desire
Beats high, and all the world of man's on fire;
When mutual ardours of the melting fair
More than repay us for whole years of care,
At Friendship's summons will my Wilkes retreat,
And see, once seen before, that ancient seat, 160
That ancient seat, where majesty displayed
Her ensigns, long before the world was made?
　Mean narrow maxims which enslave mankind,
Ne'er from its bias warp thy settled mind.
Not duped by party nor opinion's slave,
Those faculties which bounteous nature gave,
Thy honest spirit into practice brings,
Nor courts the smile, nor dreads the frown of kings.
Let rude, licentious Englishmen comply
With tumult's voice, and curse they know not why; 170
Unwilling to condemn, thy soul disdains
To wear vile faction's arbitrary chains,
And strictly weighs, in apprehension clear,
Things as they are, and not as they appear.
With thee good humour tempers lively wit;
Enthroned with judgment, candour loves to sit,

And nature gave thee, open to distress,
A heart to pity and a hand to bless.
　　Oft have I heard thee mourn the wretched lot
Of the poor, mean, despised, insulted Scot,　　　　　　180
Who, might calm reason credit idle tales,
By rancour forged where prejudice prevails,
Or starves at home, or practises, through fear
Of starving, arts which damn all conscience here.
When scribblers, to the charge by interest led,
The fierce *North Briton* foaming at their head,
Pour forth invectives, deaf to candour's call,
And, injured by one alien, rail at all;
On northern Pisgah when they take their stand,
To mark the weakness of that Holy Land,　　　　　　190
With needless truths their libels to adorn,
And hang a nation up to public scorn,
Thy generous soul condemns the frantic rage,
And hates the faithful but ill-natured page.
　　The Scots are poor, cries surly English pride;
True is the charge, nor by themselves denied.
Are they not then in strictest reason clear,
Who wisely come to mend their fortunes here?
If, by low supple arts successful grown,
They sapped our vigour to increase their own,　　　　200
If, mean in want, and insolent in power,
They only fawned more surely to devour,
Roused by such wrongs should reason take alarm,
And e'en the Muse for public safety arm;
But if they own ingenuous virtue's sway,
And follow where true honour points the way,
If they revere the hand by which they're fed,
And bless the donors for their daily bread,
Or by vast debts of higher import bound,
Are always humble, always grateful found;　　　　　210
If they, directed by Paul's holy pen,
Become discreetly all things to all men,
That all men may become all things to them,
Envy may hate, but justice can't condemn.
"Into our places, states, and beds they creep:"
They've sense to get what we want sense to keep.
　　Once, be the hour accursed, accursed the place,
I ventured to blaspheme the chosen race.
Into those traps, which men called patriots, laid,
By specious arts unwarily betrayed,　　　　　　　　220
Madly I leagued against that sacred earth,
Vile parricide! which gave a parent birth.
But shall I meanly error's path pursue,
When heavenly truth presents her friendly clue?
Once plunged in ill, shall I go farther in?
To make the oath, was rash; to keep it, sin.
Backward I tread the paths I trod before,
And calm reflection hates what passion swore.
Converted (blessed are the souls which know
Those pleasures which from true conversion flow,　　230
Whether to reason, who now rules my breast,

Or to pure faith, like Lyttelton and West),
Past crimes to expiate, be my present aim
To raise new trophies to the Scottish name;
To make (what can the proudest Muse do more?)
E'en faction's sons her brighter worth adore;
To make her glories stamped with honest rhymes,
In fullest tide roll down to latest times.
    "Presumptuous wretch! and shall a Muse like thine,
An English Muse, the meanest of the nine,   240
Attempt a theme like this? Can her weak strain
Expect indulgence from the mighty Thane?
Should he from toils of government retire,
And for a moment fan the poet's fire;
Should he of sciences the moral friend,
Each curious, each important search suspend,
Leave unassisted Hill of herbs to tell,
And all the wonders of a cockleshell,
Having the Lord's good grace before his eyes,
Would not the Home step forth and gain the prize?   250
Or if this wreath of honour might adorn
The humble brows of one in England born,
Presumptuous still thy daring must appear;
Vain all thy towering hopes whilst I am here."
    Thus spake a form, by silken smile, and tone
Dull and unvaried, for the Laureate known,
Folly's chief friend, Decorum's eldest son,
In every party found, and yet of none.
This airy substance, this substantial shade,
Abashed I heard, and with respect obeyed.   260
    From themes too lofty for a bard so mean,
Discretion beckons to an humbler scene;
The restless fever of ambition laid,
Calm I retire, and seek the sylvan shade.
Now be the Muse disrobed of all her pride,
Be all the glare of verse by truth supplied,
And if plain nature pours a simple strain,
Which Bute may praise, and Ossian not disdain,
Ossian, sublimest, simplest Bard of all,
Whom English infidels, Macpherson call,   270
Then round my head shall Honour's ensigns wave,
And pensions mark me for a willing slave.
    Two boys, whose birth, beyond all question, springs
From great and glorious, though forgotten, kings,
Shepherds, of Scottish lineage, born and bred
On the same bleak and barren mountain's head,
By niggard nature doomed on the same rocks
To spin out life, and starve themselves and flocks,
Fresh as the morning, which, enrobed in mist,
The mountain's top with usual dulness kissed,   280
Jockey and Sawney to their labours rose;
Soon clad I ween, where nature needs no clothes;
Where, from their youth enured to winter skies,
Dress and her vain refinements they despise.
    Jockey, whose manly high-boned cheeks to crown

With freckles spotted, flamed the golden down,
With meikle art could on the bag pipes play,
E'en from the rising to the setting day;
Sawney as long without remorse could bawl
Home's madrigals, and ditties from Fingal: 290
Oft at his strains, all natural though rude,
The Highland lass forgot her want of food,
And, whilst she scratched her lover into rest,
Sunk pleased, though hungry, on her Sawney's breast.

    Far as the eye could reach, no tree was seen;
Earth, clad in russet, scorned the lively green.
The plague of locusts they secure defy,
For in three hours a grasshopper must die.
No living thing, whate'er its food, feasts there,
But the cameleon, who can feast on air.   300
No birds, except as birds of passage, flew;
No bee was known to hum, no dove to coo.
No streams, as amber smooth, as amber clear,
Were seen to glide, or heard to warble here.
Rebellion's spring, which through the country ran,
Furnished, with bitter draughts, the steady clan.
No flowers embalmed the air, but one white rose,
Which, on the tenth of June, by instinct blows,
By instinct blows at morn, and when the shades
Of drizzly eve prevail, by instinct fades.   310

    One, and but one poor solitary cave,
Too sparing of her favours, nature gave;
That one alone (hard tax on Scottish pride!)
Shelter at once for man and beast supplied.
There snares without entangling briars spread,
And thistles, armed against the invader's head,
Stood in close ranks, all entrance to oppose,
Thistles now held more precious than the rose.
All creatures which, on nature's earliest plan,
Were formed to loathe, and to be loathed by man,   320
Which owed their birth to nastiness and spite,
Deadly to touch, and hateful to the sight,
Creatures, which when admitted in the ark
Their saviour shunned, and rankled in the dark,
Found place within; marking her noisome road
With poison's trail, here crawled the bloated toad;
There webs were spread of more than common size,
And half-starved spiders preyed on half-starved flies;
In quest of food, efts strove in vain to crawl;
Slugs, pinched with hunger, smeared the slimy wall;   330
The cave around with hissing serpents rung;
On the damp roof unhealthy vapour hung;
And Famine, by her children always known,
As proud as poor, here fixed her native throne.

    Here, for the sullen sky was overcast,
And summer shrunk beneath a wintry blast—
A native blast, which, armed with hail and rain,
Beat unrelenting on the naked swain—
The boys for shelter made; behind, the sheep,

Of which those shepherds every day take keep,   340
Sickly crept on, and with complainings rude,
On nature seemed to call, and bleat for food.

JOCKEY

Sith to this cave, by tempest, we're confined,
And within *ken* our flocks, under the wind,
Safe from the pelting of this perilous storm,
Are laid *emong* yon thistles, dry and warm,
What, Sawney, if by shepherds' art we try
To mock the rigour of this cruel sky?
What if we tune some merry roundelay?
Well dost thou sing, nor ill doth Jockey play.   350

SAWNEY

Ah! Jockey, ill advisest thou, *I wis*,
To think of songs at such a time as this.
Sooner shall herbage crown these barren rocks,
Sooner shall fleeces clothe these ragged flocks,
Sooner shall want seize shepherds of the south,
And we forget to live from hand to mouth,
Than Sawney, out of season, shall impart
The songs of gladness with an aching heart.

JOCKEY

Still have I known thee for a silly swain;
Of things past help what boots it to complain?   360
Nothing but mirth can conquer fortune's spite;
No sky is heavy if the heart be light:
Patience is sorrow's salve; what can't be cured,
So Donald right *areeds*, must be endured.

SAWNEY

Full silly swain, *I wot*, is Jockey now.
How didst thou bear thy Maggy's falsehood? how,
When with a foreign loon she stole away,
Didst thou forswear thy pipe and shepherd's lay?
Where was thy boasted wisdom then, when I
Applied those proverbs, which you now apply?   370

JOCKEY

O she was bonny! all the highlands round
Was there a rival to my Maggy found?
More precious (though that precious is to all)
Than the rare medicine which we brimstone call,
Or that choice plant, so grateful to the nose,
Which, in I know not what far country, grows,
Was Maggy unto me; dear do I rue
A lass so fair should ever prove untrue.

SAWNEY

Whether with pipe or song to charm the ear,
Through all the land did Jamie find a peer?   380
Cursed be that year by every honest Scot,
And in the shepherd's calendar forgot,
That fatal year, when Jamie, hapless swain,
In evil hour forsook the peaceful plain.
Jamie, when our young laird discreetly fled,
Was seized and hanged till he was dead, dead, dead.

JOCKEY

Full sorely may we all lament that day:
For all were losers in the deadly fray.
Five brothers had I; on the Scottish plains,
Well dost thou know were none more hopeful swains;   390
Five brothers there I lost, in manhood's pride;
Two in the field, the three on gibbets died;
Ah! silly swains, to follow war's alarms;
Ah! what hath shepherds' life to do with arms?

SAWNEY

Mention it not—there saw I strangers clad
In all the honours of our ravished plaid;
Saw the Ferrara, too, our nation's pride,
Unwilling grace the awkward victor's side.
There fell our choicest youth, and from that day
Mote never Sawney tune the merry lay;   400
Blessed those which fell! cursed those which still survive,
To mourn fifteen renewed in forty-five.

Thus plained the boys, when from her throne of turf,
With boils embossed, and overgrown with scurf,
Vile humours, which, in life's corrupted well,
Mixed at the birth, not abstinence could quell,
Pale Famine reared the head; her eager eyes,
Where hunger e'en to madness seemed to rise,
Speaking aloud her throes and pangs of heart,
Strained to get loose, and from their orbs to start;   410
Her hollow cheeks were each a deep-sunk cell,
Where wretchedness and horror loved to dwell;
With double rows of useless teeth supplied,
Her mouth from ear to ear extended wide,
Which, when for want of food her entrails pined,
She oped, and cursing, swallowed naught but wind;
All shrivelled was her skin; and here and there,
Making their way by force, her bones lay bare;
Such filthy sight to hide from human view,
O'er her foul limbs a tattered plaid she threw.   420
"Cease," cried the goddess, "cease, despairing swains,
And from a parent hear what Jove ordains!
"Pent in this barren corner of the isle,
Where partial fortune never deigned to smile;

Like nature's bastards, reaping for our share
What was rejected by the lawful heir;
Unknown amongst the nations of the earth,
Or only known to raise contempt and mirth;
Long free, because the race of Roman braves
Thought it not worth their while to make us slaves;   430
Then into bondage by that nation brought,
Whose ruin we for ages vainly sought,
Whom still with unslacked hate we view, and still,
The power of mischief lost, retain the will;
Considered as the refuse of mankind,
A mass till the last moment left behind,
Which frugal nature doubted, as it lay,
Whether to stamp with life or throw away;
Which, formed in haste, was planted in this nook,
But never entered in creation's book;   440
Branded as traitors who for love of gold
Would sell their God, as once their king they sold;
Long have we borne this mighty weight of ill,
These vile injurious taunts, and bear them still;
But times of happier note are now at hand,
And the full promise of a better land:
There, like the sons of Israel, having trod,
For the fixed term of years ordained by God,
A barren desert, we shall seize rich plains,
Where milk with honey flows, and plenty reigns.   450
With some few natives joined, some pliant few,
Who worship interest and our track pursue,
There shall we, though the wretched people grieve,
Ravage at large, nor ask the owners' leave.
    "For us the earth shall bring forth her increase;
For us the flocks shall wear a golden fleece;
Fat beeves shall yield us dainties not our own,
And the grape bleed a nectar yet unknown;
For our advantage shall their harvests grow,
And Scotsmen reap what they disdained to sow;   460
For us the sun shall climb the eastern hill;
For us the rain shall fall, the dew distil;
When to our wishes Nature cannot rise,
Art shall be tasked to grant us fresh supplies.
His brawny arm shall drudging Labour strain,
And for our pleasure suffer daily pain;
Trade shall for us exert her utmost powers,
Hers all the toil, and all the profit ours;
For us the oak shall from his native steep
Descend, and fearless travel through the deep;   470
The sail of commerce, for our use unfurled,
Shall waft the treasures of each distant world;
For us sublimer heights shall science reach;
For us their statesmen plot, their churchmen preach;
Their noblest limbs of council we'll disjoint,
And, mocking, new ones of our own appoint;
Devouring War, imprisoned in the north,
Shall, at our call, in horrid pomp break forth,
And when, his chariot-wheels with thunder hung,

Fell Discord braying with her brazen tongue,　　　　　　480
Death in the van, with Anger, Hate, and Fear,
And Desolation stalking in the rear,
Revenge, by Justice guided, in his train,
He drives impetuous o'er the trembling plain,
Shall, at our bidding, quit his lawful prey,
And to the meek, gentle, generous Peace give way.
　"Think not, my Sons, that this so blessed estate
Stands at a distance on the roll of fate;
Already big with hopes of future sway,
E'en from this cave I scent my destined prey.　　　　490
Think not that this dominion o'er a race
Whose former deeds shall time's last annals grace,
In the rough face of peril must be sought,
And with the lives of thousands dearly bought;
No—fooled by cunning, by that happy art
Which laughs to scorn the blundering hero's heart,
Into the snare shall our kind neighbours fall
With open eyes, and fondly give us all.
　"When Rome, to prop her sinking empire, bore
Their choicest levies to a foreign shore,　　　　　　500
What if we seized, like a destroying flood,
Their widowed plains, and filled the realm with blood,
Gave an unbounded loose to manly rage,
And, scorning mercy, spared nor sex nor age?
When, for our interest too mighty grown,
Monarchs of warlike bent possessed the throne,
What if we strove divisions to foment,
And spread the flames of civil discontent,
Assisted those who 'gainst their king made head,
And gave the traitors refuge when they fled?　　　　510
When restless Glory bade her sons advance,
And pitched her standard in the fields of France,
What if, disdaining oaths, an empty sound,
By which our nation never shall be bound,
Bravely we taught unmuzzled war to roam
Through the weak land, and brought cheap laurels home
When the bold traitors leagued for the defence
Of law, religion, liberty, and sense,
When they against their lawful monarch rose,
And dared the Lord's anointed to oppose,　　　　　520
What if we still revered the banished race,
And strove the royal vagrants to replace,
With fierce rebellions shook the unsettled state,
And greatly dared, though crossed by partial fate?
These facts, which might, where wisdom held the sway,
Awake the very stones to bar our way,
There shall be nothing, nor one trace remain
In the dull region of an English brain.
Blessed with that faith which mountains can remove,
First they shall dupes, next saints, last martyrs, prove.　530
　"Already is this game of fate begun
Under the sanction of my darling son;
That son, of nature royal as his name,
Is destined to redeem our race from shame;

His boundless power, beyond example great,
Shall make the rough way smooth, the crooked straight,
Shall for our ease the raging floods restrain,
And sink the mountain level to the plain.
Discord, whom in a cavern under ground
With massy fetters their late patriot bound,   540
Where her own flesh the furious hag might tear,
And vent her curses to the vacant air,
Where, that she never might be heard of more,
He planted Loyalty to guard the door,
For better purpose shall our chief release,
Disguise her for a time, and call her peace.
"Lured by that name, fine engine of deceit,
Shall the weak English help themselves to cheat;
To gain our love, with honours shall they grace
The old adherents of the Stuart race,   550
Who, pointed out no matter by what name,
Tories or Jacobites, are still the same;
To soothe our rage, the temporizing brood
Shall break the ties of truth and gratitude,
Against their saviour venomed falsehoods frame,
And brand with calumny our William's name;
To win our grace (rare argument of wit),
To our untainted faith shall they commit
(Our faith which, in extremest perils tried,
Disdained, and still disdains to change her side)   560
That sacred Majesty they all approve,
Who most enjoys and best deserves, their love."

                [1763, 1763]

HORACE WALPOLE (1717-1797)

The art of letter writing, which the sociable world of the eighteenth centu.y cultivated with such distinction, is inseparable from the arts of manners and friendship. Good letters spring from the desire of the writer to make himself agreeable and interesting, and he must be able to decorate, without falsifying, the commonplace texture of everyday life. A great letter writer must be first of all a charming companion. Supreme among the eighteenth century practitioners of this art stand William Cowper and, a man of very different personality and environment, Horace Walpole.

From Walpole there are extant more than three thousand letters which together constitute a vast panorama of fashionable society of the second half of the eighteenth century. He was born into that world for which his tastes and talents so eminently fitted him. He was the son of Sir Robert Walpole, the Whig prime minister who from 1721 to 1742 was the real governor of England, and who almost ruined the family fortune by building a magnificent mansion at Houghton in Norfolk and stocking it with a great collection of paintings. But the father provided for Horace, as well as for his other sons, by getting them all life appointments to sinecures in the government. Horace was also member of the House of Commons for many years, but had no political ambitions and attended sittings very irregularly. His real interests were in other directions.

His biography is largely the story of the formation of those friendships which called forth his letters. They began at Eton, especially with the "Quadruple Alliance" of Walpole, Thomas Gray, Richard West, and Thomas Ashton; others less close, who nevertheless became life-long correspondents, were his Conway cousins, the witty George Augustus Selwyn, and William Cole, the later clergyman and antiquarian who helped arouse Walpole's interest in medievalism. Many of these boyhood intimates went on to Cambridge, where Walpole also spent some time in desultory studies. In 1739 he and Gray set out on a Grand Tour through France and Italy. They were entertained in Florence by Horace Mann, the English Minister, who became henceforth one of the fortunate recipients of Walpole's letters; and among the many other new and congenial acquaintances formed in Italy should be mentioned a witty and cultivated gentleman of leisure, Mr. John Chute, who resided in Florence from 1740 to 1746. Walpole appreciated such thoroughbreds, especially as they possessed that cosmopolitanism in which the English gentleman of the eighteenth century so frequently surpassed his successor of the nineteenth. Quite fortunately for a man who lived to be eighty and therefore survived to see his friends drop off one by one, Walpole never lost the art of making new attachments. His estrangement from Gray, after their quarrel in Florence, was only temporary, and many of his later letters are addressed to William Mason, Gray's friend and biographer. In 1765, on a visit to Paris, began the strange half-romantic correspondence with the old and blind Madame du Deffand, whose letters to Walpole fill three volumes, and who bequeathed her dog Tonton to him when she died in 1780. Eight years later he met two young sisters, Mary and Agnes Berry, "the two pearls that I found in my path," whose friendship lent a peculiar happiness to his last years. In 1791 he succeeded to the title of Earl of Orford, and he died on March 2, 1797.

Paradoxically enough, this dilettante of the fashionable world contributed, with consequences he could not anticipate, to the Romantic tendencies of his time. He was not a profound student of anything, but he had acquired an enthusiasm for medieval architecture, trappings, and bric-à-brac, quite at variance with the cultivated taste of the age. He acquired in 1747 a country house, Strawberry Hill, near Twickenham, and began a long process of remodelling and enlarging which transformed the unpretentious dwelling into a fantastic pseudo-Gothic castle, the turrets and battlements made of lath and stucco, the tall pointed windows filled with stained glass, and the interior, finished in the same taste, crowded with art objects of all kinds; it was, said the witty Selwyn, "a catacomb, or, at best, a museum, rather than a habitation." The place came to be much visited by the curious and, tawdry as it was, did much to attract attention to true Gothic art, and thus bring about the renewed appreciation of it in the early nineteenth century.

Inspired by these architectural amusements, Walpole also wrote a "Gothic" romance, *The Castle of Otranto,* published anonymously in 1764, which was, however, as far from true medievalism as Strawberry Hill. It became the progenitor of the Novels of Terror which the next generation read with such delightful shudders. His antiquarian interests also led him to publish *Anecdotes of Painting in England* (3 vols., 1762, 4th vol., 1780), and the youthful Chatterton wrote to offer him a medieval manuscript on the "Historie of Peynctynge yn Englande," an offer which Walpole shrewdly declined.

Walpole's collected *Works,* excluding the letters, were published by his literary executor in five large volumes in 1798. The first attempt at a complete edition of his letters was by Peter Cunningham (9 vols., 1857-59); this was superseded by the edition of Mrs. Paget Toynbee (16 vols., 1903-05), with three supplementary volumes by Mr. Toynbee (1918, 1925). A new edition, based so far as possible on extant manuscripts, is being published by Yale University Press under the editorship of Mr. W. S. Lewis. Austin Dobson's delightful *Horace Walpole, a Memoir* should be read in the fourth edition, revised and enlarged by Paget Toynbee (Oxford, 1927). Dorothy M. Stuart has contributed a volume on Walpole to the English Men of Letters Series (London, 1927). An elaborate French study of the man and his work is Paul Yvon's *La Vie d'un Dilettante: Horace Walpole: 1717-1797; Essai de Biographie psychologique et littéraire* (Paris, 1924).

LETTERS

I. TO RICHARD WEST

From a Hamlet among the
Mountains of Savoy
Sept. 28, 1739, N. S.

Precipices, mountains, torrents, wolves, rumblings, Salvator Rosa—the pomp of our park and the meekness of our palace! Here we are, the lonely lords of glorious, desolate prospects. I have kept a sort of resolution which I made, of not writing to you as long as I staid in France; I am now a quarter of an hour out of it, and write to you. Mind, 'tis three months since we heard from you. I begin this letter among the clouds; where I shall finish, my neighbour Heaven probably knows: 'tis an odd wish in a mortal letter, to hope not to finish it on this side the atmosphere. You will have a billet tumble to you from the stars when you least think of it; and that I should write it too! Lord, how potent that sounds! But I am to undergo many transmigrations before I come to "yours ever." Yesterday I was a shepherd of Dauphiné; to-day an Alpine savage; to-morrow a Carthusian monk; and Friday a Swiss Calvinist. I have one quality which I find remains with me in all worlds and in all aethers; I brought it with me from your world, and am admired for it in

this—'tis my esteem for you: this is a common thought among you, and you will laugh at it, but it is new here: as new to remember one's friends in the world one has left, as for you to remember those you have lost.

Aix, in Savoy
Sept. 30th

We are this minute come in here, and here's an awkward abbé this minute come in to us. I asked him if he would sit down. *Oui, oui, oui.* He has ordered us a radish soup for supper, and has brought a chess-board to play with Mr. Conway. I have left 'em in the act, and am set down to write to you. Did you ever see anything like the prospect we saw yesterday? I never did. We rode three leagues to see the Grande Chartreuse; expected bad roads and the finest convent in the kingdom. We were disappointed pro and con. The building is large and plain, and has nothing remarkable but its primitive simplicity; they entertained us in the neatest manner, with eggs, pickled salmon, dried fish, conserves, cheese, butter, grapes, and figs, and pressed us mightily to lie there. We tumbled into the hands of a lay-brother, who, unluckily having the charge of the meal and bran, showed us little besides. They desired us to set down our names in the list of strangers, where, among others, we found two mottoes of our countrymen, for whose stupidity and brutality we blushed. The first was of Sir J—— D——, who had wrote down the first stanza of *Justum et tenacem,* altering the last line to *Mente quatit Carthusiana.* The second was of one D——, *Coelum ipsum petimus stultitia; et hic ventri indico bellum.* The Goth!—But the road, West, the road! winding round a prodigious mountain, and surrounded with others, all shagged with hanging woods, obscured with pines, or lost in clouds! Below, a torrent breaking through cliffs, and tumbling through fragments of rocks! Sheets of cascades forcing their silver speed down channelled precipices, and hasting into the roughened river at the bottom! Now and then an old foot-bridge, with a broken rail, a leaning cross, a cottage, or the ruin of an hermitage! This sounds too bombast and too romantic to one that has not seen it, too cold for one that has. If I could send you my letter post between two lovely tempests that echoed each other's wrath, you might have some idea of this noble roaring scene, as you were reading it. Almost on the summit, upon a fine verdure, but without any prospect, stands the Chartreuse. We staid there two hours, rode back through this charming picture, wished for a painter, wished to be poets! Need I tell you we wished for you? Good night!

. . . .

Yours ever,
HOR. WALPOLE.

II. TO JOHN CHUTE

Houghton,
August 20, 1743

Indeed, my dear sir, you certainly did not use to be stupid, and till you give me more substantial proof that you are so, I shall not believe it. As for your temperate diet and milk bringing about such a metamorphosis, I hold it impossible. I have such lamentable proofs every day before my eyes of the stupefying qualities of beef, ale, and wine, that I have contracted a most religious veneration for your spiritual nouriture. Only imagine that I here every day see men, who are mountains of roast beef, and only seem just roughly hewn out into the outlines of human form, like the giant-rock at Pratolino. I shudder when I see them brandish their knives in act to carve, and look on them as savages that devour one another. I should not stare at all more than I do, if yonder Alderman at the lower end of the table was to stick his fork into his neighbour's jolly cheek, and cut a brave slice of brown and fat. Why, I'll swear I see no difference between a country gentleman and a sirloin; whenever the first laughs, or the latter is cut, there run out just the same streams of gravy! Indeed, the sirloin does not ask quite so many questions. I have an Aunt here, a family piece of goods, an old remnant of inquisitive hospitality and economy, who, to all intents and purposes, is as beefy as her neighbours. She wore me so down yesterday with interrogatories, that I dreamt all night she was at my ear with "who's" and "why's" and "when's" and "where's," till at last in my very sleep I cried out, "For God in heaven's sake, Madam, ask me no more questions!"

Oh! my dear Sir, don't you find that nine parts in ten of the world are of no use but to make you wish yourself with that tenth part? I am so far from growing used to mankind by living amongst them, that my natural ferocity and wildness does but every day grow worse. They tire me, they fatigue me; I don't know what to do with them; I don't know what to say to them; I fling open the windows, and fancy I want air; and when I get by myself, I undress myself, and seem to have had people in my pockets, in my plaits, and on my shoulders! I indeed find this fatigue worse in the country than in town, because one can avoid it there and has more resources; but it is there too. I fear 'tis growing old;

but I literally seem to have murdered a man whose name was Ennui, for his ghost is ever before me. They say there is no English word for *ennui*; I think you may translate it most literally by what is called "entertaining people," and "doing the honours": that is, you sit an hour with somebody you don't know and don't care for, talk about the wind and the weather, and ask a thousand foolish questions, which all begin with, "I think you live a good deal in the country," or, "I think you don't love this thing or that." Oh! 'tis dreadful!

I'll tell you what is delightful—the Dominichin! My dear Sir, if ever there was a Dominichin, if there was ever an original picture, this is one. I am quite happy; for my father is as much transported with it as I am. It is hung in the gallery, where are all his most capital pictures, and he himself thinks it beats all but the two Guidos. That of the Doctors and the Octagon—I don't know if you ever saw them? What a chain of thought this leads me into! but why should I not indulge it? I will flatter myself with your, some time or other, passing a few days here with me. Why must I never expect to see anything but Beefs in a gallery which would not yield even to the Colonna! If I do not most unlimitedly wish to see you and Mr. Whithed in it this very moment, it is only because I would not take you from our dear *Miny*. Adieu! you charming people all. Is not Madam Bosville a Beef?

Yours most sincerely.

III. TO HORACE MANN

Arlington Street
April 2, 1750

You will not wonder so much at our earthquakes as at the effects they have had. All the women in town have taken them up upon the foot of *Judgments*; and the clergy, who have had no windfalls of a long season, have driven horse and foot into this opinion. There has been a shower of ser-

mons and exhortations: Secker, the jesuitical Bishop of Oxford, began the mode. He heard the women were all going out of town to avoid the next shock; and so, for fear of losing his Easter offerings, he set himself to advise them to await God's good pleasure in fear and trembling. But what is more astonishing, Sherlock, who has much better sense, and much less of the Popish confessor, has been running a race with him for the old ladies, and has written a pastoral letter, of which ten thousand were sold in two days; and fifty thousand have been subscribed for, since the two first editions. You never read so impudent, so absurd a piece! This earthquake, which has done no hurt, in a country where no earthquake ever did any, is sent, according to the Bishop, to punish bawdy prints, bawdy books (in one of which Mrs. Pilkington drew his Lordship's picture), gaming, drinking — (no, I think, drinking and avarice, those orthodox vices, are omitted) and all other sins, natural or not, which he makes a principal ingredient in the composition of an earthquake, because not having been able to answer a late piece, which Middleton has writ against him, he has turned the Doctor over to God for punishment, even in this world. Here is an epigram, which this subject put into my head:

When Whitfield preaches, and when Whis-
  ton writes,
All cry that madness dictates either's flights.
When Sherlock writes, or canting Secker
  preaches,
All think good sense inspires what either
  teaches.
Why, when all four for the same gospel fight,
Should two be crazy, two be in the right?
Plain is the reason—every son of Eve
Thinks the two madmen, what they teach,
  believe.

I told you the women talked of going out of town: several families are literally gone, and many more going to-day and to-morrow; for what adds to the absurdity, is, that the second shock having happened exactly a month after the former, it prevails that there will be a third on Thursday next, another month, which is to swallow up London. I am almost ready to burn my letter now I have begun it, lest you should think I am laughing at you: but, it is so true, that Arthur of White's told me last night, that he should put off the last ridotto, which was to be on Thursday, because he hears nobody would come to it. I have advised several who are going to keep their next earthquake in the country, to take the bark for it, as it is so periodic. Dick Leveson and Mr. Rigby, who had supped and stayed late at Bedford House the other night, knocked at several doors, and in a watchman's voice cried, "Past four o'clock, and a dreadful earthquake!" But I have done with this ridiculous panic: two pages were too much to talk of it.

We have had nothing in Parliament but trade bills, on one of which the Speaker humbled the arrogance of Sir John Barnard, who had reflected upon the proceedings of the House. It is to break up on Thursday se'nnight, and the King goes this day fortnight. He has made Lord Vere Beauclerc a baron, at the solicitation of the Pelhams, as this Lord had resigned upon a pique with Lord Sandwich. Lord Anson, who is treading in the same path, and leaving the Bedfords to follow his father-in-law, the Chancellor, is made a privy councillor, with Sir Thomas Robinson and Lord Hyndford. Lord Conway is to be an earl, and Sir John Rawdon (whose follies you remember, and whose boasted loyalty of having been kicked downstairs for not drinking the Pretender's health, though even that was false, is at last rewarded) and Sir John Vesey are to be Irish lords; and a Sir William Beauchamp Proctor, and a Mr. Loyd, Knights of the Bath.

I was entertained the other night at the house of much such a creature as Sir John Rawdon, and one whom you remember too, Naylor. He has a wife who keeps the most indecent house of all those that are called decent: every *Sunday* she has a counterband assembly: I had had a card for *Monday* a fortnight before. As the day was new, I expected a great assembly, but found scarce six persons. I asked where the company was—I was answered, "Oh! they are not come yet: they will be here presently; they all supped here last night, stayed till morning, and I suppose are not up yet." In the bedchamber I found two beds, which is too cruel to poor Naylor, to tell the whole town that he is the only man in it who does not lie with his wife!

My Lord Bolingbroke has lost his wife. When she was dying, he acted grief; flung himself upon her bed, and asked her if she could forgive him. I never saw her, but have heard her wit and parts excessively commended. Dr. Middleton told me a compliment she made him two years ago, which I thought pretty. She said she was persuaded that he was a very great writer for she understood his works better than any other English book, and that she had observed that the best writers were always the most intelligible.

Wednesday

I had not time to finish my letter on Monday. I return to the earthquake, which I had mistaken; it is to be today. This frantic terror prevails so much, that within these three days seven hundred and thirty coaches have been counted passing Hyde Park corner, with whole parties removing into the country. Here is a good advertisement which I cut out of the papers to-day:

"On Monday next will be published (price 6*d*.) a true and exact List of all the Nobility and Gentry who have left, or shall leave, this place through fear of another Earthquake."

Several women have made earthquake gowns; that is, warm gowns to sit out of doors all to-night. These are of the more courageous. One woman, still more heroic, is come to town on purpose: she says, all her friends are in London, and she will not survive them. But what will you think of Lady Catherine Pelham, Lady Frances

Arundel, and Lord and Lady Galway, who go this evening to an inn ten miles out of town, where they are to play at brag till five in the morning, and then come back—I suppose, to look for the bones of their husbands and families under the rubbish.

.   .   .   .

IV. TO GEORGE MONTAGU

Houghton,
March 25, 1761

Here I am at Houghton! and alone! in this spot, where (except two hours last month) I have not been in sixteen years! Think, what a crowd of reflections!—no, Gray, and forty churchyards, could not furnish so many; nay, I know one must feel them with greater indifference than I possess, to have patience to put them into verse. Here I am, probably for the last time of my life, though not for the last time—every clock that strikes tells me I am an hour nearer to yonder church—that church, into which I have not yet had courage to enter, where lies that mother on whom I doted, and who doted on me! There are the two rival mistresses of Houghton, neither of whom ever wished to enjoy it! There too lies he who founded its greatness, to contribute to whose fall Europe was embroiled—there he sleeps in quiet and dignity, while his friend and his foe, rather his false ally and real enemy, Newcastle and Bath, are exhausting the dregs of their pitiful lives in squabbles and pamphlets!

The surprise the pictures gave me is again renewed—accustomed for many years to see nothing but wretched daubs and varnished copies at auctions, I look at these as enchantment. My own description of them seems poor—but shall I tell you truly —the majesty of Italian ideas almost sinks before the warm nature of Flemish colouring! Alas! don't I grow old? My young imagination was fired with Guido's ideas—must they be

plump and prominent as Abishag to warm me now? Does great youth feel with poetic limbs, as well as see with poetic eyes? In one respect I am very young; I cannot satiate myself with looking—an incident contributed to make me feel this more strongly. A party arrived, just as I did, to see the house, a man and three women in riding dresses, and they rode post through the apartments—I could not hurry before them fast enough—they were not so long in *seeing* for the first time, as I could have been in one room, to examine what I knew by heart. I remember formerly being often diverted with this kind of *seers* —they come, ask what such a room is called, in which Sir Robert lay, write it down, admire a lobster or a cabbage in a market-piece, dispute whether the last room was green or purple, and then hurry to the inn for fear the fish should be over-dressed—how different my sensations! not a picture here but recalls a history; not one, but I remember in Downing Street or Chelsea where queens and crowds admired them, though *seeing* them as little as these travellers!

When I had drunk tea, I strolled into the garden—they told me it was now called the *pleasure-ground*—what a dissonant idea of pleasure—those groves, those *allées*, where I have passed so many charming moments, are now stripped up or overgrown; many fond paths I could not unravel, though with a very exact clue in my memory—I met two game-keepers, and a thousand hares! In the days when all my soul was turned to pleasure and vivacity (and you will think, perhaps, it is far from being out of tune yet), I hated Houghton and its solitude— yet I loved this garden; as now, with many regrets, I love Houghton— Houghton, I know not what to call it, a monument of grandeur or ruin! How I have wished this evening for Lord Bute! how I could preach to him! For myself, I do not want to be preached to—I have long considered, how every Balbec must wait for the chance of a Mr. Wood.

The servants wanted to lay me in the great apartment—what, to make me pass my night as I have done my evening! It were like proposing to Margaret Roper to be a duchess in the court that cut off her father's head, and imagining it would please her. I have chosen to sit in my father's little dressing-room, and am now by his scrutoire, where, in the height of his fortune, he used to receive the accounts of his farmers, and deceive himself—or us, with the thoughts of his economy—how wise a man at once, and how weak! For what has he built Houghton? for his grandson to annihilate, or for his son to mourn over! If Lord Burleigh could rise and view his representative driving the Hatfield stage, he would feel as I feel now—poor little Strawberry! at least it will not be stripped to pieces by a descendant!—You will think all these fine meditations dictated by pride, not by philosophy—pray consider through how many mediums philosophy must pass, before it is purified—

. . . how often must it weep, how often burn!

My mind was extremely prepared for all this gloom by parting with Mr. Conway yesterday morning—moral reflections on commonplaces are the livery one likes to wear, when one has just had a real misfortune.—He is going to Germany—I was glad to dress myself up in transitory Houghton, in lieu of very sensible concern. To-morrow I shall be distracted with thoughts —at least images, of very different complexion—I go to Lynn and am to be elected on Friday. I shall return hither on Saturday, again alone, to expect Burleighides on Sunday, whom I left at Newmarket—I must once in my life see him on his grandfather's throne.

Epping,
Monday night, thirty-first
No, I have not seen him, he loitered on the road, and I was kept at Lynn

till yesterday morning. It is plain I never knew for how many trades I was formed, when at this time of day I can begin electioneering, and succeed in my new vocation. Think of me, the subject of a mob, who was scarce ever before in a mob! addressing them in the town-hall, riding at the head of two thousand people through such a town as Lynn, dining with above two hundred of them, amid bumpers, huzzas, songs, and tobacco, and finishing with country dancing at a ball and sixpenny whisk! I have borne it all cheerfully; nay, have sat hours in *conversation*, the thing upon earth that I hate, have been to hear misses play on the harpsichord, and to see an alderman's copies of Reubens and Carlo Marat. Yet to do the folks justice, they are sensible, and reasonable, and civilized; their very language is polished since I lived among them. I attribute this to their more frequent intercourse with the world and the capital, by the help of good roads and post chaises, which, if they have abridged the King's dominions, have at least tamed his subjects—well! how comfortable it will be to-morrow, to see my perroquet, to play at loo, and not to be obliged to talk seriously—the Heraclitus of the beginning of this letter will be overjoyed on finishing it to sign himself

Your old friend,
DEMOCRITUS.

P. S. I forgot to tell you that my ancient aunt Hammond came over to Lynn to see me—not from any affection, but curiosity—the first thing she said to me, though we have not met these sixteen years, was, "Child, you have done a thing to-day, that your father never did in all his life; you sat as they carried you; he always stood the whole time." "Madam," said I, "when I am placed in a chair, I conclude I am to sit in it—besides, as I cannot imitate my father in great things, I am not at all ambitious of mimicking him in little ones."—I am sure she proposes to tell her remark to my uncle Horace's ghost the instant they meet.

V. TO GEORGE MONTAGU

Arlington Street,
Dec. 8, 1761

I return you the list of prints, and shall be glad you will bring me all to which I have affixed this mark X. The rest I have; yet the expense of the whole list would not ruin me. Lord Farnham, who, I believe, departed this morning, brings you the list of the Duke of Devonshire's pictures.

I had been told that Mr. Bourk's history was of England, not of Ireland—I am glad it is the latter, for I am now in Mr. Hume's England, and would fain read no more—I not only know what has been written, but what would be written. Our story is so exhausted, that to make it new, they really *make* it *new*. Mr. Hume has exalted Edward the Second, and depressed Edward the Third. The next historian, I suppose, will make James the First a hero, and geld Charles the Second.

Fingal is come out—I have not yet got through it—not but it is very fine—yet I cannot at once compass an epic poem now. It tires me to death to read how many ways a warrior is like the moon, or the sun, or a rock, or a lion, or the ocean. *Fingal* is a brave collection of similes, and will serve all the boys at Eton and Westminster for these twenty years. I will trust you with a secret, but you must not disclose it, I should be ruined with my Scotch friends—in short, I cannot believe it genuine—I cannot believe a regular poem of six books has been preserved, uncorrupted, by oral tradition, from times before Christianity was introduced into the island. What! preserved unadulterated by savages dispersed among mountains, and so often driven from their dens, so wasted by wars civil and foreign! Has one man ever got all by heart? I doubt it. Were parts preserved by some, other parts by others? Mighty lucky

that the tradition was never interrupted, nor any part lost—not a verse, not a measure, not the sense! luckier and luckier—I have been extremely qualified myself lately for this Scotch memory; we have had nothing but a coagulation of rains, fogs, and frosts, and though they have clouded all understanding, I suppose, if I had tried, I should have found that they thickened, and gave great consistence to my remembrance.

You want news—I must make it, if I send it. To change the dullness of the scene I went to the play, where I had not been this winter. They are so crowded, that though I went before six, I got no better place than a fifth row, where I heard very ill, and was pent for five hours without a soul near me that I knew. It was *Cymbeline*, and appeared to me as long as if everybody in it went really to Italy in every act, and came back again. With a few pretty passages and a scene or two, it is so absurd and tiresome, that I am persuaded Garrick . . .

VI. TO THE REV. WILLIAM COLE

Strawberry Hill,
March 9, 1765

Dear Sir,—I had time to write but a short note with the *Castle of Otranto*, as your messenger called on me at four o'clock, as I was going to dine abroad. Your partiality to me and Strawberry have, I hope, inclined you to excuse the wildness of the story. You will even have found some traits to put you in mind of this place. When you read of the picture quitting its panel, did not you recollect the portrait of Lord Falkland, all in white, in my gallery? Shall I even confess to you, what was the origin of this romance? I waked one morning in the beginning of last June, from a dream, of which, all I could recover was, that I had thought myself in an ancient castle (a very natural dream for a head filled like mine with Gothic story), and that on the uppermost banister of a great staircase I saw a gigantic hand in armour. In the evening I sat down, and began to write, without knowing in the least what I intended to say or relate. The work grew on my hands, and I grew fond of it—add that I was very glad to think of anything, rather than politics—in short, I was so engrossed with my tale, which I completed in less than two months, that one evening, I wrote from the time I had drunk my tea, about six o'clock, till half an hour after one in the morning, when my hand and fingers were so weary, that I could not hold the pen to finish the sentence, but left Matilda and Isabella talking, in the middle of a paragraph. You will laugh at my earnestness, but if I have amused you, by retracing with any fidelity the manners of ancient days, I am content, and give you leave to think me as idle as you please.

You are, as you have long been to me, exceedingly kind, and I should, with great satisfaction, embrace your offer of visiting the solitude of Blecheley, though my cold is in a manner gone, and my cough quite, if I was at liberty: but as I am preparing for my French journey, I have forty businesses upon my hands, and can only now and then purloin a day, or half a day, to come hither. You know I am not cordially disposed to *your* French journey, which is much more serious, as it is to be much more lasting. However, though I may suffer by your absence, I would not dissuade what may suit your inclination and circumstances. One thing, however, has struck me, which I must mention, though it would depend on a circumstance that would give me the most real concern. It was suggested to me by that real fondness I have for your MSS., for your kindness about which I feel the utmost gratitude. You would not, I think, leave them behind you; and are you aware of the danger they would run, if you settled entirely in France? Do you know that the King of France is heir to all strangers who die in his dominions, by what they call the Droit d'Aubaine? Sometimes

by great interest and favour, persons have obtained a remission of this right in their lifetime; and yet that, even that, has not secured their effects from being embezzled. Old Lady Sandwich had obtained this remission, and yet, though she left everything to the present Lord, her grandson, a man for whose rank one should have thought they would have had regard, the King's officers forced themselves into her house, after her death, and plundered. You see, if you go, I shall expect to have your MSS., deposited with me—seriously, you must leave them in safe custody behind you.

Lord Essex's trial is printed with the State Trials. In return for your obliging offer, I can acquaint you with a delightful publication of this winter, a collection of old ballads and poetry, in three volumes, many from Pepys's collection at Cambridge. There were three such published between thirty and forty years ago, but very carelessly, and wanting many in this set: indeed, there were others, of a looser sort, which the present editor, who is a clergyman, thought it decent to omit.

When you go into Cheshire, and upon your ramble, may I trouble you with a commission, but about which you must promise me not to go a step out of your way. Mr. Bateman has got a cloister at Old Windsor, furnished with ancient wooden chairs, most of them triangular, but all of various patterns, and carved and turned in the most uncouth and whimsical forms. He picked them up one by one, for two, three, five, or six shillings apiece, from different farmhouses in Herefordshire. I have long envied and coveted them. There may be such in poor cottages in so neighbouring a county as Cheshire. I should not grudge any expense for purchase or carriage; and should be glad even of a couple such for my cloister here. When you are copying inscriptions in a churchyard in any village, think of me, and step into the first cottage you see—but don't take farther trouble than that.

I long to know what your bundle of manuscripts from Cheshire contains.

My bower is determined, but not at all what it is to be. Though I write romances, I cannot tell how to build all that belongs to them. Madame Daunois, in the Fairy Tales, used to tapestry them with jonquils; but as that furniture will not last above a fortnight in the year, I shall prefer something more huckaback. I have decided that the outside shall be a *treillage*, which, however, I shall not commence, till I have again seen some of old Louis's old-fashioned *galanteries* at Versailles. Rosamond's bower, you, and I, and Tom Hearne know, was a labyrinth, but as my territory will admit of a very short clue, I lay aside all thoughts of a mazy habitation; though a bower is very different from an arbour, and must have more chambers than one. In short, I both know, and don't know, what it should be. I am almost afraid I must go and read Spenser, and wade through his allegories, and drawling stanzas, to get at a picture—but, good night! you see how one gossips, when one is alone, and at quiet on one's dunghill!— well! it may be trifling, yet it is such trifling as Ambition never is happy enough to know! Ambition orders palaces, but it is Content that chats for a page or two over a bower.

Yours ever,

H. WALPOLE.

VII. TO THOMAS CHATTERTON

Arlington Street,
March 28, 1769

Sir,—I cannot but think myself singularly obliged by a gentleman with whom I have not the pleasure of being acquainted, when I read your very curious and kind letter, which I have this minute received. I give you a thousand thanks for it, and for the very obliging offer you make me, of communicating your MSS. to me. What you have already sent me is very valuable, and full of information; but instead of correcting you, Sir, you are far more able to correct me. I have not the happiness of understanding the Saxon language, and without your learned notes should not have been able to comprehend Rowley's text.

As a second edition of my *Anecdotes* was published but last year, I must not flatter myself that a third will be wanted soon; but I shall be happy to lay up any notices you will be so good as to extract for me, and send me at your leisure; for, as it is uncertain when I may use them, I would by no means borrow and detain your MSS.

Give me leave to ask you where Rowley's poems are to be found? I should not be sorry to print them; or at least, a specimen of them, if they have never been printed.

The Abbot John's verses that you have given me, are wonderful for their harmony and spirit, though there are some words I do not understand. You do not point out exactly the time when he lived, which I wish to know, as I suppose it was long before John Ab Eyck's discovery of oil-painting. If so, it confirms what I had guessed, and have hinted in my *Anecdotes*, that oil-painting was known here much earlier than that discovery or revival.

I will not trouble you with more questions now, Sir, but flatter myself from the humanity and politeness you have already shown me, that you will sometimes give me leave to consult you. I hope, too, you will forgive the simplicity of my direction, as you have favoured me with no other.

I am, Sir,

Your much obliged and obedient humble Servant,

HOR. WALPOLE.

P. S. Be so good as to direct to Mr. Walpole in Arlington Street.

VIII. TO THOMAS CHATTERTON

[August, 1769]

Sir,—I do not see, I must own, how those precious MSS., of which you have sent me a few extracts, should be lost to the world by my detaining your letters. Do the originals not exist, from whence you say you copied your extracts, and from which you offered me more extracts? In truth, by your first letter I understood that the originals themselves were in your possession by the free and voluntary offer you made me of them, and which you know I did not choose to accept. If Mr. Barrett (who, give me leave to say, cannot know much of antiquity if he believes in the authenticity of those papers) intends to make use of them, would he not do better to have recourse to the originals, than to the slight fragments you have sent me? You say, Sir, you know them to be genuine; pray let me ask again, of what age are they? and how have they been transmitted? In what book of any age is there mention made either of Rowley or of the poetical monk, his ancient predecessor in such pure poetry? poetry, so resembling both Spenser and the moderns, and written in metre invented long since Rowley, and longer since the monk wrote. I doubt Mr. Barrett himself will find it difficult to solve these doubts.

For myself, I undoubtedly will never print those extracts as genuine, which I am far from believing they are. If you want them, Sir, I will have them copied, and will send you the copy. But having a little suspicion that your letters may have been designed to laugh at me, if I had fallen into the snare, you will allow me to preserve your original letters, as an ingenious contrivance, however unsuccessful. This seems the more probable, as any man would understand by your first letter, that you either was possessed of the original MSS. or had taken copies of them; whereas now you talk as if you had no copy but those written at the bottom of the very letters I have received from you.

I own I should be better diverted, if it proved that you have chosen to entertain yourself at my expense, than if you really thought these pieces ancient. The former would show you

had little opinion of my judgment; the latter, that you ought not to trust too much to your own. I should not at all take the former ill, as I am not vain of it; I should be sorry for the latter, as you say, Sir, that you are very young, and it would be pity an ingenious young man should be too early prejudiced in his own favour.

IX. TO THE REV. WILLIAM MASON

Arlington Street,
Nov. 27, 1773

Dear Sir,—Mr. Stonhewer has sent me, and I have read, your first part of Gray's Life, which I was very sorry to part with so soon. Like everything of yours, I like it ten times better upon reading it again. You have with most singular art displayed the talents of my two departed friends to the fullest advantage; and yet there is a simplicity in your manner, which, like the frame of a fine picture, seems a frame only, and yet is gold. I should say much more in praise, if, as I have told Mr. Stonhewer, I was not aware that I myself must be far more interested in the whole of the narrative than any other living mortal, and therefore may suppose it will please the world still more than it will——. And yet if wit, parts, learning, taste, sense, friendship, information, can strike or amuse mankind, must not this work have that effect?—and yet, though *me* it may affect far more strongly, self-loving certainly has no share in my affection to many parts. Of my two friends and me, I only make a most indifferent figure. I do not mean with regard to parts or talents—I never one instant of my life had the superlative vanity of ranking myself with them. They not only possessed genius, which I have not, great learning which is to be acquired, and which I never acquired; but both Gray and West had abilities marvellously premature. What wretched boyish stuff would my contemporary letters to them appear, if they existed; and which they both were so good-natured as to destroy.

What unpoetic things were mine at that age, some of which unfortunately do exist, and which I yet could never surpass; but it is not in that light I consider my own position. We had not got to Calais before Gray was dissatisfied, for I was a boy, and he, though infinitely more a man, was not enough so to make allowances. Hence am I never mentioned once with kindness in his letters to West. This hurts me for him, as well as myself. For the oblique censures on my want of curiosity, I have nothing to say. The fact was true; my eyes were not purely classic; and though I am now a dull antiquary, my age then made me taste pleasures and diversions merely modern: I say this to you, and to you only, in confidence. I do not object to a syllable. I know how trifling, how useless, how blamable I have been, and submit to hear my faults, both because I have had faults, and because I hope I have corrected some of them; and though Gray hints at my unwillingness to be told them, I can say truly that to the end of his life he neither spared the reprimand nor mollified the terms, as you and others know, and I believe have felt.

These reflections naturally arose on reading his letters again, and arose in spite of the pleasure they gave me, for self will intrude, even where self is not so much concerned. I am sorry to find I disobliged Gray so very early. I am sorry for him that it so totally obliterated all my friendship for him; a remark the world probably, and I hope, will not make, but which it is natural for me, dear Sir, to say to you. I am so sincerely zealous that all possible honour should be done to my two friends, that I care not a straw for serving as a foil to them. And as confession of faults is the only amendment I can now make to the one disobliged, I am pleased with myself for having consented, and for consenting, as I do, to that public reparation. I thank you for having revived West and his alas! stifled genius, and for having extended Gray's reputation. If the world ad-

mires them both as much as they deserved, I shall enjoy their fame; if it does not, I shall comfort myself for standing so prodigiously below them, as I do even without comparison.

There are a few false printings I could have corrected, but of no consequence, as "Grotto del Cane," for "Grotta," and a few notes I could have added, but also of little consequence. Dodsley, who is printing Lord Chesterfield's *Letters*, will hate you for this publication. I was asked to write a Preface—*Sic notus Ulysses?* I knew Ulysses too well. Besides, I have enough to burn without adding to the mass. Forgive me, if I differ with you, but I cannot think Gray's Latin poems inferior even to his English, at least as I am not a Roman. I wish too that in a note you had referred to West's Ode on the Queen in Dodsley's *Miscellanies*. Adieu! go on and prosper. My poor friends have an historian worthy of them, and who satisfies their and your friend.

HOR. WALPOLE.

X. TO THE REV. WILLIAM COLE

Arlington Street,
April 25, 1775

The least I can do, dear Sir, in gratitude for the cargo of prints I have received to-day from you, is to send you a medicine. A pair of bootikins will set out to-morrow morning in the machine that goes from the Queen's Head in Gray's Inn Lane. To be certain, you had better send for them where the machine inns, lest they should neglect delivering them at Milton. My not losing a moment shows my zeal—but if you can bear a little pain, I should not press you to use them. I have suffered so dreadfully, that I constantly wear them to diminish the stock of gout in my constitution; but as your fit is very slight, and will not last, and as you are pretty sure by its beginning so late that you will never have much; and as the gout certainly carries off other complaints, had not you better endure a little, when it is rather a remedy than a disease? I do not desire to be entirely delivered from the gout, for all reformations do but make room for some new grievance; and, in my opinion, a disorder that requires no physician is preferable to any that does. However, I have put relief in your power, and you will judge for yourself. You must tie them as tight as you can bear, the flannel next to the flesh; and when you take them off, it should be in bed. Rub your feet with a warm cloth, and put on warm stockings, for fear of catching cold while the pores are open. It would kill anybody but me, who am of adamant, to walk out into the dew in winter in my slippers in half an hour after pulling off the bootikins. A physician sent me word, good-naturedly, that there was danger of catching cold after the bootikins, unless one was careful. I thanked him, but told him my precaution was, never taking any. All the winter I pass five days in a week without walking out, and sit often by the fireside till seven in the evening. When I do go out, whatever the weather is, I go with both glasses of the coach down, and so I do at midnight out of the hottest room. I have not had a single cold, however slight, these two years.

You are too candid in submitting at once to my defence of Mr. Mason. It is true I am more charmed with his book than I almost ever was with one. I find more people like the grave letters than those of humour, and some think the latter a little affected, which is as wrong a judgment as they could make; for Gray never wrote anything easily but things of humour. Humour was his natural and original turn—and though, from his childhood, he was grave and reserved, his genius led him to see things ludicrously and satirically; and though his health and dissatisfaction gave him low spirits, his melancholy turn was much more affected than his pleasantry in writing. You knew him enough to know I am in the right—but the world in general always wants to be told how to think, as well as what to think. The print, I agree with you, though like, is a very disagreeable likeness, and the worst likeness of him. It gives the primness he had when under constraint; and there is a blackness in the countenance which was like him only the last time I ever saw him, when I was much struck with it; and, though I did not apprehend him in danger, it left an impression on me that was uneasy, and almost prophetic of what I heard but too soon after leaving him. Wilson drew the picture under much such impression, and I could not bear it in my room; Mr. Mason altered it a little, but still it is not well, nor gives any idea of the determined virtues of his heart. It just serves to help the reader to an image of the person whose genius and integrity they must admire, if they are so happy as to have a taste for either.

The peep into the gardens at Twickenham is a silly little book, of which a few little copies were printed some years ago for presents, and which now sets up for itself as a vendible book. It is a most inaccurate, superficial, blundering account of Twickenham and other places, drawn up by a Jewess, who has married twice, and turned Christian, poetess, and authoress. She has printed her poems, too, and one complimentary copy of mine, which in good breeding I could not help sending her in return for violent compliments in verse to me. I do not remember that hers were good; mine I know were very bad, and certainly never intended for the press.

I bought the first volume of Manchester, but could not read it; it was much too learned for me; and seemed rather an account of Babel than Manchester; I mean in point of antiquity. To be sure, it is very kind in an author to promise one the history of a country town, and give one a circumstantial account of the antediluvian world into the bargain. But I am simple and ignorant, and desire no more than I pay for. And then for my progenitors, Noah and the Saxons, I have no curiosity about them. Bishop Lyttelton used to plague me to death with barrows, and tumuli, and Roman camps, and all those bumps in the ground that do not amount to a most imperfect ichnography; but, in good truth, I am content with all arts when perfected, nor inquire how ingeniously people contrived to do without them—and I care still less for remains of art that retain no vestiges of art. Mr. Bryant, who is sublime in unknown knowledge, diverted me more, yet I have not finished his work, no more than he has. There is a great ingenuity in discovering all history (though it has never been written) by etymologies. Nay, he convinced me that the Greeks had totally mistaken all they went to learn in Egypt, &c., by doing, as the French do still, judge wrong by the ear—but as I have been trying now and then for above forty years to learn something, I have not time to unlearn it all again, though I allow this is our best sort of knowledge. If I should die when I am not clear in the History of the World below its first three thousand years, I should be at a sad loss on meeting with Homer and Hesiod, or any of those *moderns* in the Elysian fields, before I knew what I ought to think of them.

Pray do not betray my ignorance: the reviewers and such litterati have called me *a learned and ingenious gentleman.* I am sorry they ever heard my name, but don't let them know how irreverently I speak of the erudite, whom I dare to say they admire. These wasps, I suppose, will be very angry at the just contempt Mr. Gray had for them, and will, as insects do, attempt to sting, in hopes that their twelve-penny readers will suck a little venom from the momentary tumour they raise—but good night—and once more, thank you for the prints.

Yours ever,

H. W.

XI. TO THE REV. WILLIAM COLE

Strawberry Hill,
June 19, 1777

I thank you for your notices, dear Sir, and shall remember that on Prince William. I did see the *Monthly Review,* but hope one is not guilty of the death of every man who does not make one the dupe of a forgery. I believe Macpherson's success with *Ossian* was more the ruin of Chatterton than I. Two years passed between my doubting the authenticity of Rowley's poems and his death. I never knew he had been in London till some time after he had undone and poisoned himself there. The poems he sent me were transcripts in his own hand, and even in that circumstance he told a lie; he said he had them from the very person at Bristol to whom he had given them. If any man was to tell you that monkish rhymes had been dug up at Herculaneum, which was destroyed several centuries before there was any such poetry, should you believe it? They have all the elegance of Waller and Prior, and more than Lord Surrey—but I have no objection to anybody believing what he pleases. I think poor Chatterton was an astonishing genius—but I cannot think that Rowley foresaw metres that were invented long after he was dead, or that our language was more refined at Bristol in the reign of Henry V than it was at court under Henry VIII. One of the chaplains of the Bishop of Exeter has found a line of Rowley in *Hudibras*—the monk might foresee that too! The prematurity of Chatterton's genius is, however, full as wonderful, as that such a prodigy as Rowley should never have been heard of till the eighteenth century. The youth and industry of the former are miracles too, yet still more credible. There is not a symptom in the poems, but the old words, that savours of Rowley's age. Change the old words for modern, and the whole construction is of yesterday.

The other story you tell me is very credible and perfectly in character.

Yours ever,

H. W.

XII. TO SIR HORACE MANN

Arlington Street,
Feb. 18, 1778

I do not know how to word the following letter; how to gain credit with you! How shall I intimate to you, that you must lower your topsails, waive your imperial dignity, and strike to the colours of the thirteen United Provinces of America? Do not tremble, and imagine that Washington has defeated General Howe, and driven him out of Philadelphia; or that Gates has taken another army; or that Portsmouth is invested by an American fleet. No: no military *new* event has occasioned this revolution. The sacrifice has been made on the altar of peace. Stop again: peace is not made, it is only implored,—and I fear, only on this side of the Atlantic. In short, yesterday, *February* 17th, a most memorable era, Lord North opened his conciliatory plan,—no partial, no collusive one. In as few words as I can use, it solicits peace with the States of America: it haggles on no terms; it acknowledges the Congress, or anybody that pleases to treat; it confesses errors, misinformation, ill-success, and impossibility of conquest; it disclaims taxation, desires commerce, hopes for assistance, allows the independence of America, not verbally, yet virtually, and suspends hostilities till June 1779. It does a little more: not *verbally*, but *virtually*, it confesses that the opposition have been in the right from the beginning to the end.

The warmest American cannot deny but these gracious condescensions are ample enough to content that whole continent; and yet, my friend, such accommodating facility had one defect,—it came too late. The treaty between the high and mighty States and France is signed; and instead of peace, we must expect war with the high allies. The French army is come to the coast, and their officers here are recalled.

The House of Commons embraced the plan, and voted it *nemine contradicente*. It is to pass both Houses with a rapidity that will do everything but overtake time past. All the world is in astonishment. As my letter will not set out till the day after tomorrow, I shall have time to tell you better what is thought of this amazing step.

Feb. 20

In sooth I cannot tell you what is thought. Nobody knows what to think. To leap at once from an obstinacy of four years to a total concession of everything; to stoop so low, without hopes of being forgiven—who can understand such a transformation? I must leave you in all your wonderment; for the cloud is not dispersed. When it shall be, I doubt it will discover no serene prospect! All that remains certain is, that America is not only lost but given up. We must no longer give ourselves Continental airs! I fear even our trident will find it has lost a considerable prong.

I have lived long, but never saw such a day as last Tuesday! From the first, I augured ill of this American war; yet do not suppose that I boast of my penetration. Far was I from expecting such a conclusion! Conclusion!—*y sommes-nous?* Acts of Parliament have made a war, but cannot repeal one. They have provoked—not terrified; and Washington and Gates have respected the Speaker's mace no more than Oliver Cromwell did.

You shall hear as events arise. I disclaim all sagacity, and pretend to no foresight. It is not an Englishman's talent. Even the second sight of the Scots has proved a little purblind.

You have heard that Voltaire is actually at Paris? Perhaps soon you will learn French news earlier than I can.

What scenes my letters to you have touched on for eight-and-thirty years! I arrived here at the eve of the termination of my father's happy reign. The Rebellion, as he foresaw, followed; and much disgrace. Another war ensued, with new disgraces. And then broke forth Lord Chatham's sun; and all was glory and extensive empire. Nor tranquillity nor triumph are our lot now! The womb of time is not with child of a mouse,—but adieu! I shall probably write again before you have digested half the meditations this letter will have conjured up.

XIII. TO THE REV. WILLIAM MASON

Monday night, Feb. 19, 1781

It has not been from want of materials, if I had chosen to work them up, that I have not written to you very lately; but though I hold it delectable enough in one's dotage to prattle and gossip of the doings of the courts of one's younger days, I do not think it so decorous to invert one's Brantôme-hood and limp after and repeat the tattle of Drawing-rooms that are scarce fledged. A sovereign may be philosopher or concentrated enough in his own rays to disregard terrestrial tempests, and to be more occupied by the spots in his own orbit than by the mouldering away of his empire. For my part I have too much mortal clay about me to soar so much above matter, and to divert myself only with the music or discord of the spheres.

All this tedious proem is but to say that I have not wanted news, ay, and news that employs this whole town, if I would have condescended to tell you who has or who has not been at **Cumberland House**, or at the Queen's ball, or how King George and his brother, Duke Henry, have quarrelled about the servants of the Prince of Wales not being suffered to dine with his Royal Highness Duke Henry, and how Duke Henry was not invited to the ball at the Queen's House, with a deal of such scimble scamble stuff, which has totally obliterated the memory of all the wars that we have with all the world. Do not be surprised, if we attended to anything above such

puerilities, we should not be in the situation we are. I still do believe that distress will at last open our eyes, but I believe, too, that we shall soon shut them again. There is not energy enough left in us to produce any effect. One may judge from the *nature* of our dissipations as much as from the dissipation itself. The age that souses into every amusement and folly that is presented to it, has not imagination enough to strike out anything of itself. Mrs. Cornelys, Almack, and Dr. Graham are forced to advertise diversions by public sale, and everybody goes indolently and mechanically to them all, without choice or preference. They who are *called the people of fashion* or the *ton* have contributed nothing of their own but *being too late*; nay, actually do go to most public diversions after they are over. Your Yorkshire reformers, though not content with Mr. Burke's bill, will gather no prophetic comfort from the treatment it received to-day. I was at Mrs. Delany's this evening, when Mr. Frederic Montagu arrived from the House. They had put off the second reading till Friday, because Wednesday is the Fast Day, and Thursday Vestris's benefit. God has His day, a French dancer his, and then the national senate will be at leisure to think whether it will save three-halfpence-farthing out of eighteen millions that are to be raised in hopes of protracting the war, till we want at least eighteen millions more.

Was not you edified with the last *Gazette*? When we expected to hear that all Washington's army was catched in a drag-net, and that Lord Cornwallis had subdued and pacified all Virginia and Carolina, we were modestly told that his Lordship and his handful of men had been sick, but, thank you, are a little better; and that Colonel Ferguson was beaten, and Colonel Tarleton had had a puny advantage; all which we knew two months ago.

To-day we are very sorry for what, however, we do not care a straw about.

Well, the grand fleet, that was to fetch home Gibraltar and place it out of harm's way in the Isle of Sky, cannot sail. Governor Johnstone, the honestest man in the world, has written to Lord Hillsborough (for he would not trust Lord Sandwich, whom a fortnight ago he thought the second man in honesty in *South* Britain) complaining that the fleet is rotten, and cannot sail; nay, he has sent up a yard and a half of worm-eaten plank, which he humbly begs his Majesty himself will taste and be convinced. I do not answer for a syllable of truth in this narrative, though it was told me by a Scottish Earl who never gave a vote in his days against any court.

I have not yet been able to get you Gray's Life. My bookseller had blundered, and after trusting to him so long, he brought me the preceding volumes: but I am on a new scent, and hope at least to send you a transcript of that single Life; though I wish you to see the whole set, nay, those old ones; I dipped into them, and found that the tasteless pedant admires that wretched buffoon Dr. King, who is but a Tom Brown in rhyme; and says that *The Dispensary*, that *chef-d'oeuvre*, can scarce make itself read. This is prejudice on both sides, equal to that monkish railer Père Garasse. But Dr. Johnson has indubitably neither taste nor ear, criterion of judgment, but his old woman's prejudices; where they are wanting, he has no rule at all; he prefers Smith's poetic, but insipid and undramatic *Phaedra and Hippolitus* to Racine's *Phèdre*, the finest tragedy in my opinion of the French theatre, for, with Voltaire's leave, I think it infinitely preferable to *Iphigénie*, and so I own I do *Britannicus, Mahomet, Alzire,* and some others; but I will allow Johnson to dislike Gray, Garth, Prior—ay, and every genius we have had, when he cries up Blackmore, Thomson, Akenside, and Dr. King; nay, I am glad that the measure of our dullness is full. I would have this era

stigmatize itself in every respect, and be a proverb to the nations around, and to future ages. We want but Popery to sanctify every act of blindness. Hume should burn the works of Locke, and Johnson of Milton, and the atheist and the bigot join in the same religious rites, as they both were pensioned by the same piety. Oh, let us not have a ray of sense or throb of sensation left to distinguish us from brutes! let total stupefaction palliate our fall, and let us resemble the Jews, who when they were to elect a god, preferred a calf!

Tuesday

Upon stricter inquiry, I find that Johnson has not yet published his new *Lives,* but only given away a few copies.

An account is said to be come from New York, that above two thousand of Washington's army have left him for want of pay, but, remain encamped at some distance; have refused to join Clinton, and have sent to the Congress that they will return to Washington if they are paid; if not, that they will not disband. Governor Johnstone's remonstrance is already whittled down to a complaint of one particular ship not being ready.

2nd P. S. Lord Harcourt has got me from Taylor at Bath the method of the aquatinta, which I have sent to Mr. Stonehewer this morning to transmit to him.

XIV. TO MISS MARY BERRY

Berkeley Square,
May 26, 1791.

I am rich in letters from you: I received that by Lord Elgin's courier first, as you expected, and its elder the next day. You tell me mine entertain you; *tant mieux.* It is my wish, but my wonder; for I live so very little in the world, that I do not know the present generation by sight: for, though I pass by them in the streets, the hats with valances, the folds above the chin of the ladies, and the dirty shirts and shaggy hair of the young men, who have *levelled nobility* almost as much as the *mobility* in France have, have confounded all individuality. Besides, if I did go to public places and assemblies, which my going to roost earlier prevents, the bats and owls do not begin to fly abroad till far in the night, when they begin to see and be seen. However, one of the empresses of fashion, the Duchess of Gordon, uses fifteen or sixteen hours of her four-and-twenty. I heard her journal of last Monday. She first went to Handel's music in the Abbey; she then clambered over the benches, and went to Hastings's trial in the Hall; after dinner, to the play; then to Lady Lucan's assembly; after that to Ranelagh, and returned to Mrs. Hobart's faro-table; gave a ball herself in the evening of that morning, into which she must have got a good way; and set out for Scotland the next day. Hercules could not have achieved a quarter of her labours in the same space of time. What will the Great Duke think of our Amazons, if he has letters opened, as the Emperor was wont! One of our Camillas, but in a freer style, I hear, he saw (I fancy, just before your arrival) ; and he must have wondered at the familiarity of the dame, and the nincompoophood of her Prince. Sir W. H. is arrived—his Nymph of the Attitudes was too prudish to visit the rambling peeress.

Mrs. Cholmeley was so very good as to call on me again yesterday; Mr. French was with me, and fell in love with her understanding, and probably with her face too—but with that he did not trust me. He says we shall have Dr. Darwin's stupendous poem in a fortnight, of which you saw parts. Geo. Cholmondeley's wife, after a dreadful labour, is delivered of a dead child.

The rest of my letter must be literary; for we have no news. Boswell's book is gossiping; but, having numbers of proper names, would be more readable, at least by me, were it reduced from two volumes to one: but there are woful *longueurs*, both about his hero and himself, the *fidus Achates*; about whom one has not the smallest curiosity. But I wrong the original Achates: one is satisfied with his fidelity in keeping his master's secrets and weaknesses, which modern led-captains betray for their patron's glory and to hurt their own enemies: which Boswell has done shamefully, particularly against Mrs. Piozzi, and Mrs. Montagu, and Bishop Percy. Dr. Blagden says justly, that it is a new kind of libel, by which you may abuse anybody, by saying some dead person said so-and-so of somebody alive. Often, indeed, Johnson made the most brutal speeches to living persons; for though he was good natured at bottom, he was very ill-natured at top. He loved to dispute to show his superiority. If his opponents were weak, he told them they were fools; if they vanquished him, he was scurrilous—to nobody more than to Boswell himself, who was contemptible for flattering him so grossly, and for enduring the coarse things he was continually vomiting on Boswell's own country, Scotland. I expected, amongst the excommunicated, to find myself, but am very gently treated. I never would be in the least acquainted with Johnson; or, as Boswell calls it, had not a just value for him; which the biographer imputes to my resentment for the Doctor's putting bad arguments (purposely, out of Jacobitism) into the speeches which he wrote fifty years ago for my father in the *Gentleman's Magazine*; which I did not read then, or ever knew Johnson wrote till Johnson died, nor have looked at since. Johnson's blind Toryism and known brutality kept me aloof; nor did I ever exchange a syllable with him: nay, I do not think I ever was in a room with him six times in my days. The first time I think was at the Royal Academy. Sir Joshua said, "Let me present Dr. Goldsmith to you";

he did. "Now I will present Dr. Johnson to you." "No," said I, "Sir Joshua, for Dr. Goldsmith, pass—but you shall *not* present Dr. Johnson to me." Some time after Boswell came to me, said Dr. J. was writing the *Lives of the Poets*, and wished I would give him anecdotes of Mr. Gray. I said, very coldly, I had given what I knew to Mr. Mason. B. hummed and hawed, and then dropped, "I suppose you know Dr. J. does not admire Mr. Gray." Putting as much contempt as I could into my look and tone, I said, "Dr. Johnson don't!—humph!"—and with that monosyllable ended our interview. After the Doctor's death, Burke, Sir Joshua Reynolds, and Boswell sent an ambling circular-letter to me, begging subscriptions for a monument for him—the two last, I think, impertinently; as they could not but know my opinion, and could not suppose I would contribute to a monument, for one who had endeavoured, poor soul! to degrade my friend's superlative poetry. I would not deign to write an answer; but sent down word by my footman, as I would have done to parish officers with a brief, that I would not subscribe. In the two new volumes Johnson says, and very probably did, or is made to say, that Gray's poetry is *dull*, and that he was a *dull* man! The same oracle dislikes Prior, Swift, and Fielding. If an elephant could write a book, perhaps one that had read a great deal would say that an Arabian horse is a very clumsy, ungraceful animal. Pass to a better chapter!

Burke has published another pamphlet against the French Revolution, in which he attacks it still more grievously. The beginning is very good; but it is not equal, nor quite so injudicious as parts of its predecessor; is far less brilliant, as well as much shorter: but, were it ever so long, his mind overflows with such a torrent of images, that he cannot be tedious. His invective against Rousseau is admirable, just, and new. Voltaire he passes almost contemptuously. I wish he had dissected Mirabeau too; and I grieve that he has omitted the violation of the consciences of the clergy, nor stigmatized those universal plunderers, the National Assembly, who gorge themselves with eighteen livres a day; which to many of them would, three years ago, have been astonishing opulence.

When you return I shall lend you three volumes in quarto of another work, with which you will be delighted. They are state letters in the reigns of Henry the Eighth, Mary, Elizabeth, and James; being the correspondence of the Talbot and Howard families, given by a Duke of Norfolk to the Heralds' office, where they have lain for a century neglected, buried under dust, and unknown, till discovered by a Mr. Lodge, a genealogist, who, to gratify his passion, procured to be made a Pursuivant. Oh, how curious they are! Henry seizes an alderman who refused to contribute to a benevolence; sends him to the army on the Borders; orders him to be exposed in the front line; and if that does not do, to be treated with the utmost rigour of military discipline. His daughter Bess is not less a Tudor. The mean, unworthy treatment of the Queen of Scots is striking; and you will find how Elizabeth's jealousy of her crown and her avarice were at war, and how the more ignoble passion predominated. But the most amusing passage is one in a private letter, as it paints the awe of children for their parents a *little* differently from modern habitudes. Mr. Talbot, second son of the Earl of Shrewsbury, was a member of the House of Commons, and was married. He writes to the Earl his father, and tells him that a young woman of a very good character has been recommended to him for chambermaid to his wife, and if his Lordship does not disapprove of it, he will hire her. There are many letters of news, that are very entertaining too—but it is nine o'clock, and I must go to Lady Cecilia's.

Friday

The Conways, Mrs. Damer, the Farrens, and Lord Mount-Edgcumbe supped at the Johnstones'. Lord Mount-Edgcumbe said excellently, that "Mademoiselle D'Éon is her own widow." I wish I had seen you both in your court-*plis*, at your presentation; but that is only one wish amongst a thousand.

East winds and blights have succeeded our April spring, as you guessed, but though I have been at Strawberry every week, I have caught no cold, I kindly thank you. Adieu!

OLIVER GOLDSMITH (1730?-1774)

Although Oliver Goldsmith never had the leisure or the inclination to set down a full autobiography, every friendly reader has detected much autobiography in his work, and has sympathetically followed his own account of his childhood and careless student days in Ireland, his medical studies at Edinburgh, and his wanderings through the Low Countries, France, Switzerland, and Italy. From 1756 he was struggling to make his way in London, and soon won success as a miscellaneous contributor to periodicals, among others the *Monthly Review*, the *Critical Review*, and the *British Magazine*. After the publication of his *Enquiry into the Present State of Polite Learning* (1759) he was recognized as an able man of letters, and was fairly if not munificently paid, though his improvident habits kept him more or less at the mercy of the booksellers for whom he worked. As essayist (*Citizen of the World*, 1762), novelist (*The Vicar of Wakefield*, 1766), poet (*The Traveller*, 1764, and *The Deserted Village*, 1770), and dramatist (*The Good-Natured Man*, 1768, and *She Stoops to Conquer*, 1773), he was one of the chief ornaments of Dr. Johnson's circle. He wrote with haste and carelessness, but even his hurriedly compiled histories and biographies and his fugitive essays have some of his characteristic distinction.

Goldsmith always shows a certain docility in his work: he is imitative in his use of meters and literary forms; he is imitative in his thinking also, and is ready to acknowledge the authority of such intellectual masters as Voltaire and Johnson. It would be a mistake to set him up as an important thinker, but it would also be a mistake to accept Boswell's portrait of poor Nolly Goldsmith, the amusingly inept blunderer with a touch of genius. He is genuinely though not strenuously interested in ideas, and he contrives to set forth a pretty coherent personal attitude toward life. He is fortunate in his use of the essay (prose or verse) because that form admits an easy interplay or fusion of the personal and the impersonal. The "Prospect of Society" which he offers in *The Traveller* is soberly didactic in its plan. His essays from 1760 to 1764 indicate that during that time he was working out the idea of a survey and comparative estimate of European nationalities, and he further organizes his work around his favorite doctrine of a principle of compensation which equalizes the diverse lots of mankind (see the last paragraph of the Dedication). The "survey" in eighteenth-century verse was usually as conventional as the "progress," but we detect the quality of Goldsmith's own temperament and experiences in his descriptions of France, Italy, and England.

In *The Deserted Village*, literary convention, current social and economic ideas, and personal experience blend in a more complex way. The pastoral idealization of rural life is undeniably conventional, but it supports Goldsmith's serious attack on luxury and his portrayal of the hardships entailed by the enclosure of common lands (see Dedication and note), and it likewise supports his wistful recollections of his own youth in the Irish village of Lissoy. Professor Crane has found the germ of *The Deserted Village* in an essay of 1762 which strikingly anticipates the thought and phraseology of the poem. Here, as in the Dedication, Goldsmith insists that he has seen that of which he writes. Yet "sweet Auburn" is not exactly Lissoy or any other Irish or English village; Goldsmith's description is after all an expression of his own humor, delicacy, and grace in an idyllic mood which does not take full account of the ideas expressed in *The Traveller* and elsewhere in his writings. His considered opinion was that luxury has its attendant benefits, that the law of compensation levels out the differences between the various conditions and modes of life. A carefully formulated statement of this principle is to be found in "Asem," and in Letter XI of *The Citizen of the World*. In general, Goldsmith's characteristic attitude is that of a meditative and ingenious observer of the pageant of history (as in "A Reverie at the Boar's-Head Tavern" and *The Traveller*) and of society (as in *The Citizen of the World* and *The Deserted Village*).

Works, ed. J. W. M. Gibbs (5 vols., 1884-86); *Complete Poetical Works*, ed. A. Dobson (1906); *Plays*, ed. C. E. Doble and G. Ostler (Oxford, 1928); *New Essays*, ed. R. S. Crane (Chicago, 1927); *Collected Letters*, ed. K. C. Balderston (Cambridge, Eng., 1928); K. C. Balderston, *History and Sources of Percy's Memoir of Goldsmith* (Cambridge, 1926); John Forster, *Life and Times of Oliver Goldsmith* (2 vols., 1854); A. Dobson, *Life* (1888); Stephen Gwynn, *Oliver Goldsmith* (1935); A. L. Sells, *Les Sources françaises de Goldsmith* (Paris, 1924); H. J. Smith, *Oliver Goldsmith's The Citizen of the World* (New Haven, 1926); Arthur Friedman,

"Goldsmith and the *Weekly Magazine*," MP, XXXII (1935), 281-99; "Goldsmith's Contributions to the *Critical Review*," ibid., XLIV (1946), 23-52; Iolo A. Williams, *Seven xviii*[th] *Century Bibliographies* (1924); Temple Scott, *Oliver Goldsmith, Bibliographically and Biographically Considered* (1928); R. S. Crane in *Cambridge Bibliography of English Literature*, II [remarkably complete].

THE TRAVELLER

OR, A PROSPECT OF SOCIETY

TO THE REV. HENRY GOLDSMITH

DEAR SIR,—I am sensible that the friendship between us can acquire no new force from the ceremonies of a Dedication; and perhaps it demands an excuse thus to prefix your name to my attempts, which you decline giving with your own. But as a part of this poem was formerly written to you from Switzerland, the whole can now, with propriety, be only inscribed to you. It will also throw a light upon many parts of it, when the reader understands that it is addressed to a man, who, despising fame and fortune, has retired early to happiness and obscurity, with an income of forty pounds a year.

I now perceive, my dear brother, the wisdom of your humble choice. You have entered upon a sacred office, where the harvest is great and the laborers are but few; while you have left the field of ambition, where the laborers are many and the harvest not worth carrying away. But of all kinds of ambition, what from the refinement of the times, from differing systems of criticism, and from the divisions of party, that pursues poetical fame is the wildest.

Poetry makes a principal amusement among unpolished nations; but in a country verging to the extremes of refinement, Painting and Music come in for a share. As these offer the feeble mind a less laborious entertainment, they at first rival Poetry, and at length supplant her; they engross all that favor once shown to her, and, though but younger sisters, seize upon the elder's birthright.

Yet, however this art may be neglected by the powerful, it is still in greater danger from the mistaken efforts of the learned to improve it. What criticisms have we not heard of late in favor of blank verse, and Pindaric odes, choruses, anapests, and iambics, alliterative care and happy negligence! Every absurdity has now a champion to defend it; and as he is generally much in the wrong, so he has always much to say—for error is ever talkative.

But there is an enemy to this art still more dangerous—I mean Party. Party entirely distorts the judgment and destroys the taste. When the mind is once infected with this disease, it can only find pleasure in what contributes to increase the distemper. Like the tiger, that seldom desists from pursuing man after having once preyed upon human flesh, the reader who has once gratified his appetite with calumny makes ever after the most agreeable feast upon murdered reputation. Such readers generally admire some half-witted thing, who wants to be thought a bold man, having lost the character of a wise one. Him they dignify with the name of poet; his tawdry lampoons are called satires; his turbulence is said to be force, and his frenzy fire.

What reception a poem may find, which has neither abuse, party, nor blank verse to support it, I cannot tell, nor am I solicitous to know. My aims are right. Without espousing the cause of any party, I have attempted to moderate the rage of all. I have endeavored to show that there may be equal happiness in states that are differently governed from our own; that every state has a particular principle of happiness, and that this principle in each may be carried to a mischievous excess. There are few can judge better than yourself how far these positions are illustrated in this poem.

I am, dear sir, your most affectionate brother,

OLIVER GOLDSMITH.

Remote, unfriended, melancholy, slow,
Or by the lazy Scheldt or wandering Po;
Or onward, where the rude Carinthian boor
Against the houseless stranger shuts the door;
Or where Campania's plain forsaken lies,

A weary waste expanding to the skies;
Where'er I roam, whatever realms to see,
My heart, untravelled, fondly turns to thee,
Still to my brother turns, with ceaseless pain,
And drags at each remove a lengthening chain.   10
    Eternal blessings crown my earliest friend,
And round his dwelling guardian saints attend;
Blessed be that spot, where cheerful guests retire
To pause from toil and trim their evening fire;
Blessed that abode, where want and pain repair,
And every stranger finds a ready chair;
Blessed be those feasts with simple plenty crowned,
Where all the ruddy family around
Laugh at the jests or pranks that never fail,
Or sigh with pity at some mournful tale,   20
Or press the bashful stranger to his food,
And learn the luxury of doing good.
    But me, not destined such delights to share,
My prime of life in wandering spent, and care,
Impelled with steps unceasing to pursue
Some fleeting good, that mocks me with the view;
That, like the circle bounding earth and skies,
Allures from far, yet, as I follow, flies;
My fortune leads to traverse realms alone,
And find no spot of all the world my own.   30
    Even now, where Alpine solitudes ascend,
I sit me down a pensive hour to spend;
And, placed on high above the storm's career,
Look downward where an hundred realms appear:
Lakes, forests, cities, plains extending wide,
The pomp of kings, the shepherd's humbler pride.
    When thus creation's charms around combine,
Amidst the store, should thankless pride repine?
Say, should the philosophic mind disdain
That good which makes each humbler bosom vain?   40
Let school-taught pride dissemble all it can,
These little things are great to little man;
And wiser he, whose sympathetic mind
Exults in all the good of all mankind.
Ye glittering towns, with wealth and splendor crowned,
Ye fields, where summer spreads profusion round,
Ye lakes, whose vessels catch the busy gale,
Ye bending swains, that dress the flowery vale,
For me your tributary stores combine;
Creation's heir, the world—the world is mine!   50
    As some lone miser, visiting his store,
Bends at his treasure, counts, recounts it o'er;
Hoards after hoards his rising raptures fill,
Yet still he sighs, for hoards are wanting still;
Thus to my breast alternate passions rise,
Pleased with each good that Heaven to man supplies:
Yet oft a sigh prevails, and sorrows fall,
To see the hoard of human bliss so small;
And oft I wish, amidst the scene, to find
Some spot to real happiness consigned,   60

Where my worn soul, each wandering hope at rest,
May gather bliss, to see my fellows blessed.
　　But where to find that happiest spot below,
Who can direct, when all pretend to know?
The shuddering tenant of the frigid zone
Boldly proclaims that happiest spot his own,
Extols the treasures of his stormy seas,
And his long nights of revelry and ease:
The naked negro, panting at the line,
Boasts of his golden sands and palmy wine, 70
Basks in the glare, or stems the tepid wave,
And thanks his gods for all the good they gave.
Such is the patriot's boast, where'er we roam,
His first, best country ever is at home.
And yet, perhaps, if countries we compare,
And estimate the blessings which they share,
Though patriots flatter, still shall wisdom find
An equal portion dealt to all mankind:
As different good, by Art or Nature given,
To different nations makes their blessings even. 80
　　Nature, a mother kind alike to all,
Still grants her bliss at Labor's earnest call;
With food as well the peasant is supplied
On Idra's cliffs as Arno's shelvy side;
And though the rocky-crested summits frown,
These rocks by custom turn to beds of down.
From Art more various are the blessings sent;
Wealth, commerce, honor, liberty, content.
Yet these each other's power so strong contest
That either seems destructive of the rest. 90
Where wealth and freedom reign, contentment fails;
And honor sinks where commerce long prevails.
Hence every state, to one loved blessing prone,
Conforms and models life to that alone.
Each to the favorite happiness attends,
And spurns the plan that aims at other ends:
Till, carried to excess in each domain,
This favorite good begets peculiar pain.
　　But let us try these truths with closer eyes,
And trace them through the prospect as it lies; 100
Here for a while, my proper cares resigned,
Here let me sit in sorrow for mankind;
Like yon neglected shrub, at random cast,
That shades the steep, and sighs at every blast.
　　Far to the right, where Apennine ascends,
Bright as the summer, Italy extends;
Its uplands sloping deck the mountain's side,
Woods over woods in gay theatric pride;
While oft some temple's moldering tops between
With venerable grandeur mark the scene. 110
　　Could Nature's bounty satisfy the breast,
The sons of Italy were surely blessed.
Whatever fruits in different climes are found,
That proudly rise, or humbly court the ground;
Whatever blooms in torrid tracts appear,

Whose bright succession decks the varied year;
Whatever sweets salute the northern sky
With vernal lives, that blossom but to die;
These, here disporting, own the kindred soil,
Nor ask luxuriance from the planter's toil;   120
While sea-born gales their gelid wings expand
To winnow fragrance round the smiling land.
  But small the bliss that sense alone bestows,
And sensual bliss is all the nation knows.
In florid beauty groves and fields appear;
Man seems the only growth that dwindles here.
Contrasted faults through all his manners reign.
Though poor, luxurious; though submissive, vain;
Though grave, yet trifling; zealous, yet untrue;
And even in penance planning sins anew.   130
All evils here contaminate the mind,
That opulence departed leaves behind;
For wealth was theirs, not far removed the date,
When commerce proudly flourished through the state.
At her command the palace learned to rise;
Again the long-fallen column sought the skies;
The canvas glowed, beyond even Nature warm,
The pregnant quarry teemed with human form:
Till, more unsteady than the southern gale,
Commerce on other shores displayed her sail;   140
While naught remained of all that riches gave,
But towns unmanned and lords without a slave,
And late the nation found, with fruitless skill,
Its former strength was but plethoric ill.
  Yet, still the loss of wealth is here supplied
By arts, the splendid wrecks of former pride;
From these the feeble heart and long-fallen mind
An easy compensation seem to find.
Here may be seen, in bloodless pomp arrayed,
The pasteboard triumph and the cavalcade;   150
Processions formed for piety and love,
A mistress or a saint in every grove.
By sports like these are all their cares beguiled;
The sports of children satisfy the child;
Each nobler aim, repressed by long control,
Now sinks at last, or feebly mans the soul;
While low delights succeeding fast behind,
In happier meanness occupy the mind:
As in those domes where Caesars once bore sway,
Defaced by time, and tottering in decay,   160
There in the ruin, heedless of the dead,
The shelter-seeking peasant builds his shed;
And, wondering man could want the larger pile,
Exults, and owns his cottage with a smile.
  My soul, turn from them; turn we to survey
Where rougher climes a nobler race display,
Where the bleak Swiss their stormy mansions tread,
And force a churlish soil for scanty bread;
No product here the barren hills afford
But man and steel, the soldier and his sword;   170

No vernal blooms their torpid rocks array,
But winter lingering chills the lap of May;
No zephyr fondly sues the mountain's breast,
But meteors glare, and stormy glooms invest.
    Yet still, even here, content can spread a charm,
Redress the clime, and all its rage disarm.
Though poor the peasant's hut, his feasts though small,
He sees his little lot the lot of all;
Sees no contiguous palace rear its head,
To shame the meanness of his humble shed;   180
No costly lord the sumptuous banquet deal,
To make him loathe his vegetable meal;
But calm, and bred in ignorance and toil,
Each wish contracting, fits him to the soil.
Cheerful at morn, he wakes from short repose,
Breasts the keen air, and carols as he goes;
With patient angle trolls the finny deep,
Or drives his venturous ploughshare to the steep;
Or seeks the den where snow-tracks mark the way,
And drags the struggling savage[1] into day.   190
At night returning, every labor sped,
He sits him down the monarch of a shed;
Smiles, by his cheerful fire and round surveys
His children's looks, that brighten at the blaze;
While his loved partner, boastful of her hoard,
Displays her cleanly platter on the board;
And haply too some pilgrim, thither led,
With many a tale repays the nightly bed.
    Thus every good his native wilds impart
Imprints the patriot passion on his heart;   200
And even those ills that round his mansion rise,
Enhance the bliss his scanty fund supplies.
Dear is that shed to which his soul conforms,
And dear that hill which lifts him to the storms;
And as a child, when scaring sounds molest,
Clings close and closer to the mother's breast,
So the loud torrent and the whirlwind's roar
But bind him to his native mountains more.
    Such are the charms to barren states assigned,
Their wants but few, their wishes all confined;   210
Yet let them only share the praises due;
If few their wants, their pleasures are but few;
For every want that stimulates the breast
Becomes a source of pleasure when redressed:
Whence from such lands each pleasing science flies,
That first excites desire and then supplies;
Unknown to them, when sensual pleasures cloy,
To fill the languid pause with finer joy;
Unknown those powers that raise the soul to flame,
Catch every nerve and vibrate through the frame;   220
Their level life is but a smoldering fire,
Unquenched by want, unfanned by strong desire;
Unfit for raptures, or, if raptures cheer,
On some high festival of once a year,

[1] Wild beast.

In wild excess the vulgar breast takes fire,
Till, buried in debauch, the bliss expire.
  But not their joys alone thus coarsely flow;
Their morals, like their pleasures, are but low;
For, as refinement stops, from sire to son
Unaltered, unimproved, the manners run;   230
And love's and friendship's finely pointed dart
Fall blunted from each indurated heart.
Some sterner virtues o'er the mountain's breast
May sit, like falcons cowering on the nest;
But all the gentler morals, such as play
Through life's more cultured walks, and charm the way,
These, far dispersed, on timorous pinions fly,
To sport and flutter in a kinder sky.
  To kinder skies, where gentler manners reign,
I turn; and France displays her bright domain.   240
Gay, sprightly land of mirth and social ease,
Pleased with thyself, whom all the world can please,
How often have I led thy sportive choir,
With tuneless pipe, beside the murmuring Loire!
Where shading elms along the margin grew,
And freshened from the wave the zephyr flew.
And haply, though my harsh touch, faltering still,
But mocked all tune, and marred the dancer's skill;
Yet would the village praise my wondrous power,
And dance, forgetful of the noontide hour.   250
Alike all ages: dames of ancient days
Have led their children through the mirthful maze;
And the gay grandsire, skilled in gestic[2] lore,
Has frisked beneath the burden of threescore.
  So blessed a life these thoughtless realms display,
Thus idly busy rolls their world away;
Theirs are those arts that mind to mind endear,
For honor forms the social temper here:
Honor, that praise which real merit gains,
Or e'en imaginary worth obtains,   260
Here passes current; paid from hand to hand,
It shifts in splendid traffic round the land:
From courts to camps, to cottages it strays,
And all are taught an avarice of praise;
They please, are pleased, they give to get esteem,
Till, seeming blessed, they grow to what they seem.
  But while this softer art their bliss supplies,
It gives their follies also room to rise;
For praise too dearly loved, or warmly sought,
Enfeebles all internal strength of thought;   270
And the weak soul, within itself unblessed,
Leans for all pleasure on another's breast.
Hence Ostentation here, with tawdry art,
Pants for the vulgar praise which fools impart;
Here Vanity assumes her pert grimace,
And trims her robes of frieze with copper lace;
Here beggar Pride defrauds her daily cheer,

[2] Pertaining to bodily movement, especially dancing.

To boast one splendid banquet once a year:
The mind still turns where shifting fashion draws,
Nor weighs the solid worth of self-applause.   280
　　To men of other minds my fancy flies,
Embosomed in the deep where Holland lies.
Methinks her patient sons before me stand,
Where the broad ocean leans against the land,
And, sedulous to stop the coming tide,
Lift the tall rampire's artificial pride.
Onward, methinks, and diligently slow,
The firm connected bulwark seems to grow,
Spreads its long arms amidst the watery roar,
Scoops out an empire, and usurps the shore;   290
While the pent ocean, rising o'er the pile,
Sees an amphibious world beneath him smile:
The slow canal, the yellow-blossomed vale,
The willow-tufted bank, the gliding sail,
The crowded mart, the cultivated plain,
A new creation rescued from his reign.
　　Thus, while around the wave-subjected soil
Impels the native to repeated toil,
Industrious habits in each bosom reign,
And industry begets a love of gain.   300
Hence all the good from opulence that springs,
With all those ills superfluous treasure brings,
Are here displayed. Their much-loved wealth imparts
Convenience, plenty, elegance, and arts;
But, view them closer, craft and fraud appear;
Even liberty itself is bartered here.
At gold's superior charms all freedom flies,
The needy sell it, and the rich man buys;
A land of tyrants, and a den of slaves,
Here wretches seek dishonorable graves,   310
And calmly bent, to servitude conform,
Dull as their lakes that slumber in the storm.
　　Heavens! how unlike their Belgic sires of old!
Rough, poor, content, ungovernably bold,
War in each breast, and freedom on each brow,
How much unlike the sons of Britain now!
　　Fired at the sound, my genius spreads her wing,
And flies where Britain courts the western spring;
Where lawns extend that scorn Arcadian pride,
And brighter streams than famed Hydaspes glide;   320
There all around the gentlest breezes stray,
There gentle music melts on every spray;
Creation's mildest charms are there combined;
Extremes are only in the master's mind.
Stern o'er each bosom Reason holds her state,
With daring aims irregularly great.
Pride in their port, defiance in their eye,
I see the lords of human kind pass by;
Intent on high designs, a thoughtful band,
By forms unfashioned, fresh from Nature's hand,   330
Fierce in their native hardiness of soul,
True to imagined right, above control,

While even the peasant boasts these rights to scan,
And learns to venerate himself as man.
Thine, Freedom, thine the blessings pictured here,
Thine are those charms that dazzle and endear;
Too blessed indeed were such without alloy,
But, fostered even by Freedom, ills annoy;
That independence Britons prize too high,
Keeps man from man, and breaks the social tie;   340
The self-dependent lordlings stand alone,
All claims that bind and sweeten life unknown.
Here, by the bonds of nature feebly held,
Minds combat minds, repelling and repelled;
Ferments arise, imprisoned factions roar,
Repressed ambition struggles round her shore;
Till overwrought, the general system feels
Its motions stopped, or frenzy fire the wheels.
    Nor this the worst. As nature's ties decay,
As duty, love, and honor fail to sway,   350
Fictitious bonds, the bonds of wealth and law,
Still gather strength, and force unwilling awe.
Hence all obedience bows to these alone,
And talent sinks, and merit weeps unknown;
Till time may come, when, stripped of all her charms,
The land of scholars and the nurse of arms,
Where noble stems transmit the patriot flame,
Where kings have toiled and poets wrote for fame,
One sink of level avarice shall lie,
And scholars, soldiers, kings, unhonored die.   360
    Yet think not, thus when Freedom's ills I state,
I mean to flatter kings or court the great:
Ye powers of truth, that bid my soul aspire,
Far from my bosom drive the low desire!
And thou, fair Freedom, taught alike to feel
The rabble's rage, and tyrant's angry steel;
Thou transitory flower, alike undone
By proud contempt or favor's fostering sun,
Still may thy blooms the changeful clime endure!
I only would repress them to secure;   370
For just experience tells, in every soil,
That those who think must govern those that toil;
And all that Freedom's highest aims can reach
Is but to lay proportioned loads on each.
Hence, should one order disproportioned grow,
Its double weight must ruin all below.
    Oh, then how blind to all that truth requires,
Who think it freedom when a part aspires!
Calm is my soul, nor apt to rise to arms,
Except when fast-approaching danger warms: 380
But when contending chiefs blockade the throne,
Contracting regal power to stretch their own;
When I behold a factious band agree
To call it freedom when themselves are free;
Each wanton judge new penal statutes draw,
Laws grind the poor, and rich men rule the law;

The wealth of climes where savage nations roam,
Pillaged from slaves to purchase slaves at home;
Fear, pity, justice, indignation, start,
Tear off reserve, and bare my swelling heart;   390
Till, half a patriot, half a coward grown,
I fly from petty tyrants to the throne.
  Yes, brother, curse with me that baleful hour
When first ambition struck at regal power;
And thus polluting honor in its source,
Gave wealth to sway the mind with double force.
Have we not seen, round Britain's peopled shore,
Her useful sons exchanged for useless ore?
Seen all her triumphs but destruction haste,
Like flaring tapers brightening as they waste?   400
Seen Opulence, her grandeur to maintain,
Lead stern Depopulation in her train,
And over fields where scattered hamlets rose,
In barren solitary pomp repose?
Have ye not seen, at Pleasure's lordly call,
The smiling, long-frequented village fall?
Beheld the duteous son, the sire decayed,
The modest matron, and the blushing maid,
Forced from their homes, a melancholy train,
To traverse climes beyond the western main;   410
Where wild Oswego spreads her swamps around,
And Niagara stuns with thundering sound?
  Even now, perhaps, as there some pilgrim strays
Through tangled forests and through dangerous ways,
Where beasts with man divided empire claim,
And the brown Indian marks with murderous aim;
There, while above the giddy tempest flies,
And all around distressful yells arise,
The pensive exile, bending with his woe,
To stop too fearful, and too faint to go,   420
Casts a long look where England's glories shine,
And bids his bosom sympathize with mine.
  Vain, very vain, my weary search to find
That bliss which only centers in the mind.
Why have I strayed from pleasure and repose,
To seek a good each government bestows?
In every government, though terrors reign,
Though tyrant kings or tyrant laws restrain,
How small, of all that human hearts endure,
That part which laws or kings can cause or cure!   430
Still to ourselves in every place consigned,
Our own felicity we make or find;
With secret course which no loud storms annoy,
Glides the smooth current of domestic joy.
The lifted axe, the agonizing wheel,
Luke's iron crown, and Damiens' bed of steel,
To men remote from power but rarely known,
Leave reason, faith, and conscience all our own.

[1764]

SONG

When lovely woman stoops to folly,
And finds too late that men betray,
What charm can soothe her melancholy?
What art can wash her guilt away?

The only art her guilt to cover,
To hide her shame from every eye,
To give repentance to her lover,
And wring his bosom, is—to die.

[1766]

THE DESERTED VILLAGE

TO SIR JOSHUA REYNOLDS

DEAR SIR,—I can have no expectations in an address of this kind, either to add to your reputation, or to establish my own. You can gain nothing from my admiration, as I am ignorant of that art in which you are said to excel; and I may lose much by the severity of your judgment, as few have a juster taste in poetry than you. Setting interest therefore aside, to which I never paid much attention, I must be indulged at present in following my affections. The only dedication I ever made was to my brother, because I loved him better than most other men. He is since dead. Permit me to inscribe this poem to you.

How far you may be pleased with the versification and mere mechanical parts of this attempt, I don't pretend to inquire; but I know you will object (and indeed several of our best and wisest friends concur in the opinion) that the depopulation it deplores is nowhere to be seen, and the disorders it laments are only to be found in the poet's own imagination. To this I can scarce make any other answer, than that I sincerely believe what I have written; that I have taken all possible pains in my country excursions, for these four or five years past, to be certain of what I allege; and that all my views and inquiries have led me to believe those miseries real which I here attempt to display. But this is not the place to enter into an inquiry, whether the country be depopulating or not; the discussion would take up much room, and I should prove myself, at best, an indifferent politician, to tire the reader with a long preface, when I want his unfatigued attention to a long poem.

In regretting the depopulation of the country, I inveigh against the increase of our luxuries; and here also I expect the shout of modern politicians against me. For twenty or thirty years past it has been the fashion to consider luxury as one of the greatest national advantages, and all the wisdom of antiquity, in that particular, as erroneous. Still, however, I must remain a professed ancient on that head, and continue to think those luxuries prejudicial to states by which so many vices are introduced and so many kingdoms have been undone. Indeed so much has been poured out of late on the other side of the question, that, merely for the sake of novelty and variety, one would sometimes wish to be in the right.

I am, dear sir, your sincere friend, and ardent admirer,

OLIVER GOLDSMITH.

Sweet Auburn! loveliest village of the plain,
Where health and plenty cheered the laboring swain,
Where smiling spring its earliest visit paid,
And parting summer's lingering blooms delayed;
Dear lovely bowers of innocence and ease,
Seats of my youth, when every sport could please,
How often have I loitered o'er thy green,
Where humble happiness endeared each scene!
How often have I paused on every charm,
The sheltered cot, the cultivated farm,   10
The never-failing brook, the busy mill,
The decent church that topped the neighboring hill,
The hawthorn bush, with seats beneath the shade,
For talking age and whispering lovers made!
How often have I blessed the coming day,

When toil remitting lent its turn to play,
And all the village train, from labor free,
Led up their sports beneath the spreading tree;
While many a pastime circled in the shade,
The young contending as the old surveyed; 20
And many a gambol frolicked o'er the ground,
And sleights of art and feats of strength went round;
And still, as each repeated pleasure tired,
Succeeding sports the mirthful band inspired;
The dancing pair that simply sought renown,
By holding out to tire each other down;
The swain mistrustless of his smutted face,
While secret laughter tittered round the place;
The bashful virgin's sidelong looks of love,
The matron's glance that would those looks reprove— 30
These were thy charms, sweet village! sports like these,
With sweet succession taught even toil to please;
These round thy bowers their cheerful influence shed;
These were thy charms—but all these charms are fled.

Sweet smiling village, loveliest of the lawn,
Thy sports are fled and all thy charms withdrawn;
Amidst thy bowers the tyrant's hand is seen,
And desolation saddens all thy green;
One only master grasps the whole domain,
And half a tillage stints thy smiling plain; 40
No more thy glassy brook reflects the day,
But choked with sedges works its weedy way;
Along thy glades, a solitary guest,
The hollow-sounding bittern guards its nest;
Amidst thy desert walks the lapwing flies,
And tires their echoes with unvaried cries.
Sunk are thy bowers in shapeless ruin all,
And the long grass o'ertops the moldering wall;
And, trembling, shrinking from the spoiler's hand,
Far, far away, thy children leave the land. 50

Ill fares the land, to hastening ills a prey,
Where wealth accumulates and men decay;
Princes and lords may flourish or may fade;
A breath can make them as a breath has made:
But a bold peasantry, their country's pride,
When once destroyed, can never be supplied.

A time there was, ere England's griefs began,
When every rood of ground maintained its man;
For him light labor spread her wholesome store,
Just gave what life required, but gave no more: 60
His best companions, innocence and health;
And his best riches, ignorance of wealth.

But times are altered; trade's unfeeling train
Usurp the land, and dispossess the swain;
Along the lawn, where scattered hamlets rose,
Unwieldy wealth and cumbrous pomp repose;
And every want to opulence allied,
And every pang that folly pays to pride.
Those gentle hours that plenty bade to bloom,
Those calm desires that asked but little room. 70

Those healthful sports that graced the peaceful scene,
Lived in each look, and brightened all the green—
These, far departing, seek a kinder shore,
And rural mirth and manners are no more.
Sweet Auburn! parent of the blissful hour,
Thy glades forlorn confess the tyrant's power.
Here, as I take my solitary rounds
Amidst thy tangling walks and ruined grounds,
And, many a year elapsed, return to view
Where once the cottage stood, the hawthorn grew,   80
Remembrance wakes with all her busy train,
Swells at my breast, and turns the past to pain.
    In all my wanderings round this world of care,
In all my griefs—and God has given my share—
I still had hopes, my latest hours to crown,
Amidst these humble bowers to lay me down;
To husband out life's taper at the close,
And keep the flame from wasting by repose.
I still had hopes, for pride attends us still,
Amidst the swains to show my book-learned skill,   90
Around my fire an evening group to draw,
And tell of all I felt, and all I saw;
And, as a hare whom hounds and horns pursue,
Pants to the place from whence at first she flew,
I still had hopes, my long vexations past,
Here to return—and die at home at last.
    O blessed retirement, friend to life's decline,
Retreats from care, that never must be mine,
How happy he who crowns in shades like these
A youth of labor with an age of ease;   100
Who quits a world where strong temptations try,
And, since 'tis hard to combat, learns to fly!
For him no wretches, born to work and weep,
Explore the mine, or tempt the dangerous deep;
No surly porter stands in guilty state,
To spurn imploring famine from the gate;
But on he moves to meet his latter end,
Angels around befriending virtue's friend;
Bends to the grave with unperceived decay,
While resignation gently slopes the way;   110
And, all his prospects brightening to the last,
His heaven commences ere the world be past.
    Sweet was the sound, when oft at evening's close
Up yonder hill the village murmur rose;
There, as I passed with careless steps and slow,
The mingling notes came softened from below;
The swain responsive as the milkmaid sung,
The sober herd that lowed to meet their young,
The noisy geese that gabbled o'er the pool,
The playful children just let loose from school,   120
The watch-dog's voice that bayed the whispering wind,
And the loud laugh that spoke the vacant[1] mind—
These all in sweet confusion sought the shade,

[1] Carefree.

And filled each pause the nightingale had made.
But now the sounds of population fail,
No cheerful murmurs fluctuate in the gale,
No busy steps the grass-grown footway tread,
For all the bloomy flush of life is fled;
All but yon widowed, solitary thing,
That feebly bends beside the plashy spring;   130
She, wretched matron, forced in age, for bread,
To strip the brook with mantling cresses spread,
To pick her wintry fagot from the thorn,
To seek her nightly shed, and weep till morn—
She only left of all the harmless train,
The sad historian of the pensive plain.
    Near yonder copse, where once the garden smiled,
And still where many a garden flower grows wild,
There, where a few torn shrubs the place disclose,
The village preacher's modest mansion rose.   140
A man he was to all the country dear,
And passing rich with forty pounds a year;
Remote from towns he ran his godly race,
Nor e'er had changed, nor wished to change his place;
Unpractised he to fawn, or seek for power,
By doctrines fashioned to the varying hour;
Far other aims his heart had learned to prize,
More skilled to raise the wretched than to rise.
His house was known to all the vagrant train;
He chid their wanderings, but relieved their pain;   150
The long-remembered beggar was his guest,
Whose beard descending swept his aged breast;
The ruined spendthrift, now no longer proud,
Claimed kindred there, and has his claims allowed;
The broken soldier, kindly bade to stay,
Sat by his fire and talked the night away;
Wept o'er his wounds, or, tales of sorrow done,
Shouldered his crutch and showed how fields were won.
Pleased with his guests, the good man learned to glow,
And quite forgot their vices in their woe;   160
Careless their merits or their faults to scan,
His pity gave ere charity began.
    Thus to relieve the wretched was his pride,
And even his failings leaned to virtue's side;
But in his duty prompt at every call,
He watched and wept, he prayed and felt for all:
And, as a bird each fond endearment tries
To tempt its new-fledged offspring to the skies,
He tried each art, reproved each dull delay,
Allured to brighter worlds, and led the way.   170
    Beside the bed where parting life was laid,
And sorrow, guilt, and pain by turns dismayed,
The reverend champion stood. At his control
Despair and anguish fled the struggling soul;
Comfort came down the trembling wretch to raise,
And his last faltering accents whispered praise.
    At church, with meek and unaffected grace,
His looks adorned the venerable place;

Truth from his lips prevailed with double sway,
And fools who came to scoff remained to pray.   180
The service past, around the pious man,
With steady zeal, each honest rustic ran;
Even children followed, with endearing wile,
And plucked his gown, to share the good man's smile.
His ready smile a parent's warmth expressed,
Their welfare pleased him and their cares distressed;
To them his heart, his love, his griefs were given,
But all his serious thoughts had rest in Heaven.
As some tall cliff, that lifts its awful form,
Swells from the vale, and midway leaves the storm,   190
Though round its breast the rolling clouds are spread,
Eternal sunshine settles on its head.
　　Beside yon straggling fence that skirts the way,
With blossomed furze unprofitably gay,
There, in his noisy mansion, skilled to rule,
The village master taught his little school.
A man severe he was, and stern to view;
I knew him well, and every truant knew;
Well had the boding tremblers learned to trace
The day's disasters in his morning face;   200
Full well they laughed with counterfeited glee
At all his jokes, for many a joke had he;
Full well the busy whisper, circling round,
Conveyed the dismal tidings when he frowned;
Yet he was kind, or, if severe in aught,
The love he bore to learning was in fault;
The village all declared how much he knew;
'Twas certain he could write, and cipher too;
Lands he could measure, terms and tides presage,
And even the story ran that he could gauge: 210
In arguing, too, the parson owned his skill,
For even though vanquished, he could argue still;
While words of learned length and thundering sound
Amazed the gazing rustics ranged around;
And still they gazed, and still the wonder grew
That one small head could carry all he knew.
　　But past is all his fame. The very spot
Where many a time he triumphed is forgot.
Near yonder thorn that lifts its head on high,
Where once the sign-post caught the passing eye,   220
Low lies that house where nut-brown draughts inspired,
Where graybeard mirth and smiling toil retired,
Where village statesmen talked with looks profound,
And news much older than their ale went round.
Imagination fondly stoops to trace
The parlor splendors of that festive place;
The whitewashed wall, the nicely sanded floor,
The varnished clock that clicked behind the door;
The chest contrived a double debt to pay,
A bed by night, a chest of drawers by day;   230
The pictures placed for ornament and use,
The twelve good rules, the royal game of goose;
The hearth, except when winter chilled the day,

With aspen boughs and flowers and fennel gay;
While broken teacups, wisely kept for show,
Ranged o'er the chimney, glistened in a row.
   Vain transitory splendors! Could not all
Reprieve the tottering mansion from its fall?
Obscure it sinks, nor shall it more impart
An hour's importance to the poor man's heart;   240
Thither no more the peasant shall repair
To sweet oblivion of his daily care;
No more the farmer's news, the barber's tale,
No more the woodman's ballad shall prevail;
No more the smith his dusky brow shall clear,
Relax his ponderous strength, and lean to hear;
The host himself no longer shall be found
Careful to see the mantling bliss go round;
Nor the coy maid, half willing to be pressed,
Shall kiss the cup to pass it to the rest.   250
   Yes! let the rich deride, the proud disdain,
These simple blessings of the lowly train;
To me more dear, congenial to my heart,
One native charm, than all the gloss of art;
Spontaneous joys, where nature has its play,
The soul adopts, and owns their first-born sway;
Lightly they frolic o'er the vacant mind,
Unenvied, unmolested, unconfined.
But the long pomp, the midnight masquerade,
With all the freaks of wanton wealth arrayed,—   260
In these, ere triflers half their wish obtain,
The toiling pleasure sickens into pain;
And e'en while fashion's brightest arts decoy,
The heart distrusting asks if this be joy.
   Ye friends to truth, ye statesmen, who survey
The rich man's joys increase, the poor's decay,
'Tis yours to judge how wide the limits stand
Between a splendid and an happy land.
Proud swells the tide with loads of freighted ore,
And shouting Folly hails them from her shore;   270
Hoards even beyond the miser's wish abound,
And rich men flock from all the world around.
Yet count our gains: this wealth is but a name
That leaves our useful products still the same.
Not so the loss: the man of wealth and pride
Takes up a space that many poor supplied;
Space for his lake, his park's extended bounds,
Space for his horses, equipage, and hounds;
The robe that wraps his limbs in silken sloth
Has robbed the neighboring fields of half their growth;   280
His seat, where solitary sports are seen,
Indignant spurns the cottage from the green;
Around the world each needful product flies,
For all the luxuries the world supplies;
While thus the land, adorned for pleasure all,
In barren splendor feebly waits the fall.
   As some fair female, unadorned and plain,
Secure to please while youth confirms her reign,

Slights every borrowed charm that dress supplies,
Nor shares with art the triumph of her eyes;   290
But when those charms are past, for charms are frail,
When time advances and when lovers fail,
She then shines forth, solicitous to bless,
In all the glaring impotence of dress:
Thus fares the land, by luxury betrayed,
In nature's simplest charms at first arrayed;
But verging to decline, its splendors rise,
Its vistas strike, its palaces surprise;
While, scourged by famine from the smiling land,
The mournful peasant leads his humble band;   300
And while he sinks, without one arm to save,
The country blooms—a garden and a grave.
   Where then, ah! where shall poverty reside,
To 'scape the pressure of contiguous pride?
If to some common's fenceless limits strayed,
He drives his flock to pick the scanty blade,
Those fenceless fields the sons of wealth divide,
And even the bare-worn common is denied.
   If to the city sped—what waits him there?
To see profusion that he must not share;   310
To see ten thousand baneful arts combined
To pamper luxury, and thin mankind;
To see those joys the sons of pleasure know
Extorted from his fellow-creature's woe.
Here while the courtier glitters in brocade,
There the pale artist[2] plies the sickly trade;
Here while the proud their long-drawn pomps display,
There the black gibbet glooms beside the way;
The dome where Pleasure holds her midnight reign,
Here, richly decked, admits the gorgeous train;   320
Tumultuous grandeur crowds the blazing square,
The rattling chariots clash, the torches glare.
Sure scenes like these no troubles e'er annoy!
Sure these denote one universal joy!
Are these thy serious thoughts?—Ah, turn thine eyes
Where the poor houseless shivering female lies.
She once, perhaps, in village plenty blessed,
Has wept at tales of innocence distressed;
Her modest looks the cottage might adorn,
Sweet as the primrose peeps beneath the thorn;   330
Now lost to all—her friends, her virtue fled—
Near her betrayer's door she lays her head,
And, pinched with cold, and shrinking from the shower,
With heavy heart deplores that luckless hour,
When idly first, ambitious of the town,
She left her wheel and robes of country brown.
   Do thine, sweet Auburn, thine, the loveliest train—
Do thy fair tribes participate her pain?
Even now, perhaps, by cold and hunger led,
At proud men's doors they ask a little bread.   340
   Ah, no! To distant climes, a dreary scene,
Where half the convex world intrudes between,

[2] Artisan.

Through torrid tracts with fainting steps they go,
Where wild Altama murmurs to their woe.
Far different there from all that charmed before,
The various terrors of that horrid shore;
Those blazing suns that dart a downward ray,
And fiercely shed intolerable day;
Those matted woods where birds forget to sing,
But silent bats in drowsy clusters cling;   350
Those poisonous fields with rank luxuriance crowned,
Where the dark scorpion gathers death around;
Where at each step the stranger fears to wake
The rattling terrors of the vengeful snake;
Where crouching tigers wait their hapless prey,
And savage men more murderous still than they;
While oft in whirls the mad tornado flies,
Mingling the ravaged landscape with the skies.
Far different these from every former scene,
The cooling brook, the grassy-vested green,   360
The breezy covert of the warbling grove,
That only sheltered thefts of harmless love.
    Good Heaven! what sorrows gloomed that parting day
That called them from their native walks away;
When the poor exiles, every pleasure past,
Hung round their bowers, and fondly looked their last,
And took a long farewell, and wished in vain
For seats like these beyond the western main;
And, shuddering still to face the distant deep,
Returned and wept, and still returned to weep.   370
The good old sire the first prepared to go
To new-found worlds, and wept for others' woe;
But for himself, in conscious virtue brave,
He only wished for worlds beyond the grave.
His lovely daughter, lovelier in her tears,
The fond companion of his helpless years,
Silent went next, neglectful of her charms,
And left a lover's for a father's arms.
With louder plaints the mother spoke her woes,
And blessed the cot where every pleasure rose,   380
And kissed her thoughtless babes with many a tear,
And clasped them close, in sorrow doubly dear;
Whilst her fond husband strove to lend relief
In all the silent manliness of grief.
    O Luxury! thou cursed by Heaven's decree,
How ill exchanged are things like these for thee!
How do thy potions, with insidious joy,
Diffuse their pleasures only to destroy!
Kingdoms by thee, to sickly greatness grown,
Boast of a florid vigor not their own: 390
At every draught more large and large they grow,
A bloated mass of rank, unwieldly woe;
Till, sapped their strength, and every part unsound,
Down, down they sink, and spread a ruin round.
    Even now the devastation is begun,
And half the business of destruction done;
Even now, methinks, as pondering here I stand,

I see the rural virtues leave the land:
Down where yon anchoring vessel spreads the sail,
That idly waiting flaps with every gale,   400
Downward they move, a melancholy band,
Pass from the shore, and darken all the strand.
Contented Toil, and hospitable Care,
And kind connubial Tenderness are there;
And Piety with wishes placed above,
And steady Loyalty, and faithful Love.
And thou, sweet Poetry, thou loveliest maid,
Still first to fly where sensual joys invade,
Unfit, in these degenerate times of shame,
To catch the heart, or strike for honest fame;   410
Dear charming nymph, neglected and decried,
My shame in crowds, my solitary pride;
Thou source of all my bliss and all my woe,
That found'st me poor at first, and keep'st me so;
Thou guide by which the nobler arts excel,
Thou nurse of every virtue, fare thee well!
Farewell! and oh! where'er thy voice be tried,
On Torno's cliffs, or Pambamarca's side,
Whether where equinoctial fervors glow,
Or winter wraps the polar world in snow,   420
Still let thy voice, prevailing over time,
Redress the rigors of the inclement clime;
Aid slighted truth with thy persuasive train;
Teach erring man to spurn the rage of gain;
Teach him, that states of native strength possessed,
Though very poor, may still be very blessed;
That trade's proud empire hastes to swift decay,
As ocean sweeps the labored mole away;
While self-dependent power can time defy,
As rocks resist the billows and the sky.   430

[1770]

RETALIATION

Of old, when Scarron his companions invited,
Each guest brought his dish, and the feast was united.
If our landlord supplies us with beef and with fish,
Let each guest bring himself, and he brings the best dish:
Our Dean shall be venison, just fresh from the plains;
Our Burke shall be tongue, with a garnish of brains;
Our Will shall be wild fowl, of excellent flavor,
And Dick with his pepper, shall heighten their savor;
Our Cumberland's sweetbread its place shall obtain,
And Douglas is pudding, substantial and plain;   10
Our Garrick's a salad, for in him we see
Oil, vinegar, sugar, and saltness agree;
To make out the dinner full certain I am,
That Ridge is anchovy, and Reynolds is lamb;
That Hickey's a capon, and by the same rule,
Magnanimous Goldsmith a gooseberry fool.

At a dinner so various, at such a repast,
Who'd not be a glutton, and stick to the last?
Here, waiter, more wine, let me sit while I'm able,
Till all my companions sink under the table;   20
Then, with chaos and blunders encircling my head,
Let me ponder, and tell what I think of the dead.
  Here lies the good Dean, reunited to earth,
Who mixed reason with pleasure, and wisdom with mirth:
If he had any faults, he has left us in doubt,
At least, in six weeks I could not find 'em out;
Yet some have declared, and it can't be denied 'em,
That sly-boots was cursedly cunning to hide 'em.
  Here lies our good Edmund, whose genius was such,
We scarcely can praise it or blame it too much;   30
Who, born for the universe, narrowed his mind,
And to party gave up what was meant for mankind:
Though fraught with all learning, yet straining his throat
To persuade Tommy Townshend to lend him a vote;
Who, too deep for his hearers, still went on refining,
And thought of convincing, while they thought of dining;
Though equal to all things, for all things unfit;
Too nice for a statesman, too proud for a wit;
For a patriot too cool; for a drudge disobedient;
And too fond of the right to pursue the expedient.   40
In short, 'twas his fate, unemployed or in place, sir,
To eat mutton cold, and cut blocks with a razor.
  Here lies honest William, whose heart was a mint,
While the owner ne'er knew half the good that was in't;
The pupil of impulse, it forced him along,
His conduct still right, with his argument wrong;
Still aiming at honor, yet fearing to roam,
The coachman was tipsy, the chariot drove home.
Would you ask for his merits? alas! he had none;
What was good was spontaneous, his faults were his own.   50
  Here lies honest Richard, whose fate I must sigh at;
Alas! that such frolic should now be so quiet!
What spirits were his! what wit and what whim!
Now breaking a jest, and now breaking a limb!
Now wrangling and grumbling to keep up the ball!
Now teasing and vexing, yet laughing at all!
In short, so provoking a devil was Dick,
That we wished him full ten times a day at Old Nick;
But, missing his mirth and agreeable vein,
As often we wished to have Dick back again.   60
  Here Cumberland lies, having acted his parts,
The Terence of England, the mender of hearts;
A flattering painter, who made it his care
To draw men as they ought to be, not as they are.
His gallants are all faultless, his women divine,
And Comedy wonders at being so fine:
Like a tragedy queen he has dizened her out,
Or rather like Tragedy giving a rout.
His fools have their follies so lost in a crowd
Of virtues and feelings, that folly grows proud;   70
And coxcombs alike in their failings alone,

Adopting his portraits, are pleased with their own.
Say, where has our poet this malady caught?
Or wherefore his characters thus without fault?
Say, was it that vainly directing his view
To find out men's virtues, and finding then few,
Quite sick of pursuing each troublesome elf,
He grew lazy at last, and drew from himself?
   Here Douglas retires from his toils to relax,
The scourge of impostors, the terror of quacks: 80
Come, all ye quack bards, and ye quacking divines,
Come and dance on the spot where your tyrant reclines:
When satire and censure encircled his throne,
I feared for your safety, I feared for my own;
But now he is gone, and we want a detector;
Our Dodds shall be pious, our Kenricks shall lecture;
Macpherson write bombast, and call it a style;
Our Townshend make speeches, and I shall compile;
New Lauders and Bowers the Tweed shall cross over,
No countryman living their tricks to discover;   90
Detection her taper shall quench to a spark,
And Scotchman meet Scotchman, and cheat in the dark.
   Here lies David Garrick—describe me who can
An abridgment of all that was pleasant in man:
As an actor, confessed without rival to shine;
As a wit, if not first, in the very first line;
Yet, with talents like these, and an excellent heart,
The man had his failings—a dupe to his art.
Like an ill-judging beauty, his colors he spread,
And beplastered with rouge his own natural red.   100
On the stage he was natural, simple, affecting;
'Twas only that when he was off he was acting.
With no reason on earth to go out of his way,
He turned and he varied full ten times a day:
Though secure of our hearts, yet confoundedly sick
If they were not his own by finessing and trick:
He cast off his friends, as a huntsman his pack,
For he knew when he pleased he could whistle them back.
Of praise a mere glutton, he swallowed what came,
And the puff of a dunce, he mistook it for fame;   110
Till his relish grown callous, almost to disease,
Who peppered the highest was surest to please.
But let us be candid, and speak out our mind;
If dunces applauded, he paid them in kind.
Ye Kenricks, ye Kellys, and Woodfalls so grave,
What a commerce was yours while you got and you gave!
How did Grub Street re-echo the shouts that you raised,
While he was be-Rosciused, and you were be-praised!
But peace to his spirit, wherever it flies,
To act as an angel and mix with the skies;   120
Those poets who owe their best fame to his skill
Shall still be his flatterers, go where he will;
Old Shakespeare receive him with praise and with love,
And Beaumonts and Bens be his Kellys above.
   Here Hickey reclines, a most blunt, pleasant creature,
And slander itself must allow him good nature

He cherished his friend, and he relished a bumper;
Yet one fault he had, and that one was a thumper.
Perhaps you may ask if the man was a miser?
I answer, no, no, for he always was wiser.   130
Too courteous, perhaps, or obligingly flat?
His very worst foe can't accuse him of that.
Perhaps he confided in men as they go,
And so was too foolishly honest? Ah no!
Then what was his failing? come, tell it, and burn ye.
He was—could he help it?—a special attorney.
    Here Reynolds is laid, and, to tell you my mind,
He has not left a wiser or better behind.
His pencil was striking, resistless, and grand;
His manners were gentle, complying, and bland;   140
Still born to improve us in every part,
His pencil our faces, his manners our heart:
To coxcombs averse, yet most civilly steering,
When they judged without skill he was still hard of hearing;
When they talked of their Raphaels, Correggios, and stuff,
He shifted his trumpet and only took snuff.

[1774]

ASEM, AN EASTERN TALE; OR A VINDICATION OF THE WISDOM OF PROVIDENCE IN THE MORAL GOVERNMENT OF THE WORLD

Where Tauris lifts its head above the storm, and presents nothing to the sight of the distant traveller but a prospect of nodding rocks, falling torrents, and all the variety of tremendous Nature; on the bleak bosom of this frightful mountain, secluded from society, and detesting the ways of men, lived Asem the Man-hater.

Asem had spent his youth with men; had shared in their amusements; and had been taught to love his fellow creatures with the most ardent affection; but from the tenderness of his disposition he exhausted all his fortune in relieving the wants of the distressed. The petitioner never sued in vain; the weary traveller never passed his door; he only desisted from doing good when he had no longer the power of relieving.

From a fortune thus spent in benevolence he expected a grateful return from those he had formerly relieved; and made his application with confidence of redress: the ungrateful world soon grew weary of his importunity; for pity is but a short-lived passion. He soon therefore began to view mankind in a very different light from that in which he had before beheld them; he perceived a thousand vices he had never before suspected to exist: wherever he turned, ingratitude, dissimulation, and treachery, contributed to increase his detestation of them. Resolved, therefore, to continue no longer in a world which he hated, and which repaid his detestation with contempt, he retired to this region of sterility, in order to brood over his resentment in solitude, and converse with the only honest heart he knew, namely with his own.

A cave was his only shelter from the inclemency of the weather; fruits, gathered with difficulty from the mountain's side, his only food; and his drink was fetched with danger and toil from the headlong torrent. In this manner he lived, sequestered from society, passing the hours in meditation, and sometimes exulting that he was able to live independently of his fellow-creatures.

At the foot of the mountain an extensive lake displayed its glassy bosom, reflecting on its broad surface the impending horrors of the mountain. To this capacious mirror he would sometimes descend, and reclining on its steep banks, cast an eager look on the smooth expanse that lay before him. "How beautiful," he often cried, "is nature! How lovely even in her wildest scenes! How finely contrasted is the level plain that lies beneath me, with yon awful pile that hides its tremendous head in clouds! But the beauty of these scenes is no way comparable with their utility; from hence an hundred rivers are supplied, which distribute health and verdure to the various countries through which they flow. Every part of the universe is beautiful, just, and wise, but man: vile man is a solecism in nature; the only monster in the creation. Tempests and whirlwinds have their use; but vicious ungrateful man is a blot in the fair page of universal beauty. Why was I born of that detested species, whose vices are almost a reproach to the wisdom of the divine Creator? Were men entirely free from vice, all would be uniformity, harmony, and order. A world of moral rectitude should be the result of a perfect moral agent. Why, why then, O Alla! must I be thus confined in darkness, doubt, and despair?"

Just as he uttered the word Despair, he was going to plunge into the lake beneath him, at once to satisfy his doubts, and put a period to his anxiety; when he perceived a most majestic being walking on the surface of the water, and approaching the bank on which he stood. So unexpected an object at once checked his purpose; he stopped, contemplated, and fancied he saw something awful and divine in his aspect.

"Son of Adam," cried the Genius, "stop thy rash purpose; the Father of the faithful has seen thy justice, thy integrity, thy miseries, and hath sent me to afford and administer relief. Give me thine hand, and follow without trembling wherever I shall lead; in me behold the Genius of Conviction, kept by the Great Prophet to turn from their errors those who go astray, not from curiosity, but a rectitude of intention. Follow me and be wise."

Asem immediately descended upon the lake, and his guide conducted him along the surface of the water; till coming near the centre of the lake, they both began to sink; the waters closed over their heads; they descended several hundred fathoms, till Asem, just ready to give up his life as inevitably lost, found himself with his celestial guide in another world, at the bottom of the waters, where human foot had never trod before. His astonishment was beyond description, when he saw a sun like that he had left, a serene sky over his head, and blooming verdure under his feet.

"I plainly perceive your amazement," said the Genius; "but suspend it for a while. This world was formed by Alla, at the request, and under the inspection, of our great Prophet: who once entertained the same doubts which filled your mind when I found you, and from the consequence of which you were so lately rescued. The rational inhabitants of this world are formed agreeable to your own ideas; they are absolutely without vice. In other respects it resembles your earth, but differs from it in being wholly inhabited by men who never do wrong. If you find this world more agreeable than that you so lately left, you have free permission to spend the remainder of your days in it; but permit me for some time to attend you, that I may silence your doubts, and make you better acquainted with your company and your new habitation."

"A world without vice! Rational beings without immorality!" cried Asem in a rapture; "I thank thee, O Alla who hast at length heard my petitions; this, this indeed will produce happiness, ecstasy, and ease. O for an immortality to spend it among men who are incapable of ingratitude, injustice, fraud, violence, and a thousand other crimes, that render society miserable!"

"Cease thine acclamations," replied the Genius. "Look around thee; reflect on every object and action before us, and communicate to me the result of thine observations. Lead wherever you think proper, I shall be your attendant and instructor." Asem and his companion travelled on in silence for some time, the former being entirely lost in astonishment; but at last, recovering his former serenity, he could not help observing, that the face of the country bore a near resemblance to that he had left, except that this subterranean world still seemed to retain its primæval wildness.

"Here," cried Asem, "I perceive animals of prey, and others that seem only designed for their subsistence; it is the very same in the world over our heads. But had I been permitted to instruct our Prophet, I would have removed this defect, and formed no voracious or destructive animals which only prey on the other parts of the creation." "Your tenderness for inferior animals is, I find, remarkable," said the Genius, smiling. "But with regard to meaner creatures this world exactly resembles the other, and indeed for obvious reasons; for the earth can support a more considerable number of animals, by their thus becoming food for each other, than if they had lived entirely on the vegetable productions. So that animals of different natures thus formed, instead of lessening their multitude, subsist in the greatest number possible. But let us hasten on to the inhabited country before us, and see what that offers for instruction."

They soon gained the utmost verge of the forest, and entered the country inhabited by men without vice: and Asem anticipated in idea the rational delight he hoped to experience in such an innocent society. But they had scarce left the confines of the wood, when they beheld one of the inhabitants flying with hasty steps, and terror in his countenance, from an army of squirrels that closely pursued him. "Heavens!" cried Asem, "why does he fly? What can he fear from animals so contemptible?" He had scarcely spoke when he perceived two dogs pursuing another of the human species, who with equal terror and haste attempted to avoid them. "This," cried Asem to his guide, "is truly surprising; nor can I conceive the reason for so strange an action." "Every species of animals," replied the Genius, "has of late grown very powerful in this country; for the inhabitants at first thinking it unjust to use either fraud or force in destroying them, they have insensibly increased, and now frequently ravage their harmless frontiers." "But they should have been destroyed," cried Asem; "you see the consequence of such neglect." "Where is then that tenderness you so lately expressed for subordinate animals?" replied the Genius, smiling; "you seem to have forgot that branch of justice." I must acknowledge my mistake," returned Asem; "I am now convinced that we must be guilty of tyranny and injustice to the brute creation, if we would enjoy the world ourselves. But let us no longer observe the duty of man to these irrational creatures, but survey their connections with one another."

As they walked farther up the country, the more he was surprised to see no vestiges of handsome houses, no cities, nor any mark of elegant design. His conductor, perceiving his surprise, observed, that the inhabitants of this new world were perfectly content with their ancient simplicity; each had an house, which, though homely, was sufficient to lodge his little family; they were too good to build houses, which could only increase their own pride, and the envy of the spectator; what they built was for convenience, and not for show. "At least, then," said Asem, "they have neither architects, painters, nor statuaries, in their soci-

ety; but these are idle arts, and may be
spared. However, before I spend much
more time here, you should have my
thanks for introducing me into the
society of some of their wisest men:
there is scarcely any pleasure to me
equal to a refined conversation; there
is nothing of which I am so much
enamoured as wisdom." "Wisdom!" replied his instructor, "how ridiculous!
We have no wisdom here, for we have
no occasion for it; true wisdom is only
a knowledge of our own duty, and the
duty of others to us; but of what use
is such wisdom here? Each intuitively
performs what is right in himself, and
expects the same from others. If by wisdom you should mean vain curiosity,
and empty speculation, as such pleasures have their origin in vanity, luxury, or avarice, we are too good to pursue them." "All this may be right," says
Asem: "but methinks I observe a solitary disposition prevail among the
people; each family keeps separately
within their own precincts, without society or without intercourse." "That
indeed is true," replied the other;
"here is no established society; nor
should there be any; all societies are
made either through fear or friendship; the people we are among are too
good to fear each other; and there are
no motives to private friendship, where
all are equally meritorious." "Well
then," said the sceptic, "as I am to
spend my time here, if I am to have
neither the polite arts, nor wisdom,
nor friendship, in such a world, I
should be glad at least of an easy companion, who may tell me his thoughts,
and to whom I may communicate
mine." "And to what purpose should
either do this?" says the Genius; "flattery or curiosity are vicious motives,
and never allowed of here; and wisdom
is out of the question."

"Still however," said Asem, "the inhabitants must be happy; each is contented with his own possessions, nor
avariciously endeavours to heap up
more than is necessary for his own
subsistence: each has therefore leisure
for pitying those that stand in need

of his compassion." He had scarce
spoken when his ears were assaulted
with the lamentations of a wretch who
sat by the way-side, and in the most
deplorable distress seemed gently to
murmur at his own misery. Asem immediately ran to his relief, and found
him in the last stage of a consumption.
"Strange," cried the son of Adam,
"that men who are free from vice
should thus suffer so much misery
without relief!" "Be not surprised,"
said the wretch who was dying;
"would it not be the utmost injustice
for beings, who have only just sufficient to support themselves, and are
content with a bare subsistence, to
take it from their own mouths to put
it into mine? They never are possessed
of a single meal more than is necessary; and what is barely necessary cannot be dispensed with." "They should
have been supplied with more than is
necessary," cried Asem; "and yet I
contradict my own opinion but a moment before: all is doubt, perplexity,
and confusion. Even the want of ingratitude is no virtue here, since they
never received a favour. They have,
however, another excellence yet behind; the love of their country is still,
I hope, one of their darling virtues."
"Peace, Asem!" replied the Guardian,
with a countenance not less severe
than beautiful, "nor forfeit all thy
pretensions to wisdom; the same selfish motives, by which we prefer our
own interest to that of others, induce
us to regard our country preferably to
that of another. Nothing less than
universal benevolence is free from
vice, and that, you see, is practised
here." "Strange!" cries the disappointed pilgrim, in an agony of distress; "what sort of a world am I
now introduced to? There is scarce a
single virtue, but that of temperance,
which they practise; and in that they
are in no way superior to the very
brute creation. There is scarce an
amusement which they enjoy: fortitude, liberality, friendship, wisdom,
conversation, and love of country, all
are virtues entirely unknown here;

thus it seems that to be unacquainted with vice is not to know virtue. Take me, O my Genius, back to that very world which I have despised; a world which has Alla for its contriver is much more wisely formed than that which has been projected by Mahomet. Ingratitude, contempt, and hatred, I can now suffer, for perhaps I have deserved them. When I arraigned the wisdom of Providence, I only showed my own ignorance; henceforth let me keep from vice myself, and pity it in others."

He had scarce ended, when the Genius, assuming an air of terrible complacency, called all his thunders around him, and vanished in a whirlwind. Asem, astonished at the terror of the scene, looked for his imaginary world; when, casting his eyes around, he perceived himself in the very situation, and in the very place, where he first began to repine and despair; his right foot had been just advanced to take the fatal plunge, nor had it been yet withdrawn: so instantly did Providence strike the series of truths just imprinted on his soul. He now departed from the water-side in tranquillity, and leaving his horrid mansion, travelled to Segestan, his native city; where he diligently applied himself to commerce, and put in practice that wisdom he had learned in solitude. The frugality of a few years soon produced opulence; the number of his domestics increased; his friends came to him from every part of the city, nor did he receive them with disdain: and a youth of misery was concluded with an old age of elegance, affluence, and ease.

[1759]

A REVERIE AT THE BOAR'S-HEAD TAVERN IN EAST-CHEAP

The improvements we make in mental acquirements only render us each day more sensible of the defects of our constitution; with this in view, therefore, let us often recur to the amusements of youth; endeavour to forget age and wisdom, and, as far as innocence goes, be as much a boy as the best of them.

Let idle declaimers mourn over the degeneracy of the age; but in my opinion every age is the same. This I am sure of, that man in every season is a poor fretful being with no other means to escape the calamities of the times but by endeavouring to forget them; for if he attempts to resist, he is certainly undone. If I feel poverty and pain, I am not so hardy as to quarrel with the executioner, even while under correction: I find myself no way disposed to make fine speeches, while I am making wry faces. In a word, let me drink when the fit is on, to make me insensible; and drink when it is over, for joy that I feel pain no longer.

The character of old Falstaff, even with all his faults, gives me more consolation than the most studied efforts of wisdom: I here behold an agreeable old fellow, forgetting age, and showing me the way to be young at sixty-five. Sure I am well able to be as merry, though not so comical as he.—Is it not in my power to have, though not so much wit, at least as much vivacity?—Age, care, wisdom, reflection, be gone!—I give you to the winds. Let's have t'other bottle: here's to the memory of Shakespeare, Falstaff, and all the merry men of Eastcheap.

Such were the reflections that naturally arose while I sat at the Boar's-Head Tavern, still kept at Eastcheap. Here, by a pleasant fire, in the very room where old Sir John Falstaff cracked his jokes, in the very chair which was sometimes honoured by Prince Henry, and sometimes polluted by his immortal merry companions, I sat and ruminated on the follies of youth; wished to be young again; but was resolved to make the best of life while it lasted, and now and then compared past and present times to gether. I considered myself as the only living representative of the old knight, and transported my imagination back to the times when the prince and he gave life to the revel, and made even debauchery not disgusting. The room also conspired to throw my reflections back into antiquity; the oak floor, the Gothic windows, and the ponderous chimney-piece, had long withstood the tooth of time; the watchman had gone twelve; my companions had all stolen off; and none now remained with me but the landlord. From him I could have wished to know the history of a tavern that had such a long succession of customers. I could not help thinking that an account of this kind would be a pleasing contrast of the manners of different ages; but my landlord could give me no information. He continued to doze and sot, and tell a tedious story, as most other landlords usually do; and, though he said nothing, yet was never silent: one good joke followed another good joke; and the best joke of all was generally begun towards the end of a bottle. I found at last, however, his wine and his conversation operate by degrees. He insensibly began to alter his appearance: his cravat seemed quilled into a ruff, and his breeches swelled out into a fardingale. I now fancied him changing sexes; and as my eyes began to close in slumber, I imagined my fat landlord actually converted into as fat a landlady. However, sleep made but few changes in my situation: the tavern, the apartment, and the table, continued as before; nothing suffered mutation but my host, who was fairly altered into a gentlewoman, whom I knew to be Dame Quickly, mistress of this tavern in the days of Sir John; and the liquor we were drinking, seemed converted into sack and sugar.

"My dear Mrs. Quickly," cried I, (for I knew her perfectly well at first sight) "I am heartily glad to see you. How have you left Falstaff, Pistol, and the rest of our friends below stairs? Brave and hearty, I hope?" In good

sooth, replied she, he did deserve to live forever; but he maketh foul work on't where he hath flitted. Queen Proserpine and he have quarrelled for his attempting a rape upon her divinity; and were it not that she still had bowels of compassion, it more than seems probable he might have been now sprawling in Tartarus.

I now found that spirits still preserve the frailties of the flesh; and that, according to the laws of criticism and dreaming, ghosts have been known to be guilty of even more than platonic affection; wherefore, as I found her too much moved on such a topic to proceed, I was resolved to change the subject, and, desiring she would pledge me in a bumper, observed with a sigh, that our sack was nothing now to what it was in former days: "Ah, Mrs. Quickly, those were merry times when you drew sack for Prince Henry: men were twice as strong, and twice as wise, and much braver, and ten thousand times more charitable, than now. Those were the times! The battle of Agincourt was a victory indeed! Ever since that we have only been degenerating; and I have lived to see the day when drinking is no longer fashionable; when men wear clean shirts, and women show their necks and arms: all are degenerated, Mrs. Quickly; and we shall probably, in another century, be frittered away into beaux or monkeys. Had you been on earth to see what I have seen, it would congeal all the blood in your body (your soul, I mean). Why, our very nobility now have the intolerable arrogance, in spite of what is every day remonstrated from the press; our very nobility, I say, have the assurance to frequent assemblies, and presume to be as merry as the vulgar. See, my very friends have scarce manhood enough to sit to it till eleven; and I only am left to make a night on't. Pr'ythee do me the favour to console me a little for their absence by the story of your own adventure, or the history of the tavern where we are now sitting: I fancy the narrative may have something singular."

Observe this apartment, interrupted my companion; of neat device and excellent workmanship.—In this room I have lived, child, woman, and ghost, more than three hundred years: I am ordered by Pluto to keep an annual register of every transaction that passeth here; and I have whilom compiled three hundred tomes, which eftsoons may be submitted to thy regards: "None of your whiloms or eftsoons's, Mrs. Quickly, if you please," I replied: "I know you can talk every whit as well as I can; for, as you have lived here so long, it is but natural to suppose you should learn the conversation of the company. Believe me, dame, at best, you have neither too much sense, or too much language to spare; so give me both as well as you can; but first my service to you; old women should water their clay a little now and then; and now to your story."

The story of my own adventures, replied the vision, is but short and unsatisfactory; for believe me, Mr. Rigmarole, believe me, a woman with a butt of sack at her elbow, is never long-lived. Sir John's death afflicted me to such a degree, that I sincerely believe, to drown sorrow, I drank more liquor myself than I drew for my customers: my grief was sincere, and the sack was excellent. The prior of a neighbouring convent (for our priors then had as much power as a Middlesex justice now) he, I say, it was who gave me a licence for keeping a disorderly house; upon condition that I should never make hard bargains with the clergy, that he should have a bottle of sack every morning, and the liberty of confessing which of my girls he thought proper in private every night. I had continued for several years to pay this tribute; and he, it must be confessed, continued as rigorously to exact it. I grew old insensibly; my customers continued, however, to compliment my looks while I was by, but I could hear them say I was wearing when my back was

turned. The prior, however, still was constant, and so were half his convent: but one fatal morning he missed the usual beverage; for I had incautiously drank over-night the last bottle myself. What will you have on't?—The very next day Doll Tearsheet and I were sent to the house of correction, and accused of keeping a low bawdy-house. In short, we were so well purified there with stripes, mortification, and penance, that we were afterwards utterly unfit for worldly conversation: though sack would have killed me, had I stuck to it, yet I soon died for want of a drop of something comfortable; and fairly left my body to the care of the beadle.

Such is my own history; but that of the tavern, where I have ever since been stationed, affords greater variety. In the history of this, which is one of the oldest in London, you may view the different manners, pleasures, and follies, of men at different periods. You will find mankind neither better nor worse now than formerly; the vices of an uncivilized people are generally more detestable, though not so frequent, as those in polite society. It is the same luxury, which formerly stuffed your aldermen with plum-porridge, and now crams him with turtle. It is the same low ambition, that formerly induced a courtier to give up his religion to please his king, and now persuades him to give up his conscience to please his minister. It is the same vanity, that formerly stained our ladies' cheeks and necks with woad, and now paints them with carmine. Your ancient Briton formerly powdered his hair with red earth, like brick-dust, in order to appear frightful: your modern Briton cuts his hair on the crown, and plasters it with hog's-lard and flour; and this to make him look killing. It is the same vanity, the same folly, and the same vice, only appearing different as viewed through the glass of fashion. In a word, all mankind are ——

"Sure the woman is dreaming," interrupted I. "None of your reflections, Mrs. Quickly, if you love me; they only give me the spleen. Tell me your history at once. I love stories, but hate reasoning."

If you please, then, Sir, returned my companion, I'll read you an abstract, which I made of the three hundred volumes I mentioned just now.

My body was no sooner laid in the dust, than the prior and several of his convent came to purify the tavern from the pollutions with which they said I had filled it. Masses were said in every room, reliques were exposed upon every piece of furniture, and the whole house washed with a deluge of holy-water. My habitation was soon converted into a monastery; instead of customers now applying for sack and sugar, my rooms were crowded with images, reliques, saints, whores, and friars. Instead of being a scene of occasional debauchery, it was now filled with continual lewdness. The prior led the fashion, and the whole convent imitated his pious example. Matrons came hither to confess their sins, and to commit new. Virgins came hither who seldom went virgins away. Nor was this a convent peculiarly wicked; every convent at that period was equally fond of pleasure, and gave a boundless loose to appetite. The laws allowed it; each priest had a right to a favourite companion, and a power of discarding her as often as he pleased. The laity grumbled, quarrelled with their wives and daughters, hated their confessors, and maintained them in opulence and ease. These, these were happy times, Mr. Rigmarole; these were times of piety, bravery, and simplicity! "Not so very happy, neither, good Madam; pretty much like the present: those that labour starve; and those that do nothing wear fine clothes and live in luxury."

In this manner the fathers lived for some years without molestation; they transgressed, confessed themselves to each other, and were forgiven. One evening, however, our prior keeping a

lady of distinction somewhat too long at confession, her husband unexpectedly came upon them, and testified all the indignation which was natural upon such an occasion. The prior assured the gentleman that it was the devil who had put it into his heart; and the lady was very certain, that she was under the influence of magic, or she could never have behaved in so unfaithful a manner. The husband, however, was not to be put off by such evasions, but summoned both before the tribunal of justice. His proofs were flagrant, and he expected large damages. Such indeed he had a right to expect, were the tribunals of those days constituted in the same manner as they are now. The cause of the priest was to be tried before an assembly of priests; and a layman was to expect redress only from their impartiality and candour. What plea then do you think the prior made to obviate this accusation? He denied the fact, and challenged the plaintiff to try the merits of their cause by single combat. It was a little hard, you may be sure, upon the poor gentleman, not only to be made a cuckold, but to be obliged to fight a duel into the bargain; yet such was the justice of the times. The prior threw down his glove, and the injured husband was obliged to take it up, in token of his accepting the challenge. Upon this the priest supplied his champion, for it was not lawful for the clergy to fight; and the defendant and plaintiff, according to custom, were put in prison; both ordered to fast and pray, every method being previously used to induce both to a confession of the truth. After a month's imprisonment, the hair of each was cut, the bodies anointed with oil, the field of battle appointed and guarded by soldiers, while his majesty presided over the whole in person. Both the champions were sworn not to seek victory either by fraud or magic. They prayed and confessed upon their knees; and after these ceremonies the rest was left to the courage and conduct of the combatants. As the champion whom the prior had pitched upon had fought six or eight times upon similar occasions, it was no way extraordinary to find him victorious in the present combat. In short, the husband was discomfited; he was taken from the field of battle, stripped to his shirt, and after one of his legs had been cut off, as justice ordained in such cases, he was hanged as a terror to future offenders. These, these were the times, Mr. Rigmarole: you see how much more just, and wise, and valiant, our ancestors were than us. "I rather fancy, Madam, that the times then were pretty much like our own; where a multiplicity of laws gives a judge as much power as a want of law; since he is ever sure to find among the number some to countenance his partiality."

Our convent, victorious over their enemies, now gave a loose to every demonstration of joy. The lady became a nun, the prior was made a bishop, and three Wickliffites were burned in the illuminations and fireworks that were made on the present occasion. Our convent now began to enjoy a very high degree of reputation. There was not one in London that had the character of hating heretics so much as ours. Ladies of the first distinction chose from our convent their confessors; in short, it flourished, and might have flourished to this hour, but for a fatal accident which terminated in its overthrow. The lady whom the prior had placed in a nunnery, and whom he continued to visit for some time with great punctuality, began at last to perceive that she was quite forsaken. Secluded from conversation, as usual, she now entertained the visions of a devotee; found herself strangely disturbed; but hesitated in determining whether she was possessed by an angel or a dæmon. She was not long in suspense; for upon vomiting a large quantity of crooked pins, and finding the palms of her hands turned outwards, she quickly concluded that she was possessed by the devil. She soon lost entirely the

use of speech; and, when she seemed to speak, everybody that was present perceived that her voice was not her own, but that of the devil within her. In short, she was bewitched; and all the difficulty lay in determining who could it be that bewitched her. The nuns and the monks all demanded the magician's name, but the devil made no reply; for he knew they had no authority to ask questions. By the rules of witchcraft, when an evil spirit has taken possession, he may refuse to answer any questions asked him, unless they are put by a bishop, and to these he is obliged to reply. A bishop therefore was sent for, and now the whole secret came out: the devil reluctantly owned that he was a servant of the prior; that by his command he resided in his present habitation; and that without his command he was resolved to keep in possession. The bishop was an able exorcist; he drove the devil out by force of mystical arms; the prior was arraigned for witchcraft; the witnesses were strong and numerous against him, not less than fourteen persons being by, who heard the devil talk Latin. There was no resisting such a cloud of witnesses; the prior was condemned; and he who had assisted at so many burnings was burned himself in turn. These were times, Mr. Rigmarole; the people of those times were not infidels, as now, but sincere believers! "Equally faulty with ourselves; they believed what the devil was pleased to tell them; and we seem resolved at last to believe neither God nor devil."

After such a stain upon the convent, it was not to be supposed it could subsist any longer; the fathers were ordered to decamp, and the house was once again converted into a tavern. The king conferred it on one of his cast-off mistresses; she was constituted landlady by royal authority; and as the tavern was in the neighbourhood of the court, and the mistress a very polite woman, it began to have more business than ever, and sometimes took not less than four shillings a day.

But perhaps you are desirous of knowing what were the peculiar qualifications of women of fashion at that period; and in a description of the present landlady, you will have a tolerable idea of all the rest. This lady was the daughter of a nobleman, and received such an education in the country as became her quality, beauty, and great expectations. She could make shifts and hose for herself and all the servants of the family, when she was twelve years old. She knew the names of the four and twenty letters, so that it was impossible to bewitch her; and this was a greater piece of learning than any lady in the whole country could pretend to. She was always up early, and saw breakfast served in the great hall by six o'clock. At this scene of festivity she generally improved good-humour, by telling her dreams, relating stories of spirits, several of which she herself had seen; and one of which she was reported to have killed with a black-hafted knife. From hence she usually went to make pastry in the larder, and here she was followed by her sweet-hearts, who were much helped on in conversation by struggling with her for kisses. About ten miss generally went to play at hot-cockles and blindman's buff in the parlour; and when the young folks (for they seldom played at hot-cockles when grown old) were tired of such amusements, the gentlemen entertained miss with the history of their greyhounds, bear-baitings, and victories at cudgel-playing. If the weather was fine, they ran at the ring, shot at butts, while miss held in her hand a ribbon, with which she adorned the conqueror. Her mental qualifications were exactly fitted to her external accomplishments. Before she was fifteen she could tell the story of Jack the Giant Killer, could name every mountain that was inhabited by fairies, knew a witch at first sight, and could repeat four Latin prayers without a prompter. Her dress was perfectly fashionable; her arms and her hair were completely covered: a monstrous ruff was put round her neck; so that her head seemed like that of John the Baptist placed in a charger. In short, when completely equipped, her appearance was so very modest, that she discovered little more than her nose. These were the times, Mr. Rigmarole; when every lady that had a good nose might set up for a beauty; when every woman that could tell stories, might be cried up for a wit. "I am as much displeased at those dresses which conceal too much, as at those which discover too much: I am equally an enemy to a female dunce or a female pedant."

You may be sure that miss chose a husband with qualifications resembling her own; she pitched upon a courtier, equally remarkable for hunting and drinking, who had given several proofs of his great virility among the daughters of his tenants and domestics. They fell in love at first sight (for such was the gallantry of the times), were married, came to court, and madam appeared with superior qualifications. The king was struck with her beauty. All property was at the king's command; the husband was obliged to resign all pretensions in his wife to the sovereign, whom God had anointed to commit adultery where he thought proper. The king loved her for some time; but at length repenting of his misdeeds, and instigated by his father confessor, from a principle of conscience removed her from his levee to the bar of this tavern, and took a new mistress in her stead. Let it not surprise you to behold the mistress of a king degraded to so humble an office. As the ladies had no mental accomplishments, a good face was enough to raise them to the royal couch; and she who was this day a royal mistress, might the next, when her beauty palled upon enjoyment, be doomed to infamy and want.

Under the care of this lady the tavern grew into great reputation; the courtiers had not yet learned to game, but they paid it off by drinking; drunkenness is ever the vice of a barbarous, and gaming of a luxurious age. They had not such frequent entertainments as the moderns have, but were more expensive and more luxurious in those they had. All their fooleries were more elaborate, and more admired by the great and the vulgar than now. A courtier has been known to spend his whole fortune at a single feast, a king to mortgage his dominions to furnish out thc frippery of a tournament. There were certain days appointed for riot and debauchery, and to be sober at such times was reputed a crime. Kings themselves set the example; and I have seen monarchs in this room drunk before the entertainment was half concluded. These were the times, Sir, when kings kept mistresses, and got drunk in public; they were too plain and simple in those happy times to hide their vices, and act the hypocrite, as now. "Lord! Mrs. Quickly," interrupting her, "I expected to have heard a story, and here you are going to tell me I know not what of times and vices; pr'ythee let me entreat thee once more to waive reflections, and give thy history without deviation."

No lady upon earth, continued my visionary correspondent, knew how to put off her damaged wine or women with more art than she. When these grew flat, or those paltry, it was but changing the names; the wine became excellent, and the girls agreeable. She was also possessed of the engaging leer, the chuck under the chin, winked at a double-entendre, could nick the opportunity of calling for something comfortable, and perfectly understood the discreet moments when to withdraw. The gallants of those times pretty much resembled the bloods of ours; they were fond of pleasure, but quite ignorant of the art of refining upon it; thus a court-bawd of those times resembled the common low-lived harridan of a modern bagnio. Witness, ye powers of debauchery, how often I have been present at the various appearances of drunkenness, riot, guilt, and brutality! A tavern is a true picture of human infirmity: in history we find only one side of the age exhibited to our view; but in the accounts of a tavern we see every age equally absurd and equally vicious.

Upon this lady's decease the tavern was successfully occupied by adventurers, bullies, pimps, and gamesters. Towards the conclusion of the reign of Henry VII. gaming was more universally practised in England than even now. Kings themselves have been known to play off at primero, not only all the money and jewels they could part with, but the very images in churches. The last Henry played away, in this very room, not only the four great bells of St. Paul's cathedral, but the fine image of St. Paul, which stood upon the top of the spire, to Sir Miles Partridge, who took them down the next day, and sold them by auction. Have you then any cause to regret being born in the times you now live? or do you still believe that human nature continues to run on declining every age? If we observe the actions of the busy part of mankind, your ancestors will be found infinitely more gross, servile, and even dishonest, than you. If, forsaking history, we only trace them in their hours of amusement and dissipation, we shall find them more sensual, more entirely devoted to pleasure, and infinitely more selfish.

The last hostess of note I find upon record was Jane Rouse. She was born among the lower ranks of the people; and by frugality and extreme complaisance contrived to acquire a moderate fortune: this she might have enjoyed for many years, had she not unfortunately quarrelled with one of her neighbours, a woman who was in high repute for sanctity through the whole parish. In the times of which I speak two women seldom quarrelled, that one did not accuse the other of witchcraft, and she who first contrived to vomit crooked pins was sure to come off victorious. The scandal of a modern tea-table differs widely from the scandal of former times: the fascination of a lady's eyes at present is regarded as a compliment; but if a lady formerly should be accused of having witchcraft in her eyes, it were much better both for her soul and body that she had no eyes at all.

In short, Jane Rouse was accused of witchcraft; and though she made the best defence she could, it was all to no purpose; she was taken from her own bar to the bar of the Old Bailey, condemned, and executed accordingly. These were times indeed! when even women could not scold in safety.

Since her time the tavern underwent several revolutions, according to the spirit of the times, or the disposition of the reigning monarch. It was this day a brothel, and the next a conventicle for enthusiasts. It was one year noted for harbouring Whigs, and the next infamous for a retreat to Tories. Some years ago it was in high vogue, but at present it seems declining. This only may be remarked in general, that whenever taverns flourish most, the times are then most extravagant and luxurious.—"Lord! Mrs. Quickly," interrupted I, "you have really deceived me; I expected a romance, and here you have been this half hour giving me only a description of the spirit of the times: if you have nothing but tedious remarks to communicate, seek some other hearer. I am determined to hearken only to stories."

I had scarcely concluded, when my eyes and ears seemed opened to my landlord, who had been all this while giving me an account of the repairs he had made in the house; and was now got into the story of the cracked glass in the dining-room.

[1760]

LETTERS FROM A CITIZEN OF THE WORLD

LETTER IV. FROM LIEN CHI ALTANGI, TO THE CARE OF FIPSIHI, RESIDENT IN MOSCOW, TO BE FORWARDED BY THE RUSSIAN CARAVAN TO FUM HOAM, FIRST PRESIDENT OF THE CEREMONIAL ACADEMY AT PEKIN, IN CHINA.

ENGLISH PRIDE—LIBERTY—AN INSTANCE OF BOTH —NEWSPAPERS—POLITENESS.

The English seem as silent as the Japanese, yet vainer than the inhabitants of Siam. Upon my arrival I attributed that reserve to modesty, which I now find has its origin in pride. Condescend to address them first, and you are sure of their acquaintance; stoop to flattery, and you conciliate their friendship and esteem. They bear hunger, cold, fatigue, and all the miseries of life, without shrinking; danger only calls forth their fortitude; they even exult in calamity; but contempt is what they cannot bear. An Englishman fears contempt more than death; he often flies to death as a refuge from its pressure; and dies when he fancies the world has ceased to esteem him.

Pride seems the source not only of their national vices, but of their national virtues also. An Englishman is taught to love his king as his friend, but to acknowledge no other master than the laws which himself has contributed to enact. He despises those nations, who, that one may be free, are all content to be slaves; who first lift a tyrant into terror, and then shrink under his power as if delegated from heaven. Liberty is echoed in all their assemblies; and thousands might be found ready to offer up their lives for the sound, though perhaps not one of all the number understands its meaning. The lowest mechanic, however, looks upon it as his duty to be a watchful guardian of his country's freedom, and often uses a language that might seem haughty, even in the mouth of the great emperor who traces his ancestry to the moon.

A few days ago, passing by one of their prisons, I could not avoid stopping, in order to listen to a dialogue, which I thought might afford me some entertainment. The conversation was carried on between a debtor, through the grate of his prison, a porter, who had stopped to rest his burthen, and a soldier at the window. The subject was upon a threatened invasion from France, and each seemed extremely anxious to rescue his country from the impending danger. *For my part,* cries the prisoner, *the greatest of my apprehensions is for our freedom; if the French should conquer, what would become of English liberty? My dear friends, liberty is the Englishman's prerogative; we must preserve that at the expense of our lives; of that the French shall never deprive us. It is not to be expected that men who are slaves themselves would preserve our freedom should they happen to conquer.* "Ay, slaves," cries the porter, "they are all slaves, fit only to carry burthens, every one of them. Before I would stoop to slavery, may this be my poison (and he held the goblet in his hand), may this be my poison—but I would sooner 'list for a soldier."

The soldier, taking the goblet from his friend, with much awe fervently cried out, *It is not so much our liberties as our religion that would suffer by such a change; ay, our religion, my lads. May the devil sink me into flames* (such was the solemnity of his adjuration), *if the French should come over, but our religion would be utterly undone.* So saying, instead of a libation, he applied the goblet to his lips, and confirmed his sentiments with a ceremony of the most persevering devotion.

In short, every man here pretends to be a politician; even the fair sex are sometimes found to mix the severity of national altercation with the blandishments of love, and often become conquerors by more weapons of destruction than their eyes.

This universal passion for politics is gratified by Daily Gazettes, as with us in China. But as in ours the Emperor endeavours to instruct his people, in theirs the people endeavour to instruct the administration. You must not, however, imagine, that they who compile these papers have any actual knowledge of the politics or the government of a state; they only collect their materials from the oracle of some coffee-house, which oracle has himself gathered them the night before from a beau at a gaming-table who has pillaged his knowledge from a great man's porter, who has had his information from the great man's gentleman, who has invented the whole story for his own amuse ʼent the night preceding.

The English in general seem fonder of gaining the esteem than the love of those they converse with. This gives a formality to their amusements: their gayest conversations have something too wise for innocent relaxation: though in company you are seldom disgusted with the absurdity of a fool, you are seldom lifted into rapture by those strokes of vivacity which give instant, though not permanent, pleasure.

What they want, however, in gaiety, they make up in politeness. You smile at hearing me praise the English for their politeness; you who have heard very different accounts from the missionaries at Pekin, who have seen such a different behaviour in their merchants and seamen at home. But I must still repeat it, the English seem more polite than any of their neighbours: their great art in this respect lies in endeavouring, while they oblige, to lessen the force of the favour. Other countries are fond of obliging a stranger; but seem desirous that he should be sensible of the obligation. The English confer their kindness with an appearance of indifference, and give away benefits with an air as if they despised them.

Walking, a few days ago, between an English and a Frenchman into the suburbs of the city, we were overtaken by a heavy shower of rain. I was unprepared; but they had each large coats, which defended them from what seemed to be a perfect inundation. The Englishman, seeing me shrink from the weather, accosted me thus: *Psha, man, what dost shrink at? here, take this coat; I don't want it; I find it no way useful to me; I had as lief be without it.* The Frenchman began to show his politeness in turn. *My dear friend*, cries he, *why won't you oblige me by making use of my coat? you see how well it defends me from the rain; I should not choose to part with it to others, but to such a friend as you I could even part with my skin to do him service.*

From such minute instances as these, most reverend Fum Hoam, I am sensible your sagacity will collect instruction. The volume of nature is the book of knowledge; and he becomes most wise who makes the most judicious selection. Farewell!

LETTER XI. TO THE SAME

THE BENEFITS OF LUXURY, IN MAKING A PEOPLE MORE WISE AND HAPPY

From such a picture of nature in primeval simplicity, tell me, my much respected friend, are you in love with fatigue and solitude? Do you sigh for the severe frugality of the wandering Tartar, or regret being born amidst the luxury and dissimulation of the polite? Rather tell me, has not every kind of life vices peculiarly its own? Is it not a truth that refined countries have more vices, but those not so terrible; barbarous nations few, and they of the most hideous complexion? Perfidy and fraud are the vices of civilized nations, credulity and violence those of the inhabitants of the desert. Does the luxury of the one produce half the evils of the inhumanity of the other? Certainly those philosophers who declaim against luxury have but little understood its benefits; they seem insensible that to luxury we owe not only the greatest part of our knowledge, but even of our virtues.

It may sound fine in the mouth of a declaimer, when he talks of subduing our appetites, of teaching every sense to be content with a bare sufficiency, and of supplying only the wants of nature; but is there not more satisfaction in indulging those appetites, if with innocence and safety, than in restraining them? Am not I better pleased in enjoyment than in the sullen satisfaction of thinking that I can live without enjoyment? The more various our artificial necessities, the wider is our circle of pleasure; for all pleasure consists in obviating necessities as they rise: luxury, therefore, as it increases our wants, increases our capacity for happiness.

Examine the history of any country remarkable for opulence and wisdom; you will find they would never have been wise had they not been first luxurious; you will find poets, philosophers, and even patriots, marching in luxury's train. The reason is obvious: we then only are curious after knowledge, when we find it connected with sensual happiness. The senses ever point out the way, and reflection comments upon the discovery. Inform a native of the desert of Kobi, of the exact measure of the parallax of the moon, he finds no satisfaction at all in the information; he wonders how any could take such pains, and lay out such treasures, in order to solve so useless a difficulty: but connect it with his happiness, by showing that it improves navigation, that by such an investigation he may have a warmer coat, a better gun, or a finer knife, and he is instantly in raptures at so great an improvement. In short, we only desire to know what we desire to possess; and whatever we may talk against it, luxury adds the spur to curiosity, and gives us a desire of becoming more wise.

But not our knowledge only, but our virtues are improved by luxury. Observe the brown savage of Thibet, to whom the fruits of the spreading pomegranate supply food, and its branches an habitation. Such a character has few vices, I grant, but those he has are of the most hideous nature: rapine and cruelty are scarcely crimes in his eye; neither pity nor tenderness, which ennoble every virtue, have any place in his heart; he hates his enemies, and kills those he subdues. On the other hand, the polite Chinese and civilized European seem even to love their enemies. I have just now seen an instance where the English have succoured those enemies, whom their own countrymen actually refused to relieve.

The greater the luxuries of every country, the more closely, politically speaking, is that country united. Luxury is the child of society alone; the luxurious man stands in need of a thousand different artists to furnish out his happiness; it is more likely, therefore, that he should be a good citizen who is connected by motives of self-interest with so many, than the abstemious man who is united to none.

In whatsoever light, therefore, we consider luxury, whether as employing a number of hands naturally too feeble for more laborious employment; as finding a variety of occupation for others who might be totally idle; or as furnishing out new inlets to happiness, without encroaching on mutual property; in whatever light we regard it, we shall have reason to stand up in its defence, and the sentiment of Confucius still remains unshaken: *that we should enjoy as many of the luxuries of life as are consistent with our own safety, and the prosperity of others; and that he who finds out a new pleasure is one of the most useful members of society.*

LETTER XIII. TO THE SAME

AN ACCOUNT OF WESTMINSTER ABBEY

I am just returned from Westminster Abbey, the place of sepulture for the philosophers, heroes, and kings of England. What a gloom do monumental inscriptions, and all the venerable remains of deceased merit inspire! Imagine a temple, marked with the hand of antiquity, solemn as religious awe, adorned with all the magnificence of barbarous profusion, dim windows, fretted pillars, long colonnades, and dark ceilings. Think, then, what were my sensations at being introduced to such a scene. I stood in the midst of the temple, and threw my eyes round on the walls, filled with the statues, the inscriptions, and the monuments of the dead.

Alas, I said to myself, how does pride attend the puny child of dust even to the grave! Even humble as I am, I possess more consequence in the present scene than the greatest hero of them all: they have toiled for an hour to gain a transient immortality, and are at length retired to the grave, where they have no attendant but the worm, none to flatter but the epitaph.

As I was indulging such reflections, a gentleman, dressed in black, perceiving me to be a stranger, came up, entered into conversation, and politely offered to be my instructor and guide through the temple. "If any monument," said he, "should particularly excite your curiosity, I shall endeavour to satisfy your demands." I accepted with thanks the gentleman's offer, adding that "I was come to observe the policy, the wisdom, and the justice of the English, in conferring rewards upon deceased merit. If adulation like this," continued I, "be properly conducted, as it can no ways injure those who are flattered, so it may be a glorious incentive to those who are now capable of enjoying it. It is the duty of every good government to turn this monumental pride to its own advantage; to become strong in the aggregate from the weakness of the individual. If none but the truly great have a place in this awful repository, a temple like this will give the finest lessons of morality, and be a strong incentive to true ambition. I am told, that none have a place here but characters of the most distinguished merit." The man in black seemed impatient at my observations, so I discontinued my remarks, and we walked on together to take a view of every particular monument in order as it lay.

As the eye is naturally caught by the finest objects, I could not avoid being particularly curious about one monument, which appeared more beautiful than the rest: That, said I to my guide, I take to be the tomb of some very great man. By the peculiar excellence of the workmanship, and the magnificence of the design, this must be a trophy raised to the memory of some king who has saved his country from ruin, or lawgiver who has reduced his fellow-citizens from anarchy into just subjection.—It is not requisite, replied my companion, smiling, to have such qualifications in order to have a very fine monument here. More humble abilities will suffice. *What, I suppose then, the gaining two or three battles, or the taking half a score towns, is thought a sufficient qualification?*—Gaining battles, or taking towns, replied the man in black, may be of service: but a gentleman may have a very fine monument here without ever seeing a battle or a siege. *—This, then, is the monument of some poet, I presume of one whose wit has gained him immortality?*—No, Sir, replied my guide, the gentleman who lies here never made verses; and as for wit, he despised it in others, because he had none himself.—*Pray tell me, then, in a word,* said I, peevishly, *what is the great man who lies here particularly remarkable for?* Remarkable, Sir! said my companion; why, Sir, the gentleman that lies here is remarkable, very remarkable—for a tomb in Westminster Abbey. *But, head of my Ancestors! how has he got here? I fancy he could never bribe the guardians of the temple to give him a place. Should he not be ashamed to be seen among company, where even moderate merit would look like infamy?* I suppose, replied the man in black, the gentleman was rich, and his friends, as is usual in such a case, told him he was great. He readily believed them; the guardians of the temple, as they got by the self-delusion, were ready to believe him too; so he paid his money for a fine monument; and the workman, as you see, has made him one of the most beautiful. Think not, however, that this gentleman is singular in his desire of being buried among the

great; there are several others in the temple, who, hated and shunned by the great while alive, have come here, fully resolved to keep them company now they are dead.

As we walked along to a particular part of the temple, There, says the gentleman, pointing with his finger, that is the poet's corner; there you see the monuments of Shakespeare, and Milton, and Prior, and Drayton.—Drayton! I replied, I never heard of him before; but I have been told of one Pope, is he there?—It is time enough, replied my guide, these hundred years; he is not long dead; people have not done hating him yet.—Strange, cried I, can any be found to hate a man, whose life was wholly spent in entertaining and instructing his fellow-creatures?—Yes, says my guide, they hate him for that very reason. There are a set of men called answerers of books, who take upon them to watch the republic of letters, and distribute reputation by the sheet; they somewhat resemble the eunuchs in a seraglio, who are incapable of giving pleasure themselves, and hinder those that would. These answerers have no other employment but to cry out Dunce and Scribbler; to praise the dead, and revile the living; to grant a man of confessed abilities some small share of merit; to applaud twenty blockheads, in order to gain the reputation of candour; and to revile the moral character of the man whose writings they cannot injure. Such wretches are kept in pay by some mercenary bookseller, or more frequently, the bookseller himself takes this dirty work off their hands, as all that is required is to be very abusive and very dull. Every poet of any genius is sure to find such enemies; he feels, though he seems to despise, their malice; they make him miserable here, and in the pursuit of empty fame, at last he gains solid anxiety.

Has this been the case with every poet I see here? cried I.—Yes, with every mother's son of them, replied he, except he happened to be born a

Mandarin. If he has much money, he may buy reputation from your book-answerers, as well as a monument from the guardians of the temple.

But are there not some men of distinguished taste, as in China, who are willing to patronize men of merit, and soften the rancour of malevolent dulness?

I own there are many, replied the man in black, but alas! Sir, the book-answerers crowd about them, and call themselves the writers of books; and the patron is too indolent to distinguish: thus poets are kept at a distance, while their enemies eat up all their rewards at the Mandarin's table.

Leaving this part of the temple, we made up to an iron gate, through which my companion told me we were to pass in order to see the monuments of the kings. Accordingly, I marched up without further ceremony, and was going to enter, when a person, who held the gate in his hand, told me I must pay first. I was surprised at such a demand; and asked the man, whether the people of England kept a *show?* whether the paltry sum he demanded was not a national reproach? whether it was not more to the honour of the country to let their magnificence or their antiquities be openly seen, than thus meanly to tax a curiosity which tended to their own honour?—As for your questions, replied the gate-keeper, to be sure they may be very right, because I don't understand them; but as for that there threepence, I farm it from one, who rents it from another, who hires it from a third, who leases it from the guardians of the temple, and we all must live.—I expected, upon paying here, to see something extraordinary, since what I had seen for nothing filled me with so much surprise: but in this I was disappointed; there was little more within than black coffins, rusty armour, tattered standards, and some few slovenly figures in wax. I was sorry I had paid, but I comforted myself by considering it would be my last payment. A person attended us,

who, without once blushing, told an hundred lies: he talked of a lady who died by pricking her finger; of a king with a golden head, and twenty such pieces of absurdity. Look ye there, gentlemen, says he, pointing to an old oak chair, there's a curiosity for ye; in that chair the kings of England were crowned: you see also a stone underneath, and that stone is Jacob's pillow. I could see no curiosity either in the oak chair, or the stone: could I indeed behold one of the old kings of England seated in this, or Jacob's head laid upon the other, there might be something curious in the sight; but in the present case there was no more reason for my surprise than if I should pick a stone from their streets, and call it a curiosity, merely because one of the kings happened to tread upon it as he passed in a procession.

From hence our conductor led us through several dark walks and winding ways, uttering lies, talking to himself, and flourishing a wand which he held in his hand. He reminded me of the black magicians of Kobi. After we had been almost fatigued with a variety of objects, he at last desired me to consider attentively a certain suit of armour, which seemed to show nothing remarkable. This armour, said he, belonged to General Monk. *Very surprising, that a general should wear armour!* And pray, added he, observe this cap, this is General Monk's cap. *Very strange indeed, very strange, that a general should have a cap also! Pray, friend, what might this cap have cost originally?* That, Sir, says he, I don't know; but this cap is all the wages I have for my trouble. *A very small recompense truly,* said I. Not so very small, replied he, for every gentleman puts some money into it, and I spend the money. *What more money! still more money!* Every gentleman gives something, Sir. I'll give thee nothing, returned I; the guardians of the temple should pay your wages, friend, and not permit you to squeeze thus from every spectator. When we pay our money at the door to see a show, we never give more as we are going out. Sure the guardians of the temple can never think they get enough. Show me the gate; if I stay longer, I may probably meet with more of those ecclesiastical beggars.

Thus leaving the temple precipitately, I returned to my lodgings, in order to ruminate over what was great, and to despise what was mean, in the occurrences of the day.

LETTER XXVI. TO THE SAME

THE CHARACTER OF THE MAN IN BLACK; WITH SOME INSTANCES OF HIS INCONSISTENT CONDUCT

Though fond of many acquaintances, I desire an intimacy only with a few. The man in black, whom I have often mentioned, is one whose friendship I could wish to acquire, because he possesses my esteem. His manners, it is true, are tinctured with some strange inconsistencies, and he may be justly termed a humourist in a nation of humourists. Though he is generous even to profusion, he affects to be thought a prodigy of parsimony and prudence; though his conversation be replete with the most sordid and selfish maxims, his heart is dilated with the most unbounded love. I have known him profess himself a man-hater, while his cheek was glowing with compassion; and, while his looks were softened into pity, I have heard him use the language of the most unbounded ill-nature. Some affect humanity and tenderness, others boast of having such dispositions from Nature; but he is the only man I ever knew who seemed ashamed of his natural benevolence. He takes as much pains to hide his feelings, as any hypocrite would to conceal his indifference; but on every unguarded moment the mask drops off, and reveals him to the most superficial observer.

In one of our late excursions into the country, happening to discourse upon the provision that was made for the poor in England, he seemed amazed how any of his countrymen could be so foolishly weak as to relieve occasional objects of charity, when the laws had made such ample provision for their support. In every parish house, says he, the poor are supplied with food, clothes, fire, and a bed to lie on; they want no more, I desire no more myself; yet still they seem discontented. I am surprised at the inactivity of our magistrates, in not taking up such vagrants, who are only a weight upon the industrious; I am surprised that the people are found to relieve them, when they must be at the same time sensible that it, in some measure, encourages idleness, extravagance, and imposture. Were I to advise any man for whom I had the least regard, I would caution him by all means not to be imposed upon by their false pretences: let me assure you, Sir, they are impostors, every one of them, and rather merit a prison than relief.

He was proceeding in this strain earnestly, to dissuade me from an imprudence of which I am seldom guilty, when an old man, who still had about him the remnants of tattered finery, implored our compassion. He assured us that he was no common beggar, but forced into the shameful profession to support a dying wife and five hungry children. Being prepossessed against such falsehoods, his story had not the least influence upon me; but it was quite otherwise with the man in black; I could see it visibly operate upon his countenance, and effectually interrupt his harangue. I could easily perceive, that his heart burned to relieve the five starving children, but he seemed ashamed to discover his weakness to me. While he thus hesitated between compassion and pride, I pretended to look another way, and he seized this opportunity of giving the poor petitioner a piece of silver, bidding him at the same time, in order that I should hear, go work for his bread, and not tease passengers with such impertinent falsehoods for the future.

As he had fancied himself quite unperceived, he continued, as we proceeded, to rail against beggars with as much animosity as before: he threw in some episodes on his own amazing prudence and economy, with his profound skill in discovering impostors; he explained the manner in which he would deal with beggars were he a magistrate, hinted at enlarging some of the prisons for their reception, and told two stories of ladies that were robbed by beggarmen. He was beginning a third to the same purpose, when a sailor with a wooden leg once more crossed our walks, desiring our pity, and blessing our limbs. I was for going on without taking any notice, but my friend looking wishfully upon the poor petitioner, bade me stop, and he would show me with how much ease he could at any time detect an impostor.

He now therefore assumed a look of importance, and in an angry tone began to examine the sailor, demanding in what engagement he was thus disabled and rendered unfit for service. The sailor replied in a tone as angrily as he, that he had been an officer on board a private ship of war, and that he had lost his leg abroad in defence of those who did nothing at home. At this reply, all my friend's importance vanished in a moment; he had not a single question more to ask: he now only studied what method he should take to relieve him unobserved. He had, however, no easy part to act, as he was obliged to preserve the appearance of ill-nature before me, and yet relieve himself by relieving the sailor. Casting, therefore, a furious look upon some bundles of chips which the fellow carried in a string at his back, my friend demanded how he sold his matches; but, not waiting for a reply, desired in a surly tone to have a shilling's worth. The sailor seemed at first surprised at his demand, but soon recollected himself, and presenting his whole bundle, "Here, master," says he, "take all my cargo, and a blessing into the bargain."

It is impossible to describe with what an air of triumph my friend marched off with his new purchase; he assured me, that he was firmly of opinion that those fellows must have stolen their goods, who could thus afford to sell them for half value. He informed me of several different uses to which those chips might be applied; he expatiated largely upon the savings that would result from lighting candles with a match, instead of thrusting them into the fire. He averred, that he would as soon have parted with a tooth as his money to those vagabonds, unless for some valuable consideration. I cannot tell how long this panegyric upon frugality and matches might have continued, had not his attention been called off by another object more distressful than either of the former. A woman in rags, with one child in her arms and another on her back, was attempting to sing ballads, but with such a mournful voice, that it was difficult to determine whether she was singing or crying. A wretch, who in the deepest distress still aimed at good-humour, was an object my friend was by no means capable of withstanding: his vivacity and his discourse were instantly interrupted; upon this occasion his very dissimulation had forsaken him. Even in my presence he immediately applied his hands to his pockets, in order to relieve her; but guess his confusion when he found he had already given away all the money he carried about him to former objects. The misery painted in the woman's visage was not half so strongly expressed as the agony in his. He continued to search for some time, but to no purpose, till, at length recollecting himself, with a face of ineffable good-nature, as he had no money, he put into her hands his shilling's worth of matches.

LETTER XXVII. TO THE SAME

THE HISTORY OF THE MAN IN BLACK

As there appeared something reluc

tantly good in the character of my companion, I must own it surprised me what could be his motives for thus concealing virtues which others take such pains to display. I was unable to repress my desire of knowing the history of a man who thus seemed to act under continual restraint, and whose benevolence was rather the effect of appetite than reason.

It was not, however, till after repeated solicitations he thought proper to gratify my curiosity. "If you are fond," says he, "of hearing hairbreadth escapes, my history must certainly please; for I have been for twenty years upon the very verge of starving, without ever being starved.

"My father, the younger son of a good family, was possessed of a small living in the church. His education was above his fortune, and his generosity greater than his education. Poor as he was, he had his flatterers still poorer than himself; for every dinner he gave them, they returned an equivalent in praise; and this was all he wanted. The same ambition that actuates a monarch at the head of an army, influenced my father at the head of his table; he told the story of the ivy-tree, and that was laughed at; he repeated the jest of the two scholars and one pair of breeches, and the company laughed at that; but the story of Taffy in the sedan chair, was sure to set the table in a roar: thus his pleasure increased in proportion to the pleasure he gave; he loved all the world, and he fancied all the world loved him.

"As his fortune was but small, he lived up to the very extent of it; he had no intentions of leaving his children money, for that was dross; he was resolved they should have learning; for learning, he used to observe, was better than silver or gold. For this purpose he undertook to instruct us himself; and took as much pains to form our morals as to improve our understanding. We were told that universal benevolence was what first cemented society; we were taught to consider all the wants of mankind as our own; to regard the *human face divine* with affection and esteem; he wound us up to be mere machines of pity, and rendered us incapable of withstanding the slightest impulse made either by real or fictitious distress; in a word, we were perfectly instructed in the art of giving away thousands, before we were taught the more necessary qualifications of getting a farthing.

"I cannot avoid imagining, that thus refined by his lessons out of all my suspicion, and divested of even all the little cunning which Nature had given me, I resembled, upon my first entrance into the busy and insidious world, one of those gladiators who were exposed without armour in the amphitheatre at Rome. My father, however, who had only seen the world on one side, seemed to triumph in my superior discernment; though my whole stock of wisdom consisted in being able to talk like himself upon subjects that once were useful, because they were then topics of the busy world; but that now were utterly useless, because connected with the busy world no longer.

"The first opportunity he had of finding his expectations disappointed, was in the very middling figure I made in the university; he had flattered himself that he should soon see me rising into the foremost rank in literary reputation, but was mortified to find me utterly unnoticed and unknown. His disappointment might have been partly ascribed to his having over-rated my talents, and partly to my dislike of mathematical reasonings at a time when my imagination and memory, yet unsatisfied, were more eager after new objects, than desirous of reasoning upon those I knew. This did not, however, please my tutor, who observed, indeed, that I was a little dull; but at the same time allowed, that I seemed to be very good-natured, and had no harm in me.

"After I had resided at college seven years, my father died, and left me—

his blessing. Thus shoved from shore without ill-nature to protect, or cunning to guide, or proper stores to subsist me in so dangerous a voyage, I was obliged to embark in the wide world at twenty-two. But, in order to settle in life, my friends *advised* (for they always advise when they begin to despise us), they advised me, I say, to go into orders.

"To be obliged to wear a long wig, when I liked a short one, or a black coat, when I generally dressed in brown, I thought was such a restraint upon my liberty, that I absolutely rejected the proposal. A priest in England is not the same mortified creature with a bonze in China. With us, not he that fasts best, but eats best, is reckoned the best liver; yet I rejected a life of luxury, indolence, and ease, from no other consideration but that boyish one of dress. So that my friends were now perfectly satisfied I was undone; and yet they thought it a pity for one who had not the least harm in him, and was so very good-natured.

"Poverty naturally begets dependence, and I was admitted as flatterer to a great man. At first I was surprised that the situation of a flatterer at a great man's table could be thought disagreeable: there was no great trouble in listening attentively when his lordship spoke, and laughing when he looked round for applause. This even good manners might have obliged me to perform. I found, however, too soon, that his lordship was a greater dunce than myself; and from that very moment flattery was at an end. I now rather aimed at setting him right, than at receiving his absurdities with submission: to flatter those we do not know is an easy task; but to flatter our intimate acquaintances, all whose foibles are strongly in our eye, is drudgery insupportable. Every time I now opened my lips in praise, my falsehood went to my conscience; his lordship soon perceived me to be very unfit for service; I was therefore discharged; my patron at the same time being graciously pleased to observe,

that he believed I was tolerably good-natured, and had not the least harm in me.

"Disappointed in ambition, I had recourse to love. A young lady, who lived with her aunt, and was possessed of a pretty fortune in her own disposal, had given me, as I fancied, some reason to expect success. The symptoms by which I was guided were striking. She had always laughed with me at her awkward acquaintance, and at her aunt among the number; she always observed, that a man of sense would make a better husband than a fool, and I as constantly applied the observation in my own favour. She continually talked, in my company, of friendship and the beauties of the mind, and spoke of Mr. Shrimp my rival's high-heeled shoes with detestation. These were circumstances which I thought strongly in my favour; so, after resolving and re-resolving, I had courage enough to tell her my mind. Miss heard my proposal with serenity, seeming at the same time to study the figures of her fan. Out at last it came. There was but one small objection to complete our happiness; which was no more than—that she was married three months before to Mr. Shrimp, with high-heeled shoes! By way of consolation, however, she observed, that, though I was disappointed in her, my addresses to her aunt would probably kindle her into sensibility; as the old lady always allowed me to be very good-natured, and not to have the least share of harm in me.

"Yet, still I had friends, numerous friends, and to them I was resolved to apply. O Friendship! thou fond soother of the human breast, to thee we fly in every calamity; to thee the wretched seek for succour; on thee the care-tired son of misery fondly relies; from thy kind assistance the unfortunate always hopes relief, and may be ever sure of—disappointment! My first application was to a city-scrivener, who had frequently offered to lend me money when he knew I did not want it. I informed him that now was the time to put his friendship to the test; that I wanted to borrow a couple of hundreds for a certain occasion, and was resolved to take it up from him. 'And pray, Sir,' cried my friend, 'do you want all this money?' Indeed I never wanted it more, returned I. 'I am sorry for that,' cries the scrivener, 'with all my heart; for they who want money when they come to borrow, will always want money when they should come to pay.'

"From him I flew with indignation to one of the best friends I had in the world, and made the same request. 'Indeed, Mr. Drybone,' cries my friend, 'I always thought it would come to this. You know, Sir, I would not advise you but for your own good; but your conduct has hitherto been ridiculous in the highest degree, and some of your acquaintance always thought you a very silly fellow. Let me see—you want two hundred pounds. Do you only want two hundred, Sir, exactly?' To confess a truth, returned I, I shall want three hundred; but then I have another friend, from whom I can borrow the rest. 'Why, then,' replied my friend, 'if you would take my advice (and you know I should not presume to advise you but for your own good), I would recommend it to you to borrow the whole sum from that other friend; and then one note will serve for all, you know.'

"Poverty now began to come fast upon me; yet instead of growing more provident or cautious as I grew poor, I became every day more indolent and simple. A friend was arrested for fifty pounds; I was unable to extricate him except by becoming his bail. When at liberty he fled from his creditors, and left me to take his place. In prison I expected greater satisfactions than I had enjoyed at large. I hoped to converse with men in this new world, simple and believing like myself; but I found them as cunning and as cautious as those in the world I had left behind. They sponged up my money while it lasted, borrowed my coals and never paid for them, and cheated me when I played at cribbage. All this was done because they believed me to be very good-natured, and knew that I had no harm in me.

"Upon my first entrance into this mansion, which is to some the abode of despair, I felt no sensations different from those I experienced abroad. I was now on one side of the door, and those who were unconfined were on the other: this was all the difference between us. At first, indeed, I felt some uneasiness, in considering how I should be able to provide this week for the wants of the week ensuing; but after some time, if I found myself sure of eating one day, I never troubled my head how I was to be supplied another. I seized every precarious meal with the utmost good humour; indulged no rants of spleen at my situation; never called down heaven and all the stars to behold me dining upon an halfpenny-worth of radishes; my very companions were taught to believe that I liked salad better than mutton. I contented myself with thinking, that all my life I should either eat white bread or brown; considered that all that happened was best; laughed when I was not in pain; took the world as it went, and read Tacitus often, for want of more books and company.

"How long I might have continued in this torpid state of simplicity I cannot tell, had I not been roused by seeing an old acquaintance, whom I knew to be a prudent blockhead, preferred to a place in the government. I now found that I had pursued a wrong track, and that the true way of being able to relieve others, was first to aim at independence myself: my immediate care, therefore, was to leave my present habitation, and make an entire reformation in my conduct and behaviour. For a free, open, undesigning deportment, I put on that of closeness, prudence, and economy. One of the most heroic actions I ever performed, and for which I shall praise myself as long as I live, was the refusing half-a-crown to an old ac quaintance, at the time when he wanted it, and I had it to spare; for this alone I deserve to be decreed an ovation.

"I now, therefore, pursued a course of uninterrupted frugality, seldom wanted a dinner, and was consequently invited to twenty. I soon began to get the character of a saving hunks that had money, and insensibly grew into esteem. Neighbours have asked my advice in the disposal of their daughters, and I have always taken care not to give any. I have contracted a friendship with an alderman, only by observing, that if we take a farthing from a thousand pounds, it will be a thousand pounds no longer. I have been invited to a pawnbroker's table, by pretending to hate gravy; and am now actually upon treaty of marriage with a rich widow, for only having observed that the bread was rising. If ever I am asked a question, whether I know it or not, instead of answering, I only smile and look wise. If a charity is proposed, I go about with the hat, but put nothing in myself. If a wretch solicits my pity, I observe that the world is filled with impostors, and take a certain method of not being deceived, by never relieving. In short, I now find the truest way of finding esteem, even from the indigent, is—*to give away nothing, and thus have much in our power to give.*"

LETTER XXX. FROM THE SAME

THE PROCEEDINGS OF THE CLUB OF AUTHORS

By my last advices from Moscow, I find the caravan has not yet departed for China: I still continue to write, expecting that you may receive a large number of letters at once. In them you will find rather a minute detail of English peculiarities, than a general picture of their manners or disposition. Happy it were for mankind if all travellers would thus, instead of characterizing a people in general terms, lead us into a detail of those minute circumstances which first influenced

their opinion: the genius of a country should be investigated with a kind of experimental inquiry: by this means we should have more precise and just notions of foreign nations, and detect travellers themselves when they happened to form wrong conclusions.

My friend and I repeated our visit to the club of authors; where, upon our entrance, we found the members all assembled and engaged in a loud debate.

The poet in shabby finery, holding a manuscript in his hand, was earnestly endeavouring to persuade the company to hear him read the first book of an heroic poem, which he had composed the day before. But against this all the members very warmly objected. They knew no reason why any member of the club should be indulged with a particular hearing, when many of them had published whole volumes which had never been looked in. They insisted that the law should be observed, where reading in company was expressly noticed. It was in vain that the plaintiff pleaded the peculiar merit of his piece; he spoke to an assembly insensible to all his remonstrances; the book of laws was opened, and read by the secretary, where it was expressly enacted, "That whatsoever poet, speech-maker, critic, or historian should presume to engage the company by reading his own works, he was to lay down sixpence previous to opening the manuscript, and should be charged one shilling an hour while he continued reading: the said shilling to be equally distributed among the company as a recompense for their trouble."

Our poet seemed at first to shrink at the penalty, hesitating for some time whether he should deposit the fine, or shut up the poem; but looking round, and perceiving two strangers in the room, his love of fame outweighed his prudence, and laying down the sum by law established, he insisted on his prerogative.

A profound silence ensuing, he began by explaining his design. "Gentlemen," says he, "the present piece is not one of your common epic poems, which come from the press like paper-kites in summer: there are none of your Turnuses or Didos in it; it is an heroical description of nature. I only beg you'll endeavour to make your souls unison with mine, and hear with the same enthusiasm with which I have written. The poem begins with the description of an author's bed-chamber: the picture was sketched in my own apartment; for you must know, gentlemen, that I am myself the hero." Then putting himself into the attitude of an orator, with all the emphasis of voice and action, he proceeded:

"Where the Red Lion flaring o'er the way,
Invites each passing stranger that can pay;
Where Calvert's butt, and Parson's black
    champagne,
Regale the drabs and bloods of Drury-lane;
There in a lonely room, from bailiffs snug,
The Muse found Scroggen stretched beneath
    a rug.
A window patched with paper lent a ray,
That dimly show'd the state in which he lay;
The sanded floor that grits beneath the
    tread;
The humid wall with paltry pictures spread;
The royal game of goose was there in view,
And the twelve rules the royal martyr drew;
The seasons fram'd with listing found a
    place,
And brave Prince William show'd his lamp-
    black face;
The morn was cold, he views with keen
    desire,
The rusty grate, unconscious of a fire;
With beer and milk arrears the frieze was
    scor'd,
And five crack'd tea-cups dress'd the chim-
    ney board.
A night-cap deck'd his brows instead of bay,
A cap by night—a stocking all the day!"

With this last line he seemed so much elated, that he was unable to proceed. "There gentlemen," cries he, "there is a description for you; Rabelais' bed-chamber is but a fool to it:

" 'A cap by night—a stocking all the day!'

"there is sound and sense, and truth, and nature in the trifling compass of ten little syllables."

He was too much employed in self-admiration to observe the company; who by nods, winks, shrugs, and stifled laughter, testified every mark of contempt. He turned severally to each for their opinion, and found all, however, ready to applaud. One swore it was inimitable; another said it was damn'd fine; and a third cried out in a rapture, Carissimo! At last addressing himself to the president, "And pray, Mr. Squint," says he, "let us have your opinion." "Mine," answered the president, (taking the manuscript out of the author's hand); "may this glass suffocate me, but I think it equal to anything I have seen; and I fancy," (continued he, doubling up the poem and forcing it into the author's pocket), "that you will get great honour when it comes out; so I shall beg leave to put it in. We will not intrude upon your good-nature, in desiring to hear more of it at present; ex ungue Herculem, we are satisfied, perfectly satisfied." The author made two or three attempts to pull it out a second time, and the president made as many to prevent him. Thus, though with reluctance, he was at last obliged to sit down, contented with the commendations for which he had paid.

When this tempest of poetry and praise was blown over, one of the company changed the subject, by wondering how any man can be so dull as to write poetry at present, since prose itself would hardly pay. "Would you think it, gentlemen," continued he, "I have actually written last week sixteen prayers, twelve bawdy jests, and three sermons, all at the rate of sixpence apiece; and what is still more extraordinary, the bookseller has lost by the bargain. Such sermons would once have gained me a prebend's stall; but now, alas: we have neither piety, taste, nor humour among us. Positively, if this season does not turn out better than it has begun, unless the ministry commit some blunders to furnish us with a new topic of abuse, I shall resume my old business of working at the press, instead of finding it employment."

The whole club seemed to join in condemning the season, as one of the worst that had come for some time; a gentleman particularly observed that the nobility were never known to subscribe worse than at present. "I know not how it happens," said he, "though I follow them up as close as possible, yet I can hardly get a single subscription in a week. The houses of the great are as inaccessible as a frontier garrison at midnight. I never see a nobleman's door half-opened that some surly porter or footman does not stand full in the breach. I was yesterday to wait with a subscription-proposal upon my Lord Squash, the Creolian. I had posted myself at his door the whole morning, and just as he was getting into his coach, thrust my proposal snug into his hand, folded up in the form of a letter from myself. He just glanced at the superscription, and not knowing the hand, consigned it to his valet-de-chambre; this respectable personage treated it as his master, and put it into the hands of the porter; the porter grasped my proposal frowning; and measuring my figure from top to toe, put it back into my own hands unopened."

"To the devil I pitch all the nobility," cries a little man, in a peculiar accent: "I am sure they have of late used me most scurvily. You must know, gentlemen, some time ago, upon the arrival of a certain noble duke from his travels, I set myself down, and vamped up a fine flaunting poetical panegyric, which I had written in such a strain, that I fancied it would have even wheedled milk from a mouse. In this I represented the whole kingdom welcoming his grace to his native soil, not forgetting the loss France and Italy would sustain in their arts by his departure I expected to touch for a bank-bill at least; so folding up my verses in gilt paper, I gave my last half-crown to a genteel servant to be the bearer. My letter was safely conveyed to his grace, and the servant after four hours' absence, during which time I led the life of a fiend, returned with a letter four times as big as mine. Guess my ecstasy at the prospect of so fine a return. I eagerly took the pacquet into my hands, that trembled to receive it. I kept it some time unopened before me, brooding over the expected treasure it contained; when opening it, as I hope to be saved, gentlemen, his grace had sent me in payment for my poem no bank bills, but six copies of verse, each longer than mine, addressed to him upon the same occasion."

"A nobleman," cries a member, who had hitherto been silent, "is created as much for the confusion of us authors as the catchpole. I'll tell you a story, gentlemen, which is as true as that this pipe is made of clay. When I was delivered of my first book, I owed my tailor for a suit of clothes, but that is nothing new, you know, and may be any man's case as well as mine. Well, owing him for a suit of clothes, and hearing that my book took very well, he sent for his money, and insisted upon being paid immediately. Though I was at that time rich in fame, for my book ran like wild-fire, yet I was very short in money, and being unable to satisfy his demand, prudently resolved to keep my chamber, preferring a prison of my own choosing at home, to one of my tailor's choosing abroad. In vain the bailiffs used all their arts to decoy me from my citadel, in vain they sent to let me know that a gentleman wanted to speak with me at the next tavern, in vain they came with an urgent message from my aunt in the country; in vain I was told that a particular friend was at the point of death, and desired to take his last farewell; I was deaf, insensible, rock, adamant; the bailiffs could make no impression on my hard heart, for I effectually kept my liberty, by never stirring out of the room.

"This was very well for a fortnight; when one morning I received a most splendid message from the Earl of Doomsday, importing that he had read my book, and was in raptures with every line of it; he impatiently longed to see the author, and had some designs which might turn out greatly to my advantage. I paused upon the contents of this message, and found there could be no deceit, for the card was gilt at the edges, and the bearer, I was told, had quite the looks of a gentleman. Witness, ye powers, how my heart triumphed at my own importance! I saw a long perspective of felicity before me; I applauded the taste of the times, which never saw genius forsaken; I had prepared a set introductory speech for the occasion, five glaring compliments for his lordship, and two more modest for myself. The next morning, therefore, in order to be punctual to my appointment, I took coach, and ordered the fellow to drive to the street and house mentioned in his lordship's address. I had the precaution to pull up the window as I went along, to keep off the busy part of mankind; and, big with expectation, fancied the coach never went fast enough. At length, however, the wished-for moment of its stopping arrived; this for some time I impatiently expected, and letting down the door in a transport, in order to take a previous view of his lordship's magnificent palace and situation, I found—poison to my sight!—I found myself, not in an elegant street, but a paltry lane; not at a nobleman's door, but the door of a sponging-house. I found the coachman had all this while been just driving me to jail, and I saw the bailiff with a devil's face coming out to secure me."

To a philosopher no circumstance, however trifling, is too minute; he finds instruction and entertainment in occurrences which are passed over by the rest of mankind as low, trite, and indifferent; it is from the number of these particulars, which to many appear insignificant, that he is at last enabled to form general conclusions; this, therefore, must be my excuse for sending so far as China accounts of manners and follies, which, though

minute in their own nature, serve more truly to characterize this people than histories of their public treaties, courts, ministers, negotiations, and ambassadors. Adieu!

LETTER LXXI. TO THE SAME

THE SHABBY BEAU, THE MAN IN BLACK, THE CHINESE PHILOSOPHER, ETC., AT VAUXHALL

The people of London are as fond of walking as our friends at Pekin of riding; one of the principal entertainments of the citizens here in summer is to repair about nightfall to a garden not far from town, where they walk about, show their best clothes and best faces, and listen to a concert provided for the occasion.

I accepted an invitation a few evenings ago from my old friend, the man in black, to be one of a party that was to sup there; and at the appointed hour waited upon him at his lodgings. There I found the company assembled and expecting my arrival. Our party consisted of my friend, in superlative finery, his stockings rolled, a black velvet waistcoat which was formerly new, and a gray wig combed down in imitation of hair; a pawnbroker's widow, of whom, by-the-by, my friend was a professed admirer, dressed out in green damask, with three gold rings on every finger; Mr. Tibbs, the second-rate beau I have formerly described, together with his lady, in flimsy silk, dirty gauze instead of linen, and a hat as big as an umbrella.

Our first difficulty was in settling how we should set out. Mrs. Tibbs had a natural aversion to the water, and the widow being a little in flesh, as warmly protested against walking; a coach was therefore agreed upon, which being too small to carry five, Mr. Tibbs consented to sit in his wife's lap.

In this manner, therefore, we set forward, being entertained by the way with the bodings of Mr. Tibbs, who assured us, he did not expect to see a single creature for the evening above the degree of a cheesemonger; that this was the last night of the gardens, and that consequently we should be pestered with the nobility and gentry from Thames-street and Crooked-lane, with several other prophetic ejaculations, probably inspired by the uneasiness of his situation.

The illuminations began before we arrived, and I must confess, that upon entering the gardens, I found every sense overpaid with more than expected pleasure: the lights everywhere glimmering through the scarcely-moving trees, the full-bodied concert bursting on the stillness of the night, the natural concert of the birds in the more retired part of the grove, vying with that which was formed by art; the company gaily dressed looking satisfaction, and the tables spread with various delicacies, all conspired to fill my imagination with the visionary happiness of the Arabian lawgiver, and lifted me into an ecstasy of admiration. Head of Confucius, cried I to my friend, this is fine! this unites rural beauty with courtly magnificence; if we expect the virgins of immortality that hang on every tree, and may be plucked at every desire, I do not see how this falls short of Mahomet's Paradise!—As for virgins, cries my friend, it is true, they are a fruit that do not much abound in our gardens here; but if ladies, as plenty as apples in autumn, and as complying as any *houri* of them all, can content you, I fancy we have no need to go to Heaven for Paradise.

I was going to second his remarks, when we were called to a consultation by Mr. Tibbs and the rest of the company to know in what manner we were to lay out the evening to the greatest advantage. Mrs. Tibbs was for keeping the genteel walk of the garden, where she observed there was always the very best company; the widow, on the contrary, who came but once a season, was for securing a good standing-place to see the water-works, which she assured us would begin in less than an hour at farthest; a dispute therefore began, and as it was

managed between two of very opposite characters, it threatened to grow more bitter at every reply. Mrs. Tibbs wondered how people could pretend to know the polite world who had received all their rudiments of breeding behind a counter; to which the other replied, that though some people sat behind counters, yet they could sit at the head of their own tables too, and carve three good dishes of hot meat whenever they thought proper, which was more than some people could say for themselves, that hardly knew a rabbit and onions from a green goose and gooseberries.

It is hard to say where this might have ended, had not the husband, who probably knew the impetuosity of his wife's disposition, proposed to end the dispute by adjourning to a box, and try if there was anything to be had for supper that was supportable. To this we all consented, but here a new distress arose: Mr. and Mrs. Tibbs would sit in none but a genteel box, a box where they might see and be seen; one, as they expressed it, in the very focus of public view; but such a box was not easy to be obtained, for though we were perfectly convinced of our own gentility, and the gentility of our appearance, yet we found it a difficult matter to persuade the keepers of the boxes to be of our opinion; they chose to reserve genteel boxes for what they judged more genteel company.

At last, however, we were fixed, though somewhat obscurely, and supplied with the usual entertainment of the place. The widow found the supper excellent, but Mrs. Tibbs thought everything detestable. Come, come, my dear, cries the husband, by way of consolation, to be sure we can't find such dressing here as we have at Lord Crump's or Lady Crimp's; but for Vauxhall dressing it is pretty good; it is not their victuals indeed I find fault with, but their wine; their wine, cries he, drinking off a glass, indeed, is most abominable.

By this last contradiction the widow

was fairly conquered in point of politeness. She perceived now that she had no pretensions in the world to taste, her very senses were vulgar, since she had praised detestable custard, and smacked at wretched wine; she was therefore content to yield the victory, and for the rest of the night to listen and improve. It is true, she would now and then forget herself, and confess she was pleased, but they soon brought her back again to miserable refinement. She once praised the painting of the box in which we were sitting, but was soon convinced that such paltry pieces ought rather to excite horror than satisfaction; she ventured again to commend one of the singers, but Mrs. Tibbs soon let her know, in the style of a connoisseur, that the singer in question had neither ear, voice, nor judgment.

Mr. Tibbs, now willing to prove that his wife's pretensions to music were just, entreated her to favour the company with a song; but to this she gave a positive denial, for you know very well, my dear, says she, that I am not in voice to-day, and when one's voice is not equal to one's judgment, what signifies singing? besides, as there is no accompaniment, it would be but spoiling music. All these excuses, however, were over-ruled by the rest of the company, who, though one would think they already had music enough, joined in the entreaty. But particularly the widow, now willing to convince the company of her breeding, pressed so warmly, that she seemed determined to take no refusal. At last then the lady complied, and after humming for some minutes, began with such a voice, and such affectation, as I could perceive gave but little satisfaction to any except her husband. He sat with rapture in his eye, and beat time with his hand on the table.

You must observe, my friend, that it is the custom of this country, when a lady or gentleman happens to sing, for the company to sit as mute and motionless as statues. Every feature,

every limb, must seem to correspond in fixed attention, and while the song continues, they are to remain in a state of universal petrifaction. In this mortifying situation we had continued for some time, listening to the song, and looking with tranquillity; when the master of the box came to inform us, that the water-works were going to begin. At this information I could instantly perceive the widow bounce from her seat; but correcting herself, she sat down again, repressed by motives of good breeding. Mrs. Tibbs, who had seen the water-works a hundred times, resolving not to be interrupted, continued her song without any share of mercy, nor had the smallest pity on our impatience. The widow's face, I own, gave me high entertainment; in it I could plainly read the struggle she felt between good breeding and curiosity; she talked of the water-works the whole evening before, and seemed to have come merely in order to see them; but then she could not bounce out in the very middle of a song, for that would be forfeiting all pretensions to high life, or high-lived company, ever after. Mrs. Tibbs therefore kept on singing, and we continued to listen, till at last, when the song was just concluded, the waiter came to inform us that the water-works were over.

The water-works over! cried the widow: the water-works over already, that's impossible, they can't be over so soon!—It is not my business, replied the fellow, to contradict your ladyship, I'll run again and see. He went, and soon returned with a confirmation of the dismal tidings. No ceremony could now bind my friend's disappointed mistress, she testified her displeasure in the openest manner; in short, she now began to find fault in turn, and at last, insisted upon going home, just at the time that Mr. and Mrs. Tibbs assured the company that the polite hours were going to begin, and that the ladies would instantaneously be entertained with the horns.

Adieu!

LETTER LXXII. TO THE SAME

THE MARRIAGE ACT CENSURED

Not far from this city lives a poor tinker who has educated seven sons, all at this very time in arms and fighting for their country; and what reward do you think has the tinker from the state for such important services? None in the world; his sons, when the war is over, may probably be whipt from parish to parish as vagabonds, and the old man, when past labour, may die a prisoner in some house of correction.

Such a worthy subject in China would be held in universal reverence; his services would be rewarded if not with dignities, at least with an exemption from labour; he would take the left hand at feasts, and mandarins themselves would be proud to show their submission. The English laws punish vice; the Chinese laws do more, they reward virtue!

Considering the little encouragement given to matrimony here, I am not surprised at the discouragement given to propagation. Would you believe it, my dear Fum Hoam, there are laws made, which even forbid the people's marrying each other. By the head of Confucius, I jest not; there are such laws in being here: and yet their lawgivers have neither been instructed among the Hottentots, nor imbibed their principles of equity from the natives of Anamaboo.

There are laws which ordain, that no man shall marry a woman against her own consent. This, though contrary to what we are taught in Asia, and though in some measure a clog upon matrimony, I have no great objection to. There are laws which ordain, that no woman shall marry against her father and mother's consent, unless arrived at an age of maturity; by which is understood those years when women with us are generally past child-bearing. This must be a clog upon matrimony, as it is more difficult for the lover to please three than one, and much more diffi-

cult to please old people than young ones. The laws ordain, that the consenting couple shall take a long time to consider before they marry; this is a very great clog, because people love to have all rash actions done in a hurry. It is ordained, that all marriages shall be proclaimed before celebration; this is a severe clog, as many are ashamed to have their marriage made public, from motives of vicious modesty, and many afraid from views of temporal interest. It is ordained, that there is nothing sacred in the ceremony, but that it may be dissolved to all intents and purposes by the authority of any civil magistrate. And yet opposite to this it is ordained, that the priest shall be paid a large sum of money for granting his sacred permission.

Thus you see, my friend, that matrimony here is hedged round with so many obstructions, that those who are willing to break through or surmount them must be contented, if at last they find it a bed of thorns. The laws are not to blame, for they have deterred the people from engaging as much as they could. It is indeed become a very serious affair in England, and none but serious people are generally found willing to engage. The young, the gay, and the beautiful, who have motives of passion only to induce them, are seldom found to embark, as those inducements are taken away; and none but the old, the ugly, and the mercenary, are seen to unite, who, if they have any posterity at all, will probably be an ill-favoured race like themselves.

What gave rise to those laws might have been some such accidents as these. It sometimes happened, that a miser who had spent all his youth in scraping up money to give his daughter such a fortune as might get her a mandarin husband, found his expectations disappointed at last, by her running away with his footman: this must have been a sad shock to the poor disconsolate parent, to see his poor daughter in a one-horse chaise, when he had designed her for a coach and six. What a stroke from Providence! to see his dear money go to enrich a beggar; all nature cried out at the profanation!

It sometimes happened also, that a lady who had inherited all the titles, and all the nervous complaints of nobility, thought fit to impair her dignity and mend her constitution, by marrying a farmer: this must have been a sad shock to her inconsolable relations, to see so fine a flower snatched from a flourishing family, and planted in a dunghill; this was an absolute inversion of the first principles of things.

In order therefore to prevent the great from being thus contaminated by vulgar alliances, the obstacles to matrimony have been so contrived, that the rich only can marry amongst the rich; and the poor, who would leave celibacy, must be content to increase their poverty with a wife. Thus have their laws fairly inverted the inducements to matrimony. Nature tells us, that beauty is the proper allurement of those who are rich, and money of those who are poor; but things here are so contrived, that the rich are invited to marry by that fortune which they do not want, and the poor have no inducement, but that beauty which they do not feel.

An equal diffusion of riches through any country ever constitutes its happiness. Great wealth in the possession of one stagnates, and extreme poverty with another keeps him in unambitious indigence; but the moderately rich are generally active: not too far removed from poverty to fear its calamities, nor too near extreme wealth to slacken the nerve of labour, they remain still between both in a state of continual fluctuation. How impolitic, therefore, are those laws which promote the accumulation of wealth among the rich, more impolitic still in attempting to increase the depression on poverty!

Bacon, the English philosopher, compares money to manure: "If gath-ered in heaps," says he, "it does no good; on the contrary, it becomes offensive. But being spread, though never so thinly, over the surface of the earth, it enriches the whole country." Thus the wealth a nation possesses must expatiate, or it is of no benefit to the public; it becomes rather a grievance where matrimonial laws thus confine it to a few.

But this restraint upon matrimonial community, even considered in a physical light, is injurious. As those who rear up animals take all possible pains to cross the strain in order to improve the breed; so in those countries where marriage is most free, the inhabitants are found every age to improve in stature and in beauty; on the contrary, where it is confined to a *caste*, a *tribe* or an *horde*, as among the Gaurs, the Jews, or the Tartars, each division soon assumes a family likeness, and every tribe degenerates into peculiar deformity. From hence it may be easily inferred, that if the mandarins here are resolved only to marry among each other, they will soon produce a posterity with mandarin faces; and we shall see the heir of some honourable family scarcely equal to the abortion of a country farmer.

These are a few of the obstacles to marriage here, and it is certain, they have in some measure answered the end, for celibacy is both frequent and fashionable. Old bachelors appear abroad without a mask, and old maids, my dear Fum Hoam, have been absolutely known to ogle. To confess in friendship; if I were an Englishman, I fancy I should be an old bachelor myself; I should never find courage to run through all the adventures prescribed by the law. I could submit to court my mistress herself upon reasonable terms; but to court her father, her mother, and a long tribe of cousins, aunts, and relations, and then stand the butt of a whole country church; I would as soon turn tail and make love to her grandmother.

I can conceive no other reason for

thus loading matrimony with so many prohibitions, unless it be that the country was thought already too populous, and this was found to be the most effectual means of thinning it. If this was the motive, I cannot but congratulate the wise projectors on the success of their scheme. Hail, O ye dim-sighted politicians, ye weeders of men! 'Tis yours to clip the wing of industry, and convert Hymen to a broker. 'Tis yours to behold small objects with a microscopic eye, but to be blind to those which require an extent of vision. 'Tis yours, O ye discerners of mankind, to lay the line between society, and weaken that force by dividing, which should bind with united vigour. 'Tis yours to introduce national real distress, in order to avoid the imaginary distresses of a few. Your actions can be justified by an hundred reasons like truth, they can be opposed by but a few reasons, and those reasons are true. Farewell!

LETTER CXIX. TO THE SAME

ON THE DISTRESSES OF THE POOR; EXEMPLIFIED IN THE LIFE OF A PRIVATE SENTINEL

The misfortunes of the great, my friend, are held up to engage our attention, are enlarged upon in tones of declamation, and the world is called upon to gaze at the noble sufferers; they have at once the comfort of admiration and pity.

Yet where is the magnanimity of bearing misfortunes when the whole world is looking on? Men in such circumstances can act bravely even from motives of vanity. He only who, in the vale of obscurity, can brave adversity, who, without friends to encourage, acquaintances to pity, or even without hope to alleviate his distresses, can behave with tranquillity and indifference, is truly great: whether peasant or courtier, he deserves admiration, and should be held up for our imitation and respect.

While the slightest inconveniences of the great are magnified into calamities; while tragedy mouths out their sufferings in all the strains of eloquence, the miseries of the poor are, however, entirely disregarded; though some undergo more real hardships in one day, than the great in their whole lives. It is indeed inconceivable what difficulties the meanest English sailor or soldier endures without murmuring or regret; without passionately declaiming against Providence, or calling their fellows to be gazers on their intrepidity. Every day is to him a day of misery, and yet he bears his hard fate without repining.

With what indignation do I hear the heroes of tragedy complain of misfortunes and hardships, whose greatest calamity is founded in arrogance and pride! Their severest distresses are pleasures, compared to what many of the adventuring poor every day sustain, without murmuring. These may eat, drink, and sleep, have slaves to attend them, and are sure of subsistence for life; while many of their fellow-creatures are obliged to wander, without a friend to comfort or to assist them, find enmity in every law, and are too poor to obtain even justice.

I have been led into these reflections from accidentally meeting some days ago a poor fellow begging at one of the outlets of this town, with a wooden leg. I was curious to learn what had reduced him to his present situation; and after giving him what I thought proper, desired to know the history of his life and misfortunes, and the manner in which he was reduced to his present distress. The disabled soldier, for such he was, with an intrepidity truly British, leaning on his crutch, put himself into an attitude to comply with my request, and gave me his history as follows:

"As for misfortunes, Sir, I cannot pretend to have gone through more than others. Except the loss of my limb, and my being obliged to beg, I don't know any reason, thank Heaven, that I have to complain: there are some who have lost both legs and an eye; but, thank Heaven, it is not quite so bad with me.

"My father was a labourer in the country, and died when I was five years old; so I was put upon the parish. As he had been a wandering sort of a man, the parishioners were not able to tell to what parish I belonged, or where I was born; so they sent me to another parish, and that parish sent me to a third; till at last it was thought I belonged to no parish at all. At length, however, they fixed me. I had some disposition to be a scholar, and had actually learned my letters; but the master of the workhouse put me to business as soon as I was able to handle a mallet.

"Here I lived an easy kind of a life for five years; I only wrought ten hours in the day, and had my meat and drink provided for my labour. It is true, I was not suffered to stir far from the house, for fear I should run away: but what of that? I had the liberty of the whole house, and the yard before the door, and that was enough for me.

"I was next bound out to a farmer, where I was up both early and late, but I ate and drank well, and liked my business well enough, till he died. Being then obliged to provide for myself, I was resolved to go and seek my fortune. Thus I lived, and went from town to town, working when I could get employment, and starving when I could get none; and might have lived so still. But happening one day to go through a field belonging to a magistrate, I spied a hare crossing the path just before me. I believe the devil put it in my head to fling my stick at it: well, what will you have on't? I killed the hare, and was bringing it away in triumph, when the Justice himself met me: he called me a villain, and collaring me, desired I would give an account of myself. I began immediately to give a full account of all that I knew of my breed, seed, and generation; but though I gave a very long account, the Justice said, I could give no account of myself; so I was indicted, and found guilty of being poor, and sent to Newgate, in order to be transported to the Plantations.

"People may say this and that of being in gaol; but for my part I found Newgate as agreeable a place as ever I was in, in all my life. I had my belly-full to eat and drink, and did no work; but alas, this kind of life was too good to last forever! I was taken out of prison after five months, put on board of a ship, and sent off with two hundred more. Our passage was but indifferent, for we were all confined in the hold, and died very fast, for want of sweet air and provisions; but for my part, I did not want meat, because I had a fever all the way: Providence was kind; when provisions grew short, it took away my desire of eating. When we came ashore, we were sold to the planters. I was bound for seven years, and as I was no scholar, for I had forgot my letters, I was obliged to work among the negroes; and served out my time, as in duty bound to do.

"When my time was expired, I worked my passage home, and glad I was to see Old England again, because I loved my country. O liberty, liberty, liberty, that is the property of every Englishman, and I will die in its defence! I was afraid, however, that I should be indicted for a vagabond once more, so did not much care to go into the country, but kept about town, and did little jobs when I could get them. I was very happy in this manner for some time; till one evening, coming home from work, two men knocked me down, and then desired me to stand still. They belonged to a press-gang; I was carried before the Justice, and as I could give no account of myself (that was the thing that always hobbled me), I had my choice left, whether to go on board a man-of-war, or list for a soldier. I chose to be a soldier; and in this post of a gentleman I served two campaigns, was at the battle in Flanders, and received but one wound through the breast, which is troublesome to this day.

"When the peace came on, I was discharged; and as I could not work, because my wound was sometimes painful, I listed for a landman in the East India Company's service. I here fought the French in six pitched battles; and verily believe, that if I could read or write, our captain would have given me promotion, and have made me a corporal. But that was not my good fortune; I soon fell sick, and when I became good for nothing, got leave to return home again with forty pounds in my pocket, which I saved in the service. This was at the beginning of the present war, so I hoped to be set on shore, and to have the pleasure of spending my money; but the government wanted men, and I was pressed again, before ever I could set foot on shore.

"The boatswain found me, as he said, an obstinate fellow: he swore that I understood my business perfectly well, but that I pretended sickness merely to be idle: God knows, I knew nothing of sea-business; he beat me without considering what he was about. But still my forty pounds was some comfort to me under every beating: the money was my comfort, and the money I might have had to this day; but that our ship was taken by the French, and so I lost it all.

"Our crew was carried into a French prison, and many of them died, because they were not used to live in a gaol; but for my part, it was nothing to me, for I was seasoned. One night, however, as I was sleeping on a bed of boards, with a warm blanket about me (for I always loved to lie well) I was awaked by the boatswain, who had a dark lantern in his hand. 'Jack,' says he to me, 'will you knock out the French sentry's brains?' 'I don't care,' says I, striving to keep myself awake, 'if I lend a hand.' 'Then follow me,' says he, 'and I hope we shall do business.' So up I got, and tied my blanket, which was all the clothes I had, about my middle, and

went with him to fight the French-man. We had no arms; but one Englishman is able to beat five French at any time; so we went down to the door, where both the sentries were posted, and rushing upon them, seized their arms in a moment and knocked them down. From thence, nine of us ran together to the key, and seizing the first boat we met, got out of the harbour, and put to sea. We had not been here three days before we were taken up by an English privateer, who was glad of so many good hands; and we consented to run our chance. However, we had not so much luck as we expected. In three days we fell-in with a French man-of-war, of forty guns, while we had but twenty-three; so to it we went. The fight lasted for three hours, and I verily believe we should have taken the Frenchman, but unfortunately, we lost almost all our men, just as we were going to get the victory. I was once more in the power of the French, and I believe it would have gone hard with me, had I been brought back to my old gaol in Brest; but by good fortune, we were re-taken, and carried to England once more.

"I had almost forgot to tell you, that in this last engagement I was wounded in two places; I lost four fingers of the left hand, and my leg was shot off. Had I had the good-fortune to have lost my leg and use of my hand on board a king's ship, and not a privateer, I should have been entitled to clothing and maintenance during the rest of my life; but that was not my chance: one man is born with a silver spoon in his mouth, and another with a wooden ladle. However, blessed be God, I enjoy good health, and have no enemy in this world that I know of, but the French, and the Justice of Peace."

Thus saying, he limped off, leaving my friend and me in admiration of his intrepidity and content; nor could we avoid acknowledging, that an habitual acquaintance with misery, is the truest school of fortitude and philosophy.   Adieu!

[1762]

ESSAY ON THE THEATRE; OR, A COMPARISON BETWEEN SENTIMENTAL AND LAUGHING COMEDY

The theatre, like all other amusements, has its fashions and its prejudices; and when satiated with its excellence, mankind begin to mistake change for improvement. For some years tragedy was the reigning entertainment; but of late it has entirely given way to comedy, and our best efforts are now exerted in these lighter kinds of composition. The pompous train, the swelling phrase, and the unnatural rant, are displaced for that natural portrait of human folly and frailty, of which all are judges, because all have sat for the picture.

But, as in describing nature, it is presented with a double face, either of mirth or sadness, our modern writers find themselves at a loss which chiefly to copy from; and it is now debated, whether the exhibition of human distress is likely to afford the mind more entertainment than that of human absurdity?

Comedy is defined by Aristotle to be a picture of the frailties of the lower part of mankind, to distinguish it from tragedy, which is an exhibition of the misfortunes of the great. When comedy therefore ascends to produce the characters of princes or generals upon the stage, it is out of its walk, since low life and middle life are entirely its object. The principal question therefore is, whether in describing low or middle life, an exhibition of its follies be not preferable to a detail of its calamities? Or, in other words, which deserves the preference, the weeping sentimental comedy, so much in fashion at present, or the laughing and even low comedy, which seems to have been last exhibited by Vanbrugh and Cibber?

If we apply to authorities, all the great masters in the dramatic art have but one opinion. Their rule is, that as tragedy displays the calamities of the great, so comedy should excite our laughter, by ridiculously exhibiting the follies of the lower part of mankind. Boileau, one of the best modern critics, asserts, that comedy will not admit of tragic distress:

Le Comique, ennemi des soupirs et des pleurs,
N'admet point dans ses vers de tragiques
          douleurs.

Nor is this rule without the strongest foundation in nature, as the distresses of the mean by no means affect us so strongly as the calamities of the great. When tragedy exhibits to us some great man fallen from his height, and struggling with want and adversity, we feel his situation in the same manner as we suppose he himself must feel, and our pity is increased in proportion to the height from which he fell. On the contrary, we do not so strongly sympathize with one born in humbler circumstances, and encountering accidental distress: so that whilst we melt for Belisarius, we scarcely give halfpence to the beggar, who accosts us in the street. The one has our pity, the other our contempt. Distress therefore is the proper object of tragedy, since the great excite our pity by their fall; but not equally so of comedy, since the actors employed in it are originally so mean, that they sink but little by their fall.

Since the first origin of the stage, tragedy and comedy have run in distinct channels, and never till of late encroached upon the provinces of each other. Terence, who seems to have made the nearest approaches, always judiciously stops short before he comes to the downright pathetic; and yet he is even reproached by Cæsar for wanting the *vis comica*. All the other comic writers of antiquity aim only at rendering folly or vice ridiculous, but never exalt their characters into buskined pomp, or make what Voltaire humourously calls a *tradesman's tragedy*.

Yet notwithstanding this weight of authority, and the universal practice of former ages, a new species of dramatic composition has been introduced under the name of *sentimental* comedy, in which the virtues of private life are exhibited, rather than the vices exposed; and the distresses rather than the faults of mankind make our interest in the piece. These comedies have had of late great success, perhaps from their novelty, and also from their flattering every man in his favourite foible. In these plays almost all the characters are good, and exceedingly generous; they are lavish enough of their *tin* money on the stage; and though they want humour, have abundance of sentiment and feeling. If they happen to have faults or foibles, the spectator is taught not only to pardon, but to applaud them, in consideration of the goodness of their hearts; so that folly, instead of being ridiculed, is commended, and the comedy aims at touching our passions without the power of being truly pathetic. In this manner we are likely to lose one great source of entertainment on the stage; for while the comic poet is invading the province of the tragic muse, he leaves her lovely sister quite neglected. Of this, however, he is no way solicitous, as he measures his fame by his profits.

But it will be said, that the theatre is formed to amuse mankind, and that it matters little, if this end be answered, by what means it is obtained. If mankind find delight in weeping at comedy, it would be cruel to abridge them in that or any other innocent pleasure. If those pieces are denied the name of comedies, yet call them by any other name, and if they are delightful, they are good. Their success, it will be said, is a mark of their merit, and it is only abridging our happiness to deny us an inlet to amusement.

These objections, however, are rather specious than solid. It is true, that amusement is a great object of the theatre; and it will be allowed, that these sentimental pieces do often

amuse us; but the question is, whether the true comedy would not amuse us more? The question is, whether a character supported throughout a piece with its ridicule still attending, would not give us more delight than this species of bastard tragedy, which only is applauded because it is new?

A friend of mine, who was sitting unmoved at one of these sentimental pieces, was asked how he could be so indifferent? "Why, truly," says he, "as the hero is but a tradesman, it is indifferent to me whether he be turned out of his counting-house on Fish-Street Hill, since he will still have enough left to open shop in St. Giles's."

The other objection is as illgrounded; for though we should give these pieces another name, it will not mend their efficacy. It will continue a kind of *mulish* production, with all the defects of its opposite parents, and marked with sterility. If we are permitted to make comedy weep, we have an equal right to make tragedy laugh, and to set down in blank verse the jests and repartees of all the attendants in a funeral procession.

But there is one argument in favour of sentimental comedy which will keep it on the stage, in spite of all that can be said against it. It is of all others the most easily written. Those abilities that can hammer out a novel, are fully sufficient for the production of a sentimental comedy. It is only sufficient to raise the characters a little; to deck out the hero with a riband, or give the heroine a title; then to put an insipid dialogue, without character or humour, into their mouths, give them mighty good hearts, very fine clothes, furnish a new set of scenes, make a pathetic scene or two, with a sprinkling of tender melancholy conversation through the whole; and there is no doubt but all the ladies will cry and all the gentlemen applaud.

Humour at present seems to be departing from the stage, and it will soon happen that our comic players will have nothing left for it but a fine coat and a song. It depends upon the audience whether they will actually drive those poor merry creatures from the stage, or sit at a play as gloomy as at the Tabernacle. It is not easy to re-cover an art when once lost; and it will be but a just punishment, that when, by our being too fastidious, we have banished humour from the stage, we should ourselves be deprived of the art of laughing.

[1773]

MICHAEL BRUCE (1746-1767)

Bruce was a poor Scottish lad who died young and whose poems were posthumously published by his friend John Logan in 1770. The best piece in this volume, the *Ode to the Cuckoo*, was later included by Logan among his own poems, but it is now generally given to Bruce.

Life and Complete Works, ed. J. Mackenzie (Edinburgh, 1914); *Life and Complete Works*, ed. J. G. Barnet (1927); *Life and Works*, bicentenary ed., with an Introductory Life by E. Vernon (Perth, 1951); R. G. Snoddy, *Michael Bruce, Shepherd-Poet of the Lomond Braes, 1746-1767* (Edinburgh, 1947).

ODE TO THE CUCKOO

Hail, beauteous stranger of the wood,
  Attendant on the spring!
Now heaven repairs thy rural seat,
  And woods thy welcome sing.

Soon as the daisy decks the green,
  Thy certain voice we hear:
Hast thou a star to guide thy path,
  Or mark the rolling year?

Delightful visitant! with thee
  I hail the time of flowers,   10
When heaven is filled with music sweet
  Of birds among the bowers.

The schoolboy, wandering in the wood
  To pull the flowers so gay,
Starts, thy curious voice to hear,
  And imitates thy lay,

Soon as the pea puts on the bloom,
  Thou fly'st thy vocal vale,
An annual guest, in other lands,
  Another spring to hail.   20

Sweet bird! thy bower is ever green,
  Thy sky is ever clear;
Thou hast no sorrow in thy song,
  No winter in thy year!

Alas, sweet bird! not so my fate;
  Dark scowling skies I see
Fast gathering round, and fraught with woe
  And wintry years to me.

O could I fly, I'd fly with thee:
  We'd make, with social wing,   30
Our annual visit o'er the globe,
  Companions of the spring.

[1770]

JAMES BEATTIE (1735-1803)

James Beattie was born in Laurencekirk, Kincardineshire, distinguished himself as a student at Marischal College, Aberdeen, and from 1760 to the end of his life held the Chair of Moral Philosophy in that institution. His chief piece of professional work was his *Essay on Truth* (1770), which was much overrated in its day as a common-sense and orthodox reply to the destructive doctrines of the skeptical Hume. During the composition of the *Essay* he amused himself by writing the first canto of his most important poem, *The Minstrel,* the plan of which he thus describes in a letter of 1768:

It is a moral and descriptive poem, written in the stanza of Spenser, but not much in his style. The hint of the subject was taken from Percy's 'Essays on the English Minstrels.' The first canto is a description of a poetical visionary in a solitary country, who derives most of his acquisitions in knowledge from his own observations, with reflections and digressions so contrived [as] to diversify the subject and suggest some useful moral meditations. Here and there, too, is a little touch of satire. In the second canto I propose to introduce my Visionary to a Hermit, who is to give him sundry instructions relating to arts, literature, and human life; he (the said hermit) having been a man of the world in his youth. He will earnestly advise his pupil not to meddle with public life, nor devote himself to the unthrifty trade of the Muses. The young man is willing to follow his advice, but, being stripped of all his possessions by a hostile invasion, is obliged through necessity to take his harp on his shoulders and trudge abroad into the world in the character of a minstrel. Here endeth the second canto, and probably the poem. You will see that such is the nature of my plan, that I may either stop here or proceed to recount the adventures of my pilgrim.

As a matter of fact, Beattie ends the second canto and the poem with an account of the youthful studies of his minstrel. Beattie was in contact at Aberdeen and Edinburgh with such critics as Duff and Home, who were expounding theories of original genius and primitive inspiration, and who had just found their ideas confirmed by the appearance of Macpherson's *Ossian.* He is not, however, deeply moved by theories of primitive poetry, despite the connection of *The Minstrel* with Percy's *Reliques,* and he failed to share his countrymen's enthusiasm for *Ossian.* His treatment of the early influences that form the poet has sometimes been compared with Wordsworth's *Prelude*; it might just as fairly be said that his descriptions of Scottish scenery and his declamations in Spenserian stanza suggest Byron, or that his account of the youthful enthusiast's love of folk-lore and tradition point forward to Scott. All these anticipations, though unmistakable, are very faint indeed. Beattie has an abstract and didactic bent; his use of romantic themes in poetry falls far short of Collins and Gray; and he does not vindicate his choice of the Spenserian stanza by showing much skill as a metrist. His attitude toward romantic subject-matter appears in a remark of his about one of his own critical essays; "I believe I shall next set about finishing what I formerly threw together on romance writing and chivalry, not because it is important, but because it is amusing, and will require no deep study." He was genteel rather than enthusiastic, and represents the bookishness and timidity of pre-romanticism.

Poetical Works, ed. A. Dyce (Aldine ed., 1894); *London Diary, 1773,* ed. R. S. Walker (Aberdeen, 1946); *Day-book, 1773-1789,* ed. R. S. Walker (Aberdeen, 1948); Sir Wm. Forbes, *An Account of the Life and Writings of James Beattie* (1807); M. Forbes, *Beattie and His Friends* (1904).

THE MINSTREL; OR, THE PROGRESS OF GENIUS

THE FIRST BOOK

I

Ah! who can tell how hard it is to climb
The steep where Fame's proud temple shines afar!
Ah! who can tell how many a soul sublime
Hath felt the influence of malignant star,
And waged with Fortune an eternal war!
Checked by the scoff of Pride, by Envy's frown,
And Poverty's unconquerable bar,
In life's low vale remote hath pined alone,
Then dropped into the grave, unpitied and unknown!

II

And yet, the languor of inglorious days
Not equally oppressive is to all.
Him who ne'er listened to the voice of praise
The silence of neglect can ne'er appal.
There are, who, deaf to mad Ambition's call,
Would shrink to hear the obstreperous trump of Fame;
Supremely blessed if to their portion fall
Health, competence, and peace. Nor higher aim
Had he whose simple tale these artless lines proclaim.

III

This sapient age disclaims all classic lore;
Else I should here in cunning phrase display,
How forth the Minstrel fared in days of yore,
Right glad of heart, though homely in array,
His waving locks and beard all hoary grey;
And from his bending shoulder decent hung
His harp, the sole companion of his way,
Which to the whistling wind reponsive rung;
And ever as he went some merry lay he sung.

IV

Fret not yourselves, ye silken sons of pride,
That a poor Wanderer should inspire my strain.
The Muses fortune's fickle smile deride,
Nor ever bow the knee in Mammon's fane;
For their delights are with the village-train,
Whom Nature's laws engage, and Nature's charms:
They hate the sensual, and scorn the vain;
The parasite their influence never warms,
Nor him whose sordid soul the love of wealth alarms.

V

Though richest hues the peacock's plumes adorn,
Yet horror screams from his discordant throat.
Rise, sons of harmony, and hail the morn,
While warbling larks on russet pinions float;   40
Or seek at noon the woodland scene remote,
Where the grey linnets carol from the hill.
Oh, let them ne'er with artificial note,
To please a tyrant, strain the little bill,
But sing what Heaven inspires, and wander where they will.

VI

Liberal, not lavish, is kind Nature's hand;
Nor was perfection made for man below;
Yet all her schemes with nicest art are planned,
Good counteracting ill, and gladness woe.
With gold and gems if Chilian mountains glow,   50
If bleak and barren Scotia's hills arise,
There plague and poison, lust and rapine grow;
Here peaceful are the vales and pure the skies,
And freedom fires the soul, and sparkles in the eyes.

VII

Then grieve not, thou to whom the indulgent Muse
Vouchsafes a portion of celestial fire;
Nor blame the partial Fates, if they refuse
The imperial banquet and the rich attire.
Know thine own worth, and reverence the lyre.
Wilt thou debase the heart which God refined?   60
No; let thy heaven-taught soul to Heaven aspire,
To fancy, freedom, harmony, resigned;
Ambition's groveling crew forever left behind.

VIII

Canst thou forego the pure ethereal soul
In each fine sense so exquisitely keen,
On the dull couch of Luxury to loll,
Stung with disease, and stupefied with spleen;
Fain to implore the aid of Flattery's screen,
Even from thyself thy loathsome heart to hide,
(The mansion then no more of joy serene),   70
Where fear, distrust, malevolence, abide,
And impotent desire, and disappointed pride?

IX

Oh, how canst thou renounce the boundless store
Of charms which Nature to her votary yields?
The warbling woodland, the resounding shore,
The pomp of groves, and garniture of fields;
All that the genial ray of morning gilds,

And all that echoes to the song of even,
All that the mountain's sheltering bosom shields,
And all the dread magnificence of heaven,   80
Oh, how canst thou renounce, and hope to be forgiven?

X

These charms shall work thy soul's eternal health,
And love and gentleness and joy impart.
But these thou must renounce, if lust of wealth
E'er win its way to thy corrupted heart;
For, ah! it poisons like a scorpion's dart;
Prompting the ungenerous wish, the selfish scheme,
The stern resolve unmoved by pity's smart,
The troublous day and long distressful dream.—
Return, my roving Muse, resume thy purposed theme.   90

XI

There lived in Gothic days, as legends tell,
A shepherd-swain, a man of low degree;
Whose sires, perchance, in Fairyland might dwell,
Sicilian groves, or vales of Arcady;
But he, I ween, was of the north countrie—
A nation famed for song, and beauty's charms;
Zealous yet modest, innocent though free,
Patient of toil, serene amidst alarms,
Inflexible in faith, invincible in arms.

XII

The shepherd-swain of whom I mention made,   100
On Scotia's mountains fed his little flock;
The sickle, scythe, or plough, he never swayed;
An honest heart was almost all his stock;
His drink the living water from the rock:
The milky dams supplied his board, and lent
Their kindly fleece to baffle winter's shock;
And he, though oft with dust and sweat besprent,
Did guide and guard their wanderings, wheresoe'er they went.

XIII

From labour health, from health contentment springs.
Contentment opes the source of every joy.   110
He envied not, he never thought of kings;
Nor from those appetites sustained annoy,
Which chance may frustrate, or indulgence cloy:
Nor Fate his calm and humble hopes beguiled;
He mourned no recreant friend nor mistress coy,
For on his vows the blameless Phebe smiled,
And her alone he loved, and loved her from a child.

XIV

No jealousy their dawn of love o'ercast,
Nor blasted were their wedded days with strife;
Each season looked delightful, as it passed,   120
To the fond husband and the faithful wife.
Beyond the lowly vale of shepherd life
They never roamed; secure beneath the storm
Which in Ambition's lofty land is rife,
Where peace and love are cankered by the worm
Of pride, each bud of joy industrious to deform.

XV

The wight whose tale these artless lines unfold
Was all the offspring of this simple pair.
His birth no oracle or seer foretold;
No prodigy appeared in earth or air,   130
Nor aught that might a strange event declare.
You guess each circumstance of Edwin's birth;
The parent's transport and the parent's care;
The gossip's prayer for wealth and wit and worth;
And one long summer day of indolence and mirth.

XVI

And yet poor Edwin was no vulgar boy;
Deep thought oft seemed to fix his infant eye;
Dainties he heeded not, nor gaud, nor toy,
Save one short pipe of rudest minstrelsy.
Silent when glad; affectionate, though shy;   140
And now his look was most demurely sad,
And now he laughed aloud, yet none knew why.
The neighbours stared and sighed, yet blessed the lad:
Some deemed him wondrous wise, and some believed him mad.

XVII

But why should I his childish feats display?
Concourse and noise and toil he ever fled;
Nor cared to mingle in the clamorous fray
Of squabbling imps; but to the forest sped,
Or roamed at large the lonely mountain's head;
Or, where the maze of some bewildered stream   150
To deep untrodden groves his footsteps led,
There would he wander wild, till Phebus' beam,
Shot from the western cliff, released the weary team.

XVIII

The exploit of strength, dexterity, or speed
To him nor vanity nor joy could bring.
His heart, from cruel sport estranged, would bleed
To work the woe of any living thing,

By trap or net, by arrow or by sling;
These he detested, those he scorned to wield:
He wished to be the guardian, not the king,   160
Tyrant far less, or traitor of the field.
And sure the sylvan reign unbloody joy might yield.

XIX

Lo! where the stripling, wrapped in wonder, roves
Beneath the precipice o'erhung with pine;
And sees, on high, amidst the encircling groves,
From cliff to cliff the foaming torrents shine:
While waters, woods, and winds in concert join,
And Echo swells the chorus to the skies.
Would Edwin this majestic scene resign
For aught the huntsman's puny craft supplies?   170
Ah! no: he better knows great Nature's charms to prize.

XX

And oft he traced the uplands, to survey,
When o'er the sky advanced the kindling dawn,
The crimson cloud, blue main, and mountain grey,
And lake dim-gleaming on the smoky lawn;
Far to the west the long long vale withdrawn,
Where twilight loves to linger for a while;
And now he faintly kens the bounding fawn,
And villager abroad at early toil.—
But, lo! the sun appears! and heaven, earth, ocean, smile.   180

XXI

And oft the craggy cliff he loved to climb,
When all in mist the world below was lost.
What dreadful pleasure! there to stand sublime,
Like shipwrecked mariner on desert coast,
And view the enormous waste of vapour, tossed
In billows, lengthening to the horizon round,
Now scooped in gulfs, with mountains now embossed!
And hear the voice of mirth and song rebound,
Flocks, herds, and waterfalls, along the hoar profound!

XXII

In truth he was a strange and wayward wight,   190
Fond of each gentle and each dreadful scene.
In darkness and in storm he found delight:
Nor less than when on ocean-wave serene
The southern sun diffused his dazzling shene.
Even sad vicissitude amused his soul;
And if a sigh would sometimes intervene,
And down his cheek a tear of pity roll,
A sigh, a tear, so sweet, he wished not to control.

XXIII

"O ye wild groves, O where is now your bloom?"
(The Muse interprets thus his tender thought.)　　　　　200
"Your flowers, your verdure, and your balmy gloom,
Of late so grateful in the hour of drought?
Why do the birds, that song and rapture brought
To all your bowers, their mansions now forsake?
Ah! why hath fickle chance this ruin wrought?
For now the storm howls mournful through the brake,
And the dead foliage flies in many a shapeless flake.

XXIV

"Where now the rill, melodious, pure, and cool,
And meads, with life and mirth and beauty crowned?
Ah! see, the unsightly slime, and sluggish pool　　　　　210
Have all the solitary vale imbrowned;
Fled each fair form, and mute each melting sound.
The raven croaks forlorn on naked spray;
And, hark! the river, bursting every mound,
Down the vale thunders; and with wasteful sway
Uproots the grove, and rolls the shattered rocks away.

XXV

"Yet such the destiny of all on earth!
So flourishes and fades majestic man.
Fair is the bud his vernal morn brings forth,
And fostering gales awhile the nursling fan.　　　　　220
O smile, ye heavens, serene; ye mildews wan,
Ye blighting whirlwinds, spare his balmy prime,
Nor lessen of his life the little span.
Borne on the swift though silent wings of Time,
Old age comes on apace to ravage all the clime.

XXVI

"And be it so. Let those deplore their doom,
Whose hope still grovels in this dark sojourn.
But lofty souls, who look beyond the tomb,
Can smile at Fate, and wonder how they mourn.
Shall spring to these sad scenes no more return?　　　　　230
Is yonder wave the sun's eternal bed?—
Soon shall the orient with new lustre burn,
And spring shall soon her vital influence shed,
Again attune the grove, again adorn the mead.

XXVII

"Shall I be left abandoned in the dust,
When Fate, relenting, lets the flower revive?
Shall Nature's voice, to man alone unjust,
Bid him, though doomed to perish, hope to live?

Is it for this fair Virtue oft must strive
With disappointment, penury, and pain?—
No: Heaven's immortal spring shall yet arrive;
And man's majestic beauty bloom again,
Bright through the eternal year of Love's triumphant reign."

240

XXVIII

This truth sublime his simple sire had taught.
In sooth, 'twas almost all the shepherd knew.
No subtle nor superfluous lore he sought,
Nor ever wished his Edwin to pursue.
"Let man's own sphere," quoth he, "confine his view;
Be man's peculiar work his sole delight."
And much and oft he warned him to eschew
Falsehood and guile, and aye maintain the right,
By pleasure unseduced, unawed by lawless might.

250

XXIX

"And, from the prayer of Want and plaint of Woe,
O never, never turn away thine ear.
Forlorn, in this bleak wilderness below,
Ah! what were man, should Heaven refuse to hear!
To others do (the law is not severe)
What to thyself thou wishest to be done.
Forgive thy foes; and love thy parents dear,
And friends, and native land; nor those alone;
All human weal and woe learn thou to make thine own."

260

XXX

See, in the rear of the warm sunny shower,
The visionary boy from shelter fly!
For now the storm of summer rain is o'er,
And cool and fresh and fragrant is the sky.
And, lo! in the dark east, expanded high,
The rainbow brightens to the setting sun!
Fond fool, that deemest the streaming glory nigh,
How vain the chase thine ardour has begun!
'Tis fled afar, ere half thy purposed race be run.

270

XXXI

Yet couldst thou learn that thus it fares with age,
When pleasure, wealth, or power, the bosom warm,
This baffled hope might tame thy manhood's rage,
And Disappointment of her sting disarm.—
But why should foresight thy fond heart alarm?
Perish the lore that deadens young desire!
Pursue, poor imp, the imaginary charm,
Indulge gay Hope, and Fancy's pleasing fire:
Fancy and Hope too soon shall of themselves expire.

XXXII

When the long-sounding curfew from afar   280
Loaded with loud lament the lonely gale,
Young Edwin, lighted by the evening star,
Lingering and listening, wandered down the vale.
There would he dream of graves, and corses pale,
And ghosts that to the charnel-dungeon throng,
And drag a length of clanking chain, and wail,
Till silenced by the owl's terrific song,
Or blast that shrieks by fits the shuddering isles along.

XXXIII

Or, when the setting moon, in crimson dyed,
Hung o'er the dark and melancholy deep,   290
To haunted stream, remote from man, he hied,
Where fays of yore their revels wont to keep;
And there let Fancy roam at large, till sleep
A vision brought to his entrancèd sight.
And first, a wildly murmuring wind 'gan creep
Shrill to his ringing ear; then tapers bright,
With instantaneous gleam, illumed the vault of night.

XXXIV

Anon in view a portal's blazoned arch
Arose; the trumpet bids the valves unfold;
And forth an host of little warriors march,   300
Grasping the diamond lance and targe of gold.
Their look was gentle, their demeanour bold,
And green their helms, and green their silk attire;
And here and there, right venerably old,
The long-robed minstrels wake the warbling wire,
And some with mellow breath the martial pipe inspire.

XXXV

With merriment and song and timbrels clear,
A troop of dames from myrtle bowers advance;
The little warriors doff the targe and spear,
And loud enlivening strains provoke the dance.   310
They meet, they dart away, they wheel askance;
To right, to left, they thrid the flying maze;
Now bound aloft with vigorous spring, then glance
Rapid along; with many-coloured rays
Of tapers, gems, and gold, the echoing forests blaze.

XXXVI

The dream is fled. Proud harbinger of day,
Who scaredst the vision with thy clarion shrill,
Fell chanticleer! who oft hast reft away
My fancied good, and brought substantial ill!

Oh, to thy cursèd scream, discordant still,   320
Let Harmony aye shut her gentle ear!
Thy boastful mirth let jealous rivals spill,
Insult thy crest, and glossy pinions tear,
And ever in thy dreams the ruthless fox appear!

XXXVII

Forbear, my Muse. Let Love attune thy line.
Revoke the spell. Thine Edwin frets not so.
For how should he at wicked chance repine,
Who feels from every change amusement flow?
Even now his eyes with smiles of rapture glow,   330
As on he wanders through the scenes of morn,
Where the fresh flowers in living lustre blow,
Where thousand pearls the dewy lawns adorn,
A thousand notes of joy in every breeze are borne.

XXXVIII

But who the melodies of morn can tell?
The wild brook babbling down the mountain-side;
The lowing herd; the sheepfold's simple bell;
The pipe of early shepherd dim descried
In the lone valley; echoing far and wide
The clamorous horn along the cliffs above;
The hollow murmur of the ocean-tide;   340
The hum of bees, and linnet's lay of love,
And the full choir that wakes the universal grove.

XXXIX

The cottage curs at early pilgrim bark;
Crowned with her pail the tripping milkmaid sings;
The whistling plowman stalks afield; and, hark!
Down the rough slope the ponderous wagon rings;
Through rustling corn the hare astonished springs;
Slow tolls the village clock the drowsy hour;
The partridge bursts away on whirring wings;
Deep mourns the turtle in sequestered bower,   350
And shrill lark carols clear from her aërial tower.

XL

O Nature, how in every charm supreme!
Whose votaries feast on raptures ever new!
Oh, for the voice and fire of seraphim,
To sing thy glories with devotion due!
Blessed be the day I 'scaped the wrangling crew,
From Pyrrho's maze, and Epicurus' sty;
And held high converse with the godlike few
Who to the enraptured heart and ear and eye
Teach beauty, virtue, truth, and love, and melody.   355

XLI

Hence! ye, who snare and stupefy the mind,
Sophists, of beauty, virtue, joy, the bane!
Greedy and fell, though impotent and blind,
Who spread your filthy nets in Truth's fair fane,
And ever ply your venomed fangs amain!
Hence to dark Error's den, whose rankling slime
First gave you form! hence! lest the Muse should deign,
(Though loth on theme so mean to waste a rhyme),
With vengeance to pursue your sacrilegious crime.

XLII

But hail, ye mighty masters of the lay,   370
Nature's true sons, the friends of man and truth,
Whose song, sublimely sweet, serenely gay,
Amused my childhood, and informed my youth!
Oh, let your spirit still my bosom soothe,
Inspire my dreams, and my wild wanderings guide.
Your voice each rugged path of life can smooth;
For well I know, wherever ye reside,
There harmony and peace and innocence abide.

XLIII

Ah me! abandoned on the lonesome plain,
As yet poor Edwin never knew your lore,   380
Save when against the winter's drenching rain
And driving snow the cottage shut the door.
Then, as instructed by tradition hoar,
Her legends when the beldam 'gan impart,
Or chant the old heroic ditty o'er,
Wonder and joy ran thrilling to his heart;
Much he the tale admired, but more the tuneful art.

XLIV

Various and strange was the long-winded tale;
And halls and knights and feats of arms displayed;
Or merry swains, who quaff the nut-brown ale,   390
And sing enamoured of the nut-brown maid;
The moonlight revel of the fairy glade;
Or hags that suckle an infernal brood,
And ply in caves the unutterable trade,
'Midst fiends and spectres, quench the moon in blood,
Yell in the midnight storm, or ride the infuriate flood.

XLV

But when to horror his amazement rose,
A gentler strain the beldam would rehearse,
A tale of rural life, a tale of woes,
The orphan babes and guardian uncle fierce.   400

O cruel! will no pang of pity pierce
That heart by lust of lucre seared to stone?
For sure, if aught of virtue last, or verse,
To latest times shall tender souls bemoan
Those helpless orphan babes by thy fell arts undone.

XLVI

Behold, with berries smeared, with brambles torn,
The babes now famished lay them down to die;
'Midst the wild howl of darksome woods, forlorn,
Folded in one another's arms they lie;
Nor friend nor stranger hears their dying cry: 410
"For from the town the man returns no more."
But thou, who Heaven's just vengeance darest defy,
This deed with fruitless tears shalt soon deplore,
When Death lays waste thy house, and fiames consume thy store.

XLVII

A stifled smile of stern vindictive joy
Brightened one moment Edwin's starting tear.—
"But why should gold man's feeble mind decoy,
And Innocence thus die by doom severe?"
O Edwin, while thy heart is yet sincere,
The assaults of discontent and doubt repel: 420
Dark even at noontide is our mortal sphere;
But let us hope,—to doubt is to rebel—
Let us exalt in hope, that all shall yet be well.

XLVIII

Nor be thy generous indignation checked,
Nor checked the tender tear to Misery given;
From Guilt's contagious power shall that protect,
This soften and refine the soul for heaven.
But dreadful is their doom, whom doubt hath d·iven
To censure Fate, and pious hope forego;
Like yonder blasted boughs by lightning riven,   430
Perfection, beauty, life, they never know,
But frown on all that pass, a monument of woe.

XLIX

Shall he whose birth, maturity, and age
Scarce fill the circle of one summer day,
Shall the poor gnat with discontent and rage
Exclaim that Nature hastens to decay,
If but a cloud obstruct the solar ray,
If but a momentary shower descend?
Or shall frail man Heaven's dread decree gainsay,
Which bade the series of events extend   440
Wide through unnumbered worlds, and ages without end?

L

One part, one little part, we dimly scan
Through the dark medium of life's feverish dream;
Yet dare arraign the whole stupendous plan,
If but that little part incongruous seem.
Nor is that part perhaps what mortals deem;
Oft from apparent ill our blessings rise.
Oh, then renounce that impious self-esteem
That aims to trace the secrets of the skies:
For thou art but of dust; be humble, and be wise.   450

LI

Thus Heaven enlarged his soul in riper years.
For Nature gave him strength and fire to soar
On Fancy's wing, above this vale of tears;
Where dark cold-hearted sceptics, creeping, pore
Through microscope of metaphysic lore:
And much they grope for truth, but never hit.
For why? Their powers, inadequate before,
This art preposterous renders more unfit;
Yet deem they darkness light, and their vain blunders wit.

LII

Nor was this ancient dame a foe to mirth.   460
Her ballad, jest, and riddle's quaint device
Oft cheered the shepherds round their social hearth;
Whom levity or spleen could ne'er entice
To purchase chat or laughter at the price
Of decency. Nor let it faith exceed,
That Nature forms a rustic taste so nice.—
Ah! had they been of court or city breed,
Such delicacy were right marvelous indeed.

LIII

Oft, when the winter storm had ceased to rave,
He roamed the snowy waste at even, to view   470
The cloud stupendous, from the Atlantic wave
High-towering, sail along the horizon blue:
Where midst the changeful scenery ever new
Fancy a thousand wondrous forms descries
More wildly great than ever pencil drew,
Rocks, torrents, gulfs, and shapes of giant size,
And glittering cliffs on cliffs, and fiery ramparts rise.

LIV

Thence musing onward to the sounding shore,
The lone enthusiast oft would take his way,
Listening with pleasing dread to the deep roar   480
Of the wide-weltering waves. In black array

When sulphurous clouds rolled on the vernal day,
Even then he hastened from the haunt of man,
Along the darkening wilderness to stray,
What time the lightning's fierce career began,
And o'er heaven's rending arch the rattling thunder ran.

LV

Responsive to the sprightly pipe when all
In sprightly dance the village youth were joined,
Edwin, of melody aye held in thrall,
From the rude gambol far remote reclined,
Soothed with the soft notes warbling in the wind.
Ah, then all jollity seemed noise and folly.
To the pure soul by Fancy's fire refined
Ah, what is mirth, but turbulence unholy,
When with the charm compared of heavenly melancholy?

LVI

Is there a heart that music cannot melt?
Ah me! how is that rugged heart forlorn!
Is there who ne'er those mystic transports felt
Of solitude and melancholy born?
He needs not woo the Muse; he is her scorn.   500
The sophist's rope of cobweb he shall twine;
Mope o'er the schoolman's peevish page; or mourn,
And delve for life, in Mammon's dirty mine;
Sneak with the scoundrel fox, or grunt with glutton swine.

LVII

For Edwin, Fate a nobler doom had planned;
Song was his favourite and first pursuit.
The wild harp rang to his adventurous hand,
And languished to his breath the plaintive flute.
His infant Muse, though artless, was not mute:
Of elegance as yet he took no care;   510
For this of time and culture is the fruit;
And Edwin gained at last this fruit so rare,
As in some future verse I purpose to declare.

LVIII

Meanwhile, whate'er of beautiful or new,
Sublime or dreadful, in earth, sea, or sky,
By chance or search, was offered to his view,
He scanned with curious and romantic eye.
Whate'er of lore tradition could supply
From Gothic tale, or song, or fable old,
Roused him, still keen to listen and to pry.   520
At last, though long by penury controlled,
And solitude, his soul her graces 'gan unfold.

LIX

Thus on the chill Lapponian's dreary land,
For many a long month lost in snow profound,
When Sol from Cancer sends the season bland,
And in their northern cave the storms hath bound;
From silent mountains, straight, with startling sound,
Torrents are hurled; green hills emerge; and lo,
The trees with foliage, cliffs with flowers are crowned;
Pure rills through vales of verdure warbling go;   530
And wonder, love, and joy, the peasant's heart o'erflow.

LX

Here pause, my Gothic lyre, a little while,
The leisure hour is all that thou canst claim.
But if * * * on this labour smile,
New strains ere long shall animate thy frame.
And his applause to me is more than fame;
For still with truth accords his taste refined.
At lucre or renown let others aim;
I only wish to please the gentle mind,
Whom Nature's charms inspire, and love of humankind.   540
                                    [1766-68, 1771]

JANE ELLIOT (1727-1805)

Like some other famous Scots poems, these verses are based on an older song, originally a Jacobite lament. Scottish literature is rich in obscure writers like Jane Elliot, who worked with traditional tunes and refrains and kept to the spirit of the material which they had received. For the full history of this piece, see Scott's *Minstrelsy of the Scottish Border*, ed. Henderson (Edinburgh, 1902), iii, 402-03.

THE FLOWERS OF THE FOREST

I've heard them lilting, at our ewe-milking,
Lasses a-lilting, before the dawn of day;
But now they are moaning, on ilka green loaning;[1]
The Flowers of the Forest are a' wede[2] away.
At bughts[3] in the morning nae blythe lads are scorning;[4]
The lasses are lanely, and dowie,[5] and wae;
Nae daffing,[6] nae gabbing, but sighing and sabbing,
Ilk ane lifts her leglin,[7] and hies her away.
In hairst,[8] at the shearing, nae youths now are jeering,
The bandsters[9] are lyart,[10] and runkled and grey;   10
At fair or at preaching, nae wooing, nae fleeching[11]—
The Flowers of the Forest are a' wede away.
At e'en, in the gloaming, nae swankies[12] are roaming
'Bout stacks wi' the lasses at bogle[13] to play;
But ilk ane sits eerie, lamenting her dearie—
The Flowers of the Forest are a' wede away.

Dool and wae for the order sent our lads to the Border!
The English, for ance, by guile wan the day;
The Flowers of the Forest, that fought aye the foremost,
The prime of our land, lie cauld in the clay.   20

We'll hear nae more lilting at our ewe-milking,
Women and bairns are heartless and wae;
Sighing and moaning on ilka green loaning,
The Flowers of the Forest are a' wede away.

[1776]

[1] Lane.
[2] Passed, faded.
[3] Sheepfolds.
[4] Teasing the girls about their lovers.
[5] Melancholy; dull.
[6] Making merry.
[7] Milk pail.
[8] Harvest.
[9] Binders.
[10] Gray-haired.
[11] Beseeching.
[12] Strapping youths.
[13] A game in which the players hunt one another about the stacks of grain.

THOMAS CHATTERTON (1752-1770)

In the southern part of the busy commercial city of Bristol stands the fine old church of St. Mary Redcliffe, praised by Queen Elizabeth as "the fairest, the goodliest, and most famous parish church in England." Thomas Chatterton was the posthumous son of a humble schoolmaster in the neighborhood, but his ancestors had for generations been sextons and helpers at St. Mary's, and the great church was always the center of his imaginative life. He escaped from the dull routine of his school days and his work as a scrivener's apprentice by steeping himself in antiquarian detail. In the muniment room of St. Mary's old parchment documents lay about like so much rubbish, and his father had taken them freely for use as writing material. Chatterton studied these remains carefully and copied their spelling and handwriting. From two dictionaries of early English and a glossary to Chaucer he built up an artificial pseudo-antique poetic vocabulary. At the same time there evolved in his imagination a sort of historical romance centering about William Canynges the younger, a fifteenth century mayor of Bristol and chief benefactor of St. Mary Redcliffe. Canynges and his grandfather were important characters in local history, but Chatterton enhances their importance by making them the center of a group of learned priests and scholars, the chief of whom is the poet Rowley, to whom Chatterton attributed the poems he was now fabricating. Soon he was transmitting these documents to local antiquaries, dull and ungenerous men who gave no real sympathy or help. Though his Rowley poems may be described as "forgeries," it should be remembered that literary forgery was regarded as a comparatively innocent amusement in the eighteenth century and that Chatterton's pseudo-antique verse could not for any length of time deceive a scholar with the slightest knowledge of early English.

In 1769 Chatterton offered his Rowley manuscripts first to the publisher James Dodsley and then to Horace Walpole. Walpole invited correspondence and received more Rowley material, but was soon advised by Gray and Mason that the poems were not genuine. Failing to get any help either from Bristol citizens or from the great virtuoso, Chatterton, after a fit of despair in which he meditated suicide, set out for London in April, 1770. He had already developed a dual literary personality: he was not only Rowley but a formal eighteenth-century satirist, essayist, and literary man of all work. Valiantly he tried to make his way by youthful enthusiasm and incessant hack-work, but he continued desperately and miserably poor. On August 24, 1770, he tore up his manuscripts in despair and poisoned himself in his lodgings in Brook Street, Holborn. After his pathetic and sordid struggle came a posthumous fame; in the imagination of the greater romantics Chatterton became the supreme symbol of rebellious youthful genius foundering in a dull and cruel world. Wordsworth's lines will always come to mind here:

> I thought of Chatterton, the marvelous boy,
> The sleepless soul that perished in his pride.

Many of the Rowley poems were edited and published by Thomas Tyrwhitt in 1777. Meanwhile Thomas Warton had hesitatingly admitted Rowley to a place in the fifteenth century section of his *History of English Poetry*, adding in conclusion that he thought the poems spurious. The arguments about Ossian and Rowley ran parallel: just as Macpherson was considered incapable of writing Ossian, so, it was urged, Chatterton was incapable of writing Rowley. All this is beside the point for modern readers. If we disregard the antique spelling and ride roughshod through the peculiar vocabulary, we find here pre-romantic work of refreshing vigor. Chatterton's merit as a poet is high, even considered apart from the tragedy of his career. He does effectively what the archaizing Spenserian imitators and the artificial balladists of his time were timidly trying to do, and he shows much more metrical originality than they. His greatest debt is to Spenser rather than to Chaucer or to Percy's *Reliques*; like Scott, he sets forth medieval themes in the language of a later time. What appears to be mediaevalism in him is really poetic divination rather than scholarship or antiquarianism.

Poetical Works, ed. W. W. Skeat (2 vols., 1875; the Aldine ed.) [the text modernized]; *The Rowley Poems*, ed. M. E. Hare (Oxford, 1911) [reprint of the Tyrwhitt ed.]; E. P. Ellinger, *Thomas Chatterton* (Philadelphia, 1930); A. Watkins-Jones, "Percy, Warton, and Chatterton," *PMLA*, L (1935), 769–84; J. C. Nevill, *Thomas Chatterton* (1948).

BRISTOWE TRAGEDIE: OR, THE DETHE OF SYR CHARLES BAWDIN

The feathered songster chaunticleer
  Han wounde hys bugle horne,
And tolde the earlie villager
  The commynge of the morne:

Kynge Edwarde sawe the ruddie streakes
  Of lyghte eclypse the greie;
And herde the raven's crokynge throte
  Proclayme the fated daie.

"Thou'rt ryght," quod hee, "for, by the Godde
  That syttes enthron'd on hyghe!   10
Charles Bawdin, and hys fellowes twaine,
  To-daie shall surelie die."

Thenne wythe a jugge of nappy[1] ale
  Hys Knyghtes dydd onne hymm waite;
"Goe tell the traytour, thatt to-daie
  Hee leaves thys mortall state."

Syr Canterlone thenne bendedd lowe,
  Wythe harte brymm-fulle of woe;
Hee journey'd to the castle-gate,
  And to Syr Charles dydd goe.   20

Butt whenne hee came, hys children twaine,
  And eke hys lovynge wyfe,
Wythe brinie tears dydd wett the floore,
  For goode Syr Charleses lyfe.

"O goode Syr Charles!" sayd Canterlone,
  "Badde tydyngs I doe brynge."
"Speke boldlie, manne," sayd brave Syr Charles,
  "Whatte says thie traytor kynge?"

"I greeve to telle, before yonne sonne
  Does fromme the welkinn flye,   30
Hee hath uponne hys honour sworne,
  Thatt thou shalt surelie die."

"Wee all must die," quod brave Syr Charles;
  "Of thatte I'm not affearde;

[1] Strong.

Whatte bootes to lyve a little space?
  Thanke Jesu, I'm prepar'd:

"Butt telle thye kynge, for myne hee's not,
  I'de sooner die to-daie
Thanne lyve hys slave, as manie are,
  Tho' I shoulde lyve for aie."   40

Thenne Canterlone hee dydd goe out
  To telle the maior straite
To gett all thynges ynne reddyness
  For goode Syr Charleses fate.

Thenne Maisterr Canynge saughte the kynge,
  And felle down onne hys knee;
"I'm come," quod hee, "unto your grace
  To move your clemencye."

Thenne quod the kynge, "Youre tale speke out,
  You have been much oure friende;   50
Whatever youre request may bee,
  Wee wylle to ytte attende."

"My nobile leige! alle my request
  Ys for a nobile knyghte,
Who, tho' may hap hee has donne wronge,
  He thoughte ytte stylle was ryghte:

"Hee has a spouse and children twaine,
  Alle rewyn'd are for aie;
Yff thatt you are resolv'd to lett
  Charles Bawdin die to-daie."   60

"Speke nott of such a traytour vile,"
  The kynge ynne furie sayde;
"Before the evening starre shalle sheene,
  Bawdin shall loose hys hedde:

"Justice does loudlie for hym calle,
  And hee shalle have hys meede:
Speke, Maister Canynge! Whatte thynge else
  Att present doe you neede?"

"My nobile leige!" goode Canynge sayde,
  "Leave justice to our Godde,   70
And laye the yronne rule asyde;
  Be thyne the olyve rodde.

"Was Godde to serche our hertes and reines,
    The best were synners grete;
Christ's vycarr only knowes ne synne,
    Ynne alle thys mortall state.

"Lett mercie rule thyne infante reigne,
    'Twylle faste thye crowne fulle sure;
From race to race thy familie
    Alle sov'reigns shall endure: 80

"But yff wythe bloode and slaughter thou
    Beginne thy infante reigne,
Thy crowne uponne thy childrennes brows
    Wylle never long remayne."

"Canynge, awaie! thys traytour vile
    Has scorn'd my power and mee;
Howe canst thou thenne for such a manne
    Intreate my clemencye?"

"My nobile leige! the trulie brave
    Wylle val'rous actions prize,   90
Respect a brave and nobile mynde,
    Altho' ynne enemies."

"Canynge, awaie! By Godde ynne Heav'n
    Thatt dydd mee beinge gyve,
I wylle nott taste a bitt of breade
    Whilst thys Syr Charles dothe lyve.

"By Marie, and alle Seinctes ynne Heav'n,
    Thys sunne shall be hys laste."
Thenne Canynge dropt a brinie teare,
    And from the presence paste.   100

Wyth herte brymm-fulle of gnawynge grief,
    Hee to Syr Charles dydd goe,
And satt hymm downe uponne a stoole,
    And teares beganne to flowe.

"Wee all must die," quod brave Syr Charles;
    "Whatte bootes ytte howe or whenne;
Dethe ys the sure, the certaine fate
    Of all wee mortall menne.

"Saye why, my friend, thie honest soul
    Runns overr att thyne eye;   110
Is ytte for my most welcome doome
    Thatt thou dost child-lyke crye?"

Quod godlie Canynge, "I doe weepe,
    Thatt thou so soone must dye,
And leave thy sonnes and helpless wyfe;
    'Tys thys thatt wettes myne eye."

"Thenne drie the tears thatt out thyne eye
    From godlie fountaines sprynge;
Dethe I despise, and alle the power
    Of Edwarde, traytor kynge.   120

"Whan throgh the tyrant's welcom means
    I shall resigne my lyfe,
The Godde I serve wylle soone provyde
    For bothe mye sonnes and wyfe.

"Before I sawe the lyghtsome sunne,
    Thys was appointed mee;
Shall mortal manne repyne or grudge
    Whatt Godde ordeynes to bee?

"Howe oft ynne battaile have I stoode,
    Whan thousands dy'd arounde;   130
Whan smokynge streemes of crimson bloode
    Imbrew'd the fatten'd grounde:

"How dydd I knowe thatt ev'ry darte,
    Thatt cutte the airie waie,
Myghte nott fynde passage toe my harte,
    And close myne eyes for aie?

"And shall I nowe, forr feere of dethe,
    Looke wanne and bee dysmayde?
Ne! fromm my herte flie childyshe feere,
    Bee alle the manne display'd.   140

"Ah, goddelyke Henrie! Godde forefende,[2]
    And guarde thee and thye sonne,
Yff 'tis hys wylle; but yff 'tis nott,
    Why thenne hys wylle bee donne.

"My honest friende, my faulte has beene
    To serve Godde and mye prynce;
And thatt I no tyme-server am,
    My dethe wylle soone convynce.

"Ynne Londonne citye was I borne,
    Of parents of grette note;   150
My fadre dydd a nobile armes
    Emblazon onne hys cote:

"I make ne doubte butt hee ys gone
    Where soone I hope to goe;
Where wee for ever shall bee blest,
    From oute the reech of woe:

"Hee taughte mee justice and the laws
    Wyth pitie to unite;
And eke hee taughte mee howe to knowe
    The wronge cause fromm the ryghte: 160

[2] Defend.

"Hee taughte mee wythe a prudent hande
  To feede the hungrie poore,
Ne lett mye sarvants dryve awaie
  The hungrie fromme my doore:

"And none can saye, butt alle mye lyfe
  I have hys wordyes kept;
And summ'd the actyonns of the daie
  Eche nyghte before I slept.

"I have a spouse, goe aske of her,
  Yff I defyl'd her bedde?   170
I have a kynge, and none can laie
  Blacke treason onne my hedde.

"Ynne Lent, and onne the holie eve,
  Fromm fleshe I dydd refrayne;
Whie should I thenne appeare dismay'd
  To leave thys worlde of payne?

"Ne! hapless Henrie! I rejoyce,
  I shalle ne see thye dethe;
Moste willynglie ynne thye just cause
  Doe I resign my brethe.   180

"Oh, fickle people! rewyn'd londe!
  Thou wylt kenne peace ne moe;
Whyle Richard's sonnes exalt themselves,
  Thye brookes wythe bloude wylle flowe.

"Saie, were ye tyr'd of godlie peace,
  And godlie Henrie's reigne,
Thatt you dydd choppe[3] youre easie daies
  For those of bloude and peyne?

"Whatte tho' I onne a sledde bee drawne,
  And mangled by a hynde,   190
I doe defye the traytor's pow'r,
  Hee can ne harm my mynde;

"Whatte tho', uphoisted onne a pole,
  Mye lymbes shall rotte ynne ayre,
And ne ryche monument of brasse
  Charles Bawdin's name shall bear;

"Yett ynne the holie booke above,
  Whyche tyme can't eate awaie,
There wythe the sarvants of the Lorde
  Mye name shall lyve for aie.   200

"Thenne welcome dethe! for lyfe eterne
  I leave thys mortall lyfe:
Farewell, vayne worlde, and alle that's deare,
  Mye sonnes and lovynge wyfe!
      [3] Exchange.

"Nowe dethe as welcome to mee comes,
  As e'er the moneth of Maie;
Nor woulde I even wyshe to lyve,
  Wyth my dere wyfe to staie."

Quod Canynge, "'Tys a goodlie thynge
  To bee prepar'd to die;   210
And from thys world of peyne and grefe
  To Godde ynne Heav'n to flie."

And nowe the bell beganne to tolle,
  And claryonnes to sounde;
Syr Charles hee herde the horses feete
  A prauncyng onne the grounde:

And just before the officers,
  His lovynge wyfe came ynne,
Weepynge unfeigned teeres of woe,
  Wythe loude and dysmalle dynne.   220

"Sweet Florence! nowe I praie forbere,
  Ynne quiet lett mee die;
Praie Godde, thatt ev'ry Christian soule
  Maye looke onne dethe as I.

"Sweet Florence! why these brinie teeres?
  Theye washe my soule awaie,
And almost make mee wyshe for lyfe,
  Wyth thee, sweete dame, to staie.

"'Tys butt a journie I shalle goe
  Untoe the lande of blysse;   230
Nowe, as a proofe of husbande's love,
  Receive thys holie kysse."

Thenne Florence, fault'ring ynne her saie,
  Tremblynge these wordyes spoke,
"Ah, cruele Edwarde! bloudie kynge!
  My herte ys welle nyghe broke:

"Ah, sweete Syr Charles! why wylt thou goe,
  Wythoute thye lovynge wyfe?
The cruelle axe thatt cuttes thye necke,
  Ytte eke shall ende mye lyfe."   240

And nowe the officers came ynne
  To brynge Syr Charles awaie,
Whoe turnedd toe his lovynge wyfe,
  And thus toe her dydd saie:

"I goe to lyfe, and nott to dethe;
  Truste thou ynne Godde above,
And teache thye sonnes to feare the Lorde,
  And ynne theyre hertes hym love:

"Teache them to runne the nobile race
    Thatt I theyre fader runne: 250
Florence! shou'd dethe thee take—adieu!
    Yee officers, leade onne."

Thenne Florence rav'd as anie madde,
    And dydd her tresses teer;
"Oh! staie, mye husbande! lorde! and
        lyfe!"—
Syr Charles thenne dropt a teare.

Tyll tyredd oute wythe ravynge loud,
    Shee fallen onne the flore;
Syr Charles exerted alle hys myghte,
    And march'd fromm oute the dore.   260

Uponne a sledde hee mounted thenne,
    Wythe lookes fulle brave and swete;
Lookes, thatt enshone[4] ne moe concern
    Thanne anie ynne the strete.

Before hym went the council-menne,
    Ynne scarlett robes and golde,
And tassils spanglynge ynne the sunne,
    Muche glorious to beholde:

The Freers of Seincte Augustyne next
    Appeared to the syghte,   270
Alle cladd ynne homelie russett weedes,
    Of godlie monkysh plyghte:[5]

Ynne diffraunt partes a godlie psaume
    Moste sweetlie theye dydd chaunt;
Behynde theyre backes syx mynstrelles came,
    Who tun'd the strunge bataunt.[6]

Thenne fyve-and-twentye archers came;
    Echone the bowe dydd bende,
From rescue of kynge Henries friends
    Syr Charles forr to defend.   280

Bolde as a lyon came Syr Charles,
    Drawne onne a clothe-layde sledde,
Bye two blacke stedes ynne trappynges white,
    Wyth plumes uponne theyre hedde:

Behynde hym fyve-and-twentye moe
    Of archers stronge and stoute,
Wyth bended bowe echone ynne hande,
    Marched ynne goodlie route:

[4] Showed.
[5] Fashion.
[6] An adjective meaning "eager," wrongly used here as the name of a musical instrument.

Seincte Jameses Freers marched next,
    Echone hys parte dydd chaunt;   290
Behynde theyre backs syx mynstrelles came,
    Who tun'd the strunge bataunt:

Thenne came the maior and eldermenne,
    Ynne clothe of scarlett deck't;
And theyre attendyng menne echone,
    Lyke Easterne princes trickt:

And after them, a multitude
    Of citizenns dydd thronge;
The wyndowes were alle fulle of heddes,
    As hee dydd passe alonge.   300

And whenne hee came to the hyghe crosse,
    Syr Charles dydd turne and saie,
"O Thou, thatt savest manne fromme synne,
    Washe mye soule clean thys daie!"

Att the grete mynsterr wyndowe sat
    The kynge ynne myckle state,
To see Charles Bawdin goe alonge
    To hys most welcom fate.

Soone as the sledde drewe nyghe enowe,
    Thatt Edwarde hee myghte heare,   310
The brave Syr Charles hee dydd stande uppe,
    And thus hys wordes declare:

"Thou seest mee, Edwarde! traytour vile!
    Expos'd to infamie;
Butt bee assur'd, disloyall manne!
    I'm greaterr nowe thanne thee.

"Bye foule proceedyngs, murdre, bloude,
    Thou wearest nowe a crowne;
And hast appoynted mee to dye,
    By power nott thyne owne.   320

"Thou thynkest I shall dye to-daie;
    I have beene dede 'till nowe,
And soone shall lyve to weare a crowne
    For aie uponne my browe:

"Whylst thou, perhapps, for som few yeares,
    Shalt rule thys fickle lande,
To lett them knowe howe wyde the rule
    'Twixt kynge and tyrant hande:

"Thye pow'r unjust, thou traytour slave!
    Shall falle onne thye owne hedde"—   330
Fromm out of hearyng of the kynge
    Departed thenne the sledde.

Kynge Edwarde's soule rush'd to hys face,
  Hee turn'd hys hedde awaie,
And to hys broder Gloucester
  Hee thus dydd speke and saie:

"To hym that soe-much-dreaded dethe
  Ne ghastlie terrors brynge,
Beholde the manne! hee spake the truthe,
  Hee's greater thanne a kynge!"   340

"Soe lett hym die!" Duke Richard sayde;
  "And maye echone oure foes
Bende downe theyre neckes to bloudie axe,
  And feede the carryon crowes."

And nowe the horses gentlie drewe
  Syrr Charles uppe the hyghe hylle;
The axe dydd glysterr ynne the sunne,
  Hys pretious bloude to spylle.

Syrr Charles dydd uppe the scaffold goe,
  As uppe a gilded carre   350
Of victorye, bye val'rous chiefs
  Gayn'd ynne the bloudie warre:

And to the people hee dydd saie,
  "Beholde you see mee dye,
For servynge loyally mye kynge,
  Mye kynge most rightfullie.

"As longe as Edwarde rules thys lande,
  Ne quiet you wylle knowe;
Youre sonnes and husbandes shalle bee slayne,
  And brookes wythe bloude shalle flowe. 360

"You leave youre goode and lawfulle kynge,
  Whenne ynne adversitye;
Lyke mee, untoe the true cause stycke,
  And for the true cause dye."

Thenne hee, wyth preestes, uponne hys knees,
  A pray'r to Godde dydd make,
Beseechynge hym unto hymselfe
  Hys partynge soule to take.

Thenne, kneelynge downe, hee layd his hedde
  Most seemlie onne the blocke;   370
Whyche fromme hys bodie fayre at once
  The able heddes-manne stroke:

And oute the bloude beganne to flowe,
  And rounde the scaffolde twyne;
And teares, enow to washe't awaie,
  Dydd flowe fromme each mann's eyne.

The bloudie axe hys bodie fayre
  Ynnto foure parties cutte;
And ev'rye parte, and eke hys hedde,
  Uponne a pole was putte.   380

One parte dydd rotte onne Kynwulph-Hylle,
  One onne the mynster-tower,
And one from off the castle-gate
  The crowen dydd devoure:

The other onne Seyncte Powle's goode gate,
  A dreery spectacle;
Hys hedde was plac'd onne the hyghe crosse,
  Ynne hyghe-streete most nobile.

Thus was the ende of Bawdin's fate:
  Godde prosper longe oure kynge,   390
And grante hee maye, wyth Bawdin's soule,
  Ynne heav'n Godd's mercie synge!

[1772]

MYNSTRELLES SONGE

O! synge untoe mie roundelaie,
O! droppe the brynie teare wythe mee,
Daunce ne moe atte hallie daie,
Lycke a reynynge ryver bee;
  Mie love ys dedde,
  Gon to hys death-bedde,
  Al under the wyllowe tree.

Blacke hys cryne[1] as the wyntere nyghte,
Whyte hys rode[2] as the sommer snowe,
Rodde hys face as the mornynge lyghte,   10
Cale[3] he lyes ynne the grave belowe;
  Mie love ys dedde,
  Gon to hys deathe-bedde,
  Al under the wyllowe tree.

Swote hys tyngue as the throstles note,
Quycke ynn daunce as thoughte canne bee,
Defte hys taboure, codgelle stote,
O! hee lyes bie the wyllowe tree:
  Mie love ys dedde,
  Gonne to hys deathe-bedde,   20
  Alle underre the wyllowe tree.

Harke! the ravenne flappes hys wynge,
In the briered delle belowe;

[1] Hair.
[2] Complexion.
[3] Cold.

Harke! the dethe-owle loude dothe synge,
To the nyghte-mares as heie[4] goe;
    Mie love ys dedde,
    Gon to hys deathe-bedde,
    Al under the wyllowe tree.

See! the whyte moone sheenes onne hie;
Whyterre ys mie true loves shroude;   30
Whyterre yanne the mornynge skie,
Whyterre yanne the evenynge cloude;
    Mie love ys dedde,
    Gon to hys deathe-bedde,
    Al under the wyllowe tree.

Heere, uponne mie true loves grave,
Schalle the baren fleurs be layde,
Nee one hallie Seyncte to save
Al the celness[5] of a mayde.
    Mie love ys dedde,   40
    Gonne to hys death-bedde,
    Alle under the wyllowe tree.

    [4] They.
    [5] Coldness.

Wythe mie hondes I'lle dente[6] the brieres
Rounde his hallie corse to gre,[7]
Ouphante[8] fairie, lyghte youre fyres,
Heere mie boddie stylle schalle bee.
    Mie love ys dedde,
    Gon to hys deathe-bedde,
    Al under the wyllowe tree.

Comme, wythe acorne-coppe & thorne,   50
Drayne mie hartys blodde awaie;
Lyfe and all yttes goode I scorne,
Daunce bie nete, or feaste by daie.
    Mie love ys dedde,
    Gon to hys death-bedde,
    Al under the wyllowe tree.
Waterre wytches, crownede wythe reytes,[9]
Bere mee to yer leathalle tyde.
I die; I comme; mie true love waytes.
Thos the damselle spake, and dyed.   60

                [1777]
    [6] Plant.
    [7] Grow.
    [8] Elfin.
    [9] Reeds.

AN EXCELENTE BALADE OF CHARITIE:
AS WROTEN BIE THE GODE PRIESTE THOMAS ROWLEY,
1464

In Virgyne the sweltrie sun gan sheene,
And hotte upon the mees[1] did caste his raie;
The apple rodded[2] from its palie greene,
And the mole[3] peare did bende the leafy spraie;
The peede chelandri[4] sunge the livelong daie;
'Twas nowe the pride, the manhode of the yeare,
And eke the grounde was dighte in its mose defte[5] aumere.[6]

The sun was glemeing in the middle of daie,
Deadde still the aire, and eke the welken blue,
When from the sea arist in drear arraie   10
A hepe of cloudes of sable sullen hue,
The which full fast unto the woodlande drewe,
Hiltring attenes the sunnis fetive face,[7]
And the blacke tempeste swolne and gatherd up apace.

    [1] Meads.
    [2] Reddened.
    [3] Soft.
    [4] Pied goldfinch.
    [5] Ornamental.
    [7] Hiding at once the sun's beauteous face.

    [6] Mantel.

Beneath an holme,[8] faste by a pathwaie side,
Which dide unto Seyncte Godwine's covent lede,
A hapless pilgrim moneynge[9] did abide.
Pore in his viewe, ungentle[10] in his weede,
Longe bretful[11] of the miseries of neede,
Where from the hail-stone coulde the almer[12] flie?   20
He had no housen theere, ne anie covent nie.

Look in his glommed[13] face, his sprighte there scanne;
Howe woe-be-gone, how withered, forwynd,[14] deade!
Haste to thie church-glebe-house,[15] asshrewed[16] manne!
Haste to thie kiste,[17] thie onlie dortoure[18] bedde.
Cale, as the claie whiche will gre on thie hedde,
Is Charitie and Love aminge highe elves;
Knightis and Barons live for pleasure and themselves.

The gatherd storme is rype; the bigge drops falle;
The forswat[19] meadowes smethe,[20] and drenche[21] the raine;   30
The comyng ghastness do the cattle pall,[22]
And the full flockes are drivynge ore the plaine;
Dashde from the cloudes the waters flott[23] againe;
The welkin opes; the yellow levynne[24] flies;
And the hot fierie smothe[25] in the wide lowings[26] dies.

Liste! now the thunder's rattling clymmynge[27] sound
Cheves[28] slowlie on, and then embollen[29] clangs,
Shakes the hie spyre, and losst, dispended, drown'd,
Still on the gallard[30] eare of terroure hanges;
The windes are up; the lofty elmen swanges;   40
Again the levynne and the thunder poures,
And the full cloudes are braste attenes in stonen showers.

Spurreynge his palfrie oere the watrie plaine,
The Abbote of Seyncte Godwynes convente came;
His chapournette[31] was drented with the reine,
And his pencte[32] gyrdle met with mickle shame;
He aynewarde tolde his bederoll[33] at the same;

[8] Oak.
[9] Moaning.
[10] Beggarly.
[11] Filled.
[12] Beggar.
[13] Clouded, dejected.
[14] Dry, sapless.
[15] Grave.   [16] Accursed.
[17] Coffin.   [18] Dormitory.
[19] Sunburned.   [20] Smoke.
[21] Drink.
[22] Frighten.
[23] Fly.
[24] Lightning.
[25] Vapor.   [26] Flames.
[27] Noisy.
[28] Moves.   [29] Swollen, strengthened.
[30] Frightened.
[31] Small round hat.
[32] Bright colored.
[33] Told his beads backwards, i.e., cursed.

The storme encreasen, and he drew aside,
With the mist[34] almes-craver neere to the holme to bide.

His cope[35] was all of Lyncolne clothe so fyne,　　　　　50
With a gold button fasten'd neere his chynne;
His autremete[36] was edged with golden twynne,
And his shoone pyke a loverds mighte have binne;[37]
Full well it shewn he thoughten coste no sinne:
The trammels[38] of the palfrye pleasde his sighte,
For the horse-millanare his head with roses dighte.

"An almes, sir prieste!" the droppynge pilgrim saide,
"O! let me waite within your covente dore,
Till the sunne sheneth hie above our heade,
And the loude tempeste of the aire is oer;　　　　　60
Helpless and ould am I alas! and poor;
No house, ne friend, ne moneie in my pouche;
All yatte I call my owne is this my silver crou he."[39]

"Varlet," replyd the Abbatte, "cease your dinne;
This is no season almes and prayers to give;
Mie porter never lets a faitour[40] in;
None touch mie rynge who not in honour live."
And now the sonne with the blacke cloudes did stryve,
And shettynge on the grounde his glairie raie,
The Abbatte spurrde his steede, and eftsoones roadde awaie.　　　　　70

Once moe the skie was blacke, the thunder rolde;
Faste reyneynge oer the plaine a prieste was seen;
Ne dighte full proude, ne buttoned up in golde;
His cope and jape[41] were graie, and eke were clene;
A Limitoure[42] he was of order scene;
And from the pathwaie side then turned hee,
Where the pore almer laie binethe the holmen tree.

"An almes, sir priest!" the droppynge pilgrim sayde,
"For sweete Seyncte Marie and your order sake!"
The Limitoure then loosen'd his pouche threade,
And did thereoute a groate of silver take;
The mister pilgrim dyd for halline[43] shake.
"Here take this silver, it maie eathe[44] thie care;
We are Goddes stewards all, nete[45] of oure owne we bare.

[34] Poor, needy.
[35] Cloak.
[36] Loose white robe.
[37] His pointed shoes might have been a lord's.
[38] Shackles, used in teaching a horse to amble.
[39] Crucifix.
[40] Beggar, vagabond.
[41] Short surplice.
[42] A friar licensed to beg within certain limits.
[43] Joy.
[44] Ease.
[45] Naught.

"But ah! unhailie[46] pilgrim, lerne of me,
Scathe[47] anie give a rentrolle to their Lorde.
Here take my semecope, thou arte bare I see;
Tis thyne; the Seynctes will give me mie rewarde."
He left the pilgrim, and his waie aborde.
Virgynne and hallie Seyncte, who sitte yn gloure,[48]
Or give the mittee[49] will, or give the gode man power.

[1777]

[46] Unhappy.
[47] Scarcely.
[48] Glory.
[49] Mighty.

WILLIAM COWPER (1731-1800)

To the late eighteenth century, William Cowper was the poet of a new religious revival, Methodism, as Milton had been the poet of a sterner Puritanism in the seventeenth century. To us he is the poet and writer of inimitable letters, who celebrates with a new simplicity and affectionate fidelity to intimate detail the life of retirement in the country. Both interpretations were, and are, correct. Cowper's sometimes ecstatic, but often morbid, religious temperament and his love of all the quieter pursuits of a country life are but two related manifestations of an over-sensitive, often painfully shy temperament which caused him during his life the acutest sufferings and nervous derangements, but which was partially balanced, happily, by a delicate sense of humor and a warm human interest in other people.

His life was outwardly uneventful. He enjoyed a mildly gay young-manhood as a lawyer's apprentice at the middle Temple—a period in which he first tried his hand at verse and in which was begun the friendship with his two cousins, Theodora and Harriet, the latter of whom became the Lady Hesketh of Cowper's later correspondence. This happy interlude of a troubled spiritual life was followed, when he was thirty-two, by a period of insanity which took the form of hypochondria. Through the aid of his physician, Dr. Cotton, he emerged from this first mental illness partly through Dr. Cotton's wise ministrations to his physical being and partly through the religious conversations in which they engaged. In other words, he emerged a convert to the new evangelical religion of the day, Methodism, although his association was chiefly with the ministers of the new gospel who remained within the Established Church. Obviously unfit both physically and nervously for a professional life in the city, Cowper spent the remainder of his life in retirement in the country, living with Mrs. Unwin, his "second mother" whose life-long devotion to him is gratefully celebrated in the lines "To Mary." Most of this quiet life was spent at Olney, a rather unhealthy and unattractive village of lace-makers on the banks of the Ouse in Buckinghamshire whither Mrs. Unwin moved after the death of her husband to be near the Rev. John Newton, an evangelical preacher of force and eloquence. It is in this neighborhood, then, that the readers of Cowper's poetry and letters must think of him—living for the first years while Newton was in Olney a strenuous and, for Cowper, unwholesome pietistic life; suffering always from religious despondency and experiencing at least one serious return of his insanity, but gradually drifting nevertheless into a more genial life of gardening, of dispensing charity among the poor lace-makers, and of visiting with his neighbors. During one period he dined almost daily with Lady Austen, the inspirer of *John Gilpin* and *The Task*. He always looked forward to and cherished the visits of Lady Hesketh, and he and Mrs. Unwin walked frequently in the park and garden of their friends, the Throckmortons, to whose estate at Weston they moved in 1786. Of his life during these years Cowper once wrote, "From thirty-three to sixty I have spent my time in the country, where my reading has been only an apology for idleness, and where, when I had not either a magazine or a review in my hand, I was sometimes a carpenter, at others a bird-cage maker, or a gardener, or a drawer of landscapes. At fifty years of age I commenced an author. It is a whim that has served me longest and best, and which will probably be my last." (Letter to Thomas Park, March 10, 1792.)

The poetry that grew out of these outwardly quiet years at Olney and Weston cannot be completely understood or read with sympathy without some knowledge of the evangelical religious movement of the day and its effect on Cowper. Doctrinally there was nothing radically new in the religion preached by Whitefield and the Wesleys. It had no quarrel with the creed of the Established Church. It was a reaction, rather, against the rationalism of the Anglican Divines and the deists of the early part of the century; more emotional in nature, the evangelical sects attempted, in the words of Wesley, to bring "the life of God in the souls of men." Like the Puritanism of the seventeenth century it emphasized the *personal* relation between the individual and God in all stages of the religious experience—conviction of sin and the loss of the favor of God, repentance and re-

882

demption with its inner certainty of the forgiveness of sin and the returning grace of God. The deity of Christ was emphasized and the "witness of the Spirit." From the beginning there were two distinct branches of the new faith: the Arminian Methodists, or Wesleyans, who repudiated the doctrine of election and held out the hope of redemption to all—"You all may come, *whoever* will"; and the Calvinistic Methodists who retained the belief in predestination, although in a milder form as the century advanced. Unfortunately most of Cowper's religious advisers were of the sterner, Calvinistic branch, and Cowper's morbid self-doubts did not permit him to accept even of Newton's reassurances. Newton wrote in a letter, and his statement illustrates his moderation: "I am an avowed Calvinist. . . . But I cannot dispute; I dare not speculate. What is by some called High Calvinism I dread. I feel much more union of spirit with some Arminians than I could with some Calvinists; and if I thought a person feared sin, loved the word of God, and was seeking after Jesus, I would not walk the length of my study to proselyte to the Calvinist doctrines." (Quoted by M. J. Quinlan, *William Cowper: A Critical Life,* p. 71).

After Cowper's first attack of insanity he had lived happily enough in the faith for a number of years. These were the years of the *Olney Hymns,* which express for the most part the hope of the new religion. But the over-rigorous, pietistic life under the tutelage of Newton, and even more the subjective element in the religion itself, the constant searching of the mind and heart inspired by the fear lest the grace of God be withdrawn, proved too much for a person of Cowper's weak constitution and morbid tendency toward self-distrust. Newton said of Cowper in his funeral sermon that he had listened to his last sermon on New Year's day, 1773, twenty-seven years before his death. At that time he was seized with a conviction that the favor of God had been withdrawn from him and the conviction brought on another period of insanity. Although the insanity passed, although his humor returned and his gift of poetry developed, the conviction that God's displeasure rested on him never left him. It lies back of all his poetry, now in the gentle melancholy of much of *The Task,* now in the deep despondency of such a poem as "The Castaway." There is nowhere a more faithful and simple record of a certain type of religious experience than is to be found in the writings of Cowper. But the religious passages in his poetry are by no means exclusively subjective: strangely, Cowper's unalterable conviction that he was himself excluded from salvation did not prevent him from writing in behalf of Evangelicalism.

In other ways as well, Cowper's religion and the circumstances of his life fitted him to be the poet of England's countryside and country people. The very practice of his religion took him to the homes of the poor lace-makers of Olney and gave him an intimate knowledge of the lower classes that few poets of his or the preceding generations had had—a knowledge which he shared with the world with a new directness and simplicity. His religion gave him also a depth and breadth of sympathy for man as man irrespective of classes and nationalities that struck another new note in his poetry. Finally, the very effort to throw off his religious despondency helped to make him the whimsical and affectionate poet of the English garden and park, of the birds and hares and household pets, of the winter evening at the fireside. "If I trifle, and merely trifle," he wrote in apology, "it is because I am reduced to it by necessity—a melancholy, that nothing else so effectually disperses, engages me sometimes in the arduous task of being merry by force. And, strange as it may seem, the most ludicrous lines I ever wrote ['John Gilpin'] have been written in the saddest mood, and, but for that saddest mood, perhaps had never been written at all." It is the sympathy and humor of these narratives that give them their charm. "My descriptions are all from nature: not one of them second-handed. My delineations of the heart are from my own experience: not one of them borrowed from books, or in the least degree conjectural."

In the field of prosody, Cowper was interested in trying to free English verse from the overgreat facility of the followers of Pope. "Give me a manly rough line, with a deal of meaning in it, rather than a whole poem full of musical periods, that have nothing but their oily smoothness to recommend them." He not only captured a new fulness in his line, but in an age which was likely to imitate either Milton or Thomson in its blank verse he actually managed to achieve a delicate cadence of his own. "Blank verse," he says, "is susceptible of much greater diversification of manner, than verse in rhyme: and why the modern writers of it have all thought proper to cast their numbers alike, I know not." The many passages of the poetry of sound in his writings attest the unusual sensitiveness of his ear.

Complete Poetical Works, ed. H. S. Milford (3rd ed., 1926); *New Poems* (Oxford, 1931); *The Correspondence of William Cowper,* ed. T. Wright (1904); *Unpublished and Uncollected Letters,* ed. T. Wright (1925); G. Smith, *Cowper* (1901); T. Wright, *The Life of William*

Cowper (2nd ed., 1921) ; D. Cecil, *The Stricken Deer* (1929) ; H. I'A. Fausset, *William Cowper* (1928) ; N. Nicholson, *William Cowper* (1951) ; M. J. Quinlan, *William Cowper, a Critical Life* (Minneapolis, 1953) ; L. C. Hartley, *William Cowper, Humanitarian* (Chapel Hill, N.C., 1938) ; T. Gilbert, *William Cowper and the Eighteenth Century* (2nd ed., 1949) ; L. C. Hartley, "Cowper and the Evangelicals: A Note on Early Biographical Interpretations," *PMLA*, LXV (1950) , 719-31; L. C. Hartley, *William Cowper: A List of Critical and Biographical Studies Published from 1895 to 1949* (West Raleigh, N.C., 1950) .

OLNEY HYMNS

PRAISE FOR THE FOUNTAIN OPENED

Zech. xiii. 1

There is a fountain filled with blood
Drawn from Emmanuel's veins;
And sinners, plunged beneath that flood,
Lose all their guilty stains.

The dying thief rejoiced to see
That fountain in his day;
And there have I, as vile as he,
Washed all my sins away.

Dear dying Lamb, thy precious blood
Shall never lose its power;   10
Till all the ransomed church of God
Be saved, to sin no more.

E'er since, by faith, I saw the stream
Thy flowing wounds supply;
Redeeming love has been my theme,
And shall be till I die.

Then in a nobler sweeter song
I'll sing thy power to save:
When this poor lisping stammering tongue
Lies silent in the grave.   20

Lord, I believe thou hast prepared
(Unworthy though I be)
For me a blood-bought free reward,
A golden harp for me!

'Tis strung, and tuned, for endless years,
And formed by power divine;
To sound in God the Father's ears,
No other name but thine.

[1779]

WALKING WITH GOD

Gen. v. 24

Oh! for a closer walk with God,

A calm and heavenly frame;
A light to shine upon the road
That leads me to the Lamb!

Where is the blessedness I knew
When first I saw the Lord?
Where is the soul-refreshing view
Of Jesus, and his word?

What peaceful hours I once enjoyed!
How sweet their memory still!   10
But they have left an aching void
The world can never fill.

Return, O holy Dove, return,
Sweet messenger of rest;
I hate the sins that made thee mourn,
And drove thee from my breast.

The dearest idol I have known,
Whate'er that idol be;
Help me to tear it from thy throne,
And worship only thee.   20

So shall my walk be close with God,
Calm and serene my frame;
So purer light shall mark the road
That leads me to the Lamb.

[1779]

LIGHT SHINING OUT OF DARKNESS

God moves in a mysterious way,
His wonders to perform;
He plants his footsteps in the sea,
And rides upon the storm.

Deep in unfathomable mines
Of never failing skill,
He treasures up his bright designs,
And works his sovereign will.

Ye fearful saints fresh courage take,
The clouds ye so much dread   10
Are big with mercy, and shall break
In blessings on your head.

Judge not the Lord by feeble sense,
But trust him for his grace;
Behind a frowning providence,
He hides a smiling face.

His purposes will ripen fast,
Unfolding every hour:
The bud may have a bitter taste,
But sweet will be the flower.   20

Blind unbelief is sure to err,
And scan his work in vain;
God is his own interpreter,
And he will make it plain.

[1779]

THE HAPPY CHANGE

How blessed thy creature is, O God,
When with a single eye,
He views the lustre of thy word,
The day-spring from on high!

Through all the storms that veil the skies,
And frown on earthly things,
The Sun of righteousness he eyes,
With healing on his wings.

Struck by that light, the human heart,
A barren soil no more,   10
Sends the sweet smell of grace abroad,
Where serpents lurked before.

The soul, a dreary province once
Of Satan's dark domain,
Feels a new empire formed within,
And owns a heavenly reign.

The glorious orb, whose golden beams
The fruitful year control,
Since first, obedient to thy word,
He started from the goal;   20

Has cheered the nations, with the joys
His orient rays impart;
But Jesus, 'tis thy light alone,
Can shine upon the heart.

[1779]

THE SHRUBBERY

WRITTEN IN A TIME OF AFFLICTION

Oh, happy shades—to me unblessed!
Friendly to peace, but not to me!

How ill the scene that offers rest,
And heart that cannot rest, agree!

This glassy stream, that spreading pine,
Those alders quivering to the breeze,
Might soothe a soul less hurt than mine,
And please, if anything could please.

But fixed unalterable care
Foregoes not what she feels within,   10
Shows the same sadness everywhere,
And slights the season and the scene.

For all that pleased in wood or lawn,
While peace possessed these silent bowers,
Her animating smile withdrawn,
Has lost its beauties and its powers.

The saint or moralist should tread
This moss-grown alley, musing, slow:
They seek, like me, the secret shade,
But not, like me, to nourish woe!   20

Me fruitful scenes and prospects waste
Alike admonish not to roam;
These tell me of enjoyments past,
And those of sorrows yet to come.

[1773, 1782]

ADDRESSED TO A YOUNG LADY

Sweet stream that winds through yonder
glade,
Apt emblem of a virtuous maid—
Silent and chaste she steals along,
Far from the world's gay busy throng,
With gentle, yet prevailing force,
Intent upon her destined course;
Graceful and useful all she does,
Blessing and blessed where'er she goes,
Pure-bosomed as that watery glass,
And heaven reflected in her face.   10

[1780, 1782]

THE DIVERTING HISTORY OF JOHN GILPIN

SHOWING HOW HE WENT FARTHER THAN HE
INTENDED, AND CAME SAFE HOME AGAIN

John Gilpin was a citizen
Of credit and renown.

A train-band captain eke was he
  Of famous London town.

John Gilpin's spouse said to her dear—
  "Though wedded we have been
These twice ten tedious years, yet we
  No holiday have seen.

"To-morrow is our wedding-day,
  And we will then repair   10
Unto the Bell at Edmonton
  All in a chaise and pair.

"My sister, and my sister's child,
  Myself, and children three,
Will fill the chaise; so you must ride
  On horseback after we."

He soon replied—"I do admire
  Of womankind but one,
And you are she, my dearest dear,
  Therefore it shall be done.   20

"I am a linen-draper bold,
  As all the world doth know,
And my good friend the calender
  Will lend his horse to go."

Quoth Mrs. Gilpin—"That's well said;
  And, for that wine is dear,
We will be furnished with our own,
  Which is both bright and clear."

John Gilpin kissed his loving wife;
  O'erjoyed was he to find   30
That, though on pleasure she was bent,
  She had a frugal mind.

The morning came, the chaise was brought,
  But yet was not allowed
To drive up to the door, lest all
  Should say that she was proud.

So three doors off the chaise was stayed,
  Where they did all get in;
Six precious souls, and all agog
  To dash through thick and thin!   40

Smack went the whip, round went the wheels,
  Were never folk so glad,
The stones did rattle underneath,
  As if Cheapside were mad.

John Gilpin at his horse's side
  Seized fast the flowing mane,

And up he got, in haste to ride,
  But soon came down again;

For saddle-tree scarce reached had he,
  His journey to begin,   50
When, turning round his head, he saw
  Three customers come in.

So down he came; for loss of time,
  Although it grieved him sore,
Yet loss of pence, full well he knew,
  Would trouble him much more.

'Twas long before the customers
  Were suited to their mind,
When Betty screaming came down stairs—
  "The wine is left behind!"   60

"Good lack!" quoth he—"yet bring it me,
  My leathern belt likewise,
In which I bear my trusty sword
  When I do exercise."

Now mistress Gilpin (careful soul)!
  Had two stone bottles found,
To hold the liquor that she loved,
  And keep it safe and sound.

Each bottle had a curling ear,
  Through which the belt he drew,   70
And hung a bottle on each side,
  To make his balance true.

Then, over all, that he might be
  Equipped from top to toe,
His long red cloak, well brushed and neat,
  He manfully did throw.

Now see him mounted once again
  Upon his nimble steed,
Full slowly pacing o'er the stones,
  With caution and good heed!   80

But, finding soon a smoother road
  Beneath his well-shod feet,
The snorting beast began to trot,
  Which galled him in his seat.

So, "Fair and softly," John he cried,
  But John he cried in vain;
That trot became a gallop soon,
  In spite of curb and rein.

So stooping down, as needs he must
  Who cannot sit upright,   90

He grasped the mane with both his hands,
  And eke with all his might.

His horse, who never in that sort
  Had handled been before,
What thing upon his back had got
  Did wonder more and more.

Away went Gilpin, neck or nought;
  Away went hat and wig!—
He little dreamed, when he set out,
  Of running such a rig!   100

The wind did blow, the cloak did fly,
  Like streamer long and gay,
Till, loop and button failing both,
  At last it flew away.

Then might all people well discern
  The bottles he had slung;
A bottle swinging at each side,
  As hath been said or sung.

The dogs did bark, the children screamed,
  Up flew the windows all;   110
And every soul cried out—"Well done!"
  As loud as he could bawl.

Away went Gilpin—who but he?
  His fame soon spread around—
"He carries weight!" "He rides a race!"
  "'Tis for a thousand pound!"

And still, as fast as he drew near,
  'Twas wonderful to view
How in a trice the turnpike-men
  Their gates wide open threw.   120

And now, as he went bowing down
  His reeking head full low,
The bottles twain behind his back
  Were shattered at a blow.

Down ran the wine into the road,
  Most piteous to be seen,
Which made his horse's flanks to smoke
  As they had basted been.

But still he seemed to carry weight,
  With leathern girdle braced;   130
For all might see the bottle-necks
  Still dangling at his waist.

Thus all through merry Islington
  These gambols he did play,

And till he came unto the Wash
  Of Edmonton so gay.

And there he threw the wash about
  On both sides of the way,
Just like unto a trundling mop,
  Or a wild goose at play.   140

At Edmonton his loving wife
  From the balcony spied
Her tender husband, wondering much
  To see how he did ride.

"Stop, stop, John Gilpin!—Here's the house"—
  They all at once did cry;
"The dinner waits, and we are tired:"
  Said Gilpin—"So am I!"

But yet his horse was not a whit
  Inclined to tarry there;   150
For why?—his owner had a house
  Full ten miles off, at Ware.

So like an arrow swift he flew,
  Shot by an archer strong;
So did he fly—which brings me to
  The middle of my song.

Away went Gilpin, out of breath,
  And sore against his will,
Till at his friend the calender's
  His horse at last stood still.   160

The calender, amazed to see
  His neighbour in such trim,
Laid down his pipe, flew to the gate,
  And thus accosted him:—

"What news? what news? your tidings tell;
  Tell me you must and shall—
Say why bare-headed you are come,
  Or why you come at all?"

Now Gilpin had a pleasant wit,
  And loved a timely joke;   170
And thus unto the calender
  In merry guise he spoke:—

"I came because your horse would come;
  And, if I well forebode,
My hat and wig will soon be here—
  They are upon the road."

The calender, right glad to find
  His friend in merry pin,

Returned him not a single word,
   But to the house went in;   180

Whence straight he came with hat and wig;
   A wig that flowed behind,
A hat not much the worse for wear,
   Each comely in its kind.

He held them up, and, in his turn,
   Thus showed his ready wit—
"My head is twice as big as yours,
   They therefore needs must fit.

"But let me scrape the dirt away
   That hangs upon your face;   190
And stop and eat, for well you may
   Be in a hungry case."

Said John—"It is my wedding-day,
   And all the world would stare,
If wife should dine at Edmonton
   And I should dine at Ware!"

So, turning to his horse, he said—
   "I am in haste to dine;
'Twas for your pleasure you came here,
   You shall go back for mine."   200

Ah, luckless speech, and bootless boast!
   For which he paid full dear;
For, while he spake, a braying ass
   Did sing most loud and clear;

Whereat his horse did snort, as he
   Had heard a lion roar,
And galloped off with all his might,
   As he had done before.

Away went Gilpin, and away
   Went Gilpin's hat and wig!   210
He lost them sooner than at first—
   For why?—they were too big!

Now, mistress Gilpin, when she saw
   Her husband posting down
Into the country far away,
   She pulled out half a crown;

And thus unto the youth she said
   That drove them to the Bell—
"This shall be yours when you bring back
   My husband safe and well."   220

The youth did ride, and soon did meet
   John coming back amain;
Whom in a trice he tried to stop,
   By catching at his rein;

But, not performing what he meant,
   And gladly would have done,
The frighted steed he frighted more,
   And made him faster run.

Away went Gilpin, and away
   Went post-boy at his heels!—   230
The post-boy's horse right glad to miss
   The lumbering of the wheels.

Six gentlemen upon the road,
   Thus seeing Gilpin fly,
With post-boy scampering in the rear,
   They raised the hue and cry:

"Stop thief! stop thief!—a highwayman!"
   Not one of them was mute;
And all and each that passed that way
   Did join in the pursuit.   240

And now the turnpike gates again
   Flew open in short space;
The toll-men thinking, as before,
   That Gilpin rode a race.

And so he did—and won it too!—
   For he got first to town;
Nor stopped till where he had got up
   He did again get down.

Now let us sing—Long live the king,
   And Gilpin long live he;   250
And, when he next doth ride abroad,
   May I be there to see!

                         [1782, 1782]

THE POPLAR-FIELD

The poplars are felled; farewell to the shade
And the whispering sound of the cool colonnade;
The winds play no longer, and sing in the leaves,
Nor Ouse on his bosom their image receives.

Twelve years have elapsed since I first took a view
Of my favourite field and the bank where they grew,
And now in the grass behold they are laid,
And the tree is my seat that once lent me a shade.

The blackbird has fled to another retreat
Where the hazels afford him a screen from the heat,
And the scene where his melody charmed me before,
Resounds with his sweet-flowing ditty no more.

My fugitive years are all hasting away,
And I must ere long lie as lowly as they,
With a turf on my breast, and a stone at my head,
Ere another such grove shall arise in its stead.

'Tis a sight to engage me, if any thing can,
To muse on the perishing pleasures of man;
Though his life be a dream, his enjoyments, I see,
Have a being less durable even than he.

[*1784, 1785*]

THE TASK

BOOK III

THE GARDEN

ARGUMENT OF THE THIRD BOOK.—Self-recollection and reproof—Address to domestic happiness—
Some account of myself—The vanity of many of their pursuits who are reputed wise—Justifica·
tion of my censures—Divine illumination necessary to the most expert philosopher—The ques·
tion, What is truth? answered by other questions—Domestic happiness addressed again—Few
lovers of the country—My tame hare—Occupations of a retired gentleman in his garden—
Pruning—Framing—Greenhouse—Sowing of flower-seeds—The country preferable to the town
even in the winter—Reasons why it is deserted at that season—Ruinous effects of gaming and of
expensive improvement—Book concludes with an apostrophe to the metropolis.

As one who, long in thickets and in brakes
Entangled, winds now this way and now that
His devious course uncertain, seeking home;
Or, having long in miry ways been foiled
And sore discomfited, from slough to slough
Plunging, and half despairing of escape;
If chance at length he find a greensward smooth
And faithful to the foot, his spirits rise,
He chirrups brisk his ear-erecting steed,
And winds his way with pleasure and with ease;
So I, designing other themes, and called
To adorn the Sofa with eulogium due,
To tell its slumbers, and to paint its dreams,
Have rambled wide. In country, city, seat
Of academic fame (howe'er deserved).
Long held, and scarcely disengaged at last.
But now, with pleasant pace, a cleanlier road
I mean to tread. I feel myself at large,
Courageous, and refreshed for future toil,

If toil await me, or if dangers new.   20
   Since pulpits fail, and sounding boards reflect
Most part an empty ineffectual sound,
What chance that I, to fame so little known,
Nor conversant with men or manners much,
Should speak to purpose, or with better hope
Crack the satiric thong? 'Twere wiser far
For me, enamoured of sequestered scenes,
And charmed with rural beauty, to repose,
Where chance may throw me, beneath elm or vine,
My languid limbs, when summer sears the plains;   30
Or, when rough winter rages, on the soft
And sheltered Sofa, while the nitrous air
Feeds a blue flame, and makes a cheerful hearth;
There, undisturbed by Folly, and apprized
How great the danger of disturbing her,
To muse in silence, or at least confine
Remarks that gall so many to the few
My partners in retreat. Disgust concealed
Is oft-times proof of wisdom, when the fault
Is obstinate, and cure beyond our reach.   40
   Domestic happiness, thou only bliss
Of Paradise that has survived the fall!
Though few now taste thee unimpaired and pure,
Or, tasting, long enjoy thee; too infirm,
Or too incautious, to preserve thy sweets
Unmixed with drops of bitter, which neglect
Or temper sheds into thy crystal cup.
Thou art the nurse of Virtue—in thine arms
She smiles, appearing, as in truth she is,
Heaven-born, and destined to the skies again.   50
Thou art not known where pleasure is adored,
That reeling goddess with the zoneless waist
And wandering eyes, still leaning on the arm
Of Novelty, her fickle frail support;
For thou art meek and constant, hating change,
And finding, in the calm of truth-tried love,
Joys that her stormy raptures never yield.
Forsaking thee, what shipwreck have we made
Of honour, dignity, and fair renown!
Till prostitution elbows us aside   60
In all our crowded streets; and senates seem
Convened for purposes of empire less
Than to release the adultress from her bond.
The adultress! what a theme for angry verse!
What provocation to the indignant heart
That feels for injured love! but I disdain
The nauseous task to paint her as she is,
Cruel, abandoned, glorying in her shame!
No:—let her pass, and, charioted along
In guilty splendour, shake the public ways;   70
The frequency of crimes has washed them white!
And verse of mine shall never brand the wretch,
Whom matrons now, of character unsmirched,
And chaste themselves, are not ashamed to own.

Virtue and vice had boundaries in old time,
Not to be passed: and she that had renounced
Her sex's honour, was renounced herself
By all that prized it; not for prudery's sake,
But dignity's, resentful of the wrong.
'Twas hard, perhaps, on here and there a waif,   80
Desirous to return, and not received;
But was an wholesome rigour in the main,
And taught the unblemished to preserve with care
'That purity, whose loss was loss of all.
Men, too, were nice in honour in those days,
And judged offenders well. Then he that sharped,
And pocketed a prize by fraud obtained,
Was marked and shunned as odious. He that sold
His country, or was slack when she required
His every nerve in action and at stretch,   90
Paid with the blood that he had basely spared
The price of his default. But now—yes, now
We are become so candid and so fair,
So liberal in construction, and so rich
In Christian charity, (good-natured age!)
That they are safe, sinners of either sex,
Transgress what laws they may. Well dressed, well bred,
Well equipaged, is ticket good enough
To pass us readily through every door.
Hypocrisy, detest her as we may,   100
(And no man's hatred ever wronged her yet)
May claim this merit still—that she admits
The worth of what she mimics with such care,
And thus gives virtue indirect applause;
But she has burned her mask, not needed here,
Where vice has such allowance, that her shifts
And specious semblances have lost their use.
    I was a stricken deer, that left the herd
Long since; with many an arrow deep infixed
My panting side was charged, when I withdrew   110
To seek a tranquil death in distant shades.
There was I found by one who had himself
Been hurt by the archers. In his side he bore,
And in his hands and feet, the cruel scars.
With gentle force soliciting the darts,
He drew them forth, and healed, and bade me live.
Since then, with few associates, in remote
And silent woods I wander, far from those
My former partners of the peopled scene;
With few associates, and not wishing more.   120
Here much I ruminate, as much I may,
With other views of men and manners now
Than once, and others of a life to come.
I see that all are wanderers, gone astray
Each in his own delusions; they are lost
In chase of fancied happiness, still wooed
And never won. Dream after dream ensues;
And still they dream that they shall still succeed.
And still are disappointed. Rings the world

With the vain stir. I sum up half mankind,   130
And add two thirds of the remaining half,
And find the total of their hopes and fears
Dreams, empty dreams. The million flit as gay
As if created only like the fly,
That spreads his motley wings in the eye of noon,
To sport their season, and be seen no more.
The rest are sober dreamers, grave and wise,
And pregnant with discoveries new and rare.
Some write a narrative of wars, and feats
Of heroes little known; and call the rant   140
An history: describe the man, of whom
His own coevals took but little note;
And paint his person, character, and views,
As they had known him from his mother's womb.
They disentangle from the puzzled skein
In which obscurity has wrapped them up,
The threads of politic and shrewd design,
That ran through all his purposes, and charge
His mind with meanings that he never had,
Or, having, kept concealed. Some drill and bore   150
The solid earth, and from the strata there
Extract a register, by which we learn
That he who made it, and revealed its date
To Moses, was mistaken in its age.
Some, more acute and more industrious still,
Contrive creation; travel nature up
To the sharp peak of her sublimest height,
And tell us whence the stars; why some are fixed,
And planetary some; what gave them first
Rotation, from what fountain flowed their light.   160
Great contest follows, and much learned dust
Involves the combatants; each claiming truth,
And truth disclaiming both. And thus they spend
The little wick of life's poor shallow lamp
In playing tricks with nature, giving laws
To distant worlds, and trifling in their own.
Is it not a pity now, that tickling rheums
Should ever tease the lungs and blear the sight
Of oracles like these! Great pity too,
That, having wielded the elements, and built   170
A thousand systems, each in his own way,
They should go out in fume, and be forgot?
Ah! what is life thus spent? and what are they
But frantic who thus spend it? all for smoke—
Eternity for bubbles, proves at last
A senseless bargain. When I see such games
Played by the creatures of a power who swears
That he will judge the earth, and call the fool
To a sharp reckoning that has lived in vain;
And when I weigh this seeming wisdom well,   180
And prove it in the infallible result
So hollow and so false—I feel my heart
Dissolve in pity, and account the learned,
If this be learning, most of all deceived.

Great crimes alarm the conscience, but it sleeps
While thoughtful man is plausibly amused.
Defend me, therefore, common sense, say I,
From reveries so airy, from the toil
Of dropping buckets into empty wells,
And growing old in drawing nothing up!   1 0
" 'Twere well," says one sage erudite, profound,
Terribly arched and aquiline his nose,
And overbuilt with most impending brows,
" 'Twere well could you permit the world to live
As the world pleases. What's the world to you?"
Much. I was born of woman, and drew milk,
As sweet as charity, from human breasts.
I think, articulate, I laugh and weep,
And exercise all functions of a man.
How then should I and any man that lives   2(0/
Be strangers to each other? Pierce my vein,
Take of the crimson stream meandering there,
And catechise it well; apply thy glass,
Search it, and prove now if it be not blood
Congenial with thine own: and, if it be,
What edge of subtlety canst thou suppose
Keen enough, wise and skilful as thou art,
To cut the link of brotherhood by which,
One common Maker bound me to the kind?
True; I am no proficient, I confess,   210
In arts like yours. I cannot call the swift
And perilous lightnings from the angry clouds,
And bid them hide themselves in earth beneath;
I cannot analyse the air, nor catch
The parallax of yonder luminous point,
That seems half quenched in the immense abyss:
Such powers I boast not—neither can I rest
A silent witness of the headlong rage
Or heedless folly by which thousands die,
Bone of my bone, and kindred souls to mine.   220
    God never meant that man should scale the heavens
By strides of human wisdom. In his works
Though wondrous, he commands us in his word
To seek *him* rather, where his mercy shines.
The mind indeed, enlightened from above,
Views him in all; ascribes to the grand cause
The grand effect; acknowledges with joy
His manner, and with rapture tastes his style.
But never yet did philosophic tube
That brings the planets home into the eye   230
Of observation, and discovers, else
Not visible, his family of worlds,
Discover him that rules them; such a veil
Hangs over mortal eyes, blind from the birth,
And dark in things divine. Full often, too,
Our wayward intellect, the more we learn
Of nature, overlooks her Author more;
From instrumental causes proud to draw
Conclusions retrograde, and mad mistake.

But if his word once teach us, shoot a ray   240
Through all the heart's dark chambers, and reveal
Truths undiscerned but by that holy light,
Then all is plain. Philosophy, baptized
In the pure fountain of eternal love,
Has eyes indeed; and, viewing all she sees
As meant to indicate a God to man,
Gives *him* his praise, and forfeits not her own.
Learning has borne such fruit in other days
On all her branches: piety has found
Friends in the friends of science, and true prayer   250
Has flowed from lips wet with Castalian dews.
Such was thy wisdom, Newton, childlike sage!
Sagacious reader of the works of God,
And in his word sagacious. Such too thine,
Milton, whose genius had angelic wings,
And fed on manna! And such thine, in whom
Our British Themis gloried with just cause,
Immortal Hale! for deep discernment praised
And sound integrity, not more than famed
For sanctity of manners undefiled.   260
    All flesh is grass, and all its glory fades
Like the fair flower dishevelled in the wind;
Riches have wings, and grandeur is a dream:
The man we celebrate must find a tomb,
And we that worship him ignoble graves.
Nothing is proof against the general curse
Of vanity, that seizes all below.
The only amaranthine flower on earth
Is virtue; the only lasting treasure, truth.
But what is truth? 'twas Pilate's question, put   270
To Truth itself, that deigned him no reply.
And wherefore? will not God impart his light
To them that ask it?—Freely—'tis his joy,
His glory and his nature to impart.
But to the proud, uncandid, insincere,
Or negligent inquirer, not a spark.
What's that which brings contempt upon a book,
And him who writes it; though the style be neat,
The method clear, and argument exact?
That makes a minister in holy things   280
The joy of many, and the dread of more,
His name a theme for praise and for reproach?—
That, while it gives us worth in God's account,
Depreciates and undoes us in our own?
What pearl is it that rich men cannot buy,
That learning is too proud to gather up;
But which the poor, and the despised of all,
Seek and obtain, and often find unsought?
Tell me—and I will tell thee what is truth.
    O, friendly to the best pursuits of man,   290
Friendly to thought, to virtue, and to peace,
Domestic life in rural leisure passed!
Few know thy value, and few taste thy sweets;
Though many boast thy favours, and affect

To understand and choose thee for their own.
But foolish man foregoes his proper bliss,
Even as his first progenitor, and quits,
Though placed in paradise (for earth has still
Some traces of her youthful beauty left)
Substantial happiness for transient joy.   300
Scenes formed for contemplation and to nurse,
The growing seeds of wisdom; that suggest,
By every pleasing image they present,
Reflections such as meliorate the heart,
Compose the passions, and exalt the mind;
Scenes such as these 'tis his supreme delight
To fill with riot, and defile with blood.
Should some contagion, kind to the poor brutes
We persecute, annihilate the tribes
That draw the sportsman over hill and dale,   310
Fearless, and rapt away from all his cares;
Should never game-fowl hatch her eggs again,
Nor baited hook deceive the fish's eye;
Could pageantry and dance, and feast and song,
Be quelled in all our summer-months' retreat;
How many self-deluded nymphs and swains,
Who dream they have a taste for fields and groves,
Would find them hideous nurseries of the spleen,
And crowd the roads, impatient for the town!
They love the country, and none else, who seek   320
For their own sake its silence and its shade.
Delights which who would leave, that has a heart
Susceptible of pity, or a mind
Cultured and capable of sober thought,
For all the savage din of the swift pack,
And clamours of the field?—Detested sport,
That owes its pleasures to another's pain;
That feeds upon the sobs and dying shrieks
Of harmless nature, dumb, but yet endued
With eloquence, that agonies inspire,   330
Of silent tears and heart-distending sighs!
Vain tears, alas, and sighs, that never find
A corresponding tone in jovial souls!
Well—one at least is safe. One sheltered hare
Has never heard the sanguinary yell
Of cruel man, exulting in her woes.
Innocent partner of my peaceful home,
Whom ten long years' experience of my care
Has made at last familiar; she has lost
Much of her vigilant instinctive dread,   340
Not needful here, beneath a roof like mine.
Yes—thou mayest eat thy bread, and lick the hand
That feeds thee; thou mayest frolic on the floor
At evening, and at night retire secure
To thy straw couch, and slumber unalarmed;
For I have gained thy confidence, have pledged
All that is human in me to protect
Thine unsuspecting gratitude and love.
If I survive thee I will dig thy grave;

And, when I place thee in it, sighing, say,   350
I knew at least one hare that had a friend.
     How various his employments, whom the world
Calls idle; and who justly, in return,
Esteems that busy world an idler too!
Friends, books, a garden, and perhaps his pen,
Delightful industry enjoyed at home,
And Nature in her cultivated trim
Dressed to his taste, inviting him abroad—
Can he want occupation who has these?
Will he be idle who has much to enjoy?   360
Me, therefore, studious of laborious ease,
Not slothful; happy to deceive the time,
Not waste it; and aware that human life
Is but a loan to be repaid with use,
When he shall call his debtors to account
From whom are all our blessings; business finds
Even here: while sedulous I seek to improve,
At least neglect not, or leave unemployed,
The mind he gave me; driving it, though slack
Too oft, and much impeded in its work   370
By causes not to be divulged in vain,
To its just point—the service of mankind.
He that attends to his interior self,
That has a heart, and keeps it; has a mind
That hungers, and supplies it; and who seeks
A social, not a dissipated life;
Has business; feels himself engaged to achieve
No unimportant, though a silent, task.
A life all turbulence and noise may seem
To him that leads it, wise, and to be praised;   380
But wisdom is a pearl with most success
Sought in still water, and beneath clear skies.
He that is ever occupied in storms,
Or dives not for it, or brings up instead,
Vainly industrious, a disgraceful prize.
     The morning finds the self-sequestered man
Fresh for his task, intend what task he may;
Whether inclement seasons recommend
His warm but simple home, where he enjoys,
With her who shares his pleasures and his heart,   390
Sweet converse, sipping calm the fragrant lymph
Which neatly she prepares; then to his book,
Well chosen, and not sullenly perused
In selfish silence, but imparted oft
As aught occurs that she may smile to hear,
Or turn to nourishment, digested well:
Or, if the garden with its many cares,
All well repaid, demand him, he attends
The welcome call, conscious how much the hand
Of lubbard labour needs his watchful eye,   400
Oft loitering lazily, if not o'erseen,
Or misapplying his unskilful strength.
Nor does he govern only or direct,
But much performs himself. No works indeed

That ask robust tough sinews, bred to toil,
Servile employ; but such as may amuse,
Not tire, demanding rather skill than force.
Proud of his well-spread walls, he views his trees
That meet (no barren interval between)
With pleasure more than even their fruits afford,   410
Which, save himself who trains them, none can feel:
These, therefore, are his own peculiar charge;
No meaner hand may discipline the shoots,
None but his steel approach them. What is weak,
Distempered, or has lost prolific powers,
Impaired by age, his unrelenting hand
Dooms to the knife: nor does he spare the soft
And succulent, that feeds its giant growth,
But barren, at the expense of neighbouring twigs
Less ostentatious, and yet studded thick   420
With hopeful gems. The rest, no portion left
That may disgrace his art or disappoint
Large expectation, he disposes neat
At measured distances, that air and sun,
Admitted freely, may afford their aid,
And ventilate and warm the swelling buds.
Hence summer has her riches, autumn hence,
And hence even winter fills his withered hand
With blushing fruits, and plenty not his own:
Fair recompense of labour well bestowed,   430
And wise precaution; which a clime so rude
Makes needful still, whose Spring is but the child
Of churlish Winter, in her froward moods
Discovering much the temper of her sire.
For oft, as if in her the stream of mild
Maternal nature had reversed its course,
She brings her infants forth with many smiles;
But, once delivered, kills them with a frown.
He, therefore, timely warned, himself supplies
Her want of care, screening and keeping warm   440
The plenteous bloom, that no rough blast may sweep
His garlands from the boughs. Again, as oft
As the sun peeps and vernal airs breathe mild,
The fence withdrawn, he gives them every beam,
And spreads his hopes before the blaze of day.
      To raise the prickly and green-coated gourd,
So grateful to the palate, and when rare
So coveted, else base and disesteemed—
Food for the vulgar merely—is an art
That toiling ages have but just matured,   450
And at this moment unassayed in song.
Yet gnats have had, and frogs and mice, long since,
Their eulogy; those sang the Mantuan bard,
And these the Grecian, in ennobling strains;
And in thy numbers, Philips, shines for aye
The solitary shilling. Pardon then,
Ye sage dispensers of poetic fame,
The ambition of one, meaner far, whose powers,
Presuming an attempt not less sublime.

Pant for the praise of dressing to the taste   460
Of critic appetite, no sordid fare,
A cucumber, while costly yet and scarce.
   The stable yields a stercoraceous heap,
Impregnated with quick fermenting salts,
And potent to resist the freezing blast:
For, ere the beech and elm have cast their leaf
Deciduous, when now November dark
Checks vegetation in the torpid plant
Exposed to his cold breath, the task begins.
Warily, therefore, and with prudent heed,   470
He seeks a favoured spot; that where he builds
The agglomerated pile his frame may front
The sun's meridian disk, and at the back
Enjoy close shelter, wall, or reeds, or hedge
Impervious to the wind. First he bids spread
Dry fern or littered hay, that may imbibe
The ascending damps; then leisurely impose,
And lightly, shaking it with agile hand
From the full fork, the saturated straw.
What longest binds the closest forms secure   480
The shapely side, that as it rises takes,
By just degrees, an overhanging breadth,
Sheltering the base with its projected eaves:
The uplifted frame, compact at every joint,
And overlaid with clear translucent glass,
He settles next upon the sloping mount,
Whose sharp declivity shoots off secure
From the dashed pane the deluge as it falls.
He shuts it close, and the first labour ends.
Thrice must the voluble and restless earth   490
Spin round upon her axle, ere the warmth,
Slow gathering in the midst, through the square mass
Diffused, attain the surface: when, behold!
A pestilent and most corrosive steam,
Like a gross fog Bœotian, rising fast,
And fast condensed upon the dewy sash,
Asks egress; which obtained, the overcharged
And drenched conservatory breathes abroad,
In volumes wheeling slow, the vapour dank;
And, purified, rejoices to have lost   500
Its foul inhabitant. But to assuage
The impatient fervour which it first conceives
Within its reeking bosom, threatening death
To his young hopes, requires discreet delay.
Experience, slow preceptress, teaching oft
The way to glory by miscarriage foul,
Must prompt him, and admonish how to catch
The auspicious moment, when the tempered heat,
Friendly to vital motion, may afford
Soft fomentation, and invite the seed.   510
The seed, selected wisely, plump, and smooth,
And glossy, he commits to pots of size
Diminutive, well filled with well-prepared
And fruitful soil, that has been treasured long,

And drank no moisture from the dripping clouds:
These on the warm and genial earth, that hides
The smoking manure and o'erspreads it all,
He places lightly, and, as time subdues
The rage of fermentation, plunges deep
In the soft medium, till they stand immersed. 520
Then rise the tender germs, upstarting quick,
And spreading wide their spongy lobes; at first
Pale, wan, and livid; but assuming soon,
If fanned by balmy and nutritious air,
Strained through the friendly mats, a vivid green.
Two leaves produced, two rough indented leaves,
Cautious he pinches from the second stalk
A pimple, that portends a future sprout,
And interdicts its growth. Thence straight succeed
The branches, sturdy to his utmost wish; 530
Prolific all, and harbingers of more.
The crowded roots demand enlargement now,
And transplantation in an ampler space.
Indulged in what they wish, they soon supply
Large foliage, overshadowing golden flowers,
Blown on the summit of the apparent fruit.
These have their sexes; and, when summer shines,
The bee transports the fertilizing meal
From flower to flower, and even the breathing air
Wafts the rich prize to its appointed use. 540
Not so when winter scowls. Assistant art
Then acts in nature's office, brings to pass
The glad espousals, and insures the crop.
   Grudge not, ye rich, (since Luxury must have
His dainties, and the world's more numerous half
Lives by contriving delicates for you)
Grudge not the cost. Ye little know the cares,
The vigilance, the labour, and the skill,
That day and night are exercised, and hang
Upon the ticklish balance of suspense, 550
That ye may garnish your profuse regales
With summer fruits brought forth by wintry suns.
Ten thousand dangers lie in wait to thwart
The process. Heat and cold, and wind, and steam,
Moisture and drought, mice, worms, and swarming flies,
Minute as dust, and numberless, oft work
Dire disappointment that admits no cure,
And which no care can obviate. It were long,
Too long, to tell the expedients and the shifts
Which he that fights a season so severe 560
Devises, while he guards his tender trust;
And oft, at last, in vain. The learned and wise
Sarcastic would exclaim, and judge the song
Cold as its theme, and, like its theme, the fruit
Of too much labour, worthless when produced.
   Who loves a garden loves a greenhouse too.
Unconscious of a less propitious clime,
There blooms exotic beauty, warm and snug.
While the winds whistle and the snows descend.

The spiry myrtle with unwithering leaf   570
Shines there, and flourishes. The golden boast
Of Portugal and western India there,
The ruddier orange, and the paler lime,
Peep through their polished foliage at the storm,
And seem to smile at what they need not fear.
The amomum there with intermingling flowers
And cherries hangs her twigs. Geranium boasts
Her crimson honours, and the spangled beau,
Ficoides, glitters bright the winter long.
All plants, of every leaf, that can endure   580
The winter's frown, if screened from his shrewd bite,
Live there, and prosper. Those Ausonia claims,
Levantine regions these; the Azores send
Their jessamine, her jessamine remote
Caffraia: foreigners from many lands,
They form one social shade, as if convened
By magic summons of the Orphean lyre.
Yet just arrangement, rarely brought to pass
But by a master's hand, disposing well
The gay diversities of leaf and flower,   590
Must lend its aid to illustrate all their charms,
And dress the regular yet various scene.
Plant behind plant aspiring, in the van
The dwarfish, in the rear retired, but still
Sublime above the rest, the statelier stand.
So once were ranged the sons of ancient Rome,
A noble show! while Roscius trod the stage;
And so, while Garrick, as renowned as he,
The sons of Albion; fearing each to lose
Some note of Nature's music from his lips,   600
And covetous of Shakespeare's beauty, seen
In every flash of his far-beaming eye.
Nor taste alone and well-contrived display
Suffice to give the marshaled ranks the grace
Of their complete effect. Much yet remains
Unsung, and many cares are yet behind,
And more laborious; cares on which depends
Their vigour, injured soon, not soon restored.
The soil must be renewed, which, often washed,
Loses its treasure of salubrious salts,   610
And disappoints the roots; the slender roots
Close interwoven, where they meet the vase,
Must smooth be shorn away; the sapless branch
Must fly before the knife; the withered leaf
Must be detached, and where it strews the floor
Swept with a woman's neatness, breeding else
Contagion, and disseminating death.
Discharge but these kind offices, (and who
Would spare, that loves them, offices like these?)
Well they reward the toil. The sight is pleased,   620
The scent regaled, each odoriferous leaf,
Each opening blossom, freely breathes abroad
Its gratitude, and thanks him with its sweets.
    So manifold, all pleasing in their kind.

All healthful, are the employs of rural life,
Reiterated as the wheel of time
Runs round; still ending, and beginning still.
Nor are these all. To deck the shapely knoll,
That, softly swelled and gaily dressed, appears
A flowery island, from the dark green lawn   630
Emerging, must be deemed a labour due
To no mean hand, and asks the touch of taste.
Here also grateful mixture of well-matched
And sorted hues (each giving each relief,
And by contrasted beauty shining more)
Is needful. Strength may wield the ponderous spade,
May turn the clod, and wheel the compost home;
But elegance, chief grace the garden shows,
And most attractive, is the fair result
Of thought, the creature of a polished mind.   640
Without it all is Gothic as the scene
To which the insipid citizen resorts
Near yonder heath; where industry misspent,
But proud of his uncouth ill-chosen task,
Has made a heaven on earth; with suns and moons
Of close-rammed stones has charged the encumbered soil,
And fairly laid the zodiac in the dust.
He, therefore, who would see his flowers disposed
Sightly and in just order, ere he gives
The beds the trusted treasure of their seeds,   650
Forecasts the future whole; that, when the scene
Shall break into its preconceived display,
Each for itself, and all as with one voice
Conspiring, may attest his bright design.
Nor even then, dismissing as performed
His pleasant work, may he suppose it done.
Few self-supported flowers endure the wind
Uninjured, but expect the upholding aid
Of the smooth-shaven prop, and, neatly tied,
Are wedded thus, like beauty to old age,   660
For interest sake, the living to the dead.
Some clothe the soil that feeds them, far diffused
And lowly creeping, modest and yet fair,
Like virtue, thriving most where little seen:
Some, more aspiring, catch the neighbour shrub
With clasping tendrils, and invest his branch,
Else unadorned, with many a gay festoon
And fragrant chaplet, recompensing well
The strength they borrow with the grace they lend.
All hate the rank society of weeds,   670
Noisome, and ever greedy to exhaust
The impoverished earth; an overbearing race,
That, like the multitude made faction-mad,
Disturb good order, and degrade true worth.
    Oh, blessed seclusion from a jarring world,
Which he, thus occupied, enjoys! Retreat
Cannot indeed to guilty man restore
Lost innocence, or cancel follies past;
But it has peace, and much secures the mind

From all assaults of evil; proving still   680
A faithful barrier, not o'erleaped with ease
By vicious custom, raging uncontrolled
Abroad, and desolating public life.
When fierce temptation, seconded within
By traitor appetite, and armed with darts
Tempered in hell, invades the throbbing breast,
To combat may be glorious and success
Perhaps may crown us; but to fly is safe.
Had I the choice of sublunary good,
What could I wish that I possess not here?   690
Health, leisure, means to improve it, friendship, peace,
No loose or wanton, though a wandering, muse,
And constant occupation without care.
Thus blessed, I draw a picture of that bliss;
Hopeless, indeed, that dissipated minds,
And profligate abusers of a world
Created fair so much in vain for them,
Should seek the guiltless joys that I describe,
Allured by my report: but sure no less,
That, self-condemned, they must neglect the prize,   700
And what they will not taste must yet approve.
What we admire we praise; and, when we praise,
Advance it into notice, that, its worth
Acknowledged, others may admire it too.
I therefore recommend, though at the risk
Of popular disgust, yet boldly still,
The cause of piety and sacred truth,
And virtue, and those scenes which God ordained
Should best secure them and promote them most;
Scenes that I love, and with regret perceive   710
Forsaken, or through folly not enjoyed.
Pure is the nymph, though liberal of her smiles,
And chaste, though unconfined, whom I extol.
Not as the prince in Shushan, when he called,
Vain-glorious of her charms, his Vashti forth
To grace the full pavilion. His design
Was but to boast his own peculiar good,
Which all might view with envy, none partake.
My charmer is not mine alone; my sweets,
And she that sweetens all my bitters too,   720
Nature, enchanting Nature, in whose form
And lineaments divine I trace a hand
That errs not, and find raptures still renewed,
Is free to all men—universal prize.
Strange that so fair a creature should yet want
Admirers, and be destined to divide
With meaner objects even the few she finds!
Stripped of her ornaments, her leaves and flowers,
She loses all her influence. Cities then
Attract us, and neglected Nature pines,   730
Abandoned, as unworthy of our love.
But are not wholesome airs, though unperfumed
By roses; and clear suns, though scarcely felt;
And groves, if unharmonious, yet secure

From clamour, and whose very silence charms;
To be preferred to smoke, to the eclipse
That metropolitan volcanos make,
Whose Stygian throats breathe darkness all day long;
And to the stir of commerce, driving slow,
And thundering loud, with his ten thousand wheels?   740
They would be, were not madness in the head,
And folly in the heart; were England now
What England was; plain, hospitable, kind,
And undebauched. But we have bid farewell
To all the virtues of those better days
And all their honest pleasures. Mansions once
Knew their own masters; and laborious hinds
Who had survived the father, served the son.
Now the legitimate and rightful lord
Is but a transient guest, newly arrived,   750
And soon to be supplanted. He that saw
His patrimonial timber cast its leaf,
Sells the last scantling, and transfers the price
To some shrewd sharper, ere it buds again.
Estates are landscapes, gazed upon a while,
Then advertised, and auctioneered away.
The country starves, and they that feed the o'er-charged
And surfeited lewd town with her fair dues,
By a just judgment strip and starve themselves.
The wings that waft our riches out of sight   760
Grow on the gamester's elbows; and the alert
And nimble motion of those restless joints,
That never tire, soon fans them all away.
Improvement too, the idol of the age,
Is fed with many a victim. Lo, he comes!
The omnipotent magician, Brown, appears!
Down falls the venerable pile, the abode
Of our forefathers—a grave whiskered race,
But tasteless. Springs a palace in its stead,
But in a distant spot; where, more exposed,   770
It may enjoy the advantage of the north,
And aguish east, till time shall have transformed
Those naked acres to a sheltering grove.
He speaks. The lake in front becomes a lawn;
Woods vanish, hills subside, and valleys rise:
And streams, as if created for his use,
Pursue the track of his directing wand,
Sinuous or straight, now rapid and now slow,
Now murmuring soft, now roaring in cascades—
Even as he bids! The enraptured owner smiles.   780
'Tis finished, and yet, finished as it seems,
Still wants a grace, the loveliest it could show,
A mine to satisfy the enormous cost.
Drained to the last poor item of his wealth,
He sighs, departs, and leaves the accomplished plan
That he has touched, retouched, many a long day
Laboured, and many a night pursued in dreams,
Just when it meets his hopes, and proves the heaven
He wanted, for a wealthier to enjoy!

And now perhaps the glorious hour is come,   790
When, having no stake left, no pledge to endear
Her interests, or that gives her sacred cause
A moment's operation on his love,
He burns with most intense and flagrant zeal
To serve his country. Ministerial grace
Deals him out money from the public chest;
Or, if that mine be shut, some private purse
Supplies his need with an usurious loan,
To be refunded duly when his vote,
Well-managed, shall have earned its worthy price.   800
Oh innocent, compared with arts like these,
Crape, and cocked pistol, and the whistling ball
Sent through the traveller's temples! He that finds
One drop of heaven's sweet mercy in his cup,
Can dig, beg, rot, and perish, well content,
So he may wrap himself in honest rags
At his last gasp; but could not for a world
Fish up his dirty and dependent bread
From pools and ditches of the commonwealth,
Sordid and sickening at his own success.   810
    Ambition, avarice, penury incurred
By endless riot, vanity, the lust
Of pleasure and variety, dispatch,
As duly as the swallows disappear,
The world of wandering knights and squires to town.
London ingulfs them all! The shark is there.
And the shark's prey; the spendthrift, and the leech
That sucks him. There the sycophant, and he
Who, with bare-headed and obsequious bows,
Begs a warm office, doomed to a cold jail   820
And groat *per diem*, if his patron frown.
The levee swarms, as if, in golden pomp,
Were charactered on every statesman's door,
"BATTERED AND BANKRUPT FORTUNES MENDED HERE."
These are the charms that sully and eclipse
The charms of nature. 'Tis the cruel gripe
That lean hard-handed poverty inflicts,
The hope of better things, the chance to win,
The wish to shine, the thirst to be amused,
That at the sound of winter's hoary wing   830
Unpeople all our counties of such herds
Of fluttering, loitering, cringing, begging, loose
And wanton vagrants, as make London, vast
And boundless as it is, a crowded coop.
    Oh thou, resort and mart of all the earth,
Checkered with all complexions of mankind,
And spotted with all crimes; in whom I see
Much that I love, and more that I admire,
And all that I abhor; thou freckled fair,
That pleasest and yet shockest me, I can laugh   840
And I can weep, can hope, and can despond,
Feel wrath and pity, when I think on thee!
Ten righteous would have saved a city once,
And thou hast many righteous.—Well for thee!

That salt preserves thee; more corrupted else,
And therefore more obnoxious at this hour
Than Sodom in her day had power to be,
For whom God heard his Abraham plead in vain.

BOOK IV

THE WINTER EVENING

ARGUMENT OF THE FOURTH BOOK.—The post comes in—The newspaper is read—The world contemplated at a distance—Address to winter—The rural amusements of a winter evening compared with the fashionable ones—Address to evening—A brown study—Fall of snow in the
evening—The waggoner—A poor family-piece—The rural thief—Public houses—The multitude
of them censured—The farmer's daughter: what she was—what she is—The simplicity of country
manners almost lost—Causes of the change—Desertion of the country by the rich—Neglect of
magistrates—The militia principally in fault—The new recruit and his transformation—Reflection on bodies corporate—The love of rural objects natural to all, and never to be totally
extinguished.

Hark! 'tis the twanging horn o'er yonder bridge,
That with its wearisome but needful length
Bestrides the wintry flood, in which the moon
Sees her unwrinkled face reflected bright;—
He comes, the herald of a noisy world,
With spattered boots, strapped waist, and frozen locks;
News from all nations lumbering at his back.
True to his charge, the close-packed load behind,
Yet careless what he brings, his one concern
Is to conduct it to the destined inn: 10
And, having dropped the expected bag, pass on.
He whistles as he goes, light-hearted wretch,
Cold and yet cheerful: messenger of grief
Perhaps to thousands, and of joy to some;
To him indifferent whether grief or joy.
Houses in ashes, and the fall of stocks,
Births, deaths, and marriages, epistles wet
With tears that trickled down the writer's cheeks
Fast as the periods from his fluent quill,
Or charged with amorous sighs of absent swains   20
Or nymphs responsive, equally affect
His horse and him, unconscious of them all.
But oh the important budget! ushered in
With such heart-shaking music, who can say
What are its tidings? Have our troops awaked?
Or do they still, as if with opium drugged,
Snore to the murmurs of the Atlantic wave?
Is India free, and does she wear her plumed
And jewelled turban with a smile of peace,
Or do we grind her still? The grand debate,   30
The popular harangue, the tart reply,
The logic, and the wisdom, and the wit,
And the loud laugh—I long to know them all;
I burn to set the imprisoned wranglers free,
And give them voice and utterance once again.
   Now stir the fire, and close the shutters fast,
Let fall the curtains, wheel the sofa round,

And, while the bubbling and loud-hissing urn
Throws up a steamy column, and the cups
That cheer but not inebriate, wait on each,   40
So let us welcome peaceful evening in.
Not such his evening, who with shining face
Sweats in the crowded theatre, and, squeezed
And bored with elbow-points through both his sides,
Outscolds the ranting actor on the stage:
Nor his, who patient stands till his feet throb,
And his head thumps, to feed upon the breath
Of patriots, bursting with heroic rage,
Or placemen, all tranquillity and smiles.
This folio of four pages, happy work!   50
Which not even critics criticise; that holds
Inquisitive attention, while I read,
Fast bound in chains of silence, which the fair,
Though eloquent themselves, yet fear to break;
What is it but a map of busy life,
Its fluctuations, and its vast concerns?
Here runs the mountainous and craggy ridge
That tempts ambition. On the summit see
The seals of office glitter in his eyes;
He climbs, he pants, he grasps them! At his heels,   60
Close at his heels, a demagogue ascends,
And with a dexterous jerk soon twists him down,
And wins them, but to lose them in his turn.
Here rills of oily eloquence in soft
Meanders lubricate the course they take;
The modest speaker is ashamed and grieved
To engross a moment's notice, and yet begs,
Begs a propitious ear for his poor thoughts,
However trivial all that he conceives.
Sweet bashfulness! it claims at least this praise: 70
The dearth of information and good sense
That it foretells us always comes to pass.
Cataracts of declamation thunder here;
There forests of no meaning spread the page,
In which all comprehension wanders, lost;
While fields of pleasantry amuse us there
With merry descants on a nation's woes.
The rest appears a wilderness of strange
But gay confusion; roses for the cheeks,
And lilies for the brows of faded age,   80
Teeth for the toothless, ringlets for the bald,
Heaven, earth, and ocean, plundered of their sweets,
Nectareous essences, Olympian dews,
Sermons, and city feasts, and favourite airs,
Ethereal journeys, submarine exploits,
And Katterfelto, with his hair on end
At his own wonders, wondering for his bread.
    'Tis pleasant through the loopholes of retreat
To peep at such a world; to see the stir
Of the great Babel, and not feel the crowd;   90
To hear the roar she sends through all her gates
At a safe distance, where the dying sound

Falls a soft murmur on the uninjured ear.
Thus sitting, and surveying thus at ease
The globe and its concerns, I seem advanced
To some secure and more than mortal height,
That liberates and exempts me from them all.
It turns submitted to my view, turns round
With all its generations; I behold
The tumult, and am still. The sound of war   100
Has lost its terrors ere it reaches me;
Grieves but alarms me not. I mourn the pride
And avarice that make man a wolf to man;
Hear the faint echo of those brazen throats
By which he speaks the language of his heart,
And sigh, but never tremble at the sound.
He travels and expatiates as the bee
From flower to flower, so he from land to land;
The manners, customs, policy of all
Pay contribution to the store he gleans;   110
He sucks intelligence in every clime,
And spreads the honey of his deep research
At his return—a rich repast for me.
He travels, and I too. I tread his deck,
Ascend his topmast, through his peering eyes
Discover countries, with a kindred heart
Suffer his woes, and share in his escapes;
While fancy, like the finger of a clock,
Runs the great circuit, and is still at home.
  O Winter, ruler of the inverted year,   120
Thy scattered hair with sleet like ashes filled,
Thy breath congealed upon thy lips, thy cheeks
Fringed with a beard made white with other snows
Than those of age, thy forehead wrapped in clouds,
A leafless branch thy scepter, and thy throne
A sliding car, indebted to no wheels,
But urged by storms along its slippery way,
I love thee, all unlovely as thou seem'st,
And dreaded as thou art! Thou hold'st the sun
A prisoner in the yet undawning east,   130
Shortening his journey between morn and noon,
And hurrying him, impatient of his stay,
Down to the rosy, west; but kindly still
Compensating his loss with added hours
Of social converse and instructive ease,
And gathering, at short notice, in one group
The family dispersed, and fixing thought,
Not less dispersed by daylight and its cares.
I crown thee king of intimate delights,
Fireside enjoyments, home-born happiness,   140
And all the comforts that the lowly roof
Of undisturbed retirement and the hours
Of long uninterrupted evening know.
No rattling wheels stop short before these gates;
No powdered pert, proficient in the art
Of sounding an alarm, assaults these doors
Till the street rings; no stationary steeds

Cough their own knell, while, heedless of the sound,
The silent circle fan themselves, and quake:
But here the needle plies its busy task,　　　　　　　　　150
The pattern grows, the well-depicted flower,
Wrought patiently into the snowy lawn,
Unfolds its bosom; buds, and leaves, and sprigs,
And curling tendrils, gracefully disposed,
Follow the nimble finger of the fair—
A wreath that cannot fade, of flowers that blow
With most success when all besides decay.
The poet's or historian's page, by one
Made vocal for the amusement of the rest;
The sprightly lyre, whose treasure of sweet sounds　　160
The touch from many a trembling chord shakes out;
And the clear voice symphonious, yet distinct,
And in the charming strife triumphant still,
Beguile the night, and set a keener edge
On female industry: the threaded steel
Flies swiftly, and unfelt the task proceeds.
The volume closed, the customary rites
Of the last meal commence. A Roman meal,
Such as the mistress of the world once found
Delicious, when her patriots of high note,　　　　　170
Perhaps by moonlight, at their humble doors,
And under an old oak's domestic shade,
Enjoyed—spare feast!—a radish and an egg!
Discourse ensues, not trivial, yet not dull,
Nor such as with a frown forbids the play
Of fancy, or proscribes the sound of mirth:
Nor do we madly, like an impious world,
Who deem religion frenzy, and the God
That made them an intruder on their joys,
Start at his awful name, or deem his praise　　　　180
A jarring note—themes of a graver tone,
Exciting oft our gratitude and love,
While we retrace with memory's pointing wand,
That calls the past to our exact review,
The dangers we have escaped, the broken snare,
The disappointed foe, deliverance found
Unlooked for, life preserved and peace restored—
Fruits of omnipotent eternal love.
"Oh evenings worthy of the gods!" exclaimed
The Sabine bard. "Oh evenings," I reply,　　　　　190
"More to be prized and coveted than yours,
As more illumined, and with nobler truths,
That I, and mine, and those we love, enjoy."
　Is winter hideous in a garb like this?
Needs he the tragic fur, the smoke of lamps,
The pent-up breath of an unsavoury throng,
To thaw him into feeling; or the smart
And snappish dialogue, that flippant wits
Call comedy, to prompt him with a smile?
The self-complacent actor, when he views　　　　　200
(Stealing a side-long glance at a full house)
The slope of faces, from the floor to the roof,

(As if one master-spring controlled them all)
Relaxed into an universal grin,
Sees not a countenance there that speaks of joy
Half so refined or so sincere as ours.
Cards were superfluous here, with all the tricks
That idleness has ever yet contrived
To fill the void of an unfurnished brain,
To palliate dullness, and give time a shove.   210
Time, as he passes us, has a dove's wing,
Unsoiled, and swift, and of a silken sound;
But the world's time is time in masquerade!
Theirs, should I paint him, has his pinions fledged
With motley plumes; and, where the peacock shows
His azure eyes, is tinctured black and red
With spots quadrangular of diamond form,
Ensanguined hearts, clubs typical of strife,
And spades, the emblem of untimely graves.
What should be and what was an hourglass once,   22)
Becomes a dice-box, and a billiard mast
Well does the work of his destructive scythe.
Thus decked, he charms a world whom fashion blinds
To his true worth, most pleased when idle most,
Whose only happy are their wasted hours.
Even misses, at whose age their mothers wore
The back-string and the bib, assume the dress
Of womanhood, sit pupils in the school
Of card-devoted time, and, night by night,
Placed at some vacant corner of the board,   236
Learn every trick, and soon play all the game.
But truce with censure. Roving as I rove,
Where shall I find an end, or how proceed?
As he that travels far oft turns aside
To view some rugged rock or mouldering tower,
Which, seen, delights him not; then, coming home,
Describes and prints it, that the world may know
How far he went for what was nothing worth;
So I, with brush in hand and pallet spread,
With colours mixed for a far different use,   246
Paint cards and dolls and every idle thing
That fancy finds in her excursive flights.
   Come, Evening, once again, season of peace;
Return, sweet Evening, and continue long!
Methinks I see thee in the streaky west,
With matron-step slow-moving, while the night
Treads on thy sweeping train; one hand employed
In letting fall the curtain of repose
On bird and beast, the other charged for man
With sweet oblivion of the cares of day: 256
Not sumptuously adorned, nor needing aid,
Like homely featured night, of clustering gems;
A star or two, just twinkling on thy brow,
Suffices thee; save that the moon is thine
No less than hers, not worn indeed on high
With ostentatious pageantry, but set
With modest grandeur in thy purple zone,

Resplendent less, but of an ampler round.
Come then, and thou shalt find thy votary calm,
Or make me so. Composure is thy gift: 260
And, whether I devote thy gentle hours
To books, to music, or the poet's toil;
To weaving nets for bird-alluring fruit;
Or twining silken threads round ivory reels,
When they command whom man was born to please;
I slight thee not, but make thee welcome still.
    Just when our drawing rooms begin to blaze
With lights, by clear reflection multiplied
From many a mirror, in which he of Gath,
Goliath, might have seen his giant bulk   270
Whole, without stooping, towering crest and all,
My pleasures too begin. But me perhaps
The glowing hearth may satisfy awhile
With faint illumination, that uplifts
The shadow to the ceiling, there by fits
Dancing uncouthly to the quivering flame.
Not undelightful is an hour to me
So spent in parlour twilight; such a gloom
Suits well the thoughtful or unthinking mind,
The mind contemplative, with some new theme   280
Pregnant, or indisposed alike to all.
Laugh ye, who boast your more mercurial powers,
That never feel a stupor, know no pause,
Nor need one; I am conscious, and confess,
Fearless, a soul that does not always think.
Me oft has fancy, ludicrous and wild,
Soothed with a waking dream of houses, towers,
Trees, churches, and strange visages, expressed
In the red cinders, while with poring eye
I gazed, myself creating what I saw.   290
Nor less amused have I quiescent watched
The sooty films that play upon the bars,
Pendulous, and foreboding in the view,
Of superstition, prophesying still,
Though still deceived, some stranger's near approach.
'Tis thus the understanding takes repose
In indolent vacuity of thought,
And sleeps and is refreshed. Meanwhile the face
Conceals the mood lethargic with a mask
Of deep deliberation, as the man   300
Were tasked to his full strength, absorbed and lost.
Thus oft, reclined at ease, I lose an hour
At evening, till at length the freezing blast,
That sweeps the bolted shutter, summons home
The recollected powers; and, snapping short
The glassy threads with which the fancy weaves
Her brittle toys, restores me to myself.
How calm is my recess; and how the frost,
Raging abroad, and the rough wind, endear
The silence and the warmth enjoyed within!   310
I saw the woods and fields, at close of day,
A variegated show; the meadows green,

Though faded; and the lands, where lately waved
The golden harvest, of a mellow brown,
Upturned so lately by the forceful share.
I saw far off the weedy fallows smile
With verdure not unprofitable, grazed
By flocks, fast feeding, and selecting each
His favourite herb; while all the leafless groves,
That skirt the horizon, wore a sable hue,   320
Scarce noticed in the kindred dusk of eve.
To-morrow brings a change, a total change!
Which even now, though silently performed,
And slowly, and by most unfelt, the face
Of universal nature undergoes.
Fast falls a fleecy shower: the downy flakes,
Descending, and with never-ceasing lapse,
Softly alighting upon all below,
Assimilate all objects. Earth receives
Gladly the thickening mantle, and the green   330
And tender blade, that feared the chilling blast,
Escapes unhurt beneath so warm a veil.
    In such a world; so thorny, and where none
Finds happiness unblighted; or, if found,
Without some thistly sorrow at its side;
It seems the part of wisdom, and no sin
Against the law of love, to measure lots
With less distinguished than ourselves; that thus
We may with patience bear our moderate ills,
And sympathize with others, suffering more.   340
Ill fares the traveller now, and he that stalks
In ponderous boots beside his reeking team.
The wain goes heavily, impeded sore
By congregated loads adhering close
To the clogged wheels; and in its sluggish pace,
Noiseless, appears a moving hill of snow.
The toiling steeds expand the nostril wide,
While every breath, by respiration strong
Forced downward, is consolidated soon
Upon their jutting chests. He, formed to bear   350
The pelting brunt of the tempestuous night,
With half-shut eyes, and puckered cheeks, and teeth
Presented bare against the storm, plods on.
One hand secures his hat, save when with both
He brandishes his pliant length of whip,
Resounding oft, and never heard in vain.
Oh happy; and, in my account, denied
That sensibility of pain with which
Refinement is endued, thrice happy thou!
Thy frame, robust and hardy, feels indeed   360
The piercing cold, but feels it unimpaired.
The learned finger never need explore
Thy vigorous pulse; and the unhealthful east,
That breathes the spleen, and searches every bone
Of the infirm, is wholesome air to thee.
Thy days roll on, exempt from household care;
The wagon is thy wife; and the poor beasts

That drag the dull companion to and fro,
Thine helpless charge, dependent on thy care.
Ah, treat them kindly! rude as thou appearest,   370
Yet show that thou hast mercy! which the great,
With needless hurry whirled from place to place,
Humane as they would seem, not always show.
    Poor, yet industrious, modest, quiet, neat—
Such claim compassion in a night like this,
And have a friend in every feeling heart.
Warmed, while it lasts, by labour, all day long
They brave the season, and yet find at eve,
Ill clad and fed but sparely, time to cool.
The frugal housewife trembles when she lights   380
Her scanty stock of brushwood, blazing clear,
But dying soon, like all terrestrial joys.
The few small embers left she nurses well;
And, while her infant race, with outspread hands
And crowded knees, sit cowering o'er the sparks,
Retires, content to quake, so they be warmed.
The man feels least, as more inured than she
To winter, and the current in his veins
More briskly moved by his severer toil;
Yet he, too, finds his own distress in theirs.   390
The taper soon extinguished, which I saw
Dangled along at the cold finger's end
Just when the day declined, and the brown loaf
Lodged on the shelf, half eaten, without sauce
Of savoury cheese, or butter, costlier still;
Sleep seems their only refuge: for, alas,
Where penury is felt the thought is chained,
And sweet colloquial pleasures are but few!
With all this thrift they thrive not. All the care
Ingenious parsimony takes but just   400
Saves the small inventory, bed and stool,
Skillet, and old carved chest, from public sale.
They live, and live without extorted alms
From grudging hands; but other boast have none
To soothe their honest pride, that scorns to beg,
Nor comfort else, but in their mutual love.
I praise you much, ye meek and patient pair,
For ye are worthy; choosing rather far
A dry but independent crust, hard earned,
And eaten with a sigh, than to endure   410
The rugged frowns and insolent rebuffs
Of knaves in office, partial in the work
Of distribution: liberal of their aid
To clamorous importunity in rags,
But oft-times deaf to suppliants who would blush
To wear a tattered garb however coarse,
Whom famine cannot reconcile to filth:
These ask with painful shyness, and, refused
Because deserving, silently retire!
But be ye of good courage! Time itself   420
Shall much befriend you. Time shall give increase;
And all your numerous progeny, well-trained,

But helpless, in few years shall find their hands,
And labour too. Meanwhile ye shall not want
What, conscious of your virtues, we can spare,
Nor what a wealthier than ourselves may send.
I mean the man, who, when the distant poor
Need help, denies them nothing but his name.
   But poverty, with most who whimper forth
Their long complaints, is self-inflicted woe;
The effect of laziness or sottish waste.
Now goes the nightly thief prowling abroad
For plunder; much solicitous how best
He may compensate for a day of sloth
By works of darkness and nocturnal wrong.
Woe to the gardener's pale, the farmer's hedge,
Plashed[1] neatly, and secured with driven stakes
Deep in the loamy bank. Uptorn by strength,
Resistless in so bad a cause, but lame
To better deeds, he bundles up the spoil—
An ass's burden—and, when laden most
And heaviest, light of foot, steals fast away.
Nor does the boarded hovel better guard
The well-stacked pile of riven logs and roots
From his pernicious force. Nor will he leave
Unwrenched the door, however well secured,
Where Chanticleer amidst his harem sleeps
In unsuspecting pomp. Twitched from the perch,
He gives the princely bird, with all his wives,
To his voracious bag, struggling in vain,
And loudly wondering at the sudden change.—
Nor this to feed his own! 'Twere some excuse
Did pity of their sufferings warp aside
His principle, and tempt him into sin
For their support, so destitute.—But they
Neglected pine at home; themselves, as more
Exposed than others, with less scruple made
His victims, robbed of their defenceless all.
Cruel is all he does. 'Tis quenchless thirst
Of ruinous ebriety that prompts
His every action, and imbrutes the man.
Oh for a law to noose the villain's neck
Who starves his own, who persecutes the blood
He gave them in his children's veins, and hates
And wrongs the woman he has sworn to love!
   Pass where we may, through city or through town,
Village or hamlet of this merry land,
Though lean and beggared, ev'ry twentieth pace
Conducts the unguarded nose to such a whiff
Of stale debauch, forth-issuing from the styes
That law has licensed, as makes temperance reel.
There sit, involved and lost in curling clouds
Of Indian fume, and guzzling deep, the boor,
The lackey, and the groom: the craftsman there
Takes a Lethean leave of all his toil;
Smith, cobbler, joiner, he that plies the shears,

430

440

450

460

470

[1] With woven branches.

And he that kneads the dough; all loud alike,
All learned, and all drunk! The fiddle screams
Plaintive and piteous, as it wept and wailed
Its wasted tones and harmony unheard: 480
Fierce the dispute, whate'er the theme; while she,
Fell Discord, arbitress of such debate,
Perched on the sign-post, holds with even hand
Her undecisive scales. In this she lays
A weight of ignorance; in that, of pride;
And smiles, delighted with the eternal poise.
Dire is the frequent curse, and its twin sound
The cheek-distending oath, not to be praised
As ornamental, musical, polite,
Like those which modern senators employ,   490
Whose oath is rhetoric, and who swear for fame!
Behold the schools in which plebeian minds,
Once simple, are initiated in arts
Which some may practise with politer grace,
But none with readier skill!—'tis here they learn
The road that leads from competence and peace
To indigence and rapine; till at last
Society, grown weary of the load,
Shakes her encumbered lap, and casts them out.
But censure profits little: vain the attempt   500
To advertise in verse a public pest,
That, like the filth with which the peasant feeds
His hungry acres, stinks, and is of use.
The excise is fattened with the rich result
Of all this riot; and ten thousand casks,
Forever dribbling out their base contents,
Touched by the Midas finger of the state,
Bleed gold for ministers to sport away.
Drink, and be mad, then; 'tis your country bids!
Gloriously drunk, obey the important call!   510
Her cause demands the assistance of your throats;—
Ye all can swallow, and she asks no more.
    Would I had fallen upon those happier days
That poets celebrate; those golden times
And those Arcadian scenes that Maro sings,
And Sidney, warbler of poetic prose.
Nymphs were Dianas then, and swains had hearts
That felt their virtues: innocence, it seems,
From courts dismissed, found shelter in the groves;
The footsteps of Simplicity, impressed   520
Upon the yielding herbage (so they sing)
Then were not all effaced: then speech profane,
And manners profligate, were rarely found;
Observed as prodigies, and soon reclaimed.
Vain wish! those days were never: airy dreams
Sat for the picture; and the poet's hand,
Imparting substance to an empty shade,
Imposed a gay delirium for a truth.
Grant it:—I still must envy them an age
That favoured such a dream, in days like these   530
Impossible, when Virtue is so scarce.

That to suppose a scene where she presides,
Is tramontane, and stumbles all belief.
No: we are polished now! the rural lass,
Whom once her virgin modesty and grace,
Her artless manners, and her neat attire,
So dignified, that she was hardly less
Than the fair shepherdess of old romance,
Is seen no more. The character is lost!
Her head, adorned with lappets pinned aloft,   540
And ribands streaming gay, superbly raised,
And magnified beyond all human size,
Indebted to some smart wig-weaver's hand
For more than half the tresses it sustains;
Her elbows ruffled, and her tottering form
Ill propped upon French heels, she might be deemed
(But that the basket dangling on her arm
Interprets her more truly) of a rank
Too proud for dairy work, or sale of eggs.
Expect her soon with foot-boy at her heels,   550
No longer blushing for her awkward load,
Her train and her umbrella all her care!
   The town has tinged the country; and the stain
Appears a spot upon a vestal's robe,
The worse for what it soils. The fashion runs
Down into scenes still rural; but, alas,
Scenes rarely graced with rural manners now!
Time was when, in the pastoral retreat,
The unguarded door was safe; men did not watch
To invade another's right, or guard their own.   560
Then sleep was undisturbed by fear, unscared
By drunken howlings; and the chilling tale
Of midnight murder was a wonder heard
With doubtful credit, told to frighten babes.
But farewell now to unsuspicious nights,
And slumbers unalarmed! Now, ere you sleep,
See that your polished arms be primed with care,
And drop the night-bolt;—ruffians are abroad;
And the first larum of the cock's shrill throat
May prove a trumpet, summoning your ear   570
To horrid sounds of hostile feet within.
Even daylight has its dangers; and the walk
Through pathless wastes and woods, unconscious once
Of other tenants than melodious birds,
Or harmless flocks, is hazardous and bold.
Lamented change! to which full many a cause
Inveterate, hopeless of a cure, conspires.
The course of human things from good to ill,
From ill to worse, is fatal, never fails.
Increase of power begets increase of wealth;   580
Wealth luxury, and luxury excess;
Excess, the scrofulous and itchy plague
That seizes first the opulent, descends
To the next rank contagious, and in time
Taints downward all the graduated scale
Of order, from the chariot to the plough.

The rich, and they that have an arm to check
The license of the lowest in degree,
Desert their office; and themselves, intent
On pleasure, haunt the capital, and thus   590
To all the violence of lawless hands
Resign the scenes their presence might protect.
Authority herself not seldom sleeps,
Though resident, and witness of the wrong.
The plump convivial parson often bears
The magisterial sword in vain, and lays
His reverence and his worship both to rest
On the same cushion of habitual sloth.
Perhaps timidity restrains his arm;
When he should strike he trembles, and sets free,   600
Himself enslaved by terror of the band,
The audacious convict, whom he dares not bind.
Perhaps, though by profession ghostly pure,
He too may have his vice, and sometimes prove
Less dainty than becomes his grave outside
In lucrative concerns. Examine well
His milk-white hand; the palm is hardly clean—
But here and there an ugly smutch appears.
Foh! 'twas a bribe that left it: he has touched
Corruption! Whoso seeks an audit here   610
Propitious, pays his tribute, game or fish,
Wild-fowl or venison; and his errand speeds.
   But faster far, and more than all the rest,
A noble cause, which none who bears a spark
Of public virtue ever wished removed,
Works the deplored and mischievous effect.
'Tis universal soldiership has stabbed
The heart of merit in the meaner class.
Arms, through the vanity and brainless rage
Of those that bear them, in whatever cause,   620
Seem most at variance with all moral good,
And incompatible with serious thought.
The clown, the child of nature, without guile,
Blessed with an infant's ignorance of all
But his own simple pleasures; now and then
A wrestling-match, a foot-race, or a fair;
Is balloted, and trembles at the news:
Sheepish he doffs his hat, and, mumbling, swears
A Bible-oath to be whate'er they please,
To do he knows not what! The task performed,   630
That instant he becomes the sergeant's care,
His pupil, and his torment, and his jest.
His awkward gait, his introverted toes,
Bent knees, round shoulders, and dejected looks,
Procure him many a curse. By slow degrees,
Unapt to learn and formed of stubborn stuff,
He yet by slow degrees puts off himself,
Grows conscious of a change and likes it well:
He stands erect; his slouch becomes a walk;
He steps right onward, martial in his air,   640
His form and movement; is as smart above

As meal and larded locks can make him; wears
His hat, or his plumed helmet, with a grace;
And, his three years of heroship expired,
Returns indignant to the slighted plough.
He hates the field, in which no fife or drum
Attends him; drives his cattle to a march;
And sighs for the smart comrades he has left.
'Twere well if his exterior change were all—
But with his clumsy port the wretch has lost   650
His ignorance and harmless manners too!
To swear, to game, to drink; to show at home
By lewdness, idleness, and sabbath-breach,
The great proficiency he made abroad;
To astonish and to grieve his gazing friends,
To break some maiden's and his mother's heart;
To be a pest where he was useful once;
Are his sole aim, and all his glory, now!
   Man in society is like a flower
Blown in its native bed: 'tis there alone   660
His faculties, expanded in full bloom,
Shine out; there only reach their proper use.
But man, associated and leagued with man
By regal warrant, or self-joined by bond
For interest sake, or swarming into clans
Beneath one head for purposes of war,
Like flowers selected from the rest, and bound
And bundled close to fill some crowded vase,
Fades rapidly, and, by compression marred,
Contracts defilement not to be endured.   670
Hence chartered boroughs are such public plagues;
And burghers men immaculate perhaps,
In all their private functions, once combined,
Become a loathsome body, only fit
For dissolution, hurtful to the main.
Hence merchants, unimpeachable of sin
Against the charities of domestic life,
Incorporated, seem at once to lose
Their nature; and, disclaiming all regard
For mercy and the common rights of man,   680
Build factories with blood, conducting trade
At the sword's point, and dyeing the white robe
Of innocent commercial justice red.
Hence, too, the field of glory, as the world
Misdeems it, dazzled by its bright array,
With all its majesty of thundering pomp,
Enchanting music, and immortal wreaths,
Is but a school where thoughtlessness is taught
On principle, where foppery atones
For folly, gallantry, for every vice.   690
   But, slighted as it is, and by the great
Abandoned, and, which still I more regret,
Infected with the manners and the modes
It knew not once, the country wins me still.
I never framed a wish, or formed a plan,
That flattered me with hopes of earthly bliss,

But there I laid the scene. There early strayed
My fancy, ere yet liberty of choice
Had found me, or the hope of being free:
My very dreams were rural; rural, too,   700
The first-born efforts of my youthful Muse,
Sportive, and jingling her poetic bells
Ere yet her ear was mistress of their powers.
No bard could please me but whose lyre was tuned
To Nature's praises. Heroes and their feats
Fatigued me, never weary of the pipe
Of Tityrus, assembling, as he sang,
The rustic throng beneath his favourite beech.
Then Milton had indeed a poet's charms:
New to my taste, his Paradise surpassed   710
The struggling efforts of my boyish tongue
To speak its excellence. I danced for joy.
I marvelled much that, at so ripe an age
As twice seven years, his beauties had then first
Engaged my wonder; and, admiring still,
And still admiring, with regret supposed
The joy half lost because not sooner found.
Thee too, enamoured of the life I loved,
Pathetic in its praise, in its pursuit
Determined, and possessing it at last   720
With transports such as favoured lovers feel,
I studied, prized, and wished that I had known,
Ingenious Cowley! and, though now reclaimed
By modern lights from an erroneous taste,
I cannot but lament thy splendid wit
Entangled in the cobwebs of the schools.
I still revere thee, courtly though retired;
Though stretched at ease in Chertsey's silent bowers,
Not unemployed; and finding rich amends
For a lost world in solitude and verse.   730
'Tis born with all: the love of Nature's works
Is an ingredient in the compound, man,
Infused at the creation of the kind.
And, though the Almighty Maker has throughout
Discriminated each from each, by strokes
And touches of his hand, with so much art
Diversified, that two were never found
Twins at all points—yet this obtains in all,
That all discern a beauty in his works,
And all can taste them: minds that have been formed   740
And tutored, with a relish more exact,
But none without some relish, none unmoved.
It is a flame that dies not even there,
Where nothing feeds it: neither business, crowds,
Nor habits of luxurious city life;
Whatever else they smother of true worth
In human bosoms; quench it, or abate.
The villas with which London stands begirt,
Like a swarth Indian with his belt of beads,
Prove it. A breath of unadulterate air,   750
The glimpse of a green pasture, how they cheer

The citizen, and brace his languid frame!
Even in the stifling bosom of the town,
A garden, in which nothing thrives, has charms
That soothe the rich possessor; much consoled,
That here and there some sprigs of mournful mint,
Of nightshade, or valerian, grace the well
He cultivates. These serve him with a hint
That nature lives; that sight-refreshing green
Is still the livery she delights to wear,   760
Though sickly samples of the exuberant whole.
What are the casements lined with creeping herbs,
The prouder sashes fronted with a range
Of orange, myrtle, or the fragrant weed,
The Frenchman's darling? Are they not all proofs
That man, immured in cities, still retains
His inborn inextinguishable thirst
Of rural scenes, compensating his loss
By supplemental shifts, the best he may?
The most unfurnished with the means of life,   770
And they that never pass their brick-wall bounds
To range the fields and treat their lungs with air,
Yet feel the burning instinct— overhead
Suspend their crazy boxes, planted thick,
And watered duly. There the pitcher stands
A fragment, and the spoutless teapot there;
Sad witnesses how close-pent man regrets
The country, with what ardour he contrives
A peep at nature, when he can no more.
    Hail, therefore, patroness of health and ease   780
And contemplation, heart-consoling joys
And harmless pleasures, in the thronged abode
Of multitudes unknown! hail, rural life!
Address himself who will to the pursuit
Of honours, or emolument, or fame;
I shall not add myself to such a chase,
Thwart his attempts, or envy his success.
Some must be great. Great offices will have
Great talents. And God gives to every man
The virtue, temper, understanding, taste,   790
That lifts him into life; and lets him fall
Just in the niche he was ordained to fill.
To the deliverer of an injured land
He gives a tongue to enlarge upon, an heart
To feel, and courage to redress her wrongs;
To monarchs dignity; to judges sense;
To artists ingenuity and skill;
To me an unambitious mind, content
In the low vale of life, that early felt
A wish for ease and leisure, and ere long   800
Found here that leisure and that ease I wished.

[1785]

ON THE RECEIPT OF MY MOTHER'S PICTURE
OUT OF NORFOLK

THE GIFT OF MY COUSIN ANN BODHAM

Oh that those lips had language! Life has passed
With me but roughly since I heard thee last.
Those lips are thine—thy own sweet smiles I see,
The same that oft in childhood solaced me;
Voice only fails, else, how distinct they say,
"Grieve not, my child, chase all thy fears away!"
The meek intelligence of those dear eyes
(Blessed be the art that can immortalize,
The art that baffles time's tyrannic claim
To quench it) here shines on me still the same.   10
   Faithful remembrancer of one so dear,
O welcome guest, though unexpected, here!
Who biddest me honour with an artless song,
Affectionate, a mother lost so long,
I will obey, not willingly alone,
But gladly, as the precept were her own;
And, while that face renews my filial grief,
Fancy shall weave a charm for my relief—
Shall steep me in Elysian reverie,
A momentary dream, that thou art she.   20
   My mother! when I learned that thou wast dead,
Say, wast thou conscious of the tears I shed?
Hovered thy spirit o'er thy sorrowing son,
Wretch even then, life's journey just begun?
Perhaps thou gav'st me, though unseen, a kiss;
Perhaps a tear, if souls can weep in bliss—
Ah that maternal smile! it answers—Yes.
I heard the bell tolled on thy burial day,
I saw the hearse that bore thee slow away,
And, turning from my nursery window, drew   30
A long, long sigh, and wept a last adieu!
But was it such?—It was.—Where thou art gone
Adieus and farewells are a sound unknown.
May I but meet thee on that peaceful shore,
The parting sound shall pass my lips no more!
Thy maidens grieved themselves at my concern,
Oft gave me promise of a quick return.
What ardently I wished, I long believed,
And, disappointed still, was still deceived;
By disappointment every day beguiled,   40
Dupe of to-morrow even from a child.
Thus many a sad to-morrow came and went,
Till, all my stock of infant sorrow spent,
I learned at last submission to my lot;
But, though I less deplored thee, ne'er forgot.
   Where once we dwelt our name is heard no more,
Children not thine have trod my nursery floor;
And where the gardener Robin, day by day,
Drew me to school along the public way

Delighted with my bauble coach, and wrapped   50
In scarlet mantle warm, and velvet capped,
'Tis now become a history little known,
That once we called the pastoral house our own.
Short-lived possession! but the record fair
That memory keeps of all thy kindness there,
Still outlives many a storm that has effaced
A thousand other themes less deeply traced.
Thy nightly visits to my chamber made,
That thou might'st know me safe and warmly laid;
Thy morning bounties ere I left my home,   60
The biscuit, or confectionary plum;
The fragrant waters on my cheeks bestowed
By thy own hand, till fresh they shone and glowed;
All this, and more endearing still than all,
Thy constant flow of love, that knew no fall,
Ne'er roughened by those cataracts and brakes
That humour interposed too often makes;
All this still legible in memory's page,
And still to be so, to my latest age,
Adds joy to duty, makes me glad to pay   70
Such honours to thee as my numbers may;
Perhaps a frail memorial, but sincere,
Not scorned in heaven, though little noticed here.
   Could Time, his flight reversed, restore the hours,
When, playing with thy vesture's tissued flowers,
The violet, the pink, and jessamine,
I pricked them into paper with a pin,
(And thou wast happier than myself the while,
Would'st softly speak, and stroke my head and smile)
Could those few pleasant hours again appear,   80
Might one wish bring them, would I wish them here?
I would not trust my heart—the dear delight
Seems so to be desired, perhaps I might.—
But no—what here we call our life is such,
So little to be loved, and thou so much,
That I should ill requite thee to constrain
Thy unbound spirit into bonds again.
   Thou, as a gallant bark from Albion's coast
(The storms all weathered and the ocean crossed)
Shoots into port at some well-havened isle,   90
Where spices breathe and brighter seasons smile,
There sits quiescent on the floods that show
Her beauteous form reflected clear below,
While airs impregnated with incense play
Around her, fanning light her streamers gay—
So thou, with sails how swift! hast reached the shore
"Where tempests never beat nor billows roar,"
And thy loved consort on the dangerous tide
Of life, long since, has anchored at thy side.
But me, scarce hoping to attain that rest,   100
Always from port withheld, always distressed—
Me howling winds drive devious, tempest-tossed,
Sails ripped, seams opening wide, and compass lost,
And day by day some current's thwarting force

Sets me more distant from a prosperous course.
But oh, the thought that thou art safe, and he!
That thought is joy, arrive what may to me.
My boast is not that I deduce my birth
From loins enthroned, and rulers of the earth;
But higher far my proud pretensions rise—   110
The son of parents passed into the skies.
And now, farewell—time, unrevoked, has run
His wonted course, yet what I wished is done.
By contemplation's help, not sought in vain,
I seem to have lived my childhood o'er again;
To have renewed the joys that once were mine,
Without the sin of violating thine:
And, while the wings of fancy still are free,
And I can view this mimic show of thee,
Time has but half succeeded in his theft—   120
Thyself removed, thy power to soothe me left.

                              [*1790*, *1798*]

TO MARY

The twentieth year is well-nigh past,
Since first our sky was overcast;
Ah would that this might be the last!
                    My Mary!

Thy spirits have a fainter flow,
I see thee daily weaker grow—
'Twas my distress that brought thee low,
                    My Mary!

Thy needles, once a shining store,
For my sake restless heretofore,   10
Now rust disused, and shine no more,
                    My Mary!

For though thou gladly wouldst fulfil
The same kind office for me still,
Thy sight now seconds not thy will,
                    My Mary!

But well thou play'd'st the housewife's part,
And all thy threads with magic art
Have wound themselves about this heart,
                    My Mary! 20

Thy indistinct expressions seem
Like language uttered in a dream;
Yet me they charm, whate'er the theme,
                    My Mary!

Thy silver locks, once auburn bright,
Are still more lovely in my sight
Than golden beams of orient light,
                    My Mary!

For could I view nor them nor thee,
What sight worth seeing could I see?   30
The sun would rise in vain for me,
                    My Mary!

Partakers of thy sad decline,
Thy hands their little force resign;
Yet, gently pressed, press gently mine,
                    My Mary!

And then I feel that still I hold
A richer store ten thousandfold
Than misers fancy in their gold,
                    My Mary! 40

Such feebleness of limbs thou prov'st,
That now at every step thou mov'st
Upheld by two; yet still thou lov'st,
                    My Mary!

And still to love, though pressed with ill,
In wintry age to feel no chill,
With me is to be lovely still,
                    My Mary!

But ah! by constant heed I know
How oft the sadness that I show   50
Transforms thy smiles to looks of woe,
                    My Mary!

And should my future lot be cast
With much resemblance of the past,
Thy worn-out heart will break at last,
                    My Mary!

                              [*1793*, *1803*]

THE CASTAWAY

Obscurest night involved the sky,
　The Atlantic billows roared,
When such a destined wretch as I,
　Washed headlong from on board,
Of friends, of hope, of all bereft,
His floating home forever left.

No braver chief could Albion boast
　Than he with whom he went,
Nor ever ship left Albion's coast,
　With warmer wishes sent.　　　　　　　　10
He loved them both, but both in vain,
Nor him beheld, nor her again.

Not long beneath the whelming brine,
　Expert to swim, he lay;
Nor soon he felt his strength decline,
　Or courage die away;
But waged with death a lasting strife,
Supported by despair of life.

He shouted: nor his friends had failed
　To check the vessel's course,　　　　　　20
But so the furious blast prevailed,
　That, pitiless perforce,
They left their outcast mate behind,
And scudded still before the wind.

Some succour yet they could afford;
　And, such as storms allow,
The cask, the coop, the floated cord,
　Delayed not to bestow.
But he (they knew) nor ship, nor shore,
Whate'er they gave, should visit more.　　30

Nor, cruel as it seemed, could he
　Their haste himself condemn,
Aware that flight, in such a sea,

Alone could rescue them;
Yet bitter felt it still to die
Deserted, and his friends so nigh.

He long survives, who lives an hour
　In ocean, self-upheld;
And so long he, with unspent power,
　His destiny repelled;　　　　　　　　　　40
And ever, as the minutes flew,
Entreated help, or cried, "Adieu!"

At length, his transient respite past,
　His comrades, who before
Had heard his voice in every blast,
　Could catch the sound no more.
For then, by toil subdued, he drank
The stifling wave, and then he sank.

No poet wept him; but the page
　Of narrative sincere,　　　　　　　　　　50
That tells his name, his worth, his age,
　Is wet with Anson's tear.
And tears by bards or heroes shed
Alike immortalize the dead.

I therefore purpose not, or dream,
　Descanting on his fate,
To give the melancholy theme
　A more enduring date;
But misery still delights to trace
Its semblance in another's case.　　　　　60

No voice divine the storm allayed,
　No light propitious shone,
When, snatched from all effectual aid,
　We perished, each alone;
But I beneath a rougher sea,
And whelmed in deeper gulfs than he.

　　　　　　　　　　　　　　　　[*1799*, 1803]

LETTERS

I. TO MRS. COWPER AT THE PARK
HOUSE, HERTFORD

Huntingdon, October 20, 1766.
MY DEAR COUSIN,
　I am very sorry for poor Charles's
illness, and hope you will soon have
cause to thank God for his complete　　10
recovery. We have an epidemical fever
in this country likewise, which leaves
behind it a continual sighing, almost
to suffocation; not that I have seen
any instance of it, for, blessed be God!
our family have hitherto escaped it,
but such was the account I heard of
it this morning.
　I am obliged to you for the interest
you take in my welfare, and for your
inquiring so particularly after the
manner in which my time passes here.
As to amusements, I mean what the
world calls such, we have none; the

place indeed swarms with them, and cards and dancing are the professed business of almost all the gentle inhabitants of Huntingdon. We refuse to take part in them, or to be accessories to this way of murdering our time, and by so doing have acquired the name of Methodists. Having told you how we do not spend our time, I will next say how we do. We breakfast commonly between eight and nine; till eleven, we read either the Scripture, or the sermons of some faithful preacher of those holy mysteries; at eleven we attend divine service, which is performed here twice every day; and from twelve to three we separate and amuse ourselves as we please. During that interval I either read in my own apartment, or walk, or ride, or work in the garden. We seldom sit an hour after dinner, but, if the weather permits, adjourn to the garden, where with Mrs. Unwin and her son I have generally the pleasure of religious conversation till tea-time. If it rains, or is too windy for walking, we either converse within doors, or sing some hymns of Martin's collection, and by the help of Mrs. Unwin's harpsichord make up a tolerable concert, in which our hearts, I hope, are the best and most musical performers. After tea we sally forth to walk in good earnest. Mrs. Unwin is a good walker, and we have generally travelled about four miles before we see home again. When the days are short, we make this excursion in the former part of the day, between church-time and dinner. At night we read and converse, as before, till supper, and commonly finish the evening either with hymns or a sermon; and last of all the family are called to prayers. I need not tell *you*, that such a life as this is consistent with the utmost cheerfulness; accordingly we are all happy, and dwell together in unity as brethren. Mrs. Unwin has almost a maternal affection for me, and I have something very like a filial one for her, and her son and I are brothers. Blessed be the God of our salvation for such companions,

and for such a life; above all, for a heart to like it.

I have had many anxious thoughts about taking orders, and I believe every new convert is apt to think himself called upon for that purpose; but it has pleased God, by means which there is no need to particularize, to give me full satisfaction as to the propriety of declining it, indeed, they who have the least idea of what I have suffered from the dread of public exhibitions, will readily excuse my never attempting them hereafter. In the meantime, if it please the Almighty, I may be an instrument of turning many to the truth in a private way, and I hope that my endeavours in this way have not been entirely unsuccessful. Had I the zeal of Moses, I should want an Aaron to be my spokesman.

Yours ever, my dear cousin,

W. C.

II. TO THE REV. WILLIAM UNWIN
October 31, 1779.

MY DEAR FRIEND,

I wrote my last letter merely to inform you that I had nothing to say; in answer to which you have said nothing. I admire the propriety of your conduct, though I am a loser by it. I will endeavour to say something now, and shall hope for something in return.

I have been well entertained with Johnson's biographies, for which I thank you: with one exception, and that a swingeing one, I think he has acquitted himself with his usual good sense and sufficiency. His treatment of Milton is unmerciful to the last degree. A pensioner is not likely to spare a republican; and the Doctor, in order, I suppose, to convince his royal patron of the sincerity of his monarchical principles, has belaboured that great poet's character with the most industrious cruelty. As a man, he has hardly left him the shadow of one good quality. Churlishness in his private life, and a rancorous hatred of everything royal in his public, are the two colours with which he has smeared all the canvas. If he had any virtues, they are not to be found in the Doctor's picture of him; and it is well for Milton, that some sourness in his temper is the only vice with which his memory has been charged; it is evident enough that if his biographer could have discovered more, he would not have spared him. As a poet, he has treated him with severity enough, and has plucked one or two of the most beautiful feathers out of his Muse's wing, and trampled them under his great foot. He has passed sentence of condemnation upon *Lycidas*, and has taken occasion, from that charming poem, to expose to ridicule (what is indeed ridiculous enough), the childish prattlement of pastoral compositions, as if *Lycidas* was the prototype and pattern of them all. The liveliness of the description, the sweetness of the numbers, the classical spirit of antiquity that prevails in it, go for nothing. I am convinced, by the way, that he has no ear for poetical numbers, or that it was stopped by prejudice against the harmony of Milton's. Was there ever anything so delightful as the music of the *Paradise Lost*? It is like that of a fine organ; has the fullest and the deepest tones of majesty, with all the softness and elegance of the Dorian flute. Variety without end and never equalled, unless perhaps by Virgil. Yet the Doctor has little or nothing to say upon this copious theme, but talks something about the unfitness of the English language for blank verse, and how apt it is, in the mouth of some readers, to degenerate into declamation. Oh! I could thresh his old jacket, till I made his pension jingle in his pocket.

I could talk a good while longer, but I have no room; our love attends yourself, Mrs. Unwin, and Miss Shuttleworth, not forgetting the two miniature pictures at your elbow.

Yours affectionately,
W. C.

III. TO THE REV. JOHN NEWTON

August 21, 1780.

The following occurrence ought not to be passed over in silence, in a place where so few notable ones are to be met with. Last Wednesday night, while we were at supper, between the hours of eight and nine, I heard an unusual noise in the back parlour, as if one of the hares was entangled, and endeavouring to disengage herself. I was just going to rise from table, when it ceased. In about five minutes, a voice on the outside of the parlour door inquired if one of my hares had got away. I immediately rushed into the next room, and found that my poor favourite Puss had made her escape. She had gnawed in sunder the strings of a lattice work, with which I thought I had sufficiently secured the window, and which I preferred to any other sort of blind, because it admitted plenty of air. From thence I hastened to the kitchen, where I saw the redoubtable Thomas Freeman, who told me, that having seen her, just after she had dropped into the street, he attempted to cover her with his hat, but she screamed out, and leaped directly over his head. I then desired him to pursue as fast as possible, and added Richard Coleman to the chase, as being nimbler, and carrying less weight than Thomas; not expecting to see her again, but desirous to learn, if possible, what became of her. In something less than an hour, Richard returned, almost breathless, with the following account. That soon after he began to run, he left Tom behind him, and came in sight of a most numerous hunt of men, women, children, and dogs; that he did his best to keep back the dogs, and presently outstripped the crowd, so that the race was at last disputed between himself and Puss;—she ran right through the town, and down the lane that leads to Dropshort; a little before she came to the house, he got the start and turned her; she pushed for the town again, and soon after she entered it, sought shelter in Mr. Wagstaff's tanyard, adjoining to old Mr. Drake's. Sturges's harvest men were at supper, and saw her from the opposite side of the way. There she encountered the tanpits full of water; and while she was struggling out of one pit, and plunging into another, and almost drowned, one of the men drew her out by the ears, and secured her. She was then well washed in a bucket, to get the lime out of her coat, and brought home in a sack at ten o'clock.

This frolic cost us four shillings, but you may believe we did not grudge a farthing of it. The poor creature received only a little hurt in one of her claws, and in one of her ears, and is now almost as well as ever.

I do not call this an answer to your letter, but such as it is I send it, presuming upon that interest which I know you take in my minutest concerns, which I cannot express better than in the words of Terence a little varied—*Nihil mei a te alienum putas.*

Yours, my dear friend,

W. C.

IV. TO THE REV. JOHN NEWTON

September 18, 1784.

MY DEAR FRIEND,

Following your good example, I lay before me a sheet of my largest paper. It was this moment fair and unblemished, but I have begun to blot it, and having begun, am not likely to cease till I have spoiled it. I have sent you many a sheet that in my judgement of it has been very unworthy of your acceptance, but my conscience was in some measure satisfied by reflecting, that if it were good for nothing, at the same time it cost you nothing, except the trouble of reading it. But the case is altered now. You must pay a solid price for frothy matter, and though I do not absolutely pick your pocket, yet you lose your money, and, as the saying is, are never the wiser; a saying literally fulfilled to the reader of my epistles.

My greenhouse is never so pleasant as when we are just upon the point of being turned out of it. The gentleness of the autumnal suns, and the calmness of this latter season, make it a much more agreeable retreat than we ever find it in summer; when, the winds being generally brisk, we cannot fool it by admitting a sufficient quantity of air, without being at the same time incommoded by it. But now I sit with all the windows and the door wide open, and am regaled with the scent of every flower in a garden as full of flowers as I have known how to make it. We keep no bees, but if I lived in a hive I should hardly hear more of their music. All the bees in the neighbourhood resort to a bed of mignonette, opposite to the window, and pay me for the honey they get out of it by a hum, which, though rather monotonous, is as agreeable to my ear as the whistling of my linnets. All the sounds that nature utters are delightful, at least in this country. I should not perhaps find the roaring of lions in Africa, or of bears in Russia, very pleasing; but I know no beast in England whose voice I do not account musical, save and except always the braying of an ass. The notes of all our birds and fowls please me, without one exception. I should not, indeed, think of keeping a goose in a cage, that I might hang him up in the parlour for the sake of his melody, but a goose upon a common, or in a farmyard, is no bad performer; and as to insects, if the black beetle, and beetles indeed of all hues, will keep out of my way, I have no objection to any of the rest; on the contrary, in whatever key they sing, from the gnat's fine treble, to the bass of the humble bee, I admire them all. Seriously, however, it strikes me as a very observable instance of providential kindness to man, that such an exact accord has been contrived between his ear, and the sounds with which, at least in a rural situation, it is almost every moment visited. All the world is sensible of the uncomfortable effect that certain sounds have upon the nerves, and consequently upon the spirts:—and if a sinful world had been filled with such as would have curdled the blood, and have made the sense of hearing a perpetual inconvenience, I do not know that we should have had a right to complain. But now the fields, the woods, the gardens, have each their concert, and the ear of man is for ever regaled by creatures who seem only to please themselves. Even the ears that are deaf to the Gospel are continually entertained, though without knowing it, by sounds for which they are solely indebted to its Author. There is somewhere in infinite space a world that does not roll within the precincts of mercy, and as it is reasonable, and even scriptural, to suppose that there is music in Heaven, in those dismal regions perhaps the reverse of it is found; tones so dismal, as to make woe itself more insupportable, and to acuminate even despair. But my paper admonishes me in good time to draw the reins, and to check the descent of my fancy into deeps, with which she is but too familiar.

Our best love attends you both, with yours.

Sum ut semper, tui studiosissimus,
W. C.

V. TO THE REV. WILLIAM UNWIN

October 10, 1784.

MY DEAR WILLIAM,

I send you four quires of verse, which having sent, I shall dismiss from my thoughts, and think no more of, till I see them in print. I have not after all found time or industry enough to give the last hand to the points. I believe, however, they are not very erroneous, though in so long a work, and in a work that requires nicety in this particular, some inaccuracies will escape. Where you find any, you will oblige me by correcting them.

In some passages, especially in the second book, you will observe me very satirical. Writing on such subjects I could not be otherwise. I can write nothing without aiming at least at usefulness: it were beneath my years to do it, and still more dishonourable to my religion. I know that a reformation of such abuses as I have censured is not to be expected from the efforts of a poet; but to contemplate the world, its follies, its vices, its indifference to duty, and its strenuous attachment to what is evil, and not to reprehend, were to approve it. From this charge at least I shall be clear, for I have neither tacitly nor expressly flattered either its characters or its customs. I have paid one, and only one compliment, which was so justly due, that I did not know how to withhold it, especially having so fair an occasion;—I forget myself, there is another in the first book to Mr. Throckmorton,—but the compliment I mean is to Mr. Smith. It is, however, so managed, that nobody but himself can make the application, and you, to whom I disclose the secret; a delicacy on my part, which so much delicacy on his obliged me to the observance of.

What there is of a religious cast in the volume I have thrown towards the end of it, for two reasons; first, that I might not revolt the reader at his entrance,—and secondly, that my best impressions might be made last. Were I to write as many volumes as Lope de Vega, or Voltaire, not one of them would be without this tincture. If the world like it not, so much the worse for them. I make all the concessions I can, that I may please them, but I will not please them at the expense of conscience.

My descriptions are all from nature: not one of them second-handed. My delineations of the heart are from my own experience: not one of them borrowed from books, or in the least degree conjectural. In my numbers, which I have varied as much as I could, (for blank verse without variety of numbers is no better than bladder and string,) I have imitated nobody, though sometimes perhaps there may be an apparent resemblance; because at the same time that I would not imitate, I have not affectedly differed.

If the work cannot boast a regular plan (in which respect however I do not think it altogether indefensible), it may yet boast, that the reflections are naturally suggested always by the preceding passage, and that except the fifth book, which is rather of a political aspect, the whole has one tendency: to discountenance the modern enthusiasm after a London life, and to recommend rural ease and leisure, as friendly to the cause of piety and virtue.

If it pleases you, I shall be happy, and collect from your pleasure in it an omen of its general acceptance.

Yours, my dear friend,

W. C.

Your mother's love. She wishes that you would buy her a second-hand cream-pot, small, either kit, jug, or ewer of silver.

I shall be glad of an immediate line to apprise me of its safe arrival.

VI. TO THE REV. JOHN NEWTON

December 13, 1784.

MY DEAR FRIEND,

Having imitated no man, I may reasonably hope that I shall not incur the disadvantage of a comparison with my betters. Milton's manner was peculiar. So is Thomson's. He that should write like either of them, would, in my judgment, deserve the name of a copyist, but not of a poet. A judicious and sensible reader therefore, like yourself, will not say that my manner is not good, because it does not resemble theirs, but will rather consider what it is in itself. Blank verse is susceptible of a much greater diversification of manner, than verse in rhyme: and why the modern writers of it have all thought proper to cast their numbers alike, I know not. Certainly it was not necessity that com-

pelled them to it. I flatter myself, however, that I have avoided that sameness with others, which would entitle me to nothing but a share in one common oblivion with them all. It is possible that, as the reviewer of my former volume found cause to say that he knew not to what class of writers to refer me, the reviewer of this, whosoever he shall be, may see occasion to remark the same singularity. At any rate, though as little apt to be sanguine as most men, and more prone to fear and despond, than to overrate my own productions, I am persuaded that I shall not forfeit anything by this volume that I gained by the last.

As to the title, I take it to be the best that is to be had. It is not possible that a book, including such a variety of subjects, and in which no particular one is predominant, should find a title adapted to them all. In such a case, it seemed almost necessary to accommodate the name to the incident that gave birth to the poem; nor does it appear to me, that because I performed more than my task, therefore *The Task* is not a suitable title. A house would still be a house, though the builder of it should make it ten times as big as he at first intended. I might indeed, following the example of the Sunday newsmonger, call it the *Olio*. But I should do myself wrong; for though it have much variety, it has, I trust, no confusion.

For the same reason none of the interior titles apply themselves to the contents at large of that book to which they belong. They are, every one of them, taken either from the leading (I should say the introductory) passage of that particular book, or from that which makes the most conspicuous figure in it. Had I set off with a design to write upon a gridiron, and had I actually written near two hundred lines upon that utensil, as I have upon the Sofa, the Gridiron should have been my title. But the Sofa being, as I may say, the starting-post from which I addressed myself to the long race that I soon conceived a design to run, it acquired a just pre-eminence in my account, and was very worthily advanced to the titular honour it enjoys, its right being at least so far a good one, that no word in the language could pretend a better.

The Time-piece appears to me (though by some accident the import of that title has escaped you) to have a degree of propriety beyond the most of them. The book to which it belongs is intended to strike the hour that gives notice of approaching judgment, and dealing pretty largely in the *signs* of the *times*, seems to be denominated, as it is, with a sufficient degree of accommodation to the subject. . . .

We do not often see, or rather feel, so severe a frost before Christmas. Unexpected, at least by me, it had like to have been too much for my greenhouse, my myrtles having found themselves yesterday morning in an atmosphere so cold that the mercury was fallen eight degrees below the freezing point.

We are truly sorry for Mrs. Newton's indisposition, and shall be glad to hear of her recovery. We are most liable to colds at this season, and at this season a cold is most difficult of cure.

Be pleased to remember us to the young ladies, and to all under your roof and elsewhere, who are mindful of us.—And believe me,

Your affectionate
Wm. Cowper.

Your letters are gone to their address. The oysters were very good.

VII. TO LADY HESKETH

June 12, 1786.

I am neither young nor superannuated, yet am I a child. When I had read your letter I grumbled:—not at you, my dearest cousin, for you are in no fault, but at the whole generation of coachmakers, as you may suppose, and at yours in particular. I foresaw and foreknew that he would fail in his promise, and yet was disappointed; was, in truth, no more prepared for what I expected with so much reason, than if I had not at all expected it. I grumbled till we went to dinner, and at intervals till we had dined; and when dinner was over, with very little encouragement, I could actually have cried. And if I had, I should in truth have thought them tears as well bestowed as most that I have shed for many years. At first I numbered months, then weeks, then days, and was just beginning to number hours, and now I am thrown back to days again. My first speech was, after folding up your letter, (for I will honestly tell you all), I am crazed with Mondays, Tuesdays, and Wednesdays, and St. Alban's, and Totteridge, and Hadley. When is she to set out?—When is she to be here? Do tell me, for perhaps you understand it better than I. Why, says Mrs. Unwin, (with much more composure in her air than properly belonged to her, for she also had her feelings on the occasion), she sets out to-morrow se'nnight, and will be here on the Wednesday after. And who knows that? replied I; will the coachmaker be at all more punctual in repairing the old carriage, than in making the new one? For my part, I have no hope of seeing her this month; and if it be possible, I will not think of it, lest I should be again disappointed. And to say the truth, my dear, though hours have passed since thus I said, and I have had time for cooler consideration, the suspicion still sticks close to me, that more delays may happen. A philosopher would prepare himself for such an event, but I am no philosopher, at least when the comfort of seeing you is in question. I believe in my heart that there have been just as many true philosophers upon earth, as there have been men that have had little or no feeling, and not one more. Swift truly said—

Indifference clad in reason's guise,
All want of fortitude supplies.

When I wake in the night, I feel my spirits the lighter because you are coming. When I am not at Troy, I am either occupied in the recollection of a thousand passages of my past life, in which you were a partaker with me, or conversing about you with Mrs. Unwin. Thus my days and nights have been spent principally ever since you determined upon this journey, and especially, and almost without interruption from any other subject, since the time of your journey has seemed near at hand. While I despaired, as I did for many years, that I should ever see you more, I thought of you, indeed, and often, but with less solicitude. I used to say to myself: Providence has so ordered it, and it is my duty to submit. He has cast me at a distance from her, and from all whom I once knew. He did it, and not I; it is He who has chosen my situation for me. Have I not reason to be thankful that, since He designed me to pass a part of my life, and no inconsiderable one neither, in a state of the deepest melancholy, He appointed me a friend in Mrs. Unwin, who should share all my sorrows with me, and watch over me in my helpless condition, night and day? What, and where had I been without her? Such considerations were sufficient to reconcile me at that time to perpetual separation even from you, because perpetual I supposed it must be, and without remedy. But now every hour of your absence seems long, for this very natural reason, because the same Providence has given me a hope that you will be present with me soon. A good that seems at an immeasureable distance, and that we cannot hope to reach, has therefore the less influence on our affections. But the same good brought nearer, made to appear practicable, promised to our hopes, and almost in possession, engages all our faculties and desires. All this is according to the natural and necessary course of things in the human heart; and the philosophy that would interfere with it, is folly at least, if not

frenzy. A throne has at present but little sensible attraction for me. And why? Perhaps only because I know that should I break my heart with wishes for a throne, I should never reach one. But did I know assuredly that I should put on a crown to-morrow, perhaps I too should feel ambition, and account the interposing night tedious. The sum of the whole matter, my dear, is this: that this villainous coach-maker has mortified me monstrously, and that I tremble lest he should do so again. From you I have no fears. I see in your letter, and all the way through it, what pains you take to assure me and give me comfort. I am and will be comforted for that very reason; and will wait still other ten days with all the patience that I can muster. You, I know, will be punctual if you can, and that at least is matter of real consolation.

I approve altogether, my cousin beloved, of your sending your goods to the wagon on Saturday, and cookee by the coach on Tuesday. She will be here perhaps by four in the afternoon, at the latest by five, and will have quite time enough to find out all the cupboards and shelves in her department before you arrive. But I declare and protest that cookee shall sleep that night at our house, and get her breakfast here next morning. You will break her heart, child, if you send her into a strange house where she will find nothing that has life but the curate, who has not much neither. Servant he keeps none. A woman makes his bed, and after a fashion as they say, dresses his dinner, and then leaves him to his lucubrations. I do therefore insist on it, and so does Mrs. Unwin, that cookee shall be our guest for that time; and from this we will not depart. I tell thee besides, that I shall be more glad to see her, than ever I was in my life to see one whom I never saw before. Guess why, if you can.

You must number your miles fifty-six instead of fifty-four. The fifty-sixth mile ends but a few yards beyond the vicarage. Soon after you shall have entered Olney, you will find an opening on your right hand. It is a lane that leads to your dwelling. There your coach may stop and set down Mrs. Eaton; when she has walked about forty yards she will spy a green gate and rails on her left hand; and when she has opened the gate and reached the house-door, she will find herself at home. But we have another manœuvre to play off upon you, and in which we positively will not be opposed, or if we are, it shall be to no purpose. I have an honest fellow that works in my garden, his name is Kitchener, and we call him Kitch for brevity. He is sober, and as trusty as the day. He has a smart blue coat, that when I had worn it some years, I gave him, and he has now worn it some years himself. I shall set him on horseback, and order him to the Swan at Newport, there to wait your arrival, and if you should not stop at that place, as perhaps you may not, immediately to throw himself into your suite, and to officiate as your guide. For though the way from Newport hither is short, there are turnings that might puzzle your coachman; and he will be of use, too, in conducting you to our house, which otherwise you might not easily find, partly through the stupidity of those of whom you might inquire, and partly from its out-of-the-way situation. My brother drove up and down Olney in quest of us, almost as often as you up and down Chancery Lane in quest of the Madans, with fifty boys and girls at his tail, before he could find us. The first man, therefore, you shall see in a blue coat with white buttons, in the famous town of Newport, cry Kitch! He will immediately answer, My Lady! and from that moment you are sure not to be lost.

Your house shall be as clean as scrubbing and dry-rubbing can make it, and in all respects fit to receive you. My friend the Quaker, in all that I have seen of his doings, has acquitted himself much to my satisfaction. Some little things, he says, will perhaps be missing at first, in such a multiplicity, but they shall be produced as soon as called for. Mrs. U. has bought you six ducks, and is fatting them for you. She has also rummaged up a coop that will hold six chickens, and designs to people it for you by the first opportunity; for these things are not to be got fit for the table at Olney. Thus, my dear, are all things in the best train possible, and nothing remains but that you come and show yourself. Oh, that moment! Shall we not both enjoy it? —That we shall.

I have received an anonymous complimentary Pindaric Ode from a little poet who calls himself a schoolboy. I send you the first stanza by way of specimen. You shall see it all soon.

TO WM. COWPER, OF THE INNER TEMPLE, ESQ.

ON HIS POEMS IN THE SECOND VOLUME

In what high strains, my Muse, wilt thou
Attempt great Cowper's worth to show?
Pindaric strains shall tune the lyre,
And 'twould require
A Pindar's fire
To sing great Cowper's worth,
The lofty bard, delightful sage,
Ever the wonder of the age,
And *blessing to the earth.*

Adieu, my precious cousin, your lofty bard and delightful sage expects you with all possible affection.

Ever yours,
WM. COWPER.

I am truly sorry for your poor friend Burrows!

Our dinner hour is four o'clock. We will not surfeit you with delicacies; of that be assured. I know your palate, and am glad to know that it is easily pleased. Were it other than it is, it would stand but a poor chance to be gratified at Olney. I undertake for lettuce and cucumber, and Mrs. U. for all the rest. If she feeds you too well, you must humble her.

VIII. TO SAMUEL ROSE

Weston, July 24, 1787.

DEAR SIR,

This is the first time I have written these six months, and nothing but the constraint of obligation could induce me to write now. I cannot be so wanting to myself as not to endeavour at least to thank you both for the visits with which you have favoured me, and the poems that you sent me; in my present state of mind I taste nothing, nevertheless I read, partly from habit, and partly because it is the only thing that I am capable of.

I have therefore read Burns's poems, and have read them twice; and though they be written in a language that is new to me, and many of them on subjects much inferior to the author's ability, I think them on the whole a very extraordinary production. He is I believe the only poet these kingdoms have produced in the lower rank of life since Shakespeare (I should rather say since Prior), who need not be indebted for any part of his praise to a charitable consideration of his origin, and the disadvantages under which he has laboured. It will be pity if he should not hereafter divest himself of barbarism, and content himself with writing pure English, in which he appears perfectly qualified to excel. He who can command admiration, dishonours himself if he aims no higher than to raise a laugh.

I am, dear sir, with my best wishes for your prosperity, and with Mrs. Unwin's respects,

Your obliged and affectionate humble servant,

W. C.

IX. TO LADY HESKETH

The Lodge, March 3, 1788.

One day last week, Mrs. Unwin and I, having taken our morning walk and returning homeward through the wilderness, met the Throckmortons. A minute after we had met them, we heard the cry of hounds at no great distance, and mounting the broad stump of an elm which had been felled, and by the aid of which we were enabled to look over the wall, we saw them. They were all at that time in our orchard; presently we heard a terrier, belonging to Mrs. Throckmorton, which you may remember by the name of Fury, yelping with much vehemence, and saw her running through the thickets within a few yards of us at her utmost speed, as if in pursuit of something which we doubted not was the fox. Before we could reach the other end of the wilderness, the hounds entered also; and when we arrived at the gate which opens into the grove, there we found the whole weary cavalcade assembled. The huntsman dismounting, begged leave to follow his hounds on foot, for he was sure, he said, that they had killed him: a conclusion which I suppose he drew from their profound silence. He was accordingly admitted, and with a sagacity that would not have dishonoured the best hound in the world, pursuing precisely the same track which the fox and the dogs had taken, though he had never had a glimpse of either after their first entrance through the rails, arrived where he found the slaughtered prey. He soon produced dead reynard, and rejoined us in the grove with all his dogs about him. Having an opportunity to see a ceremony, which I was pretty sure would never fall in my way again, I determined to stay and to notice all that passed with the most minute attention. The huntsman having by the aid of a pitchfork lodged reynard on the arm of an elm, at the height of about nine feet from the ground, there left him for a considerable time. The gentlemen sat on their horses contemplating the fox, for which they had toiled so hard; and the hounds assembled at the foot of the tree, with faces not less expressive of the most rational delight, contemplated the same object. The huntsman remounted; cut off a foot, and threw it to the hounds;—one of them swallowed it whole like a bolus. He then once more alighted, and drawing down the fox by the hinder legs, desired the people, who were by this time rather numerous, to open a lane for him to the right and left. He was instantly obeyed, when throwing the fox to the distance of some yards, and screaming like a fiend, "tear him to pieces"—at least six times repeatedly, he consigned him over absolutely to the pack, who in a few minutes devoured him completely. Thus, my dear, as Virgil says, what none of the gods could have ventured to promise me, time itself, pursuing its accustomed course, has of its own accord presented me with. I have been in at the death of a fox, and you now know as much of the matter, as I, who am as well informed as any sportsman in England.

Yours,

W. C.

X. TO MRS. KING

Weston-Underwood, Oct. 11, 1788.

MY DEAR MADAM,

You are perfectly secure from all danger of being overwhelmed with presents from me. It is not much that a poet can possibly have it in his power to give. When he has presented his own works, he may be supposed to have exhausted all means of donation. They are his only superfluity. There was a time, but that time was before I commenced writer for the press, when I amused myself in a way somewhat similar to yours; allowing, I mean, for the difference between masculine and female operations. The scissors and the needle are your chief implements; mine were the chisel and the saw. In those days you might have been in some danger of too plentiful a return for your favours. Tables, such as they were, and joint-stools such as never were, might have travelled to Pertenhall in most inconvenient abundance. But I have long since discontinued this practice, and many others which I found it necessary to adopt, that I might escape the worst of all evils, both in itself and its consequences—an idle life. Many arts I have exercised with this view, for which nature never designed me; though among them were some in which I arrived at considerable proficiency, by mere dint of the most heroic perseverance. There is not a 'squire in all this country who can boast of having made better squirrel-houses, hutches for rabbits, or bird-cages, than myself; and in the article of cabbage-nets, I had no superior. I even had the hardiness to take in hand the pencil, and studied a whole year the art of drawing. Many figures were the fruit of my labours, which had, at least, the merit of being unparalleled by any production either of art or nature. But before the year was ended, I had occasion to wonder at the progress that may be made, in despite of natural deficiency, by dint alone of practice; for I actually produced three landscapes, which a lady thought worthy to be framed and glazed. I then judged it high time to exchange this occupation for another, lest, by any subsequent productions of inferior merit, I should forfeit the honour I had so fortunately acquired. But gardening was, of all employments, that in which I succeeded best; though even in this I did not suddenly attain perfection. I began with lettuces and cauliflowers: from them I proceeded to cucumbers; next to melons. I then purchased an orange-tree, to which, in due time, I added two or three myrtles. These served me day and night with employment during a whole severe winter. To defend them from the frost, in a situation that exposed them to its severity, cost me much ingenuity and much attendance. I contrived to give them a fire heat; and have waded night after night through the snow, with the bellows under my arm, just before going to bed, to give the latest possible puff to the embers, lest the frost should seize them before morning.

Very minute beginnings have sometimes important consequences. From nursing two or three little evergreens, I became ambitious of a greenhouse, and accordingly built one; which, verse excepted, afforded me amusement for a longer time than any expedient of all the many to which I have fled for refuge from the misery of having nothing to do. When I left Olney for Weston, I could no longer have a greenhouse of my own; but in a neighbour's garden I find a better, of which the sole management is consigned to me.

I had need take care, when I begin a letter, that the subject with which I set off be of some importance; for before I can exhaust it, be it what it may, I have generally filled my paper. But self is a subject inexhaustible, which is the reason that though I have said little, and nothing, I am afraid, worth your hearing, I have only room to add, that I am, my dear Madam,

Most truly yours,
WM. COWPER.

Mrs. Unwin bids me present her best compliments, and say how much she shall be obliged to you for the receipt to make that most excellent cake which came hither in its native pan. There is no production of yours that will not be always most welcome at Weston.

XI. TO SAMUEL ROSE

The Lodge, June 5, 1789.
MY DEAR FRIEND,

I am going to give you a deal of trouble, but London folks must be content to be troubled by country folks; for in London only can strange necessities be supplied. You must buy for me, if you please, a cuckoo clock; and now I will tell you where they are sold, which Londoner as you are, it is possible you may not know. They are sold, I am informed, at more houses than one, in that narrow part of Holborn which leads into Broad St. Giles's. It seems they are well-going

clocks, and cheap, which are the two best recommendations of any clock. They are made in Germany, and such numbers of them are annually imported, that they are become even a considerable article of commerce.

We are on the point of a general insurrection of Mops and Brooms, and the house for a week to come, at the least, will hardly be habitable even to ourselves.

I return you many thanks for Boswell's *Tour.* I read it to Mrs. Unwin after supper, and we find it amusing. There is much trash in it, as there must always be in every narrative that relates indiscriminately all that passed. But now and then the Doctor speaks like an oracle, and that makes amends for all. Sir John was a coxcomb, and Boswell is not less a coxcomb, though of another kind. I fancy Johnson made coxcombs of all his friends, and they in return made him a coxcomb; for, with reverence be it spoken, such he certainly was, and flattered as he was, he was sure to be so.

Thanks for your invitation to London,—but unless London can come to me, I fear we shall never meet. I was sure that you would love my friend, when you should once be well acquainted with him; and equally sure that he would take kindly to you.

Now for Homer.

W. C.

XII. TO JOHN JOHNSON

Weston, January 21, 1791.

I know that you have already been catechised by Lady Hesketh on the subject of your return hither before the winter shall be over, and shall therefore only say that, if you *can come,* we shall be happy to receive you. Remember also that nothing can excuse the non-performance of a promise but absolute necessity! In the mean time my faith in your veracity is such, that I am persuaded you will suffer nothing less than necessity to prevent it. Were you not extremely pleasant to us, and just the sort of youth that suits us, we should neither of us have said half so much, or perhaps a word on the subject.

Yours, my dear Johnny, are vagaries that I shall never see practised by any other; and whether you slap your ankle, or reel as if you were fuddled, or dance in the path before me, all is characteristic of yourself, and therefore to me delightful. I have hinted to you indeed sometimes, that you should be cautious of indulging antic habits and singularities of all sorts, and young men in general have need enough of such admonition. But yours are a sort of fairy habits, such as might belong to Puck or Robin Goodfellow, and therefore, good as the advice is, I should be half sorry should you take it.

This allowance at least I give you:—continue to take your walks, if walks they may be called, exactly in their present fashion, till you have taken orders. Then indeed, forasmuch as a skipping, curvetting, bounding divine might be a spectacle not altogether seemly, I shall consent to your adoption of a more grave demeanour.

W. C.

ROBERT BURNS (1759-1796)

"My father's generous Master died; the farm [Mount Oliphant] proved a ruinous bargain; and, to clench the curse, we fell into the hands of a Factor who sat for the picture of one in my Tale of two dogs.—My father was advanced in life when he married; I was the eldest of seven children; and he, worn out by early hardship, was unfit for labor.—My father's spirit was soon irritated, but not easily broken.—There was a freedom in his lease in two years more, and to weather these two years we retrenched expences.—We lived very poorly; I was a dextrous Ploughman for my years; and the next eldest to me was a brother, who could drive the plough very well and help me to thrash.—A Novel-Writer might perhaps have viewed these scenes with some satisfaction, but so did not I: my indignation yet boils at the recollection of the scoundrel tyrant's insolent, threatening epistles, which used to set us all in tears.—

"This kind of life, the chearless gloom of a hermit with the unceasing moil of a galley slave, brought me to my sixteenth year; a little before which period I first committed the sin of RHYME."

Thus wrote Burns in his autobiographical letter to Dr. John Moore in August, 1787, and the extract is a fair keynote to the nature of Burns's early life, so far as the mere struggle for existence was concerned. There is no space here to tell the narrative of Burns's life: the change from one ruinous lease to another—Mt. Oliphant; Lochlie, where his father died; Mossgiel, where Robert and his brother Gilbert tried to make a living for their family; Ellisland, whither Robert took Jean after his marriage. In fact the main outlines of the story are too well known to need repetition—the publishing of the Kilmarnock volume of poems in 1786, the resulting brilliant year in Edinburgh and the publishing of a fuller collection of poems there in 1787, the final years as exciseman.

Recent scholarship has tended to modify several of the early traditional features of the Burns story. Burns had been greeted in Edinburgh as the "poetical ploughman," and much was made there—and thereafter by his early biographers—of what was considered a sudden flowering of *untaught* genius. The time was ripe for enthusiasm over such a phenomenon. Burns himself was not unwilling to emphasize the meagreness of his education. At the beginning of his *Common-place Book*, begun in 1783, he wrote: "As he was but little indebted to scholastic education, and bred at a plough-tail, his performances must be strongly tinctured with his unpolished, rustic way of life; but as I believe, they are really his own, it may be some entertainment to a curious observer of human-nature to see how a Ploughman thinks, and feels . . ." As a matter of fact, Burns, judged by any standard, was far from unlettered. The educational standard even in the farmer class was very high in Scotland at that time, and William Burns was an unusually intelligent and ambitious farmer. His sons had at least the beginnings of a liberal—and theological—education, and Robert's avidity for learning added the French language and all the English literature that he could get hold of to the list of his acquirements. That he knew Scottish poetry and poetical forms will be evident from a glance at the notes to the poems in this collection. It was a man, therefore, well equipped to appreciate and make the most of Scottish literary tradition, rather than an "unlettered" ploughman, who surprised the world in 1787 with the wit and brilliance of his satire and the sweetness of his song.

Again, the double tendency on the one hand to sentimentalize some parts of Burns's story (notably the "Highland Lassie"—the Mary Campbell episode), and on the other hand to exaggerate the dissipation of other periods of his life (notably the Dumfries period when he was in the excise service) is now very much discredited. Burns's own reticence concerning Mary Campbell and the beauty of the poetry which she inspired gave plenty of excuse for the legend that early grew up about their relations, but much less excusable was the tendency on the part of early biographers to listen to the gossip of defamers and exaggerate, by innuendo and unverifiable statement, the moral laxity of certain periods of his life. That Burns was always extremely convivial, that he was disastrously susceptible to the charms of the lasses, no one would attempt to deny; but that he degenerated morally at the end of his life and virtually drank himself to death, there seems to be not one scrap of evidence to prove. On the other hand there is every evidence that he did his excise duties well and had the approval of his superiors, and that he was a responsible husband and father. His early death was the final result of the early breaking down of his constitution by great over-exertion on the farm when he was a young boy. The truth is that Burns made so many enemies by his personal satires, by his attacks on the orthodox Kirk and the narrow ethical principles of the "rigidly righteous," and by his political liberalism, that there were plenty of people ready to take their revenge in exaggerated gossip after his death; and the early biographers of Burns helped to perpetuate a Burns legend which has lived almost to the present day.

Burns made his first local reputation as a poet with his satires and epistles. He wrote at the height of the rebellion among the more liberal minded both within and without the church against the illiberal doctrines of the orthodox Presbyterian church, especially in regard to the Calvinistic doctrine of election and the impossibly rigoristic rules of conduct maintained by the church. The conservative, orthodox branch of the church was often referred to as the Auld Licht. Discipline was maintained by a series of courts, from the Kirk Session composed of the minister and two or more elders in every parish, to the Presbytery, the Synod, and the General Assembly which was the Supreme Court of the Church of Scotland. Burns came under the discipline of the Kirk Session more than once, and his friends had felt its power. He saw the spying and gossiping that it encouraged and the hypocrisy that it sheltered. In a series of satires—"The Holy Fair," "Address to the Unco Guid," "Epistle to M'Math," "Holy Willie's Prayer," and so forth—he gave such run to his wit as to make the orthodox extremely uncomfortable. As he wrote in his autobiographical letter, "Holy Willie's Prayer" so "alarmed the kirk-Session—that they held three several meetings to look over their holy artillery, if any of it was pointed against profane rhymers."

Burns is now much more widely read and loved for his songs than for any other group of his poems. Strangely enough Burns included very few songs in the editions of his poems published during his life time, "Green grow the rashes" and "I'll awa to Nanie, O" being the only notable ones. The reason may have been, as Professor F. B. Snyder suggests, that Burns thought that his songs would not be regarded as "poetry" by his readers. As a matter of fact Burns himself was passionately devoted to Scottish song, both words and music. The best of his other poems had been written by the time the 1787 Edinburgh edition was published, but it was from 1787 on that he threw himself whole-heartedly into the collecting and writing of songs. He was spurred on in this work by the enthusiasm of James Johnson who was publishing a series of volumes that he called *The Scots Musical Museum*. Burns aided very materially in the second, third, fourth, and fifth volumes. He assiduously collected old tunes and words. As the words of many of the songs had degenerated under the conditions of their *sub rosa* existence since the Reformation, he either revised many of the texts or wrote entirely new words. All together he contributed over two hundred songs either entirely of his own writing or so transformed by his genius as to be virtually his. And all this without a cent of pay at a time when he badly needed money. He similarly aided George Thomson in his *Select Collection of Original Scottish Airs*. Something of his fidelity to the spirit of the old Scottish tunes is to be gleaned from the following entry in his *Common-place Book*: "These old Scottish airs are so nobly sentimental that, when one would compose for them, to *south* the tune, as our Scotch phrase is, over and over, is the readiest way to catch the inspiration, and raise the bard into that glorious enthusiasm so strongly characteristic of our old Scotch poetry."

Poetry, ed. W. E. Henley and T. F. Henderson (The Centenary Burns, 4 vols., Edinburgh, 1896-97); *Complete Poetical Works*, ed. J. L. Robertson (3 vols., Oxford, 1916); *The Complete Writings* (10 vols., 1926-27); *Songs*, ed. J. C. Dick (1903); *Notes on Scottish Song*, ed. J. C. Dick (1908); *Scottish Poems of Robert Burns in His Native Dialect*, ed. Sir James Wilson (1925); *Letters*, ed. J. DeLancey Ferguson (2 vols., Oxford, 1931); F. B. Snyder, *Life* (1932); *Robert Burns, His Personality, His Reputation, and His Art* (Toronto, 1936); Hans Hecht, *Robert Burns: The Man and His Work* (1936); J. D. Ferguson, *Pride and Passion* (1939); *Robert Burns: His Associates and Contemporaries*, ed. R. T. Fitzhugh (Chapel Hill, N.C., 1943); *Robert Burns: Essays by Six Contemporary Writers*, ed. W. Montgomerie (Glasgow, 1947); D. Daiches, *Robert Burns* (1950); Sir James Wilson, *The Dialect of Robert Burns as Spoken in Central Ayrshire* (1923).

THE HOLY FAIR

A robe of seeming truth and trust
  Hid crafty observation;
And secret hung, with poison'd crust,
  The dirk of defamation:
A mask that like the gorget show'd,
  Dye-varying on the pigeon;
And for a mantle large and broad,
  He wrapt him in religion.
                HYPOCRISY À LA MODE.

Upon a simmer Sunday morn,
  When Nature's face is fair,
I walkèd forth to view the corn,
  An' snuff the caller[1] air.
The rising sun, owre Galston muirs,
  Wi' glorious light was glintin;
The hares were hirplin[2] down the furs,[3]
  The lav'rocks[4] they were chantin
            Fu' sweet that day.

As lightsomely I glowr'd[5] abroad,   10
  To see a scene sae gay,
Three hizzies, early at the road,
  Cam skelpin'[6] up the way.
Twa had manteeles o' dolefu' black,
  But ane wi' lyart[7] lining;
The third, that gaed a-wee a-back,
  Was in the fashion shining,
            Fu' gay that day.

The twa appear'd like sisters twin,
  In feature, form, an' claes;   20
Their visage wither'd, lang an' thin,
  An' sour as ony slaes:[8]
The third cam up, hap-step-an'-lowp,
  As light as ony lambie,
An' wi' a curchie low did stoop,
  As soon as e'er she saw me,
            Fu' kind that day.

Wi' bonnet aff, quoth I, "Sweet lass,
  I think ye seem to ken me;
I'm sure I've seen that bonie face,   30
  But yet I canna name ye."
Quo' she, an' laughin as she spak,
  An' taks me by the han's,

[1] Fresh.
[2] Hopping.
[3] Furrows.
[4] Larks.
[5] Looked.
[6] Dashing.
[7] Gray.
[8] Sloe-berries.

"Ye, for my sake, hae gi'en the feck[9]
  Of a' the ten comman's
            A screed[10] some day.

"My name is Fun—your cronie dear,
  The nearest friend ye hae;
An' this is Superstition here,
  An' that's Hypocrisy.   40
I'm gaun to Mauchline Holy Fair,
  To spend an hour in daffin:[11]
Gin ye'll go there, yon runkled[12] pair,
  We will get famous laughin
            At them this day."

Quoth I, "Wi' a' my heart, I'll do't;
  I'll get my Sunday's sark[13] on,
An' meet you on the holy spot;
  Faith, we'se hae fine remarkin!"
Then I gaed hame at crowdie-time[14]   50
  An' soon I made me ready;
For roads were clad, frae side to side,
  Wi' mony a wearie bodie,
            In droves that day.

Here farmers gash[15] in ridin' graith[16]
  Gaed hoddin'[17] by their cotters;
There swankies[18] young in braw braid-claith[19]
  Are springin owre the gutters.
The lasses, skelpin' barefit, thrang,[20]
  In silks an' scarlets glitter;   60
Wi' sweet-milk cheese, in mony a whang,[21]
  An' farls[22] bak'd wi' butter
            Fu' crump[23] that day.

When by the plate we set our nose,
  Weel heapèd up wi' ha'pence,
A greedy glow'r[24] Black Bonnet throws,
  An' we maun draw our tippence.
Then in we go to see the show,
  On ev'ry side they're gath'rin,
Some carryin' dails,[25] some chairs an' stools, 70

[9] Most.
[10] Tear.
[11] Fun.
[12] Wrinkled.
[13] Shirt.
[14] Porridge-time (breakfast).
[15] Prosperous.
[16] Gear.
[17] Riding sedately.
[18] Strapping fellows.
[19] Fine broad cloth.
[20] Thronged.
[21] Slice.
[22] Oat-cakes.
[23] Crisp.
[24] Stare.
[25] Planks.

An' some are busy blethrin[26]
        Right loud that day.

Here stands a shed to fend the show'rs,
    An' screen our countra gentry,
There racer Jess an' twa-three whores
    Are blinkin at the entry.
Here sits a raw o' tittlin'[27] jades,
    Wi' heavin' breasts an' bare neck,
An' there a batch o' wabster[28] lads,
    Blackguarding frae Kilmarnock   80
        For fun this day.

Here some are thinkin on their sins,
    An' some upo' their claes;
Ane curses feet that fyl'd[29] his shins,
    Anither sighs an' prays:
On this hand sits a chosen swatch,[30]
    Wi' screw'd up, grace-proud faces;
On that a set o' chaps at watch,
    Thrang[31] winkin' on the lasses
        To chairs that day.   90

O happy is that man an' blest!
    Nae wonder that it pride him!
Wha's ain dear lass, that he likes best,
    Comes clinkin down beside him!
Wi' arm repos'd on the chair-back
    He sweetly does compose him;
Which, by degrees, slips round her neck,
    An's loof[32] upon her bosom
        Unkenn'd that day.

Now a' the congregation o'er   100
    Is silent expectation;
For Moodie speels[33] the holy door,
    Wi' tidings o' damnation.
Should Hornie, as in ancient days,
    'Mang sons o' God present him,
The very sight o' Moodie's face
    To's ain het hame had sent him
        Wi' fright that day.

Hear how he clears the points o' faith
    Wi' rattlin' an' wi' thumpin'!   110
Now meekly calm, now wild in wrath,
    He's stampin an' he's jumpin!
His lengthen'd chin, his turned-up snout,

[26] Talking nonsense.
[27] Whispering.
[28] Weaver.
[29] Soiled.
[30] Sample.
[31] Busy.
[32] Hand.
[33] Climbs, i.e.. enters.

His eldritch[34] squeal an' gestures,
O how they fire the heart devout,
    Like cantharidian plaisters,
        On sic a day!

But, hark! the tent has chang'd its voice;
    There's peace an' rest nae langer:
For a' the real judges rise,   120
    They canna sit for anger.
Smith opens out his cauld harangues,
    On practice and on morals;
An' aff the godly pour in thrangs,
    To gie the jars an' barrels
        A lift that day.

What signifies his barren shine
    Of moral pow'rs an' reason?
His English style an' gesture fine
    Are a' clean out o' season.   130
Like Socrates or Antonine,
    Or some auld pagan heathen,
The moral man he does define,
    But ne'er a word o' faith in
        That's right that day.

In guid time comes an antidote
    Against sic poison'd nostrum;
For Peebles, frae the water-fit,[35]
    Ascends the holy rostrum:
See, up he's got the word o' God,   140
    An' meek an' mim[36] has view'd it,
While Common Sense has ta'en the road,
    An' aff, an' up the Cowgate,
        Fast, fast, that day.

Wee Miller, neist, the Guard relieves,
    An' Orthodoxy raibles,[37]
Tho' in his heart he weel believes,
    An' thinks it auld wives' fables:
But, faith! the birkie[38] wants a Manse,
    So cannilie he hums them;   150
Altho' his carnal wit an' sense
    Like hafflins-wise[39] o'ercomes him
        At times that day.

Now, butt an' ben,[40] the Change-house fills,
    Wi' yill-caup Commentators.
Here's crying out for bakes an' gills,
    An' there the pint-stowp clatters;

[34] Unearthly.
[35] River's mouth.
[36] Prim.
[37] Recites by rote.
[38] Conceited fellow.
[39] Partly.
[40] Kitchen and parlor.

While thick an' thrang, an' loud an' lang,
  Wi' logic, an' wi' Scripture,
They raise a din, that, in the end,   160
  Is like to breed a rupture
          O' wrath that day.

Leeze me on drink! it gi'es us mair
  Than either school or college:
It kindles wit, it waukens lair,[41]
  It pangs[42] us fou o' knowledge.
Be't whisky gill, or penny wheep,[43]
  Or ony stronger potion,
It never fails, on drinkin deep,
  To kittle up[44] our notion   170
          By night or day.

The lads an' lasses, blythely bent
  To mind baith saul an' body,
Sit round the table, weel content,
  An' steer about the toddy.
On this ane's dress, an' that ane's leuk,
  They're makin observations;
While some are cosy i' the neuk,
  An' formin assignations
          To meet some day.   180

But now the Lord's ain trumpet touts,
  Till a' the hills are rairin,
An' echoes back return the shouts;
  Black Russel is na sparin:
His piercing words, like Highlan' swords,
  Divide the joints an' marrow;
His talk o' Hell, whare devils dwell,
  Our very "sauls does harrow"
          Wi' fright that day.

A vast, unbottom'd, boundless pit,   190
  Fill'd fou o' lowin[45] brunstane,
Wha's ragin flame, an' scorchin heat,
  Wad melt the hardest whun-stane!
The half-asleep start up wi' fear
  An' think they hear it roarin,
When presently it does appear
  'Twas but some neebor snorin
          Asleep that day.

'Twad be owre lang a tale, to tell
  How mony stories past,   200
An' how they crowded to the yill,
  When they were a' dismist:

[41] Wakens learning.
[42] Crams.
[43] Small beer.
[44] Stimulate.
[45] Flaming.

How drink gaed round, in cogs[46] an' caups,
  Amang the furms an' benches;
An' cheese an' bread, frae women's laps,
  Was dealt about in lunches,
          An' dawds[47] that day.

In comes a gawsie,[48] gash guidwife,
  An' sits down by the fire,
Syne draws her kebbuck[49] an' her knife;   210
  The lasses they are shyer.
The auld guidmen, about the grace,
  Frae side to side they bother,
Till some ane by his bonnet lays,
  An' gi'es them't like a tether,
          Fu' lang that day.

Waesucks![50] for him that gets nae lass,
  Or lasses that hae naething!
Sma' need has he to say a grace,
  Or melvie[51] his braw claithing!   220
O wives, be mindfu', ance yoursel
  How bonie lads ye wanted,
An' dinna, for a kebbuck-heel,
  Let lasses be affronted
          On sic a day!

Now Clinkumbell, wi' rattlin' tow,[52]
  Begins to jow an' croon;[53]
Some swagger hame the best they dow,
  Some wait the afternoon.
At slaps[54] the billies halt a blink,   230
  Till lasses strip their shoon:
Wi' faith an' hope, an' love an' drink,
  They're a' in famous tune
          For crack[55] that day.

How mony hearts this day converts
  O' sinners and o' lasses!
Their hearts o' stane, gin night, are gane
  As saft as ony flesh is.
There's some are fou o' love divine;
  There's some are fou o' brandy;   240
An' mony jobs that day begin,
  May end in houghmagandie[56]
          Some ither day.

          [1785, 1786]

[46] Wooden drinking cups.
[47] Large portions.
[48] Buxom.
[49] Cheese.
[50] Alas!
[51] Soil.
[52] Rope.
[53] Peal and toll.
[54] Breaches in the fence.
[55] Talk.
[56] Fornication.

ADDRESS TO THE DEIL

O Prince, O chief of many throned pow'rs,
That led th' embattl'd Seraphim to war.

MILTON

O thou! whatever title suit thee,
Auld Hornie, Satan, Nick, or Clootie,
Wha in yon cavern grim an' sootie,
      Clos'd under hatches,
Spairges[1] about the brunstane cootie,[2]
      To scaud poor wretches!

Hear me, auld Hangie, for a wee,
An' let poor damned bodies be;
I'm sure sma' pleasure it can gie,
      Ev'n to a deil,   10
To skelp[3] an' scaud poor dogs like me,
      An' hear us squeel!

Great is thy pow'r, an' great thy fame;
Far kenn'd an' noted is thy name;
An' tho' yon lowin heugh's[4] thy hame,
      Thou travels far;
An' faith! thou's neither lag[5] nor lame,
      Nor blate[6] nor scaur.[7]

Whyles, ranging like a roarin lion
For prey, a' holes an' corners tryin;   20
Whyles on the strong-wing'd tempest flyin,
      Tirling[8] the kirks;
Whyles, in the human bosom pryin,
      Unseen thou lurks.

I've heard my reverend graunie say,
In lanely glens ye like to stray;
Or where auld ruin'd castles gray
      Nod to the moon,
Ye fright the nightly wand'rer's way,
      Wi' eldritch[9] croon.   30

When twilight did my graunie summon,
To say her pray'rs, douce,[10] honest woman!
Aft yont the dyke she's heard you bummin,[11]
      Wi' eerie drone;

Or, rustlin, thro' the boortries[12] comin,
      Wi' heavy groan.

Ae dreary, windy, winter night,
The stars shot down wi' sklentin[13] light,
Wi' you mysel I gat a fright
      Ayont the lough;[14]   40
Ye, like a rash-buss[15] stood in sight
      Wi' waving sough.[16]

The cudgel in my nieve[17] did shake,
Each bristl'd hair stood like a stake,
When, wi' an eldritch, stoor[18] quaick, quaick,
      Amang the springs,
Awa ye squatter'd, like a drake,
      On whistlin' wings.

Let warlocks[19] grim, an' wither'd hags,
Tell how wi' you on ragweed nags,   50
They skim the muirs, an' dizzy crags,
      Wi' wicked speed;
And in kirk-yards renew their leagues,
      Owre howkit[20] dead.

Thence countra wives, wi' toil an' pain,
May plunge an' plunge the kirn[21] in vain;
For, oh! the yellow treasure's taen
      By witching skill;
An' dawtit,[22] twal-pint Hawkie's[23] gaen
      As yell's the bill.[24]   60

Thence mystic knots mak great abuse
On young guidmen, fond, keen, an' crouse;[25]
When the best wark-lume[26] i' the house,
      By cantrip[27] wit,
Is instant made no worth a louse,
      Just at the bit.[28]

When thowes dissolve the snawy hoord,
An' float the jinglin icy-boord,

[1] Splashes.
[2] Small pail.
[3] Beat.
[4] Flaming pit.
[5] Slow.
[6] Shy.
[7] Afraid.
[8] Knocking for entrance at.
[9] Unearthly.
[10] Sober.
[11] Humming.
[12] Elder trees.
[13] Slanting.
[14] Pond.
[15] Clump of rushes.
[16] Moan.
[17] Fist.
[18] Harsh.
[19] Wizards.
[20] Dug up, exhumed
[21] Churn.
[22] Petted.
[23] Cow.
[24] As dry as the bull.
[25] Cocksure.
[26] Tool.
[27] Magic.
[28] Crucial moment.

Then water-kelpies haunt the foord,
  By your direction,   70
An' 'nighted trav'llers are allur'd
  To their destruction.

An' aft your moss-traversing spunkies[29]
Decoy the wight that late an' drunk is:
The bleezin,[30] curst, mischievous monkies
  Delude his eyes,
Till in some miry slough he sunk is,
  Ne'er mair to rise.

When masons' mystic word an' grip
In storms an' tempests raise you up, 80
Some cock or cat your rage maun stop,
  Or, strange to tell!
The youngest brother ye wad whip
  Aff straught to hell.

Lang syne, in Eden's bonie yard,
When youthfu' lovers first were pair'd,
And all the soul of love they shar'd,
  The raptur'd hour,
Sweet on the fragrant flow'ry swaird,
  In shady bow'r: 90

Then you, ye auld, snick-drawing dog!
Ye cam to Paradise incog,
An' play'd on man a cursed brogue,[31]
  (Black be you fa[32])
An' gied the infant warld a shog,[33]
  'Maist ruin'd a'.

D'ye mind that day, when in a bizz,[34]
Wi' reekit duds, an' reestit gizz,[35]

[29] Will-o'-the-wisp.
[30] Blazing.
[31] Trick.
[32] Lot.
[33] Shake.
[34] Flurry.
[35] Singed face.

Ye did present your smoutie phiz
  'Mang better folk,   100
An' sklented[36] on the man of Uz
  Your spitefu' joke?

An' how ye gat him i' your thrall,
An' brak him out o' house an' hal',
While scabs an' blotches did him gall
  Wi' bitter claw,
An' lows'd his ill-tongu'd, wicked scawl,[37]
  Was warst ava?

But a' your doings to rehearse,
Your wily snares an' fechtin fierce, 110
Sin' that day Michael did you pierce,
  Down to this time,
Wad ding a' Lallan tongue, or Erse,[38]
  In prose or rhyme.

An' now, auld Cloots, I ken ye're thinkin,
A certain Bardie's rantin, drinkin,
Some luckless hour will send him linkin,[39]
  To your black pit;
But faith! he'll turn a corner jinkin,[40]
  An' cheat you yet.   120

But fare you weel, auld Nickie-ben!
O wad ye tak a thought an' men'!
Ye aiblins might—I dinna ken—
  Still hae a stake—
I'm wae to think upo' yon den,
  Ev'n for your sake!

        [*1785, 1786*]

[36] Slanted, directed.
[37] Scold.
[38] Would beat a Lowland tongue, or Gaelic.
[39] Hurrying.
[40] Dodging.

THE COTTER'S SATURDAY NIGHT

INSCRIBED TO R. AIKEN, ESQ.

Let not Ambition mock their useful toil,
 Their homely joys and destiny obscure;
Nor grandeur hear, with a disdainful smile,
 The short and simple annals of the Poor.
       GRAY.

I

My lov'd, my honour'd, much respected friend!
  No mercenary bard his homage pays;
With honest pride I scorn each selfish end,
  My dearest meed a friend's esteem and praise:
  To you I sing, in simple Scottish lays,
The lowly train in life's sequester'd scene;
  The native feelings strong, the guileless ways;
What Aiken in a cottage would have been;
Ah! tho' his worth unknown, far happier there, I ween!

II

November chill blaws loud wi' angry sugh;   10
  The short'ning winter-day is near a close;
The miry beasts retreating frae the pleugh;
  The black'ning trains o' craws to their repose:
  The toil-worn Cotter frae his labour goes,
This night his weekly moil is at an end,
  Collects his spades, his mattocks, and his hoes,
Hoping the morn in ease and rest to spend,
And weary, o'er the moor, his course does hameward bend.

III

At length his lonely cot appears in view,
  Beneath the shelter of an aged tree;   20
Th' expectant wee things, toddlin, stacher[1] through
  To meet their Dad, wi' flichterin[2] noise an' glee.
  His wee bit ingle,[3] blinkin bonnilie,
His clean hearth-stane, his thrifty wifie's smile,
  The lisping infant prattling on his knee,
Does a' his weary carking care beguile,
An' makes him quite forget his labour an' his toil.

IV

Belyve[4] the elder bairns come drapping in,
  At service out, amang the farmers roun';
Some ca' the pleugh, some herd, some tentie[5] rin
  A cannie[6] errand to a neibor town:
  Their eldest hope, their Jenny, woman grown,
In youthfu' bloom, love sparkling in her e'e,
  Comes hame, perhaps, to shew a braw new gown,
Or deposite her sair-won penny-fee,
To help her parents dear, if they in hardship be.

[1] Totter.
[2] Fluttering.
[3] Fire.
[4] By and by.
[5] Heedfully.
[6] Careful.

V

With joy unfeign'd brothers and sisters meet,
  An' each for other's weelfare kindly spiers:[7]
The social hours, swift-wing'd, unnoticed fleet;
  Each tells the uncos[8] that he sees or hears;
  The parents partial eye their hopeful years;
Anticipation forward points the view.
  The mother, wi' her needle an' her sheers,
Gars[9] auld claes look amaist as weel's the new;
The father mixes a' wi' admonition due.

VI

Their master's an' their mistress's command,
  The younkers a' are warned to obey;
An' mind their labours wi' an eydent[10] hand,
  An' ne'er, tho' out o' sight, to jauk or play:
  "An' O! be sure to fear the Lord alway!
An' mind your duty, duly, morn an' night!
  Lest in temptation's path ye gang astray,
Implore His counsel and assisting might:
They never sought in vain that sought the Lord aright!"

VII

But hark! a rap comes gently to the door;
  Jenny, wha kens the meaning o' the same,
Tells how a neebor lad cam o'er the moor,
  To do some errands, and convoy her hame.
  The wily mother sees the conscious flame
Sparkle in Jenny's e'e, and flush her cheek;
  Wi' heart-struck anxious care, inquires his name,
While Jenny hafflins is afraid to speak;
Weel pleased the mother hears, it's nae wild, worthless rake.

VIII

Wi' kindly welcome, Jenny brings him ben;
  A strappin youth; he takes the mother's eye;
Blythe Jenny sees the visit's no ill ta'en;
  The father cracks of horses, pleughs, and kye.
  The youngster's artless heart o'er flows wi' joy,
But blate and laithfu',[11] scarce can weel behave;
  The mother, wi' a woman's wiles, can spy
What makes the youth sae bashfu' an' sae grave;
Weel pleased to think her bairn's respected like the lave.[12]

40

50

60

70

[7] Asks.
[8] Wonders.
[9] Makes.
[10] Diligent.
[11] Shy and sheepish.
[12] Rest.

IX

O happy love! where love like this is found!
   O heart-felt raptures! bliss beyond compare!
I've paced much this weary, mortal round,
   And sage experience bids me this declare—
   "If Heaven a draught of heavenly pleasure spare,
One cordial in this melancholy vale,
   'Tis when a youthful, loving, modest pair
In other's arms breathe out the tender tale,   80
Beneath the milk-white thorn that scents the evening gale."

X

Is there, in human form, that bears a heart—
   A wretch! a villain! lost to love and truth!
That can, with studied, sly, ensnaring art,
   Betray sweet Jenny's unsuspecting youth?
   Curse on his perjur'd arts! dissembling smooth!
Are honour, virtue, conscience, all exiled?
   Is there no pity, no relenting ruth,
Points to the parents fondling o'er their child?
Then paints the ruin'd maid, and their distraction wild!   90

XI

But now the supper crowns their simple board,
   The halesome parritch, chief of Scotia's food:
The sope their only hawkie[13] does afford,
   That 'yont the hallan[14] snugly chows her cood;
   The dame brings forth in complimental mood,
To grace the lad, her weel-hained kebbuck, fell,[15]
   An' aft he's prest, and aft he ca's it guid;
The frugal wifie, garrulous, will tell
How 'twas a towmond[16] auld, sin' lint was i' the bell.

XII

The cheerfu' supper done, wi' serious face,   100
   They round the ingle form a circle wide;
The sire turns o'er wi' patriarchal grace,
   The big ha'-bible, ance his father's pride:
   His bonnet reverently is laid aside,
His lyart haffets[17] wearing thin an' bare;
   Those strains that once did sweet in Zion glide,
He wales[18] a portion with judicious care;
And "Let us worship God!" he says with solemn air.

[13] Cow.
[14] Partition wall.
[15] Well-kept, tasty cheese.
[16] Twelve-month.
[17] Graying side-locks.
[18] Chooses.

XIII

They chant their artless notes in simple guise;
　　They tune their hearts, by far the noblest aim:　　　　　110
Perhaps Dundee's wild warbling measures rise,
　　Or plaintive Martyrs, worthy of the name;
Or noble Elgin beets[19] the heavenward flame,
　　The sweetest far of Scotia's holy lays:
　　　Compared with these, Italian trills are tame;
The tickled ears no heartfelt raptures raise;
Nae unison hae they with our Creator's praise.

XIV

The priest-like father reads the sacred page,
　　How Abram was the friend of God on high;
Or Moses bade eternal warfare wage　　　　　　　　　　120
　　With Amalek's ungracious progeny;
Or how the royal bard did groaning lie
Beneath the stroke of Heaven's avenging ire;
　　Or Job's pathetic plaint, and wailing cry;
　　Or rapt Isaiah's wild, seraphic fire;
Or other holy seers that tune the sacred lyre.

XV

Perhaps the Christian volume is the theme,
　　How guiltless blood for guilty man was shed;
How He, who bore in Heaven the second name,
　　Had not on earth whereon to lay His head:　　　　　130
　　How His first followers and servants sped;
The precepts sage they wrote to many a land:
　　How he, who lone in Patmos banishèd,
Saw in the sun a mighty angel stand
And heard great Bab'lon's doom pronounced by Heaven's command.

XVI

Then kneeling down, to Heaven's Eternal King,
　　The saint, the father, and the husband prays:
Hope "springs exulting on triumphant wing,"
　　That thus they all shall meet in future days:
　　There ever bask in uncreated rays,　　　　　　　　140
No more to sigh, or shed the bitter tear,
　　Together hymning their Creator's praise,
In such society, yet still more dear;
While circling Time moves round in an eternal sphere.

XVII

Compared with this, how poor Religion's pride,
　　In all the pomp of method and of art,
When men display to congregations wide
　　Devotion's every grace, except the heart!

[19] Kindles

The Power, incensed, the pageant will desert,
The pompous strain, the sacerdotal stole;   150
But haply, in some cottage far apart,
May hear, well pleased, the language of the soul;
And in His Book of Life the inmates poor enrol.

XVIII

Then homeward all take off their several way;
The youngling cottagers retire to rest:
The parent-pair their secret homage pay,
And proffer up to Heaven the warm request,
That He who stills the raven's clamorous nest,
And decks the lily fair in flowery pride,
Would, in the way His wisdom sees the best,   160
For them and for their little ones provide;
But chiefly, in their hearts with grace divine preside.

XIX

From scenes like these old Scotia's grandeur springs,
That makes her loved at home, revered abroad:
Princes and lords are but the breath of kings,
"An honest man's the noblest work of God":
And certes, in fair virtue's heavenly road,
The cottage leaves the palace far behind;
What is a lordling's pomp! a cumbrous load,
Disguising oft the wretch of human kind,   170
Studied in arts of hell, in wickedness refin'd!

XX

O Scotia! my dear, my native soil!
For whom my warmest wish to Heaven is sent!
Long may thy hardy sons of rustic toil
Be blest with health, and peace, and sweet content!
And, O! may Heaven their simple lives prevent
From luxury's contagion, weak and vile!
Then, howe'er crowns and coronets be rent,
A virtuous populace may rise the while,
And stand a wall of fire around their much-loved isle.   180

XXI

O Thou! who poured the patriotic tide
That streamed thro' Wallace's undaunted heart;
Who dared to nobly stem tyrannic pride,
Or nobly die, the second glorious part,
(The patriot's God, peculiarly thou art,
His friend, inspirer, guardian, and reward!)
O never, never, Scotia's realm desert;
But still the patriot, and the patriot-bard,
In bright succession raise, her ornament and guard!

[1785, 1786]

TO A MOUSE

ON TURNING HER UP IN HER NEST WITH THE PLOUGH, NOVEMBER, 1785

Wee, sleekit, cow'rin, tim'rous beastie,
O, what a panic's in thy breastie!
Thou need na start awa sae hasty,
    Wi' bickering brattle![1]
I wad be laith to rin an' chase thee,
    Wi' murd'ring pattle![2]

I'm truly sorry man's dominion
Has broken Nature's social union,
An' justifies that ill opinion
    Which makes thee startle
At me, thy poor earth-born companion, 11
    An' fellow-mortal!

I doubt na, whiles, but thou may thieve;
What then? poor beastie, thou maun live!
A daimen icker in a thrave[3]
    'S a sma' request:
I'll get a blessin wi' the lave,
    And never miss't!

Thy wee bit housie, too, in ruin!
Its silly wa's the win's are strewin! 20
An' naething, now, to big a new ane,
    O' foggage green!
An' bleak December's winds ensuin,
    Baith snell[4] an' keen!

Thou saw the fields laid bare and waste,
An' weary winter comin fast,
An' cozie here, beneath the blast,
    Thou thought to dwell,
Till crash! the cruel coulter past
    Out thro' thy cell. 30

That wee bit heap o' leaves an' stibble
Has cost thee mony a weary nibble!
Now thou's turn'd out, for a' thy trouble,
    But house or hald,[5]
To thole[6] the winter's sleety dribble,
    An' cranreuch[7] cauld!

[1] Hurrying scamper.
[2] Plough-staff.
[3] An occasional ear in twenty-four sheaves of grain.
[4] Bitter.
[5] Without house or home.
[6] Bear.
[7] Hoar-frost.

But, Mousie, thou art no thy lane,
In proving foresight may be vain:
The best laid schemes o' mice an' men
    Gang aft a-gley.[8] 40
An' lea'e us nought but grief an' pain
    For promised joy.

Still thou art blest, compared wi' me!
The present only toucheth thee:
But och! I backward cast my e'e
    On prospects drear!
An' forward, tho' I canna see,
    I guess an' fear!

        [*1785*, 1786]

TO A MOUNTAIN DAISY

ON TURNING ONE DOWN WITH THE PLOUGH, IN APRIL, 1786

Wee modest crimson-tipped flow'r,
Thou'st met me in an evil hour;
For I maun crush amang the stoure[1]
    Thy slender stem:
To spare thee now is past my pow'r,
    Thou bonnie gem.

Alas! it's no thy neibor sweet,
The bonnie lark, companion meet,
Bending thee 'mang the dewy weet
    Wie spreckled breast, 10
When upward springing, blythe to greet
    The purpling east.

Cauld blew the bitter-biting north
Upon thy early humble birth;
Yet cheerfully thou glinted forth
    Amid the storm,
Scarce rear'd above the parent-earth
    Thy tender form.

The flaunting flow'rs our gardens yield
High shelt'ring woods and wa's maun shield,
But thou, beneath the random bield[2] 21
    O' clod or stane,
Adorns the histie[3] stibble-field,
    Unseen, alane.

[8] Amiss.
[1] Dust.
[2] Shelter.
[3] Dry.

There, in thy scanty mantle clad,
Thy snawy bosom sun-ward spread,
Thou lifts thy unassuming head
                    In humble guise;
But now the share uptears thy bed,
                    And low thou lies!   30

Such is the fate of artless maid,
Sweet flow'ret of the rural shade,
By love's simplicity betrayed,
                    And guileless trust,
Till she like thee, all soiled, is laid
                    Low i' the dust.

Such is the fate of simple bard,
On life's rough ocean luckless starred:
Unskilful he to note the card
                    Of prudent lore,
Till billows rage, and gales blow hard,
                    And whelm him o'er!

Such fate to suffering worth is given,
Who long with wants and woes has striven,
By human pride or cunning driven
                    To mis'ry's brink,
Till wrench'd of ev'ry stay but Heaven,
                    He, ruin'd, sink!

Ev'n thou who mourn'st the Daisy's fate,
That fate is thine—no distant date;   50
Stern Ruin's ploughshare drives elate
                    Full on thy bloom,
Till crushed beneath the furrow's weight
                    Shall be thy doom!
                                        [1786, 1786]

EPISTLE TO JOHN LAPRAIK,
AN OLD SCOTTISH BARD

While briers an' woodbines budding green,
An' paitricks[1] scraichin' loud at e'en,
An' morning poussie whiddin[2] seen,
                    Inspire my Muse,
This freedom, in an unknown frien',
                    I pray excuse.

On Fasten-een we had a rockin,[3]
To ca' the crack[4] and weave our stockin;

And there was muckle fun and jokin,
                    Ye need na doubt;   10
At length we had a hearty yokin[5]
                    At sang about.

There was ae sang, amang the rest,
Aboon them a' it pleas'd me best,
That some kind husband had addrest
                    To some sweet wife:
It thirled the heart-strings thro' the breast,
                    A' to the life.

I've scarce heard ought described sae weel,
What gen'rous, manly bosoms feel;   20
Thought I, "Can this be Pope, or Steele,
                    Or Beattie's wark!"
They tauld me 'twas an odd kind chiel[6]
                    About Muirkirk.

It pat me fidgin' fain to hear't,
And sae about him there I spier't,[7]
Then a' that ken't him round declar'd
                    He had ingine,[8]
That nane excelled it, few cam near't,
                    It was sae fine.   30

That, set him to a pint of ale,
An' either douce or merry tale,
Or rhymes an' sangs he'd made himsel,
                    Or witty catches,
'Tween Inverness and Teviotdale,
                    He had few matches.

Then up I gat, an' swoor an aith,
Tho' I should pawn my pleugh and graith,[9]
Or die a cadger[10] pownie's death,
                    At some dyke-back   40
A pint an' gill I'd gie them baith
                    To hear your crack.

But, first an' foremost, I should tell,
Amaist as soon as I could spell,
I to the crambo-jingle[11] fell;
                    Tho' rude an' rough,
Yet crooning to a body's sel,
                    Does weel eneugh.

I am nae poet, in a sense,
But just a rhymer like by chance,   50

[5] Set-to.
[6] Good fellow.
[7] Asked.
[8] Genius.
[9] Furniture of all kinds.
[10] Hawker.
[11] Rhyming.

[1] Partridges.
[2] Hare scurrying.
[3] Party.
[4] Have a chat.

An' hae to learning nae pretence,
                    Yet, what the matter?
Whene'er my Muse does on me glance,
                    I jingle at her.

Your critic-folk may cock their nose,
And say `How can you e'er propose,
You wha ken hardly verse frae prose,
                    To mak a sang?''
But, by your leaves, my learned foes,
                    Ye're maybe wrang.   60

What's a' your jargon o' your schools,
Your Latin names for horns an' stools;
If honest nature made you fools,
                    What sairs your grammars?
Ye'd better ta'en up spades and shools,[12]
                    Or knappin'-hammers.[13]

A set o' dull, conceited hashes[14]
Confuse their brains in college classes!
They gang in stirks,[15] and come out asses,
                    Plain truth to speak;   7c
An' syne they think to climb Parnassus
                    By dint o' Greek!

Gie me ae spark o' Nature's fire,
That's a' the learning I desire;
Then tho' I drudge thro' dub an' mire
                    At pleugh or cart,
My Muse, though hamely in attire,
                    May touch the heart.

O for a spunk[16] o' Allan's glee,
Or Fergusson's, the bauld an' slee,   80
Or bright Lapraik's, my friend to be,
                    If I can hit it!
That would be lear eneugh for me,
                    If I could get it.

Now, sir, if ye hae friends enow,
Tho' real friends, I b'lieve, are few,
Yet, if your catalogue be fou,
                    I'se no insist,
But gif ye want ae friend that's true,
                    I'm on your list.   90

I winna blaw about mysel;
As ill I like my fauts to tell;

12 Shovels.
13 Hammers for breaking stones.
14 Oafs.
15 Heifers.
16 Spark

But friends, an' folks that wish me well,
                    They sometimes roose[17] me;
Tho' I maun own, as mony still
                    As far abuse me.

There's ae wee faut they whiles lay to me,
I like the lasses—Gude forgie me!
For mony a plack[18] they wheedle frae me,
                    At dance or fair;   100
Maybe some ither thing they gie me
                    They weel can spare.

But Mauchline race, or Mauchline fair,
I should be proud to meet you there;
We'se gie ae night's discharge to care,
                    If we forgather,
An' hae a swap o' rhymin'-ware
                    Wi' ane anither.

The four-gill chap, we'se gar him clatter,[19]
An' kirsen[20] him wi' reekin water;   110
Syne we'll sit down an' tak our whitter,[21]
                    To cheer our heart;
An' faith, we'se be acquainted better
                    Before we part.

Awa, ye selfish warly race,
Wha think that havins,[22] sense, an' grace,
Ev'n love an' friendship, should give place
                    To catch-the-plack!
I dinna like to see your face,
                    Nor hear your crack.   120

But ye whom social pleasure charms,
Whose hearts the tide of kindness warms,
Who hold your being on the terms,
                    "Each aid the others,''
Come to my bowl, come to my arms.
                    My friends, my brothers!

But to conclude my lang epistle,
As my auld pen's worn to the gristle;
Twa lines frae you wad gar me fissle,[23]
                    Who am, most fervent,   130
While I can either sing, or whistle,
                    Your friend and servant.
                              [1785, 1786]

17 Praise.
18 Four pennies Scots.
19 Make him rattle.
20 Christen.
21 Draught.
22 Manners.
23 Tingle with pleasure.

A BARD'S EPITAPH

Is there a whim-inspired fool,
Owre fast for thought, owre hot for rule,
Owre blate[1] to seek, owre proud to snool,[2]
    Let him draw near;
And owre this grassy heap sing dool,[3]
    And drap a tear.

Is there a bard of rustic song,
Who, noteless, steals the crowds among,
That weekly this area throng,
    O, pass not by!   10
But, with a frater-feeling strong,
    Here heave a sigh.

Is there a man whose judgment clear,
Can others teach the course to steer,
Yet runs, himself, life's mad career,
    Wild as the wave;
Here pause—and, thro' the starting tear,
    Survey this grave.

The poor inhabitant below
Was quick to learn and wise to know,   20
And keenly felt the friendly glow,
    And softer flame;
But thoughtless follies laid him low,
    And stained his name!

Reader, attend—whether thy soul
Soars fancy's flights beyond the pole,
Or darkling grubs this earthly hole,
    In low pursuit;
Know prudent, cautious self-control
    Is wisdom's root.   30
    [*1786*, 1786]

TO THE REV. JOHN M'MATH

ENCLOSING A COPY OF HOLY WILLIE'S
PRAYER, WHICH HE HAD REQUESTED

While at the stook the shearers cow'r
To shun the bitter blaudin'[1] show'r,
Or in gulravage rinnin scour;[2]
    To pass the time,

[1] Modest.
[2] Cringe.
[3] Woe.
[1] Driving.
[2] Run about in riotous play.

To you I dedicate the hour
    In idle rhyme.

My Musie, tired wi' mony a sonnet
On gown, an' ban', an' douce black bonnet,
Is grown right eerie now she's done it,
    Lest they shou'd blame her,
An' rouse their holy thunder on it,   1x
    And anathem her.

I own 'twas rash, an' rather hardy,
That I, a simple countra bardie,
Shou'd meddle wi' a pack so sturdy,
    Wha, if they ken me,
Can easy wi' a single wordie
    Lowse hell upon me.

But I gae mad at their grimaces,
Their sighin, cantin, grace-proud faces,   20
Their three-mile prayers, and half-mile graces,
    Their raxin[3] conscience,
Whase greed, revenge, an' pride disgraces
    Waur nor[4] their nonsense.

There's Gawn, misca'd waur than a beast,
Wha has mair honour in his breast
Than mony scores as guid's the priest
    Wha sae abus'd him:
An' may a bard no crack his jest
    What way they've used him?

See him, the poor man's friend in need,   3x
The gentleman in word an' deed—
An' shall his fame an' honour bleed
    By worthless skellums,
An' not a Muse erect her head
    To cowe the blellums?

O Pope, had I thy satire's darts
To gie the rascals their deserts,
I'd rip their rotten, hollow hearts,
    An' tell aloud   40
Their jugglin' hocus-pocus arts
    To cheat the crowd.

God knows I'm no the thing I shou'd be,
Nor am I even the thing I could be,
But, twenty times, I rather would be
    An atheist clean
Than under gospel colours hid be
    Just for a screen.

[3] Expanding.
[4] Worse than.

An honest man may like a glass,
An honest man may like a lass;　　50
But mean revenge an' malice fause
　　　　He'll still disdain,
An' then cry zeal for gospel laws,
　　　　Like some we ken.

They tak religion in their mouth,
They talk o' mercy, grace, an' truth:
For what? to gie their malice skouth[5]
　　　　On some puir wight;
An' hunt him down, o'er right an' ruth,
　　　　To ruin straight.　　60

All hail, Religion! Maid divine,
Pardon a Muse sae mean as mine,
Who in her rough imperfect line
　　　　Thus daurs to name thee;
To stigmatize false friends of thine
　　　　Can ne'er defame thee.

Tho' blotcht an' foul wi' monie a stain
An' far unworthy of thy train,
Wi' trembling voice I tune my strain
　　　　To join wi' those　　70
Who boldly daur thy cause maintain
　　　　In spite o' foes:

In spite o' crowds, in spite o' mobs,
In spite of undermining jobs,
In spite o' dark banditti stabs
　　　　At worth an' merit,
By scoundrels, even wi' holy robes
　　　　But hellish spirit.

O Ayr, my dear, my native ground,
Within thy presbyterial bound　　80
A candid lib'ral band is found
　　　　Of public teachers,
As men, as Christians too, renown'd,
　　　　An' manly preachers.

Sir, in that circle you are nam'd;
Sir, in that circle you are fam'd;
An' some, by whom your doctrine's blam'd
　　　　(Which gies you honour),
Even, sir, by them your heart's esteemed,
　　　　An' winning manner.　　90

Pardon this freedom I have ta'en,
An' if impertinent I've been,
Impute it not, good sir, in ane
　　　　Whase heart ne'er wrang'd ye,

[5] Play, scope.

But to his utmost would befriend
　　　　Ought that belang'd ye.
　　　　　　　　[1785, 1808]

HOLY WILLIE'S PRAYER

O Thou, wha in the Heavens dost dwell,
Wha, as it pleases best thysel',
Sends ane to heaven and ten to hell,
　　　　A' for thy glory,
And no for ony guid or ill
　　　　They've done afore thee!

I bless and praise thy matchless might,
Whan thousands thou hast left in night,
That I am here afore thy sight,
　　　　For gifts an' grace　　10
A burnin' an' a shinin light,
　　　　To a' this place.

What was I, or my generation,
That I should get sic exaltation?
I, wha deserve most just damnation,
　　　　For broken laws,
Sax thousand years 'fore my creation,
　　　　Thro' Adam's cause.

When frae my mither's womb I fell,
Thou might hae plunged me in hell,　　20
To gnash my gums, to weep and wail,
　　　　In burnin lakes,
Where damned devils roar and yell,
　　　　Chain'd to their stakes;

Yet I am here a chosen sample,
To show thy grace is great and ample;
I'm here a pillar in thy temple,
　　　　Strong as a rock,
A guide, a buckler, an example
　　　　To a' thy flock.　　30

O Lord, thou kens what zeal I bear,
When drinkers drink, and swearers swear,
And singin there and dancin here,
　　　　Wi' great an' sma':
For I am keepit by thy fear
　　　　Free frae them a'.

But yet, O Lord! confess I must
At times I'm fash'd wi' fleshy lust;
An' sometimes too, wi' warldly trust,
　　　　Vile self gets in;　　40

But thou remembers we are dust,
    Defil'd in sin.

O Lord! yestreen, thou kens, wi' Meg—
Thy pardon I sincerely beg;
O! may't ne'er be a livin' plague
    To my dishonour,
An' I'll ne'er lift a lawless leg
    Again upon her.

Besides I farther maun allow,
Wi' Lizzie's lass, three times I trow—   50
But, Lord, that Friday I was fou,[1]
    When I cam near her,
Or else thou kens thy servant true
    Wad never steer[2] her.

May be thou lets this fleshly thorn
Beset thy servant e'en and morn
Lest he owre high and proud should turn,
    That he's sae gifted;
If sae, thy hand maun e'en be borne,
    Until thou lift it.   60

Lord, bless thy chosen in this place,
For here thou hast a chosen race;
But God confound their stubborn face,
    And blast their name,
Wha bring thy elders to disgrace
    An' public shame.

Lord, mind Gawn Hamilton's deserts,
He drinks, an' swears, an' plays at cartes,
Yet has sae mony takin arts
    Wi' grit an' sma',   70
Frae God's ain priest the people's hearts
    He steals awa'.

An' when we chasten'd him therefor,
Thou kens how he bred sic a splore[3]
As set the warld in a roar
    O' laughin' at us;
Curse thou his basket and his store,
    Kail and potatoes.

Lord, hear my earnest cry an' pray'r,
Against that presbytery o' Ayr;   80
Thy strong right hand, Lord, make it bare
    Upo' their heads;
Lord, weigh it down, and dinna spare,
    For their misdeeds.

[1] Drunk.
[2] Touch.
[3] Disturbance.

O Lord my God, that glib-tongu'd Aiken,
My very heart and soul are quakin',
To think how we stood sweatin, shakin,
    An' piss'd wi' dread,
While he, wi' hingin lips and snakin,[4]
    Held up his head.   90

Lord in the day of vengeance try him;
Lord, visit them wha did employ him,
And pass not in thy mercy by them,
    Nor hear their pray'r:
But, for thy people's sake, destroy them,
    And dinna spare.

But, Lord, remember me and mine
Wi' mercies temp'ral and divine,
That I for gear and grace may shine
    Excell'd by nane,   100
And a' the glory shall be thine,
    Amen, Amen!

            [1785, 1808]

ADDRESS TO THE UNCO GUID, OR THE RIGIDLY RIGHTEOUS

My son, these maxims make a rule,
  An' lump them aye thegither:
The rigid righteous is a fool,
  The rigid wise anither:
The cleanest corn that e'er was dight[1]
  May hae some pyles o' caff in;
So ne'er a fellow-creature slight
  For random fits o' daffin.[2]
        SOLOMON (Eccles. vii. 16).

I

O ye wha are sae guid yoursel,
  Sae pious and sae holy,
Ye've nought to do but mark and tell
  Your neebour's fauts and folly!
Whase life is like a weel-gaun mill,
  Supplied wi' store o' water,
The heaped happer's ebbing still,
  And still the clap plays clatter.

II

Hear me, ye venerable core,[3]
  As counsel for poor mortals,   10

[4] Contemptuous.
[1] Winnowed.
[2] Larking.
[3] Corps.

That frequent pass douce[4] Wisdom's door
  For glaikit[5] Folly's portals;
I, for their thoughtless, careless sakes,
  Would here propone defences,
Their donsie tricks, their black mistakes,
  Their failings and mischances.

III

Ye see your state wi' their's compar'd,
  And shudder at the niffer.[6]
But cast a moment's fair regard,
  What maks the mighty differ;   20
Discount what scant occasion gave,
  That purity ye pride in,
And (what's aft mair than a' the lave)[7]
  Your better art o' hiding,

IV

Think, when your castigated pulse
  Gies now and then a wallop,
What ragings must his veins convulse,
  That still eternal gallop;
Wi' wind and tide fair i' your tail,
  Right on ye scud your sea-way;   30
But in the teeth o' baith to sail,
  It maks an unco leeway.

V

See Social life and Glee sit down,
  All joyous and unthinking,
Till, quite transmogrified, they're grown
  Debauchery and Drinking:
O would they stay to calculate
  Th' eternal consequences;
Or your more dreaded hell to state,
  Damnation of expenses!   40

VI

Ye high, exalted, virtuous Dames,
  Tied up in godly laces,
Before ye gie poor Frailty names,
  Suppose a change o' cases;
A dear lov'd lad, convenience snug,
  A treacherous inclination—
But, let me whisper i' your lug,
  Ye're aiblins nae temptation.

[4] Sober.
[5] Giddy.
[6] Exchange.
[7] Rest.

VII

Then gently scan your brother man,
  Still gentler sister woman;   50
Tho' they may gang a kennin[8] wrang,
  To step aside is human:
One point must still be greatly dark,
  The moving why they do it:
And just as lamely can ye mark
  How far perhaps they rue it.

VIII

Who made the heart, 'tis He alone
  Decidedly can try us;
He knows each chord its various tone,
  Each spring, its various bias: 60
Then at the balance let's be mute,
  We never can adjust it;
What's done we partly may compute,
  But know not what's resisted.

                              [1786, 1787]

THE JOLLY BEGGARS

A CANTATA RECITATIVO

I

When lyart[1] leaves bestrow the yird,[2]
Or, wavering like the bauckie-bird,[3]
  Bedim cauld Boreas' blast;
When hailstanes drive wi' bitter skyte,[4]
And infant frosts begin to bite,
  In hoary cranreuch[5] drest;
Ae night at e'en a merry core
  O' randie, gangrel[6] bodies
In Poosie Nansie's held the splore,[7]
  To drink their orra duddies:[8]   10
    Wi' quaffing and laughing,
      They ranted and they sang,
    Wi' jumping an thumping
      The very girdle[9] rang.

[8] Very little.
[1] Faded.
[2] Earth.
[3] Bat.
[4] Lash.
[5] Hoar-frost.
[6] Disorderly, vagrant.
[7] Carousal.
[8] Spare rags.
[9] Metal plate for frying cakes and bannocks.

II

First, niest the fire, in auld red rags
Ane sat, weel brac'd wi' mealy bags
    And knapsack a' in order;
His doxy[10] lay within his arm;
Wi' usquebae[11] an blankets warm,
    She blinket on her sodger   20
An' aye he gies the tosy[12] drab
    The tither skelpin'[13] kiss,
While she held up her greedy gab,
    Just like an aumous dish:[14]
        Ilk smack still did crack still
        Just like a cadger's whip;
        Then staggering, and swaggering,
        He roar'd this ditty up:—

AIR

Tune: *Soldier's Joy*

I

I am a son of Mars, who have been in many
    wars,
    And show my cuts and scars wherever I
        come: 30
This here was for a wench, and that other in a
    trench
    When welcoming the French at the sound
        of the drum.
                    Lal de dauble, &c.

II

My 'prenticeship I pass'd, where my leader
    breath'd his last,
    When the bloody die was cast on the heights
        of Abram;
And I served out my trade when the gallant
    game was play'd,
    And the Moro low was laid at the sound of
        the drum.

III

I lastly was with Curtis, among the floating
    batt'ries,
    And there I left for witness an arm and a
        limb;

¹⁰ Sweetheart.
¹¹ Whiskey.
¹² Tipsy.
¹³ Sounding.
¹⁴ Alms-dish.

Yet let my country need me, with Eliott to
    head me   40
I'd clatter on my stumps at the sound of a
    drum.

IV

And now tho' I must beg with a wooden arm
    and leg
    And many a tatter'd rag hanging over my
        bum,
I'm as happy with my wallet, my bottle, and
    my callet
    As when I used in scarlet to follow a drum.

V

What tho' with hoary locks I must stand the
    winter shocks,
    Beneath the woods and rocks oftentimes for
        a home?
When the t'other bag I sell, and the t'other
    bottle tell,
    I could meet a troop of hell at the sound of
        the drum.

RECITATIVO

He ended; and the kebars[15] sheuk   50
    Aboon the chorus roar;
While frighted rattons backward leuk,
    And seek the benmost bore:[16]
A fairy fiddler frae the neuk,
    He skirled out *Encore!*
But up arose the martial chuck,[17]
    An laid the loud uproar:—

AIR

Tune: *Sodger Laddie*

I

I once was a maid, tho' I cannot tell when,
And still my delight is in proper young men.
Some one of a troop of dragoons was my
    daddie: 60
No wonder I'm fond of a sodger laddie!
                    Sing, Lal de dal, &c.

II

The first of my loves was a swaggering blade,
To rattle the thundering drum was his trade;

¹⁵ Rafters.
¹⁶ Inmost chink.
¹⁷ Darling.

His leg was so tight, and his cheek was so
    ruddy,
Transported I was with my sodger laddie.

III

But the godly old chaplain left him in the
    lurch;
The sword I forsook for the sake of the church;
He risked the soul, and I ventur'd the body:
'Twas then I prov'd false to my sodger laddie.

IV

Full soon I grew sick of my sanctified sot;   71
The regiment at large for a husband I got;
From the gilded spontoon to the fife I was
    ready:
I asked no more but a sodger laddie.

V

But the peace it reduced me to beg in despair,
Till I met my old boy at a Cunningham fair;
His rags regimental they flutter'd so gaudy:
My heart it rejoic'd at a sodger laddie.

VI

And now I have liv'd—I know not how long!
And still I can join in a cup or a song;   80
But whilst with both hands I can hold the glass
    steady,
Here's to thee, my hero, my sodger laddie!

RECITATIVO

Poor Merry-Andrew in the neuk
    Sat guzzling wi' a tinkler-hizzie;
They mind't na wha the chorus teuk,
    Between themselves they were sae busy.
At length, wi' drink and courting dizzy,
He stoitered up an' made a face;
    Then turn'd an' laid a smack on Grizzy,
Syne tun'd his pipes wi' grave grimace.   90

AIR

Tune: *Auld Sir Symon*

I

Sir Wisdom's a fool when he's fou;
    Sir Knave is a fool in a session:

He's there but a prentice I trow,
    But I am a fool by profession.

II

My grannie she bought me a beuk,
    An' I held awa to the school:
I fear I my talent misteuk,
    But what will ye hae of a fool?

III

For drink I would venture my neck;
    A hizzie's the half o' my craft: 100
But what could ye other expect
    Of ane that's avowedly daft?

IV

I ance was tied up like a stirk[18]
    For civilly swearing and quaffing;
I ance was abused i' the kirk
    For towsing[19] a lass i' my daffin.

V

Poor Andrew that tumbles for sport,
    Let naebody name wi' a jeer;
There's even, I'm tauld, i' the Court
    A tumbler ca'd the Premier.   110

VI

Observ'd ye yon reverend lad
    Maks faces to tickle the mob?
He rails at our mountebank squad—
    It's rivalship just i' the job!

VII

And now my conclusion I'll tell,
    For, faith! I'm confoundedly dry:
The chiel[20] that's a fool for himsel,
    Gude Lord! he's far dafter than I.

RECITATIVO

Then niest outspak a raucle carlin,[21]
Wha kent fu' weel to cleek the sterling,[22] 120
For mony a pursie she had hooked,

[18] Young ox.
[19] Rumpling.
[20] Fellow.
[21] Rough old woman.
[22] Pinch the ready cash.

And had in mony a well been douked.
Her love had been a Highland laddie,
But weary fa' the waefu' woodie![23]
Wi' sighs and sobs, she thus began
To wail her braw John Highlandman:—

AIR

Tune: *O, An' Ye Were Dead, Guidman*

I

A Highland lad my love was born,
The Lawlan' laws he held in scorn,
But he still was faithfu' to his clan,
My gallant, braw John Highlandman.   130

CHORUS

Sing hey, my braw John Highlandman!
Sing ho, my braw John Highlandman!
There's no a lad in a' the lan'
Was match for my John Highlandman!

II

With his philibeg[24] an' tartan plaid,
And gude claymore[25] down by his side,
The ladies' hearts he did trepan,
My gallant, braw John Highlandman.

III

We rangèd a' from Tweed to Spey,
And lived like lords and ladies gay,   140
For a Lawlan' face he feared nane,
My gallant, braw John Highlandman.

IV

They banish'd him beyond the sea,
But ere the bud was on the tree,
Adown my cheeks the pearls ran,
Embracing my John Highlandman.

V

But, Och! they catch'd him at the last,
And bound him in a dungeon fast.
My curse upon them every one—   149
They've hang'd my braw John Highlandman.

[23] Gallows.
[24] Highlander's kilt.
[25] Two-handed Highland sword.

VI

And now a widow I must mourn
The pleasures that will ne'er return;
No comfort but a hearty can
When I think on John Highlandman.

RECITATIVO

I

A pigmy scraper wi' his fiddle,
Wha used at trysts and fairs to driddle,[26]
Her strappin' limb and gawsie[27] middle
    (He reach'd nae higher)
Had hol'd his heartie like a riddle,[28]
        And blawn't on fire.   160

II

Wi' hand on hainch, and upward e'e,
He croon'd his gamut, one, two, three,
Then, in an *arioso* key,
        The wee Apollo
Set aff, wi' *allegretto* glee,
        His *giga* solo.

AIR

Tune: *Whistle Owre the Lave O't*

I

Let me ryke[29] up to dight that tear;
And go wi' me and be my dear,
And then your every care and fear
    May whistle owre the lave o't.   170

CHORUS

I am a fiddler to my trade,
And a' the tunes that e'er I play'd,
The sweetest still to wife or maid
    Was *Whistle Owre the Lave O't.*

II

At kirns and weddings we'se be there,
And O, sae nicely's we will fare!
We'll bowse about till Daddie Care
Sings *Whistle Owre the Lave O't.*

[26] Scrape, saw.
[27] Plump.
[28] Sieve.
[29] Reach.

III

Sae merrily's the banes we'll pyke,
And sun oursels about the dyke;   180
And at our leisure, when ye like,
    We'll—whistle owre the lave o't!

IV

But bless me wi' your heav'n o' charms,
And while I kittle[30] hair on thairms,[31]
Hunger, cauld, an a' sic harms,
    May whistle owre the lave o't.

RECITATIVO

I

Her charms had struck a sturdy caird,[32]
    As well as poor gut-scraper;
He taks the fiddler by the beard,
    And draws a roosty rapier;   190
He swoor by a' was swearing worth
    To speet him like a pliver,[33]
Unless he would from that time forth
    Relinquish her for ever.

II

Wi' ghastly ee, poor Tweedle-Dee
    Upon his hunkers[34] bended,
And pray'd for grace wi' ruefu' face,
    And sae the quarrel ended.
But tho' his little heart did grieve
    When round the tinkler prest her,   200
He feign'd to snirtle[35] in his sleeve,
    When thus the caird address'd her:—

AIR

Tune: *Clout the Cauldron*

I

My bonie lass, I work in brass,
    A tinkler is my station;
I've travell'd round all Christian ground
    In this my occupation;
I've ta'en the gold, an' been enrolled
    In many a noble squadron;

[30] Tickle.
[31] Fiddle-strings.
[32] Tinker.
[33] Plover.
[34] Hams.
[35] Snigger.

But vain they search'd, when off I march'd
To go and clout[36] the cauldron   210

II

Despise that shrimp, that wither'd imp,
    Wi' a' his noise and cap'rin,
And tak a share wi' those that bear
    The budget[37] and the apron!
And by that stowp,[38] my faith and houpe!
    And by that dear Kilbaigie![39]
If e'er ye want, or meet wi' scant,
    May I ne'er weet my craigie![40]

RECITATIVO

I

The caird prevail'd: th' unblushing fair
    In his embraces sunk,   220
Partly wi' love o'ercome sae sair,
    An partly she was drunk.
Sir Violino, with an air
    That show'd a man o' spunk,
Wish'd unison between the pair,
    And made the bottle clunk
        To their health that night.

II

But hurchin Cupid shot a shaft,
    That play'd a dame a shavie:[41]
The fiddler rak'd her fore and aft,   230
    Behint the chicken cavie.
Her lord, a wight of Homer's craft,
    Tho' limpin' wi' the spavie,
He hirpl'd[42] up, an lap like daft,
    And shor'd[43] them "Dainty Davie"
        O' boot[44] that night.

III

He was a care-defying blade
    As ever Bacchus listed!
Tho' Fortune sair upon him laid,
    His heart, she ever miss'd it.   240
He had nae wish—but to be glad,

[36] Patch.
[37] Tinker's bag of tools.
[38] Jug.
[39] A kind of whiskey.
[40] Throat.
[41] Trick.
[42] Limped.
[43] Offered.
[44] To boot.

Nor want but—when he thirsted;
He hated nought but—to be sad,
And thus the Muse suggested
    His sang that night.

AIR

Tune: For A' That, An' A' That

I

I am a bard of no regard
  Wi' gentlefolks, and a' that,
But Homer-like, the glowrin byke,[45]
  Frae town to town I draw that.

CHORUS

For a' that, and a' that,   250
  And twice as muckle's a' that;
I've lost but ane, I've twa behin',
  I've wife eneugh for a' that.

II

I never drank the Muses' stank,[46]
  Castalia's burn, and a' that;
But there it streams, and richly reams—
  My Helicon I ca' that.

III

Great love I bear to a' the fair,
  Their humble slave, and a' that;
But lordly will, I hold it still   260
  A mortal sin to thraw[47] that.

IV

In raptures sweet this hour we meet
  Wi' mutual love, and a' that;
But for how lang the flie may stang,
  Let inclination law that.

V

Their tricks and craft hae put me daft.
  They've ta'en me in, and a' that;
But clear your decks, an' here's the sex!
  I like the jads for a' that.

For a' that, and a' that,   270
  And twice as muckle's a' that,

[45] Gazing crowd.
[46] Pool.
[47] Thwart.

My dearest bluid, to do them guid,
  They're welcome till't, for a' that!

RECITATIVO

So sung the bard, and Nansie's wa's
Shook with a thunder of applause,
  Re-echo'd from each mouth!
They toom'd[48] their pocks, an' pawn'd **their**
    duds,
They scarcely left to coor their fuds,[49]
  To quench their lowin[50] drouth.
Then owre again the jovial thrang   280
  The poet did request
To lowse his pack, an' wale[51] a sang,
  A ballad o' the best:
    He rising, rejoicing,
      Between his twa Deborahs,
    Looks round him, an' found them
      Impatient for the chorus:—

AIR

Tune: Jolly Mortals, Fill Your Glasses

I

See the smoking bowl before us!
  Mark our jovial, ragged ring!
Round and round take up the chorus,
  And in raptures let us sing: 291

CHORUS

A fig for those by law protected!
  Liberty's a glorious feast,
Courts for cowards were erected,
  Churches built to please the priest!

II

What is title, what is treasure?
  What is reputation's care?
If we lead a life of pleasure,
  'Tis no matter how or where!

III

With the ready trick and fable   300
  Round we wander all the day;
And at night, in barn or stable,
  Hug our doxies on the hay.

[48] Emptied.
[49] Cover their buttocks.
[50] Burning.
[51] Choose.

IV

Does the train-attended carriage
Thro' the country lighter rove?
Does the sober bed of marriage
Witness brighter scenes of love?

V

Life is all a variorum,
We regard not how it goes;
Let them cant about decorum   310
Who have characters to lose.

VI

Here's to budgets, bags, and wallets!
Here's to all the wandering train!
Here's our ragged brats and callets![52]
One and all, cry out, Amen!

[*1785*, 1799]

TAM O' SHANTER

Of Brownyis and of Bogillis full is this Buke.
GAWIN DOUGLAS.

When chapman billies[1] leave the street,
And drouthy[2] neebors neebors meet,
As market-days are wearing late,
An' folk begin to tak the gate;
While we sit bousing at the nappy,
An' getting fou and unco happy,
We think na on the lang Scots miles,
The mosses, waters, slaps, and styles,
That lie between us and our hame,
Where sits our sulky sullen dame,   10
Gathering her brows like gathering storm,
Nursing her wrath to keep it warm.
    This truth fand honest Tam o' Shanter,
As he frae Ayr ae night did canter,
(Auld Ayr, wham ne'er a town surpasses
For honest men and bonnie lasses).
    O Tam! hadst thou but been sae wise,
As ta'en thy ain wife Kate's advice!
She tauld thee weel thou was a skellum,[3]
A bletherin', blusterin', drunken blellum;[4]   20
That frae November till October,
Ae market-day thou was na sober;

[52] Harlots.
[1] Pedlar fellows.
[2] Thirsty.
[3] Good-for-nothing.
[4] Babbler.

That ilka melder,[5] wi' the miller
Thou sat as lang as thou had siller;[6]
That every naig was ca'd a shoe on,
The smith and thee gat roarin' fou on;
That at the Lord's house, even on Sunday,
Thou drank wi' Kirkton Jean till Monday.
She prophesied that, late or soon,
Thou would be found deep drowned in Doon;   30
Or catched wi' warlocks[7] in the mirk,[8]
By Alloway's auld haunted kirk.
    Ah, gentle dames! it gars me greet[9]
To think how mony counsels sweet,
How mony lengthened sage advices,
The husband frae the wife despises!
    But to our tale: Ae market night,
Tam had got planted unco right;
Fast by an ingle, bleezing finely,
Wi' reaming swats,[10] that drank divinely;   40
And at his elbow, Souter[11] Johnny,
His ancient, trusty, drouthy crony;
Tam lo'ed him like a vera britner;
They had been fou for weeks thegither.
The night drave on wi' sangs and clatter;
And aye the ale was growing better:
The landlady and Tam grew gracious,
Wi' favours secret, sweet, and precious:
The souter tauld his queerest stories;
The landlord's laugh was ready chorus: 50
The storm without might rair and rustle,
Tam did na mind the storm a whistle.
    Care, mad to see a man sae happy,
E'en drowned himsel amang the nappy;
As bees flee hame wi' lades o' treasure,
The minutes winged their way wi' pleasure;
Kings may be blest, but Tam was glorious,
O'er a' the ills o' life victorious!
    But pleasures are like poppies spread,
You seize the flow'r, its bloom is shed;   60
Or like the snow falls in the river,
A moment white—then melts for ever;
Or like the borealis race,
That flit ere you can point their place;
Or like the rainbow's lovely form
Evanishing amid the storm—
Nae man can tether time nor tide;
The hour approaches Tam maun ride;
That hour, o' night's black arch the key-stane,
That dreary hour, he mounts his beast in;   70
And sic a night he taks the road in,

[5] Quantity of oats ground at one time.
[6] Silver.
[7] Wizards.
[8] Dark.
[9] It makes me weep.
[10] Foaming new ale.
[11] Cobbler.

As ne'er poor sinner was abroad in.

The wind blew as 'twad blawn its last;
The rattling show'rs rose on the blast;
The speedy gleams the darkness swallowed;
Loud, deep, and lang, the thunder bellowed:
That night, a child might understand,
The Deil had business on his hand.

Weel mounted on his grey mare, Meg,
A better never lifted leg,   80
Tam skelpit on thro' dub and mire,
Despising wind, and rain, and fire;
Whiles holding fast his guid blue bonnet;
Whiles crooning o'er some auld Scots sonnet;
Whiles glow'ring round wi' prudent cares,
Lest bogles catch him unawares.
Kirk-Alloway was drawing nigh,
Whare ghaists and houlets nightly cry.

By this time he was cross the ford,
Where in the snaw the chapman smoored;[12]
And past the birks[13] and meikle stane,   91
Where drunken Charlie brak's neck-bane;
And thro' the whins,[14] and by the cairn,
Where hunters fand the murder'd bairn;
And near the thorn, aboon the well,
Where Mungo's mither hang'd hersel.
Before him Doon pours all his floods;
The doubling storm roars thro' the woods;
The lightnings flash from pole to pole;
Near and more near the thunders roll: 100
When, glimmering thro' the groaning trees,
Kirk-Alloway seem'd in a bleeze;
Thro' ilka bore[15] the beams were glancing;
And loud resounded mirth and dancing.—

Inspiring bold John Barleycorn!
What dangers thou canst make us scorn!
Wi' tippenny, we fear nae evil;
Wi' usquebae[16] we'll face the devil!—
The swats sae ream'd in Tammie's noddle,
Fair play, he cared na deils a boddle.[17]   110
But Maggie stood right sair astonished,
Till, by the heel and hand admonished,
She ventured forward on the light;
And, vow! Tam saw an unco sight!
Warlocks and witches in a dance;
Nae cotillon brent new frae France,
But hornpipes, jigs, strathspeys,[18] and reels,
Put life and mettle in their heels.

[12] Smothered.
[13] Birches.
[14] Furze.
[15] Chink.
[16] Whiskey.
[17] Copper coin worth one-sixth of English penny.
[18] Slow Highland dance.

A winnock-bunker[19] in the east,
There sat auld Nick, in shape o' beast;   120
A touzie tyke,[20] black, grim, and large!
To gie them music was his charge:
He screwed the pipes and gart them skirl,[21]
Till roof and rafters a' did dirl.—[22]
Coffins stood round like open presses,
That shaw'd the dead in their last dresses;
And by some devilish cantraip slight
Each in its cauld hand held a light,
By which heroic Tam was able
To note upon the haly table   130
A murderer's banes in gibbet-airns;
Twa span-lang, wee, unchristen'd bairns;
A thief new-cutted frae a rape,
Wi' his last gasp his gab[23] did gape;
Five tomahawks, wi' blude red-rusted;
Five scymitars, wi' murder crusted;
A garter, which a babe had strangled;
A knife, a father's throat had mangled,
Whom his ain son o' life bereft,
The gray hairs yet stack to the heft;   140
Wi' mair of horrible and awfu',
Which even to name wad be unlawfu'.

As Tammie glowr'd, amaz'd, and curious,
The mirth and fun grew fast and furious:
The piper loud and louder blew;
The dancers quick and quicker flew;
They reeled, they set, they crossed, they
        cleekit,[24]
Till ilka carlin[25] swat and reekit,
And coost[26] her duddies to the wark,
And linkit[27] at it in her sark![28]   150
Now Tam, O Tam! had thae been queans,
A' plump and strapping in their teens;
Their sarks, instead o' creeshie[29] flannen,
Been snaw-white seventeen hunder linen!
Thir breeks o' mine, my only pair,
That ance were plush, o' gude blue hair,
I wad hae gi'en them off my hurdies,
For ae blink o' the bonie burdies![30]

But wither'd beldams, auld and droll,
Rigwoodie[31] hags wad spean[32] a foal,   160

[19] Window seat.
[20] Shaggy cur.
[21] Sound shrilly.
[22] Ring.
[23] Mouth.
[24] Took hold.
[25] Beldam.
[26] Cast off.
[27] Tripped along.
[28] Shirt.
[29] Greasy.
[30] Maidens.
[31] Bony.
[32] Wean.

Louping and flinging on a crummock,[33]
I wonder didna turn thy stomach.
   But Tam kend what was what fu' brawlie
There was ae winsome wench and wawlie[34]
That night enlisted in the core,
Lang after kent on Carrick shore!
(For mony a beast to dead she shot,
And perished mony a bonie boat,
And shook baith meikle corn and bear,[35]
And kept the country-side in fear)   170
Her cutty[36] sark, o' Paisley harn,[37]
That while a lassie she had worn,
In longitude tho' sorely scanty,
It was her best, and she was vauntie.—
Ah! little kend thy reverend grannie
That sark she coft[38] for her wee Nannie
Wi' twa pund Scots ('twas a' her riches)
Wad ever graced a dance of witches!
   But here my Muse her wing maun cour;[39]
Sic flights are far beyond her pow'r—   180
To sing how Nannie lap and flang,
(A souple jade she was, and strang),
And how Tam stood, like ane bewitched,
And thought his very een enriched;
Even Satan glowr'd, and fidg'd fu' fain,
And hotched[40] and blew wi' might and main:
Till first ae caper, syne anither,
Tam tint[41] his reason a' thegither,
And roars out "Weel done, Cutty-sark!"
And in an instant all was dark!   190
And scarcely had he Maggie rallied,
When out the hellish, legion sallied.
   As bees bizz out wi' angry fyke,[42]
When plundering herds assail their byke;[43]
As open pussie's mortal foes,
When pop! she starts before their nose;
As eager runs the market-crowd,
When "Catch the thief!" resounds aloud;
So Maggie runs; the witches follow,
Wi' mony an eldritch skriech and hollow.   200
   Ah, Tam! ah, Tam! thou'll get thy fairin![44]
In hell they'll roast thee like a herrin!
In vain thy Kate awaits thy comin!
Kate soon will be a woefu' woman!
Now do thy speedy utmost, Meg,

[33] Crooked staff.
[34] Strapping.
[35] Barley.
[36] Short.
[37] Coarse cloth woven of flax.
[38] Bought.
[39] Lower.
[40] Jerked.
[41] Lost.
[42] Fret.
[43] Hive.
[44] Due.

And win the key-stane o' the brig;
There at them thou thy tail may toss,
A running stream they darena cross.
But ere the key-stane she could make,
The fient a[45] tail she had to shake!   210
For Nannie, far before the rest,
Hard upon noble Maggie prest,
And flew at Tam wi' furious ettle;[46]
But little wist she Maggie's mettle.—
Ae spring brought off her master hale,
But left behind her ain gray tail:
The carlin claught her by the rump,
And left poor Maggie scarce a stump.
   Now, wha this tale o' truth shall read,
Each man and mother's son, take heed: 220
Whene'er to drink you are inclined,
Or cutty-sarks rin in your mind,
Think! ye may buy the joys o'er dear;
Remember Tam o' Shanter's mare.

[1790, 1791]

GREEN GROW THE RASHES

Green grow the rashes, O,
   Green grow the rashes, O;
The sweetest hours that e'er I spend,
   Are spent amang the lasses, O!

I

There's nought but care on ev'ry han',
   In ev'ry hour that passes, O;
What signifies the life o' man,
   An' 'twere na for the lasses, O.

II

The warly race may riches chase,
   An' riches still may fly them, O;
An' tho' at last they catch them fast,
   Their hearts can ne'er enjoy them, O.

III

But gie me a canny hour at e'en,
   My arms about my dearie, O;
An' warly cares, an' warly men,
   May a' gae tapsalteerie,[1] O!

[45] Nothing of a.
[46] Intent.
[1] Topsy-turvy.

IV

For you sae douce, ye sneer at this,
    Ye're nought but senseless asses, O:
The wisest man the warl' saw,
    He dearly lov'd the lasses, O.   20

V

Auld Nature swears, the lovely dears
    Her noblest work she classes, O;
Her prentice han' she tried on man,
    An' then she made the lasses, O.
                [*1784*, 1787]

OF A' THE AIRTS

Of a' the airts the wind can blaw,
    I dearly like the west,
For there the bonie lassie lives,
    The lassie I lo'e best:
There's wild woods grow, and rivers row,
    And mony a hill between;
But day and night my fancy's flight
    Is ever wi' my Jean.

I see her in the dewy flowers,
    I see her sweet and fair;   10
I hear her in the tunefu' birds,
    I hear her charm the air:
There's not a bonie flower that springs
    By fountain, shaw, or green,
There's not a bonie bird that sings,
    But minds me o' my Jean.
                [*1788*, 1790]

JOHN ANDERSON MY JO

John Anderson my jo,[1] John,
    When we were first acquent,
Your locks were like the raven,
    Your bonie brow was brent;[2]
But now your brow is beld, John,
    Your locks are like the snow;
But blessings on your frosty pow,[3]
    John Anderson, my jo.

John Anderson my jo, John,

[1] Darling.
[2] High and unwrinkled.
[3] Head.

We clamb the hill thegither;   10
And mony a canty[4] day, John,
    We've had wi' ane anither:
Now we maun totter down, John,
    And hand in hand we'll go,
And sleep thegither at the foot,
    John Anderson, my jo.
                [*1789*, 1790]

HIGHLAND MARY

Ye banks, and braes, and streams around
    The castle o' Montgomery,
Green be your woods, and fair your flowers,
    Your waters never drumlie![1]
There simmer first unfauld her robes,
    And there the langest tarry;
For there I took the last fareweel
    O my sweet Highland Mary.

How sweetly bloom'd the gay green birk,
    How rich the hawthorn's blossom,   10
As underneath their fragrant shade
    I clasp'd her to my bosom!
The golden hours on angel wings
    Flew o'er me and my dearie;
For dear to me as light and life
    Was my sweet Highland Mary.

Wi' mony a vow, and lock'd embrace,
    Our parting was fu' tender;
And, pledging aft to meet again,
    We tore oursels asunder;   20
But oh! fell death's untimely frost,
    That nipt my flower sae early!—
Now green's the sod, and cauld's the clay,
    That wraps my Highland Mary!

O pale, pale now, those rosy lips,
    I aft have kiss'd sae fondly!
And closed for aye the sparkling glance,
    That dwelt on me sae kindly!
And mould'ring now in silent dust,
    That heart that lo'ed me dearly—   30
But still within my bosom's core
    Shall live my Highland Mary.
                [*1792*, 1799]

[4] Merry.
[1] Muddy.

"THOU LINGERING STAR"

Thou lingering star, with lessening ray,
　That lov'st to greet the early morn,
Again thou usherest in the day
　My Mary from my soul was torn.
O Mary! dear departed shade!
　Where is thy place of blissful rest?
Seest thou thy lover lowly laid?
　Hear'st thou the groans that rend his breast?

That sacred hour can I forget?
　Can I forget the hallow'd grove　　　　10
Where by the winding Ayr we met,
　To live one day of parting love?
Eternity will not efface
　Those records dear of transports past;
Thy image at our last embrace,
　Ah, little thought we 'twas our last!

Ayr gurgling kiss'd his pebbled shore,
　O'erhung with wild-woods thickening green;
The fragrant birch, and hawthorn hoar,
　Twin'd amorous round the raptur'd scene;
The flowers sprang wanton to be prest,　21
　The birds sang love on ev'ry spray,
Till too, too soon, the glowing west
　Proclaim'd the speed of winged day.

Still o'er these scenes my memory wakes
　And fondly broods with miser care;
Time but the impression deeper makes,
　As streams their channels deeper wear.
My Mary, dear departed shade!
　Where is thy blissful place of rest?　　30
Seest thou thy lover lowly laid?
　Hear'st thou the groans that rend his breast?

[*1789*, 1790]

AFTON WATER

Flow gently, sweet Afton, among thy green braes,
Flow gently, I'll sing thee a song in thy praise;
My Mary's asleep by thy murmuring stream,
Flow gently, sweet Afton, disturb not her dream.

Thou stock-dove whose echo resounds thro' the glen,
Ye wild whistling blackbirds in yon thorny den,
Thou green-crested lapwing, thy screaming forbear,
I charge you disturb not my slumbering fair.

How lofty, sweet Afton, thy neighbouring hills,
Far mark'd with the courses of clear winding riiis;　　10
There daily I wander as noon rises high,
My flocks and my Mary's sweet cot in my eye.

How pleasant thy banks and green valleys below,
Where wild in the woodlands the primroses blow;
There oft as mild ev'ning weeps over the lea,
The sweet-scented birk shades my Mary and me.

Thy crystal stream, Afton, how lovely it glides,
And winds by the cot where my Mary resides;
How wanton thy waters her snowy feet lave,
As gathering sweet flow'rets she stems thy clear wave.　　20

Flow gently, sweet Afton, among thy green braes,
Flow gently, sweet river, the theme of my lays;
My Mary's asleep by thy murmuring stream,
Flow gently, sweet Afton, disturb not her dream.

[*1789*, 1792]

AE FOND KISS

Ae fond kiss, and then we sever;
Ae fareweel and then for ever!
Deep in heart-wrung tears I'll pledge thee,
Warring sighs and groans I'll wage thee.
Who shall say that fortune grieves him
While the star of hope she leaves him?
Me, nae cheerfu' twinkle lights me;
Dark despair around benights me.

I'll ne'er blame my partial fancy,
Naething could resist my Nancy: 10
But to see her, was to love her,
Love but her, and love for ever.
Had we never lov'd sae kindly,
Had we never lov'd sae blindly,
Never met—or never parted,
We had ne'er been broken-hearted.

Fare thee weel, thou first and fairest!
Fare thee weel, thou best and dearest!
Thine be ilka joy and treasure,
Peace, enjoyment, love, and pleasure!   20
Ae fond kiss, and then we sever;
Ae fareweel, alas! for ever!
Deep in heart-wrung tears I'll pledge thee,
Warring sighs and groans I'll wage thee.

[*1791*, 1792]

DUNCAN GRAY

Duncan Gray came here to woo,
    Ha, ha, the wooing o't!
On blythe Yule night when we were fou,
    Ha, ha, the wooing o't!
Maggie coost her head fu' high,
Look'd asklent and unco skeigh,[1]
Gart[2] poor Duncan stand abeigh;[3]
    Ha, ha, the wooing o't.

Duncan fleech'd,[4] and Duncan pray'd,
    Ha, ha, the wooing o't!   10
Meg was deaf as Ailsa Craig,
    Ha, ha, the wooing o't!
Duncan sigh'd baith out and in,
Grat[5] his een baith bleer't and blin',

[1] Skittish.
[2] Made.
[3] Aloof.
[4] Wheedled.
[5] Wept.

Spak o' lowpin o'er a linn[6]—
    Ha, ha, the wooing o't.

Time and chance are but a tide,
    Ha, ha, the wooing o't!
Slighted love is sair to bide,
    Ha, ha, the wooing o't!   20
"Shall I, like a fool," quoth he,
"For a haughty hizzie die?
She may gae to—France for me!"—
    Ha, ha, the wooing o't!

How it comes let doctors tell,
    Ha, ha, the wooing o't!
Meg grew sick as he grew haill,
    Ha, ha, the wooing o't!
Something in her bosom wrings;
For relief a sigh she brings;   30
And O, her een they spak sic things!—
    Ha, ha, the wooing o't!

Duncan was a lad o' grace,
    Ha, ha, the wooing o't!
Maggie's was a piteous case,
    Ha, ha, the wooing o't!
Duncan couldna be her death,
Swelling pity smoor'd his wrath;
Now they're crouse[7] and cantie baith—
    Ha, ha, the wooing o't!   40

[*1792*, 1798]

A RED, RED ROSE

O my luve's like a red, red rose,
    That's newly sprung in June:
O my luve's like the melodie
    That's sweetly play'd in tune.

As fair art thou, my bonie lass,
    So deep in luve am I;
And I will luve thee still, my dear,
    Till a' the seas gang dry.

Till a' the seas gang dry, my dear,
    And the rocks melt wi' the sun: 10
And I will luve thee still, my dear,
    While the sands o' life shall run.

And fare thee weel, my only luve!
    And fare thee weel awhile!

[6] Waterfall.
[7] Merry.

And I will come again, my luve,
  Tho' it were ten thousand mile!
                    [*1794, 1796*]

AULD LANG SYNE

Should auld acquaintance be forgot,
  And never brought to mind?
Should auld acquaintance be forgot,
  And auld lang syne!

    For auld lang syne, my jo,
      For auld lang syne,
    We'll tak a cup o' kindness yet
      For auld lang syne.

And surely ye'll be your pint-stowp!
  And surely I'll be mine!   10
And we'll tak a cup o' kindness yet
  For auld lang syne.

We twa hae run about the braes,
  And pu'd the gowans fine;
But we've wander'd mony a weary fitt
  Sin auld lang syne.

We twa hae paidl'd i' the burn,[1]
  From morning sun till dine;
But seas between us braid hae roar'd,
  Sin auld lang syne.   20

And there's a hand, my trusty fiere![2]
  And gie's a hand o' thine!
And we'll tak a right guid-willie-waught,[3]
  For auld lang syne.
                    [*1788, 1796*]

YE BANKS AND BRAES

(THIRD VERSION)

Ye banks and braes o' bonie Doon,
  How can ye bloom sae fresh and fair?
How can ye chant, ye little birds,
  And I sae weary fu' o' care?
Thou'lt break my heart, thou warbling bird,
  That wantons thro' the flowering thorn:

[1] Brook.
[2] Friend.
[3] Draught.

Thou minds me o' departed joys,
  Departed never to return.

Aft hae I rov'd by bonie Doon,
  To see the rose and woodbine twine;   10
And ilka bird sang o' its luve,
  And fondly sae did I o' mine.
Wi' lightsome heart I pu'd a rose,
  Fu' sweet upon its thorny tree;
And my fause luver staw my rose—
  But ah! he left the thorn wi' me.
                    [*1792*]

GO FETCH TO ME A PINT
O' WINE

Go fetch to me a pint o' wine,
  An' fill it in a silver tassie[1];
That I may drink, before I go,
  A service to my bonie lassie.
The boat rocks at the pier o' Leith,
  Fu' loud the wind blaws frae the Ferry,
The ship rides by the Berwick-law,
  And I maun leave my bonnie Mary.

The trumpets sound, the banners fly,
  The glittering spears are rankèd ready;
The shouts o' war are heard afar,   11
  The battle closes thick and bloody;
But it's no the roar o' sea or shore
  Wad mak me langer wish to tarry;
Nor shout o' war that's heard afar,
  It's leaving thee, my bonnie Mary.
                    [*1788, 1790*]

FOR A' THAT AND A' THAT

Is there, for honest poverty,
  That hangs his head, and a' that;
The coward-slave, we pass him by,
  We dare be poor for a' that!
    For a' that, and a' that,
      Our toils obscure, and a' that,
    The rank is but the guinea stamp,
      The man's the gowd[1] for a' that.

What though on hamely fare we dine,
  Wear hoddin gray, and a' that: 10

[1] Goblet.
[1] Gold.

Gie fools their silks, and knaves their wine,
  A man's a man for a' that:
    For a' that, and a' that,
      Their tinsel show, and a' that;
  The honest man, tho' e'er sae poor,
    Is King o' men for a' that.

Ye see yon birkie,[2] ca'd a lord,
  Wha struts, and stares, and a' that;
Tho' hundreds worship at his word,
  He's but a coof[3] for a' that: 20
    For a' that, and a' that:
      His riband, star, and a' that,
  The man of independent mind,
    He looks and laughs at a' that.

A prince can mak a belted knight,
  A marquis, duke, and a' that;
But an honest man's aboon his might,
  Guid faith he mauna fa'[4] that!
    For a' that, and a' that,
      Their dignities, and a' that,   30
    The pith o' sense, and pride o' worth,
    Are higher rank than a' that.

Then let us pray that come it may,
  As come it will for a' that,
That sense and worth, o'er a' the earth,
  May bear the gree,[5] and a' that.
    For a' that and a' that,
    It's coming yet, for a' that,
    That man to man, the warld o'er,
    Shall brothers be for a' that.   40
      [*1794, 1795*]

SCOTS WHA HAE

ROBERT BRUCE'S ADDRESS TO HIS
ARMY, BEFORE THE BATTLE OF
BANNOCKBURN

Scots, wha hae wi' Wallace bled,
Scots, wham Bruce has aften led,
Welcome to your gory bed,
  Or to victorie.

Now's the day, and now's the hour;

[2] Conceited fellow.
[3] Dolt.
[4] Claim.
[5] Prize.

See the front o' battle lour;
See approach proud Edward's power—
  Chains and slaverie!

Wha will be a traitor knave?
Wha can fill a coward's grave?   10
Wha sae base as be a slave?
  Let him turn and flee!

Wha for Scotland's King and law
Freedom's sword will strongly draw,
Freeman stand, or freeman fa'?
  Let him follow me!

By oppression's woes and pains!
By your sons in servile chains!
We will drain our dearest veins,
  But they shall be free!   20

Lay the proud usurpers low!
Tyrants fall in every foe!
Liberty's in every blow!
  Let us do, or die!
      [*1793, 1794*]

O, WERT THOU IN THE CAULD BLAST

O, wert thou in the cauld blast
  On yonder lea, on yonder lea,
My plaidie to the angry airt,[1]
  I'd shelter thee, I'd shelter thee.
Or did misfortune's bitter storms
  Around thee blaw, around thee blaw,
Thy bield[2] should be my bosom,
  To share it a', to share it a'.

Or were I in the wildest waste,
  Sae black and bare, sae black and bare,
The desert were a paradise,   11
  If thou wert there, if thou wert there.
Or were I monarch o' the globe,
  Wi' thee to reign, wi' thee to reign,
The brightest jewel in my crown
  Wad be my queen, wad be my queen.
      [*1796, 1800*]

[1] Direction.
[2] Shelter.

GEORGE CRABBE (1754-1832)

To say that George Crabbe was educated to be a surgeon, but, failing in his first practice, entered the ministry instead, is to give an entirely erroneous idea of his education and preparation for the writing of poetry. He studied at no university for either profession. With only the rudiments of a classical education, he was apprenticed to a surgeon who made him help with the manual labor of his farm and sleep with the ploughboy. Although the second apprenticeship turned out better, he never acquired sufficient knowledge or skill in his profession to give him any confidence in himself. And later he passed his examinations for ordination with less than a year of reading. But this does not mean that life had not given him an education of much more value for the special service which he was to do for English poetry. He was born in the little sea-side town of Aldeburgh in Suffolk, the town which we catch glimpses of in both *The Village* and *The Borough*. Crabbe's son and biographer describes it as consisting of "two parallel and unpaved streets, running between mean and scrambling houses, the abodes of sea-faring men, pilots, and fishers." The sea and the country-side round about, bleak and windswept on the commons, marshy along the river Ald, appear in many of his poems, as do the inhabitants of the villages. "Masculine and robust frames, rude manners, stormy passions, laborious days, and, occasionally, boisterous nights of merriment,—among such accompaniments was born and reared the Poet of the Poor." Crabbe's father was a minor revenue officer and could ill afford any education for his sons. It was only a combination of George's passion for reading and his complete inefficiency in manual labor that secured for him the slight training which we have described.

It was the desperation of poverty and failure in the practice of his first profession in his native village that drove Crabbe to pack up his surgical instruments (useful later for pawning), take three pounds and his accumulated verses, and start out for London to try his literary fortunes. This venture might also have ended disastrously if a happy inspiration had not prompted him, when he was at the end of his resources, to write to Burke. Fortunately this application was more successful than those to Lords North, Shelburne, and Thurlow had been. Burke took him into his home, got Dodsley to publish *The Library*, encouraged him with the revision of *The Village*, introduced him to people like Sir Joshua Reynolds, Dr. Johnson, and the formerly reluctant Thurlow, and, finally, placed him in the church. *The Library* was published in 1781, *The Village*, a great success, in 1783, and *The Newspaper* in 1785. Crabbe was by this time well on his way toward literary fame, but then to everyone's surprise he published nothing for twenty-two years. His silence is largely to be accounted for by the fact that he was absorbed in his family and his pastoral duties. But indeed his unproductiveness was more apparent than real. He wrote, as a matter of fact, a great deal during these years, but almost all that he wrote was consigned at one time or another to those bonfires in which his small sons so gleefully assisted. Among other things, he wrote three novels, which he discarded when his wife complained that he had done the same sort of thing better in verse. It would have been of immense interest to know what this realist in verse and vehement critic of the unrealities of contemporary fiction would himself do in this genre. Certainly his gift of realistic detail was equal to the task; one questions, however, whether he had sufficient power of organization to carry through a novel of any great significance.

It was the need of more income for the education of his sons that drove Crabbe back into the publishing of poetry. In 1807 he issued a volume of poetry containing, in addition to his earlier poems and some short pieces, the significant addition of *The Parish Register*. In 1810 he published *The Borough* in which he went back to his native village for much of his material; in 1812, *Tales in Verse;* in 1819, *Tales of the Hall*. Other tales were published posthumously by his son in 1834. The popularity of these later books was even greater than that of *The Village*, and Crabbe was ranked beside Scott as one of the most significant poets of his day, Wordsworth and Coleridge not having yet achieved any widespread popularity.

There has been some tendency in recent years to restore Crabbe to a position somewhat more commensurate with that which he held before his complete eclipse by the romantic poets. He did, indeed, fight valiantly the battle of realism for poetry, as Fielding and Smollett had fought it for prose fiction. In his "Preface" to the *Tales* of 1812, he pleads for a broader conception of the poet than the current one which placed him in a land of fancy and imagination "above the grossness of actual being, into the soothing and pleasant atmosphere of supramundane existence." He asserted the poet's right to deal with "those painful realities, those every-day concerns, and those perpetually-occurring vexations," of the life about us. *The Village* was written with the sentimental pastoral, and perhaps especially, with Goldsmith's *Deserted Village* in mind, but it is more than a satire or parody. There is a fierce indignation in Crabbe's picture of the suffering and evil in *his* village that raises his poem to the level of realistic art. Later, in *The Parish Register*, Crabbe dropped all satirical reference to contemporary poetry and dealt straightforwardly and confidently with material which was uniquely his own. The plan of the latter poem, the scanning of the register of births, marriages, and deaths of a country parish, gave him ample opportunity for the sort of writing that he did best—the informal, even disjointed, survey of the various types of people found together in a community. In the fidelity and precision of some of his delineations, especially in the third part, *The Parish Register* recalls the felicity of Chaucer's Prologue to the *Canterbury Tales*, however Crabbe may fall below Chaucer in the music of his line and the sustained grace of language. There is even, in such lines as the following, something of the quiet humor of Chaucer:

> She spake, and, trembling, dropp'd upon her knees,
> Heaven in her eye, and in her hand her keys.

> A grey old cat his whiskers lick'd beside;
> A type of sadness in the house of pride.

In *The Borough*, Crabbe was once more at home in descriptions of the sea, the uplands, and the marshes about Aldborough. The poem, though uneven like all of Crabbe's poetry, contains some of his best descriptive and narrative work.

Poetical Works, with His Letters and Journals and His Life by His Son (8 vols., 1834); *Poems*, ed. A. W. Ward (3 vols., Cambridge, 1905-07); *Poetical Works*, ed. A. J. and R. M. Carlyle (1914); R. Huchon, *George Crabbe and His Times*, trans. by F. Clarke (1907); J. H. Evans, *The Poems of George Crabbe: A Literary and Historical Study* (1933); Varley Lang, "Crabbe and the Eighteenth Century," *ELH*, V (1938), 383-33.

THE VILLAGE

BOOK 1

The Subject proposed—Remarks upon Pastoral Poetry—A Tract of Country near the Coast described—An impoverished Borough—Smugglers and their Assistants—Rude Manners of the Inhabitants—Ruinous Effects of a high Tide—The Village Life more generally considered: Evils of it—The youthful Labourer—The old Man: his Soliloquy—The Parish Workhouse: its Inhabitants—The sick Poor: their Apothecary—The dying Pauper—The Village Priest.

> The village life, and every care that reigns
> O'er youthful peasants and declining swains;
> What labour yields, and what, that labour past,
> Age, in its hour of languor, finds at last;
> What form the real picture of the poor,
> Demand a song—the Muse can give no more.
> Fled are those times when, in harmonious strains,
> The rustic poet praised his native plains:
> No shepherds now, in smooth alternate verse,
> Their country's beauty or their nymphs' rehearse;
> Yet still for these we frame the tender strain,

10

Still in our lays fond Corydons complain,
And shepherds' boys their amorous pains reveal,
The only pains, alas! they never feel.
   On Mincio's banks, in Caesar's bounteous reign,
If Tityrus found the Golden Age again,
Must sleepy bards the flattering dream prolong,
Mechanic echoes of the Mantuan song?
From Truth and Nature shall we widely stray,
Where Virgil, not where Fancy, leads the way?   20
   Yes, thus the Muses sing of happy swains,
Because the Muses never knew their pains:
They boast their peasants' pipes; but peasants now
Resign their pipes and plod behind the plough;
And few, amid the rural tribe, have time
To number syllables and play with rhyme;
Save honest Duck, what son of verse could share
The poet's rapture, and the peasant's care?
Or the great labours of the field degrade,
With the new peril of a poorer trade?   30
   From this chief cause these idle praises spring,
That themes so easy few forbear to sing.
For no deep thought the trifling subjects ask;
To sing of shepherds is an easy task.
The happy youth assumes the common strain,
A nymph his mistress, and himself a swain;
With no sad scenes he clouds his tuneful prayer,
But all, to look like her, is painted fair.
   I grant indeed that fields and flocks have charms
For him that grazes or for him that farms;   40
But when amid such pleasing scenes I trace
The poor laborious natives of the place,
And see the midday sun, with fervid ray,
On their bare heads and dewy temples play;
While some, with feebler heads and fainter hearts,
Deplore their fortune, yet sustain their parts,
Then shall I dare these real ills to hide
In tinsel trappings of poetic pride?
   No; cast by Fortune on a frowning coast,
Which neither groves nor happy valleys boast;   50
Where other cares than those the Muse relates,
And other shepherds dwell with other mates;
By such examples taught, I paint the cot,
As Truth will paint it, and as bards will not:
Nor you, ye poor, of lettered scorn complain,
To you the smoothest song is smooth in vain;
O'ercome by labour, and bowed down by time,
Feel you the barren flattery of a rhyme?
Can poets soothe you, when you pine for bread,
By winding myrtles round your ruined shed?   60
Can their light tales your weighty griefs o'erpower,
Or glad with airy mirth the toilsome hour?
   Lo! where the heath, with withering brake grown o'er,
Lends the light turf that warms the neighbouring poor;
From thence a length of burning sand appears,
Where the thin harvest waves its withered ears;

Rank weeds, that every art and care defy,
Reign o'er the land, and rob the blighted rye:
There thistles stretch their prickly arms afar,
And to the ragged infant threaten war;   70
There poppies, nodding, mock the hope of toil;
There the blue bugloss paints the sterile soil;
Hardy and high, above the slender sheaf,
The slimy mallow waves her silky leaf,
O'er the young shoot the charlock throws a shade,
And clasping tares cling round the sickly blade;
With mingled tints the rocky coasts abound,
And a sad splendour vainly shines around.
So looks the nymph whom wretched arts adorn,
Betrayed by man, then left for man to scorn;   80
Whose cheek in vain assumes the mimic rose,
While her sad eyes the troubled breast disclose;
Whose outward splendour is but folly's dress,
Exposing most, when most it gilds distress.
    Here joyless roam a wild amphibious race,
With sullen woe displayed in every face;
Who, far from civil arts and social fly,
And scowl at strangers with suspicious eye.
    Here too the lawless merchant of the main
Draws from his plough the intoxicated swain;   90
Want only claimed the labour of the day,
But vice now steals his nightly rest away.
    Where are the swains, who, daily labour done,
With rural games played down the setting sun;
Who struck with matchless force the bounding ball,
Or made the ponderous quoit obliquely fall;
While some huge Ajax, terrible and strong,
Engaged some artful strippling of the throng,
And fell beneath him, foiled, while far around
Hoarse triumph rose, and rocks returned the sound?   100
Where now are these?—Beneath yon cliff they stand,
To show the freighted pinnace where to land;
To load the ready steed with guilty haste,
To fly in terror o'er the pathless waste,
Or, when detected in their straggling course,
To foil their foes by cunning or by force;
Or, yielding part (which equal knaves demand),
To gain a lawless passport through the land.
    Here, wandering long, amid these frowning fields,
I sought the simple life that Nature yields;   110
Rapine and Wrong and Fear usurped her place,
And a bold, artful, surly, savage race;
Who, only skilled to take the finny tribe,
The yearly dinner or septennial bribe,
Wait on the shore, and, as the waves run high,
On the tossed vessel bend their eager eye,
Which to their coast directs its venturous way;
Theirs, or the ocean's, miserable prey.
    As on their neighbouring beach yon swallows stand,
And wait for favouring winds to leave the land;   120
While still for flight the ready wing is spread:

So waited I the favouring hour, and fled—
Fled from these shores where guilt and famine reign,
And cried, "Ah! hapless they who still remain;
Who still remain to hear the ocean roar,
Whose greedy waves devour the lessening shore;
Till some fierce tide, with more imperious sway,
Sweeps the low hut and all it holds away;
When the sad tenant weeps from door to door,
And begs a poor protection from the poor!"　　　　　130
　　But these are scenes where Nature's niggard hand
Gave a spare portion to the famished land;
Hers is the fault, if here mankind complain
Of fruitless toil and labour spent in vain;
But yet in other scenes more fair in view,
Where Plenty smiles—alas! she smiles for few—
And those who taste not, yet behold her store,
Are as the slaves that dig the golden ore,—
The wealth around them makes them doubly poor.
　　Or will you deem them amply paid in health,　　　　　140
Labour's fair child, that languishes with wealth?
Go then! and see them rising with the sun,
Through a long course of daily toil to run;
See them beneath the dog-star's raging heat,
When the knees tremble and the temples beat;
Behold them, leaning on their scythes, look o'er
The labour past, and toils to come explore;
See them alternate suns and showers engage,
And hoard up aches and anguish for their age;
Through fens and marshy moors their steps pursue,　　　　　156
When their warm pores imbibe the evening dew;
Then own that labour may as fatal be
To these thy slaves, as thine excess to thee.
　　Amid this tribe too oft a manly pride
Strives in strong toil the fainting heart to hide;
There may you see the youth of slender frame
Contend with weakness, weariness, and shame;
Yet, urged along, and proudly loth to yield,
He strives to join his fellows of the field.
Till long-contending nature droops at last,　　　　　160
Declining health rejects his poor repast,
His cheerless spouse the coming danger sees,
And mutual murmurs urge the slow disease.
　　Yet grant them health, 'tis not for us to tell,
Though the head droops not, that the heart is well;
Or will you praise that homely, healthy fare,
Plenteous and plain, that happy peasants share?
Oh! trifle not with wants you cannot feel,
Nor mock the misery of a stinted meal;
Homely, not wholesome, plain, not plenteous, such　　　　　170
As you who praise would never deign to touch.
　　Ye gentle souls, who dream of rural ease,
Whom the smooth stream and smoother sonnet please:
Go! if the peaceful cot your praises share,
Go look within, and ask if peace be there;
If peace be his—that drooping weary sire,

Or theirs, that offspring round their feeble fire;
Or hers, that matron pale, whose trembling hand
Turns on the wretched hearth the expiring brand!
    Nor yet can time itself obtain for these   180
Life's latest comforts, due respect and ease;
For yonder see that hoary swain, whose age
Can with no cares except his own engage;
Who, propped on that rude staff, looks up to see
The bare arms broken from the withering tree,
On which, a boy, he climbed the loftiest bough,
Then his first joy, but his sad emblem now.
    He once was chief in all the rustic trade;
His steady hand the straightest furrow made;
Full many a prize he won, and still is proud   190
To find the triumphs of his youth allowed;
A transient pleasure sparkles in his eyes,
He hears and smiles, then thinks again and sighs:
For now he journeys to his grave in pain;
The rich disdain him; nay, the poor disdain:
Alternate masters now their slave command,
Urge the weak efforts of his feeble hand,
And, when his age attempts its task in vain,
With ruthless taunts, of lazy poor complain.
    Oft may you see him, when he tends the sheep,   200
His winter charge, beneath the hillock weep;
Oft hear him murmur to the winds that blow
O'er his white locks and bury them in snow,
When, roused by rage and muttering in the morn,
He mends the broken hedge with icy thorn:—
    "Why do I live, when I desire to be
At once from life and life's long labour free?
Like leaves in spring, the young are blown away,
Without the sorrows of a slow decay;
I, like yon withered leaf, remain behind,   210
Nipped by the frost and shivering in the wind;
There it abides till younger buds come on,
As I, now all my fellow-swains are gone;
Then, from the rising generation thrust,
It falls, like me, unnoticed to the dust.
    "These fruitful fields, these numerous flocks I see,
Are others' gain, but killing cares to me;
To me the children of my youth are lords,
Cool in their looks, but hasty in their words:
Wants of their own demand their care; and who   220
Feels his own want and succours others too?
A lonely, wretched man, in pain I go,
None need my help, and none relieve my woe;
Then let my bones beneath the turf be laid,
And men forget the wretch they would not aid."
    Thus groan the old, till, by disease oppressed,
They taste a final woe and then they rest.
    Theirs is yon house that holds the parish-poor,
Whose walls of mud scarce bear the broken door;
There, where the putrid vapours, flagging, play,   230
And the dull wheel hums doleful through the day;—

There children dwell who know no parents' care;
Parents who know no children's love, dwell there!
Heartbroken matrons on their joyless bed,
Forsaken wives, and mothers never wed;
Dejected widows with unheeded tears,
And crippled age with more than childhood fears;
The lame, the blind, and, far the happiest they!
The moping idiot and the madman gay.
Here too the sick their final doom receive,   240
Here brought, amid the scenes of grief, to grieve,
Where the loud groans from some sad chamber flow,
Mixed with the clamours of the crowd below;
Here, sorrowing, they each kindred sorrow scan,
And the cold charities of man to man:
Whose laws indeed for ruined age provide,
And strong compulsion plucks the scrap from pride;
But still that scrap is bought with many a sigh,
And pride embitters what it can't deny.
    Say ye, oppressed by some fantastic woes,   250
Some jarring nerve that baffles your repose;
Who press the downy couch, while slaves advance
With timid eye, to read the distant glance;
Who with sad prayers the weary doctor tease,
To name the nameless ever-new disease;
Who with mock patience dire complaints endure,
Which real pain and that alone can cure;
How would ye bear in real pain to lie,
Despised, neglected, left alone to die?
How would ye bear to draw your latest breath,   260
Where all that's wretched paves the way for death?
    Such is that room which one rude beam divides,
And naked rafters form the sloping sides;
Where the vile bands that bind the thatch are seen,
And lath and mud are all that lie between;
Save one dull pane, that, coarsely patched, gives way
To the rude tempest, yet excludes the day:
Here, on a matted flock, with dust o'erspread,
The drooping wretch reclines his languid head;
For him no hand the cordial cup applies,   270
Or wipes the tear that stagnates in his eyes;
No friends with soft discourse his pain beguile,
Or promise hope till sickness wears a smile.
    But soon a loud and hasty summons calls,
Shakes the thin roof, and echoes round the walls;
Anon, a figure enters, quaintly neat,
All pride and business, bustle and conceit;
With looks unaltered by these scenes of woe,
With speed that, entering, speaks his haste to go,
He bids the gazing throng around him fly,   280
And carries fate and physic in his eye:
A potent quack, long versed in human ills,
Who first insults the victim whom he kills;
Whose murderous hand a drowsy bench protect,
And whose most tender mercy is neglect.
    Paid by the parish for attendance here,

He wears contempt upon his sapient sneer;
In haste he seeks the bed where Misery lies,
Impatience marked in his averted eyes;
And, some habitual queries hurried o'er,   290
Without reply, he rushes on the door:
His drooping patient, long inured to pain,
And long unheeded, knows remonstrance vain;
He ceases now the feeble help to crave
Of man, and silent sinks into the grave.
 But ere his death some pious doubts arise,
Some simple fears, which "bold bad" men despise;
Fain would he ask the parish-priest to prove
His title certain to the joys above:
For this he sends the murmuring nurse, who calls 300
The holy stranger to these dismal walls.
And doth not he, the pious man, appear,
He, "passing rich with forty pounds a year?"
Ah! no; a shepherd of a different stock,
And far unlike him, feeds this little flock:
A jovial youth, who thinks his Sunday's task
As much as God or man can fairly ask;
The rest he gives to loves, and labours light,
To fields the morning, and to feasts the night;
None better skilled the noisy pack to guide, 310
To urge their chase, to cheer them or to chide;
A sportsman keen, he shoots through half the day,
And, skilled at whist, devotes the night to play:
Then, while such honours bloom around his head,
Shall he sit sadly by the sick man's bed,
To raise the hope he feels not, or with zeal
To combat fears that e'en the pious feel?
 Now once again the gloomy scene explore,
Less gloomy now; the bitter hour is o'er,
The man of many sorrows sighs no more.— 320
Up yonder hill, behold how sadly slow
The bier moves winding from the vale below;
There lie the happy dead, from trouble free,
And the glad parish pays the frugal fee.
No more, O Death! thy victim starts to hear
Churchwarden stern, or kingly overseer;
No more the farmer claims his humble bow,
Thou art his lord, the best of tyrants thou!
 Now to the church behold the mourners come,
Sedately torpid and devoutly dumb;
The village children now their games suspend,
To see the bier that bears their ancient friend;
For he was one in all their idle sport,
And like a monarch ruled their little court;
The pliant bow he formed, the flying ball,
The bat, the wicket, were his labours all;
Him now they follow to his grave, and stand
Silent and sad and gazing, hand in hand;
While bending low, their eager eyes explore
The mingled relics of the parish poor. 340
The bell tolls late, the moping owl flies round,

Fear marks the flight and magnifies the sound;
The busy priest, detained by weightier care,
Defers his duty till the day of prayer;
And, waiting long, the crowd retire distressed,
To think a poor man's bones should lie unblessed.

[1780–83, 1783]

THE PARISH REGISTER

From PART III. BURIALS

There was, 'tis said, and I believe, a time,
When humble Christians died with views sublime;
When all were ready for their faith to bleed,
But few to write or wrangle for their creed;
When lively Faith upheld the sinking heart,
And friends, assured to meet, prepared to part;
When Love felt hope, when Sorrow grew serene,
And all was comfort in the death-bed scene.
    Alas! when now the gloomy king they wait,
'Tis weakness yielding to resistless fate;   10
Like wretched men upon the ocean cast,
They labour hard and struggle to the last;
"Hope against hope," and wildly gaze around,
In search of help that never shall be found:
Nor, till the last strong billow stops the breath,
Will they believe them in the jaws of Death!
    When these my records I reflecting read,
And find what ills these numerous births succeed;
What powerful griefs these nuptial ties attend;
With what regret these painful journeys end;   20
When from the cradle to the grave I look,
Mine I conceive a melancholy book.
    Where now is perfect resignation seen?
Alas! it is not on the village-green:—
I've seldom known, though I have often read
Of happy peasants on their dying-bed;
Whose looks proclaimed that sunshine of the breast,
That more than hope, that Heaven itself expressed.
    What I behold are feverish fits of strife,
'Twixt fears of dying and desire of life: 30
Those earthly hopes, that to the last endure;
Those fears, that hopes superior fail to cure;
At best a sad submission to the doom,
Which, turning from the danger, lets it come.
    Sick lies the man, bewildered, lost, afraid,
His spirits vanquished and his strength decayed;
No hope the friend, the nurse, the doctor lend—
"Call then a priest, and fit him for his end."
A priest is called; 'tis now, alas! too late,
Death enters with him at the cottage-gate;   40
Or time allowed—he goes, assured to find
The self-commending, all-confiding mind;

And sighs to hear, what we may justly call
Death's commonplace, the train of thought in all.
   "True, I'm a sinner," feebly he begins,
"But trust in Mercy to forgive my sins:"
(Such cool confession no past crimes excite!
Such claim on Mercy seems the sinner's right!)
"I know mankind are frail, that God is just,
And pardons those who in his mercy trust;
We're sorely tempted in a world like this,
All men have done, and I like all, amiss;
But now, if spared, it is my full intent
On all the past to ponder and repent:
Wrongs against me I pardon great and small,
And if I die, I die in peace with all."
   His merits thus and not his sins confessed,
He speaks his hopes, and leaves to Heaven the rest.
Alas! are these the prospects, dull and cold,
That dying Christians to their priests unfold!
Or mends the prospect when the enthusiast cries,
"I die assured!" and in a rapture dies?
   Ah, where that humble, self-abasing mind,
With that confiding spirit, shall we find—
The mind that, feeling what repentance brings,
Dejection's terrors and Contrition's stings,
Feels then the hope, that mounts all care above,
And the pure joy that flows from pardoning love?
   Such have I seen in death, and much deplore,
So many dying—that I see no more:
Lo! now my records, where I grieve to trace,
How Death has triumphed in so short a space;
Who are the dead, how died they, I relate,
And snatch some portion of their acts from fate.
   With Andrew Collett we the year begin,
The blind, fat landlord of the Old Crown Inn,—
Big as his butt, and, for the self-same use,
To take in stores of strong fermenting juice.
On his huge chair beside the fire he sate,
In revel chief, and umpire in debate;
Each night his string of vulgar tales he told;
When ale was cheap and bachelors were bold:
His heroes all were famous in their days,
Cheats were his boast and drunkards had his praise;
"One, in three draughts, three mugs of ale took down,
As mugs were then—the champion of the Crown;
For thrice three days another lived on ale,
And knew no change but that of mild and stale;
Two thirsty soakers watched a vessel's side,
When he the tap with dexterous hand applied;
Nor from their seats departed till they found
That butt was out and heard the mournful sound."
   He praised a poacher, precious child of fun!
Who shot the keeper with his own spring-gun;
Nor less the smuggler who the exciseman tied,
And left him hanging at the birch-wood side,
There to expire;—but one who saw him hang

Cut the good cord—a traitor of the gang.
　His own exploits with boastful glee he told,
What ponds he emptied and what pikes he sold;　　　　　　100
And how, when blessed with sight alert and gay,
The night's amusements kept him through the day.
　He sang the praises of those times, when all
"For cards and dice, as for their drink, might call;
When justice winked on every jovial crew,
And ten-pins tumbled in the parson's view."
　He told, when angry wives, provoked to rail,
Or drive a third-day drunkard from his ale,
What were his triumphs, and how great the skill
That won the vexed virago to his will;　　　　　　　　110
Who raving came;—then talked in milder strain,—
Then wept, then drank, and pledged her spouse again.
　　Such were his themes: how knaves o'er laws prevail,
Or, when made captives, how they fly from jail;
The young how brave, how subtle were the old:
And oaths attested all that Folly told.
　On death like his what name shall we bestow,
So very sudden! yet so very slow?
'Twas slow:—Disease, augmenting year by year,
Showed the grim king by gradual steps brought near:　120
'Twas not less sudden; in the night he died,
He drank, he swore, he jested, and he lied;
Thus aiding folly with departing breath:—
"Beware, Lorenzo, the slow-sudden death."
　Next died the Widow Goe, an active dame,
Famed ten miles round, and worthy all her fame;
She lost her husband when their loves were young,
But kept her farm, her credit, and her tongue:
Full thirty years she ruled with matchless skill,
With guiding judgment and resistless will;　　　　　130
Advice she scorned, rebellions she suppressed,
And sons and servants bowed at her behest.
Like that great man's, who to his Saviour came,
Were the strong words of this commanding dame;—
"Come," if she said, they came; it "go," were gone;
And if "do this,"—that instant it was done.
Her maidens told she was all eye and ear,
In darkness saw and could at distance hear;—
No parish-business in the place could stir,
Without direction or assent from her;　　　　　　　140
In turn she took each office as it fell,
Knew all their duties, and discharged them well;
The lazy vagrants in her presence shook,
And pregnant damsels feared her stern rebuke;
She looked on want with judgment clear and cool,
And felt with reason and bestowed by rule;
She matched both sons and daughters to her mind,
And lent them eyes, for Love, she heard, was blind;
Yet ceaseless still she throve, alert, alive,
The working bee, in full or empty hive;　　　　　　150
Busy and careful, like that working bee,
No time for love nor tender cares had she;

But when our farmers made their amorous vows,
She :alked of market-streets and patent ploughs.
Not unemployed her evenings passed away,
Amusement closed, as business waked the day;
When to her toilet's brief concern she ran,
And conversation with her friends began,
Who all were welcome, what they saw, to share;
And joyous neighbours praised her Christmas fare,   160
That none around might, in their scorn, complain
Of Gossip Goe as greedy in her gain.
    Thus long she reigned, admired, if not approved;
Praised, if not honoured; feared, if not beloved;—
When, as the busy days of spring drew near,
That called for all the forecast of the year;
When lively hope the rising crops surveyed,
And April promised what September paid;
When strayed her lambs where gorse and greenweed grow;
When rose her grass in richer vales below;   170
When pleased she looked on all the smiling land,
And viewed the hinds who wrought at her command;
(Poultry in groups still followed where she went;)
Then dread o'ercame her,—that her days were spent.
"Bless me! I die, and not a warning given,—
With much to do on earth, and all for Heaven!—
No reparation for my soul's affairs,
No leave petitioned for the barn's repairs;
Accounts perplexed, my interest yet unpaid,
My mind unsettled, and my will unmade;—   180
A lawyer haste, and in your way, a priest;
And let me die in one good work at least."
She spake, and, trembling, dropped upon her knees,
Heaven in her eye and in her hand her keys;
And still the more she found her life decay,
With greater force she grasped those signs of sway:
Then fell and died!—In haste her sons drew near,
And dropped, in haste, the tributary tear,
Then from the adhering clasp the keys unbound,
And consolation for their sorrow found.   190
    · · · · · ·
    Down by the church-way walk and where the brook
Winds round the chancel like a shepherd's crook;
In that small house, with those green pales before,
Where jasmine trails on either side the door;
Where those dark shrubs that now grow wild at will,
Were clipped in form and tantalized with skill;
Where cockles blanched and pebbles neatly spread,
Formed shining borders for the larkspurs' bed;—
There lived a lady, wise, austere, and nice,
Who showed her virtue by her scorn of vice;   200
In the dear fashions of her youth she dressed,
A pea-green joseph[1] was her favourite vest;
Erect she stood, she walked with stately mien,
Tight was her length of stays, and she was tall and lean.
    There long she lived in maiden state immured,

[1] riding coat.

From looks of love and treacherous man secured;
Though evil fame (but that was long before)
Had blown her dubious blast at Catherine's door:
A Captain thither, rich from India came,
And though a cousin called, it touched her fame; 210
Her annual stipend rose from his behest,
And all the long-prized treasures she possessed:—
If aught like joy awhile appeared to stay
In that stern face, and chase those frowns away,
'Twas when her treasures she disposed for view,
And heard the praises to their splendour due;
Silks beyond price, so rich, they'd stand alone,
And diamonds blazing on the buckled zone;
Rows of rare pearls by curious workmen set,
And bracelets fair in box of glossy jet; 220
Bright polished amber precious from its size,
Or forms the fairest fancy could devise:
Her drawers of cedar, shut with secret springs,
Concealed the watch of gold and rubied rings;
Letters, long proofs of love, and verses fine
Round the pinked rims of crisped valentine
Her china-closet, cause of daily care,
For woman's wonder held her pencilled ware;
That pictured wealth of China and Japan,
Like its cold mistress, shunned the eye of man. 230
    Her neat small room, adorned with maiden-taste,
A clipped French puppy, first of favourites, graced:
A parrot next, but dead and stuffed with art;
(For Poll, when living, lost the Lady's heart,
And then his life; for he was heard to speak
Such frightful words as tinged his Lady's cheek:)
Unhappy bird! who had no power to prove,
Save by such speech, his gratitude and love.
A grey old cat his whiskers licked beside;
A type of sadness in the house of pride. 240
The polished surface of an India chest,
A glassy globe, in frame of ivory, pressed;
Where swam two finny creatures; one of gold,
Of silver one; both beauteous to behold:—
All these were formed the guiding taste to suit;
The beasts well-mannered and the fishes mute.
A widowed aunt was there, compelled by need
The nymph to flatter and her tribe to feed;
Who, veiling well her scorn, endured the clog,
Mute as the fish and fawning as the dog. 250
    As years increased, these treasures, her delight,
Arose in value in their owner's sight:
A miser knows that, view it as he will,
A guinea kept is but a guinea still;
And so he puts it to its proper use,
That something more this guinea may produce:
But silks and rings, in the possessor's eyes,
The oftener seen, the more in value rise,
And thus are wisely hoarded to bestow
The kind of pleasure that with years will grow. 260

But what availed their worth—if worth had they,—
In the sad summer of her slow decay?
Then we beheld her turn an anxious look
From trunks and chests, and fix it on her book,—
A rich-bound Book of Prayer the Captain gave,
(Some Princess had it, or was said to have;)
And then once more, on all her stores, look round,
And draw a sigh so piteous and profound,
That told, "Alas! how hard from these to part,
And for new hopes and habits form the heart!   20
What shall I do," she cried, "my peace of mind
To gain in dying, and to die resigned?"
"Hear," we returned; "these baubles cast aside,
Nor give thy God a rival in thy pride;
Thy closets shut, and ope thy kitchen's door;
There own thy failings, here invite the poor;
A friend of Mammon let thy bounty make;
For widows' prayers, thy vanities forsake;
And let the hungry, of thy pride, partake:
Then shall thy inward eye with joy survey   30
The angel Mercy tempering Death's delay!"
      Alas! 'twas hard; the treasures still had charms,
Hope still its flattery, sickness its alarms;
Still was the same unsettled, clouded view,
And the same plaintive cry, "What shall I do?"
      Nor change appeared: for when her race was run,
Doubtful we all exclaimed, "What has been done?"
Apart she lived, and still she lies alone;
Yon earthly heap awaits the flattering stone,
On which invention shall be long employed,   40
To show the various worth of Catherine Lloyd.
      Next to these ladies, but in nought allied,
A noble Peasant, Isaac Ashford, died.
Noble he was, contemning all things mean,
His truth unquestioned and his soul serene:
Of no man's presence Isaac felt afraid;
At no man's question Isaac looked dismayed:
Shame knew him not, he dreaded no disgrace;
Truth, simple truth, was written in his face;
Yet while the serious thought his soul approved,   50
Cheerful he seemed, and gentleness he loved:
To bliss domestic he his heart resigned,
And, with the firmest, had the fondest mind:
Were others joyful, he looked smiling on,
And gave allowance where he needed none;
Good he refused with future ill to buy,
Nor knew a joy that caused reflection's sigh,
A friend to virtue, his unclouded breast
No envy stung, no jealousy distressed;
(Bane of the poor! it wounds their weaker mind,   60
To miss one favour which their neighbours find:)
Yet far was he from stoic pride removed;
He felt humanely, and he warmly loved:
I marked his action, when his infant died,
And his old neighbour for offence was tried;

The still tears, stealing down that furrowed cheek,
Spoke pity plainer than the tongue can speak.
If pride were his, 'twas not their vulgar pride,
Who, in their base contempt, the great deride;
Nor pride in learning,—though my clerk agreed,　　　320
If fate should call him, Ashford might succeed;
Nor pride in rustic skill, although we knew
None his superior, and his equals few:—
But if that spirit in his soul had place,
It was the jealous pride that shuns disgrace;
A pride in honest fame, by virtue gained,
In sturdy boys to virtuous labours trained;
Pride in the power that guards his country's coast,
And all that Englishmen enjoy and boast;
Pride in a life that slander's tongue defied,—　　　330
In fact, a noble passion, misnamed pride.
　　He had no party's rage, no sectary's whim;
Christian and countryman was all with him:
True to his church he came; no Sunday shower
Kept him at home in that important hour;
Nor his firm feet could one persuading sect,
By the strong glare of their new light, direct;—
"On hope, in mine own sober light, I gaze,
But should be blind and lose it in your blaze."
　　In times severe, when many a sturdy swain　　　340
Felt it his pride, his comfort, to complain;
Isaac their wants would soothe, his own would hide,
And feel in that his comfort and his pride.
　　At length he found, when seventy years were run,
His strength departed and his labour done;
When he, save honest fame, retained no more,
But lost his wife and saw his children poor:
'Twas then, a spark of—say not discontent—
Struck on his mind, and thus he gave it vent:
　　"Kind are your laws, ('tis not to be denied,)　　　350
That in yon house, for ruined age, provide,
And they are just;—when young, we give you all,
And for assistance in our weakness call.—
Why then this proud reluctance to be fed,
To join your poor, and eat the parish-bread?
But yet I linger, loth with him to feed,
Who gains his plenty by the sons of need;
He who by contract all your paupers took,
And gauges stomachs with an anxious look:
On some old master I could well depend;　　　360
See him with joy and thank him as a friend;
But ill on him, who doles the day's supply,
And counts our chances, who at night may die:
Yet help me, Heaven! and let me not complain
Of what I suffer, but my fate sustain."
　　Such were his thoughts, and so resigned he grew;
Daily he placed the workhouse in his view!
But came not there, for sudden was his fate,
He dropped, expiring, at his cottage-gate.
　　I feel his absence in the hours of prayer,　　　370

And view his seat and sigh for Isaac there:
I see no more those white locks thinly spread
Round the bald polish of that honoured head,
No more that awful glance on playful wight,
Compelled to kneel and tremble at the sight,
To fold his fingers, all in dread the while,
Till Mister Ashford softened to a smile;
No more that meek and suppliant look in prayer,
Nor the pure faith (to give it force), are there:—
But he is blessed, and I lament no more   380
A wise good man contented to be poor.

[1807]

THE LETTERS OF JUNIUS (1769-1772)

On January 21, 1769, there appeared in *The Public Advertiser*, the foremost newspaper of London, a letter signed "Junius," the first of a series over a period of two years. The authorship was a secret, unknown even to Woodfall, the editor of the paper. The letters were a mixture of politics and personal scandal, aiming to expose the Duke of Grafton, then prime minister, and his political associates, including the fourth Duke of Bedford. They became a national sensation; and although Junius sometimes paints his villains with too deep a dye, he appears on the whole to have been extraordinarily well informed, and in some way or other he gained access to closely guarded secrets of government offices, of exclusive political and sporting circles, and even of the private lives of important political characters. Letter after letter was delivered by mysterious ways to the editor, but the government, failing even to find a trace of the author or his emissaries, was helpless. "How comes this Junius," asked Burke in the House of Commons, "to have broke through the cobwebs of the law, and to range uncontrolled, unpunished, through the land? The myrmidons of the court have been long, and are still, pursuing him in vain. They will not spend their time upon me, or you, or you. No; they disdain such vermin when the mighty boar of the forest, that has broke through all their toils, is before them. But what will their efforts avail? No sooner has he wounded one than he lays down another dead at his feet. . . . King, lords, and commons are but the sport of his fury." Many theories were current at the time as to who Junius was; Burke himself was mentioned, and among many others the Earl of Chesterfield, John Wilkes, the Earl of Shelburne, and Horace Walpole. A great deal of evidence points to Sir Philip Francis, then a clerk in the War Office, as the man, but even this attribution is not free from difficulties. In a famous passage in *The Vision of Judgment* Byron expressed the plausible conclusion that *no one* wrote the letters of Junius.

It was necessary to cloak the authorship with such secrecy, for Junius was conducting nothing less than an appeal to the public conscience and to public opinion against the corrupt political system fostered by George III. This monarch had been brought up by his mother and a Scotch peer, Lord Bute (the son-in-law of Lady Mary Wortley Montagu), in the political principles of Bolingbroke's *Patriot King*. He had been taught to believe that the crown could and should be the dominant influence in English politics, and he appointed a succession of subservient ministries to put his policies in effect. Power was placed in the hands of cliques, the Commons was managed by means of corruption, and the country was alarmed by the repeated violations of the spirit of the English constitution. These unhappy developments reached a climax in 1769, when the government prevented John Wilkes, duly elected member for Middlesex, from taking his seat in the House of Commons. Burke laid bare the evils inherent in the system in his *Thoughts on the Present Discontents* (1770); Junius raised the same fundamental political issues as Burke, but he also relied heavily on personalities and revelations of disreputable conduct in the inner circle of the King's political minions.

John Russell, the fourth Duke of Bedford, to whose son Burke addressed years later his invective in his *Letter to a Noble Lord* (1796), was one of the most pliable of the royal agents. Although he was enormously wealthy, he was always ready to lend his influence to his office-seeking followers, who were dubbed the "Bloomsbury gang" after the family estates in the Bloomsbury section of London. The public had no confidence in the Duke. After he had negotiated the peace with France in 1763, it was rumored that he had been bribed by the French court. In one political campaign stones were hurled at him in a village street and he was hunted out of town with a pack of bull-dogs. Junius points out the wide difference between an imaginary "independent, virtuous Duke of Bedford" and the deplorable lack of dignity and character displayed by the actual fourth Duke.

The so-called "address to the king" is not an open letter, but merely an imaginary address such as might be made "if an honest man were permitted to approach a king." This framework only adds to the sting of the satire, which invites comparison with Pope's *Epistle to Augustus,* addressed to George II. Both writers knew how to combine an exterior of cool respect with an undertone of indignation and contempt.

The best edition of Junius is by John Wade (2 vols., 1850). An excellent examination of some of the more important theories as to his identity may be found in Charles Wentworth Dilke's *Papers of a Critic* (1875). For an interesting account of the period the reader may turn to a classic of biography, *The Early History of Charles James Fox,* by George O. Trevelyan.

LETTERS

LETTER XXIII. TO HIS GRACE THE DUKE OF BEDFORD

September 19, 1769.

My Lord,

You are so little accustomed to receive any marks of respect or esteem from the public, that if in the following lines a compliment or expression of applause should escape me, I fear you would consider it as a mockery of your established character, and perhaps an insult to your understanding. You have nice feelings, my Lord, if we may judge from your resentments. Cautious, therefore, of giving offence where you have so little deserved it, I shall leave the illustration of your virtues to other hands. Your friends have a privilege to play upon the easiness of your temper, or possibly they are better acquainted with your good qualities than I am. You have done good by stealth. The rest is upon record. You have left ample room for speculation when panegyric is exhausted.

You are indeed a very considerable man. The highest rank, a splendid fortune, and a name, glorious till it was yours, were sufficient to have supported you with meaner abilities than I think you possess. From the first, you derived a constitutional claim to respect; from the second, a natural extensive authority; the last created a partial expectation of hereditary virtues. The use you have made of these uncommon advantages might have been more honourable to yourself, but could not be more instructive to mankind. We may trace it in the veneration of your country, the choice of your friends, and in the accomplish-

ment of every sanguine hope which the public might have conceived from the illustrious name of Russell.

The eminence of your station gave you a commanding prospect of your duty. The road which led to honour was open to your view. You could not lose it by mistake, and you had no temptation to depart from it by design. Compare the natural dignity and importance of the richest peer of England—the noble independence which he might have maintained in Parliament, and the real interest and respect which he might have acquired, not only in Parliament, but through the whole kingdom—compare these glorious distinctions with the ambition of holding a share in government, the emoluments of a place, the sale of a borough, or the purchase of a corporation, and though you may not regret the virtues which create respect, you may see with anguish how much real importance and authority you have lost. Consider the character of an independent, virtuous Duke of Bedford; imagine what he might be in this country, then reflect one moment upon what you are. If it be possible for me to withdraw my attention from the fact, I will tell you in theory what such a man might be.

Conscious of his own weight and importance, his conduct in Parliament would be directed by nothing but the constitutional duty of a peer. He would consider himself as a guardian of the laws. Willing to support the just measures of government, but determined to observe the conduct of the minister with suspicion, he would oppose the violence of faction with as much firmness as the encroachments of prerogative. He would be as little capable of bargaining with the minister for places for himself or his dependents as of descending to mix himself in the intrigues of opposition. Whenever an important question called for his opinion in Parliament, he would be heard by the most profligate minister with deference and respect. His authority would either sanctify or disgrace the measures of government. The people would look up to him as their protector, and a virtuous prince would have one honest man in his dominions in whose integrity and judgment he might safely confide. If it should be the will of Providence to afflict him with a domestic misfortune, he would submit to the stroke with feeling, but not without dignity. He would consider the people as his children, and receive a generous heartfelt consolation in the sympathising tears and blessings of his country.

Your Grace may probably discover something more intelligible in the negative part of this illustrious character. The man I have described would never prostitute his dignity in Parliament by an indecent violence either in opposing or defending a minister. He would not at one moment rancorously persecute, at another basely cringe to, the favourite of his sovereign. After outraging the royal dignity with peremptory conditions little short of menace and hostility, he would never descend to the humility of soliciting an interview with the favourite, and of offering to recover, at any price, the honour of his friendship. Though deceived, perhaps, in his youth, he would not, through the course of a long life, have invariably chosen his friends from among the most profligate of mankind. His own honour would have forbidden him from mixing his private pleasures or conversation with jockeys, gamesters, blasphemers, gladiators, or buffoons. He would then have never felt, much less would he have submitted to, the humiliating, dishonest necessity of engaging in the interest and intrigues of his dependents, of supplying their vices, or relieving their beggary, at the expense of his country. He would not have betrayed such ignorance or such contempt of the constitution as openly to avow, in a court of justice, the purchase and sale of a borough. He would not have thought it consistent with his rank in the state, or even with his personal importance, to be the little tyrant of a little corporation. He would never have been insulted with virtues which he had laboured to extinguish, nor suffered the disgrace of a mortifying defeat which has made him ridiculous and contemptible even to the few by whom he was not detested. I reverence the afflictions of a good man—his sorrows are sacred. But how can we take part in the distresses of a man whom we can neither love nor esteem; or feel for a calamity of which he himself is insensible? Where was the father's heart when he could look for, or find an immediate consolation for the loss of an only son, in consultations and bargains for a place at court, and even in the misery of balloting at the India House!

Admitting, then, that you have mistaken or deserted those honourable principles which ought to have directed your conduct, admitting that you have as little claim to private affection as to public esteem, let us see with what abilities, with what degree of judgment, you have carried your own system into execution. A great man in the success, and even in the magnitude, of his crimes finds a rescue from contempt. Your Grace is in every way unfortunate. Yet I will not look back to those ridiculous scenes by which, in your earlier days, you thought it an honour to be distinguished—the recorded stripes, the public infamy, your own sufferings, or Mr. Rigby's fortitude. These events undoubtedly left an impression, though not upon your mind. To *such* a mind it may, perhaps, be a pleasure to reflect that there is hardly a corner of any of His Majesty's kingdoms, except France, in which at one time or another, your valuable life has not been in danger. Amiable man! we see and acknowledge the protection of Providence, by which you have so often escaped the personal detestation of your fellow-subjects, and are still reserved for the public justice of your country.

Your history begins to be important at that auspicious period at which you were deputed to represent the Earl of Bute at the court of Versailles. It was an honourable office, and executed with the same spirit with which it was accepted. Your patrons wanted an ambassador who would submit to make concessions without daring to insist upon any honourable condition for his sovereign. Their business required a man who had as little feeling for his own dignity as for the welfare of his country; and they found him in the first rank of the nobility. Belleisle, Goree, Guadaloupe, St. Louis, Martinique, the Fishery, and the Havana, are glorious monuments of your Grace's talents for negotiation. My Lord, we are too well acquainted with your pecuniary character to think it possible that so many public sacrifices should be made without some private compensations. Your conduct carries with it an internal evidence beyond all the legal proofs of justice. Even the callous pride of Lord Egremont was alarmed. He saw and felt his own dishonour in corresponding with you; and there certainly was a moment at which he meant to have resisted, had not a fatal lethargy prevailed over his faculties, and carried all sense and memory away with it.

I will not pretend to specify the secret terms on which you were invited to support an administration which Lord Bute pretended to leave in full possession of their ministerial authority, and perfectly masters of themselves. He was not of a temper to relinquish power, though he retired from employment. Stipulations were certainly made between your Grace and him, and certainly violated. After two years submission, you thought

you had collected a strength sufficient to control his influence, and that it was your turn to be a tyrant, because you had been a slave. When you found yourself mistaken in your opinion of your gracious master's firmness, disappointment got the better of all your humble discretion, and carried you to an excess of outrage to his person, as distant from true spirit, as from all decency and respect. After robbing him of the rights of a king, you would not permit him to preserve the honour of a gentleman. It was then Lord Weymouth was nominated to Ireland, and dispatched (we well remember with what indecent hurry) to plunder the treasury of the first fruits of an employment which you well knew he was never to execute.

This sudden declaration of war against the favourite might have given you a momentary merit with the public, if it had either been adopted upon principle, or maintained with resolution. Without looking back to all your former servility, we need only observe your subsequent conduct to see upon what motives you acted. Apparently united with Mr. Grenville, you waited until Lord Rockingham's feeble administration should dissolve in its own weakness. The moment their dismission was suspected, the moment you perceived that another system was adopted in the closet, you thought it no disgrace to return to your former dependence, and solicit once more the friendship of Lord Bute. You begged an interview, at which he had spirit enough to treat you with contempt.

It would now be of little use to point out by what a train of weak, injudicious measures it became necessary, or was thought so, to call you back to a share in the administration. The friends, whom you did not in the last instance desert, were not of a character to add strength or credit to government, and at that time your alliance with the Duke of Grafton was, I presume, hardly foreseen. We must look for other stipulations to account for that sudden resolution of the closet, by which three of your dependants (whose characters, I think, cannot be less respected than they are) were advanced to offices through which you might again control the minister, and probably engross the whole direction of affairs.

The possession of absolute power is now once more within your reach. The measures you have taken to obtain and confirm it, are too gross to escape the eyes of a discerning, judicious prince. His palace is besieged; the lines of circumvallation are drawing round him; and unless he finds a resource in his own activity, or in the attachment of the real friends of his family, the best of princes must submit to the confinement of a state prisoner until your Grace's death or some less fortunate event shall raise the siege. For the present, you may safely resume that style of insult and menace which even a private gentleman cannot submit to hear without being contemptible. Mr. Mackenzie's history is not yet forgotten, and you may find precedents enough of the mode in which an imperious subject may signify his pleasures to his sovereign. Where will this gracious monarch look for assistance, when the wretched Grafton could forget his obligations to his master, and desert him for a hollow alliance with *such* a man as the Duke of Bedford!

Let us consider you, then, as arrived at the summit of worldly greatness; let us suppose that all your plans of avarice and ambition are accomplished, and your most sanguine wishes gratified in the fear as well as the hatred of the people. Can age itself forget that you are now in the last act of life? Can grey hairs make folly venerable? and is there no period to be reserved for meditation and retirement? For shame! my Lord: let it not be recorded of you, that the latest moments of your life were dedicated to the same unworthy pursuits, the same busy agitations, in which your youth and manhood were exhausted. Consider that, although you cannot disgrace your former life, you are violating the character of age, and exposing the impotent imbecility, after you have lost the vigour, of the passions.

Your friends will ask, perhaps, Whither shall this unhappy old man retire? Can he remain in the metropolis, where his life has been so often threatened, and his palace so often attacked? If he returns to Woburn, scorn and mockery await him. He must create a solitude round his estate, if he would avoid the face of reproach and derision. At Plymouth, his destruction would be more than probable: at Exeter, inevitable. No honest Englishman will ever forget his attachment, nor any honest Scotchman forgive his treachery, to Lord Bute. At every town he enters he must change his liveries and his name. Which ever way he flies, the *Hue and Cry* of the country pursues him.

In another kingdom, indeed, the blessings of his administration have been more sensibly felt; his virtues better understood; or at worst, they will not, for him alone, forget their hospitality. As well might Verres have returned to Sicily. You have twice escaped, my Lord; beware of a third experiment. The indignation of a whole people, plundered, insulted, and oppressed as they have been, will not always be disappointed.

It is in vain therefore to shift the scene. You can no more fly from your enemies than from yourself. Persecuted abroad, you look into your own heart for consolation, and find nothing but reproaches and despair. But, my Lord, you may quit the field of business, though not the field of danger; and though you cannot be safe, you may cease to be ridiculous. I fear you have listened too long to the advice of those pernicious friends with whose interests you have sordidly united your own, and for whom you have sacrificed everything that ought to be dear to a man of honour. They are still base enough to encourage the follies of your age, as they once did

the vices of your youth. As little acquainted with the rules of decorum as
with the laws of morality, they will
not suffer you to profit by experience,
nor even to consult the propriety of a
bad character. Even now they tell you,
that life is no more than a dramatic
scene, in which the hero should preserve his consistency to the last, and
that, as you live without virtue, you
should die without repentance.

JUNIUS.

LETTER XXXV. TO THE PUBLIC
ADVERTISER

(ADDRESS TO THE KING)

December 19, 1769.
When the complaints of a brave
and powerful people are observed to
increase in proportion to the wrongs
they have suffered; when, instead of
sinking into submission, they are
roused to resistance, the time will soon
arrive at which every inferior consideration must yield to the security of
the sovereign, and to the general
safety of the state. There is a moment
of difficulty and danger at which flattery and falsehood can no longer deceive, and simplicity itself can no
longer be misled. Let us suppose it
arrived. Let us suppose a gracious,
well-intentioned prince, made sensible
at last of the great duty he owes to his
people, and of his own disgraceful
situation—that he looks round him for
assistance, and asks for no advice but
how to gratify the wishes and secure
the happiness of his subjects. In these
circumstances, it may be a matter of
curious SPECULATION to consider if an
honest man were permitted to approach a king, in what terms he would
address himself to his sovereign. Let it
be imagined, no matter how improbable, that the first prejudice against
his character is removed, that the
ceremonious difficulties of an audience are surmounted, that he feels
himself animated by the purest and
most honourable affections to his king

and country, and that the great person
whom he addresses has spirit enough
to bid him speak freely, and understanding enough to listen to him with
attention. Unacquainted with the
vain impertinence of forms, he would
deliver his sentiments with dignity
and firmness, but not without respect.

Sir,—It is the misfortune of your
life, and originally the cause of every
reproach and distress which has attended your government, that you
should never have been acquainted
with the language of truth until you
heard it in the complaints of your
people. It is not, however, too late to
correct the error of your education.
We are still inclined to make an indulgent allowance for the pernicious
lessons you received in your youth,
and to form the most sanguine hopes
from the natural benevolence of your
disposition. We are far from thinking you capable of a direct, deliberate purpose to invade those original
rights of your subjects on which all
their civil and political liberties depend. Had it been possible for us to
entertain a suspicion so dishonourable to your character, we should long
since have adopted a style of remonstrance very distant from the humility
of complaint. The doctrine inculcated
by our laws, *That the king can do no
wrong*, is admitted without reluctance. We separate the amiable, good-
natured prince from the folly and
treachery of his servants, and the private virtues of the man from the vices
of his government. Were it not for this
just distinction, I know not whether
your Majesty's condition or that of
the English nation would deserve
most to be lamented. I would prepare
your mind for a favourable reception
of truth by removing every painful,
offensive idea of personal reproach.
Your subjects, Sir, wish for nothing
but that, as *they* are reasonable and
affectionate enough to separate your
person from your government, so *you*,
in your turn, should distinguish between the conduct which becomes the
permanent dignity of a king and that

which serves only to promote the temporary interest and miserable ambition of a minister.

You ascended the throne with a declared and, I doubt not, a sincere resolution of giving universal satisfaction to your subjects. You found them pleased with the novelty of a young prince whose countenance promised even more than his words, and loyal to you not only from principle but passion. It was not a cold profession of allegiance to the first magistrate, but a partial, animated attachment to a favourite prince, the native of their country. They did not await to examine your conduct, nor to be determined by experience, but gave you a generous credit for the future blessings of your reign, and paid you in advance the dearest tribute of their affections. Such, Sir, was once the disposition of a people who now surround your throne with reproaches and complaints. Do justice to yourself. Banish from your mind those unworthy opinions with which some interested persons have laboured to possess you. Distrust the men who tell you that the English are naturally light and inconstant—that they complain without a cause. Withdraw your confidence equally from all parties— from ministers, favourites, and relations; and let there be one moment in your life in which you have consulted your own understanding.

When you affectedly renounced the name of Englishman, believe me, Sir, you were persuaded to pay a very ill-judged compliment to one part of your subjects at the expense of another. While the natives of Scotland are not in actual rebellion, they are undoubtedly entitled to protection, nor do I mean to condemn the policy of giving some encouragement to the novelty of their affections for the house of Hanover. I am ready to hope for everything from their newborn zeal, and from the future steadiness of their allegiance. But hitherto they have no claim to your favour. To honour them with a determined pre-

dilection and confidence, in exclusion of your English subjects who placed your family, and in spite of treachery and rebellion have supported it, upon the throne, is a mistake too gross even for the unsuspecting generosity of youth. In this error we see a capital violation of the most obvious rules of policy and prudence. We trace it, however, to an original bias in your education, and are ready to allow for your inexperience.

To the same early influence we attribute it that you have descended to take a share not only in the narrow views and interests of particular persons, but in the fatal malignity of their passions. At your accession to the throne the whole system of government was altered, not from wisdom or deliberation, but because it had been adopted by your predecessor. A little personal motive of pique and resentment was sufficient to remove the ablest servants of the crown; but it is not in this country, Sir, that such men can be dishonoured by the frowns of a king. They were dismissed, but could not be disgraced. Without entering into a minuter discussion of the merits of the peace, we may observe, in the imprudent hurry with which the first overtures from France were accepted, in the conduct of the negotiation, and terms of the treaty, the strongest marks of that precipitate spirit of concession with which a certain part of your subjects have been at all times ready to purchase a peace with the *natural enemies* of this country. On *your* part we are satisfied that everything was honourable and sincere, and if England was sold to France, we doubt not that your Majesty was equally betrayed. The conditions of the peace were matter of grief and surprise to your subjects, but not the immediate cause of their present discontent.

Hitherto, Sir, you had been sacrificed to the prejudices and passions of others. With what firmness will you bear the mention of your own?

A man, not very honourably distinguished in the world, commences a formal attack upon your favourite, considering nothing but how he might best expose his person and principles to detestation, and the national character of his countrymen to contempt. The natives of that country, Sir, are as much distinguished by a peculiar character as by your Majesty's favour. Like another chosen people, they have been conducted into the land of plenty, where they find themselves effectually marked, and divided from mankind. There is hardly a period at which the most irregular character may not be redeemed. The mistakes of one sex find a retreat in patriotism; those of the other in devotion. Mr. Wilkes brought with him into politics the same liberal sentiments by which his private conduct had been directed, and seemed to think, that as there are few excesses in which an English gentleman may not be permitted to indulge, the same latitude was allowed him in the choice of his political principles, and in the spirit of maintaining them. I mean to state, not to defend, his conduct. In the earnestness of his zeal he suffered some unwarrantable insinuations to escape him. He said more than moderate men would justify, but not enough to entitle him to your Majesty's personal resentment. The rays of royal indignation collected upon him served only to illuminate, and could not consume. Animated by the favour of the people on one side, and heated by persecution on the other, his views and sentiments changed with his situation. Hardly serious at first, he is now an enthusiast. The coldest bodies warm with opposition, the hardest sparkle in collision. There is a holy mistaken zeal in politics as well as in religion. By persuading others, we convince ourselves. The passions are engaged, and create a maternal affection in the mind, which forces us to love the cause for which we suffer. Is this a contention worthy of a king? Are you not sensible how much the meanness of the cause gives an air of ridicule to

the serious difficulties into which you have been betrayed? the destruction of one man has been now for many years the sole object of your government; and if there can be anything still more disgraceful, we have seen for such an object the utmost influence of the executive power and every ministerial artifice exerted, without success. Nor can you ever succeed, unless *he* should be imprudent enough to forfeit the protection of those laws to which you owe your crown, or unless your ministers should persuade you to make it a question of force alone, and try the whole strength of government in opposition to the people. The lessons *he* has received from experience, will probably guard him from such excess of folly, and in your Majesty's virtues we find an unquestionable assurance that no illegal violence will be attempted.

Far from suspecting you of so horrible a design, we would attribute the continued violation of the laws, and even this last enormous attack upon the vital principles of the constitution, to an ill-advised, unworthy personal resentment. From one false step you have been betrayed into another, and as the cause was unworthy of you, your ministers were determined that the prudence of the execution should correspond with the wisdom and dignity of the design. They have reduced you to the necessity of choosing out of a variety of difficulties—to a situation so unhappy, that you can neither do wrong without ruin, nor right without affliction. These worthy servants have undoubtedly given you many singular proofs of their abilities. Not contented with making Mr. Wilkes a man of importance, they have judiciously transferred the question from the rights and interests of one man to the most important rights and interests of the people, and forced your subjects, from wishing well to the cause of an individual, to unite with him in their own. Let them proceed as they have begun, and your Majesty need not doubt that the catastrophe will do no dishonour to the conduct of the piece.

The circumstances to which you are reduced will not admit of a compromise with the English nation. Undecisive, qualifying measures will disgrace your government still more than open violence, and without satisfying the people will excite their contempt. They have too much understanding and spirit to accept of an indirect satisfaction for a direct injury. Nothing less than a repeal, as formal as the resolution itself, can heal the wound which has been given to the constitution, nor will anything less be accepted. I can readily believe that there is an influence sufficient to recall that pernicious vote. The House of Commons undoubtedly consider their duty to the crown as paramount to all other obligations. To *us* they are only indebted for an accidental existence, and have justly transferred their gratitude from their parents to their benefactors—from those who gave them birth to the minister from whose benevolence they derive the comforts and pleasures of their political life, who has taken the tenderest care of their infancy, and relieves their necessities without offending their delicacy. But, if it were possible for their integrity to be degraded to a condition so vile and abject that, compared with it, the present estimation they stand in is a state of honour and respect, consider, Sir, in what manner you will afterwards proceed. Can you conceive that the people of this country will long submit to be governed by so flexible a House of Commons? It is not in the nature of human society that any form of government, in such circumstances, can long be preserved. In ours, the general contempt of the people is as fatal as their detestation. Such, I am persuaded, would be the necessary effect of any base concession made by the present House of Commons, and, as a qualifying measure would not be accepted, it remains for you to decide whether you will, at any hazard, support a set of men who have reduced you to this unhappy dilemma, or whether you will gratify the united wishes of the whole people of England by dissolving the Parliament.

Taking it for granted, as I do very sincerely, that you have personally no design upon the constitution, nor any views inconsistent with the good of your subjects, I think you cannot hesitate long upon the choice, which it equally concerns your interest and your honour to adopt. On one side you hazard the affections of all your English subjects—you relinquish every hope of repose to yourself, and you endanger the establishment of your family for ever. All this you venture for no object whatsoever, or for such an object as it would be an affront to you to name. Men of sense will examine your conduct with suspicion, while those who are incapable of comprehending to what degree they are injured, afflict you with clamours equally insolent and unmeaning. Supposing it possible that no fatal struggle should ensue, you determine at once to be unhappy, without the hope of a compensation either from interest or ambition. If an English king be hated or despised, he *must* be unhappy; and this, perhaps, is the only political truth which he ought to be convinced of without experiment. But if the English people should no longer confine their resentment to a submissive representation of their wrongs—if, following the glorious example of their ancestors, they should no longer appeal to the creature of the constitution, but to that high Being who gave them the rights of humanity, whose gifts it were sacrilege to surrender— let me ask you, Sir, upon what part of your subjects would you rely for assistance?

The people of Ireland have been uniformly plundered and oppressed. In return, they give you every day fresh marks of their resentment. They despise the miserable governor you have sent them because he is the creature of Lord Bute; nor is it from any natural confusion in their ideas that they are so ready to confound the original of a king with the disgraceful representation of him.

The distance of the colonies would make it impossible for them to take an active concern in your affairs if they were as well affected to your government as they once pretended to be to your person. They were ready enough to distinguish between *you* and your ministers. They complained of an act of the legislature, but traced the origin of it no higher than to the servants of the crown; they pleased themselves with the hope that their sovereign, if not favourable to their cause, at least was impartial. The decisive, personal part you took against them has effectually banished that first distinction from their minds. They consider you as united with your servants against America, and know how to distinguish the sovereign and a venal Parliament on one side from the real sentiments of the English people on the other. Looking forward to independence, they might possibly receive you for their king; but, if ever you retire to America, be assured they will give you such a covenant to digest as the presbytery of Scotland would have been ashamed to offer to Charles the Second. They left their native land in search of freedom, and found it in a desert. Divided as they are into a thousand forms of policy and religion, there is one point in which they all agree—they equally detest the pageantry of a king and the supercilious hypocrisy of a bishop.

It is not then from the alienated affections of Ireland or America that you can reasonably look for assistance; still less from the people of England, who are actually contending for their rights, and in this great question are parties against you. You are not, however, destitute of every appearance of support—you have all the Jacobites, Nonjurors, Roman Catholics, and Tories of this country, and all Scotland without exception. Considering from what family you are descended, the choice of your friends has been

singularly directed; and truly, Sir, if you had not lost the Whig interest of England, I should admire your dexterity in turning the hearts of your enemies. Is it possible for you to place any confidence in men who, before they are faithful to you, must renounce every opinion and betray every principle, both in church and state, which they inherit from their ancestors, and are confirmed in by their education? whose numbers are so inconsiderable that they have long been obliged to give up the principles and language which distinguish them as a party, and to fight under the banners of their enemies? Their zeal begins with hypocrisy, and must conclude in treachery. At first they deceive—at last betray.

As to the Scotch, I must suppose your heart and understanding so biassed from your earliest infancy in their favour, that nothing less than *your own* misfortunes can undeceive you. You will not accept of the uniform experience of your ancestors; and when once a man is determined to believe, the very absurdity of the doctrine confirms him in his faith. A bigoted understanding can draw a proof of attachment to the house of Hanover from a notorious zeal for the house of Stuart, and find an earnest of future loyalty in former rebellions. Appearances are, however, in their favour; so strongly, indeed, that one would think they had forgotten that you are their lawful king, and had mistaken you for a pretender to the crown. Let it be admitted, then, that the Scotch are as sincere in their present professions as if you were in reality not an Englishman, but a Briton of the North. You would not be the first prince of their native country against whom they have rebelled, nor the first whom they have basely betrayed. Have you forgotten, Sir, or has your favourite concealed from you that part of our history when the unhappy Charles (and he too had private virtues) fled from the open avowed indignation of his English subjects, and surrendered himself at discretion to the good faith of his own countrymen? Without looking for support in their affections as subjects, he applied only to their honour as gentlemen for protection. They received him as they would your Majesty, with bows, and smiles, and falsehood, and kept him until they had settled their bargain with the English Parliament; then basely sold their native king to the vengeance of his enemies. This, Sir, was not the act of a few traitors, but the deliberate treachery of a Scotch Parliament representing the nation. A wise prince might draw from it two lessons of equal utility to himself. On one side he might learn to dread the undisguised resentment of a generous people, who dare openly assert their rights, and who, in a just cause, are ready to meet their sovereign in the field. On the other side, he would be taught to apprehend something far more formidable—a fawning treachery against which no prudence can guard, no courage defend. The insidious smile upon the cheek would warn him of the canker in the heart.

From the uses to which one part of the army has been too frequently applied, you have some reason to expect that there are no services they would refuse. Here, too, we trace the partiality of your understanding. You take the sense of the army from the conduct of the Guards, with the same justice with which you collect the sense of the people from the representations of the ministry. Your marching regiments, Sir, will not make the Guards their example either as soldiers or subjects. They feel and resent, as they ought to do, that invariable, undistinguishing favour with which the Guards are treated; while those gallant troops by whom every hazardous, every laborious service is performed, are left to perish in garrisons abroad, or pine in quarters at home, neglected and forgotten. If they had no sense of the great original duty they owe their country, their resentment would oper-

ate like patriotism, and leave your cause to be defended by those to whom you have lavished the rewards and honours of their profession. The pretorian bands, enervated and debauched as they were, had still strength enough to awe the Roman populace; but when the distant legions took the alarm, they marched to Rome and gave away the empire.

On this side, then, whichever way you turn your eyes you see nothing but perplexity and distress. You may determine to support the very ministry who have reduced your affairs to this deplorable situation—you may shelter yourself under the forms of Parliament, and set your people at defiance. But be assured, Sir, that such a resolution would be as imprudent as it would be odious. If it did not immediately shake your establishment, it would rob you of your peace of mind for ever.

On the other, how different is the prospect! How easy, how safe and honourable is the path before you! The English nation declare they are grossly injured by their representatives, and solicit your Majesty to exert your lawful prerogative, and give them an opportunity of recalling a trust which, they find, has been scandalously abused. You are not to be told that the power of the House of Commons is not original, but delegated to them for the welfare of the people from whom they received it. A question of right arises between the constituent and the representative body. By what authority shall it be decided? Will your Majesty interfere in a question in which you have properly no immediate concern? It would be a step equally odious and unnecessary. Shall the Lords be called upon to determine the rights and privileges of the Commons? They cannot do it without a flagrant breach of the constitution. Or will you refer it to the judges? They have often told your ancestors that the law of Parliament is above them. What party then remains but to leave it to the people to determine for themselves? They alone are injured; and, since there is no superior power to which the cause can be referred, they alone ought to determine.

I do not mean to perplex you with a tedious argument upon a subject already so discussed that inspiration could hardly throw a new light upon it. There are, however, two points of view in which it particularly imports your Majesty to consider the late proceedings of the House of Commons. By depriving a subject of his birthright, they have attributed to their own vote an authority equal to an act of the whole legislature; and, though perhaps not with the same motives, have strictly followed the example of the Long Parliament, which first declared the regal office useless, and soon after, with as little ceremony, dissolved the House of Lords. The same pretended power which robs an English subject of his birthright may rob an English king of his crown. In another view, the resolution of the House of Commons, apparently not so dangerous to your Majesty, is still more alarming to your people. Not contented with divesting one man of his right, they have arbitrarily conveyed that right to another. They have set aside a return as illegal, without daring to censure those officers who were particularly apprized of Mr. Wilke's incapacity, not only by the declaration of the House, but expressly by the writ directed to them, and who, nevertheless, returned him as duly elected. They have rejected the majority of votes, the only criterion by which our laws judge of the sense of the people; they have transferred the right of election from the collective to the representative body; and, by these acts, taken separately or together, they have essentially altered the original constitution of the House of Commons. Versed as your Majesty undoubtedly is in the English history, it cannot easily escape you how much it is your interest, as well as your duty, to prevent one of the three estates from encroaching upon the province of the other two, or assuming the authority of them all. When once they have departed from the great constitutional line by which all their proceedings should be directed, who will answer for their future moderation? Or what assurance will they give you that when they have trampled upon their equals they will submit to a superior? Your Majesty may learn hereafter how nearly the slave and tyrant are allied.

Some of your council, more candid than the rest, admit the abandoned profligacy of the present House of Commons, but oppose their dissolution upon an opinion, I confess not very unwarrantable, that their successors would be equally at the disposal of the treasury. I cannot persuade myself that the nation will have profited so little by experience. But if that opinion were well founded, you might then gratify our wishes at an easy rate, and appease the present clamour against your government, without offering any material injury to the favourite cause of corruption.

You still have an honourable part to act. The affections of your subjects may still be recovered. But before you subdue *their* hearts you must gain a noble victory over your own. Discard those little personal resentments which have too long directed your public conduct. Pardon this man the remainder of his punishment; and, if resentment still prevails, make it what it should have been long since— an act, not of mercy, but contempt. He will soon fall back into his natural station—a silent senator, and hardly supporting the weekly eloquence of a newspaper. The gentle breath of peace would leave him on the surface neglected and unremoved. It is only the tempest that lifts him from his place.

Without consulting your minister, call together your whole council. Let it appear to the public that you can determine and act for yourself. Come forward to your people. Lay aside the

wretched formalities of a king, and
speak to your subjects with the spirit
of a man, and in the language of a
gentleman. Tell them you have been
fatally deceived. The acknowledgment
will be no disgrace, but rather an
honour to your understanding. Tell
them you are determined to remove
every cause of complaint against your
government, that you will give your   10
confidence to no man who does not
possess the confidence of your subjects; and leave it to themselves to
determine, by their conduct at a future election, whether or no it be in
reality the general sense of the nation
that their rights have been arbitrarily
invaded by the present House of Commons, and the constitution betrayed.
They will then do justice to their rep-   20
resentatives and to themselves.

These sentiments, Sir, and the style
they are conveyed in, may be offensive,
perhaps, because they are new to you.
Accustomed to the language of courtiers, you measure their affections by
the vehemence of their expressions;
and, when they only praise you indirectly, you admire their sincerity. But
this is not a time to trifle with your   30
fortune. They deceive you, Sir, who
tell you that you have many friends
whose affections are founded upon a
principle of personal attachment. The

first foundation of friendship is not
the power of conferring benefits, but
the equality with which they are received and *may* be returned. The fortune which made you a king forbad
you to have a friend. It is a law of
nature which cannot be violated with
impunity. The mistaken prince who
looks for friendship will find a favourite, and in that favourite the ruin
of his affairs.

The people of England are loyal to
the house of Hanover, not from a vain
preference of one family to another,
but from a conviction that the establishment of that family was necessary
to the support of their civil and religious liberties. This, Sir, is a principle of allegiance equally solid and rational; fit for Englishmen to adopt,
and well worthy of your majesty's encouragement. We cannot long be deluded by nominal distinctions. The
name of Stuart, of itself, is only contemptible; armed with the sovereign
authority, their principles are formidable. The prince who imitates their
conduct should be warned by their
example; and while he plumes himself
upon the security of his title to the
crown, should remember that, as it
was acquired by one revolution, it
may be lost by another.

JUNIUS.

EDMUND BURKE (1729-1797)

John Morley said of Burke's speeches on the American policy of the ministries of George III, that "it is no exaggeration to say that they compose the most perfect manual in our literature, or in any literature, for one who approaches the study of public affairs, whether for knowledge or for practice. They are an example without fault of all the qualities which the critic, whether a theorist or an actor, of great political situations should strive by night and by day to possess." This unreserved praise is from a man whose political sagacity was proved by a long public career, but who, like Burke, understood how to raise political wisdom to the level of philosophical principle. It is the great distinction of Burke that he was a profound thinker in politics.

The comprehensiveness of his mind must have been developed to a considerable degree by his varied early experiences and education. He was born in Dublin on January 12, 1729, the son of a Protestant father and a Roman Catholic mother; and all his life he sympathized with the Irish people and strove for Catholic Emancipation. He received his early education under a Quaker whose memory he cherished with reverence to the end of his life. But his deep attachment to his own, the Anglican, church is evident in the eloquent defence of it in the *Reflections on the French Revolution*. He was educated at Trinity College, Dublin, and sent to London to study law; considering his later career, it is curious that literary interests drew him away from his legal studies, and that he was never admitted to the bar. In 1756 he published *A Vindication of Natural Society*, an ironical work purporting to show that the abstract reasoning of Lord Bolingbroke against the Christian religion would, if applied to social theory, undermine all organized society. His interest in esthetic theory led to his *Philosophical Inquiry into the Origin of our Ideas on the Sublime and Beautiful*, which had some influence on later German philosophy. In 1759 he became editor of *The Annual Register*, a task congenial to a man of his capacious memory and eager curiosity regarding political and economic matters.

He entered the House of Commons in 1765 and remained a member for twenty-nine years. During all that period he never held a ministerial position, although for a few months he was Paymaster of the Forces and reduced the incommensurate rewards of that office. His great public career was spent in opposition to the various ministries which tried to establish the "personal government" of George III, and he promoted such causes as the abolition of the slave trade, Catholic emancipation in Ireland, and protection for the misgoverned natives in India. He was a leader in the prosecution of Warren Hastings. "If I were to call for a reward," he said, "it would be for the services in which for fourteen years, without intermission, I showed the most industry and had the least success. I mean the affairs of India; they are those on which I value myself the most; most for the importance; most for the labor; most for the judgment; most for constancy and perseverance in the pursuit."

When the French Revolution broke out in 1789, a Frenchman asked Burke to write him his opinions on the new turn of affairs. In reply Burke wrote and published his *Reflections*, perhaps his greatest work. He had been stirred by a sermon preached by the Reverend Dr. Richard Price, a non-conformist minister, on November 4, 1789, at an anniversary celebration of the Revolution of 1688, in which Dr. Price had affirmed that the principles of the old and the new revolutions were identical. Burke was alarmed at this confusion, believing that the principles and sentiments of the French revolutionists were likely to destroy the most valuable elements in civilization. It is Burke's examination of political first principles, not his interpretation of the historical events of the French Revolution, that interests the reader of the *Reflections*. As a political thinker, also, Burke was consistent from the beginning to the end of his career; as Morley has admirably said, he "changed his front, but he never changed his ground." He distrusted all *a priori* theorists, whether they were subservient ministers arrogantly assuming dangerous prerogatives for the English Crown, or whether they were of the extreme opposite party, forcing abstract rights and "metaphysical politics" to revolutionary consequences. He distrusted "paper constitutions" and hastily constructed gov ernments, holding that society has more of the nature of an organism than of a machine. He objected to the theory that government is established by a contract between the governors and the governed, partly because the facts of history do not support it, but even more because he thought it implied a poor and shallow conception of a national life. Over against the bright hope that the millennium could be reached shortly if we would but emancipate our reason from the past, Burke placed a picture of "our naked and shivering human nature," needing the protection of its inheritance of institutions and traditions. In the *Reflections* Burke was therefore debating the deeper political issues that present themselves to every generation of men, and even those who disagree with his principles may read him with delight and profit.

Burke was apparently not a great orator; it is said that when he rose to speak, the members of the House of Commons went out to dinner. But his speeches were read with care by his contemporaries, and their style preserves their freshness to all later generations. They are more than reasoned argument, more than sounding eloquence. Burke's thinking was always imaginative, and his conceptions have a poetical quality about them that has reminded many readers of Shakespeare. He not only states an idea with precision, he also illuminates it, imparting to the reader the insight of a rich and profound nature.

Works (Bohn Library, 8 vols., 1853) ; *Works* (12 vols., Boston, 1865-67) ; *Select Works,* ed. Edward J. Payne (3 vols., Oxford, 1866) ; *Selected Writings and Speeches,* ed. Ross J. S. Hoffman and Paul Levack (1949) ; John Morley, *Burke* (English Men of Letters Series, 1879) ; Robert H. Murray, *Edmund Burke* (1931) ; Sir Philip Magnus, *Edmund Burke* (1939) ; A. P. I. Samuels, *The Early Life, Correspondence, and Writings of Edmund Burke* (Cambridge, Eng., 1923) ; John MacCunn, *The Political Philosophy of Edmund Burke* (1913) ; Alfred Cobban, *Edmund Burke and the Revolt Against the Eighteenth Century* (1929) ; W. G. Howard, "Burke Among the Forerunners of Lessing," *PMLA,* XXII (1907) , 608-32. For additional reading see pages 1165–1172.

FROM REFLECTIONS ON THE REVOLUTION IN FRANCE

AND

ON THE PROCEEDINGS IN CERTAIN SOCIETIES IN LONDON RELATIVE TO THAT EVENT

IN A LETTER

INTENDED TO HAVE BEEN SENT TO A GENTLEMAN IN PARIS

. . . .

You will observe, that from Magna Charta to the Declaration of Right, it has been the uniform policy of our constitution to claim and assert our liberties, as an *entailed inheritance* derived to us from our forefathers, and to be transmitted to our posterity; as an estate specially belonging to the people of this kingdom, without any reference whatever to any other more general or prior right. By this means our constitution preserves a unity in so great a diversity of its parts. We have an inheritable crown; an inheritable peerage; and a house of commons and a people inheriting privileges,

franchises, and liberties, from a long line of ancestors.

This policy appears to me to be the result of profound reflection; or rather the happy effect of following nature, which is wisdom without reflection, and above it. A spirit of innovation is generally the result of a selfish temper and confined views. People will not look forward to posterity, who never look backward to their ancestors. Besides, the people of England well know, that the idea of inheritance furnishes a sure principle of conservation and a sure principle of transmission; without at all excluding a principle of improvement. It leaves acquisition free; but it secures what it acquires. Whatever advantages are obtained by a state proceeding on these maxims, are locked fast as in a sort of family settlement; grasped as in a kind of mortmain for ever. By a constitutional policy, working after the pattern of nature, we receive, we hold, we transmit our government and our privileges, in the same manner in which we enjoy and transmit our property and our lives. The institutions of policy, the goods of fortune, the gifts of Providence, are handed down to us and from us, in the same course and order. Our political system is placed in a just correspondence and symmetry with the order of the world, and with the mode of existence decreed to a permanent body composed of transitory parts; wherein, by the disposition of a stupendous wisdom, moulding together the great mysterious incorporation of the human race, the whole at one time, is never old, or middle-aged, or young, but, in a condition of unchangeable constancy, moves on through the varied tenour of perpetual decay, fall, renovation, and progression. Thus, by preserving the method of nature in the conduct of the state, in what we improve, we are never wholly new; in what we retain we are never wholly obsolete. By adhering in this manner and on those principles to our forefathers, we are guided not by the superstition of antiquarians, but by the spirit of philosophic analogy. In this choice of inheritance we have given to our frame of polity the image of a relation in blood; binding up the constitution of our country with our dearest domestic ties; adopting our fundamental laws into the bosom of our family affections; keeping inseparable, and cherishing with the warmth of all their combined and mutually reflected charities, our state, our hearths, our sepulchres, and our altars.

Through the same plan of a conformity to nature in our artificial institutions, and by calling in the aid of her unerring and powerful instincts, to fortify the fallible and feeble contrivances of our reason, we have derived several other, and those no small benefits, from considering our liberties in the light of an inheritance. Always acting as if in the presence of canonized forefathers, the spirit of freedom, leading in itself to misrule and excess, is tempered with an awful gravity. This idea of a liberal descent inspires us with a sense of habitual native dignity, which prevents that upstart insolence almost inevitably adhering to and disgracing those who are the first acquirers of any distinction. By this means our liberty becomes a noble freedom. It carries an imposing and majestic aspect. It has a pedigree and illustrating ancestors. It has its bearings and its ensigns armorial. It has its gallery of portraits; its monumental inscriptions; its records, evidences, and titles. We procure reverence to our civil institutions on the principle upon which nature teaches us to revere individual men; on account of their age; and on account of those from whom they are descended. All your sophisters cannot produce anything better adapted to preserve a rational and manly freedom than the course that we have pursued, who have chosen our nature rather than our speculations, our breasts rather than our inventions, for the great conservatories and magazines of our rights and privileges.

You might, if you pleased, have profited of our example, and have given to your recovered freedom a correspondent dignity. Your privileges, though discontinued, were not lost to memory. Your constitution, it is true, whilst you were out of possession, suffered waste and dilapidation; but you possessed in some parts the walls, and in all the foundations, of a noble and venerable castle. You might have repaired those walls; you might have built on those old foundations. Your constitution was suspended before it was perfected; but you had the elements of a constitution very nearly as good as could be wished. In your old states you possessed that variety of parts corresponding with the various descriptions of which your community was happily composed; you had all that combination, and all that opposition of interests, you had that action and counteraction which, in the natural and in the political world, from the reciprocal struggle of discordant powers, draws out the harmony of the universe. These opposed and conflicting interests, which you considered as so great a blemish in your old and in our present constitution, interpose a salutary check to all precipitate resolutions; they render deliberation a matter not of choice, but of necessity; they make all change a subject of *compromise,* which naturally begets moderation; they produce *temperaments,* preventing the sore evil of harsh, crude, unqualified reformations; and rendering all the headlong exertions of arbitrary power, in the few or in the many, for ever impracticable. Through that diversity of members and interests, general liberty had as many securities as there were separate views in the several orders; whilst by pressing down the whole by the weight of a real monarchy, the separate parts would have been prevented from warping and starting from their allotted places.

You had all these advantages in your ancient states; but you chose to act as if you had never been moulded into civil society, and had everything to begin anew. You began ill, because you began by despising everything that belonged to you. You set up your trade without a capital. If the last generations of your country appeared without much lustre in your eyes, you might have passed them by, and derived your claims from a more early race of ancestors. Under a pious predilection for those ancestors, your imaginations would have realized in them a standard of virtue and wisdom, beyond the vulgar practice of the hour: and you would have risen with the example to whose imitation you aspired. Respecting your forefathers, you would have been taught to respect yourselves. You would not have chosen to consider the French as a people of yesterday, as a nation of low-born servile wretches until the emancipating year of 1789. In order to furnish, at the expense of your honour, an excuse to your apologists here for several enormities of yours, you would not have been content to be represented as a gang of Maroon slaves, suddenly broke loose from the house of bondage, and therefore to be pardoned for your abuse of the liberty to which you were not accustomed and ill fitted. Would it not, my worthy friend, have been wiser to have you thought, what I, for one, always thought you, a generous and gallant nation, long misled to your disadvantage by your high and romantic sentiments of fidelity, honour, and loyalty; that events had been unfavourable to you, but that you were not enslaved through any illiberal or servile disposition; that in your most devoted submission, you were actuated by a principle of public spirit, and that it was your country you worshipped, in the person of your king? Had you made it to be understood, that in the delusion of this amiable error you had gone further than your wise ancestors; that you were resolved to resume your ancient privileges, whilst you preserved the spirit of your ancient and your recent loyalty and honour; or if diffident of yourselves, and not clearly discerning the almost obliterated constitution of your ancestors, you had looked to your neighbours in this land, who had kept alive the ancient principles and models of the old common law of Europe meliorated and adapted to its present state—by following wise examples you would have given new examples of wisdom to the world. You would have rendered the cause of liberty venerable in the eyes of every worthy mind in every nation. You would have shamed despotism from the earth, by showing that freedom was not only reconcilable, but, as when well disciplined it is, auxiliary to law. You would have had an unoppressive but a productive revenue. You would have had a flourishing commerce to feed it. You would have had a free constitution; a potent monarchy; a disciplined army; a reformed and venerated clergy; a mitigated but spirited nobility, to lead your virtue, not to overlay it; you would have had a liberal order of commons, to emulate and to recruit that nobility; you would have had a protected, satisfied, laborious, and obedient people, taught to seek and to recognize the happiness that is to be found by virtue in all conditions; in which consists the true moral equality of mankind, and not in that monstrous fiction, which, by inspiring false ideas and vain expectations into men destined to travel in the obscure walk of laborious life, serves only to aggravate and embitter that real inequality, which it never can remove; and which the order of civil life establishes as much for the benefit of those whom it must leave in an humble state, as those whom it is able to exalt to a condition more splendid, but not more happy. You had a smooth and easy career of felicity and glory laid open to you, beyond anything recorded in the history of the world; but you have shown that difficulty is good for man.

Compute your gains: see what is got by those extravagant and presumptuous speculations which have taught your leaders to despise all their predecessors, and all their contemporaries, and even to despise themselves, until the moment in which they became truly despicable. By following those false lights, France has bought undisguised calamities at a higher price than any nation has purchased the most unequivocal blessings. France has bought poverty by crime! France has not sacrificed her virtue to her interest; but she has abandoned her interest, that she might prostitute her virtue. All other nations have begun the fabric of a new government, or the reformation of an old, by establishing originally, or by enforcing with greater exactness, some rites or other of religion. All other people have laid the foundations of civil freedom in severer manners, and a system of a more austere and masculine morality. France, when she let loose the reins of regal authority, doubled the licence of a ferocious dissoluteness in manners, and of an insolent irreligion in opinions and practices; and has extended through all ranks of life, as if she were communicating some privilege, or laying open some secluded benefit, all the unhappy corruptions that usually were the disease of wealth and power. This is one of the new principles of equality in France.

France, by the perfidy of her leaders, has utterly disgraced the tone of lenient council in the cabinets of princes, and disarmed it of its most potent topics. She has sanctified the dark, suspicious maxims of tyrannous distrust; and taught kings to tremble at (what will hereafter be called) the delusive plausibilities of moral politicians. Sovereigns will consider those who advise them to place an unlimited confidence in their people, as subverters of their thrones; as traitors who aim at their destruction, by leading their easy good-nature, under specious pretences, to admit combinations of bold and faithless men into a participation of their power. This alone, if there were nothing else, is an irreparable calamity to you and to mankind. Remember that your parliament of Paris told your king, that in calling the states together, he had nothing to fear but the prodigal excess of their zeal in providing for the support of the throne. It is right that these men should hide their heads. It is right that they should bear their part in the ruin which their counsel has brought on their sovereign and their country. Such sanguine declarations tend to lull authority asleep; to encourage it rashly to engage in perilous adventures of untried policy; to neglect those provisions, preparations, and precautions, which distinguish benevolence from imbecility; and without which no man can answer for the salutary effect of any abstract plan of government or of freedom. For want of these, they have seen the medicine of the state corrupted into its poison. They have seen the French rebel against a mild and lawful monarch, with more fury, outrage, and insult, than even any people has been known to rise against the most illegal usurper, or the most sanguinary tyrant. Their resistance was made to concession; their revolt was from protection; their blow was aimed at a hand holding out graces, favours, and immunities.

This was unnatural. The rest is in order. They have found their punishment in their success. Laws overturned; tribunals subverted; industry without vigour; commerce expiring; the revenue unpaid, yet the people impoverished; a church pillaged, and a state not relieved; civil and military anarchy made the constitution of the kingdom; everything human and divine sacrificed to the idol of public credit, and national bankruptcy the consequence; and to crown all, the paper securities of new, precarious, tottering power, the discredited paper securities of impoverished fraud, and beggared rapine, held out as a currency for the support of an empire, in lieu of the two great recognized species that represent the lasting conventional credit of mankind, which disappeared and hid themselves in the earth from whence they came, when the principle of property, whose creatures and representatives they are, was systematically subverted.

Were all these dreadful things necessary? Were they the inevitable results of the desperate struggle of determined patriots, compelled to wade through blood and tumult, to the quiet shore of a tranquil and prosperous liberty? No! nothing like it. The fresh ruins of France, which shock our feelings wherever we can turn our eyes, are not the devastation of civil war; they are the sad but instructive monuments of rash and ignorant counsel in time of profound peace. They are the display of inconsiderate and presumptuous, because unresisted and irresistible authority. The persons who have thus squandered away the precious treasure of their crimes, the persons who have made this prodigal and wild waste of public evils (the last stake reserved for the ultimate ransom of the state), have met in their progress with little, or rather with no opposition at all. Their whole march was more like a triumphal procession than the progress of a war. Their pioneers have gone before them, and demolished and laid everything level at their feet. Not one drop of *their* blood have they shed in the cause of the country they have ruined. They have made no sacrifices to their projects of greater consequence than their shoe-buckles, whilst they were imprisoning their king, murdering their fellow citizens, and bathing in tears, and plunging in poverty and distress, thousands of worthy men and worthy families. Their cruelty has not even been the base result of fear. It has been the effect of their sense of perfect safety, in authorizing treasons, robberies, rapes, assassinations, slaughters, and burnings, throughout their harassed land. But the cause of all was plain from the beginning.

This unforced choice, this fond election of evil, would appear perfectly unaccountable, if we did not consider the composition of the National Assembly; I do not mean its formal constitution, which, as it now stands, is exceptionable enough, but the materials of which, in a great measure, it is composed, which is of ten thousand times greater consequence than all the formalities in the world. If we were to know nothing of this Assembly but by its title and function, no colours could paint to the imagination anything more venerable. In that light the mind of an inquirer, subdued by such an awful image as that of the virtue and wisdom of a whole people collected into a focus, would pause and hesitate in condemning things even of the very worst aspect. Instead of blameable, they would appear only mysterious. But no name, no power, no function, no artificial institution whatsoever, can make the men of whom any system of authority is composed any other than God, and nature, and education, and their habits of life have made them. Capacities beyond these the people have not to give. Virtue and wisdom may be the objects of their choice; but their choice confers neither the one nor the other on those upon whom they lay their ordaining hands. They have not the engagement of nature, they have not the promise of revelation for any such powers.

. . . .

Something they must destroy, or they seem to themselves to exist for no purpose. One set is for destroying the civil power through the ecclesiastical; another for demolishing the ecclesiastic through the civil. They are aware that the worst consequences might happen to the public in accomplishing this double ruin of church and state; but they are so heated with their theories, that they give more than hints, that this ruin, with all the mischiefs that must lead to it and attend it, and which to themselves appear quite certain, would not be unacceptable to them, or very remote from their wishes. A man amongst them of great authority, and certainly of great talents, speaking of a supposed alliance between church and state, says, "perhaps *we must wait for the fall of the civil powers* before this most unnatural alliance be broken. Calamitous no doubt will that time be. But what convulsion in the political world ought to be a subject of lamentation, if it be attended with so desirable an effect?" You see with what a steady eye these gentlemen are prepared to view the greatest calamities which can befall their country!

It is no wonder therefore, that with these ideas of every thing in their constitution and government at home, either in church or state, as illegitimate and usurped, or at best as a vain mockery, they look abroad with an eager and passionate enthusiasm. Whilst they are possessed by these notions, it is vain to talk to them of the practice of their ancestors, the fundamental laws of their country, the fixed

form of a constitution, whose merits are confirmed by the solid test of long experience, and an increasing public strength and national prosperity. They despise experience as the wisdom of unlettered men; and as for the rest, they have wrought under-ground a mine that will blow up, at one grand explosion, all examples of antiquity, all precedents, charters, and acts of parliament. They have "the rights of men." Against these there can be no prescription; against these no agreement is binding: these admit no temperament, and no compromise: anything withheld from their full demand is so much of fraud and injustice. Against these their rights of men let no government look for security in the length of its continuance, or in the justice and lenity of its administration. The objections of these speculatists, if its forms do not quadrate with their theories, are as valid against such an old and beneficent government as against the most violent tyranny, or the greenest usurpation. They are always at issue with governments, not on a question of abuse, but a question of competency, and a question of title. I have nothing to say to the clumsy subtilty of their political metaphysics. Let them be their amusement in the schools.—*"Illa se jactat in aula—Æolus, et clauso ventorum carcere regnet."*—But let them not break prison to burst like a Levanter, to sweep the earth with their hurricane, and to break up the fountains of the great deep to over whelm us.

Far am I from denying in theory; full as far is my heart from withholding in practice (if I were of power to give or to withhold), the *real* rights of men. In denying their false claims of right, I do not mean to injure those which are real, and are such as their pretended rights would totally destroy. If civil society be made for the advantage of man, all the advantages for which it is made become his right. It is an institution of beneficence; and law itself is only beneficence acting by a rule. Men have a right to live by that rule; they have a right to do justice, as between their fellows, whether their fellows are in public function or in ordinary occupation. They have a right to the fruits of their industry; and to the means of making their industry fruitful. They have a right to the acquisitions of their parents; to the nourishment and improvement of their offspring; to instruction in life, and to consolation in death. Whatever each man can separately do, without trespassing upon others, he has a right to do for himself; and he has a right to a fair portion of all which society, with all its combinations of skill and force, can do in his favour. In this partnership all men have equal rights; but not to equal things. He that has but five shillings in the partnership, has as good a right to it, as he that has five hundred pounds has to his larger proportion. But he has not a right to an equal dividend in the product of the joint stock; and as to the share of power, authority, and direction which each individual ought to have in the management of the state, that I must deny to be amongst the direct original rights of man in civil society; for I have in my contemplation the civil social man, and no other. It is a thing to be settled by convention.

If civil society be the offspring of convention, that convention must be its law. That convention must limit and modify all the descriptions of constitution which are formed under it. Every sort of legislative, judicial, or executory power are its creatures. They can have no being in any other state of things; and how can any man claim, under the conventions of civil society, rights which do not so much as suppose its existence? Rights which are absolutely repugnant to it? One of the first motives to civil society, and which becomes one of its fundamental rules, is, *that no man should be judge in his own cause.* By this each person has at once divested himself of the first fundamental right of uncove-

nanted man, that is, to judge for himself, and to assert his own cause. He abdicates all right to be his own governor. He inclusively, in a great measure, abandons the right of self-defence, the first law of nature. Men cannot enjoy the rights of an uncivil and of a civil state together. That he may obtain justice he gives up his right of determining what it is in points the most essential to him. That he may secure some liberty, he makes a surrender in trust of the whole of it.

Government is not made in virtue of natural rights, which may and do exist in total independence of it; and exist in much greater clearness, and in a much greater degree of abstract perfection: but their abstract perfection is their practical defect. By having a right to every thing they want every thing. Government is a contrivance of human wisdom to provide for human *wants.* Men have a right that these wants should be provided for by this wisdom. Among these wants is to be reckoned the want, out of civil society, of a sufficient restraint upon their passions. Society requires not only that the passions of individuals should be subjected, but that even in the mass and body, as well as in the individuals, the inclinations of men should frequently be thwarted, their will controlled, and their passions brought into subjection. This can only be done *by a power out of themselves*; and not, in the exercise of its function, subject to that will and to those passions which it is its office to bridle and subdue. In this sense the restraints on men, as well as their liberties, are to be reckoned among their rights. But as the liberties and the restrictions vary with times and circumstances, and admit of infinite modifications, they cannot be settled upon any abstract rule; and nothing is so foolish as to discuss them upon that principle.

The moment you abate anything from the full rights of men, each to govern himself, and suffer any artificial positive limitation upon those rights, from that moment the whole organization of government becomes a consideration of convenience. This it is which makes the constitution of a state, and the due distribution of its powers, a matter of the most delicate and complicated skill. It requires a deep knowledge of human nature and human necessities, and of the things which facilitate or obstruct the various ends which are to be pursued by the mechanism of civil institutions. The state is to have recruits to its strength, and remedies to its distempers. What is the use of discussing a man's abstract right to food or medicine? The question is upon the method of procuring and administering them. In that deliberation I shall always advise to call in the aid of the farmer and the physician, rather than the professor of metaphysics.

The science of constructing a commonwealth, or renovating it, or reforming it, is, like every other experimental science, not to be taught à priori. Nor is it a short experience that can instruct us in that practical science; because the real effects of moral causes are not always immediate; but that which in the first instance is prejudicial may be excellent in its remoter operation; and its excellence may arise even from the ill effects it produces in the beginning. The reverse also happens; and very plausible schemes, with very pleasing commencements, have often shameful and lamentable conclusions. In states there are often some obscure and almost latent causes, things which appear at first view of little moment, on which a very great part of its prosperity or adversity may most essentially depend. The science of government being therefore so practical in itself, and intended for such practical purposes, a matter which requires experience, and even more experience than any person can gain in his whole life, however sagacious and observing he may be, it is with infinite caution that any man ought to venture upon pulling down an edifice, which has an-

swered in any tolerable degree for ages the common purposes of society, or on building it up again, without having models and patterns of approved utility before his eyes.

These metaphysic rights entering into common life, like rays of light which pierce into a dense medium, are, by the laws of nature, refracted from their straight line. Indeed in the gross and complicated mass of human passions and concerns, the primitive rights of men undergo such a variety of refractions and reflections, that it becomes absurd to talk of them as if they continued in the simplicity of their original direction. The nature of man is intricate; the objects of society are of the greatest possible complexity; and therefore no simple disposition or direction of power can be suitable either to man's nature, or to the quality of his affairs. When I hear the simplicity of contrivance aimed at and boasted of in any new political constitutions, I am at no loss to decide that the artificers are grossly ignorant of their trade, or totally negligent of their duty. The simple governments are fundamentally defective, to say no worse of them. If you were to contemplate society in but one point of view, all these simple modes of polity are infinitely captivating. In effect each would answer its single end much more perfectly than the more complex is able to attain all its complex purposes. But it is better that the whole should be imperfectly and anomalously answered, than that, while some parts are provided for with great exactness, others might be totally neglected, or perhaps materially injured, by the overcare of a favourite member.

The pretended rights of these theorists are all extremes; and in proportion as they are metaphysically true, they are morally and politically false. The rights of men are in a sort of *middle*, incapable of definition, but not impossible to be discerned. The rights of men in governments are their advantages; and these are often in balances between differences of good; in compromises sometimes between good and evil, and sometimes, between evil and evil. Political reason is a computing principle; adding, subtracting, multiplying, and dividing, morally and not metaphysically, or mathematically, true moral denominations.

By these theorists the right of the people is almost always sophistically confounded with their power. The body of the community, whenever it can come to act, can meet with no effectual resistance; but till power and right are the same, the whole body of them has no right inconsistent with virtue, and the first of all virtues, prudence. Men have no right to what is not reasonable, and to what is not for their benefit; for though a pleasant writer said, *Liceat perire poetis,* when one of them, in cold blood, is said to have leaped into the flames of a volcanic revolution, *Ardentem frigidus Ætnam insiluit,* I consider such a frolic rather as an unjustifiable poetic licence, than as one of the franchises of Parnassus; and whether he were poet, or divine, or politician, that chose to exercise this kind of right, I think that more wise, because more charitable thoughts would urge me rather to save the man, than to preserve his brazen slippers as the monuments of his folly.

The kind of anniversary sermons to which a great part of what I write refers, if men are not shamed out of their present course, in commemorating the fact, will cheat many out of the principles, and deprive them of the benefits of the revolution they commemorate. I confess to you, Sir, I never liked this continual talk of resistance and revolution, or the practice of making the extreme medicine of the constitution its daily bread. It renders the habit of society dangerously valetudinary: it is taking periodical doses of mercury sublimate, and swallowing down repeated provocatives of cantharides to our love of liberty.

This distemper of remedy, grown habitual, relaxes and wears out, by a vulgar and prostituted use, the spring of that spirit which is to be exerted on great occasions. It was in the most patient period of Roman servitude that themes of tyrannicide made the ordinary exercise of boys at school— *cum perimit sævos classis numerosa tyrannos.* In the ordinary state of things, it produces in a country like ours the worst effects, even on the cause of that liberty which it abuses with the dissoluteness of an extravagant speculation. Almost all the high-bred republicans of my time have, after a short space, become the most decided, thorough-paced courtiers; they soon left the business of a tedious, moderate, but practical resistance, to those of us whom, in the pride and intoxication of their theories, they have slighted, as not much better than Tories. Hypocrisy, of course, delights in the most sublime speculations; for, never intending to go beyond speculation, it costs nothing to have it magnificent. But even in cases where rather levity than fraud was to be suspected in these ranting speculations, the issue has been much the same. These professors, finding their extreme principles not applicable to cases which call only for a qualified, or, as I may say, civil and legal resistance, in such cases employ no resistance at all. It is with them a war or a revolution, or it is nothing. Finding their schemes of politics not adapted to the state of the world in which they live, they often come to think lightly of all public principle; and are ready, on their part, to abandon for a very trivial interest what they find of very trivial value. Some indeed are of more steady and persevering natures; but these are eager politicians out of Parliament, who have little to tempt them to abandon their favourite projects. They have some change in the church or state, or both, constantly in their view. When that is the case, they are always bad citizens, and perfectly unsure connections. For, considering their speculative designs as of infinite value, and the actual arrangement of the state as of no estimation, they are at best indifferent about it. They see no merit in the good, and no fault in the vicious management of public affairs; they rather rejoice in the latter, as more propitious to revolution. They see no merit or demerit in any man, or any action, or any political principle, any further than as they may forward or retard their design of change: they therefore take up, one day, the most violent and stretched prerogative, and another time the wildest democratic ideas of freedom, and pass from the one to the other without any sort of regard to cause, to person, or to party.

In France you are now in the crisis of a revolution, and in the transit from one form of government to another—you cannot see that character of men exactly in the same situation in which we see it in this country. With us it is militant; with you it is triumphant; and you know how it can act when its power is commensurate to its will. I would not be supposed to confine those observations to any description of men, or to comprehend all men of any description within them—No! far from it. I am as incapable of that injustice, as I am of keeping terms with those who profess principles of extremities; and who, under the name of religion teach little else than wild and dangerous politics. The worst of these politics of revolution is this: they temper and harden the breast, in order to prepare it for the desperate strokes which are sometimes used in extreme occasions. But as these occasions may never arrive, the mind receives a gratuitous taint; and the moral sentiments suffer not a little, when no political purpose is served by the depravation. This sort of people are so taken up with their theories about the rights of man, that they have totally forgotten his nature. Without opening one new avenue to the understanding, they have succeeded in stopping up those that lead

to the heart. They have perverted in themselves, and in those that attend to them, all the well-placed sympathies of the human breast.

This famous sermon of the Old Jewry breathes nothing but this spirit through all the political part. Plots, massacres, assassinations, seem to some people a trivial price for obtaining a revolution. A cheap, bloodless reformation, a guiltless liberty, appear flat and vapid to their taste. There must be a great change of scene; there must be a magnificent stage effect; there must be a grand spectacle to rouse the imagination, grown torpid with the lazy enjoyment of sixty years' security, and the still unanimating repose of public prosperity. The preacher found them all in the French Revolution. This inspires a juvenile warmth through his whole frame. His enthusiasm kindles as he advances; and when he arrives at his peroration it is in a full blaze. Then viewing, from the Pisgah of his pulpit, the free, moral, happy, flourishing, and glorious state of France, as in a bird's-eye landscape of a promised land, he breaks out into the following rapture:—

"What an eventful period is this! I am *thankful* that I have lived to it; I could almost say, *Lord, now lettest thou thy servant depart in peace, for mine eyes have seen thy salvation.*— I have lived to see a *diffusion* of knowledge which has undermined superstition and error.—I have lived to see *the rights of men* better understood than ever, and nations panting for liberty which seemed to have lost the idea of it.—I have lived to see *thirty millions of people*, indignant and resolute, spurning at slavery, and demanding liberty with an irresistible voice; *their king led in triumph, and an arbitrary monarch surrendering himself to his subjects.*"

Before I proceed further, I have to remark that Dr. Price seems rather to overvalue the great acquisitions of light which he has obtained and diffused in this age. The last century appears to me to have been quite as much enlightened. It had, though in a different place, a triumph as memorable as that of Dr. Price; and some of the great preachers of that period partook of it as eagerly as he has done in the triumph of France. On the trial of the Rev. Hugh Peters for high treason, it was deposed, that when King Charles was brought to London for his trial, the Apostle of Liberty in that day conducted the *triumph*. "I saw," says the witness, "his Majesty in the coach with six horses, and Peters riding before the king, *triumphing*." Dr. Price, when he talks as if he had made a discovery, only follows a precedent; for, after the commencement of the king's trial, this precursor, the same Dr. Peters, concluding a long prayer at the Royal Chapel at Whitehall (he had very triumphantly chosen his place), said, "I have prayed and preached these twenty years; and now I may say with old Simeon, *Lord, now lettest thou thy servant depart in peace, for mine eyes have seen thy salvation*." Peters had not the fruits of his prayer; for he neither departed so soon as he wished, nor in peace. He became (what I heartily hope none of his followers may be in this country) himself a sacrifice to the triumph which he led as pontiff. They dealt at the Restoration, perhaps, too hardly with this poor good man. But we owe it to his memory and his sufferings, that he had as much illumination, and as much zeal, and had as effectually undermined all *the superstition and error* which might impede the great business he was engaged in, as any who follow and repeat after him in this age, which would assume to itself an exclusive title to the knowledge of the rights of men, and all the glorious consequences of that knowledge.

After this sally of the preacher of the Old Jewry, which differs only in place and time, but agrees perfectly with the spirit and letter of the rapture of 1648, the Revolution Society, the fabricators of governments, the heroic band of *cashierers of monarchs*, electors of sovereigns, and leaders of kings in triumph, strutting with a proud consciousness of the diffusion of knowledge, of which every member had obtained so large a share in the donative, were in haste to make a generous diffusion of the knowledge they had thus gratuitously received. To make this bountiful communication, they adjourned from the church in the Old Jewry to the London Tavern, where the same Dr. Price, in whom the fumes of his oracular tripod were not entirely evaporated, moved and carried the resolution, or address of congratulation, transmitted by Lord Stanhope to the National Assembly of France.

I find a preacher of the Gospel profaning the beautiful and prophetic ejaculation, commonly called "*Nunc dimittis*," made on the first presentation of our Saviour in the temple, and applying it, with an inhuman and unnatural rapture, to the most horrid, atrocious, and afflicting spectacle that perhaps ever was exhibited to the pity and indignation of mankind. This "*leading in triumph*," a thing in its best form unmanly and irreligious, which fills our preacher with such unhallowed transports, must shock, I believe, the moral taste of every well-born mind. Several English were the stupefied and indignant spectators of that triumph. It was (unless we have been strangely deceived) a spectacle more resembling a procession of American savages entering into Onondaga after some of their murders called victories, and leading into hovels hung round with scalps, their captives, overpowered with the scoffs and buffets of women as ferocious as themselves, much more than it resembled the triumphal pomp of a civilized, martial nation;—if a civilized nation, or any men who had a sense of generosity, were capable of a personal triumph over the fallen and afflicted.

This, my dear Sir, was not the triumph of France. I must believe that, as a nation, it overwhelmed you with shame and horror. I must believe that the National Assembly find themselves in a state of the greatest humiliation in not being able to punish the authors of this triumph, or the actors in it, and that they are in a situation in which any inquiry they may make upon the subject must be destitute even of the appearance of liberty or impartiality. The apology of that assembly is found in their situation; but when we approve what they *must* bear, it is in us the degenerate choice of a vitiated mind.

With a compelled appearance of deliberation, they vote under the dominion of a stern necessity. They sit in the heart, as it were, of a foreign republic: they have their residence in a city whose constitution has emanated neither from the charter of their king, nor from their legislative power. There they are surrounded by an army not raised either by the authority of their crown, or by their command; and which, if they should order to dissolve itself, would instantly dissolve them. There they sit, after a gang of assassins had driven away some hundreds of the members; whilst those who held the same moderate principles, with more patience or better hope, continued every day exposed to outrageous insults and murderous threats. There a majority, sometimes real, sometimes pretended, captive itself, compels a captive king to issue as royal edicts, at third hand, the polluted nonsense of their most licentious and giddy coffee-houses. It is notorious that all their measures are decided before they are debated. It is beyond doubt, that, under the terror of the bayonet, and the lamp-post, and the torch to their houses, they are obliged to adopt all the crude and desperate measures suggested by clubs composed of a monstrous medley of all conditions, tongues, and nations. Among these are found persons in comparison of whom Catiline would be thought scrupulous, and Cethegus a man of sobriety and moderation. Nor is it in these clubs alone that the public meas-

ures are deformed into monsters. They undergo a previous distortion in academies, intended as so many seminaries for these clubs, which are set up in all the places of public resort. In these meetings of all sorts, every counsel, in proportion as it is daring, and violent, and perfidious, is taken for the mark of superior genius. Humanity and compassion are ridiculed as the fruits of superstition and ignorance. Tenderness to individuals is considered as treason to the public. Liberty is always to be estimated perfect as property is rendered insecure. Amidst assassination, massacre, and confiscation, perpetrated or meditated, they are forming plans for the good order of future society. Embracing in their arms the carcasses of base criminals, and promoting their relations on the title of their offences, they drive hundreds of virtuous persons to the same end, by forcing them to subsist by beggary or by crime.

The Assembly, their organ, acts before them the farce of deliberation with as little decency as liberty. They act like the comedians of a fair before a riotous audience; they act amidst the tumultuous cries of a mixed mob of ferocious men, and of women lost to shame, who, according to their insolent fancies, direct, control, applaud, explode them, and sometimes mix and take their seats amongst them,—domineering over them with a strange mixture of servile petulance and proud, presumptuous authority. As they have inverted order in all things, the gallery is in the place of the house. This assembly, which overthrows kings and kingdoms, has not even the physiognomy and aspect of a grave legislative body—*nec color imperii, nec frons ulla senatûs.* They have a power given to them, like that of the evil principle, to subvert and destroy, but none to construct, except such machines as may be fitted for further subversion and further destruction.

Who is it that admires, and from the heart is attached to, national representative assemblies, but must turn with horror and disgust from such a profane burlesque, and abominable perversion of that sacred institute? Lovers of monarchy, lovers of republics, must alike abhor it. The members of your Assembly must themselves groan under the tyranny of which they have all the shame, none of the direction, and little of the profit. I am sure many of the members who compose even the majority of that body must feel as I do, notwithstanding the applauses of the Revolution Society. Miserable king! miserable assembly! How must that assembly be silently scandalized with those of their members, who could call a day which seemed to blot the sun out of heaven, *"un beau jour!"* How must they be inwardly indignant at hearing others who thought fit to declare to them, "that the vessel of the state would fly forward in her course towards regeneration with more speed than ever," from the stiff gale of treason and murder which preceded our preacher's triumph! What must they have felt, whilst, with outward patience, and inward indignation, they heard of the slaughter of innocent gentlemen in their houses, that "the blood spilled was not the most pure!" What must they have felt, when they were besieged by complaints of disorders which shook their country to its foundations, at being compelled coolly to tell the complainants that they were under the protection of the law, and that they would address the king (the captive king) to cause the laws to be enforced for their protection; when the enslaved ministers of that captive king had formally notified them that there were neither law nor authority nor power left to protect! What must they have felt at being obliged, as a felicitation on the present new year, to request their captive king to forget the stormy period of the last, on account of the great good which *he* was likely to produce to his people,—to the complete attainment of which good they adjourned the practical demonstrations of their

loyalty, assuring him of their obedience, when he should no longer possess any authority to command!

This address was made with much good nature and affection, to be sure. But among the revolutions in France must be reckoned a considerable revolution in their ideas of politeness. In England we are said to learn manners at second-hand from your side of the water, and that we dress our behaviour in the frippery of France. If so, we are still in the old cut, and have not so far conformed to the new Parisian mode of good breeding, as to think it quite in the most refined strain of delicate compliment (whether in condolence or congratulation) to say, to the most humiliated creature that crawls upon the earth, that great public benefits are derived from the murder of his servants, the attempted assassination of himself and of his wife, and the mortification, disgrace, and degradation, that he has personally suffered. It is a topic of consolation which our ordinary of Newgate would be too humane to use to a criminal at the foot of the gallows. I should have thought that the hangman of Paris, now that he is liberalized by the vote of the National Assembly, and is allowed his rank and arms in the Herald's College of the rights of men, would be too generous, too gallant a man, too full of the sense of his new dignity, to employ that cutting consolation to any of the persons whom the *lèse-nation* might bring under the administration of his *executive powers*.

A man is fallen indeed, when he is thus flattered. The anodyne draught of oblivion, thus drugged, is well calculated to preserve a galling wakefulness, and to feed the living ulcer of a corroding memory. Thus to administer the opiate potion of amnesty, powdered with all the ingredients of scorn and contempt, is to hold to his lips, instead of "the balm of hurt minds," the cup of human misery full to the brim, and to force him to drink it to the dregs.

Yielding to reasons at least as forcible as those which were so delicately urged in the compliment on the new year, the king of France will probably endeavour to forget these events and that compliment. But History, who keeps a durable record of all our acts, and exercises her awful censure over the proceedings of all sorts of sovereigns, will not forget either those events, or the cra of his liberal refinement in the intercourse of mankind. History will record, that on the morning of the 6th of October, 1789, the king and queen of France, after a day of confusion, alarm, dismay, and slaughter, lay down, under the pledged security of public faith, to indulge nature in a few hours of respite, and troubled, melancholy repose. From this sleep the queen was first startled by the voice of the sentinel at her door, who cried out to her to save herself by flight, that this was the last proof of fidelity he could give, that they were upon him, and he was dead. Instantly he was cut down. A band of cruel ruffians and assassins, reeking with his blood, rushed into the chamber of the queen, and pierced with a hundred strokes of bayonets and poniards the bed, from whence this persecuted woman had but just time to fly almost naked, and, through ways unknown to the murderers, had escaped to seek refuge at the feet of a king and husband, not secure of his own life for a moment.

This king, to say no more of him, and this queen, and their infant children (who once would have been the pride and hope of a great and generous people), were then forced to abandon the sanctuary of the most splendid palace in the world, which they left swimming in blood, polluted by massacre, and strewed with scattered limbs and mutilated carcasses. Thence they were conducted into the capital of their kingdom. Two had been selected from the unprovoked, unresisted, promiscuous slaughter, which was made of the gentlemen of birth and family who composed the king's body-guard. These two gentlemen, with all the parade of an execution of justice, were cruelly and publicly dragged to the block, and beheaded in the great court of the palace. Their heads were stuck upon spears, and led the procession; whilst the royal captives who followed in the train were slowly moved along, amidst the horrid yells, and shrilling screams, and frantic dances, and infamous contumelies, and all the unutterable abominations of the furies of hell, in the abused shape of the vilest of women. After they had been made to taste, drop by drop, more than the bitterness of death, in the slow torture of a journey of twelve miles, protracted to six hours, they were, under a guard composed of those very soldiers who had thus conducted them through this famous triumph, lodged in one of the old palaces of Paris, now converted into a Bastile for kings.

Is this a triumph to be consecrated at altars, to be commemorated with grateful thanksgiving, to be offered to the divine humanity with fervent prayer and enthusiastic ejaculation?—These Theban and Thracian orgies, acted in France, and applauded only in the Old Jewry, I assure you, kindle prophetic enthusiasm in the minds but of very few people in this kingdom: although a saint and apostle, who may have revelations of his own, and who has so completely vanquished all the mean superstitions of the heart, may incline to think it pious and decorous to compare it with the entrance into the world of the Prince of Peace, proclaimed in a holy temple by a venerable sage, and not long before not worse announced by the voice of angels to the quiet innocence of shepherds.

At first I was at a loss to account for this fit of unguarded transport. I knew, indeed, that the sufferings of monarchs make a delicious repast to some sort of palates. There were reflections which might serve to keep this appetite within some bounds of temperance. But when I took one circumstance into my consideration, I was obliged to confess that much allowance ought to be made for the society, and that the temptation was too strong for common discretion: I mean, the circumstance of the Io Pæan of the triumph, the animating cry which called "for *all* the BISHOPS to be hanged on the lamp-posts," might well have brought forth a burst of enthusiasm on the foreseen consequences of this happy day. I allow to so much enthusiasm some little deviation from prudence. I allow this prophet to break forth into hymns of joy and thanksgiving on an event which appears like the precursor of the Millennium, and the projected Fifth Monarchy, in the destruction of all church establishments. There was, however (as in all human affairs there is), in the midst of this joy, something to exercise the patience of these worthy gentlemen, and to try the long-suffering of their faith. The actual murder of the king and queen, and their child, was wanting to the other auspicious circumstances of this *"beautiful day."* The actual murder of the bishops, though called for by so many holy ejaculations, was also wanting. A group of regicide and sacrilegious slaughter was indeed boldly sketched, but it was only sketched. It unhappily was left unfinished, in this great history-piece of the massacre of innocents. What hardy pencil of a great master, from the school of the rights of men, will finish it, is to be seen hereafter. The age has not yet the complete benefit of that diffusion of knowledge that has undermined superstition and error; and the king of France wants another object or two to consign to oblivion, in consideration of all the good which is to arise from his own sufferings, and the patriotic crimes of an enlightened age.

Although this work of our new light and knowledge did not go to the length that in all probability it was intended it should be carried, yet I must think that such treatment of any human creatures must be shocking to any but those who are made for accomplishing revolutions. But I cannot stop here. Influenced by the inborn feelings of my nature, and not being illuminated by a single ray of this new-sprung modern light, I confess to you, Sir, that the exalted rank of the persons suffering, and particularly the sex, the beauty, and the amiable qualities of the descendant of so many kings and emperors, with the tender age of royal infants, insensible only through infancy and innocence of the cruel outrages to which their parents were exposed, instead of being a subject of exultation, adds not a little to my sensibility on that most melancholy occasion.

I hear that the august person who was the principal object of our preacher's triumph, though he supported himself, felt much on that shameful occasion. As a man, it became him to feel for his wife and his children, and the faithful guards of his person that were massacred in cold blood about him; as a prince, it became him to feel for the strange and frightful transformation of his civilized subjects, and to be more grieved for them than solicitous for himself. It derogates little from his fortitude, while it adds infinitely to the honour of his humanity. I am very sorry to say it, very sorry indeed, that such personages are in a situation in which it is not becoming in us to praise the virtues of the great.

I hear, and I rejoice to hear, that the great lady, the other object of the triumph, has borne that day (one is interested that beings made for suffering should suffer well), and that she bears all the succeeding days, that she bears the imprisonment of her husband, and her own captivity, and the exile of her friends, and the insulting adulation of addresses, and the whole weight of her accumulated wrongs, with a serene patience, in a manner suited to her rank and race, and becoming the offspring of a sovereign distinguished for her piety and her courage; that, like her, she has lofty sentiments; that she feels with the dignity of a Roman matron; that in the last extremity she will save herself from the last disgrace; and that, if she must fall, she will fall by no ignoble hand.

It is now sixteen or seventeen years since I saw the queen of France, then the Dauphiness, at Versailles; and surely never lighted on this orb, which she hardly seemed to touch, a more delightful vision. I saw her just above the horizon, decorating and cheering the elevated sphere she just began to move in—glittering like the morning-star, full of life, and splendour and joy. Oh! what a revolution! and what a heart must I have, to contemplate without emotion that elevation and that fall! Little did I dream when she added titles of veneration to those of enthusiastic, distant, respectful love, that she should ever be obliged to carry the sharp antidote against disgrace concealed in that bosom! little did I dream that I should have lived to see such disasters fallen upon her in a nation of gallant men, in a nation of men of honour, and of cavaliers! I thought ten thousand swords must have leaped from their scabbards to avenge even a look that threatened her with insult. But the age of chivalry is gone. That of sophisters, economists, and calculators, has succeeded; and the glory of Europe is extinguished for ever. Never, never more, shall we behold that generous loyalty to rank and sex, that proud submission, that dignified obedience, that subordination of the heart, which kept alive, even in servitude itself, the spirit of an exalted freedom! The unbought grace of life, the cheap defence of nations, the nurse of manly sentiment and heroic enterprise, is gone! It is gone, that sensibility of principle, that chastity of honour, which felt a stain like a wound, which inspired courage whilst it mitigated ferocity, which ennobled whatever it touched, and under which vice itself lost half its evil, by losing all its grossness!

This mixed system of opinion and sentiment had its origin in the ancient chivalry; and the principle, though varied in its appearance by the varying state of human affairs, subsisted and influenced through a long succession of generations, even to the time we live in. If it should ever be totally extinguished, the loss I fear will be great. It is this which has given its character to modern Europe. It is this which has distinguished it under all its forms of government, and distinguished it to its advantage, from the states of Asia, and possibly from those states which flourished in the most brilliant periods of the antique world. It was this, which, without confounding ranks, had produced a noble equality, and handed it down through all the gradations of social life. It was this opinion which mitigated kings into companions, and raised private men to be fellows with kings. Without force or opposition, it subdued the fierceness of pride and power; it obliged sovereigns to submit to the soft collar of social esteem, compelled stern authority to submit to elegance, and gave a domination, vanquisher of laws, to be subdued by manners.

But now all is to be changed. All the pleasing illusions, which made power gentle and obedience liberal, which harmonized the different shades of life, and which by a bland assimilation incorporated into politics the sentiments which beautify and soften private society, are to be dissolved by this new conquering empire of light and reason. All the decent drapery of life is to be rudely torn off. All the superadded ideas, furnished from the wardrobe of a moral imagination, which the heart owns and the understanding ratifies, as necessary to cover the defects of our naked, shivering nature, and to raise it to dignity in our own estimation, are to be exploded as a ridiculous, absurd, and antiquated fashion.

On this scheme of things, a king is but a man, a queen is but a woman, a woman is but an animal,—and an animal not of the highest order. All homage paid to the sex in general as such, and without distinct views, is to be regarded as romance and folly. Regicide, and parricide, and sacrilege, are but fictions of superstition, corrupting jurisprudence by destroying its simplicity. The murder of a king, or a queen, or a bishop, or a father, are only common homicide; and if the people are by any chance or in any way gainers by it, a sort of homicide much the most pardonable, and into which we ought not to make too severe a scrutiny.

On the scheme of this barbarous philosophy, which is the offspring of cold hearts and muddy understandings, and which is as void of solid wisdom as it is destitute of all taste and elegance, laws are to be supported only by their own terrors, and by the concern which each individual may find in them from his own private speculations, or can spare to them from his own private interests. In the groves of *their* academy, at the end of every vista, you see nothing but the gallows. Nothing is left which engages the affections on the part of the commonwealth. On the principles of this mechanic philosophy, our institutions can never be embodied, if I may use the expression, in persons, so as to create in us love, veneration, admiration, or attachment. But that sort of reason which banishes the affections is incapable of filling their place. These public affections, combined with manners, are required sometimes as supplements, sometimes as correctives, always as aids to law. The precept given by a wise man, as well as a great critic, for the construction of poems, is equally true as to states:—*Non satis est pulchra esse poemata, dulcia sunto.* There ought to be a system of manners in every nation, which a well-formed mind would be disposed to relish. To make us love our country, our country ought to be lovely.

But power, of some kind or other,

will survive the shock in which manners and opinions perish; and it will find other and worse means for its support. The usurpation which, in order to subvert ancient institutions, has destroyed ancient principles, will hold power by arts similar to those by which it has acquired it. When the old feudal and chivalrous spirit of fealty, which, by freeing kings from fear, freed both kings and subjects from the precautions of tyranny, shall be extinct in the minds of men, plots and assassinations will be anticipated by preventive murder and preventive confiscation, and that long roll of grim and bloody maxims which form the political code of all power not standing on its own honour and the honour of those who are to obey it. Kings will be tyrants from policy, when subjects are rebels from principle.

When ancient opinions and rules of life are taken away, the loss cannot possibly be estimated. From that moment we have no compass to govern us, nor can we know distinctly to what port we steer. Europe, undoubtedly, taken in a mass, was in a flourishing condition the day on which your Revolution was completed. How much of that prosperous state was owing to the spirit of our old manners and opinions is not easy to say; but as such causes cannot be indifferent in their operation, we must presume, that, on the whole, their operation was beneficial.

We are but too apt to consider things in the state in which we find them, without sufficiently adverting to the causes by which they have been produced, and possibly may be upheld. Nothing is more certain than that our manners, our civilization, and all the good things which are connected with manners and with civilization, have, in this European world of ours, depended for ages upon two principles, and were indeed the result of both combined: I mean the spirit of a gentleman, and the spirit of religion. The nobility and the clergy, the one by profession, the other by patronage, kept learning in existence, even in the midst of arms and confusions, and whilst governments were rather in their causes than formed. Learning paid back what it received to nobility and to priesthood, and paid it with usury, by enlarging their ideas, and by furnishing their minds. Happy if they had all continued to know their indissoluble union, and their proper place! Happy if learning, not debauched by ambition, had been satisfied to continue the instructor, and not aspired to be the master! Along with its natural protectors and guardians, learning will be cast into the mire, and trodden down under the hoofs of a swinish multitude.

If, as I suspect, modern letters owe more than they are always willing to own to ancient manners, so do other interests which we value full as much as they are worth. Even commerce, and trade, and manufacture, the gods of our economical politicians, are themselves perhaps but creatures, are themselves but effects, which, as first causes, we choose to worship. They certainly grew under the same shade in which learning flourished. They, too, may decay with their natural protecting principles. With you, for the present at least, they all threaten to disappear together. Where trade and manufactures are wanting to a people, and the spirit of nobility and religion remains, sentiment supplies, and not always ill supplies, their place; but if commerce and the arts should be lost in an experiment to try how well a state may stand without these old fundamental principles, what sort of a thing must be a nation of gross, stupid, ferocious, and at the same time poor and sordid barbarians, destitute of religion, honour, or manly pride, possessing nothing at present, and hoping for nothing hereafter?

I wish you may not be going fast, and by the shortest cut, to that horrible and disgustful situation. Already there appears a poverty of conception,

a coarseness and vulgarity, in all the proceedings of the Assembly and of all their instructors. Their liberty is not liberal. Their science is presumptuous ignorance. Their humanity is savage and brutal.

It is not clear whether in England we learned those grand and decorous principles and manners, of which considerable traces yet remain, from you, or whether you took them from us. But to you, I think, we trace them best. You seem to me to be—*gentis incunabula nostræ.* France has always more or less influenced manners in England; and when your fountain is choked up and polluted, the stream will not run long, or not run clear, with us, or perhaps with any nation. This gives all Europe, in my opinion, but too close and connected a concern in what is done in France. Excuse me, therefore, if I have dwelt too long on the atrocious spectacle of the 6th of October, 1789, or have given too much scope to the reflections which have arisen in my mind on occasion of the most important of all revolutions, which may be dated from that day: I mean a revolution in sentiments, manners, and moral opinions. As things now stand, with everything respectable destroyed without us, and an attempt to destroy within us every principle of respect, one is almost forced to apologize for harbouring the common feelings of men.

Why do I feel so differently from the Reverend Dr. Price, and those of his lay flock who will choose to adopt the sentiments of his discourse?—For this plain reason: Because it is *natural* I should; because we are so made as to be affected at such spectacles with melancholy sentiments upon the unstable condition of mortal prosperity, and the tremendous uncertainty of human greatness; because in those natural feelings we learn great lessons; because in events like these our passions instruct our reason; because, when kings are hurled from their thrones by the Supreme Director of this great drama, and become the ob-

jects of insult to the base and of pity
to the good, we behold such disasters
in the moral as we should behold a
miracle in the physical order of things.
We are alarmed into reflection; our
minds (as it has long since been observed) are purified by terror and
pity; our weak, unthinking pride is
humbled under the dispensations of
a mysterious wisdom. Some tears 10
might be drawn from me, if such a
spectacle were exhibited on the stage.
I should be truly ashamed of finding
in myself that superficial, theatric
sense of painted distress, whilst I
could exult over it in real life. With
such a perverted mind, I could never
venture to show my face at a tragedy.
People would think the tears that
Garrick formerly, or that Siddons not 20
long since, have extorted from me,
were the tears of hypocrisy; I should
know them to be the tears of folly.

Indeed the theatre is a better school
of moral sentiments than churches
where the feelings of humanity are
thus outraged. Poets who have to deal
with an audience not yet graduated in
the school of the rights of men, and
who must apply themselves to the 30
moral constitution of the heart, would
not dare to produce such a triumph
as a matter of exultation. There,
where men follow their natural impulses, they would not bear the odious
maxims of a Machiavellian policy,
whether applied to the attainment of
monarchical or democratic tyranny.
They would reject them on the modern, as they once did on the ancient, 40
stage, where they could not bear even
the hypothetical proposition of such
wickedness in the mouth of a personated tyrant, though suitable to the
character he sustained. No theatric
audience in Athens would bear what
has been borne in the midst of the
real tragedy of his triumphal day: a
principal actor weighing, as it were in
scales hung in a shop of horrors, so 50
much actual crime against so much
contingent advantage,—and after putting in and out weights, declaring that
the balance was on the side of the

advantages. They would not bear to
see the crimes of new democracy
posted as in a ledger against the
crimes of old despotism, and the book-
keepers of politics finding democracy
still in debt, but by no means unable
or unwilling to pay the balance. In
the theatre, the first intuitive glance,
without any elaborate process of reasoning, will show that this method of
political computation would justify
every extent of crime. They would see,
that on these principles, even where
the very worst acts were not perpetrated, it was owing rather to the fortune of the conspirators, than to their
parsimony in the expenditure of
treachery and blood. They would
soon see that criminal means, once
tolerated, are soon preferred. They
present a shorter cut to the object
than through the highway of the
moral virtues. Justifying perfidy and
murder for public benefit, public
benefit would soon become the pretext, and perfidy and murder the end;
until rapacity, malice, revenge, and
fear more dreadful than revenge,
could satiate their insatiable appetites. Such must be the consequences
of losing, in the splendour of these
triumphs of the rights of men, all natural sense of wrong and right.

But the reverend pastor exults in
this "leading in triumph," because,
truly, Louis the Sixteenth was "an arbitrary monarch": that is, in other
words, neither more nor less than because he was Louis the Sixteenth, and
because he had the misfortune to be
born king of France, with the prerogatives of which a long line of ancestors,
and a long acquiescence of the people,
without any act of his, had put him in
possession. A misfortune it has indeed
turned out to him, that he was born
king of France. But misfortune is not
crime, nor is indiscretion always the
greatest guilt. I shall never think that
a prince, the acts of whose whole reign
were a series of concessions to his subjects, who was willing to relax his authority, to remit his prerogatives, to
call his people to a share of freedom

not known, perhaps not desired, by their ancestors,—such a prince, though he should be subjected to the common frailties attached to men and to princes, though he should have once thought it necessary to provide force against the desperate designs manifestly carrying on against his person, and the remnants of his authority,—though all this should be taken into consideration, I shall be led with great difficulty to think he deserves the cruel and insulting triumph of Paris, and of Dr. Price. I tremble for the cause of liberty, from such an example to kings. I tremble for the cause of humanity, in the unpunished outrages of the most wicked of mankind. But there are some people of that low and degenerate fashion of mind that they look up with a sort of complacent awe and admiration to kings who know to keep firm in their seat, to hold a strict hand over their subjects, to assert their prerogative, and, by the awakened vigilance of a severe despotism, to guard against the very first approaches of freedom. Against such as these they never elevate their voice. Deserters from principle, listed with fortune, they never see any good in suffering virtue, nor any crime in prosperous usurpation.

If it could have been made clear to me that the king and queen of France (those I mean who were such before the triumph) were inexorable and cruel tyrants, that they had formed a deliberate scheme for massacring the National Assembly (I think I have seen something like the latter insinuated in certain publications), I should think their captivity just. If this be true, much more ought to have been done, but done, in my opinion, in another manner. The punishment of real tyrants is a noble and awful act of justice; and it has with truth been said to be consolatory to the human mind. But if I were to punish a wicked king, I should regard the dignity in avenging the crime. Justice is grave and decorous, and in its punishments rather seems to submit to a

necessity than to make a choice. Had Nero, or Agrippina, or Louis the Eleventh, or Charles the Ninth, been the subject; if Charles the Twelfth of Sweden, after the murder of Patkul, or his predecessor Christina, after the murder of Monaldeschi, had fallen into your hands, Sir, or into mine, I am sure our conduct would have been different.

If the French king, or king of the French (or by whatever name he is known in the new vocabulary of your Constitution), has in his own person and that of his queen really deserved these unavowed, but unavenged, murderous attempts, and those frequent indignities more cruel than murder, such a person would ill deserve even that subordinate executory trust which I understand is to be placed in him; nor is he fit to be called chief in a nation which he has outraged and oppressed. A worse choice for such an office in a new commonwealth than that of a deposed tyrant could not possibly be made. But to degrade and insult a man as the worst of criminals, and afterwards to trust him in your highest concerns, as a faithful, honest, and zealous servant, is not consistent with reasoning, nor prudent in policy, nor safe in practice. Those who could make such an appointment must be guilty of a more flagrant breach of trust than any they have yet committed against the people. As this is the only crime in which your leading politicians could have acted inconsistently, I conclude that there is no sort of ground for these horrid insinuations. I think no better of all the other calumnies.

In England, we give no credit to them. We are generous enemies; we are faithful allies. We spurn from us with disgust and indignation the slanders of those who bring us their anecdotes with the attestation of the flower-de-luce on their shoulder. We have Lord George Gordon fast in Newgate; and neither his being a public proselyte to Judaism, nor his having in his zeal against Catholic priests and all sorts of ecclesiastics, raised a mob (excuse the term, it is still in use here) which pulled down all our prisons, have preserved to him a liberty of which he did not render himself worthy by a virtuous use of it. We have rebuilt Newgate, and tenanted the mansion. We have prisons almost as strong as the Bastile, for those who dare to libel the queens of France. In this spiritual retreat let the noble libeller remain. Let him there meditate on his Talmud, until he learns a conduct more becoming his birth and parts, and not so disgraceful to the ancient religion to which he has become a proselyte; or until some persons from your side of the water, to please your new Hebrew brethren, shall ransom him. He may then be enabled to purchase, with the old boards of the synagogue, and a very small poundage on the long compound interest of the thirty pieces of silver (Dr. Price has shown us what miracles compound interest will perform in 1790 years), the lands which are lately discovered to have been usurped by the Gallican church. Send us your Popish archbishop of Paris, and we will send you our Protestant Rabbin. We shall treat the person you send us in exchange like a gentleman and an honest man, as he is: but pray let him bring with him the fund of his hospitality, bounty, and charity; and, depend upon it, we shall never confiscate a shilling of that honourable and pious fund, nor think of enriching the Treasury with the spoils of the poor-box.

To tell you the truth, my dear Sir, I think the honour of our nation to be somewhat concerned in the disclaimer of the proceedings of this society of the Old Jewry and the London Tavern. I have no man's proxy, I speak only for myself, when I disclaim, as I do with all possible earnestness, all communion with the actors in that triumph, or with the admirers of it. When I assert anything else, as concerning the people of England, I speak from observation, not from authority; but I speak from the experience I have had in a pretty extensive and mixed communication with the inhabitants of this kingdom, of all descriptions and ranks, and after a course of attentive observation, begun early in life, and continued for nearly forty years. I have often been astonished, considering that we are divided from you but by a slender dyke of about twenty-four miles, and that the mutual intercourse between the two countries has lately been very great, to find how little you seem to know of us. I suspect that this is owing to your forming a judgment of this nation from certain publications, which do, very erroneously, if they do at all, represent the opinions and dispositions generally prevalent in England. The vanity, restlessness, petulance, and spirit of intrigue, of several petty cabals, who attempt to hide their total want of consequence in bustle and noise, and puffing, and mutual quotation of each other, makes you imagine that our contemptuous neglect of their abilities is a mark of general acquiescence in their opinions. No such thing, I assure you. Because half a dozen grasshoppers under a fern make the field ring with their importunate chink, whilst thousands of great cattle reposed beneath the shadow of the British oak chew the cud and are silent, pray do not imagine that those who make the noise are the only inhabitants of the field; that, of course, they are many in number; or that, after all, they are other than the little, shrivelled, meagre, hopping, though loud and troublesome insects of the hour.

I almost venture to affirm that not one in a hundred amongst us participates in the "triumph" of the Revolution Society. If the king and queen of France and their children were to fall into our hands by the chance of war, in the most acrimonious of all hostilities (I deprecate such an event, I deprecate such hostilities), they would be treated with another sort of triumphal entry into London. We formerly have had a king of France in that situation: you have read how he was treated by the victor in the field, and in what manner he was afterwards received in England. Four hundred years have gone over us; but I believe we are not materially changed since that period. Thanks to our sullen resistance to innovation, thanks to the cold sluggishness of our national character, we still bear the stamp of our forefathers. We have not (as I conceive) lost the generosity and dignity of thinking of the fourteenth century; nor as yet have we subtilized ourselves into savages. We are not the converts of Rousseau; we are not the disciples of Voltaire; Helvetius has made no progress amongst us. Atheists are not our preachers; madmen are not our lawgivers. We know that *we* have made no discoveries, and we think that no discoveries are to be made, in morality; nor many in the great principles of government, nor in the ideas of liberty, which were understood long before we were born altogether as well as they will be after the grave has heaped its mould upon our presumption, and the silent tomb shall have imposed its law on our pert loquacity. In England we have not yet been completely embowelled of our natural entrails: we still feel within us, and we cherish and cultivate, those inbred sentiments which are the faithful guardians, the active monitors of our duty, the true supporters of all liberal and manly morals. We have not been drawn and trussed, in order that we may be filled, like stuffed birds in a museum, with chaff and rags, and paltry, blurred shreds of paper about the rights of man. We preserve the whole of our feelings still native and entire, unsophisticated by pedantry and infidelity. We have real hearts of flesh and blood beating in our bosoms. We fear God; we look up with awe to kings, with affection to parliaments, with duty to magistrates, with reverence to priests, and with respect to nobility. Why? Because when such

ideas are brought before our minds, it is *natural* to be so affected; because all other feelings are false and spurious, and tend to corrupt our minds, to vitiate our primary morals, to render us unfit for rational liberty, and, by teaching us a servile, licentious, and abandoned insolence, to be our low sport for a few holidays, to make us perfectly fit for and justly deserving of slavery through the whole course of our lives.

You see, Sir, that in this enlightened age I am bold enough to confess that we are generally men of untaught feelings: that instead of casting away all our old prejudices, we cherish them to a very considerable degree; and, to take more shame to ourselves, we cherish them because they are prejudices; and the longer they have lasted, and the more generally they have prevailed, the more we cherish them. We are afraid to put men to live and trade each on his own private stock of reason; because we suspect that this stock in each man is small, and that the individuals would do better to avail themselves of the general bank and capital of nations and of ages. Many of our men of speculation, instead of exploding general prejudices, employ their sagacity to discover the latent wisdom which prevails in them. If they find what they seek (and they seldom fail), they think it more wise to continue the prejudice, with the reason involved, than to cast away the coat of prejudice, and to leave nothing but the naked reason; because prejudice, with its reason, has a motive to give action to that reason, and an affection which will give it permanence. Prejudice is of ready application in the emergency; it previously engages the mind in a steady course of wisdom and virtue, and does not leave the man hesitating in the moment of decision, sceptical, puzzled, and unresolved. Prejudice renders a man's virtue his habit, and not a series of unconnected acts. Through just prejudice, his duty becomes a part of his nature.

Your literary men, and your politicians, and so do the whole clan of the enlightened among us, essentially differ in these points. They have no respect for the wisdom of others; but they pay it off by a very full measure of confidence in their own. With them it is a sufficient motive to destroy an old scheme of things, because it is an old one. As to the new, they are in no sort of fear with regard to the duration of a building run up in haste; because duration is no object to those who think little or nothing has been done before their time, and who place all their hopes in discovery. They conceive, very systematically, that all things which give perpetuity are mischievous, and therefore they are at inexpiable war with all establishments. They think that government may vary like modes of dress, and with as little ill effect; that there needs no principle of attachment, except a sense of present conveniency, to any constitution of the state. They always speak as if they were of opinion that there is a singular species of compact between them and their magistrates, which binds the magistrate, but which has nothing reciprocal in it, but that the majesty of the people has a right to dissolve it without any reason but its will. Their attachment to their country itself is only so far as it agrees with some of their fleeting projects: it begins and ends with that scheme of polity which falls in with their momentary opinion.

These doctrines, or rather sentiments, seem prevalent with your new statesmen. But they are wholly different from those on which we have always acted in this country.

I hear it is sometimes given out in France, that what is doing among you is after the example of England. I beg leave to affirm that scarcely anything done with you has originated from the practice or the prevalent opinions of this people, either in the act or in the spirit of the proceeding. Let me add, that we are as unwilling to learn these lessons from France as we are sure that we never taught them to that nation. The cabals here who take a sort of share in your transactions, as yet consists of but a handful of people. If, unfortunately, by their intrigues, their sermons, their publications, and by a confidence derived from an expected union with the counsels and forces of the French nation, they should draw considerable numbers into their faction, and in consequence should seriously attempt anything here in imitation of what has been done with you, the event, I dare venture to prophesy, will be, that, with some trouble to their country, they will soon accomplish their own destruction. This people refused to change their law in remote ages from respect to the infallibility of popes, and they will not now alter it from a pious implicit faith in the dogmatism of philosophers; though the former was armed with the anathema and crusade, and though the latter should act with the libel and the lamp-iron.

Formerly your affairs were your own concern only. We felt for them as men; but we kept aloof from them, because we were not citizens of France. But when we see the model held up to ourselves, we must feel as Englishmen, and feeling, we must provide as Englishmen. Your affairs, in spite of us, are made a part of our interest,—so far at least as to keep at a distance your panacea, or your plague. If it be a panacea, we do not want it: we know the consequences of unnecessary physic. If it be a plague, it is such a plague that the precautions of the most severe quarantine ought to be established against it.

I hear on all hands that a cabal, calling itself philosophic, receives the glory of many of the late proceedings, and that their opinions and systems are the true actuating spirit of the whole of them. I have heard of no party in England, literary or political, at any time, known by such a description. It is not with you composed of those men, is it? whom the vulgar, in their blunt, homely style, commonly call atheists and infidels? If it be, I admit that we too have had writers of that description, who made some noise in their day. At present they repose in lasting oblivion. Who, born within the last forty years, has read one word of Collins, and Toland, and Tindal, and Chubb, and Morgan, and that whole race who called themselves Freethinkers? Who now reads Bolingbroke? Who ever read him through? Ask the booksellers of London what is become of all these lights of the world. In as few years their few successors will go to the family vault of "all the Capulets." But whatever they were, or are, with us, they were and are wholly unconnected individuals. With us they kept the common nature of their kind, and were not gregarious. They never acted in corps, or were known as a faction in the state, nor presumed to influence in that name or character, nor for the purposes of such a faction, on any of our public concerns. Whether they ought so to exist, and so be permitted to act, is another question. As such cabals have not existed in England, so neither has the spirit of them had any influence in establishing the original frame of our constitution, or in any one of the several reparations and improvements it has undergone. The whole has been done under the auspices, and is confirmed by the sanctions, of religion and piety. The whole has emanated from the simplicity of our national character, and from a sort of native plainness and directness of understanding, which for a long time characterized those men who have successively obtained authority amongst us. This disposition still remains; at least in the great body of the people.

We know, and what is better, we feel inwardly, that religion is the basis of civil society, and the source of all good and of all comfort. In England we are so convinced of this, that there is no rust of superstition, with which the accumulated absurdity of the human mind might have crusted it over in the course of ages, that ninety-nine in a hundred of the people of England would not prefer to impiety. We shall never be such fools as to call in an enemy to the substance of any system to remove its corruptions, to supply its defects, or to perfect its construction. If our religious tenets should ever want a further elucidation, we shall not call on Atheism to explain them. We shall not light up our temple from that unhallowed fire. It will be illuminated with other lights. It will be perfumed with other incense than the infectious stuff which is imported by the smugglers of adulterated metaphysics. If our ecclesiastical establishment should want a revision, it is not avarice or rapacity, public or private, that we shall employ for the audit or receipt or application of its consecrated revenue. Violently condemning neither the Greek nor the Armenian, nor, since heats are subsided, the Roman system of religion, we prefer the Protestant: not because we think it has less of the Christian religion in it, but because, in our judgment, it has more. We are Protestants, not from indifference, but from zeal.

We know, and it is our pride to know, that man is by his constitution a religious animal; that Atheism is against, not only our reason, but our instincts; and that it cannot prevail long. But if, in the moment of riot, and in a drunken delirium from the hot spirit drawn out of the alembic of hell, which in France is now so furiously boiling, we should uncover our nakedness, by throwing off that Christian religion which has hitherto been our boast and comfort, and one great source of civilization amongst us, and amongst many other nations, we are apprehensive (being well aware that the mind will not endure a void) that some uncouth, pernicious, and degrading superstition might take place of it.

For that reason, before we take from our establishment the natural human means of estimation, and give it up to contempt, as you have done, and in doing it have incurred the penalties you well deserve to suffer, we desire that some other may be presented to us in the place of it. We shall then form our judgment.

On these ideas, instead of quarrelling with establishments, as some do, who have made a philosophy and a religion of their hostility to such institutions, we cleave closely to them. We are resolved to keep an established church, an established monarchy, an established aristocracy, and an established democracy, each in the degree it exists, and in no greater. I shall show you presently how much of each of these we possess.

It has been the misfortune (not, as these gentlemen think it, the glory) of this age, that everything is to be discussed, as if the constitution of our country were to be always a subject rather of altercation than enjoyment. For this reason, as well as for the satisfaction of those among you (if any such you have among you) who may wish to profit of examples, I venture to trouble you with a few thoughts upon each of these establishments. I do not think they were unwise in ancient Rome, who, when they wished to new-model their laws, set commissioners to examine the best constituted republics within their reach.

First, I beg leave to speak of our church establishment, which is the first of our prejudices; not a prejudice destitute of reason, but involving in it profound and extensive wisdom. I speak of it first. It is first, and last, and midst in our minds. For, taking ground on that religious system, of which we are now in possession, we continue to act on the early received and uniformly continued sense of mankind. That sense not only, like a wise architect, hath built up the august fabric of states, but like a provident proprietor, to preserve the structure from profanation and ruin, as a sacred temple purged from all the impurities of fraud and violence and in-

justice and tyranny, hath solemnly and for ever consecrated the commonwealth, and all that officiate in it. This consecration is made, that all who administer in the government of men, in which they stand in the person of God Himself, should have high and worthy notions of their function and destination; that their hope should be full of immortality; that they should not look to the paltry pelf of the moment, nor to the temporary and transient praise of the vulgar, but to a solid, permanent existence, in the permanent part of their nature, and to a permanent fame and glory, in the example they leave as a rich inheritance to the world.

Such sublime principles ought to be infused into persons of exalted situations; and religious establishments provided, that may continually revive and enforce them. Every sort of moral, every sort of civil, every sort of politic institution, aiding the rational and natural ties that connect the human understanding and affections to the divine, are not more than necessary, in order to build up that wonderful structure, Man; whose prerogative it is, to be in a great degree a creature of his own making; and who, when made as he ought to be made, is destined to hold no trivial place in the creation. But whenever man is put over men, as the better nature ought ever to preside, in that case more particularly, he should as nearly as possible be approximated to his perfection.

The consecration of the state, by a state religious establishment, is necessary also to operate with a wholesome awe upon free citizens; because, in order to secure their freedom, they must enjoy some determinate portion of power. To them therefore a religion connected with the state, and with their duty towards it, becomes even more necessary than in such societies where the people, by the terms of their subjection, are confined to private sentiments, and the management of their own family concerns.

All persons possessing any portion of power ought to be strongly and awfully impressed with an idea that they act in trust; and that they are to account for their conduct in that trust to the one great Master, Author, and Founder of society.

This principle ought even to be more strongly impressed upon the minds of those who compose the collective sovereignty than upon those of single princes. Without instruments, these princes can do nothing. Whoever uses instruments, in finding helps, finds also impediments. Their power is therefore by no means complete; nor are they safe in extreme abuse. Such persons, however elevated by flattery, arrogance, and self-opinion, must be sensible, that, whether covered or not by positive law, in some way or other they are accountable even here for the abuse of their trust. If they are not cut off by a rebellion of their people, they may be strangled by the very janissaries kept for their security against all other rebellion. Thus we have seen the king of France sold by his soldiers for an increase of pay. But where popular authority is absolute and unrestrained, the people have an infinitely greater, because a far better founded, confidence in their own power. They are themselves in a great measure their own instruments. They are nearer to their objects. Besides, they are less under responsibility to one of the greatest controlling powers on earth, the sense of fame and estimation. The share of infamy that is likely to fall to the lot of each individual in public acts is small indeed; the operation of opinion being in the inverse ratio to the number of those who abuse power. Their own approbation of their own acts has to them the appearance of a public judgment in their favour. A perfect democracy is therefore the most shameless thing in the world. As it is the most shameless, it is also the most fearless. No man apprehends in his person that he can be made subject to punishment. Certainly the people at large never ought: for, as all punishments are for example towards the conservation of the people at large, the people at large can never become the subject of punishment by any human hand. It is therefore of infinite importance that they should not be suffered to imagine that their will, any more than that of kings, is the standard of right and wrong. They ought to be persuaded that they are full as little entitled, and far less qualified with safety to themselves, to use any arbitrary power whatsoever; that therefore they are not, under a false show of liberty, but in truth to exercise an unnatural, inverted domination, tyranically to exact, from those who officiate in the state, not an entire devotion to their interest, which is their right, but an abject submission to their occasional will: extinguishing thereby, in all those who serve them, all moral principle, all sense of dignity, all use of judgment, and all consistency of character; whilst by the very same process they give themselves up a proper, a suitable, but a most contemptible prey to the servile ambition of popular sycophants, or courtly flatterers.

When the people have emptied themselves of all the lust of selfish will, which without religion it is utterly impossible they ever should,—when they are conscious that they exercise, and exercise perhaps in a higher link of the order of delegation, the power, which to be legitimate must be according to that eternal, immutable law, in which will and reason are the same,—they will be more careful how they place power in base and incapable hands. In their nomination to office, they will not appoint to the exercise of authority, as to a pitiful job, but as to a holy function; not according to their sordid, selfish interest, nor to their wanton caprice, nor to their arbitrary will; but they will confer that power (which any man may well tremble to give or to receive) on those only in whom they may discern that predominant proportion of active virtue and wisdom, taken together and fitted to the charge, such as in the great and inevitable mixed mass of human imperfections and infirmities is to be found.

When they are habitually convinced that no evil can be acceptable, either in the act or the permission, to Him whose essence is good, they will be better able to extirpate out of the minds of all magistrates, civil, ecclesiastical, or military, anything that bears the least resemblance to a proud and lawless domination.

But one of the first and most leading principles on which the commonwealth and the laws are consecrated, is lest the temporary possessors and life-renters in it, unmindful of what they have received from their ancestors, or of what is due to their posterity, should act as if they were the entire masters; that they should not think it among their rights to cut off the entail, or commit waste on the inheritance, by destroying at their pleasure the whole original fabric of their society: hazarding to leave to those who come after them a ruin instead of an habitation,—and teaching these successors as little to respect their contrivances as they had themselves respected the institutions of their forefathers. By this unprincipled facility of changing the state as often and as much and in as many ways as there are floating fancies or fashions, the whole chain and continuity of the commonwealth would be broken. No one generation could link with the other. Men would become little better than the flies of a summer.

And first of all, the science of jurisprudence, the pride of the human intellect, which, with all its defects, redundancies, and errors, is the collected reason of ages, combining the principles of original justice with the infinite variety of human concerns, as a heap of old exploded errors, would be no longer studied. Personal self-sufficiency and arrogance (the certain attendants upon all those who have never experienced a wisdom

greater than their own) would usurp the tribunal. Of course no certain laws, establishing invariable grounds of hope and fear, would keep the actions of men in a certain course, or direct them to a certain end. Nothing stable in the modes of holding property or exercising function, could form a solid ground on which any parent could speculate in the education of his offspring, or in a choice for their future establishment in the world. No principles would be early worked into the habits. As soon as the most able instructor had completed his laborious course of institution, instead of sending forth his pupil, accomplished in a virtuous discipline, fitted to procure him attention and respect in his place in society, he would find everything altered; and that he had turned out a poor creature to the contempt and derision of the world, ignorant of the true grounds of estimation. Who would insure a tender and delicate sense of honour to beat almost with the first pulses of the heart, when no man could know what would be the test of honour in a nation, continually varying the standard of its coin? No part of life would retain its acquisitions. Barbarism with regard to science and literature, unskilfulness with regard to arts and manufactures, would infallibly succeed to the want of a steady education and settled principle; and thus the commonwealth itself would, in a few generations, crumble away, be disconnected into the dust and powder of individuality, and at length dispersed to all the winds of heaven.

To avoid, therefore, the evils of inconstancy and versatility, ten thousand times worse than those of obstinacy and the blindest prejudice, we have consecrated the state, that no man should approach to look into its defects or corruptions but with due caution; that he should never dream of beginning its reformation by its subversion; that he should approach to the faults of the state as to the wounds of a father, with pious awe and trembling solicitude. By this wise prejudice we are taught to look with horror on those children of their country, who are prompt rashly to hack that aged parent in pieces and put him into the kettle of magicians, in hopes that by their poisonous weeds and wild incantations they may regenerate the paternal constitution, and renovate their father's life.

Society is, indeed, a contract. Subordinate contracts for objects of mere occasional interest may be dissolved at pleasure; but the state ought not to be considered as nothing better than a partnership agreement in a trade of pepper and coffee, calico or tobacco, or some other such low concern, to be taken up for a little temporary interest, and to be dissolved by the fancy of the parties. It is to be looked on with other reverence; because it is not a partnership in things subservient only to the gross animal existence of a temporary and perishable nature. It is a partnership in all science; a partnership in all art; a partnership in every virtue, and in all perfection. As the ends of such a partnership cannot be obtained in many generations, it becomes a partnership not only between those who are living, but between those who are living, those who are dead, and those who are to be born. Each contract of each particular state is but a clause in the great primæval contract of eternal society, linking the lower with the higher natures, connecting the visible and invisible world, according to a fixed compact sanctioned by the inviolable oath which holds all physical and all moral natures, each in their appointed place. This law is not subject to the will of those, who by an obligation above them, and infinitely superior, are bound to submit their will to that law. The municipal corporations of that universal kingdom are not morally at liberty, at their pleasure, and on their speculations of a contingent improvement, wholly to separate and tear asunder the bands of their subordinate community, and

to dissolve it into an unsocial, uncivil, unconnected chaos of elementary principles. It is the first and supreme necessity only, a necessity that is not chosen, but chooses, a necessity paramount to deliberation, that admits no discussion, and demands no evidence, which alone can justify a resort to anarchy. This necessity is no exception to the rule; because this necessity itself is a part too of that moral and physical disposition of things, to which man must be obedient by consent or force: but if that which is only submission to necessity should be made the object of choice, the law is broken, Nature is disobeyed, and the rebellious are outlawed, cast forth, and exiled, from this world of reason, and order, and peace, and virtue, and fruitful penitence, into the antagonist world of madness, discord, vice, confusion, and unavailing sorrow. . . .

[1790]

A LETTER

FROM THE RIGHT HON. EDMUND
BURKE

TO A NOBLE LORD

On the Attacks Made Upon Him and His Pension, in the House of Lords, by the Duke of Bedford and the Earl of Lauderdale, Early in the Present Session of Parliament.

1796

My Lord,—I could hardly flatter myself with the hope that so very early in the season I should have to acknowledge obligations to the Duke of Bedford and to the Earl of Lauderdale. These noble persons have lost no time in conferring upon me that sort of honour which it is alone within their competence, and which it is certainly most congenial to their nature, and their manners, to bestow.

To be ill spoken of, in whatever language they speak, by the zealots of the new sect in philosophy and politics, of which these noble persons think so charitably, and of which others think so justly, to me is no matter of uneasiness or surprise. To have incurred the displeasure of the Duke of Orleans or the Duke of Bedford, to fall under the censure of Citizen Brissot or of his friend, the Earl of Lauderdale, I ought to consider as proofs, not the least satisfactory, that I have produced some part of the effect I proposed by my endeavours. I have laboured hard to earn what the noble Lords are generous enough to pay. Personal offence I have given them none. The part they take against me is from zeal to the cause. It is well! It is perfectly well! I have to do homage to their justice. I have to thank the Bedfords and the Lauderdales for having so faithfully and so fully acquitted towards me whatever arrear of debt was left undischarged by the Priestleys and the Paines.

Some, perhaps, may think them executors in their own wrong: I at least have nothing to complain of. They have gone beyond the demands of justice. They have been (a little, perhaps, beyond their intention) favourable to me. They have been the means of bringing out by their invectives the handsome things which Lord Grenville has had the goodness and condescension to say in my behalf. Retired as I am from the world, and from all its affairs and all its pleasures, I confess it does kindle in my nearly extinguished feelings a very vivid satisfaction to be so attacked and so commended. It is soothing to my wounded mind to be commended by an able, vigorous, and well-informed statesman, and at the very moment when he stands forth with a manliness and resolution worthy of himself and of his cause, for the preservation of the person and government of our sovereign, and therein for the security of the laws, the liberties, the morals, and the lives of his people. To be in any fair way connected with such things, is indeed a distinction. No philosophy can make me

above it: no melancholy can depress me so low as to make me wholly insensible to such an honour.

Why will they not let me remain in obscurity and inaction? Are they apprehensive that if an atom of me remains, the sect has something to fear? Must I be annihilated, lest, like old John Zisca's, my skin might be made into a drum, to animate Europe to eternal battle against a tyranny that threatens to overwhelm all Europe and all the human race?

My Lord, it is a subject of awful meditation. Before this of France, the annals of all time have not furnished an instance of a *complete* revolution. That Revolution seems to have extended even to the constitution of the mind of man. It has this of wonderful in it, that it resembles what Lord Verulam says of the operations of Nature: It was perfect, not only in its elements and principles, but in all its members and its organs from the very beginning. The moral scheme of France furnishes the only pattern ever known which they who admire will *instantly* resemble. It is, indeed, an inexhaustible repertory of one kind of examples. In my wretched condition, though hardly to be classed with the living, I am not safe from them. They have tigers to fall upon animated strength; they have hyenas to prey upon carcasses. The national menagerie is collected by the first physiologists of the time; and it is defective in no description of savage nature. They pursue even such as me into the obscurest retreats, and haul them before their revolutionary tribunals. Neither sex, nor age, nor the sanctuary of the tomb, is sacred to them. They have so determined a hatred to all privileged orders, that they deny even to the departed the sad immunities of the grave. They are not wholly without an object. Their turpitude purveys to their malice; and they unplumb the dead for bullets to assassinate the living. If all revolutionists were not proof against all caution, I should recommend it to their consideration, that no persons were ever known in history, either sacred or profane, to vex the sepulchre, and by their sorceries to call up the prophetic dead, with any other event, than the prediction of their own disastrous fate.—"Leave me, oh leave me to repose!"

In one thing I can excuse the Duke of Bedford for his attack upon me and my mortuary pension: He cannot readily comprehend the transaction he condemns. What I have obtained was the fruit of no bargain, the production of no intrigue, the result of no compromise, the effect of no solicitation. The first suggestion of it never came from me, mediately or immediately, to his Majesty or any of his ministers. It was long known that the instant my engagements would permit it, and before the heaviest of all calamities had for ever condemned me to obscurity and sorrow, I had resolved on a total retreat. I had executed that design. I was entirely out of the way of serving or of hurting any statesman, or any party, when the ministers so generously and so nobly carried into effect the spontaneous bounty of the crown. Both descriptions have acted as became them. When I could not longer serve them, the ministers have considered my situation. When I could no longer hurt them, the revolutionists have trampled on my infirmity. My gratitude, I trust, is equal to the manner in which the benefit was conferred. It came to me, indeed, at a time of life, and in a state of mind and body, in which no circumstance of fortune could afford me any real pleasure. But this was no fault in the royal donor, or in his ministers, who were pleased, in acknowledging the merits of an invalid servant of the public, to assuage the sorrows of a desolate old man.

It would ill become me to boast of anything. It would as ill become me, thus called upon, to depreciate the value of a long life spent with unexampled toil in the service of my country. Since the total body of my serv-

ices, on account of the industry which was shown in them, and the fairness of my intentions, have obtained the acceptance of my sovereign, it would be absurd in me to range myself on the side of the Duke of Bedford and the Corresponding Society, or, as far as in me lies, to permit a dispute on the rate at which the authority appointed by *our* Constitution to estimate such things has been pleased to set them.

Loose libels ought to be passed by in silence and contempt. By me they have been so always. I knew that as long as I remained in public I should live down the calumnies of malice and the judgments of ignorance. If I happened to be now and then in the wrong, (as who is not?) like all other men, I must bear the consequence of my faults and my mistakes. The libels of the present day are just of the same stuff as the libels of the past. But they derive an importance from the rank of the persons they come from, and the gravity of the place where they were uttered. In some way or other I ought to take some notice of them. To assert myself thus traduced is not vanity or arrogance. It is a demand of justice; it is a demonstration of gratitude. If I am unworthy, the ministers are worse than prodigal. On that hypothesis, I perfectly agree with the Duke of Bedford.

For whatever I have been (I am now no more) I put myself on my country. I ought to be allowed a reasonable freedom, because I stand upon my deliverance; and no culprit ought to plead in irons. Even in the utmost latitude of defensive liberty, I wish to preserve all possible decorum. Whatever it may be in the eyes of these noble persons themselves, to me their situation calls for the most profound respect. If I should happen to trespass a little, which I trust I shall not, let it always be supposed that a confusion of characters may produce mistakes,—that, in the masquerades of the grand carnival of our age, whimsical adventures happen, odd things are said and pass off. If I should fail a single point in the high respect I owe to those illustrious persons, I cannot be supposed to mean the Duke of Bedford and the Earl of Lauderdale of the House of Peers, but the Duke of Bedford and the Earl of Lauderdale, of Palace Yard,—the Dukes and Earls of Brentford. There they are on the pavement; there they seem to come nearer to my humble level, and, virtually at least, to have waived their high privilege.

Making this protestation, I refuse all revolutionary tribunals, where men have been put to death for no other reason than that they had obtained favours from the Crown. I claim, not the letter but the spirit, of the old English law,—that is, to be tried by my peers. I decline his Grace's jurisdiction as a judge. I challenge the Duke of Bedford as a juror to pass upon the value of my services. Whatever his natural parts may be, I cannot recognize in his few and idle years the competence to judge of my long and laborious life. If I can help it, he shall not be on the inquest of my *quantum meruit.* Poor rich man! He can hardly know anything of public industry in its exertions, or can estimate its compensations when its work is done. I have no doubt of his Grace's readiness in all the calculations of vulgar arithmetic; but I shrewdly suspect that he is little studied in the theory of moral proportions, and has never learned the rule of three in the arithmetic of policy and state.

His Grace thinks I have obtained too much. I answer that my exertions, whatever they have been, were such as no hopes of pecuniary reward could possibly excite; and no pecuniary compensation can possibly reward them. Between money and such services, if done by abler men than I am, there is no common principle of comparison: they are quantities incommensurable. Money is made for the comfort and convenience of animal life. It cannot be a reward for what

mere animal life must, indeed, sustain, but never can inspire. With submission to his Grace, I have not had more than sufficient. As to any noble use, I trust I know how to employ as well as he a much greater fortune than he possesses. In a more confined application, I certainly stand in need of every kind of relief and easement much more than he does. When I say I have not received more than I deserve, is this the language I hold to Majesty? No! Far, very far, from it! Before that presence, I claim no merit at all. Everything towards me is favour and bounty. One style to a gracious benefactor; another to a proud and insulting foe.

. . . .

I was not, like his Grace of Bedford, swaddled and rocked and dandled into a legislator; *"Nitor in adversum"* is the motto for a man like me. I possessed not one of the qualities nor cultivated one of the arts that recommend men to the favour and protection of the great. I was not made for a minion or a tool. As little did I follow the trade of winning the hearts by imposing on the understandings of the people. At every step of my progress in life (for in every step was I traversed and opposed), and at every turnpike I met, I was obliged to show my passport, and again and again to prove my sole title to the honour of being useful to my country, by a proof that I was not wholly unacquainted with its laws and the whole system of its interests both abroad and at home. Otherwise no rank, no toleration even, for me. I had no arts but manly arts. On them I have stood, and, please God, in spite of the Duke of Bedford and the Earl of Lauderdale, to the last gasp will I stand.

Had his Grace condescended to inquire concerning the person whom he has not thought it below him to reproach, he might have found, that, in the whole course of my life, I have never, on any pretence of economy, or on any other pretence, so much as in a single instance, stood between any man and his reward of service, or his encouragement in useful talent and pursuit, from the highest of those services and pursuits to the lowest. On the contrary, I have on an hundred occasions exerted myself with singular zeal to forward every man's even tolerable pretensions. I have more than once had good-natured reprehensions from my friends for carrying the matter to something bordering on abuse. This line of conduct, whatever its merits might be, was partly owing to natural dispositions, but I think full as much to reason and principle. I looked on the consideration of public service or public ornament to be real and very justice; and I ever held a scanty and penurious justice to partake of the nature of a wrong. I held it to be, in its consequences, the worst economy in the world. In saving money I soon can count up all the good I do; but when, by a cold penury, I blast the abilities of a nation, and stunt the growth of its active energies, the ill I may do is beyond all calculation. Whether it be too much or too little, whatever I have done has been general and systematic. I have never entered into those trifling vexations and oppressive details that have been falsely and most ridiculously laid to my charge.

Did I blame the pensions given to Mr. Barré and Mr. Dunning between the proposition and execution of my plan? No! surely no! Those pensions were within my principles. I assert it, those gentlemen deserved their pensions, their titles,—all they had; and if more they had, I should have been but pleased the more. They were men of talents; they were men of service. I put the profession of the law out of the question in one of them. It is a service that rewards itself. But their *public service*, though from their abilities unquestionably of more value than mine, in its quantity and its duration was not to be mentioned

with it. But I never could drive a hard bargain in my life, concerning any matter whatever; and least of all do I know how to haggle and huckster with merit. Pension for myself I obtained none; nor did I solicit any. Yet I was loaded with hatred for everything that was withheld, and with obloquy for everything that was given. I was thus left to support the grants of a name ever dear to me and ever venerable to the world in favour of those who were no friends of mine or of his, against the rude attacks of those who were at that time friends to the grantees and their own zealous partisans. I have never heard the Earl of Lauderdale complain of these pensions. He finds nothing wrong till he comes to me. This is impartiality, in the true, modern, revolutionary style.

Whatever I did at that time, so far as it regarded order and economy, is stable and eternal, as all principles must be. A particular order of things may be altered: order itself cannot lose its value. As to other particulars, they are variable by time and by circumstances. Laws of regulation are not fundamental laws. The public exigencies are the masters of all such laws. They rule the laws, and are not to be ruled by them. They who exercise the legislative power at the time must judge.

It may be new to his Grace, but I beg leave to tell him, that mere parsimony is not economy. It is separable in theory from it; and in fact it may or it may not be a *part* of economy, according to circumstances. Expense, and great expense, may be an essential part in true economy. If parsimony were to be considered as one of the kinds of that virtue, there is, however, another and an higher economy. Economy is a distributive virtue, and consists not in saving, but in selection. Parsimony requires no providence, no sagacity, no powers of combination, no comparison, no judgment. Mere instinct, and that not an instinct of the noblest kind, may produce this false economy in perfection. The other economy has larger views. It demands a discriminating judgment and a firm, sagacious mind. It shuts one door to impudent importunity, only to open another, and a wider, to unpresuming merit. If none but meritorious service or real talent were to be rewarded, this nation has not wanted, and this nation will not want, the means of rewarding all the service it ever will receive, and encouraging all the merit it ever will produce. No state, since the foundation of society, has been impoverished by that species of profusion. Had the economy of selection and proportion been at all times observed, we should not now have had an overgrown Duke of Bedford, to oppress the industry of humble men, and to limit by the standard of his own conceptions, the justice, the bounty, or, if he pleases, the charity of the Crown.

His Grace may think as meanly as he will of my deserts in the far greater part of my conduct in life. It is free for him to do so. There will always be some difference of opinion in the value of political services. But there is one merit of mine which he, of all men living, ought to be the last to call in question. I have supported with every great zeal, and I am told with some degree of success, those opinions, or if his Grace likes another expression better, those old prejudices, which buoy up the ponderous mass of his nobility, wealth and titles. I have omitted no exertion to prevent him and them from sinking to that level to which the meretricious French faction his Grace at least coquets with, omits no exertion to reduce both. I have done all I could to discountenance their inquiries into the fortunes of those who hold large portions of wealth without any apparent merit of their own. I have strained every nerve to keep the Duke of Bedford in that situation which alone makes him my superior. Your Lordship has been a witness of the use he makes of that preëminence.

But be it that this is virtue; be it that there is virtue in this well-selected rigour; yet all virtues are not equally becoming to all men and at all times. There are crimes, undoubtedly there are crimes, which in all seasons of our existence ought to put a generous antipathy in action; crimes that provoke an indignant justice, and call forth a warm and animated pursuit. But all things that concern what I may call the preventive police of morality, all things merely rigid, harsh, and censorial, the antiquated moralists at whose feet I was brought up would not have thought these the fittest matter to form the favourite virtues of young men of rank. What might have been well enough, and have been received with a veneration mixed with awe and terror, from an old, severe, crabbed Cato, would have wanted something of propriety in the young Scipios, the ornament of the Roman nobility, in the flower of their life. But the times, the morals, the masters, the scholars, have all undergone a thorough revolution. It is a vile illiberal school, this new French academy of the *sans-culottes*. There is nothing in it that is fit for a gentleman to learn.

Whatever its vogue may be, I still flatter myself that the parents of the growing generation will be satisfied with what is to be taught to their children in Westminster, in Eton, or in Winchester; I still indulge the hope that no *grown* gentleman or nobleman of our time will think of finishing at Mr. Thelwall's lecture whatever may have been left incomplete at the old universities of his country. I would give to Lord Grenville and Mr. Pitt for a motto, what was said of a Roman censor or prætor (or what was he?) who in virtue of a *Senatus consultum*, shut up certain academies,

Cludere ludum impudentiæ jussit.

Every honest father of a family in the

kingdom will rejoice at the break-
ing-up for the holidays, and will pray
that there may be a very long vacation, in all such schools.

The awful state of the time, and
not myself, or my own justification,
is my true object in what I now write,
or in what I shall ever write or say. It
little signifies to the world what becomes of such things as me, or even
as the Duke of Bedford. What I say
about either of us is nothing more
than a vehicle, as you, my Lord, will
easily perceive, to convey my sentiments on matters far more worthy of
your attention. It is when I stick to
my apparent first subject that I ought
to apologize, not when I depart from
it. I therefore must beg your Lordship's pardon for again resuming it
after this very short digression,—assuring you that I shall never altogether
lose sight of such matter as persons
abler than I am may turn to some
profit.

The Duke of Bedford conceives that
he is obliged to call the attention of
the House of Peers to his Majesty's
grant to me, which he considers as excessive and out of all bounds.

I know not how it has happened,
but it really seems, that, whilst his
Grace was meditating his well-con-
sidered censure upon me, he fell into
a sort of sleep. Homer nods, and the
Duke of Bedford may dream; and as
dreams (even his golden dreams) are
apt to be ill-pieced and incongruously
put together, his Grace preserved his
idea of reproach to *me*, but took the
subject-matter from the Crown grants
to his own family. This is "the stuff
of which his dreams are made." In
that way of putting things together
his Grace is perfectly in the right.
The grants to the house of Russell
were so enormous as not only to outrage economy, but even to stagger
credibility. The Duke of Bedford is
the leviathan among all the creatures
of the Crown. He tumbles about his
unwieldy bulk; he plays and frolics in
the ocean of the royal bounty. Huge
as he is, and whilst "he lies floating

many a rood," he is still a creature.
His ribs, his fins, his whalebone, his
blubber, the very spiracles through
which he spouts a torrent of brine
against his origin, and covers me all
over with the spray,—everything of
him and about him is from the
throne. Is it for *him* to question the
dispensation of the royal favour?

I really am at a loss to draw any
sort of parallel between the public
merits of his Grace, by which he justifies the grants he holds, and these
services of mine, on the favourable
construction of which I have obtained
what his Grace so much disapproves.
In private life I have not at all the
honour of acquaintance with the noble Duke; but I ought to presume,
and it costs me nothing to do so, that
he abundantly deserves the esteem
and love of all who live with him.
But as to public service, why, truly, it
would not be more ridiculous for me
to compare myself in rank, in fortune,
in splendid descent, in youth, strength,
or figure, with the Duke of Bedford,
than to make a parallel between his
services and my attempts to be useful
to my country. It would not be gross
adulation, but uncivil irony, to say
that he has any public merit of his
own to keep alive the idea of the services by which his vast landed pensions
were obtained. My merits, whatever
they are, are original and personal;
his are derivative. It is his ancestor,
the original pensioner, that has laid
up this inexhaustible fund of merit
which makes his Grace so very delicate and exceptious about the merit
of all other grantees of the Crown.
Had he permitted me to remain in
quiet, I should have said, " 'Tis his
estate: that's enough. It is his by law:
what have I to do with it or its history?" He would naturally have said
on his side, " 'Tis this man's fortune.
He is as good now as my ancestor was
two hundred and fifty years ago. I am
a young man with very old pensions;
he is an old man with very young pensions: that's all."

Why will his **Grace,** by attacking

me, force me reluctantly to compare my little merit with that which obtained from the Crown those prodigies of profuse donation by which he tramples on the mediocrity of humble and laborious individuals? I would willingly leave him to the Herald's College, which the philosophy of the *sans-culottes* (prouder by far than all the Garters, and Norroys, and Clarencieux, and Rouge-Dragons that ever pranced in a procession of what his friends call aristocrats and despots) will abolish with contumely and scorn. These historians, recorders, and blazoners of virtues and arms, differ wholly from that other description of historians who never assign any act of politicians to a good motive. These gentle historians, on the contrary, dip their pens in nothing but the milk of human kindness. They seek no further for merit than the preamble of a patent, or the inscription on a tomb. With them every man created a peer is first a hero ready-made. They judge of every man's capacity for office by the offices he has filled; and the more offices, the more ability. Every general officer with them is a Marlborough, every statesman a Burleigh, every judge a Murray or a Yorke. They who, alive, were laughed at or pitied by all their acquaintance, make as good a figure as the best of them in the pages of Guillim, Edmondson, and Collins.

To these recorders, so full of good-nature to the great and prosperous, I would willingly leave the first Baron Russell and Earl of Bedford, and the merits of his grants. But the aulnager, the weigher, the meter of grants, will not suffer us to acquiesce in the judgment of the prince reigning at the time when they were made. They are never good to those who earn them. Well then; since the new grantees have war made on them by the old, and that the word of the sovereign is not to be taken, let us turn our eyes to history, in which great men have always a pleasure in contemplating the heroic origin of their house.

The first peer of the name, the first purchaser of the grants, was a Mr. Russell, a person of an ancient gentleman's family, raised by being a minion of Henry the Eighth. As there generally is some resemblance of character to create these relations, the favourite was in all likelihood much such another as his master. The first of those immoderate grants was not taken from the ancient demesne of the Crown, but from the recent confiscation of the ancient nobility of the land. The lion, having sucked the blood of his prey, threw the offal carcass to the jackal in waiting. Having tasted once the food of confiscation, the favourites became fierce and ravenous. This worthy favourite's first grant was from the lay nobility. The second, infinitely improving on the enormity of the first, was from the plunder of the Church. In truth, his Grace is somewhat excusable for his dislike to a grant like mine, not only in its quantity, but in its kind, so different from his own.

Mine was from a mild and benevolent sovereign: his from Henry the Eighth.

Mine had not its fund in the murder of any innocent person of illustrious rank, or in the pillage of any body of unoffending men. His grants were from the aggregate and consolidated funds of judgments iniquitously legal, and from possessions voluntarily surrendered by the lawful proprietors with the gibbet at their door.

The merit of the grantee whom he derives from was that of being a prompt and greedy instrument of a *levelling* tyrant, who oppressed all descriptions of his people, but who fell with particular fury on everything that was *great and noble*. Mine has been in endeavouring to screen every man, in every class, from oppression, and particularly in defending the high and eminent, who in the bad times of confiscating princes, confiscating chief governors, or confiscating demagogues, are the most exposed to jealousy, avarice, and envy.

The merit of the original grantee of his Grace's pensions was in giving his hand to the work, and partaking the spoil, with a prince who plundered a part of the national Church of his time and country. Mine was in defending the whole of the national Church of my own time and my own country, and the whole of the national Churches of all countries, from the principles and the examples which lead to ecclesiastical pillage, thence to a contempt of *all* prescriptive titles, thence to the pillage of *all* property, and thence to universal desolation.

The merit of the origin of his Grace's fortune was in being a favourite and chief adviser to a prince who left no liberty to their native country. My endeavour was to obtain liberty for the municipal country in which I was born, and for all descriptions and denominations in it. Mine was to support with unrelaxing vigilance every right, every privilege, every franchise, in this my adopted, my dearer, and more comprehensive country; and not only to preserve those rights in this chief seat of empire, but in every nation, in every land, in every climate, language, and religion, in the vast domain that is still under the protection, and the larger that was once under the protection, of the British Crown.

His founder's merits were, by arts in which he served his master and made his fortune, to bring poverty, wretchedness, and depopulation on his country. Mine were, under a benevolent prince, in promoting the commerce, manufactures, and agriculture of his kingdom; in which his Majesty shows an eminent example, who even in his amusements is a patriot, and in hours of leisure an improver of his native soil.

His founder's merit was the merit of a gentleman raised by the arts of a court, and the protection of a Wolsey, to the eminence of a great and potent lord. His merit in that eminence was, by instigating a tyrant to injustice, to provoke a people to rebellion. My merit was, to awaken the sober part of the country, that they might put themselves on their guard against any one potent lord, or any greater number of potent lords, or any combination of great leading men of any sort, if ever they should attempt to proceed in the same courses, but in the reverse order,—that is, by instigating a corrupted populace to rebellion, and, through that rebellion, introducing a tyranny yet worse than the tyranny which his Grace's ancestor supported, and of which he profited in the manner we behold in the despotism of Henry the Eighth.

The political merit of the first pensioner of his Grace's house was that of being concerned as a counsellor of state in advising, and in his person executing, the conditions of a dishonourable peace with France,—the surrendering the fortress of Boulogne, then our outguard on the Continent. By that surrender, Calais, the key of France, and the bridle in the mouth of that power, was not many years afterwards finally lost. My merit has been in resisting the power and pride of France, under any form of its rule; but in opposing it with the greatest zeal and earnestness, when that rule appeared in the worst form it could assume,—the worst, indeed, which the prime cause and the principle of all evil could possibly give it. It was my endeavour by every means to excite a spirit in the House, where I had the honour of a seat, for carrying on with early vigour and decision the most clearly just and necessary war that this or any nation ever carried on, in order to save my country from the iron yoke of its power, and from the more dreadful contagion of its principles; to preserve, while they can be preserved, pure and untainted, the ancient, inbred integrity, piety, good-nature, and good-humour of the people of England, from the dreadful pestilence which, beginning in France, threatens to lay waste the whole moral and in a great degree the whole physical world, having done both in the focus of its most intense malignity.

The labours of his Grace's founder merited the "curses, not loud but deep," of the Commons of England, on whom *he* and his master had effected a *complete Parliamentary reform*, by making them, in their slavery and humiliation, the true and adequate representatives of a debased, degraded, and undone people. My merits were in having had an active, though not always an ostentatious share, in every one act, without exception, of undisputed constitutional utility in my time, and in having supported, on all occasions, the authority, the efficiency, and the privileges of the Commons of Great Britain. I ended my services by a recorded and fully reasoned assertion on their own journals of their constitutional rights, and a vindication of their constitutional conduct. I laboured in all things to merit their inward approbation, and (along with the assistance of the largest, the greatest, and best of my endeavours) I received their free, unbiased, public, and solemn thanks.

Thus stands the account of the comparative merits of the Crown grants which compose the Duke of Bedford's fortune as balanced against mine. In the name of common sense, why should the Duke of Bedford think that none but of the House of Russell are entitled to the favour of the Crown? Why should he imagine that no king of England has been capable of judging of merit but King Henry the Eighth? Indeed, he will pardon me, he is a little mistaken: all virtue did not end in the first Earl of Bedford; all discernment did not lose its vision when his Creator closed his eyes. Let him remit his rigour on the disproportion between merit and reward in others, and they will make no inquiry into the origin of his fortune. They will regard with much more satisfaction, as he will contemplate with infinitely more advantage, whatever in his pedigree has been

dulcified by an exposure to the influence of heaven in a long flow of generations from the hard, acidulous, metallic tincture of the spring. It is little to be doubted that several of his forefathers in that long series have degenerated into honour and virtue. Let the Duke of Bedford (I am sure he will) reject with scorn and horror the counsels of the lecturers, those wicked panders to avarice and ambition, who would tempt him, in the troubles of this country, to seek another enormous fortune from the forfeitures of another nobility and the plunder of another church. Let him (and I trust that yet he will) employ all the energy of his youth and all the resources of his wealth to crush rebellious principles which have no foundation in morals, and rebellious movements that have no provocation in tyranny.

Then will be forgot the rebellions which, by a doubtful priority in crime, his ancestor had provoked and extinguished. On such a conduct in the noble Duke, many of his countrymen might, and with some excuse might, give way to the enthusiasm of their gratitude, and, in the dashing style of some of the old declaimers, cry out, that if the fates had found no other way in which they could give a Duke of Bedford and his opulence as props to a tottering world, then the butchery of the Duke of Buckingham might be tolerated; it might be regarded even with complacency, whilst in the heir of confiscation they saw the sympathizing comforter of the martyrs who suffer under the cruel confiscation of this day, whilst they behold with admiration his zealous protection of the virtuous and loyal nobility of France, and his manly support of his brethren, the yet standing nobility and gentry of his native land. Then his Grace's merit would be pure, and new, and sharp, as fresh from the mint of honour. As he pleased, he might reflect honour on his predecessors, or throw it forward on those who were to succeed him. He might be the propagator of the stock of honour, or the root of it, as he thought proper.

Had it pleased God to continue to me the hopes of succession, I should have been, according to my mediocrity and the mediocrity of the age I live in, a sort of founder of a family: I should have left a son, who, in all the points in which personal merit can be viewed, in science, in erudition, in genius, in taste, in honour, in generosity, in humanity, in every liberal sentiment, and every liberal accomplishment, would not have shown himself inferior to the Duke of Bedford, or to any of those whom he traces in his line. His Grace very soon would have wanted all plausibility in his attack upon that provision which belonged more to mine than to me. He would soon have supplied every deficiency, and symmetrized every disproportion. It would not have been for that successor to resort to any stagnant, wasting reservoir of merit in me, or in any ancestry. He had in himself a salient, living spring of generous and manly action. Every day he lived he would have repurchased the bounty of the Crown, and ten times more, if ten times more he had received. He was made a public creature, and had no enjoyment whatever but in the performance of some duty. At this exigent moment the loss of a finished man is not easily supplied.

But a disposer whose power we are little able to resist, and whose wisdom it behooves us not at all to dispute, has ordained it in another manner, and (whatever my querulous weakness might suggest) a far better. The storm has gone over me; and I lie like one of those old oaks which the late hurricane has scattered about me. I am stripped of all my honours, I am torn up by the roots, and lie prostrate on the earth. There, and prostrate there, I most unfeignedly recognise the Divine justice, and in some degree submit to it. But whilst I humble myself before God, I do not know that it is forbidden to repel the attacks of unjust and inconsiderate men. The patience of Job is proverbial. After some of the convulsive struggles of our irritable nature, he submitted himself, and repented in dust and ashes. But even so, I do not find him blamed for reprehending, and with a considerable degree of verbal asperity, those ill-natured neighbours of his who visited his dunghill to read moral, political, and economical lectures on his misery. I am alone. I have none to meet my enemies in the gate. Indeed, my Lord, I greatly deceive myself, if in this hard season I would give a peck of refuse wheat for all that is called fame and honour in the world. This is the appetite but of a few. It is a luxury, it is a privilege, it is an indulgence for those who are at their ease. But we are all of us made to shun disgrace, as we are made to shrink from pain and poverty and disease. It is an instinct; and under the direction of reason, instinct is always in the right. I live in an inverted order. They who ought to have succeeded me are gone before me. They who should have been to me as posterity are in the place of ancestors. I owe to the dearest relation (which ever must subsist in memory) that act of piety which he would have performed to me: I owe it to him to show that he was not descended, as the Duke of Bedford would have it, from an unworthy parent.

. . . .

Am I to blame, if I attempt to pay his Grace's hostile reproaches to me with a friendly admonition to himself? Can I be blamed for pointing out to him in what manner he is likely to be affected, if the sect of the cannibal philosophers of France should proselytize any considerable part of this people, and, by their joint proselytizing arms, should conquer that government to which his Grace does not seem to me to give all the support his own security demands? Surely it is proper that he, and that others like him, should know the true genius of this sect,—what their opinions are,—what they have done,—and to whom,—and what (if a prognostic is to be formed from the dispositions and actions of men) it is certain they will do hereafter. He ought to know that they have sworn assistance, the only engagement they ever will keep, to all in this country who bear a resemblance to themselves, and who think, as such, that *the whole duty of man* consists in destruction. They are a misallied and disparaged branch of the House of Nimrod. They are the Duke of Bedford's natural hunters; and he is their natural game. Because he is not very profoundly reflecting, he sleeps in profound security: they, on the contrary, are always vigilant, active, enterprising, and, though far removed from any knowledge which makes men estimable or useful, in all the instruments and resources of evil their leaders are not meanly instructed or insufficiently furnished. In the French Revolution everything is new, and, from want of preparation to meet so unlooked-for an evil, everything is dangerous. Never before this time was a set of literary men converted into a gang of robbers and assassins. Never before did a den of bravoes and banditti assume the garb and tone of an academy of philosophers.

Let me tell his Grace that an union of such characters, monstrous as it seems, is not made for producing despicable enemies. But if they are formidable as foes, as friends they are dreadful indeed. The men of property in France confiding in a force which seemed to be irresistible because it had never been tried, neglected to prepare for a conflict with their enemies at their own weapons. They were found in such a situation as the Mexicans were, when they were attacked by the dogs, the cavalry, the iron, and the gunpowder, of a handful of bearded men, whom they did not know to exist in nature. This is a comparison that some, I think, have made; and it is just. In France they

had their enemies within their houses. They were even in the bosoms of many of them. But they had not sagacity to discern their savage character. They seemed tame, and even caressing. They had nothing but *douce humanité* in their mouth. They could not bear the punishment of the mildest laws on the greatest criminals. The slightest severity of justice made their flesh creep. The very idea that war existed in the world disturbed their repose. Military glory was no more, with them, than a splendid infamy. Hardly would they hear of self-defence, which they reduced within such bounds, as to leave it no defence at all. All this while they meditated the confiscations and massacres we have seen. Had any one told these unfortunate noblemen and gentlemen how and by whom the grand fabric of the French monarchy under which they flourished would be subverted, they would not have pitied him as a visionary, but would have turned from him as what they call a *mauvais plaisant*. Yet we have seen what has happened. The persons who have suffered from the cannibal philosophy of France are so like the Duke of Bedford, that nothing but his Grace's probably not speaking quite so good French could enable us to find out any difference. A great many of them had as pompous titles as he, and were of full as illustrious a race; some few of them had fortunes as ample; several of them, without meaning the least disparagement to the Duke of Bedford, were as wise, and as virtuous, and as valiant, and as well educated, and as complete in all the lineaments of men of honour as he is; and to all this they had added the powerful out-guard of a military profession, which, in its nature, renders men somewhat more cautious than those who have nothing to attend to but the lazy enjoyment of undisturbed possessions. But security was their ruin. They are dashed to pieces in the storm, and our shores are covered with the wrecks. If they had been aware that such a thing might happen, such a thing never could have happened.

I assure his Grace, that, if I state to him the designs of his enemies in a manner which may appear to him ludicrous and impossible, I tell him nothing that has not exactly happened, point by point, but twenty-four miles from our own shore. I assure him that the Frenchified faction, more encouraged than others are warned by what has happened in France, look at him and his landed possessions as an object at once of curiosity and rapacity. He is made for them in every part of their double character. As robbers, to them he is a noble booty; as speculatists, he is a glorious subject for their experimental philosophy. He affords matter for an extensive analysis in all the branches of their science, geometrical, physical, civil and political. These philosophers are fanatics: independent of any interest, which, if it operated alone would make them much more tractable, they are carried with such a headlong rage towards every desperate trial that they would sacrifice the whole human race to the slightest of their experiments. I am better able to enter into the character of this description of men than the noble Duke can be. I have lived long and variously in the world. Without any considerable pretensions to literature in myself, I have aspired to the love of letters. I have lived for a great many years in habitudes with those who professed them. I can form a tolerable estimate of what is likely to happen from a character chiefly dependent for fame and fortune on knowledge and talent, as well in its morbid and perverted state, as in that which is sound and natural. Naturally, men so formed and finished are the first gifts of Providence to the world. But when they have once thrown off the fear of God, which was in all ages too often the case, and the fear of man, which is now the case, and when in that state they come to understand one another, and to act in

corps, a more dreadful calamity cannot arise out of hell to scourge mankind. Nothing can be conceived more hard than the heart of a thorough-bred metaphysician. It comes nearer to the cold malignity of a wicked spirit than to the frailty and passion of man. It is like that of the Principle of Evil himself, incorporeal, pure, unmixed, dephlegmated, defecated evil. It is no easy operation to eradicate humanity from the human breast. What Shakespeare calls "the compunctious visitings of nature" will sometimes knock at their hearts, and protest against their murderous speculations. But they have a means of compounding with their nature. Their humanity is not dissolved: they only give it a long prorogation. They are ready to declare that they do not think two thousand years too long a period for the good that they pursue. It is remarkable that they never see any way to their projected good but by the road of some evil. Their imagination is not fatigued with the contemplation of human suffering through the wild waste of centuries added to centuries of misery and desolation. Their humanity is at their horizon,—and, like the horizon, it always flies before them. The geometricians and the chemists bring, the one from the dry bones of their diagrams, and the other from the soot of their furnaces, dispositions that make them worse than indifferent about those feelings and habitudes which are the supports of the moral world. Ambition is come upon them suddenly; they are intoxicated with it, and it has rendered them fearless of the danger which may from thence arise to others or to themselves. These philosophers consider men in their experiments no more than they do mice in an air-pump or in a recipient of mephitic gas. Whatever his Grace may think of himself, they look upon him, and everything that belongs to him, with no more regard than they do upon the whiskers of that little long-tailed animal that has been long the game of the grave, demure, insidious, spring-nailed, velvet-pawed, green-eyed philosophers, whether going upon two legs or upon four.

His Grace's landed possessions are irresistibly inviting to an *agrarian* experiment. They are a downright insult upon the rights of man. They are more extensive than the territory of many of the Grecian republics; and they are without comparison more fertile than most of them. There are now republics in Italy, in Germany, and in Switzerland, which do not possess anything like so fair and ample a domain. There is scope for seven philosophers to proceed in their analytical experiments upon Harrington's seven different forms of republics, in the acres of this one Duke. Hitherto they have been wholly unproductive to speculation,—fitted for nothing but to fatten bullocks, and to produce grain for beer, still more to stupefy the dull English understanding. Abbé Sieyès has whole nests of pigeon-holes full of constitutions ready-made, ticketed, sorted, and numbered, suited to every season and every fancy: some with the top of the pattern at the bottom, and some with the bottom at the top; some plain, some flowered; some distinguished for their simplicity, others for their complexity; some of blood colour; some of *boue de Paris*; some with directories, others without a direction; some with councils of elders and councils of youngsters, some without any council at all; some where the electors choose the representatives, others where the representatives choose the electors; some in long coats, and some in short cloaks; some with pantaloons, some without breeches; some with five-shilling qualifications, some totally unqualified. So that no constitution-fancier may go unsuited from his shop, provided he loves a pattern of pillage, oppression, arbitrary imprisonment, confiscation, exile, revolutionary judgment, and legalized premeditated murder, in any shapes into which they can be put. What a pity

it is that the progress of experimental philosophy should be checked by his Grace's monopoly! Such are their sentiments, I assure him; such is their language, when they dare to speak; and such are their proceedings, when they have the means to act.

.   .   .   .

Is the genius of philosophy not yet known? You may as well think the garden of the Tuileries was well protected with the cords of ribbon insultingly stretched by the National Assembly to keep the sovereign *canaille* from intruding on the retirement of the poor King of the French, as that such flimsy cobwebs will stand between the savages of the Revolution and their natural prey. Deep philosophers are no triflers; brave *sans-culottes* are no formalists. They will no more regard a Marquis of Tavistock than an Abbot of Tavistock; the Lord of Woburn will not be more respectable in their eyes than the Prior of Woburn; they will make no difference between the superior of a Covent Garden of nuns and of a Covent Garden of another description. They will not care a rush whether his coat is long or short,—whether the colour be purple or blue and buff. They will not trouble *their* heads with what part of *his* head his hair is cut from; and they will look with equal respect on a tonsure and a crop. Their only question will be that of their Legendre, or some other of their legislative butchers: How he cuts up; how he tallows in the cawl or on the kidneys.

It is not a singular phenomenon, that whilst the *sans-culotte* carcass-butchers and the philosophers of the shambles are pricking their dotted lines upon his hide, and, like the print of the poor ox that we see in the shop-windows at Charing Cross, alive as he is, and thinking no harm in the world, he is divided into rumps, and sirloins, and briskets, and into all sorts of pieces for roasting, boiling, and stewing, that, all the while they are measuring *him*, his Grace is measuring *me*,—is invidiously comparing the bounty of the Crown with the deserts of the defender of his order, and in the same moment fawning on those who have the knife half out of the sheath? Poor innocent!

Pleas'd to the last, he crops the flow'ry food,
And licks the hand just raised to shed his
    blood.

No man lives too long who lives to do with spirit and suffer with resignation what Providence pleases to command or inflict; but, indeed, they are sharp incommodities which beset old age. It was but the other day, that, on putting in order some things which had been brought here on my taking leave of London for ever, I looked over a number of fine portraits, most of them of persons now dead, but whose society, in my better days, made this a proud and happy place. Amongst these was the picture of Lord Keppel. It was painted by an artist worthy of the subject, the excellent friend of that excellent man from their earliest youth, and a common friend of us both, with whom we lived for many years without a moment of coldness, of peevishness, of jealousy, or of jar, to the day of our final separation.

I ever looked on Lord Keppel as one of the greatest and best men of his age, and I loved and cultivated him accordingly. He was much in my heart, and I believe I was in his to the very last beat. It was after his trial at Portsmouth that he gave me this picture. With what zeal and anxious affection I attended him through that his agony of glory,—what part my son [took] in the early flush and enthusiasm of his virtue, and the pious passion with which he attached himself to all my connections,—with what prodigality we both squandered ourselves in courting almost every sort of enmity for his sake, I believe he felt, just as I should have felt such friendship on such an occasion. I partook, indeed, of this honour with several of

the first and best and ablest in the kingdom, but I was behindhand with none of them; and I am sure that if, to the eternal disgrace of this nation, and to the total annihilation of every trace of honour and virtue in it, things had taken a different turn from what they did, I should have attended him to the quarter-deck with no less good will and more pride, though with far other feelings, than I partook of the general flow of national joy that attended the justice that was done to his virtue.

Pardon, my Lord, the feeble garrulity of age, which loves to diffuse itself in discourse of the departed great. At my years we live in retrospect alone; and, wholly unfitted for the society of vigorous life, we enjoy the best balm to all wounds, the consolation of friendship, in those only whom we have lost for ever. Feeling the loss of Lord Keppel at all times, at no time did I feel it so much as on the first day when I was attacked in the House of Lords.

Had he lived, that reverend form would have risen in its place, and, with a mild, parental reprehension to his nephew, the Duke of Bedford, he would have told him that the favour of that gracious Prince who had honoured his virtues with the government of the navy of Great Britain, and with a seat in the hereditary great council of his kingdom, was not undeservedly shown to the friend of the best portion of his life, and his faithful companion and counsellor under his rudest trials. He would have told him that, to whomever else these reproaches might be becoming, they were not decorous in his near kindred. He would have told him that when men in that rank lose decorum they lose everything.

On that day I had a loss in Lord Keppel. But the public loss of him in this awful crisis—! I speak from much knowledge of the person: he never would have listened to any compromise with the rabble rout of this *sans-culotterie* of France. His goodness of heart, his reason, his taste, his public duty, his principles, his prejudices, would have repelled him for ever from all connection with that horrid medley of madness, vice, impiety, and crime.

Could Keppel, who idolized the House of Nassau, who was himself given to England along with the blessings of the British and Dutch revolutions, with revolutions of stability, with revolutions which consolidated and married the liberties and the interests of the two nations for ever,—could he see the fountain of British liberty itself in servitude to France? Could he see with patience a Prince of Orange expelled, as a sort of diminutive despot, with every kind of contumely, from the country which that family of deliverers had so often rescued from slavery, and obliged to live in exile in another country, which owes its liberty to his house? Would Keppel have heard with patience that the conduct to be held on such occasions was to become short by the knees to the action of the homicides, to entreat them quietly to retire? or, if the fortune of war should drive them from their first wicked and unprovoked invasion, that no security should be taken, no arrangement made, no barrier formed, no alliance entered into for the security of that which under a foreign name is the most precious part of England? What would he have said, if it was even proposed that the Austrian Netherlands (which ought to be a barrier to Holland, and the tie of an alliance to protect her against any species of rule that might be erected or even be restored in France) should be formed into a republic under her influence, and dependent upon her power?

But above all, what would he have said, if he had heard it made a matter of accusation against me, by his nephew the Duke of Bedford, that I was the author of the war? Had I a mind to keep that high distinction to myself, (as from pride I might, but from justice I dare not,) he would have snatched his share of it from my hand, and held it with the grasp of a dying convulsion to his end.

It would be a most arrogant presumption in me to assume to myself the glory of what belongs to his Majesty, and to his ministers, and to his Parliament, and to the far greater majority of his faithful people: but had I stood alone to counsel, and that all were determined to be guided by my advice, and to follow it implicitly, then I should have been the sole author of a war. But it should have been a war on my ideas and my principles. However, let his Grace think as he may of my demerits with regard to the war with Regicide, he will find my guilt confined to that alone. He never shall, with the smallest colour of reason, accuse me of being the author of a peace with Regicide.—But that is high matter, and ought not to be mixed with anything of so little moment as what may belong to me, or even to the Duke of Bedford.

I have the honour to be, &c.

EDMUND BURKE.

[For additional reading see pages 1165–1172.]

THOMAS PAINE (1737-1809)

Tom Paine, whom his biographer and editor, Moncure Conway, has called "the great Commoner of Mankind, founder of the Republic of the World, and emancipator of the human mind and heart," was a ne'er-do-well of humble occupation until his thirty-seventh year. He and his wife agreed to separate, and he determined to start life over again in the American colonies. Carrying a letter of introduction from Benjamin Franklin, who was then in England, he arrived in Philadelphia and was fortunate enough to be made the editor of the *Pennsylvania Magazine* at a salary of fifty pounds a year. Hardly more than a year later, on January 10, 1776, he published a pamphlet, *Common Sense*, in which he proposed the formation of an independent state out of the Colonies, now on the verge of rebellion. The suggestion swept like wild-fire, the pamphlet was in everybody's hands, and Paine took a place in the front ranks of the Revolutionary leaders.

Celebrated as his career in America had made him, he was destined to play a part in a second revolution in Europe. He had returned to England to develop his project of iron bridges, when the French Revolution broke out. He became intimate with such Revolutionary sympathizers as William Godwin, John Horne Tooke, and William Blake. In reply to Burke's *Reflections* he published his *Rights of Man* (1791), which was so popular and inflammatory that the government in 1792 indicted him for high treason. He escaped to France, where he found that he had already been elected to the Convention; and during the Reign of Terror he was imprisoned for his moderation, and escaped the guillotine, according to tradition, only by the mistake of the jailer. In 1802 he returned to America, but his popularity disappeared in the storm of invective which he raised by his Deistic attack on Christianity in *The Age of Reason* (1792-95). He died in 1809. Ten years later Cobbett reverently carried his remains back to England, but they were mysteriously lost.

Paine was a journalist and publicist rather than a thinker or man of letters. His style is slip-shod and his ideas are commonplaces; but he had the eloquence and passion which stirred men to action. His voice could be heard above the noise and confusion, a power to unite and organize the minds of the multitude. Delicate phrasing and subtle distinctions are of little use for his purpose. He probably never understood Burke's conception of government as inherent in the nature of man. As a political thinker he belonged to the tradition of John Locke, and he never examined critically the theory that government is established by a contract between the governors and the governed. He was interested above all in the moral right of a people to revolution, and two revolutions made him a great man.

Complete Works, ed. Moncure D. Conway (4 vols., 1894-96); *Selections,* ed. H. H. Clarke (1944); M. D. Conway, *Life* (2 vols., 1892); F. Gould, *Thomas Paine* (Boston, 1925).

THE RIGHTS OF MAN

PART THE FIRST

Among the incivilities by which nations or individuals provoke and irritate each other, Mr. Burke's pamphlet on the French Revolution is an extraordinary instance. Neither the people of France, nor the National Assembly, were troubling themselves about the affairs of England, or the English Parliament; and that Mr. Burke should commence an unprovoked attack upon them, both in Parliament and in public, is a conduct that cannot be pardoned on the score of manners, nor justified on that of policy.

There is scarcely an epithet of abuse to be found in the English language, with which Mr. Burke has not loaded the French Nation and the National Assembly. Everything which rancour, prejudice, ignorance or knowledge could suggest, is poured forth in the copious fury of near four hundred pages. In the strain and on the plan Mr. Burke was writing, he might have written on to as many thousands. When the tongue or the pen is let loose in a frenzy of passion, it is the man, and not the subject, that becomes exhausted.

Hitherto Mr. Burke has been mistaken and disappointed in the opinions he had formed of the affairs of France; but such is the ingenuity of his hope, or the malignancy of his despair, that it furnishes him with new pretences to go on. There was a time when it was impossible to make Mr. Burke believe there would be any Revolution in France. His opinion then was, that the French had neither spirit to undertake it nor fortitude to support it; and now that there is one, he seeks an escape by condemning it.

Not sufficiently content with abusing the National Assembly, a great part of his work is taken up with abusing Dr. Price (one of the best-hearted men that lives) and the two societies in England known by the name of the Revolution Society and the Society for Constitutional Information.

Dr. Price had preached a sermon on the 4th of November, 1789, being the anniversary of what is called in England the Revolution, which took place 1688. Mr. Burke, speaking of this sermon, says, "The political Divine proceeds dogmatically to assert, that by the principles of the Revolution, the people of England have acquired three fundamental rights:

1. To choose their own governors.
2. To cashier them for misconduct.
3. To frame a government for ourselves."

Dr. Price does not say that the right to do these things exists in this or in that person, or in this or in that description of persons, but that it exists in the *whole*; that it is a right resident in the Nation. Mr. Burke, on the contrary, denies that such a right exists in the Nation, either in whole or in part, or that it exists anywhere; and,

what is still more strange and marvellous, he says, "that the people of England utterly disclaim such a right, and that they will resist the practical assertion of it with their lives and fortunes." That men should take up arms and spend their lives and fortunes, *not* to maintain their rights, but to maintain they have *not* rights, is an entirely new species of discovery, and suited to the paradoxical genius of Mr. Burke.

The method which Mr. Burke takes to prove that the people of England have no such rights, and that such rights do not now exist in the Nation, either in whole or in part, or anywhere at all, is of the same marvellous and monstrous kind with what he has already said; for his arguments are that the persons, or the generation of persons, in whom they did exist, are dead, and with them the right is dead also. To prove this, he quotes a declaration made by Parliament about a hundred years ago, to William and Mary, in these words: "The Lords Spiritual and Temporal, and Commons, do, in the name of the people aforesaid [meaning the people of England then living], most humbly and faithfully *submit* themselves, their *heirs* and *posterities*, for EVER." He also quotes a clause of another act of Parliament made in the same reign, the terms of which, he says, "bind us [meaning the people of that day], our *heirs* and our *posterity*, to the end of time."

Mr. Burke conceives his point sufficiently established by producing those clauses, which he enforces by saying that they exclude the right of the Nation for *ever*. And not yet content with making such declarations, repeated over and over again, he farther says, "that if the people of England possessed such a right before the Revolution [which he acknowledges to have been the case, not only in England, but throughout Europe, at an early period], yet that the *English Nation* did, at the time of the Revolution, most solemnly renounce and abdicate it, for themselves, and for *all their posterity, for ever."*

As Mr. Burke occasionally applies the poison drawn from his horrid principles (if it is not profanation to call them by the name of principles) not only to the English Nation, but to the French Revolution and the National Assembly, and charges that august, illuminated and illuminating body of men with the epithet of *usurpers*, I shall, *sans cérémonie,* place another system of principles in opposition to his.

The English Parliament of 1688 did a certain thing, which, for themselves and their constitutents, they had a right to do, and which it appeared right should be done: but, in addition to this right, which they possessed by delegation, *they set up another right by assumption,* that of binding and controlling posterity to the end of time. The case, therefore, divides itself into two parts; the right which they possessed by delegation, and the right which they set up by assumption. The first is admitted; but with respect to the second, I reply—

There never did, there never will, and there never can, exist a Parliament, or any description of men, or any generation of men, in any country, possessed of the right or the power of binding and controlling posterity to the *"end of time,"* or of commanding for ever how the world shall be governed, or who shall govern it; and therefore all such clauses, acts or declarations by which the makers of them attempt to do what they have neither the right nor the power to do, nor the power to execute, are in themselves null and void. Every age and generation must be as free to act for itself *in all cases* as the ages and generations which preceded it. The vanity and presumption of governing beyond the grave is the most ridiculous and insolent of all tyrannies. Man has no property in man; neither has any generation a property in the generations which are to follow. The Parliament or the people of 1688, or of any

other period, had no more right to dispose of the people of the present day, or to bind or to control them *in any shape whatever*, than the Parliament or the people of the present day have to dispose of, bind or control those who are to live a hundred or a thousand years hence. Every generation is, and must be, competent to all the purposes which its occasions require. It is the living, and not the dead, that are to be accommodated. When man ceases to be, his power and his wants cease with him; and having no longer any participation in the concerns of this world, he has no longer any authority in directing who shall be its governors, or how its government shall be organised, or how administered.

I am not contending for nor against any form of government, nor for nor against any party, here or elsewhere. That which a whole Nation chooses to do, it ha. a right to do. Mr. Burke says, No. Where, then, does the right exist? I am contending for the rights of the *living*, and against their being willed away, and controlled and contracted for, by the manuscript assumed authority of the dead; and Mr. Burke is contending for the authority of the dead over the rights and freedom of the living. There was a time when Kings disposed of their Crowns by will upon their deathbeds, and consigned the people, like beasts of the field, to whatever successor they appointed. This is now so exploded as scarcely to be remembered, and so monstrous as hardly to be believed; but the Parliamentary clauses upon which Mr. Burke builds his political church are of the same nature.

The laws of every country must be analogous to some common principle. In England no parent or master, nor all the authority of Parliament omnipotent as it has called itself, can bind or control the personal freedom even of an individual beyond the age of twenty-one years. On what ground of right, then, could the Parliament of 1688, or any other Parliament, bind all posterity for ever?

Those who have quitted the world, and those who are not yet arrived at it, are as remote from each other as the utmost stretch of mortal imagination can conceive. What possible obligation, then, can exist between them; what rule or principle can be laid down that of two non-entities, the one out of existence and the other not in, and who never can meet in this world, the one should control the other to the end of time?

In England it is said that money cannot be taken out of the pockets of the people without their consent. But who authorised, or who could authorise, the Parliament of 1688 to control and take away the freedom of posterity (who were not in existence to give or to withhold their consent), and limit and confine their right of acting in certain cases for ever?

A greater absurdity cannot present itself to the understanding of man than what Mr. Burke offers to his readers. He tells them, and he tells the world to come, that a certain body of men who existed a hundred years ago, made a law, and that there does not now exist in the Nation, nor ever will, nor ever can, a power to alter it. Under how many subtilties or absurdities has the divine right to govern been imposed on the credulity of mankind! Mr. Burke has discovered a new one, and he has shortened his journey to Rome by appealing to the power of this infallible Parliament of former days; and he produces what it has done as of divine authority, for that power must certainly be more than human which no human power to the end of time can alter. . . .

It requires but a very small glance of thought to perceive that altho' laws made in one generation often continue in force through succeeding generations, yet that they continue to derive their force from the consent of the living. A law not repealed continues in force, not because it *cannot* be repealed, but because it *is not* re-pealed; and the non-repealing passes for consent.

But Mr. Burke's clauses have not even this qualification in their favour. They become null, by attempting to become immortal. The nature of them precludes consent. They destroy the right which they *might* have, by grounding it on a right which they *cannot* have. Immortal power is not a human right, and therefore cannot be a right of Parliament. The Parliament of 1688 might as well have passed an act to have authorised themselves to live for ever, as to make their authority live for ever. All, therefore, that can be said of those clauses is that they are a formality of words, of as much import as if those who used them had addressed a congratulation to themselves, and in the oriental style of antiquity had said: O Parliament, live for ever!

The circumstances of the world are continually changing, and the opinions of men change also; and as government is for the living, and not for the dead, it is the living only that has any right in it. That which may be thought right and found convenient in one age may be thought wrong and found inconvenient in another. In such cases, Who is to decide, the living, or the dead?

As almost one hundred pages of Mr. Burke's book are employed upon these clauses, it will consequently follow that if the clauses themselves, so far as they set up an *assumed usurped* dominion over posterity for ever, are unauthoritative, and in their nature null and void; that all his voluminous inferences, and declamation drawn therefrom, or founded thereon, are null and void also; and on this ground I rest the matter.

We now come more particularly to the affairs of France. Mr. Burke's book has the appearance of being written as instruction to the French Nation; but if I may permit myself the use of an extravagant metaphor, suited to the extravagance of the case, it is darkness attempting to illuminate light.

While I am writing this there are accidentally before me some proposals for a declaration of rights by the Marquis de la Fayette (I ask his pardon for using his former address, and do it only for distinction's sake) to the National Assembly, on the 11th of July, 1789, three days before the taking of the Bastille; and I cannot but remark with astonishment how opposite the sources are from which that gentleman and Mr. Burke draw their principles. Instead of referring to musty records and mouldy parchments to prove that the rights of the living are lost, "renounced and abdicated for ever," by those who are now no more, as Mr. Burke has done, M. de la Fayette applies to the living world, and emphatically says, "Call to mind the sentiments which Nature has engraved in the heart of every citizen, and which take a new force when they are solemnly recognised by all: For a Nation to love Liberty, it is sufficient that she knows it; and to be free, it is sufficient that she wills it." How dry, barren, and obscure is the source from which Mr. Burke labours; and how ineffectual, though gay with flowers, are all his declamation and his arguments compared with these clear, concise, and soul-animating sentiments! Few and short as they are, they lead to a vast field of generous and manly thinking, and do not finish, like Mr. Burke's periods, with music in the ear, and nothing in the heart. . . .

"We have seen," says Mr. Burke, "the French rebel against a mild and lawful Monarch, with more fury, outrage, and insult, than any people has been known to rise against the most illegal usurper, or the most sanguinary tyrant." This is one among a thousand other instances, in which Mr. Burke shows that he is ignorant of the springs and principles of the French Revolution.

It was not against Louis XVI., but against the despotic principles of the government, that the Nation revolted.

These principles had not their origin in him, but in the original establishment, many centuries back; and they were become too deeply rooted to be removed, and the Augean stable of parasites and plunderers too abominably filthy to be cleansed, by anything short of a complete and universal Revolution. When it becomes necessary to do a thing, the whole heart and soul should go into the measure, or not attempt it. That crisis was then arrived, and there remained no choice but to act with determined vigour, or not to act at all. The King was known to be the friend of the Nation, and this circumstance was favourable to the enterprise. Perhaps no man bred up in the style of an absolute king, ever possessed a heart so little disposed to the exercise of that species of power as the present King of France. But the principles of the Government itself still remained the same. The Monarch and the Monarchy were distinct and separate things; and it was against the established despotism of the latter, and not against the person or principles of the former, that the revolt commenced, and the Revolution has been carried.

Mr. Burke does not attend to the distinction between *men* and *principles*; and, therefore, he does not see that a revolt may take place against the despotism of the latter, while there lies no charge of despotism against the former.

The natural moderation of Louis XVI. contributed nothing to alter the hereditary despotism of the Monarchy. All the tyrannies of former reigns, acted under that hereditary despotism, were still liable to be revived in the hands of a successor. It was not the respite of a reign that would satisfy France, enlightened as she then was become. A casual discontinuance of the *practice* of despotism, is not a discontinuance of its *principles*; the former depends on the virtue of the individual who is in immediate possession of the power; the latter, on the virtue and fortitude of the nation. In the case of Charles I. and James II. of England, the revolt was against the personal despotism of the men; whereas in France, it was against the hereditary despotism of the established government. But men who can consign over the rights of posterity for ever on the authority of a mouldy parchment, like Mr. Burke, are not qualified to judge of this Revolution. It takes in a field too vast for their views to explore, and proceeds with a mightiness or reason they cannot keep pace with.

But there are many points of view in which this Revolution may be considered. When despotism has established itself for ages in a country, as in France, it is not in the person of the King only that it resides. It has the appearance of being so in show, and in nominal authority; but it is not so in practice and in fact. It has its standard everywhere. Every office and department has its despotism, founded upon custom and usage. Every place has its Bastille, and every Bastille its despot. The original hereditary despotism resident in the person of the King, divides and subdivides itself into a thousand shapes and forms, till at last the whole of it is acted by deputation. This was the case in France: and against this species of despotism, proceeding on through an endless labyrinth of office till the source of it is scarcely perceptible, there is no mode of redress. It strengthens itself by assuming the appearance of duty, and tyrannises under the pretence of obeying.

When a man reflects on the condition which France was in from the nature of her Government, he will see other causes for revolt than those which immediately connect themselves with the person or character of Louis XVI. There were, if I may so express it, a thousand despotisms to be reformed in France, which had grown up under the hereditary despotism of the monarchy, and became so rooted as to be in great measure independent of it. Between the Monarchy, the Parliament, and the Church, there was a *rivalship* of despotism; besides the feudal despotism operating locally, and the ministerial despotism operating everywhere. But Mr. Burke, by considering the King as the only possible object of a revolt, speaks as if France was a village, in which everything that passed must be known to its commanding officer, and no oppression could be acted but what he could immediately control. Mr. Burke might have been in the Bastille his whole life, as well under Louis XVI. as Louis XIV., and neither the one nor the other have known that such a man as Mr. Burke existed. The despotic principles of the government were the same in both reigns, though the dispositions of the men were as remote as tyranny and benevolence.

What Mr. Burke considers as a reproach to the French Revolution (that of bringing it forward under a reign more mild than the preceding ones) is one of its highest honours. The Revolutions that have taken place in other European countries, have been excited by personal hatred. The rage was against the man, and he became the victim. But, in the instance of France we see a revolution generated in the rational contemplation of the rights of man, and distinguishing from the beginning between persons and principles.

But Mr. Burke appears to have no idea of principles when he is contemplating Governments. "Ten years ago," says he, "I could have felicitated France on her having a Government, without inquiring what the nature of that Government was, or how it was administered." Is this the language of a rational man? Is it the language of a heart feeling as it ought to feel for the rights and happiness of the human race? On this ground, Mr. Burke must compliment all the governments in the world, while the victims who suffer under them, whether sold into slavery, or tortured out of existence, are wholly forgotten. It is power, and not principles, that Mr

Burke venerates; and under this abominable depravity he is disqualified to judge between them. Thus much for his opinion as to the occasions of the French Revolution. I now proceed to other considerations.

I know a place in America called Point-no-Point, because as you proceed along the shore, gay and flowery as Mr. Burke's language, it continually recedes and presents itself at a distance before you; but when you have got as far as you can go, there is no point at all. Just thus it is with Mr. Burke's three hundred and fifty-six pages. It is therefore difficult to reply to him. But as the points he wishes to establish may be inferred from what he abuses, it is in his paradoxes that we must look for his arguments.

As to the tragic paintings by which Mr. Burke has outraged his own imagination, and seeks to work upon that of his readers, they are very well calculated for theatrical representation, where facts are manufactured for the sake of show, and accommodated to produce, through the weakness of sympathy, a weeping effect. But Mr. Burke should recollect that he is writing history, and not *plays,* and that his readers will expect truth, and not the spouting rant of high-toned exclamation.

When we see a man dramatically lamenting in a publication intended to be believed chat *"The age of chivalry is gone!* that *the glory of Europe is extinguished for ever!* that *the unbought grace of life* (if any one knows what it is), *the cheap defence of nations, the nurse of manly sentiment and heroic enterprise is gone!"* and all this because the Quixote age of chivalry nonsense is gone, what opinion can we form of his judgment, or what regard can we pay to his facts? In the rhapsody of his imagination he has discovered a world of windmills, and his sorrows are that there are no Quixotes to attack them. But if the age of aristocracy, like that of chivalry, should fall (and they had orig-inally some connection), Mr. Burke, the trumpeter of the Order, may continue his parody to the end, and finish with exclaiming: *"Othello's occupation's gone!"*

Notwithstanding Mr. Burke's horrid paintings, when the French Revolution is compared with the revolutions of other countries, the astonishment will be that it is marked with so few sacrifices; but this astonishment will cease when we reflect that *principles,* and not *persons,* were the meditated objects of destruction. The mind of the nation was acted upon by a higher stimulus than what the consideration of persons could inspire, and sought a higher conquest than could be produced by the downfall of an enemy. Among the few who fell there do not appear to be any that were intentionally singled out. They all of them had their fate in the circumstances of the moment, and were not pursued with that long, cold-blooded, unabated revenge which pursued the unfortunate Scotch in the affair of 1745.

Through the whole of Mr. Burke's book I do not observe that the Bastille is mentioned more than once, and that with a kind of implication as if he were sorry it was pulled down, and wished it were built up again. "We have rebuilt Newgate," says he, "and tenanted the mansion; and we have prisons almost as strong as the Bastille for those who dare to libel the Queens of France." As to what a madman like the person called Lord G—— G—— might say, to whom Newgate is rather a bedlam than a prison, it is unworthy a rational consideration. It was a madman that libelled, and that is sufficient apology; and it afforded an opportunity for confining him, which was the thing that was wished for. But certain it is that Mr. Burke, who does not call himself a madman (whatever other people may do), has libelled in the most unprovoked manner, and in the grossest style of the most vulgar abuse, the whole representative authority of

France, and yet Mr. Burke takes his seat in the British House of Commons! From his violence and his grief, his silence on some points and his excess on others, it is difficult not to believe that Mr. Burke is sorry, extremely sorry, that arbitrary power, the power of the Pope and the Bastille, are pulled down.

Not one glance of compassion, not one commiserating reflection that I can find throughout his book, has he bestowed on those who lingered out the most wretched of lives, a life without hope in the most miserable of prisons. It is painful to behold a man employing his talents to corrupt himself. Nature has been kinder to Mr. Burke than he is to her. He is not affected by the reality of distress touching his heart, but by the showy resemblance of it striking his imagination. He pities the plumage, but forgets the dying bird. Accustomed to kiss the aristocratical hand that hath purloined him from himself, he degenerates into a composition of art, and the genuine soul of nature forsakes him. His hero or his heroine must be a tragedy-victim expiring in show, and not the real prisoner of misery, sliding into death in the silence of a dungeon. . . .

PART SECOND

CHAPTER I

OF SOCIETY AND CIVILISATION

Great part of that order which reigns among mankind is not the effect of government. It has its origin in the principles of society and the natural constitution of man. It existed prior to government, and would exist if the formality of government was abolished. The mutual dependence and reciprocal interest which man has upon man, and all the parts of a civilised community upon each other, create that great chain of connection which holds it together. The landholder, the farmer, the manufacturer, the merchant, the tradesman, and every occupation, prospers by the aid which each receives from the other, and from the whole. Common interest regulates their concerns, and forms their law; and the laws which common usage ordains, have a greater influence than the laws of government. In fine, society performs for itself almost everything which is ascribed to government.

To understand the nature and quantity of government proper for man, it is necessary to attend to his character. As nature created him for social life, she fitted him for the station she intended. In all cases she made his natural wants greater than his individual powers. No one man is capable, without the aid of society, of supplying his own wants; and those wants, acting upon every individual, impel the whole of them into society, as naturally as gravitation acts to a centre.

But she has gone further. She has not only forced man into society by a diversity of wants which the reciprocal aid of each other can supply, but she has implanted in him a system of social affections, which, though not necessary to his existence, are essential to his happiness. There is no period in life when this love for society ceases to act. It begins and ends with our being.

If we examine with attention the composition and constitution of man, the diversity of his wants and talents in different men for reciprocally accommodating the wants of each other, his propensity to society, and consequently to preserve the advantages resulting from it, we shall easily discover that a great part of what is called government is mere imposition.

Government is no farther necessary than to supply the few cases to which society and civilisation are not conveniently competent; and instances are not wanting to show, that everything which government can usefully add thereto, has been performed by the common consent of society, without government.

For upwards of two years from the commencement of the American War, and to a longer period in several of the American States, there were no established forms of government. The old governments had been abolished, and the country was too much occupied in defence to employ its attention in establishing new governments; yet during this interval order and harmony were preserved as inviolate as in any country in Europe. There is a natural aptness in man, and more so in society, because it embraces a greater variety of abilities and resources, to accommodate itself to whatever situation it is in. The instant formal government is abolished, society begins to act: a general association takes place, and common interest produces common security.

So far is it from being true, as has been pretended, that the abolition of any formal government is the dissolution of society, that it acts by a contrary impulse, and brings the latter the closer together. All that part of its organization which it had committed to its government, devolves again upon itself, and acts through its medium. When men, as well from natural instinct as from reciprocal benefits, have habituated themselves to social and civilised life, there is always enough of its principles in practice to carry them through any changes they may find necessary or convenient to make in their government. In short, man is so naturally a creature of society that it is almost impossible to put him out of it.

Formal government makes but a small part of civilised life; and when even the best that human wisdom can devise is established, it is a thing more in name and idea than in fact. It is to the great and fundamental principles of society and civilisation—to the common usage universally consented to, and mutually and reciprocally maintained—to the unceasing circulation of interest, which, passing through its million channels, invigorates the whole mass of civilised man

—it is to these things, infinitely more than to anything which even the best instituted government can perform, that the safety and prosperity of the individual and of the whole depends.

The more perfect civilisation is, the less occasion has it for government, because the more it does regulate its own affairs, and govern itself; but so contrary is the practice of old governments to the reason of the case, that the expenses of them increase in the proportion they ought to diminish. It is but few general laws that civilised life requires, and those of such common usefulness, that whether they are enforced by the forms of government or not, the effect will be nearly the same. If we consider what the principles are that first condense men into society, and what the motives that regulate their mutual intercourse afterwards, we shall find, by the time we arrive at what is called government, that nearly the whole of the business is performed by the natural operation of the parts upon each other.

Man, with respect to all those matters, is more a creature of consistency than he is aware, or than governments would wish him to believe. All the great laws of society are laws of nature. Those of trade and commerce, whether with respect to the intercourse of individuals or of nations, are laws of mutual and reciprocal interests. They are followed and obeyed, because it is the interest of the parties so to do, and not on account of any formal laws their governments may impose or interpose.

But how often is the natural propensity to society disturbed or destroyed by the operations of government! When the latter, instead of being ingrafted on the principles of the former, assumes to exist for itself, and acts by partialities of favour and oppression, it becomes the cause of the mischiefs it ought to prevent.

If we look back to the riots and tumults which at various times have happened in England, we shall find that they did not proceed from the want of a government, but that government was itself the generating cause: instead of consolidating society it divided it; it deprived it of its natural cohesion, and engendered discontents and disorders which otherwise would not have existed. In those associations, which men promiscuously form for the purpose of trade, or of any concern in which government is totally out of the question, and in which they act merely on the principles of society, we see how naturally the various parties unite; and this shows, by comparison, that governments, so far from being always the cause or means of order, are often the destruction of it. The riots of 1770 had no other source than the remains of those prejudices which the Government of itself had encouraged. But with respect to England there are also other causes.

Excess and inequality of taxation, however disguised in the means, never fail to appear in their effects. As a great mass of the community are thrown thereby into poverty and discontent, they are constantly on the brink of commotion; and deprived, as they unfortunately are, of the means of information, are easily heated to outrage. Whatever the apparent cause of any riots may be, the real one is always want of happiness. It shows that something is wrong in the system of government that injures the felicity by which society is to be preserved.

But as fact is superior to reasoning, the instance of America presents itself to confirm these observations. If there is a country in the world where concord, according to common calculation, would be least expected, it is America. Made up as it is of people from different nations, accustomed to different forms and habits of government, speaking different languages, and more different in their modes of worship, it would appear that the union of such a people was impracticable; but by the simple operation of constructing government on the principles of society and the rights of man, every difficulty retires, and all the parts are brought into cordial unison. There the poor are not oppressed, the rich are not privileged. Industry is not mortified by the splendid extravagance of a Court rioting at its expense. Their taxes are few, because their government is just: and as there is nothing to render them wretched, there is nothing to engender riots and tumults.

A metaphysical man, like Mr. Burke, would have tortured his invention to discover how such a people could be governed. He would have supposed that some must be managed by fraud, others by force, and all by some contrivance; that genius must be hired to impose upon ignorance, and show and parade to fascinate the vulgar. Lost in the abundance of his researches, he would have resolved and re-resolved, and finally overlooked the plain and easy road that lay directly before him.

One of the great advantages of the American Revolution has been, that it led to a discovery of the principles, and laid open the imposition of governments. All the Revolutions till then had been worked within the small sphere of a Court, and never on the great floor of a Nation. The parties were always of the class of courtiers; and whatever was their rage for reformation, they carefully preserved the fraud of the profession.

In all cases they took care to represent government as a thing made up of mysteries, which only themselves understood; and they hid from the understanding of the Nation the only thing that was beneficial to know, namely, *that government is nothing more than a national association acting on the principles of society.*

[1791]

WILLIAM BLAKE (1757-1827)

Engraver, painter, poet, and seer of visions, William Blake has made a unique contribution to English literature. No one has completely understood his contribution; perhaps no one ever will. But it is intriguing to know that the more his difficult prophetic books are studied, the more stimulating the pattern of thought in them becomes. In the end his imagination, like Milton's, could be satisfied with nothing less than the cosmos for its field of play. That is ample reason for our difficulty in comprehending his later poems. They demand an understanding of the temperament and mind of a visionary as well as a knowledge of the currents of eighteenth-century occultism—that fascinating, half-secret undercurrent of mystical philosophy which has flowed on for centuries, but about which we know so little. His poetry, moreover, must be studied, for any intelligent understanding of it, in conjunction with his painting and engraving. These fields of knowledge are much too complex to be handled in a brief introduction; the most that can be done here is to give some idea of the direction of development of Blake's genius and to suggest in the bibliography at the end a few of the best sources of information for further study.

Outwardly Blake's life was uneventful. He was early apprenticed to an engraver, and as an engraver he earned the very modest income with which he supported himself and his wife up to the last year of his life. Practically all of these years but three were spent in some of the most uninspiring localities of London. The lovely *Songs of Innocence,* filled with sunshine and the fresh green of spring and the laughter of children, were written above a shop at 28 Poland Street. But locality meant nothing to Blake so long as he was sure of sufficient freedom to give himself to his visionary world to which he withdrew more and more as the years went on. As Mrs. Blake remarked quite simply at one time, "I have very little of Mr. Blake's company; he is always in Paradise."

For three years, 1800 to 1803, Blake had tried the experiment of living in a charming little cottage in Felpham on the Sussex coast, and for a time the change was greatly stimulating, but his patron, Hayley, a conventional, practical-minded poet and biographer for whom Blake was engraving plates for a life of Cowper, tried to exercise too much control over his mind and imagination—tried to keep him industriously working in this world of time and space. This domination Blake could not and would not tolerate. He wrote at this time to his more understanding patron, Thomas Butts, "I am not ashamed, afraid, or averse to tell you what Ought to be Told: That I am under the direction of Messengers from Heaven, Daily and Nightly; but the nature of such things is not, as some suppose, without trouble or care. Temptations are on the right hand and left; behind, the sea of time and space roars and follows swiftly; . . . But if we fear to do the dictates of our Angels, and tremble at the Tasks set before us; if we refuse to do Spiritual Acts because of Natural Fears or Natural Desires! Who can describe the dismal torments of such a state!"

Blake returned to London and gradually became reconciled to a life of comparative obscurity. "In my Brain," he wrote, "are studies and Chambers filled with books and pictures of old, which I wrote and painted in ages of Eternity before my mortal life; and those works are the delight—Study of Archangels. Why, then, should I be anxious about the riches or fame of mortality?" But as he achieved more and more fully the vast mythology of his *Prophecies* with their interpretation of the world from the creation to the apocalypse, he became less and less productive. All his best poetry was written before 1804; in fact, with the exception of the last three selections all the following poems had been written by 1794.

As only the simplest of the prophetic books are included in this selection, no attempt will be made here to interpret Blake's cosmology. His symbols will be interpreted in the notes where necessary. But perhaps an outline of some of his ideas about good and evil will make the reading of *Thel* and *The Marriage of Heaven and Hell* more interesting.

There is, according to Blake, a mental power that circumscribes the soul of man. This Blake calls reason (represented by Urizen). There is also a spiritual power which Blake calls variously energy, poetic genius, imagination, which illuminates the soul. The first is a limiting, analytical power; the second is synthetic. The former leads to destruction; the latter to salvation. Why is man so much under the domination of reason, the destructive force? Blake's answer to this question recalls the doctrines of the Gnostics and writers of the

Cabala. God being all perfect and containing everything within himself could not create anything outside of himself without a partial withdrawal or retraction of himself. The creature must therefore necessarily be less perfect than the creator, his creation being in a sense a fall from perfection. Thus Urizen, who has been given the task of the creation of man, fell from the godhead. In order to keep his fall from being infinite, it was necessary to create this limiting world of time and space and enclose the spirit in the five senses. Thus reason, the limiting, analytical power, and this material world were both necessary to the process of creation, but man must be on his guard against the domination of reason and the dogmatic, conventionalizing morality dictated by a limited view of life. Man must not be deceived by the testimony of the senses, but must keep in touch with spirit; he must learn to see not with but *through* the eye. And above all, spiritual energy, the God in man, must be free to express itself in love and creative activity. In the end it will bring about a reunion of what reason has divided, and men will live as one man, united in brotherhood.

> Mutual in one another's love and wrath all renewing,
> We live as One Man: for, contracting our Infinite senses,
> We behold multitude; or, expanding, we behold as One,
> As One Man all the Universal Family . . .

This One Man Blake often refers to as Albion. At the fall the One was divided into the Many. At the resurrection the Many will be reunited in the One. The resurrected Albion Blake often identifies with Jesus Christ who waits sorrowing for man's redemption.

This is the heart of Blake's message. It is interesting to note that Blake's revolt against reason, which was in line with a marked tendency of the latter part of the eighteenth century, did not discard reason altogether. As he says in *The Marriage of Heaven and Hell*, without contraries—reason and energy, love and hate—there is no progression. In the end of his great myth, Urizen is not destroyed but is regenerated by a union with Imagination (Los) and Passion (Luvah).

Writings, ed. G. Keynes (3 vols., 1925); *Poetry and Prose*, ed. G. Keynes (4th ed., 1948); *Prophetic Writings*, ed. D. J. Sloss and J. P. R. Wallis (2 vols., Oxford, 1926); *Pencil Drawings*, ed. G. Keynes (1927); *Engravings*, ed. G. Keynes (1950); *Note-Book*, ed. G. Keynes (1935) [facsimile]; A. Gilchrist, Life of *William Blake* (1863) [a source-book for later lives], Mona Wilson, *Life* (2nd ed., 1949); H. L. Bruce, *William Blake in this World* (1925); J. Bronowski, *William Blake, 1757-1827: A Man Without a Mask* (1944), B. Blackstone, *English Blake* (Cambridge, Eng., 1949); F. S. Damon, *William Blake: His Philosophy and Symbols* (1924, 1949); M. Plowman, *An Introduction to the Study of Blake* (1927); D. Saurat, *Blake and Modern Thought* (1929); M. O. Percival, *William Blake's Circle of Destiny* (1938); R. Lowery, *Windows of the Morning* (New Haven, 1940); M. Schorer, *William Blake: The Politics of Vision* (1946); N. Frye, *Fearful Symmetry: A Study of William Blake* (Princeton, 1947); J. G. Davis, *The Theology of William Blake* (Oxford, 1948); G. Keynes, *Blake Studies* (1949); A. VanSinderen, *Blake, the Mystic Genius* (Syracuse, 1949); H. M. Margoliouth, *William Blake* (1951); M. E. Rudd, *Divided Image* (1953); D. V. Erdman, *Blake, Prophet Against Empire* (Princeton, 1954); D. Figgis, *Paintings* (1925); L. Binyon, *Engraved Designs* (1926).

For Blake's glosses on Reynolds' *Seventh Discourse* see pages 1173-1189.

From POETICAL SKETCHES

SONG

How sweet I roamed from field to field,
  And tasted all the summer's pride,
Till I the Prince of Love beheld,
  Who in the sunny beams did glide!

He showed me lilies for my hair,
  And blushing roses for my brow;
He led me through his gardens fair,
  Where all his golden pleasures grow.

With sweet May dews my wings were wet,
  And Phoebus fired my vocal rage;   10
He caught me in his silken net,
  And shut me in his golden cage.

He loves to sit and hear me sing,
  Then, laughing, sports and plays with me;
Then stretches out my golden wing,
  And mocks my loss of liberty.
                                    [1783]

TO THE EVENING STAR

Thou fair-haired angel of the evening,
Now, while the sun rests on the mountains, light
Thy bright torch of love; thy radiant crown
Put on, and smile upon our evening bed!
Smile on our loves, and, while thou drawest the
Blue curtains of the sky, scatter thy silver dew
On every flower that shuts its sweet eyes
In timely sleep. Let thy west wind sleep on
The lake, speak silence with thy glimmering eyes,
And wash the dusk with silver. Soon, full soon,   10
Dost thou withdraw; then the wolf rages wide,
And the lion glares through the dun forest:
The fleeces of our flocks are covered with
Thy sacred dew: protect them with thine influence.
                                    [1783]

SONG

My silks and fine array,
  My smiles and languished air,
By love are driven away;
  And mournful lean Despair
Brings me yew to deck my grave:
Such end true lovers have.

His face is fair as heaven,
  When springing buds unfold;
O why to him was 't given
  Whose heart is wintry cold?   10
His breast is love's all-worshipped tomb,
Where all love's pilgrims come.

Bring me an axe and spade,
  Bring me a winding sheet;
When I my grave have made,
  Let winds and tempests beat:
Then down I'll lie, as cold as clay.
True love doth pass away!
                        [1783]

SONG

I love the jocund dance,
  The softly-breathing song,
Where innocent eyes do glance,
  And where lisps the maiden's tongue.

I love the laughing vale,
  I love the echoing hill,
Where mirth does never fail,
  And the jolly swain laughs his fill.

I love the pleasant cot,
  I love the innocent bower,   10
Where white and brown is our lot,
  Or fruit in the midday hour.

I love the oaken seat,
  Beneath the oaken tree,
Where all the old villagers meet,
  And laugh our sports to see.

I love our neighbours all,
   But, Kitty, I better love thee;
And love them I ever shall;
   But thou art all to me.   20

[1783]

SONG

Memory, hither come,
   And tune your merry notes;
And, while upon the wind
   Your music floats,
I'll pore upon the stream
Where sighing lovers dream,
And fish for fancies as they pass
   Within the watery glass.

I'll drink of the clear stream,
   And hear the linnet's song;   10
And there I'll lie and dream
   The day along:
And, when night comes, I'll go
   To places fit for woe,
Walking along the darkened valley
   With silent Melancholy.

[1783]

MAD SONG

The wild winds weep,
   And the night is a-cold;
Come hither, Sleep,
   And my griefs unfold:
But lo! the morning peeps
   Over the eastern steeps,
And the rustling birds of dawn
   The earth do scorn.

Lo! to the vault
   Of pavèd heaven,   10
With sorrow fraught
   My notes are driven:
They strike the ear of night,
   Make weep the eyes of day;
They make mad the roaring winds,
   And with tempests play.

Like a fiend in a cloud,
   With howling woe,
After night I do crowd,
   And with night will go;   20
I turn my back to the east
From whence comforts have increased;
For light doth seize my brain
   With frantic pain.

[1783]

SONG

Fresh from the dewy hill, the merry year
Smiles on my head and mounts his flaming car;
Round my young brows the laurel wreathes a shade,
And rising glories beam around my head.

My feet are winged, while o'er the dewy lawn
I meet my maiden, risen like the morn:
O bless those holy feet, like angels' feet;
O bless those limbs, beaming with heavenly light.

Like as an angel glittering in the sky
In times of innocence and holy joy,   10
The joyful shepherd stops his grateful song
To hear the music of an angel's tongue.

So when she speaks, the voice of Heaven I hear:
So when we walk, nothing impure comes near;
Each field seems Eden, and each calm retreat;
Each village seems the haunt of holy feet.

But that sweet village where my black-eyed maid
Closes her eyes in sleep beneath night's shade,
Whene'er I enter, more than mortal fire
Burns in my soul, and does my song inspire.   20

[1783]

TO THE MUSES

Whether on Ida's shady brow,
  Or in the chambers of the East,
The chambers of the sun, that now
  From ancient melody have ceased;

Whether in Heaven ye wander fair,
  Or the green corners of the earth,
Or the blue regions of the air,
  Where the melodious winds have birth;

Whether on crystal rocks ye rove,
  Beneath the bosom of the sea   10
Wandering in many a coral grove,
  Fair Nine, forsaking Poetry!

How have you left the ancient love
  That bards of old enjoyed in you!
The languid strings do scarcely move!
The sound is forced, the notes are few!
                [1783]

SONGS OF INNOCENCE AND OF EXPERIENCE

SHOWING THE TWO CONTRARY STATES OF THE HUMAN SOUL

From SONGS OF INNOCENCE

INTRODUCTION

Piping down the valleys wild,
Piping songs of pleasant glee,
On a cloud I saw a child,
And he laughing said to me:

"Pipe a song about a Lamb!"
So I piped with merry cheer.
"Piper, pipe that song again;"
So I piped: he wept to hear.

"Drop thy pipe, thy happy pipe;
Sing thy songs of happy cheer:"   10
So I sang the same again,
While he wept with joy to hear.

"Piper, sit thee down and write
In a book, that all may read."
So he vanished from my sight,
And I plucked a hollow reed,

And I made a rural pen,
And I stained the water clear,

And I wrote my happy songs
Every child may joy to hear.   20
                [1789]

THE SHEPHERD

How sweet is the Shepherd's sweet lot!
From the morn to the evening he strays;
He shall follow his sheep all the day,
And his tongue shall be filled with praise.

For he hears the lamb's innocent call,
And he hears the ewe's tender reply;
He is watchful while they are in peace,
For they know when their Shepherd is nigh.
                [1789]

THE ECHOING GREEN

The Sun does arise,
And make happy the skies;
The merry bells ring
To welcome the Spring;
The skylark and thrush,
The birds of the bush,
Sing louder around
To the bells' cheerful sound,
While our sports shall be seen
On the Echoing Green.   10

Old John, with white hair,
Does laugh away care,
Sitting under the oak,
Among the old folk.
They laugh at our play,
And soon they all say:
"Such, such were the joys
When we all, girls and boys,
In our youth time were seen
On the Echoing Green."   20

Till the little ones, weary,
No more can be merry;
The sun does descend,
And our sports have an end.
Round the laps of their mothers
Many sisters and brothers,
Like birds in their nest,
Are ready for rest,
And sport no more seen
On the darkening Green.   30
                [1789]

THE LAMB

Little Lamb, who made thee?
Dost thou know who made thee?
Gave thee life, and bid thee feed
By the stream and o'er the mead;
Gave thee clothing of delight,
Softest clothing, woolly, bright;
Gave thee such a tender voice,
Making all the vales rejoice?
  Little Lamb, who made thee?
Dost thou know who made thee? 10

Little Lamb, I'll tell thee,
  Little Lamb, I'll tell thee:
He is callèd by thy name,
For he calls himself a Lamb.
He is meek, and he is mild;
He became a little child.
I a child, and thou a lamb,
We are callèd by his name.
  Little Lamb, God bless thee!
  Little Lamb, God bless thee! 20

[1789]

THE LITTLE BLACK BOY

My mother bore me in the southern wild,
And I am black, but O! my soul is white;
White as an angel is the English child,
But I am black, as if bereaved of light.

My mother taught me underneath a tree,
And sitting down before the heat of day,
She took me on her lap and kissed me,
And, pointing to the east, began to say:

"Look on the rising sun: there God does live,
And gives his light, and gives his heat away; 10
And flowers and trees and beasts and men receive
Comfort in morning, joy in the noonday.

"And we are put on earth a little space,
That we may learn to bear the beams of love;
And these black bodies and this sunburnt face
Is but a cloud, and like a shady grove.

"For when our souls have learned the heat to bear,
The cloud will vanish; we shall hear his voice,
Saying: 'Come out from the grove, my love and care,
And round my golden tent like lambs rejoice.' " 20

Thus did my mother say, and kissed me;
And thus I say to little English boy:
When I from black and he from white cloud free,
And round the tent of God like lambs we joy,

I'll shade him from the heat, till he can bear
To lean in joy upon our Father's knee;
And then I'll stand and stroke his silver hair,
And be like him, and he will then love me.

[1789]

THE CHIMNEY SWEEPER

When my mother died I was very young,
And my father sold me while yet my tongue

Could scarcely cry " 'weep! 'weep! 'weep! 'weep!"
So your chimneys I sweep, and in soot I sleep.

There's little Tom Dacre, who cried when his head,
That curled like a lamb's back, was shaved: so I said
"Hush, Tom! never mind it, for when your head's bare
You know that the soot cannot spoil your white hair."

And so he was quiet, and that very night,
As Tom was a-sleeping, he had such a sight!   10
That thousands of sweepers, Dick, Joe, Ned, and Jack,
Were all of them locked up in coffins of black.

And by came an Angel who had a bright key,
And he opened the coffins and set them all free;
Then down a green plain leaping, laughing, they run,
And wash in a river, and shine in the sun.

Then naked and white, all their bags left behind,
They rise upon clouds and sport in the wind;
And the Angel told Tom, if he'd be a good boy,
He'd have God for his father, and never want joy.   20

And so Tom awoke; and we rose in the dark,
And got with our bags and our brushes to work.
Though the morning was cold, Tom was happy and warm;
So if all do their duty they need not fear harm.

[1789]

LAUGHING SONG

When the green woods laugh with the voice
    of joy,
And the dimpling stream runs laughing by;
When the air does laugh with our merry wit,
And the green hill laughs with the noise of it;

When the meadows laugh with lively green,
And the grasshopper laughs in the merry
    scene,
When Mary and Susan and Emily
With their sweet round mouths sing "Ha,
    Ha, He!"

When the painted birds laugh in the shade,
Where our table with cherries and nuts is
    spread,   10
Come live, and be merry, and join with me,
To sing the sweet chorus of "Ha, Ha, He!"

[1789]

A CRADLE SONG

Sweet dreams, form a shade
O'er my lovely infant's head;

Sweet dreams of pleasant streams
By happy, silent, moony beams.

Sweet sleep, with soft down
Weave thy brows an infant crown.
Sweet sleep, Angel mild,
Hover o'er my happy child.

Sweet smiles, in the night
Hover over my delight;
Sweet smiles, mother's smiles,
All the livelong night beguiles.

Sweet moans, dovelike sighs,
Chase not slumber from thy eyes.
Sweet moans, sweeter smiles,
All the dovelike moans beguiles.

Sleep, sleep, happy child,
All creation slept and smiled;
Sleep, sleep, happy sleep,
While o'er thee thy mother weep.   20

Sweet babe, in thy face
Holy image I can trace.

Sweet babe, once like thee,
Thy Maker lay and wept for me,

Wept for me, for thee, for all,
When he was an infant small.
Thou his image ever see,
Heavenly face that smiles on thee,

Smiles on thee, on me, on all;
Who became an infant small.   30
Infant smiles are his own smiles;
Heaven and earth to peace beguiles.

                    [1789]

THE DIVINE IMAGE

To Mercy, Pity, Peace, and Love
All pray in their distress;
And to these virtues of delight
Return their thankfulness.

For Mercy, Pity, Peace, and Love
Is God, our father dear,
And Mercy, Pity, Peace, and Love
Is man, his child and care.

For Mercy has a human heart,
Pity a human face,   10
And Love, the human form divine,
And Peace, the human dress.

Then every man, of every clime,
That prays in his distress,
Prays to the human form divine,
Love, Mercy, Pity, Peace.

And all must love the human form,
In heathen, Turk, or Jew;
Where Mercy, Love, and Pity dwell
There God is dwelling too.   20

                    [1789]

HOLY THURSDAY

'Twas on a Holy Thursday, their innocent faces clean,
The children walking two and two, in red and blue and green,
Grey-headed beadles walked before, with wands as white as snow,
Till into the high dome of Paul's they like Thames' waters flow.

O what a multitude they seemed, these flowers of London town!
Seated in companies they sit with radiance all their own.
The hum of multitudes was there, but multitudes of lambs,
Thousands of little boys and girls raising their innocent hands.

Now like a mighty wind they raise to Heaven the voice of song,
Or like harmonious thunderings the seats of Heaven among.
Beneath them sit the aged men, wise guardians of the poor;
Then cherish pity, lest you drive an angel from your door.

                    [1789]

NURSE'S SONG

When the voices of children are heard on the
        green
And laughing is heard on the hill,
My heart is at rest within my breast
    And everything else is still.

"Then come home, my children, the sun is
        gone down
And the dews of night arise;
Come, come, leave off play, and let us away
    Till the morning appears in the skies."

"No, no, let us play, for it is yet day,
And we cannot go to sleep;   10
Besides, in the sky the little birds fly,
    And the hills are all covered with sheep."

"Well, well, go and play till the light fades
        away,
And then go home to bed."
The little ones leaped and shouted and
        laughed
    And all the hills echoèd.

                    [1789]

INFANT JOY

"I have no name:
I am but two days old."
What shall I call thee?
"I happy am,
Joy is my name."
Sweet joy befall thee!

Pretty Joy!
Sweet Joy, but two days old,
Sweet Joy I call thee!
Thou dost smile,   16
I sing the while,
Sweet joy befall thee!

[1789]

From SONGS OF EXPERIENCE

INTRODUCTION

Hear the voice of the Bard!
Who present, past, and future, sees;
Whose ears have heard
The Holy Word
That walked among the ancient trees,

Calling the lapsèd soul,
And weeping in the evening dew;
That might control
The starry pole,
And fallen, fallen light renew!   10

"O Earth, O Earth, return!
Arise from out the dewy grass;
Night is worn,
And the morn
Rises from the slumberous mass.

"Turn away no more;
Why wilt thou turn away?
The starry floor,
The watery shore,
Is given thee till the break of day."   20

[1794]

EARTH'S ANSWER

Earth raised up her head
From the darkness dread and drear.
Her light fled,
Stony dread!
And her locks covered with grey despair.

'Prisoned on watery shore,
Starry Jealousy does keep my den:

Cold and hoar,
Weeping o'er,
I hear the Father of the Ancient Men.   10

"Selfish Father of Men!
Cruel, jealous, selfish Fear!
Can delight,
Chained in night,
The virgins of youth and morning bear?

"Does spring hide its joy
When buds and blossoms grow?
Does the sower
Sow by night,
Or the ploughman in darkness plough?   20

"Break this heavy chain
That does freeze my bones around.
Selfish! vain!
Eternal bane!
That free Love with bondage bound."

[1794]

THE CLOD AND THE PEBBLE

"Love seeketh not itself to please,
Nor for itself hath any care,
But for another gives its ease,
And builds a Heaven in Hell's despair."

So sung a little Clod of Clay,
Trodden with the cattle's feet,
But a Pebble of the brook
Warbled out these metres meet:

"Love seeketh only Self to please,
To bind another to its delight,   10
Joys in another's loss of ease,
And builds a Hell in Heaven's despite."

[1794]

HOLY THURSDAY

Is this a holy thing to see
In a rich and fruitful land,
Babes reduced to misery,
Fed with cold and usurous hand?

Is that trembling cry a song?
Can it be a song of joy?
And so many children poor?
It is a land of poverty!

And their sun does never shine,
And their fields are bleak and bare,   10

And their ways are filled with thorns:
It is eternal winter there.

For where'er the sun does shine,
And where'er the rain does fall,
Babe can never hunger there,
Nor poverty the mind appal.

[1794]

THE CHIMNEY-SWEEPER

A little black thing among the snow,
Crying " 'weep! 'weep!" in notes of woe!
"Where are thy father and mother? say?"
"They are both gone up to the church to pray.

"Because I was happy upon the heath,
And smiled among the winter's snow,
They clothed me in the clothes of death,
And taught me to sing the notes of woe.

"And because I am happy and dance and
sing,
They think they have done me no injury,   10
And are gone to praise God and his Priest and
King,
Who make up a heaven of our misery."

[1794]

NURSE'S SONG

When the voices of children are heard on the
green
And whisperings are in the dale,
The days of my youth rise fresh in my mind,
My face turns green and pale.

Then come home, my children, the sun is
gone down,
And the dews of night arise;
Your spring and your day are wasted in play,
And your winter and night in disguise.

[1794]

THE SICK ROSE

O Rose, thou art sick!
The invisible worm
That flies in the night,
In the howling storm,

Has found out thy bed
Of crimson joy,
And his dark secret love
Does thy life destroy.

[1794]

THE FLY

Little Fly,
Thy summer's play
My thoughtless hand
Has brushed away.

Am not I
A fly like thee?
Or art not thou
A man like me?

For I dance,
And drink, and sing   10
Till some blind hand
Shall brush my wing.

If thought is life
And strength and breath,
And the want
Of thought is death;

Then am I
A happy fly,
If I live
Or if I die.   20

[1794]

THE ANGEL

I dreamed a dream! what can it mean?
And that I was a maiden Queen,
Guarded by an Angel mild:
Witless woe was ne'er beguiled!

And I wept both night and day,
And he wiped my tears away,
And I wept both day and night,
And hid from him my heart's delight.

So he took his wings and fled;
Then the morn blushed rosy red;   10
I dried my tears, and armed my fears
With ten thousand shields and spears.

Soon my Angel came again:
I was armed, he came in vain;
For the time of youth was fled,
And grey hairs were on my head.

[1794]

THE TIGER

Tiger! Tiger! burning bright
In the forests of the night,
What immortal hand or eye
Could frame thy fearful symmetry?

In what distant deeps or skies
Burned the fire of thine eyes?
On what wings dare he aspire?
What the hand dare seize the fire?

And what shoulder, and what art,
Could twist the sinews of thy heart?   10
And when thy heart began to beat,
What dread hand? and what dread feet?

What the hammer? what the chain?
In what furnace was thy brain?
What the anvil? what dread grasp
Dare its deadly terrors clasp?

When the stars threw down their spears,
And watered heaven with their tears,
Did he smile his work to see?
Did he who made the Lamb make thee?   20

Tiger! Tiger! burning bright
In the forests of the night,
What immortal hand or eye,
Dare frame thy fearful symmetry?

[1794]

AH! SUNFLOWER

Ah, Sunflower! weary of time,
Who countest the steps of the sun;
Seeking after that sweet golden clime
Where the traveller's journey is done:

Where the Youth pined away with desire,
And the pale Virgin shrouded in snow
Arise from their graves, and aspire
Where my Sunflower wishes to go.

[1794]

LONDON

I wander through each chartered street,
Near where the chartered Thames does flow,
And mark in every face I meet
Marks of weakness, marks of woe.

In every cry of every Man,
In every Infant's cry of fear,
In every voice, in every ban,
The mind-forged manacles I hear.

How the chimney-sweeper's cry
Every blackening church appals;   10
And the hapless soldiers sigh
Runs in blood down palace walls.

But most through midnight streets I hear
How the youthful harlot's curse
Blasts the new-born infant's tear,
And blights with plagues the marriage hearse.

[1794]

THE HUMAN ABSTRACT

Pity would be no more
If we did not make somebody poor;
And Mercy no more could be
If all were as happy as we.

And mutual fear brings peace,
Till the selfish loves increase:
Then Cruelty knits a snare,
And spreads his baits with care.

He sits down with holy fears,
And waters the ground with tears;   10
Then Humility takes its root
Underneath his foot.

Soon spreads the dismal shade
Of Mystery over his head;
And the caterpillar and fly
Feed on the Mystery.

And it bears the fruit of Deceit,
Ruddy and sweet to eat;
And the raven his nest has made
In its thickest shade.   20

The Gods of the earth and sea
Sought through Nature to find this tree;
But their search was all in vain:
There grows one in the Human brain.

[1794]

INFANT SORROW

My mother groaned! my father wept.
Into the dangerous world I leapt:
Helpless, naked, piping loud:
Like a fiend hid in a cloud.

Struggling in my father's hands,
Striving against my swaddling-bands,
Bound and weary I thought best
To sulk upon my mother's breast.

[1794]

TO TIRZAH

Whate'er is born of mortal birth
Must be consumed with the earth

To rise from generation free:
Then what have I to do with thee?

The sexes sprung from shame and pride,
Blowed in the morn; in evening died;
But Mercy changed death into sleep;
The sexes rose to work and weep.

Thou, Mother of my mortal part,
With cruelty didst mould my heart,   10

And with false self-deceiving tears
Didst bind my nostrils, eyes, and ears;

Didst close my tongue in senseless clay,
And me to mortal life betray.
The death of Jesus set me free:
Then what have I to do with thee?

[1794]

THE BOOK OF THEL

Thel's Motto.
        Does the Eagle know what is in the pit?
        Or wilt thou go ask the Mole?
        Can Wisdom be put in a silver rod?
        Or Love in a golden bowl?

I

The daughters of [the] Seraphim led round their sunny flocks,
All but the youngest: she in paleness sought the secret air,
To fade away like morning beauty from her mortal day:
Down by the river of Adona her soft voice is heard,
And thus her gentle lamentation falls like morning dew:

"O life of this our spring! why fades the lotus of the water,   10
Why fade these children of the spring, born but to smile and fall?
Ah! Thel is like a watery bow, and like a parting cloud;
Like a reflection in a glass; like shadows in the water;
Like dreams of infants, like a smile upon an infant's face;
Like the dove's voice; like transient day; like music in the air.
Ah! gentle may I lay me down, and gentle rest my head,
And gentle sleep the sleep of death, and gentle hear the voice
Of him that walketh in the garden in the evening time."

The Lily of the Valley, breathing in the humble grass,
Answered the lovely maid and said: "I am a watery weed,   20
And I am very small, and love to dwell in lowly vales;
So weak, the gilded butterfly scarce perches on my head.
Yet I am visited from heaven, and he that smiles on all
Walks in the valley, and each morn over me spreads his hand,
Saying, 'Rejoice, thou humble grass, thou new-born lily-flower,
Thou gentle maid of silent valleys and of modest brooks;
For thou shalt be clothed in light, and fed with morning manna,
Till summer's heat melts thee beside the fountains and the springs
To flourish in eternal vales.' Then why should Thel complain?
Why should the mistress of the vales of Har utter a sigh?"   30

She ceased, and smiled in tears, then sat down in her silver shrine.

Thel answered: "O thou little Virgin of the peaceful valley,
Giving to those that cannot crave, the voiceless, the o'ertired;

Thy breath doth nourish the innocent lamb, he smells thy milky garments,
He crops thy flowers while thou sittest smiling in his face,
Wiping his mild and meeking mouth from all contagious taints.
Thy wine doth purify the golden honey; thy perfume,
Which thou dost scatter on every little blade of grass that springs,
Revives the milked cow, and tames the fire-breathing steed.
But Thel is like a faint cloud kindled at the rising sun: 20
I vanish from my pearly throne, and who shall find my place?"

"Queen of the vales," the Lily answered, "ask the tender Cloud,
And it shall tell thee why it glitters in the morning sky,
And why it scatters its bright beauty through the humid air.
Descend, O little Cloud, and hover before the eyes of Thel."

The Cloud descended, and the Lily bowed her modest head,
And went to mind her numerous charge among the verdant grass.

II

"O little Cloud," the Virgin said, "I charge thee tell to me
Why thou complainest not, when in one hour thou fade away:
Then we shall seek thee, but not find. Ah! Thel is like to thee: 50
I pass away: yet I complain, and no one hears my voice."
The Cloud then showed his golden head and his bright form emerged,
Hovering and glittering on the air before the face of Thel.

"O Virgin, knowest thou not our steeds drink of the golden springs
Where Luvah doth renew his horses? Lookest thou on my youth,
And fearest thou, because I vanish and am seen no more,
Nothing remains? O Maid, I tell thee, when I pass away,
It is to tenfold life, to love, to peace, and raptures holy:
Unseen descending, weigh my light wings upon balmy flowers,
And court the fair-eyed dew, to take me to her shining tent: 60
The weeping virgin, trembling, kneels before the risen sun,
Till we arise linked in a golden band and never part,
But walk united, bearing food to all our tender flowers."

"Dost thou, O little Cloud? I fear that I am not like thee,
For I walk through the vales of Har, and smell the sweetest flowers,
But I feed not the little flowers; I hear the warbling birds,
But I feed not the warbling birds; they fly and seek their food:
But Thel delights in these no more, because I fade away;
And all shall say, 'Without a use this shining woman lived,
Or did she only live to be at death the food of worms?'" 70

The Cloud reclined upon his airy throne, and answered thus:

"Then if thou art the food of worms, O Virgin of the skies,
How great thy use, how great thy blessing! Everything that lives
Lives not alone nor for itself. Fear not, and I will call
The weak Worm from its lowly bed, and thou shalt hear its voice.
Come forth, Worm of the silent valley, to thy pensive queen."

The helpless Worm arose, and sat upon the Lily's leaf,
And the bright Cloud sailed on, to find his partner in the vale.

III

Then Thel astonished viewed the Worm upon its dewy bed.

"Art thou a Worm? Image of weakness, art thou but a Worm?   80
I see thee like an infant wrapped in the Lily's leaf.
Ah! weep not, little voice, thou canst not speak, but thou canst weep.
Is this a Worm? I see thee lay helpless and naked, weeping,
And none to answer, none to cherish thee with mother's smile."

The Clod of Clay heard the Worm's voice and raised her pitying head:
She bowed over the weeping infant, and her life exhaled
In milky fondness: then on Thel she fixed her humble eyes.

"O Beauty of the vales of Har! we live not for ourselves.
Thou seest me, the meanest thing, and so I am indeed.
My bosom of itself is cold, and of itself is dark;   90
But he, that loves the lowly, pours his oil upon my head,
And kisses me, and binds his nuptial bands around my breast,
And says: 'Thou mother of my children, I have loved thee,
And I have given thee a crown that none can take away.'
But how this is, sweet Maid, I know not, and I cannot know;
I ponder, and I cannot ponder; yet I live and love."

The daughter of beauty wiped her pitying tears with her white veil,
And said: "Alas! I knew not this, and therefore did I weep.
That God would love a worm I knew, and punish the evil foot
That wilful bruised its helpless form; but that he cherished it   100
With milk and oil I never knew, and therefore did I weep;
And I complained in the mild air, because I fade away,
And lay me down in thy cold bed, and leave my shining lot."

"Queen of the vales," the matron Clay answered, "I heard thy sighs,
And all thy moans flew o'er my roof, but I have called them down.
Wilt thou, O Queen, enter my house? 'Tis given thee to enter
And to return: fear nothing, enter with thy virgin feet."

IV

The eternal gates' terrific Porter lifted the northern bar:
Thel entered in and saw the secrets of the land unknown.
She saw the couches of the dead, and where the fibrous roots   110
Of every heart on earth infixes deep its restless twists:
A land of sorrows and of tears where never smile was seen.

She wandered in the land of clouds through valleys dark, listening
Dolours and lamentations; waiting oft beside a dewy grave
She stood in silence, listening to the voices of the ground,
Till to her own grave-plot she came, and there she sat down,
And heard this voice of sorrow breathed from the hollow pit.

"Why cannot the Ear be closed to its own destruction?
Or the glistening Eye to the poison of a smile?
Why are Eyelids stored with arrows ready drawn,   120
Where a thousand fighting men in ambush lie?

Or an Eye of gifts and graces showering fruits and coined gold?
Why a Tongue impressed with honey from every wind?
Why an Ear, a whirlpool fierce to draw creations in?
Why a Nostril wide inhaling terror, trembling, and affright?
Why a tender curb upon the youthful, burning boy?
Why a little curtain of flesh on the bed of our desire?"

The Virgin started from her seat, and with a shriek
Fled back unhindered till she came into the vales of Har.

[1789]

THE FRENCH REVOLUTION[1]

BOOK THE FIRST

The dead brood over Europe, the cloud and vision descends over cheerful France;
O cloud well appointed! Sick, sick, the Prince on his couch, wreath'd in dim
And appalling mist, his strong hand outstretch'd, from his shoulder down the bone,
Runs aching cold into the sceptre, too heavy for mortal grasp, no more
To be swayed by visible hand, nor in cruelty bruise the mild flourishing mountains.

Sick the mountains, and all their vineyards weep, in the eyes of the kingly mourner;
Pale is the morning cloud in his visage. Rise, Necker! the ancient dawn calls us
To awake from slumbers of five thousand years. I awake, but my soul is in dreams;
From my window I see the old mountains of France, like aged men, fading away.

Troubled, leaning on Necker, descends the King to his chamber of council; shady mountains
In fear utter voices of thunder; the woods of France embosom the sound;   11
Clouds of wisdom prophetic reply, and roll over the palace roof heavy.
Forty men, each conversing with woes in the infinite shadows of his soul,
Like our ancient fathers in regions of twilight, walk, gathering round the King:
Again the loud voice of France cries to the morning; the morning prophesies to its clouds.

For the Commons convene in the Hall of the Nation. France shakes! And the heavens of France
Perplex'd vibrate round each careful countenance! Darkness of old times around them
Utters loud despair, shadowing Paris; her grey towers groan, and the Bastile trembles.
In its terrible towers the Governor stood, in dark fogs list'ning the horror;
A thousand his soldiers, old veterans of France, breathing red clouds of power and dominion.
Sudden seiz'd with howlings, despair, and black night, he stalk'd like a lion from tower   21
To tower; his howlings were heard in the Louvre; from court to court restless he dragg'd
His strong limbs; from court to court curs'd the fierce torment unquell'd,
Howling and giving the dark command; in his soul stood the purple plague,
Tugging his iron manacles, and piercing thro' the seven towers dark and sickly,
Panting over the prisoners like a wolf gorg'd; and the den nam'd Horror held a man
Chain'd hand and foot; round his neck an iron band, bound to the impregnable wall.
In his soul was the serpent coil'd round in his heart, hid from the light, as in a cleft rock:
And the man was confin'd for a writing prophetic: in the tower nam'd Darkness was a man
Pinion'd down to the stone floor, his strong bones scarce cover'd with sinews; the iron rings   30
Were forg'd smaller as the flesh decay'd, a mask of iron on his face hid the lineaments

---

[1] The text of *The French Revolution* here followed is that of Geoffrey Keynes, ed., *The Poetry and Prose of William Blake*, one volume edition, London, 1927. By kind permission of the Nonesuch Press, Ltd.

Of ancient Kings, and the frown of the eternal lion was hid from the oppressed earth.
In the tower named Bloody, a skeleton yellow remained in its chains on its couch
Of stone, once a man who refus'd to sign papers of abhorrence; the eternal worm
Crept in the skeleton. In the den nam'd Religion, a loathsome sick woman bound down
To a bed of straw; the seven diseases of earth, like birds of prey, stood on the couch
And fed on the body. She refus'd to be whore to the Minister, and with a knife smote him.
In the tower nam'd Order, an old man, whose white beard cover'd the stone floor like weeds
On margin of the sea, shrivell'd up by heat of day and cold of night; his den was short
And narrow as a grave dug for a child, with spiders' webs wove, and with slime   40
Of ancient horrors cover'd, for snakes and scorpions are his companions; harmless they breathe
His sorrowful breath: he, by conscience urg'd, in the city of Paris rais'd a pulpit,
And taught wonders to darken'd souls. In the den nam'd Destiny a strong man sat,
His feet and hands cut off, and his eyes blinded; round his middle a chain and a band
Fasten'd into the wall; fancy gave him to see an image of despair in his den,
Eternally rushing round, like a man on his hands and knees, day and night without rest:
He was friend to the favourite. In the seventh tower, nam'd the tower of God, was a man
Mad, with chains loose, which he dragg'd up and down; fed with hopes year by year, he pined
For liberty; vain hopes! his reason decay'd, and the world of attraction in his bosom
Center'd, and the rushing of chaos overwhelm'd his dark soul. He was confin'd   50
For a letter of advice to a King, and his ravings in winds are heard over Versailles.

But the dens shook and trembled: the prisoners look up and assay to shout; they listen,
Then laugh in the dismal den, then are silent, and a light walks round the dark towers:
For the Commons convene in the Hall of the Nation, like spirits of fire in the beautiful
Porches of the Sun, to plant beauty in the desert craving abyss, they gleam
On the anxious city; all children new-born first behold them; tears are fled,
And they nestle in earth-breathing bosoms. So the city of Paris, their wives and children,
Look up to the morning Senate, and visions of sorrow leave pensive streets.

But heavy-brow'd jealousies lour o'er the Louvre, and terrors of ancient Kings
Descend from the gloom and wander thro' the palace, and weep round the King and his
    Nobles.   60
While loud thunders roll, troubling the dead, Kings are sick throughout all the earth.
The voice ceas'd: the Nation sat: and the triple forg'd fetters of times were unloos'd.
The voice ceas'd: the Nation sat: but ancient darkness and trembling wander thro' the palace.

As in day of havoc and routed battle, among thick shades of discontent,
On the soul-skirting mountains of sorrow cold waving, the Nobles fold round the King;
Each stern visage lock'd up as with strong bands of iron, each strong limb bound down as
    with marble,
In flames of red wrath burning, bound in astonishment a quarter of an hour.

Then the King glow'd: his Nobles fold round, like the sun of old time quench'd in clouds;
In their darkness the King stood; his heart flam'd, and utter'd a with'ring heat, and these words
    burst forth:

'The nerves of five thousand years' ancestry tremble, shaking the heavens of France;   70
Throbs of anguish beat on brazen war foreheads, they descend and look into their graves.
I see thro' darkness, thro' clouds rolling round me, the spirits of ancient Kings
Shivering over their bleached bones; round them their counsellors look up from the dust,
Crying: "Hide from the living! Our bonds and our prisoners shout in the open field,
Hide in the nether earth! Hide in the bones! Sit obscured in the hollow scull!
Our flesh is corrupted, and we wear away. We are not numbered among the living. Let us hide
In stones, among roots of trees. The prisoners have burst their dens.
Let us hide; let us hide in the dust: and plague and wrath and tempest shall cease."'

He ceas'd, silent pond'ring; his brows folded heavy, his forehead was in affliction.
Like the central fire, from the window he saw his vast armies spread over the hills, 80
Breathing red fires from man to man, and from horse to horse: then his bosom
Expanded like starry heaven; he sat down: his Nobles took their ancient seats.

Then the ancientest Peer, Duke of Burgundy, rose from the Monarch's right hand, red as wines
From his mountains; an odour of war, like a ripe vineyard, rose from his garments,
And the chamber became as a clouded sky; o'er the Council he stretch'd his red limbs,
Cloth'd in flames of crimson; as a ripe vineyard stretches over sheaves of corn,
The fierce Duke hung over the Council; around him croud, weeping in his burning robe,
A bright cloud of infant souls; his words fall like purple autumn on the sheaves:

'Shall this marble-built heaven become a clay cottage, this earth an oak stool, and these
         mowers
From the Atlantic mountains mow down all this great starry harvest of six thousand years? 90
And shall Necker, the hind of Geneva, stretch out his crook'd sickle o'er fertile France,
Till our purple and crimson is faded to russet, and the kingdoms of earth bound in sheaves,
And the ancient forests of chivalry hewn, and the joys of the combat burnt for fuel;
Till the power and dominion is rent from the pole, sword and sceptre from sun and moon,
The law and gospel from fire and air, and eternal reason and science
From the deep and the solid, and man lay his faded head down on the rock
Of eternity, where the eternal lion and eagle remain to devour?
This to prevent—urg'd by cries in day, and prophetic dreams hovering in night,
To enrich the lean earth that craves, furrow'd with plows, whose seed is departing from her—
Thy Nobles have gather'd thy starry hosts round this rebellious city, 100
To rouze up the ancient forests of Europe, with clarions of cloud-breathing war,
To hear the horse neigh to the drum and trumpet, and the trumpet and war shout reply.
Stretch the hand that beckons the eagles of heaven; they cry over Paris, and wait
Till Fayette point his finger to Versailles; the eagles of heaven must have their prey!'

He ceas'd, and burn'd silent; red clouds roll round Necker; a weeping is heard o'er the palace.
Like a dark cloud Necker paus'd, and like thunder on the just man's burial day he paus'd;
Silent sit the winds, silent the meadows, while the husbandman and woman of weakness
And bright children look after him into the grave, and water his clay with love,
Then turn towards pensive fields; so Necker paus'd, and his visage was cover'd with clouds.

The King lean'd on his mountains, then lifted his head and look'd on his armies, that shone 110
Through heaven, tinging morning with beams of blood; then turning to Burgundy, troubled:
'Burgundy, thou wast born a lion! My soul is o'ergrown with distress
For the Nobles of France, and dark mists roll round me and blot the writing of God
Written in my bosom. Necker rise! leave the kingdom, thy life is surrounded with snares.
We have call'd an Assembly, but not to destroy; we have given gifts, not to the weak;
I hear rushing of muskets and bright'ning of swords and visages, redd'ning with war,
Frowning and looking up from brooding villages and every dark'ning city.
Ancient wonders frown over the kingdom, and cries of women and babes are heard,
And tempests of doubt roll around me, and fierce sorrows, because of the Nobles of France.
Depart! answer not! for the tempest must fall, as in years that are passed away.' 120

Dropping a tear the old man his place left, and when he was gone out
He set his face toward Geneva to flee; and the women and children of the city
Kneel'd round him and kissèd his garments and wept: he stood a short space in the street,
Then fled; and the whole city knew he was fled to Geneva, and the Senate heard it.

But the Nobles burn'd wrathful at Necker's departure, and wreath'd their clouds and waters
In dismal volumes, as, risen from beneath, the Archbishop of Paris arose
In the rushing of scales, and hissing of flames, and rolling of sulphurous smoke:

'Hearken, Monarch of France, to the terrors of heaven, and let thy soul drink of my counsel!
Sleeping at midnight in my golden tower, the repose of the labours of men
Wav'd its solemn cloud over my head. I awoke; a cold hand passed over my limbs, and behold
An aged form, white as snow, hov'ring in mist, weeping in the uncertain light.   131
Dim the form almost faded, tears fell down the shady cheeks; at his feet many cloth'd
In white robes; strewn in air censers and harps; silent they lay prostrated;
Beneath, in the awful void, myriads descending and weeping thro' dismal winds;
Endless the shady train shiv'ring descended, from the gloom where the aged form wept.
At length, trembling, the vision sighing, in a low voice like the voice of the grasshopper,
          whisper'd:
"My groaning is heard in the abbeys, and God, so long worshipp'd, departs as a lamp
Without oil; for a curse is heard hoarse thro' the land, from a godless race
Descending to beasts; they look downward, and labour, and forget my holy law;
The sound of prayer fails from lips of flesh, and the holy hymn from thicken'd tongues;   140
For the bars of Chaos are burst; her millions prepare their fiery way
Thro' the orbed abode of the holy dead, to root up and pull down and remove,
And Nobles and Clergy shall fail from before me, and my cloud and vision be no more;
The mitre become black, the crown vanish, and the sceptre and ivory staff
Of the ruler wither among bones of death; they shall consume from the thistly field,
And the sound of the bell, and voice of the sabbath, and singing of the holy choir
Is turn'd into songs of the harlot in day, and cries of the virgin in night.
They shall drop at the plow and faint at the harrow, unredeem'd, unconfess'd, unpardon'd;
The priest rot in his surplice by the lawless lover, the holy beside the accursed,
The King, frowning in purple, beside the grey plowman, and their worms embrace together."
The voice ceas'd: a groan shook my chamber; I slept, for the cloud of repose returned,   151
But morning dawn'd heavy upon me. I rose to bring my Prince heaven-utter'd counsel.
Hear my counsel, O King, and send forth thy Generals; the command of Heaven is upon thee!
Then do thou command, O King, to shut up this Assembly in their final home;
Let thy soldiers possess this city of rebels, that threaten to bathe their feet
In the blood of Nobility, trampling the heart and the head; let the Bastile devour
These rebellious seditious; seal them up, O Anointed, in everlasting chains.'
He sat down: a damp cold pervaded the Nobles, and monsters of worlds unknown
Swam round them, watching to be delivered; when Aumont, whose chaos-born soul
Eternally wand'ring a Comet and swift-falling fire, pale enter'd the chamber.   160
Before the red Council he stood, like a man that returns from hollow graves:

'Awe-surrounded, alone thro' the army, a fear and a with'ring blight blown by the north,
The Abbé de Sieyes from the Nation's Assembly, O Princes and Generals of France,
Unquestioned, unhindered! awe-struck are the soldiers; a dark shadowy man in the form
Of King Henry the Fourth walks before him in fires; the captains like men bound in chains
Stood still as he pass'd: he is come to the Louvre, O King, with a message to thee!
The strong soldiers tremble, the horses their manes bow, and the guards of thy palace are fled!'

Uprose awful in his majestic beams Bourbon's strong Duke; his proud sword from his thigh
Drawn, he threw on the earth! the Duke of Bretagne and the Earl of Bourgogne
Rose inflam'd, to and fro in the chamber, like thunder-clouds ready to burst.   170
'What damp all our fires, O spectre of Henry?' said Bourbon, 'and rend the flames
From the head of our King? Rise, Monarch of France! command me, and I will lead
This army of superstition at large, that the ardour of noble souls, quenchless,
May yet burn in France, nor our shoulders be plow'd with the furrows of poverty.'

Then Orleans, generous as mountains, arose and unfolded his robe, and put forth
His benevolent hand, looking on the Archbishop who, changed as pale as lead,
Would have risen but could not: his voice issued harsh grating; instead of words harsh hissings
Shook the chamber; he ceas'd abash'd. Then Orleans spoke; all was silent.

He breath'd on them, and said: 'O Princes of fire, whose flames are for growth, not consuming,
Fear not dreams, fear not visions, nor be you dismay'd with sorrows which flee at the morning!
Can the fires of Nobility ever be quench'd, or the stars by a stormy night?   181
Is the body diseas'd when the members are healthful? can the man be bound in sorrow
Whose ev'ry function is fill'd with its fiery desire? can the soul whose brain and heart
Cast their rivers in equal tides thro' the great Paradise, languish because the feet,
Hands, head, bosom, and parts of love follow their high breathing joy?
And can Nobles be bound when the people are free, or God weep when his children are happy?
Have you never seen Fayette's forehead, or Mirabeau's eyes, or the shoulders of Target,
Or Bailly the strong foot of France, or Clermont the terrible voice? and your robes
Still retain their own crimson: mine never yet faded, for fire delights in its form.
But go, merciless man! enter into the infinite labyrinth of another's brain   190
Ere thou measure the circle that he shall run. Go, thou cold recluse, into the fires
Of another's high flaming rich bosom, and return unconsum'd, and write laws.
If thou canst not do this, doubt thy theories, learn to consider all men as thy equals,
Thy brethren, and not as thy foot or thy hand, unless thou first fearest to hurt them.'

The Monarch stood up; the strong Duke his sword to its golden scabbard return'd;
The Nobles sat round like clouds on the mountains, when the storm is passing away:
'Let the Nation's Ambassador come among Nobles, like incense of the valley!'

Aumont went out and stood in the hollow porch, his ivory wand in his hand;
A cold orb of disdain revolv'd round him, and covered his soul with snows eternal.
Great Henry's soul shuddered, a whirlwind and fire tore furious from his angry bosom;   200
He indignant departed on horses of heav'n. Then the Abbé de Sieyes rais'd his feet
On the steps of the Louvre; like a voice of God following a storm, the Abbé follow'd
The pale fires of Aumont into the chamber; as a father that bows to his son,
Whose rich fields inheriting spread their old glory, so the voice of the people bowed
Before the ancient seat of the kingdom and mountains to be renewed.

'Hear, O Heavens of France, the voice of the people, arising from valley and hill,
O'erclouded with power. Hear the voice of valleys, the voice of meek cities,
Mourning oppressed on village and field, till the village and field is a waste.
For the husbandman weeps at blights of the fife, and blasting of trumpets consume
The souls of mild France; the pale mother nourishes her child to the deadly slaughter.   210
When the heavens were seal'd with a stone, and the terrible sun clos'd in an orb, and the moon
Rent from the nations, and each star appointed for watchers of night,
The millions of spirits immortal were bound in the ruins of sulphur, heaven
To wander enslav'd; black, depress'd in dark ignorance, kept in awe with the whip
To worship terrors, bred from the blood of revenge and breath of desire
In bestial forms, or more terrible men; till the dawn of our peaceful morning,
Till dawn, till morning, till the breaking of clouds, and swelling of winds, and the universal
        voice;
Till man raise his darken'd limbs out of the caves of night: his eyes and his heart
Expand: where is Space? where, O Sun, is thy dwelling? where thy tent, O faint slumb'rous
        Moon?
Then the valleys of France shall cry to the soldier: "Throw down thy sword and musket,   220
And run and embrace the meek peasant." Her Nobles shall hear and shall weep, and put off
The red robe of terror, the crown of oppression, the shoes of contempt, and unbuckle
The girdle of war from the desolate earth; then the Priest in his thund'rous cloud
Shall weep, bending to earth, embracing the valleys, and putting his hand to the plow,
Shall say: "No more I curse thee; but now I will bless thee: No more in deadly black
Devour thy labour; nor lift up a cloud in thy heavens, O laborious plow,
That the wild raging millions, that wander in forests, and howl in law blasted wastes,
Strength madden'd with slavery, honesty bound in the dens of superstition.

May sing in the village, and shout in the harvest, and woo in pleasant gardens
Their once savage loves, now beaming with knowledge, with gentle awe adorned;   230
And the saw, and the hammer, the chisel, the pencil, the pen, and the instruments
Of heavenly song sound in the wilds once forbidden, to teach the laborious plowman
And shepherd, deliver'd from clouds of war, from pestilence, from night-fear, from murder,
From falling, from stifling, from hunger, from cold, from slander, discontent and sloth,
That walk in beasts and birds of night, driven back by the sandy desert,
Like pestilent fogs round cities of men; and the happy earth sing in its course,
The mild peaceable nations be opened to heav'n, and men walk with their fathers in bliss."
Then hear the first voice of the morning: "Depart, O clouds of night, and no more
Return; be withdrawn cloudy war, troops of warriors depart, nor around our peaceable city
Breathe fires; but ten miles from Paris let all be peace, nor a soldier be seen!" '   240

He ended: the wind of contention arose, and the clouds cast their shadows; the Princes
Like the mountains of France, whose agèd trees utter an awful voice, and their branches
Are shatter'd till gradual a murmur is heard descending into the valley,
Like a voice in the vineyards of Burgundy when grapes are shaken on grass,
Like the low voice of the labouring man, instead of the shout of joy;
And the palace appear'd like a cloud driven abroad; blood ran down the ancient pillars.
Thro' the cloud a deep thunder, the Duke of Burgundy, delivers the King's command:

'Seest thou yonder dark castle, that moated around, keeps this city of Paris in awe?
Go, command yonder tower, saying: "Bastile, depart! and take thy shadowy course;
Overstep the dark river, thou terrible tower, and get thee up into the country ten miles.   250
And thou black southern prison, move along the dusky road to Versailles; there
Frown on the gardens"; and, if it obey and depart, then the King will disband
This war-breathing army; but, if it refuse, let the Nation's Assembly thence learn
That this army of terrors, that prison of horrors, are the bands of the murmuring kingdom.'

Like the morning star arising above the black waves, when a shipwreck'd soul sighs for morning,
Thro' the ranks, silent, walk'd the Ambassador back to the Nation's Assembly, and told
The unwelcome message; silent they heard; then a thunder roll'd round loud and louder;
Like pillars of ancient halls and ruins of times remote, they sat.
Like a voice from the dim pillars Mirabeau rose; the thunders subsided away;
A rushing of wings around him was heard as he brighten'd, and cried out aloud: 260
'Where is the General of the Nation?' The walls re-echo'd: 'Where is the General of the
     Nation?'

Sudden as the bullet wrapp'd in his fire, when brazen cannons rage in the field,
Fayette sprung from his seat saying 'Ready!' Then bowing like clouds, man toward man, the
     Assembly
Like a Council of ardours seated in clouds, bending over the cities of men,
And over the armies of strife, where their children are marshall'd together to battle,
They murmuring divide; while the wind sleeps beneath, and the numbers are counted in
     silence,
While they vote the removal of War, and the pestilence weighs his red wings in the sky.

So Fayette stood silent among the Assembly, and the votes were given, and the numbers
     numb'red;
And the vote was that Fayette should order the army to remove ten miles from Paris.

The aged Sun rises appall'd from dark mountains, and gleams a dusky beam   270
On Fayette; but on the whole army a shadow, for a cloud on the eastern hills
Hover'd, and stretch'd across the city, and across the army, and across the Louvre.
Like a flame of fire he stood before dark ranks, and before expecting captains:

On pestilent vapours around him flow frequent spectres of religious men, weeping
In winds; driven out of the abbeys, their naked souls shiver in keen open air;
Driven out by the fiery cloud of Voltaire, and thund'rous rocks of Rousseau,
They dash like foam against the ridges of the army, uttering a faint feeble cry.

Gleams of fire streak the heavens, and of sulphur the earth, from Fayette as he lifted his hand;
But silent he stood, till all the officers rush round him like waves
Round the shore of France, in day of the British flag, when heavy cannons   280
Affright the coasts, and the peasant looks over the sea and wipes a tear;
Over his head the soul of Voltaire shone fiery; and over the army Rousseau his white cloud
Unfolded, on souls of war, living terrors, silent list'ning toward Fayette.
His voice loud inspir'd by liberty, and by spirits of the dead, thus thunder'd:

'The Nation's Assembly command that the Army remove ten miles from Paris;
Nor a soldier be seen in road or in field, till the Nation command return.'

Rushing along iron ranks glittering, the officers each to his station
Depart, and the stern captain strokes his proud steed, and in front of his solid ranks
Waits the sound of trumpet; captains of foot stand each by his cloudy drum:
Then the drum beats, and the steely ranks move, and trumpets rejoice in the sky.   290
Dark cavalry, like clouds fraught with thunder, ascend on the hills, and bright infantry, rank
Behind rank, to the soul-shaking drum and shrill fife, along the roads glitter like fire.

The noise of trampling, the wind of trumpets, smote the Palace walls with a blast,
Pale and cold sat the King in midst of his peers, and his noble heart sunk, and his pulses
Suspended their motion; a darkness crept over his eyelids, and chill cold sweat
Sat round his brows faded in faint death; his Peers pale like mountains of the dead
Cover'd with dews of night, groaning, shaking forests and floods. The cold newt,
And snake, and damp toad on the kingly foot crawl, or croak on the awful knee,
Shedding their slime; in folds of the robe the crown'd adder builds and hisses
From stony brows; shaken the forests of France, sick the kings of the nations,   300
And the bottoms of the world were open'd, and the graves of archangels unseal'd:
The enormous dead lift up their pale fires and look over the rocky cliffs.

A faint heat from their fires reviv'd the cold Louvre; the frozen blood reflow'd.
Awful uprose the King; him the Peers follow'd; they saw the courts of the Palace
Forsaken, and Paris without a soldier, silent; for the noise was gone up
And follow'd the army, and the Senate in peace sat beneath morning's beam.

END OF THE FIRST BOOK

[Printed 1791]

THE MARRIAGE OF HEAVEN AND HELL

THE ARGUMENT

Rintrah roars, and shakes his fires in the
    burdened air;
Hungry clouds swag on the deep.
Once meek, and in a perilous path,
The just man kept his course along
The vale of death.

Roses are planted where thorns grow,
And on the barren heath
Sing the honey bees.

Then the perilous path was planted,
And a river and a spring   10
On every cliff and tomb,
And on the bleached bones
Red clay brought forth;
Till the villain left the paths of ease,
To walk in perilous paths, and drive
The just man into barren climes.

Now the sneaking serpent walks
In mild humility,
And the just man rages in the wilds
Where lions roam.   20

Rintrah roars, and shakes his fires in the
    burdened air;
Hungry clouds swag on the deep.

As a new heaven is begun, and it is now thirty-three years since its advent, the Eternal Hell revives. And lo! Swedenborg is the Angel sitting at the tomb: his writings are the linen clothes folded up. Now is the dominion of Edom, and the return of Adam into Paradise. See Isaiah xxxiv and xxxv chap.

Without Contraries is no progression. Attraction and Repulsion, Reason and Energy, Love and Hate, are necessary to Human existence.

From these contraries spring what the religious call Good and Evil. Good is the passive that obeys Reason. Evil is the active springing from Energy.

Good is Heaven. Evil is Hell.

THE VOICE OF THE DEVIL

All Bibles or sacred codes have been the causes of the following Errors:

1. That Man has two real existing principles: viz.: a Body and a Soul.

2. That Energy, called Evil, is alone from the Body; and that Reason, called Good, is alone from the Soul.

3. That God will torment Man in Eternity for following his Energies.

But the following Contraries to these are True:

1. Man has no Body distinct from his Soul; for that called Body is a portion of Soul discerned by the five Senses, the chief inlets of Soul in this age.

2. Energy is the only life, and is from the Body; and Reason is the bound or outward circumference of Energy.

3. Energy is Eternal Delight.

Those who restrain Desire, do so because theirs is weak enough to be restrained; and the restrainer or Reason usurps its place and governs the unwilling.

And being restrained, it by degrees becomes passive, till it is only the shadow of Desire.

The history of this is written in *Paradise Lost*, and the Governor or Reason is called Messiah.

And the original Archangel, or possessor of the command of the Heavenly Host, is called the Devil or Satan, and his children are called Sin and Death.

But in the Book of Job, Milton's Messiah is called Satan.

For this history has been adopted by both parties.

It indeed appeared to Reason as if Desire was cast out; but the Devil's account is, that the Messiah fell, and formed a Heaven of what he stole from the Abyss.

This is shown in the Gospel, where he prays to the Father to send the Comforter, or Desire, that Reason may have Ideas to build on; the Jehovah of the Bible being no other than he who dwells in flaming fire.

Know that after Christ's death, he became Jehovah.

But in Milton, the Father is Destiny, the Son a Ratio of the five senses, and the Holyghost Vacuum!

Note: The reason Milton wrote in fetters when he wrote of Angels and God, and at liberty when of Devils and Hell, is because he was a true Poet and of the Devil's party without knowing it.

A MEMORABLE FANCY

As I was walking among the fires of Hell, delighted with the enjoyments of Genius, which to Angels look like torment and insanity, I collected some of their Proverbs, thinking that as the sayings used in a nation mark its character, so the Proverbs of Hell show the nature of Infernal wisdom better than any description of buildings or garments.

When I came home: on the abyss of the five senses, where a flat-sided steep frowns over the present world, I saw a mighty Devil folded in black clouds, hovering on the sides of the rock: with corroding fires he wrote the following sentence now perceived by the minds of men, and read by them on earth:

How do you know but every Bird that cuts the airy way,
Is an immense World of Delight, closed by your senses five?

PROVERBS OF HELL

In seed time learn, in harvest teach, in winter enjoy.

Drive your cart and your plough over the bones of the dead.

The road of excess leads to the palace of wisdom.

Prudence is a rich, ugly old maid courted by incapacity.

He who desires but acts not, breeds pestilence. 10

The cut worm forgives the plough.

Dip him in the river who loves water.

A fool sees not the same tree that a wise man sees.

He whose face gives no light, shall never become a star.

Eternity is in love with the productions of time.

The busy bee has no time for sorrow.

The hours of folly are measured by the clock; but of wisdom, no clock can measure.

All wholesome food is caught without a net or a 20 trap.

Bring out number, weight and measure in a year of dearth.

No bird soars too high, if he soars with his own wings.

A dead body revenges not injuries.

The most sublime act is to set another before you.

If the fool would persist in his folly he would become wise.

Folly is the cloak of knavery.

Shame is Pride's cloak. 30

Prisons are built with stones of Law, brothels with bricks of Religion.

The pride of the peacock is the glory of God.

The lust of the goat is the bounty of God.

The wrath of the lion is the wisdom of God.

The nakedness of woman is the work of God.

Excess of sorrow laughs. Excess of joy weeps.

The roaring of lions, the howling of wolves, the raging of the stormy sea, and the destructive sword 40 are portions of eternity, too great for the eye of man.

The fox condemns the trap, not himself.

Joys impregnate. Sorrows bring forth.

Let man wear the fell of the lion, woman the fleece of the sheep.

The bird a nest, the spider a web, man friendship.

The selfish, smiling fool, and the sullen, frowning fool shall be both thought wise, that they may be a rod.

What is now proved was once only imagined.

The rat, the mouse, the fox, the rabbit watch the 50 roots; the lion, the tiger, the horse, the elephant watch the fruits.

The cistern contains: the fountain overflows.

One thought fills immensity.

Always be ready to speak your mind, and a base man will avoid you.

Everything possible to be believed is an image of truth.

The eagle never lost so much time as when he submitted to learn of the crow.

The fox provides for himself, but God provides for the lion.

Think in the morning. Act in the noon. Eat in the evening. Sleep in the night.

He who has suffered you to impose on him, knows you.

As the plough follows words, so God rewards prayers.

The tigers of wrath are wiser than the horses of instruction.

Expect poison from the standing water.

You never know what is enough unless you know what is more than enough.

Listen to the fool's reproach! it is a kingly title!

The eyes of fire, the nostrils of air, the mouth of water, the beard of earth.

The weak in courage is strong in cunning.

The apple tree never asks the beech how he shall grow, nor the lion, the horse, how he shall take his prey.

The thankful receiver bears a plentiful harvest.

If others had not been foolish, we should be so.

The soul of sweet delight can never be defiled.

When thou seest an eagle, thou seest a portion of Genius; lift up thy head!

As the caterpillar chooses the fairest leaves to lay her eggs on, so the priest lays his curse on the fairest joys.

To create a little flower is the labour of ages.

Damn braces. Bless relaxes.

The best wine is the oldest, the best water the newest.

Prayers plough not! Praises reap not!

Joys laugh not! Sorrows weep not!

The head Sublime, the heart Pathos, the genitals Beauty, the hands and feet Proportion.

As the air to a bird or the sea to a fish, so is contempt to the contemptible.

The crow wished everything was black, the owl that everything was white.

Exuberance is Beauty.

If the lion was advised by the fox, he would be cunning.

Improvement makes straight roads; but the crooked roads without improvement are roads of Genius.

Sooner murder an infant in its cradle than nurse unacted desires.

Where man is not. nature is barren.

*Truth can never be told so as to be understood
and not be believed.*

Enough! or Too much.

The ancient Poets animated all sensible objects with Gods or Geniuses, calling them by the names and adorning them with the properties of woods, rivers, mountains, lakes, cities, nations, and whatever their enlarged and numerous senses could perceive.

And particularly they studied the Genius of each city and country, placing it under its Mental Deity;

Till a System was formed, which some took advantage of, and enslaved the vulgar by attempting to realize or abstract the Mental Deities from their objects: thus began Priesthood:

Choosing forms of worship from poetic tales.

And at length they pronounced that the Gods had ordered such things.

Thus men forgot that All Deities reside in the Human breast.

A MEMORABLE FANCY

The Prophets Isaiah and Ezekiel dined with me, and I asked them how they dared so roundly to assert that God spoke to them; and whether they did not think at the time that they would be misunderstood, and so be the cause of imposition.

Isaiah answered: "I saw no God, nor heard any, in a finite organical perception; but my senses discovered the infinite in everything, and as I was then persuaded, and remain confirmed, that the voice of honest indignation is the voice of God, I cared not for consequences, but wrote."

Then I asked: "Does a firm persuasion that a thing is so, make it so?"

He replied: "All Poets believe that it does, and in ages of imagination this firm persuasion removed mountains; but many are not capable of a firm persuasion of anything."

Then Ezekiel said: "The philosophy of the East taught the first principles of human perception. Some nations held one principle for the origin, and some another: we of Israel taught that the Poetic Genius (as you now call it) was the first principle and all the others merely derivative, which was the cause of our despising the Priests and Philosophers of other countries, and prophesying that all Gods would at last be proved to originate in ours and to be the tributaries of the Poetic Genius; it was this that our great poet, King David, desired so fervently and invokes so pathetically, saying by this he conquers enemies and governs kingdoms; and we so loved our God, that we cursed in his name all the Deities of surrounding nations, and asserted that they had rebelled: from these opinions the vulgar came to think that all nations would at last be subject to the Jews."

"This," said he, "like all firm persuasions, is come to pass; for all nations believe the Jews' code and worship the Jews' god, and what greater subjection can be?"

I heard this with some wonder, and must confess my own conviction. After dinner I asked Isaiah to favour the world with his lost works; he said none of equal value was lost. Ezekiel said the same of his.

I also asked Isaiah what made him go naked and barefoot three years? He answered: "The same that made our friend Diogenes, the Grecian."

I then asked Ezekiel why he ate dung, and lay so long on his right and left side. He answered, "The desire of raising other men into a perception of the infinite: this the North American tribes practise, and is he honest who resists his genius or conscience only for the sake of present ease or gratification?"

The ancient tradition that the world will be consumed in fire at the end of six thousand years is true, as I have heard from Hell.

For the cherub with his flaming sword is hereby commanded to leave his guard at tree of life; and when he does, the whole creation will be consumed and appear infinite and holy, whereas it now appears finite and corrupt.

This will come to pass by an improvement of sensual enjoyment.

But first the notion that man has a body distinct from his soul is to be expunged; this I shall do by printing in the infernal method, by corrosives, which in Hell are salutary and medicinal, melting apparent surfaces away, and displaying the infinite which was hid.

If the doors of perception were cleansed everything would appear to man as it is, infinite.

For man has closed himself up till he sees all things through narrow chinks of his cavern.

A MEMORABLE FANCY

I was in a Printing-house in Hell, and saw the method in which knowledge is transmitted from generation to generation.

In the first chamber was a Dragon-Man, clearing away the rubbish from a cave's mouth; within, a number of Dragons were hollowing the cave.

In the second chamber was a Viper folding round the rock and the cave, and others adorning it with gold, silver, and precious stones.

In the third chamber was an Eagle with wings and feathers of air: he caused the inside of the cave to be infinite; around were numbers of Eagle-like men who built palaces in the immense cliffs.

In the fourth chamber were Lions of flaming fire, raging around and melting the metals into living fluids.

In the fifth chamber were Unnamed forms, which cast the metals into the expanse.

There they were received by Men who occupied the sixth chamber, and took the forms of books and were arranged in libraries.

The Giants who formed this world into its sensual existence, and now seem to live in it in chains, are in truth the causes of its life and the sources of all activity; but the chains are the cunning of weak and tame minds which have power to resist energy. According to the proverb, the weak in courage is strong in cunning.

Thus one portion of being is the Prolific, the other the Devouring: to the Devourer it seems as if the producer was in his chains; but it is not so, he only takes portions of existence and fancies that the whole.

But the Prolific would cease to be Prolific unless the Devourer, as a sea, received the excess of his delights.

Some will say: "Is not God alone the Prolific?" I answer: "God only Acts and Is, in existing beings or Men."

These two classes of men are always upon earth, and they should be enemies: whoever tries to reconcile them seeks to destroy existence.

Religion is an endeavour to reconcile the two.

Note: Jesus Christ did not wish to unite, but to separate them, as in the Parable of sheep and goats! And he says: "I came not to send Peace, but a Sword."

Messiah or Satan or Tempter was formerly thought to be one of the Antediluvians who are our Energies.

A MEMORABLE FANCY

An Angel came to me and said: "O pitiable foolish young man! O horrible! O dreadful state! Consider the hot burning dungeon thou art preparing for thyself to all Eternity, to which thou art going in such career."

I said: "Perhaps you will be willing to show me my eternal lot, and we will contemplate together upon it, and see whether your lot or mine is most desirable."

So he took me through a stable and through a church and down into the church vault, at the end of which was a mill: through the mill we went, and came to a cave: down the winding cavern we groped our tedious way, till a void boundless as a nether sky appeared beneath us, and we held by the roots of trees and hung over this immensity; but I said: "If you please, we will commit ourselves to this void, and see whether Providence is here also: if you will not, I will." But he answered: "Do not presume, O young man, but as we here remain, behold thy lot which will soon appear when the darkness passes away."

So I remained with him, sitting in the twisted root of an oak; he was suspended in a fungus, which hung with the head downward into the deep.

By degrees we beheld the infinite Abyss, fiery as the smoke of a burning city; beneath us, at an immense distance, was the sun, black but shining; round it were fiery tracks on which revolved vast spiders, crawling after their prey, which flew, or rather swam, in the infinite deep, in the most terrific shapes of animals sprung from corruption; and the air was full of them, and seemed composed of them: these are Devils, and are called Powers of the Air. I now asked my companion which was my eternal lot? He said: "Between the black and white spiders."

But now, from between the black and white spiders, a cloud and fire burst and rolled through the deep, blackening all beneath, so that the nether deep grew black as a sea, and rolled with a terrible noise; beneath us was nothing now to be seen but a black tempest, till looking East between the clouds and the waves, we saw a cataract of blood mixed with fire, and not many stones' throw from us appeared and sunk again the scaly fold of a monstrous serpent. At last, to the East, distant about three degrees, appeared a fiery crest above the waves. Slowly it reared like a ridge of golden rocks, till we discovered two globes of crimson fire, from which the sea fled away in clouds of smoke; and now we saw it was the head of Leviathan. His forehead was divided 10 into streaks of green and purple like those on a tiger's forehead. Soon we saw his mouth and red gills hang just above the raging foam, tinging the black deep with beams of blood, advancing toward us with all the fury of a Spiritual Existence.

My friend the Angel climbed up from his station into the mill: I remained alone; and then this appearance was no more, but I found myself sitting on a pleasant bank beside a river by moonlight, hearing a harper, who sung to the harp; and his theme was: "The man who never alters his opinion is like standing water, and breeds reptiles of the mind."

But I arose and sought for the mill, and there I found my Angel, who, surprised, asked me how I escaped.

I answered: "All that we saw was owing to your metaphysics; for when you ran away, I found myself on a bank by moonlight hearing a harper. But now we have seen my eternal lot, shall I show you yours?" He laughed at my proposal; but I by force suddenly caught him in my arms, and flew westerly through the night, till we were elevated above the earth's shadow; then I flung myself with him directly into the body of the sun; here I clothed myself 40 in white, and taking in my hand Swedenborg's volumes, sunk from the glorious clime, and passed all the planets till we came to Saturn: here I stayed to rest, and then leaped into the void between Saturn and the fixed stars.

"Here," said I, "is your lot, in this space— if space it may be called." Soon we saw the stable and the church, and I took him to the altar and opened the Bible, and lo! it was a 50 deep pit, into which I descended, driving the Angel before me. Soon we saw seven houses of brick. One we entered; in it were a number of monkeys, baboons, and all of that species, chained by the middle, grinning and snatching at one another, but withheld by the shortness of their chains. However, I saw that they sometimes grew numerous, and then the weak were caught by the strong, and with a grinning aspect, first coupled with, and then devoured, by plucking off first one limb and then another, till the body was left a helpless trunk. This, after grinning and kissing it with seeming fondness, they devoured too; and here and there I saw one savourily picking the flesh off of his own tail. As the stench terribly annoyed us both, we went into the mill, and I in my hand brought the skeleton of a body, which in the mill was Aristotle's Analytics.

So the Angel said: "Thy phantasy has imposed upon me, and thou oughtest to be ashamed."

I answered: "We impose on one another, and it is but lost time to converse with you whose works are only Analytics."

I have always found that Angels have the vanity to speak of themselves as the Only Wise; this they do with a confident insolence sprouting from systematic reasoning.

Thus Swedenborg boasts that what he writes is new: though it is only the Contents or Index of already published books.

A man carried a monkey about for a show, and because he was a little wiser than the monkey, grew vain, and conceived himself as much wiser than seven men. It is so with Swedenborg: he shows the folly of churches, and exposes hypocrites, till he imagines that all are religious, and himself the single one on earth that ever broke a net.

Now hear a plain fact: Swedenborg has not written one new truth. Now hear another: he has written all the old falsehoods.

And now hear the reason. He conversed with Angels who are all religious, and conversed not with Devils who all hate religion, for he was incapable through his conceited notions.

Thus Swedenborg's writings are a recapitulation of all superficial opinions, and an analysis of the more sublime—but no further.

Have now another plain fact. Any man of mechanical talents may, from the writings of Paracelsus or Jacob Behmen, produce ten thousand volumes of equal value with Swedenborg's, and from those of Dante or Shakespeare an infinite number.

But when he has done this, let him not say that he knows better than his master, for he only holds a candle in sunshine.

A MEMORABLE FANCY

Once I saw a Devil in a flame of fire, who arose before an Angel that sat on a cloud, and the Devil uttered these words:

"The worship of God is: Honouring his gifts in other men, each according to his genius, and loving the greatest men best: those who envy or calumniate great men hate God; for there is no other God."

The Angel hearing this became almost blue; but mastering himself he grew yellow, and at last white, pink, and smiling, and then replied: [10]

"Thou Idolater! is not God One? and is not he visible in Jesus Christ? and has not Jesus Christ given his sanction to the law of ten commandments? and are not all other men fools, sinners, and nothings?"

The Devil answered: "Bray a fool in a mortar with wheat, yet shall not his folly be beaten out of him; if Jesus Christ is the greatest man, [20] you ought to love him in the greatest degree; now hear how he has given his sanction to the law of ten commandments: did he not mock at the sabbath, and so mock the sabbath's God? murder those who were murdered because of him? turn away the law from the woman taken in adultery? steal the labour of others to support him? bear false witness when he omitted making a defence before Pilate? covet when he prayed for his disciples, and [30] when he bid them shake off the dust of their feet against such as refused to lodge them? I tell you, no virtue can exist without breaking these ten commandments. Jesus was all virtue, and acted from impulse, not from rules."

When he had so spoken, I beheld the Angel, who stretched out his arms, embracing the flame of fire, and he was consumed and arose as Elijah.

Note: This Angel, who is now become a [40] Devil, is my particular friend; we often read the Bible together in its infernal or diabolical sense, which the world shall have if they behave well.

I have also The Bible of Hell, which the world shall have whether they will or no.

One Law for the Lion and Ox is Oppression. [50]

[Etched c. 1790]

A SONG OF LIBERTY

1. The Eternal Female groaned! It was heard over all the Earth.

2. Albion's coast is sick, silent; the American meadows faint!

3. Shadows of Prophecy shiver along by the lakes and the rivers, and mutter across the ocean: France, rend down thy dungeon!

4. Golden Spain, burst the barriers of old Rome!

5. Cast thy keys, O Rome, into the deep, down falling, even to eternity down falling,

6. And weep.

7. In her trembling hands she took the new-born terror, howling.

8. On those infinite mountains of light, now barred out by the Atlantic sea, the new-born fire stood before the starry king!

9. Flagged with grey-browed snows and thunderous visages, the jealous wings waved over the deep.

10. The speary hand burned aloft, un-buckled was the shield; forth went the hand of Jealousy among the flaming hair, and hurled the new-born wonder through the starry night.

11. The fire, the fire is falling!

12. Look up! look up! O citizen of London, enlarge thy countenance! O Jew, leave counting gold! return to thy oil and wine. O African! black African! (Go, winged thought, widen his forehead!)

13. The fiery limbs, the flaming hair, shot like the sinking sun into the western sea.

14. Waked from his eternal sleep, the hoary element, roaring, fled away.

15. Down rushed, beating his wings in vain, the jealous King; his grey-browed counsellors, thunderous warriors, curled veterans, among helms, and shields, and chariots, horses, elephants, banners, castles, slings, and rocks.

16. Falling, rushing, ruining! buried in the ruins, on Urthona's dens;

17. All night beneath the ruins; then, their sullen flames faded, emerge round the gloomy King.

18. With thunder and fire, leading his starry hosts through the waste wilderness, he promulgates his ten commands, glancing his beamy eyelids over the deep in dark dismay.

19. Where the son of fire in his eastern

cloud, while the morning plumes her golden breast,

20. Spurning the clouds written with curses, stamps the stony law to dust, loosing the eternal horses from the dens of night, crying:

EMPIRE IS NO MORE! AND NOW THE LION AND WOLF SHALL CEASE.

CHORUS

Let the Priests of the Raven of dawn no longer, in deadly black, with hoarse note curse the sons of joy! Nor his accepted brethren—whom, tyrant, he calls free—lay the bound or build the roof. Nor pale Religion's lechery call that Virginity that wishes but acts not!

For everything that lives is Holy!

[1793]

AUGURIES OF INNOCENCE

To see a World in a grain of sand
And a Heaven in a wild flower,
Hold Infinity in the palm of your hand
And Eternity in an hour.

A robin redbreast in a cage
Puts all Heaven in a rage.
A dove-house filled with doves and pigeons
Shudders Hell through all its regions.
A dog starved at his master's gate
Predicts the ruin of the State.   10
A horse misused upon the road
Calls to Heaven for human blood.
Each outcry of the hunted hare
A fiber from the brain does tear.
A skylark wounded in the wing,
A cherubim does cease to sing.
The game-cock clipped and armed for fight
Does the rising sun affright.
Every wolf's and lion's howl
Raises from Hell a Human soul.   20
The wild deer, wandering here and there,
Keeps the Human soul from care.
The lamb misused breeds public strife
And yet forgives the butcher's knife.
The bat that flits at close of eve
Has left the brain that won't believe.
The owl that calls upon the night
Speaks the unbeliever's fright.

He who shall hurt the little wren
Shall never be beloved by men.   30
He who the ox to wrath has moved
Shall never be by woman loved.
The wanton boy that kills the fly
Shall feel the spider's enmity.
He who torments the chafer's sprite
Weaves a bower in endless night.
The caterpillar on the leaf
Repeats to thee thy mother's grief.
Kill not the moth nor butterfly.

For the Last Judgment draweth nigh.   40
He who shall train the horse to war
Shall never pass the polar bar.
The beggar's dog and widow's cat,
Feed them, and thou wilt grow fat.
The gnat that sings his summer's song
Poison gets from Slander's tongue.
The poison of the snake and newt
Is the sweat of Envy's foot.
The poison of the honey-bee
Is the artist's jealousy.   50
The prince's robes and beggar's rags
Are toadstools on the miser's bags.
A truth that's told with bad intent
Beats all the lies you can invent.
It is right it should be so;
Man was made for joy and woe;
And when this we rightly know
Through the world we safely go.
Joy and woe are woven fine,
A clothing for the soul divine;   60
Under every grief and pine
Runs a joy with silken twine.
The babe is more than swaddling-bands;
Throughout all these human lands
Tools were made, and born were hands,
Every farmer understands.
Every tear from every eye
Becomes a babe in Eternity;
This is caught by Females bright
And returned to its own delight.   70
The bleat, the bark, bellow, and roar
Are waves that beat on Heaven's shore.
The babe that weeps the rod beneath
Writes revenge in realms of death.
The beggar's rags, fluttering in air,
Does to rags the heavens tear.
The soldier, armed with sword and gun,
Palsied strikes the summer's sun.
The poor man's farthing is worth more
Than all the gold on Afric's shore.   80
One mite wrung from the labourer's hands
Shall buy and sell the miser's lands:

Or, if protected from on high,
Does that whole nation sell and buy.
He who mocks the infant's faith
Shall be mocked in Age and Death.
He who shall teach the child to doubt
The rotting grave shall ne'er get out.
He who respects the infant's faith
Triumphs over Hell and Death.   90
The child's toys and the old man's reasons
Are the fruits of the two seasons.
The questioner, who sits so sly,
Shall never know how to reply.
He who replies to words of Doubt
Doth put the light of knowledge out.
The strongest poison ever known
Came from Caesar's laurel crown.
Naught can deform the human race
Like to the armour's iron brace.   100
When gold and gems adorn the plough
To peaceful arts shall Envy bow.
A riddle, or the cricket's cry,
Is to Doubt a fit reply.
The emmet's inch and eagle's mile
Make lame Philosophy to smile.
He who doubts from what he sees
Will ne'er believe, do what you please.
If the Sun and Moon should doubt,
They'd immediately go out.   110
To be in a passion you good may do,
But no good if a passion is in you.
The whore and gambler, by the state
Licensed, build that nation's fate.
The harlot's cry from street to street
Shall weave Old England's winding-sheet.
The winner's shout, the loser's curse,
Dance before dead England's hearse.
Every night and every morn
Some to misery are born.   120
Every morn and every night
Some are born to sweet delight.
Some are born to sweet delight,
Some are born to endless night.
We are led to believe a lie
When we see not through the eye,
Which was born in a night, to perish in a
        night,
When the Soul slept in beams of light.
God appears and God is Light
To those poor souls who dwell in Night,   130

But does a Human Form display
To those who dwell in realms of Day.
                              [*1801–03,* 1863]

MOCK ON, MOCK ON, VOLTAIRE, ROUSSEAU

Mock on, mock on, Voltaire, Rousseau:
Mock on, mock on; 'tis all in vain!
You throw the sand against the wind,
And the wind blows it back again.

And every sand becomes a gem
Reflected in the beams divine;
Blown back they blind the mocking eye,
But still in Israel's paths they shine.

The Atoms of Democritus
And Newton's Particles of Light   10
Are sands upon the Red Sea shore,
Where Israel's tents do shine so bright.
                              [*1809–10*]

From MILTON

And did those feet in ancient time
Walk upon England's mountains green?
And was the holy Lamb of God
On England's pleasant pastures seen?

And did the Countenance Divine
Shine forth upon our clouded hills?
And was Jerusalem builded here
Among these dark Satanic Mills?

Bring me my bow of burning gold:
Bring me my arrows of desire: 10
Bring me my spear: O clouds unfold!
Bring me my chariot of fire.

I will not cease from mental fight,
Nor shall my sword sleep in my hand
Till we have built Jerusalem
In England's green and pleasant land.
                              [*1804*]

Further   Readings

&

Bibliographies

JONATHAN SWIFT (1667-1745)

THE LIFE AND GENUINE CHARACTER OF DEAN SWIFT

UPON A MAXIM IN ROCHEFOUCAULD [1]

This piece is closely connected with *Verses on the Death of Dr. Swift,* printed on pages 179-184. Swift's recent editors (Ball, Davis, Williams) accept *The Life and Character* as genuine, though it was long considered spurious. They have shown that the commonly accepted text of the *Verses* derives from an unauthorized London edition of 1739 into which someone interpolated over sixty lines from *The Life and Character.* The most nearly authentic text of the *Verses* is the Dublin edition of 1739. *The Life and Character* contains a dialogue in which one interlocutor speaks for and one against Swift; the last part of the *Verses* consists of a character of Swift given by a single speaker. The composite text usually given combines these speeches and speakers in a confusing way. Swift's plan can best be shown by reprinting both pieces. In the present edition the letters A and B have been added to indicate the two speakers in *The Life and Character.*

Wise Rochefoucauld a maxim writ,
Made up of malice, truth, and wit;
If what he says be not a joke,
We mortals are strange kind of folk.
　But hold—before we farther go,
'Tis fit the maxim we should know.
　He says, "Whenever Fortune sends
Disasters to our dearest friends,
Although we outwardly may grieve,
We oft are laughing in our sleeve." 　10
And when I think upon't this minute,
I fancy there is something in it.
　We see a comrade get a fall,
Yet laugh our hearts out one and all.
Tom for a wealthy wife looks round,
A nymph that brings ten thousand pound;
He nowhere could have better picked;
A rival comes, and Tom—is nicked!
See how behave his friends professed;
They turn the matter to a jest, 　20
Loll out their tongues, and thus they talk:

"Poor Tom has got a plaguy balk!"
　I could give instances enough,
That human friendship is but stuff.
Whene'er a flattering puppy cries
You are his dearest friend, he lies!—
To lose a guinea at piquet [2]
Would make him rage, and storm and fret,
Bring from his heart sincerer groans
Than if he heard you broke your bones. 　30
　Come, tell me truly, would you take well,
Suppose your friend and you were equal,
To see him always foremost stand,
Affect to take the upper hand,
And strive to pass in public view
For much a better man than you?
Envy, I doubt, would powerful prove,
And get the better of your love;
'Twould please your palate like a feast,
To see him mortified at least. 　40
　'Tis true, we talk of friendship much,
But who are they that can keep touch?
True friendship in two breasts requires

[1] See motto of *Verses on the Death of Dr. Swift,* page 179.

[2] A two-handed card game.

The same aversions and desires;
My friend should have, when I complain,
A fellow-feeling of my pain.
 Yet by experience oft we find
Our friends are of a different mind;
And were I tortured with the gout,
They'd laugh to see me make a rout,   50
Glad that themselves could walk about.
 Let me suppose two special friends,
And each to poetry pretends:
Would either poet take it well
To hear the other bore the bell,
His rival for the chiefest reckoned,
Himself pass only for the second?
 When you are sick, your friends, you say,
Will send their howd'ye's every day:
Alas, that gives you small relief—   60
They send for manners, not for grief:
Nor if you died would fail to go
That evening to a puppet-show;
Yet come in time to show their loves,
And get a hatband, scarf, and gloves.[3]
 To make these truths the better known,
Let me suppose the case my own.
The day will come, when't shall be said,

A.—D'ye hear the news? The Dean is dead!
 Poor man, he went all on a sudden!   70
B.—He's dropped, and given the crow a
  puddin'!
What money was behind him found?
A.—I hear about two thousand pound.
 'Tis owned he was a man of wit—
B.—Yet many a foolish thing he writ—
A.—And sure he must be deeply learned—
B.—That's more than ever I discerned!
A.—I know his nearest friends complain
 He was too airy for a dean;
 He was an honest man, I'll swear—   80
B.—Why sir, I differ from you there,
 For I have heard another story,
 He was a most confounded Tory!
A.—Yet here we had a strong report
 That he was well received at court—
B.—Why then it was, I do assert,
 Their goodness more than his desert.
 He grew, or else his comrades lied,
 Confounded dull before he died.
  He hoped to have a lucky hit,   90
 Some medals[4] sent him for his wit,
 But truly there the Dean was bit!

[3] Given to mourners at funerals.
[4] See note on *Verses on the Death of Dr.
Swift*, ll. 180–84, p. 181.

A.—And yet I think, for all your jokes,
 His claim as good as other folks'!
  Must we the Drapier then forget?
 Is not our nation in his debt?
 'Twas he that writ the *Drapier's Letters*!
B.—He should have left them for his betters;
 We had a hundred abler men,
 Nor need depend upon his pen.   100
Say what you will about his reading,
You never can defend his breeding!
Who, in his satires running riot,
Could never leave the world in quiet,
Attacking, when he took the whim,
Court, city, camp—all one to him.
  But why would he, except he slob-
  bered,
Offend our patriot, great Sir R——,
Whose counsels aid the sovereign power
To save the nation every hour?   110
What scenes of evil he unravels,
In satires, libels, lying travels!
Not sparing his own clergy-cloth,
But eats into it like a moth!
A.—If he makes mankind bad as elves,
 I answer they may thank themselves.
 If vice can ever be abashed,
 It must be ridiculed or lashed.
B.—But if I chance to make a slip,
 What right had he to hold the whip?   120
A.—If you resent it, who's to blame?
 He neither knew you nor your name.
 Should vice expect to 'scape rebuke
 Because its owner is a duke?
 Vice is a vermin; sportsmen say
 No vermin can demand fair play,
 But every hand may justly slay.
B.—I envy not the wits who write
 Merely to gratify their spite.
 Thus did the Dean; his only scope   130
 Was to be held a misanthrope.
 This into general odium drew him,
 Which if he liked, much good may do
  him;
 This gave him enemies in plenty,
 Throughout two realms nineteen in
  twenty.
 His zeal was not to lash our crimes,
 But discontent against the times;
 For had we made him timely offers,
 To raise his post or fill his coffers,
 Perhaps he might have truckled
  down,   140
 Like other brethren of the gown;
 For party he would scarce have bled;

I say no more—because he's dead.
A.—But who could charge him to his face,
    That e'er he cringed to men in place?
His principles, of ancient date,
Ill suit with those professed of late:
The Pope or Calvin he'd oppose,
And thought they both were equal foes;
That church and state had suffered
    more   150
By Calvin than the Scarlet Whore;
Thought popish and fanatic zeal
Both bitter foes to Britain's weal:
The Pope would of our faith bereave
    us,
But still our monarchy would leave us—
Not so the vile fanatic crew
That ruined church and monarch too.
    Supposing these reflections just,
We should indulge the Dean's disgust,
Who saw this factious tribe caressed, 160
And lovers of the church distressed;
The patrons of the good old cause
In senates sit at making laws;
The most malignant of the herd
In surest way to be preferred;
And preachers find the better quarter
For railing at the Royal Martyr.
Whole swarms of sects with grief he saw
More favored than the Church by law;
Thought Protestant too good a name 170
For canting hypocrites to claim,
Whose protestation hides a sting
Destructive to the Church and King,
Which might as well, in his opinion,

Become an atheist or Socinian.
A Protestant's a special clinker; 5
It serves for skeptic and free-thinker;
It serves for stubble, hay, and wood,
For everything—but what it should.
B.—What writings had he left behind? 180
A.—I hear they're of a different kind,
    A few in verse, but most in prose.
B.—Some high-flown pamphlets, I suppose—
    All scribbled in the worst of times,
    To palliate his friend Oxford's crimes,
    To praise Queen Anne, nay more, de-
        fend her,
    As never favoring the Pretender;
    Or libels yet concealed from sight,
    Against the court to show his spite;
    Perhaps his Travels, Part the Third, 190
    A lie at every second word,
    Offensive to a loyal ear,
    But—not one sermon, you may swear!
A.—Sir, our accounts are different quite,
    And your conjectures are not right.
    'Tis plain his writings were designed
    To please and to reform mankind,
    And if he often missed his aim,
    The world must own it, to their shame
    The praise is his, and theirs the
        blame.   200
        Then, since you dread no further
            lashes,
    You freely may forgive his ashes.
                                              [1733]

    5 Something that "clinches" a point or ar-
gument.

GULLIVER'S TRAVELS

Travels into Several Remote Nations of the World, by Lemuel Gulliver, to give the book its original title, is divided into four parts of which Parts I and III are omitted here. Part I, "A Voyage to Lilliput," is a social and political satire, often with particular allusion to contemporary England and Englishmen. Swift gets his satirical perspective by reducing man to one-twelfth his normal size. Part II, "A Voyage to Brobdingnag," is carefully contrasted with the "Voyage to Lilliput" throughout. The perspective is reversed, and it is Gulliver who, as representative of Man and of the English nation, is humiliated. In Part I most of the criticism of Man as Lilliputian is negative; in Part II, Swift has managed to express many of his positive social and political ideas through the Brobdingnagians. Part III, "A Voyage to Laputa," satirizes man's intellectual presumptuousness by showing us, through Gulliver's eyes, absurd devices and speculative schemes of contemporary science. In Part IV (pages 201–242), positive and negative criticism is reinforced in the opposition of the Houyhnhnms and the Yahoos. But possibly Swift's main purpose here is to answer the question of why mankind has dropped so far below the ideal. By a psychological division, that is, by making the Houyhnhnms wholly rational and the Yahoos wholly subject to passion, Swift is able to give a clear account of the origin and growth of evil among mankind as he saw it.

PART II

A VOYAGE TO BROBDINGNAG

CHAP. I

A great storm described; the long-boat sent to fetch water; the author goes with it to discover the country. He is left on shore, is seized by one of the natives, and carried to a farmer's house. His reception there, with several accidents that happened there. A description of the inhabitants.

Having been condemned by nature and fortune to an active and restless life, in two months after my return I again left my native country, and took shipping in the Downs on the 20th day of June, 1702, in the *Adventure,* Captain John Nicholas, a Cornish man, Commander, bound for Surat. We had a very prosperous gale till we arrived at the Cape of Good Hope, where we landed for fresh water, but discovering a leak we unshipped our goods and wintered there; for the Captain falling sick of an ague, we could not leave the Cape till the end of March. We then set sail, and had a good voyage till we passed the Straits of Madagascar; but having got northward of that island, and to about five degrees south latitude, the winds, which in those seas are observed to blow a constant equal gale between the north and west from the beginning of December to the beginning of May, on the 19th of April began to blow with much greater violence, and more westerly than usual, continuing so for twenty days together, during which time we were driven a little to the east of the Molucca Islands, and about three degrees northward of the Line, as our Captain found by an observation he took the 2nd of May, at which time the wind ceased, and it was a perfect calm, whereat I was not a little rejoiced. But he, being a man well experienced in the navigation of those seas, bid us all prepare against a storm, which accordingly happened the day following: for a southern wind, called the southern monsoon, began to set in.

Finding it was likely to overblow, we took in our sprit-sail, and stood

by to hand the fore-sail; but making foul weather, we looked the guns were all fast, and handed the mizen. The ship lay very broad off, so we thought it better spooning before the sea, than trying or hulling. We reeft the fore-sail and set him, we hauled aft the fore-sheet; the helm was hard a weather. The ship wore bravely. We belayed the fore-down haul; but the sail was split, and we hauled down the yard, and got the sail into the ship, and unbound all the things clear of it. It was a very fierce storm; the sea broke strange and dangerous. We hauled off upon the lanyard of the whipstaff, and helped the man at helm. We would not get down our top-mast, but let all stand, because she scudded before the sea very well, and we knew that the top-mast being aloft, the ship was the wholesomer, and made better way through the sea, seeing we had sea-room. When the storm was over, we set fore-sail and main-sail, and brought the ship to: then we set the mizen, main-top-sail, and the fore-top-sail. Our course was east-north-east, the wind was at south-west. We got the starboard tacks aboard, we cast off our weather-braces and lifts; we set in the lee-braces, and hauled forward by the weather-bowlings, and hauled them tight, and belayed them, and hauled over the mizen tack to windward, and kept her full and by as near as she would lie.

During this storm, which was followed by a strong wind west-south-west, we were carried by my computation about five hundred leagues to the east, so that the oldest sailor on board could not tell in what part of the world we were. Our provisions held out well, our ship was staunch, and our crew all in good health; but we lay in the utmost distress for water. We thought it best to hold on the same course, rather than turn more northerly, which might have brought us to the north-west parts of Great Tartary, and into the frozen sea.

On the 16th day of June, 1703, a boy on the top-mast discovered land.

On the 17th we came in full view of a great island or continent (for we knew not whether) on the south side whereof was a small neck of land jutting out into the sea, and a creek too shallow to hold a ship of above one hundred tons. We cast anchor within a league of this creek, and our Captain sent a dozen of his men well armed in the long-boat, with vessels for water if any could be found. I desired his leave to go with them, that I might see the country, and make what discoveries I could. When we came to land we saw no river or spring nor any sign of inhabitants. Our men therefore wandered on the shore to find out some fresh water near the sea, and I walked alone about a mile on the other side, where I observed the country all barren and rocky. I now began to be weary, and seeing nothing to entertain my curiosity, I returned gently down towards the creek; and the sea being full in my view, I saw our men already got into the boat, and rowing for life to the ship. I was going to hollow after them, although it had been to little purpose, when I observed a huge creature walking after them in the sea, as fast as he could: he waded not much deeper than his knees, and took prodigious strides: but our men had the start of him half a league, and the sea thereabouts being full of sharp-pointed rocks, the monster was not able to overtake the boat. This I was afterwards told, for I durst not stay to see the issue of that adventure; but ran as fast as I could the way I first went, and then climbed up a steep hill which gave me some prospect of the country. I found it fully cultivated; but that which first surprised me was the length of the grass, which in those grounds that seemed to be kept for hay, was about twenty foot high.

I fell into a high road, for so I took it to be, though it served to the inhabitants only as a footpath through a field of barley. Here I walked on for some time, but could see little on either side, it being now near harvest, and the corn rising at least forty foot. I was an hour walking to the end of this field, which was fenced in with a hedge of at least one hundred and twenty foot high, and the trees so lofty that I could make no computation of their altitude. There was a stile to pass from this field into the next. It had four steps, and a stone to cross over when you came to the uppermost. It was impossible for me to climb this stile, because every step was six foot high, and the upper stone above twenty. I was endeavouring to find some gap in the hedge, when I discovered one of the inhabitants in the next field, advancing towards the stile, of the same size with him whom I saw in the sea pursuing our boat. He appeared as tall as an ordinary spire-steeple, and took about ten yards at every stride, as near as I could guess. I was struck with the utmost fear and astonishment, and ran to hide myself in the corn, from whence I saw him at the top of the stile, looking back into the next field on the right, and heard him call in a voice many degrees louder than a speaking-trumpet; but the noise was so high in the air, that at first I certainly thought it was thunder. Whereupon seven monsters like himself came towards him with reaping-hooks in their hands, each hook about the largeness of six scythes. These people were not so well clad as the first, whose servants or labourers they seemed to be. For upon some words he spoke, they went to reap the corn in the field where I lay. I kept from them at as great a distance as I could, but was forced to move with extreme difficulty, for the stalks of the corn were sometimes not above a foot distant, so that I could hardly squeeze my body betwixt them. However, I made a shift to go forward till I came to a part of the field where the corn had been laid by the rain and wind. Here it was impossible for me to advance a step; for the stalks were so interwoven that I could not creep through, and the beards of the fallen ears so strong and pointed that they pierced through my clothes into my flesh. At the same time I heard the reapers not above an hundred yards behind me. Being quite dispirited with toil, and wholly overcome by grief and despair, I lay down between two ridges, and heartily wished I might there end my days. I bemoaned my desolate widow, and fatherless children. I lamented my own folly and wilfulness in attempting a second voyage against the advice of all my friends and relations. In this terrible agitation of mind I could not forbear thinking of Lilliput, whose inhabitants looked upon me as the greatest prodigy that ever appeared in the world; where I was able to draw an Imperial Fleet in my hand, and perform those other actions which will be recorded for ever in the chronicles of that empire, while posterity shall hardly believe them, although attested by millions. I reflected what a mortification it must prove to me to appear as inconsiderable in this nation as one single Lilliputian would be among us. But this I conceived was to be the least of my misfortunes: for as human creatures are observed to be more savage and cruel in proportion to their bulk, what could I expect but to be a morsel in the mouth of the first among these enormous barbarians that should happen to seize me? Undoubtedly philosophers are in the right when they tell us, that nothing is great or little otherwise than by comparison. It might have pleased fortune to let the Lilliputians find some nation where the people were as diminutive with respect to them as they were to me. And who knows but that even this prodigious race of mortals might be equally overmatched in some distant part of the world, whereof we have yet no discovery?

Scared and confounded as I was, I could not forbear going on with these reflections, when one of the reapers approaching within ten yards of the ridge where I lay, made me apprehend that with the next step I should be squashed to death under his foot, or cut in two with his reaping-hook. And therefore when he was again about to move, I screamed as loud as fear could make me. Whereupon the huge creature trod short, and looking round about him for some time, at last espied me as I lay on the ground. He considered a while with the caution of one who endeavours to lay hold on a small dangerous animal in such a manner that it shall not be able either to scratch or to bite him, as I myself have sometimes done with a weasel in England. At length he ventured to take me up behind by the middle between his forefinger and thumb, and brought me within three yards of his eyes, that he might behold my shape more perfectly. I guessed his meaning, and my good fortune gave me so much presence of mind that I resolved not to struggle in the least as he held me in the air about sixty foot from the ground, although he grievously pinched my sides, for fear I should slip through his fingers. All I ventured was to raise my eyes towards the sun, and place my hands together in a supplicating posture, and to speak some words in an humble melancholy tone, suitable to the condition I then was in. For I apprehended every moment that he would dash me against the ground, as we usually do any little hateful animal which we have a mind to destroy. But my good star would have it, that he appeared pleased with my voice and gestures, and began to look upon me as a curiosity, much wondering to hear me pronounce articulate words, although he could not understand them. In the mean time I was not able to forbear groaning and shedding tears, and turning my head towards my sides; letting him know, as well as I could, how cruelly I was hurt by the pressure of his thumb and finger. He seemed to apprehend my meaning; for, lifting up the lappet of his coat, he put me gently into it, and immediately ran along with me to his master, who was a substantial farmer, and the same person I had first seen in the field.

The farmer having (as I supposed by their talk) received such an account of me as his servant could give him, took a piece of a small straw, about the size of a walking staff, and therewith lifted up the lappets of my coat, which it seems he thought to be some kind of covering that nature had given me. He blew my hairs aside to take a better view of my face. He 10 called his hinds about him, and asked them (as I afterwards learned) whether they had ever seen in the fields any little creature that resembled me. He then placed me softly on the ground upon all four, but I got immediately up and walked slowly backwards and forwards, to let those people see I had no intent to run away. They all sat down in a circle 20 about me, the better to observe my motions. I pulled off my hat, and made a low bow towards the farmer. I fell on my knees, and lifted up my hands and eyes, and spoke several words as loud as I could: I took a purse of gold out of my pocket, and humbly presented it to him. He received it on the palm of his hand, then applied it close to his eye to see what 30 it was, and afterwards turned it several times with the point of a pin (which he took out of his sleeve), but could make nothing of it. Whereupon I made a sign that he should place his hand on the ground. I then took the purse, and opening it, poured all the gold into his palm. There were six Spanish pieces of four pistoles each, beside twenty or thirty smaller coins. 40 I saw him wet the tip of his little finger upon his tongue, and take up one of my largest pieces, and then another, but he seemed to be wholly ignorant what they were. He made me a sign to put them again into my purse, and the purse again into my pocket, which after offering to him several times, I thought it best to do.

The farmer by this time was con- 50 vinced I must be a rational creature. He spoke often to me, but the sound of his voice pierced my ears like that of a water-mill, yet his words were articulate enough. I answered as loud as I could, in several languages, and he often laid his ear within two yards of me, but all in vain, for we were wholly unintelligible to each other. He then sent his servants to their work, and taking his handkerchief out of his pocket he doubled and spread it on his left hand, which he placed flat on the ground, with the palm upwards, making me a sign to step into it, as I could easily do, for it was not above a foot in thickness. I thought it my part to obey, and for fear of falling, laid myself at length upon the handkerchief, with the remainder of which he lapped me up to the head for further security, and in this manner carried me home to his house. There he called his wife and showed me to her; but she screamed and ran back, as women in England do at the sight of a toad or a spider. However, when she had a while seen my behaviour, and how well I observed the signs her husband made, she was soon reconciled, and by degrees grew extremely tender of me.

It was about twelve at noon, and a servant brought in dinner. It was only one substantial dish of meat (fit for the plain condition of an husbandman) in a dish of about four-and-twenty foot diameter. The company were the farmer and his wife, three children, and an old grandmother. When they were sat down, the farmer placed me at some distance from him on the table, which was thirty foot high from the floor. I was in a terrible fright, and kept as far as I could from the edge for fear of falling. The wife minced a bit of meat, then crumbled some bread on a trencher, and placed it before me. I made her a low bow, took out my knife and fork and fell to eat, which gave them exceeding delight. The mistress sent her maid for a small dram cup, which held about three gallons, and filled it with drink; I took up the vessel with much difficulty in both hands, and in a most respectful manner drank to her ladyship's health, expressing the words as loud as I could in English, which made the company laugh so heartily that I was almost deafened with the noise. This liquor tasted like a small cyder, and was not unpleasant. Then the master made me a sign to come to his trencher side; but as I walked on the table, being in great surprise all the time as the indulgent reader will easily conceive and excuse, I happened to stumble against a crust, and fell flat on my face, but received no hurt. I got up immediately, and observing the good people to be in much concern, I took my hat (which I held under my arm out of good manners) and waving it over my head made three huzzas to show I had got no mischief by my fall. But advancing forwards toward my master (as I shall henceforth call him) his youngest son who sat next him, an arch boy of about ten years old, took me up by the legs, and held me so high in the air, that I trembled every limb; but his father snatched me from him, and at the same time gave him such a box on the left ear, as would have felled an European troop of horse to the earth, ordering him to be taken from the table. But being afraid the boy might owe me a spite, and well remembering how mischievous all children among us naturally are to sparrows, rabbits, young kittens, and puppy dogs, I fell on my knees, and pointing to the boy, made my master to understand, as well as I could, that I desired his son might be pardoned. The father complied, and the lad took his seat again; whereupon I went to him and kissed his hand, which my master took, and made him stroke me gently with it.

In the midst of dinner, my mistress's favourite cat leapt into her lap. I heard a noise behind me like that of a dozen stocking-weavers at work; and turning my head, I found it proceeded from the purring of this animal, who seemed to be three times larger than an ox, as I computed by the view of her head, and one of her paws, while her mistress was feeding and stroking her. The fierceness of this creature's

countenance altogether discomposed me; though I stood at the farther end of the table, above fifty foot off; and although my mistress held her fast for fear she might give a spring, and seize me in her talons. But it happened there was no danger; for the cat took not the least notice of me when my master placed me within three yards of her. And as I have been always told, and found true by experience in my travels, that flying, or discovering fear before a fierce animal, is a certain way to make it pursue or attack you, so I resolved in this dangerous juncture to show no manner of concern. I walked with intrepidity five or six times before the very head of the cat, and came within half a yard of her; whereupon she drew herself back, as if she were more afraid of me: I had less apprehension concerning the dogs, whereof three or four came into the room as it is usual in farmers' houses; one of which was a mastiff, equal in bulk to four elephants, and a greyhound, somewhat taller than the mastiff, but not so large.

When dinner was almost done, the nurse came in with a child of a year old in her arms, who immediately spied me, and began a squall that you might have heard from London Bridge to Chelsea, after the usual oratory of infants, to get me for a plaything. The mother out of pure indulgence took me up, and put me towards the child, who presently seized me by the middle, and got my head in his mouth, where I roared so loud that the urchin was frighted, and let me drop; and I should infallibly have broke my neck if the mother had not held her apron under me. The nurse to quiet her babe made use of a rattle, which was a kind of hollow vessel filled with great stones, and fastened by a cable to the child's waist: but all in vain, so that she was forced to apply the last remedy by giving it suck. I must confess no object ever disgusted me so much as the sight of her monstrous breast, which I cannot tell what to compare with, so as to give the curious reader an idea of its bulk, shape and color. It stood prominent six foot, and could not be less than sixteen in circumference. The nipple was about half the bigness of my head, and the hue both of that and the dug so varified with spots, pimples and freckles, that nothing could appear more nauseous: for I had a near sight of her, she sitting down the more conveniently to give suck, and I standing on the table. This made me reflect upon the fair skins of our English ladies, who appear so beautiful to us only because they are of our own size, and their defects not to be seen but through a magnifying glass, where we find by experiment that the smoothest and whitest skins look rough and coarse, and ill coloured.

I remember when I was at Lilliput, the complexions of those diminutive people appeared to me the fairest in the world; and talking upon this subject with a person of learning there, who was an intimate friend of mine, he said that my face appeared much fairer and smoother when he looked on me from the ground, than it did upon a nearer view when I took him up in my hand and brought him close, which he confessed was at first a very shocking sight. He said he could discover great holes in my skin; that the stumps of my beard were ten times stronger than the bristles of a boar, and my complexion made up of several colours altogether disagreeable: although I must beg leave to say for myself, that I am as fair as most of my sex and country, and very little sunburnt by all my travels. On the other side, discoursing of the ladies in that Emperor's court, he used to tell me one had freckles, another too wide a mouth, a third too large a nose, nothing of which I was able to distinguish. I confess this reflection was obvious enough; which however I could not forbear, lest the reader might think those vast creatures were actually deformed: for I must do them justice to say they are a comely race of people; and particularly the features

of my master's countenance, although he were but a farmer, when I beheld him from the height of sixty foot appeared very well proportioned.

When dinner was done, my master went out to his labourers, and as I could discover by his voice and gesture, gave his wife a strict charge to take care of me. I was very much tired, and disposed to sleep, which my mistress perceiving, she put me on her own bed, and covered me with a clean white handkerchief, but larger and coarser than the mainsail of a man of war.

I slept about two hours, and dreamed I was at home with my wife and children, which aggravated my sorrows when I awaked and found myself alone in a vast room, between two and three hundred foot wide, and above two hundred high, lying in a bed twenty yards wide. My mistress had gone about her household affairs, and had locked me in. The bed was eight yards from the floor. Some natural necessities required me to get down; I durst not presume to call, and if I had, it would have been in vain, with such a voice as mine, at so great a distance from the room where I lay to the kitchen where the family kept. While I was under these circumstances, two rats crept up the curtains, and ran smelling backwards and forwards on the bed. One of them came up almost to my face, whereupon I rose in a fright, and drew out my hanger to defend myself. These horrible animals had the boldness to attack me on both sides, and one of them held his fore-feet at my collar; but I had the good fortune to rip up his belly before he could do me any mischief. He fell down at my feet, and the other seeing the fate of his comrade, made his escape, but not without one good wound on the back which I gave him as he fled, and made the blood run trickling from him. After this exploit, I walked gently to and fro on the bed, to recover my breath and loss of spirits. These creatures were of the size of a large mastiff, but infinitely more nimble and fierce, so that if I had taken off my belt before I went to sleep, I must have infallibly been torn to pieces and devoured. I measured the tail of the dead rat, and found it to be two yards long, wanting an inch; but it went against my stomach to drag the carcass off the bed, where it lay still bleeding; I observed it had yet some life, but with a strong slash cross the neck, I thoroughly dispatched it.

Soon after my mistress came into the room, who seeing me all bloody, ran and took me up in her hand. I pointed to the dead rat, smiling and making other signs to show I was not hurt, whereat she was extremely rejoiced, calling the maid to take up the dead rat with a pair of tongs, and throw it out of the window. Then she set me on a table, where I showed her my hanger all bloody, and wiping it on the lappet of my coat, returned it to the scabbard. I was pressed to do more than one thing which another could not do for me, and therefore endeavoured to make my mistress understand that I desired to be set down on the floor; which after she had done, my bashfulness would not suffer me to express myself farther than by pointing to the door, and bowing several times. The good woman with much difficulty at last perceived what I would be at, and taking me up again in her hand, walked into the garden, where she set me down. I went on one side about two hundred yards, and beckoning to her not to look or to follow me, I hid myself between two leaves of sorrel and there discharged the necessities of nature.

I hope the gentle reader will excuse me for dwelling on these and the like particulars, which however insignificant they may appear to grovelling vulgar minds, yet will certainly help a philosopher to enlarge his thoughts and imagination, and apply them to the benefit of public as well as private life, which was my sole design in presenting this and other accounts of my travels to the world; wherein I have been chiefly studious of truth, without affecting any ornaments of learning or of style. But the whole scene of this voyage made so strong an impression on my mind, and is so deeply fixed in my memory, that in committing it to paper I did not omit one material circumstance: however, upon a strict review, I blotted out several passages of less moment which were in my first copy, for fear of being censured as tedious and trifling, whereof travellers are often, perhaps not without justice, accused.

CHAP. II

A description of the farmer's daughter. The author carried to a market-town, and then to the metropolis. The particulars of his journey.

My mistress had a daughter of nine years old, a child of forward parts for her age, very dexterous at her needle, and skilful in dressing her baby. Her mother and she contrived to fit up the baby's cradle for me against night: the cradle was put into a small drawer of a cabinet, and the drawer placed upon a hanging shelf for fear of the rats. This was my bed all the time I stayed with those people, though made more convenient by degrees, as I began to learn their language, and make my wants known. This young girl was so handy, that after I had once or twice pulled off my clothes before her, she was able to dress and undress me, though I never gave her that trouble when she would let me do either myself. She made me seven shirts and some other linen, of as fine cloth as could be got, which indeed was coarser than sackcloth; and these she constantly washed for me with her own hands. She was likewise my school-mistress to teach me the language: when I pointed to any thing, she told me the name of it in her own tongue, so that in a few days I was able to call for whatever I had a mind to. She was very good-natured, and not above forty foot high, being little for her age. She gave me the name of *Grildrig*, which the family took up and afterwards the whole kingdom. The word imports what the Latins call *nanunculus,* the Italians *homunceletino,* and the English *mannikin.* To her I chiefly owe my preservation in that country: we never parted while I was there; I called her my *Glumdalclitch,* or little nurse: and I should be guilty of great ingratitude if I omitted this honourable mention of her care and affection towards me, which I heartily wish it lay in my power to requite as she deserves, instead of being the innocent but unhappy instrument of her disgrace, as I have too much reason to fear.

It now began to be known and talked of in the neighbourhood, that my master had found a strange animal in the field, about the bigness of a *splacknuck,* but exactly shaped in every part like a human creature; which it likewise imitated in all its actions; seemed to speak in a little language of its own, had already learned several words of theirs, went erect upon two legs, was tame and gentle, would come when it was called, do whatever it was bid, had the finest limbs in the world, and a complexion fairer than a nobleman's daughter of three years old. Another farmer who lived hard by and was a particular friend of my master, came on a visit on purpose to enquire into the truth of this story. I was immediately produced, and placed upon a table, where I walked as I was commanded, drew my hanger, put it up again, made my reverence to my master's guest, asked him in his own language how he did, and told him he was welcome, just as my little nurse had instructed me. This man, who was old and dimsighted, put on his spectacles to behold me better, at which I could not forbear laughing very heartily, for his eyes appeared like the full moon shining into a chamber at two windows. Our people, who discovered the cause of my mirth, bore me company in laughing, at which the old fellow was fool enough to be angry and out

of countenance. He had the character of a great miser, and to my misfortune he well deserved it, by the cursed advice he gave my master to show me as a sight upon a market-day in the next town, which was half an hour's riding, about two and twenty miles from our house. I guessed there was some mischief contriving, when I observed my master and his friend whispering long together, sometimes pointing at me; and my fears made me fancy that I overheard and understood some of their words. But the next morning Glumdalclitch my little nurse told me the whole matter, which she had cunningly picked out from her mother. The poor girl laid me on her bosom, and fell a weeping with shame and grief. She apprehended some mischief would happen to me from rude vulgar folks, who might squeeze me to death, or break one of my limbs by taking me in their hands. She had also observed how modest I was in my nature, how nicely I regarded my honour, and what an indignity I should conceive it to be exposed for money as a public spectacle to the meanest of the people. She said, her papa and mamma had promised that Grildrig should be hers, but now she found they meant to serve her as they did last year, when they pretended to give her a lamb, and yet, as soon as it was fat, sold it to a butcher. For my own part, I may truly affirm that I was less concerned than my nurse. I had a strong hope which never left me, that I should one day recover my liberty; and as to the ignominy of being carried about for a monster, I considered myself to be a perfect stranger in the country, and that such a misfortune could never be charged upon me as a reproach, if ever I should return to England; since the King of Great Britain himself, in my condition, must have undergone the same distress.

My master, pursuant to the advice of his friend, carried me in a box the next market-day to the neighbouring town, and took along with him his little daughter my nurse upon a pil lion behind him. The box was close on every side, with a little door for me to go in and out, and a few gimlet-holes to let in air. The girl had been so careful to put the quilt of her baby's bed into it, for me to lie down on. However, I was terribly shaken and discomposed in this journey, though it were but of half an hour. For the horse went about forty foot at every step, and trotted so high, that the agitation was equal to the rising and falling of a ship in a great storm, but much more frequent. Our journey was somewhat further than from London to St. Albans. My master alighted at an inn which he used to frequent; and after consulting a while with the inn-keeper, and making some necessary preparations, he hired the *Grultrud,* or crier, to give notice through the town of a strange creature to be seen at the Sign of the Green Eagle, not so big as a *splacknuck* (an animal in that country very finely shaped, about six foot long) and in every part of the body resembling an human creature, could speak several words, and perform an hundred diverting tricks.

I was placed upon a table in the largest room of the inn, which might be near three hundred foot square. My little nurse stood on a low stool close to the table, to take care of me, and direct what I should do. My master, to avoid a crowd, would suffer only thirty people at a time to see me. I walked about on the table as the girl commanded: she asked me questions as far as she knew my understanding of the language reached, and I answered them as loud as I could. I turned about several times to the company, paid my humble respects, said they were welcome, and used some other speeches I had been taught. I took up a thimble filled with liquor, which Glumdalclitch had given me for a cup, and drank their health. I drew out my hanger, and flourished with it after the manner of fencers in England. My nurse gave me part of a straw, which I exercised as a pike,

having learned the art in my youth. I was that day shown to twelve sets of company, and as often forced to go over again with the same fopperies, till I was half dead with weariness and vexation. For those who had seen me made such wonderful reports, that the people were ready to break down the doors to come in. My master for his own interest would not suffer any one to touch me except my nurse; and, to prevent danger, benches were set round the table at such a distance as put me out of every body's reach. However, an unlucky school-boy aimed a hazel nut directly at my head, which very narrowly missed me; otherwise, it came with so much violence, that it would have infallibly knocked out my brains, for it was almost as large as a small pumpion: [1] but I had the satisfaction to see the young rogue well beaten, and turned out of the room.

My master gave public notice that he would show me again the next market-day, and in the meantime he prepared a more convenient vehicle for me, which he had reason enough to to do; for I was so tired with my first journey, and with entertaining company for eight hours together, that I could hardly stand upon my legs or speak a word. It was at least three days before I recovered my strength; and that I might have no rest at home, all the neighbouring gentlemen from an hundred miles round, hearing of my fame, came to see me at my master's own house. There could not be fewer than thirty persons with their wives and children (for the country is very populous) ; and my master demanded the rate of a full room whenever he showed me at home, although it were only to a single family; so that for some time I had but little ease every day of the week (except Wednesday, which is their Sabbath) although I were not carried to the town.

My master finding how profitable I was likely to be, resolved to carry me to the most considerable cities of the kingdom. Having therefore pro-

[1] Pumpkin.

vided himself with all things necessary for a long journey, and settled his affairs at home, he took leave of his wife, and upon the 17th of August, 1703, about two months after my arrival, we set out for the metropolis, situated near the middle of that empire, and about three thousand miles distance from our house. My master made his daughter Glumdalclitch ride behind him. She carried me on her lap in a box tied about her waist. The girl had lined it on all sides with the softest cloth she could get, well quilted underneath, furnished it with her baby's bed, provided me with linen and other necessaries, and made everything as convenient as she could. We had no other company but a boy of the house, who rode after us with the luggage.

My master's design was to show me in all the towns by the way, and to step out of the road for fifty or an hundred miles, to any village or person of quality's house where he might expect custom. We made easy journeys of not above seven or eight score miles a day: for Glumdalclitch, on purpose to spare me, complained she was tired with the trotting of the horse. She often took me out of my box at my own desire, to give me air and show me the country, but always held me fast by a leading-string. We passed over five or six rivers many degrees broader and deeper than the Nile or the Ganges; and there was hardly a rivulet so small as the Thames at London Bridge. We were ten weeks in our journey, and I was shown in eighteen large towns besides many villages and private families.

On the 26th day of October, we arrived at the metropolis, called in their language *Lorbrulgrud,* or Pride of the Universe. My master took a lodging in the principal street of the city, not far from the royal palace, and put out bills in the usual form, containing an exact description of my person and parts. He hired a large room between three and four hundred foot wide. He provided a table sixty foot in diameter, upon which I was to act my part, and palisadoed it round three foot from the edge, and as many high, to prevent my falling over. I was shown ten times a day to the wonder and satisfaction of all people. I could now speak the language tolerably well, and perfectly understood every word that was spoken to me. Besides, I had learnt their alphabet, and could make a shift to explain a sentence here and there; for Glumdalclitch had been my instructor while we were at home, and at leisure hours during our journey. She carried a little book in her pocket, not much larger than a Sanson's Atlas; it was a common treatise for the use of young girls, giving a short account of their religion: out of this she taught me my letters, and interpreted the words.

CHAP. III

The author sent for to Court. The Queen buys him of his master the farmer, and presents him to the King. He disputes with his Majesty's great scholars. An apartment at Court provided for the Author. He is in high favour with the Queen. He stands up for the honour of his own country. His quarrels with the Queen's dwarf.

The frequent labours I underwent every day made in a few weeks a very considerable change in my health: the more my master got by me, the more unsatiable he grew. I had quite lost my stomach, and was almost reduced to a skeleton. The farmer observed it, and concluding I soon must die, resolved to make as good a hand of me as he could. While he was thus reasoning and resolving with himself, a *Slardral,* or Gentleman Usher, came from court, commanding my master to carry me immediately thither for the diversion of the Queen and her ladies. Some of the latter had already been to see me, and reported strange things of my beauty, behaviour, and good sense. Her Majesty and those who attended her were beyond measure delighted with my demeanour. I fell on my knees, and begged the honour of kissing her Imperial foot; but this gracious princess held out her little finger towards me (after I was set on a table) which I embraced in both my arms, and put the tip of it with the utmost respect to my lips. She made me some general questions about my country and my travels, which I answered as distinctly and in as few words as I could. She asked whether I would be content to live at court. I bowed down to the board of the table, and humbly answered that I was my master's slave, but if I were at my own disposal, I should be proud to devote my life to her Majesty's service. She then asked my master whether he were willing to sell me at a good price. He, who apprehended I could not live a month, was ready enough to part with me, and demanded a thousand pieces of gold, which were ordered him on the spot, each piece being about the bigness of eight hundred moidores; but, allowing for the proportion of all things between that country and Europe, and the high price of gold among them, was hardly so great a sum as a thousand guineas would be in England. I then said to the Queen, since I was now her Majesty's most humble creature and vassal, I must beg the favour, that Glumdalclitch, who had always tended me with so much care and kindness, and understood to do it so well, might be admitted into her service, and continue to be my nurse and instructor. Her Majesty agreed to my petition, and easily got the farmer's consent, who was glad enough to have his daughter preferred at court: and the poor girl herself was not able to hide her joy. My late master withdrew, bidding me farewell, and saying he had left me in a good service; to which I replied not a word, only making him a slight bow.

The Queen observed my coldness, and when the farmer was gone out of the apartment, asked me the reason. I made bold to tell her Majesty that I owed no other obligation to my late master, than his not dashing out the brains of a poor harmless creature found by chance in his field; which

obligation was amply recompensed by the gain he had made in showing me through half the kingdom, and the price he had now sold me for. That the life I had since led was laborious enough to kill an animal of ten times my strength. That my health was much impaired by the continual drudgery of entertaining the rabble every hour of the day, and that if my master had not thought my life in danger, her Majesty perhaps would not have got so cheap a bargain. But as I was out of all fear of being ill treated under the protection of so great and good an Empress, the Ornament of Nature, the Darling of the World, the Delight of her Subjects, the Phœnix of the Creation; so I hoped my late master's apprehensions would appear to be groundless, for I already found my spirits to revive by the influence of her most august presence.

This was the sum of my speech, delivered with great improprieties and hesitation; the latter part was altogether framed in the style peculiar to that people, whereof I learned some phrases from Glumdalclitch, while she was carrying me to court.

The Queen giving great allowance for my defectiveness in speaking, was however surprised at so much wit and good sense in so diminutive an animal. She took me in her own hand, and carried me to the King, who was then retired to his cabinet. His Majesty, a prince of much gravity, and austere countenance, not well observing my shape at first view, asked the Queen after a cold manner, how long it was since she grew fond of a *splacknuck*; for such it seems he took me to be, as I lay upon my breast in her Majesty's right hand. But this princess, who hath an infinite deal of wit and humour, set me gently on my feet upon the scrutore, and commanded me to give his Majesty an account of myself, which I did in a very few words; and Glumdalclitch, who attended at the cabinet door, and could not endure I should be out of her sight, being admitted, confirmed all that had passed from my arrival at her father's house.

The King, although he be as learned a person as any in his dominions, and had been educated in the study of philosophy, and particularly mathematics; yet when he observed my shape exactly, and saw me walk erect, before I began to speak, conceived I might be a piece of clockwork, (which is in that country arrived to a very great perfection) contrived by some ingenious artist. But when he heard my voice, and found what I delivered to be regular and rational, he could not conceal his astonishment. He was by no means satisfied with the relation I gave him of the manner I came into his kingdom, but thought it a story concerted between Glumdalclitch and her father, who had taught me a set of words to make me sell at a higher price. Upon this imagination he put several other questions to me, and still received rational answers, no otherwise defective than by a foreign accent, and an imperfect knowledge in the language, with some rustic phrases which I had learned at the farmer's house, and did not suit the polite style of a court.

His Majesty sent for three great scholars who were then in their weekly waiting, according to the custom in that country. These gentlemen, after they had a while examined my shape with much nicety, were of different opinions concerning me. They all agreed that I could not be produced according to the regular laws of nature, because I was not framed with a capacity of preserving my life, either by swiftness, or climbing of trees, or digging holes in the earth. They observed by my teeth, which they viewed with great exactness, that I was a carnivorous animal; yet most quadrupeds being an overmatch for me, and field mice with some others, too nimble, they could not imagine how I should be able to support myself, unless I fed upon snails and other insects, which they offered, by many learned arguments, to evince that I

could not possibly do. One of these virtuosi seemed to think that I might be an embryo, or abortive birth. But this opinion was rejected by the other two, who observed my limbs to be perfect and finished, and that I had lived several years, as it was manifest from my beard, the stumps whereof they plainly discovered through a magnifying-glass. They would not allow me to be a dwarf, because my littleness was beyond all degrees of comparison; for the Queen's favourite dwarf, the smallest ever known in that kingdom, was nearly thirty foot high. After much debate, they concluded unanimously that I was only *replum scalcath*, which is interpreted literally, *lusus naturæ*;[2] a determination exactly agreeable to the modern philosophy of Europe, whose professors, disdaining the old evasion of *occult causes*, whereby the followers of Aristotle endeavour in vain to disguise their ignorance, have invented this wonderful solution of all difficulties, to the unspeakable advancement of human knowledge.

After this decisive conclusion, I entreated to be heard a word or two. I applied myself to the King and assured his Majesty that I came from a country which abounded with several millions of both sexes, and of my own stature; where the animals, trees, and houses were all in proportion, and where by consequence I might be as able to defend myself, and to find sustenance, as any of his Majesty's subjects could do here; which I took for a full answer to those gentlemen's arguments. To this they only replied with a smile of contempt, saying that the farmer had instructed me very well in my lesson. The King, who had a much better understanding, dismissing his learned men, sent for the farmer, who by good fortune was not yet gone out of town. Having therefore first examined him privately, and then confronted him with me and the young girl, his Majesty began to think

[2] Literally, a jest of nature; hence, a deformed person, or a freak.

that what we told him might possibly be true. He desired the Queen to order that a particular care should be taken of me, and was of opinion that Glumdalclitch should still continue in her office of tending me, because he observed we had a great affection for each other. A convenient apartment was provided for her at court; she had a sort of governess appointed to take care of her education, a maid to dress her, and two other servants for menial offices; but the care of me was wholly appropriated to herself. The Queen commanded her own cabinet-maker to contrive a box that might serve me for a bed-chamber, after the model that Glumdalclitch and I should agree upon. This man was a most ingenious artist, and according to my directions, in three weeks finished for me a wooden chamber of sixteen foot square, and twelve high, with sash-windows, a door, and two closets, like a London bed-chamber. The board that made the ceiling was to be lifted up and down by two hinges, to put in a bed ready furnished by her Majesty's upholsterer, which Glumdalclitch took out every day to air, made it with her own hands, and letting it down at night, locked up the roof over me. A nice workman, who was famous for little curiosities, undertook to make me two chairs, with backs and frames, of a substance not unlike ivory, and two tables, with a cabinet to put my things in. The room was quilted on all sides, as well as the floor and the ceiling, to prevent any accident from the carelessness of those who carried me, and to break the force of a jolt when I went in a coach. I desired a lock for my door, to prevent rats and mice from coming in: the smith, after several attempts, made the smallest that ever was seen among them, for I have known a larger at the gate of a gentleman's house in England. I made a shift to keep the key in a pocket of my own, fearing Glumdalclitch might lose it. The Queen likewise ordered the thinnest silks that could be gotten, to make me clothes,

not much thicker than an English blanket, very cumbersome till I was accustomed to them. They were after the fashion of the kingdom, partly resembling the Persian, and partly the Chinese, and are a very grave, decent habit.

The Queen became so fond of my company that she could not dine without me. I had a table placed upon the same at which her Majesty ate, just at her left elbow, and a chair to sit on. Glumdalclitch stood upon a stool on the floor, near my table, to assist and take care of me. I had an entire set of silver dishes and plates, and other necessaries, which, in proportion to those of the Queen, were not much bigger than what I have seen of the same kind in a London toy-shop, for the furniture of a baby-house: these my little nurse kept in her pocket in a silver box, and gave me at meals as I wanted them, always cleaning them herself. No person dined with the Queen but the two Princesses Royal, the elder sixteen years old, and the younger at that time thirteen and a month. Her Majesty used to put a bit of meat upon one of my dishes, out of which I carved for myself, and her diversion was to see me eat in miniature. For the Queen (who had indeed but a weak stomach) took up at one mouthful as much as a dozen English farmers could eat at a meal, which to me was for some time a very nauseous sight. She would craunch the wing of a lark, bones and all, between her teeth, although it were nine times as large as that of a full-grown turkey; and put a bit of bread into her mouth, as big as two twelve-penny loaves. She drank out of a golden cup, above a hogshead at a draught. Her knives were twice as long as a scythe set straight upon the handle. The spoons, forks, and other instruments were all in the same proportion. I remember when Glumdalclitch carried me out of curiosity to see some of the tables at court where ten or a dozen of these enormous knives and forks were lifted up together, I thought I had never till then beheld so terrible a sight.

It is the custom that every Wednesday (which, as I have before observed, was their Sabbath) the King and Queen, with the royal issue of both sexes, dine together in the apartment of his Majesty, to whom I was now become a great favourite; and at these times my little chair and table were placed at his left hand before one of the salt-cellars. This prince took a pleasure in conversing with me, inquiring into the manners, religion, laws, government, and learning of Europe; wherein I gave him the best account I was able. His apprehension was so clear, and his judgment so exact, that he made very wise reflections and observations upon all I said. But, I confess, that after I had been a little too copious in talking of my own beloved country, of our trade, and wars by sea and land, of our schisms in religion, and parties in the state, the prejudices of his education prevailed so far, that he could not forbear taking me up in his right hand, and stroking me gently with the other, after an hearty fit of laughing, asked me whether I were a Whig or a Tory. Then turning to his first minister, who waited behind him with a white staff, near as tall as the mainmast of the *Royal Sovereign*, he observed how contemptible a thing was human grandeur, which could be mimicked by such diminutive insects as I: and yet, said he, I dare engage, these creatures have their titles and distinctions of honour, they contrive little nests and burrows that they call houses and cities; they make a figure in dress and equipage; they love, they fight, they dispute, they cheat, they betray. And thus he continued on, while my colour came and went several times with indignation to hear our noble country, the mistress of arts and arms, the scourge of France, the arbitress of Europe, the seat of virtue, piety, honour and truth, the pride and envy of the world, so contemptuously treated.

But as I was not in a condition to resent injuries, so, upon mature thoughts, I began to doubt whether I were injured or no. For, after having been accustomed several months to the sight and converse of this people, and observed every object upon which I cast my eyes to be of proportionable magnitude, the horror I had first conceived from their bulk and aspect was so far worn off, that if I had then beheld a company of English lords and ladies in their finery and birth-day clothes, acting their several parts in the most courtly manner, of strutting, and bowing, and prating, to say the truth, I should have been strongly tempted to laugh as much at them as the King and his grandees did at me. Neither indeed could I forbear smiling at myself, when the Queen used to place me upon her hand towards a looking-glass, by which both our persons appeared before me in full view together; and there could be nothing more ridiculous than the comparison; so that I really began to imagine myself dwindled many degrees below my usual size.

Nothing angered and mortified me so much as the Queen's dwarf, who being of the lowest stature that was ever in that country (for I verily think he was not full thirty foot high) became insolent at seeing a creature so much beneath him, that he would always affect to swagger and look big as he passed by me in the Queen's antechamber, while I was standing on some table talking with the lords or ladies of the court, and he seldom failed of a smart word or two upon my littleness; against which I could only revenge myself by calling him brother, challenging him to wrestle, and such repartees as are usual in the mouths of court pages. One day at dinner this malicious little cub was so nettled with something I had said to him, that raising himself upon the frame of her Majesty's chair, he took me up by the middle as I was sitting down not thinking any harm, and let me drop into a large silver bowl of cream, and then ran away as fast as he could. I fell over head and ears, and if I had not been a good swimmer, it might have gone very hard with me; for Glumdalclitch in that instant happened to be at the other end of the room, and the Queen was in such a fright that she wanted presence of mind to assist me. But my little nurse ran to my relief, and took me out, after I had swallowed above a quart of cream. I was put to bed; however I received no other damage than the loss of a suit of clothes, which was utterly spoiled. The dwarf was soundly whipped, and as a farther punishment, forced to drink up the bowl of cream into which he had thrown me; neither was he ever restored to favour: for soon after the Queen bestowed him to a lady of high quality, so that I saw him no more, to my very great satisfaction; for I could not tell to what extremity such a malicious urchin might have carried his resentment.

He had before served me a scurvy trick, which set the Queen a laughing, although at the same time she were heartily vexed, and would have immediately cashiered him, if I had not been so generous as to intercede. Her Majesty had taken a marrow-bone upon her plate, and after knocking out the marrow, placed the bone again in the dish erect as it stood before; the dwarf watching his opportunity while Glumdalclitch was gone to the sideboard, mounted upon the stool she stood on to take care of me at meals, took me up in both hands, and squeezing my legs together, wedged them into the marrow-bone above my waist, where I stuck for some time, and made a very ridiculous figure. I believe it was near a minute before any one knew what was become of me, for I thought it below me to cry out. But, as princes seldom get their meat hot, my legs were not scalded, only my stockings and breeches in a sad condition. The dwarf at my entreaty had no other punishment than a sound whipping.

I was frequently rallied by the Queen upon account of my fearfulness, and she used to ask me whether the people of my country were as great cowards as myself. The occasion was this. The kingdom is much pestered with flies in summer; and these odious insects, each of them as big as a Dunstable lark, hardly gave me any rest while I sat at dinner, with their continual humming and buzzing about my ears. They would sometimes alight upon my victuals; and leave their loathsome excrement or spawn behind, which to me was very visible, though not to the natives of that country, whose large optics were not so acute as mine in viewing smaller objects. Sometimes they would fix upon my nose or forehead, where they stung me to the quick, smelling very offensively, and I could easily trace that viscous matter, which our naturalists tell us enables those creatures to walk with their feet upwards upon a ceiling. I had much ado to defend myself against these detestable animals, and could not forbear starting when they came on my face. It was the common practice of the dwarf to catch a number of these insects in his hand, as schoolboys do among us, and let them out suddenly under my nose, on purpose to frighten me and divert the Queen. My remedy was to cut them in pieces with my knife as they flew in the air, wherein my dexterity was much admired.

I remember one morning when Glumdalclitch had set me in my box upon a window, as she usually did in fair days to give me air (for I durst not venture to let the box be hung on a nail out of the window, as we do with cages in England) after I had lifted up one of my sashes and sat down at my table to eat a piece of sweet cake for my breakfast, above twenty wasps, allured by smell, came flying into the room, humming louder than the drones of as many bagpipes. Some of them seized my cake, and carried it piecemeal away, others flew about my head and face, confounding me with the noise, and putting me in the utmost terror of their stings. However I had the courage to rise and draw my hanger, and attack them in the air. I dispatched four of them, but the rest got away, and I presently shut my window. These creatures were as large as partridges: I took out their stings, found them an inch and a half long, and as sharp as needles. I carefully preserved them all, and having since shown them with some other curiosities in several parts of Europe, upon my return to England I gave three of them to Gresham College, and kept the fourth for myself.

CHAP. IV

The country described. A proposal for correcting modern maps. The King's palace, and some account of the metropolis. The author's way of travelling. The chief temple described.

I now intend to give the reader a short description of this country, as far as I travelled in it, which was not above two thousand miles round Lorbrulgrud the metropolis. For the Queen, whom I always attended, never went further when she accompanied the King in his progresses, and there stayed till his Majesty returned from viewing his frontiers. The whole extent of this prince's dominions reacheth about six thousand miles in length, and from three to five in breadth. From whence I cannot but conclude that our geographers of Europe are in a great error by supposing nothing but sea between Japan and California; for it was ever my opinion, that there must be a balance of earth to counterpoise the great continent of Tartary; and therefore they ought to correct their maps and charts, by joining this vast tract of land to the north-west parts of America, wherein I shall be ready to lend them my assistance.

The kingdom is a peninsula, terminated to the north-east by a ridge of mountains thirty miles high, which are altogether impassible by reason of the volcanoes upon the tops. Neither do the most learned know what sort of mortals inhabit beyond those mountains, or whether they be inhabited at all. On the three other sides it is bounded by the ocean. There is not one sea-port in the whole kingdom, and those parts of the coasts into which the rivers issue are so full of pointed rocks, and the sea generally so rough that there is no venturing with the smallest of their boats, so that these people are wholly excluded from any commerce with the rest of the world. But the large rivers are full of vessels, and abound with excellent fish, for they seldom get any from the sea, because the sea-fish are of the same size with those in Europe, and consequently not worth catching; whereby it is manifest, that nature, in the production of plants and animals of so extraordinary a bulk, is wholly confined to this continent, of which I leave the reasons to be determined by philosophers. However, now and then they take a whale that happens to be dashed against the rocks, which the common people feed on heartily. These whales I have known so large that a man could hardly carry one upon his shoulders; and sometimes for curiosity they are brought in hampers to Lorbrulgrud: I saw one of them in a dish at the King's table, which passed for a rarity, but I did not observe he was fond of it; for I think indeed the bigness disgusted him, although I have seen one somewhat larger in Greenland.

The country is well inhabited, for it contains fifty-one cities, near an hundred walled towns, and a great number of villages. To satisfy my curious reader, it may be sufficient to describe Lorbrulgrud. This city stands upon almost two equal parts on each side of the river that passes through. It contains above eighty thousand houses, and about six hundred thousand inhabitants. It is in length three *glonglungs* (which make about fifty-four English miles) and two and a half in breadth, as I measured it myself in the royal map made by the King's order, which was laid on the ground on purpose for me, and extended an hundred feet: I paced the diameter and circumference several times bare-foot, and computing by the scale, measured it pretty exactly.

The King's palace is no regular edifice, but an heap of buildings about seven miles round: the chief rooms are generally two hundred and forty foot high, and broad and long in proportion. A coach was allowed to Glumdalclitch and me, wherein her governess frequently took her out to see the town, or go among the shops; and I was always of the party, carried in my box; although the girl at my own desire would often take me out, and hold me in her hand that I might more conveniently view the houses and the people as we passed along the streets. I reckoned our coach to be about a square of Westminster Hall, but not altogether so high; however, I cannot be very exact. One day the governess ordered our coachman to stop at several shops, where the beggars, watching their opportunity, crowded to the sides of the coach, and gave me the most horrible spectacles that ever an English eye beheld. There was a woman with a cancer in her breast, swelled to a monstrous size, full of holes, in two or three of which I could have easily crept, and covered my whole body. There was a fellow with a wen in his neck larger than five wool-packs, and another with a couple of wooden legs, each about twenty foot high. But the most hateful sight of all was the lice crawling on their clothes. I could see distinctly the limbs of these vermin with my naked eye, much better than those of an European louse through a microscope, and their snouts with which they rooted like swine. They were the first I had ever beheld, and I should have been curious enough to dissect one of them, if I had proper instruments (which I unluckily left behind me in the ship) although indeed the sight was so nauseous, that it perfectly turned my stomach.

Besides the large box in which I was usually carried, the Queen ordered a smaller one to be made for me, of about twelve foot square, and ten high, for the convenience of travelling, because the other was somewhat too large for Glumdalclitch's lap, and cumbersome in the coach; it was made by the same artist, whom I directed in the whole contrivance. This travelling closet was an exact square with a window in the middle of three of the squares, and each window was latticed with iron wire on the outside, to prevent accidents in long journeys. On the fourth side, which had no window, two strong staples were fixed, through which the person that carried me, when I had a mind to be on horseback, put in a leathern belt, and buckled it about his waist. This was always the office of some grave trusty servant in whom I could confide, whether I attended the King and Queen in their progresses, or were disposed to see the gardens, or pay a visit to some great lady or minister of state in the court, when Glumdalclitch happened to be out of order: for I soon began to be known and esteemed among the greatest officers, I suppose more upon account of their Majesties' favour than any merit of my own. In journeys, when I was weary of the coach, a servant on horseback would buckle my box, and place it on a cushion before him; and there I had a full prospect of the country on three sides from my three windows. I had in this closet a field-bed and a hammock hung from the ceiling, two chairs and a table, neatly screwed to the floor to prevent being tossed about by the agitation of the horse or the coach. And having been long used to sea-voyages, those motions, although sometimes very violent, did not much discompose me.

Whenever I had a mind to see the town, it was always in my travelling-closet, which Glumdalclitch held in her lap in a kind of open sedan, after the fashion of the country, borne by four men, and attended by two others in the Queen's livery. The people who had often heard of me, were very curious to crowd about the sedan, and the girl was complaisant enough to make the bearers stop, and to take me in her hand that I might be more conveniently seen.

I was very desirous to see the chief temple, and particularly the tower belonging to it, which is reckoned the highest in the kingdom. Accordingly one day my nurse carried me thither, but I may truly say I came back disappointed; for the height is not above three thousand foot, reckoning from the ground to the highest pinnacle top; which allowing for the difference between the size of those people and us in Europe, is no great matter for admiration, nor at all equal in proportion (if I rightly remember) to Salisbury steeple. But, not to detract from a nation to which during my life I shall acknowledge myself extremely obliged, it must be allowed that whatever this famous tower wants in height is amply made up in beauty and strength. For the walls are near an hundred foot thick, built of hewn stone, whereof each is about forty foot square, and adorned on all sides with statues of gods and emperors cut in marble larger than the life, placed in their several niches. I measured a little finger which had fallen down from one of these statues, and lay unperceived among some rubbish, and found it exactly four foot and an inch in length. Glumdalclitch wrapped it up in a handkerchief, and carried it home in her pocket to keep among other trinkets, of which the girl was very fond, as children at her age usually are.

The King's kitchen is indeed a noble building, vaulted at top, and about six hundred foot high. The great oven is not so wide by ten paces as the cupola at St. Paul's: for I measured the latter on purpose after my return. But if I should describe the kitchen-grate, the prodigious pots and kettles, the joints of meat turning on the spits, with many other particulars, perhaps I should be hardly believed;

at least a severe critic would be apt to think I enlarged a little, as travellers are often suspected to do. To avoid which censure, I fear I have run too much into the other extreme; and that if this treatise should happen to be translated into the language of Brobdingnag (which is the general name of that kingdom) and transmitted thither, the King and his people would have reason to complain that I had done them an injury by a false and diminutive representation.

His Majesty seldom keeps above six hundred horses in his stables: they are generally from fifty-four to sixty foot high. But when he goes abroad on solemn days, he is attended for state by a militia guard of five hundred horse, which indeed I thought was the most splendid sight that could be ever beheld, till I saw part of his army in battalia, whereof I shall find another occasion to speak.

CHAP. V

Several adventures that happened to the author. The execution of a criminal. The author shows his skill in navigation.

I should have lived happy enough in that country, if my littleness had not exposed me to several ridiculous and troublesome accidents, some of which I shall venture to relate. Glumdalclitch often carried me into the gardens of the court in my smaller box, and would sometimes take me out of it and hold me in her hand, or set me down to walk. I remember, before the dwarf left the Queen, he followed us one day into those gardens, and my nurse having set me down, he and I being close together, near some dwarf apple-trees, I must needs show my wit by a silly allusion between him and the trees, which happens to hold in their language as it doth in ours. Whereupon, the malicious rogue watching his opportunity when I was walking under one of them, shook it directly over my head, by which a dozen apples, each of them near as large as a Bristol barrel, came tumbling about my ears; one of them hit me on the back as I chanced to stoop, and knocked me down flat on my face, but I received no other hurt, and the dwarf was pardoned at my desire, because I had given the provocation.

Another day Glumdalclitch left me on a smooth grass-plot to divert myself while she walked at some distance with her governess. In the meantime there suddenly fell such a violent shower of hail that I was immediately by the force of it struck to the ground: and when I was down, the hailstones gave me such cruel bangs all over the body, as if I had been pelted with tennis-balls; however I made a shift to creep on all four, and shelter myself by lying on my face on the lee-side of a border of lemon thyme, but so bruised from head to foot that I could not go abroad in ten days. Neither is this at all to be wondered at, because nature in that country observing the same proportion through all her operations, a hailstone is near eighteen hundred times as large as one in Europe, which I can assert upon experience, having been so curious to weigh and measure them.

But a more dangerous accident happened to me in the same garden, when my little nurse believing she had put me in a secure place, which I often entreated her to do that I might enjoy my own thoughts, and having left my box at home to avoid the trouble of carrying it, went to another part of the garden with her governess and some ladies of her acquaintance. While she was absent and out of hearing, a small white spaniel belonging to one of the chief gardeners, having got by accident into the garden, happened to range near the place where I lay. The dog following the scent, came directly up, and taking me in his mouth, ran straight to his master, wagging his tail, and set me gently on the ground. By good fortune he had been so well taught that I was carried between his teeth without the least hurt, or even tearing my clothes. But the poor gardener, who knew me well and had a great kindness for me, was in a terrible fright. He gently took me up in both his hands, and asked me how I did; but I was so amazed and out of breath that I could not speak a word. In a few minutes I came to myself, and he carried me safe to my little nurse, who by this time had returned to the place where she left me, and was in cruel agonies when I did not appear, nor answer when she called: she severely reprimanded the gardener on account of his dog. But the thing was hushed up and never known at court; for the girl was afraid of the Queen's anger, and truly as to myself, I thought it would not be for my reputation that such a story should go about.

This accident absolutely determined Glumdalclitch never to trust me abroad for the future out of her sight. I had been long afraid of this resolution, and therefore concealed from her some little unlucky adventures that happened in those times when I was left by myself. Once a kite hovering over the garden made a swoop at me, and if I had not resolutely drawn my hanger, and run under a thick espalier, he would have certainly carried me away in his talons. Another time walking to the top of a fresh mole-hill, I fell to my neck in the hole through which that animal had cast up the earth, and coined some lie, not worth remembering, to excuse myself for spoiling my clothes. I likewise broke my right shin against the shell of a snail, which I happened to stumble over, as I was walking alone, and thinking on poor England.

I cannot tell whether I were more pleased or mortified, to observe in those solitary walks that the smaller birds did not appear to be at all afraid of me, but would hop about within a yard distance, looking for worms and other food with as much indifference and security as if no creature at all were near them. I remembered a thrush had the confidence to snatch out of my hand with his bill a piece of cake that Glumdalclitch had just given me for my breakfast. When I attempted to catch any of these birds, they would boldly turn against me, endeavouring to pick my fingers, which I durst not venture within their reach; and then they would turn back unconcerned to hunt for worms or snails, as they did before. But one day I took a thick cudgel, and threw it with all my strength so luckily at a linnet that I knocked him down, and seizing him by the neck with both my hands, ran with him in triumph to my nurse. However, the bird, who had only been stunned, recovering himself, gave me so many boxes with his wings on both sides of my head and body, though I held him at arm's length, and was out of the reach of his claws, that I was twenty times thinking to let him go. But I was soon relieved by one of our servants, who wrung off the bird's neck, and I had him next day for dinner, by the Queen's command. This linnet, as near as I can remember, seemed to be somewhat larger than an English swan.

The Maids of Honour often invited Glumdalclitch to their apartments, and desired she would bring me along with her, on purpose to have the pleasure of seeing and touching me. They would often strip me naked from top to toes and lay me at full length in their bosoms; wherewith I was much disgusted; because, to say the truth, a very offensive smell came from their skins; which I do not mention or intend to the disadvantage of those excellent ladies, for whom I have all manner of respect; but I conceive that my sense was more acute in proportion to my littleness, and that those illustrious persons were no more disagreeable to their lovers, or to each other, than people of the same quality are with us in England. And, after all, I found their natural smell was much more supportable than when they used perfumes, under which I immediately swooned away. I cannot forget that an intimate friend of mine in Lilliput took the freedom in a warm day, when I had used a good deal of exercise, to complain of a strong smell about me, although I am as little faulty that way as most of my sex: but I suppose his faculty of smelling was as nice with regard to me, as mine was to that of this people. Upon this point, I cannot forbear doing justice to the Queen my mistress, and Glumdalclitch my nurse, whose persons were as sweet as those of any lady in England.

That which gave me most uneasiness among these Maids of Honour, when my nurse carried me to visit them, was to see them use me without any manner of ceremony, like a creature who had no sort of consequence. For they would strip themselves to the skin, and put on their smocks in my presence, while I was placed on their toilet directly before their naked bodies, which, I am sure, to me was very far from being a tempting sight, or from giving me any other emotions than those of horror and disgust. Their skins appeared so coarse and uneven, so variously coloured, when I saw them near, with a mole here and there as broad as a trencher, and hairs hanging from it thicker than pack-threads, to say nothing further concerning the rest of their persons. Neither did they at all scruple, while I was by, to discharge what they had drunk, to the quantity of at least two hogsheads, in a vessel that held above three tuns. The handsomest among these Maids of Honour, a pleasant frolicsome girl of sixteen, would sometimes set me astride upon one of her nipples, with many other tricks, wherein the reader will excuse me for not being over particular. But I was so much displeased, that I entreated Glumdalclitch to contrive some excuse for not seeing that young lady any more.

One day a young gentleman, who was nephew to my nurse's governess, came and pressed them both to see an execution. It was of a man who had murdered one of that gentleman's intimate acquaintance. Glumdalclitch was prevailed on to be of the company, very much against her inclination, for she was naturally tender-hearted: and as for myself, although I abhorred such kind of spectacles, yet my curiosity tempted me to see something that I thought must be extraordinary. The malefactor was fixed in a chair upon a scaffold erected for the purpose, and his head cut off at a blow with a sword of about forty foot long. The veins and arteries spouted up such a prodigious quantity of blood, and so high in the air, that the great *jet d'eau* at Versailles was not equal for the time it lasted; and the head, when it fell on the scaffold floor, gave such a bounce as made me start, although I were at least half an English mile distant.

The Queen, who often used to hear me talk of my sea-voyages, and took all occasions to divert me when I was melancholy, asked me whether I understood how to handle a sail or an oar, and whether a little exercise of rowing might not be convenient for my health. I answered that I understood both very well. For although my proper employment had been to be surgeon or doctor to the ship, yet often, upon a pinch, I was forced to work like a common mariner. But I could not see how this could be done in their country, where the smallest wherry was equal to a first-rate man of war among us, and such a boat as I could manage would never live in any of their rivers. Her Majesty said, if I would contrive a boat, her own joiner should make it, and she would provide a place for me to sail in. The fellow was an ingenious workman, and by my instructions in ten days finished a pleasure-boat with all its tackling, able conveniently to hold eight Europeans. When it was finished, the Queen was so delighted, that she ran with it in her lap to the King, who ordered it to be put in a cistern full of water, with me in it, by way of trial; where I could not manage my two sculls, or little oars, for want of room. But the Queen had before contrived another project. She ordered the joiner to make a wooden trough of three hundred foot long, fifty broad, and eight deep; which being well pitched to prevent leaking, was placed on the floor along the wall, in an outer room of the palace. It had a cock near the bottom to let out the water when it began to grow stale, and two servants could easily fill it in half an hour. Here I often used to row for my own diversion, as well as that of the Queen and her ladies, who thought themselves well entertained with my skill and agility. Sometimes I would put up my sail, and then my business was only to steer, while the ladies gave me a gale with their fans; and when they were weary, some of the pages would blow my sail forward with their breath, while I showed my art by steering starboard or larboard as I pleased. When I had done, Glumdalclitch always carried my boat into her closet, and hung it on a nail to dry.

In this exercise I once met an accident which had like to have cost me my life. For one of the pages having put my boat into the trough, the governess who attended Glumdalclitch very officiously lifted me up to place me in the boat, but I happened to slip through her fingers, and should have infallibly fallen down forty feet upon the floor, if by the luckiest chance in the world, I had not been stopped by a corking-pin that stuck in the good gentlewoman's stomacher; the head of the pin passed between my shirt and the waistband of my breeches, and thus I was held by the middle in the air until Glumdalclitch ran to my relief.

Another time, one of the servants, whose office it was to fill my trough every third day with fresh water, was so careless to let a huge frog (not perceiving it) slip out of his pail. The frog lay concealed till I was put into my boat, but then seeing a resting-place, climbed up, and made it lean so much on one side that I was forced to balance it with all my weight on the other, to prevent overturning.

When the frog was got in, it hopped at once half the length of the boat, and then over my head, backwards and forwards, daubing my face and clothes with its odious slime. The largeness of its features made it appear the most deformed animal that can be conceived. However, I desired Glumdalclitch to let me deal with it alone. I banged it a good while with one of my sculls, and at last forced it to leap out of the boat.

But the greatest danger I ever underwent in that kingdom was from a monkey, who belonged to one of the clerks of the kitchen. Glumdalclitch had locked me up in her closet, while she went somewhere upon business or a visit. The weather being very warm, the closet window was left open, as well as the windows in the door of my bigger box, in which I usually lived, because of its largeness and conveniency. As I sat quietly meditating at my table, I heard something bounce in at the closet window, and skip about from one side to the other; whereat, although I was much alarmed, yet I ventured to look out, but stirred not from my seat; and then I saw this frolicsome animal, frisking and leaping up and down, till at last he came to my box, which he seemed to view with great pleasure and curiosity, peeping in at the door and every window. I retreated to the farther corner of my room, or box, but the monkey looking in at every side, put me into such a fright, that I wanted presence of mind to conceal myself under the bed, as I might easily have done. After some time spent in peeping, grinning, and chattering, he at last espied me, and reaching one of his paws in at the door, as a cat does when she plays with a mouse, although I often shifted place to avoid him, he at length seized the lappet of my coat (which being made of that country cloth, was very thick and strong) and dragged me out. He took me up in his right fore-foot, and held me as a nurse does a child she is going to suckle, just as I have seen the same sort of creature do with a kitten in Europe: and when I offered to struggle, he squeezed me so hard, that I thought it more prudent to submit. I have good reason to believe that he took me for a young one of his own species, by his often stroking my face very gently with his other paw. In these diversions he was interrupted by a noise at the closet door, as if somebody were opening it; whereupon he suddenly leaped up to the window at which he had come in, and thence upon the leads and gutters, walking upon three legs, and holding me in the fourth, till he clambered up to a roof that was next to ours. I heard Glumdalclitch give a shriek at the moment he was carrying me out. The poor girl was almost distracted: that quarter of the palace was all in an uproar; the servants ran for ladders; the monkey was seen by hundreds in the court, sitting upon the ridge of a building, holding me like a baby in one of his fore-paws, and feeding me with the other, by cramming into my mouth some victuals he had squeezed out of the bag on one side of his chaps, and patting me when I would not eat; whereat many of the rabble below could not forbear laughing; neither do I think they justly ought to be blamed, for without question the sight was ridiculous enough to everybody but myself. Some of the people threw up stones, hoping to drive the monkey down; but this was strictly forbidden, or else very probably my brains had been dashed out.

The ladders were now applied, and mounted by several men, which the monkey observing, and finding himself almost encompassed, not being able to make speed enough with his three legs, let me drop on a ridge tile, and made his escape. Here I sat for some time three hundred yards from the ground, expecting every moment to be blown down by the wind, or to fall by my own giddiness, and come tumbling over and over from the ridge to the eaves; but an honest lad, one of my nurses's footmen, climbed up, and putting me in his breeches pocket, brought me down safe.

I was almost choked with the filthy stuff the monkey had crammed down my throat: but my dear little nurse picked it out of my mouth with a small needle, and then I fell a vomiting, which gave me great relief. Yet I was so weak and bruised in the sides with the squeezes given me by this odious animal that I was forced to keep my bed a fortnight. The King, Queen, and all the court, sent every day to enquire after my health, and her Majesty made me several visits during my sickness. The monkey was killed, and an order made that no such animal should be kept about the palace.

When I attended the King after my recovery, to return him thanks for his favours, he was pleased to rally me a good deal upon this adventure. He asked me what my thoughts and speculations were while I lay in the monkey's paw, how I liked the victuals he gave me, his manner of feeding, and whether the fresh air on the roof had sharpened my stomach. He desired to know what I would have done upon such an occasion in my own country. I told his Majesty that in Europe we had no monkeys, except such as were brought for curiosities from other places, and so small that I could deal with a dozen of them together, if they presumed to attack me. And as for that monstrous animal with whom I so lately engaged (it was indeed as large as an elephant), if my fears had suffered me to think so far as to make use of my hanger (looking fiercely and clapping my hand upon the hilt as I spoke) when he poked his paw into my chamber, perhaps I should have given him such a wound as would have made him glad to withdraw it with more haste than he put it in. This I delivered in a firm tone, like a person who was jealous lest his courage should be called in question. However, my speech produced nothing else besides a loud laughter, which all the respect due to his Majesty from those about him could not make them

contain. This made me reflect how vain an attempt it is for a man to endeavour doing himself honour among those who are out of all degree of equality or comparison with him. And yet I have seen the moral of my own behavior very frequent in England since my return, where a little contemptible varlet, without the least title to birth, person, wit, or common sense, shall presume to look with importance, and put himself upon a foot with the greatest persons of the kingdom.

I was every day furnishing the court with some ridiculous story; and Glumdalclitch, although she loved me to excess, yet was arch enough to inform the Queen whenever I committed any folly that she thought would be diverting to her Majesty. The girl, who had been out of order, was carried by her governess to take the air about an hour's distance, or thirty miles from town. They alighted out of the coach near a small foot-path in a field, and Glumdalclitch setting down my travelling box, I went out of it to walk. There was a cow-dung in the patch, and I must needs try my activity by attempting to leap over it. I took a run, but unfortunately jumped short, and found myself just in the middle up to my knees. I waded through with some difficulty, and one of the footmen wiped me as clean as he could with his handkerchief; for I was filthily bemired, and my nurse confined me to my box till we returned home; where the Queen was soon informed of what had passed, and the footmen spread it about the court, so that all the mirth, for some days, was at my expense.

CHAP. VI

Several contrivances of the author to please the King and Queen. He shows his skill in music. The King inquires into the state of Europe, which the author relates to him. The King's observations thereon.

I used to attend the King's levee once or twice a week, and had often seen him under the barber's hand, which indeed was at first very terrible to behold; for the razor was almost twice as long as an ordinary scythe. His Majesty, according to the custom of the country, was only shaved twice a week. I once prevailed on the barber to give me some of the suds or lather, out of which I picked forty or fifty of the strongest stumps of hair. I then took a piece of fine wood, and cut it like the back of a comb, making several holes in it at equal distance with as small a needle as I could get from Glumdalclitch. I fixed in the stumps so artificially, scraping and sloping them with my knife toward the points, that I made a very tolerable comb; which was a seasonable supply, my own being so much broken in the teeth that it was almost useless: neither did I know any artist in that country so nice and exact, as would undertake to make me another.

And this puts me in mind of an amusement wherein I spent many of my leisure hours. I desired the Queen's woman to save for me the combings of her Majesty's hair, whereof in time I got a good quantity, and consulting with my friend the cabinet-maker, who had received general orders to do little jobs for me, I directed him to make two chair-frames, no larger than those I had in my box, and then to bore little holes with a fine awl round those parts where I designed the backs and seats; through these holes I wove the strongest hairs I could pick out, just after the manner of cane-chairs in England. When they were finished, I made a present of them to her Majesty, who kept them in her cabinet, and used to show them for curiosities, as indeed they were the wonder of every one that beheld them. The Queen would have made me sit upon one of these chairs, but I absolutely refused to obey her, protesting I would rather die a thousand deaths than place a dishonorable part of my body on those precious hairs that once adorned her Majesty's head. Of these hairs (as I had always a mechanical genius) I likewise made a neat little purse above five foot long, with her Majesty's name deciphered in gold letters, which I gave to Glumdalclitch, by the Queen's consent. To say the truth, it was more for show than use, being not of strength to bear the weight of the larger coins, and therefore she kept nothing in it but some little toys that girls are fond of.

The King, who delighted in music,[3] had frequent concerts at court, to which I was sometimes carried, and set in my box on a table to hear them; but the noise was so great, that I could hardly distinguish the tunes, I am confident that all the drums and trumpets of a royal army, beating and sounding together just at your ears, could not equal it. My practice was to have my box removed from the places where the performers sat, as far as I could, then to shut the doors and windows of it, and draw the window curtains; after which I found their music not disagreeable.

I had learned in my youth to play a little upon the spinet. Glumdalclitch kept one in her chamber, and a master attended twice a week to teach her: I call it a spinet, because it somewhat resembled that instrument, and was played upon in the same manner. A fancy came into my head that I would entertain the King and Queen with an English tune upon this instrument. But this appeared extremely difficult; for the spinet was nearly sixty foot long, each key being almost a foot wide, so that, with my arms extended, I could not reach to above five keys, and to press them down required a good smart stroke with my fist, which would be too great a labour, and to no purpose. The method I contrived was this. I prepared two round sticks about the bigness of common cudgels; they were thicker at one end than the other, and I covered the thicker ends with a piece of a mouse's skin, that by rapping on them I might neither damage the tops of the keys, nor interrupt the sound. Before the spinet a

[3] May have reference to the royal enthusiasm at that time for the operas of Handel.

bench was placed, about four foot below the keys, and I was put upon the bench. I ran sideling upon it that way and this, as fast as I could, banging the proper keys with my two sticks, and made a shift to play a jig, to the great satisfaction of both their Majesties: but it was the most violent exercise I ever underwent, and yet I could not strike above sixteen keys, nor, consequently, play the bass and treble together, as other artists do; which was a great disadvantage to my performance.

The King, who, as I before observed, was a prince of excellent understanding, would frequently order that I should be brought in my box, and set upon the table in his closet. He would then command me to bring one of my chairs out of the box, and sit down within three yards distance upon the top of the cabinet, which brought me almost to a level with his face. In this manner I had several conversations with him. I one day took the freedom to tell his Majesty, that the contempt he discovered towards Europe, and the rest of the world, did not seem answerable to those excellent qualities of the mind he was master of. That reason did not extend itself with the bulk of the body: on the contrary, we observed in our country that the tallest persons were usually least provided with it. That among other animals, bees and ants had the reputation of more industry, art and sagacity, than many of the larger kinds. And that, as inconsiderable as he took me to be, I hoped I might live to do his Majesty some signal service. The King heard me with attention, and began to conceive a much better opinion of me than he had ever before. He desired I would give him as exact an account of the government of England as I possibly could; because, as fond as princes commonly are of their own customs (for so he conjectured of other monarchs, by my former discourses), he should be glad to hear of anything that might deserve immitation.

Imagine with thyself, courteous reader, how often I then wished for the tongue of Demosthenes or Cicero, that might have enabled me to celebrate the praise of my own dear native country in a style equal to its merits and felicity.

I began my discourse by informing his Majesty that our dominions consisted of two islands, which composed three mighty kingdoms under one sovereign, beside our plantations in America. I dwelt long upon the fertility of our soil, and the temperature of our climate. I then spoke at large upon the constitution of an English Parliament, partly made up of an illustrious body called the House of Peers, persons of the noblest blood, and of the most ancient and ample patrimonies. I described that extraordinary care always taken of their education in arts and arms, to qualify them for being counsellors born to the king and kingdom, to have a share in the legislature, to be members of the highest Court of Judicature, from whence there could be no appeal, and to be champions always ready for the defence of their prince and country, by their valour, conduct, and fidelity. That these were the ornament and bulwark of the kingdom, worthy followers of their most renowned ancestors, whose honour had been the reward of their virtue, from which their posterity were never once known to degenerate. To these were joined several holy persons, as part of that assembly, under the title of Bishops, whose peculiar business it is to take care of religion, and of those who instruct the people therein. These were searched and sought out through the whole nation, by the prince and his wisest counsellors, among such of the priesthood as were most deservedly distinguished by the sanctity of their lives, and the depth of their erudition; who were indeed the spiritual fathers of the clergy and the people.

That the other part of the Parliament consisted of an assembly called the House of Commons, who were all principal gentlemen, *freely* picked and culled out by the people themselves, for their great abilities and love of their country, to represent the wisdom of the whole nation. And these two bodies make up the most august assembly in Europe, to whom, in conjunction with the prince, the whole legislature is committed.

I then descended to the Courts of Justice, over which the Judges, those venerable sages and interpreters of the law, presided, for determining the disputed rights and properties of men, as well as for the punishment of vice, and protection of innocence. I mentioned the prudent management of our treasury; the valour and achievements of our forces by sea and land. I computed the number of our people, by reckoning how many millions there might be of each religious sect, or political party among us. I did not omit even our sports and pastimes, or any other particular which I thought might redound to the honour of my country. And I finished all with a brief historical account of affairs and events in England for about an hundred years past.

This conversation was not ended under five audiences, each of several hours, and the King heard the whole with great attention, frequently taking notes of what I spoke, as well as memorandums of all questions he intended to ask me.

When I had put an end to these long discourses, his Majesty in a sixth audience, consulting his notes, proposed many doubts, queries, and objections, upon every article. He asked what methods were used to cultivate the minds and bodies of our young nobility, and in what kind of business they commonly spent the first and teachable part of their lives. What course was taken to supply that assembly when any noble family became extinct. What qualifications were necessary in those who were to be created new lords. Whether the humour of the prince, a sum of money to a court lady, or a prime minister, or a design of strengthening a party opposite to the public interest, ever happened to be motives in those advancements. What share of knowledge these lords had in the laws of their country, and how they came by it, so as to enable them to decide the properties of their fellow-subjects in the last resort. Whether they were always so free from avarice, partialities, or want, that a bribe, or some other sinister view, could have no place among them. Whether those holy lords I spoke of were always promoted to that rank upon account of their knowledge in religious matters, and the sanctity of their lives, had never been compliers with the times while they were common priests, or slavish prostitute chaplains to some nobleman, whose opinions they continued servilely to follow after they were admitted into that assembly.

He then desired to know what arts were practised in electing those whom I called commoners: whether a stranger with a strong purse might not influence the vulgar voters to choose him before their own landlord, or the most considerable gentleman in the neighbourhood. How it came to pass, that people were so violently bent upon getting into this assembly, which I allowed to be a great trouble and expense, often to the ruin of their families, without any salary or pension: because this appeared such an exalted strain of virtue and public spirit, that his Majesty seemed to doubt it might possibly not be always sincere: and he desired to know whether such zealous gentlemen could have any views of refunding themselves for the charges and trouble they were at, by sacrificing the public good to the designs of a weak and vicious prince in conjunction with a corrupted ministry. He multiplied his questions, and sifted me thoroughly upon every part of this head, proposing numberless enquiries and objections, which I think it not prudent or convenient to repeat.

Upon what I said in relation to our

Courts of Justice, his Majesty desired to be satisfied in several points: and this I was the better able to do, having been formerly almost ruined by a long suit in chancery, which was decreed for me with costs. He asked, what time was usually spent in determining between right and wrong, and what degree of expense. Whether advocates and orators had liberty to plead in causes manifestly known to be unjust, vexatious, or oppressive. Whether party in religion or politics were observed to be of any weight in the scale of justice. Whether those pleading orators were persons educated in the general knowledge of equity, or only in provincial, national, and other local customs. Whether they or their judges had any part in penning those laws which they assumed the liberty of interpreting and glossing upon at their pleasure. Whether they had ever at different times pleaded for and against the same cause, and cited precedents to prove contrary opinions. Whether they were a rich or a poor corporation. Whether they received any pecuniary reward for pleading or delivering their opinions. And particularly whether they were ever admitted as members in the lower senate.

He fell next upon the management of our treasury;[4] and said he thought my memory had failed me, because I computed our taxes at about five or six millions a year, and when I came to mention the issues, he found they sometimes amounted to more than double; for the notes he had taken were very particular in this point, because he hoped, as he told me, that the knowledge of our conduct might be useful to him, and he could not be deceived in his calculations. But, if what I told him were true, he was still at a loss how a kingdom could run out of its estate like a private person.

He asked me, who were our creditors; and where we should find money to pay them. He wondered to hear me talk of such chargeable and extensive wars; that certainly we must be a quarrelsome people, or live among very bad neighbours, and that our generals must needs be richer than our kings. He asked what business we had out of our own islands, unless upon the score of trade or treaty, or to defend the coasts with our fleet. Above all, he was amazed to hear me talk of a mercenary standing army in the midst of peace, and among a free people. He said, if we were governed by our own consent in the persons of our representatives, he could not imagine of whom we were afraid, or against whom we were to fight; and would hear my opinion, whether a private man's house might not better be defended by himself, his children, and family, than by half a dozen rascals picked up at a venture in the streets, for small wages, who might get an hundred times more by cutting their throats.

He laughed at my odd kind of arithmetic (as he was pleased to call it) in reckoning the numbers of our people by a computation drawn from the several sects among us in religion and politics. He said, he knew no reason why those who entertain opinions prejudicial to the public, should be obliged to change, or should not be obliged to conceal them. And as it was tyranny in any government to require the first, so it was weakness not to enforce the second: for a man may be allowed to keep poisons in his closet, but not to vend them about for cordials.

He observed that among the diversions of our nobility and gentry I had mentioned gaming. He desired to know at what age this entertainment was usually taken up, and when it was laid down; how much of their time it employed; whether it ever went so high as to affect their fortunes; whether mean vicious people, by their dexterity in that art, might not arrive

---

[4] In this paragraph Swift deals with two matters on which the Tory party took issue with the Whigs, the national debt and the mercenary army.

at great riches, and sometimes keep our very nobles in dependence, as well as habituate them to vile companions, wholly take them from the improvement of their minds, and force them, by the losses they have received, to learn and practise that infamous dexterity upon others.

He was perfectly astonished with the historical account I gave him of our affairs during the last century, protesting it was only an heap of conspiracies, rebellions, murders, massacres, revolutions, banishments, the very worst effects that avarice, faction, hypocrisy, perfidiousness, cruelty, rage, madness, hatred, envy, lust, malice, or ambition could produce.

His Majesty in another audience was at the pains to recapitulate the sum of all I had spoken, compared the questions he made with the answers I had given, then taking me into his hands, and stroking me gently, delivered himself in these words, which I shall never forget nor the manner he spoke them in: My little friend Grildrig, you have made a most admirable panegyric upon your country; you have clearly proved that ignorance, idleness, and vice, may be sometimes the only ingredients for qualifying a legislator; that laws are best explained, interpreted, and applied by those whose interest and abilities lie in perverting, confounding, and eluding them. I observe among you some lines of an institution, which in its original might have been tolerable, but these half erased, and the rest wholly blurred and blotted by corruptions. It doth not appear from all you have said, how any one virtue is required towards the procurement of any one station among you; much less that men are ennobled on account of their virtue, that priests are advanced for their piety or learning, soldiers for their conduct or valour, judges for their integrity, senators for the love of their country, or counsellors for their wisdom. As for yourself (continued the King) who have spent the greatest part of your life in travelling,

I am well disposed to hope you may hitherto have escaped many vices of your country. But by what I have gathered from your own relation, and the answers I have with much pains wringed and extorted from you, I cannot but conclude the bulk of your natives to be the most pernicious race of little odious vermin that nature ever suffered to crawl upon the surface of the earth.

CHAP. VII

The author's love of his country. He makes a proposal of much advantage to the King, which is rejected. The King's great ignorance in politics. The learning of that country very imperfect and confined. Their laws, and military affairs, and parties in the State.

Nothing but an extreme love of truth could have hindered me from concealing this part of my story. It was in vain to discover my resentments, which were always turned into ridicule; and I was forced to rest with patience while my noble and most beloved country was so injuriously treated. I am heartily sorry as any of my readers can possibly be that such an occasion was given: but this prince happened to be so curious and inquisitive upon every particular, that it could not consist either with gratitude or good manners to refuse giving him what satisfaction I was able. Yet thus much I may be allowed to say in my own vindication, that I artfully eluded many of his questions, and gave to every point a more favourable turn by many degrees than the strictness of truth would allow. For I have always borne that laudable partiality to my own country, which Dionysius Halicarnassensis [5] with so much justice recommends to an historian. I would hide the frailties and deformities of my political mother, and place her virtues and beauties in the most advantageous light. This was my sincere endeavour in those many discourses I had with that monarch, although it unfortunately failed of success.

[5] His *Archaeologia* (*c.* 8 B.C.) gives the Greeks an idealized view of the Romans.

But great allowances should be given to a King who lives wholly secluded from the rest of the world, and must therefore be altogether unacquainted with the manners and customs that most prevail in other nations; the want of which knowledge will ever produce many prejudices, and a certain narrowness of thinking, from which we and the politer countries of Europe are wholly exempted. And it would be hard indeed, if so remote a prince's notions of virtue and vice were to be offered as a standard for all mankind.

To confirm what I have now said, and further, to show the miserable effects of a confined education, I shall here insert a passage which will hardly obtain belief. In hopes to ingratiate myself farther into his Majesty's favour, I told him of an invention discovered between three and four hundred years ago, to make a certain powder, into an heap of which the smallest spark of fire falling, would kindle the whole in a moment, although it were as big as a mountain, and make it all fly up in the air together, with a noise and agitation greater than thunder. That a proper quantity of this powder rammed into an hollow tube of brass or iron, according to its bigness, would drive a ball of iron or lead with such violence and speed, as nothing was able to sustain its force. That the largest balls thus discharged, would not only destroy whole ranks of an army at once, but batter the strongest walls to the ground, sink down ships, with a thousand men in each, to the bottom of the sea; and, when linked together by a chain, would cut through masts and rigging, divide hundreds of bodies in the middle, and lay all waste before them. That we often put this powder into large hollow balls of iron, and discharged them by an engine into some city we were besieging, which would rip up the pavements, tear the houses to pieces, burst and throw splinters on every side, dashing out the brains of all who came near. That

I knew the ingredients very well, which were cheap and common; I understood the manner of compounding them, and could direct his workmen how to make those tubes of a size proportionable to all other things in his Majesty's kingdom, and the largest need not be above an hundred foot long; twenty or thirty of which tubes charged with the proper quantity of powder and balls would batter down the walls of the strongest town in his dominions in a few hours, or destroy the whole metropolis, if ever it should pretend to dispute his absolute commands. This I humbly offered to his Majesty, as a small tribute of acknowledgment in return of so many marks that I had received of his royal favour and protection.

The King was struck with horror at the description I had given of those terrible engines, and the proposal I had made. He was amazed how so impotent and grovelling an insect as I (these were his expressions) could entertain such inhuman ideas, and in so familiar a manner as to appear wholly unmoved at all the scenes of blood and desolation which I had painted as the common effects of those destructive machines, whereof he said some evil genius, enemy to mankind, must have been the first contriver. As for himself, he protested that although few things delighted him so much as new discoveries in art or in nature, yet he would rather lose half his kingdom than be privy to such a secret, which he commanded me, as I valued my life, never to mention any more.

A strange effect of *narrow principles* and *short views!* that a prince possessed of every quality which procures veneration, love, and esteem; of strong parts, great wisdom, and profound learning, endued with admirable talents for government, and almost adored by his subjects, should from a *nice unnecessary scruple,* whereof in Europe we can have no conception, let slip an opportunity put into his hands that would have made him absolute master of the lives, the liberties, and the fortunes of his people. Neither do I say this with the least intention to detract from the many virtues of that excellent King, whose character I am sensible will on this account be very much lessened in the opinion of an English reader: but I take this defect among them to have risen from their ignorance, they not having hitherto reduced politics into a science, as the more acute wits of Europe have done. For I remember very well, in a discourse one day with the King, when I happened to say there were several thousand books among us written upon the art of government, it gave him (directly contrary to my intention) a very mean opinion of our understandings. He professed both to abominate and despise all mystery, refinement, and intrigue, either in a prince or a minister. He could not tell what I meant by secrets of state, where an enemy or some rival nation were not in the case. He confined the knowledge of governing within very narrow bounds; to common sense and reason, to justice and lenity, to the speedy determination of civil and criminal causes; with some other obvious topics, which are not worth considering. And he gave it for his opinion, that whoever could make two ears of corn or two blades of grass to grow upon a spot of ground where only one grew before, would deserve better of mankind, and do more essential service to his country than the whole race of politicians put together.

The learning of this people is very defective, consisting only in morality, history, poetry, and mathematics, wherein they must be allowed to excel. But the last of these is wholly applied to what may be useful in life, to the improvement of agriculture, and all mechanical arts; so that among us it would be little esteemed. And as to ideas, entities, abstractions, and transcendentals, I could never drive the least conception into their heads.

No law of that country must exceed in words the number of letters in their alphabet, which consists only in two and twenty. But indeed few of them extended even to that length. They are expressed in the most plain and simple terms, wherein those people are not mercurial enough to discover above one interpretation; and to write a comment upon any law is a capital crime. As to the decision of civil causes, or proceedings against criminals, their precedents are so few that they have little reason to boast of any extraordinary skill in either.

They have had the art of printing, as well as the Chinese, time out of mind. But their libraries are not very large; for that of the King's, which is reckoned the biggest, doth not amount to above a thousand volumes, placed in a gallery of twelve hundred foot long, from whence I had liberty to borrow what books I pleased. The Queen's joiner had contrived in one of Glumdalclitch's rooms a kind of wooden machine five and twenty foot high, formed like a standing ladder; the steps were each fifty foot long. It was indeed a moveable pair of stairs, the lowest end placed at ten foot distance from the wall of the chamber. The book I had a mind to read was put up leaning against the wall. I first mounted to the upper step of the ladder, and turning my face towards the book, began at the top of the page, and so walking to the right and left about eight or ten paces, according to the length of the lines, till I had gotten a little below the level of my eyes, and then descending gradually till I came to the bottom; after which I mounted again, and began the other page in the same manner, and so turned over the leaf, which I could easily do with both my hands, for it was as thick and stiff as a pasteboard, and in the largest folios not above eighteen or twenty foot long.

Their style is clear, masculine, and smooth, but not florid, for they avoid nothing more than multiplying unnecessary words, or using various expressions. I have perused many of their books, especially those in history and morality. Among the rest, I was much diverted with a little old treatise, which always lay in Glumdal-clitch's bed-chamber, and belonged to her governess, a grave elderly gentle-woman, who dealt in writings of mo-rality and devotion. The book treats of the weakness of human kind, and is in little esteem, except among the women and the vulgar. However, I was curious to see what an author of that country could say upon such a sub-ject. This writer went through all the usual topics of European moralists, showing how diminutive, contempti-ble, and helpless an animal was man in his own nature; how unable to de-fend himself from the inclemencies of the air, or the fury of wild beasts; how much he was excelled by one creature in strength, by another in speed, by a third in foresight, by a fourth in in-dustry. He added, that nature was de-generated in these latter declining ages of the world, and could now produce only small abortive births in comparison of those in ancient times. He said, it was very reasonable to think, not only that the species of men were originally much larger, but also, that there must have been giants in former ages, which, as it is asserted by history and tradition, so it hath been confirmed by huge bones and skulls casually dug up in several parts of the kingdom, far exceeding the common dwindled race of man in our days. He argued, that the very laws of nature absolutely required we should have been made in the beginning, of a size more large and robust, not so liable to destruction from every little acci-dent of a tile falling from a house, or a stone cast from the hand of a boy, or of being drowned in a little brook. From this way of reasoning the author drew several more applications useful in the conduct of life, but needless here to repeat. For my own part, I could not avoid reflecting how uni-versally this talent was spread, of drawing lectures in morality, or in-deed rather matter of discontent and repining, from the quarrels we raise with nature. And I believe, upon a

strict enquiry, those quarrels might be shown as ill grounded among us as they are among that people.

As to their military affairs, they boast that the King's army consists of an hundred and seventy-six thousand foot and thirty-two thousand horse: if that may be called an army which is made up of tradesmen in the several cities, and farmers in the country, whose commanders are only the no-bility and gentry, without pay or re-ward. They are indeed perfect enough in their exercises, and under very good discipline, wherein I saw no great merit; for how should it be otherwise, where every farmer is under the com-mand of his own landlord, and every citizen under that of the principal men in his own city, chosen after the manner of Venice by ballot?

I have often seen the militia of Lorbrulgrud drawn out to exercise in a great field near the city of twenty miles square. They were in all not above twenty-five thousand foot, and six thousand horse; but it was impos-sible for me to compute their number, considering the space of ground they took up. A cavalier mounted on a large steed, might be about an hun-dred foot high. I have seen this whole body of horse, upon a word of com-mand, draw their swords at once, and brandish them in the air. Imagination can figure nothing so grand, so sur-prising, and so astonishing. It looked as if ten thousand flashes of lightning were darting at the same time from every quarter of the sky.

I was curious to know how this prince, to whose dominions there is no access from any other country, came to think of armies, or to teach his people the practice of military discipline. But I was soon informed, both by conversation and reading their histories. For in the course of many ages they have been troubled with the same disease to which so many other governments are subject; the nobility often contending for power, the people for liberty, and the King for absolute dominion. All which, however happily tempered by the laws of the kingdom, have been sometimes violated by each of the three parties, and have once or more occasioned civil wars, the last whereof was happily put an end to by this prince's grandfather by a general composition; and the militia, then settled with common consent, hath been ever since kept in the strictest duty.   10

CHAP. VIII

The King and Queen make a progress to the frontiers. The author attends them. The manner in which he leaves the country very particularly related. He returns to England.

I had always a strong impulse that I should some time recover my liberty, though it was impossible to conjecture   20 by what means, or to form any project with the least hope of succeeding. The ship in which I sailed was the first ever known to be driven within sight of that coast, and the King had given strict orders, that if at any time another appeared, it should be taken ashore, and with all its crew and passengers brought in a tumbril to Lorbrulgrud. He was strongly bent to get   30 me a woman of my own size, by whom I might propagate the breed; but I think I should rather have died than undergone the disgrace of leaving a posterity to be kept in cages like tame canary birds, and perhaps, in time, sold about the kingdom to persons of quality for curiosities. I was, indeed, treated with much kindness; I was the favourite of a great King and Queen,   40 and the delight of the whole court, but it was upon such a foot as ill became the dignity of human kind. I could never forget those domestic pledges I had left behind me. I wanted to be among people with whom I could converse upon even terms, and walk about the streets and fields without fear of being trod to death like a frog or a young puppy. But my deliverance came sooner than I expected,   50 and in a manner not very common; the whole story and circumstances of which I shall faithfully relate.

I had now been two years in this country; and about the beginning of the third, Glumdalclitch and I attended the King and Queen in a progress to the south coast of the kingdom. I was carried, as usual, in my travelling-box, which, as I have already described, was a very convenient closet of twelve foot wide. And I had ordered a hammock to be fixed by silken ropes from the four corners at the top, to break the jolts, when a servant carried me before him on horseback, as I sometimes desired, and would often sleep in my hammock while we were upon the road. On the roof of my closet, just over the middle of the hammock, I ordered the joiner to cut out a hole of a foot square, to give me air in hot weather as I slept, which hole I shut at pleasure with a board that drew backwards and forwards through a groove.

When we came to our journey's end, the King thought proper to pass a few days at a palace he hath near Flanflasnic, a city within eighteen English miles of the seaside. Glumdalclitch and I were much fatigued; I had gotten a small cold, but the poor girl was so ill as to be confined to her chamber. I longed to see the ocean, which must be the only scene of my escape, if ever it should happen. I pretended to be worse than I really was, and desired leave to take the fresh air of the sea, with a page whom I was very fond of, and who had sometimes been trusted with me. I shall never forget with what unwillingness Glumdalclitch consented, nor the strict charge she gave the page to be careful of me, bursting at the same time into a flood of tears as if she had some foreboding of what was to happen. The boy took me out in my box about half an hour's walk from the palace, towards the rocks on the sea-shore. I ordered him to set me down, and lifting up one of my sashes, cast many a wistful melancholy look towards the sea. I found myself not very well, and told the page that I had a mind to take a nap in my hammock, which I hoped would do me good. I got in, and the boy shut the window close down to keep out the cold. I soon fell asleep, and all I can conjecture is that while I slept, the page, thinking no danger could happen, went among the rocks to look for birds' eggs, having before observed him from my window searching about, and picking up one or two in the clefts. Be that as it will, I found myself suddenly awaked with a violent pull upon the ring which was fastened at the top of my box for the conveniency of carriage. I felt my box raised very high in the air, and then borne forward with prodigious speed. The first jolt had like to have shaken me out of my hammock, but afterwards the motion was easy enough. I called out several times as loud as I could raise my voice, but all to no purpose. I looked towards my windows, and could see nothing but the clouds and sky. I heard a noise just over my head like the clapping of wings, and then began to perceive the woful condition I was in; that some eagle had got the ring of my box in his beak, with an intent to let it fall on a rock like a tortoise in a shell, and then pick out my body, and devour it. For the sagacity and smell of this bird enable him to discover his quarry at a great distance, though better concealed than I could be within a two-inch board.

In a little time I observed the noise and flutter of wings to increase very fast, and my box was tossed up and down, like a sign-post in a windy day. I heard several bangs or buffets, as I thought, given to the eagle (for such I am certain it must have been that held the ring of my box in his beak), and then all on a sudden felt myself falling perpendicularly down for above a minute, but with such incredible swiftness that I almost lost my breath. My fall was stopped by a terrible squash that sounded louder to my ears than the cataract of Niagara; after which I was quite in the dark for another minute, and then my box began to rise so high that I could see light from the tops of my windows. I now perceived that I was fallen into the sea. My box, by the weight of my body, the goods that were in, and the broad plates of iron fixed for strength at the four corners of the top and bottom, floated about five foot deep in water. I did then, and do now suppose that the eagle which flew away with my box was pursued by two or three others, and forced to let me drop while he was defending himself against the rest, who hoped to share in the prey. The plates of iron fastened at the bottom of the box (for those were the strongest) preserved the balance while it fell, and hindered it from being broken on the surface of the water. Every joint of it was well grooved, and the door did not move on hinges, but up and down like a sash, which kept my closet so tight that very little water came in. I got with much difficulty out of my hammock, having first ventured to draw back the slip-board on the roof already mentioned, contrived on purpose to let in air, for want of which I found myself almost stifled.

How often did I then wish myself with my dear Glumdalclitch, from whom one single hour had so far divided me! And I may say with truth, that in the midst of my own misfortunes I could not forbear lamenting my poor nurse, the grief she would suffer for my loss, the displeasure of the Queen, and the ruin of her fortune. Perhaps many travellers have not been under greater difficulties and distress than I was at this juncture, expecting every moment to see my box dashed in pieces, or at least overset by the first violent blast, or a rising wave. A breach in one single pane of glass would have been immediate death: nor could any thing have preserved the windows, but the strong lattice wires placed on the outside against accidents in travelling. I saw the water ooze in at several crannies, although the leaks were not considerable, and I endeavoured to stop them as well as I could. I was not able to lift up the roof of my closet, which otherwise I certainly should have done, and sat on the top of it, where I might at least preserve myself some hours longer than by being shut up, as I may call it, in the hold. Or, if I escaped these dangers for a day or two, what could I expect but a miserable death of cold and hunger! I was four hours under these circumstances, expecting and indeed wishing every moment to be my last.

I have already told the reader that there were two strong staples fixed upon that side of my box which had no window, and into which the servant who used to carry me on horseback would put a leathern belt, and buckle it about his waist. Being in this disconsolate state, I heard or at least thought I heard some kind of grating noise on that side of my box where the staples were fixed, and soon after I began to fancy that the box was pulled or towed along in the sea; for I now and then felt a sort of tugging, which made the waves rise near the tops of my windows, leaving me almost in the dark. This gave me some faint hopes of relief, although I was not able to imagine how it could be brought about. I ventured to unscrew one of my chairs, which were always fastened to the floor; and having made a hard shift to screw it down again directly under the slipping-board that I had lately opened, I mounted on the chair, and putting my mouth as near as I could to the hole, I called for help in a loud voice, and in all the languages I understood. I then fastened my handkerchief to a stick I usually carried, and thrusting it up the hole, waved it several times in the air, that if any boat or ship were near, the seamen might conjecture some unhappy mortal to be shut up in the box.

I found no effect from all I could do, but plainly perceived my closet to be moved along; and in the space of an hour, or better, that side of the box where the staples were, and had no window, struck against something that was hard. I apprehended it to be

a rock, and found myself tossed more than ever. I plainly heard a noise upon the cover of my closet, like that of a cable, and the grating of it as it passed through the ring. I then found myself hoisted up by degrees at least three foot higher than I was before. Whereupon I again thrust up my stick and handkerchief, calling for help till I was almost hoarse. In return to which, I heard a great shout repeated three times, giving me such transports of joy, as are not to be conceived but by those who feel them. I now heard a trampling over my head, and somebody calling through the hole with a loud voice in the English tongue: If there be any body below, let them speak. I answered, I was an Englishman, drawn by ill fortune into the greatest calamity that ever any creature underwent, and begged, by all that is moving, to be delivered out of the dungeon I was in. The voice replied, I was safe, for my box was fastened to their ship; and the carpenter should immediately come and saw an hole in the cover, large enough to pull me out. I answered, that was needless, and would take up too much time, for there was no more to be done, but let one of the crew put his finger into the ring, and take the box out of the sea into the ship, and so into the captain's cabin. Some of them upon hearing me talk so wildly thought I was mad; others laughed; for indeed it never came into my head that I was now got among people of my own stature and strength. The carpenter came, and in a few minutes sawed a passage about four foot square, then let down a small ladder, upon which I mounted, and from thence was taken into the ship in a very weak condition.

The sailors were all in amazement, and asked me a thousand questions, which I had no inclination to answer. I was equally confounded at the sight of so many pigmies, for such I took them to be, after having so long accustomed my eyes to the monstrous objects I had left. But the Captain, Mr. Thomas Wilcocks, an honest worthy Shropshire man, observing I was ready to faint, took me into his cabin, gave me a cordial to comfort me, and made me turn in upon his own bed, advising me to take a little rest, of which I had great need. Before I went to sleep I gave him to understand that I had some valuable furniture in my box, too good to be lost, a fine hammock, an handsome field-bed, two chairs, a table, and a cabinet; that my closet was hung on all sides, or rather quilted, with silk and cotton; that if he would let one of the crew bring my closet into his cabin, I would open it there before him, and show him my goods. The Captain hearing me utter these absurdities, concluded I was raving: however, (I suppose to pacify me) he promised to give order as I desired, and going upon deck sent some of his men down into my closet, from whence (as I afterwards found) they drew up all my goods, and stripped off the quilting; but the chairs, cabinet, and bedstead, being screwed to the floor, were much damaged by the ignorance of the seamen, who tore them up by force. Then they knocked off some of the boards for the use of the ship, and when they had got all they had a mind for, let the hull drop into the sea, which by reason of many breaches made in the bottom and sides, sunk to rights. And indeed I was glad not to have been a spectator of the havoc they made; because I am confident it would have sensibly touched me, by bringing former passages into my mind, which I had rather forget.

I slept some hours, but perpetually disturbed with dreams of the place I had left, and the dangers I had escaped. However, upon waking I found myself much recovered. It was now about eight o'clock at night, and the Captain ordered supper immediately, thinking I had already fasted too long. He entertained me with great kindness, observing me not to look wildly, or talk inconsistently: and when we were left alone, desired I would give him a relation of my travels, and by what accident I came to be set adrift in that monstrous wooden chest. He said, that about twelve o'clock at noon, as he was looking through his glass, he spied it at a distance, and thought it was a sail, which he had a mind to make, being not much out of his course, in hopes of buying some biscuit, his own beginning to fall short. That upon coming nearer, and finding his error, he sent out his long-boat to discover what I was; that his men came back in a fright, swearing they had seen a swimming house. That he laughed at their folly, and went himself in the boat, ordering his men to take a strong cable along with them. That the weather being calm, he rowed round me several times, observed my windows, and the wire lattices that defended them. That he discovered two staples upon one side, which was all of boards, without any passage for light. He then commanded his men to row up to that side, and fastening a cable to one of the staples, ordered them to tow my chest (as he called it) towards the ship. When it was there, he gave directions to fasten another cable to the ring fixed in the cover, and to raise up my chest with pulleys, which all the sailors were not able to do above two or three foot. He said they saw my stick and handkerchief thrust out of the hole, and concluded that some unhappy men must be shut up in the cavity. I asked whether he or the crew had seen any prodigious birds in the air about the time he first discovered me. To which he answered, that discoursing this matter with the sailors while I was asleep, one of them said he had observed three eagles flying towards the north, but remarked nothing of their being larger than the usual size, which I supposed must be imputed to the great height they were at; and he could not guess the reason of my question. I then asked the Captain how far he reckoned we might be from land; he said, by the best computation he could make, we were at least an hundred leagues. I assured him that he must be mistaken by almost half, for I had not left the country from whence I came above two hours before I dropt into the sea. Whereupon he began again to think that my brain was disturbed, of which he gave me a hint, and advised me to go to bed in a cabin he had provided. I assured him I was well refreshed with his good entertainment and company, and as much in my senses as ever I was in my life. He then grew serious, and desired to ask me freely whether I were not troubled in mind by the consciousness of some enormous crime, for which I was punished at the command of some prince, by exposing me in that chest, as great criminals in other countries have been forced to sea in a leaky vessel without provisions; for although he should be sorry to have taken so ill a man into his ship, yet he would engage his word to set me safe on shore in the first port where we arrived. He added that his suspicions were much increased by some very absurd speeches I had delivered at first to the sailors, and afterwards to himself, in relation to my closet or chest, as well as by my odd looks and behaviour while I was at supper.

I begged his patience to hear me tell my story, which I faithfully did from the last time I left England to the moment he first discovered me. And as truth always forceth its way into rational minds, so this honest worthy gentleman, who had some tincture of learning, and very good sense, was immediately convinced of my candour and veracity. But further to confirm all I had said, I entreated him to give order that my cabinet should be brought, of which I had the key in my pocket (for he had already informed me how the seamen disposed of my closet), I opened it in his presence and showed him the small collection of rarities I made in the country from whence I had been so strangely delivered. There was the comb I had contrived out of the stumps of the King's beard, and another of the same materials, but fixed into a paring of her Majesty's thumbnail, which served for the back. There was a collection of needles and pins from a foot to a half a yard long; four wasp-stings, like joiners' tacks; some combings of the Queen's hair; a gold ring which one day she made me a present of in a most obliging manner, taking it from her little finger, and throwing it over my head like a collar. I desired the Captain would please to accept this ring in return of his civilities, which he absolutely refused. I showed him a corn that I had cut off with my own hand, from a maid of honour's toe; it was about the bigness of a Kentish pippin, and grown so hard that when I returned to England, I got it hollowed into a cup, and set in silver. Lastly, I desired him to see the breeches I had then on, which were made of a mouse's skin.

I could force nothing on him but a footman's tooth, which I observed him to examine with great curiosity, and found he had a fancy for it. He received it with abundance of thanks, more than such a trifle could deserve. It was drawn by an unskilful surgeon, in a mistake, from one of Glumdalclitch's men, who was afflicted with the tooth-ache, but it was as sound as any in his head. I got it cleaned, and put it into my cabinet. It was about a foot long, and four inches in diameter.

The Captain was very well satisfied with this plain relation I had given him, and said he hoped when we returned to England I would oblige the world by putting it in paper and making it public. My answer was that I thought we were already overstocked with books of travels; that nothing could now pass which was not extraordinary; wherein I doubted some authors less consulted truth than their own vanity, or interest, or the diversion of ignorant readers. That my story could contain little besides common events, without those ornamental descriptions of strange plants, trees, birds, and other animals, or of the barbarous customs and idolatry of savage people, with which most writers abound. However, I thanked him for his good opinion, and promised to take the matter into my thoughts.

He said he wondered at one thing very much, which was, to hear me speak so loud, asking me whether the King or Queen of that country were thick of hearing. I told him it was what I had been used to for above two years past, and that I admired as much at the voices of him and his men, who seemed to me only to whisper, and yet I could hear them well enough. But when I spoke in that country, it was like a man talking in the street to another looking out from the top of a steeple, unless when I was placed on a table, or held in any person's hand. I told him, I had likewise observed another thing, that when I first got into the ship, and the sailors stood all about me, I thought they were the most little contemptible creatures I had ever beheld. For indeed while I was in that prince's country, I could never endure to look in a glass after my eyes had been accustomed to such prodigious objects, because the comparison gave me so despicable a conceit of myself. The Captain said that while we were at supper he observed me to look at every thing with a sort of wonder, and that I often seemed hardly able to contain my laughter, which he knew not well how to take, but imputed it to some disorder in my brain. I answered, it was very true; and I wondered how I could forbear, when I saw his dishes of the size of a silver three-pence, a leg of pork hardly a mouthful, a cup not so big as a nutshell; and so I went on, describing the rest of his household-stuff and provisions after the same manner. For, although the Queen had ordered a little equipage of all things necessary for me while I was in her service, yet my ideas were wholly taken up with what I saw on every side of me, and I winked at my own littleness as people do at their own faults. The Captain understood my raillery very well, and merrily replied with the old English proverb, that he doubted my eyes were bigger than my belly, for he did not observe my stomach so good, although I had fasted all day; and continuing in his mirth, protested he would have gladly given an hundred pounds to have seen my closet in the eagle's bill, and afterwards in its fall from so great an height into the sea; which would certainly have been a most astonishing object, worthy to have the description of it transmitted to future ages: and the comparison of Phaeton was so obvious, that he could not forbear applying it, although I did not much admire the conceit.

The Captain having been at Tonquin, was in his return to England driven north-eastward to the latitude of 44 degrees, and of longitude 143. But meeting a trade-wind two days after I came on board, we sailed southward a long time, and coasting New Holland kept our course west-southwest, and then south-south-west till we doubled the Cape of Good Hope. Our voyage was very prosperous, but I shall not trouble the reader with a journal of it. The Captain called in at one or two ports, and sent in his long-boat for provisions and fresh water, but I never went out of the ship till we came into the Downs, which was on the third day of June, 1706, about nine months after my escape. I offered to leave my goods in security for payment of my freight; but the Captain protested he would not receive one farthing. We took kind leave of each other, and I made him promise he would come to see me at my house in Redriff. I hired a horse and guide for five shillings, which I borrowed of the Captain.

As I was on the road, observing the littleness of the houses, the trees, the cattle, and the people, I began to think myself in Lilliput. I was afraid of trampling on every traveller I met, and often called aloud to have them stand out of the way, so that I had like to have gotten one or two broken heads for my impertinence.

When I came to my own house, for which I was forced to enquire, one of the servants opening the door, I bent down to go in (like a goose under a gate) for fear of striking my head. My wife ran out to embrace me, but I stooped lower than her knees, thinking she could otherwise never be able to reach my mouth. My daughter kneeled to ask my blessing, but I could not see her till she arose, having been so long used to stand with my head and eyes erect to above sixty foot; and then I went to take her up with one hand, by the waist. I looked down upon the servants and one or two friends who were in the house, as if they had been pigmies, and I a giant.

I told my wife, she had been too thrifty, for I found she had starved herself and her daughter to nothing. In short, I behaved myself so unaccountably, that they were all of the Captain's opinion when he first saw me, and concluded I had lost my wits. This I mention as an instance of the great power of habit and prejudice.

In a little time I and my family and friends came to a right understanding: but my wife protested I should never go to sea any more; although my evil destiny so ordered that she had not power to hinder me, as the reader may know hereafter. In the mean time I here conclude the second part of my unfortunate voyages.

RICHARD STEELE (1672-1729) and
JOSEPH ADDISON (1672-1719)

THE SPECTATOR

No. 10.

[Addison.] Monday, March 12, 1711.

Non aliter quam qui adverso vix flumine
lembum
Remigiis subigit, si bracchia forte remisit,
Atque illum praeceps prono rapit alveus
amni.—Virgil, *Georgics*, I, 201-03.[1]

It is with much satisfaction that I hear this great city inquiring day by day after these my papers, and receiving my morning lectures with a becoming seriousness and attention. My publisher tells me that there are already three thousand[2] of them distributed every day: so that if I allow twenty readers to every paper, which I look upon as a modest computation, I may reckon about threescore thousand disciples in London and Westminster, who I hope will take care to distinguish themselves from the thoughtless herd of their ignorant and unattentive brethren. Since I have raised to myself so great an audience, I shall spare no pains to make their instruction agreeable, and their diversion useful. For which reasons I shall endeavour to enliven morality with wit, and to temper wit with morality, that my readers may, if possible, both

ways find their account in the speculation of the day. And to the end that their virtue and discretion may not be short transient intermittent starts of thought, I have resolved to refresh their memories from day to day, till I have recovered them out of that desperate state of vice and folly into which the age is fallen. The mind that lies fallow but a single day, sprouts up in follies that are only to be killed by a constant and assiduous culture. It was said of Socrates, that he brought philosophy down from Heaven, to inhabit among men; and I shall be ambitious to have it said of me, that I have brought philosophy out of closets and libraries, schools and colleges, to dwell in clubs and assemblies, at tea-tables and in coffee-houses.

I would therefore in a very particular manner recommend these my speculations to all well regulated families, that set apart an hour in every morning for tea and bread and butter; and would earnestly advise them for their good to order this paper to be punctually served up, and to be looked upon as a part of the tea equipage.

Sir Francis Bacon[3] observes that a well-written book, compared with its rivals and antagonists, is like Moses's serpent,[4] that immediately swallowed up and devoured those of the Egyptians. I shall not be so vain as to think, that where the *Spectator* appears, the other public prints will vanish; but

---

[1] "So the boat's brawny crew the current stem,
And, slow advancing, struggle with the stream;
But if they slack their hands, or cease to strive,
Then down the flood with headlong haste they drive."
—Dryden.

[2] It has been estimated that the circulation of the *Spectator* rose at one time above 20,000 copies a day.

[3] In *Advancement of Learning*, II, introduction, 14.

[4] Exodus vii:8-12.

shall leave it to my reader's consideration, whether, Is it not much better to be let into the knowledge of one's self, than to hear what passes in Muscovy or Poland; [5] and to amuse our selves with such writings as tend to the wearing out of ignorance, passion, and prejudice, than such as naturally conduce to inflame hatreds, and make enmities irreconcileable?

In the next place, I would recommend this paper to the daily perusal of those gentlemen whom I cannot but consider as my good brothers and allies, I mean the fraternity of spectators who live in the world without having any thing to do in it; and either by an affluence of their fortunes, or laziness of their dispositions, have no other business with the rest of mankind but to look upon them. Under this class of men are comprehended all contemplative tradesmen, titular physicians, Fellows of the Royal Society, Templars [6] that are not given to be contentious, and statesmen that are out of business; in short, every one that considers the world as a theatre, and desires to form a right judgement of those who are the actors on it.

There is another set of men that I must likewise lay a claim to, whom I have lately called the blanks of society, as being altogether unfurnished with ideas, till the business and conversation of the day has supplied them. I have often considered these poor souls with an eye of great commiseration, when I have heard them asking the first man they have met with, whether there was any news stirring? and by that means gathering together materials for thinking. These needy persons do not know what to talk of, till about twelve o'clock in the morning; for by that

time they are pretty good judges of the weather, know which way the wind sits, and whether the Dutch mail be come in. As they lie at the mercy of the first man they meet, and are grave or impertinent all the day long, according to the notions which they have imbibed in the morning, I would earnestly entreat them not to stir out of their chambers till they have read this paper, and do promise them that I will daily instil into them such sound and wholesome sentiments as shall have a good effect on their conversation for the ensuing twelve hours.

But there are none to whom this paper will be more useful, than to the female world. I have often thought there has not been sufficient pains taken in finding out proper employments and diversions for the fair ones. Their amusements seem contrived for them rather as they are women, than as they are reasonable creatures; and are more adapted to the sex than to the species. The toilet is their great scene of business, and the right adjusting of their hair the principal employment of their lives. The sorting of a suit of ribbons is reckoned a very good morning's work; and if they make an excursion to a mercer's or a toy-shop, so great a fatigue makes them unfit for anything else all the day after. Their more serious occupations are sewing and embroidery, and their greatest drudgery the preparation of jellies and sweet-meats. This, I say, is the state of ordinary women; though I know there are multitudes of those of a more elevated life and conversation, that move in an exalted sphere of knowledge and virtue, that join all the beauties of the mind to the ornaments of dress, and inspire a kind of awe and respect, as well as love, into their male-beholders. I hope to increase the number of these by publishing this daily paper, which I shall always endeavour to make an innocent if not improving entertainment, and by that means at least divert the minds of my female readers

[5] In the *Tatler* Steele had drawn the portrait of a 'political' upholsterer, who was "much more inquisitive to know what passed in Poland than in his own family." Nos. 155, 160, and 178.

[6] Students of law, having chambers in the Temple, a set of buildings reserved for lawyers.

from greater trifles. At the same time, as I would fain give some finishing touches to those which are already the most beautiful pieces in human nature, I shall endeavour to point out all those imperfections that are the blemishes, as well as those virtues which are the embellishments, of the sex. In the mean while I hope these my gentle readers, who have so much time on their hands, will not grudge throwing away a quarter of an hour in a day on this paper, since they may do it without any hindrance to business.

I know several of my friends and well-wishers are in great pain for me, lest I should not be able to keep up the spirit of a paper which I oblige my self to furnish every day: but to make them easy in this particular, I will promise them faithfully to give it over as soon as I grow dull. This I know will be matter of great raillery to the small wits; who will frequently put me in mind of my promise, desire me to keep my word, assure me that it is high time to give over, with many other little pleasantries of the like nature, which men of a little smart genius cannot forbear throwing out against their best friends when they have such a handle given them of being witty. But let them remember that I do hereby enter my caveat against this piece of raillery.　　　C

No. 519.

[Addison.] Saturday, October 25, 1712.

Inde hominum pecudumque genus, vitaeque volantum,
Et quae marmoreo fert monstra sub aequore pontus.— Virgil, *Æneid*, vi, 728–29.[1]

Though there is a great deal of pleasure in contemplating the material world, by which I mean that system of bodies into which Nature has so curiously wrought the mass of dead matter, with the several relations which those bodies bear to one an-

[1] "Hence men and beasts the breath of life obtain,
And birds of air, and monsters of the main."—Dryden

other; there is still, methinks, something more wonderful and surprizing in contemplations on the world of life, by which I mean all those animals with which every part of the universe is furnished. The material world is only the shell of the universe: the world of life are its inhabitants.

If we consider those parts of the material world which lie the nearest to us, and are therefore subject to our observations and enquiries, it is amazing to consider the infinity of animals [2] with which it is stocked. Every part of matter is peopled: every green leaf swarms with inhabitants. There is scarce a single humour in the body of man, or of any other animal, in which our glasses do not discover myriads of living creatures. The surface of animals is also covered with other animals, which are in the same manner the basis of other animals that live upon it; nay, we find in the most solid bodies, as in marble itself, innumerable cells and cavities that are crowded with such imperceptible inhabitants, as are too little for the naked eye to discover. On the other hand, if we look into the more bulky parts of nature, we see the seas, lakes and rivers teeming with numberless kinds of living creatures: we find every mountain and marsh, wilderness and wood, plentifully stocked with birds and beasts, and every part of matter affording proper necessaries and conveniences for the livelihood of multitudes which inhabit it.

The author of the *Plurality of Worlds* [3] draws a very good argument from this consideration, for the peopling of every planet, as indeed it seems very probable from the analogy of reason, that if no part of matter

[2] The invention of the microscope had in its way as profound an effect on men's minds as the earlier invention of the telescope. It had been discussed by Marjorie Nicolson, *The Microscope and English Imagination* (Northampton, Mass., 1935).
[3] A famous popularization of the new astronomy by Fontenelle, published in 1686, of which English translations appeared in 1688 and 1695.

which we are acquainted with lies waste and useless, those great bodies which are at such a distance from us should not be desart and unpeopled, but rather that they should be furnished with beings adapted to their respective situations.

Existence is a blessing to those beings only which are endowed with perception, and is, in a manner, thrown away upon dead matter, any further than as it is subservient to beings which are conscious of their existence. Accordingly we find, from the bodies which lie under our observation, that matter is only made as the basis and support of animals, and that there is no more of the one than what is necessary for the existence of the other.

Infinite Goodness is of so communicative a nature, that it seems to delight in the conferring of existence upon every degree of perceptive being. As this is a speculation which I have often pursued with great pleasure to my self, I shall enlarge farther upon it, by considering that part of the scale of beings which comes within our knowledge.

There are some living creatures which are raised but just above dead matter. To mention only that species of shell-fish which are formed in the fashion of a cone, that grow to the surface of several rocks, and immediately die upon their being severed from the place where they grow. There are many other creatures but one remove from these, which have no other sense besides that of feeling and taste. Others have still an additional one of hearing; others of smell, and others of sight. It is wonderful to observe by what a gradual progress the world of life advances through a prodigious variety of species before a creature is formed that is complete in all its senses, and even among these there is such a different degree of perfection in the sense which one animal enjoys beyond what appears in another, that though the sense in different animals be distinguished by the same common

denomination, it seems almost of a different nature. If after this we look into the several inward perfections of cunning and sagacity, or what we generally call instinct, we find them rising after the same manner, imperceptibly one above another, and receiving additional improvements according to the species in which they are implanted. This progress in nature is so very gradual, that the most perfect of an inferior species comes very near to the most imperfect of that which is immediately above it.

The exuberant and overflowing goodness of the Supreme Being, whose mercy extends to all his works, is plainly seen as I have before hinted, from his having made so very little matter, at least what falls within our knowledge, that does not swarm with life: nor is his goodness less seen in the diversity than in the multitude of living creatures. Had he only made one species of animals, none of the rest would have enjoyed the happiness of existence; he has, therefore, specified in his creation every degree of life, every capacity of being. The whole chasm in nature, from a plant to a man, is filled up with diverse kinds of creatures, rising one over another, by such a gentle and easy ascent, that the little transitions and deviations from one species to another are almost insensible. This intermediate space is so well husbanded and managed, that there is scarce a degree of perception which does not appear in some one part of the world of life. Is the goodness or wisdom of the Divine Being more manifested in this his proceeding?

There is a consequence, besides those I have already mentioned, which seems very naturally deducible from the foregoing considerations. If the scale of being rises by such a regular progress so high as man, we may by a parity of reason suppose that it still proceeds gradually through those beings which are of a superior nature to him, since there is an infinitely greater space and room for different degrees of perfection between the Supreme Being and man than between man and the most despicable insect. This consequence of so great a variety of beings which are superior to us, from that variety which is inferior to us, is made by Mr. Locke, in a passage which I shall here set down, after having premised, that notwithstanding there is such infinite room between man and his Maker for the Creative Power to exert itself in, it is impossible that it should ever be filled up, since there will be still an infinite gap or distance between the highest created being and the Power which produced him.

"That there should be more species of intelligent creatures above us than there are of sensible and material below us, is probable to me from hence: that in all the visible corporeal world we see no chasm or gaps. All quite down from us, the descent is by easy steps and a continued series of things that in each remove differ very little one from the other. There are fishes that have wings and are not strangers to the airy region: and there are some birds that are inhabitants of the water, whose blood is cold as fishes, and their flesh so like in taste that the scrupulous are allowed them on fish-days. There are animals so near of kin both to birds and beasts that they are in the middle between both: amphibious animals link the terrestrial and aquatic together; seals live at land and at sea, and porpoises have the warm blood and entrails of a hog, not to mention what is confidently reported of mermaids or sea-men. There are some brutes that seem to have as much knowledge and reason as some that are called men: and the animal and vegetable kingdoms are so nearly joined that, if you will take the lowest of one and the highest of the other, there will scarce be perceived any great difference between them; and so on till we come to the lowest and most inorganical parts of matter, we shall find everywhere that the several species are linked together, and differ but in almost insensible degrees And when we consider the infinite power and wisdom of the Maker, we have reason to think that it is suitable to the magnificent harmony of the universe and the great design and infinite goodness of the Architect, that the species of creatures should also, by gentle degrees, ascend upward from us toward his infinite Perfection as we see they gradually descend from us downward: which if it be probable, we have reason then to be persuaded that there are far more species of creatures above us than there are beneath; we being in degrees of perfection much more remote from the infinite Being of God than we are from the lowest state of being and that which approaches nearest to nothing. And yet of all those distinct species we have no clear distinct ideas." [4]

In this system of being there is no creature so wonderful in its nature, and which so much deserves our particular attention, as man, who fills up the middle space between the animal and intellectual nature, the visible and invisible world, and is that link in the chain of beings which has been often termed the *nexus utriusque mundi*.[5] So that he, who in one respect is associated with angels and archangels, may look upon a Being of infinite perfection as his Father and the highest order of spirits as his brethren, and may in another respect say to *Corruption, thou art my father, and to the worm, thou art my mother and my sister*.[6]   O

[4] John Locke, *Essay concerning Human Understanding* (1690), Book III, chap. vi, sec. 12. The idea of creation as a great system of being was, of course, not original with Locke. Its history from Plato down to the eighteenth century has been traced by A. O. Lovejoy in a brilliant and erudite volume, *The Great Chain of Being* (1936). The student meets it again in Pope's *Essay on Man*. The system was thought of as essentially static; the evolution of species was not as yet known or suspected.

[5] The connecting link between two worlds; Young, in *Night Thoughts*, i, 72, put it: "Connection exquisite of distant worlds."

[6] Job xvii: 14.

ALEXANDER POPE (1688-1744)

THE DUNCIAD

Yet, yet a moment, one dim ray of light
Indulge, dread Chaos, and eternal Night!
Of darkness visible so much be lent,
As half to shew, half veil the deep intent.
Ye Powers! whose mysteries restored I sing,
To whom Time bears me on his rapid wing,
Suspend a while your force inertly strong,
Then take at once the poet and the song.
    Now flamed the Dog-star's unpropitious ray,
Smote every brain, and withered every bay;   10
Sick was the sun, the owl forsook his bower,
The moon-struck Prophet felt the madding hour:
Then rose the seed of Chaos and of Night,
To blot out order and extinguish light,
Of dull and venal a new world to mold,
And bring Saturnian days of lead and gold.
    She mounts the throne: her head a cloud concealed,
In broad effulgence all below revealed,
('Tis thus aspiring Dullness ever shines)
Soft on her lap her laureate son [1] reclines. 20
    Beneath her foot-stool, *Science* groans in chains,
And *Wit* dreads exile, penalties and pains.
There foamed rebellious *Logic,* gagged and bound,
There, stript, fair *Rhetoric* languished on the ground;
His blunted arms by *Sophistry* are borne,
And shameless *Billingsgate* her robes adorn.
Morality, by her false guardians drawn,
Chicane in furs,[2] and *Casuistry* in lawn,
Gasps, as they straiten at each end the cord,
And dies, when Dullness gives her page[3] the word.   30
Mad *Mathesis*[4] alone was unconfined,
Too mad for mere material chains to bind,
Now to pure space lifts her ecstatic stare,
Now running round the circle, finds it square.
But held in ten-fold bonds the *Muses* lie,
Watched both by Envy's and by Flattery's eye:
There to her heart sad Tragedy addrest
The dagger wont to pierce the tyrant's breast;
But sober History restrained her rage,
And promised vengeance on a barbarous age.   40
There sunk Thalia,[5] nerveless, cold, and dead,
Had not her Sister Satire held her head:
Nor could'st thou, Chesterfield! a tear refuse,
Thou wept'st, and with thee wept each gentle Muse.
    When lo! a harlot form[6] soft sliding by,
With mincing step, small voice, and languid eye;

[1] "With great judgment it is imagined by the Poet that such a colleague as Dullness had elected, should sleep on the Throne, and have very little share in the action of the poem . . ."—Scrib.

[2] In furs means in law, because of the ermine robes of the judges. *Casuistry in lawn.* The reference is to the lawn sleeves of the bishops.
[3] An allusion to Sir Francis Page, a notorious "hanging judge."
[4] Mathematics. The lines are a satirical allusion to some of the current speculations of the mathematicians about the nature of space.
[5] The Muse of comedy.
[6] "Every reader will see that from this verse to the 68th is a detached piece. We suppose it rightly inserted here, from what is said of her casting a scornful look on the *prostrate Muses:* but if any one can show us a properer place we

Foreign her air, her robe's discordant pride
In patch-work fluttering, and her head
    aside:
By singing peers upheld on either hand,
She tripped and laughed, too pretty much
    to stand;   50
Cast on the prostrate Nine a scornful look,
Then thus in quaint recitativo spoke.
    "O *Cara! Cara!* silence all that train:
Joy to great Chaos! let division reign: [7]
Chromatic tortures soon shall drive them
    hence,
Break all their nerves, and fritter all their
    sense:
One trill shall harmonize joy, grief, and
    rage,
Wake the dull church, and lull the ranting
    stage;
To the same notes thy sons shall hum, or
    snore,
And all thy yawning daughters cry,
    encore.   60
Another Phoebus, thy own Phoebus, reigns,
Joys in my jigs, and dances in my chains.
But soon, ah soon rebellion will commence,
If music meanly borrows aid from sense:
Strong in new arms, lo! giant Handel stands,
Like bold Briareus, with a hundred hands;
To stir, to rouse, to shake the soul he comes,
And Jove's own thunders follows Mars's
    drums.
Arrest him, Empress; or you sleep no
    more"—
She heard, and drove him to th' Hibernian
    shore.[8]   70
    And now had Fame's posterior trumpet
    blown,
And all the nations summoned to the
    throne.

The young, the old, who feel her inward
    sway,
One instinct seizes, and transports away.
None need a guide, by sure attraction led
And strong impulsive gravity of head:
None want a place, for all their center
    found,
Hung to the Goddess, and cohered around.
Not closer, orb in orb, conglobed are seen
The buzzing bees about their dusky
    queen.   80
    The gathering number, as it moves along,
Involves a vast involuntary throng,
Who gently drawn, and struggling less and
    less,
Roll in her vortex, and her power confess.
Not those alone who passive own her laws,
But who, weak rebels, more advance her
    cause.
Whate'er of dunce in college or in town
Sneers at another, in toupee or gown;
Whate'er of mongrel no one class admits,
A wit with dunces, and a dunce with wits. 90
    Nor absent they, no members of her
    state,
Who pay her homage in her sons, the great;
Who false to Phoebus, bow the knee to
    Baal;
Or impious, preach his word without a call.
Patrons who sneak from living worth to
    dead,
Withhold the pension, and set up the head;
Or vest dull Flattery in the sacred gown;
Or give from fool to fool the laurel crown.
And (last and worst) with all the cant of
    wit,
Without the soul, the Muse's hypocrite.[9] 100
    There marched the bard and blockhead,
    side by side,
Who rhymed for hire, and patronized for
    pride.

shall be obliged to him. The attitude given to
this phantom represents the nature and genius
of the *Italian* opera; its affected airs, its effeminate sounds, and the practice of patching up
these operas with favourite songs, incoherently
put together. These things were supported by
the subscriptions of the nobility . . ."—P.
    [7] "Alluding to the false taste of playing
tricks in music with numberless divisions, to
the neglect of that harmony which conforms
to the sense and applies to the passions . . ."
—PW.
    [8] Handel's popularity in England had suf-
fered a temporary eclipse, and for this and a
number of other reasons he was living in Ireland at this time.

    [9] ll. 75–100. "It ought to be observed that
here are three classes in this assembly. The
first of men absolutely and avowedly dull, who
naturally adhere to the Goddess, and are
imaged in the simile of the bees about their
queen. The second involuntarily drawn to
her, though not caring to own her influence;
from ver. 81 to 90. The third of such as, though
not members of her state, yet advance her service by flattering Dullness, cultivating mistaken
talents, patronizing vile scribblers, discouraging
living merit, or setting up for wits, and men
of taste in arts they understand not; from
ver. 91 to 101 . . ."—P.

Narcissus,[10] praised with all a parson's
power,
Looked a white lily sunk beneath a shower.
There moved Montalto [11] with superior air;
His stretched-out arm displayed a volume
fair;
Courtiers and patriots in two ranks divide,
Through both he passed, and bowed from
side to side:
But as in graceful act, with awful eye
Composed he stood, bold Benson [12] thrust
him by: 110
On two unequal crutches propt he came,
Milton's on this, on that one Johnston's
name.
The decent knight retired with sober rage,
Withdrew his hand, and closed the pom-
pous page.
[But (happy for him as the times went
then)
Appeared Apollo's Mayor and Aldermen,[13]
On whom three hundred gold-capt [14] youths
await,
To lug the ponderous volume off in
state.] [15]
When Dullness, smiling—"Thus revive
the Wits!
But murder first, and mince them all to
bits; 120
As erst Medea (cruel, so to save!)
A new edition of old Aeson gave,
Let standard authors thus, like trophies
born,

Appear more glorious as more hacked and
torn,
And you, my critics! in the chequered shade,
Admire new light through holes yourselves
have made.
"Leave not a foot of verse, a foot of stone,
A page, a grave, that they can call their
own;
But spread, my sons, your glory thin or
thick,
On passive paper, or on solid brick. 130
So by each Bard an Alderman shall sit,
A heavy Lord shall hang at every wit,
And while on Fame's triumphal car they
ride,
Some slave of mine be pinioned to their
side."
Now crowds on crowds around the God-
dess press,[16]
Each eager to present the first address.
Dunce scorning Dunce beholds the next
advance,
But Fop shews Fop superior complaisance.
When lo! a Spectre [17] rose, whose index-
hand
Held forth the virtue of the dreadful
wand; 140
His beavered brow a birchen garland wears,
Dropping with infant's blood, and mother's
tears.
O'er every vein a shuddering horror runs;
Eton and Winton shake through all their
sons.
All flesh is humbled, Westminster's bold
race
Shrink, and confess the genius of the place:
The pale boy-senator yet tingling stands,
And holds his breeches close with both his
hands.
Then thus. "Since Man from beast by
words is known,
Words are man's province, words we teach
alone. 150
When reason doubtful, like the Samian
letter,[18]

---

[10] Lord Hervey (see *Ep. to Dr. Arbuthnot*).
Dr. Conyers Middleton wrote a fourteen page
dedication of his *Life of Cicero* to him.
[11] Sir Thomas Hanmer, a portly gentleman
of pompous manner.
[12] "This man endeavoured to raise himself
to fame by erecting monuments, striking coins,
setting up heads, and procuring translations,
of *Milton*; and afterwards by a great passion
for *Arthur Johnston* a *Scotch* physician's version of the Psalms, of which he printed many
fine editions . . . ."—PW.
[13] Vice-Chancellor of Oxford and Heads of
the various colleges.—Sutherland, Twick. Ed.
[14] Reference is to the gold tassel on the caps
of the gentleman-commoners.—Sutherland,
Twick. Ed.
[15] ll. 115–18. The 1751 edition has this note:
"These four lines were printed in a separate
leaf by Mr. Pope in the last edition, which
he himself gave, of the Dunciad, with directions
to the printer to put this leaf into its place as
soon as Sir T. H.'s Shakespeare should be
published. B."

[16] ll. 135–336. This passage on education
may have been written earlier as part of the *Essay
on Man*.
[17] The ghost of Dr. Busby, the headmaster
of Westminster School.—Sutherland, Twick. Ed.
[18] "The letter Y, used by Pythagoras as an
emblem of the different roads of virtue and
vice . . ."—PW.

Points him two ways, the narrower is the better.
Placed at the door of learning, youth to guide,
We never suffer it to stand too wide.
To ask, to guess, to know, as they commence,
As fancy opens the quick springs of sense,
We ply the memory, we load the brain,
Bind rebel wit, and double chain on chain,
Confine the thought, to exercise the breath;
And keep them in the pale of words till death.   160
Whate'er the talents, or howe'er designed,
We hang one jingling padlock on the mind:
A poet the first day, he dips his quill;
And what the last? a very poet still.
Pity! the charm works only in our wall,
Lost, lost too soon in yonder house or hall.
There truant Wyndham [19] every Muse gave o'er,
There Talbot [20] sunk, and was a wit no more!
How sweet an Ovid, Murray [21] was our boast!
How many Martials were in Pult'ney [22] lost!   170
Else sure some bard, to our eternal praise,
In twice ten thousand rhyming nights and days,
Had reached the work, the all that mortal can;
And South beheld that master-piece of Man." [23]
  "Oh (cried the Goddess) for some pedant reign!
Some gentle James, to bless the land again;
To stick the doctor's chair into the throne,
Give law to words, or war with words alone,
Senates and courts with Greek and Latin rule,
And turn the council to a grammar school!   180
For sure, if Dullness sees a grateful day,
'Tis in the shade of arbitrary sway.
O! if my sons may learn one earthly thing,
Teach but that one, sufficient for a King;

That which my Priests, and mine alone, maintain,
Which as it dies, or lives, we fall, or reign:
May you, may Cam and Isis, preach it long!
'The Right Divine of Kings to govern wrong.' "
  Prompt at the call, around the Goddess roll
Broad hats, and hoods, and caps, a sable shoal: 100
Thick and more thick the black blockade extends,
A hundred head of Aristotle's friends.
Nor wert thou, Isis! wanting to the day,
[Tho' Christ Church long kept prudishly away.]
Each staunch Polemic, stubborn as a rock,
Each fierce Logician, still expelling Locke, [24]
Came whip and spur, and dashed thro' thin and thick
On German Crousaz, and Dutch Burgersdyck.
As many quit the streams that murm'ring fall
To lull the sons of Margaret and Clare Hall   200
Where Bentley [25] late tempestuous wont to sport
In troubled waters, but now sleeps in port.
Before them marched that awful Aristarch;
Plowed was his front with many a deep remark:
His hat, which never vailed to human pride,
Walker [26] with reverence took, and layed aside.
Low bowed the rest: he, kingly, did but nod;
So upright Quakers please both Man and God.
"Mistress! dismiss that rabble from your throne:
Avaunt——is Aristarchus yet unknown?   210
Thy mighty Scholiast, whose unwearied pains
Made Horace dull, and humbled Milton's strains.

[19] Sir William Wyndham.
[20] Charles, Baron Talbot.
[21] William, Earl of Mansfield.
[22] William Pulteney.
[23] "Viz. an *epigram*. The famous Dr. South declared a perfect epigram to be as difficult a performance as an epic poem. And the critics say, 'an epic poem is the greatest work human nature is capable of.' "—P.

[24] "In the year 1703 there was a meeting of the heads of the University of Oxford to censure Mr. Locke's Essay on Human Understanding, and to forbid the reading it . . ."—P.
[25] A scholar and theologian, and Master of Trinity College, Cambridge, from 1700 to 1742.
[26] Dr. Richard Walker, Vice-Master of Trinity College. A friend and champion of Bentley.

Turn what they will to verse, their toil is
vain,
Critics like me shall make it prose again.
Roman and Greek Grammarians! know
your better:
Author of something yet more great than
letter;
While towering o'er your alphabet, like
Saul,
Stands our Digamma, and o'er-tops them all.
'Tis true, on words is still our whole debate,
Disputes of *Me* or *Te*, of *aut* or *at*,   220
To sound or sink in *cano*, O or A,
Or give up Cicero to C or K.
Let Freind [27] affect to speak as Terence
spoke,
And Alsop [27] never but like Horace joke:
For me, what Virgil, Pliny may deny,
Manilius or Solinus [28] shall supply:
For Attic phrase in Plato let them seek,
I poach in Suidas for unlicensed Greek.
In ancient sense if any needs will deal,
Be sure I give them fragments, not a
meal;   230
What Gellius or Stobaeus hashed before,
Or chewed by blind old scholiasts o'er and
o'er.
The critic eye, that microscope of wit,
Sees hairs and pores, examines bit by bit:
How parts relate to parts, or they to whole,
The body's harmony, the beaming soul,
Are things which Kuster, Burman, Wasse
shall see,
When Man's whole frame is obvious to a
flea.
"Ah, think not, Mistress! more true dull-
ness lies
In Folly's cap, than Wisdom's grave dis-
guise.   240
Like buoys, that never sink into the flood,
On learning's surface we but lie and nod.
Thine is the genuine head of many a house,
And much divinity without a Νοῦς.
Nor could a Barrow [29] work on every block,

Nor has one Atterbury [29] spoiled the flock.
See! still thy own, the heavy canon roll,
And metaphysic smokes involve the pole.
For thee we dim the eyes, and stuff the head
With all such reading as was never read: 250
For thee explain a thing till all men doubt
it,
And write about it, Goddess, and about it:
So spins the silk-worm small its slender store,
And labours till it clouds itself all o'er.
"What though we let some better sort of
fool
Thrid every science, run through every
school?
Never by tumbler through the hoops was
shown
Such skill in passing all, and touching none.
He may indeed (if sober all this time)
Plague with dispute, or persecute with
rhyme.   260
We only furnish what he cannot use,
Or wed to what he must divorce, a Muse:
Full in the midst of Euclid dip at once,
And petrify a genius to a dunce:
Or set on metaphysic ground to prance,
Show all his paces, not a step advance.
With the same cement, ever sure to bind,
We bring to one dead level every mind.
Then take him to develop, if you can,
And hew the block off,[30] and get out the
man.   270
But wherefore waste I words? I see advance
Whore, pupil, and laced governor from
France.
Walker! our hat" [31]—nor more he deigned
to say,
But, stern as Ajax' spectre, strode away.
In flowed at once a gay embroidered race,
And tittering pushed the pedants off the
place:
Some would have spoken, but the voice was
drowned

27 *Freind, Alsop.* "Dr. Robert Freind, master
of Westminster School, and canon of Christ
Church—Dr. Anthony Alsop, a happy imitator
of the Horatian style."—PW.
28 "Some critics having had it in their choice
to comment either on Virgil or Manilius,
Pliny or Solinus, have chosen the worse author,
the more freely to display their critical capacity."—PW.
29 "Isaac Barrow, Master of Trinity, Francis
Atterbury, Dean of Christ Church, both great
genius's and eloquent preachers; one more

conversant in the sublime geometry, the other
in classical learning; but who equally made it
their care to advance the polite arts in their
several societies."—PW.
30 "A notion of Aristotle, that there was
originally in every block of marble, a statue,
which would appear on the removal of the
superfluous parts."—PW. The credit should
probably go to Michelangelo instead of Aristotle.—Sutherland, Twick. Ed.
31 Refers to a current anecdote about Bentley, in which he is said to have silenced an
irritating visitor by these words.—Sutherland,
Twick. Ed.

By the French horn, or by the opening
    hound.
The first came forwards, with as easy mien,
As if he saw St. James's and the Queen. 280
When thus th' attendant Orator begun.
"Receive, great Empress! thy accomplished
    Son:
Thine from the birth, and sacred from the
    rod,
A dauntless infant! never scared with God.
The sire saw, one by one, his virtues wake:
The mother begged the blessing of a rake.
Thou gavest that ripeness, which so soon
    began,
And ceased so soon, he ne'er was boy, nor
    man.32
Through school and college, thy kind cloud
    o'ercast,
Safe and unseen the young Aeneas past: 290
Thence bursting glorious, all at once let
    down,
Stunned with his giddy 'larum half the
    town.
Intrepid then, o'er seas and lands he flew:
Europe he saw, and Europe saw him too.
There all thy gifts and graces we display,
Thou, only thou, directing all our way!
To where the Seine, obsequious as she runs,
Pours at great Bourbon's feet her silken
    sons;
Or Tiber, now no longer Roman, rolls,
Vain of Italian arts, Italian souls: 300
To happy convents, bosomed deep in vines,
Where slumber abbots, purple as their
    wines:
To isles of fragrance, lily-silvered vales,
Diffusing languor in the panting gales:
To lands of singing, or of dancing slaves,
Love-whispering woods, and lute-resound-
    ing waves.
But chief her shrine where naked Venus
    keeps,
And cupids ride the Lion of the deeps; 33
Where, eased of fleets, the Adriatic main
Wafts the smooth eunuch and enamoured
    swain. 310

32 "Nature hath bestowed on the human
species two states or conditions, *infancy* and
manhood. Wit sometimes makes the *first*
disappear, and folly the *latter;* but true dullness annihilates *both*."—Scrib.
33 "The winged lion, the arms of Venice.
This republic heretofore the most considerable
in Europe, for her naval force and the extent
of her commerce, now illustrious for her
carnivals."—PW.

Led by my hand, he sauntered Europe
    round,
And gathered every vice on Christian
    ground;
Saw every court, heard every king declare
His royal sense, of operas or the fair;
The stews and palace equally explored,
Intrigued with glory, and with spirit
    whored;
Tried all *hors-d'oeuvres,* all *liqueurs* de-
    fined;
Judicious drank, and greatly-daring dined;
Dropt the dull lumber of the Latin store,
Spoiled his own language, and acquired no
    more; 320
All classic learning lost on classic ground;
And last turned *air,* the echo of a sound!
See now, half-cured, and perfectly well-bred,
With nothing but a solo in his head;
As much estate, and principle, and wit,
As Jansen, Fleetwood, Cibber 34 shall think
    fit;
Stolen from a duel, followed by a nun,
And, if a borough choose him,35 not un-
    done;
See, to my country happy I restore
This glorious Youth, and add one Venus
    more. 330
Her too receive (for her my soul adores)
So may the sons of sons of sons of whores,
Prop thine, O Empress! like each neighbour
    throne,
And make a long posterity thy own."
  Pleased, she accepts the Hero, and the
    Dame,
Wraps in her veil, and frees from sense of
    shame.
  Then looked, and saw a lazy, lolling sort,
Unseen at Church, at Senate, or at Court,
Of ever-listless loiterers, that attend
No cause, no trust, no duty, and no
    friend. 340
Thee too, my Paridel! she marked thee
    there,
Stretched on the rack of a too easy chair,
And heard thy everlasting yawn confess
The pains and penalties of idleness.
She pitied! but her pity only shed
Benigner influence on thy nodding head.
  But Annius, crafty seer, with ebon wand,
And well dissembled emerald on his hand,

34 All gamblers; the latter two producers of
plays.
35 If he were elected to Parliament he could
not be arrested for debt.

False as his gems, and cankered as his coins,
Came, crammed with capon, from where
    Pollio dines.   350
Soft, as the wily fox is seen to creep,
Where bask on sunny banks the simple
    sheep,
Walk round and round, now prying here,
    now there;
So he; but pious, whispered first his prayer.
    "Grant, gracious Goddess! grant me still
        to cheat,
O may thy cloud still cover the deceit!
Thy choicer mists on this assembly shed,
But pour them thickest on the noble head.
So shall each youth, assisted by our eyes,
See other Caesars, other Homers rise;   360
Through twilight ages hunt th' Athenian
    fowl,[36]
Which Chalcis gods, and mortals call an
    owl,
Now see an Attys, now a Cecrops clear,
Nay, Mahomet! the pigeon at thine ear;
Be rich in ancient brass, though not in gold,
And keep his lares, though his house be
    sold;
To headless Phoebe his fair bride postpone,
Honour a Syrian Prince above his own;
Lord of an Otho,[37] if I vouch it true;
Blest in one Niger,[37] till he knows of
    two."   370
    Mummius o'erheard him; Mummius,[38]
        fool-renowned,
Who like his Cheops stinks above the
    ground,
Fierce as a startled adder, swelled, and said,
Rattling an ancient Sistrum at his head.
    "Speak'st thou of Syrian Princes? Traitor
        base!
Mine, Goddess! mine is all the horned race.
True, he had wit, to make their value rise;
From foolish Greeks to steal them, was as
    wise;

[36] "The owl stamped on the reverse of the
ancient money of Athens."—PW.
[37] Two Roman emperors who ruled such a
short time that coins of their reigns are very
rare.—Sutherland, Twick. Ed.
[38] "This name is not merely an allusion to
the mummies he was so fond of, but probably
referred to the Roman General of that name,
who burned Corinth, and committed the curious statues to the captain of a ship, assuring
him, 'that if any were lost or broken, he should
procure others to be made in their stead:' by
which it should seem (whatever may be pretended) that Mummius was no virtuoso."—PW.

More glorious yet, from barbarous hands to
    keep,
When Sallee Rovers chased him on the
    deep.   380
Then taught by Hermes, and divinely bold,
Down his own throat he risked the Grecian
    gold;
Received each demigod, with pious care,
Deep in his entrails—I revered them there,
I bought them, shrouded in that living
    shrine,
And, at their second birth, they issue mine."
    "Witness great Ammon! by whose horns
        I swore,
(Replied soft Annius) this our paunch
    before
Still bears them, faithful; and that thus I
    eat,
Is to refund the medals with the meat.   390
To prove me, Goddess! clear of all design,
Bid me with Pollio sup, as well as dine:
There all the learned shall at the labour
    stand,
And Douglas lend his soft, obstetric hand."
    The Goddess smiling seemed to give
        consent;
So back to Pollio, hand in hand, they went.
    Then thick as locusts blackening all the
        ground,
A tribe, with weeds and shells fantastic
    crowned,
Each with some wondrous gift approached
    the Power,
A nest, a toad, a fungus, or a flower.   400
But far the foremost, two, with earnest zeal,
And aspect ardent to the throne appeal.
    The first thus opened: "Hear thy sup-
        pliant's call,
Great Queen, and common Mother of us
    all!
Fair from its humble bed I reared this
    flower,
Suckled, and cheered, with air, and sun, and
    shower,
Soft on the paper ruff its leaves I spread,
Bright with the gilded button tipt its head,
Then throned in glass, and named it
    Caroline:
Each maid cried, charming! and each youth,
    divine!   410
Did Nature's pencil ever blend such rays,
Such varied light in one promiscuous blaze?
Now prostrate! dead! behold that Caro-
    line:

No maid cries, charming! and no youth,
    divine!
And lo the wretch! whose vile, whose insect
    lust
Laid this gay daughter of the spring in dust.
Oh punish him, or to th' Elysian shades
Dismiss my soul, where no carnation fades."
    He ceased, and wept. With innocence of
        mien,
Th' accused stood forth, and thus addressed
        the Queen.   420
    "Of all th' enameled race, whose silvery
        wing
Waves to the tepid Zephyrs of the spring,
Or swims along the fluid atmosphere,
Once brightest shined this child of heat and
    air.
I saw, and started from its vernal bower
The rising game, and chased from flower to
    flower.
It fled, I followed; now in hope, now pain;
It stopt, I stopt; it moved, I moved again.
At last it fixed, 'twas on what plant it
    pleased,
And where it fixed, the beauteous bird I
    seized: 430
Rose or carnation was below my care;
I meddle, Goddess! only in my sphere.
I tell the naked fact without disguise,
And, to excuse it, need but shew the prize;
Whose spoils this paper offers to your eye,
Fair even in death! this peerless *butterfly*."
    "My sons! (she answered) both have
        done your parts:
Live happy both, and long promote our
    arts.
But hear a Mother, when she recommends
To your fraternal care, our sleeping
    friends.   440
The common soul, of Heaven's more frugal
    make,
Serves but to keep fools pert, and knaves
    awake:
A drowsy watchman, that just gives a knock,
And breaks our rest, to tell us what o'
    clock.
Yet by some object every brain is stirred;
The dull may waken to a hummingbird;
The most recluse, discreetly opened, find
Congenial matter in the cockle-kind;
The mind, in metaphysics at a loss,
May wander in a wilderness of moss;   450
The head that turns at super-lunar
    things,

Poised with a tail, may steer on Wilkins'
    wings.[39]
    "O! would the sons of men once think
        their eyes
And reason given them but to study *flies!*
See Nature in some partial narrow shape,
And let the Author of the Whole escape:
Learn but to trifle; or, who most observe,
To wonder at their Maker, not to serve."
    "Be that my task (replies a gloomy clerk,
Sworn foe to mystery, yet divinely dark;   460
Whose pious hope aspires to see the day
When moral evidence shall quite decay,
And damns implicit faith, and holy lies,
Prompt to impose, and fond to dogmatize:)
Let others creep by timid steps, and slow,
On plain experience lay foundations low,
By common sense to common knowledge
    bred,
And last, to Nature's Cause through Nature
    led.
All-seeing in thy mists, we want no guide,
Mother of arrogance, and source of
    pride!   470
We nobly take the high priori road,[40]
And reason downward, till we doubt of
    God:
Make Nature still incroach upon his plan;
And shove him off as far as e'er we can:
Thrust some mechanic cause into his place;
Or bind in matter, or diffuse in space.
Or, at one bound o'er-leaping all his laws,
Make God Man's image, Man the final
    Cause,
Find virtue local, all relation scorn,
See all in *self,* and but for self be born: 480
Of nought so certain as our *reason* still,
Of nought so doubtful as of *soul* and *will.*

[39] "One of the first projectors of the Royal Society, who, among many enlarged and useful notions, entertained the extravagant hope of a possibility to fly to the Moon; which has put some volatile genius's upon making wings for that purpose."—PW.

[40] "Those who, from the effects in this visible world, deduce the Eternal Power and Godhead of the First Cause though they cannot attain to an adequate idea of the Deity, yet discover so much of him, as enables them to see the end of their creation, and the means of their happiness: whereas they who take this high priori road (such as Hobbes, Spinoza, Descartes, and some better reasoners) for one that goes right, ten lose themselves in mists, or ramble after visions which deprive them of all sight of their end, and mislead them in the choice of wrong means."—PW.

Oh hide the God still more! and make us
        see
Such as Lucretius drew, a God like Thee:
Wrapt up in self, a God without a thought,
Regardless of our merit or default.
Or that bright image to our fancy draw,
Which Theocles [41] in raptured vision saw,
While through poetic scenes the genius
        roves,
Or wanders wild in academic groves;   490
That Nature our society adores,
Where Tindal dictates, and Silenus [42]
        snores."
    Roused at his name, up rose the bowzy
        Sire,
And shook from out his pipe the seeds of
        fire;
Then snapt his box, and stroked his belly
        down:
Rosy and reverend, though without a gown.
Bland and familiar to the throne he came,
Led up the youth, and called the Goddess
        Dame.
Then thus. "From Priest-craft happily set
        free,
Lo! every finished son returns to thee: 500
First slave to words, then vassal to a name,
Then dupe to party; child and man the
        same;
Bounded by Nature, narrowed still by art,
A trifling head, and a contracted heart.
Thus bred, thus taught, how many have I
        seen,
Smiling on all, and smiled on by a Queen.
Marked out for honours, honour'd for their
        birth,
To thee the most rebellious things on earth:
Now to thy gentle shadow all are shrunk,
All melted down, in pension, or in punk! 510
So K* so B** sneaked into the grave,
A monarch's half, and half a harlot's slave.
Poor W** nipt in Folly's broadest bloom,
Who praises now? his chaplain on his tomb.
Then take them all, oh take them to thy
        breast!

[41] One of the participants in the dialogue of
Shaftesbury's *Moralists*.
[42] "Silenus was an Epicurean philosopher,
as appears from Virgil, Eclog. 6. where he sings
the principles of that philosophy in his drink."
—PW. Silenus is thought to represent Thomas
Gordon, who had been a Walpole supporter
and who had been rewarded for his services by
being made Commissioner of the Wine Li-
censes.—Sutherland, Twick. Ed.

Thy *Magus*, Goddess! shall perform the
        rest."
    With that, a Wizard Old [43] his *cup* ex-
        tends;
Which whoso tastes, forgets his former
        friends,
Sire, ancestors, himself. One casts his eyes
Up to a *star*, and like Endymion dies: 520
A *feather* shooting from another's head,
Extracts his brain, and principle is fled,
Lost is his God, his country, every thing;
And nothing left but homage to a king!
The vulgar herd turn off to roll with hogs,
To run with horses, or to hunt with dogs;
But, sad example! never to escape
Their infamy, still keep the human shape.[44]
    But she, good Goddess, sent to every child
Firm Impudence, or Stupefaction mild; 530
And straight succeeded, leaving shame no
        room,
Cibberian forehead, or Cimmerian gloom.
    Kind Self-conceit to some her glass ap-
        plies,
Which no one looks in with another's eyes:
But as the flatterer or dependant paint,
Beholds himself a patriot, chief, or saint.
    On others Interest her gay livery flings,
Interest, that waves on party-colour'd wings:

[43] "Here beginneth the celebration of the
greater mysteries of the Goddess, which the
poet in his invocation ver. 5. promised to sing.
For when now each aspirant, as was the custom, had proved his qualification and claim to
a participation, the High Priest of Dullness
first initiateth the assembly by the usual way
of *libation*. And then each of the initiated, as
was always required, putteth on a *new nature*,
described from ver. 518 to 529. When the High
Priest and Goddess have thus done their parts,
each of them is delivered into the hands of his
conductor, and inferior minister or *hierophant*,
whose names are *Impudence, Stupefaction,
Self-conceit, Self-interest, Pleasure, Epicurism*,
etc. to lead them through the several apartments of her mystic dome or palace. When all
this is over, the sovereign Goddess, from ver.
565 to 600 conferreth her titles and degrees;
rewards inseparably attendant on the *participation* of the *mysteries* . . . Lastly the great
Mother shutteth up the solemnity with her
gracious benediction, which concludeth in
drawing the curtain, and laying all her children to rest."—Scrib.
[44] "The effects of the Magus's cup are just
contrary to that of Circe. Hers took away the
shape and left the human mind: this takes
away the mind, and leaves the human shape."
—W.

Turned to the sun, she casts a thousand
    dyes,
And, as she turns, the colours fall or
    rise.   540
  Others the Siren Sisters warble round,
And empty heads console with empty sound.
No more, alas! the voice of fame they hear,
The balm of Dullness trickling in their ear.
Great C**, H**, P**, R**, K*,
Why all your toils? your sons have learned
    to sing.
How quick ambition hastes to ridicule!
The sire is made a peer, the son a fool.
  On some, a Priest succinct in amice white
Attends; all flesh is nothing in his sight! 550
Beeves, at his touch, at once to jelly turn,
And the huge boar is shrunk into an Urn:
The board with specious miracles he loads,
Turns hares to larks, and pigeons into
    toads.
Another (for in all what one can shine?)
Explains the *seve* and *verdeur* of the vine.
What cannot copious sacrifice attone?
Thy truffles, Perigord! thy hams, Bayonne!
With French libation, and Italian strain,
Wash Bladen white, and expiate Hays's 45
    stain.   560
Knight lifts the head, for what are crowds
    undone
To three essential partridges in one?
Gone every blush, and silent all reproach,
Contending princes mount them in their
    coach.
  Next bidding all draw near on bended
    knees,
The Queen confers her *titles* and *degrees*.
Her children first of more distinguished
    sort,
Who study Shakespeare at the Inns of
    Court,
Impale a glow-worm, or vertû profess,
Shine in the dignity of F.R.S.   570
Some, deep Free-Masons, join the silent race
Worthy to fill Pythagoras's place:
Some botanists, or florists at the least,
Or issue members of an annual feast.
Nor past the meanest unregarded, one
Rose a Gregorian, one a Gormogon.46
The last, not least in honour or applause,
Isis and Cam made Doctors of her Laws.

45 "Names of gamesters . . ."—PW.
46 "A sort of lay-brothers, *slips* from the
root of the Free Masons."—PW. Founded to
ridicule the Free Masons.—Sutherland, Twick.
Ed.

  Then blessing all, "Go Children of my
    care!
To practice now from theory repair.   580
All my commands are easy, short, and full:
My Sons! be proud, be selfish, and be dull.
Guard my prerogative, assert my throne:
This nod confirms each privilege your
    own.47
The cap and switch be sacred to his grace;
With staff and pumps the marquis lead the
    race;
From stage to stage the licensed earl may
    run,
Paired with his fellow-charioteer the sun;
The learned baron butterflies design,
Or draw to silk Arachne's subtile line; 590
The judge to dance his brother sergeant
    call;
The senator at cricket urge the ball;
The bishop stow (pontific luxury!)
An hundred souls of turkeys in a pie;
The sturdy squire to Gallic masters stoop,
And drown his lands and manors in a soup.
Others import yet nobler arts from France,
Teach kings to fiddle, and make senates
    dance.
Perhaps more high 48 some daring son may
    soar,
Proud to my list to add one monarch
    more;   600
And nobly conscious, princes are but things
Born for first ministers, as slaves for kings,
Tyrant supreme! shall three estates com-
    mand,
AND MAKE ONE MIGHTY DUNCIAD OF THE
    LAND!"
  More she had spoke, but yawn'd—All
    Nature nods:
What mortal can resist the yawn of gods?
Churches and chapels instantly it reached;
(St. James's first, for leaden Gilbert
    preached)

47 "This speech of Dullness to her sons at
parting may possibly fall short of the reader's
expectation; who may imagine the Goddess
might give them a charge of more consequence,
and, from such a theory as is before delivered,
incite them to the practice of something more
extraordinary than to personate running footmen [see *staff and pumps* below], jockeys [see
cap and switch], stage coachmen, etc."—PW.
Sutherland notes that it was a fashionable
affectation about 1738–39 for young men to
appear in public in the dress of grooms,
jockeys, etc.—Twick. Ed.
48 ll. 599–604. An attack on Walpole's long
ministry, 1721 to 1742.—Sutherland, Twick. Ed.

Then catched the schools; the hall scarce
    kept awake;
The convocation gaped, but could not
    speak: 610
Lost was the nation's sense, nor could be
    found,
While the long solemn unison went round:
Wide, and more wide, it spread o'er all the
    realm;
Even Palinurus nodded at the helm:
The vapour mild o'er each committee crept;
Unfinish'd treaties in each office slept;
And chiefless armies dozed out the cam-
    paign;
And navies yawn'd for orders on the Main.
    O Muse! relate (for you can tell alone,
Wits have short memories, and dunces
    none)   620
Relate, who first, who last resigned to rest;
Whose heads she partly, whose completely
    blest;
What charms could faction, what ambition
    lull,
The venal quiet, and entrance the dull;
'Till drowned was sense, and shame, and
    right, and wrong—
O sing, and hush the nations with thy song!

   *   *   *   *   *   *

    In vain, in vain,—the all-composing hour
Resistless falls: The Muse obeys the Power.
She comes! she comes! the sable throne
    behold

Of *Night* Primaeval, and of *Chaos* old! 630
Before her, *Fancy's* gilded clouds decay,
And all its varying rainbows die away.
Wit shoots in vain its momentary fires,
The meteor drops, and in a flash expires.
As one by one, at dread Medea's strain,
The sickening stars fade off th'ethereal
    plain;
As Argus' eyes by Hermes' wand opprest,
Closed one by one to everlasting rest;
Thus at her felt approach, and secret might,
Art after *Art* goes out, and all is night. 640
See skulking *Truth* to her old cavern fled,
Mountains of casuistry heaped o'er her
    head!
Philosophy, that leaned on Heaven before,
Shrinks to her second cause, and is no more.
Physic of *Metaphysic* begs defence,
And *Metaphysic* calls for aid on *Sense!*
See *Mystery* to *Mathematics* fly!
In vain! they gaze, turn giddy, rave, and die.
Religion blushing veils her sacred fires,
And unawares *Morality* expires.   650
Nor *public* flame, nor *private,* dares to
    shine;
Nor *human* spark is left, nor glimpse
    divine!
Lo! thy dread Empire, CHAOS! is restored;
Light dies before thy uncreating word:
Thy hand, great Anarch! lets the curtain
    fall;
And universal darkness buries all.
                       [1743]

EDWARD YOUNG (1683-1765)

The history of the composition of the *Conjectures* can be traced in the Young-Richardson correspondence, *Monthly Magazine*, XLII-XLIV (1816-17). See A. D. McKillop, "Richardson, Young, and the *Conjectures*," *MP*, XXII (1925), 391-404. Young's praise of originality is based on arguments which had long been used in the controversy between the Ancients and the Moderns (see Swift's *Battle of the Books*, and note, page 1206). Young's conception of originality is twofold: (*a*) as in the advance of science, it opens up new subjects and explores new fields; (*b*) as in the Protestant tradition, it derives from the independent individual, who may be variously described as spontaneous, self-reliant, natural, or original. New matter is drawn from without; a new spirit or inspiration is drawn from within. For the religious aspects of this progressive doctrine, see R. S. Crane, "Anglican Apologetics and the Idea of Progress," *MP*, XXXI (1934), 373-74. In the eighteenth century this inner source came to be called "original genius," and critics were more and more disposed to emphasize the superiority of the natural to the learned or artificial genius, the superiority of Shakespeare to Jonson, of Homer and Ossian to Virgil. Cp. *Spectator*, No. 160, pages 285-87 above.

Young at first planned two letters, one on "original" and one on "moral" genius. The religious associations of his doctrine of originality and the moralizing inclinations of his correspondent and adviser Richardson led him to give a place of honor at the end of the *Conjectures* to the story of Addison's death. Addison is said to have called his step-son to his deathbed and exclaimed, "See in what peace a Christian can die." This conclusion, which is referred to at the opening of the *Conjectures*, is not given in the present selections.

CONJECTURES ON ORIGINAL COMPOSITION

In a Letter to the Author of *Sir Charles Grandison*

Dear Sir,—We confess the follies of youth without a blush; not so those of age. However, keep me a little in countenance by considering that age wants amusements more, though it can justify them less, than the preceding periods of life. How you may relish the pastime here sent you, I know not. It is miscellaneous in its nature, somewhat licentious in its conduct, 10 and perhaps not over-important in its end. However, I have endeavoured to make some amends by digressing into subjects more important, and more suitable to my season of life. A serious thought standing single among many of a lighter nature will sometimes strike the careless wanderer after amusement only, with useful awe; as monumental marbles scattered in a 20 wide pleasure garden (and such there are) will call to recollection those who would never have sought it in a churchyard walk of mournful yews.

To one such monument I may conduct you, in which is a hidden lustre, like the sepulchral lamps of old; but not like those will this be extinguished, but shine the brighter for being produced, after so long concealment, into open day.

You remember that your worthy patron and our common friend [1] put some questions on the serious drama, at the same time when he desired our sentiments on original and on moral composition. Though I despair of breaking through the frozen obstructions of age, and care's incumbent cloud, into that flow of thought and brightness of expression which sub-

[1] It was really Richardson himself who suggested the subject.

jects so polite require; yet will I hazard some conjectures on them.

I begin with original composition; and the more willingly as it seems an original subject to me, who have seen nothing hitherto written on it: but first, a few thoughts on composition in general. Some are of opinion that its growth at present is too luxuriant, and that the press is overcharged. Overcharged, I think, it could never be, if none were admitted but such as brought their imprimatur from sound understanding and the public good. Wit indeed, however brilliant, should not be permitted to gaze self-enamoured on its useless charms in that fountain of fame (if so I may call the press), if beauty is all that it has to boast; but, like the first Brutus,[2] it should sacrifice its most darling offspring to the sacred interests of virtue and real service of mankind.

This restriction allowed, the more composition the better. To men of letters and leisure it is not only a noble amusement but a sweet refuge; it improves their parts and promotes their peace; it opens a back-door out of the bustle of this busy and idle world into a delicious garden of moral and intellectual fruits and flowers, the key of which is denied to the rest of mankind. When stung with idle anxieties, or teased with fruitless impertinence, or yawning over insipid diversions, then we perceive the blessing of a lettered recess. With what a gust do we retire to our disinterested and immortal friends in our closet, and find our minds, when applied to some favorite theme, as naturally and as easily quieted and refreshed as a peevish child (and peevish children are we all till we fall asleep) when laid to the breast! Our happiness no longer lives on charity, nor bids fair for a fall, by leaning on that most precarious and thorny pillow, another's pleasure, for our repose. How independent of the world is he who can

2 See Thomson, *Winter,* lines 507–8 and note, page 1228.

daily find new acquaintance, that at once entertain and improve him, in the little world, the minute but fruitful creation, of his own mind!

These advantages composition affords us, whether we write ourselves or in more humble amusement peruse the works of others. While we bustle through the thronged walks of public life, it gives us a respite, at least, from care—a pleasing pause of refreshing recollection. If the country is our choice, or fate, there it rescues us from sloth and sensuality, which like obscene vermin are apt gradually to creep unperceived into the delightful bowers of our retirement and to poison all its sweets. Conscious guilt robs the rose of its scent, the lily of its lustre, and makes an Eden a deflowered and dismal scene.

Moreover, if we consider life's endless evils, what can be more prudent than to provide for consolation under them? A consolation under them the wisest of men have found in the pleasures of the pen. Witness, among many more, Thucydides, Xenophon, Tully, Ovid, Seneca, Pliny the Younger, who says, *In uxoris infirmitate, et amicorum periculo, aut morte turbatus, ad studia, unicum doloris levamentum, confugio.*[3] And why not add to these their modern equals, Chaucer, Raleigh, Bacon, Milton, Clarendon, under the same shield, unwounded by misfortune, and nobly smiling in distress?

Composition was a cordial to these under the frowns of Fortune; but evils there are which her smiles cannot prevent or cure. Among these are the languors of old age. If those are held honorable who in a hand benumbed by time have grasped the just sword in defence of their country, shall they be less esteemed whose unsteady pen vibrates to the last in the cause of re-

3 Pliny, *Letters,* VIII, xix (inaccurately quoted): "Distracted by my wife's ill health, by the dangerous illness or death of my friends, I fly to my studies, the sole consolation of my sorrows."

ligion, of virtue, of learning? Both these are happy in this, that by fixing their attention on objects most important, they escape numberless little anxieties, and that *taedium vitae* which often hangs so heavy on its evening hours. May not this insinuate some apology for my spilling ink and spoiling paper so late in life?

But there are who write with vigor and success, to the world's delight and their own renown. These are the glorious fruits where genius prevails. The mind of a man of genius is a fertile and pleasant field, pleasant as Elysium and fertile as Tempe; it enjoys a perpetual spring. Of that spring, originals are the fairest flowers: imitations are of quicker growth but fainter bloom. Imitations are of two kinds: one of nature, one of authors. The first we call originals, and confine the term imitation to the second. I shall not enter into the curious inquiry of what is or is not, strictly speaking, original, content with what all must allow, that some compositions are more so than others; and the more they are so, I say, the better. Originals are, and ought to be, great favorites, for they are great benefactors; they extend the republic of letters and add a new province to its dominion. Imitators only give us a sort of duplicates of what we had, possibly much better, before; increasing the mere drug of books, while all that makes them valuable, knowledge and genius, are at a stand. The pen of an original writer, like Armida's wand,[4] out of a barren waste calls a blooming spring. Out of that blooming spring an imitator is a transplanter of laurels, which sometimes die on removal, always languish in a foreign soil.

But suppose an imitator to be most excellent (and such there are), yet still he but nobly builds on another's foundation; his debt is at least equal to his glory, which therefore on the balance cannot be very great. On the

contrary, an original, though but indifferent (its originality being set aside), yet has something to boast; it is something to say with him in Horace,

Meo sum pauper in aere; [5]

and to share ambition with no less than Caesar, who declared he had rather be the first in a village than the second at Rome.

Still farther: an imitator shares his crown, if he has one, with the chosen object of his imitation; an original enjoys an undivided applause. An original may be said to be of a vegetable nature; it rises spontaneously from the vital root of genius; it grows, it is not made. Imitations are often a sort of manufacture wrought up by those mechanics, art and labor, out of preëxistent materials not their own.

Again: we read imitation with somewhat of his languor who listens to a twice-told tale. Our spirits rouse at an original; that is a perfect stranger, and all throng to learn what news from a foreign land; and though it comes, like an Indian prince, adorned with feathers only, having little of weight; yet of our attention it will rob the more solid, if not equally new. Thus every telescope is lifted at a new-discovered star; it makes a hundred astronomers in a moment, and denies equal notice to the sun. But if an original, by being as excellent as new, adds admiration to surprise, then are we at the writer's mercy; on the strong wing of his imagination we are snatched from Britain to Italy, from climate to climate, from pleasure to pleasure; we have no home, no thought, of our own, till the magician drops his pen. And then falling down into ourselves, we awake to flat realities, lamenting the change, like the beggar who dreamt himself a prince. It is with thoughts as it is with words, and with both as with men; they may

---

[4] Armida is the enchantress in Tasso's *Jerusalem Delivered.*

[5] Horace, *Epistles,* II, ii, 12: "I'm poor, but not in debt."

grow old and die. Words tarnished by passing through the mouths of the vulgar are laid aside as inelegant and obsolete. So thoughts, when become too common, should lose their currency; and we should send new metal to the mint, that is, new meaning to the press. The division of tongues at Babel did not more effectually debar men from making themselves a name (as the Scripture speaks), than the too great concurrence or union of tongues will do forever. We may as well grow good by another's virtue, or fat by another's food, as famous by another's thought. The world will pay its debt of praise but once; and instead of applauding, explode a second demand as a cheat.

If it is said that most of the Latin classics, and all the Greek except perhaps Homer, Pindar, and Anacreon, are in the number of imitators, yet receive our highest applause; our answer is that they, though not real, are accidental originals; the works they imitated, few excepted, are lost; they, on their father's decease, enter as lawful heirs on their estates in fame. The fathers of our copyists are still in possession, and secured in it, in spite of Goths and flames, by the perpetuating power of the press. Very late must a modern imitator's fame arrive, if it waits for their decease.

An original enters early on reputation: Fame, fond of new glories, sounds her trumpet in triumph at its birth; and yet how few are awakened by it into the noble ambition of like attempts! Ambition is sometimes no vice in life; it is always a virtue in composition. High in the towering Alps is the fountain of the Po; high in fame and in antiquity is the fountain of an imitator's undertaking; but the river and the imitation humbly creep along the vale. So few are our originals that if all other books were to be burnt, the lettered world would resemble some metropolis in flames, where a few incombustible buildings, a fortress, temple, or tower, lift their heads in melancholy grandeur amid the mighty ruin. Compared with this conflagration old Omar [6] lighted up but a small bonfire, when he heated the baths of the barbarians for eight months together with the famed Alexandrian library's inestimable spoils, that no profane book might obstruct the triumphant progress of his holy Alcoran round the globe.

But why are originals so few? Not because the writer's harvest is over, the great reapers of antiquity having left nothing to be gleaned behind them; nor because the human mind's teeming time is past, or because it is incapable of putting forth unprecedented births; but because illustrious examples engross, prejudice, and intimidate. They engross our attention and so prevent a due inspection of ourselves; they prejudice our judgment in favor of their abilities and so lessen the sense of our own; and they intimidate us with the splendor of their renown and thus under diffidence bury our strength. Nature's impossibilities and those of diffidence lie wide asunder.

Let it not be suspected that I would weakly insinuate anything in favor of the moderns, as compared with ancient authors; no, I am lamenting their great inferiority. But I think it is no necessary inferiority; that it is not from divine destination, but from some cause far beneath the moon. [7] I think that human souls through all periods are equal; that due care and exertion would set us nearer our immortal predecessors than we are at present; and he who questions and

[6] The famous Alexandrian Library, the greatest of the ancient world, was destroyed long before the capture of Alexandria by the Arabs in 641.

[7] Young's note refers to Thomas Blackwell, *Enquiry into the Life and Writings of Homer* (2nd ed., 1736), p. 76: "It has been doubted whether any influence of stars, any power of planets, or kindly aspects of the heavenly bodies might not at times reach our globe and impregnate some favorite race with a celestial spirit. Supernatural conceptions and miraculous nurslings have been contrived as a salvo for our belief, when the hero or sage achieves things which we fancy above the reach of man."

confutes this will show abilities not a little tending toward a proof of that equality which he denies.

After all, the first ancients had no merit in being originals; they could not be imitators. Modern writers have a choice to make, and therefore have a merit in their power. They may soar in the regions of liberty, or move in the soft fetters of easy imitation; and imitation has as many plausible reasons to urge as Pleasure had to offer to Hercules. Hercules made the choice of a hero,[8] and so became immortal.

Yet let not assertors of classic excellence imagine that I deny the tribute it so well deserves. He that admires not ancient authors betrays a secret he would conceal, and tells the world that he does not understand them. Let us be as far from neglecting as from copying their admirable compositions; sacred be their rights, and inviolable their fame. Let our understanding feed on theirs; they afford the noblest nourishment; but let them nourish, not annihilate, our own. When we read, let our imagination kindle at their charms; when we write, let our judgment shut them out of our thoughts; treat even Homer himself as his royal admirer was treated by the cynic; bid him stand aside, nor shade our composition from the beams of our own genius; for nothing original can rise, nothing immortal can ripen, in any other sun.

Must we then, you say, not imitate ancient authors? Imitate them by all means, but imitate aright. He that imitates the divine *Iliad* does not imitate Homer, but he who takes the same method which Homer took for arriving at a capacity of accomplishing a work so great. Tread in his steps to the sole fountain of immortality; drink where he drank, at the true Helicon, that is, at the breast of Nature; imitate, but imitate not the

composition but the man. For may not this paradox pass into a maxim?— viz., "The less we copy the renowned ancients, we shall resemble them the more."

But possibly you may reply that you must either imitate Homer or depart from Nature. Not so: for suppose you was to change place in time with Homer, then, if you write naturally, you might as well charge Homer with an imitation of you. Can you be said to imitate Homer for writing so, as you would have written if Homer had never been? As far as a regard to Nature and sound sense will permit a departure from your great predecessors, so far, ambitiously depart from them; the farther from them in similitude, the nearer are you to them in excellence; you rise by it into an original, become a noble collateral, not an humble descendant from them. Let us build our compositions with the spirit and in the taste of the ancients, but not with their materials: thus will they resemble the structures of Pericles at Athens, which Plutarch commends for having had an air of antiquity as soon as they were built.[9] All eminence and distinction lies out of the beaten road; excursion and deviation are necessary to find it; and the more remote your path from the highway the more reputable; if, like poor Gulliver (of whom anon), you fall not into a ditch in your way to glory.

What glory to come near, what glory to reach, what glory (presumptuous thought!) to surpass our predecessors! And is that then in Nature absolutely impossible? Or is it not, rather, contrary to Nature to fail in it? Nature herself sets the ladder, all wanting is our ambition to climb. For by the bounty of Nature we are as strong as our predecessors, and by the favor of time (which is but another round in Nature's scale) we stand on higher ground. As to the first, were they more than men? Or are we less? Are not our minds cast in the same mold with those before the flood? The flood af-

[8] In Xenophon's *Memorabilia*, II,i, Prodicus tells how Hercules was offered the choice between Virtue and Vice or "Pleasure," personified as two women. This became a popular educational allegory.

[9] Plutarch, *Pericles*, xiii

fected matter—mind escaped. As to the second, though we are moderns, the world is an ancient [10]—more ancient far than when they whom we most admire filled it with their fame. Have we not their beauties, as stars, to guide; their defects, as rocks, to be shunned; the judgment of ages on both, as a chart to conduct and a sure helm to steer us in our passage to greater perfection than theirs? And shall we be stopped in our rival pretensions to fame by this just reproof?

Stat contra, dicitque tibi tua pagina, fur es.
MARTIAL.[11]

It is by a sort of noble contagion, from a general familiarity with their writings, and not by any particular sordid theft, that we can be the better for those who went before us. Hope we, from plagiarism, any domination in literature, as that of Rome arose from a nest of thieves?

Rome was a powerful ally to many states; ancient authors are our powerful allies; but we must take heed that they do not succor till they enslave, after the manner of Rome. Too formidable an idea of their superiority, like a spectre, would fright us out of a proper use of our wits, and dwarf our understanding by making a giant of theirs. Too great awe for them lays genius under restraint, and denies it that free scope, that full elbow-room, which is requisite for striking its most masterly strokes. Genius is a masterworkman, learning is but an instrument; and an instrument, though most valuable, yet not always indispensable. Heaven will not admit of a partner in the accomplishment of some favorite spirits; but rejecting all human means, assumes the whole glory to itself. Have not some, though not famed for erudition, so written as almost to persuade us that they shone brighter and soared higher for escaping the boasted aid of that proud ally?

Nor is it strange; for what, for the most part, mean we by genius, but the power of accomplishing great things without the means generally reputed necessary to that end? A genius differs from a good understanding as a magician from a good architect: that raises his structure by means invisible; this by the skilful use of common tools. Hence genius has ever been supposed to partake of something divine. *Nemo unquam vir magnus fuit, sine aliquo afflatu divino.*[12]

Learning, destitute of this superior aid, is fond and proud of what has cost it much pains; is a great lover of rules, and boaster of famed examples: as beauties less perfect, who owe half their charms to cautious art, learning inveighs against natural unstudied graces and small harmless inaccuracies, and sets rigid bounds to that liberty to which genius often owes its supreme glory, but the no-genius its frequent ruin. For unprescribed beauties and unexampled excellence, which are characteristic of genius, lie without the pale of learning's authorities and laws; which pale, genius must leap to come at them; but by that leap, if genius is wanting, we break our necks; we lose that little credit which possibly we might have enjoyed before. For rules like crutches are a needful aid to the lame, though an impediment to the strong. A Homer casts them away, and like his Achilles,

Jura negat sibi nata, nihil non arrogat,[13]

by native force of mind. There is something in poetry beyond prose-reason; there are mysteries in it not to be explained but admired, which render mere prose-men infidels to their divinity. And here pardon a second paradox, viz., "Genius often then deserves most to be praised, when it is most sure to be condemned; that is, when its excellence, from mounting

[10] A familiar idea, from Bacon to Fontenelle.
[11] Martial, *Epigrams*, I, liii. "Your page confronts you and calls you 'thief.'"
[12] Cicero, *De Natura Deorum*, II, lxvi (inaccurately quoted): "No one was ever a great man without some divine inspiration."
[13] Horace, *Ars Poetica*, 122: "He denies that the laws apply to him, and claims everything for himself."

high, to weak eyes is quite out of sight."

If I might speak farther of learning and genius, I would compare genius to virtue, and learning to riches. As riches are most wanted where there is least virtue, so learning where there is least genius. As virtue without much riches can give happiness, so genius without much learning can give renown. As it is said in Terence, *Pecuniam negligere interdum maximum est lucrum*,[14] so to neglect of learning, genius sometimes owes its greater glory. Genius therefore leaves but the second place among men of letters to the learned. It is their merit and ambition to fling light on the works of genius and point out its charms. We must justly reverence their informing radius for that favor, but we must much more admire the radiant stars pointed out by them.

A star of the first magnitude among the moderns was Shakespeare; among the ancients, Pindar, who (as Vossius tells us) [15] boasted of his no-learning, calling himself the eagle, for his flight above it. And such genii as these may indeed have much reliance on their own native powers. For genius may be compared to the natural strength of the body; learning to the super-induced accoutrements of arms: if the first is equal to the proposed exploit, the latter rather encumbers than assists, rather retards than promotes the victory. *Sacer nobis inest Deus*,[16] says Seneca. With regard to the moral world, conscience, with regard to the intellectual, genius, is that god within. Genius can set us right in composition, without the rules of the learned, as conscience sets us right in life without the laws of the land: this, singly, can make us good as men; that, singly, as writers can sometimes make us great.

I say "sometimes," because there is a genius which stands in need of learning to make it shine. Of genius there are two species, an earlier and a later, or call them infantine and adult. An adult genius comes out of Nature's hand as Pallas out of Jove's head, at full growth and mature: Shakespeare's genius was of this kind; on the contrary, Swift stumbled at the threshold and set out for distinction on feeble knees: his was an infantine genius—a genius which, like other infants, must be nursed and educated, or it will come to naught: learning is its nurse and tutor, but this nurse may overlay with an indigested load which smothers common sense, and this tutor may mislead with pedantic prejudice which vitiates the best understanding. As too great admirers of the fathers of the Church have sometimes set up their authority against the true sense of Scripture, so too great admirers of the classical fathers have sometimes set up their authority or example against reason.

Neve minor, neu sit quinto productior actu Fabula.[17]

So says Horace—so says ancient example. But reason has not subscribed. I know but one book that can justify our implicit acquiescence in it; [18] and (by the way) on that book a noble disdain of undue deference to prior opinion has lately cast and is still casting a new and inestimable light.[19]

But, superstition for our predecessors set aside, the classics are forever our rightful and revered masters in composition, and our understandings bow before them—but when? When a master is wanted, which sometimes, as I have shown, is not the case. Some are pupils of nature only nor go farther to school; from such we reap

[14] Terence, *Adelphi*, ii, 216: "Sometimes the best way to make money is to disregard it."

[15] A reference to the work of the Dutch critic and scholar G. J. Vossius, *De Artis Poeticae Natura ac Constitutione* (1647), chap. v.

[16] "The Divinity is within us." A basic idea in Seneca, though not found by the editors in precisely these words. For very similar expressions, cf. Seneca, *Moral Epistles* xli, and Ovid, *Fasti* 1, "Est Deus in nobis."

[17] Horace, *Ars Poetica*, 189–90: "Let the play be neither more nor less than five acts in length."

[18] Presumably the Bible.

[19] Possibly a reference to Bishop Lowth's treatise *De Sacra Poesi Hebraeorum* (1753).

often a double advantage: they not only rival the reputation of the great ancient authors, but also reduce the number of mean ones among the moderns. For when they enter on subjects which have been in former hands, such is their superiority that like a tenth wave they overwhelm and bury in oblivion all that went before; and thus not only enrich and adorn, but remove a load, and lessen the labor of the learned world.

"But," you say, "since originals can arise from genius only, and since genius is so very rare, it is scarce worth while to labor a point so much, from which we can reasonably expect so little." To show that genius is not so very rare as you imagine, I shall point out strong instances of it in a far distant quarter from that mentioned above. The minds of the schoolmen were almost as much cloistered as their bodies; they had but little learning and few books, yet may the most learned be struck with some astonishment at their so singular natural sagacity and most exquisite edge of thought. Who would expect to find Pindar and Scotus, Shakespeare and Aquinas, of the same party? Both equally show an original unindebted energy; the *vigor igneus* and *caelestis origo* [20] burns in both, and leaves us in doubt whether genius is more evident in the sublime flights and beauteous flowers of poetry, or in the profound penetrations and marvellously keen and minute distinctions called the thorns of the schools. There might have been more able consuls called from the plough than ever arrived at that honor: many a genius probably there has been which could neither write nor read. So that genius, that supreme lustre of literature, is less rare than you conceive.

By the praise of genius we detract not from learning; we detract not from the value of gold by saying that diamond has greater still. He who disregards learning shows that he wants

[20] *Æneid,* VI, 730: "a fiery power . . . a heavenly origin."

its aid, and he that overvalues it shows that its aid has done him harm. Overvalued indeed it cannot be, if genius, as to composition, is valued more. Learning we thank, genius we revere; that gives us pleasure, this gives us rapture; that informs, this inspires and is itself inspired; for genius is from heaven, learning from man; this sets us above the low and illiterate, that above the learned and polite. Learning is borrowed knowledge; genius is knowledge innate and quite our own. Therefore, as Bacon observes, it may take a nobler name and be called wisdom, in which sense of wisdom some are born wise. [21]

But here a caution is necessary against the most fatal of errors in those automaths, those self-taught philosophers of our age, who set up genius, and often mere fancied genius, not only above human learning but divine truth. I have called genius wisdom, but let it be remembered that in the most renowned ages of the most refined heathen wisdom (and theirs is not Christian) , "the world by wisdom knew not God, and it pleased God by the foolishness of preaching to save those that believed." In the fairyland of fancy genius may wander wild; there it has a creative power, and may reign arbitrarily over its own empire of chimeras. The wide field of Nature also lies open before it, where it may range unconfined, make what discoveries it can, and sport with its infinite objects uncontrolled, as far as visible Nature extends, painting them as wantonly as it will. But what painter of the most unbounded and exalted genius can give us the true portrait of a seraph? He can give us only what by his own or others' eyes has been seen, though that indeed infinitely compounded, raised, burlesqued, dishonoured, or adorned; in like manner, who can give divine

[21] Perhaps based on *Advancement of Learning,* I, vi: "All learning is knowledge acquired, and all knowledge in God is original: and therefore we must look for it by another name, that of wisdom or sapience."

truth unrevealed? Much less should any presume to set aside divine truth when revealed, as incongruous to their own sagacities. Is this too serious for my subject? I shall be more so before I close.[22]

Having put in a caveat against the most fatal of errors, from the too great indulgence of genius, return we now to the too great suppression of it which is detrimental to composition, and endeavour to rescue the writer as well as the man. I have said that some are born wise; but they, like those that are born rich, by neglecting the cultivation and produce of their own possessions, and by running in debt, may be beggared at last; and lose their reputations, as younger brothers estates, not by being born with less abilities than the rich heir, but at too late an hour.

Many a great man has been lost to himself and the public, purely because great ones were born before him. Hermias,[23] in his collections on Homer's blindness, says that, Homer requesting the gods to grant him a sight of Achilles, that hero rose, but in armor so bright that it struck Homer blind with the blaze. Let not the blaze of even Homer's muse darken us to the discernment of our own powers, which may possibly set us above the rank of imitators, who, though most excellent and even immortal (as some of them are) yet are still but *Dii minorum gentium,* nor can expect the largest share of incense, the greatest profusion of praise, on their secondary altars.

But farther still, a spirit of imitation hath many ill effects: I shall confine myself to three. First, it deprives the liberal and politer arts of an advantage which the mechanic enjoy: in these, men are ever endeavouring to go beyond their predecessors; in the former, to follow them. And since

copies surpass not their originals, as streams rise not higher than their spring, rarely so high; hence, while arts mechanic are in perpetual progress and increase, the liberal are in retrogradation and decay. *These* resemble pyramids, are broad at bottom, but lessen exceedingly as they rise; *those* resemble rivers which from a small fountain-head are spreading ever wider and wider as they run. Hence it is evident that different portions of understanding are not (as some imagine) allotted to different periods of time, for we see in the same period understanding rising in one set of artists and declining in another. Therefore Nature stands absolved, and our inferiority in composition must be charged on ourselves.

Nay, so far are we from complying with a necessity which Nature lays us under that, secondly, by a spirit of imitation we counteract Nature and thwart her design. She brings us into the world all originals: no two faces, no two minds are just alike, but all bear Nature's evident mark of separation on them. Born originals, how comes it to pass that we die copies? That meddling ape Imitation, as soon as we come to years of indiscretion (so let me speak), snatches the pen and blots out Nature's mark of separation, cancels her kind intention, destroys all mental individuality; the lettered world no longer consists of singulars, it is a medley, a mass; and a hundred books at bottom are but one. Why are monkeys such masters of mimicry? Why receive they such a talent at imitation? Is it not as the Spartan slaves received a license for ebriety, that their betters might be ashamed of it?

The third fault to be found with a spirit of imitation is that with great incongruity it makes us poor and proud; makes us think little and write much; gives us huge folios which are little better than more reputable cushions to promote our repose. Have not some sevenfold volumes put us in mind of Ovid's sevenfold channels of the Nile at the conflagration?

[22] This long and important paragraph is substantially Richardson's.

[23] A reference to the commentary of Hermias, an Alexandrian philosopher, on Plato's *Phaedrus.*

*Pulverulenta vacant septem sine flumine
valles.*[24]

Such leaden labors are like Lycurgus'
iron money,[25] which was so much less
in value than in bulk that it required
barns for strong-boxes, and a yoke of
oxen to draw five hundred pounds.

But notwithstanding these disadvantages of imitation, imitation must
be the lot (and often an honorable lot
it is) of most writers. If there is a
famine of invention in the land, like
Joseph's brethren we must travel far
for food, we must visit the remote and
rich ancients; but an inventive genius
may safely stay at home; that, like the
widow's cruse, is divinely replenished
from within, and affords us a miraculous delight. Whether our own genius
be such or not, we diligently should
inquire, that we may not go a-begging
with gold in our purse. For there is a
mine in man which must be deeply
dug ere we can conjecture its contents. Another often sees that in us
which we see not ourselves, and may
there not be that in us which is unseen
by both? That there may, chance often
discovers, either by a luckily chosen
theme, or a mighty premium, or an
absolute necessity of exertion, or a
noble stroke of emulation from another's glory, as that on Thucydides
from hearing Herodotus repeat part
of his history at the Olympic games:
had there been no Herodotus, there
might have been no Thucydides, and
the world's admiration might have
begun at Livy for excellence in that
province of the pen. Demosthenes
had the same stimulation on hearing
Callistratus, or Tully might have been
the first of consummate renown at
the bar.

Quite clear of the dispute concerning ancient and modern learning, we
speak not of performance, but powers.
The modern powers are equal to those

before them; modern performance in
general is deplorably short. How
great are the names just mentioned!
Yet who will dare affirm that as great
may not rise up in some future, or
even in the present age? Reasons there
are why talents may not appear, none
why they may not exist as much in
one period as another. An evocation
of vegetable fruits depends on rain,
air, and sun; an evocation of the
fruits of genius no less depends on
externals. What a marvellous crop
bore it in Greece and Rome! And
what a marvellous sunshine did it
there enjoy! What encouragement
from the nature of their governments
and the spirit of their people! Virgil
and Horace owed their divine talents
to Heaven, their immortal works to
men! thank Maecenas and Augustus
for them. Had it not been for these, the
genius of those poets had lain buried
in their ashes. Athens expended on
her theatre, painting, sculpture, and
architecture, a tax levied for the support of a war.[26] Caesar dropped his
papers when Tully spoke, and Philip
trembled at the voice of Demosthenes,
and has there arisen but one Tully,
one Demosthenes, in so long a course
of years? The powerful eloquence of
them both in one stream should never
bear me down into the melancholy
persuasion that several have not been
born, though they have not emerged.
The sun as much exists in a cloudy
day as in a clear; it is outward, accidental circumstances that with regard
to genius either in nation or age

Collectas fugat nubes, solemque reducit.
                                    VIRGIL.[27]

As great, perhaps greater than those
mentioned (presumptuous as it may
sound) may possibly arise, for who
hath fathomed the mind of man? Its
bounds are as unknown as those of the
creation; since the birth of which, perhaps, not one has so far exerted as
not to leave his possibilities beyond his

[24] Ovid, *Metamorphoses*, II, 255–56: "Seven dusty mouths are empty, seven channels with-out a stream."
[25] See the account of the Spartans in Plu-tarch, *Lycurgus*, ix.

[26] See Plutarch, *Pericles*, xii.
[27] *Æneid*, I, 143: "He puts to flight the gathered clouds, and brings back the sun."

attainments, his powers beyond his exploits. Forming our judgments altogether by what *has* been done, without knowing or at all inquiring what possibly *might* have been done, we naturally enough fall into too mean an opinion of the human mind. If a sketch of the divine *Iliad* before Homer wrote had been given to mankind by some superior being, or otherwise, its execution would probably have appeared beyond the power of man. Now, to surpass it, we think impossible. As the first of these opinions would evidently have been a mistake, why may not the second be so too? Both are founded on the same bottom, on our ignorance of the possible dimensions of the mind of man.

Nor are we only ignorant of the dimensions of the human mind in general, but even of our own. That a man may be scarce less ignorant of his own powers than an oyster of its pearl or a rock of its diamond; that he may possess dormant, unsuspected abilities, till awakened by loud calls or stung up by striking emergencies, is evident from the sudden eruption of some men out of perfect obscurity into public admiration, on the strong impulse of some animating occasion— not more to the world's great surprise than their own. Few authors of distinction but have experienced something of this nature at the first beamings of their yet unsuspected genius on their hitherto dark composition: the writer starts at it, as at a lucid meteor in the night, is much surprised, can scarce believe it true. During his happy confusion it may be said to him, as to Eve at the lake,

What there thou seest, fair creature, is thyself.
MILTON.[28]

Genius in this view is like a dear friend in our company under disguise, who, while we are lamenting his absence, drops his mask, striking us at once with equal surprise and joy. This sensation which I speak of in a writer might favor and so promote the fable

[28] *Paradise Lost.* IV, 468.

of poetic inspiration: a poet of a strong imagination and stronger vanity, on feeling it, might naturally enough realize the world's mere compliment and think himself truly inspired. Which is not improbable, for enthusiasts of all kinds do no less.

Since it is plain that men may be strangers to their own abilities, and by thinking meanly of them without just cause may possibly lose a name, perhaps a name immortal, I would find some means to prevent these evils. Whatever promotes virtue promotes something more, and carries its good influence beyond the moral man. To prevent these evils I borrow two golden rules from ethics, which are no less golden in composition than in life: 1. *Know thyself.* 2. *Reverence thyself.* I design to repay ethics in a future letter by two rules from rhetoric for its service.

1. *Know thyself.* Of ourselves it may be said, as Martial says of a bad neighbor,

Nil tam prope, proculque nobis.[29]

Therefore dive deep into thy bosom; learn the depth, extent, bias, and full forte of thy mind; contract full intimacy with the stranger within thee; excite and cherish every spark of intellectual light and heat, however smothered under former negligence or scattered through the dull, dark mass of common thoughts; and collecting them into a body, let thy genius rise (if a genius thou hast) as the sun from chaos; and if I should then say, like an Indian, *Worship it*— though too bold, yet should I say little more than my second rule enjoins, viz., *Reverence thyself.*

That is, let not great examples or authorities browbeat thy reason into too great a diffidence of thyself; thyself so reverence as to prefer the native growth of thy own mind to the richest import from abroad; such borrowed riches make us poor. The man who thus reverences himself will soon

[29] Martial, *Epigrams,* I, lxxxvi: "Nothing else is so near and yet so far from us."

find the world's reverence to follow his own. His works will stand distinguished; his the sole property of them, which property alone can confer the noble title of an author; that is, of one who (to speak accurately) thinks and composes, while other invaders of the press, how voluminous and learned soever, (with due respect be it spoken) only read and write. [10]

This is the difference between those two luminaries in literature, the well-accomplished scholar and the divine-inspired enthusiast: the first is as the bright morning star, the second as the rising sun. The writer who neglects those two rules above will never stand alone; he makes one of a group and thinks in wretched unanimity with the throng; encumbered with the no- [20] tions of others and impoverished by their abundance, he conceives not the least embryo of new thought, opens not the least vista through the gloom of ordinary writers into the bright walks of rare imagination and singular design; while the true genius is crossing all public roads into fresh untrodden ground, he, up to the knees in antiquity, is treading the sacred [30] footsteps of great examples with the blind veneration of a bigot saluting the papal toe, comfortably hoping full absolution for the sins of his own understanding from the powerful charm of touching his idol's infallibility.

*   *   *   *   *   *

Bacon, under the shadow of whose [40] great name I would shelter my present attempt in favor of originals, says, "Men seek not to know their own stock and abilities, but fancy their possessions to be greater and their abilities less than they really are." [30] Which is in effect saying that we ought

[30] Perhaps connected with or paraphrased from the following in the collection called *Baconiana,* repr. in Bacon, *Works* (1765) I, [50] 570: "Men seem neither well to understand their riches, nor their strength; of the former they believe greater things than they should, and of the latter much less."

to exert more than we do, and that on exertion our probability of success is greater than we conceive.

Nor have I Bacon's opinion only but his assistance too on my side. His mighty mind traveled round the intellectual world, and with a more than eagle's eye saw, and has pointed out, blank spaces or dark spots in it [10] on which the human mind never shone: some of these have been enlightened since; some are benighted still.

Moreover, so boundless are the bold excursions of the human mind that in the vast void beyond real existence it can call forth shadowy beings and unknown worlds, as numerous, as bright, and perhaps as lasting as the [20] stars; such quite original beauties we may call paradisaical.

Natos sine semine flores.
OVID.[31]

When such an ample area for renowned adventure in original attempts lies before us, shall we be as mere leaden pipes conveying to the present age small streams of excellence from [30] its grand reservoir in antiquity, and those too perhaps muddled in the pass? Originals shine like comets; have no peer in their path; are rivaled by none, and the gaze of all. All other compositions (if they shine at all) shine in clusters, like the stars in the galaxy, where like bad neighbors all suffer from all, each particular being diminished and almost lost in the [40] throng.

If thoughts of this nature prevailed, if ancients and modern were no longer considered as masters and pupils, but as hard-matched rivals for renown, then moderns by the longevity of their labors might one day become ancients themselves; and old Time, that best weigher of merits, to keep his balance even, might have the [50] golden weight of an Augustan age in both his scales; or rather our scale might descend, and that of antiquity

[31] Ovid, *Metamorphoses,* I, 108: "Flowers brought forth without seed."

(as a modern match for it strongly speaks) might *kick the beam*.[32]

And why not? For consider, since an impartial Providence scatters talents indifferently, as through all orders of persons so through all periods of time; since a marvellous light unenjoyed of old is poured on us by revelation, with larger prospects extending our understanding, with brighter objects enriching our imagination, with an inestimable prize setting our passions on fire, thus strengthening every power that enables composition to shine; since there has been no fall in man on this side Adam, who left no works—and the works of all other ancients are our auxiliars against themselves, as being perpetual spurs to our ambition and shining lamps in our path to fame; since this world is a school as well for intellectual as moral advance, and the longer human nature is at school the better scholar it should be; since, as the moral world expects its glorious millennium, the world intellectual may hope by the rules of analogy for some superior degrees of excellence to crown her later scenes; nor may it only hope, but must enjoy them too, for Tully, Quintilian, and all true critics allow that virtue assists genius, and that the writer will be more able when better is the man—all these particulars, I say, considered, why should it seem altogether impossible that Heaven's latest editions of the human mind may be the most correct and fair, that the day may come when the moderns may proudly look back on the comparative darkness of former ages, on the children of antiquity, reputing Homer and Demosthenes as the dawn of divine genius and Athens as the cradle of infant fame? What a glorious revolution would this make in the rolls of renown!

"What a rant," say you, "is here!" I partly grant it. Yet consider, my friend, knowledge physical, mathematical, moral, and divine increases; all arts and sciences are making considerable advance; with them, all the accommodations, ornaments, delights, and glories of human life—and these are new food to the genius of a polite writer; these are as the root and composition as the flower; and as the root spreads and thrives, shall the flower fail? As well may a flower flourish when the root is dead. It is prudence to read, genius to relish, glory to surpass ancient authors; and wisdom to try our strength in an attempt in which it would be no great dishonor to fail.

Why condemned Maro his admirable epic to the flames? was it not because his discerning eye saw some length of perfection beyond it? And what he saw, may not others reach? And who bid fairer than our own countrymen for that glory? Something new may be expected from Britons particularly, who seem not to be more severed from the rest of mankind by the surrounding sea than by the current in their veins, and of whom little more appears to be required in order to give us originals than a consistency of character, and making their compositions of a piece with their lives. May our genius shine, and proclaim us in that nobler view!

—minima contentos nocte Britannos.
VIRGIL.[33]

And so it does, for in polite composition, in natural and mathematical knowledge, we have great originals already: Bacon, Boyle, Newton, Shakespeare, Milton have showed us that all the winds cannot blow the British flag farther than an original spirit can convey the British fame; their names go round the world, and what foreign genius strikes not as they pass? Why should not their posterity embark in the same bold bottom of new enterprise, and hope the same success? Hope it they may; or you must assert either that those originals which we already enjoy were written by angels,

[32] *Paradise Lost,* IV, 1004.

[33] Not in Virgil, but in Juvenal, *Satires,* I, ii, 161: "the Britons, who are satisfied with the shortest night."

or deny that we are men. As Simonides
said to Pausanias, reason should say
to the writer, "Remember thou art a
man." And for man not to grasp at all
which is laudable within his reach, is
a dishonor to human nature and a
disobedience to the divine, for as
Heaven does nothing in vain, its gift
of talents implies an injunction of
their use.

A friend of mine [34] has obeyed that
injunction; he has relied on himself,
and with a genius as well moral as
original (to speak in bold terms) has
cast out evil spirits, has made a convert to virtue of a species of composition once most its foe, as the first
Christian emperors expelled demons
and dedicated their temples to the living God.

But you, I know, are sparing in your
praise of this author; therefore I will
speak of one who is sure of your applause. Shakespeare mingled no water
with his wine. lowered his genius by
no vapid imitation. Shakespeare gave
us a Shakespeare, nor could the first
in ancient fame have given us more!
Shakespeare is not their son, but
brother—their equal, and that in spite
of all his faults. Think you this too
bold? Consider, in those ancients what
it is the world admires! Not the fewness of their faults but the number
and brightness of their beauties, and
if Shakespeare is their equal (as he
doubtless is) in that which in them
is admired, then is Shakespeare as
great as they; and not impotence, but
some other cause, must be charged
with his defects. When we are setting
these great men in competition, what
but the comparative size of their
genius is the subject of our inquiry?
And a giant loses nothing of his size,
though he should chance to trip in his
race. But it is a compliment to those
heroes of antiquity to suppose Shakespeare their equal only in dramatic
powers; therefore, though his faults
had been greater, the scale would
still turn in his favor. There is at
least as much genius on the British as

[34] Richardson.

on the Grecian stage, though the
former is not swept so clean—so clean
from violations not only of the dramatic but moral rule, for an honest
heathen, on reading some of our celebrated scenes, might be seriously concerned to see that our obligations to
the religion of Nature were canceled
by Christianity.

Jonson in the serious drama is as
much an imitator as Shakespeare is an
original. He was very learned, as Samson was very strong, to his own hurt:
blind to the nature of tragedy, he
pulled down all antiquity on his head
and buried himself under it; we see
nothing of Jonson, nor indeed of his
admired (but also murdered) ancients; for what shone in the historian
is a cloud on the poet, and *Catiline*
might have been a good play if Sallust
had never written.

Who knows whether Shakespeare
might not have thought less if he had
read more? Who knows if he might
not have labored under the load of
Jonson's learning, as Enceladus under
Aetna? [35] His mighty genius, indeed,
through the most mountainous oppression would have breathed out
some of his inextinguishable fire, yet
possibly he might not have risen up
into that giant, that much more than
common man, at which we now gaze
with amazement and delight. Perhaps
he was as learned as his dramatic
province required, for whatever other
learning he wanted, he was master of
two books unknown to many of the
profoundly read, though books which
the last conflagration alone can destroy—the book of Nature and that of
man. These he had by heart, and has
transcribed many admirable pages of
them into his immortal works. These
are the fountain-head whence the Castalian streams of original composition
flow, and these are often muddied by
other waters, though waters in their
distinct channel most wholesome and
pure, as two chemical liquors, sep-

[35] One of the giants who waged war against
the gods. He was crushed under Sicily and
Mount Aetna.

arately clear as crystal, grow foul by mixture and offend the sight. So that he had not only as much learning as his dramatic province required, but perhaps as it could safely bear. If Milton had spared some of his learning his muse would have gained more glory than he would have lost by it.

*   *   *   *   *   *

[1759]

CHRISTOPHER SMART (1722-1771)

The three selections from this poem in the text follow Mr. W. H. Bond's edition, except for the numbering of the lines and modernization of spelling and punctuation. Mr. Bond feels certain that much of the manuscript has been lost. There are two types of passage: those in which every verse begins with *Let,* and those in which the verses begin with *For.* Mr. Bond has discovered that wherever a *For* passage has been preserved that corresponds in numbering with a *Let* passage, the verses show a distinct correspondence and were probably intended to be read antiphonally. The *Let* passages are almost exclusively Biblical, whereas the *For* passages have many personal references.

The first selection in the text (ll. 1–25) comes from the section that Mr. Bond called Fragment A, ll. 1–25. There is no *For* section to match it. The second selection (ll. 26–68) comes from Fragment B1 (ll. 1–43). Here the *Let* verses have been preserved, and if Mr. Bond is correct about the antiphony, the lines would read:

> Let Elizur rejoice with the Partridge, who is a prisoner of state and is proud of his keepers;
> For I am not without authority in my jeopardy, which I derive inevitably from the glory of the name of the Lord.
> Let Shedeur rejoice with Pyrausta, who dwelleth in a medium of fire, which God hath adapted for him;
> For I bless God whose name is Jealous—and there is a zeal to deliver us from everlasting burnings.

Unfortunately Smart was running out of appropriate Biblical animals by this time, and the *Let* verses have fallen off greatly in poetical worth.

Our third selection ll. 69–142) comes from Fragment B2, and there are no *Let* verses to correspond.

The editors are greatly indebted to both Mr. Stead and Mr. Bond for the above information and for the notes which follow.

The reader who looks up the characters of the first section in the Bible will be surprised and delighted to discover how appropriate the animal associated with each man is. One of the few slips that Smart makes is in l. 16, where he confuses the Ark of Noah with the Ark of the Testimony, as Mr. Stead points out.

JUBILATE AGNO [1]

I

Rejoice in God, O ye Tongues; give the glory to the Lord, and the Lamb.
Nations, and languages, and every creature, in which is the breath of life.
Let man and beast appear before Him, and magnify His name together.
Let Noah and his company approach the throne of Grace, and do homage to the Ark of their Salvation.
Let Abraham present a Ram, and worship the God of his Redemption.
Let Isaac, the Bridegroom, kneel with his Camels, and bless the hope of his pilgrimage.
Let Jacob, and his speckled Drove adore the good Shepherd of Israel.
Let Esau offer a scape Goat for his seed, and rejoice in the blessing of God his Father.

[1] Reprinted by permission of the publishers from Christopher Smart, *Jubilate Agno,* re-edited by William Henry Bond (Cambridge Mass.: Harvard University Press, 1954) , and by permission of William Henry Bond, in whose name sections B1, lines 1–43, and B2, lines 697–770, were copyrighted in 1950.

Let Nimrod, the mighty hunter, bind a Leopard to the altar, and consecrate his spear to the Lord.

Let Ishmael dedicate a Tiger, and give praise for the liberty in which the Lord has set him at large.

Let Balaam appear with an Ass, and bless the Lord his people and his creatures for a reward eternal. 10

Let Anah, the son of Zibion, lead a Mule to the temple, and bless God who amerces the consolation of the creature for the service of Man.

Let Daniel come forth with a Lion, and praise God with all his might through faith in Christ Jesus.

Let Naphtali with an Hind give glory in the goodly words of Thanksgiving.

Let Aaron, the high priest, sanctify a Bull, and let him go free to the Lord and Giver of Life.

Let the Levites of the Lord take the Beavers of ye brook alive into the Ark of the Testimony.

Let Eleazar with the Ermine serve the Lord decently and in purity.

Let Ithamar minister with a Chamois, and bless the name of Him which clotheth the naked.

Let Gershom with a Pygarg bless the name of Him who feedeth the hungry.

Let Merari praise the wisdom and power of God with the Coney, who scoopeth the rock and archeth in the sand. 20

Let Kohath serve the Sable, and bless God in the ornaments of the Temple.

Let Jehoiada bless God with an Hare, whose mazes are determined for the health of the body and to parry the adversary.

Let Ahitub humble himself with an Ape before Almighty God, who is the maker of variety and pleasantry.

Let Abiathar with a Fox praise the name of the Lord, who balances craft against strength and skill against number.

Let Moses, the Man of God, bless with a Lizard, in the sweet majesty of good-nature and the magnimity of meekness.

    ·   ·   ·

For I am not without authority in my jeopardy,[2] which I derive inevitably from the glory of the name of the Lord.

For I bless God whose name is Jealous—and there is a zeal to deliver us from everlasting burnings.

For my existimation [3] is good even amongst the slanderers and my memory shall arise for a sweet savour unto the Lord.

For I bless the PRINCE of PEACE and pray that all the guns may be nail'd up, save such as are for the rejoicing days.

For I have abstained from the blood of the grape and that even at the Lord's table.[4] 30

For I have glorified God in GREEK and LATIN, the consecrated languages spoken by the Lord on earth.

For I meditate the peace of Europe amongst family bickerings and domestic jars.

For the HOST is in the WEST—the Lord make us thankful unto savation.

For I preach the very GOSPEL of CHRIST without comment and with this weapon shall I slay envy.

For I bless God in the rising generation, which is on my side.

---

[2] This is the first of a number of references in this section to Smart's confinement for insanity. The reader will note other statements of a personal nature in this section.

[3] This word is indistinct in the MS. Mr. Bond thinks that the word may be made up from *existimare* to mean "reputation."

[4] This is far from being a fact, but as Mr. Stead has pointed out, the phrase "even at the Lord's table" might indicate a consciousness of his former excesses and a gesture of reform.

For I have translated in the charity, which makes things better, and I shall be translated
    myself at the last.

For he that walked upon the sea hath prepared the floods with the Gospel of peace.

For the merciful man is merciful to his beast, and to the trees that give them shelter.

For he hath turned the shadow of death into the morning, the Lord is His name.

For I am come home again, but there is nobody to kill the calf or to pay the music.[5]   40

For the hour of my felicity, like the womb of Sarah, shall come at the latter end.

For I should have availed myself of waggery, had not malice been multitudinous.

For there are still serpents that can speak—God bless my head, my heart and my heel.

For I bless God that I am of the same seed with Ehud, Mutius Scaevola, and Colonel
    Draper.[6]

For the word of God is a sword on my side—no matter what other weapon a stick or a
    straw.

For I have adventured myself in the name of the Lord, and he hath marked me for his
    own.

For I bless God for the Postmaster General and all conveyancers of letters under his care,
    especially Allen and Shelvock.[7]

For my grounds in New Canaan shall infinitely compensate for the flats and mains of
    Staindrop Moor.[8]

For the praise of God can give to a mute fish the notes of a nightingale.

For I have seen the White Raven and Thomas Hall of Willingham [9] and am myself a
    greater curiosity than both.   50

For I look up to heaven which is my prospect to escape envy by surmounting it.

For if Pharaoh had known Joseph, he would have blessed God and me for the illumination
    of the people.

For I pray God to bless improvements in gardening till London be a city of palm trees.

For I pray to give his grace to the poor of England, that charity be not offended and
    that benevolence may increase.

For in my nature I quested for beauty, but God, God hath sent me to sea for pearls.

For there is a blessing from the STONE of JESUS which is founded upon hell to the
    precious jewell on the right hand of God.

For the nightly Visitor is at the window of the impenitent, while I sing a psalm of my
    own composing.

For there is a note added to the scale, which the Lord hath made fuller, stronger, and
    more glorious.

For I offer my goat as he browses the vine, bless the Lord from chambering and drunken-
    ness.

For there is a traveling for the glory of God without going to Italy or France.   60

For I bless the children of Asher [10] for the evil I did them and the good I might have
    received at their hands.

For I rejoice like a worm in the rain in him that cherishes and from him that tramples.

For I am ready for the trumpet and alarm to fight, to die, and to rise again.

For the banished of the Lord shall come about again, for so he hath prepared for them.

For sincerity is a jewel which is pure and transparent, eternal and inestimable.

For my hands and my feet are perfect as the sublimity of Naphtali and felicity of Asher.

---

[5] An obvious allusion to the parable of the Prodigal Son.

[6] The inclusion of these curiously assorted names is explained by the next line. They are all
fighters of one kind or another.

[7] Mr. Stead points out that George Shelvocke, Secretary to the Postmaster General, died on
March 12, 1760. This fact may mean that this section, at least, of *Jubilate Agno* was written
before that date.

[8] In the neighborhood in which Smart was brought up.

[9] Both prodigies to be wondered at. Thomas Hall was a "gigantic boy" who lived to be six
years old.—W. F. Stead.

[10] See *Num.*, xiii, 13, and *Judges*, v, 17, 18.

For the names and number of animals are as the names and number of the stars.
For I pray the Lord Jesus to translate my MAGNIFICAT into verse and represent it.

· · · · · · · · · ·

For I will consider my Cat Jeoffry.
For he is the servant of the Living God, duly and daily serving him.   70
For at the first glance of the glory of God in the East he worships in his way.
For is this done by wreathing his body seven times round with elegant quickness.
For then he leaps up to catch the musk,[11] which is the blessing of God upon his prayer.
For he rolls upon prank to work it in.
For having done duty and received blessing he begins to consider himself.
For this he performs in ten degrees.
For first he looks upon his fore-paws to see if they are clean.
For secondly he kicks up behind to clear away there.
For thirdly he works it upon stretch with the fore-paws extended.
For fourthly he sharpens his paws by wood.   80
For fifthly he washes himself.
For sixthly he rolls upon wash.
For seventhly he fleas himself, that he may not be interrupted upon the beat.
For eighthly he rubs himself against a post.
For ninthly he looks up for his instructions.
For tenthly he goes in quest of food.
For having considered God and himself he will consider his neighbour.
For if he meets another cat he will kiss her in kindness.
For when he takes his prey he plays with it to give it a chance.
For one mouse in seven escapes by his dallying.   90
For when his day's work is done his business more properly begins.
For he keeps the Lord's watch in the night against the adversary.
For he counteracts the powers of darkness by his electrical skin and glaring eyes.
For he counteracts the Devil, who is death, by brisking about the life.
For in his morning orisons he loves the sun and the sun loves him.
For he is of the tribe of Tiger.
For the Cherub Cat is a term of the Angel Tiger.
For he has the subtlety and hissing of a serpent, which in goodness he suppresses.
For he will not do destruction if he is well-fed, neither will he spit without provocation.
For he purrs in thankfulness when God tells him he's a good Cat.   100
For he is an instrument for the children to learn benevolence upon.
For every house is incomplete without him, and a blessing is lacking in the spirit.
For the Lord commanded Moses concerning the cats at the departure of the Children of
       Israel from Egypt.[12]
For every family had one cat at least in the bag.
For the English Cats are the best in Europe.
For he is the cleanest in the use of his fore-paws of any quadruped.
For the dexterity of his defence is an instance of the love of God to him exceedingly.
For he is the quickest to his mark of any creature.
For he is tenacious of his point.
For he is a mixture of gravity and waggery.   110
For he knows that God is his Saviour.
For there is nothing sweeter than his peace when at rest.
For there is nothing brisker than his life when in motion.

[11] There is a plant called musk. Smart may mean that the cat plays with it as he might with catnip.
[12] As Mr. Stead points out, there is no Biblical authority for supposing that the children of Israel slipped Egyptian cats into their bags as well as silver, gold, and raiment.

For he is of the Lord's poor, and so indeed is he called by benevolence perpetually—Poor
    Jeoffry! poor Jeoffry! the rat has bit thy throat.
For I bless the name of the Lord Jesus that Jeoffry is better.
For the divine spirit comes about his body to sustain it in complete cat.
For his tongue is exceeding pure so that it has in purity what it wants in music.
For he is docile and can learn certain things.
For he can sit up with gravity which is patience upon approbation.
For he can fetch and carry, which is patience in employment.   120
For he can jump over a stick which is patience upon proof positive.
For he can spraggle upon waggle at the word of command.
For he can jump from an eminence into his master's bosom.
For he can catch the cork and toss it again.
For he is hated by the hypocrite and miser.
For the former is affraid of detection.
For the latter refuses the charge.
For he camels his back to bear the first notion of business.
For he is good to think on, if a man would express himself neatly.
For he made a great figure in Egypt for his signal services.   130
For he killed the Icneumon-rat, very pernicious by land.[13]
For his ears are so acute that they sting again.
For from this proceeds the passing quickness of his attention.
For by stroking of him I have found out electricity.
For I perceived God's light about him both wax and fire.
For the electrical fire is the spiritual substance which God sends from heaven to sustain
    the bodies both of man and beast.
For God has blessed him in the variety of his movements.
For, though he cannot fly, he is an excellent clamberer.
For his motions upon the face of the earth are more than any other quadruped.
For he can tread to all the measures upon the music.   140
For he can swim for life.
For he can creep.

[13] According to Mr. Stead, Smart misunderstood the nature of the Ichneumon. It is not a rat,
but an enemy of rats.

EDMUND BURKE (1729-1797)

European interest in the esthetic problem of the sublime had been stimulated by Boileau's translation (1674) of the Greek treatise *On the Sublime,* attributed to Longinus, a Greek philosopher of the third century A.D. Before Burke there had developed an extensive discussion of the nature of the sublime and its differentiation from the beautiful. At the same time the appreciation of mountain scenery was becoming more general, poets were exploiting the thrills of the supernatural, and the "novel of terror" or Gothic novel was just about to launch on a sensational popularity. The passages from Burke's treatise illustrate his psychological approach to the problem and suggests the relation of his theory to the literary taste of the latter part of the eighteenth century. Burke's ideas greatly influenced European speculation, especially in Germany. See further, Samuel H. Monk, *The Sublime: A Study of Critical Theories in XVIII-Century England* (1935).

A PHILOSOPHICAL INQUIRY INTO THE ORIGIN OF OUR IDEAS OF THE SUBLIME AND BEAUTIFUL

PART II, SECTIONS 1–5.

The passion caused by the great and sublime in *nature,* when those causes operate most powerfully, is astonishment: and astonishment is that state of the soul in which all its motions are suspended with some degree of horror. In this case the mind is so entirely filled with its object that it [10] cannot entertain any other, nor by consequence reason on that object which employs it. Hence arises the great power of the sublime, that, far from being produced by them, it anticipates our reasonings and hurries us on by an irresistible force. Astonishment, as I have said, is the effect of the sublime in its highest degree; the inferior effects are admiration, [20] reverence, and respect.

No passion so effectually robs the mind of all its powers of acting and reasoning as fear. For fear being an apprehension of pain or death, it operates in a manner that resembles actual pain. Whatever therefore is terrible with regard to sight, is sublime too, whether this cause of terror be endued with greatness of dimensions [30] or not; for it is impossible to look on anything as trifling, or contemptible, that may be dangerous. There are many animals who, though far from being large, are yet capable of raising ideas of the sublime because they are considered as objects of terror. As serpents and poisonous animals of almost all kinds. And to things of great dimensions, if we annex an adventitious idea of terror, they become without comparison greater. A level plain of a vast extent on land is certainly no mean idea; the prospect of such a plain may be as extensive as a prospect of the ocean; but can it ever fill the mind with anything so great as the ocean itself? This is owing to several causes; but it is owing to none more than this, that the ocean is an object of no small terror. Indeed terror is in all cases whatsoever, either more openly or latently, the ruling principle of the sublime. Several languages bear a strong testimony to the affinity of these ideas. They frequently use the same word to signify indifferently the modes of astonishment or admiration and those of terror. Θάμβος is in Greek either fear or wonder; δεινός is terrible or respectable; αἰδέω to reverence or to fear. *Vereor* in Latin is what αἰδέω is in

1165

Greek. The Romans used the verb *stupeo,* a term which strongly marks the state of an astonished mind, to express the effect either of simple fear or of astonishment; the word *attonitus* (thunderstruck) is equally expressive of the alliance of these ideas; and do not the French *étonnement* and the English *astonishment* and *amazement* point out as clearly the kindred emotions which attend fear and wonder? They who have a more general knowledge of languages could produce, I make no doubt, many other and equally striking examples.

To make anything very terrible, obscurity seems in general to be necessary. When we know the full extent of any danger, when we can accustom our eyes to it, a great deal of the apprehension vanishes. Every one will be sensible of this who considers how greatly night adds to our dread in all cases of danger, and how much the notions of ghosts and goblins, of which none can form clear ideas, affect minds which give credit to the popular tales concerning such sorts of beings. Those despotic governments which are founded on the passions of men, and principally upon the passion of fear, keep their chief as much as may be from the public eye. The policy has been the same in many cases of religion. Almost all the heathen temples were dark. Even in the barbarous temples of the Americans at this day, they keep their idol in a dark part of the hut which is consecrated to his worship. For this purpose too the Druids performed all their ceremonies in the bosom of the darkest woods and in the shade of the oldest and most spreading oaks. No person seems better to have understood the secret of heightening or of setting terrible things, if I may use the expression, in their strongest light by the force of a judicious obscurity than Milton. His description of death in the second book is admirably studied; it is astonishing with what a gloomy pomp, with what a significant and expressive uncertainty of strokes and coloring,

he has finished the portrait of the king of terrors:

> The other shape,
> If shape it might be called that shape had
>   none
> Distinguishable, in member, joint, or limb;
> Or substance might be called that shadow
>   seemed;
> For each seemed either; black he stood as
>   night;
> Fierce as ten furies; terrible as hell;
> And shook a deadly dart. What seemed his
>   head
> The likeness of a kingly crown had on.[1]

In this description all is dark, uncertain, confused, terrible, and sublime to the last degree.

It is one thing to make an idea clear and another to make it *affecting* to the imagination. If I make a drawing of a palace or a temple or a landscape, I present a very clear idea of those objects; but then (allowing for the effect of imitation which is something) my picture can at most affect only as the palace, temple, or landscape would have affected in the reality. On the other hand, the most lively and spirited verbal description I can give raises a very obscure and imperfect *idea* of such objects; but then it is in my power to raise a stronger *emotion* by the description than I could do by the best painting. This experience constantly evinces. The proper manner of conveying the *affections* of the mind from one to another is by words; there is a great insufficiency in all other methods of communication; and so far is a clearness of imagery from being absolutely necessary to an influence upon the passions, that they may be considerably operated upon without presenting any image at all, by certain sounds adapted to that purpose; of which we have a sufficient proof of the acknowledged and powerful effects of instrumental music. In reality, a great clearness helps but little towards affecting the passions, as it is in some sort an enemy to all enthusiasms whatsoever.

There are two verses in Horace's Art of Poetry that seem to contradict this

[1] *Paradise Lost,* II, 666–73.

opinion; for which reason I shall take a little more pains in clearing it up. The verses are,

Segnius irritant animos demissa per aures,
Quam quæ sunt oculis subjecta fidelibus.[2]

On this the Abbé du Bos[3] founds a criticism, wherein he gives painting the preference to poetry in the article of moving the passions; principally on account of the greater clearness of the ideas it represents. I believe this excellent judge was led into this mistake (if it be a mistake) by his system; to which he found it more conformable than I imagine it will be found to experience. I know several who admire and love painting, and yet who regard the objects of their admiration in that art with coolness enough in comparison of that warmth with which they are animated by affecting pieces of poetry or rhetoric. Among the common sort of people, I never could perceive that painting had much influence on their passions. It is true that the best sorts of painting, as well as the best sorts of poetry, are not much understood in that sphere. But it is most certain that their passions are very strongly roused by a fanatic preacher, or by the ballads of Chevy Chase or the Children in the Wood, and by other little popular poems and tales that are current in that rank of life. I do not know any paintings, bad or good, that produce the same effect. So that poetry, with all its obscurity, has a more general as well as a more powerful dominion over the passions than the other art. And I think there are reasons in nature why the obscure idea, when properly conveyed, should be more affecting than the clear. It is our ignorance of things that causes all our

admiration and chiefly excites our passions. Knowledge and acquaintance make the most striking causes affect but little. It is thus with the vulgar; and all men are as the vulgar in what they do not understand. The ideas of eternity and infinity are among the most affecting we have: and yet perhaps there is nothing of which we really understand so little as of infinity and eternity. We do not anywhere meet a more sublime description than this justly-celebrated one of Milton, wherein he gives the portrait of Satan with a dignity so suitable to the subject:

> He above the rest
> In shape and gesture proudly eminent
> Stood like a tower; his form had yet not lost
> All her original brightness, nor appeared
> Less than archangel ruined, and th' excess
> Of glory obscured: as when the sun new risen
> Looks through the horizontal misty air
> Shorn of his beams; or from behind the moon
> In dim eclipse disastrous twilight sheds
> On half the nations; and with fear of change
> Perplexes monarchs.[4]

Here is a very noble picture; and in what does this poetical picture consist? In images of a tower, an archangel, the sun rising through mists, or in an eclipse, the ruin of monarchs and the revolutions of kingdoms. The mind is hurried out of itself by a crowd of great and confused images, which affect because they are crowded and confused. For separate them, and you lose much of the greatness; and join them, and you infallibly lose the clearness. The images raised by poetry are always of this obscure kind; though in general the effects of poetry are by no means to be attributed to the images it raises.[5] But painting, when we have allowed for the pleasure of imitation, can only affect simply by the images it presents; and even in painting a judicious obscurity in some things contributes to the effect of the picture; because the images in painting are exactly similar to those in nature, and in nature, dark, confused,

[2] Horace, Ars Poetica, ll. 180–81. "No doubt our minds are less vividly struck by what we hear than by what reaches us through our eyes, those dependable witnesses."

[3] Réflexions Critiques sur la Poésie et sur la Peinture (Paris, 1719), vol. I, scct. 40. An English translation by Thomas Nugent appeared in 1748.

[4] Paradise Lost, I, 589–99.
[5] Burke discusses this subject in Part V of the Treatise.

uncertain images have a greater power on the fancy to form the grander passions than those which are more clear and determinate. But where and when this observation may be applied to practice, and how far it shall be extended, will be better deduced from the nature of the subject and from the occasion than from any rule that can be given.

I am sensible that this idea has met with opposition and is likely still to be rejected by several. But let it be considered that hardly anything can strike the mind with its greatness which does not make some sort of approach towards infinity, which nothing can do whilst we are able to perceive its bounds; but to see an object distinctly and to perceive its bounds is one and the same thing. A clear idea is therefore another name for a little idea. There is a passage in the book of Job amazingly sublime, and this sublimity is principally due to the terrible uncertainty of the thing described: "In thoughts from the visions of the night, when deep sleep falleth upon men, fear came upon me and trembling, which made all my bones to shake. Then a spirit passed before my face. The hair of my flesh stood up. It stood still, *but I could not discern the form thereof:* an image was before mine eyes; there was silence; and I heard a voice,—Shall mortal man be more just than God?" [6] We are first prepared with the utmost solemnity for the vision; we are first terrified before we are let even into the obscure cause of our emotion: but when this grand cause of terror makes its appearance, what is it? Is it not wrapt up in the shades of its own incomprehensible darkness, more awful, more striking, more terrible than the liveliest description, than the clearest painting, could possibly represent it? When painters have attempted to give us clear representations of these very fanciful and terrible ideas, they have, I think, almost always failed; insomuch that I have been at a loss, in all

[6] *Job,* iv: 13–17.

the pictures I have seen of hell, to determine whether the painter did not intend something ludicrous. Several painters have handled a subject of this kind with a view of assembling as many horrid phantoms as their imagination could suggest; but all the designs I have chanced to meet of the temptations of St. Anthony were rather a sort of odd, wild grotesques than anything capable of producing a serious passion. In all these subjects poetry is very happy. Its apparitions, its chimeras, its allegorical figures, are grand and affecting; and though Virgil's Fame [7] and Homer's Discord [8] are obscure, they are magnificent figures. These figures in painting would be clear enough, but I fear they might become ridiculous.

Besides those things which *directly* suggest the idea of danger, and those which produce a similar effect from a mechanical cause, I know of nothing sublime which is not some modification of power. And this branch rises, as naturally as the other two branches, from terror, the common stock of everything that is sublime. The idea of power, at first view, seems of the class of those indifferent ones which may equally belong to pain or to pleasure. But in reality the affection arising from the idea of vast power is extremely remote from that neutral character. For first, we must remember that the idea of pain, in its highest degree, is much stronger than the highest degree of pleasure; and that it preserves the same superiority through all the subordinate gradations. From hence it is that where the chances for equal degrees of suffering or enjoyment are in any sort equal, the idea of suffering must always be prevalent. And indeed the ideas of pain, and above all of death, are so very affecting that whilst we remain in the presence of whatever is supposed to have the power of inflicting either, it is impossible to be perfectly free from *terror.* Again, we know by

[7] L. *Fama,* or Rumor. *Æneid,* iv, 173 ff.
[8] Gr. Ἔοις. *Iliad,* iv, 440 and xx. 48.

experience that, for the enjoyment of pleasure, no great efforts of power are at all necessary; nay, we know that such efforts would go a great way towards destroying our satisfaction: for pleasure must be stolen and not forced upon us; pleasure follows the will; and therefore we are generally affected with it by many things of a force greatly inferior to our own. But pain is always inflicted by a power in some way superior, because we never submit to pain willingly. So that strength, violence, pain, and terror, are ideas that rush in upon the mind together. Look at a man or any other animal of prodigious strength, and what is your idea before reflection? Is it that this strength will be subservient to you, to your ease, to your pleasure, to your interest in any sense? No; the emotion you feel is, lest this enormous strength should be employed to the purposes of rapine and destruction. That power derives all its sublimity from the terror with which it is generally accompanied, will appear evidently from its effect in the very few cases in which it may be possible to strip a considerable degree of strength of its ability to hurt. When you do this, you spoil it of everything sublime and it immediately becomes contemptible. An ox is a creature of vast strength; but he is an innocent creature, extremely serviceable and not at all dangerous; for which reason the idea of an ox is by no means grand. A bull is strong too; but his strength is of another kind; often very destructive, seldom (at least amongst us) of any use in our business; the idea of a bull is therefore great, and it has frequently a place in sublime descriptions and elevating comparisons. Let us look at another strong animal in the two distinct lights in which we may consider him. The horse in the light of an useful beast, fit for the plough, the road, the draft; in every social useful light, the horse has nothing sublime; but is it thus that we are affected with him, "whose neck is clothed with thunder, the glory of whose nostrils is terrible, who swalloweth the ground with fierceness and rage, neither believeth that it is the sound of the trumpet?" [9] In this description the useful character of the horse entirely disappears and the terrible and sublime blaze out together. We have continually about us animals of a strength that is considerable but not pernicious. Amongst these we never look for the sublime; it comes upon us in the gloomy forest, and in the howling wilderness, in the form of the lion, the tiger, the panther, or rhinoceros. Whenever strength is only useful and employed for our benefit or our pleasure, then it is never sublime; for nothing can act agreeably to us that does not act in conformity to our will; but to act agreeably to our will, it must be subject to us and therefore can never be the cause of a grand and commanding conception. The description of the wild ass, in Job, is worked up into no small sublimity merely by insisting on his freedom and his setting mankind at defiance; otherwise the description of such an animal could have had nothing noble in it. "Who hath loosed (saith he) the bands of the wild ass? whose house I have made the wilderness and the barren land his dwellings. He scorneth the multitude of the city, neither regardeth he the voice of the driver. The range of the mountains is his pasture." [10] The magnificent description of the unicorn and of leviathan in the same book is full of the same heightening circumstances: "Will the unicorn be willing to serve thee? canst thou bind the unicorn with his band in the furrow? wilt thou trust him because his strength is great? [11]—Canst thou draw out leviathan with an hook? will he make a covenant with thee? wilt thou take him for a servant forever? shall not one be cast down even at the sight of him?" [12] In short,

[9] *Job*, xxxix: 19–24.
[10] *Job*, xxxix: 5–8.
[11] *Job*, xxxix: 9–11.
[12] *Job*. xli.

wheresoever we find strength and in what light soever we look upon power, we shall all along observe the sublime the concomitant of terror, and contempt the attendant on a strength that is subservient and innoxious. The race of dogs, in many of their kinds, have generally a competent degree of strength and swiftness; and they exert these and other valuable qualities which they possess, greatly to our convenience and pleasure. Dogs are indeed the most social, affectionate, and amiable animals of the whole brute creation; but love approaches much nearer to contempt than is commonly imagined; and accordingly, though we caress dogs, we borrow from them an appellation of the most despicable kind when we employ terms of reproach; and this appellation is the common mark of the last vileness and contempt in every language. Wolves have not more strength than several species of dogs; but on account of their unmanageable fierceness the idea of a wolf is not despicable; it is not excluded from grand descriptions and similitudes. Thus we are affected by strength, which is *natural* power. The power which arises from institution in kings and commanders has the same connection with terror. Sovereigns are frequently addressed with the title of "dread majesty." And it may be observed that young persons, little acquainted with the world, and who have not been used to approach men in power, are commonly struck with an awe which takes away the free use of their faculties. "When I prepared my seat in the street (says Job), the young men saw me and hid themselves." Indeed so natural is this timidity with regard to power, and so strongly does it inhere in our constitution, that very few are able to conquer it but by mixing much in the business of the world or by using no small violence to their natural dispositions. I know some people are of opinion that no awe, no degree of terror, accompanies the idea of power; and have hazarded to affirm that we can contemplate the idea of God himself without any such emotion. I purposely avoided, when I first considered this subject, to introduce the idea of that great and tremendous Being as an example in an argument so light as this; though it frequently occurred to me, not as an objection to, but as a strong confirmation of my notions in this matter. I hope, in what I am going to say, I shall avoid presumption where it is almost impossible for any mortal to speak with strict propriety. I say then, that whilst we consider the Godhead merely as he is an object of the understanding, which forms a complex idea of power, wisdom, justice, goodness, all stretched to a degree far exceeding the bounds of our comprehension, whilst we consider the divinity in this refined and abstracted light, the imagination and passions are little or nothing affected. But because we are bound, by the condition of our nature, to ascend to these pure and intellectual ideas through the medium of sensible images, and to judge of these divine qualities by their evident acts and exertions, it becomes extremely hard to disentangle our idea of the cause from the effect by which we are led to know it. Thus, when we contemplate the Deity, his attributes and their operation, coming united on the mind, form a sort of sensible image and as such are capable of affecting the imagination. Now, though in a just idea of the Deity perhaps none of his attributes are predominant, yet to our imagination his power is by far the most striking. Some reflection, some comparing is necessary to satisfy us of his wisdom, his justice, and his goodness. To be struck with his power it is only necessary that we should open our eyes. But whilst we contemplate so vast an object, under the arm, as it were, of almighty power, and invested upon every side with omnipresence, we shrink into the minuteness of our nature and are, in a manner, annihilated before him. And though a consideration of his other attributes may relieve in some measure our apprehensions, yet no conviction of the justice with which it is exercised, nor the mercy with which it is tempered, can wholly remove the terror that naturally arises from a force which nothing can withstand. If we rejoice, we rejoice with trembling; and even whilst we are receiving benefits, we cannot but shudder at a power which can confer benefits of such mighty importance. When the prophet David contemplated the wonders of wisdom and power which are displayed in the economy of man, he seems to be struck with a sort of divine horror, and cries out, "Fearfully and wonderfully am I made!" [13] An heathen poet has a sentiment of a similar nature; Horace looks upon it as the last effort of philosophical fortitude to behold without terror and amazement this immense and glorious fabric of the universe:

Hunc solem, et stellas, et decedentia certis
Tempora momentis, sunt qui formidine nulla
Imbuti spectent.[14]

Lucretius is a poet not to be suspected of giving way to superstitious terrors; yet when he supposes the whole mechanism of nature laid open by the master of his philosophy, his transport on this magnificent view, which he has represented in the colors of such bold and lively poetry, is overcast with a shade of secret dread and horror:

His ibi me rebus quædam divina voluptas
Percipit, atque horror; quod sic natura, tua vi
Tam manifesta patens, ex omni parte recta
est.[15]

But the Scripture alone can supply ideas answerable to the majesty of this subject. In the Scripture, wherever God is represented as appearing or speaking, everything terrible in nature is called up to heighten the awe and solemnity of the Divine presence. The Psalms and the prophetical books are crowded with instances of this kind. "The earth shook (says the Psalmist), the heavens also dropped at the presence of the Lord." [16] And what is remarkable, the painting preserves the same character, not only when he is supposedly descending to take vengeance upon the wicked, but even when he exerts the like plenitude of power in acts of beneficence to mankind. "Tremble, thou earth! at the presence of the Lord; at the presence of the God of Jacob; which turned the rock into standing water, the flint into a fountain of waters." [17] It were endless to enumerate all the passages, both in the sacred and profane writers, which establish the general sentiment of mankind concerning the inseparable union of a sacred and reverential awe with our ideas of the divinity. Hence the common maxim, *Primus in orbe deos fecit timor*.[18] This maxim may be, as I believe it is, false with regard to the origin of religion. The maker of the maxim saw how inseparable these ideas were, without considering that the notion of some great power must be always precedent to our dread of it. But this dread must necessarily follow the idea of such a power when it is once excited in the mind. It is on this principle that true religion has, and must have, so large a mixture of salutary fear; and that false religions have generally nothing else but fear to support them. Before the Christian religion had, as it were, humanized the idea of the Divinity, and brought it somewhat nearer to us, there was very little said of the love of God. The followers of Plato have something of it, and only something; the other writers of pagan antiquity, whether poets or philosophers, nothing at all. And they who consider with

[13] *Psalms,* cxxxix, 14.

[14] Horace, *Epistolæ,* I, vi, 3–5. "Could there be men who contemplate, without superstitious fear, the phenomena of the sun, the stars, and the regular march of the seasons?"

[15] Lucretius, *De Rerum Natura,* iii, 28–30. 'A kind of divine pleasure, mixed with a shudder, comes over me to think that by the power [of Epicurus] the ways of nature are thus laid open to all and all aspects truly revealed."

[16] *Psalms,* xviii: 7–9.

[17] *Psalms,* cxiv: 7–8.

[18] "Man's fear created the idea of gods." The idea was at least as old as Lucretius, and was not uncommon in the eighteenth century.

what infinite attention, by what a disregard of every perishable object,
through what long habits of piety and
contemplation it is that any man is
able to attain an entire love and devotion to the Deity, will easily perceive
that it is not the first, the most natural, and the most striking effect
which proceeds from that idea. Thus
we have traced power through its sev- 10
eral gradations unto the highest of all,

where our imagination is finally lost;
and we find terror quite through the
progress, its inseparable companion
and growing along with it as far as we
can possibly trace them. Now, as
power is undoubtedly a capital source
of the sublime, this will point out evidently from whence its energy is derived and to what class of ideas we
ought to unite it.

[1757]

SIR JOSHUA REYNOLDS (1723-1792)

Among the distinguished men in the circle of Dr. Johnson none was more gentle and friendly in manner than Sir Joshua Reynolds. His paintings reflect his gracious and refined urbanity. As the fashionable portrait painter of his time he acquired the wealth to go with his social and professional distinction. When the Royal Academy was founded in 1768, he was the obvious choice for President, and in this capacity he delivered annually, to the end of his life, a discourse to instruct the young students in the principles of their art. In their polished style as well as their esthetic ideas and artistic preferences, these *Discourses* belong to the classical tradition. Reynolds admonished the young students of painting that genius, though of course a prerequisite, must submit to sound training in technique and to the discipline of correct principles. The aim of art, he explained, is not merely the self-expression of the artist, but the attainment of the perfection of ideal beauty. The Nature which he urged them to imitate was not the unselected mass of actuality, but the ideal truth which the French had called *la belle Nature*. Goethe later expressed a similar conception when he said that the true artist aims at artistic truth (*Kunstwahrheit*) and the lawless artist merely at a verisimilitude of nature (*Naturwirklichkeit*).

The artistic theories of Reynolds were subjected to a searching criticism from the Romantic point of view by William Hazlitt in his *Table Talk* (1821). William Blake, whose neglect and poverty contrasted with the prosperity of Reynolds, and who held a diametrically opposed conception of Genius, recorded his bitter condemnation of Reynolds in a copy of the 1798 edition of the *Discourses*. These marginalia were published by Edwin J. Ellis in *The Real Blake* (1907) and are included in the Nonesuch editions of Blake, edited by Geoffrey Keynes (1925 and 1927). Blake's general attitude is expressed in the following extended comment written on a flyleaf:

"I consider Reynolds's *Discourses* to the Royal Academy as the Simulations of the Hypocrite who smiles particularly when he means to Betray. His Praise of Rafael is like the Hysteric Smile of Revenge. His Softness and Candour the hidden trap, and the poisoned feast. He praises Michel Angelo for qualities which Michel Angelo abhorred: and He blames Rafael for the only qualities which Rafael Valued. Whether Reynolds knew what he was doing is nothing to me: the Mischief is the same whether a man does it Ignorantly or Knowingly. I always considered true Art and true Artists to be particularly Insulted and Degraded by the Reputation of these *Discourses*, as much as they were Degraded by the Reputation of Reynolds's Paintings, and that such Artists as Reynolds are at all times hired by the Satans for the Depression of Art. A Pretence of Art: To destroy Art."

The quotations from Blake are reprinted from *The Real Blake*, by Edwin J. Ellis, by permission of the publishers, Chatto & Windus.

Sir Joshua Reynolds, *Works*, ed. H. W. Beechey (2 vols., 1835, and reprinted); *Discourses*, ed. Roger Fry (1905); *Letters*, ed. F. W. Hilles (1929); C. R. Leslie and T. Taylor, *The Life and Times of Sir Joshua Reynolds* (2 vols., 1865); F. W. Hilles, *The Literary Career of Sir Joshua Reynolds* (1936); Louis I. Bredvold, "The Tendency toward Platonism in Neoclassical Esthetics," *ELH*, I (1934), 91–120.

THE SEVENTH
DISCOURSE [1]

Delivered to the Students of the Royal Academy, on the Distribution of the Prizes, December 10, 1776

THE REALITY OF A STANDARD OF TASTE, AS WELL AS OF CORPORAL BEAUTY—BESIDE THIS IMMEDIATE TRUTH, THERE ARE SECONDARY TRUTHS, WHICH ARE VARIABLE; BOTH REQUIRING THE ATTENTION OF THE ARTIST, IN PROPORTION TO THEIR STABILITY OR THEIR INFLUENCE

GENTLEMEN:

It has been my uniform endeavour, since I first addressed you from this place, to impress you strongly with one ruling idea. I wished you to be persuaded, that success in your art depends almost entirely on your own industry; but the industry which I principally recommended, is not the industry of the *hands,* but of the *mind.*

As our art is not a divine *gift,* so neither is it a *mechanical* trade. Its foundations are laid in solid science; and practice, though essential to perfection, can never attain that to which it aims, unless it works under the direction of principle.

Some writers upon art carry this point too far, and suppose that such a body of universal and profound learning is requisite, that the very enumeration of its kinds is enough to frighten a beginner. Vitruvius, after going through the many accomplish-

[1] The purpose of the following discourse is to Prove that Taste and Genius are not of Heavenly Origin, and that all who have supposed that they Are so, Are to be considered as Weak-headed Fanatics. The obligations which Reynolds has laid on bad Artists of all classes will at all times make them his Admirers, but most especially for this discourse, in which it is proved that the stupid are born with Faculties Equal to other Men, Only they have not Cultivated them, because they have not thought it worth the trouble. [Blake, on flyleaf.]

ments of nature, and the many acquirements of learning, necessary to an architect, proceeds with great gravity to assert that he ought to be well skilled in the civil law, that he may not be cheated in the title of the ground he builds on. But without such exaggeration, we may go so far as to assert that a painter stands in need of more knowledge than is to be picked off his palette, or collected by looking on his model, whether it be in life or in picture. He can never be a great artist who is grossly illiterate.

Every man whose business is description, ought to be tolerably conversant with the poets, in some language or other, that he may imbibe a poetical spirit, and enlarge his stock of ideas. He ought to acquire an habit of comparing and digesting his notions. He ought not to be wholly unacquainted with that part of philosophy which gives an insight into human nature, and relates to the manners, characters, passions, and affections. He ought to know *something* concerning the mind, as well as *a great deal* concerning the body of man. For this purpose, it is not necessary that he should go into such a compass of reading as must, by distracting his attention, disqualify him for the practical part of his profession, and make him sink the performer in the critic. Reading, if it can be made the favourite recreation of his leisure hours, will improve and enlarge his mind, without retarding his actual industry. What such partial and desultory reading cannot afford, may be supplied by the conversation of learned and ingenious men, which is the best of all substitutes for those who have not the means or opportunities of deep study. There are many such men in this age; and they will be pleased with communicating their ideas to artists, when they see them curious and docile, if they are treated with that respect and deference which is so justly their due. Into such society, young artists, if they make it the point of their ambition, will, by degrees, be admitted. There, without formal teaching, they will insensibly come to feel and reason like those they live with, and find a rational and systematic taste imperceptibly formed in their minds, which they will know how to reduce to a standard, by applying general truth to their own purposes, better perhaps than those to whom they owed the original sentiment.

Of these studies, and this conversation, the desire and legitimate offspring is a power of distinguishing right from wrong; which power, applied to works of art, is denominated TASTE. Let me then, without further introduction, enter upon an examination whether taste be so far beyond our reach as to be unattainable by care; or be so very vague and capricious that no care ought to be employed about it.

It has been the fate of arts to be enveloped in mysterious and incomprehensible language, as if it was thought necessary that even the terms should correspond to the idea entertained of the instability and uncertainty of the rules which they expressed.

To speak of genius and taste as in any way connected with reason or common sense, would be, in the opinion of some towering talkers, to speak like a man who possessed neither; who had never felt that enthusiasm, or, to use their own inflated language, was never warmed by that Promethean fire which animates the canvas and vivifies the marble.

If, in order to be intelligible, I appear to degrade art by bringing her down from the visionary situation in the clouds, it is only to give her a more solid mansion upon the earth. It is necessary that at some time or other we should see things as they really are, and not impose on ourselves by that false magnitude with which objects appear when viewed indistinctly as through a mist.

We will allow a poet to express his meaning, when his meaning is not well known to himself, with a certain degree of obscurity, as it is one sort of the sublime.[2] But when, in plain prose, we gravely talk of courting the Muse in shady bowers; waiting the call and inspiration of Genius, finding out where he inhabits, and where he is to be invoked with the greatest success; of attending to times and seasons when the imagination shoots with the greatest vigour, whether at the summer solstice or the vernal equinox; sagaciously observing how much the wild freedom and liberty of imagination is cramped by attention to established rules; and how this same imagination begins to grow dim in advanced age, smothered and deadened by too much judgement; when we talk such language, or entertain such sentiments as these, we generally rest contented with mere words, or at best entertain notions not only groundless but pernicious.[3]

If all this means, what it is very possible was originally intended only to be meant, that in order to cultivate an art a man secludes himself from the commerce of the world, and retires into the country at particular seasons; or that at one time of the year his body is in better health, and consequently his mind fitter for the business of hard thinking than at another time; or that the mind may be fatigued and grow confused by long and unremitted application: this I can understand. I can likewise believe that a man eminent when young for possessing poetical imagination, may, from having taken another road, so neglect its cultivation as to show less of its powers in his later life. But I am persuaded, that scarce a poet is to be found, from Homer down to Dryden, who preserved a sound mind in a sound body, and continued practising

[2] Obscurity is Neither the Source of the Sublime nor of anything Else. [Blake.]
[3] The Ancients, and the wisest of the Moderns, are of the opinion that Reynolds condemns and laughs at. [Blake.]
[4] As Replete, but not More Replete. [Blake.]

his profession to the very last, whose latter works are not as replete [4] with the fire of imagination as those which were produced in his more youthful days.

To understand literally these metaphors, or ideas expressed in poetical language, seems to be equally absurd as to conclude that because painters sometimes represent poets writing from the dictates of a little winged boy or genius, that this same genius did really inform him in a whisper what he was to write; and that he is himself but a mere machine, unconscious of the operations of his own mind.[5]

Opinions generally received and floating in the world, whether true or false, we naturally adopt and make our own; they may be considered as a kind of inheritance to which we succeed and are tenants for life, and which we leave to our posterity very nearly in the condition in which we received it; it not being much in any one man's power either to impair or improve it. The greatest part of these opinions, like current coin in its circulation, we are used to take without weighing or examining; but by this inevitable inattention many adulterated pieces are received which, when we seriously estimate our wealth, we must throw away. So the collector of popular opinions, when he embodies his knowledge, and forms a system, must separate those which are true from those which are only plausible. But it becomes more peculiarly a duty to the professors of art not to let any opinions relating to *that* art pass unexamined. The caution and circumspection required in such examination we shall presently have an opportunity of explaining.

[5] The Ancients did not mean to Impose when they affirmed their belief in Vision and Revelation. Plato was in earnest. Milton was in earnest. They believed that God did visit Man really and Truly, and not as Reynolds pretends. How very Anxious Reynolds is to Disprove and Conᵗemn Spiritual Perceptions. [Blake.]

Genius and taste, in their common acceptation, appear to be very nearly related; the difference lies only in this, that genius has superadded to it a habit or power of execution; or we may say, that taste, when this power is added, changes its name, and is called genius. They both, in the popular opinion, pretend to an entire exemption from the restraint of rules. It is supposed that their powers are intuitive; that under the name of genius great works are produced, and under the name of taste an exact judgement is given, without our knowing why, and without our being under the least obligation to reason, precept, or experience.

One can scarce state these opinions without exposing their absurdity; [6] yet they are constantly in the mouths of men, and particularly of artists. They who have thought seriously on this subject do not carry the point so far; yet I am persuaded, that even among those few who may be called thinkers, the prevalent opinion allows less than it ought to the powers of reason; and considers the principles of taste, which give all their authority to the rules of art, as more fluctuating, and as having less solid foundations, than we shall find, upon examination, they really have.[7]

The common saying, that *tastes are not to be disputed,* owes its influence, and its general reception, to the same error which leads us to imagine this faculty of too high an original to submit to the authority of an earthly tribunal. It likewise corresponds with the notions of those who consider it as a mere phantom of the imagination, so devoid of substance as to elude all criticism.

We often appear to differ in sentiments from each other, merely from

[6] Who ever said this? He states Absurdities in Company with Truths, and Calls both Absurd. [Blake.]
[7] The Artifice of the Epicurean Philosopher is to Call all other Opinions Unsolid and Unsubstantial than those which are derived from Earth. [Blake.]

the inaccuracy of terms, as we are not obliged to speak always with critical exactness.[8] Something of this too may arise from want of words in the language in which we speak, to express the more nice discrimination which a deep investigation discovers. A great deal, however, of this difference vanishes, when each opinion is tolerably explained and understood by constancy and precision in the use of terms.

We apply the term TASTE to that act of the mind by which we like or dislike, whatever be the subject. Our judgement upon an airy nothing, a fancy which has no foundation, is called by the same name which we give to our determination concerning those truths which refer to the most general and most unalterable principles of human nature: to the works which are only to be produced by the greatest efforts of the human understanding. However inconvenient this may be, we are obliged to take words as we find them; all we can do is to distinguish the things to which they are applied.[9]

We may let pass those things which are at once subjects of taste and sense, and which, having as much certainty as the senses themselves, give no occasion to inquiry or dispute. The natural appetite or taste of the human mind is for TRUTH; whether that truth results from the real agreement or equality of original ideas among themselves; from the agreement of the representation of any object with the thing represented; or from the correspondence of the several parts of any arrangement with each other. It is the very same taste which relishes a demonstration in geometry,[*] that is pleased with the resemblance of a picture to an original and touched with the harmony of music.[10]

All these have unalterable and fixed foundations in nature, and are therefore equally investigated by reason, and known by study; some with more, some with less clearness, but all exactly in the same way. A picture that is unlike, is false. Disproportionate ordonnance of parts is not right; because it cannot be true, until it ceases to be a contradiction to assert that the parts have no relation to the whole. Colouring is true, when it is naturally adapted to the eye, from brightness, from softness, from harmony, from resemblance; because these agree with their object, Nature, and therefore are true; as true as mathematical demonstration;[11] but known to be true only to those who study these things.

But besides real, there is also apparent truth, or opinion, or prejudice. With regard to real truth, when it is known, the taste which conforms to it is, and must be, uniform. With regard to the second sort of truth, which may be called truth upon sufferance, or truth by courtesy, it is not fixed, but variable. However, whilst these opinions and prejudices, on which it is founded, continue, they operate as truth; and the art, whose office it is to please the mind, as well as instruct it, must direct itself according to opinion, or it will not attain its end.

[*] Compare the sonnet by Edna St. Vincent Millay, "Euclid alone has looked on beauty bare." Roger Fry quotes from Bertrand Russell: "Mathematics rightly viewed possesses not only truth but supreme beauty—a beauty cold and austere like that of sculpture, without appeal to any part of our weaker nature, without the gorgeous trappings of painting or music, yet sublimely pure, and capable of a stern perfection such as only the greatest art can show."

[10] Demonstration, Similitude, and Harmony are Objects of Reasoning Invention. Identity and Melody are Objects of Intuition. [Blake.]

[11] God forbid that Truth should be Confined to Mathematical Demonstration. He who does not know Truth at sight is unworthy of Her Notice. [Blake.]

[8] It is not in Terms that Reynolds and I disagree. Two Contrary Opinions can never by any Language be made alike. I say Taste and Genius are not Teachable nor Acquirable, but are both born with us. Reynolds says the Contrary. [Blake.]

[9] This is False. The Fault is not in Words but in Things. Lock's Opinions on words and their Fallaciousness are hurtful opinions and Fallacious also. [Blake.]

In proportion as these prejudices are known to be generally diffused, or long received, the taste which conforms to them approaches nearer to certainty, and to a sort of resemblance to real science, even where opinions are found to be no better than prejudices.[12] And since they deserve, on account of their duration and extent, to be considered as really true, they become capable of no small degree of stability and determination, by their permanent and uniform nature.

As these prejudices become more narrow, more local, more transitory, this secondary taste becomes more and more fantastical; recedes from real science; is less to be approved by reason, and less followed by practice: though in no case perhaps to be wholly neglected, where it does not stand, as it sometimes does, in direct defiance of the most respectable opinions received amongst mankind.[13]

Having laid down these positions, I shall proceed with less method,[14] because less will serve to explain and apply them.

We will take it for granted that reason is something invariable and fixed in the nature of things;[15] and without endeavouring to go back to an account of first principles, which for ever will elude our search, we will conclude, that whatever goes under the name of taste, which we can fairly bring under the dominion of reason, must be considered as equally exempt from change.[16] If, therefore, in the course of this inquiry, we can show that there are rules for the conduct of

the artist which are fixed and invariable, it follows of course, that the art of the connoisseur, or, in other words, taste, has likewise invariable principles.

Of the judgement which we make on the works of art, and the preference that we give to one class of art over another, if a reason be demanded, the question is perhaps evaded by answering, I judge from my taste; but it does not follow that a better answer cannot be given, though, for common gazers, this may be sufficient. Every man is not obliged to investigate the cause of his approbation or dislike.

The arts would lie open for ever to caprice and casualty, if those who are to judge of their excellencies had no settled principles by which they are to regulate their decisions, and the merit or defect of performances were to be determined by unguided fancy.[17] And indeed we may venture to assert, that whatever speculative knowledge is necessary to the artist, is equally and indispensably necessary to the connoisseur.

The first idea that occurs in the consideration of what is fixed in art, or in taste, is that presiding principle of which I have so frequently spoken in former discourses,—the general idea of Nature. The beginning, the middle, and the end of everything that is valuable in taste, is comprised in the knowledge of what is truly nature; for whatever notions are not conformable to those of nature, or universal opinion, must be considered as more or less capricious.

My notion of nature comprehends not only the forms which nature produces, but also the nature and internal fabric and organization, as I may call it, of the human mind and imagination.[18] The terms beauty, or nature,

[12] Here is a great deal to do to Prove that All Truth is prejudice, for all that is Valuable in Knowledge is Superior to Demonstrative Science, such as is Weighed and Measured. [Blake.]

[13] And so he thinks he has proved that Genius and Inspiration are all a Hum. [Blake.]

[14] He calls the Above, proceeding with Method. [Blake.]

[15] Reason—or a ratio of all we have known—is not the same it shall be when we know More. He therefore takes a Falsehood for granted to set out with. [Blake.]

[16] Now this is supreme Fooling. [Blake.]

[17] He may as well say that if man does not lay down settled Principles the Sun will not rise in a Morning. [Blake.]

[18] Here is a plain Confession that he Thinks Mind and Imagination not to be above the Mortal and Perishing Nature. Such is the End of Epicurean and Newtonian Philosophy. It is Atheism. [Blake.]

which are general ideas, are but different modes of expressing the same thing, whether we apply these terms to statues, poetry, or pictures. Deformity is not nature, but an accidental deviation from her accustomed practice. This general idea, therefore, ought to be called Nature; and nothing else, correctly speaking, has a right to that name. But we are so far from speaking, in common conversation, with any such accuracy, that, on the contrary, when we criticize Rembrandt and other Dutch painters, who introduced into their historical pictures exact representations of individual objects with all their imperfections, we say,—though it is not in a good taste, yet it is nature.

This misapplication of terms must be very often perplexing to the young student. Is not art, he may say, an imitation of nature? Must he not, therefore, who imitates her with the greatest fidelity be the best artist? By this mode of reasoning Rembrandt has a higher place than Raffaelle. But a very little reflection will serve to show us that these particularities cannot be nature; for how can that be the nature of man, in which no two individuals are the same?

It plainly appears, that as a work is conducted under the influence of general ideas, or partial, it is principally to be considered as the effect of a good or a bad taste.

As beauty, therefore, does not consist in taking what lies immediately before you, so neither, in our pursuit of taste, are those opinions which we first received and adopted, the best choice, or the most natural to the mind and imagination. In the infancy of our knowledge we seize with greediness the good that is within our reach; it is by after-consideration, and in consequence of discipline, that we refuse the present for a greater good at a distance. The nobility or elevation of all arts, like the excellency of virtue itself, consists in adopting this enlarged and comprehensive idea; and all criticism built upon the more con-

fined view of what is natural, may properly be called *shallow* criticism, rather than false: its defect is, that the truth is not sufficiently extensive.

It has sometimes happened that some of the greatest men in our art have been betrayed into errors by this confined mode of reasoning. Poussin,* who, upon the whole, may be produced as an artist strictly attentive to the most enlarged and extensive ideas of nature, from not having settled principles on this point, has, in one instance at least, I think, deserted truth for prejudice. He is said to have vindicated the conduct of Julio Romano † for his inattention to the masses of light, and shade, or grouping the figures in *The Battle of Constantine,* as if designedly neglected, the better to correspond with the hurry and confusion of a battle. Poussin's own conduct in many of his pictures makes us more easily give credit to this report. That it was too much his own practice, *The Sacrifice to Silenus,* and *The Triumph of Bacchus and Ariadne,* may be produced as instances; but this principle is still more apparent, and may be said to be even more ostentatiously displayed, in his *Perseus* and *Medusa's Head.*

This is undoubtedly a subject of great bustle and tumult, and that the first effect of the picture may correspond to the subject, every principle of composition is violated; there is no principal figure, no principal light, no groups; everything is dispersed, and in such a state of confusion, that the eye finds no repose anywhere. In consequence of the forbidding appearance, I remember turning from it with disgust,[19] and should not have looked a second time, if I had not been called back to a closer inspection. I then in-

* Nicholas Poussin (1594–1665) was an eminent French painter in the classical Italian tradition.
† Giulio Romano (1492–1546) was the great successor to Raphael in the School of Rome. His *Battle of Constantine* is a fresco in the Vatican.
[19] Reynolds's Eye cannot bear Characteristic Colouring or Light and Shade. [Blake.]

deed found, what we may expect always to find in the works of Poussin, correct drawing, forcible expression, and just character; in short, all the excellencies which so much distinguish the works of this learned painter.

This conduct of Poussin I hold to be entirely improper to imitate. A picture should please at first sight,[20] and appear to invite the spectator's attention: if, on the contrary, the general effect offends the eye, a second view is not always sought, whatever more substantial and intrinsic merit it may possess.

Perhaps no apology ought to be received for offences committed against the vehicle (whether it be the organ of seeing or of hearing) by which our pleasures are conveyed to the mind. We must take care that the eye be not perplexed and distracted by a confusion of equal parts, or equal lights, or offended by an unharmonious mixture of colours, as we should guard against offending the ear by unharmonious sounds. We may venture to be more confident of the truth of this observation, since we find that Shakespeare, on a parallel occasion, has made Hamlet recommend to the players a precept of the same kind,— never to offend the ear by harsh sounds: *In the very torrent, tempest, and whirlwind of your passion,* says he, *you must acquire and beget a temperance that may give it smoothness.* And yet, at the same time, he very justly observes, *The end of playing, both at the first, and now, was and is, to hold, as 'twere, the mirror up to nature.* No one can deny that violent passions will naturally emit harsh and disagreeable tones: [21] yet this great poet and critic thought that this imitation of nature would cost too much, if purchased at the expense of disagreeable sensations, or, as he expresses it, of *splitting the ear.* The poet and

20 Please whom? Some Men Cannot see a Picture except in a Dark Corner. [Blake.]
21 Violent Passions emit the Real Good and Perfect Tones. [Blake.]

actor as well as the painter of genius, who is well acquainted with all the variety and sources of pleasure in the mind and imagination, has little regard or attention to common nature, or creeping after common sense. By overleaping those narrow bounds, he more effectually seizes the whole mind, and more powerfully accomplishes his purpose. This success is ignorantly imagined to proceed from inattention to all rules, and a defiance of reason and judgement; whereas it is in truth acting according to the best rules and the justest reason.

He who thinks nature, in the narrow sense of the word, is alone to be followed, will produce but a scanty entertainment for the imagination: everything is to be done with which it is natural for the mind to be pleased, whether it proceeds from simplicity or variety, uniformity or irregularity; whether the scenes are familiar or exotic; rude and wild, or enriched and cultivated; for it is natural for the mind to be pleased with all these in their turn. In short, whatever pleases has in it what is analogous to the mind, and is, therefore, in the highest and best sense of the word, natural.

It is the sense of nature or truth which ought more particularly to be cultivated by the professors of art: and it may be observed, that many wise and learned men, who have accustomed their minds to admit nothing for truth but what can be proved by mathematical demonstration, have seldom any relish for those arts which address themselves to the fancy, the rectitude and truth of which is known by another kind of proof; and we may add, that the acquisition of this knowledge requires as much circumspection and sagacity as is necessary to attain those truths which are more capable of demonstration. Reason must ultimately determine our choice on every occasion; but this reason may still be exerted ineffectually by applying to taste principles which, though right as far as they go, yet do not reach the object. No man, for instance, can deny that it seems at first view very reasonable that a statue, which is to carry down to posterity the resemblance of an individual, should be dressed in the fashion of the times, in the dress which he himself wore; this would certainly be true if the dress were part of the man; but after a time the dress is only an amusement for an antiquarian; and if it obstructs the general design of the piece, it is to be disregarded by the artist. Common sense must here give way to a higher sense. In the naked form, and in the disposition of the drapery, the difference between one artist and another is principally seen. But if he is compelled to exhibit the modern dress, the naked form is entirely hid, and the drapery is already disposed by the skill of the tailor. Were a Phidias to obey such absurd commands, he would please no more than an ordinary sculptor; since in the inferior parts of every art, the learned and the ignorant are nearly upon a level.

These were probably among the reasons that induced the sculptor of that wonderful figure of Laocoön, to exhibit him naked, notwithstanding he was surprised in the act of sacrificing to Apollo, and consequently ought to have been shown in his sacerdotal habits, if those greater reasons had not preponderated. Art is not yet in so high estimation with us, as to obtain so great a sacrifice as the ancients made, especially the Grecians, who suffered themselves to be represented naked, whether they were generals, lawgivers, or kings.

Under this head of balancing and choosing the greater reason, or of two evils taking the least, we may consider the conduct of Rubens in the Luxembourg gallery, where he has mixed allegorical figures with the representations of real personages, which must be acknowledged to be a fault; yet, if the artist considered himself as engaged to furnish this gallery with a rich, various, and splendid ornament, this could not be done, at least in an equal degree, without peopling the air and water with these allegorical figures: he therefore accomplished all that he purposed. In this case all lesser considerations, which tend to obstruct the great end of the work, must yield and give way.

The variety which portraits and modern dresses, mixed with allegorical figures, produce, is not to be slightly given up upon a punctilio of reason, when that reason deprives the art in a manner of its very existence. It must always be remembered that the business of a great painter is to produce a great picture; he must therefore take special care not to be cajoled by specious arguments out of his materials.

What has been so often said to the disadvantage of allegorical poetry,—that it is tedious, and uninteresting,—cannot with the same propriety be applied to painting, where the interest is of a different kind. If allegorical painting produces a greater variety of ideal beauty, a richer, a more various and delightful composition, and gives to the artist a greater opportunity of exhibiting his skill, all the interest he wishes for is accomplished: such a picture not only attracts, but fixes the attention.

If it be objected that Rubens judged ill at first in thinking it necessary to make his work so very ornamental, this puts the question upon new ground.[22] It was his peculiar style; he could paint in no other; and he was selected for that work, probably because it was his style. Nobody will dispute but some of the best of the Roman or Bolognian schools would have produced a more learned and more noble work.[23]

This leads us to another important province of taste, that of weighing the value of the different classes of the

[22] Here it is Called Ornamental that the Roman and Bolognian Schools may be Insinuated not to be Ornamental. [Blake.]

[23] Learned and Noble is Ornamental. [Blake.]

art, and of estimating them accordingly.[24]

All arts have means within them of applying themselves with success both to the intellectual and sensitive part of our natures. It cannot be disputed, supposing both these means put in practice with equal abilities, to which we ought to give the preference; to him who represents the heroic arts and more dignified passions of man, or to him who, by the help of meretricious ornaments, however elegant and graceful, captivates the sensuality, as it may be called, of our taste. Thus the Roman and Bolognian schools are reasonably preferred to the Venetian, Flemish or Dutch schools, as they address themselves to our best and noblest faculties.

Well-turned periods in eloquence, or harmony of numbers in poetry, which are in those arts what colouring is in painting, however highly we may esteem them, can never be considered as of equal importance with the art of unfolding truths that are useful to mankind, and which make us better or wiser. Nor can those works which remind us of the poverty and meanness of our nature be considered as of equal rank with what excites ideas of grandeur, or raises and dignifies humanity; or, in the words of a late poet, which makes the beholder *learn to venerate himself as man.* *

It is reason and good sense, therefore, which ranks and estimates every art, and every part of that art, according to its importance, from the painter of animated, down to inanimated nature. We will not allow a man who shall prefer the inferior style, to say it is his taste; taste here has nothing, or at least ought to have nothing, to do with the question. He wants not taste, but sense and soundness of judgement.

Indeed, perfection in an inferior style may be reasonably preferred to

mediocrity in the highest walks of art. A landscape of Claude Lorraine may be preferred to a history by Luca Giordano; but hence appears the necessity of the connoisseur's knowing in what consists the excellency of each class, in order to judge how near it approaches to perfection.

Even in works of the same kind, as in history-painting, which is composed of various parts, excellence of an inferior species, carried to a very high degree, will make a work very valuable, and in some measure compensate for the absence of the higher kinds of merit. It is the duty of the connoisseur to know and esteem, as much as it may deserve, every part of painting: he will not then think even Bassano * unworthy of his notice; who, though totally devoid of expression, sense, grace, or elegance, may be esteemed on account of his admirable taste of colours, which, in his best works, are little inferior to those of Titian.

Since I have mentioned Bassano, we must do him likewise the justice to acknowledge, that though he did not aspire to the dignity of expressing the characters and passions of men, yet, with respect to facility and truth in his manner of touching animals of all kinds, and giving them what painters call *their character,* few have excelled him.

To Bassano we may add Paul Veronese and Tintoret, for their entire inattention to what is justly thought the most essential part of our art, the expression of the passions. Notwithstanding these glaring deficiencies, we justly esteem their works; but it must be remembered, that they do not please from those defects, but from their great excellencies of another kind, and in spite of such transgressions. These excellencies, too, as far as they go, are founded in the truth of *general* nature; they tell the *truth,* though not *the whole truth.*

[24] A fool's Balance is no criterion, because though it goes down on the heaviest side, we ought to look what he puts into it. [Blake.]
* Oliver Goldsmith. [Reynolds.]

* Jacopo da Ponte Bassano (1510–1592), a Venetian painter of minor importance, who painted by preference humble subjects.

By these considerations, which can never be too frequently impressed, may be obviated two errors, which I observed to have been, formerly at least, the most prevalent, and to be most injurious to artists; that of thinking taste and genius to have nothing to do with reason, and that of taking particular living objects for nature.

I shall now say something on that part of *taste,* which, as I have hinted to you before, does not belong so much to the external form of things, but is addressed to the mind, and depends on its original frame, or, to use the expression, the organization of the soul: I mean the imagination and the passions. The principles of these are as invariable as the former, and are to be known and reasoned upon in the same manner, by an appeal to common sense deciding upon the common feelings of mankind. This sense, and these feelings appear to me of equal authority, and equally conclusive. Now this appeal implies a general uniformity and agreement in the minds of men. It would be else an idle and vain endeavour to establish rules of art; it would be pursuing a phantom to attempt to move affections with which we were entirely unacquainted. We have no reason to suspect there is a greater difference between our minds than between our forms; of which, though there are no two alike, yet there is a general similitude that goes through the whole race of mankind; and those who have cultivated their taste, can distinguish what is beautiful or deformed, or, in other words, what agrees with or deviates from the general idea of nature, in one case, as well as in the other.

The internal fabric of our minds, as well as the external form of our bodies being nearly uniform; it seems then to follow of course, that as the imagination is incapable of producing anything originally of itself, and can only vary and combine those ideas with which it is furnished by means of the senses, there will be necessarily an agreement in the imaginations, as in the senses of men. There being this agreement, it follows, that in all cases, in our lightest amusements, as well as in our most serious actions and engagements of life, we must regulate our affections of every kind by that of others. The well-disciplined mind acknowledges this authority, and submits its own opinion to the public voice. It is from knowing what are the general feelings and passions of mankind, that we acquire a true idea of what imagination is; though it appears as if we had nothing to do but to consult our own particular sensations, and these were sufficient to ensure us from all error and mistake.

A knowledge of the disposition and character of the human mind can be acquired only by experience; a great deal will be learned, I admit, by a habit of examining what passes in our bosoms, what are our own motives of action, and of what kind of sentiments we are conscious on any occasion. We may suppose an uniformity, and conclude that the same effect will be produced by the same cause in the mind of others. This examination will contribute to suggest to us matters of inquiry; but we can never be sure that our own sentiments are true and right, till they are confirmed by more extensive observation. One man opposing another determines nothing; but a general union of minds, like a general combination of the forces of all mankind, makes a strength that is irresistible. In fact, as he who does not know himself, does not know others, so it may be said with equal truth, that he who does not know others, knows himself but very imperfectly.

A man who thinks he is guarding himself against prejudices by resisting the authority of others, leaves open every avenue to singularity, vanity, self-conceit, obstinacy, and many other vices, all tending to warp the judgement, and prevent the natural operation of his faculties. This submission to others is a deference which we owe, and, indeed, are forced involuntarily

to pay. In fact, we never are satisfied
with our opinions, whatever we may
pretend, till they are ratified and confirmed by the suffrages of the rest of
mankind. We dispute and wrangle for
ever; we endeavour to get men to
come to us, when we do not go to
them.

He, therefore, who is acquainted
with the works which have pleased
different ages and different countries,
and has formed his opinion on them,
has more materials, and more means
of knowing what is analogous to the
mind of man, than he who is conversant only with the works of his
own age or country. What has pleased,
and continues to please, is likely to
please again: hence are derived the
rules of art, and on this immovable
foundation they must ever stand.

This search and study of the history of the mind ought not to be confined to one art only. It is by the analogy that one art bears to another, that
many things are ascertained, which
either were but faintly seen, or, perhaps, would not have been discovered
at all, if the inventor had not received
the first hints from the practices of a
sister art on a similar occasion. The
frequent allusions which every man
who treats of any art is obliged to
make to others, in order to illustrate
and confirm his principles, sufficiently
show their near connection and inseparable relation.

All arts having the same general
end, which is to please; and addressing themselves to the same faculties
through the medium of the senses; it
follows that their rules and principles
must have as great affinity as the different materials and the different organs or vehicles by which they pass
to the mind will permit them to retain.

We may therefore conclude that the
real substance, as it may be called, of
what goes under the name of taste, is
fixed and established in the nature of
things; that there are certain and
regular causes by which the imagination and passions of men are affected;

and that the knowledge of these
causes is acquired by a laborious and
diligent investigation of nature, and
by the same slow progress as wisdom
or knowledge of every kind, however
instantaneous its operations may appear when thus acquired.

It has been often observed, that the
good and virtuous man alone can acquire this true or just relish even of
works of art. This opinion will not
appear entirely without foundation,
when we consider that the same habit
of mind, which is acquired by our
search after truth, in the more serious duties of life, is only transferred
to the pursuit of lighter amusements.
The same disposition, the same desire
to find something steady, substantial,
and durable, on which the mind can
lean, as it were, and rest with safety,
actuates us in both cases. The subject
only is changed. We pursue the same
method in our search after the idea of
beauty and perfection in each; of virtue, by looking forwards beyond ourselves to society, and to the whole; of
arts, by extending our views in the
same manner, to all ages and all times.

Every art, like our own, has in its
composition fluctuating as well as
fixed principles. It is an attentive inquiry into their difference that will
enable us to determine how far we
are influenced by custom and habit,
and what is fixed in the nature of
things.

To distinguish how much has solid
foundation, we may have recourse to
the same proof by which some hold
that wit ought to be tried; whether it
preserves itself when translated. That
wit is false which can subsist only in
one language; and that picture which
pleases only one age or one nation
owes its reception to some local or
accidental association of ideas.

We may apply this to every custom
and habit of life. Thus, the general
principles of urbanity, politeness, or
civility have been the same in all nations; but the mode in which they are
dressed is continually varying. The
general idea of showing respect is by

making yourself less; but the manner, whether by bowing the body, kneeling, prostration, pulling off the upper part of our dress, or taking away the lower,* is a matter of custom.

Thus, in regard to ornaments,—it would be unjust to conclude that, because they were at first arbitrarily contrived, they are therefore undeserving of our attention: on the contrary, he 10 who neglects the cultivation of those ornaments, acts contrary to nature and reason. As life would be imperfect without its highest ornaments, the Arts, so these arts themselves would be imperfect without *their* ornaments. Though we by no means ought to rank these with positive and substantial beauties, yet it must be allowed, that a knowledge of both is essentially 20 requisite towards forming a complete, whole, and perfect taste. It is in reality from their ornaments that arts receive their peculiar character and complexion; we may add, that in them we find the characteristical mark of a national taste; as, by throwing up a feather in the air, we know which way the wind blows, better than by a more heavy matter. 30

The striking distinction between the works of the Roman, Bolognian, and Venetian schools, consists more in that general effect which is produced by colours, than in the more profound excellencies of the art; at least it is from thence that each is distinguished and known at first sight. Thus it is the ornaments rather than the proportions of architecture which at 40 the first glance distinguish the different orders from each other; the Doric is known by its triglyphs, the Ionic by its volutes, and the Corinthian by its acanthus.

What distinguishes oratory from a cold narration is a more liberal, though chaste, use of those ornaments which go under the name of figurative and metaphorical expressions; and poetry distinguishes itself from oratory 50

by words and expressions still more ardent and glowing. What separates and distinguishes poetry is more particularly the ornament of *verse*; it is this which gives it its character, and is essential, without which it cannot exist. Custom has appropriated different metre to different kinds of composition, in which the world is not perfectly agreed. In England the dispute is not yet settled, which is to be preferred, rhyme or blank verse. But however we disagree about what these metrical ornaments shall be, that some metre is essentially necessary, is universally acknowledged.

In poetry or eloquence, to determine how far figurative or metaphorical language may proceed, and when it begins to be affectation or beside the truth, must be determined by taste; though this taste, we must never forget, is regulated and formed by the presiding feelings of mankind,—by those works which have approved themselves to all times and all persons. Thus, though eloquence has undoubtedly an essential and intrinsic excellence, and immovable principles common to all languages, founded in the nature of our passions and affections, yet it has its ornaments and modes of address, which are merely arbitrary. What is approved in the eastern nations as grand and majestic, would be considered by the Greeks and Romans as turgid and inflated; and they, in return, would be thought by the Orientals to express themselves in a cold and insipid manner.

We may add, likewise, to the credit of ornaments, that it is by their means that Art itself accomplishes its purposes. Fresnoy * calls colouring, which is one of the chief ornaments of painting, *lena sororis*, that which procures lovers and admirers to the more valuable excellencies of the art.

It appears to be the same right turn of mind which enables a man to ac-

* "Put off thy shoes from off thy feet, for the place whereon thou standest is holy ground." Exodus, iii:5. [Reynolds.]

* Du Fresnoy's poem *De Arte Graphica* was considered a high authority in the seventeenth century. Dryden translated it in 1695, and in 1782 William Mason published a new translation with annotations by Reynolds.

quire the *truth,* or the just idea of what is right, in the ornaments, as in the more stable principles of art. It has still the same centre of perfection, though it is the centre of a smaller circle.

To illustrate this by the fashion of dress, in which there is allowed to be a good or bad taste. The component parts of dress are continually changing from great to little, from short to long; but the general form still remains; it is still the same general dress, which is comparatively fixed, though on a very slender foundation; but it is on this which fashion must rest. He who invents with the most success, or dresses in the best taste, would probably, from the same sagacity employed to greater purposes, have discovered equal skill, or have formed the same correct taste, in the highest labours of art.

I have mentioned taste in dress, which is certainly one of the lowest subjects to which this word is applied; yet, as I have before observed, there is a right even here, however narrow its foundation, respecting the fashion of any particular nation. But we have still more slender means of determining to which of the different customs of different ages, or countries, we ought to give the preference, since they seem to be all equally removed from nature. If an European, when he has cut off his beard, and put false hair on his head, or bound up his own natural hair in regular hard knots, as unlike nature as he can possibly make it; and after having rendered them immovable by the help of the fat of hogs, has covered the whole with flour, laid on by a machine with the utmost regularity; if, when thus attired, he issues forth, and meets a Cherokee Indian, who has bestowed as much time at his toilet, and laid on with equal care and attention his yellow and red ochre on particular parts of his forehead or cheeks, as he judges most becoming; whoever of these two despises the other for this attention to the fashion of his country, which ever first

feels himself provoked to laugh, is the barbarian.[25]

All these fashions are very innocent; neither worth disquisition, nor any endeavour to alter them; as the change would, in all probability, be equally distant from nature. The only circumstance against which indignation may reasonably be moved, is, where the operation is painful or destructive of health; such as some of the practices at Otaheite, and the strait-lacing of the English ladies; of the last of which practices, how destructive it must be to health and long life, the Professor of Anatomy took an opportunity of proving a few days since in this Academy.

It is in dress as in things of greater consequence. Fashions originate from those only who have the high and powerful advantages of rank, birth, and fortune. Many of the ornaments of art, those at least for which no reason can be given, are transmitted to us, are adopted, and acquire their consequence from the company in which we have been used to see them. As Greece and Rome are the fountains from whence have flowed all kinds of excellence, to that veneration which they have a right to claim for the pleasure and knowledge which they have afforded us, we voluntarily add our approbation of every ornament and every custom that belonged to them, even to the fashion of their dress. For it may be observed that, not satisfied with them in their own place, we make no difficulty of dressing statues of modern heroes or senators in the fashion of the Roman armour or peaceful robe; we go so far as hardly to bear a statue in any other drapery.

The figures of the great men of those nations have come down to us in sculpture. In sculpture remain almost all the excellent specimens of ancient art. We have so far associated personal dignity to the persons thus represented, and the truth of art to their manner of representation, that

[25] Excellent. [Blake.]

it is not in our power any longer to separate them. This is not so in painting; because having no excellent ancient portraits, that connection was never formed. Indeed we could no more venture to paint a general officer in a Roman military habit, than we could make a statue in the present uniform. But since we have no ancient portraits, to show how ready we are to adopt those kind of prejudices, we make the best authority among the moderns serve the same purpose. The great variety of excellent portraits with which Vandyke has enriched this nation, we are not content to admire for their real excellence, but extend our approbation even to the dress which happened to be the fashion of that age. We all very well remember how common it was a few years ago for portraits to be drawn in this fantastic dress; and this custom is not yet entirely laid aside. By this means it must be acknowledged very ordinary pictures acquired something of the air and effect of the works of Vandyke, and appeared therefore at first sight to be better pictures than they really were; they appeared so, however, to those only who had the means of making this association; but when made, it was irresistible. But this association is nature, and refers to that secondary truth that comes from conformity to general prejudice and opinion; it is therefore not merely fantastical. Besides the prejudice which we have in favour of ancient dresses, there may be likewise other reasons for the effect which they produce; among which we may justly rank the simplicity of them, consisting of little more than one single piece of drapery, without those whimsical capricious forms by which all other dresses are embarrassed.

Thus, though it is from the prejudice we have in favour of the ancients, who have taught us architecture, that we have adopted likewise their ornaments; and though we are satisfied that neither nature nor reason are the foundation of those beauties which we imagine we see in that art, yet if anyone, persuaded of this truth, should therefore invent new orders of equal beauty, which we will suppose to be possible, they would not please; nor ought he to complain, since the old has that great advantage of having custom and prejudice on its side. In this case we leave what has every prejudice in its favour, to take that which will have no advantage over what we have left, but novelty; which soon destroys itself, and at any rate is but a weak antagonist against custom.

Ancient ornaments, having the right of possession, ought not to be removed, unless to make room for that which not only has higher pretensions, but such pretensions as will balance the evil and confusion which innovation always brings with it.

To this we may add, that even the durability of the materials will often contribute to give a superiority to one object over another. Ornaments in buildings, with which taste is principally concerned, are composed of materials which last longer than those of which dress is composed; the former, therefore, make higher pretensions to our favour and prejudice.

Some attention is surely due to what we can no more get rid of, than we can go out of ourselves. We are creatures of prejudice; we neither can nor ought to eradicate it; we must only regulate it by reason; which kind of regulation is indeed little more than obliging the lesser, the local and temporary prejudices, to give way to those which are more durable and lasting.

He, therefore, who in his practice of portrait-painting, wishes to dignify his subject, which we will suppose to be a lady, will not paint her in the modern dress, the familiarity of which alone is sufficient to destroy all dignity. He takes care that his work shall correspond to those ideas and that imagination which he knows will regulate the judgement of others; and, therefore, dresses his figure something with the general air of the antique for the sake of dignity, and preserves something of the modern for the sake of likeness. By this conduct his works correspond with those prejudices which we have in favour of what we continually see; and the relish of the antique simplicity corresponds with what we may call the more learned and scientific prejudice.

There was a statue made not long since of Voltaire,* which the sculptor, not having that respect for the prejudices of mankind which he ought to have had, made entirely naked, and as meagre and emaciated as the original is said to be. The consequence was what might have been expected: it remained in the sculptor's shop, though it was intended as a public ornament and a public honour to Voltaire, for it was procured at the expense of his contemporary wits and admirers.

Whoever would reform a nation, supposing a bad taste to prevail in it, will not accomplish his purpose by going directly against the stream of their prejudices. Men's minds must be prepared to receive what is new to them. Reformation is a work of time. A national taste, however wrong it may be, cannot be totally changed at once; we must yield a little to the prepossession which has taken hold on the mind, and we may then bring people to adopt what would offend them, if endeavoured to be introduced by violence. When Battista Franco was employed, in conjunction with Titian, Paul Veronese and Tintoret, to adorn the library of St. Mark, his work, Vasari says, gave less satisfaction than any of the others; the dry manner of the Roman school was very ill calculated to please eyes that had been accustomed to the luxuriancy, splendour, and richness of Venetian colouring. Had the Romans been the judges of this work, probably the determina-

* This statue of the naked Voltaire is by Pigalle (1714–1785) and is in the Library of the Institute in Paris.

tion would have been just contrary; for in the more noble parts of the art Battista Franco was perhaps not inferior to any of his rivals.

GENTLEMEN,

It has been the main scope and principal end of this discourse to demonstrate the reality of a standard in taste, as well as in corporeal beauty; that a false or depraved taste is a thing as well known, as easily discovered, as anything that is deformed, misshapen, or wrong, in our form or outward make; and that this knowledge is derived from the uniformity of sentiments among mankind, from whence proceeds the knowledge of what are the general habits of nature; the result of which is an idea of perfect beauty.

If what has been advanced be true, —that beside this beauty or truth, which is formed on the uniform, eternal, and immutable laws of nature, and which of necessity can be but *one*; that beside this one immutable verity there are likewise what we have called apparent or secondary truths, proceeding from local and temporary prejudices, fancies, fashions or accidental connection of ideas; if it appears that these last have still their foundation, however slender, in the original fabric of our minds; it follows that all these truths or beauties deserve and require the attention of the artist, in proportion to their stability or duration, or as their influence is more or less extensive. And let me add, that as they ought not to pass their just bounds, so neither do they, in a well-regulated taste, at all prevent or weaken the influence of those general principles, which alone can give to art its true and permanent dignity.

To form this just taste is undoubtedly in your own power, but it is to reason and philosophy that you must have recourse: from them you must borrow the balance by which is to be weighed and estimated the value of every pretension that intrudes itself on your notice.

The general objection which is made to the introduction of Philosophy into the regions of taste, is, that it checks and restrains the flights of the imagination, and gives that timidity which an over-carefulness not to err or act contrary to reason is likely to produce. It is not so. Fear is neither reason nor philosophy. The true spirit of philosophy, by giving knowledge, gives a manly confidence, and substitutes rational firmness in the place of vain presumption. A man of real taste is always a man of judgement in other respects; and those inventions which either disdain or shrink from reason, are generally, I fear, more like the dreams of a distempered brain, than the exalted enthusiasm of a sound and true genius. In the midst of the highest flights of fancy or imagination, reason ought to preside from first to last, though I admit her more powerful operation is upon reflection.[26]

Let me add, that some of the greatest names of antiquity, and those who have most distinguished themselves in works of genius and imagination, were equally eminent for their critical skill. Plato, Aristotle, Cicero, and Horace; and among the moderns, Boileau, Corneille, Pope, and Dryden, are at least instances of genius not being destroyed by attention or subjection to rules and science. I should hope, therefore, that the natural consequence of what has been said, would be to excite in you a desire of knowing the principles and conduct of the great masters of our art, and respect and veneration for them when known.

[26] If this is True, it is a devilish Foolish Thing to be an Artist. [Blake.]

NOTES AND COMMENTS

I.

HUDIBRAS, PART I, CANTO I

2, 16. *Mirror of Knighthood.* A Spanish romance mentioned in *Don Quixote.*

2, 17-20. *That never bowed, etc.* Never, except when the king dubbed him knight.

2, 38. *Montaigne. Essays,* ii, 12.

2, 40 *Hudibras.* The name is from Spenser, *Faerie Queene,* II, ii, 17. A letter of Butler's, March 19, 1662, says that the original of Hudibras was "a west country knight, then a colonel in the Parliamentary Army and a Committee Man, with whom I became acquainted lodging in the same house with him in Holborn" (printed by R. B. Quintana, *MLN,* xlviii [1933], 1-12). Ralpho (ll. 457 ff. below) was really his clerk, Butler adds, and the disputes between them are from life. This letter supports the tradition that Sir Henry Rosewel of Devonshire was Butler's model for Hudibras.

2, 76. *committee-men.* Committees empowered by Parliament to impose penalties and exercise arbitrary authority.

2, 98. *fustian.* Coarse cloth, with the additional meaning of bombastic language.

2, 104. *leash.* Used in sporting parlance for three, as three hawks or dogs.

2, 115. *the orator.* Demosthenes.

3, 120. *Tycho Brahe.* A Danish astronomer. *Erra Pater.* Apparently a nickname for William Lilly, the famous astrologer whom Butler later satirizes as "Sidrophel."

3, 145. *entity . . . quiddity.* Being and essence, terms of scholastic philosophy.

3, 148. *Like words congealed, etc.* An old traveler's tale, found in Lucian and Rabelais and later in the *Tatler,* No. 254.

3, 152. *Irrefragable.* Alexander Hales, an English theologian of the Middle Ages, was called the Irrefragable Doctor.

3, 153. *Thomas.* Thomas Aquinas.

3, 154. *Duns.* Duns Scotus, a scholastic philosopher whose name has given us the word "dunce."

3, 155-56. *nominal . . . real.* The great division in medieval philosophy was between the nominalists, who held that general ideas were mere names, and the realists, who held that general ideas were real.

4, 232. *ass and widgeon.* The animal on which, as Mahomet dreamed, he rode to heaven, and the pigeon which was supposed to bring him divine messages.

4, 253. *heart-breakers.* Long curls, often called "love-locks."

4, 260. *Cordelier.* A member of the French branch of the Franciscans.

4, 275. *Fatal Sisters.* The Fates of Greek mythology, who spun, twisted, and cut the thread of life.

4, 281. *Taliacotius.* An Italian surgeon who wrote of amazing operations in plastic surgery.

4, 285. *Nock.* The rump, used here, perhaps, as a coarse nickname for Oliver Cromwell.

4, 289-90. *Aeneas . . . fire.* At the burning of Troy. See *Aeneid,* Book II.

4, 310-11. *Bullen . . . King Harry.* Henry VIII besieged Boulogne in 1544.

5, 359. *Toledo trusty.* Toledo, in Spain, was famous for fine swords.

5, 372. *Sergeant Bum.* A "bum-bailiff," who served warrants and made arrests.

5, 387-90. *brewer . . . score.* Oliver Cromwell had been a brewer.

5, 415 ff. The description is partly inspired by Cervantes' account of Rosinante, Don Quixote's steed.

6, 461-62. *a tailor.* Proverbially it took two, three, or nine tailors to make a man.

6, 463. *Tyrian queen.* Dido.

6, 472. *Trojan knight.* Aeneas.

6, 478. *Gift . . . New Light.* Puritan enthusiasts professed to be guided by direct inspiration, often described in these terms. Cf. ll. 503 ff., below.

6, 483. *commendation nine-pence.* Silver nine-penny pieces were bent and given as love-tokens. Cf. Gay, *Shepherd's Week, Friday,* page 420, line 129.

6, 535. *Sir Agrippa.* Cornelius Agrippa (1486-1535), German scholar, soldier, and physician, famed for his supposed skill in the occult sciences.

6, 537. *Anthroposophus.* Thomas Vaughan, author of a treatise called *Anthroposophia Theomagica, or a Discourse of the Nature of Man in the State after Death. Fludd.* Robert Fludd (1574–1637) tried to base medical science on mysticism and divine revelation.

6, 538. *Jacob Behmen.* Or Boehme (1575–1624), greatest of the German mystics.

7, 541. *Rosicrucian.* Pertaining to the Fraternity of the Rosy Cross, a supposed secret order whose members were said to claim occult powers.

7, 542. *Vere adeptus.* The title of "adept," given to one who had discovered the philosopher's stone.

7, 562. *fair of Barthol'mew.* Puppet plays of the Bible story, beginning with the Creation, were shown at Bartholomew Fair.

7, 579. *Knight o' the Post.* Men who could be hired to give false evidence.

7, 642. *Withers, Prynne, and Vicars.* Puritan pamphleteers and versifiers. Cf. Pope, *Dunciad,* page 401, line 296.

9, 826. *homoeosis.* The logical principle that if two things are alike, the same statements can be made about each of them.

9, 832. *classis.* In the Presbyterian church, the presbytery or assembly of ministers and elders.

10, 897. The gap is to be filled by the name Samuel Lake. This passage is often taken to mean that Sir Samuel Luke of Bedfordshire was the original of Hudibras. But see above, note to page 2, line 40.

10, 911. *The Phrygian knight.* Laocoön, who smote with his spear the wooden horse by which the Greeks got entrance into Troy.

10.   **CHARACTERS**

10a, 4. *Rota.* The Rota Club was a group of Commonwealth political theorists gathered in 1659–1660 about the anti-monarchical James Harrington, author of *Oceana* (1656).

11b, 40. *Amboyna.* The cruel mistreatment of the English by the Dutch on the Pacific island of Amboyna in 1622–1623. In 1652 the Cromwell regime demanded heavy indemnities and in 1672 Dryden wrote a play on the subject of the Dutch cruelties in Amboyna.

12b, 38. *Festus.* Roman procurator of Judea, before whom Paul was brought. Acts xxvi, 24.

15.   **DIARY**

15a, 7. Pepys was a member of the party that accompanied Admiral Sir Edward Montagu, Earl of Sandwich, to Holland to bring back the exiled Stuarts. The English fleet lay off Scheveningen, the port nearest to The Hague. Pepys usually refers to Sandwich as "my Lord."

15a, 10. *Sir R. Stayner.* Rear Admiral of the Fleet.

15b, 4. *The two Dukes.* The brothers of Charles II: James, Duke of York, later James II, and Henry, Duke of Gloucester, who died in 1660.

16a, 30. *Escape from Worcester.* The story of the escape of Charles after the battle of Worcester, September 3, 1651, has had a romantic appeal to all later generations, and was looked upon by some of his contemporary followers as evidence of divine protection of the king.

16b, 29. *hole.* Secret hiding place in the wall of a house.

16b, 39–42. *Thomas Killigrew,* the dramatist (1612–1683), was of a family that had always been loyal to the Stuarts. He became manager of the King's theater.

17a, 27. *General Monk.* As commander in chief of the English army, George Monk, more than any other one man, was responsible for the invitation to Charles to return to England. He was later made Duke of Albemarle.

17b, 23. *Sir J. Denham.* Sir John Denham (1615–1669) was active in pubic affairs, but is best known as a poet, especially as author of *Cooper's Hill.*

19a, 49. *Serjeant Glynne.* Sir John Glynne (1603–1666), now converted to the Stuart regime, had been Chief Justice of the Upper Bench under Cromwell. Sir John Maynard had also been in the service of Cromwell.

19b, 15. *The young ladies* of the Wardrobe were the daughters of the Earl of Sandwich.

19b, 22–23. *Bartholomew Fair.* A comedy by Ben Jonson, first produced in 1614; it was sharply satirical of the Puritans.

19b, 38–42. The Act of Uniformity, passed this year, required every clergyman and every school master to express by August 24th his complete acceptance of the Book of Common Prayer. On that day about two thousand clergymen resigned their cures for the sake of conscience, being unwilling to accept Anglicanism.

20b, 22–40. According to the *Memoirs of Grammont*, Howard and Jermyn had been rivals in a love affair with the notorious Countess of Shrewsbury. A later and more scandalous duel was fought about her by the Duke of Buckingham and others on January, 1668.

21a, 35. *The Duke of Monmouth* was the illegitimate son of Charles II by Lucy Walters. He was a young man of charming personality and early became a favorite of the public. The Whigs groomed him as a candidate for the crown in 1679, and he is the Absalom in Dryden's *Absalom and Achitophel*. He was executed in 1685 for rebellion against his uncle, James II. The Duchess of Monmouth was Lady Anne Scott of Buccleuch. Dryden refers to her gratefully for her patronage of his work.

21a, 47–48. *Lady Castlemaine*. Barbara Villiers, wife of the Earl of Castelmaine, but notoriously mistress to the king. She was made Duchess of Cleveland in 1670.

21b, 44. *Sir H. Bennet*. Later member of the "Cabal" ministry and created Earl of Arlington in 1672.

21b, 45. *Sir Charles Barkeley*. Created in 1664 Earl of Falmouth. Pepys elsewhere calls him "a most vicious person."

22a, 4–5. *My Lord Chancellor*. Edward Hyde, Earl of Clarendon (1609–1674), was Lord Chancellor and chief minister from the Restoration until his fall in 1667. His daughter, Anne, was married to the Duke of York, and became the mother of two future queens, Mary of Orange and Anne.

22b, 28. *Sir John Minnes*. Comptroller of the navy, but better known now as a wit and versificator, author of the amusing *Musarum Deliciae* (1655) and *Wit Restored* (1658).

22b, 54. *Sir W. Penn*. Penn, the father of the founder of Pennsylvania, was a commissioner of the navy.

23a, 18. *Tangier Committee*. Tangier, in northern Africa, had been acquired by England with the marriage of Charles to Catharine of Braganza. Pepys had been appointed to the Commission in 1662, through the influence of Sandwich.

24a, 12–17. *The Five Hours' Adventure*. A comedy by Sir Samuel Tuke, very popular in its day.

25a, 45. *Volpone, or The Fox*. A comedy by Ben Jonson, first acted in 1606. Pepys reflects the Restoration taste in his fondness for Ben Jonson.

25b, 26. *Lord Rochester*. John Wilmot (1647–1680), the wicked Earl of Rochester. See above, page 31.

25b, 50. Lord Hinchingbroke was son of the Earl of Sandwich.

26a, 13. In an engagement with the Dutch fleet June 1–3, the British fleet under Albermarle had been forced to run to the Thames for shelter, although the Dutch fleet was also so crippled it had to withdraw.

26a, 51. *Lady Denham*. Wife of Sir John Denham.

27b, 31. The great London Fire was one of the most spectacular of the events of this period.

30a, 14–17. Dryden's *Annus Mirabilis* deals with the Dutch War as well as the London Fire.

30a, 42. *Nell*. Nell Gwyn.

30b, 7–12. *The Silent Woman*. A comedy by Ben Jonson, first acted in 1609.

30b, 16. Hobbes's *Leviathan* had been first published in 1651.

31.   A SATIRE AGAINST MANKIND

32, 73–74. *Ingelo . . . Patrick's Pilgrim . . . Sibbs' Soliloquies*. Derisive references to edifying works: Nathaniel Ingelo's *Bentivolio and Urania* (1660), a religious romance; Simon Patrick's *Parable of the Pilgrim* (1664); and one of the devotional works of the Puritan divine Richard Sibbs.

32, 90. *philosopher*. Diogenes.

33, 120. *Meres*. Sir Thomas Meres, a Whig member of Parliament.

35.   TO SIR ROBERT HOWARD

On April 16, 1660, there was entered in the Stationers' Register a volume of poems by Sir Robert Howard, a younger son of the Earl of Berkshire. To this volume Dryden contributed a commendatory poem. It is interesting as indicating Dryden's friendship this early with such a Royalist as Sir Robert, and his sentiments on the eve of the Restoration.

36.   TO DR. CHARLETON

This commendatory poem was prefixed to *Chorea Gigantum; or, The Most Famous Antiquity of Great Britain, vulgarly called Stoneheng, standing on Salisbury Plain, restored to the Danes.*

by Walter Charleton, Dr. in Physic, and Physician in Ordinary to His Majesty (London, 1663). Dr. Charleton directed his argument against a theory of the famous architect, Inigo Jones, that Stonehenge was a work of the Romans. In spite of the date on the title-page, it is quite certain that the book was printed late in 1662, and it is probable that this poem by Dryden had something to do with his election to the Royal Society on November 19, 1662. Dryden eulogizes the great English scientists of the century, not forgetting his eminent contemporary Boyle, brother of the Earl of Orrery; his poem shows some appreciation of the principles and spirit of the newly founded Royal Society.

37.   SONGS

Dryden's lyrics have received less attention than they merit. Many of them were very popular in musical settings, and appeared frequently in song-books. There is much information about their history in *The Songs of John Dryden,* edited by Cyrus Lawrence Day, 1932.

38.   PROLOGUES AND EPILOGUES

Prologues and epilogues were a popular feature in the theatre of the time, and Dryden was a master in writing them. They were not necessarily connected with the play. Dryden sometimes turned them into broad comedy; frequently he subjected the audience to a rough badinage, which they probably enjoyed even though they were the victims of his wit; sometimes, as in the selections in this volume, Dryden chose to discuss literary theories, very likely in this way giving the wits in the audience something to carry to the coffee-houses for further argument.

Dryden also composed prologues and epilogues for other playwrights for five guineas until 1682, when he raised his price to ten guineas.

40.   ABSALOM AND ACHITOPHEL

In the summer of 1678 a rather unsavory character named Titus Oates laid before the Council a Declaration alleging that an extensive plot was on foot among the English Catholics for setting fire to the City, massacring the Protestants, assassinating the king ,and bringing England back into the fold of the Catholic church. These supposed revelations inspired terror in many English hearts, which became hysteria and panic when, in October, Sir Edmund Berry Godfrey, a justice of the peace with whom a duplicate of the Declaration had been deposited, was found murdered in the fields just outside London. The murder of Godfrey—still an unsolved problem of history— was naturally imputed to the Catholics. Many London citizens expected something like the Massacre of St. Bartholomew, or the Gunpowder Plot of 1604, or the Irish Massacre of 1641. Moreover, the papers of Coleman, the secretary of the Duke of York, were seized, and among them was found correspondence with Père La Chaise, confessor to Louis XIV, regarding the re-establishment of Catholicism in England with French aid. Coleman was convicted of treason on November 27. The inference in the public mind was naturally that the Duke of York, the heir to the throne, was also implicated in Coleman's designs.

With public feeling thus inflamed Oates and his coadjutors were able, by perjured testimony, to secure the conviction and execution of many innocent persons. But the agitation consequent upon the Popish Plot raised a definite political issue of major importance when a proposal was made in parliament for the exclusion of the Duke of York from the throne. On this issue the public divided into two parties, which came to be known as Whigs and Tories. The Whigs, led by the Earl of Shaftesbury and the Duke of Buckingham, rallied all the extreme Protestant sentiment, especially the Dissenting element which was strong in the business section of London. The Tories were more conservative, and either did not regard Catholicism as a serious danger to England or felt that the danger of setting aside the constitutional succession was greater than any that could threaten from Catholicism. The policy of Exclusion thus became the storm center of English politics from 1679 until the abatement of the excitement about 1681 or 1682.

The Whigs naturally looked about for a pretender to the throne to substitute for the Duke of York. They thought they found him in the handsome and popular Duke of Monmouth, an illegitimate son of Charles II by Lucy Walters. The King was as partial to him as the people, though the Duke's pleasing exterior concealed a weak and irresolute character. But Charles would never lend an ear to the suggestion that his son should succeed him on the throne; when an attempt was made to legitimize the Duke of Monmouth by asserting that Charles had married his mother, the King issued a statement denying that there had been any marriage. One of the merits of Charles is that, in the face of threatened civil war, he steadfastly refused to sacrifice his brother's rights and the constitutional principle of succession, when his refusal might have cost him his own undisturbed possession of the throne. But the Whigs, though they had to accept the illegitimacy of Monmouth, nevertheless went ahead with their plans to establish him as successor by parliamentary action, and in 1680 they sent him on a progress through the west of England, to stir up enthusiasm and receive the adulation of the people.

The first Exclusion Bill was introduced in May, 1679, but failed to pass. A second was introduced in the autumn of 1680 and passed the Commons, but by the heroic efforts and brilliant debating of the Marquis of Halifax, was defeated in the Lords. In January, 1681, the king issued a call for Parliament to meet in March at Oxford, away from the influence of the Whig mob of London. In the middle of March both Whigs and Tories began to gather in Oxford, with armed retainers, as though they were going to battle rather than to a legislative assembly. The third Exclusion Bill was promptly introduced in the Commons and passed, but Charles abruptly dissolved the Parliament and rode to Windsor surrounded by troops. The Whigs were stunned and panic-stricken by the abrupt maneuver. "The price of horses doubled," says Trevelyan, summarizing accounts by eye-witnesses, "as in a city about to be entered by a victorious foe. The roads to Banbury, Witney and Shotover were thick with men, in coaches and on horseback, flying for their lives, each to his far country home."

After this *débâcle* at Oxford the Whig party lost prestige, though it still continued a powerful threat. But with the inevitable reaction of public opinion in the direction of Toryism, it was safe for the government in July, 1681, to arrest Shaftesbury on a charge of high treason and lodge him in the Tower. On November 24 the bill of indictment was brought before a London grand jury, assembled by a Whig sheriff, and of course thrown out. About a week before the trial there appeared an anonymous poem called *Absalom and Achitophel,* which ran into a second edition the next month and two more in 1682.

The Biblical parallel (2 *Samuel* xiv-xviii) was an obvious one and had occurred to others before Dryden used it. Dryden deftly managed the story so as to shield the character of Absalom as much as possible and to allow of a reconciliation of father and son in the sequel; partly because of Charles' known tenderness for the Duke of Monmouth, and partly, no doubt, because of his own personal gratitude to the Duchess of Monmouth, who had been one of his early patrons.

The greatness of the poem lies, however, not in the plot but in the brilliant characterizations and in the vigorous presentation of the political tenets of both sides. Perhaps the best commentary on his satirical portraits is his own, in the *Original and Progress of Satire* (1693): "there is still a vast difference betwixt the slovenly butchering of a man, and the fineness of a stroke that separates the head from the body, and leaves it standing in its place. . . . I wish I could apply it to myself, if the reader would be kind enough to think it belongs to me. The character of Zimri in my *Absalom* is, in my opinion, worth the whole poem; it is not bloody, but it is ridiculous enough; and he, for whom it was intended [the Duke of Buckingham], was too witty to resent it as an injury. If I had railed, I might have suffered for it justly; but I managed my own work more happily, perhaps more dexterously. I avoided the mention of great crimes, and applied myself to the representing of blindsides, and little extravagances; to which, the wittier a man is, he is generally the more obnoxious. It succeeded as I wished; the jest went round, and he was laught at in his turn who began the frolic." Dryden evidently thought he paid the duke arrears for *The Rehearsal,* staged ten years earlier. In this spirit of giving sharper edge to his satire, he added to the second edition of *Absalom* lines 180 to 191, praising Shaftesbury as an upright and incorruptible judge, as a contrast to the corruption and demagoguery of his political leadership. It should be noted also that, although Dryden was wholeheartedly on the Tory side, there are some rather daring passages on Charles which must have piqued contemporary readers.

The political debate should not be lightly dismissed. Dryden had read and studied the pamphlet literature of the time, and his poem is remarkable for clarifying the whole discussion and following it up to its first principles. Dryden's conservative thought receives further statement in *The Medal,* the preface and poem of *Religio Laici,* and in *The Hind and the Panther.* For all his Toryism he must nevertheless not be supposed to favor absolutism in monarchy; "The nature of our government," he said, in dedicating *All for Love* (1778) to Danby, then Lord Treasurer, "above all others, is exactly suited to both the situation of our country, and the temper of the natives. . . . And, therefore, neither the arbitrary power of One, in a monarchy, nor of Many, in a commonwealth, could make us greater than we are." The same sentiment may be found in *The Medal,* lines 117-18 and 247-51; and in the last year of his life he again expressed them in the poem *To my honor'd Kinsman, John Driden,* which should be read in connection with *Absalom and Achitophel* and *The Medal.*

40. *Si propius stes te capiat magis:* "If you stand nearer, you will be still more attracted." Horace, *Ars Poetica,* 361–62. Dryden's motto is intriguing on the title-page of a political allegory. The main application of the allegory is clear enough: Israel is England; the Jews are the English; the Jebusites the English Catholics. Sion is London, Hebron Scotland, and the Jordan the English Channel. Michal is of course the Queen, Catharine of Braganza. Among the Whigs, Shaftesbury as Achitophel and Buckingham as Zimri receive the major attention; among the lesser figures, Balaam represents the Earl of Huntingdon, Caleb is Lord Grey; Nadab is William, Lord Howard of Escrick, who was currently accused of having taken the sacrament, when a prisoner in the Tower, in *lamb's wool*—ale poured on roasted apples and sugar. Jonas, or Sir William Jones, had as attorney-general prosecuted the victims of the Popish Plot. Shimei, or Slingsby Bethel, was one of the Whig London sheriffs elected in 1680. Corah is Titus Oates, who in the reign of James II was punished for his perjuries, but in the later reign of William III received a pension from the state.

Among the King's friends Dryden praised Barzillai, the venerable and respected old Duke of Ormond; Zadoc, William Sancroft, archbishop of Canterbury; the Sagan of Jerusalem, Henry Compton, bishop of London; Adriel, John Sheffield, Earl of Mulgrave; Jotham, George Savile, Marquis of Halifax, the brilliant orator and writer, who defeated the Exclusion Bill; Hushai, Laurence Hyde, the son of Clarendon, created in 1682 the Earl of Rochester; and Amiel, Edward Seymour, who had been speaker of the House of Commons from 1673 to 1679. All these references would have been recognized by the contemporary reader without the help of notes.

54.   THE MEDAL

After the acquittal of Shaftesbury in November, 1681, the Whigs were exultant; they struck a medal in his honor which is thus described by Scott: "The obverse presented the bust of the Earl, with the legend, *Antonio Comiti de Shaftesbury;* the reverse, a view of London, the Bridge, and the Tower; the sun is rising above the Tower, and just in the act of dispersing a cloud; the legend around the exergue is *Laetamur,* and beneath is the date of his acquittal, *24th November, 1681.* The partisans of the acquitted patriot wore these medals at their breasts, and care was taken that this emblem should be made as general as possible."

The poem was published about March 16, 1682.

54. The motto, *Per Graium populos,* etc., is from the *Æneid,* vi, 588–89, translated by Dryden thus:

> Thro' Elis and the Grecian towns he flew;
> Th' audacious wretch four fiery coursers drew;
> He wav'd a torch aloft, and, madly vain,
> Sought godlike worship from a servile train.

54, 7. *Polander.* "It was a standing joke among the opponents of Shaftesbury, that he hoped to be chosen King of Poland at the vacancy in 1673–74 when John Sobieski was elected." —Scott.

54, 11. *as he did to B.* The artist of the Whig medal was George Bower.

54, 26. *any association of men.* Among Shaftesbury's papers had been found a manuscript, not in his hand, of a project for an Association for the defense of the Protestant religion and of the king's person, and of the liberties of the subject. This was regarded by the prosecution as evidence of treasonable intent.

54, 39. *to petition in a crowd.* A statute of 1661 forbade any unauthorized petition to king or parliament of more than ten signatures.

55, 7. *your dead author.* Andrew Marvell.

55, 10. *Anyone who reads Davila.* Davila was an Italian historian, the author of a *History of the Civil Wars in France.* The story of the Holy League was regarded by the Royalists and Tories as an illuminating historical parallel to the Commonwealth and Whig movements in England. Dryden had been reading Davila already in 1660 and projected a play on the Guise story, which he took up again with the assistance of Lee in 1682. He also read eagerly in other authorities on French history of the sixteenth century; and *The Duke of Guise* and his *Vindication* of that play are important documents for understanding Dryden's views on the history of his time and on politics.

56, 28. *a rebel ere a man.* Shaftesbury raised a regiment of foot and a troop of horse for the king in 1643, when he was only twenty-two; the next year he went over to the Parliamentary side. His political prominence during the Commonwealth did not prevent him from a career under Charles: he was a member of the famous Cabal ministry, though he was not, contrary to Dryden's implication in line 65 (and in *Absalom and Achitophel,* line 175) involved in the secret breaking, in 1670, of the Protestant Triple Alliance of England, Holland, and Sweden, negotiated by Temple in 1667. Shaftesbury's character has been championed in the standard biography by W. P. Christie (1871), but a more judicious treatment will be found in the brief volume by H. D. Traill (1888).

58, 181. *The head is loyal.* A Tory, Sir John Moore, had been elected Lord Mayor of London, but there were still *two gouty hands,* the Whig sheriffs.

60, 323. *Pudet,* etc. From Ovid, *Metamorphoses,* I, 758–59, translated later by Dryden thus:

> To hear an open slander is a curse;
> But not to find an answer, is a worse.

60.   MAC FLECKNOE

This poem was published in 1682, not by Dryden's publisher, Jacob Tonson, but with the imprint of one D. Green. The text was very inaccurate, and Dryden printed a correct one in his volume of *Miscellany Poems,* 1684. Dryden acknowledged that the poem was his in the *Discourse concerning Satire* (1693). Nevertheless there have recently been ill-advised attempts to deny his authorship; for a summary of this and related discussions of the poem the reader is referred to the appendix of Mark Van Doren's *The Poetry of Dryden.*

Flecknoe was an Irish Catholic priest, who cut a ridiculous figure as a versifier. Andrew Marvell, who had seen him at Rome about 1645, has left an amusing poem about him, *Flecknoe, an English Priest at Rome.* He died in 1678, leaving his name to posterity as synonymous with bad poetry.

Thomas Shadwell (1640–1692) and Dryden had been on friendly terms during the 1670's, although Shadwell had occasionally jibed at Dryden's pension and the leisure for writing it supposedly afforded him. This, possibly together with some personal altercation of which we have no knowledge, may have been the motive for Dryden's satire on Shadwell. From the time of Malone's life of Dryden (1800) it was believed that *Mac Flecknoe* was written late in 1682, in reply to *The Medal of John Bayes,* which in turn was a reply to Dryden's *The Medal.* However, there has been recently some doubt cast on Shadwell's authorship of *The Medal of John Bayes,* and a reference to *Mac Flecknoe* has been found in *The Loyal Protestant,* a newspaper, for February 9, 1681–1682. Scholars have therefore given up the theory of a connection of the poem with the controversies of 1682. Had it been written that late, we should have expected some reference in the poem to political matters, inasmuch as Shadwell had gone with the Whigs —he was a member of the Green Ribbon Club, the centre of Whig propaganda—and Dryden had remained steadfastly a Tory. Quite possibly it was written in 1678, just after the death of Flecknoe and before the excitement over the Popish plot had developed into a political cleavage of poets as well as politicians.

Mac Flecknoe provided, of course, the inspiration for the story of Pope's *Dunciad.*

63.   RELIGIO LAICI

About the time of the publication of *The Medal,* in March, 1682, Dryden's attention was drawn to the English translation of Father Simon's *Critical History of the Old Testament,* which had just been published by the book-seller Walter Davis. The translation was by Henry Dickinson, a former student at Trinity College, Cambridge, and thus probably known to Dryden's young friend, Richard Duke. Davis's stock was taken over soon after publication by Dryden's publisher, Jacob Tonson, and put out with a new Tonson title-page and prefatory poems signed with the initials of Dryden's friends, Richard Duke, Nahum Tate and Nathaniel Lee. It was the reading of Simon's *Critical History* which stimulated the composition of *Religio Laici,* published about November 30, 1682.

Simon's *Critical History* was first printed in Paris in 1678, but suppressed before publication. An unauthorized edition was issued in Amsterdam in 1680, and this was used by Dickinson for his translation. The *Critical History* was an erudite work of "higher criticism"; it demonstrated the unreliability of the texts of the Old Testament, the impossibility of Moses having written all that is ascribed to him, and in general the great difficulty of arriving at any finality in the interpretation of the Biblical text. Dryden hints in his poem (lines 252–53) at the current suspicion that Simon was at heart not a believer in Christianity; but Simon was a good Catholic, and his efforts are to be explained in a quite different manner. His purpose was to demonstrate that the Bible, on which the Protestants depended as the unique source of religious truth, was in fact ambiguous and unintelligible; and that it must therefore be interpreted constantly by an authoritative church, which was in possession of an uninterrupted tradition. In short, Simon was trying, by his erudite labors, to undermine the authority of the Protestant religion.

But Father Simon's work was only part of a larger Catholic campaign against the position of Protestantism. Already in the sixteenth century Catholic writers were pointing out how the Protestant claim that the Bible was its unique source of religious truth really implied the ability of the individual to read and interpret the Bible correctly; that is, that the Protestants were paying a handsome compliment to the power of the human reason. They therefore set about attacking the presumption of religious rationalism, using for their purpose all the resources of philosophical dialectic which had been made available in the recently discovered writings of the Greek sceptic Sextus Empiricus. The most eminent exponent of this mode of thought was Montaigne, whose *Apology for Raymond Sebond* (1580), a classic of modern scepticism, was of course well known to Dryden, who like most other educated Englishmen of his age was very fond of Montaigne. In the seventeenth century the greatest exponent of philosophical scepticism as an ally of religious faith was Pascal; his *Pensées* (1670) were probably unknown to Dryden before their translation into English in 1688, but a knowledge of Pascal is nevertheless very helpful to a reader of Dryden's poems on religion, because both were influenced by the same intellectual traditions.

It is therefore very significant that Dryden in the preface to *Religio Laici* confesses himself "naturally inclined to scepticism in philosophy," and that he refuses his assent, not only to Deism, but even to the rationalism of some of the "philosophizing divines" of the Anglican church. The problem of religious truth and church authority troubled him greatly, and he felt strongly the desirability of an omniscient church (lines 282 ff.) In 1682 he had already gone further intellectually on the road to Catholicism than he himself realized; but he was still seeking an Anglican compromise, a *via media* between the individualism of the Sects and the submission to an infallible church.

In Dryden's mind these philosophical questions were intimately related to the political problems he had discussed in *Absalom and Achitophel* and *The Medal*. Individualism in religion was associated with factiousness and insubordination in the state. Commonwealth notions flourished among the Sects, and were given a new life in the pamphleteering of the Whigs. To the political aspect of his subject Dryden devotes considerable space both in the preface and in the poem.

Henry Crabb Robinson recorded in his diary for January 6, 1842: "Landor once said to me, Nothing was ever written in hymn equal to the beginning of Dryden's *Religio Laici*,—the first eleven lines."

73.   TO THE MEMORY OF MR. OLDHAM

John Oldham died on December 9, 1683, in his thirtieth year. He was the author of *Satires on the Jesuits* (1679). Dryden's poem was prefixed to his *Remains in Verse and Prose*, published the year after his death.

74.   TO THE MEMORY OF MRS. ANNE KILLIGREW

Anne Killigrew was the daughter of the Rev. Dr. Henry Killigrew, Master of the Savoy and a Prebendary of Westminster; she was a niece of the dramatists Thomas Killigrew and Sir William Killigrew. She was herself a poetess and, after her death in June 1685, her poems were collected in a volume which was licensed for the press on September 30 and published about November 2, though the title-page has the date 1686. Dryden's poem was prefixed to this volume.

Dryden's criticism in this poem of the licentiousness of Restoration literature is noteworthy; when Jeremy Collier in 1698 lashed the English dramatists, Dryden quite high-mindedly admitted his own errors. See the *Preface to the Fables*. But in this ode Dryden anticipated Collier's criticism by thirteen years.

77.   THE HIND AND THE PANTHER

Charles II died on February 6, 1685, and his Catholic brother, the Duke of York, succeeded to the throne as James II. The heir to the throne then became James' daughter, Mary, Princess of Orange, wife of William of Orange, the greatest leader of the Protestant cause in European politics and the redoubtable enemy of Louis XIV. William and Mary therefore became important factors in the political situation in England under James.

The dominant policy of James was to secure from Parliament the repeal of the Test Act of 1673, which prevented any English Catholic as well as any Dissenter from holding any civil or military office under the king; and also the repeal of the various Penal Laws which made Catholic worship in England a crime. James believed that the Crown had a dispensing power over the laws which enabled him to abrogate these laws by the stroke of a pen, but he chose not to exercise this power because it could only extend to the end of his own reign, whereas a repeal of the statutes by Parliament would give the Catholics security also under his Protestant successors. But as Parliament was determined not to repeal these laws, James entered on a course of political manipulation, closeting of members of the Commons, coercion and threats, which the English people regarded as a menace to their political liberties.

Among the king's advisers in these rash measures, a certain Jesuit of noble family, Father Petres, rapidly came to the front and occupied a sinister position. On the other hand the majority of old English Catholic families, with landed estates, disapproved of the violent and unconstitutional policies of the king, and expected to suffer later, on the accession of William and Mary, for every move which he made in their behalf. At one time some of the Catholics determined to petition the king for permission to sell their estates and remove to foreign countries to avoid the wrath to come; but Father Petres counselled confidence in James. Dryden refers to this episode in the fable of the swallows and the Martin in the third part of the poem. In 1687 some Catholic leaders even negotiated through the Dutch ambassador with the hope of establishing their own peace with William of Orange. English Catholics were therefore not very happy even though under a king of their own persuasion.

Dryden was evidently on the side of the moderate Catholics. From the time of Scott down it has been pointed out by editors of Dryden that his portrait of Father Petres as the Martin betrays a personal dislike of the Jesuit. The fable of the swallows was Dryden's prophecy, even though he put it in the mouth of the Panther, of the disaster which James' headstrong policies were preparing for the English Catholics.

James hoped during the first two years of his reign for Anglican support for his policy of religious freedom for the Catholics. But he was strenuously resisted by the churchmen, and when he was finally convinced that nothing was to be gained from Parliament, he, on April 4, 1687, issued his Declaration of Indulgence, exercising his Royal prerogative to suspend the Test Act and the Penal Laws against both Catholics and Dissenters. This was just one week before *The Hind and the Panther* was licensed for the press. Dryden had no love for the Dissenters, whom he had treated with hostility in the first part of his poem; but in his preface he makes an effort to adjust himself to the new policy of toleration, for which he was evidently unprepared.

On the main question of religious authority and religious truth this poem may be regarded as a resolution of the problem left unsolved in *Religio Laici*. Although Dryden has in the meantime gone over to the Catholic church, his fundamental philosophy remains the same. It is important to note this deeper consistency and continuity of his thought, in view of the frequent accusation of insincerity brought against him because of his superficial inconsistencies.

Two young wits, Charles Montague and Matthew Prior, both of whom later rose to eminence, one as a financier and founder of the Bank of England, and the other as a diplomat and poet, produced a clever parody of Dryden's poem, under the title of *The Hind and the Panther transvers'd to the Story of the Country Mouse and the City Mouse,* in which Dryden figured again as the Mr. John Bayes of Buckingham's *Rehearsal.*

77. The motto is made up of two passages from the *Æneid*: iii, 96: "Seek your ancient mother," and i, 405: "By her stately movement the goddess is known."

78, 8. *'Tis evident.* Dryden refers to a controversy in which he had become involved with the eminent Anglican divine, Stillingfleet, then Dean of St. Paul's. James II had in 1685 ordered printed some papers in defence of the Roman Catholic faith which had been found in the strong box of Charles II, among them a paper by Anne Hyde, Duchess of York, deceased first wife of James. Stillingfleet publish an attack on these papers; whereupon a *Defence* of them appeared, of which Dryden wrote that part relating to the Duchess' paper. Stillingfleet again replied, and indulged in an attack on Dryden's character. In the *Defence* Dryden urged upon Stillingfleet the "Christian virtue of humility," adding that it was a virtue not in high repute among Protestants, who had not to his knowledge produced a single treatise on humility. Stillingfleet retorted that such a treatise had recently been published in London, referring probably to one by a William Allen, but mentioning no name. Dryden supposed that he referred to a book by a certain Duncomb, which was only a translation of a Spanish Catholic treatise.

78, 1. *A milk-white Hind.* Dryden was probably influenced in his description of the Hind by Bishop Bossuet's *Exposition* of the Roman Catholic faith, which was translated into English and aroused heated discussion in England in 1685–86. Bossuet presented a statement of Catholic doctrine which did not include many of the beliefs and features of worship most objected to by Protestants; Protestants accused him of presenting a "purified" and falsified version of Catholic doctrine. Dryden was certainly familiar with this controversy.

79, 53. *False Reynard.* Dryden makes the sly fox represent the extreme rationalistic and Unitarian heresy of the Arians in antiquity, and of the Socinians in the sixteenth century. His belief (see lines 60–61) that Protestantism inevitably tended towards Socinianism shows that Dryden had considerable insight into the development of religious thought of his time. He regarded the issue of rationalism as crucial to religion, and the mention of the Socinian Fox leads him to a long discussion of the place of reason in religion.

85.   A SONG FOR ST. CECILIA'S DAY, 1687

St. Cecilia was honored as the patron saint of music. Dryden represents her as the inventress of the pipe organ. In 1683 a musical society was formed in London for performing annually a composition in her honor on November 22. Dryden wrote the poems for the festivals in 1687 and 1697. His skill in providing the composer with musical motifs for both chorus and orchestra is admirable.

86.   TO MY DEAR FRIEND MR. CONGREVE

The Double Dealer was first acted in November, 1693, when Congreve was only twenty-three years old. Dryden generously welcomed this young recruit to the ranks of literature and a warm friendship sprang up between the two. Dryden wrote to William Walsh on December 12, 1693: "His *Double Dealer* is much censured by the greater part of the Town: and is defended only by the best judges, who, you know, are commonly the fewest, yet it gains ground daily. . . . My verses which you will find before it, were written before the play was acted, but I neither altered them nor do I alter my opinion of the play." The lines requesting Congreve to defend Dryden's character after his death are moving, coming from the aged Dryden to the youthful friend. Congreve wrote the Dedication to the 1717 edition of Dryden's dramatic works.

87, 48. *Tom the first:* Thomas Shadwell, Poet Laureate and Historiographer Royal, 1688–1692. *Tom the second:* Thomas Rymer, Historiographer after 1692, whose critical writings were probably in Dryden's mind when he wrote this passage.

87.   ALEXANDER'S FEAST

See note on the *Song for St. Cecilia's Day, 1687.* On September 3, 1697, Dryden wrote to his sons at Rome: "I am writing a song for St. Cecilia's Feast, who, you know, is the patroness of music. This is troublesome, and no way beneficial; but I could not deny the stewards of the feast, who came in a body to me to desire that kindness." He took the idea of the poem from Plutarch's life of Alexander, and soon warmed to the task. Joseph Warton, in his *Essay on Pope,* records an unreliable tradition that Dryden sat up all night and finished the poem "at one sitting." Dr. Johnson believed that he had spent a couple of weeks on it. In December, after the performance of the ode, Dryden wrote to Tonson: "I am glad to hear from all hands that my Ode is esteemed the best of all my poetry, by all the town: I thought so myself when I writ it; but being old, I mistrusted my own judgment." The poem is certainly remarkable to come from a man of sixty-six, and it has enjoyed a wider popularity than any other poem by Dryden. The extreme of eulogy is perhaps to be found in the remark by Robert Louis Stevenson about Dryden's odes, "those surprising masterpieces, where there is more sustained eloquence and harmony of English numbers than in all that has been written since" (Letter to Edmund Gosse, December 6, 1880). On the other hand, Mark Van Doren says that "it is a question whether *Absalom and Achitophel* and the *Oldham* are not better poetry than *Alexander's Feast,* which perhaps is only immortal ragtime" (*Poetry of John Dryden,* p. 258).

90.   AN ESSAY OF DRAMATIC POESY

In this dialogue Dryden has the interlocutors discuss the then vital questions as to whether the Ancients were superior to the Moderns, and whether the French taste in drama should supplant the English style of the Elizabethans. The persons of the dialogue are Dryden and his friends: Crites is his brother-in-law, Sir Robert Howard; Eugenius is Charles, Lord Buckhurst, later Earl of Dorset; Lisideius is Sir Charles Sedley, and Neander is Dryden. The dialogue is of course fictitious, but presents the various sentiments and points of view of the historical persons. Frank L. Huntley has elaborately analyzed the argument in a study "On Dryden's *Essay of Dramatic Poesy*" (Ann Arbor, 1951).

90a, 18. *that memorable day.* June 3, 1666. See Pepys' *Diary,* June 10th, 1666, and note.

91a, 43. Cicero, *Pro Archia,* x, 25, narrates that once when Sulla sat on his tribunal, a poor poet passed up to him a book of wretched poetry, written in alternate hexameters and pentameters; the Dictator ordered him rewarded on condition that he should write no more.

91b, 8. *one of them.* Probably Robert Wild, author of *Iter Boreale* (1660), a labored piece of verse on General Monk.

91b, 12. *Clevelandism.* John Cleveland (1613–1658), much admired in his lifetime, represented the decadence of the "Metaphysical" style.

92a, 45. *Qui Bavium non odit.* "He who hates not the verse of Bavius, may love thine, O Maevius." Virgil, *Ecl.,* iii, 90. Both were notoriously bad Roman poets.

92b, 6. *Pace vestra.* Petronius, *Satyricon,* ii.

92b, 28. *Indignor.* Horace, *Epistles,* ii, 1, 76.

> I feel my honest indignation rise,
> When, with affected air, a coxcomb cries,
> "The work, I own, has elegance and ease,
> But sure no Modern should presume to please."—Francis.

92b, 34. *Si meliora dies.* Horace, *Epistles,* ii, 1, 34.

> But let me ask, since poetry, like wine,
> Is taught by Time to mellow and refine,
> When shall th' immortal bard begin to live?—Francis.

97b, 7. *Audita visis.* "We are more ready to praise what we have heard about, than what we have seen; we envy the present, we admire the past; we believe that the former will eclipse us, but that the latter will instruct us." Paterculus, *History of Rome,* ii, 92.

100b, 31. *Sed proavi.* Horace, *Ars Poetica,* 270.

> "And yet our Sires with joy could Plautus hear,
> Gay were his jests, his numbers charm'd their ear."
> Let me not say too lavishly they prais'd,
> But sure their judgment was full cheaply pleas'd.—Francis.

100b, 39. *Multa renascentur.* Horace, *Ars Poetica,* 70.

> Many [words] shall rise, that now forgotten lie;
> Others, in present credit, soon shall die,
> If Custom will, whose arbitrary sway,
> Words, and the Forms of Language, must obey.—Francis.

100b, 52. *Mistaque ridenti.* "The earth shall pour forth Egyptian beans with smiling acanthus intermixed." Virgil, *Ecl.,* iv, 20.

100b, 54. *seventh Æneid.* "The waves admire, the woods, unaccustomed to the sight, survey with wonder the far-gleaming shields of heroes, and the painted keels floating on the river." *Æneid,* viii, 91.

101a, 6. *quem, si verbo.* "Which, if I may be permitted so audacious an expression, I should hardly hesitate to call the Palace of highest heaven." Ovid, *Metamorphoses,* i, 175.

101a, 37. *Rebel Scot.* By John Cleveland. The next illustration is from Cleveland's *Rupertismus.*

103b, 32. *Atque ursum.* Horace, *Epistles,* ii, 1, 185.

> The little vulgar of the clamorous pit . . .
> When his most interesting scenes appear,
> Call for a prize fight, or a baited bear.—Francis.

104a, 12. *Atque ita mentitur.* Horace, *Ars Poetica,* 151.

> Then Truth and Fiction with such skill he blends,
> That equal he begins, proceeds, and ends.—Francis.

104b, 1. *Quodcunque ostendis.* Horace, *Ars Poetica,* 188.

> For while upon such monstrous scenes we gaze,
> They shock our faith, our indignation raise.—Francis.

104b, 37. *Rollo.* John Fletcher's *The Bloody Brother, or the Tragedy of Rollo, Duke of Normandy.*

106b, 28. *Segnius irritant.* Horace, *Ars Poetica,* 180–87.

> What we hear,
> With weaker passion will affect the heart,
> Than when the faithful eye beholds the part.
> But let no deed upon the stage be brought
> Which better should behind the scenes be wrought;
> Nor force th' unwilling audience to behold
> What may with grace and eloquence be told.
> Let not Medea, with unnatural rage,
> Slaughter her mangled infants on the stage;
> Nor Atreus his detested feast prepare,
> Nor Cadmus roll a snake, nor Progne wing the air.—Francis.

107a, 53. *The Scornful Lady.* By Beaumont and Fletcher.

108a, 3. *Sed ut primo.* "But as at first we are fired with a desire to overtake those whom we regard as the greatest, so when we begin to despair either to surpass or to equal them, our eagerness wanes with our hope; what it can not overtake, it ceases to follow; . . . passing over that in which we can not excell, we look for another sphere of activity." Paterculus, *History of Rome,* i, 17.

108b, 31. *The Adventures.* Diego is the comic servant in Tuke's *Adventures of Five Hours.*

113b, 26. *Quantum lenta.* "As cypresses rise above the hedgerow thorn." Virgil, *Ecl.,* i, 26.

116b, 27. *Creditur.* Horace, *Epistles,* ii, 1, 168.

> Because the comic poet forms his plays
> On Common life, they seem a work of ease;
> But, since we less indulgence must expect,
> Sure we should labor to be more correct.—Francis.

117b, 38. *ubi plura nitent.* Horace, *Ars Poetica,* 351.

> But where the Beauties more in number shine,
> I am not angry, when a casual line
> (That with some trivial faults unequal flows)
> A careless hand, or human frailty shows.—Francis.

119a, 13. *Arcades omnes.* "both Arcadians, equally ready both to sing and to answer." Virgil, *Ecl.,* vii, 4.

121b, 15. *Siege of Rhodes.* By Davenant.

122a, 44. *tentanda via est.* "I must try a way of raising myself from the ground." Virgil, *Georg.,* iii, 8.

123a, 13. *Indignatur.* Horace, *Ars Poetica,* 90.

> Nor will the direful Thyestean feast
> In comic phrase and language be debas'd.—Francis.

124b, 32. *the Water Poet.* John Taylor, a Thames waterman, who early in the seventeenth century made a name for himself by publishing a great quantity of wretched verse.

127.   OF POETRY

128b, 23 Virgil, *Eclogues,* VIII, 69–71:

> "Pale Phoebe, drawn by verse, from heav'n descends;
> And Circe chang'd with charms Ulysses' friends.
> Verse breaks the ground, and penetrates the brake,
> And in the winding cavern splits the snake."—Dryden.

129a, 25. Meric Casaubon, *Treatise concerning Enthusiasme, as it is an Effect of Nature, but is mistaken by many for either Divine Inspiration or Diabolical Possession* (1655). As the title implies, the work criticized the unintelligent religious excitement so common among Dissenters.

133a, 21. Temple, like so many of the most cultivated men of the Classical age, understood that art can not be bound by rules. Similar sentiments may be found in Dryden, Addison, and Pope, not to mention Corneille himself.

133a, 44. *Feliciter audet.* Horace, *Epistles,* II, i, 166: "He is felicitously audacious."

133a, 45. *Lusit amabiliter.* Horace, *Epistles,* II, i, 148: "He is amiably playful."

133b, 1. Horace, *Epistles,* II, i, 211–213.

133b, 39. Aristotle, *Problems,* XIX, 28.

133b, 40. Tacitus, *Germania,* II.

133b, 47. Pliny, *Natural History,* VII, 57, 14.

134b, 17. This Spanish translation of the Old Testament was published at Ferrara in 1553.

136a, 13. The translation of the original Indian fables of Bidpai, or Pilpay, was published in Paris in 1644.

136a, 25. The Greek pastoral romance, *Daphnis and Chloe,* attributed to Longus.

136b, 45. These verses of the Emperor Adrian are discussed by Steele in *Spectator,* No. 532, and translated thus: "Alas, my Soul! thou pleasing companion of this body, thou fleeting thing that art now deserting it! whither art thou flying? to what unknown region? Thou art all trembling, fearful, and pensive. Now what is become of thy former wit and humor? Thou shalt jest and be gay no more."

137b, 4. Temple's knowledge of Old Norse, rather unexpected in a cultivated gentleman of his time, was largely derived from the Latin treatises of two Danish scholars: *Literatura Runica* (1636) and *Danicorum Monumentorum libri sex* (1643) by Olaus Wormius, and *Antiquitates Danicae* (1689) by Thomas Bartholin.

137b, 47. Compare Milton's comment on rhyme in poetry in his prefatory note to *Paradise Lost.*

139a, 34. *lougaroos.* Phonetic spelling for "loups-garous."

141a, 30. Horace, *Satires,* I, iv, 81–85: "The man who calumniates his absent friend, who does not defend him when others accuse him, who seeks reputation through irresponsible pleasantry, who repeats gossip, who makes up what he has not seen, and who betrays a confidence,— such a man has a black mind; beware of him, O Roman."

141b, 14. *La Secchia Rapita.* A mock-heroic poem by Allesandro Tassoni, published in 1622.

141b, 15. Scarron's burlesque of Virgil was published in 1648–52. It was imitated by Butler in *Hudibras* and translated by Charles Cotton in 1664.

141b, 17. For Sir John Minnes, see Pepys' *Diary.* He published *Wits Recreations,* 1640, and *Musarum Deliciae,* 1655.

141b, 46. The French Academy was founded in 1634 under the patronage of Cardinal Richelieu.

142a, 29. The word *humour,* originally a medical term, came to be applied in the sixteenth century to individual eccentricities, as in Ben Jonson's comedy of "humours." Such a "humour" was serious on the part of the subject of it, but ridiculous to the spectator. The modern meaning of the word developed later. Saint-Évremond, in his essay *De la comédie anglaise* (1677), said that the English excelled all other modern nations in comedy, and with this judgment English writers of the period readily agreed. The development of the modern idea of Humor has been studied by E. N. Hooker, "Humor in the Age of Pope," *HLQ,* xi (1948), 361–85.

143a, 39. The English malady of melancholy, so familiar to us from Elizabethan drama and poetry, was in the eighteenth century attributed to the spleen, and therefore named after that organ.

143b, 26. Rosicrucian mysteries were familiar to readers of the *Comte de Gabalis* (1670), by the Abbé de Villars, which suggested to Pope the supernatural elements of *The Rape of the Lock.*

149. AN ENGLISH PADLOCK

149, 1. *Danaë* was imprisoned in a tower by her father in order that no suitors might have access to her, but Jupiter visited her in the form of a shower of gold. See Horace, *Odes,* III, xvi.

151. CLOE JEALOUS

151, 5–16. *what you late have writ, etc.* The references are to the immediately preceding pieces in Prior's *Poems on Several Occasions*—"The Question: to Lisetta," "Lisetta's Reply," "On Beauty: a Riddle," "The Lady Who Offers her Looking-glass to Venus," "The Garland." Prior's "Cloe" seems to have been a certain Anne Durham; about 1718 she was succeeded as favorite by Elizabeth Cox, the "Lisetta" of the poems.

151.   A BETTER ANSWER

152, 26. *Horace and Lydia.* See Horace, *Odes,* III, ix.

154.   TO THE ECHO

154, subtitle. *Astrop.* A town in Northamptonshire, once noted for its medicinal waters.

155.   A NOCTURNAL REVERIE

156, 19. *Salisbury.* Probably Anne Tufton, Countess of Salisbury, daughter of one of Lady Winchilsea's closest friends, Catherine Cavendish, Countess of Thanet.

158.   AN ESSAY ON PROJECTS

This work, a volume of 336 pages, was Defoe's first important prose publication. It deals chiefly with economic conditions and exhibits the author's robust common sense, his stores of information on practical matters, and his realistic thinking.

158a, 29. *Academy of Paris.* The French Academy, founded in 1634, concerned itself with the improvement of the French language as well as with directing the taste of the nation in literature.

158b, 31–34. Roscommon's *Essay on Translated Verse.*

159a, 15. *present king of England.* William III, King of England, 1688–1702, of whom Defoe was an ardent admirer and on whose behalf he later wrote his verse satire *The True-Born Englishman.* Both before and after his accession to the throne of England, William had been leader of the coalition armies against Louis XIV of France.

161a, 36. *an ingenious lady.* Mary Astell, *A Serious Proposal to the Ladies for the Advancement of Their True and Greatest Interest,* 1694, Part II, 1697.

165.   APPARITION OF MRS. VEAL

The supreme art of this ghost story lies in its dry and prosaic narration, as if the author were too unimaginative to rise above mere facts. In this respect it is characteristic of Defoe's fiction, as a whole. But, as usual, Defoe worked from a base of facts. In 1895 G. A. Aitken showed, in an article in the *Nineteenth Century,* XXXVII, 95–100, that the people concerned actually lived in Canterbury; and much additional information regarding them was published by Sir Charles Firth and Dorothy Gardiner in articles in the *Review of English Studies* VII, in 1931. There is further information in an article by Rodney M. Baine, "The Apparition of Mrs. Veal: A Neglected Account," *PMLA,* LXIX (1954), 523–41.

166a, 38. *Drelincourt upon Death.* The English translation of Charles Drelincourt's *The Christian's Defence Against the Fear of Death* was first published in 1675 and proved very popular. In editions of the eighteenth century Defoe's *Apparition of Mrs. Veal* was often printed with it.

167a, 13. *Dr. Sherlock.* The eminent divine, William Sherlock, who published, among other things, a *Practical Discourse concerning Death* (1689).

167a, 53. Anthony Horneck's *Happy Ascetick* (1681).

167b, 18. *Friendship in Perfection.* John Norris's *Damon and Pythias, or, Friendship in Perfection,* published in his *Collection of Miscellanies* (1687).

173.   BAUCIS AND PHILEMON

Swift wrote this poem in 1706, but on Addison's advice revised it extensively before publication. The story is from Ovid, *Metamorphoses,* viii, 611–724.

174.   A DESCRIPTION OF THE MORNING

Contributed to the *Tatler,* April 30, 1709.

175.   A DESCRIPTION OF A CITY SHOWER

Contributed to the *Tatler,* October 17, 1710.

176, 59–60. Starting from Smithfield Market and St. Sepulchre's Church, Newgate, the torrents flowed down Snow Hill into Fleet Ditch, which was crossed by Holborn Bridge.

176, 61–63. The conclusion burlesques the use of the triplet and the Alexandrine in heroic verse.

177. THE BEASTS' CONFESSION

179, 150. *the Excise.* Walpole's Excise Bill aroused great opposition and was withdrawn in 1733.

179, 216. *bipes et implumis.* Two-legged and without feathers—Plato's definition of a man.

179. VERSES ON THE DEATH OF DR. SWIFT

180. 59. *St. John.* Henry St. John, Viscount Bolingbroke. *Pulteney.* William Pulteney, later Earl of Bath, one of the leaders of the dissident Whigs who opposed Walpole. Cp. line 194 below.

181. 156. *to public uses.* To found a lunatic asylum.

181, 179. *Lady Suffolk.* Mrs. Howard, at one time a friend of Pope, Swift, and Gay, afterwards Countess of Suffolk, mistress of George II.

181, 180–84. *the Queen . . . medals.* On the accession of George II, Swift was on friendly terms with Queen Caroline, but he complains that she never sent him the medal she had promised as a token of her favor.

181, 189. *Chartres.* Col. Francis Chartres, infamous for his avarice and debauchery.

181, 197. *Curll.* Edmund Curll, the unscrupulous bookseller, arch-enemy of Pope, who figures so largely in the literary piracies of the day.

181, 200. *Tibbalds, Moore, and Cibber.* Lewis Theobald, James Moore-Smythe, and Colley Cibber, all attacked in the *Dunciad.* Pope's enemies were Swift's.

182, 230. *vole.* A high bid in the card game called quadrille.

182, 253. *Lintot.* Bernard Lintot, the bookseller.

182, 258. *Duck Lane.* Cp. Pope, *Essay on Criticism,* page 350, line 445.

182, 272. *Stephen Duck.* The thresher poet patronized by Queen Caroline.

182, 274. *Craftsman.* A journal published in opposition to Walpole by St. John, Pulteney, and others.

182, 278. *Mr. Henley's last oration.* "Orator" Henley, an eccentric clergyman whose extravagant and unintelligible speeches won him much notoriety.

182, 281. *Woolston's tracts.* Thomas Woolston, a deist, had been fined and imprisoned for publishing *Discourses on the Miracles of our Saviour.*

183, 378–79. *Two Kingdoms, etc.* The English government had offered a reward for the discovery of the author of *The Public Spirit of the Whigs* (1713), a pamphlet published anonymously by Swift; the Irish government had done the same thing when the fourth of his *Drapier's Letters* appeared (1724). In neither case was Swift in serious political danger.

183, 400–01. *St. John's skill . . . Ormond's valor, Oxford's cares.* Writing from the Tory point of view, Swift says that the political ability of St. John, Viscount Bolingbroke, and of Robert Harley, Earl of Oxford, and the military prestige of James Butler, second Duke of Ormond, became of no avail at the death of Queen Anne.

184, 444. *A wicked monster.* William Whitshed, Lord Chief Justice of Ireland, a relentless enemy of Swift's.

184, 447. *Scroggs,* Chief Justice in the time of Charles II, and *Tresilian* in the reign of Richard II were notorious as unfair judges.

185. THE DAY OF JUDGMENT

For what is known of the early history of this famous piece, see *Poems,* ed. Williams, pp. 576–78, and *Shenstone's Miscellany 1759–1763,* ed. Ian Gordon (Oxford, 1952), pp. 129–30, 161. Manuscript copies were in the possession of Chesterfield, Dodsley, and others. The poem seems to have been first printed in a novel called *The Friends* (1773).

185. A TALE OF A TUB

Only a complete reading of the many sections of this complicated work can give an impression of the sweep and verve of its satire, often made the more enjoyable by an irrepressible merriment. Many readers regard section ix as the greatest passage in the book; certainly it is the most searching and relentless, and there is nothing more terrible in Book IV of *Gulliver's Travels.* The nice balance of the irony should, however, not lead us to the mistaken conclusion that Swift's philosophy of life is purely nihilistic.

185a, 9. *this famous sect.* Swift had devoted an earlier section to the Æolists, or disciples of Wind. He particularly satirised the uneducated "inspiration" of some religious sects.

185b, 35. *A certain great prince.* Henri IV of France. [Swift.]

186a, 18. *a certain state-surgeon.* Ravillac, who stagged Henry the Great in his coach. [Swift.]

186a, 42. Lucretius, *De Rerum Natura*, IV, 1048, 1055. "The mind seeks the body whence it was wounded by love; whence it was smitten, thither it tends, and yearns to unite with it."

186b, 3. Horace, *Satires*, I, iii, 107: "the foulest cause of war."

186b, 5. *The other instance*. This is meant of the present French King. [Swift.]

186b, 26. *Zibeta occidentalis*. Swift, in a note added in 1710, explained this as the name given to a perfume derived by Paracelsus from human excrement.

187a, 7. *Bedlam*. Bedlam, or Bethlehem Hospital for the Insane, in London.

187a, 32. *clinamina*. Words used by Lucretius [ii, 292] to represent the Κλίσις of Epicurus, the bias or deviation from a straight line which was supposed to explain the concourse of atoms. [Nichol Smith.]

187a, 37. *his romantic system*. Descartes' theory of vortices was no longer accepted in England in Swift's time.

187b, 30. "You may well be happy that you are in a place where you appear to know something."—Cicero to Trebatius, *Epistolae ad Familiares*, VII, 10.

187b, 44. William Wotton is satirized also in *The Battle of the Books*. He published *Reflections on Ancient and Modern Learning* in 1694; to the 1705 edition he added an appendix of *Observations upon the Tale of a Tub*.

188a, 28. *cut the feather*. "Split hairs." [Nichol Smith.]

188a, 35. *Jack of Leyden*. Johann Bockholdt, a tailor of Leyden, the leader in the final struggle of Anabaptist communism. In Münster, of which the Anabaptists gained complete possession, he was crowned king of the "New Jerusalem," under the title of John of Leyden. The town was retaken on June 24th, 1535, and in January, 1536, "Jack of Leyden" was executed. [Nichol Smith.]

190a, 52. "intelligence capable of affairs."—Tacitus, *Annals*, VI, 39 and XVI, 18.

190b, 8. *Seymour, Musgrave, Bowls, How*. At that time topping Members of the House of Commons. [Swift, 1720.]

190b, 47. *green bag and papers, etc*. A lawyer's coach-hire. [Swift.]

190b, 53. *Cornuta*. Cornutus is either horned or shining, and by this term Moses is described in the vulgar Latin of the Bible. [Swift.]

191a, 51. *the society of Warwick Lane*. The Royal College of Physicians.

191.   THE BATTLE OF THE BOOKS

Although written about 1697, this satire was first published, with *A Tale of a Tub*, in 1704. It was occasioned by the famous controversy between the Ancients and the Moderns, which had been raging for some time in France and which took an acute form in England after the publication of Temple's essay on *Ancient and Modern Learning* in 1690. Much of the controversy was pedantic and personal; but Swift seizes upon the fundamental issue and gives his own interpretation of it in the episode of the spider and the bee. The bee represents the "assimilative humanism" of the party of the Ancients, whereas the spider, in its originality and self-sufficiency, represents the Moderns. In style *The Battle of the Books* is a parody of heroic narrative; it is an account of a battle between the books of St. James's Library. The episode of the spider and the bee occurs just as the books are drawn up in line for battle, and it is in a way a part of the heroic tradition of two champions meeting for single combat between the lines of the two on-looking armies; the parody is the more delightful because the combat is purely verbal.

191b, 41. *Modern way of fortification*. Fortification was one of the arts, upon the improvement of which the argument in favor of the moderns was founded by their advocates. [Scott.]

192a, 13. *Beelzebub*. Supposed to be the tutelar deity of the flies. [Scott.]

193b, 7. *borrowed shape of an ass*. Bentley was supposed to have called Boyle an *Ass*. So at least Boyle complained in his *Examination*, pp. 219, 220. But Bentley had only quoted "the old Greek Proverb, *That Leucon carries one thing, and his Ass quite another*" (*Dissertation*, p. 74); and Boyle—"voluntarily," as Bentley said—had taken this to imply that "the Writer of the Greek Epistle means differently from the *Ass* his Editor." [Nichol Smith.]

194a, 27. *sweetness and light*. A phrase well known because Matthew Arnold borrowed it as a title for one of his essays.

194.   ABOLISHING OF CHRISTIANITY IN ENGLAND

The Test Act, passed in 1672, required all those who held civil or military office under the Crown to take the communion in the Anglican Church. In the reign of Queen Anne the Whig party was disposed to repeal this Act, because the Dissenters were an influential section of the party. Swift was devoted to the Anglican Church, and published this ironical commendation of repeal at a time when he was still friendly with the Whigs.

194a, 51. *the Union.* The Union of England and Scotland into one kingdom had been achieved the preceding year, 1707.

195b, 46. *Deorum offensa.* "The insults to gods must be their own affair." Tacitus, *Annales,* I, 73.

196a, 8. *the allies.* England's allies against France were Austria, Holland, Spain, and Saxony.

196a, 37. *Asgil, Tindal, Toland, Coward.* Well-known deists, critics of Christianity and champions of natural religion.

196a, 51. *Empson and Dudley.* Ministers of Henry VII whose names had become a by-word for illegal exaction of taxes.

197b, 40. *Margarita de l'Epine, Mrs. Tofts, Valentini.* Singers in Italian opera, newly introduced.

201. GULLIVER'S TRAVELS

The *Gulliver's Travels* which children of all countries have been reading for generations is only an expurgated edition of one half of Swift's work. As Swift wrote it, the book is strong meat even for adults. It is his arraignment of mankind. But Swift also had a strong instinct of innocent playfulness, evident both in his life and work, which often softens the harshness of the satire. It is this resourceful playfulness which has so pleased children of all ages. The plan of the *Travels* was conceived before 1714, in the days of the Scriblerus Club. Swift probably wrote most of it after 1720, and it was published in 1726. It created a sensation at once, largely because of the political satire. But Swift's deeper satirical purpose, in which the modern reader is interested, is expressed in his famous letter to Pope, September 29, 1725:

". . . when you think of the world give it one lash the more at my request. I have ever hated all nations, professions, and communities, and all my love is toward individuals: for instance, I hate the tribe of lawyers, but I love Counsellor Such-a-one, and Judge Such-a-one: so with physicians—I will not speak of my own trade—soldiers, English, Scotch, French, and the rest. But principally I hate and detest that animal called man, although I heartily love John, Peter, Thomas, and so forth. This is the system upon which I have governed myself many years, but do not tell, and so I shall go on till I have done with them. I have got materials toward a treatise, proving the falsity of that definition *animal rationale,* and to show it would be only *rationis capax.* Upon this great foundation of misanthropy, though not in Timon's manner, the whole building of my Travels is erected; and I never will have peace of mind till all honest men are of my opinion."

242. A MODEST PROPOSAL

Swift did not love Ireland or the Irish, but he hated oppression; and his journalistic efforts on behalf of the Irish made him a popular hero. It is characteristic of Swift, who never liked to express his emotions directly, that he should in this tract disguise his consuming indignation beneath the cold and calculating style of economic statistics, or "political arithmetic," as it was then called. *The Modest Proposal* was published in 1729.

243a, 14. *sell themselves to the Barbadoes.* Poor people sometimes emigrated to the Colonies by agreeing to work for a period of years after their arrival to pay for their transportation.

244a, 23. It was believed in some quarters at that time that some of the natives in America were cannibals.

244b, 17. *an eminent French physician.* Rabelais. [Faulkner edition, 1735.]

245a, 49. George Psalmanazar pretended to have come from Formosa. Swift here draws upon his *Description of the Isle Formosa* (1705).

247a, 13. *Topinamboo.* A district of Brazil; no flattering comparison for the English.

247a, 31. All these are proposals advocated, of course, by Swift himself, in previous pamphlets and papers. [Temple Scott.]

249. THE TATLER

249a, 6. *Quicquid agunt homines.* "Whatever men do is the subject of our papers." This motto was used for the first forty numbers of the *Tatler* and for some of the later ones.

249b, 11. *Tuesday, Thursday, and Saturday.* These were the days on which the post left London for different parts of the country. [Aitken.]

251a, 8. *Mr. Betterton.* Thomas Betterton (1635–1710), veteran of the stage, who had distinguished himself especially in Shakespearean roles.

251a, 9. Congreve's *Love for Love* was first produced in 1695.

251b, 17. *a comedy. The Modern Prophets* by Thomas D'Urfey (1653–1723) was first produced May 3, 1709. D'Urfey's songs were popular, but not highly esteemed by educated people. Steele's comment on them is sly.

251b, 31. *Letters from the Hague.* In the earlier *Tatlers* Steele published items of news, available to him as the official writer of the *London Gazette*, the organ of the government. He tended to omit them in later numbers.

251b, 32. England did not adopt the reformed Gregorian calendar until 1752; as the new calendar made a correction of eleven days, letters written on the Continent on April 16 ("new style") would in England have been dated April 5 ("old style").

251b, 51. *a great general.* Marlborough, then in command of the Allied forces against France.

252a, 43. *the death of Mr. Partridge.* Steele is here continuing the ridicule which Swift had directed in 1708 at John Partridge, a popular almanac-maker and prophet. This is the more appropriate as Steele used for his *Tatlers* the pseudonym "Isaac Bickerstaff" under which Swift had published his papers on Partridge. Swift had prophesied the death of Partridge and then further amused the town by arguing down Partridge when he denied that he had died on the date set.

253b, 30. *"The Fox."* Ben Jonson's *Volpone, or the Fox.*

254a, 43. *the author of a play.* Viscount Grimston (1683–1756).

254b, 2. The Hon. Edward Howard, an unsuccessful playwright, was the second son of the fifth Earl of Suffolk.

254b, 21. *Goddard's Drops.* A famous patent medicine of the time.

255b, 14. *the advertisements.* The original sheets of the *Tatler* and the *Spectator*, as generally with the periodicals of the day, carried advertisements.

256.   THE SPECTATOR

256b, 40.   "One with a flash begins, and ends in smoke;
                      Another out of smoke brings glorious light,
                      And (without raising expectation high)
                      Surprises us with dazzling miracles."—Roscommon.

257b, 39. *politicians at Will's.* There is frequent reference in the literature of the time to the fact that each coffee-house tended to have its own specialized clientele.

257b, 44. *the Postman.* Then the leading Whig newspaper.

258a, 21. *blots.* A term in backgammon, for unprotected men, liable to capture.

259a, 2. *Ast alii sex, etc.* "Six more at least join their consenting voice."

262a, 5. "Admitted to the sight, would you not laugh?"

262a, 18. *Nicolini.* Addison, and other English men of letters of the time, ridiculed the absurdities of Italian opera. Nicolini was one of the most popular male sopranos imported because of the new vogue.

262b, 16. Dryden's *Sir Martin Mar-all* (1667).

262b, 40. *opera of Rinaldo.* Handel, trained in Italy, arrived in England in 1710. His opera of *Rinaldo* was acted 24 February 1711 with success.

263a, 2. *contrived by two poets.* The Italian libretto by Rossi was translated into English by Aaron Hill.

263b, 4. Boileau, *Satires*, IX, 176.

263b, 45. *London and Wise.* The leading English gardeners of the day, both practising the Dutch or formal style, which both Addison and Pope ridiculed.

264a, 2. "Poems are like pictures."

264a, 9. *written professedly upon it.* Much had been written about "wit" in the sixteenth and seventeenth centuries. But Addison is trying in this paper to make clear what a pure taste in "wit" is, and aims his criticism at the extravagances of the preceding generations, especially the "Metaphysical" style.

264a, 23. *a famous critic.* Longinus *On the Sublime*, widely read at this time.

266a, 39. "Sometimes the vulgar see and judge aright."

266b, 39. Addison's praise of Chevy Chase surprised the eighteenth-century critics and brought upon him the ridicule of John Dennis and the author of the *Comment upon the History of Tom Thumb*, a piece afterwards included in the volume known as the *Miscellaneous Works* *of Dr. William Wagstaffe.* Dr. Johnson found in the poem only "chill and lifeless imbecility." [Aitken.]

268b, 8. *Æneid,* XI, 820. Translation from Dryden.

268b, 25. *Ibid,* XII, 936.

> "The Latian chiefs have seen me beg my life;
> Thine is the conquest."—Dryden.

268b, 50. *Ibid.,* X, 821. Translation from Dryden.

271a, 16. Thucydides, II, xlv.

271a, 21. "I take it to be a principal rule of life, not to be too much addicted to any one thing."

271b, 52. *the verge of the court.* The Courts of Law.

272b, 37.

> "Here plenty's liberal horn shall pour
> Of fruits for thee a copious shower,
> Rich honors of the quiet plain."

274b, 21. "Out of breath to no purpose, and very busy about nothing."

276a, 43. . . . "I deem their breasts inspired
> With a divine sagacity."

278b, 17. "An agreeable companion upon the road is as good as a coach."

280b, 15. ". . . . That directing power,

> Who forms the genius in the natal hour:
> That God of Nature, who, within us still,
> Inclines our action, not constrains our will."—Pope.

281b, 41. *Seneca.* Epistle 95.

282b, 41.

> "The cloud, which, intercepting the clear light,
> Hangs o'er thy eyes, and blunts thy mortal sight,
> I will remove. . . ."

285b, 5.

> "On him confer the poet's sacred name,
> Whose lofty voice declares the heavenly flame."

286b, 8. *Pindarics.* The so-called Pindaric odes of the seventeenth century, such as Cowley's, were inspired by a misunderstanding of the art of Pindar.

286b, 18. "If you pretend to be mad and sane at the same time, you would not be more rash than if you think of reducing these uncertain things to any certainty by reason."

286b, 24. *the Camisars.* French Prophets, from Cevennes, who came to England in 1707. They prophesied, and said they could work miracles; and their strange actions and convulsions formed the subject of a number of pamphlets. [Aitken.]

287a, 47.

> "The whole debate in memory I retain,
> When Thyrsis argued warmly, but in vain."

287b, 1. *the old Roman fable.* Livy, *History,* Dec. I, ii, 2, and Shakespeare's *Coriolanus,* IV, i.

287b, 15. Compare another merchant, Mr. Sealand, in Steele's later play, *The Conscious Lovers,* IV, i.

289b, 21. From Winterton's *Poetae Minores Graeci,* p. 507. [G. G. Smith.] "Mirth out of season is a grievous ill."

289b, 50. *a modern philosopher.* Thomas Hobbes.

290a, 12. *words of the wise man. Eccles.,* II, 2.

291a, 1. *The Dispensary* (1699), by Sir Samuel Garth.

291a, 31. Waller, *The Countess of Carlisle in Mourning,* line 13.

291a, 39. *L'Allegro,* 11-ff.

291b, 8. "I am glad that he whom I must have loved from duty, no matter what he was, is such that I can love him from inclination."—Cicero to Trebonius, *Epist. ad Fam.,* XII, 16.

294a, 1. *new heads.* Head-dresses.

294a, 8. "Give place, ye Romans and ye Grecian writers."

294a, 10. Addison's series of papers on *Paradise Lost,* of which this is the first, were a notable contribution, not only to the popularity of Milton, but to what came later to be recognized as the Romantic conception of poetry. Their influence was especially important on German literature

294a, 22. *those who allege . . . not an heroic poem.* Neither Dryden nor Rymer would allow that *Paradise Lost* was an "heroic poem." [Aitken].

294a. 44. *Ars Poetica,* 147.

295a, 18. *The Spanish Fryar* (1680), by Dryden.

295b, 25. *Æneid,* VII, 378–84.

295b, 38. *Poetics,* VII, 4.

296b, 14.   "The blast Tartarean spreads its notes around;
                                The house astonished trembles at the sound."

296b, 24. *The Humorous Lieutenant.* A comedy by Beaumont and Fletcher.

297b, 44. In the original edition appeared this note: "Not being yet determined with whose name to fill up the gap in this dissertation, which is marked with asterisks, I shall defer it till this paper appears with others in a volume." Evidently it was never considered expedient to supply a real name.

297b, 47. *Mr. Collier.* Jeremy Collier, *Essays upon Several Moral Subjects* (1697).

298a, 22. *Almanzor.* The ranting hero of Dryden's *Conquest of Granada.*

298b, 4. "To grace each subject with enlivening wit."

298, 6. *Gracian.* Balthazar Gracian (1601–1658), whose books on literary taste and courtly manners attained European renown. His *El Oraculo Manual* (1647) was available in two English translations, *The Courtier's Oracle* (1685) and *The Art of Prudence* (1702).

301.   TO THE EARL OF WARWICK ON THE DEATH OF MR. ADDISON

301, 9–22. *Can I forget the dismal night, etc.* Addison was buried at night in the Chapel of Henry VII, Westminster Abbey, Bishop Atterbury officiating. His grave is next to that of his early friend and patron, Charles Montague, Lord Halifax.

302, 81–82. *There taught us how to live, etc.* When Addison was on his death-bed, he is said to have called the young Earl of Warwick to his side and exclaimed, "See in what peace a Christian can die!"

302, 83–94. *Thou hill, etc.* A description of the grounds of Holland House, Kensington, where Addison lived after his marriage to the Countess of Warwick.

302, 102–14. *Craggs.* James Craggs, Junior, had succeeded Addison as Secretary of State, and Tickell's edition of Addison was dedicated to him. Craggs, however, died in February, 1721, seriously involved in the South Sea crash.

302.   COLIN AND LUCY

Probably written soon after Tickell's arrival in Ireland in 1724, though there is nothing Irish about the poem except the names Leinster and Liffy. A broadside edition published in Dublin has recently been discovered. The present text is that of Dodsley's *Collection,* i (2nd ed.; 1748).

304.   THE SPLENDID SHILLING

304. 6. *Juniper's, Magpye, or Town-Hall.* Alehouses in Oxford.

304, 21. *Mundungus.* Bad tobacco.

304, 23. *Cambro-Britain.* A Welshman.

304, 27. *Cestrian.* From Chester.

304, 29. *Arvonian mart.* Arvon in Caernarvonshire.

304, 30. *Maridunum.* Town in South Wales, now Carmarthen.

304, 31. *Brechinia, Vaga.* Roman name for Brecon, South Wales; the River Wye.

304, 32. *Ariconium.* Roman town on the Wye, now Weston.

305, 34. *Massic, Setin, Falern.* Famous wines.

305, 79. *Arachne.* A Lydian maiden changed by Athena to a spider.

306, 126. *Eurus, Auster.* East and south winds.

306, 127. *Boreas.* North wind. *Cronian.* Epithet applied by Milton to north polar sea.

321.   MISCELLANY III

321b, 10. *Miscellany III* is from the section of "Miscellaneous Reflections," in which Shaftesbury assumes the role of commentator on his own essays. In the chapter included here he discusses his third treatise, *Of Soliloquy,* in which he advocates communion with oneself, rather than argument with another, as a means of rectifying the mind and arriving at truth and good taste.

323b, 25. If Shaftesbury wrote these portraits with any actual public characters in mind, they must have been Robert Harley, Earl of Oxford and Henry St. John, Viscount Bolingbroke, the leaders of the Tory ministry from 1710 to 1714. Shaftesbury was by both family tradition and inclination a Whig.

326a, 10. Juvenal, *Satires*, II, 149, 152: "That such things exist as ghosts, or realms below the earth, no one believes except small boys, too young to have paid their copper coin for a bath."

329a, 29. "You have a confessed culprit."

329. THE APOSTROPHE TO NATURE

In *The Moralists, A Philosophical Rhapsody,* the fifth treatise in the *Characteristics,* Philocles and Theocles go forth early one morning to a hill-top, hoping that the genius of the place will teach them "some celestial hymn" of Nature, and make them "feel divinity present in these solemn places of retreat." As the sun was about to rise, and the view spread before them, Theocles, "full of those divine thoughts which meet you ever in this solitude," stretched out his hands and, pointing to the landscape around, began this hymn to Nature. It was much admired in the eighteenth century, especially in Germany, and inspired J. G. von Herder's famous poem, *Naturhymnus von Shaftsburi* (1800).

331. THE GRUMBLING HIVE

332, 48. *Cross.* A small coin.

332, 62. *Dipped estates.* Mortgaged estates.

333, 163–66. *And virtue . . . was . . . made friends with vice.* Mandeville in Remark F gives the following illustration: "Thus the merchant that sends corn or cloth into foreign parts to purchase wines and brandies encourages the growth or manufactury of his own country; he is a benefactor to navigation, increases the customs, and is many ways beneficial to the public; yet it is not to be denied but that his greatest dependence is lavishness and drunkenness."

333, 173–74. *Parties directly opposite.* Mandeville gives among other illustrations the following (Remark H): "Nothing was more instrumental in forwarding the Reformation than the sloth, and stupidity of the Roman clergy; yet the same Reformation has roused them from the laziness and ignorance they then labored under."

333, 180–81. *Whilst luxury Employed a million of the poor.* Remark L on these lines contains much of Mandeville's famous defence of luxury. The following quotations will give the main drift of his argument from the economic point of view: "It is a received notion that luxury is as destructive to the wealth of the whole body politic as it is to that of every individual person who is guilty of it, and that a national frugality enriches a country in the same manner as that which is less general increases the estates of private families. I confess that though I have found men of much better understanding than myself of this opinion I cannot help dissenting from them in this point. They argue thus: We send, say they, for example to Turkey of woolen manufactory and other things of our own growth, a million's worth every year; for this we bring back silk, mohair, drugs, etc., to the value of twelve hundred thousand pounds, that are all spent in our own country. By this, say they, we get nothing; but if most of us would be content with our own growth, and so consume but half the quantity of those foreign commodities, then those in Turkey, who would still want the same quantity of our manufactures would be forced to pay ready money for the rest, and so by the balance of that trade only the nation should get six hundred thousand pounds *per Annum.* . . . We know that we could not continue long to purchase the goods of other nations if they would not take our manufactures in payment for them; and why should we judge otherwise of other nations? If those in Turkey then had not more money fall from the skies than we, let us see what would be the consequence of what we supposed. The six hundred thousand pounds in silk, mohair, etc. that are left upon their hands the first year must make those commodities fall considerably. Of this the Dutch and French will reap the benefits as much as ourselves; and if we continue to refuse taking their commodities in payment for our manufactures, they can trade no longer with us, but must content themselves with buying what they want of such nations as are willing to take what we refuse, though their goods are much worse than ours; and thus our commerce with Turkey must in few years be infallibly lost."

334, 269. *Squire Catch.* The executioner.

334, 275. *bums.* Bumbailiffs.

334, 289. *journey-bees.* Curates, "journeymen-parsons."

335, 433. In Remark Q Mandeville wrote: "Would you render a society of men strong and powerful, you must touch their passions. Divide the land, though there be never so much to spare, and their possessions will make them covetous; rouse them, though in jest, from their idleness with praises, and pride will set them to work in earnest; teach them trades and handicrafts and you'll bring envy and emulation among them; to increase their numbers, set up a variety of manufactures and leave no ground uncultivated; let property be inviolably secured, and privileges equal to all men; suffer nobody to act but what is lawful, and everybody to think what he pleases; for a country where everybody may be maintained that will be employed, and the other maxims are observed, must always be thronged and can never want people as long as there is any in the world. . . . But would you have a frugal and honest society, the best policy is to preserve men in their native simplicity, strive not to increase their numbers; let them never be acquainted with strangers or superfluities, but remove and keep from them everything that might raise their desires or improve their understanding."

336.   THE FABLE OF THE BEES

337a, 38. *Proverbs* xvi, 32.

339b, 36. Mandeville recognizes that Steele represents a view the opposite of his own. In *A Search into the Nature of Society* he directly attacks Shaftesbury because "he seems to require and expect goodness in his species, as we do a sweet taste in grapes and china oranges, of which, if any of them are sour, we boldly pronounce that they are not come to that perfection their nature is capable of."

THE POETRY OF POPE

The poetry of Pope has frequent satirical references to individuals of Pope's own time. Most of the satirical portraits, however, characterize a type as well as an individual, and the poetry can be read with appreciation without a key. A key to most of the contemporary allusions is supplied in the notes which follow, but when the person involved is obscure or the identification is uncertain, no note is given. The curious reader may consult the Twickenham Edition for the speculations of the scholars. The present editors are much indebted to the Twickenham Edition for new or expanded notes, especially for *The Dunciad*. Indebtedness for such information is indicated by the editor's name and the abbreviation, Twick. Ed.

344.   PASTORALS: SUMMER

Pope, like other poets of his day, conceived of the pastoral as a purely classical form, the main characteristics of which had been determined by Theocritus, Bion, Moschus, and Virgil. In his "Discourse on Pastoral Poetry," he thus characterizes the *genre*: "The complete character of this poem consists in simplicity, brevity, and delicacy; the two first of which render an eclogue natural, and the last delightful. If we would copy nature, it may be useful to take this idea along with us, that pastoral is an image of what they call the golden age. So that we are not to describe our shepherds as shepherds at this day really are, but as they may be conceived then to have been, when the best of men followed the employment." He adds that the modern poet may throw in a few hints of rural life as he knows it but it must seem to be "rather done by chance than on design." It is within the limits of these restrictions that one is to look for the charm of Pope's or Ambrose Philip's pastorals. Pope's pastorals were first published in the sixth part of Tonson's *Poetical Miscellanies,* 1709, in the same volume with those of Ambrose Philips. The fact that Ambrose Philips' poems received so much more recognition than Pope's—and rather more in proportion than they deserved—may account for some of the scorn with which Philips was treated in Pope's later satires.

344. 9. *Accept, O Garth.* "Dr. Samuel Garth, author of *The Dispensary* was one of the first friends of the author, whose acquaintance with him began at fourteen or fifteen. Their friendship continued from the year 1703 to 1718, which was that of his death."—Pope.

344, 16. *The woods,* etc. Pope tells us in his notes that this is a line from Spenser's *Epithalamion.*

345.   ESSAY ON CRITICISM

This poem was first published in 1711, although it may have been begun even before the death of Walsh in 1708. It is chiefly interesting for its neo-classical conception of the relation of art and nature. The student will find indispensable to a full interpretation of this conception and an understanding of its place in eighteenth-century thought the following articles: A. O. Lovejoy, "The Parallel of Deism and Classicism," *MP*, XXIX (1932), 281–99, and L. I. Bredvold, "The Tendency toward Platonism in Neo-Classical Esthetics," *ELH*, I (1934), 91–119.

345, 6. *Censure.* Judge—disapprobation not necessarily implied.

345, 17. *Wit.* This word was used in a much less confined sense in Pope's day than in ours. It means here and in other lines, intellectual capacity. At times it means something nearer to genius or imaginative power. Sometimes it means the product of intellect or genius. Only occasionally does it mean wit in the modern sense.

345, 21. *Nature.* Also a meaningful term for the eighteenth century as well as for earlier ages. It may mean, among other things, (1) the natural endowment of human beings, *i.e.*, that which is given "by nature"; (2) the endowing power or force itself; or (3) the ideal order of the universe which may be taken as a norm or pattern (see especially ll. 68 ff.). The term "nature" was usually opposed to the term "art."

345, 34. *Maevius.* A poor poet of Virgil's day.

346, 68–91. *First follow nature,* etc. Pope is here following the fundamental doctrines concerning nature of the Philosophy of the Enlightenment: the laws of nature are (1) eternal; (2) the same for all times and places; and (3) so simple and clear as to be perceptible by all men by the light of reason alone. In accordance with this philosophy, simplicity, clarity, and universality became dominant traits in the art of the neo-classical period. (See ll. 293–302.) An interesting parallel may be drawn with the abstract painters of the present time.

346, 129. *Mantuan muse.* Virgil, born near Mantua.

347, 138. *Stagirite.* Aristotle, born at Stagira in Macedonia.

347, 216. *Pierian spring.* Hippocrene on Mt. Helicon. The muses were first worshipped in Pieria on Mt. Olympus.

348, 267. *La Mancha's knight.* Don Quixote. The incident occurs in Le Sage's adaptation of Avellaneda's Second Part of *Don Quixote,* 1614.

348, 289. *Conceit.* Ingenious or fantastic conception.

349, 328. *Fungoso in the play.* A poor student in Jonson's *Every Man Out of his Humor.*

349, 356. *Alexandrine.* A line with six feet.

349, 361. *Denham; Waller.* Seventeenth-century writers of heroic couplets. Cf. Dryden: "our numbers were in their nonage until Denham and Waller appeared."

349. 374. *Timotheus.* A famous Athenian musician. Cf. Dryden's *Alexander's Feast.*

350, 445. *Duck Lane.* "A place where old and second-hand books were sold formerly, near Smithfield."—Pope.

350, 459. *parsons, critics, beaus.* Jeremy Collier, the Duke of Buckingham, Rochester, all of whom attacked Dryden.

351, 463. *Blackmores; Milbournes.* This line alludes to Blackmore's *Satire against Wit,* 1700, and Milbourne's *Notes on Dryden's Virgil,* 1698.

351, 465. *Zoilus.* A censorious critic of Homer of the fourth century B.C.

352, 544–51. In the reign of William and Mary, says Pope, unorthodox theological opinions flourished.

352, 585. *Appius.* John Dennis, author of *Appius and Virginia,* and one of Pope's most violent critics, largely, apparently, on account of this passage.

352, 617. *Durfey's Tales.* Tom D'Urfey, 1653–1723, poet and dramatist.

353, 648. *Maeonian star.* Homer.

353, 665. *Dionysius.* Dionysius of Halicarnassus, c. 57-7, B.C.

353, 667. *Petronius.* Petronius Arbiter, d. 66 A.D. "It is to be suspected that Pope had never read Petronius."—Johnson.

353, 669. *Quintilian.* Author of *Institutiones Oratoriae.*

353, 675. *Longinus.* Presumed author of *Essay on the Sublime,* a critical treatise much quoted in the eighteenth century.

353, 697. *Leo.* Leo X, 1475–1521, patron of the arts.

354, 704. *Vida.* Italian humanist, d. 1566, author of *De Arte Poetica.*

354, 714. *Boileau.* French critic and poet, 1636–1711; leader of neo-classical school.

354, 724. This line is quoted from the Duke of Buckingham's *Essay on Poetry.*

354, 725. *Roscommon.* Another contemporary of Dryden. He translated Horace's *Art of Poetry.*

354, 729. *Walsh.* William Walsh, 1663–1708, early friend and patron of Pope.

354. THE RAPE OF THE LOCK

This poem was composed, as the first few lines suggest, at the instigation of Pope's Catholic friend, John Caryll. Lord Petre, a relative of Caryll, had stolen a lock of Lady Arabella Fermor's hair, and the trifling incident had caused a coolness between two families that had long been friendly. The poem was designed to mend the breach by making light of the whole matter. The original version of the poem was composed in the summer of 1711 and published in Lintot's *Miscellany* in 1712. It was immediately popular, but Pope, conceiving the idea of making it more impersonal and more delicately mock-heroic by adding supernatural agents in imitation of the ancient epics, recast the poem, lengthened it from two to five cantos, and published the present version in 1714. The "machinery" that Pope added was suggested by the Rosicrucian sylphs and gnomes in a novel by the Abbé de Villars. Pope's own explanation in his dedicatory letter to Miss Fermor is as follows: "According to [the Rosicrucians] the four elements are inhabited by spirits, which they call sylphs, gnomes, nymphs, and salamanders. The gnomes or demons of earth delight in mischief, but the sylphs, whose habitation is in the air, are the best conditioned creatures imaginable." (See Canto I, ll. 59–67.) Pope has added a lightness of touch of his own to the Rosicrucian conception to match the delicacy of his social satire.

CANTO I

354, 22. *The morning dream.* The communication of a god with mortals by means of dreams is an epic feature.

355, 30. *Of all the nurse and all the priest.* The nurse and priest were often referred to as passing on superstitions to children.

356, 115. *Shock.* This is both the name of Belinda's dog and of the breed, a long-haired lap dog, then popular.

356, 139. *Now awful beauty puts on all its arms.* Cf. the arming of the epic hero.

CANTO II

356, 4. *the silver Thames.* This passage suggests Æneas's voyage on the Tiber.

357, 46. *the winds dispersed in empty air.* This has several epic parallels: *Iliad,* XVI, 306 ff., and *Æneid,* XI, 794.

357, 73 ff. Cf. Satan's address to his followers in *Paradise Lost,* V, 600 ff.

CANTO III

358, 27. *ombre.* A card game introduced from Spain. "The whole idea of this description of a game at ombre is taken from Vida's description of a game at chess in his poem entitled *Scacchia Ludus.*"—Warburton.

360, 165. *Atalantis. Secret Memoirs and Manners of Several Persons of Quality of Both Sexes. From the New Atalantis . . . ,* 1709, a novel of social scandal by Mrs. Manley.

CANTO IV

360, 16 ff. Parody of the descent of Æneas to the lower world.

361, 51. *Homer's tripod.* "See Hom. Iliad, xviii, of Vulcan's walking tripods."—Pope.

361, 52. *a goose-pie talks.* "Alludes to a real fact; a lady of distinction imagined herself in this condition."—Pope.

361, 56. *healing spleenwort.* Cf. the golden branch carried by Æneas.

361, 89. *Thalestris.* Mrs. Morley, sister to Sir George Brown.

361, 121. *Sir Plume.* "Sir George Brown. He was angry that the poet should make him talk nothing but nonsense: and in truth one could not well blame him."—Warburton.

CANTO V

362, 7. *Clarissa.* "A new character introduced in the subsequent editions, to open more clearly the moral of the poem, in a parody of the speech of Sarpedon to Glaucus in Homer."—Pope. The passage first appeared in the 1717 quarto edition.

363, 64. *Those eyes, etc.* "The words of a song in the opera of Camilla."—Pope.

363, 89 ff. "In imitation of the progress of Agamemnon's sceptre in Homer, Il., ii."—Pope.

364, 137. "John Partridge was a ridiculous star-gazer, who in his almanacks every year never failed to predict the downfall of the Pope, and the King of France, then at war with the English."—Pope.

364   ELEGY TO THE MEMORY OF AN UNFORTUNATE LADY

This poem was first published in 1717. No certain identification of the lady here celebrated has been made. The circumstances as related in the poem are undoubtedly largely a product of

Pope's imagination. Up to l. 74 Pope imagines the lover to be addressing the ghost of the unfortunate lady. In the conclusion Pope speaks in his own person.

365.   ELOISA TO ABELARD

Pope's *Eloisa to Abelard* was based on John Hughes' *Letters of Abelard and Heloise,* 1714, which in turn was an English translation of a French translation and adaptation of the Latin original. Pope prefaces his poem with the following remarks: "Abelard and Eloisa flourished in the twelfth century; they were two of the most distinguished persons of their age in learning and beauty, but for nothing more famous than for their unfortunate passion. After a long course of calamities, they retired each to a several convent, and consecrated the remainder of their days to religion. It was many years after this separation, that a letter of Abelard's to a friend, which contained the history of his misfortune, fell into the hands of Eloisa. This awakening all her tenderness, occasioned those celebrated letters (out of which the following is partly extracted) which give so lively a picture of the struggles of grace and nature, virtue and passion."

369, 343. *May one kind grave.* "Abelard and Eloisa were interred in the same grave, or in monuments adjoining, in the Monastery of the Paraclete; he died in the year 1142, she in 1163."—Pope.

370.   ESSAY ON MAN

The *Essay on Man* had its genesis in philosophical discussions with Lord Bolingbroke after his return from exile in France. Bolingbroke wrote in a letter to Swift, "Does Pope talk to you of the noble work, which, at my instigation he has begun in such a manner, that he must be convinced by this time, I judged better of his talents than he did?" (Aug. 2, 1731.) The *Essay on Man* was originally designed as the first of four parts of a larger work of morality. Pope said in his address "To the Reader": "This, which we first give the reader, treats of the nature and state of man with respect to the universal system. The rest will treat of him with respect to his own system, as an individual, and as a member of society, under one or other of which heads all ethics are included." (See notes to *Moral Essays, Epistle IV.*) We know from references in letters that he was working on the *Essay on Man* as early as 1729, but it was not published until 1733–34. Pope published the poem anonymously in order to avoid the virulent attacks which anything signed by his name always drew from his literary and political enemies. So published, the poem won immediate praise even from his bitterest opponents.

The *Essay on Man* embodies many of the metaphysical and moral ideas of Pope's day. The reader will find the best discussion of the idea of the Chain of Being and its far-reaching implications in A. O. Lovejoy's *The Great Chain of Being. A Study of the History of an Idea,* Cambridge, 1936, especially Chapters VI and VII. Useful also in the interpretation of the poem are the same author's "The Length of Human Infancy in Eighteenth-century Thought," *Journal of Philosophy,* XIX (1922), 381–85; and " 'Pride' in Eighteenth-century Thought," *MLN,* XXXVI (1921), 31–37. See also Maynard Mack's Introduction in the Twickenham Edition. In connection with Epistle I it is interesting to read Addison's *Spectator,* No. 519.

                              EPISTLE I

370, 1 *St. John.* Henry St. John, Viscount Bolingbroke.
370, 16. *But vindicate.* Cf. *Paradise Lost,* I, 26: "And justify the ways of God to man."
370, 33. *Great chain.* The first allusion to the Chain of Being which forms the basis of the reasoning of the first epistle. The figure of speech may have come originally from Homer's description of the golden chain upheld by Jove which supported all creation.
370, 43–44. Cf. Leibniz in his *Theodicy:* "The Supreme Wisdom, combined with a goodness no less infinite than it, must necessarily choose the best." Note the importance of the word "possible" in Pope's lines.
371, 143. *earthquakes swallow.* In 1732 there was a great earthquake followed by a tidal wave that destroyed Santiago, Chili.
372. 160. *Ammon.* Alexander the Great.
372. 193. *microscopic eye.* The suggestion for this line and the following passage comes from Locke, *Essay on the Human Understanding,* Bk. II, ch. 23, sect. 12.

                             EPISTLE II

373, 22. *Correct old time.* This may possibly refer to Sir Isaac Newton's *Chronology of Antient Kingdoms Amended.*

375, 198. *Titus.* Roman Emperor, 79–81, "The delight of mankind."

375, 200. *Decius, Curtius.* Decius, a Roman military hero in the Samnite wars. Curtius, the legendary Roman hero who leaped into the chasm made in the Forum by an earthquake.

375, 223. *Orcades.* The islands farthest north off the coast of Scotland.

375, 224. *Zembla.* Nova Zembla, an island north of Russia.

EPISTLE III

377, 68. *favoured man.* "Several of the ancients and many of the orientals since, esteemed those who were struck by lightning as sacred persons, and the particular favorites of heaven."—Pope.

377, 104. *Demoivre.* Abraham de Moivre, an eminent French mathematician, 1667–1754. He lived in London most of his life.

379, 265. *flamen.* A priest attached to the service of some particular god.

379, 268. *played the god an engine.* Made the god into an engine of war.

EPISTLE IV

381, 99. *Falkland.* A politician and *litterateur,* c. 1610–1643. He fought on the side of the Royalists and was killed at the battle of Newbury.

381, 100. *Turenne.* A celebrated French marshal, distinguished for his great care for the safety of his soldiers. He was killed in battle July 27, 1675.

381, 101. *Sidney.* Sir Philip Sidney, mortally wounded at Zutphen, 1586.

381, 104. *Digby.* The Hon. Robert Digby, d. 1726. Pope wrote his epitaph.

381, 107. *Marseille's good bishop.* M. de Belsance was bishop of Marseille during the plague year, 1720, and distinguished himself by his activity in behalf of the victims.

381, 110. *a parent.* A tribute to the poet's mother who died in 1733.

381, 123. *burning Aetna.* Empedocles and Pliny both perished by too near an approach to Aetna and Vesuvius.

381, 126. *Bethel.* Hugh Bethel, a friend of Pope who suffered from asthma.

382, 220. *Macedonia's madman to the Swede.* Alexander the Great and Charles XII of Sweden.

382, 244. *Eugene.* Prince Eugene, 1663–1736, a celebrated Austrian general.

382, 257. *Marcellus.* An opponent of Caesar and partisan of Pompey.

383, 278. *Lord Umbra, or Sir Billy.* The first name stands for any one of a number of insignificant peers. Sir Billy was Sir William Yonge, a tool of Walpole, made Knight of the Bath by him in 1725.

384.   THE UNIVERSAL PRAYER

Warburton seems to be wrong in saying that Pope composed this poem in answer to the attacks on his orthodoxy which followed the publication of the *Essay on Man.* The poet probably published it to vindicate his orthodoxy, but he may have written it as early as 1715.

385.   MORAL ESSAYS: EPISTLE IV

The *Epistles,* or *Moral Essays,* of which this is the fourth, were published in Pope's 1735 edition of his Works along with the epistles to Addison, Oxford, and Arbuthnot as Book II of the large work of which the *Essay on Man* was designated as Book I. He at that time referred to the work as *Ethic Epistles.* Later this scheme for a long work on morals and government was given up and the *Moral Essays* were separated from the *Essay on Man. Epistle IV* was first published late in 1731 and was one of the most vexatious of all his publications to Pope because of the almost immediate identification by Pope's enemies (possibly encouraged by Walpole, as Warburton asserted) of Timon as the Duke of Chandos, who, though not intimate with Pope, had extended him his hospitality, and had, some people said, no doubt falsely, made him a large gift of money. While Pope may have taken some of the details for Timon's Villa from Chandos' estate, Canons, he clearly had not intended to draw a recognizable picture either of Chandos or his seat. He had merely wanted an illustration of bad taste and was extremely annoyed and considerably injured by the personal application. (See *Epistle to Dr. Arbuthnot,* ll. 299–300 and note.)

The epistle is of importance as a further illustration (see *Essay on Criticism*) of the early eighteenth-century principles of taste founded on good sense; as a statement of the principle of use in architecture (cf. our contemporary architects of the International Style); and as an early expression of the rebellion against the formalism of the seventeenth century in what we now call landscape gardening. In connection with this last point, see Pope's essay in *The Guardian*, No. 173, also Addison's esays on the subject: *Tatler*, No. 161, *Spectator*, Nos. 412, 414, 477.

The Earl of Burlington was a patron of the arts and was especially interested in architecture and gardening. A residence in Italy in his youth had given him an enthusiasm for Palladio, and he had recently published Palladio's *Fabbriche antiche*, 1730. He helped Pope with his designs for Twickenham.

385, 7. *Topham*. "A gentleman famous for a judicious collection of drawings."—Pope.

385, 8. *Pembroke*. Henry, Earl of Pembroke, whose family seat was Wilton.

385, 9. *Hearne*. Thomas Hearne, a well known antiquary.

385, 10. *Mead, Sloane*. "Two eminent physicians; the one had an excellent library, the other the finest collection in Europe of natural curiosities; both men of great learning and humanity."—Pope.

385, 18. *Ripley*. "This man was a carpenter, employed by a first minister, who raised him to an architect, without any genius in the art; and after some wretched proofs of his insufficiency in public buildings, made him Comptroller of the Board of Works."—Pope.

385, 20. *Bubo*. George Bubb Dodington (see *Epistle to Dr. Arbuthnot*, l. 280). He had inherited Eastbury and had been required by the terms of the will to complete the house.

385, 46. *Jones and Le Nôtre*. "Inigo Jones, the celebrated architect, and M. Le Nôtre, the designer of the best gardens of France."—Pope.

386, 70. *Stowe*. "The seat and gardens of the Lord Viscount Cobham in Buckinghamshire."—Pope.

386, 75. *Or cut wide views*. "This was done in Hertfordshire, by a wealthy citizen, at the expense of above £5,000, by which means (merely to overlook a dead plain) he let in the north wind upon his house and parterre, which were before adorned and defended by beautiful woods."—Pope.

386, 78. *Nor in a hermitage*. "Dr. S. Clarke's busto placed by the Queen in the Hermitage, while the doctor duly frequented the court."—Pope.

386, 95. *boundless green*. "The two extremes in parterres, which are equally faulty; a boundless green, large and naked as a field, or a flourished carpet, where the greatness and nobleness of the piece is lessened by being divided into too many parts, with scrolled works and beds, of which the examples are frequent."—Pope.

386, 99. *Timon's Villa*. "This description is intended to comprise the principles of a false taste of magnificence, and to exemplify what was said before, that nothing but good sense can attain it."—Pope.

387, 146. *Verrio or Laguerre*. "Verrio (Antonio) painted many ceilings, etc., at Windsor, Hampton Court, etc., and Laguerre at Blenheim Castle and other places."—Pope.

387, 160. *Sancho's dread doctor*. "See *Don Quixote*, [Part II] chap. xlvii."—Pope.

387, 178. *Bathurst. Allen*, Lord Bathurst, to whom *Epistle III* was addressed.

387, 194. *Vitruvius*. M. Vitruvius, author of a famous work, *De Architectura*.

387.   EPISTLE TO DR. ARBUTHNOT

The *Epistle to Dr. Arbuthnot* is Pope's fullest apology for his satires and explanation of his attitude toward his enemies. He was, as a matter of fact, not often the aggressor in the poetical warfare, and from about 1715, when he started work on his translation of Homer, to 1727, he had paid little attention to the many attacks on him. The immediate occasion for the publication of this poem was the appearance, as he tells us in his Advertisement, of *Verses to the Imitator of Horace* and *Epistle to a Doctor of Divinity from a Nobleman at Hampton Court*. These verses attacked, as he said, "not only my writings . . . but my person, morals, and family, whereof, to those who know me not, a truer information may be requisite." The addressing of the *Epistle* to Dr. Arbuthnot was occasioned by a letter from the latter, written shortly before his death, urging Pope to "study more to reform than chastise," (July 17, 1734) to which advice Pope replied that he "took very kindly your advice concerning avoiding ill will from writing satire, and it has worked so much upon me, considering the time and state you gave it in, that I determine to address to you one of my epistles . . . wherein the question is stated, what were, and are my motives of writing, the objections to them, and my answers." (Aug. 25, 1734) In his next letter he added, "The apology is a bold one, but true." (Sept. 3, 1734)

387, 1. *good John*. The poet's servant, John Serle.

387, 3. *Dog Star rages.* Sirius. The allusion is both to the heat of late summer and to the fact that poetry was customarily rehearsed in August in the time of Juvenal.—Butt, Twick. Ed.

387, 13. *the Mint.* The neighborhood of the Mint in Southwark was exempt from all legal process and hence the resort of debtors and petty criminals.

388, 16. *A maudlin poetess.* The change from an earlier, *an Irish poetess,* was probably made to generalize the satire. The original reference might have been to a Mrs. Sykins or a Mrs. Barber.—Butt, Twick. Ed.

388, 23. *Arthur.* Arthur Moore, a politician. For other references to his son, James Moore-Smythe, see lines 98, 373.

388, 25. *Cornus.* Sir Robert Walpole, whose wife had recently left him.

388, 40. *nine years.* The advice of Horace in his *Ars Poetica.*

388, 43. *term ends.* The London season closed at the end of Trinity term, three weeks before Trinity Sunday.

388, 49. *Pitholeon.* "The name taken from a foolish poet of Rhodes, who pretended much to Greek."—Pope. The Chauncy MS has *Welsted.* Pope is again generalizing his satire. Pitholeon might also refer to Thomas Cooke.—Butt, Twick. Ed.

388, 53. *Curll.* Edmund Curll, an unscrupulous publisher.

388, 56. *A virgin tragedy.* "Alludes to a tragedy called the *Virgin Queen,* by Mr. R. Barford, published in 1729, who displeased Pope by daring to adopt the fine machinery of his sylphs in an heroi-comical poem called *The Assembly.*"—Warton.

388, 62. *Lintot.* Bernard Lintot, the publisher who brought out Pope's Homer.

388, 85. *Codrus.* Codrus, Bavius, Maevius, were conventional names for poetasters in Latin satires.

389, 97. *Colley.* Colley Cibber, the hero of *The Dunciad.*

389, 98. *Henley.* "This alludes to Henley, commonly called Orator Henley, who declaimed on Sundays on religious subjects, and on Wednesdays on the Sciences. . . . His oratory was among the butchers in Newport Market and Butcher Row."—Bowles. *his free-masons, Moore.* Moore-Smythe, a member of that society.

389, 100. *to one bishop Philips.* Bishop Boulter was Ambrose Philips' friend and patron.

389, 101. *Sappho.* Pope had already satirized Lady Mary Wortley Montagu under the name of Sappho. He had quarrelled with her in 1722.

389, 135–41. *Granville, Walsh, etc.* Pope here names some of the most prominent people of his time who had been his admirers. Most of the names we have met before in the poems. George Granville, Lord Lansdowne, to whom Pope dedicated his *Windsor Forest,* was a prominent Tory and a minor writer. Talbot, Somers, and Sheffield were patrons and friends of Dryden. Rochester was Francis Atterbury, Bishop of Rochester, one of the most eloquent preachers of his time.

389, 146. *Burnets, Oldmixons, and Cookes.* "Authors of secret and scandalous history."—Pope.

389, 151. *Gildon.* Charles Gildon, who had satirized Pope on various occasions.

389, 153. *Dennis.* See *Essay on Criticism,* l. 584, note.

389, 164. *Bentley, Tibbalds.* Richard Bentley, although a good scholar in many respects, was notorious for his emendations of Milton. For Tibbald, see the notes on *The Dunciad.*

390, 179–83. *The bard.* Ambrose Philips.

390, 190. Nahum Tate, 1652–1715, mediocre Poet Laureate.

390, 193. *Were there one, etc.* Addison. These lines on Addison had been written much earlier; Pope said, during Addison's lifetime. See A. E. Case, "Pope, Addison, and the 'Atticus' Lines," *MP,* XXXIII (1935), 187–93.

390, 230 ff. *Bufo.* Charles Montague, Earl of Halifax. A Whig leader, and opponent and satirist of Dryden.

391, 260. *Queensberry.* Gay died at the Duchess of Queensberry's house.

391, 276. *prating Balbus.* Viscount Dupplin. The reference is to "the incessant small talk of my good Lord Duplin [sic], that flows and flows as smoothly as ever, and as uninterrupted in its course."—Butt, Twick. Ed.

391, 280. *Sir Will, Bubo.* Sir William Yonge, then Secretary of War, and a leading Whig; Bubo, George Bubb Dodington, Lord Melcombe, for a time a member of Prince Frederick's circle. See *Moral Essays, Epistle IV,* l. 20.

391, 299. *the dean, and silver bell.* "Meaning the man who would have persuaded the Duke of Chandos that Mr. P. meant him in those circumstances ridiculed in the Epistle on Taste . . ."—Pope. See notes on *Moral Essays, Epistle IV.*

391, 305. *Sporus.* John, Lord Hervey, a supporter of Sir Robert Walpole. Sporus in antiquity was Nero's favorite.

392, 341. *stooped to truth. Stooped* is a term from falconry. It refers to the swoop of the bird upon its prey.

392, 353. *the pictured shape.* Refers to an illustration in one of the attacks on Pope. He is pictured as a hunchbacked ape, leaning on a pile of books.—Butt, Twick. Ed.

392, 355. *friend in exile.* Atterbury.

392, 356. *The whisper.* Hervey is the "whisperer."

392, 363. *Japhet.* Japhet Crooke, alias Sir Peter Stranger, a forger and sharper.

392, 365. *Knight of the post.* One who furnishes false evidence in court for a living.

392, 375. *Welsted's lie.* "This man had the impudence to tell in print that Mr. P. had occasioned a *lady's death,* and to name a person he never heard of. He also published that he libelled the Duke of Chandos; with whom (it was added) that he had lived in familiarity, and received from him a present of *five hundred pounds:* the falsehood of both which is known to his Grace. Mr. P. never received any present, farther than the subscription for Homer, from him, or from *any great man* whatsoever."—Pope.

392, 378. *Budgell.* Eustace Budgell charged Pope with writing for the *Grub-Street Journal.*

392, 380. *Two Curlls.* Curll the publisher and Lord Hervey.

392, 381. *His father, mother.* "In some of Curll's and other pamphlets, Mr. Pope's father was said to be a mechanic, a hatter, a farmer, nay, a bankrupt. But, what is stranger, a nobleman (if such a reflection could be thought to come from a nobleman) had dropped an allusion to that pitiful untruth, in a paper called an *Epistle to a Doctor of Divinity:* and the following line,—

Hard as thy heart, and as thy birth obscure,

had fallen from a like courtly pen, in certain *Verses to the Imitator of Horace.* Mr. Pope's father was of a gentleman's family in Oxfordshire, the head of which was the Earl of Downe, whose sole heiress married the Earl of Lindsey. His mother was the daughter of William Turnor, Esq. of York: she had three brothers, one of whom was killed, another died in the service of King Charles; the eldest following his fortunes, and becoming a general officer in Spain, left her what estate remained after the sequestrations and forfeitures of her family.—Mr. Pope died in 1717, aged 75; she in 1733, aged 93, a very few weeks after this poem was finished . . ."— Pope. Though Pope may have believed this statement about his father's family, it cannot be verified.

392, 397. *dared an oath.* "He was a nonjuror, and would not take the oath of allegiance or supremacy, or the oath against the Pope."—Bowles.

393. THE FIRST EPISTLE OF THE SECOND BOOK OF HORACE: TO AUGUSTUS

This is one of a series of imitations of the satires of Horace, and, in the opinion of most critics, the most brilliant. For a full appreciation of the adaptation of the model to English material, Pope's poem should be read in conjunction with the original. Pope very cleverly turns Horace's praise of his patron, Augustus, into withering irony in his address to George Augustus II, who was anything but a patron of literature and who, for many reasons, was especially unpopular in 1737 when the poem was published. For a further discussion of the *Imitations of Horace* see James W. Tupper, "A Study of Pope's *Imitations of Horace,*" *PMLA,* XV (1900), 181–215; see also John Butt's introduction to the poem in the Twickenham Edition.

393, 2. *open all the main.* Ironical, like all of the address to George II. The Spaniards had recently been committing depredations on English vessels.

393, 7. *Edward and Henry.* Edward III and Henry V.

393, 38. *Skelton.* John Skelton, tutor to Henry VIII and satirist of Cardinal Wolsey.

393, 40. *Christ's Kirk o' the Green.* A Scottish poem describing the revels of a Scottish fair; used as a model by Burns.

393, 42. *at the Devil.* "The Devil Tavern, where Ben Jonson held his poetical club."—Pope.

394, 66. *Stow.* John Stow's *Summary of English Chronicles,* 1561, and *Chronicles of England,* 1580, later known as *Annals, or General Chronicle of England.*

394, 75. *Cowley.* Abraham Cowley, 1618–67, a poet and essayist very popular in his own day.

394, 85. *Shadwell.* Thomas Shadwell, d. 1692, a dramatist and poet, satirized by Dryden in *Mac Flecknoe* and *Absalom and Achitopel,* Part II.

Wycherley. William Wycherley, d. 1716, one of the best of the Restoration dramatists. This line of stupid criticism is quoted almost verbatim from Rochester's *An Allusion to the Tenth Satire of the First Book of Horace.*

394, 86. *Southern sure and Rowe.* The former was best known for his play, *Oronooko, or the Royal Slave,* 1696, and the latter for *The Fair Penitent,* 1703.

394, 88. *eldest Heywood.* John Heywood, a sixteenth-century writer of interludes.

394, 91. *Gammer Gurton's Needle.* c. 1566, one of the earliest English comedies.

394, 92. *Careless Husband.* Cibber's best comedy.

394, 104. *slashing Bentley.* Alludes to Bentley's emendations of Milton.

394, 122. *Betterton.* Thomas Betterton, d. 1710, a famous actor of the Restoration stage.

394, 123. *Barton Booth,* 1681–1733, a tragedian.

394, 142. This line is quoted almost verbatim from *Progress of Beauty,* l. 174, by George Granville.

395, 149. *Lely.* Sir Peter Lely, 1618–1680, a court painter.

395, 182. *Ward.* "A famous empiric, whose pill and drop had several surprising effects, and were one of the principal subjects of writing and conversation at this time."—Pope.

395, 183. *Radcliffe's doctors.* The holders of the Radcliffe Fellowships at University College, Oxford, established by John Radcliffe, M.D.

395, 186. *Ripley.* See *Moral Essays, Epistle IV,* l. 18, note.

395, 197. *Peter.* Peter Walter, 1662–1745, a steward to certain noblemen of the time who knew how to line his own purse.

395, 215. *courtly stains.* Party writing.

395, 224. This line refers to Swift's service to the people of Ireland rendered through his *Drapier's Letters,* 1724. Pope was in danger of prosecution for this remark.

395, 230. *Hopkins and Sternhold.* These writers were known for their popular metrical versions of the Psalms, first published in 1549.

395, 236. *pope and Turk.* The opening lines of a hymn in the Queen Anne Prayer Book, 1703, were:

> Preserve us, Lord, by Thy dear word,
> From Turk and Pope defend us, Lord.

396, 277. *Otway.* Thomas Otway, 1652–85, Restoration dramatist, author of *Venice Preserved,* 1682.

396, 287. *Congreve's fools.* Congreve's wit became so subtle, especially in *The Way of the World,* 1700, that Pope's query is in a measure justified.

396, 288. *Farquhar.* George Farquhar, 1678–1707. His *Love and a Bottle* would justify the comment.

396, 289. *Van.* Sir John Vanbrugh, 1664–1726, dramatist.

396, 290. *Astraea.* "A name taken by Mrs. Behn, authoress of several obscene plays."—Pope.

396, 293. *Pinky. Tatler,* No. 188, says that William Penkethman, a low comedian, "devours a cold chick with great applause."

396, 309. *black joke.* "The Coal-black Joke," an indecent song.

397, 331. *Quin; Oldfield,* James Quin, 1693-1766, foremost tragedian between the time of Booth and Garrick. Anne Oldfield, 1683–1730, famous actress.

397, 355. *Merlin's Cave.* A grotto that Queen Caroline had had constructed at Richmond.

397, 381. *Bernini.* Giovanni Lorenzo Bernini, 1598–1680, had modelled a bust of Charles I from some portraits of Vandyke.

397, 382. *Kneller.* Sir Godfrey Kneller, 1646–1723, had painted William III.

397, 387. *Blackmore, Quarles.* Sir Richard Blackmore was knighted in 1697, not for his poetry but because he was physician in ordinary to the king. Francis Quarles, 1592–1644; see *Dunciad,* I, 140, note.

397, 417. *Eusden, Philips, Settle.* Laurence Eusden, Poet Laureate before Cibber; Ambrose Philips, who had written an "Ode to Walpole"; Elkanah Settle, City Poet in the time of Charles II and subject of much satire.

397, 419. *Bedlam and Soho.* Dealers in old books had stalls and shops near Bethlehem Hospital and in Wardour Street, Soho.

398.   THE DUNCIAD

The history of *The Dunciad* is much too complex to give in full. The main outline is as follows: An early version, the nucleus of the later poem, in the form probably of a poem on dullness in poetry, may have been in existence as early as 1725. In 1726, Theobald's uncompromising exposé of Pope's deficiency as an editor of Shakespeare in the former's *Shakespeare Restored. Or, A Specimen of the Many Errors as Well Committed, as Unamended, by Mr. Pope in his Late Edition of this Poet,* motivated the revamping of that early poem to make it into a satire on dullness not only in poetry but in pedantic learning. Theobald was made the hero. Swift, who spent the summers of 1726 and 1727 in England, was instrumental in preserving the early version of the poem when Pope was about to consign it to the fire and in helping to shape the new satire; hence the dedication to him. The satire, now known as *The Dunciad,* in three books was published in May, 1728, anonymously for safety's sake. It was widely read and went through a number of editions in 1728. In 1729 Pope was emboldened to get out *The Dunciad Variorum* with burlesqued "learned" annotations, with much prefatory material and many appendices, and with the names of the people satirized printed in full. The poem was openly acknowledged by Pope in 1735 by his inclusion of it in his *Poetical Works* of that year. In 1742 Pope published a fourth book which he called *The New Dunciad.* There is a hint in this book that he had already conceived the idea of deposing Theobald as his hero and using instead the dramatist and (since 1730) Poet Laureate, Colley Cibber. At any rate, when the four books were published together in October, 1743, the poem was sufficiently recast to make Cibber, who was indeed a more popular butt of satire than the scholarly Theobald, the King of the Dunces. It is from the final version that our selections are taken. In Book I Cibber invokes the aid of the Goddess of Dullness and is made by her King of the Dunces. Book II describes the coronation games, thereby calling to mind the coronation of George II. In Book III there is a "descent" in epic manner to Elysium where the hero is told by the former City Poet, Settle, of the glories of dullness. In Books IV Dullness triumphs and chaos and night resume their ancient sway.

Many of the following notes were supplied by Pope, or Pope in conjunction with Warburton, his friend and editor. Some, usually of a satirical nature, are signed Scriblerus. Pope says that several people contributed to the Scriblerus notes. The abbreviations, P., PW., and Scrib. will be used.

BOOK I

398, 2. *Smithfield muses.* "Smithfield is the place where Bartholomew Fair was kept, whose shows, machines, and dramatical entertainments, formerly agreeable only to the taste of the rabble, were, by the hero of this poem and of others of equal genius, brought to the theatres of Covent Garden, Lincolns Inn Fields, and the Haymarket, in the reigns of King George I and II. See Book III."—P.

398, 25. *Boeotia.* Ireland.

398, 28. *To hatch a new . . .* The new Saturnian age of lead is finally created in Book IV.

398, 30. *Monroe.* Dr. Monroe, one of the doctors of Bedlam.

398, 31. *father's hand.* "Mr. Caius Gabriel Cibber, father of the Poet Laureate. The two statues of the lunatics over the gates of Bedlam Hospital were done by him, and (as the son justly says of them) are no ill monuments of his fame as an artist."—PW.

398, 41. *hymning Tyburn.* "It is an ancient English custom for the malefactors to sing a Psalm at the execution at Tyburn; and no less customary to print elegies on their deaths, at the same time, or before."—P.

398, 57. *genial Jacob.* Jacob Tonson, a bookseller who specialized in the publishing of plays and poetry. The *third day* refers to the author's benefit performance of a play.

398, 71. *How Time himself.* Alludes to the violation of the unity of time in the current plays.

398, 74. *Zembla, Barca.* Nova Zembla, island north of Russia; Barca, in the African desert.

399, 85. *when ** rich and grave.* The name in this line was originally Thorold (Theobald), now inappropriate since Cibber is to be the hero.

399, 90. *Settle's numbers.* ". . . Settle was poet to the City of London. His office was to compose yearly panegyrics upon the lord mayors, and verses to be spoken in the pageants; but that part of the shows being at length frugally abolished, the employment of City Poet ceased; so that upon Settle's demise there was no successor to that place."—P.

399, 103. *Prynne, Daniel.* William Prynne and Daniel Defoe were both pilloried and both wrote doggerel political verse and pamphlets.

399, 104. *Eusden, Blackmore.* Laurence Eusden was Poet Laureate before Cibber; Richard Blackmore was the author of some second-rate epics.

399, 105. *Philips, Tate.* Ambrose Philips was very slow in composition. Of Nahum Tate, a former Poet Laureate, Pope remarks in his notes, "a cold writer, of no invention."

399, 109. *Bays.* Colley Cibber.

399, 110. *And act, and be a coxcomb.* Cibber's best roles were those of the fops and coxcombs on the Restoration stage.

399, 140. *Quarles.* Francis Quarles, best known for his *Emblems,* 1635, consisting of paraphrases of the scriptures and quotations from the Church Fathers.

399, 141. *Ogilby.* John Ogilby (1600–76), printer and translator, had been ridiculed by Dryden.

399, 142. *Newcastle.* Margaret, Duchess of Newcastle. "Langbaine reckons up eight folios of her Grace's which were usually adorned with gilded covers, and had her coat of arms upon them."—P.

399, 146. *Settle, Banks, and Broome.* "The poet has mentioned these three authors in particular, as they are parallel to our hero in three capacities: 1. Settle was his brother Laureate . . . 2. Banks was his rival in tragedy (though more successful) in one of his tragedies, the *Earl of Essex,* which is yet alive: *Anna Boleyn,* the *Queen of Scots,* and *Cyrus the Great,* are dead and gone . . . 3. Broome was a serving man of Ben Jonson, who once picked up a comedy from his betters, or from some cast scenes of his master, not entirely contemptible." —PW.

399, 149. *Caxton.* "A printer in the time of Edward IV, Richard III, and Henry VII; Wynkyn de Word, his successor, in that of Henry VII and VIII . . ."—P.

399, 153. *De Lyra.* "Nich. de Lyra, or Harpsfield, a very voluminous commentator, whose works, in five vast folios, were printed in 1472."—P.

399, 154. *Philemon.* "Philemon Holland, Doctor in Physic. 'He translated so many books, that a man would think he had done nothing else; insomuch that he might be called translator general of his age.'—Winstanley."—P.

399, 159. *folio commonplace.* A notebook in which, it is suggested, the author copied the material from other plays which formed the basis of his own.

400, 167. *Sir Fopling's periwig.* "The first visible cause of the passion of the town for our hero was a fair flaxen full-bottomed periwig, which, he tells us, he wore in his first play of the *Fool in Fashion* . . ."—P.

400, 188. *once betrayed me.* Refers to the *Careless Husband,* Cibber's best play.

400, 203 *the doctors.* False dice.

400, 208. *Ridpath, Mist.* "George Ridpath, author of a Whig paper, called the *Flying Post;* Nathaniel Mist, of a famous Tory journal."—P.

400, 216. *Even Ralph repents.* Ralph had become a writer against the ministry in *The Champion,* a paper which first appeared in 1739.—Sutherland, Twick. Ed.

400, 222. *Hockley Hole and Whites.* The former was an amphitheatre for bear-baiting, etc., the latter a chocolate-house.

400, 231. *gratis-given Bland.* "It was a practice so to give the Daily Gazetteer and ministerial pamphlets (in which this B. was a writer), and to send them post free to all the towns in the Kingdom."—PW.

400, 233. *Ward.* Edward Ward, a voluminous poet in Hudibrastic verse, a great number of whose works were sold in the plantations.

400, 234. *Mundungus.* Bad Tobacco.

400, 250. *Cid, Perolla, etc.* These refer to the tragedies of Cibber (not the actual titles). Cibber withdrew a play about King John before it went into rehearsal.

401, 258. *Thule.* "An unfinished poem of that name, of which one sheet was printed many years ago, by Amb. Philips, a northern author . . ."—P.

401, 270. *Quidnuncs.* Political busy bodies.

401, 286. *Ozell.* John Ozell, the translator of a number of French plays.

401, 290. *Heideggre.* "A strange bird from Switzerland, and not (as some have supposed) the name of an eminent person who was a man of parts . . ."—P. John James Heideggre came to England from Switzerland in 1708 and became first the manager of the opera house in the Haymarket and then Master of the Revels under George II.

401, 296. *Withers.* George Withers, a seventeenth-century poet who is more highly thought of now than in Pope's day.

401, 297. *Howard.* "Hon. Edward Howard, author of the *British Princes,* and a great number of wonderful pieces, celebrated by the late Earls of Dorset and Rochester, Duke of Buckingham, Mr. Waller, etc."—P.

401, 298. *Fool of Quality.* Probably Lord Hervey. See *Epistle to Dr. Arbuthnot.*

401, 309. *under Archer's wing.* Thomas Archer was groom-porter to the King.

401, 324. *pious Needham.* A notorious bawd who was set in the pillory.

401, 325. *the Devil.* "The Devil Tavern in Fleet Street . . ."—P.

401, 330. *King Log.* "See Ogilby's *Æsop's Fables,* where, in the story of the frogs and their king, this excellent hemistich is to be found . . ."—P.

402. THE GUARDIAN, NO. 173

It seems at first surprising that both Addison and Pope, representatives of Classical taste in literature, should have championed the informal, or English, style of gardening. But the student of literature must keep in mind that individuals and ages are more complex than the formulas of text-books, and that Classicists and Romanticists may have many points in common. Addison devoted *Spectator,* No. 477, to the subject of gardening, but the allusion to the gardeners, London and Wise, famous for their topiary work, in *Spectator,* No. 5, also indicated his dislike of the formal style.

402a, 5.   "The late narcissus, and the winding trail
                   Of bear's-foot, myrtles green, and ivy pale."—Dryden.

402a, 25.   "Our friend Faustinus' country seat I've seen:
                   No myrtles, placed in rows, and idly green,
                   No widowed platane, nor clipped box-tree, there
                   The useless soil unprofitably share;
                   But simple nature's hand, with nobler grace,
                   Diffuses artless beauties o'er the place."—From Chalmer's edition (1822).

402a, 51. *Georgics,* IV, 116–48.
402a, 52. *Odyssey,* VII, 78–132.
402b, 1. Temple's *Essay upon the Gardens of Epicurus.*

402b, 44.   "Here interwoven branches form a wall,
                   And from the living fence green turrets rise;
                   There ships of myrtle sail in seas of box;
                   A green encampment yonder meets the eye,
                   And loaded citrons bearing shields and spears."—From Chalmers' edition (1822).
403a, 14. The giants in the Guildhall of London are Gog and Magog.

403. PREFACE TO SHAKESPEARE

In this preface to his edition of Shakespeare (1725), Pope speaks his mind on both Shakespeare and on literary theory. Like Dryden and other important critics of that age, Pope recognizes the greatness of Shakespeare and champions his native genius against the so-called Aristotelian "rules." An excellent study of Pope's literary ideas is Austin Warren's *Alexander Pope as Critic and Humanist* (Princeton, 1929).

406a, 17. *Heminges and Condell.* Editors of the first collection of Shakespeare's plays, the folio of 1623. In their preface they said that "his mind and hand went together, and what he thought, he uttered with that easiness that we have scarce received from him a blot in his papers." But Ben Jonson, the Classicist, wrote in his *Discoveries* (1641): "I remember, the players have often mentioned it as an honour to Shakespeare that in his writing, whatsoever he penned, he never blotted out a line. My answer hath been: Would he had blotted a thousand."

406b, 51. *ethic or politic.* The virtues of private and public life.
407a, 15. *Comedy of Errors.*
407a, 17. It is unlikely that Shakespeare went so far as to Dares for his knowledge of the story of *Troilus and Cressida.*
407b, 11. "Those who laud us are our worst enemies."
407b, 17. *Eclogues,* VII, 27–28:

                   "If [Codrus] blast my Muse with envious praise,
                   Then fence my brows with amulets of bays,
                   Lest his ill arts, or his malicious tongue
                   Should poison, or bewitch my growing song."—Dryden.

407b, 29. Printed in the First Folio.
409b, 4. *Much Ado About Nothing,* Act ii. Enter Prince Leonato, Claudio, and *Jack Wilson,* instead of Balthasar. And in Act iv. *Cowley* and *Kemp,* constantly through a whole scene. Edit. Fol. of 1623 and 1632. [Pope. 1725.]

409b, 26. *Such as:* My Queen is murdered! *Ring the little bell.* His nose grew as sharp as a pen, *and a table of Greenfield's,* &c. [Pope, 1725.]

413.
ON A MISCELLANY OF POEMS

413, 12. *Jacob.* Jacob Tonson, the famous bookseller who published at various times for Dryden, Addison, Steele, and Pope.

413, 33. *Corinna.* The heroine of Ovid's *Amores.*

414, 45–47. *Buckingham . . . Sheffield.* John Sheffield, Earl of Mulgrave, afterwards Duke of Buckingham.

414. 59. *Pastora.* The poetical name for Queen Mary in Congreve's elegy, *The Morning Muse of Alexis* (1694).

414, 61. *Emma. Henry and Emma,* Prior's inferior version of the fine old poem, *The Nut-brown Maid.*

414, 63. *Hans Carvel.* A coarsely humorous tale by Prior.

414. 66. *Granville.* George Granville, Lord Lansdowne (1667–1735), poet and dramatist; early friend of Pope. He addressed amorous verses to "Myra."

414, 76. *Garth.* Dr. Samuel Garth (1661–1719), author of *The Dispensary,* a mock-epic.

414, 91. *Elzevir.* The name of a famous family of printers in Leyden.

414, 92. *Pirate Hills.* Henry Hills, in Blackfriars, was issuing boldly pirated and badly printed editions of the poems of the day. Gay's *Wine* was thus reprinted.

414, 93. *Aldus.* Aldus Manutius, a Venetian printer renowned for the beauty and correctness of his work.

414, 94. *John Morphew.* A London bookseller.

415.
THE SHEPHERD'S WEEK

Gay's Proeme, written in mock-Elizabethan prose, announces his intention of writing realistic English pastoral. "Thou wilt not find my shepherdess idly piping in oaten reeds, but milking the kine, tying up the sheaves, or if the hogs are astray driving them to their styes." His language, he adds, is neither of the court nor the country, of the past nor the present. "It is fairly certain that in the beginning *The Shepherd's Week* was burlesque of Virgil rather than ridicule of Philips."—Irving. *Thursday* imitates Virgil's *Eclogue* VIII; *Friday* is connected with *Eclogue* V, as well as Theocritus; *Saturday* is a striking imitation of *Eclogue* VI, in which Silenus sings of the wonders of Creation. Here Gay also burlesques Blackmore's *Creation* (see John Robert Moore in *JEGP,* L [1951], 83–89).

417.
FRIDAY, OR THE DIRGE

418, 17. *Gillian of Croydon.* A song by Thomas D'Urfey.

418, 18. *O'er hills and far away.* The air of Song xvi in *The Beggar's Opera.*

418, 19. *Patient Grissel.* The story of the Patient Griselda, told by Chaucer's Clerk of Oxford, was widely known in folk-tale and ballad.

420.
SATURDAY, OR THE FLIGHTS

421, 51. "Our swain had probably read Tusser, from whence he might have collected these philosophical observations."—Gay. Thomas Tusser's *Five Hundred Points of Good Husbandry,* a sixteenth-century book of country lore in doggerel verse, was long read and remembered.

422, 91. *Children in the Wood.* The famous ballad praised by Addison, *Spectator,* No. 85.

422, 99–100. *For buxom Joan, etc.* A Soldier and a Sailor, a song in Congreve's *Love for Love* 1696).

422, 102. *Chevy Chase.* The most famous of the border ballads.

423, 109. *All in the land of Essex.* By Sir John Denham.

423, 115. *Taffey Welsh.* Perhaps the broadside ballad called "The Honor of Welshmen, or the Valiant Acts of St. Taffy of Wales." See *Bagford Ballads,* p. 844. *Sawney Scot.* A song by D'Urfey, "Sawney was tall and of noble race," in *The Virtuous Wife* (1680).

423, 116. *Lillibullero.* A song in ridicule of the Irish Catholics, sung throughout England in the Revolution Year 1688. *Irish Trot.* "Printed as 'Hyde Park' by Playford in 1651."

423, 117. *Bateman.* "A Warning for Maidens, or Young Bateman." Reprinted in *Roxburghe Ballads,* iii, 193–97. *Shore.* One of the most popular broadside ballads, on Jane Shore, mistress of Edward IV.

423, 118. *Wantley's Dragon, etc.* According to this ballad, which burlesques the extravagance of the metrical romances, the dragon of Wantley was slain by "More of More Hall."

423, 119. *Rosamond.* Fair Rosamond, the mistress of Henry II.

423, 120. *And how the grass now grows, etc.* "And corn now grows where Troy Town stood," runs a line in *The Wandering Prince of Troy.* Cp. Ovid, *Heroides,* I, 53.

423. TRIVIA

Trivia is an epithet of Diana as goddess of crossroads.

423, 10. *Billingsgate.* The great fish market near London Bridge.

423, 13–16. Asses' milk was often prescribed for the sick.

423, 17–19. Street musicians and drummers volunteered their services at weddings.

424, 67. Since the houses were not numbered, the signs of shops were used in giving directions and addresses.

424, 73. *St. Giles's.* The district called Seven Dials, in the parish of St. Giles in the Fields, was formerly one of the worst slums in London.

425, 83–86. *Thesus . . . Ariadne.* When Theseus undertook to slay the Minotaur, Ariadne gave him a clue of thread to guide him out of the Cretan labyrinth.

425, 98. After this line Gay added in the second edition a long passage describing in mock-heroic myth the origins of a street-boy from the the loves of the goddess Cloacina and a scavenger.

425, 106. The sidewalks were set off by posts in the principal streets and squares.

425, 115. *the Samian.* Pythagoras, who taught the doctrine of the transmigration of souls.

425, 121. *Watling Street.* A narrow street back of St. Paul's.

425, 123–25. *that rugged street, etc.* Thames Street, running from Blackfriars to the Tower. *Fleet Ditch.* A small stream, polluted with garbage and offal, which flowed into the Thames at Blackfrairs.

426, 132. *Cornavian.* Cheshire.

426, 134. The domestic chaplain withdrew from the table before dessert.

426, 135. *Pell Mell.* Pall Mall, a fashionable street running from St. James's to the Haymarket.

426, 166. *the Mews.* Formerly on the site of Trafalgar Square, frequented by gamesters. *the thimble's cheats.* What is now known as "thimble-rigging" or "the shell game."

427, 197. *nitry.* See note on Thomson, *Winter,* page 468, lines 714–20.

427, 213. *White's.* White's Chocolate House, a fashionable gaming resort in St. James's Street.

427, 215. *'Change.* The New Exchange, in the Strand, full of dressmakers' and milliners' shops.

427, 221. *Covent Garden's famous temple.* St. Paul's, Covent Garden, designed by Inigo Jones.

428, 235–52. The great frost of 1709–10. When the Thames was frozen over, a frost fair was held on the ice.

429, 285–90. At Hockley-in-the-Hole the populace enjoyed the cruel sport of bear-baiting and bull-baiting.

430, 353. *F———.* William Fortescue, Barrister of the Inner Temple, a friend of Gay and Pope.

430, 359–70. In Elizabethan times the town houses of some of the greatest lords stood in the Strand.

430, 361–68. *Arundel's famed structure, etc.* Arundel House once contained a magnificent collection of works of art.

430, 366. *Overton.* A well known dealer in engravings and prints.

430, 369. *Essex' stately pile.* Essex House, named for Robert Devereux, Earl of Essex, the unhappy favorite of Queen Elizabeth.

430, 370. *Cecil's.* Cecil House, the residence of Sir William Cecil, Lord Burleigh, Queen Elizabeth's Lord Treasurer. *Bedford's.* Bedford House, town residence of the Earls of Bedford. *Villiers'.* York House, occupied by Francis Bacon, and later by the Dukes of Buckingham.

430, 371. *Burlington's fair palace.* Burlington House, Piccadilly, rebuilt by Lord Burlington in the neo-classical style of Palladio about 1716.

430, 375. Handel lived at Burlington House for three years.

431, 419. *seventh-born doctor.* The seventh son of a seventh son was supposed to be endowed with supernatural powers.

431, 438. *Stagyra's sage.* Aristotle.
431, 440. *D———.* John Dennis.
431, 442. *Squirts.* Squirt was the name of an apothecary in Garth's mock-heroic poem, *The Dispensary.*
431, 443. *Lintot.* Bernard Lintot published *Trivia.*
432, 452. Flemish mares were used as coach horses.

432.   SWEET WILLIAM'S FAREWELL TO BLACK-EYED SUSAN

432, 1. *the Downs.* The famous roadstead in the English Channel.

433.   TO A LADY ON HER PASSION FOR OLD CHINA

433, 23–26. *Fossils . . . Galen's soul, etc.* Presumably a hit at Dr. John Woodward, the geologist, who had been satirized as "Fossil" in Gay's *Three Hours after Marriage* (1717).

433.   SONG: O RUDDIER THAN THE CHERRY

Sung in Gay's pastoral opera *Acis and Galatea* (1732).

438.   THE YOUNG LAIRD AND EDINBURGH KATY

438, 8. *the Hill.* The Castle Hill, Edinburgh.

     THE POET'S WISH: AN ODE

438, 4. *Carse o' Gowrie's.* A fertile district in Perthshire.
438, 5. *Grampians.* The chief mountain system of Scotland, dividing Highlands and Lowlands.

439.   SANG

This song opens Act I of *The Gentle Shepherd.*

441.   THE BALLAD OF SALLY IN OUR ALLEY

Carey gives us an account of the origin of this piece:
The real occasion was this: A shoemaker's prentice, making holiday with his sweetheart, treated her with a sight of Bedlam, the puppet-shows, the flying-chairs, and all the elegancies of Moorfields; from whence proceeding to the farthing pie-house, he gave her a collation of buns, cheese-cakes, gammon of bacon, stuffed beef, and bottled ale: through all which scenes the author dodged them (charmed with the simplicity of their courtship); from whence he drew this little sketch of nature. But being then young and obscure, he was very much ridiculed by some of his acquaintance for this performance; which nevertheless made its way into the polite world, and amply recompensed him by the applause of the divine Addison, who was pleased more than once to mention it with approbation.

442.   THE BRAES OF YARROW

Yarrow is the romantic border stream famed in Scottish song. Hamilton's poem is a lyrical elaboration of a traditional ballad theme. John Logan's *Braes of Yarrow* and Wordsworth's three Yarrow poems carry on the tradition.

446.   GRONGAR HILL

At least three versions of *Grongar Hill* were circulated in 1726. First Dyer wrote the poem in the form of an irregular ode, printed in Richard Savage's *Miscellaneous Poems and Translations*, an intermediate version in octosyllabic couplets appeared in *A New Miscellany*; and the final version in David Lewis's *Miscellaneous Poems by Several Hands.* Garland Greever compares the first and the third versions in *JEGP*, XVI (1917), 274–81; Helen Sard Hughes prints the second version from the manuscript miscellany of Lady Hertford, *MP*, XXVII (1930), 312–17.

446, 1. *Silent Nymph.* The muse of painting, a sister of the muse of poetry.
446, 23. *Towy's flood.* A river in Carmarthenshire.

449.   A POEM SACRED TO THE MEMORY OF SIR ISAAC NEWTON

Newton died in March, 1727; this poem appeared in the following May.

450, 17–29. *he bound the suns, etc.* Kepler, working from the Copernican theory, had already stated the laws of the motion of the planets about the sun. Newton gave these laws their mathematical form.

450, 36–38. These lines echo the motto from Lucretius (*De Rerum Natura*, III, 28–30) on the title-page of the first edition of Thomson's poem: "At all this a kind of godlike delight mixed with shuddering awe comes over me to think that nature by thy power is laid thus visibly open, is thus unveiled on every side." Trans. H. A. J. Munro. Thomson thus applies to Newton Lucretius' praise of Epicurus.

450, 43–45. *the moons, etc.* Newton described the orbits of the moons of Jupiter and Saturn.

450, 50–56. *Her every motion clear-discerning, etc. Principia*, Proposition xxiv, Theorem xix: "That the flux and reflux of the sea arise from the actions of the sun and moon."

451, 82–88. *The heavens, etc.* In the first edition this passage reads:

> The heavens are all his own. Finished by him
> The fair discovery lies; and every eye
> May lay the useless telescope aside,
> Unless it be to hold the great acquests
> By Newton made, who from the wild domain
> Of the *French Dreamer* rescued heaven and earth.
> All Europe stood appalled; but found it vain
> To keep at odds with demonstration strong,
> And lingering to resist the awakening force
> Of truth.

"French Dreamer" is annotated "Descartes." Descartes' system of physics was widely accepted in the late seventeenth and early eighteenth centuries, until superseded by the Newtonian system.

451, 83. *vortices.* According to Descartes, the universe was full of matter and the heavenly bodies swam in vortices of matter as in a whirlpool. *spheres.* According to the Ptolemaic system, the universe consisted of a group of hollow concentric spheres.

451, 96. *Even light itself.* Newton's discovery of the solar spectrum and his theory of color were communicated to the Royal Society in 1672 and developed in his *Optics* (1704).

452, 123. *Greenwich.* The hill in Greenwich Park on which the Royal Observatory is situated commands a fine view. Thomson was especially fond of hill-views in the vicinity of London.

452, 125–28. Cp. Wordsworth's reference to the statue of Newton in the Chapel of St. John's College, Cambridge:

> The marble index of a mind forever
> Voyaging through strange seas of thought, alone. (*Prelude*, iii, 360–63)

452, 128–31. *to the source . . . ascending.* Newton tried to aid historians by applying astronomy to problems of ancient chronology.

452, 157. *Conduitt.* It was expected that John Conduitt, who married Newton's niece, would write his life.

454.   PREFACE TO *WINTER*

This Preface first appeared in the second edition (June, 1726); it was dropped in the fifth edition (1728). Thomson probably intended to incorporate it in a proposed "Essay on Descriptive Poetry" which was to serve as a general Preface to *The Seasons*, but apparently he never completed the essay.

455.   WINTER

456, 18. *Wilmington.* Sir Spencer Compton, Lord Wilmington, Speaker of the House of Commons from 1715 to 1727. Thomson flatters him.

456, 42–43. *Capricorn . . . Centaur-Archer . . . Aquarius.* The sun passes from Sagittarius (the Centaur-Archer) into Capricorn on December 21, and enters Aquarius on January 20.

458, 118–52. "The signs of coming storm are almost all from Virgil."—Macaulay. See *Georgics*, i, 351–92.

462, 359–88. *the generous band, etc.* In 1729 the philanthropist Oglethorpe headed a parliamentary committee which brought to light the shameful condition of the debtors' prisons.

463, 414–23. For the description of the avalanches in the Swiss canton of the Grisons, Thomson used a pamphlet published early in 1744, *An Account of the Glacieres or Ice Alps in Savoy.*

463, 437. *The long-lived volume.* Plutarch's *Lives.*

464, 446–52. *Solon.* The humane law-giver of Athens (c. 640–559 B.C.).

464, 453–55. *Lycurgus.* The stern law-giver of Sparta (9th century B.C.).

464, 457. *The firm devoted chief.* Leonidas.

464, 459–64. *Aristides.* Although Aristides, Athenian statesman and general, had been banished by political intrigue, he aided his "haughty rival" Themistocles (l. 464) in the campaign against the Persian invaders.

464, 466–70. *Cimon.* A follower of Aristides. After a period of youthful dissipation he became a brilliant statesman and general.

464, 473–75. *Timoleon.* His brother Timophanes set himself up as tyrant of Corinth. After pleading with him in vain, Timoleon sorrowfully consented to his assassination.

464, 476–78. *the Theban pair.* Pelopidas and Epaminondas, noble youths bound by close friendship, who led the Thebans in their campaigns against Sparta (4th century B.C.).

464, 479–85. *Phocion.* Athenian general and statesman, famed for the noble simplicity of his character; unjustly condemned to drink the hemlock (317 B.C.).

464, 486–89. *Agis.* King of Sparta, who vainly tried to restore the laws of Lycurgus and was put to death (240 B.C.).

464, 491–92. *Aratus.* Leader of the Achaean League, a confederacy of states of southern Greece against Macedonia (3rd century B.C.).

464, 493–97. *Philopoemen.* A later leader of the Achaean League.

465, 502–03. *Numa.* Numa Pompilius, the second king of Rome according to tradition, a wise and peaceable law-giver.

465, 504–05. *Servius.* Servius Tullius, the sixth king of Rome, gave a new and more democratic constitution to the city.

465, 507–08. *The public father, etc.* Lucius Junius Brutus had been instrumental in driving out the royal family of the Tarquins. As one of the first two consuls, he condemned to death his own sons for conspiring to overthrow the republic and restore the Tarquins.

465, 509–10. *Camillus.* Recalled from banishment and elected Dictator to rescue Rome from the Gauls.

465, 511. *Fabricius.* A Roman consul who refused large bribes offered him by Pyrrhus, King of Epirus.

465, 512. *Cincinnatus.* The lictors who came to summon Cincinnatus to his dictatorship found him plowing his own fields.

465, 513. *Thy willing victim, Carthage!* Regulus was taken prisoner by the Carthaginians in the first Punic War. Later he was allowed to accompany an embassy to Rome to secure peace, promising to return if the mission was not successful. At Rome he argued against concluding a peace, and went back to meet his death at Carthage.

465, 517–20. *Scipio.* The brilliant Scipio Africanus finally retired from public life and devoted himself to literary studies at Liternum, near Cumae.

465, 523. *Cato.* Cato the Younger, admired as the great exemplar of Stoic virtue, who committed suicide at Utica in Africa rather than surrender to the forces of Caesar. Cp. Addison's *Cato.*

465, 532. *the Mantuan swain.* Virgil.

466, 555–71. *Hammond.* James Hammond (1710–42), like Thomson a member of the political and literary coterie opposed to Walpole. His *Love Elegies* were published posthumously (1743).

467, 646–50. Cp. Thomas Warton, *The Pleasures of Melancholy,* page 569, lines 211–25.

467, 647. *Monimia.* The heroine of Otway's tragedy *The Orphan* (1680).

467, 648. *Belvidera.* The heroine of Otway's *Venice Preserved* (1682).

467, 655. *Bevil.* The virtuous hero of Steele's sentimental comedy *The Conscious Lovers* (1722).

468, 664. *Chesterfield.* Philip Dormer Stanhope, fourth Earl of Chesterfield, one of the most brilliant figures of the eighteenth century, whom Johnson called "a wit among lords and a lord among wits."

468, 694. *nitre.* See below, note on lines 714–20.

468, 714–20. *What art thus, Frost? etc.* A widely held theory of the nature of cold. Dr. Samuel Clark says in a note to the translation of Rohault's *Traité de physique* as *System of Natural Philosophy* (London, 1723), i, 166–67: "It is probably that cold (which is not merely comparative, as that of simply hard or liquid bodies is; but produces real effects, such as freezing, breaking in pieces, rarefaction, etc.) is owing to some particles of nitre and other salts which are of certain figures proper to excite that sensation and to produce those effects."

468, 716. *illusive fluid.* Mercury.

469, 768. *Batavia.* Holland.

470, 820–26. The hunting of the deer is from Virgil, *Georgics,* iii, 371–75.

471, 835. *Boötes.* A constellation near the Great Bear.

471, 836. *Caurus.* The northwest wind.

471, 838–42. The traditional idea of the Northern invaders who overthrew the Roman Empire and brought liberty and constitutional government to western Europe. See Sir William Temple, "Of Heroic Virtue," and Samuel Kliger, *The Goths in England* (Cambridge, Mass., 1952).

471, 843–86. *the sons of Lapland.* For this idealized picture of the Lapps and their country, Thomson drew on accounts given by Johannes Scheffer (*Lapponia* [1673]) and other northern writers.

471, 875–76. As the source for the references to Niemi and Tenglio, in Lapland, Thomson refers to a recent work by Maupertuis, translated as *The Figure of the Earth* (1738). This source also gave hints for the description of the northern skies, lines 859–62 above.

472, 887. *Tornea's lake.* In the extreme north of Sweden. Cp. *The Deserted Village,* page 816, line 418.

472, 888. *Hecla.* The great volcano of Iceland.

472, 925–35. *Such was the Briton's fate, etc.* Sir Hugh Willoughby set out with three vessels in 1553 to discover a northeast passage from Europe to India. The expedition sailed north around Norway, and two of the vessels made their way to the harbor of Arzina (930) in Lapland, where the entire crews perished.

472, 937. *Oby.* The principal river of Siberia.

473, 950–87. The progress of Russia under Peter the Great made the Czar one of the culture-heroes of the Enlightenment. Cp. *Spectator,* No. 139, and the writings of Thomson's friend Aaron Hill (*The Northern Star* [1718] and *Plain Dealer,* No. 106 [1725]).

473, 980. *The frantic Alexander of the north.* Charles XII, of Sweden. See Johnson's *Vanity of Human Wishes,* page 684, lines 189–220, and note.

473, 981. *Othman's sons.* The Turks.

475.   A HYMN

Cp. Psalm cxlviii, and the morning hymn of Adam and Eve, *Paradise Lost,* v, 153–208.

477.   RULE, BRITANNIA!

Sung by a bard in Act ii of *Alfred: A Masque* (1740). Since Thomson and David Mallet collaborated in writing *Alfred,* the authorship of this song has been much discussed, but the question has now been decided in favor of Thomson. Cp. the patriotic utterances in his *Britannia.*

478.   THE CASTLE OF INDOLENCE

481, 126. *Sybarite.* The inhabitants of Sybaris, a Greek city in southern Italy, were noted for their love of luxury. Thomson here follows the Greek author Athenaeus: "The Sybarites were also the first to forbid noise-producing crafts from being established within the city, such as blacksmiths, carpenters, and the like, their object being to have their sleep undisturbed in any way; it was not permitted even to keep a rooster inside the city."—*Deipnosophistae,* xii, 518, trans. C. B. Gulick.

482, 152. *Scipio . . . Cumaean shore.* See *Winter,* page 465, lines 517–20, and note.

482, 176–80. Cp. *Paradise Lost,* i, 775–87.

484, 240–41. *Nepenthe.* A drug which brought forgetfulness of care and sorrow. Cp. *Odyssey,* iv, 228; *Faerie Queene,* IV, iii, 43–45.

484, 262–70. A famous "romantic" stanza, inspired by Thomson's knowledge of Celtic superstition and folklore.

485, 280–88. *Come on, my Muse, etc.* Plans for epic and tragedy, partly realized in his poem *Liberty* and in such plays as *Agamemnon* (1738).

486, 341–42. *Lorrain . . . Rosa . . . Poussin.* Seventeenth century painters famed for their work in picturesque landscape. Claude Lorraine was noted for his bright and delicate style,

Salvator Rosa for his bold treatment of wild and romantic scenes, Nicolas Poussin for painting the ruins of classical antiquity.

487, 360. *the Harp of Aeolus.* "This is not an imagination of the author, there being in fact such an instrument, called Aeolus's harp, which, when placed against a little rushing or current of air, produces the effect here described."—Thomson.

488, 393. *Titian.* The greatest of the Venetian painters (1477–1576).

490, 483. *Lucifer.* The morning star.

490, 505 ff. Thomson's biographer Patrick Murdoch tells us that *The Castle of Indolence* "was at first little more than a few detached stanzas in the way of raillery on himself, and on some of his friends, who would reproach him with indolence, while he thought them at least as indolent as himself." The origins of the poem appear in this series of sketches of his friends and associates at Richmond. Some of them contributed passages or addressed verses to the poet on the subject. Thus Dr. Thomas Morell about 1742 wrote some Spenserian stanzas "To Mr. Thomson, on an unfinished plan of a poem called *The Castle of Indolence.*"

490, 505–31. Thomson's friend William Paterson.

491, 532–40. Probably Dr. John Armstrong, author of a didactic poem in blank verse, *The Art of Preserving Health.*

491, 541–49. Henry Welby?

491, 550–58. John Forbes, son of Duncan Forbes of Culloden.

492, 577–85. George, later Lord Lyttelton.

493, 595–603. *Esopus.* The name of a great tragic actor in ancient Rome, here applied to James Quin. After a year of retirement, Quin returned to the stage in 1747.

493, 604–12. *A bard here dwelt, etc.* A description of Thomson himself, written, except for the first line, by a friend (Lyttelton?).

493, 615–21. *oily man of God, etc.* The Rev. Patrick Murdoch.

494, 658 ff. The last four stanzas, written by Armstrong, were evidently inspired by the "lazar house" passage in *Paradise Lost*, XI, 477–93.

496.

THE SPLEEN

In the seventeenth century the idea grew up that the English were a particularly humorous people, that is, a nation of eccentric individuals dominated by one or the other of the four humors (blood, choler, melancholy or black bile, phlegm) of mediaeval medicine. More especially, it became a commonplace that the English were subject to a morbid melancholy called variously the "spleen," the "hyp" (hypochondria), the "vapors," or simply the "English malady." These terms might cover anything from fashionable low spirits and ennui (see *The Rape of the Lock*, Canto iv, page 360) to suicidal mania (see Blair's *Grave*, page 528, 402 ff.).

496, 15. *Gildon.* Charles Gildon, a minor critic and an enemy of Pope, published treatises on the art of poetry.

496, 24. *Raiment from naked bodies won.* Green's note quotes the following couplet as from Edward Howard's drama *The British Princes:*

> A painted vest Prince Vortiger had on,
> Which from a naked Pict his grandsire won.

But apparently Howard did not write the couplet in this form. See Boswell, *Life of Johnson* (ed. G. B. Hill), ii, 124, n. 3.

496, 31. *Moore.* Pope accused James Moore-Smythe of having plagiarized from him in his comedy *The Rival Modes*, and attacked him in *The Dunciad.*

497, 73. *Hygeia.* The goddess of health.

497, 146. *Tarantulated.* The bite of the tarantula, a poisonous spider, was supposed to cause an hysterical impulse to dance.

498, 231–33. *Blood long congealèd, etc.* A reference to the famous miracle of St. Januarius, who was beheaded in the persecution of Christians under Diocletian. The head of the saint and two phials of his blood are preserved at Naples, and it is said that the blood liquefies when brought close to the head.

498, 270. *ombre.* For details of this popular card game, see *The Rape of the Lock*, Canto iii, and notes. *quadrille.* A four-handed card game which superseded ombre in the second quarter of the eighteenth century.

498, 271. *Pam . . . loo.* See *The Rape of the Lock*, Canto iii, page 358, line 61 and note.

499, 343. *band and cloak.* The vestments of the Puritan preacher.

499, 344. *leaves of oak.* The badge of the Jacobite, symbolic of the oak in which Charles hid after the battle of Worcester.

500, 434. *a corporation.* The Charitable Corporation, founded to make small loans to the deserving poor, was plundered by unscrupulous directors. Parliament investigated and censured their conduct in 1732.

501, 543. *Psapho.* Psaphon, in order to spread his own fame, taught birds to say, "Psaphon is a god," and then let them loose.

501, 556. *a youth, etc.* Richard Glover (1712–1785), the author of dull epics and tragedies on the classical model, was a friend of Green's and wrote the preface to the posthumously published *Spleen*. Glover's epic *Leonidas* was being praised in 1737 by the opponents of Walpole (Lyttelton, Fielding, etc.).

502, 654. *Eurus.* The east wind.

503, 717. *Memmius.* Gaius Memmius, the friend to whom Lucretius addressed his great philosophical poem *De Rerum Natura.*

511.   THE COMPLAINT, OR NIGHT THOUGHTS

515, 212. *thrice my peace was slain.* Young tells us that the deaths of three members of his family, "Lucia," "Narcissa," and "Philander," within three months, inspired the *Night Thoughts.* Lucia is his wife, who died in January, 1740. His step-daughter Elizabeth had died in France in 1736; her husband, Henry Temple, died in August, 1740; and we have Young's word for it that this couple is to be identified with Narcissa and Philander, although according to the poem Narcissa died just *after* Philander. Young tells us that Narcissa was buried secretly at night, and this has been thought to refer to the difficulties he met in getting Christian burial for his step-daughter in France. Even though the poet says that the occasion of the poem was "real, not fictitious," he must have altered some of the circumstances and concealed others.

517, 321. *Lorenzo.* The libertine and infidel youth to whom Young addresses the poem, not to be identified as a real person.

520, 449. *Maeonides.* Homer.

520, 451. *his, who made Maeonides our own.* Pope.

521.   THE GRAVE

The text is based on the fourth edition, 1753.

523, 115–16. *jesters.* Cp. Hamlet's words about Yorick, *Hamlet,* V, i. Note other Shakespearean echoes in Blair.

524, 158. *sable tribe.* Mutes, hired mourners.

532, 589. *Like those of angels, etc.* Cp. Norris, *Parting:* like angels' visits, short and bright; and Thomas Campbell, *The Pleasures of Hope* (1799) ; Like angels visits, few and far between.

535, 764–67. *Thus at the shut of even, etc.* Cp. the conclusion of Parnell's *Night-Piece on Death.*

537.   THE PLEASURES OF IMAGINATION

539, 109–13. *Memnon's image, etc.* The great statue of Memnon, near Thebes in Egypt, was said to give forth a sound when struck by the rays of the rising sun.

540, 145–46. *the sublime, The wonderful, the fair.* This is Addison's doctrine that the pleasures of imagination are derived from "what is great, uncommon, or beautiful" (*Spectator,* No. 412).

540, 151. *Say, why was man so eminently rais'd, etc.* The passage is inspired by Longinus, *On the Sublime,* sect. xxxv.

541, 202. *The empyreal waste, etc.* Akenside quotes in his note Leibniz, *Théodicée,* i, 19.

541, 204–06. *unfading light, etc.* For the idea that light from distant fixed stars may have traveled since the creation without yet reaching us, Akenside refers to the great Dutch scientist Christian Huygens. Cf. *Spectator,* No. 565.

542, 297. *Penéus.* The principal river of Thessaly, flowing through the Vale of Tempe.

543, 307. *Hydra.* The many-headed monster which guarded the golden apples of the Hesperides.

543, 335. *Idalian.* See Gray, *Progress of Poesy,* page 597, line 27, and note.

544, 374. *Truth and Good are one.* In his note Akenside quotes a speech of Socrates from Xenophon's *Memorabilia,* and refers also to Shaftesbury and his disciple Francis Hutcheson.

546, 470. *bird of Juno.* The peacock.

548, 582. *the Persian tyrant.* Xerxes.

548, 591. *Lyceum's walk.* A sacred enclosure at Athens, the favorite walk of Aristotle.

548, 591–92. *the green retreats Of Academus.* The Academy, a grove outside Athens where Plato held his school.

550.   THE SCHOOLMISTRESS

There are three versions of this poem: as first published in *Poems upon Various Occasions* (Oxford, 1737) it consisted of 12 stanzas; it was successively expanded to 28 stanzas in the separate edition of 1742, and to 35 stanzas in Dodsley's *Collection of Poems*, i (2d ed., 1748). The three texts are reprinted by C. E. De Haas, *Nature and the Country in English Poetry of the First Half of the Eighteenth Century* (Amsterdam, 1928), App. ii.

551, 56. *Eol's train.* The winds, ruled by Aeolus.

551, 57. *Libs.* The west-southwest wind. *Notus, Auster.* Both names for the south wind.

552, 96. *pun-provoking thyme.* Puns could be made on *thyme* and *time.*

552, 109–13. *rosmarine.* Rosemary, highly esteemed in Elizabethan gardens.

552, 119. *Sternhold.* The metrical version of the Psalms by Sternhold and Hopkins was long the chief hymnbook of the Church of England.

552, 122–26. Psalm cxxxvii.

553, 136–39. *In elbow-chair, like that of Scottish stem, etc.* The Coronation Chair, in which every English monarch since Edward I has been crowned. Under the seat is set the Stone of Scone, brought from Scotland by Edward I in 1297.

553, 156–60. *Their books of stature small, etc.* The horn-book was a card with the alphabet, etc., mounted in a wooden frame with a handle and covered with a thin transparent sheet of horn. The back was sometimes stamped with a device of St. George and the Dragon.

553, 165. *Mulla's silver stream.* Spenser's poetical name for the Awbeg, a river near his home in Ireland.

554, 207. *y-rare.* The prefix y-, properly the sign of the past participle, was used indiscriminately by Spenser and his imitators.

555, 242. *Vernon's patriot soul.* Admiral Edward Vernon, despite his failures in the war against Spain, was set up as a hero by the enemies of Walpole and the hostile critics of the Admiralty.

555, 255. *Dennis.* See Pope, *Essay on Criticism*, ii, page 348, line 270; *Epistle to Arbuthnot*, page 389, line 153, and notes.

555, 257. *Aonian field.* Helicon, the mountain of the Muses, was situated in the plain of Aonia.

556, 304–15. Shrewsbury, on the river Severn, was famous for its cakes.

556.   WRITTEN AT AN INN AT HENLEY

Richard Graves, in his *Recollections of Shenstone* (1788), says that the last stanza of this poem was written immediately after Shenstone's return from an embarrassing and unhappy visit to his friend Anthony Whistler, of Whitchurch, Oxfordshire.

557.   SLENDER'S GHOST

See *Merry Wives of Windsor*, III, i.

560.   THE ENTHUSIAST

The text is that of the first edition, 1744.

560, 8. *Stowe.* Viscount Cobham's estate in Buckinghamshire. The most famous garden in eighteenth century England.

560, 20–21. *Egeria . . . Numa.* According to a Roman legend, Numa Pompilius, the second king of Rome, was secretly counseled by the nymph Egeria.

560, 25. *Versailles, etc.* One of the features of the great formal gardens of Louis XIV's palace at Versailles is the elaborate system of fountains, basins, and canals.

560, 30. *Anio.* A river of central Italy which once formed a famous waterfall as it flowed into the Tiber.

561, 57–64. The contrast between the shepherd and the admiral is directly from Shaftesbury, *Characteristics*, "The Moralists," Part 3, Section 2 (ed. 1738, II, 396).

561, 65–77. *Aeneas, etc.* In the *Aeneid*, viii, 347–68, Aeneas visits the rude settlement built by Evander on the future site of Rome, and is lodged in Evander's humble cottage. Warton follows the passage closely.

561, 78. *Happy the first of men, etc.* "The author has ventured to take some hints in the following lines from Lucretius' description of the uncivilized state of man, which is one of the finest pieces of poetry extant."—Warton, ed. 1744. He then quotes Lucretius, *De Rerum Natura*, v, 937–39, 955–57.

562, 119. *Yet were not myriads, etc.* "Lucretius, after beautifully describing the evils that attended the barbarous state of man, proceeds to speak of their advantages in the following lines, which are attempted to be translated."—Warton, ed. 1744. He then quotes Lucretius, v, 997 ff.

565.   THE PLEASURES OF MELANCHOLY

The text is that of the first edition, 1747.

565, 3. *Teneriff.* The peak of Tenerife, one of the Canary Islands.

565, 28. *Tempe.* A valley in Thessaly, famed for its beauty.

566, 87. *Comus, etc.* See Milton's *Comus,* lines 153–55, 520–30.

566, 97. *Eloise.* Cp. Pope, *Eloisa to Abelard,* page 369, lines 303–04.

568, 157–60. *the fated fair, etc.* Cp. Pope, *The Rape of the Lock,* ii, page 356, lines 1–4.

569, 215. *Monimia.* The heroine of Otway's *Orphan* (1680).

569, 217. *Calista.* The heroine of Rowe's *Fair Penitent* (1703).

569, 220. *Jaffeir.* A character in Otway's *Venice Preserved* (1682).

569, 246. *Hymettus.* A mountain south of Athens.

569, 260. *Persepolis.* One of the capitals of ancient Persia, laid in ruins by Alexander the Great.

570, 264. *Parian domes.* Buildings of marble from the island of Paros.

570, 284. *Euphrosyne.* One of the three Graces.

570, 302. *the nymphs of Cirrha's mossy grot.* The Muses. The town and plain of Cirrha, near Mount Parnassus, were associated with Apollo and the Muses.

570, 307. *Mona.* Angelsey, an island off the coast of Wales.

570, 314. *Meinai.* Usually Menai, a strait between Angelsey and the mainland of Wales.

571.   THE CRUSADE

571, 19. *Acon.* A city and fortress of Syria, called by the crusaders St. Jean d'Acre.

571, 64. *Kaliburn.* Excalibur, the sword of King Arthur, was supposed to have come into the possession of Richard.

572, 78. *Ashtaroth.* Hebrew name for Astarte, the Syrian love-goddess. *Termagaunt.* A name given in the mediaeval romances to the god of the Saracens.

572, 81. *Macon.* Mohammed.

572. SONNET III. WRITTEN IN A BLANK LEAF OF DUGDALE'S MONASTICON

Sir William Dugdale's *Monasticon Anglicanum* (1655–73) was a learned treatise on English monasteries.

572.   SONNET IV. WRITTEN AT STONEHENGE

These theories about the origin of Stonehenge, the great prehistoric group of stones on Salisbury Plain, may be found in Camden's *Britannia.*

572, 2. *Whether by Merlin's aid, etc.* One tradition was that the magician Merlin helped King Uther Pendragon to bring the great stones across the sea in order that he might erect a monument to the Britons treacherously slain on the plain of Amesbury (*Amber's fatal plain,* l. 3) by the Saxon chief Hengist.

572, 11. *Brutus' genuine line.* Brutus, descended from the Trojan Aeneas, was the legendary founder of the British nation.

573. SONNET VIII. ON KING ARTHUR'S ROUND TABLE AT WINCHESTER

573, 2. *Its raftered hall.* The Great Hall at Winchester, in which hangs the diagram of King Arthur's Round Table, a relic which can be traced back to the thirteenth century.

575.   A SONG FROM SHAKESPEARE'S CYMBELINE

See *Cymbeline,* IV, ii.

575. ODE TO PITY

This and the following ode were inspired by Aristotle's famous dictum in the *Poetics* that tragedy "through pity and fear effects the proper purgation of these emotions." Collins once planned to write a commentary on the *Poetics*.

575, 7. *Pella's bard.* "Euripides, of whom Aristotle pronounces, on a comparison of him with Sophocles, that he was the greater master of the tender passions, ἦν τραγικώτερος."—Collins. *Poetics* xiii, 6, inaccurately quoted.

575, 14. *Ilissus.* A river in Attica.

575, 16. *Wild Arun.* "The river Arun runs by the village [Trotton] in Sussex, where Otway had his birth."—Collins.

575. ODE TO FEAR

The *Ode to Pity* is a tribute to Euripides; this poem celebrates Aeschylus and Sophocles.

576, 22. *Collins's* note quotes Sophocles, *Electra* line 1388: "The hounds whom none escape," i.e., the Furies.

576, 30-34. Aeschylus fought at the battle of Marathon.

576, 35. *Hybla's dews.* Hybla, a town in Sicily, famous for its honey.

576, 37. *baleful grove.* The scene of Sophocles' *Oedipus at Colonus* is laid in a grove sacred to the Furies.

576, 38-41. *Wrapped in thy cloudy veil, etc.* At the end of the *Oedipus at Colonus* a thunderstorm forebodes the death of Oedipus. The voice of a god (not "the incestuous queen" Jocasta) speaks to him from the cloud, asking him why he tarries (lines 1623-28).

From l. 53 to the end, the poem is full of Miltonic and Shakespearean echoes.

577. ODE TO SIMPLICITY

For the meter, cp. Milton's *Nativity Ode.*

577, 13-14. See *Ode to Fear*, page 576, line 35, and note.

577, 16-18. *her whose lovelorn woe, etc.* "The ἀηδών, or nightingale, for which Sophocles seems to have entertained a peculiar fondness."—Collins.

577, 18. *sad Electra's poet's ear.* In the sonnet *When the Assault Was Intended to the City*, Milton uses the phrase for Euripides; Collins applies it to Sophocles.

577, 19. *Cephisus.* A river in Attica.

578. ODE ON THE POETICAL CHARACTER

Collins's most enthusiastic, difficult, and characteristic poem. The Strophe describes the girdle of Fancy; the Epode boldly connects the weaving of the girdle with the divine act of imagination by which the world was created, and thus implies that the true poet is divinely inspired in the sense that he repeats this primordial act of creation; the Antistrophe exalts Milton as the archetype of the poetical character.

578, 1-16. Cp. *The Faerie Queene*, IV, v. Collins in a note names Florimel as the "unrivaled fair" who could wear the girdle of chastity. The girdle belonged to her, but in Spenser's narrative Amoret was the maiden who could wear it.

579, 39. *thou rich-haired Youth of Morn.* The sun, according to most commentators; the poet, according to Garrod. Since the sun-god, Phoebus Apollo, was also the god of music and poetry, it may be possible to unite the two interpretations.

579, 69. *Waller's myrtle shades.* Waller, as the representative of artificial and trivial verse, is contrasted with Milton.

579. ODE WRITTEN IN THE BEGINNING OF THE YEAR 1746

Possibly in commemoration of the soldiers who fell in the battle of Falkirk, January 17, 1746, when the English were defeated by the rebel forces of the Young Pretender. Collins here uses with consummate skill the "train," or series of personifications, which eighteenth-century poets adapted from Milton. Note other examples of the "train" in Collins, Gray, and elsewhere.

579. ODE TO EVENING

First published in the *Odes*; revised version in Dodsley's *Collection of Poems*, i (2d ed., 1748). The latter is the standard text, but since some of the changes are of great interest, the readings of the *Odes* are given below.

The unrimed lyric in imitation of Milton's translation of the Fifth Ode of the First Book of Horace had been revived by the Wartons.

579, 2-3.   May hope, O pensive Eve, to soothe thine ear,
            Like thy own brawling springs,   —*Odes.*
580, 24.   Who slept in buds the day,   —*Odes.*
580, 29-32. Then let me rove some wild and heathy scene,
            Or find some ruin midst its dreary dells,
                Whose walls more awful nod
                by thy religious gleams.   —*Odes.*

580, 32. What is the antecedent of *its*? Legouis suggests that the pronoun be emended to *thy*.
580, 33-34. Or if chill blustering winds or driving rain
            Prevent my willing feet, be mine the hut   —*Odes.*

581, 49-52. So long, regardful of thy quiet rule,
            Shall Fancy, Friendship, Science, smiling Peace,
            Thy gentlest influence own,
            And love thy favorite name!   —*Odes.*

581.   THE PASSIONS: AN ODE FOR MUSIC

Cp. Dryden's *Song for St. Cecilia's Day* and *Alexander's Feast,* Pope's *Ode for Music on St. Cecilia's Day. The Passions* was set to music at Oxford in 1750, and performed there. Later it was performed at Winchester, Gloucester, and elsewhere. It was likewise a favorite piece for declamation.

581, 1-2. Collins wrote an ode, now lost, *On the Music of the Grecian Theatre.*
583, 109-18. Compare this passage with the conclusions of Dryden's St. Cecilia odes.

583.   ODE ON THE DEATH OF MR. THOMSON

James Thomson died in August, 1748, and was buried in the church at Richmond. Cp. Wordsworth's *Remembrance of Collins* (1789) and Burns's *Address to the Shade of Thomson* (1791).

583, 6. *airy harp.* "The harp of Aeolus, of which see a description in *The Castle of Indolence* [I, xl, xli]."—Collins.

584.   AN ODE ON THE POPULAR SUPERSTITIONS

Collins addressed this poem to the Scotch clergyman and dramatist John Home (pronounced "Hume"), later famous as the author of *Douglas,* who visited England in 1749 and was introduced to Collins by Thomas Barrow (the "cordial youth" of l. 5). The manuscript of the Ode was long afterwards found among Home's papers by Dr. Alexander Carlyle, communicated by him to the Royal Society of Edinburgh, and first published in the *Transactions* of the Society in 1788. This authentic version is fragmentary; an anonymously edited version published in London a little later fills in the gaps, but its authority is more than doubtful.

The Jacobite uprising of 1745 had drawn the attention of the English to the picturesque and romantic Highlands, and Collins here anticipates the important part which Highland backgrounds and traditions were to play in later literature, from Ossian to Sir Walter Scott. No doubt he got fruitful hints from the conversation of Home and perhaps other Scotch friends. He drew also from his reading of Martin Martin's *Late Voyage to St. Kilda* (1698) and *Description of the Western Islands of Scotland* (1703; revised ed. 1716).

584, 6. *Lavant's side.* The river Lavant flows through Chichester, Sussex.
584, 18. *Doric.* The language of Greek pastoral, hence *simple, natural.*
584, 23. *swart tribes.* The Brownies.
584, 27-29. *elf-shot.* The popular superstition was that disease in man or beast might come from being shot with an elf-arrow.
585, 45. *The choral dirge.* The coronach.
585, 54. *Sky.* The Isle of Skye, the largest of the Inner Hebrides, off the northwestern coast of Scotland.
585, 56. *Uist.* North Uist and South Uist are two of the Outer Hebrides.
585, 57-69. Martin tells of the Highland second sight and of witchcraft.
586, 100. *the wily monster.* The kelpie, a water-demon. See below, lines 108, 137.

586, 121–25. *For him in vain, etc.* Cp. Thomson, *Winter,* page 461, lines 311–315.

586, 142–45. Small bones, supposed to be those of pigmies, were found in a stone vault on the island of Benbecula (Martin, *Description,* p. 82).

587, 146–47. The early kings of Scotland, Ireland, and Norway were supposed to be buried on the island of Iona (Martin, *op. cit.,* pp. 260, 261).

587, 155–71. In the *Late Voyage,* pp. 131–32, Martin says that the inhabitants of St. Kilda exemplify the primitive virtues; he describes the walks along the cliffs and the hunting of the solan goose. Woodhouse has shown that Collins used both of Martin's works ([London] *Times Literary Supplement,* Dec. 20, 1928).

587, 164. *sainted spring.* St. Kilda's Well (Martin, *Late Voyage,* p. 24).

587, 171. *Nor ever vernal bee, etc.* From Martin, *op. cit.,* p. 31.

588, 192–96. Tasso, *Jerusalem Delivered,* xiii, 41–43, 46.

588, 198. *British Fairfax.* The *Jerusalem Delivered* had been translated into English by Edward Fairfax in 1600, and this version had just been reprinted in 1749. On this occasion Collins wrote and advertised for publication *An Epistle to the Editor of Fairfax His Translation of Tasso,* but apparently the poem was never actually published.

588, 214. *Jonson . . . Drummond's.* In 1619 Ben Jonson visited the Scotch poet William Drummond at Hawthornden, near Edinburgh. Drummond left a remarkable record of their conversation.

588, 215–16. *Teviot's . . . Yarrow's,* Rivers of the Scotch Border, associated with romance and balladry.

588, 219. *Lothian's plains.* The county of Lothian, in which Edinburgh is situated.

590.   SONNET ON THE DEATH OF MR. RICHARD WEST

After Milton the sonnet had practically disappeared from English poetry. This piece of Gray's is a landmark in the mid-century sonnet revival which was carried on by Thomas Edwards, Thomas Warton the Younger, Bishop Percy, and others. See Wordsworth's comments on the diction of this sonnet in the Preface to *Lyrical Ballads.* Is Wordsworth's criticism sound?

591.   ODE ON A DISTANT PROSPECT OF ETON COLLEGE

Stoke Poges, where Gray wrote this poem, is only a few miles north of Eton and Windsor, opposite one another on the Thames.

591, 4. *Henry's holy shade.* "King Henry VI, founder of the College."—Gray.

592.   HYMN TO ADVERSITY

This poem echoes Horace's *Ode to Fortune* (I, xxxv) and influenced Wordsworth's *Ode to Duty.* It won Dr. Johnson's approval.

592.   ELEGY WRITTEN IN A COUNTRY CHURCHYARD

According to Gray's friend and biographer Mason, the *Elegy* was begun in 1742, but this date is not certain. It was completed in June, 1750, and passed about in manuscript. Gray had it published anonymously in February, 1751, in order to forestall some unscrupulous editors who were about to print an unauthorized version in the *Magazine of Magazines.*

593, 21–24. *For them no more, etc.* Cp. Thomson, *Winter,* page 461, lines 311–15, but the passage goes back to Lucretius (*De Rerum Natura,* iii, 894–96) and Horace (*Epode,* ii, 39 ff.) as well.

593, 33–36. *The boast of heraldry, etc.* Cp. Richard West's *Monody on the Death of Queen Caroline:*

> Ah me! what boots us all our boasted power,
> Our golden treasure, and our purple state?
> They cannot ward the inevitable hour,
> Nor stay the fearful violence of Fate.

593, 35. *Hour* is the subject of *awaits.*

594, 57. *Hampden.* John Hampden, a leader of the opposition to the taxes unconstitutionally imposed by Charles I. Gray at first wrote "Cato" for Hampden, "Tully" for Milton, and "Caesar" for Cromwell.

594, 72. After this line, in the rough draft known as the Eton MS., stand the following four stanzas.

> The thoughtless world to Majesty may bow,
> Exalt the brave, and idolize success;
> But more to Innocence their safety owe
> Than Power and Genius e'er conspired to bless.
>
> And thou, who mindful of the unhonored dead
> Dost in these notes their artless tale relate,
> By night and lonely contemplation led
> To linger in the gloomy walks of fate,
>
> Hark, how the sacred Calm that broods around
> Bids every fierce tumultuous passion cease,
> In still small accents whispering from the ground
> A grateful earnest of eternal peace.
>
> No more with Reason and thyself at strife,
> Give anxious cares and endless wishes room;
> But through the cool, sequestered vale of life
> Pursue the silent tenor of thy doom.

These stanzas, according to Mason, were originally intended to conclude the poem. They may be taken to refer to Gray himself. In the final text (ll. 97–128) the description given by the "hoary-headed swain" and the Epitaph present the imaginary figure of a young poet, colored by Gray's temperament as well as by the literary tradition of solitude and melancholy. For interesting discussions, see Odell Shepard, "A Youth to Fortune and to Fame Unknown," *MP*, xx (1923), 47–73; H. W. Starr, "A Youth to Fortune and to Fame Unknown, A Reconstruction," *JEGP*, xlviii (1949), 97–107; F. H. Ellis, "Gray's *Elegy*," *PMLA*, lxvi (1951), 971–1008.

595, 95–96. In the Eton MS. these lines have for their equivalent:

> If chance that e'er some pensive spirit more,
> By sympathetic musings here delayed,
> With vain, though kind, inquiry shall explore
> Thy once-loved haunt, this long-deserted shade.

595, 100. After this line the Eton MS. has the following stanza:

> Him have we seen the greenwood side along,
> While o'er the heath we hied, our labors done,
> Oft as the woodlark piped her farewell song,
> With wistful eyes pursue the setting sun.

595, 116. After this line the Eton MS. and several editions after the second have the following stanza:

> There scattered oft, the earliest of the year,
> By hands unseen, are showers of violets found;
> The red-breast loves to build and warble there,
> And little footsteps lightly print the ground.

595. STANZAS TO MR. BENTLEY

Written about 1752; first published by Mason. Richard Bentley, son of the famous scholar, illustrated the beautiful edition of Gray's poems published in 1753.

596, 26–28. "A corner of the only manuscript copy which Mr. Gray left of this fragment is unfortunately torn."—Mason.

596. THE PROGRESS OF POESY

The Pindaric ode, according to the practice of Ben Jonson and Cowley, was supposed to be lofty in style and irregular in meter. Between 1660 and 1750 poets often essayed the form and usually failed. In particular it was associated with the theme of the power of music (see Collins's *Passions,* above, page 581, note) and with the idea of the superior poetical inspiration of primitive times. The scholarly Gray tried to follow the exact construction of the Pindaric ode by laying out three parts, each consisting of strophe, antistrophe, and epode. The strophes exactly correspond with one another in meter, and so with the antistrophes and epodes. But Gray himself wrote of this scheme (to Wharton, March 9, 1755): "Setting aside the difficulties, methinks it has little or no effect upon the ear, which scarce perceives the regular return of meters at so great a distance from one another. To make it succeed, I am persuaded the stanzas must not consist of above nine lines each at the most. Pindar has several such odes."

596, 1. *Aeolian lyre.* Pindar often applies the term *Aeolian* to his poetry. In Greek music, the Aeolian mode was joyous and festive.

596, 3-12. "The various sources of poetry, which gives life and lustre to all it touches, are here described; its quiet majestic progress enriching every subject (otherwise dry and barren) with a pomp of diction and luxuriant harmony of numbers; and its more rapid and irresistible course, when swollen and hurried away by the conflict of tumultuous passions."—Gray.

596, 13. "Power of harmony to calm the turbulent sallies of the soul. The thoughts are borrowed from the first Pythian of Pindar."—Gray.

596, 17. *the Lord of War.* Ares or Mars, particularly associated with Thrace.

596, 21. *the feathered king.* Jove's bird, the eagle.

596, 25. "Power of harmony to produce all the graces of motion in the body."—Gray.

597, 27. *Idalia's velvet-green.* The birth of Aphrodite from the foam of the Aegean sea was associated both with the island of Cyprus, where the goddess was worshiped at Idalia, and with the island of Cythera (hence *Cytherea,* l. 29).

597, 39. *gliding state.* The *incessus* or gliding gait of the gods.

597, 53. *Hyperion.* A Titan, the sun-god.

597, 54. "Extensive influence of poetic genius over the remotest and most uncivilized nations; its connection with liberty, and the virtues that naturally attend on it. (See the Erse, Norwegian, and Welsh fragments, the Lapland and American songs.)"—Gray. Cp. selections from James Macpherson, below and notes; Gray's own Norwegian and Welsh fragments; F. E. Farley, "Three Lapland Songs," *PMLA,* xxi (1906), 1-39.

597, 66-82. "Progress of poetry from Greece to Italy, and from Italy to England."—Gray.

597, 66. *Delphi's steep.* Delphi, the oracle of Apollo, was at the foot of Mount Parnassus, in central Greece.

597, 68. *Ilissus.* A river flowing through Athens.

597, 69. *Maeander.* A winding river in Asia Minor.

598, 78-81. *Latian . . . Latium.* "The word 'Latium' seems to do duty both for declining Rome and for the land of the Renaissance."—Elton.

598, 84. *Nature's darling.* Shakespeare.

598, 95. *Nor second he, etc.* Milton.

598, 98. *the flaming bounds.* "The flaming walls of the world."—Lucretius, i, 74.

598, 99. *Ezekiel* i, 20, 26, 28.

598, 105-06. *Two coursers, etc.* "Meant to express the stately march and sounding energy of Dryden's rhymes."—Gray. Cp. Pope, *Imitations of Horace,* II, i, 267-69.

598, 112. *what daring spirit.* Gray himself.

598, 115. *the Theban Eagle.* Pindar.

599. THE BARD

Gray prefixed a brief Advertisement: "The following ode is founded on a tradition current in Wales, that Edward I, when he completed the conquest of that country, ordered all the bards that fell into his hands to be put to death." He found this tradition in the second volume of Carte's *History of England.* For an account of his Celtic studies, see E. D. Snyder, *The Celtic Revival in English Literature, 1760-1800* (Cambridge, U. S. A., 1923), and the monographs of R. Martin and W. P. Jones.

Gray's note-book outlines the poem thus: "The army of Edward I, as they march through a deep valley, are suddenly stopped by the appearance of a venerable figure seated on the summit of an inaccessible rock, who, with a voice more than human, reproaches the King with all the misery and desolation which he has brought on his country; foretells the misfortunes of the Norman race, and with prophetic spirit declares that all his cruelty shall never extinguish the noble ardor of poetic genius in this island; and that men shall never be wanting to celebrate true virtue and valor in immortal strains, to expose vice and infamous pleasure, and boldly censure tyranny and oppression. His song ended, he precipitates himself from the mountain, and is swallowed up by the river that rolls at its foot."

599, 8. *Cambria.* Wales.

599, 11. *Snowdon.* A mountain-group in North Wales

599, 13. *Glo'ster*. Gilbert de Clare, Earl of Gloucester and Hertford, son-in-law of Edward I.

599, 14. *Mortimer*. Edmond de Mortimer, Lord of Wigmore.

599, 16. *Conway*. A river in North Wales.

599, 19. "The image was taken from a well-known picture of Raphael, representing the Supreme Being in the vision of Ezekiel."—Gray. He saw copies of this picture at Paris and at Florence; the actual painting is that of a follower of Raphael. Later Gray referred to Parmegiano's picture of Moses breaking the Tables as his principal model (see Sir Joshua Reynolds, *Discourses*, xv).

599, 28. *Hoel*. A prince and bard. *Llewellyn*. He was praised by Welsh poets as a mild prince, but perhaps Gray thought of him as a bard.

599, 29–31. *Cadwallo . . . Urien*. Bards.

599, 33. *Modred*. No bard of this name is known. Perhaps Gray drew the name from the story of King Arthur.

599, 34. *Plinlimmon*. A mountain in Wales.

600, 35. *Arvon*. Carnarvonshire, a county in Wales.

600, 49–100. Chanted by a chorus of the spirits of the slain bards.

600, 48–49. The image of weaving is from Norse poetry. See *The Fatal Sisters*, page 602.

600, 54–56. "Edward II, cruelly butchered in Berkeley Castle."—Gray.

600, 57. "Isabel of France, Edward II's adulterous Queen."—Gray.

600, 59. "Triumphs of Edward III in France."—Gray.

600, 63–64. "Death of that King, abandoned by his children, and even robbed in his last moments by his courtiers and his mistress."—Gray.

600, 67. "Edward the Black Prince, dead some time before his father."—Gray.

600, 71. "Magnificence of Richard II's reign."—Gray.

600, 77–82. Gray's note cites authority for the story that Richard II was starved to death.

601, 83–86. "Ruinous civil wars of York and Lancaster."—Gray.

601, 87. "Henry VI, George Duke of Clarence, Edward V, Richard Duke of York, etc., believed to be murdered secretly in the Tower of London. The oldest part of that structure is vulgarly attributed to Julius Caesar."—Gray.

601, 89. *his consort*. Margaret of Anjou, Henry VI's queen. *his father*. Henry V.

601, 90. *meek usurper*. Henry VI.

601, 91–92. "The white and red roses, devices of York and Lancaster."—Gray.

601, 93. *Boar*. Richard III. *infant gore*. Richard III murdered the two young princes, sons of Edward IV, in the Tower.

601, 99. Eleanor of Castile, Edward's queen, died a few years after the conquest of Wales.

601, 102. An early draft gave the bard's name as Caradoc in this line.

601, 109. "It was the common belief of the Welsh nation, that King Arthur was still alive in Fairyland, and should return again to reign over Britain."—Gray.

601, 110. "Both Merlin and Taliessin had prophesied that the Welsh should regain their sovereignty over this island, which seemed to be accomplished in the House of Tudor."—Gray. Henry VII was the grandson of a Welsh nobleman, Owen Tudor.

601, 115. *a form divine!* Queen Elizabeth.

601, 121. *Taliessin*. "Taliessin, chief of the bards flourished in the sixth century."—Gray.

601, 126. "Fierce wars and faithful loves shall moralize my song."—Spenser, Proeme to *The Faerie Queene*.

602, 128. Shakespearean tragedy.

602, 131. *A voice, etc.* Milton.

602, 133. *And distant warblings, etc.* "The succession of poets after Milton's time."—Gray.

602.   THE FATAL SISTERS

Gray's Norse and Celtic pieces were intended to illustrate a history of English poetry, a project which he did not carry far. The two Norse poems were taken from the Latin versions given by Thomas Bartholin in his learned treatise *De Causis Contemptae Mortis* (1689), an important work on Scandinavian antiquities. Gray's prefatory note refers to the *Orcades* of Thormodus Torfaeus, but the latter took this first piece from Bartholin. See G. L. Kittredge, "Gray's Knowledge of Old Norse," in *Selections from Gray*, ed. Phelps (Boston, 1894). Gray's Preface to *The Fatal Sisters*, taken from Torfaeus, follows:

"In the eleventh century, Sigurd, Earl of the Orkney Islands, went with a fleet of ships and a considerable body of troops into Ireland, to the assistance of *Sictryg with the silken beard*, who was then making war on his father-in-law Brian, King of Dublin; the Earl and all his forces were cut to pieces, and Sictryg was in danger of a total defeat, but the enemy had a greater loss by the death of Brian, their king, who fell in action. On Christmas Day, the day of the battle, a native of Caithness in Scotland saw at a distance a number of persons on horseback riding full speed towards a hill, and seeming to enter into it. Curiosity led him to follow them, till looking through an opening in the rocks he saw twelve gigantic figures resembling women: they were all employed about a loom; and, as they wove, they sung the following dreadful song, which when they had finished, they tore the web into twelve pieces, and (each taking her portion) galloped six to the north and as many to the south."

For the survival of this legend in the Orkneys, see Sir Walter Scott's entry in his diary, printed in Lockhart's *Life* under date of August 14, 1814, and given also in Scott's note to *The Pirate*, ch. ii.

Gray adds a note in general explanation of title and contents: "The *Valkyriur* were female divinities, servants of Odin or Woden in the Gothic mythology. Their name signifies *choosers of the slain*. They were mounted on swift horses, with drawn swords in their hands; and in the throng of battle selected such as were destined to slaughter, and conducted them to Valhalla, the hall of Odin or paradise of the brave, where they attended the banquet and served the departed heroes with horns of mead and ale."

602, 8. *Randver's bane.* "Gray here follows Bartholin's Latin, which misrepresents the original. The Icelandic has 'the friends of the slayer of Randverr,' *i.e.*, 'the friends of Odin,' *i.e.*, 'the valkyrjur,'—a typical skaldic phrase."—Note in Phelps's edition.

602, 32. *the youthful king.* Sigtrygg.

602, 41. *the dauntless earl.* Sigurd.

602, 44. *a king.* Brian.

603.   THE DESCENT OF ODIN

See note to *The Fatal Sisters*, above. The original, known as *The Song of Vegtamr* (Odin) or as *Balder's Dreams* is found in the great collection of Old Norse poetry called the *Elder* or *Poetic Edda*. Balder, the god of light, has had a threatening dream. As the poem opens, Odin goes down to the lower world to find out the truth about the impending danger. For the whole story, see Matthew Arnold's *Balder Dead*.

603, 4. *Hela.* "*Niflheimr*, the hell of the Gothic nations, consisted of nine worlds [see l. 16], to which were devoted all such as died of sickness, old age, or by any other means than in battle. Over it presided Hela, the goddess of death."—Gray.

603, 37. *traveller.* Odin assumes the name *Vegtamr*, wanderer or traveller.

603, 55-56. *In Hoder's hand, etc.* Frigga, the mother of Balder, had made all things swear not to hurt her son, but had passed over the insignificant mistletoe. The malevolent Loki persuaded Hoder, Balder's blind brother, to cast mistletoe at him, and thus brought about his death.

603, 63-70. Vali, son of Odin and Rinda, when only one day old killed Hoder.

603, 75-79. *What virgins these, etc.* Odin betrays his identity; no mortal could behold the Norns, or Fates.

604, 90. *Lok.* "Lok [Loki] is the evil being, who continues in chains till the *Twilight of the Gods* approaches, when he shall break his bonds; the human race, the stars, and sun shall disappear; the earth sink in the seas, and fire consume the skies; even Odin himself and his kindred deities shall perish."—Gray.

604.   LETTERS

604a, 38. Isaiah, xxxiv, 13-15.

604b, 21. *hyp.* Hypochondria.

605a, 22. *forest.* Burnham Beeches, in Buckinghamshire.

605b, 11. *Isabella and Oroonoko.* The title characters in two plays by Thomas Southerne, first published in 1694 and 1696.

605b, 18. For "N.S." (New Style) and "O.S." (Old Style), see note to Steele's *Tatler*, No. 1.

607b, 25. *Douâniers.* Customs officers.

607b, 51. "Representation of a damned soul."

609b, 1. Horace, *Odes*, I, vii, 13-14: "The rapids of the Anio, the grove of Tiburnus, and the orchards moist from the flowing waters."

609b, 13. *andava il detto Signor.* "The aforesaid gentleman went to amuse himself with this same Horace."

609b, 51. "most splendid gift."

610a, 25. *Pretendente.* The "Old Pretender," James Francis Edward Stuart, son of James II, born in 1688.

610a, 29. "Then came to birth an elegant ball."

610a, 33. *rinfrescatives.* Gray anglicizes the Italian word for refreshments.

610b, 26. *fresco.* Italian word, meaning "the coolness of the air."

610b, 46. *Portici.* Herculaneum.

612a, 4. Some of the words here listed by Gray have since his time become popularized in prose and speech.

612a, 31. *Richard III,* I, i, 14–21.

612b, 10. *una litura.* "a single erasure."

612b, 21. "to live one's life without knowledge and without the arts."

612b, 35. The *Elegy* was published by Dodsley a few days later, on February 16, twelve days before the *Magazine of Magazines* appeared.

613a, 15. *Hurd.* Richard Hurd was already well known as a man of letters as well as a churchman. Gray had sent him a copy of his Pindaric odes, published earlier the same year. Hurd, who became bishop in 1774, published some *Letters on Chivalry and Romance* (1762), of considerable influence in the revival of medieval interests.

616a, 34. Macpherson published *Fragments of Ancient Poetry Collected in the Highlands* in 1760.

616b, 15–21. This Latin dissertation was later included in Evans's *Specimens of the Poetry of the Antient Welsh Bards* (1764).

616b, 41. George Colman the Elder (1732–1794).

616b, 49. *Tristram.* The first two volumes of Sterne's *Tristram Shandy* were published in London on January 1, 1760, and his sermons in May of the same year.

619.   THE LIFE OF JOHNSON

620a, 10. *Rambler,* No. 60. [Boswell.]

620a, 39. *a former occasion.* Boswell's *Journal of a Tour in the Hebrides with Dr. Johnson,* published in 1785.

620b, 15. *Plutarch.* Plutarch's *Life of Alexander,* Langhorne's translation. [Boswell.]

620b, 33. *Rambler,* No. 60. [Boswell.]

622a, 13. Bacon's *Advancement of Learning.* Book I. [Boswell.]

622a, 33. Richard Savage, who died in 1743, claimed to be the illegitimate son of the fourth Earl Rivers. He blackmailed his supposed father, and in a poem satirized his supposed mother. He was condemned to death for murder in 1727, but was pardoned. Johnson's biography of him is one of his most popular and interesting works.

623a, 37. *Respicere exemplar.* Horace, *Ars Poetica,* 317: "I shall bid you look upon a model of life and morals."

627a, 47. "The conqueror of the conqueror of the world." Boileau, *L'Art Poétique,* III, 272.

627b, 19. *shepherd in Virgil.* Virgil, *Eclogues,* VIII, 44–46.

627b, 31. *solitary.* Dr. Johnson's wife died in 1752.

628a, 24. See *The Vanity of Human Wishes,* page 683, lines 159–160.

632a, 30–32. *one who . . . attacked, etc.* John Wilkes.

632a, 46. Mr. Sheridan [the father of the dramatist] was then reading lectures upon Oratory at Bath, where Derrick was Master of the Ceremonies; or, as the phrase is, King. [Boswell.]

633a, 54. *Smart.* Christopher Smart (1722–1771), a remarkable minor poet, best known for his *Song to David.*

635a, 6. Charles Churchill (1731–1764), the friend of John Wilkes, published a number of very personal satires. His *Rosciad* (1761) attacked the leading actors of the time.

639a, 28. *pension.* When I mentioned the same idle clamour to him several years afterwards, he said, with a smile, "I wish my pension were twice as large, that they might make twice as much noise." [Boswell.]

639a, 48. He used to tell with great humour, from my relation to him, the following little story of my early years, which was literally true: "Boswell, in the year 1745, was a fine boy, wore a white cockade, and prayed for King James, till one of his uncles (General Cochran) gave him a shilling on condition that he should pray for King George, which he accordingly did. So you see (says Boswell) that *Whigs of all ages are made the same way.*" [Boswell.]

640a, 32–33. *an impudent fellow from Scotland.* James Macpherson.

642b, 6. *Rousseau's treatise.* Jean Jacques Rousseau first became famous by his *Discourse on the Sciences and the Arts* in 1750. His *Discourse on the Origin of Inequality,* here referred to, appeared in 1754.

644a, 27–28. *a gentleman, etc.* George Dempster, M.P., a friend of Boswell's.
644a, 34. *a noted infidel.* David Hume.
654a, 49. Goldsmith's couplet on Burke in his *Retaliation.*
657b, 8. Horace, *Ars Poetica,* 142: "the customs and cities of many nations."
658b, 31. *his Majesty.* George III.
659b, 35. *Dr. Warburton.* The Rev. Mr. Strahan clearly recollects having been told by Johnson, that the King observed that Pope made Warburton a Bishop. "True, Sir, (said Johnson) but Warburton did more for Pope; he made him a Christian": alluding, no doubt, to his ingenious Comments on the *Essay on Man.* [Boswell.]
660a, 32. *Dr. Hill.* A notorious quack doctor and satirist. Garrick described him in a couplet:

> "For physic and farce, his equal there scarce is;
> His farces are physic; his physic a farce is."

661b, 20. *a lady.* Lady Diana Beauclerk, wife of Topham Beauclerk, one of Johnson's circle.
664a, 2. *Elwal.* An ironmonger at Wolverhampton who had been prosecuted for publishing a book against the doctrine of the Trinity. He and Johnson were both from Staffordshire.
665a, 16. *Toplady.* The Rev. Augustus Toplady was a sharp controversialist, but is now best known as the author of the hymn *Rock of Ages.*
666a, 37. Johnson would naturally not want to associate with a man so notorious for loose morals and radical politics as John Wilkes. Boswell, however, had cultivated Wilkes's acquaintance during his tour on the Continent.
666a, 38. *Jack Ketch.* The public executioner at Tyburn.
667a, 36. Johnson's *London, a Poem,* 145. [Boswell.]
668a, 1. *Foote.* Samuel Foote (1727–1777), an actor and mimic who impersonated well-known persons on the stage.
668b, 16. *Scrub.* The comic servant in Farquhar's *The Beaux' Stratagem,* a part Garrick frequently played.
668b, 54. *Swinney.* Owen MacSwinney managed the Haymarket and Drury Lane theaters early in the eighteenth century.
674a, 5. Jonathan Edwards (1703–1757), whose principal philosophical work, *The Freedom of the Will* (1754), is here referred to.

679. PROLOGUE . . . DRURY LANE, 1747

679, 9. *Then Jonson came, etc.* It was a commonplace of criticism to contrast the spontaneity of Shakespeare with the labored art of Ben Jonson.
680, 36. *great Faustus.* The long vogue of pantomime on the English stage began in 1723, when Rich produced "The Necromancer, or The History of Dr. Faustus."
680, 42. *New Behns, new Durfeys.* Aphra Behn (1640–1689), dramatist and novelist. Thomas D'Urfey (1653–1723), writer of numerous comedies and songs.
680, 46. *Hunt.* Edward Hunt, a lightweight boxer. *Mahomet.* A rope-dancer at Covent Garden.

680. THE VANITY OF HUMAN WISHES

681, 49. *Democritus.* Called the "laughing philosopher."
682, 84. *Palladium.* The image of the goddess Pallas, on which depended the safety of the city of Troy.
682, 97. *septennial ale.* Ale distributed by candidates at parliamentary elections, held at least once every seven years.
682, 99. *Wolsey.* Cp. Shakespeare's *Henry VIII.*
682, 102. After this line the editions up to 1755 have the following couplet:

> Turned by his nod the stream of honor flows,
> His smile alone security bestows.

683, 127. *Villiers.* George Villiers, Duke of Buckingham, assassinated in 1628.
683, 128. *Harley.* Robert Harley, first Earl of Oxford, Tory minister under Queen Anne.
683, 129. *Wentworth.* Thomas Wentworth, Earl of Strafford, the most powerful of the supporters of Charles I in his struggle with Parliament, executed in 1641. *Hyde.* Edward Hyde, Earl of Clarendon, Lord Chancellor after the Restoration, lost popularity and was driven into exile in 1667.
683, 137. *Bodley's dome.* The Bodleian Library, Oxford.

683, 138. *Bacon's mansion.* A note in Dodsley's *Collection,* iv (1755), refers to an Oxford tradition that the study of Roger Bacon, "built on an arch over the bridge, will fall when a man greater than Bacon shall pass under it."

683, 158. *the patron.* Johnson substituted *patron* for the original reading *garret,* alluding to his disappointment in Chesterfield's "fallacious patronage."

683, 162. *Lydiat's life.* Thomas Lydiat (1572–1646), an Oxford scholar who suffered as a Royalist. *Galileo's end.* Galileo (1564–1642) was imprisoned by the Inquisition in 1633; though this sentence was commuted to a mild banishment, the last years of his life were marred by blindness and ill health.

683, 166. *Laud.* The High Church Archbishop of Charles I's reign, executed in 1644. But it was not his learning that led him to the block.

684, 177. *the rapid Greek.* Alexander the Great.

684, 180. *Danube . . . Rhine.* In the war of the Spanish Succession the English armies under Marlborough campaigned in the valleys of the Danube and the Rhine.

684, 190–220. *Swedish Charles, etc.* After a series of triumphant campaigns against Denmark, Poland, and Russia, Charles XII of Sweden was defeated by the Russians at Pultowa (1709). He then fled to Turkey, in the vain hope of enlisting aid against Aussia (ll. 209–12). Later he made his way back to Sweden, and in a campaign against Norway was shot at the "petty fortress" of Frederikshald. Johnson once planned to write a play on Charles XII.

684, 225–38. *Great Xerxes, etc.* When Xerxes was preparing to invade Greece, a storm destroyed the bridges he had built over the Hellespont, whereupon, says Herodotus, he "bade them scourge the Hellespont with three hundred strokes of the lash, and let down into the sea a pair of fetters." Herodotus also says that according to one story Xerxes tried to return to Asia in a Phoenician ship which was almost lost in a storm.

685, 239–52. *The bold Bavarian, etc.* Charles Albert, Elector of Bavaria, claimed the crown of the Empire in opposition to Maria Theresa (*fair Austria,* l. 243) and the war of the Austrian Succession ensued (1740–48). The Elector was chosen Emperor in 1742, but three years later he died, worn out by the struggle.

685, 247. *Croatian . . . Hussar.* The forces of Maria Theresa.

686, 311–12. *Lydia's monarch, etc.* When Croesus, King of Lydia, was at the height of his prosperity, the philosopher Solon warned him that no man was to be counted happy till after his death.

686, 315. *Marlborough's eyes, etc.* The great Duke of Marlborough was reported to be broken in mind and body from 1716 to his death in 1722.

686, 316. *Swift expires, etc.* Swift died insane in 1745.

686, 319. *Vane.* Anne Vane, mistress of Frederick, Prince of Wales.

686, 320. *Sedley.* Catharine Sedley, Countess of Dorchester, mistress of the Duke of York, afterwards James II.

687.   LINES WRITTEN IN RIDICULE, ETC.

The poems ridiculed were Thomas Warton's. This impromptu was first published in Mrs. Piozzi's *Anecdotes of the Late Samuel Johnson* (1786).

687.   ON THE DEATH OF MR. ROBERT LEVET

Robert Levet or Levett, an unlicensed practioner of medicine, lived for many years in Johnson's house. He died January 17, 1782.

688.   THE RAMBLER

688a, 5. *The Rambler* appeared as an essay periodical on Tuesdays and Saturdays from March 20, 1750 to March 1, 1752, and later was published in volume form. It added greatly to Johnson's reputation as a teacher of wisdom and piety.

688a, 10. Johnson here obviously has in mind the popular works of fiction which had appeared recently: Richardson's *Clarissa* (1747–48), Smollett's *Roderick Random* (1748), and Fielding's *Tom Jones* (1749).

688a, 34. Julius Caesar Scaliger (1484–1538) comments on Pontanus, his contemporary, in his *Poetics,* V, iv.

691.   THE IDLER

The essays under this title, somewhat lighter in style than the *Ramblers,* were published every Saturday from April 15, 1758, to April 5, 1760.

691b, 13. *Dick Minim* is a satire on the superficial critic who pronounces judgements which, whether right or wrong, he does not understand. Such a critic is likely to try, above everything, to be safe, and Dick Minim rehearses many of the standard doctrines of the preceding age.

692b, 5. *Phædra and Hippolytus.* A heavy tragedy by Edmund Smith, a friend of Addison, which was a famous failure in the theatre.

693a, 16–25. Butler, *Hudibras,* I, i, 11–12, and II, ii, 385–88.

695. RASSELAS

Johnson wrote *Rasselas* at great speed in January, 1759, between the 13th, when he learned of his mother's serious illness, and the 23rd, when she was buried. It came out in two small volumes in April. Johnson wrote it under the pressure of financial need and the stress of anxiety over his mother in Lichfield. It is not a cheerful work, but nevertheless witty and entertaining, and of all his writings the most bracing and tonic. He had learned about the "Happy Valley" when, as a young man, he had translated from the French the *Voyage to Abyssinia* by a Portuguese Jesuit, Father Lobo. The same tradition appears in Milton, *Paradise Lost,* IV, 280–84. But our interest in *Rasselas* is not in the geographical background, but in the consummate irony with which the author leads his innocents to discover the futility of one recipe for happiness after another. Voltaire's *Candide,* which appeared the same year, was likewise directed against this fashionable Deistic optimism. For all this identity of purpose, the two works are as different as the two men, and make an excellent study in similarities and contrasts.

753. A SONG TO DAVID

753, 26. *Samuel's horn.* Samuel anointed David. See I Samuel, xvi.

754, 35. *Against the boaster, etc.* For the combat of David and Goliath, see I Samuel, xvii.

754, 38. *the famous temple.* I Chronicles, xxviii.

754, 47. *En-gedi's conscious cave.* I Samuel, xxiv.

754, 48. *Shimei's blunted dart.* II Samuel, xvi, 5–14; xix, 16–23.

754, 69. *Kidron.* A brook near Bethlehem.

754, 77. *lion . . . bear.* I Samuel, xvii, 34–35.

754, 83. *Ziba . . . Mephibosheth.* Mephibosheth was the son of Jonathan, the son of Saul and David's beloved friend. Ziba was a servant of the house of Saul. After the death of Saul and Jonathan, David placed Ziba in the service of Mephibosheth. See II Samuel, ix, xvi.

754, 88. *ephod.* The vestment of the Hebrew high priest.

754, 101. *Michael.* David's first wife, daughter of Saul.

754, 102. *Abishag.* Abishag the Shunammite ministered to David in his old age. See I Kings, i, 1–4, 15.

754, 112. *Michael.* Revelations, xii, 7.

755, 162. *The frantic throes of Saul.* I Samuel, xvi, 23. See also Browning's *Saul.*

755, 175. *The seven pillars of wisdom* (Proverbs, ix, 1) are here correlated with the days of the creative week and given the names of letters of the Greek alphabet. The symbolism of the passage has never been fully explained; for Alpha and Omega, see Revelation, xxii, 13.

756, 228. *lion . . . bee.* See Samson's riddle, Judges, xiv, 18.

756, 235. *Tell them I am.* Exodus, iii, 14.

756, 267. *ass and bull.* Deuteronomy, xxii, 10.

756, 270. *flax with wool.* Deuteronomy, xxii, 11.

757, 316. *Ivis.* "The humming-bird."—Smart.

757, 319. *vinous syrups.* Psalm civ, 16.

757, 320. *rocks . . . honey.* Psalm lxxxi, 16.

757, 328. *beasts embark.* Smart's note refers to the beaver: "There is a large quadruped that preys upon fish and provides himself with a species of timber for that purpose, with which he is very handy."

757, 329. *halcyon's ark.* The nest of the kingfisher. According to the Greek legend, the sea was always calm at the time of the winter solstice, when the kingfisher was breeding.

757, 331. *fig.* Micah, iv, 4.

757, 341. *silverlings.* Tarpons.

757, 341. *crusions.* Fish of the carp family.

757, 356. *thyine woods.* Revelation, xvii, 12.

757, 393. *The Dog, the Ram, and Rose.* Constellations. The cluster of stars near the tail of the Lion was sometimes called the Rose, but more commonly *enices.* See *The Rape of the Lock,* v, page 364, line 129.

757, 394. *planet's ring.* Saturn's ring.

757, 397. *strings.* A reference to the Aeolian harp.

757, 404. *bezoar.* Originally a stone or concretion found in the stomach or intestines of some animals, and used as an antidote against poison; later employed generally to mean either antidote or precious stone.

757, 408. *galbanum.* A resinous gum.

758, 422–24. *sparrows . . . swallow.* Psalm lxxxiv, 3.

758, 445–56. With the whole passage, cp. Job, xxxix.

758, 450. *xiphias.* The sword-fish.

758, 485. *alba's.* The white stone of Revelation, ii, 17.

767. THE PROPHECY OF FAMINE

767, 47. *Theocrite.* Theocritus, writer of Sicilian pastorals.

767, 67. *Mason.* William Mason (1724–97); mediocre poet, friend and biographer of Gray.

768, 70. *Gisbal.* "Gisbal, a Hyperborean tale, translated from the fragments of Ossian, the son of Fingal."—Tooke.

768, 71. *Lord* ——. Lord Lyttelton, a political enemy. His monody to his wife is here satirized.

768, 110. An ironical allusion to the Scottish loyalty to the Pretender in the rebellion of 1745.

768, 116. *Stuarts.* "Stuart, the family name of Lord Bute; it was noticed by the opposition papers of the day that out of sixteen names in one list of gazette promotions there were eleven Stuarts and four M'Kenzies."—Tooke.

769, 122. The Scots had delivered up Charles I to the English Parliament.

769, 125. *Ramsay.* A portrait painter, son of the author of *The Gentle Shepherd.*

769, 127. *Home.* The author of the successful tragedy *Douglas*; he resigned from the ministry to become private secretary to Lord Bute.

769, 129. *Macpherson.* See selection from James Macpherson, page 760.

769, 131. *Malloch.* David Malloch (changed to Mallet), a Scottish writer who was regarded as a friend to infidelity because he had brought out the posthumous edition of Bolingbroke's works. His political services to Bute had just been rewarded by a government appointment.

770, 186. *North Briton.* The weekly periodical edited by John Wilkes between June, 1762, and May, 1763, with which Churchill was intimately connected.

770, 222. There is a tradition that Churchill's mother was Scottish.

771, 232. "George Lord Lyttelton, author of the history of Henry II, and Gilbert West, the translator of Pindar. The former, who had been a skeptic in his earlier years, received at Wickham in Kent, in the house of Mr. West, the conviction which produced his celebrated *Observations on the Conversion and Apostleship of St. Paul.*"—Tooke.

771, 242. *The mighty Thane.* Bute.

771, 247. *Hill.* John Hill, an apothecary with dramatic aspirations. Under the patronage of Bute he wrote *The Vegetable Kingdom*, in twenty-six volumes.

771, 256. *the Laureate.* William Whitehead.

772, 307. "The white rose, the emblem of the Jacobites, was worn by them on the 10th of June, in honor of the young Pretender's birthday."—Tooke.

779. LETTERS

779a, 7. Gray's letter to his mother on October 13, 1739, gives his account of the same mountain tour. See page 606.

780a, 5. *the first stanza.* Horace, *Odes,* III, iii.

780a, 43. *Houghton.* The country seat of Sir Robert Walpole, who had gathered there a notable collection of paintings.

781a, 41. *Horace Mann.* Walpole and Gray had spent many months at Florence as the guests of Horace Mann, the British minister there from 1740 to his death in 1786.

781a, 42. *Arlington Street.* Walpole's residence in London.

781b, 9. *Sherlock.* Then Bishop of London.

781b, 31. Conyers Middleton (1683–1750), a rather heterodox scholar and writer on religion.

783a, 34. *There too lies he.* Horace's father, Sir Robert Walpole.

784a, 2. *Mr. Wood.* The author of *Ruins of Baalbek* (1757), an account of the city known in antiquity as Heliopolis.

784a, 30. Heraclitus was the "Weeping Philosopher" and Democritus the "Laughing Philosopher."

785a, 3v. *Fingal.* Compare Gray's opinion in his letter to Wharton in 1760. See page 615.

785b, 7. The remainder of this letter is missing.

786b, 21. *a collection of old ballads.* Percy's *Reliques of Ancient Poetry* (1765).

787a, 39. Thomas Chatterton (1752–1770), the boy poet of remarkable gifts, who forged a whole series of medieval manuscripts, including the work of a supposed medieval poet Rowley. He tried to sell Walpole an account of a series of great painters of medieval Bristol, but Walpole was suspicious. Walpole had already published part of his *Anecdotes of Painting in England* (1762–1780).

787b, 49. The following note was appended by Horace Walpole to this letter: "N.B. The above letter I had begun to write to Chatterton on his re-demanding his MSS., but not choosing to enter into a controversy with him, did not finish it, and, only folding up his papers, returned them." [Toynbee.]

788b, 17. *Gray's life.* Mason published his *Life and Letters of Gray* in 1775.

790b, 2. *The print.* The portrait prefixed to the quarto edition of the memoirs of Gray.

790b, 43. *The History of Manchester,* by John Whitaker. [Toynbee.]

791b, 7. An article in the *Monthly Review* for May, 1777, blamed Chatterton's suicide on Walpole's alleged harsh treatment of him.

794a, 20. *Gray's life.* Dr. Johnson's biography in the *Lives of the Poets.*

794b, 40. Mary Berry (1763–1852), a protégée of the aging wit. She edited his posthumous works.

795a, 37. *Nymph.* Lady Hamilton.

795a, 45. *Darwin's poem.* Erasmus Darwin's *Botanic Garden* (1791).

795a, 51. *Boswell's book.* The *Life of Samuel Johnson* had just been published.

796a, 42. *another pamphlet.* The *Letter to a Member of the National Assembly.* The more famous *Reflections on the Revolution in France* was published in 1790.

799.   THE TRAVELLER

799, 28. *some half-witted thing, etc.* This passage is probably directed against Charles Churchill.

799, 2. *Scheldt.* The Schelde, a river flowing through Holland and Belgium. *Po.* The chief river of northern Italy.

799, 3. *Carinthian.* Carinthia is a mountainous district in southern Austria.

799, 5. *Campania.* The Roman Campagna.

801, 84. *Idra.* A town in Jugoslavia, noted for quicksilver mines. *Arno.* A river in Tuscany.

802, 169–70. Swiss soldiers were famous as mercenaries.

805, 320. *Hydaspes.* The *fabulosus Hydaspes* of Horace, the modern Jhelam or Jhelum, a river in India.

807, 397–412. Cp. the theme of *The Deserted Village.*

807, 411. *Oswego.* A river in northern New York.

807, 429–38. This passage except ll. 435–36, was written by Dr. Johnson.

807, 436. *Luke's iron crown.* The brothers George and Luke Dosa led a rebellion in Hungary in 1513. It was George, not Luke, who suffered the torture of the red-hot iron crown. *Damiens's bed of steel.* Damiens, who tried to assassinate Louis XV in 1757, was tortured on an iron bed before being torn to pieces by four horses.

808.   THE DESERTED VILLAGE

808, 10. *the depopulation it deplores, etc.* In the eighteenth century English agriculture finally abandoned the open-field system, in which meadows and pasture-land were held in common. These lands were now "enclosed" and controlled by individual owners. Numerous Enclosure Acts were passed, and the process was complete by the beginning of the nineteenth century. The change was to the advantage of the large landowners and the more energetic farmers generally, but the small yeomen and cottagers could not adapt themselves so easily to the new conditions. The loss of common pasture-land was keenly felt by the poor (see lines 305–08 below). Although Goldsmith idealizes the life of the village, the plight of the inhabitants of Auburn was not a mere figment of his imagination.

812, 209. *terms.* "Days in the year fixed for payment of rent, wages, and other dues, beginning and end of tenancy, etc."—*N.E.D.* *tides.* Seasons or days in the church calendar. Cp.

William Cobbett, quoted in *N.E.D.*: "The country people in England go to this day by the tides, and in some cases by the movable tides."

812, 232. *twelve good rules.* "King Charles's Twelve Good Rules" were printed in broadside form and hung on the wall. *game of goose.* A game in which the players moved their men on a board according to the throw of the dice.

815, 344. *Altama.* The Altamaha River in Georgia.

816, 418. *Torno.* The river Tornio, in the extreme north of Sweden Cp. Thomson's *Winter*, line 887. *Pambamarca.* A mountain in Ecuador.

816, 426–30. Boswell says that Dr. Johnson wrote these lines.

816. RETALIATION

When the members of the Club were once amusing themselves at Goldsmith's expense, Garrick extemporized the following epitaph for him:

> Here lies Nolly Goldsmith, for shortness called Noll,
> Who wrote like an angel, but talked like poor Poll.

Goldsmith made no answer at the time, but later made an effective rejoinder by writing and circulating these verses, in detached fragments.

816, 1. *Scarron.* Paul Scarron, witty French burlesque writer.

816, 3. *our landlord.* The proprietor of St. James's Coffee House, where the Club met.

816, 5. *Our Dean.* Thomas Barnard, Dean of Derry.

816, 6. *Burke,* Edmund Burke.

816, 7. *Will.* William Burke, a member of Parliament.

816, 8. *Dick.* Richard Burke, younger brother of Edmund Burke.

816, 9. *Cumberland.* Richard Cumberland, best known as a writer of sentimental comedy.

816, 10. *Douglas.* Dr. John Douglas, Canon of Windsor, later Bishop of Salisbury.

816, 14. *Ridge.* John Ridge, an Irish lawyer.

816, 15. *Hickey.* An attorney known as "honest Tom Hickey."

816, 16. *gooseberry fool.* A dish of gooseberries and cream, but a pun is of course intended

817, 34. *Tommy Townshend.* M.P. for Whitchurch, afterwards Lord Sydney.

817, 61–78. Goldsmith slyly satirizes sentimental comedy.

818, 80. *The scourge of imposters, etc.* Dr. Douglas had exposed the frauds of Archibald Bower, secretly a Jesuit, who wrote a *History of the Popes,* and of William Lauder, who by means of forged texts tried to prove Milton a plagiarist (see l. 89 below).

818, 86. *Our Dodds.* Dr. William Dodd, a disreputable clergyman, later executed for forgery. *our Kenricks.* Dr. William Kenrick, an unscrupulous hack-writer, was lecturing at the Devil Tavern.

818, 87. *Macpherson.* Goldsmith was of course no lover of *Ossian.*

818, 115. *Kenricks.* Garrick had been grossly libeled by Kenrick, but treated him in a conciliatory way. *Kellys.* Hugh Kelly, a writer of sentimental comedy, with some pretensions as a dramatic critic; Garrick had taken him up in opposition to Goldsmith. *Woodfalls.* William Woodfall, editor and dramatic critic, had recently written provocative letters to Garrick (*Private Correspondence of David Garrick* [London, 1831], 1, 583–85). The point of Goldsmith's criticism is that Garrick was showing too much deference to inferior men who attacked or threatened to attack him.

818, 118. *be-Rosciused.* Praised as the equal of Roscius, the great Roman actor.

819, 146. Sir Joshua Reynolds used an ear-trumpet.

819. ASEM, AN EASTERN TALE

First printed in the *Royal Magazine,* December, 1759. The tale with an Oriental setting was popular in this century as a vehicle for moral philosophy.

823. A REVERIE AT THE BOAR'S-HEAD TAVERN

First printed in the *British Magazine* for February, March, and April, 1760. The essay is inspired, of course, by Shakespeare's *Henry IV.*

825b, 41. *woad.* A blue vegetable dye.

830a, 18. *conventicle.* A meeting-house for nonconformists, who were often referred to as "enthusiasts," or fanatics.

830.   LETTERS FROM A CITIZEN OF THE WORLD

Goldsmith utilizes in these *Letters* a literary device which had been popular for some time, of having a foreigner from a remote country express his naive comments on European manners and customs. The device permits of a delightful combination of amusement at the foreigner and refreshing satire of the country he is visiting. Among the more famous series of this type may be mentioned Montesquieu's *Persian Letters* (1721) and D'Argens' *Chinese Letters* (1750). Goldsmith began his *Letters* on January 24, 1760, in a newspaper, *The Public Ledger*, usually two a week. In 1762 they were collected in two volumes under the present title.

832a, 21. Letter X gives a picture of the religion of the Daures, a primitive people visited by Lien Chi Altangi on his way to Europe. The question of luxury versus simplicity was being argued much in England during this period.

841a, 40. This Club of Authors had been described by Goldsmith in the preceding letter, No. XXIX.

842a, 30–31. *Royal game of goose . . . twelve rules. Deserted Village*, line 232.

842b, 23. *ex ungue Herculem.* "You may know Hercules by his finger nail."

843b, 18. *Catchpole.* A sheriff's officer who makes arrests for debt.

844a, 38. *Sponging-house.* "A victualling-house, where persons arrested for debt are kept for some time, either till they agree with their adversary, or are removed to closer confinement." —Bailey's *Dictionary* (6th ed., 1733).

847a, 2. *Marriage Act.* Possibly Lord Hardwick's Act of 1753, which did away with the Fleet marriages and some other abuses, but was for a time very unpopular. [Gibbs.]

847a, 12. *The war.* The Seven Years War (1756–63).

852.   ESSAY ON THE THEATRE

First printed in the *Westminster Magazine*, January, 1773.

In this essay, as in his comedies, Goldsmith set himself squarely against the sentimental movement of the age. His definition of the ethical weakness of sentimentalism might be compared with Mandeville's remarks on Sir Richard Steele (see above, page 339, line 36 and note).

852b, 11. *L'Art Poétique,* III, 401–02.

853a, 5. The word *sentimental* was coined in the eighteenth century, and became current after 1740.

854a, 6. *the Tabernacle.* The famous Methodist chapel where George Whitefield preached, in Tottenham Court Road.

857.   THE MINSTREL

859, 95. *of the north countrie.* "There is scarce an old historical song or ballad wherein a minstrel or harper appears, but he is characterized by way of eminence to have been of the north countreye."—Percy, "Essay on the Ancient Minstrels." Beattie applies the phrase to Scotland.

865, 357. *Pyrrho's maze.* The philosophy of the Greek Pyrrho (4th century B.C.) was a thorough-going skepticism. *Epicurus' sty.* The phrase is from Horace, *Epistles,* ii, 4, 16. Epicurus taught that refined pleasure, not mere sensual indulgence, was the highest good; but his doctrine was often misunderstood and misrepresented. At this time Beattie was writing his answer to the skeptic Hume, to whom the entire line alludes. In similar vein, William Mason called Hume "the fattest hog of Epicurus' sty" (*Heroic Epistle to Sir William Chambers*, 1773).

866, 398. *a gentler strain, etc.* The ballad of *The Babes in the Wood.*

870, 534. Beattie at first planned to fill the blank with the surname of his intimate friend Robert Arbuthnot. In 1783–84 the line was changed to read, "But on this verse if Montagu should smile"—in compliment to Mrs. Elizabeth Montagu, a famous literary lady.

873.   BRISTOWE TRAGEDIE

873, 11. *Charles Bawdin.* Sir Baldwin Fulford, a Lancastrian knight, was executed at Bristol in 1461, at the beginning of the reign of the Yorkist king Edward IV (cp. line 5 above).

873, 45. *Maisterr Canynge.* William Canynges the younger. See biographical sketch of Chatterton.

874, 141. *goddelyke Henrie.* Henry VI, a pious but weak king, had just been deposed by Edward.

875, 183. *Richard's sonnes.* Two of the sons of Richard, Duke of York—Edward IV, and Richard, Duke of Gloucester, afterwards Richard III.

876, 269–71. *The Freers of Seincte Augustyne, etc.* "The canons (not Friars) of St. Augustine did not wear russet, but black."—Skeat. Bristol Cathedral was originally the church of an abbey of the Augustinian canons.

877, 355. *Gloucester.* See above, line 183 note.

877. MYNSTRELLES SONGE

Sung by a group of minstrels in the lyrical drama called *Aella, a Tragycal Enterlude.*

878. AN EXCELENTE BALADE OF CHARITIE

Chatterton sent this poem to the editor of the *Town and Country Magazine* in July, 1770. He may have written it in London, or brought it with him from Bristol. It is based on the parable of the Good Samaritan.

Sub-title. "Thomas Rowley, the author, was born at Norton Mal-reward in Somersetshire, educated at the Convent of St. Kenna at Keynesham, and died at Westbury in Gloucestershire." —Chatterton.

879, 44. "It would have been *charitable*, if the author had not pointed at personal characters in this Ballad of Charity. The Abbot of St. Godwin's at the time of the writing of this was Ralph de Bellomont, a great stickler for the Lancastrian family. Rowley was a Yorkist."— Chatterton.

884. OLNEY HYMNS

Cowper's *Olney Hymns* were written in conjunction with the Rev. John Newton, chiefly in 1771 and 1772 before the attack of insanity of 1773. They were published in 1779. Cowper contributed 67 hymns to the collection. While the hymns express for the most part the more serene and beautiful side of Cowper's religious experience, there are forebodings of the gathering storm of self-doubt, as in "Light Shining Out of Darkness" which is reputed to have been written after a frustrated attempt at suicide early in 1773. "The Happy Change" is a typical description of the experience of conversion.

885. THE SHRUBBERY

Written, as the title suggests, during a period of derangement—that of 1773.

885. ADDRESSED TO A YOUNG LADY

Written in 1780 to Mrs. Shuttleworth, sister-in-law of the Rev. William Unwin, Mrs. Mary Unwin's son.

885. JOHN GILPIN

This poem, written in 1782, retells in ballad stanza a story which Lady Austen had told Cowper of the ride of John Beyer, linen-draper, of No. 3 Cheapside. Concerning the great popularity of the poem, he said, "A serious poem is like a swan, it flies heavily, and never far; but a jest has the wings of a swallow, that never tire, and that carry it into every nook and corner."

Cowper writes of the ballad form: "The ballad is a species of poetry, I believe, peculiar to this country, equally adapted to the drollest and the most tragical subjects. Simplicity and ease are its proper characteristics. Our forefathers excelled in it; but we moderns have lost the art. . . . It is a sort of composition I was ever fond of, and if graver matters had not called me another way, should have addicted myself to it more than to any other."

889. THE TASK

Cowper, in his Advertisement to the first edition of the volume of poems containing *The Task,* thus describes the genesis of the poem: "The history of the following production is briefly this:— A lady, fond of blank verse, demanded a poem of that kind from the author, and gave him the Sofa for a subject. He obeyed; and, having much leisure, connected another subject with it; and, pursuing the train of thought to which his situation and turn of mind led him, brought forth at length, instead of the trifle which he at first intended, a serious affair—a Volume!" The "lady" is, of course, Lady Austen. The subject of the sofa gave Cowper the starting point, suited to his genius, for a meditative poem that flowed easily and informally from a mind filled with the love of the country and its pursuits, and troubled by the state of the world. Cowper

was, however, temperamentally incapable of producing any extended piece of writing without
a serious purpose, and especially without a religious cast. "Were I to write as many volumes as
Lope de Vega, or Voltaire," he said, "not one of them would be without this tincture. If the
world like it or not, so much the worse for them." For in Cowper's mind "The earth is a grain
of sand, but the spiritual interests of man are commensurate with the Heavens." In a letter to
the Rev. William Unwin, he stated that his purpose was "to discountenance the modern enthusiasm after a London life, and to recommend rural ease and leisure, as friendly to the cause
of piety and virtue." While this theme sounds prosy, and even illiberal, the poem is far from
being either, for, however austere Cowper's purpose might be, his intimate knowledge of the
country and its people, and his love of whimsical detail are responsible for passage after passage
of delicacy and beauty.

889. *Book III. The Garden.* On the love of his garden at Olney, Cowper wrote to Newton,
July 27, 1783: "In former years I have known sorrow, and before I had ever tasted of spiritual
trouble. The effect was an abhorrence of the scene in which I had suffered so much, and a
weariness of those objects which I had so long looked at with an eye of despondency and dejection. But it is otherwise with me now . . . The very stones in the garden-walls are my intimate
acquaintance. I should miss almost the minutest object, and be disagreeably affected by its
removal, and am persuaded that were it possible I could leave this incommodious nook for a
twelvemonth, I should return to it again with rapture, and be transported with the sight of
objects which to all the world beside would be at least indifferent."

891, 108–20. One of Cowper's most poetic descriptions of his conversion.

892, 139–260. It is interesting to compare Cowper's distrust of the pretensions of science
and learning with Pope's ridicule of the same thing in *Essay on Man,* Book II, lines 1–52. For
a contrasting passage on man of great force and beauty, see Shelley's *Prometheus Unbound,*
Act IV, lines 376–423. In lines 242–60 Cowper qualifies, to a certain extent, his criticism of
natural philosophers who, like Sir Isaac Newton, approach their subject in a pious spirit. It is
an interesting anomaly that Sir Isaac Newton, whose physics helped to make possible a purely
mechanistic interpretation of the universe, was himself an extremely pious man and was idolized
by the pious of the eighteenth century for having given to the world a fuller appreciation of the
wisdom of God in the design of the Universe.

The following lines of Cowper's earlier poem, *Charity,* further illustrate a more liberal attitude toward philosophy:

> Philosophy, that does not dream or stray,
> Walks arm in arm with nature all his way;
> Compasses earth, dives into it, ascends
> Whatever steep inquiry recommends,
> Sees planetary wonders smoothly roll
> Round other systems under her control,
> Drinks wisdom at the milky stream of light
> That cheers the silent journey of the night,
> And brings, at his return, a bosom charged
> With rich instruction, and a soul enlarged.
> The treasured sweets of the capacious plan
> That heaven spreads wide before the view of man,
> All prompt his pleased pursuit, and to pursue
> Still prompt him, with a pleasure always new;
> He, too, has a connecting power, and draws
> Man to the centre of the common cause;
> Aiding a dubious and deficient sight
> With a new medium, and a purer light.
> All truth is precious, if not all divine;
> And what dilates the powers must needs refine.

894, 258. Sir Matthew Hale, 1609–76, was Chief Justice of England from 1671 to 1675, and
the author of many treatises on law, religion, and science, although his scientific treatises were
considered of little value even in his own day.

895, 334. *One sheltered hare.* See Cowper's charming description of "Puss" in the notes to
"Epitaph on a Hare."

897, 455–56. *Philips.* John Philips, author of *The Splendid Shilling.*

903, 765ff. *Brown.* "Capability Brown," a popular landscape gardener.

905. *Book IV. The Winter Evening.* "I see the winter approaching without much concern," Cowper wrote to Joseph Hill, Oct. 20, 1783, "though a passionate lover of fine weather and the pleasant scenes of summer; but the long evenings have their comforts too, and there is hardly to be found upon the earth, I suppose, so snug a creature as an Englishman by his fireside in the winter."

906, 86–87. *Katterfelto.* A conjuror and quack doctor from Prussia, who first visited London in 1782. He headed his advertisements in the newspapers with the words, "Wonders! wonders!"

907, 107–19. Cowper was a great lover of travel literature. In a letter to John Newton, October 6, 1783, he wrote, "I am much obliged to you for the voyages [Hawkesworth's], which I received, and began to read last night. My imagination is so captivated upon these occasions that I seem to partake with the navigators in all the dangers they encountered. I lose my anchor; my mainsail is rent into shreds; I kill a shark, and by signs converse with a Patagonian, and all this without moving from the fireside. The principal fruits of these circuits, that have been made around the globe, seem likely to be the amusement of those that stayed at home."

909, 243–66. Compare with Collins's "Ode to Evening."

911, 341–428. The sympathy, simplicity, and realism of these lines would be hard to match before Wordsworth. Lines 427–28 refer to Mr. Robert Smith of Nottingham whose charities Cowper had the grateful task of dispensing.

914, 513–52. Again Cowper permits himself to long for the fancied simplicity of a primitive age without quite accepting the ideas of the golden age held by the more radical primitivists.

918, 718–30. Abraham Cowley, 1618–67.

920.   ON THE RECEIPT OF MY MOTHER'S PICTURE

Although Cowper's mother had died when he was not quite six, he wrote to his friend Joseph Hill in November, 1784, "I can truly say that not a week passes (perhaps I might with equal veracity say a day), in which I do not think of her. Such was the impression her tenderness made upon me, though the opportunity she had of showing it was so short."

921, 97. From Garth, *Dispensary,* iii, line 226 .

922.   TO MARY

Written in 1793 in honor of Mrs. Unwin.

923.   THE CASTAWAY

In this poem, the last that he wrote (March 20, 1799), Cowper draws a parallel between himself and a sailor on Anson's ship who had been washed overboard on one of Anson's voyages of discovery. The poem is an expression of the profound religious despair of the closing years of Cowper's life. "Cowper's Spiritual Diary," written in 1795 and edited by Kenneth Povey, *London Mercury,* XV (1927), 493–96, is of interest in this connection.

923.   LETTERS

923a, 4. *Mrs. Cowper.* Frances Maria Cowper, cousin of the poet.
923a, 8. *Charles.* The son of Mrs. Mary Unwin.
924b, 38. *Johnson's biographies.* Johnson's *Lives of the Poets* were published in 1779–1781.
925b, 1. *The Rev. John Newton.* A clergyman of evangelical zeal who had in earlier days been captain of a slave-ship. He exercised a stern discipline over his spiritual charges. In 1767 Cowper and Mrs. Unwin had moved to Olney to be near him. In 1779 he had left Olney for a parish in London.
926a, 27. "You consider nothing concerning me foreign to you."
926a, 46. *it cost you nothing.* At this time the recipient of mail paid the postage.
927a, 32. "I am, as ever, your most zealous friend."
927a, 40. *four quires of verse.* The manuscript of *The Task,* published the following June.
927a, 46. *points.* Punctuation.
927b, 22. *to Mr. Throckmorton. The Task,* I, 262.
927b, 24. *to Mr. Smith. The Winter Evening,* 427–428.
928b, 6. *reviewer of my former volume.* Cowper published a volume of *Poems* in 1782, which was reviewed in the *Monthly Review* for October, 1782.
928b, 36. *Olio.* A miscellany.
929a, 43. *Lady Hesketh.* Cowper's cousin Harriet, widow of Sir Thomas Hesketh.
930a, 3. *when I am not at Troy.* Cowper was at this time engaged in translating Homer.

931a, 30. *Newport.* A village five miles from Olney. Cowper and Mrs. Unwin had in 1786 moved to the neighboring village of Weston-Underwood. Cowper had also had a recurrence of his mental derangement.

933a, 15. *as Virgil says.* In the *Æneid,* IX, 6–7.

933a, 28. *Mrs. King.* The wife of the Rev. Mr. John King, rector of Pertenhall, Bedfordshire.

933b, 28. *a lady.* Lady Austen, whose suggestion led to the composition of *The Task.*

934b, 12. *Boswell's Tour.* The *Tour to the Hebrides* had been published in 1785.

934b, 20. *Sir John.* Sir John Hawkins, a bristling and unamiable member of Johnson's circle, published a life of Johnson in 1787.

934b, 36. *John Johnson.* A young kinsman who was devoted to the poet.

938.   THE HOLY FAIR

The stanza of "The Holy Fair" is an adaptation of the old "Christis Kirk on the Green" stanza:

> Was nevir in Scotland hard nor sene
>   Sic dansing nor deray,
> Nowther at Faulkland on the grene
>   Nor Peblis at the play,
> As wes of wowaris, as I wene,
>   At Chryst kirk on ane day.
> Thair come out Kitteis, weschin clene,
>   In thair new Kirtillis of gray
>   Fu' gay
> At Christis Kirk on the Grene that day.

The Holy Fair was the name used in western Scotland for the annual celebration of the Lord's Supper. The tent-preaching went on outside of the church while the Communion service was held within.

941.   ADDRESS TO THE DEIL

Burns often in his correspondence referred to his "favourite hero, Milton's Satan." "I have bought a pocket Milton," he wrote to his friend William Nicol, in June, 1787, "which I carry perpetually about with me, in order to study the sentiments—the dauntless magnanimity; the intrepid unyielding independence; the desperate daring, and noble defiance of hardship, in that great personage, Satan." But it was chiefly the illiberal and often hypocritical attitude toward wrong-doing and wrong-doers on the part of the Kirk that instigated Burns's playful and sympathetic address. Incidentally the subject gives him an opportunity to recount the picturesque devil-lore of the folk. The 6 line stanza in *rime couée,* which is a favorite with him, was a very old stanzaic form which had been vigorously revived in the eighteenth century.

942.   THE COTTER'S SATURDAY NIGHT

This is one of the most Scottish in feeling and English in form and phrasing of Burns's poems. Burns is here using the Spenserian stanza which he got from Shenstone or Beattie. He took the hint for the poem from Fergusson's "Farmer's Ingle."

943, 1. *My . . . much respected friend.* Robert Aiken, Solicitor in Ayr. Burns called him in 1786 "my chief patron." He was among other things a noted elocutionist. Burns said of him that he "read him into fame."

948.   TO A MOUSE

Said by Gilbert Burns actually to have been composed while Burns was ploughing. The reader will find an excellent account of the growing sympathy for animals in eighteenth-century England in D. Harwood, *Love for Animals and How it Developed in Great Britain,* 1928. Burns and Cowper are the two poets of the later part of the century who did most toward creating a poetry of familiar but neglected animal life.

949.   EPISTLE TO JOHN LAPRAIK

John Lapraik, 1727–1807, was inspired by Burns's success to publish his own *Poems on Several Occasions,* 1788.

951. TO THE REVEREND JOHN M'MATH

This poem and "Holy Willie's Prayer" following were, for prudential reasons, withheld from publication during Burns's lifetime. They first appeared in Cromek's edition of 1808. The occasion for "Holy Willie's Prayer" was explained by Burns in a preface in the *Glenriddell Book* at Liverpool: "Argument.—Holy Willie [William Fisher] was a rather oldish bachelor elder, in the parish of Mauchline, and much and justly famed for that polemical chattering which ends in tippling orthodoxy, and for that spiritualized bawdry which refines to liquorish devotion. In a sessional process with a gentleman in Mauchline—a Mr. Gavin Hamilton—*Holy Willie* and his priest, Father Auld, after a full hearing in the Presbytery of Ayr, came off but second best, owing partly to the oratorical powers of Mr. Robert Aiken, Mr. Hamilton's counsel; but chiefly to Mr. Hamilton's being one of the most irreproachable and truly respectable characters in the country. On losing his process, the muse overheard him at his devotions, as follows."

The poem is a brilliant satire on the Calvinistic doctrine of election as it was then understood by the Scottish orthodox.

954. THE JOLLY BEGGARS

"The Jolly Beggars," by some considered Burns's masterpiece, was written in 1785 after a visit, tradition has it, to Poosie Nansie's brothel in Mauchline. There is some evidence that Burns had hoped to include the poem in the 1787 edition but was dissuaded, partly by Dr. Hugh Blair. At any rate the cantata remained unpublished until 1799 when it was included in the *Poetical Miscellany* published by Stewart and Meikle. An excellent summary of the beggar tradition in literature as well as the use of the opera or operetta form for its expression is to be found in *The Centenary Burns,* II, 291–304. Here, as nearly always, Burns has taken old poetical forms and themes and has transmuted them into pure art by the vigor of his genius and the breadth of his sympathy. In his *Commonplace Book,* he wrote, "I have often coveted the acquaintance of that part of mankind commonly known by the ordinary phrase of Blackguards, sometimes farther than was consistent with the safety of my character; those who by thoughtless prodigality, or headstrong passions have been driven to ruin;—though disgraced by follies, nay sometimes 'stained with guilt, and crimsoned o'er with crimes'; I have yet found among them, not a few instances, some of the noblest Virtues, Magnanimity, Generosity, disinterested friendship and even Modesty, in the highest perfection."

955, 35. *the heights of Abram.* The battle of the plains of Abraham, at Quebec, 1759.

955, 37. *Moro.* At Santiago de Cuba, 1762.

955, 38. *Curtis.* Sir Roger Curtis destroyed the Spanish floating batteries at the siege of Gibraltar, 1782.

955, 40. *Eliott.* George Augustus Eliott held Gibraltar in the famous siege of 1779–1782.

960. TAM O'SHANTER

Burns lived in the neighborhood of Alloway Kirk, a picturesque ruin. When Captain Grose was in Ayr collecting materials for his *Antiquities of Scotland,* Burns suggested a sketch of the church. "The Captain," Gilbert says, "agreed to the request, provided the poet would furnish a witch story to be printed along with it." Burns first sent Captain Grose in a letter, June, 1790, three current stories of the church, and later, "Tam o'Shanter." The poem was likewise published in the *Edinburgh Magazine* for March, 1791. Besides the old legend of which Burns has made use, he may have drawn a suggestion for his hero from Douglas Graham, a tenant of the farm of Shanter and owner of a boat named Tam o'Shanter. He was a noted tipler of the neighborhood.

Burns wrote to Mrs. Dunlop, April 11, 1791, "Indeed I look on your little Namesake [one of Burns's sons] to be my *chef d'oeuvre* in that species of manufacture, as I look on 'Tam o'Shanter' to be my standard performance in the Poetical line. 'Tis true, both the one and the other discover a spice of roguish waggery that might perhaps be as well spared; but then they also show in my opinion a force of genius and a finishing polish that I despair of ever excelling."

962. GREEN GROW THE RASHES

Suggested by an old song, a fragment of which Burns may have seen in Herd's *Ancient and Modern Scottish Songs:*

> Green grows the rashes—O
> Green grows the rashes—O

The feather-bed is no sae saft
As a bed amang the rashes.

963.   OF A' THE AIRTS

Note by Burns: "This air is by Marshall; the song I composed out of compliment to Mrs. Burns. N.B. It was during the honeymoon."

963.   HIGHLAND MARY

Burns wrote to George Thomson, November, 1792: "The foregoing Song pleases myself; I think it is in my happiest manner: you will see at first glance that it suits the air.—The Subject of the Song is one of the most interesting passages of my youthful days; and I own that I should be much flattered to see the verses set to an Air which would insure celebrity.—Perhaps, after all, 'tis the still glowing prejudice of my heart, that throws a borrowed lustre over the merits of the Composition."

For a discussion of Burns's relations to Mary Campbell, the subject of the poem, see F. B. Snyder, *op. cit.*, 129–46; Robert T. Fitzhugh, "Burns' Highland Mary," *PMLA*, LIJ (1937), 829–34 .

964.   THOU LINGERING STAR

This is another of the Mary Campbell poems. The occasion for the poem is thus described by Burns:

"My Highland lassie was as warm-hearted, charming young creature as ever blessed a man with generous love. After a pretty long tract of the most ardent reciprocal attachment, we met by appointment, on the second Sunday of May, in a sequestered spot by the banks of Ayr, where we spent the day in taking farewell, before she should embark for the West Highlands to arrange matters among her friends for our projected change of life. At the close of Autumn following she crossed the sea to meet me at Greenock, where she had scarce landed when she was seized with a malignant fever, which hurried my dear girl to the grave in a few days, before I could even hear of her illness."

964.   AFTON WATER

In a letter to Mrs. Dunlop, February 5, 1789, in which Burns enclosed a copy of this poem, he wrote. "There is a small river, Afton, that falls into Nith, near New Cumnock; which has some charming, wild, romantic scenery on its banks.—I have a particular pleasure in those little pieces of poetry such as our Scots songs &c. where the names and landskip-features of rivers, lakes or woodlands, that one knows, are introduced.—I attempted a compliment of that kind, to Afton. . . ."

965.   AE FOND KISS

Written to "Clarinda" (Mrs. McLehose) on the occasion of her departure in December of 1791 to join her husband in the West Indies.

965.   MY LUVE IS LIKE A RED RED ROSE

This song, like so many of Burns's, is made up from parts of several old songs. *The Centenary Burns* cites among others the following possible sources:

The Wanton Wife of Castle Gate

Her cheeks are like the Roses
That blossom fresh in June,
O, she's like a new-strung instrument
That's newly put in tune.

*The Loyal Lover's Faithful Promise to His Sweetheart at
His Going a Long Journey*

Altho' I go a thousand miles
I vow thy face to see,
Altho' I go ten thousand miles
I'll come again to thee, dear Love,
I'll come again to thee.

The day shall turn to Night, dear Love,
And the Rocks melt with the Sun,
Before that I prove false to thee
Before my Life is gone, dear Love,
Before my Life is gone.

The Young Man's Farewell to His Love

The seas they shall run dry,
And rocks melt into sands;
Then I'll love you still, my dear,
When all those things are done.

966.   AULD LANG SYNE

For a discussion of Burns's probable part in the composition of this famous song, see J. C. Dick, *The Songs of Robert Burns,* London, 1903, 433-40.

966.   GO FETCH TO ME A PINT O' WINE

Of this poem Burns wrote: "This air is Oswald's; the first stanza of the song is old, *the rest mine.*"

967.   SCOTS WHA HAE

Burns wrote to Thomson about August 30, 1793, "You know that my pretensions to musical taste are merely a few of Nature's instincts, untaught and untutored by Art.—For this reason, many musical compositions, particularly where much of the merit lies in Counterpoint, however they may transport and ravish the ears of you, Connoisseurs, affect my simple lug no otherwise than merely as melodious Din.—On the other hand, by way of amends, I am delighted with many little melodies, which the learned Musician despises as silly and insipid.—I do not know whether the old air, 'Hey tutti taitie,' may rank among this number; but well I know that, with Fraser's Hautboy, it has often filled my eyes with tears.—There is a tradition, which I have met with in many places of Scotland, that it was Robert Bruce's March at the battle of Bannockburn.—This thought, in my yesternight's evening walk, warmed me to a pitch of enthusiasm on the theme of Liberty and Independence, which I threw into a kind of Scots Ode, fitted to the Air, that one might suppose to be the gallant Royal Scot's Address to his heroic followers on that eventful morning.—

"So may God ever defend the cause of Truth and Liberty, as he did that day!—Amen.
                                                                "R. B.
"P. S. I showed the air to Urbani, who was highly pleased with it, and begged me to make soft verses for it; but I had no idea of giving myself any trouble on the subject, till the accidental recollection of that glorious struggle for Freedom, associated with the glowing ideas of some other struggles on the same nature, *not quite so ancient,* roused my rhyming Mania. . . ."

967.   O WERT THOU IN THE CAULD BLAST

Said to have been written during Burns's last illness.

969.   THE VILLAGE

In his "Preface" to the 1807 edition of his poems, Crabbe included the following note about *The Village:* "No man can, I think, publish a work without some expectation of satisfying those who are to be judge of its merit: but I can, with the utmost regard to veracity, speak my fears, as predominating over every pre-indulged thought of a more favorable nature, when I was told that a judge so discerning [as Dr. Johnson] had consented to read and give his opinion of *The Village,* the poem I had prepared for publication. The time of suspense was not long protracted. I was soon favored with a few words from Sir Joshua, who observed—'If I knew how cautious Doctor Johnson is in giving commendation, I should be well satisfied with the portion dealt to me in his letter.'—Of that letter the following is a copy:
    SIR,
I have sent you back Mr. Crabbe's poem; which I read with great delight. It is original, vigorous, and elegant. The alterations which I have made, I do not require him to adopt; for my lines are, perhaps, not often better [than] his own: but he may take mine and his own together,

and perhaps, between them, produce something better than either.—He is not to think his copy wantonly defaced: a wet sponge will wash all the red lines away, and leave the pages clean. —His Dedication will be least liked: it were better to contract it into a short sprightly address. —I do not doubt of Mr. Crabbe's success.

I am, Sir, your most humble servant,
SAM: JOHNSON.

March 4, 1783."

970, 27. *Save honest Duck.* Stephen Duck, the poetical thresher, who was made by Queen Caroline Keeper of her library at Richmond.

975, 303. From Goldsmith, *The Deserted Village;* see page 811, line 142.

976.   THE PARISH REGISTER

In the "Preface" to the 1807 edition of his poems, Crabbe makes the following statement about *The Parish Register:* "In the *Parish Register,* he will find an endeavor once more to describe village manners, not by adopting the notion of pastoral simplicity or assuming ideas of rustic barbarity, but by more natural views of the peasantry, considered as a mixed body of persons, sober or profligate, and hence, in a great measure, contented or miserable. To this more general description are added the various characters which occur in the three parts of a Register: Baptism, Marriages, and Burials."

978, 124. From Young, *Night Thoughts;* see page 518, line 387.

985.   LETTERS OF JUNIUS

985b, 21. *purchase of a corporation.* Corruption of a parliamentary constituency.

986a, 16. *domestic misfortune.* The duke's son had lately been killed by a fall from his horse. This son was the father of the fifth Duke of Bedford, to whom Burke addressed his *Letter to a Noble Lord.*

986a, 37. *interview.* At this interview, which passed at the house of the late Lord Eglintoun, Lord Bute told the duke that he was determined never to have any connection with a man who had so basely betrayed him. [Junius.]

986b, 6. *sale of a borough.* In an answer in Chancery, in a suit against him to recover a large sum paid him by a person whom he had undertaken to return to Parliament for one of his Grace's boroughs. He was compelled to repay the money. [Junius.]

986b, 9. *little corporation.* Of Bedford, where the tyrant was held in such contempt and detestation, that, in order to deliver themselves from him, they admitted a great number of strangers to the freedom. To make his defeat truly ridiculous, he tried his whole strength against Mr. Horne, and was beaten upon his own ground. [Junius.]

986b, 45. *recorded stripes.* Mr. Heston Homphrey, a country attorney, horsewhipped the duke with equal justice, severity, and perseverance, on the course at Lichfield. Rigby and Lord Trentham were also cudgelled in a most exemplary manner. [Junius.]

987a, 35. *Lord Egremont.* This man, notwithstanding his pride and Tory principles, had some English stuff in him. Upon an official letter he wrote to the Duke of Bedford, the duke desired to be recalled, and it was with the utmost difficulty that Lord Bute could appease him. [Junius].

987a, 45. *an administration.* Mr. Grenville, Lord Halifax, and Lord Egremont. [Junius.]

987b, 11. *all decency and respect.* The ministry having endeavored to exclude the Dowager out of the Regency Bill, the Earl of Bute determined to dismiss them. Upon this the Duke of Bedford demanded an audience of the King, reproached him in plain terms with his duplicity, baseness, falsehood, treachery, and hypocrisy—repeatedly gave him the lie, and left him in convulsions. [Junius.]

987b, 18. *plunder the treasury.* He received three thousand pounds for plate and equipage money. [Junius.]

987b, 42–46. When Earl Gower was appointed president of the council, the King, with his usual sincerity, assured him that he had not had one happy moment since the Duke of Bedford left him. [Junius.]

988a, 1. *dependants.* Lords Gower, Weymouth, and Sandwich. [Junius.]

988a, 26. *Mackenzie.* Bedford's domineering use of his political power was illustrated in 1765, when he successfully insisted upon the dismissal of Lord Bute's own brother, Stuart Mackenzie, from an office which the King had solemnly promised him for life.

989b, 19. *pernicious lessons.* The plan of tutelage and future dominion over the heir-apparent, laid many years ago at Carlton House, between the Princess Dowager and her favorite, the Earl of Bute, was as gross and palpable as that which was concerted between Anne of Austria and Cardinal Mazarin, to govern Louis the Fourteenth and in effect to prolong his minority until the end of their lives. [Junius.]

990a, 38. *renounced the name of Englishman.* "Born and educated in this country, I glory in the name of Briton, and the peculiar happiness of my life will ever consist in promoting the welfare of a people whose loyalty and warm affection to me I consider as the greatest and most permanent security of my throne."—Speech of the King, November 18, 1760.

990a, 48. *novelty of their affections.* Alluding to the popularity in Scotland of the pretensions of the Stuarts, as late as the Rebellion of 1745.

990b, 24. *remove the ablest servants.* One of the first acts of the present reign was to dismiss Mr. Legge, because he had some years before refused to yield his interest in Hampshire to a Scotchman recommended by Lord Bute. This was the reason publicly assigned by his lordship. [Junius.]

991a, 2. *formal attack.* John Wilkes in his short-lived periodical, the *North Briton* (1763). By arresting him and expelling him from Parliament, the government succeeded only in making the profligate and hitherto obscure Wilkes into one of the great and popular martyrs of English liberty.

991b, 27. *enormous attack.* In 1769, to the cry of "Wilkes and Liberty," Middlesex elected him to the House of Commons, but a servile house ejected him. The government was then charged with violating the constitutional right of free representation.

992b, 51. *miserable governor.* Viscount Townshend, sent over on the plan of being resident governor. The history of his ridiculous administrations shall not be lost to the public. [Junius.]

993a, 18. *personal part.* In the King's speech of November 8, 1768, it was declared "That the spirit of faction had broken out afresh in some of the colonies, and, in one of them, proceeded to acts of violence and resistance to the execution of the laws;—that Boston was in a state of disobedience to all law and government, and had proceeded to measures subversive of the constitution, and attended with circumstances that manifested a disposition to throw off their dependence on Great Britain." [Junius.]

993b, 52. *unhappy Charles.* Junius is alluding to the history of Charles I in 1646 and 1647.

995b, 37. *Pardon this man.* Wilkes was then in prison.

998.   REFLECTIONS ON THE REVOLUTION IN FRANCE

998a, 10. *a letter.* The *Reflections,* although in form a printed letter to a "gentleman in Paris," becomes in places an address to the French people.

1003b, 35. Virgil, *Æneid,* I, 140: "In that palace let Æolus proudly boast and exercise sway in the close prison of the winds."

1006a, 22–26. Horace, *Ars Poetica,* 465–66: "[Empedocles, ambitious of being esteemed an immortal god,] leaped in cold blood into burning Ætna. Let poets have the licence to perish as they please."

1006b, 9. Juvenal, VII, 151: "[What iron bowels must the teacher of rhetoric have] when the school-boys [in their orations] slay the cruel tyrants!"

1007b, 49. Another of these reverend gentlemen, who was witness to some of the spectacles which Paris has lately exhibited, expresses himself thus:—"*A king dragged in submissive triumph by his conquering subjects,* is one of those appearances of grandeur which seldom rise in the prospect of human affairs, and which, during the remainder of my life, I shall think of with wonder and gratification." These gentlemen agree marvellously in their feelings. [Burke.]

1008a, 7. *Peters. State Trials,* vol. ii, pp. 360, 363. [Burke.] The Rev. Hugh Peters, a Dissenting preacher, who rose to prominence during the Civil War, and was tried and executed along with other regicides in 1660.

1009b, 45. Lucan, *Pharsalia,* IX, 207: "Neither pretence of military authority nor any appearance of being a senate."

1010a, 18. *a day.* 6th of October, 1789. [Burke.]

1010b, 39. *Lèse-nation.* Violation of the dignity of the people. Burke implies that the new democracy is as intolerant and oppressive as the old law of *lèse-majesté.*

1012a, 8. Tous les Évêques à la lanterne. [Burke.]

1012b, 52. *a sovereign.* Maria Theresa, Empress of Austria.

1014a, 47. Horace, *Ars Poetica,* 99: "It is not enough that poems be beautiful: let them be tender and affecting."

1015b, 13. Virgil, *Æneid,* III, 105: "the cradle of our race."

1017b, 51. *Lord George Gordon*. A fanatic, who led the "No-Popery" riots of 1780, for which he was charged with high treason, but acquitted. In 1787 he was convicted of libelling the Queen of France and the French ambassador, and sentenced to five years' imprisonment in Newgate. He had recently become a proselyte to Judaism.

1019a, 45–54. The English are, I conceive, misrepresented in a letter published in one of the papers, by a gentleman thought to be a dissenting minister. When writing to Dr. Price of the spirit which prevails in Paris, he says: "The spirit of the people in this place has abolished all the proud *distinctions* which the *king* and *nobles* had usurped in their minds: whether they talk of *the king, the noble, or the priest*, their whole language is that of the most *enlightened and liberal amongst the English.*" If this gentleman means to confine the terms *enlightened and liberal* to one set of men in England, it may be true. It is not generally so. [Burke.]

1023b, 4. *people at large*. Quicquid multis peccatur inultum. [Burke, quoting Lucan, *Pharsalia*, V, 260: "The sin of the multitude always goes unpunished."]

1025.   A LETTER TO A NOBLE LORD

In 1794, with the close of the trial of Hastings, Burke, in his sixty-fourth year, retired from the House of Commons, and his son Richard was nominated for his place. It was proposed to raise Burke to the peerage, with the title of Lord Beaconsfield. But Richard died in August, 1794, in the midst of these preparations. Burke, left childless and desolate, had no further interest in titular honors, but he accepted as a reward for his life of service to his country, a pension, conferred by the Crown and, to Burke's chagrin, not submitted to Parliament for ratification. Francis Russell (1762–1802), fifth Duke of Bedford, who as a follower of Charles James Fox declared himself in sympathy with the French Revolution and opposed the government, attacked Burke's pension in the House of Lords. Burke took up the gage of the Duke, to whose grandfather Junius had directed some of his most scathing letters. The veteran dealt with the imprudent young peer in his *Letter to a Noble Lord*, which Morley has called "the most splendid repartee in the English language."

1026a, 5. *Duke of Orleans*. He had gone over to the Revolution and voted for the death of Louis XVI, his cousin.

1026a, 7. *Brissot*. A leader of the Girondist party, guillotined after his fall from power in October, 1793.

1026a, 23. *Priestleys*. Dr. Joseph Priestley, a political liberal, also remembered as the discoverer of oxygen; his house in Birmingham was burned by a mob in 1791.

1026b, 9. *made into a drum*. John Zisca (1360–1424), leader of the Hussites, desired that upon his death his skin should be made into drum-heads and so continue to molest his enemies.

1026b, 51. *unplumb*. The revolutionists dug up graves for lead coffins, with which to make bullets.

1027b, 7. *Corresponding Society*. This organization, with local branches in many English cities, was active in spreading revolutionary doctrines.

1028a, 9. *Brentford*. For the "two Kings of Brentford," ridiculous puppets without individuality, see Buckingham's play, *The Rehearsal* (1671).

1028a, 30. "How much was it worth." Familiar Latin of the law courts.

1028b, 23. Ovid, *Metamorphoses*, II, 72: "I struggle against opposition."

1029a, 39. Both Barré and Dunning were granted pensions in 1782 by the Rockingham ministry.

1029b, 11. *a name ever dear to me*. The Marquis of Rockingham.

1030b, 32. *sans-culottes*: "without breeches." Ragged and slovenly dress became an affectation among the more radical groups of the French Revolution, and even such an English dandy as Charles James Fox assumed slovenliness to indicate his Revolutionary sympathies.

1030b, 51. Tacitus, *De Oratoribus*, 35: "He ordered closed this school of impudence."

1031a, 54. *Paradise Lost*, I, 196.

1032a, 7. *Herald's College*. Keeps records of the armorial bearings and genealogies of families entitled to them. The Garters, Norroys, etc., are officers of the College.

1032a, 36. *Guillim, Edmondson, and Collins*. English authorities on the peerage.

1032a, 42. *Aulnager*. Inspector of weight and quality of wool.

1032b, 31. *murder*. See the history of the melancholy catastrophe of the Duke of Buckingham. Temp. Henry VIII. [Burke.]

1037b, 5. *metaphysician*. Burke distrusted *a priori* political theorists.

1038a, 18. James Harrington (1611–77), a friend of Milton, Described an ideal commonwealth in his *Oceana*.

1038a, 26. *Abbé Sieyès.* One of the philosophers and doctrinaire constitution-makers of the French Revolution.

1038a, 36. *Boue de Paris.* Paris mud.

1038b, 23–30. Burke is, of course, alluding to the titles and possessions of the wealthy Duke of Bedford.

1038b, 39. Legendre (1752–1833), an eminent mathematician.

1039a, 9–10. Pope, *Essay on Man,* I, 83–84.

1039a, 25. *Lord Keppel.* Admiral in the Seven Years' War. After an unsuccessful battle with the French in 1778, Keppel was tried by a court-martial in 1779 and acquitted, but ordered to strike his flag. He died in 1786.

1040a, 19–26. In 1795 the French army overran the Netherlands, expelled the reigning house and established a republic. Burke refers to William III of England (1688–1702), whose arrival from Holland made possible the Revolution of 1688.

1040b, 36. *peace with Regicide.* Louis XVI was executed on January 21, 1793; on February 1, the Convention declared war against England and Holland. Burke's enemies contended that his *Reflections* had so inflamed public opinion as to make the war inevitable.

1041.   THE RIGHTS OF MAN

1046b, 39–44. Burke asked "could I, in common sense, ten years ago, have felicitated France," *etc.?* Paine perverted the passage.

1047b, 41. *Lord George Gordon.* Burke alluded to him in the *Reflections.* See page 1017.

1053.   POETICAL SKETCHES

The poems of this collection were printed in 1783. They are said by the Rev. Henry Mathew, who wrote a kindly, if patronizing, preface to the book, to have been written by Blake between the ages of twelve and twenty. They show interesting experiments in rhythm and rhyme. Note especially the experiment in approximate rhyming in the song beginning, "Fresh from the dewy hill," and the metrical felicity of "Mad Song." While there are many echoes of the Elizabethans and even of Chatterton and Macpherson in the *Poetical Sketches,* such lines as

> Let thy west wind sleep on
> The lake; speak silence with thy glimmering eyes,
> And wash the dusk with silver,

show a remarkable and original command of both imagery and lyric movement.

                                    TO THE EVENING STAR

1053, 2. *while.* For this reading instead of *whilst,* see G. Keynes, *Blake Studies,* p. 33.

                                    MAD SONG

1054, 4. *infold.* For this reading instead of the former *unfold,* as well as *birds* of dawn (l. 7) instead of *beds* of dawn, see G. Keynes, *op. cit.,* pp. 30–32.

1055.   SONGS OF INNOCENCE AND OF EXPERIENCE

These two books are usually printed together because Blake so combined them in 1794, although the *Songs of Innocence* had been etched in 1789 and other poems had intervened before the etching of *Songs of Experience.* These two books, like so many of Blake's, were printed by him by hand from copper plates on which both the text and marginal designs were etched in relief. The sheets were then colored, some by Blake and some by his wife. The coloring is different in different copies and the order of the plates varies. Since it is impossible to reproduce the plates in this volume, perhaps Swinburne's description of them may in some measure fill their place and suggest their beauty and importance: ". . . the infinite delight of those drawings, sweeter to see than music to hear, where herb and stem break into grace of shape and blossom of form, and the branch-work is full of little flames and flowers, catching as it were from the verse enclosed the fragrant heat and delicate sound they seem to give back; where colour lapses into light and light assumes feature in colour. If elsewhere the artist's strange strength of thought and hand is more visible, nowhere is there such pure sweetness and singleness of design in his work. All the tremulous and tender splendour of spring is mixed into the written word and coloured draught; every page has the smell of April. Over all things given, the sleep of flocks and the growth of leaves, the laughter in dividing lips of flowers and the music at the moulded mouth of the flute player, there is cast a pure fine veil of light, softer than sleep and keener than sunshine. The sweetness of sky and leaf, of grass and water—the bright light life of bird and child and beast—is so to speak kept fresh by some graver sense of faithful and mysterious love, explained and vivified by a conscience and purpose in the Artist's hand and mind. Such a fiery outbreak of spring, such an insurrection of fierce floral life and radiant riot of childish power and pleasure, no poet or painter ever gave before: such lustre of green leaves and flushed limbs, kindled cloud and fervent fleece, was never wrought into speech or shape."

1055.   SONGS OF INNOCENCE

There is an excellent discussion of this book in P. Berger, *William Blake, Poet and Mystic,* 284–304.

1059.   SONGS OF EXPERIENCE

The clue to the interpretation of the *Songs of Experience* lies in Blake's subtitle, "Shewing the Two Contrary States of the Human Soul." Some of these songs cast on the love and faith and imagination of childhood the sinister light of experience; others tell what happens to childhood when it encounters the world of selfishness and materialism. They are a protest against every form of tyranny. If one bears in mind Blake's ideas about the limitations of reason and the holiness of imagination, explained in the introduction, there will be little difficulty in the interpretation of the symbols.

1059.   INTRODUCTION AND EARTH'S ANSWER

As the stars are usually associated with Urizen, the "Father of the Ancient Men," the "starry floor" would seem to mean the barrier that shuts man off from eternity. "The wat'ry shore," is an allusion to the sea of time and space, or of materialism.

1060.   THE SICK ROSE

The rose symbolizes love; the worm, the flesh; the night, experience; the storm, materialism.

1060.   THE TIGER

As Mr. Damon has pointed out, this poem raises in Blake's most magnificent imagery the problem of good and evil in relation to God. The Tiger represents the wrath of God. The question stated is, how are the wrath of God and the punishment of sin to be reconciled with the forgiveness of sin (the Lamb)?

It is interesting to compare the final version of the poem with this earlier version:

> Tyger, Tyger, burning bright
> In the forests of the night,
> What immortal hand or eye
> Dare frame thy fearful symmetry?
>
> Burnt in distant deeps or skies
> The cruel fire of thine eyes?
> On what wings dare he aspire?
> What the hand dare sieze the fire?
>
> And what shoulder and what art
> Could twist the sinews of thy heart?
> And when thy heart began to beat
> What dread hand and what dread feet
>
> Could fetch it from the furnace deep
> And in thy horrid ribs dare steep
> In the well of sanguine woe?
> In what clay and in what mould
> Were thy eyes of fury rolled?

Where the hammer? Where the chain?
In what furnace was thy brain?
What the anvil? What dread grasp
Dare its deadly terrors clasp?

When the stars threw down their spears
And watered heaven with their tears
Dare he laugh his work to see?
Dare he who made the lamb make thee?

Tyger, Tyger, burning bright
In the forests of the night,
What immortal hand and eye
Dare frame thy fearful symmetry?

1061.   TO TIRZAH

Tirzah is one of Blake's names for Nature, thought of as the mother of man. This poem gives expression to Blake's idea that the creation of man was a descent and a limiting of eternal spirit. Salvation can only come to man through following the example of the perfect love and selflessness of Christ.

1062.   THE BOOK OF THEL

This poem, which was engraved in 1789, is usually not included in the symbolic books because it merely touches the outer kingdoms of Blake's mythological world. It contains, however, some of his most characteristic ideas. Thel, in her spirit state, shrinks from descent into transient mortal form. The Lily of the Valley, the Cloud, the Worm, and the Clod of Clay give her the answer, found often in Blake's poetry, that, however transient the life of the body may be, salvation of the spirit is possible through the sacrifice of the self to the service of others, all life being interdependent. Section IV is the only one that offers any difficulty of interpretation. At the invitation of the Clod of Clay, Thel enters the material world to view her own future grave-plot (the body), but, instead of being reassured, she flees from the terror and the wonder of the five senses by which her spirit is to be enclosed, and through which she, in her mortal state, would find passion (symbolized by Luvah in the poem). For Thel is the "virgin" and therefore, in Blake's ideology, not the perfect woman. She is not yet ready, Blake would seem to suggest by the prefatory motto, to sacrifice herself through passion to find her immortality in an endless chain of generation.

1065.   THE FRENCH REVOLUTION

Book I of *The French Revolution* was set up in type by the bookseller, Joseph Johnson, in 1791, but it apparently did not get beyond page proof. It was first published in 1913 by Dr. Sampson in the Oxford edition of Blake. It was called "A Poem in Seven Books" but no trace of the other books has been found.

1065, 7. *Necker*. Controller General; represented by Blake as the idol of the people.

1065, 16. *For the Commons convene in the Hall of the Nation.* On June 17, 1789 the Third Estate called itself the National Assembly.

1067, 83. *Duke of Burgundy.* Represents the spirit of war.

1071.   THE MARRIAGE OF HEAVEN AND HELL

When Blake speaks in this poem of a "new heaven" begun thirty-three years ago, he is referring to a declaration of Swedenborg made in 1757. On this internal evidence *The Marriage of Heaven and Hell* is sometimes dated 1790. Mr. Geoffrey Keynes, however, dates it about 1793.

The Song of Liberty is bound with it in all of the known copies. By some editors the former is thought to be of later date than *The Marriage of Heaven and Hell*, but Max Plowman has given reason to believe that it was intended by Blake as the culminating song of triumph.

The Marriage of Heaven and Hell has been one of the most popular of Blake's prophetic books partly because it is one of the most lucid and straightforward statements of his concept of good and evil—an invaluable document for the understanding of the rest of Blake—and partly for the pungency of its expression and challenge of its paradoxical ideas. To quote from Swinburne, "the humour is of that fierce grave sort, whose cool insanity of manner is more horrible and more obscure to the Philistine than any sharp edge of burlesque or glitter of irony; it is huge, swift, inexplicable; hardly laughable through its enormity of laughter, hardly significant through its condensation of meaning; but as true and thoughtful as the greatest humourist's. The variety and audacity of thoughts and words are incomparable: not less so their fervour and beauty."

The scheme of the whole is really simple although it looks complex. The first section which includes the "Proverbs of Hell" announces and elaborates the theme, the theory of contraries. What is called good is merely conventionalized morality, negative at best, hypocritical and cruel at its worst. The just man, finding his gentleness hypocritically assumed by the evil man, is forced to assume rage in self-defense. This theme, announced in the "Argument," and interpreted in conjunction with Blake's conception of reason, gives one the clue to the interpretation of the opposition of reason and energy and the paradoxical handling of the terms good and evil throughout.

The second section, which extends to (but not through) the "Memorable Fancy" beginning "An Angel came to me," deals with the development of religious thought. The chief difficulty is in the description of the "Printing-house in Hell" which seems to be an exposition of the creative process rather than the process of dissemination of knowledge. The Dragons probably symbolize the instincts; the Viper, reason; the Eagle, inspiration; the Lions, just wrath.

In the "Memorable Fancy" devoted to the revelation of the Angel, Blake associates the Angel with the barren metaphysician who can produce "only Analytics." He can reveal to Blake therefore nothing but darkness and commotion, whereas the simple faith of the poet, left to itself, sees only beauty and peace.

After a digression in criticism of Swedenborg, Blake gives a statement of the true religion. *A Song of Liberty* which follows is an ecstatic prophecy of the fall of reason and jealousy, and the triumph of love and imagination. The poem opens with a description of the ominous condition of the world. Into this world comes the "new-born terror," probably Orc, passion informed by imagination. Urizen, terrified, casts out Orc, who falls into the "western sea" and gives rise to revolution, first in America, then in Europe. Urizen is finally defeated and his "stony law" is stamped to dust. The reign of universal brotherhood succeeds.

1078. AUGURIES OF INNOCENCE

This succession of proverbs from the Pickering MS was probably jotted down by Blake without much thought about its arrangement. The title may not have been intended to apply to the whole collection.

1079. LINES FROM MILTON

These lines are Blake's most beautiful expression of his beliefs about the ancient Druids. Blake adopted and adapted these ideas from the cult known in his day as Druidism. He believed that the Druids were the first men, symbolized by him as Albion. Their home was in the British Isles. From them came all civilization and all religion. He says in his *Descriptive Catalogue*, "Adam was a Druid, and Noah also; Abraham was called to succeed the Druidical Age." At the fall the Jews were separated from Albion and founded Jerusalem. At the regeneration of man they will return and help humanity (now symbolized by Christ) build a new Jerusalem in "England's green and pleasant land." See M. Saurat's *Blake and Modern Thought*, 51–85.

BIBLIOGRAPHY

The following selective list of books and articles is intended to supplement the list given at the end of the introduction to each author in the body of the book. When the place of publication of a volume is omitted, it is either London or New York. The following abbreviations have been used:

ELH, Journal of English Literary History
ES, Englische Studien
HLQ, Huntington Library Quarterly
JEGP, Journal of English and Germanic Philology
JHI, Journal of History of Ideas
MLN, Modern Language Notes
MLQ, Modern Language Quarterly
MP, Modern Philology
N&Q, Notes and Queries
PMLA, Publications of the Modern Language Association of America
PQ, Philological Quarterly
RES, Review of English Studies
SP, Studies in Philology
TLS, Times Literary Supplement (London)

I. BIBLIOGRAPHICAL AIDS

ANNUAL BIBLIOGRAPHY OF ENGLISH LANGUAGE AND LITERATURE. Edited for the Modern Humanities Research Association. Cambridge, Eng. 1920 and later.

BIBLIOGRAPHY OF BRITISH HISTORY: THE EIGHTEENTH CENTURY 1714-1789. Edited by Stanley Pargellis and D. J. Medley. Oxford. 1951.

CAMBRIDGE BIBLIOGRAPHY OF ENGLISH LITERATURE. Edited by F. W. Bateson. 4 Vols. Cambridge, 1940.

ENGLISH LITERATURE 1660-1800: A BIBLIOGRAPHY OF MODERN STUDIES COMPILED FOR PHILOLOGICAL QUARTERLY. By Ronald S. Crane, Louis I. Bredvold, Richmond P. Bond, Arthur Friedman, and Louis A. Landa. Vol. I: 1926-1938. Princeton. 1950. Vol II: 1939-1950. Princeton, 1952. Continued annually in *PQ* (Iowa City, Iowa).

NORTHUP, CLARK S. A Register of Bibliographies of English Language and Literature. New Haven. 1925.

TOBIN, JAMES E. Eighteenth Century English Literature and Its Cultural Background. 1939.

II. LITERARY CRITICISM AND HISTORY

THE AGE OF JOHNSON: ESSAYS PRESENTED TO CHAUNCEY BREWSTER TINKER. New Haven. 1949.

ALDEN, R. M. The Rise of Formal Satire in England. Philadelphia. 1899.

ALLEN, B. SPRAGUE. Tides in English Taste (1619-1800). 2 vols. Cambridge, Mass. 1937.

ARTHOS, JOHN. The Language of Natural Description in Eighteenth-Century Poetry. (*University of Michigan Publications: Language and Literature,* XXIV.) Ann Arbor, Mich. 1949.

AUBIN, R. Topographical Poetry in Eighteenth-Century England. 1936.

BABBITT, IRVING. The New Laocoon: An Essay on the Confusion of the Arts. 1910.

BALDWIN, EDWARD C. The Relation of the Seventeenth Century Character to the Periodical Essay. *PMLA,* XIX (1904), 75-114.

BATE, WALTER J. From Classic to Romantic: Premises of Taste in Eighteenth-Century England. Cambridge, Mass. 1946.

BEERS, HENRY A. A History of English Romanticism in the Eighteenth Century. 1898.

BELJAME, ALEXANDRE. Men of Letters and the English Public in the Eighteenth Century, 1660-1744. Edited by Bonamy Dobrée, translated by E. O. Lorimer. 1948.

BERNBAUM, ERNEST. Guide through the Romantic Movement. Revised edition. 1949.

BOND, RICHMOND P. English Burlesque Poetry, 1700-1750. Cambridge, Mass. 1932.
BRAY, RENÉ. La formation de la doctrine classique en France. Paris. 1927.
BREDVOLD, LOUIS I. The Literature of the Restoration and the Eighteenth Century, 1660-1798. Book III in *A History of English Literature*. Edited by Hardin Craig. 1950.
BROWN, WALLACE C. The Triumph of Form; A Study of the Later Masters of the Heroic Couplet. Chapel Hill, N.C. 1948.
BUTT, JOHN E. The Augustan Age. 1950.
CAZAMIAN, LOUIS. L'évolution psychologique et la littérature en Angleterre. Paris. 1920.
CHARLANNE, L. L'influence française en Angleterre au dix-septième siècle. Paris. 1906.
CLARK, A. F. B. Boileau and the French Classical Critics in England (1660-1800). Paris. 1925.
CLARK, KENNETH. The Gothic Revival. 1928.
CLIFFORD, JAMES L., and LOUIS A. LANDA (eds.). Pope and His Contemporaries: Essays Presented to George Sherburn. Oxford. 1949.
COLLINS, A. S. Authorship in the Days of Johnson, 1726-1780. 1927.
————. The Profession of Letters, 1780-1832. 1927.
————. Some Aspects of Copyright from 1700 to 1780. *Library*, VII (1926), 67-81.
CONANT, MARTHA. The Oriental Tale in England in the Eighteenth Century. 1908.
CONGLETON, J. E. Theories of Pastoral Poetry in England, 1684-1798. Gainesville, Fla. 1952.
COURTHOPE, W. J. History of English Poetry. Vols. IV, V, VI. 1903, 1905, 1910.
————. Life in Poetry: Law in Taste. 1901.
CRANE, RONALD S. Neo-Classical Criticism, in *Dictionary of World Literature*, edited by J. T. Shipley. 1943.
CROLL, MORRIS W. Attic Prose in the Seventeenth Century. *SP*, XVIII (1921), 79-128.
————. The Baroque Style in Prose. [Klaeber] *Studies in English Philology*. Minneapolis. 1929. Pp. 427-55.
DE MAAR, HARKO G. A History of Modern English Romanticism. Vol. I. 1924.
DENNIS, JOHN. The Age of Pope. 1901.
DOBSON, AUSTIN. Eighteenth Century Vignettes. First series, 1892; second series, 1894; third series, 1896.
————. A Paladin of Philanthropy. 1899.
————. Side-Walk Studies. 1902.
————. At Prior Park. 1912.
DURHAM, WILLARD H. Critical Essays of the Eighteenth Century. New Haven. 1915.
DURLING, DWIGHT L. The Georgic Tradition in English Poetry. 1935.
DYSON, H. V. D., and JOHN E. BUTT. Augustans and Romantics, 1689-1830. 1940.
ELTON, OLIVER. The Augustan Ages. 1899.
————. A Survey of English Literature, 1730-1780. 2 vols. 1928.
————. A Survey of English Literature, 1780-1832. 2 vols. 1912.
ESSAYS IN THE EIGHTEENTH CENTURY PRESENTED TO DAVID NICHOL SMITH. Oxford, 1945.
FAIRCHILD, HOXIE N. The Noble Savage: A Study in Romantic Naturalism. 1928.
————. Religious Trends in English Poetry. 3 vols. 1939-1949.
FARLEY, FRANK E. Scandinavian Influences in the English Romantic Movement. Boston. 1903.
FOLKIERSKI, WLADYSLAW. Entre le classicisme et le romantisme: Étude sur l'esthétique et les esthéticiens du dix-huitième Siècle. Paris. 1925.
FRANTZ, R. W. The English Traveller and the Movement of Ideas, 1660-1732. Lincoln, Nebraska. 1934.
GARNETT, RICHARD. The Age of Dryden. 1897, 1907.
GILLOT, HUBERT. La querelle des Anciens et des Modernes en France. Paris. 1914.
GOSSE, EDMUND. From Shakespeare to Pope: an inquiry into the causes and phenomena of the rise of classical poetry in England. Cambridge. 1885.
————. A History of Eighteenth Century Literature (1660-1780). 1888.
GRAHAM, WALTER. English Literary Periodicals. 1930.
GREENOUGH, CHESTER N. The Development of the *Tatler* Particularly in Regard to News. *PMLA*, XXXI (1916), 633-62.
GRIERSON, H. J. C. Classical and Romantic. Cambridge. 1923. (Reprinted in *The Background of English Literature*. 1925.)
————. Cross Currents in English Literature of the XVIIth Century; or the World, the Flesh, and the Spirit, Their Actions and Reactions. 1929.
HAFERKORN, REINHARD. Gotik und Ruine in der Englischen Dichtung des achtzehnten Jahrhunderts. (*Beiträge zur Englischen Philologie*, IV.) Leipzig. 1924.

HAMELIUS, PAUL. Die Kritik in der Englischen Literatur des 17. und 18. Jahrhunderts. Leipzig. 1897.

HAVENS, RAYMOND D. The Influence of Milton on English Poetry. Cambridge, Mass. 1922.

HAZLITT, WILLIAM. Lectures on the English Comic Writers. 1819.

HETTNER, HERMANN. Geschichte der Englischen Literatur von der Wiederherstellung des Königthums bis in die zweite Hälfte des achtzehnten Jahrhunderts, 1660-1770. Braunschweig, 6th edition. 1912.

HOOKER, EDWARD N. The Discussion of Taste, from 1750 to 1770, and the New Trends in Literary Criticism. *PMLA*, XLIX (1934), 577-92.

——. Humour in the Age of Pope. *HLQ*, XI (1948), 361-85.

——. The Reviewers and the New Criticism, 1754-1770. *PQ*, XII (1934), 189-202.

HUSSEY, CHRISTOPHER. The Picturesque. Studies in a Point of View. 1927.

JACK, IAN. Augustan Satire: Intention and Idiom in English Poetry, 1660-1750. Oxford. 1952.

JONES, HOWARD M. American Prose Style: 1700-1770. *Huntington Library Bulletin*, no. vi (1934), 115-151.

JONES, RICHARD F. and OTHERS WRITING IN HIS HONOR. Studies in the History of English Thought and Literature from Bacon to Pope. Stanford, Calif. 1951.

KITCHIN, GEORGE. A Survey of Burlesque and Parody in English. Edinburgh. 1931.

LEMONNIER, LÉON. Les Poètes anglais du dix-huitième siècle. Paris. 1947.

LEONARD, S. A. The Doctrine of Correctness in English Usage, 1700-1800. (*University of Wisconsin Studies in Language and Literature*, no. 25.) Madison, Wis. 1929.

LONGAKER, MARK. English Biography in the Eighteenth Century. Philadelphia. 1931.

LOVEJOY, ARTHUR O. Essays in the History of Ideas. Baltimore. 1948.

McCUTCHEON, ROGER P. Eighteenth Century English Literature. 1949.

McKILLOP, ALAN D. English Literature from Dryden to Burns. 1948.

MANWARING, ELIZABETH W. Italian Landscape in Eighteenth Century England. 1925.

MARR, G. S. The Periodical Essayists of the Eighteenth Century. 1924.

MILLAR, JOHN H. The Mid-Eighteenth Century. Edinburgh. 1902.

MINTO, WILLIAM. The Literature of the Georgian Era. (Ed. Knight.) 1895.

MITCHELL, W. FRASER. English Pulpit Oratory from Andrewes to Tillotson. A Study of its Literary Aspects. 1932.

MONK, SAMUEL H. The Sublime: A Study of Critical Theories in XVIII-Century England. 1935.

MOORE, CECIL A. Backgrounds of English Literature 1700-1760. Minneapolis, Minn. 1953.

MORE, PAUL ELMER. With the Wits. (Shelburne Essays, tenth series.) 1919.

MORISON, STANLEY. The English Newspaper: Some account of the physical development of journals printed in London between 1622 and the present day. Cambridge, Eng. 1932.

NICHOLS, JOHN. Literary Anecdotes of the Eighteenth Century. 9 vols. 1812-1816.

——. Illustrations of the Literary History of the Eighteenth Century. 8 vols. 1817-1858.

OMOND, T. S. English Metrists in the Eighteenth and Nineteenth Centuries. 1907.

PERRY, THOMAS S. English Literature in the Eighteenth Century. 1883.

PHELPS, WILLIAM LYON. The Beginnings of the English Romantic Movement. Boston. 1893.

PREVITÉ-ORTON, C. W. Political Satire in English Poetry. Cambridge, Eng. 1910.

QUAYLE, THOMAS. Poetic Diction: A Study of Eighteenth Century Verse. 1924.

READ, HERBERT. English Prose Style. 1928.

——. Reason and Romanticism. 1926.

ROBERTSON, JOHN G. Studies in the Genesis of Romantic Theory in the Eighteenth Century. Cambridge, Eng. 1923.

SAINTSBURY, GEORGE. A History of English Prosody. 3 vols. Vol. II. 1908.

——. The Peace of the Augustans. 1916.

SCHELLING, FELIX E. Ben Jonson and the Classical School. *PMLA*, XIII (1898), 221-49.

SCHÖFFLER, HERBERT. Protestantismus und Literatur. Leipzig. 1922.

SECCOMBE, THOMAS. The Age of Johnson. 1900.

SHERBURN, GEORGE. The Restoration and Eighteenth Century (1660-1789). Book III in *A Literary History of England*. Edited by Albert C. Baugh. 1948.

SMITH, D. NICHOL. Some Observations on Eighteenth Century Poetry. 1937.

SMITH, LOGAN PEARSALL. Four Words: Romantic, Originality, Creative, Genius. Oxford. 1924. (Also in *Words and Idioms*. 1925.)

SNYDER, E. D. The Celtic Revival in English Literature, 1760-1800. Cambridge, Mass. 1923.

SPINGARN, J. E. (ed.). Critical Essays of the Seventeenth Century. 3 vols. Oxford, 1908-09.

STAUFFER, D. A. The Art of Biography in Eighteenth Century England. 2 vols. Princeton. 1941.

SUTHERLAND, JAMES. A Preface to Eighteenth Century Poetry. Oxford. 1948.
SWEDENBERG, H. T., JR. The Theory of the Epic in England, 1650-1800. *(University of California Publications in English,* XV.) Berkeley and Los Angeles. 1944.
THACKERAY, WILLIAM M. English Humorists of the Eighteenth Century. 1853.
THORPE, CLARENCE D. Addison and Hutcheson on the Imagination. *ELH,* II (1935), 215-34.
TURNER, F. M. C. The Element of Irony in English Literature. Cambridge, Eng. 1926.
VAN TIEGHEM, PAUL. Le Préromantisme. Etudes d'Histoire Littéraire Européenne. Paris. 1924. Second series. 1930.
VAUGHAN, CHARLES E. The Romantic Revolt. 1907.
VINES, SHERARD. The Course of English Classicism. 1930.
WALLERSTEIN, RUTH C. The Development of the Rhetoric and Metre of the Heroic Couplet, especially in 1625-1645. *PMLA,* L (1935), 166-209.
WENDELL, BARRETT. The Temper of the Seventeenth Century in English Literature. 1904.
WILLIAMSON, GEORGE. The Rhetorical Pattern of Neo-Classical Wit. *MP,* XXXIII (1935), 55-81.
———. Senecan Style in the Seventeenth Century. *PQ,* XV (1936), 321-51.
WOOD, PAUL S. Native Elements in English Neo-Classicism. *MP,* XXIV (1926), 201-08.

III. SOCIAL AND POLITICAL HISTORY

ASHTON, JOHN. Social Life in the Reign of Queen Anne. 1883.
BESANT, SIR WALTER. London in the Eighteenth Century. 1902.
BOTSFORD, JAY B. English Society in the Eighteenth Century. 1924.
BRYANT, ARTHUR. The England of Charles II. 1934.
The Cambridge Modern History, Vols. V and VI. Cambridge. 1908, 1909.
CHANCELLOR, E. B. The Eighteenth Century in London. 1920.
CLARK, G. N. The Seventeenth Century. Oxford. 1929.
———. The Later Stuarts, 1660-1714. Oxford. 1934.
COLLINS, A. S. The Growth of the Reading Public during the Eighteenth Century. *RES,* II (1926), 284-93; 428-38.
———. The Growth of the Reading Public: 1780-1800. *Nineteenth Century,* CI (1927), 749-58.
FEILING, KEITH. A History of the Tory Party, 1640-1714. 1924.
———. The Second Tory Party, 1714-1832. 1938.
GEORGE, M. DOROTHY. London Life in the XVIIIth Century. 1930.
GOOCH, G. P. The History of English Democratic Ideas in the Seventeenth Century. Cambridge, Eng. 1912.
GRAY, B. KIRKMAN. A History of English Philanthropy. 1905.
GREEN, JOHN R. A Short History of the English People. 4 vols. 1877-1880.
HEARNSHAW, F. J. C. (ed.). The Social and Political Ideas of Some English Thinkers of the Augustan Age. 1928.
HILLHOUSE, JAMES T. The Grub-Street Journal. Durham, N. C. 1928.
HUNT, WILLIAM. The History of England from the Accession of George III to the Close of Pitt's First Administration (1760-1801). 1921.
LEADAM, I. S. The History of England from the Accession of Anne to the Death of George II. (1702-1760). 1921.
LECKY, WILLIAM E. H. A History of England in the Eighteenth Century. 2 vols. 1878-1890. Cabinet edition, 7 vols. 1916-1917.
LIPSON, E. The Economic History of England. Vols. II and III: The Age of Mercantilism. 1931.
LOCKITT, C. H. The Relations between French and English Society, 1763-1793. 1920.
MACAULAY, THOMAS B. History of England from the Accession of James II. 5 vols. 1849-1861. Edited by Sir Charles Firth, 6 vols. 1913-1915.
McLACHLAN, H. English Education under the Test Acts, being the history of the Nonconformist Academies, 1662-1820. Manchester. 1931.
MANTOUX, PAUL. The Industrial Revolution in the Eighteenth Century. Rev. ed., translated by Marjorie Vernon. 1928.
MOORE, C. A. Whig Panegyric Verse, 1700-1760. *PMLA,* XLI (1926), 362-401.
MOWAT, R. B. England in the Eighteenth Century. 1932.
OGG, DAVID. England in the Reign of Charles II. 2 vols. Oxford. 1934.
OVERTON, J. H. Life in the English Church, 1660-1717. 1885.
———. The Nonjurors. 1902.
PATTON, JULIA. The English Village, 1750-1850. 1919.

BIBLIOGRAPHY 1267

QUINLAN, M. J. Victorian Prelude: A History of English Manners, 1700-1830. 1941.
REYNOLDS, MYRA. The Learned Lady in England, 1650-1760. Boston. 1920.
SALMON, DAVID P. The Education of the Poor in the Eighteenth Century. 1908.
SCHÜCKING, L. I. Die Familie im Puritanismus. Leipzig. 1929.
STRAUS, RALPH. The Unspeakable Curll. 1927.
TINKER, CHAUNCEY B. The Salon and English Letters. 1915.
TREVELYAN, GEORGE M. England under Queen Anne. 3 vols. 1930-1934.
TURBERVILLE, A. S. English Men and Manners in the Eighteenth Century. 1926.
—— (ed.). Johnson's England. An Account of the Life and Manners of the Age. 2 vols. Oxford. 1933.
WARNER, W. J. The Wesleyan Movement and the Industrial Revolution. 1930.
WHITING, C. E. Studies in English Puritanism from the Restoration to the Revolution 1660-1688. 1931.
WILLIAMS, BASIL. The Whig Supremacy, 1714-1760. Oxford. 1939.
WINSTANLEY, D. A. The University of Cambridge in the Eighteenth Century. Cambridge, Eng. 1921.
WRIGHT, THOMAS. Caricature History of the Georges. 1904.
——. England under the House of Hanover, Illustrated from Caricatures and Satires. 1848.

IV. INTELLECTUAL BACKGROUND

BABBITT, IRVING. Rousseau and Romanticism. 1919.
BECKER, CARL. The Heavenly City of the Eighteenth Century Philosophers. New Haven. 1932.
BENN, ALFRED W. A History of English Rationalism. 2 vols. 1906.
BONAR, JAMES. Moral Sense. 1930.
BREDVOLD, LOUIS I. The Tendency toward Platonism in Neo-Classical Esthetics. ELH, I (1934), 91-120.
BRYSON, GLADYS. Mind and Society. The Scottish Inquiry of the Eighteenth Century. Princeton. 1945.
BURTT, EDWIN A. The Metaphysical Foundations of Modern Physical Science. 1925.
BURY, J. B. The Idea of Progress. 1920.
CASSIRER, ERNST. The Philosophy of the Enlightenment. Translated by F. C. A. Koelln and J. P. Pettegrove. Princeton. 1951.
CHANCELLOR, E. B. A History of Political Theories from Rousseau to Spencer. 1920.
CLARK, HENRY W. A History of English Non-Conformity. Vol. II. From the Restoration to the Close of the Nineteenth Century. 1913.
CRANE, RONALD S. Anglican Apologetics and the Idea of Progress. MP, XXXI (1934), 273-306; 349-82.
——. Suggestions toward a Genealogy of the "Man of Feeling." ELH, I (1934), 205-30.
CREED, J. M., and JOHN S. BOYS SMITH. Religious Thought in the Eighteenth Century. Cambridge, Eng. 1934.
CRU, R. LOYALTY. Diderot as a Disciple of English Thought. 1913.
DUNCAN, CARSON S. The New Science and English Literature in the Classical Period. Menasha, Wis. 1913.
DUNNING, WILLIAM A. A History of Political Ideas from Rousseau to Spencer. 1920.
ELTON, OLIVER. Reason and Enthusiasm in the Eighteenth Century. English Association, Essays and Studies, X. 1924.
GREEN, F. C. Minuet: A Critical Survey of French and English Literary Ideas in the Eighteenth Century. 1935.
HECKSCHER, ELI F. Mercantilism. Translated by Mendel Shapiro. 2 vols. 1935.
HUNT, JOHN. Religious Thought in England to the End of the Eighteenth Century. 3 vols. 1870-1873.
HUTTON, WILLIAM H. The English Church from the Accession of Charles I to the Death of Anne. 1903.
JONES, HOWARD M. Albrecht von Haller and English Philosophy. PMLA, XL (1925), 103-27.
JONES, RICHARD F. Ancients and Moderns: A Study of the Background of the 'Battle of the Books.' (Washington University Studies in Language and Literature, no. 6.) St. Louis, Mo. 1936.
LOVEJOY, ARTHUR O. The Great Chain of Being. A Study in the History of an Idea. Cambridge, Mass. 1936.
——, and GEORGE BOAS. Primitivism and Related Ideas in Antiquity. Baltimore. 1935.

MORNET, DANIEL. French Thought in the Eighteenth Century. Translated by L. M. Levin. 1929.

MOSSNER, ERNEST C. Bishop Butler and the Age of Reason. 1936.

NICOLSON, MARJORIE. The Breaking of the Circle; Studies in the Effect of the "New Science" upon Seventeenth Century Poetry. Evanston, Ill. 1950.

———. The Microscope and English Imagination. (*Smith College Studies in Modern Languages*, Vol. XVI, no. 4.) Northampton, Mass. 1935.

———. The "New Astronomy" and English Literary Imagination, *SP*, XXXII (1935), 428-62.

———. The Telescope and Imagination. *MP*, XXXII (1935), 233-60.

ROBERTSON, H. M. Aspects of the Rise of Economic Individualism: A Criticism of Max Weber and his School. Cambridge, Eng. 1933.

SMITH, PRESERVED. A History of Modern Culture. Vol. II, The Enlightenment, 1687-1776. 1934.

STEPHEN, SIR LESLIE. History of English Thought in the Eighteenth Century. 2 vols. 3rd ed. 1902.

TAWNEY, R. H. Religion and the Rise of Capitalism: A Historical Study. 1926.

TEXTE, J. Rousseau et les origines du cosmopolitisme littéraire. Paris. 1895. Translated by J. W. Matthews. 1899.

TINKER, CHAUNCEY B. Nature's Simple Plan. Princeton, 1922.

TORREY, NORMAN L. Voltaire and the English Deists. New Haven. 1930.

WHITNEY, LOIS. Primitivism and the Idea of Progress in English Popular Literature of the Eighteenth Century. Baltimore. 1934.

WILLEY, BASIL. The Eighteenth Century Background. 1940.

———. The Seventeenth Century Background. 1934.

WOLF, ABRAHAM. History of Science, Technology, and Philosophy in the Sixteenth and Seventeenth Centuries. 1935.

———. History of Science, Technology, and Philosophy in the Eighteenth Century. 1939.

FURTHER BIBLIOGRAPHIES

BUTLER (See also page 1)
Dan Gibson, "Samuel Butler," in *Seventeenth Century Studies*, ed. Robert Shafer (Princeton, 1933); Ricardo Quintana, "Samuel Butler: A Restoration Figure in a Modern Light," *ELH* XVIII (1951), 7-31.

ROCHESTER (See also page 31)
More easily accessible is Vivian de Sola Pinto's edition of the Works (Cambridge, Mass., 1954); *The Rochester-Saville Letters, 1671-1680*, ed. J. H. Wilson (Columbus, 1941); Kenneth B. Murdock, *The Sun at Noon* (1939).

DRYDEN (See also pages 35-36)
The Noyes volume was revised 1950; *Poetical Works*, ed. W. D. Christie (1870); D. Nichol Smith, *John Dryden* (Cambridge, Eng., 1950); T. S. Eliot, *Homage to Dryden* (1924) and *John Dryden: the Poet, the Dramatist, the Critic* (1932); James M. Osborn, *John Dryden: Some Biographical Facts and Problems* (1940); Ruth Wallerstein, "To Madness Near Allied," *HLQ*, VI (1943), 445-71; and "On the Death of Mrs. Killigrew: The Perfecting of a Genre," *SP*, XLIV (1947), 519-28; S. H. Monk, "Dryden Studies: A Survey, 1920-1945," *ELH*, XIV (1947), 46-63; and *John Dryden: A List of Critical Studies Published from 1895 to 1948* (Minneapolis, 1950); Hugh Macdonald, *John Dryden, A Bibliography* (Oxford, 1939).

TEMPLE (See also page 127)
Homer E. Woodbridge, *Sir William Temple: The Man and His Work* (1940).

DEFOE (See also pages 157-58)
Romances and Narratives, ed. G. A. Aitken (16 vols., 1895); *Novels and Selected Writings* (14 vols., Oxford, 1927-28); *Journal of the Plague Year and Other Pieces*, ed. A. W. Secord (1935); Dottin's *Daniel Defoe et ses romans* is available in an English translation by L. Ragan (New York, 1929); John R. Moore, "The Character of Daniel Defoe," *RES*, XIV (1938), 68-71; *Defoe in the Pillory and Other Studies* (Bloomington, 1939).

SWIFT (See also pages 171-72)
Martin Price, *Swift's Rhetorical Art* (New Haven, 1953); W. B. Ewald, Jr., *The Masks of Jonathan Swift* (Oxford, 1954); Herbert Davis, "Swift's View of Poetry," in *Studies in*

English by Members of University College (Toronto, 1931) ; M. O. Johnson, *The Sin of Wit: Jonathan Swift as a Poet* (Syracuse, 1950) ; Sir Charles Firth, "The Political Significance of Gulliver's Travels," *Proceedings of the British Academy* IX (1919-20) , 237-59, repr. in *Essays, Historical and Literary* (Oxford, 1938) ; W. A. Eddy, *Gulliver's Travels: A Critical Study* (Princeton, 1923) ; Marjorie Nicolson and Nora M. Mohler, "The Scientific Background of Swift's Voyage to Laputa," *Annals of Science,* II (1937) , 299-334, 405-30; A. E. Case, *Four Essays on Gulliver's Travels* (Princeton, 1945) ; Harold Williams, *The Text of Gulliver's Travels* (Cambridge, Eng., 1952; L. A. Landa, "*A Modest Proposal* and Populousness," *MP,* XL (1942) , 161-70; "Jonathan Swift and Charity," *JEGP,* XLIV (1945) , 337-50; "Swift, the Mysteries, and Deism," *University of Texas Studies in English* (1944) , pp. 239-56; H. Teerink, *Bibliography of the Writings in Prose and Verse* (The Hague, 1937) ; L. A. Landa and J. E. Tobin, *Jonathan Swift: A List of Critical Studies Published from 1895 to 1945* (1945) .

STEELE AND ADDISON (See also pages 248-49)
   Austin Dobson, *Richard Steele* (1886) ; Willard Connely, *Sir Richard Steele* (1934) ; Addison's *Works,* ed. H. G. Bohn (6 vols., 1882-83) ; *Selections,* ed. B. Wendell and C. N. Greenough (Boston, 1905) ; *Letters,* ed. Walter Graham (Oxford, 1941) ; Peter Smithers, *Addison* (Oxford, 1954) ; C. S. Lewis, "Addison," in *Essays on the Eighteenth Century Presented to David Nichol Smith* (Oxford, 1945) .

SHAFTESBURY (See also page 309)
   R. L. Brett, *The Third Earl of Shaftesbury: A Study in Eighteenth-Century Literary Theory* (1951) ; Moore's article on the return to Nature is reprinted in *Backgrounds of English Literature* (Minneapolis, 1953) ; A. O. Aldridge, "Shaftesbury and the Deist Manifesto," *Transactions of the American Philosophical Society,* N. S., XLI (1951) , Part 2.

JOHN GAY (See also page 412)
   Trivia, ed. W. H. Williams (1922) ; *The Shepherd's Week,* ed. H. F. B. Brett-Smith (Oxford, 1924) ; W. H. Irving, *John Gay, Favorite of the Wits* (Durham, 1940) ; James Sutherland, "John Gay," in *Pope and His Contemporaries* (Oxford, 1949) , pp. 201-14.

ALLAN RAMSAY (See also page 437)
   Poetical Works, ed. C. Mackay (2 vols.; 1866-68) ; *Works,* ed. Burns Martin and John W. Oliver; I, *Poems, 1721* (Edinburgh, 1951) ; *Bibliography of Allan Ramsay* (Glasgow, 1931) .

ISAAC WATTS (See also page 505)
   Bernard Lord Manning, *The Hymns of Wesley and Watts* (1942, repr. 1954) ; Arthur P. Davis, *Isaac Watts* (1943) ; Robert Stevenson, "Dr. Watts' 'Flights of Fancy,' " *Harvard Theological Review,* XLII (1949) , 235-53; Norman Nicholson, "Wesley and Watts," *TLS* (August 6, 1954) , xliv-xlv.

CHARLES WESLEY (See also page 509)
   Henry Bett, *The Hymns of Methodism* (1913, rev ed. 1945) ; T. W. Herbert, *John Wesley as Editor and Author* (Princeton, 1940) ; J. E. Rattenbury, *The Evangelical Doctrines of Charles Wesley's Hymns* (1941) . See also the references under Watts.

MARK AKENSIDE (See also page 536)
   C. T. Houpt, *Mark Akenside: A Biographical and Critical Study* (Philadelphia, 1944) ; A. O. Aldridge, "The Eclecticism of Mark Akenside's 'The Pleasures of Imagination,' " *JHI,* V (1944) , 293-314; "Akenside and Imagination," *SP,* XLII (1945) , 769-92.

JOSEPH WARTON (See also page 559)
   D. H. Bishop, "The Father of the Wartons," *South Atlantic Quarterly,* XVI (1917) , 357-68; John Wooll, *Biographical Memoirs of Joseph Warton* (1806) ; Thomas Warton the Younger, *History of English Poetry,* ed. W. C. Hazlitt (4 vols., 1871) ; *Poetical Works,* ed. R. Mant (2 vols., Oxford, 1802) ; R. D. Havens, "Thomas Warton and the Eighteenth-Century Dilemma," *SP,* XXV (1928) , 36-50; René Wellek, *The Rise of English Literary History* (Chapel Hill, 1941) [for Thomas Warton's *History of English Poetry*].

BOSWELL (See also page 618)
   P. H. Houston, *Dr. Johnson : A Study in Eighteenth-Century Humanism* (Cambridge, Mass., 1923) ; W. B. C. Watkins, *Johnson and English Poetry before 1660* (Princeton, 1936) ; W. K. Wimsatt, Jr., *The Prose Style of Samuel Johnson* (New Haven, 1941) ; *Philosophic Words* (New

Haven, 1948) [for Johnson's diction]; J. W. Krutch, *Samuel Johnson* (1944); B. H. Bronson, *Johnson and Boswell* (Berkeley, 1944); J. H. Hagstrum, *Samuel Johnson's Literary Criticism* (Minneapolis, 1952); W. R. Keast, "The Theoretical Foundations of Johnson's Criticism," in *Critics and Criticism*, ed. R. S. Crane (Chicago, 1952); W. P. Courtney and D. Nichol Smith, *Bibliography* (revised ed., Oxford, 1925); R. W. Chapman and A. T. Hazen, "Supplement to Courtney," *Oxford Bibliographical Society*, V (1938), 119-66; *The R. B. Adam Library Relating to Dr. Samuel Johnson and His Era* (3 vols., 1929); J. L. Clifford, *Johnsonian Studies 1887-1950* (Minneapolis, 1951).

HORACE WALPOLE, (See also pages 778–79)
Robert W. Ketton-Cremer, *Horace Walpole, a Biography* (1940).

INDEX OF AUTHORS, TITLES, AND FIRST LINES OF POEMS

Authors' names are set in italic type, titles are set in capitals, and first lines of poems are set in body type. Entry is by first line only when the title repeats the first line.